GRAND CORDON de Mumm.

THE WINE SPECTATOR'S

Ultimate Guide to Buying Wine

Premier Edition

1992

Vol. 1

WINE SPECTATOR PRESS
San Francisco, California

Editor and Publisher..........Marvin R. Shanken
President....................Gregory S. Walter
Managing Editor.....................Jim Gordon
Project Editor.......................Liza Gross
Wine Research Coordinator..........Mark Norris
Tasting Coordinator...................Ray Bush
Art Director...................Kathy McGilvery
Production Manager.......Donna Marianno Morris
Art/Production Staff...........Kim M. Viniconis,
   Jane Van Ginkel, Kevin Mulligan, Jennifer Salazar,
               Shawn Wilson, Larry Hughes
Senior Vice President, Sales...........Jeff Diskin
Vice President,
   Director of Advertising....Miriam Morgenstern
Vice President,
   Advertising Services......Constance McGilvray
Western Advertising Manager......Leslie P. Motto
Advertising Services Manager....Elizabeth Ferrero
Assistant Advertising Manager.....Virginia Juliano
Senior Vice President, Marketing.......Jay Morris
Retail Sales Director.............Christine Carroll
Special Accounts Director........Mark A. Mazotti
Sales Representatives.......Gabriella Spelda (NY),
                           Clark Harris (SF)
Operations Manager................Gina Miranda
Information Systems Manager.........Dave Budai

The Wine Spectator's Ultimate Guide to Buying Wine, 1992 Edition

ISBN 0-918076-81-1
ISSN 1058-5729

Published by Wine Spectator Press, a division of M. Shanken Communications, Inc./West, Opera Plaza Suite 2014, 601 Van Ness Ave., San Francisco, CA 94102, (415) 673-2040, (415) 673-0103 (fax).

M. Shanken Communications, Inc. also publishes *The Wine Spectator, Impact, Impact International, Market Watch, Food Arts, Impact Research Reports, Leaders, Impact Yearbook, Impact International Directory, The Wine Spectator's Great Restaurant Wine Lists, The Wine Spectator's Wine Country Guide,* and sponsors the *Impact* Marketing Seminars and the California and New York Wine Experiences. Headquarters offices are at 387 Park Avenue South, New York, NY 10016, (212) 684-4224, (212) 684-5424 (fax).

Manufactured in the United States

Contents

fleur

FLEUR DE CHAMPAGNE

CHAMPAGNE

PERRIER-JOUËT

He knew that he was behaving like a schoolboy, but no matter how hard he tried, he couldn't stop looking at her. So after a while he simply gave up and stare

TATION

Perrier-Jouët *fleur* de Champagne

FROM THE PUBLISHER

Open a bottle of Champagne and join us!

With the publication of our first annual "Ultimate Guide to Buying Wine," the staff of *The Wine Spectator* has much reason to rejoice.

We have been building toward this publication date for 12 years. Over the years we have received hundreds upon hundreds of letters from readers asking for summary compilations of all our wine ratings. We almost came out with the book you now hold in your hands two years ago, but after considerable internal discussion, decided we were not yet ready.

We wanted this book to be especially valuable to wine lovers and collectors as well as members of the wine trade—so valuable that its users would refer to it week after week during the year. We wanted to play a role in your various wine decisions—buy, sell, drink or hold. We decided then that in order to make the "Ultimate Guide to Buying Wine" vital, the wines listed must have current market prices in addition to our ratings. We hope that you agree.

For the past two years, we have had a specially trained research team compiling wine prices from every conceivable source (more than 100 of them) including retailer ads from newspapers and magazines, retailer catalogs, state price books, auction hammer prices from major wine auctions both in the United States and Europe, and many other sources. More than 125,000 prices have been entered into our databases. Some of the more popular "investment grade" wines have more than 200 price entries for a single vintage (the highest to date was 1970 Château Mouton-Rothschild at 240 entries). All of this data was used to arrive at one current average price per wine. Thank heaven for the computer age!

This book contains an incredible 24,000 wine ratings, most of them from our weekly blind tastings, others from our senior editors' tastings on location in the wine regions of the world. You will also note that the compilations are indexed in two useful ways—alphabetically by country, type and producer, as well as by country, type, vintage and score.

While we are proud of this new data book for wine, we know that with your help we will be able to make significant improvements in its format and content in time for next year's edition. We ask that as you use Volume I and come upon any flaws or omissions, please take the time to write us about your observations and suggestions. With your help, we can make next year's "Ultimate Guide to Buying Wine" even more valuable and useful to you.

Marvin R. Shanken

CHATEAU ST. JEAN FOR FIFTEEN VINTAGES, ONLY THE FINEST.

FIRST GROWTH*

1988 Robert Young Vineyards: Continues in the successful Robert Young tradition, offering ripe, gentle melon, pear, spice and toast flavors that are more supple and forward than the 1987, but still very pleasing. May be ready to drink before the 1985 through 1987 vintages. 91

SECOND GROWTH*

1988 Belle Terre Vineyards: Extends the Belle Terre streak of excellence, and with time may rank as one of the best. Plenty of pretty ripe apple, pear, peach, fig and spice flavors that are rich and crisp, with a measure of elegance and finesse. 90

From California's Great Chardonnays, by James Laube, Wine Spectator Press, 1990.

FOR WINERY AND VINEYARD INFORMATION, CALL THE CHATEAU ST. JEAN WINELINE AT 1-800-332-WINE.

FOREWORD

This book is, we believe, the largest and most complete collection of wine ratings anywhere. It was designed for anyone interested in buying wine—from the sophisticated collector evaluating purchases for his growing collection, to the new wine lover buying wines for his own consumption.

Our goal was to provide in one easy-to-use reference book compelling and useful information and advice on topics such as vintage charts, proper wine storage and inventory tracking, serving tips, wine auctions, matching wine and food, and much more.

We hope that you feel we have accomplished that goal.

This project was possible through the efforts of the entire *Wine Spectator* team. In particular, special thanks go to project editor Liza Gross for her thorough, methodical coordination, and to wine research coordinator Mark Norris for his computer wizardry and just plain hard work. Thanks to tasting coordinator Ray Bush, who worked long hours helping to prepare and verify the data. Thanks also to art director Kathy McGilvery and her assistant Kim Viniconis for their design efforts, and to production manager Donna Marianno Morris and her staff: Jane Van Ginkel, Shawn Wilson, Kevin Mulligan and Jenny Salazar for their dedication and high-quality work.

Thanks also go to the book's contributors and fellow *Wine Spectator* staffers for their help and advice: managing editor Jim Gordon, editor at large Harvey Steiman, senior editors James Laube and Thomas Matthews, and free-lance contributors Steve Heimoff and J. Patrick Forden.

There is only one caveat that I would bring to your attention at this point. As you will read later in ''How to Use This Book,'' the data in this book is cumulative; that is, it has been drawn from past issues of *The Wine Spectator*. Nearly 65 percent, or more than 15,500 ratings, come from issues published in the last three years. The balance of the ratings come from earlier issues. These older ratings are provided primarily for historical reference. When using the wine ratings, please pay special attention to the date at the end of each listing, and use the most recent rating as your guide.

All of us hope that this book helps you make the best and most enjoyable use of your wine buying dollars.

Gregory S. Walter
President

Santa Rita Medalla Real Cabernet Sauvignon and Chardonnay, photographed at The River Café in New York City.

Viña Santa Rita

Medalla Real is the top of the line, the "royal medal" winner of Santa Rita wines.

Winner of the Gault-Millau World Wine Olympiad in 1987, Santa Rita's Medalla Real Cabernet brought the world's attention to the wines of Chile.

"Santa Rita is one of the stars of the new wave of Chilean wineries . . . The Medalla Real Cabernet Sauvignon is reminiscent of some of the better small chateaux of Bordeaux."

Frank J. Prial
The New York Times

"In its determination to put quality before quantity, Santa Rita is tapping more fully than any other firm Chile's fund of natural resources."

Harrod's Book of Fine Wines

Vineyard Brands, Inc.
ROBERT HAAS SELECTIONS

How to Use This Book

The pages that follow contain a lot of data—more than 350 pages of more than 24,000 wine ratings, plus vintage charts, price analyses and useful "how-to" feature articles. This book is designed as an easy-to-use reference to the wine ratings published in *The Wine Spectator*. This chapter will provide you with the necessary background to help you best apply the information contained here.

How the Book Is Organized

The information presented in "*The Wine Spectator*'s Ultimate Guide to Buying Wine" is divided into three main sections. The first, Section A, contains many useful feature articles on various aspects of wine and wine buying. Section B begins the list of wine ratings with the first index, organized by producer. Section C is the second index, listing wines by vintage then score. Here is a detailed look at each section.

SECTION A: A SPECIAL REPORT ON BUYING WINE—This section begins with "The Tasters," a personal look at the senior editors who taste the wines, their credentials and qualifications, plus background on the tasting program at *The Wine Spectator* (page A-15). Next is "Wine-Buying Strategies," by senior editor James Laube (page A-21). Laube looks at the basics of buying wine from the standpoint of a casual consumer, as well as that of a serious collector, and gives his "10 Tips to Better Wine Buying."

Harvey Steiman, editor-at-large of *The Wine Spectator*, tracks wine-pricing trends in "Spiraling Prices Put Wine Lovers in a Bind." You will find his analysis of prices helpful in deciding how to make your purchases count (page A-23). For those readers interested in the burgeoning auction market, New York bureau chief Thomas Matthews delivers a complete primer on buying wine at auction both in the United States and abroad (page A-27). Matching wine and food need not be a vexing challenge according to Harvey Steiman, who presents his ideas in "Choosing a Wine for Dinner," (page A-31). Managing editor Jim Gordon sorts out some of the more confusing aspects of wine service in "Shapes, Sizes and Degrees," with a look at bottle sizes, glassware and serving temperatures (page A-37).

In "Vintage Charts" (page A-38), we present our vintage ratings for the major wine-producing regions. In some cases, we have rated as many as three decades of vintages. "The Top 100" (page A-41) is a look at a popular annual feature in the magazine. The Top 100 are the 100 most interesting wines of the year, as chosen by our board of editors. In this section we list the Top 100 from each of the last three years for your perusal. In "Keeping Track of Inventory" (page A-47), frequent *Wine Spectator* contributor Steve Heimoff looks at several methods for keeping your wine cellar in order. "Special Ratings" (page A-48) provides lists by score of our special wine ratings: Spectator Selection, Cellar Selection and Best Buy.

SECTION B: ALL WINES LISTED BY PRODUCER—This section, beginning on page B-1, contains wine ratings organized in alphabetical order, first by country, then by type and then by producer.

SECTION C: ALL WINES LISTED BY VINTAGE —This section, beginning on page C-1, contains wine ratings organized in alphabetical order, first by country, then by type, then by vintage and then by score.

The Wine Ratings

The wine ratings contained in sections B and C are a compilation of the tasting results that have been published in *The Wine Spectator* over the past decade. Therefore, while there are ratings in this book that are quite recent—15,500 in the past three years—there are also ratings that are from an earlier period.

We feel that these older ratings can be very useful in that they present, in many cases, a nearly complete vertical representation of a particular wine. To determine the age of the rating, pay particular attention to the date at the end of each listing.

Another situation that will arise in your use of this book is that you will find multiple ratings for the same vintage of the same wine. In general, you will see one rating from *The Wine Spectator*'s tasting panel, and then generally no more than two other ratings with initials at the end of the listing in parentheses. These additional ratings come from one of two sources: individual tasting reports by senior editors, or tastings conducted by a senior editor as part of the research for one of the three Wine Spectator Press books currently on the market. After long deliberations on the question of whether to include the non-tasting panel ratings, we decided that rather than simply average the scores to come up with one rating per wine, we felt that more information was better than less.

There is one other type of rating you will see in this book, primarily in the sections for red Bordeaux, red Burgundy and California Cabernet. These are ratings based on barrel tastings. Barrel tastings are tastings conducted on wines still in the barrel—before they are bottled and released for sale. These are, by definition, preliminary scores and should be treated as such. Many things can happen to a wine between the time it is tasted in barrel and the time when you purchase it at your local store. Wines can improve or decline during that period, and can even show signs of poor shipping or storage conditions. We have included these barrel-tasting results again because we feel it gives you a better picture of our total, evolutionary experience with a particular wine. We hope that this additional information helps you make a better buying decision. We have used the initials ''BT'' in parentheses to indicate a barrel-tasting listing. In addition, these wines will have a plus (+) next to the score to indicate a preliminary range.

THE RATINGS: PIECE BY PIECE

Because of the very large number of ratings presented here, we had to make each wine listing as brief as possible. Therefore, we have used abbreviations and shortcuts throughout this book. For your convenience we have included a key to those abbreviations called ''Key to Symbols'' in the lower left-hand corner of every other page in sections B and C. Below are two typical wine listings, and definitions for each of the key pieces.

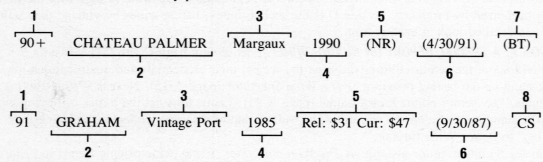

1. SCORE —This is the number, from *The Wine Spectator*'s 100-point scale, that represents the taster's evaluation of the wine's quality. For a detailed discussion of our 100-point scale, please see the next chapter, ''The Tasters.'' When you see a plus (+) next to the wine's score, this indicates a preliminary, and therefore approximate rating. If the plus is used in conjunction with the initials ''BT'' then the rating is from a barrel tasting.

2. PRODUCER'S NAME —This is the name of the winery or producer. We have set it in all capital letters to set it off from the rest of the wine's information.

3. WINE TYPE/DESCRIPTION —This will generally contain the type of wine and any varietal name, appellation, or any other vineyard or special designation (i.e. Sonoma Valley or Martha's Vineyard or Cask 23).

4. VINTAGE —This is the year the wine was harvested and vinified.

5. PRICE DATA —This is the wine's price information and can come in four distinct forms. (NR) means that the wine has not been released and no official price had been set at the time of tasting. (NA) means that no price data was available. This occurs typically with older wines. A single price ($37) signifies that the only price available was the suggested retail price on release. Two prices (Rel: $31 Cur: $47) show the price on release, and the current market price for the wine. A word on the current market prices in this book: *The Wine Spectator* maintains a price-tracking department whose sole job is to track wine prices from many sources—auctions, retailer advertisements and catalogs, wholesale price books, etc. The current market prices represent a weighted average of all price sources, and as such are our ''best educated guess.''

6. ISSUE PUBLISHED —This date represents the issue of *The Wine Spectator* in which the rating was first published. For ratings included from one of the three Wine Spectator Press books, the following format is used: (CA-date) for ''California's Great Cabernets'' by James Laube, (CH-date) for ''California's Great Chardonnays'' by James Laube, and (VP-date) for ''Vintage Port'' by James Suckling.

7. TASTER'S INITIALS —Unless noted with one of the initials here, all wine ratings in this book are the results of blind tastings conducted by a panel of senior editors. The taster's initials are used to indicate a rating that was done outside of the tasting panel. The initials used are: (JG) for Jim Gordon, (HS) for Harvey Steiman, (JL) for James Laube, (JS) for James Suckling, (TM) for Thomas Matthews, (TR) for Terry Robards, and (BT) for barrel tasting (these wines were tasted blind from barrel samples).

8. SPECIAL DESIGNATIONS —These are used to indicate special ratings given by the tasting panel. For a detailed look at these special designations, please see ''Special Ratings'' page A-48. The special designations used here are: SS for Spectator Selection, CS for Cellar Selection and BB for Best Buy.

If
YOU'VE
EVER
BEEN
WRAPPED
IN SILK
you
ALREADY
KNOW

THE
FEELING
of
COGNAC
HENNESSY

COGNAC
Hennessy

ESTᴰ 1765

A short course in Napa Valley geography.

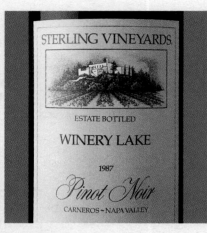
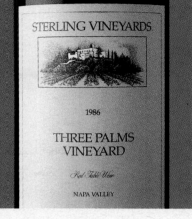

The vineyard-designated wines of Sterling offer not only enjoyment but a measure of insight as well. They reflect both the Napa Valley's diverse geography and Sterling's uncompromising winemaking philosophy.

Our winemaker, Bill Dyer, embarks upon every wine he creates with a specific goal in mind. For our family of estate-bottled varietals, that goal is to express the true character of each grape variety as produced in our Napa Valley vineyards. For our vineyard-designated wines, his mission is significantly different. With these, his overriding concern is to capture the unique character of the vineyards themselves. Of course, there is little point in achieving this unless the vineyards possess character that is indeed unique. Those described below are three which meet that qualification.

Winery Lake Vineyard

At the southern reach of the valley, in the highly-regarded Carneros

region, Winery Lake has become one of Napa's most celebrated vineyards. Cooling breezes from nearby San Francisco Bay plus a 30-acre lake on the vineyard itself maintain ideal temperatures throughout the growing season. Winery Lake's soil is a lime-rich mixture of marine deposits and volcanic spill in a shallow layer over rolling hills and flat land. Such conditions produce exquisite, critically-acclaimed wines. A notable example is our Winery Lake Pinot Noir. It captures the vineyard's earthiness, with an intense spicy aroma and crisp, well-defined fruit on the palate. Our lush Winery Lake Chardonnay also says much about the vineyard's character.

Three Palms Vineyard

This historic site on the valley floor lies just a half-mile southeast of

the Sterling Winery, from which its trio of namesake palms are clearly visible. For centuries, Selby Creek has carried volcanic stone from Dutch Henry Canyon across the Silverado

Trail and deposited it in layers over Three Palms' 75 acres. The growing conditions thus produced are unique, and Three Palms has earned renown as one of Napa's select vineyards. Its Cabernet Sauvignon and Merlot are distinctive in their deep color, intense aroma, and rich flavor. The two are blended with balance and complexity under Sterling's Three Palms label.*

Diamond Mountain Ranch

In the valley's northwest sector, the dramatic terraces of our Diamond Mountain Ranch have been carved into austere, volcanic slopes. They climb from 1200 to 1700 feet high along a steep ridge of the Mayacamas Range facing 4,000 foot Mount St. Helena. This unique juxtaposition forms a natural trap for ocean breezes from the nearby Pacific Coast, cooling the vines on Diamond Mountain on warm summer afternoons. The wines grown here are big, mountain-styled,

and intense–suitable for long-aging. We bottle Diamond Mountain Ranch Cabernet Sauvignon and Diamond Mountain Ranch Chardonnay.

The best way to appreciate the distinctiveness of these Sterling vineyards, of course, is to sample the wines bearing their designation.

We believe you'll find that to be by far the most palatable geography lesson you've ever experienced.

The Wines of Sterling Vineyards.

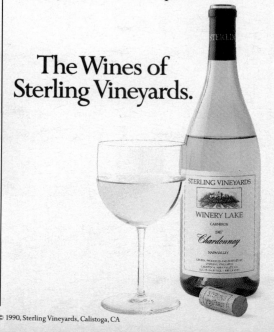

© 1990, Sterling Vineyards, Calistoga, CA

The Tasters

The wine ratings and other data contained in this book are the result of hundreds of tastings by the senior editors of *The Wine Spectator*. There are two types of tastings used to review wines for the magazine, and by extension, this book. First are the regular, twice-weekly tastings of new wine releases by *The Wine Spectator*'s tasting panel. Second are the special tastings conducted by our senior editors of a particular type or vintage of wine, frequently conducted on location around the world.

HOW WE TASTE WINE

Wines selected for review in *The Wine Spectator* (and for inclusion in this book) are tasted blind. Bottles are bagged and coded by an independent tasting coordinator. All capsules and corks are removed from the bottles prior to tasting, and corks are substituted to ensure that the wines remain anonymous. Tasters are told only the general type of wine (varietal or region) and vintage. In scoring, price is not taken into account. Wines are sampled one at a time, but tasters often compare several close-scoring wines of a similar type before removing the bags.

Wines are chosen for tasting from those sent to our office for review and from wines purchased at retail. Since *The Wine Spectator* serves a national audience, we prefer to review wines that are widely available and, therefore, wider interest among our readers.

Wines scoring below 60 are automatically retasted. We also retaste wines that score lower than their reputations suggest. The higher score prevails.

ABOUT THE WINE SPECTATOR'S 100-POINT SCALE

Tasters for *The Wine Spectator* score wines using our 100-point scale. Ratings reflect how highly our tasting panel regards each wine relative to other wines.

Ratings are based on potential quality, as well as on how good the wines will be when they are at their peak, regardless of how soon that will be.

THE WINE SPECTATOR 100-POINT SCALE

95-100 — Classic, a great wine.
90-94 — Outstanding, superior character and style.
80-89 — Good to very good, a wine with special qualities.
70-79 — Average, drinkable wine that may have minor flaws.
60-69 — Below average, drinkable but not recommended.
50-59 — Poor, undrinkable, not recommended.

"+"—With a score indicates a range; used primarily to indicate a preliminary score.

Unless otherwise indicated, the wine ratings in this book are from our tasting panel. Reviews from individual tasters are signed with their initials. A brief look at the backgrounds and credentials of our senior tasters begins on the next page.

The Wine Spectator
Tasting Panel

Marvin R. Shanken
Editor and Publisher

Marvin Shanken, 47, has been involved in beverage-industry publishing for 18 years, but his involvement in wine goes back more than 20 years.

In the early 1970s, while he was a partner in a Wall Street investment firm, Shanken bought *Impact*, then a little-known wine and spirits industry newsletter. In 1975, he left Wall Street to enter the world of publishing and run *Impact* full-time. His interest in wine led him to purchase *The Wine Spectator* in 1979. Today, *The Wine Spectator* is the largest and most influential wine publication in the world. Shanken continues to shape the editorial direction of *The Wine Spectator* through his work with the magazine's editors and also writes his column "From the Editor" in each issue.

In addition to his editorial duties, Shanken is chairman of M. Shanken Communications, Inc., publisher of *Impact, Impact International, Market Watch* and *Food Arts*, and event chairman of the New York and California Wine Experiences.

Shanken earned a bachelor's degree in business and finance from the University of Miami, and an M.B.A. in real estate and finance from the American University in Washington, D.C.

He lives with his wife, Hazel, and his daughter, Jessica, in New York. He has two daughters, Samantha and Allison, from a previous marriage.

Jim Gordon
Managing Editor

Jim Gordon, 39, is a career journalist with 16 years of experience writing and editing for newspapers and magazines. He joined *The Wine Spectator* in 1984 as associate editor, later became news editor and was named managing editor in 1987.

Gordon manages a staff of editors, writers and photographers from editorial offices in San Francisco. His writing and wine-tasting assignments have included reports from Bordeaux, Burgundy, the Rhône Valley, Italy, California and Germany. He has been a member of *The Wine Spectator*'s tasting panel since 1984.

Before joining *The Wine Spectator*, Gordon was managing editor of the *St. Helena Star* newspaper for five years in the Napa Valley. He began his professional journalism career in 1977 as a reporter and photographer with the *Madison Press* (London, Ohio). Gordon earned a bachelor's degree in English from Denison University in Ohio.

He, his wife, Catherine, and their son, Lucas, live in Fairfax, Calif.

Harvey Steiman
Editor at Large

Harvey Steiman, 44, has been with *The Wine Spectator* since 1984, first as managing editor, later as executive editor. His columns, features and extensive tasting reports have covered the wines from many diverse wine regions including California, France, Italy, and the Pacific Northwest. Steiman also creates a regular monthly menu matching food and wine. He has been a member of the tasting panel since 1984.

Steiman is also the host of "In the Kitchen with Harvey" on KNBR radio, San Francisco. He was host of a similar program on KCBS San Francisco from 1982 to 1990. A book of recipes from that program, "Harvey Steiman's California Kitchen," was published in 1990 by Chronicle Books. He is the author of two previous cookbooks, "Great Recipes From San Francisco," (Tarcher 1979) and, with chef Ken Hom, "Chinese Technique," (Simon and Schuster 1980).

A music major at UCLA, he began a career in journalism in 1968 as the sports editor of the *Inglewood Daily News* (in California). He joined *The Miami Herald* in 1969, and in 1973 became its food editor. In 1977, he was named food-and-wine editor of the *San Francisco Examiner*.

He lives in San Francisco with his wife, Carol, and his daughter, Katherine.

James Laube
Senior Editor

James Laube, 40, has spent the last decade traveling, tasting and writing about the wines of the world.

Laube began writing for *The Wine Spectator* in 1980. In 1983, he joined the staff full-time as its first senior editor. He has written regularly on assignment about the wines of Bordeaux, Burgundy, the Loire, the Rhône, Germany, Italy, Spain, Australia, Oregon, Washington, Long Island and California.

In 1989, Laube finished his first book, "California's Great Cabernets" (Wine Spectator Press), which was an immediate success. His second book, "California's Great Chardonnays" (Wine Spectator Press), followed one year later. Prior to joining *The Wine Spectator*, Laube was the Napa bureau chief of the *Vallejo Times-Herald* (in California) for four years, and earlier worked at the *Anaheim Bulletin* (in California) and the Colorado Springs *Gazette-Telegraph*. He earned a bachelor's and master's degree in history from San Diego State University.

He lives with his wife, Cheryl, and their two children, Dwight and Margaux, in Napa, Calif.

James Suckling
Senior Editor/European Bureau Chief

James Suckling, 33, joined *The Wine Spectator* in 1981 after spending three years as a reporter for daily newspapers in Madison, Wis., and Washington, D.C. He attended Utah State University, earning a bachelor's degree in journalism and political science and finished course work for a master's degree at the University of Wisconsin-Madison School of Journalism.

In 1984, Suckling was transferred to Paris to cover the European wine scene. In 1986, he was promoted to European bureau chief in London, where he now lives in Greenwich with his wife, Catherine.

In 1990, Suckling finished his first book, ''Vintage Port'' (Wine Spectator Press), which has been well received on both sides of the Atlantic.

Per-Henrik Mansson
Senior Editor

Per-Henrik Mansson, 40, was born in Sweden and grew up in French-speaking Switzerland near vineyards that overlook Lake Geneva.

In 1987, Mansson joined *The Wine Spectator* as news editor in San Francisco. He was promoted to senior editor and transferred to the London bureau to report on the European wine scene in 1989.

Mansson attended college in Sweden, where he earned a bachelor's degree in economics. He came to the United States in 1974 and earned a master's degree in international relations at Johns Hopkins University's School of Advanced International Studies in Washington, D.C. Mansson was admitted to the Columbia University School of Journalism in New York where he earned a master's degree in 1978. He moved to Northern California where he worked as a journalist for the *San Francisco Examiner, Wall Street Journal Europe* and other publications.

Mansson lives in London with his wife, Lynda, and son, Nicholas.

Thomas Matthews
Senior Editor/New York Bureau Chief

Thomas Matthews, 38, began writing for *The Wine Spectator* in 1987, while living in a village in the vineyards near Bordeaux. In 1988, he joined the magazine's staff as a reporter in the London bureau, moving back to the United States in 1989 to become *The Wine Spectator*'s New York bureau chief.

Matthews got his start in the wine business in 1979 picking grapes in Bordeaux and Cognac. From 1982 to 1986, he worked in New York City as the wine buyer for Odeon Restaurant and Café Luxembourg. He has a bachelor's degree in literature and philosophy from Bennington College and a master's degree in political science from Yale University.

Matthews lives in New York with his wife, Sara.

Ray Bush
Tasting Coordinator

Ray Bush, 38, has been *The Wine Spectator*'s tasting coordinator since 1985. He is responsible for all the behind-the-scenes duties and research that creates each issue's Buying Guide and the many special tastings.

Prior to joining *The Wine Spectator*, Bush worked in wine retail sales in San Francisco, from 1983 to 1986, and was the cellarmaster for the 1984, 1985 and 1986 San Francisco Fair and Exposition Wine Competition.

Bush has been a member of the following tasting panels: the *San Francisco Examiner*'s 1983 ''California Living'' panel, the 1986 University of San Francisco Alumni Association, the 1986 Foothill Counties Wine Show (Calaveras County) and the San Francisco Symphony (1986 to 1991). He also came in third place in the First Annual California Wine Tasting Olympics in 1983.

In 1978, Bush earned a bachelor's degree from Georgia State University.

Bush was born in East Point, Georgia, and lives in San Francisco.

Warehouse Wine Storage

BY STEVE HEIMOFF

In some wine lovers' homes, it's a familiar story: The Bordeaux has taken over the bedroom, the basement is bursting with Burgundy, there's no more room for the Rhônes and you're sleeping on a cot in the kitchen.

Who you gonna call? A wine-storage company, that's who. Today, home wine-storage systems are readily available for those who have the money to buy them.

Just a few years ago, collectors with more wine than could easily be stored in a closet had few options. A massive credenza filled with wine is the last thing collectors who live in small apartments need. And those who own thousands of bottles would need an entire roomful of the gizmos to hold their collections.

For these people, wine storage companies represent the ideal solution, and they're springing up all around the country. *The Wine Spectator* recently completed its latest census of such facilities, and while the list is certainly not complete, a search through your local Yellow Pages should turn up something.

If you're planning to buy a storage facility, there are a few things you should consider before choosing one. Storage conditions are the first and foremost consideration—the temperature should be constant and low (less than about 62 Fahrenheit), with high humidity, darkness and little or no vibration.

But security is also a factor. After all, you wouldn't want some midnight caller waltzing off with your Warre's.

Another thing to consider is access. Storage facilities permit you to get to your wines only during business hours, and business hours vary. In addition, a few facilities require advance notice if you want to withdraw your stash.

Another factor is whether the customer has access to his own locker. Some facilities operate like banks: When you're ready to withdraw your goodies, you put in your request at a "teller's" counter and someone else goes into the storeroom to get your bottles. That means the owners themselves don't get to visit their own collections, a treat many collectors might miss.

A final consideration is cost. Like other businesses, some storage facilities charge more than others without necessarily providing a greater array of services. A number of them make you pay a handling fee each time you deposit or remove a few bottles. And many of the companies rent space on a per-locker basis rather than a per-

Steve Heimoff is a free-lance writer in Oakland, Calif.

case basis, meaning you might be paying for a space that holds 24 cases even if you're storing only five or 10.

While all storage facilities are security conscious and equipped with sprinkler systems, they're not invulnerable. Since none of the ones we contacted insures the wines it holds, collectors should take out extra insurance on their wines, which can usually be done on a homeowner's policy.

In general, there are three types of storage facilities. Many general storage companies permit wine to be stored on-premises, and these can be good, inexpensive choices. Almost every city has a general storage facility, so we've included only a sampling on our list. Try to find one that's had experience storing wine.

More wine shops are also offering long-term storage. Some of them allow their cellars to be used only by their own customers, but the ones we've included service the general public.

The professional, wine-only storage companies are the newest options. Many of them offer an array of personal services. Some will provide a signed affidavit testifying to the wine's provenance, which can be important in reselling. These facilities often offer the most sophisticated climate-control systems as well as elaborate security systems.

All these extras usually make the wine-only facilities a bit pricier than general storage facilities, but, after all, you get what you pay for. □

Wine Storage Facilities
WO=wine only, RO=retail outlet, GS=general storage

CHICAGO

Kent Cellars *WO.* Open Tuesday to Friday, 4 to 7 p.m. and Saturday 10 a.m. to 6 p.m. Two locker sizes: 16 case/$115 per year and 32 case/$230 per year. A few half-lockers available. (312) 528-5445.

The Strong Box Wine Cellar *WO.* Open Monday to Friday, 9 a.m. to 6 p.m.; Saturday, 10 a.m. to 4 p.m.; Sunday, noon to 4 p.m. $80 per year for eight-case unit minimum, up to 100 cases for $825 per year. (312) 787-2800.

DALLAS

La Cave Warehouse *RO.* Access by appointment only; same day OK. Prices range from $100 per year for a slot holding 12 cases to a locker holding 23 cases for $320 per year. (214) 979-9463.

DENVER

The Vineyard *RO.* Open Monday to Saturday, 9:30 a.m. to 6 p.m. $1 per case per month; five-plus cases are 90 cents per month and 25-plus cases are 75 cents per month. (303) 355-8324.

DETROIT

The Merchant of Vino *RO.* Open Monday to Saturday, 10 a.m. to 7 p.m.; Sunday, noon to 5 p.m. Cages holding up to 150 cases for $600 per year. For smaller amounts, $1 per case per month. (313) 433-3000.

GLENDALE, CALIF.

The Wine Vault Open Tuesday to Saturday, 11 a.m. to 7 p.m. Temperature and humidity controlled. No access fee. Many sizes from $95 to $3,300 per year. Ultra-strong facilities for earthquake protection. (818) 545-9463.

LONG ISLAND

North Fork Wine Storage/Aging Warehouse *WO.* Open Monday to Friday, 8 a.m. to 5 p.m. $1 per case per month. Deposit charge of 45 cents per case. No out charge. 1-800-955-9463.

LOS ANGELES AREA

Trader Joe's *RO.* Open seven days a week from 2 to 6 p.m., except holidays. Four-case locker is $16.80 per year, up to 150-case locker for $630 per year. (818) 990-7751.

The Wine Box *WO.* Open Friday, 4 to 9 p.m.; Saturday, 10 a.m. to 4 p.m., but arrangements can be made for other times. A 12-case locker is $112 per year; 24-case locker is $169 per year; 36-case locker is $218 per year, up to a walk-in holding 150 cases for $874 per

year. Waiting list. (818) 703-0090.

The Wine Cellar *WO.* Open Tuesday to Saturday, 10:30 a.m. to 6:30 p.m.; Sunday, 11:30 a.m. to 5:30 p.m. Minimum 12-case locker is $112, up to walk-ins for $1,700 per year. (213) 477-9463.

The Wine House *RO.* Open Monday to Saturday, 10 a.m. to 7 p.m. $150 per year minimum for a 15-case locker, with varying sizes and prices above that. (213) 479-3731.

The Wine Merchant *RO.* Open Monday to Saturday, 10 a.m. to 6 p.m. Prices range from 16-case locker for $128 per year to a 225-case walk-in for $1,800 per year, with other sizes in between. (213) 278-7322.

NEW YORK CITY

Liberty Warehouse *WO.* Open Monday to Friday, 9 a.m. to 5 p.m. $20 per month per cage holding 15 cases, or $60 per month per cage holding 45 cases. (212) 580-4755.

Morgan Manhattan *WO.* Open Monday to Friday, 8 a.m. to 5 p.m. Advance notice of 24 hours required. $15 per month minimum for up to 11 cases. Beyond that, $1.30 per case per month. $1.75 per case for new deposits, with a $5 minimum. Courier service available for extra charge. (212) 353-8230.

Vintage Wine Warehouse *WO.* Open Monday to Saturday, 9 a.m. to 6:30 p.m. Advance notice of 24 hours required. $1.20 per case per month, $15 minimum. $1.50 per case access charge. Delivery $4 per case. (212) 688-9370.

MIAMI

International Wine Storage *WO.* Open Monday to Saturday, 9 a.m. to 6 p.m.; Sunday, noon to 6 p.m. $25 per month for a shelf holding up to 18 cases. Half-shelves available. (305) 856-1208.

MILLBRAE, CALIF.

La Cave *WO.* Open seven days, 9 a.m. to 6 p.m. $1 per case per month. Minimum 12 cases for 6 months. 1-800-288-4246.

MINNEAPOLIS

Haskell's Inc. *RO.* Open Monday to Thursday, 9 a.m. to 8 p.m.; Friday and Saturday, 9 a.m. to 10 p.m. Prefer 24 hours' notice. $1 per case per month. No access fee for full case withdrawal, but less than that is $5. (612) 544-4456.

NAPA, CALIF.

RCI Wine Warehouse *WO.* Open Monday

to Friday, 8:30 a.m. to 4:30 p.m. Advance notice of 24 hours required. 28-case units, $300 per year. No access charge for monthly withdrawals; otherwise $10 each. (707) 252-8686.

OAKLAND, CALIF.

Subterraneum Private Wine Storage *WO.* Open Tuesday to Saturday 9 a.m. to 4 p.m. 12-16 case locker: $12 per month. Large locker than can hold up to 40 cases: $28 per month. (415) 451-3939.

Walkup Drayage & Warehouse Co. *GS.* Open Monday to Friday, 8 a.m. to 4 p.m. 100 cases, $36 per month; 200 cases, $52 per month; 300 cases, $68 per month. For fewer than 100 cases, inquire. $3.50 withdrawal charge. (415) 444-6093.

PORTLAND, ORE.

Liner & Elsen Wine Merchants Open Monday to Saturday, 10 a.m. to 7 p.m. Three locker sizes: 12 cases/$144, 20 cases/$240, 30 cases/$360 per year. (503) 241-WINE.

SAN FRANCISCO

Connoisseur Wine Imports *RO.* Open Tuesday to Friday, 9:30 a.m. to 6:30 p.m.; Saturday, 10 a.m. to 5 p.m. Many different locker sizes and prices available, including up to 15 cases for $72 for six months and 1,000 cases for $1,400 every six months. (415) 433-0825.

John Walker & Co. *RO.* Open Monday to Friday, 8:30 a.m. to 2:30 p.m. Advance notice of 24 hours required. If purchased from store, $12.50 per case per year for one to nine cases; 10-plus cases is $10 per case per year. Slightly higher if purchased elsewhere. (415) 986-2707.

VAN NUYS, CALIF.

The Wine Locker *WO.* Open Tuesday to Saturday, 2 to 7 p.m. Two locker sizes available: 16 cases for $109 per year and 24 cases for $198 per year. (818) 781-1600.

WASHINGTON, D.C.

Security Storage Co. *GS.* Open Monday to Friday, 8:30 a.m. to 4 p.m. 75 cents per case per month, minimum of $15 a month. Handling charge of 75 cents per case in and out, with a minimum of $8. (202) 797-5610.

The Wine Rack *WO.* Open Tuesday, 6:15 to 7:30 p.m.; Saturday, 10:30 a.m. to 1:30 p.m. One case, $18 per year; 10 cases, $135 per year; 26 cases, $285 per year; 50 cases, $485 per year; 70 cases, $565 per year. (202) 337-7270.

CRESO

King Croesus ruled the ancient nation of Lydia more than 2500 years ago. And yet the legend of Croesus' vast wealth lives with us today. His name still represents that which is rich, exquisite and perfect. Now, the legend lives in Creso. A proprietary wine which rightfully takes its name from that illustrious sovereign.

Bolla's most commanding creation, Creso, has been honored with gold medals at the 1989 VinExpo at Bordeaux and the 1989 Banco d'Assaggio di Torgiano, Italy's most prestigious wine competition.

Rich in color. Exquisite in taste. Perfectly balanced. Live the legend that has been masterfully captured in Creso – the only wine worthy to bear the name of one of history's greatest kings.

BOLLA

Il vino classico d'Italia

The American Protegé of a Champagne Aristocrat

Domaine Carneros
By Taittinger
Carneros, California

Wine-Buying Strategies

REGARDLESS

OF YOUR LEVEL OF

INTEREST IN WINE,

YOU'RE IN FOR FUN

AND CHALLENGES

BY JAMES LAUBE

10 TIPS TO BETTER WINE BUYING

1. Always taste before you buy. Don't get trapped buying what your friends or critics call the best. Trust your own palate. Taste a bottle before you buy six or a case.
2. Diversify your collection. You may have passions for one kind of wine or another, but variety is the spice of life with wine, so shop around for different styles of wines.
3. Shop for values. Go out of your way to look for best buys to get the most mileage out of your wine dollar.
4. Drink your wines before they get too old. Even the most age-worthy reds from Bordeaux or California reach drinkability in 10 years. You've paid good money for your wines; don't let them slide over the hill.
5. Keep costs in perspective. A few fine wines are expensive, but far too many well-made, reasonably prices wines are ignored because they lack the image and prestige of higher-priced wines.
6. Buy wine by the case. Most retailers give you a 10 percent discount—or one bottle free.
7. Beware of last year's superstar. Last year's hero could be this year's goat.
8. Stockpile wines you like so that you don't run out or hesitate to open the last bottle.
9. Investing in futures can be risky business.
10. Assemble your wines with rhyme and reason. Think about your needs before parting with your cash.

If you're new to wine, devising a buying strategy can be as simple as choosing a few brands you like and sticking with them. Or it can be as complex as collecting verticals of the world's greatest wines or buying wine futures, where you pay a discounted price in advance of a wine's delivery.

For many wine drinkers, maintaining brand loyalty is a tried-and-true way to keep your cellar stocked with reliable wines that suit your taste and budget. More daring collectors expand their hobby of wine collecting into a more sophisticated enterprise. They keep tabs on new wines and vintages from old-guard producers in Bordeaux, Burgundy, Italy, Spain or Germany, as well as a watchful eye on up-and-coming producers from the New World, such as California, Oregon, Washington, Australia, New Zealand and Chile.

Regardless of your level of interest in wine, you're in for some fun and challenges. Wine is a living thing and constantly changing. Every year consumers are presented with an endless stream of new wines, producers, appellations and vintages. Even when you find a winery or style of wine that appeals to you, your tastes will likely change with time. You'll also discover something new that appeals to your taste. The combination of possibilities is endless.

Rule No. 1 of buying wine is to trust your own taste. No one knows your taste preferences better than you, so it's important early on to be comfortable deciding which wines you like and which ones you don't. Taste a wine by buying a single bottle before you commit to several bottles or more. The importance of this rule is further magnified for expensive wines. It makes no sense to pay $20, $30 or $40 for a wine you've never tried. There's a big world to choose from, with literally thousands of different wines. Even if your friends or wine critics rave about a wine, there's no guarantee that you'll like it.

Gaining experience with the world's fine wines takes time, but it is a fascinating journey and you'll learn just as much from your mistakes as you will from your triumphs. A great part of the fun of wine is learning where and how it's grown and vinified in different parts of the world, which food types match well with different wines, and which wine types improve with cellaring and bottle age.

Before you start buying wine, it's important to assess your needs. How much wine do you drink and on what occasions? Do you want to cellar young wines for drinking in a few years? You'll also need a budget to determine how much money you can realistically afford to spend on wine. It's easy for some people to identify their wine needs. For others it's wiser to plan a strategy before heading to the wine shop. Remember, it's easier to buy a case of wine than to drink it.

It's also easy to buy more types of wines than you realistically need. Buying wine on a whim can be fun, particularly when you spot a special bottle you've been looking for. But fanciful buying also increases the odds that you'll return home with a wine you may not need for which you may have paid too much. Planning ahead allows you to set aside a specific amount of money for buying wine by the case. Many retailers and wineries offer a 10 percent discount for case purchases.

Discount stores, however, usually pass along the 10 percent discount on all purchases.

Once you've outlined your needs, you'll need a place to shop. Years ago, about the only place to buy fine wine was at the traditional fine-wine merchant. Today your options abound. You see fine wine in scores of discount chain stores and upscale supermarkets, some of which present a dazzling selection of rare, fine wines. Retailers have also become more aggressive with sales promotions, selling wine through ads in newspapers and magazines via telephone and toll-free "800" numbers. A growing list of retailers publish catalogs, especially during the holiday season, offering hundreds of wines and special gift packages. There are even mail order wine-of-the-month clubs. Once you join, the club selects wines for you and ships them to your home for you to sample. Most of the time, though, you'll be purchasing wine at a retail store, so it helps to get to know your local wine stores and merchants, what kinds of wines they stock and their pricing strategies.

A well-informed retailer is an excellent source of sound buying advice and tips about what's new and interesting in his store. Retailers can also come in handy ordering special bottles of wines that may be hard to find. Some retail stores even do the shopping for their customers. When a special wine comes in, they set aside a few bottles or a case and bill the customer, holding the wine until it's picked up.

While you're visiting wine shops, take special notice of how the wines are stored and if the temperature is cool. Light and heat are enemies of wine. Wine shops that are warm or hot in summer months may not be the best place to buy your wines. It's also wise to examine wine bottles to make sure the fill level is good—up to the neck of the bottle—and that wine hasn't leaked through the cork. If wine leaks out, that means air is getting into the bottle and oxidizing the wine. Pass on bottles with low fills or leaks.

As wine gets costlier, it makes greater sense to develop a buying strategy. One fun way to defray costs and taste a broad selection of wines is to join a club or group that tastes wines regularly. This way you can spread out some of the costs and taste expensive wines like Château Lafite-Rothschild, Romanée-Conti, Gaja or Château Yquem. Each member brings a bottle of wine to the tasting and shares it among six, eight or 12 people. Some wine syndicates even order cases of wines together, another way to cut costs (with a 10 percent discount) and broaden your exposure to the world of fine wines.

For those who like to take risks, buying wine futures is one way to obtain hard-to-get wines, presumably at reduced prices. Buying futures works this way: Young unbottled wines are sold at discounted prices through retailers or wineries. Once the wine is bottled and ready for sale, it is delivered to the consumer. Most of the time, consumers pay less for futures and futures can be a good way to obtain hard-to-get wines or larger-sized bottles.

Others buy wine futures for speculation purposes. They hope the price they pay for futures is sufficiently lower than the price on release. If that's true, they can resell the wine at a profit. But there are risks in buying futures. The major danger is that you're buying a wine you haven't tried. Unless you're intimately familiar with the producer, vintage or style of wine, you're gambling. You could also pay more for a wine than is necessary. If the economy sours, the price on release may be far less than anticipated. Finally, in buying futures you may tie up your money with one or two producers and miss out on some of the other bargains once that vintage is released. There's also the possibility that your retailer may go out of business in the mean time, making your wine and your money difficult to recover.

When you're on the road touring wine country, you'll also discover that many wineries have specialty wines or older vintages no longer on the market that they sell only at the winery. Be on the lookout for some of those rarities, but don't necessarily expect to find great bargains. Most wineries give a 10 percent discount on sales, but they mark their wines up to full retail price. You can often find them less expensive at your local retail outlet.

James Laube is a senior editor of The Wine Spectator *and author of two books on California wine.*

THE WORLD ACCORDING TO
RUFFINO

Bring Tuscany home in a bottle.

CONSUMERS COPE BY BUYING LESS
OF THE BEST OR TRADING DOWN
TO LOWER-PRICED CHOICES

Spiraling Prices Put Wine Lovers In a Bind

BY HARVEY STEIMAN

By his own calculations, Chris Tally spends about $12,000 a year on wine. He is an eclectic collector, filling his cellar with French, California, Italian and Australian wines. But now, he says, a trip to the wine shop is not as much fun as it used to be.

"There were very few wines I had to think twice about buying," he says, "but now ..." his voice trails off. "I'm starting to become much more conservative. There is probably a good reason for all these high prices, but I have to say, it feels like they're taking it to us. These prices are just out of proportion."

Tally, 35, says he is thinking hard before spending $25 a bottle on the 1987 vintage of a California Cabernet Sauvignon he used to buy for $11 on sale only three years ago. "I like B.R. Cohn Cabernet, but I'm giving it a pass," he says. He knows 1989 Château Haut-Brion may be the wine of the vintage, but at $1,300 a case for

Harvey Steiman is editor at large of The Wine Spectator.

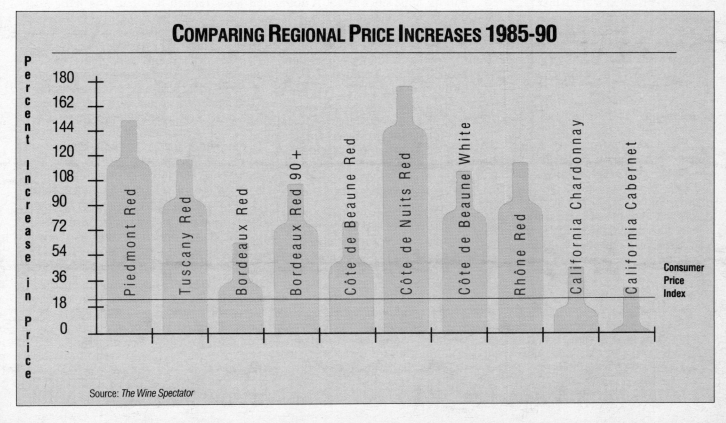

COMPARING REGIONAL PRICE INCREASES 1985-90

Percent Increase in Price

180
162
144
120
108
90
72
54
36
18
0

Piedmont Red
Tuscany Red
Bordeaux Red
Bordeaux Red 90+
Côte de Beaune Red
Côte de Nuits Red
Côte de Beaune White
Rhône Red
California Chardonnay
California Cabernet

Consumer Price Index

Source: *The Wine Spectator*

The average price of a bottle of wine we reviewed rose 43 percent from 1985 through 1990. For outstanding wines, those rated 90 or above, the jump was 52 percent

futures, he has decided to forgo it as well. "The '88 Burgundies I've tasted are great wines, but so far all I've bought is a case of Leroy Vosne-Romanée. It was $72 a bottle."

He limits himself to a few bottles of wines he used to purchase in case lots. And he is looking for alternatives, wines that offer value. "I'm finding I really like German wines," he says. "You can get great things for pretty fair prices."

Tally, who is in the textile business in Los Angeles, readily admits he could live off the contents of his cellar for years without having to replace a single bottle. "But I like to collect things," he says. "I like to be in the wine shops. I like to visit the cellars in wine country. If I could afford it, I would collect Ferraris. I collect antique toys, and I own a lot of books. I just hope I can still afford to collect wine."

Tally's attitude appears to be fairly typical of today's upscale wine consumers—and, on a different scale, all quality-oriented wine drinkers. "People who have cellars full of good vintages can afford to miss the latest hot wine," says Sterling Pratt, wine director of Schaefer's in Chicago. Pratt says his customers look for lower-priced alternatives.

It is no illusion that wine prices are going up. And prices are going up fastest for the best wines.

The average price of a bottle of wine reviewed by *The Wine Spectator* rose 43 percent from 1985 through 1990. For outstanding wines, those rated 90 or above on *The Wine Spectator* 100-point scale, the jump was 52 percent—exactly double the rise in the U.S. urban Consumer Price Index during the same six years.

For this report, *The Wine Spectator* analyzed prices for wines of greatest interest to its readers. This is an atypical view, but we believe it reflects the taste of consumers who are willing to pay higher prices for better quality if necessary. The survey covered prices for 15,236 wines during the calendar years 1985 through 1990.

The most pleasant surprise was the performance of California wines. Despite steep increases among the most highly publicized wines, prices for the 1,926 California bottlings reviewed in 1990 averaged only 31 percent higher than those reviewed in 1985. That rate's just a little faster than inflation over the same period, but it pales next to the big jumps recorded by the top European wines.

Burgundy reds from the Côte de Nuits, for example, have almost tripled in price. Rhône reds have more than doubled. Bordeaux reds scoring 90 or above have doubled. Italian reds from Piedmont have gone up 151 percent, those from Tuscany 120 percent. Spanish wines are up 142 percent. (These figures reflect reviews of 633 Côte de Nuits wines, 331 Rhône reds, 755 Italian reds and 391 Spanish bottlings.)

Blame some of these price increases on a dollar that has lost nearly half its value since 1985. A dollar that bought 9.7 francs in January 1985 sank to 5.1 in January 1991. To put that another way, if French wine prices in francs remained the same, all French wines would cost 90 percent more in dollars.

In 1985, a strong dollar was buying 1982 Bordeaux at prices that made this most highly praised vintage seem almost affordable in retrospect. In 1988, halfway through the dollar's slide, prices for 1985 Bordeaux were 50 percent higher.

The dollar's fluctuations lend perspective to one perplexing aspect of Bordeaux: how a relatively modest vintage such as 1987 can cost more than better vintages. The average price for Bordeaux we reviewed in 1990 (mostly 1987s) was the highest yet. Although prices of individual châteaux's wines were down, the average price still rose slightly. Many lesser châteaux were not imported to the United States, so the ones that arrived tended to be the more expensive bottlings.

Not all of the blame for price increases can be pinned on the falling dollar, however. Even if you take out the effects of the dollar's slide, Côte de Nuits and Piedmont reds have still doubled in price. Tuscan reds are up 67 percent beyond the rise of the lira.

Today, a weak dollar is putting the squeeze on 1988 Bordeaux prices and, even more dramatically, those of the 1988 red Burgundies. Both groups of wines are arriving at their highest prices ever. In the past few months some wine shops were refusing to buy their allotments of 1988 DRC Burgundies as the prices per bottle soared beyond $500.

Too many good vintages from too many regions are backing up in the supply pipeline for prices to remain as high as they are for all wines. The consensus of retailers and wine marketers was that consumers can expect to see prices come down, but it will not be an across-the-board phenomenon.

Traditional market categories do not begin to explain the forces affecting wine prices today. Wine marketers like to talk about premium and super-premium wines, fighting varietals and jug wines, dividing the market into neat price categories. Within each of these categories, some wines always seem to be on sale while others are in short supply.

What really affects prices, therefore, has as much to do with the desirability of any given wine, the reviews it receives from influential publications and the reputation it enjoys in the public's mind. As Larry Seibel of the Wine House in Los Angeles puts it, "If something has a name, they overlook the price."

Heitz Cellars restricts its Martha's Vineyard Cabernet Sauvignon 1986 ($60) to six bottles per customer, while Grgich Hills 1985 (rated 92 by James Laube in his book, *California's Great Cabernets*) can be found on sale for 20 percent or 30 percent off its list price of $20. Beringer Cabernet Sauvignon Private Reserve 1986 was $30 when it was ranked No. 1 in *The Wine Spectator* Top 100 last December. Today it sells for $50 and up.

These are extreme examples, but they illustrate a fact of life for consumers looking for the best quality. The most desirable wines are going to remain pricey and hard to get, especially if they are produced in relatively small quantities. Value-minded consumers will look for wines on the next rung down, wines that earn good ratings but fail to stir up quite as much excitement as the megabuck choices.

Several retailers echoed the observation that savvy wine consumers are buying as much wine as they always have, only trading down to lower-priced choices.

"They're buying down, but they're still buying," reports Don Zacharia, owner of Zachys in Scarsdale, N.Y. "The first-growth customer is buying third growths. We're selling a lot of California wines at around $10 a bottle."

"The person who was asking me for a $15 Chardonnay a year ago is asking me for a $10 Chardonnay today. Last year's $10 Chardonnay is now asking me for something around $7.99," says Seibel. "Last year I was selling cases of items that cost $150 a bottle. This year I have to sell it by the bottle. The average ticket has gone down, but people are still buying."

"The buying pattern is changing from the high-ticket items to the short-term drinking wines," says Shaefer's Sterling Pratt. Pratt pointed to an unusual event his store organized in January. It was a three-day warehouse sale, in which slower-selling wines from the store and from several local distributors were priced low.

"We had Hungarian varietals in magnum for $1.57, Grand-Puy-Lacoste 1986 for $16.97, Warre's 1983 Vintage Port for $16.97, Jaboulet Côte de Ventoux 1988 for $2.97, Bahans-Haut-Brion 1986 [the second label of Château Haut-Brion] for $11.97," recalls Pratt. "Everything was available for tasting. We sent out 17,000 postcards and sold wine to 2,000 people.

"The interesting thing to me was the same people who come in during the week in three-piece suits came to this in jeans, buying 10, 15 cases of wine at a crack," Pratt says. "It remains to be seen how quickly they burn that up and come back for more, but there's no question they're still buying when the price is right."

On the other hand, the same store reports that sales of high-priced 1988 red Burgundies have been brisk. Muses Pratt, "I guess that proves that there are people who will pay any price to get the great wines."

But he also noticed that a Bourgogne rouge or simple village wine from the same producers can sit on the shelf for two or three years before someone finally buys it. That suggests that a person may be willing to pay $75 to $100 for a *grand cru* because it offers something unique. A simple village wine lacks the distinction to make its $25-to-$50 price tag as appealing. Other, less costly wines can fill that need.

And that brings up the issue of how American wines compare in value with European wines. As French and Italian wine prices escalate, many consumers perceive American wines as reasonable alternatives. The top Cabernet Sauvignons seem to be keeping pace with ever-rising Bordeaux prices, while Chardonnays are lagging well behind the faster-rising white Burgundies.

Tempting as it is to suggest that American Cabernets are better than American Chardonnays, the real explanation centers around quantity rather than quality. Many of the best Cabernets are made in limited quantities while big-name Bordeaux châteaux produce 10,000 to 30,000 cases annually. There is plenty of each château's wine to go around, and that at least slows down the inevitable rise in prices. The upward pressure on the limited-production Cabernets can be greater.

Chardonnays, by contrast, come to

market in waves of 10,000 cases or more. On the other side of the Atlantic, few big-name red or white Burgundies exceed 1,000 cases. Demand, therefore, puts more pressure on the supply of each individual Burgundy. With many more cases to sell of each Chardonnay, wineries tend to keep their prices moderate.

"Wineries like Grgich Hills are putting out as much Chardonnay as the entire village of Puligny," says Fred Ek of Classic Wine Imports in Brookline, Mass. For the record, Grgich Hills made 33,000 cases of its 1987 Chardonnay and 20,000 cases its 1988. "That keeps the lid on what you can charge."

That doesn't stop an aggressively priced wine from leading a rush to higher prices. One example that kept coming up in discussions with retailers was Far Niente, whose California Chardonnay is priced at $26.

"Winery representatives keep coming to me with these expensive Chardonnays, and when I complain about the price they point to Far Niente," says Seibel, the Los Angeles retailer. "They say, 'If Far Niente is worth $26, then my wine is worth at least $15 or $20.' If a new winery is releasing a wine at an exorbitant price, I am saying no. Some other store can have the bragging rights."

Pricing a wine high to achieve immediate prestige is a tactic that has gained momentum in the past decade. One of the more prominent examples is Opus One, at the time of its debut in 1983 the most expensive wine in California at $50 a bottle. Ceretto's 1982 Barolo Bricco Rocche Bricco Rocche came out at $100 a bottle, making it the most expensive Italian wine. In Spain, Pesquera debuted a special bottling called Janus at $75.

Although few wines attempted to match these prices, they served as trendsetters. They created a vacuum that gradually filled with more and more aggressively priced bottles.

"That is a spiral that has no end," says Agustin Huneeus, president of Franciscan Vineyards in California. "If I came out with a $100 wine tomorrow, it would be written about. It is a fast way to make an impression.

"This is fine if the market will bear the level we want," he adds. "But I think we have too high a platform for wines in California. Are we telling the consumer that if he wants to drink a reasonably good wine and impress his guests he has to spend $15 for a bottle of Chardonnay? That's crazy."

Huneeus thinks the American wine consumer has become sophisticated enough to prefer a well-made $10 wine to a overly hyped $20 bottle. And that, he believes, may end the dreams of some financially wobbly California wineries. Napa Valley vintners whisper among themselves that as many as 30 wineries may close their doors or sell the farm this year or next.

"Some of these new wineries are based on a calculated risk," explains Huneeus. "They can only pay back their loans if they can get $15 or $18 a bottle for their wines. That's hard to do in a market as crowded as ours. Some of them are going to fail."

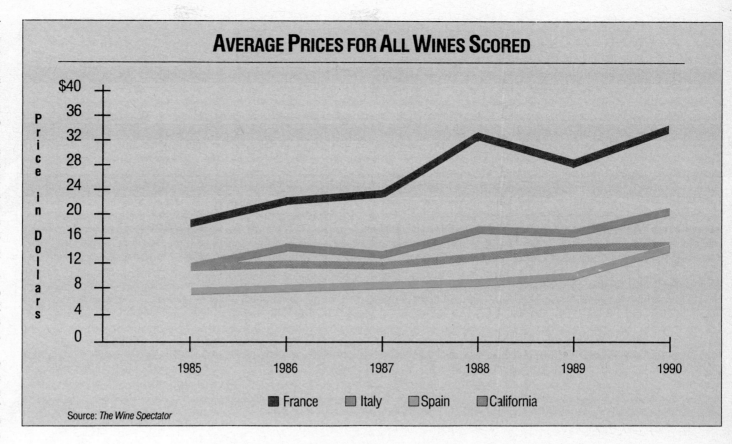

AVERAGE PRICES FOR ALL WINES SCORED

Price in Dollars (y-axis): 0, 4, 8, 12, 16, 20, 24, 28, 32, 36, $40

Years (x-axis): 1985, 1986, 1987, 1988, 1989, 1990

■ France   □ Italy   □ Spain   □ California

Source: *The Wine Spectator*

"If you buy a winery for $40 million, you owe $4 million in debt before you make the first bottle," points out Tony Terlato, president of Paterno Imports in Chicago. But very expensive wines are not priced according to how much it cost to make them, or how much the winery has to pay its bank.

"In a ballpark, there are sky boxes that sell for $1 million and there are bleacher seats that cost $3. The price is not based on how much it cost to build the ballpark. The price is based on how many people are waiting to buy it. I've been to plenty of ball games where there were open seats in the bleachers but the sky boxes were full."

That's the situation in the wine market today. The prestige wines are the sky boxes and the inexpensive jug wines are the bleachers. Prices are dropping on inexpensive wines because demand is falling, while prestige wines keep getting more expensive.

Producers, exporters and importers defend the higher prices as the inevitable result of supply and demand. The market for fine wine has become international. American consumers are competing for a few thousand cases of the best wines with German, Swiss, Japanese, French and British counterparts, all of whose currencies are stronger than the floundering U.S. dollar. Demand outstrips supply, so prices must rise, goes the reasoning.

No one can produce figures to back up this theory, however. On the other side are those who point to the 1988, 1989 and 1990 vintages in the fine-wine regions of Europe. Three ex-. cellent to outstanding vintages in succession should mean that France, Germany and Italy will have an excess of high-quality wine to sell. Theoretically, prices should come down. So far, though, that has not happened.

Ironically, prices for top-shelf wines are rising at the same time that overall demand for wine is falling. The

U.S. table-wine market declined by an estimated 2 percent in volume in 1990, according to *Impact* newsletter. Imports were down 12 percent. If there is a decline in consumption, it seems to be taking place among those who buy lower-priced wines, not among those who stock their cellars with Cabernet and Bordeaux.

"I think it's the sophisticated buyer whose favorite $11 wine has gone up to $17 or $18 who is looking for alternatives," says Terlato. "For the person who is looking for the best wine of the vintage, he's going to buy it whether it is $25, $35 or $45. He'll complain about it, but he wants to own these signature wines."

Terlato has been criticized for raising the price of some of his imported wines. When he took on the Barbarescos of Marchese di Gresy, for example, he doubled the prices. The 1985s are priced at $56 to $66 a bottle.

"I think wine should be priced for what it is," explains Terlato. "When we took on Frescobaldi, they were cutting corners to make price points. I told them to make me wines that I could sell and let me find the markets for them. Now we have some of their wines at $6, some at $12 and some at $20.

"Martinenga [Gresy's vineyard] is a unique property, a monopole, something really special. It deserves to be recognized for what it is."

At least one retailer believes that prestige wines still represent an affordable luxury, even at today's prices.

"Wine stores give American consumers value, and they know it," says N.Y. wine shop owner Zacharia. "That's why they keep buying. It's not like buying an automobile for $75,000. Or even a men's suit for $800. Consumers know they're going to see that same suit on sale for $300 next year. That does not happen with wine. The consumer is smart."

Restaurants report that business has slowed in the past six months as the recession and war jitters dampen

diners' spirits.

"People are buying less of everything—liquor, food and wine," says Raymond Wellington, wine director for the New York Restaurant Group, which includes Smith & Wollensky, the Port House and La Cité. "It's not a dramatic drop, just softer. People are still drinking the same wines they did a year ago, just less of them."

Although most New York restaurants have raised wine prices $1 to $3 a bottle to make up the shortfall, Wellington has kept prices at his restaurants the same. "We're drawing on inventory," he says. "It will be a long time before those wines run out. Anyone investing in wine in January 1991 is either under the care of a therapist or has the only solvent restaurant business this side of the Rockies."

At least one retailer, who did not want to be identified, suggested that a slow time for restaurants means a livelier time for retail shops. "The restaurants' loss is our gain," he says. "Those people are eating at home and maybe they drink a few more bottles of wine because it costs less than it would in a restaurant."

"A small but growing number of people are looking for something different," says Ek, the Brookline, Mass., importer and retailer. "There does seem to be an interest in other wines from France—the Languedoc, Minervois, Anjou, Côteaux de Layon."

German wines, long shunned by American consumers, are beginning to pick up momentum in some circles. Seibel's Los Angeles store offers tasting classes titled "German Wine Without Angst."

"The trick is to get people to taste the wines," says Pratt, whose store ran the giant warehouse sale. "If it's priced right and it tastes good, I just stand back and watch 'em buy."

"You can still buy terrific wines at around $200 a case," says Zacharia. "You give me $200 a case and I'll give you wines that knock your socks off." □

Domecq, Spain's premier wine and spirits family for over 260 years, produces the critically acclaimed Marques de Arienzo wines from Spain's renowned Rioja region.

Because Domecq grows all their own grapes on their own vineyards, they have meticulous control over their quality. This, combined with the expertise and technical innovation of the eighth gene-ration Domecq winemaker, José Ignacio Domecq, Jr., ensures the continued high quality of these fine, elegant wines.

DOMECQ ESTATES

The Ups and Downs of Buying Wine at Auction

DESPITE COMPLICATED BIDDING PROCEDURES, AUCTION NEWCOMERS ENJOY THE THRILL OF THE CHASE

BY THOMAS MATTHEWS

Going going GONE!'' The hammer comes down, and another bidder owns a wine he wants for a price he judges fair. And, if he's lucky, perhaps for less than he expected to spend.

Château Clerc-Milon 1975 for $9 per bottle. Léoville-Barton 1979 for $18. Gruaud-Larose 1970 for $29. These may look like prices from some dusty archive, but all came at recent auctions. Rare old wines can sell for thousands of dollars. But most auctions concentrate on mature wines from reputable producers—the wines most wine drinkers want to drink.

Buying wine at auction, if you are unfamiliar with it, can be complicated compared with shopping in a retail store. Prices can vary widely. It only takes two determined bidders to drive any wine far beyond its real worth. But auctions are the archetype of the free market: No one ever has to pay more than he thinks an object is worth. In addition to scarce wines at fair prices, auctions offer another benefit—the thrill of the chase. That's why new bidders are constantly raising paddles at wine auctions across America, according to auctioneers.

Wine auctions have a short track record here. Regularly scheduled live auctions by established auction houses date only to the mid-1980s. Only two states, California and Illinois, make it legal and practical to hold commercial wine auctions. There are two main players in the United States. Christie's offers six to eight wine auctions per year in Chicago and Los Angeles; Butterfield & Butterfield, in San Francisco and Los Angeles, holds six main sales. In all, they add up to more than 10,000 lots a year. It's enough to turn growing numbers of wine lovers into auction bidders.

AUCTION HOUSES AND HOW THEY WORK

London has always been the center of the wine-auction market in Europe, and Christie's is considered its leading

Thomas Matthews is New York bureau chief of The Wine Spectator.

Auction Prices Take a Tumble

Single-bottle prices for auctions in London and San Francisco in June and July 1991

		LATEST RESULTS		PAST AVERAGES		
	House	Bottles Sold	Price	Jan.-May 1991	1990	1989
BORDEAUX						
'47 Cheval Blanc	Christie's	3	$ 822	$1,078	$ 804	$ 753
'61 Gruaud-Larose	Christie's	12	140	161	172	145
'61 Lafite	Butterfield	5	253	340	374	319
'61 Lynch-Bages	Sotheby's	9	89	138	162	142
'61 Margaux	Butterfield	6	293	334	349	295
'61 Mouton	Sotheby's	11	380	461	461	387
'61 Palmer	Christie's	12	308	342	420	333
'61 Pétrus	Christie's	2	1,324	1,511	1,233	1,194
'75 La Mission	Butterfield	4	236	233	221	174
'82 Lafite	Sotheby's	12	104	124	126	100
'82 Latour	Christie's	36	123	122	123	99
'82 Léoville	Christie's	24	61	66	67	51
'82 Mouton	Christie's	56	129	140	143	115
'85 Margaux	Christie's	36	52	64	62	55
'85 Mouton	Christie's	36	53	66	66	58
PORT						
'77 Dow	Christie's	120	$ 26	$ 31	$ 35	$ 32
'77 Fonseca	Sotheby's	72	34	43	45	47
'77 Taylor Fladgate	Christie's	120	37	46	46	43
CALIFORNIA CABERNET SAUVIGNON						
'68 BV Private Res.	Butterfield	4	$ 110	$ 98	$ 134	$ 134
'68 Mondavi Unfined	Butterfield	8	52	46	NA	65
'78 Diamond Creek Volcanic Hill	Butterfield	12	69	71	62	48
'78 Heitz Martha's Vineyard	Butterfield	23	72	90	81	52
'82 Spottswoode	Butterfield	11	95	79	NA	NA
'82 Mondavi Reserve	Christie's	12	29	24	NA	17

Butterfield & Butterfield sales held in San Francisco; Sotheby's and Christie's sales held in London. May-June 1991, 1990, 1989 prices are averages of sales from all houses. Prices include 10 percent buyer's premium. ''NA'' means price not available.

SOURCE: *THE WINE SPECTATOR*

auction house. James Christie included wine in his first auction, in 1766, and it remained an important element in English sales through the 19th century. After a pause due to the world wars, Christie's revived wine auctions in 1966 with a separate wine department headed by J. Michael Broadbent, who is still firmly in charge.

Christie's holds a variety of regularly scheduled wine auctions in London. The most important venue is King Street, where twice-monthly sales serve as the stock market of wine, establishing what amount to commodity prices for the most widely traded wines. Many wine merchants buy and sell there, so the chances of great bargains are slim. In the 1990-1991 auction season, which runs from September through July, King Street sold almost 12,500 lots, each lot an average of 1.5 cases, for a total of nearly $8 million.

Christie's also covers the high and low ends of the market. Their finest and rarest sales may include 18th-century rarities such as the 1787 Lafite-Rothschild, which may once have belonged to Thomas Jefferson. It sold for $156,000 in 1985, still a world record for a single bottle. Regular sales in South Kensington, London, cater to a more casual crowd, and feature smaller lots of everyday wines. This more accessible market grew 15 percent this year, according to Christie's, who see it as an indication that the consumer base for wine auctions is continuing to grow.

Christie's main U.K. competitor is Sotheby's, whose wine department is directed by author and merchant Serena Sutcliffe. Sutcliffe joined Sotheby's late in 1990 replacing Patrick Grubb. She has oriented the sales more toward consumers, offering many mixed and smaller lots, and adding her own tasting notes to many wines.

There are smaller auction houses based in the United Kingdom that offer periodic wine sales, such as Phillips in Oxford. Wine auctions are also held in many European countries; Christie's organizes regular sales in Geneva and Amsterdam.

Prices for certain categories of wines, such as vintage Port, generally run lower in European markets than in U.S. auctions. But the logistics and expenses of transporting wine overseas are daunting. Shipping adds $50 or more to each case of wine, and there is much obligatory and confusing paperwork. When the dollar is exceptionally strong against foreign currencies, however, Americans may find it worthwhile to bid abroad. If so, it may be advisable to store the wine where it is purchased until it is either resold or can be consolidated into larger, less expensive shipments.

For the most part, however, and especially for beginners, U.S. sales probably offer the best introduction to wine auctions.

Christie's U.S. wine operation is based in Chicago and run by Michael Davis. Its six-to-eight sales a year generally alternate between Chicago and Los Angeles. The sales are large, often running over 1,200 lots. Most of the stock comes from private collectors, though retailers and restaurateurs are

What's a Wine Worth?
Lowest 1990 price per bottle

	AUCTIONS			RETAIL	
	Christie's Chicago	Butterfield & Butterfield	Christie's London	New York	California
1983 Château d'Yquem	$165	$174	$148	$185	$179
1982 Château la Mission Haut-Brion	$ 86	$ 71	$ 62	$ 65	$ 68
1978 Beaulieu Private Reserve	$ 58	$ 32	$ 35	$ 45	$ 40
1977 Graham's Vintage Port	$ 48	$ 58	$ 32	$ 45	$ 54
1970 Château Lafite-Rothschild	$108	$ 90	$122	$200	$150

other sources. Most of the buyers are consumers, according to Davis. In the 1990-1991 season, Christie's Chicago sold 4,500 lots for more than $3.3 million.

Butterfield & Butterfield, a smaller auction house based in San Francisco, offers an average of six wine auctions a year. Bruce Kaiser is director of the wine department, which had sales of around $1 million in 1990-1991. Butterfield's also holds regular auctions of more affordable wines at its Butterfield's West location. The sales are held in San Francisco; major auctions are simulcast in Los Angeles.

Very few other options are open to Americans who want to buy or sell wine at auction. The Chicago Wine Company, which specializes in silent auctions and also operates as a retail outlet, holds two live auctions a year. In 1990, it staged a live commercial auction in Boston, which may lead to other commercial auctions in Massachusetts.

The procedures for either buying or selling wine at auction are simple in concept but more complicated in detail. The auction houses themselves are the best sources of information for interested wine buffs. But here is an outline of the process.

Collectors who want to sell will generally contact the auction houses directly, usually with a list of the wines they want to sell. If the auction house is interested, a more formal inventory and appraisal will be made. The auction house may assist with packing and transportation, but most costs are generally borne by the seller. A reserve price is set, below which the auction house will not sell the wines, and a description of the wines along with an estimate is entered in the catalog. The seller agrees to pay the auction house a commission, usually 15 percent but sometimes negotiable, on the hammer price of any wines sold.

Catalogs are sent worldwide to collectors and trade members. Several hundred may actually attend the auction, while others will bid over the telephone or by mail. Absentee buyers will specify lot numbers and maximum bids. The auctioneers will bid for them, promising not to bid higher than necessary to win the lot, or dropping out if the maximum is reached. Successful bidders agree to pay a buyer's premium, usually 10 percent, to the auction house as a commission.

The wines are then personally picked

up or shipped to the purchaser. Buyers who live close enough to the auction houses to pick up their own wines have few problems. Those who require shipping, especially out of state, will find the logistics more difficult.

The laws regulating the sale and transport of alcoholic beverages are complicated, and while auction houses can help make arrangements for transportation and the legal paperwork, the buyer is responsible for final legal clearance and all charges. Charges range from $25 to $50 or more per case, depending on distance and method and speed of shipment. About half the buyers at any given U.S. auction are from out-of-state, and many of those are out of the country, so the barriers can be overcome.

Charity wine auctions are increasing even more rapidly than commercial auctions. More and more organizations are turning to wine auctions, often accompanied by tastings and gala dinners, to raise money for such causes as cancer research, special schools and cultural organizations. Some have developed into premier social events in their communities and raise hundreds of thousands of dollars. Others are more low-key. Charity auctions permit donors and buyers to take limited tax deductions related to the value of the wines. Prices are generally higher than normal market value, but some special bottles, such as large-format, specially etched limited editions, are only available in such settings.

The wine-auction scene is relatively young and still underdeveloped in America, but in contrast to many aspects of the wine market, it continues to grow.

The Wine Spectator regularly provides full coverage of this dynamic area in its Auction News section, which includes regular reports of both commercial and charity auctions, in-depth market analysis and a full calendar of events. Wine auctions can't satisfy all the needs of most wine buffs, but they offer an alternative market that can supply fine wines at reasonable prices and spice the purchase with the thrill of the chase.

BUYING AND SELLING AT AUCTION

Auctions are poor sources for many wines, but excellent places to buy some of the wines connoisseurs want most.

Variety is not an auction's strong suit. The only white wines regularly offered at auction are top Burgundies,

WINE AUCTIONS CAN'T SATISFY ALL THE NEEDS OF MOST WINE BUFFS, BUT THEY OFFER AN ALTERNATIVE MARKET THAT CAN SUPPLY FINE WINES AT REASONABLE PRICES AND SPICE THE PURCHASE WITH THE THRILL OF THE CHASE

vintage Champagnes, dessert wines and California Chardonnays. Red wines from various countries, such as Australia and Spain, rarely appear at auction. Country wines, "fighting varietals," and wines made for early drinking are also uncommon in most auction catalogs.

Auctions concentrate on the wines that make up the heart of most wine cellars: Bordeaux, vintage Port, red Burgundy, California Cabernet Sauvignon. These wines make up 80 percent to 90 percent of an average sale. The rest will be red Rhônes, other red California varietals, old Madeira and an occasional surprise such as vintage Tokay.

Within these few red- and white-wine categories, however, there is plenty of variety and depth. A recent sale offered 20 vintages of Lafite, from 1854 to 1981. Another included 28 different Bordeaux from the fine, relatively inexpensive 1979 vintage. While most retail stores might offer one or two young vintages of Heitz Martha's Vineyard Cabernet Sauvignon, one of California's most collectible wines, a sale in June 1991 offered a dozen, from 1967 to 1980.

The rare wines bring high prices and wide publicity. The 1854 Lafite sold for $3,520, well above the $2,420 another bottle from that vintage fetched earlier in the year. It probably made a tidy profit for the seller and filled a difficult hole for some collector.

Most prices are more accessible. The average lot at Butterfield & Butterfield sells for around $350 for about 10 bottles, roughly $35 per bottle. Many wines sell for less. Caymus Zinfandel 1978 at $14 per bottle, 1980 Mondavi Cabernet Reserve at $22 and 1979 Ducru-Beaucaillou at $32 are all near or below the release prices for current vintages. In effect, the auction buyer is getting their tasting track records and the carrying costs of maturing them for free.

There are risks in buying at auction. The condition of older wines is crucial to quality, and poor storage can ruin the best wine. Without a physical inspection—which is rarely possible for auction stock—the buyer is gambling on the purchase. Most retailers will take back a bad bottle. Auction house policy is "buyer beware." Most catalogs are conscientious in listing any visible problems with ullage level, label quality or other defects, and will trumpet an impeccable provenance. But the older the wine, the more fragile it is. Buyers should make every effort to learn as much as they can about the wine's condition and storage history.

Of course there are no buyers without sellers. In general, U.S. law doesn't make it easy for a wine collector to change his mind. Once he's bought the wine, he's stuck with it. Only a few states permit a private individual to sell wines to a local retailer, and sales among private individuals are generally prohibited. Bottles donated to charity, to some degree, are eligible for tax write-offs, but overall, wine is hardly an asset with liquidity.

THE CURRENT MARKET

Before a bidder ever raises his paddle, he should study the state of the wine market, becoming familiar with both current auction and retail prices for the wines they want to buy.

The bulk of the wine on offer, and the most consistent prices, will be claret, the red wines of Bordeaux. While prewar, and even pre-phylloxera, wines are not uncommon at auction, the majority of the claret will come from good vintages over the past twenty years. In England, wines as young as 1986 and 1987 are occasionally offered, but legal restrictions in the United States keep younger wines mostly off the auction market.

This year has seen little increase in most Bordeaux prices, and many vintages have lost value. Comparing auction prices from 1990 and 1991 for vintages from 1945 to 1986, Château

1981 Bordeaux
Auction Price Appreciation
Average Price Per Bottle

	1989	1990	1991	Change 1989-1991
Lynch-Bages	$22	$25	$33	50%
Haut-Brion	41	47	57	39%
Pichon-Lalande	30	37	42	40%
Léoville Las-Cases	27	31	36	33%
Mouton-Rothschild	48	51	48	0%
Cos d'Estournel	26	26	27	3%

SOURCE: *THE WINE SPECTATOR*

Latour, one of wine's true blue-chip stocks, saw average prices decrease for 17 vintages and increase for only three. Margaux slipped in 17 out of 21 years and Pichon-Lalande in 11 of 17. This is bad news for impatient speculators banking on rapid returns, but good news for wine lovers who plan to drink what they buy.

The highest-priced recent vintages for Bordeaux are 1982, 1975 and 1970, and even these are trading at or below the offering prices for 1989 futures from the same châteaux. Because of the phenomenal succession of high-quality, high-quantity harvests since 1979, the prices for other vintages have tended to flatten out. Even though their original release prices varied considerably, the 1979, '81, '83, '85 and '86 vintages of any given estate are all trading for roughly similar prices. For example, 1991 average auction prices for Léoville-Las Cases, per bottle, run like this: '79—$32, '81—$34, '83—$26, '85—$30 and '86—$37.

Vintage Port is a puzzle. It represents only a tiny fraction of total Port production, the very best of the best. It's offered at prices that compare favorably to equivalent Bordeaux, and lives for decades. Yet its market has all but collapsed. Prices have not moved, except downward, for three years in England. Tighter supplies in the United States result in higher prices, but appreciation is still slow and chancy.

According to *The Wine Spectator* auction database, no widely traded Port vintage rose in price from 1990 to 1991. The 1963s, one of the top vintages of the century and now at its peak, dropped an average of 18 percent on the year. The 1977s, another classic vintage with decades of life left, slipped 11 percent. The only Port brand that showed consistent appreciation over the past year is Nacional from Quinta do Noval. Only about 200 cases of Nacional are produced in any declared vintage, from a tiny plot of old, ungrafted vines. It rarely comes up at auction, but could be considered an investment-grade wine. Few others, despite their undoubted quality, can make the same claim.

California Cabernet Sauvignons present the least predictable market of all the major auction categories. The track record is too short and the buyer base too small to keep prices in consistent patterns. The wines are almost never traded in London, the heart of the auction market, but appear frequently in the U.S. auction catalogs.

Among the best-known wineries, Heitz has shown the strongest growth. Its Martha's Vineyard bottlings command prices that range from $50 per bottle for the 1980 to more than $300 for the fully mature 1968. Most vintages trade for significantly higher prices now than they did in 1989.

Prices for other producers have been more erratic. Even big, reliable wineries such as Beaulieu and Mondavi have not achieved consistent appreciation at auction. On the other hand, smaller, newer estates sometimes catch fire and prices skyrocket. Forman 1985 shot from $32 per bottle in 1990 to $53 this year. Dunn and Spottswoode have also achieved impressive growth. It's too early to know, however, if they can maintain these levels, or whether this growth is due to speculative fever.

No summary can do justice to the wide range of other wines and spirits offered at auction. A wine buff devoted to Vega Sicilia or Vosne-Romanée or Veuve Clicquot should follow the sales, taste as many wines as possible, and submit conservative bids hoping that lightning will strike. These wines may or may not show rapid appreciation, but a timely bid may stock one's cellar at very attractive prices.

Does it make sense to approach wine as an investment? Can auctions serve buyers who are looking principally for financial return on resale, hoping cases will outperform other collectibles or the consumer index?

No one can guarantee that prices will rise. Wine is particularly risky because it varies so much. In any given vintage, some producers will outperform others, and these variations may not become apparent for some time. Every vintage follows its own pattern of development. Only the longest-lived have a real chance for significant appreciation. Even a great wine in a great vintage will vary from bottle to bottle, depending primarily on storage conditions, but also on chance factors such as the condition of the original cork. And the structure of the wine market also works against the speculator, because the laws regarding trade are so complex that the market is kept relatively limited and static.

Despite these obstacles, however, many wines have outperformed the inflation rate. Some have shown stronger appreciation than other collectibles, such as coins or even gold, over specific periods. And a few have been

bonanzas for early buyers. A case of Château Latour 1961 could have been purchased for about $100 as a futures offering in 1963. Today, the average case price is $6,000, and sales of wines from particularly good provenance have reached $10,000 per case. Château Mouton-Rothschild 1982 was initially offered at around $60 per bottle; it now sells for $130.

We at *The Wine Spectator* believe that wine's primary purpose is for drinking. A careful buyer can realize significant savings by buying at auction, either by purchasing wines relatively young and cellaring them, or by finding undervalued older wines for current consumption. If prices subsequently rise, the satisfaction of financial growth can intensify the pleasure of the palate. □

THERE ARE RISKS IN BUYING AT AUCTION. THE CONDITION OF OLDER WINES IS CRUCIAL TO QUALITY, AND POOR STORAGE CAN RUIN THE BEST WINE. WITHOUT A PHYSICAL INSPECTION—WHICH IS RARELY POSSIBLE FOR AUCTION STOCK —THE BUYER IS GAMBLING ON THE PURCHASE

MASI

MASI
BARDOLINO 1988

MASI
SOAVE 1989

MASI
VALPOLICELLA 1988

REVOLUTIONIZING THE ART OF VERONESE WINE MAKING

PATERNO IMPORTS

Choosing a Wine for Dinner

THE FIRST

THING TO

REMEMBER

ABOUT MATCHING

FOOD AND WINE

IS TO FORGET

THE RULES

BY HARVEY STEIMAN

PHOTO BY RICK MARIANI / STYLING BY ROBERT SKOTNICKI

T he first thing to remember about matching food and wine is to forget the rules. Forget about shoulds and shouldn'ts. Forget about complicated systems for selecting the right wine with the food on the table. This is not rocket science. It's common sense. Follow your intincts.

The most important rule is to choose a wine that you want to drink by itself. Despite all the hoopla about matching wine and food, you will probably drink most of the wine without the benefit of food—either before the food is served or after you've finished your meal. Therefore, you will not go too far wrong if you make sure the food is good and the wine is, too. Even if the match is not perfect, you will still have an enjoyable wine to drink.

Some of today's food-and-wine pontificators suggest that mediocre wines can be improved by serving them with the right food. The flaw in that reasoning, however, is the scenario described above. If the match does not

quite work as well as you hope, you're stuck with a mediocre wine. So don't try to get too fancy. First pick a good wine.

As for which (good) wine to choose, that's where common sense comes in. The old rule about white wine with fish and red wine with meat made perfect sense in the days when white wines were light and fruity and red wines were tannic and weighty. But today, when most California Chardonnays are heavier and fuller-bodied than most California Pinot Noirs, and even some Cabernets, color coding does not always work.

Color affects the food matchup only on two counts: tannins—many red wines have them, few white wines do—and flavors. Although white and red wines share many common flavors, both can be spicy, buttery, leathery, earthy or floral. But the apple, pear and citrus flavors in many white wines seldom show up in reds, and the currant, cherry and stone fruit flavors

of red grapes usually do not appear in whites.

In the wine-and-food matching game, these flavor differences come under the heading of subtleties. You can make better wine choices by focusing on a wine's size and weight. Like human beings, wines come in all dimensions. To match them with food, it's useful to know where they fit in a spectrum, with the lightest wines at one end and fuller-bodied wines toward the other end.

A SPECTRUM OF WINES

To help put the world of wines into perspective, consult the following lists, which arrange many of the most commonly encountered wines into a hierarchy based on size, from lightest to weightiest. If you balance the wine with the food by choosing one that will seem about the same weight as the food, you raise the odds dramatically that the match will succeed.

Yes, purists, some Champagnes

Choose a full-bodied white wine with lots of concentration to match black bean-goat cheese tortillas, above

are more delicate than some Rieslings and some Sauvignon Blancs are bigger than some Chardonnays, but we're trying to paint with broad strokes here for a reason. When you're searching for a lightish wine to go with dinner, pick one from the top end of the list. When you want a bigger wine, look toward the end.

Selected dry and off-dry white wines, lightest to weightiest:
Soave, Orvieto
Off-dry German wines (other than Riesling)
Off-dry Riesling (United States, Australian, German)
Dry Riesling (Alsace, United States)
Muscadet
Champagne
Chenin Blanc (including Vouvray)

HEARTY FOOD NEEDS A HEARTY WINE, BECAUSE IT WILL MAKE A LIGHTER WINE TASTE INSIPID

PHOTO BY RICK MARIANI; STYLING BY ROBERT SKOTNICKI

Pouilly-Fumé, Sancerre
French Chablis (and other unoaked
    Chardonnays)
U.S. Sauvignon Blanc
White Bordeaux
Gavi
Mâcon (including Pouilly-Fuissé)
U.S. Gewürztraminer
Alsace Gewürztraminer
California barrel-fermented or
    barrel-aged Chardonnay
Meursault, Puligny-Montrachet,
    Chassagne-Montrachet
White Rhône

Selected red wines, lightest to
    weightiest:
Beaujolais
Valpolicella
Dolcetto
Burgundy Côte de Beaune
Rioja
St.-Emilion, Pomerol
California Pinot Noir
Burgundy Côte de Nuits
Italian, U.S. Barbera
Chianti Classico
Washington Merlot
California Merlot
Zinfandel
California, Washington Cabernet
Rhône, U.S. Syrah
Barbaresco
Brunello di Montalcino
Barolo

More common sense: Hearty food
needs a hearty wine, because it will
make a lighter wine taste insipid. With

lighter food, you have more leeway.
Lighter wines will balance nicely, of
course, but heartier wines will still
show you all they have. Purists may
complain that full-bodied wines ''over-
whelm'' less hearty foods, but the truth
is that anything but the blandest food
still tastes fine after a sip of a
heavyweight wine.

These are the secrets behind some
of the classic wine-and-food matches.
Muscadet washes down a plate of
oysters because it's just weighty
enough to match the delicacy of a raw
bivalve. Cabernet complements lamb
chops or roast lamb because they're
equally vigorous. Pinot Noir or
Burgundy makes a better match with
roast beef because the richness of texture is the same in both.

To make your own classic matches,
follow the same path as the first person who tried Muscadet with oysters.
Try a dry Champagne or a dry Riesling, which are on either side of
Muscadet on our weight list, for a
similar effect. Don't get stuck on
Cabernet with lamb. Try Zinfandel or
Côtes du Rhône. Instead of Burgundy
or Pinot Noir with roast beef, try a little St.-Emilion or Barbera. That's the
way to put a little variety into your wine
life without straying too far from the
original purpose.

At this point, let us interject a few
words about sweetness. Some wine
drinkers recoil at the thought of drinking an off-dry wine with dinner, in-
sisting that any hint of sweetness in a

wine destroys its ability to complement
food. In practice, nothing can be further from the truth. How many
Americans drink sweetened iced tea
with dinner? Lemonade? Or sugary
soft drinks? Why should wine be different? The secret is balance. So long
as a wine balances its sugar with
enough natural acidity, a match can
work. This opens plenty of avenues for
fans of German Rieslings, Vouvrays
and White Zinfandel.

One of the classic wine-and-food
matches is Sauternes, a sweet dessert
wine, with *foie gras*—which blows the
sugarphobes' theory completely. The
match works because the wine builds
richness upon richness. The moral of
the story is not to let some arbitrary
rules spoil your fun. If you like a wine,
drink it with food you like, and you're
bound to be satisfied.

The following examples put these
wine-and-food ideas into practice. The
recipes are selected from recent *Wine
Spectator* Menus, a monthly feature in
which we taste a variety of wines with
fresh and original dishes to identify the
wines that perform best.

Match 1: OFF-DRY WHITE

In this dish, an off-dry white wine
offers a combination of sweetness, fruit
flavors and crisp texture that fits a
rustic salad of green beans, white beans
and sweet grilled onions. It's precise-
ly the light sweetness of a California
Chenin Blanc that made the match in
a July 1990 menu. Drier wines lose out

**Above, braised short ribs and
full-bodied reds make an extraordinary
combination**

to the sweetness of the onions.

GRILLED RED ONION AND BEAN SALAD

1 pound fresh Blue Lake green beans
1 can (15 ounces) small white beans
    or flageolets
1/3 cup extra virgin or virgin olive oil
2 tablespoons balsamic vinegar
1 to 2 tablespoons chopped fresh
    tarragon
Salt, pepper to taste
1 large, flattish red onion, 8 to 10
    ounces

Trim the ends off the green beans
and cut them into 1-1/2-inch lengths.
Bring a large pot of water to a boil, add
2 teaspoons salt per quart, and boil the
green beans 5 minutes. Drain them
well and cool them quickly under cold
running water.

Drain and rinse the canned beans
well. In a large bowl, combine the
green beans and white beans. Toss with
1/4 cup of the oil and the remaining ingredients, except the onion, and let
them marinate at least 1 hour.

Peel the onion and cut off the stem
and flower ends. Cut it crosswise into
1/2-inch slices. If you are using a
barbecue grill for anything else, grill
the onions before you cook the re-
mainder of the food. Brush the onion
slices with some of the olive oil,

SELLING THE WINE SPECTATOR SELLS WINE
See How We're The Talk Of The Trade

"It's the most informative, up-to-date periodical on wine there is. My customers buy the SPECTATOR's recommendations."

Mike Goldstein, Park Avenue Liquor Shop, New York, N.Y.

"We've never had a publication anywhere close to the quality of THE WINE SPECTATOR. Our customers buy based on the SPECTATOR's recommendations."

Steve Wallace, Wally's, Los Angeles, California

"We find THE WINE SPECTATOR to be an excellent aid for selling. Our customers read about wines and in turn buy them from us."

Larry Shapiro, Marty's, Dallas, Texas

"An informed wine customer buys more wine. THE WINE SPECTATOR is a major part of our in-store marketing and merchandising."

Fred Rosen, Sam's , Chicago, Illinois

*I*t's a proven fact: the more informed your customers are about wine, the more they'll buy.

So why not whet your customers' appetite with America's most informative wine publication: THE WINE SPECTATOR. Each big issue has sparkling articles on how to select, store and serve fine wines, and the latest news in the wine industry. Better still, our Buying Guide includes ratings, tasting notes and recommendations to drive up sales.

When you offer THE WINE SPECTATOR, you'll make money on every issue you sell — but that's just the beginning. Because readers of THE WINE SPECTATOR buy more wine, more often. And that means more wine profits for you.

GET A FREE DISPLAY RACK!
Increase sales when you display THE WINE SPECTATOR. Stores ordering 12 or more copies will receive — **FREE** — an attractive plexiglass counter rack. Or, we'll provide a clip strip — **also free of charge**— for hanging issues on a wine rack or shelf.

Join over 1500 retailers who successfully sell THE WINE SPECTATOR in their stores. Minimum purchase is five copies. You are billed, in advance, on a quarterly basis.

To order, or for more information, call Christine Carroll or Gaby Spelda at **1-800-344-0763**

10 Food-and-Wine Ideas

from selected Wine Spectator *Menus*

FETTUCCINE WITH RED PEPPERS AND ONIONS
Bonfio Chianti Riserva La Portine 1985
(4/15/90)

LOBSTER CHUNKS AND ASPARAGUS
Dauvissat-Camus Chablis Premier Cru La Forest 1988
(6/15/91)

PROSCIUTTO-WRAPPED PRAWNS
Ca' Ronseca Collio del Friuli Sauvignon Podere di Ipplis 1989
(5/15/91)

LOBSTER POT STICKERS
Château Ste. Michelle Gewürztraminer Columbia Valley 1989
(9/15/90)

RISOTTO WITH SCALLOPS AND ASPARAGUS
Jermann Chardonnay de Friuli Venezia Giulia 1989
(5/15/91)

SEA BASS BAKED IN WHITE WINE
Terruzi & Puthod Terre di Tufo 1989
(5/15/91)

ROAST SQUAB IN PORT WINE SAUCE
Leroy Chambertin 1980
(10/15/90)

CANTONESE ROAST DUCK
Clos du Bois Cabernet Sauvignon Briarcrest 1986
(9/15/90)

LAMB STEW WITH WHITE BEANS AND GARLIC
Marcel Martin Chinon Les Bernières 1989
(6/15/91)

GRILLED TENDERLOIN OF BEEF
Paul Jaboulet Crozes-Hermitage Domaine Thalabert 1988
(7/15/90)

---

sprinkle with salt and brown them lightly on both sides, about 5 minutes per side. Or brush the slices with some of the olive oil and broil them in the oven until they char slightly. Cut the slices in quarters and toss them with the beans. Makes 6 to 8 servings.

Match 2: FULL-BODIED WHITE

One of the pervasive myths about wine is that it is too fragile to drink with spicy food. This next dish exposes that lie. Extremely hot and spicy dishes may go better with beer (or just water) but if the dish is balanced toward the mild or medium end of the spectrum, richer, fuller-bodied wines can stand up to them quite well.

The key to finding a Chardonnay to match with this dish (from a March 1991 menu featuring Southwestern American food), is intensity of flavor.

Save the delicate, floral Chardonnays for another occasion. Choose something with lots of concentration. A wine with ripe fruit was especially good with the dusky flavors of the food. Earthier flavors in other wines tended to turn spicy, not bad, but we liked the fruit better.

BLACK BEAN-GOAT CHEESE TORTILLAS

6 corn tortillas
4 tablespoons vegetable oil
3 cups cooked black beans (see note)
1 teaspoon diced serrano chile
1/2 teaspoon ground cumin
1/2 to 1 cup liquid from the black beans
Salt to taste
6 ounces fresh goat cheese (chèvre)
Cilantro cream (recipe below)

Fry the tortillas for 15 to 20 seconds each in 2 tablespoons of the oil in a skillet. Drain them well on paper and arrange them in a single layer on a baking sheet. Discard the oil.

Purée the black beans with the serrano chile and cumin. Season with salt to taste. In the remaining 2 tablespoons oil, cook the black bean purée for 2 to 3 minutes, just until the oil is absorbed. Add the reserved bean liquid to keep the beans moist. Don't let the mixture become too dry.

Preheat the broiler. Divide the bean mixture among the six tortillas. Crumble the goat cheese and divide among the tortillas as well. Broil 1 to 2 minutes, or just enough to melt the goat cheese. Transfer the tortillas to individual plates. Finally, drizzle some of the cilantro cream over the tortillas in a zigzag pattern. Garnish with additional cilantro sprigs. Makes 6 servings.

CILANTRO CREAM

1/3 cup whipping cream
3 tablespoons finely chopped cilantro (fresh coriander leaf)
Salt to taste
Pinch of cayenne
2 tablespoons cream cheese

In a blender or food processor, make a purée of all the ingredients. Put the mixture in a squeeze bottle (like the kind used for ketchup and mustard).

Match 3: LIGHT TO MEDIUM REDS

Here is a good dish to show off all sorts of red wines. In sampling a variety of wines for the May 1990 menu featuring the wines and foods of Tuscany, the pork in the following recipe brings out the fruit in a firm and spicy Chianti Rufina, emphasizes the juicy fruity flavors in a single-vineyard Chianti, smoothes the edges of a tannic and leathery Brunello di Montalcino Riserva and lets a barrique-aged Sangiovese show off its oak flavors and rich tannins. Try it with a light- to medium-bodied red and see what emerges.

MARINATED ROAST PORK

1 pork rib or loin roast, about 3 pounds
1/2 to 2/3 bottle red wine
2 onions, roughly sliced
4 to 6 cloves garlic, crushed
3 bay leaves, crumbled
1/2 bunch fresh sage (about 3 dozen leaves), crumbled
1/4 cup extra virgin olive oil
Salt, freshly ground pepper

Combine all the ingredients except the salt and pepper in a large glass, enamel or stainless steel bowl. Let the meat marinate in this mixture at room temperature for one to two hours, or longer in the refrigerator. For best flavor, marinate overnight.

Remove the pork from the marinade and preheat the oven to 450 degrees Fahrenheit. Place the pork on a rack in a roasting pan. Dry it well with paper towels and season it lightly with salt and more generously with pepper. Strain about 2 cups of the marinade into the bottom of the pan.

Place the pan in the preheated oven and lower the temperature to 350 degrees. Roast the pork approximately 80 to 90 minutes, or until the internal temperature reaches at least 150 degrees. Let the roast stand at least 20 minutes before carving. Serves six.

While the roast is resting, strain and defast the juices left in the roasting pan. Dilute with veal broth, chicken broth or water to make 1 cup. Moisten the slices of pork with this juice.

Match 4: FULL-BODIED, MATURE REDS

When you want to show off a mature, full-bodied red wine, such as a 12- or 15-year-old California Cabernet Sauvignon, the best course to follow is to make the food as simple and elegant as possible. Following that reasoning, braised short ribs would not be the first thought. For some such a dish may not seem fancy enough, but in devising a menu for mature Cabernets (February 1991), the combination turned out to be extraordinary.

To make the short ribs look a little fancier, we devised a simple presentation that looks dramatic but is easy to execute. Rest the ribs on a bed of sautéed cabbage and surround them with noodles dressed with butter and grated Parmesan cheese. The ribs can be prepared a day ahead and reheated for the meal, which makes them especially convenient.

SHORT RIBS BRAISED IN CABERNET

6 pounds beef short ribs
Oil for browning
Salt and freshly ground pepper
1 large onion, sliced thin
1/2 cup Cabernet Sauvignon (see note below)
2 cloves garlic
1 tablespoon fresh thyme leaves
Pinch of nutmeg
1/2 cup beef broth, or 1 bouillon cube and 1/2 cup water
1 can (35 ounces) plum tomatoes, drained
2 ounces diced ham

Note: If you decant the dinner wine well in advance, use the dregs and enough additional wine—not necessarily the aged wine—to make 1/2 cup.)

Preheat the oven to 325 degrees Fahrenheit.

In a large skillet, brown the short ribs on all sides in enough oil to film the bottom of the pan. Season them lightly with salt and pepper while they brown. Transfer the ribs to a shallow roasting pan. Spoon off all but 2 tablespoons fat from the pan. Brown the onions in the remaining fat and add them to the pan with short ribs. Final-

ly, add the wine to the pan, scraping up any remaining browned bits. Pour this over the ribs.

Meanwhile, in a blender, purée the garlic, thyme, nutmeg, broth and 1 cup of the tomatoes. Mix this with the remaining tomatoes and the ham. Pour this mixture over the ribs. Cover the pan with foil and bake 2 1/2 to 3 hours, or until the meat is very tender.

Skim the fat from the pan sauce and serve it with the short ribs and buttered noodles. Makes 6 servings.

Individual presentation: Make a "nest" of the noodles around the edge of the plate. Spoon some cabbage in the middle and place the short ribs on top. Sprinkle with chopped parsley or a mixture of parsley and thyme. Moisten with some of the sauce and pass the rest in a sauceboat.

SAUTEED CABBAGE

2 heads round or Savoy cabbage
3 tablespoons butter or olive oil
3/4 cup water
Salt and freshly ground pepper

Cut the core from the cabbage. Quarter the cabbage lengthwise and cut it crosswise into 1/4-inch slices. Put these in a medium-size saucepan with the butter or oil, the water, and a light sprinkling of salt and pepper. Cover the pan and bring to a boil. Uncover the pan and let the cabbage cook, stirring it occasionally, for 8 to 10 minutes or just until tender. Drain well and serve as a side dish. Makes 6 servings.

BUTTERED AND PARMESANED NOODLES

1 pound wide egg noodles
3 tablespoons butter
1/4 cup freshly grated Parmesan
Freshly ground pepper to taste

Boil the noodles in plenty of salted water according to package directions until they are cooked to your taste. Drain them well and toss with the remaining ingredients. Serve immediately. Makes 6 servings.

Match 5: DESSERT WINES

The secret to matching dessert wines with dessert is to make sure that the wine tastes sweeter than the food. Desserts made from fruits and nuts tend to meld better with wine than those dishes that depend on cream or eggs for their flavors and textures. This is a great stand-by dessert because its sweetness level is modest enough to show off a great range of sweet wines.

FRESH BERRIES WITH SECRET SOUR CREAM SAUCE

3 to 4 cups mixed fresh berries, rinsed well
1 cup sour cream
1 tablespoon powdered sugar
2 tablespoons Sambuca Romana, anisette or other anise-flavored liqueur
Milk, if needed

Arrange the berries in individual coupes, bowls or wine glasses. In a mixing bowl, using a wire whisk, blend the remaining ingredients, adding milk only if necessary to make a thick, barely pourable sauce. Add a dash of vanilla (optional). Pour over the berries. Garnish with mint sprigs. Makes 6 servings.

Gloria Ferrer, Gloria Ferrer, Gloria Ferrer. The name is so familiar. Gloria Ferrer. Wait, I went to school with her. I had a crush on her. Fifth grade. We were in Mrs. Peterson's home room. One day Gloria set her desk on fire. This couldn't be the same Gloria Ferrer.

Gloria Ferrer is a Sonoma County méthode champenoise that many feel rivals the great sparkling wines of Champagne, France.

Timeless. By Design.

Great style is more than just passing fancy. So is great wine. Classically designed
and elegantly textured. The masterful crafting of experienced winemakers.
Benziger of Glen Ellen.

1883 London Ranch Road, Glen Ellen, CA 95442 · (707) 935–3000

Shapes, Sizes and Degrees

A BIT OF FINE TUNING CAN ENHANCE YOUR ENJOYMENT OF CERTAIN WINE TYPES

By Jim Gordon

Sherry   Red Bordeaux   Champagne   Red Burgundy   White Wine   Port

Different wine glasses are traditionally used to augment the special qualities of regional wines

Knowing a few basic terms and standards can aid your appreciation of wine. In this section you will find an explanation of several popular types of wine glasses, the traditional terminology for wine bottles of varying sizes and tips on the preferred temperatures at which to serve different wines.

WINE GLASSES

There is no right or wrong glass for wine. But certain shapes and sizes have become traditional over the years, and often for practical reasons. In general, wine is best appreciated when drunk from a clear, smooth-surfaced, stemmed glass. Colored or faceted wine glasses don't afford the best view of a wine's color and clarity. Holding a wine glass by its stem gets your hand out of the way so you can see the wine, and it enables you to give the wine a slight swirl to release more aromas into the air.

Sherry and Port glasses traditionally are small. This is because Port and Sherry are fortified wines, usually drunk in small quantities.

You can drink Champagne out of the stemmed, flat saucer that was popular in the past, but the tall Champagne glasses, called flutes, are now in vogue. They make it less likely your Champagne will spill out of the glass during a wild party.

The white wine glass pictured on this page is probably the best all-around wine glass to have. Glasses much like this are used by many professional wine tasters when they analyze wines. Remember that it's wise not to fill a wine glass more than half full. That will leave enough air space to let the aromas come out. The standard white wine glass's narrow opening concentrates the bouquet.

Generally, glasses for red table wines are wider than those for white, but beyond that it's really up to your personal preference. Don't spend much time worrying about the choices; try one style and see if it suits you.

BOTTLE SIZES

A great majority of the world's premium wines are sold in a standard bottle that holds 750 milliliters. Standard-bottle heights, shapes and colors vary from region to region and wine variety to wine variety, but they all hold 750 milliliters, or about 25 ounces. That equals five to six good-sized pours. Some people still call this size a fifth, recalling the days when bottles about this size held one fifth of a gallon.

The other two sizes most frequently found in wine shops and on restaurant wine lists are the half-bottle and the magnum. Half-bottles, sometimes called tenths, hold 375 milliliters. Even smaller than a half-bottle is a split, or quarter-bottle, used mostly for sparkling wines. Magnums hold as much wine as two standard bottles, or 1.5 liters. Double magnums hold the equivalent of four bottles, or 3 liters.

You rarely encounter a bottle larger than a double magnum. These behemoths carry Biblical-sounding names. They start with the jeroboam, holding the equivalent of about six bottles, or 5 liters. (In Champagne, however, a jeroboam is a 3-liter bottle.) Imperials and methuselahs are both eight-bottle sizes, and a salmanazar holds the equivalent of an entire 12-bottle case. A balthazar holds the same as 16 bottles. And the king of wine bottles, holding the equivalent of 15 to 20 bottles, is named nebuchadnezzar.

Wine-bottle designations include, from left, half-bottle, bottle, magnum and double magnum, and imperial

SERVING TEMPERATURES

The best temperature at which to serve wines is another topic, like choosing the proper wine glass, where the rules can get confusing. In general, sparkling wines should be served as cold as you can get them. It takes at least an hour in the refrigerator to bring one down from room temperature. Most white wines are also best when served cold, at refrigerator temperature or a bit warmer, to preserve their freshness and fruitiness and to make their impression on the palate more refreshing. For most red wines, connoisseurs prefer to serve them at cellar temperature, about 55 to 65 degrees Fahrenheit.

With that said, there's a bit of fine tuning that can enhance your enjoyment of certain wine types. In the whites, rich, full-bodied wines such as white Burgundy, Chardonnay and Sémillon often show more of their complexity when served warmer than other whites. Cellar temperature is good. If you don't have a really cool cellar, about 40 minutes in the fridge should do it. Most sweet dessert wines will be at their best using the same rule.

Pouring a red wine at room temperature can be a mistake, especially in the summer when rooms are quite warm. A warm red wine seems to lose some of its flavor, and the tannins tend to feel rough. The idea of room temperature was appropriate in drafty, damp English manors in the 19th century, but not in most homes today.

Light, fresh-tasting red wines such as Beaujolais and many Pinot Noirs can be good when moderately chilled. Half an hour in the refrigerator should be plenty of time. Most rosés and blush wines are best when served at refrigerator temperature like the majority of white wines.

Vintage Charts

The best guarantee of satisfaction in evaluating a wine for purchase is the quality behind a producer's name. Once you've picked a producer with a track record for quality, in many cases, the next question is "which vintage should I buy?"

Knowing the relative merits of each vintage can help you make more informed buying decisions. This section will present our qualitative ratings of vintages in the world's major wine regions for the last 20-30 years.

Vintage charts are by necessity general in nature. Ratings listed are averages for the years and regions. Many good wines are produced in "bad" years, just as bad wines are produced in "good" years. Use our vintage charts as a general guide to overall quality.

The vintages in this section are rated on *The Wine Spectator*'s 100-point scale. For each vintage you will find the score, our rating, a comment on the characteristics of the vintage or the wines from that vintage, and our drinkability recommendation.

THE WINE SPECTATOR 100-POINT SCALE

95-100 — Classic, a great wine.

90-94 — Outstanding, superior character and style.

80-89 — Good to very good, a wine with special qualities.

70-79 — Average, a drinkable wine that may have minor flaws.

60-69 — Below average, drinkable but not recommended.

50-59 — Poor, undrinkable, not recommended.

"+"—With a score indicates a range; used primarily to indicate a preliminary score.

FRANCE/ALSACE

Vintage	Score	Rating	Comment	Drinkability
1989	96	Classic	Super dessert wines, rich and round	Hold
1988	95	Classic	Excellent balance, firm and opulant	Drink
1987	85	Very Good	Steely, lean, and fresh	Drink
1986	84	Good	Light, elegant and delicious	Drink
1985	90	Outstanding	Concentrated, intensely fruity, good backbone	Drink or Hold
1984	74	Average	Slightly unripe, thin and simple	Drink
1983	93	Outstanding	Very rich, superbly structured; many dessert wines	Drink or Hold
1982	80	Good	Large production; fruity and simple	Drink
1981	89	Very Good	Racy, classy, elegant; some great wines	Drink
1980	72	Average	Unripe, meager; most past their primes	Drink

FRANCE/BORDEAUX RED

Vintage	Score	Rating	Comment	Drinkability
1990	95	Classic	Firm structure, opulent fruit, intense flavors	Not Released
1989	98	Classic	Bold, rich, tannic, long aging; applies to top estates	Not Released
1988	92	Outstanding	Rich, concentrated, classic structure	Hold
1987	73	Average	Light, simple, quick maturing	Drink
1986	96	Classic	Powerful, intense and tannic; best in Médoc	Hold
1985	94	Outstanding	Ripe, supple, balanced, consistently fine quality	Hold
1984	70	Average	Unripe, tough, tannic; mediocre quality	Drink
1983	86	Very Good	Balanced, rich, fruity, some are simple	Drink or Hold
1982	94	Outstanding	Huge crop; extremely ripe, opulent, concentrated, stunning	Drink or Hold
1981	82	Good	Classic claret, elegant, balanced, charming	Drink or Hold
1980	78	Average	Light, pleasant wines for early drinking	Drink
1979	83	Good	Supple, fruity and delicate; perfect now	Drink
1978	86	Very Good	Structured, fleshy and complex; best are improving	Drink or Hold
1977	60	Below Average	Poor, unripe and acidic; well past their primes	Drink
1976	80	Good	Early promise unfulfilled; fully matured now	Drink
1975	85	Very Good	Hard, tannic, slowly evolving; time will tell	Drink
1974	58	Poor	Unripe and diluted; never worth much	Drink
1973	68	Below Average	Early maturing, luncheon wines; mostly faded	Drink
1972	60	Poor	Acidic, light wines; never very interesting	Drink
1971	85	Very Good	Uneven quality; Médoc and Graves fading quickly	Drink
1970	91	Outstanding	Excellent all-around vintage; structured, with lots of fruit	Drink or Hold
1966	89	Very Good	Classic but hard wines; best are still improving	Drink or Hold
1964	80	Good	Uneven quality; outstanding Pomerols, St.-Emilions	Drink
1961	98	Classic	Best since '45; great concentration, structure, longevity	Drink or Hold

FRANCE/BURGUNDY RED

Vintage	Score	Rating	Comment	Drinkability
1989	87	Very Good	Charming, early drinking	Hold
1988	94	Outstanding	Classic structure, concentration	Hold

FRANCE/BURGUNDY RED (continued)

Vintage	Score	Rating	Comment	Drinkability
1987	83	Good	Flavorful, early drinking	Drink or Hold
1986	79	Average	Aromatic but very tannic	Hold
1985	97	Classic	Plush, complex, seductive	Drink or Hold
1984	73	Average	Many thin, watery wines	Drink
1983	85	Very Good	Inconsistent; rot spoiled some	Drink or Hold
1982	80	Good	Good vintage at its peak	Drink
1981	74	Average	Light, thin	Drink
1980	79	Average	Was good, past its peak	Drink
1979	80	Good	Was good, past its peak	Drink
1978	92	Outstanding	Big wines, flavorful	Drink or Hold
1977	65	Below Average	Past its peak	Drink
1976	87	Very Good	Tough wines coming around	Drink or Hold
1975	65	Below Average	Past its peak	Drink
1974	65	Below Average	Past its peak	Drink
1973	69	Below Average	Lighter style but charming	Drink
1972	81	Good	Lean wines with style	Drink
1971	89	Very Good	Best wines are still evolving	Drink
1970	81	Good	Forgotten vintage, holding up	Drink
1969	93	Outstanding	Classic structure, flavorful	Drink

FRANCE/BURGUNDY WHITE

Vintage	Score	Rating	Comment	Drinkability
1989	94	Outstanding	Rich, opulent, with masses of fruit and flavor; should age well	Hold
1988	86	Very Good	Firm and fruity, with good concentration and balance	Drink or Hold
1986	92	Outstanding	Excellent acidity and focused fruit; many marked by botrytis	Drink
1987	84	Good	Fresh and simple, with medium-term aging potential	Drink
1985	96	Classic	Bold, powerful; exuberant fruit, firm acidity, great potential	Drink or Hold
1984	78	Average	Light and very simple; very high in green acidity	Drink
1983	85	Very Good	Uneven quality, but some outstanding and powerful wines made	Drink or Hold
1982	83	Good	Some surprises, but generally light, slightly diluted wines	Drink
1981	82	Good	Difficult vintage; high acidity, but top producers very good	Drink
1980	73	Average	Mostly unripe and diluted wines produced	Drink

FRANCE/CHAMPAGNE

Vintage	Score	Rating	Comment	Drinkability
1986	86	Very Good	Good quality; lean and firm	Drink
1985	96	Classic	Superb balance, great structure, ripe fruit	Drink or Hold
1984	83	Good	Large harvest; pleasant, early drinking	Drink
1983	83	Good	Large harvest; pleasant	Drink
1982	94	Outstanding	Rich, complex, abundant fruit	Drink or Hold
1981	84	Good	Angular, hard, clean fruit, some surprises	Drink or Hold
1980	82	Good	Generous, very fruity, average structure	Drink
1979	91	Outstanding	Classy, elegant, firm, aging well	Drink

FRANCE/SAUTERNES

Vintage	Score	Rating	Comment	Drinkability
1989	98	Classic	Incredibly rich; lots of botrytis; built for aging	Hold
1988	95	Classic	Concentrated, well balanced, extremely fine and firm	Hold
1987	75	Average	Light, simple, sweet wines; many taste diluted	Drink
1986	90	Outstanding	Intense, focused, honeyed; lively acidity	Hold
1985	79	Average	Slight botrytis; clean and sweet	Drink or Hold
1984	68	Below Average	Few good wines; a wet, difficult harvest	Drink
1983	95	Classic	Thick, powerful, abundant botrytis, a classic year	Hold
1982	77	Average	Mostly sweet, fat and alcoholic; Suduiraut is an exception	Drink or Hold
1981	83	Good	Medium richness, fine balance	Drink
1980	82	Good	Good year; balanced, lightly botrytised	Drink

GERMANY/RIESLING

Vintage	Score	Rating	Comment	Drinkability
1989	96	Classic	Super botrytised, massive, rich, round	Hold
1988	94	Outstanding	Classic, balanced, firm; best in Middle Mosel	Hold
1987	82	Good	Fresh, light; surprisingly good	Drink or Hold
1986	86	Very Good	Aromatic, elegant, fruity	Drink
1985	83	Good	Racy, well structured; problems in Rheingau, Rheinpfalz	Drink or Hold
1984	74	Average	Unripe, aggresive acidity; only top producers drinkable	Drink
1983	93	Outstanding	Super fruity, ripe, round, little botrytis	Drink or Hold
1982	78	Average	Overproduction; diluted, soft; very good Ausleses	Drink
1981	81	Good	Clean, lean, light	Drink
1980	65	Below Average	Very green, unripe, thin	Drink
1979	88	Very Good	Small crop; fresh, well structured	Drink
1978	70	Average	Green, thin but drinkable	Drink
1977	75	Average	Difficult, light, elegant, most consumed	Drink
1976	97	Classic	Huge, ripe, powerful; plenty of botrytis	Drink
1975	94	Outstanding	Superb class, great balance, firm structure	Drink
1974	66	Below Average	Mean, no harmony, little fruit	Drink
1973	82	Good	Better than expected, ripe acidity, good fruit	Drink
1972	70	Average	High acidity, lean; most past their primes	Drink
1971	98	Classic	Powerful, elegant, superb structure, long-lived	Drink

ITALY/CHIANTI

Vintage	Score	Rating	Comment	Drinkability
1987	79	Average	Soft, light	Drink
1986	83	Good	Firm, somewhat tannic	Drink or Hold
1985	91	Outstanding	Concentrated; Riservas can be tannic	Drink or Hold
1984	64	Below Average	Thin, acidic	Drink
1983	86	Very Good	Powerful, tannic	Drink or Hold
1982	80	Good	Smooth, elegant	Drink
1981	74	Average	Light, somewhat acidic	Drink
1980	68	Below Average	Most wines past their primes	Drink
1979	80	Good	Best wines still rich and supple	Drink
1978	87	Very Good	Tough and tannic, starting to come around	Drink or Hold

ITALY/TUSCANY VINO DA TAVOLA

Vintage	Score	Rating	Comment	Drinkability
1989	79	Average	Some light, pleasant wines; others very diluted	Hold
1988	96	Classic	Balanced, with excellent concentration, firm acidity, fine tannins	Hold
1987	82	Good	Variable quality but some surprises; medium-structured wines	Hold
1986	86	Very Good	Slightly lean but solid wines with good fruit	Drink or Hold
1985	94	Outstanding	Hot, super-ripe year; big and rich wines with tons of fruit	Drink or Hold
1984	75	Average	Light, difficult vintage; most wines insipid	Drink
1983	86	Very Good	Pretty wines, with good intensity and backbone	Drink or Hold
1982	93	Outstanding	Very ripe fruit, with plenty of tannin; rich, round wines	Drink or Hold
1981	85	Very Good	Focused fruit, firm tannins; some exceptional wines	Drink
1980	77	Average	Tricky weather for most of vintage; uneven quality, unique wines	Drink

PORTUGAL/VINTAGE PORT

Vintage	Score	Rating	Comment	Drinkability
1987	88	Very Good	Balanced, elegant, good finesse	Hold
1986	80	Good	Firm, gutsy, a little simple	Hold
1985	96	Classic	Opulent, intense, solid backbone	Hold
1984	81	Good	Lean, linear, one-dimensional	Drink or Hold
1983	92	Outstanding	Powerful, tannic, ageworthy	Hold
1982	84	Good	Sweet, raisiny, unbalanced	Drink or Hold
1980	87	Very Good	Solid, well structured, focused fruit	Drink or Hold
1979	74	Average	Light, sweet, insipid	Drink
1978	84	Good	Fruity, soft, ready	Drink
1977	97	Classic	Tough, tannic, complex, ageless	Hold
1976	76	Average	Simple, variable, short	Drink
1975	80	Good	Light, one-dimensional, fruity	Drink

PORTUGAL/VINTAGE PORT (continued)

Vintage	Score	Rating	Comment	Drinkability
1974	74	Average	Aromatic, angular; small production	Drink
1972	79	Average	Light, fragrant, easy to drink	Drink
1970	95	Classic	Harmonious, well structured, intense fruit	Drink or Hold
1969	72	Average	Light, simple; tiny production	Drink
1968	77	Average	One-dimensional, fruity; small crop	Drink
1967	88	Very Good	Focused fruit, angular, elegant	Drink
1966	93	Outstanding	Iron backbone, good concentration, fresh flavors	Drink or Hold
1965	80	Good	Rich focused fruit; tiny production	Drink
1964	81	Good	Appealing fruit, stylish, soft, round	Drink
1963	98	Classic	Copious fruit, forceful, extremely ageworthy	Drink or Hold
1962	82	Good	Pleasant, fruity, soft	Drink
1961	80	Good	Very ripe, roasted flavors, sweet	Drink
1960	87	Very Good	Balanced, sweet, elegant, peaked	Drink
1945	98	Classic	Youthful, concentrated, superlative quality	Drink or Hold
1935	95	Classic	Aromatic, refined, firmly structured	Drink
1927	100	Classic	Superb concentration, balance, breeding, large production	Drink
1912	98	Classic	Concentrated, powerful, superbly structured	Drink

UNITED STATES/CALIFORNIA CABERNET SAUVIGNON

Vintage	Score	Rating	Comment	Drinkability
1990	90+	Outstanding	Rich, deep, supple, complex	Not Released
1989	87	Very Good	Ripe, harmonious, but uneven	Not Released
1988	86	Very Good	Ripe, elegant, balanced	Not Released
1987	90	Outstanding	Deep, rich, complex, tannic	Hold
1986	95	Classic	Classic structure, ageworthy	Hold
1985	97	Classic	One of California's finest; elegant, stylish	Hold
1984	94	Outstanding	Rich, fruity, opulent	Hold
1983	81	Good	Lean, tannic, uneven quality	Hold
1982	78	Average	Austere, structured, uneven quality	Hold
1981	85	Very Good	Supple, charming, balanced	Drink or Hold
1980	84	Good	Ripe, opulent, balanced	Drink or Hold
1979	88	Very Good	Austere, but ageworthy	Drink
1978	93	Outstanding	Ripe, flavorful, ageworthy	Drink
1977	82	Good	Elegant, charming	Drink
1976	75	Average	Ripe, but awkward	Drink
1975	86	Very Good	Charming, supple, elegant, balanced	Drink
1974	91	Outstanding	Bold, rich, opulent, dramatic	Drink or Hold
1973	87	Very Good	Elegant, charming, subtle, balanced	Drink
1972	67	Below Average	Rainy; simple, watery, uninspired	Drink
1971	68	Below Average	Rainy harvest, poor quality, mediocre	Drink
1970	95	Classic	Deep, complex, elegant, ageworthy	Drink
1969	92	Outstanding	Elegant, supple, balanced, charming	Drink
1968	96	Classic	Rich, concentrated, powerful, tannic	Drink or Hold
1967	82	Good	Elegant, supple, balanced, early charm	Drink
1966	91	Outstanding	Rich, complex, balanced, delightful	Drink
1965	83	Good	Ripe, balanced, charming, serviceable	Drink
1964	91	Outstanding	Ripe, complex, balanced, enduring	Drink
1963	69	Below Average	Frost, short crop; uneven quality, not memorable	Drink
1962	69	Below Average	Frost damage, mediocre vintage, uninspiring	Drink
1961	71	Average	Severe frosts, decent quality; wines past their primes	Drink
1960	84	Good	Fruity, elegant, balanced, commendable	Drink
1958	95	Classic	Amazingly youthful, complex, elegant, ageworthy	Drink or Hold

UNITED STATES/CALIFORNIA CHARDONNAY

Vintage	Score	Rating	Comment	Drinkability
1990	90+	Outstanding	Ripe, rich, concentrated	Not Released
1989	85	Very Good	Uneven quality, but some are superb	Drink
1988	89	Very Good	Ripe, balanced, delicate, forward	Drink or Hold
1987	85	Very Good	Hard, austere; uneven quality but some are fine	Drink
1986	91	Outstanding	Deep, rich, concentrated, complex	Drink
1985	92	Outstanding	Ripe, elegant, concentrated, complex	Drink
1984	87	Very Good	Very ripe, fleshy, early maturing	Drink
1983	81	Good	Austere; uneven quality, most have faded	Drink
1982	79	Average	Huge crop, very ripe, but unbalanced	Drink
1981	87	Very Good	Ripe, forward, charming when young	Drink
1980	86	Very Good	Very rich, ripe, full-bodied	Drink
1979	89	Very Good	Austere, elegant, balanced, ageworthy	Drink
1978	85	Very Good	Ripe, intense, powerful	Drink
1977	84	Good	Drought year; elegant, balanced, charming	Drink
1976	77	Average	Drought year; very ripe, unbalanced	Drink
1975	85	Very Good	Ripe, elegant, balanced, charming	Drink
1974	88	Very Good	Ripe, rich, bold, balanced	Drink
1973	85	Very Good	Elegant, subtle, balanced, charming	Drink
1972	67	Below Average	Rainy; simple, watery, uninspired	Drink
1971	68	Below Average	Rainy harvest, poor quality	Drink
1970	89	Very Good	Complex, elegant, balanced	Drink

SOURCE: *THE WINE SPECTATOR, CALIFORNIA'S GREAT CABERNETS, CALIFORNIA'S GREAT CHARDONNAYS, VINTAGE PORT*

GOLD at the PEAK

GEYSER PEAK WINERY

19 Gold Medals in 1990
25 Silver Medals in 1990
40 Bronze Medals in 1990

'85 Reserve Alexandre
GOLD-*SpringFest Wine Festival*

'86 Reserve Alexandre
GOLD-*SpringFest Wine Festival*
GOLD-*Internat'l Eastern Wine Competition*
GOLD-*Indiana State Fair*

'87 Reserve Alexandre
GOLD-*Sonoma County Harvest Fair*

'87 Cabernet Sauvignon
GOLD-*Indiana State Fair*

'86 Reserve Cabernet Sauvignon
GOLD-*Indiana State Fair*

'89 Semchard
GOLD-*Orange County Fair*

'89 Soft Johannisberg Riesling
GOLD-*Orange County Fair*
GOLD-*Cloverdale Citrus Fair*
GOLD-*Tasters Guild Wine Competition*
GOLD-*Florida State Fair*

'88 Chenin Blanc
GOLD-*Tennessee Wine Festival*

'89 Chenin Blanc
GOLD-*Orange County Fair*
GOLD-*Indiana State Fair*

'89 Soft Gewurztraminer
GOLD-*Tasters Guild Wine Competition*
GOLD-*San Diego Nat'l Wine Competition*
GOLD-*Indiana State Fair*

'89 Pinot Noir Blanc
GOLD-*Orange County Fair*

Geyser Peak Winery, Geyserville, CA 95441

The Top 100

BY HARVEY STEIMAN

Each year the editors of *The Wine Spectator* choose 100 of the most exciting wines from the thousands reviewed to present our Top 100 wines of the year. All of the wines considered for our Top 100 come from blind tastings by two or more tasters in our San Francisco editorial offices and on location in Europe. The result each year, we believe, is 100 choices that would make splendid drinking for even the toughest wine critic.

We could have simply given you a list of the highest-scoring wines, but that would only be part of the story. Many of the most exciting wines we review set our pulses racing because they show a special style or made a real contribution to the great diversity that makes wine so much fun. We call this the "excitement factor."

It is for this reason that the Top 100 is not simply a list of the highest-scoring wines from a particular year. A wine's score only reflects how good it is, regardless of price or where it comes from. For the Top 100, absolute quality is only one factor. We also consider:

OVERALL VALUE—We expect more of higher-priced wines. In other words, a $50 Cabernet had better deliver. It makes our spines tingle when a wine strikes us as just as impressive as those that cost several times its price. That's why, for example, we ranked the 1985 Château Lynch-Bages No. 1 in our 1988 ranking. It rates right up there with the first-growth Bordeaux at a fraction of the price.

RELATIVE VALUE WITHIN ITS TYPE—The Top 100 favors highly rated wines that are priced below average for the type. In other words, a $35 Chassagne-Montrachet is a *relatively* good value. A $35 Italian Chardonnay is not.

AVAILABILITY—The Top 100 favors wines that are not in extremely limited supply. However, some wines made in tiny quantities, such as *cru* Burgundies, were so highly rated and reasonably priced in their categories that we decided that they are well worth searching for. We made exceptions to the rule for these.

RARITY OF EXCELLENCE WITHIN ITS TYPE—We like to find outstanding wines in categories that don't usually produce such good wines. For example, the best Sauvignon Blanc may make the list ahead of the 15th-best Chardonnay, even if both wines are rated the same.

On the following pages are the Top 100 lists for 1990, 1989 and 1988. Over the years, the editors have found it difficult to narrow each of these lists to only 100 wines and to decide their order. For one example, how do you differentiate between similarly priced wines with the same high scores? We shuffled the wines around several different ways until we agreed among ourselves on the lists you see. There are a lot of terrific wines on these lists, and finally, one may rank ahead of another because it has broader appeal.

A GRAND COLLECTION.

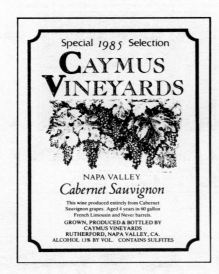

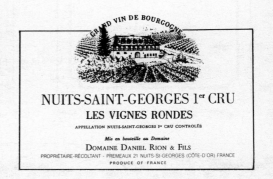

THE TOP 100: 1990's BEST WINES

1   95   BERINGER Cabernet Sauvignon Napa Valley Private Reserve 1986 Rel: $35 Cur: $39 (9/15/90) CS

2   99   CAYMUS Cabernet Sauvignon Napa Valley Special Selection 1985 Rel: $50 Cur: $127 (4/30/90)

3   96   CHARTRON & TREBUCHET Chassagne-Montrachet Les Morgeots 1988 $34 (2/28/90)

4   95   POGGIO ANTICO Brunello di Montalcino 1985 $36 (11/30/90) CS

5   98   HEITZ Cabernet Sauvignon Napa Valley Martha's Vineyard 1985 Rel: $60 Cur: $118 (4/30/90)

6   97   OPUS ONE Napa Valley 1987 Rel: $68 Cur: $69 (11/15/90) CS

7   95   DOMAINE DANIEL RION Nuits-St.-Georges Les Vignes Rondes 1987 $35 (4/30/90)

8   98   JOH. JOS. PRUM Spätlese Mosel-Saar-Ruwer Wehlener Sonnenuhr (Cask 2) 1988 $24 (9/30/89)

9   96   SPOTTSWOODE Cabernet Sauvignon Napa Valley 1987 Rel: $36 Cur: $56 (9/15/90) SS

10   95   WOODWARD CANYON Cabernet Sauvignon Columbia Valley 1987 $18.50 (12/31/90)

11   95   DUCKHORN Cabernet Sauvignon Napa Valley 1987 Rel: $20 Cur: $27 (6/30/90) CS

12   96   C. VON SCHUBERT Spätlese Mosel-Saar-Ruwer Maximin Grunhauser Abtsberg 1988 $18 (9/30/89)

13   95   WILLIAM HILL Cabernet Sauvignon Napa Valley Reserve 1987 Rel: $24 Cur: $25 (11/15/90) SS

14   95   ZILLIKEN Spätlese Mosel-Saar-Ruwer Saarburger Rausch 1988 $17 (9/30/89)

15   96   SILVERADO Cabernet Sauvignon Napa Valley Limited Reserve 1986 Rel: $35 Cur: $38 (12/15/90) CS

16   95   LA JOTA Cabernet Sauvignon Howell Mountain 1987 Rel: $25 Cur: $28 (7/31/90) SS

17   96   BOLLINGER Brut Champagne Grand Année 1985 $45 (12/31/90)

18   95   DUNN Cabernet Sauvignon Howell Mountain 1986 Rel: $30 Cur: $91 (7/31/90) CS

19   95   GROTH Cabernet Sauvignon Napa Valley Reserve 1985 Rel: $30 Cur: $166 (4/15/90)

20   96   EMMANUEL ROUGET Echézeaux 1988 $81 (11/15/90)

21   95   BODEGAS VEGA SICILIA Ribera del Duero Unico 1979 Rel: $75 Cur: $80 (3/31/90)

22   95   DOPFF AU MOULIN Riesling Alsace Grand Cru Schoenenberg 1988 $19 (10/15/89)

23   94   ST. FRANCIS Merlot Sonoma Valley Reserve 1986 $20 (1/31/90)

24   94   CAYMUS Cabernet Sauvignon Napa Valley 1986 Rel: $22 Cur: $29 (3/15/90) SS

25   94   SANFORD Chardonnay Santa Barbara County Barrel Select 1988 Rel: $25 Cur: $28 (8/31/90)

26   94   KISTLER Chardonnay Sonoma Valley Kistler Estate 1988 $26 (4/30/90)

27   94   GIUSEPPE MASCARELLO & FIGLIO Barolo Santo Stefano di Perno 1985 $35 (10/15/90)

28   94   SIMI Cabernet Sauvignon Alexander Valley Reserve 1985 Rel: $25 Cur: $28 (8/31/90) SS

29   94   SILVER OAK Cabernet Sauvignon Napa Valley 1986 Rel: $26 Cur: $54 (10/31/90) CS

30   93   CHATEAU LA TOUR MARTILLAC Blanc Pessac-Léognan 1987 $15 (1/31/90)

31   93   BENZIGER Cabernet Sauvignon Sonoma County 1987 $10 (9/30/90) SS

32   95   STERLING Reserve Napa Valley 1986 Rel: $35 Cur: $43 (3/15/90) CS

33   94   DOMAINE JEAN CHARTRON Puligny-Montrachet Les Folatières 1988 $38 (3/15/90)

34   92   SILVERADO Cabernet Sauvignon Napa Valley 1987 Rel: $14 Cur: $18 (4/15/90) SS

35   93   LANSON Brut Champagne 1985 $37 (12/31/90)

36   92   SILVERADO Merlot Napa Valley 1987 $14 (4/15/90)

37   92   FRANCISCAN Chardonnay Napa Valley Oakville Estate Reserve 1987 $15 (6/15/90)

38   91   LAR DE BARROS Tierra de Barros Tinto Reserva 1986 $8 (10/15/90) SS

39   90   ROSEMOUNT Shiraz Hunter Valley 1988 $8 (1/31/90) SS

40   93   CAYMUS Cabernet Sauvignon Napa Valley 1987 Rel: $16 Cur: $19 (9/15/90)

41   93   FERRARI-CARANO Chardonnay Alexander Valley 1988 Rel: $18 Cur: $18 (5/31/90) SS

42   93   ARGYLE Chardonnay Oregon Barrel Fermented 1987 $18.50 (12/31/90)

43   93   MERRYVALE Chardonnay Napa Valley 1987 $19 (2/15/90)

44   92   RUTHERFORD RANCH Cabernet Sauvignon Napa Valley 1985 Rel: $11 Cur: $11 (5/15/90) SS

45   92   BYRON Chardonnay Santa Barbara County 1988 $12 (4/30/90) SS

46   93   FATTORIA DI FELSINA Chianti Classico Berardenga Vigneto Rancia Riserva 1985 Rel: $23 Cur: $23 (4/30/90) CS

47   93   LOUIS M. MARTINI Cabernet Sauvignon Sonoma Valley Monte Rosso 1987 Rel: $20 Cur: $23 (11/15/90)

48   93   MAZZOCCO Cabernet Sauvignon Alexander Valley Claret Style 1987 $20 (8/31/90)

49   93   SILVER OAK Cabernet Sauvignon Alexander Valley 1986 Rel: $26 Cur: $37 (10/31/90) SS

50   93   DOMAINE GEOFFROY Gevrey-Chambertin Clos Prieur 1987 $29 (3/31/90)

51   94   CHATEAU MAGDELAINE St.-Emilion 1986 Rel: $48 Cur: $48 (2/15/90)

52   93   CLOS DU BOIS Chardonnay Alexander Valley Winemaker's Reserve 1987 Rel: $24 Cur: $24 (2/28/90)

53   93   OLIVIER LEFLAIVE FRERES Puligny-Montrachet 1987 $33 (6/30/90)

54   93   PODERE IL POGGIOLO Brunello di Montalcino 1985 $34 (11/30/90)

55   93   MICHEL BOUZEREAU Meursault Genevrières 1988 $37 (7/15/90)

56   93   CHATEAU ST. JEAN Chardonnay Alexander Valley Robert Young Vineyards Reserve 1.5L 1985 Rel: $40 Cur: $40 (9/30/90)

57   95   E. GUIGAL Côte-Rôtie La Turque 1986 Rel: $99 Cur: $340 (10/15/90) CS

58   93   JEAN GROS Richebourg 1987 Rel: $99 Cur: $170 (3/31/90)

59   94   GAJA Cabernet Sauvignon Darmagi 1986 Rel: $76 Cur: $76 (1/31/90)

60   96   CHATEAU D'YQUEM Sauternes 1984 Rel: $149 Cur: $151 (3/31/90)

61   92   WILLIAMS SELYEM Pinot Noir Sonoma Coast 1988 $40 (5/31/90)

62   92   VITICCIO Prunaio 1986 $19 (3/31/90) SS

63   91   SNOQUALMIE Merlot Columbia Valley Reserve 1987 $12 (9/30/90)

64   91   CAPEZZANA Ghiaie della Furba 1985 $20 (1/31/90)

65   92   DOMAINE AUFFRAY Chablis Les Clos 1988 $38 (3/31/90)

66   92   DOMAINE DAUVISSAT-CAMUS Chablis Les Clos 1988 $41 (7/31/90)

67   92   BODEGAS VEGA SICILIA Valbuena Ribera del Duero 3.0 1985 $40 (10/15/90)

68   91   SAINTSBURY Pinot Noir Carneros 1988 $15 (12/15/90) SS

69   91   EDMUNDS ST. JOHN Les Fleurs du Chaparral Napa Valley 1987 $15 (8/31/90)

70   91   BROWN BROTHERS Chardonnay King Valley Family Reserve 1987 $15.50 (7/15/90) SS

71   92   FREEMARK ABBEY Johannisberg Riesling Late Harvest Napa Valley Edelwein Gold 1989 $22/375ml (7/15/90)

72   92   LUCIANO SANDRONE Barolo Cannubi Boschis 1985 $30 (1/31/90)

73   92   ELIO ALTARE Barolo 1985 $24 (1/31/90)

74   92   CLERICO Barolo Ciabot Mentin Ginestra 1985 Rel: $27 Cur: $40 (4/15/90) CS

75   92   PESQUERA Ribera del Duero Reserva 1986 $26 (9/30/90)

76   92   VILLA BANFI Brunello di Montalcino 1985 Rel: $30 Cur: $30 (10/15/90)

77   91   BRIDGEHAMPTON Chardonnay Long Island Grand Vineyard Selection 1988 $18 (3/31/90)

78   90   CLINE Oakley Cuvée Contra Costa County 1988 $12 (2/28/90)

79   91   TRIMBACH Riesling Alsace Cuvée Frédéric Emile 1988 $15 (10/15/89)

80   91   SELVAPIANA Chianti Rufina Vigneto Bucerchiale Riserva 1985 $19 (9/15/90)

81   91   PONZI Pinot Noir Willamette Valley Reserve 1987 $20 (2/15/90)

82   91   LEONETTI Cabernet Sauvignon Washington 1987 $22 (6/15/90)

83   91   DOMAINE MUMM Brut Carneros Winery Lake Cuvée Napa 1987 $22 (11/15/90)

84   92   E. GUIGAL Hermitage 1986 Rel: $32 Cur: $32 (2/28/90) CS

85   92   PRINCE FLORENT DE MERODE Corton Renardes 1987 $36 (3/31/90)

86   92   CA'ROME Barbaresco Maria di Brun 1985 $37 (1/31/90)

87   90   SIMI Sauvignon Blanc Sonoma County 1988 $8 (10/31/90)

88   90   SILVERADO Sauvignon Blanc Napa Valley 1988 $8.50 (2/15/90) SS

89   90   KENDALL-JACKSON Sauvignon Blanc Lake County Vintner's Reserve 1989 $9 (10/31/90)

90   90   BODEGAS BERBERANA Rioja Reserva 1985 $10 (2/28/90)

91   90   A. RAFANELLI Zinfandel Dry Creek Valley 1988 $9.75 (9/15/90)

92   90   GRGICH HILLS Fumé Blanc Napa Valley 1988 $10 (3/31/90)

93   90   SNOQUALMIE Cabernet Sauvignon Columbia Valley 1987 $10 (9/30/90)

94   90   DOMAINE DU GOUR DE CHAULE Gigondas 1986 $13 (9/15/90)

95   90   VALFIERI Barolo 1985 $13.50 (10/15/90)

96   90   LYTTON SPRINGS Zinfandel Sonoma County 1988 $12 (7/31/90)

97   90   PRODUTTORI DEL BARBARESCO Barbaresco 1986 $12 (10/31/90)

98   90   J.J. VINCENT Pouilly-Fuissé 1988 $15 (10/31/90)

99   90   DOMAINES SCHLUMBERGER Riesling Alsace Kitterlé 1988 $14 (10/15/89)

100   91   N. JOLY Savennières Clos de la Coulée de Serrant 1989 $33 (11/30/90)

THE TOP 100: 1989's BEST WINES

1   98   CAYMUS Cabernet Sauvignon Napa Valley Special Selection 1984 Rel: $35 Cur: $118 (7/15/89) CS
2   97   CHATEAU CLERC-MILON Pauillac 1986 Rel: $23 Cur: $32 (5/31/89)
3   97   HEITZ Cabernet Sauvignon Napa Valley Martha's Vineyard 1984 Rel: $40 Cur: $77 (3/15/89) SS
4   97   CHATEAU PICHON-BARON Pauillac 1986 Rel: $31 Cur: $58 (5/31/89)
5   97   KENDALL-JACKSON Cabernet Sauvignon California Cardinale 1985 $45 (11/15/89)
6   98   CHATEAU MARGAUX Margaux 1986 Rel: $80 Cur: $100 (6/15/89) CS
7   98   CHATEAU CHEVAL BLANC St.-Emilion 1986 Rel: $80 Cur: $85 (6/30/89) CS
8   98   CHATEAU MOUTON-ROTHSCHILD Pauillac 1986 Rel: $102 Cur: $114 (5/31/89) CS
9   97   CHATEAU PICHON-LALANDE Pauillac 1986 Rel: $50 Cur: $57 (5/31/89)
10   96   PENFOLDS Shiraz South Australia Grange Hermitage Bin 95 1982 Rel: $60 Cur: $68 (9/30/89) CS
11   98   ROMANEE-CONTI Romanée-St.-Vivant 1986 Rel: $195 Cur: $195 (8/31/89)
12   98   ROMANEE-CONTI La Tâche 1986 Rel: $250 Cur: $250 (8/31/89) CS
13   95   JOHNSON TURNBULL Cabernet Sauvignon Napa Valley Vineyard Selection 82 1986 Rel: $14.50 Cur: $25 (8/31/89)
14   96   STERLING Reserve Napa Valley 1985 Rel: $30 Cur: $38 (7/15/89) SS
15   95   SEPPELT Tawny Port Australia Old Trafford NV $15 (3/15/89)
16   95   DOMAINE MEO-CAMUZET Vosne-Romanée Aux Brûlées 1987 $63 (12/15/89)
17   95   DOMAINE MEO-CAMUZET Vosne-Romanée Au Cros-Parantoux 1987 $63 (12/15/89)
18   95   DUNN Cabernet Sauvignon Napa Valley 1986 Rel: $27 Cur: $55 (10/15/89) CS
19   95   CHATEAU LA DOMINIQUE St.-Emilion 1986 Rel: $29 Cur: $29 (6/30/89)
20   95   SPOTTSWOODE Cabernet Sauvignon Napa Valley 1986 Rel: $30 Cur: $71 (9/15/89)
21   95   KENWOOD Cabernet Sauvignon Sonoma Valley Artist Series 1986 Rel: $30 Cur: $31 (11/30/89) CS
22   95   BERINGER Cabernet Sauvignon Napa Valley Private Reserve 1985 Rel: $30 Cur: $42 (12/15/89) SS
23   95   ROBERT MONDAVI Cabernet Sauvignon Napa Valley Reserve 1986 Rel: $35 Cur: $39 (11/15/89)
24   94   LAUREL GLEN Cabernet Sauvignon Sonoma Mountain Counterpoint 1987 $13 (10/31/89)
25   94   SILVERADO Cabernet Sauvignon Napa Valley 1986 Rel: $13.50 Cur: $18 (8/31/89) SS
26   94   CUVAISON Cabernet Sauvignon Napa Valley 1986 Rel: $15 Cur: $20 (7/31/89)
27   94   FROG'S LEAP Cabernet Sauvignon Napa Valley 1987 Rel: $15 Cur: $20 (12/31/89) SS
28   92   ROSEMOUNT Shiraz Hunter Valley 1986 $9 (4/15/89)
29   92   CARNEROS CREEK Pinot Noir Carneros Fleur de Carneros 1987 $9 (2/28/89) SS
30   94   FERRARI-CARANO Chardonnay Alexander Valley 1987 Rel: $16 Cur: $23 (5/31/89)
31   94   B.R. COHN Cabernet Sauvignon Sonoma Valley Olive Hill Vineyard 1986 Rel: $18 Cur: $27 (5/31/89)
32   94   DUCKHORN Cabernet Sauvignon Napa Valley 1986 Rel: $18 Cur: $24 (7/31/89) SS
33   94   BUENA VISTA Cabernet Sauvignon Carneros Private Reserve 1985 Rel: $18 Cur: $23 (10/15/89) SS
34   94   CLOS RENE Pomerol 1986 Rel: $19 Cur: $25 (6/15/89) SS
35   94   BERINGER Cabernet Sauvignon Napa Valley Private Reserve 1984 Rel: $25 Cur: $38 (2/15/89) CS
36   94   CASTELLARE DI CASTELLINA I Sodi di San Niccolo 1986 Rel: $25 Cur: $29 (11/30/89)
37   94   FATTORIA DI AMA Chianti Classico Castello di Ama Vigneto Bellavista 1985 Rel: $30 Cur: $30 (7/31/89)
38   95   ROBERT MONDAVI Cabernet Sauvignon Napa Valley Reserve 1985 Rel: $40 Cur: $43 (11/15/89) SS
39   95   DIAMOND CREEK Cabernet Sauvignon Napa Valley Volcanic Hill 1987 Rel: $40 Cur: $41 (12/15/89)
40   96   STAG'S LEAP WINE CELLARS Cask 23 Napa Valley 1985 Rel: $75 Cur: $141 (11/30/89)
41   95   SASSICAIA 1986 Rel: $50 Cur: $50 (12/15/89)
42   95   OPUS ONE Napa Valley 1985 Rel: $55 Cur: $69 (6/15/89)
43   94   GAJA Cabernet Sauvignon Darmagi 1985 Rel: $70 Cur: $70 (3/15/89) CS
44   90   VALLANA Barbera 1986 $6 (2/15/89) BB
45   90   SAUSAL Zinfandel Alexander Valley 1986 $6.75 (3/31/89) SS
46   90   HOGUE Johannisberg Riesling Yakima Valley 1988 $6 (10/15/89) BB
47   93   STRAUS Merlot Napa Valley 1986 $11 (2/28/89)
48   93   ROSEMOUNT Cabernet Sauvignon Hunter Valley 1986 $11 (1/31/89) SS

49   93   GUNDLACH BUNDSCHU Merlot Sonoma Valley Rhinefarm Vineyards 1987 Rel: $13 Cur: $16 (10/31/89) SS
50   93   MOUNT EDEN Chardonnay Edna Valley MEV MacGregor Vineyard 1987 Rel: $14 Cur: $20 (4/30/89) SS
51   93   CHATEAU OLIVIER Graves 1985 Rel: $15 Cur: $24 (2/15/89) SS
52   93   KEENAN Cabernet Sauvignon Napa Valley 1986 Rel: $16.50 Cur: $17 (8/31/89)
53   93   SHAFER Cabernet Sauvignon Stags Leap District 1986 Rel: $16 Cur: $20 (9/30/89) SS
54   94   DOM RUINART Brut Blanc de Blancs Champagne 1982 Rel: $61 Cur: $70 (12/31/89)
55   93   WOODWARD CANYON Cabernet Sauvignon Columbia Valley 1986 $18.50 (10/15/89)
56   93   NAVARRO Gewürztraminer Late Harvest Anderson Valley Vineyard Selection 1986 $18.50 (2/28/89)
57   93   DOMAINE AUFFRAY Chablis Vaillons 1988 $20 (12/15/89)
58   93   ORNELLAIA 1986 Rel: $25 Cur: $41 (12/15/89) CS
59   92   NALLE Zinfandel Dry Creek Valley 1987 Rel: $10 Cur: $10 (5/31/89) SS
60   92   LE MASSE Chianti Classico 1985 $12 (7/15/89)
61   93   CHATEAU MOUTON-BARONNE-PHILIPPE Pauillac 1986 Rel: $23 Cur: $23 (5/31/89)
62   92   WILLIAMS SELYEM Pinot Noir Russian River Valley Allen Vineyard 1987 $20 (5/31/89)
63   93   KUMEU RIVER Chardonnay Kumeu 1987 $29 (3/31/89)
64   93   BERNARD BURGAUD Côte-Rôtie 1986 $31 (1/31/89)
65   93   OLIVIER LEFLAIVE FRERES Puligny-Montrachet Les Chalumeaux 1986 $36 (4/15/89)
66   93   JOSEPH PHELPS Insignia Napa Valley 1985 Rel: $40 Cur: $46 (7/31/89) CS
67   93   DOMAINE DANIEL RION Vosne-Romanée Les Chaumes 1986 Rel: $47 Cur: $54 (4/30/89) CS
68   91   A. RAFANELLI Cabernet Sauvignon Dry Creek Valley 1986 $9.50 (9/30/89)
69   90   HESS Chardonnay California Hess Select 1988 $9 (11/30/89) SS
70   92   DOMAINE RASPAIL-AY Gigondas 1986 $15 (1/31/89)
71   92   CHATEAU DE MARBUZET St.-Estèphe 1986 Rel: $15 Cur: $16 (6/30/89)
72   92   BURGESS Cabernet Sauvignon Napa Valley Vintage Selection 1985 Rel: $18 Cur: $23 (7/15/89)
73   91   KIONA Chardonnay Yakima Valley Barrel Fermented 1987 $10 (10/15/89)
74   92   ROBERT MONDAVI Pinot Noir Napa Valley Reserve 1985 Rel: $19 Cur: $22 (4/15/89) SS
75   92   MATANZAS CREEK Merlot Sonoma County 1986 Rel: $20 Cur: $20 (6/30/89)
76   92   CHATEAU MONTELENA Cabernet Sauvignon Napa Valley 1985 Rel: $25 Cur: $44 (11/15/89) CS
77   92   CHANSON PERE & FILS Beaune Clos des Fèves 1985 Rel: $25 Cur: $33 (1/31/89)
78   92   E. GUIGAL Côte-Rôtie Côtes Brune et Blonde 1985 Rel: $30 Cur: $34 (1/31/89)
79   91   RIDGE Zinfandel Sonoma County Lytton Springs 1987 Rel: $11 Cur: $11 (10/31/89)
80   91   EDMUNDS ST. JOHN Syrah Sonoma County 1986 $12 (4/15/89)
81   92   CHATEAU MONTELENA Cabernet Sauvignon Napa Valley 1985 Rel: $25 Cur: $44 (11/15/89) CS
82   91   MICHEL TRIBAUT Brut Monterey County 1985 $13 (5/31/89)
83   90   RIDGE Zinfandel Sonoma County Geyserville 1987 Rel: $14 Cur: $14 (10/31/89)
84   92   KISTLER Chardonnay Sonoma Valley Kistler Estate Vineyard 1987 Rel: $22 Cur: $55 (7/15/89)
85   92   FERRARI-CARANO Chardonnay California Reserve 1986 Rel: $28 Cur: $42 (5/31/89)
86   90   LATAH CREEK Merlot Washington Limited Bottling 1987 $10 (10/15/89)
87   90   CASTELLO DI VOLPAIA Chianti Classico 1985 $10 (6/30/89) SS
88   91   BUENA VISTA Cabernet Sauvignon Carneros 1986 $11 (10/15/89)
89   91   TUDAL Cabernet Sauvignon Napa Valley 1986 Rel: $14.50 Cur: $20 (12/15/89)
90   91   BERNARD PRADEL Cabernet Sauvignon Napa Valley 1985 $12 (4/30/89)
91   91   CHATEAU LA LOUVIERE Pessac-Léognan 1986 Rel: $15 Cur: $25 (6/15/89)
92   92   CHATEAU ST.-PIERRE St.-Julien 1986 Rel: $17 Cur: $21 (9/15/89) SS
93   91   COLUMBIA Cabernet Sauvignon Yakima Valley Otis Vineyard 1985 $15 (10/15/89)
94   91   PESQUERA Ribera del Duero 1986 $26 (4/30/89)
95   90   GRGICH HILLS Johannisberg Riesling Napa Valley 1987 $7.75 (8/31/89)
96   90   FREEMARK ABBEY Johannisberg Riesling Napa Valley 1988 $8 (8/31/89)
97   91   SIMI Cabernet Sauvignon Sonoma County 1985 Rel: $13 Cur: $18 (9/30/89)
98   91   COSENTINO Chardonnay Napa Valley 1987 $11.50 (3/15/89)
99   91   ROBERT MONDAVI Pinot Noir Napa Valley Reserve 1986 Rel: $22 Cur: $23 (10/15/89)
100   90   KENDALL-JACKSON Syrah Sonoma Valley Durell Vineyard 1987 $17 (12/15/89)

THE TOP 100: 1988'S BEST WINES

1	97	CHATEAU LYNCH-BAGES Pauillac 1985 Rel: $37 Cur: $45 (4/30/88) CS
2	99	CHATEAU MARGAUX Margaux 1985 Rel: $76 Cur: $92 (4/30/88)
3	100	ROMANEE-CONTI Richebourg 1985 Rel: $210 Cur: $310 (2/29/88)
4	97	TOLLOT-BEAUT Corton 1985 Rel: $49 Cur: $49 (3/15/88)
5	97	GAJA Barbaresco Sori Tildin 1985 Rel: $94 Cur: $125 (12/15/88)
6	96	CASTELLARE DI CASTELLINA I Sodi di San Niccolo 1985 Rel: $25 Cur: $31 (5/31/88)
7	95	LOUIS JADOT Beaune Clos des Ursules 1985 Rel: $30 Cur: $30 (3/15/88) SS
8	95	SPOTTSWOODE Cabernet Sauvignon Napa Valley 1985 Rel: $25 Cur: $94 (11/15/88)
9	97	CHATEAU D'YQUEM Sauternes 1983 Rel: $180 Cur: $229 (1/31/88)
10	97	JOSEPH DROUHIN Montrachet Marquis de Laguiche 1986 Rel: $200 Cur: $244 (10/31/88)
11	98	LOUIS LATOUR Romanée-St.-Vivant Les Quatre Journaux 1985 Rel: $99 Cur: $110 (3/15/88)
12	98	CHATEAU PETRUS Pomerol 1985 Rel: $160 Cur: $350 (5/31/88)
13	96	GAJA Barbaresco Costa Russi 1985 Rel: $83 Cur: $100 (12/15/88)
14	96	GAJA Barbaresco Sori San Lorenzo 1985 Rel: $88 Cur: $102 (12/15/88)
15	95	RIDGE Cabernet Sauvignon Santa Cruz Mountains Monte Bello 1985 Rel: $40 Cur: $89 (7/15/88) CS
16	95	CHATEAU BEYCHEVELLE St.-Julien 1985 Rel: $35 Cur: $39 (8/31/88) CS
17	95	CHATEAU PICHON-LALANDE Pauillac 1985 Rel: $40 Cur: $53 (2/29/88) CS
18	95	CHATEAU DUCRU-BEAUCAILLOU St.-Julien 1985 Rel: $50 Cur: $51 (6/15/88)
19	95	DOMAINE DAUVISSAT-CAMUS Chablis Les Clos 1986 $40 (9/15/88)
20	95	GAJA Barbaresco 1985 Rel: $45 Cur: $58 (12/15/88) CS
21	93	FRESCOBALDI Pomino Tenuta di Pomino 1985 Rel: $12 Cur: $16 (9/15/88) SS
22	92	BONNY DOON Le Cigare Volant California 1986 Rel: $13.50 Cur: $25 (11/15/88)
23	92	KENDALL-JACKSON Syrah Sonoma Valley Durell Vineyard 1986 $14 (11/30/88)
24	92	ANTINORI Chianti Classico Pèppoli 1985 Rel: $16 Cur: $16 (5/31/88)
25	94	TORRES Chardonnay Penedès Milmanda 1987 $35 (12/15/88)
26	93	PENFOLDS Shiraz South Australia Grange Hermitage Bin 95 1981 Rel: $49 Cur: $62 (12/31/88) CS
27	94	PESQUERA Ribera del Duero Janus Reserva Especial 1982 Rel: $75 Cur: $75 (9/15/88)
28	92	SAN FELICE Predicato di Biturica 1982 Rel: $19 Cur: $19 (1/31/88) SS
29	90	BONNY DOON Pinot Noir Oregon Bethel Heights Vineyard 1985 Rel: $18 (6/15/88)
30	91	CLERICO Arte 1985 $22 (1/31/88)
31	94	B.R. COHN Cabernet Sauvignon Sonoma Valley Olive Hill Vineyard 1985 Rel: $16 Cur: $35 (11/15/88)
32	94	ARROWOOD Cabernet Sauvignon Sonoma County 1985 Rel: $19 Cur: $25 (12/15/88)
33	97	DOMAINE MEO-CAMUZET Richebourg 1985 Rel: $150 Cur: $235 (3/31/88)
34	97	CHATEAU LAFITE-ROTHSCHILD Pauillac 1985 Rel: $80 Cur: $99 (5/31/88) CS
35	97	CHATEAU LATOUR Pauillac 1985 Rel: $82 Cur: $95 (4/30/88)
36	96	CHATEAU HAUT-BRION Graves 1985 Rel: $70 Cur: $84 (4/30/88)
37	98	ROMANEE-CONTI La Tâche 1985 Rel: $225 Cur: $310 (2/29/88)
38	94	CHATEAU PICHON-BARON Pauillac 1985 Rel: $32 Cur: $36 (4/30/88)
39	91	CHATEAU MUSAR Lebanon 1980 Rel: $11 Cur: $18 (7/31/88)
40	92	CA' DEL BOSCO Maurizio Zanella 1985 Rel: $38 Cur: $38 (9/15/88)
41	95	KENDALL-JACKSON Cabernet Sauvignon California Proprietor's Reserve 1985 $20 (12/15/88)
42	96	LOUIS JADOT Nuits-St.-Georges Clos des Corvées 1985 Rel: $44 Cur: $46 (3/15/88)
43	96	JAFFELIN Clos de Vougeot 1985 $49 (6/15/88)
44	94	FROG'S LEAP Cabernet Sauvignon Napa Valley 1986 Rel: $14 Cur: $20 (12/31/88)
45	94	ROBERT MONDAVI Cabernet Sauvignon Napa Valley 1985 Rel: $15 Cur: $20 (12/15/88) SS
46	94	DUNN Cabernet Sauvignon Napa Valley 1985 Rel: $20 Cur: $64 (9/15/88) CS
47	94	CHATEAU MONTELENA Cabernet Sauvignon Napa Valley 1984 Rel: $20 Cur: $39 (10/15/88)
48	95	LOUIS JADOT Bonnes Mares 1985 Rel: $48 Cur: $78 (3/15/88)

49	95	DOMAINE DANIEL RION Vosne-Romanée Beaux-Monts 1985 Rel: $38 Cur: $55 (2/29/88)
50	95	CHATEAU CLIMENS Barsac 1983 Rel: $50 Cur: $50 (1/31/88) CS
51	95	CHATEAU FIGEAC St.-Emilion 1985 Rel: $37 Cur: $53 (5/15/88)
52	95	CHATEAU LA MISSION HAUT-BRION Graves 1985 Rel: $70 Cur: $73 (4/30/88)
53	94	OPUS ONE Napa Valley 1984 Rel: $50 Cur: $70 (5/31/88)
54	94	BIONDI-SANTI Brunello di Montalcino Riserva 1982 Rel: $80 Cur: $98 (10/15/88) CS
55	93	FERRARI-CARANO Chardonnay Alexander Valley 1986 Rel: $16 Cur: $28 (7/15/88)
56	93	GIRARD Chardonnay Napa Valley 1986 Rel: $13.50 Cur: $28 (8/31/88) SS
57	93	KENDALL-JACKSON Merlot Alexander Valley 1986 $16 (12/31/88)
58	93	CHATEAU DU TERTRE Margaux 1985 Rel: $14 Cur: $23 (6/30/88) SS
59	93	POMMERY Brut Champagne 1982 $24 (2/15/88)
60	93	PIERRE GELIN Gevrey-Chambertin 1985 $25 (4/15/88)
61	93	PAUL JABOULET AINE Côte-Rôtie Les Jumelles 1985 Rel: $35 Cur: $35 (9/30/88)
62	92	CHATEAU MEYNEY St.-Estèphe 1985 Rel: $16 Cur: $17 (8/31/88)
63	92	AVIGNONESI Chardonnay Il Marzocco 1986 $16 (2/15/88)
64	92	CLOS RENE Pomerol 1985 Rel: $17 Cur: $20 (3/15/88)
65	93	CHATEAU LARMANDE St.-Emilion 1985 Rel: $23 Cur: $23 (5/15/88)
66	93	CHATEAU LA CROIX Pomerol 1985 Rel: $25 Cur: $25 (5/15/88)
67	93	CHATEAU L'EGLISE-CLINET Pomerol 1985 Rel: $30 Cur: $57 (2/29/88)
68	93	BOLLINGER Brut Champagne Grand Année 1982 $30 (7/15/88)
69	94	CHATEAU RIEUSSEC Sauternes 1983 Rel: $52 Cur: $57 (1/31/88)
70	94	PRINCE FLORENT DE MERODE Pommard Clos de la Platière 1985 Rel: $45 Cur: $45 (3/15/88)
71	94	MOILLARD Echézeaux 1985 $47 (4/15/88)
72	94	DOMAINE JEAN CHARTRON Puligny-Montrachet Clos de la Pucelle 1986 $50 (5/31/88)
73	93	CHATEAU RAYAS Châteauneuf-du-Pape Réserve 1985 Rel: $41 Cur: $49 (7/31/88)
74	91	TORRES Penedès Gran Sangre de Toro Reserva 1983 $9.50 (6/15/88) SS
75	90	CASTELLO DEI RAMPOLLA Chianti Classico 1985 $8 (9/15/88)
76	93	STERLING Three Palms Vineyard Napa Valley 1985 Rel: $20 Cur: $22 (12/31/88)
77	95	JEAN-NOEL GAGNARD Bâtard-Montrachet 1986 $93 (12/31/88)
78	92	A. RAFANELLI Zinfandel Dry Creek Valley 1986 $7 (9/15/88)
79	92	CAYMUS Cabernet Sauvignon Napa Valley Cuvée 1985 $12 (7/15/88)
80	92	CORBANS Chardonnay Marlborough 1986 $10 (6/15/88)
81	91	INGLENOOK Gravion Napa Valley 1986 $9.50 (4/30/88) SS
82	91	PRESTON Sirah-Syrah Dry Creek Valley 1985 $9.50 (1/31/88)
83	91	INGLENOOK Merlot Napa Valley Reserve 1985 Rel: $10.50 Cur: $14 (10/15/88) SS
84	91	ALSACE WILLM Gewürztraminer Alsace 1985 $11 (7/15/88)
85	91	SILVERADO Chardonnay Napa Valley 1986 Rel: $12 Cur: $16 (4/30/88)
86	92	SAINTSBURY Pinot Noir Carneros 1986 $14 (6/15/88)
87	92	COSENTINO Cabernet Franc North Coast 1986 $14 (7/31/88)
88	90	ANTINORI Chianti Classico Santa Cristina 1985 $6 (10/31/88) BB
89	90	HUSCH Gewürztraminer Anderson Valley 1987 $7 (9/15/88)
90	90	BUENA VISTA Sauvignon Blanc Lake County 1987 $7.50 (6/15/88)
91	90	NAVARRO White Riesling Anderson Valley 1986 $7.50 (4/30/88)
92	90	CHRISTIAN BROTHERS Cabernet Sauvignon Napa Valley 1985 $8 (6/15/88)
94	92	CHATEAU ST. JEAN Chardonnay Alexander Valley Belle Terre Vineyards 1986 Rel: $16 Cur: $20 (7/15/88)
95	92	KISTLER Chardonnay Russian River Valley Dutton Ranch 1987 Rel: $18 Cur: $45 (12/31/88)
96	91	BERINGER Chardonnay Napa Valley Private Reserve 1986 Rel: $16 Cur: $22 (4/15/88)
97	91	PAUL JABOULET AINE Hermitage La Chapelle 1986 Rel: $35 Cur: $35 (9/30/88)
98	90	NALLE Zinfandel Dry Creek Valley 1986 $9 Cur: $9 (6/30/88)
99	91	ZACA MESA Pinot Noir Santa Barbara County Reserve 1986 $15 (6/15/88)
100	93	DOM PERIGNON Brut Champagne 1982 Rel: $75 Cur: $84 (10/15/88)

Ferdinand and Isabella; Artist Unknown; 1492; Chantilly, Musée Condé

500 years before Ferdinand and Isabella discovered Columbus, we had discovered a new world of our own—brandy.

In 1492, Ferdinand and Isabella approved Christopher Columbus's voyage. Five centuries earlier there was another great discovery in Spain: distilled wine spirits. These were the grandfather of today's grandest spirit. Brandy.

Today, you can enjoy the finest in Spanish brandies: Brandies de Jerez Solera Gran Reserva. These brandies blend young spirits with older ones. And they are aged a minimum of 3 years, most averaging 10-15 years. There is no smoother, more consistent flavor anywhere.

Discover eight distinctive tasting brandies with 1,000 years of history behind them. They're well worth exploring. For a brochure and a list of retailers, call 1-800-BE-THERE.

Brandy de Jerez Solera Gran Reserva

Great brandies from Spain, the country that invented brandy.

Conde de Osborne • Lepanto
Cardenal Mendoza • Terry Primero
Carlos I • Gran Duque de Alba
Gran Capitán • Gran Garvey

© 1990 Wines of Spain, New York, NY

Keeping Track of Inventory

BY STEVE HEIMOFF

Losing, and years later finding, three bottles of Château Pétrus in one's own cellar may not be the sort of thing that happens to most of us, but that may be because we do not have wine collections the size of Marvin Overton's.

The Fort Worth, Texas, neurosurgeon-rancher has so many bottles (he won't say how many) that it's quite understandable how a few of them could occasionally get lost in the shuffle. These things happen. Stacy Childs, a Birmingham, Ala., physician, recently rediscovered four bottles of 1974 Heitz Martha's Vineyard in his 6,000-bottle cellar years after he thought he'd run out of it, and Sid Cross, a Vancouver, Wash., attorney, has friends who found some 1961 Château Palmer lurking in the shadows long after they thought it was history.

All three were serendipitous finds; the wines were fantastic when opened. The ending might not have been so happy had the wines not been Methuselahs. It makes you wonder if there's a foolproof way of keeping track of your goodies down in the cellar so this sort of thing won't happen.

Right up front, let's admit there isn't. If you have 1,000 bottles, that's 1,000 more things to stay on top of, added to all the other minutiae of existence, and human nature rebels against keeping track of every sparrow that falls to earth. Besides, one could argue that keeping statistics on wine isn't the point; enjoying it is.

But keeping track of your inventory can be a good idea, and not just to avoid having good wines go bad on you. There are other reasons for keeping a log, particularly if you include some kind of tasting notes in addition to the number crunching. Collectors with particularly large collections say that, starting at about 1,000 bottles, keeping track becomes necessary simply to know where things are. Others, with personalities that tend to be organized (such as lawyers), find that record keeping is just something they gravitate toward naturally. Still others say that record keeping enables them to record their drinking patterns. And collectors who go so far as to record their tasting observations say notes help them understand what styles of wine they like, and how their taste evolves over time.

There seem to be three basic schools of thought on keeping records: the do-it-by-handers, the techies and the to-hell-with-its. Eugene Wong, a Honolulu physician, is a do-it-by-hander. He keeps a looseleaf binder that's divided into different sections, such as white Burgundy and Sauternes. Whenever something goes into or out of his 3,500-bottle cellar, a notation goes into the binder, just like a ledger book.

Childs use to have a manual system, but went high tech a few years ago when he transferred his inventory to a computer program called Lotus 1-2-3. That has its advantages; you can get up-to-the-minute printouts on the state of the cellar, and computer users are particularly enamored of the various "sort" options by which they can arrange the contents of their collections. Moreover, pecking away at a PC feels great, if you enjoy that sort of thing (but that's a different story).

But there's one huge disadvantage to computers. "It's cumbersome to boot the computer up every time you want to enter something. In the middle of a dinner party, you go down and get two more bottles and you don't want to take the time to put it in the computer," Childs says.

Childs found a solution for that. "I print out a copy of my wine list every six months, keep it in the cellar and pencil in every time I do something. Then, once or twice a year, I take the marked-up list and enter it into the computer. That makes it really easy."

Maybe so, but in actuality, points out Cross, you're then keeping two separate systems, and that doesn't make much sense. Cross prefers to keep his inventory in a looseleaf binder because "it's more personal and hands on, rather than a distant, computer-type feel." He has another, more practical reason for his hands-on approach. "It

takes more discipline, which makes you reflect on your inventory as to which [wines] are coming into drinkability and which are drinking up now."

Andy Lawlor, a Dexter, Mich., collector with 7,000 bottles, also attempts to keep inventory on his personal computer, but runs into the same kind of problem Childs does. "I must say it doesn't get updated too often. New purchases, everyday drinking and giving to charity often don't get listed, so it's always out of date." Lawlor keeps purchase receipts in a manila folder in the cellar and usually gets around to entering them in the computer at some point, but consumption rarely gets recorded as a debit. But Lawlor claims he possesses a vinous memory "that keeps things from getting too far out of kilter."

Vinous memory is a phenomenon noted by many wine lovers who shun record keeping. Even those who can't remember where they put the car keys last night say they have an uncanny knack for recalling the whereabouts of each bottle, or the taste of a Zinfandel they had back in 1979. Wong doesn't bother to keep tasting notes, he says, "because I have a good memory to keep track of tastings in my head." Jeff Zell, a Potomac, Md., collector with 2,000 bottles, says, "I pick sections of my cellar and memorize them pretty easily, so I have a visual of the entire cellar. I can give you a rough estimate of 90 percent of it from memory." Zell does put neck tags on his bottles.

Back to Overton. He admits he's tried computers, cellar logs, scratch pads and everything else you can think of to keep track of his collection, "but nothing works. In fact," he adds, "I think it's impossible to keep track. I don't know how it happens, but you don't really completely know how many bottles you have at any one time." It might be possible, he speculates, but not without putting in more time and effort than is worth the candle.

Maybe that's true when you start getting up to collections the size of Overton's. Those of us with more modest cellars will no doubt find the going easier, but it's a trade-off—we're not likely to experience the thrill of finding long-lost bottles of Pétrus at the bottom of the trove. □

Steve Heimoff is a free-lance writer in Oakland, Calif.

Special Ratings

The editors of *The Wine Spectator* meet twice a week to taste and evaluate wines for each issue of the magazine. And while the Buying Guide in each issue contains reviews and ratings of more than 100 wines, the editors always find several wines that they believe deserve special recognition.

Typically, the reviews of these wines are placed on the opening page of the Buying Guide and are given one of four special designations: Spectator Selection, Cellar Selection, Highly Recommended and Best Buy. Here are the criteria for these special designations:

SPECTATOR SELECTION—Our highest recommendation in each issue. Although it is not necessarily the highest scoring wine, it is the wine we think would make the most outstanding purchase. High quality balanced against value is the key to this rating. More expensive wines must be especially good to earn this distinction.

CELLAR SELECTION—This, as the name implies, is the wine we believe is the best candidate for addition to your cellar. We belive it will improve most from additional bottle aging and shows the greatest potential as a collectible.

HIGHLY RECOMMENDED—These especially noteworthy wines are selected from those scoring 90 or above. Expanded lists of these wines are not included in this section because of space considerations.

BEST BUYS—Wines carrying this designation are chosen because the editors feel that they show outstanding quality at modest prices. Because of their extremely attractive prices, these wines tend to disappear from retail shelves very quickly.

In this section, we present for you the cumulative lists of three of these special designations: Spectator Selection, Cellar Selection and Best Buy. They are listed on the following pages in order by score. First are lists of wines receiving our Spectator Selection designation. Next are those earning our Cellar Selection designation. Since the lists of Spectator and Cellar Selections go back as far as 1984, we have provided you with a release price, and where available, a verified current price. Finally, we list the Best Buys from 1990 and 1991.

SPECTATOR SELECTIONS BY SCORE

Score	Winery	Type/Appellation/Vineyard/Vintage	Release Price	Current Price	Percent Change	Issue Published
99	CHATEAU MARGAUX	Margaux 1983	$70	$100	42.86%	4/16/86
97	A. CHARBAUT	Brut Blanc de Blancs Champagne Certificate 1976	$63	—	—	2/01/86
97	CHATEAU PICHON-LALANDE	Pauillac 1983	$44	$53	20.45%	3/01/86
97	DUNN	Cabernet Sauvignon Napa Valley 1982	$13	$95	630.77%	11/01/85
97	HEITZ	Cabernet Sauvignon Napa Valley Martha's Vineyard 1984	$40	$77	92.50%	3/15/89
96	CAYMUS	Cabernet Sauvignon Napa Valley Special Selection 1980	$30	$128	326.67%	3/16/86
96	CERETTO	Barolo Zonchera 1980	$9.50	$16	68.42%	2/16/86
96	CHATEAU MONTROSE	St.-Estèphe 1986	$31	—	—	5/15/89
96	F. CHAUVENET	Chassagne-Montrachet 1985	$35	$43	22.86%	3/15/87
96	GRGICH HILLS	Chardonnay Napa Valley 1983	$17	$33	94.12%	10/01/85
96	MOILLARD	Echézeaux 1984	$21.50	$28	30.23%	11/15/86
96	NEWTON	Cabernet Sauvignon Napa Valley 1983	$12.50	$36	188%	4/15/87
96	SIMI	Chardonnay Sonoma County Reserve 1982	$22	$60	172.73%	5/01/86
96	SPOTTSWOODE	Cabernet Sauvignon Napa Valley 1987	$36	$56	55.56%	9/15/90
96	STERLING	Reserve Napa Valley 1985	$30	$38	26.67%	7/15/89
95	ACACIA	Pinot Noir Carneros Napa Valley 1984	$11	—	—	12/15/86
95	BELVEDERE	Cabernet Sauvignon Alexander Valley Robert Young Vineyards 1982	$12	—	—	12/01/85
95	BERINGER	Cabernet Sauvignon Napa Valley Private Reserve 1985	$30	$42	40%	12/15/89
95	CHATEAU COS D'ESTOURNEL	St.-Estèphe 1983	$29	$54	86.21%	5/16/86
95	CHATEAU HAUT-BRION	Graves 1983	$86.50	$87	.58%	9/30/86
95	CHATEAU PICHON-BARON	Pauillac 1988	$30	—	—	3/31/91
95	DUNN	Cabernet Sauvignon Napa Valley 1983	$15	$85	466.67%	10/31/86
95	FROG'S LEAP	Cabernet Sauvignon Napa Valley 1984	$10	$25	150%	3/31/87
95	WILLIAM HILL	Cabernet Sauvignon Napa Valley Reserve 1987	$24	$25	4.17%	11/15/90
95	LA JOTA	Cabernet Sauvignon Howell Mountain 1987	$25	$28	12%	7/31/90
95	LOUIS JADOT	Beaune Clos des Ursules 1985	$30	—	—	3/15/88
95	PIGNAN	Châteauneuf-du-Pape Réserve 1985	$14	—	—	8/31/87
95	RAVENSWOOD	Cabernet Sauvignon Sonoma County 1982	$11	$18	63.64%	4/01/86
95	ROBERT MONDAVI	Cabernet Sauvignon Napa Valley Reserve 1985	$40	$43	7.50%	11/15/89
95	SAN FELICE	Vigorello 1980	$12	—	—	2/28/87
95	SONOMA-CUTRER	Chardonnay Russian River Valley Russian River Ranches 1983	$10.50	$25	138.10%	11/16/85
94	BUENA VISTA	Cabernet Sauvignon Carneros Private Reserve 1985	$18	$23	27.78%	10/15/89
94	CAYMUS	Cabernet Sauvignon Napa Valley 1986	$22	$29	31.82%	3/15/90
94	CHATEAU CLERC-MILON	Pauillac 1988	$26	—	—	4/30/91
94	CHATEAU LA LOUVIERE	Graves 1982	$11.50	$25	117.39%	10/16/85
94	CHATEAU PICHON-LALANDE	Pauillac 1982	$29	$89	206.90%	2/01/85
94	CLOS RENE	Pomerol 1986	$19	$25	31.58%	6/15/89
94	DEHLINGER	Merlot Sonoma County 1984	$12	$18	50%	6/15/87
94	DOM PERIGNON	Brut Champagne 1980	$60	$94	56.67%	9/15/86
94	DUCKHORN	Cabernet Sauvignon Napa Valley 1986	$18	$24	33.33%	7/31/89
94	DUCKHORN	Merlot Napa Valley 1984	$15	$40	166.67%	12/31/86
94	FROG'S LEAP	Cabernet Sauvignon Napa Valley 1987	$15	$20	33.33%	12/31/89
94	GAJA	Nebbiolo d'Alba Vignaveja 1983	$16	$28	75%	2/15/87
94	HEITZ	Cabernet Sauvignon Napa Valley Martha's Vineyard 1979	$25	$71	184%	2/15/84
94	HESS	Cabernet Sauvignon Napa Valley 1987	$17	—	—	4/15/91
94	WILLIAM HILL	Cabernet Sauvignon Napa Valley Gold Label 1982	$18	$32	77.78%	6/16/86
94	KEENAN	Cabernet Sauvignon Napa Valley 1984	$13.50	$30	122.22%	10/15/87
94	KNUDSEN ERATH	Pinot Noir Yamhill County Vintage Select 1983	$35	—	—	7/01/86
94	ROBERT MONDAVI	Cabernet Sauvignon Napa Valley 1985	$15	$20	33.33%	12/15/88
94	ROBERT PECOTA	Sauvignon Blanc Napa Valley 1985	$9.25	—	—	10/15/86
94	JOSEPH PHELPS	Scheurebe Late Harvest Napa Valley 1985	$15	$21	40%	8/31/86
94	PINE RIDGE	Chardonnay Napa Valley Pine Ridge Stags Leap Vineyard 1983	$16	$25	56.25%	12/16/85
94	SILVERADO	Cabernet Sauvignon Napa Valley 1986	$13.50	$18	33.33%	8/31/89
94	SIMI	Cabernet Sauvignon Alexander Valley Reserve 1985	$25	$28	12%	8/31/90
93	ALEXANDER VALLEY	Cabernet Sauvignon Alexander Valley 1984	$10.50	$18	71.43%	5/15/87
93	BEAULIEU	Cabernet Sauvignon Napa Valley Georges de Latour Private Reserve 1979	$21	$53	152.38%	3/01/84
93	BEAULIEU	Cabernet Sauvignon Napa Valley Georges de Latour Private Reserve 1980	$24	$48	100%	9/16/85
93	BENZIGER	Cabernet Sauvignon Sonoma County 1987	$10	—	—	9/30/90
93	BUEHLER	Cabernet Sauvignon Napa Valley 1983	$12	$23	91.67%	7/16/86
93	CAYMUS	Cabernet Sauvignon Napa Valley Special Selection 1979	$30	$165	450%	6/01/85
93	CHATEAU DU TERTRE	Margaux 1985	$14	$23	64.29%	6/30/88
93	CHATEAU OLIVIER	Graves 1985	$15	$24	60%	2/15/89
93	CLOS DU BOIS	Chardonnay Alexander Valley Calcaire Vineyard 1984	$12	$30	150%	6/01/86
93	DOMAINE PIERRE AMIOT	Clos de la Roche 1982	$27.50	—	—	6/16/85
93	FERRARI-CARANO	Chardonnay Alexander Valley 1985	$14	$30	114.29%	9/15/87
93	FERRARI-CARANO	Chardonnay Alexander Valley 1988	$18	—	—	5/31/90
93	FRESCOBALDI	Pomino Tenuta di Pomino 1985	$12	$16	33.33%	9/15/88
93	GIRARD	Chardonnay Napa Valley 1986	$13.50	$28	107.41%	8/31/88
93	GUNDLACH BUNDSCHU	Merlot Sonoma Valley Rhinefarm Vineyards 1987	$13	$16	23.08%	10/31/89
93	CHARLES HEIDSIECK	Brut Champagne 1982	$33	$36	9.09%	12/31/88
93	LAUREL GLEN	Cabernet Sauvignon Sonoma Mountain 1981	$12.50	$42	236%	2/16/85
93	MANZANITA	Chardonnay Napa Valley 1983	$12.50	—	—	1/01/86
93	MOUNT EDEN	Chardonnay Edna Valley MEV MacGregor Vineyard 1987	$14	$20	42.86%	4/30/89
93	PAVILLON ROUGE DU CHATEAU MARGAUX	Margaux 1985	$23	$26	13.04%	4/15/88
93	PODERE IL PALAZZINO	Chianti Classico 1985	$11	—	—	11/30/87
93	ROBERT STEMMLER	Pinot Noir Sonoma County 1983	$15	—	—	3/16/85
93	ROSEMOUNT	Cabernet Sauvignon Hunter Valley 1986	$11	—	—	1/31/89
93	ST. ANDREW'S WINERY	Chardonnay Napa Valley 1985	$7.50	—	—	11/30/86
93	SHAFER	Cabernet Sauvignon Napa Valley 1984	$14	$25	78.57%	12/15/87
93	SHAFER	Cabernet Sauvignon Stags Leap District 1986	$16	$20	25%	9/30/89
93	SILVER OAK	Cabernet Sauvignon Alexander Valley 1986	$26	$37	42.31%	10/31/90
93	SONOMA-CUTRER	Chardonnay Sonoma Valley Les Pierres 1985	$17.50	$30	71.43%	9/30/87
93	VEUVE CLICQUOT	Brut Champagne 1982	$32	$41	28.13%	5/31/87
92	ALEXANDER VALLEY	Cabernet Sauvignon Alexander Valley 1982	$10	$16	60%	11/01/84
92	BICHOT	Volnay Hospices de Beaune Cuvée Blondeau 1982	$26	$38	46.15%	8/01/84

Without Black, it would all be flat.

Ultimately, there's Black.

Score	Winery	Type/Appellation/Vineyard/Vintage	Release Price	Current Price	Percent Change	Issue Published
92	BOLLINGER	Brut Champagne Spécial Cuvée NV	$25	—	—	12/31/87
92	BYRON	Chardonnay Santa Barbara County 1988	$12	—	—	4/30/90
92	CARNEROS CREEK	Pinot Noir Carneros Fleur de Carneros 1987	$9	—	—	2/28/89
92	CHATEAU DE FRANCE	Pessac-Léognan 1988	$18	—	—	2/28/91
92	CHATEAU DE MARBUZET	St.-Estèphe 1988	$15	—	—	7/15/91
92	CHATEAU ST. JEAN	Cabernet Sauvignon Alexander Valley 1987	$16	—	—	6/30/91
92	CHATEAU ST. JEAN	Johannisberg Riesling Late Harvest Alexander Valley Robert Young 1983 (375 ml)	$25	—	—	8/01/85
92	CHATEAU ST.-PIERRE	St.-Julien 1986	$17	$21	23.53%	9/15/89
92	CLOS DU BOIS	Chardonnay Dry Creek Valley Flintwood Vineyard 1983	$10.50	$37	252.38%	7/01/85
92	CLOS DU BOIS	Merlot Sonoma County 1985	$10	$16	60%	10/31/87
92	COLLI MONFORTESI	Barolo 1982	$15	—	—	4/30/87
92	GEORGES DUBOEUF	Moulin-à-Vent 1986	$10	—	—	7/31/87
92	DUCKHORN	Merlot Napa Valley 1982	$13	$52	300%	12/16/84
92	FAR NIENTE	Chardonnay Napa Valley 1983	$22	$38	72.73%	4/01/85
92	GUNDLACH BUNDSCHU	Merlot Sonoma Valley Rhinefarm Vineyards 1985	$12	$20	66.67%	2/29/88
92	HACIENDA	Chardonnay Sonoma County Clair de Lune 1986	$12	$18	50%	7/15/88
92	IL POGGIONE	Brunello di Montalcino Riserva 1978	$35	$47	34.29%	7/01/84
92	LAKESPRING	Cabernet Sauvignon Napa Valley Reserve Selection 1984	$15	$21	40%	10/31/88
92	MATANZAS CREEK	Merlot Sonoma County 1987	$25	$32	28%	6/15/90
92	MARKHAM	Chardonnay Napa Valley 1989	$12	—	—	6/15/91
92	MONTICELLO	Chardonnay Napa Valley Corley Reserve 1988	$17.25	—	—	1/31/91
92	GEORGES MUGNERET	Ruchottes-Chambertin 1982	$26	—	—	9/01/85
92	NALLE	Zinfandel Dry Creek Valley 1987	$10	—	—	5/31/89
92	ROUND HILL	Merlot Napa Valley 1983	$7.50	—	—	1/31/87
92	ROBERT MONDAVI	Pinot Noir Napa Valley Reserve 1985	$19	$22	15.79%	4/15/89
92	RUTHERFORD RANCH	Cabernet Sauvignon Napa Valley 1985	$11	—	—	5/15/90
92	SAN FELICE	Predicato di Biturica 1982	$19	—	—	1/31/88
92	SILVERADO	Cabernet Sauvignon Napa Valley 1987	$14	$18	28.57%	4/15/90
92	SONOMA-CUTRER	Chardonnay Russian River Valley Russian River Ranches 1982	$10	$24	140%	10/16/84
92	VITICCIO	Prunaio 1986	$19	—	—	3/31/90
91	BROWN BROTHERS	Chardonnay King Valley Family Reserve 1987	$15.50	—	—	7/15/90
91	BUENA VISTA	Sauvignon Blanc Lake County 1986	$7.25	—	—	7/15/87
91	CHATEAU HAUT-MARBUZET	St.-Estèphe 1988	$25	—	—	12/31/90
91	CHATEAU MOUTON-BARONNE-PHILIPPE	Pauillac 1985	$18	$26	44.44%	5/15/88
91	CLOS DU VAL	Cabernet Sauvignon Napa Valley Reserve 1979	$25	$55	120%	9/01/84
91	CUVAISON	Chardonnay Carneros Napa Valley 1988	$15	$17	13.33%	2/28/90
91	JOSEPH DROUHIN	Savigny-lès-Beaune 1985	$21	$23	9.52%	11/15/87
91	DRY CREEK	Cabernet Sauvignon Sonoma County 1985	$11	$16	45.45%	5/31/88
91	GRGICH HILLS	Zinfandel Alexander Valley 1982	$10	$17	70%	5/16/85
91	E. GUIGAL	Gigondas 1985	$12.50	$15	20%	9/30/88
91	INGLENOOK	Gravion Napa Valley 1986	$9.50	—	—	4/30/88
91	INGLENOOK	Merlot Napa Valley Reserve 1985	$10.50	$14	33.33%	10/15/88
91	KEENAN	Chardonnay Napa Valley 1988	$15	—	—	6/30/90
91	LAKESPRING	Merlot Napa Valley 1985	$12	$15	25%	3/31/88
91	LAR DE BARROS	Tierra de Barros Tinto Reserva 1986	$8	—	—	10/15/90
91	PINE RIDGE	Merlot Napa Valley Selected Cuvée 1985	$13	$18	38.46%	2/15/88
91	JOH. JOS. PRUM	Kabinett Mosel-Saar-Ruwer Wehlener Klosterberg 1983	$9	—	—	11/16/84
91	JOH. JOS. PRUM	Spätlese Mosel-Saar-Ruwer Wehlener Sonnenuhr 1983	$13	—	—	5/01/85
91	RIDGE	Zinfandel Napa County York Creek 1982	$10.50	—	—	7/16/85
91	ROSEMOUNT	Shiraz Hunter Valley 1989	$8	—	—	2/15/91
91	SAINTSBURY	Pinot Noir Carneros 1988	$15	—	—	12/15/90
91	SIMI	Cabernet Sauvignon Alexander Valley 1979	$9	$28	211.11%	4/01/84
91	SILVERADO	Cabernet Sauvignon Napa Valley 1985	$12.50	$20	60%	11/15/88
91	STAG'S LEAP WINE CELLARS	Cabernet Sauvignon Napa Valley Stag's Leap Vineyards Cask 23 1977	$30	$75	150%	10/01/83
91	TALTARNI	Shiraz Victoria 1985	$10	—	—	11/30/88
91	TORRES	Penedès Gran Sangre de Toro Reserva 1983	$9.50	—	—	6/15/88
91	VICHON	Chevrignon Napa Valley 1983	$9.60	—	—	1/01/85
90	BOUCHAINE	Chardonnay Napa Valley 1982	$14.50	$15	3.45%	6/16/84
90	BURGESS	Cabernet Sauvignon Napa Valley Vintage Selection 1980	$16	$39	143.75%	5/01/84
90	CASTELLO DI VOLPAIA	Chianti Classico 1985	$10	—	—	6/30/89
90	CHATEAU ST. JEAN	Fumé Blanc Sonoma County 1983	$9.75	—	—	4/16/84
90	CHALK HILL	Chardonnay Chalk Hill 1989	$14	—	—	5/15/91
90	CHIMNEY ROCK	Cabernet Sauvignon Napa Valley Stags Leap District 1987	$18	—	—	7/31/91
90	CLOS DU VAL	Sémillon California 1983	$7.50	—	—	3/01/85
90	DOMAINE DE LA ROQUETTE	Châteauneuf-du-Pape 1985	$13	—	—	7/31/88
90	FRANCISCAN	Merlot Napa Valley Oakville Estate 1984	$8.50	$15	76.47%	6/30/87
90	HESS	Chardonnay California Hess Select 1988	$9	—	—	11/30/89
90	J. LOHR	Chardonnay Monterey Riverstone 1989	$12	—	—	3/15/91
90	MASTROBERARDINO	Lacryma Christi del Vesuvio 1979	$6.25	—	—	1/01/84
90	RIDGE	Zinfandel Sonoma County Geyserville 1988	$14	—	—	11/30/90
90	ROSEMOUNT	Shiraz Hunter Valley 1988	$8	—	—	1/31/90
90	ST. CLEMENT	Chardonnay Napa Valley 1989	$16	—	—	5/31/91
90	SAUSAL	Zinfandel Alexander Valley 1986	$6.75	—	—	3/31/89
90	SILVERADO	Sauvignon Blanc Napa Valley 1988	$8.50	—	—	2/15/90
90	STERLING	Cabernet Sauvignon Napa Valley Reserve 1978	$27.50	$57	107.27%	12/01/82
90	VILLA BANFI	Brunello di Montalcino 1979	$18	—	—	4/16/85
89	KENWOOD	Cabernet Sauvignon Sonoma Valley Artist Series 1981	$25	$55	120%	9/16/84
89	JOSEPH PHELPS	Cabernet Sauvignon Napa Valley Backus Vineyard 1978	$16.50	$55	233.33%	4/01/82
89	PINE RIDGE	Chardonnay Napa Valley Oak Knoll Cuvée 1982	$13	$19	46.15%	3/16/84
89	PIO CESARE	Barolo Riserva 1978	$19	$28	47.37%	10/01/84
89	ST. CLEMENT	Cabernet Sauvignon Napa Valley 1981	$12.50	$24	92%	6/01/84
88	BOUCHARD PERE & FILS	Côte de Beaune-Villages 1982	$18.50	—	—	5/16/84
88	MATANZAS CREEK	Chardonnay Sonoma Valley Estate 1982	$18	$25	38.89%	7/16/84
88	TREFETHEN	Cabernet Sauvignon Napa Valley 1981	$11	$36	227.27%	12/16/84

TOOLS ARE MADE, BUT

BORN ARE HANDS.

WILLIAM BLAKE

POET & ARTIST

1757 - 1827

THE HANDS OF
CLOS DU BOIS
GENERAL MANAGER,
TOM HOBART.

Why cite an 18th-century humanist to

describe 20th-century Clos du Bois?

Because we know that our craft's "tools"—

from majestic vineyards to the distinctive

French oak cooperage—are merely material

prerequisites for elegant, graceful wines.

What sets them apart, however, is an intan-

gible yet essential human touch. It is born

of pride, dedication, even inspiration. The

heart and soul of Clos du Bois is a remark-

able group of people whose spirit, humanity,

and very hands nurture all our wines.

CLOS DU BOIS

CELLAR SELECTION BY SCORE

Score	Winery	Type/Appellation/Vineyard/Vintage	Release Price	Current Price	Percent Change	Issue Published
98	CAYMUS	Cabernet Sauvignon Napa Valley Special Selection 1986	$50	—	—	1/31/91
98	CAYMUS	Cabernet Sauvignon Napa Valley Special Selection 1984	$35	$118	237.14%	7/15/89
98	CHATEAU CHEVAL BLANC	St.-Emilion 1986	$80	$85	6.25%	6/30/89
98	CHATEAU MARGAUX	Margaux 1986	$80	$100	25%	6/15/89
98	CHATEAU MOUTON ROTHSCHILD	Pauillac 1986	$102	$114	11.76%	5/31/89
98	ROMANEE-CONTI	La Tâche 1986	$250	—	—	8/31/89
98	TAYLOR FLADGATE	Vintage Port 1977	$17	$75	341.18%	12/16/83
97	CHATEAU LAFITE-ROTHSCHILD	Pauillac 1985	$80	$99	23.75%	5/31/88
97	CHATEAU LYNCH-BAGES	Pauillac 1985	$37	$45	21.62%	4/30/88
97	CHATEAU MARGAUX	Margaux 1988	$75	—	—	3/31/91
97	JOSEPH DROUHIN	Montrachet Marquis de Laguiche 1986	$200	$244	22%	10/31/88
97	OPUS ONE	Napa Valley 1987	$68	$69	1.47%	11/15/90
96	CHATEAU CHEVAL BLANC	St.-Emilion 1982	$69	$143	107.25%	2/16/85
96	CHATEAU LAFITE-ROTHSCHILD	Pauillac 1988	$100	—	—	4/30/91
96	CHATEAU LEOVILLE-LAS CASES	St.-Julien 1986	$44	$61	38.64%	9/15/89
96	CHATEAU MARGAUX	Margaux 1982	$60	$138	130%	6/16/85
96	CHATEAU PALMER	Margaux 1988	$65	—	—	2/28/91
96	F. CHAUVENET	Chassagne-Montrachet Morgeot 1985	$37	$52	40.54%	5/15/87
96	PENFOLDS	Shiraz South Australia Grange Hermitage Bin 95 1982	$60	$68	13.33%	9/30/89
96	SILVER OAK	Cabernet Sauvignon Napa Valley 1982	$19	$53	178.95%	2/15/87
96	SILVERADO	Cabernet Sauvignon Napa Valley Limited Reserve 1986	$35	$38	8.57%	12/15/90
95	ACACIA	Pinot Noir Carneros Napa Valley St. Clair Vineyard 1983	$15	$30	100%	10/01/85
95	BERINGER	Cabernet Sauvignon Napa Valley Private Reserve 1986	$35	$39	11.43%	9/15/90
95	CAYMUS	Cabernet Sauvignon Napa Valley Special Selection 1978	$30	$225	650%	6/16/84
95	CHATEAU BEYCHEVELLE	St.-Julien 1985	$35	$39	11.43%	8/31/88
95	CHATEAU CLIMENS	Barsac 1983	$50	—	—	1/31/88
95	CHATEAU COS D'ESTOURNEL	St.-Estèphe 1988	$30	—	—	7/15/91
95	CHATEAU D'ANGLUDET	Margaux 1982	$15	$27	80%	12/01/85
95	CHATEAU D'YQUEM	Sauternes 1983	$180	$229	27.22%	10/15/87
95	CHATEAU LA FLEUR DE GAY	Pomerol 1986	$43	$48	11.63%	10/31/89
95	CHATEAU LYNCH-BAGES	Pauillac 1988	$35	—	—	3/15/91
95	CHATEAU PICHON-LALANDE	Pauillac 1985	$40	$53	32.50%	2/29/88
95	CHATEAU LE PIN	Pomerol 1988	$65	—	—	6/30/91
95	DIAMOND CREEK	Cabernet Sauvignon Napa Valley Red Rock Terrace 1984	$25	$65	160%	9/30/86
95	DUCKHORN	Cabernet Sauvignon Napa Valley 1987	$20	$27	35%	6/30/90
95	DUNN	Cabernet Sauvignon Howell Mountain 1986	$30	$91	203.33%	7/31/90
95	DUNN	Cabernet Sauvignon Napa Valley 1986	$27	$55	103.70%	10/15/89
95	GAJA	Barbaresco 1985	$45	$58	28.89%	12/15/88
95	E. GUIGAL	Côte-Rôtie La Turque 1986	$99	$340	243.43%	10/15/90
95	HEITZ	Cabernet Sauvignon Napa Valley Martha's Vineyard 1986	$60	—	—	4/15/91
95	INGLENOOK	Reunion Napa Valley 1983	$33	$38	15.15%	11/30/87
95	KENWOOD	Cabernet Sauvignon Sonoma Valley Artist Series 1986	$30	$31	3.33%	11/30/89
95	MARCHESI DI GRESY	Barbaresco Gaiun Martinenga 1985	$55	$73	32.73%	1/31/89
95	MOILLARD	Clos de Vougeot 1983	$26	$45	73.08%	10/16/85
95	MOILLARD	Vosne-Romanée Malconsorts 1984	$24	$28	16.67%	12/15/86
95	POGGIO ANTICO	Brunello di Montalcino 1985	$36	—	—	11/30/90
95	RIDGE	Cabernet Sauvignon Santa Cruz Mountains Monte Bello 1985	$40	$89	122.50%	7/15/88
95	RIDGE	Cabernet Sauvignon Santa Cruz Mountains Monte Bello 1984	$35	$80	128.57%	9/15/87
95	SPOTTSWOODE	Cabernet Sauvignon Napa Valley 1985	$25	$94	276%	11/15/88
95	STERLING	Reserve Napa Valley 1986	$35	$43	22.86%	3/15/90
94	BERINGER	Cabernet Sauvignon Napa Valley Private Reserve 1984	$25	$38	52%	2/15/89
94	BIONDI-SANTI	Brunello di Montalcino Riserva 1982	$80	$98	22.50%	10/15/88
94	CAYMUS	Cabernet Sauvignon Napa Valley 1983	$15	$42	180%	11/30/86
94	CHATEAU L'ANGELUS	St.-Emilion 1985	$26	$34	30.77%	3/31/88
94	CHATEAU LA CROIX DE GAY	Pomerol 1983	$16	$23	43.75%	7/01/86
94	CHATEAU LYNCH-BAGES	Pauillac 1982	$27.50	$54	96.36%	3/01/85
94	CHATEAU PICHON-LALANDE	Pauillac 1984	$27	$34	25.93%	1/31/87
94	COL D'ORCIA	Brunello di Montalcino 1979	$15.50	$26	67.74%	9/15/86
94	DOM RUINART	Brut Blanc de Blancs Champagne 1982	$61	$70	14.75%	12/31/89
94	DUCKHORN	Merlot Napa Valley 1983	$15	$45	200%	11/01/85
94	DUNN	Cabernet Sauvignon Napa Valley 1985	$20	$64	220%	9/15/88
94	GAJA	Cabernet Sauvignon Darmagi 1985	$70	—	—	3/15/89
94	HEITZ	Cabernet Sauvignon Napa Valley Martha's Vineyard 1982	$30	$65	116.67%	4/15/87
94	HENRI JAYER	Echézeaux 1982	$41	$150	265.85%	6/16/86
94	KEENAN	Merlot Napa Valley 1984	$16.50	$20	21.21%	7/31/87
94	OPUS ONE	Napa Valley 1981	$50	$91	82%	5/16/85
94	ROBERT MONDAVI	Cabernet Sauvignon Napa Valley Reserve 1981	$30	$34	13.33%	2/16/86
94	SILVER OAK	Cabernet Sauvignon Napa Valley 1986	$26	$54	107.69%	10/31/90
94	STERLING	Cabernet Sauvignon Napa Valley Diamond Mountain Ranch 1982	$15	$37	146.67%	11/16/85
94	WARRE	Vintage Port 1983	$28	$43	53.57%	12/31/86
93	BEAULIEU	Cabernet Sauvignon Napa Valley Georges de Latour Private Reserve 1982	$24	$39	62.50%	3/15/87
93	BERINGER	Cabernet Sauvignon Napa Valley Private Reserve Lemmon-Chabot Vineyard 1980	$20	$42	110%	8/01/84
93	CHATEAU CHEVAL BLANC	St.-Emilion 1988	$105	—	—	12/31/90
93	CHATEAU COS D'ESTOURNEL	St.-Estèphe 1982	$23	$77	234.78%	7/16/85
93	CHATEAU LA FLEUR-PETRUS	Pomerol 1986	$52	—	—	2/15/90
93	CHATEAU MARGAUX	Margaux 1984	$35	$62	77.14%	2/28/87
93	CHATEAU MONTELENA	Cabernet Sauvignon Napa Valley 1983	$18	$28	55.56%	11/15/87
93	CHATEAU RIEUSSEC	Sauternes 1983	$52	$57	9.62%	3/16/86
93	CHATEAU ST.-PIERRE	St.-Julien 1982	$15	$23	53.33%	12/16/85
93	DIAMOND CREEK	Cabernet Sauvignon Napa Valley Gravelly Meadow 1983	$20	$40	100%	2/01/86
93	DOMAINE DANIEL RION	Vosne-Romanée Les Chaumes 1986	$47	$54	14.89%	4/30/89
93	DUCKHORN	Merlot Napa Valley 1985	$16	$38	137.50%	12/31/87
93	FATTORIA DI FELSINA	Chianti Classico Berardenga Vigneto Rancia Riserva 1985	$23	—	—	4/30/90
93	FREEMARK ABBEY	Cabernet Sauvignon Napa Valley Bosché 1982	$15	$41	173.33%	5/16/86
93	GIUSEPPE MASCARELLO & FIGLIO	Barolo Belvedere 1985	$35	—	—	6/15/90

Score	Winery	Type/Appellation/Vineyard/Vintage	Release Price	Current Price	Percent Change	Issue Published
93	E. GUIGAL	Côte-Rôtie La Landonne 1987	$125	—	—	7/31/91
93	HEITZ	Cabernet Sauvignon Napa Valley Martha's Vineyard 1980	$30	$65	116.67%	7/01/85
93	PAUL JABOULET AINE	Hermitage La Chapelle 1982	$17.50	$50	185.71%	11/01/84
93	MOILLARD	Chambertin Clos de Bèze 1983	$37	$60	62.16%	9/16/85
93	OPUS ONE	Napa Valley 1982	$50	$83	66%	5/01/86
93	ORNELLAIA	1986	$25	$41	64%	12/15/89
93	PARIGOT PERE & FILS	Pommard Les Charmots 1985	$24	$34	41.67%	6/15/87
93	PENFOLDS	Shiraz South Australia Grange Hermitage Bin 95 1981	$49	$62	26.53%	12/31/88
93	ROBERT PEPI	Cabernet Sauvignon Napa Valley Vine Hill Ranch 1981	$14	$20	42.86%	1/01/86
93	JOSEPH PHELPS	Insignia Napa Valley 1986	$40	$40	—	8/31/90
93	JOSEPH PHELPS	Insignia Napa Valley 1985	$40	$46	15%	7/31/89
93	PINE RIDGE	Cabernet Sauvignon Napa Valley Andrus Vineyards Reserve 1980	$30	$60	100%	12/01/84
93	RENATO RATTI	Barolo 1982	$17	$28	64.71%	6/30/87
93	STRUZZIERO	Taurasi Riserva 1977	$22.50	$24	6.67%	8/31/86
92	BERINGER	Cabernet Sauvignon Napa Valley Private Reserve 1981	$18	$30	66.67%	6/01/86
92	BODEGAS VEGA SICILIA	Valbuena 3.0 Ribera del Duero 1985	$40	$55	37.50%	3/31/90
92	CHATEAU LAFITE-ROTHSCHILD	Pauillac 1978	$60	$161	168.33%	9/01/83
92	CHATEAU MONTELENA	Cabernet Sauvignon Napa Valley 1985	$25	$44	76%	11/15/89
92	CHATEAU SUDUIRAUT	Sauternes 1979	$19	$40	110.53%	2/16/84
92	CLERICO	Barolo Ciabot Mentin Ginestra 1985	$27	$40	48.15%	4/15/90
92	COCKBURN	Vintage Port 1983	$22	$45	104.55%	8/31/87
92	DIAMOND CREEK	Cabernet Sauvignon Napa Valley Volcanic Hill 1982	$20	$68	240%	12/16/84
92	DOMAINE DE CHEVALIER	Graves 1985	$43	$56	30.23%	9/30/88
92	F. CHAUVENET	Meursault Hospices de Beaune Cuvée Loppin 1982	$33	$65	96.97%	1/01/85
92	GAJA	Barbaresco 1986	$47	—	—	1/31/90
92	E. GUIGAL	Côte-Rôtie Côtes Brune et Blonde 1983	$21	$34	61.90%	4/30/87
92	E. GUIGAL	Hermitage 1986	$32	—	—	2/28/90
92	E. GUIGAL	Hermitage 1985	$33	—	—	4/15/89
92	HEITZ	Cabernet Sauvignon Napa Valley Bella Oaks Vineyard 1985	$25	$32	28%	5/15/90
92	KENWOOD	Cabernet Sauvignon Sonoma Valley Artist Series 1983	$30	$38	26.67%	11/15/86
92	MASTROBERARDINO	Taurasi Riserva 1977	$28	$51	82.14%	10/16/84
92	MOILLARD	Pommard Clos des Epeneaux 1985	$40	$45	12.50%	6/30/88
92	ROBERT MONDAVI	Cabernet Sauvignon Napa Valley Reserve 1978	$40	$70	75%	8/01/83
92	ST. CLEMENT	Cabernet Sauvignon Napa Valley 1982	$13.50	$20	48.15%	3/16/85
92	SAN FELICE	Brunello di Montalcino Campogiovanni 1982	$22	—	—	7/31/88
92	SASSICAIA	1985	$48	$84	75%	5/15/89
92	STERLING	Cabernet Sauvignon Napa Valley Reserve 1984	$25	$38	52%	3/31/89
92	TAITTINGER	Brut Champagne Collection Arman 1981	$80	$85	6.25%	5/31/87
92	J. VIDAL-FLEURY	Crozes-Hermitage 1985	$11	$13	18.18%	10/31/87
92	VILLA BANFI	Brunello di Montalcino 1981	$23	$32	39.13%	3/31/87
92	WARRE	Vintage Port 1980	$16	$36	125%	10/01/84
92	WHITEHALL LANE	Merlot Knights Valley 1982	$10	$19	90%	6/01/85
91	ACACIA	Pinot Noir Carneros Napa Valley Iund Vineyard 1982	$15	$29	93.33%	7/16/84
91	ANTINORI	Tignanello 1982	$37	—	—	7/15/87
91	ADRIEN BELLAND	Santenay Comme 1982	$12	$25	108.33%	8/01/85
91	BOUCHAINE	Pinot Noir Napa Valley Los Carneros Winery Lake Vineyard 1982	$15	$18	20%	3/01/86
91	CHATEAU LA CROIX DE GAY	Pomerol 1985	$33	—	—	3/15/88
91	CHATEAU LA TOUR HAUT-BRION	Pessac-Léognan 1988	$37	—	—	6/15/91
91	F. CHAUVENET	Pommard Hospices de Beaune Cuvée Dames-de-la-Charite 1982	$36	$60	66.67%	2/01/85
91	DOMAINE LONG DEPAQUIT	Chablis Les Vaudésirs 1984	$20	$30	50%	10/15/86
91	DOMAINE DU VIEUX-TELEGRAPHE	Châteauneuf-du-Pape 1986	$17	—	—	11/30/88
91	JOSEPH DROUHIN	Charmes-Chambertin 1986	$56	$60	7.14%	2/28/89
91	DUCKHORN	Cabernet Sauvignon Napa Valley 1985	$17.50	$38	117.14%	6/15/88
91	GRAHAM	Vintage Port 1985	$31	$47	51.61%	9/30/87
91	GRAHAM	Vintage Port 1977	$15	$66	340%	3/16/84
91	E. GUIGAL	Hermitage 1980	$13	$37	184.62%	9/01/84
91	HEITZ	Cabernet Sauvignon Napa Valley Martha's Vineyard 1981	$30	$61	103.33%	4/16/86
91	WILLIAM HILL	Cabernet Sauvignon Napa Valley Reserve 1984	$18.25	$26	42.47%	4/15/88
91	JAFFELIN	Corton 1983	$33	$45	36.36%	4/01/86
91	ROBERT MONDAVI	Cabernet Sauvignon Napa Valley Reserve 1988	$45	—	—	5/31/91
91	OPUS ONE	Napa Valley 1980	$50	$134	168%	4/01/84
91	PAOLO CORDERO DI MONTEZEMOLO	Barolo 1980	$16.50	$20	21.21%	12/15/87
91	PINE RIDGE	Cabernet Sauvignon Napa Valley Pine Ridge Stags Leap Vineyard 1982	$20	$34	70%	10/31/86
91	RAYMOND	Cabernet Sauvignon Napa Valley Private Reserve 1985	$24	$25	4.17%	7/15/90
91	RIDGE	Cabernet Sauvignon Santa Cruz Mountains Monte Bello 1978	$30	$94	213.33%	10/16/83
91	SHAFER	Cabernet Sauvignon Stags Leap District Hillside Select 1985	$24.50	$28	14.29%	5/31/90
91	STAG'S LEAP WINE CELLARS	Cabernet Sauvignon Napa Valley Stag's Leap Vineyards Cask 23 1977	$30	$75	150%	12/01/83
91	STELTZNER	Cabernet Sauvignon Napa Valley 1982	$14	$26	85.71%	9/01/85
90	CHATEAU PALMER	Margaux 1983	$45	$77	71.11%	7/16/86
90	CHATEAU MARGAUX	Margaux 1980	$30	$66	120%	5/01/84
90	CHATEAU PICHON-LALANDE	Pauillac 1980	$14	$36	157.14%	3/01/84
90	CLOS DU VAL	Zinfandel Napa Valley 1981	$9	$18	100%	5/16/84
90	DOMINUS	Napa Valley 1984	$40	$55	37.50%	5/15/88
90	FONTANAFREDDA	Barolo Vigna la Rosa 1982	$40	$45	12.50%	2/15/88
90	INGLENOOK	Cabernet Sauvignon Napa Valley Reserve Cask 1985	$16	—	—	2/15/91
90	JORDAN	Cabernet Sauvignon Alexander Valley 1981	$17	$44	158.82%	5/01/85
90	LAUREL GLEN	Cabernet Sauvignon Sonoma Mountain 1988	$30	—	—	5/15/91
90	JOSEPH PHELPS	Insignia Napa Valley 1980	$25	$52	108%	7/01/84
90	JOSEPH PHELPS	Scheurebe Late Harvest Napa Valley 1982	$15	$21	40%	4/16/84
90	STAG'S LEAP WINE CELLARS	Cabernet Sauvignon Napa Valley Stag's Leap Vineyards 1981	$15	$35	133.33%	9/16/84
90	STERLING	Cabernet Sauvignon Napa Valley Reserve 1980	$27.50	$43	56.36%	11/01/84
89	CHATEAU LA MISSION HAUT-BRION	Graves 1979	$48	$70	45.83%	9/16/83
88	CHATEAU DUCRU-BEAUCAILLOU	St.-Julien 1980	$13.50	$23	70.37%	5/01/84
88	CLOS DU VAL	Cabernet Sauvignon Napa Valley 1980	$12.50	$28	124%	2/01/84
88	GRAHAM	Vintage Port 1980	$18	$42	133.33%	4/16/85

Henri Forner, Bodegas Marqués de Cáceres

Jean Bachelet-Ramonet and Robert Haas

Prince Florent de Merode

Edgard Leyrat

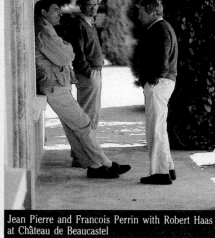

Jean Girardin of Château de la Charrière

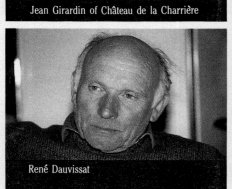
René Dauvissat

Louis Michel

Jean Pierre and Francois Perrin with Robert Haas at Château de Beaucastel

Vincent Delaporte   Jean-Marie Ponsot

Bernard Morey

IMPORTED BY
VINEYARD
BRANDS, INC.
CHESTER, VT

SHIPPED BY
ROBERT HAAS
SELECTIONS
BORDEAUX ★ BEAUNE

Colette Faller of Domaine Weinbach

Robert Haas in the cellars at Domaine Trapet

Photographs by Kindra Clineff and Gerry Dawes

James Symington at Warre's & Co., Ltd.

Jean Mongeard and Robert Haas at Domaine Mongeard-Mugneret

Michel Gouges, Domaine Henri Gouges

Jean Trapet, Domaine Louis Trapet

Robert Haas travels the wine cellars of France, Spain and Portugal regularly to taste and select the best estate-bottled wines from some of the finest winemakers in the world.

ROBERT HAAS SELECTIONS

Imported by Vineyard Brands, Inc., Chester, Vermont

BEST BUYS 1990-1991 BY SCORE

Score / Winery / Type/Appellation/Vineyard/Vintage / Release / Issue Published

91 WYNDHAM Cabernet Shiraz Hunter Valley 1987 $7 1/31/90
89 CASETTA Barbera d'Alba Vigna Lazaretto 1987 $9 3/15/91
89 CHATEAU ST. JEAN Pinot Blanc Alexander Valley Robert Young Vineyards 1988 $9 5/31/91
89 HANDLEY Gewürztraminer Anderson Valley 1988 $7 1/31/90
89 ISOLE E OLENA Chianti Classico 1988 $9 11/30/90
89 NAVARRO Gewürztraminer Anderson Valley 1989 $8.50 4/30/91
89 ROUND HILL Zinfandel Napa Valley 1988 $6.50 2/15/91
88 BON MARCHE Chardonnay Alexander Valley 1989 $8 3/31/91
88 BONNY DOON Grenache California Clos de Gilroy Cuvée Tremblement de Terre 1989 $7.50 2/15/90
88 COLUMBIA CREST Cabernet Sauvignon Columbia Valley 1986 $8 1/31/91
88 COVEY RUN Johannisberg Riesling Yakima Valley 1989 $7 8/31/90
88 TENUTA FARNETA Chianti di Collalto 1988 $6 12/15/90
88 GEYSER PEAK Cabernet Sauvignon Sonoma County 1987 $8.50 11/30/90
88 GUNDLACH BUNDSCHU Zinfandel Sonoma Valley 1988 $7 5/31/90
88 HERZOG Vin de Pays d'Oc NV $7 3/31/91
88 MARCHESI DI BAROLO Dolcetto d'Alba Madonna di Como 1989 $9 12/31/90
88 NAPA RIDGE Chardonnay North Coast Coastal 1989 $7 6/30/91
88 DOMAINE DE LA QUILLA Muscadet de Sèvre & Maine Sur Lie 1989 $7 11/30/90
88 RIDGE Zinfandel Sonoma County 1988 $8.50 2/15/91
88 TALOSA Chianti Colli Senesi 1988 $8 11/30/90
88 TYRRELL'S Cabernet Sauvignon Hunter Valley Classic 1984 $7 9/15/90
88 TYRRELL'S Cabernet Sauvignon Merlot Hunter Valley 1986 $8 1/31/90
88 STEPHEN ZELLERBACH Chardonnay Sonoma County 1988 $4 4/15/90
87 VINA BERCEO Rioja Crianza 1986 $7 9/30/90
87 BON MARCHE Cabernet Sauvignon Alexander Valley 1989 $8 2/28/91
87 BONNY DOON Grenache California Clos de Gilroy 1990 $8 2/15/91
87 DESSILANI Barbera del Piemonte 1986 $7 3/15/91
87 GEORGES DUBOEUF Beaujolais-Villages 1989 $8 11/15/90
87 GEYSER PEAK Semchard California 1989 $8 2/15/91
87 HARDY'S Shiraz McLaren Vale 1987 $7.50 7/15/90
87 INGLENOOK Chardonnay Napa Valley 1989 $7.50 2/28/91
87 CHARLES KRUG Pinot Noir Carneros 1987 $8.50 2/28/91
87 MARKHAM Sauvignon Blanc Napa Valley 1989 $7 10/31/90
87 JOSEPH PHELPS Grenache Rosé California Vin du Mistral 1990 $9 6/15/91
87 STRATFORD Chardonnay California 1989 $10 7/15/91
87 MIGUEL TORRES Cabernet Sauvignon Curicó 1988 $4.50 9/15/90
87 TRIMBACH Pinot Blanc Alsace 1988 $8 11/15/90
87 UNDURRAGA Cabernet Sauvignon Maipo Valley 1987 $5.25 2/15/90
87 LA VIEILLE FERME Côtes du Rhône Réserve 1989 $9 3/15/91
86 DOMAINE BRUSSET Côtes du Rhône-Villages Côteaux des Trabers 1988 $7.75 12/15/90
86 CALITERRA Cabernet Sauvignon Maipo 1987 $6 9/15/90
86 LAS CAMPANAS Navarra 1984 $6 3/31/90
86 CARNEROS CREEK Chardonnay Carneros Fleur de Carneros 1989 $9 6/30/91
86 COLUMBIA CREST Chardonnay Columbia Valley 1989 $7 9/30/90
86 COLUMBIA CREST Merlot Columbia Valley 1987 $8 9/30/90
86 COLUMBIA CREST Columbia Valley 1990 $6 7/15/91
86 GEORGES DUBOEUF Beaujolais 1989 $7 11/15/90
86 GERARD GELIN Beaujolais-Villages Domaine des Nugues 1989 $8 11/15/90
86 HILL-SMITH Shiraz Barossa Valley 1986 $9 2/28/91
86 MANZANITA RIDGE Chardonnay Sonoma County Barrel Fermented 1989 $8 6/30/91
86 MITCHELTON Shiraz Goulburn Valley 1988 $8 3/15/91
86 PENFOLDS Cabernet Sauvignon Shiraz South Australia 1987 $7.50 2/28/91
86 PENFOLDS Sémillon Chardonnay Koonunga Hill South Australia 1989 $6 9/15/91
86 SANTA MONICA Cabernet Sauvignon Rancagua 1988 $6 3/15/90
86 STONE CREEK Merlot Columbia Valley 1989 $5 5/31/91
86 RODNEY STRONG Chardonnay Sonoma County 1989 $9 7/15/91
86 MARK SWANN Cabernet Sauvignon South Australia Proprietor's Reserve 1988 $5.50 2/28/91
86 TAFT STREET Chardonnay Sonoma County 1989 $8.50 7/15/91
86 DOMAINE DU TARIQUET Vin de Pays des Côtes de Gascogne 1989 $5.75 11/15/90
86 TYRRELL'S Long Flat White Hunter Valley 1989 $5 10/31/90
86 LOS VASCOS Cabernet Sauvignon Colchagua 1987 $5 9/15/90
86 VINTERRA Cabernet Sauvignon Maipo-Napa Valleys NV $7 2/15/90
85 ANTINORI Santa Cristina 1988 $6.50 1/31/91
85 VILLA BANFI Rosso di Montalcino Centine 1987 $8 6/15/90
85 BLACK OPAL Cabernet Sauvignon South Eastern Australia 1987 $8 2/28/91
85 CHATEAU BONNET Entre-Deux-Mers 1990 $9 7/31/91
85 BODEGAS BRANAVIEJA Navarra Pleno 1988 $6 12/15/90
85 CELLIER DE LA DONA Côtes du Roussillon-Villages 1988 $8.50 10/15/90
85 CHATEAU STE. MICHELLE Riesling Columbia Valley Dry River Ridge Vineyard 1990 $7 6/15/91
85 CLOS DU VAL Le Clos Napa Valley NV $5.50 8/31/90
85 COLLAVINI Grave del Friuli Cabernet Sauvignon 1984 $8 4/15/90
85 COUSINO-MACUL Chardonnay Maipo 1987 $6 3/31/90
85 J. DIAZ Madrid 1985 $5.75 3/31/90
85 JOSEPH DROUHIN Bourgogne Pinot Noir Laforet 1989 $9 4/30/91
85 ESTANCIA Chardonnay Monterey 1989 $8 3/31/91
85 FETZER Johannisberg Riesling California 1990 $6.75 5/15/91
85 FREEMARK ABBEY Johannisberg Riesling Napa Valley 1990 $8 4/30/91
85 FREMONT CREEK Cabernet Sauvignon Mendocino-Napa Counties 1986 $8 4/30/91
85 HIDDEN CELLARS Johannisberg Riesling Potter Valley 1990 $7.50 6/30/91
85 HOP KILN Marty Griffin's Big Red Russian River Valley 1988 $7.50 11/30/90
85 INGLENOOK Cabernet Sauvignon Napa Valley 1986 $7.50 2/28/91
85 PIERRE JEAN St.-Emilion 1988 $10 6/30/91
85 LINDEMANS Chardonnay South Eastern Australia Bin 65 1990 $7 2/28/91
85 LINDEMANS Chardonnay South Eastern Australia Bin 65 1989 $6 4/30/90
85 LOUIS M. MARTINI Pinot Noir Los Carneros 1988 $8 7/15/91

Score / Winery / Type/Appellation/Vineyard/Vintage / Release / Issue Published

85 VINA MAYOR Ribera del Duero Tinto 1989 $7 3/31/91
85 LOUIS METAIREAU Muscadet de Sèvre & Maine Sur Lie Carte Noire 1988 $8 11/30/90
85 MOILLARD Côtes du Rhône Les Violettes 1989 $7.50 5/31/91
85 NAPA CELLARS Chardonnay Napa Valley 1989 $7 4/15/91
85 OLIVET LANE Pinot Noir Russian River Valley 1988 $9 6/30/91
85 ORLANDO Cabernet Sauvignon South Eastern Australia Jacob's Creek 1987 $7 7/31/90
85 OXFORD LANDING Chardonnay South Australia 1990 $7 2/28/91
85 PARDUCCI Pinot Noir Mendocino County 1988 $7.50 4/15/90
85 J. PEDRONCELLI Cabernet Sauvignon Dry Creek Valley 1987 $8.50 11/15/90
85 CHATEAU PLAISANCE Premières Côtes de Blaye Cuvée Spéciale 1989 $9 2/28/91
85 LA RIOJA ALTA Rioja Viña Alberdi 1985 $8 3/15/91
85 SANTA MONICA Sauvignon Blanc Rancagua 1988 $6 3/31/90
85 SEGHESIO Zinfandel Northern Sonoma 1987 $6.50 7/31/90
85 SUTTER HOME Zinfandel California 1989 $5 5/15/91
85 DR. COSIMO TAURINO Salice Salentino Riserva 1985 $8 2/15/91
85 TIJSSELING Cabernet Sauvignon Mendocino 1986 $8 1/31/90
85 UNDURRAGA Cabernet Sauvignon Maipo Valley Reserve Selection 1985 $7.75 3/15/91
85 VINA SAN PEDRO Cabernet Sauvignon Lontue Gato de Oro 1986 $4.50 2/15/90
85 WALNUT CREST Merlot Rapel 1987 $4 6/30/90
85 WYNDHAM Merlot Hunter Valley 1986 $8 1/31/90
85 WYNDHAM Shiraz Hunter Valley Bin 555 1986 $7 1/31/90
85 STEPHEN ZELLERBACH Chardonnay Sonoma County 1989 $8.50 11/30/90
84 BARTON & GUESTIER Bordeaux Merlot 1988 $6 2/15/90
84 BODEGAS BERBERANA Rioja Carta de Plata 1987 $7.50 12/15/90
84 BONNY DOON Blush California Vin Gris de Cigare 1990 $7 7/15/91
84 BONNY DOON Chardonnay California Grahm Crew 1989 $9 9/30/90
84 BONNY DOON Malvasia Bianca Ca' del Solo Monterey 1990 $8 6/15/91
84 BRAREN PAULI Cabernet Sauvignon Mendocino 1987 $8.50 3/31/91
84 CANEPA Cabernet Sauvignon Maipo Valley Reserva 1988 $6.50 6/15/90
84 LES CAVES ST.-PIERRE Côtes du Rhône-Villages Les Lissandres 1988 $7.25 12/15/90
84 CHATEAU STE. MICHELLE Columbia Valley 1990 $6 7/15/91
84 CLOS DE BEAUREGARD Muscadet de Sèvre & Maine Sur Lie 1988 $6.75 4/15/91
84 CODORNIU Brut Blanc de Blancs Cava 1988 $9 12/31/90
84 COLTERENZIO Alto Adige Chardonnay 1989 $8 1/31/91
84 CORBETT CANYON Chardonnay Central Coast Coastal Classic 1989 $7/1L 7/15/91
84 JOSEPH DROUHIN Bourgogne Pinot Noir Laforet 1988 $10 3/31/91
84 CHATEAU DUCLA Entre-Deux-Mers 1990 $7 6/15/91
84 FINCA FLICHMAN Argenta Mendoza 1988 $4 3/15/91
84 JOSE MARIA DA FONSECA Periquita 1987 $5.75 12/31/90
84 CHATEAU GOFFRETEAU Bordeaux Rouge 1989 $8 5/15/91
84 DOMAINE DE LA GUICHARDE Côtes du Rhône 1988 $7 3/15/91
84 MAURICE JOSSERAND Mâcon-Péronne Domaine du Mortier 1988 $8 12/31/90
84 PETER LEHMANN Shiraz Barossa Valley 1987 $8 4/15/91
84 J. LOHR Cabernet Sauvignon California 1987 $7 2/15/90
84 LUPE-CHOLET Bourgogne Chardonnay Comtesse de Lupé 1988 $9 4/30/91
84 DOMAINE DE MARTINOLES Brut Blanquette de Limoux NV $8 4/15/90
84 MONTES Cabernet Sauvignon Curicó Valley 1987 $7 2/15/90
84 MOREAU Bourgogne Chardonnay 1988 $8 4/30/91
84 MOUNTAIN VIEW Chardonnay Monterey County 1989 $6 4/15/91
84 ORLANDO Chardonnay South Eastern Australia Jacob's Creek 1990 $7 5/15/91
84 J. PEDRONCELLI Fumé Blanc Dry Creek Valley 1989 $7 4/30/91
84 J. PEDRONCELLI Pinot Noir Dry Creek Valley 1988 $8 2/28/91
84 J. PEDRONCELLI Zinfandel Dry Creek Valley 1988 $7 11/30/90
84 R.H. PHILLIPS Cuvée Rouge Night Harvest California NV $6 5/31/91
84 QUINTA DO CARDO Douro Castelo Rodrigo 1989 $7 12/31/90
84 RAVENSWOOD Merlot Sonoma County Vintner's Blend 1989 $9 3/31/91
84 ROSEMOUNT Sémillon-Chardonnay South Eastern Australia 1990 $7 5/31/91
84 ROSEMOUNT Shiraz Cabernet South Eastern Australia 1990 $7 7/15/91
84 ROUND HILL Gewürztraminer Napa Valley 1988 $6.25 1/31/90
84 ROUND HILL Zinfandel Napa Valley Select 1987 $6 3/31/91
84 CASTELLO DI SALLE Montepulciano d'Abruzzo 1985 $15 6/15/90
84 STEVENOT White Zinfandel Amador County 1989 $5 12/31/90
84 MARK SWANN Cabernet Sauvignon Coonawarra 1987 $7 2/28/91
84 DR. COSIMO TAURINO Salice Salentino Rosato 1988 $7.25 3/15/91
84 JEAN-CLAUDE THEVENET Mâcon-Pierreclos 1988 $6.25 7/15/90
84 TYRRELL'S Cabernet Merlot Australia 1988 $7.50 3/31/91
84 TYRRELL'S Chardonnay Hunter Valley 1989 $7 10/15/90
84 TYRRELL'S Shiraz Hunter Valley Classic 1986 $8 1/31/90
84 VALLE DE SAN FERNANDO Cabernet Sauvignon San Fernando Valley 1988 $6 9/15/90
84 VALLFORMOSA Penedès Vall Fort 1984 $7 3/31/91
84 LA VIEILLE FERME Côtes du Rhône Réserve 1988 $8 12/15/90
84 VINA SAN PEDRO Merlot Lontue Valley 1988 $5 12/31/90
84 VINTERRA Chardonnay Maipo-Napa Valleys NV $7 3/31/90
84 WEIBEL Cabernet Sauvignon Mendocino County 1987 $8 2/28/91
84 WHITEHALL LANE Chardonnay Napa Valley Le Petit 1988 $8 4/30/90
84 YALUMBA Tawny Port South Australia Clocktower NV $8.50 4/15/91
83 VILLA BIANCHI Verdicchio dei Castelli di Jesi Classico 1989 $7 6/30/91
83 BODEGAS MARTINEZ BUJANDA Rioja Valdemar Vino Tinto 1989 $7 6/30/91
83 BODEGAS CAMPO VIEJO Rioja 1985 $6.50 3/15/90
83 CHRISTOPHE Chardonnay California 1988 $7.50 4/30/90
83 DOMAINE ST. GEORGE Cabernet Sauvignon Sonoma County 1988 $6 11/15/90
83 ERRAZURIZ PANQUEHUE Chardonnay Maule Reserva 1989 $7 9/15/90
83 ESTANCIA Chardonnay Alexander Valley 1988 $8 4/30/90
83 FINCA FLICHMAN Chardonnay Mendoza Proprietor's Private Reserve 1990 $6 4/30/91
83 JOSE MARIA DA FONSECA Pasmados 1984 $7.25 4/30/91
83 VITTORIO INNOCENTI Chianti 1987 $7 5/15/90
83 KONOCTI Merlot Lake County 1988 $9.50 3/31/91

THE ART OF ANTICIPATION.

COGNAC. L'ART DE MARTELL.

Score / Winery / Type/Appellation/Vineyard/Vintage / Release / Issue Published

83 CHARLES KRUG Zinfandel Napa Valley 1989 $6 12/15/90
83 PETER LEHMANN Sémillon Late Harvest Barossa Valley Botrytis Sauternes 1988 $6/375ml 4/15/91
83 LIBERTY SCHOOL Three Valley Select Series One California 1989 $4.50 6/15/91
83 LUPE-CHOLET Bourgogne Pinot Noir Comte de Lupé 1988 $9 2/28/90
83 LUPE-CHOLET Crozes-Hermitage 1987 $8 3/31/90
83 MADDALENA Chardonnay Central Coast 1989 $8 4/30/91
83 LOUIS M. MARTINI Barbera California 1987 $6 12/31/90
83 MONTEREY VINEYARD Cabernet Sauvignon Monterey County Classic 1987 $6 1/31/91
83 ANTONIO & ELIO MONTI Montepulciano d'Abruzzo 1988 $6.25 2/15/91
83 MONTPELLIER Cabernet Sauvignon California 1988 $7 7/31/91
83 MONTROSE Chardonnay South Eastern Australia Bin 747 1989 $8 2/28/90
83 NAPA RIDGE Chardonnay Central Coast 1989 $7 11/15/90
83 BODEGAS OLARRA Rioja Añares 1987 $6.50 3/31/90
83 ORLANDO Cabernet Sauvignon South Eastern Australia Jacob's Creek 1988 $7 7/15/91
83 PARDUCCI Chardonnay Mendocino County 1989 $9.50 7/15/91
83 R.H. PHILLIPS Chardonnay California 1990 $8 7/15/91
83 R.H. PHILLIPS Chardonnay California 1989 $7 4/30/91
83 CHATEAU PITRAY Côtes de Castillon 1988 $7 3/31/90
83 BODEGAS PRINCIPE DE VIANA Cabernet Sauvignon Navarra 1989 $8 3/31/91
83 RAVENSWOOD Zinfandel North Coast Vintner's Blend 1989 $7.50 7/31/91
83 BARONE RICASOLI Chianti 1989 $7 4/15/91
83 RICHMOND GROVE Chardonnay Hunter Valley French Cask 1989 $7 5/15/91
83 BODEGAS RIOJANAS Rioja Monte Real Reserva 1983 $7.50 3/31/90
83 ROSEMOUNT Dry Red Diamond Reserve Hunter Valley 1988 $6.50 2/28/90
83 ROUND HILL Chardonnay California House 1989 $6.50 7/15/91
83 ROUND HILL Chardonnay California House 1988 $5.50 4/15/90
83 ROUND HILL Fumé Blanc Napa Valley House 1989 $5.75 11/30/90
83 RUFFINO Chianti Classico 1987 $7 4/30/90
83 SENORIO DE SARRIA Navarra 1984 $5 2/28/90
83 TRAPICHE Malbec Mendoza Reserve 1987 $5 9/15/90
83 UNDURRAGA Cabernet Sauvignon Maipo Valley 1988 $5.25 9/15/90
83 UNDURRAGA Cabernet Sauvignon Maipo Valley Reserve Selection 1986 $8 6/15/91
83 LOS VASCOS Sauvignon Blanc Colchagua 1988 $4.75 3/31/90
83 VINA DEL MAR Cabernet Sauvignon Curicó Selección Especial 35 1987 $6 9/15/90
82 BADIA A COLTIBUONO Chianti Cetamura 1988 $7 12/15/90
82 BOEGER Hangtown Red California 1987 $5.25 2/28/90
82 CHATEAU DU BOIS DE LA GARDE Côtes du Rhône 1988 $7 10/31/90
82 BONNY DOON Grahm Crew Vin Rouge California 1989 $7.50 10/31/90
82 BOSCAINI Soave Classico Monteleone 1988 $6 6/30/91
82 BOUCHARD PERE & FILS Côtes du Rhône 1989 $8.50 7/15/91
82 CANTERBURY Chardonnay California 1989 $7.50 7/15/91
82 CHATEAU DE BAUN Château Blanc Reserve Sonoma County 1989 $5 6/15/91
82 COLDRIDGE Sémillon Chardonnay Victoria 1990 $6 4/15/91
82 COUSINO-MACUL Chardonnay Maipo Reserva 1988 $7.75 4/30/90
82 CUNE Rioja Clarete 1986 $7 2/28/90
82 CHATEAU LA DECELLE Côteaux du Tricastin 1989 $7.50 7/15/91
82 DOMAINE BRETON Chardonnay California 1989 $8 2/28/91
82 JOSEPH DROUHIN Bourgogne Chardonnay Laforet 1989 $9 4/30/91
82 ESTANCIA Chardonnay Monterey 1988 $8 4/30/90
82 ESTANCIA Sauvignon Blanc Alexander Valley 1988 $6 5/15/90
82 FETZER Chardonnay California Sundial 1989 $8 4/30/90
82 E.&J. GALLO Cabernet Sauvignon Northern Sonoma Reserve 1982 $6 5/31/91
82 E.&J. GALLO Sauvignon Blanc California Reserve 1989 $4 7/31/91
82 CHATEAU DE LA GRAVE Bordeaux Supérieur 1988 $8 7/15/90
82 HARDY'S Chardonnay Sunraysia 1988 $7 7/31/90
82 ISOLE E OLENA Antiche Tenute 1989 $6 10/31/90
82 CHATEAU LAGARENNE Bordeaux Supérieur 1988 $8 7/31/90
82 CHATEAU LAGRAVE PARAN Bordeaux 1988 $6 7/15/90
82 LOUIS M. MARTINI Pinot Noir Carneros 1987 $7 2/28/91
82 MASI Bardolino Classico Superiore 1988 $6 5/15/91
82 MCDOWELL Grenache Rosé McDowell Valley Les Vieux Cépages 1990 $7.50 6/15/91
82 MCDOWELL Grenache Rosé McDowell Valley Les Vieux Cépages 1989 $6.50 10/31/90
82 MONTEREY PENINSULA California NV $6.50 7/15/91
82 MOUNTAIN VIEW Pinot Noir Monterey-Napa Counties 1989 $6 2/28/91
82 BODEGAS MUGA-VILLFRANCA Navarra Mendiani 1989 $4 6/15/91
82 ALEJANDRO HERNANDEZ MUNOZ Cabernet Sauvignon Maipo Viña Portal del Alto Gran Reserva Tinto 1983 $4 9/15/90
82 NAPA RIDGE Pinot Noir North Coast Coastal 1989 $7.50 7/31/91
82 NICOLAS Beaujolais-Villages 1989 $8 11/15/90
82 BODEGAS OLARRA Rioja Añares Blanco Seco 1988 $7 3/31/90
82 OXFORD LANDING Chardonnay South Australia 1989 $7 10/15/90
82 R.H. PHILLIPS Cabernet Sauvignon California 1989 $8 7/31/91
82 RABBIT RIDGE Mystique Sonoma County 1989 $7 6/30/91
82 CHATEAU ROC MIGNON D'ADRIEN Bordeaux Supérieur 1989 $6 2/28/91
82 SAN MARTIN Petite Sirah Baja California International Series 1987 $4 8/31/90
82 DOMAINE ST.-CHARLES Beaujolais-Villages Château du Bluizard 1988 $8 11/15/90
82 TORRES Penedès Sangre de Toro 1988 $6.50 3/31/91
82 MIGUEL TORRES Cabernet Sauvignon Curicó 1989 $7 6/15/91
82 CHATEAU VAL JOANIS Côtes du Lubéron 1988 $7 6/30/90
82 M.G. VALLEJO Cabernet Sauvignon California 1986 $5 6/15/90
82 VARICHON & CLERC Demi-Sec NV $7 1/31/90
82 LOS VASCOS Cabernet Sauvignon Colchagua 1988 $7 6/15/91
82 VINA DEL MAR Merlot Curicó Selección Especial 12 1988 $6 9/15/90
82 WEIBEL Chardonnay Mendocino County 1989 $8 3/31/91
82 XENIUS Cava NV $7.50 7/15/90
82 STEPHEN ZELLERBACH Sauvignon Blanc Sonoma County 1989 $5.50 12/31/90
81 CAVE DES COTEAUX CAIRANNE Côtes du Rhône-Villages 1988 $6.50 2/28/90
81 BODEGAS CAMPO VIEJO Rioja 1987 $6.50 9/30/90
81 CASAL THAULERO Montepulciano d'Abruzzo 1989 $6 6/30/91
81 CHANTOVENT Vin de Pays d'Oc 1988 $6 3/15/90
81 CAVE DE CHARDONNAY Mâcon-Chardonnay Chardonnay de Chardonnay 1988 $9 7/15/90
81 BODEGAS EL COTO Rioja 1985 $5 3/31/90
81 BODEGAS EL COTO Rioja 1984 $7 3/31/90

Score / Winery / Type/Appellation/Vineyard/Vintage / Release / Issue Published

81 FETZER Cabernet Sauvignon California 1988 $8 1/31/91
81 FINCA FLICHMAN Cabernet Sauvignon Mendoza Proprietor's Private Reserve 1987 $6 3/15/91
81 E.&J. GALLO Chardonnay North Coast Reserve 1989 $6.50 7/15/91
81 CASA GIRELLI Trentino Chardonnay I Mesi 1989 $8 2/15/91
81 CHATEAU GOFFRETEAU Bordeaux Supérieur 1988 $6 2/28/91
81 CHATEAU HAUT-RIAN Premières Côtes de Bordeaux 1988 $7 5/15/90
81 JAFFELIN Bourgogne Chardonnay 1990 $9 7/31/91
81 PIERRE JEAN Bordeaux Blanc de Blancs 1990 $7 6/15/91
81 LINDEMANS Sémillon Chardonnay Bin 77 South Eastern Australia 1988 $6 4/15/91
81 MARIETTA Old Vine Red Lot No. Eight Sonoma County NV $5.50 5/31/91
81 LOUIS M. MARTINI Cabernet Sauvignon Sonoma County 1988 $9 4/30/91
81 MIRASSOU Pinot Noir Monterey County Fifth Generation Family Selection 1988 $7.50 4/30/91
81 MIRASSOU Zinfandel California Lot No. 4 NV $5.50 7/31/91
81 ROBERT MONDAVI Cabernet Sauvignon California Woodbridge 1988 $6 2/28/91
81 MOUNTAIN VIEW Chardonnay Monterey County 1988 $6.50 4/30/90
81 MOUTON-CADET Bordeaux 1988 $9 4/30/91
81 J. PEDRONCELLI White Riesling Dry Creek Valley 1989 $5.50 9/30/90
81 RAVENSWOOD Zinfandel North Coast Vintner's Blend 1988 $7.25 10/15/90
81 BARONE RICASOLI Orvieto Classico Secco 1989 $8 4/15/91
81 ROSEMOUNT Cabernet Shiraz South Eastern Australia 1989 $6 7/31/91
81 ROUND HILL Chardonnay California 1988 $7.50 2/28/91
81 ARMAND ROUX Côtes du Rhône La Berberine 1988 $7.50 10/31/90
81 STE. CHAPELLE Johannisberg Riesling Idaho Johannisberg 1989 $6 12/15/90
81 SAN MARTIN Chardonnay Maipo Valley International Series 1988 $4.50 4/30/91
81 SANTA MONICA Sémillon Rancagua Seaborne 1988 $5 3/31/90
81 SUTTER HOME Cabernet Sauvignon California 1988 $5 11/15/90
81 TORRES Penedès Coronas 1988 $7 6/15/91
81 TREFETHEN Eschol White Napa Valley NV $6.50 1/31/91
81 VALLE DE SAN FERNANDO Cabernet Sauvignon San Fernando Gran Reserva 1984 $6 9/15/90
81 M.G. VALLEJO Fumé Blanc California 1988 $5 5/15/90
81 VEGA DE MORIZ Valdepeñas Cencibel 1989 $5.50 6/15/91
81 VINA DEL MAR Cabernet Sauvignon Curicó Selección Especial 35 1988 $6 6/15/91
80 RENE BARBIER Red Table Wine 1983 $3 3/31/90
80 BEAULIEU Burgundy Napa Valley 1987 $5 1/31/91
80 BELVEDERE Chardonnay Sonoma County Discovery Series 1989 $6 12/31/90
80 CHATEAU BONNET Entre-Deux-Mers 1988 $7 5/31/90
80 BODEGAS MARTINEZ BUJANDA Rioja Conde de Valdemar 1986 $7 6/30/90
80 LE CARDINALE Brut NV $5.25 6/15/90
80 BODEGAS JAIME CARRERAS Valencia 1985 $4 3/31/90
80 CASAL THAULERO Montepulciano d'Abruzzo 1988 $5 5/31/90
80 CHANTEFLEUR Vin de Pays de l'Ardèche 1988 $6 5/31/90
80 CHATEAU ST. JEAN Vin Blanc Sonoma County 1989 $5 2/15/91
80 ABEL CLEMENT Côtes du Rhône 1988 $6 2/28/91
80 CONCHA Y TORO Cabernet Sauvignon-Merlot Rapel 1986 $4.25 9/15/90
80 GEORGES DUBOEUF Côtes du Rhône 1989 $6 10/15/90
80 GEORGES DUBOEUF Vin de Pays d'Oc 1989 $6.50 11/15/90
80 ESTANCIA Cabernet Sauvignon Alexander Valley 1987 $7 7/15/90
80 GLEN ELLEN Cabernet Sauvignon California Proprietor's Reserve 1990 $6 7/31/91
80 HAWK CREST Sauvignon Blanc California 1989 $6 8/31/90
80 CHATEAU LAGRAVE PARAN Bordeaux 1987 $7 5/15/90
80 ROBERT MONDAVI Sauvignon Blanc California Woodbridge 1989 $5 4/30/90
80 BODEGAS MONTECILLO Viña Cumbrero Rioja 1989 $6 7/15/91
80 MOUNTAIN VIEW Cabernet Sauvignon North Coast 1988 $6 4/30/91
80 CHATEAU LES OLLIEUX Corbières 1988 $5.25 11/30/90
80 FREDERICO PATERNINA Banda Azul Rioja 1985 $5 3/15/90
80 DOMAINE DE POUY Vin de Pays des Côtes de Gascogne 1989 $5 11/30/90
80 ST.-JOVIAN Bordeaux Supérieur Premium 1988 $5.50 7/31/91
80 SANTA RITA Merlot Maipo Valley 120 1989 $7 6/15/91
80 SEGHESIO Zinfandel Northern Sonoma 1986 $6.50 5/15/90
80 SUTTER HOME Chardonnay California 1989 $5 11/15/90
80 TAJA Jumilla 1987 $6 3/31/90
80 TORRES Coronas Penedès 1987 $6.50 10/15/90
80 VIGNE TOSCANE Chianti Terre Toscane 1989 $5 11/30/90
80 VALLFORMOSA Brut Cava NV $10 12/31/90
80 LA VIEILLE FERME Côtes du Lubéron 1989 $7 4/30/91
80 VINA DEL MAR Cabernet Sauvignon Lontue Selección Especial 17 1986 $6 2/15/91
80 VINA DEL MAR Merlot Curicó Selección Especial 12 1989 $6 6/15/91
80 WALNUT CREST Cabernet Sauvignon Maipo 1985 $4 6/30/90
80 ZONIN Montepulciano d'Abruzzo 1988 $6 6/30/91
79 VIGNERONS ARDECHOIS Vin de Pays des Côteaux de l'Ardeche 1988 $4.50 4/30/90
79 CANEPA Merlot Maipo Valley 1988 $6 6/30/90
79 FINCA FLICHMAN Selection Mendoza 1988 $4.50 3/15/91
79 HARDY'S Premium Classic Dry White South Australia 1988 $5.25 6/15/90
79 ARMAND ROUX Bordeaux Verdillac 1988 $6.25 7/15/90
78 HARDY'S Premium Classic Dry Red South Australia 1988 $5.25 7/31/90
78 MOCERI Vin de Pays de l'Aude 1987 $4 6/30/90
78 ROSEMOUNT Sémillon-Chardonnay South Eastern Australia 1988 $6 6/15/90
78 SAN MARTIN Cabernet Sauvignon Maipo Valley International Series 1987 $4.50 6/15/90
78 L. DE VALLOUIT Vin de Pays des Collines Rhodanienn Les Sables 1988 $4.75 6/30/90
77 MOCERI Vin de Pays de l'Aude 1987 $4 6/30/90

Beaulieu Vineyard

For more than fifty vintages, the Private Collector's Private Reserve

Georges de Latour

1936

The first Private Reserve was from a vintage noted for the most severe frost on record. The wine is complex, the nose still rich. Showing some age, but still well balanced, with good flavors and a long finish. **18**

1937

The quality of the vintage was poor, and no Private Reserve was produced.

1938

Another difficult vintage. It is believed that little, if any, Private Reserve was produced, although the Cabernet juice was used to produce Burgundy and Claret.

1939

The growing season saw less rain than normal and only light frost. The wine from this vintage is well-balanced and rich. Now fully mature, it still has a remarkable nose, good flavors and a long finish. **82 ★★**

1940

The year began with a flood in February and the greatest annual rainfall on record. A mild growing season and absence of frost produced a somewhat lighter wine than in 1939. Showing its age, but still pleasant. **16**

1941

Said to be one of the best vintages ever produced at Beaulieu. A big, ripe wine, it required considerable bottle aging when young. Now mature, but with a flowery bouquet and spicy, anise flavors. **85 ★★**

1942

A cold, wet winter followed by a cool and rainy spring delayed bud break and produced a wine slightly lighter than the previous year, but of similar quality. Tasted in 1989, the wine surprised all with its complexity, life and rich fruit flavors. **87**

1943

Weather conditions similar to those of the previous vintage again produced a light-bodied wine.

1944

A late, short spring led to a cool, dry growing season. Judged superior to the previous vintage, the 1944 Private Reserve is fully mature, but still offers a bouquet of anise and plum. In recent years, the wine has been extremely scarce, due to limited production and loss of wine in the 1947 fire. **87 ★★★★**

1945

A very good vintage of good grape yields produced a medium-bodied wine with firm tannin and deep Cabernet fruit that was well-liked by everyone at Beaulieu.

1946

Ideal growing conditions, free from spring frosts, led to a vintage rated excellent in the Napa Valley. It was the year of both the legendary Beaumont Pinot Noir and a superb Private Reserve of ripe, rich fruit flavors. **15.5 88**

1947

The growing season began with early bud break, followed by generally mild and fair weather and ending in an excellent vintage. Crop size was rather low. The wine is medium-bodied, with rich flavors, fine balance and a long finish. This was the year of the fire at Beaulieu, which destroyed two buildings and over 800,000 gallons of wine. Consequently, 10,000 gallons of older Private Reserve was transferred to Rutherford Cabernet to keep up with sales demands. **16 93 ★★★★ (★)**

1948

Considered a poor vintage, with grapes never fully reaching maturity and repeated rains during harvest. The Cabernet crop itself was nearly double that of the previous year. Still, the vintage produced a pleasant, though light-bodied, Private Reserve that drew favorable comments in later years. **85 ★★**

1949

A mild growing season followed a winter of abundant rainfall and the coldest temperatures on record. The crop size was rather small, but of good quality and only Private Reserve Cabernet was produced. The wine has medium body, rich flavors and a long finish. **17**

1950

An excellent vintage, with Cabernet sugars averaging 22 degrees Brix, although crop size was small due to below-average rainfall and a May frost. The wine is elegant, with a perfumed, faintly cedary nose. **16**

1951

Among the finest Private Reserve vintages, from a superb growing season and medium-sized crop. An elegant, complex wine with lovely flavors and balance, which should continue to hold for 20 years. Perhaps the best California Cabernet ever made, say some experts. **19 90 ★★★★**

1952

After some damage due to a late spring frost, the vintage was a very good one, with dry weather during harvest allowing grapes to reach optimum maturity. The wine is somewhat light, but has some fruit and vanilla flavors and is holding well. **15**

1953

An extremely cold winter was followed by an April frost which caused substantial crop damage. A very small amount of Private Reserve is believed to have been made and the wine is delicate and elegant.

1954

A very favorable growing season produced a large crop of Cabernet and the grapes from BV Vineyard No. 1 were sold. The Private Reserve from this vintage was good to excellent, with medium structure, good flavors and finish. **16**

1955

A spring marked by frost and a rainy September produced a Private Reserve that was light in body and color, but still complex, with good flavors and a fine finish.

1956

Ample winter rainfall and little spring frost led to a nearly ideal growing season and the Cabernet grapes were harvested in good condition and at desired sugar levels. The wine is complex and intriguing, with a perfumed nose and rounded, faintly spicy flavors with hints of tea leaves and vanilla. **18 88 ★★★**

1957

A generally favorable growing season produced a medium-large crop. The Private Reserve was above average quality, a delicate wine that is now fully mature.

1958

An exceptional vintage and large crop produced a big, richly-textured Private Reserve of tremendous structure and complexity, excellent flavors and a long finish. Once magnificent, this wine is still a great vintage, although it is aging now. **18 96 ★★★★★**

1959

Below average rainfall and moderate summer temperatures produced a large crop of very good quality. Somewhat less concentrated than the '58, this wine is more subtle and elegant, with good fruit and toasty, minty undertones. **17 89**

1960

Another very good vintage produced a medium-bodied wine that was the last Private Reserve produced from the original plantings made by Georges de Latour. Tasted in 1989, it was rated "astonishingly good," well-balanced and elegant, with good flavors and a long finish. **17**

1961

A disastrous series of spring frosts, followed by a cool summer, reduced crop size dramatically and prompted Beaulieu to initiate an aggressive policy of frost protection. Harvest rains further slowed ripening and the Private Reserve produced was of average quality; elegant, with nice fruit. **16.5 78 ★★★(★)**

1962

A mild spring was followed by a cold and humid growing season, and the danger of mildew led to grapes harvested at lower sugar levels and with higher acid. Consequently, the Private Reserve produced was light-bodied, with distinct tea-like aromas. **73**

1963

A fair vintage in the Napa Valley, with severe heat in September followed by heavy rains during harvest. Only the Private Reserve grapes attained desirable sugar levels and produced a light-bodied wine that still retains some pleasant fruit flavors. **15 70**

1964

A warm summer and autumn led to a ripe vintage. Although crop size was somewhat short due to spring frosts, it was of excellent quality, and the Private Reserve was full-bodied and rich in extract, although it is showing age now. **84 ★★★**

1965

A very good vintage, despite extreme heat during harvest, which pushed temperatures to 111 degrees in Rutherford and generated numerous forest and grass fires with accompanying winds. The Private Reserve was of very good quality with medium body and great harmony between nose and palate. **15.5 85 ★★★★(★)**

1966

A dry spring was followed by a moderate growing season and early harvest of a light Cabernet crop of superb quality. Exemplifying the classic Beaulieu style, the '66 Private Reserve is a wine of finesse and elegance, still complex with a soft richness and very good flavors leading to a long finish. **16 87 ★★★★**

1967

A cold year produced grapes with lower sugar levels at harvest and a lighter wine that is slightly more tannic than previous vintages. The nose is rather austere and the wine is quite subtle, with some Cabernet fruit on the palate. **85**

1968

A classic vintage. Warm spring weather was followed by a warm summer and autumn without damaging temperature extremes, conditions ideally suited for producing grapes of optimum sugar levels and balance. The Private Reserve is superb, with excellent color, a lovely nose and complex fruit flavors; full-bodied, with a lingering finish. It should hold for some years. **18.5 91 ★★★★**

1969

Cool growing conditions produced a Private Reserve that was somewhat Bordeaux-like in its initial austerity. A fine balance between the Cabernet varietal fruit and American oak flavors along with higher tannin have enabled this vintage to gain complexity and develop into an excellent wine. **18 90**

1970

An outstanding vintage and a crop reduced to one-third normal size by severe spring frosts and heat-induced shatter during bloom resulted in Cabernet grapes of extreme concentration, deep color and intense flavor. The wine is powerful but elegant with deep color, intense aroma and rich varietal fruit flavors with undertones of the classic Rutherford dust. Should hold for many years. **18.5 95 ★★★(★)**

1971

A cooler growing season led to a late harvest with grapes picked at lower sugar levels. The wine is elegant with much finesse, good varietal character and pleasant. **17 67**

1972

Above average rainfall and cool temperatures again produced a lighter style of Private Reserve with subtle aroma, flavors and smooth body. **16 73**

1973

Warm, even temperatures during the growing season recalled the 1968 vintage and crop size was good — an unusual combination of quality and quantity. A "typical" Private Reserve — with an element of tea in the nose, good flavors, balance and a long finish. **16.5 79**

1974

Near-perfect growing conditions of warm days and cool nights permitted optimum maturation of the Cabernet fruit with excellent sugars and acid levels. The wine is rich and elegant with classic structure, fruit and Cabernet character. Now fully mature. **17 79 ★★★(★★)**

1975

A cool spring delayed bud break and was followed by a cool growing season ending in the latest harvest on record. The Private Reserve grapes, however, were of excellent quality and produced a wine of deep color, with medium body and a strong Beaulieu "house" character. **79**

1976

A very dry winter followed by a hot spring induced stress in the Cabernet vines, producing a small crop of small-sized, intensely flavored grapes. The wine is ripe without being raisiny, with deep color and rich in varietal intensity. It should continue to age well. **15 86**

1977

The second of two drought years, although some spring rain and moderate summer temperatures allowed a normal yield of Cabernet grapes with intense varietal character. Deep in color with strong character, the wine has the tannins to age well. **79**

1978

Ample winter rainfall provided vineyards with adequate moisture and excellent summer growing conditions produced a Cabernet crop of both large quantity and very good quality. Similar in style to the '68 vintage, this Private Reserve is rich and concentrated with black cherry and plum flavors. It is still developing. **15.5 91**

1979

Growing conditions were excellent and the Private Reserve grapes were fortunately harvested at desired sugar levels before heavy rains fell in late October. The resulting wine is intensely dark, with rich, concentrated flavors, firm back-bone and complexities that are still developing. **16.5 90**

1980

A long, cool growing season ended with a warm, dry harvest period that brought grapes to an excellent sugar-acid balance. The Private Reserve has a deep color and good varietal character, with flavors of currant and black cherry and undertones of mint. It has the potential to develop beautifully for the next decade. **18 93**

1981

A mild, rather dry winter led to a warm spring and an early bud break, followed by an extremely warm June and early harvest of Cabernet grapes of high natural acidity and excellent balance. While less concentrated than the 1980, this wine has excellent fruit, delicate balance and the potential to improve with age. **87**

1982

Abundant rainfall followed by a warm summer produced a large Cabernet crop of very good quality. The Private Reserve grapes were harvested at optimum maturity prior to heavy autumn rains. A wine of intense color and flavors, this vintage has the firm tannins to cellar a decade or more. **17 88**

1983

A warm summer and cool September, preceeded by ample rainfall, again produced a large crop of very good quality. The Private Reserve is somewhat lean with good structure, varietal fruit and herbal flavors that should develop with additional aging. **82**

1984

Warm summer days and cool nights led to the earliest harvest in Beaulieu history, with Cabernet berries of small size and intense varietal character. The resulting wine is rich and opulent with currant, black cherry and anise flavors and the potential to age very well. **91**

1985

A classic vintage, with the optimum balance of early season warmth followed by a cool, extended maturation period. The resulting Private Reserve is superb, with rich, ripe varietal fruit, excellent balance and a lingering finish. Excellent now, this wine has the potential to develop for at least 20 years. **95**

1986

A long and cool growing season allowed slow maturation of grapes with optimum varietal character, producing the third consecutive superlative vintage of Private Reserve. A rich and concentrated Cabernet with intense black currant, cedar and berry aromas, this wine is tightly knit and has excellent cellaring potential. **93**

1987

A warm spring followed by a summer of moderate temperatures again permitted an extended growing season, while low rainfall produced small berries of intense flavor. Tasted in barrel, the wine promises to rate among the finest Private Reserves. **90***

1988

The growing season was atypical, beginning with an unseasonably warm early spring, followed by a period of rain and cool temperatures. Mid-summer brought the onset of extremely warm weather, leading to an early and rapid harvest.

Ratings

20 point scale from "The Underground Wine Journal"

100 point scale from "California's Great Cabernets" by James Laube (Senior Editor, The Wine Spectator)

★ ratings from "The Great Vintage Book" by Michael Broadbent

* ratings from Robert Parker, "The Wine Advocate"

Today's Best Wine Buy!
Ratings On Over 24,000 Wines For Only $14.95

Today's best wine buy, the *Ultimate Guide to Buying Wine,* is a comprehensive 300-page plus listing of wines of the world, complete with ratings and selected price information. It's the ultimate source for selecting and buying wine.

Buy Wine With Confidence.
Extensive ratings on over 24,000 wines, using the 100 point rating system perfected by the senior editors of The Wine Spectator over years of tastings.

Enjoy Wines From Every Major Wine-Producing Region.
Compiled from over 200 issues of The Wine Spectator, the *Ultimate Guide to Buying Wine* features wines from 21 countries covering 130 vintages, through 1990.

Easily Select Wines That Suit Your Palate — And Your Budget.
Ratings are indexed in two ways for easy access, first by country of origin and producer, and second by country of origin, vintage and score.

Make Solid Investment Decisions For Your Cellar.
Complete listings of all Spectator Selection and Cellar Selection wines, plus an analysis of the price performance and current value — information you won't find anywhere else!

Plus, you'll find useful information on buying wine at auction...dos and don'ts on serving and storing...keys to matching wine with food...wine bottle shapes and sizes...even proper glassware and decanters.

Order Your Copy Now!
You can examine this book — FREE — for 10 days. If you are not completely satisfied, simply return it within 10 days of receipt for a full refund! To order your copy of the *Ultimate Guide to Buying Wine* for only $14.95 plus postage and handling, simply complete and return the coupon below.

Or call toll-free: 1-800-622-2062

ATTENTION RETAILERS: FOR WHOLESALE ORDERS AND INFORMATION, CALL 1-800-344-0763.

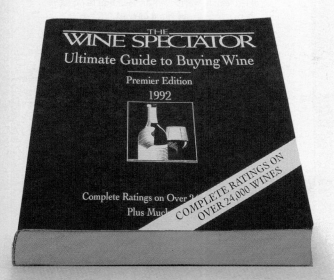

Yes! Please send me The Wine Spectator's ULTIMATE GUIDE TO BUYING WINE. This spectacular premier edition is just $14.95* (plus $3.50** for postage and handling). If I'm not completely satisfied, I'll return it within 10 days for a full refund.

Name (please print)_____ Company_____

Address_____ City_____ State____ Zip_____

Please send me _____ copy(ies). ☐ Payment enclosed.
Charge to: ☐ VISA ☐ MASTERCARD ☐ AMEX

Card #_____ Exp_____

Signature_____

☐ Please also enter a subscription to THE WINE SPECTATOR in my name.
One year—22 issues—for $40 (U.S. only).

Make check payable to: THE WINE SPECTATOR, 601 Van Ness Avenue, Suite 2014, San Francisco, CA 94102. Please allow 4-6 weeks for delivery.
*CA and NY residents add sales tax. **On foreign orders, add $15 for postage and handling.

W5U

SECTION B: WINES LISTED BY COUNTRY/TYPE/PRODUCER

AUSTRALIA
CABERNET SAUVIGNON

83 BAROSSA VALLEY Cabernet Sauvignon South Australia 1987 $11 (1/31/90)
76 BERRI Cabernet Sauvignon Barossa Valley 1985 $7 (4/30/88)
81 BLACK OPAL Cabernet Sauvignon Hunter Valley 1985 $8 (7/15/88) BB
85 BLACK OPAL Cabernet Sauvignon South Eastern Australia 1987 $8 (2/28/90) BB
76 WOLF BLASS Cabernet Sauvignon South Australia President's Selection 1983 $13.50 (4/30/88)
78 WOLF BLASS Cabernet Sauvignon South Australia Yellow Label 1984 $10 (4/30/89)
86 WOLF BLASS Cabernet Sauvignon South Australia Yellow Label 1983 $9 (12/15/87)
89 BLUE PYRENEES Cabernet Sauvignon Australia 1982 $20 (5/31/87)
83 BROWN BROTHERS Cabernet Sauvignon Victoria Family Reserve 1987 $11.50 (9/15/90)
82 BROWN BROTHERS Cabernet Sauvignon Victoria Family Selection 1987 $9.50 (7/15/90)
76 BROWN BROTHERS Cabernet Sauvignon Victoria Family Selection 1985 $7.50 (5/15/89)
86 BROWN BROTHERS Cabernet Sauvignon Victoria St.-George Vineyard 1984 $8 (5/31/87)
84 CAPE MENTELLE Cabernet Sauvignon Western Australia 1987 $18.50 (3/31/91)
83 CASSEGRAIN Cabernet Sauvignon Pokolbin 1986 $18 (3/31/91)
86 CHATEAU REYNELLA Cabernet Sauvignon Coonawarra 1988 $8.50 (4/30/91)
80 CHATEAU REYNELLA Cabernet Sauvignon Coonawarra 1984 $7.50 (4/30/88)
84 CHATEAU REYNELLA Cabernet Sauvignon Coonawarra 1980 $15 (5/31/87)
87 CHATEAU TAHBILK Cabernet Sauvignon Goulburn Valley 1988 $12 (3/31/91)
89 CHATEAU TAHBILK Cabernet Sauvignon Goulburn Valley 1987 $11 (7/31/90)
88 CHATEAU TAHBILK Cabernet Sauvignon Goulburn Valley 1986 $10 (3/31/89)
81 CHATEAU TAHBILK Cabernet Sauvignon Goulburn Valley 1984 $7.50 (11/15/87)
79 CLYDE PARK Cabernet Sauvignon Geelong 1984 $15 (3/15/88)
84 COLDSTREAM HILLS Cabernet Sauvignon Lilydale 1987 $20 (1/31/90)
76 DENMAN Cabernet Sauvignon Hunter Valley 1983 $5 (11/15/87)
73 GRANTS Cabernet Sauvignon Barossa Valley 1984 $8 (11/15/87)
81 HARDY'S Cabernet Sauvignon Coonawarra 1987 $10.50 (7/15/90)
79 HARDY'S Cabernet Sauvignon Keppoch 1986 $7.50 (7/15/90)
80 HARDY'S Cabernet Sauvignon Keppoch 1985 $7.25 (10/31/88)
81 HARDY'S Cabernet Sauvignon Keppoch Bird Series 1985 $6 (9/30/88) BB
75 HARDY'S Cabernet Sauvignon McLaren Vale Captain's Selection 1985 $4.50 (7/15/88)
76 HARDY'S Cabernet Sauvignon McLaren Vale The Hardy Collection No. Eight 1986 $10.50 (1/31/89)
83 HARDY'S Cabernet Sauvignon South Australia The Hardy Collection 1988 $10 (2/15/91)
91 HENSCHKE Cabernet Sauvignon Barossa Valley Cyril Henschke 1986 $23 (9/15/89)
90 HENSCHKE Cabernet Sauvignon Barossa Valley Cyril Henschke 1985 $21 (1/31/89)
94 HENSCHKE Cabernet Sauvignon Barossa Valley Cyril Henschke 1984 $18.50 (12/15/87)
75 HILL-SMITH Cabernet Sauvignon Barossa Valley 1984 $9.50 (8/31/87)
82 HILL-SMITH Cabernet Sauvignon Barossa Valley 1981 $9.50 (7/16/86)
78 HOUGHTON Cabernet Sauvignon Frankland River Wildflower Ridge 1988 $9 (7/15/91)
79 HUNGERFORD HILL Cabernet Sauvignon Coonawarra 1984 $11 (3/15/88)
84 KOALA RIDGE Cabernet Sauvignon Barossa Valley 1985 $9 (1/31/89)
83 LEASINGHAM Cabernet Sauvignon Australia Bin 49 Winemakers Selection 1982 $7.25 (11/15/87)
86 LEEUWIN Cabernet Sauvignon Margaret River 1983 $18 (5/31/88)
79 LEEUWIN Cabernet Sauvignon Margaret River 1979 $20 (9/15/89)
80 PETER LEHMANN Cabernet Sauvignon Barossa Valley 1987 $8 (3/31/91)
85 PETER LEHMANN Cabernet Sauvignon Barossa Valley 1986 $9 (1/31/90)
81 PETER LEHMANN Cabernet Sauvignon Barossa Valley 1983 $9 (7/01/87)
83 LINDEMANS Cabernet Sauvignon Coonawarra 1986 $14 (10/31/90)
86 LINDEMANS Cabernet Sauvignon Coonawarra 1985 $14 (4/30/89)
84 LINDEMANS Cabernet Sauvignon Coonawarra 1984 $12 (2/15/88)
79 LINDEMANS Cabernet Sauvignon Coonawarra 1982 $8 (9/30/86)
80 LINDEMANS Cabernet Sauvignon Coonawarra St.-George Vineyard 1985 $21 (4/30/89)
88 LINDEMANS Cabernet Sauvignon Coonawarra St.-George Vineyard 1984 $15 (1/31/88)
88 LINDEMANS Cabernet Sauvignon Coonawarra St.-George Vineyard NV $15 (5/31/87)
79 LINDEMANS Cabernet Sauvignon South Australia Bin 45 1985 $6 (1/31/88)
73 LONGLEAT Cabernet Sauvignon Goulburn Valley Revi Resco 1986 $9 (9/30/89)
90 MILDARA Cabernet Sauvignon Coonawarra 1986 $10 (1/31/89)
89 MILDARA Cabernet Sauvignon Coonawarra 1985 $8 (4/15/88) BB
77 MILDARA Cabernet Sauvignon Coonawarra 1984 $6.50 (4/30/87)
85 MILDARA Cabernet Sauvignon McLaren Vale Private Reserve 1985 $13 (1/31/89)
80 MILDARA Cabernet Sauvignon Murray River Valley 1986 $8 (1/31/89)
86 MITCHELTON Cabernet Sauvignon Goulburn Valley 1988 $13 (4/15/91)
73 MITCHELTON Cabernet Sauvignon Goulburn Valley 1986 $13 (1/31/90)
81 MONTROSE Cabernet Sauvignon Mudgee 1987 $10 (2/28/91)
86 MONTROSE Cabernet Sauvignon Mudgee 1986 $8 (7/31/89)
88 MONTROSE Cabernet Sauvignon Mudgee 1984 $10 (4/30/88)
80 MONTROSE Cabernet Sauvignon Mudgee Special Reserve 1985 $16 (1/31/90)
78 ORLANDO Cabernet Sauvignon Coonawarra St.-Hugo 1987 $15 (5/31/91)
81 ORLANDO Cabernet Sauvignon Coonawarra St.-Hugo 1986 $8 (2/28/91)
90 ORLANDO Cabernet Sauvignon Coonawarra St.-Hugo 1985 $15 (4/30/89)
83 ORLANDO Cabernet Sauvignon South Eastern Australia Jacob's Creek 1988 $7 (7/15/91) BB
85 ORLANDO Cabernet Sauvignon South Eastern Australia Jacob's Creek 1987 $7 (7/31/90) BB
87 ORLANDO Cabernet Sauvignon South Eastern Australia Jacob's Creek 1986 $7 (5/15/89) BB
83 PENFOLDS Cabernet Sauvignon South Australia Bin 707 1987 $38 (5/31/91)
90 PENFOLDS Cabernet Sauvignon South Australia Bin 707 1986 $28 (9/30/89)
90 PENFOLDS Cabernet Sauvignon South Australia Bin 707 1981 $18 (7/01/87)
91 PETALUMA Cabernet Sauvignon Coonawarra 1984 $18 (5/31/87)
74 REDBANK Cabernet Sauvignon South Eastern Australia Long Paddock 1986 $13 (1/31/90)
74 REDBANK Cabernet Sauvignon South Eastern Australia Long Paddock 1985 $7 (7/15/91)
89 REDBANK Cabernet Sauvignon South Eastern Australia Redbank Cabernet 1986 $54 (1/31/90)
89 ROO'S LEAP Cabernet Sauvignon McLaren Vale 1985 $10 (11/30/88)
85 ROO'S LEAP Cabernet Sauvignon McLaren Vale Limited Edition 1986 $9.50 (1/31/90)
88 ROSEMOUNT Cabernet Sauvignon Coonawarra Kirri Billi Vineyard 1986 $19.50 (10/31/90)
89 ROSEMOUNT Cabernet Sauvignon Coonawarra Show Reserve 1988 $16 (5/31/91)
88 ROSEMOUNT Cabernet Sauvignon Coonawarra Show Reserve 1987 $15 (2/28/91)
82 ROSEMOUNT Cabernet Sauvignon Coonawarra Show Reserve 1985 $14 (1/31/89)
86 ROSEMOUNT Cabernet Sauvignon Coonawarra Show Reserve 1984 $13.50 (2/28/87)
76 ROSEMOUNT Cabernet Sauvignon Hunter Valley 1988 $10 (1/31/90)
83 ROSEMOUNT Cabernet Sauvignon Hunter Valley 1987 $10 (7/31/89)
93 ROSEMOUNT Cabernet Sauvignon Hunter Valley 1986 $11 (1/31/89) SS
85 ROSEMOUNT Cabernet Sauvignon Hunter Valley 1985 $9 (1/31/88)
78 ROSEMOUNT Cabernet Sauvignon Hunter Valley 1984 $9.50 (4/30/87)
84 ROUGE HOMME Cabernet Sauvignon Coonawarra 1984 $12 (2/15/88)
84 ST.-HUBERTS Cabernet Sauvignon Yarra Valley 1984 $13 (11/15/87)
79 SALTRAM Cabernet Sauvignon Hazelwood 1985 $8.50 (7/31/89)
88 SEAVIEW Cabernet Sauvignon South Australia 1986 $10 (7/31/90)
81 SEPPELT Cabernet Sauvignon Padthaway Black Label 1988 $12 (3/31/91)
64 SEPPELT Cabernet Sauvignon South Eastern Australia Black Label 1985 $11 (4/30/88)
78 SEPPELT Cabernet Sauvignon South Eastern Australia Black Label 1982 $12.50 (4/01/86)
77 SEPPELT Cabernet Sauvignon South Eastern Australia Murray River 1987 $5 (4/15/88)
82 SEPPELT Cabernet Sauvignon South Eastern Australia Reserve Bin 1988 $9 (7/15/91)
84 MARK SWANN Cabernet Sauvignon Coonawarra 1987 $7 (2/28/91) BB
88 MARK SWANN Cabernet Sauvignon Coonawarra 1985 $7 (10/31/88) BB
77 MARK SWANN Cabernet Sauvignon Coonawarra 1984 $8 (8/31/87)
78 MARK SWANN Cabernet Sauvignon Coonawarra 1982 $7.50 (3/16/84)
86 MARK SWANN Cabernet Sauvignon South Australia Proprietor's Reserve 1988 $5.50 (2/28/91) BB
81 MARK SWANN Cabernet Sauvignon South Australia Proprietor's Reserve 1987 $5.50 (7/31/89) BB
78 MARK SWANN Cabernet Sauvignon South Australia Proprietor's Reserve 1986 $5 (10/31/88)
85 TALTARNI Cabernet Sauvignon Victoria 1984 $9.25 (11/15/87)
84 TALTARNI Cabernet Sauvignon Victoria 1982 $9.25 (4/30/87)
80 TALTARNI Cabernet Sauvignon Victoria 1981 $7.50 (5/16/85)
81 TALTARNI Cabernet Sauvignon Victoria 1980 $6.75 (3/01/84)
88 TYRRELL'S Cabernet Sauvignon Hunter Valley Classic 1984 $7 (9/15/90) BB
87 TYRRELL'S Cabernet Sauvignon Hunter Valley Premier Selection 1983 $8 (4/30/88) BB
68 VIRGIN HILLS Cabernet Sauvignon Bendigo 1984 $17 (4/30/88)
84 WIRRA WIRRA Cabernet Sauvignon McLaren Vale 1984 $14 (1/31/88)
82 WYNDHAM Cabernet Sauvignon Hunter Valley Bin 444 1983 $6.50 (7/15/88) BB
90 WYNNS Cabernet Sauvignon Coonawarra 1982 $15 (11/30/88)
73 YARRA YERING Cabernet Sauvignon Coldstream Dry Red Wine No. 1 1984 $14 (5/31/88)

CABERNET BLENDS

86 BAROSSA VALLEY Shiraz Cabernet Barossa Valley Sauvignon 1985 $8 (9/30/89) BB
89 BERRI Cabernet Shiraz Australia 1985 $10 (7/01/87)
80 BERRI Shiraz Cabernet South Australia Vintage Selection 1986 $9.50 (3/15/88)
77 WOLF BLASS Cabernet Merlot South Australia Black Label 1983 $25 (4/30/89)
89 WOLF BLASS Cabernet Shiraz Australia Black Label 1980 $18 (7/01/87)
87 WOLF BLASS Cabernet Shiraz Australia Yellow Label 1983 $8 (7/01/87)
88 WOLF BLASS Cabernet Shiraz Clare-Barossa Valleys Black Label 1982 $25 (4/15/88)
90 WOLF BLASS Cabernet Shiraz Langhorne Creek 1981 $18 (7/01/87)
87 BROWN BROTHERS Shiraz Mondeuse Cabernet Australia 1983 $10 (7/01/87)
87 CULLENS Cabernet Merlot Margaret River 1985 $15 (11/15/87)
86 ELDERTON Cabernet Sauvignon Merlot Barossa Valley 1984 $11 (4/30/88)
83 GOVERNOR PHILLIP Cabernet Sauvignon Shiraz Barossa Valley 1986 $6 (7/31/89) BB
76 HARDY'S Cabernet Sauvignon Malbec Reynella McLaren Vale Hardy Collection No. 9 1984 $6.50 (7/15/88)
79 HENSCHKE Shiraz Cabernet Malbec Barossa Valley Keyneton Estate 1985 $11.50 (3/31/89)
85 HENSCHKE Shiraz Cabernet Malbec Barossa Valley Keyneton Estate 1984 $12 (2/15/88)
72 HOLLICK Cabernet Merlot Coonawarra 1985 $16 (5/31/88)
88 HOUGHTON Cabernet Shiraz McLaren Vale Wildflower Ridge 1985 $9 (12/31/88)
80 HUNGERFORD HILL Cabernet Merlot Hunter Valley 1985 $10 (2/28/90) (JL)
75 JOHNSTONE Cabernet Shiraz Hunter Valley 1988 $6.50 (7/15/91)
80 JUD'S HILL Cabernet Sauvignon Merlot Australia 1985 $13 (4/30/88)
89 KRONDORF Cabernet Sauvignon Cabernet Franc McLaren Vale 1984 $9 (4/15/87) BB
80 LAKE'S FOLLY Cabernet Hunter Valley 1985 $15.50 (3/31/89)
84 LEASINGHAM Cabernet Malbec Australia Bin 56 Winemakers Selection 1984 $7.25 (11/15/87)
79 LEASINGHAM Cabernet Shiraz Australia Bin 68 1983 $5.25 (11/15/87)
81 LEASINGHAM Shiraz Cabernet Australia Hutt Creek Malbec 1984 $4 (9/30/87) BB
78 PETER LEHMANN Shiraz Cabernet Barossa Valley 1986 $8 (2/28/91)
83 PETER LEHMANN Shiraz Cabernet Sauvignon Barossa Valley 1985 $7 (1/31/90)
87 LINDEMANS Cabernet Shiraz Coonawarra Limestone Ridge 1984 $15 (7/01/87)
78 LINDEMANS Coonawarra Pyrus 1986 $24 (7/31/90)
87 LINDEMANS Coonawarra Pyrus 1985 $20 (5/31/88)
70 LINDEMANS Shiraz Cabernet Coonawarra Limestone Ridge Lindemans Classic 1982 $38 (7/31/90)
84 LINDEMANS Shiraz Cabernet Coonawarra Limestone Ridge Vineyard 1986 $24 (7/31/90)
68 LINDEMANS Shiraz Cabernet Coonawarra Limestone Ridge Vineyard 1985 $21 (7/31/89)
80 MILDARA Cabernet Sauvignon Merlot Coonawarra 1985 $5.50 (1/31/88) BB
82 MILDARA Cabernet Sauvignon Merlot Coonawarra 1984 $5 (6/15/87) BB
80 MILDARA Cabernet Sauvignon Merlot Murray River Valley 1986 $7.50 (3/31/89)
78 MITCHELTON Cabernet Sauvignon Merlot Australia Print Label 1985 $17 (1/31/90)
86 MITCHELTON Cabernet Shiraz Merlot Victoria 1987 $9 (1/31/90)
73 OXFORD LANDING Cabernet Sauvignon Shiraz South Australia 1988 $7 (9/15/90)
88 PENFOLDS Cabernet Shiraz South Australia Bin 389 1987 $14 (2/28/91)
83 PENFOLDS Cabernet Shiraz South Australia Bin 389 1986 $15 (1/31/90)
86 PENFOLDS Cabernet Shiraz South Australia Bin 389 1985 $14 (12/31/88)
91 PENFOLDS Cabernet Shiraz South Australia Bin 389 1983 $15 (7/01/87)
86 PENFOLDS Cabernet Sauvignon Shiraz South Australia Koonunga Hill 1987 $7.50 (2/28/91) BB
78 PENFOLDS Cabernet Sauvignon Shiraz South Australia Koonunga Hill 1986 $7.50 (5/15/89)
89 PENFOLDS Cabernet Sauvignon Shiraz South Australia Koonunga Hill 1984 $7 (7/01/87)
87 PETALUMA Cabernet Merlot Coonawarra 1986 $25 (5/31/91)
92 PETALUMA Cabernet Merlot Coonawarra 1984 $18 (5/31/87)
89 PETALUMA Cabernet Merlot Coonawarra 1982 $16 (7/01/87)
86 REDBANK South Eastern Australia Sally's Paddock 1986 $32 (1/31/90)
84 ROSEMOUNT Shiraz Cabernet Sauvignon South Eastern Australia 1990 $7 (7/15/91) BB
81 ROSEMOUNT Shiraz Cabernet Sauvignon South Eastern Australia 1989 $6 (7/31/90) BB
89 SALTRAM Cabernet Sauvignon Shiraz Barossa Valley 1984 $12 (1/31/90)
84 SEAVIEW Cabernet Shiraz South Australia 1987 $8 (7/31/90)
82 SEPPELT Cabernet Shiraz South Eastern Australia 1986 $8 (1/31/90)

Key to Symbols

The scores reported here are the results of blind tastings conducted by our panel of senior editors. Wines that carry the initials below are results of individual tastings.

THE WINE SPECTATOR 100-POINT SCALE *95-100*—Classic, a great wine; *90-94*—Outstanding, superior character and style; *80-89*—Good to very good, a wine with special qualities; *70-79*—Average, drinkable wine that may have minor flaws; *60-69*—Below average, drinkable but not recommended; *50-59*—Poor, undrinkable, not recommended. "+"—With a score indicates a range; used primarily with barrel tastings to indicate a preliminary score.

SPECIAL DESIGNATIONS SS—Spectator Selection, CS—Cellar Selection, BB—Best Buy.

TASTER'S INITIALS (JG)—Jim Gordon, (HS)—Harvey Steiman, (JL)—James Laube, (JS)—James Suckling, (TM)—Thomas Matthews, (TR)—Terry Robards, (BT)—Barrel Tasting (these wines were tasted blind from barrel samples), (CA-date)—*California's Great Cabernets* by James Laube, (CH-date)—*California's Great Chardonnays* by James Laube, (VP-date)—*Vintage Port* by James Suckling.

DATE TASTED Dates in parentheses represent the issue in which the rating was published.

AUSTRALIA

CABERNET BLENDS

78 STANLEY Shiraz Cabernet Sauvignon Coonawarra Private Reserve 1985 $4 (12/15/87)
84 TYRRELL'S Cabernet Merlot Australia Old Winery 1988 $7.50 (3/31/91) BB
79 TYRRELL'S Cabernet Sauvignon Merlot Hunter Valley 1987 $7 (9/15/90)
88 TYRRELL'S Cabernet Sauvignon Merlot Hunter Valley 1986 $8 (1/31/90) BB
84 TYRRELL'S Cabernet Sauvignon Merlot Hunter Valley 1985 $9 (7/31/89)
82 TYRRELL'S Cabernet Sauvignon Merlot Hunter Valley 1984 $9 (7/15/88)
84 TYRRELL'S Cabernet Merlot New South Wales Victoria 1983 $8 (3/15/88)
89 WIRRA WIRRA Cabernet Shiraz Merlot McLaren Vale Church Block 1985 $11 (3/15/88)
91 WYNDHAM Cabernet Shiraz Hunter Valley 1987 $7 (1/31/90) BB
87 WYNDHAM Cabernet Shiraz Hunter Valley 1986 $6.50 (12/31/88) BB
87 WYNDHAM Cabernet Shiraz Hunter Valley 1985 $6.50 (3/15/88) BB
79 WYNNS Cabernet Hermitage Coonawarra 1984 $10 (12/31/88)
67 YALUMBA Cabernet Shiraz Coonawarra 1985 $6.50 (9/30/89)
78 YALUMBA Cabernet Shiraz Coonawarra 1984 $6 (1/31/88)

CHARDONNAY

74 BALGOWNIE Chardonnay Coonawarra Series One Premier Cuvée 1987 $6.50 (9/30/88)
81 BAROSSA VALLEY Chardonnay South Australia 1988 $11 (3/15/90)
89 BERRI Chardonnay Barossa Valley 1986 $12 (5/31/87)
89 BERRI Chardonnay South Australia Vintage Selection 1986 $7.75 (2/15/88)
85 BLACK OPAL Chardonnay Hunter Valley 1987 $9 (7/31/89)
79 BLACK OPAL Chardonnay Hunter Valley 1986 $8 (12/31/87)
87 BLACK OPAL Chardonnay Hunter Valley 1985 $8 (5/15/87) BB
82 WOLF BLASS Chardonnay South Australia Première Release 1987 $9 (4/15/89)
81 WOLF BLASS Chardonnay South Australia Première Release 1986 $10 (5/15/88)
86 BROWN BROTHERS Chardonnay Australia Family Reserve NV $9 (5/31/87)
84 BROWN BROTHERS Chardonnay King Valley 1987 $11 (7/31/89)
91 BROWN BROTHERS Chardonnay King Valley Family Reserve 1987 $15.50 (7/15/90) SS
80 BROWN BROTHERS Chardonnay King Valley Family Selection 1988 $11.50 (7/15/90)
85 BROWN BROTHERS Chardonnay Victoria Estate Selection 1985 $8 (8/31/87)
72 LEO BURNING Chardonnay South Australia 1987 $7 (5/31/88)
80 CAPE MENTELLE Chardonnay Margaret River 1989 $20 (3/31/91)
89 CASSEGRAIN Chardonnay Hastings Valley Fromenteau Vineyard 1989 $25 (3/31/91)
87 CASSEGRAIN Chardonnay South Eastern Australia 1989 $14.50 (3/31/91)
85 CHATEAU REYNELLA Chardonnay McLaren Vale 1988 $9 (7/31/90)
82 CHATEAU REYNELLA Chardonnay McLaren Vale 1987 $11.50 (12/31/88)
89 CHATEAU REYNELLA Chardonnay McLaren Vale 1985 $7 (5/15/88) BB
90 CLYDE PARK Chardonnay Geelong 1986 $15 (2/15/88)
87 COLDSTREAM HILLS Chardonnay Lilydale Three Vineyards Blend 1987 $20 (1/31/90)
72 COLDSTREAM HILLS Chardonnay Lilydale Three Vineyards Blend 1986 $18 (5/31/88)
87 COLDSTREAM HILLS Chardonnay Lilydale Yarra Ridge Vineyard 1987 $19 (10/15/90)
68 COLDSTREAM HILLS Chardonnay Lilydale Yarra Ridge Vineyard 1986 $18 (5/31/88)
83 CULLENS Chardonnay Western Australia Margaret River 1985 $18 (11/15/87)
80 DENMAN Chardonnay Hunter Valley Private Bin 1985 $6 (12/31/87)
78 EVANS FAMILY Chardonnay Hunter Valley 1985 $13 (4/15/87)
88 EVANS FAMILY Chardonnay Hunter Valley Vintage Selection 1986 $14 (2/15/88)
80 ANDREW GARRETT Chardonnay South Australia 1986 $9.75 (12/31/87)
77 GRANTS Chardonnay McLaren Vale 1986 $8 (12/15/87)
86 HARDY'S Chardonnay Australia NV $10 (5/31/87)
72 HARDY'S Chardonnay Padthaway Hardy Collection No. 1 1987 $7 (5/31/88)
69 HARDY'S Chardonnay Padthaway Hardy Collection No. 1 1987 $11.50 (2/15/89)
80 HARDY'S Chardonnay Padthaway Clare Valley The Hardy Collection 1988 $10.50 (7/15/90)
69 HARDY'S Chardonnay South Eastern Australia 1987 $7.50 (7/15/90)
75 HARDY'S Chardonnay South Eastern Australia Bird Series 1987 $6 (5/31/88)
82 HARDY'S Chardonnay Sunraysia 1988 $7 (7/31/90) BB
83 HEGGIES Chardonnay Barossa Valley 1987 $14 (1/31/90)
69 HEGGIES Chardonnay Barossa Valley 1985 $13 (12/15/87)
73 HILL-SMITH Chardonnay Barossa Valley 1986 $8 (11/15/87)
72 HILL-SMITH Chardonnay Barossa Valley 1985 $9.50 (5/15/87)
86 HOLLICK Chardonnay Coonawarra 1986 $16 (5/15/88)
69 HOUGHTON Chardonnay Western Australia Gold Reserve 1987 $10 (10/31/90)
86 HUNGERFORD HILL Chardonnay Hunter Valley 1986 $12 (2/15/88)
85 KOALA RIDGE Chardonnay Barossa Valley 1989 $9 (5/31/91)
80 KOALA RIDGE Chardonnay Barossa Valley 1987 $7 (3/15/90)
84 KOALA RIDGE Chardonnay Barossa Valley 1986 $8 (2/15/89)
85 KRONDORF Chardonnay Australia 1985 $13 (4/15/87)
87 KRONDORF Chardonnay Barossa Valley 1986 $8 (3/31/87) BB
83 LEASINGHAM Chardonnay Clare Valley Domaine 1989 $8.50 (10/15/90)
84 LEEUWIN Chardonnay Margaret River Second Release 1983 $24 (5/31/88)
81 PETER LEHMANN Chardonnay Barossa Valley 1988 $11 (7/31/89)
81 LINDEMANS Chardonnay Padthaway 1988 $15 (7/31/90)
87 LINDEMANS Chardonnay Padthaway 1986 $12 (12/31/87)
81 LINDEMANS Chardonnay Padthaway 1985 $9 (2/28/87)
77 LINDEMANS Chardonnay South Australia Bin 65 1985 $6 (2/28/87)
85 LINDEMANS Chardonnay South Eastern Australia Bin 65 1990 $7 (2/28/91) BB
85 LINDEMANS Chardonnay South Eastern Australia Bin 65 1989 $6 (4/30/90) BB
87 LINDEMANS Chardonnay South Eastern Australia Bin 65 1988 $6 (5/15/89) BB
83 LINDEMANS Chardonnay Victoria Bin 65 1987 $6 (2/15/88) BB
75 MILDARA Chardonnay Barossa Valley 1989 $7.50 (2/28/91)
88 MILDARA Chardonnay Barossa Valley 1987 $12 (12/31/88)
84 MILDARA Chardonnay Coonawarra 1985 $7.50 (4/15/87)
79 MILDARA Chardonnay Merbian Church Hill 1987 $5.50 (2/15/88)
82 MILDARA Chardonnay Merbian Church Hill 1986 $5 (6/15/87) BB
70 MILDARA Chardonnay Murray River Valley 1987 $8 (2/15/89)
90 MITCHELTON Chardonnay Goulburn Valley Reserve 1988 $14 (3/15/90)
84 MITCHELTON Chardonnay Goulburn Valley Wood Matured Reserve 1989 $15 (3/31/91)
80 MITCHELTON Chardonnay Victoria 1989 $8 (4/15/91)
79 MITCHELTON Chardonnay Victoria 1988 $10 (3/15/90)
91 MONTROSE Chardonnay Australia Show Reserve 1986 $14 (5/31/87)
85 MONTROSE Chardonnay Mudgee 1989 $10 (2/28/91)
84 MONTROSE Chardonnay Mudgee 1988 $9 (6/15/90)
78 MONTROSE Chardonnay Mudgee 1987 $8 (7/31/89)
81 MONTROSE Chardonnay Mudgee 1986 $10 (2/15/88)
89 MONTROSE Chardonnay Mudgee Special Reserve 1984 $15 (5/15/87)
87 MONTROSE Chardonnay Mudgee Stoney Creek Vineyard Special Reserve 1986 $13 (3/15/90)
83 MONTROSE Chardonnay South Eastern Australia Bin 747 1989 $8 (2/28/91) BB
90 MOUNTADAM Chardonnay Eden Valley 1989 $25 (3/31/91)
77 MOUNTADAM Chardonnay Eden Valley High Eden Ridge 1986 $17 (5/15/88)
68 ORLANDO Chardonnay McLaren Vale St.-Hugo 1986 $15 (7/31/90)
91 ORLANDO Chardonnay McLaren Vale St.-Hugo 1985 $15 (7/31/89)
84 ORLANDO Chardonnay South Eastern Australia Jacob's Creek 1990 $7 (5/15/91) BB
76 ORLANDO Chardonnay South Eastern Australia Jacob's Creek 1989 $7 (6/15/90)
80 ORLANDO Chardonnay South Eastern Australia Jacob's Creek 1988 $7 (1/31/90)
83 ORLANDO Chardonnay South Eastern Australia Jacob's Creek 1987 $6.50 (3/15/89) BB
85 OXFORD LANDING Chardonnay South Australia 1990 $7 (2/28/91) BB
82 OXFORD LANDING Chardonnay South Australia 1989 $7 (10/15/90) BB
73 PEACOCK HILL Chardonnay Hunter Valley 1987 $11 (5/31/88)
83 PENFOLDS Chardonnay South Australia 1988 $9.50 (1/31/90)
80 PENFOLDS Chardonnay South Australia 1987 $8 (2/15/89)
88 PETALUMA Chardonnay Australia 1987 $21 (5/31/91)
90 PETALUMA Chardonnay Australia 1986 $18 (5/31/87)
86 PIPERS BROOK Chardonnay Tasmania 1989 $25 (3/31/91)
86 PIPERS BROOK Chardonnay Tasmania 1988 $25 (3/31/91)
83 RICHMOND GROVE Chardonnay Hunter Valley French Cask 1989 $7 (5/15/91) BB
88 RIDDOCH Chardonnay Victoria 1987 $9 (10/15/90)
69 RIDDOCH Chardonnay Victoria 1986 $9 (5/31/88)
88 ROO'S LEAP Chardonnay Hunter Valley Barrel Fermented 1987 $10 (2/15/89)
80 ROSEMOUNT Chardonnay Hunter Valley Giants Creek Vineyard 1987 $20 (3/15/90)
88 ROSEMOUNT Chardonnay Hunter Valley Matured in Oak Casks 1990 $9 (5/15/91)
80 ROSEMOUNT Chardonnay Hunter Valley Matured in Oak Casks 1989 $9 (4/30/90)
82 ROSEMOUNT Chardonnay Hunter Valley Matured in Oak Casks 1988 $10 (3/15/90)
87 ROSEMOUNT Chardonnay Hunter Valley Matured in Oak Casks 1987 $10.50 (3/15/89)
87 ROSEMOUNT Chardonnay Hunter Valley Matured in Oak Casks 1986 $9 (5/31/88)
83 ROSEMOUNT Chardonnay Hunter Valley Matured in Oak Casks 1985 $10 (4/15/87)
91 ROSEMOUNT Chardonnay Hunter Valley Roxburgh 1986 $25 (5/31/87)
88 ROSEMOUNT Chardonnay Hunter Valley Roxburgh 1985 $25 (8/31/87)
92 ROSEMOUNT Chardonnay Hunter Valley Show Reserve 1989 $16 (5/31/91)
85 ROSEMOUNT Chardonnay Hunter Valley Show Reserve 1988 $16 (3/15/90)
92 ROSEMOUNT Chardonnay Hunter Valley Show Reserve 1987 $16.50 (2/15/89)
90 ROSEMOUNT Chardonnay Hunter Valley Show Reserve 1986 $16 (12/31/87)
88 ROSEMOUNT Chardonnay Hunter Valley Show Reserve 1985 $15 (4/15/87)
69 ROTHBURY Chardonnay Hunter Valley 1984 $8 (7/01/86)
84 ROTHBURY Chardonnay Hunter Valley Brokenback Vineyard 1989 $9 (10/15/90)
89 ROTHBURY Chardonnay Hunter Valley Brokenback Vineyard 1988 $10 (3/15/89)
88 ROTHBURY Chardonnay Hunter Valley Brokenback Vineyard 1987 $7.50 (2/15/88)
90 ROTHBURY Chardonnay Hunter Valley Brokenback Vineyard 1986 $9.50 (5/31/87)
85 ROTHBURY Chardonnay Hunter Valley Reserve 1988 $18.50 (10/15/90)
89 ROTHBURY Chardonnay Hunter Valley Reserve 1987 $19 (2/15/89)
83 ROTHBURY Chardonnay Hunter Valley Reserve 1986 $15 (2/15/88)
92 ROTHBURY Chardonnay Hunter Valley Reserve 1985 $25 (5/31/87)
66 ST.-HUBERTS Chardonnay Yarra Valley 1985 $13.25 (12/31/87)
82 SALTRAM Chardonnay Hazelwood 1987 $8.50 (7/31/89)
82 SALTRAM Chardonnay McLaren Vale Hunter Valley Mamre Brook 1987 $12 (7/31/89)
71 SEAVIEW Chardonnay South Australia 1988 $10 (7/15/90)
89 SEPPELT Chardonnay Barooga Padthaway Black Label 1989 $14 (3/31/91)
79 SEPPELT Chardonnay Barooga Padthaway Black Label Great Western Vineyards 1987 $15 (7/31/89)
88 SEPPELT Chardonnay South Eastern Australia Reserve Bin 1989 $10 (7/31/90)
80 SEPPELT Chardonnay South Eastern Australia Reserve Bin 1987 $9 (5/31/88)
87 SEPPELT Chardonnay South Eastern Australia Reserve Bin 1986 $8 (2/15/88)
74 SEPPELT Chardonnay South Eastern Australia Reserve Bin 1985 $8 (9/30/86)
84 SEPPELT Chardonnay South Eastern Australia Reserve Bin 1984 $8.50 (2/01/86)
79 MARK SWANN Chardonnay Barossa Valley 1989 $7 (2/28/91)
81 MARK SWANN Chardonnay McLaren Vale 1983 $11 (9/16/84)
79 MARK SWANN Chardonnay South Australia Proprietor's Reserve 1987 $5 (2/15/89)
78 MARK SWANN Chardonnay Victoria Proprietor's Reserve 1989 $7 (5/31/91)
92 TARRA WARRA Chardonnay Yarra Glen 1988 $25 (12/31/90)
84 TYRRELL'S Chardonnay Hunter Valley 1989 $7 (10/15/90) BB
68 TYRRELL'S Chardonnay Hunter Valley 1988 $9 (7/31/89)
82 TYRRELL'S Chardonnay Hunter Valley 1986 $7.50 (5/15/88)
70 TYRRELL'S Pinot Chardonnay Hunter Valley Vat 47 1989 $13 (10/15/90)
77 TYRRELL'S Pinot Chardonnay Hunter Valley Vat 47 1988 $16 (7/31/89)
85 TYRRELL'S Pinot Chardonnay Hunter Valley Vat 47 1986 $12 (5/15/88)
64 WIRRA WIRRA Chardonnay McLaren Vale David Paxton's Hillstowe Vineyard 1985 $14 (12/31/87)
78 WOODLEY Chardonnay South Eastern Australia Queen Adelaide 1987 $8 (5/31/88)
85 WYNDHAM Chardonnay Hunter Valley 1989 $11.50 (5/15/91)
71 WYNDHAM Chardonnay Hunter Valley 1987 $7.75 (1/31/90)
83 WYNDHAM Chardonnay Hunter Valley Bin 222 1988 $7 (1/31/90)
84 WYNNS Chardonnay Coonawarra 1987 $16 (12/31/88)
85 YALUMBA Chardonnay Barossa Valley 1987 $8 (3/15/89)
78 YALUMBA Chardonnay Eden Valley 1986 $7 (12/31/87)

DESSERT

77 BROWN BROTHERS Muscat of Alexandria Victoria Lexia 1986 $8 (5/15/89)
73 BROWN BROTHERS Muscat of Alexandria Victoria Lexia Family Selection 1987 $8.50 (7/31/90)
84 BROWN BROTHERS Port Victoria Family Selection 1987 $12.50 (7/31/90)
92 CAMPBELLS Muscat Rutherglen Old NV $15 (7/01/87)
91 CAMPBELLS Muscat Rutherglen Old NV $15 (7/01/87)
72 HARDY'S Port Australia 1982 $15 (7/31/90)
83 HARDY'S Tawny Port Australia Tall Ships NV $11 (7/31/90)
92 HEGGIES Rhine Riesling Barossa Valley Late Harvest Botrytis 1986 $8/375ml (2/15/88)
84 HILL-SMITH Sémillon Barossa Valley Late Harvest Botrytis 1986 $10/375ml (3/15/89)

Key to Symbols

The scores reported here are the results of blind tastings conducted by our panel of senior editors. Wines that carry the initials below are results of individual tastings.

THE WINE SPECTATOR 100-POINT SCALE *95-100*—Classic, a great wine; *90-94*—Outstanding, superior character and style; *80-89*—Good to very good, a wine with special qualities; *70-79*—Average, drinkable wine that may have minor flaws; *60-69*—Below average, drinkable but not recommended; *50-59*—Poor, undrinkable, not recommended. "+"—With a score indicates a range; used primarily with barrel tastings to indicate a preliminary score.

SPECIAL DESIGNATIONS SS—Spectator Selection, CS—Cellar Selection, BB—Best Buy.

TASTER'S INITIALS (JG)—Jim Gordon, (HS)—Harvey Steiman, (JL)—James Laube, (JS)—James Suckling, (TM)—Thomas Matthews, (TR)—Terry Robards, (BT)—Barrel Tasting (these wines were tasted blind from barrel samples), (CA-date)—*California's Great Cabernets* by James Laube, (CH-date)—*California's Great Chardonnays* by James Laube, (VP-date)—*Vintage Port* by James Suckling.

DATE TASTED Dates in parentheses represent the issue in which the rating was published.

88 HILL-SMITH Sémillon Barossa Valley Late Harvest Botrytis 1985 $8/375ml (2/15/88)
84 HILL-SMITH Sémillon Barossa Valley Late Harvest Botrytis 1983 $8/375ml (8/31/86)
83 PETER LEHMANN Sémillon Sauternes Barossa Valley Late Harvest Botrytis 1988 $6/375ml (4/15/91) BB
89 PETER LEHMANN Sémillon Sauternes Barossa Valley Late Harvest Botrytis 1987 $8/375ml (10/31/89)
89 PETER LEHMANN Sémillon Sauternes Barossa Valley Late Harvest Botrytis 1984 $15 (7/01/87)
83 LINDEMANS Sémillon Griffith Padthaway Late Harvest Botrytis 1988 $12/375ml (7/31/90)
91 LINDEMANS Sémillon Griffith Padthaway Late Harvest Botrytis 1987 $12/375ml (10/31/89)
84 LINDEMANS Tawny Port Macquarie Very Special Wood Matured NV $11 (7/31/90)
92 MORRIS Tokay Australia Show Reserve NV $15 (7/01/87)
88 PENFOLDS Rhine Riesling South Australia Late Harvest 1987 $5.50/375ml (3/15/89) BB
84 PENFOLDS Sémillon South Australia Late Harvest 1987 $6.50/375ml (3/15/89)
90 PEWSEY VALE Rhine Riesling Barossa Valley Late Harvest Botrytis 1986 $8/375ml (2/15/88)
71 PEWSEY VALE Rhine Riesling Barossa Valley Late Harvest Botrytis Individual Vineyard Selection 1987 $9/375ml (10/31/89)
91 ROSEWOOD Muscat Australia Liqueur NV $50 (7/01/87)
90 ROSEWOOD Muscat Rutherglen Old Liqueur NV $40 (7/01/87)
91 ROSEWOOD Muscat Rutherglen Special Liqueur NV $30 (7/01/87)
92 SEPPELT Port Barossa Valley Para Bin 109 NV $25 (2/15/88)
70 SEPPELT Port McLaren Flat Barossa 1978 $15 (2/15/88)
95 SEPPELT Tawny Port Australia Old Trafford NV $15 (3/15/89)
78 SEPPELT Tawny Port Barossa Valley Mount Rufus NV $12 (2/15/88)
79 SEPPELT Tawny Port Barossa Valley Para No. 110 NV $25 (3/15/89)
78 MARK SWANN Port Australia 1980 $10 (4/16/84)
92 MARK SWANN Dessert Rutherglen Gold Vintner's Select NV $10/375ml (12/31/88)
91 YALUMBA Muscat Rutherglen Museum Show Reserve NV $10/375ml (4/15/91)
95 YALUMBA Port Barossa Valley Galway Pipe NV $10.50 (1/31/87)
91 YALUMBA Port Barossa Valley Galway Pipe NV $18 (4/15/91)
90 YALUMBA Tawny Port South Australia Clocktower NV $6 (5/31/87) BB
84 YALUMBA Tawny Port South Australia Clocktower NV $8.50 (4/15/91) BB
83 YALUMBA Sémillon Barossa Valley Late Harvest Botrytis Affected 1984 $5.50/375ml (3/15/89)

Pinot Noir

73 BANNOCKBURN Pinot Noir Geelong 1986 $26 (1/31/90)
74 BANNOCKBURN Pinot Noir Geelong 1985 $16.50 (3/15/88)
83 BROWN BROTHERS Pinot Noir Victoria 1983 $9 (7/01/87)
74 HUNGERFORD HILL Pinot Noir Hunter Valley 1986 $12 (2/28/90)
70 HUNGERFORD HILL Pinot Noir Hunter Valley 1984 $11 (3/15/88)
73 LINDEMANS Pinot Noir Padthaway 1986 $12 (9/15/89)
82 LINDEMANS Pinot Noir Padthaway 1984 $12 (2/15/88)
86 MOUNTADAM Pinot Noir Eden Valley 1988 $25 (3/31/91)
86 ROO'S LEAP Pinot Noir McLaren Vale 1988 $8 (2/28/91)
84 ROSEMOUNT Pinot Noir Hunter Valley Giants Creek Vineyard 1987 $20 (2/28/90)
84 ROSEMOUNT Pinot Noir Hunter Valley 1985 $9.50 (4/30/87)
80 ROSEMOUNT Pinot Noir Hunter Valley NV $9 (7/01/87)
87 ROTHBURY Pinot Noir Hunter Valley 1983 $10 (7/01/87)
89 ROTHBURY Pinot Noir Hunter Valley Director's Reserve 1983 $15 (7/01/87)
80 ST.-HUBERTS Pinot Noir Yarra Valley 1985 $11.50 (11/15/87)
86 TARRA WARRA Pinot Noir Yarra Glen 1988 $25 (12/31/90)
81 TERRACE VALE Pinot Noir Hunter Valley 1986 $9.25 (3/15/88)
76 TOLLEY'S Pinot Noir Barossa Valley Selected Harvest 1983 $5 (11/15/87)
68 TYRRELL'S Pinot Noir Hunter River 1988 $14 (1/31/90)
87 TYRRELL'S Pinot Noir Hunter River 1985 $10 (7/01/87)

Riesling

90 HARDY'S Rhine Riesling Australia NV $7 (5/31/87)
86 PETALUMA Rhine Riesling Australia 1986 $8 (5/31/87)
76 PEWSEY VALE Rhine Riesling Adelaide Hills Individual Vineyard Selection 1990 $9.50 (7/15/91)
79 PEWSEY VALE Rhine Riesling Barossa Valley Individual Vineyard Selection 1987 $5.50 (3/15/89)
84 PEWSEY VALE Rhine Riesling Barossa Valley Individual Vineyard Selection 1986 $6 (2/15/88)

Sauvignon Blanc

71 BERRI Fumé Blanc South Australia Vintage Selection 1987 $6.50 (3/15/88)
77 WOLF BLASS Sauvignon Blanc South Australia 1987 $9 (2/15/88)
87 BROWN BROTHERS Sauvignon Blanc Victoria Estate Selection 1985 $7.50 (8/31/87)
80 DE BORTOLI Sauvignon Blanc Australia Riverina 1985 $6 (2/28/87)
84 HARDY'S Fumé Blanc Padthaway Hardy Collection No. 6 1986 $6 (9/30/88) BB
77 HARDY'S Fumé Blanc South Australia Captain's Selection 1985 $4.50 (9/30/88)
84 HILL-SMITH Fumé Blanc Barossa Valley 1986 $6.25 (7/15/87) BB
72 KATNOOK Sauvignon Blanc Coonawarra 1985 $9.50 (5/15/87)
68 KOALA RIDGE Sauvignon Blanc Barossa Valley 1987 $8 (10/31/89)
69 LINDEMANS Sauvignon Blanc Padthaway 1985 $12 (2/15/88)
82 LINDEMANS Sauvignon Blanc South Australia Bin 95 1985 $5 (2/15/87) BB
67 LINDEMANS Sauvignon Blanc Victoria Bin 95 1986 $6 (2/15/88)
76 MILDARA Fumé Blanc Coonawarra 1986 $5 (5/15/87)
75 MILDARA Fumé Blanc Victoria 1987 $5.50 (2/15/88)
78 MONTROSE Fumé Blanc Mudgee 1985 $7.50 (5/15/87)
85 ROSEMOUNT Fumé Blanc Australia 1986 $7 (5/31/87)
83 MARK SWANN Sauvignon Blanc Australia Proprietor's Reserve NV $4.50 (8/31/87) BB
76 TALTARNI Sauvignon Blanc Victoria 1989 $10 (11/30/90)
89 TALTARNI Sauvignon Blanc Victoria 1988 $15 (9/15/89)
78 YALUMBA Sauvignon Blanc Barossa Valley Fumé Style 1986 $6 (2/15/88)

Sémillon

70 DENMAN Sémillon Hunter Valley Bin 3 1985 $5 (12/15/87)
80 HENSCHKE Sémillon Barossa Valley Matured in French Oak 1986 $12 (2/15/88)
71 PETER LEHMANN Sémillon Barossa Valley 1984 $5 (5/15/87)
86 LINDEMANS Sémillon Hunter Valley 1986 $11 (5/31/88)
64 LINDEMANS Sémillon South Australia Bin 77 1984 $5 (8/31/86)
80 MONTROSE Sémillon Mudgee 1986 $8 (5/31/88)
84 ROSEMOUNT Sémillon Hunter Valley Wood Matured 1987 $9 (10/31/89)
72 ROSEMOUNT Sémillon Hunter Valley Wood Matured 1986 $8 (12/15/87)

87 ROTHBURY Sémillon Hunter Valley 1986 $7 (5/31/87)
86 ROTHBURY Sémillon Hunter Valley 1984 $10 (5/31/87)
77 ROTHBURY Sémillon Hunter Valley Brokenback Vineyard 1986 $8 (12/15/87)
62 MARK SWANN Sémillon Australia Dry 1982 $5.50 (3/16/84)
85 TOLLEY'S Sémillon Barossa Valley Wood Aged Selected Harvest 1983 $5 (12/31/87)
84 TYRRELL'S Sémillon Hunter Valley 1985 $7 (5/31/87)
80 TYRRELL'S Sémillon Hunter Valley Classic 1988 $7 (4/15/91)
86 WYNDHAM Sémillon Hunter Valley Bin 777 1986 $6.50 (5/31/88) BB
77 YARRA YERING Sémillon Coldstream 1986 $17 (5/31/88)

Sémillon Blends

69 CHATEAU TAHBILK Sémillon Sauvignon Blanc Goulburn Valley 1986 $8.25 (2/15/88)
82 COLDRIDGE Sémillon Chardonnay Victoria 1990 $6 (4/15/91) BB
86 HARDY'S Sauvignon Blanc Sémillon Australia 1986 $7 (5/31/87)
70 HILL-SMITH Sémillon Chenin Blanc Barossa Valley Varietal White 1986 $4 (12/15/87)
78 LINDEMANS Sémillon Chardonnay New South Wales Bin 77 1987 $6 (5/31/88)
81 LINDEMANS Sémillon Chardonnay South Eastern Australia Bin 77 1988 $6 (4/15/91) BB
86 PENFOLDS Sémillon Chardonnay South Australia Koonunga Hill 1989 $6 (9/15/90) BB
87 ROSEMOUNT Sémillon Chardonnay Hunter Valley 1985 $9.50 (2/28/87)
82 ROSEMOUNT Sémillon Chardonnay Hunter Valley 1987 $9 (7/31/89)
84 ROSEMOUNT Sémillon Chardonnay South Eastern Australia 1990 $7 (5/31/91) BB
78 ROSEMOUNT Sémillon Chardonnay South Eastern Australia 1988 $6 (6/15/90) BB
87 ROTHBURY Chardonnay Sémillon Hunter Valley NV $9 (5/31/87)
79 YALUMBA Sémillon Chardonnay Eden Valley 1987 $7.50 (4/15/89)
73 YALUMBA Sémillon Chardonnay Eden Valley 1986 $6 (2/15/88)

Shiraz

81 BANNOCKBURN Shiraz Geelong 1984 $13 (10/31/89)
85 BERRI Shiraz Barossa Valley 1985 $9.25 (2/15/88)
92 BROWN BROTHERS Shiraz Australia 1983 $9 (7/01/87)
83 BROWN BROTHERS Shiraz Victoria 1985 $7 (5/15/89) BB
85 BROWN BROTHERS Shiraz Victoria Family Selection 1986 $8 (7/15/90)
88 CAPE MENTELLE Shiraz Margaret River 1988 $15 (2/28/91)
87 CASSEGRAIN Shiraz Pokolbin Leonard Select Vineyard 1987 $20 (3/15/91)
87 CHATEAU TAHBILK Shiraz Goulburn Valley 1987 $11 (3/15/91)
77 CHATEAU TAHBILK Shiraz Goulburn Valley 1984 $6 (11/15/87)
88 CHATEAU TAHBILK Shiraz Victoria 1986 $10 (3/31/89)
80 ANDREW GARRETT Shiraz South Australia Clarendon Estate 1982 $8.75 (11/15/87)
87 HARDY'S Shiraz McLaren Vale 1987 $7.50 (7/15/90) BB
89 HARDY'S Shiraz McLaren Vale 1986 $7.50 (12/31/88) BB
79 HARDY'S Shiraz McLaren Vale Padthaway Bird Series 1984 $5.50 (7/15/88)
86 HENSCHKE Shiraz Australia Keyneton Mount Edelstone 1987 $16.50 (5/31/91)
87 HENSCHKE Shiraz Barossa Valley Hill of Grace 1986 $26 (9/30/89)
90 HENSCHKE Shiraz Barossa Valley Mount Edelstone 1986 $17 (10/31/89) HR
81 HENSCHKE Shiraz Barossa Valley Mount Edelstone 1985 $14.50 (3/31/89)
90 HENSCHKE Shiraz Barossa Valley Mount Edelstone 1984 $14 (2/15/90)
86 HILL-SMITH Shiraz Barossa Valley 1986 $9 (2/28/91) BB
82 HILL-SMITH Shiraz Barossa Valley 1984 $6.25 (5/15/87)
88 HOUGHTON Shiraz McLaren Vale Wildflower Ridge 1985 $9 (12/31/88)
80 HUNGERFORD HILL Shiraz Hunter Valley 1988 $10 (2/28/90)
79 LEASINGHAM Shiraz Australia Bin 61 1982 $4.25 (12/15/87)
84 PETER LEHMANN Shiraz Barossa Valley 1987 $8 (4/15/91) BB
81 PETER LEHMANN Shiraz Barossa Valley 1983 $7 (7/01/87)
84 PETER LEHMANN Shiraz Barossa Valley Dry Red 1985 $7.25 (7/31/89) BB
79 PETER LEHMANN Shiraz Barossa Valley Dry Red 1983 $5 (4/30/87)
83 LINDEMANS Shiraz Barossa Valley 1986 $12 (5/15/89)
81 LINDEMANS Shiraz Hunter Valley 1987 $10 (2/15/91)
96 LINDEMANS Shiraz Hunter Valley Bin 3110 Lindemans Classic 1965 $95 (9/15/89)
89 LINDEMANS Shiraz Hunter Valley Bin 4110 Lindemans Classic 1970 $60 (9/15/89)
73 LINDEMANS Shiraz Hunter Valley Bin 5910 Lindemans Classic 1980 $30 (7/31/90)
78 LINDEMANS Shiraz South Australia Bin 50 1986 $5.50 (5/15/89)
84 LINDEMANS Shiraz South Eastern Australia Bin 50 1987 $5.50 (7/15/90) BB
89 MILDARA Shiraz Coonawarra 1986 $9 (12/31/88)
86 MITCHELTON Shiraz Goulburn Valley 1988 $8 (3/15/91) BB
78 MONTROSE Shiraz Mudgee 1988 $9 (3/15/91)
87 MONTROSE Shiraz Mudgee 1984 $10 (7/01/87)
86 MONTROSE Shiraz Mudgee 1983 $7 (3/15/88)
92 PENFOLDS Grange Hermitage South Australia Bin 95 1983 Rel: $80 Cur: $80 (3/15/91)
96 PENFOLDS Grange Hermitage South Australia Bin 95 1982 $60 (9/30/89) CS
93 PENFOLDS Grange Hermitage South Australia Bin 95 1981 $49 (12/31/88) CS
89 PENFOLDS Grange Hermitage South Australia Bin 95 1980 Cur: $98 (10/29/87) (JL)
95 PENFOLDS Grange Hermitage South Australia Bin 95 1967 Cur: $67 (10/29/87) (JL)
92 PENFOLDS Grange Hermitage South Australia Bin 95 1966 Cur: $100 (10/29/87) (JL)
87 PENFOLDS Shiraz South Australia Magill Estate Vineyard 1985 $45 (7/31/89)
91 ROSEMOUNT Shiraz Hunter Valley 1989 $8 (2/15/91) SS
90 ROSEMOUNT Shiraz Hunter Valley 1988 $8 (1/31/90) SS
87 ROSEMOUNT Shiraz Hunter Valley 1987 $9 (7/31/89)
92 ROSEMOUNT Shiraz Hunter Valley 1986 $9 (4/15/89)
80 ROSEMOUNT Shiraz Hunter Valley 1985 $8 (2/15/88)
83 ROSEMOUNT Shiraz Hunter Valley 1984 $7.50 (4/30/87)
85 ROTHBURY Shiraz Hunter Valley Herlstone Vineyard 1987 $9.50 (5/31/91)
76 ROTHBURY Shiraz Hunter Valley Herlstone Vineyard 1986 $10.50 (7/31/89)
78 ROTHBURY Shiraz Hunter Valley Herlstone Vineyard 1985 $10.50 (3/31/89)
90 ROTHBURY Shiraz Hunter Valley Herlstone Vineyard 1984 $9.50 (5/15/87)
81 SALTRAM Shiraz Hazelwood 1984 $8.50 (7/31/89)
87 SEPPELT Shiraz South Eastern Australia Black Label 1984 $12 (12/31/88)
74 SEPPELT Shiraz South Eastern Australia Black Label 1983 $10 (2/15/88)
80 MARK SWANN Shiraz Eden Valley 1980 $6.50 (3/16/84)
84 TALTARNI Shiraz Victoria 1986 $10 (10/31/90)
91 TALTARNI Shiraz Victoria 1985 $10 (11/30/88) SS
75 TALTARNI Shiraz Victoria 1984 $9.25 (2/15/88)
86 TALTARNI Shiraz Victoria 1982 $9.25 (4/30/87)
77 TALTARNI Shiraz Victoria 1980 $6.75 (3/16/84)
73 TERRACE VALE Shiraz Hunter Valley Bin 6 1986 $9.50 (3/15/88)
75 TYRRELL'S Shiraz Hunter Valley 1982 $7 (7/15/88)
84 TYRRELL'S Shiraz Hunter Valley Classic 1986 $8 (1/31/90) BB
85 WYNDHAM Shiraz Hunter Valley Bin 555 1986 $7 (1/31/90) BB

AUSTRALIA
SPARKLING

76 ANGAS Brut Australia NV $8 (12/31/87)
78 ANGAS Brut Rosé Australia NV $8 (12/31/87)
87 LASSETER Brut Australia 1985 $17 (10/31/89)
84 LASSETER Brut Australia NV $10 (12/31/88)
85 SEPPELT Brut Australia Fleur de Lys 1985 $18 (12/31/88)
82 SEPPELT Brut South Eastern Australia Imperial NV $10 (1/31/90)
82 TYRRELL'S Brut Pinot Noir Hunter Valley 1983 $19 (9/30/88)
84 YALUMBA Brut de Brut Australia 1984 $8.25 (3/15/88)
84 YALUMBA Brut Rosé South Australia Angas NV $9 (12/31/90)
78 YALUMBA Brut South Australia Angas NV $9 (12/31/90)

OTHER AUSTRALIA RED

82 GOVERNOR PHILLIP Australian Red Australia Classic NV $5 (7/31/89) BB
75 HARDY'S Classic Dry Red McLaren Vale Premium 1986 $6 (5/15/89)
78 HARDY'S Classic Dry Red South Australia Premium 1988 $5.25 (7/31/90) BB
75 HILL-SMITH Varietal Red Barossa Valley 1985 $4 (1/31/88)
80 KOALA RIDGE Hermitage Barossa Valley 1985 $9 (1/31/90)
71 KOALA RIDGE Hermitage Barossa Valley 1984 $8.50 (8/31/87)
83 ROSEMOUNT Dry Red Hunter Valley Diamond Reserve 1988 $6.50 (2/28/90) BB
83 ROSEMOUNT Dry Red Hunter Valley Diamond Reserve 1988 $6.50 (9/15/87) BB (JL)
86 ROSEMOUNT Hunter Valley Dry Red Diamond Reserve 1986 $6.50 (9/15/87) BB

90 ROTHBURY Hermitage Hunter Valley 1984 $10 (7/01/87)
90 ROTHBURY Hermitage Hunter Valley 1983 $15 (7/01/87)
84 TYRRELL'S Hermitage Hunter River 1982 $8 (7/01/87)
79 TYRRELL'S Long Flat Red Hunter Valley 1986 $6 (1/31/90)
81 TYRRELL'S Long Flat Red Hunter Valley 1985 $5.25 (7/31/89) BB
83 TYRRELL'S Long Flat Red Hunter Valley 1984 $6 (9/30/88) BB
79 TYRRELL'S Long Flat Red Hunter Valley 1983 $6 (4/15/88)
85 WYNDHAM Merlot Hunter Valley 1986 $8 (1/31/90) BB

OTHER AUSTRALIA WHITE

75 BERRI Columbard Chardonnay South Australia Vintage Selection 1987 $6.50 (3/15/88)
80 CHATEAU TAHBILK Marsanne Goulburn Valley 1989 $10 (7/15/91)
75 CHATEAU TAHBILK Marsanne Goulburn Valley 1985 $6 (2/15/88)
79 HARDY'S Classic Dry White South Australia Premium 1988 $5.25 (6/15/90) BB
79 HARDY'S Classic Dry White South Australia Premium 1988 $6 (5/15/89)
78 HILL-SMITH Sémillon Chenin Blanc Barossa Valley Varietal White 1984 $4 (11/15/86) BB
68 ROSEMOUNT Dry White Hunter Valley Diamond Reserve 1987 $6.50 (7/31/89)
83 ROSEMOUNT Dry White Hunter Valley Diamond Reserve 1986 $6.50 (9/15/87) BB
86 TYRRELL'S Long Flat White Hunter Valley 1989 $5 (10/31/90) BB
80 TYRRELL'S Long Flat White Hunter Valley 1986 $6 (3/15/88) BB
84 TYRRELL'S Long Flat White Hunter Valley NV $4 (5/31/87)

CHILE
CABERNET SAUVIGNON

77 ALAMEDA Cabernet Sauvignon Maipo Valley 1988 $7 (6/15/91)
86 CALITERRA Cabernet Sauvignon Maipo 1987 $6 (9/15/90) BB
85 CALITERRA Cabernet Sauvignon Maipo 1986 $6 (7/31/89) BB
75 CANEPA Cabernet Sauvignon Maipo 1985 $4 (11/15/87)
75 CANEPA Cabernet Sauvignon Maipo Valley 1986 $6 (6/15/90)
76 CANEPA Cabernet Sauvignon Maipo Valley Finisimo 1983 $9 (6/30/90)
84 CANEPA Cabernet Sauvignon Maipo Valley Reserva 1988 $6.50 (6/15/90) BB
78 CARTA VIEJA Cabernet Sauvignon Maule Valley 1987 $6 (6/15/91)
75 CARTA VIEJA Cabernet Sauvignon Maule Valley 1986 $4 (6/15/90)
68 CARTA VIEJA Cabernet Sauvignon Maule Valley 1985 $3 (7/31/89)
75 CARTA VIEJA Cabernet Sauvignon Maule Valley Antiqua Selection 1986 $8 (6/15/91)
60 CHATEAU ANDREW Cabernet Sauvignon Colchagua 1983 $6 (12/01/85)
69 CONCHA Y TORO Cabernet Sauvignon Maipo 1985 $5 (9/15/90)
89 CONCHA Y TORO Cabernet Sauvignon Maipo 1984 $5.50 (4/30/88) BB
85 CONCHA Y TORO Cabernet Sauvignon Maipo Puente Alto Vineyard Private Reserve Don Melchor 1987 $13 (6/30/90)
85 CONCHA Y TORO Cabernet Sauvignon Maipo Reserva Special Casillero del Diablo 1984 $7 (11/15/87)
80 CONCHA Y TORO Cabernet Sauvignon Maipo Special Reserve 1981 $6.75 (4/30/88)
75 CONCHA Y TORO Cabernet Sauvignon Maipo Valley 1985 $5 (3/15/90)
75 CONCHA Y TORO Cabernet Sauvignon Maipo Valley Puente Alto Vineyard Special Reserve 1983 $8 (9/15/90)
65 CONCHA Y TORO Cabernet Sauvignon Maipo Valley Puente Alto Vineyard Special Reserve 1983 $8 (2/15/90)
71 COUSINO-MACUL Cabernet Sauvignon Maipo 1987 $6 (9/15/90)
72 COUSINO-MACUL Cabernet Sauvignon Maipo 1986 $8 (9/15/90)
86 COUSINO-MACUL Cabernet Sauvignon Maipo 1984 $5.50 (2/15/89) BB
85 COUSINO-MACUL Cabernet Sauvignon Maipo 1983 $6 (5/15/88) BB
77 COUSINO-MACUL Cabernet Sauvignon Maipo Antiguas Reservas 1984 $9 (9/15/90)
80 COUSINO-MACUL Cabernet Sauvignon Maipo Antiguas Reservas 1981 $9 (2/15/89)
80 COUSINO-MACUL Cabernet Sauvignon Maipo Antiguas Reservas 1980 $8 (5/15/88)
82 ERRAZURIZ PANQUEHUE Cabernet Sauvignon Aconcagua 1987 $9 (9/15/90)
82 ERRAZURIZ PANQUEHUE Cabernet Sauvignon Aconcagua 1985 $5.50 (9/15/88)
87 ERRAZURIZ PANQUEHUE Cabernet Sauvignon Aconcagua Antigua Reserva Don Maximiano 1984 $7.50 (9/15/88) BB
68 ERRAZURIZ PANQUEHUE Cabernet Sauvignon Aconcagua Antigua Reserva Don Maximiano 1980 $6 (11/15/87)
79 LA PLAYA Cabernet Sauvignon Maipo Valley 1988 $5 (6/15/91)
74 LA PLAYA Cabernet Sauvignon Maipo Valley 1986 $4.50 (3/15/90)
80 LIBERTY SCHOOL Cabernet Sauvignon Lontue NV $6 (9/15/88) BB
73 MONTES Cabernet Sauvignon Curicó Valley 1988 $4.50 (2/15/90)
84 MONTES Cabernet Sauvignon Curicó Valley 1987 $7 (2/15/90) BB
84 MONTES Cabernet Sauvignon Curicó Valley Special Selection 1987 $12 (9/15/90)
77 ALEJANDRO HERNANDEZ MUNOZ Cabernet Sauvignon Maipo Cabernet Viña Portal Del Alto Gran Vino 1984 $3.50 (3/15/90)
82 ALEJANDRO HERNANDEZ MUNOZ Cabernet Sauvignon Maipo Viña Portal del Alto Gran Reserva Tinto 1983 $4 (9/15/90) BB
69 LOS PUMAS Cabernet Sauvignon Curicó Valley 1988 $4 (9/15/90)
75 ST. MORILLON Cabernet Sauvignon Lontue 1985 $4 (9/15/90)
73 SAN JOSE DE SANTIAGO Cabernet Sauvignon Colchagua Valley 1990 $3 (6/15/91)
78 SAN MARTIN Cabernet Sauvignon Maipo Valley International Series 1987 $4.50 (6/15/90) BB
76 SANTA CAROLINA Cabernet Sauvignon Maipo Valley Estrella de Oro 1982 $8 (3/15/90)
78 SANTA CAROLINA Cabernet Sauvignon Maipo Valley Santa Rosa Vineyard 1986 $4 (4/30/88)
86 SANTA MONICA Cabernet Sauvignon Rancagua 1988 $6 (3/15/90) BB
83 SANTA RITA Cabernet Sauvignon Maipo Valley 120 1986 $5 (5/15/89) BB
78 SANTA RITA Cabernet Sauvignon Maipo Valley 120 Medalla Real 1987 $11 (6/15/90)
87 SANTA RITA Cabernet Sauvignon Maipo Valley 120 Medalla Real 1984 $9 (7/15/87)
85 SANTA RITA Cabernet Sauvignon Maipo Valley 120 Medalla Real 1984 $9 (11/15/87)
82 SANTA RITA Cabernet Sauvignon Maipo Valley Medalla Real 1987 $12 (6/15/91)
78 SANTA RITA Cabernet Sauvignon Maipo Valley Medalla Real 1986 $5 (3/15/90)
75 SANTA RITA Cabernet Sauvignon Maipo Valley Medalla Real 1985 $8 (3/31/88)
84 SANTA RITA Cabernet Sauvignon Maipo Valley Reserva 1988 $9.75 (6/15/91)
85 SANTA RITA Cabernet Sauvignon Maipo Valley Reserva 1987 $11.50 (9/15/90)
87 SANTA RITA Cabernet Sauvignon Maipo Valley Reserva 1986 $6.25 (5/15/89) BB
82 MIGUEL TORRES Cabernet Sauvignon Curicó 1989 $7 (6/15/91) BB
87 MIGUEL TORRES Cabernet Sauvignon Curicó 1988 $4.50 (9/15/90) BB
73 MIGUEL TORRES Cabernet Sauvignon Curicó 1985 $5 (3/31/88)
79 MIGUEL TORRES Cabernet Sauvignon Curicó 1984 $4.50 (1/31/87)
83 UNDURRAGA Cabernet Sauvignon Maipo Valley 1988 $5.25 (9/15/90) BB
87 UNDURRAGA Cabernet Sauvignon Maipo Valley 1987 $5.25 (2/15/90) BB
83 UNDURRAGA Cabernet Sauvignon Maipo Valley Reserve Selection 1986 $8 (6/15/91) BB
85 UNDURRAGA Cabernet Sauvignon Maipo Valley Reserve Selection 1985 $7.75 (3/15/90) BB
78 UNDURRAGA Cabernet Sauvignon Maipo Valley Santa Ana 1985 $5 (11/15/87)
81 VALDIVIESO Cabernet Sauvignon Maipo Valley 1984 $7 (9/15/90)
79 VALLE DE SAN FERNANDO Cabernet Sauvignon San Fernando 1985 $7 (7/31/89)
77 VALLE DE SAN FERNANDO Cabernet Sauvignon San Fernando 1983 $4 (11/15/88)
81 VALLE DE SAN FERNANDO Cabernet Sauvignon San Fernando Gran Reserva 1984 $6 (9/15/90) BB
83 VALLE DE SAN FERNANDO Cabernet Sauvignon San Fernando Gran Reserva 1984 $6 (7/31/89) BB
81 VALLE DE SAN FERNANDO Cabernet Sauvignon San Fernando Gran Reserva 1982 $6 (11/15/88) BB
84 VALLE DE SAN FERNANDO Cabernet Sauvignon San Fernando Valley 1988 $6 (9/15/90) BB
82 LOS VASCOS Cabernet Sauvignon Colchagua 1988 $7 (6/15/91) BB
86 LOS VASCOS Cabernet Sauvignon Colchagua 1987 $5 (9/15/90) BB
84 LOS VASCOS Cabernet Sauvignon Colchagua 1985 $5 (11/15/87)
88 LOS VASCOS Cabernet Sauvignon Colchagua 1984 $4.50 (4/30/88) BB
81 VINA DEL MAR Cabernet Sauvignon Curicó Selección Especial 35 1988 $6 (6/15/91) BB
83 VINA DEL MAR Cabernet Sauvignon Curicó Selección Especial 35 1987 $6 (9/15/90) BB
86 VINA DEL MAR Cabernet Sauvignon Lontue 1985 $6 (4/30/88) BB
80 VINA DEL MAR Cabernet Sauvignon Lontue Selección Especial 17 1986 $6 (2/15/90) BB
78 VINA SAN PEDRO Cabernet Sauvignon Lontue Castillo de Molina 1982 $7.50 (2/15/89)
83 VINA SAN PEDRO Cabernet Sauvignon Lontue Castillo de Molina 1981 $7.50 (11/15/87) BB
81 VINA SAN PEDRO Cabernet Sauvignon Lontue Castillo de Molina 1979 $7.50 (3/15/87)
80 VINA SAN PEDRO Cabernet Sauvignon Lontue Gato Negro 1986 $4.50 (11/15/88) BB
83 VINA SAN PEDRO Cabernet Sauvignon Lontue Gato Negro 1984 $4.50 (5/15/88) BB
76 VINA SAN PEDRO Cabernet Sauvignon Lontue Gato Negro 1983 $4.50 (3/15/87)

85 VINA SAN PEDRO Cabernet Sauvignon Lontue Gato de Oro 1986 $4.50 (2/15/90) BB
86 VINTERRA Cabernet Sauvignon Maipo-Napa Valleys NV $7 (2/15/90) BB
80 WALNUT CREST Cabernet Sauvignon Maipo 1985 $4 (6/30/90) BB

CHARDONNAY

78 CALITERRA Chardonnay Curicó 1990 $6 (6/15/91)
79 CALITERRA Chardonnay Curicó 1989 $7 (9/15/90)
81 CANEPA Chardonnay Maipo 1986 $4 (11/15/87)
72 CANEPA Chardonnay Maipo Valley 1989 $6.50 (6/30/90)
65 CONCHA Y TORO Chardonnay Maipo 1983 $5 (11/15/87)
67 CONCHA Y TORO Chardonnay Maipo Valley 1987 $5 (4/30/90)
76 COUSINO-MACUL Chardonnay Maipo 1989 $7 (9/15/90)
85 COUSINO-MACUL Chardonnay Maipo 1987 $6 (3/31/90) BB
82 COUSINO-MACUL Chardonnay Maipo 1986 $6 (5/15/88)
75 COUSINO-MACUL Chardonnay Maipo 1986 $5 (11/15/87)
82 COUSINO-MACUL Chardonnay Maipo Reserva 1988 $7.75 (4/30/90) BB
74 ERRAZURIZ PANQUEHUE Chardonnay Aconcagua 1986 $5 (11/15/87)
83 ERRAZURIZ PANQUEHUE Chardonnay Maule Reserva 1989 $7 (9/15/90) BB
70 LIBERTY SCHOOL Chardonnay Maule 1987 $6 (9/15/88)
81 SAN MARTIN Chardonnay Maipo Valley International Series 1988 $4.50 (4/30/90) BB
80 SANTA CAROLINA Chardonnay Maipo Valley Los Toros Vineyard 1986 $4 (3/31/88) BB
71 SANTA CAROLINA Chardonnay Maipo Valley NV $5 (3/31/90)
70 SANTA MONICA Chardonnay Rancagua 1988 $6 (3/31/90)
82 SANTA RITA Chardonnay Maipo Valley Medalla Real 1990 $11.50 (6/15/91)
86 SANTA RITA Chardonnay Maipo Valley Medalla Real 1986 $8 (3/31/88)
78 SANTA RITA Chardonnay Maipo Valley Reserva 1989 $9.50 (6/30/90)
79 SANTA RITA Chardonnay Maipo Valley Reserva 1987 $7.50 (3/31/90)
75 MIGUEL TORRES Chardonnay Curicó 1989 $7.50 (3/31/90)
81 VINA SAN PEDRO Chardonnay Lontue Gato de Oro 1986 $7.50 (2/28/87) BB
73 VINA SAN PEDRO Chardonnay Lontue Gato de Oro Gran Reserva 1987 $7 (5/15/88)
84 VINTERRA Chardonnay Maipo-Napa Valleys NV $7 (3/31/90) BB
74 WALNUT CREST Chardonnay Maipo 1988 $4 (4/30/90)

MERLOT

77 ROBERT ALLISON Merlot Maipo Valley 1987 $5 (6/30/90)
79 CANEPA Merlot Maipo Valley 1988 $6 (6/30/90) BB
76 CONCHA Y TORO Merlot Rapel 1986 $4.50 (3/15/90)
68 LA PLAYA Merlot Maipo Valley 1988 $5 (6/15/91)
75 LA PLAYA Merlot Maipo Valley 1987 $4.50 (3/15/90)
79 MONTES Merlot Curicó Valley 1989 $7 (9/15/90)
80 SANTA RITA Merlot Maipo Valley 120 1989 $7 (6/15/91) BB
80 VINA DEL MAR Merlot Curicó Selección Especial 12 1989 $6 (6/15/91) BB
82 VINA DEL MAR Merlot Curicó Selección Especial 12 1988 $6 (9/15/90) BB
80 VINA DEL MAR Merlot Lontue 1988 $6 (7/31/89) BB
81 VINA SAN PEDRO Merlot Lontue Gato de Oro 1987 $6 (2/15/89) BB
84 VINA SAN PEDRO Merlot Lontue Valley 1988 $5 (12/31/90) BB
85 WALNUT CREST Merlot Rapel 1987 $4 (6/30/90) BB

SAUVIGNON BLANC

70 CANEPA Sauvignon Blanc Maipo 1986 $4 (11/15/87)
87 ERRAZURIZ PANQUEHUE Sauvignon Blanc Maule 1988 $5.50 (9/15/88) BB
82 LIBERTY SCHOOL Sauvignon Blanc Maule 1987 $5 (9/15/88) BB
69 VALLE DE SAN FERNANDO Sauvignon Blanc San Fernando 1987 $4 (9/15/88)
85 SANTA MONICA Sauvignon Blanc Rancagua 1988 $6 (3/31/90) BB
83 SANTA RITA Sauvignon Blanc Maipo 120 Tres Medallas 1985 $7 (11/15/87)
71 SANTA RITA Sauvignon Blanc Maipo Medalla Real 1985 $4.50 (3/15/88)
77 SANTA RITA Sauvignon Blanc Maipo Valley 120 Tres Medallas NV $5 (7/15/87)
82 MIGUEL TORRES Sauvignon Blanc Curicó 1987 $4.50 (3/15/88) BB
74 MIGUEL TORRES Sauvignon Blanc Curicó 1985 $4 (10/31/87)
74 MIGUEL TORRES Sauvignon Blanc Curicó District 1985 $4 (10/31/87)
75 UNDURRAGA Sauvignon Blanc Maipo Valley 1989 $5.25 (3/31/90)
83 LOS VASCOS Sauvignon Blanc Colchagua 1988 $4.75 (3/31/90) BB
79 LOS VASCOS Sauvignon Blanc Colchagua 1987 $4 (11/15/87)
70 VILLA RICA Sauvignon Blanc Aconcagua 1986 $5 (11/15/87)
86 VINA SAN PEDRO Fumé Blanc Lontue 1986 $6 (11/15/87)
84 VINA SAN PEDRO Sauvignon Blanc Lontue Gato Blanco 1987 $5 (11/15/87)
75 VINA SAN PEDRO Sauvignon Blanc Lontue Gato Blanco 1986 $4.50 (9/15/88)
77 VINA SAN PEDRO Sauvignon Blanc Lontue Gato Blanco 1985 $4.50 (4/30/88)
70 VINA SAN PEDRO Sauvignon Blanc Lontue Gato Blanco 1984 $4.25 (11/15/87)
76 VINA SAN PEDRO Fumé Blanc Lontue Gran Reserva 1987 $6.25 (9/15/88)
68 VINA SAN PEDRO Sauvignon Blanc Lontue San Pedro 1984 $7 (2/28/87)

OTHER CHILE RED

74 ALEJANDRO HERNANDEZ MUNOZ Pinot Noir Maipo Viña Portal del Alto Gran Vino 1984 $3.50 (3/15/90)
74 CANEPA Maipo Cabernet Sauvignon Malbec 1984 $4 (3/15/88)
80 CONCHA Y TORO Rapel Cabernet Sauvignon Merlot 1986 $4.25 (9/15/90) BB
69 SANTA CAROLINA Reserva de Familia 1979 $9 (11/15/87)
78 MIGUEL TORRES Santa Digna 1983 (NA) (2/16/86)

OTHER CHILE WHITE

48 CHATEAU ANDREW Colchagua Chevrier 1984 $5.25 (5/16/86)
76 MIGUEL TORRES Santa Digna 1985 (NA) (2/16/86)
81 SANTA MONICA Sémillon Rancagua Seaborne 1988 $5 (3/31/90) BB

FRANCE
ALSACE/GEWÜRZTRAMINER

93   DOMAINE LUCIEN ALBRECHT Gewürztraminer Alsace Sélection de Grains Nobles 1989 (NA) (11/15/90)

85   DOMAINE LUCIEN ALBRECHT Gewürztraminer Alsace Vendange Tardive 1989 (NA) (11/15/90)

78   J. BECKER Gewürztraminer Alsace 1986 $13 (7/15/88)

76   J. BECKER Gewürztraminer Alsace Frohen 1986 $16.50 (7/15/88)

90   LEON BEYER Gewürztraminer Alsace 1989 (NA) (11/15/90)

85   LEON BEYER Gewürztraminer Alsace 1988 $11.50 (10/15/89)

91   LEON BEYER Gewürztraminer Alsace Comtes d'Eguisheim 1989 (NA) (11/15/90)

89   LEON BEYER Gewürztraminer Alsace Cuvée des Comtes d'Eguisheim 1988 $25 (10/15/89)

96   LEON BEYER Gewürztraminer Alsace Sélection de Grains Nobles 1989 (NA) (11/15/90)

75   LEON BEYER Gewürztraminer Alsace Vendange Tardive 1989 (NA) (11/15/90)

87   BOTT FRERES Gewürztraminer Alsace Cuvée Exceptionnelle 1989 $13.50 (6/30/91)

88   BOTT FRERES Gewürztraminer Alsace Réserve Personnelle 1989 $17 (6/30/91)

63   BOTT FRERES Gewürztraminer Alsace Vendange Tardive 1988 $40 (7/31/91)

82   DOPFF AU MOULIN Gewürztraminer Alsace 1989 (NA) (11/15/90)

84   DOPFF AU MOULIN Gewürztraminer Alsace 1988 (NA) (10/15/89)

81   DOPFF AU MOULIN Gewürztraminer Alsace 1985 $10.50 (7/15/88)

82   DOPFF AU MOULIN Gewürztraminer Alsace Brand 1988 (NA) (10/15/89)

87   DOPFF AU MOULIN Gewürztraminer Alsace Réserve 1989 (NA) (11/15/90)

94   DOPFF AU MOULIN Gewürztraminer Alsace Sélection de Grains Nobles 1989 (NA) (11/15/90)

81   DOPFF AU MOULIN Gewürztraminer Alsace Vendange Tardive 1989 (NA) (11/15/90)

90   DOPFF AU MOULIN Gewürztraminer Alsace Vendange Tardive 1988 (NA) (10/15/89)

81   DOPFF & IRION Gewürztraminer Alsace 1989 (NA) (11/15/90)

82   DOPFF & IRION Gewürztraminer Alsace 1988 $11 (10/15/89)

58   DOPFF & IRION Gewürztraminer Alsace 1985 $9 (3/15/87)

80   DOPFF & IRION Gewürztraminer Alsace Cuvée René Dopff 1989 (NA) (11/15/90)

60   DOPFF & IRION Gewürztraminer Alsace Les Sorcières Château de Riquewihr 1985 $13 (3/15/87)

83   DOPFF & IRION Gewürztraminer Alsace Les Sorcières Château de Riquewihr 1985 $34 (3/15/87)

76   DOPFF & IRION Gewürztraminer Alsace Vendange Tardives 1983 $26 (3/15/87)

87   ROLLY GASSMAN Gewürztraminer Alsace Brandhurst 1985 $17 (7/15/88)

85   HUGEL Gewürztraminer Alsace 1989 (NA) (11/15/90)

83   HUGEL Gewürztraminer Alsace 1988 $14.25 (10/15/89)

87   HUGEL Gewürztraminer Alsace 1986 $11 (7/15/88)

90   HUGEL Gewürztraminer Alsace 1985 $12.25 (8/31/87)

85   HUGEL Gewürztraminer Alsace Réserve Personnelle 1983 $19 (10/15/87)

89   HUGEL Gewürztraminer Alsace Sélection de Grains Nobles ''R'' 1989 (NA) (11/15/90)

96   HUGEL Gewürztraminer Alsace Sélection de Grains Nobles ''S'' 1989 (NA) (11/15/90)

91   HUGEL Gewürztraminer Alsace Sélection de Grains Nobles ''T'' 1989 (NA) (11/15/90)

95   HUGEL Gewürztraminer Alsace Sélection de Grains Nobles 1983 (NA) (4/30/87) (JS)

93   HUGEL Gewürztraminer Alsace Sélection de Grains Nobles 1981 (NA) (4/30/87) (JS)

90   HUGEL Gewürztraminer Alsace Sélection de Grains Nobles 1976 (NA) (4/30/87) (JS)

98   HUGEL Gewürztraminer Alsace Sélection de Grains Nobles 1961 (NA) (4/30/87) (JS)

90   HUGEL Gewürztraminer Alsace Vendange Tardive 1989 (NA) (11/15/90)

95   HUGEL Gewürztraminer Alsace Vendange Tardive 1983 (NA) (4/30/87) (JS)

88   HUGEL Gewürztraminer Alsace Vendange Tardive 1976 (NA) (4/30/87) (JS)

75   HUGEL Gewürztraminer Alsace Vendange Tardive 1966 (NA) (4/30/87) (JS)

83   JOSMEYER Gewürztraminer Alsace Cuvée des Folastries 1989 $16 (11/15/90)

90   JOSMEYER Gewürztraminer Alsace Hengst 1989 (NA) (11/15/90)

85   JOSMEYER Gewürztraminer Alsace Sélection de Grains Nobles 1989 (NA) (11/15/90)

88   JOSMEYER Gewürztraminer Alsace Vendange Tardive 1989 (NA) (11/15/90)

79   MARC KREYDENWEISS Gewürztraminer Alsace Kritt 1989 $19 (11/15/90)

86   MARC KREYDENWEISS Gewürztraminer Alsace Kritt 1988 $19 (10/15/89)

83   MARC KREYDENWEISS Gewürztraminer Alsace Vendange Tardive Kritt 1989 (NA) (11/15/90)

86   KUENTZ-BAS Gewürztraminer Alsace 1989 (NA) (11/15/90)

84   KUENTZ-BAS Gewürztraminer Alsace Cuvée Tradition 1988 (NA) (10/15/89)

93   KUENTZ-BAS Gewürztraminer Alsace Eichberg 1989 (NA) (11/15/90)

84   KUENTZ-BAS Gewürztraminer Alsace Réserve Personnelle 1989 (NA) (11/15/90)

86   KUENTZ-BAS Gewürztraminer Alsace Vendange Tardive Eichberg 1989 (NA) (11/15/90)

80   CUVEE LEON Gewürztraminer Alsace 1988 $11 (3/31/91)

85   GUSTAVE LORENTZ Gewürztraminer Alsace 1989 (NA) (11/15/90)

89   GUSTAVE LORENTZ Gewürztraminer Alsace 1988 (NA) (10/15/89)

86   GUSTAVE LORENTZ Gewürztraminer Alsace 1986 $11 (7/31/89)

85   GUSTAVE LORENTZ Gewürztraminer Alsace Altenberg 1989 (NA) (11/15/90)

79   GUSTAVE LORENTZ Gewürztraminer Alsace Réserve 1989 (NA) (11/15/90)

91   GUSTAVE LORENTZ Gewürztraminer Alsace Sélection de Grains Nobles 1988 (NA) (10/15/89)

75   MURE Gewürztraminer Alsace 1986 $7.50 (7/15/88)

64   MURE Gewürztraminer Alsace 1985 $7 (6/15/87)

70   MURE Gewürztraminer Alsace Clos St.-Landelin Vorbourg 1985 $12 (6/15/87)

84   MURE Gewürztraminer Alsace Zinnkoepflé 1989 (NA) (11/15/90)

86   DOMAINE OSTERTAG Gewürztraminer Alsace 1988 (NA) (10/15/89)

90   DOMAINE OSTERTAG Gewürztraminer Alsace Vignoble d'Epfig 1989 $14 (11/15/90)

74   DOMAINE OSTERTAG Gewürztraminer Alsace Vignoble de Nothalten 1986 $14 (7/15/88)

90   SALZMANN Gewürztraminer Alsace 1985 $16 (6/15/87)

85   SALZMANN Gewürztraminer Alsace Cuvée Réservee 1986 $14 (7/15/88)

73   DOMAINES SCHLUMBERGER Gewürztraminer Alsace 1989 (NA) (11/15/90)

78   DOMAINES SCHLUMBERGER Gewürztraminer Alsace 1988 (NA) (10/15/89)

90   DOMAINES SCHLUMBERGER Gewürztraminer Alsace Fleur de Guebwiller 1985 $14.50 (7/15/88)

87   DOMAINES SCHLUMBERGER Gewürztraminer Alsace Fleur de Guebwiller 1983 $11.50 (8/31/87)

90   DOMAINES SCHLUMBERGER Gewürztraminer Alsace Kessler 1989 (NA) (11/15/90)

78   DOMAINES SCHLUMBERGER Gewürztraminer Alsace Kitterlé 1989 (NA) (11/15/90)

79   DOMAINES SCHLUMBERGER Gewürztraminer Alsace Sélection de Grains Nobles 1989 (NA) (11/15/90)

78   DOMAINES SCHLUMBERGER Gewürztraminer Alsace Sélection de Grains Nobles 1988 (NA) (10/15/89)

59   RENE SCHMIDT Gewürztraminer Alsace Cuvée Particulière Réserve 1983 $9 (6/01/86)

68   LOUIS SIPP Gewürztraminer Alsace 1985 $9 (7/15/88)

79   PIERRE SPARR Gewürztraminer Alsace 1989 (NA) (11/15/90)

88   PIERRE SPARR Gewürztraminer Alsace Brand 1989 (NA) (11/15/90)

83   PIERRE SPARR Gewürztraminer Alsace Cuvée Centenaire Mambourg 1985 $17.50 (7/15/88)

87   PIERRE SPARR Gewürztraminer Alsace Sélection de Grains Nobles Cuvée Centenaire Mambo 1989 (NA) (11/15/90)

68   PIERRE SPARR Gewürztraminer Alsace Vendange Tardive Mambourg Cuvée Centenaire 1989 (NA) (11/15/90)

86   TRIMBACH Gewürztraminer Alsace 1989 (NA) (11/15/90)

83   TRIMBACH Gewürztraminer Alsace 1988 $8.50 (10/15/89)

83   TRIMBACH Gewürztraminer Alsace 1986 $12 (7/15/88)

82   TRIMBACH Gewürztraminer Alsace 1983 $7 (9/01/85)

85   TRIMBACH Gewürztraminer Alsace Carte d'Or 1989 (NA) (11/15/90)

92   TRIMBACH Gewürztraminer Alsace Réserve 1989 (NA) (11/15/90)

97   TRIMBACH Gewürztraminer Alsace Sélection de Grains Nobles Hors Choix 1989 (NA) (11/15/90)

97   TRIMBACH Gewürztraminer Alsace Vendange Tardive 1989 (NA) (11/15/90)

87   TRIMBACH Gewürztraminer Alsace Vendange Tardive 1988 (NA) (10/15/89)

89   DOMAINE WEINBACH Gewürztraminer Alsace Clos des Capucins 1985 $21 (7/15/88)

79   DOMAINE WEINBACH Gewürztraminer Alsace Clos des Capucins (Cask 21) 1989 (NA) (11/15/90)

79   DOMAINE WEINBACH Gewürztraminer Alsace Clos des Capucins Cuvée Laurence (Cask 8) 1989 $50 (11/15/90)

80   DOMAINE WEINBACH Gewürztraminer Alsace Clos des Capucins Cuvée Laurence (Cask 17) 1989 $50 (11/15/90)

80   DOMAINE WEINBACH Gewürztraminer Alsace Clos des Capucins Personnelle 1985 $16 (7/15/88)

84   DOMAINE WEINBACH Gewürztraminer Alsace Clos des Capucins Réserve Personnelle Théo Faller 1988 $21 (6/30/91)

83   DOMAINE WEINBACH Gewürztraminer Alsace Cuvée Laurence 1988 $34 (10/15/89)

85   DOMAINE WEINBACH Gewürztraminer Alsace Cuvée Théo 1988 (NA) (10/15/89)

87   DOMAINE WEINBACH Gewürztraminer Alsace Sélection de Grains Nobles Clos des Capucins Quintes 1989 $275 (11/15/90)

92   DOMAINE WEINBACH Gewürztraminer Alsace Vendange Tardive 1988 $67.50 (10/15/89)

69   ALSACE WILLM Gewürztraminer Alsace 1989 (NA) (11/15/90)

91   ALSACE WILLM Gewürztraminer Alsace 1985 $11 (7/15/88)

83   ALSACE WILLM Gewürztraminer Alsace Clos Gaensbroennel Kirchberg de Barr 1989 (NA) (11/15/90)

86   ALSACE WILLM Gewürztraminer Alsace Sélection de Grains Nobles 1989 (NA) (11/15/90)

80   ALSACE WILLM Gewürztraminer Alsace Vendange Tardive Gaensbroennel 1989 (NA) (11/15/90)

83   DOMAINE ZIND HUMBRECHT Gewürztraminer Alsace 1988 (NA) (10/15/89)

84   DOMAINE ZIND HUMBRECHT Gewürztraminer Alsace 1986 $10 (7/15/88)

83   DOMAINE ZIND HUMBRECHT Gewürztraminer Alsace Clos Windsbuhl 1989 $36 (11/15/90)

81   DOMAINE ZIND HUMBRECHT Gewürztraminer Alsace Goldert Vendage Tardive 1985 $40 (9/15/87)

94   DOMAINE ZIND HUMBRECHT Gewürztraminer Alsace Guebershwihr Vendange Tardive 1985 $40 (9/15/87)

91   DOMAINE ZIND HUMBRECHT Gewürztraminer Alsace Hengst 1985 $29 (9/15/87)

84   DOMAINE ZIND HUMBRECHT Gewürztraminer Alsace Herrenweg Turckheim 1989 $25 (11/15/90)

88   DOMAINE ZIND HUMBRECHT Gewürztraminer Alsace Herrenweg Turckheim 1985 $14 (7/31/87)

85   DOMAINE ZIND HUMBRECHT Gewürztraminer Alsace Vendange Tardive Rangen 1988 (NA) (10/15/89)

PINOT BLANC

75   DOMAINE LUCIEN ALBRECHT Pinot Blanc Alsace 1989 $7 (11/15/90)

81   J. BECKER Pinot Blanc Alsace 1986 $9.50 (7/15/88)

78   LEON BEYER Pinot Blanc Alsace 1989 (NA) (11/15/90)

79   LEON BEYER Pinot Blanc Alsace Blanc de Blancs 1988 $8.75 (10/15/89)

84   LEON BEYER Pinot Blanc Alsace de Blancs 1987 $9 (7/31/89)

84   DOPFF & IRION Pinot Blanc Alsace 1989 (NA) (11/15/90)

82   DOPFF & IRION Pinot Blanc Alsace Cuvée René Dopff 1988 (NA) (10/15/89)

82   DOPFF & IRION Pinot Blanc Alsace de Blancs 1985 $7 (2/28/87)

86   HUGEL Pinot Blanc Alsace 1989 (NA) (11/15/90)

83   HUGEL Pinot Blanc Alsace 1988 $9 (10/15/89)

71   HUGEL Pinot Blanc Alsace Cuvée les Amours 1986 $7.75 (7/15/88)

75   HUGEL Pinot Blanc Alsace Cuvée les Amours 1985 $9 (5/31/87)

80   HUGEL Pinot Blanc Alsace Cuvée les Amours 1982 $6 (10/16/84)

85   JOSMEYER Pinot Blanc Alsace Les Lutins 1989 $15 (11/15/90)

89   JOSMEYER Pinot Blanc Alsace Pinot Auxerrois ''H'' Vieilles Vignes 1989 (NA) (11/15/90)

83   MARC KREYDENWEISS Pinot Blanc Alsace Kritt 1989 $14 (11/15/90)

87   MARC KREYDENWEISS Pinot Blanc Alsace Kritt 1988 $13 (10/15/89)

86   MARC KREYDENWEISS Pinot Blanc Alsace Kritt Klevner 1989 $17 (11/15/90)

73   KUENTZ-BAS Pinot Blanc Alsace 1989 (NA) (11/15/90)

84   KUENTZ-BAS Pinot Blanc Alsace Cuvée Tradition 1988 (NA) (10/15/89)

83   CUVEE LEON Pinot Blanc Alsace Cuvée Pinot Blanc 1988 $10 (3/31/91)

83   GUSTAVE LORENTZ Pinot Blanc Alsace 1989 $11 (11/15/90)

79   GUSTAVE LORENTZ Pinot Blanc Alsace 1988 $12 (10/15/89)

78   GUSTAVE LORENTZ Pinot Blanc Alsace Réserve 1986 $7 (7/31/89)

81   DOMAINE OSTERTAG Pinot Blanc Alsace Barriques 1989 $14 (7/31/91)

84   DOMAINES SCHLUMBERGER Pinot Blanc Alsace 1988 (NA) (10/15/89)

83   DOMAINES SCHLUMBERGER Pinot Blanc Alsace 1986 $8.75 (7/15/88)

82   DOMAINES SCHLUMBERGER Pinot Blanc Alsace 1983 $8 (6/15/87)

86   TRIMBACH Pinot Blanc Alsace 1989 (NA) (11/15/90)

87   TRIMBACH Pinot Blanc Alsace 1988 $8 (11/15/90) BB

83   TRIMBACH Pinot Blanc Alsace 1988 $7 (10/15/89)

86   TRIMBACH Pinot Blanc Alsace 1986 $9 (7/15/88)

86   TRIMBACH Pinot Blanc Alsace Sélection 1989 (NA) (11/15/90)

88 DOMAINE WEINBACH Pinot Blanc Alsace 1989 (NA) (11/15/90)

80 DOMAINE WEINBACH Pinot Blanc Alsace Clos des Capucins 1988 (NA) (10/15/89)

74 DOMAINE WEINBACH Pinot Blanc Alsace Clos des Capucins Réserve Particulière 1988 $19 (10/15/89)

83 ALSACE WILLM Pinot Blanc Alsace 1989 (NA) (11/15/90)

78 ALSACE WILLM Pinot Blanc Alsace Cordon d'Alsace 1985 $7.75 (7/15/88)

76 DOMAINE ZIND HUMBRECHT Pinot Blanc Alsace 1989 (NA) (11/15/90)

87 DOMAINE ZIND HUMBRECHT Pinot Blanc Alsace 1988 (NA) (10/15/89)

RIESLING

87 DOMAINE LUCIEN ALBRECHT Riesling Alsace Sélection de Grains Nobles Pfingstberg 1989 (NA) (11/15/90)

77 J. BECKER Riesling Alsace 1986 $11 (7/15/88)

84 LEON BEYER Riesling Alsace 1989 (NA) (11/15/90)

80 LEON BEYER Riesling Alsace 1988 $10.50 (10/15/89)

92 LEON BEYER Riesling Alsace Cuvée Particulière 1989 (NA) (11/15/90)

76 LEON BEYER Riesling Alsace Réserve 1987 $13 (7/31/89)

80 LEON BEYER Riesling Alsace Sélection de Grains Nobles 1989 (NA) (11/15/90)

87 LEON BEYER Riesling Alsace Sélection de Grains Nobles 1988 $25 (10/15/89)

79 LEON BEYER Riesling Alsace Vendange Tardive 1989 (NA) (11/15/90)

81 BOTT FRERES Riesling Alsace Cuvée Exceptionnelle 1989 $13 (7/31/91)

84 DOPFF AU MOULIN Riesling Alsace 1988 (NA) (10/15/89)

79 DOPFF AU MOULIN Riesling Alsace Propre Récolte 1989 (NA) (11/15/90)

80 DOPFF AU MOULIN Riesling Alsace Réserve 1989 (NA) (11/15/90)

78 DOPFF AU MOULIN Riesling Alsace Schoenenbourg 1989 (NA) (11/15/90)

95 DOPFF AU MOULIN Riesling Alsace Sélection de Grains Nobles 1989 (NA) (11/15/90)

86 DOPFF AU MOULIN Riesling Alsace Vendange Tardive 1989 (NA) (11/15/90)

83 DOPFF AU MOULIN Riesling Alsace Vendange Tardive 1988 (NA) (10/15/89)

81 DOPFF & IRION Riesling Alsace 1989 (NA) (11/15/90)

84 DOPFF & IRION Riesling Alsace 1985 $8 (4/30/87)

85 DOPFF & IRION Riesling Alsace Cuvée René Dopff 1988 $9.25 (10/15/89)

80 DOPFF & IRION Riesling Alsace Les Murailles Château de Riquewihr 1989 (NA) (11/15/90)

79 DOPFF & IRION Riesling Alsace Les Murailles Château de Riquewihr 1985 $12 (3/15/87)

79 DOPFF & IRION Riesling Alsace Les Murailles 1988 (NA) (10/15/89)

81 DOPFF & IRION Riesling Alsace Schoenenbourg 1989 (NA) (11/15/90)

79 DOPFF & IRION Riesling Alsace Les Sorcières Château de Riquewihr 1985 $12 (3/15/87)

87 DOPFF & IRION Riesling Alsace Vendange Tardive 1988 (NA) (10/15/89)

84 DOPFF & IRION Riesling Alsace Vendange Tardive 1983 $23 (3/15/87)

76 DOMAINE FERNAND GRESSER Riesling Alsace Andlau 1986 $15 (7/15/88)

87 HUGEL Riesling Alsace 1989 (NA) (11/15/90)

87 HUGEL Riesling Alsace 1988 $12.50 (10/15/89)

80 HUGEL Riesling Alsace 1985 $10.50 (10/15/87)

86 HUGEL Riesling Alsace Cuvée Tradition 1989 (NA) (11/15/90)

89 HUGEL Riesling Alsace Cuvée Tradition 1988 (NA) (10/15/89)

90 HUGEL Riesling Alsace Jubilée Réserve Personnelle 1989 (NA) (11/15/90)

98 HUGEL Riesling Alsace Sélection de Grains Nobles 1976 (NA) (4/30/87) (JS)

90 HUGEL Riesling Alsace Vendange Tardive 1989 (NA) (11/15/90)

88 HUGEL Riesling Alsace Vendange Tardive 1983 (NA) (4/30/87) (JS)

80 HUGEL Riesling Alsace Vendange Tardive 1981 (NA) (4/30/87) (JS)

92 HUGEL Riesling Alsace Vendange Tardive 1976 (NA) (4/30/87) (JS)

95 HUGEL Riesling Alsace Vendange Tardive 1961 (NA) (4/30/87) (JS)

90 JOSMEYER Riesling Alsace Hengst 1989 (NA) (11/15/90)

86 JOSMEYER Riesling Alsace La Kottabe 1989 (NA) (11/15/90)

86 MARC KREYDENWEISS Riesling Alsace 1988 $15.50 (10/15/89)

83 MARC KREYDENWEISS Riesling Alsace Andlau 1989 $18 (11/15/90)

84 MARC KREYDENWEISS Riesling Alsace Grand Cru Weibelsberg 1988 $23 (10/15/89)

82 MARC KREYDENWEISS Riesling Alsace Kastelberg 1989 (NA) (11/15/90)

95 MARC KREYDENWEISS Riesling Alsace Sélection de Grains Nobles Weibelsberg 1988 (NA) (10/15/89)

90 MARC KREYDENWEISS Riesling Alsace Vendange Tardive Kastelberg 1988 $26 (10/15/89)

79 MARC KREYDENWEISS Riesling Alsace Vendange Tardive Weibelsberg 1989 (NA) (11/15/90)

84 MARC KREYDENWEISS Riesling Alsace Weibelsberg 1989 (NA) (11/15/90)

69 KUENTZ-BAS Riesling Alsace 1989 (NA) (11/15/90)

84 KUENTZ-BAS Riesling Alsace Cuvée Tradition 1988 (NA) (10/15/89)

83 KUENTZ-BAS Riesling Alsace Pfersigberg 1989 (NA) (11/15/90)

79 KUENTZ-BAS Riesling Alsace Réserve Personelle 1989 (NA) (11/15/90)

84 KUENTZ-BAS Riesling Alsace Réserve Personelle 1988 (NA) (10/15/89)

74 GUSTAVE LORENTZ Riesling Alsace 1989 $15 (11/15/90)

85 GUSTAVE LORENTZ Riesling Alsace 1988 $15 (10/15/89)

88 GUSTAVE LORENTZ Riesling Alsace Altenberg 1989 (NA) (11/15/90)

84 GUSTAVE LORENTZ Riesling Alsace Altenberg de Bergheim 1988 (NA) (10/15/89)

75 GUSTAVE LORENTZ Riesling Alsace Réserve 1989 (NA) (11/15/90)

79 GUSTAVE LORENTZ Riesling Alsace Réserve 1986 $9.50 (7/31/89)

87 MURE Riesling Alsace Clos St.-Landelin Vorbourg 1989 (NA) (11/15/90)

69 MURE Riesling Alsace Clos St.-Landelin Vorbourg 1985 $11.50 (5/31/87)

89 MURE Riesling Alsace Sélection de Grains Nobles Clos St.-Landelin Vorbour 1989 (NA) (11/15/90)

78 MURE Riesling Alsace Vendange Tardive Clos St.-Landelin Vorbourg 1989 (NA) (11/15/90)

89 DOMAINE OSTERTAG Riesling Alsace 1988 (NA) (10/15/89)

76 DOMAINE OSTERTAG Riesling Alsace 1985 $10 (7/15/88)

85 DOMAINE OSTERTAG Riesling Alsace en Barriques Heissenberg 1989 $24 (7/31/91)

87 DOMAINE OSTERTAG Riesling Alsace Fronholz 1989 $24 (7/31/91)

88 DOMAINE OSTERTAG Riesling Alsace Muenchberg 1989 $33 (7/31/91)

81 DOMAINE OSTERTAG Riesling Alsace Muenchberg 1988 $28 (10/15/89)

87 DOMAINE OSTERTAG Riesling Alsace Vignoble d'Epfig 1989 $14 (7/31/91)

86 DOMAINES SCHLUMBERGER Riesling Alsace 1989 (NA) (11/15/90)

85 DOMAINES SCHLUMBERGER Riesling Alsace 1988 (NA) (10/15/89)

89 DOMAINES SCHLUMBERGER Riesling Alsace Grand Cru Kitterlé 1989 (NA) (11/15/90)

74 DOMAINES SCHLUMBERGER Riesling Alsace des Princes Abbes 1986 $10.50 (7/15/88)

90 DOMAINES SCHLUMBERGER Riesling Alsace Kitterlé 1988 (NA) (10/15/89)

82 DOMAINES SCHLUMBERGER Riesling Alsace Saering 1988 (NA) (10/15/89)

79 DOMAINES SCHLUMBERGER Riesling Alsace Saering 1985 $14.50 (7/15/88)

62 RENE SCHMIDT Riesling Alsace Schoenenberg Cuvée Particulière Réserve 1983 $9 (4/01/86)

79 PIERRE SPARR Riesling Alsace Altenbourg Cuvée Centenaire 1989 (NA) (11/15/90)

86 PIERRE SPARR Riesling Alsace Schlossberg Cuvée Réserve 1989 (NA) (11/15/90)

86 TRIMBACH Riesling Alsace 1989 (NA) (11/15/90)

86 TRIMBACH Riesling Alsace 1988 $7.50 (10/15/89)

79 TRIMBACH Riesling Alsace 1986 $10 (7/15/88)

74 TRIMBACH Riesling Alsace 1982 $6.50 (1/01/85)

91 TRIMBACH Riesling Alsace Clos Ste.-Hune 1986 (NA) (5/15/89) (JS)

90 TRIMBACH Riesling Alsace Clos Ste.-Hune 1985 Cur: $50 (5/15/89) (JS)

95 TRIMBACH Riesling Alsace Clos Ste.-Hune 1983 (NA) (5/15/89) (JS)

85 TRIMBACH Riesling Alsace Clos Ste.-Hune 1982 $24 (5/15/89) (JS)

91 TRIMBACH Riesling Alsace Clos Ste.-Hune 1981 (NA) (5/15/89) (JS)

87 TRIMBACH Riesling Alsace Clos Ste.-Hune 1979 (NA) (5/15/89) (JS)

91 TRIMBACH Riesling Alsace Clos Ste.-Hune 1976 (NA) (5/15/89) (JS)

95 TRIMBACH Riesling Alsace Clos Ste.-Hune 1975 (NA) (5/15/89) (JS)

82 TRIMBACH Riesling Alsace Clos Ste.-Hune 1973 (NA) (5/15/89) (JS)

94 TRIMBACH Riesling Alsace Clos Ste.-Hune 1971 (NA) (5/15/89) (JS)

85 TRIMBACH Riesling Alsace Clos Ste.-Hune 1967 (NA) (5/15/89) (JS)

94 TRIMBACH Riesling Alsace Clos Ste.-Hune 1966 (NA) (5/15/89) (JS)

92 TRIMBACH Riesling Alsace Cuvée Frédéric Emile 1989 (NA) (11/15/90)

91 TRIMBACH Riesling Alsace Cuvée Frédéric Emile 1988 (NA) (10/15/89)

90 TRIMBACH Riesling Alsace Réserve 1989 (NA) (11/15/90)

90 TRIMBACH Riesling Alsace Sélection de Grains Nobles Frédéric Emile 1989 (NA) (11/15/90)

96 TRIMBACH Riesling Alsace Vendange Tardive Clos Ste.-Hune 1989 (NA) (11/15/90)

97 TRIMBACH Riesling Alsace Vendange Tardive Clos Ste.-Hune Hors Choix 1989 (NA) (11/15/90)

95 TRIMBACH Riesling Alsace Vendange Tardive Cuvée Frédéric Emile 1989 (NA) (11/15/90)

80 DOMAINE WEINBACH Riesling Alsace Clos des Capucins Cuvée Ste.-Catherine 1989 $43 (11/15/90)

88 DOMAINE WEINBACH Riesling Alsace Clos des Capucins Cuvée Théo 1989 $31 (11/15/90)

86 DOMAINE WEINBACH Riesling Alsace Clos des Capucins Réserve Personnelle 1989 $23 (11/15/90)

81 DOMAINE WEINBACH Riesling Alsace Clos des Capucins Réserve Personnelle Théo Faller 1989 $23 (7/31/91)

78 DOMAINE WEINBACH Riesling Alsace Clos des Capucins Réserve Personnelle Théo Faller 1988 $18 (7/31/91)

84 DOMAINE WEINBACH Riesling Alsace Clos des Capucins Schlossberg 1989 $31 (11/15/90)

82 DOMAINE WEINBACH Riesling Alsace Clos des Capucins Schlossberg 1985 $18 (7/15/88)

87 DOMAINE WEINBACH Riesling Alsace Cuvée Ste.-Catherine 1988 $30 (10/15/89)

80 DOMAINE WEINBACH Riesling Alsace Cuvée Théo 1988 (NA) (10/15/89)

96 DOMAINE WEINBACH Riesling Alsace Sélection de Grains Nobles Clos des Capucins 1989 (NA) (11/15/90)

85 ALSACE WILLM Riesling Alsace 1989 (NA) (11/15/90)

75 ALSACE WILLM Riesling Alsace 1985 $10 (7/15/88)

80 ALSACE WILLM Riesling Alsace Cuvée Emile Willm 1989 (NA) (11/15/90)

82 ALSACE WILLM Riesling Alsace Kirchberg de Barr 1989 (NA) (11/15/90)

71 WOLFBERGER Riesling Alsace 1987 $8 (7/31/89)

87 DOMAINE ZIND HUMBRECHT Riesling Alsace 1988 (NA) (10/15/89)

80 DOMAINE ZIND HUMBRECHT Riesling Alsace 1986 $12.50 (7/15/88)

86 DOMAINE ZIND HUMBRECHT Riesling Alsace Clos St.-Urbain 1985 $26 (9/15/87)

86 DOMAINE ZIND HUMBRECHT Riesling Alsace Clos St.-Urbain Rangen 1989 $45 (11/15/90)

89 DOMAINE ZIND HUMBRECHT Riesling Alsace Herrenweg 1989 $24 (11/15/90)

86 DOMAINE ZIND HUMBRECHT Riesling Alsace Rangen 1988 (NA) (10/15/89)

70 DOMAINE ZIND HUMBRECHT Riesling Alsace Réserve 1985 $11 (7/31/87)

85 DOMAINE ZIND HUMBRECHT Riesling Alsace Vendange Tardive 1985 $19 (9/15/87)

87 DOMAINE ZIND HUMBRECHT Riesling Alsace Vendange Tardive Brand 1989 (NA) (11/15/90)

TOKAY PINOT GRIS

80 DOMAINE LUCIEN ALBRECHT Tokay Pinot Gris Alsace Pfingstberg 1989 (NA) (11/15/90)

80 DOMAINE LUCIEN ALBRECHT Tokay Pinot Gris Alsace Réserve du Domaine 1989 (NA) (11/15/90)

88 DOMAINE LUCIEN ALBRECHT Tokay Pinot Gris Alsace Vendange Tardive 1989 (NA) (11/15/90)

78 LEON BEYER Tokay Pinot Gris Alsace Cuvée Particulière 1988 $12 (10/15/89)

84 LEON BEYER Tokay Pinot Gris Alsace Réserve 1989 (NA) (11/15/90)

93 LEON BEYER Tokay Pinot Gris Alsace Sélection de Grains Nobles 1989 (NA) (11/15/90)

77 LEON BEYER Tokay Pinot Gris Alsace Vendange Tardive 1989 (NA) (11/15/90)

86 DOPFF AU MOULIN Tokay Pinot Gris Alsace 1988 (NA) (10/15/89)

87 DOPFF AU MOULIN Tokay Pinot Gris Alsace Sélection de Grains Nobles 1989 (NA) (11/15/90)

87 DOPFF AU MOULIN Tokay Pinot Gris Alsace Sélection de Grains Nobles 1988 (NA) (10/15/89)

85 DOPFF & IRION Tokay Pinot Gris Alsace Cuvée René Dopff 1989 (NA) (11/15/90)

79 DOPFF & IRION Tokay Pinot Gris Alsace Cuvée René Dopff 1988 $10 (10/15/89)

87 DOPFF & IRION Tokay Pinot Gris Alsace Les Maquisards 1989 (NA) (11/15/90)

94 HUGEL Tokay Pinot Gris Alsace Sélection de Grains Nobles 1989 (NA) (11/15/90)

92 HUGEL Tokay Pinot Gris Alsace Sélection de Grains Nobles 1989 (NA) (11/15/90)

87 HUGEL Tokay Pinot Gris Alsace Sélection de Grains Nobles 1976 (NA) (4/30/87) (JS)

86 HUGEL Tokay Pinot Gris Alsace Tradition 1988 (NA) (10/15/89)

90 HUGEL Tokay Pinot Gris Alsace Vendange Tardive 1989 (NA) (11/15/90)

86 HUGEL Tokay Pinot Gris Alsace Vendange Tardive 1983 (NA) (4/30/87) (JS)

80 HUGEL Tokay Pinot Gris Alsace Vendange Tardive 1976 (NA) (4/30/87) (JS)

86 JOSMEYER Tokay Pinot Gris Alsace 1989 (NA) (11/15/90)

86 JOSMEYER Tokay Pinot Gris Alsace Sélection de Grains Nobles Hengst 1989 (NA) (11/15/90)

86 MARC KREYDENWEISS Tokay Pinot Gris Alsace 1988 $23 (10/15/89)

90 MARC KREYDENWEISS Tokay Pinot Gris Alsace Sélection de Grains Nobles Moenchberg 1989 (NA) (11/15/90)

88 MARC KREYDENWEISS Tokay Pinot Gris Alsace Vendange Tardive Grand Cru Moenchberg 1989 (NA) (11/15/90)

86 KUENTZ-BAS Tokay Pinot Gris Alsace Cuvée Tradition 1989 (NA) (11/15/90)

81 KUENTZ-BAS Tokay Pinot Gris Alsace Cuvée Tradition 1988 (NA) (10/15/89)

81 KUENTZ-BAS Tokay Pinot Gris Alsace Réserve Personelle 1989 (NA) (11/15/90)

86 KUENTZ-BAS Tokay Pinot Gris Alsace Réserve Personelle 1988 (NA) (10/15/89)

90 KUENTZ-BAS Tokay Pinot Gris Alsace Sélection de Grains Nobles Cuvée Jeremy 1989 (NA) (11/15/90)

82 GUSTAVE LORENTZ Tokay Pinot Gris Alsace 1989 $15 (11/15/90)

87 GUSTAVE LORENTZ Tokay Pinot Gris Alsace 1988 $14 (10/15/89)

83 GUSTAVE LORENTZ Tokay Pinot Gris Alsace Altenberg de Bergheim 1988 (NA) (10/15/89)

82 GUSTAVE LORENTZ Tokay Pinot Gris Alsace Réserve 1989 (NA) (11/15/90)

86 GUSTAVE LORENTZ Tokay Pinot Gris Alsace Sélection de Grains Nobles 1989 (NA) (11/15/90)

82 MURE Tokay Pinot Gris Alsace Clos St.-Landelin Vorbourg 1989 (NA) (11/15/90)

74 MURE Tokay Pinot Gris Alsace Clos St.-Landelin Vorbourg 1985 $11.50 (5/31/87)

86 MURE Tokay Pinot Gris Alsace Sélection de Grains Nobles Clos St.-Landelin Vorbour 1989 (NA) (11/15/90)

FRANCE
ALSACE/TOKAY PINOT GRIS

90	MURE Tokay Pinot Gris Alsace Vendange Tardive Clos St.-Landelin Vorbourg 1989 (NA) (11/15/90)
84	DOMAINE OSTERTAG Tokay Pinot Gris Alsace Moenchberg 1988 (NA) (10/15/89)
81	DOMAINES SCHLUMBERGER Tokay Pinot Gris Alsace 1988 (NA) (10/15/89)
78	DOMAINES SCHLUMBERGER Tokay Pinot Gris Alsace Vendange Tardive 1989 (NA) (11/15/90)
88	PIERRE SPARR Tokay Pinot Gris Alsace Carte d'Or 1989 (NA) (11/15/90)
89	PIERRE SPARR Tokay Pinot Gris Alsace Prestige Tête de Cuvée 1989 (NA) (11/15/90)
78	PIERRE SPARR Tokay Pinot Gris Alsace Vendange Tardive Cuvée Centenaire 1989 (NA) (11/15/90)
83	TRIMBACH Tokay Pinot Gris Alsace 1988 $9 (10/15/89)
85	TRIMBACH Tokay Pinot Gris Alsace Réserve Tradition 1989 (NA) (11/15/90)
86	TRIMBACH Tokay Pinot Gris Alsace Réserve Tradition 1988 (NA) (10/15/89)
99	TRIMBACH Tokay Pinot Gris Alsace Sélection de Grains Nobles Hors Choix 1989 (NA) (11/15/90)
90	TRIMBACH Tokay Pinot Gris Alsace Sélection de Grains Nobles Réserve 1989 (NA) (11/15/90)
90	DOMAINE WEINBACH Tokay Pinot Gris Alsace Clos des Capucins Cuvée Ste.-Catherine 1989 $43 (11/15/90)
79	DOMAINE WEINBACH Tokay Pinot Gris Alsace Clos des Capucins Cuvée Ste.-Catherine Théo Faller 1988 $35 (7/31/91)
95	DOMAINE WEINBACH Tokay Pinot Gris Alsace Sélection de Grains Nobles Clos des Capucins 1989 (NA) (11/15/90)
86	DOMAINE WEINBACH Tokay Pinot Gris Alsace Vendange Tardive Clos des Capucins 1989 (NA) (11/15/90)
87	ALSACE WILLM Tokay Pinot Gris Alsace 1989 (NA) (11/15/90)
90	ALSACE WILLM Tokay Pinot Gris Alsace Sélection de Grains Nobles 1989 (NA) (11/15/90)
82	DOMAINE ZIND HUMBRECHT Tokay Pinot Gris Alsace 1988 (NA) (10/15/89)
90	DOMAINE ZIND HUMBRECHT Tokay Pinot Gris Alsace Clos Jebsal 1988 (NA) (10/15/89)
86	DOMAINE ZIND HUMBRECHT Tokay Pinot Gris Alsace Clos St.-Urbain Rangen de Thann 1986 $35 (7/15/88)
85	DOMAINE ZIND HUMBRECHT Tokay Pinot Gris Alsace Sélection de Grains Nobles Clos St.-Urbain Rangen 1989 (NA) (11/15/90)
91	DOMAINE ZIND HUMBRECHT Tokay Pinot Gris Alsace Vendange Tardive Clos Windsbuhl 1989 (NA) (11/15/90)
85	DOMAINE ZIND HUMBRECHT Tokay Pinot Gris Alsace Vieille Vigne 1986 $15 (7/15/88)

OTHER ALSACE

87	LEON BEYER Pinot Gris Alsace Sélection de Grains Nobles 1983 $48/375ml (7/31/89)
80	BOTT FRERES Tokay d'Alsace Alsace Cuvée Exceptionnelle 1989 $13.50 (7/31/91)
76	DOPFF & IRION Pinot Gris Alsace Les Maquisards Château de Riquewihr 1985 $12 (2/28/87)
73	HUGEL Sylvaner Alsace 1985 $7.25 (7/15/88)
68	KLUG Muscat Alsace 1983 $4.75 (12/16/85)
49	KLUG Pinot d'Alsace Alsace 1983 $4.50 (12/01/85)
84	DOMAINE OSTERTAG Pinot Gris Alsace Barriques 1989 $24 (7/31/91)
72	DOMAINE OSTERTAG Sylvaner Alsace 1985 $8.75 (7/15/88)
77	DOMAINE OSTERTAG Sylvaner Alsace Vieilles Vignes 1989 $12 (7/31/91)
80	SALZMANN Tokay d'Alsace Alsace Schlossberg 1985 $12.25 (5/31/87)
78	TRIMBACH Pinot Gris Alsace 1986 $12.50 (7/15/88)
88	TRIMBACH Pinot Gris Alsace Réserve 1982 $7 (1/01/85)
81	TRIMBACH Sylvaner Alsace Sélection 1989 (NA) (11/15/90)
78	TRIMBACH Sylvaner Alsace 1985 $8 (7/15/88)
78	DOMAINE WEINBACH Muscat Alsace Clos des Capucins Théo Faller 1988 $23 (7/31/91)
74	DOMAINE ZIND HUMBRECHT Pinot d'Alsace Alsace 1986 $9 (7/15/88)
80	DOMAINE ZIND HUMBRECHT Sylvaner Alsace 1986 $7.50 (7/15/88)

BEAUJOLAIS

55	ALIGNE Moulin-à-Vent 1985 $12 (3/15/87)
82	PHILIPPE ANTOINE Brouilly 1988 $11.50 (5/31/89) (TM)
77	PHILIPPE ANTOINE Beaujolais-Villages 1988 $5.50 (5/31/89) (TM)
75	PHILIPPE ANTOINE Beaujolais-Villages 1986 $6.50 (3/15/88)
84	PHILIPPE ANTOINE Fleurie 1988 $11.50 (5/31/89) (TM)
85	PHILIPPE ANTOINE Juliénas 1988 $11.50 (5/31/89) (TM)
88	PHILIPPE ANTOINE Moulin-à-Vent 1988 $11.50 (5/31/89) (TM)
81	PHILIPPE ANTOINE Régnié 1988 $11.50 (5/31/89) (TM)
82	BARTON & GUESTIER Brouilly 1988 $11 (5/31/89) (TM)
77	BARTON & GUESTIER Beaujolais-Villages 1988 $9 (5/31/89) (TM)
75	BARTON & GUESTIER Beaujolais-Villages St.-Louis 1988 $7.50 (5/31/89) (TM)
84	BARTON & GUESTIER Moulin-à-Vent 1988 $13 (5/31/89) (TM)
81	BICHOT Brouilly 1984 $7 (2/01/86)
77	JEAN CLAUDE BOISSET Beaujolais 1988 $6.75 (11/15/90)
76	JEAN CLAUDE BOISSET Beaujolais-Villages 1988 $7.50 (11/15/90)
75	LOUIS CHAMPAGNON Chénas 1984 $7 (5/01/86)
68	LOUIS CHAMPAGNON Moulin-à-Vent 1984 $7.25 (5/01/86)
86	GEORGES DUBOEUF Beaujolais 1989 $7 (11/15/90) BB
87	GEORGES DUBOEUF Beaujolais-Villages 1989 $8 (11/15/90) BB
83	GEORGES DUBOEUF Beaujolais-Villages 1988 $8 (5/31/89) (TM)
83	GEORGES DUBOEUF Brouilly 1988 $11 (5/31/89) (TM)
90	GEORGES DUBOEUF Brouilly 1986 $9 (7/31/87)
82	GEORGES DUBOEUF Brouilly 1985 $12 (12/15/86)
89	GEORGES DUBOEUF Brouilly Château de Nervers 1988 $11 (5/31/89) (TM)
85	GEORGES DUBOEUF Chénas 1988 $10 (5/31/89) (TM)

85	GEORGES DUBOEUF Chénas 1986 $8.50 (7/31/87)
81	GEORGES DUBOEUF Chénas 1985 $9 (12/15/86)
84	GEORGES DUBOEUF Chiroubles 1988 $11 (5/31/89) (TM)
87	GEORGES DUBOEUF Chiroubles 1986 $9.50 (7/31/87)
78	GEORGES DUBOEUF Chiroubles 1985 $9 (12/15/86)
90	GEORGES DUBOEUF Côte-de-Brouilly 1986 $9 (7/31/87)
89	GEORGES DUBOEUF Fleurie 1988 $14.50 (5/31/89) (TM)
87	GEORGES DUBOEUF Fleurie 1986 $10 (7/31/87)
69	GEORGES DUBOEUF Fleurie 1985 $10 (12/15/86)
84	GEORGES DUBOEUF Juliénas 1986 $9 (7/31/87)
87	GEORGES DUBOEUF Morgon 1988 $10.75 (5/31/89) (TM)
88	GEORGES DUBOEUF Morgon 1986 $9 (7/31/87)
87	GEORGES DUBOEUF Morgon 1985 $10 (12/15/86)
90	GEORGES DUBOEUF Morgon Jean Descombes 1988 $11.25 (5/31/89) (TM)
87	GEORGES DUBOEUF Moulin-à-Vent 1988 $12.25 (5/31/89) (TM)
92	GEORGES DUBOEUF Moulin-à-Vent 1986 $10 (7/31/87) SS
87	GEORGES DUBOEUF Moulin-à-Vent 1985 $10 (12/15/86)
93	GEORGES DUBOEUF Moulin-à-Vent New Barrel Aged 1988 $12.25 (5/31/89) (TM)
83	GEORGES DUBOEUF Régnié 1988 $8 (5/31/89) (TM)
87	GEORGES DUBOEUF St.-Amour 1986 $9.50 (7/31/87)
83	GEORGES DUBOEUF St.-Amour 1985 $8 (12/15/86)
81	PIERRE FERRAUD & FILS Beaujolais-Villages Cuvée Ensorceleuse 1988 $10 (5/31/89) (TM)
84	PIERRE FERRAUD & FILS Brouilly Domaine Rolland 1988 $16 (5/31/89) (TM)
89	PIERRE FERRAUD & FILS Chénas Cuvée Jean-Michel 1988 $10 (5/31/89) (TM)
79	PIERRE FERRAUD & FILS Chiroubles Domaine de la Chapelle du Bois 1988 $12 (5/31/89) (TM)
83	PIERRE FERRAUD & FILS Côte-de-Brouilly 1988 $16 (5/31/89) (TM)
87	PIERRE FERRAUD & FILS Fleurie 1988 $15 (5/31/89) (TM)
86	PIERRE FERRAUD & FILS Fleurie Château de Grand Pre 1988 $16 (5/31/89) (TM)
73	PIERRE FERRAUD & FILS Juliénas 1988 $12 (5/31/89) (TM)
89	PIERRE FERRAUD & FILS Morgon Domaine de l'Eveque 1988 $16 (5/31/89) (TM)
83	PIERRE FERRAUD & FILS Moulin-à-Vent 1988 $16 (5/31/89) (TM)
81	PIERRE FERRAUD & FILS Régnié 1988 $10 (5/31/89) (TM)
85	PIERRE FERRAUD & FILS St.-Amour 1988 $12 (5/31/89) (TM)
87	SYLVAIN FESSY Brouilly Domaine de Chavannes 1985 $8 (12/15/86)
72	SYLVAIN FESSY Côte-de-Brouilly Domaine de Chavannes 1985 $8 (12/15/86)
71	SYLVAIN FESSY Juliénas Cuvée Michel Tête 1986 $7 (12/31/87)
86	SYLVAIN FESSY Juliénas Cuvée Michel Tête 1985 $8.50 (12/15/86)
74	SYLVAIN FESSY Morgon Cuvée André Gauthier 1986 $7 (12/31/87)
76	SYLVAIN FESSY Morgon Cuvée André Gauthier 1985 $8.50 (12/15/86)
87	DOMAINE JEAN GAUDET Morgon 1988 $10 (5/31/89) (TM)
86	GERARD GELIN Beaujolais-Villages Domaine des Nugues 1989 $8 (11/15/90) BB
84	DOMAINE DE L'INSTITUT PASTEUR Côte-de-Brouilly 1988 $10 (5/31/89) (TM)
79	LOUIS JADOT Beaujolais Jadot 1989 $6 (11/15/90)
81	LOUIS JADOT Brouilly 1987 $8.50 (7/15/88)
79	LOUIS JADOT Fleurie 1987 $11 (7/15/88)
68	LOUIS JADOT Fleurie 1983 $9 (11/01/85)
80	LOUIS JADOT Juliénas 1987 $8.50 (7/15/88)
83	LOUIS JADOT Moulin-à-Vent 1987 $10.50 (7/15/88)
79	JAFFELIN Beaujolais-Villages Domaine de Riberolles 1987 $7 (4/15/89)
85	JAFFELIN Fleurie 1985 $9.75 (12/15/86)
89	JAFFELIN Moulin-à-Vent 1985 $9.75 (12/15/86)
85	PAUL JANIN Moulin-à-Vent 1985 $12.75 (10/31/87)
83	PAUL JANIN Moulin-à-Vent 1983 $9 (11/01/85)
81	MOILLARD Fleurie Grumage 1985 $8 (12/15/86)
78	MOMMESSIN Beaujolais-Villages Château de Montmelas 1988 $9.50 (5/31/89) (TM)
81	MOMMESSIN Brouilly Château de Briante 1988 $11.50 (5/31/89) (TM)
83	MOMMESSIN Chiroubles Château de Raosset 1988 $11.25 (5/31/89) (TM)
87	MOMMESSIN Fleurie 1988 $13.50 (5/31/89) (TM)
81	MOMMESSIN Juliénas Domaine de la Conseillere 1988 $10.50 (5/31/89) (TM)
86	MOMMESSIN Morgon 1988 $10 (5/31/89) (TM)
88	MOMMESSIN Morgon Domaine de Lathevalle 1988 $10 (5/31/89) (TM)
91	MOMMESSIN Moulin-à-Vent Domaine de Champ de Cour 1988 $12.50 (5/31/89) (TM)
85	MOMMESSIN Régnié 1988 $10.50 (5/31/89) (TM)
84	MOMMESSIN St.-Amour Domaine de Monreve 1988 $12 (5/31/89) (TM)
74	CHARLES MONCAUT Fleurie 1984 $6.75 (12/01/85)
76	DOMAINE DU MONT VERRIER Beaujolais-Villages 1988 $10 (5/31/89) (TM)
82	NICOLAS Beaujolais-Villages 1989 $8 (11/15/90) BB
83	PELLERIN Brouilly 1987 $8.50 (4/15/89)
88	DOMAINE DE PETIT-CHENE Moulin-à-Vent 1988 $10 (5/31/89) (TM)
78	CHATEAU DES RAVATYS Brouilly 1988 $10 (5/31/89) (TM)
85	DOMAINE DE ROBERT Fleurie 1983 $8 (12/16/85)
91	DOMAINE DE LA ROCHELLE Moulin-à-Vent 1988 $10 (5/31/89) (TM)
75	ANTONIN RODET Beaujolais-Villages Rodet 1988 $8 (11/15/90)
81	ROMANECHE-THORINS Moulin-à-Vent Château des Jacques 1985 $10 (3/15/88)
82	DOMAINE ST.-CHARLES Beaujolais-Villages Château du Bluizard 1988 $8 (11/15/90) BB
79	THORIN Beaujolais-Villages 1988 $7 (5/31/89) (TM)
88	THORIN Moulin-à-Vent Château des Jacques 1988 $16 (5/31/89) (TM)
78	TRENEL & FILS Beaujolais-Villages 1988 $9 (5/31/89) (TM)
86	TRENEL & FILS Chénas 1988 $14 (5/31/89) (TM)
83	TRENEL & FILS Chiroubles 1988 $12 (5/31/89) (TM)
86	TRENEL & FILS Fleurie 1988 $14 (5/31/89) (TM)
92	TRENEL & FILS Morgon Côte de Py 1988 $17 (5/31/89) (TM)
90	TRENEL & FILS Moulin-à-Vent La Rochelle 1988 $17 (5/31/89) (TM)
83	TRENEL & FILS Régnié 1988 $12 (5/31/89) (TM)
87	TRENEL & FILS St.-Amour 1988 $15 (5/31/89) (TM)
76	ROGER VERGE Fleurie 1986 $9.25 (12/31/87)
83	ROGER VERGE Juliénas 1986 $9.25 (12/31/87)
79	ROGER VERGE Moulin-à-Vent 1986 $12 (12/31/87)

BORDEAUX RED/BORDEAUX

70	CHATEAU LES ALOUETTES Bordeaux Kosher 1986 $10 (3/31/90)
73	BARTON & GUESTIER Bordeaux Cabernet Sauvignon 1988 $6 (2/15/90)
84	BARTON & GUESTIER Bordeaux Merlot 1988 $6 (2/15/90) BB
81	BEAU MAYNE Bordeaux 1983 $5 (3/31/87) BB
53	CHATEAU BOIS-VERT Bordeaux 1983 $3.75 (11/16/85)
80+	CHATEAU BONNET Bordeaux 1989 (NR) (4/30/91) (BT)

77   CHATEAU BONNET Bordeaux 1988 $7.50 (4/30/91)
78   CHATEAU BONNET Bordeaux Reserve 1988 $11 (7/15/91)
79   CHATEAU BONNET Bordeaux 1987 $7 (4/15/90)
73   CHATEAU BONNET Bordeaux 1986 $6 (5/15/89)
72   CHATEAU BONNET Bordeaux 1983 $4.75 (5/01/86)
73   CHATEAU BONNET Bordeaux 1982 $4.50 (4/16/85)
80   LE BORDEAUX PRESTIGE Bordeaux 1985 $9.50 (9/30/88)
75   CHATEAU BRIOT Bordeaux 1985 $4 (5/15/87)
82   LA CAVE TROISGROS Bordeaux Rouge 1989 $9.50 (5/15/91)
78   CHATEAU DU CHALET Bordeaux 1987 $6 (4/15/90)
74   CHARTRON LA FLEUR Bordeaux 1986 $4.50 (5/15/89)
78   DOMAINE DE CHEVAL BLANC Bordeaux 1985 $5 (5/15/88)
80   CHEVALIER DUCLA Bordeaux 1986 $5.50 (5/15/89) BB
77   CHEVALIER VEDRINES Bordeaux 1986 $6 (6/30/88)
74   LA COMBE DES DAMES Bordeaux 1985 $6.50 (3/15/88)
75   CHATEAU LES CONFRERIES Bordeaux 1985 $3.50 (2/15/88)
77   LA COUR PAVILLON Bordeaux 1986 $7.25 (2/28/91)
67   LA COUR PAVILLON Bordeaux 1985 $6.75 (7/15/88)
68   LA COUR PAVILLON Bordeaux 1983 $7 (8/31/87)
79   CHATEAU DAVRIL Bordeaux 1987 $5 (9/30/89)
79   LES DOUELLES Bordeaux 1982 $3 (10/01/85) BB
77   CHATEAU L'ESPERANCE Bordeaux 1986 $7 (9/30/89)
79   CHATEAU FAURIE-PASCAUD Bordeaux 1986 $5 (6/30/88)
84   CHATEAU GOFFRETEAU Bordeaux Rouge 1989 $8 (5/15/91) BB
79   CHATEAU LAGRAVE PARAN Bordeaux 1989 $8 (2/28/91)
82   CHATEAU LAGRAVE PARAN Bordeaux 1988 $6 (7/15/90) BB
80   CHATEAU LAGRAVE PARAN Bordeaux 1987 $7 (5/15/90) BB
75+ CHATEAU LAMARTINE Bordeaux 1989 (NR) (4/30/91) (BT)
79   CHATEAU LAURETAN Bordeaux 1986 $5 (5/15/89)
75   MICHEL LYNCH Bordeaux 1983 $6.75 (10/15/87)
84   MAITRE D'ESTOURNEL Bordeaux 1985 $7.25 (5/31/88)
70   CHATEAU MAROTTE Bordeaux 1986 $3.50 (4/30/88)
78   MARQUIS DES TOURS Bordeaux 1988 $5 (2/28/91)
72   YVON MAU Bordeaux Officiel du Bicentenaire de la Revolution Française 1986 $4.50 (6/30/89)
68   YVON MAU Bordeaux Officiel du Bicentenaire de la Revolution Française 1986 $4.50 (5/15/89)
73   CHATEAU DU MOULIN DE PEYRONIN Bordeaux 1986 $10 (3/31/90)
81   MOUTON-CADET Bordeaux 1988 $9 (4/30/91) BB
79   MOUTON-CADET Bordeaux 1987 $7.50 (4/15/90)
81   MOUTON-CADET Bordeaux 1986 $7.25 (2/15/89) BB
80   MOUTON-CADET Bordeaux 1985 $6.50 (5/15/88)
77   PONTALLIER JOHNSON Bordeaux Merlot 1982 $8 (10/15/87)
72   CHATEAU RAUZAN DESPAGNE Bordeaux 1985 $5.75 (2/15/88)
79   ARMAND ROUX Bordeaux Verdillac 1988 $6.25 (7/15/90) BB
77   DOMAINE SAINTE-ANNE Bordeaux 1987 $5 (5/15/90)
75   ST.-JOVIAN Bordeaux 1985 $4.50 (5/15/88)
78   ST.-JOVIAN Bordeaux Cabernet Sauvignon 1986 $4.50 (7/31/88)
76   ST.-JOVIAN Bordeaux Merlot 1986 $5 (5/15/89)
73   CHATEAU ST.-SULPICE Bordeaux 1982 $6 (5/15/87)
74   CHATEAU TALMONT Bordeaux 1989 $8 (2/28/91)

BORDEAUX SUPÉRIEUR

79   BEAUCLAIRE Bordeaux Supérieur 1988 $6 (12/31/90)
70   CHATEAU BELLERIVE Bordeaux Supérieur 1985 $7 (11/15/87)
72   CHATEAU BELLERIVE Bordeaux Supérieur 1982 $8 (12/16/85)
80   CHATEAU BRASSAC Bordeaux Supérieur 1986 $5.50 (8/31/88) BB
78   CHATEAU CANDELAY Bordeaux Supérieur 1986 $5 (6/15/89)
71   CHATEAU LES CHARMILLES Bordeaux Supérieur 1985 $8 (2/15/88)
76   CHATEAU LA CROIX DE GIRON Bordeaux Supérieur 1986 $5.25 (5/15/89)
81   CHATEAU LA CROIX ST.-JEAN Bordeaux Supérieur 1986 $6 (11/30/88) BB
81   CHATEAU GOFFRETEAU Bordeaux Supérieur 1988 $6 (2/28/91) BB
82   CHATEAU GOFFRETEAU Bordeaux Supérieur 1986 $6 (6/15/89) BB
77   CHATEAU LES GRANDS JAYS Bordeaux Supérieur 1986 $6 (5/15/89)
82   CHATEAU DE LA GRAVE Bordeaux Supérieur 1988 $8 (7/15/90) BB
76   CHATEAU HAUT MALLET Bordeaux Supérieur 1987 $7.50 (4/15/90)
71   CHATEAU HAUT-COLAS NOUET Bordeaux Supérieur 1985 $4 (11/15/87)
70   CHATEAU JALOUSIE-BEAULIEU Bordeaux Supérieur 1985 $7 (12/31/88)
65   CHATEAU JONQUEYRES Bordeaux Supérieur Cuvée Vieilles Vignes 1988 $12 (3/31/91)
82   CHATEAU LAGARENNE Bordeaux Supérieur 1988 $8 (7/31/90) BB
76   CHATEAU LAMARTINE Bordeaux Supérieur 1984 $9 (5/15/87)
81   CHATEAU LANDEREAU Bordeaux Supérieur 1985 $6.75 (2/15/88) BB
81   CHATEAU LESCALLE Bordeaux Supérieur 1986 $8 (6/30/89)
71   CHATEAU DE LUCAT Bordeaux Supérieur 1982 $4 (10/01/85)
74   G. MICHELOT Bordeaux Supérieur 1982 $5 (1/01/86) BB
81   CHATEAU DE PARENCHERE Bordeaux Supérieur 1986 $9 (6/30/89)
75   PIERRE JEAN Bordeaux Supérieur 1988 $8 (7/31/91)
83   CHATEAU REYNIER Bordeaux Supérieur 1983 $3.50 (10/16/85) BB
82   CHATEAU ROC MIGNON D'ADRIEN Bordeaux Supérieur 1989 $6 (2/28/91) BB
80   ST.-JOVIAN Bordeaux Supérieur Premium 1988 $5.50 (7/31/91) BB
78   CHATEAU DE SOURS Bordeaux Supérieur 1986 $7 (9/30/89)
79   CHATEAU LA TERRASSE Bordeaux Supérieur 1989 $8 (3/31/91)
76   CHATEAU LA TERRASSE Bordeaux Supérieur 1988 $8 (6/30/89)
78   CHATEAU LA TERRASSE Bordeaux Supérieur 1985 $6 (11/15/87)
74   CHATEAU LA TERRASSE Bordeaux Supérieur 1982 $4.50 (11/16/85)
77   CHATEAU TOUR DE BELLEGARDE Bordeaux Supérieur 1986 $4.75 (5/15/89)
84   CHATEAU VIEUX GABRIAN Bordeaux Supérieur 1988 $11 (4/30/91)

CÔTES DE FRANCS

80+ CHATEAU LA CLAVERIE Côtes de Francs 1988 $18 (8/31/90) (BT)
70+ CHATEAU LA CLAVERIE Côtes de Francs 1988 $18 (6/30/89) (BT)
75+ CHATEAU FRANCS Côtes de Francs 1989 (NR) (4/30/90) (BT)
80+ CHATEAU FRANCS Côtes de Francs 1988 (NR) (8/31/90) (BT)
70+ CHATEAU FRANCS Côtes de Francs 1988 (NR) (6/30/89) (BT)
73   LAURIOL Côtes de Francs 1986 $8 (6/15/89)
78   LAURIOL Côtes de Francs 1985 $6.50 (6/30/88)
70+ CHATEAU LA PRADE Côtes de Francs 1988 (NR) (6/30/89) (BT)
80+ CHATEAU PUYGUERAUD Côtes de Francs 1989 (NR) (4/30/90) (BT)
80+ CHATEAU PUYGUERAUD Côtes de Francs 1988 $15 (8/31/90) (BT)
80+ CHATEAU PUYGUERAUD Côtes de Francs 1988 $15 (6/30/89) (BT)

84   CHATEAU PUYGUERAUD Côtes de Francs 1986 Rel: $12 Cur: $12 (6/15/89)
83   CHATEAU PUYGUERAUD Côtes de Francs 1985 Rel: $9 Cur: $9 (6/30/88)
82   CHATEAU PUYGUERAUD Côtes de Francs 1983 Rel: $7.50 Cur: $8 (10/16/85)

FRONSAC/CANON-FRONSAC

80+ CHATEAU CANON (FRONSAC) Canon-Fronsac 1990 (NR) (4/30/91) (BT)
80+ CHATEAU CANON (FRONSAC) Canon-Fronsac 1989 (NR) (4/30/91) (BT)
80+ CHATEAU CANON (FRONSAC) Canon-Fronsac 1989 (NR) (4/30/90) (BT)
75+ CHATEAU CANON DE BREM Canon-Fronsac 1990 (NR) (4/30/91) (BT)
80+ CHATEAU CANON DE BREM Canon-Fronsac 1989 (NR) (4/30/91) (BT)
80+ CHATEAU CANON DE BREM Canon-Fronsac 1989 (NR) (4/30/90) (BT)
80+ CHATEAU CANON DE BREM Canon-Fronsac 1988 $13 (6/30/89) (BT)
80+ CHATEAU CANON DE BREM Canon-Fronsac 1987 $14 (6/30/89) (BT)
70+ CHATEAU CANON DE BREM Canon-Fronsac 1986 $15 (5/15/87) (BT)
80+ CHATEAU CANON DE BREM Canon-Fronsac 1985 Cur: $18 (5/15/87) (BT)
70+ CHATEAU CANON DE BREM Canon-Fronsac 1985 Cur: $18 (4/16/86) (BT)
80+ CHATEAU CANON MOUEIX Canon-Fronsac 1990 (NR) (4/30/91) (BT)
70+ CHATEAU CANON MOUEIX Canon-Fronsac 1989 (NR) (4/30/91) (BT)
80+ CHATEAU CANON MOUEIX Canon-Fronsac 1989 (NR) (4/30/90) (BT)
85+ CHATEAU CANON MOUEIX Canon-Fronsac 1988 $16 (8/31/90) (BT)
75+ CHATEAU CANON MOUEIX Canon-Fronsac 1987 $14 (6/30/89) (BT)
75+ CHATEAU CANON MOUEIX Canon-Fronsac 1987 $14 (6/30/88) (BT)
80+ CHATEAU CANON MOUEIX Canon-Fronsac 1986 $15 (5/15/89) (BT)
80+ CHATEAU CANON MOUEIX Canon-Fronsac 1986 Rel: $15 Cur: $20 (5/15/87) (BT)
80+ CHATEAU CANON MOUEIX Canon-Fronsac 1985 Rel: $15 Cur: $20 (5/15/87) (BT)
80+ CHATEAU DE CARLES Fronsac 1989 (NR) (4/30/91) (BT)
80+ CHATEAU DE LA DAUPHINE Fronsac 1990 (NR) (4/30/91) (BT)
80+ CHATEAU DE LA DAUPHINE Fronsac 1989 (NR) (4/30/91) (BT)
80+ CHATEAU DE LA DAUPHINE Fronsac 1989 (NR) (4/30/90) (BT)
80+ CHATEAU DE LA DAUPHINE Fronsac 1988 (NR) (8/31/90) (BT)
75+ CHATEAU DE LA DAUPHINE Fronsac 1988 (NR) (6/30/89) (BT)
75+ CHATEAU DE LA DAUPHINE Fronsac 1987 $17 (6/30/89) (BT)
75+ CHATEAU DE LA DAUPHINE Fronsac 1987 $17 (6/30/88) (BT)
75+ CHATEAU DE LA DAUPHINE Fronsac 1986 $20 (6/30/88) (BT)
70+ CHATEAU DE LA DAUPHINE Fronsac 1986 $20 (5/15/87) (BT)
84   CHATEAU DE LA DAUPHINE Fronsac 1985 $20 (9/30/88)
80+ CHATEAU DE LA DAUPHINE Fronsac 1985 $20 (5/15/87) (BT)
60+ CHATEAU DE LA DAUPHINE Fronsac 1985 $20 (4/16/86) (BT)
85+ CHATEAU FONTENIL Fronsac 1989 (NR) (4/30/91) (BT)
76   CHATEAU FONTENIL Fronsac 1986 $14 (2/15/90)
70+ CHATEAU FONTENIL Fronsac 1986 $14 (5/15/87) (BT)
87   CHATEAU FONTENIL Fronsac 1985 $14 (9/30/88)
80+ CHATEAU MAZERIS Canon-Fronsac 1990 (NR) (4/30/91) (BT)
85+ CHATEAU MAZERIS Canon-Fronsac 1989 (NR) (4/30/91) (BT)
85+ CHATEAU MAZERIS Canon-Fronsac 1989 (NR) (4/30/90) (BT)
75+ CHATEAU MAZERIS Canon-Fronsac 1988 $18 (6/30/89) (BT)
75+ CHATEAU MAZERIS Canon-Fronsac 1987 $12.50 (6/30/89) (BT)
70+ CHATEAU MAZERIS Canon-Fronsac 1987 $12.50 (6/30/88) (BT)
80+ CHATEAU MAZERIS Canon-Fronsac 1986 $12.50 (6/30/88) (BT)
70+ CHATEAU MAZERIS Canon-Fronsac 1986 $12.50 (5/15/87) (BT)
80+ CHATEAU MAZERIS Canon-Fronsac 1985 $12.50 (5/15/87) (BT)
83   A. MOUEIX Fronsac 1985 $9.50 (9/30/88)
78   CHATEAU MOULIN HAUT-LAROQUE Fronsac 1986 $11 (11/15/89)
81   CHATEAU LA VALADE Fronsac 1986 $5.25 (5/15/89) BB
75+ CHATEAU LA VIEILLE CURE Fronsac 1989 (NR) (4/30/91) (BT)
82   CHATEAU LA VIEILLE CURE Fronsac 1987 $14 (5/15/90)
81   CHATEAU LA VIEILLE CURE Fronsac 1986 $15 (5/15/91)
88   CHATEAU LA VIEILLE CURE Fronsac 1985 $15 (12/31/88)

GRAVES/PESSAC-LÉOGNAN

90+ CHATEAU BAHANS-HAUT-BRION Pessac-Léognan 1989 (NR) (4/30/91) (BT)
80+ CHATEAU BAHANS-HAUT-BRION Pessac-Léognan 1988 $20 (8/31/90) (BT)
80+ CHATEAU BAHANS-HAUT-BRION Pessac-Léognan 1988 $20 (6/30/89) (BT)
75+ CHATEAU BAHANS-HAUT-BRION Pessac-Léognan 1987 $19 (6/30/89) (BT)
86   CHATEAU BAHANS-HAUT-BRION Pessac-Léognan 1986 $22 (9/15/89)
80+ CHATEAU BAHANS-HAUT-BRION Pessac-Léognan 1986 $22 (6/30/88) (BT)
80+ CHATEAU BAHANS-HAUT-BRION Pessac-Léognan 1986 $22 (5/15/87) (BT)
80+ CHATEAU BAHANS-HAUT-BRION Graves 1985 $20 (5/15/87) (BT)
90+ CHATEAU BARET Pessac-Léognan 1989 (NR) (4/30/91) (BT)
85+ CHATEAU BARET Pessac-Léognan 1989 (NR) (4/30/90) (BT)
70+ CHATEAU BARET Pessac-Léognan 1988 $15 (6/30/89) (BT)
75+ CHATEAU BARET Pessac-Léognan 1987 $14 (6/30/89) (BT)
70+ CHATEAU BARET Pessac-Léognan 1986 $16 (5/15/87) (BT)
87   CHATEAU LE BONNAT Graves 1988 $18 (12/31/90)
83   CHATEAU LE BONNAT Graves 1987 $12 (4/15/90)
84   CHATEAU BONNET Graves 1985 $5.50 (4/15/88) BB
90+ CHATEAU BOUSCAUT Pessac-Léognan 1990 (NR) (4/30/91) (BT)
90+ CHATEAU BOUSCAUT Pessac-Léognan 1989 (NR) (4/30/91) (BT)
87   CHATEAU BOUSCAUT Pessac-Léognan 1988 $20 (4/30/91)
75+ CHATEAU BOUSCAUT Pessac-Léognan 1988 $20 (6/30/89) (BT)
80+ CHATEAU BOUSCAUT Pessac-Léognan 1987 Rel: $10 Cur: $10 (6/30/89) (BT)
80+ CHATEAU BOUSCAUT Pessac-Léognan 1987 Rel: $10 Cur: $10 (6/30/88) (BT)
78   CHATEAU BOUSCAUT Pessac-Léognan 1986 Rel: $9 Cur: $12 (2/15/89)
90   CHATEAU BOUSCAUT Graves 1985 Rel: $15 Cur: $15 (12/31/88)
80+ CHATEAU BOUSCAUT Graves 1985 Rel: $15 Cur: $15 (5/15/87) (BT)
86   CHATEAU BOUSCAUT Graves 1981 Rel: $12.50 Cur: $13 (5/01/84)
80+ CHATEAU BROWN Pessac-Léognan 1988 $17 (6/30/89) (BT)
75+ CHATEAU BROWN Pessac-Léognan 1987 $15 (6/30/89) (BT)
80+ CHATEAU BROWN Pessac-Léognan 1986 $19 (5/15/87) (BT)
90+ CHATEAU CARBONNIEUX Pessac-Léognan 1990 (NR) (4/30/91) (BT)
80+ CHATEAU CARBONNIEUX Pessac-Léognan 1989 $22 (4/30/91) (BT)
85+ CHATEAU CARBONNIEUX Pessac-Léognan 1989 $22 (4/30/90) (BT)
86   CHATEAU CARBONNIEUX Pessac-Léognan 1988 $20 (2/28/91)
80+ CHATEAU CARBONNIEUX Pessac-Léognan 1988 $20 (8/31/90) (BT)
80+ CHATEAU CARBONNIEUX Pessac-Léognan 1988 $20 (6/30/89) (BT)
80   CHATEAU CARBONNIEUX Pessac-Léognan 1987 $15 (5/15/90)
80+ CHATEAU CARBONNIEUX Pessac-Léognan 1987 $15 (6/30/89) (BT)
80+ CHATEAU CARBONNIEUX Pessac-Léognan 1987 $15 (6/30/88) (BT)
87   CHATEAU CARBONNIEUX Pessac-Léognan 1986 $18 (9/15/89)
85+ CHATEAU CARBONNIEUX Pessac-Léognan 1986 $18 (6/30/88) (BT)

FRANCE

BORDEAUX RED/*GRAVES/PESSAC-LÉOGNAN*

87 CHATEAU CARBONNIEUX Graves 1985 $16 (11/30/88)
75+ CHATEAU CARMES-HAUT-BRION Pessac-Léognan 1988 $22 (6/30/89) (BT)
75+ CHATEAU CARMES-HAUT-BRION Pessac-Léognan 1987 $20 (6/30/89) (BT)
75+ CHATEAU CARMES-HAUT-BRION Pessac-Léognan 1987 $20 (6/30/88) (BT)
80+ CHATEAU CARMES-HAUT-BRION Pessac-Léognan 1986 $26 (6/30/88) (BT)
65+ CHATEAU CHENE VERT Pessac-Léognan 1987 (NR) (6/30/89) (BT)
90+ DOMAINE DE CHEVALIER Pessac-Léognan 1990 (NR) (4/30/91) (BT)
90+ DOMAINE DE CHEVALIER Pessac-Léognan 1989 (NR) (4/30/91) (BT)
90+ DOMAINE DE CHEVALIER Pessac-Léognan 1989 (NR) (4/30/90) (BT)
91 DOMAINE DE CHEVALIER Pessac-Léognan 1988 $37 (7/15/91)
90+ DOMAINE DE CHEVALIER Pessac-Léognan 1988 $37 (6/30/89) (BT)
80+ DOMAINE DE CHEVALIER Pessac-Léognan 1987 Rel: $29 Cur: $29 (6/30/89) (BT)
80+ DOMAINE DE CHEVALIER Pessac-Léognan 1987 Rel: $29 Cur: $29 (6/30/88) (BT)
89 DOMAINE DE CHEVALIER Pessac-Léognan 1986 Rel: $33 Cur: $38 (6/15/89)
90+ DOMAINE DE CHEVALIER Pessac-Léognan 1986 Rel: $33 Cur: $38 (6/30/88) (BT)
90+ DOMAINE DE CHEVALIER Pessac-Léognan 1986 Rel: $33 Cur: $38 (5/15/87) (BT)
92 DOMAINE DE CHEVALIER Graves 1985 Rel: $43 Cur: $56 (9/30/88) CS
90+ DOMAINE DE CHEVALIER Graves 1985 Rel: $43 Cur: $56 (5/15/87) (BT)
90 DOMAINE DE CHEVALIER Graves 1984 Rel: $20 Cur: $34 (8/31/87)
87 DOMAINE DE CHEVALIER Graves 1979 Cur: $40 (10/15/89) (JS)
76 DOMAINE DE CHEVALIER Graves 1961 Cur: $150 (3/16/86) (JL)
97 DOMAINE DE CHEVALIER Graves 1959 Cur: $100 (10/15/90) (JS)
59 DOMAINE DE CHEVALIER Graves 1945 Cur: $180 (3/16/86) (JL)
85+ CHATEAU DE CRUZEAU Pessac-Léognan 1989 (NR) (4/30/91) (BT)
87 CHATEAU DE CRUZEAU Pessac-Léognan 1988 $14 (2/28/91)
75+ CHATEAU DE CRUZEAU Pessac-Léognan 1987 $12 (6/30/89) (BT)
87 CHATEAU DE CRUZEAU Pessac-Léognan 1986 $10 (6/30/89)
85 CHATEAU DE CRUZEAU Graves 1985 $9 (6/15/88) BB
84 CHATEAU DE CRUZEAU Graves 1982 $7 (12/16/85)
75 CHATEAU FERRANDE Graves 1981 $7.50 (3/16/85)
95+ CHATEAU DE FIEUZAL Pessac-Léognan 1990 (NR) (4/30/91) (BT)
95+ CHATEAU DE FIEUZAL Pessac-Léognan 1989 (NR) (4/30/90) (BT)
91 CHATEAU DE FIEUZAL Pessac-Léognan 1988 $32 (4/30/91)
95+ CHATEAU DE FIEUZAL Pessac-Léognan 1988 $32 (8/31/90) (BT)
90+ CHATEAU DE FIEUZAL Pessac-Léognan 1988 $32 (6/30/89) (BT)
81 CHATEAU DE FIEUZAL Pessac-Léognan 1987 Rel: $18 Cur: $18 (5/15/90)
85+ CHATEAU DE FIEUZAL Pessac-Léognan 1987 Rel: $18 Cur: $18 (6/30/89) (BT)
80+ CHATEAU DE FIEUZAL Pessac-Léognan 1987 Rel: $18 Cur: $18 (6/30/88) (BT)
90 CHATEAU DE FIEUZAL Pessac-Léognan 1986 Rel: $21 Cur: $23 (6/30/89)
90+ CHATEAU DE FIEUZAL Pessac-Léognan 1986 Rel: $21 Cur: $23 (6/30/88) (BT)
70+ CHATEAU DE FIEUZAL Pessac-Léognan 1986 Rel: $21 Cur: $23 (5/15/87) (BT)
90 CHATEAU DE FIEUZAL Graves 1985 Rel: $24 Cur: $24 (6/15/88)
80+ CHATEAU DE FIEUZAL Graves 1985 Rel: $24 Cur: $24 (5/15/87) (BT)
81 CHATEAU DE FIEUZAL Graves 1982 Rel: $12 Cur: $22 (5/01/85)
81 CHATEAU DE FIEUZAL Graves 1982 Rel: $12 Cur: $22 (2/01/85)
83 CHATEAU DE FIEUZAL Graves 1979 Cur: $25 (10/15/89) (JS)
85+ CHATEAU DE FRANCE Pessac-Léognan 1989 (NR) (4/30/91) (BT)
92 CHATEAU DE FRANCE Pessac-Léognan 1988 $18 (2/28/91) SS
80+ CHATEAU DE FRANCE Pessac-Léognan 1988 $18 (6/30/89) (BT)
80+ CHATEAU DE FRANCE Pessac-Léognan 1987 $15 (6/30/89) (BT)
70+ CHATEAU DE FRANCE Pessac-Léognan 1987 $15 (6/30/88) (BT)
80+ CHATEAU DE FRANCE Pessac-Léognan 1986 $15 (6/30/88) (BT)
90+ CHATEAU DE FRANCE Pessac-Léognan 1986 $15 (5/15/87) (BT)
75+ CHATEAU LA GARDE Pessac-Léognan 1988 $15 (6/30/89) (BT)
70+ CHATEAU LA GARDE Pessac-Léognan 1987 $13 (6/30/89) (BT)
70+ CHATEAU LA GARDE Pessac-Léognan 1986 $14 (5/15/87) (BT)
80 DOMAINE DE GRAND MAISON Pessac-Léognan 1986 $8.50 (4/15/90)
85+ CHATEAU HAUT-BAILLY Pessac-Léognan 1990 (NR) (4/30/91) (BT)
80+ CHATEAU HAUT-BAILLY Pessac-Léognan 1989 (NR) (4/30/90) (BT)
94 CHATEAU HAUT-BAILLY Pessac-Léognan 1988 $30 (4/30/91)
90+ CHATEAU HAUT-BAILLY Pessac-Léognan 1988 $30 (8/31/90) (BT)
85+ CHATEAU HAUT-BAILLY Pessac-Léognan 1987 Rel: $20 Cur: $20 (6/30/88) (BT)
91 CHATEAU HAUT-BAILLY Pessac-Léognan 1986 Rel: $23 Cur: $28 (6/15/89)
90+ CHATEAU HAUT-BAILLY Pessac-Léognan 1986 Rel: $23 Cur: $28 (6/30/88) (BT)
90+ CHATEAU HAUT-BAILLY Pessac-Léognan 1986 Rel: $23 Cur: $28 (5/15/87) (BT)
89 CHATEAU HAUT-BAILLY Graves 1985 Rel: $28 Cur: $28 (6/15/88)
80+ CHATEAU HAUT-BAILLY Graves 1985 Rel: $28 Cur: $28 (5/15/87) (BT)
87 CHATEAU HAUT-BAILLY Graves 1984 Rel: $15 Cur: $19 (6/15/87)
86 CHATEAU HAUT-BAILLY Graves 1983 Rel: $21 Cur: $21 (4/16/86)
87 CHATEAU HAUT-BAILLY Graves 1981 Rel: $13.50 Cur: $21 (6/01/84)
84 CHATEAU HAUT-BAILLY Graves 1979 Cur: $23 (10/15/89) (JS)
94 CHATEAU HAUT-BAILLY Graves 1945 Cur: $200 (3/16/86) (JL)
85+ CHATEAU HAUT-BERGEY Pessac-Léognan 1989 (NR) (4/30/91) (BT)
80+ CHATEAU HAUT-BERGEY Pessac-Léognan 1988 $12 (6/30/89) (BT)
65+ CHATEAU HAUT-BERGEY Pessac-Léognan 1987 $10 (6/30/89) (BT)
80+ CHATEAU HAUT-BERGEY Pessac-Léognan 1986 $12 (6/30/88) (BT)
80+ CHATEAU HAUT-BERGEY Pessac-Léognan 1986 $12 (5/15/87) (BT)
95+ CHATEAU HAUT-BRION Pessac-Léognan 1990 (NR) (4/30/91) (BT)
95+ CHATEAU HAUT-BRION Pessac-Léognan 1989 (NR) (4/30/91) (BT)
95+ CHATEAU HAUT-BRION Pessac-Léognan 1989 (NR) (4/30/90) (BT)
98 CHATEAU HAUT-BRION Pessac-Léognan 1988 $95 (4/30/91)
95+ CHATEAU HAUT-BRION Pessac-Léognan 1988 $95 (8/31/90) (BT)
95+ CHATEAU HAUT-BRION Pessac-Léognan 1988 $95 (6/30/89) (BT)
90 CHATEAU HAUT-BRION Pessac-Léognan 1987 Rel: $70 Cur: $70 (10/15/90)
85+ CHATEAU HAUT-BRION Pessac-Léognan 1987 Rel: $70 Cur: $70 (6/30/89) (BT)
85+ CHATEAU HAUT-BRION Pessac-Léognan 1987 Rel: $70 Cur: $70 (6/30/88) (BT)
92 CHATEAU HAUT-BRION Pessac-Léognan 1986 Rel: $88 Cur: $88 (6/30/89)
95+ CHATEAU HAUT-BRION Pessac-Léognan 1986 Rel: $88 Cur: $88 (6/30/88) (BT)
90+ CHATEAU HAUT-BRION Pessac-Léognan 1986 Rel: $88 Cur: $88 (5/15/87) (BT)
96 CHATEAU HAUT-BRION Graves 1985 Rel: $70 Cur: $84 (4/30/88)
90+ CHATEAU HAUT-BRION Graves 1985 Rel: $70 Cur: $84 (5/15/87) (BT)
90+ CHATEAU HAUT-BRION Graves 1985 Rel: $70 Cur: $84 (4/16/86) (BT)
80 CHATEAU HAUT-BRION Graves 1984 Rel: $36 Cur: $53 (7/31/87)
95 CHATEAU HAUT-BRION Graves 1983 Rel: $86.50 Cur: $87 (9/30/86) SS
92 CHATEAU HAUT-BRION Graves 1982 Rel: $60 Cur: $117 (7/01/85)
92 CHATEAU HAUT-BRION Graves 1981 Rel: $56 Cur: $65 (5/01/89)
94 CHATEAU HAUT-BRION Graves 1979 Cur: $88 (10/15/89) (JS)
67 CHATEAU HAUT-BRION Graves 1970 Cur: $150 (4/01/86)
70 CHATEAU HAUT-BRION Graves 1962 Cur: $157 (11/30/87) (JS)
84 CHATEAU HAUT-BRION Graves 1961 Cur: $440 (3/16/86) (JL)
99 CHATEAU HAUT-BRION Graves 1945 Cur: $860 (3/16/86) (JL)
91 CHATEAU HAUT-GARDERE Pessac-Léognan 1986 $11 (9/30/89)
80+ CHATEAU HAUT-GARDERE Pessac-Léognan 1986 $11 (5/15/87) (BT)
77 CHATEAU HAUT-GARDERE Graves 1985 $15 (7/31/88)
75+ CHATEAU LES HAUTS DE SMITH Pessac-Léognan 1988 (NR) (6/30/89) (BT)
70+ CHATEAU LES HAUTS DE SMITH Pessac-Léognan 1987 (NR) (6/30/89) (BT)
85+ CHATEAU LARRIVET-HAUT-BRION Pessac-Léognan 1989 (NR) (4/30/91) (BT)
94 CHATEAU LARRIVET-HAUT-BRION Pessac-Léognan 1988 $25 (4/30/91)
70+ CHATEAU LARRIVET-HAUT-BRION Pessac-Léognan 1988 $25 (6/30/89) (BT)
75+ CHATEAU LARRIVET-HAUT-BRION Pessac-Léognan 1987 $17 (6/30/89) (BT)
75+ CHATEAU LARRIVET-HAUT-BRION Pessac-Léognan 1987 $17 (6/30/88) (BT)
82 CHATEAU LARRIVET-HAUT-BRION Pessac-Léognan 1986 $17 (6/15/89)
80+ CHATEAU LARRIVET-HAUT-BRION Pessac-Léognan 1986 $17 (6/30/88) (BT)
80+ CHATEAU LARRIVET-HAUT-BRION Pessac-Léognan 1986 $17 (5/15/87) (BT)
90+ CHATEAU LA LOUVIERE Pessac-Léognan 1990 (NR) (4/30/91) (BT)
90+ CHATEAU LA LOUVIERE Pessac-Léognan 1989 (NR) (4/30/91) (BT)
90+ CHATEAU LA LOUVIERE Pessac-Léognan 1989 (NR) (4/30/90) (BT)
85+ CHATEAU LA LOUVIERE Pessac-Léognan 1988 $20 (8/31/90) (BT)
80+ CHATEAU LA LOUVIERE Pessac-Léognan 1988 $20 (6/30/89) (BT)
80+ CHATEAU LA LOUVIERE Pessac-Léognan 1987 Rel: $20 Cur: $20 (6/30/89) (BT)
80+ CHATEAU LA LOUVIERE Pessac-Léognan 1987 Rel: $20 Cur: $20 (6/30/88) (BT)
91 CHATEAU LA LOUVIERE Pessac-Léognan 1986 Rel: $15 Cur: $25 (6/15/89)
85+ CHATEAU LA LOUVIERE Pessac-Léognan 1986 Rel: $15 Cur: $25 (6/30/88) (BT)
80+ CHATEAU LA LOUVIERE Pessac-Léognan 1986 Rel: $15 Cur: $25 (5/15/87) (BT)
87 CHATEAU LA LOUVIERE Graves 1985 Rel: $16 Cur: $16 (6/30/88)
78 CHATEAU LA LOUVIERE Graves 1983 Rel: $11 Cur: $16 (11/30/86)
94 CHATEAU LA LOUVIERE Graves 1982 Rel: $11.50 Cur: $25 (10/16/85) SS
78 CHATEAU MAGNEAU Graves 1987 $12 (5/15/90)
80+ CHATEAU MALARTIC-LAGRAVIERE Pessac-Léognan 1989 (NR) (4/30/90) (BT)
84 CHATEAU MALARTIC-LAGRAVIERE Pessac-Léognan 1988 $20 (7/15/91)
85+ CHATEAU MALARTIC-LAGRAVIERE Pessac-Léognan 1988 $20 (6/30/89) (BT)
80+ CHATEAU MALARTIC-LAGRAVIERE Pessac-Léognan 1987 Rel: $18 Cur: $18 (6/30/89) (BT)
90 CHATEAU MALARTIC-LAGRAVIERE Pessac-Léognan 1986 Rel: $18 Cur: $23 (6/15/89)
80+ CHATEAU MALARTIC-LAGRAVIERE Pessac-Léognan 1986 Rel: $18 Cur: $23 (6/30/88) (BT)
70+ CHATEAU MALARTIC-LAGRAVIERE Pessac-Léognan 1986 Rel: $18 Cur: $23 (5/15/87) (BT)
90+ CHATEAU MALARTIC-LAGRAVIERE Graves 1985 Rel: $22.50 Cur: $23 (5/15/87) (BT)
76 CHATEAU MERIC Graves 1988 $17 (4/30/91)
95+ CHATEAU LA MISSION-HAUT-BRION Pessac-Léognan 1990 (NR) (4/30/91) (BT)
95+ CHATEAU LA MISSION-HAUT-BRION Pessac-Léognan 1989 (NR) (4/30/91) (BT)
95+ CHATEAU LA MISSION-HAUT-BRION Pessac-Léognan 1989 (NR) (4/30/90) (BT)
87 CHATEAU LA MISSION-HAUT-BRION Pessac-Léognan 1988 $90 (4/30/91)
95+ CHATEAU LA MISSION-HAUT-BRION Pessac-Léognan 1988 $90 (8/31/90) (BT)
95+ CHATEAU LA MISSION-HAUT-BRION Pessac-Léognan 1988 $90 (6/30/89) (BT)
89 CHATEAU LA MISSION-HAUT-BRION Pessac-Léognan 1987 Rel: $39 Cur: $41 (5/15/90)
85+ CHATEAU LA MISSION-HAUT-BRION Pessac-Léognan 1987 Rel: $39 Cur: $41 (6/30/89) (BT)
85+ CHATEAU LA MISSION-HAUT-BRION Pessac-Léognan 1987 Rel: $39 Cur: $41 (6/30/88) (BT)
94 CHATEAU LA MISSION-HAUT-BRION Pessac-Léognan 1986 Rel: $50 Cur: $60 (6/15/89)
90+ CHATEAU LA MISSION-HAUT-BRION Pessac-Léognan 1986 Rel: $50 Cur: $60 (6/30/88) (BT)
90+ CHATEAU LA MISSION-HAUT-BRION Pessac-Léognan 1986 Rel: $50 Cur: $60 (5/15/87) (BT)
95 CHATEAU LA MISSION-HAUT-BRION Graves 1985 Rel: $70 Cur: $73 (4/30/88)
90+ CHATEAU LA MISSION-HAUT-BRION Graves 1985 Rel: $70 Cur: $73 (5/15/87) (BT)
90+ CHATEAU LA MISSION-HAUT-BRION Graves 1985 Rel: $70 Cur: $73 (4/16/86) (BT)
89 CHATEAU LA MISSION-HAUT-BRION Graves 1984 Rel: $55 Cur: $55 (5/01/89)
90 CHATEAU LA MISSION-HAUT-BRION Graves 1983 Rel: $63 Cur: $63 (4/16/86)
96 CHATEAU LA MISSION-HAUT-BRION Graves 1982 Cur: $85 (5/01/85)
91 CHATEAU LA MISSION-HAUT-BRION Graves 1981 Cur: $56 (5/01/85)
81 CHATEAU LA MISSION-HAUT-BRION Graves 1980 Cur: $40 (5/01/85)
89 CHATEAU LA MISSION-HAUT-BRION Graves 1979 Rel: $48 Cur: $70 (10/15/89) (JS)
89 CHATEAU LA MISSION-HAUT-BRION Graves 1979 Rel: $48 Cur: $70 (5/01/85)
88 CHATEAU LA MISSION-HAUT-BRION Graves 1978 Cur: $120 (5/01/85)
68 CHATEAU LA MISSION-HAUT-BRION Graves 1962 Cur: $157 (11/30/87) (JS)
92 CHATEAU LA MISSION-HAUT-BRION Graves 1961 Cur: $450 (3/16/86) (JL)
85 CHATEAU LA MISSION-HAUT-BRION Graves 1959 Cur: $390 (10/15/90) (JS)
70 CHATEAU LA MISSION-HAUT-BRION Graves 1945 Cur: $690 (3/16/86) (JL)
90+ CHATEAU OLIVIER Pessac-Léognan 1990 (NR) (4/30/91) (BT)
90+ CHATEAU OLIVIER Pessac-Léognan 1989 (NR) (4/30/91) (BT)
90+ CHATEAU OLIVIER Pessac-Léognan 1989 (NR) (4/30/90) (BT)
91 CHATEAU OLIVIER Pessac-Léognan 1988 $23 (2/15/91)
90+ CHATEAU OLIVIER Pessac-Léognan 1988 $23 (8/31/90) (BT)
75+ CHATEAU OLIVIER Pessac-Léognan 1988 $23 (6/30/89) (BT)
80+ CHATEAU OLIVIER Pessac-Léognan 1987 Rel: $20 Cur: $24 (6/30/89) (BT)
80+ CHATEAU OLIVIER Pessac-Léognan 1987 Rel: $20 Cur: $24 (6/30/88) (BT)
85+ CHATEAU OLIVIER Pessac-Léognan 1986 Rel: $16 Cur: $19 (6/30/88) (BT)
93 CHATEAU OLIVIER Graves 1985 Rel: $15 Cur: $24 (2/15/89) SS
92 CHATEAU OLIVIER Graves 1983 Rel: $15 Cur: $20 (5/01/89)
89 CHATEAU OLIVIER Graves 1982 Rel: $17.50 Cur: $26 (3/15/87)
86 CHATEAU OLIVIER Graves 1981 Rel: $14 Cur: $14 (10/16/85)
60+ CHATEAU LE PAPE Pessac-Léognan 1988 (NR) (6/30/89) (BT)
75+ CHATEAU LE PAPE Pessac-Léognan 1987 (NR) (6/30/89) (BT)
95+ CHATEAU PAPE-CLEMENT Pessac-Léognan 1990 (NR) (4/30/91) (BT)
95+ CHATEAU PAPE-CLEMENT Pessac-Léognan 1989 (NR) (4/30/91) (BT)
85+ CHATEAU PAPE-CLEMENT Pessac-Léognan 1989 (NR) (4/30/90) (BT)
93 CHATEAU PAPE-CLEMENT Pessac-Léognan 1988 $40 (12/31/90)

Key to Symbols

The scores reported here are the results of blind tastings conducted by our panel of senior editors. Wines that carry the initials below are results of individual tastings.

THE WINE SPECTATOR 100-POINT SCALE ***95-100***—Classic, a great wine; ***90-94***—Outstanding, superior character and style; ***80-89***—Good to very good, a wine with special qualities; ***70-79***—Average, drinkable wine that may have minor flaws; ***60-69***—Below average, drinkable but not recommended; ***50-59***—Poor, undrinkable, not recommended. "+"—With a score indicates a range; used primarily with barrel tastings to indicate a preliminary score.

SPECIAL DESIGNATIONS SS—Spectator Selection, CS—Cellar Selection, BB—Best Buy.

TASTER'S INITIALS (JG)—Jim Gordon, (HS)—Harvey Steiman, (JL)—James Laube, (JS)—James Suckling, (TM)—Thomas Matthews, (TR)—Terry Robards, (BT)—Barrel Tasting (these wines were tasted blind from barrel samples), (CA-date)—*California's Great Cabernets* by James Laube, (CH-date)—*California's Great Chardonnays* by James Laube, (VP-date)—*Vintage Port* by James Suckling.

DATE TASTED Dates in parentheses represent the issue in which the rating was published.

95+ CHATEAU PAPE-CLEMENT Pessac-Léognan 1988 $40 (6/30/89) (BT)
84 CHATEAU PAPE-CLEMENT Pessac-Léognan 1987 Rel: $24 Cur: $25 (5/15/90)
80+ CHATEAU PAPE-CLEMENT Pessac-Léognan 1987 Rel: $24 Cur: $25 (6/30/89) (BT)
85+ CHATEAU PAPE-CLEMENT Pessac-Léognan 1987 Rel: $24 Cur: $25 (6/30/88) (BT)
92 CHATEAU PAPE-CLEMENT Pessac-Léognan 1986 Rel: $36 Cur: $36 (6/30/89)
90+ CHATEAU PAPE-CLEMENT Pessac-Léognan 1986 Rel: $36 Cur: $36 (6/30/88) (BT)
80+ CHATEAU PAPE-CLEMENT Pessac-Léognan 1986 Rel: $36 Cur: $36 (5/15/87) (BT)
83 CHATEAU PAPE-CLEMENT Graves 1985 Rel: $44 Cur: $47 (6/30/88)
80+ CHATEAU PAPE-CLEMENT Graves 1985 Rel: $44 Cur: $47 (5/15/87) (BT)
89 CHATEAU PAPE-CLEMENT Graves 1983 Rel: $20 Cur: $30 (3/31/87)
84 CHATEAU PAPE-CLEMENT Graves 1982 Rel: $24 Cur: $31 (2/01/85)
77 CHATEAU PAPE-CLEMENT Graves 1981 Rel: $17.50 Cur: $19 (6/01/84)
84 CHATEAU PAPE-CLEMENT Graves 1979 Cur: $22 (10/15/89) (JS)
90 CHATEAU PAPE-CLEMENT Graves 1962 Cur: $120 (11/30/87) (JS)
77 CHATEAU PAPE-CLEMENT Graves 1961 Cur: $160 (3/16/86) (JL)
80 CHATEAU PAPE-CLEMENT Graves 1959 Cur: $125 (10/15/90) (JS)
75+ CHATEAU PIQUE-CAILLOU Pessac-Léognan 1988 (NR) (6/30/89) (BT)
70+ CHATEAU PIQUE-CAILLOU Pessac-Léognan 1987 (NR) (6/30/89) (BT)
70+ CHATEAU PIQUE-CAILLOU Pessac-Léognan 1987 (NR) (6/30/88) (BT)
80+ CHATEAU PIQUE-CAILLOU Pessac-Léognan 1986 (NR) (6/30/88) (BT)
60+ CHATEAU PIQUE-CAILLOU Pessac-Léognan 1986 (NR) (5/15/87) (BT)
83 CHATEAU RAHOUL Graves 1986 $18 (12/31/90)
80+ CHATEAU RAHOUL Graves 1986 $18 (5/15/87) (BT)
85 CHATEAU RESPIDE-MEDEVILLE Graves 1985 $12.50 (2/29/88)
85+ CHATEAU DE ROCHEMORIN Pessac-Léognan 1989 (NR) (4/30/91) (BT)
75+ CHATEAU DE ROCHEMORIN Pessac-Léognan 1988 (NR) (6/30/89) (BT)
75+ CHATEAU DE ROCHEMORIN Pessac-Léognan 1987 (NR) (6/30/89) (BT)
84 CHATEAU DE ROCHEMORIN Pessac-Léognan 1986 Rel: $10 Cur: $10 (6/15/89)
70+ CHATEAU DE ROCHEMORIN Pessac-Léognan 1986 Rel: $10 Cur: $10 (5/15/87) (BT)
85 CHATEAU DE ROCHEMORIN Graves 1985 Rel: $9 Cur: $9 (6/15/88)
75+ CHATEAU LE SARTRE Pessac-Léognan 1987 (NR) (6/30/89) (BT)
85+ CHATEAU SMITH-HAUT-LAFITE Pessac-Léognan 1990 (NR) (4/30/91) (BT)
85+ CHATEAU SMITH-HAUT-LAFITE Pessac-Léognan 1989 (NR) (4/30/91) (BT)
85+ CHATEAU SMITH-HAUT-LAFITE Pessac-Léognan 1989 (NR) (4/30/90) (BT)
80+ CHATEAU SMITH-HAUT-LAFITE Pessac-Léognan 1988 $15 (6/30/89) (BT)
84 CHATEAU SMITH-HAUT-LAFITE Pessac-Léognan 1987 Rel: $15 Cur: $15 (5/15/90)
80+ CHATEAU SMITH-HAUT-LAFITE Pessac-Léognan 1987 Rel: $15 Cur: $15 (6/30/89) (BT)
85+ CHATEAU SMITH-HAUT-LAFITE Pessac-Léognan 1986 Rel: $15 Cur: $15 (6/30/88) (BT)
70+ CHATEAU SMITH-HAUT-LAFITE Pessac-Léognan 1986 Rel: $15 Cur: $15 (5/15/87) (BT)
89 CHATEAU SMITH-HAUT-LAFITE Graves 1985 Rel: $15 Cur: $23 (11/30/88)
79 CHATEAU SMITH-HAUT-LAFITE Graves 1981 Rel: $12.50 Cur: $13 (6/01/84)
69 CHATEAU SMITH-HAUT-LAFITE Graves 1979 Cur: $20 (10/15/89) (JS)
85+ CHATEAU LA TOUR-HAUT-BRION Pessac-Léognan 1989 (NR) (4/30/91) (BT)
91 CHATEAU LA TOUR-HAUT-BRION Pessac-Léognan 1988 $37 (6/15/91) CS
85+ CHATEAU LA TOUR-HAUT-BRION Pessac-Léognan 1988 $37 (8/31/90) (BT)
80+ CHATEAU LA TOUR-HAUT-BRION Pessac-Léognan 1988 $37 (6/30/89) (BT)
87 CHATEAU LA TOUR-HAUT-BRION Pessac-Léognan 1987 Rel: $22 Cur: $22 (5/15/90)
80+ CHATEAU LA TOUR-HAUT-BRION Pessac-Léognan 1987 Rel: $22 Cur: $22 (6/30/89) (BT)
80+ CHATEAU LA TOUR-HAUT-BRION Pessac-Léognan 1987 Rel: $22 Cur: $22 (6/30/88) (BT)
85+ CHATEAU LA TOUR-HAUT-BRION Pessac-Léognan 1986 Cur: $34 (6/30/88) (BT)
80+ CHATEAU LA TOUR-HAUT-BRION Pessac-Léognan 1986 Cur: $34 (5/15/87) (BT)
86 CHATEAU LA TOUR-HAUT-BRION Graves 1985 Rel: $42 Cur: $42 (2/15/89)
80+ CHATEAU LA TOUR-HAUT-BRION Graves 1985 Rel: $42 Cur: $42 (5/15/87) (BT)
70+ CHATEAU LA TOUR-HAUT-BRION Graves 1985 Rel: $42 Cur: $42 (4/16/86) (BT)
90 CHATEAU LA TOUR-HAUT-BRION Graves 1983 Rel: $25 Cur: $33 (3/15/87)
86 CHATEAU LA TOUR-HAUT-BRION Graves 1979 Cur: $30 (10/15/89) (JS)
85 CHATEAU LA TOUR-HAUT-BRION Graves 1962 Cur: $40 (11/30/87) (JS)
67 CHATEAU LA TOUR-HAUT-BRION Graves 1945 Cur: $520 (3/16/86) (JL)
70+ CHATEAU LA TOUR-LEOGNAN Pessac-Léognan 1987 $10 (6/30/89) (BT)
85 CHATEAU LA TOUR-LEOGNAN Pessac-Léognan 1986 $11 (2/15/89)
85+ CHATEAU LA TOUR-MARTILLAC Pessac-Léognan 1989 (NR) (4/30/91) (BT)
88 CHATEAU LA TOUR-MARTILLAC Pessac-Léognan 1988 $24 (2/28/91)
85+ CHATEAU LA TOUR-MARTILLAC Pessac-Léognan 1988 $24 (8/31/90) (BT)
80+ CHATEAU LA TOUR-MARTILLAC Pessac-Léognan 1988 $24 (6/30/89) (BT)
75+ CHATEAU LA TOUR-MARTILLAC Pessac-Léognan 1987 $15 (6/30/88) (BT)
90 CHATEAU LA TOUR-MARTILLAC Pessac-Léognan 1986 $15 (2/15/90)
80+ CHATEAU LA TOUR-MARTILLAC Pessac-Léognan 1986 $15 (6/30/88) (BT)
80+ CHATEAU LA TOUR-MARTILLAC Pessac-Léognan 1986 $15 (5/15/87) (BT)
87 CHATEAU LA TOUR-MARTILLAC Graves 1985 $19.50 (8/31/88)

HAUT-MÉDOC

80+ CHATEAU D'AGASSAC Haut-Médoc 1989 (NR) (4/30/91) (BT)
85+ CHATEAU ARNAULD Haut-Médoc 1989 (NR) (4/30/91) (BT)
84 CHATEAU ARNAULD Haut-Médoc 1988 $15 (4/30/91)
80+ CHATEAU ARNAULD Haut-Médoc 1988 $15 (6/30/89) (BT)
79 CHATEAU ARNAULD Haut-Médoc 1987 Rel: $13 Cur: $13 (11/30/89) (JS)
75+ CHATEAU ARNAULD Haut-Médoc 1987 Rel: $13 Cur: $13 (6/30/89) (BT)
82 CHATEAU ARNAULD Haut-Médoc 1986 Cur: $18 (11/30/89) (JS)
82 CHATEAU ARNAULD Haut-Médoc 1985 Rel: $15 Cur: $15 (2/15/88)
75 CHATEAU ARNAULD Haut-Médoc 1983 Rel: $8 Cur: $15 (1/01/86)
71 CHATEAU ARNAULD Haut-Médoc 1982 Cur: $17 (11/30/89) (JS)
70+ CHATEAU D'ARSAC Haut-Médoc 1988 $7 (6/30/89) (BT)
70+ CHATEAU D'ARSAC Haut-Médoc 1987 $6 (6/30/89) (BT)
75 CHATEAU D'ARSAC Haut-Médoc 1985 $5.75 (2/15/89)
78 CHATEAU BARREYRES Haut-Médoc 1986 $8.25 (6/30/89)
82 CHATEAU LA BATISSE Haut-Médoc 1985 $10 (6/30/88)
85+ CHATEAU BEAUMONT Haut-Médoc 1989 (NR) (4/30/91) (BT)
82 CHATEAU BEAUMONT Haut-Médoc 1988 $15 (7/15/91)
75+ CHATEAU BEAUMONT Haut-Médoc 1988 $15 (6/30/89) (BT)
75+ CHATEAU BEAUMONT Haut-Médoc 1987 $13 (6/30/89) (BT)
75+ CHATEAU BEAUMONT Haut-Médoc 1987 $13 (6/30/88) (BT)
84 CHATEAU BEAUMONT Haut-Médoc 1986 $9 (6/30/89)
80+ CHATEAU BEAUMONT Haut-Médoc 1986 $9 (6/30/88) (BT)
70+ CHATEAU BEAUMONT Haut-Médoc 1986 $9 (5/15/87) (BT)
74 CHATEAU BEAUMONT Haut-Médoc 1985 $8.50 (4/30/88)
85 CHATEAU BEL-AIR Haut-Médoc 1988 $15 (4/30/91)
88 CHATEAU BEL-AIR Haut-Médoc 1986 $9 (11/15/89) BB
80 CHATEAU BEL-AIR Haut-Médoc 1985 $5 (3/15/88) BB
83 CHATEAU BEL-AIR Haut-Médoc 1983 $6 (12/31/86)
72 CHATEAU BEL-AIR Haut-Médoc 1981 $6 (5/01/84)
79 CHATEAU BELGRAVE Haut-Médoc 1988 $28 (7/31/91)
75+ CHATEAU BELGRAVE Haut-Médoc 1988 $28 (6/30/89) (BT)
81 CHATEAU BELGRAVE Haut-Médoc 1986 Rel: $16 Cur: $16 (3/31/90)
80+ CHATEAU DE CAMENSAC Haut-Médoc 1989 (NR) (4/30/90) (BT)
55 CHATEAU DE CAMENSAC Haut-Médoc 1988 $16 (7/15/91)
80+ CHATEAU DE CAMENSAC Haut-Médoc 1988 $16 (6/30/89) (BT)
75+ CHATEAU DE CAMENSAC Haut-Médoc 1987 Rel: $12 Cur: $12 (6/30/89) (BT)
75+ CHATEAU DE CAMENSAC Haut-Médoc 1987 Rel: $12 Cur: $12 (6/30/88) (BT)
83 CHATEAU DE CAMENSAC Haut-Médoc 1986 Rel: $14 Cur: $14 (6/30/89)
80+ CHATEAU DE CAMENSAC Haut-Médoc 1986 Rel: $14 Cur: $14 (5/15/87) (BT)
90+ CHATEAU DE CAMENSAC Haut-Médoc 1985 Rel: $16 Cur: $18 (5/15/87) (BT)
82 CHATEAU DE CAMENSAC Haut-Médoc 1979 Cur: $22 (10/15/89) (JS)
78 CHATEAU CANTELAUDE Haut-Médoc 1986 $17 (6/30/89)
80+ CHATEAU CANTEMERLE Haut-Médoc 1990 (NR) (4/30/91) (BT)
90+ CHATEAU CANTEMERLE Haut-Médoc 1989 (NR) (4/30/91) (BT)
90+ CHATEAU CANTEMERLE Haut-Médoc 1989 (NR) (4/30/90) (BT)
85 CHATEAU CANTEMERLE Haut-Médoc 1988 $25 (3/15/91)
75+ CHATEAU CANTEMERLE Haut-Médoc 1988 $25 (6/30/89) (BT)
87 CHATEAU CANTEMERLE Haut-Médoc 1987 Rel: $21 Cur: $21 (5/15/90)
80+ CHATEAU CANTEMERLE Haut-Médoc 1987 Rel: $21 Cur: $21 (6/30/89) (BT)
85+ CHATEAU CANTEMERLE Haut-Médoc 1987 Rel: $21 Cur: $21 (6/30/88) (BT)
89 CHATEAU CANTEMERLE Haut-Médoc 1986 Rel: $30 Cur: $30 (6/30/89)
85+ CHATEAU CANTEMERLE Haut-Médoc 1986 Rel: $30 Cur: $30 (6/30/88) (BT)
90+ CHATEAU CANTEMERLE Haut-Médoc 1986 Rel: $30 Cur: $30 (5/15/87) (BT)
88 CHATEAU CANTEMERLE Haut-Médoc 1985 Rel: $30 Cur: $30 (8/31/88)
85 CHATEAU CANTEMERLE Haut-Médoc 1984 Rel: $17 Cur: $17 (6/15/87)
92 CHATEAU CANTEMERLE Haut-Médoc 1982 Rel: $30 Cur: $30 (5/01/89)
70 CHATEAU CANTEMERLE Haut-Médoc 1981 Rel: $13.50 Cur: $17 (5/01/84)
78 CHATEAU CANTEMERLE Haut-Médoc 1979 Cur: $20 (10/15/89) (JS)
90 CHATEAU CANTEMERLE Haut-Médoc 1962 Cur: $101 (11/30/87) (JS)
78 CHATEAU CANTEMERLE Haut-Médoc 1961 Cur: $151 (3/16/86) (JL)
92 CHATEAU CANTEMERLE Haut-Médoc 1945 Cur: $300 (3/16/86) (JL)
80+ CHATEAU CARONNE-STE.-GEMME Haut-Médoc 1989 (NR) (4/30/91) (BT)
75+ CHATEAU CARONNE-STE.-GEMME Haut-Médoc 1988 (NR) (6/30/89) (BT)
75+ CHATEAU CARONNE-STE.-GEMME Haut-Médoc 1987 (NR) (6/30/89) (BT)
81 CHATEAU CISSAC Haut-Médoc 1987 Rel: $14 Cur: $14 (11/30/89) (JS)
79 CHATEAU CISSAC Haut-Médoc 1986 Rel: $20 Cur: $20 (11/30/89) (JS)
79 CHATEAU CISSAC Haut-Médoc 1985 Rel: $16 Cur: $16 (7/31/88)
81 CHATEAU CISSAC Haut-Médoc 1982 Cur: $24 (11/30/89) (JS)
85+ CHATEAU CITRAN Haut-Médoc 1990 (NR) (4/30/91) (BT)
90+ CHATEAU CITRAN Haut-Médoc 1989 (NR) (4/30/91) (BT)
90+ CHATEAU CITRAN Haut-Médoc 1989 (NR) (4/30/90) (BT)
91 CHATEAU CITRAN Haut-Médoc 1988 $15 (4/30/91)
90+ CHATEAU CITRAN Haut-Médoc 1988 $15 (8/31/90) (BT)
90+ CHATEAU CITRAN Haut-Médoc 1988 $15 (6/30/89) (BT)
75+ CHATEAU CITRAN Haut-Médoc 1987 Rel: $14 Cur: $14 (6/30/89) (BT)
80+ CHATEAU CITRAN Haut-Médoc 1987 Rel: $14 Cur: $14 (6/30/88) (BT)
82 CHATEAU CITRAN Haut-Médoc 1983 Rel: $10 Cur: $11 (4/01/86)
78 CHATEAU CITRAN Haut-Médoc 1982 Rel: $6 Cur: $11 (4/01/85)
70+ CHATEAU CLEMENT-PICHON Haut-Médoc 1988 $15 (6/30/89) (BT)
73 CHATEAU CLEMENT-PICHON Haut-Médoc 1987 $14 (11/30/89) (JS)
85 CHATEAU CLEMENT-PICHON Haut-Médoc 1986 $11 (11/30/89) (JS)
76 CHATEAU CLEMENT-PICHON Haut-Médoc 1986 $11 (9/30/89)
60 LES CLOCHERS DU HAUT-MEDOC Haut-Médoc 1983 $7 (6/15/87)
85+ CHATEAU COUFRAN Haut-Médoc 1990 (NR) (4/30/91) (BT)
85+ CHATEAU COUFRAN Haut-Médoc 1989 (NR) (4/30/91) (BT)
80+ CHATEAU COUFRAN Haut-Médoc 1989 (NR) (4/30/90) (BT)
84 CHATEAU COUFRAN Haut-Médoc 1988 $15 (4/30/91)
85+ CHATEAU COUFRAN Haut-Médoc 1988 $15 (8/31/90) (BT)
80+ CHATEAU COUFRAN Haut-Médoc 1988 $15 (6/30/89) (BT)
81 CHATEAU COUFRAN Haut-Médoc 1987 Rel: $12 Cur: $12 (11/30/89) (JS)
80+ CHATEAU COUFRAN Haut-Médoc 1987 Rel: $12 Cur: $12 (6/30/89) (BT)
80+ CHATEAU COUFRAN Haut-Médoc 1987 Rel: $12 Cur: $12 (6/30/88) (BT)
82 CHATEAU COUFRAN Haut-Médoc 1986 Rel: $13 Cur: $15 (11/30/89) (JS)
85 CHATEAU COUFRAN Haut-Médoc 1986 Rel: $13 Cur: $15 (6/30/89)
80+ CHATEAU COUFRAN Haut-Médoc 1986 Rel: $13 Cur: $15 (6/30/88) (BT)
85 CHATEAU COUFRAN Haut-Médoc 1985 Rel: $11 Cur: $15 (6/30/88)
83 CHATEAU COUFRAN Haut-Médoc 1982 Rel: $9 Cur: $15 (11/30/89) (JS)
70+ CHATEAU LA FLEUR BECADE Haut-Médoc 1988 (NR) (6/30/89) (BT)
70+ CHATEAU FONTESTEAU Haut-Médoc 1988 (NR) (6/30/89) (BT)
70+ CHATEAU FONTESTEAU Haut-Médoc 1987 (NR) (6/30/89) (BT)
76 CHATEAU FOURNAS-BERNADOTTE Haut-Médoc 1988 $18 (6/15/91)
70+ CHATEAU FOURNAS-BERNADOTTE Haut-Médoc 1988 $18 (6/30/89) (BT)
65+ CHATEAU FOURNAS-BERNADOTTE Haut-Médoc 1987 $13 (6/30/89) (BT)
63 CHATEAU GRAND-MOULIN Haut-Médoc 1983 $6.75 (4/16/86)
80+ CHATEAU HANTEILLAN Haut-Médoc 1989 (NR) (4/30/91) (BT)
75+ CHATEAU HANTEILLAN Haut-Médoc 1988 $17 (6/30/89) (BT)
75 CHATEAU HANTEILLAN Haut-Médoc 1987 Rel: $13 Cur: $13 (11/30/89) (JS)
75+ CHATEAU HANTEILLAN Haut-Médoc 1987 Rel: $13 Cur: $13 (6/30/89) (BT)
81 CHATEAU HANTEILLAN Haut-Médoc 1986 Rel: $15 Cur: $15 (11/30/89) (JS)
81 CHATEAU HANTEILLAN Haut-Médoc 1982 Cur: $12 (11/30/89) (JS)
72 CHATEAU LABAT Haut-Médoc 1981 $7 (4/01/85)
75+ CHATEAU LACHESNAYE Haut-Médoc 1988 $24 (6/30/89) (BT)
75+ CHATEAU LACHESNAYE Haut-Médoc 1987 $19 (6/30/89) (BT)
85+ CHATEAU LA LAGUNE Haut-Médoc 1989 (NR) (4/30/90) (BT)
91 CHATEAU LA LAGUNE Haut-Médoc 1988 $24 (4/30/91)
90+ CHATEAU LA LAGUNE Haut-Médoc 1988 $24 (8/31/90) (BT)
90+ CHATEAU LA LAGUNE Haut-Médoc 1988 $24 (6/30/89) (BT)
89 CHATEAU LA LAGUNE Haut-Médoc 1987 Rel: $20 Cur: $20 (5/15/90)
85+ CHATEAU LA LAGUNE Haut-Médoc 1987 Rel: $20 Cur: $20 (6/30/89) (BT)
89 CHATEAU LA LAGUNE Haut-Médoc 1986 Rel: $22 Cur: $26 (6/30/89)
89 CHATEAU LA LAGUNE Haut-Médoc 1985 Rel: $22 Cur: $27 (5/15/88)
86 CHATEAU LA LAGUNE Haut-Médoc 1984 Rel: $13.50 Cur: $21 (3/31/87)
85 CHATEAU LA LAGUNE Haut-Médoc 1983 Rel: $20 Cur: $28 (4/16/86)
97 CHATEAU LA LAGUNE Haut-Médoc 1982 Rel: $28 Cur: $43 (5/01/89)
82 CHATEAU LA LAGUNE Haut-Médoc 1981 Rel: $25 Cur: $31 (5/01/89)
86 CHATEAU LA LAGUNE Haut-Médoc 1979 Cur: $29 (10/15/89) (JS)

FRANCE

BORDEAUX RED/*HAUT-MÉDOC*

80 CHATEAU LA LAGUNE Haut-Médoc 1962 Cur: $65 (11/30/87) (JS)
87 CHATEAU LA LAGUNE Haut-Médoc 1945 Cur: $200 (3/16/86) (JL)
86 CHATEAU DE LAMARQUE Haut-Médoc 1988 $20 (4/30/91)
85+ CHATEAU DE LAMARQUE Haut-Médoc 1988 $20 (8/31/90) (BT)
75+ CHATEAU DE LAMARQUE Haut-Médoc 1988 $20 (6/30/89) (BT)
74 CHATEAU DE LAMARQUE Haut-Médoc 1987 Rel: $10 Cur: $10 (11/30/89) (JS)
75+ CHATEAU DE LAMARQUE Haut-Médoc 1987 Rel: $10 Cur: $10 (6/30/89) (BT)
70+ CHATEAU DE LAMARQUE Haut-Médoc 1987 Rel: $10 Cur: $10 (6/30/88) (BT)
75 CHATEAU DE LAMARQUE Haut-Médoc 1986 Rel: $12 Cur: $12 (11/30/89) (JS)
80+ CHATEAU DE LAMARQUE Haut-Médoc 1986 Rel: $12 Cur: $12 (6/30/88) (BT)
70+ CHATEAU DE LAMARQUE Haut-Médoc 1986 Rel: $12 Cur: $12 (5/15/87) (BT)
79 CHATEAU DE LAMARQUE Haut-Médoc 1982 Rel: $9 Cur: $14 (11/30/89) (JS)
80+ CHATEAU LAMOTHE-BERGERON Haut-Médoc 1988 $15 (6/30/89) (BT)
70+ CHATEAU LAMOTHE-BERGERON Haut-Médoc 1987 Rel: $10 Cur: $10 (6/30/89) (BT)
74 CHATEAU LAMOTHE-CISSAC Haut-Médoc 1987 $10 (11/30/89) (JS)
69 CHATEAU LAMOTHE-CISSAC Haut-Médoc 1986 $12 (11/30/89) (JS)
73 CHATEAU LANDAT Haut-Médoc 1987 $7 (11/30/89) (JS)
77 CHATEAU LANDAY Haut-Médoc 1982 $6.75 (2/16/85)
72 CHATEAU LANDAY Haut-Médoc 1981 $6.50 (2/16/85)
80+ CHATEAU LANESSAN Haut-Médoc 1990 (NR) (4/30/91) (BT)
75+ CHATEAU LANESSAN Haut-Médoc 1989 (NR) (4/30/91) (BT)
85+ CHATEAU LANESSAN Haut-Médoc 1989 (NR) (4/30/90) (BT)
80 CHATEAU LANESSAN Haut-Médoc 1988 $25 (7/31/91)
85+ CHATEAU LANESSAN Haut-Médoc 1988 $25 (8/31/90) (BT)
80+ CHATEAU LANESSAN Haut-Médoc 1988 $25 (6/30/89) (BT)
70+ CHATEAU LANESSAN Haut-Médoc 1987 Rel: $14 Cur: $14 (6/30/89) (BT)
70+ CHATEAU LANESSAN Haut-Médoc 1987 Rel: $14 Cur: $14 (6/30/88) (BT)
80+ CHATEAU LANESSAN Haut-Médoc 1986 Rel: $16 Cur: $16 (6/30/88) (BT)
87 CHATEAU LANESSAN Haut-Médoc 1985 Rel: $16.50 Cur: $17 (4/30/88)
75+ CHATEAU LAROSE-TRINTAUDON Haut-Médoc 1990 (NR) (4/30/91) (BT)
75+ CHATEAU LAROSE-TRINTAUDON Haut-Médoc 1989 (NR) (4/30/91) (BT)
80+ CHATEAU LAROSE-TRINTAUDON Haut-Médoc 1989 (NR) (4/30/90) (BT)
84 CHATEAU LAROSE-TRINTAUDON Haut-Médoc 1988 $12 (4/30/91)
80+ CHATEAU LAROSE-TRINTAUDON Haut-Médoc 1988 $12 (6/30/89) (BT)
71 CHATEAU LAROSE-TRINTAUDON Haut-Médoc 1987 Rel: $9 Cur: $9 (11/30/89) (JS)
75+ CHATEAU LAROSE-TRINTAUDON Haut-Médoc 1987 Rel: $9 Cur: $9 (6/30/89) (BT)
75+ CHATEAU LAROSE-TRINTAUDON Haut-Médoc 1987 Rel: $9 Cur: $9 (6/30/88) (BT)
78 CHATEAU LAROSE-TRINTAUDON Haut-Médoc 1986 Rel: $10 Cur: $10 (11/30/89) (JS)
85 CHATEAU LAROSE-TRINTAUDON Haut-Médoc 1986 Rel: $10 Cur: $10 (11/15/89)
70+ CHATEAU LAROSE-TRINTAUDON Haut-Médoc 1986 Rel: $10 Cur: $10 (5/15/87) (BT)
84 CHATEAU LAROSE-TRINTAUDON Haut-Médoc 1985 Rel: $8.50 Cur: $9 (11/30/88) BB
73 CHATEAU LAROSE-TRINTAUDON Haut-Médoc 1983 Rel: $7 Cur: $13 (10/15/86)
79 CHATEAU LAROSE-TRINTAUDON Haut-Médoc 1982 Rel: $6 Cur: $11 (11/30/89) (JS)
81 CHATEAU LAROSE-TRINTAUDON Haut-Médoc 1982 Rel: $6 Cur: $11 (2/16/86) BB
76 CHATEAU LAROSE-TRINTAUDON Haut-Médoc 1979 Rel: $5 Cur: $15 (10/15/89) (JS)
74 CHATEAU LESTAGE-SIMON Haut-Médoc 1987 Rel: $13 Cur: $13 (11/30/89) (JS)
85 CHATEAU LESTAGE-SIMON Haut-Médoc 1986 Rel: $13 Cur: $13 (11/30/89) (JS)
84 CHATEAU LESTAGE-SIMON Haut-Médoc 1982 Rel: $10 Cur: $14 (11/30/89) (JS)
90+ CHATEAU LIVERSAN Haut-Médoc 1989 (NR) (4/30/91) (BT)
87 CHATEAU LIVERSAN Haut-Médoc 1988 $14 (7/31/91)
75+ CHATEAU LIVERSAN Haut-Médoc 1988 $14 (6/30/89) (BT)
75+ CHATEAU LIVERSAN Haut-Médoc 1987 Rel: $13 Cur: $13 (6/30/89) (BT)
90 CHATEAU LIVERSAN Haut-Médoc 1985 Rel: $16 Cur: $18 (4/30/88)
80+ CHATEAU MAGNOL Haut-Médoc 1988 (NR) (6/30/89) (BT)
75+ CHATEAU MAGNOL Haut-Médoc 1987 (NR) (6/30/89) (BT)
77 CHATEAU MAGNOL Haut-Médoc 1983 $9.50 (7/31/87)
69 CHATEAU MAGNOL Haut-Médoc 1981 $8.75 (8/31/87)
80+ CHATEAU MALESCASSE Haut-Médoc 1990 (NR) (4/30/91) (BT)
80+ CHATEAU MALESCASSE Haut-Médoc 1989 (NR) (4/30/91) (BT)
70+ CHATEAU MALESCASSE Haut-Médoc 1989 (NR) (4/30/90) (BT)
85+ CHATEAU MALESCASSE Haut-Médoc 1988 $14 (6/30/89) (BT)
74 CHATEAU MALESCASSE Haut-Médoc 1987 Rel: $9 Cur: $9 (11/30/89) (JS)
75+ CHATEAU MALESCASSE Haut-Médoc 1987 Rel: $9 Cur: $9 (6/30/89) (BT)
75+ CHATEAU MALESCASSE Haut-Médoc 1987 Rel: $9 Cur: $9 (6/30/88) (BT)
88 CHATEAU MALESCASSE Haut-Médoc 1986 Rel: $9 Cur: $9 (11/30/89) (JS)
85 CHATEAU MALESCASSE Haut-Médoc 1986 Rel: $9 Cur: $9 (6/30/89)
80+ CHATEAU MALESCASSE Haut-Médoc 1986 Rel: $9 Cur: $9 (6/30/88) (BT)
70+ CHATEAU MALESCASSE Haut-Médoc 1986 Rel: $9 Cur: $9 (5/15/87) (BT)
82 CHATEAU MALESCASSE Haut-Médoc 1982 Rel: $7 Cur: $10 (11/30/89) (JS)
77 CHATEAU DE MALLERET Haut-Médoc 1981 $5.99 (3/01/85)
74 CHATEAU MOULIN-ROUGE Haut-Médoc 1987 Rel: $12 Cur: $12 (11/30/89) (JS)
87 CHATEAU MOULIN-ROUGE Haut-Médoc 1986 Rel: $14 Cur: $14 (11/30/89) (JS)
83 CHATEAU MOULIN-ROUGE Haut-Médoc 1983 Rel: $10 Cur: $10 (7/31/87)
80 CHATEAU MOULIN-ROUGE Haut-Médoc 1982 Rel: $9 Cur: $13 (11/30/89) (JS)
85 CHATEAU PICHON Haut-Médoc 1985 $13 (8/31/88)
60+ CHATEAU PROCHE PONTET Haut-Médoc 1988 (NR) (6/30/89) (BT)
85+ CHATEAU RAMAGE LA BATISSE Haut-Médoc 1989 (NR) (4/30/91) (BT)
82 CHATEAU RAMAGE LA BATISSE Haut-Médoc 1987 Rel: $12 Cur: $12 (11/30/89) (JS)
82 CHATEAU RAMAGE LA BATISSE Haut-Médoc 1986 Rel: $14 Cur: $14 (11/30/89) (JS)
68 CHATEAU RAMAGE LA BATISSE Haut-Médoc 1982 Rel: $11 Cur: $11 (11/30/89) (JS)
75 BARONS EDMOND & BENJAMIN ROTHSCHILD Haut-Médoc 1987 $24 (3/31/91)
76 BARONS EDMOND & BENJAMIN ROTHSCHILD Haut-Médoc 1986 $48 (3/31/91)
82 CHATEAU SEGUR Haut-Médoc 1988 $15 (12/31/90)
75 CHATEAU SEGUR Haut-Médoc 1982 $6 (4/16/85)
85+ CHATEAU SENEJAC Haut-Médoc 1989 (NR) (4/30/91) (BT)
78 CHATEAU SENEJAC Haut-Médoc 1988 $11.50 (4/30/91)
80+ CHATEAU SENEJAC Haut-Médoc 1988 $11.50 (6/30/89) (BT)
70+ CHATEAU SENEJAC Haut-Médoc 1987 Rel: $9 Cur: $9 (6/30/89) (BT)
85+ CHATEAU SOCIANDO-MALLET Haut-Médoc 1990 (NR) (4/30/91) (BT)
90+ CHATEAU SOCIANDO-MALLET Haut-Médoc 1989 (NR) (4/30/91) (BT)
85+ CHATEAU SOCIANDO-MALLET Haut-Médoc 1989 (NR) (4/30/90) (BT)
87 CHATEAU SOCIANDO-MALLET Haut-Médoc 1988 $26 (3/31/91)
85+ CHATEAU SOCIANDO-MALLET Haut-Médoc 1988 $26 (8/31/90) (BT)
85+ CHATEAU SOCIANDO-MALLET Haut-Médoc 1988 $26 (6/30/89) (BT)
88 CHATEAU SOCIANDO-MALLET Haut-Médoc 1987 Rel: $15 Cur: $15 (5/15/90)
86 CHATEAU SOCIANDO-MALLET Haut-Médoc 1987 Rel: $15 Cur: $15 (11/30/89) (JS)
70+ CHATEAU SOCIANDO-MALLET Haut-Médoc 1987 Rel: $15 Cur: $15 (6/30/89) (BT)
94 CHATEAU SOCIANDO-MALLET Haut-Médoc 1986 Rel: $25 Cur: $25 (11/30/89) (JS)
84 CHATEAU SOCIANDO-MALLET Haut-Médoc 1986 Rel: $25 Cur: $25 (6/30/89)
85 CHATEAU SOCIANDO-MALLET Haut-Médoc 1985 Rel: $17 Cur: $21 (4/30/88)
84 CHATEAU SOCIANDO-MALLET Haut-Médoc 1984 Rel: $11 Cur: $17 (3/31/87)
77 CHATEAU SOCIANDO-MALLET Haut-Médoc 1983 Rel: $15 Cur: $18 (4/16/86)
92 CHATEAU SOCIANDO-MALLET Haut-Médoc 1982 Cur: $37 (11/30/89) (JS)
85+ CHATEAU SOUDARS Haut-Médoc 1990 (NR) (4/30/91) (BT)
75+ CHATEAU SOUDARS Haut-Médoc 1989 (NR) (4/30/91) (BT)
80+ CHATEAU SOUDARS Haut-Médoc 1989 (NR) (4/30/90) (BT)
88 CHATEAU SOUDARS Haut-Médoc 1988 $15 (4/30/91)
80+ CHATEAU SOUDARS Haut-Médoc 1988 $15 (8/31/90) (BT)
70+ CHATEAU SOUDARS Haut-Médoc 1988 $15 (6/30/89) (BT)
77 CHATEAU SOUDARS Haut-Médoc 1987 $12 (11/30/89) (JS)
70+ CHATEAU SOUDARS Haut-Médoc 1987 $12 (6/30/89) (BT)
79 CHATEAU SOUDARS Haut-Médoc 1986 $13 (11/30/89) (JS)
76 CHATEAU LA TONNELLE Haut-Médoc 1987 (NR) (11/30/89) (JS)
70 CHATEAU LA TONNELLE Haut-Médoc 1986 $11 (11/30/89) (JS)
77 CHATEAU LA TONNELLE Haut-Médoc 1985 $10 (2/15/89)
75+ CHATEAU LA TOUR CARNET Haut-Médoc 1990 (NR) (4/30/91) (BT)
85+ CHATEAU LA TOUR CARNET Haut-Médoc 1988 $23 (8/31/90) (BT)
80+ CHATEAU LA TOUR CARNET Haut-Médoc 1986 Rel: $22 Cur: $22 (5/15/87) (BT)
71 CHATEAU LA TOUR CARNET Haut-Médoc 1985 Rel: $22 Cur: $22 (12/31/88)
90+ CHATEAU LA TOUR CARNET Haut-Médoc 1985 Rel: $22 Cur: $22 (5/15/87) (BT)
69 CHATEAU LA TOUR CARNET Haut-Médoc 1983 Rel: $13 Cur: $13 (2/29/88)
88 CHATEAU LA TOUR CARNET Haut-Médoc 1945 Cur: $130 (3/16/86) (JL)
88 CHATEAU TOUR DU HAUT-MOULIN Haut-Médoc 1988 $20 (4/30/91)
80 CHATEAU TOUR DU HAUT-MOULIN Haut-Médoc 1987 Rel: $15 Cur: $15 (11/30/89) (JS)
90 CHATEAU TOUR DU HAUT-MOULIN Haut-Médoc 1986 Rel: $16 Cur: $16 (11/30/89) (JS)
84 CHATEAU TOUR DU HAUT-MOULIN Haut-Médoc 1986 Rel: $16 Cur: $16 (6/30/89)
84 CHATEAU TOUR DU HAUT-MOULIN Haut-Médoc 1985 Rel: $15 Cur: $15 (2/15/89)
84 CHATEAU TOUR DU HAUT-MOULIN Haut-Médoc 1982 Cur: $17 (11/30/89) (JS)
83 CHATEAU TOUR-DU-MIRAIL Haut-Médoc 1987 Rel: $10 Cur: $10 (11/30/89) (JS)
79 CHATEAU TOUR-DU-MIRAIL Haut-Médoc 1986 Rel: $12 Cur: $12 (11/30/89) (JS)
79 CHATEAU TOUR-DU-MIRAIL Haut-Médoc 1982 Rel: $9 Cur: $9 (11/30/89) (JS)
74 CHATEAU TOUR-DU-ROC Haut-Médoc 1987 Rel: $10 Cur: $10 (11/30/89) (JS)
76 CHATEAU TOUR-DU-ROC Haut-Médoc 1986 Rel: $11 Cur: $11 (11/30/89) (JS)
67 CHATEAU TOUR-DU-ROC Haut-Médoc 1986 Rel: $11 Cur: $11 (9/30/89)
84 CHATEAU TOUR-DU-ROC Haut-Médoc 1982 Rel: $9 Cur: $12 (11/30/89) (JS)
85+ CHATEAU VERDIGNAN Haut-Médoc 1990 (NR) (4/30/91) (BT)
75+ CHATEAU VERDIGNAN Haut-Médoc 1989 (NR) (4/30/91) (BT)
80+ CHATEAU VERDIGNAN Haut-Médoc 1989 (NR) (4/30/90) (BT)
86 CHATEAU VERDIGNAN Haut-Médoc 1988 $15 (4/30/91)
80+ CHATEAU VERDIGNAN Haut-Médoc 1988 $15 (8/31/90) (BT)
75+ CHATEAU VERDIGNAN Haut-Médoc 1988 $15 (6/30/89) (BT)
78 CHATEAU VERDIGNAN Haut-Médoc 1987 Rel: $15 Cur: $15 (11/30/89) (JS)
65+ CHATEAU VERDIGNAN Haut-Médoc 1987 Rel: $15 Cur: $15 (6/30/89) (BT)
76 CHATEAU VERDIGNAN Haut-Médoc 1986 Rel: $15 Cur: $15 (11/30/89) (JS)
83 CHATEAU VERDIGNAN Haut-Médoc 1986 Rel: $15 Cur: $15 (6/30/89)
81 CHATEAU VERDIGNAN Haut-Médoc 1985 Rel: $13 Cur: $14 (2/15/88)
69 CHATEAU VERDIGNAN Haut-Médoc 1983 Rel: $8 Cur: $17 (4/01/86)
76 CHATEAU VERDIGNAN Haut-Médoc 1982 Rel: $7.50 Cur: $15 (11/30/89) (JS)
83 CHATEAU VERDIGNAN Haut-Médoc 1982 Rel: $7.50 Cur: $15 (2/16/85) BB
80+ CHATEAU VILLEGEORGE Haut-Médoc 1988 $15 (6/30/89) (BT)
75+ CHATEAU VILLEGEORGE Haut-Médoc 1987 Rel: $12 Cur: $12 (6/30/89) (BT)
70+ CHATEAU VILLEGEORGE Haut-Médoc 1986 Rel: $13 Cur: $13 (5/15/87) (BT)
80+ CHATEAU VILLEGEORGE Haut-Médoc 1985 Rel: $13 Cur: $13 (5/15/87) (BT)

LISTRAC

81 CHATEAU CLARKE Listrac 1988 $18 (4/30/91)
80+ CHATEAU CLARKE Listrac 1988 $18 (6/30/89) (BT)
75+ CHATEAU CLARKE Listrac 1987 $15 (6/30/89) (BT)
90 CHATEAU CLARKE Listrac 1986 $17 (11/15/89)
70+ CHATEAU CLARKE Listrac 1986 $17 (5/15/87) (BT)
68 CHATEAU CLARKE Listrac 1982 $13 (10/15/86)
79 CHATEAU DUCLUZEAU Listrac 1987 $7 (11/30/89) (JS)
83 CHATEAU DUCLUZEAU Listrac 1986 $11 (11/30/89) (JS)
80 CHATEAU DUCLUZEAU Listrac 1982 Cur: $12 (11/30/89) (JS)
85+ CHATEAU FONREAUD Listrac 1989 (NR) (4/30/91) (BT)
82 CHATEAU FONREAUD Listrac 1988 $15 (4/30/91)
70+ CHATEAU FONREAUD Listrac 1988 $15 (6/30/89) (BT)
65+ CHATEAU FONREAUD Listrac 1987 $10 (6/30/89) (BT)
65+ CHATEAU FONREAUD Listrac 1987 $10 (6/30/88) (BT)
70+ CHATEAU FONREAUD Listrac 1986 $10 (6/30/88) (BT)
85+ CHATEAU FOURCAS-DUPRE Listrac 1989 (NR) (4/30/91) (BT)
83 CHATEAU FOURCAS-DUPRE Listrac 1988 $22 (4/30/91)
70+ CHATEAU FOURCAS-DUPRE Listrac 1988 $22 (6/30/89) (BT)
75+ CHATEAU FOURCAS-DUPRE Listrac 1987 Rel: $15 Cur: $15 (6/30/89) (BT)
75+ CHATEAU FOURCAS-DUPRE Listrac 1987 Rel: $15 Cur: $15 (6/30/88) (BT)
75+ CHATEAU FOURCAS-DUPRE Listrac 1986 Rel: $15 Cur: $15 (6/30/88) (BT)
60+ CHATEAU FOURCAS-DUPRE Listrac 1986 Rel: $15 Cur: $15 (5/15/87) (BT)
89 CHATEAU FOURCAS-DUPRE Listrac 1983 Rel: $9 Cur: $15 (10/31/86)
85+ CHATEAU FOURCAS-HOSTEN Listrac 1990 (NR) (4/30/91) (BT)
85+ CHATEAU FOURCAS-HOSTEN Listrac 1989 (NR) (4/30/91) (BT)
75+ CHATEAU FOURCAS-HOSTEN Listrac 1989 (NR) (4/30/90) (BT)
82 CHATEAU FOURCAS-HOSTEN Listrac 1988 $13.50 (7/15/91)
80+ CHATEAU FOURCAS-HOSTEN Listrac 1988 $13.50 (8/31/90) (BT)
70+ CHATEAU FOURCAS-HOSTEN Listrac 1988 $13.50 (6/30/89) (BT)

Key to Symbols

The scores reported here are the results of blind tastings conducted by our panel of senior editors. Wines that carry the initials below are results of individual tastings.

THE WINE SPECTATOR 100-POINT SCALE ***95-100***—Classic, a great wine; ***90-94***—Outstanding, superior character and style; ***80-89***—Good to very good, a wine with special qualities; ***70-79***—Average, drinkable wine that may have minor flaws; ***60-69***—Below average, drinkable but not recommended; ***50-59***—Poor, undrinkable, not recommended. "+"—With a score indicates a range; used primarily with barrel tastings to indicate a preliminary score.

SPECIAL DESIGNATIONS SS—Spectator Selection, CS—Cellar Selection, BB—Best Buy.

TASTER'S INITIALS (JG)—Jim Gordon, (HS)—Harvey Steiman, (JL)—James Laube, (JS)—James Suckling, (TM)—Thomas Matthews, (TR)—Terry Robards, (BT)—Barrel Tasting (these wines were tasted blind from barrel samples), (CA-date)—*California's Great Cabernets* by James Laube, (CH-date)—*California's Great Chardonnays* by James Laube, (VP-date)—*Vintage Port* by James Suckling.

DATE TASTED Dates in parentheses represent the issue in which the rating was published.

70+ CHATEAU FOURCAS-HOSTEN Listrac 1987 Rel: $11 Cur: $11 (6/30/89) (BT)
70+ CHATEAU FOURCAS-HOSTEN Listrac 1987 Rel: $11 Cur: $11 (6/30/88) (BT)
79 CHATEAU FOURCAS-HOSTEN Listrac 1986 Rel: $13.50 Cur: $14 (11/15/89)
75+ CHATEAU FOURCAS-HOSTEN Listrac 1986 Rel: $13.50 Cur: $14 (6/30/88) (BT)
70+ CHATEAU FOURCAS-HOSTEN Listrac 1986 Rel: $13.50 Cur: $14 (5/15/87) (BT)
83 CHATEAU FOURCAS-HOSTEN Listrac 1983 Rel: $11 Cur: $16 (10/15/86)
83 CHATEAU FOURCAS-LOUBANEY Listrac 1988 $17 (2/28/91)

MARGAUX

85+ CHATEAU D'ANGLUDET Margaux 1990 (NR) (4/30/91) (BT)
90+ CHATEAU D'ANGLUDET Margaux 1989 (NR) (4/30/90) (BT)
85 CHATEAU D'ANGLUDET Margaux 1988 $22 (2/28/91)
85+ CHATEAU D'ANGLUDET Margaux 1988 $22 (8/31/90) (BT)
85+ CHATEAU D'ANGLUDET Margaux 1988 $22 (6/30/89) (BT)
78 CHATEAU D'ANGLUDET Margaux 1987 Rel: $13 Cur: $14 (5/15/90)
84 CHATEAU D'ANGLUDET Margaux 1987 Rel: $13 Cur: $14 (11/30/89) (JS)
75+ CHATEAU D'ANGLUDET Margaux 1987 Rel: $13 Cur: $14 (6/30/89) (BT)
75+ CHATEAU D'ANGLUDET Margaux 1987 Rel: $13 Cur: $14 (6/30/88) (BT)
90 CHATEAU D'ANGLUDET Margaux 1986 Rel: $17 Cur: $25 (11/30/89) (JS)
91 CHATEAU D'ANGLUDET Margaux 1986 Rel: $17 Cur: $25 (6/15/89)
90+ CHATEAU D'ANGLUDET Margaux 1986 Rel: $17 Cur: $25 (6/30/88) (BT)
70+ CHATEAU D'ANGLUDET Margaux 1986 Rel: $17 Cur: $25 (5/15/87) (BT)
90 CHATEAU D'ANGLUDET Margaux 1985 Rel: $17 Cur: $21 (4/15/88)
80+ CHATEAU D'ANGLUDET Margaux 1985 Rel: $17 Cur: $21 (5/15/87) (BT)
93 CHATEAU D'ANGLUDET Margaux 1983 Rel: $17.50 Cur: $23 (10/15/86)
90 CHATEAU D'ANGLUDET Margaux 1982 Rel: $15 Cur: $27 (11/30/89) (JS)
95 CHATEAU D'ANGLUDET Margaux 1982 Rel: $15 Cur: $27 (12/01/85) CS
75 BARTON & GUESTIER Margaux 1985 $12 (4/30/88)
85+ CHATEAU BOYD-CANTENAC Margaux 1988 $20 (6/30/89) (BT)
75+ CHATEAU BOYD-CANTENAC Margaux 1987 Rel: $15 Cur: $15 (6/30/89) (BT)
80+ CHATEAU BOYD-CANTENAC Margaux 1986 Rel: $15 Cur: $15 (5/15/87) (BT)
90 CHATEAU BOYD-CANTENAC Margaux 1985 Rel: $22 Cur: $22 (4/15/88)
70+ CHATEAU BOYD-CANTENAC Margaux 1985 Rel: $22 Cur: $22 (5/15/87) (BT)
86 CHATEAU BOYD-CANTENAC Margaux 1983 Rel: $19 Cur: $19 (4/16/86)
91 CHATEAU BOYD-CANTENAC Margaux 1982 Rel: $14.75 Cur: $25 (5/01/85)
65 CHATEAU BOYD-CANTENAC Margaux 1961 Cur: $100 (3/16/86) (JL)
80+ CHATEAU BRANE-CANTENAC Margaux 1988 $42 (6/30/89) (BT)
80+ CHATEAU BRANE-CANTENAC Margaux 1987 Rel: $25 Cur: $25 (6/30/89) (BT)
80+ CHATEAU BRANE-CANTENAC Margaux 1987 Rel: $25 Cur: $25 (6/30/88) (BT)
87 CHATEAU BRANE-CANTENAC Margaux 1986 Rel: $26 Cur: $30 (6/15/89)
90+ CHATEAU BRANE-CANTENAC Margaux 1986 Rel: $26 Cur: $30 (6/30/88) (BT)
80+ CHATEAU BRANE-CANTENAC Margaux 1986 Rel: $26 Cur: $30 (5/15/87) (BT)
89 CHATEAU BRANE-CANTENAC Margaux 1985 Rel: $24 Cur: $31 (6/30/88)
90+ CHATEAU BRANE-CANTENAC Margaux 1985 Rel: $24 Cur: $31 (5/15/87) (BT)
94 CHATEAU BRANE-CANTENAC Margaux 1983 Rel: $19 Cur: $30 (4/16/86)
88 CHATEAU BRANE-CANTENAC Margaux 1982 Rel: $22 Cur: $30 (5/01/85)
80 CHATEAU BRANE-CANTENAC Margaux 1979 Cur: $21 (10/15/89) (JS)
60 CHATEAU BRANE-CANTENAC Margaux 1962 Cur: $65 (11/30/87) (JS)
64 CHATEAU BRANE-CANTENAC Margaux 1961 Cur: $135 (3/16/86) (JL)
87 CHATEAU BRANE-CANTENAC Margaux 1945 Cur: $200 (3/16/86) (JL)
95+ CHATEAU CANTENAC-BROWN Margaux 1990 (NR) (4/30/91) (BT)
90+ CHATEAU CANTENAC-BROWN Margaux 1989 (NR) (4/30/91) (BT)
70+ CHATEAU CANTENAC-BROWN Margaux 1989 (NR) (4/30/90) (BT)
89 CHATEAU CANTENAC-BROWN Margaux 1988 $25 (4/30/91)
90+ CHATEAU CANTENAC-BROWN Margaux 1988 $25 (8/31/90) (BT)
80+ CHATEAU CANTENAC-BROWN Margaux 1988 $25 (6/30/89) (BT)
78 CHATEAU CANTENAC-BROWN Margaux 1987 Rel: $18 Cur: $22 (2/15/90)
70+ CHATEAU CANTENAC-BROWN Margaux 1987 Rel: $18 Cur: $22 (6/30/89) (BT)
80+ CHATEAU CANTENAC-BROWN Margaux 1987 Rel: $18 Cur: $22 (6/30/88) (BT)
85+ CHATEAU CANTENAC-BROWN Margaux 1986 Rel: $24 Cur: $27 (6/30/88) (BT)
85 CHATEAU CANTENAC-BROWN Margaux 1984 Rel: $19 Cur: $19 (5/15/87)
91 CHATEAU CANTENAC-BROWN Margaux 1982 Rel: $12 Cur: $18 (5/01/85)
91 CHATEAU CANTENAC-BROWN Margaux 1981 Rel: $12 Cur: $12 (3/01/85)
89 CHATEAU CANTENAC-BROWN Margaux 1959 Cur: $100 (10/15/90) (JS)
75 CHATEAU CANTENAC-BROWN Margaux 1945 Cur: $150 (3/16/86) (JL)
90+ CHATEAU CANUET Margaux 1990 (NR) (4/30/91) (BT)
75+ CHATEAU CANUET Margaux 1989 (NR) (4/30/91) (BT)
90+ CHATEAU CANUET Margaux 1989 (NR) (4/30/90) (BT)
85+ CHATEAU CANUET Margaux 1988 $15 (8/31/90) (BT)
74 CHATEAU CANUET Margaux 1987 $12.50 (5/15/90)
79 CHATEAU CANUET Margaux 1987 $12.50 (11/30/89) (JS)
88 CHATEAU CANUET Margaux 1986 $15 (11/30/89) (JS)
79 CHATEAU DE CLAIREFONT Margaux 1985 $9.25 (4/30/88)
86 CHATEAU DE LA DAME Margaux 1988 $15 (2/15/91)
85+ CHATEAU DAUZAC Margaux 1989 (NR) (4/30/91) (BT)
80+ CHATEAU DAUZAC Margaux 1989 (NR) (4/30/90) (BT)
90 CHATEAU DAUZAC Margaux 1988 $20 (6/30/91)
75+ CHATEAU DAUZAC Margaux 1988 $20 (6/30/89) (BT)
70+ CHATEAU DAUZAC Margaux 1987 Rel: $15 Cur: $15 (6/30/89) (BT)
70+ CHATEAU DAUZAC Margaux 1987 Rel: $15 Cur: $15 (6/30/88) (BT)
70+ CHATEAU DAUZAC Margaux 1986 Cur: $20 (6/30/88) (BT)
70+ CHATEAU DAUZAC Margaux 1986 Cur: $20 (5/15/87) (BT)
87 CHATEAU DAUZAC Margaux 1985 Rel: $21 Cur: $21 (9/30/88)
80+ CHATEAU DAUZAC Margaux 1985 Rel: $21 Cur: $21 (5/15/87) (BT)
80+ CHATEAU DESMIRAIL Margaux 1988 $25 (6/30/89) (BT)
70+ CHATEAU DESMIRAIL Margaux 1987 $18 (6/30/89) (BT)
90 CHATEAU DESMIRAIL Margaux 1986 Rel: $22 Cur: $22 (6/30/89)
70+ CHATEAU DESMIRAIL Margaux 1986 Rel: $22 Cur: $22 (5/15/87) (BT)
80+ CHATEAU DESMIRAIL Margaux 1985 Rel: $20 Cur: $20 (5/15/87) (BT)
75+ CHATEAU DURFORT-VIVENS Margaux 1988 $40 (6/30/89) (BT)
75+ CHATEAU DURFORT-VIVENS Margaux 1987 Rel: $24 Cur: $24 (6/30/89) (BT)
75+ CHATEAU DURFORT-VIVENS Margaux 1987 Rel: $24 Cur: $24 (6/30/88) (BT)
90 CHATEAU DURFORT-VIVENS Margaux 1986 Rel: $25 Cur: $25 (6/15/89)
85+ CHATEAU DURFORT-VIVENS Margaux 1986 Rel: $25 Cur: $25 (6/30/88) (BT)
80+ CHATEAU DURFORT-VIVENS Margaux 1986 Rel: $25 Cur: $25 (5/15/87) (BT)
80+ CHATEAU DURFORT-VIVENS Margaux 1985 Rel: $20 Cur: $20 (5/15/87) (BT)
85+ CHATEAU GISCOURS Margaux 1990 (NR) (4/30/91) (BT)
85+ CHATEAU GISCOURS Margaux 1989 (NR) (4/30/91) (BT)
85+ CHATEAU GISCOURS Margaux 1989 (NR) (4/30/90) (BT)
89 CHATEAU GISCOURS Margaux 1988 $30 (4/30/91)
80+ CHATEAU GISCOURS Margaux 1988 $30 (6/30/89) (BT)
75+ CHATEAU GISCOURS Margaux 1987 Rel: $20 Cur: $20 (6/30/89) (BT)
80+ CHATEAU GISCOURS Margaux 1987 Rel: $20 Cur: $20 (6/30/88) (BT)
83 CHATEAU GISCOURS Margaux 1986 Rel: $30 Cur: $30 (6/15/89)
90+ CHATEAU GISCOURS Margaux 1986 Rel: $30 Cur: $30 (6/30/88) (BT)
70+ CHATEAU GISCOURS Margaux 1986 Rel: $30 Cur: $30 (5/15/87) (BT)
86 CHATEAU GISCOURS Margaux 1985 Rel: $35 Cur: $35 (9/30/88)
70+ CHATEAU GISCOURS Margaux 1985 Rel: $35 Cur: $35 (5/15/87) (BT)
80+ CHATEAU GISCOURS Margaux 1985 Rel: $35 Cur: $35 (4/16/86) (BT)
78 CHATEAU GISCOURS Margaux 1983 Cur: $26 (5/01/89)
88 CHATEAU GISCOURS Margaux 1982 Rel: $26 Cur: $34 (12/01/85)
82 CHATEAU GISCOURS Margaux 1981 Rel: $12.50 Cur: $40 (6/01/84)
80 CHATEAU GISCOURS Margaux 1980 Cur: $23 (2/16/84)
87 CHATEAU GISCOURS Margaux 1979 Cur: $34 (10/15/89) (JS)
88 CHATEAU GISCOURS Margaux 1979 Cur: $34 (2/16/84)
87 CHATEAU GISCOURS Margaux 1978 Cur: $59 (2/16/84)
83 CHATEAU GISCOURS Margaux 1976 Cur: $45 (2/16/84)
81 CHATEAU GISCOURS Margaux 1970 Cur: $73 (2/16/84)
89 CHATEAU GISCOURS Margaux 1964 Cur: $116/1.5L (2/16/84)
68 CHATEAU GISCOURS Margaux 1962 Cur: $33 (11/30/87) (JS)
78 CHATEAU GISCOURS Margaux 1961 Cur: $100 (3/16/86) (JL)
90+ CHATEAU LA GURGUE Margaux 1989 (NR) (4/30/90) (BT)
90 CHATEAU LA GURGUE Margaux 1988 $29 (4/30/91)
75+ CHATEAU LA GURGUE Margaux 1988 $29 (8/31/90) (BT)
75+ CHATEAU LA GURGUE Margaux 1988 $29 (6/30/89) (BT)
81 CHATEAU LA GURGUE Margaux 1987 Rel: $13 Cur: $13 (5/15/90)
82 CHATEAU LA GURGUE Margaux 1987 Rel: $13 Cur: $13 (11/30/89) (JS)
80+ CHATEAU LA GURGUE Margaux 1987 Rel: $13 Cur: $13 (6/30/89) (BT)
85 CHATEAU LA GURGUE Margaux 1986 Rel: $22 Cur: $23 (11/30/89) (JS)
86 CHATEAU LA GURGUE Margaux 1986 Rel: $22 Cur: $23 (6/15/89)
90 CHATEAU LA GURGUE Margaux 1985 Rel: $17 Cur: $17 (2/15/88)
90 CHATEAU LA GURGUE Margaux 1983 Rel: $9.75 Cur: $10 (1/01/86)
85 CHATEAU LA GURGUE Margaux 1982 Cur: $24 (11/30/89) (JS)
82 CHATEAU HAUT-BRETON-LARIGAUDIERE Margaux 1985 $16.50 (2/15/88)
90+ CHATEAU D'ISSAN Margaux 1990 (NR) (4/30/91) (BT)
85+ CHATEAU D'ISSAN Margaux 1989 (NR) (4/30/91) (BT)
80+ CHATEAU D'ISSAN Margaux 1989 (NR) (4/30/90) (BT)
88 CHATEAU D'ISSAN Margaux 1988 $30 (4/30/91)
90+ CHATEAU D'ISSAN Margaux 1988 $30 (8/31/90) (BT)
80+ CHATEAU D'ISSAN Margaux 1988 $30 (6/30/89) (BT)
76 CHATEAU D'ISSAN Margaux 1987 Rel: $20 Cur: $20 (5/15/90)
75+ CHATEAU D'ISSAN Margaux 1987 Rel: $20 Cur: $20 (6/30/89) (BT)
85+ CHATEAU D'ISSAN Margaux 1987 Rel: $20 Cur: $20 (6/30/88) (BT)
83 CHATEAU D'ISSAN Margaux 1986 Rel: $22 Cur: $23 (6/15/89)
90+ CHATEAU D'ISSAN Margaux 1986 Rel: $22 Cur: $23 (6/30/88) (BT)
70+ CHATEAU D'ISSAN Margaux 1986 Rel: $22 Cur: $23 (5/15/87) (BT)
88 CHATEAU D'ISSAN Margaux 1985 Rel: $23 Cur: $27 (4/15/88)
60+ CHATEAU D'ISSAN Margaux 1985 Rel: $23 Cur: $27 (5/15/87) (BT)
86 CHATEAU D'ISSAN Margaux 1984 Rel: $10 Cur: $19 (3/31/87)
91 CHATEAU D'ISSAN Margaux 1983 Rel: $24 Cur: $28 (4/16/86)
85+ CHATEAU KIRWAN Margaux 1990 (NR) (4/30/91) (BT)
75+ CHATEAU KIRWAN Margaux 1989 (NR) (4/30/91) (BT)
70+ CHATEAU KIRWAN Margaux 1989 (NR) (4/30/90) (BT)
87 CHATEAU KIRWAN Margaux 1988 $28 (4/30/91)
75+ CHATEAU KIRWAN Margaux 1988 $28 (6/30/89) (BT)
70+ CHATEAU KIRWAN Margaux 1987 Rel: $22 Cur: $22 (6/30/89) (BT)
80+ CHATEAU KIRWAN Margaux 1987 Rel: $22 Cur: $22 (6/30/88) (BT)
82 CHATEAU KIRWAN Margaux 1986 Rel: $25 Cur: $25 (6/30/89)
85+ CHATEAU KIRWAN Margaux 1986 Rel: $25 Cur: $25 (6/30/88) (BT)
70+ CHATEAU KIRWAN Margaux 1986 Rel: $25 Cur: $25 (5/15/87) (BT)
90 CHATEAU KIRWAN Margaux 1985 Rel: $29 Cur: $33 (2/15/89)
90+ CHATEAU KIRWAN Margaux 1985 Rel: $29 Cur: $33 (5/15/87) (BT)
86 CHATEAU KIRWAN Margaux 1983 Rel: $16 Cur: $22 (7/16/86)
88 CHATEAU KIRWAN Margaux 1945 Cur: $150 (3/16/86) (JL)
77 CHATEAU LABEGORCE Margaux 1987 $30 (3/31/91)
86 CHATEAU LABEGORCE Margaux 1986 $15 (2/15/90)
85+ CHATEAU LABEGORCE-ZEDE Margaux 1990 (NR) (4/30/91) (BT)
95+ CHATEAU LABEGORCE-ZEDE Margaux 1989 (NR) (4/30/91) (BT)
85+ CHATEAU LABEGORCE-ZEDE Margaux 1989 (NR) (4/30/90) (BT)
83 CHATEAU LABEGORCE-ZEDE Margaux 1988 $20 (4/30/91)
84 CHATEAU LABEGORCE-ZEDE Margaux 1987 Rel: $16 Cur: $16 (11/30/89) (JS)
91 CHATEAU LABEGORCE-ZEDE Margaux 1986 Rel: $18 Cur: $22 (11/30/89) (JS)
87 CHATEAU LABEGORCE-ZEDE Margaux 1986 Rel: $18 Cur: $22 (6/15/89)
84 CHATEAU LABEGORCE-ZEDE Margaux 1985 Rel: $13 Cur: $13 (2/29/88)
88 CHATEAU LABEGORCE-ZEDE Margaux 1983 Rel: $15 Cur: $15 (10/15/86)
87 CHATEAU LABEGORCE-ZEDE Margaux 1982 Cur: $18 (11/30/89) (JS)
75+ CHATEAU LAMOUROUX Margaux 1988 (NR) (6/30/89) (BT)
70+ CHATEAU LAMOUROUX Margaux 1987 (NR) (6/30/89) (BT)
80+ CHATEAU LASCOMBES Margaux 1989 (NR) (4/30/90) (BT)
85+ CHATEAU LASCOMBES Margaux 1988 $25 (6/30/89) (BT)
80+ CHATEAU LASCOMBES Margaux 1987 Rel: $24 Cur: $24 (6/30/89) (BT)
85+ CHATEAU LASCOMBES Margaux 1987 Rel: $24 Cur: $24 (6/30/88) (BT)
80+ CHATEAU LASCOMBES Margaux 1986 Cur: $24 (6/30/88) (BT)
70+ CHATEAU LASCOMBES Margaux 1986 Cur: $24 (5/15/87) (BT)
80+ CHATEAU LASCOMBES Margaux 1985 Rel: $20 Cur: $20 (5/15/87) (BT)
84 CHATEAU LASCOMBES Margaux 1983 Rel: $32 Cur: $32 (2/15/88)
85 CHATEAU LASCOMBES Margaux 1981 Rel: $19 Cur: $31 (5/16/85)
84 CHATEAU LASCOMBES Margaux 1979 Cur: $15 (10/15/89) (JS)
85+ CHATEAU MALESCOT-ST.-EXUPERY Margaux 1989 (NR) (4/30/90) (BT)
89 CHATEAU MALESCOT-ST.-EXUPERY Margaux 1988 $23 (4/30/91)
85+ CHATEAU MALESCOT-ST.-EXUPERY Margaux 1988 $23 (6/30/89) (BT)
70+ CHATEAU MALESCOT-ST.-EXUPERY Margaux 1987 Rel: $20 Cur: $20 (6/30/89) (BT)
88 CHATEAU MALESCOT-ST.-EXUPERY Margaux 1986 Rel: $26 Cur: $29 (6/15/89)
87 CHATEAU MALESCOT-ST.-EXUPERY Margaux 1985 Rel: $24 Cur: $24 (9/30/88)
82 CHATEAU MALESCOT-ST.-EXUPERY Margaux 1983 Rel: $16 Cur: $22 (9/30/86)
87 CHATEAU MALESCOT-ST.-EXUPERY Margaux 1981 Rel: $13 Cur: $22 (5/01/89)
65 CHATEAU MALESCOT-ST.-EXUPERY Margaux 1962 Cur: $80 (11/30/87) (JS)
66 CHATEAU MALESCOT-ST.-EXUPERY Margaux 1961 Cur: $135 (3/16/86) (JL)
87 CHATEAU MALESCOT-ST.-EXUPERY Margaux 1959 Cur: $150 (10/15/90) (JS)
81 CHATEAU MALESCOT-ST.-EXUPERY Margaux 1945 Cur: $200 (3/16/86) (JL)

FRANCE
BORDEAUX RED/MARGAUX

95+ CHATEAU MARGAUX Margaux 1990 (NR) (4/30/91) (BT)
95+ CHATEAU MARGAUX Margaux 1989 (NR) (4/30/91) (BT)
95+ CHATEAU MARGAUX Margaux 1989 (NR) (4/30/90) (BT)
97   CHATEAU MARGAUX Margaux 1988 $75 (3/31/91) CS
95+ CHATEAU MARGAUX Margaux 1988 $75 (8/31/90) (BT)
95+ CHATEAU MARGAUX Margaux 1988 $75 (6/30/89) (BT)
87   CHATEAU MARGAUX Margaux 1987 Rel: $55 Cur: $55 (5/15/90)
85+ CHATEAU MARGAUX Margaux 1987 Rel: $55 Cur: $55 (6/30/89) (BT)
85+ CHATEAU MARGAUX Margaux 1987 Rel: $55 Cur: $55 (6/30/88) (BT)
98   CHATEAU MARGAUX Margaux 1986 Rel: $80 Cur: $100 (12/15/89) (JS)
98   CHATEAU MARGAUX Margaux 1986 Rel: $80 Cur: $100 (6/15/89) CS
95+ CHATEAU MARGAUX Margaux 1986 Rel: $80 Cur: $100 (6/30/88) (BT)
90+ CHATEAU MARGAUX Margaux 1986 Rel: $80 Cur: $100 (5/15/87) (BT)
97   CHATEAU MARGAUX Margaux 1985 Rel: $76 Cur: $92 (12/15/89) (JS)
99   CHATEAU MARGAUX Margaux 1985 Rel: $76 Cur: $92 (4/30/88)
90+ CHATEAU MARGAUX Margaux 1985 Rel: $76 Cur: $92 (5/15/87) (BT)
91   CHATEAU MARGAUX Margaux 1984 Rel: $35 Cur: $62 (7/15/87) (HS)
93   CHATEAU MARGAUX Margaux 1984 Rel: $35 Cur: $62 (2/28/87) CS
92   CHATEAU MARGAUX Margaux 1983 Rel: $70 Cur: $100 (12/15/89) (JS)
99   CHATEAU MARGAUX Margaux 1983 Rel: $70 Cur: $100 (4/16/86) SS
98   CHATEAU MARGAUX Margaux 1982 Rel: $60 Cur: $138 (12/15/89) (JS)
96   CHATEAU MARGAUX Margaux 1982 Rel: $60 Cur: $138 (6/16/85) CS
97   CHATEAU MARGAUX Margaux 1981 Cur: $94 (7/15/87) (HS)
80   CHATEAU MARGAUX Margaux 1980 Rel: $30 Cur: $66 (7/15/87) (HS)
90   CHATEAU MARGAUX Margaux 1980 Rel: $30 Cur: $66 (5/01/84) CS
91   CHATEAU MARGAUX Margaux 1979 Cur: $118 (12/15/89) (JS)
93   CHATEAU MARGAUX Margaux 1979 Cur: $118 (10/15/89) (JS)
94   CHATEAU MARGAUX Margaux 1979 Cur: $118 (7/15/87) (HS)
92   CHATEAU MARGAUX Margaux 1978 Cur: $175 (12/15/89) (JS)
92   CHATEAU MARGAUX Margaux 1978 Cur: $175 (7/15/87) (HS)
75   CHATEAU MARGAUX Margaux 1977 Cur: $34 (7/15/87) (HS)
81   CHATEAU MARGAUX Margaux 1976 Cur: $90 (7/15/87) (HS)
88   CHATEAU MARGAUX Margaux 1975 Cur: $119 (7/15/87) (HS)
77   CHATEAU MARGAUX Margaux 1971 Cur: $76 (7/15/87) (HS)
70   CHATEAU MARGAUX Margaux 1970 Cur: $144 (7/15/87) (HS)
84   CHATEAU MARGAUX Margaux 1967 Cur: $58 (7/15/87) (HS)
90   CHATEAU MARGAUX Margaux 1966 Cur: $161 (7/15/87) (HS)
86   CHATEAU MARGAUX Margaux 1964 Cur: $115 (7/15/87) (HS)
86   CHATEAU MARGAUX Margaux 1962 Cur: $376/1.5 (12/15/89) (JS)
85   CHATEAU MARGAUX Margaux 1962 Cur: $179 (7/15/87) (HS)
98   CHATEAU MARGAUX Margaux 1961 Cur: $1,050/1.5L (12/15/89) (JS)
94   CHATEAU MARGAUX Margaux 1961 Cur: $500 (7/15/87) (HS)
93   CHATEAU MARGAUX Margaux 1959 Cur: $380 (10/15/90) (JS)
95   CHATEAU MARGAUX Margaux 1959 Cur: $380 (12/15/89) (JS)
95   CHATEAU MARGAUX Margaux 1959 Cur: $380 (7/15/87) (HS)
90   CHATEAU MARGAUX Margaux 1957 Cur: $200 (7/15/87) (HS)
79   CHATEAU MARGAUX Margaux 1955 Cur: $233 (7/15/87) (HS)
84   CHATEAU MARGAUX Margaux 1953 Cur: $410 (12/15/89) (HS)
94   CHATEAU MARGAUX Margaux 1953 Cur: $850/1.5L (7/15/87) (HS)
90   CHATEAU MARGAUX Margaux 1953 Cur: $410 (7/15/87) (HS)
85   CHATEAU MARGAUX Margaux 1952 Cur: $500/1.5L (7/15/87) (HS)
89   CHATEAU MARGAUX Margaux 1950 Cur: $600/1.5L (7/15/87) (HS)
95   CHATEAU MARGAUX Margaux 1949 Cur: $207 (7/15/87) (HS)
96   CHATEAU MARGAUX Margaux 1947 Cur: $360 (7/15/87) (HS)
90   CHATEAU MARGAUX Margaux 1945 Cur: $800 (3/16/86) (JL)
78   CHATEAU MARGAUX Margaux 1943 Cur: $320 (7/15/87) (HS)
82   CHATEAU MARGAUX Margaux 1937 Cur: $340 (7/15/87) (HS)
88   CHATEAU MARGAUX Margaux 1934 Cur: $272 (7/15/87) (HS)
83   CHATEAU MARGAUX Margaux 1929 Cur: $750 (7/15/87) (HS)
73   CHATEAU MARGAUX Margaux 1928 Cur: $830 (7/15/87) (HS)
84   CHATEAU MARGAUX Margaux 1928 Cur: $1,750/1.5L (7/15/87) (HS)
77   CHATEAU MARGAUX Margaux 1926 Cur: $300 (7/15/87) (HS)
73   CHATEAU MARGAUX Margaux 1924 Cur: $380 (7/15/87) (HS)
81   CHATEAU MARGAUX Margaux 1923 Cur: $330 (7/15/87) (HS)
79   CHATEAU MARGAUX Margaux 1920 Cur: $420 (7/15/87) (HS)
80   CHATEAU MARGAUX Margaux 1918 Cur: $500 (7/15/87) (HS)
62   CHATEAU MARGAUX Margaux 1917 Cur: $300 (7/15/87) (HS)
65   CHATEAU MARGAUX Margaux 1909 Cur: $480 (7/15/87) (HS)
85   CHATEAU MARGAUX Margaux 1908 Cur: $530 (7/15/87) (HS)
64   CHATEAU MARGAUX Margaux 1905 Cur: $300 (7/15/87) (HS)
93   CHATEAU MARGAUX Margaux 1900 Cur: $2,000 (7/15/87) (HS)
94   CHATEAU MARGAUX Margaux 1899 Cur: $1,700 (7/15/87) (HS)
75   CHATEAU MARGAUX Margaux 1898 Cur: $2,070 (7/15/87) (HS)
95   CHATEAU MARGAUX Margaux 1893 Cur: $2,000 (7/15/87) (HS)
80   CHATEAU MARGAUX Margaux 1892 Cur: $750 (7/15/87) (HS)
81   CHATEAU MARGAUX Margaux 1887 Cur: $760 (7/15/87) (HS)
100 CHATEAU MARGAUX Margaux 1875 $15,000/3L (12/15/88) (JS)
89   CHATEAU MARGAUX Margaux 1870 Cur: $3,300 (7/15/87) (HS)
69   CHATEAU MARGAUX Margaux 1868 Cur: $2,000 (7/15/87) (HS)
97   CHATEAU MARGAUX Margaux 1865 Cur: $5,000 (7/15/87) (HS)
98   CHATEAU MARGAUX Margaux 1864 Cur: $3,500 (7/15/87) (HS)
95   CHATEAU MARGAUX Margaux 1848 Cur: $10,000 (7/15/87) (HS)
96   CHATEAU MARGAUX Margaux 1847 Cur: $52,500/1.5L (7/15/87) (HS)
97   CHATEAU MARGAUX Margaux 1791 (NA) (7/15/87) (HS)

99   CHATEAU MARGAUX Margaux 1771 (NA) (7/15/87) (HS)
75+ CHATEAU MARQUIS D'ALESME BECKER Margaux 1988 $20 (6/30/89) (BT)
70+ CHATEAU MARQUIS D'ALESME BECKER Margaux 1987 Rel: $15 Cur: $15 (6/30/89) (BT)
84   CHATEAU MARQUIS D'ALESME BECKER Margaux 1985 Rel: $19 Cur: $30 (6/30/88)
69   CHATEAU MARQUIS D'ALESME BECKER Margaux 1984 Rel: $16.50 Cur: $17 (6/15/87)
84   CHATEAU MARQUIS D'ALESME BECKER Margaux 1983 Rel: $15 Cur: $15 (12/31/86)
92   CHATEAU MARQUIS DE TERME Margaux 1988 $23 (4/30/91)
80+ CHATEAU MARQUIS DE TERME Margaux 1988 $23 (6/30/89) (BT)
75+ CHATEAU MARQUIS DE TERME Margaux 1987 Rel: $20 Cur: $20 (6/30/89) (BT)
79   CHATEAU MARQUIS DE TERME Margaux 1986 Rel: $23 Cur: $25 (6/30/89)
75+ CHATEAU MARSAC-SEGUINEAU Margaux 1988 (NR) (6/30/89) (BT)
65+ CHATEAU MARSAC-SEGUINEAU Margaux 1987 Rel: $10 Cur: $10 (6/30/89) (BT)
68   CHATEAU MARSAC-SEGUINEAU Margaux 1983 Rel: $9 Cur: $9 (9/30/86)
90+ CHATEAU MONBRISON Margaux 1990 (NR) (4/30/91) (BT)
90+ CHATEAU MONBRISON Margaux 1989 (NR) (4/30/91) (BT)
90+ CHATEAU MONBRISON Margaux 1989 (NR) (4/30/90) (BT)
92   CHATEAU MONBRISON Margaux 1988 $20 (2/28/91)
90+ CHATEAU MONBRISON Margaux 1988 $20 (8/31/90) (BT)
85+ CHATEAU MONBRISON Margaux 1988 $20 (6/30/89) (BT)
85   CHATEAU MONBRISON Margaux 1987 Rel: $20 Cur: $20 (5/15/90)
86   CHATEAU MONBRISON Margaux 1987 Rel: $20 Cur: $20 (11/30/89) (JS)
80+ CHATEAU MONBRISON Margaux 1987 Rel: $20 Cur: $20 (6/30/89) (BT)
80+ CHATEAU MONBRISON Margaux 1987 Rel: $20 Cur: $20 (6/30/88) (BT)
92   CHATEAU MONBRISON Margaux 1986 Rel: $20 Cur: $20 (11/30/89) (JS)
85+ CHATEAU MONBRISON Margaux 1986 Rel: $20 Cur: $20 (6/30/88) (BT)
78   CHATEAU MONBRISON Margaux 1984 Rel: $15 Cur: $15 (5/15/87)
90   CHATEAU MONBRISON Margaux 1982 Rel: $14 Cur: $20 (11/30/89) (JS)
90+ CHATEAU PALMER Margaux 1990 (NR) (4/30/91) (BT)
90+ CHATEAU PALMER Margaux 1989 (NR) (4/30/91) (BT)
90+ CHATEAU PALMER Margaux 1989 (NR) (4/30/90) (BT)
96   CHATEAU PALMER Margaux 1988 $65 (2/28/91) CS
90+ CHATEAU PALMER Margaux 1988 $65 (8/31/90) (BT)
90+ CHATEAU PALMER Margaux 1988 $65 (6/30/89) (BT)
84   CHATEAU PALMER Margaux 1987 Rel: $28 Cur: $29 (5/15/90)
85+ CHATEAU PALMER Margaux 1987 Rel: $28 Cur: $29 (6/30/89) (BT)
85+ CHATEAU PALMER Margaux 1987 Rel: $28 Cur: $29 (6/30/88) (BT)
94   CHATEAU PALMER Margaux 1986 Rel: $40 Cur: $53 (6/15/89)
90   CHATEAU PALMER Margaux 1985 Rel: $40 Cur: $55 (4/15/88)
84   CHATEAU PALMER Margaux 1984 Rel: $41 Cur: $41 (10/15/87)
90   CHATEAU PALMER Margaux 1983 Rel: $45 Cur: $77 (7/16/86) CS
95   CHATEAU PALMER Margaux 1982 Cur: $65 (5/01/85)
90   CHATEAU PALMER Margaux 1981 Rel: $24.50 Cur: $50 (5/01/85)
86   CHATEAU PALMER Margaux 1981 Rel: $24.50 Cur: $50 (5/15/84)
86   CHATEAU PALMER Margaux 1980 Cur: $23 (5/01/85)
90   CHATEAU PALMER Margaux 1979 Cur: $67 (10/15/89) (JS)
87   CHATEAU PALMER Margaux 1979 Cur: $67 (5/01/85)
81   CHATEAU PALMER Margaux 1978 Rel: $35 Cur: $91 (5/01/85)
80   CHATEAU PALMER Margaux 1962 Cur: $150 (11/30/87) (JS)
93   CHATEAU PALMER Margaux 1961 Cur: $480 (3/16/86) (JL)
98   CHATEAU PALMER Margaux 1959 Cur: $247 (10/15/90) (JS)
90   CHATEAU PALMER Margaux 1945 Cur: $400 (3/16/86) (JL)
85+ PAVILLON ROUGE DU CHATEAU MARGAUX Margaux 1990 (NR) (4/30/91) (BT)
88   PAVILLON ROUGE DU CHATEAU MARGAUX Margaux 1988 $30 (4/30/91)
79   PAVILLON ROUGE DU CHATEAU MARGAUX Margaux 1987 Rel: $19 Cur: $21 (5/15/90)
84   PAVILLON ROUGE DU CHATEAU MARGAUX Margaux 1986 Rel: $24 Cur: $30 (6/30/89)
93   PAVILLON ROUGE DU CHATEAU MARGAUX Margaux 1985 Rel: $23 Cur: $26 (4/15/88) SS
80   PAVILLON ROUGE DU CHATEAU MARGAUX Margaux 1983 Rel: $25 Cur: $26 (6/30/87)
85   PAVILLON ROUGE DU CHATEAU MARGAUX Margaux 1982 Cur: $28 (7/15/87) (HS)
87   PAVILLON ROUGE DU CHATEAU MARGAUX Margaux 1981 Cur: $25 (7/15/87) (HS)
76   PAVILLON ROUGE DU CHATEAU MARGAUX Margaux 1980 Cur: $20 (7/15/87) (HS)
78   PAVILLON ROUGE DU CHATEAU MARGAUX Margaux 1979 Cur: $34 (7/15/87) (HS)
63   PAVILLON ROUGE DU CHATEAU MARGAUX Margaux 1916 (NA) (7/15/87) (HS)
85+ CHATEAU POUGET Margaux 1988 $18 (6/30/89) (BT)
70+ CHATEAU POUGET Margaux 1987 Rel: $15 Cur: $15 (6/30/89) (BT)
70+ CHATEAU POUGET Margaux 1986 Rel: $16 Cur: $16 (5/15/87) (BT)
70+ CHATEAU POUGET Margaux 1985 Rel: $14 Cur: $17 (5/15/87) (BT)
86   CHATEAU POUGET Margaux 1983 Rel: $11.25 Cur: $19 (2/15/87)
85+ CHATEAU PRIEURE-LICHINE Margaux 1990 (NR) (4/30/91) (BT)
85+ CHATEAU PRIEURE-LICHINE Margaux 1989 (NR) (4/30/91) (BT)
85+ CHATEAU PRIEURE-LICHINE Margaux 1989 (NR) (4/30/90) (BT)
90   CHATEAU PRIEURE-LICHINE Margaux 1988 $30 (4/30/91)
90+ CHATEAU PRIEURE-LICHINE Margaux 1988 $30 (8/31/90) (BT)
80+ CHATEAU PRIEURE-LICHINE Margaux 1988 $30 (6/30/89) (BT)
78   CHATEAU PRIEURE-LICHINE Margaux 1987 Rel: $13.50 Cur: $17 (2/15/90)
70+ CHATEAU PRIEURE-LICHINE Margaux 1987 Rel: $13.50 Cur: $17 (6/30/89) (BT)
80+ CHATEAU PRIEURE-LICHINE Margaux 1987 Rel: $13.50 Cur: $17 (6/30/88) (BT)
92   CHATEAU PRIEURE-LICHINE Margaux 1986 Rel: $21 Cur: $23 (6/15/89)
85+ CHATEAU PRIEURE-LICHINE Margaux 1986 Rel: $21 Cur: $23 (6/30/88) (BT)
90+ CHATEAU PRIEURE-LICHINE Margaux 1986 Rel: $21 Cur: $23 (5/15/87) (BT)
82   CHATEAU PRIEURE-LICHINE Margaux 1985 Rel: $24 Cur: $24 (2/15/88)
80+ CHATEAU PRIEURE-LICHINE Margaux 1985 Rel: $24 Cur: $24 (5/15/87) (BT)
70+ CHATEAU PRIEURE-LICHINE Margaux 1985 Rel: $24 Cur: $24 (4/16/86) (BT)
80   CHATEAU PRIEURE-LICHINE Margaux 1984 Rel: $14 Cur: $15 (11/30/86)
96   CHATEAU PRIEURE-LICHINE Margaux 1983 Rel: $18 Cur: $26 (4/16/86)
89   CHATEAU PRIEURE-LICHINE Margaux 1982 Rel: $15 Cur: $27 (5/01/85)
86   CHATEAU PRIEURE-LICHINE Margaux 1981 Rel: $12 Cur: $24 (11/01/84)
80   CHATEAU PRIEURE-LICHINE Margaux 1959 Cur: $50 (10/15/90) (JS)
85+ CHATEAU RAUSAN-SEGLA Margaux 1990 (NR) (4/30/91) (BT)
90+ CHATEAU RAUSAN-SEGLA Margaux 1989 (NR) (4/30/91) (BT)
90+ CHATEAU RAUSAN-SEGLA Margaux 1989 (NR) (4/30/90) (BT)
92   CHATEAU RAUSAN-SEGLA Margaux 1988 $40 (3/15/91)
85+ CHATEAU RAUSAN-SEGLA Margaux 1988 $40 (6/30/89) (BT)
87   CHATEAU RAUSAN-SEGLA Margaux 1986 Rel: $28 Cur: $38 (9/15/89)

85+ CHATEAU RAUSAN-SEGLA Margaux 1986 Rel: $28 Cur: $38 (6/30/88) (BT)
80+ CHATEAU RAUSAN-SEGLA Margaux 1986 Rel: $28 Cur: $38 (5/15/87) (BT)
92 CHATEAU RAUSAN-SEGLA Margaux 1985 Rel: $24 Cur: $24 (5/31/88)
80+ CHATEAU RAUSAN-SEGLA Margaux 1985 Rel: $24 Cur: $24 (5/15/87) (BT)
86 CHATEAU RAUSAN-SEGLA Margaux 1981 Rel: $16 Cur: $23 (10/16/84)
90 CHATEAU RAUSAN-SEGLA Margaux 1981 Rel: $16 Cur: $23 (5/01/84)
69 CHATEAU RAUSAN-SEGLA Margaux 1979 Cur: $28 (10/15/89) (JS)
63 CHATEAU RAUSAN-SEGLA Margaux 1961 Cur: $146 (3/16/86) (JL)
73 CHATEAU RAUSAN-SEGLA Margaux 1945 Cur: $150 (3/16/86) (JL)
80+ CHATEAU RAUZAN-GASSIES Margaux 1990 (NR) (4/30/91) (BT)
80+ CHATEAU RAUZAN-GASSIES Margaux 1989 (NR) (4/30/91) (BT)
70+ CHATEAU RAUZAN-GASSIES Margaux 1987 Rel: $20 Cur: $20 (6/30/88) (BT)
88 CHATEAU RAUZAN-GASSIES Margaux 1986 Rel: $24 Cur: $25 (6/30/89)
70+ CHATEAU RAUZAN-GASSIES Margaux 1986 Rel: $24 Cur: $25 (6/30/88) (BT)
73 CHATEAU RAUZAN-GASSIES Margaux 1959 Cur: $93 (10/15/90) (JS)
91 CHATEAU RAUZAN-GASSIES Margaux 1945 Cur: $300 (3/16/86) (JL)
78 CHATEAU RICHETERRE Margaux 1986 $12.50 (2/15/89)
75+ CHATEAU SEGONNES Margaux 1988 $18 (6/30/89) (BT)
70+ CHATEAU SEGONNES Margaux 1987 Rel: $15 Cur: $15 (6/30/89) (BT)
85+ CHATEAU SIRAN Margaux 1990 (NR) (4/30/91) (BT)
90+ CHATEAU SIRAN Margaux 1989 (NR) (4/30/91) (BT)
90+ CHATEAU SIRAN Margaux 1989 (NR) (4/30/90) (BT)
88 CHATEAU SIRAN Margaux 1988 $19 (6/30/91)
85+ CHATEAU SIRAN Margaux 1988 $19 (8/31/90) (BT)
75+ CHATEAU SIRAN Margaux 1988 $19 (6/30/89) (BT)
75+ CHATEAU SIRAN Margaux 1987 $14 (6/30/89) (BT)
90 CHATEAU SIRAN Margaux 1985 $15.50 (9/30/88)
85+ CHATEAU DU TERTRE Margaux 1990 (NR) (4/30/91) (BT)
85+ CHATEAU DU TERTRE Margaux 1989 (NR) (4/30/91) (BT)
85+ CHATEAU DU TERTRE Margaux 1989 (NR) (4/30/90) (BT)
86 CHATEAU DU TERTRE Margaux 1988 $40 (6/30/91)
90+ CHATEAU DU TERTRE Margaux 1988 $40 (6/30/89) (BT)
70+ CHATEAU DU TERTRE Margaux 1987 Rel: $18 Cur: $18 (6/30/89) (BT)
70+ CHATEAU DU TERTRE Margaux 1987 Rel: $18 Cur: $18 (6/30/88) (BT)
89 CHATEAU DU TERTRE Margaux 1986 Rel: $22 Cur: $22 (6/15/89)
80+ CHATEAU DU TERTRE Margaux 1986 Rel: $22 Cur: $22 (6/30/88) (BT)
80+ CHATEAU DU TERTRE Margaux 1986 Rel: $22 Cur: $22 (5/15/87) (BT)
93 CHATEAU DU TERTRE Margaux 1985 Rel: $14 Cur: $23 (6/30/88) SS
80+ CHATEAU DU TERTRE Margaux 1985 Rel: $14 Cur: $23 (5/15/87) (BT)
91 CHATEAU DU TERTRE Margaux 1983 Rel: $14.25 Cur: $30 (7/16/86)
80+ CHATEAU LA TOUR DE MONS Margaux 1989 (NR) (4/30/91) (BT)
90 CHATEAU LA TOUR DE MONS Margaux 1986 $19 (11/30/89) (JS)
90 CHATEAU LA TOUR DE MONS Margaux 1986 $19 (6/15/89)
90 CHATEAU LA TOUR DE MONS Margaux 1982 Cur: $16 (11/30/89) (JS)
89 CHATEAU LA TOUR DE MONS Margaux 1945 Cur: $200 (3/16/86) (JL)

MÉDOC

79 CHATEAU BELLERIVE Médoc 1986 $4.50 (2/15/89)
84 CHATEAU LE BOSCQ Médoc 1988 $20 (4/30/91)
75 CHATEAU LE BOSCQ Médoc 1986 $10 (6/30/89)
70 CHATEAU LE BOSCQ Médoc 1983 $8 (1/01/86)
76 CHATEAU LE BOSCQ Médoc 1982 $6 (10/01/85) BB
80+ CHATEAU LA CARDONNE Médoc 1989 (NR) (4/30/91) (BT)
70+ CHATEAU LA CARDONNE Médoc 1987 Rel: $10 Cur: $10 (6/30/88) (BT)
84 CHATEAU LA CARDONNE Médoc 1986 Rel: $10 Cur: $10 (2/15/90)
75+ CHATEAU LA CARDONNE Médoc 1986 Rel: $10 Cur: $10 (6/30/88) (BT)
83 CHATEAU LA CARDONNE Médoc 1985 Rel: $9 Cur: $9 (12/31/88)
79 CHATEAU LA CARDONNE Médoc 1983 Rel: $7 Cur: $7 (10/15/86)
75+ CHATEAU LA CROIX-LANDON Médoc 1988 (NR) (6/30/89) (BT)
80+ CHATEAU GREYSAC Médoc 1990 (NR) (4/30/91) (BT)
85+ CHATEAU GREYSAC Médoc 1989 (NR) (4/30/91) (BT)
75+ CHATEAU GREYSAC Médoc 1989 (NR) (4/30/90) (BT)
87 CHATEAU GREYSAC Médoc 1988 $15 (4/30/91)
75+ CHATEAU GREYSAC Médoc 1988 $15 (6/30/89) (BT)
75+ CHATEAU GREYSAC Médoc 1987 Rel: $9 Cur: $9 (6/30/89) (BT)
85 CHATEAU GREYSAC Médoc 1986 Rel: $10 Cur: $10 (11/30/89) (JS)
60+ CHATEAU GREYSAC Médoc 1986 Rel: $10 Cur: $10 (5/15/87) (BT)
77 CHATEAU GREYSAC Médoc 1985 Rel: $9 Cur: $9 (12/31/88)
65 CHATEAU GREYSAC Médoc 1983 Rel: $8.50 Cur: $9 (7/31/87)
80 CHATEAU GREYSAC Médoc 1982 Rel: $8 Cur: $10 (11/30/89) (JS)
77 CHATEAU GREYSAC Médoc 1981 Rel: $8 Cur: $8 (6/01/84)
85+ CHATEAU LOUDENNE Médoc 1989 (NR) (4/30/91) (BT)
75 CHATEAU LOUDENNE Médoc 1987 Rel: $10 Cur: $10 (11/30/89) (JS)
74 CHATEAU LOUDENNE Médoc 1986 Rel: $12 Cur: $12 (11/30/89) (JS)
75 CHATEAU LOUDENNE Médoc 1985 Rel: $13.50 Cur: $14 (11/30/88)
74 CHATEAU LOUDENNE Médoc 1982 Rel: $10 Cur: $12 (11/30/89) (JS)
84 CHATEAU LOUDENNE Médoc 1981 Rel: $10.75 Cur: $11 (9/01/84)
84 CHATEAU LES ORMES SORBET Médoc 1988 $20 (4/30/91)
75+ CHATEAU LES ORMES SORBET Médoc 1988 $20 (6/30/89) (BT)
75+ CHATEAU LES ORMES SORBET Médoc 1987 Rel: $14 Cur: $14 (6/30/89) (BT)
80 CHATEAU PATACHE D'AUX Médoc 1988 $10 (4/30/91)
83 CHATEAU PATACHE D'AUX Médoc 1982 Rel: $5 Cur: $18 (5/01/85)
85+ CHATEAU PLAGNAC Médoc 1989 (NR) (4/30/91) (BT)
79 CHATEAU PLAGNAC Médoc 1988 $8.50 (4/30/91)
77 CHATEAU PLAGNAC Médoc 1987 $8 (11/30/89) (JS)
82 CHATEAU PLAGNAC Médoc 1986 $9 (11/30/89) (JS)
79 CHATEAU PLAGNAC Médoc 1986 $9 (6/30/89)
70+ CHATEAU PLAGNAC Médoc 1986 $9 (5/15/87) (BT)
68 CHATEAU PLAGNAC Médoc 1985 $9 (8/31/88)
72 CHATEAU POTENSAC Médoc 1987 Rel: $9.50 Cur: $12 (5/15/90)
70+ CHATEAU POTENSAC Médoc 1987 Rel: $9.50 Cur: $12 (6/30/88) (BT)
86 CHATEAU POTENSAC Médoc 1986 Rel: $15 Cur: $15 (11/30/89) (JS)
80+ CHATEAU POTENSAC Médoc 1986 Rel: $15 Cur: $15 (6/30/88) (BT)
70+ CHATEAU POTENSAC Médoc 1986 Rel: $15 Cur: $15 (5/15/87) (BT)
80+ CHATEAU POTENSAC Médoc 1985 Rel: $11 Cur: $16 (5/15/87) (BT)
75 CHATEAU POTENSAC Médoc 1983 Rel: $9 Cur: $15 (10/15/86)
63 CHATEAU ROQUEGRAVE Médoc 1983 $6 (4/01/86)
79 CHATEAU ST.-BONNET Médoc 1985 $9 (4/15/88)
77 CHATEAU ST.-BONNET Médoc 1985 $9 (2/15/88)

82 CHATEAU ST.-CHRISTOPHE Médoc 1985 $6.50 (7/31/88) BB
70 CHATEAU ST.-SEVE Médoc 1985 $6 (11/15/87)
72 ALFRED SCHYLER Médoc 1985 $8.50 (6/30/88)
75+ CHATEAU LA TOUR DE BY Médoc 1989 (NR) (4/30/91) (BT)
86 CHATEAU LA TOUR DE BY Médoc 1988 $12.50 (6/15/91)
75+ CHATEAU LA TOUR DE BY Médoc 1988 $12.50 (6/30/89) (BT)
79 CHATEAU LA TOUR DE BY Médoc 1987 Rel: $10 Cur: $10 (11/30/89) (JS)
70+ CHATEAU LA TOUR DE BY Médoc 1987 Rel: $10 Cur: $10 (6/30/89) (BT)
70+ CHATEAU LA TOUR DE BY Médoc 1987 Rel: $10 Cur: $10 (6/30/88) (BT)
80 CHATEAU LA TOUR DE BY Médoc 1986 Rel: $12 Cur: $12 (11/30/89) (JS)
84 CHATEAU LA TOUR DE BY Médoc 1986 Rel: $12 Cur: $12 (2/15/89)
80+ CHATEAU LA TOUR DE BY Médoc 1986 Rel: $12 Cur: $12 (6/30/88) (BT)
78 CHATEAU LA TOUR DE BY Médoc 1983 Rel: $7 Cur: $7 (10/16/85)
80 CHATEAU LA TOUR DE BY Médoc 1982 Rel: $5.50 Cur: $10 (11/30/89) (JS)
86 CHATEAU LA TOUR DE BY Médoc 1982 Rel: $5.50 Cur: $10 (2/01/85) BB
80+ CHATEAU LA TOUR-HAUT-CAUSSAN Médoc 1989 (NR) (4/30/91) (BT)
79 CHATEAU LA TOUR-HAUT-CAUSSAN Médoc 1988 $12.50 (7/15/91)
80+ CHATEAU LA TOUR-HAUT-CAUSSAN Médoc 1988 $12.50 (6/30/89) (BT)
80 CHATEAU LA TOUR-HAUT-CAUSSAN Médoc 1987 Rel: $11 Cur: $11 (11/30/89) (JS)
80+ CHATEAU LA TOUR-HAUT-CAUSSAN Médoc 1987 Rel: $11 Cur: $11 (6/30/89) (BT)
88 CHATEAU LA TOUR-HAUT-CAUSSAN Médoc 1986 Rel: $14 Cur: $14 (11/30/89) (JS)
80 CHATEAU LA TOUR-HAUT-CAUSSAN Médoc 1984 Rel: $10 Cur: $10 (2/15/88)
83 CHATEAU LA TOUR-HAUT-CAUSSAN Médoc 1982 Cur: $10 (11/30/89) (JS)
83 CHATEAU LA TOUR-ST.-BONNET Médoc 1985 $9 (6/30/88)

MOULIS

80+ CHATEAU BRILLETTE Moulis 1988 $15 (6/30/89) (BT)
72 CHATEAU BRILLETTE Moulis 1987 $15 (11/30/89) (JS)
75+ CHATEAU BRILLETTE Moulis 1987 $15 (6/30/89) (BT)
78 CHATEAU BRILLETTE Moulis 1986 $14 (11/30/89) (JS)
78 CHATEAU BRILLETTE Moulis 1986 $14 (6/30/89)
85 CHATEAU BRILLETTE Moulis 1982 Cur: $18 (11/30/89) (JS)
85+ CHATEAU CHASSE-SPLEEN Moulis 1990 (NR) (4/30/91) (BT)
90+ CHATEAU CHASSE-SPLEEN Moulis 1989 (NR) (4/30/91) (BT)
90+ CHATEAU CHASSE-SPLEEN Moulis 1989 (NR) (4/30/90) (BT)
89 CHATEAU CHASSE-SPLEEN Moulis 1988 $26 (3/31/91)
85+ CHATEAU CHASSE-SPLEEN Moulis 1988 $26 (8/31/90) (BT)
85+ CHATEAU CHASSE-SPLEEN Moulis 1988 $26 (6/30/89) (BT)
78 CHATEAU CHASSE-SPLEEN Moulis 1987 Rel: $15 Cur: $16 (2/15/90)
82 CHATEAU CHASSE-SPLEEN Moulis 1987 Rel: $15 Cur: $16 (11/30/89) (JS)
80+ CHATEAU CHASSE-SPLEEN Moulis 1987 Rel: $15 Cur: $16 (6/30/89) (BT)
85+ CHATEAU CHASSE-SPLEEN Moulis 1987 Rel: $15 Cur: $16 (6/30/88) (BT)
90 CHATEAU CHASSE-SPLEEN Moulis 1986 Rel: $26 Cur: $26 (11/30/89) (JS)
85 CHATEAU CHASSE-SPLEEN Moulis 1986 Rel: $26 Cur: $26 (6/30/89)
90+ CHATEAU CHASSE-SPLEEN Moulis 1986 Rel: $26 Cur: $26 (6/30/88) (BT)
86 CHATEAU CHASSE-SPLEEN Moulis 1985 Rel: $22 Cur: $28 (5/15/88)
74 CHATEAU CHASSE-SPLEEN Moulis 1984 Rel: $13 Cur: $15 (6/15/87)
87 CHATEAU CHASSE-SPLEEN Moulis 1983 Rel: $16.50 Cur: $23 (4/16/86)
90 CHATEAU CHASSE-SPLEEN Moulis 1982 Rel: $14.75 Cur: $36 (11/30/89) (JS)
90 CHATEAU CHASSE-SPLEEN Moulis 1982 Rel: $14.75 Cur: $36 (2/16/85)
71 CHATEAU DUPLESSIS-FABRE Moulis 1987 $7 (11/30/89) (JS)
74 CHATEAU DUPLESSIS-FABRE Moulis 1986 $7 (11/30/89) (JS)
79 CHATEAU DUPLESSIS-FABRE Moulis 1982 Cur: $10 (11/30/89) (JS)
82 CHATEAU MAUCAILLOU Moulis 1988 $14 (7/31/91)
80+ CHATEAU MAUCAILLOU Moulis 1988 $14 (6/30/89) (BT)
70+ CHATEAU MAUCAILLOU Moulis 1987 Rel: $14 Cur: $14 (6/30/89) (BT)
80+ CHATEAU MAUCAILLOU Moulis 1987 Rel: $14 Cur: $14 (6/30/88) (BT)
85+ CHATEAU MAUCAILLOU Moulis 1986 Rel: $18 Cur: $18 (6/30/88) (BT)
88 CHATEAU MAUCAILLOU Moulis 1985 Rel: $18 Cur: $18 (8/31/88)
87 CHATEAU MAUCAILLOU Moulis 1983 Rel: $16 Cur: $16 (3/15/87)
90 CHATEAU MAUCAILLOU Moulis 1982 Rel: $15 Cur: $25 (11/30/89) (JS)
90 CHATEAU MAUCAILLOU Moulis 1982 Rel: $15 Cur: $25 (4/16/86)
88 CHATEAU MAUCAILLOU Moulis 1981 Rel: $12 Cur: $14 (10/01/85)
81 CHATEAU LA MOULINE Moulis 1988 $20 (2/15/91)
85+ CHATEAU POUJEAUX Moulis 1990 (NR) (4/30/91) (BT)
90+ CHATEAU POUJEAUX Moulis 1989 (NR) (4/30/91) (BT)
85+ CHATEAU POUJEAUX Moulis 1989 (NR) (4/30/90) (BT)
88 CHATEAU POUJEAUX Moulis 1988 $15 (2/28/91)
80+ CHATEAU POUJEAUX Moulis 1988 $15 (6/30/89) (BT)
74 CHATEAU POUJEAUX Moulis 1987 Rel: $15 Cur: $15 (5/15/90)
81 CHATEAU POUJEAUX Moulis 1987 Rel: $15 Cur: $15 (11/30/89) (JS)
80+ CHATEAU POUJEAUX Moulis 1987 Rel: $15 Cur: $15 (6/30/89) (BT)
80+ CHATEAU POUJEAUX Moulis 1987 Rel: $15 Cur: $15 (6/30/88) (BT)
88 CHATEAU POUJEAUX Moulis 1986 Rel: $22 Cur: $22 (11/30/89) (JS)
83 CHATEAU POUJEAUX Moulis 1986 Rel: $22 Cur: $22 (6/30/89)
85+ CHATEAU POUJEAUX Moulis 1986 Rel: $22 Cur: $22 (6/30/88) (BT)
70+ CHATEAU POUJEAUX Moulis 1986 Rel: $22 Cur: $22 (5/15/87) (BT)
87 CHATEAU POUJEAUX Moulis 1985 Rel: $18.50 Cur: $19 (9/30/88)
79 CHATEAU POUJEAUX Moulis 1983 Rel: $13 Cur: $19 (10/31/86)
88 CHATEAU POUJEAUX Moulis 1982 Cur: $23 (11/30/89) (JS)

PAUILLAC

81 DOMAINES BARONS DE ROTHSCHILD Pauillac Réserve Spéciale 1987 $12 (12/31/90)
85 DOMAINES BARONS DE ROTHSCHILD Pauillac Réserve Spéciale NV $12 (2/15/90)
85+ CHATEAU BATAILLEY Pauillac 1990 (NR) (4/30/91) (BT)
85+ CHATEAU BATAILLEY Pauillac 1989 (NR) (4/30/91) (BT)
85+ CHATEAU BATAILLEY Pauillac 1989 (NR) (4/30/90) (BT)
90 CHATEAU BATAILLEY Pauillac 1988 $23 (4/30/91)
85+ CHATEAU BATAILLEY Pauillac 1988 $23 (6/30/89) (BT)
75+ CHATEAU BATAILLEY Pauillac 1987 Rel: $18 Cur: $18 (6/30/89) (BT)
75+ CHATEAU BATAILLEY Pauillac 1987 Rel: $18 Cur: $18 (6/30/88) (BT)
80+ CHATEAU BATAILLEY Pauillac 1986 Cur: $36 (6/30/88) (BT)
84 CHATEAU BATAILLEY Pauillac 1961 Cur: $127 (3/16/86) (JL)
87 CHATEAU BATAILLEY Pauillac 1945 Cur: $300 (3/16/86) (JL)
80+ CHATEAU BERNADOTTE Pauillac 1988 $20 (6/30/89) (BT)
79 CHATEAU BERNADOTTE Pauillac 1987 $20 (11/30/89) (JS)
75+ CHATEAU BERNADOTTE Pauillac 1987 $20 (6/30/89) (BT)
92 CHATEAU BERNADOTTE Pauillac 1986 $20 (11/30/89) (JS)
89 CHATEAU BERNADOTTE Pauillac 1985 $19 (3/31/88)
90 CHATEAU BERNADOTTE Pauillac 1983 $14.50 (2/15/87)

FRANCE
BORDEAUX RED/*PAUILLAC*

80+ CARRUADES DE LAFITE Pauillac 1990 (NR) (4/30/91) (BT)
85+ CARRUADES DE LAFITE Pauillac 1989 (NR) (4/30/91) (BT)
85+ CARRUADES DE LAFITE Pauillac 1989 (NR) (4/30/90) (BT)
80+ CARRUADES DE LAFITE Pauillac 1988 $19 (8/31/90) (BT)
75+ CARRUADES DE LAFITE Pauillac 1987 Cur: $19 (6/30/89) (BT)
70+ CARRUADES DE LAFITE Pauillac 1986 Cur: $30 (5/15/87) (BT)
82 CARRUADES DE LAFITE Pauillac 1967 Cur: $37 (11/30/87)
81 CARRUADES DE LAFITE Pauillac 1964 Cur: $45 (11/30/87)
75 CARRUADES DE LAFITE Pauillac 1962 Cur: $76 (11/30/87) (JS)
84 CARRUADES DE LAFITE Pauillac 1959 Cur: $100 (10/15/90) (JS)
88 CARRUADES DE LAFITE Pauillac 1959 Cur: $100 (11/30/87)
77 CARRUADES DE LAFITE Pauillac 1937 Cur: $125 (11/30/87)
84 CARRUADES DE LAFITE Pauillac 1934 Cur: $145 (11/30/87)
80 CARRUADES DE LAFITE Pauillac 1902 Cur: $275 (11/30/87)
90+ CHATEAU CLERC-MILON Pauillac 1990 (NR) (4/30/91) (BT)
85+ CHATEAU CLERC-MILON Pauillac 1989 (NR) (4/30/91) (BT)
90+ CHATEAU CLERC-MILON Pauillac 1989 (NR) (4/30/90) (BT)
94 CHATEAU CLERC-MILON Pauillac 1988 $26 (4/30/91) SS
90+ CHATEAU CLERC-MILON Pauillac 1988 $26 (8/31/90) (BT)
85+ CHATEAU CLERC-MILON Pauillac 1988 $26 (6/30/89) (BT)
80+ CHATEAU CLERC-MILON Pauillac 1987 Cur: $19 (6/30/89) (BT)
80+ CHATEAU CLERC-MILON Pauillac 1987 Cur: $19 (6/30/88) (BT)
97 CHATEAU CLERC-MILON Pauillac 1986 Rel: $23 Cur: $32 (5/31/89)
90+ CHATEAU CLERC-MILON Pauillac 1986 Rel: $23 Cur: $32 (6/30/88) (BT)
80+ CHATEAU CLERC-MILON Pauillac 1986 Rel: $23 Cur: $32 (5/15/87) (BT)
91 CHATEAU CLERC-MILON Pauillac 1985 Rel: $18.50 Cur: $24 (5/15/88)
80+ CHATEAU CLERC-MILON Pauillac 1985 Rel: $18.50 Cur: $24 (5/15/87) (BT)
90+ CHATEAU CLERC-MILON Pauillac 1985 Rel: $18.50 Cur: $24 (4/16/86) (BT)
78 CHATEAU CLERC-MILON Pauillac 1984 Rel: $18 Cur: $18 (6/15/87)
91 CHATEAU CLERC-MILON Pauillac 1983 Rel: $16.50 Cur: $18 (4/01/86)
86 CHATEAU CLERC-MILON Pauillac 1982 Rel: $15 Cur: $27 (4/01/85)
85+ CHATEAU CROIZET-BAGES Pauillac 1990 (NR) (4/30/91) (BT)
80+ CHATEAU CROIZET-BAGES Pauillac 1989 (NR) (4/30/91) (BT)
60+ CHATEAU CROIZET-BAGES Pauillac 1987 Rel: $15 Cur: $15 (6/30/88) (BT)
78 CHATEAU CROIZET-BAGES Pauillac 1986 Rel: $15 Cur: $15 (6/30/89)
65+ CHATEAU CROIZET-BAGES Pauillac 1986 Rel: $15 Cur: $15 (6/30/88) (BT)
83 CHATEAU CROIZET-BAGES Pauillac 1962 Cur: $60 (11/30/87) (JS)
85+ CHATEAU DUHART-MILON Pauillac 1990 (NR) (4/30/91) (BT)
90+ CHATEAU DUHART-MILON Pauillac 1989 (NR) (4/30/91) (BT)
90+ CHATEAU DUHART-MILON Pauillac 1989 (NR) (4/30/90) (BT)
85+ CHATEAU DUHART-MILON Pauillac 1988 $20 (8/31/90) (BT)
80+ CHATEAU DUHART-MILON Pauillac 1988 $20 (6/30/89) (BT)
79 CHATEAU DUHART-MILON Pauillac 1987 Rel: $22 Cur: $22 (5/15/90)
80+ CHATEAU DUHART-MILON Pauillac 1987 Rel: $22 Cur: $22 (6/30/89) (BT)
80+ CHATEAU DUHART-MILON Pauillac 1987 Rel: $22 Cur: $22 (6/30/88) (BT)
90 CHATEAU DUHART-MILON Pauillac 1986 Rel: $30 Cur: $30 (5/31/89)
90+ CHATEAU DUHART-MILON Pauillac 1986 Rel: $30 Cur: $30 (6/30/88) (BT)
60+ CHATEAU DUHART-MILON Pauillac 1986 Rel: $30 Cur: $30 (5/15/87) (BT)
87 CHATEAU DUHART-MILON Pauillac 1985 Rel: $34 Cur: $34 (6/30/88)
80+ CHATEAU DUHART-MILON Pauillac 1985 Rel: $34 Cur: $34 (5/15/87) (BT)
86 CHATEAU DUHART-MILON Pauillac 1979 Cur: $26 (10/15/89) (JS)
75+ CHATEAU FONBADET Pauillac 1988 $16 (6/30/89) (BT)
75+ CHATEAU FONBADET Pauillac 1987 $15 (6/30/89) (BT)
86 CHATEAU FONBADET Pauillac 1982 $16 (8/01/85)
80+ LES FORTS DE LATOUR Pauillac 1990 (NR) (4/30/91) (BT)
85+ LES FORTS DE LATOUR Pauillac 1989 (NR) (4/30/91) (BT)
75+ LES FORTS DE LATOUR Pauillac 1987 (NR) (6/30/89) (BT)
70+ LES FORTS DE LATOUR Pauillac 1986 (NR) (5/15/87) (BT)
80+ LES FORTS DE LATOUR Pauillac 1985 $40 (5/15/87) (BT)
85 LES FORTS DE LATOUR Pauillac 1983 Rel: $32 Cur: $32 (10/15/90)
86 LES FORTS DE LATOUR Pauillac 1982 Rel: $55 Cur: $55 (10/15/90)
87 LES FORTS DE LATOUR Pauillac 1979 Cur: $35 (10/15/89) (JS)
89 CHATEAU GRAND-PUY-DUCASSE Pauillac 1988 $21 (4/30/91)
80+ CHATEAU GRAND-PUY-DUCASSE Pauillac 1988 $21 (6/30/89) (BT)
75+ CHATEAU GRAND-PUY-DUCASSE Pauillac 1987 Rel: $18 Cur: $18 (6/30/89) (BT)
85 CHATEAU GRAND-PUY-DUCASSE Pauillac 1986 Rel: $22 Cur: $24 (6/30/89)
90 CHATEAU GRAND-PUY-DUCASSE Pauillac 1985 Rel: $19 Cur: $20 (2/29/88)
90+ CHATEAU GRAND-PUY-LACOSTE Pauillac 1989 (NR) (4/30/91) (BT)
85+ CHATEAU GRAND-PUY-LACOSTE Pauillac 1989 (NR) (4/30/90) (BT)
90 CHATEAU GRAND-PUY-LACOSTE Pauillac 1988 $33 (4/30/91)
85+ CHATEAU GRAND-PUY-LACOSTE Pauillac 1988 $33 (8/31/90) (BT)
85+ CHATEAU GRAND-PUY-LACOSTE Pauillac 1988 $33 (6/30/89) (BT)
77 CHATEAU GRAND-PUY-LACOSTE Pauillac 1987 Rel: $22 Cur: $22 (5/15/90)
80+ CHATEAU GRAND-PUY-LACOSTE Pauillac 1987 Rel: $22 Cur: $22 (6/30/88) (BT)
88 CHATEAU GRAND-PUY-LACOSTE Pauillac 1986 Rel: $25 Cur: $27 (5/31/89)
85+ CHATEAU GRAND-PUY-LACOSTE Pauillac 1986 Rel: $25 Cur: $27 (6/30/88) (BT)
80+ CHATEAU GRAND-PUY-LACOSTE Pauillac 1986 Rel: $25 Cur: $27 (5/15/87) (BT)
91 CHATEAU GRAND-PUY-LACOSTE Pauillac 1985 Rel: $23 Cur: $30 (6/30/88)
80+ CHATEAU GRAND-PUY-LACOSTE Pauillac 1985 Rel: $23 Cur: $30 (4/16/86) (BT)
83 CHATEAU GRAND-PUY-LACOSTE Pauillac 1984 Rel: $24.50 Cur: $25 (10/15/87)
88 CHATEAU GRAND-PUY-LACOSTE Pauillac 1979 Cur: $33 (10/15/89) (JS)
96 CHATEAU GRAND-PUY-LACOSTE Pauillac 1961 Cur: $181 (3/16/86) (JL)
80 CHATEAU GRAND-PUY-LACOSTE Pauillac 1945 Cur: $380 (3/16/86) (JL)
85+ CHATEAU HAUT-BAGES-AVEROUS Pauillac 1990 (NR) (4/30/91) (BT)
85+ CHATEAU HAUT-BAGES-AVEROUS Pauillac 1989 (NR) (4/30/91) (BT)
90+ CHATEAU HAUT-BAGES-AVEROUS Pauillac 1989 (NR) (4/30/90) (BT)
93 CHATEAU HAUT-BAGES-AVEROUS Pauillac 1988 $23 (4/30/91)
85+ CHATEAU HAUT-BAGES-AVEROUS Pauillac 1988 $23 (8/31/90) (BT)
80+ CHATEAU HAUT-BAGES-AVEROUS Pauillac 1988 $23 (6/30/89) (BT)
85 CHATEAU HAUT-BAGES-AVEROUS Pauillac 1987 Rel: $15 Cur: $15 (11/30/89) (JS)
75+ CHATEAU HAUT-BAGES-AVEROUS Pauillac 1987 Rel: $15 Cur: $15 (6/30/89) (BT)
75+ CHATEAU HAUT-BAGES-AVEROUS Pauillac 1987 Rel: $15 Cur: $15 (6/30/88) (BT)
90 CHATEAU HAUT-BAGES-AVEROUS Pauillac 1986 Rel: $15 Cur: $19 (11/30/89) (JS)
85 CHATEAU HAUT-BAGES-AVEROUS Pauillac 1986 Rel: $15 Cur: $19 (5/31/89)
80+ CHATEAU HAUT-BAGES-AVEROUS Pauillac 1986 Rel: $15 Cur: $19 (6/30/88) (BT)
70+ CHATEAU HAUT-BAGES-AVEROUS Pauillac 1986 Rel: $15 Cur: $19 (5/15/87) (BT)
82 CHATEAU HAUT-BAGES-AVEROUS Pauillac 1985 Rel: $17 Cur: $17 (4/30/88)
70+ CHATEAU HAUT-BAGES-AVEROUS Pauillac 1985 Rel: $17 Cur: $17 (5/15/87) (BT)
60+ CHATEAU HAUT-BAGES-AVEROUS Pauillac 1985 Rel: $17 Cur: $17 (4/16/86) (BT)
89 CHATEAU HAUT-BAGES-AVEROUS Pauillac 1982 Cur: $25 (11/30/89) (JS)
84 CHATEAU HAUT-BAGES-AVEROUS Pauillac 1979 Cur: $18 (10/15/89) (JS)
90+ CHATEAU HAUT-BAGES-LIBERAL Pauillac 1989 (NR) (4/30/90) (BT)
88 CHATEAU HAUT-BAGES-LIBERAL Pauillac 1988 $17.50 (3/15/91)
70+ CHATEAU HAUT-BAGES-LIBERAL Pauillac 1988 $17.50 (8/31/90) (BT)
80+ CHATEAU HAUT-BAGES-LIBERAL Pauillac 1988 $17.50 (6/30/89) (BT)
75+ CHATEAU HAUT-BAGES-LIBERAL Pauillac 1987 Rel: $14 Cur: $14 (6/30/89) (BT)
75+ CHATEAU HAUT-BAGES-LIBERAL Pauillac 1987 Rel: $14 Cur: $14 (6/30/88) (BT)
91 CHATEAU HAUT-BAGES-LIBERAL Pauillac 1986 Rel: $17 Cur: $22 (5/31/89)
80+ CHATEAU HAUT-BAGES-LIBERAL Pauillac 1986 Rel: $17 Cur: $22 (6/30/88) (BT)
88 CHATEAU HAUT-BAGES-LIBERAL Pauillac 1985 Rel: $16 Cur: $23 (4/30/88)
67 CHATEAU HAUT-BAGES-LIBERAL Pauillac 1984 Rel: $19 Cur: $19 (6/15/87)
67 CHATEAU HAUT-BAGES-LIBERAL Pauillac 1983 Rel: $18 Cur: $18 (5/01/86)
85 CHATEAU HAUT-BAGES-LIBERAL Pauillac Belgian Bottled 1959 Cur: $55 (10/15/90) (JS)
85+ CHATEAU HAUT-BAGES-MONPELOU Pauillac 1989 (NR) (4/30/90) (BT)
90+ CHATEAU HAUT-BATAILLEY Pauillac 1990 (NR) (4/30/91) (BT)
85+ CHATEAU HAUT-BATAILLEY Pauillac 1989 (NR) (4/30/91) (BT)
95+ CHATEAU HAUT-BATAILLEY Pauillac 1989 (NR) (4/30/90) (BT)
85+ CHATEAU HAUT-BATAILLEY Pauillac 1988 $26 (6/30/89) (BT)
86 CHATEAU HAUT-BATAILLEY Pauillac 1987 Rel: $17 Cur: $17 (5/15/90)
80+ CHATEAU HAUT-BATAILLEY Pauillac 1987 Rel: $17 Cur: $17 (6/30/88) (BT)
85 CHATEAU HAUT-BATAILLEY Pauillac 1986 Rel: $23 Cur: $23 (5/31/89)
80+ CHATEAU HAUT-BATAILLEY Pauillac 1986 Rel: $23 Cur: $23 (5/15/87) (BT)
81 CHATEAU HAUT-BATAILLEY Pauillac 1985 Rel: $17 Cur: $21 (11/30/88)
80+ CHATEAU HAUT-BATAILLEY Pauillac 1985 Rel: $17 Cur: $21 (5/15/87) (BT)
70+ CHATEAU HAUT-BATAILLEY Pauillac 1985 Rel: $17 Cur: $21 (4/16/86) (BT)
82 CHATEAU HAUT-BATAILLEY Pauillac 1979 Cur: $28 (10/15/89) (JS)
91 CHATEAU HAUT-BATAILLEY Pauillac 1961 Cur: $95 (3/16/86) (JL)
89 CHATEAU LACOSTE-BORIE Pauillac 1988 $19 (4/30/91)
84 CHATEAU LACOSTE-BORIE Pauillac 1986 $15 (6/30/89)
60+ CHATEAU LACOSTE-BORIE Pauillac 1986 $15 (5/15/87) (BT)
75 CHATEAU LACOSTE-BORIE Pauillac 1983 $7.50 (6/15/87)
95+ CHATEAU LAFITE-ROTHSCHILD Pauillac 1990 (NR) (4/30/91) (BT)
95+ CHATEAU LAFITE-ROTHSCHILD Pauillac 1989 (NR) (4/30/91) (BT)
95+ CHATEAU LAFITE-ROTHSCHILD Pauillac 1989 (NR) (4/30/90) (BT)
96 CHATEAU LAFITE-ROTHSCHILD Pauillac 1988 $100 (4/30/91) CS
95+ CHATEAU LAFITE-ROTHSCHILD Pauillac 1988 $100 (8/31/90) (BT)
95+ CHATEAU LAFITE-ROTHSCHILD Pauillac 1988 $100 (6/30/89) (BT)
85 CHATEAU LAFITE-ROTHSCHILD Pauillac 1987 Rel: $60 Cur: $60 (5/15/90)
85+ CHATEAU LAFITE-ROTHSCHILD Pauillac 1987 Rel: $60 Cur: $60 (6/30/89) (BT)
85+ CHATEAU LAFITE-ROTHSCHILD Pauillac 1987 Rel: $60 Cur: $60 (6/30/88) (BT)
95 CHATEAU LAFITE-ROTHSCHILD Pauillac 1986 Rel: $102 Cur: $102 (5/31/89)
96 CHATEAU LAFITE-ROTHSCHILD Pauillac 1986 Rel: $102 Cur: $102 (3/31/89) (JS)
90+ CHATEAU LAFITE-ROTHSCHILD Pauillac 1986 Rel: $102 Cur: $102 (6/30/88) (BT)
90+ CHATEAU LAFITE-ROTHSCHILD Pauillac 1986 Rel: $102 Cur: $102 (5/15/87) (BT)
94 CHATEAU LAFITE-ROTHSCHILD Pauillac 1985 Rel: $80 Cur: $99 (3/31/89) (JS)
97 CHATEAU LAFITE-ROTHSCHILD Pauillac 1985 Rel: $80 Cur: $99 (5/31/88) CS
90+ CHATEAU LAFITE-ROTHSCHILD Pauillac 1985 Rel: $80 Cur: $99 (5/15/87) (BT)
87 CHATEAU LAFITE-ROTHSCHILD Pauillac 1984 Rel: $51 Cur: $68 (5/01/89)
93 CHATEAU LAFITE-ROTHSCHILD Pauillac 1984 Rel: $51 Cur: $68 (3/31/87)
84 CHATEAU LAFITE-ROTHSCHILD Pauillac 1983 Rel: $60 Cur: $94 (5/01/89)
90 CHATEAU LAFITE-ROTHSCHILD Pauillac 1983 Rel: $60 Cur: $94 (3/31/89) (JS)
94 CHATEAU LAFITE-ROTHSCHILD Pauillac 1983 Rel: $60 Cur: $94 (12/15/88) (TR)
91 CHATEAU LAFITE-ROTHSCHILD Pauillac 1982 Rel: $120 Cur: $172 (5/01/89)
95 CHATEAU LAFITE-ROTHSCHILD Pauillac 1982 Rel: $120 Cur: $172 (3/31/89) (JS)
90 CHATEAU LAFITE-ROTHSCHILD Pauillac 1981 Rel: $75 Cur: $131 (5/01/89)
81 CHATEAU LAFITE-ROTHSCHILD Pauillac 1980 Cur: $52 (12/15/88) (TR)
92 CHATEAU LAFITE-ROTHSCHILD Pauillac 1979 Cur: $116 (10/15/89) (JS)
88 CHATEAU LAFITE-ROTHSCHILD Pauillac 1979 Cur: $116 (12/15/88) (TR)
92 CHATEAU LAFITE-ROTHSCHILD Pauillac 1978 Cur: $161 (12/15/88) (TR)
76 CHATEAU LAFITE-ROTHSCHILD Pauillac 1977 Cur: $47 (12/15/88) (TR)
92 CHATEAU LAFITE-ROTHSCHILD Pauillac 1976 Cur: $160 (3/31/89) (JS)
86 CHATEAU LAFITE-ROTHSCHILD Pauillac 1976 Cur: $160 (12/15/88) (TR)
88 CHATEAU LAFITE-ROTHSCHILD Pauillac 1975 Cur: $190 (12/15/88) (TR)
75 CHATEAU LAFITE-ROTHSCHILD Pauillac 1974 Cur: $56 (12/15/88) (TR)
80 CHATEAU LAFITE-ROTHSCHILD Pauillac 1973 Cur: $54 (12/15/88) (TR)
78 CHATEAU LAFITE-ROTHSCHILD Pauillac 1972 Cur: $58 (12/15/88) (TR)
87 CHATEAU LAFITE-ROTHSCHILD Pauillac 1971 Cur: $109 (12/15/88) (TR)
91 CHATEAU LAFITE-ROTHSCHILD Pauillac 1970 Cur: $187 (12/15/88) (TR)
83 CHATEAU LAFITE-ROTHSCHILD Pauillac 1969 Cur: $32 (12/15/88) (TR)
71 CHATEAU LAFITE-ROTHSCHILD Pauillac 1968 Cur: $35 (12/15/88) (TR)
85 CHATEAU LAFITE-ROTHSCHILD Pauillac 1967 Cur: $79 (12/15/88) (TR)
93 CHATEAU LAFITE-ROTHSCHILD Pauillac 1966 Cur: $192 (12/15/88) (TR)
76 CHATEAU LAFITE-ROTHSCHILD Pauillac 1965 Cur: $45 (12/15/88) (TR)
84 CHATEAU LAFITE-ROTHSCHILD Pauillac 1964 Cur: $96 (12/15/88) (TR)
78 CHATEAU LAFITE-ROTHSCHILD Pauillac 1963 Cur: $290 (12/15/88) (TR)
87 CHATEAU LAFITE-ROTHSCHILD Pauillac 1962 Cur: $205 (12/15/88) (TR)
94 CHATEAU LAFITE-ROTHSCHILD Pauillac 1961 Cur: $580 (12/15/88) (TR)
86 CHATEAU LAFITE-ROTHSCHILD Pauillac 1960 Cur: $90 (12/15/88) (TR)
90 CHATEAU LAFITE-ROTHSCHILD Pauillac 1959 Cur: $550 (10/15/90) (JS)
95 CHATEAU LAFITE-ROTHSCHILD Pauillac 1959 Cur: $550 (12/15/88) (TR)
89 CHATEAU LAFITE-ROTHSCHILD Pauillac 1958 Cur: $105 (12/15/88) (TR)
86 CHATEAU LAFITE-ROTHSCHILD Pauillac 1957 Cur: $125 (12/15/88) (TR)
86 CHATEAU LAFITE-ROTHSCHILD Pauillac 1956 Cur: $250 (12/15/88) (TR)
84 CHATEAU LAFITE-ROTHSCHILD Pauillac 1955 Cur: $330 (12/15/88) (TR)

Key to Symbols

The scores reported here are the results of blind tastings conducted by our panel of senior editors. Wines that carry the initials below are results of individual tastings.

THE WINE SPECTATOR 100-POINT SCALE ***95-100***—Classic, a great wine; ***90-94***—Outstanding, superior character and style; ***80-89***—Good to very good, a wine with special qualities; ***70-79***—Average, drinkable wine that may have minor flaws; ***60-69***—Below average, drinkable but not recommended; ***50-59***—Poor, undrinkable, not recommended. "+"—With a score indicates a range; used primarily with barrel tastings to indicate a preliminary score.

SPECIAL DESIGNATIONS SS—Spectator Selection, CS—Cellar Selection, BB—Best Buy.

TASTER'S INITIALS (JG)—Jim Gordon, (HS)—Harvey Steiman, (JL)—James Laube, (JS)—James Suckling, (TM)—Thomas Matthews, (TR)—Terry Robards, (BT)—Barrel Tasting (these wines were tasted blind from barrel samples), (CA-date)—*California's Great Cabernets* by James Laube, (CH-date)—*California's Great Chardonnays* by James Laube, (VP-date)—*Vintage Port* by James Suckling.

DATE TASTED Dates in parentheses represent the issue in which the rating was published.

84 CHATEAU LAFITE-ROTHSCHILD Pauillac 1954 Cur: $290 (12/15/88) (TR)
87 CHATEAU LAFITE-ROTHSCHILD Pauillac 1953 Cur: $460 (12/15/88) (TR)
84 CHATEAU LAFITE-ROTHSCHILD Pauillac 1952 Cur: $193 (12/15/88) (TR)
83 CHATEAU LAFITE-ROTHSCHILD Pauillac 1951 Cur: $150 (12/15/88) (TR)
84 CHATEAU LAFITE-ROTHSCHILD Pauillac 1950 Cur: $300 (12/15/88) (TR)
88 CHATEAU LAFITE-ROTHSCHILD Pauillac 1949 Cur: $480 (12/15/88) (TR)
84 CHATEAU LAFITE-ROTHSCHILD Pauillac 1948 Cur: $600 (12/15/88) (TR)
86 CHATEAU LAFITE-ROTHSCHILD Pauillac 1947 Cur: $410 (12/15/88) (TR)
90 CHATEAU LAFITE-ROTHSCHILD Pauillac 1946 Cur: $450 (12/15/88) (TR)
92 CHATEAU LAFITE-ROTHSCHILD Pauillac 1945 Cur: $850 (3/16/86) (JL)
80 CHATEAU LAFITE-ROTHSCHILD Pauillac 1943 Cur: $320 (12/15/88) (TR)
80 CHATEAU LAFITE-ROTHSCHILD Pauillac 1942 Cur: $320 (12/15/88) (TR)
78 CHATEAU LAFITE-ROTHSCHILD Pauillac 1941 Cur: $500 (12/15/88) (TR)
77 CHATEAU LAFITE-ROTHSCHILD Pauillac 1940 Cur: $700 (12/15/88) (TR)
78 CHATEAU LAFITE-ROTHSCHILD Pauillac 1939 Cur: $320 (12/15/88) (TR)
76 CHATEAU LAFITE-ROTHSCHILD Pauillac 1938 Cur: $225 (12/15/88) (TR)
80 CHATEAU LAFITE-ROTHSCHILD Pauillac 1937 Cur: $250 (12/15/88) (TR)
87 CHATEAU LAFITE-ROTHSCHILD Pauillac 1934 Cur: $360 (12/15/88) (TR)
79 CHATEAU LAFITE-ROTHSCHILD Pauillac 1933 Cur: $200 (12/15/88) (TR)
76 CHATEAU LAFITE-ROTHSCHILD Pauillac 1931 Cur: $550 (12/15/88) (TR)
88 CHATEAU LAFITE-ROTHSCHILD Pauillac 1929 Cur: $860 (12/15/88) (TR)
83 CHATEAU LAFITE-ROTHSCHILD Pauillac 1928 Cur: $700 (12/15/88) (TR)
74 CHATEAU LAFITE-ROTHSCHILD Pauillac 1925 Cur: $193 (12/15/88) (TR)
79 CHATEAU LAFITE-ROTHSCHILD Pauillac 1924 Cur: $530 (12/15/88) (TR)
84 CHATEAU LAFITE-ROTHSCHILD Pauillac 1923 Cur: $292 (12/15/88) (TR)
77 CHATEAU LAFITE-ROTHSCHILD Pauillac 1921 Cur: $500 (12/15/88) (TR)
75 CHATEAU LAFITE-ROTHSCHILD Pauillac 1920 Cur: $580 (12/15/88) (TR)
77 CHATEAU LAFITE-ROTHSCHILD Pauillac 1919 Cur: $740 (12/15/88) (TR)
79 CHATEAU LAFITE-ROTHSCHILD Pauillac 1918 Cur: $580 (12/15/88) (TR)
83 CHATEAU LAFITE-ROTHSCHILD Pauillac 1916 Cur: $450 (12/15/88) (TR)
75 CHATEAU LAFITE-ROTHSCHILD Pauillac 1914 Cur: $560 (12/15/88) (TR)
77 CHATEAU LAFITE-ROTHSCHILD Pauillac 1913 Cur: $500 (12/15/88) (TR)
76 CHATEAU LAFITE-ROTHSCHILD Pauillac 1912 Cur: $520 (12/15/88) (TR)
81 CHATEAU LAFITE-ROTHSCHILD Pauillac 1911 Cur: $400 (12/15/88) (TR)
77 CHATEAU LAFITE-ROTHSCHILD Pauillac 1910 Cur: $570 (12/15/88) (TR)
79 CHATEAU LAFITE-ROTHSCHILD Pauillac 1907 Cur: $700 (12/15/88) (TR)
78 CHATEAU LAFITE-ROTHSCHILD Pauillac 1906 Cur: $350 (12/15/88) (TR)
82 CHATEAU LAFITE-ROTHSCHILD Pauillac 1905 Cur: $420 (12/15/88) (TR)
80 CHATEAU LAFITE-ROTHSCHILD Pauillac 1904 Cur: $660 (12/15/88) (TR)
79 CHATEAU LAFITE-ROTHSCHILD Pauillac 1902 Cur: $510 (12/15/88) (TR)
78 CHATEAU LAFITE-ROTHSCHILD Pauillac 1899 Cur: $2,200 (12/15/88) (TR)
79 CHATEAU LAFITE-ROTHSCHILD Pauillac 1898 Cur: $1,300 (12/15/88) (TR)
81 CHATEAU LAFITE-ROTHSCHILD Pauillac 1897 Cur: $1,400 (12/15/88) (TR)
79 CHATEAU LAFITE-ROTHSCHILD Pauillac 1896 Cur: $1,200 (12/15/88) (TR)
89 CHATEAU LAFITE-ROTHSCHILD Pauillac 1895 Cur: $2,050 (12/15/88) (TR)
75 CHATEAU LAFITE-ROTHSCHILD Pauillac 1894 Cur: $1,000 (12/15/88) (TR)
84 CHATEAU LAFITE-ROTHSCHILD Pauillac 1893 Cur: $1,200 (12/15/88) (TR)
85 CHATEAU LAFITE-ROTHSCHILD Pauillac 1892 Cur: $1,300 (12/15/88) (TR)
84 CHATEAU LAFITE-ROTHSCHILD Pauillac 1891 Cur: $1,100 (12/15/88) (TR)
83 CHATEAU LAFITE-ROTHSCHILD Pauillac 1890 Cur: $1,100 (12/15/88) (TR)
85 CHATEAU LAFITE-ROTHSCHILD Pauillac 1889 Cur: $750 (12/15/88) (TR)
82 CHATEAU LAFITE-ROTHSCHILD Pauillac 1888 Cur: $900 (12/15/88) (TR)
88 CHATEAU LAFITE-ROTHSCHILD Pauillac 1886 Cur: $1,100 (12/15/88) (TR)
82 CHATEAU LAFITE-ROTHSCHILD Pauillac 1882 Cur: $800 (12/15/88) (TR)
85 CHATEAU LAFITE-ROTHSCHILD Pauillac 1881 Cur: $720 (12/15/88) (TR)
82 CHATEAU LAFITE-ROTHSCHILD Pauillac 1880 Cur: $1,500 (12/15/88) (TR)
83 CHATEAU LAFITE-ROTHSCHILD Pauillac 1879 Cur: $2,800 (12/15/88) (TR)
83 CHATEAU LAFITE-ROTHSCHILD Pauillac 1878 Cur: $2,500 (12/15/88) (TR)
88 CHATEAU LAFITE-ROTHSCHILD Pauillac 1877 Cur: $2,500 (12/15/88) (TR)
84 CHATEAU LAFITE-ROTHSCHILD Pauillac 1876 Cur: $1,310 (12/15/88) (TR)
91 CHATEAU LAFITE-ROTHSCHILD Pauillac 1875 Cur: $4,000 (12/15/88) (TR)
97 CHATEAU LAFITE-ROTHSCHILD Pauillac 1875 Cur: $8,400/1.5L (12/15/88) (TR)
84 CHATEAU LAFITE-ROTHSCHILD Pauillac 1874 Cur: $2,500 (12/15/88) (TR)
95 CHATEAU LAFITE-ROTHSCHILD Pauillac 1870 Cur: $4,000 (12/15/88) (TR)
82 CHATEAU LAFITE-ROTHSCHILD Pauillac 1869 Cur: $2,410 (12/15/88) (TR)
86 CHATEAU LAFITE-ROTHSCHILD Pauillac 1868 Cur: $2,000 (12/15/88) (TR)
84 CHATEAU LAFITE-ROTHSCHILD Pauillac 1865 Cur: $3,800 (12/15/88) (TR)
84 CHATEAU LAFITE-ROTHSCHILD Pauillac 1864 Cur: $4,700 (12/15/88) (TR)
96 CHATEAU LAFITE-ROTHSCHILD Pauillac 1858 Cur: $4,000 (12/15/88) (TR)
92 CHATEAU LAFITE-ROTHSCHILD Pauillac 1848 Cur: $10,000 (12/15/88) (TR)
83 CHATEAU LAFITE-ROTHSCHILD Pauillac 1846 Cur: $9,000 (12/15/88) (TR)
84 CHATEAU LAFITE-ROTHSCHILD Pauillac 1844 Cur: $5,700 (12/15/88) (TR)
82 CHATEAU LAFITE-ROTHSCHILD Pauillac 1832 Cur: $9,000 (12/15/88) (TR)
83 CHATEAU LAFITE-ROTHSCHILD Pauillac 1806 $25,000 (12/15/88) (TR)
95+ CHATEAU LATOUR Pauillac 1990 (NR) (4/30/91) (BT)
95+ CHATEAU LATOUR Pauillac 1989 (NR) (4/30/91) (BT)
90+ CHATEAU LATOUR Pauillac 1989 (NR) (4/30/90) (BT)
93 CHATEAU LATOUR Pauillac 1988 $90 (4/30/91)
90+ CHATEAU LATOUR Pauillac 1988 $90 (8/31/90) (BT)
90+ CHATEAU LATOUR Pauillac 1988 $90 (6/30/89) (BT)
80 CHATEAU LATOUR Pauillac 1987 Rel: $60 Cur: $60 (10/15/90)
85+ CHATEAU LATOUR Pauillac 1987 Rel: $60 Cur: $60 (6/30/89) (BT)
85+ CHATEAU LATOUR Pauillac 1987 Rel: $60 Cur: $60 (6/30/88) (BT)
93 CHATEAU LATOUR Pauillac 1986 Rel: $90 Cur: $90 (3/31/90) (HS)
93 CHATEAU LATOUR Pauillac 1986 Rel: $90 Cur: $90 (5/31/89)
90+ CHATEAU LATOUR Pauillac 1986 Rel: $90 Cur: $90 (6/30/88) (BT)
90+ CHATEAU LATOUR Pauillac 1986 Rel: $90 Cur: $90 (5/15/87) (BT)
96 CHATEAU LATOUR Pauillac 1985 Rel: $82 Cur: $95 (3/31/90) (HS)
97 CHATEAU LATOUR Pauillac 1985 Rel: $82 Cur: $95 (4/30/88)
90+ CHATEAU LATOUR Pauillac 1985 Rel: $82 Cur: $95 (5/15/87) (BT)
92 CHATEAU LATOUR Pauillac 1984 Rel: $40 Cur: $61 (3/31/87)
93 CHATEAU LATOUR Pauillac 1983 Rel: $72 Cur: $85 (3/31/90) (HS)
97 CHATEAU LATOUR Pauillac 1983 Rel: $72 Cur: $85 (3/01/86)
99 CHATEAU LATOUR Pauillac 1982 Cur: $150 (3/31/90) (HS)
97 CHATEAU LATOUR Pauillac 1982 Cur: $150 (5/01/89)
90 CHATEAU LATOUR Pauillac 1981 Cur: $81 (3/31/90) (HS)
92 CHATEAU LATOUR Pauillac 1981 Cur: $81 (5/01/89)
90 CHATEAU LATOUR Pauillac 1979 Cur: $92 (3/31/90) (HS)
84 CHATEAU LATOUR Pauillac 1979 Cur: $92 (10/15/89) (JS)
94 CHATEAU LATOUR Pauillac 1978 Cur: $139 (3/31/90) (HS)
87 CHATEAU LATOUR Pauillac 1976 Cur: $92 (3/31/90) (HS)
93 CHATEAU LATOUR Pauillac 1975 Cur: $149 (3/31/90) (HS)
84 CHATEAU LATOUR Pauillac 1971 Cur: $127 (3/31/90) (HS)
97 CHATEAU LATOUR Pauillac 1970 Cur: $197 (3/31/90) (HS)
79 CHATEAU LATOUR Pauillac 1967 Cur: $100 (3/31/90) (HS)
93 CHATEAU LATOUR Pauillac 1966 Cur: $222 (3/31/90) (HS)
74 CHATEAU LATOUR Pauillac 1965 Cur: $135 (3/31/90) (HS)
86 CHATEAU LATOUR Pauillac 1964 Cur: $180 (3/31/90) (HS)
88 CHATEAU LATOUR Pauillac 1964 Cur: $378/1.5L (3/31/90) (HS)
77 CHATEAU LATOUR Pauillac 1963 Cur: $135 (3/31/90) (HS)
92 CHATEAU LATOUR Pauillac 1962 Cur: $525/1.5L (3/31/90) (HS)
98 CHATEAU LATOUR Pauillac 1962 Cur: $250 (11/30/87) (JS)
99 CHATEAU LATOUR Pauillac 1961 Cur: $640 (3/31/90) (HS)
97 CHATEAU LATOUR Pauillac 1961 Cur: $640 (3/16/86) (JL)
88 CHATEAU LATOUR Pauillac 1960 Cur: $275 (3/31/90) (HS)
98 CHATEAU LATOUR Pauillac 1959 Cur: $450 (10/15/90) (JS)
95 CHATEAU LATOUR Pauillac 1959 Cur: $450 (3/31/90) (HS)
95 CHATEAU LATOUR Pauillac 1959 Cur: $945/1.5L (3/31/90) (HS)
81 CHATEAU LATOUR Pauillac 1958 Cur: $140 (3/31/90) (HS)
62 CHATEAU LATOUR Pauillac 1956 Cur: $248 (3/31/90) (HS)
90 CHATEAU LATOUR Pauillac 1955 Cur: $320 (3/31/90) (HS)
80 CHATEAU LATOUR Pauillac 1953 Cur: $279 (3/31/90) (HS)
91 CHATEAU LATOUR Pauillac 1952 Cur: $260 (3/31/90) (HS)
79 CHATEAU LATOUR Pauillac 1950 Cur: $340 (3/31/90) (HS)
94 CHATEAU LATOUR Pauillac 1949 Cur: $520 (3/31/90) (HS)
84 CHATEAU LATOUR Pauillac 1948 Cur: $390 (3/31/90) (HS)
91 CHATEAU LATOUR Pauillac 1947 Cur: $400 (3/31/90) (HS)
98 CHATEAU LATOUR Pauillac 1945 Cur: $1,150 (3/31/90) (HS)
98 CHATEAU LATOUR Pauillac 1945 Cur: $1,150 (3/16/86) (JL)
70 CHATEAU LATOUR Pauillac 1944 Cur: $330 (3/31/90) (HS)
67 CHATEAU LATOUR Pauillac 1943 Cur: $238 (3/31/90) (HS)
59 CHATEAU LATOUR Pauillac 1942 Cur: $330 (3/31/90) (HS)
64 CHATEAU LATOUR Pauillac 1940 Cur: $370 (3/31/90) (HS)
89 CHATEAU LATOUR Pauillac 1937 Cur: $360 (3/31/90) (HS)
75 CHATEAU LATOUR Pauillac 1936 Cur: $400 (3/31/90) (HS)
83 CHATEAU LATOUR Pauillac 1934 Cur: $340 (3/31/90) (HS)
95 CHATEAU LATOUR Pauillac 1929 Cur: $2,300/1.5L (3/31/90) (HS)
91 CHATEAU LATOUR Pauillac 1928 Cur: $2,300/1.5L (3/31/90) (HS)
87 CHATEAU LATOUR Pauillac 1926 Cur: $780 (3/31/90) (HS)
91 CHATEAU LATOUR Pauillac 1924 Cur: $750 (3/31/90) (HS)
50 CHATEAU LATOUR Pauillac 1920 Cur: $530 (3/31/90) (HS)
75 CHATEAU LATOUR Pauillac 1918 Cur: $580 (3/31/90) (HS)
90 CHATEAU LATOUR Pauillac 1900 Cur: $2,000 (3/31/90) (HS)
94 CHATEAU LATOUR Pauillac 1899 Cur: $1,900 (3/31/90) (HS)
50 CHATEAU LATOUR Pauillac 1899 Cur: $4,000/1.5L (3/31/90) (HS)
67 CHATEAU LATOUR Pauillac 1893 Cur: $4,500 (3/31/90) (HS)
63 CHATEAU LATOUR Pauillac 1892 Cur: $1,200 (3/31/90) (HS)
77 CHATEAU LATOUR Pauillac 1875 Cur: $1,800 (3/31/90) (HS)
95 CHATEAU LATOUR Pauillac 1875 Cur: $3,780/1.5L (12/15/88)
97 CHATEAU LATOUR Pauillac 1874 Cur: $3,220 (3/31/90) (HS)
94 CHATEAU LATOUR Pauillac 1870 Cur: $4,000 (3/31/90) (HS)
94 CHATEAU LATOUR Pauillac 1865 Cur: $14,700/1.5L (3/31/90) (HS)
59 CHATEAU LATOUR Pauillac 1864 $10,000/1.5L (3/31/90) (HS)
93 CHATEAU LATOUR Pauillac 1847 $18,000/1.5L (3/31/90) (HS)
90+ CHATEAU LYNCH-BAGES Pauillac 1990 (NR) (4/30/91) (BT)
95+ CHATEAU LYNCH-BAGES Pauillac 1989 (NR) (4/30/91) (BT)
95+ CHATEAU LYNCH-BAGES Pauillac 1989 (NR) (4/30/90) (BT)
95 CHATEAU LYNCH-BAGES Pauillac 1988 $35 (3/15/91) CS
90+ CHATEAU LYNCH-BAGES Pauillac 1988 $35 (8/31/90) (BT)
90+ CHATEAU LYNCH-BAGES Pauillac 1988 $35 (6/30/89) (BT)
86 CHATEAU LYNCH-BAGES Pauillac 1987 Rel: $27 Cur: $27 (2/15/90)
87 CHATEAU LYNCH-BAGES Pauillac 1987 Rel: $27 Cur: $27 (10/31/89) (JS)
80+ CHATEAU LYNCH-BAGES Pauillac 1987 Rel: $27 Cur: $27 (6/30/89) (BT)
80+ CHATEAU LYNCH-BAGES Pauillac 1987 Rel: $27 Cur: $27 (6/30/88) (BT)
94 CHATEAU LYNCH-BAGES Pauillac 1986 Rel: $37 Cur: $37 (10/31/89) (JS)
93 CHATEAU LYNCH-BAGES Pauillac 1986 Rel: $37 Cur: $37 (5/31/89)
90+ CHATEAU LYNCH-BAGES Pauillac 1986 Rel: $37 Cur: $37 (6/30/88) (BT)
80+ CHATEAU LYNCH-BAGES Pauillac 1986 Rel: $37 Cur: $37 (5/15/87) (BT)
93 CHATEAU LYNCH-BAGES Pauillac 1985 Rel: $37 Cur: $45 (10/31/89) (JS)
97 CHATEAU LYNCH-BAGES Pauillac 1985 Rel: $37 Cur: $45 (4/30/88) CS
90+ CHATEAU LYNCH-BAGES Pauillac 1985 Rel: $37 Cur: $45 (5/15/87) (BT)
80+ CHATEAU LYNCH-BAGES Pauillac 1985 Rel: $37 Cur: $45 (4/16/86) (BT)
87 CHATEAU LYNCH-BAGES Pauillac 1984 Rel: $19 Cur: $27 (10/31/89) (JS)
90 CHATEAU LYNCH-BAGES Pauillac 1984 Rel: $19 Cur: $27 (3/31/87)
88 CHATEAU LYNCH-BAGES Pauillac 1983 Rel: $25 Cur: $45 (10/31/89) (JS)
90 CHATEAU LYNCH-BAGES Pauillac 1983 Rel: $25 Cur: $45 (3/01/86)
90 CHATEAU LYNCH-BAGES Pauillac 1982 Rel: $27.50 Cur: $54 (10/31/89) (JS)
94 CHATEAU LYNCH-BAGES Pauillac 1982 Rel: $27.50 Cur: $54 (3/01/85) CS
90 CHATEAU LYNCH-BAGES Pauillac 1981 Rel: $15.50 Cur: $37 (10/31/89) (JS)
92 CHATEAU LYNCH-BAGES Pauillac 1981 Rel: $15.50 Cur: $37 (6/01/84)
88 CHATEAU LYNCH-BAGES Pauillac 1980 Cur: $24 (10/31/89) (JS)
87 CHATEAU LYNCH-BAGES Pauillac 1979 Cur: $40 (10/31/89) (JS)
91 CHATEAU LYNCH-BAGES Pauillac 1979 Cur: $40 (10/15/89) (JS)
92 CHATEAU LYNCH-BAGES Pauillac 1978 Cur: $52 (10/31/89) (JS)
78 CHATEAU LYNCH-BAGES Pauillac 1977 Cur: $25 (10/31/89) (JS)
70 CHATEAU LYNCH-BAGES Pauillac 1976 Cur: $55 (10/31/89) (JS)
90 CHATEAU LYNCH-BAGES Pauillac 1975 Cur: $70 (10/31/89) (JS)
82 CHATEAU LYNCH-BAGES Pauillac 1973 Cur: $30 (10/31/89) (JS)
67 CHATEAU LYNCH-BAGES Pauillac 1971 Cur: $28 (10/31/89) (JS)
90 CHATEAU LYNCH-BAGES Pauillac 1970 Cur: $115 (10/31/89) (JS)
79 CHATEAU LYNCH-BAGES Pauillac 1967 Cur: $55 (10/31/89) (JS)
90 CHATEAU LYNCH-BAGES Pauillac 1966 Cur: $125 (10/31/89) (JS)
76 CHATEAU LYNCH-BAGES Pauillac 1964 Cur: $90 (10/31/89) (JS)
94 CHATEAU LYNCH-BAGES Pauillac 1962 Cur: $124 (10/31/89) (JS)
80 CHATEAU LYNCH-BAGES Pauillac 1962 Cur: $124 (11/30/87) (JS)
86 CHATEAU LYNCH-BAGES Pauillac 1961 Cur: $225 (10/31/89) (JS)
96 CHATEAU LYNCH-BAGES Pauillac 1961 Cur: $225 (3/16/86) (JL)
76 CHATEAU LYNCH-BAGES Pauillac 1960 Cur: $55 (10/31/89) (JS)
95 CHATEAU LYNCH-BAGES Pauillac 1959 Cur: $195 (10/15/90) (JS)
95 CHATEAU LYNCH-BAGES Pauillac 1959 Cur: $195 (10/31/89) (JS)

FRANCE
BORDEAUX RED/*PAUILLAC*

79 CHATEAU LYNCH-BAGES Pauillac 1958 Cur: $60 (10/31/89) (JS)
88 CHATEAU LYNCH-BAGES Pauillac 1957 Cur: $95 (10/31/89) (JS)
92 CHATEAU LYNCH-BAGES Pauillac 1955 Cur: $245 (10/31/89) (JS)
74 CHATEAU LYNCH-BAGES Pauillac 1954 Cur: $75 (10/31/89) (JS)
77 CHATEAU LYNCH-BAGES Pauillac 1953 Cur: $320 (10/31/89) (JS)
83 CHATEAU LYNCH-BAGES Pauillac 1952 Cur: $100 (10/31/89) (JS)
84 CHATEAU LYNCH-BAGES Pauillac 1949 Cur: $175 (10/31/89) (JS)
90 CHATEAU LYNCH-BAGES Pauillac 1947 Cur: $350 (10/31/89) (JS)
80 CHATEAU LYNCH-BAGES Pauillac (Bottled in Denmark) 1945 Cur: $230 (10/31/89) (JS)
65 CHATEAU LYNCH-BAGES Pauillac 1945 Cur: $350 (3/16/86) (JL)
85+ CHATEAU LYNCH-MOUSSAS Pauillac 1990 (NR) (4/30/91) (BT)
85+ CHATEAU LYNCH-MOUSSAS Pauillac 1989 (NR) (4/30/91) (BT)
80+ CHATEAU LYNCH-MOUSSAS Pauillac 1988 $25 (6/30/89) (BT)
70+ CHATEAU LYNCH-MOUSSAS Pauillac 1987 Rel: $17 Cur: $17 (6/30/89) (BT)
65+ CHATEAU LYNCH-MOUSSAS Pauillac 1987 Rel: $17 Cur: $17 (6/30/88) (BT)
86 CHATEAU LYNCH-MOUSSAS Pauillac 1986 Rel: $18 Cur: $18 (6/30/89)
75+ CHATEAU LYNCH-MOUSSAS Pauillac 1986 Rel: $18 Cur: $18 (6/30/88) (BT)
86 CHATEAU LYNCH-MOUSSAS Pauillac 1959 Cur: $101 (10/15/90) (JS)
80+ MOULIN DE DUHART Pauillac 1989 (NR) (4/30/90) (BT)
70+ MOULIN DE DUHART Pauillac 1987 (NR) (6/30/89) (BT)
88 MOULIN DES CARRUADES Pauillac 1983 $14 (10/31/86)
85+ CHATEAU MOUTON-BARONNE-PHILIPPE Pauillac 1990 (NR) (4/30/91) (BT)
90+ CHATEAU MOUTON-BARONNE-PHILIPPE Pauillac 1989 (NR) (4/30/91) (BT)
90+ CHATEAU MOUTON-BARONNE-PHILIPPE Pauillac 1989 (NR) (4/30/90) (BT)
90 CHATEAU MOUTON-BARONNE-PHILIPPE Pauillac 1988 $25 (4/30/91)
85+ CHATEAU MOUTON-BARONNE-PHILIPPE Pauillac 1988 $25 (8/31/90) (BT)
80+ CHATEAU MOUTON-BARONNE-PHILIPPE Pauillac 1988 $25 (6/30/89) (BT)
80+ CHATEAU MOUTON-BARONNE-PHILIPPE Pauillac 1987 Rel: $16 Cur: $16 (6/30/89) (BT)
80+ CHATEAU MOUTON-BARONNE-PHILIPPE Pauillac 1987 Rel: $16 Cur: $16 (6/30/88) (BT)
93 CHATEAU MOUTON-BARONNE-PHILIPPE Pauillac 1986 Rel: $23 Cur: $23 (5/31/89)
85+ CHATEAU MOUTON-BARONNE-PHILIPPE Pauillac 1986 Rel: $23 Cur: $23 (6/30/88) (BT)
70+ CHATEAU MOUTON-BARONNE-PHILIPPE Pauillac 1986 Rel: $23 Cur: $23 (5/15/87) (BT)
91 CHATEAU MOUTON-BARONNE-PHILIPPE Pauillac 1985 Rel: $18 Cur: $26 (5/15/88) SS
70+ CHATEAU MOUTON-BARONNE-PHILIPPE Pauillac 1985 Rel: $18 Cur: $26 (5/15/87) (BT)
70+ CHATEAU MOUTON-BARONNE-PHILIPPE Pauillac 1985 Rel: $18 Cur: $26 (4/16/86) (BT)
64 CHATEAU MOUTON-BARONNE-PHILIPPE Pauillac 1984 Rel: $17.50 Cur: $18 (6/15/87)
88 CHATEAU MOUTON-BARONNE-PHILIPPE Pauillac 1983 Rel: $16.50 Cur: $17 (3/01/86)
86 CHATEAU MOUTON-BARONNE-PHILIPPE Pauillac 1982 Rel: $15 Cur: $27 (4/01/85)
81 CHATEAU MOUTON-BARONNE-PHILIPPE Pauillac 1981 Rel: $12 Cur: $15 (6/01/84)
62 CHATEAU MOUTON-BARONNE-PHILIPPE Pauillac 1961 Cur: $125 (3/16/86) (JL)
80 CHATEAU MOUTON-BARONNE-PHILIPPE Pauillac 1945 Cur: $390 (3/16/86) (JL)
95+ CHATEAU MOUTON-ROTHSCHILD Pauillac 1990 (NR) (4/30/91) (BT)
95+ CHATEAU MOUTON-ROTHSCHILD Pauillac 1989 (NR) (4/30/91) (BT)
95+ CHATEAU MOUTON-ROTHSCHILD Pauillac 1989 (NR) (4/30/90) (BT)
100 CHATEAU MOUTON-ROTHSCHILD Pauillac 1988 $105 (4/30/91)
95+ CHATEAU MOUTON-ROTHSCHILD Pauillac 1988 $105 (8/31/90) (BT)
95+ CHATEAU MOUTON-ROTHSCHILD Pauillac 1988 $105 (6/30/89) (BT)
89 CHATEAU MOUTON-ROTHSCHILD Pauillac 1987 Rel: $56 Cur: $69 (5/15/90)
90+ CHATEAU MOUTON-ROTHSCHILD Pauillac 1987 Rel: $56 Cur: $69 (6/30/89) (BT)
90+ CHATEAU MOUTON-ROTHSCHILD Pauillac 1987 Rel: $56 Cur: $69 (6/30/88) (BT)
97 CHATEAU MOUTON-ROTHSCHILD Pauillac 1986 Rel: $102 Cur: $114 (5/15/91) (PM)
98 CHATEAU MOUTON-ROTHSCHILD Pauillac 1986 Rel: $102 Cur: $114 (5/31/89) CS
90+ CHATEAU MOUTON-ROTHSCHILD Pauillac 1986 Rel: $102 Cur: $114 (6/30/88) (BT)
90+ CHATEAU MOUTON-ROTHSCHILD Pauillac 1986 Rel: $102 Cur: $114 (5/15/87) (BT)
94 CHATEAU MOUTON-ROTHSCHILD Pauillac 1985 Rel: $90 Cur: $90 (4/30/88)
90+ CHATEAU MOUTON-ROTHSCHILD Pauillac 1985 Rel: $90 Cur: $90 (5/15/87) (BT)
90+ CHATEAU MOUTON-ROTHSCHILD Pauillac 1985 Rel: $90 Cur: $90 (4/16/86) (BT)
92 CHATEAU MOUTON-ROTHSCHILD Pauillac 1984 Rel: $40 Cur: $63 (3/31/87)
96 CHATEAU MOUTON-ROTHSCHILD Pauillac 1983 Rel: $57 Cur: $86 (3/01/86)
93 CHATEAU MOUTON-ROTHSCHILD Pauillac 1982 Cur: $176 (5/15/91) (PM)
85 CHATEAU MOUTON-ROTHSCHILD Pauillac 1982 Cur: $176 (6/16/86) (TR)
86 CHATEAU MOUTON-ROTHSCHILD Pauillac 1981 Rel: $40 Cur: $84 (6/16/86) (TR)
67 CHATEAU MOUTON-ROTHSCHILD Pauillac 1980 Cur: $85 (6/16/86) (TR)
96 CHATEAU MOUTON-ROTHSCHILD Pauillac 1979 Cur: $91 (10/15/89) (JS)
85 CHATEAU MOUTON-ROTHSCHILD Pauillac 1979 Cur: $91 (6/16/86) (TR)
92 CHATEAU MOUTON-ROTHSCHILD Pauillac 1978 Cur: $127 (5/15/91) (PM)
88 CHATEAU MOUTON-ROTHSCHILD Pauillac 1978 Cur: $127 (6/16/86) (TR)
68 CHATEAU MOUTON-ROTHSCHILD Pauillac 1977 Cur: $82 (6/16/86) (TR)
85 CHATEAU MOUTON-ROTHSCHILD Pauillac 1976 Cur: $96 (6/16/86) (TR)
89 CHATEAU MOUTON-ROTHSCHILD Pauillac 1975 Cur: $153 (5/15/91) (PM)
86 CHATEAU MOUTON-ROTHSCHILD Pauillac 1975 Cur: $153 (6/16/86) (TR)
67 CHATEAU MOUTON-ROTHSCHILD Pauillac 1974 Cur: $145 (6/16/86) (TR)
75 CHATEAU MOUTON-ROTHSCHILD Pauillac 1973 Cur: $119 (6/16/86) (TR)
55 CHATEAU MOUTON-ROTHSCHILD Pauillac 1972 Cur: $138 (6/16/86) (TR)

Key to Symbols

The scores reported here are the results of blind tastings conducted by our panel of senior editors. Wines that carry the initials below are results of individual tastings.

THE WINE SPECTATOR 100-POINT SCALE ***95-100***—Classic, a great wine; ***90-94***—Outstanding, superior character and style; ***80-89***—Good to very good, a wine with special qualities; ***70-79***—Average, drinkable wine that may have minor flaws; ***60-69***—Below average, drinkable but not recommended; ***50-59***—Poor, undrinkable, not recommended. "+"—With a score indicates a range; used primarily with barrel tastings to indicate a preliminary score.

SPECIAL DESIGNATIONS SS—Spectator Selection, CS—Cellar Selection, BB—Best Buy.

TASTER'S INITIALS (JG)—Jim Gordon, (HS)—Harvey Steiman, (JL)—James Laube, (JS)—James Suckling, (TM)—Thomas Matthews, (TR)—Terry Robards, (BT)—Barrel Tasting (these wines were tasted blind from barrel samples), (CA-date)—*California's Great Cabernets* by James Laube, (CH-date)—*California's Great Chardonnays* by James Laube, (VP-date)—*Vintage Port* by James Suckling.

DATE TASTED Dates in parentheses represent the issue in which the rating was published.

78 CHATEAU MOUTON-ROTHSCHILD Pauillac 1971 Cur: $102 (6/16/86) (TR)
84 CHATEAU MOUTON-ROTHSCHILD Pauillac 1970 Cur: $195 (5/15/91) (PM)
85 CHATEAU MOUTON-ROTHSCHILD Pauillac 1970 Cur: $195 (6/16/86) (TR)
78 CHATEAU MOUTON-ROTHSCHILD Pauillac 1969 Cur: $269 (6/16/86) (TR)
64 CHATEAU MOUTON-ROTHSCHILD Pauillac 1968 Cur: $480 (6/16/86) (TR)
87 CHATEAU MOUTON-ROTHSCHILD Pauillac 1967 Cur: $100 (6/16/86) (TR)
88 CHATEAU MOUTON-ROTHSCHILD Pauillac 1966 Cur: $224 (5/15/91) (PM)
86 CHATEAU MOUTON-ROTHSCHILD Pauillac 1966 Cur: $224 (6/16/86) (TR)
61 CHATEAU MOUTON-ROTHSCHILD Pauillac 1965 Cur: $840 (6/16/86) (TR)
84 CHATEAU MOUTON-ROTHSCHILD Pauillac 1964 Cur: $124 (6/16/86) (TR)
77 CHATEAU MOUTON-ROTHSCHILD Pauillac 1963 Cur: $1,160 (6/16/86) (TR)
93 CHATEAU MOUTON-ROTHSCHILD Pauillac 1962 Cur: $273 (5/15/91) (PM)
98 CHATEAU MOUTON-ROTHSCHILD Pauillac 1962 Cur: $273 (11/30/87) (JS)
90 CHATEAU MOUTON-ROTHSCHILD Pauillac 1961 Cur: $650 (5/15/91) (PM)
94 CHATEAU MOUTON-ROTHSCHILD Pauillac 1961 Cur: $650 (6/16/86) (TR)
84 CHATEAU MOUTON-ROTHSCHILD Pauillac 1960 Cur: $540 (6/16/86) (TR)
98 CHATEAU MOUTON-ROTHSCHILD Pauillac 1959 Cur: $460 (5/15/91) (PM)
99 CHATEAU MOUTON-ROTHSCHILD Pauillac 1959 Cur: $460 (10/15/90) (JS)
88 CHATEAU MOUTON-ROTHSCHILD Pauillac 1959 Cur: $460 (6/16/86) (TR)
68 CHATEAU MOUTON-ROTHSCHILD Pauillac 1958 Cur: $770 (6/16/86) (TR)
86 CHATEAU MOUTON-ROTHSCHILD Pauillac 1957 Cur: $450 (6/16/86) (TR)
85 CHATEAU MOUTON-ROTHSCHILD Pauillac 1956 Cur: $2,430 (6/16/86) (TR)
95 CHATEAU MOUTON-ROTHSCHILD Pauillac 1955 Cur: $430 (5/15/91) (PM)
92 CHATEAU MOUTON-ROTHSCHILD Pauillac 1955 Cur: $430 (6/16/86) (TR)
81 CHATEAU MOUTON-ROTHSCHILD Pauillac 1954 Cur: $4,000 (6/16/86) (TR)
94 CHATEAU MOUTON-ROTHSCHILD Pauillac 1953 Cur: $680 (5/15/91) (PM)
90 CHATEAU MOUTON-ROTHSCHILD Pauillac 1952 Cur: $400 (6/16/86) (TR)
84 CHATEAU MOUTON-ROTHSCHILD Pauillac 1951 Cur: $1,850 (6/16/86) (TR)
83 CHATEAU MOUTON-ROTHSCHILD Pauillac 1950 Cur: $870 (6/16/86) (TR)
87 CHATEAU MOUTON-ROTHSCHILD Pauillac 1949 Cur: $1,160 (5/15/91) (PM)
94 CHATEAU MOUTON-ROTHSCHILD Pauillac 1949 Cur: $1,160 (6/16/86) (TR)
87 CHATEAU MOUTON-ROTHSCHILD Pauillac 1948 Cur: $1,900 (6/16/86) (TR)
75 CHATEAU MOUTON-ROTHSCHILD Pauillac 1947 Cur: $1,310 (5/15/91) (PM)
95 CHATEAU MOUTON-ROTHSCHILD Pauillac 1947 Cur: $1,310 (6/16/86) (TR)
77 CHATEAU MOUTON-ROTHSCHILD Pauillac 1946 Cur: $5,720 (6/16/86) (TR)
100 CHATEAU MOUTON-ROTHSCHILD Pauillac 1945 Cur: $1,850 (5/15/91) (PM)
95 CHATEAU MOUTON-ROTHSCHILD Pauillac 1945 Cur: $1,850 (3/16/86) (JL)
86 CHATEAU MOUTON-ROTHSCHILD Pauillac 1944 Cur: $950 (6/16/86) (TR)
78 CHATEAU MOUTON-ROTHSCHILD Pauillac 1943 Cur: $480 (6/16/86) (TR)
77 CHATEAU MOUTON-ROTHSCHILD Pauillac 1940 Cur: $530 (6/16/86) (TR)
55 CHATEAU MOUTON-ROTHSCHILD Pauillac 1939 Cur: $500 (6/16/86) (TR)
73 CHATEAU MOUTON-ROTHSCHILD Pauillac 1938 Cur: $500 (6/16/86) (TR)
91 CHATEAU MOUTON-ROTHSCHILD Pauillac 1937 Cur: $440 (5/15/91) (PM)
95 CHATEAU MOUTON-ROTHSCHILD Pauillac 1937 Cur: $440 (12/15/88) (JS)
63 CHATEAU MOUTON-ROTHSCHILD Pauillac 1936 Cur: $246 (6/16/86) (TR)
90 CHATEAU MOUTON-ROTHSCHILD Pauillac 1934 Cur: $450 (5/15/91) (PM)
78 CHATEAU MOUTON-ROTHSCHILD Pauillac 1933 Cur: $300/375ml (6/16/86) (TR)
75 CHATEAU MOUTON-ROTHSCHILD Pauillac 1929 Cur: $800 (5/15/91) (PM)
86 CHATEAU MOUTON-ROTHSCHILD Pauillac 1929 Cur: $800 (6/16/86) (TR)
89 CHATEAU MOUTON-ROTHSCHILD Pauillac 1928 Cur: $950 (5/15/91) (PM)
65 CHATEAU MOUTON-ROTHSCHILD Pauillac 1926 Cur: $800 (6/16/86) (TR)
40 CHATEAU MOUTON-ROTHSCHILD Pauillac 1925 Cur: $1,100 (6/16/86) (TR)
69 CHATEAU MOUTON-ROTHSCHILD Pauillac 1924 Cur: $1,910 (6/16/86) (TR)
80 CHATEAU MOUTON-ROTHSCHILD Pauillac 1921 Cur: $500 (5/15/91) (PM)
84 CHATEAU MOUTON-ROTHSCHILD Pauillac 1921 Cur: $500 (6/16/86) (TR)
75 CHATEAU MOUTON-ROTHSCHILD Pauillac 1920 Cur: $700 (6/16/86) (TR)
79 CHATEAU MOUTON-ROTHSCHILD Pauillac 1919 Cur: $600 (5/15/91) (PM)
83 CHATEAU MOUTON-ROTHSCHILD Pauillac 1918 Cur: $1,640 (5/15/91) (PM)
67 CHATEAU MOUTON-ROTHSCHILD Pauillac 1916 Cur: $420 (6/16/86) (TR)
65 CHATEAU MOUTON-ROTHSCHILD Pauillac 1914 Cur: $400 (6/16/86) (TR)
62 CHATEAU MOUTON-ROTHSCHILD Pauillac 1912 Cur: $400 (6/16/86) (TR)
76 CHATEAU MOUTON-ROTHSCHILD Pauillac 1910 Cur: $400 (5/15/91) (PM)
65 CHATEAU MOUTON-ROTHSCHILD Pauillac 1909 Cur: $700 (6/16/86) (TR)
50 CHATEAU MOUTON-ROTHSCHILD Pauillac 1908 Cur: $700 (6/16/86) (TR)
50 CHATEAU MOUTON-ROTHSCHILD Pauillac 1907 Cur: $600 (6/16/86) (TR)
66 CHATEAU MOUTON-ROTHSCHILD Pauillac 1906 Cur: $800 (6/16/86) (TR)
88 CHATEAU MOUTON-ROTHSCHILD Pauillac 1905 Cur: $970 (5/15/91) (PM)
90 CHATEAU MOUTON-ROTHSCHILD Pauillac 1900 Cur: $1,800 (5/15/91) (PM)
82 CHATEAU MOUTON-ROTHSCHILD Pauillac 1899 Cur: $1,900 (6/16/86) (TR)
60 CHATEAU MOUTON-ROTHSCHILD Pauillac 1888 Cur: $1,100 (6/16/86) (TR)
60 CHATEAU MOUTON-ROTHSCHILD Pauillac 1886 Cur: $1,200 (6/16/86) (TR)
74 CHATEAU MOUTON-ROTHSCHILD Pauillac 1881 Cur: $1,380 (6/16/86) (TR)
99 CHATEAU MOUTON-ROTHSCHILD Pauillac 1878 Cur: $3,200 (5/15/91) (PM)
95 CHATEAU MOUTON-ROTHSCHILD Pauillac 1874 Cur: $2,500 (5/15/91) (PM)
73 CHATEAU MOUTON-ROTHSCHILD Pauillac 1874 Cur: $2,500 (6/16/86) (TR)
87 CHATEAU MOUTON-ROTHSCHILD Pauillac 1870 Cur: $3,500 (5/15/91) (PM)
78 CHATEAU MOUTON-ROTHSCHILD Pauillac 1870 Cur: $3,500 (6/16/86) (TR)
40 CHATEAU MOUTON-ROTHSCHILD Pauillac 1869 Cur: $1,700 (6/16/86) (TR)
40 CHATEAU MOUTON-ROTHSCHILD Pauillac 1867 Cur: $2,100 (6/16/86) (TR)
80+ CHATEAU PEDESCLAUX Pauillac 1988 $20 (6/30/89) (BT)
79 CHATEAU PEDESCLAUX Pauillac 1986 Rel: $18 Cur: $18 (2/15/90)
90+ CHATEAU PIBRAN Pauillac 1990 (NR) (4/30/91) (BT)
95+ CHATEAU PIBRAN Pauillac 1989 (NR) (4/30/91) (BT)
90+ CHATEAU PIBRAN Pauillac 1989 (NR) (4/30/90) (BT)
85+ CHATEAU PIBRAN Pauillac 1988 $27 (8/31/90) (BT)
85+ CHATEAU PIBRAN Pauillac 1988 $27 (6/30/89) (BT)
85 CHATEAU PIBRAN Pauillac 1987 Rel: $20 Cur: $20 (11/30/89) (JS)
80+ CHATEAU PIBRAN Pauillac 1987 Rel: $20 Cur: $20 (6/30/89) (BT)
75+ CHATEAU PIBRAN Pauillac 1987 Rel: $20 Cur: $20 (6/30/88) (BT)
88 CHATEAU PIBRAN Pauillac 1986 Rel: $18 Cur: $18 (11/30/89) (JS)
90 CHATEAU PIBRAN Pauillac 1982 Cur: $15 (11/30/89) (JS)
95+ CHATEAU PICHON-BARON Pauillac 1990 (NR) (4/30/91) (BT)
90+ CHATEAU PICHON-BARON Pauillac 1989 (NR) (4/30/91) (BT)
95+ CHATEAU PICHON-BARON Pauillac 1989 (NR) (4/30/90) (BT)
95 CHATEAU PICHON-BARON Pauillac 1988 $30 (3/31/91) SS
95+ CHATEAU PICHON-BARON Pauillac 1988 $30 (8/31/90) (BT)
85+ CHATEAU PICHON-BARON Pauillac 1988 $30 (6/30/89) (BT)
88 CHATEAU PICHON-BARON Pauillac 1987 Rel: $20 Cur: $41 (10/15/90)
85+ CHATEAU PICHON-BARON Pauillac 1987 Rel: $20 Cur: $41 (6/30/89) (BT)
85+ CHATEAU PICHON-BARON Pauillac 1987 Rel: $20 Cur: $41 (6/30/88) (BT)

97	CHATEAU PICHON-BARON Pauillac 1986 Rel: $31 Cur: $58 (5/31/89)
85+	CHATEAU PICHON-BARON Pauillac 1986 Rel: $31 Cur: $58 (6/30/88) (BT)
94	CHATEAU PICHON-BARON Pauillac 1985 Rel: $32 Cur: $36 (4/30/88)
78	CHATEAU PICHON-BARON Pauillac 1984 Rel: $23 Cur: $24 (9/30/88)
94	CHATEAU PICHON-BARON Pauillac 1983 Rel: $18 Cur: $35 (3/01/86)
78	CHATEAU PICHON-BARON Pauillac 1982 Rel: $12.50 Cur: $37 (9/30/88)
84	CHATEAU PICHON-BARON Pauillac 1981 Rel: $13.50 Cur: $33 (9/30/88)
79	CHATEAU PICHON-BARON Pauillac 1980 Cur: $17 (9/30/88)
88	CHATEAU PICHON-BARON Pauillac 1979 Cur: $29 (10/15/89) (JS)
84	CHATEAU PICHON-BARON Pauillac 1979 Cur: $29 (9/30/88)
80	CHATEAU PICHON-BARON Pauillac 1978 Cur: $39 (9/30/88)
76	CHATEAU PICHON-BARON Pauillac 1977 Cur: $13 (9/30/88)
73	CHATEAU PICHON-BARON Pauillac 1976 Cur: $20 (9/30/88)
74	CHATEAU PICHON-BARON Pauillac 1975 Cur: $59 (9/30/88)
78	CHATEAU PICHON-BARON Pauillac 1974 Cur: $20 (9/30/88)
78	CHATEAU PICHON-BARON Pauillac 1973 Cur: $13 (9/30/88)
68	CHATEAU PICHON-BARON Pauillac 1972 Cur: $13 (9/30/88)
71	CHATEAU PICHON-BARON Pauillac 1971 Cur: $31 (9/30/88)
83	CHATEAU PICHON-BARON Pauillac 1970 Cur: $69 (9/30/88)
78	CHATEAU PICHON-BARON Pauillac 1969 Cur: $21 (9/30/88)
80	CHATEAU PICHON-BARON Pauillac 1967 Cur: $46 (9/30/88)
80	CHATEAU PICHON-BARON Pauillac 1966 Cur: $59 (9/30/88)
88	CHATEAU PICHON-BARON Pauillac 1964 Cur: $63 (9/30/88)
88	CHATEAU PICHON-BARON Pauillac 1962 Cur: $85 (9/30/88)
84	CHATEAU PICHON-BARON Pauillac 1961 Cur: $164 (9/30/88)
81	CHATEAU PICHON-BARON Pauillac 1960 Cur: $50 (9/30/88)
94	CHATEAU PICHON-BARON Pauillac 1959 Cur: $174 (10/15/90) (JS)
88	CHATEAU PICHON-BARON Pauillac 1959 Cur: $174 (9/30/88)
79	CHATEAU PICHON-BARON Pauillac 1958 Cur: $95 (9/30/88)
76	CHATEAU PICHON-BARON Pauillac 1957 Cur: $110 (9/30/88)
81	CHATEAU PICHON-BARON Pauillac 1955 Cur: $122 (9/30/88)
80	CHATEAU PICHON-BARON Pauillac 1954 Cur: $95 (9/30/88)
80	CHATEAU PICHON-BARON Pauillac 1953 Cur: $200 (9/30/88)
84	CHATEAU PICHON-BARON Pauillac 1952 Cur: $105 (9/30/88)
83	CHATEAU PICHON-BARON Pauillac 1950 Cur: $150 (9/30/88)
87	CHATEAU PICHON-BARON Pauillac 1949 Cur: $175 (9/30/88)
80	CHATEAU PICHON-BARON Pauillac 1947 Cur: $200 (9/30/88)
75	CHATEAU PICHON-BARON Pauillac 1945 Cur: $370 (9/30/88)
85+	CHATEAU PICHON-LALANDE Pauillac 1990 (NR) (4/30/91) (BT)
90+	CHATEAU PICHON-LALANDE Pauillac 1989 (NR) (4/30/91) (BT)
90+	CHATEAU PICHON-LALANDE Pauillac 1989 (NR) (4/30/90) (BT)
91	CHATEAU PICHON-LALANDE Pauillac 1988 $50 (4/30/91)
90+	CHATEAU PICHON-LALANDE Pauillac 1988 $50 (8/31/90) (BT)
85+	CHATEAU PICHON-LALANDE Pauillac 1988 $50 (6/30/89) (BT)
87	CHATEAU PICHON-LALANDE Pauillac 1987 Rel: $30 Cur: $30 (2/15/90)
85+	CHATEAU PICHON-LALANDE Pauillac 1987 Rel: $30 Cur: $30 (6/30/89) (BT)
85+	CHATEAU PICHON-LALANDE Pauillac 1987 Rel: $30 Cur: $30 (6/30/88) (BT)
97	CHATEAU PICHON-LALANDE Pauillac 1986 Rel: $50 Cur: $57 (5/31/89)
90+	CHATEAU PICHON-LALANDE Pauillac 1986 Rel: $50 Cur: $57 (6/30/88) (BT)
90+	CHATEAU PICHON-LALANDE Pauillac 1986 Rel: $50 Cur: $57 (5/15/87) (BT)
95	CHATEAU PICHON-LALANDE Pauillac 1985 Rel: $40 Cur: $53 (2/29/88) CS
90+	CHATEAU PICHON-LALANDE Pauillac 1985 Rel: $40 Cur: $53 (5/15/87) (BT)
90+	CHATEAU PICHON-LALANDE Pauillac 1985 Rel: $40 Cur: $53 (4/16/86) (BT)
94	CHATEAU PICHON-LALANDE Pauillac 1984 Rel: $27 Cur: $34 (1/31/87) CS
97	CHATEAU PICHON-LALANDE Pauillac 1983 Rel: $44 Cur: $53 (3/01/86) SS
94	CHATEAU PICHON-LALANDE Pauillac 1982 Rel: $29 Cur: $89 (2/01/85) SS
93	CHATEAU PICHON-LALANDE Pauillac 1981 Rel: $21 Cur: $56 (5/01/85)
92	CHATEAU PICHON-LALANDE Pauillac 1980 Rel: $14 Cur: $36 (5/01/85)
90	CHATEAU PICHON-LALANDE Pauillac 1980 Rel: $14 Cur: $36 (3/01/84) CS
90	CHATEAU PICHON-LALANDE Pauillac 1979 Cur: $64 (5/01/85)
91	CHATEAU PICHON-LALANDE Pauillac 1978 Cur: $89 (5/01/85)
85	CHATEAU PICHON-LALANDE Pauillac 1962 Cur: $125 (11/30/87) (JS)
79	CHATEAU PICHON-LALANDE Pauillac 1961 Cur: $225 (3/16/86) (JL)
97	CHATEAU PICHON-LALANDE Pauillac 1959 Cur: $175 (10/15/90) (JS)
80	CHATEAU PICHON-LALANDE Pauillac 1945 Cur: $400 (3/16/86) (JL)
80+	CHATEAU PONTET-CANET Pauillac 1990 (NR) (4/30/91) (BT)
90+	CHATEAU PONTET-CANET Pauillac 1989 (NR) (4/30/91) (BT)
80+	CHATEAU PONTET-CANET Pauillac 1988 (NR) (6/30/89) (BT)
75+	CHATEAU PONTET-CANET Pauillac 1987 Cur: $14 (6/30/89) (BT)
75+	CHATEAU PONTET-CANET Pauillac 1987 Cur: $14 (6/30/88) (BT)
89	CHATEAU PONTET-CANET Pauillac 1986 Rel: $21 Cur: $21 (5/31/89)
80+	CHATEAU PONTET-CANET Pauillac 1986 Rel: $21 Cur: $21 (6/30/88) (BT)
70+	CHATEAU PONTET-CANET Pauillac 1986 Rel: $21 Cur: $21 (5/15/87) (BT)
80+	CHATEAU PONTET-CANET Pauillac 1985 Cur: $20 (5/15/87) (BT)
66	CHATEAU PONTET-CANET Pauillac 1961 Cur: $95 (3/16/86) (JL)
60	CHATEAU PONTET-CANET Pauillac 1945 Cur: $250 (3/16/86) (JL)
88	RESERVE DE LA COMTESSE Pauillac 1988 $23 (3/15/91)
82	RESERVE DE LA COMTESSE Pauillac 1987 Rel: $14 Cur: $16 (5/15/90)
90	RESERVE DE LA COMTESSE Pauillac 1986 Rel: $20 Cur: $25 (5/31/89)
82	RESERVE DE LA COMTESSE Pauillac 1983 Rel: $18 Cur: $21 (3/01/86)
90+	LES TOURELLS DE LONGUEVILLE Pauillac 1990 (NR) (4/30/91) (BT)
90+	LES TOURELLS DE LONGUEVILLE Pauillac 1989 (NR) (4/30/91) (BT)
90+	LES TOURELLS DE LONGUEVILLE Pauillac 1989 (NR) (4/30/90) (BT)
85+	LES TOURELLS DE LONGUEVILLE Pauillac 1988 $25 (8/31/90) (BT)
80+	LES TOURELLS DE LONGUEVILLE Pauillac 1988 $25 (6/30/89) (BT)
75+	LES TOURELLS DE LONGUEVILLE Pauillac 1987 $17 (6/30/89) (BT)

POMEROL

90	CHATEAU BEAUREGARD Pomerol 1988 $36 (7/31/91)
87	CHATEAU BEAUREGARD Pomerol 1986 Rel: $22 Cur: $24 (6/15/89)
89	CHATEAU BEAUREGARD Pomerol 1982 Rel: $16 Cur: $21 (5/15/89) (TR)
85+	CHATEAU BONALGUE Pomerol 1989 (NR) (4/30/91) (BT)
85+	CHATEAU BONALGUE Pomerol 1988 (NR) (6/30/89) (BT)
80+	CHATEAU BONALGUE Pomerol 1987 Rel: $18 Cur: $18 (6/30/89) (BT)
75+	CHATEAU BONALGUE Pomerol 1987 Rel: $18 Cur: $18 (6/30/88) (BT)
85+	CHATEAU BONALGUE Pomerol 1986 Cur: $26 (6/30/88) (BT)
85+	CHATEAU LE BON-PASTEUR Pomerol 1990 (NR) (4/30/91) (BT)
85+	CHATEAU LE BON-PASTEUR Pomerol 1989 (NR) (4/30/91) (BT)
85+	CHATEAU LE BON-PASTEUR Pomerol 1989 (NR) (4/30/90) (BT)

85	CHATEAU LE BON-PASTEUR Pomerol 1988 $23 (2/28/91)
90+	CHATEAU LE BON-PASTEUR Pomerol 1988 $23 (8/31/90) (BT)
90+	CHATEAU LE BON-PASTEUR Pomerol 1988 $23 (6/30/89) (BT)
81	CHATEAU LE BON-PASTEUR Pomerol 1987 Rel: $22 Cur: $22 (5/15/90)
85+	CHATEAU LE BON-PASTEUR Pomerol 1987 Rel: $22 Cur: $22 (6/30/89) (BT)
80+	CHATEAU LE BON-PASTEUR Pomerol 1987 Rel: $22 Cur: $22 (6/30/88) (BT)
92	CHATEAU LE BON-PASTEUR Pomerol 1986 Rel: $22 Cur: $25 (6/15/89)
90+	CHATEAU LE BON-PASTEUR Pomerol 1986 Rel: $22 Cur: $25 (6/30/88) (BT)
80+	CHATEAU LE BON-PASTEUR Pomerol 1986 Rel: $22 Cur: $25 (5/15/87) (BT)
92	CHATEAU LE BON-PASTEUR Pomerol 1985 Rel: $20 Cur: $49 (5/15/88)
80+	CHATEAU LE BON-PASTEUR Pomerol 1985 Rel: $20 Cur: $49 (5/15/87) (BT)
60+	CHATEAU LE BON-PASTEUR Pomerol 1985 Rel: $20 Cur: $49 (4/16/86) (BT)
86	CHATEAU LE BON-PASTEUR Pomerol 1984 Rel: $12.50 Cur: $23 (6/15/87)
86	CHATEAU LE BON-PASTEUR Pomerol 1983 Rel: $22.50 Cur: $35 (6/16/86)
91	CHATEAU LE BON-PASTEUR Pomerol 1982 Cur: $50 (5/15/89) (TR)
91	CHATEAU LE BON-PASTEUR Pomerol 1979 Cur: $28 (10/15/89) (JS)
85+	CHATEAU BOURGNEUF-VAYRON Pomerol 1990 (NR) (4/30/91) (BT)
80+	CHATEAU BOURGNEUF-VAYRON Pomerol 1989 (NR) (4/30/91) (BT)
85+	CHATEAU BOURGNEUF-VAYRON Pomerol 1989 (NR) (4/30/90) (BT)
90	CHATEAU BOURGNEUF-VAYRON Pomerol 1988 $19 (6/30/91)
85+	CHATEAU BOURGNEUF-VAYRON Pomerol 1988 $19 (6/30/89) (BT)
75+	CHATEAU BOURGNEUF-VAYRON Pomerol 1987 Rel: $13 Cur: $13 (6/30/89) (BT)
75+	CHATEAU BOURGNEUF-VAYRON Pomerol 1987 Rel: $13 Cur: $13 (6/30/88) (BT)
80+	CHATEAU BOURGNEUF-VAYRON Pomerol 1986 Rel: $22 Cur: $25 (6/30/88) (BT)
70+	CHATEAU BOURGNEUF-VAYRON Pomerol 1986 Rel: $22 Cur: $25 (5/15/87) (BT)
86	CHATEAU BOURGNEUF-VAYRON Pomerol 1985 Rel: $28 Cur: $28 (11/30/88)
90+	CHATEAU BOURGNEUF-VAYRON Pomerol 1985 Rel: $28 Cur: $28 (5/15/87) (BT)
70+	CHATEAU BOURGNEUF-VAYRON Pomerol 1985 Rel: $28 Cur: $28 (4/16/86) (BT)
83	CHATEAU BOURGNEUF-VAYRON Pomerol 1982 Cur: $23 (5/15/89) (TR)
85+	CHATEAU LA CABANNE Pomerol 1989 (NR) (4/30/91) (BT)
80+	CHATEAU LA CABANNE Pomerol 1987 $20 (6/30/89) (BT)
75+	CHATEAU LA CABANNE Pomerol 1987 $20 (6/30/88) (BT)
85+	CHATEAU LA CABANNE Pomerol 1986 Cur: $30 (6/30/88) (BT)
70+	CHATEAU LA CABANNE Pomerol 1986 Cur: $30 (5/15/87) (BT)
80+	CHATEAU LA CABANNE Pomerol 1985 Cur: $30 (5/15/87) (BT)
85+	CHATEAU CERTAN DE MAY Pomerol 1990 (NR) (4/30/91) (BT)
90+	CHATEAU CERTAN DE MAY Pomerol 1989 (NR) (4/30/91) (BT)
90	CHATEAU CERTAN DE MAY Pomerol 1988 $66 (6/30/91)
90+	CHATEAU CERTAN DE MAY Pomerol 1988 $66 (6/30/89) (BT)
85+	CHATEAU CERTAN DE MAY Pomerol 1987 Rel: $50 Cur: $50 (6/30/89) (BT)
93	CHATEAU CERTAN DE MAY Pomerol 1986 Rel: $53 Cur: $70 (9/15/89)
90+	CHATEAU CERTAN DE MAY Pomerol 1986 Rel: $53 Cur: $70 (5/15/87) (BT)
86	CHATEAU CERTAN DE MAY Pomerol 1985 Rel: $70 Cur: $85 (4/30/88)
90+	CHATEAU CERTAN DE MAY Pomerol 1985 Rel: $70 Cur: $85 (5/15/87) (BT)
92	CHATEAU CERTAN DE MAY Pomerol 1982 Cur: $114 (5/15/89) (TR)
90	CHATEAU CERTAN DE MAY Pomerol 1979 Cur: $65 (10/15/89) (JS)
89	CHATEAU CERTAN-GIRAUD Pomerol 1988 $23 (2/28/91)
80+	CHATEAU CERTAN-GIRAUD Pomerol 1988 $23 (6/30/89) (BT)
75+	CHATEAU CERTAN-GIRAUD Pomerol 1987 Rel: $18 Cur: $18 (6/30/89) (BT)
86	CHATEAU CERTAN-GIRAUD Pomerol 1986 Rel: $22 Cur: $22 (6/30/89)
85	CHATEAU CERTAN-GIRAUD Pomerol 1985 Rel: $25 Cur: $25 (4/30/88)
90	CHATEAU CERTAN-GIRAUD Pomerol 1982 Cur: $37 (5/15/89) (TR)
90+	CHATEAU CLINET Pomerol 1990 (NR) (4/30/91) (BT)
90+	CHATEAU CLINET Pomerol 1989 (NR) (4/30/91) (BT)
95+	CHATEAU CLINET Pomerol 1989 (NR) (4/30/90) (BT)
92	CHATEAU CLINET Pomerol 1988 $31 (2/28/91)
95+	CHATEAU CLINET Pomerol 1988 $31 (8/31/90) (BT)
85+	CHATEAU CLINET Pomerol 1988 $31 (6/30/89) (BT)
90+	CHATEAU CLINET Pomerol 1987 Rel: $25 Cur: $25 (6/30/89) (BT)
85+	CHATEAU CLINET Pomerol 1987 Rel: $25 Cur: $25 (6/30/88) (BT)
78	CHATEAU CLINET Pomerol 1986 Rel: $25 Cur: $27 (9/15/89)
90+	CHATEAU CLINET Pomerol 1986 Rel: $25 Cur: $27 (6/30/88) (BT)
90+	CHATEAU CLINET Pomerol 1986 Rel: $25 Cur: $27 (5/15/87) (BT)
91	CHATEAU CLINET Pomerol 1985 Rel: $34 Cur: $34 (4/30/88)
80+	CHATEAU CLINET Pomerol 1985 Rel: $34 Cur: $34 (5/15/87) (BT)
78	CHATEAU CLINET Pomerol 1982 Cur: $38 (5/15/89) (TR)
83	CLOS DES LITANIES Pomerol 1982 (NA) (5/15/89) (TR)
85+	CLOS DU CLOCHER Pomerol 1989 (NR) (4/30/91) (BT)
80+	CLOS DU CLOCHER Pomerol 1988 $22 (6/30/89) (BT)
80+	CLOS DU CLOCHER Pomerol 1987 Rel: $18 Cur: $18 (6/30/89) (BT)
70+	CLOS DU CLOCHER Pomerol 1987 Rel: $18 Cur: $18 (6/30/88) (BT)
80+	CLOS DU CLOCHER Pomerol 1986 Rel: $20 Cur: $20 (6/30/88) (BT)
88	CLOS DU CLOCHER Pomerol 1985 Rel: $17 Cur: $20 (2/29/88)
83	CLOS DU CLOCHER Pomerol 1982 Cur: $33 (5/15/89) (TR)
90+	CLOS L'EGLISE Pomerol 1990 (NR) (4/30/91) (BT)
95+	CLOS L'EGLISE Pomerol 1989 (NR) (4/30/91) (BT)
80+	CLOS L'EGLISE Pomerol 1989 (NR) (4/30/90) (BT)
83	CLOS L'EGLISE Pomerol 1988 $24 (6/30/91)
80+	CLOS L'EGLISE Pomerol 1988 $24 (6/30/89) (BT)
75+	CLOS L'EGLISE Pomerol 1987 Rel: $20 Cur: $20 (6/30/89) (BT)
86	CLOS L'EGLISE Pomerol 1986 Rel: $28 Cur: $28 (2/15/90)
90+	CLOS L'EGLISE Pomerol 1986 Rel: $28 Cur: $28 (5/15/87) (BT)
80+	CLOS L'EGLISE Pomerol 1985 Rel: $21 Cur: $25 (5/15/87) (BT)
88	CLOS L'EGLISE Pomerol 1982 Cur: $27 (5/15/89) (TR)
63	CLOS L'EGLISE Pomerol 1961 Cur: $75 (3/16/86) (JL)
87	CLOS L'EGLISE Pomerol 1945 Cur: $225 (3/16/86) (JL)
88	CLOS RENE Pomerol 1988 $24 (4/30/91)
80+	CLOS RENE Pomerol 1988 $24 (6/30/89) (BT)
75+	CLOS RENE Pomerol 1987 $20 (6/30/89) (BT)
94	CLOS RENE Pomerol 1986 Rel: $19 Cur: $25 (6/15/89) SS
92	CLOS RENE Pomerol 1985 Rel: $17 Cur: $20 (3/15/88)
70+	CLOS RENE Pomerol 1985 Rel: $17 Cur: $20 (4/16/86) (BT)
91	CLOS RENE Pomerol 1983 Rel: $17 Cur: $23 (3/16/86)
87	CLOS RENE Pomerol 1982 Cur: $24 (5/15/89) (TR)
60	CLOS RENE Pomerol 1962 Cur: $35 (11/30/87) (JS)
88	CLOS RENE Pomerol 1959 Cur: $50 (10/15/90) (JS)
79	CLOS RENE Pomerol 1945 Cur: $100 (3/16/86) (JL)
90+	CHATEAU LA CONSEILLANTE Pomerol 1990 (NR) (4/30/91) (BT)
85+	CHATEAU LA CONSEILLANTE Pomerol 1989 (NR) (4/30/91) (BT)
90	CHATEAU LA CONSEILLANTE Pomerol 1988 $56 (3/31/91)

FRANCE
BORDEAUX RED/POMEROL

85+ CHATEAU LA CONSEILLANTE Pomerol 1988 $56 (6/30/89) (BT)	80+ CHATEAU LA FLEUR-PETRUS Pomerol 1987 Rel: $36 Cur: $36 (6/30/89) (BT)
86 CHATEAU LA CONSEILLANTE Pomerol 1987 Rel: $35 Cur: $35 (5/15/90)	93 CHATEAU LA FLEUR-PETRUS Pomerol 1986 Rel: $52 Cur: $52 (2/15/90) CS
80+ CHATEAU LA CONSEILLANTE Pomerol 1987 Rel: $35 Cur: $35 (6/30/89) (BT)	86 CHATEAU LA FLEUR-PETRUS Pomerol 1985 Rel: $50 Cur: $54 (6/30/88)
85+ CHATEAU LA CONSEILLANTE Pomerol 1987 Rel: $35 Cur: $35 (6/30/88) (BT)	90+ CHATEAU LA FLEUR-PETRUS Pomerol 1985 Rel: $50 Cur: $54 (4/16/86) (BT)
93 CHATEAU LA CONSEILLANTE Pomerol 1986 Rel: $40 Cur: $54 (6/15/89)	88 CHATEAU LA FLEUR-PETRUS Pomerol 1982 Cur: $85 (5/15/89) (TR)
90+ CHATEAU LA CONSEILLANTE Pomerol 1986 Rel: $40 Cur: $54 (6/30/88) (BT)	92 CHATEAU LA FLEUR-PETRUS Pomerol (Bottled in England) 1959 Cur: $150 (10/15/90) (JS)
93 CHATEAU LA CONSEILLANTE Pomerol 1985 Rel: $50 Cur: $63 (2/29/88)	63 CHATEAU LA FLEUR-PETRUS Pomerol 1945 Cur: $300 (3/16/86) (JL)
70+ CHATEAU LA CONSEILLANTE Pomerol 1985 Rel: $50 Cur: $63 (4/16/86) (BT)	90+ CHATEAU LA FLEUR DE GAY Pomerol 1990 (NR) (4/30/91) (BT)
93 CHATEAU LA CONSEILLANTE Pomerol 1984 Rel: $26 Cur: $38 (3/31/87)	95+ CHATEAU LA FLEUR DE GAY Pomerol 1989 (NR) (4/30/91) (BT)
84 CHATEAU LA CONSEILLANTE Pomerol 1983 Rel: $33 Cur: $40 (11/15/86)	95+ CHATEAU LA FLEUR DE GAY Pomerol 1989 (NR) (4/30/90) (BT)
96 CHATEAU LA CONSEILLANTE Pomerol 1982 Rel: $29.50 Cur: $70 (5/15/89) (TR)	94 CHATEAU LA FLEUR DE GAY Pomerol 1988 $57 (6/30/91)
93 CHATEAU LA CONSEILLANTE Pomerol 1982 Rel: $29.50 Cur: $70 (2/16/85)	90+ CHATEAU LA FLEUR DE GAY Pomerol 1988 $57 (8/31/90) (BT)
60 CHATEAU LA CONSEILLANTE Pomerol 1962 Cur: $55 (11/30/87) (JS)	95+ CHATEAU LA FLEUR DE GAY Pomerol 1988 $57 (6/30/89) (BT)
88 CHATEAU LA CONSEILLANTE Pomerol 1959 Cur: $150 (10/15/90) (JS)	85+ CHATEAU LA FLEUR DE GAY Pomerol 1987 $38 (6/30/89) (BT)
90+ CHATEAU LA CROIX Pomerol 1990 (NR) (4/30/91) (BT)	85+ CHATEAU LA FLEUR DE GAY Pomerol 1987 $38 (6/30/88) (BT)
90+ CHATEAU LA CROIX Pomerol 1989 (NR) (4/30/91) (BT)	95 CHATEAU LA FLEUR DE GAY Pomerol 1986 Rel: $43 Cur: $48 (10/31/89) CS
82 CHATEAU LA CROIX Pomerol 1988 $19 (7/31/91)	90+ CHATEAU LA FLEUR DE GAY Pomerol 1986 Rel: $43 Cur: $48 (6/30/88) (BT)
70+ CHATEAU LA CROIX Pomerol 1988 $19 (6/30/89) (BT)	88 CHATEAU LA FLEUR DE GAY Pomerol 1982 Cur: $45 (5/15/89) (TR)
75+ CHATEAU LA CROIX Pomerol 1987 Rel: $15 Cur: $15 (6/30/89) (BT)	90+ CHATEAU LE GAY Pomerol 1990 (NR) (4/30/91) (BT)
75+ CHATEAU LA CROIX Pomerol 1987 Rel: $15 Cur: $15 (6/30/88) (BT)	95+ CHATEAU LE GAY Pomerol 1989 (NR) (4/30/91) (BT)
80+ CHATEAU LA CROIX Pomerol 1986 Rel: $25 Cur: $25 (6/30/88) (BT)	90+ CHATEAU LE GAY Pomerol 1989 (NR) (4/30/90) (BT)
93 CHATEAU LA CROIX Pomerol 1985 Rel: $25 Cur: $25 (5/15/88)	83 CHATEAU LE GAY Pomerol 1988 $30 (4/30/91)
84 CHATEAU LA CROIX Pomerol 1983 Rel: $14 Cur: $19 (11/30/86)	90+ CHATEAU LE GAY Pomerol 1988 $30 (8/31/90) (BT)
89 CHATEAU LA CROIX Pomerol 1982 Rel: $23 Cur: $23 (5/15/89) (TR)	90+ CHATEAU LE GAY Pomerol 1988 $30 (6/30/89) (BT)
86 CHATEAU LA CROIX Pomerol 1982 Rel: $23 Cur: $23 (5/01/89)	60+ CHATEAU LE GAY Pomerol 1985 Cur: $26 (4/16/86) (BT)
72 CHATEAU LA CROIX Pomerol 1981 Rel: $13.75 Cur: $14 (5/01/89)	89 CHATEAU LE GAY Pomerol 1982 Cur: $40 (5/15/89) (TR)
60 CHATEAU LA CROIX Pomerol 1979 Rel: $11 Cur: $22 (4/01/84)	90+ CHATEAU GAZIN Pomerol 1990 (NR) (4/30/91) (BT)
80+ CHATEAU LA CROIX DE GAY Pomerol 1990 (NR) (4/30/91) (BT)	90+ CHATEAU GAZIN Pomerol 1989 (NR) (4/30/91) (BT)
89 CHATEAU LA CROIX DE GAY Pomerol 1988 $26 (6/30/91)	90+ CHATEAU GAZIN Pomerol 1989 (NR) (4/30/90) (BT)
85+ CHATEAU LA CROIX DE GAY Pomerol 1988 $26 (8/31/90) (BT)	87 CHATEAU GAZIN Pomerol 1988 $30 (6/30/91)
85+ CHATEAU LA CROIX DE GAY Pomerol 1988 $26 (6/30/89) (BT)	90+ CHATEAU GAZIN Pomerol 1988 $30 (8/31/90) (BT)
80+ CHATEAU LA CROIX DE GAY Pomerol 1987 Rel: $20 Cur: $20 (6/30/89) (BT)	90+ CHATEAU GAZIN Pomerol 1988 $30 (6/30/89) (BT)
85+ CHATEAU LA CROIX DE GAY Pomerol 1987 Rel: $20 Cur: $20 (6/30/88) (BT)	80+ CHATEAU GAZIN Pomerol 1987 Rel: $22 Cur: $22 (6/30/89) (BT)
90+ CHATEAU LA CROIX DE GAY Pomerol 1986 Rel: $20 Cur: $22 (6/30/88) (BT)	80+ CHATEAU GAZIN Pomerol 1986 Rel: $21 Cur: $23 (5/15/87) (BT)
80+ CHATEAU LA CROIX DE GAY Pomerol 1986 Rel: $20 Cur: $22 (5/15/87) (BT)	90 CHATEAU GAZIN Pomerol 1985 Rel: $21 Cur: $28 (9/30/88)
91 CHATEAU LA CROIX DE GAY Pomerol 1985 Rel: $33 Cur: $33 (3/15/88) CS	70+ CHATEAU GAZIN Pomerol 1985 Rel: $21 Cur: $28 (5/15/87) (BT)
80+ CHATEAU LA CROIX DE GAY Pomerol 1985 Rel: $33 Cur: $33 (5/15/87) (BT)	88 CHATEAU GAZIN Pomerol 1982 Cur: $30 (5/15/89) (TR)
94 CHATEAU LA CROIX DE GAY Pomerol 1983 Rel: $16 Cur: $23 (7/01/86) CS	83 CHATEAU GAZIN Pomerol 1961 Cur: $120 (3/16/86) (JL)
91 CHATEAU LA CROIX DE GAY Pomerol 1982 Rel: $16.25 Cur: $17 (5/15/89) (TR)	70+ CHATEAU GOMBAUDE-GUILLOT Pomerol 1987 Rel: $17 Cur: $17 (6/30/89) (BT)
70 CHATEAU LA CROIX DE GAY Pomerol 1945 Cur: $370 (3/16/86) (JL)	83 CHATEAU GOMBAUDE-GUILLOT Pomerol 1982 Cur: $28 (5/15/89) (TR)
90+ CHATEAU LA CROIX DU CASSE Pomerol 1989 (NR) (4/30/91) (BT)	90+ CHATEAU LA GRAVE-TRIGANT DE BOISSET Pomerol 1990 (NR) (4/30/91) (BT)
85+ CHATEAU LA CROIX DU CASSE Pomerol 1988 $20 (6/30/89) (BT)	90+ CHATEAU LA GRAVE-TRIGANT DE BOISSET Pomerol 1989 (NR) (4/30/91) (BT)
75+ CHATEAU LA CROIX DU CASSE Pomerol 1987 Rel: $17 Cur: $17 (6/30/88) (BT)	80+ CHATEAU LA GRAVE-TRIGANT DE BOISSET Pomerol 1989 (NR) (4/30/90) (BT)
82 CHATEAU LA CROIX DU CASSE Pomerol 1985 Rel: $25 Cur: $25 (5/15/88)	90+ CHATEAU LA GRAVE-TRIGANT DE BOISSET Pomerol 1988 $24 (8/31/90) (BT)
80 CHATEAU LA CROIX-TOULIFAUT Pomerol 1982 (NA) (5/15/89) (TR)	85+ CHATEAU LA GRAVE-TRIGANT DE BOISSET Pomerol 1988 $24 (6/30/89) (BT)
91 CHATEAU L'EGLISE-CLINET Pomerol 1988 $47 (12/31/90)	80+ CHATEAU LA GRAVE-TRIGANT DE BOISSET Pomerol 1987 Rel: $21 Cur: $21 (6/30/89) (BT)
83 CHATEAU L'EGLISE-CLINET Pomerol 1987 Rel: $22 Cur: $23 (2/15/90)	80+ CHATEAU LA GRAVE-TRIGANT DE BOISSET Pomerol 1987 Rel: $21 Cur: $21 (6/30/88) (BT)
91 CHATEAU L'EGLISE-CLINET Pomerol 1986 Rel: $29 Cur: $45 (6/15/89)	89 CHATEAU LA GRAVE-TRIGANT DE BOISSET Pomerol 1986 Rel: $35 Cur: $35 (3/31/90)
93 CHATEAU L'EGLISE-CLINET Pomerol 1985 Rel: $30 Cur: $57 (2/29/88)	85+ CHATEAU LA GRAVE-TRIGANT DE BOISSET Pomerol 1986 Rel: $35 Cur: $35 (6/30/88) (BT)
70+ CHATEAU L'EGLISE-CLINET Pomerol 1985 Rel: $30 Cur: $57 (4/16/86) (BT)	90+ CHATEAU LA GRAVE-TRIGANT DE BOISSET Pomerol 1986 Rel: $35 Cur: $35 (5/15/87) (BT)
88 CHATEAU L'EGLISE-CLINET Pomerol 1983 Rel: $19 Cur: $24 (3/16/86)	80+ CHATEAU LA GRAVE-TRIGANT DE BOISSET Pomerol 1985 Cur: $29 (5/15/87) (BT)
87 CHATEAU L'EGLISE-CLINET Pomerol 1982 Rel: $18 Cur: $27 (5/15/89) (TR)	91 CHATEAU LA GRAVE-TRIGANT DE BOISSET Pomerol 1982 Cur: $40 (5/15/89) (TR)
92 CHATEAU L'EGLISE-CLINET Pomerol 1982 Rel: $18 Cur: $27 (5/01/85)	90 CHATEAU LA GRAVE-TRIGANT DE BOISSET Pomerol 1979 Cur: $25 (10/15/89) (JS)
90+ DOMAINE DE L'EGLISE Pomerol 1990 (NR) (4/30/91) (BT)	85+ CHATEAU HAUT-MAILLET Pomerol 1989 (NR) (4/30/91) (BT)
90+ DOMAINE DE L'EGLISE Pomerol 1989 (NR) (4/30/90) (BT)	83 CHATEAU HERMITAGE Pomerol 1982 (NA) (5/15/89) (TR)
85 CHATEAU L'ENCLOS Pomerol 1988 $17 (3/15/91)	95+ CHATEAU LAFLEUR Pomerol 1989 (NR) (4/30/91) (BT)
80+ CHATEAU L'ENCLOS Pomerol 1987 Rel: $15 Cur: $15 (6/30/89) (BT)	90+ CHATEAU LAFLEUR Pomerol 1989 (NR) (4/30/90) (BT)
92 CHATEAU L'ENCLOS Pomerol 1986 Rel: $20 Cur: $20 (6/15/89)	90+ CHATEAU LAFLEUR Pomerol 1988 (NR) (8/31/90) (BT)
83 CHATEAU L'ENCLOS Pomerol 1984 Rel: $16 Cur: $20 (3/31/87)	95+ CHATEAU LAFLEUR Pomerol 1988 (NR) (6/30/89) (BT)
86 CHATEAU L'ENCLOS Pomerol 1982 Rel: $20 Cur: $25 (5/15/89) (TR)	90 CHATEAU LAFLEUR Pomerol 1986 Rel: $100 Cur: $138 (10/31/89)
78 CHATEAU L'ENCLOS Pomerol 1945 Cur: $100 (3/16/86) (JL)	95 CHATEAU LAFLEUR Pomerol 1985 Cur: $135 (5/01/89)
84 CHATEAU ENCLOS-HAUT-MAZEYRES Pomerol 1982 (NA) (5/15/89) (TR)	94 CHATEAU LAFLEUR Pomerol 1982 Cur: $237 (5/15/89) (TR)
90+ CHATEAU L'EVANGILE Pomerol 1990 (NR) (4/30/91) (BT)	91 CHATEAU LAFLEUR Pomerol 1982 Cur: $237 (5/01/89)
87 CHATEAU L'EVANGILE Pomerol 1988 $38 (6/30/91)	80 CHATEAU LAFLEUR Pomerol 1981 Rel: $22 Cur: $110 (6/01/84)
80+ CHATEAU L'EVANGILE Pomerol 1988 $38 (6/30/89) (BT)	96 CHATEAU LAFLEUR Pomerol 1979 Cur: $175 (10/15/89) (JS)
80+ CHATEAU L'EVANGILE Pomerol 1987 Rel: $25 Cur: $31 (6/30/89) (BT)	64 CHATEAU LAFLEUR Pomerol 1945 Cur: $400 (3/16/86) (JL)
80+ CHATEAU L'EVANGILE Pomerol 1987 Rel: $25 Cur: $31 (6/30/88) (BT)	58 CHATEAU LAFLEUR-GAZIN Pomerol 1945 (NA) (3/16/86) (JL)
88 CHATEAU L'EVANGILE Pomerol 1986 Rel: $62 Cur: $62 (9/15/89)	83 CHATEAU LAFLEUR DU ROY Pomerol 1982 (NA) (5/15/89) (TR)
90+ CHATEAU L'EVANGILE Pomerol 1986 Rel: $62 Cur: $62 (6/30/88) (BT)	90+ CHATEAU LAGRANGE Pomerol 1990 (NR) (4/30/91) (BT)
92 CHATEAU L'EVANGILE Pomerol 1985 Rel: $55 Cur: $73 (2/29/88)	85+ CHATEAU LAGRANGE Pomerol 1989 (NR) (4/30/91) (BT)
79 CHATEAU L'EVANGILE Pomerol 1984 Rel: $31 Cur: $75 (2/15/87)	85+ CHATEAU LAGRANGE Pomerol 1989 (NR) (4/30/90) (BT)
92 CHATEAU L'EVANGILE Pomerol 1983 Rel: $42 Cur: $51 (3/16/86)	85+ CHATEAU LAGRANGE Pomerol 1988 $25 (6/30/89) (BT)
93 CHATEAU L'EVANGILE Pomerol 1982 Rel: $55 Cur: $85 (5/15/89) (TR)	80+ CHATEAU LAGRANGE Pomerol 1985 Cur: $22 (4/16/86) (BT)
90 CHATEAU L'EVANGILE Pomerol 1982 Rel: $55 Cur: $85 (5/01/89)	84 CHATEAU LAGRANGE Pomerol 1982 Cur: $30 (5/15/89) (TR)
77 CHATEAU L'EVANGILE Pomerol 1961 Cur: $253 (3/16/86) (JL)	90+ CHATEAU LATOUR A POMEROL Pomerol 1990 (NR) (4/30/91) (BT)
90+ CHATEAU FEYTIT-CLINET Pomerol 1989 (NR) (4/30/91) (BT)	90+ CHATEAU LATOUR A POMEROL Pomerol 1989 (NR) (4/30/91) (BT)
88 CHATEAU FEYTIT-CLINET Pomerol 1985 Rel: $30 Cur: $30 (4/30/88)	80+ CHATEAU LATOUR A POMEROL Pomerol 1989 (NR) (4/30/90) (BT)
70 CHATEAU FEYTIT-CLINET Pomerol 1983 Rel: $13 Cur: $17 (7/16/86)	95+ CHATEAU LATOUR A POMEROL Pomerol 1988 $55 (6/30/89) (BT)
91 CHATEAU FEYTIT-CLINET Pomerol 1982 Rel: $14.75 Cur: $20 (5/15/89) (TR)	80+ CHATEAU LATOUR A POMEROL Pomerol 1987 Rel: $35 Cur: $35 (6/30/89) (BT)
87 CHATEAU FEYTIT-CLINET Pomerol 1982 Rel: $14.75 Cur: $20 (3/16/85)	90+ CHATEAU LATOUR A POMEROL Pomerol 1986 Cur: $39 (5/15/87) (BT)
90+ CHATEAU LA FLEUR-PETRUS Pomerol 1990 (NR) (4/30/91) (BT)	90+ CHATEAU LATOUR A POMEROL Pomerol 1985 Cur: $61 (5/15/87) (BT)
95+ CHATEAU LA FLEUR-PETRUS Pomerol 1989 (NR) (4/30/91) (BT)	92 CHATEAU LATOUR A POMEROL Pomerol 1982 Cur: $81 (5/15/89) (TR)
85+ CHATEAU LA FLEUR-PETRUS Pomerol 1989 (NR) (4/30/90) (BT)	94 CHATEAU LATOUR A POMEROL Pomerol 1961 Cur: $1,100 (3/16/86) (JL)
85+ CHATEAU LA FLEUR-PETRUS Pomerol 1988 $63 (6/30/89) (BT)	90 CHATEAU LATOUR A POMEROL Pomerol 1959 Cur: $580 (10/15/90) (JS)
	77 CHATEAU LA LOUBIERE Pomerol 1983 Rel: $15 Cur: $15 (6/16/86)
	88 CHATEAU LA LOUBIERE Pomerol 1982 Rel: $13 Cur: $13 (5/15/89) (TR)
	56 CHATEAU LA MADELEINE Pomerol 1985 $10 (3/15/88)
	90+ CHATEAU MAZEYRES Pomerol 1989 (NR) (4/30/91) (BT)
	70+ CHATEAU MAZEYRES Pomerol 1986 (NR) (6/30/88) (BT)
	85+ CHATEAU MONTVIEL Pomerol 1989 (NR) (4/30/91) (BT)
	80+ CHATEAU MONTVIEL Pomerol 1987 $20 (6/30/89) (BT)
	75+ CHATEAU MONTVIEL Pomerol 1987 $20 (6/30/88) (BT)
	80+ CHATEAU MONTVIEL Pomerol 1986 $29 (6/30/88) (BT)
	90+ CHATEAU MOULINET Pomerol 1989 (NR) (4/30/91) (BT)

88 CHATEAU MOULINET Pomerol 1988 $17 (7/31/91)
80+ CHATEAU MOULINET Pomerol 1988 $17 (6/30/89) (BT)
75+ CHATEAU MOULINET Pomerol 1987 Rel: $15 Cur: $15 (6/30/89) (BT)
75+ CHATEAU MOULINET Pomerol 1987 Rel: $15 Cur: $15 (6/30/88) (BT)
80+ CHATEAU MOULINET Pomerol 1986 Rel: $15 Cur: $15 (6/30/88) (BT)
87 CHATEAU MOULINET Pomerol 1982 Rel: $9.75 Cur: $10 (5/15/89) (TR)
86 CHATEAU MOULINET Pomerol 1982 Rel: $9.75 Cur: $10 (4/01/85)
75+ CHATEAU NENIN Pomerol 1987 Rel: $20 Cur: $20 (6/30/88) (BT)
84 CHATEAU NENIN Pomerol 1986 Rel: $22 Cur: $22 (6/30/89)
75+ CHATEAU NENIN Pomerol 1986 Rel: $22 Cur: $22 (6/30/88) (BT)
89 CHATEAU NENIN Pomerol 1982 Cur: $30 (5/15/89) (TR)
88 CHATEAU NENIN Pomerol 1959 Cur: $96 (10/15/90) (JS)
74 CHATEAU NENIN Pomerol 1945 Cur: $250 (3/16/86) (JL)
90+ CHATEAU PETIT-VILLAGE Pomerol 1990 (NR) (4/30/91) (BT)
85+ CHATEAU PETIT-VILLAGE Pomerol 1989 (NR) (4/30/91) (BT)
85+ CHATEAU PETIT-VILLAGE Pomerol 1989 (NR) (4/30/90) (BT)
90+ CHATEAU PETIT-VILLAGE Pomerol 1988 $26 (8/31/90) (BT)
85+ CHATEAU PETIT-VILLAGE Pomerol 1988 $26 (6/30/89) (BT)
80+ CHATEAU PETIT-VILLAGE Pomerol 1987 Rel: $22 Cur: $22 (6/30/89) (BT)
85+ CHATEAU PETIT-VILLAGE Pomerol 1987 Rel: $22 Cur: $22 (6/30/88) (BT)
90+ CHATEAU PETIT-VILLAGE Pomerol 1986 Rel: $24 Cur: $25 (6/30/88) (BT)
80+ CHATEAU PETIT-VILLAGE Pomerol 1986 Rel: $24 Cur: $25 (5/15/87) (BT)
92 CHATEAU PETIT-VILLAGE Pomerol 1982 Cur: $48 (5/15/89) (TR)
86 CHATEAU PETIT-VILLAGE Pomerol 1959 Cur: $80 (10/15/90) (JS)
78 LA PETITE EGLISE Pomerol 1986 Rel: $15 Cur: $15 (9/15/89)
73 LA PETITE EGLISE Pomerol 1986 Rel: $15 Cur: $15 (6/30/89)
95+ CHATEAU PETRUS Pomerol 1990 (NR) (4/30/91) (BT)
95+ CHATEAU PETRUS Pomerol 1989 (NR) (4/30/91) (BT)
95+ CHATEAU PETRUS Pomerol 1989 (NR) (4/30/90) (BT)
95+ CHATEAU PETRUS Pomerol 1988 $221 (8/31/90) (BT)
95+ CHATEAU PETRUS Pomerol 1988 $221 (6/30/89) (BT)
85 CHATEAU PETRUS Pomerol 1987 Rel: $175 Cur: $175 (2/15/91) (JS)
84 CHATEAU PETRUS Pomerol 1987 Rel: $175 Cur: $175 (10/15/90)
85+ CHATEAU PETRUS Pomerol 1987 Rel: $175 Cur: $175 (6/30/89) (BT)
85+ CHATEAU PETRUS Pomerol 1987 Rel: $175 Cur: $175 (6/30/88) (BT)
96 CHATEAU PETRUS Pomerol 1986 Rel: $200 Cur: $285 (2/15/91) (JS)
95 CHATEAU PETRUS Pomerol 1986 Rel: $200 Cur: $285 (11/15/89)
95+ CHATEAU PETRUS Pomerol 1986 Rel: $200 Cur: $285 (6/30/88) (BT)
90+ CHATEAU PETRUS Pomerol 1986 Rel: $200 Cur: $285 (5/15/87) (BT)
97 CHATEAU PETRUS Pomerol 1985 Rel: $160 Cur: $350 (2/15/91) (JS)
98 CHATEAU PETRUS Pomerol 1985 Rel: $160 Cur: $350 (5/31/88)
90+ CHATEAU PETRUS Pomerol 1985 Rel: $160 Cur: $350 (5/15/87) (BT)
83 CHATEAU PETRUS Pomerol 1984 Rel: $125 Cur: $187 (2/15/91) (JS)
90 CHATEAU PETRUS Pomerol 1984 Rel: $125 Cur: $187 (9/15/87)
91 CHATEAU PETRUS Pomerol 1983 Rel: $125 Cur: $285 (2/15/91) (JS)
94 CHATEAU PETRUS Pomerol 1983 Rel: $125 Cur: $285 (2/15/87)
96 CHATEAU PETRUS Pomerol 1982 Cur: $530 (2/15/91) (JS)
92 CHATEAU PETRUS Pomerol 1982 Cur: $530 (5/15/89) (TR)
93 CHATEAU PETRUS Pomerol 1982 Cur: $530 (5/01/89)
90 CHATEAU PETRUS Pomerol 1981 Cur: $310 (2/15/91) (JS)
86 CHATEAU PETRUS Pomerol 1980 Cur: $185 (2/15/91) (JS)
90 CHATEAU PETRUS Pomerol 1979 Cur: $330 (2/15/91) (JS)
93 CHATEAU PETRUS Pomerol 1979 Cur: $330 (10/15/89) (JS)
89 CHATEAU PETRUS Pomerol 1978 Cur: $380 (2/15/91) (JS)
86 CHATEAU PETRUS Pomerol 1976 Cur: $290 (2/15/91) (JS)
93 CHATEAU PETRUS Pomerol 1975 Cur: $500 (2/15/91) (JS)
78 CHATEAU PETRUS Pomerol 1973 Cur: $240 (2/15/91) (JS)
94 CHATEAU PETRUS Pomerol 1971 Cur: $480 (2/15/91) (JS)
92 CHATEAU PETRUS Pomerol 1970 Cur: $550 (2/15/91) (JS)
79 CHATEAU PETRUS Pomerol 1968 Cur: $200 (2/15/91) (JS)
87 CHATEAU PETRUS Pomerol 1967 Cur: $310 (2/15/91) (JS)
93 CHATEAU PETRUS Pomerol 1966 Cur: $500 (2/15/91) (JS)
94 CHATEAU PETRUS Pomerol 1964 Cur: $580 (2/15/91) (JS)
94 CHATEAU PETRUS Pomerol 1962 Cur: $570 (2/15/91) (JS)
90 CHATEAU PETRUS Pomerol 1962 Cur: $570 (11/30/87) (JS)
100 CHATEAU PETRUS Pomerol 1961 Cur: $2,000 (2/15/91) (JS)
92 CHATEAU PETRUS Pomerol 1961 Cur: $2,000 (3/16/86) (JL)
96 CHATEAU PETRUS Pomerol 1959 Cur: $930 (2/15/91) (JS)
97 CHATEAU PETRUS Pomerol 1959 Cur: $930 (10/15/90) (JS)
96 CHATEAU PETRUS Pomerol 1959 Cur: $930 (12/15/88)
85 CHATEAU PETRUS Pomerol 1958 Cur: $460 (2/15/91) (JS)
91 CHATEAU PETRUS Pomerol 1955 Cur: $580 (2/15/91) (JS)
92 CHATEAU PETRUS Pomerol 1953 Cur: $780 (2/15/91) (JS)
89 CHATEAU PETRUS Pomerol 1952 Cur: $570 (2/15/91) (JS)
99 CHATEAU PETRUS Pomerol 1950 Cur: $850 (2/15/91) (JS)
98 CHATEAU PETRUS Pomerol 1949 Cur: $1,200 (2/15/91) (JS)
91 CHATEAU PETRUS Pomerol 1948 Cur: $1,200 (2/15/91) (JS)
97 CHATEAU PETRUS Pomerol 1947 Cur: $1,700 (2/15/91) (JS)
100 CHATEAU PETRUS Pomerol 1945 Cur: $2,700 (2/15/91) (JS)
84 CHATEAU PETRUS Pomerol 1945 Cur: $2,700 (3/16/86) (JL)
95+ CHATEAU LE PIN Pomerol 1989 (NR) (4/30/90) (BT)
95 CHATEAU LE PIN Pomerol 1988 $65 (6/30/91) CS
90+ CHATEAU LE PIN Pomerol 1988 $65 (6/30/89) (BT)
85+ CHATEAU LE PIN Pomerol 1987 Rel: $45 Cur: $53 (6/30/89) (BT)
95 CHATEAU LE PIN Pomerol 1986 Rel: $55 Cur: $105 (6/15/89)
95 CHATEAU LE PIN Pomerol 1982 Cur: $217 (5/15/89) (TR)
85+ CHATEAU PLINCE Pomerol 1990 (NR) (4/30/91) (BT)
80+ CHATEAU PLINCE Pomerol 1989 (NR) (4/30/91) (BT)
80+ CHATEAU PLINCE Pomerol 1989 (NR) (4/30/90) (BT)
75+ CHATEAU PLINCE Pomerol 1987 Rel: $16 Cur: $21 (6/30/89) (BT)
70+ CHATEAU PLINCE Pomerol 1985 Rel: $17 Cur: $17 (5/15/87) (BT)
92 CHATEAU PLINCE Pomerol 1982 Cur: $25 (5/15/89) (TR)
95+ CHATEAU LA POINTE Pomerol 1989 (NR) (4/30/91) (BT)
85+ CHATEAU LA POINTE Pomerol 1989 (NR) (4/30/90) (BT)
83 CHATEAU LA POINTE Pomerol 1988 $35 (7/31/91)
80+ CHATEAU LA POINTE Pomerol 1988 $35 (6/30/89) (BT)
70+ CHATEAU LA POINTE Pomerol 1987 Rel: $21 Cur: $21 (6/30/88) (BT)
90 CHATEAU LA POINTE Pomerol 1986 Rel: $21 Cur: $21 (6/15/89)
75+ CHATEAU LA POINTE Pomerol 1986 Rel: $21 Cur: $21 (6/30/88) (BT)
50+ CHATEAU LA POINTE Pomerol 1985 Rel: $16 Cur: $16 (4/16/86) (BT)

85 CHATEAU LA POINTE Pomerol 1982 Cur: $22 (5/15/89) (TR)
80 CHATEAU LA POINTE Pomerol 1962 Cur: $35 (11/30/87) (JS)
78 CHATEAU LA POINTE Pomerol 1945 Cur: $250 (3/16/86) (JL)
90+ CHATEAU PRIEURS DE LA COMMANDERIE Pomerol 1989 (NR) (4/30/91) (BT)
70+ CHATEAU PRIEURS DE LA COMMANDERIE Pomerol 1987 (NR) (6/30/88) (BT)
75+ CHATEAU PRIEURS DE LA COMMANDERIE Pomerol 1986 (NR) (6/30/88) (BT)
93 CHATEAU PRIEURS DE LA COMMANDERIE Pomerol 1985 Rel: $27 Cur: $27 (9/30/88)
79 CHATEAU PRIEURS DE LA COMMANDERIE Pomerol 1983 Rel: $25 Cur: $25 (9/30/86)
85 CHATEAU LA ROSE-FIGEAC Pomerol 1982 Cur: $25 (5/15/89) (TR)
90+ CHATEAU ROUGET Pomerol 1990 (NR) (4/30/91) (BT)
85+ CHATEAU ROUGET Pomerol 1989 (NR) (4/30/91) (BT)
85+ CHATEAU ROUGET Pomerol 1989 (NR) (4/30/90) (BT)
86 CHATEAU ROUGET Pomerol 1982 Cur: $19 (5/15/89) (TR)
75+ CHATEAU DE SALES Pomerol 1990 (NR) (4/30/91) (BT)
90+ CHATEAU DE SALES Pomerol 1989 (NR) (4/30/91) (BT)
85+ CHATEAU DE SALES Pomerol 1989 (NR) (4/30/90) (BT)
70+ CHATEAU DE SALES Pomerol 1988 (NR) (6/30/89) (BT)
86 CHATEAU DE SALES Pomerol 1986 Rel: $20 Cur: $20 (6/30/89)
87 CHATEAU DE SALES Pomerol 1985 Rel: $14 Cur: $18 (6/30/88)
88 CHATEAU DE SALES Pomerol 1982 Cur: $23 (5/15/89) (TR)
91 CHATEAU TAILHAS Pomerol 1988 $20 (4/30/91)
82 CHATEAU TAILHAS Pomerol 1982 Rel: $15 Cur: $15 (5/15/89) (TR)
90+ CHATEAU TAILLEFER Pomerol 1989 (NR) (4/30/91) (BT)
87 CHATEAU TAILLEFER Pomerol 1988 $22 (6/30/91)
70+ CHATEAU TAILLEFER Pomerol 1988 $22 (6/30/89) (BT)
75+ CHATEAU TAILLEFER Pomerol 1987 Rel: $18 Cur: $18 (6/30/89) (BT)
70+ CHATEAU TAILLEFER Pomerol 1987 Rel: $18 Cur: $18 (6/30/88) (BT)
80+ CHATEAU TAILLEFER Pomerol 1986 Rel: $20 Cur: $20 (6/30/88) (BT)
81 CHATEAU TAILLEFER Pomerol 1985 Rel: $19 Cur: $19 (6/30/88)
85 CHATEAU TAILLEFER Pomerol 1982 (NA) (5/15/89) (TR)
95+ CHATEAU TROTANOY Pomerol 1990 (NR) (4/30/91) (BT)
95+ CHATEAU TROTANOY Pomerol 1989 (NR) (4/30/91) (BT)
90+ CHATEAU TROTANOY Pomerol 1989 (NR) (4/30/90) (BT)
95+ CHATEAU TROTANOY Pomerol 1988 $48 (8/31/90) (BT)
90+ CHATEAU TROTANOY Pomerol 1988 $48 (6/30/89) (BT)
85+ CHATEAU TROTANOY Pomerol 1987 Rel: $45 Cur: $45 (6/30/89) (BT)
88 CHATEAU TROTANOY Pomerol 1987 Rel: $45 Cur: $45 (10/15/88) (JS)
85+ CHATEAU TROTANOY Pomerol 1987 Rel: $45 Cur: $45 (6/30/88) (BT)
83 CHATEAU TROTANOY Pomerol 1986 Rel: $68 Cur: $68 (10/31/89)
90+ CHATEAU TROTANOY Pomerol 1986 Rel: $68 Cur: $68 (6/30/88) (BT)
90+ CHATEAU TROTANOY Pomerol 1986 Rel: $68 Cur: $68 (5/15/87) (BT)
93 CHATEAU TROTANOY Pomerol 1985 Rel: $70 Cur: $85 (4/30/88)
90+ CHATEAU TROTANOY Pomerol 1985 Rel: $70 Cur: $85 (5/15/87) (BT)
88 CHATEAU TROTANOY Pomerol 1983 Cur: $58 (10/15/88) (JS)
90 CHATEAU TROTANOY Pomerol 1982 Cur: $162 (5/15/89) (TR)
95 CHATEAU TROTANOY Pomerol 1982 Cur: $162 (10/15/88) (JS)
95 CHATEAU TROTANOY Pomerol 1981 Cur: $61 (10/15/88) (JS)
83 CHATEAU TROTANOY Pomerol 1980 Cur: $42 (10/15/88) (JS)
88 CHATEAU TROTANOY Pomerol 1979 Cur: $65 (10/15/89) (JS)
83 CHATEAU TROTANOY Pomerol 1978 Cur: $70 (10/15/88) (JS)
86 CHATEAU TROTANOY Pomerol 1976 Cur: $83 (10/15/88) (JS)
84 CHATEAU TROTANOY Pomerol 1975 Cur: $138 (10/15/88) (JS)
90 CHATEAU TROTANOY Pomerol 1971 Cur: $180 (10/15/88) (JS)
95 CHATEAU TROTANOY Pomerol 1970 Cur: $176 (10/15/88) (JS)
84 CHATEAU TROTANOY Pomerol 1967 Cur: $62 (10/15/88) (JS)
92 CHATEAU TROTANOY Pomerol 1966 Cur: $144 (10/15/88) (JS)
88 CHATEAU TROTANOY Pomerol 1962 Cur: $139 (10/15/88) (JS)
96 CHATEAU TROTANOY Pomerol 1961 Cur: $550 (10/15/88) (JS)
90 CHATEAU TROTANOY Pomerol 1959 Cur: $192 (10/15/90) (JS)
92 CHATEAU TROTANOY Pomerol 1959 Cur: $192 (10/15/88) (JS)
94 CHATEAU TROTANOY Pomerol 1955 Cur: $192 (10/15/88) (JS)
86 CHATEAU TROTANOY Pomerol 1953 Cur: $300 (10/15/88) (JS)
83 CHATEAU TROTANOY Pomerol 1952 Cur: $138 (10/15/88) (JS)
80 CHATEAU TROTANOY Pomerol 1947 Cur: $550 (10/15/88) (JS)
98 CHATEAU TROTANOY Pomerol 1945 Cur: $500 (10/15/88) (JS)
60 CHATEAU TROTANOY Pomerol 1934 Cur: $350 (10/15/88) (JS)
95 CHATEAU TROTANOY Pomerol 1928 Cur: $600 (10/15/88) (JS)
89 CHATEAU TROTANOY Pomerol 1926 Cur: $650 (10/15/88) (JS)
91 VIEUX CHATEAU CERTAN Pomerol 1988 $60 (3/31/91)
85+ VIEUX CHATEAU CERTAN Pomerol 1988 $60 (8/31/90) (BT)
84 VIEUX CHATEAU CERTAN Pomerol 1987 Rel: $30 Cur: $30 (5/15/90)
85+ VIEUX CHATEAU CERTAN Pomerol 1987 Rel: $30 Cur: $30 (6/30/89) (BT)
85+ VIEUX CHATEAU CERTAN Pomerol 1987 Rel: $30 Cur: $30 (6/30/88) (BT)
93 VIEUX CHATEAU CERTAN Pomerol 1986 Rel: $40 Cur: $54 (6/15/89)
95+ VIEUX CHATEAU CERTAN Pomerol 1986 Rel: $40 Cur: $54 (6/30/88) (BT)
90+ VIEUX CHATEAU CERTAN Pomerol 1986 Rel: $40 Cur: $54 (5/15/87) (BT)
90 VIEUX CHATEAU CERTAN Pomerol 1985 Rel: $38 Cur: $56 (6/30/88)
83 VIEUX CHATEAU CERTAN Pomerol 1983 Rel: $33 Cur: $36 (3/16/86)
89 VIEUX CHATEAU CERTAN Pomerol 1982 Rel: $29 Cur: $59 (5/15/89) (TR)
85 VIEUX CHATEAU CERTAN Pomerol 1982 Rel: $29 Cur: $59 (2/16/85)
87 VIEUX CHATEAU CERTAN Pomerol 1979 Cur: $48 (10/15/89) (JS)
60 VIEUX CHATEAU CERTAN Pomerol 1962 Cur: $65 (11/30/87) (JS)
90 VIEUX CHATEAU CERTAN Pomerol 1961 Cur: $229 (3/16/86) (JL)
91 VIEUX CHATEAU CERTAN Pomerol 1959 Cur: $120 (10/15/90) (JS)
50 VIEUX CHATEAU CERTAN Pomerol 1945 Cur: $900 (3/16/86) (JL)
82 CHATEAU VIEUX-FERRAND Pomerol 1982 (NA) (5/15/89) (TR)
88 CHATEAU VIOLETTE Pomerol 1982 Cur: $25 (5/15/89) (TR)
79 CHATEAU LA VIOLETTE Pomerol 1979 Cur: $25 (10/15/89) (JS)

St.-Emilion

85+ CHATEAU L'ANGELUS St.-Emilion 1990 (NR) (4/30/91) (BT)
85+ CHATEAU L'ANGELUS St.-Emilion 1989 (NR) (4/30/91) (BT)
93 CHATEAU L'ANGELUS St.-Emilion 1988 $41 (3/31/91)
80+ CHATEAU L'ANGELUS St.-Emilion 1988 $41 (6/30/89) (BT)
85 CHATEAU L'ANGELUS St.-Emilion 1987 Rel: $30 Cur: $30 (5/15/90)
80+ CHATEAU L'ANGELUS St.-Emilion 1987 Rel: $30 Cur: $30 (6/30/89) (BT)
75+ CHATEAU L'ANGELUS St.-Emilion 1987 Rel: $30 Cur: $30 (6/30/88) (BT)
94 CHATEAU L'ANGELUS St.-Emilion 1986 Rel: $26 Cur: $30 (6/30/89)

FRANCE
BORDEAUX RED/*ST.-EMILION*

80+ CHATEAU L'ANGELUS St.-Emilion 1986 Rel: $26 Cur: $30 (6/30/88) (BT)
80+ CHATEAU L'ANGELUS St.-Emilion 1986 Rel: $26 Cur: $30 (5/15/87) (BT)
94 CHATEAU L'ANGELUS St.-Emilion 1985 Rel: $26 Cur: $34 (3/31/88) CS
92 CHATEAU L'ANGELUS St.-Emilion 1983 Rel: $22 Cur: $24 (3/16/86)
88 CHATEAU L'ANGELUS St.-Emilion 1982 Rel: $20.50 Cur: $32 (5/15/89) (TR)
85 CHATEAU L'ANGELUS St.-Emilion 1982 Rel: $20.50 Cur: $32 (3/16/85)
82 CHATEAU L'ANGELUS St.-Emilion 1979 Cur: $22 (10/15/89) (JS)
68 CHATEAU L'ANGELUS St.-Emilion 1962 Cur: $45 (11/30/87) (JS)
94 CHATEAU L'ARROSEE St.-Emilion 1988 $34 (3/15/91)
82 CHATEAU L'ARROSEE St.-Emilion 1987 Rel: $25 Cur: $25 (5/15/90)
87 CHATEAU L'ARROSEE St.-Emilion 1986 Rel: $31 Cur: $37 (2/15/89)
85 CHATEAU L'ARROSEE St.-Emilion 1985 Rel: $24 Cur: $40 (2/29/88)
87 CHATEAU L'ARROSEE St.-Emilion 1983 Rel: $20 Cur: $33 (5/16/86)
91 CHATEAU L'ARROSEE St.-Emilion 1982 Cur: $40 (5/15/89) (TR)
90+ CHATEAU AUSONE St.-Emilion 1990 (NR) (4/30/91) (BT)
95+ CHATEAU AUSONE St.-Emilion 1989 (NR) (4/30/91) (BT)
90+ CHATEAU AUSONE St.-Emilion 1989 (NR) (4/30/90) (BT)
95+ CHATEAU AUSONE St.-Emilion 1988 $76 (8/31/90) (BT)
95+ CHATEAU AUSONE St.-Emilion 1988 $76 (6/30/89) (BT)
85+ CHATEAU AUSONE St.-Emilion 1987 $55 (6/30/89) (BT)
85+ CHATEAU AUSONE St.-Emilion 1987 $55 (6/30/88) (BT)
85 CHATEAU AUSONE St.-Emilion 1986 Rel: $90 Cur: $98 (6/30/89)
90+ CHATEAU AUSONE St.-Emilion 1986 Rel: $90 Cur: $98 (6/30/88) (BT)
90+ CHATEAU AUSONE St.-Emilion 1986 Rel: $90 Cur: $98 (5/15/87) (BT)
87 CHATEAU AUSONE St.-Emilion 1985 Rel: $100 Cur: $121 (5/31/88)
94 CHATEAU AUSONE St.-Emilion 1985 Rel: $100 Cur: $121 (11/30/87) (TR)
90+ CHATEAU AUSONE St.-Emilion 1985 Rel: $100 Cur: $121 (5/15/87) (BT)
90+ CHATEAU AUSONE St.-Emilion 1985 Rel: $100 Cur: $121 (4/16/86) (BT)
96 CHATEAU AUSONE St.-Emilion 1983 Cur: $123 (11/30/87) (TR)
93 CHATEAU AUSONE St.-Emilion 1982 Cur: $167 (5/15/89) (TR)
84 CHATEAU AUSONE St.-Emilion 1982 Cur: $167 (11/30/87) (TR)
90 CHATEAU AUSONE St.-Emilion 1981 Cur: $88 (11/30/87) (TR)
86 CHATEAU AUSONE St.-Emilion 1980 Cur: $29 (11/30/87) (TR)
92 CHATEAU AUSONE St.-Emilion 1979 Cur: $83 (10/15/89) (JS)
94 CHATEAU AUSONE St.-Emilion 1979 Cur: $83 (11/30/87) (TR)
93 CHATEAU AUSONE St.-Emilion 1978 Cur: $71 (11/30/87) (TR)
83 CHATEAU AUSONE St.-Emilion 1977 Cur: $29 (11/30/87) (TR)
89 CHATEAU AUSONE St.-Emilion 1976 Cur: $117 (11/30/87) (TR)
76 CHATEAU AUSONE St.-Emilion 1974 Cur: $28 (11/30/87) (TR)
77 CHATEAU AUSONE St.-Emilion 1973 Cur: $35 (11/30/87) (TR)
75 CHATEAU AUSONE St.-Emilion 1972 Cur: $30 (11/30/87) (TR)
83 CHATEAU AUSONE St.-Emilion 1971 Cur: $118 (11/30/87) (TR)
82 CHATEAU AUSONE St.-Emilion 1970 Cur: $125 (11/30/87) (TR)
76 CHATEAU AUSONE St.-Emilion 1969 Cur: $27 (11/30/87) (TR)
79 CHATEAU AUSONE St.-Emilion 1967 Cur: $68 (11/30/87) (TR)
85 CHATEAU AUSONE St.-Emilion 1966 Cur: $162 (11/30/87) (TR)
78 CHATEAU AUSONE St.-Emilion 1964 Cur: $87 (11/30/87) (TR)
85 CHATEAU AUSONE St.-Emilion 1962 Cur: $130 (11/30/87) (JS)
82 CHATEAU AUSONE St.-Emilion 1961 Cur: $310 (11/30/87) (TR)
79 CHATEAU AUSONE St.-Emilion 1959 Cur: $275 (10/15/90) (JS)
76 CHATEAU AUSONE St.-Emilion 1959 Cur: $275 (11/30/87) (TR)
79 CHATEAU AUSONE St.-Emilion 1958 Cur: $95 (11/30/87) (TR)
74 CHATEAU AUSONE St.-Emilion 1957 Cur: $200 (11/30/87) (TR)
86 CHATEAU AUSONE St.-Emilion 1956 Cur: $175 (11/30/87) (TR)
91 CHATEAU AUSONE St.-Emilion 1955 Cur: $275 (11/30/87) (TR)
87 CHATEAU AUSONE St.-Emilion 1954 Cur: $180 (11/30/87) (TR)
78 CHATEAU AUSONE St.-Emilion 1953 Cur: $253 (11/30/87) (TR)
85 CHATEAU AUSONE St.-Emilion 1952 Cur: $180 (11/30/87) (TR)
78 CHATEAU AUSONE St.-Emilion 1950 Cur: $217 (11/30/87) (TR)
91 CHATEAU AUSONE St.-Emilion 1949 Cur: $265 (11/30/87) (TR)
83 CHATEAU AUSONE St.-Emilion 1947 Cur: $275 (11/30/87) (TR)
75 CHATEAU AUSONE St.-Emilion 1945 Cur: $320 (3/16/86) (JL)
84 CHATEAU AUSONE St.-Emilion 1943 Cur: $350 (11/30/87) (TR)
81 CHATEAU AUSONE St.-Emilion 1942 Cur: $250 (11/30/87) (TR)
83 CHATEAU AUSONE St.-Emilion 1937 Cur: $200 (11/30/87) (TR)
82 CHATEAU AUSONE St.-Emilion 1936 Cur: $300 (11/30/87) (TR)
83 CHATEAU AUSONE St.-Emilion 1929 Cur: $290 (11/30/87) (TR)
83 CHATEAU AUSONE St.-Emilion 1928 Cur: $330 (11/30/87) (TR)
82 CHATEAU AUSONE St.-Emilion 1926 Cur: $249 (11/30/87) (TR)
75 CHATEAU AUSONE St.-Emilion 1925 Cur: $200 (11/30/87) (TR)
95 CHATEAU AUSONE St.-Emilion 1924 Cur: $225 (11/30/87) (TR)
76 CHATEAU AUSONE St.-Emilion 1923 Cur: $200 (11/30/87) (TR)
94 CHATEAU AUSONE St.-Emilion 1921 Cur: $250 (11/30/87) (TR)
87 CHATEAU AUSONE St.-Emilion 1918 Cur: $480 (11/30/87) (TR)
86 CHATEAU AUSONE St.-Emilion 1916 Cur: $480 (11/30/87) (TR)
79 CHATEAU AUSONE St.-Emilion 1914 Cur: $380 (11/30/87) (TR)
81 CHATEAU AUSONE St.-Emilion 1913 Cur: $380 (11/30/87) (TR)
79 CHATEAU AUSONE St.-Emilion 1912 Cur: $380 (11/30/87) (TR)
82 CHATEAU AUSONE St.-Emilion 1905 Cur: $600 (11/30/87) (TR)
83 CHATEAU AUSONE St.-Emilion 1902 Cur: $500 (11/30/87) (TR)
78 CHATEAU AUSONE St.-Emilion 1900 Cur: $1,000 (11/30/87) (TR)
77 CHATEAU AUSONE St.-Emilion 1899 Cur: $1,500 (11/30/87) (TR)
85 CHATEAU AUSONE St.-Emilion 1894 Cur: $800 (11/30/87) (TR)
93 CHATEAU AUSONE St.-Emilion 1879 Cur: $700 (11/30/87) (TR)

Key to Symbols

The scores reported here are the results of blind tastings conducted by our panel of senior editors. Wines that carry the initials below are results of individual tastings.

THE WINE SPECTATOR 100-POINT SCALE ***95-100***—Classic, a great wine; ***90-94***—Outstanding, superior character and style; ***80-89***—Good to very good, a wine with special qualities; ***70-79***—Average, drinkable wine that may have minor flaws; ***60-69***—Below average, drinkable but not recommended; ***50-59***—Poor, undrinkable, not recommended. "+"—With a score indicates a range; used primarily with barrel tastings to indicate a preliminary score.

SPECIAL DESIGNATIONS SS—Spectator Selection, CS—Cellar Selection, BB—Best Buy.

TASTER'S INITIALS (JG)—Jim Gordon, (HS)—Harvey Steiman, (JL)—James Laube, (JS)—James Suckling, (TM)—Thomas Matthews, (TR)—Terry Robards, (BT)—Barrel Tasting (these wines were tasted blind from barrel samples), (CA-date)—*California's Great Cabernets* by James Laube, (CH-date)—*California's Great Chardonnays* by James Laube, (VP-date)—*Vintage Port* by James Suckling.

DATE TASTED Dates in parentheses represent the issue in which the rating was published.

92 CHATEAU AUSONE St.-Emilion 1877 Cur: $2,200 (11/30/87) (TR)
80+ CHATEAU BALESTARD LA TONNELLE St.-Emilion 1990 (NR) (4/30/91) (BT)
85+ CHATEAU BALESTARD LA TONNELLE St.-Emilion 1989 (NR) (4/30/91) (BT)
91 CHATEAU BALESTARD LA TONNELLE St.-Emilion 1988 $25 (4/30/91)
80+ CHATEAU BALESTARD LA TONNELLE St.-Emilion 1988 $25 (6/30/89) (BT)
75+ CHATEAU BALESTARD LA TONNELLE St.-Emilion 1987 Rel: $20 Cur: $20 (6/30/89) (BT)
75+ CHATEAU BALESTARD LA TONNELLE St.-Emilion 1987 Rel: $20 Cur: $20 (6/30/88) (BT)
80+ CHATEAU BALESTARD LA TONNELLE St.-Emilion 1986 Rel: $22 Cur: $22 (6/30/88) (BT)
83 CHATEAU BALESTARD LA TONNELLE St.-Emilion 1982 Cur: $25 (5/15/89) (TR)
87 CHATEAU BEAUSEJOUR St.-Emilion 1988 $20 (4/30/91)
87 CHATEAU BEAU-SEJOUR-BECOT St.-Emilion 1988 $21 (6/30/91)
79 CHATEAU BEAU-SEJOUR-BECOT St.-Emilion 1986 Rel: $22 Cur: $22 (7/31/89)
85 CHATEAU BEAU-SEJOUR-BECOT St.-Emilion 1982 Cur: $25 (5/15/89) (TR)
95+ CHATEAU BEAUSEJOUR-DUFFAU-LAGARROSSE St.-Emilion 1990 (NR) (4/30/91) (BT)
90+ CHATEAU BEAUSEJOUR-DUFFAU-LAGARROSSE St.-Emilion 1989 (NR) (4/30/91) (BT)
75+ CHATEAU BEAUSEJOUR-DUFFAU-LAGARROSSE St.-Emilion 1989 (NR) (4/30/90) (BT)
90+ CHATEAU BEAUSEJOUR-DUFFAU-LAGARROSSE St.-Emilion 1988 $32 (8/31/90) (BT)
85+ CHATEAU BEAUSEJOUR-DUFFAU-LAGARROSSE St.-Emilion 1988 $32 (6/30/89) (BT)
85+ CHATEAU BEAUSEJOUR-DUFFAU-LAGARROSSE St.-Emilion 1987 $20 (6/30/89) (BT)
91 CHATEAU BEAUSEJOUR-DUFFAU-LAGARROSSE St.-Emilion 1986 Rel: $27 Cur: $29 (6/30/89)
90 CHATEAU BEAUSEJOUR-DUFFAU-LAGARROSSE St.-Emilion 1982 Cur: $30 (5/15/89) (TR)
81 CHATEAU DU BEAU-VALLON St.-Emilion 1987 $10 (5/15/90)
84 CHATEAU DU BEAU-VALLON St.-Emilion 1986 $10 (9/30/89)
82 CHATEAU DU BEAU-VALLON St.-Emilion 1985 $8.50 (9/30/88)
85+ CHATEAU BELAIR St.-Emilion 1990 (NR) (4/30/91) (BT)
90+ CHATEAU BELAIR St.-Emilion 1989 (NR) (4/30/91) (BT)
85+ CHATEAU BELAIR St.-Emilion 1989 (NR) (4/30/90) (BT)
80+ CHATEAU BELAIR St.-Emilion 1988 $28 (8/31/90) (BT)
85+ CHATEAU BELAIR St.-Emilion 1988 $28 (6/30/89) (BT)
85+ CHATEAU BELAIR St.-Emilion 1987 Rel: $25 Cur: $25 (6/30/89) (BT)
80+ CHATEAU BELAIR St.-Emilion 1987 Rel: $25 Cur: $25 (6/30/88) (BT)
82 CHATEAU BELAIR St.-Emilion 1986 Rel: $26 Cur: $35 (3/31/90)
85+ CHATEAU BELAIR St.-Emilion 1986 Rel: $26 Cur: $35 (6/30/88) (BT)
80+ CHATEAU BELAIR St.-Emilion 1986 Rel: $26 Cur: $35 (5/15/87) (BT)
80+ CHATEAU BELAIR St.-Emilion 1985 Cur: $33 (4/16/86) (BT)
90 CHATEAU BELAIR St.-Emilion 1982 Cur: $26 (5/15/89) (TR)
75 CHATEAU BELAIR St.-Emilion 1961 Cur: $113 (3/16/86) (JL)
80+ CHATEAU BERGAT St.-Emilion 1989 (NR) (4/30/90) (BT)
90 CHATEAU BERLIQUET St.-Emilion 1983 $12 (12/31/86)
80+ CHATEAU CADET-PIOLA St.-Emilion 1989 (NR) (4/30/91) (BT)
89 CHATEAU CADET-PIOLA St.-Emilion 1988 $20 (7/15/91)
75+ CHATEAU CADET-PIOLA St.-Emilion 1988 $20 (6/30/89) (BT)
70+ CHATEAU CADET-PIOLA St.-Emilion 1987 Rel: $16 Cur: $16 (6/30/89) (BT)
88 CHATEAU CADET-PIOLA St.-Emilion 1982 Cur: $23 (5/15/89) (TR)
90+ CHATEAU CANON St.-Emilion 1990 (NR) (4/30/91) (BT)
90+ CHATEAU CANON St.-Emilion 1989 (NR) (4/30/91) (BT)
90 CHATEAU CANON St.-Emilion 1988 $40 (6/30/91)
85+ CHATEAU CANON St.-Emilion 1988 $40 (8/31/90) (BT)
90+ CHATEAU CANON St.-Emilion 1988 $40 (6/30/89) (BT)
79 CHATEAU CANON St.-Emilion 1987 Rel: $32 Cur: $32 (5/15/90)
85+ CHATEAU CANON St.-Emilion 1987 Rel: $32 Cur: $32 (6/30/89) (BT)
90+ CHATEAU CANON St.-Emilion 1987 Rel: $32 Cur: $32 (6/30/88) (BT)
86 CHATEAU CANON St.-Emilion 1986 Rel: $45 Cur: $45 (3/31/90)
93 CHATEAU CANON St.-Emilion 1986 Rel: $45 Cur: $45 (6/30/89)
95 CHATEAU CANON St.-Emilion 1986 Rel: $45 Cur: $45 (5/15/89) (TM)
95+ CHATEAU CANON St.-Emilion 1986 Rel: $45 Cur: $45 (6/30/88) (BT)
91 CHATEAU CANON St.-Emilion 1985 Rel: $34 Cur: $47 (5/15/89) (TM)
90 CHATEAU CANON St.-Emilion 1985 Rel: $34 Cur: $47 (3/31/88)
70+ CHATEAU CANON St.-Emilion 1985 Rel: $34 Cur: $47 (4/16/86) (BT)
88 CHATEAU CANON St.-Emilion 1983 Rel: $31 Cur: $42 (5/15/89) (TM)
73 CHATEAU CANON St.-Emilion 1983 Rel: $31 Cur: $42 (3/16/86)
91 CHATEAU CANON St.-Emilion 1982 Cur: $60 (5/15/89) (TM)
94 CHATEAU CANON St.-Emilion 1982 Cur: $60 (5/15/89) (TR)
82 CHATEAU CANON St.-Emilion 1981 Cur: $31 (5/15/89) (TM)
80 CHATEAU CANON St.-Emilion 1980 Cur: $19 (5/15/89) (TM)
89 CHATEAU CANON St.-Emilion 1979 Cur: $40 (5/15/89) (TM)
84 CHATEAU CANON St.-Emilion 1978 Cur: $59 (5/15/89) (TM)
84 CHATEAU CANON St.-Emilion 1975 Cur: $38 (5/15/89) (TM)
85 CHATEAU CANON St.-Emilion 1971 Cur: $53 (5/15/89) (TM)
93 CHATEAU CANON St.-Emilion 1970 Cur: $60 (5/15/89) (TM)
91 CHATEAU CANON St.-Emilion 1966 Cur: $69 (5/15/89) (TM)
89 CHATEAU CANON St.-Emilion 1964 Cur: $60 (5/15/89) (TM)
93 CHATEAU CANON St.-Emilion 1962 Cur: $100 (5/15/89) (TM)
88 CHATEAU CANON St.-Emilion 1961 Cur: $100 (5/15/89) (TM)
95 CHATEAU CANON St.-Emilion 1959 Cur: $125 (5/15/89) (TM)
88 CHATEAU CANON St.-Emilion 1955 Cur: $110 (5/15/89) (TM)
88 CHATEAU CANON St.-Emilion 1953 Cur: $125 (5/15/89) (TM)
91 CHATEAU CANON St.-Emilion 1947 Cur: $250 (5/15/89) (TM)
90+ CHATEAU CANON-LA-GAFFELIERE St.-Emilion 1990 (NR) (4/30/91) (BT)
85+ CHATEAU CANON-LA-GAFFELIERE St.-Emilion 1989 (NR) (4/30/91) (BT)
95+ CHATEAU CANON-LA-GAFFELIERE St.-Emilion 1989 (NR) (4/30/90) (BT)
86 CHATEAU CANON-LA-GAFFELIERE St.-Emilion 1988 $30 (6/30/91)
85+ CHATEAU CANON-LA-GAFFELIERE St.-Emilion 1988 $30 (8/31/90) (BT)
85+ CHATEAU CANON-LA-GAFFELIERE St.-Emilion 1988 $30 (6/30/89) (BT)
70+ CHATEAU CANON-LA-GAFFELIERE St.-Emilion 1987 Cur: $15 (6/30/89) (BT)
75+ CHATEAU CANON-LA-GAFFELIERE St.-Emilion 1987 Cur: $15 (6/30/88) (BT)
91 CHATEAU CANON-LA-GAFFELIERE St.-Emilion 1986 Rel: $21 Cur: $28 (6/30/89)
80+ CHATEAU CANON-LA-GAFFELIERE St.-Emilion 1986 Rel: $21 Cur: $28 (6/30/88) (BT)
90+ CHATEAU CANON-LA-GAFFELIERE St.-Emilion 1986 Rel: $21 Cur: $28 (5/15/87) (BT)
90+ CHATEAU CANON-LA-GAFFELIERE St.-Emilion 1985 Rel: $20 Cur: $37 (5/15/87) (BT)
85+ CHATEAU CAP DE MOURLIN St.-Emilion 1989 (NR) (4/30/91) (BT)
84 CHATEAU CAP DE MOURLIN St.-Emilion 1988 $20 (4/30/91)
80+ CHATEAU CAP DE MOURLIN St.-Emilion 1988 $20 (6/30/89) (BT)
70+ CHATEAU CAP DE MOURLIN St.-Emilion 1987 $15 (6/30/89) (BT)
75+ CHATEAU CAP DE MOURLIN St.-Emilion 1987 $15 (6/30/88) (BT)
87 CHATEAU CAP DE MOURLIN St.-Emilion 1986 Rel: $18 Cur: $18 (6/30/89)
80+ CHATEAU CAP DE MOURLIN St.-Emilion 1986 Rel: $18 Cur: $18 (6/30/88) (BT)
80+ CHATEAU CAP DE MOURLIN St.-Emilion 1985 Rel: $15 Cur: $15 (5/15/87) (BT)

86 CHATEAU CAP DE MOURLIN (JACQUES) St.-Emilion 1982 (NA) (5/15/89) (TR)
81 CHATEAU CAP DE MOURLIN (JEAN) St.-Emilion 1982 (NA) (5/15/89) (TR)
79 CHATEAU CARTEYRON St.-Emilion 1982 $7.25 (9/01/85)
84 CHATEAU DU CAUZE St.-Emilion 1986 $15 (6/30/89)
84 CHATEAU CHAUVIN St.-Emilion 1988 $20 (6/30/91)
75 CHATEAU CHAUVIN St.-Emilion 1986 $15 (6/30/89)
90+ CHATEAU CHEVAL BLANC St.-Emilion 1990 (NR) (4/30/91) (BT)
95+ CHATEAU CHEVAL BLANC St.-Emilion 1989 (NR) (4/30/91) (BT)
95+ CHATEAU CHEVAL BLANC St.-Emilion 1989 (NR) (4/30/90) (BT)
93 CHATEAU CHEVAL BLANC St.-Emilion 1988 $105 (12/31/90) CS
90+ CHATEAU CHEVAL BLANC St.-Emilion 1988 $105 (8/31/90) (BT)
90+ CHATEAU CHEVAL BLANC St.-Emilion 1988 $105 (6/30/89) (BT)
82 CHATEAU CHEVAL BLANC St.-Emilion 1987 Rel: $57 Cur: $57 (2/15/91) (JS)
87 CHATEAU CHEVAL BLANC St.-Emilion 1987 Rel: $57 Cur: $57 (5/15/90)
81 CHATEAU CHEVAL BLANC St.-Emilion 1987 Rel: $57 Cur: $57 (3/31/90)
80+ CHATEAU CHEVAL BLANC St.-Emilion 1987 Rel: $57 Cur: $57 (6/30/89) (BT)
80+ CHATEAU CHEVAL BLANC St.-Emilion 1987 Rel: $57 Cur: $57 (6/30/88) (BT)
93 CHATEAU CHEVAL BLANC St.-Emilion 1986 Rel: $80 Cur: $85 (2/15/91) (JS)
98 CHATEAU CHEVAL BLANC St.-Emilion 1986 Rel: $80 Cur: $85 (6/30/89) CS
95+ CHATEAU CHEVAL BLANC St.-Emilion 1986 Rel: $80 Cur: $85 (6/30/88) (BT)
98 CHATEAU CHEVAL BLANC St.-Emilion 1985 Rel: $80 Cur: $91 (2/15/91) (JS)
94 CHATEAU CHEVAL BLANC St.-Emilion 1985 Rel: $80 Cur: $91 (2/29/88)
85 CHATEAU CHEVAL BLANC St.-Emilion 1984 Rel: $69 Cur: $69 (2/15/91) (HS)
78 CHATEAU CHEVAL BLANC St.-Emilion 1984 Rel: $69 Cur: $69 (2/15/91) (JS)
88 CHATEAU CHEVAL BLANC St.-Emilion 1984 Rel: $69 Cur: $69 (5/15/87)
91 CHATEAU CHEVAL BLANC St.-Emilion 1984 Rel: $69 Cur: $69 (3/31/87)
96 CHATEAU CHEVAL BLANC St.-Emilion 1983 Rel: $63 Cur: $80 (2/15/91) (JS)
85 CHATEAU CHEVAL BLANC St.-Emilion 1983 Rel: $63 Cur: $80 (3/16/86)
97 CHATEAU CHEVAL BLANC St.-Emilion 1982 Rel: $69 Cur: $143 (2/15/91) (JS)
96 CHATEAU CHEVAL BLANC St.-Emilion 1982 Rel: $69 Cur: $143 (5/15/89) (TR)
96 CHATEAU CHEVAL BLANC St.-Emilion 1982 Rel: $69 Cur: $143 (5/01/85)
96 CHATEAU CHEVAL BLANC St.-Emilion 1982 Rel: $69 Cur: $143 (2/16/85) CS
90 CHATEAU CHEVAL BLANC St.-Emilion 1981 Rel: $46 Cur: $78 (2/15/91) (JS)
88 CHATEAU CHEVAL BLANC St.-Emilion 1981 Rel: $46 Cur: $78 (5/01/89)
84 CHATEAU CHEVAL BLANC St.-Emilion 1980 Cur: $48 (2/15/91) (JS)
88 CHATEAU CHEVAL BLANC St.-Emilion 1979 Cur: $76 (2/15/91) (JS)
85 CHATEAU CHEVAL BLANC St.-Emilion 1979 Cur: $76 (10/15/89) (JS)
94 CHATEAU CHEVAL BLANC St.-Emilion 1978 Cur: $120 (2/15/91) (JS)
74 CHATEAU CHEVAL BLANC St.-Emilion 1977 Cur: $38 (2/15/91) (JS)
88 CHATEAU CHEVAL BLANC St.-Emilion 1976 Cur: $80 (2/15/91) (JS)
91 CHATEAU CHEVAL BLANC St.-Emilion 1975 Cur: $140 (2/15/91) (JS)
83 CHATEAU CHEVAL BLANC St.-Emilion 1974 Cur: $43 (2/15/91) (JS)
83 CHATEAU CHEVAL BLANC St.-Emilion 1973 Cur: $60 (2/15/91) (JS)
82 CHATEAU CHEVAL BLANC St.-Emilion 1972 Cur: $40 (2/15/91) (JS)
89 CHATEAU CHEVAL BLANC St.-Emilion 1971 Cur: $130 (2/15/91) (JS)
88 CHATEAU CHEVAL BLANC St.-Emilion 1970 Cur: $165 (2/15/91) (JS)
75 CHATEAU CHEVAL BLANC St.-Emilion 1969 Cur: $68 (2/15/91) (JS)
85 CHATEAU CHEVAL BLANC St.-Emilion 1967 Cur: $102 (2/15/91) (JS)
87 CHATEAU CHEVAL BLANC St.-Emilion 1966 Cur: $140 (2/15/91) (JS)
94 CHATEAU CHEVAL BLANC St.-Emilion 1964 Cur: $220 (2/15/91) (HS)
85 CHATEAU CHEVAL BLANC St.-Emilion 1964 Cur: $220 (2/15/91) (JS)
85 CHATEAU CHEVAL BLANC St.-Emilion 1962 Cur: $150 (2/15/91) (JS)
75 CHATEAU CHEVAL BLANC St.-Emilion 1962 Cur: $150 (11/30/87) (JS)
96 CHATEAU CHEVAL BLANC St.-Emilion 1961 Cur: $420 (2/15/91) (JS)
78 CHATEAU CHEVAL BLANC St.-Emilion 1961 Cur: $420 (3/16/86) (JL)
81 CHATEAU CHEVAL BLANC St.-Emilion 1960 Cur: $150 (2/15/91) (JS)
90 CHATEAU CHEVAL BLANC St.-Emilion 1959 Cur: $340 (2/15/91) (JS)
96 CHATEAU CHEVAL BLANC St.-Emilion 1959 Cur: $340 (10/15/90) (JS)
86 CHATEAU CHEVAL BLANC St.-Emilion 1958 Cur: $180 (2/15/91) (JS)
94 CHATEAU CHEVAL BLANC St.-Emilion 1955 Cur: $200 (2/15/91) (JS)
87 CHATEAU CHEVAL BLANC St.-Emilion 1953 Cur: $390 (2/15/91) (JS)
91 CHATEAU CHEVAL BLANC St.-Emilion 1952 Cur: $268 (2/15/91) (JS)
76 CHATEAU CHEVAL BLANC St.-Emilion 1951 Cur: $150 (2/15/91) (JS)
95 CHATEAU CHEVAL BLANC St.-Emilion 1950 Cur: $275 (2/15/91) (HS)
89 CHATEAU CHEVAL BLANC St.-Emilion 1950 Cur: $275 (2/15/91) (JS)
93 CHATEAU CHEVAL BLANC St.-Emilion 1949 Cur: $570 (2/15/91) (HS)
84 CHATEAU CHEVAL BLANC St.-Emilion 1949 Cur: $570 (2/15/91) (JS)
97 CHATEAU CHEVAL BLANC St.-Emilion 1948 Cur: $300 (2/15/91) (JS)
100 CHATEAU CHEVAL BLANC St.-Emilion 1947 Cur: $1,230 (2/15/91) (JS)
87 CHATEAU CHEVAL BLANC St.-Emilion 1946 Cur: $340 (2/15/91) (JS)
95 CHATEAU CHEVAL BLANC St.-Emilion 1945 Cur: $590 (3/16/86) (JL)
85 CHATEAU CHEVAL BLANC St.-Emilion 1943 Cur: $185 (2/15/91) (JS)
71 CHATEAU CHEVAL BLANC St.-Emilion 1941 Cur: $175 (2/15/91) (JS)
83 CHATEAU CHEVAL BLANC St.-Emilion 1940 Cur: $500 (2/15/91) (JS)
75 CHATEAU CHEVAL BLANC St.-Emilion 1938 Cur: $150 (2/15/91) (JS)
93 CHATEAU CHEVAL BLANC St.-Emilion 1937 Cur: $400 (2/15/91) (JS)
81 CHATEAU CHEVAL BLANC St.-Emilion 1936 Cur: $275 (2/15/91) (JS)
93 CHATEAU CHEVAL BLANC St.-Emilion 1934 Cur: $325 (2/15/91) (JS)
88 CHATEAU CHEVAL BLANC St.-Emilion 1933 Cur: $275 (2/15/91) (JS)
72 CHATEAU CHEVAL BLANC St.-Emilion 1931 Cur: $225 (2/15/91) (JS)
82 CHATEAU CHEVAL BLANC St.-Emilion 1930 Cur: $275 (2/15/91) (JS)
90 CHATEAU CHEVAL BLANC St.-Emilion 1929 Cur: $450 (2/15/91) (JS)
92 CHATEAU CHEVAL BLANC St.-Emilion 1928 Cur: $475 (2/15/91) (JS)
85 CHATEAU CHEVAL BLANC St.-Emilion 1926 Cur: $400 (2/15/91) (JS)
69 CHATEAU CHEVAL BLANC St.-Emilion 1924 Cur: $450 (2/15/91) (JS)
65 CHATEAU CHEVAL BLANC St.-Emilion 1923 Cur: $200 (2/15/91) (JS)
100 CHATEAU CHEVAL BLANC St.-Emilion 1921 Cur: $500 (2/15/91) (JS)
70 CHATEAU CHEVAL BLANC St.-Emilion 1919 Cur: $500 (2/15/91) (JS)
70 CHATEAU CHEVAL BLANC St.-Emilion 1917 Cur: $500 (2/15/91) (JS)
71 CHATEAU CHEVAL BLANC St.-Emilion 1916 Cur: $500 (2/15/91) (JS)
72 CHATEAU CHEVAL BLANC St.-Emilion 1915 Cur: $500 (2/15/91) (JS)
71 CHATEAU CHEVAL BLANC St.-Emilion 1908 Cur: $500 (2/15/91) (JS)
70 CHATEAU CHEVAL BLANC St.-Emilion 1905 Cur: $600 (2/15/91) (JS)
90 CHATEAU CHEVAL BLANC St.-Emilion 1899 Cur: $1,200 (2/15/91) (JS)
80+ CLOS DE L'ORATOIRE St.-Emilion 1989 (NR) (4/30/91) (BT)
75+ CLOS DE L'ORATOIRE St.-Emilion 1988 (NR) (6/30/89) (BT)
75+ CLOS DE L'ORATOIRE St.-Emilion 1987 (NR) (6/30/89) (BT)
78 CLOS DE L'ORATOIRE St.-Emilion 1982 (NA) (5/15/89) (TR)
95+ CHATEAU CLOS DES JACOBINS St.-Emilion 1989 (NR) (4/30/90) (BT)
90 CHATEAU CLOS DES JACOBINS St.-Emilion 1988 $26 (4/15/91)
73 CHATEAU CLOS DES JACOBINS St.-Emilion 1987 Rel: $23.50 Cur: $24 (5/15/90)
94 CHATEAU CLOS DES JACOBINS St.-Emilion 1986 Rel: $34 Cur: $34 (6/30/89)
80+ CHATEAU CLOS DES JACOBINS St.-Emilion 1986 Rel: $34 Cur: $34 (5/15/87) (BT)
89 CHATEAU CLOS DES JACOBINS St.-Emilion 1985 Rel: $31 Cur: $31 (9/30/88)
83 CHATEAU CLOS DES JACOBINS St.-Emilion 1984 Rel: $20 Cur: $20 (5/15/87)
83 CHATEAU CLOS DES JACOBINS St.-Emilion 1982 Cur: $38 (5/15/89) (TR)
81 CHATEAU CLOS DES JACOBINS St.-Emilion 1981 Rel: $16 Cur: $31 (6/01/84)
85+ CLOS FOURTET St.-Emilion 1990 (NR) (4/30/91) (BT)
90+ CLOS FOURTET St.-Emilion 1989 (NR) (4/30/91) (BT)
85+ CLOS FOURTET St.-Emilion 1989 (NR) (4/30/90) (BT)
85+ CLOS FOURTET St.-Emilion 1988 $20 (8/31/90) (BT)
90+ CLOS FOURTET St.-Emilion 1988 $20 (6/30/89) (BT)
80+ CLOS FOURTET St.-Emilion 1987 Rel: $20 Cur: $20 (6/30/89) (BT)
80 CLOS FOURTET St.-Emilion 1986 Rel: $29 Cur: $35 (6/30/89)
87 CLOS FOURTET St.-Emilion 1982 Rel: $20 Cur: $29 (5/15/89) (TR)
88 CLOS FOURTET St.-Emilion 1982 Rel: $20 Cur: $29 (6/01/85)
66 CLOS FOURTET St.-Emilion 1961 Cur: $106 (3/16/86) (JL)
68 CLOS FOURTET St.-Emilion 1945 Cur: $175 (3/16/86) (JL)
77 CLOS J. KANON St.-Emilion 1987 $10 (5/15/90)
91 CLOS J. KANON St.-Emilion 1986 $17 (11/15/89)
82 CLOS LABARDE St.-Emilion 1986 $15 (6/30/89)
83 CHATEAU CLOS LA MADELAINE St.-Emilion 1982 (NA) (5/15/89) (TR)
85+ CLOS LARCIS St.-Emilion 1989 (NR) (4/30/91) (BT)
85+ CHATEAU CLOS ST.-MARTIN St.-Emilion 1989 (NR) (4/30/91) (BT)
90+ CHATEAU CLOS ST.-MARTIN St.-Emilion 1988 (NR) (6/30/89) (BT)
80+ CHATEAU CLOS ST.-MARTIN St.-Emilion 1987 (NR) (6/30/89) (BT)
87 CHATEAU LA CLOTTE St.-Emilion 1985 $27 (5/15/88)
68 CHATEAU LA CLOTTE St.-Emilion 1983 $12 (5/16/86)
80+ CHATEAU LA CLUSIERE St.-Emilion 1989 (NR) (4/30/91) (BT)
65+ CHATEAU LA CLUSIERE St.-Emilion 1988 $20 (6/30/89) (BT)
88 CHATEAU LA CLUSIERE St.-Emilion 1982 Cur: $20 (5/15/89) (TR)
79 CHATEAU LA COMMANDERIE St.-Emilion 1983 $10.50 (1/01/86)
88 CHATEAU CORBIN St.-Emilion 1986 $15 (6/30/89)
86 CHATEAU CORBIN St.-Emilion 1985 $15 (5/31/88)
72 CHATEAU CORBIN-MICHOTTE St.-Emilion 1988 $15 (7/15/91)
85 CHATEAU CORMEIL-FIGEAC St.-Emilion 1988 $20 (4/30/91)
75 CHATEAU CORMEIL-FIGEAC St.-Emilion 1986 $12 (6/30/89)
81 CHATEAU COUVENT DES JACOBINS St.-Emilion 1988 $28 (3/31/91)
84 CHATEAU COUVENT DES JACOBINS St.-Emilion 1985 Rel: $27 Cur: $27 (3/31/88)
95 CHATEAU COUVENT DES JACOBINS St.-Emilion 1983 Rel: $18 Cur: $27 (3/16/86)
78 CHATEAU LE COUVENT St.-Emilion 1982 $13 (6/16/86)
83 CHATEAU CROQUE MICHOTTE St.-Emilion 1982 Cur: $24 (5/15/89) (TR)
84 CHATEAU CURE-BON-LA-MADELAINE St.-Emilion 1982 Cur: $30 (5/15/89) (TR)
85+ CHATEAU DASSAULT St.-Emilion 1989 (NR) (4/30/91) (BT)
83 CHATEAU DASSAULT St.-Emilion 1988 $16 (7/15/91)
65+ CHATEAU DASSAULT St.-Emilion 1988 $16 (6/30/89) (BT)
75+ CHATEAU DASSAULT St.-Emilion 1987 Rel: $14 Cur: $14 (6/30/89) (BT)
90 CHATEAU DASSAULT St.-Emilion 1982 Cur: $20 (5/15/89) (TR)
81 CHATEAU DESTIEUX St.-Emilion 1988 $19 (6/30/91)
84 CHATEAU DESTIEUX St.-Emilion 1985 $14 (3/31/88)
90+ CHATEAU LA DOMINIQUE St.-Emilion 1990 (NR) (4/30/91) (BT)
90+ CHATEAU LA DOMINIQUE St.-Emilion 1989 (NR) (4/30/91) (BT)
86 CHATEAU LA DOMINIQUE St.-Emilion 1988 $25 (6/30/91)
75+ CHATEAU LA DOMINIQUE St.-Emilion 1988 $25 (6/30/89) (BT)
80+ CHATEAU LA DOMINIQUE St.-Emilion 1987 Rel: $20 Cur: $20 (6/30/89) (BT)
95 CHATEAU LA DOMINIQUE St.-Emilion 1986 Rel: $29 Cur: $29 (6/30/89)
83 CHATEAU LA DOMINIQUE St.-Emilion 1985 Rel: $30 Cur: $32 (3/31/88)
88 CHATEAU LA DOMINIQUE St.-Emilion 1983 Rel: $18 Cur: $29 (5/16/86)
81 CHATEAU LA DOMINIQUE St.-Emilion 1979 Cur: $27 (10/15/89) (JS)
79 CHATEAU DURAND-LAPLAGNE St.-Emilion 1982 $7.50 (9/16/85)
87 CHATEAU JEAN FAURE St.-Emilion 1983 $17 (3/31/87)
85 CHATEAU JEAN FAURE St.-Emilion 1982 $14 (11/16/85)
80+ CHATEAU FAURIE-DE-SOUCHARD St.-Emilion 1989 (NR) (4/30/91) (BT)
75+ CHATEAU FAURIE-DE-SOUCHARD St.-Emilion 1988 $22 (6/30/89) (BT)
70+ CHATEAU FAURIE-DE-SOUCHARD St.-Emilion 1987 $19 (6/30/89) (BT)
85+ CHATEAU FIGEAC St.-Emilion 1990 (NR) (4/30/91) (BT)
95+ CHATEAU FIGEAC St.-Emilion 1989 (NR) (4/30/91) (BT)
95+ CHATEAU FIGEAC St.-Emilion 1989 (NR) (4/30/90) (BT)
93 CHATEAU FIGEAC St.-Emilion 1988 $45 (6/30/91)
85+ CHATEAU FIGEAC St.-Emilion 1988 $45 (8/31/90) (BT)
85+ CHATEAU FIGEAC St.-Emilion 1988 $45 (6/30/89) (BT)
84 CHATEAU FIGEAC St.-Emilion 1987 Rel: $35 Cur: $35 (5/15/90)
80+ CHATEAU FIGEAC St.-Emilion 1987 Rel: $35 Cur: $35 (6/30/89) (BT)
80+ CHATEAU FIGEAC St.-Emilion 1987 Rel: $35 Cur: $35 (6/30/88) (BT)
89 CHATEAU FIGEAC St.-Emilion 1986 Rel: $45 Cur: $45 (6/30/89)
90+ CHATEAU FIGEAC St.-Emilion 1986 Rel: $45 Cur: $45 (6/30/88) (BT)
95 CHATEAU FIGEAC St.-Emilion 1985 Rel: $37 Cur: $53 (5/15/88)
80+ CHATEAU FIGEAC St.-Emilion 1985 Rel: $37 Cur: $53 (5/15/87) (BT)
83 CHATEAU FIGEAC St.-Emilion 1984 Rel: $26 Cur: $30 (3/31/87)
77 CHATEAU FIGEAC St.-Emilion 1983 Rel: $37 Cur: $43 (5/16/86)
92 CHATEAU FIGEAC St.-Emilion 1982 Cur: $54 (5/15/89) (TR)
92 CHATEAU FIGEAC St.-Emilion 1982 Cur: $54 (5/01/85)
86 CHATEAU FIGEAC St.-Emilion 1981 Cur: $34 (5/01/85)
90 CHATEAU FIGEAC St.-Emilion 1980 Cur: $30 (5/01/85)
82 CHATEAU FIGEAC St.-Emilion 1979 Cur: $38 (10/15/89) (JS)
80 CHATEAU FIGEAC St.-Emilion 1979 Cur: $38 (5/01/85)
83 CHATEAU FIGEAC St.-Emilion 1978 Cur: $51 (5/01/85)
90 CHATEAU FIGEAC St.-Emilion 1962 Cur: $66 (11/30/87) (JS)
84 CHATEAU FIGEAC St.-Emilion 1961 Cur: $176 (3/16/86) (JL)
82 CHATEAU LA FLEUR St.-Emilion 1986 $13.50 (2/15/90)
75+ CHATEAU FLEUR-POURRET St.-Emilion 1989 (NR) (4/30/90) (BT)
75+ CHATEAU FLEUR-POURRET St.-Emilion 1988 (NR) (8/31/90) (BT)
75+ CHATEAU FLEUR-POURRET St.-Emilion 1987 (NR) (6/30/88) (BT)
86 CHATEAU FOMBRAUGE St.-Emilion 1986 Rel: $19 Cur: $19 (6/30/89)
87 CHATEAU FOMBRAUGE St.-Emilion 1985 Rel: $15 Cur: $17 (5/15/88)
85+ CHATEAU FONPLEGADE St.-Emilion 1989 (NR) (4/30/91) (BT)
85 CHATEAU FONPLEGADE St.-Emilion 1988 $18 (6/30/91)
75+ CHATEAU FONPLEGADE St.-Emilion 1988 $18 (6/30/89) (BT)
70+ CHATEAU FONPLEGADE St.-Emilion 1987 Rel: $15 Cur: $15 (6/30/89) (BT)
70+ CHATEAU FONPLEGADE St.-Emilion 1987 Rel: $15 Cur: $15 (6/30/88) (BT)

FRANCE
BORDEAUX RED/*ST.-EMILION*

80+ CHATEAU FONPLEGADE St.-Emilion 1986 Rel: $15 Cur: $15 (6/30/88) (BT)
70+ CHATEAU FONPLEGADE St.-Emilion 1986 Rel: $15 Cur: $15 (5/15/87) (BT)
70+ CHATEAU FONPLEGADE St.-Emilion 1985 Rel: $15 Cur: $15 (5/15/87) (BT)
77 CHATEAU FONPLEGADE St.-Emilion 1982 Cur: $25 (5/15/89) (TR)
80+ CHATEAU FONROQUE St.-Emilion 1990 (NR) (4/30/91) (BT)
85+ CHATEAU FONROQUE St.-Emilion 1989 (NR) (4/30/91) (BT)
85+ CHATEAU FONROQUE St.-Emilion 1989 (NR) (4/30/90) (BT)
90+ CHATEAU FONROQUE St.-Emilion 1988 $18 (8/31/90) (BT)
80+ CHATEAU FONROQUE St.-Emilion 1988 $18 (6/30/89) (BT)
75+ CHATEAU FONROQUE St.-Emilion 1987 Rel: $15 Cur: $15 (6/30/89) (BT)
75+ CHATEAU FONROQUE St.-Emilion 1987 Rel: $15 Cur: $15 (6/30/88) (BT)
80+ CHATEAU FONROQUE St.-Emilion 1986 Cur: $19 (6/30/88) (BT)
80+ CHATEAU FONROQUE St.-Emilion 1986 Cur: $19 (5/15/87) (BT)
80+ CHATEAU FONROQUE St.-Emilion 1985 Cur: $23 (5/15/87) (BT)
70+ CHATEAU FONROQUE St.-Emilion 1985 Cur: $23 (4/16/86) (BT)
78 CHATEAU FONROQUE St.-Emilion 1982 Cur: $17 (5/15/89) (TR)
91 CHATEAU FRANC-BIGAROUX St.-Emilion 1988 $24 (7/31/91)
85+ CHATEAU DE FRANC-MAYNE St.-Emilion 1990 (NR) (4/30/91) (BT)
80+ CHATEAU DE FRANC-MAYNE St.-Emilion 1989 (NR) (4/30/91) (BT)
90+ CHATEAU DE FRANC-MAYNE St.-Emilion 1989 (NR) (4/30/90) (BT)
83 CHATEAU DE FRANC-MAYNE St.-Emilion 1988 $15 (7/15/91)
85+ CHATEAU DE FRANC-MAYNE St.-Emilion 1988 $15 (8/31/90) (BT)
75+ CHATEAU DE FRANC-MAYNE St.-Emilion 1987 $13 (6/30/88) (BT)
65+ CHATEAU DE FRANC-MAYNE St.-Emilion 1986 Rel: $16 Cur: $16 (6/30/88) (BT)
84 CHATEAU FUMET-PEYROUTAS St.-Emilion 1985 $7.25 (7/31/88) BB
60+ CHATEAU LA GAFFELIERE St.-Emilion 1990 (NR) (4/30/91) (BT)
90+ CHATEAU LA GAFFELIERE St.-Emilion 1989 (NR) (4/30/91) (BT)
70+ CHATEAU LA GAFFELIERE St.-Emilion 1989 (NR) (4/30/90) (BT)
84 CHATEAU LA GAFFELIERE St.-Emilion 1988 $36 (4/30/91)
80+ CHATEAU LA GAFFELIERE St.-Emilion 1988 $36 (6/30/89) (BT)
75+ CHATEAU LA GAFFELIERE St.-Emilion 1987 Rel: $20 Cur: $20 (6/30/89) (BT)
80+ CHATEAU LA GAFFELIERE St.-Emilion 1986 Cur: $22 (5/15/87) (BT)
80+ CHATEAU LA GAFFELIERE St.-Emilion 1985 Cur: $35 (5/15/87) (BT)
88 CHATEAU LA GAFFELIERE St.-Emilion 1982 Cur: $25 (5/15/89) (TR)
81 CHATEAU LA GAFFELIERE St.-Emilion 1979 Cur: $43 (10/15/89) (JS)
88 CHATEAU LA GAFFELIERE St.-Emilion 1962 Cur: $60 (11/30/87) (JS)
76 CHATEAU LA GAFFELIERE St.-Emilion 1961 Cur: $125 (3/16/86) (JL)
82 CHATEAU LA GAFFELIERE St.-Emilion 1959 Cur: $95 (10/15/90) (JS)
85 CHATEAU LA GAFFELIERE St.-Emilion 1945 Cur: $140 (3/16/86) (JL)
72 CHATEAU GRAND-BARRAIL-LAMARZELLE-FIGEAC St.-Emilion 1986 Rel: $15 Cur $15 (6/30/89)
85 CHATEAU GRAND-BARRAIL-LAMARZELLE-FIGEAC St.-Emilion 1982 Cur: $24 (5/15/89) (TR)
70 CHATEAU GRAND-CORBIN-DESPAGNE St.-Emilion 1945 Cur: $100 (3/16/86) (JL)
87 CHATEAU GRAND-MAYNE St.-Emilion 1988 $20 (7/15/91)
89 CHATEAU GRAND-MAYNE St.-Emilion 1988 $20 (4/30/91)
87 CHATEAU GRAND-MAYNE St.-Emilion 1986 $16 (6/30/89)
86 CHATEAU GRAND-PONTET St.-Emilion 1988 $21 (7/15/91)
83 CHATEAU GRAND-PONTET St.-Emilion 1982 Cur: $26 (5/15/89) (TR)
81 CHATEAU GRANDES-MURAILLES St.-Emilion 1982 (NA) (5/15/89) (TR)
75+ CHATEAU GUADET-ST.-JULIEN St.-Emilion 1989 (NR) (4/30/91) (BT)
75+ CHATEAU GUADET-ST.-JULIEN St.-Emilion 1988 (NR) (6/30/89) (BT)
70+ CHATEAU GUADET-ST.-JULIEN St.-Emilion 1987 (NR) (6/30/89) (BT)
73 CHATEAU HAUT-CADET St.-Emilion 1981 $6.50 (4/01/85)
90+ CHATEAU HAUT-CORBIN St.-Emilion 1989 (NR) (4/30/90) (BT)
70+ CHATEAU HAUT-CORBIN St.-Emilion 1986 $14 (5/15/87) (BT)
85+ CHATEAU HAUT-SARPE St.-Emilion 1989 (NR) (4/30/91) (BT)
83 CHATEAU HAUT-SARPE St.-Emilion 1988 $16 (6/30/91)
80+ CHATEAU HAUT-SARPE St.-Emilion 1988 $16 (6/30/89) (BT)
75+ CHATEAU HAUT-SARPE St.-Emilion 1987 Rel: $14 Cur: $14 (6/30/89) (BT)
87 CHATEAU HAUT-SARPE St.-Emilion 1982 Cur: $20 (5/15/89) (TR)
78 CHATEAU HAUT-SARPE St.-Emilion 1979 Rel: $11 Cur: $11 (4/01/84)
78 CHATEAU JACQUES-BLANC St.-Emilion Cuvée du Maitre 1988 $23 (4/30/91)
85 PIERRE JEAN St.-Emilion 1988 $10 (6/30/91) BB
70+ CHATEAU LE JURAT St.-Emilion 1986 (NR) (5/15/87) (BT)
70+ CHATEAU LAFLEUR-POURRET St.-Emilion 1989 (NR) (4/30/91) (BT)
95+ CHATEAU LAFLEUR-ST.-EMILION St.-Emilion 1990 (NR) (4/30/91) (BT)
85+ CHATEAU LAFLEUR-ST.-EMILION St.-Emilion 1989 (NR) (4/30/91) (BT)
75+ CHATEAU LAFLEUR-ST.-EMILION St.-Emilion 1989 (NR) (4/30/90) (BT)
82 CHATEAU LARCIS-DUCASSE St.-Emilion 1988 $20 (4/30/91)
75+ CHATEAU LARCIS-DUCASSE St.-Emilion 1988 $20 (6/30/89) (BT)
75+ CHATEAU LARCIS-DUCASSE St.-Emilion 1987 Rel: $17 Cur: $17 (6/30/89) (BT)
70+ CHATEAU LARCIS-DUCASSE St.-Emilion 1987 Rel: $17 Cur: $17 (6/30/88) (BT)
80+ CHATEAU LARCIS-DUCASSE St.-Emilion 1986 Rel: $20 Cur: $25 (6/30/88) (BT)
85 CHATEAU LARCIS-DUCASSE St.-Emilion 1982 Cur: $25 (5/15/89) (TR)
85+ CHATEAU LARMANDE St.-Emilion 1990 (NR) (4/30/91) (BT)
90+ CHATEAU LARMANDE St.-Emilion 1989 (NR) (4/30/91) (BT)
95+ CHATEAU LARMANDE St.-Emilion 1989 (NR) (4/30/90) (BT)
86 CHATEAU LARMANDE St.-Emilion 1988 $23 (4/30/91)
85+ CHATEAU LARMANDE St.-Emilion 1988 $23 (8/31/90) (BT)
80+ CHATEAU LARMANDE St.-Emilion 1988 $23 (6/30/89) (BT)
80+ CHATEAU LARMANDE St.-Emilion 1987 Rel: $17 Cur: $17 (6/30/89) (BT)
75+ CHATEAU LARMANDE St.-Emilion 1987 Rel: $17 Cur: $17 (6/30/88) (BT)
91 CHATEAU LARMANDE St.-Emilion 1986 Rel: $19 Cur: $26 (6/30/89)
80+ CHATEAU LARMANDE St.-Emilion 1986 Rel: $19 Cur: $26 (6/30/88) (BT)
80+ CHATEAU LARMANDE St.-Emilion 1986 Rel: $19 Cur: $26 (5/15/87) (BT)
93 CHATEAU LARMANDE St.-Emilion 1985 Rel: $23 Cur: $23 (5/15/88)
87 CHATEAU LARMANDE St.-Emilion 1983 Rel: $13 Cur: $16 (3/16/86)
91 CHATEAU LARMANDE St.-Emilion 1982 Cur: $13 (5/15/89) (TR)
76 CHATEAU LARMANDE St.-Emilion 1981 Rel: $10.50 Cur: $11 (8/01/84)
64 CHATEAU LAROQUE St.-Emilion 1983 $12.50 (2/15/88)
84 CHATEAU LEYDET-FIGEAC St.-Emilion 1985 $18 (9/30/88)
90+ CHATEAU MAGDELAINE St.-Emilion 1990 (NR) (4/30/91) (BT)
85+ CHATEAU MAGDELAINE St.-Emilion 1989 (NR) (4/30/91) (BT)
80+ CHATEAU MAGDELAINE St.-Emilion 1989 (NR) (4/30/90) (BT)
85+ CHATEAU MAGDELAINE St.-Emilion 1988 $50 (8/31/90) (BT)
75+ CHATEAU MAGDELAINE St.-Emilion 1988 $50 (6/30/89) (BT)
80+ CHATEAU MAGDELAINE St.-Emilion 1987 Cur: $32 (6/30/89) (BT)
80+ CHATEAU MAGDELAINE St.-Emilion 1987 Cur: $32 (6/30/88) (BT)
94 CHATEAU MAGDELAINE St.-Emilion 1986 Rel: $48 Cur: $48 (2/15/90)
90+ CHATEAU MAGDELAINE St.-Emilion 1986 Rel: $48 Cur: $48 (6/30/88) (BT)
90+ CHATEAU MAGDELAINE St.-Emilion 1986 Rel: $48 Cur: $48 (5/15/87) (BT)
90 CHATEAU MAGDELAINE St.-Emilion 1985 Rel: $40 Cur: $41 (6/30/88)
90+ CHATEAU MAGDELAINE St.-Emilion 1985 Rel: $40 Cur: $41 (5/15/87) (BT)
95 CHATEAU MAGDELAINE St.-Emilion 1982 Cur: $53 (5/15/89) (TR)
89 CHATEAU MAGDELAINE St.-Emilion 1979 Cur: $40 (10/15/89) (JS)
86 CHATEAU MAGDELAINE St.-Emilion 1961 Cur: $250 (3/16/86) (JL)
89 CHATEAU MAGDELAINE St.-Emilion 1959 Cur: $150 (10/15/90) (JS)
80 CHATEAU MATRAS St.-Emilion 1982 (NA) (5/15/89) (TR)
87 CHATEAU MAUVINON St.-Emilion 1983 $10 (11/30/86)
78 A. MOUEIX St.-Emilion 1981 $7.50 (9/01/85)
80+ CHATEAU MOULIN DU CADET St.-Emilion 1990 (NR) (4/30/91) (BT)
85+ CHATEAU MOULIN DU CADET St.-Emilion 1989 (NR) (4/30/91) (BT)
80+ CHATEAU MOULIN DU CADET St.-Emilion 1988 (NR) (6/30/89) (BT)
75+ CHATEAU MOULIN DU CADET St.-Emilion 1987 (NR) (6/30/89) (BT)
90+ CHATEAU PAVIE St.-Emilion 1990 (NR) (4/30/91) (BT)
85+ CHATEAU PAVIE St.-Emilion 1989 (NR) (4/30/91) (BT)
89 CHATEAU PAVIE St.-Emilion 1988 $46 (3/31/91)
80+ CHATEAU PAVIE St.-Emilion 1988 $46 (6/30/89) (BT)
82 CHATEAU PAVIE St.-Emilion 1987 Rel: $30 Cur: $31 (5/15/90)
85+ CHATEAU PAVIE St.-Emilion 1987 Rel: $30 Cur: $31 (6/30/89) (BT)
80+ CHATEAU PAVIE St.-Emilion 1987 Rel: $30 Cur: $31 (6/30/88) (BT)
93 CHATEAU PAVIE St.-Emilion 1986 Rel: $35 Cur: $35 (6/30/89)
85+ CHATEAU PAVIE St.-Emilion 1986 Rel: $35 Cur: $35 (6/30/88) (BT)
92 CHATEAU PAVIE St.-Emilion 1985 Rel: $38 Cur: $38 (5/15/88)
92 CHATEAU PAVIE St.-Emilion 1983 Rel: $23 Cur: $27 (3/16/86)
89 CHATEAU PAVIE St.-Emilion 1982 Rel: $23.50 Cur: $37 (5/15/89) (TR)
90 CHATEAU PAVIE St.-Emilion 1982 Rel: $23.50 Cur: $37 (3/16/85)
84 CHATEAU PAVIE St.-Emilion 1981 Rel: $15.50 Cur: $21 (6/01/84)
86 CHATEAU PAVIE St.-Emilion 1979 Cur: $34 (10/15/89) (JS)
62 CHATEAU PAVIE St.-Emilion 1961 Cur: $125 (3/16/86) (JL)
90+ CHATEAU PAVIE-DECESSE St.-Emilion 1990 (NR) (4/30/91) (BT)
85+ CHATEAU PAVIE-DECESSE St.-Emilion 1989 (NR) (4/30/91) (BT)
94 CHATEAU PAVIE-DECESSE St.-Emilion 1988 $27 (3/31/91)
75+ CHATEAU PAVIE-DECESSE St.-Emilion 1988 $27 (6/30/89) (BT)
75+ CHATEAU PAVIE-DECESSE St.-Emilion 1987 Rel: $21 Cur: $21 (6/30/89) (BT)
75+ CHATEAU PAVIE-DECESSE St.-Emilion 1987 Rel: $21 Cur: $21 (6/30/88) (BT)
93 CHATEAU PAVIE-DECESSE St.-Emilion 1986 Rel: $33 Cur: $33 (6/30/89)
85+ CHATEAU PAVIE-DECESSE St.-Emilion 1986 Rel: $33 Cur: $33 (6/30/88) (BT)
89 CHATEAU PAVIE-DECESSE St.-Emilion 1985 Rel: $27 Cur: $27 (3/31/88)
92 CHATEAU PAVIE-DECESSE St.-Emilion 1983 Rel: $17 Cur: $17 (3/16/86)
89 CHATEAU PAVIE-DECESSE St.-Emilion 1982 Cur: $30 (5/15/89) (TR)
89 CHATEAU PAVIE-MACQUIN St.-Emilion 1982 (NA) (5/15/89) (TR)
89 LE PETIT CHEVAL St.-Emilion 1987 $35 (3/31/91)
75+ CHATEAU PETIT-FAURIE-DE-SOUTARD St.-Emilion 1989 (NR) (4/30/91) (BT)
82 CHATEAU PETIT-FAURIE-DE-SOUTARD St.-Emilion 1988 $20 (4/30/91)
70+ CHATEAU PETIT-FAURIE-DE-SOUTARD St.-Emilion 1988 $20 (6/30/89) (BT)
75+ CHATEAU PETIT-FAURIE-DE-SOUTARD St.-Emilion 1987 Rel: $15 Cur: $15 (6/30/89) (BT)
80 CHATEAU PETIT-FAURIE-DE-SOUTARD St.-Emilion 1986 Rel: $15 Cur: $15 (6/30/89)
70+ CHATEAU PETIT-FIGEAC St.-Emilion 1989 (NR) (4/30/91) (BT)
75+ CHATEAU PETIT-FIGEAC St.-Emilion 1989 (NR) (4/30/90) (BT)
85+ CHATEAU PETIT-FIGEAC St.-Emilion 1988 $17 (8/31/90) (BT)
85+ CHATEAU PUY-BLANQUET St.-Emilion 1990 (NR) (4/30/91) (BT)
85+ CHATEAU PUY-BLANQUET St.-Emilion 1989 (NR) (4/30/91) (BT)
80+ CHATEAU PUY-BLANQUET St.-Emilion 1989 (NR) (4/30/90) (BT)
75+ CHATEAU PUY-BLANQUET St.-Emilion 1988 $15 (6/30/89) (BT)
75+ CHATEAU PUY-BLANQUET St.-Emilion 1987 Rel: $14 Cur: $14 (6/30/88) (BT)
80+ CHATEAU PUY-BLANQUET St.-Emilion 1986 Rel: $16 Cur: $16 (6/30/88) (BT)
70+ CHATEAU PUY-BLANQUET St.-Emilion 1986 Rel: $16 Cur: $16 (5/15/87) (BT)
60+ CHATEAU PUY-BLANQUET St.-Emilion 1985 Rel: $13 Cur: $13 (4/16/86) (BT)
76 CHATEAU PUY-BLANQUET St.-Emilion 1983 Rel: $9.50 Cur: $10 (12/31/86)
88 CHATEAU RIPEAU St.-Emilion 1982 Cur: $18 (5/15/89) (TR)
73 CHATEAU DU ROCHER St.-Emilion 1983 $11 (5/15/87)
80+ CHATEAU DU ROCHER-BELLEVUE-FIGEAC St.-Emilion 1989 (NR) (4/30/90) (BT)
87 CHATEAU DU ROCHER-BELLEVUE-FIGEAC St.-Emilion 1988 $13.50 (4/30/91)
80+ CHATEAU DU ROCHER-BELLEVUE-FIGEAC St.-Emilion 1986 Rel: $12 Cur: $16 (5/15/87) (BT)
79 CHATEAU ROLAND St.-Emilion 1986 $11.25 (6/30/89)
85 BARON PHILIPPE DE ROTHSCHILD St.-Emilion 1985 $10.50 (9/30/88)
89 CHATEAU DE ROUFFLIAC St.-Emilion 1985 $15 (9/30/88)
85+ CHATEAU LA SERRE St.-Emilion 1989 (NR) (4/30/91) (BT)
80 CHATEAU LA SERRE St.-Emilion 1988 $18 (6/15/91)
80+ CHATEAU LA SERRE St.-Emilion 1988 $18 (6/30/89) (BT)
75+ CHATEAU LA SERRE St.-Emilion 1987 $15 (6/30/89) (BT)
91 CHATEAU LA SERRE St.-Emilion 1985 Rel: $15 Cur: $15 (5/15/88)
85 CHATEAU SOUTARD St.-Emilion 1985 Rel: $20 Cur: $20 (5/15/88)
84 CHATEAU SOUTARD St.-Emilion 1982 Cur: $30 (5/15/89) (TR)
90 CHATEAU DU TERTRE St.-Emilion 1988 $40 (6/15/91)
85 CHATEAU TERTRE-DAUGAY St.-Emilion 1988 $20 (4/30/91)
80+ CHATEAU TERTRE-DAUGAY St.-Emilion 1985 Rel: $15 Cur: $18 (5/15/87) (BT)
90 CHATEAU TERTRE-ROTEBOEUF St.-Emilion 1988 $40 (6/15/91)
79 CHATEAU TERTRE-ROTEBOEUF St.-Emilion 1988 $40 (3/31/91)

Key to Symbols

The scores reported here are the results of blind tastings conducted by our panel of senior editors. Wines that carry the initials below are results of individual tastings.

THE WINE SPECTATOR 100-POINT SCALE ***95-100***—Classic, a great wine; ***90-94***—Outstanding, superior character and style; ***80-89***—Good to very good, a wine with special qualities; ***70-79***—Average, drinkable wine that may have minor flaws; ***60-69***—Below average, drinkable but not recommended; ***50-59***—Poor, undrinkable, not recommended. "+"—With a score indicates a range; used primarily with barrel tastings to indicate a preliminary score.

SPECIAL DESIGNATIONS SS—Spectator Selection, CS—Cellar Selection, BB—Best Buy.

TASTER'S INITIALS (JG)—Jim Gordon, (HS)—Harvey Steiman, (JL)—James Laube, (JS)—James Suckling, (TM)—Thomas Matthews, (TR)—Terry Robards, (BT)—Barrel Tasting (these wines were tasted blind from barrel samples), (CA-date)—*California's Great Cabernets* by James Laube, (CH-date)—*California's Great Chardonnays* by James Laube, (VP-date)—*Vintage Port* by James Suckling.

DATE TASTED Dates in parentheses represent the issue in which the rating was published.

83 CHATEAU TERTRE-ROTEBOEUF St.-Emilion 1987 Rel: $15 Cur: $23 (2/15/90)
90 CHATEAU TERTRE-ROTEBOEUF St.-Emilion 1986 Rel: $25 Cur: $34 (6/30/89)
89 CHATEAU TERTRE-ROTEBOEUF St.-Emilion 1985 Rel: $23 Cur: $25 (6/30/88)
81 CHATEAU TERTRE-ROTEBOEUF St.-Emilion 1983 Rel: $11.50 Cur: $20 (5/16/86)
85 CHATEAU TERTRE-ROTEBOEUF St.-Emilion 1982 Rel: $10 Cur: $17 (9/16/85)
82 CHATEAU TOUR-BALADOZ St.-Emilion 1985 $11.50 (2/29/88)
81 CHATEAU LA TOUR DU PIN St.-Emilion 1982 $12 (5/01/85)
85+ CHATEAU LA TOUR-DU-PIN-FIGEAC-MOUEIX St.-Emilion 1989 (NR) (4/30/91) (BT)
77 CHATEAU LA TOUR-DU-PIN-FIGEAC-MOUEIX St.-Emilion 1988 $24 (7/15/91)
80+ CHATEAU LA TOUR-DU-PIN-FIGEAC-MOUEIX St.-Emilion 1988 $24 (6/30/89) (BT)
80+ CHATEAU LA TOUR-DU-PIN-FIGEAC-MOUEIX St.-Emilion 1987 Rel: $17 Cur: $17 (6/30/89) (BT)
88 CHATEAU LA TOUR-DU-PIN-FIGEAC-MOUEIX St.-Emilion 1982 Cur: $26 (5/15/89) (TR)
82 CHATEAU LA TOUR-DU-PIN-FIGEAC-BELIVIER St.-Emilion 1982 (NA) (5/15/89) (TR)
85+ CHATEAU LA TOUR-FIGEAC St.-Emilion 1989 (NR) (4/30/91) (BT)
70+ CHATEAU LA TOUR-FIGEAC St.-Emilion 1988 $17 (6/30/89) (BT)
75+ CHATEAU LA TOUR-FIGEAC St.-Emilion 1987 Rel: $14 Cur: $14 (6/30/89) (BT)
89 CHATEAU LA TOUR-FIGEAC St.-Emilion 1982 Cur: $22 (5/15/89) (TR)
79 CHATEAU TOUR-GRAND-FAURIE St.-Emilion 1985 $9.75 (2/15/89)
91 CHATEAU TRIMOULET St.-Emilion 1988 $16 (6/15/91)
81 CHATEAU TRIMOULET St.-Emilion 1982 (NA) (5/15/89) (TR)
90+ CHATEAU TROPLONG-MONDOT St.-Emilion 1990 (NR) (4/30/91) (BT)
90+ CHATEAU TROPLONG-MONDOT St.-Emilion 1989 (NR) (4/30/91) (BT)
90+ CHATEAU TROPLONG-MONDOT St.-Emilion 1989 (NR) (4/30/90) (BT)
85 CHATEAU TROPLONG-MONDOT St.-Emilion 1988 $21 (7/15/91)
80+ CHATEAU TROPLONG-MONDOT St.-Emilion 1988 $21 (8/31/90) (BT)
80+ CHATEAU TROPLONG-MONDOT St.-Emilion 1988 $21 (6/30/89) (BT)
80+ CHATEAU TROPLONG-MONDOT St.-Emilion 1987 Rel: $16 Cur: $16 (6/30/89) (BT)
80+ CHATEAU TROPLONG-MONDOT St.-Emilion 1987 Rel: $16 Cur: $16 (6/30/88) (BT)
88 CHATEAU TROPLONG-MONDOT St.-Emilion 1986 Rel: $20 Cur: $23 (6/30/89)
85+ CHATEAU TROPLONG-MONDOT St.-Emilion 1986 Rel: $20 Cur: $23 (6/30/88) (BT)
80+ CHATEAU TROPLONG-MONDOT St.-Emilion 1986 Rel: $20 Cur: $23 (5/15/87) (BT)
88 CHATEAU TROPLONG-MONDOT St.-Emilion 1985 Rel: $21 Cur: $21 (6/30/88)
90+ CHATEAU TROTTEVIEILLE St.-Emilion 1990 (NR) (4/30/91) (BT)
90+ CHATEAU TROTTEVIEILLE St.-Emilion 1989 (NR) (4/30/91) (BT)
85+ CHATEAU TROTTEVIEILLE St.-Emilion 1989 (NR) (4/30/90) (BT)
85 CHATEAU TROTTEVIEILLE St.-Emilion 1988 $20 (4/30/91)
80+ CHATEAU TROTTEVIEILLE St.-Emilion 1988 $20 (6/30/89) (BT)
80+ CHATEAU TROTTEVIEILLE St.-Emilion 1987 Rel: $15 Cur: $15 (6/30/89) (BT)
87 CHATEAU TROTTEVIEILLE St.-Emilion 1982 Cur: $35 (5/15/89) (TR)
75 CHATEAU TROTTEVIEILLE St.-Emilion 1962 Cur: $30 (11/30/87) (JS)
80 VIEUX CHATEAU GUIBEAU St.-Emilion 1982 $8 (9/16/85)
83 CHATEAU VIEUX SARPE St.-Emilion 1982 (NA) (5/15/89) (TR)
75 CHATEAU VILLADIERE St.-Emilion 1982 $8 (9/01/85)
90+ CHATEAU VILLEMAURINE St.-Emilion 1989 (NR) (4/30/91) (BT)
75+ CHATEAU VILLEMAURINE St.-Emilion 1987 (NR) (6/30/88) (BT)
80+ CHATEAU VILLEMAURINE St.-Emilion 1986 (NR) (6/30/88) (BT)
83 CHATEAU VILLEMAURINE St.-Emilion 1982 (NA) (5/15/89) (TR)
87 CHATEAU YON-FIGEAC St.-Emilion 1982 $23 (5/15/89) (TR)

ST.-EMILION SATELLITES

71 CHATEAU DU CHEVALIER Montagne-St.-Emilion 1986 $19 (3/31/91)
75 CHATEAU FAIZEAU Montagne-St.-Emilion 1983 $9 (11/15/87)
73 CHATEAU DE LUSSAC Lussac-St.-Emilion 1982 $6.75 (5/01/84)
80 CHATEAU MAISON-BLANCHE Montagne-St.-Emilion 1985 $13 (2/15/89)
78 CHATEAU MAISON-NEUVE Montagne-St.-Emilion 1985 $7 (3/15/88)
64 CHATEAU LE MAYNE Puisseguin-St.-Emilion 1982 $7.50 (12/01/85)
80+ CHATEAU ST.-ANDRE-CORBIN St.-Georges-St.-Emilion 1990 (NR) (4/30/91) (BT)
80+ CHATEAU ST.-ANDRE-CORBIN St.-Georges-St.-Emilion 1989 (NR) (4/30/91) (BT)
75+ CHATEAU ST.-ANDRE-CORBIN St.-Georges-St.-Emilion 1989 (NR) (4/30/90) (BT)
80+ CHATEAU ST.-ANDRE-CORBIN St.-Georges-St.-Emilion 1988 (NR) (6/30/89) (BT)
75+ CHATEAU ST.-ANDRE-CORBIN St.-Georges-St.-Emilion 1987 (NR) (6/30/89) (BT)
77 CHATEAU ST.-ANDRE-CORBIN St.-Georges-St.-Emilion 1986 Rel: $22 Cur: $22 (3/31/90)
70+ CHATEAU ST.-ANDRE-CORBIN St.-Georges-St.-Emilion 1986 Rel: $22 Cur: $22 (5/15/87) (BT)
80+ CHATEAU ST.-ANDRE-CORBIN St.-Georges-St.-Emilion 1985 (NR) (5/15/87) (BT)
87 CHATEAU ST.-GEORGES St.-Georges-St.-Emilion 1986 $14 (7/15/90)
87 CHATEAU ST.-GEORGES St.-Georges-St.-Emilion 1985 $11 (7/31/89)
81 CHATEAU TOUR CALON Montagne-St.-Emilion 1986 $10 (9/30/89)

ST.-ESTÈPHE

90+ CHATEAU BEAU-SITE St.-Estèphe 1990 (NR) (4/30/91) (BT)
90+ CHATEAU BEAU-SITE St.-Estèphe 1989 (NR) (4/30/91) (BT)
90+ CHATEAU BEAU-SITE St.-Estèphe 1989 (NR) (4/30/90) (BT)
80+ CHATEAU BEAU-SITE St.-Estèphe 1988 $14 (6/30/89) (BT)
81 CHATEAU BEAU-SITE St.-Estèphe 1987 Rel: $12 Cur: $12 (11/30/89) (JS)
75+ CHATEAU BEAU-SITE St.-Estèphe 1987 Rel: $12 Cur: $12 (6/30/89) (BT)
86 CHATEAU BEAU-SITE St.-Estèphe 1986 Rel: $15 Cur: $15 (11/30/89) (JS)
86 CHATEAU BEAU-SITE St.-Estèphe 1982 Cur: $15 (11/30/89) (JS)
85+ CHATEAU CALON-SEGUR St.-Estèphe 1990 (NR) (4/30/91) (BT)
85+ CHATEAU CALON-SEGUR St.-Estèphe 1989 (NR) (4/30/91) (BT)
80+ CHATEAU CALON-SEGUR St.-Estèphe 1989 (NR) (4/30/90) (BT)
85 CHATEAU CALON-SEGUR St.-Estèphe 1988 $30 (7/15/91)
80+ CHATEAU CALON-SEGUR St.-Estèphe 1988 $30 (6/30/89) (BT)
75+ CHATEAU CALON-SEGUR St.-Estèphe 1987 Rel: $25 Cur: $25 (6/30/89) (BT)
80+ CHATEAU CALON-SEGUR St.-Estèphe 1987 Rel: $25 Cur: $25 (6/30/88) (BT)
86 CHATEAU CALON-SEGUR St.-Estèphe 1986 Rel: $32 Cur: $32 (5/31/89)
85+ CHATEAU CALON-SEGUR St.-Estèphe 1986 Rel: $32 Cur: $32 (6/30/88) (BT)
80+ CHATEAU CALON-SEGUR St.-Estèphe 1986 Rel: $32 Cur: $32 (5/15/87) (BT)
88 CHATEAU CALON-SEGUR St.-Estèphe 1985 Rel: $30 Cur: $30 (5/31/88)
80+ CHATEAU CALON-SEGUR St.-Estèphe 1985 Rel: $30 Cur: $30 (5/15/87) (BT)
83 CHATEAU CALON-SEGUR St.-Estèphe 1983 Rel: $16.50 Cur: $26 (10/31/86)
70 CHATEAU CALON-SEGUR St.-Estèphe 1962 Cur: $69 (11/30/87) (JS)
84 CHATEAU CALON-SEGUR St.-Estèphe 1961 Cur: $134 (3/16/86) (JL)
82 CHATEAU CALON-SEGUR St.-Estèphe 1959 Cur: $162 (10/15/90) (JS)
94 CHATEAU CALON-SEGUR St.-Estèphe 1945 Cur: $310 (3/16/86) (JL)
90+ CHATEAU CAPBERN-GASQUETON St.-Estèphe 1989 (NR) (4/30/91) (BT)

75+ CHATEAU CAPBERN-GASQUETON St.-Estèphe 1988 (NR) (6/30/89) (BT)
76 CHATEAU CAPBERN-GASQUETON St.-Estèphe 1986 Rel: $20 Cur: $20 (11/30/89) (JS)
85 CHATEAU CAPBERN-GASQUETON St.-Estèphe 1985 Rel: $18 Cur: $18 (8/31/88)
66 CHATEAU CAPBERN-GASQUETON St.-Estèphe 1983 Rel: $19 Cur: $19 (2/15/88)
83 CHATEAU CAPBERN-GASQUETON St.-Estèphe 1982 Rel: $11 Cur: $28 (11/30/89) (JS)
91 CHATEAU CAPBERN-GASQUETON St.-Estèphe 1982 Rel: $11 Cur: $28 (9/16/85)
90+ CHATEAU CHAMBERT-MARBUZET St.-Estèphe 1990 (NR) (4/30/91) (BT)
85+ CHATEAU CHAMBERT-MARBUZET St.-Estèphe 1989 (NR) (4/30/91) (BT)
80+ CHATEAU CHAMBERT-MARBUZET St.-Estèphe 1989 (NR) (4/30/90) (BT)
75+ CHATEAU CHAMBERT-MARBUZET St.-Estèphe 1988 $26 (8/31/90) (BT)
79 CHATEAU CHAMBERT-MARBUZET St.-Estèphe 1987 Rel: $18 Cur: $18 (11/30/89) (JS)
89 CHATEAU CHAMBERT-MARBUZET St.-Estèphe 1986 Rel: $25 Cur: $28 (11/30/89) (JS)
81 CHATEAU CHAMBERT-MARBUZET St.-Estèphe 1986 Rel: $25 Cur: $28 (5/31/89)
87 CHATEAU CHAMBERT-MARBUZET St.-Estèphe 1985 Rel: $28 Cur: $31 (6/30/88)
77 CHATEAU CHAMBERT-MARBUZET St.-Estèphe 1983 Rel: $15 Cur: $15 (9/30/86)
88 CHATEAU CHAMBERT-MARBUZET St.-Estèphe 1982 Cur: $30 (11/30/89) (JS)
75+ CHATEAU LA COMMANDERIE St.-Estèphe 1988 (NR) (6/30/89) (BT)
90+ CHATEAU COS D'ESTOURNEL St.-Estèphe 1990 (NR) (4/30/91) (BT)
95+ CHATEAU COS D'ESTOURNEL St.-Estèphe 1989 (NR) (4/30/91) (BT)
95+ CHATEAU COS D'ESTOURNEL St.-Estèphe 1989 (NR) (4/30/90) (BT)
95 CHATEAU COS D'ESTOURNEL St.-Estèphe 1988 $30 (7/15/91) CS
95+ CHATEAU COS D'ESTOURNEL St.-Estèphe 1988 $30 (8/31/90) (BT)
95+ CHATEAU COS D'ESTOURNEL St.-Estèphe 1988 $30 (6/30/89) (BT)
81 CHATEAU COS D'ESTOURNEL St.-Estèphe 1987 Rel: $30 Cur: $30 (5/15/90)
83 CHATEAU COS D'ESTOURNEL St.-Estèphe 1987 Rel: $30 Cur: $30 (5/15/90) (HS)
85+ CHATEAU COS D'ESTOURNEL St.-Estèphe 1987 Rel: $30 Cur: $30 (6/30/89) (BT)
85+ CHATEAU COS D'ESTOURNEL St.-Estèphe 1987 Rel: $30 Cur: $30 (6/30/88) (BT)
92 CHATEAU COS D'ESTOURNEL St.-Estèphe 1986 Rel: $40 Cur: $45 (5/15/90) (HS)
93 CHATEAU COS D'ESTOURNEL St.-Estèphe 1986 Rel: $40 Cur: $45 (5/31/89)
90+ CHATEAU COS D'ESTOURNEL St.-Estèphe 1986 Rel: $40 Cur: $45 (6/30/88) (BT)
90+ CHATEAU COS D'ESTOURNEL St.-Estèphe 1986 Rel: $40 Cur: $45 (5/15/87) (BT)
95 CHATEAU COS D'ESTOURNEL St.-Estèphe 1985 Rel: $33 Cur: $51 (5/15/90) (HS)
92 CHATEAU COS D'ESTOURNEL St.-Estèphe 1985 Rel: $33 Cur: $51 (4/30/88)
90+ CHATEAU COS D'ESTOURNEL St.-Estèphe 1985 Rel: $33 Cur: $51 (5/15/87) (BT)
81 CHATEAU COS D'ESTOURNEL St.-Estèphe 1984 Rel: $29 Cur: $29 (5/15/90) (HS)
93 CHATEAU COS D'ESTOURNEL St.-Estèphe 1984 Rel: $29 Cur: $29 (3/31/87)
85 CHATEAU COS D'ESTOURNEL St.-Estèphe 1983 Rel: $29 Cur: $54 (5/15/90) (HS)
95 CHATEAU COS D'ESTOURNEL St.-Estèphe 1983 Rel: $29 Cur: $54 (5/16/86) SS
92 CHATEAU COS D'ESTOURNEL St.-Estèphe 1982 Rel: $23 Cur: $77 (5/15/90) (HS)
93 CHATEAU COS D'ESTOURNEL St.-Estèphe 1982 Rel: $23 Cur: $77 (7/16/85) CS
87 CHATEAU COS D'ESTOURNEL St.-Estèphe 1981 Rel: $23.50 Cur: $41 (5/15/90) (HS)
89 CHATEAU COS D'ESTOURNEL St.-Estèphe 1981 Rel: $23.50 Cur: $41 (6/01/84)
83 CHATEAU COS D'ESTOURNEL St.-Estèphe 1980 Cur: $38 (5/15/90) (HS)
92 CHATEAU COS D'ESTOURNEL St.-Estèphe 1979 Cur: $47 (5/15/90) (HS)
87 CHATEAU COS D'ESTOURNEL St.-Estèphe 1979 Cur: $47 (10/15/89) (JS)
93 CHATEAU COS D'ESTOURNEL St.-Estèphe 1978 Cur: $53 (5/15/90) (HS)
85 CHATEAU COS D'ESTOURNEL St.-Estèphe 1977 Cur: $30 (5/15/90) (HS)
84 CHATEAU COS D'ESTOURNEL St.-Estèphe 1976 Cur: $46 (5/15/90) (HS)
88 CHATEAU COS D'ESTOURNEL St.-Estèphe 1975 Cur: $61 (5/15/90) (HS)
82 CHATEAU COS D'ESTOURNEL St.-Estèphe 1973 Cur: $31 (5/15/90) (HS)
91 CHATEAU COS D'ESTOURNEL St.-Estèphe 1971 Cur: $50 (5/15/90) (HS)
89 CHATEAU COS D'ESTOURNEL St.-Estèphe 1970 Cur: $92 (5/15/90) (HS)
58 CHATEAU COS D'ESTOURNEL St.-Estèphe 1969 Cur: $18 (5/15/90) (HS)
82 CHATEAU COS D'ESTOURNEL St.-Estèphe 1967 Cur: $34 (5/15/90) (HS)
74 CHATEAU COS D'ESTOURNEL St.-Estèphe 1966 Cur: $100 (5/15/90) (HS)
84 CHATEAU COS D'ESTOURNEL St.-Estèphe 1964 Cur: $75 (5/15/90) (HS)
79 CHATEAU COS D'ESTOURNEL St.-Estèphe 1962 Cur: $124 (5/15/90) (HS)
85 CHATEAU COS D'ESTOURNEL St.-Estèphe 1962 Cur: $124 (11/30/87) (JS)
87 CHATEAU COS D'ESTOURNEL St.-Estèphe 1961 Cur: $217 (5/15/90) (HS)
79 CHATEAU COS D'ESTOURNEL St.-Estèphe 1960 Cur: $85 (5/15/90) (HS)
90 CHATEAU COS D'ESTOURNEL St.-Estèphe 1959 Cur: $215 (10/15/90) (JS)
83 CHATEAU COS D'ESTOURNEL St.-Estèphe 1959 Cur: $215 (5/15/90) (HS)
89 CHATEAU COS D'ESTOURNEL St.-Estèphe 1958 Cur: $95 (5/15/90) (HS)
79 CHATEAU COS D'ESTOURNEL St.-Estèphe 1956 Cur: $60 (5/15/90) (HS)
90 CHATEAU COS D'ESTOURNEL St.-Estèphe 1955 Cur: $137 (5/15/90) (HS)
81 CHATEAU COS D'ESTOURNEL St.-Estèphe 1954 Cur: $80 (5/15/90) (HS)
91 CHATEAU COS D'ESTOURNEL St.-Estèphe 1953 Cur: $262 (5/15/90) (HS)
95 CHATEAU COS D'ESTOURNEL St.-Estèphe 1952 Cur: $120 (5/15/90) (HS)
86 CHATEAU COS D'ESTOURNEL St.-Estèphe 1950 Cur: $100 (5/15/90) (HS)
80 CHATEAU COS D'ESTOURNEL St.-Estèphe 1949 Cur: $195 (5/15/90) (HS)
91 CHATEAU COS D'ESTOURNEL St.-Estèphe 1947 Cur: $300 (5/15/90) (HS)
77 CHATEAU COS D'ESTOURNEL St.-Estèphe 1945 Cur: $360 (5/15/90) (HS)
87 CHATEAU COS D'ESTOURNEL St.-Estèphe 1945 Cur: $360 (3/16/86) (JL)
85 CHATEAU COS D'ESTOURNEL St.-Estèphe 1943 Cur: $220 (5/15/90) (HS)
78 CHATEAU COS D'ESTOURNEL St.-Estèphe 1942 Cur: $110 (5/15/90) (HS)
64 CHATEAU COS D'ESTOURNEL St.-Estèphe 1937 Cur: $260 (5/15/90) (HS)
88 CHATEAU COS D'ESTOURNEL St.-Estèphe 1934 Cur: $175 (5/15/90) (HS)
92 CHATEAU COS D'ESTOURNEL St.-Estèphe 1929 Cur: $580 (5/15/90) (HS)
90 CHATEAU COS D'ESTOURNEL St.-Estèphe 1928 Cur: $460 (5/15/90) (HS)
77 CHATEAU COS D'ESTOURNEL St.-Estèphe 1926 Cur: $300 (5/15/90) (HS)
82 CHATEAU COS D'ESTOURNEL St.-Estèphe 1924 Cur: $300 (5/15/90) (HS)
65 CHATEAU COS D'ESTOURNEL St.-Estèphe 1921 Cur: $200 (5/15/90) (HS)
93 CHATEAU COS D'ESTOURNEL St.-Estèphe 1920 Cur: $350 (5/15/90) (HS)
73 CHATEAU COS D'ESTOURNEL St.-Estèphe 1917 Cur: $250 (5/15/90) (HS)
65 CHATEAU COS D'ESTOURNEL St.-Estèphe 1905 Cur: $250 (5/15/90) (HS)
63 CHATEAU COS D'ESTOURNEL St.-Estèphe 1904 Cur: $210 (5/15/90) (HS)
87 CHATEAU COS D'ESTOURNEL St.-Estèphe 1899 Cur: $940 (5/15/90) (HS)
72 CHATEAU COS D'ESTOURNEL St.-Estèphe 1898 Cur: $500 (5/15/90) (HS)
69 CHATEAU COS D'ESTOURNEL St.-Estèphe 1890 Cur: $330 (5/15/90) (HS)
90 CHATEAU COS D'ESTOURNEL St.-Estèphe 1870 Cur: $1,240 (5/15/90) (HS)
82 CHATEAU COS D'ESTOURNEL St.-Estèphe 1869 Cur: $1,200 (5/15/90) (HS)
85+ CHATEAU COS-LABORY St.-Estèphe 1990 (NR) (4/30/91) (BT)
90+ CHATEAU COS-LABORY St.-Estèphe 1989 (NR) (4/30/91) (BT)
90+ CHATEAU COS-LABORY St.-Estèphe 1989 (NR) (4/30/90) (BT)
85 CHATEAU COS-LABORY St.-Estèphe 1988 $20 (4/30/91)
85+ CHATEAU COS-LABORY St.-Estèphe 1988 $20 (8/31/90) (BT)
85+ CHATEAU COS-LABORY St.-Estèphe 1988 $20 (6/30/89) (BT)
65+ CHATEAU COS-LABORY St.-Estèphe 1987 Rel: $15 Cur: $15 (6/30/88) (BT)
75+ CHATEAU COS-LABORY St.-Estèphe 1986 Rel: $16 Cur: $16 (6/30/88) (BT)
87 CHATEAU COS-LABORY St.-Estèphe 1985 Rel: $16 Cur: $17 (4/30/88)

FRANCE
BORDEAUX RED/ST.-ESTÈPHE

73 CHATEAU COS-LABORY St.-Estèphe 1984 Rel: $12 Cur: $12 (6/15/87)
86 CHATEAU COS-LABORY St.-Estèphe 1983 Rel: $9.50 Cur: $17 (5/16/86)
79 CHATEAU LE CROCK St.-Estèphe 1987 $16 (11/30/89) (JS)
92 CHATEAU LE CROCK St.-Estèphe 1986 $18 (11/30/89) (JS)
88 CHATEAU LE CROCK St.-Estèphe 1986 $18 (6/30/89)
79 CHATEAU LE CROCK St.-Estèphe 1985 $16.50 (2/15/88)
81 CHATEAU LE CROCK St.-Estèphe 1983 $9.50 (12/16/85)
80 CHATEAU LE CROCK St.-Estèphe 1982 Cur: $20 (11/30/89) (JS)
81 CHATEAU HAUT-COUTELIN St.-Estèphe 1982 $12.50 (2/15/88)
95+ CHATEAU HAUT-MARBUZET St.-Estèphe 1990 (NR) (4/30/91) (BT)
90+ CHATEAU HAUT-MARBUZET St.-Estèphe 1989 (NR) (4/30/91) (BT)
90+ CHATEAU HAUT-MARBUZET St.-Estèphe 1989 (NR) (4/30/90) (BT)
91 CHATEAU HAUT-MARBUZET St.-Estèphe 1988 $25 (12/31/90) SS
85+ CHATEAU HAUT-MARBUZET St.-Estèphe 1988 $25 (8/31/90) (BT)
90+ CHATEAU HAUT-MARBUZET St.-Estèphe 1988 $25 (6/30/89) (BT)
85 CHATEAU HAUT-MARBUZET St.-Estèphe 1987 Rel: $20 Cur: $20 (5/15/90)
82 CHATEAU HAUT-MARBUZET St.-Estèphe 1987 Rel: $20 Cur: $20 (11/30/89) (JS)
75+ CHATEAU HAUT-MARBUZET St.-Estèphe 1987 Rel: $20 Cur: $20 (6/30/89) (BT)
92 CHATEAU HAUT-MARBUZET St.-Estèphe 1986 Rel: $30 Cur: $30 (11/30/89) (JS)
93 CHATEAU HAUT-MARBUZET St.-Estèphe 1986 Rel: $30 Cur: $30 (5/31/89)
91 CHATEAU HAUT-MARBUZET St.-Estèphe 1985 Rel: $25 Cur: $47 (6/30/88)
92 CHATEAU HAUT-MARBUZET St.-Estèphe 1982 Cur: $57 (11/30/89) (JS)
85 CHATEAU HAUT-MARBUZET St.-Estèphe 1979 Cur: $30 (10/15/89) (JS)
70 CHATEAU HAUT-MARBUZET St.-Estèphe 1962 Cur: $50 (11/30/87) (JS)
83 CHATEAU HAUT-MARBUZET St.-Estèphe (Bottled in England) 1959 Cur: $60 (10/15/90) (JS)
80 CHATEAU LES HAUTS DE BRAME St.-Estèphe 1986 $22 (3/31/91)
82 CHATEAU LES HAUTS DE BRAME St.-Estèphe 1986 $18.50 (10/31/89)
74 CHATEAU LAFFITTE-CARCASSET St.-Estèphe 1981 $7 (3/16/85)
85+ CHATEAU LAFON-ROCHET St.-Estèphe 1990 (NR) (4/30/91) (BT)
90+ CHATEAU LAFON-ROCHET St.-Estèphe 1989 (NR) (4/30/91) (BT)
90+ CHATEAU LAFON-ROCHET St.-Estèphe 1989 (NR) (4/30/90) (BT)
85+ CHATEAU LAFON-ROCHET St.-Estèphe 1988 $17 (6/30/89) (BT)
80+ CHATEAU LAFON-ROCHET St.-Estèphe 1987 Cur: $13 (6/30/89) (BT)
80+ CHATEAU LAFON-ROCHET St.-Estèphe 1987 Cur: $13 (6/30/88) (BT)
85+ CHATEAU LAFON-ROCHET St.-Estèphe 1986 Cur: $18 (6/30/88) (BT)
80+ CHATEAU LAFON-ROCHET St.-Estèphe 1986 Cur: $18 (5/15/87) (BT)
70+ CHATEAU LAFON-ROCHET St.-Estèphe 1985 Cur: $16 (5/15/87) (BT)
58 CHATEAU LAFON-ROCHET St.-Estèphe 1961 Cur: $80 (3/16/86) (JL)
75 CHATEAU LAFON-ROCHET St.-Estèphe 1945 Cur: $100 (3/16/86) (JL)
85+ CHATEAU LILIAN-LADOUYS St.-Estèphe 1989 (NR) (4/30/91) (BT)
92 CHATEAU DE MARBUZET St.-Estèphe 1988 $15 (7/15/91) SS
85+ CHATEAU DE MARBUZET St.-Estèphe 1988 $15 (6/30/89) (BT)
80 CHATEAU DE MARBUZET St.-Estèphe 1987 Rel: $14 Cur: $14 (11/30/89) (JS)
70+ CHATEAU DE MARBUZET St.-Estèphe 1987 Rel: $14 Cur: $14 (6/30/89) (BT)
70+ CHATEAU DE MARBUZET St.-Estèphe 1987 Rel: $14 Cur: $14 (6/30/88) (BT)
86 CHATEAU DE MARBUZET St.-Estèphe 1986 Rel: $15 Cur: $16 (11/30/89) (JS)
92 CHATEAU DE MARBUZET St.-Estèphe 1986 Rel: $15 Cur: $16 (6/30/89)
80+ CHATEAU DE MARBUZET St.-Estèphe 1986 Rel: $15 Cur: $16 (5/15/87) (BT)
87 CHATEAU DE MARBUZET St.-Estèphe 1985 Rel: $11.50 Cur: $21 (6/30/88)
80+ CHATEAU DE MARBUZET St.-Estèphe 1985 Rel: $11.50 Cur: $21 (5/15/87) (BT)
91 CHATEAU DE MARBUZET St.-Estèphe 1983 Rel: $9 Cur: $22 (10/15/86)
86 CHATEAU DE MARBUZET St.-Estèphe 1982 Cur: $22 (11/30/89) (JS)
80+ CHATEAU MEYNEY St.-Estèphe 1990 (NR) (4/30/91) (BT)
90+ CHATEAU MEYNEY St.-Estèphe 1989 (NR) (4/30/91) (BT)
90+ CHATEAU MEYNEY St.-Estèphe 1989 (NR) (4/30/90) (BT)
88 CHATEAU MEYNEY St.-Estèphe 1988 $17 (3/15/91)
80+ CHATEAU MEYNEY St.-Estèphe 1988 $17 (6/30/89) (BT)
87 CHATEAU MEYNEY St.-Estèphe 1987 Rel: $14 Cur: $14 (5/15/90)
83 CHATEAU MEYNEY St.-Estèphe 1987 Rel: $14 Cur: $14 (11/30/89) (JS)
75+ CHATEAU MEYNEY St.-Estèphe 1987 Rel: $14 Cur: $14 (6/30/89) (BT)
88 CHATEAU MEYNEY St.-Estèphe 1986 Rel: $19 Cur: $19 (11/30/89) (JS)
90 CHATEAU MEYNEY St.-Estèphe 1986 Rel: $19 Cur: $19 (6/30/89)
70+ CHATEAU MEYNEY St.-Estèphe 1986 Rel: $19 Cur: $19 (5/15/87) (BT)
92 CHATEAU MEYNEY St.-Estèphe 1985 Rel: $16 Cur: $17 (8/31/88)
79 CHATEAU MEYNEY St.-Estèphe 1984 Rel: $10 Cur: $11 (5/15/87)
92 CHATEAU MEYNEY St.-Estèphe 1983 Rel: $11 Cur: $18 (10/15/86)
86 CHATEAU MEYNEY St.-Estèphe 1982 Cur: $22 (11/30/89) (JS)
87 CHATEAU MEYNEY St.-Estèphe 1979 Cur: $18 (10/15/89) (JS)
90+ CHATEAU MONTROSE St.-Estèphe 1990 (NR) (4/30/91) (BT)
90+ CHATEAU MONTROSE St.-Estèphe 1989 (NR) (4/30/91) (BT)
90+ CHATEAU MONTROSE St.-Estèphe 1989 (NR) (4/30/90) (BT)
87 CHATEAU MONTROSE St.-Estèphe 1988 $41 (3/31/91)
80+ CHATEAU MONTROSE St.-Estèphe 1988 $41 (8/31/90) (BT)
95+ CHATEAU MONTROSE St.-Estèphe 1988 $41 (6/30/89) (BT)
80 CHATEAU MONTROSE St.-Estèphe 1987 Rel: $17 Cur: $18 (2/15/90)
80+ CHATEAU MONTROSE St.-Estèphe 1987 Rel: $17 Cur: $18 (6/30/88) (BT)
96 CHATEAU MONTROSE St.-Estèphe 1986 Rel: $31 Cur: $31 (5/15/89) SS
90+ CHATEAU MONTROSE St.-Estèphe 1986 Rel: $31 Cur: $31 (6/30/88) (BT)
90+ CHATEAU MONTROSE St.-Estèphe 1986 Rel: $31 Cur: $31 (5/15/87) (BT)
90 CHATEAU MONTROSE St.-Estèphe 1985 Rel: $33 Cur: $33 (4/30/88)
90+ CHATEAU MONTROSE St.-Estèphe 1985 Rel: $33 Cur: $33 (5/15/87) (BT)
80+ CHATEAU MONTROSE St.-Estèphe 1985 Rel: $33 Cur: $33 (4/16/86) (BT)
88 CHATEAU MONTROSE St.-Estèphe 1984 Rel: $14 Cur: $25 (3/31/87)
87 CHATEAU MONTROSE St.-Estèphe 1983 Rel: $18.50 Cur: $46 (5/16/86)
92 CHATEAU MONTROSE St.-Estèphe 1982 Rel: $18 Cur: $39 (5/01/85)
90 CHATEAU MONTROSE St.-Estèphe 1981 Rel: $14 Cur: $29 (12/01/84)
81 CHATEAU MONTROSE St.-Estèphe 1979 Cur: $32 (10/15/89) (JS)
80 CHATEAU MONTROSE St.-Estèphe 1970 Cur: $92 (4/01/86)
90 CHATEAU MONTROSE St.-Estèphe 1962 Cur: $100 (11/30/87) (JS)
87 CHATEAU MONTROSE St.-Estèphe 1961 Cur: $230 (3/16/86) (JL)
90 CHATEAU MONTROSE St.-Estèphe 1959 Cur: $131 (10/15/90) (JS)
88 CHATEAU MONTROSE St.-Estèphe 1945 Cur: $300 (3/16/86) (JL)
95+ CHATEAU LES ORMES DE PEZ St.-Estèphe 1990 (NR) (4/30/91) (BT)
90+ CHATEAU LES ORMES DE PEZ St.-Estèphe 1989 (NR) (4/30/91) (BT)
85+ CHATEAU LES ORMES DE PEZ St.-Estèphe 1989 (NR) (4/30/90) (BT)
88 CHATEAU LES ORMES DE PEZ St.-Estèphe 1988 $21 (4/30/91)
80+ CHATEAU LES ORMES DE PEZ St.-Estèphe 1988 $21 (6/30/89) (BT)
83 CHATEAU LES ORMES DE PEZ St.-Estèphe 1987 Rel: $15 Cur: $15 (5/15/90)
86 CHATEAU LES ORMES DE PEZ St.-Estèphe 1987 Rel: $15 Cur: $15 (11/30/89) (JS)
75+ CHATEAU LES ORMES DE PEZ St.-Estèphe 1987 Rel: $15 Cur: $15 (6/30/89) (BT)
75+ CHATEAU LES ORMES DE PEZ St.-Estèphe 1987 Rel: $15 Cur: $15 (6/30/88) (BT)
87 CHATEAU LES ORMES DE PEZ St.-Estèphe 1986 Rel: $21 Cur: $21 (11/30/89) (JS)
90 CHATEAU LES ORMES DE PEZ St.-Estèphe 1986 Rel: $21 Cur: $21 (5/31/89)
85+ CHATEAU LES ORMES DE PEZ St.-Estèphe 1986 Rel: $21 Cur: $21 (6/30/88) (BT)
70+ CHATEAU LES ORMES DE PEZ St.-Estèphe 1986 Rel: $21 Cur: $21 (5/15/87) (BT)
89 CHATEAU LES ORMES DE PEZ St.-Estèphe 1985 Rel: $16 Cur: $18 (4/30/88)
80+ CHATEAU LES ORMES DE PEZ St.-Estèphe 1985 Rel: $16 Cur: $18 (5/15/87) (BT)
50+ CHATEAU LES ORMES DE PEZ St.-Estèphe 1985 Rel: $16 Cur: $18 (4/16/86) (BT)
86 CHATEAU LES ORMES DE PEZ St.-Estèphe 1983 Rel: $17 Cur: $17 (10/15/86)
87 CHATEAU LES ORMES DE PEZ St.-Estèphe 1982 Cur: $23 (11/30/89) (JS)
83 CHATEAU DE PEZ St.-Estèphe 1988 $19 (6/15/91)
90 CHATEAU DE PEZ St.-Estèphe 1986 Rel: $17 Cur: $17 (6/30/89)
90 CHATEAU DE PEZ St.-Estèphe 1985 Rel: $15 Cur: $22 (6/30/88)
90 CHATEAU DE PEZ St.-Estèphe 1982 Rel: $12 Cur: $21 (4/01/86)
85+ CHATEAU PHELAN-SEGUR St.-Estèphe 1990 (NR) (4/30/91) (BT)
85+ CHATEAU PHELAN-SEGUR St.-Estèphe 1989 (NR) (4/30/91) (BT)
87 CHATEAU PHELAN-SEGUR St.-Estèphe 1988 $20 (7/15/91)
80+ CHATEAU PHELAN-SEGUR St.-Estèphe 1988 $20 (8/31/90) (BT)
80+ CHATEAU PHELAN-SEGUR St.-Estèphe 1988 $20 (6/30/89) (BT)
82 CHATEAU PHELAN-SEGUR St.-Estèphe 1987 Rel: $16 Cur: $16 (11/30/89) (JS)
75+ CHATEAU PHELAN-SEGUR St.-Estèphe 1987 Rel: $16 Cur: $16 (6/30/89) (BT)
86 CHATEAU PHELAN-SEGUR St.-Estèphe 1986 Rel: $19 Cur: $19 (11/30/89) (JS)
77 CHATEAU PHELAN-SEGUR St.-Estèphe 1986 Rel: $19 Cur: $19 (6/30/89)
80+ CHATEAU PHELAN-SEGUR St.-Estèphe 1986 Rel: $19 Cur: $19 (5/15/87) (BT)
88 CHATEAU PHELAN-SEGUR St.-Estèphe 1982 Cur: $25 (11/30/89) (JS)
67 CHATEAU PHELAN-SEGUR St.-Estèphe 1961 Cur: $43 (3/16/86) (JL)
90+ CHATEAU TRONQUOY-LALANDE St.-Estèphe 1989 (NR) (4/30/90) (BT)
84 CHATEAU TRONQUOY-LALANDE St.-Estèphe 1988 $14 (7/15/91)
80+ CHATEAU TRONQUOY-LALANDE St.-Estèphe 1988 $14 (6/30/89) (BT)
84 CHATEAU TRONQUOY-LALANDE St.-Estèphe 1987 Rel: $13 Cur: $13 (11/30/89) (JS)
75+ CHATEAU TRONQUOY-LALANDE St.-Estèphe 1987 Rel: $13 Cur: $13 (6/30/89) (BT)
92 CHATEAU TRONQUOY-LALANDE St.-Estèphe 1986 Rel: $15 Cur: $16 (11/30/89) (JS)
86 CHATEAU TRONQUOY-LALANDE St.-Estèphe 1982 Cur: $18 (11/30/89) (JS)

ST.-JULIEN

83 BARTON & GUESTIER St.-Julien 1985 $12.50 (2/15/88)
85+ CHATEAU BEYCHEVELLE St.-Julien 1990 (NR) (4/30/91) (BT)
85+ CHATEAU BEYCHEVELLE St.-Julien 1989 (NR) (4/30/91) (BT)
85+ CHATEAU BEYCHEVELLE St.-Julien 1989 (NR) (4/30/90) (BT)
93 CHATEAU BEYCHEVELLE St.-Julien 1988 $40 (4/30/91)
95+ CHATEAU BEYCHEVELLE St.-Julien 1988 $40 (6/30/89) (BT)
79 CHATEAU BEYCHEVELLE St.-Julien 1987 Rel: $28 Cur: $28 (5/15/90)
85+ CHATEAU BEYCHEVELLE St.-Julien 1987 Rel: $28 Cur: $28 (6/30/89) (BT)
80+ CHATEAU BEYCHEVELLE St.-Julien 1987 Rel: $28 Cur: $28 (6/30/88) (BT)
93 CHATEAU BEYCHEVELLE St.-Julien 1986 Rel: $37 Cur: $37 (5/31/89)
90+ CHATEAU BEYCHEVELLE St.-Julien 1986 Rel: $37 Cur: $37 (5/15/87) (BT)
95 CHATEAU BEYCHEVELLE St.-Julien 1985 Rel: $35 Cur: $39 (8/31/88) CS
90+ CHATEAU BEYCHEVELLE St.-Julien 1985 Rel: $35 Cur: $39 (4/16/86) (BT)
78 CHATEAU BEYCHEVELLE St.-Julien 1984 Rel: $32 Cur: $32 (5/15/87)
88 CHATEAU BEYCHEVELLE St.-Julien 1983 Rel: $25 Cur: $30 (3/01/86)
89 CHATEAU BEYCHEVELLE St.-Julien 1982 Rel: $35 Cur: $44 (12/31/89) (TM)
81 CHATEAU BEYCHEVELLE St.-Julien 1981 Rel: $17.50 Cur: $27 (5/01/84)
92 CHATEAU BEYCHEVELLE St.-Julien 1979 Cur: $38 (10/15/89) (JS)
86 CHATEAU BEYCHEVELLE St.-Julien 1978 Cur: $41 (12/31/89) (TM)
85 CHATEAU BEYCHEVELLE St.-Julien 1971 Cur: $50 (12/31/89) (TM)
83 CHATEAU BEYCHEVELLE St.-Julien 1967 Cur: $36 (12/31/89) (TM)
95 CHATEAU BEYCHEVELLE St.-Julien 1962 Cur: $89 (11/30/87) (JS)
68 CHATEAU BEYCHEVELLE St.-Julien 1961 Cur: $158 (3/16/86) (JL)
80 CHATEAU BEYCHEVELLE St.-Julien 1959 Cur: $155 (10/15/90) (JS)
92 CHATEAU BEYCHEVELLE St.-Julien 1948 Cur: $175 (12/31/89) (TM)
88 CHATEAU BEYCHEVELLE St.-Julien 1945 Cur: $420 (3/16/86) (JL)
95 CHATEAU BEYCHEVELLE St.-Julien 1929 Cur: $500 (12/31/89) (TM)
80+ CHATEAU BRANAIRE-DUCRU St.-Julien 1990 (NR) (4/30/91) (BT)
85+ CHATEAU BRANAIRE-DUCRU St.-Julien 1989 (NR) (4/30/91) (BT)
90+ CHATEAU BRANAIRE-DUCRU St.-Julien 1989 (NR) (4/30/90) (BT)
85+ CHATEAU BRANAIRE-DUCRU St.-Julien 1988 $16 (8/31/90) (BT)
90+ CHATEAU BRANAIRE-DUCRU St.-Julien 1988 $16 (6/30/89) (BT)
80+ CHATEAU BRANAIRE-DUCRU St.-Julien 1987 Rel: $15 Cur: $15 (6/30/89) (BT)
65+ CHATEAU BRANAIRE-DUCRU St.-Julien 1987 Rel: $15 Cur: $15 (6/30/88) (BT)
85+ CHATEAU BRANAIRE-DUCRU St.-Julien 1986 Rel: $16 Cur: $20 (6/30/88) (BT)
90+ CHATEAU BRANAIRE-DUCRU St.-Julien 1986 Rel: $16 Cur: $20 (5/15/87) (BT)
89 CHATEAU BRANAIRE-DUCRU St.-Julien 1985 Rel: $25 Cur: $25 (6/30/88)
88 CHATEAU BRANAIRE-DUCRU St.-Julien 1983 Rel: $24 Cur: $24 (3/01/86)
79 CHATEAU BRANAIRE-DUCRU St.-Julien 1961 Cur: $114 (3/16/86) (JL)
86 CHATEAU BRANAIRE-DUCRU St.-Julien 1959 Cur: $127 (10/15/90) (JS)
67 CHATEAU BRANAIRE-DUCRU St.-Julien 1945 Cur: $175 (3/16/86) (JL)
79 CLOS DU MARQUIS St.-Julien 1987 Rel: $12 Cur: $14 (5/15/90)
80+ CLOS DU MARQUIS St.-Julien 1987 Rel: $12 Cur: $14 (6/30/88) (BT)
84 CLOS DU MARQUIS St.-Julien 1986 Rel: $17 Cur: $20 (9/15/89)
85+ CLOS DU MARQUIS St.-Julien 1986 Rel: $17 Cur: $20 (6/30/88) (BT)
80+ CLOS DU MARQUIS St.-Julien 1986 Rel: $17 Cur: $20 (5/15/87) (BT)
84 CLOS DU MARQUIS St.-Julien 1985 Rel: $14 Cur: $20 (9/30/88)
80+ CLOS DU MARQUIS St.-Julien 1985 Rel: $14 Cur: $20 (5/15/87) (BT)
95+ CHATEAU DUCRU-BEAUCAILLOU St.-Julien 1990 (NR) (4/30/91) (BT)

Key to Symbols

The scores reported here are the results of blind tastings conducted by our panel of senior editors. Wines that carry the initials below are results of individual tastings.

THE WINE SPECTATOR 100-POINT SCALE ***95-100***—Classic, a great wine; ***90-94***—Outstanding, superior character and style; ***80-89***—Good to very good, a wine with special qualities; ***70-79***—Average, drinkable wine that may have minor flaws; ***60-69***—Below average, drinkable but not recommended; ***50-59***—Poor, undrinkable, not recommended. "+"—With a score indicates a range; used primarily with barrel tastings to indicate a preliminary score.

SPECIAL DESIGNATIONS SS—Spectator Selection, CS—Cellar Selection, BB—Best Buy.

TASTER'S INITIALS (JG)—Jim Gordon, (HS)—Harvey Steiman, (JL)—James Laube, (JS)—James Suckling, (TM)—Thomas Matthews, (TR)—Terry Robards, (BT)—Barrel Tasting (these wines were tasted blind from barrel samples), (CA-date)—*California's Great Cabernets* by James Laube, (CH-date)—*California's Great Chardonnays* by James Laube, (VP-date)—*Vintage Port* by James Suckling.

DATE TASTED Dates in parentheses represent the issue in which the rating was published.

90+ CHATEAU DUCRU-BEAUCAILLOU St.-Julien 1989 (NR) (4/30/91) (BT)
90+ CHATEAU DUCRU-BEAUCAILLOU St.-Julien 1989 (NR) (4/30/90) (BT)
92 CHATEAU DUCRU-BEAUCAILLOU St.-Julien 1988 $48 (4/30/91)
90+ CHATEAU DUCRU-BEAUCAILLOU St.-Julien 1988 $48 (8/31/90) (BT)
85+ CHATEAU DUCRU-BEAUCAILLOU St.-Julien 1988 $48 (6/30/89) (BT)
86 CHATEAU DUCRU-BEAUCAILLOU St.-Julien 1987 Rel: $35 Cur: $35 (5/15/90)
80+ CHATEAU DUCRU-BEAUCAILLOU St.-Julien 1987 Rel: $35 Cur: $35 (6/30/88) (BT)
91 CHATEAU DUCRU-BEAUCAILLOU St.-Julien 1986 Rel: $52 Cur: $52 (6/30/89)
90+ CHATEAU DUCRU-BEAUCAILLOU St.-Julien 1986 Rel: $52 Cur: $52 (6/30/88) (BT)
90+ CHATEAU DUCRU-BEAUCAILLOU St.-Julien 1986 Rel: $52 Cur: $52 (5/15/87) (BT)
95 CHATEAU DUCRU-BEAUCAILLOU St.-Julien 1985 Rel: $50 Cur: $51 (6/15/88)
90+ CHATEAU DUCRU-BEAUCAILLOU St.-Julien 1985 Rel: $50 Cur: $51 (5/15/87) (BT)
90+ CHATEAU DUCRU-BEAUCAILLOU St.-Julien 1985 Rel: $50 Cur: $51 (4/16/86) (BT)
87 CHATEAU DUCRU-BEAUCAILLOU St.-Julien 1984 Rel: $24 Cur: $31 (8/31/87)
90 CHATEAU DUCRU-BEAUCAILLOU St.-Julien 1983 Rel: $27 Cur: $42 (6/16/86)
92 CHATEAU DUCRU-BEAUCAILLOU St.-Julien 1982 Rel: $28 Cur: $76 (5/01/85)
93 CHATEAU DUCRU-BEAUCAILLOU St.-Julien 1981 Rel: $25 Cur: $49 (5/01/85)
88 CHATEAU DUCRU-BEAUCAILLOU St.-Julien 1980 Rel: $13.50 Cur: $23 (5/01/84) CS
87 CHATEAU DUCRU-BEAUCAILLOU St.-Julien 1979 Cur: $48 (10/15/89) (JS)
81 CHATEAU DUCRU-BEAUCAILLOU St.-Julien 1979 Cur: $48 (5/01/85)
91 CHATEAU DUCRU-BEAUCAILLOU St.-Julien 1978 Cur: $75 (5/01/85)
80 CHATEAU DUCRU-BEAUCAILLOU St.-Julien 1962 Cur: $120 (11/30/87) (JS)
94 CHATEAU DUCRU-BEAUCAILLOU St.-Julien 1961 Cur: $320 (3/16/86) (JL)
90 CHATEAU DUCRU-BEAUCAILLOU St.-Julien 1959 Cur: $250 (10/15/90) (JS)
79 CHATEAU DUCRU-BEAUCAILLOU St.-Julien 1945 Cur: $470 (3/16/86) (JL)
85+ LES FIEFS DE LAGRANGE St.-Julien 1989 (NR) (4/30/91) (BT)
92 LES FIEFS DE LAGRANGE St.-Julien 1988 $17 (4/30/91)
70+ LES FIEFS DE LAGRANGE St.-Julien 1987 Rel: $14 Cur: $14 (6/30/88) (BT)
80+ LES FIEFS DE LAGRANGE St.-Julien 1986 Rel: $17 Cur: $17 (6/30/88) (BT)
70+ LES FIEFS DE LAGRANGE St.-Julien 1985 Rel: $17 Cur: $18 (5/15/87) (BT)
85 LES FIEFS DE LAGRANGE St.-Julien 1983 Rel: $10 Cur: $13 (5/01/86)
80+ CHATEAU DU GLANA St.-Julien 1989 (NR) (4/30/91) (BT)
75+ CHATEAU DU GLANA St.-Julien 1988 (NR) (6/30/89) (BT)
81 CHATEAU DU GLANA St.-Julien 1987 (NR) (11/30/89) (JS)
75+ CHATEAU DU GLANA St.-Julien 1987 (NR) (6/30/89) (BT)
84 CHATEAU DU GLANA St.-Julien 1986 $17 (11/30/89) (JS)
85 CHATEAU DU GLANA St.-Julien 1982 Cur: $12 (11/30/89) (JS)
85+ CHATEAU GLORIA St.-Julien 1990 (NR) (4/30/91) (BT)
85+ CHATEAU GLORIA St.-Julien 1989 (NR) (4/30/91) (BT)
90+ CHATEAU GLORIA St.-Julien 1989 (NR) (4/30/90) (BT)
90 CHATEAU GLORIA St.-Julien 1988 $23 (3/31/91)
85+ CHATEAU GLORIA St.-Julien 1988 $23 (8/31/90) (BT)
80+ CHATEAU GLORIA St.-Julien 1988 $23 (6/30/89) (BT)
80 CHATEAU GLORIA St.-Julien 1987 Rel: $14.50 Cur: $15 (5/15/90)
84 CHATEAU GLORIA St.-Julien 1987 Rel: $14.50 Cur: $15 (11/30/89) (JS)
80+ CHATEAU GLORIA St.-Julien 1987 Rel: $14.50 Cur: $15 (6/30/89) (BT)
89 CHATEAU GLORIA St.-Julien 1986 Rel: $18 Cur: $18 (11/30/89) (JS)
89 CHATEAU GLORIA St.-Julien 1986 Rel: $18 Cur: $18 (5/31/89)
89 CHATEAU GLORIA St.-Julien 1985 Rel: $14 Cur: $20 (4/15/88)
60+ CHATEAU GLORIA St.-Julien 1985 Rel: $14 Cur: $20 (4/16/86) (BT)
87 CHATEAU GLORIA St.-Julien 1984 Rel: $8 Cur: $14 (3/15/87) BB
83 CHATEAU GLORIA St.-Julien 1983 Rel: $10 Cur: $18 (10/15/86)
83 CHATEAU GLORIA St.-Julien 1982 Rel: $14.75 Cur: $29 (11/30/89) (JS)
81 CHATEAU GLORIA St.-Julien 1982 Rel: $14.75 Cur: $29 (2/16/85)
82 CHATEAU GLORIA St.-Julien 1981 Rel: $10 Cur: $22 (6/01/84)
83 CHATEAU GLORIA St.-Julien 1979 Cur: $18 (10/15/89) (JS)
90+ CHATEAU GRUAUD-LAROSE St.-Julien 1990 (NR) (4/30/91) (BT)
90+ CHATEAU GRUAUD-LAROSE St.-Julien 1989 (NR) (4/30/91) (BT)
85+ CHATEAU GRUAUD-LAROSE St.-Julien 1989 (NR) (4/30/90) (BT)
84 CHATEAU GRUAUD-LAROSE St.-Julien 1988 $31 (3/31/91)
89 CHATEAU GRUAUD-LAROSE St.-Julien 1988 Rel: $31 Cur: $31 (2/28/91) (TR)
90+ CHATEAU GRUAUD-LAROSE St.-Julien 1988 $31 (8/31/90) (BT)
85+ CHATEAU GRUAUD-LAROSE St.-Julien 1988 $31 (6/30/89) (BT)
83 CHATEAU GRUAUD-LAROSE St.-Julien 1987 Rel: $22 Cur: $22 (2/28/91) (TR)
78 CHATEAU GRUAUD-LAROSE St.-Julien 1987 Rel: $22 Cur: $22 (5/15/90)
85+ CHATEAU GRUAUD-LAROSE St.-Julien 1987 Rel: $22 Cur: $22 (6/30/89) (BT)
80+ CHATEAU GRUAUD-LAROSE St.-Julien 1987 Rel: $22 Cur: $22 (6/30/88) (BT)
89 CHATEAU GRUAUD-LAROSE St.-Julien 1986 Rel: $34 Cur: $34 (2/28/91) (TR)
93 CHATEAU GRUAUD-LAROSE St.-Julien 1986 Rel: $34 Cur: $34 (5/31/89)
85+ CHATEAU GRUAUD-LAROSE St.-Julien 1986 Rel: $34 Cur: $34 (6/30/88) (BT)
90+ CHATEAU GRUAUD-LAROSE St.-Julien 1986 Rel: $34 Cur: $34 (5/15/87) (BT)
93 CHATEAU GRUAUD-LAROSE St.-Julien 1985 Rel: $31 Cur: $33 (2/28/91) (TR)
90 CHATEAU GRUAUD-LAROSE St.-Julien 1985 Rel: $31 Cur: $33 (4/30/88)
83 CHATEAU GRUAUD-LAROSE St.-Julien 1984 Rel: $21.50 Cur: $23 (2/28/91) (TR)
88 CHATEAU GRUAUD-LAROSE St.-Julien 1984 Rel: $21.50 Cur: $23 (5/15/87)
85 CHATEAU GRUAUD-LAROSE St.-Julien 1983 Rel: $19 Cur: $32 (2/28/91) (TR)
88 CHATEAU GRUAUD-LAROSE St.-Julien 1983 Rel: $19 Cur: $32 (7/16/86)
89 CHATEAU GRUAUD-LAROSE St.-Julien 1982 Rel: $40 Cur: $51 (2/28/91) (TR)
90 CHATEAU GRUAUD-LAROSE St.-Julien 1982 Rel: $40 Cur: $51 (5/01/89)
90 CHATEAU GRUAUD-LAROSE St.-Julien 1981 Rel: $18.50 Cur: $35 (2/28/91) (TR)
87 CHATEAU GRUAUD-LAROSE St.-Julien 1981 Rel: $18.50 Cur: $35 (6/01/84)
83 CHATEAU GRUAUD-LAROSE St.-Julien 1980 Cur: $25 (2/28/91) (TR)
89 CHATEAU GRUAUD-LAROSE St.-Julien 1979 Cur: $30 (2/28/91) (TR)
83 CHATEAU GRUAUD-LAROSE St.-Julien 1979 Cur: $30 (10/15/89) (JS)
91 CHATEAU GRUAUD-LAROSE St.-Julien 1978 Cur: $43 (2/28/91) (TR)
71 CHATEAU GRUAUD-LAROSE St.-Julien 1977 Cur: $33 (2/28/91) (TR)
85 CHATEAU GRUAUD-LAROSE St.-Julien 1976 Cur: $34 (2/28/91) (TR)
89 CHATEAU GRUAUD-LAROSE St.-Julien 1975 Cur: $52 (2/28/91) (TR)
63 CHATEAU GRUAUD-LAROSE St.-Julien 1974 Cur: $28 (2/28/91) (TR)
65 CHATEAU GRUAUD-LAROSE St.-Julien 1974 Cur: $28 (2/28/91) (TR)
76 CHATEAU GRUAUD-LAROSE St.-Julien 1973 Cur: $28 (2/28/91) (TR)
85 CHATEAU GRUAUD-LAROSE St.-Julien 1971 Cur: $31 (2/28/91) (TR)
89 CHATEAU GRUAUD-LAROSE St.-Julien 1970 Cur: $74 (2/28/91) (TR)
50 CHATEAU GRUAUD-LAROSE St.-Julien 1969 Cur: $15 (2/28/91) (TR)
65 CHATEAU GRUAUD-LAROSE St.-Julien 1968 Cur: $15 (2/28/91) (TR)
78 CHATEAU GRUAUD-LAROSE St.-Julien 1967 Cur: $33 (2/28/91) (TR)
87 CHATEAU GRUAUD-LAROSE St.-Julien 1966 Cur: $115 (2/28/91) (TR)
88 CHATEAU GRUAUD-LAROSE St.-Julien 1964 Cur: $70 (2/28/91) (TR)
94 CHATEAU GRUAUD-LAROSE St.-Julien 1962 Cur: $95 (2/28/91) (TR)
88 CHATEAU GRUAUD-LAROSE St.-Julien 1962 Cur: $95 (11/30/87) (JS)
95 CHATEAU GRUAUD-LAROSE St.-Julien 1961 Cur: $243 (2/28/91) (TR)
86 CHATEAU GRUAUD-LAROSE St.-Julien 1961 Cur: $243 (3/16/86) (JL)
85 CHATEAU GRUAUD-LAROSE St.-Julien 1959 Cur: $145 (2/28/91) (TR)
78 CHATEAU GRUAUD-LAROSE St.-Julien 1957 Cur: $65 (2/28/91) (TR)
87 CHATEAU GRUAUD-LAROSE St.-Julien 1955 Cur: $150 (2/28/91) (TR)
88 CHATEAU GRUAUD-LAROSE St.-Julien 1953 Cur: $150 (2/28/91) (TR)
85 CHATEAU GRUAUD-LAROSE St.-Julien 1952 Cur: $157 (2/28/91) (TR)
83 CHATEAU GRUAUD-LAROSE St.-Julien 1950 Cur: $250 (2/28/91) (TR)
85 CHATEAU GRUAUD-LAROSE St.-Julien 1949 Cur: $255 (2/28/91) (TR)
88 CHATEAU GRUAUD-LAROSE St.-Julien 1947 Cur: $285 (2/28/91) (TR)
96 CHATEAU GRUAUD-LAROSE St.-Julien 1945 Cur: $380 (2/28/91) (TR)
86 CHATEAU GRUAUD-LAROSE St.-Julien 1945 Cur: $380 (3/16/86) (JL)
83 CHATEAU GRUAUD-LAROSE St.-Julien 1943 Cur: $200 (2/28/91) (TR)
87 CHATEAU GRUAUD-LAROSE St.-Julien 1937 Cur: $150 (2/28/91) (TR)
83 CHATEAU GRUAUD-LAROSE St.-Julien 1934 Cur: $150 (2/28/91) (TR)
85 CHATEAU GRUAUD-LAROSE St.-Julien 1929 Cur: $550 (2/28/91) (TR)
94 CHATEAU GRUAUD-LAROSE St.-Julien 1928 Cur: $500 (2/28/91) (TR)
95 CHATEAU GRUAUD-LAROSE St.-Julien 1926 Cur: $250 (2/28/91) (TR)
89 CHATEAU GRUAUD-LAROSE St.-Julien 1924 Cur: $250 (2/28/91) (TR)
87 CHATEAU GRUAUD-LAROSE St.-Julien 1921 Cur: $250 (2/28/91) (TR)
85 CHATEAU GRUAUD-LAROSE St.-Julien 1920 Cur: $300 (2/28/91) (TR)
78 CHATEAU GRUAUD-LAROSE St.-Julien 1918 Cur: $300 (2/28/91) (TR)
72 CHATEAU GRUAUD-LAROSE St.-Julien 1907 Cur: $255 (2/28/91) (TR)
85 CHATEAU GRUAUD-LAROSE St.-Julien 1906 Cur: $300 (2/28/91) (TR)
83 CHATEAU GRUAUD-LAROSE St.-Julien 1899 Cur: $600 (2/28/91) (TR)
78 CHATEAU GRUAUD-LAROSE St.-Julien 1893 Cur: $500 (2/28/91) (TR)
71 CHATEAU GRUAUD-LAROSE St.-Julien 1887 Cur: $400 (2/28/91) (TR)
83 CHATEAU GRUAUD-LAROSE St.-Julien 1878 Cur: $500 (2/28/91) (TR)
87 CHATEAU GRUAUD-LAROSE St.-Julien 1870 Cur: $2300 (2/28/91) (TR)
65 CHATEAU GRUAUD-LAROSE St.-Julien 1865 Cur: $1800 (2/28/91) (TR)
85 CHATEAU GRUAUD-LAROSE St.-Julien 1844 (NA) (2/28/91) (TR)
83 CHATEAU GRUAUD-LAROSE St.-Julien 1834 (NA) (2/28/91) (TR)
89 CHATEAU GRUAUD-LAROSE St.-Julien 1819 (NA) (2/28/91) (TR)
90+ CHATEAU LAGRANGE St.-Julien 1990 (NR) (4/30/91) (BT)
90+ CHATEAU LAGRANGE St.-Julien 1989 (NR) (4/30/91) (BT)
96 CHATEAU LAGRANGE St.-Julien 1988 $26 (4/30/91)
75+ CHATEAU LAGRANGE St.-Julien 1987 Rel: $25 Cur: $25 (6/30/88) (BT)
86 CHATEAU LAGRANGE St.-Julien 1986 Rel: $20 Cur: $28 (2/15/90)
85+ CHATEAU LAGRANGE St.-Julien 1986 Rel: $20 Cur: $28 (6/30/88) (BT)
83 CHATEAU LAGRANGE St.-Julien 1985 Rel: $23 Cur: $27 (9/30/88)
80+ CHATEAU LAGRANGE St.-Julien 1985 Rel: $23 Cur: $27 (5/15/87) (BT)
67 CHATEAU LAGRANGE St.-Julien 1961 Cur: $90 (3/16/86) (JL)
85+ CHATEAU LALANDE-BORIE St.-Julien 1989 (NR) (4/30/91) (BT)
87 CHATEAU LALANDE-BORIE St.-Julien 1988 $17 (4/30/91)
81 CHATEAU LALANDE-BORIE St.-Julien 1987 Rel: $15 Cur: $15 (11/30/89) (JS)
91 CHATEAU LALANDE-BORIE St.-Julien 1986 Rel: $17 Cur: $17 (11/30/89) (JS)
84 CHATEAU LALANDE-BORIE St.-Julien 1986 Rel: $17 Cur: $17 (11/15/89)
70+ CHATEAU LALANDE-BORIE St.-Julien 1986 Rel: $17 Cur: $17 (5/15/87) (BT)
92 CHATEAU LALANDE-BORIE St.-Julien 1982 Rel: $15 Cur: $17 (11/30/89) (JS)
76 CHATEAU LALANDE-BORIE St.-Julien 1982 Rel: $15 Cur: $17 (10/15/86)
90+ CHATEAU LANGOA-BARTON St.-Julien 1990 (NR) (4/30/91) (BT)
90+ CHATEAU LANGOA-BARTON St.-Julien 1989 (NR) (4/30/91) (BT)
85+ CHATEAU LANGOA-BARTON St.-Julien 1989 (NR) (4/30/90) (BT)
86 CHATEAU LANGOA-BARTON St.-Julien 1988 $25 (7/15/91)
85+ CHATEAU LANGOA-BARTON St.-Julien 1988 $25 (8/31/90) (BT)
80+ CHATEAU LANGOA-BARTON St.-Julien 1988 $25 (6/30/89) (BT)
75+ CHATEAU LANGOA-BARTON St.-Julien 1987 Rel: $17 Cur: $17 (6/30/89) (BT)
80+ CHATEAU LANGOA-BARTON St.-Julien 1987 Rel: $17 Cur: $17 (6/30/88) (BT)
85+ CHATEAU LANGOA-BARTON St.-Julien 1986 Rel: $22 Cur: $25 (6/30/88) (BT)
70+ CHATEAU LANGOA-BARTON St.-Julien 1986 Rel: $22 Cur: $25 (5/15/87) (BT)
91 CHATEAU LANGOA-BARTON St.-Julien 1985 Rel: $20 Cur: $22 (6/15/88)
70+ CHATEAU LANGOA-BARTON St.-Julien 1985 Rel: $20 Cur: $22 (4/16/86) (BT)
63 CHATEAU LANGOA-BARTON St.-Julien 1961 Cur: $113 (3/16/86) (JL)
71 CHATEAU LANGOA-BARTON St.-Julien 1945 Cur: $250 (3/16/86) (JL)
80+ LADY LANGOA St.-Julien 1989 (NR) (4/30/91) (BT)
95+ CHATEAU LEOVILLE-BARTON St.-Julien 1990 (NR) (4/30/91) (BT)
90+ CHATEAU LEOVILLE-BARTON St.-Julien 1989 (NR) (4/30/91) (BT)
95+ CHATEAU LEOVILLE-BARTON St.-Julien 1989 (NR) (4/30/90) (BT)
91 CHATEAU LEOVILLE-BARTON St.-Julien 1988 $20 (3/31/91)
85+ CHATEAU LEOVILLE-BARTON St.-Julien 1988 $20 (8/31/90) (BT)
85+ CHATEAU LEOVILLE-BARTON St.-Julien 1988 $20 (6/30/89) (BT)
80 CHATEAU LEOVILLE-BARTON St.-Julien 1987 Rel: $20 Cur: $20 (5/15/90)
80+ CHATEAU LEOVILLE-BARTON St.-Julien 1987 Rel: $20 Cur: $20 (6/30/89) (BT)
90 CHATEAU LEOVILLE-BARTON St.-Julien 1986 Rel: $24 Cur: $28 (5/31/89)
90+ CHATEAU LEOVILLE-BARTON St.-Julien 1986 Rel: $24 Cur: $28 (6/30/88) (BT)
90+ CHATEAU LEOVILLE-BARTON St.-Julien 1986 Rel: $24 Cur: $28 (5/15/87) (BT)
92 CHATEAU LEOVILLE-BARTON St.-Julien 1985 Rel: $24 Cur: $31 (4/15/88)
80+ CHATEAU LEOVILLE-BARTON St.-Julien 1985 Rel: $24 Cur: $31 (4/16/86) (BT)
92 CHATEAU LEOVILLE-BARTON St.-Julien 1983 Rel: $24 Cur: $26 (3/01/86)
70 CHATEAU LEOVILLE-BARTON St.-Julien 1962 Cur: $80 (11/30/87) (JS)
76 CHATEAU LEOVILLE-BARTON St.-Julien 1961 Cur: $125 (3/16/86) (JL)
85 CHATEAU LEOVILLE-BARTON St.-Julien 1959 Cur: $125 (10/15/90) (JS)
73 CHATEAU LEOVILLE-BARTON St.-Julien 1945 Cur: $340 (3/16/86) (JL)
84 CHATEAU LEOVILLE-LAS CASES St.-Julien 1987 Cur: $32 (2/15/90) (PM)
85+ CHATEAU LEOVILLE-LAS CASES St.-Julien 1987 Cur: $32 (6/30/88) (BT)
96 CHATEAU LEOVILLE-LAS CASES St.-Julien 1986 Rel: $44 Cur: $61 (2/15/90) (PM)
96 CHATEAU LEOVILLE-LAS CASES St.-Julien 1986 Rel: $44 Cur: $61 (9/15/89) CS
90+ CHATEAU LEOVILLE-LAS CASES St.-Julien 1986 Rel: $44 Cur: $61 (6/30/88) (BT)
94 CHATEAU LEOVILLE-LAS CASES St.-Julien 1985 Rel: $45 Cur: $55 (2/15/90) (PM)
90 CHATEAU LEOVILLE-LAS CASES St.-Julien 1985 Rel: $45 Cur: $55 (8/31/88)
90+ CHATEAU LEOVILLE-LAS CASES St.-Julien 1985 Rel: $45 Cur: $55 (5/15/87) (BT)
82 CHATEAU LEOVILLE-LAS CASES St.-Julien 1984 Rel: $33 Cur: $33 (2/15/90) (PM)
78 CHATEAU LEOVILLE-LAS CASES St.-Julien 1984 Rel: $33 Cur: $33 (10/15/87)
85 CHATEAU LEOVILLE-LAS CASES St.-Julien 1983 Rel: $26 Cur: $44 (2/15/90) (PM)
84 CHATEAU LEOVILLE-LAS CASES St.-Julien 1983 Rel: $26 Cur: $44 (3/31/87)
98 CHATEAU LEOVILLE-LAS CASES St.-Julien 1982 Rel: $59 Cur: $93 (2/15/90) (PM)
93 CHATEAU LEOVILLE-LAS CASES St.-Julien 1982 Rel: $59 Cur: $93 (5/01/89)
86 CHATEAU LEOVILLE-LAS CASES St.-Julien 1981 Rel: $23.50 Cur: $50 (2/15/90) (PM)
91 CHATEAU LEOVILLE-LAS CASES St.-Julien 1981 Rel: $23.50 Cur: $50 (6/01/84)
84 CHATEAU LEOVILLE-LAS CASES St.-Julien 1980 Cur: $71/1.5L (2/15/90) (PM)

FRANCE
BORDEAUX RED/ST.-JULIEN

90   CHATEAU LEOVILLE-LAS CASES St.-Julien 1979 Cur: $51 (2/15/90) (PM)
95   CHATEAU LEOVILLE-LAS CASES St.-Julien 1979 Cur: $51 (10/15/89) (JS)
94   CHATEAU LEOVILLE-LAS CASES St.-Julien 1978 Cur: $73 (2/15/90) (PM)
76   CHATEAU LEOVILLE-LAS CASES St.-Julien 1971 Cur: $66 (4/01/86)
89   CHATEAU LEOVILLE-LAS CASES St.-Julien 1970 Cur: $89 (2/15/90) (PM)
85   CHATEAU LEOVILLE-LAS CASES St.-Julien 1962 Cur: $92 (11/30/87) (JS)
88   CHATEAU LEOVILLE-LAS CASES St.-Julien 1961 Cur: $245 (3/16/86) (JL)
96   CHATEAU LEOVILLE-LAS CASES St.-Julien 1959 Cur: $208 (10/15/90) (JS)
75   CHATEAU LEOVILLE-LAS CASES St.-Julien 1945 Cur: $460 (3/16/86) (JL)
95+ CHATEAU LEOVILLE-POYFERRE St.-Julien 1990 (NR) (4/30/91) (BT)
90+ CHATEAU LEOVILLE-POYFERRE St.-Julien 1989 (NR) (4/30/91) (BT)
85+ CHATEAU LEOVILLE-POYFERRE St.-Julien 1989 (NR) (4/30/90) (BT)
81   CHATEAU LEOVILLE-POYFERRE St.-Julien 1988 $23 (7/15/91)
80+ CHATEAU LEOVILLE-POYFERRE St.-Julien 1988 $23 (8/31/90) (BT)
85+ CHATEAU LEOVILLE-POYFERRE St.-Julien 1988 $23 (6/30/89) (BT)
86   CHATEAU LEOVILLE-POYFERRE St.-Julien 1987 Rel: $24 Cur: $24 (5/15/90)
85+ CHATEAU LEOVILLE-POYFERRE St.-Julien 1987 Rel: $24 Cur: $24 (6/30/89) (BT)
85+ CHATEAU LEOVILLE-POYFERRE St.-Julien 1987 Rel: $24 Cur: $24 (6/30/88) (BT)
86   CHATEAU LEOVILLE-POYFERRE St.-Julien 1986 Rel: $24 Cur: $27 (5/31/89)
85+ CHATEAU LEOVILLE-POYFERRE St.-Julien 1986 Rel: $24 Cur: $27 (6/30/88) (BT)
92   CHATEAU LEOVILLE-POYFERRE St.-Julien 1985 Rel: $19 Cur: $27 (4/30/88)
70+ CHATEAU LEOVILLE-POYFERRE St.-Julien 1985 Rel: $19 Cur: $27 (4/16/86) (BT)
85   CHATEAU LEOVILLE-POYFERRE St.-Julien 1984 Cur: $24.50 Cur: $25 (10/15/87)
83   CHATEAU LEOVILLE-POYFERRE St.-Julien 1983 Rel: $20 Cur: $25 (3/01/86)
89   CHATEAU LEOVILLE-POYFERRE St.-Julien 1982 Rel: $20 Cur: $43 (6/01/85)
88   CHATEAU LEOVILLE-POYFERRE St.-Julien 1981 Rel: $12.50 Cur: $25 (6/01/84)
77   CHATEAU LEOVILLE-POYFERRE St.-Julien 1961 Cur: $125 (3/16/86) (JL)
80   CHATEAU LEOVILLE-POYFERRE St.-Julien 1945 Cur: $206 (3/16/86) (JL)
76   CHATEAU DU MOULIN DE LA BRIDAN St.-Julien 1983 $11.25 (4/01/86)
79   CHATEAU MOULIN-RICHE St.-Julien 1987 Rel: $18 Cur: $18 (11/30/89) (JS)
88   CHATEAU MOULIN-RICHE St.-Julien 1986 Rel: $20 Cur: $20 (11/30/89) (JS)
83   CHATEAU MOULIN-RICHE St.-Julien 1985 Rel: $20 Cur: $20 (6/15/88) (JS)
90   CHATEAU MOULIN-RICHE St.-Julien 1982 Cur: $22 (11/30/89) (JS)
85+ CHATEAU ST.-PIERRE St.-Julien 1990 (NR) (4/30/91) (BT)
90+ CHATEAU ST.-PIERRE St.-Julien 1989 (NR) (4/30/91) (BT)
90+ CHATEAU ST.-PIERRE St.-Julien 1989 (NR) (4/30/90) (BT)
85   CHATEAU ST.-PIERRE St.-Julien 1988 $32 (4/30/91)
90+ CHATEAU ST.-PIERRE St.-Julien 1988 $32 (8/31/90) (BT)
85+ CHATEAU ST.-PIERRE St.-Julien 1988 $32 (6/30/89) (BT)
89   CHATEAU ST.-PIERRE St.-Julien 1987 Rel: $17.50 Cur: $18 (5/15/90)
80+ CHATEAU ST.-PIERRE St.-Julien 1987 Rel: $17.50 Cur: $18 (6/30/89) (BT)
92   CHATEAU ST.-PIERRE St.-Julien 1986 Rel: $17 Cur: $21 (9/15/89) SS
70+ CHATEAU ST.-PIERRE St.-Julien 1985 Cur: $21 (4/16/86) (BT)
93   CHATEAU ST.-PIERRE St.-Julien 1982 Rel: $15 Cur: $23 (12/16/85) CS
84   CHATEAU ST.-PIERRE St.-Julien 1979 Cur: $24 (10/15/89) (JS)
68   CHATEAU ST.-PIERRE St.-Julien 1962 Cur: $55 (11/30/87) (JS)
90+ CHATEAU TALBOT St.-Julien 1990 (NR) (4/30/91) (BT)
90+ CHATEAU TALBOT St.-Julien 1989 (NR) (4/30/91) (BT)
95+ CHATEAU TALBOT St.-Julien 1989 (NR) (4/30/90) (BT)
90   CHATEAU TALBOT St.-Julien 1988 $25 (3/15/91)
90+ CHATEAU TALBOT St.-Julien 1988 $25 (6/30/89) (BT)
85   CHATEAU TALBOT St.-Julien 1987 Rel: $23.50 Cur: $24 (5/15/90)
80+ CHATEAU TALBOT St.-Julien 1987 Rel: $23.50 Cur: $24 (6/30/89) (BT)
80+ CHATEAU TALBOT St.-Julien 1987 Rel: $23.50 Cur: $24 (6/30/88) (BT)
91   CHATEAU TALBOT St.-Julien 1986 Rel: $32 Cur: $32 (5/31/89)
85+ CHATEAU TALBOT St.-Julien 1986 Rel: $32 Cur: $32 (6/30/88) (BT)
80+ CHATEAU TALBOT St.-Julien 1986 Rel: $32 Cur: $32 (5/15/87) (BT)
87   CHATEAU TALBOT St.-Julien 1985 Rel: $26 Cur: $26 (4/30/88)
80   CHATEAU TALBOT St.-Julien 1984 Rel: $19 Cur: $20 (5/15/87)
89   CHATEAU TALBOT St.-Julien 1983 Rel: $22 Cur: $26 (9/30/86)
88   CHATEAU TALBOT St.-Julien 1982 Rel: $26 Cur: $34 (5/01/89)
83   CHATEAU TALBOT St.-Julien 1981 Rel: $17 Cur: $30 (6/01/84)
84   CHATEAU TALBOT St.-Julien 1979 Cur: $26 (10/15/89) (JS)
55   CHATEAU TALBOT St.-Julien 1962 Cur: $63 (11/30/87) (JS)
86   CHATEAU TALBOT St.-Julien 1959 Cur: $110 (10/15/90) (JS)
81   CHATEAU TALBOT St.-Julien 1945 Cur: $310 (3/16/86) (JL)
85+ CHATEAU TERREY-GROS-CAILLOUX St.-Julien 1989 (NR) (4/30/91) (BT)
80+ CHATEAU TERREY-GROS-CAILLOUX St.-Julien 1988 $14 (6/30/89) (BT)
85   CHATEAU TERREY-GROS-CAILLOUX St.-Julien 1987 $12 (11/30/89) (JS)
75+ CHATEAU TERREY-GROS-CAILLOUX St.-Julien 1987 $12 (6/30/89) (BT)
87   CHATEAU TERREY-GROS-CAILLOUX St.-Julien 1986 $12 (11/30/89) (JS)

OTHER BORDEAUX RED

80   CHATEAU BEAUSEJOUR Côtes de Castillon 1986 Rel: $5 Cur: $5 (6/15/89) BB
85   CHATEAU DE BEL-AIR Lalande-de-Pomerol 1985 $18 (9/30/88)
76   CHATEAU DE BELCIER Côtes de Castillon 1985 $5 (6/30/88)
85   CHATEAU BERTINERIE Premières Côtes de Blaye 1988 $10 (7/15/90)
76   CHATEAU CAYLA Premières Côtes de Bordeaux 1986 $7 (6/30/89)
73   CHATEAU CAYLA Premières Côtes de Bordeaux 1985 $4 (5/31/88)
78   CHATEAU CHANGROLLE Lalande-de-Pomerol 1982 $6 (12/16/84)
76   CHATEAU CLAIRAC Premières Côtes de Blaye 1985 $4.50 (4/15/88)
79   CHATEAU LA CROIX DE MILLORIT Côtes de Bourg 1986 $9/375ml (5/15/91)
75   CHATEAU DUPLESSY Premières Côtes de Bordeaux 1985 $6 (5/31/88)
76   CHATEAU GRAND-CHEMIN Côtes de Bourg 1985 $8 (6/15/89)

78   CHATEAU GRAND-CLARET Premières Côtes de Bordeaux 1988 $7 (HS) (7/31/91)
88   CHATEAU GRAND-ORMEAU Lalande-de-Pomerol 1985 $16 (5/31/88)
70   CHATEAU DE LA GRAVE Côtes de Bourg 1982 $5.25 (2/16/85)
74   CHATEAU DE LA GRAVE Côtes de Bourg 1981 $4.99 (2/16/85)
69   CHATEAU LA GROLET Côtes de Bourg 1985 $7 (5/15/88)
74   CHATEAU LA GROLET Côtes de Bourg 1985 $7 (2/15/88)
81   CHATEAU HAUT-RIAN Premières Côtes de Bordeaux 1988 $7 (5/15/90) BB
79   CHATEAU LEON Côtes de Bordeaux 1983 $5.50 (11/15/86)
72   CHATEAU LEZONGARS Premières Côtes de Bordeaux 1985 $7 (11/15/87)
81   CHATEAU MAYNE-DAVID Côtes de Castillon 1985 $6 (2/28/87) BB
76   CHATEAU DE LA MEULIERE Premières Côtes de Bordeaux 1988 $9 (2/28/91)
78   CHATEAU PERENNE Premières Côtes de Blaye 1989 $9 (3/31/91)
82   CHATEAU PERENNE Premières Côtes de Blaye 1986 $7 (6/30/89)
80   CHATEAU PERENNE Premières Côtes de Blaye 1985 $7 (2/15/88)
79   CHATEAU PERENNE Premières Côtes de Blaye 1982 $5 (11/16/85) BB
79   CHATEAU PERENNE Premières Côtes de Blaye 1982 $5 (5/01/85)
80   CHATEAU PEYRAUD Premières Côtes de Blaye 1988 $8 (3/31/91)
77   CHATEAU LA PIERRIERE Côtes de Castillon 1986 $6 (12/31/88)
83   CHATEAU PITRAY Côtes de Castillon 1988 $7 (2/28/91) BB
81   CHATEAU PITRAY Côtes de Castillon 1986 $6 (9/30/89) BB
85   CHATEAU PLAISANCE Premières Côtes de Blaye Cuvée Spéciale 1989 $9 (2/28/91) BB
71   CHATEAU DE PRIEURE Premières Côtes de Bordeaux 1985 $4.50 (5/31/88)
81   CHATEAU SAUVAGE Premières Côtes de Bordeaux 1988 $9 (4/15/90)
79   CHATEAU SEGONZAC Premières Côtes de Blaye 1986 $9.75 (6/30/89)
85   CHATEAU SEGONZAC Premières Côtes de Blaye 1985 $9 (2/15/88)
80+ CHATEAU SIAURAC Lalande-de-Pomerol 1989 (NR) (4/30/91) (BT)
70+ CHATEAU SIAURAC Lalande-de-Pomerol 1989 (NR) (4/30/90) (BT)
75+ CHATEAU SIAURAC Lalande-de-Pomerol 1988 $20 (6/30/89) (BT)
75+ CHATEAU SIAURAC Lalande-de-Pomerol 1987 Rel: $17 Cur: $17 (6/30/89) (BT)
72   DOMAINE LA TUQUE BEL-AIR Côtes de Castillon 1985 $8.50 (9/30/88)

BORDEAUX WHITE/GRAVES/PESSAC-LÉOGNAN

80+ CHATEAU BARET Pessac-Léognan 1988 $19 (6/30/89) (BT)
75+ CHATEAU BARET Pessac-Léognan 1987 $15 (6/30/89) (BT)
84   CHATEAU LE BONNAT Graves 1988 $17 (3/31/90)
80+ CHATEAU BOUSCAUT Pessac-Léognan 1988 $15 (6/30/89) (BT)
85+ CHATEAU BOUSCAUT Pessac-Léognan 1987 $13 (6/30/89) (BT)
81   CHATEAU CARBONNIEUX Pessac-Léognan 1989 $22 (2/28/91)
80+ CHATEAU CARBONNIEUX Pessac-Léognan 1988 $20 (6/30/89) (BT)
80+ CHATEAU CARBONNIEUX Pessac-Léognan 1987 $15 (6/30/89) (BT)
80+ CHATEAU CARBONNIEUX Pessac-Léognan 1987 $15 (7/15/88) (BT)
81   CHATEAU CARBONNIEUX Graves 1985 $13 (3/31/87)
81   CHATEAU CARBONNIEUX Graves 1984 $11.50 (2/15/84)
77   CHATEAU CHERCHY Graves 1986 $6.50 (5/31/88)
80   CHATEAU CHERCHY Graves 1985 $5 (6/30/87) BB
90+ DOMAINE DE CHEVALIER Pessac-Léognan 1988 (NR) (6/30/89) (BT)
95+ DOMAINE DE CHEVALIER Pessac-Léognan 1987 Cur: $49 (6/30/89) (BT)
90+ DOMAINE DE CHEVALIER Pessac-Léognan 1987 Cur: $49 (7/15/88) (BT)
90+ DOMAINE DE CHEVALIER Graves 1985 Cur: $85 (5/15/87) (BT)
86   DOMAINE DE CHEVALIER Graves 1983 $65 (11/15/87)
89   CHATEAU COUHINS-LURTON Pessac-Léognan 1989 $25 (7/31/91)
83   CHATEAU COUHINS-LURTON Pessac-Léognan 1988 $28 (5/31/90)
85+ CHATEAU COUHINS-LURTON Pessac-Léognan 1988 $28 (6/30/89) (BT)
90+ CHATEAU COUHINS-LURTON Pessac-Léognan 1987 $25 (6/30/89) (BT)
88   CHATEAU COUHINS-LURTON Pessac-Léognan 1986 $22.50 (8/31/88)
74   CHATEAU COUHINS-LURTON Graves 1983 $11.50 (7/16/86)
56   CHATEAU COUHINS-LURTON Graves 1983 $11.50 (12/16/85)
90   CHATEAU DE CRUZEAU Pessac-Léognan 1989 $16 (6/15/91)
82   CHATEAU DE CRUZEAU Pessac-Léognan 1988 $13 (5/31/90)
80+ CHATEAU DE CRUZEAU Pessac-Léognan 1988 $13 (6/30/89) (BT)
82   CHATEAU DE CRUZEAU Pessac-Léognan 1987 $9 (7/31/89)
80+ CHATEAU DE CRUZEAU Pessac-Léognan 1987 $9 (6/30/89) (BT)
82   CHATEAU DE CRUZEAU Pessac-Léognan 1986 $8 (4/30/88)
70   CHATEAU DOMS Graves 1985 $7 (4/30/87)
95+ CHATEAU DE FIEUZAL Pessac-Léognan 1988 $45 (6/30/89) (BT)
90+ CHATEAU DE FIEUZAL Pessac-Léognan 1987 $40 (6/30/89) (BT)
85+ CHATEAU DE FIEUZAL Pessac-Léognan 1987 $40 (7/15/88) (BT)
90   CHATEAU DE FIEUZAL Graves 1985 $39 (11/15/87)
85+ CHATEAU LA GARDE Pessac-Léognan 1988 (NR) (6/30/89) (BT)
80+ CHATEAU LA GARDE Pessac-Léognan 1987 (NR) (6/30/89) (BT)
57   CHATEAU DU GRAND-ABORD Graves 1984 $4 (6/01/86)
87   CHATEAU HAUT-BRION Pessac-Léognan 1988 $84 (12/15/90)
95+ CHATEAU HAUT-BRION Pessac-Léognan 1988 Rel: $84 Cur: $110 (6/30/89) (BT)
78   CHATEAU HAUT-BRION Pessac-Léognan 1987 $70 (1/31/90)
95+ CHATEAU HAUT-BRION Pessac-Léognan 1987 $70 (6/30/89) (BT)
90+ CHATEAU HAUT-BRION Pessac-Léognan 1987 $70 (7/15/88) (BT)
79   CHATEAU HAUT-BRION Graves 1985 $81 (11/15/87)
90+ CHATEAU HAUT-BRION Graves 1985 $81 (5/15/87) (BT)
80+ CHATEAU LARRIVET-HAUT-BRION Pessac-Léognan 1987 (NR) (7/15/88) (BT)
85   CHATEAU LAVILLE-HAUT-BRION Pessac-Léognan 1988 $64 (12/15/90)
95+ CHATEAU LAVILLE-HAUT-BRION Pessac-Léognan 1988 $64 (6/30/89) (BT)
85   CHATEAU LAVILLE-HAUT-BRION Pessac-Léognan 1988 $50 (1/31/90)
95+ CHATEAU LAVILLE-HAUT-BRION Pessac-Léognan 1987 $50 (6/30/89) (BT)
90+ CHATEAU LAVILLE-HAUT-BRION Pessac-Léognan 1987 $50 (7/15/88) (BT)
90+ CHATEAU LAVILLE-HAUT-BRION Graves 1985 Cur: $66 (5/15/87) (BT)
86   CHATEAU LAVILLE-HAUT-BRION Graves 1983 $57 (11/15/87)
83   CHATEAU LA LOUVIERE Pessac-Léognan 1988 $15 (5/31/90)
83   CHATEAU LA LOUVIERE Pessac-Léognan 1988 $15 (5/15/90)
85+ CHATEAU LA LOUVIERE Pessac-Léognan 1988 $15 (6/30/89) (BT)
85   CHATEAU LA LOUVIERE Pessac-Léognan 1987 $15 (7/31/89)
85+ CHATEAU LA LOUVIERE Pessac-Léognan 1987 $15 (6/30/89) (BT)
85+ CHATEAU LA LOUVIERE Pessac-Léognan 1987 $15 (7/15/88) (BT)
87   CHATEAU LA LOUVIERE Pessac-Léognan 1986 $20 (8/31/88)
88   CHATEAU LA LOUVIERE Graves 1983 $9.75 (9/16/85)
79   CHATEAU MALARTIC-LAGRAVIERE Pessac-Léognan 1988 $31 (7/31/91)
85+ CHATEAU MALARTIC-LAGRAVIERE Pessac-Léognan 1988 $31 (6/30/89) (BT)
90+ CHATEAU MALARTIC-LAGRAVIERE Pessac-Léognan 1987 $30 (6/30/89) (BT)
84   CHATEAU MALARTIC-LAGRAVIERE Graves 1985 $22.50 (11/15/87)

78 CHATEAU DU MAYNE Graves 1983 $6 (9/16/85)
74 CHATEAU LE MERLE Graves 1984 $6 (12/01/85)
82 CHATEAU OLIVIER Pessac-Léognan 1988 $23 (3/31/91)
80+ CHATEAU OLIVIER Pessac-Léognan 1988 $23 (6/30/89) (BT)
75+ CHATEAU OLIVIER Pessac-Léognan 1987 $20 (6/30/89) (BT)
75+ CHATEAU OLIVIER Pessac-Léognan 1987 $20 (7/15/88) (BT)
88 CHATEAU OLIVIER Pessac-Léognan 1986 $16 (3/31/89)
73 CHATEAU OLIVIER Graves 1984 $15 (3/31/87)
80 CHATEAU PIRON Graves 1984 $7.50 (7/16/86)
73 CHATEAU PIRON Graves 1983 $6.50 (5/16/85)
71 CHATEAU PIRON Graves 1982 $6.75 (3/01/84)
80 LES PLANTIERS DU HAUT-BRION Graves 1974 $24 (3/31/89)
78 CHATEAU R Graves Dry 1983 $6 (2/01/85)
84 CHATEAU RAHOUL Graves 1988 $20 (3/31/91)
84 CHATEAU RESPIDE-MEDEVILLE Graves 1984 $7.50 (7/16/86)
90 CHATEAU DE ROCHEMORIN Pessac-Léognan 1989 $17 (6/15/91)
82 CHATEAU DE ROCHEMORIN Pessac-Léognan 1988 $15 (5/31/90)
80+ CHATEAU DE ROCHEMORIN Pessac-Léognan 1988 $15 (6/30/89) (BT)
80 CHATEAU DE ROCHEMORIN Pessac-Léognan 1987 $9 (7/31/89)
85+ CHATEAU DE ROCHEMORIN Pessac-Léognan 1987 $9 (6/30/89) (BT)
86 CHATEAU DE ROCHEMORIN Pessac-Léognan 1986 $10 (8/31/88)
88 CHATEAU LE SARTRE Pessac-Léognan 1989 $13.50 (3/31/91)
80+ CHATEAU LE SARTRE Pessac-Léognan 1988 $12 (6/30/89) (BT)
80+ CHATEAU SMITH-HAUT-LAFITE Pessac-Léognan 1988 (NR) (6/30/89) (BT)
85+ CHATEAU SMITH-HAUT-LAFITE Pessac-Léognan 1987 $17 (6/30/89) (BT)
80+ CHATEAU SMITH-HAUT-LAFITE Pessac-Léognan 1987 $17 (7/15/88) (BT)
80+ CHATEAU LA TOUR-LEOGNAN Pessac-Léognan 1988 (NR) (6/30/89) (BT)
86 CHATEAU LA TOUR-MARTILLAC Pessac-Léognan 1989 $28 (2/28/91)
90+ CHATEAU LA TOUR-MARTILLAC Pessac-Léognan 1988 $30 (6/30/89) (BT)
93 CHATEAU LA TOUR-MARTILLAC Pessac-Léognan 1987 $15 (1/31/90)
85+ CHATEAU LA TOUR-MARTILLAC Pessac-Léognan 1987 $15 (6/30/89) (BT)
80+ CHATEAU LA TOUR-MARTILLAC Pessac-Léognan 1987 $15 (7/15/88) (BT)

OTHER BORDEAUX WHITE

84 ALPHA Bordeaux 1989 $16 (2/28/91)
75 AUGEY Bordeaux 1984 $4.50 (10/15/86)
71 CHATEAU BALLUE-MONDON Bordeaux Sauvignon Blanc Sec 1988 $8 (3/31/90)
78 BARTON & GUESTIER Bordeaux Sauvignon Blanc 1988 $6 (3/31/90)
80 BEAU MAYNE Bordeaux 1985 $5 (4/30/87)
85 CHATEAU BONNET Entre-Deux-Mers 1990 $9 (7/31/91) BB
80 CHATEAU BONNET Entre-Deux-Mers 1988 $7 (5/31/90) BB
84 CHATEAU BONNET Entre-Deux-Mers 1988 $7 (5/15/89) BB
79 CHATEAU BONNET Entre-Deux-Mers 1987 $6 (8/31/88)
79 CHATEAU BONNET Entre-Deux-Mers 1986 $4.50 (4/30/88)
84 CHATEAU BONNET Entre-Deux-Mers Oak Aged 1989 $13 (6/15/91)
75 LA CAVE TROISGROS Bordeaux Blanc 1990 $9 (6/15/91)
76 CHATEAU CHEVAL BLANC Bordeaux 1989 $5 (7/31/91)
77 CHEVALIER VEDRINES Bordeaux Sauvignon Blanc 1986 $6 (5/31/88)
70 CHATEAU COTES DES CHARIS Bordeaux Sauvignon Blanc Sec 1990 $10 (6/15/91)
78 LA COUR PAVILLON Bordeaux Sec 1989 $7.25 (3/31/91)
71 LA COUR PAVILLON Bordeaux Sec 1986 $7 (3/31/89)
63 LA COUR PAVILLON Bordeaux Sec 1984 $7 (7/15/87)
83 PIERRE DOURTHE Bordeaux 1987 $10 (9/30/88)
75 PIERRE DOURTHE Bordeaux Sémillon 1990 $4 (6/15/91)
84 CHATEAU DUCLA Entre-Deux-Mers 1990 $7 (6/15/91) BB
81 CHATEAU DUCLA Entre-Deux-Mers 1987 $5 (9/30/88) BB
72 CHATEAU LE GORRE Bordeaux Blanc Sec 1988 $9 (3/31/90)
81 PIERRE JEAN Bordeaux Blanc de Blancs 1990 $7 (6/15/91) BB
71 CHATEAU LAMOTHE Bordeaux 1985 $5 (10/15/87)
79 CHATEAU LARROQUE Bordeaux 1985 $3.75 (10/15/87) BB
85 CHATEAU LARROQUE Bordeaux 1984 $3.75 (12/15/86) BB
78 CHATEAU LARROQUE Bordeaux Sec 1987 $5 (3/31/89)
78 CHATEAU LAURETAN Bordeaux 1986 $5.50 (8/31/88)
70 ALEXIS LICHINE Bordeaux Blanc 1986 $4.50 (3/31/89)
72 CHATEAU LOUDENNE Bordeaux 1986 $12 (3/31/89)
73 CHATEAU LOUDENNE Bordeaux 1985 $10.50 (7/15/87)
77 MICHEL LYNCH Bordeaux 1986 $6 (10/15/87)
83 MAITRE D'ESTOURNEL Bordeaux 1987 $7 (8/31/88) BB
84 MAITRE D'ESTOURNEL Bordeaux 1985 $5 (12/31/86) BB
54 M. DE MALLE Bordeaux 1983 $6.25 (7/01/86)
73 CHATEAU MAROTTE Bordeaux 1986 $3.50 (3/31/88)
77 YVON MAU Bordeaux Officiel du Bicentenaire de la Revolution Française 1988 $4.50 (7/31/89)
86 A. MOUEIX Bordeaux 1984 $2.50 (4/16/86) BB
75 MOUTON-CADET Bordeaux 1986 $5.50 (5/31/88)
70 MOUTON-CADET Bordeaux Blanc 1987 $7.25 (7/31/89)
69 CHATEAU NICOT Haut-Benauge 1984 $4 (11/16/85)
86 PAVILLON BLANC DU CHATEAU MARGAUX Bordeaux 1983 Cur: $44 (7/15/87) (HS)
91 PAVILLON BLANC DU CHATEAU MARGAUX Bordeaux 1979 Rel: $49 Cur: $49 (7/15/87) (HS)
80 PAVILLON BLANC DU CHATEAU MARGAUX Bordeaux 1978 Cur: $50 (7/15/87) (HS)
78 PAVILLON BLANC DU CHATEAU MARGAUX Bordeaux 1961 Cur: $122 (7/15/87) (HS)
86 PAVILLON BLANC DU CHATEAU MARGAUX Bordeaux 1928 Cur: $300 (7/15/87) (HS)
92 PAVILLON BLANC DU CHATEAU MARGAUX Bordeaux 1926 Cur: $300 (7/15/87) (HS)
76 CHATEAU LE REY Bordeaux 1986 $4 (9/30/88)
62 CHATEAU REYNIER Entre-Deux-Mers 1984 $3.25 (12/16/85)
76 ST.-JOVIAN Bordeaux Premium 1990 $5.50 (6/15/91)
69 ST.-JOVIAN Bordeaux Sauvignon Blanc 1987 $4 (8/31/88)
75 CHATEAU TALBOT Bordeaux 1985 $9 (4/30/87)
77 CHATEAU TAREY DU CASTEL Bordeaux NV $3.25 (5/31/88)
78 CHATEAU THIEULEY Bordeaux 1985 $4 (5/31/88)
78 LE SEC DE LA TOUR-BLANCHE Bordeaux Sauvignon Blanc 1989 $9 (3/31/91)
78 VALMAISON Bordeaux 1986 $4 (11/15/87) BB

BURGUNDY RED/*CÔTE DE BEAUNE*/ALOXE-CORTON

92 MAISON AMBROISE Corton Le Rognet 1988 $43 (11/30/90)
90 MAISON AMBROISE Corton Le Rognet 1987 $38 (3/31/90)
88 PIERRE ANDRE Corton Clos du Roi 1985 $45 (7/15/88)
90 PIERRE ANDRE Corton Pougets 1985 $45 (7/15/88)
92 DR. BAROLET Aloxe-Corton Villamont 1952 (NA) (8/31/90) (TR)
87 ADRIEN BELLAND Corton Grèves 1982 $16.50 (9/01/85)
68 BICHOT Aloxe-Corton 1983 $18 (11/30/86)
78 PIERRE BITOUZET Aloxe-Corton Valozières 1986 $18.50 (8/31/90)
91 BONNEAU DU MARTRAY Corton 1985 $62 (10/15/88)
95+ BOUCHARD PERE & FILS Corton Le Corton Domaines du Château de Beaune 1989 $77 (7/15/90) (BT)
91 BOUCHARD PERE & FILS Corton Le Corton Domaines du Château de Beaune 1988 $77 (3/31/91)
90+ BOUCHARD PERE & FILS Corton Le Corton Domaines du Château de Beaune 1988 $77 (7/15/90) (BT)
85 BOUCHARD PERE & FILS Corton Le Corton Domaines du Château de Beaune 1986 $47 (7/31/88)
83 BOUCHARD PERE & FILS Corton Le Corton Domaines du Château de Beaune 1983 $37 (9/15/86)
92 CAPTAIN-GAGNEROT Corton Les Renardes 1985 $70 (12/31/88)
87 JEANNE-MARIE DE CHAMPS Corton Hospices de Beaune Cuvée Charlotte-Dumay 1985 $76 (10/15/88)
84 DOMAINE CHANDON DE BRIAILLES Aloxe-Corton 1983 $25 (9/15/86)
89 DOMAINE CHANDON DE BRIAILLES Corton Bressandes 1988 $75 (2/28/91)
88 DOMAINE CHANDON DE BRIAILLES Corton Bressandes 1986 $43 (2/28/90)
85 DOMAINE CHANDON DE BRIAILLES Corton Clos du Roi 1986 $47 (2/28/90)
90 CHANSON PERE & FILS Corton 1986 $30 (4/30/89)
87 F. CHAUVENET Corton 1986 $50 (7/31/88)
96 F. CHAUVENET Corton 1985 $53 (7/31/87)
90+ F. CHAUVENET Corton Bressandes 1988 $58 (7/15/90) (BT)
97 F. CHAUVENET Corton Hospices de Beaune Docteur-Peste 1985 $133 (7/15/88)
85 CHEVALIER PERE & FILS Aloxe-Corton 1983 $19 (9/15/86)
90+ DOMAINE DU CLOS FRANTIN Corton 1989 (NR) (7/15/90) (BT)
75+ DOMAINE DU CLOS FRANTIN Corton 1988 $52 (7/15/90) (BT)
83 EDMOND CORNU Aloxe-Corton Les Moutottes 1987 $35 (12/31/90)
90 EDMOND CORNU Corton Les Bressandes 1987 $53 (12/31/90)
86 DOUDET-NAUDIN Corton Renardes 1945 (NA) (8/31/90) (TR)
75+ JOSEPH DROUHIN Aloxe-Corton 1988 $37 (7/15/90) (BT)
83 JOSEPH DROUHIN Aloxe-Corton 1986 $25 (4/30/89)
90 JOSEPH DROUHIN Aloxe-Corton 1985 $23 (11/15/87)
85+ JOSEPH DROUHIN Corton 1988 $64 (7/15/90) (BT)
92 JOSEPH DROUHIN Corton 1985 $48 (11/15/87)
92 JOSEPH DROUHIN Corton Bressandes 1988 $60 (11/15/90)
90 JOSEPH DROUHIN Corton Bressandes 1986 $45 (4/30/89)
75+ DUBREUIL-FONTAINE Aloxe-Corton 1988 (NR) (7/15/90) (BT)
85+ DUBREUIL-FONTAINE Corton Bressandes 1989 (NR) (7/15/90) (BT)
86 DUBREUIL-FONTAINE Corton Bressandes 1985 $50 (1/31/89)
85 DUBREUIL-FONTAINE Corton Bressandes 1982 $24 (10/16/85)
85 DUBREUIL-FONTAINE Corton Clos du Roi 1987 $34 (12/31/90)
90 DUBREUIL-FONTAINE Corton Clos du Roi 1985 Rel: $49 Cur: $63 (7/15/88)
86 DUBREUIL-FONTAINE Corton Clos du Roi 1982 $25 (9/16/85)
90+ FAIVELEY Corton Clos des Cortons 1989 (NR) (7/15/90) (BT)
90 FAIVELEY Corton Clos des Cortons 1988 $120 (3/31/91)
92 FAIVELEY Corton Clos des Cortons 1987 $50 (3/31/90)
79 FAIVELEY Corton Clos des Cortons 1985 Rel: $80 Cur: $103 (3/15/88)
80 MACHARD DE GRAMONT Aloxe-Corton Les Morais 1985 $34 (7/15/88)
90+ LOUIS JADOT Corton Pougets 1989 (NR) (7/15/90) (BT)
93 LOUIS JADOT Corton Pougets 1988 $61 (3/31/91)
80+ LOUIS JADOT Corton Pougets 1988 $61 (7/15/90) (BT)
87 LOUIS JADOT Corton Pougets 1987 $39 (6/15/90)
86 LOUIS JADOT Corton Pougets 1986 $42 (4/30/89)
86 LOUIS JADOT Corton Pougets 1986 $42 (7/31/88)
89 LOUIS JADOT Corton Pougets 1985 $47 (3/15/88)
87 JAFFELIN Corton 1986 $45 (12/31/88)
91 JAFFELIN Corton 1983 Rel: $33 Cur: $45 (4/01/86) CS
85 LOUIS LATOUR Aloxe-Corton 1955 (NA) (8/31/90) (TR)
76 LOUIS LATOUR Aloxe-Corton Les Chaillots 1985 $37 (4/15/88)
89 LOUIS LATOUR Corton Château Corton Grancey 1985 Rel: $46 Cur: $64 (3/15/88)
89 LOUIS LATOUR Corton Château Corton Grancey 1959 Cur: $130 (8/31/90) (TR)
91 LOUIS LATOUR Corton Château Corton Grancey 1953 Cur: $195 (8/31/90) (TR)
85 LOUIS LATOUR Corton Château Corton Grancey 1947 Cur: $96 (8/31/90) (TR)
89 LOUIS LATOUR Corton Clos de la Vigne au Saint 1985 $43 (3/15/88)
90 LOUIS LATOUR Corton Domaine Latour 1985 $38 (3/15/88)
88 OLIVIER LEFLAIVE FRERES Corton Bressandes 1986 $45 (7/31/88)
86 DOMAINE LEQUIN-ROUSSOT Corton Les Languettes 1985 $39 (7/15/88)
84 LUPE-CHOLET Aloxe-Corton 1985 $18 (3/15/88)
89 DOMAINE MEO-CAMUZET Corton 1986 $50 (10/31/88)
87 PRINCE FLORENT DE MERODE Aloxe-Corton 1987 $30 (2/28/91)
92 PRINCE FLORENT DE MERODE Corton Bressandes 1987 $42 (3/31/91)
84 PRINCE FLORENT DE MERODE Corton Bressandes 1986 $38 (8/31/89)
93 PRINCE FLORENT DE MERODE Corton Bressandes 1985 $52 (2/15/88)
87 PRINCE FLORENT DE MERODE Corton Clos du Roi 1987 $44 (3/31/90)
80 PRINCE FLORENT DE MERODE Corton Clos du Roi 1986 $49 (8/31/89)
88 PRINCE FLORENT DE MERODE Corton Maréchaudes 1987 $36 (8/31/90)
82 PRINCE FLORENT DE MERODE Corton Maréchaudes 1986 $33 (8/31/89)
81 PRINCE FLORENT DE MERODE Corton Maréchaudes 1985 $49 (3/15/88)
92 PRINCE FLORENT DE MERODE Corton Renardes 1987 $36 (3/31/90)
76 PRINCE FLORENT DE MERODE Corton Renardes 1986 $38 (8/31/89)
92 MOILLARD Corton Clos des Vergennes 1985 $36 (5/31/87)
88 MOILLARD Corton Clos des Vergennes 1983 $19 (10/01/85)
87 MOILLARD Corton Clos du Roi 1984 $24 (5/31/87)
91 MOMMESSIN Corton 1985 $28 (2/15/88)
90+ MOMMESSIN Corton Bressandes 1988 $30 (7/15/90) (BT)
88 GASTON & PIERRE RAVAUT Aloxe-Corton 1985 $35 (7/31/88)
92 GASTON & PIERRE RAVAUT Corton Hautes-Mourottes 1985 $46 (7/31/88)
85+ TOLLOT-BEAUT Aloxe-Corton 1988 $35 (7/15/90) (BT)
89 TOLLOT-BEAUT Aloxe-Corton 1985 $35 (3/15/88)
80+ TOLLOT-BEAUT Corton 1988 $55 (7/15/90) (BT)
87 TOLLOT-BEAUT Corton 1986 $45 (8/31/89)
97 TOLLOT-BEAUT Corton 1985 $49 (3/15/88)
90+ TOLLOT-BEAUT Corton Bressandes 1988 $55 (7/15/90) (BT)
84 CHARLES VIENOT Corton Maréchaude 1985 $57 (7/15/88)

FRANCE

BURGUNDY RED/*CÔTE DE BEAUNE*/BEAUNE

82 BICHOT Beaune 1988 $15 (8/31/90)
80 BICHOT Beaune Bressandes 1986 $24 (7/31/88)
88 JEAN-MARC BOILLOT Beaune Montrevenots 1988 $37 (5/15/91)
85+ BOUCHARD PERE & FILS Beaune Clos de la Mousse Domaines du Château de Beaune 1989 $36 (7/15/90) (BT)
78 BOUCHARD PERE & FILS Beaune Clos de la Mousse Domaines du Château de Beaune 1986 $33 (7/31/88)
95+ BOUCHARD PERE & FILS Beaune Grèves Vigne de l'Enfant Jésus 1989 $59 (7/15/90) (BT)
91 BOUCHARD PERE & FILS Beaune Grèves Vigne de l'Enfant Jésus 1988 $59 (4/30/91)
80+ BOUCHARD PERE & FILS Beaune Grèves Vigne de l'Enfant Jésus 1988 $59 (7/15/90) (BT)
82 BOUCHARD PERE & FILS Beaune Grèves Vigne de l'Enfant Jésus 1986 $47 (7/31/88)
91 BOUCHARD PERE & FILS Beaune Grèves Vigne de l'Enfant Jésus 1985 $61 (1/31/89)
85 BOUCHARD PERE & FILS Beaune Grèves Vigne de l'Enfant Jésus 1983 $30 (9/15/86)
80+ BOUCHARD PERE & FILS Beaune Marconnets Domaines du Château de Beaune 1989 $41 (7/15/90) (BT)
83 BOUCHARD PERE & FILS Beaune Marconnets Domaines du Château de Beaune 1986 $24 (7/31/88)
89 BOUCHARD PERE & FILS Beaune Marconnets Domaines du Château de Beaune 1985 $35 (1/31/89)
70+ BOUCHARD PERE & FILS Beaune Teurons Domaines du Château de Beaune 1988 $36 (7/15/90) (BT)
81 BOUCHARD PERE & FILS Beaune Teurons Domaines du Château de Beaune 1986 $32 (7/31/88)
85 BOUCHARD PERE & FILS Beaune Teurons Domaines du Château de Beaune 1985 $35 (1/31/89)
71 BOUCHARD PERE & FILS Beaune Teurons Domaines du Château de Beaune 1983 $21.25 (9/15/86)
88 PIERRE BOUREE FILS Beaune Epenottes 1987 $35 (6/15/90)
84 CHANSON PERE & FILS Beaune Clos des Fèves 1988 $35 (8/31/90)
85 CHANSON PERE & FILS Beaune Clos des Fèves 1987 $23 (7/31/89)
92 CHANSON PERE & FILS Beaune Clos des Fèves 1985 $25 (1/31/89)
81 CHANSON PERE & FILS Beaune Clos des Marconnets 1986 $20 (5/31/89)
88 DOMAINE JEAN CHARTRON Beaune Hospices de Beaune Cuvée Cyrot-Chaudron 1988 $40 (2/15/91)
82 F. CHAUVENET Beaune Clos des Mouches 1986 $27 (12/31/88)
82 F. CHAUVENET Beaune Clos des Mouches 1986 $27 (7/31/88)
85+ F. CHAUVENET Beaune Grèves 1988 $25 (7/15/90) (BT)
79 F. CHAUVENET Beaune Grèves 1986 $25 (12/31/88)
90 F. CHAUVENET Beaune Grèves 1986 $25 (7/31/88)
91 F. CHAUVENET Beaune Hospices de Beaune Rosseau-Deslandes 1980 $36 (6/16/86)
70+ F. CHAUVENET Beaune Theurons 1988 $25 (7/15/90) (BT)
88 F. CHAUVENET Beaune Theurons 1985 $23 (7/31/87)
90 A.R. CHOPPIN Beaune Bressandes 1985 $32 (9/30/87)
81 A.R. CHOPPIN Beaune Cent Vignes 1985 $32 (10/31/87)
79 A.R. CHOPPIN Beaune Grèves 1985 $32 (9/30/87)
87 A.R. CHOPPIN Beaune Teurons 1987 $30 (2/28/90)
87 A.R. CHOPPIN Beaune Teurons 1985 $32 (10/31/87)
83 A.R. CHOPPIN Beaune Toussaints 1987 $30 (2/28/90)
81 DOMAINE HENRI CLERC & FILS Beaune Chaume Gaufriot 1985 $29 (11/15/88)
85+ JOSEPH DROUHIN Beaune Clos des Mouches 1989 $62 (7/15/90) (BT)
88 JOSEPH DROUHIN Beaune Clos des Mouches 1988 $50 (2/15/91)
80+ JOSEPH DROUHIN Beaune Clos des Mouches 1988 $54 (7/15/90) (BT)
83 JOSEPH DROUHIN Beaune Clos des Mouches 1987 $47 (6/15/90)
94+ JOSEPH DROUHIN Beaune Clos des Mouches 1986 $38 (11/15/87) (BT)
80 JOSEPH DROUHIN Beaune Grèves 1959 (NA) (8/31/90) (TR)
85 DOMAINE DUCHET Beaune Cent-Vignes 1985 $27 (3/15/88)
86 FAIVELEY Beaune Champs-Pimont 1985 $36 (3/15/88)
86 JEAN GARAUDET Beaune Clos des Mouches 1988 $40 (11/15/90)
85+ JACQUES GERMAIN Beaune Les Boucherottes 1989 (NR) (7/15/90) (BT)
85+ JACQUES GERMAIN Beaune Cent Vignes 1989 (NR) (7/15/90) (BT)
90+ JACQUES GERMAIN Beaune Cent Vignes 1988 (NR) (7/15/90) (BT)
85+ JACQUES GERMAIN Beaune Les Crâs 1989 $42 (7/15/90) (BT)
90+ JACQUES GERMAIN Beaune Les Crâs 1988 (NR) (7/15/90) (BT)
80+ JACQUES GERMAIN Beaune Les Teurons 1989 (NR) (7/15/90) (BT)
90 JACQUES GERMAIN Beaune Les Teurons 1988 $42 (2/15/91)
85+ JACQUES GERMAIN Beaune Les Teurons 1988 (NR) (7/15/90) (BT)
70 JACQUES GERMAIN Beaune Les Teurons 1986 $33 (7/31/88)
85+ JACQUES GERMAIN Beaune Vigne-Franches 1989 (NR) (7/15/90) (BT)
90+ JACQUES GERMAIN Beaune Vignes-Franches 1988 (NR) (7/15/90) (BT)
71 DOMAINE ALETH GIRARDIN Beaune Clos des Mouches 1988 $36 (7/15/91)
89 MACHARD DE GRAMONT Beaune Les Chouacheux 1985 $34 (5/31/88)
69 DOMAINE JEAN GUITTON Beaune Les Sizies 1986 $19 (5/31/89)
85+ LOUIS JADOT Beaune Boucherottes 1989 (NR) (7/15/90) (BT)
92 LOUIS JADOT Beaune Boucherottes 1988 $33 (3/31/91)
85+ LOUIS JADOT Beaune Boucherottes 1988 $33 (7/15/90) (BT)
91 LOUIS JADOT Beaune Boucherottes 1985 $30 (3/15/88)
80+ LOUIS JADOT Beaune Bressandes 1989 (NR) (7/15/90) (BT)
80+ LOUIS JADOT Beaune Bressandes 1988 $26 (7/15/90) (BT)
90 LOUIS JADOT Beaune Bressandes 1986 $24 (5/31/89)
87 LOUIS JADOT Beaune Bressandes 1985 $30 (3/15/88)
85+ LOUIS JADOT Beaune Clos des Couchereaux 1989 (NR) (7/15/90) (BT)
90 LOUIS JADOT Beaune Clos des Couchereaux 1988 $33 (3/31/91)
90+ LOUIS JADOT Beaune Clos des Couchereaux 1988 $33 (7/15/90) (BT)
91 LOUIS JADOT Beaune Clos des Couchereaux 1985 $30 (3/15/88)
95+ LOUIS JADOT Beaune Clos des Ursules 1989 (NR) (7/15/90) (BT)
91 LOUIS JADOT Beaune Clos des Ursules 1988 $40 (3/31/91)
85+ LOUIS JADOT Beaune Clos des Ursules 1988 $40 (7/15/90) (BT)
81 LOUIS JADOT Beaune Clos des Ursules 1987 $27 (6/15/90)
88 LOUIS JADOT Beaune Clos des Ursules 1986 $27 (3/15/89) (JS)
91 LOUIS JADOT Beaune Clos des Ursules 1985 Rel: $30 Cur: $35 (3/15/89) (JS)
95 LOUIS JADOT Beaune Clos des Ursules 1985 Rel: $30 Cur: $35 (3/15/88) SS
93 LOUIS JADOT Beaune Clos des Ursules 1983 Cur: $25 (3/15/89) (JS)
83 LOUIS JADOT Beaune Clos des Ursules 1980 Cur: $26 (3/15/89) (JS)
89 LOUIS JADOT Beaune Clos des Ursules 1978 Cur: $47 (3/15/89) (JS)
85 LOUIS JADOT Beaune Clos des Ursules 1976 Cur: $40 (3/15/89) (JS)
86 LOUIS JADOT Beaune Clos des Ursules 1973 (NA) (3/15/89) (JS)
78 LOUIS JADOT Beaune Clos des Ursules 1971 Cur: $60 (3/15/89) (JS)
90 LOUIS JADOT Beaune Clos des Ursules 1969 Cur: $120 (3/15/89) (JS)
90 LOUIS JADOT Beaune Clos des Ursules 1966 Cur: $130 (3/15/89) (JS)
86 LOUIS JADOT Beaune Clos des Ursules 1964 (NA) (3/15/89) (JS)
79 LOUIS JADOT Beaune Clos des Ursules 1962 (NA) (3/15/89) (JS)
88 LOUIS JADOT Beaune Clos des Ursules 1961 (NA) (3/15/89) (JS)
98 LOUIS JADOT Beaune Clos des Ursules 1959 (NA) (3/15/89) (JS)
89 LOUIS JADOT Beaune Clos des Ursules 1957 (NA) (3/15/89) (JS)
81 LOUIS JADOT Beaune Clos des Ursules 1954 (NA) (3/15/89) (JS)
87 LOUIS JADOT Beaune Clos des Ursules 1952 (NA) (3/15/89) (JS)
86 LOUIS JADOT Beaune Clos des Ursules 1949 (NA) (3/15/89) (JS)
95 LOUIS JADOT Beaune Clos des Ursules 1947 (NA) (3/15/89) (JS)
84 LOUIS JADOT Beaune Clos des Ursules 1945 (NA) (3/15/89) (JS)
92 LOUIS JADOT Beaune Clos des Ursules 1937 (NA) (3/15/89) (JS)
80 LOUIS JADOT Beaune Clos des Ursules 1933 (NA) (3/15/89) (JS)
97 LOUIS JADOT Beaune Clos des Ursules 1928 (NA) (3/15/89) (JS)
88 LOUIS JADOT Beaune Clos des Ursules 1926 (NA) (3/15/89) (JS)
78 LOUIS JADOT Beaune Clos des Ursules 1923 (NA) (3/15/89) (JS)
90 LOUIS JADOT Beaune Clos des Ursules 1919 (NA) (3/15/89) (JS)
95 LOUIS JADOT Beaune Clos des Ursules 1915 (NA) (3/15/89) (JS)
81 LOUIS JADOT Beaune Clos des Ursules 1911 (NA) (3/15/89) (JS)
92 LOUIS JADOT Beaune Clos des Ursules 1906 (NA) (3/15/89) (JS)
88 LOUIS JADOT Beaune Clos des Ursules 1904 (NA) (3/15/89) (JS)
80 LOUIS JADOT Beaune Clos des Ursules 1895 (NA) (3/15/89) (JS)
90 LOUIS JADOT Beaune Clos des Ursules 1887 (NA) (3/15/89) (JS)
85+ LOUIS JADOT Beaune Les Chouacheux 1989 (NR) (7/15/90) (BT)
90+ LOUIS JADOT Beaune Les Chouacheux 1988 $25 (7/15/90) (BT)
85 LOUIS JADOT Beaune Les Chouacheux 1986 $24 (5/31/89)
91 LOUIS JADOT Beaune Les Chouacheux 1985 $30 (3/15/88)
90 LOUIS JADOT Beaune Hospices de Beaune Cuvée Dames-Hospitalier 1985 $85 (3/15/88)
92 LOUIS JADOT Beaune Hospices de Beaune Cuvée Nicolas-Rolin 1985 $85 (3/15/88)
90+ JAFFELIN Beaune Les Champimonts 1989 (NR) (7/15/90) (BT)
75+ JAFFELIN Beaune Les Champimonts 1988 $30 (7/15/90) (BT)
68 JAFFELIN Beaune Les Champimonts 1983 $17.50 (9/15/86)
77 JAFFELIN Beaune du Châpitre 1986 $18 (12/31/88)
85 JAFFELIN Beaune Hospices de Beaune Cuvée Clos des Avaux 1986 $65 (12/31/88)
90+ DOMAINE PIERRE LABET Beaune Coucherias 1989 (NR) (7/15/90) (BT)
90 LOUIS LATOUR Beaune Vignes Franches 1985 Rel: $31 Cur: $41 (3/15/88)
87 LIGER-BELAIR Beaune Les Avaux 1947 (NA) (8/31/90) (TR)
89 LUPE-CHOLET Beaune Avaux 1986 (NA) (7/31/88)
87 CHATEAU DE MEURSAULT Beaune Cent-Vignes 1985 $31 (2/28/90)
68 MOILLARD Beaune 1983 $10 (10/16/85)
89 MOILLARD Beaune Grèves 1985 $25 (3/15/87)
87 MOILLARD Beaune Grèves 1984 $11.50 (2/15/87)
80 MOILLARD Beaune Grèves Domaine Thomas-Moillard 1986 $14 (12/31/88)
90+ MOMMESSIN Beaune Les Epenottes 1989 (NR) (7/15/90) (BT)
89 DOMAINE RENE MONNIER Beaune Cent Vignes 1985 $25 (10/31/87)
85 DOMAINE MARC MOREY Beaune Les Paules 1988 $24 (8/31/90)
84 DOMAINE MARC MOREY Beaune Les Paules 1985 $15 (12/31/88)
87 ALBERT MOROT Beaune Bressandes 1988 $30 (3/31/91)
91 ALBERT MOROT Beaune Cent-Vignes 1988 $30 (4/30/91)
86 ALBERT MOROT Beaune Grèves 1988 $32 (7/15/91)
80 ALBERT MOROT Beaune Teurons 1988 $33 (7/15/91)
86 DOMAINE MUSSY Beaune Epenottes 1986 $28 (5/31/89)
86 DOMAINE MUSSY Beaune Montremenots 1986 $28 (5/31/89)
88 PARIGOT PERE & FILS Beaune Grèves 1987 $26 (2/28/90)
86 PAUL PERNOT Beaune Teurons 1988 $33 (3/31/91)
88 POTHIER-RIEUSSET Beaune Boucherottes 1988 $35 (11/30/90)
88 POTHIER-RIEUSSET Beaune Boucherottes 1986 $19 (5/31/89)
82 DOMAINE PRIEUR-BRUNET Beaune Clos du Roy 1988 $30 (12/31/90)
90 REMOISSENET Beaune Grèves 1988 $30 (11/30/90)
86 TOLLOT-BEAUT Beaune Clos du Roi 1988 $53 (2/28/91)
85+ TOLLOT-BEAUT Beaune Clos du Roi 1988 $53 (7/15/90) (BT)
85+ TOLLOT-BEAUT Beaune Grèves 1988 $35 (7/15/90) (BT)
90 LEON VOILLAND Beaune Clos du Roy 1945 (NA) (8/31/90) (TR)

CHASSAGNE-MONTRACHET

85 BOUCHARD PERE & FILS Chassagne-Montrachet 1988 $22 (4/30/91)
85 FONTAINE-GAGNARD Chassagne-Montrachet 1985 $15.50 (12/31/88)
83 JEAN-CHARLES FORNEROT Chassagne-Montrachet Les Champs Gain 1985 $19 (7/31/89)
86 JEAN-CHARLES FORNEROT Chassagne-Montrachet La Maltroie 1985 $19 (7/31/89)
86 JEAN-NOEL GAGNARD Chassagne-Montrachet Morgeot 1988 $20 (12/31/90)
79 JEAN-NOEL GAGNARD Chassagne-Montrachet Morgeot 1985 $18 (11/30/87)
80+ LOUIS JADOT Chassagne-Montrachet Morgeot Clos de la Chapelle Domaine Duc de Magenta 1989 (NR) (7/15/90) (BT)
85 LOUIS JADOT Chassagne-Montrachet Morgeot Clos de la Chapelle Domaine Duc de Magenta 1988 $20 (3/31/91)
80+ LOUIS JADOT Chassagne-Montrachet Morgeot Clos de la Chapelle Domaine Duc de Magenta 1988 $18 (7/15/90) (BT)
77 LOUIS JADOT Chassagne-Montrachet Morgeot Clos de la Chapelle Domaine Duc de Magenta 1986 $17.50 (10/31/89)
83 LOUIS JADOT Chassagne-Montrachet Morgeot Clos de la Chapelle Domaine Duc de Magenta 1985 $19 (4/15/88)
80+ JAFFELIN Chassagne-Montrachet 1989 (NR) (7/15/90) (BT)
80+ JAFFELIN Chassagne-Montrachet 1988 $20 (7/15/90) (BT)
80+ OLIVIER LEFLAIVE FRERES Chassagne-Montrachet 1989 (NR) (7/15/90) (BT)
89 OLIVIER LEFLAIVE FRERES Chassagne-Montrachet 1986 $26 (2/29/88)
83 OLIVIER LEFLAIVE FRERES Chassagne-Montrachet 1985 $32 (10/31/88)

Key to Symbols

The scores reported here are the results of blind tastings conducted by our panel of senior editors. Wines that carry the initials below are results of individual tastings.

THE WINE SPECTATOR 100-POINT SCALE ***95-100***—Classic, a great wine; ***90-94***—Outstanding, superior character and style; ***80-89***—Good to very good, a wine with special qualities; ***70-79***—Average, drinkable wine that may have minor flaws; ***60-69***—Below average, drinkable but not recommended; ***50-59***—Poor, undrinkable, not recommended. "+"—With a score indicates a range; used primarily with barrel tastings to indicate a preliminary score.

SPECIAL DESIGNATIONS SS—Spectator Selection, CS—Cellar Selection, BB—Best Buy.

TASTER'S INITIALS (JG)—Jim Gordon, (HS)—Harvey Steiman, (JL)—James Laube, (JS)—James Suckling, (TM)—Thomas Matthews, (TR)—Terry Robards, (BT)—Barrel Tasting (these wines were tasted blind from barrel samples), (CA-date)—*California's Great Cabernets* by James Laube, (CH-date)—*California's Great Chardonnays* by James Laube, (VP-date)—*Vintage Port* by James Suckling.

DATE TASTED Dates in parentheses represent the issue in which the rating was published.

86   DOMAINE LEQUIN-ROUSSOT Chassagne-Montrachet Morgeot 1985 $24 (5/31/88)
86   CHATEAU DE LA MALTROYE Chassagne-Montrachet Boudriottes 1985 $17 (10/15/88)
89   CHATEAU DE LA MALTROYE Chassagne-Montrachet Clos St.-Jean 1985 $19 (10/15/88)
65   CHATEAU DE LA MALTROYE Chassagne-Montrachet Clos St.-Jean 1983 $12.50 (11/16/85)
88   HENRI MEURGEY Chassagne-Montrachet Clos de la Boudriotte 1985 $40 (10/31/88)
84   MOILLARD Chassagne-Montrachet Morgeot 1985 $15 (5/31/87)
75+ MOMMESSIN Chassagne-Montrachet 1989 (NR) (7/15/90) (BT)
61   BERNARD MOREAU Chassagne-Montrachet Morgeot La Cardeuse 1986 $15.50 (12/31/88)
75   BERNARD MOREY Chassagne-Montrachet 1987 $20 (10/31/89)
84   PAUL PILLOT Chassagne-Montrachet Clos St.-Jean 1986 $23 (2/28/90)
86   PAUL PILLOT Chassagne-Montrachet Clos St.-Jean 1985 $24 (11/15/88)
83   DOMAINE PRIEUR-BRUNET Chassagne-Montrachet Morgeot 1988 $17 (11/15/90)
86   DOMAINE ROUX PERE & FILS Chassagne-Montrachet Clos St.-Jean 1983 $13 (9/16/85)

PERNAND-VERGELESSES

83   DOMAINE CHANDON DE BRIAILLES Pernand-Vergelesses Ile des Vergelesses 1988 $35 (2/28/91)
85   CHANSON PERE & FILS Pernand-Vergelesses Les Vergelesses 1988 $24 (8/31/90)
82   DOMAINE DELARCHE Pernand-Vergelesses 1989 $15/375ml (4/30/91)
89   DOMAINE DELARCHE Pernand-Vergelesses Ile des Vergelesses 1985 $23 (10/15/88)
91   JOSEPH DROUHIN Pernand-Vergelesses 1985 $17 (11/15/87)
70+ DUBREUIL-FONTAINE Pernand-Vergelesses Ile des Vergelesses 1989 (NR) (7/15/90) (BT)
78   DUBREUIL-FONTAINE Pernand-Vergelesses Ile des Vergelesses 1982 $18 (10/16/85)
80+ LOUIS JADOT Pernand-Vergelesses 1989 (NR) (7/15/90) (BT)
80+ LOUIS JADOT Pernand-Vergelesses 1988 $16 (7/15/90) (BT)
85   LOUIS JADOT Pernand-Vergelesses 1985 $18 (4/15/88)
86   LOUIS JADOT Pernand-Vergelesses Clos de la Croix de Pierre 1988 $16.50 (3/31/91)
79   LOUIS JADOT Pernand-Vergelesses Clos de la Croix de Pierre 1987 $15 (11/15/90)
85   LOUIS JADOT Pernand-Vergelesses Clos de la Croix de Pierre 1986 $17 (7/31/89)
83   LOUIS JADOT Pernand-Vergelesses Clos de la Croix de Pierre 1985 $18 (4/15/88)
79   DOMAINE RAPET Pernand-Vergelesses 1988 $31 (2/28/91)

POMMARD

90   COMTE ARMAND Pommard Clos des Epeneaux 1988 $46 (2/28/91)
81   COMTE ARMAND Pommard Clos des Epeneaux 1987 $41 (8/31/90)
91   COMTE ARMAND Pommard Clos des Epeneaux 1985 $44 (3/15/88)
81   BARTON & GUESTIER Pommard 1985 $21 (11/30/87)
87   BICHOT Pommard 1988 $25 (8/31/90)
79   BICHOT Pommard 1986 $20 (9/15/89)
83   BICHOT Pommard 1983 $19 (9/15/86)
91   BICHOT Pommard Hospices de Beaune Cuvée Cyrot-Chaudron 1985 $60 (10/31/88)
80+ BICHOT Pommard Rugiens 1988 $40 (7/15/90) (BT)
77   JEAN-MARC BOILLOT Pommard Saucilles 1988 $47 (5/15/91)
78   JEAN CLAUDE BOISSET Pommard 1985 $28 (4/30/88)
76   JEAN CLAUDE BOISSET Pommard Rugiens 1985 $33 (3/15/88)
80+ BOUCHARD PERE & FILS Pommard 1989 $38 (7/15/90) (BT)
90   BOUCHARD PERE & FILS Pommard 1988 $37 (4/30/91)
74   BOUCHARD PERE & FILS Pommard 1983 $23 (9/15/86)
89   BOUCHARD PERE & FILS Pommard Premier Cru Domaines du Château de Beaune 1988 $53 (3/31/91)
90+ BOUCHARD PERE & FILS Pommard Premier Cru Domaines du Château de Beaune 1988 $53 (7/15/90) (BT)
87   BOUCHARD PERE & FILS Pommard Premier Cru Domaines du Château de Beaune 1986 $41 (7/31/88)
63   DOMAINE JEAN-MARC BOULEY Pommard Les Rugiens 1987 $34 (11/15/90)
92   DOMAINE JEAN-MARC BOULEY Pommard Les Rugiens 1985 $30 (10/31/88)
88   DOMAINE F. BUFFET Pommard Rugiens 1985 $40 (10/15/88)
79   ROGER CAILLOT Pommard 1987 $35 (9/15/89)
87   CHARTRON & TREBUCHET Pommard Les Epenots 1988 $45 (2/28/91)
85+ F. CHAUVENET Pommard Chanlins 1988 $55 (7/15/90) (BT)
95   F. CHAUVENET Pommard Epenots 1985 $48 (7/31/87)
91   F. CHAUVENET Pommard Hospices de Beaune Cuvée Dames-de-la-Charité 1982 $36 (2/01/85) CS
90   F. CHAUVENET Pommard Les Chanlins 1986 $40 (7/31/88)
70+ MAURICE CHENU Pommard 1989 (NR) (7/15/90) (BT)
75+ MAURICE CHENU Pommard 1988 (NR) (7/15/90) (BT)
76   DOMAINE COSTE-CAUMARTIN Pommard 1987 $21 (11/15/90)
79   DOMAINE COSTE-CAUMARTIN Pommard Les Fremiers 1987 $26 (11/15/90)
89   DOMAINE DE COURCEL Pommard Clos des Epeneaux 1985 $37 (4/30/88)
92   DOMAINE DE COURCEL Pommard Rugiens 1985 $40 (4/30/88)
80+ JOSEPH DROUHIN Pommard 1989 $46 (7/15/90) (BT)
85+ JOSEPH DROUHIN Pommard 1988 $40 (7/15/90) (BT)
87   JOSEPH DROUHIN Pommard 1986 $27 (4/30/89)
93   JOSEPH DROUHIN Pommard 1985 $33 (11/15/87)
83   JOSEPH DROUHIN Pommard 1981 $27.75 (9/01/84)
80+ JOSEPH DROUHIN Pommard Epenots 1989 $60 (7/15/90) (BT)
85+ JOSEPH DROUHIN Pommard Epenots 1988 $55 (7/15/90) (BT)
83   JOSEPH DROUHIN Pommard Epenots 1986 $40 (7/31/88)
95   JOSEPH DROUHIN Pommard Epenots 1985 $41 (11/15/87)
88   JEAN GARAUDET Pommard 1988 $37 (11/15/90)
88   JEAN GARAUDET Pommard 1987 $25 (12/15/90)
90   JEAN GARAUDET Pommard Les Charmots 1988 $46 (11/15/90)
88   JEAN GARAUDET Pommard Les Charmots 1987 $30 (9/15/89)
87   DOMAINE ALETH GIRARDIN Pommard Charmots 1988 $44 (7/15/91)
83   LOUIS JADOT Pommard 1988 $36 (3/31/91)
91   LOUIS JADOT Pommard Chaponnières 1985 $39 (3/15/88)
86   LOUIS JADOT Pommard Grands Epenots 1988 $38 (3/31/91)
80+ LOUIS JADOT Pommard Grands Epenots 1988 $38 (7/15/90) (BT)
79   JAFFELIN Pommard 1986 $26 (4/30/89)
89   JAFFELIN Pommard 1985 $38 (3/15/88)
81   JAFFELIN Pommard 1983 $19 (9/15/86)
79   LABOURE-ROI Pommard Les Bertins 1985 $29 (3/15/88)
89   LOUIS LATOUR Pommard Epenots 1985 $46 (3/15/88)
80+ OLIVIER LEFLAIVE FRERES Pommard 1989 (NR) (7/15/90) (BT)

75+ OLIVIER LEFLAIVE FRERES Pommard 1988 $31 (7/15/90) (BT)
88   LEROY Pommard Les Vignots 1988 $84 (4/30/91)
88   DOMAINE CHANTAL LESCURE Pommard Les Bertins 1988 $40 (11/30/90)
86   LUPE-CHOLET Pommard Les Boucherottes 1983 $19 (6/16/86)
82   ROBERT MAX Pommard 1982 $15.50 (12/16/84)
76   PRINCE FLORENT DE MERODE Pommard Clos de la Platière 1987 $36 (8/31/90)
86   PRINCE FLORENT DE MERODE Pommard Clos de la Platière 1986 $35 (7/31/89)
94   PRINCE FLORENT DE MERODE Pommard Clos de la Platière 1985 Rel: $45 Cur: $45 (3/15/88)
71   PRINCE FLORENT DE MERODE Pommard Clos de la Platière 1984 $23 (2/15/88)
78   JEAN MICHELOT Pommard 1987 $33 (8/31/90)
87   MICHELOT Pommard 1985 $29 (4/30/88)
78   MICHELOT Pommard 1983 $21 (6/16/86)
92   MOILLARD Pommard Clos des Epeneaux 1985 Rel: $40 Cur: $45 (6/30/88) CS
85   MOILLARD Pommard Rugiens 1985 $40 (6/30/88)
89   DOMAINE RENE MONNIER Pommard Les Vignots 1985 $30 (11/15/88)
81   DOMAINE RENE MONNIER Pommard Les Vignots 1982 $16.50 (7/01/85)
66   DOMAINE MUSSY Pommard 1986 $32 (4/30/89)
86   DOMAINE MUSSY Pommard 1985 $35 (10/15/88)
86   DOMAINE MUSSY Pommard Premier Cru 1986 $35 (4/30/89)
83   DOMAINE PARENT Pommard 1982 $18 (11/01/85)
94   DOMAINE PARENT Pommard Les Epenots 1959 (NA) (8/31/90) (TR)
87   PARIGOT PERE & FILS Pommard Les Charmots 1987 $28 (7/31/89)
93   PARIGOT PERE & FILS Pommard Les Charmots 1985 Rel: $24 Cur: $35 (6/15/87) CS
78   DOMAINE JEAN PASCAL Pommard La Chanière 1986 $30 (10/15/88)
88   CHATEAU DE POMMARD Pommard 1979 $33 (9/01/85)
76   POTHIER-RIEUSSET Pommard 1986 $25 (9/15/89)
87   POTHIER-RIEUSSET Pommard Clos de Verger 1986 $33 (9/15/89)
72   POTHIER-RIEUSSET Pommard Rugiens 1986 $35 (9/15/89)
70   LA POUSSE D'OR Pommard Les Jarollières 1986 $45 (4/30/89)
87   LA POUSSE D'OR Pommard Les Jarollières 1985 $39 (3/15/88)
83   CHATEAU DE PULIGNY-MONTRACHET Pommard 1988 $34 (8/31/90)
75   THORIN Pommard 1986 $24 (2/28/90)
81   CHARLES VIENOT Pommard 1985 $33 (4/30/88)

SANTENAY

78   ADRIEN BELLAND Santenay Comme 1987 $22 (11/15/90)
91   ADRIEN BELLAND Santenay Comme 1982 Rel: $12 Cur: $25 (8/01/85) CS
78   BICHOT Santenay 1986 $12 (10/15/89)
70+ BICHOT Santenay Clos Rousseau 1988 $20 (7/15/90) (BT)
66   BICHOT Santenay Les Gravières 1985 $15 (3/15/88)
88   PIERRE BOUREE FILS Santenay Gravières 1985 $30 (5/31/88)
84   F. CHAUVENET Santenay 1985 $18 (7/31/87)
88   LOUIS CLAIR Santenay Gravières Domaine de L'Abbaye 1985 $16.50 (10/15/87)
88   JOSEPH DROUHIN Santenay 1985 $17 (11/15/87)
84   JEAN-NOEL GAGNARD Santenay Clos de Tavannes 1988 $25 (11/15/90)
87   DOMAINE JEAN GIRARDIN Santenay Clos Rousseau Château de la Charrière 1987 $25 (2/28/91)
83   DOMAINE JEAN GIRARDIN Santenay Comme Château de la Charrière 1987 $25 (2/28/91)
80   DOMAINE JEAN GIRARDIN Santenay Comme Château de la Charrière 1986 $23 (10/15/89)
80+ LOUIS JADOT Santenay Clos de Malte 1989 (NR) (7/15/90) (BT)
84   JAFFELIN Santenay La Maladière 1985 $22 (3/15/88)
86   JESSIAUME PERE & FILS Santenay Gravières 1988 $21 (3/31/91)
81   OLIVIER LEFLAIVE FRERES Santenay 1986 $17 (7/31/88)
76   DOMAINE LEQUIN-ROUSSOT Santenay 1987 $15 (11/15/90)
78   DOMAINE LEQUIN-ROUSSOT Santenay 1985 $18 (5/31/88)
85   DOMAINE LEQUIN-ROUSSOT Santenay La Comme 1985 $24 (5/31/88)
85   PROSPER MAUFOUX Santenay Les Gravières 1985 $18 (10/15/89)
87   PROSPER MAUFOUX Santenay Les Gravières 1985 $18 (10/15/88)
80+ MOMMESSIN Santenay Grand Clos Rousseau 1989 (NR) (7/15/90) (BT)
75+ MOMMESSIN Santenay Grand Clos Rousseau 1988 $23 (7/15/90) (BT)
87   BERNARD MOREY Santenay Grand Clos Rousseau 1987 $24 (10/15/90)
78   LA POUSSE D'OR Santenay Clos Tavannes 1986 $27 (6/15/89)
67   LA POUSSE D'OR Santenay Clos Tavannes 1985 $22 (3/15/88)
80   DOMAINE PRIEUR-BRUNET Santenay Maladière 1988 $20 (11/15/90)
83   DOMAINE ROUX PERE & FILS Santenay 1985 $21 (10/31/87)

SAVIGNY-LÈS-BEAUNE

85   PIERRE ANDRE Savigny-lès-Beaune Clos des Guettes 1985 $19.50 (7/31/88)
80+ BICHOT Savigny-lès-Beaune 1988 $17 (7/15/90) (BT)
81   BICHOT Savigny-lès-Beaune 1986 $10 (10/15/89)
87   PIERRE BITOUZET Savigny-lès-Beaune Lavières 1986 $14.50 (3/31/90)
67   PIERRE BITOUZET Savigny-lès-Beaune Lavières 1985 $19 (3/15/88)
80+ BOUCHARD PERE & FILS Savigny-lès-Beaune Les Lavières Domaines du Château de Beaune 1989 $29 (7/15/90) (BT)
83   BOUCHARD PERE & FILS Savigny-lès-Beaune Les Lavières Domaines du Château de Beaune 1988 $29 (4/30/91)
75+ BOUCHARD PERE & FILS Savigny-lès-Beaune Les Lavières Domaines du Château de Beaune 1988 $29 (7/15/90) (BT)
78   BOUCHARD PERE & FILS Savigny-lès-Beaune Les Lavières Domaines du Château de Beaune 1986 $25 (7/31/88)
83   VALENTIN BOUCHOTTE Savigny-lès-Beaune Hauts-Jarrons 1988 $31 (2/28/91)
86   DOMAINE CHANDON DE BRIAILLES Savigny-lès-Beaune Les Lavières 1988 $31 (2/28/91)
75+ MAURICE CHENU Savigny-lès-Beaune 1989 (NR) (7/15/90) (BT)
75+ MAURICE CHENU Savigny-lès-Beaune 1988 (NR) (7/15/90) (BT)
79   A.R. CHOPPIN Savigny-lès-Beaune Vergelesses 1987 $32 (2/28/90)
87   A.R. CHOPPIN Savigny-lès-Beaune Vergelesses 1985 $25 (10/31/87)
80   BRUNO CLAIR Savigny-lès-Beaune La Dominode 1985 $24 (3/15/88)
80+ JOSEPH DROUHIN Savigny-lès-Beaune 1989 $25 (7/15/90) (BT)
80+ JOSEPH DROUHIN Savigny-lès-Beaune 1988 $22 (7/15/90) (BT)
91   JOSEPH DROUHIN Savigny-lès-Beaune 1985 Rel: $21 Cur: $25 (11/15/87) SS
79   JOSEPH DROUHIN Savigny-lès-Beaune 1981 $15.75 (9/01/84)
80+ DUBREUIL-FONTAINE Savigny-lès-Beaune Les Vergelesses 1989 (NR) (7/15/90) (BT)
75+ DUBREUIL-FONTAINE Savigny-lès-Beaune Les Vergelesses 1988 (NR) (7/15/90) (BT)
88   DUBREUIL-FONTAINE Savigny-lès-Beaune Les Vergelesses 1985 $24 (1/31/89)
80   MAURICE ECARD Savigny-lès-Beaune Les Serpentières 1987 $17 (10/15/89)
89   MACHARD DE GRAMONT Savigny-lès-Beaune Les Guettes 1985 $25 (7/31/88)

FRANCE
BURGUNDY RED/CÔTE DE BEAUNE/SAVIGNY-LÈS-BEAUNE

83 LUPE-CHOLET Savigny-lès-Beaune Les Serpentières 1985 $17 (3/15/88)
80 MOMMESSIN Savigny-lès-Beaune 1985 $16.50 (7/31/88)
86 ALBERT MOROT Savigny-lès-Beaune Vergelesses La Bataillère 1988 $26 (3/31/91)
84 JEAN-MARC PAVELOT Savigny-lès-Beaune 1986 $17.50 (10/15/89)
89 JEAN-MARC PAVELOT Savigny-lès-Beaune Les Guettes 1985 $20 (2/15/88)
85+ TOLLOT-BEAUT Savigny-lès-Beaune Lavières 1988 $28 (7/15/90) (BT)
80 HENRI DE VILLAMONT Savigny-lès-Beaune Le Village 1988 $18 (3/31/91)

VOLNAY

84 BICHOT Volnay 1988 $25 (8/31/90)
80+ BICHOT Volnay 1988 $25 (7/15/90) (BT)
68 BICHOT Volnay 1983 $18 (9/15/86)
88 BICHOT Volnay Hospices de Beaune Cuvée Blondeau 1985 $53 (4/30/89)
92 BICHOT Volnay Hospices de Beaune Cuvée Blondeau 1982 Rel: $26 Cur: $38 (8/01/84) SS
84 BICHOT Volnay Premier Cru 1986 $25 (7/31/88)
77 BICHOT Volnay-Santenots 1986 $22 (10/31/39)
80 BITOUZET-PRIEUR Volnay Clos des Chênes 1987 $36 (12/31/90)
91 BITOUZET-PRIEUR Volnay Pitures 1985 $36 (7/31/88)
86 DOMAINE LUCIEN BOILLOT Volnay Les Angles 1985 $33 (7/15/88)
85 PIERRE BOILLOT Volnay-Santenots 1988 $37 (8/31/90)
86 PIERRE BOILLOT Volnay-Santenots 1987 $37 (6/15/90)
86 JEAN CLAUDE BOISSET Volnay Clos des Chênes 1985 $28 (4/15/88)
85+ BOUCHARD PERE & FILS Volnay Caillerets Ancienne Cuvée Carnot Domaines du Château de Beaune 1989 $50 (7/15/90) (BT)
87 BOUCHARD PERE & FILS Volnay Caillerets Ancienne Cuvée Carnot Domaines du Château de Beaune 1988 $47 (3/31/91)
83 BOUCHARD PERE & FILS Volnay Caillerets Ancienne Cuvée Carnot Domaines du Château de Beaune 1986 $34 (7/31/88)
87 BOUCHARD PERE & FILS Volnay Caillerets Ancienne Cuvée Carnot Domaines du Château de Beaune 1985 $44 (1/31/89)
88 BOUCHARD PERE & FILS Volnay Frémiets Clos de la Rougeotte Domaines du Château de Beaune 1985 $35 (1/31/89)
85+ BOUCHARD PERE & FILS Volnay Taillepieds Domaines du Château de Beaune 1989 $50 (7/15/90) (BT)
88 BOUCHARD PERE & FILS Volnay Taillepieds Domaines du Château de Beaune 1988 $50 (3/31/91)
90+ BOUCHARD PERE & FILS Volnay Taillepieds Domaines du Château de Beaune 1988 $50 (7/15/90) (BT)
90 DOMAINE JEAN-MARC BOULEY Volnay Caillerets 1985 $27 (10/15/88)
87 DOMAINE JEAN-MARC BOULEY Volnay Clos des Chênes 1985 $27 (10/15/88)
91 DOMAINE F. BUFFET Volnay Champans 1985 $35 (10/15/88)
91 DOMAINE F. BUFFET Volnay Clos de la Rougeotte 1985 $35 (10/15/88)
80+ JOSEPH DROUHIN Volnay 1989 $43 (7/15/90) (BT)
80+ JOSEPH DROUHIN Volnay 1988 $36 (7/15/90) (BT)
88 JOSEPH DROUHIN Volnay 1985 $29 (11/15/87)
85 JOSEPH DROUHIN Volnay Clos des Chênes 1988 $45 (2/15/91)
85 JOSEPH DROUHIN Volnay Clos des Chênes 1987 $30 (6/15/90)
80 JOSEPH DROUHIN Volnay Clos des Chênes 1986 $31 (4/30/89)
87 REMY GAUTHIER Volnay Santenots 1985 $27 (3/15/88)
88 CHATEAU DES HERBEUX Volnay Santenots 1988 $36 (11/30/90)
80+ JAFFELIN Volnay 1989 (NR) (7/15/90) (BT)
85+ JAFFELIN Volnay 1988 $31 (7/15/90) (BT)
86 JAFFELIN Volnay 1986 $27 (4/30/89)
88 JAFFELIN Volnay 1985 $30 (3/15/88)
92 JAFFELIN Volnay 1983 $17 (10/16/85)
90 DOMAINE MICHEL LAFARGE Volnay Clos des Chênes 1988 $65 (7/15/91)
90 DOMAINE MICHEL LAFARGE Volnay Clos du Château des Ducs 1988 $65 (7/15/91)
87 DOMAINE MICHEL LAFARGE Volnay Premier Cru 1988 $44 (7/15/91)
86 PIERRE LATOUR Volnay Caillerets 1953 (NA) (8/31/90) (TR)
90 PIERRE LATOUR Volnay Caillerets 1952 (NA) (8/31/90) (TR)
78 OLIVIER LEFLAIVE FRERES Volnay 1987 $27 (8/31/90)
85+ OLIVIER LEFLAIVE FRERES Volnay Clos de la Barre 1989 (NR) (7/15/90) (BT)
85+ OLIVIER LEFLAIVE FRERES Volnay Clos de la Barre 1988 $40 (7/15/90) (BT)
89 OLIVIER LEFLAIVE FRERES Volnay Clos de la Barre 1986 $28 (7/31/88)
91 LUPE-CHOLET Volnay Hospices de Beaune Cuvée Blondeau 1986 (NA) (7/31/88)
80 MARQUIS D'ANGERVILLE Volnay Clos des Ducs 1985 $35 (3/15/88)
87 CHATEAU DE MEURSAULT Volnay Clos des Chênes 1988 $47 (7/15/91)
89 MOILLARD Volnay Clos des Chênes 1985 $32 (7/15/88)
75 MOILLARD Volnay Clos des Chênes 1983 $15 (12/01/85)
85+ MOMMESSIN Volnay Le Clos des Chênes 1988 $38 (7/15/90) (BT)
91 MOMMESSIN Volnay Hospices de Beaune Cuvée General-Muteau 1985 $80 (3/15/88)
87 MONTHELIE-DOUHAIRET Volnay Champans 1985 $25 (7/15/88)
85 POTHIER-EMONIN Volnay 1986 $24 (4/30/89)
93 POTHIER-RIEUSSET Volnay 1985 $21 (2/15/88)
90 LA POUSSE D'OR Volnay Les Caillerets 1985 $35 (3/15/88)
82 LA POUSSE D'OR Volnay Les Caillerets Clos ces 60 Ouvrées 1987 $29 (6/15/90)
83 LA POUSSE D'OR Volnay Les Caillerets Clos ces 60 Ouvrées 1986 $41 (4/30/89)
86 LA POUSSE D'OR Volnay Les Caillerets Clos ces 60 Ouvrées 1985 $39 (3/15/88)
75 LA POUSSE D'OR Volnay Clos de la Bousse d'Or 1986 $46 (4/30/89)
85 DOMAINE PRIEUR-BRUNET Volnay-Santenots 1988 $35 (11/30/90)
92 ROSSIGNOL-FEVRIER Volnay 1988 $32 (3/31/91)
86 DOMAINE ROUX PERE & FILS Volnay en Champans 1988 $35 (3/31/90)
92 DOMAINE ROUX PERE & FILS Volnay en Champans 1985 $35 (3/15/87)
91 ARMAND ROUX Volnay Hospices de Beaune Général Muteau 1959 (NA) (8/31/90) (TR)

89 JACQUES THEVENOT-MACHAL Volnay-Santenots 1988 $36 (11/15/90)

OTHER CÔTE DE BEAUNE RED

86 BICHOT Monthélie Hospices de Beaune Cuvée Lebelin 1985 $52 (10/15/87)
86 JEAN CLAUDE BOISSET Côte de Beaune-Villages 1982 $5 (7/01/85) BB
88 BOUCHARD PERE & FILS Côte de Beaune-Villages 1982 $18.50 (5/16/84) SS
82 BOUCHARD PERE & FILS Côte de Beaune-Villages Clos des Topes Bizot 1983 $21.25 (9/15/86)
85+ DOMAINE JEAN CHARTRON Puligny-Montrachet Clos du Caillerets 1989 (NR) (7/15/90) (BT)
85+ DOMAINE JEAN CHARTRON Puligny-Montrachet Clos du Caillerets 1988 (NR) (7/15/90) (BT)
79 CHARTRON & TREBUCHET Côte de Beaune-Villages 1988 $16 (2/28/91)
84 F. CHAUVENET Côte de Beaune-Villages 1985 $16 (7/31/87)
81 F. CHAUVENET Puligny-Montrachet 1985 $16 (6/15/87)
85+ MAURICE CHENU Côte de Beaune-Villages 1989 (NR) (7/15/90) (BT)
80+ MAURICE CHENU Côte de Beaune-Villages 1988 (NR) (7/15/90) (BT)
87 J.-F. COCHE-DURY Auxey-Duresses 1987 $30 (2/28/90)
80 J.-F. COCHE-DURY Meursault 1987 $30 (2/28/90)
78 EDMOND CORNU Ladoix 1987 $18 (2/28/91)
78 JOSEPH DROUHIN Côte de Beaune-Villages 1986 $12.50 (6/15/89)
85 JOSEPH DROUHIN Côte de Beaune-Villages 1985 $13.50 (11/15/87)
82 JEAN-CHARLES FORNEROT St.-Aubin Les Perrières 1985 $15 (7/31/89)
88 JEAN GARAUDET Monthélie 1988 $23 (11/15/90)
80 JACQUES GERMAIN Chorey-lès-Beaune Château de Chorey-lès-Beaune 1986 $16 (7/31/89)
75 JACQUES GERMAIN Chorey-lès-Beaune Château de Chorey-lès-Beaune 1986 $16 (7/31/88)
84 MACHARD DE GRAMONT Chorey-lès-Beaune Les Beaumonts 1985 $22 (7/31/88)
75+ LOUIS JADOT Côte de Beaune-Villages 1989 (NR) (7/15/90) (BT)
75+ LOUIS JADOT Côte de Beaune-Villages 1988 $13.50 (7/15/90) (BT)
78 LOUIS JADOT Côte de Beaune-Villages 1986 $15 (6/15/89)
79 LOUIS JADOT Côte de Beaune-Villages 1985 $16.50 (4/15/88)
80+ JAFFELIN Monthélie 1989 (NR) (7/15/90) (BT)
80+ JAFFELIN Monthélie 1988 $21 (7/15/90) (BT)
79 JAFFELIN Monthélie 1986 $15 (6/15/89)
88 JAYER-GILLES Bourgogne Hautes Côtes de Beaune 1988 $26 (5/15/91)
85 LEROY Auxey-Duresses Les Clous 1988 $52 (5/15/91)
78 LUPE-CHOLET Bourgogne Clos de la Roche 1986 $10 (7/31/88)
69 LUPE-CHOLET Monthélie 1983 $9 (9/15/86)
73 M & G Côte de Beaune-Villages 1987 $20 (3/31/91)
79 DOMAINE RENE MANUEL Meursault Clos de La Baronne 1988 $18 (3/31/91)
77 PRINCE FLORENT DE MERODE Ladoix Les Chaillots 1987 $18 (11/15/90)
74 PRINCE FLORENT DE MERODE Ladoix Les Chaillots 1986 $17.50 (8/31/89)
83 MOILLARD Bourgogne Hautes Côtes de Beaune Les Alouettes 1988 $15 (7/15/91)
85 MOMMESSIN Côte de Beaune-Villages 1985 $13 (2/15/88)
81 MONTHELIE-DOUHAIRET Monthélie 1985 $16 (6/30/88)
63 DOMAINE JEAN MORETEAUX Côte de Beaune-Villages 1983 $8.50 (3/16/86)
76 DOMAINE DU MOULIN AUX MOINES Auxey-Duresses 1983 $10 (3/15/87)
83 DOMAINE PONNELLE Côte de Beaune Les Pierres Blanches 1987 $14 (3/31/91)
84 PRUNIER Auxey-Duresses Clos du Val 1987 $25 (11/15/89)
77 CHATEAU DE PULIGNY-MONTRACHET Monthélie 1988 $16 (11/15/90)
88 GASTON & PIERRE RAVAUT Ladoix Les Corvées 1985 $26 (7/31/88)
88 TOLLOT-BEAUT Chorey-lès-Beaune 1988 $25 (12/31/90)
83 TOLLOT-BEAUT Chorey-Côte-de-Beaune 1985 $18 (4/15/88)

CÔTE DE NUITS/CHAMBOLLE-MUSIGNY

91 ARLAUD Bonnes Mares 1983 $30 (12/01/85)
88 GHISLAINE BARTHOD Chambolle-Musigny 1988 $50 (3/15/91)
83 GHISLAINE BARTHOD Chambolle-Musigny Les Beaux-Bruns 1988 $45 (2/28/91)
87 GHISLAINE BARTHOD Chambolle-Musigny Les Crâs 1988 $45 (2/28/91)
81 GHISLAINE BARTHOD Chambolle-Musigny Les Véroilles 1988 $45 (2/28/91)
82 G. BARTHOD-NOELLAT Chambolle-Musigny Charmes 1984 $27 (10/31/87)
88 G. BARTHOD-NOELLAT Chambolle-Musigny Les Crâs 1985 $37 (7/31/88)
89 DOMAINE BERTHEAU Bonnes Mares 1987 $55 (6/15/90)
80 DOMAINE BERTHEAU Chambolle-Musigny 1987 $25 (6/15/90)
84 DOMAINE BERTHEAU Chambolle-Musigny Les Amoureuses 1987 $50 (6/15/90)
81 DOMAINE BERTHEAU Chambolle-Musigny Les Charmes 1987 $35 (6/15/90)
85+ BOUCHARD PERE & FILS Chambolle-Musigny 1989 (NR) (7/15/90) (BT)
73 BOUCHARD PERE & FILS Chambolle-Musigny 1986 $29 (7/31/88)
91 PIERRE BOUREE FILS Bonnes Mares 1985 $85 (5/31/88)
82 PIERRE BOUREE FILS Chambolle-Musigny 1987 $44 (6/15/90)
82 PIERRE BOUREE FILS Chambolle-Musigny Charmes 1987 $56 (6/15/90)
87 GUY CASTAGNIER Bonnes Mares 1988 $67 (7/15/91)
91 GUY CASTAGNIER Bonnes Mares 1986 $50 (4/15/89)
84 GUY CASTAGNIER Chambolle-Musigny 1986 $31 (7/15/89)
91 DOMAINE CECI Chambolle-Musigny Aux Echanges 1988 $33 (7/15/91)
72 DOMAINE CECI Chambolle-Musigny Les Echanges 1987 $20 (3/31/90)
83 F. CHAUVENET Chambolle-Musigny Les Charmes 1982 $33 (4/30/87)
91 DOMAINE DES CHEZEAUX Chambolle-Musigny Les Charmes 1985 $75 (6/15/88)
78 MICHEL CLERGET Chambolle-Musigny 1986 $23 (8/31/89)
73 MICHEL CLERGET Chambolle-Musigny 1985 $38 (5/15/88)
76 MICHEL CLERGET Chambolle-Musigny Les Charmes 1986 $33 (8/31/89)
83 MICHEL CLERGET Chambolle-Musigny Les Charmes 1985 $56 (5/15/88)
85+ JOSEPH DROUHIN Chambolle-Musigny 1988 $38 (7/15/90) (BT)
88 JOSEPH DROUHIN Chambolle-Musigny 1986 $27 (7/31/88)
93 JOSEPH DROUHIN Chambolle-Musigny 1985 $33 (11/15/87)
87 JOSEPH DROUHIN Chambolle-Musigny Les Amoureuses 1988 $76 (12/31/90)
65 JOSEPH DROUHIN Chambolle-Musigny Les Amoureuses 1955 (NA) (8/31/90) (TR)
93 DROUHIN-LAROZE Bonnes Mares 1988 $81 (12/31/90)
89 DROUHIN-LAROZE Bonnes Mares 1987 $38 (3/31/90)
75+ DOMAINE DUJAC Bonnes Mares 1989 (NR) (7/15/90) (BT)
90+ DOMAINE DUJAC Bonnes Mares 1988 $86 (7/15/90) (BT)
91 DOMAINE DUJAC Bonnes Mares 1987 $62 (3/31/90)
85 DOMAINE DUJAC Bonnes Mares 1986 $60 (4/15/89)
82 DOMAINE DUJAC Bonnes Mares 1986 $60 (6/15/90)
93 DOMAINE DUJAC Chambolle-Musigny Les Gruenchers 1987 $47 (3/31/90)
76 DOMAINE DUJAC Chambolle-Musigny Les Gruenchers 1986 $48 (7/31/88)
74 DOMAINE DUJAC Chambolle-Musigny Les Gruenchers 1985 $43 (3/31/88)
89 FAIVELEY Chambolle-Musigny 1985 $45 (5/15/88)
88 FAIVELEY Chambolle-Musigny 1981 $24 (5/01/86)
92 FAIVELEY Musigny Le Musigny 1949 (NA) (8/31/90) (TR)

85 JEAN GRIVOT Chambolle-Musigny La Combe d'Orvaux 1987 $47 (6/15/90)
90 DOMAINE ROBERT GROFFIER Bonnes Mares 1988 $80 (11/15/90)
89 DOMAINE ROBERT GROFFIER Bonnes Mares 1987 $67 (7/31/89)
93 DOMAINE ROBERT GROFFIER Chambolle-Musigny Amoureuses 1988 $66 (11/15/90)
86 DOMAINE ROBERT GROFFIER Chambolle-Musigny Amoureuses 1987 $51 (8/31/89)
84 DOMAINE ROBERT GROFFIER Chambolle-Musigny Amoureuses 1986 $50 (2/28/89)
89 DOMAINE ROBERT GROFFIER Chambolle-Musigny Les Sentiers 1988 $45 (11/15/90)
87 DOMAINE ROBERT GROFFIER Chambolle-Musigny Les Sentiers 1987 $37 (8/31/89)
90 DOMAINE ROBERT GROFFIER Chambolle-Musigny Les Sentiers 1986 $36 (2/28/89)
73 HAEGELEN-JAYER Chambolle-Musigny 1988 $39 (5/15/91)
83 CHATEAU DES HERBEUX Musigny 1988 $75 (12/31/90)
88 LOUIS JADOT Bonnes Mares 1988 $65 (3/15/91)
91 LOUIS JADOT Bonnes Mares 1987 $52 (6/15/90)
89 LOUIS JADOT Bonnes Mares 1986 $57 (4/15/89)
83 LOUIS JADOT Bonnes Mares 1986 $57 (7/31/88)
95 LOUIS JADOT Bonnes Mares 1985 Rel: $48 Cur: $78 (3/15/88)
78 LOUIS JADOT Chambolle-Musigny 1986 $30 (7/15/89)
91 LOUIS JADOT Chambolle-Musigny 1985 $33 (5/15/88)
85+ LOUIS JADOT Musigny Le Musigny 1989 (NR) (7/15/90) (BT)
85+ LOUIS JADOT Musigny Le Musigny 1988 Rel: $82 Cur: $92 (7/15/90) (BT)
77 LOUIS JADOT Musigny Le Musigny 1986 $70 (4/15/89)
88 LOUIS JADOT Musigny Le Musigny 1985 $74 (3/31/88)
88 JAFFELIN Chambolle-Musigny 1988 $32 (12/31/90)
81 JAFFELIN Chambolle-Musigny 1983 $21 (3/16/86)
86 LABOURE-ROI Chambolle-Musigny 1988 $35 (2/28/91)
88 OLIVIER LEFLAIVE FRERES Bonnes Mares 1987 $50 (9/30/90)
92 GEORGES LIGNIER Bonnes Mares 1987 $75 (3/31/90)
77 GEORGES LIGNIER Chambolle-Musigny 1987 $32 (6/15/90)
90+ LUPE-CHOLET Bonnes Mares 1988 (NR) (7/15/90) (BT)
81 LUPE-CHOLET Chambolle-Musigny 1986 $20 (7/31/88)
85 CLAUDE MARCHAND Chambolle-Musigny 1986 $32 (7/15/89)
92 MOILLARD Bonnes Mares 1984 $35 (5/31/87)
86 MOILLARD Bonnes Mares Domaine Thomas-Moillard 1986 $45 (11/15/88)
89 MOILLARD Chambolle-Musigny 1984 $15 (11/30/86)
92 MOILLARD Musigny 1984 $38 (5/31/87)
90+ MOMMESSIN Chambolle-Musigny Les Charmes 1988 $42 (7/15/90) (BT)
86 GEORGES MUGNERET Chambolle-Musigny Les Feusselottes 1988 $54 (11/15/90)
92 GEORGES MUGNERET Chambolle-Musigny Les Feusselottes 1987 $41 (10/15/89)
90 GEORGES MUGNERET Chambolle-Musigny Les Feusselottes 1986 $45 (11/15/88)
89 GEORGES MUGNERET Chambolle-Musigny Les Feusselottes 1986 $45 (7/31/88)
86 JACQUES-FREDERIC MUGNIER Chambolle-Musigny 1988 $48 (5/15/91)
86 JACQUES-FREDERIC MUGNIER Chambolle-Musigny Les Amoureuses 1988 $80 (5/15/91)
89 JACQUES-FREDERIC MUGNIER Chambolle-Musigny Les Fuées 1988 $60 (5/15/91)
75 NICOLAS Bonnes Mares 1959 (NA) (8/31/90) (TR)
92 DOMAINE PONSOT Chambolle-Musigny Les Charmes 1988 $58 (4/30/91)
94 DOMAINE PONSOT Chambolle-Musigny Les Charmes 1985 $75 (6/15/88)
84 REMOISSENET Bonnes Mares 1988 $80 (12/31/90)
82 REMOISSENET Bonnes Mares 1985 $88 (3/15/88)
87 DOMAINE DANIEL RION Chambolle-Musigny Les Beaux Bruns 1988 $37 (1/31/91)
90+ DOMAINE DANIEL RION Chambolle-Musigny Les Beaux Bruns 1988 $37 (7/15/90) (BT)
86 DOMAINE DANIEL RION Chambolle-Musigny Les Beaux Bruns 1986 $39 (4/15/89)
90 DOMAINE DANIEL RION Chambolle-Musigny Les Beaux Bruns 1986 $39 (7/31/88)
88 DOMAINE DANIEL RION Chambolle-Musigny Les Beaux Bruns 1985 $33 (3/31/88)
89 DOMAINE G. ROUMIER Chambolle-Musigny 1988 $30 (7/15/91)
87 DOMAINE G. ROUMIER Chambolle-Musigny 1985 $26 (2/15/88)
82 HERVE ROUMIER Chambolle-Musigny 1986 $29 (8/31/89)
89 HERVE ROUMIER Chambolle-Musigny Les Amoureuses 1985 $65 (3/31/88)
84 DOMAINE B. SERVEAU Chambolle-Musigny Les Amoureuses 1988 $66 (2/28/91)
91 DOMAINE B. SERVEAU Chambolle-Musigny Les Amoureuses 1985 $75 (6/15/88)
86 DOMAINE B. SERVEAU Chambolle-Musigny Les Chabiots 1988 $39 (2/28/91)
78 DOMAINE B. SERVEAU Chambolle-Musigny Les Chabiots 1987 $30 (6/15/90)
90 DOMAINE B. SERVEAU Chambolle-Musigny Les Chabiots 1985 $39 (6/15/88)
91 DOMAINE B. SERVEAU Chambolle-Musigny Les Chabiots 1984 $23 (4/15/87)
79 DOMAINE B. SERVEAU Chambolle-Musigny Les Sentiers 1988 $39 (2/28/91)
83 HENRI DE VILLAMONT Chambolle-Musigny 1988 $39 (2/15/91)
89 COMTE DE VOGUE Bonnes Mares 1988 $93 (3/31/91)
87 COMTE DE VOGUE Bonnes Mares 1987 $69 (7/15/90)
88 COMTE DE VOGUE Bonnes Mares 1979 Cur: $48 (11/16/84) (HS)
90 COMTE DE VOGUE Bonnes Mares 1976 Cur: $68 (11/16/84) (HS)
79 COMTE DE VOGUE Bonnes Mares 1972 Cur: $125 (11/16/84) (HS)
88 COMTE DE VOGUE Bonnes Mares 1971 Cur: $164 (11/16/84) (HS)
83 COMTE DE VOGUE Bonnes Mares 1959 Cur: $179 (11/16/84) (HS)
87 COMTE DE VOGUE Bonnes Mares Avery Bottling 1959 Cur: $179 (11/16/84) (HS)
91 COMTE DE VOGUE Bonnes Mares 1955 Cur: $285 (11/16/84) (HS)
90 COMTE DE VOGUE Bonnes Mares 1949 Cur: $600/1.5L (11/16/84) (HS)
82 COMTE DE VOGUE Bonnes Mares Grivolet 1934 Cur: $400 (11/16/84) (HS)
89 COMTE DE VOGUE Chambolle-Musigny Les Amoureuses 1988 $93 (2/28/91)
87 COMTE DE VOGUE Chambolle-Musigny Les Amoureuses 1987 $74 (3/31/90)
86 COMTE DE VOGUE Chambolle-Musigny Les Amoureuses 1971 Cur: $85 (11/16/84) (HS)
78 COMTE DE VOGUE Chambolle-Musigny Les Amoureuses 1970 Cur: $55 (11/16/84) (HS)
90 COMTE DE VOGUE Musigny Cuvée Vieilles Vignes 1988 $134 (2/28/91)
93 COMTE DE VOGUE Musigny Cuvée Vieilles Vignes 1988 $134 (12/31/90)
87 COMTE DE VOGUE Musigny Cuvée Vieilles Vignes 1987 Rel: $100 Cur: $105 (3/31/90)
92 COMTE DE VOGUE Musigny Cuvée Vieilles Vignes 1985 Rel: $125 Cur: $140 (3/31/88)
87 COMTE DE VOGUE Musigny Vieilles Vignes 1979 Cur: $114 (11/16/84) (HS)
86 COMTE DE VOGUE Musigny Vieilles Vignes 1976 Cur: $119 (11/16/84) (HS)
80 COMTE DE VOGUE Musigny Vieilles Vignes 1972 Cur: $122 (11/16/84) (HS)
90 COMTE DE VOGUE Musigny Vieilles Vignes 1971 Cur: $235 (11/16/84) (HS)
65 COMTE DE VOGUE Musigny Vieilles Vignes 1969 Cur: $220 (11/16/84) (HS)
92 COMTE DE VOGUE Musigny Vieilles Vignes 1966 Cur: $210 (11/16/84) (HS)
90 COMTE DE VOGUE Musigny Vieilles Vignes 1962 Cur: $550/1.5L (11/16/84) (HS)
93 COMTE DE VOGUE Musigny Vieilles Vignes 1961 Cur: $350 (11/16/84) (HS)
89 COMTE DE VOGUE Musigny Vieilles Vignes 1959 Cur: $440 (11/16/84) (HS)
95 COMTE DE VOGUE Musigny Vieilles Vignes 1957 Cur: $255 (8/31/90) (TR)
80 COMTE DE VOGUE Musigny Vieilles Vignes 1957 Cur: $255 (11/16/84) (HS)
81 COMTE DE VOGUE Musigny 1953 Cur: $200 (11/16/84) (HS)
85 COMTE DE VOGUE Musigny 1952 Cur: $200 (11/16/84) (HS)
98 COMTE DE VOGUE Musigny 1949 Cur: $610 (11/16/84) (HS)
96 COMTE DE VOGUE Musigny 1945 Cur: $1,600/1.5L (11/16/84) (HS)
93 COMTE DE VOGUE Musigny 1937 Cur: $660 (11/16/84) (HS)
95 COMTE DE VOGUE Musigny 1934 Cur: $610 (11/16/84) (HS)
78 VOLPATO-COSTAILLE Chambolle-Musigny 1988 $34 (2/28/91)

FIXIN

71 CLEMANCEY FRERES Fixin Les-Hervelets 1985 $21 (4/30/88)
82 GELIN & MOLIN Fixin Clos du Châpitre Domaine Marion 1985 $25 (5/01/88)
76 PIERRE GELIN Fixin Clos Napolèon 1985 $25 (4/30/88)
90 JEHAN JOLIET Fixin Clos de la Perrière 1985 $25 (7/31/88)
79 MOILLARD Fixin Clos d'Entre Deux Velles 1985 $16 (5/31/87)
78 MOILLARD Fixin Clos d'Entre Deux Velles 1984 $11 (11/30/86)
85 MOILLARD Fixin Clos de la Perrière 1986 $18 (2/28/89)
78 MOILLARD Fixin Clos de la Perrière 1983 $12 (10/16/85)
75+ MOMMESSIN Fixin 1988 $19 (7/15/90) (BT)
84 MONGEARD-MUGNERET Fixin 1986 $19 (10/15/89)
94 PIERRE PONNELLE Fixin Hervelets 1959 (NA) (8/31/90) (TR)

GEVREY-CHAMBERTIN

89 DOMAINE PIERRE AMIOT Gevrey-Chambertin Les Combottes 1988 $64 (3/15/91)
88 DOMAINE PIERRE AMIOT Gevrey-Chambertin Les Combottes 1987 $42 (12/15/89)
87 DOMAINE BACHELET Charmes-Chambertin Vieilles Vignes 1986 $43 (7/15/89)
83 DOMAINE BACHELET Gevrey-Chambertin Les Corbeaux Vieilles Vignes 1986 $30 (7/15/89)
88 DOMAINE BACHELET Gevrey-Chambertin Vieilles Vignes 1986 $24 (7/15/89)
89 BARTON & GUESTIER Gevrey-Chambertin 1985 $21 (4/30/88)
91 BEAULT-FORGEOT Mazis-Chambertin Hospice de Beaune Cuvée Madeleine-Collignon 1980 $56 (7/01/84)
58 BICHOT Gevrey-Chambertin 1983 $13 (2/01/86)
85 DOMAINE LUCIEN BOILLOT Gevrey-Chambertin Les Cherbaudes 1987 $25 (5/31/90)
74 JEAN CLAUDE BOISSET Gevrey-Chambertin 1982 $9 (6/01/85)
84 BOUCHARD AINE Chambertin Clos de Bèze 1959 (NA) (8/31/90) (TR)
90+ BOUCHARD PERE & FILS Chambertin 1989 (NR) (7/15/90) (BT)
81 BOUCHARD PERE & FILS Chambertin 1986 $78 (7/31/88)
89 BOUCHARD PERE & FILS Chambertin Clos de Bèze 1988 $82 (4/30/91)
80 BOUCHARD PERE & FILS Gevrey-Chambertin 1982 $18 (6/16/84)
90 PIERRE BOUREE FILS Chambertin 1987 $100 (5/31/90)
92 PIERRE BOUREE FILS Chambertin 1985 $113 (5/31/88)
89 PIERRE BOUREE FILS Charmes-Chambertin 1988 $75 (3/31/91)
87 PIERRE BOUREE FILS Charmes-Chambertin 1987 $66 (5/31/90)
88 PIERRE BOUREE FILS Charmes-Chambertin 1985 $68 (5/31/88)
80 PIERRE BOUREE FILS Gevrey-Chambertin Les Cazetiers 1987 $66 (5/31/90)
91 PIERRE BOUREE FILS Gevrey-Chambertin Les Cazetiers 1985 $67 (5/31/88)
85 PIERRE BOUREE FILS Gevrey-Chambertin Clos de la Justice 1985 $51 (5/31/88)
86 PIERRE BOUREE FILS Gevrey-Chambertin Clos St.-Jacques 1987 $56 (5/31/90)
98 PIERRE BOUREE FILS Latricières-Chambertin 1959 (NA) (8/31/90) (TR)
88 ALAIN BURGUET Gevrey-Chambertin Vieilles Vignes 1988 $45 (12/31/90)
84 ALAIN BURGUET Gevrey-Chambertin Vieilles Vignes 1986 $33 (7/15/89)
93 GUY CASTAGNIER Latricières-Chambertin 1988 $63 (7/15/91)
91 GUY CASTAGNIER Mazis-Chambertin 1988 $63 (7/15/91)
64 CHARLOPIN-PARIZOT Gevrey-Chambertin 1985 $22 (11/30/87)
79 CHARLOPIN-PARIZOT Gevrey-Chambertin Cuvée Vieilles Vignes 1988 $31 (12/31/90)
90+ F. CHAUVENET Charmes-Chambertin 1988 $78 (7/15/90) (BT)
90 F. CHAUVENET Charmes-Chambertin 1986 $65 (7/31/88)
97 F. CHAUVENET Charmes-Chambertin 1985 $72 (7/31/87)
88 F. CHAUVENET Charmes-Chambertin 1983 $24 (9/15/86)
88 F. CHAUVENET Gevrey-Chambertin Charreux 1985 $33 (10/15/87)
85 F. CHAUVENET Gevrey-Chambertin Clos St.-Jacques 1986 $35 (7/31/88)
89 F. CHAUVENET Gevrey-Chambertin Estournel St.-Jacques 1986 $35 (7/31/88)
70+ F. CHAUVENET Gevrey-Chambertin Lavaux St.-Jacques 1988 $48 (7/15/90) (BT)
86 F. CHAUVENET Gevrey-Chambertin Lavaux St.-Jacques 1986 $35 (7/31/88)
70+ F. CHAUVENET Gevrey-Chambertin Petite Chapelle 1988 $40 (7/15/90) (BT)
72 F. CHAUVENET Mazis-Chambertin 1983 $27 (6/30/87)
90 DOMAINE DES CHEZEAUX Griotte-Chambertin 1988 $110 (5/15/91)
91 DOMAINE DES CHEZEAUX Griotte-Chambertin 1985 $100 (6/15/88)
90 DOMAINE DU CLOS FRANTIN Chambertin 1986 $63 (2/28/89)
88 DOMAINE DU CLOS FRANTIN Chambertin 1986 $63 (7/31/88)
80+ DOMAINE DU CLOS FRANTIN Gevrey-Chambertin 1989 (NR) (7/15/90) (BT)
87 DOMAINE DU CLOS FRANTIN Gevrey-Chambertin 1988 $37 (7/15/90)
85 DOMAINE DU CLOS FRANTIN Gevrey-Chambertin 1988 $37 (7/15/90)
82 DOMAINE DU CLOS FRANTIN Gevrey-Chambertin 1987 $20 (3/31/90)
87 DOMAINE CLAUDINE DESCHAMPS Gevrey-Chambertin Bel-Air 1985 $28 (3/31/88)
94 JOSEPH DROUHIN Chambertin 1988 $112 (2/15/91)
90 JOSEPH DROUHIN Chambertin 1986 $80 (2/28/89)
95 JOSEPH DROUHIN Chambertin 1985 Rel: $75 Cur: $107 (11/15/87)
90+ JOSEPH DROUHIN Charmes-Chambertin 1989 $85 (7/15/90) (BT)
93 JOSEPH DROUHIN Charmes-Chambertin 1988 $65 (11/15/90)
91 JOSEPH DROUHIN Charmes-Chambertin 1986 Rel: $56 Cur: $60 (2/28/89) CS
91 JOSEPH DROUHIN Charmes-Chambertin 1986 Rel: $56 Cur: $60 (7/31/88)
89 JOSEPH DROUHIN Charmes-Chambertin 1985 $60 (11/15/87)
75+ JOSEPH DROUHIN Gevrey-Chambertin 1988 $41 (7/15/90) (BT)
83 JOSEPH DROUHIN Gevrey-Chambertin 1986 $27 (2/28/89)
91 JOSEPH DROUHIN Gevrey-Chambertin 1985 $33 (11/15/87)
95+ JOSEPH DROUHIN Griotte-Chambertin 1989 $95 (7/15/90) (BT)
91 JOSEPH DROUHIN Griotte-Chambertin 1988 $81 (11/15/90)
90+ JOSEPH DROUHIN Griotte-Chambertin 1988 $81 (7/15/90) (BT)
92 JOSEPH DROUHIN Griotte-Chambertin 1986 $81 (7/31/88)
95 JOSEPH DROUHIN Griotte-Chambertin 1985 $68 (11/15/87)
87 JOSEPH DROUHIN Latricières-Chambertin 1988 $72 (2/15/91)
92 DROUHIN-LAROZE Chambertin Clos de Bèze 1988 $88 (12/31/90)
90 DROUHIN-LAROZE Chambertin Clos de Bèze 1987 $40 (3/31/90)
92 DROUHIN-LAROZE Chambertin Clos de Bèze 1985 Rel: $70 Cur: $110 (10/15/88)
88 DROUHIN-LAROZE Chapelle-Chambertin 1988 $68 (12/31/90)
88 DROUHIN-LAROZE Gevrey-Chambertin Clos Prieur 1988 $44 (12/31/90)
80 DROUHIN-LAROZE Gevrey-Chambertin Lavaux-St.-Jacques 1988 $44 (12/31/90)
91 DROUHIN-LAROZE Latricières-Chambertin 1988 $68 (12/31/90)
88 DROUHIN-LAROZE Latricières-Chambertin 1987 $36 (3/31/90)
90 DROUHIN-LAROZE Mazis-Chambertin 1985 $47 (10/15/88)
90+ DOMAINE DUJAC Charmes-Chambertin 1989 (NR) (7/15/90) (BT)
85 DOMAINE DUJAC Charmes-Chambertin 1988 $66 (3/31/91)
90+ DOMAINE DUJAC Charmes-Chambertin 1988 $66 (7/15/90) (BT)
85 DOMAINE DUJAC Charmes-Chambertin 1986 $50 (7/31/88)

FRANCE
BURGUNDY RED/CÔTE DE NUITS/GEVREY-CHAMBERTIN

95 DOMAINE DUJAC Charmes-Chambertin 1985 $100 (3/15/88)
86 DOMAINE DUJAC Gevrey-Chambertin Aux Combottes 1988 $54 (3/31/91)
80 DOMAINE DUJAC Gevrey-Chambertin Aux Combottes 1987 $42 (5/31/90)
87 DOMAINE MICHEL ESMONIN Gevrey-Chambertin Clos-St.-Jacques 1987 $44 (3/31/90)
84 DOMAINE MICHEL ESMONIN Gevrey-Chambertin Estournelles St.-Jacques 1988 $40 (3/31/91)
95+ FAIVELEY Chambertin Clos de Bèze 1988 $114 (7/15/90) (BT)
83 FAIVELEY Chambertin Clos de Bèze 1987 $70 (3/31/90)
88 FAIVELEY Chambertin Clos de Bèze 1986 $66 (7/15/89)
96 FAIVELEY Chambertin Clos de Bèze 1985 $105 (3/15/88)
90 FAIVELEY Gevrey-Chambertin 1985 $38 (4/15/88)
89 FAIVELEY Gevrey-Chambertin Les Cazetiers 1988 $57 (3/31/91)
92 FAIVELEY Gevrey-Chambertin Les Cazetiers 1985 $53 (3/31/88)
88 FAIVELEY Latricières-Chambertin 1985 $77 (3/15/88)
92 FAIVELEY Mazis-Chambertin 1985 $81 (3/15/88)
94 FORTNUM & MASON Charmes-Chambertin (Bottled in England) 1947 (NA) (8/31/90) (TR)
84 PIERRE GELIN Chambertin Clos de Bèze 1985 $77 (3/15/88)
93 PIERRE GELIN Gevrey-Chambertin 1985 $25 (4/15/88)
80 PIERRE GELIN Gevrey-Chambertin 1982 $18.75 (3/16/85)
90 PIERRE GELIN Mazis-Chambertin 1985 $25 (3/15/88)
85 DOMAINE GEOFFROY Gevrey-Chambertin Les Champeaux 1986 $36 (7/15/89)
93 DOMAINE GEOFFROY Gevrey-Chambertin Clos Prieur 1987 $29 (3/31/90)
89 DOMAINE GEOFFROY Gevrey-Chambertin Clos Prieur 1986 $29 (7/15/89)
79 DOMAINE GEOFFROY Gevrey-Chambertin Les Escorvées 1986 $26 (7/15/89)
92 DOMAINE GEOFFROY Mazis-Chambertin 1987 $48 (3/31/90)
88 DOMAINE ROBERT GROFFIER Chambertin Clos de Bèze 1987 $45 (7/31/89)
85 DOMAINE ROBERT GROFFIER Gevrey-Chambertin 1986 $27 (2/28/89)
87 CHATEAU DES HERBEUX Chambertin 1988 $75 (12/31/90)
90 BERNARD HERESZTYN Gevrey-Chambertin Les Goulots 1988 $44 (7/15/91)
83 STANISLAS HERESZTYN Gevrey-Chambertin 1987 $25 (3/31/90)
82 STANISLAS HERESZTYN Gevrey-Chambertin Les Champonnets 1988 $37 (12/31/90)
86 R. HERESZTYN-BAILLY Gevrey-Chambertin 1986 $20 (7/15/89)
82 R. HERESZTYN-BAILLY Gevrey-Chambertin Les Goulots 1986 $28 (10/15/89)
90+ LOUIS JADOT Chambertin Clos de Bèze 1989 (NR) (7/15/90) (BT)
96 LOUIS JADOT Chambertin Clos de Bèze 1988 $97 (3/15/91)
90+ LOUIS JADOT Chambertin Clos de Bèze 1988 $97 (7/15/90) (BT)
89 LOUIS JADOT Chambertin Clos de Bèze 1987 $65 (7/15/90)
90 LOUIS JADOT Chambertin Clos de Bèze 1986 $63 (7/15/89)
89 LOUIS JADOT Chambertin Clos de Bèze 1985 Rel: $66 Cur: $80 (3/15/88)
85+ LOUIS JADOT Chapelle-Chambertin 1989 (NR) (7/15/90) (BT)
93 LOUIS JADOT Chapelle-Chambertin 1988 $75 (3/15/91)
85+ LOUIS JADOT Chapelle-Chambertin 1988 $75 (7/15/90) (BT)
90 LOUIS JADOT Chapelle-Chambertin 1985 $54 (3/15/88)
77 LOUIS JADOT Gevrey-Chambertin 1986 $25 (7/15/89)
85+ LOUIS JADOT Gevrey-Chambertin Clos St.-Jacques 1989 (NR) (7/15/90) (BT)
88 LOUIS JADOT Gevrey-Chambertin Clos St.-Jacques 1988 $52 (3/15/91)
85+ LOUIS JADOT Gevrey-Chambertin Clos St.-Jacques 1988 $52 (7/15/90) (BT)
84 LOUIS JADOT Gevrey-Chambertin Clos St.-Jacques 1986 $44 (7/15/89)
89 LOUIS JADOT Gevrey-Chambertin Clos St.-Jacques 1986 $44 (7/31/88)
94 LOUIS JADOT Gevrey-Chambertin Clos St.-Jacques 1985 $45 (3/31/88)
91 LOUIS JADOT Gevrey-Chambertin Estournelles St.-Jacques 1988 $50 (3/15/91)
80+ LOUIS JADOT Gevrey-Chambertin Estournelles St.-Jacques 1988 $50 (7/15/90) (BT)
87 LOUIS JADOT Gevrey-Chambertin Estournelles St.-Jacques 1986 $40 (7/15/89)
86 LOUIS JADOT Gevrey-Chambertin Estournelles St.-Jacques 1985 $41 (3/31/88)
94 LOUIS JADOT Griotte-Chambertin 1988 $75 (3/15/91)
80 LOUIS JADOT Griotte-Chambertin 1987 $50 (7/15/90)
92 LOUIS JADOT Mazis-Chambertin 1987 $50 (5/31/90)
91 LOUIS JADOT Ruchottes-Chambertin 1988 $75 (3/15/91)
89 JAFFELIN Chambertin Le Chambertin 1986 $65 (12/31/88)
93 JAFFELIN Chambertin Le Chambertin 1983 $48 (4/16/86)
90+ JAFFELIN Charmes-Chambertin 1988 $68 (7/15/90) (BT)
77 JAFFELIN Charmes-Chambertin 1986 $45 (12/31/88)
85 JAFFELIN Gevrey-Chambertin 1986 $49 (2/28/89)
77 JAFFELIN Gevrey-Chambertin 1983 $17 (10/01/85)
81 LABOURE-ROI Gevrey-Chambertin 1988 $35 (12/31/90)
95 LOUIS LATOUR Chambertin Cuvée Héritiers Latour 1985 Rel: $76 Cur: $87 (3/15/88)
85 LOUIS LATOUR Charmes-Chambertin 1985 $50 (3/15/88)
77 LOUIS LATOUR Gevrey-Chambertin 1985 $36 (10/15/88)
96 LEBEGUE-BICHOT Chambertin Clos de Bèze 1945 (NA) (8/31/90) (TR)
90 PHILIPPE LECLERC Gevrey-Chambertin 1984 $26 (7/15/87)
82 PHILIPPE LECLERC Gevrey-Chambertin Les Cazetiers 1988 $80 (7/15/91)
85 PHILIPPE LECLERC Gevrey-Chambertin Les Cazetiers 1987 $63 (5/31/90)
89 PHILIPPE LECLERC Gevrey-Chambertin Les Cazetiers 1985 $64 (10/15/88)
83 PHILIPPE LECLERC Gevrey-Chambertin Les Cazetiers 1984 $38 (8/31/87)
68 PHILIPPE LECLERC Gevrey-Chambertin Les Cazetiers 1982 Rel: $21 Cur: $45 (11/16/85)
79 PHILIPPE LECLERC Gevrey-Chambertin Les Champeaux 1985 $55 (10/31/88)
76 PHILIPPE LECLERC Gevrey-Chambertin La Combe-aux-Moines 1987 $68 (5/31/90)
92 PHILIPPE LECLERC Gevrey-Chambertin La Combe-aux-Moines 1985 $70 (10/15/88)
82 PHILIPPE LECLERC Gevrey-Chambertin La Combe-aux-Moines 1984 $42 (8/31/87)
82 PHILIPPE LECLERC Gevrey-Chambertin La Combe-aux-Moines 1988 $80 (7/15/91)
74 PHILIPPE LECLERC Gevrey-Chambertin Les Platières 1988 $45 (7/15/91)
81 PHILIPPE LECLERC Gevrey-Chambertin Les Platières 1987 $35 (5/31/90)
90 PHILIPPE LECLERC Gevrey-Chambertin Les Platières 1985 Rel: $38 Cur: $56 (10/15/88)
82 DOMAINE RENE LECLERC Gevrey-Chambertin Combes-aux-Moines 1985 $55 (10/31/88)

Key to Symbols

The scores reported here are the results of blind tastings conducted by our panel of senior editors. Wines that carry the initials below are results of individual tastings.

THE WINE SPECTATOR 100-POINT SCALE *95-100*—Classic, a great wine; *90-94*—Outstanding, superior character and style; *80-89*—Good to very good, a wine with special qualities; *70-79*—Average, drinkable wine that may have minor flaws; *60-69*—Below average, drinkable but not recommended; *50-59*—Poor, undrinkable, not recommended. "+"—With a score indicates a range; used primarily with barrel tastings to indicate a preliminary score.

SPECIAL DESIGNATIONS SS—Spectator Selection, CS—Cellar Selection, BB—Best Buy.

TASTER'S INITIALS (JG)—Jim Gordon, (HS)—Harvey Steiman, (JL)—James Laube, (JS)—James Suckling, (TM)—Thomas Matthews, (TR)—Terry Robards, (BT)—Barrel Tasting (these wines were tasted blind from barrel samples), (CA-date)—*California's Great Cabernets* by James Laube, (CH-date)—*California's Great Chardonnays* by James Laube, (VP-date)—*Vintage Port* by James Suckling.

DATE TASTED Dates in parentheses represent the issue in which the rating was published.

88 OLIVIER LEFLAIVE FRERES Charmes-Chambertin 1986 $50 (7/31/88)
75+ OLIVIER LEFLAIVE FRERES Gevrey-Chambertin 1989 (NR) (7/15/90) (BT)
80+ OLIVIER LEFLAIVE FRERES Gevrey-Chambertin 1988 $35 (7/15/90) (BT)
84 GEORGES LIGNIER Gevrey-Chambertin 1987 $29 (5/31/90)
87 GEORGES LIGNIER Gevrey-Chambertin Les Combottes 1987 $34 (5/31/90)
59 LUPE-CHOLET Gevrey-Chambertin Lavaux St.-Jacques 1983 $27 (11/30/86)
73 M & G Gevrey-Chambertin 1987 $40 (3/31/91)
81 HENRI MAGNIEN Gevrey-Chambertin 1985 $25 (10/15/87)
68 HENRI MAGNIEN Gevrey-Chambertin 1983 $13 (2/01/86)
89 HENRI MAGNIEN Gevrey-Chambertin 1982 $12 (7/01/85)
88 HENRI MAGNIEN Gevrey-Chambertin Les Cazetiers 1985 $35 (10/15/87)
72 HENRI MAGNIEN Gevrey-Chambertin Les Cazetiers 1983 $17.50 (12/16/85)
80 HENRI MAGNIEN Gevrey-Chambertin Les Cazetiers 1982 $16 (5/01/84)
80 HENRI MAGNIEN Gevrey-Chambertin Premier Cru 1985 $29 (10/15/87)
92 CLAUDE MARCHAND Charmes-Chambertin 1986 $50 (7/15/89)
81 CLAUDE MARCHAND Gevrey-Chambertin 1987 $22 (7/15/90)
89 CLAUDE MARCHAND Gevrey-Chambertin 1986 $28 (7/15/89)
76 DOMAINE JEAN-PHILIPPE MARCHAND Charmes-Chambertin 1987 $60 (12/31/90)
82 DOMAINE JEAN-PHILIPPE MARCHAND Gevrey-Chambertin Les Combottes 1987 $30 (7/15/90)
76 DOMAINE MARCHAND-GRILLOT Gevrey-Chambertin Petite Chapelle 1986 $30 (10/15/89)
86 DOMAINE MAUME Charmes-Chambertin 1988 $60 (7/15/91)
77 DOMAINE MAUME Gevrey-Chambertin 1987 $25 (3/31/90)
80 DOMAINE MAUME Gevrey-Chambertin en Pallud 1987 $36 (3/31/90)
74 DOMAINE MAUME Mazis-Chambertin 1987 $56 (3/31/90)
76 MOILLARD Chambertin 1984 $42 (5/31/87)
80 MOILLARD Chambertin Clos de Bèze 1984 $42 (5/31/87)
93 MOILLARD Chambertin Clos de Bèze 1983 Rel: $37 Cur: $60 (9/16/85) CS
94 MOILLARD Charmes-Chambertin 1985 $55 (5/31/88)
66 MOILLARD Gevrey-Chambertin 1987 $20 (3/31/90)
83 MOMMESSIN Charmes-Chambertin 1985 $45 (2/15/88)
90 MOMMESSIN Gevrey-Chambertin 1985 $25 (2/15/88)
80+ MOMMESSIN Gevrey-Chambertin Estournelles St.-Jacques 1989 (NR) (7/15/90) (BT)
87 CHARLES MORTET Chambertin 1987 $69 (3/31/90)
91 CHARLES MORTET Chambertin 1986 $62 (2/28/89)
90 CHARLES MORTET Chambertin 1985 $64 (6/15/88)
89 CHARLES MORTET Gevrey-Chambertin 1988 $35 (2/15/91)
86 CHARLES MORTET Gevrey-Chambertin 1987 $28 (3/31/90)
87 CHARLES MORTET Gevrey-Chambertin 1986 $24 (2/28/89)
87 CHARLES MORTET Gevrey-Chambertin Les Champeaux 1988 $46 (3/15/91)
81 CHARLES MORTET Gevrey-Chambertin Les Champeaux 1987 $36 (3/31/90)
86 CHARLES MORTET Gevrey-Chambertin Les Champeaux 1986 $33 (2/28/89)
91 CHARLES MORTET Gevrey-Chambertin Clos Prieur 1988 $41 (2/15/91)
83 CHARLES MORTET Gevrey-Chambertin Clos Prieur 1987 $32 (3/31/90)
84 CHARLES MORTET Gevrey-Chambertin Clos Prieur 1986 $30 (2/28/89)
92 CHARLES MORTET Gevrey-Chambertin Clos Prieur 1985 $29 (7/31/88)
92 GEORGES MUGNERET Ruchottes-Chambertin 1988 $80 (11/15/90)
93 GEORGES MUGNERET Ruchottes-Chambertin 1987 $56 (10/15/89)
91 GEORGES MUGNERET Ruchottes-Chambertin 1986 $55 (11/15/88)
90 GEORGES MUGNERET Ruchottes-Chambertin 1986 $55 (7/31/88)
92 GEORGES MUGNERET Ruchottes-Chambertin 1985 $63 (2/15/88)
83 GEORGES MUGNERET Ruchottes-Chambertin 1984 $34 (3/15/87)
92 GEORGES MUGNERET Ruchottes-Chambertin 1982 $26 (9/01/85) SS
80 PHILIPPE NADDEF Gevrey-Chambertin 1988 $25 (7/15/91)
86 PHILIPPE NADDEF Gevrey-Chambertin 1987 $19 (3/31/90)
94 PHILIPPE NADDEF Gevrey-Chambertin 1985 $25 (4/15/88)
88 PHILIPPE NADDEF Gevrey-Chambertin Les Cazetiers 1987 $35 (3/31/90)
90 PHILIPPE NADDEF Gevrey-Chambertin Les Champeaux 1987 $28 (3/31/90)
80 PHILIPPE NADDEF Gevrey-Chambertin Les Champeaux 1985 $29 (3/31/88)
69 PHILIPPE NADDEF Mazis-Chambertin 1988 $60 (7/15/91)
89 PHILIPPE NADDEF Mazis-Chambertin 1987 $50 (3/31/90)
89 DOMAINE PONSOT Griotte-Chambertin 1988 $150 (5/15/91)
91 DOMAINE PONSOT Latricières-Chambertin 1988 $150 (5/15/91)
91 REMOISSENET Chambertin 1985 $100 (3/15/88)
86 ANTONIN RODET Gevrey-Chambertin 1986 $25 (7/15/90)
92 ANTONIN RODET Gevrey-Chambertin Lavaux St.-Jacques 1982 $35 (6/30/87)
69 PHILIPPE ROSSIGNOL Gevrey-Chambertin 1987 $23 (5/31/90)
93 ARMAND ROUSSEAU Chambertin 1988 $201 (5/15/91)
97 ARMAND ROUSSEAU Chambertin 1985 Rel: $100 Cur: $120 (3/15/88)
95 ARMAND ROUSSEAU Chambertin Clos de Bèze 1988 $188 (5/15/91)
86 ARMAND ROUSSEAU Charmes-Chambertin 1985 $63 (10/15/88)
92 ARMAND ROUSSEAU Gevrey-Chambertin Clos St.-Jacques 1985 $80 (10/15/88)
85 ARMAND ROUSSEAU Mazy-Chambertin 1985 $61 (10/15/88)
68 DOMAINE ROY PERE & FILS Gevrey-Chambertin Clos Prieur 1988 $35 (12/31/90)
72 DOMAINE ROY PERE & FILS Gevrey-Chambertin Vieilles Vignes 1988 $30 (12/31/90)
92 SERAFIN PERE & FILS Gevrey-Chambertin 1988 $35 (3/31/91)
91 SERAFIN PERE & FILS Gevrey-Chambertin Les Cazetiers 1988 $53 (5/15/91)
92 SERAFIN PERE & FILS Gevrey-Chambertin Le Fonteny 1988 $50 (5/15/91)
91 SERAFIN PERE & FILS Gevrey-Chambertin Vieilles Vignes 1987 $35 (3/31/90)
66 LEONARD DE ST.-AUBIN Gevrey-Chambertin 1985 $25 (11/30/87)
94 DOMAINE TORTOCHOT Chambertin 1985 $90 (12/31/88)
92 LOUIS TRAPET Chambertin 1988 $111 (7/15/91)
91 LOUIS TRAPET Chambertin 1987 $75 (5/31/90)
88 LOUIS TRAPET Chambertin 1985 Rel: $80 Cur: $101 (3/15/88)
89 LOUIS TRAPET Chambertin Cuvée Vieilles Vignes 1988 $133 (7/15/91)
89 LOUIS TRAPET Chapelle-Chambertin 1988 $84 (7/15/91)
84 LOUIS TRAPET Chapelle-Chambertin 1985 $64 (3/15/88)
79 LOUIS TRAPET Chapelle-Chambertin Réserve Jean Trapet 1987 $62 (3/15/91)
81 LOUIS TRAPET Gevrey-Chambertin 1988 $40 (7/15/91)
74 LOUIS TRAPET Gevrey-Chambertin 1987 $30 (7/15/90)
79 LOUIS TRAPET Gevrey-Chambertin 1985 $40 (5/31/88)
84 LOUIS TRAPET Latricières-Chambertin 1988 $84 (7/15/91)
88 LOUIS TRAPET Latricières-Chambertin 1987 $62 (5/31/90)
85 G. VACHET-ROUSSEAU Gevrey-Chambertin 1988 $30 (12/31/90)
64 G. VACHET-ROUSSEAU Gevrey-Chambertin 1983 $16 (5/01/86)
87 CHARLES VIENOT Gevrey-Chambertin 1985 $32 (4/30/88)

MOREY-ST.-DENIS

86 DOMAINE PIERRE AMIOT Clos de la Roche 1988 $75 (3/15/91)

86 DOMAINE PIERRE AMIOT Clos de la Roche 1987 $49 (12/15/89)
93 DOMAINE PIERRE AMIOT Clos de la Roche 1982 $27.50 (6/16/85) SS
88 DOMAINE PIERRE AMIOT Morey-St.-Denis Aux Charmes 1982 $18 (7/01/85)
80 DOMAINE PIERRE AMIOT Morey-St.-Denis Les Ruchots 1988 $57 (2/28/91)
91 PIERRE BOUREE FILS Clos de la Roche 1988 $85 (3/31/91)
85 PIERRE BOUREE FILS Clos de la Roche 1987 $86 (6/15/90)
74 PIERRE BOUREE FILS Morey-St.-Denis 1987 $35 (5/15/90)
91 GUY CASTAGNIER Clos de la Roche 1988 $63 (7/15/91)
75 GUY CASTAGNIER Clos de la Roche 1986 $43 (7/15/89)
89 GUY CASTAGNIER Clos St.-Denis 1988 $63 (7/15/91)
84 GUY CASTAGNIER Clos St.-Denis 1986 $43 (7/15/89)
66 GUY CASTAGNIER Morey-St.-Denis 1986 $28 (7/15/89)
85+ F. CHAUVENET Clos St.-Denis 1988 $48 (7/15/90) (BT)
90 F. CHAUVENET Clos St.-Denis 1986 $50 (2/28/89)
88 F. CHAUVENET Clos St.-Denis 1986 $50 (7/31/88)
94 F. CHAUVENET Clos St.-Denis 1985 $67 (7/31/87)
73 BRUNO CLAIR Morey-St.-Denis 1985 $20 (5/15/88)
90+ JOSEPH DROUHIN Clos de la Roche 1989 $81 (7/15/90) (BT)
93 JOSEPH DROUHIN Clos de la Roche 1988 $73 (2/15/91)
85+ JOSEPH DROUHIN Clos de la Roche 1988 $73 (7/15/90) (BT)
83 JOSEPH DROUHIN Clos de la Roche 1986 $53 (7/15/89)
85 JOSEPH DROUHIN Clos de la Roche 1986 $53 (7/31/88)
97 JOSEPH DROUHIN Clos de la Roche 1985 $60 (11/15/87)
92 JOSEPH DROUHIN Morey-St.-Denis Monts-Luisants 1988 $38 (2/28/91)
85+ DOMAINE DUJAC Clos de la Roche Clos la Roche 1989 (NR) (7/15/90) (BT)
90 DOMAINE DUJAC Clos de la Roche Clos la Roche 1988 $75 (3/31/91)
85+ DOMAINE DUJAC Clos de la Roche Clos la Roche 1988 $75 (7/15/90) (BT)
86 DOMAINE DUJAC Clos de la Roche Clos la Roche 1987 $53 (3/31/90)
79 DOMAINE DUJAC Clos de la Roche Clos la Roche 1986 $56 (7/31/88)
95 DOMAINE DUJAC Clos de la Roche Clos la Roche 1985 $85 (3/15/88)
85 DOMAINE DUJAC Clos St.-Denis 1987 $58 (3/31/90)
89 DOMAINE DUJAC Clos St.-Denis 1986 $56 (7/31/88)
91 DOMAINE DUJAC Clos St.-Denis 1985 $89 (3/15/88)
82 FAIVELEY Clos de la Roche 1986 $55 (7/15/89)
78 FAIVELEY Clos de la Roche 1985 $88 (3/15/88)
85+ JAFFELIN Morey-St.-Denis Les Ruchots 1989 (NR) (7/15/90) (BT)
80+ JAFFELIN Morey-St.-Denis Les Ruchots 1988 $31 (7/15/90) (BT)
90+ OLIVIER LEFLAIVE FRERES Clos de la Roche 1988 $60 (7/15/90) (BT)
90+ OLIVIER LEFLAIVE FRERES Morey-St.-Denis 1989 (NR) (7/15/90) (BT)
89 GEORGES LIGNIER Clos St.-Denis 1987 $49 (5/15/90)
91 GEORGES LIGNIER Clos St.-Denis 1985 $54 (3/15/88)
90 GEORGES LIGNIER Clos de la Roche 1987 $55 (3/31/90)
85 GEORGES LIGNIER Clos de la Roche 1985 $63 (3/15/88)
82 GEORGES LIGNIER Morey-St.-Denis 1987 $25 (5/15/90)
82 GEORGES LIGNIER Morey-St.-Denis 1985 $23 (3/15/88)
88 GEORGES LIGNIER Morey-St.-Denis Clos des Ormes 1987 $32 (5/15/90)
86 GEORGES LIGNIER Morey-St.-Denis Clos des Ormes 1985 $28 (3/15/88)
80 CLAUDE MARCHAND Morey-St.-Denis 1987 $30 (9/30/90)
69 CLAUDE MARCHAND Morey-St.-Denis Clos des Ormes 1987 $30 (9/30/90)
85 CLAUDE MARCHAND Morey-St.-Denis Clos des Ormes 1986 $33 (7/15/89)
91 MOILLARD Morey-St.-Denis Monts Luisants 1988 $30 (12/15/90)
87 MOILLARD Morey-St.-Denis Monts Luisants 1985 $21.50 (5/31/87)
80+ MOMMESSIN Clos de Tart 1989 (NR) (7/15/90) (BT)
95+ MOMMESSIN Clos de Tart 1988 $112 (7/15/90) (BT)
91 MOMMESSIN Clos de Tart 1985 $95 (2/15/88)
78 MOMMESSIN Clos de Tart 1950 Cur: $125 (8/31/90) (TR)
73 DOMAINE PONSOT Clos de la Roche 1984 Rel: $29 Cur: $48 (2/15/88)
88 DOMAINE PONSOT Clos de la Roche Cuvée Vieilles Vignes 1988 $185 (5/15/91)
90 DOMAINE PONSOT Clos de la Roche Cuvée Vieilles Vignes 1985 $200 (6/15/88)
89 DOMAINE PONSOT Clos de la Roche Cuvée William 1988 $150 (5/15/91)
85 DOMAINE PONSOT Clos St.-Denis Cuvée Vieilles Vignes 1988 $165 (7/15/91)
85 DOMAINE PONSOT Morey-St.-Denis Monts-Luisants 1988 $40 (4/30/91)
91 REMOISSENET Clos de la Roche 1985 $72 (3/15/88)
83 DOMAINE G. ROUMIER Morey-St.-Denis Clos de la Bussière 1988 $30 (7/15/91)
92 DOMAINE G. ROUMIER Morey-St.-Denis Clos de la Bussière 1985 $27 (4/30/88)
91 ARMAND ROUSSEAU Clos de la Roche 1988 $75 (5/15/91)
91 DOMAINE FABIEN & LOUIS SAIER Clos des Lambrays 1988 $75 (3/31/91)
78 DOMAINE FABIEN & LOUIS SAIER Clos des Lambrays Domaine des Lambrays 1985 $55 (2/15/88)
88 DOMAINE B. SERVEAU Morey-St.-Denis Les Sorbets 1988 $35 (2/28/91)
83 DOMAINE B. SERVEAU Morey-St.-Denis Les Sorbets 1987 $30 (5/15/90)
88 DOMAINE B. SERVEAU Morey-St.-Denis Les Sorbets 1985 $39 (6/15/88)
87 DOMAINE B. SERVEAU Morey-St.-Denis Les Sorbets 1984 $22.50 (3/15/87)

NUITS-ST.-GEORGES

93 BERTRAND AMBROISE Nuits-St.-Georges En Rue de Chaux 1988 $40 (5/15/91)
87 DOMAINE DE L'ARLOT Nuits-St.-Georges Clos de L'Arlot 1988 $43 (3/31/91)
85 DOMAINE DE L'ARLOT Nuits-St.-Georges Clos des Forets St.-Georges 1988 $53 (3/31/91)
83 DOMAINE DE L'ARLOT Nuits-St.-Georges Clos des Forets St.-Georges 1987 $43 (3/31/90)
83 BEAULT-FORGEOT Nuits-St.-Georges Les Plateaux 1981 $17 (7/01/84)
91 JULES BELIN Nuits-St.-Georges Les St.-Georges 1943 (NA) (8/31/90) (TR)
85 DOMAINE BERTAGNA Nuits-St.-Georges Aux Murgers 1985 $41 (2/28/89)
77 BICHOT Nuits-St.-Georges Les Boudots Hospices de Nuits Cuvée Mesny de Boissea 1986 $36 (3/31/90)
75 BICHOT Nuits-St.-Georges Les Maladières Hospices de Nuits 1986 $33 (2/28/89)
80 BICHOT Nuits-St.-Georges Les Maladières Hospices de Nuits Cuvée Grangier 1986 $33 (3/31/90)
85 BICHOT Nuits-St.-Georges Les Vignerondes Hospices de Nuits Cuvée Richard de Bligny 1986 $40 (2/28/89)
88 DOMAINE LUCIEN BOILLOT Nuits-St.-Georges Les Pruliers 1987 $25 (7/15/90)
79 JEAN CLAUDE BOISSET Nuits-St.-Georges 1985 $25 (4/30/88)
68 BOUCHARD PERE & FILS Nuits-St.-Georges 1983 $21.25 (9/15/86)
85+ BOUCHARD PERE & FILS Nuits-St.-Georges Clos St.-Marc 1989 $57 (7/15/90) (BT)
75+ BOUCHARD PERE & FILS Nuits-St.-Georges Clos St.-Marc 1988 $52 (7/15/90) (BT)
87 BOUCHARD PERE & FILS Nuits-St.-Georges Clos-St.-Marc 1985 $53 (2/28/89)
74 BOUCHARD PERE & FILS Nuits-St.-Georges Clos-St.-Marc 1983 $33 (9/15/86)
87 BOUCHARD PERE & FILS Nuits-St.-Georges Les Cailles 1959 (NA) (8/31/90) (TR)
93 PIERRE BOUREE FILS Nuits-St.-Georges Les Vaucrains 1985 $68 (5/31/88)
77 CATHIARD-MOLINIER Nuits-St.-Georges Les Meurgers 1986 $22.50 (2/28/89)
83 JEANNE-MARIE DE CHAMPS Nuits-St.-Georges Les Didiers Hospices de Nuits Cuvée Cabet 1988 $49 (9/30/90)
89 JEANNE-MARIE DE CHAMPS Nuits-St.-Georges Les Didiers Hospices de Nuits Cuvée Jacques Duret 1988 $49 (9/30/90)
96 JEANNE-MARIE DE CHAMPS Nuits-St.-Georges Les Didiers Hospices de Nuits Cuvée Cabet 1985 $53 (3/15/88)
90 JEANNE-MARIE DE CHAMPS Nuits-St.-Georges Les Terres Blanches 1988 $39 (7/15/91)
80+ F. CHAUVENET Nuits-St.-Georges Les Chaignots 1988 $38 (7/15/90) (BT)
87 F. CHAUVENET Nuits-St.-Georges Les Chaignots 1986 $40 (7/31/88)
80 F. CHAUVENET Nuits-St.-Georges Les Perrières 1985 $48 (7/31/87)
84 F. CHAUVENET Nuits-St.-Georges Les Plateaux 1985 $34 (7/31/87)
78 F. CHAUVENET Nuits-St.-Georges Les Plateaux 1982 $16 (1/01/85)
88 JEAN CHAUVENET Nuits-St.-Georges Les Bousselots 1985 $49 (5/31/88)
84 CHEVALIER DE BEAUBASSIN Nuits-St.-Georges 1985 $31 (4/30/88)
87 DENIS CHEVILLON Nuits-St.-Georges Les Chaignots 1987 $33 (7/15/90)
84 DENIS CHEVILLON Nuits-St.-Georges Les Pruliers 1987 $38 (7/15/90)
74 ROBERT CHEVILLON Nuits-St.-Georges 1986 $37 (12/15/89)
85 ROBERT CHEVILLON Nuits-St.-Georges 1985 $40 (4/30/88)
91 A. CHOPIN Nuits-St.-Georges Aux Murgers 1988 $28 (7/15/90)
85 A. CHOPIN Nuits-St.-Georges Aux Murgers 1987 $26 (12/15/89)
78 A. CHOPIN Nuits-St.-Georges Aux Murgers 1986 $29 (10/15/88)
80+ DOMAINE DU CLOS FRANTIN Nuits-St.-Georges 1989 (NR) (7/15/90) (BT)
80+ DOMAINE DU CLOS FRANTIN Nuits-St.-Georges 1988 $37 (7/15/90) (BT)
82 DOMAINE DU CLOS FRANTIN Nuits-St.-Georges 1986 $20 (11/15/88)
83 DOMAINE DU CLOS FRANTIN Nuits-St.-Georges 1983 $18 (2/01/86)
85+ JOSEPH DROUHIN Nuits-St.-Georges 1989 $43 (7/15/90) (BT)
86 JOSEPH DROUHIN Nuits-St.-Georges 1986 $25 (4/30/89)
92 JOSEPH DROUHIN Nuits-St.-Georges 1985 $29 (11/15/87)
85 JOSEPH DROUHIN Nuits-St.-Georges Les Roncières 1986 $38 (4/30/89)
93 JOSEPH DROUHIN Nuits-St.-Georges Les Roncières 1985 $38 (11/15/87)
90 FAIVELEY Nuits-St.-Georges 1985 $40 (3/15/88)
70+ FAIVELEY Nuits-St.-Georges Clos de la Maréchale 1989 (NR) (7/15/90) (BT)
76 FAIVELEY Nuits-St.-Georges Clos de la Maréchale 1988 $50 (3/15/91)
85 FAIVELEY Nuits-St.-Georges Clos de la Maréchale 1985 $51 (3/15/88)
84 FAIVELEY Nuits-St.-Georges Clos de la Maréchale 1982 $20 (5/01/86)
85 FAIVELEY Nuits-St.-Georges Les Damodes 1988 $52 (3/31/91)
90+ FAIVELEY Nuits-St.-Georges Les Porets St.-Georges 1988 $54 (7/15/90) (BT)
76 FAIVELEY Nuits-St.-Georges Les Porets St.-Georges 1985 $47 (3/15/88)
84 DOMAINE HENRI GOUGES Nuits-St.-Georges 1986 $30 (7/31/88)
90 DOMAINE HENRI GOUGES Nuits-St.-Georges Les Chaignots 1986 $40 (7/31/88)
80+ DOMAINE HENRI GOUGES Nuits-St.-Georges Clos des Porrets-St.-Georges 1988 $50 (7/15/90) (BT)
80+ DOMAINE HENRI GOUGES Nuits-St.-Georges Clos des Porrets-St.-Georges 1989 (NR) (7/15/90) (BT)
75+ DOMAINE HENRI GOUGES Nuits-St.-Georges Les Pruliers 1989 (NR) (7/15/90) (BT)
85+ DOMAINE HENRI GOUGES Nuits-St.-Georges Les St.-Georges 1989 (NR) (7/15/90) (BT)
75+ DOMAINE HENRI GOUGES Nuits-St.-Georges Les St.-Georges 1988 $54 (7/15/90) (BT)
68 DOMAINE HENRI GOUGES Nuits-St.-Georges Les St.-Georges 1985 $45 (2/15/88)
86 MACHARD DE GRAMONT Nuits-St.-Georges Les Allots 1985 $35 (5/31/88)
84 MACHARD DE GRAMONT Nuits-St.-Georges Les Hauts Poirets 1985 $41 (6/15/88)
90 MACHARD DE GRAMONT Nuits-St.-Georges Les Hauts Pruliers 1985 $36 (2/15/88)
89 MACHARD DE GRAMONT Nuits-St.-Georges En la Perrière Noblot 1985 $41 (5/31/88)
78 MACHARD DE GRAMONT Nuits-St.-Georges Les Vallerots 1985 $47 (5/31/88)
87 JEAN GRIVOT Nuits-St.-Georges Les Boudots 1988 $54 (4/30/91)
81 JEAN GRIVOT Nuits-St.-Georges Les Charmois 1987 $47 (7/15/90)
89 JEAN GRIVOT Nuits-St.-Georges Les Pruliers 1988 $53 (4/30/91)
71 JEAN GRIVOT Nuits-St.-Georges Les Pruliers 1987 $55 (7/15/90)
88 JEAN GRIVOT Nuits-St.-Georges Les Roncières 1987 $55 (7/15/90)
81 JEAN GROS Nuits-St.-Georges 1988 $42 (2/28/91)
85 JEAN GROS Nuits-St.-Georges 1985 $36 (7/31/88)
89 HAEGELEN-JAYER Nuits-St.-Georges Les Damodes 1988 $39 (5/15/91)
80+ LOUIS JADOT Nuits-St.-Georges 1989 (NR) (7/15/90) (BT)
75+ LOUIS JADOT Nuits-St.-Georges 1988 $27 (7/15/90) (BT)
91 LOUIS JADOT Nuits-St.-Georges 1985 $30 (4/15/88)
80+ LOUIS JADOT Nuits-St.-Georges Clos des Corvées 1989 (NR) (7/15/90) (BT)
89 LOUIS JADOT Nuits-St.-Georges Clos des Corvées 1988 $49 (2/28/91)
85+ LOUIS JADOT Nuits-St.-Georges Clos des Corvées 1988 $49 (7/15/90) (BT)
84 LOUIS JADOT Nuits-St.-Georges Clos des Corvées 1987 $35 (4/30/90)
83 LOUIS JADOT Nuits-St.-Georges Clos des Corvées 1986 $37 (4/30/89)
96 LOUIS JADOT Nuits-St.-Georges Clos des Corvées 1985 $44 (3/15/88)
88 LOUIS JADOT Nuits-St.-Georges Les Boudots 1988 $49 (2/28/91)
85 LOUIS JADOT Nuits-St.-Georges Les Boudots 1986 $38 (4/30/89)
75 LOUIS JADOT Nuits-St.-Georges Les Boudots 1985 $42 (3/15/88)
80 JAFFELIN Nuits-St.-Georges 1986 $28 (2/28/89)
72 JAFFELIN Nuits-St.-Georges 1983 $18.50 (9/15/86)
88 J. JAYER Nuits-St.-Georges Les Lavières 1985 $38 (3/15/88)
87 LAROCHE Nuits-St.-Georges 1988 $28 (11/15/90)
75 DOMAINE LEQUIN-ROUSSOT Nuits-St.-Georges 1985 $39 (4/15/88)
85 LEROY Nuits-St.-Georges Aux Allots 1988 $84 (4/30/91)
93 LEROY Nuits-St.-Georges Aux Boudots 1988 $230 (4/30/91)
82 LEROY Nuits-St.-Georges Aux Lavières 1988 $84 (4/30/91)
85+ LUPE-CHOLET Nuits-St.-Georges Château Gris 1989 (NR) (7/15/90) (BT)
90+ LUPE-CHOLET Nuits-St.-Georges Château Gris 1988 $50 (7/15/90) (BT)
84 LUPE-CHOLET Nuits-St.-Georges Château Gris 1987 $38 (3/31/90)
86 LUPE-CHOLET Nuits-St.-Georges Château Gris 1986 $33 (7/31/88)
88 LUPE-CHOLET Nuits-St.-Georges Château Gris 1985 $39 (2/15/88)
77 LUPE-CHOLET Nuits-St.-Georges Château Gris 1983 $24 (6/16/86)
91 LUPE-CHOLET Nuits-St.-Georges Les Vignes Rondex Hospice de Nuits 1986 (NA) (7/31/88)
82 BERTRAND MACHARD DE GRAMONT Nuits-St.-Georges Les Allots 1987 $30 (7/15/90)
88 BERTRAND MACHARD DE GRAMONT Nuits-St.-Georges Les Hauts Pruliers 1988 $37 (7/15/91)
85 BERTRAND MACHARD DE GRAMONT Nuits-St.-Georges Les Hauts Pruliers 1987 $32 (4/30/90)
77 BERTRAND MACHARD DE GRAMONT Nuits-St.-Georges Les Hauts Pruliers 1986 $22 (12/15/89)
91 DOMAINE MEO-CAMUZET Nuits-St.-Georges 1988 $50 (11/30/90)
86 DOMAINE MEO-CAMUZET Nuits-St.-Georges 1987 $42 (12/15/89)
90 DOMAINE MEO-CAMUZET Nuits-St.-Georges 1986 $32 (11/15/88)
92 DOMAINE MEO-CAMUZET Nuits-St.-Georges Aux Boudots 1988 $80 (11/30/90)
88 DOMAINE MEO-CAMUZET Nuits-St.-Georges Aux Boudots 1987 $56 (12/15/89)

FRANCE
BURGUNDY RED/CÔTE DE NUITS/NUITS-ST.-GEORGES

92   DOMAINE MEO-CAMUZET Nuits-St.-Georges Aux Boudots 1986 $46 (11/15/88)
91   DOMAINE MEO-CAMUZET Nuits-St.-Georges Aux Murgers 1988 $80 (11/30/90)
93   DOMAINE MEO-CAMUZET Nuits-St.-Georges Aux Murgers 1987 $56 (12/15/89)
90   DOMAINE MEO-CAMUZET Nuits-St.-Georges Aux Murgers 1986 $48 (11/15/88)
91   DOMAINE MEO-CAMUZET Nuits-St.-Georges Aux Murgers 1986 $48 (7/31/88)
90   DOMAINE MEO-CAMUZET Nuits-St.-Georges Aux Murgers 1985 Rel: $50 Cur: $73 (4/15/88)
91   ALAIN MICHELOT Nuits-St.-Georges 1988 $39 (7/15/91)
86   ALAIN MICHELOT Nuits-St.-Georges 1982 $17 (5/01/84)
83   ALAIN MICHELOT Nuits-St.-Georges Les Cailles 1988 $54 (5/15/91)
90   ALAIN MICHELOT Nuits-St.-Georges Les Cailles 1982 $19.50 (7/16/85)
90   ALAIN MICHELOT Nuits-St.-Georges Les Chaignots 1988 $56 (5/15/91)
81   ALAIN MICHELOT Nuits-St.-Georges Les Champs-Perdrix 1986 $30 (12/15/89)
83   ALAIN MICHELOT Nuits-St.-Georges Les Porets-St.-Georges 1988 $56 (5/15/91)
89   ALAIN MICHELOT Nuits-St.-Georges Les Richemone 1988 $54 (5/15/91)
87   ALAIN MICHELOT Nuits-St.-Georges Les Vaucrains 1988 $56 (5/15/91)
88   ALAIN MICHELOT Nuits-St.-Georges Les Vaucrains 1986 $30 (12/15/89)
89   MOILLARD Nuits-St.-Georges Clos de Thorey 1985 $38 (5/31/87)
84   MOILLARD Nuits-St.-Georges Clos de Thorey 1984 $24.50 (5/31/87)
84   MOILLARD Nuits-St.-Georges Clos de Thorey 1983 $19 (9/16/85)
88   MOILLARD Nuits-St.-Georges Clos de Thorey Domaine Thomas-Moillard 1987 $27 (12/15/89)
78   MOILLARD Nuits-St.-Georges Clos de Thorey Domaine Thomas-Moillard 1986 $28 (11/15/88)
89   MOILLARD Nuits-St.-Georges Les Thorey 1988 $50 (12/31/90)
80+   MOMMESSIN Nuits-St.-Georges Les Vaucrains 1989 (NR) (7/15/90) (BT)
90   CHARLES MONCAUT Nuits-St.-Georges Les Argillières 1984 $32 (6/15/87)
81   MONGEARD-MUGNERET Nuits-St.-Georges Les Boudots 1987 $32 (4/30/90)
78   MONGEARD-MUGNERET Nuits-St.-Georges Les Boudots 1984 $23 (2/15/88)
80   GEORGES MUGNERET Nuits-St.-Georges Les Chaignots 1988 $47 (11/15/90)
87   GEORGES MUGNERET Nuits-St.-Georges Les Chaignots 1987 $41 (10/15/89)
89   GEORGES MUGNERET Nuits-St.-Georges Les Chaignots 1986 $40 (11/15/88)
89   GEORGES MUGNERET Nuits-St.-Georges Les Chaignots 1984 $26 (3/15/87)
76   GERARD MUGNERET Nuits-St.-Georges Les Boudots 1988 $48 (2/28/91)
88   GERARD MUGNERET Nuits-St.-Georges Les Boudots 1987 $40 (7/15/90)
87   REMOISSENET Nuits-St.-Georges Aux Argilats 1985 $34 (10/15/88)
84   GILLES REMORIQUET Nuits-St.-Georges 1982 $18.50 (7/16/85)
81   HENRI & GILLES REMORIQUET Nuits-St.-Georges Rue de Chaux 1985 $21.50 (7/31/88)
85   DOMAINE DANIEL RION Nuits-St.-Georges 1986 $31 (4/30/89)
85   DOMAINE DANIEL RION Nuits-St.-Georges 1985 $28 (3/15/88)
91   DOMAINE DANIEL RION Nuits-St.-Georges Clos des Argillières 1988 $54 (1/31/91)
80+   DOMAINE DANIEL RION Nuits-St.-Georges Clos des Argillières 1988 $54 (7/15/90) (BT)
92   DOMAINE DANIEL RION Nuits-St.-Georges Clos des Argillières 1987 $30 (4/30/90)
90   DOMAINE DANIEL RION Nuits-St.-Georges Clos des Argillières 1986 $47 (4/30/89)
89   DOMAINE DANIEL RION Nuits-St.-Georges Clos des Argillières 1986 $47 (7/31/88)
94   DOMAINE DANIEL RION Nuits-St.-Georges Clos des Argillières 1985 Rel: $44 Cur: $75 (3/15/88)
85+   DOMAINE DANIEL RION Nuits-St.-Georges Grandes Vignes 1989 (NR) (7/15/90) (BT)
85+   DOMAINE DANIEL RION Nuits-St.-Georges Grandes Vignes 1988 (NR) (7/15/90) (BT)
91   DOMAINE DANIEL RION Nuits-St.-Georges Hauts Pruliers 1988 $54 (1/31/91)
90+   DOMAINE DANIEL RION Nuits-St.-Georges Hauts Pruliers 1988 $54 (7/15/90) (BT)
91   DOMAINE DANIEL RION Nuits-St.-Georges Hauts Pruliers 1987 $35 (4/30/90)
91   DOMAINE DANIEL RION Nuits-St.-Georges Hauts Pruliers 1986 $45 (4/30/89)
92   DOMAINE DANIEL RION Nuits-St.-Georges Hauts Pruliers 1986 $45 (7/31/88)
88   DOMAINE DANIEL RION Nuits-St.-Georges Hauts Pruliers 1985 $43 (3/15/88)
93   DOMAINE DANIEL RION Nuits-St.-Georges Les Lavières 1988 $33 (2/15/91)
87   DOMAINE DANIEL RION Nuits-St.-Georges Les Lavières 1987 $21 (4/30/90)
90+   DOMAINE DANIEL RION Nuits-St.-Georges Les Vignes Rondes 1989 (NR) (7/15/90) (BT)
92   DOMAINE DANIEL RION Nuits-St.-Georges Les Vignes Rondes 1988 $54 (1/31/91)
95+   DOMAINE DANIEL RION Nuits-St.-Georges Les Vignes Rondes 1988 $54 (7/15/90) (BT)
95   DOMAINE DANIEL RION Nuits-St.-Georges Les Vignes Rondes 1987 $35 (4/30/90)
88   DOMAINE DANIEL RION Nuits-St.-Georges Les Vignes Rondes 1986 $43 (4/30/89)
88   DOMAINE DANIEL RION Nuits-St.-Georges Les Vignes Rondes 1986 $43 (7/31/88)
91   DOMAINE DANIEL RION Nuits-St.-Georges Les Vignes Rondes 1985 $40 (3/15/88)
79   RION PERE & FILS Nuits-St.-Georges Les Murgers 1987 $31 (3/31/90)
86   EMMANUEL ROUGET Nuits-St.-Georges 1987 $32 (3/31/90)
84   DOMAINE B. SERVEAU Nuits-St.-Georges Chaines Carteaux 1988 $39 (3/31/91)
86   DOMAINE B. SERVEAU Nuits-St.-Georges Chaines Carteaux 1985 $39 (6/15/87)
71   LEONARD DE ST.-AUBIN Nuits-St.-Georges 1985 $25 (11/30/87)

VOSNE-ROMANÉE

91   ROBERT ARNOUX Romanée-St.-Vivant 1988 $250 (11/15/90)
80   ROBERT ARNOUX Vosne-Romanée Les Chaumes 1988 $62 (2/28/91)
60   ROBERT ARNOUX Vosne-Romanée Les Chaumes 1988 $62 (12/31/90)
86   ROBERT ARNOUX Vosne-Romanée Les Suchots 1988 $76 (2/28/91)
60   ROBERT ARNOUX Vosne-Romanée Les Suchots 1988 $76 (12/31/90)
90   ROBERT ARNOUX Vosne-Romanée Les Suchots 1985 $52 (7/31/88)
82   DOMAINE BERTAGNA Vosne-Romanée Les Beaux Monts Bas 1985 $35 (10/15/88)
87   BICHOT Vosne-Romanée Les Beaux Monts 1988 $34 (7/15/90)
90+   BOUCHARD PERE & FILS Echézeaux 1989 (NR) (7/15/90) (BT)
90+   BOUCHARD PERE & FILS La Romanée Château de Vosne-Romanée 1989 (NR) (7/15/90) (BT)
90+   BOUCHARD PERE & FILS La Romanée Château de Vosne-Romanée 1988 $238 (7/15/90) (BT)

91   BOUCHARD PERE & FILS La Romanée Château de Vosne-Romanée 1986 $200 (7/31/88)
85+   BOUCHARD PERE & FILS Vosne-Romanée Aux Reignots Château de Vosne-Romanée 1989 (NR) (7/15/90) (BT)
70+   BOUCHARD PERE & FILS Vosne-Romanée Aux Reignots Château de Vosne-Romanée 1988 $50 (7/15/90) (BT)
89   BOUCHARD PERE & FILS Vosne-Romanée Aux Reignots Château de Vosne-Romanée 1986 $50 (7/31/88)
90   BOUCHARD PERE & FILS Vosne-Romanée Aux Reignots Château de Vosne-Romanée 1985 $51 (2/28/89)
68   PIERRE BOUREE FILS Vosne-Romanée 1987 $44 (7/15/90)
87   CHANSON PERE & FILS Vosne-Romanée Suchots 1988 $55 (9/30/90)
90+   F. CHAUVENET Echézeaux 1988 $50 (7/15/90) (BT)
89   F. CHAUVENET Echézeaux 1985 $47 (7/31/87)
92   F. CHAUVENET Vosne-Romanée Les Suchots 1985 $46 (7/31/87)
71   GEORGES CLERGET Vosne-Romanée Les Violettes 1986 $23 (8/31/89)
85   MICHEL CLERGET Echézeaux 1986 $31 (8/31/89)
82   MICHEL CLERGET Echézeaux 1985 $51 (7/31/88)
80+   DOMAINE DU CLOS FRANTIN Echézeaux 1989 (NR) (7/15/90) (BT)
95+   DOMAINE DU CLOS FRANTIN Echézeaux 1988 $56 (7/15/90) (BT)
90   DOMAINE DU CLOS FRANTIN Echézeaux 1986 $30 (11/30/88)
91   DOMAINE DU CLOS FRANTIN Echézeaux 1986 $30 (7/31/88)
96   DOMAINE DU CLOS FRANTIN Echézeaux 1985 $37 (9/15/87)
86   DOMAINE DU CLOS FRANTIN Grands Echézeaux 1987 $56 (7/15/90)
87   DOMAINE DU CLOS FRANTIN Grands Echézeaux 1986 $60 (2/28/89)
86   DOMAINE DU CLOS FRANTIN Grands Echézeaux 1986 $60 (7/31/88)
88   DOMAINE DU CLOS FRANTIN Richebourg 1986 $100 (8/31/89)
70+   DOMAINE DU CLOS FRANTIN Vosne-Romanée 1989 (NR) (7/15/90) (BT)
80   DOMAINE DU CLOS FRANTIN Vosne-Romanée 1986 $19 (12/31/88)
89   DOMAINE DU CLOS FRANTIN Vosne-Romanée 1986 $19 (7/31/88)
91   DOMAINE DU CLOS FRANTIN Vosne-Romanée 1985 $29 (10/15/87)
85+   DOMAINE DU CLOS FRANTIN Vosne-Romanée Les Malconsorts 1989 (NR) (7/15/90) (BT)
85+   DOMAINE DU CLOS FRANTIN Vosne-Romanée Les Malconsorts 1988 $58 (7/15/90) (BT)
88   DOMAINE DU CLOS FRANTIN Vosne-Romanée Les Malconsorts 1987 $30 (7/15/90)
79   DOMAINE DU CLOS FRANTIN Vosne-Romanée Les Malconsorts 1986 $30 (10/31/88)
90   DOMAINE DU CLOS FRANTIN Vosne-Romanée Les Malconsorts 1986 $30 (7/31/88)
95   DOMAINE DU CLOS FRANTIN Vosne-Romanée Les Malconsorts 1985 Rel: $40 Cur: $55 (9/30/87)
93   JOSEPH DROUHIN Echézeaux 1988 $60 (11/15/90)
92   JOSEPH DROUHIN Echézeaux 1986 $60 (7/31/88)
90+   JOSEPH DROUHIN Grands Echézeaux 1989 $120 (7/15/90) (BT)
93   JOSEPH DROUHIN Grands Echézeaux 1985 $75 (11/15/87)
80+   JOSEPH DROUHIN Vosne-Romanée Les Beaumonts 1989 (NR) (7/15/90) (BT)
80   JOSEPH DROUHIN Vosne-Romanée Les Beaumonts 1988 $56 (3/31/91)
93   JOSEPH DROUHIN Vosne-Romanée Les Beaumonts 1985 $42 (11/15/87)
90   JOSEPH DROUHIN Vosne-Romanée Les Suchots 1988 $57 (2/28/91)
75+   JOSEPH DROUHIN Vosne-Romanée Les Suchots 1988 $64 (7/15/90) (BT)
94   JOSEPH DROUHIN Vosne-Romanée Les Suchots 1985 $42 (11/15/87)
90   DOMAINE DUJAC Echézeaux 1988 $70 (3/31/91)
82   DOMAINE DUJAC Echézeaux 1987 $56 (5/15/90)
89   DOMAINE DUJAC Echézeaux 1986 $52 (4/30/89)
92   RENE ENGEL Echézeaux 1988 $56 (3/31/91)
78   RENE ENGEL Echézeaux 1986 $38 (11/30/88)
90   RENE ENGEL Echézeaux 1985 $32 (10/15/87)
71   RENE ENGEL Grands Echézeaux 1986 $50 (11/30/88)
86   RENE ENGEL Grands Echézeaux 1985 $43 (10/15/87)
81   RENE ENGEL Vosne-Romanée 1988 $30 (7/15/90)
75   RENE ENGEL Vosne-Romanée 1986 $29 (2/28/89)
77   RENE ENGEL Vosne-Romanée 1985 $24 (10/15/87)
67   RENE ENGEL Vosne-Romanée 1983 $19.50 (2/16/86)
89   RENE ENGEL Vosne-Romanée Les Brûlées 1988 $45 (2/28/91)
68   RENE ENGEL Vosne-Romanée Les Brûlées 1986 $32 (10/31/88)
85   RENE ENGEL Vosne-Romanée Les Brûlées 1985 $28 (10/15/87)
78   RENE ENGEL Vosne-Romanée Les Brûlées 1983 $22 (3/16/86)
80   FAIVELEY Echézeaux 1987 $53 (3/31/90)
89   FAIVELEY Echézeaux 1985 $74 (3/31/88)
68   FAIVELEY Echézeaux 1981 $40 (5/01/86)
87   JEAN GRIVOT Vosne-Romanée 1985 $31 (4/30/88)
94   DOMAINE GROS FRERE & SOEUR Grands Echézeaux 1988 $110 (3/15/91)
71   DOMAINE GROS FRERE & SOEUR Grands Echézeaux 1985 $75 (3/31/88)
91   DOMAINE GROS FRERE & SOEUR Richebourg 1988 $192 (2/28/91)
89   DOMAINE GROS FRERE & SOEUR Vosne-Romanée 1988 $46 (3/31/91)
70   DOMAINE GROS FRERE & SOEUR Vosne-Romanée 1985 $35 (4/15/88)
91   A.-F. GROS Echézeaux 1988 $84 (2/15/91)
97   A.-F. GROS Richebourg 1988 $190 (2/15/91)
71   A.-F. GROS Vosne-Romanée Aux Réas 1988 $41 (2/28/91)
98   JEAN GROS Richebourg 1988 $190 (2/28/91)
95   JEAN GROS Richebourg 1987 Rel: $99 Cur: $170 (3/31/90)
90   JEAN GROS Vosne-Romanée 1988 $38 (2/28/91)
89   JEAN GROS Vosne-Romanée 1987 $32 (4/30/90)
94   JEAN GROS Vosne-Romanée Clos des Réas 1988 $50 (2/28/91)
93   JEAN GROS Vosne-Romanée Clos des Réas 1987 $37 (4/30/90)
90   JEAN GROS Vosne-Romanée Clos des Réas 1986 $36 (2/28/89)
87   JEAN GROS Vosne-Romanée Clos des Réas 1985 $55 (7/31/88)
71   ALAIN GUYARD Vosne-Romanée Aux Réas 1987 $29 (7/15/90)
86   LOUIS JADOT Vosne-Romanée 1985 $33 (3/31/88)
86   JAFFELIN Echézeaux 1986 $45 (12/31/88)
90   JAFFELIN Echézeaux 1983 $30 (5/01/86)
79   JAFFELIN Vosne-Romanée 1986 $30 (2/28/89)
94   HENRI JAYER Echézeaux 1982 Rel: $41 Cur: $150 (6/16/86) CS
91   J. JAYER Echézeaux 1988 $100 (3/15/91)
80   J. JAYER Vosne-Romanée Les Rouges 1985 $44 (3/15/88)
58   JAYER-GILLES Echézeaux 1982 $23 (11/01/85)
87   DOMAINE FRANCOIS LAMARCHE Echézeaux 1987 $48 (9/30/90)
91   DOMAINE FRANCOIS LAMARCHE Vosne-Romanée La Grande Rue 1987 $68 (9/30/90)
89   DOMAINE FRANCOIS LAMARCHE Vosne-Romanée La Grande Rue 1985 $60 (10/15/88)
84   DOMAINE FRANCOIS LAMARCHE Vosne-Romanée La Grande Rue 1984 $45 (10/15/88)
91   DOMAINE FRANCOIS LAMARCHE Vosne-Romanée Suchots 1985 $36 (10/15/88)
87   LOUIS LATOUR Echézeaux 1985 $49 (3/15/88)
98   LOUIS LATOUR Romanée-St.-Vivant Les Quatre Journaux 1985 Rel: $99 Cur: $110 (3/15/88)
94   LOUIS LATOUR Romanée-St.-Vivant Les Quatre Journaux 1953 Cur: $225 (8/31/90) (TR)

86 LOUIS LATOUR Vosne-Romanée Beaumonts 1985 $36 (3/15/88)
96 LEROY Richebourg 1988 $325 (4/30/91)
95 LEROY Romanée-St.-Vivant 1988 $325 (4/30/91)
93 LEROY Vosne-Romanée Les Beaux Monts 1988 $180 (4/30/91)
89 BERTRAND MACHARD DE GRAMONT Vosne-Romanée Les Réas 1988 $32 (7/15/91)
96 DOMAINE MEO-CAMUZET Richebourg 1988 $253 (11/30/90)
96 DOMAINE MEO-CAMUZET Richebourg 1987 $165 (12/15/89)
90 DOMAINE MEO-CAMUZET Richebourg 1986 $160 (10/31/88)
97 DOMAINE MEO-CAMUZET Richebourg 1986 $160 (7/31/88)
97 DOMAINE MEO-CAMUZET Richebourg 1985 Rel: $150 Cur: $235 (3/31/88)
87 DOMAINE MEO-CAMUZET Vosne-Romanée 1988 $50 (12/31/90)
90 DOMAINE MEO-CAMUZET Vosne-Romanée 1987 $35 (12/15/89)
88 DOMAINE MEO-CAMUZET Vosne-Romanée 1986 $30 (10/31/88)
94 DOMAINE MEO-CAMUZET Vosne-Romanée Au Cros-Parantoux 1988 $84 (11/30/90)
95 DOMAINE MEO-CAMUZET Vosne-Romanée Au Cros-Parantoux 1987 $63 (12/15/89)
93 DOMAINE MEO-CAMUZET Vosne-Romanée Au Cros-Parantoux 1986 $60 (7/31/88)
89 DOMAINE MEO-CAMUZET Vosne-Romanée Aux Brûlées 1988 $84 (11/30/90)
95 DOMAINE MEO-CAMUZET Vosne-Romanée Aux Brûlées 1987 $63 (12/15/89)
88 DOMAINE MEO-CAMUZET Vosne-Romanée Les Chaumes 1988 $60 (11/30/90)
83 DOMAINE MEO-CAMUZET Vosne-Romanée Les Chaumes 1986 $38 (12/31/88)
83 DOMAINE MEO-CAMUZET Vosne-Romanée Les Chaumes 1986 $38 (7/31/88)
92 DOMAINE MEO-CAMUZET Vosne-Romanée Les Chaumes 1985 $80 (3/31/88)
94 MOILLARD Echézeaux 1985 $47 (4/15/88)
96 MOILLARD Echézeaux 1984 Rel: $22 Cur: $40 (11/15/86) SS
90 MOILLARD Grands Echézeaux 1984 $39 (5/31/87)
87 MOILLARD Romanée-St.-Vivant 1984 $42 (5/31/87)
90 MOILLARD Vosne-Romanée Malconsorts 1985 $21 (12/15/86)
80 MOILLARD Vosne-Romanée Malconsorts 1984 Rel: $24 Cur: $30 (5/31/87)
95 MOILLARD Vosne-Romanée Malconsorts 1984 Rel: $24 Cur: $30 (12/15/86) CS
88 MOILLARD Vosne-Romanée Malconsorts Domaine Thomas-Moillard 1988 $50 (3/31/91)
91 MOILLARD Vosne-Romanée Malconsorts Domaine Thomas-Moillard 1987 $30 (8/31/89)
88 MOILLARD Vosne-Romanée Malconsorts Domaine Thomas-Moillard 1986 $29 (10/31/88)
95 MOILLARD Vosne-Romanée Malconsorts Domaine Thomas-Moillard 1985 $47 (7/31/88)
80+ MOMMESSIN Echézeaux 1989 (NR) (7/15/90) (BT)
86 MOMMESSIN Echézeaux 1979 $18.50 (2/16/86)
62 CHARLES MONCAUT Vosne-Romanée Cuvée Particulière 1983 $16 (9/15/86)
68 MONGEARD-MUGNERET Echézeaux 1984 $28 (2/15/88)
88 MONGEARD-MUGNERET Echézeaux Vieille Vigne 1988 $61 (2/15/91)
86 MONGEARD-MUGNERET Echézeaux Vieille Vigne 1987 $42 (5/15/90)
90 MONGEARD-MUGNERET Echézeaux Vieille Vigne 1986 $44 (8/31/89)
85 MONGEARD-MUGNERET Grands Echézeaux 1987 $65 (5/15/90)
92 MONGEARD-MUGNERET Grands Echézeaux 1986 $73 (8/31/89)
92 MONGEARD-MUGNERET Richebourg 1985 $123 (3/15/88)
79 MONGEARD-MUGNERET Vosne-Romanée 1986 $26 (8/31/89)
62 MONGEARD-MUGNERET Vosne-Romanée Les Orveaux 1987 $35 (7/15/90)
82 MONGEARD-MUGNERET Vosne-Romanée Les Orveaux 1986 $34 (8/31/89)
82 MONGEARD-MUGNERET Vosne-Romanée Les Orveaux 1985 $32 (3/15/88)
68 MONGEARD-MUGNERET Vosne-Romanée Les Orveaux 1984 $18 (2/15/88)
74 MONGEARD-MUGNERET Vosne-Romanée Les Petits Monts 1987 $35 (4/30/90)
82 MONGEARD-MUGNERET Vosne-Romanée Les Suchots 1987 $35 (6/15/90)
86 GERARD MUGNERET Vosne-Romanée 1988 $37 (2/28/91)
79 GERARD MUGNERET Vosne-Romanée 1987 $32 (7/15/90)
84 GERARD MUGNERET Vosne-Romanée Les Suchots 1988 $57 (2/28/91)
82 GERARD MUGNERET Vosne-Romanée Les Suchots 1987 $42 (7/15/90)
90 RENE MUGNERET Vosne-Romanée 1985 $27 (4/30/88)
73 RENE MUGNERET Vosne-Romanée 1983 $16 (11/16/85)
86 RENE MUGNERET Vosne-Romanée 1982 $17 (7/16/85)
89 MUGNERET-GIBOURG Echézeaux 1988 $84 (11/15/90)
93 MUGNERET-GIBOURG Echézeaux 1987 $50 (10/15/89)
83 MUGNERET-GIBOURG Echézeaux 1986 $55 (11/30/88)
87 MUGNERET-GIBOURG Echézeaux 1986 $55 (7/31/88)
93 MUGNERET-GIBOURG Echézeaux 1985 $57 (2/29/88)
85 MUGNERET-GIBOURG Echézeaux 1984 $32 (3/15/87)
64 MUGNERET-GIBOURG Vosne-Romanée 1988 $34 (12/31/90)
90 MUGNERET-GIBOURG Vosne-Romanée 1987 $30 (10/15/89)
81 MUGNERET-GIBOURG Vosne-Romanée 1986 $33 (12/31/88)
84 MUGNERET-GIBOURG Vosne-Romanée 1986 $33 (7/31/88)
85 MUGNERET-GIBOURG Vosne-Romanée 1985 $33 (2/29/88)
91 B. MUGNERET-GOUACHON Echézeaux 1985 $29 (12/31/88)
61 A. PERNIN-ROSSIN Vosne-Romanée 1988 $31 (2/28/89)
75 REMOISSENET Echézeaux 1985 $73 (3/15/88)
91 REMOISSENET Richebourg 1985 $138 (3/15/88)
95 REMOISSENET Vosne-Romanée Clos de Réas 1949 (NA) (8/31/90) (TR)
91 REMOISSENET Vosne-Romanée Les Suchots 1985 $75 (3/15/88)
85+ DOMAINE DANIEL RION Vosne-Romanée 1988 $32 (7/15/90) (BT)
89 DOMAINE DANIEL RION Vosne-Romanée 1987 $21 (4/30/90)
87 DOMAINE DANIEL RION Vosne-Romanée 1986 $31 (4/30/89)
86 DOMAINE DANIEL RION Vosne-Romanée 1986 $31 (7/31/88)
78 DOMAINE DANIEL RION Vosne-Romanée 1985 $28 (2/29/88)
63 DOMAINE DANIEL RION Vosne-Romanée Clos 1985 $19 (2/01/86)
92 DOMAINE DANIEL RION Vosne-Romanée Beaux-Monts 1988 $53 (2/15/91)
80+ DOMAINE DANIEL RION Vosne-Romanée Beaux-Monts 1988 $53 (7/15/90) (BT)
91 DOMAINE DANIEL RION Vosne-Romanée Beaux-Monts 1986 $43 (4/30/89)
88 DOMAINE DANIEL RION Vosne-Romanée Beaux-Monts 1986 $43 (7/31/88)
95 DOMAINE DANIEL RION Vosne-Romanée Beaux-Monts 1985 Rel: $38 Cur: $55 (2/29/88)
93 DOMAINE DANIEL RION Vosne-Romanée Les Chaumes 1988 $54 (1/31/91)
90+ DOMAINE DANIEL RION Vosne-Romanée Les Chaumes 1988 $54 (7/15/90) (BT)
88 DOMAINE DANIEL RION Vosne-Romanée Les Chaumes 1987 $35 (4/30/90)
93 DOMAINE DANIEL RION Vosne-Romanée Les Chaumes 1986 $47 (4/30/89) CS
95 DOMAINE DANIEL RION Vosne-Romanée Les Chaumes 1986 $47 (7/31/88)
92 ROMANEE-CONTI Echézeaux 1988 $225 (4/30/91)
92 ROMANEE-CONTI Echézeaux 1987 $98 (9/30/90)
92 ROMANEE-CONTI Echézeaux 1986 $110 (8/31/89)
96 ROMANEE-CONTI Echézeaux 1985 Rel: $95 Cur: $126 (2/29/88)
90 ROMANEE-CONTI Echézeaux 1984 Rel: $52 Cur: $68 (2/28/87)
63 ROMANEE-CONTI Echézeaux 1983 Rel: $75 Cur: $96 (11/30/86)
97 ROMANEE-CONTI Echézeaux 1952 Cur: $96 (8/31/90) (TR)
92 ROMANEE-CONTI Grands Echézeaux 1988 $315 (4/30/91)
89 ROMANEE-CONTI Grands Echézeaux 1987 $145 (9/30/90)
94 ROMANEE-CONTI Grands Echézeaux 1986 $160 (8/31/89)

94 ROMANEE-CONTI Grands Echézeaux 1985 Rel: $140 Cur: $178 (2/29/88)
88 ROMANEE-CONTI Grands Echézeaux 1984 Rel: $64 Cur: $88 (2/28/87)
64 ROMANEE-CONTI Grands Echézeaux 1983 $100 (11/30/86)
93 ROMANEE-CONTI Grands Echézeaux 1942 Cur: $230 (8/31/90) (TR)
98 ROMANEE-CONTI La Tâche 1988 $450 (4/30/91)
92 ROMANEE-CONTI La Tâche 1987 Rel: $225 Cur: $320 (9/30/90)
98 ROMANEE-CONTI La Tâche 1986 $250 (8/31/89) CS
98 ROMANEE-CONTI La Tâche 1985 Rel: $225 Cur: $310 (2/29/88)
95 ROMANEE-CONTI La Tâche 1984 Rel: $105 Cur: $150 (2/28/87)
61 ROMANEE-CONTI La Tâche 1983 Rel: $150 Cur: $168 (11/30/86)
94 ROMANEE-CONTI Richebourg 1988 $400 (4/30/91)
93 ROMANEE-CONTI Richebourg 1987 $190 (9/30/90)
94 ROMANEE-CONTI Richebourg 1986 $230 (8/31/89)
100 ROMANEE-CONTI Richebourg 1985 Rel: $210 Cur: $320 (2/29/88)
91 ROMANEE-CONTI Richebourg 1984 $102 (2/28/87)
52 ROMANEE-CONTI Richebourg 1983 $150 (11/30/86)
88 ROMANEE-CONTI Richebourg 1954 Cur: $175 (8/31/90) (TR)
65 ROMANEE-CONTI Richebourg 1947 Cur: $760 (8/31/90) (TR)
98 ROMANEE-CONTI Romanée-Conti 1988 $600 (4/30/91)
89 ROMANEE-CONTI Romanée-Conti 1987 Rel: $350 Cur: $620 (9/30/90)
95 ROMANEE-CONTI Romanée-Conti 1986 Rel: $400 Cur: $620 (8/31/89)
99 ROMANEE-CONTI Romanée-Conti 1985 Rel: $375 Cur: $1,080 (1/31/90) (JS)
96 ROMANEE-CONTI Romanée-Conti 1985 Rel: $375 Cur: $1,080 (2/29/88)
94 ROMANEE-CONTI Romanée-Conti 1984 Cur: $640 (1/31/90) (JS)
78 ROMANEE-CONTI Romanée-Conti 1983 Rel: $250 Cur: $750 (1/31/90) (JS)
65 ROMANEE-CONTI Romanée-Conti 1983 Rel: $250 Cur: $750 (11/30/86)
85 ROMANEE-CONTI Romanée-Conti 1982 Cur: $450 (1/31/90) (JS)
90 ROMANEE-CONTI Romanée-Conti 1979 Cur: $790 (1/31/90) (JS)
95 ROMANEE-CONTI Romanée-Conti 1978 Cur: $1,480 (1/31/90) (JS)
82 ROMANEE-CONTI Romanée-Conti 1975 Cur: $780 (1/31/90) (JS)
98 ROMANEE-CONTI Romanée-Conti 1964 Cur: $1,160 (1/31/90) (JS)
50 ROMANEE-CONTI Romanée-Conti 1963 Cur: $1,210 (1/31/90) (JS)
68 ROMANEE-CONTI Romanée-Conti 1959 Cur: $1,820 (1/31/90) (JS)
93 ROMANEE-CONTI Romanée-Conti 1953 Cur: $2,070 (1/31/90) (JS)
50 ROMANEE-CONTI Romanée-Conti 1937 Cur: $1,950 (1/31/90) (JS)
94 ROMANEE-CONTI Romanée-Conti 1937 Cur: $1,950 (12/15/88)
50 ROMANEE-CONTI Romanée-Conti 1935 Cur: $600 (1/31/90) (JS)
66 ROMANEE-CONTI Romanée-Conti 1934 Cur: $2,060 (1/31/90) (JS)
50 ROMANEE-CONTI Romanée-Conti 1929 Cur: $2,340 (1/31/90) (JS)
97 ROMANEE-CONTI Romanée-St.-Vivant 1988 $360 (4/30/91)
89 ROMANEE-CONTI Romanée-St.-Vivant 1987 $175 (9/30/90)
98 ROMANEE-CONTI Romanée-St.-Vivant 1986 $195 (8/31/89)
88 ROMANEE-CONTI Romanée-St.-Vivant 1985 $175 (2/29/88)
96 ROMANEE-CONTI Romanée-St.-Vivant 1984 Rel: $70 Cur: $93 (2/28/87)
66 ROMANEE-CONTI Romanée-St.-Vivant 1983 $125 (11/30/86)
96 EMMANUEL ROUGET Echézeaux 1988 $81 (11/15/90)
88 EMMANUEL ROUGET Echézeaux 1987 $55 (3/31/90)
87 EMMANUEL ROUGET Echézeaux 1986 $55 (12/31/88)
91 EMMANUEL ROUGET Vosne-Romanée 1987 $32 (3/31/90)
89 EMMANUEL ROUGET Vosne-Romanée Les Beaumonts 1986 $40 (12/31/88)
94 ARMAND ROUX Echézeaux 1959 (NA) (8/31/90) (TR)
91 ARMAND ROUX Richebourg 1959 (NA) (8/31/90) (TR)

VOUGEOT

78 ROBERT ARNOUX Clos Vougeot 1988 $70 (3/15/91)
84 THOMAS BASSOT Clos de Vougeot 1942 (NA) (8/31/90) (TR)
87 DOMAINE BERTAGNA Vougeot Clos de la Perrière 1985 $40 (4/15/89)
85 DOMAINE BERTAGNA Vougeot Les Crâs 1985 $30 (3/31/88)
85 BOUCHARD PERE & FILS Clos de Vougeot 1959 (NA) (8/31/90) (TR)
86 CAPTAIN-GAGNEROT Clos Vougeot 1985 $67 (12/31/88)
93 DOMAINE CECI Clos de Vougeot 1988 $48 (7/15/91)
82 DOMAINE CECI Clos de Vougeot 1987 $40 (3/31/90)
79 F. CHAUVENET Clos de Vougeot 1986 $57 (12/31/88)
87 F. CHAUVENET Clos de Vougeot 1985 $57 (7/31/88)
87 CHOPIN-GROFFIER Clos Vougeot 1988 $70 (5/15/91)
92 CHOPIN-GROFFIER Vougeot 1988 $32 (5/15/91)
85 DOMAINE DU CLOS FRANTIN Clos de Vougeot 1987 $56 (7/15/90)
87 DOMAINE DU CLOS FRANTIN Clos de Vougeot 1986 $37 (11/30/88)
90 DOMAINE DU CLOS FRANTIN Clos de Vougeot 1986 $37 (7/31/88)
90 JOSEPH DROUHIN Clos de Vougeot 1988 $85 (2/15/91)
85+ JOSEPH DROUHIN Clos de Vougeot 1988 $93 (7/15/90) (BT)
86 JOSEPH DROUHIN Clos de Vougeot 1986 $55 (4/15/89)
86 JOSEPH DROUHIN Clos de Vougeot 1986 $55 (7/31/88)
94 JOSEPH DROUHIN Clos de Vougeot 1985 $57 (11/15/87)
89 DROUHIN-LAROZE Clos de Vougeot 1988 $81 (12/31/90)
79 DROUHIN-LAROZE Clos de Vougeot 1987 $38 (3/31/90)
88 DROUHIN-LAROZE Clos de Vougeot 1985 $60 (10/15/88)
91 RENE ENGEL Clos Vougeot 1988 $75 (3/15/91)
81 RENE ENGEL Clos Vougeot 1986 $50 (11/30/88)
85 RENE ENGEL Clos Vougeot 1985 $43 (10/15/87)
80 RENE ENGEL Clos Vougeot 1983 $30 (2/16/86)
85+ FAIVELEY Clos de Vougeot 1989 (NR) (7/15/90) (BT)
90+ FAIVELEY Clos de Vougeot 1988 $92 (7/15/90) (BT)
85 JEAN GRIVOT Clos de Vougeot 1988 $70 (4/30/91)
81 JEAN GRIVOT Clos de Vougeot 1985 $62 (4/30/88)
92 DOMAINE GROS FRERE & SOEUR Clos Vougeot Musigny 1988 $95 (3/31/91)
75 DOMAINE GROS FRERE & SOEUR Clos de Vougeot Musigny 1985 $70 (3/31/88)
73 HAEGELEN-JAYER Clos de Vougeot 1988 $69 (5/15/91)
90 HAEGELEN-JAYER Clos de Vougeot 1985 $64 (4/15/88)
86 CHATEAU DES HERBEUX Clos Vougeot 1988 $65 (11/30/90)
85+ LOUIS JADOT Clos Vougeot 1989 (NR) (7/15/90) (BT)
80+ LOUIS JADOT Clos Vougeot 1988 $52 (7/15/90) (BT)
87 LOUIS JADOT Clos Vougeot 1986 $50 (4/15/89)
82 LOUIS JADOT Clos Vougeot 1985 Rel: $53 Cur: $85 (3/31/88)
77 JAFFELIN Clos de Vougeot 1988 $45 (12/31/88)
96 JAFFELIN Clos de Vougeot 1985 $49 (6/15/88)
85+ J. LABET & N. DECHELETTE Clos Vougeot Château de la Tour 1989 (NR) (7/15/90) (BT)
91 J. LABET & N. DECHELETTE Clos Vougeot Château de la Tour 1988 $50 (11/30/90)
84 J. LABET & N. DECHELETTE Clos Vougeot Château de la Tour 1987 $50 (2/15/91)
90 J. LABET & N. DECHELETTE Clos Vougeot Château de la Tour 1985 $53 (6/15/88)

FRANCE
BURGUNDY RED/CÔTE DE NUITS/VOUGEOT

66 J. LABET & N. DECHELETTE Clos Vougeot Château de la Tour 1979 $40 (9/01/84)
90+ J. LABET & N. DECHELETTE Clos Vougeot Château de la Tour 1988 $50 (7/15/90) (BT)
86 DOMAINE FRANCOIS LAMARCHE Clos de Vougeot 1987 $55 (9/30/90)
90 DOMAINE FRANCOIS LAMARCHE Clos de Vougeot 1985 $48 (10/15/88)
89 LEROY Clos de Vougeot 1988 $260 (4/30/91)
92 DOMAINE MEO-CAMUZET Clos de Vougeot 1988 $95 (11/30/90)
91 DOMAINE MEO-CAMUZET Clos de Vougeot 1986 $55 (11/30/88)
93 DOMAINE MEO-CAMUZET Clos de Vougeot 1985 Rel: $65 Cur: $105 (3/31/88)
90 MOILLARD Clos de Vougeot 1984 $32 (5/31/87)
95 MOILLARD Clos de Vougeot 1983 Rel: $26 Cur: $45 (10/16/85) CS
81 MONGEARD-MUGNERET Clos de Vougeot 1987 $53 (5/15/90)
87 MONGEARD-MUGNERET Clos de Vougeot 1986 $56 (7/31/89)
84 CHARLES MORTET Clos Vougeot 1986 $43 (4/15/89)
84 GEORGES MUGNERET Clos Vougeot 1988 $90 (11/15/90)
91 GEORGES MUGNERET Clos Vougeot 1987 $68 (10/15/89)
90 GEORGES MUGNERET Clos Vougeot 1986 $73 (11/30/88)
90 GEORGES MUGNERET Clos Vougeot 1986 $73 (7/31/88)
49 HENRI REBOURSEAU Clos de Vougeot 1983 $25 (11/16/85)
92 DOMAINE DANIEL RION Clos Vougeot 1988 $75 (1/31/91)
75+ DOMAINE DANIEL RION Clos Vougeot 1988 $75 (7/15/90) (BT)
90 DOMAINE DANIEL RION Clos Vougeot 1986 $70 (4/15/89)
85 DOMAINE DANIEL RION Clos Vougeot 1986 $70 (7/31/88)
86 RION PERE & FILS Clos Vougeot 1987 $48 (11/15/90)
70 JEAN TARDY Clos de Vougeot 1987 $49 (3/31/90)

OTHER CÔTE DE NUITS RED

82 MAISON AMBROISE Côte de Nuits-Villages 1987 $15 (2/28/90)
80 DOMAINE DE L'ARLOT Côte de Nuits-Villages Clos du Châpeau 1988 $21 (3/31/91)
78 JEAN CLAUDE BOISSET Côte de Nuits-Villages 1983 $13 (2/01/86)
83 A. CHOPIN Côte de Nuits-Villages 1985 $9 (10/31/87) BB
86 JOSEPH DROUHIN Côte de Nuits-Villages 1985 $19.50 (11/15/87)
80 A.-F. GROS Bourgogne Hautes Côtes de Nuits 1988 $22 (3/31/91)
78 MICHEL GROS Hautes Côtes de Nuits 1987 $14 (2/28/90)
77 LOUIS JADOT Marsannay 1986 $11.50 (6/15/89)
76 MOILLARD Hautes Côtes de Nuits 1983 $6.50 (11/01/85)
85 MOMMESSIN Côte de Nuits-Villages 1985 $17 (7/31/88)
82 CHATEAU DE PULIGNY-MONTRACHET Côte de Nuits-Villages 1988 $17 (3/31/91)
81 DOMAINE DANIEL RION Côte de Nuits-Villages 1986 $15 (7/31/88)
89 PHILIPPE ROSSIGNOL Côte de Nuits-Villages 1985 $24 (7/31/88)
83 DOMAINE SIRUGUE Côte de Nuits-Villages Clos de la Belle Marguerite 1988 $16 (3/31/91)
78 LOUIS TRAPET Marsannay 1987 $17 (3/31/91)

CHALLONAISE

68 MICHEL BRIDAY Rully Champ Clou 1987 $16 (12/31/90)
78 CHANSON PERE & FILS Givry 1988 $13 (12/31/90)
70 JEAN CHOFFLET Givry 1985 $12 (11/15/87)
83 JOSEPH DROUHIN Mercurey 1985 $17 (11/15/87)
82 DUVERNAY Rully Les Cloux 1988 $18 (12/31/90)
75 FAIVELEY Mercurey Clos des Myglands 1985 $20 (4/30/88)
68 FAIVELEY Mercurey Clos des Myglands 1981 $11 (6/16/86)
84 FAIVELEY Mercurey Clos du Roy 1988 $22 (3/31/91)
81 FAIVELEY Mercurey Clos du Roy 1985 $23 (4/30/88)
81 FAIVELEY Mercurey Domaine de la Croix Jacquelet 1988 $17.50 (3/31/91)
83 FAIVELEY Rully 1986 $17.50 (6/15/89)
77 JAFFELIN Rully 1986 $13 (6/15/89)
84 DOMAINE JOBLOT Givry Clos du Cellier aux Moines 1988 $19 (12/31/90)
56 DOMAINE DU CHATEAU DE MERCEY Mercurey 1983 $10.25 (5/01/86)
68 REMOISSENET Givry du Domaine Thénard 1988 $19 (3/31/91)
77 REMOISSENET Givry du Domaine Thénard 1985 $18 (4/30/88)
83 REMOISSENET Mercurey Clos Fortoul 1988 $17 (3/31/91)
83 DOMAINE FABIEN & LOUIS SAIER Mercurey Les Champs Martins 1985 $20 (3/31/88)
67 DOMAINE FABIEN & LOUIS SAIER Mercurey Les Chenelots 1988 $17 (4/30/91)
85 CHARLES VIENOT Mercurey 1985 $12.50 (4/30/88)

OTHER BURGUNDY RED

82 GHISLAINE BARTHOD Bourgogne 1988 $20 (3/31/91)
81 BICHOT Bourgogne Le Bourgogne Bichot Pinot Noir 1985 $8 (11/15/87)
77 BICHOT Bourgogne Croix St.-Louis 1986 $6 (10/31/88)
76 HENRI BOILLOT Bourgogne 1985 $13 (12/31/88)
78 LIONEL J. BRUCK Bourgogne St.-Vincent Pinot Noir 1983 $10 (2/15/87)
75 CAVE DES VIGNERONS DE BUXY Bourgogne Pinot Noir Grande Réserve 1985 $7 (6/30/88)
73 CAVE DES VIGNERONS DE BUXY Bourgogne Pinot Noir Grande Réserve 1983 $5 (2/01/86)
75+ DOMAINE JEAN CHARTRON Bourgogne Pinot Noir L'Orme 1988 (NR) (7/15/90) (BT)
75+ CHARTRON & TREBUCHET Bourgogne 1989 (NR) (7/15/90) (BT)
80 F. CHAUVENET Bourgogne Pinot Noir Château Marguerite de Bourgogne 1985 $10 (6/30/88)
79 J.-F. COCHE-DURY Bourgogne Pinot Noir 1987 $25 (2/28/90)
76 CHATEAU DE DRACY Bourgogne 1986 $6.50 (12/31/88)
68 CHATEAU DE DRACY Bourgogne Pinot Noir 1988 $8 (2/28/90)
85 JOSEPH DROUHIN Bourgogne Pinot Noir Laforet 1989 $9 (4/30/91) BB
84 JOSEPH DROUHIN Bourgogne Pinot Noir Laforet 1988 $10 (3/31/91) BB
78 JOSEPH DROUHIN Bourgogne Pinot Noir Laforet 1987 $8.75 (6/15/89)
78 JOSEPH DROUHIN Bourgogne Pinot Noir Laforet 1985 $8.50 (11/15/87)
71 JOSEPH DROUHIN Bourgogne Pinot Noir Laforet 1983 $7.50 (11/01/85)
75 FAIVELEY Bourgogne Cuvée Joseph Faiveley 1979 $8 (4/16/86) BB

Key to Symbols

The scores reported here are the results of blind tastings conducted by our panel of senior editors. Wines that carry the initials below are results of individual tastings.

THE WINE SPECTATOR 100-POINT SCALE *95-100*—Classic, a great wine; *90-94*—Outstanding, superior character and style; *80-89*—Good to very good, a wine with special qualities; *70-79*—Average, drinkable wine that may have minor flaws; *60-69*—Below average, drinkable but not recommended; *50-59*—Poor, undrinkable, not recommended. "+"—With a score indicates a range; used primarily with barrel tastings to indicate a preliminary score.

SPECIAL DESIGNATIONS SS—Spectator Selection, CS—Cellar Selection, BB—Best Buy.

TASTER'S INITIALS (JG)—Jim Gordon, (HS)—Harvey Steiman, (JL)—James Laube, (JS)—James Suckling, (TM)—Thomas Matthews, (TR)—Terry Robards, (BT)—Barrel Tasting (these wines were tasted blind from barrel samples), (CA-date)—*California's Great Cabernets* by James Laube, (CH-date)—*California's Great Chardonnays* by James Laube, (VP-date)—*Vintage Port* by James Suckling.

DATE TASTED Dates in parentheses represent the issue in which the rating was published.

81 MACHARD DE GRAMONT Bourgogne Pinot Noir Domaine de la Vierge Romaine 1985 $13 (6/30/88)
70+ LOUIS JADOT Bourgogne 1989 (NR) (7/15/90) (BT)
70+ LOUIS JADOT Bourgogne Pinot Noir 1988 (NR) (7/15/90) (BT)
78 LOUIS JADOT Bourgogne Pinot Noir Jadot 1985 $11 (4/30/88)
84 JEAN-LUC JOILLOT Bourgogne Tastevinage 1985 $14.50 (6/30/88)
83 LABOURE-ROI Bourgogne 1988 $12 (3/31/91)
73 LEROY Bourgogne d'Auvenay 1985 $12 (3/31/88)
87 LEROY Bourgogne Leroy d'Auvenay 1988 $14.50 (4/30/91)
79 LUPE-CHOLET Bourgogne Clos de Lupé 1985 $15 (3/31/88)
83 LUPE-CHOLET Bourgogne Pinot Noir Comte de Lupé 1988 $9 (2/28/90) BB
78 LUPE-CHOLET Bourgogne Hautes Côtes de Beaune 1987 $10 (4/15/90)
84 DOMAINE MEO-CAMUZET Bourgogne Passetoutgrains 1989 $17 (7/15/91)
81 MOILLARD Bourgogne Hautes Côtes de Nuits Les Hameaux 1986 $11 (12/31/88)
78 MOILLARD Bourgogne Pinot Noir 1985 $7 (3/31/88)
61 MOMMESSIN Bourgogne Pinot Noir 1983 $5 (2/16/86)
77 DOMAINE JEAN MORETEAUX Bourgogne Pinot Noir Les Clous 1985 $9 (11/15/87)
79 CHARLES MORTET Bourgogne 1986 $15 (6/15/89)
79 POTHIER-RIEUSSET Bourgogne Rouge 1986 $10 (6/15/89)
83 POTHIER-RIEUSSET Bourgogne Rouge 1985 $7.50 (6/30/88) BB
80 DOMAINE RAPET Bourgogne en Bully 1988 $18.50 (3/31/91)
76 DOMAINE B. SERVEAU Bourgogne Rouge 1985 $13 (11/15/87)
78 CHARLES VIENOT Bourgogne 1985 $9 (6/15/89)
75 CHARLES VIENOT Bourgogne 1983 $6.50 (12/16/85)
52 CHARLES VIENOT Bourgogne 1982 $6 (11/01/85)
78 HENRI DE VILLAMONT Bourgogne Pinot Noir 1989 $11 (3/31/91)
73 JEAN-CLAUDE VOLPATO Bourgogne Passetoutgrain 1988 $12.50 (3/31/91)

BURGUNDY WHITE/CÔTE DE BEAUNE/ALOXE-CORTON

89 JEAN-CLAUDE BELLAND Corton-Charlemagne 1986 $58 (3/31/89)
87 BICHOT Corton-Charlemagne 1985 $63 (3/15/88)
91 PIERRE BITOUZET Corton-Charlemagne 1988 $75 (12/31/90)
92 PIERRE BITOUZET Corton-Charlemagne 1987 $68 (11/15/89)
95 PIERRE BITOUZET Corton-Charlemagne 1986 $72 (9/30/88)
88 BONNEAU DU MARTRAY Corton-Charlemagne 1986 Rel: $60 Cur: $66 (2/28/90)
84 BONNEAU DU MARTRAY Corton-Charlemagne 1985 Rel: $65 Cur: $69 (5/31/88)
84 DOMAINE CHANDON DE BRIAILLES Corton 1988 $88 (2/28/91)
85 CHARTRON & TREBUCHET Corton-Charlemagne 1989 $105 (2/28/91)
95 CHARTRON & TREBUCHET Corton-Charlemagne 1988 $70 (2/28/90)
91 CHARTRON & TREBUCHET Corton-Charlemagne 1987 $79 (3/31/89)
95 CHARTRON & TREBUCHET Corton-Charlemagne 1986 $92 (5/31/88)
96 F. CHAUVENET Corton-Charlemagne 1985 $70 (4/30/87)
96 F. CHAUVENET Corton-Charlemagne Hospices de Beaune Cuvée François de Salins 1985 $140 (7/31/87)
95 F. CHAUVENET Corton Vergennes Hospices de Beaune Cuvée Paul Chanson 1982 $83 (8/01/85)
71 DOMAINE DU CLOS FRANTIN Corton-Charlemagne 1988 $66 (4/30/91)
87 DOMAINE DU CLOS FRANTIN Corton-Charlemagne 1986 $55 (3/31/89)
88 J.-F. COCHE-DURY Corton-Charlemagne 1987 $122 (2/28/90)
85 DOMAINE DELARCHE Corton-Charlemagne 1986 $65 (9/30/88)
94 MARIUS DELARCHE PERE & FILS Corton-Charlemagne 1988 $60 (7/31/90)
91 JOSEPH DROUHIN Corton-Charlemagne 1989 $92 (2/28/91)
90 JOSEPH DROUHIN Corton-Charlemagne 1987 Rel: $90 Cur: $90 (3/31/89)
90 JOSEPH DROUHIN Corton-Charlemagne 1986 Rel: $98 Cur: $98 (12/15/88)
94 JOSEPH DROUHIN Corton-Charlemagne 1985 Rel: $78 Cur: $78 (4/30/87)
93 LOUIS JADOT Corton-Charlemagne 1988 $98 (4/30/91)
92 LOUIS JADOT Corton-Charlemagne 1986 Rel: $92 Cur: $92 (5/31/89)
86 JAFFELIN Corton-Charlemagne 1984 $60 (5/01/86)
84 MICHEL JUILLOT Corton-Charlemagne 1987 $77 (2/28/90)
90 LABOURE-ROI Corton-Charlemagne 1988 $50 (10/15/90)
95 LOUIS LATOUR Corton-Charlemagne 1988 Rel: $85 Cur: $86 (10/15/90)
96 LOUIS LATOUR Corton-Charlemagne 1985 Rel: $88 Cur: $95 (11/15/87)
82 LOUIS LATOUR Corton-Charlemagne 1982 Rel: $65 Cur: $79 (12/01/85)
83 OLIVIER LEFLAIVE FRERES Corton-Charlemagne 1986 $67 (7/31/90)
90 A. LIGERET Corton-Charlemagne 1987 $83 (10/15/90)
90 MOILLARD Corton-Charlemagne 1986 $70 (5/31/88)
90 MOILLARD Corton-Charlemagne 1984 $51 (5/31/87)
92 MOILLARD Corton-Charlemagne 1983 $34 (10/01/85)
92 REINE PEDAUQUE Corton-Charlemagne 1985 $60 (11/15/89)
73 REINE PEDAUQUE Corton-Charlemagne 1982 $33 (8/01/85)
82 REMOISSENET Corton-Charlemagne Diamond Jubilee 1986 $82 (12/15/88)
90 REMOISSENET Corton-Charlemagne Diamond Jubilee 1985 $100 (3/15/88)

CHASSAGNE-MONTRACHET

70 AMIOT-BONFILS Chassagne-Montrachet Les Caillerets 1988 $27 (5/15/90)
86 AMIOT-BONFILS Chassagne-Montrachet Les Champs-Gains 1988 $27 (3/31/90)
86 AMIOT-PONSOT Chassagne-Montrachet Les Champs-Gains 1987 $42 (5/31/89)
80 BACHELET-RAMONET Chassagne-Montrachet 1988 $37 (4/30/91)
78 BACHELET-RAMONET Chassagne-Montrachet 1987 $36 (11/15/89)
87 BACHELET-RAMONET Chassagne-Montrachet Caillerets 1987 $35 (5/15/90)
91 BACHELET-RAMONET Chassagne-Montrachet Caillerets 1985 $41 (2/29/88)
92 BACHELET-RAMONET Chassagne-Montrachet Caillerets 1985 $41 (11/15/87)
69 C. BERGERET Chassagne-Montrachet 1985 $31 (8/31/87)
71 C. BERGERET Chassagne-Montrachet Morgeot 1985 $35 (8/31/87)
82 BICHOT Chassagne-Montrachet Morgeot-Vignes-Blanches 1988 $40 (2/15/91)
90 BICHOT Chassagne-Montrachet La Romanée 1986 $32 (4/30/88)
88 BLAIN-GAGNARD Chassagne-Montrachet Caillerets 1985 $45 (5/31/88)
86 JEAN CLAUDE BOISSET Chassagne-Montrachet 1988 $28 (2/15/91)
88 BOUCHARD PERE & FILS Chassagne-Montrachet 1989 $17 (4/30/91)
80 BOUCHARD PERE & FILS Chassagne-Montrachet 1982 $17.50 (7/01/84)
93 HUBERT BOUZEREAU Chassagne-Montrachet 1985 $35 (8/31/87)
77 PHILIPPE BOUZEREAU Chassagne-Montrachet Les Meix Goudard 1986 $29 (11/15/88)
88 CHARTRON & TREBUCHET Chassagne-Montrachet 1989 $46 (2/15/91)
91 CHARTRON & TREBUCHET Chassagne-Montrachet 1988 $26 (2/28/90)
94 CHARTRON & TREBUCHET Chassagne-Montrachet Les Morgeots 1989 $54 (2/15/91)
96 CHARTRON & TREBUCHET Chassagne-Montrachet Les Morgeots 1988 $34 (2/28/90)
90 CHARTRON & TREBUCHET Chassagne-Montrachet Les Morgeots 1987 $40 (3/15/89)
96 F. CHAUVENET Chassagne-Montrachet 1985 $35 (3/15/87) SS

86 F. CHAUVENET Chassagne-Montrachet 1982 $13 (3/16/85)
87 F. CHAUVENET Chassagne-Montrachet Clos St.-Marc 1986 $38 (6/30/88)
91 F. CHAUVENET Chassagne-Montrachet Clos St.-Marc 1985 $43 (6/15/87)
93 F. CHAUVENET Chassagne-Montrachet Morgeot 1986 $45 (5/31/88)
96 F. CHAUVENET Chassagne-Montrachet Morgeot 1985 $37 (5/15/87) CS
94 FERNAND COFFINET Chassagne-Montrachet 1985 $25 (5/15/87)
86 MICHEL COLIN-DELEGER Chassagne-Montrachet 1988 $40 (2/28/91)
90 MICHEL COLIN-DELEGER Chassagne-Montrachet Les Chaumées 1988 $48 (2/28/91)
88 MICHEL COLIN-DELEGER Chassagne-Montrachet Morgeot 1987 $43 (5/31/89)
90 MICHEL COLIN-DELEGER Chassagne-Montrachet Les Remilly 1988 $30 (5/15/90)
93 MICHEL COLIN-DELEGER Chassagne-Montrachet Les Remilly 1986 $38 (10/31/88)
88 MICHEL COLIN-DELEGER Chassagne-Montrachet Les Vergers 1988 $48 (5/15/90)
90 MICHEL COLIN-DELEGER Chassagne-Montrachet Les Vergers 1987 $42 (11/15/89)
83 MADAME FRANCOIS COLIN Chassagne-Montrachet Clos Devant 1988 $26 (5/15/90)
83 CORON PERE Chassagne-Montrachet 1985 $20 (8/31/87)
89 GEORGES DELEGER Chassagne-Montrachet 1986 $82 (12/15/88)
87 JOSEPH DROUHIN Chassagne-Montrachet 1988 $39 (3/31/90)
82 JOSEPH DROUHIN Chassagne-Montrachet 1987 $39 (3/15/89)
84 JOSEPH DROUHIN Chassagne-Montrachet 1986 $35 (6/30/88)
87 JOSEPH DROUHIN Chassagne-Montrachet 1982 $21.75 (10/01/84)
90 JOSEPH DROUHIN Chassagne-Montrachet Marquis de Laguiche 1989 $58 (2/15/91)
84 JOSEPH DROUHIN Chassagne-Montrachet Marquis de Laguiche 1987 Rel: $48 Cur: $61 (3/15/89)
91 JOSEPH DROUHIN Chassagne-Montrachet Marquis de Laguiche 1986 Rel: $43 Cur: $43 (5/31/88)
93 JOSEPH DROUHIN Chassagne-Montrachet Marquis de Laguiche 1985 Rel: $40 Cur: $40 (2/29/88)
91 JOSEPH DROUHIN Chassagne-Montrachet Marquis de Laguiche 1983 Rel: $35 Cur: $35 (2/29/88)
71 FONTAINE-GAGNARD Chassagne-Montrachet Morgeot 1985 $45 (5/31/88)
83 JEAN-NOEL GAGNARD Chassagne-Montrachet 1986 $36 (3/15/89)
92 JEAN-NOEL GAGNARD Chassagne-Montrachet 1985 $40 (9/15/87)
96 JEAN-NOEL GAGNARD Chassagne-Montrachet 1984 $32 (4/30/87)
87 JEAN-NOEL GAGNARD Chassagne-Montrachet 1983 $25 (10/01/85)
94 JEAN-NOEL GAGNARD Chassagne-Montrachet Les Caillerets 1985 $45 (9/15/87)
80 JEAN-NOEL GAGNARD Chassagne-Montrachet Morgeot 1988 $54 (11/15/90)
89 JEAN-NOEL GAGNARD Chassagne-Montrachet Morgeot 1986 $54 (11/15/88)
86 JEAN-NOEL GAGNARD Chassagne-Montrachet Morgeot 1985 $45 (9/15/87)
91 JEAN-NOEL GAGNARD Chassagne-Montrachet Première Cru 1988 $50 (10/15/90)
74 JEAN-NOEL GAGNARD Chassagne-Montrachet Première Cru 1986 $47 (12/15/88)
83 HENRI GERMAIN Chassagne-Montrachet Morgeot 1988 $43 (4/30/91)
78 HENRI GERMAIN Chassagne-Montrachet Morgeot 1988 $43 (2/15/91)
86 HENRI GERMAIN Chassagne-Montrachet Morgeot 1986 $39 (3/15/89)
89 JEAN GERMAIN Chassagne-Montrachet 1985 $35 (9/15/87)
93 JEAN GERMAIN Chassagne-Montrachet 1983 $18 (9/01/85)
91 LOUIS JADOT Chassagne-Montrachet 1986 $32 (5/31/89)
91 LOUIS JADOT Chassagne-Montrachet 1985 $32 (2/29/88)
81 LOUIS JADOT Chassagne-Montrachet 1984 $30 (2/29/88)
89 LOUIS JADOT Chassagne-Montrachet 1983 $28 (2/29/88)
88 LOUIS JADOT Chassagne-Montrachet Morgeot 1984 $38 (2/29/88)
86 LOUIS JADOT Chassagne-Montrachet Morgeot 1983 $34 (2/29/88)
89 LOUIS JADOT Chassagne-Montrachet Morgeot Clos de la Chapelle Domaine du Duc de Magenta 1988 $43 (4/30/91)
85 LOUIS JADOT Chassagne-Montrachet Morgeot Clos de la Chapelle Domaine de la Duc de Magent 1986 $41 (5/31/89)
89 LOUIS JADOT Chassagne-Montrachet Morgeot Clos de la Chapelle Domaine du Duc de Magenta 1985 $38 (2/29/88)
83 JAFFELIN Chassagne-Montrachet 1987 $30 (3/15/89)
91 JAFFELIN Chassagne-Montrachet Les Caillerets 1983 $20 (6/01/85)
91 LABOURE-ROI Chassagne-Montrachet 1985 $31.50 (8/31/87)
90 LAROCHE Chassagne-Montrachet 1989 $45 (2/28/91)
83 LAROCHE Chassagne-Montrachet 1988 $33 (2/15/91)
90 LAROCHE Chassagne-Montrachet Première Cru 1988 $39 (2/15/91)
90 LOUIS LATOUR Chassagne-Montrachet 1986 $38 (9/30/88)
87 LOUIS LATOUR Chassagne-Montrachet 1986 $38 (2/29/88)
88 LOUIS LATOUR Chassagne-Montrachet 1985 $33 (2/29/88)
85 LOUIS LATOUR Chassagne-Montrachet 1985 $33 (6/15/87)
78 LOUIS LATOUR Chassagne-Montrachet 1984 $33 (2/29/88)
88 LOUIS LATOUR Chassagne-Montrachet 1982 $33 (2/29/88)
92 LOUIS LATOUR Chassagne-Montrachet Première Cru 1986 $43 (2/29/88)
95 OLIVIER LEFLAIVE FRERES Chassagne-Montrachet Les Baudines 1986 $38 (10/15/90)
86 LEROY Chassagne-Montrachet Les Chenevottes 1988 $116 (4/30/91)
90 LEROY Chassagne-Montrachet Les Ruchottes 1988 $116 (4/30/91)
84 A. LIGERET Chassagne-Montrachet Réserve Antonin Toursier 1988 $45 (2/15/91)
73 LUPE-CHOLET Chassagne-Montrachet Morgeot Vignes Blanches 1987 $45 (11/15/89)
85 LUPE-CHOLET Chassagne-Montrachet La Romanée 1986 $26 (2/29/88)
80 CHATEAU DE LA MALTROYE Chassagne-Montrachet Clos de la Maltroye 1983 $21 (6/01/86)
86 CHATEAU DE LA MALTROYE Chassagne-Montrachet Grandes Ruchottes 1989 $40 (2/28/91)
74 CHATEAU DE LA MALTROYE Chassagne-Montrachet Maltroie-Crets 1986 $27 (10/31/88)
86 CHATEAU DE LA MALTROYE Chassagne-Montrachet Morgeot-Fairendes 1986 $26 (9/30/88)
79 CHATEAU DE LA MALTROYE Chassagne-Montrachet Morgeot-Fairendes 1983 $19 (11/16/85)
87 CHATEAU DE LA MALTROYE Chassagne-Montrachet Morgeot Vigne Blanche 1989 $40 (2/28/91)
90 CHATEAU DE LA MALTROYE Chassagne-Montrachet Morgeot Vigne Blanche 1986 $29 (9/30/88)
88 CHATEAU DE LA MALTROYE Chassagne-Montrachet Morgeot Vigne Blanche 1983 $17 (6/16/85)
89 PROSPER MAUFOUX Chassagne-Montrachet 1985 $31 (4/30/88)
71 PROSPER MAUFOUX Chassagne-Montrachet Les Chenevottes 1987 $37 (2/28/91)
74 MOILLARD Chassagne-Montrachet La Romanée 1987 $31 (11/15/89)
88 MOILLARD Chassagne-Montrachet La Romanée 1986 $40 (4/30/88)
91 BERNARD MOREAU Chassagne-Montrachet Grandes Ruchottes 1986 $38 (9/30/88)
86 BERNARD MOREY Chassagne-Montrachet 1982 $11.25 (3/01/85)
88 BERNARD MOREY Chassagne-Montrachet Les Baudines 1986 $41 (12/15/88)
91 BERNARD MOREY Chassagne-Montrachet Les Baudines 1986 $41 (2/29/88)
91 BERNARD MOREY Chassagne-Montrachet Les Embrazées 1986 $40 (12/15/88)
88 BERNARD MOREY Chassagne-Montrachet Morgeot 1987 $42 (5/31/89)
88 BERNARD MOREY Chassagne-Montrachet Morgeot 1986 $35 (12/15/88)
88 JEAN-MARC MOREY Chassagne-Montrachet Champs-Gains 1986 $38 (12/15/88)
75 JEAN-MARC MOREY Chassagne-Montrachet Champs-Gains 1985 $30 (10/31/87)
85 JEAN-MARC MOREY Chassagne-Montrachet Les Caillerets 1986 $39 (12/15/88)
90 JEAN-MARC MOREY Chassagne-Montrachet Les Chaumées 1986 $38 (12/15/88)
86 JEAN-MARC MOREY Chassagne-Montrachet Les Chênevottes 1986 $34 (12/15/88)
83 DOMAINE MARC MOREY Chassagne-Montrachet 1986 $34 (9/30/88)
94 DOMAINE MARC MOREY Chassagne-Montrachet Morgeot 1986 $37 (9/30/88)
91 DOMAINE MARC MOREY Chassagne-Montrachet Virondot 1986 $42 (12/15/88)
90 FERNAND PILLOT Chassagne-Montrachet Grandes Ruchottes 1988 $43 (5/15/90)
91 FERNAND PILLOT Chassagne-Montrachet Morgeot 1988 $35 (5/15/90)
87 FERNAND PILLOT Chassagne-Montrachet Les Vergers 1988 $35 (5/15/90)
85 FERNAND PILLOT Chassagne-Montrachet Les Vergers 1985 $28 (5/31/89)
88 JEAN PILLOT Chassagne-Montrachet Les Caillerets 1988 $39 (2/28/91)
84 PAUL PILLOT Chassagne-Montrachet Les Caillerets 1985 $30 (10/31/87)
91 PAUL PILLOT Chassagne-Montrachet Les Grandes Ruchottes 1987 $38 (2/28/90)
91 PAUL PILLOT Chassagne-Montrachet Les Grandes Ruchottes 1986 $30 (11/15/88)
88 PAUL PILLOT Chassagne-Montrachet Les Grandes Ruchottes 1985 $30 (10/31/87)
91 PAUL PILLOT Chassagne-Montrachet La Romanée 1987 $48 (2/28/90)
86 DOMAINE PONAVOY Chassagne-Montrachet 1988 $40 (2/15/91)
86 DOMAINE RAMONET Chassagne-Montrachet 1988 $43 (2/28/91)
92 DOMAINE RAMONET Chassagne-Montrachet Morgeot 1988 $59 (2/28/91)
79 DOMAINE RAMONET Chassagne-Montrachet Morgeot 1987 $49 (2/28/90)
86 DOMAINE RAMONET Chassagne-Montrachet Les Ruchottes 1987 $52 (2/28/90)
90 REMOISSENET Chassagne-Montrachet Les Caillerets 1985 $63 (2/29/88)
58 ANTONIN RODET Chassagne-Montrachet 1981 $14 (12/01/84)
89 DOMAINE ROUX PERE & FILS Chassagne-Montrachet 1989 $45 (2/28/91)
88 DOMAINE ROUX PERE & FILS Chassagne-Montrachet 1988 $35 (2/28/90)
90 DOMAINE ROUX PERE & FILS Chassagne-Montrachet 1986 $34 (2/29/88)
86 DOMAINE ROUX PERE & FILS Chassagne-Montrachet 1985 $32 (8/31/87)
88 DOMAINE ROUX PERE & FILS Chassagne-Montrachet 1985 $32 (2/28/87)
88 DOMAINE ROUX PERE & FILS Chassagne-Montrachet Morgeot 1989 $55 (2/28/91)
86 DOMAINE ROUX PERE & FILS Chassagne-Montrachet Morgeot 1988 $39 (2/28/90)
79 DOMAINE ROUX PERE & FILS Chassagne-Montrachet Morgeot 1987 $43 (5/31/89)
91 DOMAINE ROUX PERE & FILS Chassagne-Montrachet Morgeot 1986 $36 (2/29/88)
91 DOMAINE ETIENNE SAUZET Chassagne-Montrachet 1988 $38 (2/15/91)
76 LEONARD DE ST.-AUBIN Chassagne-Montrachet 1986 $25 (12/31/87)
81 HENRI DE VILLAMONT Chassagne-Montrachet Les Vergers 1986 $29 (12/15/88)

MEURSAULT

77 R. BALLOT-MILLOT & FILS Meursault Charmes 1987 $34 (8/31/90)
88 R. BALLOT-MILLOT & FILS Meursault Les Criots 1985 $34 (4/30/88)
75 BICHOT Meursault 1987 $24 (9/30/89)
92 BICHOT Meursault Charmes 1988 $40 (7/15/90)
82 BICHOT Meursault Charmes 1986 $37 (3/15/88)
93 BICHOT Meursault Charmes 1985 $30 (2/15/88)
92 BICHOT Meursault Hospices de Beaune Cuvée Goureau 1986 $55 (2/15/88)
85 BICHOT Meursault Poruzot 1988 $36 (7/15/90)
86 BITOUZET-PRIEUR Meursault 1987 $28 (7/15/90)
87 BITOUZET-PRIEUR Meursault Charmes 1987 $41 (2/28/91)
87 BITOUZET-PRIEUR Meursault Clos du Cromin 1987 $34 (8/31/90)
91 GUY BOCARD Meursault Charmes 1985 $32 (4/30/87)
69 GUY BOCARD Meursault Les Grands Charrons 1986 $27 (10/15/88)
84 GUY BOCARD Meursault Limozin 1986 $28 (10/15/88)
85 GUY BOCARD Meursault Limozin 1985 $28 (4/30/87)
87 PIERRE BOILLOT Meursault 1988 $37 (8/31/90)
90 PIERRE BOILLOT Meursault Charmes 1988 $47 (8/31/90)
79 PIERRE BOILLOT Meursault Charmes 1987 $44 (8/31/90)
83 JEAN CLAUDE BOISSET Meursault 1988 $28 (5/31/91)
81 JEAN CLAUDE BOISSET Meursault 1988 $27 (5/15/90)
83 BOUCHARD PERE & FILS Meursault 1989 $37 (4/30/91)
75 BOUCHARD PERE & FILS Meursault 1983 $20 (4/30/87)
83 BOUCHARD PERE & FILS Meursault Clos des Corvées de Citeaux 1986 $26 (3/15/89)
77 BOUCHARD PERE & FILS Meursault Genevrières Domaines du Château de Beaune 1986 $44 (3/15/89)
88 HUBERT BOUZEREAU Meursault Limozin 1985 $27 (8/31/87)
73 HUBERT BOUZEREAU Meursault Les Narvaux 1985 $25 (4/30/87)
70 HUBERT BOUZEREAU Meursault Les Tessons 1985 $25 (5/31/88)
93 MICHEL BOUZEREAU Meursault Genevrières 1989 $46 (5/31/91)
93 MICHEL BOUZEREAU Meursault Genevrières 1988 $37 (7/15/90)
90 MICHEL BOUZEREAU Meursault Les Grands Charrons 1989 $33 (5/31/91)
91 MICHEL BOUZEREAU Meursault Les Grands Charrons 1988 $25 (8/31/90)
87 MICHEL BOUZEREAU Meursault Les Tessons 1989 $35 (5/31/91)
90 MICHEL BOUZEREAU Meursault Les Tessons 1988 $28 (8/31/90)
75 PHILIPPE BOUZEREAU Meursault Charmes 1987 $37 (11/15/89)
80 PHILIPPE BOUZEREAU Meursault Genevrières 1987 $37 (7/15/90)
81 PHILIPPE BOUZEREAU Meursault Les Narvaux 1986 $31 (3/15/89)
83 PHILIPPE BOUZEREAU Meursault Poruzot 1987 $36 (11/15/89)
60 BOYER-MARTENOT Meursault Les Narvaux 1983 $15 (2/16/86)
88 CHARTRON & TREBUCHET Meursault 1989 $41 (2/28/91)
87 CHARTRON & TREBUCHET Meursault Charmes 1986 $45 (5/31/88)
91 CHARTRON & TREBUCHET Meursault Les Charmes 1989 $57 (2/28/91)
91 CHARTRON & TREBUCHET Meursault Genevrières Hospices de Beaune Cuvée Baudot 1987 $87 (3/15/89)
77 F. CHAUVENET Meursault Les Boucheres 1986 $40 (6/30/88)
84 F. CHAUVENET Meursault Les Casse Têtes 1985 $32 (8/31/87)
71 F. CHAUVENET Meursault Les Casse Têtes 1984 $19 (7/16/86)
82 F. CHAUVENET Meursault Les Casse Têtes 1982 $11 (3/01/85)
86 F. CHAUVENET Meursault Charmes Hospices de Beaune Cuvée de Bahèzre-de-Lanlay 1985 $141 (3/15/89)
85 F. CHAUVENET Meursault Les Genevrières 1986 $40 (4/30/88)
88 F. CHAUVENET Meursault Genevrières Hospices de Beaune Cuvée Baudot 1983 $55 (11/01/85)
91 F. CHAUVENET Meursault Hospices de Beaune Cuvée Jehan-Humblot 1985 $90 (7/31/87)
92 F. CHAUVENET Meursault Hospices de Beaune Cuvée Loppin 1982 $33 (1/01/85) CS
86 F. CHAUVENET Meursault Les Perrières 1986 $40 (4/30/88)
92 F. CHAUVENET Meursault Les Poruzots 1986 $40 (4/30/88)
81 CHEVALIER DE BEAUBASSIN Meursault 1985 $24 (4/30/88)
86 DENIS CHEVILLON Meursault Charmes 1959 (NA) (8/31/90) (TR)

FRANCE
BURGUNDY WHITE/CÔTE DE BEAUNE/MEURSAULT

86 J.-F. COCHE-DURY Meursault 1987 $33 (2/28/90)
91 J.-F. COCHE-DURY Meursault Les Chevalières 1987 $36 (2/28/90)
90 J.-F. COCHE-DURY Meursault Les Rougeots 1987 $33 (2/28/90)
90 J.-F. COCHE-DURY Meursault Perrières 1987 $50 (2/28/90)
64 CORON PERE Meursault 1985 $18 (8/31/87)
89 JOSEPH DROUHIN Meursault 1988 $34 (3/31/90)
83 JOSEPH DROUHIN Meursault 1986 $29 (5/31/88)
84 JOSEPH DROUHIN Meursault Perrières 1989 $60 (2/28/91)
88 JOSEPH DROUHIN Meursault Perrières 1988 $48 (3/31/90)
80 JOSEPH DROUHIN Meursault Perrières 1987 $44 (4/30/89)
88 JOSEPH DROUHIN Meursault Perrières 1986 $41 (5/31/88)
87 JOSEPH DROUHIN Meursault Perrières 1985 $40 (4/30/87)
91 HENRI GERMAIN Meursault 1988 $35 (2/28/91)
88 HENRI GERMAIN Meursault 1986 $27 (4/30/89)
89 HENRI GERMAIN Meursault Charmes 1988 $42 (5/15/90)
86 HENRI GERMAIN Meursault Charmes 1986 $39 (4/30/89)
90 ALBERT GRIVAULT Meursault Clos des Perrières 1984 $50 (8/31/87)
92 CHATEAU DES HERBEUX Meursault Perrières 1988 $42 (7/15/90)
90 LOUIS JADOT Meursault Perrières 1988 $57 (4/30/91)
83 JAFFELIN Meursault 1987 $25 (3/15/89)
86 JAFFELIN Meursault 1983 $16.50 (6/01/85)
76 FRANCOIS JOBARD Meursault 1987 $25 (7/15/90)
82 FRANCOIS JOBARD Meursault 1986 $30 (9/30/89)
85 FRANCOIS JOBARD Meursault Blagny 1987 $37 (7/15/90)
80 FRANCOIS JOBARD Meursault Charmes 1987 $34 (8/31/90)
75 FRANCOIS JOBARD Meursault Genevrières 1987 $34 (8/31/90)
76 FRANCOIS JOBARD Meursault Poruzot 1987 $40 (7/15/90)
73 FRANCOIS JOBARD Meursault Poruzot 1985 $28 (11/15/87)
87 LABOURE-ROI Meursault 1988 $35 (8/31/90)
86 LABOURE-ROI Meursault 1986 $28 (4/30/88)
70 LABOURE-ROI Meursault 1985 $32 (11/15/86)
89 DOMAINE LAROCHE Meursault Poruzot 1986 $27 (10/31/88)
82 LAROCHE Meursault 1988 $28 (8/31/90)
82 LAROCHE Meursault Perrières 1986 $20 (10/31/88)
86 LOUIS LATOUR Meursault 1985 $25 (11/15/87)
83 LOUIS LATOUR Meursault 1984 $28 (4/30/87)
45 LOUIS LATOUR Meursault Blagny Château de Blagny 1982 Rel: $65 Cur: $79 (12/01/85)
83 LOUIS LATOUR Meursault Première Cru 1983 $24 (11/16/85)
82 OLIVIER LEFLAIVE FRERES Meursault 1984 $22 (7/16/86)
87 LEROY Meursault Les Narvaux 1988 $100 (4/30/91)
89 LEROY Meursault Perrières 1988 $150 (4/30/91)
83 A. LIGERET Meursault Les Narvaux 1988 $45 (10/15/90)
80 LUPE-CHOLET Meursault 1986 $26 (2/15/88)
90 LUPE-CHOLET Meursault 1984 $20 (10/31/86)
69 LUPE-CHOLET Meursault Charmes 1988 $40 (2/28/90)
89 LUPE-CHOLET Meursault Hospices de Beaune Cuvée Goureau 1986 $45 (2/15/88)
75 M & G Meursault Les Forges 1987 $42 (3/31/91)
86 DOMAINE RENE MANUEL Meursault Clos des Bouches Chères 1988 $50 (8/31/90)
93 DOMAINE RENE MANUEL Meursault Clos des Bouches Chères 1985 $39 (8/31/87)
85 DOMAINE RENE MANUEL Meursault Poruzot 1985 $37 (8/31/87)
81 DOMAINE JOSEPH MATROT Meursault 1987 $30 (5/15/90)
73 DOMAINE JOSEPH MATROT Meursault 1987 $30 (7/31/89)
65 DOMAINE JOSEPH MATROT Meursault Les Chevalières 1986 $36 (12/15/88)
75 PIERRE MATROT Meursault 1985 $27.50 (12/31/87)
86 PROSPER MAUFOUX Meursault 1987 $27 (5/15/90)
64 MAZILLY PERE Meursault 1984 $17.50 (4/30/87)
79 MESTRE-MICHELOT Meursault Charmes 1987 $50 (8/31/90)
86 MESTRE-MICHELOT Meursault Le Limozin 1986 $39 (3/15/89)
83 MESTRE-MICHELOT Meursault Sous la Velle 1988 $40 (2/28/91)
94 CHATEAU DE MEURSAULT Meursault 1986 S55 (7/31/91)
95 CHATEAU DE MEURSAULT Meursault 1985 Rel: $50 Cur: $50 (12/31/87)
84 C. MICHELOT Meursault Charmes 1988 $55 (2/28/91)
82 C. MICHELOT Meursault Grands Charrons 1987 $41 (8/31/90)
78 C. MICHELOT Meursault Les Tillets 1987 $32 (8/31/90)
91 G. MICHELOT Meursault Clos du Cromin 1986 $39 (3/15/89)
88 JEAN MICHELOT Meursault 1988 $33 (5/15/90)
90 JEAN MICHELOT Meursault 1986 $27 (12/15/88)
81 MICHELOT-BUISSON Meursault 1987 $37 (8/31/90)
85 MICHELOT-BUISSON Meursault Charmes 1986 $50 (3/15/89)
93 MICHELOT-BUISSON Meursault Genevrières 1988 $55 (2/28/91)
78 MICHELOT-BUISSON Meursault Genevrières 1987 $50 (8/31/90)
72 MICHELOT-BUISSON Meursault Genevrières 1986 $50 (3/15/89)
93 MICHELOT-BUISSON Meursault Le Limozin 1985 $37 (8/31/87)
63 MOILLARD Meursault 1987 $24 (11/15/89)
74 MOILLARD Meursault Charmes 1987 $33 (9/30/89)
74 MOILLARD Meursault Charmes 1986 $37 (5/31/88)
95 MOILLARD Meursault Charmes 1985 $30 (11/30/86)
88 MOILLARD Meursault Clos du Cromin 1986 $28 (10/15/88)
86 MOILLARD Meursault Poruzot 1986 $37 (5/31/88)
66 CHARLES MONCAUT Meursault 1983 $16 (6/01/86)
87 DOMAINE RENE MONNIER Meursault Charmes 1985 $39 (12/15/88)
89 DOMAINE RENE MONNIER Meursault Les Chevalires 1986 $34 (10/15/88)
89 DOMAINE RENE MONNIER Meursault Le Limozin 1986 $32 (12/15/88)
87 PIERRE MOREY Meursault Charmes 1987 $41 (2/28/90)

89 PIERRE MOREY Meursault Charmes 1986 $47 (12/15/88)
91 PIERRE MOREY Meursault Genevrières 1987 $41 (11/15/89)
92 PIERRE MOREY Meursault Perrières 1986 $47 (12/15/88)
90 PIERRE MOREY Meursault Les Tessons 1986 $35 (12/15/88)
76 PIERRE MOREY Meursault Les Tessons 1983 $17.25 (10/16/85)
77 NOIROT-CARRIERE Meursault Perrières 1986 $39 (2/28/90)
88 PATRIARCHE Meursault Réserve St.-Anne 1985 $23 (9/30/89)
88 MICHEL POUHIN-SEURRE Meursault Le Limosin 1986 $25 (2/15/88)
85 DOMAINE PRIEUR-BRUNET Meursault Charmes 1988 $35 (8/31/90)
90 DOMAINE PRIEUR-BRUNET Meursault Charmes 1986 $30 (4/30/89)
89 DOMAINE PRIEUR-BRUNET Meursault Chevalières 1988 $30 (2/28/91)
82 CHATEAU DE PULIGNY-MONTRACHET Meursault 1989 $42 (2/28/91)
91 CHATEAU DE PULIGNY-MONTRACHET Meursault Les Perrières 1989 $57 (2/28/91)
79 CHATEAU DE PULIGNY-MONTRACHET Meursault Les Poruzots 1988 $52 (7/15/90)
90 CHATEAU DE PULIGNY-MONTRACHET Meursault Les Poruzots 1989 $55 (2/28/91)
68 REMOISSENET Meursault Charmes 1986 $49 (12/15/88)
65 REMOISSENET Meursault Cuvée Maurice Chevalier 1986 $35 (3/15/89)
75 REMOISSENET Meursault Cuvée Maurice Chevalier 1985 $42 (3/15/88)
91 REMOISSENET Meursault Genevrières 1986 $49 (12/15/88)
89 REMOISSENET Meursault Genevrières 1985 $60 (3/15/88)
90 DOMAINE ROUGEOT-LATOUR Meursault Charmes 1986 $38 (6/30/88)
69 DOMAINE ROUGEOT-LATOUR Meursault Les Pellans 1986 $25 (10/15/88)
87 DOMAINE GUY ROULOT Meursault Les Meix Chavaux 1988 $33 (5/15/90)
91 DOMAINE GUY ROULOT Meursault Les Tessons Clos de Mon Plaisir 1988 $35 (5/15/90)
82 DOMAINE ROUX PERE & FILS Meursault 1985 $27.50 (2/28/87)
87 ROLAND THEVENIN Meursault Les Casse Têtes 1985 $20 (4/30/87)
81 JACQUES THEVENOT-MACHAL Meursault Poruzot 1987 $38 (7/31/89)
86 JACQUES THEVENOT-MACHAL Meursault Poruzot 1986 $38 (3/15/89)
84 THORIN Meursault 1987 $25 (12/15/88)
90 VINCENT VIAL Meursault 1947 (NA) (8/31/90) (TR)
71 HENRI DE VILLAMONT Meursault Les Genevrières 1986 $29 (12/15/88)

MONTRACHET

90 AMIOT-BONFILS Montrachet 1988 $135 (2/28/90)
93 BACHELET-RAMONET Bienvenues-Bâtard-Montrachet 1979 (NA) (2/29/88)
90 BICHOT Bâtard-Montrachet 1983 $60 (2/29/88)
68 BOUCHARD PERE & FILS Chevalier-Montrachet Domaines du Château de Beaune 1986 Rel: $92 Cur: $92 (2/28/89)
91 BOUCHARD PERE & FILS Chevalier-Montrachet Domaines du Château de Beaune 1986 Rel: $92 Cur: $92 (2/29/88)
93 ROGER CAILLOT Bâtard-Montrachet 1985 $90 (5/31/88)
94 DOMAINE JEAN CHARTRON Chevalier-Montrachet 1989 $125 (2/28/91)
97 DOMAINE JEAN CHARTRON Chevalier-Montrachet 1988 Rel: $95 Cur: $106 (2/28/90)
92 DOMAINE JEAN CHARTRON Chevalier-Montrachet 1987 Rel: $100 Cur: $100 (2/28/89)
95 DOMAINE JEAN CHARTRON Chevalier-Montrachet 1986 Rel: $125 Cur: $125 (5/31/88)
91 DOMAINE JEAN CHARTRON Chevalier-Montrachet 1985 Rel: $75 Cur: $75 (10/31/87)
92 CHARTRON & TREBUCHET Bâtard-Montrachet 1989 $120 (2/28/91)
95 CHARTRON & TREBUCHET Bâtard-Montrachet 1988 $90 (2/28/91)
92 CHARTRON & TREBUCHET Bâtard-Montrachet 1987 $100 (3/31/89)
93 CHARTRON & TREBUCHET Montrachet Le Montrachet 1987 $240 (2/28/89)
90 DOMAINE HENRI CLERC & FILS Bâtard-Montrachet 1986 $104 (3/31/89)
90 DOMAINE HENRI CLERC & FILS Bienvenues-Bâtard-Montrachet 1986 $69 (2/29/88)
90 JOSEPH DROUHIN Bâtard-Montrachet 1987 Rel: $98 Cur: $98 (3/31/89)
94 JOSEPH DROUHIN Bâtard-Montrachet 1986 Rel: $113 Cur: $113 (12/31/88)
92 JOSEPH DROUHIN Bâtard-Montrachet 1986 Rel: $113 Cur: $113 (2/29/88)
95 JOSEPH DROUHIN Bâtard-Montrachet 1985 Rel: $95 Cur: $95 (2/29/88)
92 JOSEPH DROUHIN Bâtard-Montrachet 1984 Rel: $65 Cur: $65 (2/29/88)
84 JOSEPH DROUHIN Chevalier-Montrachet 1985 $100 (4/30/87)
95 JOSEPH DROUHIN Montrachet Marquis de Laguiche 1988 $180 (2/28/91)
95 JOSEPH DROUHIN Montrachet Marquis de Laguiche 1987 Rel: $180 Cur: $209 (10/15/90)
97 JOSEPH DROUHIN Montrachet Marquis de Laguiche 1986 Rel: $200 Cur: $244 (10/31/88) CS
100 JOSEPH DROUHIN Montrachet Marquis de Laguiche 1985 Rel: $142 Cur: $265 (2/29/88)
97 JOSEPH DROUHIN Montrachet Marquis de Laguiche 1979 Cur: $250 (2/29/88)
95 JEAN-NOEL GAGNARD Bâtard-Montrachet 1986 $93 (12/31/88)
90 CHATEAU DES HERBEUX Chevalier-Montrachet 1988 $100 (7/31/90)
78 CHATEAU DES HERBEUX Montrachet 1988 $165 (7/31/90)
93 LOUIS JADOT Bâtard-Montrachet 1986 $99 (5/31/89)
94 LOUIS JADOT Bâtard-Montrachet 1985 $88 (2/29/88)
92 LOUIS JADOT Bâtard-Montrachet 1983 $80 (2/29/88)
92 LOUIS JADOT Chevalier-Montrachet Les Demoiselles 1988 $127 (5/31/91)
94 LOUIS JADOT Chevalier-Montrachet Les Demoiselles 1985 Rel: $150 Cur: $166 (2/29/88)
92 LOUIS JADOT Chevalier-Montrachet Les Demoiselles 1984 Rel: $95 Cur: $95 (2/29/88)
98 LOUIS JADOT Montrachet 1973 Cur: $300 (2/29/88)
84 JAFFELIN Bâtard-Montrachet 1984 $77 (6/01/86)
87 LAROCHE Criots-Bâtard-Montrachet 1986 $63 (10/31/88)
89 LOUIS LATOUR Bâtard-Montrachet 1987 Rel: $82 Cur: $83 (2/28/90)
93 LOUIS LATOUR Bâtard-Montrachet 1985 Rel: $93 Cur: $93 (11/15/87)
94 LOUIS LATOUR Chevalier-Montrachet Les Demoiselles 1986 Rel: $150 Cur: $150 (10/31/88)
93 LOUIS LATOUR Montrachet 1988 Rel: $200 Cur: $200 (10/15/90)
95 LOUIS LATOUR Montrachet 1986 Rel: $125 Cur: $179 (10/31/88)
88 LOUIS LATOUR Montrachet 1979 Cur: $200 (2/29/88)
83 DOMAINE LEFLAIVE Bienvenues-Bâtard-Montrachet 1987 $79 (12/31/90)
95 DOMAINE LEFLAIVE Bienvenues-Bâtard-Montrachet 1979 Cur: $137 (2/29/88)
94 DOMAINE LEFLAIVE Chevalier-Montrachet 1987 $99 (12/31/90)
97 DOMAINE LEFLAIVE Chevalier-Montrachet 1983 Cur: $150 (2/29/88)
85 DOMAINE LEQUIN-ROUSSOT Bâtard-Montrachet 1987 $79 (7/31/90)
94 MOILLARD Bâtard-Montrachet 1986 $70 (5/31/88)
93 PAUL PERNOT Bâtard-Montrachet 1989 $160 (2/28/91)
92 DOMAINE JACQUES PRIEUR Montrachet 1986 $165 (2/28/89)
87 DOMAINE PRIEUR-BRUNET Bâtard-Montrachet 1988 $75 (7/31/90)
95 DOMAINE RAMONET Bâtard-Montrachet 1988 $190 (2/28/91)
87 DOMAINE RAMONET Bâtard-Montrachet 1987 Rel: $119 Cur: $119 (2/29/90)
96 DOMAINE RAMONET Montrachet 1988 $590 (2/28/91)
81 REMOISSENET Bâtard-Montrachet 1986 $87 (2/29/88)
95 REMOISSENET Bienvenues-Bâtard-Montrachet 1986 $100 (11/15/88)
82 REMOISSENET Bienvenues-Bâtard-Montrachet 1986 $87 (2/29/88)
85 REMOISSENET Montrachet Le Montrachet du Domaine Thénard 1986 Rel: $125 Cur: $166 (12/31/88)
91 REMOISSENET Montrachet Le Montrachet du Domaine Thénard 1986 Rel: $125 Cur: $166 (2/29/88)

91 REMOISSENET Montrachet Le Montrachet du Domaine Thénard 1985 Cur: $155 (2/29/88)
94 ROMANEE-CONTI Montrachet 1988 $600 (4/30/91)
94 ROMANEE-CONTI Montrachet 1987 $525 (12/31/90)
96 ROMANEE-CONTI Montrachet 1985 Cur: $640 (2/28/87) (HS)
93 ROMANEE-CONTI Montrachet 1984 Cur: $460 (2/28/87) (HS)
95 ROMANEE-CONTI Montrachet 1983 Cur: $730 (2/28/87) (HS)
93 ROMANEE-CONTI Montrachet 1982 Cur: $600 (2/28/87) (HS)
91 ROMANEE-CONTI Montrachet 1981 Cur: $480 (2/28/87) (HS)
88 ROMANEE-CONTI Montrachet 1980 Cur: $410 (2/28/87) (HS)
89 ROMANEE-CONTI Montrachet 1979 Cur: $610 (2/28/87) (HS)
98 ROMANEE-CONTI Montrachet 1978 Cur: $640 (2/28/87) (HS)
90 ROMANEE-CONTI Montrachet 1977 Cur: $217 (2/28/87) (HS)
94 ROMANEE-CONTI Montrachet 1976 Cur: $510 (2/28/87) (HS)
89 ROMANEE-CONTI Montrachet 1975 Cur: $430 (2/28/87) (HS)
87 ROMANEE-CONTI Montrachet 1974 Cur: $430 (2/28/87) (HS)
99 ROMANEE-CONTI Montrachet 1973 Cur: $500 (2/28/87) (HS)
92 ROMANEE-CONTI Montrachet 1972 Cur: $580 (2/28/87) (HS)
94 ROMANEE-CONTI Montrachet 1971 Cur: $760 (2/28/87) (HS)
86 ROMANEE-CONTI Montrachet 1970 Cur: $680 (2/28/87) (HS)
88 ROMANEE-CONTI Montrachet 1969 Cur: $990 (2/28/87) (HS)
85 ROMANEE-CONTI Montrachet 1968 Cur: $830 (2/28/87) (HS)
85 ROMANEE-CONTI Montrachet 1967 Cur: $1280 (2/28/87) (HS)
95 ROMANEE-CONTI Montrachet 1966 Cur: $810 (2/28/87) (HS)
82 ROMANEE-CONTI Montrachet 1964 Cur: $660 (2/28/87) (HS)
93 DOMAINE ETIENNE SAUZET Bâtard-Montrachet 1988 $92 (2/28/91)
94 DOMAINE ETIENNE SAUZET Bâtard-Montrachet 1988 $92 (12/31/90)
90 DOMAINE ETIENNE SAUZET Bâtard-Montrachet 1986 $85 (2/29/88)
93 DOMAINE BARON THENARD Montrachet 1988 $180 (12/31/90)

PULIGNY-MONTRACHET

87 AMIOT-BONFILS Puligny-Montrachet Les Demoiselles 1988 $33 (3/15/90)
89 ADRIEN BELLAND Puligny-Montrachet 1985 $35 (9/15/87)
75 ADRIEN BELLAND Puligny-Montrachet 1984 $27.25 (1/31/87)
88 ADRIEN BELLAND Puligny-Montrachet 1983 $20 (9/16/85)
77 BICHOT Puligny-Montrachet 1987 $28 (9/30/89)
76 BICHOT Puligny-Montrachet Les Chalumeaux 1988 $39 (6/30/90)
75 HENRI BOILLOT Puligny-Montrachet Clos de la Moushere 1986 $36 (9/30/88)
92 JEAN-MARC BOILLOT Puligny-Montrachet Les Pucelles 1986 $43 (9/30/88)
81 JEAN CLAUDE BOISSET Puligny-Montrachet 1988 $29 (6/30/90)
70 JEAN CLAUDE BOISSET Puligny-Montrachet 1987 $33 (7/31/89)
87 BOUCHARD PERE & FILS Puligny-Montrachet 1986 $31 (2/28/89)
87 BOUCHARD PERE & FILS Puligny-Montrachet 1982 $17.95 (6/16/84)
90 BOUCHARD PERE & FILS Puligny-Montrachet Les Folatières 1986 $33 (2/28/89)
85 BOUCHARD PERE & FILS Puligny-Montrachet Les Folatières 1985 $33 (2/29/88)
88 MICHEL BOUZEREAU Puligny-Montrachet 1985 $30 (5/31/88)
91 MICHEL BOUZEREAU Puligny-Montrachet Les Champs-Gains 1989 $42 (5/31/91)
90 MICHEL BOUZEREAU Puligny-Montrachet Les Champs-Gains 1988 $32 (7/31/90)
86 PHILIPPE BOUZEREAU Puligny-Montrachet Les Champs-Gains 1986 $38 (11/15/88)
94 PHILIPPE BOUZEREAU Puligny-Montrachet Les Champs-Gains 1985 $34 (4/15/87)
73 ROGER CAILLOT Puligny-Montrachet Les Folatières 1988 $40 (6/30/90)
85 LOUIS CARILLON Puligny-Montrachet 1988 $36 (2/28/91)
82 LOUIS CARILLON Puligny-Montrachet 1987 $36 (9/30/89)
88 LOUIS CARILLON Puligny-Montrachet Les Perrières 1988 $39 (2/28/91)
71 CHANSON PERE & FILS Puligny-Montrachet 1988 $44 (10/15/90)
89 DOMAINE JEAN CHARTRON Puligny-Montrachet Clos du Cailleret 1989 $79 (2/28/91)
88 DOMAINE JEAN CHARTRON Puligny-Montrachet Clos de la Pucelle 1989 $69 (2/28/91)
85 DOMAINE JEAN CHARTRON Puligny-Montrachet Clos de la Pucelle 1988 $40 (3/15/90)
81 DOMAINE JEAN CHARTRON Puligny-Montrachet Clos de la Pucelle 1987 $45 (2/28/89)
94 DOMAINE JEAN CHARTRON Puligny-Montrachet Clos de la Pucelle 1986 $50 (5/31/88)
74 DOMAINE JEAN CHARTRON Puligny-Montrachet Clos de la Pucelle 1985 $39 (11/15/87)
88 DOMAINE JEAN CHARTRON Puligny-Montrachet Les Folatières 1989 $62 (2/28/91)
94 DOMAINE JEAN CHARTRON Puligny-Montrachet Les Folatières 1988 $38 (3/15/90)
88 DOMAINE JEAN CHARTRON Puligny-Montrachet Les Folatières 1987 $45 (2/28/89)
88 DOMAINE JEAN CHARTRON Puligny-Montrachet Les Folatières 1986 $50 (5/31/88)
90 DOMAINE JEAN CHARTRON Puligny-Montrachet Les Folatières 1986 $50 (2/28/88)
90 CHARTRON & TREBUCHET Puligny-Montrachet 1988 $30 (3/15/90)
91 CHARTRON & TREBUCHET Puligny-Montrachet Les Garennes 1988 $38 (3/15/90)
90 CHARTRON & TREBUCHET Puligny-Montrachet Les Garennes 1987 $40 (2/28/89)
93 CHARTRON & TREBUCHET Puligny-Montrachet Les Garennes 1986 $49 (5/31/88)
90 CHARTRON & TREBUCHET Puligny-Montrachet Les Garennes 1986 $49 (2/29/88)
89 CHARTRON & TREBUCHET Puligny-Montrachet Les Referts 1988 $35 (3/15/90)
79 CHARTRON & TREBUCHET Puligny-Montrachet Les Referts 1987 $40 (2/28/89)
91 CHARTRON & TREBUCHET Puligny-Montrachet Les Referts 1986 $46 (5/31/88)
88 F. CHAUVENET Puligny-Montrachet Champs-Gains 1984 $40 (4/30/87)
88 F. CHAUVENET Puligny-Montrachet Champs-Gains 1982 $17 (3/16/85)
66 F. CHAUVENET Puligny-Montrachet Reuchaux 1985 $35 (2/28/87)
85 F. CHAUVENET Puligny-Montrachet Reuchaux 1982 $20 (9/16/85)
82 GERARD CHAVY Puligny-Montrachet 1985 $27.50 (12/31/87)
69 GERARD CHAVY Puligny-Montrachet 1984 $22 (11/15/87)
91 GERARD CHAVY Puligny-Montrachet Les Pucelles 1986 $30 (12/15/88)
75 DOMAINE HENRI CLERC & FILS Puligny-Montrachet Les Combettes 1987 $41 (7/31/89)
79 DOMAINE HENRI CLERC & FILS Puligny-Montrachet Les Folatières 1987 $41 (7/31/89)
93 DOMAINE HENRI CLERC & FILS Puligny-Montrachet Les Folatières 1986 $44 (11/15/88)
89 MADAME FRANCOIS COLIN Puligny-Montrachet Les Demoiselles 1988 $47 (6/30/90)
78 JOSEPH DROUHIN Puligny-Montrachet 1988 $39 (3/15/90)
87 JOSEPH DROUHIN Puligny-Montrachet 1987 $38 (4/15/89)
88 JOSEPH DROUHIN Puligny-Montrachet 1986 $34 (2/29/88)
83 JOSEPH DROUHIN Puligny-Montrachet 1984 $27 (2/29/88)
81 JOSEPH DROUHIN Puligny-Montrachet Clos de la Garenne 1987 $44 (4/15/89)
89 JOSEPH DROUHIN Puligny-Montrachet Clos de la Garenne 1986 $40 (6/15/88)
78 JOSEPH DROUHIN Puligny-Montrachet Les Folatières 1987 $44 (4/15/89)
91 JOSEPH DROUHIN Puligny-Montrachet Les Folatières 1986 $40 (5/31/88)
93 JOSEPH DROUHIN Puligny-Montrachet Les Folatières 1986 $40 (2/29/88)
88 JOSEPH DROUHIN Puligny-Montrachet Les Folatières 1985 $35 (2/29/88)
90 JOSEPH DROUHIN Puligny-Montrachet Les Pucelles 1989 $68 (2/28/91)
90 JOSEPH DROUHIN Puligny-Montrachet Les Pucelles 1986 $50 (2/29/88)
92 JOSEPH DROUHIN Puligny-Montrachet Les Pucelles 1985 $50 (4/30/87)
90 JEAN GERMAIN Puligny-Montrachet 1983 $12 (9/01/85)
96 JEAN GERMAIN Puligny-Montrachet Les Champs-Gains 1983 $27 (3/01/86)
73 MACHARD DE GRAMONT Puligny-Montrachet Les Houillères 1985 $47 (5/31/88)

89 CHATEAU DES HERBEUX Puligny-Montrachet Les Combettes 1986 $21 (2/28/89)
87 LOUIS JADOT Puligny-Montrachet 1988 $36 (5/31/91)
83 LOUIS JADOT Puligny-Montrachet 1985 $33 (2/29/88)
90 LOUIS JADOT Puligny-Montrachet 1985 $33 (2/29/88)
89 LOUIS JADOT Puligny-Montrachet 1984 $30 (2/29/88)
66 LOUIS JADOT Puligny-Montrachet 1983 $25 (2/29/88)
91 LOUIS JADOT Puligny-Montrachet Clos de la Garenne Domaine du duc de Magenta 1988 $52 (4/30/91)
91 LOUIS JADOT Puligny-Montrachet Clos de la Garenne Domaine du duc de Magenta 1986 $57 (5/31/89)
92 LOUIS JADOT Puligny-Montrachet Clos de la Garenne Domaine du duc de Magenta 1985 $50 (2/29/88)
93 LOUIS JADOT Puligny-Montrachet Les Combettes 1985 $45 (2/29/88)
89 LOUIS JADOT Puligny-Montrachet Les Combettes 1984 $37 (2/29/88)
87 LOUIS JADOT Puligny-Montrachet Les Combettes 1983 $34 (2/29/88)
84 JAFFELIN Puligny-Montrachet 1989 $42 (5/31/91)
92 JAFFELIN Puligny-Montrachet 1985 $33 (4/15/87)
92 JAFFELIN Puligny-Montrachet 1983 $20.75 (2/01/86)
85 JAFFELIN Puligny-Montrachet Champ Canet 1986 $40 (12/15/88)
90 JAFFELIN Puligny-Montrachet Les Folatières 1983 $20 (6/16/85)
81 LABOURE-ROI Puligny-Montrachet 1985 $23 (11/15/86)
84 DOMAINE LAROCHE Puligny-Montrachet Folatières 1988 $39 (6/30/90)
92 DOMAINE LAROCHE Puligny-Montrachet Château de Puligny-Montrachet 1986 $60 (9/30/88)
80 LAROCHE Puligny-Montrachet 1989 $47 (2/28/91)
82 LOUIS LATOUR Puligny-Montrachet 1986 $41 (9/30/88)
87 LOUIS LATOUR Puligny-Montrachet 1986 $41 (2/29/88)
89 LOUIS LATOUR Puligny-Montrachet 1985 $30 (2/29/88)
88 LOUIS LATOUR Puligny-Montrachet 1985 $37 (4/15/87)
90 LOUIS LATOUR Puligny-Montrachet 1983 $35 (2/29/88)
86 LOUIS LATOUR Puligny-Montrachet Les Folatières 1982 $38 (2/29/88)
88 DOMAINE LEFLAIVE Puligny-Montrachet 1985 $40 (2/29/88)
90 DOMAINE LEFLAIVE Puligny-Montrachet Clavoillon 1985 Cur: $64 (2/29/88)
91 DOMAINE LEFLAIVE Puligny-Montrachet Les Folatières 1985 Cur: $52 (2/29/88)
92 DOMAINE LEFLAIVE Puligny-Montrachet Les Pucelles 1985 Cur: $75 (2/29/88)
94 DOMAINE LEFLAIVE Puligny-Montrachet Les Pucelles 1982 Cur: $72 (2/29/88)
95 DOMAINE LEFLAIVE Puligny-Montrachet Les Pucelles 1979 Cur: $100 (2/29/88)
93 OLIVIER LEFLAIVE FRERES Puligny-Montrachet 1987 $33 (6/30/90)
88 OLIVIER LEFLAIVE FRERES Puligny-Montrachet 1986 $30 (7/31/89)
90 OLIVIER LEFLAIVE FRERES Puligny-Montrachet 1986 $29 (2/29/88)
83 OLIVIER LEFLAIVE FRERES Puligny-Montrachet 1984 $25 (6/01/86)
93 OLIVIER LEFLAIVE FRERES Puligny-Montrachet Les Chalumeaux 1986 $36 (4/15/89)
87 OLIVIER LEFLAIVE FRERES Puligny-Montrachet Les Champs-Gains 1986 $36 (2/29/88)
90 OLIVIER LEFLAIVE FRERES Puligny-Montrachet Les Combettes 1986 $46 (2/29/88)
91 OLIVIER LEFLAIVE FRERES Puligny-Montrachet Les Folatières 1986 $36 (2/29/88)
93 OLIVIER LEFLAIVE FRERES Puligny-Montrachet Les Pucelles 1986 $65 (9/30/88)
92 A. LIGERET Puligny-Montrachet Les Referts 1988 $51 (12/31/90)
82 LUPE-CHOLET Puligny-Montrachet Les Chalumeaux 1987 $46 (11/15/89)
83 DOMAINE MAROSLAVAC Puligny-Montrachet Clos du Vieux Château 1988 $40 (7/31/90)
88 PIERRE MATROT Puligny-Montrachet Les Combettes 1986 $37 (12/15/88)
90 PROSPER MAUFOUX Puligny-Montrachet 1988 $31 (4/30/90)
68 PROSPER MAUFOUX Puligny-Montrachet 1986 $36 (5/31/89)
80 C. MICHELOT Puligny-Montrachet 1987 $41 (6/30/90)
88 MOILLARD Puligny-Montrachet 1986 $33 (5/31/88)
81 DOMAINE RENE MONNIER Puligny-Montrachet Les Folatières 1986 $44 (11/15/88)
93 DOMAINE JEAN PASCAL Puligny-Montrachet Hameau de Blagny 1986 $40 (6/15/88)
91 DOMAINE JEAN PASCAL Puligny-Montrachet Les Chalumeaux 1986 $40 (6/15/88)
92 DOMAINE JEAN PASCAL Puligny-Montrachet Les Champs-Gains 1985 $31 (9/15/87)
90 PATRIARCHE Puligny-Montrachet 1985 $30 (9/30/89)
80 PAUL PERNOT Puligny-Montrachet 1989 $52 (2/28/91)
72 PAUL PERNOT Puligny-Montrachet 1988 $40 (2/28/91)
89 PAUL PERNOT Puligny-Montrachet Folatières 1989 $70 (2/28/91)
93 PAUL PERNOT Puligny-Montrachet Folatières 1988 $74 (12/31/90)
89 PAUL PERNOT Puligny-Montrachet Folatières 1986 $50 (2/28/89)
90 PAUL PERNOT Puligny-Montrachet Les Pucelles 1988 $74 (12/31/90)
76 JEAN PILLOT Puligny-Montrachet 1989 $42 (4/30/91)
74 CHATEAU DE PULIGNY-MONTRACHET Puligny-Montrachet 1989 $66 (2/28/91)
81 CHATEAU DE PULIGNY-MONTRACHET Puligny-Montrachet 1986 $60 (2/29/88)
79 CHATEAU DE PULIGNY-MONTRACHET Puligny-Montrachet 1985 $55 (2/29/88)
92 REMOISSENET Puligny-Montrachet Les Combettes 1986 $57 (11/15/88)
85 REMOISSENET Puligny-Montrachet Les Folatières 1986 $50 (11/15/88)
79 REMOISSENET Puligny-Montrachet Les Folatières 1985 $56 (2/29/88)
82 J. RIGER-BRISET Puligny-Montrachet 1987 $35 (3/15/90)
83 DOMAINE ROUX PERE & FILS Puligny-Montrachet Champs-Gains 1989 $55 (2/28/91)
92 DOMAINE ROUX PERE & FILS Puligny-Montrachet Champs-Gains 1988 $40 (3/15/90)
92 DOMAINE ROUX PERE & FILS Puligny-Montrachet Les Enseignères 1986 $36 (2/29/88)
88 DOMAINE ROUX PERE & FILS Puligny-Montrachet Les Enseignères 1985 $34 (9/15/87)
83 DOMAINE ROUX PERE & FILS Puligny-Montrachet La Garenne 1987 $44 (4/15/89)
89 DOMAINE ROUX PERE & FILS Puligny-Montrachet La Garenne 1986 $37.50 (12/31/87)
92 DOMAINE ROUX PERE & FILS Puligny-Montrachet La Garenne 1985 $30 (4/15/87)
92 DOMAINE ETIENNE SAUZET Puligny-Montrachet 1986 $40 (4/30/88)
88 DOMAINE ETIENNE SAUZET Puligny-Montrachet 1986 $40 (2/29/88)
91 DOMAINE ETIENNE SAUZET Puligny-Montrachet Champ Canet 1988 $50 (12/31/90)
91 DOMAINE ETIENNE SAUZET Puligny-Montrachet Champ Canet 1986 $48 (4/30/88)
90 DOMAINE ETIENNE SAUZET Puligny-Montrachet Champ Canet 1986 $50 (2/29/88)
90 DOMAINE ETIENNE SAUZET Puligny-Montrachet Champ Canet 1985 $37 (10/15/87)
93 DOMAINE ETIENNE SAUZET Puligny-Montrachet Les Combettes 1988 $56 (12/31/90)
93 DOMAINE ETIENNE SAUZET Puligny-Montrachet Les Combettes 1986 $50 (4/30/88)
90 DOMAINE ETIENNE SAUZET Puligny-Montrachet Les Combettes 1985 $50 (2/29/88)
90 DOMAINE ETIENNE SAUZET Puligny-Montrachet Les Perrières 1988 $70 (2/28/91)
93 DOMAINE ETIENNE SAUZET Puligny-Montrachet Les Perrières 1985 $39 (10/15/87)
92 DOMAINE ETIENNE SAUZET Puligny-Montrachet Les Referts 1988 $47 (12/31/90)
87 DOMAINE ETIENNE SAUZET Puligny-Montrachet Les Referts 1986 $45 (2/29/88)
93 DOMAINE ETIENNE SAUZET Puligny-Montrachet Les Truffières 1986 $45 (2/29/88)
91 DOMAINE ETIENNE SAUZET Puligny-Montrachet Les Truffières 1985 $42 (2/29/88)
87 LEONARD DE ST.-AUBIN Puligny-Montrachet 1986 $25 (11/15/87)
84 BERNARD THEVENOT Puligny-Montrachet 1982 $15 (10/16/84)
82 JACQUES THEVENOT-MACHAL Puligny-Montrachet Les Charmes 1986 $35 (2/29/88)
88 JACQUES THEVENOT-MACHAL Puligny-Montrachet Les Folatières au Chaniot 1988 $40 (12/31/90)

FRANCE
BURGUNDY WHITE/CÔTE DE BEAUNE/PULIGNY-MONTRACHET

78 JACQUES THEVENOT-MACHAL Puligny-Montrachet Les Folatières au Chaniot 1987 $43 (4/15/89)
81 JACQUES THEVENOT-MACHAL Puligny-Montrachet Les Folatières au Chaniot 1986 $38 (2/29/88)
87 THORIN Puligny-Montrachet 1987 $32 (11/15/89)
63 CHARLES VIENOT Puligny-Montrachet 1984 $30.50 (2/28/87)
79 CHARLES VIENOT Puligny-Montrachet Champs Gain 1987 $38 (7/31/89)
85 HENRI DE VILLAMONT Puligny-Montrachet Les Folatières 1986 $30 (12/15/88)

OTHER CÔTE DE BEAUNE WHITE

81 BOUCHARD PERE & FILS Beaune Clos St.-Landry Domaines du Château de Beaune 1986 $33 (2/28/89)
79 CHANSON PERE & FILS Pernand-Vergelesses 1986 $16 (7/31/89)
72 CHANSON PERE & FILS Pernand-Vergelesses Les Caradeux 1988 $25 (8/31/90)
83 CHARTRON & TREBUCHET Beaune 1987 $30 (2/28/89)
83 CHARTRON & TREBUCHET Pernand-Vergelesses 1988 $18 (3/15/90)
86 CHARTRON & TREBUCHET St.-Aubin La Chatenière 1989 $24 (2/28/91)
85 CHARTRON & TREBUCHET St.-Aubin La Chatenière 1988 $18 (3/15/90)
83 CHARTRON & TREBUCHET St.-Aubin La Chatenière 1987 $20 (4/15/89)
85 CHARTRON & TREBUCHET St.-Romain 1989 $20 (2/28/91)
87 CHARTRON & TREBUCHET Santenay Sous la Fée 1988 $18 (3/15/90)
79 CHARTRON & TREBUCHET Santenay Sous la Fée 1987 $23 (4/30/89)
87 JOSEPH DROUHIN Auxey-Duresses 1989 $22 (2/28/91)
90 JOSEPH DROUHIN Beaune Clos des Mouches 1988 Rel: $64 Cur: $64 (7/31/90)
81 JOSEPH DROUHIN Beaune Clos des Mouches 1987 Rel: $48 Cur: $53 (4/30/89)
87 JOSEPH DROUHIN Beaune Clos des Mouches 1986 Rel: $56 Cur: $56 (12/15/88)
86 JOSEPH DROUHIN Pernand-Vergelesses 1989 $23 (2/28/91)
81 JOSEPH DROUHIN St.-Aubin 1987 $21 (4/15/89)
82 JOSEPH DROUHIN St.-Aubin 1986 $20 (10/15/88)
73 DUBREUIL-FONTAINE Pernand-Vergelesses Ile des Vergelesses 1985 $22 (2/28/89)
77 JEAN GERMAIN St.-Romain Clos le Château 1984 $14.50 (7/16/86)
83 JEAN GERMAIN St.-Romain Clos Sous le Château 1983 $12 (9/16/85)
88 LOUIS JADOT Auxey-Duresses Domaine du Duc de Magenta 1988 $23 (4/30/91)
85 LOUIS JADOT Pernand-Vergelesses 1988 $21 (4/30/91)
80 LOUIS JADOT Savigny-lès-Beaune Blanc 1988 $24 (4/30/91)
79 JAFFELIN Auxey-Duresses 1985 $13 (3/31/87)
79 JAFFELIN Auxey-Duresses 1983 $11 (11/01/85)
88 JAFFELIN Santenay Les Gravières 1989 $25 (5/31/91)
84 JAFFELIN St.-Aubin 1985 $13 (3/31/87)
84 JAYER-GILLES Bourgogne Hautes Côtes de Beaune 1988 $22 (6/15/91)
73 JAYER-GILLES Bourgogne Hautes Côtes de Beaune 1988 $22 (2/28/91)
75 JEAN LAFOUGE Auxey-Duresses 1985 $16 (6/15/87)
80 LUPE-CHOLET Bourgogne Hautes Côtes de Beaune 1988 $10 (4/30/90)
83 LUPE-CHOLET Pernand-Vergelesses 1988 $15 (3/15/90)
78 LUPE-CHOLET Savigny-lès-Beaune 1985 $10 (11/15/86)
75 PROSPER MAUFOUX Auxey-Duresses 1988 $18 (4/30/91)
78 MOILLARD Bourgogne Hautes Côtes de Beaune Les Alouettes 1989 $15 (6/15/91)
68 DOMAINE PONNELLE Côte de Beaune Les Pierres Blanches 1988 $18 (2/28/91)
84 PRUNIER Auxey-Duresses 1986 $25 (11/15/90)
82 CHATEAU DE PULIGNY-MONTRACHET Monthélie Chardonnay 1989 $26 (2/28/91)
85 DOMAINE ROUX PERE & FILS St.-Aubin La Pucelle 1989 $26 (2/28/91)
85 DOMAINE ROUX PERE & FILS St.-Aubin La Pucelle 1988 $18.50 (3/15/90)
69 ROLAND THEVENIN Auxey-Duresses Chanterelle 1984 $10 (3/31/87)
78 CHARLES VIENOT St.-Aubin 1984 $13 (3/31/87)

CHALONNAISE

50 BICHOT Rully 1984 $8 (6/01/86)
79 JEAN-MARC BOILLOT Montagny Premier Cru 1988 $22 (8/31/90)
85 CHATEAU DE CHAMIREY Mercurey 1985 $13.50 (1/31/87)
69 CHARTRON & TREBUCHET Mercurey 1986 $20 (5/31/88)
78 CHARTRON & TREBUCHET Rully La Chaume 1989 $18 (4/30/91)
88 CHARTRON & TREBUCHET Rully La Chaume 1988 $14 (3/15/90)
74 CHARTRON & TREBUCHET Rully La Chaume 1987 $15 (4/30/89)
83 JOSEPH DROUHIN Montagny 1986 $15 (6/15/88)
86 JOSEPH DROUHIN Rully 1989 $17.50 (2/28/91)
81 JOSEPH DROUHIN Rully 1987 $15 (4/30/89)
88 JOSEPH DROUHIN Rully 1986 $14 (6/15/88)
87 DUVERNAY Mercurey La Chiquette 1988 $17 (4/30/91)
62 FAIVELEY Mercurey Blanc Clos de la Rochette 1983 $14 (3/31/87)
86 FAIVELEY Mercurey Clos Rochette 1988 $22 (4/30/91)
74 FAIVELEY Rully 1983 $10.25 (8/31/86)
86 JAFFELIN Rully Barrel Fermented 1988 $13 (3/15/90)
82 JAFFELIN Rully Blanc 1987 $13 (3/15/89)
87 JAFFELIN Rully Blanc 1986 $12 (2/15/88)
88 JAFFELIN Rully Blanc 1985 $11 (3/31/87)
80 OLIVIER LEFLAIVE FRERES Montagny Premier Cru 1987 $15.50 (8/31/90)
81 OLIVIER LEFLAIVE FRERES Rully Premier Cru 1989 $20 (7/31/91)
80 LUPE-CHOLET Rully Marissou 1988 $16 (3/15/90)
56 PROSPER MAUFOUX Montagny 1984 $11 (3/31/87)
65 ANTONIN RODET Montagny Les Chagnots 1985 $10 (11/15/86)
83 ALAIN ROY-THEVENIN Montagny Château de la Saule 1988 $12 (8/31/90)
83 DOMAINE FABIEN & LOUIS SAIER Mercurey Blanc Les Chenelots 1988 $17 (4/30/91)
83 JEAN VACHET Montagny Les Coeres 1986 $16 (1/31/89)

MÂCONNAIS/MÂCON

63 LES ACACIAS Mâcon-Villages 1984 $5.25 (11/16/85)
71 LES ACACIAS Mâcon-Villages Cave de Viré 1989 $11 (2/28/91)
76 LES ACACIAS Mâcon-Viré Vieilles Vignes 1988 $9 (8/31/90)
69 PHILIPPE ANTOINE Mâcon-Villages 1986 $8 (4/15/88)
75 ARTISAN CRU Mâcon-Villages 1984 $7 (9/15/86)
81 BARTON & GUESTIER Mâcon-Villages 1988 $9 (9/30/90)
83 BICHOT Mâcon-Villages 1989 $9 (7/15/90)
82 BICHOT Mâcon-Villages 1987 $6 (1/31/89) BB
76 JEAN CLAUDE BOISSET Mâcon-Blanc-Villages 1988 $9 (12/31/90)
76 JEAN CLAUDE BOISSET Mâcon-Blanc-Villages 1987 $8.50 (9/15/89)
67 JEAN CLAUDE BOISSET Mâcon-Blanc-Villages 1986 $7.75 (10/31/87)
75 JEAN CLAUDE BOISSET Mâcon-Blanc-Villages 1984 $7.75 (11/15/86)
71 BOUCHARD PERE & FILS Mâcon-Villages Le Chamville 1984 $8.50 (3/31/87)
81 CAVE DE CHARDONNAY Mâcon-Chardonnay Chardonnay de Chardonnay 1988 $9 (7/15/90) BB
80 F. CHAUVENET Mâcon-Villages Les Jumelles 1987 $7 (10/31/88)
79 F. CHAUVENET Mâcon-Villages Les Jumelles 1986 $8 (10/31/87)
78 F. CHAUVENET Mâcon-Villages Les Jumelles 1985 $8 (3/31/87)
62 LES CHAZELLES Mâcon-Villages 1984 $8.25 (9/15/86)
76 CHEVALIER DE BEAUBASSIN Mâcon-Blanc-Villages 1986 $9 (4/15/88)
75 RAOUL CLERGET Mâcon-Villages 1985 $5.75 (10/15/88)
72 CORON PERE Mâcon-Fuissé St.-Jacques 1984 $8.50 (3/31/87)
78 CORON PERE Mâcon-Villages Blanc 1985 $8 (3/31/87)
72 JOSEPH DROUHIN Mâcon-Villages 1986 $8.75 (6/15/88)
84 GEORGES DUBOEUF Mâcon-Lugny Fête des Fleurs 1989 $9 (10/31/90)
81 GEORGES DUBOEUF Mâcon-Villages 1989 $8.50 (10/31/90)
79 GEORGES DUBOEUF Mâcon-Villages 1988 $8 (9/30/89)
79 GEORGES DUBOEUF Mâcon-Villages 1987 $7 (6/30/88)
73 GEORGES DUBOEUF Mâcon-Villages 1986 $7 (7/31/87)
83 GEORGES DUBOEUF Mâcon-Villages 1985 $8.50 (3/31/87)
77 GEORGES DUBOEUF Mâcon-Villages La Coupe Perration 1988 $8 (9/30/89)
80 DOMAINE EMILIAN GILLET Mâcon-Clessé Quintaine 1988 $17 (8/31/90)
71 SYLVAIN FESSY Mâcon-Clessé Les Jumelles 1986 $7.50 (2/15/88)
69 GEORGES BLANC Mâcon-Clessé 1986 $8 (3/15/88)
79 LES GIRAUDIERES Mâcon-Villages 1986 $7.25 (10/31/87)
81 LE GRAND CHENEAU Mâcon-Viré 1986 $6.50 (6/30/88) BB
78 LE GRAND CHENEAU Mâcon-Viré Chardonnay 1985 $6 (3/31/87)
84 LOUIS JADOT Mâcon-Villages La Fontaine 1988 $9 (9/15/89)
71 LOUIS JADOT Mâcon-Villages La Fontaine 1985 $7.50 (3/31/87)
71 JAFFELIN Mâcon-Villages 1985 $9.25 (3/31/87)
74 PIERRE JANNY Mâcon-Villages Domaine du Prieuré 1987 $7 (1/31/89)
77 PIERRE JANNY Mâcon-Villages Domaine du Prieuré 1986 $6.50 (2/15/88)
84 MAURICE JOSSERAND Mâcon-Péronne Domaine du Mortier 1988 $8 (12/31/90) BB
79 LABOURE-ROI Mâcon-Lugny 1986 $9 (4/15/88)
80 LABOURE-ROI Mâcon-Villages 1989 $10 (4/30/91)
76 LACHARME Mâcon-La Roche Vineuse 1985 $9 (9/15/86)
79 LAROCHE Mâcon-Villages 1988 $8.50 (7/15/90)
76 LOUIS LATOUR Mâcon-Villages Chameroy 1985 $11 (3/31/87)
70 ALEXIS LICHINE Mâcon-Villages Pinot Chardonnay 1985 $6.75 (3/31/87)
84 CAVE DE LUGNY Mâcon-Lugny Les Charmes Pinot Chardonnay 1985 $7.50 (3/31/87)
55 LUPE-CHOLET Mâcon-Villages Les Roches 1985 $6.75 (9/15/86)
78 M & G Mâcon-Villages 1988 $14 (3/31/91)
84 MANCIAT-PONCET Mâcon-Charnay Domaine des Crays 1986 $11.50 (4/15/88)
92 MANCIAT-PONCET Mâcon-Charnay Domaine des Crays 1985 $9.50 (12/15/86)
82 PROSPER MAUFOUX Mâcon-Villages 1988 $10.50 (7/15/90)
77 PROSPER MAUFOUX Mâcon-Villages 1984 $9.25 (3/31/87)
80 PROSPER MAUFOUX Mâcon-Viré Château de Viré 1985 $11 (4/30/88)
63 PROSPER MAUFOUX Mâcon-Viré Château de Viré 1984 $9.25 (3/31/87)
77 MOILLARD Mâcon-Villages Domaine de Montbellet 1989 $10.50 (4/30/91)
81 MOMMESSIN Mâcon Chardonnay 1984 $5 (12/16/85) BB
65 MOMMESSIN Mâcon-Villages Le Beau Champ 1985 $6.75 (3/31/87)
65 MOREAU Mâcon-Vinzelles Chardonnay Réserve La Couronne 1983 $9.50 (5/01/86)
76 REINE PEDAUQUE Mâcon-Villages Coupées 1988 $9.50 (9/30/89)
84 CAVE DE PRISSE Mâcon-Prissé Les Clochettes 1986 $8.50 (1/31/89)
76 DOMAINE DES ROCHES Mâcon-Igé 1989 $9 (10/31/90)
84 DOMAINE DES ROCHES Mâcon-Igé 1987 $7 (5/15/89) BB
81 ROBERT SARRAU Mâcon-Villages 1989 $8 (10/31/90)
84 LOUIS-RENE SAVIN Mâcon-Villages 1984 $8 (3/31/87)
78 DOMAINE TALMARD Mâcon-Chardonnay 1989 $10 (10/31/90)
80 DOMAINE TALMARD Mâcon-Chardonnay 1988 $9 (7/15/90)
60 DOMAINE TALMARD Mâcon-Chardonnay 1985 $6 (3/31/87)
90 DOMAINE TALMARD Mâcon-Chardonnay 1984 $6 (11/01/85) BB
84 JEAN-CLAUDE THEVENET Mâcon-Pierreclos 1988 $6.25 (7/15/90) BB
74 THORIN Mâcon-Villages 1987 $8.50 (1/31/89)
82 DOMAINE DU VIEUX ST.-SORLIN Mâcon-La Roche Vineuse 1989 $13.50 (2/28/91)
86 DOMAINE DU VIEUX SAINT-SORLIN Mâcon-La Roche Vineuse Eleve en futs de Chêne 1988 $11 (7/15/90)
75 VIGNERONS Mâcon-Villages Pinot Chardonnay 1985 $7.50 (3/31/87)
79 J.J. VINCENT Mâcon-Villages 1988 $7 (10/31/90)
83 J.J. VINCENT Mâcon-Villages 1984 $7 (2/16/86)
77 J.J. VINCENT Mâcon-Villages Pièce d'Or 1987 $7 (5/15/89)

POUILLY

79 PHILIPPE ANTOINE Pouilly-Fuissé 1986 $15 (4/30/88)
78 CHATEAU DE BEAUREGARD Pouilly-Fuissé 1983 $14.50 (3/16/85)
86 ANDRE BESSON Pouilly-Fuissé Domaine de Pouilly 1988 $15 (7/31/90)
73 BICHOT Pouilly-Fuissé 1988 $13 (12/31/90)
59 BICHOT Pouilly-Fuissé 1988 $13 (8/31/90)
84 BICHOT Pouilly-Fuissé 1987 $10 (4/30/89)
79 BICHOT Pouilly-Fuissé 1986 $11 (3/15/88)
85 BICHOT Pouilly-Fuissé 1985 $16 (3/31/87)
80 BICHOT Pouilly-Fuissé 1985 $16 (8/31/86)
90 JEAN CLAUDE BOISSET Pouilly-Fuissé 1986 $10 (9/30/87)
77 JEAN CLAUDE BOISSET Pouilly-Fuissé 1985 $16.50 (3/31/87)
87 BOUCHARD AINE Pouilly-Fuissé Réserve 1985 $17.50 (3/31/87)
85 BOUCHARD PERE & FILS Pouilly-Fuissé 1989 $25 (4/30/91)
87 BOUCHARD PERE & FILS Pouilly-Fuissé 1984 $20 (3/31/87)
79 BOUCHARD PERE & FILS Pouilly-Vinzelles 1984 $12.50 (3/31/87)

76 F. CHAUVENET Pouilly-Fuissé 1982 $8.50 (3/01/84)
78 F. CHAUVENET Pouilly-Fuissé Clos de France 1987 $13 (4/30/89)
79 F. CHAUVENET Pouilly-Fuissé Clos de France 1986 $14 (10/15/87)
67 RAOUL CLERGET Pouilly-Fuissé 1986 $10 (10/15/88)
86 LOUIS CURVEUX Pouilly-Fuissé Les Menestrières 1988 $23 (7/31/90)
84 DOMAINE DELACOUR Pouilly-Fuissé 1984 $18 (3/31/87)
83 JOSEPH DROUHIN Pouilly-Fuissé 1987 $18 (4/30/89)
76 JOSEPH DROUHIN Pouilly-Fuissé 1986 $17.50 (6/30/88)
86 GEORGES DUBOEUF Pouilly-Fuissé 1989 $15 (10/31/90)
84 GEORGES DUBOEUF Pouilly-Fuissé 1988 $12 (9/30/89)
81 GEORGES DUBOEUF Pouilly-Fuissé 1987 $12 (6/15/88)
82 GEORGES DUBOEUF Pouilly-Fuissé 1986 $14 (7/31/87)
80 GEORGES DUBOEUF Pouilly-Fuissé 1985 $14.50 (3/31/87)
82 J.A. FERRET Pouilly-Fuissé Les Perrières Cuvée Spéciale 1986 $30 (7/31/90)
82 HENRY FESSY Pouilly-Fuissé 1986 $10 (10/15/88)
86 SYLVAIN FESSY Pouilly-Fuissé Cuvée Gilles Guérrin 1986 $12 (12/31/87)
81 THIERRY GUERIN Pouilly-Fuissé 1985 $18.50 (3/31/87)
89 THIERRY GUERIN Pouilly-Fuissé Clos de France 1988 $23 (7/31/90)
85 LOUIS JADOT Pouilly-Fuissé 1988 $16 (9/30/89)
90 LOUIS JADOT Pouilly-Fuissé 1985 $19.25 (3/31/87)
87 LOUIS JADOT Pouilly-Fuissé Cuvée Réserve Spéciale 1989 $21 (7/31/91)
83 JAFFELIN Pouilly-Fuissé 1990 $18 (7/31/91)
89 JAFFELIN Pouilly-Fuissé 1985 $18.50 (4/15/87)
89 JAFFELIN Pouilly-Fuissé 1984 $18.50 (3/31/87)
89 LABOURE-ROI Pouilly-Fuissé 1988 $18 (10/31/90)
92 LABOURE-ROI Pouilly-Fuissé 1985 $18 (3/31/87)
90 DOMAINE LAPIERRE Pouilly-Fuissé 1985 $13.50 (3/31/87)
90 ROGER LASSARAT Pouilly-Fuissé Clos de France 1986 $26 (4/30/88)
88 ROGER LASSARAT Pouilly-Fuissé Clos de France 1985 $23 (12/31/87)
68 LOUIS LATOUR Pouilly-Fuissé Latour 1984 $25 (4/30/87)
55 CHATEAU DE LAYE Pouilly-Vinzelles 1983 $8 (12/01/85)
70 A. LIGERET Pouilly-Fuissé 1988 $21 (2/15/91)
70 LUPE-CHOLET Pouilly-Fuissé 1987 $12.50 (4/30/89)
64 LUPE-CHOLET Pouilly-Fuissé 1984 $19.25 (8/31/86)
88 MANCIAT-PONCET Pouilly-Fuissé La Roche 1985 $20 (2/15/88)
78 PROSPER MAUFOUX Pouilly-Fuissé 1984 $16.50 (3/31/87)
62 CHARLES MONCAUT Pouilly-Fuissé 1985 $18 (6/15/87)
76 REINE PEDAUQUE Pouilly-Fuissé Griselles 1988 $16 (9/30/89)
75 PELLERIN Pouilly-Fuissé 1987 $12 (4/30/89)
80 ANTONIN RODET Pouilly-Fuissé Rodet 1985 $19 (10/15/87)
91 ROGER SAUMAIZE Pouilly-Fuissé Clos de la Roche 1989 $28 (7/31/91)
89 ROGER SAUMAIZE Pouilly-Fuissé Les Ronchevats 1989 $31 (7/31/91)
84 ROLAND THEVENIN Pouilly-Fuissé Les Moulins 1985 $19 (3/31/87)
79 ROGER VERGE Pouilly-Fuissé 1986 $15 (3/15/88)
75 CHARLES VIENOT Pouilly-Fuissé 1987 $13.50 (4/30/89)
80 CHARLES VIENOT Pouilly-Fuissé 1984 $19 (3/31/87)
70 CHARLES VIENOT Pouilly-Vinzelles 1985 $16 (3/31/87)
79 J.J. VINCENT Pouilly-Fuissé 1989 $15 (4/30/91)
90 J.J. VINCENT Pouilly-Fuissé 1988 $15 (10/31/90)
71 J.J. VINCENT Pouilly-Fuissé 1984 $17 (2/16/86)
77 M. VINCENT Pouilly-Fuissé Château Fuissé 1987 $27 (11/30/90)
89 M. VINCENT Pouilly-Fuissé Château Fuissé 1986 $29 (10/31/90)

ST.-VÉRAN

75 ANCIEN DOMAINE DU CHAPITRE DE MACON St.-Véran Les Colombières 1988 $12 (8/31/90)
83 PHILIPPE ANTOINE St.-Véran 1986 $10 (4/30/88)
68 JEAN CLAUDE BOISSET St.-Véran 1989 $12 (7/31/91)
81 JEAN CLAUDE BOISSET St.-Véran 1988 $9.50 (7/31/90)
68 JEAN CLAUDE BOISSET St.-Véran 1984 $10 (3/31/87)
81 F. CHAUVENET St.-Véran 1985 $12 (3/31/87)
62 F. CHAUVENET St.-Véran 1983 $6 (12/16/85)
85 JOSEPH DROUHIN St.-Véran 1989 $15.50 (2/28/91)
85 GEORGES DUBOEUF St.-Véran 1989 $10 (10/31/90)
82 GEORGES DUBOEUF St.-Véran 1988 $9 (9/30/89)
77 GEORGES DUBOEUF St.-Véran 1987 $9 (10/15/88)
79 GEORGES DUBOEUF St.-Véran 1986 $9 (7/31/87)
87 GEORGES DUBOEUF St.-Véran 1985 $10 (3/31/87)
80 GEORGES DUBOEUF St.-Véran Coupe Louis Dailly 1988 $9 (9/30/89)
80 GEORGES DUBOEUF St.-Véran Coupe Louis Dailly 1987 $9 (10/15/88)
75 SYLVAIN FESSY St.-Véran Cuvée Prissé 1986 $8 (2/15/88)
72 GEORGES BLANC St.-Véran 1986 $10 (12/31/87)
79 THIERRY GUERIN St.-Véran 1989 $9 (3/31/91)
80 THIERRY GUERIN St.-Véran La Côte Rôtie 1987 $8.50 (4/30/89)
79 THIERRY GUERIN St.-Véran La Côte Rôtie 1986 $11.50 (10/15/88)
72 THIERRY GUERIN St.-Véran La Côte Rôtie 1985 $10 (3/31/87)
81 LOUIS JADOT St.-Véran 1984 $9 (3/31/87)
80 JAFFELIN St.-Véran 1989 $14 (7/31/91)
88 JAFFELIN St.-Véran 1985 $9.25 (3/31/87)
81 LAROCHE St.-Véran 1988 $10 (7/31/90)
73 ROGER LASSARAT St.-Véran La Côte Rôtie 1986 $13 (4/30/88)
77 ROGER LASSARAT St.-Véran Cuvée Prestige 1988 $15 (8/31/90)
82 PROSPER MAUFOUX St.-Véran 1988 $12 (7/31/90)
67 PROSPER MAUFOUX St.-Véran 1985 $12 (3/31/87)
76 MOMMESSIN St.-Véran Domaine de l'Evèque 1985 $10.50 (3/31/87)
75 CHARLES MONCAUT St.-Véran 1985 $10.25 (6/15/87)
92 CAVE DE PRISSE St.-Véran Les Blanchettes 1985 $10 (3/31/87)
82 VIGNERONS St.-Véran 1983 $7 (10/16/85) BB
85 J.J. VINCENT St.-Véran 1988 $10 (10/31/90)
87 J.J. VINCENT St.-Véran 1985 $12 (3/31/87)

OTHER BURGUNDY WHITE

84 DOMAINE DE L'ARLOT Nuits-St.-Georges Clos de L'Arlot 1988 $27/375ml (4/30/91)
76 BICHOT Bourgogne Le Bourgogne Bichot 1988 $8 (4/30/90)
79 BICHOT Bourgogne Le Bourgogne Bichot 1987 $8 (5/15/89)
75 PIERRE BOILLOT Bourgogne Aligoté 1987 $13 (7/31/90)
79 LIONEL J. BRUCK Bourgogne St.-Vincent Pinot Chardonnay 1984 $10 (3/31/87)
83 CALVET Bourgogne Chardonnay Première 1987 $10 (4/30/89)
70 CHARTRON & TREBUCHET Bourgogne Aligoté Les Equinces 1985 $9 (4/30/87)
83 CHARTRON & TREBUCHET Bourgogne Blanc Hommage à Victor Hugo 1988 $10 (3/31/90)
78 CHARTRON & TREBUCHET Bourgogne Blanc Hommage à Victor Hugo 1987 $13 (3/15/89)
70 CHARTRON & TREBUCHET Bourgogne Blanc Hommage à Victor Hugo 1986 $13 (5/31/88)
78 CHARTRON & TREBUCHET Bourgogne Chardonnay 1989 $10 (2/28/91)
68 DOMAINE HENRI CLERC & FILS Bourgogne Blanc 1984 $10 (3/31/87)
65 A. & P. DE VILLAINE Bourgogne Les Clous Bouzeron 1986 $16 (1/31/89)
82 JOSEPH DROUHIN Bourgogne Chardonnay Laforet 1989 $9 (4/30/91) BB
79 JOSEPH DROUHIN Bourgogne Chardonnay Laforet 1988 $8.75 (9/30/89)
81 JOSEPH DROUHIN Bourgogne Chardonnay Laforet 1986 $8.50 (1/31/88)
85 JOSEPH DROUHIN Bourgogne Chardonnay Laforet 1985 $8.25 (3/31/87)
84 JOSEPH DROUHIN Bourgogne Chardonnay Laforet 1985 $8.25 (8/31/86) BB
61 JOSEPH DROUHIN Bourgogne Chardonnay Laforet 1983 $7.50 (6/01/86)
80 DOMAINE DUJAC Morey-St.-Denis Vin Gris de Pinot Noir 1986 $13 (4/15/89)
74 FAIVELEY Bourgogne Chardonnay 1988 $14 (7/31/90)
71 FAIVELEY Bourgogne Chardonnay Cuvée Joseph Faiveley 1985 $13.50 (3/31/87)
61 FAIVELEY Bourgogne Chardonnay Cuvée Joseph Faiveley 1983 $7.50 (5/01/86)
81 LOUIS JADOT Bourgogne Chardonnay 1988 $9.50 (9/30/89)
78 LOUIS JADOT Bourgogne Chardonnay 1986 $10 (10/15/88)
74 LOUIS JADOT Bourgogne Chardonnay 1986 $10 (2/15/88)
65 LOUIS JADOT Bourgogne Chardonnay 1985 $9 (3/31/87)
85 JAFFELIN Bourgogne Blanc 1988 $9 (3/31/90)
81 JAFFELIN Bourgogne Chardonnay 1990 $9 (7/31/91) BB
76 JAFFELIN Bourgogne Chardonnay du Châpitre 1987 $9.50 (3/15/89)
80 JAFFELIN Bourgogne Chardonnay du Châpitre 1985 $9.50 (3/31/87)
74 JAFFELIN Bourgogne Chardonnay du Châpitre 1983 $6.25 (1/01/85)
80 DOMAINE LAROCHE Bourgogne Clos du Château 1986 $16 (1/31/89)
79 LOUIS LATOUR Bourgogne Chardonnay Latour 1985 $11 (3/31/87)
79 DOMAINE LATOUR GIRAUD Bourgogne Chardonnay 1985 $11 (3/31/87)
79 OLIVIER LEFLAIVE FRERES Bourgogne Les Sétilles 1987 $8.50 (3/31/90)
87 OLIVIER LEFLAIVE FRERES Bourgogne Les Sétilles 1985 $12 (3/31/87)
76 LEROY Bourgogne d'Auvenay 1988 $14.50 (4/30/91)
84 LEROY Bourgogne d'Auvenay 1986 $17 (9/15/89)
79 LEROY Bourgogne d'Auvenay 1983 $14.50 (12/31/87)
84 LUPE-CHOLET Bourgogne Chardonnay Comtesse de Lupé 1988 $9 (4/30/90) BB
80 LUPE-CHOLET Bourgogne Chardonnay Comtesse de Lupé 1987 $8.25 (3/15/89) BB
72 CHATEAU MARQUERITE DE BOURGOGNE Bourgogne Chardonnay 1985 $14 (6/30/87)
76 DOMAINE JOSEPH MATROT Bourgogne Chardonnay 1988 $15.50 (4/30/91)
78 DOMAINE JOSEPH MATROT Bourgogne Chardonnay 1987 $16 (4/15/90)
80 DOMAINE JOSEPH MATROT Bourgogne Chardonnay 1987 $16 (9/15/89)
78 PROSPER MAUFOUX Bourgogne Aligoté 1989 $12 (7/31/91)
71 DOMAINE DU CHATEAU DE MERCEY Bourgogne Blanc Côtes de Beaune 1985 $8.50 (3/31/87)
83 CHATEAU DE MEURSAULT Bourgogne Chardonnay Clos du Château 1988 $23 (4/30/91)
82 CHATEAU DE MEURSAULT Bourgogne Chardonnay Clos du Château 1985 $20 (3/31/90)
84 JEAN MICHELOT Bourgogne Aligoté 1988 $11.50 (7/31/90)
78 MOILLARD Hautes Côtes de Nuits 1986 $12 (1/31/89)
84 MOREAU Bourgogne Chardonnay 1988 $8 (4/30/91) BB
64 MOREAU Bourgogne Chardonnay 1983 $6.50 (6/01/86)
74 PIERRE MOREY Bourgogne Aligoté 1985 $9.75 (2/15/88)
83 PAUL PERNOT Bourgogne Chardonnay Champerrier 1989 $16 (4/30/91)
87 DOMAINE PONSOT Morey-St.-Denis Monts-Luisants 1988 $50 (5/31/91)
81 CHATEAU DE PULIGNY-MONTRACHET Bourgogne Clos du Château 1988 $19 (7/31/90)
83 CHATEAU DE PULIGNY-MONTRACHET Côte de Nuits-Villages 1989 $27 (2/28/91)
80 DOMAINE ROUGEOT-LATOUR Bourgogne Chardonnay Clos des Six Ouvrées 1986 $15 (10/15/88)
73 DOMAINE B. SERVEAU Bourgogne Chardonnay 1989 $16 (4/30/91)
76 ROLAND THEVENIN Bourgogne Chardonnay Réserve Roland Thévenin 1985 $8 (3/31/87)
72 THEVENOT-LE-BRUN Bourgogne Aligoté 1988 $11.50 (7/31/90)

CHABLIS

66 DOMAINE AUFFRAY Chablis 1986 $12.95 (11/15/87)
86 DOMAINE AUFFRAY Chablis Champs Royaux 1989 $19 (1/31/91)
79 DOMAINE AUFFRAY Chablis Champs Royaux 1988 $12 (3/31/90)
88 DOMAINE AUFFRAY Chablis Champs Royaux 1986 $17 (9/15/88)
85 DOMAINE AUFFRAY Chablis Fourchaume 1986 $24 (9/15/88)
92 DOMAINE AUFFRAY Chablis Les Clos 1989 $50 (1/31/91)
92 DOMAINE AUFFRAY Chablis Les Clos 1988 $38 (3/31/90)
70 DOMAINE AUFFRAY Chablis Les Clos 1986 $36 (10/15/88)
88 DOMAINE AUFFRAY Chablis Les Preuses 1986 $36 (9/15/88)
92 DOMAINE AUFFRAY Chablis Les Preuses 1984 $30 (4/15/87)
74 DOMAINE AUFFRAY Chablis Montée de Tonnerre 1989 $25 (2/28/91)
87 DOMAINE AUFFRAY Chablis Montée de Tonnerre 1988 $21 (3/31/90)
75 DOMAINE AUFFRAY Chablis Montée de Tonnerre 1986 $24 (10/15/88)
88 DOMAINE AUFFRAY Chablis Vaillons 1989 $27 (1/31/91)
93 DOMAINE AUFFRAY Chablis Vaillons 1988 $20 (12/15/89)
80 DOMAINE AUFFRAY Chablis Valmur 1988 $32 (12/15/89)
84 BICHOT Chablis 1988 $17 (3/31/90)
85 BICHOT Chablis 1987 $11 (3/31/89)
65 BICHOT Chablis 1984 $9 (2/16/86)
82 BICHOT Chablis Les Vaillons 1988 $17 (12/15/89)
72 J. BILLAUD-SIMON Chablis Montée de Tonnerre 1985 $19.50 (9/30/87)
75 JEAN CLAUDE BOISSET Chablis 1985 $14 (1/31/87)
65 JEAN CLAUDE BOISSET Chablis Grenouilles 1982 $15 (6/16/85)
83 BOUCHARD PERE & FILS Chablis 1985 $15 (10/15/87)
86 JEAN-MARC BROCARD Chablis Domaine Ste.-Claire 1989 $13 (1/31/91)
90 DOMAINE ANTOINE CHAPUIS Chablis Montée de Tonnerre 1985 $21 (8/31/87)
82 F. CHAUVENET Chablis Montmains 1982 $10 (7/01/85)
82 JEAN DAUVISSAT Chablis Les Preuses 1986 $30 (7/15/90)
91 JEAN DAUVISSAT Chablis Vaillons 1987 $22 (1/31/91)
82 JEAN DAUVISSAT Chablis Vaillons 1986 $19 (7/15/90)
85 JEAN DAUVISSAT Chablis Vaillons Vieilles Vignes 1986 $24 (7/15/90)
74 DOMAINE DAUVISSAT-CAMUS Chablis La Forest 1988 $25 (7/31/90)
83 DOMAINE DAUVISSAT-CAMUS Chablis La Forest 1987 $22 (10/15/89)
85 DOMAINE DAUVISSAT-CAMUS Chablis La Forest 1986 $25 (9/15/88)
74 DOMAINE DAUVISSAT-CAMUS Chablis La Forest 1985 $28 (11/15/87)
92 DOMAINE DAUVISSAT-CAMUS Chablis Les Clos 1988 $41 (7/31/90)
88 DOMAINE DAUVISSAT-CAMUS Chablis Les Clos 1987 $37 (10/15/89)
95 DOMAINE DAUVISSAT-CAMUS Chablis Les Clos 1986 $40 (9/15/88)
86 DOMAINE DAUVISSAT-CAMUS Chablis Les Preuses 1988 $41 (7/31/90)

FRANCE
CHABLIS

87 DOMAINE DAUVISSAT-CAMUS Chablis Les Preuses 1987 $37 (10/15/89)
94 DOMAINE DAUVISSAT-CAMUS Chablis Les Preuses 1986 $40 (9/15/88)
91 DOMAINE DAUVISSAT-CAMUS Chablis Vaillons 1988 $25 (7/15/90)
78 DOMAINE DAUVISSAT-CAMUS Chablis Vaillons 1987 $22 (10/15/89)
84 DOMAINE DAUVISSAT-CAMUS Chablis Vaillons 1986 $24.50 (9/15/88)
88 DOMAINE DAUVISSAT-CAMUS Chablis Vaillons 1985 $28 (11/15/87)
67 M. DEOLIVEIRA Chablis Les Clos 1985 $34 (8/31/87)
85 JEAN-PAUL DROIN Chablis Fourchaume 1986 $17 (7/15/88)
87 JEAN-PAUL DROIN Chablis Les Clos 1986 $32 (5/15/88)
90 JEAN-PAUL DROIN Chablis Montée de Tonnerre 1986 $21 (5/15/88)
72 JOSEPH DROUHIN Chablis 1988 $18 (3/31/90)
84 JOSEPH DROUHIN Chablis 1987 $14 (3/31/89)
87 JOSEPH DROUHIN Chablis Première Cru 1987 $20 (3/31/89)
83 JOSEPH DROUHIN Chablis 1986 $14 (5/15/88)
85 JOSEPH DROUHIN Chablis Première Cru 1986 $19.50 (5/15/88)
87 JOSEPH DROUHIN Chablis Bougros 1986 $33 (5/15/88)
86 JOSEPH DROUHIN Chablis Montmains 1989 $23 (2/28/91)
83 JOSEPH DROUHIN Chablis Montmains 1988 $23 (3/31/89)
89 JOSEPH DROUHIN Chablis Vaudésir 1989 $54 (2/28/91)
87 JOSEPH DROUHIN Chablis Vaudésir 1988 $38 (3/31/90)
92 JOSEPH DROUHIN Chablis Vaudésir 1986 $34 (5/15/88)
88 DOMAINE DE L'EGLANTIERE Chablis 1985 $14.25 (1/31/87)
85 YVONNE FEBVRE Chablis Blanchot 1988 $23 (1/31/91)
73 YVONNE FEBVRE Chablis Montée de Tonnerre 1984 $14.75 (1/31/87)
89 CHATEAU GRENOUILLES Chablis Grenouille 1985 $34 (8/31/87)
86 JAFFELIN Chablis Fourchaume 1983 $14.50 (10/16/85)
70 LABOURE-ROI Chablis Fourchaumes 1988 $22 (7/31/90)
88 LAROCHE Chablis 1986 $12 (5/15/88)
80 LAROCHE Chablis Fourchaume 1988 $23 (7/31/90)
87 DOMAINE LAROCHE Chablis 1988 $15.50 (7/31/90)
85 DOMAINE LAROCHE Chablis 1988 $15.50 (3/31/90)
74 DOMAINE LAROCHE Chablis 1987 $26 (3/31/91)
91 DOMAINE LAROCHE Chablis 1983 $13 (11/15/86)
87 DOMAINE LAROCHE Chablis Cuvée Première 1989 $25 (1/31/91)
83 DOMAINE LAROCHE Chablis Laroche Cuvée Première 1988 $16 (12/15/89)
79 DOMAINE LAROCHE Chablis Les Beauroys 1984 $19 (10/31/87)
87 DOMAINE LAROCHE Chablis Les Blanchots 1989 $57 (1/31/91)
93 DOMAINE LAROCHE Chablis Les Blanchots 1984 $27.25 (2/28/87)
88 DOMAINE LAROCHE Chablis Les Blanchots Vieilles Vignes 1989 $72 (1/31/91)
86 DOMAINE LAROCHE Chablis Les Blanchots Vieilles Vignes 1988 $58 (7/31/90)
86 DOMAINE LAROCHE Chablis Les Bouguerots 1985 $33 (6/15/87)
83 DOMAINE LAROCHE Chablis Les Clos 1988 $49 (12/15/89)
89 DOMAINE LAROCHE Chablis Les Clos 1986 $50 (12/31/88)
88 DOMAINE LAROCHE Chablis Les Fourchaumes 1988 $23 (12/15/89)
86 DOMAINE LAROCHE Chablis Les Fourchaumes 1986 $29 (5/15/88)
85 DOMAINE LAROCHE Chablis Les Fourchaumes 1984 $18 (1/31/87)
84 DOMAINE LAROCHE Chablis Les Montmains 1988 $25 (7/31/90)
86 DOMAINE LAROCHE Chablis Les Vaillons 1989 $33 (1/31/91)
88 DOMAINE LAROCHE Chablis Les Vaillons 1988 $22 (12/15/89)
86 DOMAINE LAROCHE Chablis Les Vaillons 1986 $29 (12/31/88)
82 DOMAINE LAROCHE Chablis Les Vaillons 1986 $29 (9/15/88)
66 DOMAINE LAROCHE Chablis Les Vaillons 1983 $15 (2/15/86)
87 DOMAINE LAROCHE Chablis Les Vaudevey 1988 $24 (7/31/90)
80 DOMAINE LAROCHE Chablis Les Vaudevey 1985 $19 (6/15/87)
75 DOMAINE LAROCHE Chablis Les Vaudevey 1984 $17 (1/31/87)
77 DOMAINE LAROCHE Chablis Les Vaudevey 1983 $15 (12/01/85)
82 DOMAINE LAROCHE Chablis St.-Martin 1989 $21 (2/28/91)
90 DOMAINE LAROCHE Chablis St.-Martin 1988 $15 (12/15/89)
86 DOMAINE LAROCHE Chablis St.-Martin 1986 $16 (12/31/88)
83 DOMAINE LAROCHE Chablis St.-Martin 1985 $16 (6/30/87)
68 ROLAND LAVANTUREUX Chablis 1986 $16 (1/31/89)
80 ROLAND LAVANTUREUX Chablis 1985 $17 (5/15/88)
75 ROLAND LAVANTUREUX Chablis Petit 1986 $11 (5/15/88)
83 DOMAINE LONG-DEPAQUIT Chablis 1987 $12 (3/31/89)
71 DOMAINE LONG-DEPAQUIT Chablis 1986 $15 (5/15/88)
80 DOMAINE LONG-DEPAQUIT Chablis 1985 $14 (11/15/87)
67 DOMAINE LONG-DEPAQUIT Chablis Les Beugnons 1984 $12 (7/16/86)
88 DOMAINE LONG-DEPAQUIT Chablis Les Blanchots 1988 $36 (1/31/91)
88 DOMAINE LONG-DEPAQUIT Chablis Les Blanchots 1987 $29 (3/31/89)
87 DOMAINE LONG-DEPAQUIT Chablis Les Blanchots 1986 $28 (3/31/88)
76 DOMAINE LONG-DEPAQUIT Chablis Les Blanchots 1984 $20 (9/15/86)
90 DOMAINE LONG-DEPAQUIT Chablis Les Clos 1988 $42 (7/15/90)
90 DOMAINE LONG-DEPAQUIT Chablis Les Clos 1986 $32 (3/31/88)
88 DOMAINE LONG-DEPAQUIT Chablis Les Clos 1985 $32 (8/31/87)
85 DOMAINE LONG-DEPAQUIT Chablis Les Lys 1987 $15 (12/31/88)
90 DOMAINE LONG-DEPAQUIT Chablis Les Preuses 1987 $30 (3/31/89)
87 DOMAINE LONG-DEPAQUIT Chablis Les Vaillons 1988 $20 (7/31/90)
86 DOMAINE LONG-DEPAQUIT Chablis Les Vaillons 1987 $15 (12/31/88)
77 DOMAINE LONG-DEPAQUIT Chablis Les Vaillons 1986 $18 (5/15/88)
80 DOMAINE LONG-DEPAQUIT Chablis Les Vaillons 1984 $21 (6/30/87)
87 DOMAINE LONG-DEPAQUIT Chablis Les Vaudésirs 1988 $40 (7/31/90)
85 DOMAINE LONG-DEPAQUIT Chablis Les Vaudésirs 1986 $28 (3/31/88)
86 DOMAINE LONG-DEPAQUIT Chablis Les Vaudésirs 1985 $30 (6/30/87)
91 DOMAINE LONG-DEPAQUIT Chablis Les Vaudésirs 1984 $20 (10/15/86) CS

92 DOMAINE LONG-DEPAQUIT Chablis Moutonne 1988 $47 (7/31/90)
85 DOMAINE LONG-DEPAQUIT Chablis Moutonne 1987 $36 (3/31/89)
88 DOMAINE LONG-DEPAQUIT Chablis Moutonne 1986 $35 (3/31/88)
87 DOMAINE LONG-DEPAQUIT Chablis Moutonne 1985 $35 (11/15/87)
87 DOMAINE LONG-DEPAQUIT Chablis Moutonne 1983 $20 (12/16/85)
67 DOMAINE LONG-DEPAQUIT Chablis Vaucopins 1986 $18 (5/15/88)
86 DOMAINE LONG-DEPAQUIT Chablis Vaudésirs 1987 $30 (3/31/89)
82 LUPE-CHOLET Chablis Château de Viviers 1988 $15 (3/31/90)
81 DOMAINE DE LA MALADIERE Chablis 1988 $13 (2/28/91)
76 CHATEAU DE MALIGNY Chablis 1988 $15 (7/31/90)
71 CHATEAU DE MALIGNY Chablis Fourchaume 1988 $22 (7/31/90)
85 CHATEAU DE MALIGNY Chablis Fourchaume 1986 $18 (3/31/89)
77 LOUIS MICHEL & FILS Chablis 1988 $16.50 (7/15/90)
86 LOUIS MICHEL & FILS Chablis Montée de Tonnerre 1988 $26 (7/31/90)
87 LOUIS MICHEL & FILS Chablis Montée de Tonnerre 1987 $20 (7/15/90)
80 LOUIS MICHEL & FILS Chablis Montmain 1987 $20 (7/15/90)
89 LOUIS MICHEL & FILS Chablis Vaudésir 1987 $31 (7/15/90)
81 MOILLARD Chablis 1989 $26 (2/28/91)
86 MOILLARD Chablis 1987 $17 (10/15/89)
68 MOILLARD Chablis 1985 $14 (5/31/87)
89 MOILLARD Chablis Vaillons 1985 $16 (5/31/87)
62 MOREAU Chablis 1983 $9.50 (12/01/85)
88 MOREAU Chablis Domaine de Bieville 1988 $15 (2/28/91)
84 MOREAU Chablis Domaine de Bieville 1985 $13.50 (4/15/87)
84 MOREAU Chablis Les Clos 1987 $38 (2/28/91)
91 MOREAU Chablis Les Clos 1986 $36 (5/15/88)
89 MOREAU Chablis Les Clos Clos des Hospices 1987 $60 (2/28/91)
78 MOREAU Chablis Les Clos Clos des Hospices 1986 $35 (10/15/88)
87 MOREAU Chablis Montmain 1986 $21 (2/28/91)
87 MOREAU Chablis Vaillon 1989 $20 (2/28/91)
90 MOREAU Chablis Valmur 1986 $38 (2/28/91)
86 MOREAU Chablis Les Clos Clos des Hospices 1987 $52 (10/15/89)
79 PATRIARCHE Chablis Cuvée des Quatre Vents 1986 $13 (10/15/89)
87 BARON PATRICK Chablis 1979 $12.75 (6/16/84)
79 ALBERT PIC & FILS Chablis 1986 $16 (9/15/88)
77 ALBERT PIC & FILS Chablis Bougros 1986 $38 (9/15/88)
84 ALBERT PIC & FILS Chablis Les Clos 1986 $40 (9/15/88)
88 ALBERT PIC & FILS Chablis Les Preuses 1986 $37 (9/15/88)
78 ALBERT PIC & FILS Chablis Valmur 1986 $40 (10/15/88)
83 ALBERT PIC & FILS Chablis Vaudésir 1986 $40 (9/15/88)
92 FRANCOIS RAVENEAU Chablis Blanchot 1987 $40 (3/31/90)
90 FRANCOIS RAVENEAU Chablis Clos 1987 $50 (3/31/90)
90 FRANCOIS RAVENEAU Chablis Montée de Tonnerre 1987 $35 (3/31/90)
90 JEAN-MARIE RAVENEAU Chablis Chapelot 1987 $25 (3/31/90)
88 JEAN-MARIE RAVENEAU Chablis Vaillons 1987 $25 (3/31/90)
92 JEAN-MARIE RAVENEAU Chablis Valmur 1987 $40 (3/31/90)
83 A. REGNARD & FILS Chablis Fourchaume 1986 $22 (9/15/88)
79 A. REGNARD & FILS Chablis Fourchaume 1983 $11 (11/01/84)
78 A. REGNARD & FILS Chablis Mont de Milieu 1986 $20 (10/15/88)
70 A. REGNARD & FILS Chablis Montée de Tonnerre 1986 $21 (10/15/88)
70 A. REGNARD & FILS Chablis Montmains 1986 $20 (9/15/88)
86 A. REGNARD & FILS Chablis Vaillons 1986 $20 (9/15/88)
83 GUY ROBIN Chablis Vaudésir 1986 $37 (2/28/91)
74 DOMAINE MICHEL-ROBIN Chablis Blanchots 1985 $34 (8/31/87)
79 DOMAINE MICHEL-ROBIN Chablis Vaillons 1985 $21.50 (8/31/87)
88 ANTONIN RODET Chablis Montmains 1985 $20 (4/15/87)
79 DOMAINE SEGUINOT Chablis 1988 $16 (2/28/91)
68 SIMONNET-FEBVRE Chablis 1986 $12 (5/15/88)
55 SIMONNET-FEBVRE Chablis Les Clos 1986 $29 (7/15/88)
76 SIMONNET-FEBVRE Chablis Vaillons 1986 $17 (5/15/88)
90 PHILIPPE TESTUT Chablis 1984 $12.50 (4/15/87)
91 THORIN Chablis Fourchaume 1987 $24 (10/15/89)
86 THORIN Chablis Fourchaume 1986 $23 (2/15/89)
68 DOMAINE TRIBAUT-DAUVISSAT Chablis 1987 $15 (10/15/89)
87 LAURENT TRIBUT Chablis 1988 $17 (7/31/90)
89 LAURENT TRIBUT Chablis Beauroy 1988 $17 (7/15/90)
84 DOMAINE TRIBUT-DAUVISSAT Chablis 1988 $18 (1/31/91)
62 ANDRE VANNIER Chablis Les Clos 1986 $32 (9/15/88)
63 ANDRE VANNIER Chablis Les Clos 1983 $17.50 (3/16/85)
87 ANDRE VANNIER Chablis Les Preuses 1986 $33 (5/15/88)
90 ANDRE VANNIER Chablis Les Preuses 1983 $17.50 (3/01/85)
89 CHARLES VIENOT Chablis Vauignot 1987 $20 (3/31/89)
72 CHATEAU DE VIVIERS Chablis 1984 $11.75 (7/16/86)

CHAMPAGNE/BLANC DE BLANCS

90 AYALA Brut Blanc de Blancs Champagne 1985 $57 (12/31/90)
82 AYALA Brut Blanc de Blancs Champagne 1985 $57 (12/31/89)
85 AYALA Brut Blanc de Blancs Champagne 1982 $29 (4/15/88)
71 BARANCOURT Brut Blanc de Blancs Champagne Cramant NV $20 (5/31/87)
85 BARANCOURT Brut Blanc de Blancs Champagne Cramant Grand Cru NV $30 (12/31/90)
85 BEAUMET Brut Blanc de Blancs Champagne NV $30 (12/31/90)
74 BEAUMET Brut Blanc de Blancs Champagne NV $25 (12/31/89)
86 BEAUMET Brut Blanc de Blancs Champagne NV $25 (5/31/87)
85 BEAUMET Brut Blanc de Blancs Champagne Cuvée Malakoff 1982 $41 (4/15/90)
91 BEAUMET Brut Blanc de Blancs Champagne Cuvée Malakoff 1982 $41 (12/31/90)
89 BEAUMET Brut Blanc de Blancs Champagne Cuvée Malakoff 1979 $30 (5/31/87)
88 BILLECART-SALMON Brut Blanc de Blancs Champagne 1983 $50 (12/31/89)
90 BILLECART-SALMON Brut Blanc de Blancs Champagne 1983 $50 (5/15/88)
86 BILLECART-SALMON Brut Blanc de Blancs Champagne 1982 $43 (5/31/87)
83 BONNAIRE Brut Blanc de Blancs Champagne Cramant 1985 $42 (12/31/89)
87 BONNAIRE Brut Blanc de Blancs Champagne Cramant 1983 $38 (2/29/88)
86 BONNAIRE Brut Blanc de Blancs Champagne Cramant 1979 $40 (5/31/87)
90 BONNAIRE Brut Blanc de Blancs Champagne Cramant NV $30 (12/31/89)
90 BONNAIRE Brut Blanc de Blancs Champagne Cramant NV $30 (5/31/87)
85 BRICOUT Brut Blanc de Blancs Champagne NV $21 (12/31/87)
65 BRICOUT Brut Blanc de Blancs Champagne NV $21 (12/31/86)
84 DE CASTELLANE Brut Blanc de Blancs Champagne 1981 $33 (4/15/88)
91 DE CASTELLANE Brut Blanc de Blancs Champagne 1980 $22 (5/31/87)

90 DE CASTELLANE Brut Blanc de Blancs Champagne Brut Chardonnay 1983 (NA) (12/31/90)
81 DE CASTELLANE Brut Blanc de Blancs Champagne Brut Chardonnay NV $26 (12/31/90)
90 A. CHARBAUT Brut Blanc de Blancs Champagne 1982 $43 (4/15/90)
96 A. CHARBAUT Brut Blanc de Blancs Champagne 1979 $34 (5/31/87)
83 A. CHARBAUT Brut Blanc de Blancs Champagne NV $40 (12/31/90)
86 A. CHARBAUT Brut Blanc de Blancs Champagne NV $32 (12/31/88)
87 A. CHARBAUT Brut Blanc de Blancs Champagne Certificate 1982 $82 (12/31/89)
92 A. CHARBAUT Brut Blanc de Blancs Champagne Certificate 1979 $80 (7/15/88)
87 A. CHARBAUT Brut Blanc de Blancs Champagne Certificate 1976 $63 (5/31/87)
97 A. CHARBAUT Brut Blanc de Blancs Champagne Certificate 1976 $63 (2/01/86) SS
84 DELAMOTTE Blanc de Blancs Champagne 1982 $28 (4/15/88)
79 DELAMOTTE Blanc de Blancs Champagne NV $24 (12/31/87)
83 DEUTZ Brut Blanc de Blancs Champagne 1985 $42 (12/31/90)
90 DEUTZ Brut Blanc de Blancs Champagne 1982 $39 (5/31/87)
76 ANDRE DRAPPIER Brut Blanc de Blancs Champagne NV $30 (5/31/87)
86 ANDRE DRAPPIER Brut Blanc de Blancs Champagne Signature NV $23 (2/01/86)
86 DUVAL-LEROY Brut Blanc de Blancs Champagne NV (NA) (12/31/90)
90 ELLNER Brut Blanc de Blancs Champagne NV $32 (7/31/89)
89 H. GERMAINE Blanc de Blancs Crémant Champagne 1983 $24 (12/31/90)
77 H. GERMAINE Blanc de Blancs Crémant Champagne 1982 $53 (5/31/87)
86 GEORGE GOULET Blanc de Blancs Crémant Champagne 1982 $30 (7/31/88)
74 GEORGE GOULET Brut Blanc de Blancs Champagne Cuvée "G" NV $26 (7/31/88)
84 CHARLES HEIDSIECK Brut Blanc de Blancs Champagne NV (NA) (12/31/90)
78 CHARLES HEIDSIECK Brut Blanc de Blancs Champagne Brut de Chardonnay 1981 $30 (5/31/87)
85 HENRIOT Brut Blanc de Blancs Champagne de Chardonnay NV (NA) (12/31/90)
85 JACQUART Brut Blanc de Blancs Champagne NV $25 (12/31/90)
89 JACQUESSON Blanc de Blancs Champagne NV $40 (12/31/90)
85 JACQUESSON Blanc de Blancs Champagne NV $25 (5/31/87)
77 JEAN-MARIE Brut Blanc de Blancs Champagne NV (NA) (12/31/90)
84 KRUG Brut Blanc de Blancs Champagne Clos du Mesnil 1982 Rel: $120 Cur: $195 (12/31/90)
87 KRUG Brut Blanc de Blancs Champagne Clos du Mesnil 1981 Rel: $120 Cur: $162 (12/31/90)
87 KRUG Brut Blanc de Blancs Champagne Clos du Mesnil 1981 Rel: $120 Cur: $162 (12/31/89)
80 KRUG Brut Blanc de Blancs Champagne Clos du Mesnil 1980 Rel: $100 Cur: $160 (5/31/87)
92 GUY LARMANDIER Brut Blanc de Blancs Champagne Cramant NV $26.50 (5/31/87)
89 LECHERE Brut Blanc de Blancs Champagne NV $25 (12/31/87)
86 LECHERE Brut Blanc de Blancs Champagne Cuvée Orient Express NV $45 (12/31/90)
81 LECHERE Brut Blanc de Blancs Champagne Première Cru NV $30 (5/31/87)
75 R & L LEGRAS Brut Blanc de Blancs Champagne NV $24 (5/31/87)
85 R & L LEGRAS Brut Blanc de Blancs Champagne Cuvée St.-Vincent 1976 $33 (5/31/87)
85 R & L LEGRAS Brut Blanc de Blancs Champagne Présidence 1982 $29 (5/31/87)
86 MARQUIS DE SADE Brut Blanc de Blancs Champagne Grand Cru NV $41 (12/31/90)
91 G.H. MUMM Brut Blanc de Blancs Champagne Mumm de Cramant NV $43 (12/31/90)
86 G.H. MUMM Brut Blanc de Blancs Champagne Mumm de Cramant NV $43 (1/31/89)
74 OUDINOT Brut Blanc de Blancs Champagne NV $25 (12/31/90)
94 BRUNO PAILLARD Brut Blanc de Blancs Champagne 1983 $40 (5/31/87)
70 BRUNO PAILLARD Brut Blanc de Blancs Champagne 1975 $42 (5/31/87)
85 BRUNO PAILLARD Blanc de Blancs Crémant Champagne NV $36 (12/31/90)
75 BRUNO PAILLARD Blanc de Blancs Crémant Champagne NV $25 (5/31/87)
88 JOSEPH PERRIER Brut Blanc de Blancs Champagne Cuvée Royale NV $37 (12/31/90)
80 JOSEPH PERRIER Brut Blanc de Blancs Champagne Cuvée Royale NV $31 (12/31/89)
86 JOSEPH PERRIER Brut Blanc de Blancs Champagne Cuvée Royale NV $34 (5/31/87)
88 BATISTE PERTOIS Brut Blanc de Blancs Champagne Cramant Cuvée de Réserve NV $24 (12/31/89)
92 PHILIPPONNAT Brut Blanc de Blancs Champagne 1980 $26 (5/31/87)
89 PHILIPPONNAT Brut Blanc de Blancs Champagne Cuvée Première 1980 $39 (12/31/88)
87 PHILIPPONNAT Brut Blanc de Blancs Champagne Grand Blanc 1985 $40 (12/31/90)
83 LOUIS ROEDERER Brut Blanc de Blancs Champagne 1983 $45 (12/31/90)
94 LOUIS ROEDERER Brut Blanc de Blancs Champagne 1979 $39 (5/31/87)
91 POL ROGER Brut Blanc de Blancs Champagne Blanc de Chardonnay 1982 $50 (12/31/90)
90 POL ROGER Brut Blanc de Blancs Champagne Blanc de Chardonnay 1982 $50 (12/31/88)
84 POL ROGER Brut Blanc de Blancs Champagne Blanc de Chardonnay 1979 $41 (12/31/90)
72 POL ROGER Brut Blanc de Blancs Champagne Blanc de Chardonnay 1979 $35 (5/31/87)
87 DOM RUINART Brut Blanc de Blancs Champagne 1983 Rel: $60 (12/31/90)
90 DOM RUINART Brut Blanc de Blancs Champagne 1982 $61 (12/31/90)
94 DOM RUINART Brut Blanc de Blancs Champagne 1982 Rel: $61 (12/31/89) CS
90 DOM RUINART Brut Blanc de Blancs Champagne 1981 Rel: $61 Cur: $67 (12/31/89)
91 DOM RUINART Brut Blanc de Blancs Champagne 1979 Rel: $39 Cur: $52 (10/31/86)
87 DOM RUINART Brut Blanc de Blancs Champagne 1978 Rel: $40 Cur: $50 (5/16/86)
84 DOM RUINART Brut Blanc de Blancs Champagne 1976 Rel: $30 Cur: $45 (10/01/84)
90 SALON Brut Blanc de Blancs Champagne Le Mesnil 1982 $119 (12/31/90)
89 SALON Brut Blanc de Blancs Champagne Le Mesnil 1982 $119 (12/31/89)
93 SALON Brut Blanc de Blancs Champagne Le Mesnil 1979 Disgorged Summer 1988 $119 (12/31/89)
92 SALON Brut Blanc de Blancs Champagne Le Mesnil 1979 $119 (12/31/88)
91 SALON Brut Blanc de Blancs Champagne Le Mesnil 1976 $225/1.5L (12/31/88)
89 SALON Brut Blanc de Blancs Champagne Le Mesnil 1976 Rel: $71 Cur: $105 (5/31/87)
85 MARIE STUART Brut NV $22 (12/31/87)
87 MARIE STUART Brut Blanc de Blancs Champagne 1979 $25 (12/31/87)
82 MARIE STUART Brut Blanc de Blancs Champagne NV $22 (12/31/87)
82 TAILLEVENT Brut Blanc de Blancs Champagne 1983 $33 (12/31/89)
92 TAITTINGER Brut Blanc de Blancs Champagne Comtes de Champagne 1985 (NA) (12/31/90)
93 TAITTINGER Brut Blanc de Blancs Champagne Comtes de Champagne 1983 $92 (12/31/90)
95 TAITTINGER Brut Blanc de Blancs Champagne Comtes de Champagne 1982 Rel: $83 Cur: $83 (12/31/89)
93 TAITTINGER Brut Blanc de Blancs Champagne Comtes de Champagne 1981 Rel: $69 Cur: $72 (4/15/88)
92 TAITTINGER Brut Blanc de Blancs Champagne Comtes de Champagne 1979 Rel: $65 Cur: $65 (5/31/87)
83 TAITTINGER Brut Blanc de Blancs Champagne Comtes de Champagne 1976 Rel: $66 Cur: $126 (5/16/86)
86 DE VENOGE Brut Blanc de Blancs Champagne NV $38 (12/31/90)

BRUT

90 HENRI ABELE Brut Champagne Grande Marque Impériale 1982 $29 (7/31/87)
79 HENRI ABELE Brut Champagne Le Sourire de Reims NV $24 (7/31/87)
89 AYALA Brut Champagne 1985 $57 (12/31/90)
80 AYALA Brut Champagne 1983 $30 (12/31/89)
86 AYALA Brut Champagne 1982 $27 (4/15/88)
83 AYALA Brut Champagne NV $23 (4/15/88)
78 AYALA Brut Champagne Extra Quality NV $28 (12/31/87)
84 AYALA Brut Champagne Grand Cuvée 1985 $57 (12/31/89)
87 AYALA Brut Champagne Grand Cuvée 1982 $52 (4/15/88)
89 PAUL BARA Brut Champagne 1982 $34 (12/31/88)
90 BARANCOURT Champagne Cuvée de Fondateurs 1985 (NA) (12/31/90)
84 BEAUMET Brut Champagne NV $22 (12/31/89)
89 BILLECART-SALMON Brut Champagne 1983 $47 (12/31/89)
91 BILLECART-SALMON Brut Champagne NV $30 (12/31/87)
94 BOLLINGER Brut Champagne Extra RD 1979 Rel: $79 Cur: $87 (12/31/89)
88 BOLLINGER Brut Champagne Extra RD 1976 Rel: $59 Cur: $73 (4/15/88)
89 BOLLINGER Brut Champagne Extra RD 1975 Rel: $64 Cur: $93 (5/16/86)
96 BOLLINGER Brut Champagne Grand Année 1985 $45 (12/31/90)
86 BOLLINGER Brut Champagne Grand Année 1983 $43 (12/31/89)
87 BOLLINGER Brut Champagne Grand Année 1983 $43 (12/31/88)
93 BOLLINGER Brut Champagne Grand Année 1982 $30 (7/15/88)
92 BOLLINGER Brut Champagne Spécial Cuvée NV $25 (12/31/87) SS
81 BRICOUT Brut Champagne 1985 (NA) (12/31/90)
75 BRICOUT Brut Champagne Carte d'Or Prestige 1983 $25 (12/31/89)
90 BRICOUT Brut Champagne Carte d'Or Prestige 1983 $25 (12/31/88)
78 BRICOUT Brut Champagne Carte d'Or Prestige 1983 $25 (12/31/87)
69 BRICOUT Brut Champagne Carte d'Or Prestige NV $19 (12/31/86)
82 BRICOUT Brut Champagne Carte Noire Réserve NV $20 (12/31/88)
79 BRICOUT Brut Champagne Carte Noire Réserve NV $20 (12/31/87)
85 BRICOUT Brut Champagne Elegance de Bricout 1985 (NA) (12/31/90)
90 BRICOUT Brut Champagne Elegance de Bricout 1982 $50 (12/31/88)
85 CANARD-DUCHENE Brut Champagne Cuvée Bicentenaire NV $39 (12/31/89)
85 CANARD-DUCHENE Brut Champagne Cuvée Spéciale de Charles VII NV $75 (12/31/89)
80 CANARD-DUCHENE Brut Champagne Patrimoine 1983 $42 (12/31/89)
89 CANARD-DUCHENE Brut Champagne Patrimoine NV $35 (12/31/89)
84 DE CASTELLANE Brut Champagne 1985 $27 (12/31/90)
80 DE CASTELLANE Brut Champagne NV $24 (4/15/88)
87 DE CASTELLANE Champagne Cuvée Commodore 1981 $50 (4/15/88)
88 DE CASTELLANE Brut Champagne Cuvée Florens de Castellane 1982 $59 (12/31/90)
82 CATTIER Brut Champagne NV $17 (12/31/89)
89 CATTIER Brut Champagne Clos du Moulin NV $37 (12/31/89)
94 A. CHARBAUT Brut Champagne 1985 $49 (12/31/90)
94 A. CHARBAUT Brut Champagne 1985 $49 (12/31/90)
74 A. CHARBAUT Brut Champagne 1979 $23 (2/01/86)
77 A. CHARBAUT Brut Champagne NV $24 (12/31/88)
93 VEUVE CLICQUOT Brut Champagne 1982 $32 (5/31/87) SS
88 VEUVE CLICQUOT Brut Champagne 1979 $50 (12/16/85)
91 VEUVE CLICQUOT Brut Champagne NV $27 (12/31/87)
90 VEUVE CLICQUOT Brut Champagne Gold Label 1983 $42 (12/31/90)
85 VEUVE CLICQUOT Brut Champagne Gold Label 1982 $37 (12/31/88)
91 VEUVE CLICQUOT Brut Champagne La Grande Dame 1985 Rel: $72 Cur: $82 (12/31/90)
92 VEUVE CLICQUOT Brut Champagne La Grande Dame 1983 Rel: $79 Cur: $79 (12/31/89)
86 VEUVE CLICQUOT Brut Champagne La Grande Dame 1983 Rel: $79 Cur: $79 (7/31/89)
96 VEUVE CLICQUOT Brut Champagne La Grande Dame 1979 Rel: $61 Cur: $74 (5/16/86)
89 COMTE AUDOIN DE DAMPIERRE Brut Champagne Grande Année 1983 $32 (12/31/90)
78 DELAMOTTE Brut Champagne NV $20 (12/31/87)
83 DEUTZ Brut Champagne 1985 $40 (12/31/90)
81 DEUTZ Brut Champagne NV $28 (12/31/87)
79 DEUTZ Brut Champagne 150 Anniversaire NV $50 (12/31/88)
87 DEUTZ Brut Champagne Cuvée Georges Mathieu 1982 $34 (10/15/88)
80 DEUTZ Brut Champagne Cuvée Lallier Gold Lack NV $33 (12/31/90)
89 DEUTZ Brut Champagne Cuvée Lallier Gold Lack NV $25 (12/31/88)
85 DEUTZ Brut Champagne Cuvée William Deutz 1982 Rel: $61 Cur: $72 (12/31/89)
90 DEUTZ Brut Champagne Cuvée William Deutz 1982 Rel: $61 Cur: $72 (12/31/88)
90 DEUTZ Brut Champagne Cuvée William Deutz 1979 Rel: $35 Cur: $47 (7/16/85)
89 DEUTZ Brut Champagne George Mathieu 1982 $40 (12/31/89)
86 DEUTZ Brut Champagne George Mathieu Réserve 1985 $46 (12/31/90)
84 DUVAL-LEROY Champagne Cuvée des Roys 1985 (NA) (12/31/90)
91 ELLNER Brut Champagne 1982 $38 (7/31/89)
87 ELLNER Brut Champagne Réserve NV $30 (7/31/89)
86 SERGE FAUST Brut Champagne Cuvée de Réserve à Vandières NV $33 (12/31/90)
73 NICHOLAS FEUILLATTE Brut Champagne Réserve Particulière NV $17 (12/31/87)
89 GOSSET Brut Champagne Grande Millésime 1985 Rel: $72 Cur: $90 (4/30/91)
91 GOSSET Brut Champagne Grande Millésime 1985 Rel: $72 Cur: $90 (12/31/90)
90 GOSSET Brut Champagne Grande Millésime 1982 Rel: $60 Cur: $64 (12/31/90)
85 GOSSET Brut Champagne Grande Millésime 1982 Rel: $60 Cur: $64 (12/31/88)
96 GOSSET Brut Champagne Grande Millésime 1979 Rel: $45 Cur: $84 (7/15/87)
90 GOSSET Brut Champagne Grande Réserve NV $39 (12/31/90)
92 GOSSET Brut Champagne Grande Réserve NV $39 (12/31/87)
90 GOSSET Brut Champagne Réserve NV $34 (12/31/90)
78 GOSSET Brut Champagne Réserve NV $34 (12/31/88)
90 GEORGE GOULET Brut Champagne 1982 $30 (7/31/88)
83 GEORGE GOULET Brut Champagne NV $21 (7/31/88)
87 GEORGE GOULET Brut Champagne Cuvée du Centenaire 1982 $47 (7/31/88)
92 ALFRED GRATIEN Brut Champagne 1979 $28 (9/16/85)
93 ALFRED GRATIEN Brut Champagne NV $23 (11/01/85)
93 CHARLES HEIDSIECK Brut Champagne 1985 $50 (12/31/90)
90 CHARLES HEIDSIECK Brut Champagne 1983 $41 (3/31/91)
93 CHARLES HEIDSIECK Brut Champagne 1982 $33 (12/31/88) SS
87 CHARLES HEIDSIECK Brut Champagne Millésime 1983 $38 (12/31/89)
85 CHARLES HEIDSIECK Brut Champagne Réserve NV $25 (12/31/88)
89 HEIDSIECK MONOPOLE Brut Champagne Diamant Bleu 1982 Rel: $40 Cur: $62 (11/30/87)
93 HEIDSIECK MONOPOLE Brut Champagne Diamant Bleu 1979 Rel: $39 Cur: $39 (5/16/86)
90 HEIDSIECK MONOPOLE Brut Champagne Diamant Rosé 1982 Rel: $55 Cur: $55 (11/30/87)
90 HEIDSIECK MONOPOLE Brut Champagne Dry Monopole 1985 (NA) (12/31/90)
88 HEIDSIECK MONOPOLE Brut Champagne Dry Monopole 1982 $37.50 (12/31/88)
86 HEIDSIECK MONOPOLE Brut Champagne Dry Monopole NV $35 (12/31/88)
86 HENRIOT Brut Champagne NV $21 (7/01/86)
70 HENRIOT Brut Champagne Cuvée du Soleil NV $27 (12/31/87)
88 JACQUART Brut Champagne 1983 $43 (4/15/90)
90 JACQUART Brut Champagne 1982 $39 (12/31/88)
83 JACQUART Brut Champagne NV $24 (12/31/88)
90 JACQUART Brut Champagne La Cuvée Renommée 1982 $64 (12/31/88)
84 JACQUESSON Brut Champagne Perfection 1985 (NA) (12/31/90)
88 JACQUESSON Brut Champagne Perfection NV $24 (12/31/88)
93 JACQUESSON Brut Champagne Signature 1979 $34 (7/31/87)

FRANCE
CHAMPAGNE/BRUT

75	JEAN-MARIE Brut Champagne 1985 (NA) (12/31/90)
92	KRUG Brut Champagne 1982 Rel: $135 Cur: $135 (12/31/89)
91	KRUG Brut Champagne 1981 Rel: $85 Cur: $102 (12/31/88)
93	KRUG Brut Champagne 1976 Rel: $70 Cur: $123 (5/16/86)
91	KRUG Brut Champagne Grande Cuvée NV $88 (12/31/89)
94	KRUG Brut Champagne Grande Cuvée NV $88 (12/31/87)
93	LANSON Brut Champagne 1985 $37 (12/31/90)
85	LANSON Brut Champagne 1983 $30 (12/31/89)
92	LANSON Brut Champagne 1982 $27 (10/15/88)
89	LANSON Champagne 225th Anniversary Cuvée 1981 $43 (10/15/88)
95	LANSON 225th Anniversary Spécial Cuvée 1980 $43 (11/30/86)
79	LANSON Brut Champagne Black Label NV $21 (12/31/88)
88	LANSON Brut Champagne Black Label Cuvée NV $29 (12/31/88)
92	LANSON Brut Champagne Black Label Cuvée NV $29 (1/31/87)
87	LAURENT-PERRIER Brut Champagne 1985 $40 (12/31/90)
93	LAURENT-PERRIER Brut Champagne 1982 $36 (12/31/88)
90	LAURENT-PERRIER Brut Champagne NV $23 (12/31/87)
92	LAURENT-PERRIER Brut Champagne Cuvée Grand Siècle 1982 $70 (12/31/88)
90	LAURENT-PERRIER Brut Champagne Cuvée Grand Siècle 1979 $45 (2/15/88)
85	LAURENT-PERRIER Brut Champagne L.P. NV $15 (12/31/90)
73	LAURENT-PERRIER Brut Champagne Ultra Cuvée Sans Dosage NV $27 (1/31/88)
85	LECLERC-BRIANT Brut Champagne 1979 $31 (3/15/88)
80	LECLERC-BRIANT Brut Champagne Réserve NV $23 (3/15/88)
83	LECLERC-BRIANT Brut Champagne Spécial Club 1983 $35 (12/31/89)
88	MARQUIS DE SADE Brut Champagne Private Reserve 1985 $50 (12/31/90)
89	MARQUIS DE SADE Brut Champagne Private Reserve 1981 $56 (12/31/90)
87	MOET & CHANDON Brut Champagne Impérial 1986 $40 (12/31/90)
87	MOET & CHANDON Brut Champagne Impérial 1985 $57 (12/31/90)
86	MOET & CHANDON Brut Champagne Impérial 1985 $57 (12/31/89)
69	MOET & CHANDON Brut Champagne Impérial 1983 $40 (12/31/89)
83	MOET & CHANDON Brut Champagne Impérial 1983 $40 (12/31/88)
84	MOET & CHANDON Brut Champagne Impérial 1982 $33 (4/15/88)
91	MOET & CHANDON Brut Champagne Impérial 1980 $30 (3/16/85)
84	MOET & CHANDON Brut Champagne Impérial NV $25.50 (5/16/86)
86	G.H. MUMM Brut Champagne Cordon Rouge 1985 $34 (12/31/90)
85	G.H. MUMM Brut Champagne Cordon Rouge 1982 $37 (12/31/88)
93	G.H. MUMM Brut Champagne Cordon Rouge 1979 $24 (2/16/86)
81	G.H. MUMM Brut Champagne Cordon Rouge NV $25 (12/31/87)
86	G.H. MUMM Brut Champagne René Lalou 1985 $58 (12/31/90)
90	G.H. MUMM Brut Champagne René Lalou 1982 Rel: $55 Cur: $61 (9/30/88)
95	G.H. MUMM Brut Champagne René Lalou 1979 Rel: $56 Cur: $68 (5/16/86)
90	OUDINOT Brut Champagne 1985 $28 (12/31/90)
90	BRUNO PAILLARD Brut Champagne 1985 $40 (12/31/90)
93	DOM PERIGNON Brut Champagne 1982 Rel: $75 Cur: $84 (10/15/88)
94	DOM PERIGNON Brut Champagne 1980 Rel: $60 Cur: $94 (9/15/86) SS
88	DOM PERIGNON Brut Champagne 1978 Rel: $61 Cur: $120 (5/16/86)
90	PERRIER-JOUET Brut Champagne 1955 (NA)/1.5L (10/15/87) (JS)
85	PERRIER-JOUET Brut Champagne 1947 (NA)/1.5L (10/15/87) (JS)
97	PERRIER-JOUET Brut Champagne 1928 (NA) (10/15/87) (JS)
55	PERRIER-JOUET Brut Champagne 1914 (NA) (10/15/87) (JS)
95	PERRIER-JOUET Brut Champagne 1911 (NA) (10/15/87) (JS)
97	PERRIER-JOUET Brut Champagne 1900 (NA) (10/15/87) (JS)
80	PERRIER-JOUET Brut Champagne 1893 (NA) (10/15/87) (JS)
95	PERRIER-JOUET Brut Champagne 1825 (NA) (10/15/87) (JS)
86	PERRIER-JOUET Brut Champagne Fleur de Champagne 1985 $75 (12/31/90)
88	PERRIER-JOUET Brut Champagne Fleur de Champagne 1983 $65 (12/31/89)
88	PERRIER-JOUET Brut Champagne Fleur de Champagne 1982 $65 (12/31/88)
93	PERRIER-JOUET Brut Champagne Fleur de Champagne 1979 $50 (2/01/86)
84	PERRIER-JOUET Brut Champagne Grand Brut NV $22 (12/31/89)
91	PERRIER-JOUET Brut Champagne Grand Brut NV $25 (12/31/87)
82	JOSEPH PERRIER Brut Champagne 1985 $37 (12/31/90)
87	JOSEPH PERRIER Brut Champagne 1979 $22 (10/01/85)
92	JOSEPH PERRIER Brut Champagne NV $19 (11/16/85)
93	JOSEPH PERRIER Brut Champagne Cuvée Josephine 1982 $100 (12/31/90)
82	JOSEPH PERRIER Brut Champagne Cuvée Josephine 1982 $100 (12/31/89)
82	JOSEPH PERRIER Brut Champagne Cuvée Royale 1985 $37 (12/31/90)
89	JOSEPH PERRIER Brut Champagne Cuvée Royale 1982 $35 (12/31/89)
88	JOSEPH PERRIER Brut Champagne Cuvée Royale NV $30 (12/31/90)
83	JOSEPH PERRIER Brut Champagne Cuvée Royale NV $30 (4/15/90)
90	JOSEPH PERRIER Brut Champagne Cuvée Royale NV $30 (1/31/89)
85	PHILIPPONNAT Brut Champagne Clos des Goisses 1985 (NA) (12/31/90)
84	PHILIPPONNAT Brut Champagne Clos des Goisses 1982 $89 (12/31/88)
84	PHILIPPONNAT Brut Champagne Grand Blanc 1982 $38 (12/31/88)
82	PHILIPPONNAT Brut Champagne Royale Réserve NV $24 (12/31/88)
88	PIPER-HEIDSIECK Brut Champagne 1985 (NA) (12/31/90)
86	PIPER-HEIDSIECK Brut Champagne 1982 $32 (12/31/88)
89	PIPER-HEIDSIECK Brut Champagne Cuvée NV $22 (12/31/89)
78	PIPER-HEIDSIECK Brut Champagne Extra NV $26 (12/31/87)
80	PIPER-HEIDSIECK Champagne Rare 1985 (NA) (12/31/90)
89	PIPER-HEIDSIECK Champagne Rare 1979 $65 (3/15/87)
88	PIPER-HEIDSIECK Champagne Rare 1976 $66 (8/01/85)
89	PIPER-HEIDSIECK Brut Champagne Sauvage 1982 $30 (12/31/89)
87	POMMERY Brut Champagne 1985 $40 (12/31/90)
93	POMMERY Brut Champagne 1982 $24 (2/15/88)

79	POMMERY Brut Champagne NV $23 (12/31/87)
78	POMMERY Brut Champagne NV $23 (5/16/86)
85	LOUIS ROEDERER Brut Champagne 1985 $50 (12/31/90)
93	LOUIS ROEDERER Brut Champagne 1982 $45 (12/31/88)
82	LOUIS ROEDERER Brut Champagne NV $25 (5/16/86)
88	LOUIS ROEDERER Brut Champagne Cristal 1983 Rel: $120 Cur: $120 (12/31/89)
90	LOUIS ROEDERER Brut Champagne Cristal 1983 Rel: $120 Cur: $120 (12/31/88)
92	LOUIS ROEDERER Brut Champagne Cristal 1982 Rel: $106 Cur: $106 (9/30/87)
91	LOUIS ROEDERER Brut Champagne Cristal 1981 Rel: $85 Cur: $100 (5/16/86)
78	LOUIS ROEDERER Brut Champagne Premier NV $27 (12/31/87)
90	POL ROGER Brut Champagne 1979 $23 (9/01/85)
89	POL ROGER Brut Champagne NV $24 (12/31/87)
92	POL ROGER Brut Champagne Cuvée Sir Winston Churchill 1982 $63 (4/15/90)
92	POL ROGER Brut Champagne Extra Cuvée de Réserve 1982 $30 (12/31/90)
86	POL ROGER Brut Champagne Réserve 1985 $35 (12/31/90)
92	POL ROGER Brut Champagne Réserve NV $30 (12/31/88)
84	MARIE STUART Brut Champagne Cuvée de la Reine NV $26 (12/31/87)
91	TAILLEVENT Brut Champagne Grande Réserve NV $23 (12/31/89)
89	TAITTINGER Brut Champagne 1985 (NA) (12/31/90)
84	TAITTINGER Brut Champagne 1983 Rel: $35 Cur: $37 (12/31/89)
89	TAITTINGER Brut Champagne NV $26 (12/31/87)
92	TAITTINGER Brut Champagne Collection Arman 1981 Rel: $80 Cur: $85 (5/31/87) CS
90	TAITTINGER Brut Champagne Collection Masson 1982 Rel: $96 Cur: $96 (12/31/88)
89	TAITTINGER Brut Champagne Collection Vieira da Silva 1983 Rel: $95 Cur: $95 (12/31/89)
85	TAITTINGER Brut Champagne La Française NV $27 (12/31/89)
83	TAITTINGER Brut Champagne La Française NV $27 (7/15/88)
89	TAITTINGER Brut Champagne Millésime 1982 Rel: $38 Cur: $38 (12/31/88)
73	TAITTINGER Brut Champagne Réserve NV $24 (5/16/86)
78	JULIEN TARIN Brut Champagne NV $25 (2/15/87)
86	DE VENOGE Brut Champagne 1985 $38 (12/31/90)

ROSÉ

77	HENRI ABELE Brut Rosé Champagne NV $29 (7/31/87)
85	AYALA Brut Rosé Champagne NV $26 (4/15/88)
80	AYALA Brut Rosé Champagne Extra Quality NV $20 (5/31/87)
90	BEAUMET Brut Rosé Champagne 1983 $30 (12/31/89)
79	BEAUMET Brut Rosé Champagne 1979 $16.50 (12/16/85)
80	BILLECART-SALMON Brut Rosé Champagne NV $28 (12/16/85)
89	BOLLINGER Brut Rosé Champagne Grand Année 1983 $50 (12/31/89)
84	BOLLINGER Brut Rosé Champagne Grand Année 1983 $50 (12/31/88)
80	BOLLINGER Brut Rosé Champagne Grand Année 1982 $35 (7/15/88)
94	BOLLINGER Brut Rosé Champagne Grand Année 1979 $40 (12/16/85)
90	BRICOUT Brut Rosé Champagne NV $28 (12/31/88)
81	BRICOUT Brut Rosé Champagne NV $28 (12/31/87)
88	DE CASTELLANE Brut Rosé Champagne NV $31 (12/31/90)
89	DE CASTELLANE Brut Rosé Champagne NV $31 (4/15/88)
86	A. CHARBAUT Brut Rosé Champagne NV $32 (12/31/88)
88	A. CHARBAUT Brut Rosé Champagne Certificate 1982 $82 (12/31/89)
89	A. CHARBAUT Brut Rosé Champagne Certificate 1979 $80 (7/15/88)
86	VEUVE CLICQUOT Brut Rosé Champagne 1983 $47 (12/31/89)
89	VEUVE CLICQUOT Brut Rosé Champagne 1979 $35 (7/16/86)
82	VEUVE CLICQUOT Brut Rosé Champagne 1978 $60 (12/16/85)
91	DELAMOTTE Rosé Champagne Spécial NV $28 (12/31/87)
88	DEUTZ Brut Rosé Champagne 1985 $46 (12/31/90)
88	DEUTZ Brut Rosé Champagne 1985 $46 (12/31/89)
86	DEUTZ Brut Rosé Champagne 1982 $35 (12/31/87)
67	DEUTZ Brut Rosé Champagne 1981 $27 (12/16/85)
89	DIEBOLT-VALLOIS Brut Rosé Champagne Cramant NV $21 (10/31/87)
72	ANDRE DRAPPIER Brut Rosé Champagne Val des Demoiselles 1981 $23 (12/16/85)
89	MICHEL GONET Brut Rosé Champagne NV $21 (12/16/85)
88	GOSSET Brut Rosé Champagne 1982 $75 (12/31/88)
85	GOSSET Brut Rosé Champagne NV $37 (12/31/90)
95	GOSSET Brut Rosé Champagne NV $37 (12/16/85)
85	GEORGE GOULET Brut Rosé Champagne 1982 $31 (7/31/88)
81	ALFRED GRATIEN Rosé Champagne NV $24 (10/01/85)
89	CHARLES HEIDSIECK Brut Rosé Champagne 1983 $49 (3/31/91)
91	CHARLES HEIDSIECK Brut Rosé Champagne 1982 $40 (12/31/88)
61	CHARLES HEIDSIECK Brut Rosé Champagne 1976 $25 (12/16/85)
75	HEIDSIECK MONOPOLE Brut Rosé Champagne 1983 $40 (12/31/89)
84	HEIDSIECK MONOPOLE Brut Rosé Champagne 1982 $43 (12/31/88)
72	HEIDSIECK MONOPOLE Brut Rosé Champagne 1979 $27 (12/16/85)
93	HENRIOT Brut Rosé Champagne 1981 $28 (7/01/86)
90	JACQUART Brut Rosé Champagne NV $38 (12/31/88)
88	JACQUART Brut Rosé Champagne La Cuvée Renommée 1982 $74 (12/31/88)
84	JACQUESSON Brut Rosé Champagne Perfection NV $27 (12/31/88)
93	KRUG Brut Rosé Champagne NV $115 (12/31/89)
96	KRUG Brut Rosé Champagne NV $115 (12/16/85)
88	LANSON Brut Rosé Champagne 1982 $35 (12/31/88)
73	LANSON Brut Rosé Champagne NV $24 (12/31/86)
84	GUY LARMANDIER Brut Rosé Champagne NV $20 (12/31/89)
92	LAURENT-PERRIER Brut Rosé Champagne Cuvée NV $28 (3/15/88)
91	LAURENT-PERRIER Brut Rosé Champagne Grand Siècle Cuvée Alexandra 1982 $125 (12/31/89)
84	LECLERC-BRIANT Brut Rosé Champagne NV $28 (3/15/88)
88	MOET & CHANDON Brut Rosé Champagne Impérial 1983 $40 (12/31/89)
90	MOET & CHANDON Brut Rosé Champagne Impérial 1982 $36 (4/15/88)
70	MOET & CHANDON Brut Rosé Champagne Impérial 1978 $55 (12/16/85)
87	G.H. MUMM Brut Rosé Champagne Cordon Rosé 1985 $35 (12/31/89)
81	G.H. MUMM Brut Rosé Champagne Cordon Rosé 1983 $30 (12/31/89)
86	G.H. MUMM Brut Rosé Champagne Cordon Rosé 1983 $30 (7/31/89)
83	G.H. MUMM Brut Rosé Champagne Cordon Rosé 1982 $30 (12/31/88)
88	OUDINOT Brut Rosé Champagne 1983 $25 (12/31/89)
88	DOM PERIGNON Brut Rosé Champagne 1978 Rel: $89 Cur: $199 (10/15/86)
93	DOM PERIGNON Brut Rosé Champagne 1975 Rel: $85 Cur: $85 (12/16/85)
88	PERRIER-JOUET Brut Rosé Champagne Fleur de Champagne 1985 Rel: $70 Cur: $79 (12/31/90)
89	PERRIER-JOUET Brut Rosé Champagne Fleur de Champagne 1982 Rel: $57 Cur: $64 (11/15/87)
90	PERRIER-JOUET Brut Rosé Champagne Fleur de Champagne 1978 Rel: $55 Cur: $55 (12/16/85)

86 JOSEPH PERRIER Brut Rosé Champagne Cuvée Royale NV $40 (12/31/90)
85 JOSEPH PERRIER Brut Rosé Champagne Cuvée Royale NV $40 (12/31/89)
72 PHILIPPONNAT Brut Rosé Champagne NV $26 (12/16/85)
89 PHILIPPONNAT Brut Rosé Champagne Royale Réserve NV $38 (12/31/88)
84 PIPER-HEIDSIECK Brut Rosé Champagne 1982 $38 (12/31/88)
86 POMMERY Brut Rosé Champagne NV $27 (12/16/85)
79 LOUIS ROEDERER Brut Rosé Champagne NV $37 (12/16/85)
69 LOUIS ROEDERER Brut Rosé Champagne Cristal 1979 $87 (12/16/85)
80 POL ROGER Rosé Champagne 1982 $34 (12/31/88)
88 POL ROGER Rosé Champagne 1979 $28 (12/16/85)
67 POL ROGER Rosé Champagne 1975 $33 (12/16/85)
92 DOM RUINART Brut Rosé Champagne 1979 Rel: $55 Cur: $55 (9/30/88)
91 DOM RUINART Brut Rosé Champagne 1978 Rel: $40 Cur: $40 (9/30/86)
61 DOM RUINART Brut Rosé Champagne 1976 Rel: $35 Cur: $60 (12/16/85)
   DOM RUINART Brut Rosé Champagne 1975 Rel: $35 Cur: $35 (2/01/84) SS
80 MARIE STUART Brut Rosé Champagne NV $23 (12/31/87)
82 TAILLEVENT Brut Rosé Champagne Phantom of the Opera NV $32 (12/31/89)
92 TAITTINGER Brut Rosé Champagne Comtes de Champagne 1982 Rel: $100 Cur: $100 (12/31/89)
90 TAITTINGER Brut Rosé Champagne Comtes de Champagne 1976 Rel: $70 Cur: $85 (12/16/85)
88 DE VENOGE Rosé Champagne Crémant NV $26 (12/31/88)
53 GEORGES VESSELLE Brut Rosé Champagne de Noirs NV $30 (12/16/85)

OTHER CHAMPAGNE

90 BEAUMET Brut Blanc de Noirs Champagne 1985 $30 (12/31/90)
89 BEAUMET Brut Blanc de Noirs Champagne 1983 $30 (12/31/89)
87 A. CHARBAUT Extra Dry Champagne NV $22 (12/31/88)
86 HEIDSIECK MONOPOLE Extra Dry Champagne NV $35 (12/31/88)
89 JACQUART Extra Dry Champagne NV $23 (12/31/88)
86 LANSON Extra Dry Champagne Ivory Label NV $19 (12/31/88)
70 LANSON Extra Dry Champagne White Label NV $19 (12/31/88)
90 G.H. MUMM Extra Dry Champagne NV $26 (1/31/89)
85 G.H. MUMM Extra Dry Champagne Cordon Vert NV $23 (4/15/90)
74 MARIE STUART Extra Dry Champagne NV $19 (12/31/87)

LOIRE RED

78 PIERRE CHAINIER SELECTION Bourgueil 1985 $7.75 (9/30/88)
83 PIERRE CHAINIER SELECTION Chinon 1985 $7.75 (9/30/88)
86 CLOS DE L'ABBAYE Bourgueil 1986 $16 (8/31/89)
72 COULY-DUTHEIL Chinon Les Gravieres d'Amador Abbe de Turpennay 1986 $10 (4/30/88)
86 COULY-DUTHEIL Chinon Les Gravieres d'Amador Abbe de Turpennay 1985 $9.25 (2/28/87)
86 COULY-DUTHEIL Chinon Domaine de Versailles 1981 $12.25 (3/15/87)
87 COULY-DUTHEIL Saumur Champigny La Vigneronne 1985 $10 (2/15/87)
82 GILBERT DELAGOUTTIERE St.-Nicolas de Bourgueil 1987 $9 (12/31/88)
86 DOMAINE DESSERRE Chinon 1987 $9 (12/31/88)
83 DOMAINE DU GRAND CLOS Bourgueil 1985 $9 (9/30/87)
79 HAUT POITOU Haut Poitou Cabernet 1986 $6 (10/31/88)
78 DOMAINE MORIN HER Chinon 1986 $7.50 (12/31/88)
89 CHARLES JOGUET Chinon Cuvée du Clos de la Dioterie 1986 $21 (12/31/88)
82 CHARLES JOGUET Chinon Cuvée des Varennes du Grand Clos 1986 $15 (4/30/88)
85 DOMAINE HENRY PELLE Menetou-Salon Morogues 1987 $11 (7/15/89)
71 JOEL & CLARRISE TALUAU St.-Nicolas de Bourgueil 1985 $12 (4/15/89)

LOIRE WHITE/*MUSCADET DE SÈVRE & MAINE*

74 DOMAINE DE L'ALOUETTE Muscadet de Sèvre & Maine Sur Lie 1989 $7 (11/30/90)
77 ANDRE-MICHEL BREGEON Muscadet de Sèvre & Maine Sur Lie 1988 $6.75 (11/15/90)
76 CHATEAU DU CLERAY Muscadet de Sèvre & Maine Sur Lie 1985 $7 (5/15/87)
84 CLOS DE BEAUREGARD Muscadet de Sèvre & Maine Sur Lie 1988 $6.75 (4/15/90) BB
83 CLOS DES BOURGUIGNONS Muscadet de Sèvre & Maine Sur Lie 1985 $5 (6/15/87) BB
78 LES FRERES COUILLAUD Muscadet de Sèvre & Maine Château de la Ragotière 1986 $9.75 (4/15/88)
77 LES FRERES COUILLAUD Muscadet de Sèvre & Maine Château de la Ragotière Sur Lie 1987 $10 (7/15/89)
88 CHATEAU DE LA MERCREDIERE Muscadet de Sèvre & Maine Sur Lie 1985 $6 (9/30/86) BB
85 LOUIS METAIREAU Muscadet de Sèvre & Maine Sur Lie Carte Noire 1988 $8 (11/30/90) BB
80 LOUIS METAIREAU Muscadet de Sèvre & Maine Sur Lie Carte Noire 1986 $8.75 (2/28/89)
83 LOUIS METAIREAU Muscadet de Sèvre & Maine Sur Lie Carte Noire 1985 $8.25 (10/31/87)
85 LOUIS METAIREAU Muscadet de Sèvre & Maine Sur Lie Carte Noire 1983 $6.50 (4/16/85) BB
81 LOUIS METAIREAU Muscadet de Sèvre & Maine Sur Lie Cuvée One 1987 $11 (7/15/89)
89 LOUIS METAIREAU Muscadet de Sèvre & Maine Sur Lie Cuvée One 1983 $9.75 (5/01/84)
80 LOUIS METAIREAU Muscadet de Sèvre & Maine Sur Lie Grand Mouton 1984 $8.50 (11/15/87)
68 CHATEAU DE LA MOUCHETIERE Muscadet de Sèvre & Maine 1985 $5 (10/15/86)
82 DOMAINE DE LA POMMERAYE Muscadet de Sèvre & Maine Sur Lie 1986 $6 (12/31/88) BB
88 DOMAINE DE LA QUILLA Muscadet de Sèvre & Maine Sur Lie 1989 $7 (11/30/90) BB
84 CHATEAU DE LA RAGOTIERE Muscadet de Sèvre & Maine Sur Lie 1990 $14.50 (6/15/91)
78 CHATEAU DE LA RAGOTIERE Muscadet de Sèvre & Maine Sur Lie 1988 $10 (4/15/90)

POUILLY-FUMÉ

81 PHILIPPE CHASE Pouilly-Fumé 1983 $11.50 (10/15/86)
87 JEAN-CLAUDE CHATELAIN Pouilly-Fumé Domaine des Chailloux 1989 $18 (3/31/91)
87 JEAN-CLAUDE CHATELAIN Pouilly-Fumé Domaine des Chailloux 1988 $17.50 (9/15/90)
88 PAUL FIGEAT Pouilly-Fumé 1988 $14 (4/15/90)
85 DOMAINE DENIS GAUDRY Pouilly-Fumé Côteaux du Petit Boisgibault 1989 $15 (3/31/91)
77 DOMAINE DENIS GAUDRY Pouilly-Fumé Côteaux du Petit Boisgibault 1986 $14 (5/31/88)
84 JEAN-CLAUDE GUYOT Pouilly-Fumé Les Loges 1988 $11 (3/31/91)
88 PASCAL JOLIVET Pouilly-Fumé Cuvée Pascal Jolivet 1987 $29 (9/15/90)
86 DE LADOUCETTE Pouilly-Fumé 1989 $22 (4/30/91)
91 DE LADOUCETTE Pouilly-Fumé 1984 $10.50 (3/31/87)
88 DE LADOUCETTE Pouilly-Fumé Baron de L 1988 $49 (5/31/91)
90 DE LADOUCETTE Pouilly-Fumé Baron de L 1985 $40 (7/15/89)
82 DE LADOUCETTE Pouilly-Fumé La Ladoucette 1988 $18 (9/15/90)
84 DOMAINE J.-M. MASSON-BLONDELET Pouilly-Fumé Les Angelots 1989 $20 (3/31/91)

90 DOMAINE J.-M. MASSON-BLONDELET Pouilly-Fumé Les Bascoins 1989 $20 (3/31/91)
78 F. TINEL-BLONDELET Pouilly-Fumé 1987 $12.50 (2/28/89)
86 F. TINEL-BLONDELET Pouilly-Fumé L'Arret Buffatte 1987 $14.50 (2/28/89)

SANCERRE

76 LA BOURGEOISE Sancerre Chavignol 1985 $13 (10/31/87)
86 CHERRIER PERE Sancerre Domaine des Chasseignes 1989 $16 (3/31/91)
83 CHERRIER PERE Sancerre Domaine des Chasseignes 1986 $12.50 (5/31/88)
80 CHEVALIER DE BEAUBASSIN Sancerre 1986 $12.50 (5/31/88)
84 COMPTE LAFOND Sancerre Omina Pro Petri Sede 1988 $16 (11/15/90)
85 PAUL COTAT Sancerre Chavignol Les Culs de Beaujeu 1989 $22 (2/28/91)
77 PAUL COTAT Sancerre Chavignol Les Culs de Beaujeu 1988 $15 (4/15/90)
89 PAUL COTAT Sancerre Chavignol Les Culs de Beaujeu 1985 $12.25 (2/15/87)
86 PAUL COTAT Sancerre Chavignol La Grande Côte 1989 $25 (2/28/91)
85 PAUL COTAT Sancerre Chavignol La Grande Côte 1988 $18 (4/15/90)
91 PAUL COTAT Sancerre Chavignol La Grande Côte 1985 $13 (3/15/87)
82 PAUL COTAT Sancerre Chavignol Réserve des Monts Damnés 1989 $19 (2/28/91)
72 PAUL COTAT Sancerre Chavignol Réserve des Monts Damnés 1985 $13 (2/15/87)
83 LUCIEN CROCHET Sancerre Clos Chêne Marchand 1984 $11.25 (3/01/86)
75 ETIENNE HENRI Sancerre 1988 $35 (2/28/91)
75 GITTON PERE Sancerre De la Vigne du Larrey 1983 $9.50 (3/01/86)
79 GITTON PERE Sancerre Les Romains 1983 $8 (3/01/86)
84 PASCAL JOLIVET Sancerre 1988 $15.50 (9/15/90)
82 PASCAL JOLIVET Sancerre Domaine du Colombier 1988 $18 (9/15/90)
88 COMTE LAFOND Sancerre 1989 $21 (4/30/91)
76 DOMAINE LAPORTE Sancerre Domaine du Rochoy 1988 $16 (4/15/90)
85 DOMAINE LAPORTE Sancerre Domaine du Rochoy 1987 $13.50 (2/28/89)
76 PROSPER MAUFOUX Sancerre 1988 $15 (4/15/90)
68 DOMAINE ALPHONSE MELLOT Sancerre 1987 $16 (3/31/91)
71 MICHEL NATHAN Sancerre Domaine des Grandes Pierres 1985 $12.50 (9/30/87)
76 DOMAINE DU NOZAY Sancerre 1985 $10.25 (6/15/87)
82 JEAN PAUL PICARD Sancerre 1989 $14.50 (4/30/91)
88 HIPPOLYTE REVERDY Sancerre Les Perriers 1987 $13 (2/28/89)
85 HIPPOLYTE REVERDY Sancerre Les Perriers 1986 $10 (12/15/87)
85 REVERDY-DUCROUX Sancerre Clos les Perriers 1986 $10 (2/15/88)
85 DOMAINE JEAN-MAX ROGER Sancerre Le Chêne Marchand 1988 $17.50 (9/15/90)
71 JEAN VATAN Sancerre Les Perriers 1986 $10 (2/15/88)

SAVENNIÈRES

78 DOMAINE DES BAUMARD Savennières 1988 $8.75 (4/15/90)
85 DOMAINE DES BAUMARD Savennières Clos du Papillon 1988 $9.50 (4/15/90)
86 A. JOLY Savennières Clos de la Coulée de Serrant 1987 $36 (2/15/89) (TM)
87 A. JOLY Savennières Clos de la Coulée de Serrant 1986 $38 (7/15/89)
87 A. JOLY Savennières Clos de la Coulée de Serrant 1982 (NA) (2/15/89) (TM)
93 A. JOLY Savennières Clos de la Coulée de Serrant 1976 (NA) (2/15/89) (TM)
91 N. JOLY Savennières Clos de la Coulée de Serrant 1989 $33 (11/30/90)
83 PIERRE & YVES SOULEZ Savennières Château de Chamboureau 1986 $12 (2/28/89)
84 PIERRE & YVES SOULEZ Savennières Clos du Papillon 1986 $15 (2/28/89)
80 PIERRE & YVES SOULEZ Savennières Clos du Papillon 1985 $12 (9/30/87)
77 PIERRE & YVES SOULEZ Savennières Roche aux Moines Château de Chamboureau 1986 $18.50 (2/28/89)

OTHER LOIRE WHITE

81 DOMAINE DES BAUMARD Côteaux du Layon Clos de Ste.-Catherine 1988 $10.50 (4/15/90)
82 DOMAINE DES BAUMARD Quarts de Chaume 1988 $20 (4/15/90)
87 MARC BREDIF Vouvray 1988 $11 (4/30/91)
84 DOMAINE CHAVET Menetou-Salon 1987 $9.50 (7/15/89)
88 DOMAINE DU CLOS NAUDIN Vouvray Demi-Sec 1989 $19.50 (3/31/91)
83 DOMAINE DU CLOS NAUDIN Vouvray Sec 1989 $17.50 (3/31/91)
77 COULY-DUTHEIL Touraine Sauvignon 1985 $8 (3/15/87)
79 HAUT POITOU Haut Poitou Chardonnay 1987 $6 (12/31/88)
72 LANGLOIS-CHATEAU Saumur 1987 $6 (12/31/88)
75 LANGLOIS-CHATEAU Vin de Pays du Jardin de la France Chardonnay 1987 $7 (10/15/88)
77 ROBERT MICHELE Vouvray Les Trois Fils 1989 $9 (4/30/91)
90 DOMAINE LE PEU DE LA MORIETTE Vouvray 1989 $12 (4/30/91)
69 DOMAINE LE PEU DE LA MORIETTE Vouvray 1987 $10 (2/28/89)
84 PIERRE & YVES SOULEZ Quarts de Chaume L'Amandier 1988 $28 (11/30/90)

RHÔNE RED/*CHÂTEAUNEUF-DU-PAPE*

84 PIERRE ANDRE Châteauneuf-du-Pape 1988 $23 (3/31/91)
92 PERE ANSELME Châteauneuf-du-Pape 1983 $12.50 (9/30/87)
88 PERE ANSELME Châteauneuf-du-Pape La Fiole 1984 $12 (10/31/87)
74 PERE ANSELME Châteauneuf-du-Pape La Fiole Grand Cuvée 1984 $13 (10/31/87)
86 PERE ANSELME Châteauneuf-du-Pape La Fiole du Pape NV $14 (9/30/89)
82 PERE ANSELME Châteauneuf-du-Pape La Fiole du Pape Uno Bono Fiolo NV $13 (1/31/88)
67 ARNAUD-DAUMEN Châteauneuf-du-Pape Domaine de la Vieille Julienne 1978 $20 (11/15/87)
73 ARNAUD-DAUMEN Châteauneuf-du-Pape Domaine de la Vieille Julienne 1972 $20 (11/15/87)
86 PAUL AVRIL Châteauneuf-du-Pape Clos des Papes 1988 $19 (9/30/90)
87 DOMAINE LUCIEN BARROT Châteauneuf-du-Pape 1981 $16 (9/30/87)
74 BARTON & GUESTIER Châteauneuf-du-Pape 1983 $11 (9/30/87)
88 CHATEAU DE BEAUCASTEL Châteauneuf-du-Pape 1988 $28 (3/31/91)
83 CHATEAU DE BEAUCASTEL Châteauneuf-du-Pape 1987 $17 (11/30/89) (HS)
86 CHATEAU DE BEAUCASTEL Châteauneuf-du-Pape 1987 $17 (9/30/90)
88 CHATEAU DE BEAUCASTEL Châteauneuf-du-Pape 1986 $25 (11/30/89) (HS)
89 CHATEAU DE BEAUCASTEL Châteauneuf-du-Pape 1986 $25 (10/15/88)
90 CHATEAU DE BEAUCASTEL Châteauneuf-du-Pape 1985 $16 (11/30/89) (HS)
89 CHATEAU DE BEAUCASTEL Châteauneuf-du-Pape 1985 $16 (9/30/87)
89 CHATEAU DE BEAUCASTEL Châteauneuf-du-Pape 1984 $12.50 (11/30/89) (HS)
82 CHATEAU DE BEAUCASTEL Châteauneuf-du-Pape 1984 $12.50 (9/30/87)
85 CHATEAU DE BEAUCASTEL Châteauneuf-du-Pape 1983 Rel: $17.50 Cur: $28 (11/30/89) (HS)
87 CHATEAU DE BEAUCASTEL Châteauneuf-du-Pape 1983 Rel: $17.50 Cur: $28 (9/30/87)
92 CHATEAU DE BEAUCASTEL Châteauneuf-du-Pape 1982 Cur: $30 (11/30/89) (HS)
88 CHATEAU DE BEAUCASTEL Châteauneuf-du-Pape 1981 Cur: $39 (11/30/89) (HS)
83 CHATEAU DE BEAUCASTEL Châteauneuf-du-Pape 1980 Cur: $32 (11/30/89) (HS)

FRANCE
RHÔNE RED/*CHÂTEAUNEUF-DU-PAPE*

79 DOMAINE DE BEAURENARD Châteauneuf-du-Pape 1985 $16 (10/31/87)
85 DOMAINE DE BEAURENARD Châteauneuf-du-Pape 1982 $9 (4/01/85) BB
84 BICHOT Châteauneuf-du-Pape 1988 $13 (9/30/90)
82 BICHOT Châteauneuf-du-Pape 1987 $10 (3/15/90)
86 BICHOT Châteauneuf-du-Pape 1986 $9 (11/30/88)
86 BICHOT Châteauneuf-du-Pape 1985 $12 (11/15/87)
79 HENRI BOIRON Châteauneuf-du-Pape 1983 $11 (8/31/86)
76 HENRI BOIRON Châteauneuf-du-Pape Les Relagnes 1984 $12.75 (11/15/87)
62 DOMAINE DU BOIS DAUPHIN Châteauneuf-du-Pape 1983 $12 (11/15/87)
80 JEAN CLAUDE BOISSET Châteauneuf-du-Pape 1986 $12 (11/30/88)
82 HENRI BONNEAU Châteauneuf-du-Pape Réserve des Celestins 1986 $19.50 (5/31/89)
82 BOSQUET DES PAPES Châteauneuf-du-Pape 1985 $18 (1/31/89)
91 BOSQUET DES PAPES Châteauneuf-du-Pape 1984 $17 (11/15/87)
82 BOUCHARD PERE & FILS Châteauneuf-du-Pape 1985 $11.50 (9/30/87)
81 BOURGOGNE ST.-VINCENT Châteauneuf-du-Pape 1983 $8.50 (7/16/85)
89 LUCIEN & ANDRE BRUNEL Châteauneuf-du-Pape Les Cailloux Sélection Reflets 1986 $14 (5/31/89)
82 CHATEAU CABRIERES Châteauneuf-du-Pape 1988 $17 (11/30/90)
86 DOMAINE DU CAILLOU Châteauneuf-du-Pape 1988 $22 (3/31/91)
87 LES CAVES ST.-PIERRE Châteauneuf-du-Pape Clefs des Prelats 1988 $13 (1/31/91)
82 DOMAINE CHANTE PERDRIX Châteauneuf-du-Pape 1988 $17 (5/31/91)
89 M. CHAPOUTIER Châteauneuf-du-Pape La Bernardine 1985 $25 (3/15/90)
89 M. CHAPOUTIER Châteauneuf-du-Pape La Bernardine 1984 $15 (9/30/87)
81 M. CHAPOUTIER Châteauneuf-du-Pape La Bernardine 1983 $15 (6/01/86)
87 CLOS DE L'ORATOIRE DES PAPES Châteauneuf-du-Pape 1985 $10 (7/31/88)
85 JACQUES CORTENAY Châteauneuf-du-Pape 1985 $8 (9/30/87) BB
91 DELAS Châteauneuf-du-Pape 1985 $17 (10/31/87)
79 DELAS Châteauneuf-du-Pape Cuvée de Haute Pierre 1988 $17 (11/30/90)
78 DOMAINE JEAN DEYDIER & FILS Châteauneuf-du-Pape Les Clefs d'Or 1983 $16 (10/31/87)
88 REMY DIFFONTY Châteauneuf-du-Pape Réserve du Vatican 1983 $12 (9/30/87)
78 DOMAINE DURIEU Châteauneuf-du-Pape 1984 $13 (11/15/87)
85 CHATEAU DES FINES ROCHES Châteauneuf-du-Pape 1986 $14 (9/30/90)
80 CHATEAU DES FINES ROCHES Châteauneuf-du-Pape 1985 $12 (10/31/87)
89 CHATEAU DES FINES ROCHES Châteauneuf-du-Pape 1984 $12 (9/30/87)
88 DOMAINE FONT DE MICHELLE Châteauneuf-du-Pape 1988 $18 (9/30/90)
86 DOMAINE FONT DE MICHELLE Châteauneuf-du-Pape 1985 $13.50 (10/31/87)
87 CHATEAU FORTIA Châteauneuf-du-Pape 1983 Rel: $13.50 Cur: $24 (12/31/87)
82 DOMAINE LOU FREJAU Châteauneuf-du-Pape 1988 $17 (3/31/91)
87 DOMAINE LOU FREJAU Châteauneuf-du-Pape 1986 $15.50 (1/31/89)
87 CHATEAU DE LA GARDINE Châteauneuf-du-Pape 1985 $15 (12/31/87)
78 CHATEAU DE LA GARDINE Châteauneuf-du-Pape 1984 $15 (12/31/87)
87 CHATEAU DE LA GARDINE Châteauneuf-du-Pape 1983 $12 (9/30/87)
86 ROBERT GIRARD Châteauneuf-du-Pape Le Boucou Cuvée du Belvedere 1986 $16 (1/31/89)
93 ROBERT GIRARD Châteauneuf-du-Pape Le Boucou Cuvée du Belvedere 1985 $18 (2/15/88)
62 ROBERT GIRARD Châteauneuf-du-Pape Le Boucou Cuvée du Belvedere 1983 $16 (11/15/87)
77 DOMAINE ALAIN GRANGEON Châteauneuf-du-Pape 1986 $16 (1/31/89)
90 E. GUIGAL Châteauneuf-du-Pape 1988 $20 (11/30/90)
87 E. GUIGAL Châteauneuf-du-Pape 1986 $19 (3/15/90)
87 E. GUIGAL Châteauneuf-du-Pape 1985 $18 (10/15/88)
87 E. GUIGAL Châteauneuf-du-Pape 1983 $18 (11/30/87)
85 DOMAINE DU HAUT DES TERRES BLANCHES Châteauneuf-du-Pape 1988 $16 (7/15/91)
82 PAUL JABOULET AINE Châteauneuf-du-Pape 1983 $10 (9/30/87)
91 PAUL JABOULET AINE Châteauneuf-du-Pape Les Cédres 1989 $23 (7/15/91)
71 DOMAINE FRANCOIS LAGET Châteauneuf-du-Pape 1985 $14 (9/30/87)
76 DOMAINE FRANCOIS LAGET Châteauneuf-du-Pape 1984 $14 (12/31/87)
89 DOMAINE FRANCOIS LAGET Châteauneuf-du-Pape 1983 $12 (9/30/87)
58 LANCON PERE & FILS Châteauneuf-du-Pape Domaine de la Solitude 1983 $14 (12/31/87)
92 DOMAINE DE MARCOUX Châteauneuf-du-Pape Vieilles Vignes 1989 $24 (7/15/91)
86 CHATEAU MAUCOIL Châteauneuf-du-Pape Réserve Suzeraine 1985 $12.50 (11/15/87)
91 LUCIEN MICHEL Châteauneuf-du-Pape Le Vieux Donjon 1986 $15.50 (11/30/88)
79 LUCIEN MICHEL Châteauneuf-du-Pape Le Vieux Donjon 1985 $16 (2/15/88)
79 LUCIEN MICHEL Châteauneuf-du-Pape Le Vieux Donjon 1984 $14 (10/31/87)
83 DOMAINE DE MONPERTUIS Châteauneuf-du-Pape 1987 $14 (6/30/90)
73 DOMAINE DE MONPERTUIS Châteauneuf-du-Pape 1986 $18 (9/30/89)
88 CHATEAU MONT-REDON Châteauneuf-du-Pape 1985 $11.50 (10/15/88)
92 CHATEAU MONT-REDON Châteauneuf-du-Pape 1984 $10.50 (9/30/87)
75 LOUIS MOUSSET Châteauneuf-du-Pape 1982 $6 (12/16/84)
85 DU PELOUX Châteauneuf-du-Pape 1986 $12 (4/15/89)
87 PIGNAN Châteauneuf-du-Pape Réserve 1986 $22 (9/30/90)
95 PIGNAN Châteauneuf-du-Pape Réserve 1985 $14 (8/31/87) SS
87 PIGNAN Châteauneuf-du-Pape Réserve 1980 $12.75 (10/15/86)
86 CHATEAU RAYAS Châteauneuf-du-Pape Réserve 1988 $71 (3/31/91)
88 CHATEAU RAYAS Châteauneuf-du-Pape Réserve 1986 $48 (12/15/89)
93 CHATEAU RAYAS Châteauneuf-du-Pape Réserve 1985 $41 (7/31/88)
92 CHATEAU RAYAS Châteauneuf-du-Pape Réserve 1983 Rel: $30 Cur: $43 (8/31/86)
90 DOMAINE DE LA ROQUETTE Châteauneuf-du-Pape 1985 $13 (7/31/88) SS
82 JOSEPH SABON Châteauneuf-du-Pape Clos du Mont-Olivet 1988 $18.50 (1/31/91)
74 JOSEPH SABON Châteauneuf-du-Pape Clos du Mont-Olivet 1985 $15 (7/31/88)
83 JOSEPH SABON Châteauneuf-du-Pape Clos du Mont-Olivet 1983 $13.50 (1/31/87)
91 JOSEPH SABON Châteauneuf-du-Pape Clos du Mont-Olivet 1982 $12 (3/16/86)
88 DOMAINE ROGER SABON & FILS Châteauneuf-du-Pape 1988 $20 (9/30/90)

85 DOMAINE ROGER SABON & FILS Châteauneuf-du-Pape Cuvée Prestige 1988 $23 (9/30/90)
80 DOMAINE ROGER SABON & FILS Châteauneuf-du-Pape Cuvée Réserve 1988 $20 (9/30/90)
87 CHATEAU ST.-ANDRE Châteauneuf-du-Pape 1988 $16 (11/30/90)
85 DOMAINE DES SENECHAUX Châteauneuf-du-Pape 1985 $17 (10/15/88)
86 CHATEAU SIMIAN Châteauneuf-du-Pape 1988 $20 (7/15/91)
87 THORIN Châteauneuf-du-Pape 1986 $13 (11/30/88)
72 CHATEAU DE VAUDIEU Châteauneuf-du-Pape 1984 $12.50 (11/15/87)
89 DOMAINE DU VIEUX LAZARET Châteauneuf-du-Pape 1986 $13.50 (1/31/89)
85 DOMAINE DU VIEUX LAZARET Châteauneuf-du-Pape 1985 $12 (11/15/87)
81 DOMAINE DU VIEUX TELEGRAPHE Châteauneuf-du-Pape 1988 $20 (3/31/91)
81 DOMAINE DU VIEUX TELEGRAPHE Châteauneuf-du-Pape 1987 $17 (9/30/90)
91 DOMAINE DU VIEUX TELEGRAPHE Châteauneuf-du-Pape 1986 $17 (11/30/88) CS
90 DOMAINE DU VIEUX TELEGRAPHE Châteauneuf-du-Pape 1985 $17 (11/30/87)
89 DOMAINE DU VIEUX TELEGRAPHE Châteauneuf-du-Pape 1984 $12.50 (9/30/87)
77 DOMAINE DU VIEUX TELEGRAPHE Châteauneuf-du-Pape 1983 Rel: $17 Cur: $31 (9/30/87)

CORNAS

81 GUY DE BARJAC Cornas 1985 $17 (10/15/88)
88 A. CLAPE Cornas 1986 $22 (1/31/89)
78 A. CLAPE Cornas 1984 $12.50 (8/31/87)
84 JEAN-LUC COLOMBO Cornas Les Ruchets 1987 $50 (1/31/91)
83 MARCEL JUGE Cornas 1986 $23 (11/30/90)
89 MARCEL JUGE Cornas 1986 $23 (1/31/89)
85 MARCEL JUGE Cornas Cuvée C 1986 $25 (6/15/89)
87 MARCEL JUGE Cornas Cuvée S C 1986 $30 (6/15/89)
90 JEAN LIONNET Cornas 1987 $23 (3/31/90)
87 JEAN LIONNET Cornas 1986 $23 (1/31/89)
83 JEAN LIONNET Cornas Cuvée Rochepertuis 1988 $28 (1/31/91)
89 CAVE DE TAIN L'HERMITAGE Cornas Michel Courtial 1986 $11 (7/31/89)
88 NOEL VERSET Cornas 1987 $23 (3/31/90)
86 NOEL VERSET Cornas 1986 $25 (1/31/89)
85 J. VIDAL-FLEURY Cornas 1988 $20 (1/31/91)

CÔTE-RÔTIE

68 PERE ANSELME Côte-Rôtie Tête de Cuvée 1982 $13 (10/15/87)
84 PIERRE BARGE Côte-Rôtie 1988 $42 (7/31/91)
78 GUY BERNARD Côte-Rôtie 1988 $30 (10/15/90)
87 BERNARD BURGAUD Côte-Rôtie 1988 $40 (3/31/91)
85 BERNARD BURGAUD Côte-Rôtie 1987 $29 (2/28/90)
93 BERNARD BURGAUD Côte-Rôtie 1986 $31 (1/31/89)
90 BERNARD BURGAUD Côte-Rôtie 1984 $22 (10/15/87)
92 BERNARD BURGAUD Côte-Rôtie 1983 $18 (5/01/86)
84 LES CAVES ST.-PIERRE Côte-Rôtie Marquis de Tournelles 1987 $23 (1/31/91)
86 M. CHAPOUTIER Côte-Rôtie 1989 $30 (7/31/91)
85 GILBERT CLUSEL Côte-Rôtie La Viallière 1986 $23 (4/15/89)
87 GEORGES DUBOEUF Côte-Rôtie Domaine de la Rousse 1988 $18 (7/31/91)
90 PIERRE GAILLARD Côte-Rôtie Côte Brune et Blonde 1988 $30 (11/30/90)
82 PIERRE GAILLARD Côte-Rôtie Côte Brune et Blonde 1987 $24 (8/31/89)
86 PIERRE GAILLARD Côte-Rôtie Côte Brune et Blonde 1986 $25 (11/30/88)
73 GENTAZ-DERVIEUX Côte-Rôtie Côte Brune Cuvée Réserve 1987 $40 (6/30/90)
70 FRANCOIS GERARD Côte-Rôtie 1988 $36 (7/31/91)
77 FRANCOIS GERARD Côte-Rôtie 1987 $30 (10/15/90)
90 E. GUIGAL Côte-Rôtie Côtes Brune et Blonde 1987 $25 (1/31/91)
90 E. GUIGAL Côte-Rôtie Côtes Brune et Blonde 1986 $28 (2/28/90)
91 E. GUIGAL Côte-Rôtie Côtes Brune et Blonde 1985 $30 (3/15/90) (HS)
92 E. GUIGAL Côte-Rôtie Côtes Brune et Blonde 1985 $30 (1/31/89)
83 E. GUIGAL Côte-Rôtie Côtes Brune et Blonde 1984 $25 (11/30/87)
94 E. GUIGAL Côte-Rôtie Côtes Brune et Blonde 1983 Rel: $21 Cur: $34 (3/15/90) (HS)
92 E. GUIGAL Côte-Rôtie Côtes Brune et Blonde 1983 Rel: $21 Cur: $34 (4/30/87) CS
89 E. GUIGAL Côte-Rôtie Côtes Brune et Blonde 1982 Cur: $40 (3/15/90) (HS)
89 E. GUIGAL Côte-Rôtie Côtes Brune et Blonde 1980 Rel: $13 Cur: $32 (9/16/84)
95 E. GUIGAL Côte-Rôtie Côtes Brune et Blonde 1978 Cur: $78 (3/15/90) (HS)
88 E. GUIGAL Côte-Rôtie Côtes Brune et Blonde 1976 Cur: $65 (3/15/90) (HS)
93 E. GUIGAL Côte-Rôtie Côtes Brune et Blonde 1969 Cur: $100 (3/15/90) (HS)
88 E. GUIGAL Côte-Rôtie Côtes Brune et Blonde 1966 Cur: $145 (3/15/90) (HS)
92 E. GUIGAL Côte-Rôtie Côtes Brune et Blonde 1964 Cur: $100 (3/15/90) (HS)
89 E. GUIGAL Côte-Rôtie Côtes Brune et Blonde 1962 Cur: $100 (3/15/90) (HS)
82 E. GUIGAL Côte-Rôtie Côtes Brune et Blonde 1961 Cur: $100 (3/15/90) (HS)
93 E. GUIGAL Côte-Rôtie La Landonne 1987 $125 (7/31/91) CS
91 E. GUIGAL Côte-Rôtie La Landonne 1986 Rel: $99 Cur: $140 (10/15/90)
90 E. GUIGAL Côte-Rôtie La Landonne 1985 $370 (3/15/90) (HS)
86 E. GUIGAL Côte-Rôtie La Landonne 1984 Cur: $111 (3/15/90) (HS)
94 E. GUIGAL Côte-Rôtie La Landonne 1983 Cur: $310 (3/15/90) (HS)
90 E. GUIGAL Côte-Rôtie La Landonne 1982 Cur: $210 (3/15/90) (HS)
82 E. GUIGAL Côte-Rôtie La Landonne 1981 Cur: $156 (3/15/90) (HS)
84 E. GUIGAL Côte-Rôtie La Landonne 1980 Cur: $170 (3/15/90) (HS)
91 E. GUIGAL Côte-Rôtie La Landonne 1979 Cur: $260 (3/15/90) (HS)
95 E. GUIGAL Côte-Rôtie La Landonne 1978 Cur: $410 (3/15/90) (HS)
92 E. GUIGAL Côte-Rôtie La Mouline 1987 $115 (7/31/91)
93 E. GUIGAL Côte-Rôtie La Mouline 1986 Rel: $99 Cur: $135 (10/15/90)
98 E. GUIGAL Côte-Rôtie La Mouline 1985 Cur: $370 (3/15/90) (HS)
94 E. GUIGAL Côte-Rôtie La Mouline 1983 Cur: $310 (3/15/90) (HS)
92 E. GUIGAL Côte-Rôtie La Mouline 1982 Cur: $210 (3/15/90) (HS)
90 E. GUIGAL Côte-Rôtie La Mouline 1981 Cur: $151 (3/15/90) (HS)
85 E. GUIGAL Côte-Rôtie La Mouline 1979 Cur: $260 (3/15/90) (HS)
96 E. GUIGAL Côte-Rôtie La Mouline 1978 Cur: $430 (3/15/90) (HS)
75 E. GUIGAL Côte-Rôtie La Mouline 1977 Cur: $263 (3/15/90) (HS)
87 E. GUIGAL Côte-Rôtie La Mouline 1976 Cur: $330 (3/15/90) (HS)
75 E. GUIGAL Côte-Rôtie La Mouline 1975 Cur: $225 (3/15/90) (HS)
89 E. GUIGAL Côte-Rôtie La Mouline 1974 Cur: $300 (3/15/90) (HS)
84 E. GUIGAL Côte-Rôtie La Mouline 1973 Cur: $242 (3/15/90) (HS)
88 E. GUIGAL Côte-Rôtie La Mouline 1971 Cur: $300 (3/15/90) (HS)
74 E. GUIGAL Côte-Rôtie La Mouline 1970 Cur: $300 (3/15/90) (HS)
90 E. GUIGAL Côte-Rôtie La Mouline 1969 Cur: $900 (3/15/90) (HS)
82 E. GUIGAL Côte-Rôtie La Mouline 1968 Cur: $300 (3/15/90) (HS)
86 E. GUIGAL Côte-Rôtie La Mouline 1967 Cur: $510 (3/15/90) (HS)
88 E. GUIGAL Côte-Rôtie La Mouline 1966 Cur: $760 (3/15/90) (HS)

95 E. GUIGAL Côte-Rôtie La Turque 1987 $145 (7/31/91)
95 E. GUIGAL Côte-Rôtie La Turque 1986 Rel: $99 Cur: $340 (10/15/90) CS
98 E. GUIGAL Côte-Rôtie La Turque 1985 Cur: $660 (3/15/90) (HS)
87 BERNARD GUY Côte-Rôtie 1987 $25 (8/31/89)
89 BERNARD GUY Côte-Rôtie 1986 $29 (9/30/88)
93 PAUL JABOULET AINE Côte-Rôtie Les Jumelles 1985 $35 (9/30/88)
88 JOSEPH JAMET Côte-Rôtie 1985 $33 (4/15/89)
89 JASMIN Côte-Rôtie 1988 $32 (12/31/90)
90 JASMIN Côte-Rôtie 1987 $30 (6/30/90)
88 ANDRE PASSAT Côte-Rôtie 1985 $25 (10/15/87)
86 R. ROSTAING Côte-Rôtie Côte Blonde 1987 $40 (6/30/90)
75 L. DE VALLOUIT Côte-Rôtie 1985 $20 (10/15/87)
73 J. VIDAL-FLEURY Côte-Rôtie Côte Blonde La Chatillonne 1984 $26 (10/31/87)
88 J. VIDAL-FLEURY Côte-Rôtie Côtes Brune et Blonde 1988 $30 (10/15/90)
90 J. VIDAL-FLEURY Côte-Rôtie Côtes Brune et Blonde 1985 $25 (3/15/90) (HS)
85 J. VIDAL-FLEURY Côte-Rôtie Côtes Brune et Blonde 1945 Cur: $175 (3/15/90) (HS)
85 J. VIDAL-FLEURY Côte-Rôtie Côtes Brune et Blonde 1934 Cur: $300 (3/15/90) (HS)

CÔTES DU RHÔNE

73 CHATEAU D'AIGUEVILLE Côtes du Rhône 1987 $5 (1/31/89)
68 CHATEAU D'AIGUEVILLE Côtes du Rhône 1984 $4.50 (10/15/87)
74 ALIGNE Côtes du Rhône 1985 $6 (2/28/87)
72 DOMAINE DE L'AMEILLAUD Côtes du Rhône 1984 $4.50 (6/01/86)
75 PERE ANSELME Côtes du Rhône-Villages Marescal 1985 $5.25 (12/31/87)
72 PERE ANSELME Côtes du Rhône-Villages Seguret 1986 $5.25 (5/15/89)
75 DOMAINE LES AUSSELONS Côtes du Rhône Vinsobres 1987 $8 (6/30/90)
79 G. BAROUX Côtes du Rhône Château de Bourdines 1988 $8 (12/15/90)
77 DOMAINE MICHEL BERNARD Côtes du Rhône Domaine de la Serrière 1987 $7 (3/15/91)
72 BICHOT Côtes du Rhône 1987 $3.50 (11/15/88)
75 BICHOT Côtes du Rhône 1985 $5.75 (12/15/87)
83 CHATEAU DU BOIS DE LA GARDE Côtes du Rhône 1989 $8 (5/31/91)
82 CHATEAU DU BOIS DE LA GARDE Côtes du Rhône 1988 $7 (10/31/90) BB
78 JEAN CLAUDE BOISSET Côtes du Rhône 1987 $4.50 (1/31/89)
73 JEAN CLAUDE BOISSET Côtes du Rhône 1986 $4 (10/31/87)
77 JEAN CLAUDE BOISSET Côtes du Rhône 1985 $3.75 (11/30/86) BB
68 BOKOBSA Côtes du Rhône Cuvée du Centenaire 1986 $6.50 (2/28/90)
74 CHATEAU LA BORIE Côtes du Rhône Cuvée de Prestige 1986 $7 (7/15/87)
87 CHATEAU LA BORIE Côtes du Rhône Cuvée de Prestige 1983 $4 (3/16/85) BB
82 BOUCHARD PERE & FILS Côtes du Rhône 1989 $8.50 (7/15/91) BB
80 LAURENT CHARLES BROTTE Côtes du Rhône-Villages Seguret 1986 $6 (9/30/89) BB
61 DOMAINE BRUSSET Côtes du Rhône-Villages Cairanne Côteaux des Trabers 1986 $7 (6/15/89)
86 DOMAINE BRUSSET Côtes du Rhône-Villages Côteaux des Trabers 1988 $7.75 (12/15/90) BB
86 CAVE DES COTEAUX CAIRANNE Côtes du Rhône 1986 $7.25 (7/31/88)
85 CAVE DES COTEAUX CAIRANNE Côtes du Rhône Domaine le Château 1985 $6.25 (8/31/87) BB
77 CAVE DES COTEAUX CAIRANNE Côtes du Rhône Le Château a Cairanne 1987 $7 (12/15/89)
82 CAVE DES COTEAUX CAIRANNE Côtes du Rhône Le Château a Cairanne 1986 $6 (7/31/88) BB
81 CAVE DES COTEAUX CAIRANNE Côtes du Rhône-Villages 1988 $6.50 (2/28/90) BB
76 CAVE DES COTEAUX CAIRANNE Côtes du Rhône-Villages Cairanne 1988 $6.25 (6/30/90)
84 LES CAVES ST.-PIERRE Côtes du Rhône-Villages Les Lissandres 1988 $7.25 (12/15/90) BB
82 DOMAINE DES CEDRES Côtes du Rhône Pons Dominique 1986 $10 (3/31/90)
87 M. CHAPOUTIER Côtes du Rhône Cuvée de Belleruche 1986 $12 (12/15/89)
79 CAVE DES VIGNERONS A CHUSCLAN Côtes du Rhône Prieure St.-Julien 1985 $4.25 (12/31/87)
80 ABEL CLEMENT Côtes du Rhône 1988 $6 (2/28/90) BB
78 ABEL CLEMENT Côtes du Rhône 1985 $5 (1/31/87) BB
76 CRU DE COUDELET Côtes du Rhône 1987 $12 (12/15/89)
84 CRU DE COUDELET Côtes du Rhône 1986 $15 (9/30/88)
85 CRU DE COUDELET Côtes du Rhône 1985 $12 (4/30/88)
84 DELAS Côtes du Rhône St.-Esprit 1988 $6.75 (12/15/90) BB
80 DELAS Côtes du Rhône St.-Esprit 1985 $5.50 (12/15/87) BB
80 GEORGES DUBOEUF Côtes du Rhône 1989 $6 (10/15/90) BB
78 DOMAINE DURIEU Côtes du Rhône-Villages 1988 $6 (3/15/91)
87 CHATEAU DE FONSALETTE Côtes du Rhône Réserve 1985 $15.50 (9/30/88)
73 DOMAINE LOU FREJAU Côtes du Rhône 1986 $8 (5/31/89)
78 DOMAINE LES GOUBERT Côtes du Rhône 1986 $6.75 (3/31/88)
81 DOMAINE LES GOUBERT Côtes du Rhône-Villages Beaumes de Venise 1987 $9 (7/31/89)
80 DOMAINE LES GOUBERT Côtes du Rhône-Villages Beaumes de Venise 1985 $9.25 (4/30/88)
76 DOMAINE LES GOUBERT Côtes du Rhône-Villages Sablet 1985 $8.25 (4/30/88)
84 DOMAINE DE LA GUICHARDE Côtes du Rhône 1988 $7 (3/15/91) BB
81 E. GUIGAL Côtes du Rhône 1988 $11.50 (7/15/91)
84 E. GUIGAL Côtes du Rhône 1986 $9 (2/28/90)
85 E. GUIGAL Côtes du Rhône 1985 $8 (9/30/88)
84 E. GUIGAL Côtes du Rhône 1984 $7 (12/15/87) BB
85 E. GUIGAL Côtes du Rhône 1982 $6 (5/01/86) BB
86 E. GUIGAL Côtes du Rhône 1981 $5 (5/01/84) BB
85 E. GUIGAL Côtes du Rhône 1980 $4.50 (5/01/84) BB
84 PAUL JABOULET AINE Côtes du Rhône Parallele 45 1988 $6.50 (12/15/89) BB
73 PAUL JABOULET AINE Côtes du Rhône Parallele 45 1985 $6.50 (4/30/88)
79 JEAN LIONNET Côtes du Rhône Cépage Syrah 1986 $10 (9/30/88)
83 KERMIT LYNCH Côtes du Rhône 1985 $9 (1/31/89)
84 PROSPER MAUFOUX Côtes du Rhône 1989 $9 (5/31/91)
79 PROSPER MAUFOUX Côtes du Rhône 1988 $6.50 (6/30/90)
74 PROSPER MAUFOUX Côtes du Rhône 1987 $6.25 (6/15/89)
85 MOILLARD Côtes du Rhône Les Violettes 1988 $7.50 (5/31/91) BB
84 MOILLARD Côtes du Rhône Les Violettes 1986 $8 (8/31/89) BB
85 MOILLARD Côtes du Rhône Les Violettes 1985 $4.50 (11/15/86) BB
82 MOMMESSIN Côtes du Rhône 1986 $4.75 (4/30/88) BB
68 DOMAINE DE LA MORDOREE Côtes du Rhône 1988 $5.50 (2/28/90)
81 LOUIS MOUSSET Côtes du Rhône 1983 $2.50 (12/16/84) BB
74 J.Y. MULTIER Côtes du Rhône Cépage Syrah 1988 $10 (12/15/90)
77 CHATEAU D'ORSAN Côtes du Rhône 1987 $4 (11/15/88)
81 CHATEAU D'ORSAN Côtes du Rhône 1986 $4 (2/29/88) BB
79 CHATEAU D'ORSAN Côtes du Rhône 1985 $6.75 (12/15/87)
77 PATRIARCHE Côtes du Rhône-Villages Cuvée Leblanc-Vatel 1985 $5.50 (8/31/89)

75 DU PELOUX Côtes du Rhône 1986 $4.50 (5/15/89)
78 DU PELOUX Côtes du Rhône-Villages 1986 $5.50 (5/15/89)
81 DOMAINE RABASSE CHARAVIN Côtes du Rhône 1985 $6 (8/31/87) BB
84 LA RAMILLADE Côtes du Rhône 1982 $5 (11/01/85) BB
84 DOMAINE DE LA RENJARDIERE Côtes du Rhône 1983 $4.50 (3/16/86) BB
80 PAR E. REYNAUD Côtes du Rhône Château des Tours 1989 $12 (3/15/91)
78 DOMAINE DES RICHARDS Côtes du Rhône-Villages 1987 $4 (1/31/89)
81 ARMAND ROUX Côtes du Rhône La Berberine 1988 $7.50 (10/31/90) BB
89 CHARLES ROUX Côtes du Rhône-Villages Rasteau 1985 $10 (2/28/90)
79 DOMAINE ROGER SABON & FILS Côtes du Rhône 1988 $11 (10/31/90)
75 DOMAINE ST.-GAYAN Côtes du Rhône 1988 $8 (10/31/90)
75 DOMAINE ST.-GAYAN Côtes du Rhône 1985 $6 (4/30/88)
80 DOMAINE STE.-ANNE Côtes du Rhône-Villages Cuvée Notre-Dame des Cellettes 1987 $7.50 (1/31/89)
78 SERRE DE LAUZIERE Côtes du Rhône-Villages 1988 $7 (10/31/90)
SICHEL Côtes du Rhône 1979 $5 (12/16/81) SS
82 DOMAINE LA SOUMADE Côtes du Rhône-Villages Rasteau 1986 $11 (2/28/90)
69 DOMAINE LA SOUMADE Côtes du Rhône-Villages Rasteau Cuvée Réservee 1982 $5.50 (10/31/87)
67 THORIN Côtes du Rhône L'Escalou 1987 $6 (1/31/89)
80 CHATEAU DU TRIGNON Côtes du Rhône-Villages Rasteau 1986 $9 (12/15/90)
85 J. VIDAL-FLEURY Côtes du Rhône 1988 $9 (12/15/90)
88 J. VIDAL-FLEURY Côtes du Rhône 1985 $7.50 (10/31/87) BB
87 LA VIEILLE FERME Côtes du Rhône Réserve 1989 $9 (3/15/91) BB
84 LA VIEILLE FERME Côtes du Rhône Réserve 1988 $8 (12/15/90) BB
86 LA VIEILLE FERME Côtes du Rhône Réserve 1988 $8 (12/31/89) BB
80 LA VIEILLE FERME Côtes du Rhône Réserve 1987 $6.50 (6/15/89) BB
85 LA VIEILLE FERME Côtes du Rhône Réserve 1985 $7 (11/15/88) BB
79 VIGNOBLE DE LA JASSE Côtes du Rhône 1986 $8 (12/15/90)

CROZES-HERMITAGE

80 PERE ANSELME Crozes-Hermitage 1986 $7.75 (7/31/89)
84 PERE ANSELME Crozes-Hermitage 1983 $7.50 (10/15/87) BB
78 BERNARD CHAVE Crozes-Hermitage 1988 $14 (2/15/91)
86 BERNARD CHAVE Crozes-Hermitage 1985 $12.25 (11/30/88)
89 CHATEAU CURSON Crozes-Hermitage 1989 $17 (7/15/91)
78 DELAS Crozes-Hermitage 1985 $7.50 (12/15/87)
84 DESMEURE Crozes-Hermitage Domaine des Remizières Cuvée Particulaire 1986 $8 (5/31/89) BB
85 GEORGES DUBOEUF Crozes-Hermitage 1988 $9 (1/31/91)
85 FERRATON PERE Crozes-Hermitage La Matinière 1988 $14 (6/30/90)
88 ALAIN GRAILLOT Crozes-Hermitage 1989 $13.50 (3/31/91)
88 ALAIN GRAILLOT Crozes-Hermitage 1988 $9.75 (4/15/89)
90 PAUL JABOULET AINE Crozes-Hermitage Domaine de Thalabert 1989 $18 (7/15/91)
83 PAUL JABOULET AINE Crozes-Hermitage Domaine de Thalabert 1988 $13 (10/15/90)
83 PAUL JABOULET AINE Crozes-Hermitage Domaine de Thalabert 1987 $10 (3/31/90)
88 PAUL JABOULET AINE Crozes-Hermitage Domaine de Thalabert 1986 $13.50 (9/30/88)
85 PAUL JABOULET AINE Crozes-Hermitage Domaine de Thalabert 1985 Rel: $13.50 Cur: $30 (9/30/88)
83 LUPE-CHOLET Crozes-Hermitage 1987 $8 (3/31/90) BB
77 CAVE DE TAIN L'HERMITAGE Crozes-Hermitage Michel Courtial 1986 $6 (5/15/89)
86 J. VIDAL-FLEURY Crozes-Hermitage 1988 $13.50 (12/31/90)
78 J. VIDAL-FLEURY Crozes-Hermitage 1986 $10 (5/31/88)
92 J. VIDAL-FLEURY Crozes-Hermitage 1985 $11 (10/31/87) CS
70 WILLI'S WINE BAR Crozes-Hermitage Cuvée Anniversaire 1980-1990 1988 $11 (3/31/91)

GIGONDAS

90 DANIEL BRUSSET Gigondas Les Hauts de Montmirail 1988 $16.50 (9/30/90)
79 GEORGES DUBOEUF Gigondas 1988 $10 (9/30/90)
93 MICHEL FARAUD Gigondas Domaine du Cayron 1985 $15.75 (11/30/88)
86 DOMAINE DE FONT-SANE Gigondas 1985 $13 (1/31/89)
81 DOMAINE LES GOUBERT Gigondas 1986 $13 (3/15/90)
89 DOMAINE LES GOUBERT Gigondas 1985 $11.50 (4/30/88)
92 DOMAINE LES GOUBERT Gigondas Cuvée Florence 1986 $24 (4/30/88)
90 DOMAINE DU GOUR DE CHAULE Gigondas 1986 $13 (9/15/90)
85 E. GUIGAL Gigondas 1988 $13 (3/31/91)
87 E. GUIGAL Gigondas 1986 $15 (11/30/90)
91 E. GUIGAL Gigondas 1985 $12.50 (9/30/88) SS
86 E. GUIGAL Gigondas 1984 $13 (11/30/87)
91 E. GUIGAL Gigondas 1983 $12.50 (7/31/87)
84 PAUL JABOULET AINE Gigondas 1989 $18 (7/15/91)
65 PROSPER MAUFOUX Gigondas 1985 $11 (4/30/88)
78 CHATEAU DE MONTMIRAIL Gigondas Cuvée de Beauchamp 1985 $14 (9/30/88)
90 CHATEAU DE MONTMIRAIL Gigondas Cuvée de Beauchamp 1983 $11 (11/30/86)
75 LOUIS MOUSSET Gigondas 1983 $6 (12/01/84)
86 DOMAINE LES PALLIERES Gigondas 1984 $14 (9/30/89)
85 DOMAINE LES PALLIERES Gigondas 1983 $15 (1/31/89)
89 DOMAINE LES PALLIERES Gigondas 1982 $11 (5/31/87)
90 DOMAINE LES PALLIERES Gigondas 1981 $10.25 (3/15/87)
92 DOMAINE RASPAIL-AY Gigondas 1986 $15 (1/31/89)
86 J. VIDAL-FLEURY Gigondas 1985 $13 (10/31/87)

HERMITAGE

88 LES CAVES ST.-PIERRE Hermitage Tertre des Carmes 1988 $23 (12/31/90)
88 M. CHAPOUTIER Hermitage Le Pavillon NV $60 (1/31/89)
83 M. CHAPOUTIER Hermitage M. de la Sizeranne 1983 $19 (5/01/86)
88 M. CHAPOUTIER Hermitage M. de la Sizeranne 1981 $10 (11/01/84)
83 M. CHAPOUTIER Hermitage M. de la Sizeranne Grande Cuvée NV $14 (5/01/86)
86 BERNARD CHAVE Hermitage 1986 $32 (11/30/88)
89 J.L. CHAVE Hermitage 1987 $48 (6/30/90)
89 J.L. CHAVE Hermitage 1984 $25 (8/31/87)
83 J.L. CHAVE Hermitage 1980 Rel: $25 Cur: $37 (5/01/86)
68 DESMEURE Hermitage Domaine des Remizières 1986 $19 (4/15/90)
86 E. GUIGAL Hermitage 1987 $29 (1/31/91)
92 E. GUIGAL Hermitage 1985 $33 (4/15/89) CS
87 E. GUIGAL Hermitage 1984 $23 (4/30/87)
91 E. GUIGAL Hermitage 1982 Rel: $18 Cur: $29 (5/01/86)
91 E. GUIGAL Hermitage 1980 Rel: $13 Cur: $37 (9/01/84) CS
91 E. GUIGAL Hermitage 1978 Cur: $71 (3/15/90) (HS)
80 E. GUIGAL Hermitage 1976 Cur: $75 (3/15/90) (HS)

FRANCE
RHÔNE RED/*HERMITAGE*

84 E. GUIGAL Hermitage 1969 Cur: $100 (3/15/90) (HS)
90 E. GUIGAL Hermitage 1966 Cur: $100 (3/15/90) (HS)
93 E. GUIGAL Hermitage 1964 Cur: $100 (3/15/90) (HS)
88 DOMAINE DE L'HERMITE Hermitage 1983 $9.50 (5/01/86)
84 DOMAINE DE L'HERMITE Hermitage 1980 $12.25 (5/01/86)
92 PAUL JABOULET AINE Hermitage La Chapelle 1988 $40 (3/31/91)
89 PAUL JABOULET AINE Hermitage La Chapelle 1986 $35 (11/15/89) (JS)
91 PAUL JABOULET AINE Hermitage La Chapelle 1986 $35 (9/30/88)
93 PAUL JABOULET AINE Hermitage La Chapelle 1985 $50 (11/15/89) (JS)
90 PAUL JABOULET AINE Hermitage La Chapelle 1985 $50 (12/31/87)
80 PAUL JABOULET AINE Hermitage La Chapelle 1984 Cur: $17 (11/15/89) (JS)
94 PAUL JABOULET AINE Hermitage La Chapelle 1983 Cur: $63 (11/15/89) (JS)
89 PAUL JABOULET AINE Hermitage La Chapelle 1982 Rel: $17.50 Cur: $50 (11/15/89) (JS)
93 PAUL JABOULET AINE Hermitage La Chapelle 1982 Rel: $17.50 Cur: $50 (11/01/84) CS
83 PAUL JABOULET AINE Hermitage La Chapelle 1981 Cur: $30 (11/15/89) (JS)
79 PAUL JABOULET AINE Hermitage La Chapelle 1980 Cur: $28 (11/15/89) (JS)
86 PAUL JABOULET AINE Hermitage La Chapelle 1979 Cur: $50 (11/15/89) (JS)
98 PAUL JABOULET AINE Hermitage La Chapelle 1978 Cur: $181 (11/15/89) (JS)
87 PAUL JABOULET AINE Hermitage La Chapelle 1976 Cur: $142 (11/15/89) (JS)
81 PAUL JABOULET AINE Hermitage La Chapelle 1975 Cur: $35 (11/15/89) (JS)
85 PAUL JABOULET AINE Hermitage La Chapelle 1974 Cur: $128 (11/15/89) (JS)
89 PAUL JABOULET AINE Hermitage La Chapelle 1973 Cur: $58 (11/15/89) (JS)
90 PAUL JABOULET AINE Hermitage La Chapelle 1972 Cur: $135 (11/15/89) (JS)
85 PAUL JABOULET AINE Hermitage La Chapelle 1971 Cur: $175 (11/15/89) (JS)
86 PAUL JABOULET AINE Hermitage La Chapelle 1971 Cur: $175 (10/29/87)
93 PAUL JABOULET AINE Hermitage La Chapelle 1970 Cur: $215 (11/15/89) (JS)
92 PAUL JABOULET AINE Hermitage La Chapelle 1969 Cur: $195 (11/15/89) (JS)
95 PAUL JABOULET AINE Hermitage La Chapelle 1969 Cur: $195 (10/29/87)
83 PAUL JABOULET AINE Hermitage La Chapelle 1967 Cur: $65 (11/15/89) (JS)
95 PAUL JABOULET AINE Hermitage La Chapelle 1966 Cur: $175 (11/15/89) (JS)
93 PAUL JABOULET AINE Hermitage La Chapelle 1964 Cur: $330 (11/15/89) (JS)
91 PAUL JABOULET AINE Hermitage La Chapelle 1962 Cur: $150 (11/15/89) (JS)
100 PAUL JABOULET AINE Hermitage La Chapelle 1961 Cur: $590 (11/15/89) (JS)
77 PAUL JABOULET AINE Hermitage La Chapelle 1959 Cur: $510 (11/15/89) (JS)
88 PAUL JABOULET AINE Hermitage La Chapelle 1955 Cur: $330 (11/15/89) (JS)
90 PAUL JABOULET AINE Hermitage La Chapelle 1953 Cur: $560 (11/15/89) (JS)
77 PAUL JABOULET AINE Hermitage La Chapelle 1952 Cur: $460 (11/15/89) (JS)
77 PAUL JABOULET AINE Hermitage La Chapelle 1949 Cur: $810 (11/15/89) (JS)
93 PAUL JABOULET AINE Hermitage La Chapelle 1944 Cur: $810 (11/15/89) (JS)
50 PAUL JABOULET AINE Hermitage La Chapelle 1937 Cur: $860 (11/15/89) (JS)
87 H. SORREL Hermitage 1985 $29 (7/31/88)
84 H. SORREL Hermitage Le Greal 1983 $19.50 (5/01/86)
74 H. SORREL Hermitage Le Meal 1980 $25 (5/01/86)
82 CAVE DE TAIN L'HERMITAGE Hermitage 1986 $15.50 (7/15/89)
89 CAVE DE TAIN L'HERMITAGE Hermitage Michel Courtial 1986 $15 (3/31/90)
79 L. DE VALLOUIT Hermitage 1983 $12 (5/01/86)
89 J. VIDAL-FLEURY Hermitage 1985 $22.50 (10/31/87)
80 J. VIDAL-FLEURY Hermitage 1945 Cur: $175 (3/15/90) (HS)
91 J. VIDAL-FLEURY Hermitage 1937 Cur: $135 (3/15/90) (HS)

OTHER RHÔNE RED

75 JEAN CLAUDE BOISSET Côtes du Ventoux 1988 $4 (10/15/90)
79 LA BOUVERIE Costières de Nimes 1989 $6 (7/15/91)
83 DOMAINE LE CLOS DES CAZAUX Vacqueyras Cuvée des Templiers 1983 $11 (1/31/87)
83 DOMAINE LE COUROULU Vacqueyras 1985 $8 (1/31/89) BB
76 CUILLERON St.-Joseph 1983 $12.50 (2/16/86)
80 CUILLERON St.-Joseph Cuvée de la Côte 1987 $16 (11/30/90)
76 GEORGES DUBOEUF St.-Joseph 1988 $11 (11/30/90)
87 PIERRE GAILLARD St.-Joseph Clos de Cuminaille 1988 $15 (12/31/90)
87 PIERRE GAILLARD St.-Joseph Clos de Cuminaille 1987 $14 (3/15/90)
86 PAUL JABOULET AINE St.-Joseph Le Grand Pompée 1985 $11.25 (10/15/88)
84 DOMAINE DES LONES Côteaux du Tricastin 1988 $11 (5/31/91)
78 DOMAINE DES LONES Côteaux du Tricastin 1988 $7.50 (10/15/90)
82 DOMAINE DES LONES Côteaux du Tricastin 1986 $7.25 (10/15/88)
83 CHATEAU DE MILLE Côtes du Lubéron 1985 $8.50 (12/15/88)
88 DOMAINE DE LA MORDOREE Lirac 1986 $11 (9/30/88)
88 CHATEAU DES ROQUES Vacqueyras Cuvée de Noe 1986 $7.50 (12/15/89) BB
82 DOMAINE ST.-SAUVEUR Côtes du Ventoux 1988 $5.50 (9/30/89) BB
79 CAVE DE TAIN L'HERMITAGE St.-Joseph Michel Courtial 1986 $8 (7/31/89)
82 CHATEAU VAL JOANIS Côtes du Lubéron 1988 $7 (6/30/90) BB
78 L. DE VALLOUIT Vin de Pays des Collines Rhodanienn Les Sables 1988 $4.75 (6/30/90) BB
84 J. VIDAL-FLEURY St.-Joseph 1988 $14 (1/31/91)
89 J. VIDAL-FLEURY Vacqueyras 1988 $13.50 (12/15/90)
78 LA VIEILLE FERME Côtes du Ventoux 1988 $8 (6/30/90)
81 LA VIEILLE FERME Côtes du Ventoux 1987 $5.75 (6/15/89) BB
83 LA VIEILLE FERME Côtes du Ventoux 1986 $6 (10/15/88) BB

RHÔNE WHITE/*CHÂTEAUNEUF-DU-PAPE*

84 PIERRE ANDRE Châteauneuf-du-Pape 1984 $16.50 (10/01/85)
84 CHATEAU DE BEAUCASTEL Châteauneuf-du-Pape 1986 $29 (2/29/88)
82 CHATEAU DE BEAUCASTEL Châteauneuf-du-Pape 1985 $27 (11/15/87)
87 CHATEAU DE BEAUCASTEL Châteauneuf-du-Pape Roussanne Vieille Vigne 1988 $46 (12/31/90)
74 LAURENT CHARLES BROTTE Châteauneuf-du-Pape 1987 $14 (10/31/89)
73 DELAS Châteauneuf-du-Pape 1985 $18 (11/15/87)
74 DOMAINE JEAN DEYDIER & FILS Châteauneuf-du-Pape Les Clefs d'Or 1986 $17 (11/15/87)
81 DOMAINE FONT DE MICHELLE Châteauneuf-du-Pape 1985 $15 (11/15/87)
87 DOMAINE DE MONPERTUIS Châteauneuf-du-Pape 1988 $29 (3/31/91)
80 DOMAINE DE MONPERTUIS Châteauneuf-du-Pape 1988 $22 (11/30/90)
79 CHATEAU MONT-REDON Châteauneuf-du-Pape 1987 $20 (10/31/89)
85 CHATEAU RAYAS Châteauneuf-du-Pape Réserve 1986 $44 (3/15/89)
81 DOMAINE DU VIEUX LAZARET Châteauneuf-du-Pape 1986 $14.50 (3/15/89)
77 DOMAINE DU VIEUX TELEGRAPHE Châteauneuf-du-Pape 1986 $15 (11/15/87)

OTHER RHÔNE WHITE

76 JEAN CLAUDE BOISSET Côtes du Rhône 1988 $4.50 (10/31/90)
70 JEAN CLAUDE BOISSET Côtes du Rhône 1986 $4.50 (11/15/87)
79 LA BOUVERIE Costières de Nimes 1989 $6 (7/15/91)
77 DOMAINE DE LA CAVALE Côtes du Lubéron 1987 $7 (2/15/89)
80 M. CHAPOUTIER Hermitage Chante Alouette 1985 $23 (3/15/90)
70 M. CHAPOUTIER Hermitage Chante Alouette 1983 $16 (5/01/86)
83 M. CHAPOUTIER Hermitage Spécial Cuvée 180th Anniversary 1986 $24 (12/31/90)
81 J.L. CHAVE Hermitage 1983 Rel: $20 Cur: $48 (5/01/86)
91 CUILLERON Condrieu 1988 $34 (12/31/90)
81 CUILLERON St.-Joseph Blanc 1988 $17 (12/31/90)
81 VINCENT L. DARNAT Côtes du Rhône Blanc 1985 $5.50 (2/29/88) BB
87 DEZORMEAUX Condrieu Viognier Côteaux du Colombier 1987 $37 (3/15/89)
80 CHATEAU DE FONSALETTE Côtes du Rhône 1986 $18.50 (3/15/89)
87 PIERRE GAILLARD Côtes du Rhône Viognier Clos de Cuminaille 1986 $25 (3/15/89)
68 DOMAINE LES GOUBERT Côtes du Rhône-Villages Sablet 1986 $7 (3/31/88)
80 CHATEAU GRILLET Château-Grillet 1986 $75 (11/30/90)
87 CHATEAU GRILLET Château-Grillet 1986 $75 (3/15/89)
89 E. GUIGAL Condrieu Viognier 1987 $48 (3/15/89)
83 E. GUIGAL Côtes du Rhône 1989 $10 (3/31/91)
83 E. GUIGAL Côtes du Rhône 1988 $9 (3/15/90)
87 E. GUIGAL Hermitage 1988 $23 (3/31/91)
88 E. GUIGAL Hermitage 1986 $27 (3/15/90) (HS)
76 E. GUIGAL Hermitage 1985 $23 (12/15/87)
64 E. GUIGAL Hermitage 1981 $15 (5/01/86)
80 E. GUIGAL Tavel 1989 $15 (3/31/91)
70 PAUL JABOULET AINE Crozes-Hermitage Moute Blanche 1987 $11.50 (10/15/88)
78 PAUL JABOULET AINE Hermitage Le Chevalier de Sterimberg 1983 $11 (5/01/86)
67 PROSPER MAUFOUX Côtes du Rhône 1989 $8 (3/31/91)
81 PROSPER MAUFOUX Côtes du Rhône 1987 $6 (7/15/89)
86 CHATEAU MONT-REDON Côtes du Rhône 1987 $8 (10/31/89) BB
68 CHATEAU DES ROQUES Côtes du Rhône-Villages Cuvée Bethleem 1988 $7.50 (3/31/90)
81 CHATEAU DE SEGRIES Lirac 1985 $10 (12/15/89)
83 H. SORREL Hermitage Les Rocoules 1984 $20 (5/01/86)
84 CAVE DE TAIN L'HERMITAGE Crozes-Hermitage Michel Courtial 1986 $8.50 (3/15/90)
81 GEORGES VERNAY Condrieu 1988 $40 (10/31/89)
85 GEORGES VERNAY Condrieu 1987 $36 (3/15/89)
77 GEORGES VERNAY Condrieu Côteau de Vernon 1987 $43 (10/31/89)
80 LA VIEILLE FERME Côtes du Lubéron 1989 $7 (4/30/91) BB
78 LA VIEILLE FERME Côtes du Lubéron 1988 $6.50 (3/15/90)
71 LA VIEILLE FERME Côtes du Lubéron 1986 $6 (4/15/88)
85 LA VIEILLE FERME Côtes du Rhône Réserve 1988 $8 (10/31/89)

SAUTERNES

87 CHATEAU D'ARCHE Sauternes 1988 $20/375ml (4/30/91)
90+ CHATEAU D'ARCHE Sauternes 1988 Rel: $20 Cur: $28 (6/15/90) (BT)
85 CHATEAU D'ARCHE Sauternes 1987 (NA) (6/15/90)
85 CHATEAU D'ARCHE Sauternes 1986 Rel: $32 Cur: $32 (12/31/89)
90+ CHATEAU D'ARCHE Sauternes 1986 Rel: $32 Cur: $32 (6/30/88) (BT)
93 CHATEAU D'ARCHE Sauternes 1983 Rel: $23 Cur: $43 (1/31/88)
75+ CHATEAU D'ARCHE-PUGNEAU Sauternes 1989 (NR) (6/15/90) (BT)
75+ CHATEAU D'ARCHE-PUGNEAU Sauternes 1988 (NR) (6/15/90) (BT)
71 CHATEAU D'ARCHE-PUGNEAU Sauternes 1987 (NA) (6/15/90)
90+ CHATEAU D'ARMAJAN-DES-ORMES Sauternes 1989 (NR) (6/15/90) (BT)
72 CHATEAU D'ARMAJAN-DES-ORMES Sauternes 1987 (NA) (6/15/90)
85+ DOMAINE DE BARJUNEAU-CHAUVIN Sauternes 1989 (NR) (6/15/90) (BT)
74 DOMAINE DE BARJUNEAU-CHAUVIN Sauternes 1987 (NA) (6/15/90)
75 BARTON & GUESTIER Sauternes 1985 $12 (5/31/88)
95+ CHATEAU BASTOR-LAMONTAGNE Sauternes 1989 (NR) (6/15/90) (BT)
82 CHATEAU BASTOR-LAMONTAGNE Sauternes 1988 $18 (2/15/91)
85+ CHATEAU BASTOR-LAMONTAGNE Sauternes 1988 $18 (6/15/90) (BT)
67 CHATEAU BASTOR-LAMONTAGNE Sauternes 1987 (NA) (6/15/90)
82 CHATEAU BASTOR-LAMONTAGNE Sauternes 1985 $20 (5/31/88)
82 CHATEAU BASTOR-LAMONTAGNE Sauternes 1983 $20 (1/31/88)
80+ CHATEAU BECHEREAU Sauternes 1989 (NR) (6/15/90) (BT)
70+ CHATEAU BOUYOT Barsac 1988 (NR) (6/15/90) (BT)
74 CHATEAU BOUYOT Barsac 1987 (NA) (6/15/90)
90+ CHATEAU BROUSTET Barsac 1989 (NR) (6/15/90) (BT)
83 CHATEAU BROUSTET Barsac 1988 $19/375ml (3/31/91)
80+ CHATEAU BROUSTET Barsac 1988 $19 (6/15/90) (BT)
75+ CHATEAU BROUSTET Barsac 1986 (NR) (6/30/88) (BT)
95+ CHATEAU CAILLOU Barsac 1989 (NR) (6/15/90) (BT)
85+ CHATEAU CAILLOU Barsac 1988 Rel: $37 Cur: $37 (6/15/90) (BT)
85 CHATEAU CAILLOU Barsac 1987 (NA) (6/15/90)
75+ CHATEAU CAILLOU Barsac 1986 Rel: $30 Cur: $30 (6/30/88) (BT)
76 CHATEAU CAILLOU Barsac 1983 Rel: $22 Cur: $22 (1/31/88)
85+ CHATEAU CAMERON Sauternes 1989 (NR) (6/15/90) (BT)
85+ CHATEAU CAMERON Sauternes 1988 (NR) (6/15/90) (BT)
82 CHATEAU CAMERON Sauternes 1987 (NA) (6/15/90)
85+ CHATEAU CANTEGRIL Barsac 1989 (NR) (6/15/90) (BT)
81 DOMAINE DE CAPLANE Sauternes 1985 $11 (9/30/88)
80+ CHATEAU DE LA CHARTREUSE Sauternes 1988 (NR) (6/15/90) (BT)
77 CHATEAU DE LA CHARTREUSE Sauternes 1987 (NA) (6/15/90)
90 CHATEAU DE LA CHARTREUSE Sauternes 1983 $10 (1/31/88)

Key to Symbols

The scores reported here are the results of blind tastings conducted by our panel of senior editors. Wines that carry the initials below are results of individual tastings.

THE WINE SPECTATOR 100-POINT SCALE *95-100*—Classic, a great wine; *90-94*—Outstanding, superior character and style; *80-89*—Good to very good, a wine with special qualities; *70-79*—Average, drinkable wine that may have minor flaws; *60-69*—Below average, drinkable but not recommended; *50-59*—Poor, undrinkable, not recommended. "+"—With a score indicates a range; used primarily with barrel tastings to indicate a preliminary score.

SPECIAL DESIGNATIONS SS—Spectator Selection, CS—Cellar Selection, BB—Best Buy.

TASTER'S INITIALS (JG)—Jim Gordon, (HS)—Harvey Steiman, (JL)—James Laube, (JS)—James Suckling, (TM)—Thomas Matthews, (TR)—Terry Robards, (BT)—Barrel Tasting (these wines were tasted blind from barrel samples), (CA-date)—*California's Great Cabernets* by James Laube, (CH-date)—*California's Great Chardonnays* by James Laube, (VP-date)—*Vintage Port* by James Suckling.

DATE TASTED Dates in parentheses represent the issue in which the rating was published.

90+ CHATEAU CLIMENS Barsac 1989 (NR) (6/15/90) (BT)
90+ CHATEAU CLIMENS Barsac 1988 $48 (6/15/90) (BT)
84 CHATEAU CLIMENS Barsac 1986 $48 (12/31/89)
85+ CHATEAU CLIMENS Barsac 1986 $48 (6/30/88) (BT)
95 CHATEAU CLIMENS Barsac 1983 $50 (1/31/88) CS
80+ CHATEAU CLOS HAUT-PEYRAGUEY Sauternes 1989 (NR) (6/15/90) (BT)
85+ CHATEAU CLOS HAUT-PEYRAGUEY Sauternes 1988 $26 (6/15/90) (BT)
83 CHATEAU CLOS HAUT-PEYRAGUEY Sauternes 1987 (NA) (6/15/90)
80+ CHATEAU CLOS HAUT-PEYRAGUEY Sauternes 1986 $23 (6/30/88) (BT)
95+ CHATEAU COUTET Barsac 1989 (NR) (6/15/90) (BT)
90+ CHATEAU COUTET Barsac 1988 Rel: $47 Cur: $47 (6/15/90) (BT)
80 CHATEAU COUTET Barsac 1987 (NA) (6/15/90)
80+ CHATEAU COUTET Barsac 1986 Cur: $30 (6/30/88) (BT)
86 CHATEAU COUTET Barsac 1983 Rel: $30 Cur: $35 (1/31/88)
85+ CHATEAU DOISY DAENE Sauternes 1989 (NR) (6/15/90) (BT)
85+ CHATEAU DOISY DAENE Sauternes 1988 Rel: $34 Cur: $34 (6/15/90) (BT)
68 CHATEAU DOISY DAENE Sauternes 1986 Rel: $35 Cur: $35 (12/31/89)
73 CHATEAU DOISY DAENE Sauternes 1985 Rel: $24 Cur: $24 (5/31/88)
87 CHATEAU DOISY DAENE Sauternes 1983 Rel: $21 Cur: $31 (1/31/88)
90+ CHATEAU DOISY DUBROCA Barsac 1989 (NR) (6/15/90) (BT)
85+ CHATEAU DOISY DUBROCA Barsac 1988 Rel: $30 Cur: $30 (6/15/90) (BT)
90+ CHATEAU DOISY-VEDRINES Sauternes 1989 (NR) (6/15/90) (BT)
90+ CHATEAU DOISY-VEDRINES Sauternes 1988 Rel: $31 Cur: $31 (6/15/90) (BT)
86 CHATEAU DOISY-VEDRINES Sauternes 1986 Rel: $19 Cur: $19 (12/31/89)
80+ CHATEAU DOISY-VEDRINES Sauternes 1986 Rel: $19 Cur: $19 (6/30/88) (BT)
73 CHATEAU DOISY-VEDRINES Sauternes 1983 Rel: $18 Cur: $24 (1/31/88)
60+ CHATEAU DUDON Barsac 1989 (NR) (6/15/90) (BT)
85+ CHATEAU FARLURET Barsac 1988 (NR) (6/15/90) (BT)
85+ CHATEAU FILHOT Sauternes 1989 (NR) (6/15/90) (BT)
85+ CHATEAU FILHOT Sauternes 1988 Rel: $25 Cur: $25 (6/15/90) (BT)
68 CHATEAU FILHOT Sauternes 1987 Rel: $19 Cur: $19 (6/15/90)
83 CHATEAU FILHOT Sauternes 1986 Rel: $19 Cur: $24 (12/31/89)
95+ CHATEAU FILHOT Sauternes 1986 Rel: $19 Cur: $24 (6/30/88) (BT)
86 CHATEAU FILHOT Sauternes 1983 Rel: $21 Cur: $35 (1/31/88)
80 CHATEAU FILHOT Sauternes 1980 Rel: $11.50 Cur: $25 (5/01/84)
90+ CHATEAU GRAVES Barsac 1989 (NR) (6/15/90) (BT)
85+ CHATEAU GUIRAUD Sauternes 1989 (NR) (6/15/90) (BT)
85+ CHATEAU GUIRAUD Sauternes 1988 Rel: $38 Cur: $38 (6/15/90) (BT)
72 CHATEAU GUIRAUD Sauternes 1987 (NA) (6/15/90)
89 CHATEAU GUIRAUD Sauternes 1986 Rel: $48 Cur: $48 (12/31/89)
90+ CHATEAU GUIRAUD Sauternes 1986 Rel: $48 Cur: $48 (6/30/88) (BT)
76 CHATEAU GUIRAUD Sauternes 1983 Rel: $30 Cur: $41 (1/31/88)
62 CHATEAU GUIRAUD Sauternes 1983 Rel: $30 Cur: $41 (4/30/87)
72 CHATEAU GUIRAUD Sauternes Le Dauphin 1987 Rel: $11 Cur: $11 (12/31/89)
90+ CHATEAU HAUT-BERGERON Sauternes 1989 (NR) (6/15/90) (BT)
90+ CHATEAU HAUT-BERGERON Sauternes 1988 (NR) (6/15/90) (BT)
81 CHATEAU HAUT-BERGERON Sauternes 1987 (NA) (6/15/90)
85+ CHATEAU HAUT-BOMMES Sauternes 1989 (NR) (6/15/90) (BT)
75+ CHATEAU HAUT-BOMMES Sauternes 1988 (NR) (6/15/90) (BT)
74 CHATEAU HAUT-BOMMES Sauternes 1987 (NA) (6/15/90)
85+ CHATEAU HAUT-CLAVERIE Sauternes 1988 (NR) (6/15/90) (BT)
85+ CHATEAU LES JUSTICES Sauternes 1989 (NR) (6/15/90) (BT)
87 CHATEAU LES JUSTICES Sauternes 1988 $28 (2/15/91)
95+ CHATEAU LES JUSTICES Sauternes 1988 $28 (6/15/90) (BT)
75 CHATEAU LES JUSTICES Sauternes 1987 (NA) (6/15/90)
85 CHATEAU LES JUSTICES Sauternes 1986 $16 (12/31/89)
67 CHATEAU LES JUSTICES Sauternes 1983 $15 (1/31/88)
95+ CHATEAU LAFAURIE-PEYRAGUEY Sauternes 1989 (NR) (6/15/90) (BT)
85 CHATEAU LAFAURIE-PEYRAGUEY Sauternes 1988 $35 (4/30/91)
90+ CHATEAU LAFAURIE-PEYRAGUEY Sauternes 1988 Rel: $35 Cur: $35 (6/15/90) (BT)
87 CHATEAU LAFAURIE-PEYRAGUEY Sauternes 1987 Rel: $27 Cur: $27 (6/15/90)
86 CHATEAU LAFAURIE-PEYRAGUEY Sauternes 1986 Rel: $27 Cur: $35 (12/31/89)
85+ CHATEAU LAFAURIE-PEYRAGUEY Sauternes 1986 Rel: $27 Cur: $35 (6/30/88) (BT)
92 CHATEAU LAFAURIE-PEYRAGUEY Sauternes 1985 Rel: $32 Cur: $35 (9/30/88)
91 CHATEAU LAFAURIE-PEYRAGUEY Sauternes 1983 Rel: $24 Cur: $40 (1/31/88)
84 CHATEAU LAMOTHE Sauternes 1988 $16/375ml (3/31/91)
85 CHATEAU LAMOTHE Sauternes 1986 $29 (12/31/89)
80+ CHATEAU LAMOTHE Sauternes 1986 $29 (6/30/88) (BT)
85+ CHATEAU LAMOTHE-DESPUJOLS Sauternes 1989 (NR) (6/15/90) (BT)
84 CHATEAU LAMOTHE-DESPUJOLS Sauternes 1987 (NA) (6/15/90)
85+ CHATEAU LAMOTHE-GUIGNARD Sauternes 1989 (NR) (6/15/90) (BT)
85+ CHATEAU LAMOTHE-GUIGNARD Sauternes 1988 $35 (6/15/90) (BT)
77 CHATEAU LAMOTHE-GUIGNARD Sauternes 1987 (NA) (6/15/90)
75+ CHATEAU LAMOTHE-GUIGNARD Sauternes 1986 $30 (6/30/88) (BT)
80+ CHATEAU LANGE Sauternes 1988 (NR) (6/15/90) (BT)
78 CHATEAU LANGE Sauternes 1987 (NA) (6/15/90)
85+ CHATEAU LIOT Barsac 1989 (NR) (6/15/90) (BT)
80+ CHATEAU LIOT Barsac 1988 $25 (6/15/90) (BT)
87 CHATEAU LIOT Barsac 1986 $22 (12/31/89)
84 CHATEAU LIOT Barsac 1985 $9.25 (5/31/88)
56 CHATEAU LIOT Barsac 1983 $11.25 (4/01/86)
85+ CHATEAU DE MALLE Sauternes 1989 (NR) (6/15/90) (BT)
85+ CHATEAU DE MALLE Sauternes 1988 (NR) (6/15/90) (BT)
81 CHATEAU DE MALLE Sauternes 1987 (NA) (6/15/90)
85+ CHATEAU DE MALLE Sauternes 1986 (NR) (6/30/88) (BT)
84 CHATEAU DE MALLE Sauternes Comte de Bournazel 1981 $13 (8/31/86)
80+ CHATEAU MENOTA Barsac 1988 (NR) (6/15/90) (BT)
78 CHATEAU MENOTA Barsac 1987 (NA) (6/15/90)
75+ CHATEAU MONT-JOYE Barsac 1989 (NR) (6/15/90) (BT)
63 CHATEAU MONT-JOYE Barsac 1987 (NA) (6/15/90)
80+ DOMAINE DE MONTEILS Sauternes 1988 (NR) (6/15/90) (BT)
72 DOMAINE DE MONTEILS Sauternes 1987 (NA) (6/15/90)
85+ CHATEAU NAIRAC Barsac 1989 (NR) (6/15/90) (BT)
85+ CHATEAU NAIRAC Barsac 1988 $30 (6/15/90) (BT)
81 CHATEAU NAIRAC Barsac 1987 $31 (6/15/90)
77 CHATEAU NAIRAC Barsac 1986 $31 (12/31/89)
85+ CHATEAU NAIRAC Barsac 1986 $31 (6/30/88) (BT)
92 CHATEAU NAIRAC Barsac 1983 $15 (4/15/87)
62 CHATEAU PAJOT Sauternes 1983 $8 (1/31/88)
78 CHATEAU PASCAUD-VILLEFRANCHE Sauternes 1986 $24 (12/31/89)

65 CHATEAU PASCAUD-VILLEFRANCHE Sauternes 1983 $10 (1/31/88)
70 CHATEAU PIADA Barsac 1983 $11 (1/31/88)
85+ CHATEAU PIADA Sauternes 1989 (NR) (6/15/90) (BT)
90+ CHATEAU PIADA Sauternes 1988 (NR) (6/15/90) (BT)
86 CHATEAU PIADA Sauternes 1987 $35 (3/31/91)
76 CHATEAU PIADA Sauternes 1987 (NA) (6/15/90)
85+ CHATEAU PIOT-DAVID Barsac 1989 (NR) (6/15/90) (BT)
70+ CHATEAU PROST Barsac 1989 (NR) (6/15/90) (BT)
85+ CHATEAU RABAUD-PROMIS Sauternes 1989 (NR) (6/15/90) (BT)
95+ CHATEAU RABAUD-PROMIS Sauternes 1988 $35 (6/15/90) (BT)
83 CHATEAU RABAUD-PROMIS Sauternes 1987 (NA) (6/15/90)
95+ CHATEAU RABAUD-PROMIS Sauternes 1986 $28 (6/30/88) (BT)
90 CHATEAU RABAUD-PROMIS Sauternes 1983 $54 (1/31/88)
93 CHATEAU RAYMOND-LAFON Sauternes 1983 Rel: $38 Cur: $60 (1/31/88)
80+ CHATEAU DE RAYNE-VIGNEAU Sauternes 1989 (NR) (6/15/90) (BT)
85+ CHATEAU DE RAYNE-VIGNEAU Sauternes 1988 Cur: $31 (6/15/90) (BT)
77 CHATEAU DE RAYNE-VIGNEAU Sauternes 1987 (NA) (6/15/90)
86 CHATEAU DE RAYNE-VIGNEAU Sauternes 1986 Rel: $49 Cur: $49 (12/31/89)
80+ CHATEAU DE RAYNE-VIGNEAU Sauternes 1986 Rel: $49 Cur: $49 (6/30/88) (BT)
77 CHATEAU DE RAYNE-VIGNEAU Sauternes 1983 Rel: $17 Cur: $20 (1/31/88)
90+ CHATEAU RIEUSSEC Sauternes 1989 (NR) (6/15/90) (BT)
95+ CHATEAU RIEUSSEC Sauternes 1988 Rel: $50 Cur: $50 (6/15/90) (BT)
89 CHATEAU RIEUSSEC Sauternes 1987 Rel: $31 Cur: $31 (6/15/90)
80 CHATEAU RIEUSSEC Sauternes 1986 Rel: $50 Cur: $50 (12/31/89)
86 CHATEAU RIEUSSEC Sauternes 1985 Rel: $38 Cur: $38 (5/31/88)
94 CHATEAU RIEUSSEC Sauternes 1983 Rel: $52 Cur: $57 (1/31/88)
93 CHATEAU RIEUSSEC Sauternes 1983 Rel: $52 Cur: $57 (3/16/86) CS
86 CHATEAU RIEUSSEC Sauternes 1982 Rel: $6.50 Cur: $25/375ml (2/01/85)
90 CHATEAU RIEUSSEC Sauternes 1981 Rel: $14.50 Cur: $32 (12/01/84)
80+ CHATEAU ROLLAND Barsac 1988 (NR) (6/15/90) (BT)
77 CHATEAU ROLLAND Barsac 1987 (NA) (6/15/90)
80+ CHATEAU ROMER DU HAYOT Sauternes 1989 (NR) (6/15/90) (BT)
72 CHATEAU ROMER DU HAYOT Sauternes 1988 $17/375ml (4/30/91)
85+ CHATEAU ROMER DU HAYOT Sauternes 1988 $17 (6/15/90) (BT)
78 CHATEAU ROMER DU HAYOT Sauternes 1986 $22 (12/31/89)
85+ CHATEAU ROMER DU HAYOT Sauternes 1986 $22 (6/30/88) (BT)
72 CHATEAU ROMER DU HAYOT Sauternes 1983 $19 (1/31/88)
67 CHATEAU ROMER DU HAYOT Sauternes 1983 $19 (10/15/86)
82 CHATEAU ROMER DU HAYOT Sauternes 1982 $13 (10/16/85)
85+ CHATEAU ROUMIEU-LACOSTE Barsac 1989 (NR) (6/15/90) (BT)
90+ CHATEAU SIGALAS RABAUD Sauternes 1989 (NR) (6/15/90) (BT)
77 CHATEAU SIGALAS RABAUD Sauternes 1986 Rel: $42 Cur: $42 (12/31/89)
82 CHATEAU SIGALAS RABAUD Sauternes 1985 Rel: $41 Cur: $41 (7/15/91)
88 CHATEAU SIGALAS RABAUD Sauternes 1983 Rel: $24 Cur: $29 (1/31/88)
85+ CHATEAU ST.-MARC Barsac 1989 (NR) (6/15/90) (BT)
69 CHATEAU ST.-MARC Barsac 1987 (NA) (6/15/90)
85+ CHATEAU SUAU Barsac 1989 (NR) (6/15/90) (BT)
80+ CHATEAU SUAU Barsac 1988 (NR) (6/15/90) (BT)
85+ CHATEAU SUAU Barsac 1986 (6/30/88) (BT)
90+ CHATEAU SUDUIRAUT Sauternes 1989 (NR) (6/15/90) (BT)
85+ CHATEAU SUDUIRAUT Sauternes 1988 Rel: $45 Cur: $45 (6/15/90) (BT)
85 CHATEAU SUDUIRAUT Sauternes 1986 Rel: $35 Cur: $35 (12/31/89)
81 CHATEAU SUDUIRAUT Sauternes 1985 Cur: $32 (11/30/88) (JS)
81 CHATEAU SUDUIRAUT Sauternes 1984 Cur: $22 (11/30/88) (JS)
85 CHATEAU SUDUIRAUT Sauternes 1983 Rel: $30 Cur: $38 (11/30/88) (JS)
82 CHATEAU SUDUIRAUT Sauternes 1983 Rel: $30 Cur: $38 (1/31/88)
83 CHATEAU SUDUIRAUT Sauternes 1982 Cur: $43 (11/30/88) (JS)
86 CHATEAU SUDUIRAUT Sauternes 1979 Rel: $19 Cur: $40 (11/30/88) (JS)
92 CHATEAU SUDUIRAUT Sauternes 1979 Rel: $19 Cur: $40 (2/16/84) CS
78 CHATEAU SUDUIRAUT Sauternes 1978 Cur: $42 (11/30/88) (JS)
77 CHATEAU SUDUIRAUT Sauternes 1976 Cur: $79 (11/30/88) (JS)
84 CHATEAU SUDUIRAUT Sauternes 1975 Cur: $51 (11/30/88) (JS)
77 CHATEAU SUDUIRAUT Sauternes 1972 Cur: $25 (11/30/88) (JS)
81 CHATEAU SUDUIRAUT Sauternes 1970 Cur: $56 (11/30/88) (JS)
88 CHATEAU SUDUIRAUT Sauternes 1969 Cur: $70 (11/30/88) (JS)
93 CHATEAU SUDUIRAUT Sauternes 1959 Cur: $200 (11/30/88) (JS)
93 CHATEAU SUDUIRAUT Sauternes 1928 Cur: $500 (11/30/88) (JS)
90 CHATEAU SUDUIRAUT Sauternes Cuvée Madame 1982 (NA) (11/30/88) (JS)
85+ CHATEAU LA TOUR BLANCHE Sauternes 1989 (NR) (6/15/90) (BT)
85+ CHATEAU LA TOUR BLANCHE Sauternes 1988 $29 (6/15/90) (BT)
82 CHATEAU LA TOUR BLANCHE Sauternes 1987 (NA) (5/15/90)
79 CHATEAU LA TOUR BLANCHE Sauternes 1986 $26 (12/31/89)
85+ CHATEAU LA TOUR BLANCHE Sauternes 1986 $26 (6/30/88) (BT)
85 CHATEAU LA TOUR BLANCHE Sauternes 1985 $25 (7/15/88)
87 CHATEAU LA TOUR BLANCHE Sauternes 1983 $32 (1/31/88)
79 CHATEAU LA VIOLETTE Sauternes 1987 (NA) (6/15/90)
87 CHATEAU D'YQUEM Sauternes 1986 $310 (2/28/91)
94 CHATEAU D'YQUEM Sauternes 1985 Rel: $225 Cur: $225 (3/31/90)
96 CHATEAU D'YQUEM Sauternes 1984 Rel: $149 Cur: $151 (3/31/90)
97 CHATEAU D'YQUEM Sauternes 1983 Rel: $180 Cur: $229 (1/31/88)
95 CHATEAU D'YQUEM Sauternes 1983 Rel: $180 Cur: $229 (10/15/87) CS
94 CHATEAU D'YQUEM Sauternes 1976 Cur: $290 (12/15/88)
93 CHATEAU D'YQUEM Sauternes 1937 Cur: $2,163/1.5L (12/15/88)

OTHER FRANCE DESSERT

76 CHATEAU LE BARRADIS Monbazillac 1988 $20 (7/15/91)
75 MARC BREDIF Vouvray Vin Moelleux Nectar 1985 $9/375ml (6/15/91)
83 DOMAINE DU CLOS NAUDIN Vouvray Moelleux 1989 $34 (4/30/91)
89 DOMAINE DU CLOS NAUDIN Vouvray Moelleux Réserve 1989 $54 (3/31/91)
86 DOMAINE DE DURBAN Muscat de Beaumes-de-Venise 1988 $15 (3/31/91)
84 PAUL JABOULET AINE Muscat de Beaumes-de-Venise Vin Doux Naturel 1986 $17 (10/15/88)
78 CHATEAU LAURETTE Ste.-Croix-de-Mont 1985 $8.50 (9/30/88)
82 LEYRAT Pineau des Charentes Grande Réserve Sélection Robert Hass NV $23 (3/31/91)
81 M & G Vouvray Moelleux 1988 $10 (3/31/91)
80 DOMAINE DU MAS BLANC Banyuls Vendanges Tardives 1982 $26 (2/28/91)
82 DOMAINE DU MAS BLANC Banyuls Vieilles Vignes 1982 $27 (2/28/91)
85 DOMAINE DU MAS BLANC Banyuls Vieilles Vignes 1976 $40 (2/28/91)

FRANCE
OTHER FRANCE DESSERT

82 DOMAINE DU MAS BLANC Collioure Cuvée Cosprons Levants 1988 $21 (3/31/91)
88 PROSPER MAUFOUX Muscat de Beaumes-de-Venise NV $16 (8/31/89)
87 DOMAINE DE LA MELOTERIE Vouvray Demi-Sec 1989 $9 (6/15/91)
80 DOMAINE LE PEU DE LA MORIETTE Vouvray Moelleux Cuvée Exceptionelle 1989 $19 (6/15/91)
80 CHATEAU DE RICAUD Loupiac 1986 $17/375ml (12/31/89)
80 DOMAINE ST.-SAUVEUR Muscat de Beaumes-de-Venise Vin Doux Naturel 1988 $17 (3/31/91)

OTHER FRANCE RED

78 GILBERT ALQUIER Faugères 1985 $7 (9/30/87)
78 PERE ANSELME Merlot Vin de Pays des Côteaux d'Enserune NV $5.50 (7/15/89)
79 VIGNERONS ARDECHOIS Vin de Pays des Côteaux de l'Ardeche 1988 $4.50 (4/30/90) BB
85 CHATEAU DE BEAUREGARD Côteaux du Languedoc 1986 $3.75 (5/31/88) BB
72 CHATEAU BELLEVUE LA FORET Côtes du Frontonnais 1985 $6 (11/15/87)
83 DANIEL BESSIERE Côteaux du Languedoc 1987 $5 (9/30/89) BB
73 DANIEL BESSIERE Faugères 1987 $6 (9/15/89)
81 DANIEL BESSIERE Minervois 1986 $6 (9/15/89) BB
79 DANIEL BESSIERE St.-Chinian 1987 $6 (8/31/89)
75 BICHOT Vin Rouge NV $3 (8/31/89)
68 BICHOT Vin Rouge NV $3 (2/16/86)
72 BOUCHARD AINE Merlot Vin de Pays de l'Aude NV $5 (6/30/90)
82 DOMAINE DE LA BOUSQUETTE St.-Chinian 1986 $8 (3/31/90)
69 CHATEAU CANET Minervois Cuvée Elevée en Futs Grande Réserve 1988 $6 (5/31/90)
77 CHATEAU CAPENDU Corbières Cuvée Elevée en Futs Grande Réserve 1988 $6 (5/31/90)
81 CHATEAU DU CAYROU Cahors 1985 $8.75 (12/31/88)
75 DOMAINE DU CEDRE Cahors Le Prestige 1987 $14 (3/15/90)
80 DOMAINE DU CEDRE Cahors Le Prestige 1985 $9 (12/31/88)
85 CELLIER DE LA DONA Côtes du Roussillon-Villages 1988 $8.50 (10/15/90) BB
87 CHATEAU DE CHAMBERT Cahors 1986 $12 (8/31/89)
75 CHANTEFLEUR Merlot Vin de Pays d'Oc 1988 $6 (5/31/90)
80 CHANTEFLEUR Cabernet Sauvignon Vin de Pays de l'Ardèche 1988 $6 (5/31/90) BB
81 CHANTOVENT Cabernet Sauvignon Vin de Pays d'Oc Prestige 1988 $6 (3/15/90) BB
78 CHANTOVENT Cabernet Sauvignon Vin de Pays d'Oc Prestige 1987 $5 (10/31/89)
79 CHANTOVENT Cabernet Sauvignon Vin de Pays d'Oc Prestige 1986 $6.50 (5/15/89)
73 CHANTOVENT Merlot Vin de Pays d'Oc Prestige 1988 $6 (3/15/90)
69 CHANTOVENT Merlot Vin de Pays d'Oc Prestige 1986 $6.50 (5/15/89)
76 CHATEAU DE CHARRON 1982 $5 (7/01/85)
74 GUY CHEVALIER Vin de Pays de l'Aude Le Texas 1989 $9 (7/15/91)
79 CHEVALIER DE BEAUBASSIN Cuvée Montgolfier NV $4 (3/31/88)
79 RAOUL CLERGET Prestige de Raoul Clerget NV $3 (7/15/88)
77 CLOS STE. NICOLE Cabernet Sauvignon French-California Cuvée NV $5 (10/31/89)
79 CLOS STE. NICOLE Merlot French-California Cuvée NV $5 (10/31/89)
80 CLOS TRIGUEDINA Cahors 1983 $11 (2/28/91)
82 CLOS TRIGUEDINA Cahors Prince Probus 1985 $17 (2/28/91)
79 CLOS TRIGUEDINA Cahors Prince Probus 1983 $14.25 (12/31/88)
66 JEAN CORDIER Rouge NV $3 (12/15/88)
75 JEAN CORDIER Vin de Table Rouge Français NV $3 (12/15/90)
82 CHATEAU LA DECELLE Côteaux du Tricastin 1989 $7.50 (7/15/91) BB
77 DOMAINE DONA BAISSAS Côtes du Roussillon-Villages 1988 $7 (10/15/90)
77 CHATEAU ETANG DES COLOMBES Corbières Cuvée du Bicentenaire 1986 $9 (3/31/91)
73 CHATEAU ETANG DES COLOMBES Corbières Cuvée du Bicentenaire 1985 $6 (4/15/88)
72 CHATEAU FABAS Minervois 1986 $5.50 (9/15/89)
77 DOMAINE DE FONTSAINTE Corbières Réserve La Demoiselle 1986 $7 (8/31/89)
83 DOMAINE DE FONTSAINTE Corbières Rouge Réserve La Demoiselle 1984 $8 (10/31/87)
70 FORTANT Cabernet Sauvignon Vin de Pays d'Oc 1988 $6 (4/30/91)
70 FORTANT Merlot Vin de Pays d'Oc 1988 $6 (5/31/91)
72 DOMAINES GAVOTY Côtes de Provence Cuvée Clarendon 1987 $8.50 (3/31/90)
67 HERZOG Cabernet Sauvignon Vin de Pays d'Oc 1988 $6 (3/15/90)
88 HERZOG Cabernet Sauvignon Vin de Pays d'Oc NV $7 (3/31/91) BB
75 HERZOG Merlot Vin de Pays d'Oc NV $7 (3/31/91)
76 DOMAINE DES JOUGLA St.-Chinian 1986 $6.75 (5/15/89)
67 DOMAINES LAFRAN-VEYROLLES Bandol 1983 (NA) (8/31/86)
78 LAJOLIE Cabernet Sauvignon Vin de Pays d'Oc 1987 $6 (10/31/88)
81 ROGER MARES Syrah Mas des Bressades 1988 $10.50 (10/31/90)
81 ROGER MARES Syrah Mas des Bressades 1988 $10.50 (10/31/90)
77 MARILYN MERLOT Merlot Vin de Pays de l'Aude 1987 $6 (3/15/90)
85 MAS DE DAUMAS GASSAC Vin de Pays de l'Herault 1987 $23 (10/31/89)
81 MAS DE DAUMAS GASSAC Vin de Pays de l'Herault 1986 $25 (12/31/88)
70 MAS DE GOURGONNIER Côteaux des Baux en Provence 1983 $3.75 (12/16/85)
79 MAS DE GOURGONNIER Côteaux des Baux en Provence Les Baux de Provence 1988 $8.50 (4/30/91)
82 MAS DE GOURGONNIER Côteaux des Baux en Provence Côteaux d'Aix 1984 $5.50 (3/15/87) BB
72 DOMAINE DU MEUNIER Côtes de Gascogne 1985 $5 (5/31/88)
77 CHATEAU MILLEGRAND Minervois 1988 $5 (4/30/90)
77 MOCERI Cabernet Sauvignon Vin de Pays de l'Aude 1987 $4 (6/30/90) BB
78 MOCERI Merlot Vin de Pays de l'Aude 1987 $4 (6/30/90) BB
81 MOILLARD Moillard Rouge NV $4.50 (5/31/88) BB
79 LES PRODUCTEURS DU MONT TAUCH Fitou 1985 $6 (4/15/89)
79 CHATEAU MONTUS Madiran 1985 $10 (4/15/89)
80 CHATEAUX DE MOUJAN Côteaux du Languedoc 1987 $4 (8/31/89)
80 CHATEAU LES MUTS Côtes de Bergerac 1983 $6.50 (11/15/86)
80 CHATEAU LES OLLIEUX Corbières 1988 $5.25 (11/30/90) BB

68 CHATEAU L'OREE DU BOIS 1983 $4 (5/01/86)
79 CHATEAU L'OREE DU BOIS 1982 $4 (3/16/85)
77 DOMAINE D'ORMESSON Vin de Pays d'Oc 1985 $4 (4/15/89)
78 DOMAINES OTT Côtes de Provence Société Civile des Domaines Ott Frères 1987 $22 (5/31/91)
79 CHATEAU DE PADERE Buzet 1986 $5.75 (12/15/88)
63 CHATEAU LA PALME Côtes du Frontonnais 1988 $7 (7/31/91)
80 CHATEAU DE PARAZA Minervois 1985 $6.25 (2/29/88)
67 CHATEAU DE PARAZA Minervois Cuvée Spéciale 1988 $7 (5/31/91)
76 CHATEAU DE PARAZA Minervois Cuvée Spéciale 1986 $6 (10/15/88)
78 CHATEAU PECH DE JAMMES Cahors 1987 $9 (6/30/90)
77 CHATEAU PECH DE JAMMES Cahors 1983 $9.50 (10/15/88)
77 DOMAINE PERRIERE Vin de Pays de l'Aude Les Amandiers 1988 $4.50 (4/15/90)
76 CHATEAU PETIT CHOLET 1983 $3.25 (4/16/85)
75 CHATEAU DE PIBARNON Bandol 1987 $17 (3/15/90)
79 CHATEAU DE PIBARNON Bandol 1985 $17.25 (10/15/88)
70 CHATEAU DE PIBARNON Bandol 1984 (NA) (8/31/86)
75 CHATEAU DE PIBARNON Bandol 1982 $9.75 (10/01/85)
78 PLACE D'ARGENT Cabernet Sauvignon Vin de Pays de l'Aude 1985 $5.50 (4/15/89)
77 PLACE D'ARGENT Merlot Vin de Pays de l'Aude 1987 $5 (4/30/90)
80 PLACE D'ARGENT Merlot Vin de Pays de l'Aude 1985 $5.50 (12/15/88) BB
83 CHATEAU PRADEAUX Bandol 1986 $17.50 (10/31/90)
58 CHATEAU PRADEAUX Bandol Réserve 1981 (NA) (8/31/86) (JS)
76 DOMAINE DU PUGET Merlot Vin de Pays de l'Aude 1988 $4 (6/30/90)
78 PAR E. REYNAUD Vin de Pays de Vaucluse Domaine des Tours 1989 $8 (3/31/91)
75 DOMAINE RICHEAUME Cabernet Sauvignon Côtes de Provence 1988 $15 (10/31/90)
73 DOMAINE RICHEAUME Syrah Côtes de Provence 1988 $15 (10/31/90)
83 LA ROGUE Bandol 1987 $10.50 (11/30/90)
78 DOMAINE LA ROSIERE Syrah Côteaux des Baronnies 1988 $6.50 (2/28/90)
65 MAS DE LA ROUVIERE Bandol 1983 (NA) (8/31/86)
73 MAS DE LA ROUVIERE Bandol 1982 (NA) (8/31/86)
80 MAS DE LA ROUVIERE Bandol 1979 (NA) (8/31/86)
85 LA SABONITE Vin de Table Français NV $5.50 (9/30/88) BB
72 ST.-CESAIRE Vin de Pays des Bouches du Rhône NV $4.25 (6/30/90)
75 ST.-FLORANT Cabernet Sauvignon 1984 $5 (2/28/87)
60 DOMAINE SARDA-MALET Côtes du Roussillon 1986 $7.50 (10/15/90)
74 DOMAINE DE SAULT Corbières 1988 $5 (6/30/90)
79 DOMAINE TEMPIER Bandol 1984 $15 (12/15/87)
78 DOMAINE TEMPIER Bandol 1983 $16 (8/31/87)
73 DOMAINE TEMPIER Bandol 1981 (NA) (8/31/86)
88 DOMAINE TEMPIER Bandol Cuvée Spéciale Cabassaou 1987 $23 (10/31/90)
86 DOMAINE TEMPIER Bandol Cuvée Spéciale La Migoua 1987 $22 (10/31/90)
82 DOMAINE TEMPIER Bandol Cuvée Spéciale La Tourtine 1987 $22 (10/31/90)
60 DOMAINE DE TERREBRUNE Bandol 1982 (NA) (8/31/86)
82 CHATEAU DE TIREGAND Pécharmant 1985 $8 (10/31/88)
78 DOMAINE DE TREVALLON Côteaux d'Aix en Provence Les Baux 1987 $18 (3/31/90)
87 DOMAINE DE TREVALLON Côteaux d'Aix en Provence Les Baux 1986 $21 (4/15/89)
82 DOMAINE DE TREVALLON Côteaux d'Aix en Provence Les Baux 1985 $13 (2/29/88)
71 CHATEAU TRINITE VALROSE Ile de Patires 1985 $6 (11/15/87)
76 TROUBADOUR Merlot Vin de Pays de l'Aude 1987 $5 (8/31/89)
74 CHATEAU DE LA TUILERIE Costières du Gard 1986 $4.75 (6/30/88)
77 CHATEAU DE LA TUILERIE Costières du Gard 1985 $6 (2/15/87) BB
67 CHATEAU VANNIERES Bandol 1986 $15 (9/15/89)
80 CHATEAU VANNIERES Bandol 1983 (NA) (8/31/86) (JS)
80 CHATEAU VANNIERES Côtes de Provence La Provence de Vannières 1986 $15 (8/31/89)
89 CHATEAU VIGNELAURE Côteaux d'Aix en Provence 1981 $10 (10/01/84)
78 CLOS DE VILLEMAJOU Corbières 1988 $6 (4/30/90)
71 CLOS DE VILLEMAJOU Corbières 1985 $7.50 (5/31/90)
68 DOMAINE DE LA VIVONNE Bandol 1981 (NA) (8/31/86)

OTHER FRANCE SPARKLING

78 LES ACACIAS Brut Crémant de Bourgogne Cépage Chardonnay NV $11 (6/15/90)
61 AUBEL Brut Blanc de Blancs NV $6 (6/01/86)
70 COMTE DE BAILLY Brut Crémant de Bourgogne 1983 $8 (10/15/86)
84 DOMAINE DU BICHERON Blanc de Blancs Crémant de Bourgogne NV $12 (3/31/90)
81 MAISTRE BLANQUETIER Brut Blanquette de Limoux Le Berceau NV $9 (4/15/90)
70 BLANQUETTE DE LIMOUX Brut Blanc de Blancs Blanquette de Limoux Cuvée Réserve NV $9 (5/31/87)
81 BOUVET Brut Saumur Ladubay Tresor NV $44 (10/15/90)
84 BOUVET Brut Saumur Saphir 1985 $14 (6/15/90)
87 BOUVET Brut Saumur Saphir 1985 $14 (10/15/88)
75 BOUVET Brut Saumur Signature NV $11.50 (6/15/90)
85 BOUVET Brut Saumur Signature NV $11.50 (10/15/88)
80 BOUVET Brut Rosé NV $10 (6/15/90)
80 BOUVET Brut Rosé Excellence NV $12 (6/15/90)
85 BOUVET Brut Rosé Excellence NV $12 (10/15/88)
72 BOUVET Rubis NV $12 (6/15/90)
86 BOUVET Rubis NV $12 (9/30/88)
79 BRUMMELL Blanc de Blancs Carte Noir NV $7.25 (6/15/90)
80 LE CARDINALE Brut NV $5.25 (6/15/90) BB
70 BARON CHAGALE Brut Blanc de Blancs NV $6 (6/15/90)
74 PAUL CHAMBLAIN Brut Blanc de Blancs NV $6.75 (6/15/90)
79 CHARBAUT FRERES Brut Blanc de Blancs Crémant de Bourgogne 1986 $11.50 (12/31/90)
79 CHARBAUT FRERES Brut Rosé Crémant de Bourgogne 1986 $11.50 (12/31/90)
82 DARGENT Brut Blanc de Blancs Côtes du Jura 1984 $10 (3/31/88)
83 DARGENT Brut Blanc de Blancs Côtes du Jura Chardonnay 1988 $10.50 (6/15/90)
86 DARGENT Brut Rosé Côtes du Jura 1984 $10 (3/31/88)
79 BERNARD DELMAS Brut Blanquette de Limoux NV $14 (3/31/90)
88 CHARLES DE FERE Brut Tradition NV $12 (6/15/90)
77 CHARLES DE FERE Brut Blanc de Blancs Réserve NV $10 (6/15/90)
70 CHARLES DE FERE Brut Rosé NV $10 (6/15/90)
63 LA FOLIE Brut Blanc de Blancs Réserve NV $5.50 (6/15/90)
83 GEORGES BLANC Blanc de Blanc NV $9 (12/31/87)
76 GRAND IMPERIAL Brut NV $4.50 (6/15/90)
82 GRANDIN Brut Ingrandes-Sur-Loire NV $10 (6/15/90)
74 GRATIEN Saumur Rouge NV $12 (7/15/88)
83 GRATIEN Brut Saumur NV $9.25 (6/15/90)
74 PHILIPPE HERARD Brut Blanc de Blancs NV $9.50 (6/15/90)
81 DE JESSY Extra Dry NV $9 (6/15/90)
57 KRITER Blanc de Blancs Brut de Brut 1985 $9 (6/15/90)

83	KRITER Brut Blanc de Blancs Extra Leger 1983 $6 (5/31/87) BB
57	KRITER Brut Blanc de Blancs Imperial 1983 $12 (6/15/90)
71	KRITER Brut Rosé NV $9 (6/15/90)
71	KRITER Demi-Sec NV $9 (6/15/90)
83	KRITER Demi-Sec Délicatesse NV $12 (6/15/90)
84	LANGLOIS-CHATEAU Brut Crémant de Loire NV $10.50 (7/15/88)
86	LANGLOIS-CHATEAU Rosé Saumur Crémant NV $10.50 (7/15/88)
81	LAURENS Blanc de Blancs Blanquette de Limoux Clos des Demoiselles 1986 $11 (12/31/90)
84	DOMAINE DE MARTINOLES Brut Blanquette de Limoux NV $8 (4/15/90) BB
82	MONMOUSSIN Brut Touraine Etoile 1986 $13 (12/31/90)
79	MONMOUSSIN Brut Touraine Monmousseau 1983 $11 (2/15/88)
69	MONMOUSSIN Brut Vouvray Cuvée du Centenaire 1983 $11 (1/31/88)
81	MONMOUSSIN Extra Dry Vouvray 1985 $13 (12/31/90)
65	MURE Crémant d'Alsace Réserve NV $11.50 (5/31/87)
79	MURE Brut Crémant d'Alsace Réserve NV $7 (6/15/90)
80	JEAN PHILIPPE Brut Blanquette de Limoux 1986 $10.25 (6/15/90)
80	JEAN PHILIPPE Brut Blanquette de Limoux NV $9.75 (1/31/88)
84	CHATEAU DE POCE Brut Crémant de Loire 1982 $12 (7/31/88)
81	CHATEAU DE POCE Brut Touraine Crémant de Blancs NV $10.75 (10/15/88)
78	DOMAINE ROBERT Brut Blanc de Blancs Blanquette de Limoux 1986 $8.75 (6/15/90)
77	DOMAINE ROBERT Brut Blanc de Blancs Blanquette de Limoux 1983 $8 (1/31/88)
85	SILVER CLOUD Brut Blanc de Blancs Blanquette de Limoux 1985 $9 (4/15/90)
87	VARICHON & CLERC Brut Blanc de Blancs NV $7 (12/31/89) BB
82	VARICHON & CLERC Demi-Sec NV $7 (1/31/90) BB
78	VEUVE AMIOT Brut Saumur Cuvée Haute Tradition NV $13 (3/31/90)
83	ALSACE WILLM Brut Crémant d'Alsace NV $10.50 (4/15/90)
83	WOLFBERGER Crémant d'Alsace NV $12 (7/31/89)

OTHER FRANCE WHITE

70	PHILIPPE ANTOINE Chardonnay 1986 $5 (3/31/88)
75	DOMAINE AUFFRAY Chardonnay Vin de Pays de l'Yonne 1988 $8 (4/15/90)
77	BICHOT Côtes de Duras 1987 $4 (5/15/89)
75	BICHOT Côtes de Duras 1986 $3.50 (12/31/88)
74	BOUCHARD AINE Chardonnay Vin de Pays de l'Aude 1987 $6.50 (9/30/88)
75	BOUCHARD PERE & FILS Chardonnay Vin de Pays d'Oc Première 1989 $9 (4/30/91)

79	CHANTEFLEUR Chardonnay Vin de Pays d'Oc 1988 $6 (4/30/90)
75	CHEVALIER DE BEAUBASSIN Cuvée Montgolfier NV $3.75 (5/31/88)
68	CHEVALIER DE BEAUBASSIN Chardonnay Vin de Pays d'Oc 1986 $4.75 (4/15/88)
75	CLOS STE. MAGDELEINE Cassis 1984 $12 (11/15/87)
72	JEAN CORDIER Vin de Table Blanc Français NV $3 (12/31/90)
80	GEORGES DUBOEUF Beaujolais Blanc 1989 $9 (11/30/90)
69	GEORGES DUBOEUF Beaujolais Blanc 1986 $8.50 (7/31/87)
58	GEORGES DUBOEUF Beaujolais Blanc 1985 $9.50 (3/31/87)
80	GEORGES DUBOEUF Chardonnay Vin de Pays d'Oc 1989 $6.50 (11/15/90) BB
64	GEORGES DUBOEUF Chardonnay Vin de Pays d'Oc 1986 $5 (7/31/87)
46	CHATEAU DE FONTBLANCHE Cassis E. Bodin 1983 $6.50 (11/16/85)
73	DOMAINE DE FONTSAINTE Corbières Gris de Gris NV $7 (10/31/87)
69	FORTANT Chardonnay Vin de Pays d'Oc 1989 $6 (5/31/91)
76	HERZOG Chardonnay Vin de Pays d'Oc 1989 $9 (3/31/91)
76	LOUIS JADOT Beaujolais Blanc Le Bienvenu 1985 $11 (3/31/87)
80	DOMAINE DES JOUGLA Limoux 1988 $8 (3/31/90)
80	LABOURE-ROI Chardonnay Vin de Pays d'Oc 1986 $7 (3/31/88) BB
73	LAROCHE Chardonnay 1987 $7 (3/31/88)
70	LAROCHE Chardonnay 1986 $7 (8/31/87)
73	LAROCHE Chardonnay Vin de Pays l'Ile de Beaute 1987 $7 (10/31/89)
72	LOUIS LATOUR Chardonnay Vin de Pays des Côteaux de l'Ardeche 1986 $8.50 (12/31/88)
78	PROSPER MAUFOUX Beaujolais Blanc 1984 $7.75 (3/31/87)
85	MAS DE DAUMAS GASSAC Vin de Pays de l'Herault NV $37 (3/31/90)
68	LES PRODUCTEURS DU MONT TAUCH Corbières 1987 $5 (2/15/89)
74	DOMAINE DU MONTMARIN Vin de Pays des Côtes de Thongue Cépage Marsanne 1987 $5 (2/15/89)
75	MOREAU Moreau Blanc NV $4 (3/31/87)
74	DOMAINE DE PETIT ROUBIE Sauvignon Blanc Côteaux du Languedoc Picpoul de Pinet 1988 $7 (3/31/90)
80	DOMAINE DE POUY Vin de Pays des Côtes de Gascogne Cépage Ugni Blanc 1989 $5 (11/30/90) BB
65	ST.-FLORANT Chardonnay 1985 $5 (2/15/87)
82	DOMAINE ST. MARTIN DE LA GARRIGUE Chardonnay Vin de Pays des Côteaux de Bessilles 1989 $12 (4/30/91)
86	DOMAINE DU TARIQUET Vin de Pays des Côtes de Gascogne 1989 $5.75 (11/15/90) BB
73	CHATEAU DE LA TUILERIE Costières du Gard 1985 $4.50 (1/31/87)

GERMANY
RIESLING/MOSEL-SAAR-RUWER

86 BAUM Eiswein Mosel-Saar-Ruwer Ockenheimer St. Rochuskapelle 1983 $24.50 (10/01/84)
79 BAUM Qualitätswein Mosel-Saar-Ruwer Piesporter Michelsberg 1983 $4 (4/01/84)
85 BAUM Spätlese Mosel-Saar-Ruwer Piesporter Goldtropchen 1983 $11 (10/01/84)
77 BAUM Spätlese Mosel-Saar-Ruwer Weingartener Trappenberg 1983 $5 (10/01/84)
78 BISCHOFLICHE WEINGUTER Auslese Mosel-Saar-Ruwer Drhoner Hofberger 1988 (NA) (9/30/89) (JS)
90 BISCHOFLICHE WEINGUTER Auslese Mosel-Saar-Ruwer Kassler Neis'chen 1988 (NA) (9/30/89) (JS)
86 BISCHOFLICHE WEINGUTER Auslese Mosel-Saar-Ruwer Kassler Neis'chen 1983 $10.50 (4/01/85)
79 BISCHOFLICHE WEINGUTER Kabinett Mosel-Saar-Ruwer Trittenheimer Apotheke 1983 $8 (5/01/85)
84 BISCHOFLICHE WEINGUTER Spätlese Mosel-Saar-Ruwer Ayler Kupp 1988 (NA) (9/30/89) (JS)
76 BISCHOFLICHE WEINGUTER Spätlese Mosel-Saar-Ruwer Kaseler Nies'chen 1983 $8.50 (5/01/85)
85 BISCHOFLICHE WEINGUTER Spätlese Mosel-Saar-Ruwer Trittenheimer Apotheke 1988 (NA) (9/30/89) (JS)
86 BISCHOFLICHES PRIESTERSEMINAR Auslese Mosel-Saar-Ruwer Erdener Treppchen 1985 $14 (11/30/87)
92 JOH. JOS. CHRISTOFFEL Auslese Mosel-Saar-Ruwer Erdener Treppchen 1988 (NA) (9/30/89) (JS)
89 JOH. JOS. CHRISTOFFEL Auslese Mosel-Saar-Ruwer Erdener Treppchen 1988 (NA) (9/30/89) (JS)
84 JOH. JOS. CHRISTOFFEL Spätlese Mosel-Saar-Ruwer Erdener Treppchen 1988 $10 (9/30/89) (JS)
85 JOH. JOS. CHRISTOFFEL Spätlese Mosel-Saar-Ruwer Urziger Würzgarten 1988 (NA) (9/30/89) (JS)
85 WEGELER DEINHARD Auslese Mosel-Saar-Ruwer Bernkasteler Graben 1989 $22 (12/15/90) (JS)
85 WEGELER DEINHARD Auslese Mosel-Saar-Ruwer Wehlener Sonnenuhr 1988 $17.50 (9/30/89) (JS)
83 WEGELER DEINHARD Kabinett Mosel-Saar-Ruwer Bernkasteler Badstube 1989 $10.50 (12/15/90) (JS)
79 WEGELER DEINHARD Kabinett Mosel-Saar-Ruwer Bernkasteler Badstube 1988 $9 (9/30/89) (JS)
86 WEGELER DEINHARD Kabinett Mosel-Saar-Ruwer Wehlener Sonnenuhr 1989 $13.50 (12/15/90) (JS)
73 WEGELER DEINHARD Kabinett Mosel-Saar-Ruwer Wehlener Sonnenuhr 1985 $10 (10/15/87)
91 WEGELER DEINHARD Spätlese Mosel-Saar-Ruwer Bernkasteler Doctor 1986 (NA) (4/15/89) (JS)
81 WEGELER DEINHARD Spätlese Mosel-Saar-Ruwer Bernkasteler Graben 1989 $17 (12/15/90) (JS)
84 WEGELER DEINHARD Spätlese Mosel-Saar-Ruwer Bernkasteler Graben 1988 $14.50 (9/30/89) (JS)
83 WEGELER DEINHARD Spätlese Mosel-Saar-Ruwer Graacher Himmelreich 1989 $17 (12/15/90) (JS)
87 WEGELER DEINHARD Spätlese Mosel-Saar-Ruwer Wehlener Sonnenuhr 1989 $17 (12/15/90) (JS)
88 WEGELER DEINHARD Spätlese Mosel-Saar-Ruwer Wehlener Sonnenuhr 1988 $15 (9/30/89) (JS)
88 WEGELER DEINHARD Spätlese Mosel-Saar-Ruwer Wehlener Sonnenuhr 1986 (NA) (4/15/89) (JS)
84 WEGELER DEINHARD Spätlese Mosel-Saar-Ruwer Wehlener Sonnenuhr 1985 (NA) (4/15/89) (JS)
90 DR. FISCHER Auslese Mosel-Saar-Ruwer Ockfener Bockstein 1983 $12 (3/16/85)
94 DR. FISCHER Auslese Mosel-Saar-Ruwer Wawerner Herrenberg 1988 (NA) (9/30/89) (JS)
85 DR. FISCHER Kabinett Mosel-Saar-Ruwer Ockfener Bockstein 1988 $13 (9/30/89) (JS)
81 DR. FISCHER Qualitätswein Mosel-Saar-Ruwer Ockfener Bockstein 1988 $6 (9/30/89) (JS)
83 DR. FISCHER Spätlese Mosel-Saar-Ruwer Ockfener Bockstein 1988 $15 (9/30/89) (JS)
88 DR. FISCHER Spätlese Mosel-Saar-Ruwer Ockfener Bockstein 1985 $13 (5/15/87)
81 FRIEDRICH-WILHELM-GYMNASIUM Auslese Mosel-Saar-Ruwer Graacher Himmelreich 1988 (NA) (9/30/89) (JS)
82 FRIEDRICH-WILHELM-GYMNASIUM Auslese Mosel-Saar-Ruwer Mehringer Blattenberg 1989 (NA) (12/15/90) (JS)
95 FRIEDRICH-WILHELM-GYMNASIUM Auslese Mosel-Saar-Ruwer Mehringer Goldkupp 1988 $30 (9/30/89) (JS)
82 FRIEDRICH-WILHELM-GYMNASIUM Auslese Mosel-Saar-Ruwer Trittenheimer Apotheke 1989 $19 (12/15/90) (JS)
90 FRIEDRICH-WILHELM-GYMNASIUM Beerenauslese Mosel-Saar-Ruwer Graacher Himmelreich 1989 $150 (12/15/90) (JS)
84 FRIEDRICH-WILHELM-GYMNASIUM Kabinett Mosel-Saar-Ruwer Graacher Himmelreich 1989 $10 (12/15/90) (JS)
83 FRIEDRICH-WILHELM-GYMNASIUM Spätlese Mosel-Saar-Ruwer Falkensteiner Hofberg 1989 (NA) (12/15/90) (JS)
80 FRIEDRICH-WILHELM-GYMNASIUM Spätlese Mosel-Saar-Ruwer Oberemmeler Rosenberg 1989 (NA) (12/15/90) (JS)
74 GEBERT Qualitätswein Mosel-Saar-Ruwer Ockfener Bockstein 1986 $6 (11/30/87)
82 GEBERT Qualitätswein Mosel-Saar-Ruwer Ockfener Bockstein 1985 $6.50 (5/15/87)
85 GOLDENER OKTOBER Qualitätswein Mosel-Saar-Ruwer Piesporter Michelsberg 1987 $7 (11/30/88)
81 FRITZ HAAG Auslese Mosel-Saar-Ruwer Brauneberger Juffer-Sonnenuhr 1989 $150 (12/15/90) (JS)

86 FRITZ HAAG Auslese Mosel-Saar-Ruwer Brauneberger Juffer-Sonnenuhr 1988 (NA) (9/30/89) (JS)
85 FRITZ HAAG Auslese Mosel-Saar-Ruwer Brauneberger Juffer-Sonnenuhr (AP16) 1988 (NA) (9/30/89) (JS)
90 FRITZ HAAG Auslese Mosel-Saar-Ruwer Brauneberger Juffer-Sonnenuhr Gold Cap 1989 $150 (12/15/90) (JS)
92 FRITZ HAAG Auslese Mosel-Saar-Ruwer Brauneberger Juffer-Sonnenuhr Long Gold Cap 1989 $150 (12/15/90) (JS)
85 FRITZ HAAG Kabinett Mosel-Saar-Ruwer Brauneberger Juffer-Sonnenuhr 1989 $18 (12/15/90) (JS)
83 FRITZ HAAG Kabinett Mosel-Saar-Ruwer Brauneberger Juffer-Sonnenuhr 1988 (NA) (9/30/89) (JS)
70 FRITZ HAAG Kabinett Mosel-Saar-Ruwer Brauneberger Juffer-Sonnenuhr 1985 $9 (6/30/87)
86 FRITZ HAAG Spätlese Mosel-Saar-Ruwer Brauneberger Juffer-Sonnenuhr 1989 $27 (12/15/90) (JS)
86 FRITZ HAAG Spätlese Mosel-Saar-Ruwer Brauneberger Juffer-Sonnenuhr 1988 (NA) (9/30/89) (JS)
91 FRITZ HAAG Spätlese Mosel-Saar-Ruwer Brauneberger Juffer-Sonnenuhr 1986 (NA) (4/15/89) (JS)
97 FRITZ HAAG Spätlese Mosel-Saar-Ruwer Brauneberger Juffer-Sonnenuhr 1985 (NA) (4/15/89) (JS)
88 REINHOLD HAART Auslese Mosel-Saar-Ruwer Piesporter Goldtröpfchen 1988 (NA) (9/30/89) (JS)
88 REINHOLD HAART Kabinett Mosel-Saar-Ruwer Piesporter Goldtröpfchen 1988 (NA) (9/30/89) (JS)
92 REINHOLD HAART Spätlese Mosel-Saar-Ruwer Piesporter Goldtröpfchen 1988 (NA) (9/30/89) (JS)
91 REINHOLD HAART Spätlese Mosel-Saar-Ruwer Piesporter Goldtröpfchen (AP6) 1988 (NA) (9/30/89) (JS)
78 REINHOLD HAART Spätlese Mosel-Saar-Ruwer Piesporter Goldtröpfchen 1985 (NA) (4/15/89) (JS)
68 HAVEMEYER Spätlese Mosel-Saar-Ruwer Piesporter Goldtröpfchen 1985 $17 (11/30/87)
81 DR. HEIDEMANNS-BERGWEILER Auslese Mosel-Saar-Ruwer Bernkasteler Alte Badstube am Doctorberg 1988 (NA) (9/30/89) (JS)
79 DR. HEIDEMANNS-BERGWEILER Auslese Mosel-Saar-Ruwer Graacher Himmelreich 1988 (NA) (9/30/89) (JS)
85 DR. HEIDEMANNS-BERGWEILER Spätlese Mosel-Saar-Ruwer Bernkasteler Badstube 1988 (NA) (9/30/89) (JS)
85 DR. HEIDEMANNS-BERGWEILER Spätlese Mosel-Saar-Ruwer Bernkasteler Doctor 1986 (NA) (4/15/89) (JS)
88 DR. HEIDEMANNS-BERGWEILER Spätlese Mosel-Saar-Ruwer Wehlener Sonnenuhr 1988 (NA) (9/30/89) (JS)
96 IMMICH-BATTERIEBERG Auslese Mosel-Saar-Ruwer 1988 (NA) (9/30/89) (JS)
96 IMMICH-BATTERIEBERG Spätlese Mosel-Saar-Ruwer Enkircher Batterieberg 1988 (NA) (9/30/89) (JS)
79 KARL JOSTOCK-THUL Kabinett Mosel-Saar-Ruwer Piesporter Treppchen 1983 $4.75 (11/01/84)
84 HERIBERT KERPEN Auslese Mosel-Saar-Ruwer Wehlener Sonnenuhr (AP12) 1988 $15 (9/30/89) (JS)
90 HERIBERT KERPEN Spätlese Mosel-Saar-Ruwer Wehlener Sonnenuhr 1988 $12 (9/30/89) (JS)
86 KESSELSTATT Auslese Mosel-Saar-Ruwer Josephshöfer 1989 $39 (12/15/90)
92 KESSELSTATT Auslese Mosel-Saar-Ruwer Oberemmeler Karlsberg 1989 $32 (12/15/90)
87 KESSELSTATT Auslese Mosel-Saar-Ruwer Scharzhofberger 1989 $25 (12/15/90)
92 KESSELSTATT Auslese Mosel-Saar-Ruwer Scharzhofberger Gold Cap 1989 $48 (12/15/90)
94 KESSELSTATT Beerenauslese Mosel-Saar-Ruwer Scharzhofberger 1989 $220 (12/15/90)
90 KESSELSTATT Eiswein Mosel-Saar-Ruwer Oberemmeler Karlsberg 1983 $150 (4/30/89)
77 KESSELSTATT Kabinett Mosel-Saar-Ruwer Graacher Himmelreich 1988 $10 (12/15/90)
87 KESSELSTATT Kabinett Mosel-Saar-Ruwer Josephshöfer 1989 $8.50 (12/15/90)
90 KESSELSTATT Kabinett Mosel-Saar-Ruwer Josephshöfer 1988 $14 (9/30/89) (JS)
84 KESSELSTATT Kabinett Mosel-Saar-Ruwer Piesporter Goldtröpfchen 1988 (NA) (9/30/89) (JS)
84 KESSELSTATT Kabinett Mosel-Saar-Ruwer Scharzhofberger 1989 $11 (12/15/90)
82 KESSELSTATT Qualitätswein Mosel-Saar-Ruwer Berkastler Badstube 1989 $8 (12/15/90)
83 KESSELSTATT Qualitätswein Mosel-Saar-Ruwer Josephshöfer 1989 $7 (12/15/90)
85 KESSELSTATT Spätlese Mosel-Saar-Ruwer Bernkastler Lay 1989 $13 (12/15/90)
84 KESSELSTATT Spätlese Mosel-Saar-Ruwer Josephshöfer 1989 $14 (12/15/90)
94 KESSELSTATT Spätlese Mosel-Saar-Ruwer Kaseler Nies'chen 1988 $20 (9/30/89) (JS)
82 KESSELSTATT Spätlese Mosel-Saar-Ruwer Ockfener Bockstein 1989 $16 (12/15/90)
86 KESSELSTATT Spätlese Mosel-Saar-Ruwer Piesporter Goldtröpfchen 1989 $15 (12/15/90)
90 KESSELSTATT Spätlese Mosel-Saar-Ruwer Scharzhofberger 1989 $13 (12/15/90)
94 KESSELSTATT Trockenbeerenauslese Mosel-Saar-Ruwer Scharzhofberger 1989 $150 (12/15/90)
84 LEONARD KREUSCH Kabinett Mosel-Saar-Ruwer Bereich Bernkastel 1986 $6 (11/30/88)
84 LEONARD KREUSCH Kabinett Mosel-Saar-Ruwer Zeltinger Himmelreich 1986 $5.75 (11/30/88)
83 J. LAUERBURG Spätlese Mosel-Saar-Ruwer Bernkasteler Doctor 1986 (NA) (4/15/89) (JS)
82 J. LAUERBURG Spätlese Mosel-Saar-Ruwer Bernkasteler Doctor 1985 (NA) (4/15/89) (JS)
78 J. LAUERBURG Spätlese Mosel-Saar-Ruwer Bernkasteler Lay 1985 (NA) (4/15/89) (JS)
83 JOSEFINENGRUND LEIWEN Auslese Mosel-Saar-Ruwer Leiwener Laurentiuslay 1985 $11 (1/31/87)
82 JOSEFINENGRUND LEIWEN Kabinett Mosel-Saar-Ruwer Leiwener Klostergarten 1985 $6 (1/31/87)
88 LINGENFELDER Auslese Mosel-Saar-Ruwer Grosskarlbacher Burgweg Scheurebe 1989 $20/375ml (12/15/90) (JS)
88 LINGENFELDER Beerenauslese Mosel-Saar-Ruwer Grosskarlbacher Burgweg Scheurebe 1989 $65/375ml (12/15/90) (JS)
90 LINGENFELDER Spätlese Mosel-Saar-Ruwer Grosskarlbacher Burgweg Scheurebe 1989 $14 (12/15/90) (JS)
88 DR. MEYER Qualitätswein Mosel-Saar-Ruwer Piesporter Michelsberg 1987 $4 (10/15/88) BB
91 MILZ Auslese Mosel-Saar-Ruwer Drhoner Hofberger 1988 (NA) (9/30/89) (JS)
78 MILZ Auslese Mosel-Saar-Ruwer Trittenheimer Felsenkopf 1988 (NA) (9/30/89) (JS)
83 MILZ Spätlese Mosel-Saar-Ruwer Piesporter Hofberg 1988 (NA) (9/30/89) (JS)
83 MILZ Spätlese Mosel-Saar-Ruwer Trittenheimer Altärchen 1988 (NA) (9/30/89) (JS)
90 MONCHHOF Kabinett Mosel-Saar-Ruwer Urziger Würzgarten 1988 $15 (9/30/89) (JS)
86 MONCHHOF Spätlese Mosel-Saar-Ruwer Erdener Treppchen 1988 (NA) (9/30/89) (JS)
84 MONCHHOF Spätlese Mosel-Saar-Ruwer Urziger Würzgarten 1988 (NA) (9/30/89) (JS)
83 MONCHHOF Spätlese Mosel-Saar-Ruwer Wehlener Klosterberg 1988 (NA) (9/30/89) (JS)
89 EGON MULLER Auslese Mosel-Saar-Ruwer Le Gallais Wiltingener Braune Kupp 1989 (NA) (12/15/90) (JS)

93 EGON MULLER Auslese Mosel-Saar-Ruwer Scharzhofberger 1989 (NA) (12/15/90) (JS)
97 EGON MULLER Auslese Mosel-Saar-Ruwer Scharzhofberger Gold Cap 1989 $385 (12/15/90) (JS)
91 EGON MULLER Beerenauslese Mosel-Saar-Ruwer Le Gallais Wiltingener Braune Kupp 1989 (NA) (12/15/90) (JS)
95 EGON MULLER Beerenauslese Mosel-Saar-Ruwer Scharzhofberger 1989 (NA) (12/15/90) (JS)
99 EGON MULLER Beerenauslese Mosel-Saar-Ruwer Scharzhofberger 1988 $70 (9/30/89) (JS)
97 EGON MULLER Eiswein Mosel-Saar-Ruwer Scharzhofberger 1989 (NA) (12/15/90) (JS)
92 EGON MULLER Eiswein Mosel-Saar-Ruwer Scharzhofberger 1988 (NA) (9/30/89) (JS)
86 EGON MULLER Kabinett Mosel-Saar-Ruwer Scharzhofberger 1989 $25 (12/15/90) (JS)
92 EGON MULLER Kabinett Mosel-Saar-Ruwer Scharzhofberger 1988 $13 (9/30/89) (JS)
85 EGON MULLER Spätlese Mosel-Saar-Ruwer Le Gallais Wiltingener Braune Kupp 1989 $29 (12/15/90) (JS)
94 EGON MULLER Spätlese Mosel-Saar-Ruwer Scharzhofberger 1989 $31 (12/15/90) (JS)
95 EGON MULLER Trockenbeerenauslese Mosel-Saar-Ruwer Le Gallais Wiltingener Braune Kupp 1989 (NA) (12/15/90) (JS)
100 EGON MULLER Trockenbeerenauslese Mosel-Saar-Ruwer Scharzhofberger 1989 (NA) (12/15/90) (JS)
83 RUDOLF MULLER Kabinett Mosel-Saar-Ruwer Ockfener Bockstein 1985 $7 (4/15/87)
90 RUDOLF MULLER Kabinett Mosel-Saar-Ruwer Piesporter Goldtröpfchen 1985 $9.50 (4/15/87)
90 RUDOLF MULLER Kabinett Mosel-Saar-Ruwer Piesporter Goldtröpfchen 1983 $7.50 (6/16/85)
78 RUDOLF MULLER Kabinett Mosel-Saar-Ruwer Piesporter Treppchen 1986 $6.75 (1/31/88)
79 RUDOLF MULLER Kabinett Mosel-Saar-Ruwer Piesporter Treppchen 1985 $6 (4/15/87)
76 RUDOLF MULLER Kabinett Mosel-Saar-Ruwer Reiler Mullay-Hofberg 1986 $7.25 (1/31/88)
74 RUDOLF MULLER Kabinett Mosel-Saar-Ruwer Scharzhofberger 1985 $8 (4/15/87)
84 RUDOLF MULLER Qualitätswein Mosel-Saar-Ruwer Scharzhofberger 1985 $6.50 (5/15/87)
72 RUDOLF MULLER Spätlese Mosel-Saar-Ruwer Ockfener Bockstein 1983 $9.25 (5/15/87)
80 RUDOLF MULLER Spätlese Mosel-Saar-Ruwer Piesporter Treppchen 1986 $8.25 (11/30/87)
83 RUDOLF MULLER Spätlese Mosel-Saar-Ruwer Wehlener Sonnenuhr 1986 $8.25 (11/30/87)
92 RUDOLF MULLER Spätlese Mosel-Saar-Ruwer Wehlener Sonnenuhr 1985 $7.50 (3/31/87)
83 PETER NICOLAY Auslese Mosel-Saar-Ruwer Erdener Prälat 1986 $21 (1/31/88)
89 PETER NICOLAY Auslese Mosel-Saar-Ruwer Urziger Goldwingert 1989 $30 (12/15/90) (JS)
79 PETER NICOLAY Auslese Mosel-Saar-Ruwer Urziger Goldwingert 1985 $10 (1/31/87)
83 PETER NICOLAY Auslese Mosel-Saar-Ruwer Urziger Würzgarten 1989 $30 (12/15/90) (JS)
94 PETER NICOLAY Eiswein Mosel-Saar-Ruwer Urziger Würzgarten 1985 $66 (11/30/87)
77 PETER NICOLAY Kabinett Mosel-Saar-Ruwer Erdener Treppchen Artist 1986 $40/1.5L (9/15/88)
85 PETER NICOLAY Kabinett Mosel-Saar-Ruwer Urziger Goldwingert 1988 (NA) (9/30/89) (JS)
90 PETER NICOLAY Kabinett Mosel-Saar-Ruwer Urziger Würzgarten 1986 $10 (11/30/87)
85 PETER NICOLAY Kabinett Mosel-Saar-Ruwer Urziger Würzgarten 1985 $7 (11/15/86)
68 PETER NICOLAY Spätlese Mosel-Saar-Ruwer Erdener Treppchen 1985 $8 (11/15/86)
86 PETER NICOLAY Spätlese Mosel-Saar-Ruwer Urziger Goldwingert 1986 (NA) (4/15/89) (JS)
84 PETER NICOLAY Spätlese Mosel-Saar-Ruwer Urziger Goldwingert 1986 (NA) (4/15/89) (JS)
91 PETER NICOLAY Trockenbeerenauslese Mosel-Saar-Ruwer Urziger Würzgarten 1989 $325 (12/15/90) (JS)
80 DR. PAULY-BERGWEILER Auslese Mosel-Saar-Ruwer Bernkasteler alte Badstube am Doctorberg 1989 $45 (12/15/90) (JS)
91 DR. PAULY-BERGWEILER Auslese Mosel-Saar-Ruwer Bernkasteler alte Badstube am Doctorberg 1985 $30 (1/31/88)
85 DR. PAULY-BERGWEILER Auslese Mosel-Saar-Ruwer Bernkasteler Lay 1985 $14 (1/31/87)
80 DR. PAULY-BERGWEILER Auslese Mosel-Saar-Ruwer Graacher Himmelreich 1988 (NA) (9/30/89) (JS)
82 DR. PAULY-BERGWEILER Auslese Mosel-Saar-Ruwer Wehlener Sonnenuhr 1983 $15.50 (9/01/85)
86 DR. PAULY-BERGWEILER Beerenauslese Mosel-Saar-Ruwer Bernkasteler Badstube 1989 $60 (12/15/90) (JS)
83 DR. PAULY-BERGWEILER Beerenauslese Mosel-Saar-Ruwer Wehlener Sonnenuhr 1989 $70 (12/15/90) (JS)
87 DR. PAULY-BERGWEILER Eiswein Mosel-Saar-Ruwer Bernkasteler Badstube 1985 $100 (9/15/88)
81 DR. PAULY-BERGWEILER Eiswein Mosel-Saar-Ruwer Graacher Himmelreich 1989 $100 (12/15/90) (JS)
87 DR. PAULY-BERGWEILER Eiswein Mosel-Saar-Ruwer Graacher Himmelreich 1983 $90 (9/16/85)
76 DR. PAULY-BERGWEILER Kabinett Mosel-Saar-Ruwer Bernkasteler Alte Badstube am Doctorberg 1988 (NA) (9/30/89) (JS)
82 DR. PAULY-BERGWEILER Kabinett Mosel-Saar-Ruwer Graacher Himmelreich 1985 $8 (11/15/86)
84 DR. PAULY-BERGWEILER Kabinett Mosel-Saar-Ruwer Wehlener Sonnenuhr 1989 $18 (12/15/90) (JS)
80 DR. PAULY-BERGWEILER Spätlese Mosel-Saar-Ruwer Bernkasteler Alte Badstube am Doctorberg 1989 $30 (12/15/90) (JS)
86 DR. PAULY-BERGWEILER Spätlese Mosel-Saar-Ruwer Bernkasteler Alte Badstube am Doctorberg 1986 $24 (10/15/88)
82 DR. PAULY-BERGWEILER Spätlese Mosel-Saar-Ruwer Bernkasteler Alte Badstube am Doctorberg 1986 $24 (4/15/89) (JS)
86 DR. PAULY-BERGWEILER Spätlese Mosel-Saar-Ruwer Bernkasteler Alte Badstube am Doctorberg 1985 (NA) (4/15/89) (JS)
90 DR. PAULY-BERGWEILER Spätlese Mosel-Saar-Ruwer Bernkasteler Badstube 1985 $10 (9/30/86)
78 DR. PAULY-BERGWEILER Spätlese Mosel-Saar-Ruwer Bernkasteler Badstube 1983 $9.50 (10/01/85)
86 DR. PAULY-BERGWEILER Spätlese Mosel-Saar-Ruwer Bernkasteler Lay 1988 (NA) (9/30/89) (JS)
70 DR. PAULY-BERGWEILER Spätlese Mosel-Saar-Ruwer Brauneberger Juffer 1983 $9.50 (10/01/85)
86 DR. PAULY-BERGWEILER Spätlese Mosel-Saar-Ruwer Wehlener Sonnenuhr 1986 $13 (11/30/87)
74 DR. F. PRUM Spätlese Mosel-Saar-Ruwer Graacher Domprobst 1985 $12 (10/15/87)
92 JOH. JOS. PRUM Auslese Mosel-Saar-Ruwer Wehlener Sonnenuhr 1989 $35 (12/15/90) (JS)
90 JOH. JOS. PRUM Auslese Mosel-Saar-Ruwer Wehlener Sonnenuhr 1988 $33 (9/30/89) (JS)
90 JOH. JOS. PRUM Auslese Mosel-Saar-Ruwer Wehlener Sonnenuhr 1985 $20 (5/31/87)
98 JOH. JOS. PRUM Auslese Mosel-Saar-Ruwer Wehlener Sonnenuhr Gold Cap 1988 $80 (9/30/89) (JS)
94 JOH. JOS. PRUM Auslese Mosel-Saar-Ruwer Wehlener Sonnenuhr Long Gold Cap 1989 $249 (12/15/90) (JS)

95 JOH. JOS. PRUM Beerenauslese Mosel-Saar-Ruwer Wehlener Sonnenuhr 1989 (NA) (12/15/90) (JS)
91 JOH. JOS. PRUM Kabinett Mosel-Saar-Ruwer Wehlener Klosterberg 1983 $9 (11/16/84) SS
87 JOH. JOS. PRUM Kabinett Mosel-Saar-Ruwer Wehlener Nonnenberg 1983 $9 (5/01/85)
91 JOH. JOS. PRUM Kabinett Mosel-Saar-Ruwer Wehlener Sonnenuhr 1989 $21 (12/15/90) (JS)
76 JOH. JOS. PRUM Kabinett Mosel-Saar-Ruwer Wehlener Sonnenuhr 1985 $11.50 (4/15/87)
50 JOH. JOS. PRUM Spätlese Mosel-Saar-Ruwer Bernkasteler Badstube 1983 $11 (11/16/85)
91 JOH. JOS. PRUM Spätlese Mosel-Saar-Ruwer Graacher Himmelreich 1985 $15.50 (4/15/89) (JS)
77 JOH. JOS. PRUM Spätlese Mosel-Saar-Ruwer Graacher Himmelreich 1985 $15.50 (5/15/87)
91 JOH. JOS. PRUM Spätlese Mosel-Saar-Ruwer Wehlener Sonnenuhr 1989 $29 (12/15/90) (JS)
92 JOH. JOS. PRUM Spätlese Mosel-Saar-Ruwer Wehlener Sonnenuhr 1986 (NA) (4/15/89) (JS)
88 JOH. JOS. PRUM Spätlese Mosel-Saar-Ruwer Wehlener Sonnenuhr 1985 (NA) (4/15/89) (JS)
91 JOH. JOS. PRUM Spätlese Mosel-Saar-Ruwer Wehlener Sonnenuhr 1983 $13 (5/01/85) SS
97 JOH. JOS. PRUM Spätlese Mosel-Saar-Ruwer Wehlener Sonnenuhr (Cask 1) 1988 $20 (9/30/89) (JS)
98 JOH. JOS. PRUM Spätlese Mosel-Saar-Ruwer Wehlener Sonnenuhr (Cask 2) 1988 $20 (9/30/89) (JS)
94 S.A. PRUM Auslese Mosel-Saar-Ruwer Graacher Himmelreich 1988 $25 (9/30/89) (JS)
85 S.A. PRUM Auslese Mosel-Saar-Ruwer Wehlener Sonnenuhr 1988 $29 (9/30/89) (JS)
81 S.A. PRUM Kabinett Mosel-Saar-Ruwer Graacher Himmelreich 1988 (NA) (9/30/89) (JS)
88 S.A. PRUM Spätlese Mosel-Saar-Ruwer Bernkasteler Graben 1988 $17.50 (9/30/89) (JS)
81 S.A. PRUM Spätlese Mosel-Saar-Ruwer Graacher Himmelreich 1988 $18 (9/30/89) (JS)
83 S.A. PRUM Spätlese Mosel-Saar-Ruwer Wehlener Sonnenuhr 1988 $18 (9/30/89) (JS)
81 ZACH. BERGWEILER PRUM-ERBEN Qualitätswein Mosel-Saar-Ruwer Bernkasteler Badstube Dr. Heidemanns Bergweiler 1987 $11 (4/30/89)
80 MAX FERD. RICHTER Auslese Mosel-Saar-Ruwer Brauneberger Juffer 1989 $17 (12/15/90)
87 MAX FERD. RICHTER Auslese Mosel-Saar-Ruwer Brauneberger Juffer-Sonnenuhr 1988 (NA) (9/30/89) (JS)
87 MAX FERD. RICHTER Auslese Mosel-Saar-Ruwer Mülheimer Helenenkloster 1989 $20 (12/15/90)
80 MAX FERD. RICHTER Auslese Mosel-Saar-Ruwer Veldenzer Elisenberg 1989 $16 (12/15/90)
82 MAX FERD. RICHTER Eiswein Mosel-Saar-Ruwer Mülheimer Helenenkloster 1989 $50/375ml (12/15/90)
84 MAX FERD. RICHTER Kabinett Mosel-Saar-Ruwer Brauneberger Juffer 1989 $11 (12/15/90)
85 MAX FERD. RICHTER Kabinett Mosel-Saar-Ruwer Graacher Himmelreich 1989 $11 (12/15/90)
85 MAX FERD. RICHTER Kabinett Mosel-Saar-Ruwer Wehlener Sonnenuhr 1989 $11 (12/15/90)
83 MAX FERD. RICHTER Qualitätswein Halbtrocken Mosel-Saar-Ruwer Dr. Richter 1989 $8 (12/15/90)
84 MAX FERD. RICHTER Spätlese Mosel-Saar-Ruwer Brauneberger Juffer 1989 $13 (12/15/90)
94 MAX FERD. RICHTER Spätlese Mosel-Saar-Ruwer Brauneberger Juffer-Sonnenuhr 1988 (NA) (9/30/89) (JS)
94 MAX FERD. RICHTER Spätlese Mosel-Saar-Ruwer Veldenzer Elisenberg 1988 (NA) (9/30/89) (JS)
81 MAX FERD. RICHTER Spätlese Mosel-Saar-Ruwer Wehlener Sonnenuhr 1989 $13 (12/15/90)
88 MAX FERD. RICHTER Spätlese Mosel-Saar-Ruwer Wehlener Sonnenuhr 1988 (NA) (9/30/89) (JS)
92 MAX FERD. RICHTER Trockenbeerenauslese Mosel-Saar-Ruwer Mülheimer Sonnenlay 1989 $100/375ml (12/15/90)
88 SCHLOSS SAARSTEIN (EBERT) Auslese Mosel-Saar-Ruwer Serriger Schloss Saarsteiner Gold Cup 1988 $25 (9/30/89) (JS)
83 SCHLOSS SAARSTEIN (EBERT) Kabinett Mosel-Saar-Ruwer Serriger Schloss Saarsteiner (AP10) 1988 (NA) (9/30/89) (JS)
90 SCHLOSS SAARSTEIN (EBERT) Kabinett Mosel-Saar-Ruwer Serriger Schloss Saarsteiner (AP15) 1988 (NA) (9/30/89) (JS)
85 SCHLOSS SAARSTEIN (EBERT) Spätlese Mosel-Saar-Ruwer Serriger Schloss Saarsteiner 1988 (NA) (9/30/89) (JS)
90 DR. LOOSEN ST. JOHANNISHOF Auslese Mosel-Saar-Ruwer Erdener Prälat Gold Cap 1988 (NA) (9/30/89) (JS)
92 DR. LOOSEN ST. JOHANNISHOF Auslese Mosel-Saar-Ruwer Erdener Prälat 1985 $20 (11/15/86)
93 DR. LOOSEN ST. JOHANNISHOF Auslese Mosel-Saar-Ruwer Wehlener Sonnenuhr Gold Cap 1988 (NA) (9/30/89) (JS)
78 DR. LOOSEN ST. JOHANNISHOF Kabinett Mosel-Saar-Ruwer Bernkasteler Badstube 1983 $6.50 (4/01/85)
85 DR. LOOSEN ST. JOHANNISHOF Kabinett Mosel-Saar-Ruwer Erdener Treppchen 1983 $7 (3/16/85)
84 DR. LOOSEN ST. JOHANNISHOF Kabinett Mosel-Saar-Ruwer Wehlener Sonnenuhr 1988 (NA) (9/30/89) (JS)
81 DR. LOOSEN ST. JOHANNISHOF Kabinett Mosel-Saar-Ruwer Wehlener Sonnenuhr 1985 $8 (1/31/87)
78 DR. LOOSEN ST. JOHANNISHOF Kabinett Mosel-Saar-Ruwer Wehlener Sonnenuhr 1983 $6 (4/01/85)
82 DR. LOOSEN ST. JOHANNISHOF Spätlese Mosel-Saar-Ruwer Bernkasteler Doctor 1986 (NA) (4/15/89) (JS)
90 DR. LOOSEN ST. JOHANNISHOF Spätlese Mosel-Saar-Ruwer Erdener Prälat 1988 (NA) (9/30/89) (JS)
85 DR. LOOSEN ST. JOHANNISHOF Spätlese Mosel-Saar-Ruwer Erdener Prälat 1986 (NA) (4/15/89) (JS)
85 DR. LOOSEN ST. JOHANNISHOF Spätlese Mosel-Saar-Ruwer Erdener Treppchen 1985 $11 (1/31/87)
87 DR. LOOSEN ST. JOHANNISHOF Spätlese Mosel-Saar-Ruwer Erdener Treppchen 1983 $9 (3/01/85)
80 WILLI SCHAEFER Auslese Mosel-Saar-Ruwer Graacher Domprobst 1988 $13 (9/30/89) (JS)
81 WILLI SCHAEFER Kabinett Mosel-Saar-Ruwer Graacher Himmelreich 1988 $8 (9/30/89) (JS)
80 WILLI SCHAEFER Spätlese Mosel-Saar-Ruwer Graacher Domprobst 1988 $10 (9/30/89) (JS)
87 WILLI SCHAEFER Spätlese Mosel-Saar-Ruwer Wehlener Sonnenuhr 1988 $10 (9/30/89) (JS)
91 SELBACH-OSTER Auslese Mosel-Saar-Ruwer Zeltinger Sonnenuhr (AP5) 1988 $22 (9/30/89) (JS)
91 SELBACH-OSTER Beerenauslese Mosel-Saar-Ruwer Zeltingen-Rachtiger Sonnenuhr 1989 $56/375ml (12/15/90)
76 SELBACH-OSTER Eiswein Mosel-Saar-Ruwer Zeltinger Himmelreich 1986 $40/375ml (4/30/89)
83 SELBACH-OSTER Eiswein Mosel-Saar-Ruwer Zeltinger Himmelreich 1985 $35/375ml (4/30/89)
84 SELBACH-OSTER Kabinett Mosel-Saar-Ruwer Bernkasteler Badstube 1989 $10 (12/15/90)

GERMANY

RIESLING/*MOSEL-SAAR-RUWER*

80 SELBACH-OSTER Kabinett Mosel-Saar-Ruwer Graacher Himmelreich 1985 $10 (10/15/88)
86 SELBACH-OSTER Kabinett Mosel-Saar-Ruwer Wehlener Klosterberg 1986 $8 (11/30/88)
81 SELBACH-OSTER Kabinett Mosel-Saar-Ruwer Wehlener Sonnenuhr 1989 $10 (12/15/90)
81 SELBACH-OSTER Kabinett Mosel-Saar-Ruwer Zeltinger Himmelreich 1988 $8.50 (9/30/89) (JS)
81 SELBACH-OSTER Mosel-Saar-Ruwer Hochgewächs Graacher Himmelreich 1986 $6 (10/15/88)
87 SELBACH-OSTER Spätlese Mosel-Saar-Ruwer Bernkasteler Badstube 1989 $11.50 (12/15/90)
84 SELBACH-OSTER Spätlese Mosel-Saar-Ruwer Bernkasteler Badstube 1989 $11.50 (12/15/90)
90 SELBACH-OSTER Spätlese Mosel-Saar-Ruwer Bernkasteler Badstube 1985 $9.50 (9/15/88)
82 SELBACH-OSTER Spätlese Mosel-Saar-Ruwer Graacher Himmelreich 1985 $8 (9/15/88)
84 SELBACH-OSTER Spätlese Mosel-Saar-Ruwer Wehlener Klosterberg 1988 $11 (9/30/89) (JS)
81 SELBACH-OSTER Spätlese Mosel-Saar-Ruwer Wehlener Sonnenuhr 1989 $10 (12/15/90)
86 SELBACH-OSTER Spätlese Mosel-Saar-Ruwer Zeltingen-Rachtiger Himmelreich 1989 $11.50 (12/15/90)
85 SELBACH-OSTER Spätlese Mosel-Saar-Ruwer Zeltingen-Rachtiger Sonnenuhr 1989 $18 (12/15/90)
93 SELBACH-OSTER Spätlese Mosel-Saar-Ruwer Zeltinger Sonnenuhr 1988 $12.50 (9/30/89) (JS)
97 SELBACH-OSTER Trockenbeerenauslese Mosel-Saar-Ruwer Zeltingen-Rachtiger Sonnenuhr 1989 $100/375ml (12/15/90)
84 J&H SELBACH Kabinett Mosel-Saar-Ruwer Brauneberger Mandelgraben 1983 $4.50 (11/16/84) BB
86 J&H SELBACH Kabinett Mosel-Saar-Ruwer Zeltinger Himmelreich 1985 $7.50 (10/15/88)
78 J&H SELBACH Mosel-Saar-Ruwer Hochgewächs 1987 $7 (10/15/88)
89 J&H SELBACH Spätlese Mosel-Saar-Ruwer Piesporter Goldtröpfchen 1985 $14 (9/15/88)
84 BERT SIMON Auslese Mosel-Saar-Ruwer Kaseler Gold Cap 1989 $32 (12/15/90)
86 BERT SIMON Auslese Mosel-Saar-Ruwer Patheiger Kaseler Kehrnagel Long Gold Cap 1989 $24/375ml (12/15/90)
85 BERT SIMON Auslese Mosel-Saar-Ruwer Serringer Herrenberg 1989 $21 (12/15/90)
87 BERT SIMON Auslese Mosel-Saar-Ruwer Serriger Würtzberg 1988 (NA) (9/30/89) (JS)
86 BERT SIMON Auslese Mosel-Saar-Ruwer Serriger Würtzberg Gold Cap 1989 $31 (12/15/90)
93 BERT SIMON Beerenauslese Mosel-Saar-Ruwer Serriger Würtzberg 1989 $53/375ml (12/15/90)
87 BERT SIMON Kabinett Mosel-Saar-Ruwer Eitelsbacher Marienholz 1989 $13 (12/15/90)
85 BERT SIMON Kabinett Mosel-Saar-Ruwer Serringer Herrenberg 1989 $11.50 (12/15/90)
84 BERT SIMON Kabinett Mosel-Saar-Ruwer Serriger Würtzberg 1989 $13 (12/15/90)
82 BERT SIMON Kabinett Mosel-Saar-Ruwer Serriger Würtzberg 1988 (NA) (9/30/89) (JS)
79 BERT SIMON Kabinett Halbtrocken Mosel-Saar-Ruwer Mertesdorfer Herrenberg 1989 $13 (12/15/90)
84 BERT SIMON Qualitätswein Mosel-Saar-Ruwer 1988 $6 (9/30/89) (JS)
85 BERT SIMON Spätlese Mosel-Saar-Ruwer Kastel-Staadt Maximiner Prälat 1989 $13 (12/15/90)
78 BERT SIMON Spätlese Mosel-Saar-Ruwer Patheiger Kaseler Kehrnagel 1989 $15 (12/15/90)
87 BERT SIMON Spätlese Mosel-Saar-Ruwer Serriger Würtzberg 1989 $15 (12/15/90)
90 BERT SIMON Spätlese Mosel-Saar-Ruwer Serriger Würtzberg 1988 (NA) (9/30/89) (JS)
95+ BERT SIMON Trockenbeerenauslese Mosel-Saar-Ruwer Serriger Würtzberg 1989 $96/375ml (12/15/90) (BT)
90 STAATLICHEN WEINBAUDOMANEN Auslese Mosel-Saar-Ruwer Schlossböckelheimer Kupfergrube 1989 $19 (12/15/90)
85 STAATLICHEN WEINBAUDOMANEN Qualitätswein Mosel-Saar-Ruwer Schlossböckelheimer Kupfergrube 1989 $9 (12/15/90)
90 STAATLICHEN WEINBAUDOMANEN Spätlese Mosel-Saar-Ruwer Schlossböckelheimer Kupfergrube 1989 (NA) (12/15/90)
80 STAATLICHEN WEINBAUDOMANEN Spätlese Mosel-Saar-Ruwer Serriger Vogelsang 1983 $7 (11/01/84)
88 STAATLICHEN WEINBAUDOMANEN Trockenbeerenauslese Mosel-Saar-Ruwer Schlossböckelheimer Kupfergrube 1989 $150 (12/15/90)
86 STUDERT-PRUM Auslese Mosel-Saar-Ruwer Wehlener Sonnenuhr 1988 (NA) (9/30/89) (JS)
82 THANISCH (KNABBEN-SPIER) Auslese Mosel-Saar-Ruwer Bernkasteler Badstube 1988 $25 (9/30/89) (JS)
92 THANISCH (KNABBEN-SPIER) Auslese Mosel-Saar-Ruwer Bernkasteler Lay 1988 (NA) (9/30/89) (JS)
90 THANISCH (KNABBEN-SPIER) Spätlese Mosel-Saar-Ruwer Bernkasteler Doctor 1988 $15 (9/30/89) (JS)
79 THANISCH (KNABBEN-SPIER) Spätlese Mosel-Saar-Ruwer Bernkasteler Doctor 1986 (NA) (4/15/89) (JS)
89 THANISCH (KNABBEN-SPIER) Spätlese Mosel-Saar-Ruwer Bernkasteler Lay 1988 $12 (9/30/89) (JS)
82 THANISCH (KNABBEN-SPIER) Spätlese Mosel-Saar-Ruwer Bernkasteler Lay 1985 (NA) (4/15/89) (JS)
85 THANISCH (KNABBEN-SPIER) Spätlese Mosel-Saar-Ruwer Graacher Himmelreich 1985 (NA) (4/15/89) (JS)
90 DR. H. THANISCH (MULLER-BURGGRAEFF) Auslese Mosel-Saar-Ruwer Bernkasteler Doctor 1988 (NA) (9/30/89) (JS)
85 DR. H. THANISCH (MULLER-BURGGRAEFF) Auslese Mosel-Saar-Ruwer Brauneberger Juffer-Sonnenuhr 1989 $25 (12/15/90) (JS)
85 DR. H. THANISCH (MULLER-BURGGRAEFF) Auslese Mosel-Saar-Ruwer Brauneberger Juffer-Sonnenuhr 1988 (NA) (9/30/89) (JS)
91 DR. H. THANISCH (MULLER-BURGGRAEFF) Beerenauslese Mosel-Saar-Ruwer Bernkasteler Doctor 1989 $240 (12/15/90) (JS)
88 DR. H. THANISCH (MULLER-BURGGRAEFF) Eiswein Mosel-Saar-Ruwer Bernkasteler Doctor 1989 $190 (12/15/90) (JS)
74 DR. H. THANISCH (MULLER-BURGGRAEFF) Kabinett Halbtrocken Mosel-Saar-Ruwer Bernkasteler Doctor 1989 (NA) (12/15/90) (JS)

Key to Symbols

The scores reported here are the results of blind tastings conducted by our panel of senior editors. Wines that carry the initials below are results of individual tastings.

THE WINE SPECTATOR 100-POINT SCALE *95-100*—Classic, a great wine; *90-94*—Outstanding, superior character and style; *80-89*—Good to very good, a wine with special qualities; *70-79*—Average, drinkable wine that may have minor flaws; *60-69*—Below average, drinkable but not recommended; *50-59*—Poor, undrinkable, not recommended. "+"—With a score indicates a range; used primarily with barrel tastings to indicate a preliminary score.

SPECIAL DESIGNATIONS SS—Spectator Selection, CS—Cellar Selection, BB—Best Buy.

TASTER'S INITIALS (JG)—Jim Gordon, (HS)—Harvey Steiman, (JL)—James Laube, (JS)—James Suckling, (TM)—Thomas Matthews, (TR)—Terry Robards, (BT)—Barrel Tasting (these wines were tasted blind from barrel samples), (CA-date)—*California's Great Cabernets* by James Laube, (CH-date)—*California's Great Chardonnays* by James Laube, (VP-date)—*Vintage Port* by James Suckling.

DATE TASTED Dates in parentheses represent the issue in which the rating was published.

72 DR. H. THANISCH (MULLER-BURGGRAEFF) Kabinett Mosel-Saar-Ruwer Bernkasteler Badstube 1986 $11 (11/30/87)
88 DR. H. THANISCH (MULLER-BURGGRAEFF) Kabinett Mosel-Saar-Ruwer Bernkasteler Badstube 1985 $11.25 (4/15/87)
84 DR. H. THANISCH (MULLER-BURGGRAEFF) Kabinett Mosel-Saar-Ruwer Bernkasteler Doctor 1986 $29 (11/30/87)
81 DR. H. THANISCH (MULLER-BURGGRAEFF) Kabinett Mosel-Saar-Ruwer Bernkastler Lay 1989 $13.50 (12/15/90) (JS)
79 DR. H. THANISCH (MULLER-BURGGRAEFF) Kabinett Mosel-Saar-Ruwer Graacher Himmelreich 1989 $14 (12/15/90) (JS)
87 DR. H. THANISCH (MULLER-BURGGRAEFF) Kabinett Mosel-Saar-Ruwer Lieserer Niederberg-Heldenberg 1989 $14 (12/15/90) (JS)
86 DR. H. THANISCH (MULLER-BURGGRAEFF) Kabinett Mosel-Saar-Ruwer Lieserer Niederberg-Heldenberg 1988 (NA) (9/30/89) (JS)
71 DR. H. THANISCH (MULLER-BURGGRAEFF) Spätlese Mosel-Saar-Ruwer Bernkasteler Doctor 1989 (NA) (12/15/90) (JS)
64 DR. H. THANISCH (MULLER-BURGGRAEFF) Spätlese Mosel-Saar-Ruwer Bernkasteler Doctor 1986 (NA) (4/15/89) (JS)
77 DR. H. THANISCH (MULLER-BURGGRAEFF) Spätlese Mosel-Saar-Ruwer Bernkasteler Doctor 1985 (NA) (4/15/89) (JS)
88 DR. H. THANISCH (MULLER-BURGGRAEFF) Spätlese Mosel-Saar-Ruwer Bernkasteler Kurfurstlay 1986 $12 (11/30/87)
72 DR. H. THANISCH (MULLER-BURGGRAEFF) Spätlese Mosel-Saar-Ruwer Bernkasteler Kurfurstlay 1985 $9.50 (4/15/89) (JS)
80 DR. H. THANISCH (MULLER-BURGGRAEFF) Spätlese Mosel-Saar-Ruwer Bernkasteler Kurfurstlay 1985 $9.50 (4/15/87)
78 DR. H. THANISCH (MULLER-BURGGRAEFF) Spätlese Mosel-Saar-Ruwer Brauneberger Juffer-Sonnenuhr 1989 $19 (12/15/90) (JS)
81 DR. H. THANISCH (MULLER-BURGGRAEFF) Spätlese Mosel-Saar-Ruwer Lieserer Niederberg-Helden 1989 $15 (12/15/90) (JS)
70 DR. H. THANISCH (MULLER-BURGGRAEFF) Spätlese Mosel-Saar-Ruwer Lieserer Niederberg-Helden 1988 (NA) (9/30/89) (JS)
80 H. THAPRICH Spätlese Mosel-Saar-Ruwer Bernkasteler Badstube 1983 $8.50 (4/01/85)
78 H. THAPRICH Spätlese Mosel-Saar-Ruwer Bernkasteler Lay 1983 $8.25 (3/16/85)
85 TYRELL Kabinett Mosel-Saar-Ruwer Karthäuserhofberg (AP3) 1988 (NA) (9/30/89) (JS)
85 TYRELL Kabinett Mosel-Saar-Ruwer Karthäuserhofberg (AP9) 1988 (NA) (9/30/89) (JS)
86 TYRELL Spätlese Mosel-Saar-Ruwer Karthäuserhofberg 1988 (NA) (9/30/89) (JS)
85 TYRELL Spätlese Mosel-Saar-Ruwer Karthäuserhofberg (AP8) 1988 (NA) (9/30/89) (JS)
95 TYRELL Spätlese Mosel-Saar-Ruwer Karthäuserhofberg (AP10) 1988 (NA) (9/30/89) (JS)
90 VEREINIGTE HOSPITIEN Auslese Mosel-Saar-Ruwer Piesporter Schubertslay 1988 (NA) (9/30/89) (JS)
90 VEREINIGTE HOSPITIEN Auslese Mosel-Saar-Ruwer Wehlener Sonnenuhr 1988 (NA) (9/30/89) (JS)
79 VEREINIGTE HOSPITIEN Kabinett Mosel-Saar-Ruwer Serriger Schloss Saarfelser Schlossberger 1988 (NA) (9/30/89) (JS)
83 VEREINIGTE HOSPITIEN Spätlese Mosel-Saar-Ruwer Wiltinger Hölle 1988 (NA) (9/30/89) (JS)
86 VON HOVEL Auslese Mosel-Saar-Ruwer Oberemmeler Hütte 1989 $27 (12/15/90)
92 VON HOVEL Auslese Mosel-Saar-Ruwer Oberemmeler Hütte Gold Cap 1989 $45/375ml (12/15/90)
81 VON HOVEL Auslese Mosel-Saar-Ruwer Oberemmeler Hütte Gold Cap 1988 (NA) (9/30/89) (JS)
93 VON HOVEL Beerenauslese Mosel-Saar-Ruwer Oberemmeler Hütte 1989 $88/375ml (12/15/90)
87 VON HOVEL Eiswein Mosel-Saar-Ruwer Oberemmeler Hütte 1989 $147/375ml (12/15/90)
80 VON HOVEL Kabinett Mosel-Saar-Ruwer Oberemmeler Hütte 1989 $12 (12/15/90)
80 VON HOVEL Kabinett Mosel-Saar-Ruwer Oberemmeler Hütte 1985 $8 (10/15/87)
86 VON HOVEL Kabinett Mosel-Saar-Ruwer Scharzhofberger 1989 $12 (12/15/90)
90 VON HOVEL Kabinett Mosel-Saar-Ruwer Scharzhofberger 1988 $12 (9/30/89) (JS)
90 VON HOVEL Spätlese Mosel-Saar-Ruwer Oberemmeler Hütte 1989 $16 (12/15/90)
89 VON HOVEL Spätlese Mosel-Saar-Ruwer Oberemmeler Hütte 1988 $15 (9/30/89) (JS)
82 VON HOVEL Spätlese Mosel-Saar-Ruwer Scharzhofberger 1989 $16 (12/15/90)
85 C. VON SCHUBERT Auslese Mosel-Saar-Ruwer Maximin Grunhauser Abtsberg 1989 $40 (12/15/90)
95 C. VON SCHUBERT Auslese Mosel-Saar-Ruwer Maximin Grunhauser Abtsberg (Cask 96) 1989 (NA) (12/15/90)
90 C. VON SCHUBERT Auslese Mosel-Saar-Ruwer Maximin Grunhauser Abtsberg (Cask 98) 1989 $45 (12/15/90)
90 C. VON SCHUBERT Auslese Mosel-Saar-Ruwer Maximin Grunhauser Abtsberg (Cask 133) 1989 $70 (12/15/90)
86 C. VON SCHUBERT Auslese Mosel-Saar-Ruwer Maximin Grunhauser Herrenberg 1989 $40 (12/15/90)
91 C. VON SCHUBERT Auslese Mosel-Saar-Ruwer Maximin Grunhauser Herrenberg (Cask 93) 1989 $80 (12/15/90)
95 C. VON SCHUBERT Auslese Mosel-Saar-Ruwer Maximin Grunhauser Herrenberg (AP153) 1988 $30 (9/30/89) (JS)
99 C. VON SCHUBERT Beerenauslese Mosel-Saar-Ruwer Maximin Grunhauser Abtsberg 1989 (NA) (12/15/90)
78 C. VON SCHUBERT Kabinett Mosel-Saar-Ruwer Brüderberg 1989 $9.50 (12/15/90)
90 C. VON SCHUBERT Kabinett Mosel-Saar-Ruwer Maximin Grunhauser Abtsberg 1989 $20 (12/15/90)
89 C. VON SCHUBERT Kabinett Mosel-Saar-Ruwer Maximin Grunhauser Herrenberg 1988 $10 (9/30/89) (JS)
82 C. VON SCHUBERT Kabinett Mosel-Saar-Ruwer Maximin Grunhauser Herrenberg 1987 $12 (4/30/89)
80 C. VON SCHUBERT Qualitätswein Mosel-Saar-Ruwer Maximin Grunhauser Abtsberg 1988 $10 (9/30/89) (JS)
87 C. VON SCHUBERT Qualitätswein Mosel-Saar-Ruwer Maximin Grunhauser Abtsberg 1987 $13 (4/30/89)
80 C. VON SCHUBERT Qualitätswein Mosel-Saar-Ruwer Maximin Grunhauser Herrenberg 1989 $13 (12/15/90)
90 C. VON SCHUBERT Spätlese Mosel-Saar-Ruwer Maximin Grunhauser Abtsberg 1989 $28 (12/15/90)
96 C. VON SCHUBERT Spätlese Mosel-Saar-Ruwer Maximin Grunhauser Abtsberg 1988 (NA) (9/30/89) (JS)
96 C. VON SCHUBERT Trockenbeerenauslese Mosel-Saar-Ruwer Maximin Grunhauser Herrenberg 1989 (NA) (12/15/90)
86 DR. WEINS-PRUM Auslese Mosel-Saar-Ruwer Erdener Prälat 1988 (NA) (9/30/89) (JS)
84 DR. WEINS-PRUM Kabinett Mosel-Saar-Ruwer Wehlener Sonnenuhr 1988 (NA) (9/30/89) (JS)

82 DR. WEINS-PRUM Spätlese Mosel-Saar-Ruwer Urziger Würzgarten 1988 (NA) (9/30/89) (JS)
84 DR. WEINS-PRUM Spätlese Mosel-Saar-Ruwer Wehlener Sonnenuhr 1988 (NA) (9/30/89) (JS)
86 WELLER-LEHNERT Auslese Mosel-Saar-Ruwer Piesporter Goldtröpfchen 1988 (NA) (9/30/89) (JS)
86 WOLFGANG ZAHN Spätlese Mosel-Saar-Ruwer Piesporter Goldtröpfchen 1983 $10 (5/16/85)
90 DR. ZENZEN Beerenauslese Mosel-Saar-Ruwer Erdener Treppchen 1976 $90 (2/01/86)
70 DR. ZENZEN Kabinett Mosel-Saar-Ruwer Erdener Treppchen 1981 $8 (4/01/86)
74 DR. ZENZEN Spätlese Mosel-Saar-Ruwer Valwiger Herrenberg 1982 $12 (2/01/86)
88 ZILLIKEN Auslese Mosel-Saar-Ruwer Saarburger Rausch 1989 $35 (12/15/90)
95 ZILLIKEN Auslese Mosel-Saar-Ruwer Saarburger Rausch Long Gold Cap 1989 $64 (12/15/90)
96 ZILLIKEN Eiswein Mosel-Saar-Ruwer Saarburger Rausch 1989 (NA) (12/15/90)
97 ZILLIKEN Eiswein Mosel-Saar-Ruwer Saarburger Rausch 1988 (NA) (9/30/89) (JS)
81 ZILLIKEN Kabinett Mosel-Saar-Ruwer Ockfener Bockstein 1989 $14 (12/15/90)
77 ZILLIKEN Kabinett Mosel-Saar-Ruwer Saarburger Rausch (AP5) 1989 $14 (12/15/90)
85 ZILLIKEN Kabinett Mosel-Saar-Ruwer Saarburger Rausch (AP12) 1989 $14 (12/15/90)
78 ZILLIKEN Kabinett Mosel-Saar-Ruwer Saarburger Rausch (AP5) 1988 $9 (9/30/89) (JS)
79 ZILLIKEN Kabinett Mosel-Saar-Ruwer Saarburger Rausch (AP7) 1988 $9 (9/30/89) (JS)
79 ZILLIKEN Spätlese Mosel-Saar-Ruwer Ockfener Bockstein 1989 $18 (12/15/90)
85 ZILLIKEN Spätlese Mosel-Saar-Ruwer Saarburger Rausch 1989 $19 (12/15/90)
84 ZILLIKEN Spätlese Mosel-Saar-Ruwer Saarburger Rausch (AP6) 1989 $19 (12/15/90)
95 ZILLIKEN Spätlese Mosel-Saar-Ruwer Saarburger Rausch 1988 (NA) (9/30/89) (JS)
78 ZILLIKEN Spätlese Mosel-Saar-Ruwer Saarburger Rausch 1985 $9.25 (5/15/87)

NAHE

91 HANS CRUSIUS & SOHN Auslese Nahe Schlossböckelheimer Felsenberg Gold Capsule 1989 $35 (12/15/90)
88 HANS CRUSIUS & SOHN Auslese Nahe Traisener Rotenfels 1989 $24 (12/15/90)
85 HANS CRUSIUS & SOHN Kabinett Nahe Traisener Rotenfels 1989 $14 (12/15/90)
82 HANS CRUSIUS & SOHN Qualitätswein Halbtrocken Nahe 1989 $11 (12/15/90)
78 HANS CRUSIUS & SOHN Spätlese Nahe Traisener Rotenfels 1989 $17 (12/15/90)
86 STAATLICHEN WEINBAUDOMANEN Auslese Nahe Münsterer Dautenpflänzer 1989 $14 (12/15/90)
86 STAATLICHEN WEINBAUDOMANEN Auslese Nahe Niederhausener Hermannshöhle 1989 $25 (12/15/90)
91 STAATLICHEN WEINBAUDOMANEN Beerenauslese Nahe Münsterer Pittersberg 1989 $41 (12/15/90)
87 STAATLICHEN WEINBAUDOMANEN Beerenauslese Nahe Niederhausener Hermannsberg 1989 $65 (12/15/90)
78 STAATLICHEN WEINBAUDOMANEN Kabinett Nahe Altenbamberger Rothenberg 1989 $10 (12/15/90)
80 STAATLICHEN WEINBAUDOMANEN Kabinett Nahe Niederhausener Steinberg 1989 $9 (12/15/90)
86 STAATLICHEN WEINBAUDOMANEN Spätlese Nahe Niederhausener Kertz 1989 $14 (12/15/90)

RHEINGAU

79 GEHEIMRAT ASCHROTT Kabinett Rheingau Hochheimer Kirchenstüch 1988 (NA) (9/30/89) (JS)
87 GEHEIMRAT ASCHROTT Kabinett Rheingau Hochheimer Stielweg 1988 (NA) (9/30/89) (JS)
92 GEHEIMRAT ASCHROTT Spätlese Halbtrocken Rheingau Hochheimer Hölle 1988 (NA) (9/30/89) (JS)
85 GEHEIMRAT ASCHROTT Spätlese Rheingau Hochheimer Hölle 1988 (NA) (9/30/89) (JS)
83 GEORG BREUER Kabinett Halbtrocken Rheingau Rüdesheimer Berg Schlossberg Charta 1988 $22.40 (9/30/89) (JS)
82 GEORG BREUER Kabinett Halbtrocken Rheingau Rüdesheimer Bischofsberg Charta 1988 $16 (9/30/89) (JS)
81 GEORG BREUER Qualitätswein Rheingau Charta 1988 $14 (9/30/89) (JS)
85 GEORG BREUER Qualitätswein Rheingau Rüdesheimer Berg Roseneck Charta 1988 $14 (9/30/89) (JS)
85 GEORG BREUER Qualitätswein Rheingau Rüdesheimer Berg Rottland Charta 1988 $14 (9/30/89) (JS)
92 WEGELER DEINHARD Kabinett Halbtrocken Rheingau Winkeler Hasensprung Charta 1988 $15 (9/30/89) (JS)
88 WEGELER DEINHARD Kabinett Rheingau Rüdesheimer Berg Rottland 1988 (NA) (9/30/89) (JS)
89 WEGELER DEINHARD Spätlese Rheingau Mittelheimer St. Nikolaus 1988 (NA) (9/30/89) (JS)
81 WEGELER DEINHARD Spätlese Rheingau Rüdesheimer Berg Rottland 1988 (NA) (9/30/89) (JS)
67 JAKOB DEMMER Rheingau Dry 1986 $4 (11/30/88)
59 DOMAINE CLEMENS Qualitätswein Rheingau Bereich Johannisberg 1983 $6 (9/01/85)
74 DOMAINE CLEMENS Qualitätswein Rheingau Bereich Johannisberg 1982 $6 (9/16/84)
82 FREIHERR ZU KNYPHAUSEN Kabinett Halbtrocken Rheingau Erbacher Marcobrunn Charta 1988 (NA) (9/30/89) (JS)
86 FREIHERR ZU KNYPHAUSEN Kabinett Halbtrocken Rheingau Erbacher Steinmorgen 1988 (NA) (9/30/89) (JS)
87 FREIHERR ZU KNYPHAUSEN Kabinett Rheingau Erbacher Steinmorgen 1988 (NA) (9/30/89) (JS)
84 FREIHERR ZU KNYPHAUSEN Kabinett Rheingau Kiedricher Sandgrub 1988 (NA) (9/30/89) (JS)
85 FURST VON METTERNICH Kabinett Halbtrocken Rheingau Schloss Johannisberg 1988 $15 (9/30/89) (JS)
75 FURST VON METTERNICH Qualitätswein Rheingau Schloss Johannisberg 1988 $15 (9/30/89) (JS)
91 FURST VON METTERNICH Rheingau Extra Trocken 1981 $13 (4/01/84)
85 SCHLOSS GROENESTEYN Auslese Rheingau Rüdesheimer Berg Rottland 1989 $40 (12/15/90)
83 SCHLOSS GROENESTEYN Kabinett Rheingau Kiedricher Gräfenberg 1989 $12 (12/15/90)
91 SCHLOSS GROENESTEYN Kabinett Rheingau Kiedricher Gräfenberg 1988 (NA) (9/30/89) (JS)
81 SCHLOSS GROENESTEYN Kabinett Rheingau Kiedricher Sandgrub 1989 $12 (12/15/90)
89 SCHLOSS GROENESTEYN Kabinett Rheingau Kiedricher Sandgrub 1988 (NA) (9/30/89) (JS)
74 SCHLOSS GROENESTEYN Kabinett Rheingau Rüdesheimer Berg Rottland 1988 (NA) (9/30/89) (JS)

78 SCHLOSS GROENESTEYN Kabinett Rheingau Rüdesheimer Berg Rottland 1985 $9 (10/15/87)
86 SCHLOSS GROENESTEYN Kabinett Rheingau Rüdesheimer Berg Rottland 1983 $5.75 (1/01/85) BB
82 SCHLOSS GROENESTEYN Kabinett Rheingau Rüdesheimer Klosterlay 1988 (NA) (9/30/89) (JS)
78 SCHLOSS GROENESTEYN Spätlese Rheingau Kiedricher Gräfenberg 1989 $16 (12/15/90)
83 SCHLOSS GROENESTEYN Spätlese Rheingau Kiedricher Sandgrub 1989 $16 (12/15/90)
80 SCHLOSS GROENESTEYN Spätlese Rheingau Rüdesheimer Berg Rottland 1989 $15 (12/15/90)
86 SCHLOSS JOHANNISBERGER Kabinett Rheingau 1989 (NA) (12/15/90)
88 SCHLOSS JOHANNISBERGER Kabinett Rheingau Rotlack 1983 $12 (8/01/85)
84 SCHLOSS JOHANNISBERGER Qualitätswein Rheingau 1989 (NA) (12/15/90)
90 SCHLOSS JOHANNISBERGER Spätlese Rheingau Grunlack 1983 $20 (8/01/85)
80 LANDGRAF VON HESSEN Kabinett Halbtrocken Rheingau Winkeler Jesuitengarten 1988 (NA) (9/30/89) (JS)
81 LANDGRAF VON HESSEN Kabinett Rheingau Johannisberger Klaus 1988 (NA) (9/30/89) (JS)
80 LANDGRAF VON HESSEN Kabinett Rheingau Prinz von Hessen 1988 (NA) (9/30/89) (JS)
89 LANDGRAF VON HESSEN Spätlese Rheingau Eltville Sonnenberg 1988 (NA) (9/30/89) (JS)
94 LANGWERTH VON SIMMERN Auslese Rheingau Hattenheimer Mannberg 1989 $50 (12/15/90)
91 LANGWERTH VON SIMMERN Auslese Rheingau Hattenheimer Nussbrunnen 1989 $57 (12/15/90)
80 LANGWERTH VON SIMMERN Kabinett Rheingau Eltviller Sonnberg 1989 $11 (12/15/90)
83 LANGWERTH VON SIMMERN Kabinett Rheingau Erbacher Marcobrunn 1989 $16 (12/15/90)
84 LANGWERTH VON SIMMERN Kabinett Rheingau Hattenheimer Mannberg 1989 $25 (12/15/90)
83 LANGWERTH VON SIMMERN Kabinett Rheingau Hattenheimer Mannberg 1985 $8.50 (1/31/87)
88 LANGWERTH VON SIMMERN Kabinett Rheingau Hattenheimer Nussbrunnen 1989 $13.50 (12/15/90)
80 LANGWERTH VON SIMMERN Kabinett Rheingau Kiedricher Sandgrub 1988 (NA) (9/30/89) (JS)
87 LANGWERTH VON SIMMERN Spätlese Rheingau Erbacher Marcobrunn 1989 $25 (12/15/90)
84 LANGWERTH VON SIMMERN Spätlese Rheingau Hattenheimer Nussbrunnen 1989 $25 (12/15/90)
84 LANGWERTH VON SIMMERN Spätlese Rheingau Hattenheimer Nussbrunnen 1988 (NA) (9/30/89) (JS)
76 LANGWERTH VON SIMMERN Spätlese Rheingau Hattenheimer Nussbrunnen 1983 $12 (4/01/85)
87 LANGWERTH VON SIMMERN Spätlese Rheingau Rauenthaler Baiken 1989 $25 (12/15/90)
90 LANGWERTH VON SIMMERN Spätlese Rheingau Rauenthaler Baiken 1988 (NA) (9/30/89) (JS)
99 LANGWERTH VON SIMMERN Trockenbeerenauslese Rheingau Erbacher Marcobrunn 1989 (NA) (12/15/90)
81 MADRIGAL Qualitätswein Rheingau Bereich Johannisberg 1983 $5.50 (10/01/84)
92 SCHLOSS REINHARTSHAUSEN Auslese Rheingau Erbacher Siegelsberg 1989 (NA) (12/15/90)
86 SCHLOSS REINHARTSHAUSEN Qualitätswein Rheingau Erbacher Schlossberg 1989 (NA) (12/15/90)
89 SCHLOSS REINHARTSHAUSEN Spätlese Rheingau Erbacher Siegelsberg 1989 (NA) (12/15/90)
95 SCHLOSS REINHARTSHAUSEN Trockenbeerenauslese Rheingau Erbacher Markobrunn 1937 (NA) (12/15/88)
89 BALTHASAR RESS Kabinett Halbtrocken Rheingau Geisenheimer Kläuserweg Charta 1988 $9.50 (9/30/89) (JS)
78 BALTHASAR RESS Kabinett Halbtrocken Rheingau Hattenheimer Nussbrunnen Charta 1988 $9.50 (9/30/89) (JS)
89 BALTHASAR RESS Spätlese Halbtrocken Rheingau Rüdesheimer Berg Rottland 1988 $14 (9/30/89) (JS)
84 BALTHASAR RESS Spätlese Rheingau Rüdesheimer Berg Schlossberg 1988 $13.50 (9/30/89) (JS)
87 SCHLOSS SCHONBORN Auslese Rheingau Hattenheimer Nussbrunnen 1989 (NA) (12/15/90)
90 SCHLOSS SCHONBORN Auslese Rheingau Rüdeshemier Berg Schlossberg 1989 (NA) (12/15/90)
81 SCHLOSS SCHONBORN Kabinett Halbtrocken Rheingau Geisenheimer Schlossberg 1988 (NA) (9/30/89) (JS)
81 SCHLOSS SCHONBORN Kabinett Rheingau Bereich Johannisberg 1985 $10.50 (1/31/88)
83 SCHLOSS SCHONBORN Kabinett Rheingau Johannisberger Klaus 1989 $10 (12/15/90)
92 SCHLOSS SCHONBORN Kabinett Rheingau Winkeler Gutenberg 1989 (NA) (12/15/90)
89 SCHLOSS SCHONBORN Spätlese Halbtrocken Rheingau Hochheimer Hölle 1988 (NA) (9/30/89) (JS)
87 SCHLOSS SCHONBORN Spätlese Halbtrocken Rheingau Hochheimer Kirchenstück 1989 (NA) (12/15/90)
88 SCHLOSS SCHONBORN Spätlese Halbtrocken Rheingau Rüdesheimer Bischofsberg 1988 (NA) (9/30/89) (JS)
86 SCHLOSS SCHONBORN Spätlese Rheingau 1989 (NA) (12/15/90)
93 SCHLOSS SCHONBORN Spätlese Rheingau Erbacher Marcobrunn 1989 (NA) (12/15/90)
90 SCHLOSS SCHONBORN Spätlese Rheingau Hattenheimer Nussbrunnen 1989 (NA) (12/15/90)
86 SCHLOSS SCHONBORN Spätlese Rheingau Hattenheimer Nussbrunnen 1988 $21 (9/30/89) (JS)
91 SCHLOSS SCHONBORN Spätlese Rheingau Hattenheimer Pfaffenberg 1989 (NA) (12/15/90)
84 SCHLOSS SCHONBORN Spätlese Rheingau Hochheimer Kirchenstück 1989 (NA) (12/15/90)
88 STAATSWEINGUTER Kabinett Halbtrocken Rheingau Eltville Hochheimer Kirchenstück 1988 $8 (9/30/89) (JS)
79 STAATSWEINGUTER Kabinett Rheingau Eltville Rauenthaler Baiken 1988 $7.50 (9/30/89) (JS)
78 STAATSWEINGUTER Kabinett Rheingau Eltville Rauenthaler Gehrn 1988 $8 (9/30/89) (JS)
89 STAATSWEINGUTER Spätlese Rheingau Eltville Rauenthaler Baiken 1988 $25 (9/30/89) (JS)
80 SCHLOSS VOLLRADS Kabinett Rheingau 1983 $8 (3/01/85)
78 SCHLOSS VOLLRADS Kabinett Rheingau Blaugold 1985 $11.50 (5/15/87)
89 SCHLOSS VOLLRADS Qüalitätswein Rheingau Grungold 1985 $8.50 (5/15/87)
83 DR. WEIL Auslese Rheingau Kiedricher Gräfenberg 1989 (NA) (12/15/90)
98 DR. WEIL Beerenauslese Rheingau 1989 (NA) (12/15/90)
84 DR. WEIL Kabinett Halbtrocken Rheingau Kiedricher Wasseros Charta 1988 (NA) (9/30/89) (JS)

GERMANY
RIESLING/*RHEINGAU*

83	DR. WEIL Kabinett Rheingau Kiedricher Gräfenberg 1989 (NA) (12/15/90)
91	DR. WEIL Spätlese Halbtrocken Rheingau 1989 (NA) (12/15/90)
78	DR. WEIL Spätlese Rheingau 1989 (NA) (12/15/90)
84	DR. WEIL Spätlese Rheingau Kiedricher Gräfenberg 1988 (NA) (9/30/89) (JS)
93	DR. WEIL Trockenbeerenauslese Rheingau 1989 (NA) (12/15/90)
88	DOMDECHANT WERNER'SCHES Auslese Rheingau Hochheimer 1989 (NA) (12/15/90)
79	DOMDECHANT WERNER'SCHES Beerenauslese Rheingau Hochheimer 1989 (NA) (12/15/90)
79	DOMDECHANT WERNER'SCHES Kabinett Rheingau Hochheimer Domdechaney 1989 (NA) (12/15/90)
88	DOMDECHANT WERNER'SCHES Kabinett Rheingau Hochheimer Domdechaney 1989 (NA) (12/15/90)
87	DOMDECHANT WERNER'SCHES Kabinett Rheingau Hochheimer Hölle 1988 $10.50 (9/30/89) (JS)
86	DOMDECHANT WERNER'SCHES Kabinett Rheingau Hochheimer Hölle (AP989) 1989 (NA) (12/15/90)
83	DOMDECHANT WERNER'SCHES Kabinett Rheingau Hochheimer Hölle (AP1,490) 1989 (NA) (12/15/90)
84	DOMDECHANT WERNER'SCHES Kabinett Halbtrocken Rheingau Hochheimer Stein 1989 (NA) (12/15/90)
87	DOMDECHANT WERNER'SCHES Kabinett Halbtrocken Rheingau Werner Hochheimer Stein 1988 $10.50 (9/30/89) (JS)
77	DOMDECHANT WERNER'SCHES Qualitätswein Rheingau Hochheimer 1989 (NA) (12/15/90)
93	DOMDECHANT WERNER'SCHES Spätlese Halbtrocken Rheingau Hochheimer Hölle 1988 $12.50 (9/30/89) (JS)
83	DOMDECHANT WERNER'SCHES Spätlese Rheingau Hochheimer Domdechaney 1989 $16 (12/15/90)
93	DOMDECHANT WERNER'SCHES Spätlese Rheingau Hochheimer Domdechaney 1988 $12.50 (9/30/89) (JS)
84	DOMDECHANT WERNER'SCHES Trockenbeerenauslese Rheingau Hochheimer 1989 (NA) (12/15/90)

RHEINHESSEN

80	BALBACH Auslese Rheinhessen Niersteiner Hipping 1989 (NA) (12/15/90) (JS)
84	BALBACH Auslese Rheinhessen Niersteiner Pettenthal 1989 (NA) (12/15/90) (JS)
79	BALBACH Auslese Rheinhessen Niersteiner Pettenthal 1985 $16.25 (1/31/87)
84	BALBACH Beerenauslese Rheinhessen Niersteiner Pettenthal 1989 (NA) (12/15/90) (JS)
69	BALBACH Kabinett Rheinhessen 1989 (NA) (12/15/90) (JS)
80	BALBACH Kabinett Rheinhessen Niersteiner Bildstock 1983 $7 (3/01/85)
60	BALBACH Kabinett Rheinhessen Niersteiner Klostergarten 1985 $8 (1/31/87)
82	BALBACH Kabinett Rheinhessen Niersteiner Rehbach 1988 $9 (9/30/89) (JS)
84	BALBACH Spätlese Rheinhessen Niersteiner Hipping 1989 (NA) (12/15/90) (JS)
85	BALBACH Spätlese Rheinhessen Niersteiner Hipping 1988 $12 (9/30/89) (JS)
85	BALBACH Spätlese Rheinhessen Niersteiner Pettenthal 1989 (NA) (12/15/90) (JS)
86	BALBACH Spätlese Rheinhessen Niersteiner Pettenthal 1988 $12 (9/30/89) (JS)
61	BALBACH Spätlese Rheinhessen Niersteiner Pettenthal 1985 $10 (1/31/87)
83	BALBACH Spätlese Rheinhessen Niersteiner Pattenthal 1983 $9 (4/16/85)
88	BALBACH Spätlese Rheinhessen Niersteiner Rehbach 1989 (NA) (12/15/90) (JS)
88	BALBACH Spätlese Rheinhessen Niersteiner Rehbach 1988 $12 (9/30/89) (JS)
81	BALBACH Spätlese Rheinhessen Niersteiner Spiegelberg 1989 (NA) (12/15/90) (JS)
82	BAUM Kabinett Rheinhessen Mainzer Domherr 1985 $5 (10/15/86) BB
76	BAUM Qualitätswein Rheinhessen Niersteiner Gutes Domtal 1984 $4.50 (5/16/85)
91	LOUIS GUNTRUM Auslese Rheinhessen Oppenheimer Schützenhütte 1989 (NA) (12/15/90)
84	LOUIS GUNTRUM Auslese Trocken Rheinhessen Niersteiner Pettenthal 1989 (NA) (12/15/90)
86	LOUIS GUNTRUM Beerenauslese Rheinhessen Niersteiner Pettenthal 1989 (NA) (12/15/90)
88	LOUIS GUNTRUM Kabinett Halbtrocken Rheinhessen Oppenheimer Herrenberg 1988 (NA) (9/30/89) (JS)
84	LOUIS GUNTRUM Kabinett Rheinhessen Niersteiner Bergkirche 1989 (NA) (12/15/90)
86	LOUIS GUNTRUM Kabinett Trocken Rheinhessen Classic Niersteiner Olberg 1989 (NA) (12/15/90)
86	LOUIS GUNTRUM Kabinett Trocken Rheinhessen Classic Oppenheimer Sackträger 1989 (NA) (12/15/90)
91	LOUIS GUNTRUM Spätlese Rheinhessen Heiligenbaum 1988 (NA) (9/30/89) (JS)
74	LOUIS GUNTRUM Spätlese Rheinhessen Oppenheimer Herrenberg 1989 (NA) (12/15/90)
82	LOUIS GUNTRUM Spätlese Trocken Rheinhessen Niersteiner Pettenthal 1989 (NA) (12/15/90)
79	LOUIS GUNTRUM Spätlese Trocken Rheinhessen Oppenheimer Kreuz 1989 (NA) (12/15/90)
85	LOUIS GUNTRUM Trockenbeerenauslese Rheinhessen Oppenheimer Sackträger 1989 (NA) (12/15/90)
88	HEYL ZU HERRNSHEIM Auslese Rheinhessen Niersteiner Olberg 1989 $25 (12/15/90)
91	HEYL ZU HERRNSHEIM Kabinett·Halbtrocken Rheinhessen Niersteiner Pettenthal 1988 (NA) (9/30/89) (JS)
85	HEYL ZU HERRNSHEIM Kabinett Rheinhessen Niersteiner Olberg 1989 $12 (12/15/90)
90	HEYL ZU HERRNSHEIM Kabinett Rheinhessen Niersteiner Olberg 1988 (NA) (9/30/89) (JS)
85	HEYL ZU HERRNSHEIM Kabinett Rheinhessen Niersteiner Pettenthal 1989 $11 (12/15/90)
95	HEYL ZU HERRNSHEIM Spätlese Halbtrocken Rheinhessen Niersteiner Pettenthal 1988 (NA) (9/30/89) (JS)
86	HEYL ZU HERRNSHEIM Spätlese Rheinhessen Niersteiner Brudersberg 1989 $15 (12/15/90)
84	HEYL ZU HERRNSHEIM Spätlese Rheinhessen Niersteiner Olberg 1989 $15 (12/15/90)
89	HEYL ZU HERRNSHEIM Spätlese Rheinhessen Niersteiner Olberg 1988 (NA) (9/30/89) (JS)
84	HEYL ZU HERRNSHEIM Spätlese Rheinhessen Niersteiner Pettenthal 1989 $15 (12/15/90)
90	HEYL ZU HERRNSHEIM Trockenbeerenauslese Rheinhessen Niersteiner Olberg 1989 $50 (12/15/90)
51	KURFURSTENHOF Spätlese Rheinhessen Bornheimer Adelberg 1983 $4.50 (12/01/85)

Key to Symbols

The scores reported here are the results of blind tastings conducted by our panel of senior editors. Wines that carry the initials below are results of individual tastings.

THE WINE SPECTATOR 100-POINT SCALE   95-100—Classic, a great wine; *90-94*—Outstanding, superior character and style; *80-89*—Good to very good, a wine with special qualities; *70-79*—Average, drinkable wine that may have minor flaws; *60-69*—Below average, drinkable but not recommended; *50-59*—Poor, undrinkable, not recommended. "*+*"—With a score indicates a range; used primarily with barrel tastings to indicate a preliminary score.

SPECIAL DESIGNATIONS   SS—Spectator Selection, CS—Cellar Selection, BB—Best Buy.

TASTER'S INITIALS   (JG)—Jim Gordon, (HS)—Harvey Steiman, (JL)—James Laube, (JS)—James Suckling, (TM)—Thomas Matthews, (TR)—Terry Robards, (BT)—Barrel Tasting (these wines were tasted blind from barrel samples), (CA-date)—*California's Great Cabernets* by James Laube, (CH-date)—*California's Great Chardonnays* by James Laube, (VP-date)—*Vintage Port* by James Suckling.

DATE TASTED   Dates in parentheses represent the issue in which the rating was published.

81	DR. MEYER Kabinett Rheinhessen Bereich Nierstein 1987 $4 (10/15/88) BB
75	DR. MEYER Qualitätswein Rheinhessen Zeller Schwarze Katz 1987 $4 (11/30/88)
81	DR. MEYER Rheinhessen Liebfraumilch 1987 $3 (11/30/88) BB
82	DR. MEYER Spätlese Rheinhessen Mainzer Domherr 1986 $5 (11/30/88) BB
64	RUDOLF MULLER Kabinett Rheinhessen Niersteiner Spiegelberg 1986 $5.75 (11/30/87)
81	RUDOLF MULLER Rheinhessen Liebfraumilch Mariengold 1987 $4 (11/30/88) BB
85	REINHOLD SENFTER Kabinett Rheinhessen Niersteiner Oelberg 1986 $8.25 (1/31/88)

RHEINPFALZ

87	BASSERMANN-JORDAN Auslese Rheinpfalz Deddesheimer Hohenmorgen 1989 (NA) (12/15/90)
89	BASSERMANN-JORDAN Kabinett Rheinpfalz Deddesheimer 1989 $9 (12/15/90)
74	BASSERMANN-JORDAN Kabinett Rheinpfalz Deddesheimer Herrgottsaker 1983 $7 (3/16/85)
86	BASSERMANN-JORDAN Kabinett Rheinpfalz Deddesheimer Hohenmorgen 1989 $10 (12/15/90)
94	DR. BURKLIN-WOLF Auslese Rheinpfalz Forster Pechstein 1989 $25 (12/15/90)
95	DR. BURKLIN-WOLF Auslese Rheinpfalz Wachenheimer Gerümpel 1989 $34 (12/15/90)
95	DR. BURKLIN-WOLF Beerenauslese Rheinpfalz Wachenheimer Gerümpel 1989 (NA) (12/15/90)
87	DR. BURKLIN-WOLF Beerenauslese Rheinpfalz Wachenheimer Goldbächel 1988 $30 (9/30/89) (JS)
93	DR. BURKLIN-WOLF Beerenauslese Rheinpfalz Wachenheimer Rechbächel 1989 $95/375ml (12/15/90)
85	DR. BURKLIN-WOLF Kabinett Halbtrocken Rheinpfalz 1988 $8 (9/30/89) (JS)
61	DR. BURKLIN-WOLF Kabinett Rheinpfalz Deidesheimer Hohenmorgen 1985 $6.25 (6/30/87)
87	DR. BURKLIN-WOLF Kabinett Rheinpfalz Ruppertsberger Hoheburg 1989 (NA) (12/15/90)
83	DR. BURKLIN-WOLF Kabinett Rheinpfalz Wachenheimer Gerümpel 1989 $9 (12/15/90)
78	DR. BURKLIN-WOLF Kabinett Rheinpfalz Wachenheimer Rechbächel 1989 (NA) (12/15/90)
84	DR. BURKLIN-WOLF Spätlese Rheinpfalz Deidesheimer Hohenmorgen 1989 $14 (12/15/90)
90	DR. BURKLIN-WOLF Spätlese Rheinpfalz Forster Jusuitgarten 1989 $18 (12/15/90)
85	DR. BURKLIN-WOLF Spätlese Rheinpfalz Wachenheimer Gerümpel 1989 $15 (12/15/90)
80	DR. BURKLIN-WOLF Spätlese Trocken Rheinpfalz Geheimrat Dr. Albert Bürklin-Wolf 1989 (NA) (12/15/90)
88	DR. BURKLIN-WOLF Spätlese Trocken Rheinpfalz Wachenheimer Gerümpel 1988 $10 (9/30/89) (JS)
79	DR. BURKLIN-WOLF Trockenbeerenauslese Rheinpfalz Ruppertsberger Linsenbusch 1988 $9 (9/30/89) (JS)
95	DR. BURKLIN-WOLF Trockenbeerenauslese Rheinpfalz Wachenheimer Luginsland 1989 $165 (12/15/90)
87	MESSMER BURRWEILER Kabinett Halbtrocken Rheinpfalz Schlossgarten 1988 $8 (9/30/89) (JS)
90	MESSMER BURRWEILER Kabinett Rheinpfalz Schlossgarten 1988 (NA) (9/30/89) (JS)
87	MESSMER BURRWEILER Spätlese Rheinpfalz Schäwer 1988 $9 (9/30/89) (JS)
94	MESSMER BURRWEILER Spätlese Trocken Rheinpfalz Schlossgarten 1988 $10 (9/30/89) (JS)
85	WEGELER DEINHARD Auslese Rheinpfalz Deidesheimer Herrgottsacker 1989 $17 (12/15/90) (JS)
82	WEGELER DEINHARD Kabinett Rheinpfalz Deidesheimer Herrgottsacker 1989 $10 (12/15/90) (JS)
87	WEGELER DEINHARD Spätlese Rheinpfalz Deidesheimer Herrgottsacker 1989 $13 (12/15/90) (JS)
84	WEGELER DEINHARD Spätlese Rheinpfalz Deidesheimer Herrgottsacker 1988 $11 (9/30/89) (JS)
86	WEGELER DEINHARD Spätlese Rheinpfalz Forster Ungeheuer 1988 $12 (9/30/89) (JS)
85	WEGELER DEINHARD Spätlese Trocken Rheinpfalz Deidesheimer Herrgottsacker 1988 (NA) (9/30/89) (JS)
93	WEGELER DEINHARD Trockenbeerenauslese Rheinpfalz Deidesheimer Herrgottsacker 1989 (NA) (12/15/90) (JS)
88	JAKOB DEMMER Spätlese Rheinpfalz Weingartener Trappenberg 1986 $5 (11/30/88) BB
90	LINGENFELDER Spätlese Rheinpfalz Freinsheimer Goldberg 1989 $15 (12/15/90) (JS)
89	LINGENFELDER Spätlese Rheinpfalz Freinsheimer Goldberg 1988 $12 (9/30/89) (JS)
88	LINGENFELDER Spätlese Trocken Rheinpfalz Freinsheimer Goldberg 1989 $15 (12/15/90) (JS)
91	LINGENFELDER Spätlese Trocken Rheinpfalz Freinsheimer Goldberg 1988 $12 (9/30/89) (JS)
96	LINGENFELDER Trockenbeerenauslese Rheinpfalz Freinsheimer Goldberg 1989 $100/375ml (12/15/90) (JS)
92	LINGENFELDER Trockenbeerenauslese Rheinpfalz Grosskarlbacher Osterberg 1989 $85/375ml (12/15/90) (JS)
92	MULLER-CATOIR Kabinett Halbtrocken Rheinpfalz Haardter Bürgergarten 1988 $9 (9/30/89) (JS)
92	MULLER-CATOIR Spätlese Trocken Rheinpfalz Mussbacher Eselshaut 1988 $14 (9/30/89) (JS)
72	K. NECKERAUER Kabinett Halbtrocken Rheinpfalz Weisenheimer Hasenzeile 1988 $7 (9/30/89) (JS)
81	K. NECKERAUER Spätlese Trocken Rheinpfalz Weisenheimer Altenberg 1988 $8 (9/30/89) (JS)
82	K. NECKERAUER Spätlese Trocken Rheinpfalz Weisenheimer Hahnen 1988 $8 (9/30/89) (JS)
85	PFEFFINGEN Auslese Rheinpfalz Ungsteiner Herrenberg 1989 $25 (12/15/90)
85	PFEFFINGEN Auslese Rheinpfalz Ungsteiner Weilberg 1989 $25 (12/15/90)
85	PFEFFINGEN Auslese Trocken Rheinpfalz Ungsteiner Herrenberg Scheurebe 1989 $25 (12/15/90)
92	PFEFFINGEN Kabinett Halbtrocken Rheinpfalz Ungsteiner Hönigsäckel 1988 (NA) (9/30/89) (JS)
81	PFEFFINGEN Kabinett Rheinpfalz Ungsteiner Hönigsäckel 1989 $16 (12/15/90)
88	PFEFFINGEN Kabinett Rheinpfalz Ungsteiner Hönigsäckel 1988 $15 (9/30/89) (JS)
85	PFEFFINGEN Spätlese Halbtrocken Rheinpfalz Ungsteiner Herrenberg 1989 $16 (12/15/90)
90	PFEFFINGEN Spätlese Halbtrocken Rheinpfalz Ungsteiner Herrenberg 1988 $16 (9/30/89) (JS)
84	PFEFFINGEN Spätlese Halbtrocken Rheinpfalz Ungsteiner Herrenberg Scheurebe 1989 $16 (12/15/90)
90	PFEFFINGEN Spätlese Rheinpfalz Ungsteiner Herrenberg 1989 $16 (12/15/90)
94	PFEFFINGEN Spätlese Rheinpfalz Ungsteiner Herrenberg 1988 $16 (9/30/89) (JS)
81	PFEFFINGEN Spätlese Rheinpfalz Ungsteiner Herrenberg Scheurebe 1989 $16 (12/15/90)
84	PFEFFINGEN Spätlese Trocken Rheinpfalz Ungsteiner Weilberg 1989 $16 (12/15/90)
92	SICHEL Beerenauslese Rheinpfalz Deidesheimer Hofstuck 1988 $9.75/375ml (3/15/90)

SPARKLING

84	RUDOLF MULLER Mosel-Saar-Ruwer Mosel-Riesling Sekt 1986 $7.50 (10/15/88)
72	DR. H. THANISCH Mosel-Saar-Ruwer Brut 1985 $12.50 (1/31/88)
81	DEINHARD Riesling Lila Imperial NV $7 (8/31/89) BB
72	HENKELL Trocken Feinertrockner Sekt NV $10 (10/15/88)
66	RUDOLF MULLER Splendid Sektkellerei Gold NV $6.25 (6/30/87)
85	SICHEL Novum 1987 $7.50 (10/15/88)

ITALY
DESSERT

73 ABBAZIA DI ROSAZZO Ronco della Abbazia 1988 $11/375ml (7/15/91)
83 ABBAZIA DI ROSAZZO Colli Orientali del Friuli Verduzzo 1986 $22 (10/15/88)
92 AVIGNONESI Vin Santo 1977 $18 (10/01/85)
87 MARCO DE BARTOLI Marsala Superiore Vigna la Miccia 1985 $16 (3/31/90)
87 MARCO DE BARTOLI Moscato di Pantelleria 1987 $16 (3/31/90)
85 BENI DI BATASIOLO Moscato d'Asti 1989 $14 (7/15/91)
68 CAPEZZANA Vin Santo di Carmignano 1981 $16 (10/31/86)
83 CASTELCOSA Picolit 1983 (NA) (9/15/88)
88 CASTELLARE DI CASTELLINA Vin Santo 1984 $28/375ml (9/30/90)
87 FRESCOBALDI Pomino Tenuta di Pomino Vin Santo 1981 $20 (10/15/88)
78 CASTELLO DI GABBIANO Vin Santo 1985 $20 (3/15/91)
85 CARLO HAUNER Malvasia delle Lipari 1984 $15/375ml (12/31/88)
93 ISOLE E OLENA Vin Santo NV $17/375ml (3/31/90)
81 JERMANN Moscato Rosa del FVG Vigna Bellina 1989 $26 (3/15/91)
85 JERMANN Moscato Rosa del FVG Vigna Bellina 1987 $20 (9/15/88)
79 LUNGAROTTI Vin Santo 1985 $7/375ml (3/15/91)
81 LUNGAROTTI Vin Santo 1983 $9.50 (3/15/89)
91 MACULAN Torcolato 1988 $35 (4/15/91)
84 MACULAN Torcolato 1985 $15/375ml (3/31/89)
82 MACULAN Torcolato 1983 $29 (11/15/87)
96 MARTINI DI CIGALA San Giusto a Rentennano Vin Santo 1982 $18/375ml (12/31/88)
89 MARTINI DI CIGALA San Giusto a Rentennano Vin Santo 1981 $25 (12/31/87)
83 MONTE VERTINE Vino Bianco Lungamente M 1983 $20 (2/15/87)
89 MONTE VERTINE Vin Santo NV $20 (2/15/87)
92 CASTELLO DI MONTEGROSSI Vin Santo 1982 $19/375ml (3/31/90)
85 BARONE RICASOLI Vin Santo Brolio 1977 $13 (3/31/90)
76 RUSSIZ SUPERIORE Verduzzo 1987 (NA) (9/15/88)
89 I SELVATICI Vin Santo 1984 $16/375ml (4/30/91)

PIEDMONT RED/*BARBARESCO DOCG*

83 BAVA Barbaresco 1982 $23 (4/30/91)
79 BERSANO Barbaresco 1983 $7.75 (1/31/89)
76 BERSANO Barbaresco 1975 (NA) (9/15/88) (HS)
78 BERSANO Barbaresco 1971 (NA) (9/15/88) (HS)
85 BERSANO Barbaresco 1964 (NA) (9/15/88) (HS)
87 LA CA'NOVA Barbaresco 1986 $14.50 (10/31/90)
88 CA'ROME Barbaresco 1985 $28 (1/31/90)
92 CA'ROME Barbaresco Maria di Brun 1985 $37 (1/31/90)
90 CAVALOTTO Barbaresco Vigna San Giuseppe Riserva 1985 $22 (2/28/91)
58 CERETTO Barbaresco 1981 $9.50 (5/16/86)
86 CERETTO Barbaresco Asij 1987 $22 (7/15/91)
64 CERETTO Barbaresco Asij 1985 $15 (1/31/90)
89 CERETTO Barbaresco Bricco Asili Bricco Asili 1987 $40 (4/30/91)
85 CERETTO Barbaresco Bricco Asili Bricco Asili 1986 $35 (4/15/90)
89 CERETTO Barbaresco Bricco Asili Bricco Asili 1985 $35 (8/31/89)
90 CERETTO Barbaresco Bricco Asili Bricco Asili 1985 $35 (9/15/88) (HS)
80 CERETTO Barbaresco Bricco Asili Bricco Asili 1984 $15 (9/15/88) (HS)
87 CERETTO Barbaresco Bricco Asili Bricco Asili 1982 Rel: $19 Cur: $54 (9/15/88) (HS)
90 CERETTO Barbaresco Bricco Asili Bricco Asili 1978 Cur: $75 (3/01/86) (JS)
89 CERETTO Barbaresco Bricco Asili Bricco Asili 1976 (NA) (9/15/88) (HS)
90 CERETTO Barbaresco Bricco Asili Bricco Asili 1974 (NA) (3/01/86) (JS)
89 CERETTO Barbaresco Bricco Asili Faset 1987 $31 (7/15/91)
87 CERETTO Barbaresco Bricco Asili Faset 1985 $31 (1/31/90)
84 CERETTO Barbaresco Bricco Asili Faset 1985 $31 (9/15/88) (HS)
68 PIO CESARE Barbaresco Riserva 1980 $15.50 (12/16/85)
86 FRATELLI CIGLIUTI Barbaresco Serraboella 1986 $20 (8/31/89)
79 LE COLLINE Barbaresco Riserva Spéciale 1979 $15 (7/31/87)
85 GIUSEPPE CORTESE Barbaresco 1982 $19 (12/15/88)
89 GIUSEPPE CORTESE Barbaresco Rabajà 1986 $19 (9/15/90)
79 GIUSEPPE CORTESE Barbaresco Spéciale 1983 $13 (8/31/89)
75 GIUSEPPE CORTESE Barbaresco Vigna in Rabata 1983 $18 (1/31/90)
72 GIUSEPPE CORTESE Barbaresco Vigna in Rabata 1981 $12 (8/31/89)
80 FONTANAFREDDA Barbaresco 1983 $11.50 (9/15/88) (HS)
81 FONTANAFREDDA Barbaresco 1982 (NA) (9/15/88) (HS)
86 FONTANAFREDDA Barbaresco 1978 (NA) (9/15/88) (HS)
63 DE FORVILLE Barbaresco 1981 $14 (2/16/86)
92 GAJA Barbaresco 1986 $47 (1/31/90) CS
95 GAJA Barbaresco 1985 Rel: $45 Cur: $58 (9/15/89) (HS)
95 GAJA Barbaresco 1985 Rel: $45 Cur: $58 (12/15/88) CS
93 GAJA Barbaresco 1983 Rel: $35 Cur: $53 (9/15/89) (HS)
90 GAJA Barbaresco 1983 Rel: $35 Cur: $53 (7/31/87)
93 GAJA Barbaresco 1982 Cur: $103 (9/15/89) (HS)
90 GAJA Barbaresco 1981 Cur: $110 (9/15/89) (HS)
88 GAJA Barbaresco 1980 Rel: $14 Cur: $75 (7/01/85)
89 GAJA Barbaresco 1979 Cur: $130 (9/15/89) (HS)
93 GAJA Barbaresco 1978 Cur: $130 (9/15/89) (HS)
91 GAJA Barbaresco 1976 Cur: $130 (9/15/89) (HS)
89 GAJA Barbaresco 1974 Cur: $145 (9/15/89) (HS)
86 GAJA Barbaresco 1971 Cur: $156 (9/15/89) (HS)
83 GAJA Barbaresco 1967 Cur: $170 (9/15/89) (HS)
87 GAJA Barbaresco 1964 Cur: $195 (9/15/89) (HS)
92 GAJA Barbaresco 1961 Cur: $270 (9/15/89) (HS)
89 GAJA Barbaresco Costa Russi 1986 Rel: $85 Cur: $126 (1/31/90)
96 GAJA Barbaresco Costa Russi 1985 Rel: $83 Cur: $100 (12/15/88)
91 GAJA Barbaresco Costa Russi 1982 Cur: $93 (9/15/88) (HS)
91 GAJA Barbaresco Sori San Lorenzo 1986 Rel: $89 Cur: $106 (1/31/90)
96 GAJA Barbaresco Sori San Lorenzo 1985 Rel: $88 Cur: $102 (12/15/88)
90 GAJA Barbaresco Sori San Lorenzo 1983 Cur: $99 (9/15/88) (HS)
93 GAJA Barbaresco Sori Tildin 1986 Rel: $94 Cur: $109 (1/31/90)
98 GAJA Barbaresco Sori Tildin 1985 Rel: $94 Cur: $125 (9/15/89) (HS)
97 GAJA Barbaresco Sori Tildin 1985 Rel: $94 Cur: $125 (12/15/88)
88 GAJA Barbaresco Sori Tildin 1983 Cur: $97 (9/15/89) (HS)
94 GAJA Barbaresco Sori Tildin 1982 Cur: $140 (9/15/89) (HS)
87 GAJA Barbaresco Sori Tildin 1981 Cur: $150 (9/15/89) (HS)
89 GAJA Barbaresco Sori Tildin 1979 Cur: $225 (9/15/89) (HS)
90 GAJA Barbaresco Sori Tildin 1978 Cur: $220 (9/15/89) (HS)
88 GAJA Barbaresco Sori Tildin 1973 Cur: $156 (9/15/89) (HS)
91 GAJA Barbaresco Sori Tildin 1971 Cur: $200 (9/15/89) (HS)
78 GAJA Barbaresco Sori Tildin 1970 Cur: $220 (9/15/89) (HS)
84 BRUNO GIACOSA Barbaresco 1985 $42 (8/31/89)
88 BRUNO GIACOSA Barbaresco 1983 $24 (7/31/87)
92 BRUNO GIACOSA Barbaresco Santo Stefano 1982 $57 (9/15/88)
90 BRUNO GIACOSA Barbaresco Santo Stefano di Neive Riserva 1982 $60 (9/15/88) (HS)
87 GIACOSA FRATELLI Barbaresco 1986 $17 (7/15/91)
72 GIACOSA FRATELLI Barbaresco Suri Secondine 1986 $11.50 (10/31/90)
92 MARCHESI DI GRESY Barbaresco Camp Gros Martinenga 1985 Rel: $58 Cur: $73 (1/31/89)
88 MARCHESI DI GRESY Barbaresco Camp Gros Martinenga 1983 Rel: $30 Cur: $85 (9/15/88) (HS)
89 MARCHESI DI GRESY Barbaresco Camp Gros Martinenga 1982 Cur: $75 (9/15/88) (HS)
88 MARCHESI DI GRESY Barbaresco Camp Gros Martinenga 1979 Cur: $40 (9/15/88) (HS)
90 MARCHESI DI GRESY Barbaresco Gaiun Martinenga 1986 Rel: $64 Cur: $96 (9/15/90)
95 MARCHESI DI GRESY Barbaresco Gaiun Martinenga 1985 Rel: $55 Cur: $73 (1/31/89) CS
84 MARCHESI DI GRESY Barbaresco Gaiun Martinenga 1983 Rel: $30 Cur: $83 (9/15/88) (HS)
87 MARCHESI DI GRESY Barbaresco Gaiun Martinenga 1982 Cur: $75 (9/15/88) (HS)
88 MARCHESI DI GRESY Barbaresco Martinenga 1986 Rel: $56 Cur: $84 (9/15/90)
90 MARCHESI DI GRESY Barbaresco Martinenga 1985 Rel: $39 Cur: $57 (1/31/89)
84 MARCHESI DI GRESY Barbaresco Martinenga 1984 Rel: $20 Cur: $36 (9/15/88) (HS)
87 MARCHESI DI GRESY Barbaresco Martinenga 1983 Rel: $20 Cur: $68 (9/15/88) (HS)
86 MARCHESI DI GRESY Barbaresco Martinenga 1982 Rel: $20 Cur: $68 (9/15/88) (HS)
81 MARCHESI DI GRESY Barbaresco Martinenga 1979 Cur: $30 (9/15/88) (HS)
89 MARCHESI DI GRESY Barbaresco Martinenga 1978 Cur: $40 (9/15/88) (HS)
85 GIUSEPPE MASCARELLO & FIGLIO Barbaresco Marcarini 1985 $29.50 (8/31/89)
89 MOCCAGATTA Barbaresco Bric Balin 1987 $28 (7/15/91)
86 MOCCAGATTA Barbaresco Vigneto Basarin 1987 $23 (7/15/91)
79 CASTELLO DI NEIVE Barbaresco Vigneto Santo Stefano 1987 $20 (12/31/90)
86 CASTELLO DI NEIVE Barbaresco Vigneto Santo Stefano 1982 $27 (9/15/88) (HS)
84 ODDERO Barbaresco 1982 $15 (9/15/88)
88 ELIA PASQUERO Barbaresco Sori'Paitin 1985 $14 (3/31/90)
90 PRODUTTORI DEL BARBARESCO Barbaresco 1986 $12 (10/31/90)
80 PRODUTTORI DEL BARBARESCO Barbaresco 1984 $12 (9/15/88) (HS)
85 PRODUTTORI DEL BARBARESCO Barbaresco 1983 $12 (9/15/88) (HS)
87 PRODUTTORI DEL BARBARESCO Barbaresco 1982 $12 (9/15/88) (HS)
90 PRODUTTORI DEL BARBARESCO Barbaresco 1979 $12 (9/15/88) (HS)
92 PRODUTTORI DEL BARBARESCO Barbaresco Asili Riserva 1985 $27 (10/31/90)
89 PRODUTTORI DEL BARBARESCO Barbaresco Asili Riserva 1982 $22 (9/15/88) (HS)
89 PRODUTTORI DEL BARBARESCO Barbaresco Moccagatta 1982 $22 (9/15/88) (HS)
85 PRODUTTORI DEL BARBARESCO Barbaresco Montefico 1982 $22 (9/15/88) (HS)
92 PRODUTTORI DEL BARBARESCO Barbaresco Montefico 1978 $30 (9/15/88) (HS)
88 PRODUTTORI DEL BARBARESCO Barbaresco Montestefano 1982 $18 (9/15/88) (HS)
82 PRODUTTORI DEL BARBARESCO Barbaresco Montestefano Riserva 1985 $25 (10/31/90)
86 PRODUTTORI DEL BARBARESCO Barbaresco Ovello 1982 $22 (9/15/88) (HS)
86 PRODUTTORI DEL BARBARESCO Barbaresco Ovello Riserva 1985 $25 (10/31/90)
91 PRODUTTORI DEL BARBARESCO Barbaresco Paje 1982 $22 (9/15/88) (HS)
91 PRODUTTORI DEL BARBARESCO Barbaresco Pora 1982 $18 (9/15/88) (HS)
91 PRODUTTORI DEL BARBARESCO Barbaresco Pora 1979 $24 (9/15/88) (HS)
89 PRODUTTORI DEL BARBARESCO Barbaresco Rabajà 1982 $22 (9/15/88) (HS)
87 PRODUTTORI DEL BARBARESCO Barbaresco Rio Sordo 1982 $22 (9/15/88) (HS)
86 PRUNOTTO Barbaresco Montestefano 1986 $37 (12/31/90)
87 PRUNOTTO Barbaresco Montestefano 1985 $29 (3/31/90)
81 PRUNOTTO Barbaresco Rabajà Riserva 1982 $19 (7/31/87)
87 FRANCESCO RINALDI & FIGLI Barbaresco 1985 $23 (9/15/90)
79 FRANCESCO RINALDI & FIGLI Barbaresco 1983 $16 (1/31/89)
86 ALFREDO & GIOVANNI ROAGNA Barbaresco 1986 $26 (7/15/91)
89 ALFREDO & GIOVANNI ROAGNA Barbaresco 1985 $37 (2/28/89)
84 SCARPA Barbaresco 1981 $20 (9/15/88) (HS)
90 SCARPA Barbaresco 1979 $20 (9/15/88) (HS)
90 SCARPA Barbaresco 1978 $27 (9/15/88) (HS)
89 SCARPA Barbaresco 1974 (NA) (9/15/88) (HS)
83 SCARPA Barbaresco I Tetti di Neive 1978 $27 (3/15/87)
77 LE TERRE FORTI Barbaresco 1982 $19 (9/15/90)
86 TRAVERSA Barbaresco Sori Ciabot 1985 $23 (9/15/90)
82 VALFIERI Barbaresco 1986 $12 (9/15/90)
70 VALFIERI Barbaresco 1985 $8.25 (7/31/89)
81 VIETTI Barbaresco 1985 $28 (7/31/89)
84 VIETTI Barbaresco 1982 $15 (7/31/87)
87 VIETTI Barbaresco Della Località Rabajà 1986 $18 (10/31/90)

BARBERA DOC

91 ELIO ALTARE Barbera d'Alba 1989 $13 (3/15/91)
84 ELIO ALTARE Barbera d'Alba 1988 $10 (3/31/90)
92 ELIO ALTARE Barbera d'Alba 1987 $11.50 (8/31/89)
88 BENI DI BATASIOLO Barbera d'Alba 1988 $10.50 (4/15/91)
87 BAVA Barbera d'Asti 1985 $13 (3/15/91)
80 BERSANO Barbera d'Asti 1987 $9 (3/15/91)
78 LUIGI CALDI Barbera d'Asti 1985 $7 (7/31/89)
89 CASETTA Barbera d'Alba Vigna Lazaretto 1987 $9 (3/15/91) BB
81 PIO CESARE Barbera d'Alba 1987 $12.50 (4/15/91)
78 PIO CESARE Barbera d'Alba 1985 $11.50 (11/15/88)
86 MICHELE CHIARLO Barbera d'Asti Superiore 1986 $18 (3/15/91)
89 FRATELLI CIGLIUTI Barbera d'Alba Serraboella 1989 $13.50 (3/15/91)
84 CLERICO Barbera d'Alba 1988 $12 (3/15/91)
85 CLERICO Barbera d'Alba 1987 $8 (8/31/89)
84 CLERICO Barbera d'Alba 1985 $8.25 (11/30/87)
86 CONTERNO FANTINO Barbera d'Alba Vignota 1989 $20 (3/15/91)
88 LUIGI COPPO Barbera d'Asti Camp du Rouss 1988 $21 (3/15/91)
87 LUIGI COPPO Barbera d'Asti Camp du Rouss 1986 $19 (3/31/90)
90 LUIGI COPPO Barbera d'Asti Pomorosso 1987 $41 (3/15/91)
84 LUIGI COPPO Barbera d'Asti Pomorosso 1986 $41 (3/15/91)
86 GIUSEPPE CORTESE Barbera d'Alba 1989 $11 (7/15/91)
86 GIUSEPPE CORTESE Barbera d'Alba 1988 $9 (3/15/91)
84 RICCARDO FENOCCHIO Barbera d'Alba Pianpolvere Soprano 1988 $10 (3/15/91)
75 RICCARDO FENOCCHIO Barbera d'Alba Pianpolvere Soprano 1987 $10 (3/15/91)
83 RICCARDO FENOCCHIO Barbera d'Alba Pianpolvere Soprano 1986 $8.50 (3/15/89)
86 RICCARDO FENOCCHIO Barbera d'Alba Pianpolvere Soprano 1985 $15 (3/15/91)
88 GAJA Barbera d'Alba Vignarey 1987 $35 (4/15/91)
88 GAJA Barbera d'Alba Vignarey 1986 $27.50 (3/15/91)
82 GAJA Barbera d'Alba Vignarey 1984 $13.50 (2/15/87)
73 BRUNO GIACOSA Barbera d'Alba Altavilla d'Alba 1987 $12.50 (3/15/91)
77 BRUNO GIACOSA Barbera d'Alba Altavilla d'Alba 1986 $12.50 (3/15/91)

ITALY
PIEDMONT RED/BARBERA DOC

86 GIACOSA FRATELLI Barbera d'Alba Maria Gioana 1986 $22 (3/15/91)
90 MARCARINI Barbera d'Alba Ciabot Camerano 1988 $18 (3/15/91)
82 MARCHESI DI BAROLO Barbera del Monferrato 1985 $5 (9/15/87) BB
78 MARCHESI DI BAROLO Barbera del Monferrato Le Lune 1988 $6 (7/15/91)
80 GIUSEPPE MASCARELLO & FIGLIO Barbera d'Alba Fasana 1987 $10 (3/15/91)
85 GIUSEPPE MASCARELLO & FIGLIO Barbera d'Alba Fasana 1985 $9 (11/30/87)
85 GIUSEPPE MASCARELLO & FIGLIO Barbera d'Alba Superiore Ginestra 1987 $11 (3/15/91)
83 GIUSEPPE MASCARELLO & FIGLIO Barbera d'Alba Superiore Santo Stefano di Perno 1987 $13 (9/15/90)
74 FATTORIA MASSARA Barbera d'Alba 1987 $7.75 (9/15/90)
83 MIRAFIORE Barbera d'Alba 1987 $12.50 (4/15/91)
89 MOCCAGATTA Barbera d'Alba 1989 $14 (3/15/91)
88 NEGRO Barbera d'Alba Nicolon 1989 $11.50 (3/15/91)
83 CASTELLO DI NEIVE Barbera d'Alba Vigneto Messoirano 1988 $11 (7/15/91)
69 CASTELLO DI NEIVE Barbera d'Alba Vigneto Messoirano 1987 $11 (4/15/91)
77 ODDERO Barbera d'Alba 1985 $9 (7/15/88)
85 PARUSSO Barbera d'Alba 1988 $12 (3/15/91)
83 ELIA PASQUERO Barbera d'Alba Sori'Paitin 1988 $8 (3/15/91)
76 LIVIO PAVESE Barbera d'Asti Superiore 1986 $9 (3/15/91)
85 PRUNOTTO Barbera d'Alba 1987 $9.50 (3/31/90)
81 PRUNOTTO Barbera d'Alba 1985 $8 (7/15/88)
89 PRUNOTTO Barbera d'Alba 1983 $6 (7/15/87) BB
81 PRUNOTTO Barbera d'Alba Pian Romualdo 1987 $14.50 (9/15/90)
87 FRANCESCO RINALDI & FIGLI Barbera d'Alba 1987 $10 (3/15/91)
88 FRANCESCO RINALDI & FIGLI Barbera d'Alba 1986 $9 (2/15/89)
90 ROCCHE COSTAMAGNA Barbera d'Alba 1988 $11.50 (3/15/91)
88 SCARPA Barbera d'Asti 1985 $12 (8/31/89)
83 G.D. VAJRA Barbera d'Alba Bricco delle Viole Riserva 1985 $22 (7/31/89)
69 VALFIERI Barbera d'Alba 1987 $7 (9/15/90)
86 VIETTI Barbera d'Alba Della Localita Scarrone 1987 $11 (8/31/89)
79 VIETTI Barbera d'Alba Pianromualdo 1988 $15 (3/15/91)
85 VIETTI Barbera d'Alba Scarrone 1989 $13 (3/15/91)

BAROLO DOCG

92 ELIO ALTARE Barolo 1985 $24 (1/31/90)
88 ELIO ALTARE Barolo 1982 $13 (6/30/87)
87 ELIO ALTARE Barolo Vigneto Arborina 1982 $15 (9/15/87)
81 AZELIA Barolo Bricco Fiasco 1985 $30 (7/15/91)
89 AZELIA Barolo Bricco Fiasco 1985 $30 (9/15/90)
92 AZELIA Barolo Bricco Punta 1982 $23 (11/15/88)
84 BENI DI BATASIOLO Barolo 1985 $14.50 (3/31/90)
79 BENI DI BATASIOLO Barolo Riserva 1982 $17 (3/31/90)
83 BAVA Barolo 1985 $19 (4/30/91)
85 BEL COLLE Barolo Riserva 1982 $15 (3/31/90)
87 BEL COLLE Barolo Vigna Monvigliero 1985 $20 (10/15/90)
79 BERSANO Barolo 1985 $10 (10/15/90)
81 BERSANO Barolo 1983 $9 (11/15/88)
79 BERSANO Barolo 1974 (NA) (9/15/88) (HS)
77 BERSANO Barolo 1971 (NA) (9/15/88) (HS)
80 BERSANO Barolo 1964 (NA) (9/15/88) (HS)
89 CA'ROME Barolo 1985 $35 (10/15/90)
86 CARRETTA Barolo Poderi Cannubi 1985 $22 (10/15/90)
62 CARRETTA Barolo Poderi Cannubi 1980 $14 (9/15/87)
91 CEREQUIO Barolo 1982 $18.50 (11/15/88)
69 CEREQUIO Barolo 1979 $13 (7/31/89)
80 CEREQUIO Barolo Riserva 1980 $13 (7/31/89)
89 CERETTO Barolo Bricco Rocche Rocche 1986 $119 (4/30/91)
86 CERETTO Barolo Bricco Rocche Bricco Rocche 1985 Rel: $56 Cur: $103 (3/31/90)
94 CERETTO Barolo Bricco Rocche Bricco Rocche 1985 Rel: $56 Cur: $103 (9/15/88) (HS)
91 CERETTO Barolo Bricco Rocche Bricco Rocche 1982 Cur: $100 (9/15/88) (HS)
90 CERETTO Barolo Bricco Rocche Bricco Rocche 1980 Cur: $60 (3/01/86) (JS)
80 CERETTO Barolo Bricco Rocche Brunate 1986 $40 (4/30/91)
92 CERETTO Barolo Bricco Rocche Brunate 1985 $41 (1/31/90)
89 CERETTO Barolo Bricco Rocche Brunate 1985 $41 (9/15/88) (HS)
85 CERETTO Barolo Bricco Rocche Brunate 1983 Rel: $27 Cur: $37 (7/31/89)
86 CERETTO Barolo Bricco Rocche Brunate 1979 Cur: $42 (3/01/86) (JS)
86 CERETTO Barolo Bricco Rocche Brunate 1978 Cur: $92 (9/15/88) (HS)
90 CERETTO Barolo Bricco Rocche Brunate 1967 (NA) (10/20/87)
91 CERETTO Barolo Bricco Rocche Prapò 1986 $50 (2/28/91)
78 CERETTO Barolo Bricco Rocche Prapò 1985 $50 (3/31/90)
91 CERETTO Barolo Bricco Rocche Prapò 1985 $50 (9/15/88) (HS)
86 CERETTO Barolo Bricco Rocche Prapò 1983 $31 (7/31/89)
95 CERETTO Barolo Bricco Rocche Prapò 1978 $95 (3/01/86) (JS)
82 CERETTO Barolo Bricco Rocche Prapò 1976 Cur: $70 (9/15/88) (HS)
88 CERETTO Barolo Bricco Rocche Prapò 1971 Cur: $100 (10/30/87)
85 CERETTO Barolo Cannubi 1971 (NA) (3/01/86) (JS)
82 CERETTO Barolo Zonchera 1985 $16 (6/15/90)
83 CERETTO Barolo Zonchera 1984 $16 (9/15/88) (HS)
90 CERETTO Barolo Zonchera 1982 $16 (6/30/87)
96 CERETTO Barolo Zonchera 1980 Rel: $9.50 Cur: $17 (2/16/86) SS
89 PIO CESARE Barolo 1985 $38 (5/15/91)
88 PIO CESARE Barolo 1983 Cur: $33 (9/15/88) (HS)
91 PIO CESARE Barolo 1982 Cur: $36 (9/15/88) (HS)
87 PIO CESARE Barolo 1981 Cur: $25 (9/15/88) (HS)

85 PIO CESARE Barolo 1978 Cur: $18 (9/15/88) (HS)
77 PIO CESARE Barolo 1974 Cur: $40 (9/15/88) (HS)
80 PIO CESARE Barolo 1971 Cur: $38 (9/15/88) (HS)
91 PIO CESARE Barolo Ornato Riserva 1985 $48 (5/15/91)
86 PIO CESARE Barolo Riserva 1982 $31 (11/15/88)
72 PIO CESARE Barolo Riserva 1980 $18.50 (2/15/87)
89 PIO CESARE Barolo Riserva 1978 Rel: $19 Cur: $28 (10/01/84) SS
89 MICHELE CHIARLO Barolo Granduca 1985 $20 (2/28/91)
87 MICHELE CHIARLO Barolo Rocche di Castiglione Riserva 1985 $44 (2/28/91)
78 MICHELE CHIARLO Barolo Rocche di Castiglione Riserva 1983 $30 (2/28/91)
81 MICHELE CHIARLO Barolo Vigna Rionda di Serralunga Riserva 1985 $39 (2/28/91)
87 MICHELE CHIARLO Barolo Vigna Rionda di Serralunga Riserva 1983 $36 (2/28/91)
89 MICHELE CHIARLO Barolo Vigna Rionda di Serralunga Riserva 1982 $32 (1/31/90)
85 CLERICO Barolo 1984 $13 (8/31/88)
92 CLERICO Barolo Ciabot Mentin Ginestra 1985 Rel: $27 Cur: $40 (4/15/90) CS
88 CLERICO Barolo Ciabot Mentin Ginestra 1983 $19 (12/15/87)
86 CLERICO Barolo Vigna Bricotto della Bussia 1980 $8.25 (9/01/85) BB
90 ALDO CONTERNO Barolo Bricco Bussia Vigna Cicala 1985 $40 (6/15/90)
86 ALDO CONTERNO Barolo Bricco Bussia Vigna Cicala 1982 $20 (9/15/87)
84 ALDO CONTERNO Barolo Bricco Bussia Vigna Colonnello 1985 $40 (6/15/90)
87 ALDO CONTERNO Barolo Bussia Soprana 1985 $40 (9/15/90)
85 ALDO CONTERNO Barolo Bussia Soprana 1983 $25 (9/15/88) (HS)
85 ALDO CONTERNO Barolo Bussia Soprana 1982 Rel: $17.50 Cur: $33 (9/15/87)
86 ALDO CONTERNO Barolo Bussia Soprana 1980 Cur: $35 (9/15/88) (HS)
92 ALDO CONTERNO Barolo Bussia Soprana 1978 Cur: $64 (9/15/88) (HS)
90 ALDO CONTERNO Barolo Bussia Soprana 1974 Cur: $60 (9/15/88) (HS)
87 ALDO CONTERNO Barolo Bussia Soprana 1971 Cur: $50 (9/15/88) (HS)
93 ALDO CONTERNO Barolo Granbussia 1982 (NA) (9/15/88) (HS)
87 GIACOMO CONTERNO Barolo 1985 $23 (4/15/90)
88 GIACOMO CONTERNO Barolo 1983 $23 (9/15/88) (HS)
90 GIACOMO CONTERNO Barolo 1982 $25 (9/15/88) (HS)
83 GIACOMO CONTERNO Barolo Riserva Spéciale 1978 (NA) (9/15/88) (HS)
88 GIACOMO CONTERNO Barolo Riserva Spéciale 1970 (NA) (9/15/88) (HS)
84 CONTERNO FANTINO Barolo Sori'Ginestra Riserva 1982 $24 (1/31/90)
75 CONTRATTO Barolo 1983 $10 (3/31/90)
76 CONTRATTO Barolo 1979 $9 (9/30/86)
86 CONTRATTO Barolo del Centenario Riserva 1978 $18 (5/16/86)
91 PAOLO CORDERO DI MONTEZEMOLO Barolo 1980 Rel: $16.50 Cur: $20 (12/15/87) CS
86 PAOLO CORDERO DI MONTEZEMOLO Barolo Enrico VI 1983 $20 (9/15/88) (HS)
88 PAOLO CORDERO DI MONTEZEMOLO Barolo Enrico VI 1982 $25 (9/15/88) (HS)
88 PAOLO CORDERO DI MONTEZEMOLO Barolo Enrico VI 1981 Cur: $25 (9/15/88) (HS)
85 PAOLO CORDERO DI MONTEZEMOLO Barolo Enrico VI 1980 (NA) (9/15/88) (HS)
88 PAOLO CORDERO DI MONTEZEMOLO Barolo Monfalletto 1984 (NA) (9/15/88) (HS)
85 PAOLO CORDERO DI MONTEZEMOLO Barolo Monfalletto 1983 $17 (2/28/89)
87 PAOLO CORDERO DI MONTEZEMOLO Barolo Monfalletto 1983 $17 (9/15/88) (HS)
91 PAOLO CORDERO DI MONTEZEMOLO Barolo Monfalletto 1980 $10.75 (1/31/87)
82 PAOLO CORDERO DI MONTEZEMOLO Barolo Monfalletto 1979 Cur: $33 (9/15/88) (HS)
84 PAOLO CORDERO DI MONTEZEMOLO Barolo Monfalletto 1978 (NA) (9/15/88) (HS)
69 PAOLO CORDERO DI MONTEZEMOLO Barolo Monfalletto 1977 (NA) (9/15/88) (HS)
77 PAOLO CORDERO DI MONTEZEMOLO Barolo Monfalletto 1975 (NA) (9/15/88) (HS)
65 PAOLO CORDERO DI MONTEZEMOLO Barolo Monfalletto 1973 (NA) (9/15/88) (HS)
85 PAOLO CORDERO DI MONTEZEMOLO Barolo Monfalletto 1971 (NA) (9/15/88) (HS)
81 LUIGI EINAUDI Barolo 1982 $22.50 (6/30/87)
62 RICCARDO FENOCCHIO Barolo Pianpolvere Soprano 1984 $15 (7/31/89)
74 RICCARDO FENOCCHIO Barolo Pianpolvero Soprano 1982 $26 (7/31/89)
92 EREDI VIRGINIA FERRERO Barolo S. Rocco 1982 $22 (7/15/88)
67 EREDI VIRGINIA FERRERO Barolo S. Rocco Riserva 1979 $19 (7/31/89)
83 FONTANAFREDDA Barolo 1983 $16 (9/15/88) (HS)
84 FONTANAFREDDA Barolo 1982 $16 (9/15/88) (HS)
80 FONTANAFREDDA Barolo 1978 $12.75 (2/15/84)
90 FONTANAFREDDA Barolo Lazarito 1982 $42 (9/15/88) (HS)
85 FONTANAFREDDA Barolo San Pietro 1982 $42 (9/15/88) (HS)
89 FONTANAFREDDA Barolo Vigna la Rosa 1982 Rel: $40 Cur: $45 (9/15/88) (HS)
90 FONTANAFREDDA Barolo Vigna la Rosa 1982 Rel: $40 Cur: $45 (2/15/88) CS
79 FRANCO-FIORINA Barolo 1982 $22 (5/31/88)
78 BRUNO GIACOSA Barolo 1980 $19 (9/15/87)
88 BRUNO GIACOSA Barolo 1978 $31 (9/16/84)
86 BRUNO GIACOSA Barolo Collina Rionda di Serralunga 1985 $50 (4/30/91)
72 BRUNO GIACOSA Barolo Riserva 1982 $65 (1/31/90)
90 BRUNO GIACOSA Barolo Rocche 1982 $41 (9/15/88)
80 BRUNO GIACOSA Barolo Le Rocche di Castiglione Falletto 1982 $38 (7/31/89)
85 BRUNO GIACOSA Barolo Villero di Castiglione 1983 $29 (1/31/89)
90 MARCARINI Barolo Brunate 1985 $35 (3/31/90)
89 MARCARINI Barolo Brunate 1983 $23 (9/15/88) (HS)
90 MARCARINI Barolo Brunate 1982 $18 (9/15/88) (HS)
88 MARCARINI Barolo Brunate 1979 Cur: $29 (9/15/88) (HS)
80 MARCARINI Barolo Brunate 1978 Cur: $44 (9/15/88) (HS)
89 MARCARINI Barolo Brunate 1971 Cur: $60 (9/15/88) (HS)
96 MARCARINI Barolo Brunate 1964 (NA) (9/15/88) (HS)
87 MARCARINI Barolo La Serra 1983 $17 (9/15/88) (HS)
91 MARCARINI Barolo La Serra 1982 $18 (9/15/88) (HS)
89 MARCARINI Barolo La Serra 1980 $9.50 (4/16/86)
79 MARCARINI Barolo La Serra 1978 $18 (9/16/84)
85 MARCHESI DI BAROLO Barolo Brunate 1985 $29 (10/15/90)
89 MARCHESI DI BAROLO Barolo Brunate 1982 $13.50 (2/15/89)
88 MARCHESI DI BAROLO Barolo Cannubi 1985 $29 (10/15/90)
86 MARCHESI DI BAROLO Barolo Coste di Rosé 1985 $29 (10/15/90)
87 MARCHESI DI BAROLO Barolo Riserva 1982 $13.50 (2/15/89)
86 MARCHESI DI BAROLO Barolo Riserva 1978 $20 (2/28/89)
88 MARCHESI DI BAROLO Barolo Valletta 1985 $29 (10/15/90)
88 BARTOLO MASCARELLO Barolo 1983 $27 (5/31/88)
81 GIUSEPPE MASCARELLO & FIGLIO Barolo 1982 $28 (6/30/87)
91 GIUSEPPE MASCARELLO & FIGLIO Barolo 1978 $19.50 (9/16/84)
93 GIUSEPPE MASCARELLO & FIGLIO Barolo Belvedere 1985 $35 (6/15/90) CS
87 GIUSEPPE MASCARELLO & FIGLIO Barolo Dardi 1982 $18 (9/15/87)
86 GIUSEPPE MASCARELLO & FIGLIO Barolo Monprivato 1985 $53 (6/15/90)
86 GIUSEPPE MASCARELLO & FIGLIO Barolo Monprivato 1983 $28 (9/15/88) (HS)
89 GIUSEPPE MASCARELLO & FIGLIO Barolo Monprivato 1982 $22 (9/15/88) (HS)
84 GIUSEPPE MASCARELLO & FIGLIO Barolo Monprivato 1981 Cur: $23 (9/15/88) (HS)
76 GIUSEPPE MASCARELLO & FIGLIO Barolo Monprivato 1980 Cur: $23 (9/15/88) (HS)

83	GIUSEPPE MASCARELLO & FIGLIO Barolo Monprivato 1979 Cur: $28 (9/15/88) (HS)
86	GIUSEPPE MASCARELLO & FIGLIO Barolo Monprivato 1978 Cur: $42 (9/15/88) (HS)
91	GIUSEPPE MASCARELLO & FIGLIO Barolo Monprivato 1974 Cur: $90 (9/15/88) (HS)
81	GIUSEPPE MASCARELLO & FIGLIO Barolo Monprivato 1971 Cur: $73 (9/15/88) (HS)
80	GIUSEPPE MASCARELLO & FIGLIO Barolo Monprivato 1970 Cur: $60 (9/15/88) (HS)
88	GIUSEPPE MASCARELLO & FIGLIO Barolo Monprivato Falletto 1986 $47 (7/15/91)
80	GIUSEPPE MASCARELLO & FIGLIO Barolo Monprivato Falletto 1983 $23 (7/31/89)
94	GIUSEPPE MASCARELLO & FIGLIO Barolo Santo Stefano di Perno 1985 $35 (10/15/90)
77	GIUSEPPE MASCARELLO & FIGLIO Barolo Villero 1983 $17 (10/15/88)
80	FATTORIA MASSARA Barolo 1985 $20 (6/15/90)
87	MAURO MOLINO Barolo Vigna Conca 1986 $29 (2/28/91)
82	MAURO MOLINO Barolo Vigna Conca 1985 $25 (3/31/90)
92	COLLI MONFORTESI Barolo 1982 $15 (4/30/87) SS
85	ODDERO Barolo 1983 $15 (9/15/88) (HS)
92	ODDERO Barolo 1982 $14 (9/15/88) (HS)
73	ODDERO Barolo 1980 $7 (5/16/86)
84	PARUSSO Barolo 1985 $27 (4/30/91)
83	PARUSSO Barolo Mariondino 1986 $23 (4/30/91)
90	LIVIO PAVESE Barolo Riserva Spéciale 1978 $12 (9/16/84)
82	PRUNOTTO Barolo 1985 $31 (3/31/90)
92	PRUNOTTO Barolo Bussia 1985 $38 (9/15/90)
88	PRUNOTTO Barolo Bussia 1983 $23 (9/15/88) (HS)
91	PRUNOTTO Barolo Bussia 1982 $25 (9/15/88) (HS)
86	PRUNOTTO Barolo Bussia 1978 Cur: $50 (9/15/88) (HS)
80	PRUNOTTO Barolo Bussia 1974 Cur: $65 (9/15/88) (HS)
90	PRUNOTTO Barolo Bussia 1971 Cur: $75 (9/15/88) (HS)
82	PRUNOTTO Barolo Bussia 1967 Cur: $49 (9/15/88) (HS)
80	PRUNOTTO Barolo Bussia 1964 Cur: $85 (9/15/88) (HS)
91	PRUNOTTO Barolo Bussia 1961 Cur: $110 (9/15/88) (HS)
85	PRUNOTTO Barolo Cannubi 1985 $32 (3/31/90)
85	PRUNOTTO Barolo Cannubi 1983 (NA) (9/15/88) (HS)
75	PRUNOTTO Barolo Cannubi 1982 $25 (9/15/88) (HS)
78	PRUNOTTO Barolo Cannubi 1978 (NA) (9/15/88) (HS)
65	PRUNOTTO Barolo Riserva 1980 $12.50 (6/30/87)
78	PRUNOTTO Barolo Riserva Ginestra di Monforte d'Alba 1980 $13.50 (6/30/87)
85	RENATO RATTI Barolo 1985 $23 (9/15/90)
87	RENATO RATTI Barolo 1983 $20 (10/15/88)
93	RENATO RATTI Barolo 1982 Rel: $17 Cur: $28 (6/30/87) CS
83	RENATO RATTI Barolo 1980 $10 (2/15/87)
89	RENATO RATTI Barolo 1979 $8.50 (1/01/86)
82	RENATO RATTI Barolo Marcenasco 1985 $37 (10/15/90)
90	RENATO RATTI Barolo Marcenasco 1982 Rel: $23 Cur: $37 (6/30/87)
84	RENATO RATTI Barolo Marcenasco 1981 $14.50 (6/30/87)
86	RENATO RATTI Barolo Marcenasco Rocche 1983 $30 (1/31/89)
88	RENATO RATTI Barolo Marcenasco Rocche 1981 $19 (6/30/87)
86	GIOVANNI & BATTISTA RINALDI Barolo 1983 (NA) (9/15/88) (HS)
84	GIOVANNI & BATTISTA RINALDI Barolo 1982 (NA) (9/15/88) (HS)
83	FRANCESCO RINALDI & FIGLI Barolo 1986 $22 (7/15/91)
84	FRANCESCO RINALDI & FIGLI Barolo 1983 $20 (9/15/88) (HS)
83	FRANCESCO RINALDI & FIGLI Barolo 1982 Rel: $16 Cur: $50 (9/15/88) (HS)
89	FRANCESCO RINALDI & FIGLI Barolo 1978 Rel: $12 Cur: $69 (9/16/84)
89	FRANCESCO RINALDI & FIGLI Barolo La Brunata 1985 $24 (7/15/91)
86	FRANCESCO RINALDI & FIGLI Barolo La Brunata 1985 $24 (6/15/90)
79	FRANCESCO RINALDI & FIGLI Barolo La Brunata Riserva 1982 $27 (6/30/87)
78	FRANCESCO RINALDI & FIGLI Barolo Cannubbio 1985 $25 (6/15/90)
75	FRANCESCO RINALDI & FIGLI Barolo Cannubbio 1982 $16 (10/31/87)
72	ROCCHE COSTAMAGNA Barolo Rocche di la Morra 1985 $25 (2/28/91)
82	LUCIANO SANDRONE Barolo 1984 $13.50 (8/31/88)
90	LUCIANO SANDRONE Barolo 1983 $20 (12/15/87)
94	LUCIANO SANDRONE Barolo 1982 $15 (6/30/87)
89	LUCIANO SANDRONE Barolo Cannubi Boschis 1986 $34 (12/31/90)
92	LUCIANO SANDRONE Barolo Cannubi Boschis 1985 $30 (1/31/90)
90	SCARPA Barolo 1985 (NA) (9/15/88) (HS)
88	SCARPA Barolo 1982 (NA) (9/15/88) (HS)
89	SCARPA Barolo 1978 $27 (9/15/88) (HS)
81	SCARPA Barolo Le Coste di Monforte 1978 $27 (3/15/87)
88	PAOLO SCAVINO Barolo 1985 $21 (10/15/90)
85	PAOLO SCAVINO Barolo 1983 (NA) (9/15/88) (HS)
88	PAOLO SCAVINO Barolo 1982 (NA) (9/15/88) (HS)
90	PAOLO SCAVINO Barolo Brico dell Fiasco 1985 $39 (6/15/90)
74	PAOLO SCAVINO Barolo Cannubi 1985 $30 (1/31/90)
90	SEBASTE Barolo 1985 (NA) (9/15/88) (HS)
85	SEBASTE Barolo 1984 (NA) (9/15/88) (HS)
86	SEBASTE Barolo 1983 (NA) (9/15/88) (HS)
91	SEBASTE Barolo 1982 (NA) (9/15/88) (HS)
85	SEBASTE Barolo 1979 (NA) (9/15/88) (HS)
84	SEBASTE Barolo Bussia Riserva 1984 $17 (7/31/89)
90	SEBASTE Barolo Bussia Riserva 1982 $15 (11/15/87)
83	AURELIO SETTIMO Barolo Vigna Rocche 1982 $19 (5/31/88)
73	AURELIO SETTIMO Barolo Vigna Rocche 1980 $17 (5/31/88)
67	AURELIO SETTIMO Barolo Vigna Rocche 1979 $25 (5/31/88)
91	G.D. VAJRA Barolo 1982 $14 (3/15/87)
91	G.D. VAJRA Barolo Bricco delle Viole 1982 $19 (8/31/88)
91	G.D. VAJRA Barolo Fossati Vineyard 1985 $34 (12/31/90)
90	VALFIERI Barolo 1985 $13.50 (10/15/90)
84	VIETTI Barolo 1978 $12 (9/16/84)
89	VIETTI Barolo Bussia 1982 $20 (9/15/87)
85	VIETTI Barolo Rocche 1982 Rel: $45 Cur: $60 (7/31/89)
90	VIETTI Barolo Rocche 1982 Rel: $45 Cur: $60 (9/15/88) (HS)
87	VIETTI Barolo Rocche 1980 Cur: $30 (9/15/88) (HS)
79	VIETTI Barolo Rocche 1979 (NA) (9/15/88) (HS)
92	VIETTI Barolo Rocche 1978 Cur: $60 (9/15/88) (HS)
86	VIETTI Barolo Rocche 1971 Cur: $70 (9/15/88) (HS)
93	VIETTI Barolo Rocche 1961 Cur: $100 (9/15/88) (HS)
89	VIETTI Barolo Villero Riserva 1982 $45 (9/15/88) (HS)
73	VILLADORIA Barolo Riserva Spéciale 1978 $14 (8/31/86)
87	VOERZIO Barolo 1985 $18 (1/31/90)
88	VOERZIO Barolo 1983 $15 (9/15/88) (HS)
90	VOERZIO Barolo 1982 $12 (9/15/88) (HS)
91	VOERZIO Barolo La Serra di La Morra 1982 $12 (7/31/87)

DOLCETTO DOC

79	ABBAZIA DI VALLE CHIARA Dolcetto d'Ovada 1989 $13 (7/15/91)
81	ELIO ALTARE Dolcetto d'Alba 1989 $12 (7/15/91)
82	ELIO ALTARE Dolcetto d'Alba 1988 $10 (3/31/90)
90	ELIO ALTARE Dolcetto d'Alba 1987 $9 (2/28/89)
85	AZELIA Dolcetto d'Alba 1987 $7 (3/15/89)
79	AZELIA Dolcetto d'Alba Bricco dell'Oriolo 1989 $9.25 (7/15/91)
78	AZELIA Dolcetto d'Alba Cascina Nuova 1986 $8.50 (12/31/87)
82	BENI DI BATASIOLO Dolcetto d'Alba 1989 $12 (7/15/91)
85	BENI DI BATASIOLO Dolcetto d'Alba 1988 $10.50 (12/31/90)
80	BEL COLLE Dolcetto d'Alba 1986 $7.50 (4/15/88)
84	CASCINA BORDINO Dolcetto d'Alba 1988 $9.50 (3/31/90)
83	CAVALOTTO Dolcetto d'Alba Mallera 1987 $10 (3/15/89)
79	CERETTO Dolcetto d'Alba Rossana 1989 $16 (4/30/91)
86	CERETTO Dolcetto d'Alba Rossana 1987 $12 (3/15/89)
74	CERETTO Dolcetto d'Alba Rossana 1985 $8.75 (12/31/87)
77	CERETTO Dolcetto d'Alba Vigna 1985 $11 (3/15/89)
71	PIO CESARE Dolcetto d'Alba 1985 $10 (10/31/86)
88	PIO CESARE Dolcetto d'Alba 1984 $7.50 (11/16/85)
87	CHIONETTI Dolcetto di Dogliani Briccolero 1989 $15.50 (4/30/91)
87	CLERICO Dolcetto d'Alba 1987 $7.50 (8/31/88)
80	CLERICO Dolcetto d'Alba 1986 $7.75 (12/31/87)
68	CLERICO Dolcetto d'Alba 1984 $4 (9/15/87)
82	ELVIO COGNO Dolcetto d'Alba 1984 $5.50 (2/16/86)
84	ALDO CONTERNO Dolcetto d'Alba 1987 $12 (9/15/90)
77	ALDO CONTERNO Dolcetto d'Alba 1985 $10 (5/15/87)
81	LUIGI COPPO Dolcetto d'Alba 1989 $10.50 (7/15/91)
83	GIUSEPPE CORTESE Dolcetto d'Alba 1989 $9.75 (12/31/90)
78	GIUSEPPE CORTESE Dolcetto d'Alba 1988 $8 (3/31/90)
58	LUIGI EINAUDI Dolcetto di Dogliani 1983 $7 (9/30/86)
81	DE FORVILLE Dolcetto d'Alba Vigneto Loreto 1989 $12 (2/28/91)
83	FRANCO-FIORINA Dolcetto d'Alba 1989 $13 (4/30/91)
76	FRANCO-FIORINA Dolcetto d'Alba 1987 $8.75 (7/31/89)
88	BRUNO GIACOSA Dolcetto d'Alba 1989 $12 (2/28/91)
77	BRUNO GIACOSA Dolcetto d'Alba Plinet di Trezzo Tinella 1985 $8 (12/31/87)
76	EILO GRASSO Dolcetto d'Alba Gavarini Vigna dei Grassi 1989 $18 (7/15/91)
81	MARCHESI DI GRESY Dolcetto d'Alba Monte Aribaldo 1986 $8 (10/31/88)
89	MARCARINI Dolcetto d'Alba Boschi di Berri 1989 $23 (4/30/91)
86	MARCARINI Dolcetto d'Alba Boschi di Berri 1988 $17 (3/31/90)
89	MARCARINI Dolcetto d'Alba Boschi di Berri 1987 $13 (3/15/89)
84	MARCARINI Dolcetto d'Alba Fontanazza 1989 $13.50 (4/30/91)
87	MARCARINI Dolcetto d'Alba Fontanazza 1988 $11 (3/31/90)
78	MARCARINI Dolcetto d'Alba Fontanazza 1987 $9.75 (3/15/89)
82	MARCARINI Dolcetto d'Alba Fontanazza 1985 $7.50 (2/15/87)
88	MARCHESI DI BAROLO Dolcetto d'Alba Madonna di Como 1989 $9 (12/31/90) BB
87	MARCHESI DI BAROLO Dolcetto d'Alba Madonna di Como 1987 $8 (2/15/89)
88	GIUSEPPE MASCARELLO & FIGLIO Dolcetto d'Alba Bricco Falletto 1987 $9 (3/15/89)
82	GIUSEPPE MASCARELLO & FIGLIO Dolcetto d'Alba Bricco Ravera 1988 $10 (9/15/90)
85	GIUSEPPE MASCARELLO & FIGLIO Dolcetto d'Alba Gagliassi 1989 $13 (7/15/91)
80	GIUSEPPE MASCARELLO & FIGLIO Dolcetto d'Alba Gagliassi 1987 $10 (3/31/90)
82	GIUSEPPE MASCARELLO & FIGLIO Dolcetto d'Alba Gagliassi Monforte 1987 $9 (3/15/89)
80	GIUSEPPE MASCARELLO & FIGLIO Dolcetto d'Alba Venora 1985 $7 (12/31/87)
87	MAURO MOLINO Dolcetto d'Alba 1989 $14 (2/28/91)
82	MAURO MOLINO Dolcetto d'Alba 1988 $12 (3/31/90)
80	CASTELLO DI NEIVE Dolcetto d'Alba Vigneto Basarin 1989 $12 (2/28/91)
80	CASTELLO DI NEIVE Dolcetto d'Alba Vigneto Basarin 1987 $11 (3/15/89)
73	CASTELLO DI NEIVE Dolcetto d'Alba Vigneto Valtorta 1986 $12 (3/15/89)
73	CASTELLO DI NEIVE Dolcetto d'Alba Vigneto Valtorta 1986 $12 (8/31/88)
78	ODDERO Dolcetto d'Alba 1989 $8.75 (4/30/91)
78	ODDERO Dolcetto d'Alba 1987 $9.50 (3/15/89)
85	ODDERO Dolcetto d'Alba 1986 $9.50 (3/15/89)
83	ODDERO Dolcetto d'Alba 1986 $9.50 (8/31/88)
84	PRUNOTTO Dolcetto d'Alba 1985 $10 (3/15/89)
88	PRUNOTTO Dolcetto d'Alba Gagliassi di Monforte Riserva 1985 $11.50 (3/15/89)
90	RENATO RATTI Dolcetto d'Alba Vigna Colombe 1985 $9.25 (2/28/87)
80	FRANCESCO RINALDI & FIGLI Dolcetto d'Alba 1989 $12 (7/15/91)
78	FRANCESCO RINALDI & FIGLI Dolcetto d'Alba Roussot 1988 $10 (7/15/91)
86	FRANCESCO RINALDI & FIGLI Dolcetto d'Alba Roussot 1988 $10 (9/15/90)
86	FRANCESCO RINALDI & FIGLI Dolcetto d'Alba Roussot Alto 1987 $9 (3/31/90)
83	ROCCHE COSTAMAGNA Dolcetto d'Alba 1989 $12 (4/30/91)
87	LUCIANO SANDRONE Dolcetto d'Alba 1989 $12 (7/15/91)
80	LUCIANO SANDRONE Dolcetto d'Alba 1986 $8.75 (12/31/87)
87	LUCIANO SANDRONE Dolcetto d'Alba 1985 $6.50 (7/31/87) BB
81	VALFIERI Dolcetto d'Alba 1988 $8.50 (12/31/90)
78	VALFIERI Dolcetto d'Alba 1987 $5.75 (3/15/89)
85	VIETTI Dolcetto d'Alba Bussia 1989 $12 (2/28/91)
87	VIETTI Dolcetto d'Alba Della Località Disa 1988 $12 (9/15/90)
74	VIETTI Dolcetto d'Alba Disa 1985 $7 (9/15/87)
65	VILLADORIA Dolcetto d'Alba 1987 $6 (3/15/89)
87	VOERZIO Dolcetto d'Alba Priavino 1988 $11 (12/31/90)

VINO DA TAVOLA

65	ACCOMASSO Nebbiolo delle Langhe 1982 $14 (7/31/89)
85	ELIO ALTARE 1989 $11.50 (7/15/91)
84	ELIO ALTARE Nebbiolo Vigna Arborina 1987 $32 (9/15/90)
90	ELIO ALTARE Nebbiolo Vigna Arborina 1986 $20 (2/28/89)
89	ELIO ALTARE Nebbiolo Vigna Larigi 1987 $28 (5/31/90)
81	ELIO ALTARE Nebbiolo delle Langhe 1988 $10 (3/31/90)
85	ELIO ALTARE Nebbiolo delle Langhe 1987 $9 (7/31/89)
88	BERSANO Castellengo 1986 $16 (4/15/91)
92	GIACOMO BOLOGNA Barbera Bricco della Bigotta 1988 $40 (3/15/91)
88	GIACOMO BOLOGNA Barbera Bricco della Bigotta 1987 $34 (3/15/91)
88	GIACOMO BOLOGNA Barbera Bricco della Bigotta 1986 $34 (3/15/91)
91	GIACOMO BOLOGNA Bricco dell' Uccellone Barbera 1988 $45 (3/15/91)
88	GIACOMO BOLOGNA Bricco dell' Uccellone Barbera 1987 $45 (3/15/91)
89	GIACOMO BOLOGNA Bricco dell' Uccellone Barbera 1986 $38 (3/15/91)
88	GIACOMO BOLOGNA Bricco dell' Uccellone Barbera 1985 $33 (8/31/89)
79	BRICCO DEL DRAGO Vigna 'd le Mace 1985 $22 (1/31/89)
84	BRICCO DEL DRAGO Vigna 'd le Mace 1982 $14 (11/30/87)

ITALY
PIEDMONT RED/VINO DA TAVOLA

89 CASAL THAULERO Abbazia di Propezzano 1986 $19 (7/15/91)
61 CASCINACASTLE'T Passum 1984 $25 (12/31/88)
88 PIO CESARE Nebbiolo 1983 $8 (2/16/86)
82 PIO CESARE Ornato 1983 $15.50 (3/31/88)
80 MICHELE CHIARLO Barilot 1986 $27 (2/28/91)
90 CLERICO Arte 1988 $26 (2/28/91)
78 CLERICO Arte 1987 $22 (1/31/90)
88 CLERICO Arte 1986 $22 (2/15/89)
91 CLERICO Arte 1985 $22 (1/31/88)
84 ALDO CONTERNO Nebbiolo Il Favot Monforte Bussia 1983 $12.50 (5/31/90)
83 ALDO CONTERNO Nebbiolo Il Favot Monforte Bussia NV $10 (5/31/90)
85 ALDO CONTERNO Nebbiolo delle Langhe Bussia Conca Tre Pile 1985 $13 (11/15/88)
91 CONTERNO FANTINO Monprá 1988 $27 (3/15/91)
87 LUIGI COPPO Mondaccione 1987 $13.50 (3/31/90)
80 GIUSEPPE CORTESE Vigna in Rabajà 1988 $12.50 (2/28/91)
87 DESSILANI Barbera del Piemonte 1986 $7 (3/15/91) BB
79 DESSILANI Caramino Riserva 1985 $13 (9/15/90)
70 LUIGI EINAUDI Nebbiolo delle Langhe 1983 $8 (7/01/86)
94 GAJA Cabernet Sauvignon Darmagi 1986 $76 (1/31/90)
94 GAJA Cabernet Sauvignon Darmagi 1985 $70 (3/15/89) CS
91 GAJA Cabernet Sauvignon Darmagi 1983 Rel: $51 Cur: $68 (7/15/88)
83 EILO GRASSO Gavarini 1989 $20 (7/15/91)
82 MARCHESI DI GRESY Nebbiolo Martinenga 1986 $11 (10/15/88)
84 MARCARINI Lasarin Nebbiolo delle Langhe 1989 $9.50 (4/30/91)
84 MARCARINI Nebbiolo delle Langhe 1988 $10 (3/31/90)
86 MAURO MOLINO Nebbiolo delle Langhe 1989 $14 (2/28/91)
84 MAURO MOLINO Nebbiolo delle Langhe 1988 $12 (3/31/90)
80 LUIGI & ITALO NERVI Spanna 1988 $9 (7/15/91)
82 PRODUTTORI DEL BARBARESCO Nebbiolo Langhe 1988 $9 (2/28/91)
76 ALFREDO & GIOVANNI ROAGNA Opera Prima IV NV $23 (7/31/89)
82 ALFREDO & GIOVANNI ROAGNA Opera Prima Imbottigliato il 15 Novembre 1986 NV $17 (12/31/87)
85 ROCCHE COSTAMAGNA Roccardo Nebbiolo delle Langhe 1989 $13 (4/30/91)
89 SEBASTE Bricco Viole 1986 $16 (1/31/89)
91 SEBASTE Bricco Viole 1985 $13 (10/31/87)
83 TRAVAGLINI Spanna 1988 $10 (7/15/91)
88 VALLANA Barbera 1988 $8 (3/15/91)
80 VALLANA Barbera 1988 $7 (3/31/90)
90 VALLANA Barbera 1986 $6 (2/15/89) BB
85 VIETTI Fioretto 1987 $17 (6/15/90)

OTHER PIEDMONT RED DOC

84 GIACOMO BOLOGNA Brachetto d'Acqui 1987 $16 (3/31/90)
69 LUIGI CALDI Gattinara 1982 $12 (1/31/90)
81 CERETTO Nebbiolo d'Alba Lantasco 1988 $18 (4/30/91)
74 LE COLLINE Gattinara Monsecco 1976 $13.50 (8/31/87)
78 FRANCO-FIORINA Freisa delle Langhe 1989 $16 (7/15/91)
80 FRANCO-FIORINA Nebbiolo d'Alba 1985 $9.25 (8/31/88)
87 GAJA Nebbiolo d'Alba Vignaveja 1985 $30 (2/15/89)
94 GAJA Nebbiolo d'Alba Vignaveja 1983 $16 (2/15/87) SS
78 MARCHISIO Roero Vigneti Mongalletto 1987 $10 (3/31/90)
75 GIUSEPPE MASCARELLO & FIGLIO Grignolino del Monferrato Casalese Besso 1988 $9.50 (1/31/90)
85 GIUSEPPE MASCARELLO & FIGLIO Nebbiolo d'Alba San Rocco 1986 $15 (9/15/90)
63 LUIGI & ITALO NERVI Gattinara 1983 $11 (5/31/90)
68 LUIGI & ITALO NERVI Gattinara Vigneto Molsino 1983 $15 (5/31/90)
77 LUIGI & ITALO NERVI Gattinara Vigneto Valferana 1983 $15 (5/31/90)
72 GIUSEPPE POGGIO Bricco Trionzo 1985 $10 (3/15/89)
62 PRUNOTTO Nebbiolo d'Alba 1983 $8 (7/15/87)
82 PRUNOTTO Roero 1986 $10 (6/30/88)
88 PRUNOTTO Roero 1985 $9 (7/31/87)
81 RENATO RATTI Nebbiolo d'Alba 1983 $7 (6/16/86) BB
63 TRAVAGLINI Gattinara 1980 $8.75 (12/16/85)
76 VALLANA Gattinara 1983 $10 (1/31/90)
69 VIETTI Nebbiolo d'Alba San Michele 1983 $7 (9/15/87)

PIEDMONT WHITE/VINO DA TAVOLA

79 BENI DI BATASIOLO Chardonnay delle Langhe 1989 $14 (7/15/91)
82 BENI DI BATASIOLO Chardonnay delle Langhe Vigneto Morino 1989 $27 (7/15/91)
87 BENI DI BATASIOLO Chardonnay Vigneto Morino 1988 $25 (12/31/90)
76 BOLLA Chardonnay 1989 $6 (4/30/90)
82 BOLLA Chardonnay 1988 $6 (9/15/89)
82 CERETTO Arneis Blange' 1989 $19 (7/15/91)
92 PIO CESARE Chardonnay 1987 $29 (9/15/89)
88 PIO CESARE Chardonnay 1986 $29 (9/15/89)
90 PIO CESARE Chardonnay 1986 $29 (10/15/88)
75 DE FORVILLE Chardonnay 1989 $12 (2/15/91)
83 FRANCO-FIORINA Chardonnay 1989 $21 (3/31/91)
70 FRANCO-FIORINA Freisa delle Langhe 1989 $15.50 (4/15/91)
75 FRANCO-FIORINA Favorita delle Langhe 1988 $12 (4/30/90)
86 GAJA Chardonnay Gaia & Rey 1988 $68 (12/31/90)
95 GAJA Chardonnay Gaia & Rey 1987 $43 (9/15/89)

---

88 GAJA Chardonnay Gaia & Rey 1987 $43 (3/31/89)
90 GAJA Chardonnay Gaia & Rey 1986 $37 (6/30/88)
98 GAJA Chardonnay Gaia & Rey 1985 Rel: $45 Cur: $65 (9/15/89)
85 GAJA Chardonnay Rossj-Bass 1988 $45 (3/31/90)
85 MARCHESI DI GRESY Chardonnay 1987 $37 (9/15/89) (HS)
75 MOCCAGATTA Chardonnay Bric Buschet 1987 (NA) (9/15/89)
74 MOCCAGATTA Chardonnay Vigneto Buschet 1988 (NA) (9/15/89)
72 CASTELLO DI NEIVE Arneis Delle Langhe 1986 $18 (10/15/88)
89 ALFREDO & GIOVANNI ROAGNA Chardonnay 1987 $20 (9/15/89)
74 SEBASTE Arneis 1986 $11.50 (11/15/87)

WHITE DOC

83 VILLA BANFI Gavi Principessa 1989 $12 (12/31/90)
86 VILLA BANFI Gavi Principessa 1987 $12 (12/31/88)
80 VILLA BANFI Gavi Principessa 1986 $11 (3/31/88)
82 VILLA BANFI Gavi Principessa 1985 $10 (10/15/86)
85 VILLA BANFI Gavi Principessa 1983 $10 (4/16/85)
83 LA BATTISTINA Gavi 1987 $18 (4/30/90)
80 LA BATTISTINA Gavi Bricco Battistina 1985 $24 (12/31/88)
78 BAVA Gavi 1989 $13 (7/15/91)
81 BOLLA Gavi di Gavi 1987 $8 (10/15/89)
75 BOLLA Gavi di Gavi 1986 $8.50 (10/15/88)
86 PIO CESARE Cortese di Gavi 1986 $15 (10/15/88)
85 PIO CESARE Cortese di Gavi 1985 $13 (11/30/86)
84 MICHELE CHIARLO Gavi Granduca 1989 $12 (1/31/91)
70 CONTRATTO Gavi 1984 $8 (10/15/86)
61 FONTANAFREDDA Gavi 1984 $6.75 (4/16/86)
71 GIACOSA FRATELLI Gavi 1989 $14 (7/15/91)
77 GIACOSA FRATELLI Roero Arneis 1989 $17 (7/15/91)
82 NEIRANO Gavi 1985 $5 (10/15/86)
80 LA SCOLCA Gavi La Scolca 1986 $23 (6/30/88)
75 LA SCOLCA Gavi Villa Scolca 1986 $14 (6/30/88)
79 VALFIERI Gavi 1987 $5.75 (7/31/89)
83 VALFIERI Gavi Villa Montersino Vigneti Borghero 1989 $16 (7/15/91)

SPARKLING

68 ANTINORI Nature NV $18 (12/31/86)
81 VILLA BANFI Brut 1985 $15.50 (6/30/90)
90 VILLA BANFI Brut 1984 $14 (3/31/88)
88 VILLA BANFI Brut 1982 $13 (12/31/86)
82 BELLAVISTA Brut Cuvée NV $17.50 (12/31/86)
84 BELLAVISTA Brut Franciacorta Gran Cuvée 1982 $27 (12/31/86)
83 BERA Asti Spumante NV $15 (7/15/91)
84 BERA Moscato d'Asti NV $14 (7/15/91)
80 GUIDO BERLUCCHI Brut Cuvée Impériale 1981 $14.50 (12/31/86)
81 GUIDO BERLUCCHI Brut Cuvée Impériale NV $12.50 (9/15/89)
80 GUIDO BERLUCCHI Brut Cuvée Impériale NV $13 (12/31/86)
75 GUIDO BERLUCCHI Cuvée Impériale Pas Dose NV $13 (12/31/86)
76 BONARDI Asti Spumante NV $9.75 (2/15/87)
81 BONARDI Moscato d'Asti NV $12 (3/31/90)
88 CA' DEL BOSCO Franciacorta Brut NV $25 (10/15/88)
82 CA' DEL BOSCO Franciacorta Crémant NV $29 (10/15/88)
87 CA' DEL BOSCO Franciacorta Dosage Zero NV $25 (10/15/88)
79 BRENTA D'ORO Asti Spumante Vezza d'Alba NV $7 (5/31/87)
75 BURATI Asti Spumante NV $6.50 (3/15/89)
80 CASCINETTA Moscato d'Asti 1987 $9 (12/31/90)
77 CELLA Asti Spumante NV $7.50 (1/31/88)
78 CINZANO Dry Chardonnay NV $7 (2/01/86)
84 CINZANO Dry Pinot Nature NV $7 (2/16/86) BB
83 CINZANO Dry Sauvignon Blanc NV $7 (3/16/86) BB
78 CINZANO Pas Dose 1983 $30 (12/31/86)
84 CINZANO Pinot Nature NV $7 (12/31/86)
78 CONTE BALDUINO Extra Brut Riccadonna 1981 $13.50 (12/31/86)
75 CONTRATTO Asti Spumante Fermentazione Naturale NV $8 (10/31/86)
82 CONTRATTO Brut Classico Dégorgement Winter 1989 NV $10 (6/15/90)
64 CONTRATTO Brut Classico Riserva Dégorgement Spring 1985 1981 $19 (12/31/86)
60 CONTRATTO Classico Reserve for England Dégorgement Spring 1985 NV $15 (12/31/86)
84 GIROLAMO DORIGO Cuvée Pinot Pas Dose Montsclapade 1984 $22 (3/31/88)
78 EQUIPE 5 Brut NV $15 (12/31/86)
83 EQUIPE 5 Brut Riserva NV $20 (12/31/86)
82 FAZI-BATTAGLIA Brut NV $10 (12/31/86)
88 FERRARI Brut NV $20 (12/31/90)
84 FERRARI Brut de Brut 1981 $22 (5/31/87)
97 FERRARI Brut de Brut 1981 $22 (12/31/86)
90 FERRARI Brut de Brut NV $16 (12/31/86)
88 FERRARI Brut Perle' 1985 $30 (12/31/90)
86 GIULIO FERRARI Riserva del Fondatore 1982 $50 (12/31/90)
86 FONTANAFREDDA Asti Spumante The Royal Preserves NV $10.50 (1/31/88)
68 FONTANAFREDDA Contessa Rosa NV $5.75 (12/31/86)
86 FRESCOBALDI Brut 1985 $12 (12/31/90)
84 GANCIA Asti Spumante NV $12.50 (8/31/90)
82 GANCIA Brut Chardonnay NV $11 (12/31/90)
86 GANCIA Brut Chardonnay NV $11 (12/31/89) BB
75 GANCIA Brut Chardonnay NV $11 (12/31/86)
82 GANCIA Crémant Gran Riserva NV $15 (12/31/86)
85 GANCIA Dei Gancia NV $10 (12/31/86)
82 GANCIA Extra Brut NV $6.25 (12/31/86)
85 GANCIA Gran Cuvée NV $10.50 (12/31/86)
80 GANCIA Pinot di Pinot NV $12 (12/31/86)
82 LUNGAROTTI Brut NV $23 (3/15/89)
75 CARPENE MALVOLTI Brut 1982 $14 (12/31/86)
84 FOSS MARAI Brut Chardonnay NV $8 (3/15/89) BB
78 FOSS MARAI Prosecco di Valdobbiadene NV $11 (12/31/90)
83 FOSS MARAI Prosecco di Valdobbiadene 1986 $7 (12/31/88) BB
72 MARTINI & ROSSI Brut Montelera Riserva NV $15 (12/31/86)
62 MARTINI & ROSSI Brut Montelera Riserva NV $12.50 (12/31/86)
90 MONTE ROSSA Brut Franciacorta NV (NA) (12/31/86)
92 MONTE ROSSA Franciacorta Non Docato NV (NA) (12/31/86)

Key to Symbols

The scores reported here are the results of blind tastings conducted by our panel of senior editors. Wines that carry the initials below are results of individual tastings.

THE WINE SPECTATOR 100-POINT SCALE   95-100—Classic, a great wine; *90-94*—Outstanding, superior character and style; *80-89*—Good to very good, a wine with special qualities; *70-79*—Average, drinkable wine that may have minor flaws; *60-69*—Below average, drinkable but not recommended; *50-59*—Poor, undrinkable, not recommended. "*+*"—With a score indicates a range; used primarily with barrel tastings to indicate a preliminary score.

SPECIAL DESIGNATIONS SS—Spectator Selection, CS—Cellar Selection, BB—Best Buy.

TASTER'S INITIALS (JG)—Jim Gordon, (HS)—Harvey Steiman, (JL)—James Laube, (JS)—James Suckling, (TM)—Thomas Matthews, (TR)—Terry Robards, (BT)—Barrel Tasting (these wines were tasted blind from barrel samples), (CA-date)—*California's Great Cabernets* by James Laube, (CH-date)—*California's Great Chardonnays* by James Laube, (VP-date)—*Vintage Port* by James Suckling.

DATE TASTED Dates in parentheses represent the issue in which the rating was published.

75 RICCADONNA Presidente Extra Seco NV $5.75 (12/31/86)
68 RICCADONNA Riserva Privata 1981 $12.50 (12/31/86)
91 VENEGAZZU Brut di Venegazzu 1982 $12 (12/15/86)
83 LA VERSA Brut Metodo Classico 1982 (NA) (12/31/86)
75 ZONIN 1989 $7 (7/15/91)

TUSCANY RED/*BRUNELLO DI MONTALCINO DOCG*

85 ALTESINO Brunello di Montalcino 1982 $22 (9/15/86)
80 ALTESINO Brunello di Montalcino 1981 $22 (9/15/86)
91 ALTESINO Brunello di Montalcino 1980 $18 (9/15/86)
82 ALTESINO Brunello di Montalcino 1979 $20 (9/15/86)
86 ALTESINO Brunello di Montalcino Riserva 1983 $29 (11/30/89)
91 ALTESINO Brunello di Montalcino Vigna Altesino 1985 $32 (9/30/90)
84 ALTESINO Brunello di Montalcino Vigna Altesino 1983 $26 (1/31/90)
63 ALTESINO Brunello di Montalcino Vigna Altesino 1983 $26 (9/30/89)
77 ARGIANO Brunello di Montalcino 1979 $11.25 (9/15/86)
68 ARGIANO Brunello di Montalcino Riserva 1978 $12.50 (9/15/86)
67 ARGIANO Brunello di Montalcino Riserva 1977 $12.50 (9/15/86)
92 VILLA BANFI Brunello di Montalcino 1985 $30 (10/15/90)
89 VILLA BANFI Brunello di Montalcino 1982 Rel: $28 Cur: $38 (12/15/87)
92 VILLA BANFI Brunello di Montalcino 1981 Rel: $23 Cur: $32 (3/31/87) CS
90 VILLA BANFI Brunello di Montalcino 1980 Rel: $20 Cur: $33 (9/15/86)
90 VILLA BANFI Brunello di Montalcino 1979 Rel: $18 Cur: $35 (4/16/85) SS
78 FATTORIA DEI BARBI Brunello di Montalcino 1982 $20 (3/15/89)
80 FATTORIA DEI BARBI Brunello di Montalcino 1982 $20 (9/15/86)
85 FATTORIA DEI BARBI Brunello di Montalcino 1981 $20 (9/15/86)
81 FATTORIA DEI BARBI Brunello di Montalcino Blue Label 1981 $20 (1/31/91)
86 FATTORIA DEI BARBI Brunello di Montalcino Riserva 1977 $20 (9/15/86)
64 FATTORIA DEI BARBI Brunello di Montalcino Vigna del Fiore 1982 Rel: $23 Cur: $32 (3/15/89)
91 BIONDI-SANTI Brunello di Montalcino Il Greppo 1983 $66 (11/30/89)
92 BIONDI-SANTI Brunello di Montalcino Il Greppo 1982 $45 (10/15/88)
92 BIONDI-SANTI Brunello di Montalcino Il Greppo 1982 $45 (9/15/86)
93 BIONDI-SANTI Brunello di Montalcino Il Greppo 1981 Rel: $40 Cur: $53 (9/15/86)
88 BIONDI-SANTI Brunello di Montalcino Il Greppo 1980 $40 (9/15/86)
70 BIONDI-SANTI Brunello di Montalcino Il Greppo 1978 $45 (9/15/86)
94 BIONDI-SANTI Brunello di Montalcino Riserva 1982 Rel: $80 Cur: $98 (10/15/88) CS
98 BIONDI-SANTI Brunello di Montalcino Riserva 1982 Rel: $80 Cur: $98 (9/15/86)
93 CASTIGLIONE DEL BOSCO Brunello di Montalcino 1979 $14 (4/30/87)
72 CAMIGLIANO Brunello di Montalcino 1980 $8.50 (9/15/86)
85 CAMIGLIANO Brunello di Montalcino Riserva 1977 $11 (8/01/85)
83 CAPARZO Brunello di Montalcino 1985 $34 (7/15/91)
95 CAPARZO Brunello di Montalcino 1982 Cur: $31 (9/15/86)
90 CAPARZO Brunello di Montalcino 1981 $18 (9/15/86)
88 CAPARZO Brunello di Montalcino 1980 $23 (9/15/86)
88 CAPARZO Brunello di Montalcino La Casa 1985 $53 (7/15/91)
67 CAPARZO Brunello di Montalcino La Casa 1982 $50 (11/30/89)
83 CAPARZO Brunello di Montalcino La Casa 1981 $50 (6/15/90)
89 CAPARZO Brunello di Montalcino La Casa 1979 $27 (9/15/86)
70 CAPARZO Brunello di Montalcino Riserva 1981 $23 (6/15/90)
83 S. CARLO Brunello di Montalcino 1983 $23 (6/15/90)
86 IL CASELLO Brunello di Montalcino 1982 $18 (7/31/88)
84 IL CASELLO Brunello di Montalcino 1981 $15 (10/31/87)
80 IL CASELLO Brunello di Montalcino 1981 $15 (9/15/86)
56 LA CHIESA DI S. RESTITUTA Brunello di Montalcino 1982 $23 (3/15/89)
91 CIACCI PICCOLOMINI D'ARAGONA Brunello di Montalcino 1984 $25 (6/15/90)
88 COL D'ORCIA Brunello di Montalcino 1985 $23 (11/30/90)
70 COL D'ORCIA Brunello di Montalcino 1981 $22.50 (9/15/86)
94 COL D'ORCIA Brunello di Montalcino 1979 Rel: $15.50 Cur: $22 (9/15/86) CS
89 COL D'ORCIA Brunello di Montalcino Poggio al Vento Riserva 1982 $40 (4/15/91)
89 COL D'ORCIA Brunello di Montalcino Riserva 1981 $22.50 (7/31/88)
65 COL D'ORCIA Brunello di Montalcino Riserva 1978 $18.50 (9/15/86)
88 CONTI D'ATTIMIS Brunello di Montalcino Ferrante 1983 $35 (9/30/90)
81 EMILIO COSTANTI Brunello di Montalcino 1982 $32 (7/31/88)
83 EMILIO COSTANTI Brunello di Montalcino 1982 $32 (9/15/86)
80 EMILIO COSTANTI Brunello di Montalcino 1981 $20 (9/15/86)
89 EMILIO COSTANTI Brunello di Montalcino 1980 $17 (9/15/86)
80 GEOGRAFICO Brunello di Montalcino 1985 $30 (7/15/91)
90 GREPPONE MAZZI Brunello di Montalcino 1982 (NA) (9/15/86)
70 GREPPONE MAZZI Brunello di Montalcino 1981 (NA) (9/15/86)
73 LISINI Brunello di Montalcino 1983 $22 (7/31/89)
84 LISINI Brunello di Montalcino 1982 $25 (1/31/89)
78 LISINI Brunello di Montalcino 1975 $30 (9/15/86)
87 MASTROIANNI Brunello di Montalcino 1982 $17.50 (6/15/90)
72 MASTROIANNI Brunello di Montalcino 1979 $17.50 (9/15/86)
91 VILLA NICOLA Brunello di Montalcino 1985 $32 (11/30/90)
75 VILLA NICOLA Brunello di Montalcino Riserva 1981 $14 (9/15/88)
77 PERTIMALI Brunello di Montalcino 1982 $25 (1/31/88)
83 PERTIMALI Brunello di Montalcino Riserva 1985 $41 (11/30/90)
90 PIAN DI CONTE Brunello di Montalcino 1982 (NA) (9/15/86)
88 PIAN DI CONTE Brunello di Montalcino 1981 (NA) (9/15/86)
93 PODERE IL POGGIOLO Brunello di Montalcino 1985 $34 (11/30/90)
69 LA PODERINA Brunello di Montalcino 1979 $12.50 (2/16/86)
91 IL PODERUCCIO Brunello di Montalcino I Due Cipressi 1985 $22 (4/15/91)
95 POGGIO ANTICO Brunello di Montalcino 1985 $36 (11/30/90) CS
92 POGGIO ANTICO Brunello di Montalcino 1982 $25 (11/30/89)
72 POGGIO ANTICO Brunello di Montalcino 1979 $12.50 (9/15/86)
88 POGGIO SALVI Brunello di Montalcino 1981 $20 (10/15/88)
78 IL POGGIONE Brunello di Montalcino 1982 $30 (7/31/88)
95 IL POGGIONE Brunello di Montalcino 1982 $30 (9/15/86)
93 IL POGGIONE Brunello di Montalcino 1981 $28 (9/15/86)
79 IL POGGIONE Brunello di Montalcino Riserva 1979 Rel: $35 Cur: $42 (9/15/86)
92 IL POGGIONE Brunello di Montalcino Riserva 1978 Rel: $35 Cur: $47 (7/01/84) SS
89 DEI ROSETI Brunello di Montalcino 1982 $20 (7/31/89)
88 DEI ROSETI Brunello di Montalcino 1979 $10 (8/31/86)
83 POGGIO SALVI Brunello di Montalcino 1985 $30 (11/30/90)
88 POGGIO SALVI Brunello di Montalcino 1979 $15 (3/15/87)
85 POGGIO SALVI Brunello di Montalcino Riserva 1981 $35 (11/30/90)
85 SAN FELICE Brunello di Montalcino Campogiovanni 1985 $24 (9/30/90)
92 SAN FELICE Brunello di Montalcino Campogiovanni 1982 Rel: $22 Cur: $22 (7/31/88) CS
89 SOLDERA Brunello di Montalcino 1985 $90 (7/15/91)
78 LA TORRE Brunello di Montalcino 1985 $30 (4/15/91)
88 VAL DI SUGA Brunello di Montalcino 1985 $23 (9/30/90)
89 VAL DI SUGA Brunello di Montalcino Riserva 1982 $20 (11/30/89)
67 VAL DI SUGA Brunello di Montalcino Riserva 1978 $13.50 (3/15/87)
90 VAL DI SUGA Brunello di Montalcino Vigna del Lago 1985 $52 (7/15/91)

CHIANTI DOCG

85 CASTELLO D'ALBOLA Chianti Classico 1986 $7.50 (11/30/89)
76 CASTELLO D'ALBOLA Chianti Classico Riserva 1985 $12 (11/30/89)
87 FATTORIA DI AMA Chianti Classico 1987 $9 (11/30/89) (HS)
87 FATTORIA DI AMA Chianti Classico Castello di Ama 1988 $18.50 (4/15/91)
87 FATTORIA DI AMA Chianti Classico Castello di Ama 1986 $8 (1/31/89)
90 FATTORIA DI AMA Chianti Classico Castello di Ama Vigneto Bellavista 1986 $36 (11/30/89) (HS)
94 FATTORIA DI AMA Chianti Classico Castello di Ama Vigneto Bellavista 1985 $30 (7/31/89)
90 FATTORIA DI AMA Chianti Classico Castello di Ama Vigneto Bellavista 1983 $25 (12/15/87)
87 FATTORIA DI AMA Chianti Classico Castello di Ama Vigneto La Casuccia 1986 $40 (11/30/89) (HS)
91 FATTORIA DI AMA Chianti Classico Castello di Ama Vigneto La Casuccia 1985 $35 (7/31/89)
84 FATTORIA DI AMA Chianti Classico Castello di Ama Vigneto San Lorenzo 1986 $36 (11/30/89) (HS)
86 FATTORIA DI AMA Chianti Classico Castello di Ama Vigneto San Lorenzo 1985 $32 (11/30/89) (HS)
83 ANTINORI Chianti Classico Pèppoli 1987 $17.50 (5/15/90)
90 ANTINORI Chianti Classico Pèppoli 1986 $17 (7/15/89)
92 ANTINORI Chianti Classico Pèppoli 1985 $16 (5/31/88)
89 ANTINORI Chianti Classico Riserva 1985 $9 (10/15/89)
87 ANTINORI Chianti Classico Riserva 1982 $10 (11/30/89) (HS)
87 ANTINORI Chianti Classico Riserva 1982 $10 (9/15/87)
79 ANTINORI Chianti Classico Riserva Villa Antinori 1983 $9.25 (3/31/89)
90 ANTINORI Chianti Classico Santa Cristina 1985 $6 (10/31/88) BB
88 ANTINORI Chianti Classico Tenute Marchese Antinori Riserva 1987 (NA) (11/30/89) (HS)
92 ANTINORI Chianti Classico Tenute Marchese Antinori Riserva 1985 $21 (11/30/89) (HS)
90 ANTINORI Chianti Classico Tenute Marchese Antinori Riserva 1983 $16 (11/30/89) (HS)
90 ANTINORI Chianti Classico Tenute Marchese Antinori Riserva 1982 $16 (5/31/89)
90 ANTINORI Chianti Classico Tenute Marchese Antinori Riserva 1980 $16 (9/15/87)
78 B. ARRIGONI Chianti Putto 1987 $4.50 (11/30/89)
82 BADIA A COLTIBUONO Chianti Cetamura 1988 $7 (12/15/90) BB
85 BADIA A COLTIBUONO Chianti Classico 1987 $8 (11/30/89) (HS)
86 BADIA A COLTIBUONO Chianti Classico Riserva 1985 Cur: $18 (11/30/89) (HS)
78 BADIA A COLTIBUONO Chianti Classico Riserva 1983 Cur: $15 (11/30/89) (HS)
88 BADIA A COLTIBUONO Chianti Classico Riserva 1982 $13 (7/31/88)
85 VILLA BANFI Chianti 1987 $7.50/1L (11/30/89) BB
86 VILLA BANFI Chianti Classico Riserva 1985 $9 (5/15/90)
83 VILLA BANFI Chianti Classico Riserva 1982 $7 (12/15/87)
80 VILLA BANFI Chianti Classico Riserva 1981 $7 (8/31/86)
73 FEDERICO BONFIO Chianti Il Poggiolo Riserva 1982 $7 (11/15/87)
76 FEDERICO BONFIO Chianti Le Poggiolo Riserva 1985 $10.50 (3/31/90)
85 FEDERICO BONFIO Chianti Le Portine Riserva 1985 $9.50 (3/31/90)
79 FEDERICO BONFIO Chianti Le Portine Riserva 1982 $9 (11/15/87)
85 FEDERICO BONFIO Chianti Proprietor's Reserve 1985 $15 (3/31/90)
71 BORGIANNI Chianti Classico 1982 $3.50 (4/01/85)
78 BOSCARELLI Chianti Colli Senesi 1986 $8 (1/31/89)
72 BOSCARELLI Chianti Colli Senesi 1984 $6 (9/15/87)
77 VILLA BROTINI Chianti Classico Villa Brotini 1984 $5.75 (12/31/87)
85 BRUGNANO Chianti Colli Fiorentini 1986 $5 (1/31/89) BB
86 CASTELLO DI CACCHIANO Chianti Classico 1986 $8 (5/15/90)
86 CASTELLO DI CACCHIANO Chianti Classico 1986 $8 (11/30/89)
87 CASTELLO DI CACCHIANO Chianti Classico 1985 $10 (10/31/88)
73 CASTELLO DI CACCHIANO Chianti Classico 1983 $6 (9/15/87)
80 CASTELLO DI CACCHIANO Chianti Classico Millennio Riserva 1985 $18 (9/15/90)
83 VILLA CAFAGGIO Chianti Classico 1988 $10 (11/30/90)
86 VILLA CAFAGGIO Chianti Classico 1987 $9 (9/15/89)
89 VILLA CAFAGGIO Chianti Classico 1986 $9 (3/31/90)
84 VILLA CAFAGGIO Chianti Classico 1985 $8 (5/31/88)
91 VILLA CAFAGGIO Chianti Classico 1983 $10.50 (9/15/87)
66 VILLA CAFAGGIO Chianti Classico 1982 $4 (10/16/85)
86 VILLA CAFAGGIO Chianti Classico Riserva 1986 $18 (12/15/90)
88 VILLA CAFAGGIO Chianti Classico Riserva 1985 $13 (9/15/89)
80 VILLA CAFAGGIO Chianti Classico Riserva 1983 $10 (5/31/88)
77 CAMIGLIANO Chianti Colli Senesi 1985 $3.50 (12/15/87)
82 CAMIGLIANO Chianti Colli Senesi 1983 $2.75 (5/16/85) BB
83 CAPEZZANA Chianti Montalbano 1983 $6 (9/15/86) BB
77 CARATELLO Chianti Classico 1988 $9 (12/15/90)
68 CARATELLO Chianti Classico 1986 $6.75 (1/31/89)
70 CARATELLO Chianti Classico 1983 $4 (8/31/86)
85 CARATELLO Chianti Classico 1982 $3.50 (3/01/86) BB
81 CASA FRANCESCO Chianti Classico 1982 $6 (11/30/89)
79 CASTELL'IN VILLA Chianti Classico 1986 $13 (9/15/90)
86 CASTELL'IN VILLA Chianti Classico 1985 $11.50 (6/30/89)
87 CASTELL'IN VILLA Chianti Classico 1983 $7 (9/15/87)
86 CASTELL'IN VILLA Chianti Classico Riserva 1982 $18 (11/30/90)
82 CASTELLARE DI CASTELLINA Chianti Classico 1988 $12.50 (11/30/90)
81 CASTELLARE DI CASTELLINA Chianti Classico 1987 $11 (11/30/89)
82 CASTELLARE DI CASTELLINA Chianti Classico 1986 $11 (10/15/89)
85 CASTELLARE DI CASTELLINA Chianti Classico 1985 $11 (3/31/88)
86 CASTELLARE DI CASTELLINA Chianti Classico Riserva 1986 $11 (11/30/89) (HS)
86 CASTELLARE DI CASTELLINA Chianti Classico Riserva 1985 $16 (11/30/89)
85 CASTELVECCHI Chianti Classico Riserva 1982 $13 (5/15/90)
80 CECCHI Chianti 1986 $5 (1/31/89)
86 CECCHI Chianti Classico 1986 $7 (7/15/89)
91 CELLOLE Chianti Classico Riserva 1985 $13 (11/30/89)
74 FATTORIA DEL CERRO Chianti Colli Senesi 1987 $5 (7/31/89)
85 VILLA CILNIA Chianti Colli Aretini 1989 $10 (4/30/91)
89 VILLA CILNIA Chianti Colli Aretini 1988 $10 (4/15/91)
76 VILLA CILNIA Chianti Colli Aretini 1987 $8.25 (10/15/89)

ITALY
TUSCANY RED/*CHIANTI DOCG*

87 VILLA CILNIA Chianti Colli Aretini 1986 $9 (5/31/89) BB
76 COLI Chianti 1987 $6 (11/30/89)
82 CONTI D'ATTIMIS Chianti Classico Ermanno 1987 $11 (9/15/90)
84 CONTI D'ATTIMIS Chianti Classico Ermanno Riserva 1985 $13 (9/15/90)
78 CONTI D'ATTIMIS Chianti Classico Odorico 1988 $10 (11/30/90)
91 DIEVOLE Chianti Classico Dieulele 1988 $22 (4/15/91)
82 DIEVOLE Chianti Classico Vigna Campi Nuovi 1988 $15 (4/15/91)
84 DIEVOLE Chianti Classico Vigna Campi Nuovi 1987 $10 (11/30/90)
83 DIEVOLE Chianti Classico Villa Dievole 1987 $8 (12/15/90)
88 TENUTA FARNETA Chianti di Collalto 1988 $6 (12/15/90) BB
86 FATTORIA DI FELSINA Chianti Classico 1988 $13 (11/30/89) (BT) (HS)
83 FATTORIA DI FELSINA Chianti Classico 1987 $10 (11/30/89) (HS)
78 FATTORIA DI FELSINA Chianti Classico 1986 $7.50 (11/30/89) (HS)
83 FATTORIA DI FELSINA Chianti Classico Berardenga 1987 $8 (5/15/90)
72 FATTORIA DI FELSINA Chianti Classico Berardenga 1986 $7.50 (12/15/88)
86 FATTORIA DI FELSINA Chianti Classico Berardenga Riserva 1985 $11 (5/15/90)
89 FATTORIA DI FELSINA Chianti Classico Berardenga Riserva 1985 $11 (11/30/89) (BT) (HS)
87 FATTORIA DI FELSINA Chianti Classico Berardenga Riserva 1983 $12 (11/30/89) (HS)
93 FATTORIA DI FELSINA Chianti Classico Berardenga Vigneto Rancia Riserva 1985 $23 (4/30/90) CS
95+ FATTORIA DI FELSINA Chianti Classico Berardenga Vigneto Rancia Riserva 1985 $23 (11/30/89) (BT) (HS)
91 FATTORIA DI FELSINA Chianti Classico Berardenga Vigneto Rancia Riserva 1983 Rel: $17 Cur: $23 (12/15/88)
87 FATTORIA DI FELSINA Chianti Classico Berardenga Vigneto Rancia Riserva 1983 Rel: $17 Cur: $23 (12/15/88)
67 FATTORIA DI FOGNANO Chianti Colli Senesi 1985 $6.50 (5/15/89)
85 CASTELLO DI FONTERUTOLI Chianti Classico 1988 $14 (11/30/90)
85+ CASTELLO DI FONTERUTOLI Chianti Classico 1988 $14 (11/30/89) (BT) (HS)
90 CASTELLO DI FONTERUTOLI Chianti Classico 1987 $11 (11/30/89)
85 CASTELLO DI FONTERUTOLI Chianti Classico 1986 $11 (1/31/89)
88 CASTELLO DI FONTERUTOLI Chianti Classico 1985 $11 (11/30/89) (HS)
88 CASTELLO DI FONTERUTOLI Chianti Classico Riserva 1983 $15 (11/30/89) (HS)
88 CASTELLO DI FONTERUTOLI Chianti Classico Ser Lapo Riserva 1986 $25 (11/30/90)
91 CASTELLO DI FONTERUTOLI Chianti Classico Ser Lapo Riserva 1985 $18 (11/30/89)
88 CASTELLO DI FONTERUTOLI Chianti Classico Ser Lapo Riserva 1983 $15 (1/31/89)
81 FONTODI Chianti Classico 1987 $11 (11/30/89)
90 FONTODI Chianti Classico 1987 $11 (11/30/89) (HS)
74 FONTODI Chianti Classico 1986 $9 (1/31/89)
85 FONTODI Chianti Classico Riserva 1985 $12 (11/30/89)
87 FONTODI Chianti Classico Riserva 1983 $8.75 (9/15/87)
87 FONTODI Chianti Classico Riserva 1982 $7.50 (9/15/87)
92 FONTODI Chianti Classico Riserva Vigna del Sorbo 1985 $18 (11/30/89) (HS)
70 FRESCOBALDI Chianti 1989 $5.50 (4/15/91)
85 FRESCOBALDI Chianti 1988 $5 (11/30/89) BB
75 FRESCOBALDI Chianti 1987 $4.50 (5/15/89)
75 FRESCOBALDI Chianti 1986 $3.50 (12/15/87)
90+ FRESCOBALDI Chianti Rufina Castello di Nipozzano Riserva 1988 (NR) (11/30/89) (BT) (HS)
82 FRESCOBALDI Chianti Rufina Castello di Nipozzano Riserva 1986 $11 (9/15/90)
88 FRESCOBALDI Chianti Rufina Castello di Nipozzano Riserva 1985 $11 (11/30/89)
85 FRESCOBALDI Chianti Rufina Castello di Nipozzano Riserva 1985 $11 (11/30/89) (HS)
89 FRESCOBALDI Chianti Rufina Castello di Nipozzano Riserva 1983 $10 (11/30/89) (HS)
83 FRESCOBALDI Chianti Rufina Castello di Nipozzano Riserva 1983 $10 (10/31/88)
87+ FRESCOBALDI Chianti Rufina Montesodi 1988 (NR) (11/30/89) (BT) (HS)
90 FRESCOBALDI Chianti Rufina Montesodi 1985 Cur: $32 (11/30/89) (HS)
86 FRESCOBALDI Chianti Rufina Montesodi 1982 $28 (12/15/88)
81 CASTELLO DI GABBIANO Chianti Classico 1987 $7 (11/30/89)
82 CASTELLO DI GABBIANO Chianti Classico 1986 $7.75 (5/31/89) BB
82 CASTELLO DI GABBIANO Chianti Classico 1986 $7.75 (9/15/88)
72 CASTELLO DI GABBIANO Chianti Classico 1985 $7 (2/15/88)
85 CASTELLO DI GABBIANO Chianti Classico 1983 $6 (5/31/87) BB
68 CASTELLO DI GABBIANO Chianti Classico 1982 $6.25 (1/01/86)
84 CASTELLO DI GABBIANO Chianti Classico Riserva 1982 $10.50 (7/31/88)
79 CASTELLO DI GABBIANO Chianti Classico Riserva Gold Label 1982 $21 (11/30/89)
81 CASTELLO DI GABBIANO Chianti Classico Riserva Gold Label 1981 $18 (2/15/88)
83 VITTORIO INNOCENTI Chianti 1987 $7 (5/15/90) BB
77 VITTORIO INNOCENTI Chianti 1986 $7 (3/31/90)
89 ISOLE E OLENA Chianti Classico 1988 $9 (11/30/90) BB
88 ISOLE E OLENA Chianti Classico 1987 $9 (9/15/89)
86 ISOLE E OLENA Chianti Classico 1986 $7.50 (7/31/88)
89 ISOLE E OLENA Chianti Classico 1985 $7.50 (5/31/88) BB
85 ISOLE E OLENA Chianti Classico 1983 $5 (12/15/86) BB
90 LAMOLE DI LAMOLE Chianti Classico Vigneto di Campolungo 1985 $20 (4/30/90)
68 LANCIOLA II Chianti Colli Fiorentini 1987 $7.75 (5/15/89)
81 LILLIANO Chianti Classico 1988 $10 (11/30/90)
86 LILLIANO Chianti Classico 1987 $8.50 (11/30/89)
70 LILLIANO Chianti Classico 1986 $7.75 (5/15/89)
74 LILLIANO Chianti Classico 1985 $6 (10/31/87)
89 LILLIANO Chianti Classico Riserva 1985 $14 (11/30/89)
76 FATTORIA DI LUCIGNANO Chianti Colli Fiorentini 1987 $6 (6/30/89)
71 LUIANO Chianti Classico Riserva 1978 $6 (8/31/86)
79 VILLA MARCIALLA Chianti Colli Fiorentini 1986 $6 (10/15/89)
74 MARTINI DI CIGALA Chianti Classico San Giusto a Rentennano 1987 $9 (3/31/90)
79 MARTINI DI CIGALA Chianti Classico San Giusto a Rentennano 1986 $8 (1/31/89)
87 MARTINI DI CIGALA Chianti Classico San Giusto a Rentennano 1985 $8 (11/30/87)
80 MARTINI DI CIGALA Chianti Classico San Giusto a Rentennano 1983 $6.25 (9/15/87)
91 MARTINI DI CIGALA Chianti Classico San Giusto a Rentennano Riserva 1985 $17 (11/30/89)
87 MARTINI DI CIGALA Chianti Classico San Giusto a Rentennano Riserva 1983 $11 (11/15/87)
87 LE MASSE Chianti Classico 1988 $12.50 (4/30/91)
92 LE MASSE Chianti Classico 1985 $12 (7/15/89)
90 LE MASSE Chianti Classico Riserva 1985 $18 (9/15/90)
80 MELINI Chianti Classico 1987 $7 (4/30/90)
83 MELINI Chianti Classico 1986 $6 (10/31/88) BB
82 MELINI Chianti Classico 1985 $5 (7/31/88) BB
87 MELINI Chianti Classico Riserva Vigneti la Selvanella 1985 $7 (11/30/89) BB
80 MONSANTO Chianti Classico Il Poggio Vineyard Riserva 1985 $25 (3/31/90)
86 MONSANTO Chianti Classico Il Poggio Vineyard Riserva 1983 $23 (11/30/89) (HS)
93 MONSANTO Chianti Classico Il Poggio Vineyard Riserva 1982 $23 (11/30/89) (HS)
88 MONSANTO Chianti Classico Il Poggio Vineyard Riserva 1982 $23 (6/30/89)
82 MONSANTO Chianti Classico Il Poggio Vineyard Riserva 1981 $17 (11/30/89) (HS)
93 MONSANTO Chianti Classico Il Poggio Vineyard Riserva 1979 $16 (9/15/87)
85 MONSANTO Chianti Classico Riserva 1986 $15 (4/15/91)
89 MONSANTO Chianti Classico Riserva 1985 $10 (11/30/89) (HS)
72 MONSANTO Chianti Classico Riserva 1982 $10 (2/15/88)
67 MONSANTO Chianti Classico Riserva 1981 $10 (12/15/87)
83 MONSANTO Chianti Classico Riserva 1979 $9.50 (11/01/84)
85 VECCHIE TERRE DI MONTEFILI Chianti Classico 1986 $14 (4/30/90)
89 CASTELLO DI MONTEGROSSI Chianti Classico 1986 $8 (7/15/89)
86 CASTELLO DI MONTEGROSSI Chianti Classico 1985 $7.25 (9/15/88)
78 CASTELLO DI MONTEGROSSI Chianti Classico 1985 $7.25 (2/15/88)
83 FATTORIA MONTELLORI Chianti Putto 1988 $6 (11/30/89)
85 MONTE VERTINE Chianti Classico 1983 $15 (2/15/87)
72 NOZZOLE Chianti Classico Riserva 1981 $7 (10/31/87)
76 PAGLIARESE Chianti Classico 1985 $6 (3/31/88)
82 PAGLIARESE Chianti Classico Boscardini Riserva 1981 $9.25 (5/31/88)
85 PAGLIARESE Chianti Classico Boscardini Riserva 1980 $9.50 (3/15/87)
85 PODERE IL PALAZZINO Chianti Classico 1987 $9 (11/30/89) (HS)
86 PODERE IL PALAZZINO Chianti Classico 1986 $9 (11/30/89) (HS)
93 PODERE IL PALAZZINO Chianti Classico Riserva 1985 $11 (11/30/89) (HS)
78 PASOLINI Chianti 1986 $6.50 (12/15/90)
79 PASOLINI Chianti 1985 $5 (9/15/88)
76 PLACIDO Chianti 1989 $6 (7/15/91)
67 PODERE IL PALAZZINO Chianti Classico 1987 $12 (3/31/90)
86 PODERE IL PALAZZINO Chianti Classico 1986 $9 (1/31/89)
93 PODERE IL PALAZZINO Chianti Classico 1985 $11 (11/30/87) SS
78 PODERE IL PALAZZINO Chianti Classico 1983 $5 (9/16/85)
79 PODERE IL PALAZZINO Chianti Classico Riserva 1985 $22 (3/31/90)
80 PODERE IL PALAZZINO Chianti Classico Riserva 1983 $21 (11/15/87)
69 PODERE IL PALAZZINO Chianti Classico Riserva 1981 $6.25 (4/16/86)
83 POGGIARELLO Chianti Classico De Rham I Riservati "4" 1985 $6 (10/31/88) BB
83 FATTORIA LA QUERCE Chianti 1985 $9.50 (11/30/87)
86+ FATTORIA LA QUERCE Chianti Classico 1988 $9 (11/30/89) (BT) (HS)
80 FATTORIA LA QUERCE Chianti Classico 1987 $7 (11/30/89) (HS)
81 FATTORIA LA QUERCE Chianti Classico 1986 $7 (11/30/89) (HS)
68 FATTORIA LA QUERCE Chianti Classico Caratello 1986 $6.75 (11/30/89) (HS)
70 FATTORIA LA QUERCE Chianti Classico Caratello 1983 $4 (11/30/89) (HS)
91 FATTORIA LA QUERCE Chianti Classico Riserva 1985 $16 (11/30/89)
84 CASTELLO DEI RAMPOLLA Chianti Classico 1987 $15 (4/15/91)
90 CASTELLO DEI RAMPOLLA Chianti Classico 1985 $8 (9/15/88)
84 CASTELLO DEI RAMPOLLA Chianti Classico 1983 $7 (7/31/87) BB
64 CASTELLO DEI RAMPOLLA Chianti Classico 1982 $6 (10/16/85)
81 CASTELLO DEI RAMPOLLA Chianti Classico Riserva 1985 $16 (4/30/90)
83 BARONE RICASOLI Chianti 1989 $7 (4/15/91) BB
84 BARONE RICASOLI Chianti Ricasoli 1986 $5.50 (5/15/89) BB
77 BARONE RICASOLI Chianti Classico Brolio 1986 $8 (11/30/90)
84 BARONE RICASOLI Chianti Classico Brolio 1986 $8 (11/30/89) (HS)
85 BARONE RICASOLI Chianti Classico Brolio 1985 $7 (11/30/89) (HS)
87 BARONE RICASOLI Chianti Classico Brolio 1985 $7 (10/31/88) BB
73 BARONE RICASOLI Chianti Classico Brolio 1984 $4 (9/15/87)
81 BARONE RICASOLI Chianti Classico Brolio Riserva 1985 $12 (9/15/90)
80 BARONE RICASOLI Chianti Classico Brolio Riserva 1983 $10 (5/15/90)
83 BARONE RICASOLI Chianti Classico Brolio Riserva 1983 $10 (3/31/89) BB
85 BARONE RICASOLI Chianti Classico Brolio Riserva del Barone 1983 $11 (11/30/89) (HS)
90 BARONE RICASOLI Chianti Classico Brolio Riserva del Barone 1978 $10.50 (6/01/85)
79 BARONE RICASOLI Chianti Classico Ricasoli 1987 $6 (11/30/89) (HS)
83 BARONE RICASOLI Chianti Classico Ricasoli Riserva 1983 $8 (11/30/89) (HS)
79 BARONE RICASOLI Chianti Classico San Ripolo 1987 $10 (4/15/91)
89 RIECINE Chianti Classico 1988 $22 (4/30/91)
83 RIECINE Chianti Classico 1987 $20 (4/30/91)
82 ROCCA DELLE MACIE Chianti Classico 1987 (NA) (11/30/89) (HS)
80 ROCCA DELLE MACIE Chianti Classico 1986 (NA) (11/30/89) (HS)
89 ROCCA DELLE MACIE Chianti Classico Riserva di Fizzano 1987 (NA) (11/30/89) (HS)
88 ROCCA DELLE MACIE Chianti Classico Riserva di Fizzano 1985 $16 (11/30/89) (HS)
87 ROCCA DELLE MACIE Chianti Classico Riserva di Fizzano 1982 $15.50 (3/31/89)
83 RUFFINO Chianti Classico 1987 $7 (4/30/90) BB
78 RUFFINO Chianti Classico 1984 $5 (11/30/86)
85 RUFFINO Chianti Classico Aziano 1986 $8 (5/31/89) BB
80 RUFFINO Chianti Classico Aziano 1985 $9 (8/31/88)
88 RUFFINO Chianti Classico Nozzole Vigneto La Forra 1987 (NA) (11/30/89) (BT) (HS)
90 RUFFINO Chianti Classico Nozzole Vigneto La Forra 1985 (NA) (11/30/89) (HS)
90 RUFFINO Chianti Classico Riserva Ducale 1985 $13 (5/15/90)
85 RUFFINO Chianti Classico Riserva Ducale 1985 $13 (11/30/89) (HS)
84 RUFFINO Chianti Classico Riserva Ducale 1983 $17 (11/30/89) (HS)
80 RUFFINO Chianti Classico Riserva Ducale 1982 $20 (5/31/89)
66 RUFFINO Chianti Classico Riserva Ducale 1981 $9 (10/31/86)
70 RUFFINO Chianti Classico Riserva Ducale 1979 $16 (9/30/86)
80 RUFFINO Chianti Classico Riserva Ducale 1979 $16 (9/16/85)
82 RUFFINO Chianti Classico Riserva Ducale 1978 Cur: $55 (11/30/89) (HS)
89 RUFFINO Chianti Classico Riserva Ducale 1977 Cur: $39 (9/16/85) (JS)
86 RUFFINO Chianti Classico Riserva Ducale 1975 Cur: $57 (9/16/85) (JS)
85 RUFFINO Chianti Classico Riserva Ducale 1971 Cur: $61 (9/16/85) (JS)
68 RUFFINO Chianti Classico Riserva Ducale 1962 Cur: $75 (9/16/85) (JS)
82 RUFFINO Chianti Classico Riserva Ducale 1958 Cur: $144 (9/16/85) (JS)

Key to Symbols

The scores reported here are the results of blind tastings conducted by our panel of senior editors. Wines that carry the initials below are results of individual tastings.

THE WINE SPECTATOR 100-POINT SCALE *95-100*—Classic, a great wine; *90-94*—Outstanding, superior character and style; *80-89*—Good to very good, a wine with special qualities; *70-79*—Average, drinkable wine that may have minor flaws; *60-69*—Below average, drinkable but not recommended; *50-59*—Poor, undrinkable, not recommended. "+"—With a score indicates a range; used primarily with barrel tastings to indicate a preliminary score.

SPECIAL DESIGNATIONS SS—Spectator Selection, CS—Cellar Selection, BB—Best Buy.

TASTER'S INITIALS (JG)—Jim Gordon, (HS)—Harvey Steiman, (JL)—James Laube, (JS)—James Suckling, (TM)—Thomas Matthews, (TR)—Terry Robards, (BT)—Barrel Tasting (these wines were tasted blind from barrel samples), (CA-date)—*California's Great Cabernets* by James Laube, (CH-date)—*California's Great Chardonnays* by James Laube, (VP-date)—*Vintage Port* by James Suckling.

DATE TASTED Dates in parentheses represent the issue in which the rating was published.

75 SACCARDI Chianti Classico 1987 $10 (5/15/90)
89 SACCARDI Chianti Classico 1985 $6 (11/30/87) BB
87 SACCARDI Chianti Classico Riserva 1983 $12 (5/15/90)
79 SACCARDI Chianti Classico Riserva 1983 $12 (3/31/89)
81 SACCARDI Chianti Classico Riserva 1981 $9 (11/30/87)
89 SAN FELICE Chianti Classico Il Grigio Riserva 1985 $10 (11/30/89) (HS)
86 SAN FELICE Chianti Classico Il Grigio Riserva 1985 $10 (9/15/90)
85 SAN FELICE Chianti Classico Il Grigio Riserva 1983 $12 (11/30/89) (HS)
90 SAN FELICE Chianti Classico Il Grigio Riserva 1982 $11 (11/30/89) (HS)
90 SAN FELICE Chianti Classico Il Grigio Riserva 1982 $11 (5/31/88)
89 SAN FELICE Chianti Classico Poggio Rosso Riserva 1985 (NA) (11/30/89) (BT) (HS)
87 SAN FELICE Chianti Classico Poggio Rosso Riserva 1983 (NA) (11/30/89) (HS)
81 SAN FELICE Chianti Classico Poggio Rosso Riserva 1982 $15 (9/15/90)
84 SAN FELICE Chianti Classico Poggio Rosso Riserva 1982 $15 (11/30/89) (HS)
87 SAN FELICE Chianti Classico Poggio Rosso Riserva 1981 $15 (11/30/89) (HS)
87 SAN FELICE Chianti Classico Poggio Rosso Riserva 1981 $15 (8/31/88)
73 SAN FELICE Chianti Classico Poggio Rosso Riserva 1978 $14 (3/15/87)
87 SAN LEONINO Chianti Classico 1988 $10 (12/15/90)
67 CASTELLO DI SAN POLO IN ROSSO Chianti Classico 1985 $10 (11/30/89)
78 CASTELLO DI SAN POLO IN ROSSO Chianti Classico Riserva 1985 $14 (11/30/89)
80 VILLA SANTINA Chianti 1987 $5 (11/30/89) BB
72 VILLA SANTINA Chianti Classico 1984 $5 (11/15/87)
70 A. SARDELLI Chianti Classico Bartenura 1987 $9 (3/31/91)
86 A. SARDELLI Chianti Classico Bartenura 1987 $7 (10/15/89) BB
82 SELVAPIANA Chianti Classico 1986 $5 (11/30/89) (HS)
89 SELVAPIANA Chianti Classico Riserva 1985 $11 (11/30/89) (HS)
86 SELVAPIANA Chianti Classico Riserva 1983 $10 (11/30/89) (HS)
87 SELVAPIANA Chianti Classico Riserva 1982 $10 (11/30/89) (HS)
91 SELVAPIANA Chianti Rufina Bucerchiale Riserva 1985 $15 (11/30/89) (HS)
91 SELVAPIANA Chianti Rufina Vigneto Bucerchiale Riserva 1985 $19 (9/15/90)
88 TALOSA Chianti Colli Senesi 1988 $8 (11/30/90) BB
78 CASTELLO DI TIZZANO Chianti Classico Riserva 1982 $18 (7/15/89)
80 VIGNE TOSCANE Chianti Terre Toscane 1989 $5 (11/30/90) BB
88 VIGNAMAGGIO Chianti Classico 1988 (NA) (11/30/89) (BT) (HS)
85 VIGNAMAGGIO Chianti Classico 1986 $12 (5/15/90)
83 VIGNAMAGGIO Chianti Classico 1986 $12 (11/30/89) (HS)
86 VIGNAMAGGIO Chianti Classico 1985 $11 (8/31/88)
86 VIGNAMAGGIO Chianti Classico Riserva 1987 (NA) (11/30/89) (BT) (HS)
85 VIGNAMAGGIO Chianti Classico Riserva 1986 (NA) (11/30/89) (BT) (HS)
90 VIGNAMAGGIO Chianti Classico Riserva 1985 $17 (5/15/90)
89 VIGNAMAGGIO Chianti Classico Riserva 1985 $17 (11/30/89) (HS)
85 VIGNAMAGGIO Chianti Classico Riserva 1983 $15 (5/15/90)
88 VIGNAMAGGIO Chianti Classico Riserva 1983 $15 (7/31/88)
85 VIGNETI LA SELVANELLA Chianti Classico Riserva 1982 $6 (6/30/88) BB
84 VILLA CERNA Chianti Classico Riserva 1983 $8.25 (3/31/89) BB
89 VISTARENNI Chianti Classico 1987 $10 (10/15/89)
78 VISTARENNI Chianti Classico 1986 $18 (7/31/89)
78 VITICCIO Chianti Classico 1987 $9 (4/30/90)
88 VITICCIO Chianti Classico 1986 $8 (3/31/89) BB
74 VITICCIO Chianti Classico 1984 $5.75 (11/15/87)
85 VITICCIO Chianti Classico Riserva 1985 $11 (11/30/89)
80 VITICCIO Chianti Classico Riserva 1983 $12 (11/30/89)
77 VITICCIO Chianti Classico Viticcio Riserva 1983 $8 (11/15/87)
84 VITICCIO Chianti Classico Viticcio Riserva 1982 $8.75 (11/15/87)
78 VITICCIO Chianti Classico Viticcio Riserva 1978 $12.50 (11/30/87)
71 VITICCIO Chianti Classico Viticcio Riserva 1975 $13.50 (11/15/87)
85 CASTELLO DI VOLPAIA Chianti Classico 1987 $16 (11/30/89) (HS)
75 CASTELLO DI VOLPAIA Chianti Classico 1986 $10 (3/31/90)
90 CASTELLO DI VOLPAIA Chianti Classico 1986 $10 (11/30/89) (HS)
90 CASTELLO DI VOLPAIA Chianti Classico 1985 $10 (6/30/89) SS
88 CASTELLO DI VOLPAIA Chianti Classico 1983 $9 (9/15/87) (HS)
78 CASTELLO DI VOLPAIA Chianti Classico Riserva 1985 $13 (3/31/90)
88 CASTELLO DI VOLPAIA Chianti Classico Riserva 1985 $13 (11/30/89) (HS)
87 CASTELLO DI VOLPAIA Chianti Classico Riserva 1983 $11.50 (5/31/89)
84 CASTELLO DI VOLPAIA Chianti Classico Riserva 1982 $11 (9/15/87) (HS)
86 CASTELLO DI VOLPAIA Chianti Classico Riserva 1981 (NA) (9/15/87) (HS)
81 CASTELLO DI VOLPAIA Chianti Classico Riserva 1977 (NA) (9/15/87) (HS)
85 CASTELLO DI VOLPAIA Chianti Classico Riserva 1970 (NA) (9/15/87) (HS)

ROSSO DI MONTALCINO DOC

73 ALTESINO Rosso di Montalcino 1988 $14.50 (7/15/91)
80 ALTESINO Rosso di Montalcino 1986 $10 (7/15/89)
85 VILLA BANFI Rosso di Montalcino Centine 1987 $8 (6/15/90) BB
87 VILLA BANFI Rosso di Montalcino Centine 1986 $7 (11/30/89) BB
88 VILLA BANFI Rosso di Montalcino Centine 1985 $7 (11/30/87) BB
89 VILLA BANFI Rosso di Montalcino Centine 1983 $7 (4/30/87) BB
82 BIONDI-SANTI Rosso di Montalcino Il Greppo 1984 $23 (11/30/90)
83 BIONDI-SANTI Rosso di Montalcino Il Greppo 1984 $23 (8/31/88)
82 CASTIGLIONE DEL BOSCO Rosso di Montalcino 1988 $11 (7/15/91)
81 CAPARZO Rosso di Montalcino 1988 $14 (4/30/91)
86 CAPARZO Rosso di Montalcino 1986 $10 (9/30/89)
78 CAPRILI Rosso di Montalcino 1986 $10 (1/31/89)
82 S. CARLO Rosso di Montalcino 1986 $10 (7/15/89)
83 LA CHIESA DI S. RESTITUTA Rosso di Montalcino 1986 $9.50 (5/31/88)
82 CIACCI PICCOLOMINI D'ARAGONA Rosso di Montalcino 1988 $16 (4/30/91)
84 COL D'ORCIA Rosso di Montalcino 1988 $9 (4/30/91)
80 COL D'ORCIA Rosso di Montalcino 1985 $7.50 (6/30/88)
76 COL D'ORCIA Rosso di Montalcino 1983 $6 (6/30/87)
79 LISINI Rosso di Montalcino 1988 $14 (4/30/91)
79 MASTROIANNI Rosso di Montalcino 1988 $10 (7/15/91)
84 MASTROIANNI Rosso di Montalcino 1987 $10 (6/15/90)
89 VILLA NICOLA Rosso di Montalcino 1988 $15 (1/31/91)
84 PERTIMALI Rosso di Montalcino 1988 $12.50 (1/31/91)
84 PERTIMALI Rosso di Montalcino 1987 $12.50 (11/30/89)
87 LA PODERINA Rosso di Montalcino 1983 $6.50 (12/01/85) BB
83 IL PODERUCCIO Rosso di Montalcino I Due Cipressi 1988 $9.50 (4/30/91)
85 IL POGGIONE Rosso di Montalcino 1985 $17 (3/31/88)
87 DEI ROSETI Rosso di Montalcino 1988 $13 (1/31/91)
78 DEI ROSETI Rosso di Montalcino 1985 $9 (7/15/89)
79 DEI ROSETI Rosso di Montalcino 1985 $9 (9/15/88)

68 SAN FILIPPO Rosso di Montalcino 1987 $11 (4/30/91)
87 VAL DI SUGA Rosso di Montalcino 1988 $10 (4/30/91)
81 VAL DI SUGA Rosso di Montalcino 1986 $9 (11/30/89)

VINO NOBILE DI MONTEPULCIANO DOCG

86 AVIGNONESI Vino Nobile di Montepulciano 1985 $12 (2/15/88)
86 AVIGNONESI Vino Nobile di Montepulciano 1981 $7.25 (10/01/85)
85 AVIGNONESI Vino Nobile di Montepulciano 1980 $6.75 (7/01/85)
87 CANTINE BAIOCCHI Vino Nobile di Montepulciano 1986 $15 (3/15/91)
85 CANTINE BAIOCCHI Vino Nobile di Montepulciano Riserva 1985 $10 (11/30/89)
81 BIGI Vino Nobile di Montepulciano 1985 $11.50 (11/30/90)
77 BIGI Vino Nobile di Montepulciano Riserva 1982 $9 (1/31/88)
84 BIGI Vino Nobile di Montepulciano Riserva 1980 $8 (9/01/85)
68 BINDELLA Vino Nobile di Montepulciano Riserva 1985 $27 (10/31/90)
71 BOSCARELLI Vino Nobile di Montepulciano 1981 $10 (7/01/86)
76 BOSCARELLI Vino Nobile di Montepulciano Riserva 1985 $15 (6/15/90)
70 BOSCARELLI Vino Nobile di Montepulciano Riserva 1981 $11 (10/31/86)
86 E. CASASLTE Vino Nobile di Montepulciano 1983 $9 (11/30/87)
82 CECCHI Vino Nobile di Montepulciano 1987 $9 (11/30/90)
77 CECCHI Vino Nobile di Montepulciano 1983 $9 (5/15/89)
75 CONTI D'ATTIMIS Vino Nobile di Montepulciano Varnero 1987 $14 (9/15/90)
85 DEI Vino Nobile di Montepulciano Riserva 1985 $13 (4/15/90)
86 FASSATI Vino Nobile di Montepulciano Riserva 1985 $22 (11/30/89)
73 FASSATI Vino Nobile di Montepulciano Riserva 1978 $8.50 (7/01/86)
85 FATTORIA DI FOGNANO Vino Nobile di Montepulciano Riserva Talosa 1983 $7 (5/15/89) BB
76 FATTORIA DI FOGNANO Vino Nobile di Montepulciano Riserva Talosa 1981 $8.50 (5/15/89)
81 CANTINA GATTAVECCHI Vino Nobile di Montepulciano Riserva 1985 $11 (11/30/89)
85 GEOGRAFICO Vino Nobile di Montepulciano Vigneti alla Cerraia 1986 $14.50 (7/15/91)
77 VITTORIO INNOCENTI Vino Nobile di Montepulciano 1985 $10 (3/31/90)
82 MELINI Vino Nobile di Montepulciano 1985 $10 (4/15/90)
74 MELINI Vino Nobile di Montepulciano Riserva 1983 $7.50 (6/30/88)
84 POLIZIANO Vino Nobile di Montepulciano 1987 $12 (3/15/91)
89 POLIZIANO Vino Nobile di Montepulciano 1985 $13 (9/15/88)
86 SANGUINETO Vino Nobile di Montepulciano Riserva 1980 $9 (10/31/86)
84 TALOSA Vino Nobile di Montepulciano Riserva 1986 $15 (7/15/91)
72 TALOSA Vino Nobile di Montepulciano Riserva 1982 $8.50 (4/15/88)
80 TENUTA TREROSE Vino Nobile di Montepulciano 1986 $16 (7/15/91)
90 TENUTA TREROSE Vino Nobile di Montepulciano 1985 $11 (11/15/88)
85 TENUTA TREROSE Vino Nobile di Montepulciano Riserva 1985 $19 (7/15/91)

VINO DA TAVOLA

84 CASTELLO D'ALBOLA Acciaiolo 1988 $50 (4/15/91)
85 ALTESINO Alte d'Altesi 1986 $32 (7/15/89)
82 ALTESINO Palazzo Altesi 1985 $23 (10/31/90)
88 ALTESINO Palazzo Altesi 1983 $17.50 (2/15/88)
82 FATTORIA DI AMA Colline di Ama 1986 $9 (11/15/87)
87 FATTORIA DI AMA Vigna l'Apparita Merlot 1986 (NA) (11/30/89) (HS)
92 FATTORIA DI AMA Vigna l'Apparita Merlot 1985 (NA) (11/30/89) (HS)
76 AMBRA Barco Reale 1985 $7 (4/15/88)
80 ANTINORI Santa Cristina 1989 $7 (7/15/91)
85 ANTINORI Santa Cristina 1988 $6.50 (1/31/91) BB
81 ANTINORI Santa Cristina 1987 $6 (4/30/89) BB
92 ANTINORI Solàia 1985 Rel: $62 Cur: $96 (12/15/89)
81 ANTINORI Solàia 1982 $62 (7/31/87)
87 ANTINORI Tignanello 1985 $30 (4/15/90)
88 ANTINORI Tignanello 1983 $25 (12/15/89)
91 ANTINORI Tignanello 1982 $37 (7/15/87) CS
86 AVIGNONESI Grifi 1987 $21 (4/15/91)
86 AVIGNONESI Grifi 1986 $18 (1/31/89)
85 AVIGNONESI Grifi 1985 Rel: $16.50 Cur: $27 (2/15/88)
91 AVIGNONESI Grifi 1983 Rel: $12 Cur: $22 (6/01/86)
87 AVIGNONESI Grifi 1982 Rel: $10 Cur: $10 (6/16/85)
81 BADIA A COLTIBUONO Coltibuono Rosso 1986 $6.75 (7/31/88)
85 BADIA A COLTIBUONO Sangioveto 1985 (NA) (11/30/89) (HS)
84 BADIA A COLTIBUONO Sangioveto 1983 $20 (11/30/89) (HS)
93 BADIA A COLTIBUONO Sangioveto 1983 $20 (9/15/87) (HS)
87 BADIA A COLTIBUONO Sangioveto 1982 $21 (11/30/89) (HS)
83 BADIA A COLTIBUONO Sangioveto 1982 $21 (9/15/88)
87 BADIA A COLTIBUONO Sangioveto 1981 $21 (9/15/87) (HS)
84 FATTORIA BAGGIOLINO Poggio Brandi 1985 $19 (9/15/89)
89 VILLA BANFI Cabernet Sauvignon Tavernelle 1984 $18 (1/31/88)
88 VILLA BANFI Cabernet Sauvignon Tavernelle 1982 $15 (8/01/85)
80 FATTORIA DEI BARBI Brusco dei Barbi 1988 $9.50 (10/31/90)
79 FATTORIA DEI BARBI Brusco dei Barbi 1986 $9 (4/30/89)
85 FATTORIA DEI BARBI Brusco dei Barbi 1985 $9 (10/15/88)
92 BOSCARELLI 1985 $30 (2/15/89)
85 BOSCARELLI Vino da Tavola Tuscany 1983 $29 (6/30/88)
85 CASTELLO DI CACCHIANO RF 1986 $16.50 (6/15/90)
91 CASTELLO DI CACCHIANO RF 1985 $15.50 (8/31/88)
79 VILLA CAFAGGIO San Martino 1985 $20 (9/30/89)
80 VILLA CAFAGGIO Solatio Basilica 1985 $22 (9/30/89)
82 S. FABIANO CALCINAIA Cerviolo 1986 $18.50 (3/31/90)
77 CAPARZO Ca' del Pazzo 1985 $28 (5/15/90)
78 CAPEZZANA Barco Reale 1987 $11.50 (7/15/91)
91 CAPEZZANA Ghiaie della Furba 1985 $20 (1/31/90)
87 CASTELLARE DI CASTELLINA Coniale di Castellare 1987 $31 (10/31/90)
86 CASTELLARE DI CASTELLINA I Sodi di San Niccolo 1987 $32 (4/15/91)
94 CASTELLARE DI CASTELLINA I Sodi di San Niccolo 1986 $25 (11/30/89)
96 CASTELLARE DI CASTELLINA I Sodi di San Niccolo 1985 $25 (5/31/88)
87 CASTELLARE DI CASTELLINA I Sodi di San Niccolo 1983 $18 (5/31/88)
89 CASTELLARE DI CASTELLINA I Sodi di San Niccolo 1982 (NA) (9/15/87) (HS)
87 CASTELLARE DI CASTELLINA I Sodi di San Niccolo 1981 (NA) (9/15/87) (HS)
75 CECCHI Spargolo Predicato di Cardisco 1983 $25 (3/15/91)
68 CECCHI Spargolo Predicato di Cardisco 1982 $12 (9/30/89)
90 VILLA CILNIA Le Vignacce 1986 $19 (11/30/89)
88 VILLA CILNIA Le Vignacce 1985 $20 (7/15/89)
86 VILLA CILNIA Vocato 1986 $10.50 (5/15/89)
86 FATTORIA LE CORTI Masso Tondo 1985 $20 (4/30/89)
79 EMILIO COSTANTI Vermiglio 1981 $7.50 (10/31/86)

ITALY
TUSCANY RED/VINO DA TAVOLA

91	FATTORIA DI FELSINA Fontalloro 1985 $24 (9/15/88)
70	MARSILIO FICINO Poggio Il Pino 1986 $6 (7/31/89)
87	CASTELLO DI FONTERUTOLI Concerto di Fonterutoli 1986 $35 (3/15/91)
84	CASTELLO DI FONTERUTOLI Concerto di Fonterutoli 1985 $25 (2/15/89)
86	CASTELLO DI FONTERUTOLI Concerto di Fonterutoli 1983 $15 (11/30/89) (HS)
88	FONTODI Flaccianello 1986 $29 (1/31/90)
90	FONTODI Flaccianello 1986 $29 (11/30/89) (HS)
91	FONTODI Flaccianello 1985 Rel: $23 Cur: $33 (1/31/89)
95	FONTODI Flaccianello 1983 $19 (7/15/87)
93	FRESCOBALDI Mormoreto Predicato di Biturica 1988 (NR) (11/30/89) (HS)
86	FRESCOBALDI Mormoreto Predicato di Biturica 1983 $27 (11/30/89) (HS)
88	FRESCOBALDI Mormoreto Predicato di Biturica 1983 $34 (2/15/89)
86	FRESCOBALDI Mormoreto Predicato di Biturica 1983 $27 (1/31/88)
86	CASTELLO DI GABBIANO Merlot 1988 $55 (7/15/91)
93	CASTELLO DI GABBIANO Ania 1985 $30 (1/31/90)
83	CASTELLO DI GABBIANO Ania 1983 $25 (7/15/87)
90	CASTELLO DI GABBIANO R & R 1986 $38 (1/31/91)
91	CASTELLO DI GABBIANO R & R 1985 $30 (3/31/90)
80	VITTORIO INNOCENTI Acerone 1988 $13 (7/15/91)
78	VITTORIO INNOCENTI Acerone 1985 $9 (9/15/89)
82	ISOLE E OLENA Antiche Tenute 1989 $6 (10/31/90) BB
83	ISOLE E OLENA Antiche Tenute 1988 $6 (9/15/89) BB
81	ISOLE E OLENA Antiche Tenute 1987 $4.50 (1/31/89) BB
78	ISOLE E OLENA Antiche Tenute 1986 $5 (11/15/88)
86	ISOLE E OLENA Cepparello 1986 $20 (9/30/89)
87	ISOLE E OLENA Cepparello 1985 $15 (11/15/88)
86	LILLIANO Anagallis 1985 $34 (3/31/90)
88	MARTINI DI CIGALA San Giusto a Rentennano Percarlo 1986 $24 (11/30/89)
92	MARTINI DI CIGALA San Giusto a Rentennano Percarlo 1985 $25 (2/15/89)
77	MARTINI DI CIGALA San Giusto a Rentennano Percarlo 1983 $13 (9/15/87)
87	MONSANTO Cabernet Sauvignon Nemo 1983 $28 (9/15/90)
88	MONSANTO Tinscvil 1985 $22 (9/15/90)
91	MONSANTO Tinscvil 1985 $22 (11/30/89) (HS)
85	CASTELLO DI MONTE ANTICO 1985 $6.75 (6/30/88)
82	CASTELLO DI MONTE ANTICO 1982 $3.75 (4/01/86) BB
87	MONTE VERTINE Il Sodaccio 1987 $32 (1/31/91)
90	MONTE VERTINE Il Sodaccio 1986 $30 (9/30/89)
91	MONTE VERTINE Il Sodaccio 1985 $25 (3/15/89)
93	MONTE VERTINE Il Sodaccio 1983 $19.50 (2/15/87)
90	MONTE VERTINE Le Pergole Torte 1987 $41 (1/31/91)
90	MONTE VERTINE Le Pergole Torte 1986 $36 (9/30/89)
88	MONTE VERTINE Le Pergole Torte 1985 $33 (4/30/89)
90	MONTE VERTINE Le Pergole Torte 1983 $24.50 (2/15/87)
90	MONTE VERTINE Le Pergole Torte 1982 $16.50 (7/16/86)
87	MONTE VERTINE Le Pergole Torte 1981 $11.25 (7/16/85)
91	MONTE VERTINE Riserva 1987 $30 (3/15/91)
86	MONTE VERTINE Riserva 1986 $26 (9/30/89)
84	MONTE VERTINE Riserva 1982 $18 (2/15/87)
90	MONTE VERTINE Riserva 1981 $15 (8/31/86)
89	MONTE VERTINE Sangioveto 1985 $17 (8/31/88)
89	ORNELLAIA 1987 $46 (11/30/90)
93	ORNELLAIA 1986 Rel: $25 Cur: $40 (12/15/89) CS
95	PODERE IL PALAZZINO Grosso Sanese 1988 $29 (11/30/89) (HS)
88	PODERE IL PALAZZINO Grosso Sanese 1988 $29 (3/15/91)
90	PODERE IL PALAZZINO Grosso Sanese 1987 $25 (11/30/89) (HS)
87	PODERE IL PALAZZINO Grosso Sanese 1986 $22 (2/15/89)
94	PODERE IL PALAZZINO Grosso Sanese 1985 $13 (12/15/87)
93	FATTORIA LA QUERCE La Corte 1985 $20 (11/30/89)
93	FATTORIA LA QUERCE La Corte 1985 $20 (11/30/89) (HS)
83	FATTORIA LA QUERCE La Corte 1983 $17 (11/30/89) (HS)
85	FATTORIA LA QUERCE Querciolaia 1986 (NA) (11/30/89) (HS)
85	FATTORIA LA QUERCE Querciolaia 1985 $30 (11/30/89) (HS)
85	FATTORIA LA QUERCE Querciolaia 1985 $30 (2/15/89)
76	CASTELLO DEI RAMPOLLA Sammarco 1986 $46 (3/15/91)
90	CASTELLO DEI RAMPOLLA Sammarco 1985 (NA) (11/30/89) (HS)
88	CASTELLO DEI RAMPOLLA Sammarco 1983 $28 (9/15/88)
82	RIECINE La Gioia di Riecine 1987 $45 (4/30/91)
90	ROCCA DELLE MACIE Ser Gioveto 1987 $17 (11/30/89) (HS)
84	ROCCA DELLE MACIE Ser Gioveto 1986 $14.50 (2/15/89)
88	ROCCA DELLE MACIE Ser Gioveto 1985 $15 (11/30/89) (HS)
85	DEI ROSETI Belconvento 1987 $24 (3/15/91)
86	DEI ROSETI Belconvento 1985 $23 (7/15/89)
90	RUFFINO Cabreo Il Borgo Predicato di Biturica 1985 $21 (9/30/89)
87	SAN FELICE Predicato di Biturica 1985 $25 (9/15/90)
89	SAN FELICE Predicato di Biturica 1985 $25 (11/30/89) (HS)
87	SAN FELICE Predicato di Biturica 1983 $22 (11/30/89) (HS)
92	SAN FELICE Predicato di Biturica 1982 $19 (1/31/88) SS
89	SAN FELICE Vigorello 1985 $18 (9/15/90)
91	SAN FELICE Vigorello 1985 $18 (11/30/89) (HS)
90	SAN FELICE Vigorello 1983 $17 (11/30/89) (HS)
87	SAN FELICE Vigorello 1982 $15 (11/30/89) (HS)
84	SAN FELICE Vigorello 1982 $15 (8/31/88)
84	SAN FELICE Vigorello 1981 $13 (1/31/88)
95	SAN FELICE Vigorello 1980 $12 (2/28/87) SS

82	SASSICAIA 1987 $45 (3/15/91)
95	SASSICAIA 1986 $50 (12/15/89)
92	SASSICAIA 1985 Rel: $48 Cur: $84 (5/15/89) CS
85	SASSICAIA 1984 $57 (3/15/89)
84	SASSICAIA 1982 Rel: $45 Cur: $110 (7/31/87)
83	TERRICCI Antiche Terre de'Ricci 1986 $23 (5/15/90)
91	TERRICCI Antiche Terre de'Ricci 1985 $22.50 (3/15/89)
68	TERUZZI & PUTHOD Vigna Peperino 1986 $11 (1/31/90)
92	TERUZZI & PUTHOD Vigna Peperino 1985 $10.50 (10/31/88)
79	TOSCOLO Red Tuscan Table Wine 1986 $4.25 (1/31/89)
92	VIGNAMAGGIO Gherardino 1987 (NA) (11/30/89) (HS)
91	VIGNAMAGGIO Gherardino 1986 (NA) (11/30/89) (HS)
91	VIGNAMAGGIO Gherardino 1985 (NA) (11/30/89) (HS)
91	VINATIERRI Rosso 1985 (NA) (9/15/87) (HS)
84	VINATIERRI Rosso 1983 $14 (9/15/87) (HS)
90	VISTARENNI Codirosso 1986 $22 (11/30/89)
92	VITICCIO Prunaio 1986 $19 (3/31/90) SS
88	VITICCIO Prunaio 1985 $18 (4/30/89)
89	CASTELLO DI VOLPAIA Balifico 1987 (NA) (11/30/89) (HS)
83	CASTELLO DI VOLPAIA Balifico 1986 $19 (4/30/89)
91	CASTELLO DI VOLPAIA Balifico 1985 $21 (11/30/89) (HS)
86	CASTELLO DI VOLPAIA Coltassala 1986 (NA) (11/30/89) (HS)
88	CASTELLO DI VOLPAIA Coltassala 1985 $19 (11/30/89) (HS)
75	CASTELLO DI VOLPAIA Coltassala 1985 $19 (4/30/89)
86	CASTELLO DI VOLPAIA Coltassala 1983 $22 (9/15/88)
87	CASTELLO DI VOLPAIA Coltassala 1982 (NA) (9/15/87) (HS)
90	CASTELLO DI VOLPAIA Coltassala 1981 (NA) (9/15/87) (HS)

OTHER TUSCANY RED DOC

80	AMBRA Carmignano 1986 $12.50 (5/15/89)
83	AMBRA Carmignano 1985 $10.50 (4/15/88)
79	AMBRA Carmignano 1984 $8.75 (12/31/87)
88	AMBRA Carmignano 1983 $9 (7/16/86) BB
83	AVIGNONESI Rosso di Montepulciano 1989 $12 (4/30/91)
81	CAPEZZANA Carmignano 1986 $15 (7/15/91)
83	CAPEZZANA Carmignano Riserva 1985 $25 (7/15/91)
81	IL COLLE Rosso delle Colline Lucchesi 1986 $7.50 (3/31/90)
87	FRESCOBALDI Pomino Tenuta di Pomino 1986 $14 (1/31/90)
93	FRESCOBALDI Pomino Tenuta di Pomino 1985 Rel: $12 Cur: $15 (9/15/88) SS
80	VILLA IL POGGIOLO Carmignano Riserva 1985 $16 (5/15/90)
87	MORBELLI Carema 1982 $21 (11/30/89)
86	LE PUPILLE Morellino di Scansano Riserva 1986 $16 (6/30/91)

TUSCANY WHITE/VINO DA TAVOLA

90	CASTELLO D'ALBOLA Chardonnay 1989 $50 (2/15/91)
82	FATTORIA DI AMA Chardonnay Colline di Ama 1988 $17 (9/15/89)
82	FATTORIA DI AMA Chardonnay Colline di Ama 1987 $17 (9/15/89)
79	FATTORIA DI AMA Chardonnay Colline di Ama 1986 $17 (9/15/89)
88	FATTORIA DI AMA Chardonnay Colline di Ama 1986 $17 (11/15/87)
85	ANTINORI Bianco Toscano 1988 $6.50 (10/15/89) BB
79	ANTINORI Galestro 1989 $7 (12/31/90)
74	ANTINORI Galestro 1987 $6 (10/15/88)
65	ANTINORI Galestro 1986 $6 (11/15/87)
77	ANTINORI Galestro 1985 $4 (4/30/87)
90	AVIGNONESI Chardonnay Il Marzocco 1987 $18 (9/15/89)
82	AVIGNONESI Chardonnay Il Marzocco 1987 $18 (3/31/89)
92	AVIGNONESI Chardonnay Il Marzocco 1986 $16 (2/15/88)
87	AVIGNONESI Sauvignon Blanc Il Vignola 1988 $20 (10/15/89)
83	AVIGNONESI Terre di Cortona 1987 $18 (3/31/89)
87	AVIGNONESI Terre di Cortona 1986 $9.50 (2/15/88)
78	VILLA BANFI Chardonnay Centine 1988 $8 (4/30/90)
84	VILLA BANFI Chardonnay Centine 1987 $8 (3/31/89)
81	VILLA BANFI Chardonnay Centine 1986 $7 (12/31/87)
86	VILLA BANFI Chardonnay Fontanelle 1988 $11 (12/31/90)
80	VILLA BANFI Chardonnay Fontanelle 1987 $16.50 (9/15/89)
86	VILLA BANFI Chardonnay Fontanelle 1986 $16.50 (9/15/89)
87	VILLA BANFI Chardonnay Fontanelle 1986 $16.50 (10/15/88)
84	VILLA BANFI Chardonnay Fontanelle 1984 $10 (1/31/87)
75	VILLA BANFI Pinot Grigio San Angelo 1987 $12 (11/15/88)
77	VILLA BANFI Pinot Grigio San Angelo 1986 $10 (12/15/87)
79	LA CADALORA Chardonnay della Vallagarina 1988 $11.25 (9/15/89)
84	LA CADALORA Chardonnay della Vallagarina 1987 $8.25 (3/31/89)
79	S. FABIANO CALCINAIA Cerviolo 1987 $18.50 (3/31/90)
84	CAPEZZANA Chardonnay 1988 $14 (9/15/89)
82	CAPEZZANA Chardonnay 1987 $14 (9/15/89)
72	CAPEZZANA Chardonnay 1984 $11 (10/15/86)
79	CASTELLARE DI CASTELLINA Canonico di Castellare 1988 $18 (12/31/90)
80	VILLA CILNIA Poggio Garbato 1989 $9.25 (7/15/91)
86	FATTORIA DI FELSINA Berardenga I Sistri 1988 $24 (3/31/90)
82	FONTODI Meriggio 1987 $17 (3/31/90)
88	FONTODI Meriggio 1987 $17 (12/31/88)
68	FRESCOBALDI Bianco NV $3.50 (12/15/87)
78	FRESCOBALDI Vergena Predicato del Selvante 1985 $25 (11/15/88)
78	CASTELLO DI GABBIANO Bianco del Castello 1987 $8 (12/31/90)
83	CASTELLO DI GABBIANO Chardonnay Ariella 1988 $23 (1/31/91)
87	CASTELLO DI GABBIANO Chardonnay Ariella 1987 $23 (3/31/90)
69	CASTELLO DI GABBIANO Chardonnay Ariella 1985 $25 (8/31/87)
87	ISOLE E OLENA Chardonnay Collezione de Marchi 1989 $23 (7/15/91)
73	ISOLE E OLENA Chardonnay Collezione de Marchi 1988 $17 (3/31/90)
87	ISOLE E OLENA Chardonnay Collezione de Marchi 1988 $17 (9/15/89)
86	NOZZOLE Chardonnay Vigneto Le Bruniche 1988 $9.25 (3/31/90)
84	NOZZOLE Chardonnay Vigneto Le Bruniche 1988 $10 (9/15/89)
74	PLACIDO Chardonnay 1989 $6 (7/15/91)
90	RUFFINO Cabreo Vigneto La Pietra 1986 $18 (9/15/89)
83	RUFFINO Cabreo Vigneto La Pietra 1985 $18 (9/15/89)
82	RUFFINO Cabreo la Pietra Predicato del Muschio 1985 $17 (10/15/88)
90	RUFFINO Cabreo la Pietra Predicato del Muschio 1983 $17 (3/31/87)
78	RUFFINO Libaio 1987 $8.50 (9/15/89)

79   RUFFINO Libaio 1986 $8 (11/15/87)
79   TOSCOLO Tuscan Table Wine 1987 $4.25 (12/31/88)

WHITE DOC

82   CECCHI Vernaccia di San Gimignano 1987 $6 (5/15/89) BB
62   IL CIPRESSINO Vernaccia di San Gimignano 1982 $5 (8/31/87)
71   RICCARDO FALCHINI Vernaccia di San Gimignano 1985 $5 (4/30/87)
85   FRESCOBALDI Pomino Tenuta di Pomino Il Benefizio 1986 $20 (3/31/90)
79   FRESCOBALDI Pomino Tenuta di Pomino Il Benefizio 1985 $18.50 (10/15/88)
63   FRESCOBALDI Pomino Tenuta di Pomino Il Benefizio 1983 $15 (6/30/87)
78   MELINI Vernaccia di San Gimignano Lydia 1989 $8 (7/15/91)
75   TONI PAOLA Vernaccia di San Gimignano Ambra delle Torri 1989 $9.75 (7/15/91)
82   BARONE RICASOLI Vernaccia di San Gimignano 1989 $9 (4/15/91)
77   SALVUCCI Vernaccia di San Gimignano 1987 $5.50 (5/15/89)
78   SAN QUIRICO Vernaccia di San Gimignano 1989 $8.50 (7/15/91)
87   TERUZZI & PUTHOD Vernaccia di San Gimignano Riserva 1986 $7.50 (11/15/88) BB
84   TERUZZI & PUTHOD Vernaccia di San Gimignano Terre di Tufo 1989 $26 (12/31/90)
88   TERUZZI & PUTHOD Vernaccia di San Gimignano Terre di Tufo 1987 $11.50 (10/15/88)
81   ANGELO DEL TUFO Vernaccia di San Gimignano 1988 $7.50 (4/30/90)
61   ZONIN Vernaccia di San Gimignano 1983 $5 (4/16/86)

OTHER ITALY NORTH RED/CABERNET DOC

73   BOLLINI Cabernet Sauvignon Grave del Friuli 1983 $6.25 (7/31/87)
85   COLLAVINI Cabernet Sauvignon Grave del Friuli 1984 $8 (4/15/90) BB
76   ENO-FRIULIA Cabernet Sauvignon Collio 1988 $12 (7/15/91)
80   FANTINEL Cabernet Sauvignon Grave del Friuli 1985 $7 (7/31/87)
84   LIVIO FELLUGA Cabernet Franc Collio 1988 $15 (6/30/91)
75   LIVIO FELLUGA Cabernet Franc Collio 1986 $14 (9/15/88) (TM)
92   MACULAN Breganze Cabernet Fratta 1986 $29 (3/31/89)
85   MACULAN Breganze Rosso Brentino 1986 $9.50 (3/31/89)
85   PLOZNER Cabernet Sauvignon Grave del Friuli 1985 $6 (9/15/88) (TM)
80   PLOZNER Cabernet Sauvignon Grave del Friuli Bollini 1983 $6 (9/15/88) (TM)
83   RUSSIZ SUPERIORE Cabernet Franc Collio 1986 $15 (9/15/88) (TM)
87   SANTA MARGHERITA Cabernet Sauvignon Pramaggiore 1982 $5.50 (12/01/85) BB
84   TIEFENBRUNNER Cabernet Alto Adige 1987 $9 (3/31/89)

RECIOTO DELLA VALPOLICELLA DOC

85   ALLEGRINI Recioto della Valpolicella Classico Amarone Superiore 1980 $13 (12/31/87)
86   ANSELMI Recioto della Valpolicella Amarone 1985 $19 (6/30/91)
83   BOLLA Recioto della Valpolicella Amarone 1985 $16 (10/31/88)
80   LA COLOMBAIA Recioto della Valpolicella Amarone 1979 $12 (7/01/86)
70   REMO FARINA Recioto della Valpolicella Amarone Classico 1983 $12.50 (3/31/90)
85   MASI Recioto della Valpolicella Amarone Campolongo 1983 $26 (4/15/88)
84   MASI Recioto della Valpolicella Amarone Classico 1981 $15 (10/31/88)
88   MASI Recioto della Valpolicella Amarone Mazzano 1980 $26 (10/31/88)
90   LUIGI RIGHETTI Recioto della Valpolicella Amarone Capitel de' Roari 1983 $16 (2/15/89)
83   SANTI Recioto della Valpolicella Amarone 1985 $20 (6/30/91)
79   SARTORI Recioto della Valpolicella Amarone Classico Superiore 1982 $11 (11/15/88)
62   SCAMPERLE Recioto della Valpolicella Amarone Classico 1981 $11 (8/01/85)
77   SCAMPERLE Recioto della Valpolicella Amarone Classico 1978 $9.50 (9/01/84)
81   ZENATO Recioto della Valpolicella Amarone Classico 1981 $11 (3/15/89)

VALPOLICELLA DOC

78   ALLEGRINI Valpolicella Classico Superiore Palazzo della Torre 1983 $7 (12/31/87)
71   BOLLA Valpolicella 1986 $6 (12/15/89)
77   BOLLA Valpolicella 1985 $5.50 (10/31/88)
78   BOLLA Valpolicella Vigneti di Jago Classico 1986 $12 (12/31/90)
81   BOSCAINI Valpolicella Classico Superiore Marano 1985 $6 (9/15/88) BB
71   MASI Valpolicella Classico Serego Alighieri 1983 $9.50 (5/15/87)
78   MASI Valpolicella Classico Superiore 1987 $7.25 (12/31/90)
76   MASI Valpolicella Classico Superiore 1985 $5 (5/31/88)
79   GUERRIERI RIZZARDI Valpolicella Classico Superiore 1987 $6.50 (3/31/90)
82   GUERRIERI RIZZARDI Valpolicella Poiega Classico 1988 $9 (12/15/89)
80   SARTORI Valpolicella Classico Superiore 1985 $4.75 (11/15/88) BB

VINO DA TAVOLA

85   ABBAZIA DI ROSAZZO Pignolo 1987 $36 (6/30/91)
86   ABBAZIA DI ROSAZZO Pignolo 1985 $22 (9/15/88) (TM)
87   ABBAZIA DI ROSAZZO Ronco dei Roseti 1987 $35 (7/15/91)
85   ABBAZIA DI ROSAZZO Ronco dei Roseti 1986 $22 (3/15/89)
87   ABBAZIA DI ROSAZZO Ronco dei Roseti 1983 $20 (9/15/88) (TM)
86   ANTONUTTI Poggio Alto 1986 $15 (4/15/90)
92   BELLAVISTA Solesine 1986 $30 (5/15/89)
86   BERTANI Catullo 1984 $9 (2/15/89)
81   BERTANI Catullo 1983 $9 (6/30/88)
88   BOLLA Creso Rosso 1986 $25 (4/15/90)
88   CA' DEL BOSCO Maurizio Zanella 1987 Rel: $40 Cur: $43 (12/31/90)
92   CA' DEL BOSCO Maurizio Zanella 1987 Rel: $40 Cur: $43 (4/15/90)
92   CA' DEL BOSCO Maurizio Zanella 1985 Rel: $38 Cur: $38 (9/15/88)
82   CA' DEL BOSCO Pinot Noir Pinero 1987 $69 (6/15/90)
82   CASTELCOSA Refosco 1985 (NA) (9/15/88) (TM)
74   FARALTA Rosso del Friuli-Venezia Giulia 1986 $12.50 (4/15/90)
76   BARONE FINI Cabernet Sauvignon Cabernello 1988 $10 (7/15/91)
85   BARONE FINI Cabernet Sauvignon Cabernello 1985 $9.75 (4/15/88)
84   FRANCESCO GRAVNER Rujno 1985 (NA) (9/15/88) (TM)
81   LIVON Schioppettino 1987 $18 (4/15/90)
71   MACULAN Palazzotto 1986 $19 (3/31/89)
77   MASI Campo Fiorin 1985 $11.50 (9/15/90)
81   MASI Campo Fiorin 1983 $7.50 (5/15/89) BB
88   MASI Campo Fiorin 1981 $8 (4/15/88) BB
84   MASO CANTANGHEL Pinot Nero Altesino Riserva 1988 $33 (2/15/91)
82   PIGHIN Blended Red 1987 (NA) (9/15/88) (TM)
84   RONCHI DI CIALLA Schioppettino di Cialla 1983 $25 (3/31/89)
80   RONCO DEL GNEMIZ Rosso 1986 $15 (3/31/89)
84   TEDESCHI Capitel San Rocco 1983 $11 (2/15/89)
84   VALLE SELEZIONE ARALDICA L'Araldo Collina Friulana 1985 $20 (5/15/91)
91   VENEGAZZU Della Casa 1985 $25 (3/31/90)
86   VENEGAZZU Della Casa 1983 $25 (2/15/89)

82   VENEGAZZU Della Casa 1982 $15 (7/15/87)
72   VENEGAZZU Della Casa 1980 $10 (2/15/87)
80   VIGNALTA Merlot 1988 $18 (4/15/91)

OTHER RED DOC

74   BOLLA Bardolino 1982 $5.50 (10/31/88)
82   BOSCAINI Bardolino Classico Superiore Le Canne 1985 $6 (7/31/88) BB
77   CA' DEL BOSCO Franciacorta 1987 $16 (12/31/90)
83   CA' DEL BOSCO Franciacorta 1985 $11 (9/15/88)
81   TENUTA IL BOSCO Pinot Nero Oltrepò Pavese 1988 $9.50 (6/30/91)
75   JOSEF BRIGL Santa Maddalena 1986 $6.75 (10/15/88)
84   BORGO CONVENTI Merlot Collio 1987 $15 (3/31/89)
80   GIROLAMO DORIGO Merlot Colli Orientali del Friuli Montsclapade 1985 $10 (4/15/88)
70   GIROLAMO DORIGO Pinot Nero Colli Orientali del Friuli Montsclapade 1985 $10 (4/15/88)
82   GIOVANNI DRI Refosco Colli Orientali del Friuli 1986 $11 (9/15/89)
82   ENO-FRIULIA Merlot Collio 1988 $12 (4/30/91)
83   FANTINEL Merlot Grave del Friuli 1985 $7 (7/31/87)
84   LIVIO FELLUGA Merlot Collio 1988 $16 (7/15/91)
81   CASA GIRELLI Pinot Nero Trentino i Mesi 1988 $10 (2/15/91)
77   MASI Bardolino Classico 1985 $5 (5/31/88)
80   MASI Bardolino Classico 1984 $5 (5/15/87) BB
82   MASI Bardolino Classico Superiore 1988 $6 (5/15/91) BB
82   TENUTA MAZZOLINO Oltrepò Pavese Barbera 1989 $10 (4/15/91)
64   PLOZNER Merlot Grave del Friuli 1983 $5.50 (7/01/86)
79   RONCHI DI CIALLA Refosco Colli Orientali del Friuli dal Peduncolo Rosso di Cialla 1983 $23 (3/31/89)
80   RUSSIZ SUPERIORE Merlot Collio 1986 $14 (9/15/88) (TM)
68   SARTORI Bardolino Classico Superiore 1985 $4.75 (11/15/88)
80   SARTORI Merlot Grave del Friuli 1986 $6.25 (11/15/88)
79   TORRESELLA Merlot Lison-Pramaggiore 1986 $5.75 (10/31/88)
78   ZENATO Bardolino Classico Superiore 1989 $7.75 (7/15/91)

OTHER ITALY NORTH WHITE/CHARDONNAY DOC

85   BOLLINI Chardonnay Trentino di Mezzocorona 1988 $7 (9/15/89)
84   BOLLINI Chardonnay Trentino di Mezzocorona 1987 $7.25 (9/15/89)
85   CA' DEL BOSCO Chardonnay Franciacorta 1986 $38 (9/15/89)
86   CA' DEL BOSCO Chardonnay Franciacorta 1985 $38 (10/15/88)
77   JOSEF BRIGL Chardonnay Alto Adige 1989 $10 (7/15/91)
65   JOSEF BRIGL Chardonnay Alto Adige 1986 $8 (10/15/88)
84   CAVIT Chardonnay Trentino 1988 $6 (9/15/89)
84   COLTERENZIO Chardonnay Alto Adige 1989 $8 (1/31/91) BB
58   CONSORZIO VITICOLTORI ALTO ADIGE Chardonnay Alto Adige 1983 $4 (11/01/85)
81   CASA GIRELLI Chardonnay Trentino i Mesi 1989 $8 (2/15/91) BB
83   HOSTATTER Chardonnay Alto Adige 1988 (NA) (9/15/89)
80   ISTITUTO AGRARIO PROVINCIALE Chardonnay Trentino 1987 $10 (9/15/89)
80   ISTITUTO AGRARIO PROVINCIALE Chardonnay Trentino 1982 $10.50 (9/15/89)
84   KETTMEIR Chardonnay Alto Adige 1988 $11 (9/15/89)
88   ALOIS LAGEDER Chardonnay Alto Adige Buchholz 1988 $13 (9/15/89)
82   ALOIS LAGEDER Chardonnay Alto Adige Loewengang 1986 $19 (9/15/89)
90   ALOIS LAGEDER Chardonnay Alto Adige Loewengang 1985 $19 (9/15/89)
82   LIVON Chardonnay Grave del Friuli Vigneto Medeuzza 1988 $14 (12/31/90)
85   MALPAGA Chardonnay Trentino 1988 $8 (9/15/89)
75   MALPAGA Chardonnay Trentino 1987 $8 (9/15/89)
79   MASI Chardonnay Trentino Rosabel 1987 (NA) (9/15/89)
75   CANTINE MEZZACORONA Chardonnay Trentino 1986 $6 (12/31/87)
85   PIGHIN Chardonnay Grave del Friuli 1988 $8 (9/15/89)
80   PIGHIN Chardonnay Grave del Friuli Pighin di Capriva 1988 $9.25 (9/15/89)
78   PLOZNER Chardonnay Grave del Friuli 1988 $6 (9/15/89)
81   PLOZNER Chardonnay Grave del Friuli 1986 $8 (9/15/89)
85   PLOZNER Chardonnay Grave del Friuli Riserva 1986 $6 (9/15/88)
84   POJER E SANDRI Chardonnay Trentino 1987 $8 (9/15/89)
82   POJER E SANDRI Chardonnay Trentino 1985 $7.50 (9/15/89)
78   SAN MICHELE Chardonnay Alto Adige 1986 $8.50 (10/15/88)
60   CASTEL SAN VALENTINO Chardonnay Alto Adige Egart 1986 $6.25 (12/15/87)
75   SANTA MARGHERITA Chardonnay Alto Adige 1989 $13 (12/31/90)
71   SANTA MARGHERITA Chardonnay Alto Adige 1985 $8.50 (11/15/87)
79   SANTA MARGHERITA Chardonnay Alto Adige 1984 $6.50 (12/16/85)
70   SARTORI Chardonnay Grave del Friuli 1987 $6.25 (11/15/88)
82   TIEFENBRUNNER Chardonnay Alto Adige 1989 $10 (7/15/91)
84   VENICA Chardonnay Dolegna del Collio 1989 $17 (1/31/91)
85   ZENI Chardonnay Trentino 1988 $12 (9/15/89)

CHARDONNAY VINO DA TAVOLA

82   ABBAZIA DI ROSAZZO Chardonnay 1986 $12 (4/15/88)
83   BELLAVISTA Chardonnay Uccellanda 1987 $30 (9/15/89)
92   BELLAVISTA Chardonnay Uccellanda 1986 $30 (9/15/89)
87   BORTOLUZZI Chardonnay 1988 $11 (9/15/89)
72   BORTOLUZZI Chardonnay 1987 $11 (5/15/89)
79   LA CADALORA Chardonnay della Vallagarina 1988 $11.25 (9/15/89)
84   LA CADALORA Chardonnay della Vallagarina 1987 $8.25 (3/31/89)
82   CASTELCOSA Chardonnay 1987 $12.50 (9/15/89)
85   CASTELCOSA Chardonnay 1986 $9.50 (9/15/89)
83   CASTELCOSA Chardonnay Pra di Pradis 1986 $13 (9/15/89)
86   LA CASTELLADA Chardonnay 1988 $14 (3/31/90)
80   ENO-FRIULIA Chardonnay 1989 $12 (3/31/91)
61   FANTINEL Chardonnay 1985 $7 (6/30/87)
82   MARCO FELLUGA Chardonnay 1988 $9 (9/15/89)
80   MARCO FELLUGA Chardonnay 1987 $9 (9/15/89)
83   STELIO GALLO Chardonnay 1987 (NA) (9/15/89)
81   STELIO GALLO Chardonnay 1986 (NA) (9/15/89)
90   FRANCESCO GRAVNER Chardonnay di Oslavia 1986 (NA) (9/15/88)
80   JERMANN Chardonnay 1989 $17.50 (3/31/91)
85   JERMANN Chardonnay 1987 $15 (9/15/89)
80   JERMANN Chardonnay 1987 $15 (9/15/88)
79   JERMANN Chardonnay 1986 $12 (10/15/88)
91   JERMANN Chardonnay 1985 $12 (9/15/89)
86   JERMANN Chardonnay Dreams 1988 $40 (4/30/90)
92   JERMANN Chardonnay Dreams NV $34 (3/31/90)

ITALY
OTHER ITALY NORTH WHITE/*CHARDONNAY VINO DA TAVOLA*

90	MACULAN Chardonnay Ferrata 1987 $22 (9/15/89)
89	MACULAN Chardonnay Ferrata 1987 $240/3L (9/15/89)
87	MACULAN Chardonnay 1986 $18 (9/15/89)
87	MACULAN Chardonnay Ferrata 1986 $18 (9/15/89)
87	MACULAN Chardonnay 1985 $22 (9/15/89)
87	MACULAN Chardonnay Ferrata 1985 $22 (9/15/89)
87	MACULAN Chardonnay Ferrata 1984 $25 (9/15/89)
89	MASO CANTANGHEL Chardonnay Altesino Vigna Piccola 1989 $25 (1/31/91)
82	VOLPE PASINI Chardonnay 1987 (NA) (9/15/89)
73	FRANCESCO PECORARI Chardonnay Vigna di S. Lorenzo 1986 $10 (12/15/87)
76	PIGHIN Chardonnay 1987 $8.50 (9/15/88)
51	POJER E SANDRI Chardonnay di Faedo 1983 $6.50 (6/16/86)
84	PUIATTI Chardonnay 1989 $17 (3/31/91)
80	GUERRIERI RIZZARDI Chardonnay 1988 (NA) (9/15/89)
88	RONCO DEL GNEMIZ Chardonnay 1989 $27 (7/15/91)
90	RONCO DEL GNEMIZ Chardonnay 1987 $18 (9/15/89)
80	RONCO DEL GNEMIZ Chardonnay 1986 $12.50 (4/15/88)
84	MARIN RONCO FORNAZ Chardonnay 1988 (NA) (9/15/89)
83	CA' RONESCA Chardonnay 1988 $11 (9/15/88)
78	TORRE ROSAZZA Chardonnay 1989 $15 (2/15/91)
81	TORRE ROSAZZA Chardonnay 1988 (NA) (9/15/89)
83	TORRESELLA Chardonnay 1988 $6 (9/15/89)
79	TORRESELLA Chardonnay 1986 $5.75 (3/31/89)
77	VENEGAZZU Chardonnay 1988 $8.50 (9/15/89)
80	VIGNALTA Chardonnay Selezione Vendemmia 1988 $18 (2/15/91)
84	VIGNE DAL LEON Chardonnay Tullio Zamò 1989 $27 (7/15/91)
79	TENUTA VILLANOVA Chardonnay 1987 $7 (11/15/88)

PINOT GRIGIO DOC

77	ABBAZIA DI ROSAZZO Pinot Grigio Colli Orientali del Friuli 1987 $15 (9/15/88)
80	ABBAZIA DI ROSAZZO Pinot Grigio Colli Orientali del Friuli 1986 $12 (4/15/88)
78	BOLLA Pinot Grigio Alto Adige 1986 $8.50 (10/15/88)
82	BOLLINI Pinot Grigio Valdadige 1986 $6.50 (3/31/88) BB
69	BOLLINI Pinot Grigio Valdadige 1985 $6.25 (4/30/87)
86	BOLLINI Pinot Grigio Valdadige 1984 $5.50 (2/01/86) BB
73	LA COLOMBAIA Pinot Grigio Valdadige 1985 $7 (4/30/87)
79	COLTERENZIO Pinot Grigio Alto Adige 1989 $10 (3/31/91)
80	ENO-FRIULIA Pinot Grigio Collio 1989 $12 (3/31/91)
74	FANTINEL Pinot Grigio Grave del Friuli 1985 $7 (6/30/87)
78	LIVIO FELLUGA Pinot Grigio Colli Orientali del Friuli 1989 $18 (3/31/91)
77	LIVIO FELLUGA Pinot Grigio Colli Orientali del Friuli 1987 $15 (9/15/88)
78	BARONE FINI Pinot Grigio Valdadige 1986 $6 (3/31/88)
76	CANTINE MEZZACORONA Pinot Grigio Trentino 1986 $10 (3/31/88)
74	CANTINE MEZZACORONA Pinot Grigio Trentino 1986 $10 (12/31/87)
82	PIGHIN Pinot Grigio Grave del Friuli 1987 $9 (9/15/88)
78	PLOZNER Pinot Grigio Grave del Friuli 1984 $4.50 (11/16/85) BB
85	PUIATTI Pinot Grigio Collio 1989 $17 (3/31/91)
78	RONCO DEL GNEMIZ Pinot Grigio Colli Orientali del Friuli 1986 $12.50 (4/15/88)
81	CA' RONESCA Pinot Grigio Colli Orientali del Friuli 1989 $19 (3/31/91)
74	CA' RONESCA Pinot Grigio Collio 1987 $14.50 (9/15/88)
75	SAN MICHELE Pinot Grigio Alto Adige 1986 $9 (10/15/88)
75	CASTEL SAN VALENTINO Pinot Grigio Alto Adige di Magre 1986 $6.50 (12/15/87)
80	CASTEL SAN VALENTINO Pinot Grigio Alto Adige di Magre 1985 $6.25 (11/15/87)
77	SANTA MARGHERITA Pinot Grigio Alto Adige 1985 $12 (2/28/87)
70	SANTA MARGHERITA Pinot Grigio Alto Adige 1984 $9 (4/16/86)
73	STEVERJAN Pinot Grigio Collio 1985 $9.50 (2/28/87)
79	SUBIDA DI MONTE Pinot Grigio Collio 1989 $10.50 (7/15/91)
83	TIEFENBRUNNER Pinot Grigio Alto Adige 1989 $10 (6/30/91)

SAUVIGNON BLANC DOC

83	ABBAZIA DI ROSAZZO Sauvignon Colli Orientali del Friuli 1989 $19 (7/15/91)
83	ABBAZIA DI ROSAZZO Sauvignon Colli Orientali del Friuli 1987 $15 (9/15/88)
83	ABBAZIA DI ROSAZZO Sauvignon Colli Orientali del Friuli 1986 $12 (4/15/88)
65	CA' BOLANI Sauvignon Aqueileia 1984 $5.25 (6/16/86)
80	LIVIO FELLUGA Sauvignon Blanc Colli Orientali del Friuli 1987 $15 (9/15/88)
86	FRANCESCO GRAVNER Sauvignon Blanc Collio 1986 (NA) (9/15/88)
81	PIGHIN Sauvignon Blanc Collio 1987 $12.50 (9/15/88)
84	CA' RONESCA Sauvignon Colli Orientali del Friuli del Podere 1989 $19 (4/15/91)
85	CA' RONESCA Sauvignon Colli Orientali del Friuli del Podere 1987 $15 (9/15/88)
85	CA' RONESCA Sauvignon Blanc Collio 1987 (NA) (9/15/88)
83	RUSSIZ SUPERIORE Sauvignon Blanc Collio 1987 (NA) (9/15/88)
87	SUBIDA DI MONTE Sauvignon Collio 1989 $11 (7/15/91)
83	LA VIARTE Sauvignon Colli Orientali del Friuli 1989 $19.50 (7/15/91)

TOCAI FRIULANO DOC

80	ABBAZIA DI ROSAZZO Tocai Friulano Colli Orientali del Friuli 1987 $14 (9/15/88)
85	LE DUE TERRE Tocai Friulano Colli Orientali del Friuli 1987 $10 (9/15/88)
81	LIVIO FELLUGA Tocai Friulano Colli Orientali del Friuli 1989 $15.50 (4/15/91)
82	LIVIO FELLUGA Tocai Friulano Colli Orientali del Friuli 1987 $13 (9/15/88)
82	LIVON Tocai Friulano Collio Vigneto di Ruttars 1988 $15 (12/31/90)
72	FRANCESCO PECORARI Tocai Friulano Collio Vigna di S. Lorenzo 1986 $9 (12/15/87)
78	DORO PRINCIC Tocai Friulano Collio 1986 $11 (4/15/88)
75	RONCO DEL GNEMIZ Tocai Friulano Colli Orientali del Friuli 1986 $11 (4/15/88)
88	CA' RONESCA Tocai Friulano Collio 1987 (NA) (9/15/88)

85	SCHIOPETTO Tocai Friulano Collio 1987 (NA) (9/15/88)
82	VENICA Tocai Friulano Collio 1989 $15 (2/15/91)
77	VIGNE DAL LEON Tocai Friulano Colli Orientali del Friuli 1989 $18.50 (7/15/91)

OTHER VINO DA TAVOLA

89	ABBAZIA DI ROSAZZO Ronco delle Acacie 1989 $36 (7/15/91)
86	ABBAZIA DI ROSAZZO Ronco delle Acacie 1987 (NA) (9/15/88)
91	ABBAZIA DI ROSAZZO Ronco delle Acacie 1985 (NA) (9/15/88)
84	ABBAZIA DI ROSAZZO Ronco di Corte 1989 $27 (7/15/91)
86	BERTANI Catullo 1987 $8 (3/31/89)
86	CONTE CE CUCCANEA Collavini 1985 (NA) (9/15/88)
85	LIVIO FELLUGA Terre Alta 1986 $15 (9/15/88)
82	FOSSI Chardonnay dell' Alto Adige 1988 $11.50 (7/15/91)
81	FRANCO FURLAN Tai di Castelcosa NV $16 (4/30/90)
84	STELIO GALLO Sauvignon Blanc 1985 (NA) (9/15/88)
82	FRANCESCO GRAVNER Vinograd Breg 1987 (NA) (9/15/88)
87	JERMANN Pinot Bianco 1989 $17.50 (4/15/91)
79	JERMANN Pinot Bianco 1986 $10 (10/15/88)
82	JERMANN Pinot Grigio 1989 $17.50 (3/31/91)
78	JERMANN Pinot Grigio 1987 $15 (9/15/88)
84	JERMANN Sauvignon 1989 $17.50 (4/15/91)
88	JERMANN Traminer 1987 (NA) (9/15/88)
79	JERMANN Vinnae 1987 (NA) (9/15/88)
84	JERMANN Vinnae da Vinnaioli 1989 $17.50 (4/15/91)
88	JERMANN Vintage Tunina 1986 $26 (9/15/88)
84	MACULAN Dindarello 1989 $24 (7/15/91)
83	MACULAN Prato di Canzio 1987 $17 (10/15/89)
78	MASI Masianco 1987 $6.75 (5/15/89)
79	MASI Masianco 1986 $6.75 (10/15/88)
62	MASI Masianco 1985 $6 (4/30/87)
74	MONTEVINO Pinot Grigio del Veneto 1989 $6.50 (7/15/91)
79	DORO PRINCIC Riesling 1986 $11 (4/15/88)
82	RONCO DEL GNEMIZ Müller Thurgau 1989 $18.50 (7/15/91)
85	RUSSIZ SUPERIORE Roncuz 1987 (NA) (9/15/88)
73	SANTA MARGHERITA Cuvée Margherita del Veneto Orientale 1988 $11 (12/31/90)
86	SANTA MARGHERITA Luna del Feldi di Rovere 1984 $12.50 (1/01/86)

OTHER WHITE DOC

79	ABBAZIA DI ROSAZZO Ribolla Gialla Colli Orientali del Friuli 1986 $12 (4/15/88)
76	ANSELMI Soave Classico Capitel Foscarino 1989 $20 (7/15/91)
81	ANSELMI Soave Classico Superiore 1989 $8 (7/15/91)
81	BOLLA Soave Classico Vigneti di Castellaro 1989 $12 (12/31/90)
82	BOSCAINI Soave Classico Monteleone 1989 $8 (6/30/91) BB
78	CA' DEL BOSCO Franciacorta 1988 $16.50 (4/30/90)
85	CA' DEL BOSCO Franciacorta 1986 $13 (10/15/88)
78	CAMPAGNOLA Soave Classico 1985 $3.25 (4/15/87) BB
79	FRANCESCO GRAVNER Ribolla Gialla Collio 1987 (NA) (9/15/88)
77	FRANCESCO GRAVNER Riesling Collio Italico 1987 (NA) (9/15/88)
85	MACULAN Breganze Bianco Breganze di Breganze 1987 $7.50 (5/15/89) BB
78	FOSS MARAI Prosecco di Valdobbiadene 1989 $7.50 (12/31/90)
70	MASI Soave Classico Col Baraca 1985 $8 (4/30/87)
62	MASI Soave Classico Col Baraca 1984 $7.50 (4/16/86)
74	PIEROPAN Soave Classico 1985 $7.25 (4/30/87)
78	DORO PRINCIC Pinot Bianco Collio 1989 $14 (7/15/91)
74	DORO PRINCIC Pinot Bianco Collio 1986 $11 (4/15/88)
85	PUIATTI Pinot Bianco Collio 1989 $17 (4/15/91)
84	CA' RONESCA Pinot Bianco Collio 1987 (NA) (9/15/88)
84	RUSSIZ SUPERIORE Pinot Bianco Collio 1987 (NA) (9/15/88)
77	CASTEL SAN VALENTINO Pinot Bianco Alto Adige Tenuta Schulthaus 1986 $6.25 (12/15/87)
86	SCHIOPETTO Pinot Bianco Collio 1986 (NA) (9/15/88)
76	CA' VESCOVO Chardonnay Aqueileia 1989 $8 (7/15/91)
85	LA VIARTE Colli Orientali del Friuli Ribolla 1988 $18 (12/31/90)
80	ZENATO Bianco di Custoza Sole del Benaco 1989 $9 (6/30/91)

OTHER ITALY RED/*RED DOC*

84	ADANTI Montefalco d'Arquata 1985 $7.75 (7/31/88)
77	ADANTI Montefalco Sagrantino d'Arquata 1983 $12.25 (10/15/88)
70	D'ANGELO Aglianico del Vulture 1985 $18 (9/15/89)
70	ARPA CLASSICA Sangiovese di Romagna 1985 $4 (12/31/87)
81	CASAL THAULERO Montepulciano d'Abruzzo 1989 $6 (6/30/91) BB
80	CASAL THAULERO Montepulciano d'Abruzzo 1988 $5 (5/31/90) BB
86	CASAL THAULERO Montepulciano d'Abruzzo 1983 $6.50 (6/30/87) BB
79	CITRA Montepulciano d'Abruzzo 1985 $4.50 (7/31/87)
65	CITRA Montepulciano d'Abruzzo Rubino 1979 $5.75 (7/31/87)
84	CONSORZIO VITICOLTORI DEL VULTURE Aglianico del Vulture 1982 $6 (9/15/88) BB
78	BARONE CORNACCHIA Montepulciano d'Abruzzo 1988 $5 (12/31/90)
83	LUNGAROTTI Torgiano Rubesco 1987 $11 (5/15/91)
74	LUNGAROTTI Torgiano Rubesco 1985 $11 (9/15/89)
77	LUNGAROTTI Torgiano Rubesco 1979 $8.50 (1/01/86)
84	LUNGAROTTI Torgiano Rubesco Monticchio Riserva 1980 $27 (7/15/91)
82	LUNGAROTTI Torgiano Rubesco Monticchio Riserva 1978 $23 (9/15/89)
83	LUNGAROTTI Torgiano Torre di Giano 1989 $11 (7/15/91)
89	MASTROBERARDINO Lacryma Christi del Vesuvio 1989 $14 (7/15/91)
87	MASTROBERARDINO Taurasi 1986 $18 (7/15/91)
75	MASTROBERARDINO Taurasi 1982 $13 (7/15/91)
84	MASTROBERARDINO Taurasi Riserva 1985 $21.50 (6/30/91)
78	MASTROBERARDINO Taurasi Riserva 1981 Rel: $21 Cur: $21 (2/15/89)
75	MASTROBERARDINO Taurasi Riserva 1980 Rel: $15 Cur: $15 (9/15/89)
92	MASTROBERARDINO Taurasi Riserva 1977 Rel: $28 Cur: $51 (10/16/84) CS
83	ANTONIO & ELIO MONTI Montepulciano d'Abruzzo 1988 $6.25 (2/15/91) BB
80	CAMILLO MONTORI Montepulciano d'Abruzzo 1987 $8 (3/31/90)
74	BRUNO NICODEMI Montepulciano d'Abruzzo Dei Colli Venia 1984 $5.50 (11/15/87)
85	FATTORIA PARADISO Sangiovese di Romagna Riserva Superiore Vigna delle Lepri 1987 $16 (7/15/91)
83	RIVERA Castel del Monte Il Falcone Riserva 1985 $16.50 (12/31/90)
75	UMANI RONCHI Montepulciano d'Abruzzo 1989 $5 (2/15/91)
84	CASTELLO DI SALLE Montepulciano d'Abruzzo 1985 $15 (6/15/90) BB
83	SASSO Aglianico del Vulture 1985 $11 (3/15/89)

93 STRUZZIERO Taurasi Riserva 1977 Rel: $22.50 Cur: $24 (8/31/86) CS
85 DR. COSIMO TAURINO Brindisi Patriglione 1981 $14 (12/31/90)
82 DR. COSIMO TAURINO Brindisi Patriglione Riserva 1979 $12 (3/31/89)
82 DR. COSIMO TAURINO Salice Salentino 1982 $6 (3/31/89) BB
85 DR. COSIMO TAURINO Salice Salentino Riserva 1985 $8 (2/15/91) BB
81 DR. COSIMO TAURINO Salice Salentino Riserva 1981 $6 (3/31/88) BB
84 DR. COSIMO TAURINO Salice Salentino Riserva 1980 $5 (12/15/87) BB
84 DR. COSIMO TAURINO Salice Salentino Rosato 1988 $7.25 (3/15/91) BB
84 DR. COSIMO TAURINO Salice Salentino Rosato 1987 $6.50 (12/31/89) BB
81 DR. COSIMO TAURINO Salice Salentino Rosso Riserva 1983 $6.50 (12/15/89) BB
80 VALENTINI Montepulciano d'Abruzzo 1979 $28 (2/15/89)
80 ZONIN Montepulciano d'Abruzzo 1988 $6 (6/30/91) BB
78 ZONIN Montepulciano d'Abruzzo 1987 $4.50 (3/31/90)
81 ZONIN Montepulciano d'Abruzzo 1983 $4 (5/16/86) BB

VINO DA TAVOLA

92 CORVO Duca di Salaparuta Duca Enrico 1984 $27 (9/15/89)
71 CORVO Rosso 1985 $5.75 (9/15/88)
84 GIROLAMO DORIGO Montsclapade 1987 $25 (2/15/91)
85 LUNGAROTTI Cabernet Sauvignon di Miralduolo 1983 $18 (5/15/91)
79 LUNGAROTTI Cabernet Sauvignon 1979 $11 (2/15/87)
77 LUNGAROTTI San Giorgio Rosso 1982 $34 (7/15/91)
75 LUNGAROTTI San Giorgio Rosso 1979 $18 (3/15/87)
84 LUNGAROTTI San Giorgio Rosso 1978 $18.50 (4/16/85)
87 MASTROBERARDINO Avellanio 1989 $10.50 (7/15/91)
76 VILLA MATILDE Falerno 1983 $5 (5/15/87)
80 PAOLA DI MAURO Colle Picchioni 1986 $15 (3/31/90)
83 PAOLA DI MAURO Vigna del Vassalle 1986 $12 (3/31/90)
72 MIRAFIORE Z 1985 $4 (1/31/87)
80 FATTORIA PARADISO Barbarossa 1983 $13.50 (3/15/89)
77 REGALEALI Rosso 1987 $11 (12/15/89)
84 REGALEALI Rosso del Conte 1984 $19 (7/31/89)
74 RIGALEALI Conte Tasca d'Almerita 1985 $7.25 (4/15/88)
73 SOLICHIATA Torrepalino 1987 $5.75 (4/15/90)
80 DR. COSIMO TAURINO Notarpanaro 1978 $8 (3/31/89)
78 DR. COSIMO TAURINO Notarpanaro 1975 $8 (4/15/88)
86 DR. COSIMO TAURINO Notarpanaro 1981 $9 (5/15/91)
82 TORRE GAIA Il Dugentino 1986 $5 (9/15/88)
70 VALLANIA Terre Rosse 1985 $9 (3/31/90)

OTHER ITALY WHITE/VINO DA TAVOLA

73 ADANTI Arquata de Bevagna 1986 $6.50 (10/15/88)
86 ANTINORI Castello della Sala Borro della Sala 1989 $11.50 (1/31/91)
77 ANTINORI Castello della Sala Borro della Sala 1987 $10 (10/15/89)
89 ANTINORI Castello della Sala Cervaro della Sala 1988 $21 (1/31/91)
83 ANTINORI Castello della Sala Cervaro della Sala 1987 $20 (4/30/90)
76 ANTINORI Castello della Sala Cervaro della Sala 1986 $6 (12/31/87)
90 ANTINORI Castello della Sala Cervaro della Sala 1985 $18 (12/15/87)
79 FABIO BERIN Berin 1983 $9.75 (10/15/86)
71 CORVO Bianco 1984 $5 (11/01/85)
81 CORVO Duca di Salaparuta Bianca di Valguarnera 1987 $34 (12/31/90)
76 FOLONARI Chardonnay 1987 $5 (9/15/89)
81 CARLO HAUNER Salina Bianco 1989 $11.50 (7/15/91)
77 LUNGAROTTI Chardonnay 1989 $11 (3/31/91)
82 LUNGAROTTI Chardonnay 1988 $10 (9/15/89)
83 LUNGAROTTI Chardonnay 1987 $10.50 (9/15/89)
87 LUNGAROTTI Chardonnay I Palazzi 1985 $16 (9/15/89)
68 LUNGAROTTI Chardonnay I Palazzi 1983 $16 (2/28/87)
81 LUNGAROTTI Pinot Grigio 1989 $11 (3/31/91)
84 MASTROBERARDINO Plinius D'Irpinia Bianco 1989 $17 (7/15/91)
75 VILLA MATILDE Falerno 1985 $5 (2/28/87)
83 FATTORIA PARADISO Chardonnay Emilia-Romagna 1988 $10 (9/15/89)
79 FATTORIA PARADISO Pagadebit di Romagna Secco Vigna Dello Spungone 1989 $13 (7/15/91)
79 PRATOSCURO 1989 $18 (12/31/90)
82 REGALEALI Nozze d'Oro 1989 $20 (7/15/91)
79 SETTESOLI Bianco 1990 $7 (7/15/91)
80 SETTESOLI Bianco Feudo dei Fiori 1990 $9 (6/30/91)
84 TORREBIANCO Chardonnay 1988 $12.50 (9/15/88)
78 TORREBIANCO Chardonnay 1987 $12.50 (12/31/90)
84 TORREBIANCO Chardonnay 1987 $12.50 (9/15/88)

WHITE DOC

78 ANTINORI Orvieto Classico 1987 $5 (5/15/89)
72 ANTINORI Orvieto Classico 1985 $5 (4/30/87)
80 ANTINORI Orvieto Classico Campogrande Secco 1989 $7.25 (7/15/91)
83 VILLA BIANCHI Verdicchio dei Castelli di Jesi Classico 1989 $7 (6/30/91) BB
73 BUCCI Verdicchio dei Castelli di Jesi Classico 1988 $14 (12/31/90)
74 CASTELLUCCI Verdicchio dei Castelli di Jesi 1984 $4 (6/16/86)
89 COLLE DEI BARDELLINI Vermentino Riviera Ligure di Ponent Vigna ''U Munte'' 1989 $18 (1/31/91)
78 COTTI Orvieto Classico 1984 $5.50 (1/01/86)
     COTTI Orvieto Classico 1980 $4 (1/01/82) SS
77 FALESCO Est! Est!! Est!!! di Montefiascone Poggio dei Gelsi 1989 $12 (7/15/91)
82 FONTANA CANDIDA Frascati Superiore 1984 $5 (1/01/86) BB
72 MACHIAVELLI Orvieto Classico 1985 $4 (4/30/87)
79 MASTROBERARDINO Fiano di Avellino Apianum Vigna d'Oro 1988 $25 (4/30/90)
84 MASTROBERARDINO Fiano di Avellino Vignadora 1989 $30 (7/15/91)
78 MASTROBERARDINO Fiano di Avellino Vignadora 1986 $22.50 (10/15/89)
83 MASTROBERARDINO Fiano di Avellino Vignadora 1985 $25 (5/31/87)
79 MASTROBERARDINO Greco di Tufo Vignadangelo 1986 $15 (10/15/89)
86 MASTROBERARDINO Greco di Tufo Vignadangelo 1985 $13.50 (5/31/87)
76 MASTROBERARDINO Lacryma Christi del Vesuvio 1989 $13 (7/15/91)
89 MASTROBERARDINO Lacryma Christi del Vesuvio 1987 $9 (3/31/89)
90 MASTROBERARDINO Lacryma Christi del Vesuvio 1979 $6.25 (1/01/84) SS
81 FATTORIA PARADISO Albana di Romagna Secco Vigna Dell'Olivo 1989 $13 (7/15/91)
81 BARONE RICASOLI Orvieto Classico Secco 1989 $8 (4/15/91) BB
78 RUFFINO Orvieto Classico 1987 $6.25 (5/15/89)

82 RUFFINO Orvieto Classico 1985 $5 (10/31/86) BB
63 VILLA SIMONE Frascati Superiore 1984 $6.50 (6/16/86)
91 STRUZZIERO Greco di Tufo 1984 $7.50 (9/15/86)
80 VALENTINI Trebbiano d'Abruzzo 1984 $20 (3/31/89)
75 VASELLI Orvieto Classico Secco 1989 $7.75 (7/15/91)
71 VASELLI Orvieto Classico Secco 1984 $4.50 (7/01/86)
76 VASELLI Orvieto Classico Torre Sant' Andrea 1989 $14 (7/15/91)
83 VASELLI Orvieto Classico Torre Sant' Andrea 1989 $11 (12/31/90)
77 ZENATO Lugana San Benedetto 1989 $9.25 (7/15/91)

PORTUGAL
VINTAGE PORT

81	BARROS Vintage Port 1987 Rel: $28 Cur: $28 (VP-1/90)
80	BARROS Vintage Port 1985 Rel: $24 Cur: $29 (VP-1/90)
76	BARROS Vintage Port 1983 Rel: $8 Cur: $33 (VP-1/90)
75	BARROS Vintage Port 1978 Rel: $7 Cur: $30 (VP-1/90)
74	BARROS Vintage Port 1974 Cur: $40 (VP-1/90)
82	BARROS Vintage Port 1970 Cur: $60 (VP-1/90)
70	BORGES Vintage Port 1985 Rel: $15 Cur: $15 (VP-5/90)
70	BORGES Vintage Port 1983 Rel: $12 Cur: $29 (VP-5/90)
79	BORGES Vintage Port 1982 Rel: $12 Cur: $30 (VP-5/90)
70	BORGES Vintage Port 1980 Rel: $11 Cur: $23 (VP-5/90)
65	BORGES Vintage Port 1979 Rel: $11 Cur: $22 (VP-5/90)
59	BORGES Vintage Port 1970 Cur: $86 (VP-5/90)
93	BURMESTER Vintage Port 1985 Rel: $25 Cur: $25 (VP-1/90)
87	BURMESTER Vintage Port 1985 Rel: $25 Cur: $25 (12/31/88)
84	BURMESTER Vintage Port 1984 (NA) (VP-1/90)
88	BURMESTER Vintage Port 1980 Rel: $18 Cur: $33 (VP-1/90)
82	BURMESTER Vintage Port 1977 Rel: $11 Cur: $37 (VP-1/90)
86	BURMESTER Vintage Port 1970 Cur: $55 (VP-1/90)
83	BURMESTER Vintage Port 1963 Cur: $131 (VP-1/90)
88	CALEM Vintage Port 1985 Rel: $25 Cur: $38 (VP-6/90)
84	CALEM Vintage Port 1985 Rel: $25 Cur: $38 (9/30/87)
84	CALEM Vintage Port 1983 Rel: $18 Cur: $40 (VP-6/90)
78	CALEM Vintage Port 1980 Rel: $14 Cur: $38 (VP-6/90)
69	CALEM Vintage Port 1977 Rel: $11 Cur: $66 (VP-11/89)
86	CALEM Vintage Port 1975 Cur: $50 (VP-2/90)
80	CALEM Vintage Port 1970 Cur: $50 (VP-11/89)
82	CALEM Vintage Port 1966 Cur: $65 (VP-11/89)
82	CALEM Vintage Port 1963 Cur: $85 (VP-12/89)
84	CALEM Vintage Port Quinta do Foz 1987 Rel: $28 Cur: $28 (VP-6/90)
82	CALEM Vintage Port Quinta do Foz 1982 Rel: $12 Cur: $37 (VP-6/90)
86	CHAMPALIMAUD Vintage Port 1982 Rel: $20 Cur: $20 (VP-2/90)
81	CHURCHILL Vintage Port 1985 Rel: $22 Cur: $39 (VP-2/90)
84	CHURCHILL Vintage Port 1985 Rel: $22 Cur: $39 (9/30/87)
78	CHURCHILL Vintage Port 1982 (NA) (VP-6/90)
83	CHURCHILL Vintage Port Agua Alta 1987 Rel: $37 Cur: $37 (4/15/91)
83	CHURCHILL Vintage Port Agua Alta 1987 Rel: $37 Cur: $37 (VP-5/90)
69	CHURCHILL Vintage Port Agua Alta 1983 Rel: $22 Cur: $41 (VP-7/90)
78	CHURCHILL Vintage Port Fojo 1986 (NR) (VP-2/90)
79	CHURCHILL Vintage Port Fojo 1984 (NA) (VP-2/90)
90	COCKBURN Vintage Port 1985 Rel: $33 Cur: $46 (VP-6/90)
93	COCKBURN Vintage Port 1985 Rel: $33 Cur: $46 (10/31/88)
97	COCKBURN Vintage Port 1983 Rel: $22 Cur: $45 (VP-6/90)
91	COCKBURN Vintage Port 1983 Rel: $22 Cur: $45 (10/31/88)
92	COCKBURN Vintage Port 1983 Rel: $22 Cur: $45 (8/31/87) CS
77	COCKBURN Vintage Port 1975 Cur: $47 (VP-1/90)
75	COCKBURN Vintage Port 1975 Cur: $47 (10/31/88)
86	COCKBURN Vintage Port 1970 Cur: $78 (VP-12/89)
87	COCKBURN Vintage Port 1970 Cur: $78 (10/31/88)
85	COCKBURN Vintage Port 1967 Cur: $74 (VP-12/89)
87	COCKBURN Vintage Port 1967 Cur: $74 (10/31/88)
91	COCKBURN Vintage Port 1966 (NA) (10/31/88)
88	COCKBURN Vintage Port 1963 Cur: $110 (VP-12/89)
91	COCKBURN Vintage Port 1963 Cur: $110 (10/31/88)
82	COCKBURN Vintage Port 1960 Cur: $98 (10/31/88)
80	COCKBURN Vintage Port 1960 Cur: $98 (VP-8/88)
84	COCKBURN Vintage Port 1958 (NA) (VP-11/89)
90	COCKBURN Vintage Port 1955 Cur: $155 (VP-11/89)
76	COCKBURN Vintage Port 1950 Cur: $100 (VP-11/89)
90	COCKBURN Vintage Port 1947 Cur: $191 (VP-11/89)
92	COCKBURN Vintage Port 1935 Cur: $330 (VP-2/90)
89	COCKBURN Vintage Port 1931 (NA) (VP-11/89)
91	COCKBURN Vintage Port 1927 Cur: $340 (VP-12/89)
91	COCKBURN Vintage Port 1912 Cur: $350 (VP-10/87)
89	COCKBURN Vintage Port 1908 Cur: $400 (VP-10/87)
75	COCKBURN Vintage Port 1904 Cur: $390 (VP-10/87)
82	COCKBURN Vintage Port 1896 Cur: $400 (VP-2/90)
81	CROFT Vintage Port 1985 Rel: $30 Cur: $42 (VP-6/90)
92	CROFT Vintage Port 1985 Rel: $30 Cur: $42 (10/31/88)
69	CROFT Vintage Port 1982 Rel: $22 Cur: $41 (VP-4/90)
82	CROFT Vintage Port 1982 Rel: $22 Cur: $41 (10/31/88)
85	CROFT Vintage Port 1977 Rel: $14 Cur: $63 (VP-4/90)
93	CROFT Vintage Port 1977 Rel: $14 Cur: $63 (10/31/88)
80	CROFT Vintage Port 1975 Cur: $45 (10/31/88)
76	CROFT Vintage Port 1975 Cur: $45 (VP-8/88)
89	CROFT Vintage Port 1970 Cur: $76 (VP-12/89)
90	CROFT Vintage Port 1970 Cur: $76 (10/31/88)
90	CROFT Vintage Port 1966 Cur: $83 (VP-12/89)
84	CROFT Vintage Port 1966 Cur: $83 (10/31/88)
91	CROFT Vintage Port 1963 Cur: $122 (VP-12/89)
86	CROFT Vintage Port 1963 Cur: $122 (10/31/88)
90	CROFT Vintage Port 1960 Cur: $93 (VP-9/89)
90	CROFT Vintage Port 1960 Cur: $93 (10/31/88)
84	CROFT Vintage Port 1955 Cur: $184 (VP-11/89)
77	CROFT Vintage Port 1950 Cur: $170 (VP-4/90)

99	CROFT Vintage Port 1945 Cur: $380 (VP-11/89)
93	CROFT Vintage Port 1935 Cur: $320 (VP-2/90)
87	CROFT Vintage Port 1927 Cur: $460 (VP-12/89)
79	CROFT Vintage Port Quinta da Roeda 1987 (NR) (VP-2/90)
85	CROFT Vintage Port Quinta da Roeda 1983 Rel: $22 Cur: $22 (VP-2/90)
75	CROFT Vintage Port Quinta da Roeda 1980 Rel: $25 Cur: $30 (VP-2/90)
83	CROFT Vintage Port Quinta da Roeda 1978 Rel: $22 Cur: $29 (VP-2/90)
85	CROFT Vintage Port Quinta da Roeda 1967 Cur: $60 (VP-1/90)
80	C. DA SILVA Vintage Port Presidential 1987 (NR) (VP-2/90)
78	C. DA SILVA Vintage Port Presidential 1985 Rel: $30 Cur: $30 (VP-2/90)
77	C. DA SILVA Vintage Port Presidential 1978 Cur: $37 (VP-2/90)
72	C. DA SILVA Vintage Port Presidential 1977 Cur: $39 (VP-2/90)
75	C. DA SILVA Vintage Port Presidential 1970 Cur: $46 (VP-2/90)
81	DELAFORCE Vintage Port 1985 Rel: $24 Cur: $41 (VP-6/90)
69	DELAFORCE Vintage Port 1982 Rel: $20 Cur: $27 (VP-6/90)
80	DELAFORCE Vintage Port 1977 Rel: $11 Cur: $62 (VP-2/90)
76	DELAFORCE Vintage Port 1975 Cur: $43 (VP-2/90)
89	DELAFORCE Vintage Port 1970 Cur: $57 (VP-2/90)
85	DELAFORCE Vintage Port 1966 Cur: $65 (VP-2/90)
93	DELAFORCE Vintage Port 1963 Cur: $100 (VP-2/90)
87	DELAFORCE Vintage Port Quinta da Corte 1987 (NR) (VP-2/90)
84	DELAFORCE Vintage Port Quinta da Corte 1984 (NR) (VP-2/90)
81	DELAFORCE Vintage Port Quinta da Corte 1980 (NA) (VP-2/90)
80	DELAFORCE Vintage Port Quinta da Corte 1978 Rel: $24 Cur: $24 (VP-2/90)
82	DIEZ HERMANOS Vintage Port 1977 (NA) (VP-4/90)
89	DOW Vintage Port 1985 Rel: $30 Cur: $37 (VP-6/90)
91	DOW Vintage Port 1985 Rel: $30 Cur: $37 (9/30/87)
94	DOW Vintage Port 1983 Rel: $20 Cur: $36 (VP-6/90)
88	DOW Vintage Port 1983 Rel: $20 Cur: $36 (10/31/88)
90	DOW Vintage Port 1980 Rel: $15 Cur: $39 (VP-6/90)
89	DOW Vintage Port 1980 Rel: $15 Cur: $39 (10/31/88)
94	DOW Vintage Port 1977 Rel: $12 Cur: $61 (VP-4/90)
92	DOW Vintage Port 1977 Rel: $12 Cur: $61 (10/31/88)
80	DOW Vintage Port 1975 Cur: $46 (VP-4/89)
75	DOW Vintage Port 1975 Cur: $46 (10/31/88)
79	DOW Vintage Port 1972 Cur: $39 (VP-1/90)
94	DOW Vintage Port 1970 Cur: $73 (VP-12/89)
90	DOW Vintage Port 1970 Cur: $73 (10/31/88)
94	DOW Vintage Port 1966 Cur: $90 (VP-12/89)
90	DOW Vintage Port 1966 Cur: $90 (10/31/88)
92	DOW Vintage Port 1963 Cur: $132 (VP-2/90)
90	DOW Vintage Port 1963 Cur: $132 (10/31/88)
88	DOW Vintage Port 1960 Cur: $89 (VP-2/90)
94	DOW Vintage Port 1960 Cur: $89 (10/31/88)
91	DOW Vintage Port 1955 Cur: $219 (VP-4/90)
86	DOW Vintage Port 1950 Cur: $110 (VP-11/89)
88	DOW Vintage Port 1947 Cur: $249 (VP-11/89)
89	DOW Vintage Port 1945 Cur: $440 (VP-11/89)
79	DOW Vintage Port 1935 Cur: $300 (VP-6/90)
84	DOW Vintage Port 1934 Cur: $350 (VP-6/90)
87	DOW Vintage Port 1927 Cur: $480 (VP-4/90)
86	DOW Vintage Port Quinta do Bomfim 1987 (NR) (VP-2/90)
82	DOW Vintage Port Quinta do Bomfim 1986 (NR) (VP-2/90)
86	DOW Vintage Port Quinta do Bomfim 1984 (NR) (VP-2/90)
82	DOW Vintage Port Quinta do Bomfim 1982 (NR) (VP-2/90)
81	DOW Vintage Port Quinta do Bomfim 1979 Rel: $28 Cur: $28 (VP-2/90)
85	DOW Vintage Port Quinta do Bomfim 1978 Rel: $27 Cur: $30 (VP-2/90)
88	DOW Vintage Port Quinta do Bomfim 1978 Rel: $27 Cur: $30 (11/30/88)
87	DOW Vintage Port Quinta do Bomfim 1965 (NA) (VP-6/90)
72	FEIST Vintage Port 1985 Rel: $20 Cur: $25 (VP-1/90)
78	FEIST Vintage Port 1982 (NA) (VP-1/90)
78	FEIST Vintage Port 1978 (NA) (VP-1/90)
88	FERREIRA Vintage Port 1987 (NR) (VP-11/89)
85	FERREIRA Vintage Port 1985 Rel: $20 Cur: $28 (VP-11/89)
92	FERREIRA Vintage Port 1985 Rel: $20 Cur: $28 (10/31/88)
81	FERREIRA Vintage Port 1982 Rel: $14 Cur: $32 (VP-11/89)
85	FERREIRA Vintage Port 1982 Rel: $14 Cur: $32 (10/31/88)
80	FERREIRA Vintage Port 1980 Rel: $13 Cur: $21 (VP-11/89)
84	FERREIRA Vintage Port 1980 Rel: $13 Cur: $21 (10/31/88)
89	FERREIRA Vintage Port 1978 Rel: $11 Cur: $28 (VP-11/89)
86	FERREIRA Vintage Port 1977 Rel: $11 Cur: $51 (VP-11/89)
90	FERREIRA Vintage Port 1977 Rel: $11 Cur: $51 (10/31/88)
81	FERREIRA Vintage Port 1975 Cur: $41 (VP-11/89)
84	FERREIRA Vintage Port 1975 Cur: $41 (10/31/88)
86	FERREIRA Vintage Port 1970 Cur: $45 (VP-4/89)
85	FERREIRA Vintage Port 1966 Cur: $81 (VP-11/89)
87	FERREIRA Vintage Port 1966 Cur: $81 (10/31/88)
90	FERREIRA Vintage Port 1963 Cur: $110 (10/31/88)
85	FERREIRA Vintage Port 1963 Cur: $110 (VP-8/88)
86	FERREIRA Vintage Port 1960 Cur: $95 (10/31/88)
80	FERREIRA Vintage Port 1960 Cur: $95 (VP-8/88)
85	FERREIRA Vintage Port 1955 Cur: $119 (VP-11/89)
79	FERREIRA Vintage Port 1950 Cur: $90 (VP-11/89)
81	FERREIRA Vintage Port 1945 Cur: $225 (VP-11/89)
93	FERREIRA Vintage Port 1935 Cur: $200 (VP-2/90)
91	FERREIRA Vintage Port Quinta do Seixo 1983 Rel: $14 Cur: $26 (VP-11/89)
87	FERREIRA Vintage Port Quinta do Seixo 1983 Rel: $14 Cur: $26 (10/31/88)
91	FERREIRA Vintage Port Quinta do Seixo 1983 Rel: $14 Cur: $26 (3/31/87)
72	FEUERHEERD Vintage Port 1985 (NR) (VP-1/90)
76	FEUERHEERD Vintage Port 1980 (NA) (VP-1/90)
69	FEUERHEERD Vintage Port 1977 Cur: $17 (VP-1/90)
80	FEUERHEERD Vintage Port 1970 Cur: $45 (VP-1/90)
95	FONSECA Vintage Port 1985 Rel: $32 Cur: $40 (VP-6/90)
91	FONSECA Vintage Port 1985 Rel: $32 Cur: $40 (9/30/87)
90	FONSECA Vintage Port 1983 Rel: $24 Cur: $40 (VP-6/90)
89	FONSECA Vintage Port 1983 Rel: $24 Cur: $40 (10/31/88)
89	FONSECA Vintage Port 1983 Rel: $24 Cur: $40 (3/31/87)
74	FONSECA Vintage Port 1980 Rel: $22 Cur: $40 (VP-6/90)
85	FONSECA Vintage Port 1980 Rel: $22 Cur: $40 (3/31/87) (JS)
100	FONSECA Vintage Port 1977 Rel: $16 Cur: $70 (VP-4/90)

91 FONSECA Vintage Port 1977 Rel: $16 Cur: $70 (10/31/88)
81 FONSECA Vintage Port 1975 Cur: $50 (10/31/88)
79 FONSECA Vintage Port 1975 Cur: $50 (VP-8/88)
96 FONSECA Vintage Port 1970 Cur: $76 (VP-12/89)
94 FONSECA Vintage Port 1970 Cur: $76 (10/31/88)
97 FONSECA Vintage Port 1966 Cur: $84 (VP-2/90)
87 FONSECA Vintage Port 1966 Cur: $84 (10/31/88)
98 FONSECA Vintage Port 1963 Cur: $162 (VP-12/89)
97 FONSECA Vintage Port 1963 Cur: $162 (10/31/88)
81 FONSECA Vintage Port 1960 Cur: $95 (10/31/88)
80 FONSECA Vintage Port 1960 Cur: $95 (VP-8/88)
96 FONSECA Vintage Port 1955 Cur: $214 (VP-8/88)
100 FONSECA Vintage Port 1948 Cur: $340 (VP-11/89)
91 FONSECA Vintage Port 1945 Cur: $660 (VP-11/89)
91 FONSECA Vintage Port 1934 Cur: $330 (VP-2/90)
100 FONSECA Vintage Port 1927 Cur: $430 (VP-12/89)
90 FONSECA Vintage Port Guimaraens 1987 (NR) (VP-2/90)
86 FONSECA Vintage Port Guimaraens 1986 (NR) (VP-2/90)
85 FONSECA Vintage Port Guimaraens 1984 (NR) (VP-2/90)
82 FONSECA Vintage Port Guimaraens 1982 (NR) (VP-2/90)
80 FONSECA Vintage Port Guimaraens 1978 Rel: $32 Cur: $35 (VP-2/90)
89 FONSECA Vintage Port Guimaraens 1976 Rel: $32 Cur: $38 (VP-2/90)
84 FONSECA Vintage Port Guimaraens 1974 Rel: $40 (VP-1/90)
75 FONSECA Vintage Port Guimaraens 1972 Cur: $43 (VP-2/90)
84 FONSECA Vintage Port Guimaraens 1968 Cur: $51 (VP-2/90)
90 FONSECA Vintage Port Guimaraens 1967 Cur: $56 (VP-2/90)
78 FONSECA Vintage Port Guimaraens 1967 Cur: $56 (3/31/87) (JS)
89 FONSECA Vintage Port Guimaraens 1965 Cur: $64 (VP-2/90)
90 FONSECA Vintage Port Guimaraens 1964 Cur: $60 (VP-2/90)
88 FONSECA Vintage Port Guimaraens 1962 Cur: $70 (VP-2/90)
85 FONSECA Vintage Port Guimaraens 1961 Cur: $70 (VP-2/90)
88 FONSECA Vintage Port Guimaraens 1958 Cur: $90 (VP-2/90)
82 FONSECA Vintage Port Quinta do Panascal 1987 (NR) (VP-2/90)
79 FONSECA Vintage Port Quinta do Panascal 1986 (NR) (VP-2/90)
78 FONSECA Vintage Port Quinta do Panascal 1985 (NR) (VP-2/90)
70 FONSECA Vintage Port Quinta do Panascal 1984 (NR) (VP-2/90)
79 FONSECA Vintage Port Quinta do Panascal 1983 (NR) (VP-2/90)
85 GOULD CAMPBELL Vintage Port 1985 Rel: $23 Cur: $33 (VP-6/90)
81 GOULD CAMPBELL Vintage Port 1985 Rel: $23 Cur: $33 (9/30/87)
90 GOULD CAMPBELL Vintage Port 1983 Rel: $22 Cur: $34 (VP-6/90)
88 GOULD CAMPBELL Vintage Port 1983 Rel: $22 Cur: $34 (3/31/87)
86 GOULD CAMPBELL Vintage Port 1980 Rel: $15 Cur: $44 (VP-2/90)
93 GOULD CAMPBELL Vintage Port 1977 Rel: $11 Cur: $50 (VP-2/90)
76 GOULD CAMPBELL Vintage Port 1975 Cur: $33 (VP-2/90)
88 GOULD CAMPBELL Vintage Port 1970 Cur: $54 (VP-2/90)
84 GOULD CAMPBELL Vintage Port 1966 Cur: $70 (VP-2/90)
96 GRAHAM Vintage Port 1985 Rel: $31 Cur: $47 (VP-6/90)
92 GRAHAM Vintage Port 1985 Rel: $31 Cur: $47 (10/31/88)
91 GRAHAM Vintage Port 1985 Rel: $31 Cur: $47 (9/30/87) CS
93 GRAHAM Vintage Port 1983 Rel: $30 Cur: $43 (VP-6/90)
95 GRAHAM Vintage Port 1983 Rel: $30 Cur: $43 (10/31/88)
90 GRAHAM Vintage Port 1980 Rel: $18 Cur: $42 (VP-6/90)
87 GRAHAM Vintage Port 1980 Rel: $18 Cur: $42 (10/31/88)
88 GRAHAM Vintage Port 1980 Rel: $18 Cur: $42 (4/16/85) CS
90 GRAHAM Vintage Port 1977 Rel: $15 Cur: $66 (VP-4/90)
94 GRAHAM Vintage Port 1977 Rel: $15 Cur: $66 (10/31/88)
91 GRAHAM Vintage Port 1977 Rel: $15 Cur: $66 (3/16/84) CS
78 GRAHAM Vintage Port 1975 Cur: $49 (VP-2/89)
78 GRAHAM Vintage Port 1975 Cur: $49 (10/31/88)
94 GRAHAM Vintage Port 1970 Cur: $83 (VP-12/89)
91 GRAHAM Vintage Port 1970 Cur: $83 (10/31/88)
93 GRAHAM Vintage Port 1966 Cur: $88 (VP-12/89)
94 GRAHAM Vintage Port 1966 Cur: $88 (10/31/88)
97 GRAHAM Vintage Port 1963 Cur: $159 (VP-12/89)
92 GRAHAM Vintage Port 1963 Cur: $159 (10/31/88)
88 GRAHAM Vintage Port 1960 Cur: $102 (10/31/88)
84 GRAHAM Vintage Port 1960 Cur: $102 (VP-8/88)
94 GRAHAM Vintage Port 1955 Cur: $210 (VP-11/89)
91 GRAHAM Vintage Port 1954 Cur: $187 (VP-2/90)
95 GRAHAM Vintage Port 1948 Cur: $290 (VP-11/89)
95 GRAHAM Vintage Port 1945 Cur: $510 (VP-11/89)
89 GRAHAM Vintage Port 1942 Cur: $420 (VP-4/90)
94 GRAHAM Vintage Port 1935 Cur: $400 (VP-4/90)
94 GRAHAM Vintage Port 1927 Cur: $570 (VP-2/90)
93 GRAHAM Vintage Port Malvedos 1988 Rel: $26 Cur: $27 (1/31/91)
91 GRAHAM Vintage Port Malvedos 1987 (NR) (VP-2/90)
84 GRAHAM Vintage Port Malvedos 1986 Rel: $35 Cur: $35/375ml (3/31/90)
85 GRAHAM Vintage Port Malvedos 1986 Rel: $35 Cur: $35 (VP-2/90)
83 GRAHAM Vintage Port Malvedos 1984 (NR) (VP-2/90)
90 GRAHAM Vintage Port Malvedos 1982 (NR) (VP-2/90)
74 GRAHAM Vintage Port Malvedos 1979 (NA) (VP-2/90)
82 GRAHAM Vintage Port Malvedos 1978 Rel: $30 Cur: $34 (VP-2/90)
81 GRAHAM Vintage Port Malvedos 1978 Rel: $30 Cur: $34 (11/30/88)
74 GRAHAM Vintage Port Malvedos 1976 Rel: $17 Cur: $31 (VP-2/90)
70 GRAHAM Vintage Port Malvedos 1968 Cur: $50 (VP-2/90)
79 GRAHAM Vintage Port Malvedos 1965 Cur: $58 (VP-2/90)
82 GRAHAM Vintage Port Malvedos 1964 Cur: $54 (VP-2/90)
89 GRAHAM Vintage Port Malvedos 1962 Cur: $65 (VP-2/90)
87 GRAHAM Vintage Port Malvedos 1961 Cur: $65 (VP-2/90)
79 GRAHAM Vintage Port Malvedos 1958 Cur: $65 (VP-2/90)
84 GRAHAM Vintage Port Malvedos 1957 Cur: $70 (VP-2/90)
85 GRAHAM Vintage Port Malvedos 1952 Cur: $125 (VP-11/89)
80 HOOPER Vintage Port 1985 Rel: $15 Cur: $20 (VP-6/90)
84 HOOPER Vintage Port 1985 Rel: $15 Cur: $20 (9/30/87)
60 HOOPER Vintage Port 1983 Cur: $16 (VP-3/90)
68 HOOPER Vintage Port 1982 Cur: $18 (VP-5/90)
67 HOOPER Vintage Port 1980 Cur: $22 (VP-5/90)
69 HUTCHESON Vintage Port 1979 Cur: $40 (VP-1/90)
79 HUTCHESON Vintage Port 1970 Cur: $50 (VP-1/90)
86 KOPKE Vintage Port 1987 Rel: $24 Cur: $24 (VP-1/90)

90 KOPKE Vintage Port 1985 Rel: $18 Cur: $21 (VP-1/90)
85 KOPKE Vintage Port 1983 Rel: $18 Cur: $23 (VP-1/90)
83 KOPKE Vintage Port 1982 Rel: $16 Cur: $26 (VP-1/90)
71 KOPKE Vintage Port 1980 Rel: $16 Cur: $31 (VP-1/90)
69 KOPKE Vintage Port 1979 (NA) (VP-1/90)
70 KOPKE Vintage Port 1978 Cur: $29 (VP-1/90)
68 KOPKE Vintage Port 1977 (NA) (VP-1/90)
82 KOPKE Vintage Port 1975 Cur: $28 (VP-1/90)
74 KOPKE Vintage Port 1974 (NA) (VP-1/90)
82 KOPKE Vintage Port 1970 Cur: $41 (VP-1/90)
81 KOPKE Vintage Port 1966 Cur: $65 (VP-1/90)
87 KOPKE Vintage Port 1960 Cur: $65 (VP-1/90)
84 MARTINEZ Vintage Port 1987 (NR) (VP-5/90)
89 MARTINEZ Vintage Port 1985 Rel: $21 Cur: $29 (VP-6/90)
87 MARTINEZ Vintage Port 1985 Rel: $21 Cur: $29 (9/30/87)
82 MARTINEZ Vintage Port 1982 Rel: $17 Cur: $28 (VP-6/90)
75 MARTINEZ Vintage Port 1975 Cur: $40 (VP-2/90)
89 MARTINEZ Vintage Port 1970 Cur: $60 (VP-2/90)
93 MARTINEZ Vintage Port 1967 Cur: $56 (VP-2/90)
82 MARTINEZ Vintage Port 1963 Cur: $95 (VP-2/90)
86 MARTINEZ Vintage Port 1955 Cur: $120 (VP-11/89)
67 MESSIAS Vintage Port 1985 Rel: $12 Cur: $14 (VP-2/90)
78 MESSIAS Vintage Port 1984 Rel: $11 Cur: $15 (VP-2/90)
72 MESSIAS Vintage Port 1982 Rel: $7 Cur: $12 (VP-2/90)
71 MESSIAS Vintage Port 1963 Cur: $40 (VP-2/90)
77 MESSIAS Vintage Port Quinta do Cachão 1983 Rel: $8 Cur: $11 (VP-2/90)
60 MESSIAS Vintage Port Quinta do Cachão 1977 Rel: $7 Cur: $19 (VP-2/90)
87 MESSIAS Vintage Port Quinta do Cachão 1970 Cur: $50 (VP-2/90)
84 MESSIAS Vintage Port Quinta do Cachão 1966 Cur: $30 (VP-2/90)
85 MORGAN Vintage Port 1985 (NR) (VP-2/90)
78 MORGAN Vintage Port 1977 (NR) (VP-1/90)
88 MORGAN Vintage Port 1970 (NR) (VP-2/90)
80 MORGAN Vintage Port 1966 (NR) (VP-2/90)
86 MORGAN Vintage Port 1963 (NR) (VP-2/90)
91 NIEPOORT Vintage Port 1987 Rel: $27 Cur: $27 (VP-11/89)
92 NIEPOORT Vintage Port 1985 Rel: $25 Cur: $33 (VP-6/90)
89 NIEPOORT Vintage Port 1985 Rel: $25 Cur: $33 (1/31/88)
84 NIEPOORT Vintage Port 1983 Rel: $14 Cur: $33 (VP-6/90)
90 NIEPOORT Vintage Port 1982 Rel: $13 Cur: $39 (VP-6/90)
93 NIEPOORT Vintage Port 1982 Rel: $13 Cur: $39 (3/31/87)
87 NIEPOORT Vintage Port 1980 Rel: $12 Cur: $35 (VP-6/90)
81 NIEPOORT Vintage Port 1978 Rel: $11 Cur: $32 (VP-11/89)
89 NIEPOORT Vintage Port 1977 Rel: $11 Cur: $50 (VP-4/90)
79 NIEPOORT Vintage Port 1975 Cur: $37 (VP-11/89)
93 NIEPOORT Vintage Port 1970 Cur: $55 (VP-1/90)
89 NIEPOORT Vintage Port 1966 Cur: $70 (VP-11/89)
90 NIEPOORT Vintage Port 1963 Cur: $90 (VP-11/89)
98 NIEPOORT Vintage Port 1955 Cur: $175 (VP-8/88)
97 NIEPOORT Vintage Port 1945 Cur: $250 (VP-2/90)
93 NIEPOORT Vintage Port 1942 Cur: $240 (VP-4/90)
97 NIEPOORT Vintage Port 1927 Cur: $260 (VP-4/90)
84 OFFLEY Vintage Port 1987 (NR) (VP-1/90)
88 OFFLEY Vintage Port Boa Vista 1987 (NR) (VP-1/90)
89 OFFLEY Vintage Port Boa Vista 1985 Rel: $22 Cur: $31 (VP-6/90)
85 OFFLEY Vintage Port Boa Vista 1985 Rel: $22 Cur: $31 (9/30/87)
91 OFFLEY Vintage Port Boa Vista 1983 Rel: $22 Cur: $28 (VP-1/90)
84 OFFLEY Vintage Port Boa Vista 1982 Rel: $18 Cur: $23 (VP-6/90)
90 OFFLEY Vintage Port Boa Vista 1980 Rel: $14 Cur: $30 (VP-4/90)
88 OFFLEY Vintage Port Boa Vista 1977 Rel: $11 Cur: $49 (VP-1/90)
75 OFFLEY Vintage Port Boa Vista 1975 Cur: $27 (VP-2/89)
79 OFFLEY Vintage Port Boa Vista 1972 Cur: $30 (VP-2/89)
81 OFFLEY Vintage Port Boa Vista 1970 Cur: $60 (VP-2/89)
90 OFFLEY Vintage Port Boa Vista 1966 Cur: $70 (VP-2/89)
80 OFFLEY Vintage Port Boa Vista 1963 Cur: $110 (VP-2/89)
78 OFFLEY Vintage Port Boa Vista 1960 Cur: $60 (VP-2/89)
76 OSBORNE Vintage Port 1985 Rel: $20 Cur: $26 (VP-2/89)
72 OSBORNE Vintage Port 1982 Rel: $13 Cur: $26 (VP-1/90)
77 OSBORNE Vintage Port 1970 Cur: $50 (VP-1/90)
82 OSBORNE Vintage Port 1960 Cur: $60 (VP-1/90)
69 A. PINTOS DOS SANTOS Vintage Port 1985 (NR) (VP-1/90)
70 A. PINTOS DOS SANTOS Vintage Port 1982 (NR) (VP-1/90)
70 A. PINTOS DOS SANTOS Vintage Port 1980 (NA) (VP-1/90)
70 A. PINTOS DOS SANTOS Vintage Port 1970 (NA) (VP-1/90)
85 POCAS JUNIOR Vintage Port 1985 Rel: $17 Cur: $19 (VP-2/90)
74 POCAS JUNIOR Vintage Port 1975 Cur: $42 (VP-2/90)
84 POCAS JUNIOR Vintage Port 1970 Cur: $52 (VP-2/90)
82 POCAS JUNIOR Vintage Port 1963 Cur: $100 (VP-2/90)
82 POCAS JUNIOR Vintage Port 1960 Cur: $80 (VP-2/90)
85 QUARLES HARRIS Vintage Port 1985 Rel: $21 Cur: $30 (VP-6/90)
87 QUARLES HARRIS Vintage Port 1985 Rel: $21 Cur: $30 (9/30/87)
89 QUARLES HARRIS Vintage Port 1983 Rel: $18 Cur: $33 (VP-2/90)
90 QUARLES HARRIS Vintage Port 1983 Rel: $18 Cur: $33 (3/31/87)
83 QUARLES HARRIS Vintage Port 1980 Rel: $13 Cur: $29 (VP-2/90)
89 QUARLES HARRIS Vintage Port 1977 Rel: $11 Cur: $43 (VP-2/90)
73 QUARLES HARRIS Vintage Port 1975 Cur: $38 (VP-4/90)
89 QUARLES HARRIS Vintage Port 1970 Cur: $52 (VP-2/90)
74 QUARLES HARRIS Vintage Port 1966 Cur: $78 (VP-2/90)
85 QUARLES HARRIS Vintage Port 1963 Cur: $110 (VP-2/90)
86 QUINTA DA EIRA VELHA Vintage Port 1987 (NR) (VP-2/90)
81 QUINTA DA EIRA VELHA Vintage Port 1982 (NR) (VP-3/90)
85 QUINTA DA EIRA VELHA Vintage Port 1978 Rel: $22 Cur: $30 (VP-3/90)
81 QUINTA DA ROMANEIRA Vintage Port 1987 (NR) (VP-1/90)
78 QUINTA DA ROMANEIRA Vintage Port 1985 Rel: $29 Cur: $29 (VP-1/90)
90 QUINTA DA ROMANEIRA Vintage Port 1935 (NA) (VP-2/90)
78 QUINTA DE LA ROSA Vintage Port 1988 (NR) (VP-5/90)
76 QUINTA DE LA ROSA Vintage Port 1972 (NA) (VP-10/89)
82 QUINTA DE LA ROSA Vintage Port 1966 (NA) (VP-10/89)
85 QUINTA DE LA ROSA Vintage Port 1963 (NA) (VP-10/89)
88 QUINTA DE LA ROSA Vintage Port 1960 (NA) (VP-10/89)
87 QUINTA DE LA ROSA Vintage Port Feuerheerd Quinta de la Rosa 1927 (NA) (VP-12/89)

PORTUGAL
VINTAGE PORT

83 QUINTA DE VAL FIGUEIRA Vintage Port 1987 (NR) (VP-2/90)
80 QUINTA DO CRASTO Vintage Port 1987 (NR) (VP-1/90)
71 QUINTA DO CRASTO Vintage Port 1985 Rel: $24 Cur: $24 (VP-1/90)
70 QUINTA DO CRASTO Vintage Port 1978 (NA) (VP-1/90)
79 QUINTA DO CRASTO Vintage Port 1958 (NA) (VP-8/90)
76 QUINTA DO INFANTADO Vintage Port 1985 Rel: $33 Cur: $33 (VP-7/90)
70 QUINTA DO INFANTADO Vintage Port 1982 Rel: $35 Cur: $35 (VP-7/90)
75 QUINTA DO INFANTADO Vintage Port 1978 (NA) (VP-7/90)
89 QUINTA DO NOVAL Vintage Port 1987 (NR) (VP-1/90)
86 QUINTA DO NOVAL Vintage Port 1985 Rel: $22 Cur: $35 (VP-6/90)
91 QUINTA DO NOVAL Vintage Port 1985 Rel: $22 Cur: $35 (10/31/88)
78 QUINTA DO NOVAL Vintage Port 1982 Rel: $23 Cur: $36 (VP-6/90)
85 QUINTA DO NOVAL Vintage Port 1982 Rel: $23 Cur: $36 (10/31/88)
72 QUINTA DO NOVAL Vintage Port 1978 Rel: $18 Cur: $39 (VP-11/89)
78 QUINTA DO NOVAL Vintage Port 1978 Rel: $18 Cur: $39 (10/31/88)
78 QUINTA DO NOVAL Vintage Port 1977 Cur: $50 (10/31/88)
81 QUINTA DO NOVAL Vintage Port 1975 Cur: $60 (VP-11/89)
79 QUINTA DO NOVAL Vintage Port 1975 Cur: $60 (10/31/88)
89 QUINTA DO NOVAL Vintage Port 1970 Cur: $71 (VP-11/89)
87 QUINTA DO NOVAL Vintage Port 1970 Cur: $71 (10/31/88)
88 QUINTA DO NOVAL Vintage Port 1967 Cur: $52 (VP-12/89)
88 QUINTA DO NOVAL Vintage Port 1967 Cur: $52 (10/31/88)
91 QUINTA DO NOVAL Vintage Port 1966 Cur: $87 (VP-12/89)
90 QUINTA DO NOVAL Vintage Port 1966 Cur: $87 (10/31/88)
84 QUINTA DO NOVAL Vintage Port 1963 Cur: $123 (VP-12/89)
89 QUINTA DO NOVAL Vintage Port 1963 Cur: $123 (10/31/88)
82 QUINTA DO NOVAL Vintage Port 1960 Cur: $84 (VP-11/89)
87 QUINTA DO NOVAL Vintage Port 1960 Cur: $84 (10/31/88)
82 QUINTA DO NOVAL Vintage Port 1958 Cur: $100 (VP-11/89)
88 QUINTA DO NOVAL Vintage Port 1955 Cur: $156 (VP-8/90)
85 QUINTA DO NOVAL Vintage Port 1950 Cur: $240 (VP-11/89)
93 QUINTA DO NOVAL Vintage Port 1947 Cur: $280 (VP-11/89)
92 QUINTA DO NOVAL Vintage Port 1945 Cur: $310 (VP-11/89)
86 QUINTA DO NOVAL Vintage Port 1942 Cur: $200 (VP-4/90)
50 QUINTA DO NOVAL Vintage Port 1941 Cur: $70 (VP-9/85)
71 QUINTA DO NOVAL Vintage Port 1938 Cur: $110 (VP-9/85)
98 QUINTA DO NOVAL Vintage Port 1934 Cur: $310 (VP-2/90)
99 QUINTA DO NOVAL Vintage Port 1931 Cur: $1,000 (VP-11/89)
93 QUINTA DO NOVAL Vintage Port 1927 Cur: $450 (VP-12/89)
94 QUINTA DO NOVAL Vintage Port Nacional 1987 (NR) (VP-1/90)
95 QUINTA DO NOVAL Vintage Port Nacional 1985 Cur: $200 (VP-11/89)
86 QUINTA DO NOVAL Vintage Port Nacional 1982 Cur: $190 (VP-11/89)
90 QUINTA DO NOVAL Vintage Port Nacional 1982 Cur: $190 (11/01/85) (JS)
80 QUINTA DO NOVAL Vintage Port Nacional 1980 Cur: $280 (VP-2/90)
77 QUINTA DO NOVAL Vintage Port Nacional 1978 Cur: $242 (VP-11/89)
91 QUINTA DO NOVAL Vintage Port Nacional 1978 Cur: $242 (11/01/85) (JS)
86 QUINTA DO NOVAL Vintage Port Nacional 1975 Cur: $285 (VP-11/89)
88 QUINTA DO NOVAL Vintage Port Nacional 1975 Cur: $285 (11/01/85) (JS)
98 QUINTA DO NOVAL Vintage Port Nacional 1970 Cur: $370 (VP-11/89)
89 QUINTA DO NOVAL Vintage Port Nacional 1970 Cur: $370 (11/01/85) (JS)
95 QUINTA DO NOVAL Vintage Port Nacional 1967 Cur: $380 (VP-11/89)
88 QUINTA DO NOVAL Vintage Port Nacional 1967 Cur: $380 (11/01/85) (JS)
98 QUINTA DO NOVAL Vintage Port Nacional 1966 Cur: $310 (VP-11/89)
89 QUINTA DO NOVAL Vintage Port Nacional 1966 Cur: $310 (11/01/85) (JS)
84 QUINTA DO NOVAL Vintage Port Nacional 1964 Cur: $350 (VP-11/89)
100 QUINTA DO NOVAL Vintage Port Nacional 1963 Cur: $750 (VP-11/89)
95 QUINTA DO NOVAL Vintage Port Nacional 1963 Cur: $750 (11/01/85) (JS)
86 QUINTA DO NOVAL Vintage Port Nacional 1962 Cur: $350 (VP-11/89)
84 QUINTA DO NOVAL Vintage Port Nacional 1960 Cur: $350 (VP-11/89)
88 QUINTA DO NOVAL Vintage Port Nacional 1960 Cur: $350 (11/01/85) (JS)
90 QUINTA DO NOVAL Vintage Port Nacional 1950 Cur: $850 (VP-11/89)
100 QUINTA DO NOVAL Vintage Port Nacional 1931 Cur: $3,700 (VP-11/89)
85 RAMOS-PINTO Vintage Port 1985 Rel: $21 Cur: $32 (VP-11/89)
89 RAMOS-PINTO Vintage Port 1983 Rel: $17 Cur: $32 (VP-11/89)
79 RAMOS-PINTO Vintage Port 1982 Rel: $12 Cur: $31 (VP-11/89)
74 RAMOS-PINTO Vintage Port 1980 Rel: $11 Cur: $25 (VP-11/89)
81 RAMOS-PINTO Vintage Port 1970 Cur: $100 (VP-11/89)
83 RAMOS-PINTO Vintage Port 1963 Cur: $80 (VP-11/89)
81 REBELLO-VALENTE Vintage Port 1985 Rel: $23 Cur: $42 (VP-6/90)
84 REBELLO-VALENTE Vintage Port 1985 Rel: $23 Cur: $42 (9/30/87)
78 REBELLO-VALENTE Vintage Port 1983 Rel: $23 Cur: $36 (VP-6/90)
80 REBELLO-VALENTE Vintage Port 1980 Rel: $16 Cur: $50 (VP-2/90)
89 REBELLO-VALENTE Vintage Port 1977 Rel: $12 Cur: $47 (VP-2/90)
75 REBELLO-VALENTE Vintage Port 1975 Cur: $53 (VP-2/90)
83 REBELLO-VALENTE Vintage Port 1972 Cur: $53 (VP-1/90)
92 REBELLO-VALENTE Vintage Port 1970 Cur: $50 (VP-2/90)
91 REBELLO-VALENTE Vintage Port 1967 Cur: $77 (VP-2/90)
82 REBELLO-VALENTE Vintage Port 1966 Cur: $70 (VP-2/90)
85 REBELLO-VALENTE Vintage Port 1963 Cur: $92 (VP-2/90)
85 REBELLO-VALENTE Vintage Port 1960 Cur: $55 (VP-11/88)
92 REBELLO-VALENTE Vintage Port 1945 Cur: $245 (VP-5/90)
75 REBELLO-VALENTE Vintage Port 1942 Cur: $140 (VP-2/85)
88 ROCHA Vintage Port 1985 $32 (4/15/91)
81 ROCHA Vintage Port 1977 $19 (4/30/91)
80 ROYAL OPORTO Vintage Port 1987 Rel: $12 Cur: $14 (VP-11/89)
71 ROYAL OPORTO Vintage Port 1985 Rel: $12 Cur: $17 (VP-6/90)
65 ROYAL OPORTO Vintage Port 1984 Rel: $11 Cur: $16 (VP-11/89)
76 ROYAL OPORTO Vintage Port 1983 Rel: $9 Cur: $15 (VP-6/90)
60 ROYAL OPORTO Vintage Port 1982 Rel: $9 Cur: $19 (VP-6/90)
60 ROYAL OPORTO Vintage Port 1980 Rel: $8 Cur: $20 (VP-6/90)
68 ROYAL OPORTO Vintage Port 1978 Rel: $8 Cur: $24 (VP-11/89)
74 ROYAL OPORTO Vintage Port 1977 Rel: $8 Cur: $30 (VP-11/89)
75 ROYAL OPORTO Vintage Port 1970 Cur: $36 (VP-11/89)
72 ROYAL OPORTO Vintage Port 1967 Cur: $30 (VP-11/89)
73 ROYAL OPORTO Vintage Port 1963 Cur: $55 (VP-11/89)
98 ROYAL OPORTO Vintage Port 1871 (NA) (VP-11/89)
86 ROZES Vintage Port 1987 (NR) (VP-6/90)
81 ROZES Vintage Port 1985 Rel: $16 Cur: $21 (VP-5/90)
75 ROZES Vintage Port 1982 (NR) (VP-6/90)
83 SANDEMAN Vintage Port 1985 Rel: $22 Cur: $33 (VP-6/90)
80 SANDEMAN Vintage Port 1985 Rel: $22 Cur: $33 (9/30/87)
82 SANDEMAN Vintage Port 1982 Rel: $19 Cur: $36 (VP-6/90)
85 SANDEMAN Vintage Port 1982 Rel: $19 Cur: $36 (10/31/88)
85 SANDEMAN Vintage Port 1980 Rel: $19 Cur: $46 (VP-6/90)
86 SANDEMAN Vintage Port 1980 Rel: $19 Cur: $46 (10/31/88)
85 SANDEMAN Vintage Port 1977 Rel: $15 Cur: $74 (VP-6/90)
88 SANDEMAN Vintage Port 1977 Rel: $15 Cur: $74 (10/31/88)
78 SANDEMAN Vintage Port 1975 Cur: $49 (VP-3/90)
75 SANDEMAN Vintage Port 1975 Cur: $49 (10/31/88)
83 SANDEMAN Vintage Port 1970 Cur: $74 (VP-3/90)
82 SANDEMAN Vintage Port 1970 Cur: $74 (10/31/88)
90 SANDEMAN Vintage Port 1967 Cur: $58 (VP-3/90)
89 SANDEMAN Vintage Port 1967 Cur: $58 (10/31/88)
90 SANDEMAN Vintage Port 1966 Cur: $89 (7/15/90) (JS)
92 SANDEMAN Vintage Port 1966 Cur: $89 (VP-3/90)
93 SANDEMAN Vintage Port 1966 Cur: $89 (10/31/88)
96 SANDEMAN Vintage Port 1963 Cur: $112 (7/15/90) (JS)
96 SANDEMAN Vintage Port 1963 Cur: $112 (VP-3/90)
95 SANDEMAN Vintage Port 1963 Cur: $112 (10/31/88)
79 SANDEMAN Vintage Port 1960 Cur: $80 (7/15/90) (JS)
79 SANDEMAN Vintage Port 1960 Cur: $80 (VP-3/90)
80 SANDEMAN Vintage Port 1960 Cur: $80 (10/31/88)
82 SANDEMAN Vintage Port 1958 Cur: $75 (VP-3/90)
85 SANDEMAN Vintage Port 1957 (NA) (VP-10/88)
94 SANDEMAN Vintage Port 1955 Cur: $159 (VP-3/90)
87 SANDEMAN Vintage Port 1950 Cur: $170 (VP-3/90)
90 SANDEMAN Vintage Port 1947 Cur: $196 (VP-3/90)
95 SANDEMAN Vintage Port 1945 Cur: $350 (VP-3/90)
88 SANDEMAN Vintage Port 1942 Cur: $210 (VP-3/90)
92 SANDEMAN Vintage Port 1935 Cur: $460 (VP-3/90)
94 SANDEMAN Vintage Port 1934 Cur: $300 (VP-3/90)
92 SANDEMAN Vintage Port 1927 Cur: $400 (VP-3/90)
78 SANDEMAN Vintage Port 1920 Cur: $300 (VP-3/90)
88 SANDEMAN Vintage Port 1917 Cur: $300 (VP-3/90)
82 SANDEMAN Vintage Port 1911 Cur: $282 (VP-6/90)
75 SANDEMAN Vintage Port 1908 Cur: $320 (VP-3/90)
88 SANDEMAN Vintage Port 1904 Cur: $420 (VP-3/90)
81 SANDEMAN Vintage Port 1896 Cur: $600 (VP-3/90)
74 SANDEMAN Vintage Port 1887 Cur: $600 (VP-3/90)
98 SANDEMAN Vintage Port 1870 Cur: $700 (VP-3/90)
89 SMITH WOODHOUSE Vintage Port 1985 Rel: $22 Cur: $34 (VP-6/90)
87 SMITH WOODHOUSE Vintage Port 1985 Rel: $22 Cur: $34 (9/30/87)
92 SMITH WOODHOUSE Vintage Port 1983 Rel: $22 Cur: $33 (VP-6/90)
95 SMITH WOODHOUSE Vintage Port 1983 Rel: $22 Cur: $33 (3/31/87)
90 SMITH WOODHOUSE Vintage Port 1980 Rel: $15 Cur: $33 (VP-6/90)
84 SMITH WOODHOUSE Vintage Port 1980 Rel: $15 Cur: $33 (5/01/84)
89 SMITH WOODHOUSE Vintage Port 1977 Rel: $11 Cur: $50 (VP-2/90)
80 SMITH WOODHOUSE Vintage Port 1975 Cur: $40 (VP-2/90)
86 SMITH WOODHOUSE Vintage Port 1970 Cur: $58 (VP-2/90)
83 SMITH WOODHOUSE Vintage Port 1966 Cur: $88 (VP-2/90)
89 SMITH WOODHOUSE Vintage Port 1963 Cur: $110 (VP-2/90)
90 TAYLOR FLADGATE Vintage Port 1985 Rel: $32 Cur: $53 (VP-6/90)
91 TAYLOR FLADGATE Vintage Port 1985 Rel: $32 Cur: $53 (10/31/88)
89 TAYLOR FLADGATE Vintage Port 1983 Rel: $25 Cur: $45 (VP-6/90)
88 TAYLOR FLADGATE Vintage Port 1983 Rel: $25 Cur: $45 (10/31/88)
97 TAYLOR FLADGATE Vintage Port 1983 Rel: $25 Cur: $45 (3/31/87)
88 TAYLOR FLADGATE Vintage Port 1980 Rel: $21 Cur: $41 (VP-6/90)
85 TAYLOR FLADGATE Vintage Port 1980 Rel: $21 Cur: $41 (10/31/88)
98 TAYLOR FLADGATE Vintage Port 1977 Rel: $17 Cur: $75 (VP-4/90)
92 TAYLOR FLADGATE Vintage Port 1977 Rel: $17 Cur: $75 (10/31/88)
78 TAYLOR FLADGATE Vintage Port 1975 Cur: $47 (VP-12/89)
81 TAYLOR FLADGATE Vintage Port 1975 Cur: $47 (10/31/88)
98 TAYLOR FLADGATE Vintage Port 1970 Cur: $81 (VP-12/89)
89 TAYLOR FLADGATE Vintage Port 1970 Cur: $81 (10/31/88)
89 TAYLOR FLADGATE Vintage Port 1966 Cur: $95 (VP-12/89)
88 TAYLOR FLADGATE Vintage Port 1966 Cur: $95 (10/31/88)
97 TAYLOR FLADGATE Vintage Port 1963 Cur: $159 (VP-12/89)
90 TAYLOR FLADGATE Vintage Port 1963 Cur: $159 (10/31/88)
84 TAYLOR FLADGATE Vintage Port 1960 Cur: $100 (10/31/88)
80 TAYLOR FLADGATE Vintage Port 1960 Cur: $100 (VP-8/88)
88 TAYLOR FLADGATE Vintage Port 1955 Cur: $206 (VP-11/89)
99 TAYLOR FLADGATE Vintage Port 1948 Cur: $330 (VP-11/89)
97 TAYLOR FLADGATE Vintage Port 1945 Cur: $680 (VP-11/89)
78 TAYLOR FLADGATE Vintage Port 1942 Cur: $275 (VP-4/90)
79 TAYLOR FLADGATE Vintage Port 1938 Cur: $265 (VP-4/90)
88 TAYLOR FLADGATE Vintage Port 1935 Cur: $390 (VP-2/90)
95 TAYLOR FLADGATE Vintage Port 1927 Cur: $440 (VP-12/89)
93 TAYLOR FLADGATE Vintage Port Quinta de Vargellas 1987 (NR) (VP-2/90)
88 TAYLOR FLADGATE Vintage Port Quinta de Vargellas 1986 (NR) (VP-2/90)
87 TAYLOR FLADGATE Vintage Port Quinta de Vargellas 1984 (NR) (VP-2/90)
81 TAYLOR FLADGATE Vintage Port Quinta de Vargellas 1982 (NR) (VP-2/90)
85 TAYLOR FLADGATE Vintage Port Quinta de Vargellas 1978 Rel: $29 Cur: $34 (VP-2/90)
81 TAYLOR FLADGATE Vintage Port Quinta de Vargellas 1976 Rel: $29 Cur: $42 (VP-2/90)
78 TAYLOR FLADGATE Vintage Port Quinta de Vargellas 1974 Rel: $27 Cur: $41 (VP-2/90)

Key to Symbols

The scores reported here are the results of blind tastings conducted by our panel of senior editors. Wines that carry the initials below are results of individual tastings.

THE WINE SPECTATOR 100-POINT SCALE ***95-100***—Classic, a great wine; ***90-94***—Outstanding, superior character and style; ***80-89***—Good to very good, a wine with special qualities; ***70-79***—Average, drinkable wine that may have minor flaws; ***60-69***—Below average, drinkable but not recommended; ***50-59***—Poor, undrinkable, not recommended. "+"—With a score indicates a range; used primarily with barrel tastings to indicate a preliminary score.

SPECIAL DESIGNATIONS SS—Spectator Selection, CS—Cellar Selection, BB—Best Buy.

TASTER'S INITIALS (JG)—Jim Gordon, (HS)—Harvey Steiman, (JL)—James Laube, (JS)—James Suckling, (TM)—Thomas Matthews, (TR)—Terry Robards, (BT)—Barrel Tasting (these wines were tasted blind from barrel samples), (CA-date)—*California's Great Cabernets* by James Laube, (CH-date)—*California's Great Chardonnays* by James Laube, (VP-date)—*Vintage Port* by James Suckling.

DATE TASTED Dates in parentheses represent the issue in which the rating was published.

85   TAYLOR FLADGATE Vintage Port Quinta de Vargellas 1974 Rel: $27 Cur: $41 (3/31/87) (JS)
84   TAYLOR FLADGATE Vintage Port Quinta de Vargellas 1972 Cur: $48 (VP-2/90)
85   TAYLOR FLADGATE Vintage Port Quinta de Vargellas 1969 Cur: $50 (VP-2/90)
82   TAYLOR FLADGATE Vintage Port Quinta de Vargellas 1968 Cur: $61 (VP-2/90)
80   TAYLOR FLADGATE Vintage Port Quinta de Vargellas 1968 Cur: $61 (3/31/87) (JS)
82   TAYLOR FLADGATE Vintage Port Quinta de Vargellas 1967 Cur: $66 (VP-2/90)
80   TAYLOR FLADGATE Vintage Port Quinta de Vargellas 1965 Cur: $60 (VP-2/90)
75   TAYLOR FLADGATE Vintage Port Quinta de Vargellas 1964 Cur: $50 (VP-7/90)
68   TAYLOR FLADGATE Vintage Port Quinta de Vargellas 1961 Cur: $45 (VP-2/90)
68   TAYLOR FLADGATE Vintage Port Quinta de Vargellas 1958 Cur: $50 (VP-2/90)
80   VAN ZELLER Vintage Port 1985 (NR) (VP-1/90)
84   VAN ZELLER Vintage Port 1983 Rel: $22 Cur: $36 (VP-1/90)
87   VAN ZELLER Vintage Port Quinta do Roriz 1985 (NR) (VP-7/90)
84   VAN ZELLER Vintage Port Quinta do Roriz 1983 $22 (VP-7/90)
86   VAN ZELLER Vintage Port Quinta do Roriz 1970 (NA) (VP-7/90)
83   VAN ZELLER Vintage Port Quinta do Roriz 1960 (NA) (VP-7/90)
74   VASCONCELLOS Vintage Port Butler & Nephew 1975 Cur: $37 (VP-7/90)
76   VASCONCELLOS Vintage Port Butler & Nephew 1970 Cur: $50 (VP-7/90)
81   VASCONCELLOS Vintage Port Gonzalez Byass 1970 Cur: $50 (VP-6/90)
87   VASCONCELLOS Vintage Port Gonzalez Byass 1963 Cur: $82 (VP-7/90)
70   VIEIRA DE SOUSA Vintage Port 1985 (NR) (VP-1/90)
70   VIEIRA DE SOUSA Vintage Port 1980 (NA) (VP-1/90)
74   VIEIRA DE SOUSA Vintage Port 1978 (NA) (VP-1/90)
71   VIEIRA DE SOUSA Vintage Port 1970 (NA) (VP-1/90)
91   WARRE Vintage Port 1985 Rel: $28 Cur: $38 (VP-6/90)
93   WARRE Vintage Port 1985 Rel: $28 Cur: $38 (10/31/88)
88   WARRE Vintage Port 1983 Rel: $28 Cur: $43 (VP-6/90)
84   WARRE Vintage Port 1983 Rel: $28 Cur: $43 (10/31/88)
94   WARRE Vintage Port 1983 Rel: $28 Cur: $43 (12/31/86) CS
88   WARRE Vintage Port 1980 Rel: $16 Cur: $36 (VP-6/90)
90   WARRE Vintage Port 1980 Rel: $16 Cur: $36 (10/31/88)
92   WARRE Vintage Port 1980 Rel: $16 Cur: $36 (10/01/84) CS
92   WARRE Vintage Port 1977 Rel: $15 Cur: $61 (VP-4/90)
89   WARRE Vintage Port 1977 Rel: $15 Cur: $61 (10/31/88)
74   WARRE Vintage Port 1975 Cur: $43 (10/31/88)
75   WARRE Vintage Port 1975 Cur: $43 (VP-8/88)
88   WARRE Vintage Port 1970 Cur: $74 (VP-12/89)
89   WARRE Vintage Port 1970 Cur: $74 (10/31/88)
91   WARRE Vintage Port 1966 Cur: $85 (VP-6/89)
93   WARRE Vintage Port 1966 Cur: $85 (10/31/88)
92   WARRE Vintage Port 1963 Cur: $132 (VP-12/89)
97   WARRE Vintage Port 1963 Cur: $132 (10/31/88)
90   WARRE Vintage Port 1960 Cur: $91 (10/31/88)
82   WARRE Vintage Port 1960 Cur: $91 (VP-8/88)
81   WARRE Vintage Port 1958 Cur: $99 (VP-11/89)
86   WARRE Vintage Port 1955 Cur: $191 (VP-11/89)
88   WARRE Vintage Port 1947 Cur: $237 (VP-11/89)
87   WARRE Vintage Port 1945 Cur: $360 (VP-11/89)
87   WARRE Vintage Port 1934 Cur: $285 (VP-2/90)
93   WARRE Vintage Port 1927 Cur: $400 (VP-12/89)
79   WARRE Vintage Port 1900 Cur: $430 (VP-11/89)
86   WARRE Vintage Port Quinta da Cavadinha 1987 (NR) (VP-2/90)
85   WARRE Vintage Port Quinta da Cavadinha 1986 (NR) (VP-2/90)
81   WARRE Vintage Port Quinta da Cavadinha 1984 (NR) (VP-2/90)
86   WARRE Vintage Port Quinta da Cavadinha 1982 (NR) (VP-2/90)
82   WARRE Vintage Port Quinta da Cavadinha 1979 Rel: $25 Cur: $25 (7/31/90)
82   WARRE Vintage Port Quinta da Cavadinha 1979 Rel: $25 Cur: $25 (VP-2/90)
83   WARRE Vintage Port Quinta da Cavadinha 1978 Rel: $28 Cur: $28 (VP-2/90)
90   WARRE Vintage Port Quinta da Cavadinha 1978 Rel: $28 Cur: $28 (11/30/88)
81   WIESE & KROHN Vintage Port 1985 Rel: $21 Cur: $32 (VP-1/90)
86   WIESE & KROHN Vintage Port 1984 Rel: $13 Cur: $20 (VP-1/90)
83   WIESE & KROHN Vintage Port 1982 Rel: $13 Cur: $32 (VP-1/90)
85   WIESE & KROHN Vintage Port 1982 Rel: $13 Cur: $32 (12/31/88)
84   WIESE & KROHN Vintage Port 1978 Rel: $11 Cur: $37 (VP-1/90)
80   WIESE & KROHN Vintage Port 1975 Cur: $49 (VP-1/90)
74   WIESE & KROHN Vintage Port 1970 Cur: $75 (VP-1/90)
75   WIESE & KROHN Vintage Port 1967 Cur: $65 (VP-1/90)
85   WIESE & KROHN Vintage Port 1965 Cur: $100 (VP-1/90)
87   WIESE & KROHN Vintage Port 1963 Cur: $145 (VP-1/90)
85   WIESE & KROHN Vintage Port 1961 Cur: $125 (VP-1/90)
89   WIESE & KROHN Vintage Port 1960 Cur: $115 (VP-1/90)
87   WIESE & KROHN Vintage Port 1958 Cur: $180 (VP-1/90)

OTHER PORT

77   AVERY Club NV $9.50 (3/31/88)
96   BARROS Tawny Port 20 Year Old NV $35 (2/28/90) (JS)
95   BURMESTER Tawny Port 20 Year Old NV $40 (2/28/90) (JS)
83   CALEM Tawny Port 20 Años NV $35 (4/15/90) (JS)
83   CHURCHILL Tawny Port 20 Años Finest Vintage Character NV $18.50 (4/15/91)
86   COCKBURN Fine Ruby Port NV $35 (2/28/90) (JS)
85   COCKBURN Fine Ruby Port NV $10 (3/31/88)
85   COCKBURN Fine Ruby Port NV $8 (3/31/88)
76   CROFT Tawny Port 20 Year Old NV $38 (2/28/90) (JS)
89   DELAFORCE Fine Ruby Port NV $8.50 (3/31/88)
86   DELAFORCE Fine Ruby Port NV $9 (4/16/85)
82   DOW Tawny Port 20 Year Old NV $23 (2/28/90) (JS)
89   DOW Tawny Port 20 Year Old NV $10 (3/31/88)
80   FERREIRA Tawny Port 20 Year Old Duque de Bragança 20 Year Old Port NV $38 (2/28/90) (JS)
83   FERREIRA Tawny Port 20 Year Old Duque de Bragança 20 Year Old Port NV $7 (3/31/88)
87   FERREIRA Tawny Port 20 Year Old Duque de Bragança 20 Year Old Port NV $30 (3/31/87)
90   FONSECA Tawny Port 20 Year Old Duque de Bragança 20 Year Old Port Bin 27 NV $40 (2/28/90) (JS)
88   FONSECA Tawny Port 20 Year Old Duque de Bragança 20 Year Old Port Bin 27 NV $16 (3/31/88)
84   GRAHAM Fine Ruby Port NV $36 (2/28/90) (JS)
74   GRAHAM Fine Ruby Port NV $7 (3/31/88)
80   GRAHAM Fine Ruby Port NV $15/375ml (3/31/88)
78   HOOPER Tawny Port 20 Year Old NV $35 (2/28/90) (JS)

88   KOPKE Tawny Port 20 Year Old NV $30 (2/28/90) (JS)
72   KOPKE Tawny Port 20 Year Old NV $6.50 (3/31/88)
93   MARTINEZ Tawny Port 20 Year Old Directors NV $25 (2/28/90) (JS)
79   NIEPOORT Ruby Port NV $7 (3/31/88)
75   OFFLEY Ruby Port Boa Vista Special Reserve NV $9.75 (3/31/88)
89   OFFLEY Ruby Port Boa Vista Special Reserve NV $35 (2/28/90) (JS)
78   C. PINTO Ruby Port Boa Vista Special Reserve Vinho do Porto Consolador NV $7.50 (3/31/88)
89   POCAS JUNIOR Tawny Port 20 Year Old NV $35 (2/28/90) (JS)
72   QUARLES HARRIS Ruby Port Club NV $7.50 (3/31/88)
96   QUARLES HARRIS Ruby Port Club 1940 $70 (1/31/88)
82   QUINTA DO NOVAL Tawny Port 20 Year Old NV $32 (2/28/90) (JS)
79   RAMOS-PINTO Ruby Port NV $8.75 (3/31/88)
84   RAMOS-PINTO Ruby Port NV $39 (2/28/90) (JS)
77   ROBERTSON Fine Ruby Port NV $9.75 (3/31/88)
81   ROBERTSON Fine Ruby Port NV $33 (2/28/90) (JS)
68   ROYAL OPORTO Ruby Port NV $7.25 (3/31/88)
77   ROYAL OPORTO Ruby Port NV $25 (2/28/90) (JS)
87   SANDEMAN Fine Ruby Port NV $29 (2/28/90) (JS)
78   SANDEMAN Fine Ruby Port NV $8.25 (3/31/88)
86   SANDEMAN Fine Ruby Port NV $12.50 (3/31/88)
76   SANDEMAN Fine Ruby Port NV $13 (1/01/85)
74   SMITH WOODHOUSE Fine Ruby Port Oporto Portugal Bicentennial NV $8 (3/31/88)
79   SMITH WOODHOUSE Fine Ruby Port Oporto Portugal Bicentennial NV $9.50 (6/01/85)
85   TAYLOR FLADGATE Fine Ruby Port Oporto Portugal Bicentennial Special Club NV $38 (2/28/90) (JS)
78   TAYLOR FLADGATE Fine Ruby Port Oporto Portugal Bicentennial Special Club NV $8 (3/31/88)
84   TAYLOR FLADGATE Fine Ruby Port Oporto Portugal Bicentennial Special Club NV $12.95 (2/16/85)
83   WARRE Fine Ruby Port Oporto Portugal Bicentennial Special Club 10 Year Old Sir William NV $20 (4/30/91)
85   WARRE Fine Ruby Port Oporto Portugal Bicentennial Special Club 10 Year Old Sir William NV $24 (4/15/91)
84   WARRE Fine Ruby Port Oporto Portugal Bicentennial Special Club 10 Year Old Sir William NV $38 (2/28/90) (JS)
84   WARRE Fine Ruby Port Oporto Portugal Bicentennial Special Club 10 Year Old Sir William NV $8.25 (3/31/88)
82   WARRE Fine Ruby Port Oporto Portugal Bicentennial Special Club 10 Year Old Sir William NV $11.50 (1/31/87)
88   WIESE & KROHN Tawny Port 20 Year Old NV $33 (2/28/90) (JS)

OTHER PORTUGAL

78   CAVES ALIANCA Garrafeira 1984 $8 (7/15/91)
77   CAVES ALIANCA Reserva 1987 $5 (7/15/91)
84   CAVES ALIANCA Garrafeira 1982 $9 (7/15/91)
74   CAVES ALIANCA Vinho Tinto 1984 $8 (7/15/91)
76   ESTEVA 1984 $5 (12/15/87)
83   JOSE MARIA DA FONSECA Garrafeira CO 1982 $13.50 (12/31/90)
88   JOSE MARIA DA FONSECA Garrafeira RA 1982 $13.50 (12/31/90)
83   JOSE MARIA DA FONSECA Pasmados 1984 $7.25 (4/30/91) BB
84   JOSE MARIA DA FONSECA Periquita 1987 $5.75 (12/31/90) BB
82   JOSE MARIA DA FONSECA Tinto Velho Requengos de Monsarax Colheita 1986 $9.75 (12/31/90)
84   QUINTA DO CARDO Castelo Rodrigo 1989 $7 (12/31/90) BB
81   QUINTA DO COTTO Grande Escolha 1987 $18 (12/31/90)
74   QUINTA DO COTTO Vinho Tinto 1987 $9 (4/30/91)
65   CORADO Vinho Verde White Periquita NV $4.50 (9/30/86)

SPAIN
SPAIN RED/*NAVARRA*

85 BODEGAS BRANAVIEJA Navarra Pleno 1988 $6 (12/15/90) BB
86 LAS CAMPANAS Navarra Crianza 1984 $6 (3/31/90) BB
78 FINO ALAIZ Navarra NV $4 (10/31/88)
81 BODEGAS IRACHE Navarra Castillo Irache Reserva 1978 $12 (3/31/90)
73 BODEGAS MAGANA Navarra 1982 $14 (3/31/90)
77 VINA MAGANA Navarra 1982 $16 (11/15/87)
82 BODEGAS MUGA-VILLFRANCA Navarra Mendiani 1989 $4 (6/15/91) BB
80 VINICOLA NAVARRA Navarra Castillo de Tiebas Reserva 1976 $7 (1/31/88)
77 VINICOLA NAVARRA Navarra Las Campanas Tino Tinto 1982 $5 (1/31/88)
73 OCHOA Navarra 1986 $5.50 (4/15/89)
82 OCHOA Navarra 1984 $7.50 (4/15/89)
85 OCHOA Navarra Reserva 1980 $10.50 (4/15/89)
83 BODEGAS PRINCIPE DE VIANA Cabernet Sauvignon Navarra 1989 $8 (3/31/91) BB
83 SENORIO DE SARRIA Navarra 1984 $5 (2/28/90) BB
65 SENORIO DE SARRIA Navarra Gran Reserva 1981 $11 (3/31/90)
77 SENORIO DE SARRIA Navarra 1985 $5 (7/31/89)

PENEDES

77 RENE BARBIER Penedès 1982 $3 (1/31/87)
74 RENE BARBIER Cabernet Sauvignon Penedès 1981 $5 (3/31/90)
69 RENE BARBIER Cabernet Sauvignon Penedès 1981 $5 (1/31/87)
77 RENE BARBIER Penedès Reserva 1978 $4.50 (3/31/90)
73 RENE BARBIER Penedès Reserva 1978 $4.50 (1/31/87)
68 GRAN CAUS Penedès 1984 $12 (9/15/88)
77 GRAN CAUS Cabernet Sauvignon-Cabernet Franc-Merlot Penedès 1986 $12 (4/30/89)
77 GRAN CAUS Cabernet Sauvignon-Cabernet Franc-Merlot Penedès 1985 $11.75 (10/15/88)
78 GRAN CAUS Penedès Can Ràfols dels Caus 1987 $11 (10/15/90)
77 JEAN LEON Cabernet Sauvignon Penedès 1984 $12 (3/31/91)
85 JEAN LEON Cabernet Sauvignon Penedès 1983 $8.50 (3/31/90)
66 JEAN LEON Cabernet Sauvignon Penedès 1978 $6.50 (4/16/84)
83 MONT-MARCAL Penedès Tinto 1988 $8 (3/31/91)
81 TORRES Penedès Coronas 1988 $7 (6/15/91) BB
80 TORRES Penedès Coronas 1987 $6.50 (10/15/90) BB
78 TORRES Penedès Coronas 1986 $6.25 (11/30/89)
86 TORRES Penedès Coronas 1985 $5.50 (11/30/88) BB
84 TORRES Penedès Coronas 1983 $4.50 (6/30/87) BB
76 TORRES Penedès Coronas 1982 $4.50 (2/16/86) (JS)
89 TORRES Penedès Gran Coronas 1985 $11 (11/30/88)
75 TORRES Penedès Gran Coronas 1979 $9 (2/16/86) (JS)
85 TORRES Penedès Gran Coronas Más la Plana Reserva 1985 $32 (10/15/90)
85 TORRES Penedès Gran Coronas Más la Plana Reserva 1983 $26 (3/31/90)
82 TORRES Penedès Gran Coronas Black Label Reserva 1983 $26 (11/30/88)
85 TORRES Penedès Gran Coronas Black Label Reserva 1982 $27 (6/15/88)
88 TORRES Penedès Gran Coronas Black Label Reserva 1982 $27 (2/16/86)
83 TORRES Penedès Gran Coronas Black Label Reserva 1981 $18 (10/15/87)
85 TORRES Penedès Gran Coronas Black Label Reserva 1978 Cur: $65 (2/16/86)
86 TORRES Penedès Gran Coronas Reserva 1986 $12 (11/30/89)
77 TORRES Penedès Gran Coronas Reserva 1985 $12 (3/31/90)
78 TORRES Penedès Gran Sangre de Toro 1984 $9 (9/15/88)
79 TORRES Penedès Gran Sangre de Toro 1979 $9 (2/16/86) (JS)
83 TORRES Penedès Gran Sangre de Toro Reserva 1986 $10 (10/15/90)
87 TORRES Penedès Gran Sangre de Toro Reserva 1985 $9 (11/30/89)
91 TORRES Penedès Gran Sangre de Toro Reserva 1983 $9.50 (6/15/88) SS
80 TORRES Penedès Gran Sangre de Toro Reserva 1981 $5.50 (6/15/87)
79 TORRES Penedès Más Borras 1988 $18 (10/15/90)
82 TORRES Penedès Sangre de Toro 1988 $6.50 (3/31/91) BB
82 TORRES Penedès Sangre de Toro 1987 $5.25 (11/30/89) BB
80 TORRES Penedès Sangre de Toro 1986 $4.75 (12/15/88) BB
81 TORRES Penedès Sangre de Toro 1985 $5.50 (6/15/88) BB
79 TORRES Penedès Sangre de Toro 1983 $4 (6/15/87)
83 TORRES Penedès Sangre de Toro 1982 $4 (2/16/86) (JS)
82 TORRES Merlot Penedès Viña Las Torres 1989 $13 (10/15/90)
83 TORRES Merlot Penedès Viña Las Torres 1988 $10 (3/31/90)
76 TORRES Penedès Viña Magdala 1984 $11 (7/31/89)
74 TORRES Penedès Viña Magdala 1983 $9.50 (6/15/88)
72 TORRES Penedès Viña Magdala 1979 (NA) (2/16/86) (JS)
76 VALLFORMOSA Penedès Vall Fort 1986 $7 (5/31/91)
84 VALLFORMOSA Penedès Vall Fort 1984 $7 (3/31/91) BB
84 VALLFORMOSA Penedès Vall Reserva Tinto Propia 1980 $10 (3/31/91)

RIBERA DEL DUERO

60 BODEGAS ISMAEL ARROYO Ribera del Duero Mesoñeros de Castilla 1986 $6 (4/30/88)
81 BODEGAS BALBAS Ribera del Duero 1987 $14 (9/30/90)
87 BODEGAS BALBAS Ribera del Duero 1986 $15 (7/31/89)
83 BODEGAS BALBAS Ribera del Duero 1985 $13 (9/15/88)
75 BODEGAS BALBAS Ribera del Duero Reserva 1985 (NA) (3/31/90) (TM)
82 BODEGAS MAURO Ribera del Duero 1987 $17 (10/15/90)
76 BODEGAS MAURO Ribera del Duero 1986 $17 (3/31/90)
88 BODEGAS MAURO Ribera del Duero 1985 $15 (3/31/90)
78 BODEGAS MAURO Ribera del Duero 1984 $16 (3/31/90) (TM)
85 BODEGAS MAURO Ribera del Duero 1984 $16 (9/15/88)
82 BODEGAS MAURO Ribera del Duero 1983 $15 (10/15/87)
85 VINA MAYOR Ribera del Duero Tinto 1989 $7 (3/31/91) BB
82 BODEGA HNOS. PEREZ PASCUAS Ribera del Duero Viña Pedrosa 1988 $16.50 (5/31/91)

77 BODEGA HNOS. PEREZ PASCUAS Ribera del Duero Viña Pedrosa 1987 $15 (9/30/90)
88 BODEGA HNOS. PEREZ PASCUAS Ribera del Duero Viña Pedrosa 1986 $14 (3/31/90)
82 BODEGA HNOS. PEREZ PASCUAS Ribera del Duero Viña Pedrosa 1986 $14 (7/31/89)
83 BODEGA HNOS. PEREZ PASCUAS Ribera del Duero Viña Pedrosa 1985 $16 (9/15/88)
86 PENALBA Ribera del Duero 1983 $12 (2/28/90)
87 PENALBA Ribera del Duero Crianza 1985 $9 (2/28/90)
73 PENALBA Ribera del Duero Gran Reserva 1980 (NA) (3/31/90) (TM)
70 PENALBA Ribera del Duero Reserva 1982 (NA) (3/31/90) (TM)
84 PESQUERA Ribera del Duero 1987 $17 (9/30/90)
91 PESQUERA Ribera del Duero 1986 $26 (4/30/89)
89 PESQUERA Ribera del Duero 1985 $16 (4/30/88)
89 PESQUERA Ribera del Duero 1984 $14 (11/15/87) (JL)
86 PESQUERA Ribera del Duero 1984 $14 (10/15/87)
94 PESQUERA Ribera del Duero 1983 $12 (11/15/87) (JL)
93 PESQUERA Ribera del Duero 1983 $12 (12/31/86)
89 PESQUERA Ribera del Duero 1982 (NA) (11/15/87) (JL)
90 PESQUERA Ribera del Duero 1979 (NA) (11/15/87) (JL)
89 PESQUERA Ribera del Duero 1978 (NA) (11/15/87) (JL)
88 PESQUERA Ribera del Duero 1975 (NA) (11/15/87) (JL)
92 PESQUERA Ribera del Duero Janus Reserva Especial 1982 $75 (3/31/90)
94 PESQUERA Ribera del Duero Janus Reserva Especial 1982 $75 (9/15/88)
92 PESQUERA Ribera del Duero Reserva 1986 $26 (9/30/90)
91 PESQUERA Ribera del Duero Reserva 1986 $26 (3/31/90) (TM)
89 PESQUERA Ribera del Duero Reserva 1985 $16 (3/31/90) (TM)
81 SENORIO DE NAVA Ribera del Duero 1986 $8 (11/15/89)
95 BODEGAS VEGA SICILIA Ribera del Duero Unico 1979 $75 (3/31/90)
91 BODEGAS VEGA SICILIA Ribera del Duero Unico 1976 Rel: $60 Cur: $83 (4/30/89)
90 BODEGAS VEGA SICILIA Ribera del Duero Unico 1973 Cur: $82 (3/31/90) (TM)
89 BODEGAS VEGA SICILIA Ribera del Duero Unico 1962 $106 (3/31/90)
79 BODEGAS VEGA SICILIA Ribera del Duero Unico Reserva Especial NV $156 (3/31/90)
90 BODEGAS VEGA SICILIA Ribera del Duero Valbuena 1982 $25 (10/15/88)
90 BODEGAS VEGA SICILIA Ribera del Duero Valbuena 3 Años 1986 $47 (12/15/90)
92 BODEGAS VEGA SICILIA Ribera del Duero Valbuena 3 Años 1985 Rel: $40 Cur: $55 (3/31/90) CS
79 BODEGAS VEGA SICILIA Ribera del Duero Valbuena 3 Años 1984 $28 (4/30/89)
88 BODEGAS VEGA SICILIA Ribera del Duero Valbuena 3 Años 1983 $22.50 (10/15/88)
90 BODEGAS VEGA SICILIA Ribera del Duero Valbuena 5 Años 1984 $49 (3/31/90)
91 BODEGAS VEGA SICILIA Ribera del Duero Valbuena 5 Años 1982 $37 (3/31/90)
91 BODEGAS VEGA SICILIA Ribera del Duero Valbuena 5 Años 1982 $36 (10/15/88)

RIOJA

88 ANARES Rioja Reserva 1981 $8 (9/30/86)
81 MARQUES DE ARIENZO Rioja 1986 $8 (3/31/90) (TM)
78 MARQUES DE ARIENZO Rioja 1985 $7.50 (3/15/90)
84 MARQUES DE ARIENZO Rioja 1985 $8 (7/31/89) BB
81 MARQUES DE ARIENZO Rioja 1983 $5 (6/30/88) BB
83 MARQUES DE ARIENZO Rioja Gran Reserva 1981 $18 (5/31/91)
78 MARQUES DE ARIENZO Rioja Gran Reserva 1978 $18 (3/31/90) (TM)
72 MARQUES DE ARIENZO Rioja Gran Reserva 1976 $18 (3/31/90)
70 MARQUES DE ARIENZO Rioja Gran Reserva 1976 $18 (11/15/87)
84 MARQUES DE ARIENZO Rioja Reserva 1983 $12 (5/31/91)
84 MARQUES DE ARIENZO Rioja Reserva 1983 $13 (3/31/90) (TM)
83 MARQUES DE ARIENZO Rioja Reserva 1981 $12 (7/31/89)
76 MARQUES DE ARIENZO Rioja Reserva 1980 $8 (6/30/88)
80 ARTADI Rioja Alavesa 1987 $6 (4/30/88)
87 BODEGAS BERBERANA Rioja Berberana Reserva 1983 $7 (4/30/89) BB
81 BODEGAS BERBERANA Rioja Carta de Oro 1986 $8 (3/31/90)
78 BODEGAS BERBERANA Rioja Carta de Oro 1985 $6 (7/31/89)
84 BODEGAS BERBERANA Rioja Carta de Plata 1987 $7.50 (12/15/90) BB
88 BODEGAS BERBERANA Rioja Carta de Plata 1986 $6 (5/15/89) BB
89 BODEGAS BERBERANA Rioja Carta de Plata 1985 $6 (10/31/88) BB
82 BODEGAS BERBERANA Rioja Gran Reserva 1980 $9 (10/31/88)
90 BODEGAS BERBERANA Rioja Reserva 1985 $10 (2/28/90)
86 BODEGAS BERBERANA Rioja Reserva 1983 $9 (11/15/89)
82 BODEGAS BERBERANA Rioja Reserva 1982 $10 (12/15/88)
70 VINA BERCEO Rioja 1988 $5 (9/30/90)
77 VINA BERCEO Rioja 1988 $5 (11/15/89)
86 VINA BERCEO Rioja 1987 $5 (4/15/89) BB
87 VINA BERCEO Rioja Crianza 1986 $7 (9/30/90) BB
70 VINA BERCEO Rioja Crianza 1986 $7 (11/15/89)
76 VINA BERCEO Rioja Reserva 1985 $10 (3/31/90)
69 VINA BERCEO Rioja Reserva 1983 $10 (11/15/89)
76 VINA BERCEO Rioja Tinto Crianza 1984 $5.75 (10/15/88)
76 VINA BERCEO Rioja Tinto Reserva 1982 $8.50 (10/15/88)
77 VINA BERCEO Rioja Tinto Reserva 1980 $8.50 (10/15/88)
82 BODEGAS BERONIA Rioja Reserva 1982 $12 (3/31/90) (TM)
79 BODEGAS BILBAINAS Rioja Viña Pomal 1983 $8 (6/30/90)
88 BODEGAS BILBAINAS Rioja Viña Pomal Gran Reserva 1978 $20 (3/31/90)
85 BODEGAS BRETON Rioja Lorinon Crianza 1985 $9 (3/31/90)
80 BODEGAS MARTINEZ BUJANDA Rioja Conde de Valdemar 1986 $7 (6/30/90) BB
89 BODEGAS MARTINEZ BUJANDA Rioja Conde de Valdemar 1985 $7 (12/15/88) BB
79 BODEGAS MARTINEZ BUJANDA Rioja Conde de Valdemar Reserva 1982 (NA) (11/15/87) (JL)
83 BODEGAS MARTINEZ BUJANDA Rioja Valdemar Viño Tinto 1989 $7 (6/30/90) BB
82 MARQUES DE CACERES Rioja 1986 $9 (5/31/91)
80 MARQUES DE CACERES Rioja 1985 $9.50 (3/31/90)
82 MARQUES DE CACERES Rioja 1985 $9.50 (12/15/88)
87 MARQUES DE CACERES Rioja 1982 $7.50 (11/15/87) (JL)
88 MARQUES DE CACERES Rioja 1981 $5.50 (11/01/85) BB
69 MARQUES DE CACERES Rioja Reserva 1981 $20 (3/31/90)
67 MARQUES DE CACERES Rioja Reserva 1975 $9.50 (12/01/85)
81 BODEGAS CAMPO VIEJO Rioja 1987 $6.50 (9/30/90) BB
82 BODEGAS CAMPO VIEJO Rioja 1984 $5.25 (1/31/88) BB
83 BODEGAS CAMPO VIEJO Rioja Crianza 1985 $6.50 (3/15/90) BB
83 BODEGAS CAMPO VIEJO Rioja Gran Reserva 1978 $13.50 (9/30/90)
78 BODEGAS CAMPO VIEJO Rioja Gran Reserva 1978 $13.50 (11/15/88)
82 BODEGAS CAMPO VIEJO Rioja Reserva 1985 $9 (9/30/90)
78 BODEGAS CAMPO VIEJO Rioja Reserva 1981 $7.25 (11/15/88)
85 BODEGAS CAMPO VIEJO Rioja Viña Alcorta 1985 $10 (9/30/90)
76 BODEGAS CAMPO VIEJO Rioja Viña Alcorta 1981 $7.25 (10/31/88)

---

64 BODEGAS CAMPO VIEJO Rioja Viña Alcorta (Tempranillo) 1981 $7 (3/31/90)
87 BODEGAS CAMPO VIEJO Rioja Viña Alcorta Reserva 1982 (NA) (11/15/87) (JL)
78 CODICE Rioja 1988 $6 (6/15/91)
83 CONDE DE VALDEMAR Rioja Reserva 1985 $9 (11/15/89)
79 BODEGAS CORRAL Rioja Don Jacobo 1985 $8 (3/31/90)
79 BODEGAS CORRAL Rioja Don Jacobo 1982 $7 (11/15/87) (JL)
86 BODEGAS CORRAL Rioja Don Jacobo Reserva 1981 $10.50 (3/31/90)
81 BODEGAS EL COTO Rioja 1985 $5 (3/31/90) BB
67 BODEGAS EL COTO Rioja Crianza 1985 $5.50 (3/31/90)
81 BODEGAS EL COTO Rioja 1984 $7 (3/31/90) BB
81 BODEGAS EL COTO Rioja Coto de Imaz Reserva 1981 $9 (3/31/90)
86 BODEGAS EL COTO Rioja Gran Reserva 1982 (NA) (11/15/87) (JL)
88 CUNE Rioja 1985 $17 (3/31/90) (TM)
78 CUNE Rioja 1978 $5.50 (6/16/85)
82 CUNE Rioja Clarete 1986 $7 (2/28/90) BB
85 CUNE Rioja Clarete 1985 $6 (4/15/89) BB
80 CUNE Rioja Clarete 1984 $6 (10/15/88) BB
83 CUNE Rioja Clarete 1982 $4.50 (6/01/85)
88 CUNE Rioja Contino Reserva 1985 $14 (12/15/90)
84 CUNE Rioja Contino Reserva 1984 $12 (3/31/90)
81 CUNE Rioja Contino Reserva 1982 $12 (4/30/89)
83 CUNE Rioja Contino Reserva 1980 $10.75 (1/31/87)
86 CUNE Rioja Imperial Gran Reserva 1981 $21 (3/31/90)
70 CUNE Rioja Imperial Gran Reserva 1978 $15 (3/31/90)
84 CUNE Rioja Imperial Gran Reserva 1975 $24 (3/31/90)
85 CUNE Rioja Imperial Gran Reserva 1973 (NA) (3/31/90) (TM)
85 CUNE Rioja Reserva 1985 $8.50 (3/31/90)
81 CUNE Rioja Viña Real 1986 $8 (3/31/90)
75 CUNE Rioja Viña Real 1980 $5.50 (6/01/85)
85 CUNE Rioja Viña Real Crianza 1985 $7 (3/31/90) (TM)
88 CUNE Rioja Viña Real Gran Reserva 1981 $17 (3/31/90)
88 BODEGAS DOMECQ Rioja Gran Reserva 1976 $19 (11/15/89)
88 FAUSTINO I Rioja Gran Reserva 1981 $12 (10/31/88)
83 FAUSTINO V Rioja 1985 $7.50 (10/15/88)
80 GRAN CONDAL Rioja 1987 $6.50 (3/31/90)
79 GRAN CONDAL Rioja Gran Reserva 1982 $10 (11/15/87) (JL)
80 GRAN CONDAL Rioja Gran Reserva 1981 $8 (11/30/87)
82 GRAN CONDAL Rioja Reserva 1980 $7 (11/30/87) BB
85 GURPEGUI Rioja Viña Berceo Reserva 1982 (NA) (11/15/87) (JL)
70 R. LOPEZ DE HEREDIA Rioja Bosconia 1982 $6 (12/31/87)
72 R. LOPEZ DE HEREDIA Rioja Bosconia Gran Reserva 1976 $14 (3/31/90)
80 R. LOPEZ DE HEREDIA Rioja Bosconia Gran Reserva 1973 $14 (3/31/90)
75 R. LOPEZ DE HEREDIA Rioja Bosconia Gran Reserva 1973 $15 (12/31/87)
78 R. LOPEZ DE HEREDIA Rioja Bosconia Reserva 1983 $5.50 (3/31/90)
84 R. LOPEZ DE HEREDIA Rioja Bosconia Reserva 1982 $5.50 (11/15/87) (JL)
70 R. LOPEZ DE HEREDIA Rioja Cubillo 1984 $5.50 (3/31/90)
78 R. LOPEZ DE HEREDIA Rioja Tondonia 1981 $6 (12/31/87)
83 R. LOPEZ DE HEREDIA Rioja Tondonia Gran Reserva 1976 $14 (3/31/90)
79 R. LOPEZ DE HEREDIA Rioja Tondonia Gran Reserva 1973 $15 (12/31/87)
79 R. LOPEZ DE HEREDIA Rioja Tondonia Reserva 1983 $5.50 (3/31/90)
73 MONTE VELAZ Rioja 1981 $4 (10/15/87)
85 BODEGAS MONTECILLO Rioja Especial Gran Reserva 1978 $30 (3/31/90)
85 BODEGAS MONTECILLO Rioja Gran Reserva 1975 $29 (12/15/88)
66 BODEGAS MONTECILLO Rioja Viña Cumbrero 1986 $5 (3/31/90)
59 BODEGAS MONTECILLO Rioja Viña Cumbrero 1985 $5 (3/31/90)
80 BODEGAS MONTECILLO Rioja Viña Cumbrero 1985 $5 (11/15/88) BB
69 BODEGAS MONTECILLO Rioja Viña Cumbrero 1984 $4 (11/30/87)
79 BODEGAS MONTECILLO Rioja Viña Cumbrero 1982 $4 (11/15/87) (JL)
89 BODEGAS MONTECILLO Rioja Viña Cumbrero 1982 $4 (12/31/86) BB
73 BODEGAS MONTECILLO Rioja Viña Cumbrero 1981 $4 (6/01/86) BB
81 BODEGAS MONTECILLO Rioja Viña Monty 1978 $7 (9/30/86)
70 BODEGAS MONTECILLO Rioja Viña Monty 1976 $6 (5/16/86)
86 BODEGAS MONTECILLO Rioja Viña Monty Gran Reserva 1981 $9.25 (7/31/89)
78 BODEGAS MONTECILLO Rioja Viña Monty Gran Reserva 1981 $5 (11/15/88)
79 BODEGAS MONTECILLO Rioja Viña Monty Gran Reserva 1980 $7 (11/30/87)
77 BODEGAS MUERZA Rioja Rioja Vega 1989 $7 (3/31/91)
75 BODEGAS MUERZA Rioja Rioja Vega Crianza 1986 $10 (3/31/91)
82 BODEGAS MUGA Rioja 1984 $8.50 (4/30/89)
77 BODEGAS MUGA Rioja 1982 $7 (11/15/87) (JL)
81 BODEGAS MUGA Rioja Crianza 1986 $12 (5/31/91)
83 BODEGAS MUGA Rioja Crianza 1985 (NA) (3/31/90) (TM)
77 BODEGAS MUGA Rioja Gran Reserva 1976 (NA) (3/31/90) (TM)
79 BODEGAS MUGA Rioja Prado Enea Gran Reserva 1981 (NA) (3/31/90) (TM)
84 BODEGAS MUGA Rioja Prado Enea Gran Reserva 1976 (NA) (3/31/90) (TM)
80 BODEGAS MUGA Rioja Prado Enea Reserva 1981 $20 (4/30/89)
79 BODEGAS MUGA Rioja Prado Enea Reserva 1978 $18 (3/31/90)
87 MARQUES DE MURRIETA Rioja 1985 $17 (2/28/90)
92 MARQUES DE MURRIETA Rioja Castillo Ygay Gran Reserva 1968 Rel: $85 Cur: $98 (3/31/90)
94 MARQUES DE MURRIETA Rioja Castillo Ygay Gran Reserva 1952 $150 (3/31/90)
89 MARQUES DE MURRIETA Rioja Gran Reserva 1978 $29 (3/31/90)
87 MARQUES DE MURRIETA Rioja Gran Reserva 1975 $33 (3/31/90)
84 MARQUES DE MURRIETA Rioja Reserva 1983 $13 (3/31/90)
83 MARQUES DE MURRIETA Rioja Reserva 1980 $27 (3/31/90)
84 NUESTRA SENORA DE LA ANTIGUA Rioja 1982 (NA) (11/15/87) (JL)
86 BODEGAS OLARRA Rioja 1982 (NA) (11/15/87) (JL)
83 BODEGAS OLARRA Rioja Añares 1987 $6.50 (3/31/90) BB
82 BODEGAS OLARRA Rioja Añares 1985 $6 (2/28/90) BB
76 BODEGAS OLARRA Rioja Añares 1983 $6.50 (2/28/90)
84 BODEGAS OLARRA Rioja Añares Gran Reserva 1981 $16 (3/31/90)
73 BODEGAS OLARRA Rioja Añares Reserva 1983 $12 (2/28/90)
70 BODEGAS OLARRA Rioja Cerro Añon 1984 $4.50 (12/01/85)
75 BODEGAS OLARRA Rioja Cerro Añon 1980 $4.50 (4/01/85)
74 BODEGAS OLARRA Rioja Cerro Añon Gran Reserva 1981 $13.50 (3/31/90)
61 BODEGAS OLARRA Rioja Cerro Añon Reserva 1983 $10.50 (3/31/90)
78 BODEGAS OLARRA Rioja Cerro Añon Reserva 1981 $8 (9/30/86)
83 BODEGAS OLARRA Rioja Cerro Añon Reserva 1980 $8 (3/01/85)
82 BODEGAS OLARRA Rioja Reserva 1978 $7.50 (3/16/85)
87 BODEGAS OLARRA Rioja Tinto 1983 $5 (9/30/86) BB
87 BODEGAS OLARRA Rioja Tinto 1980 $4.50 (3/16/85) BB
80 BODEGAS ONDARRE Rioja Ondarre 1984 $5 (11/15/88) BB

84 BODEGAS ONDARRE Rioja Reserva 1981 $7 (12/15/88) BB
78 BODEGAS ONDARRE Rioja Tidon 1986 $4.50 (12/15/88)
83 BODEGAS PALACIO Rioja Cosme Palacio y Hermanos 1987 (NA) (3/31/90) (TM)
88 BODEGAS PALACIO Rioja Cosme Palacio y Hermanos 1986 $9 (2/28/89)
80 BODEGAS PALACIO Rioja Glorioso 1986 $8 (3/31/90) (TM)
85 BODEGAS PALACIO Rioja Glorioso 1985 $7 (2/28/89) BB
75 BODEGAS PALACIO Rioja Glorioso Gran Reserva 1981 (NA) (3/31/90) (TM)
88 BODEGAS PALACIO Rioja Glorioso Gran Reserva 1978 $15 (2/28/89)
79 BODEGAS PALACIO Rioja Glorioso Reserva 1982 $18 (3/31/90) (TM)
83 BODEGAS PALACIO Rioja Glorioso Reserva 1981 $10 (2/28/89)
90 BODEGAS PALACIOS REMONDO Rioja 1982 (NA) (11/15/87) (JL)
81 BODEGAS PALACIOS REMONDO Rioja Herencia 1985 (NA) (3/31/90) (TM)
80 FREDERICO PATERNINA Rioja Banda Azul 1985 $5 (3/15/90) BB
76 PRIVILEGIO DEL RAY SANCHO Rioja 1978 $3 (4/01/84)
78 MARQUES DEL PUERTO Rioja 1984 $7 (2/28/90)
78 MARQUES DEL PUERTO Rioja 1982 $6 (11/15/87) (JL)
85 MARQUES DEL PUERTO Rioja Gran Reserva 1978 $20 (3/31/90)
87 REMELLURI Rioja 1986 $11 (12/15/90)
88 REMELLURI Rioja 1985 $10 (3/31/90) (TM)
77 REMELLURI Rioja 1984 $9 (3/31/90) (TM)
77 REMELLURI Rioja 1983 $11.50 (3/31/90)
82 REMELLURI Rioja 1982 $12 (3/31/90) (TM)
84 REMELLURI Rioja Alavesa Labastida 1982 $8 (9/30/86)
83 LA RIOJA ALTA Rioja Reserva 890 Gran Reserva 1973 Cur: $54 (3/31/90) (TM)
90 LA RIOJA ALTA Rioja Reserva 904 Gran Reserva 1976 Cur: $26 (3/31/90) (TM)
84 LA RIOJA ALTA Rioja Reserva 904 Gran Reserva 1973 $10 (9/30/86)
85 LA RIOJA ALTA Rioja Viña Alberdi 1985 $8 (3/15/90) BB
79 LA RIOJA ALTA Rioja Viña Ardanza 1985 $15 (3/31/90)
76 LA RIOJA ALTA Rioja Viña Ardanza Reserva 1983 $21 (12/15/90)
84 LA RIOJA ALTA Rioja Viña Ardanza Reserva 1982 $15 (3/31/90)
65 LA RIOJA ALTA Rioja Viña Ardanza Reserva 1978 $6 (9/30/86)
75 BODEGAS RIOJANAS Rioja Canchales 1987 $4 (3/15/90)
83 BODEGAS RIOJANAS Rioja Monte Real Reserva 1983 $7.50 (3/31/90) BB
68 BODEGAS RIOJANAS Rioja Viña Albina 1983 $7.50 (3/31/90)
80 BODEGAS RIOJANAS Rioja Viña Albina Gran Reserva 1982 $10 (11/15/87) (JL)
58 MARQUES DE RISCAL Rioja 1984 $9 (3/31/90)
68 MARQUES DE RISCAL Rioja 1984 $9 (11/15/88)
84 MARQUES DE RISCAL Rioja 1982 $7 (11/15/87) (JL)
74 MARQUES DE RISCAL Rioja 1982 $7 (6/15/87)
62 MARQUES DE RISCAL Rioja Reserva 1985 $9.50 (3/31/90)
87 MARQUIS DE VILLAMAGNA Rioja Gran Reserva 1975 $19 (10/31/88)
77 VINADRIAN Rioja Tinto 1986 $3.75 (10/15/88)

OTHER SPAIN RED

83 MARQUES DE CARO Valencia Vinedos del Valle de Albaida Reserva Garnacha Tintorera 1982 $6.50 (12/15/88) BB
80 BODEGAS JAIME CARRERAS Valencia 1985 $4 (3/31/90) BB
82 CASA DE LA VINA Valdepeñas Cencibel 1985 $6.50 (3/31/90)
74 CASTILLO DE ALMANSA Almansa Crianza 1983 $7 (3/31/90)
77 COLEGIATA Toro Gran Colegiata Tinto de Crianza 1986 $7 (11/30/89)
82 COLEGIATA Toro Tinto 1986 $5 (11/30/89) BB
88 COLEGIATA Toro Tinto 1985 $5 (11/30/89) BB
82 BODEGAS C. AUGUSTO EGLI Utiel-Requena Casa lo Alto 1983 $9 (7/31/89)
87 ESTOLA La Mancha Reserva 1982 $6 (11/15/89) BB
84 BODEGAS INVIOSA Tierra de Barros Lar de Lares Gran Reserva 1982 $12 (3/31/90)
75 CASTILLO JUMILLA Jumilla 1985 $5 (7/31/89)
91 LAR DE BARROS Tierra de Barros Tinto Reserva 1986 $8 (10/15/90) SS
77 LAR DE BARROS Tierra de Barros Tinto Reserva 1983 $7.50 (10/15/87)
87 LAR DE BARROS Tierra de Barros Tinto Reserva 1982 $5.50 (5/15/87) BB
90 LAR DE LARES Tierra de Barros Gran Reserva 1982 $14 (6/15/91)
85 MONTE DUCAY Cariñena Gran Reserva 1982 $8 (11/30/89)
82 MONTE DUCAY Cariñena Vinedos Propios Tinto Gran Reserva 1978 $8.50 (10/31/88)
81 MONTESIERRA Somontano 1988 $6 (3/31/90)
78 MONTESIERRA Somontano 1988 $6 (5/15/89)
80 MONTESIERRA Somontano 1987 $5.50 (9/15/88)
77 MONTESIERRA Somontano 1986 $5 (11/15/87)
74 BODEGAS PIQUERAS Almansa Castello de Almansa 1983 $7 (3/31/90)
83 BODEGAS PIQUERAS Almansa Castello de Almansa 1983 $6 (10/31/88) BB
70 BODEGAS PIQUERAS Almansa Castillo de Almansa Vino de Crianza 1985 $7.50 (4/30/91)
88 BODEGAS PIQUERAS Almansa Castillo de Almansa Vino de Crianza 1983 $6.50 (7/31/89) BB
84 BODEGAS PORTO Toro Tinto Colegiata 1985 $4 (12/31/87) BB
85 BODEGAS PORTO Toro Tinto de Crianza Gran Colegiata 1985 $5 (12/31/87)
78 BODEGAS PORTO Toro Tinto de Crianza Gran Colegiata 1982 $5.50 (11/30/87)
81 RAIMAT Cabernet Sauvignon Costers del Segre 1986 $10 (3/31/90)
84 RAIMAT Costers del Segre Abadia 1987 $9 (3/31/90)
81 BODEGA SAN VALERO Cariñena Don Mendo Tinto Especial 1987 $5 (11/30/89) BB
80 TAJA Jumilla 1987 $6 (3/31/90) BB
81 VEGA DE MORIZ Valdepeñas Cencibel 1989 $5.50 (6/15/91) BB

SPAIN WHITE/PENEDÈS

75 BALADA Penedès Macabeo Gran Blanc 1988 $8 (3/31/90)
81 GRAN CAUS Chardonnay Chenin Blanc Penedès Xarel-lo 1987 $10 (5/15/89)
88 JEAN LEON Chardonnay Penedès 1988 $34 (1/31/91)
81 NAVERAN Penedès NV $9 (12/31/88)
79 TORRES Penedès Fransola 1988 $14.50 (3/31/90)
81 TORRES Penedès Fransola (Green Label) 1990 $16 (7/15/91)
86 TORRES Penedès Fransola Reserva 1987 $12.50 (12/15/88)
80 TORRES Penedès Gran Viña Sol 1989 $10 (12/15/90)
83 TORRES Penedès Gran Viña Sol 1987 $8 (3/31/90)
81 TORRES Penedès Gran Viña Sol 1987 $8 (12/15/88)
83 TORRES Penedès Gran Viña Sol 1985 $5 (4/30/87) BB
80 TORRES Penedès Gran Viña Sol 1984 $5 (2/16/86)
87 TORRES Penedès Gran Viña Sol Green Label 1986 $14 (10/15/88)
78 TORRES Penedès Gran Viña Sol Green Label 1984 $12 (2/16/86)
75 TORRES Penedès Gran Viña Sol Reserva 1984 $12 (11/15/87)
93 TORRES Penedès Milmanda 1989 $40 (12/15/90)
80 TORRES Penedès Milmanda 1988 $35 (3/31/90)
94 TORRES Penedès Milmanda 1987 $35 (12/15/88)
74 TORRES Penedès San Valentin 1985 (NA) (2/16/86) (JS)

SPAIN
SPAIN WHITE/*PENEDÈS*

84 TORRES Penedès Viña Esmeralda 1990 $10.50 (7/15/91)
84 TORRES Penedès Viña Esmeralda 1989 $9 (3/31/90)
74 TORRES Penedès Viña Esmeralda 1987 $8.50 (6/15/88)
75 TORRES Penedès Viña Esmeralda 1985 $7.50 (2/16/86) (JS)
73 TORRES Penedès Viña Sol 1989 $7 (7/15/91)
72 TORRES Penedès Viña Sol 1988 $5.25 (3/31/90)
78 TORRES Penedès Viña Sol 1984 $4.50 (2/16/86) (JS)

RIOJA

78 MARQUES DE CACERES Rioja 1988 $7.50 (3/31/90)
83 MARQUES DE CACERES Rioja 1987 $6.75 (12/15/88)
59 MARQUES DE CACERES Rioja 1984 $4.25 (5/16/86)
79 CUNE Rioja Blanco 1984 $6.75 (2/15/88)
76 FAUSTINO V Rioja 1986 $7.50 (11/30/88)
62 R. LOPEZ DE HEREDIA Rioja Tondonia 1984 $6 (2/15/88)
80 BODEGAS MONTECILLO Rioja Viña Cumbrero 1989 $6 (7/15/91) BB
72 BODEGAS MONTECILLO Rioja Viña Cumbrero 1988 $5 (3/31/90)
70 BODEGAS MONTECILLO Rioja Viña Cumbrero 1986 $4 (2/15/88)
76 BODEGAS MONTECILLO Rioja Viña Cumbrero 1985 $4 (10/15/86) BB
68 BODEGAS MONTECILLO Rioja Viña Cumbrero 1984 $4 (5/01/86)
88 MARQUES DE MURRIETA Rioja 1985 $14 (3/31/90)
85 MARQUES DE MURRIETA Rioja 1984 $13 (3/31/90)
91 MARQUES DE MURRIETA Rioja Gran Reserva 1978 $29 (3/31/90)
82 BODEGAS OLARRA Rioja Añares Blanco Seco 1988 $7 (3/31/90) BB
75 BODEGAS ONDARRE Rioja Ondarre 1986 $5 (11/30/88)
69 FREDERICO PATERNINA Rioja Banda Dorada 1987 $5 (3/31/90)

OTHER SPAIN WHITE

80 MARQUES DE ALLELLA Alella 1989 $17 (12/15/90)
77 HIJOS DE ANTONIO BARCELO Rueda Vino Blanco Santorcal 1989 $6 (7/15/91)
84 CARBALLO DO REI CONDADO Rias Baixas 1990 $14 (7/15/91)
85 MORGADIO ALBARINO Rias Baixas 1990 $22 (7/15/91)
82 RAIMAT Chardonnay Costers del Segre 1989 $10 (12/15/90)
70 MARQUES DE RISCAL Rueda 1987 $5 (10/15/88)
81 MARQUES DE RISCAL Sauvignon Blanc Rueda 1988 $7.50 (3/31/90)
85 MARQUES DE RISCAL Sauvignon Blanc Rueda 1987 $7.25 (12/15/88)
77 ANGEL RODRIGUEZ VIDAL Rueda Martinsancho Verdejo 1988 $9 (3/31/90)

SPARKLING

79 CADIZ Brut Cava Reserva NV $7 (5/31/88)
78 CASTELLBLANCH Brut Cava Extra NV $5.25 (5/31/88)
73 CASTELLBLANCH Brut Cava Zero 1985 $6 (12/31/88)
81 CASTELLBLANCH Brut Cava Zero 1982 $6 (5/31/88)
83 CAVAS HILL Blanc de Blancs Cava Reserva Oro Seco NV $8 (5/31/88)
69 PAUL CHENEAU Brut Cava Vintage Cuvée Spéciale 1981 $9 (5/31/88)
75 PAUL CHENEAU Brut Blanc de Blancs Cava NV $7.25 (5/31/88)
72 CODORNIU Blanc de Blancs Cava 1984 $9.25 (5/31/88)
79 CODORNIU Brut Cava 1985 $7.25 (5/31/88)
78 CODORNIU Brut Cava Anna de Codorniu 1988 $8 (12/31/90)
75 CODORNIU Brut Cava Anna de Codorniu 1987 $7 (8/31/90)
76 CODORNIU Brut Cava Anna de Codorniu 1985 $6.50 (7/31/89)
73 CODORNIU Brut Cava Anna de Codorniu 1984 $7.50 (5/31/88)
84 CODORNIU Brut Cava Chardonnay 1986 $12 (7/31/89)
82 CODORNIU Brut Cava Clasico 1986 $6 (5/15/89) BB
55 CODORNIU Brut Cava Clasico 1983 $6 (4/01/86)
73 CODORNIU Brut Cava Gran Reserve 1983 $14 (5/31/88)
84 CODORNIU Brut Blanc de Blancs Cava 1988 $9 (12/31/90) BB
77 CODORNIU Brut Blanc de Blancs Cava 1986 $8 (7/31/89)
72 CODORNIU Extra Dry Cava 1985 $7.25 (5/31/88)
70 DUBOSC Brut Cava NV $8 (4/30/88)
67 FERRET Brut Cava NV $11 (9/30/87)
78 FERRET Brut Nature Cava 1984 $14 (5/31/88)
78 FERRET Brut Nature Cava NV $11.50 (9/30/87)
85 FERRET Brut Nature Cava Rosat 1984 $15 (5/31/88)
77 FREIXENET Blanc de Blancs Cava Extra Dry Seco NV $6.25 (5/31/88)
78 FREIXENET Brut Cava Carta Nevada NV $7 (12/31/90)
85 FREIXENET Brut Cava Carta Nevada NV $7 (5/31/88)
78 FREIXENET Brut Cava Cordon Negro NV $7.75 (12/31/90)
74 FREIXENET Brut Cava Cordon Negro NV $7.75 (5/31/88)
81 FREIXENET Brut Nature Cava 1985 $10 (12/31/90)
75 FREIXENET Brut Nature Cava 1984 $8.50 (5/31/88)
82 FREIXENET Brut Rosé Cava NV $7 (5/31/88)
71 FREIXENET Semi-Seco Cava Carta Nevada NV $7 (12/31/90)
84 FREIXENET Semi-Seco Cava Carta Nevada NV $7 (5/31/88)
74 JUVE Y CAMPS Brut Cava Grand Cru NV $12.50 (5/31/88)
79 JUVE Y CAMPS Brut Cava Natural Reserva de la Familia 1983 $10 (5/31/88)
80 JUVE Y CAMPS Brut Cava Natural Reserva de la Familia 1981 $10 (7/16/86)
85 LEMBEY Cava Première Cuvée 1985 $12 (7/15/91)
74 LEMBEY Brut Cava 1985 $6.50 (5/31/88)
70 LEMBEY Brut Cava 1984 $6.50 (5/31/88)
72 LEMBEY Brut Cava 1982 $6 (12/16/85) BB
79 LEMBEY Brut Cava Pedro Domecq 1986 $7.25 (7/15/90)
79 MARQUES DE MONISTROL Brut Blanc de Blancs Cava NV $7.25 (5/31/88)
78 MONT-MARCAL Brut Cava NV $8 (7/15/90)

86 MONT-MARCAL Brut Cava Gran Reserva NV $13 (5/31/88)
81 MONT-MARCAL Brut Cava Tradición NV $7 (5/31/88)
81 BODEGAS ONDARRE Brut Rioja Ondarre NV $11 (12/31/88)
83 ROVELLATS Brut Cava Imperial NV $13 (12/31/90)
78 ROVELLATS Brut Nature Cava Gran Reserva NV $17 (12/31/90)
78 SEGURA VIUDAS Brut Cava 1983 $7 (5/31/88)
87 SEGURA VIUDAS Brut Cava 1981 $7 (11/30/86) BB
72 SEGURA VIUDAS Brut Cava Reserva NV $6.50 (5/31/88)
74 SEGURA VIUDAS Brut Cava Reserva NV $6.50 (10/15/86) BB
81 SEGURA VIUDAS Brut Cava Reserva Heredad NV $12 (5/31/88)
73 SEGURA VIUDAS Brut Cava Reserva Heredad NV $12 (12/31/86)
70 SEGURA VIUDAS Brut Blanc de Blancs Cava NV $6.75 (5/31/88)
80 VALLFORMOSA Brut Cava NV $10 (12/31/90) BB
79 VALLFORMOSA Brut Cava NV $10 (10/15/88)
82 VALLFORMOSA Brut Penedès NV $7.50 (4/30/88)
79 VALLFORMOSA Brut Nature Cava NV $11 (12/31/90)
87 VALLFORMOSA Brut Nature Cava NV $11 (10/15/88)
82 XENIUS Cava NV $7.50 (7/15/90) BB
74 XIPELLA Blanc de Blancs Conca de Barbera 1988 $6 (3/31/90)

OTHER INTERNATIONAL
ARGENTINA

77   VALENTIN BIANCHI Cabernet Sauvignon Mendoza Elsa's Vineyard 1987 $7 (7/15/91)
76   VALENTIN BIANCHI Malbec Mendoza Elsa's Vineyard 1985 $6 (7/15/91)
68   FINCA FLICHMAN Cabernet Sauvignon Mendoza Caballero de la Cepa 1985 $8 (3/15/91)
81   FINCA FLICHMAN Cabernet Sauvignon Mendoza Proprietor's Private Reserve 1987 $6 (3/15/91) BB
78   FINCA FLICHMAN Chardonnay Mendoza Caballero de la Cepa 1990 $8 (7/15/91)
83   FINCA FLICHMAN Chardonnay Mendoza Proprietor's Private Reserve 1990 $6 (4/30/91) BB
66   FINCA FLICHMAN Mendoza Merlot Proprietor's Private Reserve 1988 $6 (3/15/91)
84   FINCA FLICHMAN Red Mendoza Argenta 1988 $4 (3/15/91) BB
79   FINCA FLICHMAN Red Mendoza Selection 1988 $4.50 (3/15/91) BB
76   FINCA FLICHMAN White Mendoza 1990 $4 (7/15/91)
79   FINCA FLICHMAN White Mendoza Selection Flichman 1990 $4.50 (7/15/91)
76   FOND DE CAVE Cabernet Sauvignon Mendoza 1982 $7 (2/15/89)
79   NAVARRO CORREAS Cabernet Sauvignon Mendoza 1981 $8.50 (2/15/89)
79   PASCUAL TOSO Cabernet Sauvignon Mendoza 1988 $7 (3/15/91)
81   TRAPICHE Cabernet Sauvignon Mendoza 1982 $4 (2/15/89) BB
77   TRAPICHE Cabernet Sauvignon Mendoza Reserve 1986 $5.50 (9/15/90)
69   TRAPICHE Cabernet Sauvignon Mendoza Vintner's Selection Oak Cask Reserve 1986 $8 (7/15/91)
78   TRAPICHE Chardonnay Mendoza Reserve 1989 $5.50 (9/15/90)
83   TRAPICHE Malbec Mendoza Reserve 1987 $5 (9/15/90) BB
74   TRAPICHE Malbec Mendoza Vintner's Selection Oak Cask Reserve 1988 $8 (7/15/91)

AUSTRIA

77   STEGENDORF Burgenland Kabinett 1985 $5 (8/31/87)

BRAZIL

78   MARCUS JAMES White Zinfandel Aurora Valley 1987 $4 (6/15/89)

BULGARIA

58   BALKAN CREST Cabernet Sauvignon Stara Zagora Oriahovitza Vineyards Reserve 1985 $6 (7/15/91)
79   BALKAN CREST Chardonnay Shoumen Khan Krum Vineyards Reserve 1987 $6 (7/15/91)

GREECE

78   ODYSSEY North Greece Cava Premium Dry 1981 $3.50 (12/15/87)

ISRAEL

69   CARMEL Cabernet Sauvignon Israel Galil 1981 $7 (6/30/87)
78   CARMEL Cabernet Sauvignon Samson 1986 $7.50 (3/31/91)
72   CARMEL Chenin Blanc Galil 1989 $6 (3/31/91)
75   GAMLA Cabernet Sauvignon Galil 1987 $9.50 (3/31/91)
83   GAMLA Cabernet Sauvignon Galil Special Reserve 1986 $12 (3/31/91)
66   GAMLA Chardonnay Galil Special Reserve 1988 $11 (3/31/91)
75   GAMLA Late Harvest Sauvignon Blanc Galil 1988 $14 (3/31/91)
75   GAMLA Sauvignon Blanc Galil 1988 $9 (3/31/91)
74   GAMLA Sauvignon Blanc Galil Special Reserve 1988 $10 (3/31/91)
85   GOLAN Cabernet Sauvignon Galil 1986 $11 (3/31/91)
72   GOLAN Sauvignon Blanc Galil 1988 $8 (3/31/91)
79   YARDEN Cabernet Sauvignon Galil 1986 $14 (6/30/90)
82   YARDEN Cabernet Sauvignon Galil 1985 $14 (6/30/90)
84   YARDEN Chardonnay Galil 1989 $10 (3/31/91)
77   YARDEN Merlot Galil Special Reserve 1988 $14 (3/31/91)
79   YARDEN Merlot Galil Special Reserve 1986 $12 (6/30/90)
70   YARDEN Mt. Hermon Red Galil 1989 $7 (3/31/91)
77   YARDEN Mt. Hermon White Galil 1989 $6 (3/31/91)
79   YARDEN Sauvignon Blanc Galil 1989 $9 (3/31/91)

LEBANON

86   CHATEAU MUSAR Lebanon 1983 $17 (7/15/91)
87   CHATEAU MUSAR Lebanon 1982 $15 (7/15/91)
84   CHATEAU MUSAR Lebanon 1981 $18 (7/15/91)
91   CHATEAU MUSAR Lebanon 1980 Rel: $11 Cur: $18 (7/31/88)

MADEIRA

78   BLANDYS Rainwater NV $6.99 (6/01/85)

MEXICO

82   SAN MARTIN Petite Sirah Baja California International Series 1987 $4 (8/31/90) BB
73   PINSON Chardonnay 1987 $4.50 (6/30/90)

NEW ZEALAND

74   BABICH Cabernet Sauvignon Hawke's Bay 1989 $10 (7/15/91)
88   BABICH Chardonnay Hawke's Bay Irongate 1989 $17 (3/31/91)
86   BABICH Chardonnay Henderson Valley 1986 $10 (5/15/88)
84   BABICH Sauvignon Blanc Hawke's Bay 1986 $11 (5/15/88)
92   CORBANS Chardonnay Marlborough 1986 $10 (5/15/88)
87   CORBANS Sauvignon Blanc Marlborough 1986 $10 (5/15/88)
73   GOLDWATER ESTATE Cabernet Merlot Franc Waiheke Island 1985 $27 (7/15/88)
82   HOUSE OF NOBILO Pinotage Huapai Valley (Pinot Noir Clone) 1988 $15 (7/15/91)
87   HUNTER'S Chardonnay Marlborough 1986 $13 (2/15/88)
88   HUNTER'S Chardonnay Marlborough 1985 $9.25 (3/15/87)
80   HUNTER'S Müller-Thurgau Marlborough 1986 $6.50 (4/30/87)
71   HUNTER'S Sauvignon Blanc Marlborough 1986 $8.50 (2/15/88)
87   KUMEU RIVER Merlot Cabernet Kumeu 1987 $18 (12/31/90)
91   KUMEU RIVER Chardonnay Kumeu 1989 $27 (12/31/90)
93   KUMEU RIVER Chardonnay Kumeu 1987 $29 (3/31/89)
82   LONGRIDGE Chardonnay Hawke's Bay 1989 $10 (7/15/91)
83   MORTON Chardonnay Hawke's Bay 1990 $10 (7/15/91)
78   MORTON Chardonnay Hawke's Bay Winemaker's Selection 1988 $13 (7/15/91)
90   MORTON Chardonnay Hawke's Bay Winemaker's Selection 1986 $12 (2/15/88)
90   MORTON Chardonnay New Zealand Winery Reserve 1986 $38 (5/15/88)
82   MORTON Sauvignon Blanc Hawke's Bay Winemaker's Selection 1987 $9 (2/15/88)
78   NAUTILUS Sauvignon Blanc Hawke's Bay 1986 $11.50 (2/15/88)
86   STONELEIGH Chardonnay Marlborough 1989 $11 (7/15/91)
74   VILLA MARIA Cabernet Sauvignon Auckland Reserve 1986 $30 (7/15/88)

ROMANIA

55   PREMIAT Brut Transylvania Méthode Champenoise NV $6 (6/01/86)

YUGOSLAVIA

77   AVIA Cabernet Sauvignon Yugoslavia Primorska Region 1985 $3 (3/31/89)
75   AVIA Merlot Yugoslavia Primorska Hrvatska-Istria 1985 $3 (3/31/89)
81   CANTERBURY Cabernet Sauvignon Yugoslavia Istria 1985 $5.50 (9/30/89) BB
64   LE SABLE Cabernet Sauvignon Primorska Region 1986 $4.50 (3/31/91)
70   LE SABLE Pinot Noir Oplenac 1987 $4.50 (3/31/91)

UNITED STATES
CALIFORNIA/BLUSH

74   BANDIERA White Zinfandel California 1988 $5.25 (6/15/89)
70   BANDIERA White Zinfandel North Coast 1986 $4 (3/31/87)
79   BARON HERZOG White Zinfandel California 1989 $7 (3/31/91)
80   BARON HERZOG White Zinfandel California 1988 $6 (6/15/89)
72   WILLIAM BATES White Zinfandel California 1988 $4 (6/15/89)
83   BEL ARBRES White Zinfandel California 1988 $5.25 (6/15/89)
84   BEL ARBRES White Zinfandel California 1986 $5 (3/31/87)
78   BELVEDERE White Zinfandel California Discovery Series 1988 $4 (6/15/89)
70   BELVEDERE White Zinfandel California Discovery Series 1985 $3.25 (2/16/86)
72   BERINGER White Zinfandel North Coast 1988 $7.50 (6/15/89)
79   BLOSSOM HILL White Zinfandel California 1988 $7/1.5L (6/15/89)
65   BOEGER White Zinfandel El Dorado 1988 $7.50 (6/15/89)
84   BONNY DOON Vin Gris de Cigare California 1990 $7 (7/15/91) BB
78   BONNY DOON Vin Gris de Cigare California 1989 $7.50 (10/31/90)
89   BONNY DOON Vin Gris de Cigare California 1988 $6.75 (7/31/89) BB
84   BONNY DOON Vin Gris de Cigare California 1987 $6.50 (4/15/89)
69   BRUTOCAO White Zinfandel Mendocino 1987 $7 (6/15/89)
88   BUEHLER White Zinfandel Napa Valley 1988 $6 (6/15/89)
65   BUEHLER White Zinfandel Napa Valley 1986 $5.50 (3/31/87)
85   BUEHLER White Zinfandel Napa Valley 1985 $8 (2/16/86)
82   BUENA VISTA Pinot Noir Blanc Carneros 1986 $4.75 (10/31/87) BB
85   BUENA VISTA Pinot Noir Blanc Carneros Steelhead Run 1985 $5.50 (7/01/86) BB
67   CASTORO White Zinfandel San Luis Obispo 1988 $6 (6/15/89)
77   CHATEAU SOUVERAIN White Zinfandel California 1988 $5.75 (6/15/89)
77   CHRISTIAN BROTHERS White Zinfandel Napa Valley 1988 $5.50 (6/15/89)
68   CHRISTIAN BROTHERS White Zinfandel Napa Valley 1986 $5 (3/31/87)
86   CRESTON MANOR White Zinfandel San Luis Obispo 1988 $7 (6/15/89)
77   DE LOACH White Zinfandel Russian River Valley 1990 $7.50 (3/31/91)
82   DE LOACH White Zinfandel Russian River Valley 1988 $7.50 (6/15/89)
73   DE LOACH White Zinfandel Russian River Valley 1986 $6 (3/31/87)
81   DE LOACH White Zinfandel Russian River Valley 1985 $5.50 (4/16/86)
73   DELICATO White Zinfandel California 1988 $5.25 (6/15/89)
67   DOMAINE SAN MARTIN White Zinfandel Central Coast 1985 $4 (3/31/87)
80   FENESTRA White Zinfandel Livermore Valley 1987 $5 (6/15/89)
85   FETZER White Zinfandel California 1988 $7 (6/15/89)
74   FIRESTONE Rosé of Cabernet Sauvignon Santa Ynez Valley 1984 $4.50 (2/01/86)
79   E.&J. GALLO White Zinfandel California 1988 $5 (6/15/89)
72   E.&J. GALLO White Zinfandel California 1987 $3.50 (4/15/89)
75   GARLAND RANCH White Zinfandel Monterey 1987 $6 (6/15/89)
80   GLEN ELLEN White Zinfandel California Proprietor's Reserve 1989 $5 (12/31/90)
84   GLEN ELLEN White Zinfandel California Proprietor's Reserve 1988 $5.75 (6/15/89)
73   GLEN ELLEN White Zinfandel California Proprietor's Reserve 1985 $4 (2/16/86)
73   GRAND CRU White Zinfandel California 1988 $5 (6/15/89)
74   HAGAFEN Pinot Noir Blanc California 1989 $6 (3/31/91)
88   HOP KILN White Zinfandel Russian River Valley 1988 $6.75 (6/15/89)
69   INGLENOOK-NAVELLE White Zinfandel California NV $7.50/1.5L (6/15/89)
76   KARLY White Zinfandel Amador County 1988 $7 (6/15/89)
86   KENWOOD White Zinfandel Sonoma Valley 1988 $6.75 (6/15/89)
80   KENWOOD White Zinfandel Sonoma Valley 1986 $5.75 (3/31/87)
72   CHARLES KRUG White Zinfandel North Coast 1988 $6 (6/15/89)
70   LA CREMA Pinot Noir Blanc California Vin Gris 1986 $8 (10/31/87)
61   CHARLES LEFRANC White Zinfandel California 1985 $5 (5/01/86)
61   LOS HERMANOS White Zinfandel California 1988 $8/1.5L (6/15/89)
76   MADRONA White Zinfandel El Dorado 1988 $5.25 (6/15/89)
77   MANISCHEWITZ White Zinfandel Sonoma County 1989 $6 (3/31/91)
81   LOUIS M. MARTINI White Zinfandel Napa Valley 1988 $5.50 (6/15/89)
74   PAUL MASSON White Zinfandel California 1988 $7/1.5L (6/15/89)
82   MCDOWELL Grenache Rosé McDowell Valley Les Vieux Cépages 1990 $7.50 (6/15/91) BB
82   MCDOWELL Grenache Rosé McDowell Valley Les Vieux Cépages 1989 $6.50 (10/31/90) BB
75   MIRASSOU White Zinfandel California 1988 $6.50 (6/15/89)
85   CK MONDAVI White Zinfandel California 1988 $5.25 (6/15/89)
80   ROBERT MONDAVI Rosé California 1986 $5 (3/31/87)
80   ROBERT MONDAVI White Zinfandel California 1988 $5.50 (6/15/89)
78   ROBERT MONDAVI White Zinfandel California 1986 $4 (10/31/87)
74   ROBERT MONDAVI White Zinfandel California 1985 $3.75 (9/30/86)
69   ROBERT MONDAVI White Zinfandel California 1985 $5.75 (6/16/86)
63   MONTEVINA White Zinfandel Shenandoah Valley 1985 $5 (2/16/86)
73   J.W. MORRIS White Zinfandel California 1988 $5 (6/15/89)
75   NAPA RIDGE White Zinfandel Lodi 1988 $6 (6/15/89)
68   NORTH COAST CELLARS White Zinfandel North Coast 1987 $6 (6/15/89)
87   J. PEDRONCELLI White Zinfandel Sonoma County 1988 $6 (6/15/89)
82   J. PEDRONCELLI White Zinfandel Sonoma County 1986 $4.50 (3/31/87)
80   J. PEDRONCELLI White Zinfandel Sonoma County 1985 $3.50 (7/16/86)
83   J. PEDRONCELLI White Zinfandel Sonoma County 1985 $4.50 (2/16/86) BB
87   JOSEPH PHELPS Grenache Rosé California Vin du Mistral 1990 $9 (6/15/91) BB
84   JOSEPH PHELPS Grenache Rosé California Vin du Mistral 1989 $9 (11/30/90)
66   REDWOOD VALLEY White Zinfandel California 1987 $6/1.5L (6/15/89)
80   RIVERSIDE FARM White Zinfandel California 1988 $5.25 (6/15/89)
87   SANTINO White Zinfandel Amador County 1988 $5 (6/15/89)
70   SAUSAL White Zinfandel Alexander Valley 1988 $6 (6/15/89)
65   AUGUST SEBASTIANI White Zinfandel California 1988 $7.50/1.5L (6/15/89)
69   SEBASTIANI White Zinfandel California 1988 $5 (6/15/89)
84   SEGHESIO White Zinfandel Northern Sonoma 1988 $5.50 (6/15/89)
70   CHARLES SHAW Gamay Blanc Napa Valley 1986 $4.50 (3/31/87)

81   SHENANDOAH White Zinfandel Amador County 1988 $6 (6/15/89)
82   SHENANDOAH White Zinfandel Amador County 1986 $5 (3/31/87)
81   SIMI Rosé of Cabernet Sauvignon Sonoma County 1988 $7 (11/15/89)
81   SIMI Rosé of Cabernet Sauvignon Sonoma County 1985 $7 (7/16/86)
78   ST. FRANCIS Pinot Noir Blanc Sonoma Valley 1986 $5.50 (10/31/87)
86   STERLING Cabernet Blanc Napa Valley 1985 $6.25 (4/01/86)
84   STEVENOT White Zinfandel Amador County 1989 $5 (12/31/90) BB
77   SUTTER HOME White Zinfandel California 1990 $5.50 (3/31/91)
68   SUTTER HOME White Zinfandel California 1989 $4.50 (12/31/90)
77   SUTTER HOME White Zinfandel California 1988 $5.25 (6/15/89)
70   SUTTER HOME White Zinfandel California 1986 $4.75 (3/31/87)
62   SUTTER HOME White Zinfandel California 1985 $4.50 (2/16/86)
85   IVAN TAMAS White Zinfandel Mendocino 1988 $5.75 (6/15/89)
80   VENTANA White Zinfandel Monterey Primrose Ventana Vineyards 1986 $5 (10/31/87)
65   WEIBEL White Zinfandel Mendocino 1988 $5 (6/15/89)
75   WEINSTOCK White Zinfandel Sonoma County 1989 $8 (3/31/91)
84   WILLIAM WHEELER White Zinfandel Sonoma County Young Vines 1988 $6 (6/15/89)
83   WILLIAM WHEELER White Zinfandel Sonoma County Young Vines 1986 $5.50 (3/31/87)
80   ZACA MESA White Zinfandel Santa Barbara County 1985 $5.50 (3/31/87)

CABERNET FRANC

76   AUSTIN Cabernet Franc Santa Barbara County 1988 $12 (11/15/90)
85   CHATEAU CHEVRE Cabernet Franc Napa Valley 1985 $16 (7/31/88)
88   CONGRESS SPRINGS Cabernet Franc Santa Cruz Mountains 1986 $18 (7/31/89)
75   COSENTINO Cabernet Franc Napa County 1987 $12.50 (9/30/89)
85+   COSENTINO Cabernet Franc North Coast 1987 $12.50 (4/15/89) (BT)
92   COSENTINO Cabernet Franc North Coast 1986 $14 (7/31/88)
90+   COSENTINO Cabernet Franc North Coast 1986 $14 (4/15/88) (BT)
84   DEHLINGER Cabernet Franc Russian River Valley 1988 $13 (4/30/91)
70   GUENOC Cabernet Franc Lake County 1985 $15 (2/15/89)
89   GUNDLACH BUNDSCHU Cabernet Franc Sonoma Valley Rhinefarm Vineyards 1987 $12 (9/15/90)
85+   IRON HORSE Cabernet Franc Alexander Valley 1987 (NR) (4/15/91) (BT)
83   KONOCTI Cabernet Franc Lake County 1988 $9.50 (2/28/91)
81   LA JOTA Cabernet Franc Howell Mountain 1986 $25 (10/15/89)
79   NELSON ESTATE Cabernet Franc Sonoma County 1987 $16 (4/30/91)
79   NEYERS Cabernet Franc Napa Valley 1987 $16 (11/15/90)
77   SEBASTIANI ESTATES Cabernet Franc California 1988 $8.50 (7/15/91)
88   WHITEHALL LANE Cabernet Franc Napa Valley 1988 $18.50 (11/15/90)

CABERNET SAUVIGNON & BLENDS

89   ABREU Cabernet Sauvignon Napa Valley Madrona Ranch 1987 $25 (7/31/91)
75   ACACIA Cabernet Sauvignon Napa Valley 1984 $15 (12/15/86)
89   ADELAIDA Cabernet Sauvignon Paso Robles 1987 $14 (2/28/91)
75   ADELAIDA Cabernet Sauvignon Paso Robles 1983 $12 (12/15/89)
88   ADELAIDA Cabernet Sauvignon Paso Robles 1981 $7.25 (3/01/84)
74   ADLER FELS Cabernet Sauvignon Napa Valley 1980 $10 (10/01/84)
90+   ALEXANDER VALLEY Cabernet Sauvignon Alexander Valley 1990 (NR) (5/15/91) (BT)
85+   ALEXANDER VALLEY Cabernet Sauvignon Alexander Valley 1989 (NR) (5/15/91) (BT)
90+   ALEXANDER VALLEY Cabernet Sauvignon Alexander Valley 1988 $12 (4/30/90) (BT)
87   ALEXANDER VALLEY Cabernet Sauvignon Alexander Valley 1987 Rel: $12 Cur: $13 (5/31/90)
88   ALEXANDER VALLEY Cabernet Sauvignon Alexander Valley 1986 Rel: $11.50 Cur: $12 (CA-3/89)
89   ALEXANDER VALLEY Cabernet Sauvignon Alexander Valley 1986 Rel: $11.50 Cur: $12 (12/31/88)
85+   ALEXANDER VALLEY Cabernet Sauvignon Alexander Valley 1986 Rel: $11.50 Cur: $12 (4/15/88) (BT)
88   ALEXANDER VALLEY Cabernet Sauvignon Alexander Valley 1985 Rel: $11 Cur: $15 (CA-3/89)
92   ALEXANDER VALLEY Cabernet Sauvignon Alexander Valley 1985 Rel: $11 Cur: $15 (11/15/87)
92   ALEXANDER VALLEY Cabernet Sauvignon Alexander Valley 1984 Rel: $10.50 Cur: $18 (CA-3/89)
93   ALEXANDER VALLEY Cabernet Sauvignon Alexander Valley 1984 Rel: $10.50 Cur: $18 (5/15/87) SS
90   ALEXANDER VALLEY Cabernet Sauvignon Alexander Valley 1983 Rel: $10.50 Cur: $18 (CA-3/89)
87   ALEXANDER VALLEY Cabernet Sauvignon Alexander Valley 1983 Rel: $10.50 Cur: $18 (1/01/86)
90   ALEXANDER VALLEY Cabernet Sauvignon Alexander Valley 1982 Rel: $10 Cur: $16 (CA-3/89)
84   ALEXANDER VALLEY Cabernet Sauvignon Alexander Valley 1982 Rel: $10 Cur: $16 (2/01/85)
92   ALEXANDER VALLEY Cabernet Sauvignon Alexander Valley 1982 Rel: $10 Cur: $16 (11/01/84) SS
87   ALEXANDER VALLEY Cabernet Sauvignon Alexander Valley 1981 Rel: $9 Cur: $18 (CA-3/89)
89   ALEXANDER VALLEY Cabernet Sauvignon Alexander Valley 1981 Rel: $9 Cur: $18 (2/01/86)
89   ALEXANDER VALLEY Cabernet Sauvignon Alexander Valley 1981 Rel: $9 Cur: $18 (2/01/85)
83   ALEXANDER VALLEY Cabernet Sauvignon Alexander Valley 1980 Rel: $9 Cur: $16 (CA-3/89)
80   ALEXANDER VALLEY Cabernet Sauvignon Alexander Valley 1980 Rel: $9 Cur: $16 (2/01/86)
80   ALEXANDER VALLEY Cabernet Sauvignon Alexander Valley 1980 Rel: $9 Cur: $16 (2/01/85)
86   ALEXANDER VALLEY Cabernet Sauvignon Alexander Valley 1979 Rel: $7 Cur: $18 (CA-3/89)
84   ALEXANDER VALLEY Cabernet Sauvignon Alexander Valley 1979 Rel: $7 Cur: $18 (2/01/86)
84   ALEXANDER VALLEY Cabernet Sauvignon Alexander Valley 1979 Rel: $7 Cur: $18 (2/01/85)
80   ALEXANDER VALLEY Cabernet Sauvignon Alexander Valley 1978 Rel: $6.50 Cur: $20 (CA-3/89)
88   ALEXANDER VALLEY Cabernet Sauvignon Alexander Valley 1978 Rel: $6.50 Cur: $20 (2/01/86)
88   ALEXANDER VALLEY Cabernet Sauvignon Alexander Valley 1978 Rel: $6.50 Cur: $20 (2/01/85)

60   ALEXANDER VALLEY Cabernet Sauvignon Alexander Valley 1976 Rel: $5.50 Cur: $18 (CA-3/89)

75   ALEXANDER VALLEY Cabernet Sauvignon Alexander Valley 1975 Rel: $5.50 Cur: $20 (CA-3/89)

80   ALMADEN Cabernet Sauvignon Monterey County 1981 $5.85 (7/01/84)
      ALMADEN Cabernet Sauvignon Monterey County 1979 $5.50 (8/01/82) SS

74   ALMADEN Cabernet Sauvignon Monterey County Vintage Classic Selection 1983 $5 (10/15/87)

70   AMIZETTA Cabernet Sauvignon Napa Valley 1985 $16 (5/31/88)

90+ S. ANDERSON Cabernet Sauvignon Napa Valley Stags Leap District Richard Chambers Vineyard 1990 (NR) (5/15/91) (BT)

90+ S. ANDERSON Cabernet Sauvignon Napa Valley Stags Leap District Richard Chambers Vineyard 1989 (NR) (5/15/91) (BT)

80   ARCIERO Cabernet Sauvignon Paso Robles 1986 $9 (11/15/90)

79   ARCIERO Cabernet Sauvignon Paso Robles 1986 $9 (12/31/89)

77   ARCIERO Cabernet Sauvignon Paso Robles 1985 $6 (12/31/87)

87   ARROWOOD Cabernet Sauvignon Sonoma County 1987 $22 (11/15/90)

85+ ARROWOOD Cabernet Sauvignon Sonoma County 1987 $22 (4/15/89) (BT)

92   ARROWOOD Cabernet Sauvignon Sonoma County 1986 Rel: $20 Cur: $24 (10/15/89)

90+ ARROWOOD Cabernet Sauvignon Sonoma County 1986 Rel: $20 Cur: $24 (4/15/88) (BT)

94   ARROWOOD Cabernet Sauvignon Sonoma County 1985 Rel: $19 Cur: $25 (12/15/88)

91   VINCENT ARROYO Cabernet Sauvignon Napa Valley 1987 $12 (11/15/90)

77   AUDUBON Cabernet Sauvignon Napa Valley 1985 $11 (6/15/88)

74   AUSTIN A Genoux Santa Barbara County 1986 $15 (12/15/89)

86   BALDINELLI Cabernet Sauvignon Shenandoah Valley 1983 $7.75 (11/30/88)

86   BALVERNE Cabernet Sauvignon Chalk Hill Laurel Vineyard 1983 $13 (2/15/89)

88   BALVERNE Cabernet Sauvignon Sonoma County 1982 $12 (8/31/88)

85   BANDIERA Cabernet Sauvignon Napa Valley 1986 $6.50 (10/31/89) BB

79   LAWRENCE J. BARGETTO Cabernet Sauvignon Sonoma County Cypress 1985 $8.50 (11/15/89)

73   BARON HERZOG Cabernet Sauvignon Sonoma County 1989 $11 (3/31/91)

74   BARON HERZOG Cabernet Sauvignon Sonoma County Special Reserve 1986 $16 (3/31/91)

83   BARON HERZOG Cabernet Sauvignon Sonoma County Special Reserve 1986 $14 (11/15/89)

79   BEAULIEU Cabernet Sauvignon Napa Valley Beau Tour 1988 $7 (9/30/90)

81   BEAULIEU Cabernet Sauvignon Napa Valley Beau Tour 1987 $8 (5/31/89) BB

83   BEAULIEU Cabernet Sauvignon Napa Valley Beau Tour 1986 $7 (10/31/88)

83   BEAULIEU Cabernet Sauvignon Napa Valley Beau Tour 1985 $7 (6/15/88)

64   BEAULIEU Cabernet Sauvignon Napa Valley Beau Tour 1982 $7.50 (10/15/86)

85+ BEAULIEU Cabernet Sauvignon Napa Valley Georges de Latour Private Reserve 1990 (NR) (5/15/91) (BT)

85+ BEAULIEU Cabernet Sauvignon Napa Valley Georges de Latour Private Reserve 1989 (NR) (5/15/91) (BT)

90+ BEAULIEU Cabernet Sauvignon Napa Valley Georges de Latour Private Reserve 1987 $35 (4/15/89) (BT)

93   BEAULIEU Cabernet Sauvignon Napa Valley Georges de Latour Private Reserve 1986 Rel: $31 Cur: $39 (3/31/91) (JL)

89   BEAULIEU Cabernet Sauvignon Napa Valley Georges de Latour Private Reserve 1986 Rel: $31 Cur: $39 (11/15/90)

93   BEAULIEU Cabernet Sauvignon Napa Valley Georges de Latour Private Reserve 1986 Rel: $31 Cur: $39 (CA-3/89)

95   BEAULIEU Cabernet Sauvignon Napa Valley Georges de Latour Private Reserve 1985 Rel: $25 Cur: $29 (3/31/91) (JL)

91   BEAULIEU Cabernet Sauvignon Napa Valley Georges de Latour Private Reserve 1985 Rel: $25 Cur: $29 (12/31/89)

95   BEAULIEU Cabernet Sauvignon Napa Valley Georges de Latour Private Reserve 1985 Rel: $25 Cur: $29 (CA-3/89)

85+ BEAULIEU Cabernet Sauvignon Napa Valley Georges de Latour Private Reserve 1985 Rel: $25 Cur: $29 (6/15/87) (BT)

92   BEAULIEU Cabernet Sauvignon Napa Valley Georges de Latour Private Reserve 1984 Rel: $25 Cur: $28 (3/31/91) (JL)

91   BEAULIEU Cabernet Sauvignon Napa Valley Georges de Latour Private Reserve 1984 Rel: $25 Cur: $28 (CA-3/89)

91   BEAULIEU Cabernet Sauvignon Napa Valley Georges de Latour Private Reserve 1984 Rel: $25 Cur: $28 (12/31/88)

82   BEAULIEU Cabernet Sauvignon Napa Valley Georges de Latour Private Reserve 1983 Rel: $24 Cur: $28 (3/31/91) (JL)

82   BEAULIEU Cabernet Sauvignon Napa Valley Georges de Latour Private Reserve 1983 Rel: $24 Cur: $28 (CA-3/89)

77   BEAULIEU Cabernet Sauvignon Napa Valley Georges de Latour Private Reserve 1983 Rel: $24 Cur: $28 (5/31/88)

90   BEAULIEU Cabernet Sauvignon Napa Valley Georges de Latour Private Reserve 1982 Rel: $24 Cur: $39 (3/31/91) (JL)

88   BEAULIEU Cabernet Sauvignon Napa Valley Georges de Latour Private Reserve 1982 Rel: $24 Cur: $39 (CA-3/89)

93   BEAULIEU Cabernet Sauvignon Napa Valley Georges de Latour Private Reserve 1982 Rel: $24 Cur: $39 (3/15/87) CS

86   BEAULIEU Cabernet Sauvignon Napa Valley Georges de Latour Private Reserve 1981 Rel: $24 Cur: $36 (3/31/91) (JL)

87   BEAULIEU Cabernet Sauvignon Napa Valley Georges de Latour Private Reserve 1981 Rel: $24 Cur: $36 (CA-3/89)

80   BEAULIEU Cabernet Sauvignon Napa Valley Georges de Latour Private Reserve 1981 Rel: $24 Cur: $36 (8/31/86)

93   BEAULIEU Cabernet Sauvignon Napa Valley Georges de Latour Private Reserve 1980 Rel: $24 Cur: $48 (3/31/91) (JL)

93   BEAULIEU Cabernet Sauvignon Napa Valley Georges de Latour Private Reserve 1980 Rel: $24 Cur: $48 (CA-3/89)

93   BEAULIEU Cabernet Sauvignon Napa Valley Georges de Latour Private Reserve 1980 Rel: $24 Cur: $48 (9/16/85) SS

87   BEAULIEU Cabernet Sauvignon Napa Valley Georges de Latour Private Reserve 1979 Rel: $21 Cur: $53 (3/31/91) (JL)

90   BEAULIEU Cabernet Sauvignon Napa Valley Georges de Latour Private Reserve 1979 Rel: $21 Cur: $53 (CA-3/89)

93   BEAULIEU Cabernet Sauvignon Napa Valley Georges de Latour Private Reserve 1979 Rel: $21 Cur: $53 (3/01/84) SS

90   BEAULIEU Cabernet Sauvignon Napa Valley Georges de Latour Private Reserve 1978 Rel: $19 Cur: $57 (3/31/91) (JL)

91   BEAULIEU Cabernet Sauvignon Napa Valley Georges de Latour Private Reserve 1978 Rel: $19 Cur: $57 (CA-3/89)

92   BEAULIEU Cabernet Sauvignon Napa Valley Georges de Latour Private Reserve 1978 Rel: $19 Cur: $57 (4/30/87)

79   BEAULIEU Cabernet Sauvignon Napa Valley Georges de Latour Private Reserve 1977 Rel: $16 Cur: $46 (3/31/91) (JL)

79   BEAULIEU Cabernet Sauvignon Napa Valley Georges de Latour Private Reserve 1977 Rel: $16 Cur: $46 (CA-3/89)

88   BEAULIEU Cabernet Sauvignon Napa Valley Georges de Latour Private Reserve 1976 Rel: $19 Cur: $60 (3/31/91) (JL)

86   BEAULIEU Cabernet Sauvignon Napa Valley Georges de Latour Private Reserve 1976 Rel: $19 Cur: $60 (CA-3/89)

90   BEAULIEU Cabernet Sauvignon Napa Valley Georges de Latour Private Reserve 1976 Rel: $19 Cur: $60 (6/01/85) (JL)

83   BEAULIEU Cabernet Sauvignon Napa Valley Georges de Latour Private Reserve 1975 Rel: $16 Cur: $57 (3/31/91) (JL)

79   BEAULIEU Cabernet Sauvignon Napa Valley Georges de Latour Private Reserve 1975 Rel: $16 Cur: $57 (CA-3/89)

79   BEAULIEU Cabernet Sauvignon Napa Valley Georges de Latour Private Reserve 1974 Rel: $12 Cur: $81 (3/31/91) (JL)

87   BEAULIEU Cabernet Sauvignon Napa Valley Georges de Latour Private Reserve 1974 Rel: $12 Cur: $81 (2/15/90) (JG)

79   BEAULIEU Cabernet Sauvignon Napa Valley Georges de Latour Private Reserve 1974 Rel: $12 Cur: $81 (CA-3/89)

91   BEAULIEU Cabernet Sauvignon Napa Valley Georges de Latour Private Reserve 1974 Rel: $12 Cur: $81 (6/01/85) (JL)

75   BEAULIEU Cabernet Sauvignon Napa Valley Georges de Latour Private Reserve 1973 Rel: $9 Cur: $55 (3/31/91) (JL)

79   BEAULIEU Cabernet Sauvignon Napa Valley Georges de Latour Private Reserve 1973 Rel: $9 Cur: $55 (CA-3/89)

71   BEAULIEU Cabernet Sauvignon Napa Valley Georges de Latour Private Reserve 1972 Rel: $6 Cur: $45 (3/31/91) (JL)

73   BEAULIEU Cabernet Sauvignon Napa Valley Georges de Latour Private Reserve 1972 Rel: $6 Cur: $45 (CA-3/89)

79   BEAULIEU Cabernet Sauvignon Napa Valley Georges de Latour Private Reserve 1971 Rel: $8 Cur: $60 (3/31/91) (JL)

67   BEAULIEU Cabernet Sauvignon Napa Valley Georges de Latour Private Reserve 1971 Rel: $8 Cur: $60 (CA-3/89)

93   BEAULIEU Cabernet Sauvignon Napa Valley Georges de Latour Private Reserve 1970 Rel: $8 Cur: $130 (3/31/91) (JL)

95   BEAULIEU Cabernet Sauvignon Napa Valley Georges de Latour Private Reserve 1970 Rel: $8 Cur: $130 (CA-3/89)

95   BEAULIEU Cabernet Sauvignon Napa Valley Georges de Latour Private Reserve 1970 Rel: $8 Cur: $130 (6/01/85) (JL)

92   BEAULIEU Cabernet Sauvignon Napa Valley Georges de Latour Private Reserve 1969 Rel: $6.50 Cur: $100 (3/31/91) (JL)

90   BEAULIEU Cabernet Sauvignon Napa Valley Georges de Latour Private Reserve 1969 Rel: $6.50 Cur: $100 (CA-3/89)

92   BEAULIEU Cabernet Sauvignon Napa Valley Georges de Latour Private Reserve 1968 Rel: $6 Cur: $153 (3/31/91) (JL)

91   BEAULIEU Cabernet Sauvignon Napa Valley Georges de Latour Private Reserve 1968 Rel: $6 Cur: $153 (CA-3/89)

93   BEAULIEU Cabernet Sauvignon Napa Valley Georges de Latour Private Reserve 1968 Rel: $6 Cur: $153 (6/01/85) (JL)

82   BEAULIEU Cabernet Sauvignon Napa Valley Georges de Latour Private Reserve 1967 Rel: $5.25 Cur: $110 (3/31/91) (JL)

85   BEAULIEU Cabernet Sauvignon Napa Valley Georges de Latour Private Reserve 1967 Rel: $5.25 Cur: $110 (CA-3/89)

87   BEAULIEU Cabernet Sauvignon Napa Valley Georges de Latour Private Reserve 1966 Rel: $5.25 Cur: $145 (3/31/91) (JL)

87   BEAULIEU Cabernet Sauvignon Napa Valley Georges de Latour Private Reserve 1966 Rel: $5.25 Cur: $145 (CA-3/89)

91   BEAULIEU Cabernet Sauvignon Napa Valley Georges de Latour Private Reserve 1966 Rel: $5.25 Cur: $145 (6/01/85) (JL)

77   BEAULIEU Cabernet Sauvignon Napa Valley Georges de Latour Private Reserve 1965 Rel: $5.25 Cur: $130 (3/31/91) (JL)

85   BEAULIEU Cabernet Sauvignon Napa Valley Georges de Latour Private Reserve 1965 Rel: $5.25 Cur: $130 (CA-3/89)

72   BEAULIEU Cabernet Sauvignon Napa Valley Georges de Latour Private Reserve 1964 Rel: $4.25 Cur: $145 (3/31/91) (JL)

84   BEAULIEU Cabernet Sauvignon Napa Valley Georges de Latour Private Reserve 1964 Rel: $4.25 Cur: $145 (CA-3/89)

74   BEAULIEU Cabernet Sauvignon Napa Valley Georges de Latour Private Reserve 1963 Rel: $3.50 Cur: $120 (3/31/91) (JL)

70   BEAULIEU Cabernet Sauvignon Napa Valley Georges de Latour Private Reserve 1963 Rel: $3.50 Cur: $120 (CA-3/89)

75   BEAULIEU Cabernet Sauvignon Napa Valley Georges de Latour Private Reserve 1962 Rel: $3.50 Cur: $125 (3/31/91) (JL)

73   BEAULIEU Cabernet Sauvignon Napa Valley Georges de Latour Private Reserve 1962 Rel: $3.50 Cur: $125 (CA-3/89)

77   BEAULIEU Cabernet Sauvignon Napa Valley Georges de Latour Private Reserve 1961 Rel: $3.50 Cur: $210 (3/31/91) (JL)

78   BEAULIEU Cabernet Sauvignon Napa Valley Georges de Latour Private Reserve 1961 Rel: $3.50 Cur: $210 (CA-3/89)

85   BEAULIEU Cabernet Sauvignon Napa Valley Georges de Latour Private Reserve 1960 Rel: $3.50 Cur: $150 (3/31/91) (JL)

89   BEAULIEU Cabernet Sauvignon Napa Valley Georges de Latour Private Reserve 1959 Rel: $3.50 Cur: $340 (3/31/91) (JL)

89   BEAULIEU Cabernet Sauvignon Napa Valley Georges de Latour Private Reserve 1959 Rel: $3.50 Cur: $340 (CA-3/89)

97   BEAULIEU Cabernet Sauvignon Napa Valley Georges de Latour Private Reserve 1958 Rel: $3 Cur: $490 (3/31/91) (JL)

96   BEAULIEU Cabernet Sauvignon Napa Valley Georges de Latour Private Reserve 1958 Rel: $3 Cur: $490 (CA-3/89)

86   BEAULIEU Cabernet Sauvignon Napa Valley Georges de Latour Private Reserve 1958 Rel: $3 Cur: $490 (2/28/87) (JL)

69   BEAULIEU Cabernet Sauvignon Napa Valley Georges de Latour Private Reserve 1957 Rel: $2.50 Cur: $240 (3/31/91) (JL)

88   BEAULIEU Cabernet Sauvignon Napa Valley Georges de Latour Private Reserve 1956 Rel: $2.50 Cur: $600 (3/31/91) (JL)

88   BEAULIEU Cabernet Sauvignon Napa Valley Georges de Latour Private Reserve 1956 Rel: $2.50 Cur: $600 (CA-3/89)

85   BEAULIEU Cabernet Sauvignon Napa Valley Georges de Latour Private Reserve 1955 Rel: $2.50 Cur: $550 (3/31/91) (JL)

UNITED STATES
CALIFORNIA/*CABERNET SAUVIGNON & BLENDS*

86 BEAULIEU Cabernet Sauvignon Napa Valley Georges de Latour Private Reserve 1954 Rel: $2.50 Cur: $330 (3/31/91) (JL)

91 BEAULIEU Cabernet Sauvignon Napa Valley Georges de Latour Private Reserve 1953 Rel: $2.50 Cur: $600 (3/31/91) (JL)

91 BEAULIEU Cabernet Sauvignon Napa Valley Georges de Latour Private Reserve 1952 Rel: $2.50 Cur: $600 (3/31/91) (JL)

92 BEAULIEU Cabernet Sauvignon Napa Valley Georges de Latour Private Reserve 1951 Rel: $1.82 Cur: $1,000 (3/31/91) (JL)

90 BEAULIEU Cabernet Sauvignon Napa Valley Georges de Latour Private Reserve 1951 Rel: $1.82 Cur: $1,000 (CA-3/89)

98 BEAULIEU Cabernet Sauvignon Napa Valley Georges de Latour Private Reserve 1951 Rel: $1.82 Cur: $1,000 (2/28/87) (JL)

88 BEAULIEU Cabernet Sauvignon Napa Valley Georges de Latour Private Reserve 1950 Rel: $1.82 Cur: $800 (3/31/91) (JL)

88 BEAULIEU Cabernet Sauvignon Napa Valley Georges de Latour Private Reserve 1949 Rel: $1.82 Cur: $950 (3/31/91) (JL)

79 BEAULIEU Cabernet Sauvignon Napa Valley Georges de Latour Private Reserve 1948 Rel: $1.82 Cur: $1,040 (3/31/91) (JL)

85 BEAULIEU Cabernet Sauvignon Napa Valley Georges de Latour Private Reserve 1948 Rel: $1.82 Cur: $1,040 (CA-3/89)

89 BEAULIEU Cabernet Sauvignon Napa Valley Georges de Latour Private Reserve 1947 Rel: $1.82 Cur: $1,350 (3/31/91) (JL)

93 BEAULIEU Cabernet Sauvignon Napa Valley Georges de Latour Private Reserve 1947 Rel: $1.82 Cur: $1,350 (CA-3/89)

87 BEAULIEU Cabernet Sauvignon Napa Valley Georges de Latour Private Reserve 1946 Rel: $1.47 Cur: $1,000 (3/31/91) (JL)

88 BEAULIEU Cabernet Sauvignon Napa Valley Georges de Latour Private Reserve 1946 Rel: $1.47 Cur: $1,000 (CA-3/89)

70 BEAULIEU Cabernet Sauvignon Napa Valley Georges de Latour Private Reserve 1945 Rel: $1.47 Cur: $700 (3/31/91) (JL)

75 BEAULIEU Cabernet Sauvignon Napa Valley Georges de Latour Private Reserve 1944 Rel: $1.47 Cur: $680 (3/31/91) (JL)

87 BEAULIEU Cabernet Sauvignon Napa Valley Georges de Latour Private Reserve 1944 Rel: $1.47 Cur: $680 (CA-3/89)

87 BEAULIEU Cabernet Sauvignon Napa Valley Georges de Latour Private Reserve 1943 Rel: $1.45 Cur: $500 (3/31/91) (JL)

85 BEAULIEU Cabernet Sauvignon Napa Valley Georges de Latour Private Reserve 1942 Rel: $1.45 Cur: $1,300 (3/31/91) (JL)

87 BEAULIEU Cabernet Sauvignon Napa Valley Georges de Latour Private Reserve 1942 Rel: $1.45 Cur: $1,300 (CA-3/89)

89 BEAULIEU Cabernet Sauvignon Napa Valley Georges de Latour Private Reserve 1941 Rel: $1.45 Cur: $1,200 (3/31/91) (JL)

85 BEAULIEU Cabernet Sauvignon Napa Valley Georges de Latour Private Reserve 1941 Rel: $1.45 Cur: $1,200 (CA-3/89)

89 BEAULIEU Cabernet Sauvignon Napa Valley Georges de Latour Private Reserve 1940 Rel: $1.45 Cur: $1,200 (3/31/91) (JL)

91 BEAULIEU Cabernet Sauvignon Napa Valley Georges de Latour Private Reserve 1939 Rel: $1.45 Cur: $1,500 (3/31/91) (JL)

82 BEAULIEU Cabernet Sauvignon Napa Valley Georges de Latour Private Reserve 1939 Rel: $1.45 Cur: $1,500 (CA-3/89)

86 BEAULIEU Cabernet Sauvignon Napa Valley Georges de Latour Private Reserve 1936 Rel: $1.45 Cur: $1,500 (3/31/91) (JL)

85+ BEAULIEU Cabernet Sauvignon Napa Valley Rutherford 1990 (NR) (5/15/91) (BT)

85+ BEAULIEU Cabernet Sauvignon Napa Valley Rutherford 1989 (NR) (5/15/91) (BT)

86 BEAULIEU Cabernet Sauvignon Napa Valley Rutherford 1988 $11 (7/15/91)

85 BEAULIEU Cabernet Sauvignon Napa Valley Rutherford 1987 $10 (12/15/90)

85 BEAULIEU Cabernet Sauvignon Napa Valley Rutherford 1986 Rel: $11.25 Cur: $12 (9/15/89)

85 BEAULIEU Cabernet Sauvignon Napa Valley Rutherford 1985 Rel: $9.50 Cur: $10 (6/15/88)

80+ BEAULIEU Cabernet Sauvignon Napa Valley Rutherford 1985 Rel: $9.50 Cur: $10 (6/15/87) (BT)

78 BEAULIEU Cabernet Sauvignon Napa Valley Rutherford 1984 Rel: $9.50 Cur: $10 (8/31/87)

80 BEAULIEU Cabernet Sauvignon Napa Valley Rutherford 1983 Rel: $6.50 Cur: $12 (6/15/87)

81 BEAULIEU Cabernet Sauvignon Napa Valley Rutherford 1982 Rel: $8.50 Cur: $14 (4/16/86)

81 BEAULIEU Cabernet Sauvignon Napa Valley Rutherford 1981 Rel: $9 Cur: $20 (5/16/85)

88 BEAULIEU Cabernet Sauvignon Napa Valley Rutherford 1980 Rel: $9 Cur: $30 (6/01/85) (JL)

89 BEAULIEU Cabernet Sauvignon Napa Valley Rutherford 1979 Rel: $9 Cur: $25 (6/01/85) (JL)

90 BEAULIEU Cabernet Sauvignon Napa Valley Rutherford 1970 Cur: $67 (6/01/85) (JL)

83 BELLEROSE Cuvée Bellerose Sonoma County 1986 $18 (1/31/90)

82 BELLEROSE Cuvée Bellerose Sonoma County 1985 $16 (12/15/88)

77 BELLEROSE Cuvée Bellerose Sonoma County 1984 $14 (11/15/87)

74 BELLEROSE Cuvée Bellerose Sonoma County 1983 $12 (1/31/87)

79 BELLEROSE Cuvée Bellerose Sonoma County 1980 $10.50 (11/01/84)

85+ BELVEDERE Cabernet Sauvignon Alexander Valley Robert Young Vineyards 1986 (NR) (4/15/88) (BT)

81 BELVEDERE Cabernet Sauvignon Alexander Valley Robert Young Vineyard Gifts of the Land 1985 $16 (1/31/91)

80 BELVEDERE Cabernet Sauvignon Alexander Valley Robert Young Vineyard Gifts of the Land 1985 $15 (11/30/89)

88 BELVEDERE Cabernet Sauvignon Alexander Valley Robert Young Vineyards 1984 $13 (7/15/88)

88 BELVEDERE Cabernet Sauvignon Alexander Valley Robert Young Vineyards 1983 $12 (5/15/87)

95 BELVEDERE Cabernet Sauvignon Alexander Valley Robert Young Vineyards 1982 $12 (12/01/85) SS

80 BELVEDERE Cabernet Sauvignon Lake County Discovery Series 1982 $4 (4/01/85) BB

71 BELVEDERE Cabernet Sauvignon Napa Valley Discovery Series 1982 $4 (2/16/86)

75 BELVEDERE Cabernet Sauvignon Sonoma County Discovery Series 1987 $6 (6/15/90)

85+ BELVEDERE Cabernet Sauvignon Napa Valley York Creek 1986 (NR) (4/15/88) (BT)

79 BELVEDERE Cabernet Sauvignon Napa Valley York Creek Vineyard 1983 $12 (12/31/87)

72 BELVEDERE Cabernet Sauvignon Napa Valley York Creek Vineyard 1982 $12 (9/15/86)

75+ BELVEDERE Cabernet Sauvignon Sonoma County Bradford Mountain 1986 (NR) (4/15/88) (BT)

93 BENZIGER Cabernet Sauvignon Sonoma County 1987 $10 (9/30/90) SS

82 BENZIGER Cabernet Sauvignon Sonoma County 1986 $10 (7/31/89)

85 BENZIGER Cabernet Sauvignon Sonoma Valley Estate Bottled 1987 $12 (11/15/90)

78 BENZIGER Cabernet Sauvignon Sonoma Valley 1986 $17 (4/30/90)

83 BENZIGER Cabernet Sauvignon Sonoma Valley 1985 $16 (12/15/88)

85 BENZIGER A Tribute Sonoma Mountain 1987 $20 (12/31/90)

85+ BERINGER Cabernet Sauvignon Knights Valley 1989 (NR) (5/15/91) (BT)

90+ BERINGER Cabernet Sauvignon Knights Valley 1988 (NR) (4/30/90) (BT)

90 BERINGER Cabernet Sauvignon Knights Valley 1987 $15.50 (11/15/90)

87 BERINGER Cabernet Sauvignon Knights Valley 1985 $12 (5/31/88)

85+ BERINGER Cabernet Sauvignon Knights Valley 1985 $12 (6/15/87) (BT)

83 BERINGER Cabernet Sauvignon Knights Valley 1983 $9 (4/15/87)

90 BERINGER Cabernet Sauvignon Knights Valley 1982 $9 (4/15/87)

86 BERINGER Cabernet Sauvignon Knights Valley 1981 $9 (10/01/85)

88 BERINGER Cabernet Sauvignon Knights Valley 1980 $8 (2/15/84)

85+ BERINGER Cabernet Sauvignon Napa Valley Chabot Vineyard 1989 (NR) (5/15/91) (BT)

90+ BERINGER Cabernet Sauvignon Napa Valley Chabot Vineyard 1988 (NR) (4/30/90) (BT)

90+ BERINGER Cabernet Sauvignon Napa Valley Chabot Vineyard 1987 (NR) (4/15/89) (BT)

93 BERINGER Cabernet Sauvignon Napa Valley Chabot Vineyard 1986 (NR) (CA-3/89)

85+ BERINGER Cabernet Sauvignon Napa Valley Chabot Vineyard 1986 (NR) (4/15/88) (BT)

91 BERINGER Cabernet Sauvignon Napa Valley Chabot Vineyard 1985 Rel: $30 Cur: $30 (CA-3/89)

85 BERINGER Cabernet Sauvignon Napa Valley Chabot Vineyard 1984 Rel: $30 Cur: $32 (9/15/90)

87 BERINGER Cabernet Sauvignon Napa Valley Chabot Vineyard 1984 Rel: $30 Cur: $32 (CA-3/89)

85 BERINGER Cabernet Sauvignon Napa Valley Chabot Vineyard 1983 Rel: $27 Cur: $33 (CA-3/89)

89 BERINGER Cabernet Sauvignon Napa Valley Chabot Vineyard 1982 Rel: $25 Cur: $40 (CA-3/89)

87 BERINGER Cabernet Sauvignon Napa Valley Chabot Vineyard 1981 Rel: $23 Cur: $42 (CA-3/89)

85+ BERINGER Cabernet Sauvignon Napa Valley Private Reserve 1989 (NR) (5/15/91) (BT)

95+ BERINGER Cabernet Sauvignon Napa Valley Private Reserve 1988 (NR) (4/30/90) (BT)

95+ BERINGER Cabernet Sauvignon Napa Valley Private Reserve 1987 (NR) (4/15/89) (BT)

95 BERINGER Cabernet Sauvignon Napa Valley Private Reserve 1986 Rel: $35 Cur: $39 (9/15/90) CS

96 BERINGER Cabernet Sauvignon Napa Valley Private Reserve 1986 Rel: $35 Cur: $39 (CA-3/89)

95+ BERINGER Cabernet Sauvignon Napa Valley Private Reserve 1986 Rel: $35 Cur: $39 (4/15/88) (BT)

95 BERINGER Cabernet Sauvignon Napa Valley Private Reserve 1985 Rel: $30 Cur: $42 (12/15/89) SS

96 BERINGER Cabernet Sauvignon Napa Valley Private Reserve 1985 Rel: $30 Cur: $42 (CA-3/89)

95+ BERINGER Cabernet Sauvignon Napa Valley Private Reserve 1985 Rel: $30 Cur: $42 (6/15/87) (BT)

94 BERINGER Cabernet Sauvignon Napa Valley Private Reserve 1984 Rel: $25 Cur: $38 (CA-3/89)

94 BERINGER Cabernet Sauvignon Napa Valley Private Reserve 1984 Rel: $25 Cur: $38 (2/15/89) CS

89 BERINGER Cabernet Sauvignon Napa Valley Private Reserve 1983 Rel: $19 Cur: $33 (CA-3/89)

90 BERINGER Cabernet Sauvignon Napa Valley Private Reserve 1983 Rel: $19 Cur: $33 (4/15/87)

92 BERINGER Cabernet Sauvignon Napa Valley Private Reserve 1982 Rel: $19 Cur: $43 (CA-3/89)

94 BERINGER Cabernet Sauvignon Napa Valley Private Reserve 1982 Rel: $19 Cur: $43 (4/15/87)

91 BERINGER Cabernet Sauvignon Napa Valley Private Reserve 1981 Rel: $18 Cur: $30 (CA-3/89)

93 BERINGER Cabernet Sauvignon Napa Valley Private Reserve 1981 Rel: $18 Cur: $30 (4/15/87)

92 BERINGER Cabernet Sauvignon Napa Valley Private Reserve 1981 Rel: $18 Cur: $30 (6/01/86) CS

93 BERINGER Cabernet Sauvignon Napa Valley Private Reserve Lemmon-Chabot Vineyard 1981 Rel: $23 Cur: $42 (4/15/87)

89 BERINGER Cabernet Sauvignon Napa Valley Private Reserve Lemmon-Chabot Vineyard 1980 Rel: $20 Cur: $42 (CA-3/89)

93 BERINGER Cabernet Sauvignon Napa Valley Private Reserve Lemmon-Chabot Vineyard 1980 Rel: $20 Cur: $42 (8/01/84) CS

85 BERINGER Cabernet Sauvignon Napa Valley Private Reserve State Lane Vineyard 1980 Rel: $15 Cur: $40 (CA-3/89)

88 BERINGER Cabernet Sauvignon Napa Valley Private Reserve State Lane Vineyard 1980 Rel: $15 Cur: $40 (8/01/84)

89 BERINGER Cabernet Sauvignon Napa Valley Private Reserve State Lane Vineyard 1979 Rel: $15 Cur: $42 (CA-3/89)

92 BERINGER Cabernet Sauvignon Napa Valley Private Reserve Lemmon Ranch Vineyard 1978 Rel: $15 Cur: $36 (CA-3/89)

92 BERINGER Cabernet Sauvignon Napa Valley Private Reserve Lemmon Ranch Vineyard 1978 Rel: $15 Cur: $36 (4/30/87)

92 BERINGER Cabernet Sauvignon Napa Valley Private Reserve Lemmon Ranch Vineyard 1978 Rel: $15 Cur: $36 (4/30/87)

88 BERINGER Cabernet Sauvignon Napa Valley Private Reserve Lemmon Ranch Vineyard 1977 Rel: $12 Cur: $75 (CA-3/89)

87 BLACK MOUNTAIN Cabernet Sauvignon Alexander Valley Fat Cat 1985 $18 (4/30/90)

85 BOEGER Cabernet Sauvignon El Dorado 1987 $11 (3/15/91)

77 BOEGER Cabernet Sauvignon El Dorado 1985 $11 (2/15/89)

81 BOEGER Cabernet Sauvignon El Dorado 1984 $10.50 (5/31/88)

82 BOEGER Cabernet Sauvignon El Dorado 1983 $10 (8/31/87)

76 BOEGER Cabernet Sauvignon El Dorado 1980 $8.50 (4/16/84)

72 JEAN CLAUDE BOISSET Cabernet Sauvignon Napa Valley 1984 $7 (12/31/87)

Key to Symbols

The scores reported here are the results of blind tastings conducted by our panel of senior editors. Wines that carry the initials below are results of individual tastings.

THE WINE SPECTATOR 100-POINT SCALE 95-100—Classic, a great wine; *90-94*—Outstanding, superior character and style; *80-89*—Good to very good, a wine with special qualities; *70-79*—Average, drinkable wine that may have minor flaws; *60-69*—Below average, drinkable but not recommended; *50-59*—Poor, undrinkable, not recommended. *"+"*—With a score indicates a range; used primarily with barrel tastings to indicate a preliminary score.

SPECIAL DESIGNATIONS SS—Spectator Selection, CS—Cellar Selection, BB—Best Buy.

TASTER'S INITIALS (JG)—Jim Gordon, (HS)—Harvey Steiman, (JL)—James Laube, (JS)—James Suckling, (TM)—Thomas Matthews, (TR)—Terry Robards, (BT)—Barrel Tasting (these wines were tasted blind from barrel samples), (CA-date)—*California's Great Cabernets* by James Laube, (CH-date)—*California's Great Chardonnays* by James Laube, (VP-date)—*Vintage Port* by James Suckling.

DATE TASTED Dates in parentheses represent the issue in which the rating was published.

80 JEAN CLAUDE BOISSET Cabernet Sauvignon Napa Valley 1981 $9 (5/01/85)
87 BON MARCHE Cabernet Sauvignon Alexander Valley 1989 $8 (2/28/91) BB
84 BRAREN PAULI Cabernet Sauvignon Mendocino 1987 $8.50 (3/31/91) BB
79 DAVID BRUCE Cabernet Sauvignon California Vintner's Select 1983 $12.50 (9/30/86)
83 BRUTOCAO Cabernet Sauvignon Mendocino 1982 $9 (11/30/88)
80+ BUEHLER Cabernet Sauvignon Napa Valley 1988 (NR) (4/30/90) (BT)
85 BUEHLER Cabernet Sauvignon Napa Valley 1987 Rel: $16 Cur: $19 (7/31/90)
90+ BUEHLER Cabernet Sauvignon Napa Valley 1987 Rel: $16 Cur: $19 (4/15/89) (BT)
85 BUEHLER Cabernet Sauvignon Napa Valley 1986 Rel: $15 Cur: $15 (4/30/89)
91 BUEHLER Cabernet Sauvignon Napa Valley 1986 Rel: $15 Cur: $15 (CA-3/89)
80+ BUEHLER Cabernet Sauvignon Napa Valley 1986 Rel: $15 Cur: $15 (4/15/88) (BT)
93 BUEHLER Cabernet Sauvignon Napa Valley 1985 Rel: $14 Cur: $16 (CA-3/89)
89 BUEHLER Cabernet Sauvignon Napa Valley 1985 Rel: $14 Cur: $16 (4/30/88)
87 BUEHLER Cabernet Sauvignon Napa Valley 1984 Rel: $13 Cur: $23 (CA-3/89)
92 BUEHLER Cabernet Sauvignon Napa Valley 1984 Rel: $13 Cur: $23 (5/31/87)
91 BUEHLER Cabernet Sauvignon Napa Valley 1983 Rel: $12 Cur: $23 (CA-3/89)
93 BUEHLER Cabernet Sauvignon Napa Valley 1983 Rel: $12 Cur: $23 (7/16/86) SS
88 BUEHLER Cabernet Sauvignon Napa Valley 1982 Rel: $12 Cur: $30 (CA-3/89)
85 BUEHLER Cabernet Sauvignon Napa Valley 1981 Rel: $11 Cur: $20 (CA-3/89)
82 BUEHLER Cabernet Sauvignon Napa Valley 1980 Rel: $10 Cur: $25 (CA-3/89)
87 BUEHLER Cabernet Sauvignon Napa Valley 1978 Rel: $10 Cur: $35 (CA-3/89)
85+ BUENA VISTA Cabernet Sauvignon Carneros 1988 $13 (4/30/90) (BT)
83 BUENA VISTA Cabernet Sauvignon Carneros 1987 $13 (10/15/90)
80+ BUENA VISTA Cabernet Sauvignon Carneros 1987 $13 (4/15/89) (BT)
91 BUENA VISTA Cabernet Sauvignon Carneros 1986 $11 (10/15/89)
85+ BUENA VISTA Cabernet Sauvignon Carneros 1986 $11 (4/15/88) (BT)
84 BUENA VISTA Cabernet Sauvignon Carneros 1985 $10 (11/15/88)
94 BUENA VISTA Cabernet Sauvignon Carneros 1984 $10 (8/31/87)
77 BUENA VISTA Cabernet Sauvignon Carneros 1983 $9.75 (6/15/87)
85 BUENA VISTA Cabernet Sauvignon Carneros 1982 $11 (9/16/85)
89 BUENA VISTA Cabernet Sauvignon Carneros 1981 $11 (2/16/85)
90 BUENA VISTA Cabernet Sauvignon Carneros 1981 $11 (12/16/84)
89 BUENA VISTA Cabernet Sauvignon Carneros Private Reserve 1986 $25 (3/15/91)
93 BUENA VISTA Cabernet Sauvignon Carneros Private Reserve 1986 $25 (10/15/90)
93 BUENA VISTA Cabernet Sauvignon Carneros Private Reserve 1986 $25 (CA-3/89)
85+ BUENA VISTA Cabernet Sauvignon Carneros Private Reserve 1986 $25 (4/15/88) (BT)
94 BUENA VISTA Cabernet Sauvignon Carneros Private Reserve 1985 Rel: $18 Cur: $23 (10/15/89) SS
93 BUENA VISTA Cabernet Sauvignon Carneros Private Reserve 1985 Rel: $18 Cur: $23 (CA-3/89)
90 BUENA VISTA Cabernet Sauvignon Carneros Private Reserve 1984 Rel: $18 Cur: $18 (CA-3/89)
87 BUENA VISTA Cabernet Sauvignon Carneros Private Reserve 1983 Rel: $18 Cur: $25 (CA-3/89)
90 BUENA VISTA Cabernet Sauvignon Carneros Private Reserve 1983 Rel: $18 Cur: $25 (2/15/88)
85 BUENA VISTA Cabernet Sauvignon Carneros Private Reserve 1982 Rel: $18 Cur: $30 (CA-3/89)
87 BUENA VISTA Cabernet Sauvignon Carneros Private Reserve 1982 Rel: $18 Cur: $30 (2/15/87)
86 BUENA VISTA Cabernet Sauvignon Carneros Private Reserve Special Selection 1981 Rel: $18 Cur: $30 (CA-3/89)
88 BUENA VISTA Cabernet Sauvignon Carneros Private Reserve Special Selection 1981 Rel: $18 Cur: $30 (7/01/86)
84 BUENA VISTA Cabernet Sauvignon Carneros Special Selection 1980 Rel: $18 Cur: $30 (CA-3/89)
92 BUENA VISTA Cabernet Sauvignon Carneros Special Selection 1979 Rel: $18 Cur: $35 (CA-3/89)
90 BUENA VISTA Cabernet Sauvignon Carneros Special Selection 1978 Rel: $18 Cur: $35 (CA-3/89)
96 BUENA VISTA Cabernet Sauvignon Carneros Special Selection 1978 Rel: $18 Cur: $35 (6/01/86)
94 BUENA VISTA Cabernet Sauvignon Sonoma Valley 1978 $12 (6/01/86)
66 BUENA VISTA Cabernet Sauvignon Sonoma Valley 1976 $12 (CA-3/89)
64 BUENA VISTA Cabernet Sauvignon Sonoma Valley 1975 $12 (CA-3/89)
72 BUENA VISTA Cabernet Sauvignon Sonoma Valley Cask 34 1977 Rel: $12 Cur: $40 (CA-3/89)
68 BUENA VISTA Cabernet Sauvignon Sonoma Valley Cask 25 1974 Rel: $12 Cur: $40 (CA-3/89)
90 BUENA VISTA Cabernet Sauvignon Sonoma County 1986 $11 (11/15/89)
87 BUENA VISTA L'Année Carneros 1986 $35 (2/28/91)
88 BUENA VISTA L'Année Carneros 1984 $32/1.5L (2/15/88)
88 BURGESS Cabernet Sauvignon Napa Valley Vintage Selection 1986 Rel: $20 Cur: $22 (7/15/90)
91 BURGESS Cabernet Sauvignon Napa Valley Vintage Selection 1986 Rel: $20 Cur: $22 (CA-3/89)
85+ BURGESS Cabernet Sauvignon Napa Valley Vintage Selection 1986 Rel: $20 Cur: $22 (4/15/88) (BT)
92 BURGESS Cabernet Sauvignon Napa Valley Vintage Selection 1985 Rel: $18 Cur: $23 (7/15/89)
93 BURGESS Cabernet Sauvignon Napa Valley Vintage Selection 1985 Rel: $18 Cur: $23 (CA-3/89)
85+ BURGESS Cabernet Sauvignon Napa Valley Vintage Selection 1985 Rel: $18 Cur: $23 (6/15/87) (BT)
93 BURGESS Cabernet Sauvignon Napa Valley Vintage Selection 1984 Rel: $17 Cur: $25 (CA-3/89)
92 BURGESS Cabernet Sauvignon Napa Valley Vintage Selection 1984 Rel: $17 Cur: $25 (7/31/88)
87 BURGESS Cabernet Sauvignon Napa Valley Vintage Selection 1983 Rel: $17 Cur: $21 (CA-3/89)
85 BURGESS Cabernet Sauvignon Napa Valley Vintage Selection 1983 Rel: $17 Cur: $21 (10/15/87)
88 BURGESS Cabernet Sauvignon Napa Valley Vintage Selection 1982 Rel: $16 Cur: $23 (CA-3/89)
81 BURGESS Cabernet Sauvignon Napa Valley Vintage Selection 1982 Rel: $16 Cur: $23 (10/15/86)
88 BURGESS Cabernet Sauvignon Napa Valley Vintage Selection 1981 Rel: $16 Cur: $25 (CA-3/89)
87 BURGESS Cabernet Sauvignon Napa Valley Vintage Selection 1981 Rel: $16 Cur: $25 (9/16/85)
88 BURGESS Cabernet Sauvignon Napa Valley Vintage Selection 1980 Rel: $16 Cur: $39 (CA-3/89)
90 BURGESS Cabernet Sauvignon Napa Valley Vintage Selection 1980 Rel: $16 Cur: $39 (5/01/84) SS
87 BURGESS Cabernet Sauvignon Napa Valley Vintage Selection 1979 Rel: $16 Cur: $35 (CA-3/89)
93 BURGESS Cabernet Sauvignon Napa Valley Vintage Selection 1978 Rel: $14 Cur: $34 (CA-3/89)
92 BURGESS Cabernet Sauvignon Napa Valley Vintage Selection 1977 Rel: $12 Cur: $45 (CA-3/89)
87 BURGESS Cabernet Sauvignon Napa Valley Vintage Selection 1976 Rel: $12 Cur: $40 (CA-3/89)
88 BURGESS Cabernet Sauvignon Napa Valley Vintage Selection 1975 Rel: $9 Cur: $45 (CA-3/89)
86 BURGESS Cabernet Sauvignon Napa Valley Vintage Selection 1974 Rel: $9 Cur: $70 (CA-3/89)
71 DAVIS BYNUM Cabernet Sauvignon Napa Valley Reserve Bottling 1984 $7 (12/15/87)
79 DAVIS BYNUM Cabernet Sauvignon Sonoma County 1987 $10.50 (11/15/90)
84 DAVIS BYNUM Cabernet Sauvignon Sonoma County 1986 $10 (11/15/89)
76 BYRON Cabernet Sauvignon Central Coast 1985 $14 (12/15/89)
84 CAFARO Cabernet Sauvignon Napa Valley 1987 $20 (11/15/90)
93 CAFARO Cabernet Sauvignon Napa Valley 1986 $18 (11/15/89)
85 CAIN Cabernet Sauvignon Napa Valley 1986 $16 (8/31/90)
81 CAIN Cabernet Sauvignon Napa Valley 1985 $16 (4/15/89)
79 CAIN Cabernet Sauvignon Napa Valley 1984 $14 (5/31/88)
75 CAIN Cabernet Sauvignon Napa Valley 1983 $14 (8/31/87)
78 CAIN Cabernet Sauvignon Napa Valley 1982 $11 (9/30/86)
92 CAIN Cabernet Sauvignon Napa Valley Estate 1987 $25 (10/15/90)
90+ CAIN Five Napa Valley 1990 (NR) (5/15/91) (BT)
90+ CAIN Five Napa Valley 1989 (NR) (5/15/91) (BT)
91 CAIN Five Napa Valley 1987 $30 (4/30/91)
91 CAIN Five Napa Valley 1986 $30 (2/15/90)
87 CAIN Five Napa Valley 1985 $26 (6/15/89)
90 CAKEBREAD Cabernet Sauvignon Napa Valley 1987 Rel: $18 Cur: $18 (10/15/90)
90 CAKEBREAD Cabernet Sauvignon Napa Valley 1986 Rel: $18 Cur: $18 (8/31/89)
89 CAKEBREAD Cabernet Sauvignon Napa Valley 1986 Rel: $18 Cur: $18 (CA-3/89)
84 CAKEBREAD Cabernet Sauvignon Napa Valley 1985 Rel: $17 Cur: $19 (CA-3/89)
90 CAKEBREAD Cabernet Sauvignon Napa Valley 1985 Rel: $17 Cur: $19 (4/15/88)
89 CAKEBREAD Cabernet Sauvignon Napa Valley 1984 Rel: $16 Cur: $25 (CA-3/89)
87 CAKEBREAD Cabernet Sauvignon Napa Valley 1984 Rel: $16 Cur: $25 (9/30/87)
77 CAKEBREAD Cabernet Sauvignon Napa Valley 1983 Rel: $16 Cur: $25 (CA-3/89)
93 CAKEBREAD Cabernet Sauvignon Napa Valley 1983 Rel: $16 Cur: $25 (11/30/86)
86 CAKEBREAD Cabernet Sauvignon Napa Valley 1982 Rel: $16 Cur: $28 (CA-3/89)
70 CAKEBREAD Cabernet Sauvignon Napa Valley 1982 Rel: $16 Cur: $28 (7/16/86)
88 CAKEBREAD Cabernet Sauvignon Napa Valley 1981 Rel: $16 Cur: $30 (CA-3/89)
84 CAKEBREAD Cabernet Sauvignon Napa Valley 1980 Rel: $14 Cur: $30 (CA-3/89)
82 CAKEBREAD Cabernet Sauvignon Napa Valley 1979 Rel: $13 Cur: $30 (CA-3/89)
85 CAKEBREAD Cabernet Sauvignon Napa Valley 1978 Rel: $12 Cur: $35 (CA-3/89)
85 CAKEBREAD Cabernet Sauvignon Napa Valley Rutherford Reserve 1985 $40 (CA-3/89)
85 CAKEBREAD Cabernet Sauvignon Napa Valley Rutherford Reserve 1984 Rel: $35 Cur: $38 (2/15/90)
88 CAKEBREAD Cabernet Sauvignon Napa Valley Rutherford Reserve 1983 Rel: $35 Cur: $35 (CA-3/89)
86 CAKEBREAD Cabernet Sauvignon Napa Valley Lot 2 1978 Rel: $12 Cur: $50 (CA-3/89)
60 CAMBIASO Cabernet Sauvignon Dry Creek Valley 1981 $4.75 (6/16/84)
80 CAPARONE Cabernet Sauvignon Santa Maria Valley Tepusquet Vineyard 1981 $10 (3/16/84)
83 J. CAREY Cabernet Sauvignon Santa Ynez Valley 1985 $10 (11/15/89)
72 J. CAREY Cabernet Sauvignon Santa Ynez Valley 1984 $9 (3/31/88)
76 J. CAREY Cabernet Sauvignon Santa Ynez Valley Alamo Pintado Vineyard 1981 $9.50 (6/16/84)
83 J. CAREY Cabernet Sauvignon Santa Ynez Valley La Cuesta Vineyard 1983 $9.50 (12/15/89)
81 J. CAREY Cabernet Sauvignon Santa Ynez Valley La Cuesta Vineyard Reserve 1987 $16 (5/31/91)
85+ CARMENET Sonoma Valley 1989 (NR) (5/15/91) (BT)
90+ CARMENET Sonoma Valley 1988 (NR) (4/30/90) (BT)
89 CARMENET Sonoma Valley 1987 Rel: $20 Cur: $20 (11/15/90)
90+ CARMENET Sonoma Valley 1987 Rel: $20 Cur: $20 (4/15/89) (BT)
91 CARMENET Sonoma Valley 1986 Rel: $20 Cur: $21 (7/31/89)
93 CARMENET Sonoma Valley 1986 Rel: $20 Cur: $21 (CA-3/89)
90+ CARMENET Sonoma Valley 1986 Rel: $20 Cur: $21 (4/15/88) (BT)
91 CARMENET Sonoma Valley 1985 Rel: $18.50 Cur: $23 (CA-3/89)
91 CARMENET Sonoma Valley 1985 Rel: $18.50 Cur: $23 (12/31/88)
90+ CARMENET Sonoma Valley 1985 Rel: $18.50 Cur: $23 (6/15/87) (BT)
92 CARMENET Sonoma Valley 1984 Rel: $16 Cur: $30 (CA-3/89)
93 CARMENET Sonoma Valley 1984 Rel: $16 Cur: $30 (5/31/87)
85 CARMENET Sonoma Valley 1983 Rel: $18 Cur: $23 (CA-3/89)
84 CARMENET Sonoma Valley 1983 Rel: $18 Cur: $23 (9/30/86)
87 CARMENET Sonoma Valley 1982 Rel: $16 Cur: $31 (CA-3/89)
93 CARMENET Sonoma Valley 1982 Rel: $16 Cur: $31 (10/16/85)
90 CARNEROS CREEK Cabernet Sauvignon Los Carneros 1985 $15 (10/31/89)
86 CARNEROS CREEK Cabernet Sauvignon Napa Valley 1983 $10.50 (8/31/87)
71 CARNEROS CREEK Cabernet Sauvignon Napa Valley 1982 $11 (2/16/86)
77 CARNEROS CREEK Cabernet Sauvignon Napa Valley 1981 $12 (12/16/84)
70 CARNEROS CREEK Cabernet Sauvignon Napa Valley Fay Vineyard 1982 $13.50 (5/15/87)
83 CARNEROS CREEK Cabernet Sauvignon Napa Valley Reserve 1983 $13.50 (10/15/88)
80 CASTORO Cabernet Sauvignon Paso Robles Hope Farms 1986 $8.50 (12/15/89)
93 CAYMUS Cabernet Sauvignon Napa Valley 1987 Rel: $16 Cur: $19 (9/15/90)
90+ CAYMUS Cabernet Sauvignon Napa Valley 1987 Rel: $16 Cur: $19 (4/15/89) (BT)
94 CAYMUS Cabernet Sauvignon Napa Valley 1986 Rel: $22 Cur: $29 (3/15/90) SS
92 CAYMUS Cabernet Sauvignon Napa Valley 1986 Rel: $22 Cur: $29 (CA-3/89)
85+ CAYMUS Cabernet Sauvignon Napa Valley 1986 Rel: $22 Cur: $29 (4/15/88) (BT)
92 CAYMUS Cabernet Sauvignon Napa Valley 1985 Rel: $18 Cur: $38 (CA-3/89)
90 CAYMUS Cabernet Sauvignon Napa Valley 1985 Rel: $18 Cur: $38 (11/15/88)
90+ CAYMUS Cabernet Sauvignon Napa Valley 1985 Rel: $18 Cur: $38 (6/15/87) (BT)
91 CAYMUS Cabernet Sauvignon Napa Valley 1984 Rel: $16 Cur: $42 (CA-3/89)
90 CAYMUS Cabernet Sauvignon Napa Valley 1984 Rel: $16 Cur: $42 (12/31/87)
87 CAYMUS Cabernet Sauvignon Napa Valley 1983 Rel: $15 Cur: $42 (CA-3/89)
94 CAYMUS Cabernet Sauvignon Napa Valley 1983 Rel: $15 Cur: $42 (11/30/86) CS
90 CAYMUS Cabernet Sauvignon Napa Valley 1982 Rel: $14 Cur: $43 (CA-3/89)
94 CAYMUS Cabernet Sauvignon Napa Valley 1982 Rel: $14 Cur: $43 (4/01/86)

UNITED STATES
CALIFORNIA/CABERNET SAUVIGNON & BLENDS

94	CAYMUS Cabernet Sauvignon Napa Valley 1982 Rel: $14 Cur: $43 (2/01/85)
88	CAYMUS Cabernet Sauvignon Napa Valley 1981 Rel: $14 Cur: $55 (CA-3/89)
93	CAYMUS Cabernet Sauvignon Napa Valley 1981 Rel: $14 Cur: $55 (2/01/86)
93	CAYMUS Cabernet Sauvignon Napa Valley 1981 Rel: $14 Cur: $55 (2/01/85)
90	CAYMUS Cabernet Sauvignon Napa Valley 1980 Rel: $12.50 Cur: $53 (CA-3/89)
94	CAYMUS Cabernet Sauvignon Napa Valley 1980 Rel: $12.50 Cur: $53 (2/01/86)
94	CAYMUS Cabernet Sauvignon Napa Valley 1980 Rel: $12.50 Cur: $53 (2/01/85)
92	CAYMUS Cabernet Sauvignon Napa Valley 1979 Rel: $12 Cur: $55 (CA-3/89)
90	CAYMUS Cabernet Sauvignon Napa Valley 1979 Rel: $12 Cur: $55 (2/01/86)
90	CAYMUS Cabernet Sauvignon Napa Valley 1979 Rel: $12 Cur: $55 (2/01/85)
87	CAYMUS Cabernet Sauvignon Napa Valley 1978 Rel: $12 Cur: $60 (CA-3/89)
91	CAYMUS Cabernet Sauvignon Napa Valley 1978 Rel: $12 Cur: $60 (2/01/85)
77	CAYMUS Cabernet Sauvignon Napa Valley 1977 Rel: $10 Cur: $41 (CA-3/89)
85	CAYMUS Cabernet Sauvignon Napa Valley 1976 Rel: $10 Cur: $63 (CA-3/89)
89	CAYMUS Cabernet Sauvignon Napa Valley 1975 Rel: $8.50 Cur: $87 (CA-3/89)
91	CAYMUS Cabernet Sauvignon Napa Valley 1974 Rel: $7 Cur: $110 (2/15/90) (JG)
87	CAYMUS Cabernet Sauvignon Napa Valley 1974 Rel: $7 Cur: $110 (CA-3/89)
93	CAYMUS Cabernet Sauvignon Napa Valley 1973 Rel: $6 Cur: $126 (CA-3/89)
86	CAYMUS Cabernet Sauvignon Napa Valley 1972 Rel: $4.50 Cur: $110 (CA-3/89)
90	CAYMUS Cabernet Sauvignon Napa Valley Cuvée 1986 $15 (8/31/89)
92	CAYMUS Cabernet Sauvignon Napa Valley Cuvée 1985 $12 (7/15/88)
80+	CAYMUS Cabernet Sauvignon Napa Valley Cuvée 1985 $12 (6/15/87) (BT)
88	CAYMUS Cabernet Sauvignon Napa Valley Cuvée 1984 $12 (8/31/87)
98	CAYMUS Cabernet Sauvignon Napa Valley Special Selection 1986 $50 (1/31/91) CS
98	CAYMUS Cabernet Sauvignon Napa Valley Special Selection 1986 $50 (CA-3/89)
99	CAYMUS Cabernet Sauvignon Napa Valley Special Selection 1985 Rel: $50 Cur: $127 (4/30/90)
99	CAYMUS Cabernet Sauvignon Napa Valley Special Selection 1985 Rel: $50 Cur: $127 (CA-3/89)
98	CAYMUS Cabernet Sauvignon Napa Valley Special Selection 1984 Rel: $35 Cur: $118 (7/15/89) CS
98	CAYMUS Cabernet Sauvignon Napa Valley Special Selection 1984 Rel: $35 Cur: $118 (CA-3/89)
91	CAYMUS Cabernet Sauvignon Napa Valley Special Selection 1983 Rel: $35 Cur: $115 (CA-3/89)
90	CAYMUS Cabernet Sauvignon Napa Valley Special Selection 1983 Rel: $35 Cur: $115 (5/31/88)
92	CAYMUS Cabernet Sauvignon Napa Valley Special Selection 1982 Rel: $35 Cur: $100 (CA-3/89)
90	CAYMUS Cabernet Sauvignon Napa Valley Special Selection 1982 Rel: $35 Cur: $100 (11/30/87)
93	CAYMUS Cabernet Sauvignon Napa Valley Special Selection 1981 Rel: $35 Cur: $115 (CA-3/89)
94	CAYMUS Cabernet Sauvignon Napa Valley Special Selection 1981 Rel: $35 Cur: $115 (11/30/86)
92	CAYMUS Cabernet Sauvignon Napa Valley Special Selection 1980 Rel: $30 Cur: $128 (CA-3/89)
96	CAYMUS Cabernet Sauvignon Napa Valley Special Selection 1980 Rel: $30 Cur: $128 (3/16/86) SS
97	CAYMUS Cabernet Sauvignon Napa Valley Special Selection 1979 Rel: $30 Cur: $165 (CA-3/89)
93	CAYMUS Cabernet Sauvignon Napa Valley Special Selection 1979 Rel: $30 Cur: $165 (6/01/85) SS
97	CAYMUS Cabernet Sauvignon Napa Valley Special Selection 1978 Rel: $30 Cur: $230 (CA-3/89)
98	CAYMUS Cabernet Sauvignon Napa Valley Special Selection 1978 Rel: $30 Cur: $230 (4/30/87)
95	CAYMUS Cabernet Sauvignon Napa Valley Special Selection 1978 Rel: $30 Cur: $230 (6/16/84) CS
90	CAYMUS Cabernet Sauvignon Napa Valley Special Selection 1976 Rel: $35 Cur: $220 (CA-3/89)
92	CAYMUS Cabernet Sauvignon Napa Valley Special Selection 1975 Rel: $22 Cur: $250 (CA-3/89)
83	CECCHETTI SEBASTIANI Cabernet Sauvignon Alexander Valley 1986 $8.50 (4/15/89)
76	CECCHETTI SEBASTIANI Cabernet Sauvignon Sonoma County 1983 $12.50 (9/30/86)
87	CHALK HILL Cabernet Sauvignon Chalk Hill 1988 $12 (6/15/91)
78	CHALK HILL Cabernet Sauvignon Sonoma County 1983 $10 (11/15/86)
66	CHALK HILL Cabernet Sauvignon Sonoma County 1982 $9 (11/01/85)
83	CHALK HILL Cabernet Sauvignon Sonoma County 1981 $8 (4/01/84)
85+	CHAPPELLET Cabernet Sauvignon Napa Valley 1987 (NR) (4/15/89) (BT)
92	CHAPPELLET Cabernet Sauvignon Napa Valley Reserve 1986 Rel: $18 Cur: $20 (CA-3/89)
80+	CHAPPELLET Cabernet Sauvignon Napa Valley Reserve 1986 Rel: $18 Cur: $20 (4/15/88) (BT)
84	CHAPPELLET Cabernet Sauvignon Napa Valley Reserve 1985 Rel: $20 Cur: $21 (2/15/90)
70	CHAPPELLET Cabernet Sauvignon Napa Valley Reserve 1985 Rel: $20 Cur: $21 (5/31/89)
88	CHAPPELLET Cabernet Sauvignon Napa Valley Reserve 1985 Rel: $20 Cur: $21 (CA-3/89)
87	CHAPPELLET Cabernet Sauvignon Napa Valley Reserve 1984 Rel: $18 Cur: $23 (CA-3/89)
88	CHAPPELLET Cabernet Sauvignon Napa Valley 1984 Rel: $18 Cur: $23 (7/31/88)
77	CHAPPELLET Cabernet Sauvignon Napa Valley 1983 Rel: $12 Cur: $16 (CA-3/89)
80	CHAPPELLET Cabernet Sauvignon Napa Valley 1982 Rel: $9.25 Cur: $16 (CA-3/89)
79	CHAPPELLET Cabernet Sauvignon Napa Valley 1981 Rel: $11 Cur: $23 (CA-3/89)
81	CHAPPELLET Cabernet Sauvignon Napa Valley 1981 Rel: $11 Cur: $23 (12/16/84)
91	CHAPPELLET Cabernet Sauvignon Napa Valley 1980 Rel: $18 Cur: $29 (CA-3/89)
79	CHAPPELLET Cabernet Sauvignon Napa Valley 1979 Rel: $13 Cur: $29 (CA-3/89)
88	CHAPPELLET Cabernet Sauvignon Napa Valley 1978 Rel: $13 Cur: $36 (CA-3/89)
82	CHAPPELLET Cabernet Sauvignon Napa Valley 1977 Rel: $12 Cur: $33 (CA-3/89)
76	CHAPPELLET Cabernet Sauvignon Napa Valley 1976 Rel: $12 Cur: $41 (CA-3/89)
78	CHAPPELLET Cabernet Sauvignon Napa Valley 1975 Rel: $10 Cur: $45 (CA-3/89)
78	CHAPPELLET Cabernet Sauvignon Napa Valley 1974 Rel: $7.50 Cur: $66 (2/15/90) (JG)
70	CHAPPELLET Cabernet Sauvignon Napa Valley 1974 Rel: $7.50 Cur: $66 (CA-3/89)
69	CHAPPELLET Cabernet Sauvignon Napa Valley 1973 Rel: $7.50 Cur: $68 (CA-3/89)
67	CHAPPELLET Cabernet Sauvignon Napa Valley 1972 Rel: $6.50 Cur: $41 (CA-3/89)
65	CHAPPELLET Cabernet Sauvignon Napa Valley 1971 Rel: $7.50 Cur: $80 (CA-3/89)
93	CHAPPELLET Cabernet Sauvignon Napa Valley 1970 Rel: $7.50 Cur: $95 (CA-3/89)
87	CHAPPELLET Cabernet Sauvignon Napa Valley 1969 Rel: $10 Cur: $125 (CA-3/89)
88	CHAPPELLET Cabernet Sauvignon Napa Valley 1968 Rel: $5.50 Cur: $100 (CA-3/89)
82	CHATEAU CHEVALIER Cabernet Sauvignon Napa Valley 1980 $11.25 (1/01/84)
88	CHATEAU CHEVRE Chevrè Reserve Napa Valley 1986 $25 (7/31/89)
82	CHATEAU DIANA Cabernet Sauvignon Central Coast Limited Edition 1984 $6 (11/30/88) BB
90+	CHATEAU MONTELENA Cabernet Sauvignon Napa Valley 1987 (NR) (4/15/89) (BT)
93	CHATEAU MONTELENA Cabernet Sauvignon Napa Valley 1986 Rel: $25 Cur: $30 (10/15/90)
93	CHATEAU MONTELENA Cabernet Sauvignon Napa Valley 1986 Rel: $25 Cur: $30 (CA-3/89)
90+	CHATEAU MONTELENA Cabernet Sauvignon Napa Valley 1986 Rel: $25 Cur: $30 (4/15/88) (BT)
92	CHATEAU MONTELENA Cabernet Sauvignon Napa Valley 1985 Rel: $25 Cur: $44 (11/15/89) CS
92	CHATEAU MONTELENA Cabernet Sauvignon Napa Valley 1985 Rel: $25 Cur: $44 (11/15/89) CS
95	CHATEAU MONTELENA Cabernet Sauvignon Napa Valley 1985 Rel: $25 Cur: $44 (CA-3/89)
90+	CHATEAU MONTELENA Cabernet Sauvignon Napa Valley 1985 Rel: $25 Cur: $44 (6/15/87) (BT)
94	CHATEAU MONTELENA Cabernet Sauvignon Napa Valley 1984 Rel: $20 Cur: $39 (CA-3/89)
94	CHATEAU MONTELENA Cabernet Sauvignon Napa Valley 1984 Rel: $20 Cur: $39 (10/15/88)
92	CHATEAU MONTELENA Cabernet Sauvignon Napa Valley 1983 Rel: $18 Cur: $28 (CA-3/89)
93	CHATEAU MONTELENA Cabernet Sauvignon Napa Valley 1983 Rel: $18 Cur: $28 (11/15/87) CS
92	CHATEAU MONTELENA Cabernet Sauvignon Napa Valley 1982 Rel: $16 Cur: $41 (CA-3/89)
79	CHATEAU MONTELENA Cabernet Sauvignon Napa Valley 1982 Rel: $16 Cur: $41 (10/15/86)
80	CHATEAU MONTELENA Cabernet Sauvignon Napa Valley 1981 Rel: $16 Cur: $37 (CA-3/89)
86	CHATEAU MONTELENA Cabernet Sauvignon Napa Valley 1980 Rel: $16 Cur: $54 (CA-3/89)
83	CHATEAU MONTELENA Cabernet Sauvignon Napa Valley 1980 Rel: $16 Cur: $54 (10/01/84)
87	CHATEAU MONTELENA Cabernet Sauvignon Napa Valley 1979 Rel: $16 Cur: $45 (CA-3/89)
	CHATEAU MONTELENA Cabernet Sauvignon Napa Valley 1979 Rel: $16 Cur: $45 (11/01/83) SS
93	CHATEAU MONTELENA Cabernet Sauvignon Napa Valley 1978 Rel: $16 Cur: $79 (CA-3/89)
87	CHATEAU MONTELENA Cabernet Sauvignon Napa Valley 1978 Rel: $16 Cur: $79 (4/30/87)
94	CHATEAU MONTELENA Cabernet Sauvignon Napa Valley 1977 Rel: $12 Cur: $70 (CA-3/89)
90	CHATEAU MONTELENA Cabernet Sauvignon North Coast 1976 Rel: $10 Cur: $75 (CA-3/89)
86	CHATEAU MONTELENA Cabernet Sauvignon North Coast 1975 Rel: $9 Cur: $100 (CA-3/89)
90	CHATEAU MONTELENA Cabernet Sauvignon Napa Valley 1974 Rel: $9 Cur: $100 (2/15/90) (JG)
90	CHATEAU MONTELENA Cabernet Sauvignon Napa Valley 1974 Rel: $9 Cur: $100 (CA-3/89)
88	CHATEAU MONTELENA Cabernet Sauvignon Alexander Valley Sonoma 1979 Rel: $14 Cur: $45 (CA-3/89)
87	CHATEAU MONTELENA Cabernet Sauvignon Alexander Valley Sonoma 1978 Rel: $12 Cur: $68 (CA-3/89)
91	CHATEAU MONTELENA Cabernet Sauvignon Alexander Valley Sonoma 1977 Rel: $12 Cur: $65 (CA-3/89)
87	CHATEAU MONTELENA Cabernet Sauvignon Alexander Valley Sonoma 1974 Rel: $9 Cur: $100 (CA-3/89)
87	CHATEAU MONTELENA Cabernet Sauvignon Alexander Valley Sonoma 1973 Rel: $8 Cur: $100 (CA-3/89)
85	CHATEAU NAPA-BEAUCANON Cabernet Sauvignon Napa Valley 1986 $15 (12/31/88)
84	CHATEAU POTELLE Cabernet Sauvignon Alexander Valley 1986 $14.50 (10/31/90)
83	CHATEAU POTELLE Cabernet Sauvignon Alexander Valley 1984 $13 (12/31/88)
85+	CHATEAU SOUVERAIN Cabernet Sauvignon Alexander Valley 1990 (NR) (5/15/91) (BT)
90+	CHATEAU SOUVERAIN Cabernet Sauvignon Alexander Valley 1989 (NR) (5/15/91) (BT)
87	CHATEAU SOUVERAIN Cabernet Sauvignon Alexander Valley 1987 $9.50 (11/15/90)
85	CHATEAU SOUVERAIN Cabernet Sauvignon Alexander Valley 1986 $8.50 (11/15/89) BB
83	CHATEAU SOUVERAIN Cabernet Sauvignon Alexander Valley Private Reserve 1987 $15 (5/15/91)
83	CHATEAU SOUVERAIN Cabernet Sauvignon North Coast Vintage Selection 1980 $13 (9/16/85)
87	CHATEAU SOUVERAIN Cabernet Sauvignon Sonoma County 1985 $8 (11/30/88)
83	CHATEAU SOUVERAIN Cabernet Sauvignon Sonoma County 1984 $8.50 (8/31/87)
84	CHATEAU SOUVERAIN Cabernet Sauvignon Sonoma County Vintage Selection 1974 Cur: $50 (2/15/90) (JG)
92	CHATEAU ST. JEAN Cabernet Sauvignon Alexander Valley 1987 $16 (6/30/91) SS
90	CHATEAU ST. JEAN Cabernet Sauvignon Alexander Valley 1986 Rel: $19 Cur: $20 (10/15/89)
85+	CHATEAU ST. JEAN Cabernet Sauvignon Alexander Valley 1986 Rel: $19 Cur: $20 (4/15/88) (BT)
86	CHATEAU ST. JEAN Cabernet Sauvignon Alexander Valley 1985 Rel: $19 Cur: $23 (11/15/88)
72	CHATEAU ST. JEAN Cabernet Sauvignon Sonoma County 1981 Rel: $15 Cur: $20 (11/30/86)

82 CHATEAU ST. JEAN Cabernet Sauvignon Sonoma Valley Wildwood Vineyards 1980 Rel: $17 Cur: $18 (9/01/85)
76 CHATEAU ST. JEAN Cabernet Sauvignon Sonoma Valley Wildwood Vineyards 1979 Rel: $17 Cur: $18 (7/01/84)
91 CHESTNUT HILL Cabernet Sauvignon Napa Valley 1983 $7 (10/31/86) BB
80 CHESTNUT HILL Cabernet Sauvignon Sonoma County 1987 $9 (3/31/90)
77 CHESTNUT HILL Cabernet Sauvignon Sonoma County 1985 $7.75 (10/15/88)
80+ CHIMNEY ROCK Cabernet Sauvignon Napa Valley Stags Leap District 1988 (NR) (4/30/90) (BT)
90 CHIMNEY ROCK Cabernet Sauvignon Napa Valley Stags Leap District 1987 $18 (7/31/91) SS
85+ CHIMNEY ROCK Cabernet Sauvignon Napa Valley Stags Leap District 1987 $18 (4/15/89) (BT)
87 CHIMNEY ROCK Cabernet Sauvignon Napa Valley Stags Leap District 1986 Rel: $15 Cur: $17 (9/30/89)
86 CHIMNEY ROCK Cabernet Sauvignon Napa Valley Stags Leap District 1986 Rel: $15 Cur: $17 (CA-3/89)
87 CHIMNEY ROCK Cabernet Sauvignon Napa Valley Stags Leap District 1985 Rel: $15 Cur: $19 (CA-3/89)
88 CHIMNEY ROCK Cabernet Sauvignon Napa Valley Stags Leap District 1985 Rel: $15 Cur: $19 (10/31/88)
82 CHIMNEY ROCK Cabernet Sauvignon Napa Valley Stags Leap District 1984 Rel: $15 Cur: $18 (CA-3/89)
87 CHIMNEY ROCK Cabernet Sauvignon Napa Valley Stags Leap District 1984 Rel: $15 Cur: $18 (4/30/88)
90+ CHRISTIAN BROTHERS Cabernet Sauvignon Napa Valley 1987 (NR) (4/15/89) (BT)
88 CHRISTIAN BROTHERS Cabernet Sauvignon Napa Valley 1986 $9.50 (11/15/90)
85+ CHRISTIAN BROTHERS Cabernet Sauvignon Napa Valley 1986 $9.50 (4/15/88) (BT)
90 CHRISTIAN BROTHERS Cabernet Sauvignon Napa Valley 1985 $8 (6/15/88)
87 CHRISTIAN BROTHERS Cabernet Sauvignon Napa Valley 1984 $7 (10/15/87) BB
58 CHRISTIAN BROTHERS Cabernet Sauvignon Napa Valley 1980 $6.75 (10/01/85)
84 CHRISTIAN BROTHERS Montage Premier Cuvée Bordeaux-Napa Valley NV $15 (10/15/88)
83 CHRISTOPHE Cabernet Sauvignon California 1988 $9 (3/31/91)
85 CHRISTOPHE Cabernet Sauvignon California 1982 $4.50 (12/16/85) BB
78 CHRISTOPHE Cabernet Sauvignon Napa Valley Reserve 1986 $12 (11/15/90)
74 CHRISTOPHE Cabernet Sauvignon Napa Valley Reserve 1985 $12.50 (11/15/89)
82 CHRISTOPHE Cabernet Sauvignon Napa Valley Reserve 1983 $9.50 (3/31/88)
84 CINNABAR Cabernet Sauvignon Santa Cruz Mountains 1987 $18 (3/31/91)
93 CINNABAR Cabernet Sauvignon Santa Cruz Mountains 1986 $15 (11/15/89)
77 CLOS DU BOIS Cabernet Sauvignon Alexander Valley 1988 $14 (7/15/91)
86 CLOS DU BOIS Cabernet Sauvignon Alexander Valley 1987 $11 (2/15/90)
86 CLOS DU BOIS Cabernet Sauvignon Alexander Valley 1986 $12 (5/31/89)
85+ CLOS DU BOIS Cabernet Sauvignon Alexander Valley 1986 $12 (4/15/88) (BT)
87 CLOS DU BOIS Cabernet Sauvignon Alexander Valley 1985 $10.50 (4/15/88)
87 CLOS DU BOIS Cabernet Sauvignon Alexander Valley 1984 $10 (6/15/87)
91 CLOS DU BOIS Cabernet Sauvignon Alexander Valley 1981 $9 (3/01/86)
81 CLOS DU BOIS Cabernet Sauvignon Sonoma County 1980 $9 (7/01/84)
87 CLOS DU BOIS Cabernet Sauvignon Alexander Valley Briarcrest Vineyard 1986 Rel: $17 Cur: $18 (8/31/90)
86 CLOS DU BOIS Cabernet Sauvignon Alexander Valley Briarcrest Vineyard 1985 Rel: $16 Cur: $20 (6/15/89)
82 CLOS DU BOIS Cabernet Sauvignon Alexander Valley Briarcrest Vineyard 1985 Rel: $16 Cur: $20 (CA-3/89)
87 CLOS DU BOIS Cabernet Sauvignon Alexander Valley Briarcrest Vineyard 1984 Rel: $16 Cur: $24 (CA-3/89)
90 CLOS DU BOIS Cabernet Sauvignon Alexander Valley Briarcrest Vineyard 1984 Rel: $16 Cur: $24 (7/15/88)
74 CLOS DU BOIS Cabernet Sauvignon Alexander Valley Briarcrest Vineyard 1983 Rel: $12 Cur: $28 (CA-3/89)
66 CLOS DU BOIS Cabernet Sauvignon Alexander Valley Briarcrest Vineyard 1982 Rel: $12 Cur: $35 (CA-3/89)
91 CLOS DU BOIS Cabernet Sauvignon Alexander Valley Briarcrest Vineyard 1982 Rel: $12 Cur: $35 (7/31/87)
88 CLOS DU BOIS Cabernet Sauvignon Alexander Valley Briarcrest Vineyard 1981 Rel: $12 Cur: $37 (CA-3/89)
80 CLOS DU BOIS Cabernet Sauvignon Alexander Valley Briarcrest Vineyard 1980 Rel: $12 Cur: $32 (CA-3/89)
66 CLOS DU BOIS Cabernet Sauvignon Alexander Valley Briarcrest Vineyard 1980 Rel: $12 Cur: $32 (4/16/86)
88 CLOS DU BOIS Cabernet Sauvignon Dry Creek Valley Proprietor's Reserve 1982 $19 (9/15/87)
74 CLOS DU BOIS Cabernet Sauvignon Sonoma County Dry Creek 1974 Cur: $40 (2/15/90) (JG)
90 CLOS DU BOIS Marlstone Vineyard Alexander Valley 1987 $20 (7/31/91)
85 CLOS DU BOIS Marlstone Vineyard Alexander Valley 1986 Rel: $20 Cur: $21 (8/31/90)
81 CLOS DU BOIS Marlstone Vineyard Alexander Valley 1985 Rel: $19.50 Cur: $23 (6/15/89)
88 CLOS DU BOIS Marlstone Vineyard Alexander Valley 1985 Rel: $19.50 Cur: $23 (CA-3/89)
89 CLOS DU BOIS Marlstone Vineyard Alexander Valley 1984 Rel: $19.50 Cur: $27 (CA-3/89)
85 CLOS DU BOIS Marlstone Vineyard Alexander Valley 1984 Rel: $19.50 Cur: $27 (5/15/88)
70 CLOS DU BOIS Marlstone Vineyard Alexander Valley 1983 Rel: $20 Cur: $25 (CA-3/89)
88 CLOS DU BOIS Marlstone Vineyard Alexander Valley 1983 Rel: $20 Cur: $25 (9/15/87)
79 CLOS DU BOIS Marlstone Vineyard Alexander Valley 1982 Rel: $16 Cur: $26 (CA-3/89)
86 CLOS DU BOIS Marlstone Vineyard Alexander Valley 1982 Rel: $16 Cur: $26 (9/30/86)
85 CLOS DU BOIS Marlstone Vineyard Alexander Valley 1981 Rel: $15 Cur: $32 (CA-3/89)
96 CLOS DU BOIS Marlstone Vineyard Alexander Valley 1981 Rel: $15 Cur: $32 (3/16/86)
77 CLOS DU BOIS Marlstone Vineyard Alexander Valley 1980 Rel: $15 Cur: $29 (CA-3/89)
75 CLOS DU BOIS Marlstone Vineyard Alexander Valley 1979 Rel: $16 Cur: $30 (CA-3/89)
72 CLOS DU BOIS Marlstone Vineyard Alexander Valley 1978 Rel: $16 Cur: $30 (CA-3/89)
82 CLOS DU VAL Cabernet Sauvignon Napa Valley 1976 Rel: $9 Cur: $55 (CA-3/89)
82 CLOS DU VAL Cabernet Sauvignon Napa Valley Joli Val 1988 $13 (7/31/91)
87 CLOS DU VAL Cabernet Sauvignon Napa Valley Joli Val 1986 Rel: $12.50 Cur: $13 (12/15/89)
91 CLOS DU VAL Cabernet Sauvignon Napa Valley Joli Val 1986 Rel: $12.50 Cur: $13 (CA-3/89)
85+ CLOS DU VAL Cabernet Sauvignon Napa Valley Stags Leap District 1989 (NR) (5/15/91) (BT)
92 CLOS DU VAL Cabernet Sauvignon Napa Valley Stags Leap District 1987 $17 (6/30/91)
80+ CLOS DU VAL Cabernet Sauvignon Napa Valley Stags Leap District 1987 $17 (4/15/89) (BT)
91 CLOS DU VAL Cabernet Sauvignon Napa Valley Stags Leap District 1986 Rel: $17.50 Cur: $18 (5/31/90)
92 CLOS DU VAL Cabernet Sauvignon Napa Valley Stags Leap District 1986 Rel: $17.50 Cur: $18 (CA-3/89)
90 CLOS DU VAL Cabernet Sauvignon Napa Valley Stags Leap District 1985 Rel: $16 Cur: $25 (6/15/89)
93 CLOS DU VAL Cabernet Sauvignon Napa Valley Stags Leap District 1985 Rel: $16 Cur: $25 (CA-3/89)
92 CLOS DU VAL Cabernet Sauvignon Napa Valley Stags Leap District 1984 Rel: $15 Cur: $17 (CA-3/89)
86 CLOS DU VAL Cabernet Sauvignon Napa Valley Stags Leap District 1984 Rel: $15 Cur: $17 (4/15/88)
86 CLOS DU VAL Cabernet Sauvignon Napa Valley Stags Leap District 1983 Rel: $15 Cur: $18 (CA-3/89)
77 CLOS DU VAL Cabernet Sauvignon Napa Valley Stags Leap District 1983 Rel: $15 Cur: $18 (9/15/87)
88 CLOS DU VAL Cabernet Sauvignon Napa Valley Stags Leap District 1982 Rel: $13.25 Cur: $24 (CA-3/89)
91 CLOS DU VAL Cabernet Sauvignon Napa Valley Stags Leap District 1982 Rel: $13.25 Cur: $24 (7/01/86)
88 CLOS DU VAL Cabernet Sauvignon Napa Valley Stags Leap District 1982 Rel: $13.25 Cur: $24 (2/01/85)
82 CLOS DU VAL Cabernet Sauvignon Napa Valley Stags Leap District 1981 Rel: $12.50 Cur: $18 (CA-3/89)
89 CLOS DU VAL Cabernet Sauvignon Napa Valley Stags Leap District 1981 Rel: $12.50 Cur: $18 (2/01/86)
89 CLOS DU VAL Cabernet Sauvignon Napa Valley Stags Leap District 1981 Rel: $12.50 Cur: $18 (2/01/85)
88 CLOS DU VAL Cabernet Sauvignon Napa Valley Stags Leap District 1980 Rel: $12.50 Cur: $28 (CA-3/89)
83 CLOS DU VAL Cabernet Sauvignon Napa Valley Stags Leap District 1980 Rel: $12.50 Cur: $28 (2/01/86)
83 CLOS DU VAL Cabernet Sauvignon Napa Valley Stags Leap District 1980 Rel: $12.50 Cur: $28 (2/01/85)
90 CLOS DU VAL Cabernet Sauvignon Napa Valley Stags Leap District 1979 Rel: $12.50 Cur: $40 (CA-3/89)
93 CLOS DU VAL Cabernet Sauvignon Napa Valley Stags Leap District 1979 Rel: $12.50 Cur: $40 (2/01/86)
93 CLOS DU VAL Cabernet Sauvignon Napa Valley Stags Leap District 1979 Rel: $12.50 Cur: $40 (2/01/85)
92 CLOS DU VAL Cabernet Sauvignon Napa Valley Stags Leap District 1978 Rel: $12 Cur: $36 (CA-3/89)
90 CLOS DU VAL Cabernet Sauvignon Napa Valley Stags Leap District 1978 Rel: $12 Cur: $36 (6/01/86)
84 CLOS DU VAL Cabernet Sauvignon Napa Valley Stags Leap District 1978 Rel: $12 Cur: $36 (2/01/85)
89 CLOS DU VAL Cabernet Sauvignon Napa Valley Stags Leap District 1977 Rel: $10 Cur: $40 (CA-3/89)
89 CLOS DU VAL Cabernet Sauvignon Napa Valley Stags Leap District 1975 Rel: $9 Cur: $65 (CA-3/89)
91 CLOS DU VAL Cabernet Sauvignon Napa Valley Stags Leap District 1974 Rel: $7.50 Cur: $75 (CA-3/89)
86 CLOS DU VAL Cabernet Sauvignon Napa Valley Stags Leap District 1973 Rel: $6 Cur: $75 (CA-3/89)
90 CLOS DU VAL Cabernet Sauvignon Napa Valley Stags Leap District 1972 Rel: $6 Cur: $75 (CA-3/89)
81 CLOS DU VAL Cabernet Sauvignon Napa Valley Stags Leap District 1972 Rel: $6 Cur: $75 (4/01/86)
88 CLOS DU VAL Cabernet Sauvignon Napa Valley Stags Leap District Gran Val 1985 $8.50 (5/31/88)
85 CLOS DU VAL Cabernet Sauvignon Napa Valley Stags Leap District Gran Val 1984 $8.50 (2/15/87) BB
88 CLOS DU VAL Cabernet Sauvignon Napa Valley Stags Leap District Gran Val 1982 $7.50 (4/16/84)
94 CLOS DU VAL Napa Valley Stags Leap District Reserve 1985 $45 (11/15/90)
92 CLOS DU VAL Napa Valley Stags Leap District Reserve 1985 $45 (11/15/89)
94 CLOS DU VAL Napa Valley Stags Leap District Reserve 1985 $45 (CA-3/89)
90 CLOS DU VAL Napa Valley Stags Leap District Reserve 1982 Rel: $28 Cur: $37 (CA-3/89)
88 CLOS DU VAL Napa Valley Stags Leap District Reserve 1982 Rel: $28 Cur: $37 (11/15/87)
92 CLOS DU VAL Cabernet Sauvignon Napa Valley Stags Leap District Reserve 1979 Rel: $25 Cur: $55 (CA-3/89)
91 CLOS DU VAL Cabernet Sauvignon Napa Valley Stags Leap District Reserve 1979 Rel: $25 Cur: $55 (9/01/84) SS
94 CLOS DU VAL Cabernet Sauvignon Napa Valley Stags Leap District Reserve 1978 Rel: $30 Cur: $50 (CA-3/89)
85 CLOS DU VAL Cabernet Sauvignon Napa Valley Stags Leap District Reserve 1978 Rel: $30 Cur: $50 (4/30/87)
87 CLOS DU VAL Cabernet Sauvignon Napa Valley Stags Leap District Reserve 1977 Rel: $20 Cur: $53 (CA-3/89)
90 CLOS DU VAL Cabernet Sauvignon Napa Valley Stags Leap District Reserve 1973 Rel: $10 Cur: $100 (CA-3/89)
88 CLOS PEGASE Cabernet Sauvignon Napa Valley 1986 $16.50 (9/30/90)
86 CLOS PEGASE Cabernet Sauvignon Napa Valley 1985 $17 (5/31/88)
71 CLOS ROBERT Cabernet Sauvignon Napa Valley Proprietor's Reserve 1984 $7 (12/31/87)
85+ B.R. COHN Cabernet Sauvignon Sonoma Valley Olive Hill Vineyard 1990 (NR) (5/15/91) (BT)
85+ B.R. COHN Cabernet Sauvignon Sonoma Valley Olive Hill Vineyard 1989 (NR) (5/15/91) (BT)
89 B.R. COHN Cabernet Sauvignon Sonoma Valley Olive Hill Vineyard 1988 $25 (5/15/91)
92 B.R. COHN Cabernet Sauvignon Sonoma Valley Olive Hill Vineyard 1987 Rel: $25 Cur: $27 (6/30/90)
94 B.R. COHN Cabernet Sauvignon Sonoma Valley Olive Hill Vineyard 1986 Rel: $18 Cur: $27 (5/31/89)
94 B.R. COHN Cabernet Sauvignon Sonoma Valley Olive Hill Vineyard 1986 Rel: $18 Cur: $27 (CA-3/89)
94 B.R. COHN Cabernet Sauvignon Sonoma Valley Olive Hill Vineyard 1985 Rel: $16 Cur: $35 (CA-3/89)
94 B.R. COHN Cabernet Sauvignon Sonoma Valley Olive Hill Vineyard 1985 Rel: $16 Cur: $35 (11/15/88)
93 B.R. COHN Cabernet Sauvignon Sonoma Valley Olive Hill Vineyard 1984 Rel: $15 Cur: $35 (CA-3/89)
89 B.R. COHN Cabernet Sauvignon Sonoma Valley Olive Hill Vineyard 1984 Rel: $15 Cur: $35 (6/30/88)
89 B.R. COHN Cabernet Sauvignon Sonoma Valley Olive Hill Vineyard 1984 Rel: $15 Cur: $35 (6/30/88)
89 COLONY Cabernet Sauvignon Sonoma County 1982 $7 (3/16/86) BB

UNITED STATES
CALIFORNIA/*CABERNET SAUVIGNON & BLENDS*

77 CONCANNON Cabernet Sauvignon Livermore Valley 1983 $11.50 (6/15/87)
82 CONCANNON Cabernet Sauvignon Livermore Valley 1981 $12 (12/16/84)
83 CONCANNON Cabernet Sauvignon Livermore Valley Reserve 1987 $16 (7/15/91)
87 CONCANNON Cabernet Sauvignon Livermore Valley Reserve 1985 $13.50 (2/15/89)
87 CONN CREEK Cabernet Sauvignon Napa Valley Barrel Select 1987 $17 (7/15/91)
90+ CONN CREEK Cabernet Sauvignon Napa Valley Barrel Select 1987 $17 (4/15/89) (BT)
55 CONN CREEK Cabernet Sauvignon Napa Valley Barrel Select 1986 $15 (2/28/91)
87 CONN CREEK Cabernet Sauvignon Napa Valley Barrel Select 1986 $15 (CA-3/89)
85+ CONN CREEK Cabernet Sauvignon Napa Valley Barrel Select 1986 $15 (4/15/88) (BT)
90 CONN CREEK Cabernet Sauvignon Napa Valley Barrel Select 1985 Rel: $15 Cur: $18 (9/15/90)
85 CONN CREEK Cabernet Sauvignon Napa Valley Barrel Select 1985 Rel: $15 Cur: $18 (CA-3/89)
86 CONN CREEK Cabernet Sauvignon Napa Valley Barrel Select Lot 79 1984 Rel: $13 Cur: $20 (CA-3/89)
86 CONN CREEK Cabernet Sauvignon Napa Valley Barrel Select Lot 79 1984 Rel: $13 Cur: $20 (12/31/88)
82 CONN CREEK Cabernet Sauvignon Napa Valley Barrel Select 1983 Rel: $13 Cur: $15 (CA-3/89)
88 CONN CREEK Cabernet Sauvignon Napa Valley Barrel Select 1983 Rel: $13 Cur: $15 (12/31/88)
85 CONN CREEK Cabernet Sauvignon Napa Valley Barrel Select 1982 Rel: $12 Cur: $20 (CA-3/89)
85 CONN CREEK Cabernet Sauvignon Napa Valley 1981 Rel: $14 Cur: $18 (CA-3/89)
85 CONN CREEK Cabernet Sauvignon Napa Valley 1981 Rel: $14 Cur: $18 (12/16/84)
88 CONN CREEK Cabernet Sauvignon Napa Valley 1980 Rel: $13 Cur: $28 (CA-3/89)
86 CONN CREEK Cabernet Sauvignon Napa Valley 1980 Rel: $13 Cur: $28 (2/15/84)
77 CONN CREEK Cabernet Sauvignon Napa Valley 1979 Rel: $13 Cur: $25 (CA-3/89)
90 CONN CREEK Cabernet Sauvignon Napa Valley 1977 Rel: $12 Cur: $40 (CA-3/89)
86 CONN CREEK Cabernet Sauvignon Napa Valley 1976 Rel: $12 Cur: $45 (CA-3/89)
90 CONN CREEK Cabernet Sauvignon Napa Valley 1974 Rel: $9 Cur: $198 (2/15/90) (JG)
94 CONN CREEK Cabernet Sauvignon Napa Valley 1974 Rel: $9 Cur: $198 (CA-3/89)
92 CONN CREEK Cabernet Sauvignon Napa Valley Stags Leap District 1973 Rel: $9 Cur: $70 (CA-3/89)
90+ CONN CREEK Cabernet Sauvignon Napa Valley Barrel Select Private Reserve 1987 (NR) (4/15/89) (BT)
91 CONN CREEK Cabernet Sauvignon Napa Valley Barrel Select Private Reserve 1986 $37 (12/15/90)
80+ CONN CREEK Cabernet Sauvignon Napa Valley Barrel Select Private Reserve 1986 $37 (4/15/88) (BT)
91 CONN CREEK Cabernet Sauvignon Napa Valley Barrel Select Private Reserve 1985 Rel: $30 Cur: $34 (9/15/90)
87 CONN CREEK Cabernet Sauvignon Napa Valley Barrel Select Private Reserve 1985 Rel: $30 Cur: $34 (CA-3/89)
90+ CONN CREEK Cabernet Sauvignon Napa Valley Reserve 1985 Rel: $30 Cur: $34 (6/15/87) (BT)
94 CONN CREEK Cabernet Sauvignon Napa Valley Collins Vineyard Private Reserve 1984 Rel: $23 Cur: $30 (3/31/89)
88 CONN CREEK Cabernet Sauvignon Napa Valley Collins Vineyard Private Reserve 1984 Rel: $23 Cur: $30 (CA-3/89)
87 CONN CREEK Cabernet Sauvignon Napa Valley Collins Vineyard Proprietor's Special Selection 1983 Cur: $70 (CA-3/89)
85 CONN CREEK Cabernet Sauvignon Napa Valley Collins Vineyard Proprietor's Special Selection 1982 Cur: $70 (CA-3/89)
86 CONN CREEK Cabernet Sauvignon Napa Valley Collins Vineyard Proprietor's Special Selection 1981 Cur: $70 (CA-3/89)
93 CONN CREEK Cabernet Sauvignon Napa Valley Collins Vineyard Proprietor's Special Selection 1980 Cur: $70 (CA-3/89)
86 CONN CREEK Cabernet Sauvignon Napa Valley Lot 1 1978 Rel: $12 Cur: $35 (CA-3/89)
92 CONN CREEK Cabernet Sauvignon Napa Valley Lot 2 1978 Rel: $12 Cur: $35 (CA-3/89)
86 CONN CREEK Cabernet Sauvignon Napa Valley Lot 1 1978 Rel: $12 Cur: $35 (4/30/87)
80 CORBETT CANYON Cabernet Sauvignon Central Coast 1983 $7 (5/16/86) BB
80 CORBETT CANYON Cabernet Sauvignon Central Coast Coastal Classic 1986 $6.50/1.5L (12/15/89)
82 CORBETT CANYON Cabernet Sauvignon Central Coast Select 1984 $8 (2/15/87)
79 CORBETT CANYON Cabernet Sauvignon Santa Barbara-San Luis Obispo Counties Select 1985 $10 (5/31/88)
90+ CORISON Cabernet Sauvignon Napa Valley 1990 (NR) (5/15/91) (BT)
85+ CORISON Cabernet Sauvignon Napa Valley 1989 (NR) (5/15/91) (BT)
92 CORISON Cabernet Sauvignon Napa Valley 1987 $20 (11/15/90)
85+ COSENTINO Cabernet Sauvignon North Coast 1989 (NR) (5/15/91) (BT)
88 COSENTINO Cabernet Sauvignon North Coast 1988 $15 (5/31/91)
80 COSENTINO Cabernet Sauvignon North Coast 1987 $16 (6/30/90)
90+ COSENTINO Cabernet Sauvignon North Coast 1987 $16 (4/15/89) (BT)
75+ COSENTINO Cabernet Sauvignon North Coast 1986 $13 (4/15/88) (BT)
84 COSENTINO Cabernet Sauvignon North Coast 1985 $10.50 (9/15/88)
86 COSENTINO Cabernet Sauvignon North Coast Reserve 1987 $28 (2/28/91)
90 COSENTINO Cabernet Sauvignon North Coast Reserve 1986 $18 (5/15/90)
81 COSENTINO Cabernet Sauvignon North Coast Reserve 1985 $18 (4/30/89)
78 COSENTINO Cabernet Sauvignon North Coast Reserve Edition 1984 $14 (3/31/88)
85+ COSENTINO The Poet California 1989 (NR) (5/15/91) (BT)
85 COSENTINO The Poet California 1988 $27 (5/31/91)
85 COSENTINO The Poet California 1987 $25 (9/15/90)
90+ COSENTINO The Poet California 1987 $25 (4/15/89) (BT)

Key to Symbols

The scores reported here are the results of blind tastings conducted by our panel of senior editors. Wines that carry the initials below are results of individual tastings.

THE WINE SPECTATOR 100-POINT SCALE ***95-100***—Classic, a great wine; ***90-94***—Outstanding, superior character and style; ***80-89***—Good to very good, a wine with special qualities; ***70-79***—Average, drinkable wine that may have minor flaws; ***60-69***—Below average, drinkable but not recommended; ***50-59***—Poor, undrinkable, not recommended. "+"—With a score indicates a range; used primarily with barrel tastings to indicate a preliminary score.

SPECIAL DESIGNATIONS SS—Spectator Selection, CS—Cellar Selection, BB—Best Buy.

TASTER'S INITIALS (JG)—Jim Gordon, (HS)—Harvey Steiman, (JL)—James Laube, (JS)—James Suckling, (TM)—Thomas Matthews, (TR)—Terry Robards, (BT)—Barrel Tasting (these wines were tasted blind from barrel samples), (CA-date)—*California's Great Cabernets* by James Laube, (CH-date)—*California's Great Chardonnays* by James Laube, (VP-date)—*Vintage Port* by James Suckling.

DATE TASTED Dates in parentheses represent the issue in which the rating was published.

86 COSENTINO The Poet California 1986 $22 (7/31/89)
79 COSENTINO The Poet California 1985 $18 (8/31/88)
75 CRESTON MANOR Cabernet Sauvignon Central Coast Winemaker's Selection 1985 $16.50 (12/15/89)
71 CRESTON MANOR Cabernet Sauvignon Central Coast Winemaker's Selection 1984 $16 (12/15/87)
68 CRESTON MANOR Cabernet Sauvignon San Luis Obispo County 1985 $12 (12/15/89)
89 CRONIN Cabernet Sauvignon Merlot Robinson Vineyard Napa Valley 1987 $17 (2/28/91)
88 CRONIN Cabernet Sauvignon Merlot Shaw-Cronin Cuvée San Mateo County 1986 $15 (2/28/91)
88 CRONIN Cabernet Sauvignon Merlot Robinson Vineyard Napa Valley 1986 $16 (2/15/90)
85 CRUVINET Cabernet Sauvignon Alexander Valley 1985 $7 (9/15/88) BB
89 CRYSTAL VALLEY Cabernet Sauvignon North Coast 1983 $8.50 (8/31/86) BB
75 CRYSTAL VALLEY Cabernet Sauvignon North Coast Reserve Edition 1984 $14 (10/15/87)
85 CUTLER Satyre Sonoma Valley 1986 $20 (2/28/91)
86 CUTLER Cabernet Sauvignon Sonoma Valley Batto Ranch 1986 $17 (11/15/90)
91 CUTLER Cabernet Sauvignon Sonoma Valley Batto Ranch 1985 $20 (7/31/89)
92 CUVAISON Cabernet Sauvignon Napa Valley 1987 Rel: $17.50 Cur: $19 (10/31/90)
94 CUVAISON Cabernet Sauvignon Napa Valley 1986 Rel: $15 Cur: $20 (7/15/89)
93 CUVAISON Cabernet Sauvignon Napa Valley 1986 Rel: $15 Cur: $20 (CA-3/89)
90+ CUVAISON Cabernet Sauvignon Napa Valley 1986 Rel: $15 Cur: $20 (4/15/88) (BT)
91 CUVAISON Cabernet Sauvignon Napa Valley 1985 Rel: $14 Cur: $20 (3/31/89)
90 CUVAISON Cabernet Sauvignon Napa Valley 1985 Rel: $14 Cur: $20 (CA-3/89)
89 CUVAISON Cabernet Sauvignon Napa Valley 1984 Rel: $14 Cur: $18 (CA-3/89)
75 CUVAISON Cabernet Sauvignon Napa Valley 1983 Rel: $12 Cur: $15 (CA-3/89)
82 CUVAISON Cabernet Sauvignon Napa Valley 1982 Rel: $11 Cur: $18 (CA-3/89)
90 CUVAISON Cabernet Sauvignon Napa Valley 1982 Rel: $11 Cur: $18 (10/15/87)
74 CUVAISON Cabernet Sauvignon Napa Valley 1981 Rel: $11 Cur: $18 (CA-3/89)
89 CUVAISON Cabernet Sauvignon Napa Valley 1981 Rel: $11 Cur: $18 (11/30/86)
77 CUVAISON Cabernet Sauvignon Napa Valley 1980 Rel: $11 Cur: $18 (CA-3/89)
85 CUVAISON Cabernet Sauvignon Napa Valley 1980 Rel: $11 Cur: $18 (2/16/85)
75 CUVAISON Cabernet Sauvignon Napa Valley 1979 Rel: $11 Cur: $20 (CA-3/89)
72 CUVAISON Cabernet Sauvignon Napa Valley 1978 Rel: $10 Cur: $30 (CA-3/89)
65 CUVAISON Cabernet Sauvignon Napa Valley 1978 Rel: $10 Cur: $30 (5/16/84)
79 CUVAISON Cabernet Sauvignon Napa Valley 1977 Rel: $10 Cur: $30 (CA-3/89)
79 CUVAISON Cabernet Sauvignon Napa Valley 1976 Rel: $10 Cur: $30 (CA-3/89)
79 CUVAISON Cabernet Sauvignon Napa Valley 1975 Rel: $10 Cur: $33 (CA-3/89)
88 CUVAISON Cabernet Sauvignon Napa Valley Philip Togni Signature 1975 Rel: $40 Cur: $60 (CA-3/89)
85 DALLA VALLE Cabernet Sauvignon Napa Valley 1986 $20 (6/30/90)
89 DANIEL Cabernet Sauvignon Napa Valley 1984 $21 (7/15/88)
79 DANIEL Cabernet Sauvignon Napa Valley 1983 $20 (4/30/89)
89 DE LOACH Cabernet Sauvignon Dry Creek Valley 1984 $11 (12/15/87)
85 DE LOACH Cabernet Sauvignon Dry Creek Valley 1983 $11 (9/30/86)
80 DE LOACH Cabernet Sauvignon Dry Creek Valley 1981 $11 (4/01/85)
85 DE LOACH Cabernet Sauvignon Russian River Valley O.F.S. 1987 $22 (10/15/90)
84 DE LORIMIER Mosaic Alexander Valley 1986 $16 (10/31/89)
79 DE MOOR Cabernet Sauvignon Napa Valley 1985 Rel: $14 Cur: $14 (CA-3/89)
88 DE MOOR Cabernet Sauvignon Napa Valley 1984 Rel: $14 Cur: $16 (CA-3/89)
89 DE MOOR Cabernet Sauvignon Napa Valley 1984 Rel: $14 Cur: $16 (8/31/88)
86 DE MOOR Cabernet Sauvignon Napa Valley 1983 Rel: $12 Cur: $16 (CA-3/89)
86 DE MOOR Cabernet Sauvignon Napa Valley 1982 Rel: $12 Cur: $18 (CA-3/89)
86 DE MOOR Cabernet Sauvignon Napa Valley Napa Cellars 1981 Rel: $12 Cur: $25 (CA-3/89)
95 DE MOOR Cabernet Sauvignon Napa Valley Napa Cellars 1981 Rel: $12 Cur: $25 (4/16/86)
80 DE MOOR Cabernet Sauvignon Napa Valley Napa Cellars 1980 Rel: $12 Cur: $20 (CA-3/89)
85 DE MOOR Cabernet Sauvignon Napa Valley Napa Cellars 1979 Rel: $10 Cur: $25 (CA-3/89)
89 DE MOOR Cabernet Sauvignon Napa Valley Napa Cellars 1978 Rel: $10 Cur: $28 (CA-3/89)
78 DE MOOR Cabernet Sauvignon Napa Valley Owner's Select 1986 $16 (2/28/91)
88 DE MOOR Cabernet Sauvignon Napa Valley Owner's Select 1982 Rel: $12 Cur: $19 (CA-3/89)
72 DEER VALLEY Cabernet Sauvignon Monterey 1985 $5.50 (12/31/87)
88 DEHLINGER Cabernet Sauvignon Russian River Valley 1987 $13 (2/28/91)
90 DEHLINGER Cabernet Sauvignon Russian River Valley 1986 $13 (3/15/90)
90+ DEHLINGER Cabernet Sauvignon Russian River Valley 1986 $13 (4/15/88) (BT)
74 DEHLINGER Cabernet Sauvignon Russian River Valley 1985 $13 (5/31/89)
76 DEHLINGER Cabernet Sauvignon Russian River Valley 1984 $12 (2/15/88)
85 DEHLINGER Cabernet Sauvignon Russian River Valley 1983 $11 (6/15/87)
73 DEHLINGER Cabernet Sauvignon Russian River Valley 1982 $11 (8/31/86)
87 DEHLINGER Cabernet Sauvignon Sonoma County 1981 $9 (5/16/85)
66 DELICATO Cabernet Sauvignon California 1985 $6 (6/30/88)
72 DELICATO Cabernet Sauvignon Carneros Napa Valley 1983 $10 (6/15/87)
83 DEVLIN Cabernet Sauvignon Sonoma County 1981 $6 (8/01/85)
80+ DIAMOND CREEK Cabernet Sauvignon Napa Valley 1985 $30 (6/15/87) (BT)
85+ DIAMOND CREEK Cabernet Sauvignon Napa Valley Gravelly Meadow 1990 (NR) (5/15/91) (BT)
85+ DIAMOND CREEK Cabernet Sauvignon Napa Valley Gravelly Meadow 1989 (NR) (5/15/91) (BT)
87 DIAMOND CREEK Cabernet Sauvignon Napa Valley Gravelly Meadow 1988 $40 (11/15/90)
90+ DIAMOND CREEK Cabernet Sauvignon Napa Valley Gravelly Meadow 1988 $40 (4/30/90) (BT)
90 DIAMOND CREEK Cabernet Sauvignon Napa Valley Gravelly Meadow 1987 Rel: $40 Cur: $43 (12/15/89)
90+ DIAMOND CREEK Cabernet Sauvignon Napa Valley Gravelly Meadow 1987 Rel: $40 Cur: $43 (4/15/89) (BT)
94 DIAMOND CREEK Cabernet Sauvignon Napa Valley Gravelly Meadow 1986 Rel: $30 Cur: $48 (CA-3/89)
91 DIAMOND CREEK Cabernet Sauvignon Napa Valley Gravelly Meadow 1986 Rel: $30 Cur: $48 (12/31/88)
92 DIAMOND CREEK Cabernet Sauvignon Napa Valley Gravelly Meadow 1985 Rel: $30 Cur: $56 (CA-3/89)
89 DIAMOND CREEK Cabernet Sauvignon Napa Valley Gravelly Meadow 1985 Rel: $30 Cur: $56 (11/30/87)
80+ DIAMOND CREEK Cabernet Sauvignon Napa Valley Gravelly Meadow 1985 Rel: $30 Cur: $56 (6/15/87) (BT)
94 DIAMOND CREEK Cabernet Sauvignon Napa Valley Gravelly Meadow 1984 Rel: $25 Cur: $65 (CA-3/89)
93 DIAMOND CREEK Cabernet Sauvignon Napa Valley Gravelly Meadow 1984 Rel: $25 Cur: $65 (11/15/86)
89 DIAMOND CREEK Cabernet Sauvignon Napa Valley Gravelly Meadow 1983 Rel: $20 Cur: $40 (CA-3/89)

93 DIAMOND CREEK Cabernet Sauvignon Napa Valley Gravelly Meadow 1983 Rel: $20 Cur: $40 (2/01/86) CS
89 DIAMOND CREEK Cabernet Sauvignon Napa Valley Gravelly Meadow 1982 Rel: $20 Cur: $58 (CA-3/89)
91 DIAMOND CREEK Cabernet Sauvignon Napa Valley Gravelly Meadow 1982 Rel: $20 Cur: $58 (12/16/84)
89 DIAMOND CREEK Cabernet Sauvignon Napa Valley Gravelly Meadow 1981 Rel: $20 Cur: $58 (CA-3/89)
92 DIAMOND CREEK Cabernet Sauvignon Napa Valley Gravelly Meadow 1980 Rel: $20 Cur: $66 (CA-3/89)
91 DIAMOND CREEK Cabernet Sauvignon Napa Valley Gravelly Meadow 1979 Rel: $15 Cur: $94 (CA-3/89)
93 DIAMOND CREEK Cabernet Sauvignon Napa Valley Gravelly Meadow 1978 Rel: $12.50 Cur: $95 (CA-3/89)
88 DIAMOND CREEK Cabernet Sauvignon Napa Valley Gravelly Meadow 1978 Rel: $12.50 Cur: $95 (4/30/87)
89 DIAMOND CREEK Cabernet Sauvignon Napa Valley Gravelly Meadow 1977 Rel: $10 Cur: $80 (CA-3/89)
85 DIAMOND CREEK Cabernet Sauvignon Napa Valley Gravelly Meadow 1976 Rel: $9 Cur: $90 (CA-3/89)
85 DIAMOND CREEK Cabernet Sauvignon Napa Valley Gravelly Meadow 1975 Rel: $7.50 Cur: $80 (CA-3/89)
96 DIAMOND CREEK Cabernet Sauvignon Napa Valley Gravelly Meadow 1974 Rel: $7.50 Cur: $140 (2/15/90) (JG)
88 DIAMOND CREEK Cabernet Sauvignon Napa Valley Gravelly Meadow 1974 Rel: $7.50 Cur: $140 (CA-3/89)
84 DIAMOND CREEK Cabernet Sauvignon Napa Valley Gravelly Meadow Special Selection 1982 Rel: $20 Cur: $40 (CA-3/89)
91 DIAMOND CREEK Cabernet Sauvignon Napa Valley Lake 1987 $100 (11/15/90)
92 DIAMOND CREEK Cabernet Sauvignon Napa Valley Lake 1984 Rel: $50 Cur: $250 (CA-3/89)
99 DIAMOND CREEK Cabernet Sauvignon Napa Valley Lake 1978 Rel: $25 Cur: $350 (CA-3/89)
85+ DIAMOND CREEK Cabernet Sauvignon Napa Valley Red Rock Terrace 1990 (NR) (5/15/91) (BT)
85+ DIAMOND CREEK Cabernet Sauvignon Napa Valley Red Rock Terrace 1989 (NR) (5/15/91) (BT)
89 DIAMOND CREEK Cabernet Sauvignon Napa Valley Red Rock Terrace 1988 $40 (11/15/90)
90+ DIAMOND CREEK Cabernet Sauvignon Napa Valley Red Rock Terrace 1988 $40 (4/30/91) (BT)
94 DIAMOND CREEK Cabernet Sauvignon Napa Valley Red Rock Terrace 1987 Rel: $40 Cur: $42 (12/15/89)
90+ DIAMOND CREEK Cabernet Sauvignon Napa Valley Red Rock Terrace 1987 Rel: $40 Cur: $42 (4/15/89) (BT)
96 DIAMOND CREEK Cabernet Sauvignon Napa Valley Red Rock Terrace 1986 Rel: $30 Cur: $46 (CA-3/89)
93 DIAMOND CREEK Cabernet Sauvignon Napa Valley Red Rock Terrace 1986 Rel: $30 Cur: $46 (12/31/88)
85+ DIAMOND CREEK Cabernet Sauvignon Napa Valley Red Rock Terrace 1986 Rel: $30 Cur: $46 (4/15/88) (BT)
93 DIAMOND CREEK Cabernet Sauvignon Napa Valley Red Rock Terrace 1985 Rel: $30 Cur: $51 (CA-3/89)
91 DIAMOND CREEK Cabernet Sauvignon Napa Valley Red Rock Terrace 1985 Rel: $30 Cur: $51 (11/30/87)
85+ DIAMOND CREEK Cabernet Sauvignon Napa Valley Red Rock Terrace 1985 Rel: $30 Cur: $51 (6/15/87) (BT)
96 DIAMOND CREEK Cabernet Sauvignon Napa Valley Red Rock Terrace 1984 Rel: $25 Cur: $65 (CA-3/89)
95 DIAMOND CREEK Cabernet Sauvignon Napa Valley Red Rock Terrace 1984 Rel: $25 Cur: $65 (9/30/86) CS
88 DIAMOND CREEK Cabernet Sauvignon Napa Valley Red Rock Terrace 1983 Rel: $20 Cur: $37 (CA-3/89)
89 DIAMOND CREEK Cabernet Sauvignon Napa Valley Red Rock Terrace 1983 Rel: $20 Cur: $37 (2/01/86)
87 DIAMOND CREEK Cabernet Sauvignon Napa Valley Red Rock Terrace 1982 Rel: $20 Cur: $66 (CA-3/89)
86 DIAMOND CREEK Cabernet Sauvignon Napa Valley Red Rock Terrace 1982 Rel: $20 Cur: $66 (1/01/85)
91 DIAMOND CREEK Cabernet Sauvignon Napa Valley Red Rock Terrace 1981 Rel: $20 Cur: $55 (CA-3/89)
86 DIAMOND CREEK Cabernet Sauvignon Napa Valley Red Rock Terrace 1980 Rel: $20 Cur: $57 (CA-3/89)
92 DIAMOND CREEK Cabernet Sauvignon Napa Valley Red Rock Terrace 1979 Rel: $15 Cur: $90 (CA-3/89)
92 DIAMOND CREEK Cabernet Sauvignon Napa Valley Red Rock Terrace 1978 Rel: $12.50 Cur: $104 (CA-3/89)
88 DIAMOND CREEK Cabernet Sauvignon Napa Valley Red Rock Terrace First Pick 1977 Rel: $10 Cur: $72 (CA-3/89)
85 DIAMOND CREEK Cabernet Sauvignon Napa Valley Red Rock Terrace 1976 Rel: $9 Cur: $95 (CA-3/89)
88 DIAMOND CREEK Cabernet Sauvignon Napa Valley Red Rock Terrace 1975 Rel: $7.50 Cur: $88 (CA-3/89)
74 DIAMOND CREEK Cabernet Sauvignon Napa Valley Red Rock Terrace 1972 Rel: $7.50 Cur: $200 (CA-3/89)
80 DIAMOND CREEK Cabernet Sauvignon Napa Valley Red Rock Terrace Special Selection 1982 Rel: $20 Cur: $35 (CA-3/89)
75 DIAMOND CREEK Cabernet Sauvignon Napa Valley Red Rock Terrace Second Pick 1977 Rel: $10 Cur: $45 (CA-3/89)
89 DIAMOND CREEK Cabernet Sauvignon Napa Valley Three Vineyard Blend 1985 Rel: $50 Cur: $100 (CA-3/89)
89 DIAMOND CREEK Cabernet Sauvignon Napa Valley Three Vineyard Blend 1984 Rel: $50 Cur: $100 (CA-3/89)
90 DIAMOND CREEK Cabernet Sauvignon Napa Valley Three Vineyard Blend 1981 Rel: $20 Cur: $100 (CA-3/89)
85+ DIAMOND CREEK Cabernet Sauvignon Napa Valley Volcanic Hill 1990 (NR) (5/15/91) (BT)
90+ DIAMOND CREEK Cabernet Sauvignon Napa Valley Volcanic Hill 1989 (NR) (5/15/91) (BT)
88 DIAMOND CREEK Cabernet Sauvignon Napa Valley Volcanic Hill 1988 $40 (11/15/90)
90+ DIAMOND CREEK Cabernet Sauvignon Napa Valley Volcanic Hill 1988 $40 (4/30/91) (BT)
95 DIAMOND CREEK Cabernet Sauvignon Napa Valley Volcanic Hill 1987 Rel: $40 Cur: $41 (12/15/89)

85+ DIAMOND CREEK Cabernet Sauvignon Napa Valley Volcanic Hill 1987 Rel: $40 Cur: $41 (4/15/89) (BT)
96 DIAMOND CREEK Cabernet Sauvignon Napa Valley Volcanic Hill 1986 Rel: $30 Cur: $52 (CA-3/89)
91 DIAMOND CREEK Cabernet Sauvignon Napa Valley Volcanic Hill 1986 Rel: $30 Cur: $52 (12/31/88)
90+ DIAMOND CREEK Cabernet Sauvignon Napa Valley Volcanic Hill 1986 Rel: $30 Cur: $52 (4/15/88) (BT)
93 DIAMOND CREEK Cabernet Sauvignon Napa Valley Volcanic Hill 1985 Rel: $30 Cur: $50 (CA-3/89)
88 DIAMOND CREEK Cabernet Sauvignon Napa Valley Volcanic Hill 1985 Rel: $30 Cur: $50 (11/30/87)
94 DIAMOND CREEK Cabernet Sauvignon Napa Valley Volcanic Hill 1984 Rel: $25 Cur: $62 (CA-3/89)
94 DIAMOND CREEK Cabernet Sauvignon Napa Valley Volcanic Hill 1984 Rel: $25 Cur: $62 (11/15/86)
89 DIAMOND CREEK Cabernet Sauvignon Napa Valley Volcanic Hill 1983 Rel: $20 Cur: $35 (CA-3/89)
87 DIAMOND CREEK Cabernet Sauvignon Napa Valley Volcanic Hill 1983 Rel: $20 Cur: $35 (2/01/86)
89 DIAMOND CREEK Cabernet Sauvignon Napa Valley Volcanic Hill 1982 Rel: $20 Cur: $68 (CA-3/89)
92 DIAMOND CREEK Cabernet Sauvignon Napa Valley Volcanic Hill 1982 Rel: $20 Cur: $68 (12/16/84) CS
92 DIAMOND CREEK Cabernet Sauvignon Napa Valley Volcanic Hill 1981 Rel: $20 Cur: $49 (CA-3/89)
90 DIAMOND CREEK Cabernet Sauvignon Napa Valley Volcanic Hill 1980 Rel: $20 Cur: $75 (CA-3/89)
95 DIAMOND CREEK Cabernet Sauvignon Napa Valley Volcanic Hill First Pick 1979 Rel: $15 Cur: $90 (CA-3/89)
95 DIAMOND CREEK Cabernet Sauvignon Napa Valley Volcanic Hill 1978 Rel: $12.50 Cur: $90 (CA-3/89)
84 DIAMOND CREEK Cabernet Sauvignon Napa Valley Volcanic Hill 1977 Rel: $10 Cur: $66 (CA-3/89)
87 DIAMOND CREEK Cabernet Sauvignon Napa Valley Volcanic Hill 1976 Rel: $9 Cur: $90 (CA-3/89)
93 DIAMOND CREEK Cabernet Sauvignon Napa Valley Volcanic Hill 1975 Rel: $7.50 Cur: $80 (CA-3/89)
95 DIAMOND CREEK Cabernet Sauvignon Napa Valley Volcanic Hill 1974 Rel: $7.50 Cur: $135 (2/15/90) (JG)
87 DIAMOND CREEK Cabernet Sauvignon Napa Valley Volcanic Hill 1974 Rel: $7.50 Cur: $135 (CA-3/89)
80 DIAMOND CREEK Cabernet Sauvignon Napa Valley Volcanic Hill 1973 Rel: $7.50 Cur: $200 (CA-3/89)
85 DIAMOND CREEK Cabernet Sauvignon Napa Valley Volcanic Hill 1972 Rel: $7.50 Cur: $200 (CA-3/89)
82 DIAMOND CREEK Cabernet Sauvignon Napa Valley Volcanic Hill Second Pick 1979 Rel: $15 Cur: $45 (CA-3/89)
79 DIAMOND CREEK Cabernet Sauvignon Napa Valley Volcanic Hill Special Selection 1982 Rel: $20 Cur: $35 (CA-3/89)
88 DOLAN Cabernet Sauvignon Mendocino 1984 $12 (5/31/88)
86 DOLAN Cabernet Sauvignon Mendocino 1983 $12 (2/29/88)
76 DOMAIN SAN MARTIN Cabernet Sauvignon Central Coast 1981 $7.75 (10/01/85)
82 DOMAINE LAURIER Cabernet Sauvignon Sonoma County Green Valley 1982 $12 (2/16/85)
85+ DOMAINE MICHEL Cabernet Sauvignon Sonoma County 1989 $15 (5/15/91) (BT)
84 DOMAINE MICHEL Cabernet Sauvignon Sonoma County 1987 $19.50 (3/31/91)
75 DOMAINE MICHEL Cabernet Sauvignon Sonoma County 1986 $19 (6/30/90)
86 DOMAINE MICHEL Cabernet Sauvignon Sonoma County 1984 $19 (9/15/87)
85+ DOMAINE MICHEL Cabernet Sauvignon Sonoma County Reserve 1989 $20 (5/15/91) (BT)
81 DOMAINE DE NAPA Cabernet Sauvignon Napa Valley 1985 $12 (12/15/88)
87 DOMAINE PHILIPPE Cabernet Sauvignon Napa Valley Select Cuvée 1984 $6.50 (5/15/88) BB
79 DOMAINE ST. GEORGE Cabernet Sauvignon Russian River Valley Select Reserve 1986 $9 (5/31/90)
83 DOMAINE ST. GEORGE Cabernet Sauvignon Sonoma County 1988 $6 (11/15/90) BB
90+ DOMINUS Napa Valley 1987 (NR) (4/15/89) (BT)
91 DOMINUS Napa Valley 1986 $45 (2/28/91)
93 DOMINUS Napa Valley 1986 $45 (3/01/89)
84 DOMINUS Napa Valley 1985 Rel: $45 Cur: $50 (2/15/90)
95 DOMINUS Napa Valley 1985 Rel: $45 Cur: $50 (3/01/89)
90+ DOMINUS Napa Valley 1985 Rel: $45 Cur: $50 (6/15/87) (BT)
90 DOMINUS Napa Valley 1984 Rel: $40 Cur: $55 (3/01/89)
90 DOMINUS Napa Valley 1984 Rel: $40 Cur: $55 (5/15/88) CS
86 DOMINUS Napa Valley 1983 Rel: $43 Cur: $50 (4/15/89)
87 DOMINUS Napa Valley 1983 Rel: $43 Cur: $50 (3/01/89)
64 DORE Cabernet Sauvignon California 1984 $5 (12/31/87)
81 DRY CREEK Cabernet Sauvignon Sonoma County 1988 $14 (5/31/91)
84 DRY CREEK Cabernet Sauvignon Sonoma County 1987 $12.50 (4/15/90)
85+ DRY CREEK Cabernet Sauvignon Sonoma County 1987 $12.50 (4/15/89) (BT)
88 DRY CREEK Cabernet Sauvignon Sonoma County 1986 $11 (3/31/89)
80+ DRY CREEK Cabernet Sauvignon Sonoma County 1986 $11 (4/15/88) (BT)
91 DRY CREEK Cabernet Sauvignon Sonoma County 1985 Rel: $16 (5/31/88) SS
85 DRY CREEK Cabernet Sauvignon Sonoma County 1984 $10 (5/15/87)
81 DRY CREEK Cabernet Sauvignon Sonoma County 1982 $9.50 (2/01/85)
78 DRY CREEK Cabernet Sauvignon Sonoma County 1980 $9.50 (4/16/84)
78 DRY CREEK Cabernet Sauvignon Sonoma County Special Reserve 1980 $13 (5/01/86)
84 DRY CREEK Meritage Dry Creek Valley 1987 $24 (7/31/91)
90+ DRY CREEK Meritage Dry Creek Valley 1987 $24 (4/15/89) (BT)
80 DRY CREEK Meritage Dry Creek Valley 1986 $22 (9/15/90)
89 DRY CREEK Meritage Dry Creek Valley 1985 $22 (11/15/89)
88 DRY CREEK David S. Stare Vintner's Reserve Sonoma County 1984 $18 (5/31/88)
74 DRY CREEK David S. Stare Vintner's Selection Dry Creek Valley 1983 $15 (12/31/86)
85 DUCKHORN Cabernet Sauvignon Napa Valley 1988 $20 (7/31/91)
95 DUCKHORN Cabernet Sauvignon Napa Valley 1987 Rel: $20 Cur: $27 (6/30/90) CS
85+ DUCKHORN Cabernet Sauvignon Napa Valley 1987 Rel: $20 Cur: $27 (4/15/89) (BT)
94 DUCKHORN Cabernet Sauvignon Napa Valley 1986 Rel: $18 Cur: $24 (7/31/89) SS
94 DUCKHORN Cabernet Sauvignon Napa Valley 1986 Rel: $18 Cur: $24 (CA-3/89)
92 DUCKHORN Cabernet Sauvignon Napa Valley 1985 Rel: $17.50 Cur: $38 (CA-3/89)
91 DUCKHORN Cabernet Sauvignon Napa Valley 1985 Rel: $17.50 Cur: $38 (6/15/88) CS
92 DUCKHORN Cabernet Sauvignon Napa Valley 1984 Rel: $17 Cur: $32 (CA-3/89)

UNITED STATES

CALIFORNIA/*CABERNET SAUVIGNON & BLENDS*

87 DUCKHORN Cabernet Sauvignon Napa Valley 1984 Rel: $17 Cur: $32 (6/15/87)
88 DUCKHORN Cabernet Sauvignon Napa Valley 1983 Rel: $16 Cur: $44 (CA-3/89)
89 DUCKHORN Cabernet Sauvignon Napa Valley 1983 Rel: $16 Cur: $44 (7/01/86)
90 DUCKHORN Cabernet Sauvignon Napa Valley 1982 Rel: $15 Cur: $53 (CA-3/89)
86 DUCKHORN Cabernet Sauvignon Napa Valley 1982 Rel: $15 Cur: $53 (5/16/85)
87 DUCKHORN Cabernet Sauvignon Napa Valley 1981 Rel: $15 Cur: $68 (CA-3/89)
91 DUCKHORN Cabernet Sauvignon Napa Valley 1980 Rel: $14 Cur: $69 (CA-3/89)
92 DUCKHORN Cabernet Sauvignon Napa Valley 1978 Rel: $10.50 Cur: $85 (CA-3/89)
90+ DUNN Cabernet Sauvignon Howell Mountain 1990 (NR) (5/15/91) (BT)
90+ DUNN Cabernet Sauvignon Howell Mountain 1989 (NR) (5/15/91) (BT)
95+ DUNN Cabernet Sauvignon Howell Mountain 1988 (NR) (4/30/91) (BT)
94 DUNN Cabernet Sauvignon Howell Mountain 1987 $36 (4/15/91)
90+ DUNN Cabernet Sauvignon Howell Mountain 1987 $36 (4/15/89) (BT)
95 DUNN Cabernet Sauvignon Howell Mountain 1986 Rel: $30 Cur: $91 (7/31/90) CS
94 DUNN Cabernet Sauvignon Howell Mountain 1986 Rel: $30 Cur: $91 (CA-3/89)
90+ DUNN Cabernet Sauvignon Howell Mountain 1986 Rel: $30 Cur: $91 (4/15/88) (BT)
88 DUNN Cabernet Sauvignon Howell Mountain 1985 Rel: $30 Cur: $112 (4/15/89)
89 DUNN Cabernet Sauvignon Howell Mountain 1985 Rel: $30 Cur: $112 (CA-3/89)
85+ DUNN Cabernet Sauvignon Howell Mountain 1985 Rel: $30 Cur: $112 (6/15/87) (BT)
97 DUNN Cabernet Sauvignon Howell Mountain 1984 Rel: $25 Cur: $128 (CA-3/89)
93 DUNN Cabernet Sauvignon Howell Mountain 1984 Rel: $25 Cur: $128 (3/31/88)
92 DUNN Cabernet Sauvignon Howell Mountain 1983 Rel: $18 Cur: $116 (CA-3/89)
95 DUNN Cabernet Sauvignon Howell Mountain 1983 Rel: $18 Cur: $116 (5/15/87)
95 DUNN Cabernet Sauvignon Howell Mountain 1982 Rel: $15 Cur: $160 (CA-3/89)
90 DUNN Cabernet Sauvignon Howell Mountain 1981 Rel: $14 Cur: $157 (CA-3/89)
93 DUNN Cabernet Sauvignon Howell Mountain 1981 Rel: $14 Cur: $157 (12/16/84)
92 DUNN Cabernet Sauvignon Howell Mountain 1980 Rel: $13 Cur: $172 (CA-3/89)
87 DUNN Cabernet Sauvignon Howell Mountain 1980 Rel: $13 Cur: $172 (3/16/84)
91 DUNN Cabernet Sauvignon Howell Mountain 1979 Rel: $12.50 Cur: $230 (CA-3/89)
90+ DUNN Cabernet Sauvignon Napa Valley 1990 (NR) (5/15/91) (BT)
85+ DUNN Cabernet Sauvignon Napa Valley 1989 (NR) (5/15/91) (BT)
90+ DUNN Cabernet Sauvignon Napa Valley 1988 (NR) (4/30/91) (BT)
93 DUNN Cabernet Sauvignon Napa Valley 1987 $33 (11/15/90)
90+ DUNN Cabernet Sauvignon Napa Valley 1987 $33 (4/15/89) (BT)
95 DUNN Cabernet Sauvignon Napa Valley 1986 Rel: $27 Cur: $55 (10/15/89) CS
93 DUNN Cabernet Sauvignon Napa Valley 1986 Rel: $27 Cur: $55 (CA-3/89)
90+ DUNN Cabernet Sauvignon Napa Valley 1986 Rel: $27 Cur: $55 (4/15/88) (BT)
94 DUNN Cabernet Sauvignon Napa Valley 1985 Rel: $20 Cur: $64 (CA-3/89)
94 DUNN Cabernet Sauvignon Napa Valley 1985 Rel: $20 Cur: $64 (9/15/88) CS
93 DUNN Cabernet Sauvignon Napa Valley 1984 Rel: $18 Cur: $65 (CA-3/89)
90 DUNN Cabernet Sauvignon Napa Valley 1984 Rel: $18 Cur: $65 (11/30/87)
95 DUNN Cabernet Sauvignon Napa Valley 1983 Rel: $15 Cur: $85 (CA-3/89)
95 DUNN Cabernet Sauvignon Napa Valley 1983 Rel: $15 Cur: $85 (10/31/86) SS
94 DUNN Cabernet Sauvignon Napa Valley 1982 Rel: $13 Cur: $95 (CA-3/89)
97 DUNN Cabernet Sauvignon Napa Valley 1982 Rel: $13 Cur: $95 (11/01/85) SS
73 DUNNEWOOD Cabernet Sauvignon California 1986 $7 (6/15/90)
82 DUNNEWOOD Cabernet Sauvignon Napa Valley Napa Reserve 1986 $10.50 (6/15/90)
85 DUNNEWOOD Cabernet Sauvignon Napa Valley Reserve 1984 $10.50 (12/31/88)
82 DURNEY Cabernet Sauvignon Carmel Valley 1981 $12.50 (9/01/84)
86 DURNEY Cabernet Sauvignon Carmel Valley Private Reserve 1983 $20 (4/30/91)
80+ EBERLE Cabernet Sauvignon Paso Robles 1988 (NR) (4/30/91) (BT)
85 EBERLE Cabernet Sauvignon Paso Robles 1986 Rel: $12 Cur: $12 (11/15/89)
85 EBERLE Cabernet Sauvignon Paso Robles 1986 Rel: $12 Cur: $12 (CA-3/89)
80+ EBERLE Cabernet Sauvignon Paso Robles 1986 Rel: $12 Cur: $12 (4/15/88) (BT)
89 EBERLE Cabernet Sauvignon Paso Robles 1985 Rel: $12 Cur: $17 (CA-3/89)
82 EBERLE Cabernet Sauvignon Paso Robles 1985 Rel: $12 Cur: $17 (2/15/89)
86 EBERLE Cabernet Sauvignon Paso Robles 1984 Rel: $12 Cur: $17 (CA-3/89)
84 EBERLE Cabernet Sauvignon Paso Robles 1983 Rel: $10 Cur: $18 (CA-3/89)
79 EBERLE Cabernet Sauvignon Paso Robles 1983 Rel: $10 Cur: $18 (6/15/87)
72 EBERLE Cabernet Sauvignon Paso Robles 1982 Rel: $10 Cur: $24 (CA-3/89)
87 EBERLE Cabernet Sauvignon Paso Robles 1982 Rel: $10 Cur: $24 (9/30/86)
85 EBERLE Cabernet Sauvignon Paso Robles 1981 Rel: $10 Cur: $24 (CA-3/89)
87 EBERLE Cabernet Sauvignon Paso Robles 1981 Rel: $10 Cur: $24 (4/16/85)
78 EBERLE Cabernet Sauvignon Paso Robles 1980 Rel: $10 Cur: $24 (CA-3/89)
82 EBERLE Cabernet Sauvignon San Luis Obispo 1979 Rel: $10 Cur: $25 (CA-3/89)
71 EBERLE Cabernet Sauvignon Paso Robles Reserve 1982 Rel: $25 Cur: $30 (CA-3/89)
80 EBERLE Cabernet Sauvignon Paso Robles Reserve 1981 Rel: $25 Cur: $35 (CA-3/89)
91 EDMUNDS ST. JOHN Les Fleurs du Chaparral Napa Valley 1987 $15 (8/31/90)
79 EHLERS LANE Cabernet Sauvignon Napa Valley 1983 $12 (6/15/87)
81 ESTANCIA Cabernet Sauvignon Alexander Valley 1988 $9 (5/31/91)
80 ESTANCIA Cabernet Sauvignon Alexander Valley 1987 $7 (7/15/90) BB
85 ESTANCIA Cabernet Sauvignon Alexander Valley 1986 $8 (4/15/89) BB
87 ESTANCIA Cabernet Sauvignon Alexander Valley 1985 $6.50 (6/15/88) BB
79 ESTANCIA Cabernet Sauvignon Alexander Valley 1984 $6.50 (12/31/87)
87 ESTANCIA Cabernet Sauvignon Alexander Valley 1982 $6 (4/15/87) BB
88 ESTANCIA Meritage Alexander Valley 1987 $12 (1/31/91)
67 ESTRELLA RIVER Cabernet Sauvignon Paso Robles 1985 $9 (11/15/89)
80 ESTRELLA RIVER Cabernet Sauvignon Paso Robles 1983 $8 (4/15/88)
85 ESTRELLA RIVER Cabernet Sauvignon Paso Robles 1982 $10 (6/15/87)
88 ESTRELLA RIVER Cabernet Sauvignon Paso Robles 1981 $9 (5/01/85)
65 ESTRELLA RIVER Cabernet Sauvignon Paso Robles Founders Epic Collection 1983 $12 (12/15/89)
77 ESTRELLA RIVER Cabernet Sauvignon San Luis Obispo County 1980 $10 (3/16/85)
84 ESTRELLA RIVER Cabernet Sauvignon San Luis Obispo County 1979 $6 (3/01/84) BB

Key to Symbols

The scores reported here are the results of blind tastings conducted by our panel of senior editors. Wines that carry the initials below are results of individual tastings.

THE WINE SPECTATOR 100-POINT SCALE ***95-100***—Classic, a great wine; ***90-94***—Outstanding, superior character and style; ***80-89***—Good to very good, a wine with special qualities; ***70-79***—Average, drinkable wine that may have minor flaws; ***60-69***—Below average, drinkable but not recommended; ***50-59***—Poor, undrinkable, not recommended. "+"—With a score indicates a range; used primarily with barrel tastings to indicate a preliminary score.

SPECIAL DESIGNATIONS SS—Spectator Selection, CS—Cellar Selection, BB—Best Buy.

TASTER'S INITIALS (JG)—Jim Gordon, (HS)—Harvey Steiman, (JL)—James Laube, (JS)—James Suckling, (TM)—Thomas Matthews, (TR)—Terry Robards, (BT)—Barrel Tasting (these wines were tasted blind from barrel samples), (CA-date)—*California's Great Cabernets* by James Laube, (CH-date)—*California's Great Chardonnays* by James Laube, (VP-date)—*Vintage Port* by James Suckling.

DATE TASTED Dates in parentheses represent the issue in which the rating was published.

92 ETUDE Cabernet Sauvignon California 1985 Rel: $16 Cur: $16 (12/15/88)
85 ETUDE Cabernet Sauvignon Napa Valley 1987 $24 (10/31/90)
92 ETUDE Cabernet Sauvignon Napa Valley 1986 $20 (9/30/89)
85+ ETUDE Cabernet Sauvignon Napa Valley 1986 $20 (4/15/88) (BT)
90+ FAR NIENTE Cabernet Sauvignon Napa Valley 1988 (NR) (4/30/90) (BT)
88 FAR NIENTE Cabernet Sauvignon Napa Valley 1987 $33 (11/15/90)
90+ FAR NIENTE Cabernet Sauvignon Napa Valley 1987 $33 (4/15/89) (BT)
91 FAR NIENTE Cabernet Sauvignon Napa Valley 1986 Rel: $30 Cur: $30 (9/30/89)
91 FAR NIENTE Cabernet Sauvignon Napa Valley 1986 Rel: $30 Cur: $30 (CA-3/89)
92 FAR NIENTE Cabernet Sauvignon Napa Valley 1985 Rel: $28 Cur: $28 (CA-3/89)
90 FAR NIENTE Cabernet Sauvignon Napa Valley 1985 Rel: $28 Cur: $28 (12/31/88)
90+ FAR NIENTE Cabernet Sauvignon Napa Valley 1985 Rel: $28 Cur: $28 (6/15/87) (BT)
92 FAR NIENTE Cabernet Sauvignon Napa Valley 1984 Rel: $25 Cur: $30 (CA-3/89)
92 FAR NIENTE Cabernet Sauvignon Napa Valley 1984 Rel: $25 Cur: $30 (10/15/87)
87 FAR NIENTE Cabernet Sauvignon Napa Valley 1983 Rel: $25 Cur: $32 (CA-3/89)
93 FAR NIENTE Cabernet Sauvignon Napa Valley 1983 Rel: $25 Cur: $32 (6/16/86)
82 FAR NIENTE Cabernet Sauvignon Napa Valley 1982 Rel: $25 Cur: $35 (CA-3/89)
84 FAR NIENTE Cabernet Sauvignon Napa Valley 1982 Rel: $25 Cur: $35 (9/16/85)
87 GARY FARRELL Cabernet Sauvignon Sonoma County 1987 $16 (10/31/90)
78 FELTA SPRINGS Cabernet Sauvignon Sonoma County 1983 $5 (3/31/87)
84 FERRARI-CARANO Cabernet Sauvignon Alexander Valley 1987 $17.50 (7/15/91)
80 FERRARI-CARANO Cabernet Sauvignon Alexander Valley 1986 $17.50 (9/15/90)
81 FETZER Cabernet Sauvignon California 1988 $8 (1/31/91) BB
85+ FETZER Cabernet Sauvignon California 1986 (NR) (4/15/88) (BT)
87 FETZER Cabernet Sauvignon California Reserve 1985 $17 (11/15/89)
82 FETZER Cabernet Sauvignon Lake County 1985 $6.50 (8/31/87) BB
74 FETZER Cabernet Sauvignon Lake County 1984 $8 (5/15/87)
83 FETZER Cabernet Sauvignon Lake County 1983 $5.50 (5/01/86)
78 FETZER Cabernet Sauvignon Lake County 1982 $5.50 (5/16/84)
90 FETZER Cabernet Sauvignon Mendocino Barrel Select 1986 $11 (4/15/90)
85 FETZER Cabernet Sauvignon Mendocino Barrel Select 1985 $10 (12/15/88)
82 FETZER Cabernet Sauvignon Mendocino Barrel Select 1984 $9 (11/30/87)
70 FETZER Cabernet Sauvignon California Barrel Select 1983 $8 (6/15/87)
73 FETZER Cabernet Sauvignon Mendocino Barrel Select 1982 $7 (2/01/85)
86 FETZER Cabernet Sauvignon Mendocino County 1981 $7 (12/16/84)
85+ FETZER Cabernet Sauvignon Mendocino Special Reserve 1987 (NR) (4/15/89) (BT)
86 FETZER Cabernet Sauvignon Sonoma County Reserve 1985 $24 (8/31/90)
85 FETZER Cabernet Sauvignon Mendocino Special Reserve 1984 $14 (12/31/88)
85 FIELD STONE Cabernet Sauvignon Alexander Valley 1987 $14 (2/28/91)
74 FIELD STONE Cabernet Sauvignon Alexander Valley 1983 $11 (10/15/88)
70 FIELD STONE Cabernet Sauvignon Alexander Valley Home Ranch Vineyard 1985 $14 (4/15/89)
85 FIELD STONE Cabernet Sauvignon Alexander Valley Hoot Owl Reserve 1986 $20 (12/15/90)
87 FIELD STONE Cabernet Sauvignon Alexander Valley Hoot Owl Creek Vineyards 1985 $20 (3/31/89)
82 FIELD STONE Cabernet Sauvignon Alexander Valley Hoot Owl Creek Vineyards 1984 $14 (10/15/88)
84 FIELD STONE Cabernet Sauvignon Alexander Valley Turkey Hill Vineyard 1985 $18 (2/28/91)
88 FIELD STONE Cabernet Sauvignon Alexander Valley Turkey Hill Vineyard 1984 $16 (12/31/88)
78 FIELD STONE Cabernet Sauvignon Alexander Valley Turkey Hill Vineyard 1982 $12 (3/16/86)
82 FIRESTONE Cabernet Sauvignon Santa Ynez Valley 1987 $11 (5/31/90)
81 FIRESTONE Cabernet Sauvignon Santa Ynez Valley 1986 $10 (12/15/89)
85+ FIRESTONE Cabernet Sauvignon Santa Ynez Valley 1986 $10 (4/15/88) (BT)
72 FIRESTONE Cabernet Sauvignon Santa Ynez Valley 1985 $9.50 (8/31/88)
72 FIRESTONE Cabernet Sauvignon Santa Ynez Valley 1984 $9.50 (3/31/88)
77 FIRESTONE Cabernet Sauvignon Santa Ynez Valley 1983 $9 (6/15/87)
89 FIRESTONE Cabernet Sauvignon Santa Ynez Valley 1981 $8 (3/01/85)
84 FIRESTONE Cabernet Sauvignon Santa Ynez Valley Reserve 1988 $18 (2/28/91)
77 FIRESTONE Cabernet Sauvignon Santa Ynez Valley Special Release 1977 $9.50 (4/16/85)
67 FIRESTONE Cabernet Sauvignon Santa Ynez Valley Vintage Reserve 1985 $25 (12/15/89)
73 FIRESTONE Cabernet Sauvignon Santa Ynez Valley Vintage Reserve 1979 $12 (3/16/86)
73 FISHER Cabernet Sauvignon Sonoma County 1983 $12.50 (6/15/87)
88 FISHER Cabernet Sauvignon Sonoma County 1982 $12.50 (11/01/85)
85 FISHER Cabernet Sauvignon Sonoma County 1981 $12 (12/01/84)
90+ FISHER Cabernet Sauvignon Sonoma County Coach Insignia 1990 (NR) (5/15/91) (BT)
85+ FISHER Cabernet Sauvignon Sonoma County Coach Insignia 1989 (NR) (5/15/91) (BT)
85+ FISHER Cabernet Sauvignon Sonoma County Coach Insignia 1988 (NR) (4/30/91) (BT)
85 FISHER Cabernet Sauvignon Sonoma-Napa Counties Coach Insignia 1987 Rel: $20 Cur: $22 (9/30/90)
85+ FISHER Cabernet Sauvignon Sonoma County Coach Insignia 1987 Rel: $20 Cur: $22 (4/15/89) (BT)
87 FISHER Cabernet Sauvignon Sonoma County Coach Insignia 1986 Rel: $20 Cur: $21 (1/31/90)
90 FISHER Cabernet Sauvignon Sonoma County Coach Insignia 1986 Rel: $20 Cur: $21 (CA-3/89)
85+ FISHER Cabernet Sauvignon Sonoma County Coach Insignia 1986 Rel: $20 Cur: $21 (4/15/88) (BT)
90 FISHER Cabernet Sauvignon Sonoma County Coach Insignia 1985 Rel: $18 Cur: $20 (CA-3/89)
91 FISHER Cabernet Sauvignon Sonoma County Coach Insignia 1985 Rel: $18 Cur: $20 (9/15/88)
80+ FISHER Cabernet Sauvignon Sonoma County Coach Insignia 1985 Rel: $18 Cur: $20 (6/15/87) (BT)
89 FISHER Cabernet Sauvignon Sonoma County Coach Insignia 1984 Rel: $18 Cur: $25 (CA-3/89)
90 FISHER Cabernet Sauvignon Sonoma County Coach Insignia 1984 Rel: $18 Cur: $25 (11/15/87)
74 FITCH MOUNTAIN Cabernet Sauvignon Napa Valley 1985 $9 (4/15/89)
87 FIVE PALMS Cabernet Sauvignon Napa Valley 1984 $6 (3/31/87) BB
90+ FLORA SPRINGS Cabernet Sauvignon Napa Valley 1990 (NR) (5/15/91) (BT)
85+ FLORA SPRINGS Cabernet Sauvignon Napa Valley 1989 (NR) (5/15/91) (BT)
90+ FLORA SPRINGS Cabernet Sauvignon Napa Valley 1988 (NR) (4/30/90) (BT)
91 FLORA SPRINGS Cabernet Sauvignon Napa Valley Cellar Select 1987 $25 (11/15/90)
90+ FLORA SPRINGS Cabernet Sauvignon Napa Valley Cellar Select 1987 $25 (4/15/89) (BT)
85 FLORA SPRINGS Cabernet Sauvignon Napa Valley 1986 Rel: $15 Cur: $16 (3/15/90)
77 FLORA SPRINGS Cabernet Sauvignon Napa Valley 1986 Rel: $15 Cur: $16 (CA-3/89)
85+ FLORA SPRINGS Cabernet Sauvignon Napa Valley 1986 Rel: $15 Cur: $16 (4/15/88) (BT)
90 FLORA SPRINGS Cabernet Sauvignon Napa Valley 1985 Rel: $15 Cur: $18 (7/31/89)
88 FLORA SPRINGS Cabernet Sauvignon Napa Valley 1985 Rel: $15 Cur: $18 (CA-3/89)

85+ FLORA SPRINGS Cabernet Sauvignon Napa Valley 1985 Rel: $15 Cur: $18 (6/15/87) (BT)
85 FLORA SPRINGS Cabernet Sauvignon Napa Valley 1984 Rel: $13 Cur: $18 (CA-3/89)
71 FLORA SPRINGS Cabernet Sauvignon Napa Valley 1984 Rel: $13 Cur: $18 (7/31/88)
79 FLORA SPRINGS Cabernet Sauvignon Napa Valley 1983 Rel: $13 Cur: $15 (12/15/86)
78 FLORA SPRINGS Cabernet Sauvignon Napa Valley 1982 Rel: $9 Cur: $9 (10/15/86)
82 FLORA SPRINGS Cabernet Sauvignon Napa Valley 1981 Rel: $12 Cur: $12 (12/16/84)
85 FLORA SPRINGS Cabernet Sauvignon Napa Valley 1980 Rel: $12 Cur: $28 (CA-3/89)
90+ FLORA SPRINGS Trilogy Napa Valley 1990 (NR) (5/15/91) (BT)
90+ FLORA SPRINGS Trilogy Napa Valley 1989 (NR) (5/15/91) (BT)
90+ FLORA SPRINGS Trilogy Napa Valley 1988 $30 (4/30/90) (BT)
90 FLORA SPRINGS Trilogy Napa Valley 1987 $35 (5/15/91)
84 FLORA SPRINGS Trilogy Napa Valley 1987 $35 (1/31/91)
94 FLORA SPRINGS Trilogy Napa Valley 1986 Rel: $33 Cur: $33 (2/15/90)
85 FLORA SPRINGS Trilogy Napa Valley 1986 Rel: $33 Cur: $33 (CA-3/89)
88 FLORA SPRINGS Trilogy Napa Valley 1985 Rel: $30 Cur: $43 (CA-3/89)
87 FLORA SPRINGS Trilogy Napa Valley 1985 Rel: $30 Cur: $43 (2/15/89)
84 FLORA SPRINGS Trilogy Napa Valley 1984 Rel: $30 Cur: $32 (CA-3/89)
73 FLORA SPRINGS Trilogy Napa Valley 1984 Rel: $30 Cur: $32 (2/29/88)
70 THOMAS FOGARTY Cabernet Sauvignon Napa Valley 1985 $15 (7/15/91)
92 FOLIE A DEUX Cabernet Sauvignon Napa Valley 1987 $18 (11/15/90)
85 FOLIE A DEUX Cabernet Sauvignon Napa Valley 1986 $16.50 (4/15/90)
88 FOLIE A DEUX Cabernet Sauvignon Napa Valley 1984 $14.50 (5/31/88)
71 FOPPIANO Cabernet Sauvignon Russian River Valley 1985 $9 (6/30/89)
77 FOPPIANO Cabernet Sauvignon Russian River Valley 1984 $8.50 (4/30/88)
81 FOPPIANO Cabernet Sauvignon Russian River Valley 1981 $7.75 (4/16/85)
79 FOPPIANO Cabernet Sauvignon Sonoma County 1986 $9 (11/15/90)
93 FORMAN Cabernet Sauvignon Napa Valley 1987 Rel: $26 Cur: $44 (9/30/90)
93 FORMAN Cabernet Sauvignon Napa Valley 1986 Rel: $20 Cur: $48 (6/15/89)
93 FORMAN Cabernet Sauvignon Napa Valley 1986 Rel: $20 Cur: $48 (CA-3/89)
85+ FORMAN Cabernet Sauvignon Napa Valley 1986 Rel: $20 Cur: $48 (4/15/88) (BT)
93 FORMAN Cabernet Sauvignon Napa Valley 1985 Rel: $18 Cur: $68 (CA-3/89)
92 FORMAN Cabernet Sauvignon Napa Valley 1985 Rel: $18 Cur: $68 (6/15/88)
92 FORMAN Cabernet Sauvignon Napa Valley 1984 Rel: $18 Cur: $71 (CA-3/89)
92 FORMAN Cabernet Sauvignon Napa Valley 1984 Rel: $18 Cur: $71 (4/30/87)
90 FORMAN Cabernet Sauvignon Napa Valley 1983 Rel: $15.50 Cur: $70 (CA-3/89)
75 FOX MOUNTAIN Cabernet Sauvignon Russian River Valley Reserve 1985 $19 (9/15/89)
85 FOX MOUNTAIN Cabernet Sauvignon Russian River Valley Reserve 1984 $18 (3/15/89)
77 FOX MOUNTAIN Cabernet Sauvignon Russian River Valley Reserve 1982 $18 (12/31/87)
79 FOX MOUNTAIN Cabernet Sauvignon Russian River Valley Reserve 1981 $16 (12/15/86)
86 FRANCISCAN Cabernet Sauvignon Alexander Valley 1980 $7.50 (10/16/84)
79 FRANCISCAN Cabernet Sauvignon Napa Valley 1979 Rel: $8.50 Cur: $18 (CA-3/89)
88 FRANCISCAN Cabernet Sauvignon Napa Valley Library Selection 1985 Rel: $17.50 Cur: $20 (CA-3/89)
85+ FRANCISCAN Cabernet Sauvignon Napa Valley Oakville Estate 1988 (NR) (4/30/90) (BT)
89 FRANCISCAN Cabernet Sauvignon Napa Valley Oakville Estate 1987 $12 (2/15/91)
85+ FRANCISCAN Cabernet Sauvignon Napa Valley Oakville Estate 1987 $12 (4/15/89) (BT)
84 FRANCISCAN Cabernet Sauvignon Napa Valley Oakville Estate 1986 $11 (7/15/90)
80+ FRANCISCAN Cabernet Sauvignon Napa Valley Oakville Estate 1986 $11 (4/15/88) (BT)
86 FRANCISCAN Cabernet Sauvignon Napa Valley Oakville Estate 1985 $11 (5/15/89)
84 FRANCISCAN Cabernet Sauvignon Napa Valley Oakville Estate 1984 $9.50 (9/15/88)
75 FRANCISCAN Cabernet Sauvignon Napa Valley Oakville Estate 1983 $9 (4/30/87)
88 FRANCISCAN Cabernet Sauvignon Napa Valley Oakville Estate Reserve 1985 Rel: $17.50 Cur: $20 (5/31/90)
87 FRANCISCAN Cabernet Sauvignon Napa Valley Oakville Estate Reserve 1985 Rel: $17.50 Cur: $20 (CA-3/89)
87 FRANCISCAN Cabernet Sauvignon Napa Valley Private Reserve 1984 Rel: $9 Cur: $15 (CA-3/89)
85 FRANCISCAN Cabernet Sauvignon Napa Valley Private Reserve 1983 Rel: $8.50 Cur: $15 (CA-3/89)
78 FRANCISCAN Cabernet Sauvignon Napa Valley Reserve 1978 Rel: $15 Cur: $23 (CA-3/89)
82 FRANCISCAN Cabernet Sauvignon Napa Valley Reserve 1975 Rel: $12 Cur: $32 (CA-3/89)
90+ FRANCISCAN Meritige Napa Valley 1988 (NR) (4/30/90) (BT)
87 FRANCISCAN Meritage Napa Valley 1987 $17 (4/30/91)
85+ FRANCISCAN Meritige Napa Valley 1987 $17 (4/15/89) (BT)
79 FRANCISCAN Meritage Napa Valley 1986 Rel: $15 Cur: $18 (7/31/90)
90 FRANCISCAN Meritage Napa Valley 1985 Rel: $20 Cur: $20 (3/31/90)
89 FRANCISCAN Meritage Napa Valley 1985 Rel: $20 Cur: $20 (CA-3/89)
76 FREEMARK ABBEY Cabernet Sauvignon Napa Valley Bosché 1986 Rel: $24 Cur: $25 (7/31/90)
90 FREEMARK ABBEY Cabernet Sauvignon Napa Valley Bosché 1986 Rel: $24 Cur: $25 (CA-3/89)
90 FREEMARK ABBEY Cabernet Sauvignon Napa Valley Bosché 1985 Rel: $24 Cur: $24 (7/31/89)
93 FREEMARK ABBEY Cabernet Sauvignon Napa Valley Bosché 1985 Rel: $24 Cur: $24 (CA-3/89)
80+ FREEMARK ABBEY Cabernet Sauvignon Napa Valley Bosché 1985 Rel: $24 Cur: $24 (6/15/87) (BT)
88 FREEMARK ABBEY Cabernet Sauvignon Napa Valley Bosché 1984 Rel: $20 Cur: $25 (CA-3/89)
80 FREEMARK ABBEY Cabernet Sauvignon Napa Valley Bosché 1984 Rel: $20 Cur: $25 (4/30/88)
86 FREEMARK ABBEY Cabernet Sauvignon Napa Valley Bosché 1983 Rel: $18 Cur: $38 (CA-3/89)
80 FREEMARK ABBEY Cabernet Sauvignon Napa Valley Bosché 1983 Rel: $18 Cur: $38 (6/15/87)
88 FREEMARK ABBEY Cabernet Sauvignon Napa Valley Bosché 1982 Rel: $15 Cur: $41 (CA-3/89)
93 FREEMARK ABBEY Cabernet Sauvignon Napa Valley Bosché 1982 Rel: $15 Cur: $41 (5/16/86) CS
86 FREEMARK ABBEY Cabernet Sauvignon Napa Valley Bosché 1981 Rel: $14 Cur: $36 (CA-3/89)
89 FREEMARK ABBEY Cabernet Sauvignon Napa Valley Bosché 1981 Rel: $14 Cur: $36 (7/01/85)
88 FREEMARK ABBEY Cabernet Sauvignon Napa Valley Bosché 1980 Rel: $14.50 Cur: $38 (CA-3/89)
84 FREEMARK ABBEY Cabernet Sauvignon Napa Valley Bosché 1980 Rel: $14.50 Cur: $38 (2/01/86)
84 FREEMARK ABBEY Cabernet Sauvignon Napa Valley Bosché 1980 Rel: $14.50 Cur: $38 (2/01/85)
93 FREEMARK ABBEY Cabernet Sauvignon Napa Valley Bosché 1979 Rel: $12 Cur: $34 (CA-3/89)
86 FREEMARK ABBEY Cabernet Sauvignon Napa Valley Bosché 1979 Rel: $12 Cur: $34 (2/01/86)
93 FREEMARK ABBEY Cabernet Sauvignon Napa Valley Bosché 1978 Rel: $12.50 Cur: $50 (CA-3/89)
92 FREEMARK ABBEY Cabernet Sauvignon Napa Valley Bosché 1978 Rel: $12.50 Cur: $50 (4/30/87)
80 FREEMARK ABBEY Cabernet Sauvignon Napa Valley Bosché 1978 Rel: $12.50 Cur: $50 (2/01/85)
88 FREEMARK ABBEY Cabernet Sauvignon Napa Valley Bosché 1977 Rel: $12.50 Cur: $31 (CA-3/89)
85 FREEMARK ABBEY Cabernet Sauvignon Napa Valley Bosché 1976 Rel: $12.50 Cur: $45 (CA-3/89)
90 FREEMARK ABBEY Cabernet Sauvignon Napa Valley Bosché 1975 Rel: $10 Cur: $57 (CA-3/89)
91 FREEMARK ABBEY Cabernet Sauvignon Napa Valley Bosché 1974 Rel: $7.75 Cur: $76 (CA-3/89)
88 FREEMARK ABBEY Cabernet Sauvignon Napa Valley Bosché 1973 Rel: $8 Cur: $70 (CA-3/89)
80 FREEMARK ABBEY Cabernet Sauvignon Napa Valley Bosché 1972 Rel: $6 Cur: $30 (CA-3/89)
86 FREEMARK ABBEY Cabernet Sauvignon Napa Valley Bosché 1971 Rel: $6.75 Cur: $50 (CA-3/89)
91 FREEMARK ABBEY Cabernet Sauvignon Napa Valley Bosché 1970 Rel: $8.75 Cur: $117 (CA-3/89)
70 FREEMARK ABBEY Cabernet Sauvignon Napa Valley 1988 $15 (12/31/90)
86 FREEMARK ABBEY Cabernet Sauvignon Napa Valley 1987 $16 (7/31/91)
83 FREEMARK ABBEY Cabernet Sauvignon Napa Valley 1986 $15 (11/15/90)
79 FREEMARK ABBEY Cabernet Sauvignon Napa Valley 1985 Rel: $15 Cur: $15 (10/31/89)
75+ FREEMARK ABBEY Cabernet Sauvignon Napa Valley 1985 Rel: $15 Cur: $15 (6/15/87) (BT)
84 FREEMARK ABBEY Cabernet Sauvignon Napa Valley 1984 Rel: $14 Cur: $14 (2/15/89)
68 FREEMARK ABBEY Cabernet Sauvignon Napa Valley 1983 Rel: $12 Cur: $12 (2/15/88)
84 FREEMARK ABBEY Cabernet Sauvignon Napa Valley 1982 Rel: $12 Cur: $12 (2/15/87)
79 FREEMARK ABBEY Cabernet Sauvignon Napa Valley 1981 Rel: $10.50 Cur: $11 (10/01/85)
84 FREEMARK ABBEY Cabernet Sauvignon Napa Valley 1980 Rel: $14.50 Cur: $22 (5/16/84)
89 FREEMARK ABBEY Cabernet Sauvignon Napa Valley 1979 Rel: $10.50 Cur: $25 (1/01/84)
68 FREEMARK ABBEY Cabernet Sauvignon Napa Valley 1969 Cur: $57 (4/01/86)
88 FREEMARK ABBEY Cabernet Sauvignon Napa Valley Sycamore Vineyards 1985 $25 (10/31/89)
75+ FREEMARK ABBEY Cabernet Sauvignon Napa Valley Sycamore Vineyards 1985 $25 (6/15/87) (BT)
91 FREEMARK ABBEY Cabernet Sauvignon Napa Valley Sycamore Vineyards 1984 $20 (12/15/88)
85 FREMONT CREEK Cabernet Sauvignon Mendocino & Napa Counties 1986 $8 (4/30/91) BB
76 FREMONT CREEK Cabernet Sauvignon Mendocino & Napa Counties 1986 $8 (11/15/89)
78 FREMONT CREEK Cabernet Sauvignon Mendocino & Napa Counties 1985 $9.50 (3/31/88)
57 J FRITZ Cabernet Sauvignon Alexander Valley 1985 $10 (12/31/88)
88 FROG'S LEAP Cabernet Sauvignon Napa Valley 1988 $17 (12/15/90)
94 FROG'S LEAP Cabernet Sauvignon Napa Valley 1987 Rel: $15 Cur: $20 (12/31/89) SS
94 FROG'S LEAP Cabernet Sauvignon Napa Valley 1986 Rel: $14 Cur: $20 (CA-3/89)
94 FROG'S LEAP Cabernet Sauvignon Napa Valley 1986 Rel: $14 Cur: $20 (12/31/88)
85 FROG'S LEAP Cabernet Sauvignon Napa Valley 1985 Rel: $12 Cur: $18 (CA-3/89)
82 FROG'S LEAP Cabernet Sauvignon Napa Valley 1985 Rel: $12 Cur: $18 (12/31/87)
92 FROG'S LEAP Cabernet Sauvignon Napa Valley 1984 Rel: $10 Cur: $25 (CA-3/89)
95 FROG'S LEAP Cabernet Sauvignon Napa Valley 1984 Rel: $10 Cur: $25 (3/31/87) SS
80 FROG'S LEAP Cabernet Sauvignon Napa Valley 1983 Rel: $10 Cur: $20 (CA-3/89)
85 FROG'S LEAP Cabernet Sauvignon Napa Valley 1983 Rel: $10 Cur: $20 (5/16/86)
87 FROG'S LEAP Cabernet Sauvignon Napa Valley 1982 Rel: $9 Cur: $25 (CA-3/89)
82 GAINEY Cabernet Sauvignon Santa Barbara County 1987 $13 (11/15/90)
89 GAINEY Cabernet Sauvignon Santa Barbara County Limited Selection 1986 $15 (12/15/89)
78 E.&J. GALLO Cabernet Sauvignon California Limited Release Reserve 1980 $8 (11/15/86)
75 E.&J. GALLO Cabernet Sauvignon Limited Release 1981 $5 (12/31/88)
82 E.&J. GALLO Cabernet Sauvignon Northern Sonoma Reserve 1982 $6 (5/31/91) BB
90 GAN EDEN Cabernet Sauvignon Alexander Valley 1987 $18 (3/31/91)
81 GAN EDEN Cabernet Sauvignon Alexander Valley 1987 $18 (11/15/90)
86 GAN EDEN Cabernet Sauvignon Alexander Valley 1986 $15 (2/15/89)
70 GARLAND RANCH Cabernet Sauvignon Central Coast 1986 $6.75 (10/31/89)
84 GARLAND RANCH Cabernet Sauvignon Monterey County 1984 $6.75 (8/31/88) BB
85+ GEYSER PEAK Cabernet Sauvignon Alexander Valley 1986 (NR) (4/15/88) (BT)
77 GEYSER PEAK Cabernet Sauvignon Alexander Valley 1984 $7.50 (3/15/88)
87 GEYSER PEAK Cabernet Sauvignon Alexander Valley 1983 $7 (3/15/87) BB
68 GEYSER PEAK Cabernet Sauvignon Alexander Valley 1982 $7 (9/15/86)
57 GEYSER PEAK Cabernet Sauvignon Alexander Valley 1980 $6.50 (1/01/85)
89 GEYSER PEAK Cabernet Sauvignon Alexander Valley Estate Reserve 1987 $14 (6/15/91)
85 GEYSER PEAK Cabernet Sauvignon Alexander Valley Estate Reserve 1986 $15 (9/30/90)
77 GEYSER PEAK Cabernet Sauvignon Alexander Valley Estate Reserve 1985 $15 (5/15/89)
88 GEYSER PEAK Cabernet Sauvignon Sonoma County 1987 $8.50 (11/30/90) BB
83 GEYSER PEAK Cabernet Sauvignon Sonoma County 1981 $7 (6/16/85)
90 GEYSER PEAK Réserve Alexandre Alexander Valley 1987 $18 (6/15/91)
89 GEYSER PEAK Réserve Alexandre Alexander Valley 1986 $20 (9/30/90)
88 GEYSER PEAK Réserve Alexandre Alexander Valley 1985 $19 (9/30/89)
89 GEYSER PEAK Réserve Alexandre Alexander Valley 1984 $19 (8/31/88)
80 GEYSER PEAK Réserve Alexandre Alexander Valley 1983 $15 (4/30/87)
90+ GIRARD Cabernet Sauvignon Napa Valley 1990 (NR) (5/15/91) (BT)
85+ GIRARD Cabernet Sauvignon Napa Valley 1989 (NR) (5/15/91) (BT)
85+ GIRARD Cabernet Sauvignon Napa Valley 1988 (NR) (4/30/90) (BT)
86 GIRARD Cabernet Sauvignon Napa Valley 1987 $16 (11/15/90)
90+ GIRARD Cabernet Sauvignon Napa Valley 1987 $16 (4/15/89) (BT)
89 GIRARD Cabernet Sauvignon Napa Valley 1986 Rel: $16 Cur: $17 (11/15/89)
88 GIRARD Cabernet Sauvignon Napa Valley 1985 Rel: $15 Cur: $18 (9/15/88)
85+ GIRARD Cabernet Sauvignon Napa Valley 1985 Rel: $15 Cur: $18 (6/15/87) (BT)
88 GIRARD Cabernet Sauvignon Napa Valley 1984 Rel: $11 Cur: $12 (11/30/87)
71 GIRARD Cabernet Sauvignon Napa Valley 1983 Rel: $12 Cur: $13 (12/15/86)
87 GIRARD Cabernet Sauvignon Napa Valley 1982 Rel: $12.50 Cur: $30 (CA-3/89)
89 GIRARD Cabernet Sauvignon Napa Valley 1982 Rel: $12.50 Cur: $30 (2/16/86)
86 GIRARD Cabernet Sauvignon Napa Valley 1981 Rel: $12.50 Cur: $20 (CA-3/89)
89 GIRARD Cabernet Sauvignon Napa Valley 1981 Rel: $12.50 Cur: $20 (8/01/85)
92 GIRARD Cabernet Sauvignon Napa Valley 1980 Rel: $11 Cur: $25 (CA-3/89)
90+ GIRARD Cabernet Sauvignon Napa Valley Reserve 1990 (NR) (5/15/91) (BT)

UNITED STATES

CALIFORNIA/*CABERNET SAUVIGNON & BLENDS*

90+ GIRARD Cabernet Sauvignon Napa Valley Reserve 1989 (NR) (5/15/91) (BT)
85+ GIRARD Cabernet Sauvignon Napa Valley Reserve 1988 (NR) (4/30/90) (BT)
90+ GIRARD Cabernet Sauvignon Napa Valley Reserve 1987 (NR) (4/15/89) (BT)
87 GIRARD Cabernet Sauvignon Napa Valley Reserve 1986 $25 (11/15/90)
91 GIRARD Cabernet Sauvignon Napa Valley Reserve 1986 $25 (CA-3/89)
90+ GIRARD Cabernet Sauvignon Napa Valley Reserve 1986 $25 (4/15/88) (BT)
86 GIRARD Cabernet Sauvignon Napa Valley Reserve 1985 Rel: $25 Cur: $41 (2/15/90)
89 GIRARD Cabernet Sauvignon Napa Valley Reserve 1985 Rel: $25 Cur: $41 (CA-3/89)
92 GIRARD Cabernet Sauvignon Napa Valley Reserve 1984 Rel: $25 Cur: $45 (CA-3/89)
93 GIRARD Cabernet Sauvignon Napa Valley Reserve 1984 Rel: $25 Cur: $45 (12/15/88)
87 GIRARD Cabernet Sauvignon Napa Valley Reserve 1983 Rel: $18 Cur: $25 (CA-3/89)
86 GIRARD Cabernet Sauvignon Napa Valley Reserve 1983 Rel: $18 Cur: $25 (12/15/87)
79 GLEN ELLEN Cabernet Sauvignon California Proprietor's Reserve 1987 $6 (1/31/91)
82 GLEN ELLEN Cabernet Sauvignon California Proprietor's Reserve 1986 $4.50 (7/15/88) BB
82 GLEN ELLEN Cabernet Sauvignon Sonoma Valley Benziger Family Selection 1984 $14 (10/15/87)
91 GLEN ELLEN Cabernet Sauvignon Sonoma Valley Benziger Family Selection 1983 $9.75 (5/15/87)
85 GLEN ELLEN Cabernet Sauvignon Sonoma Valley Glen Ellen Estate 1982 $9.75 (2/01/85)
86 GLEN ELLEN Cabernet Sauvignon Sonoma Valley Imagery Series 1985 $12.50 (2/15/89)
90+ GRACE FAMILY Cabernet Sauvignon Napa Valley 1990 (NR) (5/15/91) (BT)
85+ GRACE FAMILY Cabernet Sauvignon Napa Valley 1989 (NR) (5/15/91) (BT)
92 GRACE FAMILY Cabernet Sauvignon Napa Valley 1988 $63 (6/30/91)
90+ GRACE FAMILY Cabernet Sauvignon Napa Valley 1988 $63 (4/30/90) (BT)
97 GRACE FAMILY Cabernet Sauvignon Napa Valley 1987 Rel: $56 Cur: $200 (6/30/90)
95+ GRACE FAMILY Cabernet Sauvignon Napa Valley 1987 Rel: $56 Cur: $200 (4/15/89) (BT)
93 GRACE FAMILY Cabernet Sauvignon Napa Valley 1986 Rel: $40 Cur: $250 (CA-3/89)
90+ GRACE FAMILY Cabernet Sauvignon Napa Valley 1986 Rel: $40 Cur: $250 (4/15/88) (BT)
95 GRACE FAMILY Cabernet Sauvignon Napa Valley 1985 Rel: $50 Cur: $250 (CA-3/89)
93 GRACE FAMILY Cabernet Sauvignon Napa Valley 1985 Rel: $50 Cur: $250 (12/15/88)
85+ GRACE FAMILY Cabernet Sauvignon Napa Valley 1985 Rel: $50 Cur: $250 (6/15/87) (BT)
92 GRACE FAMILY Cabernet Sauvignon Napa Valley 1984 Rel: $38 Cur: $290 (CA-3/89)
90 GRACE FAMILY Cabernet Sauvignon Napa Valley 1984 Rel: $38 Cur: $290 (4/15/88)
91 GRACE FAMILY Cabernet Sauvignon Napa Valley 1983 Rel: $38 Cur: $330 (CA-3/89)
85 GRACE FAMILY Cabernet Sauvignon Napa Valley 1983 Rel: $38 Cur: $330 (6/15/87)
89 GRACE FAMILY Cabernet Sauvignon Napa Valley 1982 Rel: $31 Cur: $250 (CA-3/89)
88 GRACE FAMILY Cabernet Sauvignon Napa Valley 1981 Rel: $28 Cur: $300 (CA-3/89)
92 GRACE FAMILY Cabernet Sauvignon Napa Valley 1980 Rel: $25 Cur: $350 (CA-3/89)
92 GRACE FAMILY Cabernet Sauvignon Napa Valley 1979 Rel: $20 Cur: $400 (CA-3/89)
86 GRACE FAMILY Cabernet Sauvignon Napa Valley 1978 Rel: $20 Cur: $500 (CA-3/89)
85 GRAND CRU Cabernet Sauvignon Alexander Valley Collector's Reserve 1986 $22 (5/15/90)
81 GRAND CRU Cabernet Sauvignon Alexander Valley Collector's Reserve 1985 $18 (7/15/89)
70 GRAND CRU Cabernet Sauvignon Alexander Valley Collector's Reserve 1982 $15 (9/30/87)
85 GRAND CRU Cabernet Sauvignon Alexander Valley Collector's Reserve 1980 $14.50 (11/01/84)
79 GRAND CRU Cabernet Sauvignon Sonoma County Premium Selection 1986 $12 (4/30/90)
79 GRAND CRU Cabernet Sauvignon Sonoma County Premium Selection 1985 $9 (6/15/89)
75 GRAND CRU Cabernet Sauvignon Sonoma County 1984 $8.50 (12/31/87)
68 GRAND CRU Cabernet Sauvignon Sonoma County 1983 $8.50 (11/16/85)
95+ GRGICH HILLS Cabernet Sauvignon Napa Valley 1987 (NR) (4/15/89) (BT)
91 GRGICH HILLS Cabernet Sauvignon Napa Valley 1986 $20 (CA-3/89)
85+ GRGICH HILLS Cabernet Sauvignon Napa Valley 1986 $20 (4/15/88) (BT)
90 GRGICH HILLS Cabernet Sauvignon Napa Valley 1985 Rel: $20 Cur: $23 (10/31/90)
92 GRGICH HILLS Cabernet Sauvignon Napa Valley 1985 Rel: $20 Cur: $23 (CA-3/89)
87 GRGICH HILLS Cabernet Sauvignon Napa Valley 1984 Rel: $17 Cur: $24 (4/30/89)
94 GRGICH HILLS Cabernet Sauvignon Napa Valley 1984 Rel: $17 Cur: $24 (CA-3/89)
88 GRGICH HILLS Cabernet Sauvignon Napa Valley 1983 Rel: $17 Cur: $26 (CA-3/89)
90 GRGICH HILLS Cabernet Sauvignon Napa Valley 1983 Rel: $17 Cur: $26 (4/30/88)
87 GRGICH HILLS Cabernet Sauvignon Napa Valley 1982 Rel: $17 Cur: $29 (CA-3/89)
92 GRGICH HILLS Cabernet Sauvignon Napa Valley 1982 Rel: $17 Cur: $29 (4/15/87)
86 GRGICH HILLS Cabernet Sauvignon Napa Valley 1981 Rel: $17 Cur: $35 (CA-3/89)
90 GRGICH HILLS Cabernet Sauvignon Napa-Sonoma Counties 1980 Rel: $16 Cur: $33 (CA-3/89)
90+ GROTH Cabernet Sauvignon Napa Valley 1990 (NR) (5/15/91) (BT)
90+ GROTH Cabernet Sauvignon Napa Valley 1989 (NR) (5/15/91) (BT)
90+ GROTH Cabernet Sauvignon Napa Valley 1988 (NR) (4/30/90) (BT)
81 GROTH Cabernet Sauvignon Napa Valley 1987 Rel: $20 Cur: $21 (10/31/90)
90+ GROTH Cabernet Sauvignon Napa Valley 1987 Rel: $20 Cur: $21 (4/15/89) (BT)
92 GROTH Cabernet Sauvignon Napa Valley 1986 Rel: $18 Cur: $25 (11/15/89)
92 GROTH Cabernet Sauvignon Napa Valley 1986 Rel: $18 Cur: $25 (CA-3/89)
85+ GROTH Cabernet Sauvignon Napa Valley 1986 Rel: $18 Cur: $25 (4/15/88) (BT)
91 GROTH Cabernet Sauvignon Napa Valley 1985 Rel: $16 Cur: $32 (CA-3/89)
93 GROTH Cabernet Sauvignon Napa Valley 1985 Rel: $16 Cur: $32 (11/15/88)
90+ GROTH Cabernet Sauvignon Napa Valley 1985 Rel: $16 Cur: $32 (6/15/87) (BT)
92 GROTH Cabernet Sauvignon Napa Valley 1984 Rel: $14 Cur: $39 (CA-3/89)
86 GROTH Cabernet Sauvignon Napa Valley 1984 Rel: $14 Cur: $39 (2/15/88)
88 GROTH Cabernet Sauvignon Napa Valley 1983 Rel: $13 Cur: $22 (CA-3/89)
85 GROTH Cabernet Sauvignon Napa Valley 1983 Rel: $13 Cur: $22 (8/31/86)
88 GROTH Cabernet Sauvignon Napa Valley 1982 Rel: $13 Cur: $35 (CA-3/89)
84 GROTH Cabernet Sauvignon Napa Valley 1982 Rel: $13 Cur: $35 (11/01/84)
91 GROTH Cabernet Sauvignon Napa Valley Reserve 1986 $40 (4/30/91)
93 GROTH Cabernet Sauvignon Napa Valley Reserve 1986 $40 (CA-3/89)
95 GROTH Cabernet Sauvignon Napa Valley Reserve 1985 Rel: $30 Cur: $166 (4/15/90)
93 GROTH Cabernet Sauvignon Napa Valley Reserve 1985 Rel: $30 Cur: $166 (CA-3/89)

Key to Symbols

The scores reported here are the results of blind tastings conducted by our panel of senior editors. Wines that carry the initials below are results of individual tastings.

THE WINE SPECTATOR 100-POINT SCALE *95-100*—Classic, a great wine; *90-94*—Outstanding, superior character and style; *80-89*—Good to very good, a wine with special qualities; *70-79*—Average, drinkable wine that may have minor flaws; *60-69*—Below average, drinkable but not recommended; *50-59*—Poor, undrinkable, not recommended. "+"—With a score indicates a range; used primarily with barrel tastings to indicate a preliminary score.

SPECIAL DESIGNATIONS SS—Spectator Selection, CS—Cellar Selection, BB—Best Buy.

TASTER'S INITIALS (JG)—Jim Gordon, (HS)—Harvey Steiman, (JL)—James Laube, (JS)—James Suckling, (TM)—Thomas Matthews, (TR)—Terry Robards, (BT)—Barrel Tasting (these wines were tasted blind from barrel samples), (CA-date)—*California's Great Cabernets* by James Laube, (CH-date)—*California's Great Chardonnays* by James Laube, (VP-date)—*Vintage Port* by James Suckling.

DATE TASTED Dates in parentheses represent the issue in which the rating was published.

84 GROTH Cabernet Sauvignon Napa Valley Reserve 1984 Rel: $25 Cur: $90 (4/15/89)
94 GROTH Cabernet Sauvignon Napa Valley Reserve 1984 Rel: $25 Cur: $90 (CA-3/89)
92 GROTH Cabernet Sauvignon Napa Valley Reserve 1983 Rel: $25 Cur: $90 (CA-3/89)
92 GROTH Cabernet Sauvignon Napa Valley Reserve 1983 Rel: $25 Cur: $90 (12/15/88)
92 GUENOC Cabernet Sauvignon Napa Valley Beckstoffer Reserve 1987 $24 (6/30/91)
84 GUENOC Cabernet Sauvignon Guenoc Valley Premier Cuvée 1985 $17.50 (10/15/90)
87 GUENOC Cabernet Sauvignon Guenoc Valley Premier Cuvée 1985 $17.50 (12/15/88)
89 GUENOC Cabernet Sauvignon Lake County 1987 $12 (7/15/91)
78 GUENOC Cabernet Sauvignon Lake County 1986 $12.50 (4/30/91)
89 GUENOC Cabernet Sauvignon Lake County 1983 $9.75 (9/30/86)
78 GUENOC Cabernet Sauvignon Lake County 1981 $8.50 (12/16/84)
88 GUENOC Langtry Meritage Lake-Napa Counties 1987 $35 (4/15/91)
87 GUNDLACH BUNDSCHU Cabernet Sauvignon Sonoma Valley 1986 $9.50 (11/15/89)
84 GUNDLACH BUNDSCHU Cabernet Sauvignon Sonoma Valley 1981 $7 (3/01/89)
85 GUNDLACH BUNDSCHU Cabernet Sauvignon Sonoma Valley 1981 $7 (5/16/85)
79 GUNDLACH BUNDSCHU Cabernet Sauvignon Sonoma Valley Batto Ranch 1984 Rel: $14 Cur: $16 (CA-3/89)
77 GUNDLACH BUNDSCHU Cabernet Sauvignon Sonoma Valley Batto Ranch 1983 Rel: $14 Cur: $15 (CA-3/89)
74 GUNDLACH BUNDSCHU Cabernet Sauvignon Sonoma Valley Batto Ranch 1983 Rel: $14 Cur: $15 (2/15/88)
70 GUNDLACH BUNDSCHU Cabernet Sauvignon Sonoma Valley Batto Ranch 1982 Rel: $12 Cur: $18 (CA-3/89)
89 GUNDLACH BUNDSCHU Cabernet Sauvignon Sonoma Valley Batto Ranch 1982 Rel: $12 Cur: $18 (6/16/85)
88 GUNDLACH BUNDSCHU Cabernet Sauvignon Sonoma Valley Batto Ranch 1981 Rel: $10 Cur: $18 (CA-3/89)
80 GUNDLACH BUNDSCHU Cabernet Sauvignon Sonoma Valley Batto Ranch 1980 Rel: $8 Cur: $20 (CA-3/89)
80 GUNDLACH BUNDSCHU Cabernet Sauvignon Sonoma Valley Batto Ranch 1979 Rel: $8 Cur: $22 (CA-3/89)
89 GUNDLACH BUNDSCHU Cabernet Sauvignon Sonoma Valley Batto Ranch 1977 Rel: $8 Cur: $24 (CA-3/89)
90+ GUNDLACH BUNDSCHU Cabernet Sauvignon Sonoma Valley Rhinefarm Vineyards 1988 (NR) (4/30/90) (BT)
85 GUNDLACH BUNDSCHU Cabernet Sauvignon Sonoma Valley Rhinefarm Vineyards 1987 Rel: $15 Cur: $15 (5/15/91)
85+ GUNDLACH BUNDSCHU Cabernet Sauvignon Sonoma Valley Rhinefarm Vineyards 1987 Rel: $15 Cur: $15 (4/15/89) (BT)
89 GUNDLACH BUNDSCHU Cabernet Sauvignon Sonoma Valley Rhinefarm Vineyards 1986 Rel: $12 Cur: $12 (3/01/89)
78 GUNDLACH BUNDSCHU Cabernet Sauvignon Sonoma Valley Rhinefarm Vineyards 1985 Rel: $9 Cur: $12 (3/31/89)
91 GUNDLACH BUNDSCHU Cabernet Sauvignon Sonoma Valley Rhinefarm Vineyards 1985 Rel: $9 Cur: $12 (3/01/89)
85 GUNDLACH BUNDSCHU Cabernet Sauvignon Sonoma Valley Rhinefarm Vineyards 1984 Rel: $9 Cur: $12 (3/01/89)
84 GUNDLACH BUNDSCHU Cabernet Sauvignon Sonoma Valley Rhinefarm Vineyards 1984 Rel: $9 Cur: $12 (9/30/88)
73 GUNDLACH BUNDSCHU Cabernet Sauvignon Sonoma Valley Rhinefarm Vineyards 1983 Rel: $9 Cur: $14 (3/01/89)
65 GUNDLACH BUNDSCHU Cabernet Sauvignon Sonoma Valley Rhinefarm Vineyards 1982 Rel: $9 Cur: $13 (3/01/89)
71 GUNDLACH BUNDSCHU Cabernet Sauvignon Sonoma Valley Rhinefarm Vineyards Reserve 1982 Rel: $20 Cur: $21 (9/15/87)
90 GUNDLACH BUNDSCHU Cabernet Sauvignon Sonoma Valley Rhinefarm Vineyards Reserve 1981 Rel: $20 Cur: $26 (3/01/89)
88 GUNDLACH BUNDSCHU Cabernet Sauvignon Sonoma Valley Rhinefarm Vineyards Reserve 1981 Rel: $20 Cur: $26 (11/30/86)
91 HACIENDA Antares Sonoma County 1987 $28 (11/15/90)
91 HACIENDA Antares Sonoma County 1986 $28 (7/31/89)
83 HACIENDA Cabernet Sauvignon Sonoma County 1985 $15 (9/30/90)
87 HACIENDA Cabernet Sauvignon Sonoma Valley Estate Reserve 1984 $18 (5/31/91)
86 HACIENDA Cabernet Sauvignon Sonoma Valley 1983 $11 (5/31/88)
86 HACIENDA Cabernet Sauvignon Sonoma Valley Selected Reserve 1982 $18 (3/31/87)
63 HACIENDA Cabernet Sauvignon Sonoma Valley 1982 $11 (9/01/85)
88 HAGAFEN Cabernet Sauvignon Napa Valley 1988 $20 (3/31/91)
88 HAGAFEN Cabernet Sauvignon Napa Valley 1987 $20 (4/30/90)
80 HANNA Cabernet Sauvignon Sonoma County 1987 $16 (8/31/90)
87 HANNA Cabernet Sauvignon Sonoma County 1986 $16 (7/31/89)
86 HANNA Cabernet Sauvignon Sonoma Valley 1985 $14 (6/30/88)
90 HANZELL Cabernet Sauvignon Sonoma Valley 1986 Rel: $22 Cur: $27 (10/31/90)
76 HANZELL Cabernet Sauvignon Sonoma Valley 1982 Rel: $20 Cur: $30 (3/31/87)
84 HAWK CREST Cabernet Sauvignon Mendocino 1981 $5 (3/16/85) BB
79 HAWK CREST Cabernet Sauvignon North Coast 1987 $8 (3/31/90)
82 HAWK CREST Cabernet Sauvignon North Coast 1986 $7.50 (10/15/88) BB
75 HAWK CREST Cabernet Sauvignon North Coast 1985 $6.50 (7/31/88)
76 HAWK CREST Cabernet Sauvignon North Coast 1984 $7 (10/15/87)
65 HAWK CREST Cabernet Sauvignon North Coast 1981 $5 (2/01/86)
85+ HAYWOOD Cabernet Sauvignon Sonoma Valley 1988 (NR) (4/30/90) (BT)
80+ HAYWOOD Cabernet Sauvignon Sonoma Valley Los Chamizal Vineyards 1987 $16 (4/15/87) (BT)
92 HAYWOOD Cabernet Sauvignon Sonoma Valley 1986 Rel: $16 Cur: $16 (11/15/89)
91 HAYWOOD Cabernet Sauvignon Sonoma Valley 1986 Rel: $16 Cur: $16 (CA-3/89)
90+ HAYWOOD Cabernet Sauvignon Sonoma Valley 1986 Rel: $16 Cur: $16 (4/15/88) (BT)
89 HAYWOOD Cabernet Sauvignon Sonoma Valley 1985 Rel: $14.50 Cur: $17 (CA-3/89)
91 HAYWOOD Cabernet Sauvignon Sonoma Valley 1985 Rel: $14.50 Cur: $17 (3/15/88)
85+ HAYWOOD Cabernet Sauvignon Sonoma Valley 1985 Rel: $14.50 Cur: $17 (6/15/87) (BT)
88 HAYWOOD Cabernet Sauvignon Sonoma Valley 1984 Rel: $12.50 Cur: $20 (CA-3/89)
93 HAYWOOD Cabernet Sauvignon Sonoma Valley 1984 Rel: $12.50 Cur: $20 (10/31/87)
77 HAYWOOD Cabernet Sauvignon Sonoma Valley 1983 Rel: $12.50 Cur: $20 (CA-3/89)
77 HAYWOOD Cabernet Sauvignon Sonoma Valley 1983 Rel: $12.50 Cur: $20 (5/15/87)
79 HAYWOOD Cabernet Sauvignon Sonoma Valley 1982 Rel: $11 Cur: $20 (CA-3/89)
85 HAYWOOD Cabernet Sauvignon Sonoma Valley 1981 Rel: $11 Cur: $20 (CA-3/89)
84 HAYWOOD Cabernet Sauvignon Sonoma Valley 1981 Rel: $11 Cur: $20 (9/01/84)
86 HAYWOOD Cabernet Sauvignon Sonoma Valley 1980 Rel: $9.75 Cur: $12 (CA-3/89)
78 HAYWOOD Cabernet Sauvignon Sonoma Valley 1980 Rel: $9.75 Cur: $12 (2/15/84)
88 HEITZ Cabernet Sauvignon Napa Valley 1986 $18 (4/15/91)
80 HEITZ Cabernet Sauvignon Napa Valley 1985 Rel: $18 Cur: $21 (5/15/90)
89 HEITZ Cabernet Sauvignon Napa Valley 1984 Rel: $15 Cur: $18 (1/31/90) (JL)

86 HEITZ Cabernet Sauvignon Napa Valley 1984 Rel: $15 Cur: $18 (5/15/89)
85 HEITZ Cabernet Sauvignon Napa Valley 1983 Rel: $13 Cur: $18 (1/31/90) (JL)
80 HEITZ Cabernet Sauvignon Napa Valley 1983 Rel: $13 Cur: $18 (4/30/88)
80 HEITZ Cabernet Sauvignon Napa Valley 1982 Rel: $13.50 Cur: $21 (1/31/90) (JL)
74 HEITZ Cabernet Sauvignon Napa Valley 1982 Rel: $13.50 Cur: $21 (6/15/87)
86 HEITZ Cabernet Sauvignon Napa Valley 1981 Rel: $13.25 Cur: $25 (1/31/90) (JL)
75 HEITZ Cabernet Sauvignon Napa Valley 1981 Rel: $13.25 Cur: $25 (5/16/86)
88 HEITZ Cabernet Sauvignon Napa Valley 1980 Rel: $12 Cur: $24 (1/31/90) (JL)
82 HEITZ Cabernet Sauvignon Napa Valley 1980 Rel: $12 Cur: $24 (6/01/85)
86 HEITZ Cabernet Sauvignon Napa Valley 1979 Rel: $11.25 Cur: $45 (1/31/90) (JL)
81 HEITZ Cabernet Sauvignon Napa Valley 1979 Rel: $11.25 Cur: $45 (2/16/84) (HS)
90 HEITZ Cabernet Sauvignon Napa Valley 1978 Rel: $11 Cur: $30 (1/31/90) (JL)
83 HEITZ Cabernet Sauvignon Napa Valley 1977 Rel: $11 Cur: $48 (1/31/90) (JL)
73 HEITZ Cabernet Sauvignon Napa Valley 1977 Rel: $11 Cur: $48 (2/16/84) (HS)
78 HEITZ Cabernet Sauvignon Napa Valley 1973 Cur: $38 (1/31/90) (JL)
74 HEITZ Cabernet Sauvignon Napa Valley 1970 Cur: $78 (1/31/90) (JL)
68 HEITZ Cabernet Sauvignon Napa Valley NV (NA) (1/31/90) (JL)
75 HEITZ Cabernet Sauvignon Napa Valley MZ-1 NV (NA) (1/31/90) (JL)
90 HEITZ Cabernet Sauvignon Napa Valley Z-91 NV (NA) (1/31/90) (JL)
89 HEITZ Cabernet Sauvignon Napa Valley Bella Oaks Vineyard 1986 $21.50 (4/15/91)
92 HEITZ Cabernet Sauvignon Napa Valley Bella Oaks Vineyard 1985 Rel: $25 Cur: $32 (5/15/90) CS
92 HEITZ Cabernet Sauvignon Napa Valley Bella Oaks Vineyard 1985 Rel: $25 Cur: $32 (CA-3/89)
86 HEITZ Cabernet Sauvignon Napa Valley Bella Oaks Vineyard 1984 Rel: $25 Cur: $32 (5/15/89)
86 HEITZ Cabernet Sauvignon Napa Valley Bella Oaks Vineyard 1984 Rel: $25 Cur: $32 (CA-3/89)
86 HEITZ Cabernet Sauvignon Napa Valley Bella Oaks Vineyard 1983 Rel: $15 Cur: $27 (CA-3/89)
90 HEITZ Cabernet Sauvignon Napa Valley Bella Oaks Vineyard 1983 Rel: $15 Cur: $27 (4/30/88)
85 HEITZ Cabernet Sauvignon Napa Valley Bella Oaks Vineyard 1982 Rel: $16 Cur: $31 (CA-3/89)
91 HEITZ Cabernet Sauvignon Napa Valley Bella Oaks Vineyard 1982 Rel: $16 Cur: $31 (4/30/87)
90 HEITZ Cabernet Sauvignon Napa Valley Bella Oaks Vineyard 1981 Rel: $16 Cur: $50 (CA-3/89)
79 HEITZ Cabernet Sauvignon Napa Valley Bella Oaks Vineyard 1981 Rel: $16 Cur: $50 (4/16/86)
93 HEITZ Cabernet Sauvignon Napa Valley Bella Oaks Vineyard 1980 Rel: $20 Cur: $51 (CA-3/89)
90 HEITZ Cabernet Sauvignon Napa Valley Bella Oaks Vineyard 1980 Rel: $20 Cur: $51 (7/16/85)
89 HEITZ Cabernet Sauvignon Napa Valley Bella Oaks Vineyard 1978 Rel: $15 Cur: $60 (CA-3/89)
90 HEITZ Cabernet Sauvignon Napa Valley Bella Oaks Vineyard 1978 Rel: $15 Cur: $60 (2/16/84) (HS)
91 HEITZ Cabernet Sauvignon Napa Valley Bella Oaks Vineyard 1977 Rel: $30 Cur: $66 (CA-3/89)
89 HEITZ Cabernet Sauvignon Napa Valley Bella Oaks Vineyard 1977 Rel: $30 Cur: $66 (2/16/84) (HS)
85 HEITZ Cabernet Sauvignon Napa Valley Bella Oaks Vineyard 1976 Rel: $30 Cur: $62 (CA-3/89)
92 HEITZ Cabernet Sauvignon Napa Valley Bella Oaks Vineyard 1976 Rel: $30 Cur: $62 (2/16/84) (HS)
80 HEITZ Cabernet Sauvignon Napa Valley Fay Vineyard 1978 Rel: $12.75 Cur: $32 (2/16/84) (HS)
78 HEITZ Cabernet Sauvignon Napa Valley Fay Vineyard 1977 Rel: $17.50 Cur: $32 (2/16/84) (HS)
95 HEITZ Cabernet Sauvignon Napa Valley Martha's Vineyard 1986 $60 (4/15/91) CS
98 HEITZ Cabernet Sauvignon Napa Valley Martha's Vineyard 1985 Rel: $60 Cur: $118 (4/30/90)
98 HEITZ Cabernet Sauvignon Napa Valley Martha's Vineyard 1985 Rel: $60 Cur: $118 (CA-3/89)
97 HEITZ Cabernet Sauvignon Napa Valley Martha's Vineyard 1984 Rel: $40 Cur: $77 (3/15/89) SS
97 HEITZ Cabernet Sauvignon Napa Valley Martha's Vineyard 1984 Rel: $40 Cur: $77 (CA-3/89)
89 HEITZ Cabernet Sauvignon Napa Valley Martha's Vineyard 1983 Rel: $32.50 Cur: $53 (CA-3/89)
90 HEITZ Cabernet Sauvignon Napa Valley Martha's Vineyard 1983 Rel: $32.50 Cur: $53 (4/30/88)
88 HEITZ Cabernet Sauvignon Napa Valley Martha's Vineyard 1982 Rel: $30 Cur: $65 (CA-3/89)
94 HEITZ Cabernet Sauvignon Napa Valley Martha's Vineyard 1982 Rel: $30 Cur: $65 (4/15/87) CS
89 HEITZ Cabernet Sauvignon Napa Valley Martha's Vineyard 1981 Rel: $30 Cur: $61 (CA-3/89)
91 HEITZ Cabernet Sauvignon Napa Valley Martha's Vineyard 1981 Rel: $30 Cur: $61 (4/16/86) CS
89 HEITZ Cabernet Sauvignon Napa Valley Martha's Vineyard 1980 Rel: $30 Cur: $65 (CA-3/89)
93 HEITZ Cabernet Sauvignon Napa Valley Martha's Vineyard 1980 Rel: $30 Cur: $65 (7/01/85) CS
93 HEITZ Cabernet Sauvignon Napa Valley Martha's Vineyard 1979 Rel: $25 Cur: $71 (CA-3/89)
94 HEITZ Cabernet Sauvignon Napa Valley Martha's Vineyard 1979 Rel: $25 Cur: $71 (2/15/84) SS
91 HEITZ Cabernet Sauvignon Napa Valley Martha's Vineyard 1978 Rel: $22 Cur: $110 (CA-3/89)
91 HEITZ Cabernet Sauvignon Napa Valley Martha's Vineyard 1978 Rel: $22 Cur: $110 (2/16/84) (HS)
90 HEITZ Cabernet Sauvignon Napa Valley Martha's Vineyard 1977 Rel: $30 Cur: $75 (1/31/90) (JL)
90 HEITZ Cabernet Sauvignon Napa Valley Martha's Vineyard 1977 Rel: $30 Cur: $75 (CA-3/89)
88 HEITZ Cabernet Sauvignon Napa Valley Martha's Vineyard 1977 Rel: $30 Cur: $75 (2/16/84) (HS)
85 HEITZ Cabernet Sauvignon Napa Valley Martha's Vineyard 1976 Rel: $30 Cur: $86 (CA-3/89)
94 HEITZ Cabernet Sauvignon Napa Valley Martha's Vineyard 1976 Rel: $30 Cur: $86 (2/16/84) (HS)
92 HEITZ Cabernet Sauvignon Napa Valley Martha's Vineyard 1975 Rel: $25 Cur: $100 (CA-3/89)
90 HEITZ Cabernet Sauvignon Napa Valley Martha's Vineyard 1975 Rel: $25 Cur: $100 (2/16/84) (HS)
94 HEITZ Cabernet Sauvignon Napa Valley Martha's Vineyard 1974 Rel: $25 Cur: $240 (2/15/90) (JG)
99 HEITZ Cabernet Sauvignon Napa Valley Martha's Vineyard 1974 Rel: $25 Cur: $240 (CA-3/89)
92 HEITZ Cabernet Sauvignon Napa Valley Martha's Vineyard 1973 Rel: $11 Cur: $120 (CA-3/89)
79 HEITZ Cabernet Sauvignon Napa Valley Martha's Vineyard 1972 Rel: $12.75 Cur: $114 (CA-3/89)
98 HEITZ Cabernet Sauvignon Napa Valley Martha's Vineyard 1970 Rel: $12.75 Cur: $280 (CA-3/89)
93 HEITZ Cabernet Sauvignon Napa Valley Martha's Vineyard 1969 Rel: $12.75 Cur: $280 (CA-3/89)
99 HEITZ Cabernet Sauvignon Napa Valley Martha's Vineyard 1968 Rel: $9.50 Cur: $390 (CA-3/89)
86 HEITZ Cabernet Sauvignon Napa Valley Martha's Vineyard 1967 Rel: $7.50 Cur: $300 (CA-3/89)
92 HEITZ Cabernet Sauvignon Napa Valley Martha's Vineyard 1966 Rel: $8 Cur: $470 (CA-3/89)
85+ HESS Cabernet Sauvignon Napa Valley 1990 (NR) (5/15/91) (BT)
90+ HESS Cabernet Sauvignon Napa Valley 1989 (NR) (5/15/91) (BT)
90+ HESS Cabernet Sauvignon Napa Valley 1988 (NR) (4/30/90) (BT)
94 HESS Cabernet Sauvignon Napa Valley 1987 $17 (4/15/91) SS
90+ HESS Cabernet Sauvignon Napa Valley 1987 $17 (4/15/89) (BT)
90 HESS Cabernet Sauvignon Napa Valley 1986 Rel: $14 Cur: $17 (11/15/89)
91 HESS Cabernet Sauvignon Napa Valley 1986 Rel: $14 Cur: $17 (CA-3/89)
96 HESS Cabernet Sauvignon Napa Valley 1985 Rel: $13 Cur: $40 (CA-3/89)
91 HESS Cabernet Sauvignon Napa Valley 1985 Rel: $13 Cur: $40 (11/15/88)
84 HESS Cabernet Sauvignon Napa Valley 1983 Rel: $13 Cur: $18 (CA-3/89)
82 HESS Cabernet Sauvignon Napa Valley 1983 Rel: $13 Cur: $18 (11/15/87)
93 HESS Cabernet Sauvignon Napa Valley Reserve 1986 Rel: $33 Cur: $45 (9/15/90)
93 HESS Cabernet Sauvignon Napa Valley Reserve 1986 Rel: $33 Cur: $45 (CA-3/89)
93 HESS Cabernet Sauvignon Napa Valley Reserve 1984 Rel: $22 Cur: $110 (CA-3/89)
92 HESS Cabernet Sauvignon Napa Valley Reserve 1984 Rel: $22 Cur: $110 (11/15/88)
88 HESS Cabernet Sauvignon Napa Valley Reserve 1983 Rel: $22 Cur: $98 (CA-3/89)
89 HESS Cabernet Sauvignon Napa Valley Reserve 1983 Rel: $22 Cur: $98 (9/15/88)
88 HIDDEN CELLARS Cabernet Sauvignon Mendocino County Mountanos Vineyard 1984 $12 (8/31/88)
85 WILLIAM HILL Cabernet Sauvignon Napa Valley Silver Label 1987 $14 (11/15/90)
85+ WILLIAM HILL Cabernet Sauvignon Napa Valley Silver Label 1986 $13 (4/15/88) (BT)
90 WILLIAM HILL Cabernet Sauvignon Napa Valley Silver Label 1985 $12 (4/30/88)
80+ WILLIAM HILL Cabernet Sauvignon Napa Valley Reserve 1990 (NR) (5/15/91) (BT)
85+ WILLIAM HILL Cabernet Sauvignon Napa Valley Reserve 1989 (NR) (5/15/91) (BT)
95 WILLIAM HILL Cabernet Sauvignon Napa Valley Reserve 1987 Rel: $24 Cur: $25 (11/15/90) SS
90+ WILLIAM HILL Cabernet Sauvignon Napa Valley Reserve 1987 Rel: $24 Cur: $25 (4/15/89) (BT)
91 WILLIAM HILL Cabernet Sauvignon Napa Valley Reserve 1986 Rel: $24.50 Cur: $25 (11/15/89)
95 WILLIAM HILL Cabernet Sauvignon Napa Valley Reserve 1986 Rel: $24.50 Cur: $25 (CA-3/89)
95+ WILLIAM HILL Cabernet Sauvignon Napa Valley Reserve 1986 Rel: $24.50 Cur: $25 (4/15/88) (BT)
94 WILLIAM HILL Cabernet Sauvignon Napa Valley Reserve 1985 Rel: $22.50 Cur: $27 (CA-3/89)
92 WILLIAM HILL Cabernet Sauvignon Napa Valley Reserve 1985 Rel: $22.50 Cur: $27 (11/15/88)
90+ WILLIAM HILL Cabernet Sauvignon Napa Valley Reserve 1985 Rel: $22.50 Cur: $27 (6/15/87) (BT)
91 WILLIAM HILL Cabernet Sauvignon Napa Valley Reserve 1984 Rel: $18.25 Cur: $26 (CA-3/89)
91 WILLIAM HILL Cabernet Sauvignon Napa Valley Reserve 1984 Rel: $18.25 Cur: $26 (4/15/88) CS
85 WILLIAM HILL Cabernet Sauvignon Napa Valley Gold Label 1983 Rel: $18.25 Cur: $25 (CA-3/89)
89 WILLIAM HILL Cabernet Sauvignon Napa Valley Gold Label 1983 Rel: $18.25 Cur: $25 (8/31/87)
90 WILLIAM HILL Cabernet Sauvignon Napa Valley Gold Label 1982 Rel: $18 Cur: $32 (CA-3/89)
94 WILLIAM HILL Cabernet Sauvignon Napa Valley Gold Label 1982 Rel: $18 Cur: $32 (6/16/86) SS
85 WILLIAM HILL Cabernet Sauvignon Napa Valley Gold Label 1981 Rel: $16.25 Cur: $28 (CA-3/89)
88 WILLIAM HILL Cabernet Sauvignon Napa Valley Gold Label 1981 Rel: $16.25 Cur: $28 (12/15/84)
87 WILLIAM HILL Cabernet Sauvignon Napa Valley Gold Label 1980 Rel: $18.25 Cur: $32 (CA-3/89)
93 WILLIAM HILL Cabernet Sauvignon Napa Valley Gold Label 1979 Rel: $18 Cur: $45 (CA-3/89)
95 WILLIAM HILL Cabernet Sauvignon Napa Valley Gold Label 1978 Rel: $16.25 Cur: $46 (CA-3/89)
95 WILLIAM HILL Cabernet Sauvignon Napa Valley Gold Label 1978 Rel: $16.25 Cur: $46 (4/30/87)
77 HOP KILN Cabernet Sauvignon Alexander Valley 1984 $10 (3/31/88)
69 HOP KILN Cabernet Sauvignon Dry Creek Valley 1986 $12 (6/15/89)
75 HOP KILN Cabernet Sauvignon Dry Creek Valley 1985 $10 (10/15/88)
63 HOUTZ Cabernet Sauvignon Santa Ynez Valley 1985 $8 (12/15/89)
84 HUSCH Cabernet Sauvignon Mendocino 1986 $12 (2/15/90)
84 HUSCH Cabernet Sauvignon Mendocino La Ribera Cabernet 1985 $5 (11/30/87) BB
86 HUSCH Cabernet Sauvignon Mendocino La Ribera Vineyards 1988 $12 (6/30/91)
90 HUSCH Cabernet Sauvignon Mendocino La Ribera Vineyards 1987 $12 (11/15/90)
73 HUSCH Cabernet Sauvignon Mendocino La Ribera Vineyards 1984 $10 (12/31/87)
87 HUSCH Cabernet Sauvignon Mendocino North Field Select 1987 $16 (11/15/90)
85 INGLENOOK Cabernet Sauvignon Napa Valley 1986 $7.50 (2/28/91) BB
83 INGLENOOK Cabernet Sauvignon Napa Valley 1985 $9.50 (3/31/89)
80 INGLENOOK Cabernet Sauvignon Napa Valley 1983 $9.50 (3/15/88)
87 INGLENOOK Cabernet Sauvignon Napa Valley 1980 $8 (2/15/84)
89 INGLENOOK Cabernet Sauvignon Napa Valley 1960 Cur: $135 (6/01/85) (JL)
88 INGLENOOK Cabernet Sauvignon Napa Valley 1958 Cur: $140 (6/01/85) (JL)
90+ INGLENOOK Cabernet Sauvignon Napa Valley Reserve Cask 1987 (NR) (4/15/89) (BT)
92 INGLENOOK Cabernet Sauvignon Napa Valley Reserve Cask 1986 (NR) (CA-3/89)
90+ INGLENOOK Cabernet Sauvignon Napa Valley Reserve Cask 1986 (NR) (4/15/88) (BT)

UNITED STATES

CALIFORNIA/*CABERNET SAUVIGNON & BLENDS*

90 INGLENOOK Cabernet Sauvignon Napa Valley Reserve Cask 1985 $16 (2/15/91) CS
95 INGLENOOK Cabernet Sauvignon Napa Valley Reserve Cask 1985 $16 (CA-3/89)
90+ INGLENOOK Cabernet Sauvignon Napa Valley Reserve Cask 1985 $16 (6/15/87) (BT)
90 INGLENOOK Cabernet Sauvignon Napa Valley Reserve Cask 1984 Rel: $22 Cur: $17 (7/31/90)
92 INGLENOOK Cabernet Sauvignon Napa Valley Reserve Cask 1984 Rel: $22 Cur: $17 (CA-3/89)
89 INGLENOOK Cabernet Sauvignon Napa Valley Reserve Cask 1983 Rel: $15.50 Cur: $19 (CA-3/89)
88 INGLENOOK Cabernet Sauvignon Napa Valley Reserve Cask 1983 Rel: $15.50 Cur: $19 (9/15/87)
91 INGLENOOK Cabernet Sauvignon Napa Valley Reserve Cask 1982 Rel: $22 Cur: $28 (CA-3/89)
93 INGLENOOK Cabernet Sauvignon Napa Valley Reserve Cask 1982 Rel: $22 Cur: $28 (2/15/87)
93 INGLENOOK Cabernet Sauvignon Napa Valley Reserve Cask 1981 Rel: $15.50 Cur: $22 (CA-3/89)
92 INGLENOOK Cabernet Sauvignon Napa Valley Reserve Cask 1981 Rel: $15.50 Cur: $22 (10/15/86)
88 INGLENOOK Cabernet Sauvignon Napa Valley Cask 1980 Rel: $15.50 Cur: $22 (CA-3/89)
89 INGLENOOK Cabernet Sauvignon Napa Valley Cask 1980 Rel: $15.50 Cur: $22 (9/16/84)
77 INGLENOOK Cabernet Sauvignon Napa Valley Cask 1979 Rel: $10.75 Cur: $23 (CA-3/89)
86 INGLENOOK Cabernet Sauvignon Napa Valley Cask 1978 Rel: $9.25 Cur: $25 (CA-3/89)
90 INGLENOOK Cabernet Sauvignon Napa Valley Cask 1978 Rel: $9.25 Cur: $25 (4/30/87)
84 INGLENOOK Cabernet Sauvignon Napa Valley Cask 1977 Rel: $8.75 Cur: $25 (CA-3/89)
92 INGLENOOK Cabernet Sauvignon Napa Valley Cask 1977 Rel: $8.75 Cur: $25 (6/01/85) (JL)
72 INGLENOOK Cabernet Sauvignon Napa Valley Cask 1976 Rel: $8.75 Cur: $19 (CA-3/89)
86 INGLENOOK Cabernet Sauvignon Napa Valley Cask 1974 Rel: $9 Cur: $46 (CA-3/89)
79 INGLENOOK Cabernet Sauvignon Napa Valley Cask A8 1974 Rel: $9 Cur: $46 (2/15/90) (JG)
94 INGLENOOK Cabernet Sauvignon Napa Valley Cask 1974 Rel: $9 Cur: $46 (6/01/85) (JL)
67 INGLENOOK Cabernet Sauvignon Napa Valley Cask 1973 Rel: $8 Cur: $39 (CA-3/89)
67 INGLENOOK Cabernet Sauvignon Napa Valley Cask 1972 Rel: $7 Cur: $44 (CA-3/89)
73 INGLENOOK Cabernet Sauvignon Napa Valley Cask 1971 Rel: $6.50 Cur: $50 (CA-3/89)
85 INGLENOOK Cabernet Sauvignon Napa Valley Cask 1970 Rel: $6.50 Cur: $75 (CA-3/89)
90 INGLENOOK Cabernet Sauvignon Napa Valley Cask 1970 Rel: $6.50 Cur: $75 (6/01/85) (JL)
80 INGLENOOK Cabernet Sauvignon Napa Valley Cask 1969 Rel: $6.50 Cur: $80 (CA-3/89)
85 INGLENOOK Cabernet Sauvignon Napa Valley Cask 1968 Rel: $6 Cur: $90 (CA-3/89)
73 INGLENOOK Cabernet Sauvignon Napa Valley Cask 1967 Rel: $6 Cur: $84 (CA-3/89)
73 INGLENOOK Cabernet Sauvignon Napa Valley Cask 1966 Rel: $5.75 Cur: $114 (CA-3/89)
84 INGLENOOK Cabernet Sauvignon Napa Valley Cask 1966 Rel: $5.75 Cur: $114 (6/01/85) (JL)
80 INGLENOOK Cabernet Sauvignon Napa Valley Cask 1960 Rel: $2.75 Cur: $140 (CA-3/89)
94 INGLENOOK Cabernet Sauvignon Napa Valley Cask 1958 Rel: $2.50 Cur: $250 (CA-3/89)
79 INGLENOOK Cabernet Sauvignon Napa Valley Cask F-11 1958 Rel: $2.50 Cur: $250 (2/28/87)
93 INGLENOOK Cabernet Sauvignon Napa Valley Cask 1955 Rel: $1.85 Cur: $400 (CA-3/89)
93 INGLENOOK Cabernet Sauvignon Napa Valley Cask 1955 Rel: $1.85 Cur: $400 (6/01/85) (JL)
92 INGLENOOK Cabernet Sauvignon Napa Valley Cask 1949 Rel: $1.49 Cur: $750 (CA-3/89)
87 INGLENOOK Cabernet Sauvignon Napa Valley 1946 Rel: $1.49 Cur: $900 (CA-3/89)
91 INGLENOOK Cabernet Sauvignon Napa Valley 1943 Rel: $1.49 Cur: $970 (CA-3/89)
100 INGLENOOK Cabernet Sauvignon Napa Valley 1941 Rel: $1.49 Cur: $1,790 (CA-3/89)
95 INGLENOOK Cabernet Sauvignon Napa Valley 1941 Rel: $1.49 Cur: $1,790 (6/01/85) (JL)
95 INGLENOOK Cabernet Sauvignon Napa Valley 1933 Rel: $1.30 Cur: $1,600 (CA-3/89)
87 INGLENOOK Cabernet Sauvignon California Claret-Medoc Type 1897 (NA) (CA-3/89)
85+ INGLENOOK Niebaum Claret Napa Valley 1987 (NR) (4/15/89) (BT)
74 INGLENOOK Niebaum Claret Napa Valley 1986 $12.50 (6/30/91)
82 INGLENOOK Niebaum Claret Napa Valley 1985 $12 (3/15/89)
88 INGLENOOK Niebaum Claret Napa Valley 1983 $12 (11/30/87)
92 INGLENOOK Reunion Napa Valley 1986 (NR) (CA-3/89)
91 INGLENOOK Reunion Napa Valley 1985 Rel: $35 Cur: $36 (7/15/89)
94 INGLENOOK Reunion Napa Valley 1985 Rel: $35 Cur: $36 (CA-3/89)
92 INGLENOOK Reunion Napa Valley 1984 Rel: $35 Cur: $35 (CA-3/89)
87 INGLENOOK Reunion Napa Valley 1984 Rel: $35 Cur: $35 (10/15/88)
93 INGLENOOK Reunion Napa Valley 1983 Rel: $33 Cur: $38 (CA-3/89)
95 INGLENOOK Reunion Napa Valley 1983 Rel: $33 Cur: $38 (11/30/87) CS
84 INNISFREE Cabernet Sauvignon Napa Valley 1988 $11 (4/30/91)
73 INNISFREE Cabernet Sauvignon Napa Valley 1986 $10.50 (6/30/90)
86 INNISFREE Cabernet Sauvignon Napa Valley 1985 $9 (3/15/89)
68 INNISFREE Cabernet Sauvignon Napa Valley 1984 $9 (12/15/87)
82 INNISFREE Cabernet Sauvignon Napa Valley 1983 $9 (11/15/86)
80 INNISFREE Cabernet Sauvignon Napa Valley 1982 $9 (12/16/85)
80+ IRON HORSE Cabernets Alexander Valley 1988 (NR) (4/30/90) (BT)
86 IRON HORSE Cabernets Alexander Valley 1987 $18.50 (3/15/91)
90+ IRON HORSE Cabernets Alexander Valley 1987 $18.50 (4/15/89) (BT)
90 IRON HORSE Cabernets Alexander Valley 1986 Rel: $17.50 Cur: $18 (4/15/90)
88 IRON HORSE Cabernets Alexander Valley 1986 Rel: $17.50 Cur: $18 (CA-3/89)
80+ IRON HORSE Cabernets Alexander Valley 1986 Rel: $17.50 Cur: $18 (4/15/88) (BT)
87 IRON HORSE Cabernets Alexander Valley 1985 Rel: $16 Cur: $17 (CA-3/89)
88 IRON HORSE Cabernets Alexander Valley 1985 Rel: $16 Cur: $17 (12/31/88)
86 IRON HORSE Cabernet Sauvignon Alexander Valley 1984 Rel: $14 Cur: $16 (CA-3/89)
82 IRON HORSE Cabernet Sauvignon Alexander Valley 1983 Rel: $12 Cur: $16 (CA-3/89)
83 IRON HORSE Cabernet Sauvignon Alexander Valley 1982 Rel: $12 Cur: $18 (CA-3/89)
79 IRON HORSE Cabernet Sauvignon Alexander Valley 1981 Rel: $12 Cur: $16 (CA-3/89)

Key to Symbols

The scores reported here are the results of blind tastings conducted by our panel of senior editors. Wines that carry the initials below are results of individual tastings.

THE WINE SPECTATOR 100-POINT SCALE ***95-100***—Classic, a great wine; ***90-94***—Outstanding, superior character and style; ***80-89***—Good to very good, a wine with special qualities; ***70-79***—Average, drinkable wine that may have minor flaws; ***60-69***—Below average, drinkable but not recommended; ***50-59***—Poor, undrinkable, not recommended. "+"—With a score indicates a range; used primarily with barrel tastings to indicate a preliminary score.

SPECIAL DESIGNATIONS SS—Spectator Selection, CS—Cellar Selection, BB—Best Buy.

TASTER'S INITIALS (JG)—Jim Gordon, (HS)—Harvey Steiman, (JL)—James Laube, (JS)—James Suckling, (TM)—Thomas Matthews, (TR)—Terry Robards, (BT)—Barrel Tasting (these wines were tasted blind from barrel samples), (CA-date)—*California's Great Cabernets* by James Laube, (CH-date)—*California's Great Chardonnays* by James Laube, (VP-date)—*Vintage Port* by James Suckling.

DATE TASTED Dates in parentheses represent the issue in which the rating was published.

92 IRON HORSE Cabernet Sauvignon Alexander Valley 1981 Rel: $12 Cur: $16 (12/16/84)
86 IRON HORSE Cabernet Sauvignon Alexander Valley 1980 Rel: $12 Cur: $20 (CA-3/89)
91 IRON HORSE Cabernet Sauvignon Alexander Valley 1979 Rel: $12 Cur: $25 (CA-3/89)
80 IRON HORSE Cabernet Sauvignon Alexander Valley 1978 Rel: $12 Cur: $25 (CA-3/89)
75 JADE MOUNTAIN Cabernet Sauvignon Alexander Valley Icaria Creek Vineyard deCarteret 1984 $8.75 (6/30/88)
83 JEKEL Cabernet Sauvignon Arroyo Seco 1986 $13 (11/15/90)
63 JEKEL Cabernet Sauvignon Arroyo Seco Home Vineyard 1980 $25 (2/01/86)
63 JEKEL Cabernet Sauvignon Monterey 1984 $12 (7/31/89)
67 JEKEL Cabernet Sauvignon Monterey 1983 $8 (2/15/89)
71 JEKEL Cabernet Sauvignon Monterey 1982 $11 (1/31/87)
69 JEKEL Cabernet Sauvignon Monterey Home Vineyard Private Reserve 1982 Rel: $20 Cur: $20 (2/01/86)
76 JEKEL Cabernet Sauvignon Monterey Home Vineyard Private Reserve 1981 Rel: $20 Cur: $18 (2/01/86)
77 JEKEL Cabernet Sauvignon Monterey Home Vineyard Private Reserve 1979 $18 (2/01/86)
70 JEKEL Cabernet Sauvignon Monterey Home Vineyard Private Reserve 1978 $16 (2/01/86)
85+ JOHNSON TURNBULL Cabernet Sauvignon Napa Valley 1988 (NR) (4/30/90) (BT)
80 JOHNSON TURNBULL Cabernet Sauvignon Napa Valley 1987 $16 (11/15/90)
95+ JOHNSON TURNBULL Cabernet Sauvignon Napa Valley 1986 Rel: $14.50 Cur: $25 (4/15/88) (BT)
83 JOHNSON TURNBULL Cabernet Sauvignon Napa Valley 1985 Rel: $14.50 Cur: $18 (CA-3/89)
88 JOHNSON TURNBULL Cabernet Sauvignon Napa Valley 1985 Rel: $14.50 Cur: $18 (7/15/88)
80+ JOHNSON TURNBULL Cabernet Sauvignon Napa Valley 1985 Rel: $14.50 Cur: $18 (6/15/87) (BT)
90 JOHNSON TURNBULL Cabernet Sauvignon Napa Valley 1984 Rel: $14.50 Cur: $23 (CA-3/89)
73 JOHNSON TURNBULL Cabernet Sauvignon Napa Valley 1984 Rel: $14.50 Cur: $23 (7/31/87)
88 JOHNSON TURNBULL Cabernet Sauvignon Napa Valley 1983 Rel: $12.50 Cur: $18 (CA-3/89)
86 JOHNSON TURNBULL Cabernet Sauvignon Napa Valley 1983 Rel: $12.50 Cur: $18 (9/15/86)
82 JOHNSON TURNBULL Cabernet Sauvignon Napa Valley 1982 Rel: $12.50 Cur: $20 (CA-3/89)
86 JOHNSON TURNBULL Cabernet Sauvignon Napa Valley 1982 Rel: $12.50 Cur: $20 (10/16/85)
87 JOHNSON TURNBULL Cabernet Sauvignon Napa Valley 1981 Rel: $12 Cur: $26 (CA-3/89)
76 JOHNSON TURNBULL Cabernet Sauvignon Napa Valley 1981 Rel: $12 Cur: $26 (4/16/84)
87 JOHNSON TURNBULL Cabernet Sauvignon Napa Valley 1980 Rel: $12 Cur: $29 (CA-3/89)
85 JOHNSON TURNBULL Cabernet Sauvignon Napa Valley 1979 Rel: $10.50 Cur: $29 (CA-3/89).
90+ JOHNSON TURNBULL Cabernet Sauvignon Napa Valley Vineyard Selection 67 1990 (NR) (5/15/91) (BT)
85+ JOHNSON TURNBULL Cabernet Sauvignon Napa Valley Vineyard Selection 67 1989 (NR) (5/15/91) (BT)
85+ JOHNSON TURNBULL Cabernet Sauvignon Napa Valley Vineyard Selection 67 1988 (NR) (4/30/90) (BT)
89 JOHNSON TURNBULL Cabernet Sauvignon Napa Valley Vineyard Selection 67 1987 $22 (6/30/91)
90+ JOHNSON TURNBULL Cabernet Sauvignon Napa Valley Vineyard Selection 67 1987 $22 (4/15/89) (BT)
86 JOHNSON TURNBULL Cabernet Sauvignon Napa Valley Vineyard Selection 67 1986 Rel: $20 Cur: $30 (4/15/90)
87 JOHNSON TURNBULL Cabernet Sauvignon Napa Valley Vineyard Selection 67 1986 Rel: $20 Cur: $30 (CA-3/89)
95 JOHNSON TURNBULL Cabernet Sauvignon Napa Valley Vineyard Selection 82 1986 Rel: $14.50 Cur: $25 (8/31/89)
95 JOHNSON TURNBULL Cabernet Sauvignon Napa Valley Vineyard Selection 82 1986 Rel: $14.50 Cur: $25 (CA-3/89)
85+ JORDAN Cabernet Sauvignon Alexander Valley 1988 (NR) (4/30/90) (BT)
88 JORDAN Cabernet Sauvignon Alexander Valley 1986 $22 (11/15/90)
88 JORDAN Cabernet Sauvignon Alexander Valley 1986 $22 (CA-3/89)
88 JORDAN Cabernet Sauvignon Alexander Valley 1985 Rel: $19.50 Cur: $25 (9/15/89)
85 JORDAN Cabernet Sauvignon Alexander Valley 1985 Rel: $19.50 Cur: $25 (CA-3/89)
86 JORDAN Cabernet Sauvignon Alexander Valley 1984 Rel: $19 Cur: $39 (CA-3/89)
86 JORDAN Cabernet Sauvignon Alexander Valley 1984 Rel: $19 Cur: $39 (7/15/88)
78 JORDAN Cabernet Sauvignon Alexander Valley 1983 Rel: $18 Cur: $32 (CA-3/89)
81 JORDAN Cabernet Sauvignon Alexander Valley 1983 Rel: $18 Cur: $32 (7/15/87)
73 JORDAN Cabernet Sauvignon Alexander Valley 1982 Rel: $18 Cur: $39 (CA-3/89)
84 JORDAN Cabernet Sauvignon Alexander Valley 1982 Rel: $18 Cur: $39 (2/01/86)
84 JORDAN Cabernet Sauvignon Alexander Valley 1982 Rel: $18 Cur: $39 (2/01/85)
84 JORDAN Cabernet Sauvignon Alexander Valley 1981 Rel: $17 Cur: $44 (CA-3/89)
89 JORDAN Cabernet Sauvignon Alexander Valley 1981 Rel: $17 Cur: $44 (2/01/86)
90 JORDAN Cabernet Sauvignon Alexander Valley 1981 Rel: $17 Cur: $44 (5/01/85) CS
89 JORDAN Cabernet Sauvignon Alexander Valley 1981 Rel: $17 Cur: $44 (2/01/85)
80 JORDAN Cabernet Sauvignon Alexander Valley 1980 Rel: $17 Cur: $46 (CA-3/89)
82 JORDAN Cabernet Sauvignon Alexander Valley 1980 Rel: $17 Cur: $46 (2/01/86)
82 JORDAN Cabernet Sauvignon Alexander Valley 1980 Rel: $17 Cur: $46 (2/01/85)
79 JORDAN Cabernet Sauvignon Alexander Valley 1979 Rel: $16 Cur: $57 (CA-3/89)
81 JORDAN Cabernet Sauvignon Alexander Valley 1979 Rel: $16 Cur: $57 (2/01/86)
81 JORDAN Cabernet Sauvignon Alexander Valley 1979 Rel: $16 Cur: $57 (2/01/85)
81 JORDAN Cabernet Sauvignon Alexander Valley 1978 Rel: $16 Cur: $61 (CA-3/89)
89 JORDAN Cabernet Sauvignon Alexander Valley 1978 Rel: $16 Cur: $61 (4/30/87)
78 JORDAN Cabernet Sauvignon Alexander Valley 1978 Rel: $16 Cur: $61 (2/01/85)
77 JORDAN Cabernet Sauvignon Alexander Valley 1977 Rel: $14 Cur: $70 (CA-3/89)
79 JORDAN Cabernet Sauvignon Alexander Valley 1976 Rel: $10 Cur: $76 (CA-3/89)
81 JOULLIAN Cabernet Sauvignon Carmel Valley 1987 $14 (7/31/91)
90+ JUDD'S HILL Cabernet Sauvignon Napa Valley 1990 (NR) (5/15/91) (BT)
90+ JUDD'S HILL Cabernet Sauvignon Napa Valley 1989 (NR) (5/15/91) (BT)
90 JUSTIN Reserve Paso Robles 1987 $20 (2/15/91)
83 KALIN Cabernet Sauvignon Sonoma County Reserve 1985 $23 (4/15/91)
86 KEENAN Cabernet Sauvignon Napa Valley 1987 Rel: $18 Cur: $19 (5/31/90)
95+ KEENAN Cabernet Sauvignon Napa Valley 1987 Rel: $18 Cur: $19 (4/15/89) (BT)
93 KEENAN Cabernet Sauvignon Napa Valley 1986 Rel: $16.50 Cur: $17 (8/31/89)
94 KEENAN Cabernet Sauvignon Napa Valley 1986 Rel: $16.50 Cur: $17 (CA-3/89)
90+ KEENAN Cabernet Sauvignon Napa Valley 1986 Rel: $16.50 Cur: $17 (4/15/88) (BT)
79 KEENAN Cabernet Sauvignon Napa Valley 1985 Rel: $15 Cur: $21 (3/31/89)

86	KEENAN Cabernet Sauvignon Napa Valley 1985 Rel: $15 Cur: $21 (CA-3/89)
92	KEENAN Cabernet Sauvignon Napa Valley 1984 Rel: $13.50 Cur: $30 (CA-3/89)
94	KEENAN Cabernet Sauvignon Napa Valley 1984 Rel: $13.50 Cur: $30 (10/15/87) SS
87	KEENAN Cabernet Sauvignon Napa Valley 1983 Rel: $11 Cur: $18 (CA-3/89)
87	KEENAN Cabernet Sauvignon Napa Valley 1983 Rel: $11 Cur: $18 (2/15/87)
88	KEENAN Cabernet Sauvignon Napa Valley 1982 Rel: $10 Cur: $24 (CA-3/89)
91	KEENAN Cabernet Sauvignon Napa Valley 1982 Rel: $10 Cur: $24 (1/01/86)
84	KEENAN Cabernet Sauvignon Napa Valley 1981 Rel: $13.50 Cur: $22 (CA-3/89)
80	KEENAN Cabernet Sauvignon Napa Valley 1980 Rel: $13.50 Cur: $40 (CA-3/89)
85	KEENAN Cabernet Sauvignon Napa Valley 1980 Rel: $13.50 Cur: $40 (1/01/84)
74	KEENAN Cabernet Sauvignon Napa Valley 1979 Rel: $12 Cur: $38 (CA-3/89)
74	KEENAN Cabernet Sauvignon Napa Valley 1978 Rel: $12 Cur: $40 (CA-3/89)
69	KEENAN Cabernet Sauvignon Napa Valley 1977 Rel: $12 Cur: $40 (CA-3/89)
91	KENDALL-JACKSON Cabernet Sauvignon California Cardinale 1986 $65 (11/15/90)
97	KENDALL-JACKSON Cabernet Sauvignon California Cardinale 1985 $45 (11/15/89)
84	KENDALL-JACKSON Cardinale California 1984 $12 (7/31/87)
82	KENDALL-JACKSON Cardinale California 1983 $9 (10/16/85)
85	KENDALL-JACKSON Cabernet Sauvignon California The Proprietor's 1986 $24 (3/15/90)
95	KENDALL-JACKSON Cabernet Sauvignon California The Proprietor's Reserve 1985 $20 (12/15/88)
85	KENDALL-JACKSON Cabernet Sauvignon California Vintner's Reserve 1986 $11 (12/31/88)
74	KENDALL-JACKSON Cabernet Sauvignon Lake County 1986 $7.75 (7/31/88)
81	KENDALL-JACKSON Cabernet Sauvignon Lake County 1984 $7.50 (11/15/87) BB
69	KENDALL-JACKSON Cabernet Sauvignon Lake County 1983 $7 (5/01/86)
89	KATHRYN KENNEDY Cabernet Sauvignon Santa Cruz Mountains 1987 $45 (1/31/91)
81	KATHRYN KENNEDY Cabernet Sauvignon Santa Cruz Mountains 1986 $30 (3/15/90)
93	KATHRYN KENNEDY Cabernet Sauvignon Santa Cruz Mountains 1985 $25 (12/15/88)
87	KATHRYN KENNEDY Lateral California 1988 $14.50 (10/15/90)
90	KENWOOD Cabernet Sauvignon Sonoma Valley 1987 $15 (7/15/91)
86	KENWOOD Cabernet Sauvignon Sonoma Valley 1986 $15 (9/30/89)
91	KENWOOD Cabernet Sauvignon Sonoma Valley 1985 $14.50 (2/15/89)
83	KENWOOD Cabernet Sauvignon Sonoma Valley 1984 $12 (5/31/88)
85	KENWOOD Cabernet Sauvignon Sonoma Valley 1983 $10 (2/15/88)
88	KENWOOD Cabernet Sauvignon Sonoma Valley Artist Series 1987 $35 (11/15/90)
95	KENWOOD Cabernet Sauvignon Sonoma Valley Artist Series 1986 Rel: $30 Cur: $31 (11/30/89) CS
94	KENWOOD Cabernet Sauvignon Sonoma Valley Artist Series 1986 Rel: $30 Cur: $31 (CA-3/89)
91	KENWOOD Cabernet Sauvignon Sonoma Valley Artist Series 1985 Rel: $30 Cur: $31 (CA-3/89)
91	KENWOOD Cabernet Sauvignon Sonoma Valley Artist Series 1985 Rel: $30 Cur: $31 (2/15/89)
93	KENWOOD Cabernet Sauvignon Sonoma Valley Artist Series 1984 Rel: $30 Cur: $35 (CA-3/89)
93	KENWOOD Cabernet Sauvignon Sonoma Valley Artist Series 1984 Rel: $30 Cur: $35 (11/30/87)
87	KENWOOD Cabernet Sauvignon Sonoma Valley Artist Series 1983 Rel: $30 Cur: $38 (CA-3/89)
92	KENWOOD Cabernet Sauvignon Sonoma Valley Artist Series 1983 Rel: $30 Cur: $38 (11/15/86) CS
87	KENWOOD Cabernet Sauvignon Sonoma Valley Artist Series 1982 Rel: $25 Cur: $42 (CA-3/89)
89	KENWOOD Cabernet Sauvignon Sonoma Valley Artist Series 1982 Rel: $25 Cur: $42 (11/01/85)
89	KENWOOD Cabernet Sauvignon Sonoma Valley Artist Series 1981 Rel: $25 Cur: $55 (CA-3/89)
89	KENWOOD Cabernet Sauvignon Sonoma Valley Artist Series 1981 Rel: $25 Cur: $55 (9/16/84) SS
80	KENWOOD Cabernet Sauvignon Sonoma Valley Artist Series 1980 Rel: $20 Cur: $55 (CA-3/89)
91	KENWOOD Cabernet Sauvignon Sonoma Valley Artist Series 1979 Rel: $20 Cur: $70 (CA-3/89)
90	KENWOOD Cabernet Sauvignon Sonoma Valley Artist Series 1978 Rel: $20 Cur: $95 (CA-3/89)
94	KENWOOD Cabernet Sauvignon Sonoma Valley Artist Series 1978 Rel: $20 Cur: $95 (4/30/87)
82	KENWOOD Cabernet Sauvignon Sonoma Valley Artist Series 1977 Rel: $15 Cur: $175 (CA-3/89)
77	KENWOOD Cabernet Sauvignon Sonoma County Artist Series 1976 Rel: $10 Cur: $160 (CA-3/89)
73	KENWOOD Cabernet Sauvignon Sonoma County Artist Series 1975 Rel: $6.50 Cur: $500 (CA-3/89)
92	KENWOOD Cabernet Sauvignon Sonoma Valley Jack London Vineyard 1987 $18 (1/31/91)
90	KENWOOD Cabernet Sauvignon Sonoma Valley Jack London Vineyard 1986 Rel: $18 Cur: $18 (9/15/89)
89	KENWOOD Cabernet Sauvignon Sonoma Valley Jack London Vineyard 1985 Rel: $18 Cur: $19 (10/15/88)
80+	KENWOOD Cabernet Sauvignon Sonoma Valley Jack London Vineyard 1985 Rel: $18 Cur: $19 (6/15/87) (BT)
91	KENWOOD Cabernet Sauvignon Sonoma Valley Jack London Vineyard 1984 Rel: $16 Cur: $21 (11/30/87)
86	KENWOOD Cabernet Sauvignon Sonoma Valley Jack London Vineyard 1983 Rel: $15 Cur: $21 (2/15/87)
80	KENWOOD Cabernet Sauvignon Sonoma Valley Jack London Vineyard 1980 Rel: $12.50 Cur: $15 (5/16/84)
83	KISTLER Cabernet Sauvignon Sonoma Valley Kistler Estate Vineyard 1987 $25 (2/28/91)
84	KISTLER Cabernet Sauvignon Sonoma Valley Kistler Estate Vineyard 1986 Rel: $20 Cur: $30 (9/30/89)
91	KISTLER Cabernet Sauvignon Sonoma Valley Kistler Estate Vineyard 1986 Rel: $20 Cur: $30 (CA-3/89)
93	KISTLER Cabernet Sauvignon Sonoma Valley Kistler Estate Vineyard 1985 Rel: $16 Cur: $30 (CA-3/89)
92	KISTLER Cabernet Sauvignon Sonoma Valley Kistler Estate Vineyard 1985 Rel: $16 Cur: $30 (5/31/88)
78	KISTLER Cabernet Sauvignon Napa Valley Veeder Hills Vineyard 1983 Rel: $13.50 Cur: $25 (CA-3/89)
61	KISTLER Cabernet Sauvignon Napa Valley Veeder Hills Vineyard 1983 Rel: $13.50 Cur: $25 (1/31/87)
86	KISTLER Cabernet Sauvignon Napa Valley Veeder Hills Vineyard 1982 Rel: $12 Cur: $26 (CA-3/89)

87	KISTLER Cabernet Sauvignon Napa Valley Veeder Hills-Veeder Peak 1981 Rel: $12 Cur: $32 (CA-3/89)
85	KISTLER Cabernet Sauvignon Napa Valley Veeder Hills-Veeder Peak 1980 Rel: $16 Cur: $45 (CA-3/89)
84	KISTLER Cabernet Sauvignon Sonoma Valley Glen Ellen Vineyard 1980 Rel: $16 Cur: $45 (CA-3/89)
87	KLEIN Cabernet Sauvignon Santa Cruz Mountains 1987 $19 (10/15/90)
89	KLEIN Cabernet Sauvignon Santa Cruz Mountains 1986 $22 (9/30/89)
80	KONOCTI Cabernet Sauvignon Lake County 1986 $9 (4/30/90)
89	KONOCTI Cabernet Sauvignon Lake County 1985 $7.50 (11/15/89) BB
76	KONOCTI Cabernet Sauvignon Lake County 1984 $7.50 (2/15/89)
84	KONOCTI Cabernet Sauvignon Lake County 1983 $6 (6/15/87) BB
78	KONOCTI Cabernet Sauvignon Lake County 1982 $7 (11/15/86)
85	KONOCTI Meritage Red Clear Lake 1987 $17 (4/15/91)
87	CHARLES KRUG Cabernet Sauvignon Napa Valley 1986 $10.50 (2/28/91)
77	CHARLES KRUG Cabernet Sauvignon Napa Valley 1985 $10.50 (1/31/90)
79	CHARLES KRUG Cabernet Sauvignon Napa Valley 1982 $7 (10/31/87)
74	CHARLES KRUG Cabernet Sauvignon Napa Valley 1965 Cur: $35 (7/16/85) (JL)
84	CHARLES KRUG Cabernet Sauvignon Napa Valley 1962 Cur: $60 (7/16/85) (JL)
84	CHARLES KRUG Cabernet Sauvignon Napa Valley 1961 Cur: $105 (7/16/85) (JL)
86	CHARLES KRUG Cabernet Sauvignon Napa Valley 1952 Cur: $250 (7/16/85) (JL)
80	CHARLES KRUG Cabernet Sauvignon Napa Valley 1951 Cur: $250 (7/16/85) (JL)
89	CHARLES KRUG Cabernet Sauvignon Napa Valley 1947 Cur: $300 (7/16/85) (JL)
85+	CHARLES KRUG Cabernet Sauvignon Napa Valley Slinsen Ranch 1986 (NR) (4/15/88) (BT)
87	CHARLES KRUG Cabernet Sauvignon Napa Valley Vintage Select 1986 (NR) (CA-3/89)
84	CHARLES KRUG Cabernet Sauvignon Napa Valley Vintage Select 1985 (NA) (CA-3/89)
87	CHARLES KRUG Cabernet Sauvignon Napa Valley Vintage Select 1984 Rel: $20 Cur: $24 (6/30/90)
87	CHARLES KRUG Cabernet Sauvignon Napa Valley Vintage Select 1984 Rel: $20 Cur: $24 (CA-3/89)
81	CHARLES KRUG Cabernet Sauvignon Napa Valley Vintage Select 1983 Rel: $20 Cur: $26 (6/30/90)
82	CHARLES KRUG Cabernet Sauvignon Napa Valley Vintage Select 1983 Rel: $20 Cur: $26 (CA-3/89)
90	CHARLES KRUG Cabernet Sauvignon Napa Valley Vintage Select 1981 Rel: $20 Cur: $24 (9/30/90)
82	CHARLES KRUG Cabernet Sauvignon Napa Valley Vintage Select 1981 Rel: $20 Cur: $24 (CA-3/89)
79	CHARLES KRUG Cabernet Sauvignon Napa Valley Vintage Select 1980 Rel: $15 Cur: $23 (CA-3/89)
82	CHARLES KRUG Cabernet Sauvignon Napa Valley Vintage Select 1979 Rel: $12.50 Cur: $20 (CA-3/89)
78	CHARLES KRUG Cabernet Sauvignon Napa Valley Vintage Select 1978 Rel: $11 Cur: $22 (CA-3/89)
74	CHARLES KRUG Cabernet Sauvignon Napa Valley Vintage Select 1977 Rel: $10 Cur: $22 (CA-3/89)
87	CHARLES KRUG Cabernet Sauvignon Napa Valley Vintage Select 1974 Rel: $9 Cur: $50 (2/15/90) (JG)
86	CHARLES KRUG Cabernet Sauvignon Napa Valley Vintage Select 1974 Rel: $9 Cur: $50 (6/01/85) (JL)
88	CHARLES KRUG Cabernet Sauvignon Napa Valley Vintage Select Lot F-1 1974 Rel: $9 Cur: $50 (CA-3/89)
91	CHARLES KRUG Cabernet Sauvignon Napa Valley Vintage Select Lot F-1 1974 Rel: $9 Cur: $50 (6/01/85) (JL)
73	CHARLES KRUG Cabernet Sauvignon Napa Valley Vintage Select 1973 Rel: $9 Cur: $40 (CA-3/89)
77	CHARLES KRUG Cabernet Sauvignon Napa Valley Vintage Select 1972 Rel: $9 Cur: $45 (CA-3/89)
79	CHARLES KRUG Cabernet Sauvignon Napa Valley Vintage Select 1971 Rel: $7.50 Cur: $42 (CA-3/89)
75	CHARLES KRUG Cabernet Sauvignon Napa Valley Vintage Select 1970 Rel: $7.50 Cur: $60 (CA-3/89)
81	CHARLES KRUG Cabernet Sauvignon Napa Valley Vintage Select 1969 Rel: $6.50 Cur: $55 (CA-3/89)
85	CHARLES KRUG Cabernet Sauvignon Napa Valley Vintage Select 1969 Rel: $6.50 Cur: $55 (6/01/85) (JL)
80	CHARLES KRUG Cabernet Sauvignon Napa Valley Vintage Select 1968 Rel: $6.50 Cur: $90 (CA-3/89)
88	CHARLES KRUG Cabernet Sauvignon Napa Valley Vintage Select 1968 Rel: $6.50 Cur: $90 (6/01/85) (JL)
87	CHARLES KRUG Cabernet Sauvignon Napa Valley Vintage Select 1966 Rel: $6 Cur: $88 (6/01/85) (JL)
87	CHARLES KRUG Cabernet Sauvignon Napa Valley Vintage Select 1965 Rel: $5 Cur: $86 (CA-3/89)
90	CHARLES KRUG Cabernet Sauvignon Napa Valley Vintage Select 1965 Rel: $5 Cur: $86 (6/01/85) (JL)
86	CHARLES KRUG Cabernet Sauvignon Napa Valley Vintage Select 1964 Rel: $4 Cur: $75 (CA-3/89)
86	CHARLES KRUG Cabernet Sauvignon Napa Valley Vintage Select 1964 Rel: $4 Cur: $75 (7/16/85) (JL)
74	CHARLES KRUG Cabernet Sauvignon Napa Valley Vintage Select 1963 Rel: $3.50 Cur: $77 (CA-3/89)
79	CHARLES KRUG Cabernet Sauvignon Napa Valley Vintage Select 1963 Rel: $3.50 Cur: $77 (7/16/85) (JL)
78	CHARLES KRUG Cabernet Sauvignon Napa Valley Vintage Select 1962 Rel: $3.50 Cur: $113 (CA-3/89)
78	CHARLES KRUG Cabernet Sauvignon Napa Valley Vintage Select 1962 Rel: $3.50 Cur: $113 (7/16/85) (JL)
89	CHARLES KRUG Cabernet Sauvignon Napa Valley Vintage Select 1961 Rel: $3.50 Cur: $140 (CA-3/89)
88	CHARLES KRUG Cabernet Sauvignon Napa Valley Vintage Select 1961 Rel: $3.50 Cur: $140 (7/16/85) (JL)
79	CHARLES KRUG Cabernet Sauvignon Napa Valley Vintage Select 1960 Rel: $2.25 Cur: $70 (CA-3/89)
89	CHARLES KRUG Cabernet Sauvignon Napa Valley Vintage Select 1960 Rel: $2.25 Cur: $70 (7/16/85) (JL)
85	CHARLES KRUG Cabernet Sauvignon Napa Valley Vintage Select 1959 Rel: $2.25 Cur: $140 (CA-3/89)
78	CHARLES KRUG Cabernet Sauvignon Napa Valley Vintage Select 1959 Rel: $2.25 Cur: $140 (7/16/85) (JL)

UNITED STATES

CALIFORNIA/CABERNET SAUVIGNON & BLENDS

88 CHARLES KRUG Cabernet Sauvignon Napa Valley Vintage Select 1958 Rel: $2 Cur: $310 (CA-3/89)
91 CHARLES KRUG Cabernet Sauvignon Napa Valley Vintage Select 1958 Rel: $2 Cur: $310 (7/16/85) (JL)
81 CHARLES KRUG Cabernet Sauvignon Napa Valley Vintage Select 1957 Rel: $2 Cur: $280 (7/16/85) (JL)
90 CHARLES KRUG Cabernet Sauvignon Napa Valley Vintage Select 1956 Rel: $1.40 Cur: $430 (CA-3/89)
85 CHARLES KRUG Cabernet Sauvignon Napa Valley Vintage Select 1956 Rel: $1.40 Cur: $430 (7/16/85) (JL)
92 CHARLES KRUG Cabernet Sauvignon Napa Valley Vintage Select 1952 Rel: $1.26 Cur: $530 (CA-3/89)
90 CHARLES KRUG Cabernet Sauvignon Napa Valley Vintage Select 1952 Rel: $1.26 Cur: $530 (7/16/85) (JL)
85 CHARLES KRUG Cabernet Sauvignon Napa Valley Vintage Select 1951 Rel: $1.25 Cur: $450 (CA-3/89)
88 CHARLES KRUG Cabernet Sauvignon Napa Valley Vintage Select 1951 Rel: $1.25 Cur: $450 (7/16/85) (JL)
79 CHARLES KRUG Cabernet Sauvignon Napa Valley Vintage Select 1950 Rel: $1.25 Cur: $500 (CA-3/89)
82 CHARLES KRUG Cabernet Sauvignon Napa Valley Vintage Select 1950 Rel: $1.25 Cur: $500 (7/16/85) (JL)
88 CHARLES KRUG Cabernet Sauvignon Napa Valley Vintage Select 1946 Rel: $1 Cur: $750 (CA-3/89)
90 CHARLES KRUG Cabernet Sauvignon Napa Valley Vintage Select 1946 Rel: $1 Cur: $750 (7/16/85) (JL)
88 CHARLES KRUG Cabernet Sauvignon Napa Valley 1944 Rel: $0.95 Cur: $420 (CA-3/89)
95 CHARLES KRUG Cabernet Sauvignon Napa Valley 1944 Rel: $0.95 Cur: $420 (7/16/85)
80 LA FERRONNIERE Cabernet Sauvignon Napa Valley 1985 $14 (1/31/90)
90+ LA JOTA Cabernet Sauvignon Howell Mountain 1990 (NR) (5/15/91) (BT)
90+ LA JOTA Cabernet Sauvignon Howell Mountain 1989 (NR) (5/15/91) (BT)
90+ LA JOTA Cabernet Sauvignon Howell Mountain 1988 $28 (4/30/90) (BT)
95 LA JOTA Cabernet Sauvignon Howell Mountain 1987 Rel: $25 Cur: $28 (7/31/90) SS
90+ LA JOTA Cabernet Sauvignon Howell Mountain 1987 Rel: $25 Cur: $28 (4/15/89) (BT)
85 LA JOTA Cabernet Sauvignon Howell Mountain 1986 Rel: $21 Cur: $27 (10/15/89)
92 LA JOTA Cabernet Sauvignon Howell Mountain 1986 Rel: $21 Cur: $27 (CA-3/89)
90+ LA JOTA Cabernet Sauvignon Howell Mountain 1986 Rel: $21 Cur: $27 (4/15/88) (BT)
88 LA JOTA Cabernet Sauvignon Howell Mountain 1985 Rel: $18 Cur: $36 (CA-3/89)
91 LA JOTA Cabernet Sauvignon Howell Mountain 1985 Rel: $18 Cur: $36 (11/15/88)
85+ LA JOTA Cabernet Sauvignon Howell Mountain 1985 Rel: $18 Cur: $36 (6/15/87) (BT)
88 LA JOTA Cabernet Sauvignon Howell Mountain 1984 Rel: $15 Cur: $32 (CA-3/89)
84 LA JOTA Cabernet Sauvignon Howell Mountain 1984 Rel: $15 Cur: $32 (11/15/87)
84 LA JOTA Cabernet Sauvignon Howell Mountain 1983 Rel: $15 Cur: $30 (CA-3/89)
90 LA JOTA Cabernet Sauvignon Howell Mountain 1983 Rel: $15 Cur: $30 (3/31/87)
84 LA JOTA Cabernet Sauvignon Howell Mountain 1982 Rel: $13.50 Cur: $28 (CA-3/89)
81 LA VIEILLE MONTAGNE Cabernet Sauvignon Napa Valley 1987 $14 (6/15/91)
84 LA VIEILLE MONTAGNE Cabernet Sauvignon Napa Valley 1986 $14 (6/30/90)
80+ LAKESPRING Cabernet Sauvignon Napa Valley 1987 $14 (4/15/89) (BT)
88 LAKESPRING Cabernet Sauvignon Napa Valley 1986 Rel: $14 Cur: $18 (CA-3/89)
88 LAKESPRING Cabernet Sauvignon Napa Valley 1985 Rel: $12 Cur: $12 (CA-3/89)
92 LAKESPRING Cabernet Sauvignon Napa Valley 1985 Rel: $12 Cur: $12 (7/15/88)
92 LAKESPRING Cabernet Sauvignon Napa Valley Reserve Selection 1984 Rel: $15 Cur: $21 (CA-3/89)
92 LAKESPRING Cabernet Sauvignon Napa Valley Reserve Selection 1984 Rel: $15 Cur: $21 (10/31/88) SS
85 LAKESPRING Cabernet Sauvignon Napa Valley 1983 Rel: $11 Cur: $13 (CA-3/89)
77 LAKESPRING Cabernet Sauvignon Napa Valley 1983 Rel: $11 Cur: $13 (12/15/86)
88 LAKESPRING Cabernet Sauvignon Napa Valley Vintage Selection 1982 Rel: $14 Cur: $24 (CA-3/89)
94 LAKESPRING Cabernet Sauvignon Napa Valley Vintage Selection 1982 Rel: $14 Cur: $24 (12/15/86)
86 LAKESPRING Cabernet Sauvignon Napa Valley 1981 Rel: $11 Cur: $20 (CA-3/89)
87 LAKESPRING Cabernet Sauvignon Napa Valley 1981 Rel: $11 Cur: $20 (9/16/84)
88 LAKESPRING Cabernet Sauvignon Napa Valley 1980 Rel: $10 Cur: $21 (CA-3/89)
80 LAMBERT BRIDGE Cabernet Sauvignon Sonoma County 1984 $10 (4/15/87)
75 LAMBERT BRIDGE Cabernet Sauvignon Sonoma County 1981 $12 (1/01/85)
71 LAURA'S Cabernet Sauvignon Paso Robles 1985 $12 (12/15/89)
80 LAURA'S Cabernet Sauvignon Paso Robles 1983 $8.50 (12/31/87)
90+ LAUREL GLEN Cabernet Sauvignon Sonoma Mountain 1990 (NR) (5/15/91) (BT)
90+ LAUREL GLEN Cabernet Sauvignon Sonoma Mountain 1989 (NR) (5/15/91) (BT)
90 LAUREL GLEN Cabernet Sauvignon Sonoma Mountain 1988 $30 (5/15/91) CS
90+ LAUREL GLEN Cabernet Sauvignon Sonoma Mountain 1988 $30 (4/30/90) (BT)
90 LAUREL GLEN Cabernet Sauvignon Sonoma Mountain 1987 Rel: $22 Cur: $25 (9/15/90)
90+ LAUREL GLEN Cabernet Sauvignon Sonoma Mountain 1987 Rel: $22 Cur: $25 (4/15/89) (BT)
87 LAUREL GLEN Cabernet Sauvignon Sonoma Mountain 1986 Rel: $20 Cur: $27 (5/15/89)
89 LAUREL GLEN Cabernet Sauvignon Sonoma Mountain 1986 Rel: $20 Cur: $27 (CA-3/89)
90+ LAUREL GLEN Cabernet Sauvignon Sonoma Mountain 1986 Rel: $20 Cur: $27 (4/15/88) (BT)
93 LAUREL GLEN Cabernet Sauvignon Sonoma Mountain 1985 Rel: $18 Cur: $39 (CA-3/89)
91 LAUREL GLEN Cabernet Sauvignon Sonoma Mountain 1985 Rel: $18 Cur: $39 (4/30/88)
90+ LAUREL GLEN Cabernet Sauvignon Sonoma Mountain 1985 Rel: $18 Cur: $39 (6/15/87) (BT)
89 LAUREL GLEN Cabernet Sauvignon Sonoma Mountain 1984 Rel: $15 Cur: $45 (CA-3/89)

Key to Symbols

The scores reported here are the results of blind tastings conducted by our panel of senior editors. Wines that carry the initials below are results of individual tastings.

THE WINE SPECTATOR 100-POINT SCALE *95-100*—Classic, a great wine; *90-94*—Outstanding, superior character and style; *80-89*—Good to very good, a wine with special qualities; *70-79*—Average, drinkable wine that may have minor flaws; *60-69*—Below average, drinkable but not recommended; *50-59*—Poor, undrinkable, not recommended. "+"—With a score indicates a range; used primarily with barrel tastings to indicate a preliminary score.

SPECIAL DESIGNATIONS SS—Spectator Selection, CS—Cellar Selection, BB—Best Buy.

TASTER'S INITIALS (JG)—Jim Gordon, (HS)—Harvey Steiman, (JL)—James Laube, (JS)—James Suckling, (TM)—Thomas Matthews, (TR)—Terry Robards, (BT)—Barrel Tasting (these wines were tasted blind from barrel samples), (CA-date)—*California's Great Cabernets* by James Laube, (CH-date)—*California's Great Chardonnays* by James Laube, (VP-date)—*Vintage Port* by James Suckling.

DATE TASTED Dates in parentheses represent the issue in which the rating was published.

87 LAUREL GLEN Cabernet Sauvignon Sonoma Mountain 1984 Rel: $15 Cur: $45 (4/30/87)
59 LAUREL GLEN Cabernet Sauvignon Sonoma Mountain 1983 Rel: $11 Cur: $12 (CA-3/89)
85 LAUREL GLEN Cabernet Sauvignon Sonoma Mountain 1982 Rel: $12.50 Cur: $35 (CA-3/89)
83 LAUREL GLEN Cabernet Sauvignon Sonoma Mountain 1982 Rel: $12.50 Cur: $35 (6/01/86)
92 LAUREL GLEN Cabernet Sauvignon Sonoma Mountain 1981 Rel: $12.50 Cur: $42 (CA-3/89)
93 LAUREL GLEN Cabernet Sauvignon Sonoma Mountain 1981 Rel: $12.50 Cur: $42 (2/16/85) SS
83 LAUREL GLEN Cabernet Sauvignon Sonoma County Counterpoint 1988 $13 (7/15/91)
94 LAUREL GLEN Cabernet Sauvignon Sonoma Mountain Counterpoint 1987 $13 (10/31/89)
89 LAUREL GLEN Cabernet Sauvignon Sonoma Mountain Counterpoint Cuvée 85-86 NV $11 (5/31/88)
85 LAUREL GLEN Terra Rosa Napa Valley 1988 $12 (11/15/90)
86 LAUREL GLEN Terra Rosa Napa Valley 1987 $14 (7/31/90)
84 LEEWARD Cabernet Sauvignon Alexander Valley 1987 $13 (11/15/90)
79 LEEWARD Cabernet Sauvignon Alexander Valley 1986 $12 (10/15/89)
83 LEEWARD Cabernet Sauvignon Alexander Valley 1985 $12 (10/31/87)
76 CHARLES LEFRANC Cabernet Sauvignon Monterey County 1981 $8.50 (9/16/85)
80 CHARLES LEFRANC Cabernet Sauvignon Napa County 1984 $12 (10/15/87)
64 LIBERTY SCHOOL Cabernet Sauvignon Alexander Valley Lot 13 NV $6 (1/01/86)
73 LIBERTY SCHOOL Cabernet Sauvignon California Lot 17 NV $6 (2/29/88)
81 LIBERTY SCHOOL Cabernet Sauvignon California Lot 18 NV $7.50 (4/30/89) BB
77 LIBERTY SCHOOL Cabernet Sauvignon California Lot 19 NV $7.50 (11/15/89)
90+ LIVINGSTON Cabernet Sauvignon Napa Valley Moffett Vineyard 1990 (NR) (5/15/91) (BT)
85+ LIVINGSTON Cabernet Sauvignon Napa Valley Moffett Vineyard 1989 (NR) (5/15/91) (BT)
90+ LIVINGSTON Cabernet Sauvignon Napa Valley Moffett Vineyard 1988 $30 (4/30/90) (BT)
94 LIVINGSTON Cabernet Sauvignon Napa Valley Moffett Vineyard 1987 $24 (11/15/90)
90+ LIVINGSTON Cabernet Sauvignon Napa Valley Moffett Vineyard 1987 $24 (4/15/89) (BT)
88 LIVINGSTON Cabernet Sauvignon Napa Valley Moffett Vineyard 1986 Rel: $24 Cur: $28 (11/30/89)
90 LIVINGSTON Cabernet Sauvignon Napa Valley Moffett Vineyard 1986 Rel: $24 Cur: $28 (CA-3/89)
86 LIVINGSTON Cabernet Sauvignon Napa Valley Moffett Vineyard 1985 Rel: $18 Cur: $30 (CA-3/89)
85 LIVINGSTON Cabernet Sauvignon Napa Valley Moffett Vineyard 1985 Rel: $18 Cur: $30 (10/15/88)
90+ LIVINGSTON Cabernet Sauvignon Napa Valley Moffett Vineyard 1985 Rel: $18 Cur: $30 (6/15/87) (BT)
87 LIVINGSTON Cabernet Sauvignon Napa Valley Moffett Vineyard 1984 Rel: $18 Cur: $29 (CA-3/89)
86 LIVINGSTON Cabernet Sauvignon Napa Valley Moffett Vineyard 1984 Rel: $18 Cur: $29 (11/15/87)
85+ LIVINGSTON Cabernet Sauvignon Napa Valley Stanley's Selection 1990 (NR) (5/15/91) (BT)
85+ LIVINGSTON Cabernet Sauvignon Napa Valley Stanley's Selection 1989 (NR) (5/15/91) (BT)
79 LLORDS & ELWOOD Cabernet Sauvignon Napa Valley 1982 $8 (12/15/87)
84 J. LOHR Cabernet Sauvignon California 1987 $7 (2/15/90) BB
84 J. LOHR Cabernet Sauvignon California 1986 $6.50 (4/15/89) BB
82 J. LOHR Cabernet Sauvignon California 1984 $5 (11/30/86) BB
89 J. LOHR Cabernet Sauvignon Napa Valley Carol's Vineyard Reserve 1985 $14.50 (12/15/88)
88 J. LOHR Cabernet Sauvignon Napa Valley Carol's Vineyard Reserve Lot 2 1985 $17.50 (9/30/90)
86 J. LOHR Cabernet Sauvignon Paso Robles Seven Oaks 1987 $12 (4/30/91)
83 LOLONIS Cabernet Sauvignon Mendocino County Private Reserve 1986 $15 (5/15/90)
90+ LONG Cabernet Sauvignon Napa Valley 1990 (NR) (5/15/91) (BT)
90+ LONG Cabernet Sauvignon Napa Valley 1989 (NR) (5/15/91) (BT)
86 LONG Cabernet Sauvignon Napa Valley 1986 Rel: $40 Cur: $45 (CA-3/89)
92 LONG Cabernet Sauvignon Napa Valley 1985 Rel: $36 Cur: $50 (CA-3/89)
80+ LONG Cabernet Sauvignon Napa Valley 1985 Rel: $36 Cur: $50 (6/15/87) (BT)
88 LONG Cabernet Sauvignon Napa Valley 1984 Rel: $32 Cur: $48 (CA-3/89)
88 LONG Cabernet Sauvignon Napa Valley 1984 Rel: $32 Cur: $48 (12/15/88)
78 LONG Cabernet Sauvignon Napa Valley 1983 Rel: $32 Cur: $40 (CA-3/89)
72 LONG Cabernet Sauvignon Napa Valley 1983 Rel: $32 Cur: $40 (8/31/87)
91 LONG Cabernet Sauvignon Napa Valley 1980 Rel: $32 Cur: $50 (CA-3/89)
90 LONG Cabernet Sauvignon Napa Valley 1979 Rel: $32 Cur: $59 (CA-3/89)
85+ LYETH Red Alexander Valley 1988 (NR) (4/30/90) (BT)
88 LYETH Red Alexander Valley 1986 $23 (11/15/90)
86 LYETH Red Alexander Valley 1985 Rel: $22 Cur: $22 (5/31/89)
92 LYETH Red Alexander Valley 1985 Rel: $22 Cur: $22 (CA-3/89)
80+ LYETH Red Alexander Valley 1985 Rel: $22 Cur: $22 (6/15/87) (BT)
90 LYETH Red Alexander Valley 1984 Rel: $18 Cur: $26 (CA-3/89)
91 LYETH Red Alexander Valley 1984 Rel: $18 Cur: $26 (3/15/88)
78 LYETH Red Alexander Valley 1983 Rel: $17 Cur: $23 (CA-3/89)
91 LYETH Red Alexander Valley 1983 Rel: $17 Cur: $23 (6/30/87)
85 LYETH Red Alexander Valley 1982 Rel: $16 Cur: $35 (CA-3/89)
86 LYETH Red Alexander Valley 1982 Rel: $16 Cur: $35 (6/16/86)
77 LYETH Red Alexander Valley 1981 Rel: $15 Cur: $31 (CA-3/89)
88 LYTTON SPRINGS Cabernet Sauvignon Mendocino County Private Reserve 1987 $18 (9/15/90)
77 MADDALENA Cabernet Sauvignon Alexander Valley Reserve 1986 $10 (3/31/90)
78 MADDALENA Cabernet Sauvignon Alexander Valley Reserve 1985 $11 (6/30/89)
74 MADDALENA Cabernet Sauvignon Sonoma County 1985 $6 (5/31/88)
82 MADDALENA Cabernet Sauvignon Sonoma County Vintner's Reserve 1984 $9 (3/31/87)
87 MARIETTA Cabernet Sauvignon Sonoma County 1987 $10 (2/28/91)
83 MARIETTA Cabernet Sauvignon Sonoma County 1985 $10 (6/30/90)
78 MARIETTA Cabernet Sauvignon Sonoma County 1984 $10 (12/31/87)
78 MARIETTA Cabernet Sauvignon Sonoma County 1981 $9 (6/16/84)
62 MARION Cabernet Sauvignon California 1985 $5.50 (12/31/87)
85+ MARKHAM Cabernet Sauvignon Napa Valley 1990 (NR) (5/15/91) (BT)
85+ MARKHAM Cabernet Sauvignon Napa Valley 1989 (NR) (5/15/91) (BT)
85+ MARKHAM Cabernet Sauvignon Napa Valley 1988 (NR) (4/30/90) (BT)
87 MARKHAM Cabernet Sauvignon Napa Valley 1986 $13 (4/30/91)
91 MARKHAM Cabernet Sauvignon Napa Valley 1986 $13 (CA-3/89)
93 MARKHAM Cabernet Sauvignon Napa Valley 1985 Rel: $13 Cur: $16 (4/15/90)
88 MARKHAM Cabernet Sauvignon Napa Valley 1985 Rel: $13 Cur: $16 (CA-3/89)
91 MARKHAM Cabernet Sauvignon Napa Valley 1984 Rel: $12 Cur: $18 (CA-3/89)
87 MARKHAM Cabernet Sauvignon Napa Valley 1984 Rel: $12 Cur: $18 (10/31/88)
90 MARKHAM Cabernet Sauvignon Napa Valley 1983 Rel: $13 Cur: $15 (7/31/89)
89 MARKHAM Cabernet Sauvignon Napa Valley 1983 Rel: $13 Cur: $15 (CA-3/89)
90 MARKHAM Cabernet Sauvignon Napa Valley 1982 Rel: $13 Cur: $18 (CA-3/89)
92 MARKHAM Cabernet Sauvignon Napa Valley 1982 Rel: $13 Cur: $18 (11/15/87)
86 MARKHAM Cabernet Sauvignon Napa Valley 1981 Rel: $13 Cur: $20 (CA-3/89)

89 MARKHAM Cabernet Sauvignon Napa Valley 1980 Rel: $13 Cur: $26 (CA-3/89)
88 MARKHAM Cabernet Sauvignon Napa Valley 1979 Rel: $13 Cur: $31 (CA-3/89)
85 MARKHAM Cabernet Sauvignon Napa Valley 1978 Rel: $13 Cur: $35 (CA-3/89)
87 LOUIS M. MARTINI Cabernet Sauvignon Napa Valley Reserve 1987 $14 (10/15/90)
80 LOUIS M. MARTINI Cabernet Sauvignon North Coast 1986 $9.25 (9/15/89)
76 LOUIS M. MARTINI Cabernet Sauvignon North Coast 1985 $8.25 (10/31/88)
69 LOUIS M. MARTINI Cabernet Sauvignon North Coast 1983 $7 (3/31/87)
83 LOUIS M. MARTINI Cabernet Sauvignon North Coast 1981 $6.50 (3/01/85)
85 LOUIS M. MARTINI Cabernet Sauvignon North Coast Special Selection 1984 (NA) (CA-3/89)
84 LOUIS M. MARTINI Cabernet Sauvignon North Coast Special Selection 1980 Rel: $12 Cur: $15 (CA-3/89)
78 LOUIS M. MARTINI Cabernet Sauvignon North Coast Special Selection 1980 Rel: $12 Cur: $15 (12/15/86)
86 LOUIS M. MARTINI Cabernet Sauvignon California Special Selection 1978 Rel: $9 Cur: $29 (CA-3/89)
70 LOUIS M. MARTINI Cabernet Sauvignon California Special Selection 1977 Rel: $9 Cur: $20 (CA-3/89)
86 LOUIS M. MARTINI Cabernet Sauvignon California Special Selection 1976 Rel: $9 Cur: $32 (CA-3/89)
77 LOUIS M. MARTINI Cabernet Sauvignon California Special Selection 1974 Rel: $10 Cur: $41 (CA-3/89)
88 LOUIS M. MARTINI Cabernet Sauvignon California Special Selection 1974 Rel: $10 Cur: $41 (6/01/85) (JL)
63 LOUIS M. MARTINI Cabernet Sauvignon California Special Selection 1972 Rel: $5 Cur: $50 (CA-3/89)
88 LOUIS M. MARTINI Cabernet Sauvignon California Special Selection 1970 Rel: $8 Cur: $60 (CA-3/89)
90 LOUIS M. MARTINI Cabernet Sauvignon California Special Selection 1968 Rel: $6 Cur: $75 (CA-3/89)
90 LOUIS M. MARTINI Cabernet Sauvignon California Special Selection 1968 Rel: $6 Cur: $75 (6/01/85) (JL)
87 LOUIS M. MARTINI Cabernet Sauvignon California Special Selection 1966 Rel: $6 Cur: $150 (CA-3/89)
85 LOUIS M. MARTINI Cabernet Sauvignon California Special Selection 1964 Rel: $6 Cur: $100 (CA-3/89)
86 LOUIS M. MARTINI Cabernet Sauvignon California Special Selection 1964 Rel: $6 Cur: $100 (6/01/85) (JL)
73 LOUIS M. MARTINI Cabernet Sauvignon California Private Reserve 1962 Rel: $3.50 Cur: $80 (CA-3/89)
80 LOUIS M. MARTINI Cabernet Sauvignon California Special Selection 1961 Rel: $4 Cur: $160 (CA-3/89)
87 LOUIS M. MARTINI Cabernet Sauvignon California Special Selection 1959 Rel: $4.50 Cur: $140 (CA-3/89)
88 LOUIS M. MARTINI Cabernet Sauvignon California Special Selection 1958 Rel: $4.50 Cur: $200 (CA-3/89)
91 LOUIS M. MARTINI Cabernet Sauvignon California Special Selection 1957 Rel: $3.50 Cur: $175 (CA-3/89)
92 LOUIS M. MARTINI Cabernet Sauvignon California Special Selection 1957 Rel: $3.50 Cur: $175 (6/01/85) (JL)
77 LOUIS M. MARTINI Cabernet Sauvignon California Private Reserve 1956 Rel: $2.50 Cur: $80 (CA-3/89)
87 LOUIS M. MARTINI Cabernet Sauvignon California Special Selection 1955 Rel: $2.50 Cur: $190 (CA-3/89)
89 LOUIS M. MARTINI Cabernet Sauvignon California Special Selection 1955 Rel: $2.50 Cur: $190 (6/01/85) (JL)
93 LOUIS M. MARTINI Cabernet Sauvignon California Private Reserve 1952 Rel: $2.50 Cur: $350 (2/28/87) (HS)
93 LOUIS M. MARTINI Cabernet Sauvignon California Special Selection 1952 Rel: $2.50 Cur: $350 (CA-3/89)
87 LOUIS M. MARTINI Cabernet Sauvignon California Special Selection 1951 Rel: $2 Cur: $280 (CA-3/89)
90 LOUIS M. MARTINI Cabernet Sauvignon California Special Selection 1951 Rel: $2 Cur: $280 (2/28/87) (HS)
90 LOUIS M. MARTINI Cabernet Sauvignon California Special Selection 1947 Rel: $1.50 Cur: $700 (CA-3/89)
75 LOUIS M. MARTINI Cabernet Sauvignon California Special Selection 1945 Rel: $1.50 Cur: $400 (CA-3/89)
75 LOUIS M. MARTINI Cabernet Sauvignon California Special Selection 1945 Rel: $1.50 Cur: $400 (6/01/85) (JL)
70 LOUIS M. MARTINI Cabernet Sauvignon California Private Reserve Villa del Rey 1943 Rel: $1.50 Cur: $400 (CA-3/89)
77 LOUIS M. MARTINI Cabernet Sauvignon California Private Reserve Villa del Rey 1943 Rel: $1.50 Cur: $400 (6/01/85) (JL)
90 LOUIS M. MARTINI Cabernet Sauvignon California Special Reserve 1939 Rel: $1.25 Cur: $1,000 (CA-3/89)
90 LOUIS M. MARTINI Cabernet Sauvignon California Special Reserve 1939 Rel: $1.25 Cur: $1,000 (6/01/85) (JL)
81 LOUIS M. MARTINI Cabernet Sauvignon Sonoma County 1988 $9 (4/30/91) BB
85+ LOUIS M. MARTINI Cabernet Sauvignon Sonoma Valley Monte Rosso 1989 (NR) (5/15/91) (BT)
80+ LOUIS M. MARTINI Cabernet Sauvignon Sonoma Valley Monte Rosso 1988 (NR) (4/30/90) (BT)
93 LOUIS M. MARTINI Cabernet Sauvignon Sonoma Valley Monte Rosso 1987 Rel: $20 Cur: $23 (11/15/90)
90+ LOUIS M. MARTINI Cabernet Sauvignon Sonoma Valley Monte Rosso 1987 Rel: $20 Cur: $23 (4/15/89) (BT)
86 LOUIS M. MARTINI Cabernet Sauvignon Sonoma Valley Monte Rosso 1986 Rel: $20 Cur: $22 (CA-3/89)
85+ LOUIS M. MARTINI Cabernet Sauvignon Sonoma Valley Monte Rosso 1986 Rel: $20 Cur: $22 (4/15/88) (BT)
80 LOUIS M. MARTINI Cabernet Sauvignon Sonoma Valley Monte Rosso 1985 Rel: $22 Cur: $23 (CA-3/89)
89 LOUIS M. MARTINI Cabernet Sauvignon Sonoma Valley Monte Rosso 1984 Rel: $22 Cur: $23 (CA-3/89)
86 LOUIS M. MARTINI Cabernet Sauvignon Sonoma Valley Monte Rosso 1983 Rel: $22 Cur: $22 (CA-3/89)
85 LOUIS M. MARTINI Cabernet Sauvignon Sonoma Valley Monte Rosso 1982 Rel: $22 Cur: $22 (CA-3/89)
90 LOUIS M. MARTINI Cabernet Sauvignon Sonoma Valley Monte Rosso 1981 Rel: $25 Cur: $25 (12/15/86)

83 LOUIS M. MARTINI Cabernet Sauvignon Sonoma Valley Monte Rosso Los Niños 1983 Rel: $25 Cur: $25 (CA-3/89)
82 LOUIS M. MARTINI Cabernet Sauvignon Sonoma Valley Monte Rosso Los Niños 1982 Rel: $25 Cur: $25 (CA-3/89)
85 LOUIS M. MARTINI Cabernet Sauvignon Sonoma Valley Monte Rosso Los Niños 1981 Rel: $25 Cur: $25 (CA-3/89)
84 LOUIS M. MARTINI Cabernet Sauvignon Sonoma Valley Monte Rosso Lot 2 1979 Rel: $10 Cur: $19 (CA-3/89)
79 MASSON Cabernet Sauvignon Monterey County Vintage Selection 1986 $9 (11/15/89)
78 MASSON Cabernet Sauvignon Monterey County Vintage Selection 1985 $8 (9/15/88)
84 PAUL MASSON Cabernet Sauvignon California Vintner's Selection 1986 $6 (6/30/89)
75 MATANZAS CREEK Cabernet Sauvignon Sonoma Valley 1983 $14 (7/16/86)
88 MATANZAS CREEK Cabernet Sauvignon Sonoma Valley 1982 $14 (8/01/85)
84 MATANZAS CREEK Cabernet Sauvignon Sonoma Valley 1981 $16 (4/16/84)
86 MAYACAMAS Cabernet Sauvignon Napa Valley 1986 $25 (CA-3/89)
92 MAYACAMAS Cabernet Sauvignon Napa Valley 1985 Rel: $25 Cur: $30 (1/31/90)
92 MAYACAMAS Cabernet Sauvignon Napa Valley 1985 Rel: $25 Cur: $30 (CA-3/89)
80 MAYACAMAS Cabernet Sauvignon Napa Valley 1984 Rel: $20 Cur: $26 (4/15/89)
90 MAYACAMAS Cabernet Sauvignon Napa Valley 1984 Rel: $20 Cur: $26 (CA-3/89)
90 MAYACAMAS Cabernet Sauvignon Napa Valley 1983 Rel: $20 Cur: $26 (CA-3/89)
80 MAYACAMAS Cabernet Sauvignon Napa Valley 1983 Rel: $20 Cur: $26 (9/15/88)
77 MAYACAMAS Cabernet Sauvignon Napa Valley 1982 Rel: $20 Cur: $27 (CA-3/89)
77 MAYACAMAS Cabernet Sauvignon Napa Valley 1982 Rel: $20 Cur: $27 (3/31/87)
91 MAYACAMAS Cabernet Sauvignon Napa Valley 1981 Rel: $18 Cur: $27 (CA-3/89)
92 MAYACAMAS Cabernet Sauvignon Napa Valley 1980 Rel: $18 Cur: $38 (CA-3/89)
95 MAYACAMAS Cabernet Sauvignon Napa Valley 1979 Rel: $18 Cur: $44 (CA-3/89)
94 MAYACAMAS Cabernet Sauvignon Napa Valley 1978 Rel: $18 Cur: $60 (CA-3/89)
75 MAYACAMAS Cabernet Sauvignon Napa Valley 1978 Rel: $18 Cur: $60 (4/30/87)
92 MAYACAMAS Cabernet Sauvignon Napa Valley 1977 Rel: $15 Cur: $60 (CA-3/89)
84 MAYACAMAS Cabernet Sauvignon Napa Valley 1976 Rel: $15 Cur: $50 (CA-3/89)
89 MAYACAMAS Cabernet Sauvignon Napa Valley 1975 Rel: $12 Cur: $64 (CA-3/89)
97 MAYACAMAS Cabernet Sauvignon Napa Valley 1974 Rel: $9.50 Cur: $115 (2/15/90) (JG)
95 MAYACAMAS Cabernet Sauvignon Napa Valley 1974 Rel: $9.50 Cur: $115 (CA-3/89)
87 MAYACAMAS Cabernet Sauvignon Napa Valley 1973 Rel: $9 Cur: $90 (CA-3/89)
82 MAYACAMAS Cabernet Sauvignon Napa Valley 1972 Rel: $8 Cur: $70 (CA-3/89)
86 MAYACAMAS Cabernet Sauvignon Napa Valley 1971 Rel: $8 Cur: $75 (CA-3/89)
87 MAYACAMAS Cabernet Sauvignon Napa Valley 1971 Rel: $8 Cur: $75 (4/01/86)
96 MAYACAMAS Cabernet Sauvignon Napa Valley 1970 Rel: $8 Cur: $130 (CA-3/89)
89 MAYACAMAS Cabernet Sauvignon California 1969 Rel: $6.50 Cur: $108 (CA-3/89)
88 MAYACAMAS Cabernet Sauvignon California 1968 Rel: $4.50 Cur: $125 (CA-3/89)
65 MAYACAMAS Cabernet Sauvignon California 1967 Rel: $4 Cur: $125 (CA-3/89)
75 MAYACAMAS Cabernet Sauvignon California 1966 Rel: $3.50 Cur: $125 (CA-3/89)
65 MAYACAMAS Cabernet Sauvignon California 1965 Rel: $2.75 Cur: $200 (CA-3/89)
69 MAYACAMAS Cabernet Sauvignon California 1963 Rel: $2 Cur: $150 (CA-3/89)
68 MAYACAMAS Cabernet Sauvignon California 1962 Rel: $2 Cur: $150 (CA-3/89)
93 MAZZOCCO Cabernet Sauvignon Alexander Valley Claret Style 1987 $20 (8/31/90)
78 MAZZOCCO Cabernet Sauvignon Alexander Valley Claret Style 1986 $20 (7/31/89)
78 MCDOWELL Cabernet Sauvignon California 1987 $9 (11/15/90)
70 MCDOWELL Cabernet Sauvignon McDowell Valley 1986 $8 (4/30/90)
76 MCDOWELL Cabernet Sauvignon McDowell Valley 1983 $11 (4/15/88)
89 MCDOWELL Cabernet Sauvignon McDowell Valley 1982 $11 (12/15/86)
78 MCDOWELL Cabernet Sauvignon McDowell Valley 1981 $11 (12/16/84)
72 MEEKER Cabernet Sauvignon Dry Creek Valley 1986 $18.50 (2/15/90)
76 MEEKER Cabernet Sauvignon Dry Creek Valley 1985 $18 (4/30/89)
78 MEEKER Cabernet Sauvignon Dry Creek Valley 1984 $18 (6/15/88)
61 MENDOCINO ESTATE Cabernet Sauvignon Mendocino 1985 $5.50 (2/15/88)
78 MENDOCINO ESTATE Cabernet Sauvignon Mendocino 1984 $4.75 (6/15/87)
87 MENDOCINO ESTATE Cabernet Sauvignon Mendocino 1982 $4.25 (10/15/86) BB
73 MENDOCINO VINEYARDS Cabernet Sauvignon Mendocino County NV $6 (4/15/89)
84 MERLION Cabernet Sauvignon Napa Valley 1986 $16.50 (11/15/90)
85 MERLION Cabernet Sauvignon Napa Valley 1985 $13.50 (8/31/88)
86 MERRYVALE Cabernet Sauvignon Napa Valley 1988 $18 (7/15/91)
90+ MERRYVALE Profile Napa Valley 1990 (NR) (5/15/91) (BT)
85 MERRYVALE Profile Napa Valley 1989 (NR) (5/15/91) BT
85+ MERRYVALE Profile Napa Valley 1988 (NR) (4/30/90) (BT)
86 MERRYVALE Red Table Wine Napa Valley 1986 Rel: $25 Cur: $25 (10/15/90)
89 MERRYVALE Red Table Wine Napa Valley 1986 Rel: $25 Cur: $25 (CA-3/89)
91 MERRYVALE Red Table Wine Napa Valley 1985 Rel: $24 Cur: $24 (CA-3/89)
87 MERRYVALE Red Table Wine Napa Valley 1985 Rel: $24 Cur: $24 (11/15/88)
86 MERRYVALE Red Table Wine Napa Valley 1984 Rel: $24 Cur: $28 (CA-3/89)
90 MERRYVALE Red Table Wine Napa Valley 1984 Rel: $24 Cur: $28 (10/31/87)
88 MERRYVALE Red Table Wine Napa Valley 1983 Rel: $18 Cur: $28 (CA-3/89)
94 MERRYVALE Red Table Wine Napa Valley 1983 Rel: $18 Cur: $28 (2/15/87)
75 MICHAEL'S Cabernet Sauvignon Napa Valley Summit Vineyard Reserve 1984 $15 (3/31/88)
78 RICHARD MICHAELS Cabernet Sauvignon California 1985 $10 (9/30/88)
80 MILANO Cabernet Sauvignon Mendocino County Sanel Valley Vineyard 1985 $18 (9/30/89)
83 MILANO Cabernet Sauvignon Mendocino County Sanel Valley Vineyard 1982 $12.50 (12/15/87)
68 MILL CREEK Cabernet Sauvignon Dry Creek Valley 1982 $9.50 (6/15/88)
81 MILL CREEK Cabernet Sauvignon Dry Creek Valley 1982 $9.50 (12/31/87)
83 MIRASSOU Cabernet Sauvignon California Fifth Generation Family Selection 1986 $9.75 (5/31/91)
60 MIRASSOU Cabernet Sauvignon Monterey County Fifth Generation Harvest Reserve 1986 $12.50 (7/31/91)
81 MIRASSOU Cabernet Sauvignon Napa Valley Fifth Generation Harvest Reserve 1985 $12 (11/15/89)
67 MIRASSOU Cabernet Sauvignon Napa Valley Fifth Generation Harvest Reserve 1983 $12 (12/15/86)
82 MIRASSOU Cabernet Sauvignon Napa Valley Harvest Reserve 1982 $12 (4/16/86)
82 MIRASSOU Cabernet Sauvignon North Coast 1982 $7 (10/16/85) BB
72 MISSION VIEW Cabernet Sauvignon Paso Robles 1986 $12 (12/15/89)
65 CK MONDAVI Cabernet Sauvignon Napa Valley 1983 $4.50 (10/15/87)
81 ROBERT MONDAVI Cabernet Sauvignon California Woodbridge 1988 $6 (2/28/91) BB
74 ROBERT MONDAVI Cabernet Sauvignon California Woodbridge 1987 $6 (9/15/89)
80 ROBERT MONDAVI Cabernet Sauvignon California Cabernet 1986 $5.50 (12/15/88) BB
78 ROBERT MONDAVI Cabernet Sauvignon California Cabernet 1985 $4.25 (10/31/87) BB
90+ ROBERT MONDAVI Cabernet Sauvignon Napa Valley 1990 (NR) (5/15/91) (BT)
87 ROBERT MONDAVI Cabernet Sauvignon Napa Valley 1987 Rel: $20 Cur: $21 (5/31/90)
93 ROBERT MONDAVI Cabernet Sauvignon Napa Valley 1986 Rel: $18 Cur: $22 (7/31/89)
94 ROBERT MONDAVI Cabernet Sauvignon Napa Valley 1985 Rel: $15 Cur: $20 (12/15/88) SS

UNITED STATES
CALIFORNIA/CABERNET SAUVIGNON & BLENDS

80   ROBERT MONDAVI Cabernet Sauvignon Napa Valley 1984 Rel: $13 Cur: $34 (12/31/87)
94   ROBERT MONDAVI Cabernet Sauvignon Napa Valley 1983 Rel: $12 Cur: $26 (4/15/87)
90   ROBERT MONDAVI Cabernet Sauvignon Napa Valley 1982 Rel: $11 Cur: $20 (7/01/85)
90   ROBERT MONDAVI Cabernet Sauvignon Napa Valley 1981 Rel: $11 Cur: $27 (12/16/84)
85   ROBERT MONDAVI Cabernet Sauvignon Napa Valley 1979 Cur: $25 (7/16/85) (JL)
88   ROBERT MONDAVI Cabernet Sauvignon Napa Valley 1978 Cur: $38 (6/01/86)
89   ROBERT MONDAVI Cabernet Sauvignon Napa Valley 1977 Cur: $30 (7/16/85) (JL)
84   ROBERT MONDAVI Cabernet Sauvignon Napa Valley 1976 Cur: $43 (7/16/85) (JL)
79   ROBERT MONDAVI Cabernet Sauvignon Napa Valley 1975 Cur: $38 (7/16/85) (JL)
79   ROBERT MONDAVI Cabernet Sauvignon Napa Valley 1974 Cur: $50 (2/15/90) (JG)
90   ROBERT MONDAVI Cabernet Sauvignon Napa Valley 1974 Cur: $50 (7/16/85) (JL)
86   ROBERT MONDAVI Cabernet Sauvignon Napa Valley 1973 Cur: $35 (7/16/85) (JL)
75   ROBERT MONDAVI Cabernet Sauvignon Napa Valley 1972 Rel: $6 Cur: $45 (CA-3/89)
80   ROBERT MONDAVI Cabernet Sauvignon Napa Valley 1972 Rel: $6 Cur: $45 (7/16/85) (JL)
87   ROBERT MONDAVI Cabernet Sauvignon Napa Valley 1971 Rel: $6 Cur: $43 (7/16/85) (JL)
86   ROBERT MONDAVI Cabernet Sauvignon Napa Valley 1969 Cur: $86 (7/16/85) (JL)
84   ROBERT MONDAVI Cabernet Sauvignon Napa Valley 1967 Rel: $5 Cur: $100 (CA-3/89)
83   ROBERT MONDAVI Cabernet Sauvignon Napa Valley 1967 Rel: $5 Cur: $100/1.5L (7/16/85) (JL)
80   ROBERT MONDAVI Cabernet Sauvignon Napa Valley 1966 Rel: $5 Cur: $165 (CA-3/89)
78   ROBERT MONDAVI Cabernet Sauvignon Napa Valley 1966 Rel: $5 Cur: $165 (7/16/85) (JL)
79   ROBERT MONDAVI Cabernet Sauvignon Napa Valley 1966 Rel: $5 Cur: $165/1.5L (7/16/85) (JL)
90+   ROBERT MONDAVI Cabernet Sauvignon Napa Valley Reserve 1990 (NR) (5/15/91) (BT)
90+   ROBERT MONDAVI Cabernet Sauvignon Napa Valley Reserve 1989 (NR) (5/15/91) (BT)
91   ROBERT MONDAVI Cabernet Sauvignon Napa Valley Reserve 1988 $45 (5/31/91) CS
90+   ROBERT MONDAVI Cabernet Sauvignon Napa Valley Reserve 1988 $45 (4/30/90) (BT)
90   ROBERT MONDAVI Cabernet Sauvignon Napa Valley Reserve 1987 Rel: $43 Cur: $47 (8/31/90)
90+   ROBERT MONDAVI Cabernet Sauvignon Napa Valley Reserve 1987 Rel: $43 Cur: $47 (4/15/89) (BT)
95   ROBERT MONDAVI Cabernet Sauvignon Napa Valley Reserve 1986 Rel: $35 Cur: $39 (11/15/89)
95   ROBERT MONDAVI Cabernet Sauvignon Napa Valley Reserve 1986 Rel: $35 Cur: $39 (CA-3/89)
90+   ROBERT MONDAVI Cabernet Sauvignon Napa Valley Reserve 1986 Rel: $35 Cur: $39 (4/15/88) (BT)
95   ROBERT MONDAVI Cabernet Sauvignon Napa Valley Reserve 1985 Rel: $40 Cur: $43 (11/15/89) SS
95   ROBERT MONDAVI Cabernet Sauvignon Napa Valley Reserve 1985 Rel: $40 Cur: $43 (CA-3/89)
90+   ROBERT MONDAVI Cabernet Sauvignon Napa Valley Reserve 1985 Rel: $40 Cur: $43 (6/15/87) (BT)
92   ROBERT MONDAVI Cabernet Sauvignon Napa Valley Reserve 1984 Rel: $37 Cur: $38 (CA-3/89)
90   ROBERT MONDAVI Cabernet Sauvignon Napa Valley Reserve 1984 Rel: $37 Cur: $38 (12/31/88)
83   ROBERT MONDAVI Cabernet Sauvignon Napa Valley Reserve 1983 Rel: $30 Cur: $36 (CA-3/89)
91   ROBERT MONDAVI Cabernet Sauvignon Napa Valley Reserve 1983 Rel: $30 Cur: $36 (11/30/87)
82   ROBERT MONDAVI Cabernet Sauvignon Napa Valley Reserve 1982 Rel: $30 Cur: $39 (CA-3/89)
95   ROBERT MONDAVI Cabernet Sauvignon Napa Valley Reserve 1982 Rel: $30 Cur: $39 (2/15/87)
92   ROBERT MONDAVI Cabernet Sauvignon Napa Valley Reserve 1982 Rel: $30 Cur: $39 (2/01/85)
83   ROBERT MONDAVI Cabernet Sauvignon Napa Valley Reserve 1981 Rel: $30 Cur: $34 (CA-3/89)
94   ROBERT MONDAVI Cabernet Sauvignon Napa Valley Reserve 1981 Rel: $30 Cur: $34 (2/16/86) CS
89   ROBERT MONDAVI Cabernet Sauvignon Napa Valley Reserve 1981 Rel: $30 Cur: $34 (2/01/85)
79   ROBERT MONDAVI Cabernet Sauvignon Napa Valley Reserve 1980 Rel: $30 Cur: $37 (CA-3/89)
91   ROBERT MONDAVI Cabernet Sauvignon Napa Valley Reserve 1980 Rel: $30 Cur: $37 (2/01/86)
91   ROBERT MONDAVI Cabernet Sauvignon Napa Valley Reserve 1980 Rel: $30 Cur: $37 (2/01/85)
92   ROBERT MONDAVI Cabernet Sauvignon Napa Valley Reserve 1979 Rel: $25 Cur: $46 (CA-3/89)
90   ROBERT MONDAVI Cabernet Sauvignon Napa Valley Reserve 1979 Rel: $25 Cur: $46 (2/01/86)
90   ROBERT MONDAVI Cabernet Sauvignon Napa Valley Reserve 1979 Rel: $25 Cur: $46 (2/01/85)
92   ROBERT MONDAVI Cabernet Sauvignon Napa Valley Reserve 1978 Rel: $40 Cur: $70 (CA-3/89)
97   ROBERT MONDAVI Cabernet Sauvignon Napa Valley Reserve 1978 Rel: $40 Cur: $70 (6/01/86)
83   ROBERT MONDAVI Cabernet Sauvignon Napa Valley Reserve 1978 Rel: $40 Cur: $70 (2/01/85)
84   ROBERT MONDAVI Cabernet Sauvignon Napa Valley Reserve 1977 Rel: $35 Cur: $45 (CA-3/89)

91   ROBERT MONDAVI Cabernet Sauvignon Napa Valley Reserve 1977 Rel: $35 Cur: $45 (7/16/85) (JL)
84   ROBERT MONDAVI Cabernet Sauvignon Napa Valley Reserve 1976 Rel: $25 Cur: $55 (CA-3/89)
90   ROBERT MONDAVI Cabernet Sauvignon Napa Valley Reserve 1976 Rel: $25 Cur: $55 (7/16/85) (JL)
86   ROBERT MONDAVI Cabernet Sauvignon Napa Valley Reserve 1975 Rel: $30 Cur: $65 (CA-3/89)
89   ROBERT MONDAVI Cabernet Sauvignon Napa Valley Reserve 1975 Rel: $30 Cur: $65 (7/16/85) (JL)
92   ROBERT MONDAVI Cabernet Sauvignon Napa Valley Reserve 1974 Rel: $30 Cur: $96 (2/15/90) (JG)
92   ROBERT MONDAVI Cabernet Sauvignon Napa Valley Reserve 1974 Rel: $30 Cur: $96 (CA-3/89)
94   ROBERT MONDAVI Cabernet Sauvignon Napa Valley Reserve 1974 Rel: $30 Cur: $96 (7/16/85) (JL)
82   ROBERT MONDAVI Cabernet Sauvignon Napa Valley Reserve 1973 Rel: $12 Cur: $80 (CA-3/89)
91   ROBERT MONDAVI Cabernet Sauvignon Napa Valley Reserve 1973 Rel: $12 Cur: $80 (7/16/85) (JL)
93   ROBERT MONDAVI Cabernet Sauvignon Napa Valley Reserve 1971 Rel: $12 Cur: $130 (CA-3/89)
90   ROBERT MONDAVI Cabernet Sauvignon Napa Valley Reserve 1971 Rel: $12 Cur: $130 (7/16/85) (JL)
89   ROBERT MONDAVI Cabernet Sauvignon Napa Valley Unfined 1970 Rel: $12 Cur: $105 (CA-3/89)
93   ROBERT MONDAVI Cabernet Sauvignon Napa Valley Unfiltered 1970 Rel: $12 Cur: $105 (7/16/85) (JL)
93   ROBERT MONDAVI Cabernet Sauvignon Napa Valley Unfined 1970 Rel: $12 Cur: $105 (7/16/85) (JL)
86   ROBERT MONDAVI Cabernet Sauvignon Napa Valley Unfined 1969 Rel: $12 Cur: $140 (CA-3/89)
92   ROBERT MONDAVI Cabernet Sauvignon Napa Valley Unfined 1969 Rel: $12 Cur: $140 (7/16/85) (JL)
83   ROBERT MONDAVI Cabernet Sauvignon Napa Valley Unfined 1968 Rel: $8.50 Cur: $135 (CA-3/89)
87   MONT ST. JOHN Cabernet Sauvignon Napa Valley 1986 $14 (4/30/91)
78   MONT ST. JOHN Cabernet Sauvignon Napa Valley 1983 $15 (7/31/89)
82   MONT ST. JOHN Cabernet Sauvignon Napa Valley 1982 $15 (3/15/89)
75   MONT ST. JOHN Cabernet Sauvignon Napa Valley Private Reserve 1980 $11.50 (5/16/84)
80   MONTE VERDE Cabernet Sauvignon California Proprietor's Reserve 1987 $6.50/1.5L (12/15/89)
81   MONTEREY PENINSULA Cabernet Sauvignon Monterey Doctors' Reserve 1984 $16 (2/28/91)
83   MONTEREY PENINSULA Cabernet Sauvignon Monterey Doctors' Reserve Lot II 1982 $14 (6/15/87)
74   MONTEREY PENINSULA Cabernet Sauvignon Monterey County 1982 $11 (3/31/87)
83   MONTEREY VINEYARD Cabernet Sauvignon Monterey County Classic 1987 $6 (1/31/91) BB
76   MONTEREY VINEYARD Cabernet Sauvignon Monterey County Classic 1986 $5.50 (10/31/89)
83   MONTEREY VINEYARD Cabernet Sauvignon Monterey County Limited Release 1986 $10 (11/15/89)
75   MONTEREY VINEYARD Cabernet Sauvignon Monterey County Limited Release 1985 $10 (8/31/88)
73   MONTEREY VINEYARD Cabernet Sauvignon Monterey-Sonoma-San Luis Obispo County Classic 1985 $5 (2/15/89)
77   MONTEVINA Cabernet Sauvignon California 1988 $8.50 (2/15/90)
86   MONTEVINA Cabernet Sauvignon Shenandoah Valley Limited Release 1984 $7.50 (8/31/88) BB
85+   MONTICELLO Cabernet Sauvignon Napa Valley Corley Reserve 1990 (NR) (5/15/91) (BT)
90+   MONTICELLO Cabernet Sauvignon Napa Valley Corley Reserve 1989 (NR) (5/15/91) (BT)
90   MONTICELLO Cabernet Sauvignon Napa Valley Corley Reserve 1987 $25 (11/15/90)
85+   MONTICELLO Cabernet Sauvignon Napa Valley Corley Reserve 1987 $25 (4/15/89) (BT)
92   MONTICELLO Cabernet Sauvignon Napa Valley Corley Reserve 1986 Rel: $24 Cur: $24 (3/15/90)
88   MONTICELLO Cabernet Sauvignon Napa Valley Corley Reserve 1986 Rel: $24 Cur: $24 (CA-3/89)
75+   MONTICELLO Cabernet Sauvignon Napa Valley Corley Reserve 1986 Rel: $24 Cur: $24 (4/15/88) (BT)
92   MONTICELLO Cabernet Sauvignon Napa Valley Corley Reserve 1985 Rel: $22.50 Cur: $30 (7/31/89)
88   MONTICELLO Cabernet Sauvignon Napa Valley Corley Reserve 1985 Rel: $22.50 Cur: $30 (CA-3/89)
75+   MONTICELLO Cabernet Sauvignon Napa Valley Corley Reserve 1985 Rel: $22.50 Cur: $30 (6/15/87) (BT)
91   MONTICELLO Cabernet Sauvignon Napa Valley Corley Reserve 1984 Rel: $18.50 Cur: $28 (CA-3/89)
90   MONTICELLO Cabernet Sauvignon Napa Valley Corley Reserve 1984 Rel: $18.50 Cur: $28 (11/30/87)
88   MONTICELLO Cabernet Sauvignon Napa Valley Corley Reserve 1983 Rel: $24 Cur: $26 (CA-3/89)
90   MONTICELLO Cabernet Sauvignon Napa Valley Corley Reserve 1982 Rel: $15 Cur: $32 (CA-3/89)
92   MONTICELLO Cabernet Sauvignon Napa Valley Corley Reserve 1982 Rel: $15 Cur: $32 (12/16/85)
90   MONTICELLO Cabernet Sauvignon Napa Valley Jefferson Cuvée 1987 $14 (9/30/90)
85+   MONTICELLO Cabernet Sauvignon Napa Valley Jefferson Cuvée 1987 $14 (4/15/89) (BT)
89   MONTICELLO Cabernet Sauvignon Napa Valley Jefferson Cuvée 1986 $14 (4/15/89)
87   MONTICELLO Cabernet Sauvignon Napa Valley Jefferson Cuvée 1985 $12 (2/29/88)
85+   MONTICELLO Cabernet Sauvignon Napa Valley Jefferson Cuvée 1985 $12 (6/15/87) (BT)
90   MONTICELLO Cabernet Sauvignon Napa Valley Jefferson Cuvée 1984 $11 (11/30/87)
77   MONTICELLO Cabernet Sauvignon Napa Valley Jefferson Cuvée 1983 $10 (11/30/86)
91   MONTICELLO Cabernet Sauvignon Napa Valley Jefferson Cuvée 1982 $10 (2/01/86)
74   MONTICELLO Cabernet Sauvignon Napa Valley 1981 $13.50 (7/16/84)
76   MONTPELLIER Cabernet Sauvignon California 1988 $7 (10/31/89)
83   MONTPELLIER Cabernet Sauvignon California 1988 $7 (7/31/91) BB
92   MORGAN Cabernet Sauvignon Carmel Valley 1987 $16 (9/30/90)
90   MORGAN Cabernet Sauvignon Carmel Valley 1986 $16 (9/15/89)
74   J.W. MORRIS Cabernet Sauvignon Alexander Valley 1985 $8 (2/15/89)

Key to Symbols

The scores reported here are the results of blind tastings conducted by our panel of senior editors. Wines that carry the initials below are results of individual tastings.

THE WINE SPECTATOR 100-POINT SCALE 95-100—Classic, a great wine; *90-94*—Outstanding, superior character and style; *80-89*—Good to very good, a wine with special qualities; *70-79*—Average, drinkable wine that may have minor flaws; *60-69*—Below average, drinkable but not recommended; *50-59*—Poor, undrinkable, not recommended. "*+*"—With a score indicates a range; used primarily with barrel tastings to indicate a preliminary score.

SPECIAL DESIGNATIONS SS—Spectator Selection, CS—Cellar Selection, BB—Best Buy.

TASTER'S INITIALS   (JG)—Jim Gordon, (HS)—Harvey Steiman, (JL)—James Laube, (JS)—James Suckling, (TM)—Thomas Matthews, (TR)—Terry Robards, (BT)—Barrel Tasting (these wines were tasted blind from barrel samples), (CA-date)—*California's Great Cabernets* by James Laube, (CH-date)—*California's Great Chardonnays* by James Laube, (VP-date)—*Vintage Port* by James Suckling.

DATE TASTED   Dates in parentheses represent the issue in which the rating was published.

83 J.W. MORRIS Cabernet Sauvignon California Private Reserve 1987 $8 (3/31/90)
85+ MOUNT EDEN Cabernet Sauvignon Santa Cruz Mountains 1988 (NR) (4/30/90) (BT)
65 MOUNT EDEN Cabernet Sauvignon Santa Cruz Mountains 1987 $28 (4/30/91)
85+ MOUNT EDEN Cabernet Sauvignon Santa Cruz Mountains 1987 $28 (4/15/89) (BT)
83 MOUNT EDEN Cabernet Sauvignon Santa Cruz Mountains 1986 Rel: $28 Cur: $28 (8/31/90)
85 MOUNT EDEN Cabernet Sauvignon Santa Cruz Mountains 1986 Rel: $28 Cur: $28 (CA-3/89)
81 MOUNT EDEN Cabernet Sauvignon Santa Cruz Mountains 1985 Rel: $28 Cur: $29 (11/15/89)
86 MOUNT EDEN Cabernet Sauvignon Santa Cruz Mountains 1985 Rel: $28 Cur: $29 (CA-3/89)
84 MOUNT EDEN Cabernet Sauvignon Santa Cruz Mountains 1984 Rel: $22 Cur: $26 (CA-3/89)
90 MOUNT EDEN Cabernet Sauvignon Santa Cruz Mountains 1984 Rel: $22 Cur: $26 (10/31/88)
79 MOUNT EDEN Cabernet Sauvignon Santa Cruz Mountains 1983 Rel: $20 Cur: $21 (CA-3/89)
70 MOUNT EDEN Cabernet Sauvignon Santa Cruz Mountains 1982 Rel: $18 Cur: $20 (CA-3/89)
86 MOUNT EDEN Cabernet Sauvignon Santa Cruz Mountains 1981 Rel: $18 Cur: $25 (CA-3/89)
81 MOUNT EDEN Cabernet Sauvignon Santa Cruz Mountains 1981 Rel: $18 Cur: $25 (11/01/84)
85 MOUNT EDEN Cabernet Sauvignon Santa Cruz Mountains 1980 Rel: $30 Cur: $35 (CA-3/89)
69 MOUNT EDEN Cabernet Sauvignon Santa Cruz Mountains 1979 Rel: $25 Cur: $45 (CA-3/89)
88 MOUNT EDEN Cabernet Sauvignon Santa Cruz Mountains 1978 Rel: $25 Cur: $55 (CA-3/89)
91 MOUNT EDEN Cabernet Sauvignon Santa Cruz Mountains 1977 Rel: $20 Cur: $54 (CA-3/89)
83 MOUNT EDEN Cabernet Sauvignon Santa Cruz Mountains 1976 Rel: $20 Cur: $68 (CA-3/89)
90 MOUNT EDEN Cabernet Sauvignon Santa Cruz Mountains 1975 Rel: $20 Cur: $70 (CA-3/89)
87 MOUNT EDEN Cabernet Sauvignon Santa Cruz Mountains 1974 Rel: $20 Cur: $120 (2/15/90) (JG)
87 MOUNT EDEN Cabernet Sauvignon Santa Cruz Mountains 1974 Rel: $20 Cur: $120 (CA-3/89)
91 MOUNT EDEN Cabernet Sauvignon Santa Cruz Mountains 1973 Rel: $14 Cur: $120 (CA-3/89)
84 MOUNT EDEN Cabernet Sauvignon Santa Cruz Mountains 1972 Rel: $20 Cur: $60 (CA-3/89)
87 MOUNT EDEN Cabernet Sauvignon Santa Cruz Mountains Lathweisen Ridge 1988 $12 (4/30/91)
85 MOUNT EDEN Cabernet Sauvignon Santa Cruz Mountains Young Vine Cuvée 1987 $12 (4/15/90)
85 MOUNT VEEDER Cabernet Sauvignon Napa Valley 1987 $20 (4/30/91)
83 MOUNT VEEDER Cabernet Sauvignon Napa Valley 1986 $18 (11/15/90)
87 MOUNT VEEDER Cabernet Sauvignon Napa Valley 1986 $18 (CA-3/89)
85+ MOUNT VEEDER Cabernet Sauvignon Napa Valley 1986 $18 (4/15/88) (BT)
87 MOUNT VEEDER Cabernet Sauvignon Napa Valley 1985 Rel: $18 Cur: $23 (CA-3/89)
85+ MOUNT VEEDER Cabernet Sauvignon Napa Valley 1985 Rel: $18 Cur: $23 (6/15/87) (BT)
88 MOUNT VEEDER Cabernet Sauvignon Napa Valley 1984 Rel: $14 Cur: $18 (CA-3/89)
83 MOUNT VEEDER Cabernet Sauvignon Napa Valley 1984 Rel: $14 Cur: $18 (11/15/88)
84 MOUNT VEEDER Cabernet Sauvignon Napa Valley 1983 Rel: $14 Cur: $22 (CA-3/89)
75 MOUNT VEEDER Cabernet Sauvignon Napa Valley 1983 Rel: $14 Cur: $22 (10/31/87)
68 MOUNT VEEDER Cabernet Sauvignon Napa Valley 1982 Rel: $12.50 Cur: $17 (CA-3/89)
64 MOUNT VEEDER Cabernet Sauvignon Napa Valley 1982 Rel: $12.50 Cur: $17 (6/15/87)
77 MOUNT VEEDER Cabernet Sauvignon Napa Valley 1981 Rel: $12.50 Cur: $25 (CA-3/89)
81 MOUNT VEEDER Cabernet Sauvignon Napa Valley 1981 Rel: $12.50 Cur: $25 (7/16/86)
87 MOUNT VEEDER Cabernet Sauvignon Napa Valley Bernstein Vineyards 1980 Rel: $13.50 Cur: $30 (CA-3/89)
85 MOUNT VEEDER Cabernet Sauvignon Napa Valley Bernstein Vineyards 1980 Rel: $13.50 Cur: $30 (5/16/84)
92 MOUNT VEEDER Cabernet Sauvignon Napa Valley Bernstein Vineyards 1979 Rel: $13.50 Cur: $43 (CA-3/89)
89 MOUNT VEEDER Cabernet Sauvignon Napa Valley Bernstein Vineyards 1978 Rel: $12.75 Cur: $40 (CA-3/89)
85 MOUNT VEEDER Cabernet Sauvignon Napa Valley Bernstein Vineyards 1977 Rel: $11 Cur: $50 (CA-3/89)
77 MOUNT VEEDER Cabernet Sauvignon Napa Valley Bernstein Vineyards 1976 Rel: $11 Cur: $35 (CA-3/89)
83 MOUNT VEEDER Cabernet Sauvignon Napa Valley Bernstein Vineyards 1975 Rel: $11 Cur: $35 (CA-3/89)
89 MOUNT VEEDER Cabernet Sauvignon Napa Valley 1974 Rel: $8 Cur: $65 (2/15/90) (JG)
80 MOUNT VEEDER Cabernet Sauvignon Napa Valley 1974 Rel: $8 Cur: $65 (CA-3/89)
90 MOUNT VEEDER Cabernet Sauvignon Napa Valley 1973 Rel: $8 Cur: $70 (CA-3/89)
93 MOUNT VEEDER Meritage Napa Valley 1986 (NR) (CA-3/89)
85+ MOUNT VEEDER Meritage Napa Valley 1986 (NR) (4/15/88) (BT)
86 MOUNT VEEDER Cabernet Sauvignon Napa Valley Sidehill Ranch 1978 Rel: $13.50 Cur: $40 (CA-3/89)
88 MOUNT VEEDER Cabernet Sauvignon Napa Valley Niebaum-Coppola 1977 Rel: $9.75 Cur: $60 (CA-3/89)
79 MOUNTAIN VIEW Cabernet Sauvignon Mendocino County 1986 $6.50 (3/31/90)
77 MOUNTAIN VIEW Cabernet Sauvignon Mendocino County 1985 $6 (2/15/89)
80 MOUNTAIN VIEW Cabernet Sauvignon North Coast 1988 $6 (4/30/91) BB
62 MOUNTAIN VIEW Cabernet Sauvignon North Coast 1980 $5 (4/16/84)
89 MURPHY-GOODE Cabernet Sauvignon Alexander Valley 1987 $16.50 (5/31/90)
90 MURPHY-GOODE Cabernet Sauvignon Alexander Valley Premier Vineyard 1986 $16 (11/15/89)
80 MURPHY-GOODE Cabernet Sauvignon Alexander Valley Goode-Ready The Second Cabernet 1989 $10 (6/15/91)
89 NALLE Cabernet Sauvignon Dry Creek Valley 1987 $18 (1/31/91)
74 NAPA RIDGE Cabernet Sauvignon North Coast 1987 $7 (11/15/90)
72 NAPA RIDGE Cabernet Sauvignon North Coast 1982 $5.75 (3/31/87)
75 NAPA SUN Cabernet Sauvignon Napa Valley 1980 $5.99 (3/16/84)
87 NAVARRO Cabernet Sauvignon Mendocino 1985 $14 (11/15/90)
89 NEWLAN Cabernet Sauvignon Napa Valley 1986 $15 (4/30/91)
87 NEWLAN Cabernet Sauvignon Napa Valley 1985 $15 (3/31/90)
85+ NEWTON Cabernet Sauvignon Napa Valley 1988 (NR) (4/30/90) (BT)
90+ NEWTON Cabernet Sauvignon Napa Valley 1987 (NR) (4/15/89) (BT)
91 NEWTON Cabernet Sauvignon Napa Valley 1986 Rel: $16 Cur: $18 (5/31/90)
91 NEWTON Cabernet Sauvignon Napa Valley 1986 Rel: $16 Cur: $18 (CA-3/89)
90+ NEWTON Cabernet Sauvignon Napa Valley 1986 Rel: $16 Cur: $18 (4/15/88) (BT)
89 NEWTON Cabernet Sauvignon Napa Valley 1985 Rel: $15.25 Cur: $18 (CA-3/89)
89 NEWTON Cabernet Sauvignon Napa Valley 1985 Rel: $15.25 Cur: $18 (1/31/89)
87 NEWTON Cabernet Sauvignon Napa Valley 1984 Rel: $13.50 Cur: $22 (CA-3/89)
91 NEWTON Cabernet Sauvignon Napa Valley 1984 Rel: $13.50 Cur: $22 (9/30/87)
92 NEWTON Cabernet Sauvignon Napa Valley 1983 Rel: $12.50 Cur: $36 (CA-3/89)
96 NEWTON Cabernet Sauvignon Napa Valley 1983 Rel: $12.50 Cur: $36 (4/15/87) SS
66 NEWTON Cabernet Sauvignon Napa Valley 1982 Rel: $12.50 Cur: $21 (CA-3/89)
83 NEWTON Cabernet Sauvignon Napa Valley 1981 Rel: $12.50 Cur: $21 (CA-3/89)
91 NEWTON Cabernet Sauvignon Napa Valley 1981 Rel: $12.50 Cur: $21 (12/16/84)
55 NEWTON Cabernet Sauvignon Napa Valley 1980 Rel: $12 Cur: $30 (CA-3/89)
85 NEWTON Cabernet Sauvignon Napa Valley 1979 Rel: $12 Cur: $30 (CA-3/89)
89 NEWTON Claret Napa Valley 1988 $11 (3/15/91)
85+ NEYERS Cabernet Sauvignon Napa Valley 1987 (NR) (4/15/89) (BT)
85+ NEYERS Cabernet Sauvignon Napa Valley 1986 (NR) (4/15/88) (BT)
83 NEYERS Cabernet Sauvignon Napa Valley 1985 $14 (7/15/89)
90+ NEYERS Cabernet Sauvignon Napa Valley 1985 $14 (6/15/87) (BT)
75 NEYERS Cabernet Sauvignon Napa Valley 1984 $12.50 (4/30/88)
79 NEYERS Cabernet Sauvignon Napa Valley 1983 $12 (8/31/87)
89 GUSTAVE NIEBAUM Cabernet Sauvignon Napa Valley Reference 1985 $13.50 (10/31/89)
93 GUSTAVE NIEBAUM Cabernet Sauvignon Napa Valley Tench Vineyard 1986 $16 (10/15/89)
85+ NIEBAUM-COPPOLA Rubicon Napa Valley 1989 (NR) (5/15/91) (BT)
85+ NIEBAUM-COPPOLA Rubicon Napa Valley 1988 (NR) (4/30/90) (BT)
92 NIEBAUM-COPPOLA Rubicon Napa Valley 1986 (NR) (CA-3/89)
87 NIEBAUM-COPPOLA Rubicon Napa Valley 1985 $28 (11/15/90)
91 NIEBAUM-COPPOLA Rubicon Napa Valley 1985 $28 (CA-3/89)
85 NIEBAUM-COPPOLA Rubicon Napa Valley 1984 (NR) (CA-3/89)
88 NIEBAUM-COPPOLA Rubicon Napa Valley 1982 Rel: $40 Cur: $40 (10/15/89)
89 NIEBAUM-COPPOLA Rubicon Napa Valley 1982 Rel: $40 Cur: $40 (CA-3/89)
87 NIEBAUM-COPPOLA Rubicon Napa Valley 1981 Rel: $35 Cur: $35 (CA-3/89)
89 NIEBAUM-COPPOLA Rubicon Napa Valley 1981 Rel: $35 Cur: $35 (11/15/88)
87 NIEBAUM-COPPOLA Rubicon Napa Valley 1980 Rel: $30 Cur: $35 (CA-3/89)
92 NIEBAUM-COPPOLA Rubicon Napa Valley 1980 Rel: $30 Cur: $35 (10/15/87)
75 NIEBAUM-COPPOLA Rubicon Napa Valley 1979 Rel: $25 Cur: $40 (CA-3/89)
81 NIEBAUM-COPPOLA Rubicon Napa Valley 1979 Rel: $25 Cur: $40 (2/28/87) (JG)
88 NIEBAUM-COPPOLA Rubicon Napa Valley 1978 Rel: $25 Cur: $25 (CA-3/89)
85 NIEBAUM-COPPOLA Rubicon Napa Valley 1978 Rel: $25 Cur: $25 (2/28/87) (JG)
93 NIEBAUM-COPPOLA Rubicon Napa Valley 1977 (NR) (2/28/87) (JG)
91 OAKFORD Cabernet Sauvignon Napa Valley 1987 $25 (11/15/90)
83 OCTOPUS MOUNTAIN Cabernet Sauvignon Anderson Valley Dennison Vineyards 1989 $12.50 (7/31/91)
92 OPTIMA Cabernet Sauvignon Sonoma County 1987 $22 (12/15/90)
91 OPTIMA Cabernet Sauvignon Sonoma County 1986 $22 (2/15/90)
93 OPTIMA Cabernet Sauvignon Sonoma County 1985 $18.50 (12/15/88)
90 OPTIMA Cabernet Sauvignon Sonoma County 1984 $16.50 (2/29/88)
97 OPUS ONE Napa Valley 1987 Rel: $68 Cur: $69 (11/15/90) CS
95 OPUS ONE Napa Valley 1986 Rel: $55 Cur: $60 (11/30/89)
95 OPUS ONE Napa Valley 1986 Rel: $55 Cur: $60 (CA-3/89)
95 OPUS ONE Napa Valley 1985 Rel: $55 Cur: $69 (6/15/89)
95 OPUS ONE Napa Valley 1985 Rel: $55 Cur: $69 (CA-3/89)
94 OPUS ONE Napa Valley 1984 Rel: $50 Cur: $70 (CA-3/89)
94 OPUS ONE Napa Valley 1984 Rel: $50 Cur: $70 (5/31/88)
89 OPUS ONE Napa Valley 1983 Rel: $50 Cur: $66 (6/15/87)
89 OPUS ONE Napa Valley 1983 Rel: $50 Cur: $66 (CA-3/89)
90 OPUS ONE Napa Valley 1982 Rel: $50 Cur: $83 (CA-3/89)
93 OPUS ONE Napa Valley 1982 Rel: $50 Cur: $83 (5/01/86) CS
88 OPUS ONE Napa Valley 1981 Rel: $50 Cur: $91 (CA-3/89)
94 OPUS ONE Napa Valley 1981 Rel: $50 Cur: $91 (5/16/85) CS
93 OPUS ONE Napa Valley 1980 Rel: $50 Cur: $134 (CA-3/89)
92 OPUS ONE Napa Valley 1980 Rel: $50 Cur: $134 (7/16/85)
91 OPUS ONE Napa Valley 1980 Rel: $50 Cur: $134 (4/01/84) CS
90 OPUS ONE Napa Valley 1979 Rel: $50 Cur: $194 (CA-3/89)
90 OPUS ONE Napa Valley 1979 Rel: $50 Cur: $194 (7/16/85)
95+ PAHLMEYER Caldwell Vineyard Napa Valley 1990 (NR) (5/15/91) (BT)
85+ PAHLMEYER Caldwell Vineyard Napa Valley 1989 (NR) (5/15/91) (BT)
85+ PAHLMEYER Caldwell Vineyard Napa Valley 1988 $30 (4/30/90) (BT)
91 PAHLMEYER Caldwell Vineyard Napa Valley 1987 $28 (11/15/90)
89 PAHLMEYER Caldwell Vineyard Napa Valley 1986 $25 (11/15/89)
85+ PAHLMEYER Caldwell Vineyard Napa Valley 1986 $25 (4/15/88) (BT)
74 PARDUCCI Cabernet Sauvignon Mendocino County 1984 $8.50 (7/31/88)
73 PARDUCCI Cabernet Sauvignon Mendocino County 1981 $6.50 (2/01/86)
79 PARDUCCI Cabernet Sauvignon Mendocino County 1980 $6.25 (2/01/86)
69 PARDUCCI Cabernet Sauvignon Mendocino County 1979 $8 (2/01/86)
75 PARDUCCI Cabernet Sauvignon Mendocino County 1978 $5.50 (2/01/86)
80 PARDUCCI Cabernet Sauvignon North Coast 1987 $9.50 (4/30/91)
79 PARDUCCI Cabernet Merlot Cellarmaster Selection Mendocino County 1986 $15 (4/30/91)
75 PARDUCCI Cabernet Merlot Cellarmaster Selection Mendocino County 1978 $12 (2/01/86)
75 PARSONS CREEK Cabernet Sauvignon Sonoma County 1986 $13 (11/15/89)
76 PARSONS CREEK Cabernet Sauvignon Sonoma County 1985 $13 (6/30/89)
70 PAT PAULSEN Cabernet Sauvignon Alexander Valley 1984 $11 (4/30/87)
84 PAT PAULSEN Cabernet Sauvignon Alexander Valley 1983 $11 (7/01/86)
85 PAT PAULSEN Cabernet Sauvignon Alexander Valley 1982 $10 (3/01/85) BB
78 PAT PAULSEN Cabernet Sauvignon Sonoma County 1985 $11 (12/31/87)
78 PAT PAULSEN Cabernet Sauvignon Sonoma County 1981 $8 (1/01/84)
90+ ROBERT PECOTA Cabernet Sauvignon Napa Valley Kara's Vineyard 1990 (NR) (5/15/91) (BT)
90+ ROBERT PECOTA Cabernet Sauvignon Napa Valley Kara's Vineyard 1989 (NR) (5/15/91) (BT)
90 ROBERT PECOTA Cabernet Sauvignon Napa Valley Kara's Vineyard 1987 Rel: $16 Cur: $17 (10/15/90)
85+ ROBERT PECOTA Cabernet Sauvignon Napa Valley Kara's Vineyard 1987 Rel: $16 Cur: $17 (4/15/89) (BT)
86 ROBERT PECOTA Cabernet Sauvignon Napa Valley Kara's Vineyard 1986 Rel: $16 Cur: $16 (9/15/89)
88 ROBERT PECOTA Cabernet Sauvignon Napa Valley Kara's Vineyard 1986 Rel: $16 Cur: $16 (CA-3/89)
85+ ROBERT PECOTA Cabernet Sauvignon Napa Valley Kara's Vineyard 1986 Rel: $16 Cur: $16 (4/15/88) (BT)
86 ROBERT PECOTA Cabernet Sauvignon Napa Valley Kara's Vineyard 1985 Rel: $16 Cur: $20 (CA-3/89)
89 ROBERT PECOTA Cabernet Sauvignon Napa Valley Kara's Vineyard 1985 Rel: $16 Cur: $20 (12/15/88)
85 ROBERT PECOTA Cabernet Sauvignon Napa Valley Kara's Vineyard 1984 Rel: $14 Cur: $20 (CA-3/89)
91 ROBERT PECOTA Cabernet Sauvignon Napa Valley Kara's Vineyard 1984 Rel: $14 Cur: $20 (10/15/87)
85 ROBERT PECOTA Cabernet Sauvignon Napa Valley 1982 Rel: $12 Cur: $20 (CA-3/89)
85 J. PEDRONCELLI Cabernet Sauvignon Dry Creek Valley 1987 $8.50 (11/15/90) BB
83 J. PEDRONCELLI Cabernet Sauvignon Dry Creek Valley 1986 $7 (9/15/89) BB
90+ J. PEDRONCELLI Cabernet Sauvignon Dry Creek Valley 1986 $7 (4/15/88) (BT)
79 J. PEDRONCELLI Cabernet Sauvignon Dry Creek Valley 1985 $7 (10/15/88)
75 J. PEDRONCELLI Cabernet Sauvignon Dry Creek Valley 1983 $6.50 (8/31/87)

UNITED STATES
CALIFORNIA/*CABERNET SAUVIGNON & BLENDS*

80 J. PEDRONCELLI Cabernet Sauvignon Dry Creek Valley 1981 $6 (12/01/84) BB
85 J. PEDRONCELLI Cabernet Sauvignon Dry Creek Valley Reserve 1985 $14 (3/31/90)
73 J. PEDRONCELLI Cabernet Sauvignon Dry Creek Valley Reserve 1982 $13 (10/15/89)
87 PEJU Cabernet Sauvignon Napa Valley HB Vineyard 1987 $20 (11/15/90)
92 PEJU Cabernet Sauvignon Napa Valley HB Vineyard 1986 $20 (11/15/89)
82 PELLEGRINI FAMILY Cabernet Sauvignon Alexander Valley Cloverdale Ranch Estate Cuvée 1988 $12 (6/15/91)
85+ ROBERT PEPI Cabernet Sauvignon Napa Valley Vine Hill Ranch 1988 (NR) (4/30/90) (BT)
90 ROBERT PEPI Cabernet Sauvignon Napa Valley Vine Hill Ranch 1987 $20 (4/30/91)
88 ROBERT PEPI Cabernet Sauvignon Napa Valley Vine Hill Ranch 1986 Rel: $18 Cur: $24 (10/31/90)
85+ ROBERT PEPI Cabernet Sauvignon Napa Valley Vine Hill Ranch 1986 Rel: $18 Cur: $24 (4/15/88) (BT)
85 ROBERT PEPI Cabernet Sauvignon Napa Valley Vine Hill Ranch 1985 Rel: $18 Cur: $23 (7/31/90)
90 ROBERT PEPI Cabernet Sauvignon Napa Valley Vine Hill Ranch 1985 Rel: $18 Cur: $23 (CA-3/89)
80 ROBERT PEPI Cabernet Sauvignon Napa Valley Vine Hill Ranch 1984 Rel: $16 Cur: $21 (8/31/89)
87 ROBERT PEPI Cabernet Sauvignon Napa Valley Vine Hill Ranch 1984 Rel: $16 Cur: $21 (CA-3/89)
80 ROBERT PEPI Cabernet Sauvignon Napa Valley Vine Hill Ranch 1983 Rel: $16 Cur: $21 (CA-3/89)
89 ROBERT PEPI Cabernet Sauvignon Napa Valley Vine Hill Ranch 1983 Rel: $16 Cur: $21 (5/31/88)
88 ROBERT PEPI Cabernet Sauvignon Napa Valley Vine Hill Ranch 1982 Rel: $14 Cur: $17 (CA-3/89)
84 ROBERT PEPI Cabernet Sauvignon Napa Valley Vine Hill Ranch 1982 Rel: $14 Cur: $17 (3/31/87)
86 ROBERT PEPI Cabernet Sauvignon Napa Valley Vine Hill Ranch 1981 Rel: $14 Cur: $20 (CA-3/89)
93 ROBERT PEPI Cabernet Sauvignon Napa Valley Vine Hill Ranch 1981 Rel: $14 Cur: $20 (1/01/86) CS
83 MARIO PERELLI-MINETTI Cabernet Sauvignon Napa Valley 1987 $12 (4/30/91)
84 PESENTI Cabernet Sauvignon San Luis Obispo County Family Reserve 1987 $8 (12/15/89)
77 PESENTI Cabernet Sauvignon San Luis Obispo County Family Reserve 1985 $13 (12/15/89)
85+ JOSEPH PHELPS Cabernet Sauvignon Napa Valley 1990 (NR) (5/15/91) (BT)
85+ JOSEPH PHELPS Cabernet Sauvignon Napa Valley 1989 (NR) (5/15/91) (BT)
75 JOSEPH PHELPS Cabernet Sauvignon Napa Valley 1987 $14.50 (7/15/91)
85+ JOSEPH PHELPS Cabernet Sauvignon Napa Valley 1986 Rel: $15 Cur: $18 (4/15/88) (BT)
84 JOSEPH PHELPS Cabernet Sauvignon Napa Valley 1985 Rel: $14 Cur: $19 (5/15/89)
91 JOSEPH PHELPS Cabernet Sauvignon Napa Valley 1984 Rel: $14 Cur: $25 (10/31/88)
84 JOSEPH PHELPS Cabernet Sauvignon Napa Valley 1983 Rel: $13 Cur: $14 (8/31/87)
82 JOSEPH PHELPS Cabernet Sauvignon Napa Valley 1982 Rel: $12 Cur: $17 (12/15/86)
86 JOSEPH PHELPS Cabernet Sauvignon Napa Valley 1981 Rel: $11 Cur: $24 (9/01/85)
89 JOSEPH PHELPS Cabernet Sauvignon Napa Valley 1980 Rel: $10.75 Cur: $31 (7/01/84)
90+ JOSEPH PHELPS Cabernet Sauvignon Napa Valley Backus Vineyard 1990 (NR) (5/15/91) (BT)
90+ JOSEPH PHELPS Cabernet Sauvignon Napa Valley Backus Vineyard 1989 (NR) (5/15/91) (BT)
88 JOSEPH PHELPS Cabernet Sauvignon Napa Valley Backus Vineyard 1987 $30 (7/15/91)
85+ JOSEPH PHELPS Cabernet Sauvignon Napa Valley Backus Vineyard 1987 $30 (4/15/89) (BT)
83 JOSEPH PHELPS Cabernet Sauvignon Napa Valley Backus Vineyard 1986 Rel: $22 Cur: $35 (1/31/90)
93 JOSEPH PHELPS Cabernet Sauvignon Napa Valley Backus Vineyard 1986 Rel: $22 Cur: $35 (CA-3/89)
90+ JOSEPH PHELPS Cabernet Sauvignon Napa Valley Backus Vineyard 1986 Rel: $22 Cur: $35 (4/15/88) (BT)
90 JOSEPH PHELPS Cabernet Sauvignon Napa Valley Backus Vineyard 1985 Rel: $27.50 Cur: $32 (CA-3/89)
91 JOSEPH PHELPS Cabernet Sauvignon Napa Valley Backus Vineyard 1985 Rel: $27.50 Cur: $32 (12/31/88)
90+ JOSEPH PHELPS Cabernet Sauvignon Napa Valley Backus Vineyard 1985 Rel: $27.50 Cur: $32 (6/15/87) (BT)
86 JOSEPH PHELPS Cabernet Sauvignon Napa Valley Backus Vineyard 1984 Rel: $20 Cur: $39 (CA-3/89)
88 JOSEPH PHELPS Cabernet Sauvignon Napa Valley Backus Vineyard 1984 Rel: $20 Cur: $39 (12/31/87)
85 JOSEPH PHELPS Cabernet Sauvignon Napa Valley Backus Vineyard 1983 Rel: $16.50 Cur: $28 (CA-3/89)
85 JOSEPH PHELPS Cabernet Sauvignon Napa Valley Backus Vineyard 1983 Rel: $16.50 Cur: $28 (6/15/87)
91 JOSEPH PHELPS Cabernet Sauvignon Napa Valley Backus Vineyard 1981 Rel: $15 Cur: $50 (CA-3/89)
90 JOSEPH PHELPS Cabernet Sauvignon Napa Valley Backus Vineyard 1981 Rel: $15 Cur: $50 (4/16/85)
89 JOSEPH PHELPS Cabernet Sauvignon Napa Valley Backus Vineyard 1978 Rel: $16.50 Cur: $55 (CA-3/89)
86 JOSEPH PHELPS Cabernet Sauvignon Napa Valley Backus Vineyard 1977 Rel: $15 Cur: $63 (CA-3/89)
90+ JOSEPH PHELPS Cabernet Sauvignon Napa Valley Eisele Vineyard 1989 (NR) (5/15/91) (BT)
75+ JOSEPH PHELPS Cabernet Sauvignon Napa Valley Eisele Vineyard 1987 Rel: $40 Cur: $41 (4/15/89) (BT)
77 JOSEPH PHELPS Cabernet Sauvignon Napa Valley Eisele Vineyard 1986 Rel: $40 Cur: $41 (8/31/90)

Key to Symbols

The scores reported here are the results of blind tastings conducted by our panel of senior editors. Wines that carry the initials below are results of individual tastings.

THE WINE SPECTATOR 100-POINT SCALE *95-100*—Classic, a great wine; *90-94*—Outstanding, superior character and style; *80-89*—Good to very good, a wine with special qualities; *70-79*—Average, drinkable wine that may have minor flaws; *60-69*—Below average, drinkable but not recommended; *50-59*—Poor, undrinkable, not recommended. "+"—With a score indicates a range; used primarily with barrel tastings to indicate a preliminary score.

SPECIAL DESIGNATIONS SS—Spectator Selection, CS—Cellar Selection, BB—Best Buy.

TASTER'S INITIALS (JG)—Jim Gordon, (HS)—Harvey Steiman, (JL)—James Laube, (JS)—James Suckling, (TM)—Thomas Matthews, (TR)—Terry Robards, (BT)—Barrel Tasting (these wines were tasted blind from barrel samples), (CA-date)—*California's Great Cabernets* by James Laube, (CH-date)—*California's Great Chardonnays* by James Laube, (VP-date)—*Vintage Port* by James Suckling.

DATE TASTED Dates in parentheses represent the issue in which the rating was published.

95 JOSEPH PHELPS Cabernet Sauvignon Napa Valley Eisele Vineyard 1986 Rel: $40 Cur: $41 (CA-3/89)
90+ JOSEPH PHELPS Cabernet Sauvignon Napa Valley Eisele Vineyard 1986 Rel: $40 Cur: $41 (4/15/88) (BT)
81 JOSEPH PHELPS Cabernet Sauvignon Napa Valley Eisele Vineyard 1985 Rel: $40 Cur: $43 (5/31/89)
94 JOSEPH PHELPS Cabernet Sauvignon Napa Valley Eisele Vineyard 1985 Rel: $40 Cur: $43 (CA-3/89)
85+ JOSEPH PHELPS Cabernet Sauvignon Napa Valley Eisele Vineyard 1985 Rel: $40 Cur: $43 (6/15/87) (BT)
87 JOSEPH PHELPS Cabernet Sauvignon Napa Valley Eisele Vineyard 1984 Rel: $35 Cur: $39 (CA-3/89)
88 JOSEPH PHELPS Cabernet Sauvignon Napa Valley Eisele Vineyard 1984 Rel: $35 Cur: $39 (3/15/88)
86 JOSEPH PHELPS Cabernet Sauvignon Napa Valley Eisele Vineyard 1983 Rel: $25 Cur: $36 (CA-3/89)
76 JOSEPH PHELPS Cabernet Sauvignon Napa Valley Eisele Vineyard 1983 Rel: $25 Cur: $36 (8/31/87)
85 JOSEPH PHELPS Cabernet Sauvignon Napa Valley Eisele Vineyard 1982 Rel: $30 Cur: $39 (CA-3/89)
84 JOSEPH PHELPS Cabernet Sauvignon Napa Valley Eisele Vineyard 1982 Rel: $30 Cur: $39 (12/15/86)
89 JOSEPH PHELPS Cabernet Sauvignon Napa Valley Eisele Vineyard 1981 Rel: $30 Cur: $44 (CA-3/89)
78 JOSEPH PHELPS Cabernet Sauvignon Napa Valley Eisele Vineyard 1981 Rel: $30 Cur: $44 (11/16/85)
92 JOSEPH PHELPS Cabernet Sauvignon Napa Valley Eisele Vineyard 1979 Rel: $30 Cur: $54 (CA-3/89)
86 JOSEPH PHELPS Cabernet Sauvignon Napa Valley Eisele Vineyard 1979 Rel: $30 Cur: $54 (2/16/84) (HS)
97 JOSEPH PHELPS Cabernet Sauvignon Napa Valley Eisele Vineyard 1978 Rel: $30 Cur: $90 (CA-3/89)
96 JOSEPH PHELPS Cabernet Sauvignon Napa Valley Eisele Vineyard 1978 Rel: $30 Cur: $90 (4/30/87)
82 JOSEPH PHELPS Cabernet Sauvignon Napa Valley Eisele Vineyard 1977 Rel: $25 Cur: $56 (CA-3/89)
97 JOSEPH PHELPS Cabernet Sauvignon Napa Valley Eisele Vineyard 1975 Rel: $15 Cur: $162 (CA-3/89)
90+ JOSEPH PHELPS Insignia Napa Valley 1990 (NR) (5/15/91) (BT)
85+ JOSEPH PHELPS Insignia Napa Valley 1989 (NR) (5/15/91) (BT)
93 JOSEPH PHELPS Insignia Napa Valley 1986 Rel: $40 Cur: $40 (8/31/90) CS
96 JOSEPH PHELPS Insignia Napa Valley 1986 Rel: $40 Cur: $40 (CA-3/89)
85+ JOSEPH PHELPS Insignia Napa Valley 1986 Rel: $40 Cur: $40 (4/15/88) (BT)
93 JOSEPH PHELPS Insignia Napa Valley 1985 Rel: $40 Cur: $46 (7/31/89) CS
89 JOSEPH PHELPS Insignia Napa Valley 1984 Rel: $30 Cur: $35 (CA-3/89)
91 JOSEPH PHELPS Insignia Napa Valley 1984 Rel: $30 Cur: $35 (11/15/88)
89 JOSEPH PHELPS Insignia Napa Valley 1983 Rel: $25 Cur: $35 (CA-3/89)
88 JOSEPH PHELPS Insignia Napa Valley 1983 Rel: $25 Cur: $35 (10/31/87)
85 JOSEPH PHELPS Insignia Napa Valley 1982 Rel: $25 Cur: $35 (CA-3/89)
92 JOSEPH PHELPS Insignia Napa Valley 1982 Rel: $25 Cur: $35 (10/31/87)
92 JOSEPH PHELPS Insignia Napa Valley 1981 Rel: $25 Cur: $47 (CA-3/89)
90 JOSEPH PHELPS Insignia Napa Valley 1981 Rel: $25 Cur: $47 (10/31/87)
90 JOSEPH PHELPS Insignia Napa Valley 1980 Rel: $25 Cur: $52 (CA-3/89)
90 JOSEPH PHELPS Insignia Napa Valley 1980 Rel: $25 Cur: $52 (10/31/87)
90 JOSEPH PHELPS Insignia Napa Valley 1980 Rel: $25 Cur: $52 (7/01/84) CS
90 JOSEPH PHELPS Insignia Napa Valley 1979 Rel: $25 Cur: $55 (CA-3/89)
81 JOSEPH PHELPS Insignia Napa Valley 1979 Rel: $25 Cur: $55 (10/31/87)
87 JOSEPH PHELPS Insignia Napa Valley 1978 Rel: $25 Cur: $86 (CA-3/89)
87 JOSEPH PHELPS Insignia Napa Valley 1978 Rel: $25 Cur: $86 (10/31/87)
91 JOSEPH PHELPS Insignia Napa Valley 1977 Rel: $25 Cur: $75 (CA-3/89)
91 JOSEPH PHELPS Insignia Napa Valley 1977 Rel: $25 Cur: $75 (10/31/87)
93 JOSEPH PHELPS Insignia Napa Valley 1976 Rel: $20 Cur: $120 (CA-3/89)
85 JOSEPH PHELPS Insignia Napa Valley 1976 Rel: $20 Cur: $120 (10/31/87)
85 JOSEPH PHELPS Insignia Napa Valley 1975 Rel: $15 Cur: $113 (CA-3/89)
91 JOSEPH PHELPS Insignia Napa Valley 1975 Rel: $15 Cur: $113 (10/31/87)
90 JOSEPH PHELPS Insignia Napa Valley 1974 Rel: $12 Cur: $200 (CA-3/89)
93 JOSEPH PHELPS Insignia Napa Valley 1974 Rel: $12 Cur: $200 (10/31/87)
82 R.H. PHILLIPS Cabernet Sauvignon California 1989 $8 (7/31/91) BB
80 R.H. PHILLIPS Cabernet Sauvignon California 1985 $6 (11/30/88)
83 R.H. PHILLIPS Cabernet Sauvignon California Night Harvest NV $4 (11/30/88) BB
80+ PINE RIDGE Cabernet Sauvignon Napa Valley Andrus Reserve 1990 (NR) (5/15/91) (BT)
80+ PINE RIDGE Cabernet Sauvignon Napa Valley Andrus Reserve 1988 (NR) (4/30/90) (BT)
85+ PINE RIDGE Cabernet Sauvignon Napa Valley Andrus Reserve 1987 (NR) (4/15/89) (BT)
80 PINE RIDGE Cabernet Sauvignon Napa Valley Andrus Reserve 1986 Rel: $40 Cur: $40 (5/15/90)
92 PINE RIDGE Cabernet Sauvignon Napa Valley Andrus Reserve 1986 Rel: $40 Cur: $40 (CA-3/89)
92 PINE RIDGE Cabernet Sauvignon Napa Valley Andrus Reserve Cuvée Duet 1985 Rel: $40 Cur: $45 (CA-3/89)
83 PINE RIDGE Cabernet Sauvignon Napa Valley Andrus Reserve Cuvée Duet 1985 Rel: $40 Cur: $45 (10/15/88)
90+ PINE RIDGE Cabernet Sauvignon Napa Valley Andrus Reserve Cuvée Duet 1985 Rel: $40 Cur: $45 (6/15/87) (BT)
93 PINE RIDGE Cabernet Sauvignon Napa Valley Andrus Reserve 1984 Rel: $37 Cur: $40 (CA-3/89)
90 PINE RIDGE Cabernet Sauvignon Napa Valley Andrus Reserve 1984 Rel: $37 Cur: $40 (6/30/88)
88 PINE RIDGE Cabernet Sauvignon Napa Valley Andrus Reserve 1983 Rel: $35 Cur: $40 (CA-3/89)
96 PINE RIDGE Cabernet Sauvignon Napa Valley Andrus Reserve 1980 Rel: $30 Cur: $60 (CA-3/89)
93 PINE RIDGE Cabernet Sauvignon Napa Valley Andrus Reserve 1980 Rel: $30 Cur: $60 (12/01/84) CS
85+ PINE RIDGE Cabernet Sauvignon Napa Valley Diamond Mountain 1989 (NR) (5/15/91) (BT)
80+ PINE RIDGE Cabernet Sauvignon Napa Valley Diamond Mountain 1988 (NR) (4/30/90) (BT)
84 PINE RIDGE Cabernet Sauvignon Napa Valley Diamond Mountain 1987 $35 (11/15/90)
85+ PINE RIDGE Cabernet Sauvignon Napa Valley Diamond Mountain 1987 $35 (4/15/89) (BT)
92 PINE RIDGE Cabernet Sauvignon Napa Valley Diamond Mountain 1986 Rel: $30 Cur: $30 (11/30/89)

91	PINE RIDGE Cabernet Sauvignon Napa Valley Diamond Mountain 1986 Rel: $30 Cur: $30 (CA-3/89)
90+	PINE RIDGE Cabernet Sauvignon Napa Valley Diamond Mountain 1986 Rel: $30 Cur: $30 (4/15/88) (BT)
85+	PINE RIDGE Cabernet Sauvignon Napa Valley Rutherford Cuvée 1990 (NR) (5/15/91) (BT)
90+	PINE RIDGE Cabernet Sauvignon Napa Valley Rutherford Cuvée 1989 (NR) (5/15/91) (BT)
80+	PINE RIDGE Cabernet Sauvignon Napa Valley Rutherford Cuvée 1988 (NR) (4/30/90) (BT)
80	PINE RIDGE Cabernet Sauvignon Napa Valley Rutherford Cuvée 1987 $16.50 (11/15/90)
90+	PINE RIDGE Cabernet Sauvignon Napa Valley Rutherford Cuvée 1987 $16.50 (4/15/89) (BT)
90	PINE RIDGE Cabernet Sauvignon Napa Valley Rutherford Cuvée 1986 Rel: $16 Cur: $17 (5/31/90)
90	PINE RIDGE Cabernet Sauvignon Napa Valley Rutherford Cuvée 1986 Rel: $16 Cur: $17 (CA-3/89)
85+	PINE RIDGE Cabernet Sauvignon Napa Valley Rutherford Cuvée 1986 Rel: $16 Cur: $17 (4/15/88) (BT)
93	PINE RIDGE Cabernet Sauvignon Napa Valley Rutherford Cuvée 1985 Rel: $16 Cur: $19 (CA-3/89)
88	PINE RIDGE Cabernet Sauvignon Napa Valley Rutherford Cuvée 1985 Rel: $16 Cur: $19 (2/15/89)
90+	PINE RIDGE Cabernet Sauvignon Napa Valley Rutherford Cuvée 1985 Rel: $16 Cur: $19 (6/15/87) (BT)
90	PINE RIDGE Cabernet Sauvignon Napa Valley Rutherford Cuvée 1984 Rel: $14 Cur: $29 (CA-3/89)
87	PINE RIDGE Cabernet Sauvignon Napa Valley Rutherford Cuvée 1984 Rel: $14 Cur: $29 (8/31/87)
84	PINE RIDGE Cabernet Sauvignon Napa Valley Rutherford Cuvée 1983 Rel: $14 Cur: $18 (CA-3/89)
81	PINE RIDGE Cabernet Sauvignon Napa Valley Rutherford Cuvée 1983 Rel: $14 Cur: $18 (4/30/87)
90	PINE RIDGE Cabernet Sauvignon Napa Valley Rutherford Cuvée 1982 Rel: $13 Cur: $24 (CA-3/89)
86	PINE RIDGE Cabernet Sauvignon Napa Valley Rutherford Cuvée 1982 Rel: $13 Cur: $24 (10/01/85)
88	PINE RIDGE Cabernet Sauvignon Napa Valley Rutherford Cuvée 1981 Rel: $13 Cur: $28 (CA-3/89)
93	PINE RIDGE Cabernet Sauvignon Napa Valley Rutherford Cuvée 1981 Rel: $13 Cur: $28 (12/16/84)
91	PINE RIDGE Cabernet Sauvignon Napa Valley Rutherford District 1980 Rel: $12 Cur: $37 (CA-3/89)
85	PINE RIDGE Cabernet Sauvignon Napa Valley Rutherford District 1979 Rel: $9 Cur: $45 (CA-3/89)
89	PINE RIDGE Cabernet Sauvignon Napa Valley Rutherford District 1978 Rel: $7.50 Cur: $50 (CA-3/89)
90	PINE RIDGE Cabernet Sauvignon Napa Valley Rutherford District 1978 Rel: $7.50 Cur: $50 (4/30/87)
85+	PINE RIDGE Cabernet Sauvignon Napa Valley Stags Leap District Pine Ridge Stags Leap Vineyard 1990 (NR) (5/15/91) (BT)
80+	PINE RIDGE Cabernet Sauvignon Napa Valley Stags Leap District Pine Ridge Stags Leap Vineyard 1989 (NR) (5/15/91) (BT)
80+	PINE RIDGE Cabernet Sauvignon Napa Valley Stags Leap District Pine Ridge Stags Leap Vineyard 1988 (NR) (4/30/90) (BT)
85+	PINE RIDGE Cabernet Sauvignon Napa Valley Stags Leap District Pine Ridge Stags Leap Vineyard 1987 (NR) (4/15/89) (BT)
91	PINE RIDGE Cabernet Sauvignon Napa Valley Stags Leap District Pine Ridge Stags Leap Vineyard 1986 Cur: $29 (CA-3/89)
80+	PINE RIDGE Cabernet Sauvignon Napa Valley Stags Leap District Pine Ridge Stags Leap Vineyard 1986 Rel: $29 Cur: $29 (4/15/88) (BT)
94	PINE RIDGE Cabernet Sauvignon Napa Valley Stags Leap District Pine Ridge Stags Leap Vineyard 1985 Rel: $26 Cur: $26 (CA-3/89)
90+	PINE RIDGE Cabernet Sauvignon Napa Valley Stags Leap District Pine Ridge Stags Leap Vineyard 1985 Rel: $26 Cur: $26 (6/15/87) (BT)
93	PINE RIDGE Cabernet Sauvignon Napa Valley Stags Leap District Pine Ridge Stags Leap Vineyard 1984 Rel: $25 Cur: $39 (CA-3/89)
91	PINE RIDGE Cabernet Sauvignon Napa Valley Stags Leap District Pine Ridge Stags Leap Vineyard 1984 Rel: $25 Cur: $39 (2/15/88)
85	PINE RIDGE Cabernet Sauvignon Napa Valley Stags Leap District Pine Ridge Stags Leap Vineyard 1983 Rel: $20 Cur: $27 (CA-3/89)
79	PINE RIDGE Cabernet Sauvignon Napa Valley Stags Leap District Pine Ridge Stags Leap Vineyard 1983 Rel: $20 Cur: $27 (7/15/87)
90	PINE RIDGE Cabernet Sauvignon Napa Valley Stags Leap District Pine Ridge Stags Leap Vineyard 1982 Rel: $20 Cur: $34 (CA-3/89)
91	PINE RIDGE Cabernet Sauvignon Napa Valley Stags Leap District Pine Ridge Stags Leap Vineyard 1982 Rel: $20 Cur: $34 (10/31/86) CS
92	PINE RIDGE Cabernet Sauvignon Napa Valley Stags Leap District Pine Ridge Stags Leap Vineyard 1981 Rel: $20 Cur: $50 (CA-3/89)
88	PINE RIDGE Cabernet Sauvignon Napa Valley Stags Leap District Stags Leap Cuvée 1981 Rel: $20 Cur: $50 (2/01/85)
92	PLAM Cabernet Sauvignon Napa Valley 1986 $24 (9/15/89)
91	PLAM Cabernet Sauvignon Napa Valley 1985 $24 (6/30/88)
78	POPPY HILL Cabernet Sauvignon California 1987 $7.50 (5/31/91)
86	BERNARD PRADEL Cabernet Sauvignon Napa Valley 1987 $20 (10/15/90)
82	BERNARD PRADEL Cabernet Sauvignon Napa Valley 1986 $12 (1/31/90)
91	BERNARD PRADEL Cabernet Sauvignon Napa Valley 1985 $12 (4/30/89)
88	BERNARD PRADEL Cabernet Sauvignon Napa Valley 1984 $11 (2/29/88)
90+	PRESTON Cabernet Sauvignon Dry Creek Valley 1988 $15 (4/30/90) (BT)
88	PRESTON Cabernet Sauvignon Dry Creek Valley 1987 Rel: $14 Cur: $14 (10/31/90)
87	PRESTON Cabernet Sauvignon Dry Creek Valley 1986 Rel: $11 Cur: $15 (3/15/90)
88	PRESTON Cabernet Sauvignon Dry Creek Valley 1986 Rel: $11 Cur: $15 (CA-3/89)
80+	PRESTON Cabernet Sauvignon Dry Creek Valley 1986 Rel: $11 Cur: $15 (4/15/88) (BT)
89	PRESTON Cabernet Sauvignon Dry Creek Valley 1985 Rel: $11 Cur: $15 (CA-3/89)
86	PRESTON Cabernet Sauvignon Dry Creek Valley 1985 Rel: $11 Cur: $15 (9/30/88)
87	PRESTON Cabernet Sauvignon Dry Creek Valley 1984 Rel: $11 Cur: $15 (CA-3/89)
91	PRESTON Cabernet Sauvignon Dry Creek Valley 1984 Rel: $11 Cur: $15 (10/15/87)
86	PRESTON Cabernet Sauvignon Dry Creek Valley 1983 Rel: $11 Cur: $15 (CA-3/89)
86	PRESTON Cabernet Sauvignon Dry Creek Valley 1983 Rel: $11 Cur: $15 (7/16/86)
87	PRESTON Cabernet Sauvignon Dry Creek Valley 1982 Rel: $11 Cur: $18 (CA-3/89)
84	PRESTON Cabernet Sauvignon Dry Creek Valley 1982 Rel: $11 Cur: $18 (7/01/85)
89	QUAIL RIDGE Cabernet Sauvignon Napa Valley 1986 $15 (11/15/90)
82	QUAIL RIDGE Cabernet Sauvignon Napa Valley 1985 $15 (7/31/89)
88	QUAIL RIDGE Cabernet Sauvignon Napa Valley 1984 $15 (3/31/89)
86	QUAIL RIDGE Cabernet Sauvignon Napa Valley 1982 $13 (9/16/85)
87	QUIVIRA Cabernet Sauvignon Dry Creek Valley 1987 $15 (11/15/90)
91	A. RAFANELLI Cabernet Sauvignon Dry Creek Valley 1987 $12 (8/31/90)
91	A. RAFANELLI Cabernet Sauvignon Dry Creek Valley 1986 $9.50 (9/30/89)
78	A. RAFANELLI Cabernet Sauvignon Dry Creek Valley 1985 $8 (9/15/88)
73	RANCHO SISQUOC Cabernet Sauvignon Santa Maria Valley 1986 $10 (12/15/89)
90+	KENT RASMUSSEN Cabernet Sauvignon Napa Valley 1987 $20 (4/15/87) (BT)
89	RAVENSWOOD Cabernet Sauvignon Sonoma Valley 1988 $14 (3/15/91)
84	RAVENSWOOD Cabernet Sauvignon Sonoma Valley 1987 Rel: $11 Cur: $13 (5/31/90)
90+	RAVENSWOOD Cabernet Sauvignon Sonoma Valley 1987 Rel: $11 Cur: $13 (4/15/89) (BT)
86	RAVENSWOOD Cabernet Sauvignon Sonoma County 1986 Rel: $12 Cur: $16 (CA-3/89)
88	RAVENSWOOD Cabernet Sauvignon Sonoma County 1986 Rel: $12 Cur: $16 (12/31/88)
85	RAVENSWOOD Cabernet Sauvignon Sonoma County 1985 Rel: $12 Cur: $17 (CA-3/89)
83	RAVENSWOOD Cabernet Sauvignon Sonoma County 1985 Rel: $12 Cur: $17 (5/31/88)
80	RAVENSWOOD Cabernet Sauvignon Sonoma County 1984 Rel: $12 Cur: $25 (CA-3/89)
76	RAVENSWOOD Cabernet Sauvignon Sonoma County 1983 Rel: $9.50 Cur: $19 (CA-3/89)
84	RAVENSWOOD Cabernet Sauvignon Sonoma County 1982 Rel: $11 Cur: $18 (CA-3/89)
95	RAVENSWOOD Cabernet Sauvignon Sonoma County 1982 Rel: $11 Cur: $18 (4/01/86) SS
79	RAVENSWOOD Cabernet Sauvignon Sonoma County 1980 Rel: $10.50 Cur: $16 (CA-3/89)
83	RAVENSWOOD Cabernet Sauvignon Sonoma Valley Olive Hill 1978 Rel: $10.50 Cur: $24 (CA-3/89)
59	RAVENSWOOD Cabernet Sauvignon California 1979 Rel: $8 Cur: $8 (CA-3/89)
81	RAVENSWOOD Cabernet Sauvignon California 1978 Rel: $10 Cur: $20 (CA-3/89)
82	RAVENSWOOD Cabernet Sauvignon El Dorado County Madrona Vineyards 1977 Rel: $8.50 Cur: $9 (CA-3/89)
80+	RAVENSWOOD Pickberry Vineyards Sonoma Mountain 1989 (NR) (5/15/91) (BT)
82	RAVENSWOOD Pickberry Vineyards Sonoma Mountain 1988 $27 (4/30/91)
89	RAVENSWOOD Pickberry Vineyards Sonoma Mountain 1986 Rel: $25 Cur: $28 (CA-3/89)
78	RAVENSWOOD Pickberry Vineyards Sonoma Mountain 1986 Rel: $25 Cur: $28 (2/15/89)
85+	RAVENSWOOD Pickberry Vineyards Sonoma Mountain 1986 Rel: $25 Cur: $28 (4/15/88) (BT)
85+	RAYMOND Cabernet Sauvignon Napa Valley 1988 (NR) (4/30/90) (BT)
83	RAYMOND Cabernet Sauvignon Napa Valley 1987 $17 (2/28/91)
90	RAYMOND Cabernet Sauvignon Napa Valley 1986 Rel: $16 Cur: $17 (5/31/90)
84	RAYMOND Cabernet Sauvignon Napa Valley 1985 Rel: $15 Cur: $16 (12/15/89)
80+	RAYMOND Cabernet Sauvignon Napa Valley 1985 Rel: $15 Cur: $16 (6/15/87) (BT)
90	RAYMOND Cabernet Sauvignon Napa Valley 1984 Rel: $13 Cur: $17 (2/15/89)
89	RAYMOND Cabernet Sauvignon Napa Valley 1983 Rel: $13 Cur: $20 (2/15/88)
91	RAYMOND Cabernet Sauvignon Napa Valley 1982 Rel: $12 Cur: $16 (11/15/86)
85	RAYMOND Cabernet Sauvignon Napa Valley 1981 Rel: $11 Cur: $17 (CA-3/89)
77	RAYMOND Cabernet Sauvignon Napa Valley 1981 Rel: $11 Cur: $17 (5/01/85)
82	RAYMOND Cabernet Sauvignon Napa Valley 1980 Rel: $12 Cur: $19 (CA-3/89)
81	RAYMOND Cabernet Sauvignon Napa Valley 1980 Rel: $12 Cur: $19 (1/01/84)
85	RAYMOND Cabernet Sauvignon Napa Valley 1979 Rel: $12 Cur: $20 (CA-3/89)
82	RAYMOND Cabernet Sauvignon Napa Valley 1978 Rel: $10 Cur: $30 (CA-3/89)
84	RAYMOND Cabernet Sauvignon Napa Valley 1977 Rel: $8.50 Cur: $27 (CA-3/89)
78	RAYMOND Cabernet Sauvignon Napa Valley 1976 Rel: $6 Cur: $35 (CA-3/89)
78	RAYMOND Cabernet Sauvignon Napa Valley 1974 Rel: $5.50 Cur: $60 (CA-3/89)
90+	RAYMOND Cabernet Sauvignon Napa Valley Private Reserve 1988 (NR) (4/30/90) (BT)
86	RAYMOND Cabernet Sauvignon Napa Valley Private Reserve 1986 Rel: $26 Cur: $26 (CA-3/89)
91	RAYMOND Cabernet Sauvignon Napa Valley Private Reserve 1985 Rel: $24 Cur: $25 (7/15/90) CS
88	RAYMOND Cabernet Sauvignon Napa Valley Private Reserve 1985 Rel: $24 Cur: $25 (CA-3/89)
87	RAYMOND Cabernet Sauvignon Napa Valley Private Reserve 1984 Rel: $20 Cur: $22 (7/15/89)
89	RAYMOND Cabernet Sauvignon Napa Valley Private Reserve 1984 Rel: $20 Cur: $22 (CA-3/89)
84	RAYMOND Cabernet Sauvignon Napa Valley Private Reserve 1983 Rel: $18 Cur: $25 (CA-3/89)
91	RAYMOND Cabernet Sauvignon Napa Valley Private Reserve 1983 Rel: $18 Cur: $25 (6/30/88)
85	RAYMOND Cabernet Sauvignon Napa Valley Private Reserve 1982 Rel: $16 Cur: $27 (CA-3/89)
88	RAYMOND Cabernet Sauvignon Napa Valley Private Reserve 1982 Rel: $16 Cur: $27 (6/15/87)
87	RAYMOND Cabernet Sauvignon Napa Valley Private Reserve 1981 Rel: $16 Cur: $35 (CA-3/89)
92	RAYMOND Cabernet Sauvignon Napa Valley Private Reserve 1981 Rel: $16 Cur: $35 (8/31/86)
85	RAYMOND Cabernet Sauvignon Napa Valley Private Reserve 1980 Cur: $34 (CA-3/89)
83	RENAISSANCE Cabernet Sauvignon North Yuba 1986 $15 (7/15/91)
78	RICHARDSON Cabernet Sauvignon Sonoma Valley 1985 $12 (11/30/88)
83	RIDGE Cabernet Sauvignon Howell Mountain 1983 $12 (3/16/86)
88	RIDGE Cabernet Sauvignon Howell Mountain 1982 $12 (6/01/85)
63	RIDGE Cabernet Sauvignon Napa County 1981 $12 (2/15/84)
88	RIDGE Cabernet Sauvignon Napa County York Creek 1986 $18 (CA-3/89)
92	RIDGE Cabernet Sauvignon Napa County York Creek 1985 Rel: $16 Cur: $18 (CA-3/89)
88	RIDGE Cabernet Sauvignon Napa County York Creek 1984 Rel: $14 Cur: $16 (CA-3/89)
78	RIDGE Cabernet Sauvignon Napa County York Creek 1984 Rel: $14 Cur: $16 (2/15/87)
73	RIDGE Cabernet Sauvignon Napa County York Creek 1983 Rel: $12 Cur: $16 (CA-3/89)
73	RIDGE Cabernet Sauvignon Napa County York Creek 1982 Rel: $12 Cur: $16 (CA-3/89)
76	RIDGE Cabernet Sauvignon Napa County York Creek 1981 Rel: $12 Cur: $20 (CA-3/89)
89	RIDGE Cabernet Sauvignon Napa County York Creek 1981 Rel: $12 Cur: $20 (12/16/84)
88	RIDGE Cabernet Sauvignon Napa County York Creek 1980 Rel: $12 Cur: $30 (CA-3/89)
88	RIDGE Cabernet Sauvignon Napa County York Creek 1979 Rel: $12 Cur: $30 (CA-3/89)
87	RIDGE Cabernet Sauvignon Napa County York Creek 1978 Rel: $12 Cur: $35 (CA-3/89)
88	RIDGE Cabernet Sauvignon Napa County York Creek 1977 Rel: $12 Cur: $35 (CA-3/89)
68	RIDGE Cabernet Sauvignon Napa County York Creek 1976 Rel: $10 Cur: $36 (CA-3/89)
87	RIDGE Cabernet Sauvignon Napa County York Creek 1975 Rel: $10 Cur: $53 (CA-3/89)
87	RIDGE Cabernet Sauvignon Napa County York Creek 1974 Rel: $6.75 Cur: $54 (CA-3/89)
83	RIDGE Cabernet Sauvignon Santa Barbara County Tepusquet Vineyard 1981 $9 (4/16/84)
68	RIDGE Cabernet Sauvignon Santa Cruz Mountains 1986 $15 (10/31/89)
64	RIDGE Cabernet Sauvignon Santa Cruz Mountains 1985 $12 (6/15/89)
64	RIDGE Cabernet Sauvignon Santa Cruz Mountains 1984 $12 (6/15/87)
87	RIDGE Cabernet Sauvignon Santa Cruz Mountains Jimsomare 1985 $16 (2/15/89)
69	RIDGE Cabernet Sauvignon Santa Cruz Mountains Jimsomare 1984 $16 (10/31/87)
78	RIDGE Cabernet Sauvignon Santa Cruz Mountains Jimsomare 1983 $10 (11/30/86)
87	RIDGE Cabernet Sauvignon Santa Cruz Mountains Jimsomare-Monte Bello 1981 $12 (1/01/85)

UNITED STATES
CALIFORNIA/CABERNET SAUVIGNON & BLENDS

90+ RIDGE Cabernet Sauvignon Santa Cruz Mountains Monte Bello 1990 (NR) (5/15/91) (BT)

85+ RIDGE Cabernet Sauvignon Santa Cruz Mountains Monte Bello 1988 (NR) (4/30/90) (BT)

88 RIDGE Cabernet Sauvignon Santa Cruz Mountains Monte Bello 1987 $45 (11/15/90)

80+ RIDGE Cabernet Sauvignon Santa Cruz Mountains Monte Bello 1987 $45 (4/15/89) (BT)

82 RIDGE Cabernet Sauvignon Santa Cruz Mountains Monte Bello 1986 Rel: $35 Cur: $45 (9/15/89)

85 RIDGE Cabernet Sauvignon Santa Cruz Mountains Monte Bello 1986 Rel: $35 Cur: $45 (CA-3/89)

85+ RIDGE Cabernet Sauvignon Santa Cruz Mountains Monte Bello 1986 Rel: $35 Cur: $45 (4/15/88) (BT)

95 RIDGE Cabernet Sauvignon Santa Cruz Mountains Monte Bello 1985 Rel: $40 Cur: $89 (CA-3/89)

95 RIDGE Cabernet Sauvignon Santa Cruz Mountains Monte Bello 1985 Rel: $40 Cur: $89 (7/15/88) CS

90+ RIDGE Cabernet Sauvignon Santa Cruz Mountains Monte Bello 1985 Rel: $40 Cur: $89 (6/15/87) (BT)

97 RIDGE Cabernet Sauvignon Santa Cruz Mountains Monte Bello 1984 Rel: $35 Cur: $80 (CA-3/89)

95 RIDGE Cabernet Sauvignon Santa Cruz Mountains Monte Bello 1984 Rel: $35 Cur: $80 (9/15/87) CS

84 RIDGE Cabernet Sauvignon Santa Cruz Mountains 1983 Rel: $12 Cur: $15 (CA-3/89)

75 RIDGE Cabernet Sauvignon Santa Cruz Mountains Monte Bello 1982 Rel: $18 Cur: $26 (CA-3/89)

75 RIDGE Cabernet Sauvignon Santa Cruz Mountains Monte Bello 1982 Rel: $18 Cur: $26 (11/30/86)

92 RIDGE Cabernet Sauvignon Santa Cruz Mountains Monte Bello 1981 Rel: $25 Cur: $65 (CA-3/89)

89 RIDGE Cabernet Sauvignon Santa Cruz Mountains Monte Bello 1981 Rel: $25 Cur: $65 (8/01/85)

80 RIDGE Cabernet Sauvignon Santa Cruz Mountains Monte Bello 1980 Rel: $30 Cur: $45 (CA-3/89)

70 RIDGE Cabernet Sauvignon Santa Cruz Mountains Monte Bello 1980 Rel: $30 Cur: $45 (4/01/85)

91 RIDGE Cabernet Sauvignon Santa Cruz Mountains Monte Bello 1978 Rel: $30 Cur: $94 (CA-3/89)

94 RIDGE Cabernet Sauvignon Santa Cruz Mountains Monte Bello 1977 Rel: $40 Cur: $100 (CA-3/89)

83 RIDGE Cabernet Sauvignon Santa Cruz Mountains Monte Bello 1976 Rel: $15 Cur: $65 (CA-3/89)

88 RIDGE Cabernet Sauvignon Santa Cruz Mountains Monte Bello 1975 Rel: $10 Cur: $95 (CA-3/89)

92 RIDGE Cabernet Sauvignon Santa Cruz Mountains Monte Bello 1974 Rel: $12 Cur: $155 (2/15/90) (JG)

93 RIDGE Cabernet Sauvignon Santa Cruz Mountains Monte Bello 1974 Rel: $12 Cur: $155 (CA-3/89)

87 RIDGE Cabernet Sauvignon Santa Cruz Mountains Monte Bello 1973 Rel: $10 Cur: $110 (CA-3/89)

84 RIDGE Cabernet Sauvignon Santa Cruz Mountains Monte Bello 1972 Rel: $10 Cur: $100 (CA-3/89)

85 RIDGE Cabernet Sauvignon Santa Cruz Mountains Monte Bello 1971 Rel: $10 Cur: $164 (CA-3/89)

85 RIDGE Cabernet Sauvignon Santa Cruz Mountains Monte Bello 1971 Rel: $10 Cur: $164 (4/01/86)

96 RIDGE Cabernet Sauvignon Santa Cruz Mountains Monte Bello 1970 Rel: $10 Cur: $197 (CA-3/89)

92 RIDGE Cabernet Sauvignon Santa Cruz Mountains Monte Bello 1969 Rel: $7.50 Cur: $200 (CA-3/89)

87 RIDGE Cabernet Sauvignon Santa Cruz Mountains Monte Bello 1968 Rel: $7.50 Cur: $200 (CA-3/89)

86 RIDGE Cabernet Sauvignon Santa Cruz Mountains Monte Bello 1965 Rel: $6.50 Cur: $280 (CA-3/89)

90 RIDGE Cabernet Sauvignon Santa Cruz Mountains Monte Bello 1964 Rel: $6.50 Cur: $310 (CA-3/89)

70 RIDGE Cabernet Sauvignon Santa Cruz Mountains Monte Bello 1963 Rel: $5 Cur: $490 (CA-3/89)

75 RIVER OAKS Cabernet Sauvignon North Coast 1984 $6 (10/15/87)

75 RIVER OAKS Cabernet Sauvignon Sonoma County 1983 $6 (12/15/86)

82 RIVER OAKS Cabernet Sauvignon Sonoma County 1982 $6 (4/01/85) BB

76 RIVER OAKS Cabernet Sauvignon Sonoma County 1981 $6 (7/01/84)

72 RIVERSIDE FARM Cabernet Sauvignon California 1985 $4.50 (5/31/88)

77 RIVERSIDE FARM Cabernet Sauvignon North Coast 1983 $3.75 (9/15/86)

86 ROLLING HILLS Cabernet Sauvignon California 1987 $7 (12/15/89) BB

88 ROMBAUER Cabernet Sauvignon Napa Valley 1986 Rel: $15 Cur: $16 (4/15/90)

86 ROMBAUER Cabernet Sauvignon Napa Valley 1986 Rel: $15 Cur: $16 (CA-3/89)

85 ROMBAUER Cabernet Sauvignon Napa Valley 1985 Rel: $14.75 Cur: $17 (4/30/89)

85 ROMBAUER Cabernet Sauvignon Napa Valley 1985 Rel: $14.75 Cur: $17 (CA-3/89)

75 ROMBAUER Cabernet Sauvignon Napa Valley 1985 Rel: $14.75 Cur: $17 (2/15/89)

84 ROMBAUER Cabernet Sauvignon Napa Valley 1984 Rel: $13.50 Cur: $21 (CA-3/89)

80 ROMBAUER Cabernet Sauvignon Napa Valley 1984 Rel: $13.50 Cur: $21 (2/15/88)

73 ROMBAUER Cabernet Sauvignon Napa Valley 1983 Rel: $13.50 Cur: $19 (CA-3/89)

73 ROMBAUER Cabernet Sauvignon Napa Valley 1983 Rel: $13.50 Cur: $19 (9/15/87)

83 ROMBAUER Cabernet Sauvignon Napa Valley 1982 Cur: $33 (CA-3/89)

91 ROMBAUER Cabernet Sauvignon Napa Valley 1982 Cur: $33 (2/16/86)

82 ROMBAUER Cabernet Sauvignon Napa Valley 1981 Cur: $24 (CA-3/89)

88 ROMBAUER Cabernet Sauvignon Napa Valley 1981 Rel: $12 Cur: $24 (12/16/84)

86 ROMBAUER Cabernet Sauvignon Napa Valley 1980 Rel: $10 Cur: $25 (CA-3/89)

84 ROMBAUER Le Meilleur du Chai Napa Valley 1986 $35 (5/15/91)

89 ROMBAUER Le Meilleur du Chai Napa Valley 1986 $35 (CA-3/89)

90 ROMBAUER Le Meilleur du Chai Napa Valley 1985 Rel: $37.50 Cur: $42 (10/31/89)

90 ROMBAUER Le Meilleur du Chai Napa Valley 1985 Rel: $37.50 Cur: $42 (CA-3/89)

94 ROMBAUER Le Meilleur du Chai Napa Valley 1984 Rel: $32.50 Cur: $47 (3/31/89)

90 ROMBAUER Le Meilleur du Chai Napa Valley 1984 Rel: $32.50 Cur: $47 (CA-3/89)

90 ROMBAUER Le Meilleur du Chai Napa Valley 1983 Rel: $30 Cur: $45 (CA-3/89)

81 ROUDON-SMITH Cabernet Sauvignon Santa Cruz Mountains 1986 $12 (3/15/91)

78 ROUDON-SMITH Cabernet Sauvignon Santa Cruz Mountains 1984 $12 (6/30/88)

76 ROUND HILL Cabernet Sauvignon California House Lot 5 NV $5 (9/30/86) BB

72 ROUND HILL Cabernet Sauvignon California House Lot 6 NV $5 (10/15/87)

78 ROUND HILL Cabernet Sauvignon California House Lot 7 NV $6.25 (2/15/89)

79 ROUND HILL Cabernet Sauvignon California Lot 7 NV $6 (10/31/90)

82 ROUND HILL Cabernet Sauvignon Napa Valley 1986 $8 (10/15/88)

84 ROUND HILL Cabernet Sauvignon Napa Valley 1984 $8.50 (5/31/88)

88 ROUND HILL Cabernet Sauvignon Napa Valley 1982 $9 (5/16/86)

86 ROUND HILL Cabernet Sauvignon Napa Valley 1981 $9 (3/16/85)

81 ROUND HILL Cabernet Sauvignon Napa Valley 1980 $7.50 (4/16/84)

80 ROUND HILL Cabernet Sauvignon Napa Valley Reserve 1986 $9 (6/30/90)

86 ROUND HILL Cabernet Sauvignon Napa Valley Reserve 1985 $10.50 (5/31/88)

88 ROUND HILL Cabernet Sauvignon Napa Valley Reserve 1984 $10 (10/31/87)

92 ROUND HILL Cabernet Sauvignon Napa Valley Reserve 1983 $9.50 (12/15/86)

79 ROUND HILL Cabernet Sauvignon California House Lot 8 NV $6.25 (7/31/91)

72 RUTHERFORD ESTATE Cabernet Sauvignon Napa Valley 1984 $5 (11/15/87)

68 RUTHERFORD HILL Cabernet Sauvignon Napa Valley 1986 $14 (2/28/91)

75+ RUTHERFORD HILL Cabernet Sauvignon Napa Valley 1986 $14 (4/15/88) (BT)

82 RUTHERFORD HILL Cabernet Sauvignon Napa Valley 1985 Rel: $14 Cur: $16 (4/30/90)

80+ RUTHERFORD HILL Cabernet Sauvignon Napa Valley 1985 Rel: $14 Cur: $16 (6/15/87) (BT)

88 RUTHERFORD HILL Cabernet Sauvignon Napa Valley 1984 Rel: $12.50 Cur: $15 (CA-3/89)

88 RUTHERFORD HILL Cabernet Sauvignon Napa Valley 1984 Rel: $12.50 Cur: $15 (8/31/88)

83 RUTHERFORD HILL Cabernet Sauvignon Napa Valley 1983 Rel: $12.50 Cur: $16 (CA-3/89)

83 RUTHERFORD HILL Cabernet Sauvignon Napa Valley 1983 Rel: $12.50 Cur: $16 (9/15/87)

83 RUTHERFORD HILL Cabernet Sauvignon Napa Valley 1982 Rel: $12.50 Cur: $23 (CA-3/89)

88 RUTHERFORD HILL Cabernet Sauvignon Napa Valley 1982 Rel: $12.50 Cur: $23 (11/15/84)

85 RUTHERFORD HILL Cabernet Sauvignon Napa Valley 1981 Rel: $11.50 Cur: $19 (CA-3/89)

90 RUTHERFORD HILL Cabernet Sauvignon Napa Valley 1981 Rel: $11.50 Cur: $19 (6/01/86)

82 RUTHERFORD HILL Cabernet Sauvignon Napa Valley 1980 Rel: $11.50 Cur: $21 (CA-3/89)

82 RUTHERFORD HILL Cabernet Sauvignon Napa Valley 1980 Rel: $11.50 Cur: $21 (10/16/84)

88 RUTHERFORD HILL Cabernet Sauvignon Napa Valley Cask Lot 2 Limited Edition 1980 Rel: $11.50 Cur: $21 (CA-3/89)

92 RUTHERFORD HILL Cabernet Sauvignon Napa Valley Cask Lot 2 Limited Edition 1980 Rel: $11.50 Cur: $21 (7/31/87)

87 RUTHERFORD HILL Cabernet Sauvignon Napa Valley 1979 Rel: $11.50 Cur: $22 (CA-3/89)

82 RUTHERFORD HILL Cabernet Sauvignon Napa Valley 1978 Rel: $12 Cur: $25 (CA-3/89)

72 RUTHERFORD HILL Cabernet Sauvignon Napa Valley 1977 Rel: $10 Cur: $18 (CA-3/89)

73 RUTHERFORD HILL Cabernet Sauvignon Napa Valley 1976 Rel: $9 Cur: $17 (CA-3/89)

69 RUTHERFORD HILL Cabernet Sauvignon Napa Valley 1975 Rel: $9 Cur: $18 (CA-3/89)

88 RUTHERFORD HILL Cabernet Sauvignon Napa Valley XVS 1986 (NR) (CA-3/89)

88 RUTHERFORD HILL Cabernet Sauvignon Napa Valley XVS 1985 Rel: $25 Cur: $27 (4/30/89)

89 RUTHERFORD HILL Cabernet Sauvignon Napa Valley XVS 1985 Rel: $25 Cur: $27 (CA-3/89)

83 RUTHERFORD RANCH Cabernet Sauvignon Napa Valley 1987 $13 (4/30/91)

92 RUTHERFORD RANCH Cabernet Sauvignon Napa Valley 1985 Rel: $11 Cur: $11 (5/15/90) SS

85 RUTHERFORD RANCH Cabernet Sauvignon Napa Valley 1984 Rel: $12.50 Cur: $13 (5/31/89)

83 RUTHERFORD RANCH Cabernet Sauvignon Napa Valley 1983 Rel: $10.25 Cur: $11 (12/31/87)

84 RUTHERFORD RANCH Cabernet Sauvignon Napa Valley 1982 Rel: $9 Cur: $9 (6/15/87)

87 ST. ANDREW'S WINERY Cabernet Sauvignon Napa Valley 1986 $14.50 (4/30/90)

80+ ST. ANDREW'S WINERY Cabernet Sauvignon Napa Valley 1986 $14.50 (4/15/88) (BT)

89 ST. ANDREW'S WINERY Cabernet Sauvignon Napa Valley 1985 $10.50 (5/15/88)

90 ST. CLEMENT Cabernet Sauvignon Napa Valley 1986 Rel: $18 Cur: $18 (9/30/90)

87 ST. CLEMENT Cabernet Sauvignon Napa Valley 1986 Rel: $18 Cur: $18 (CA-3/89)

90 ST. CLEMENT Cabernet Sauvignon Napa Valley 1985 Rel: $17 Cur: $19 (3/15/90)

93 ST. CLEMENT Cabernet Sauvignon Napa Valley 1985 Rel: $17 Cur: $19 (CA-3/89)

90+ ST. CLEMENT Cabernet Sauvignon Napa Valley 1985 Rel: $17 Cur: $19 (6/15/87) (BT)

89 ST. CLEMENT Cabernet Sauvignon Napa Valley 1984 Rel: $15 Cur: $17 (CA-3/89)

90 ST. CLEMENT Cabernet Sauvignon Napa Valley 1984 Rel: $15 Cur: $17 (10/15/88)

91 ST. CLEMENT Cabernet Sauvignon Napa Valley 1983 Rel: $14.50 Cur: $17 (CA-3/89)

89 ST. CLEMENT Cabernet Sauvignon Napa Valley 1983 Rel: $14.50 Cur: $17 (6/01/86)

91 ST. CLEMENT Cabernet Sauvignon Napa Valley 1982 Rel: $13.50 Cur: $20 (CA-3/89)

92 ST. CLEMENT Cabernet Sauvignon Napa Valley 1982 Rel: $13.50 Cur: $20 (3/16/85) CS

85 ST. CLEMENT Cabernet Sauvignon Napa Valley 1981 Rel: $12.50 Cur: $24 (CA-3/89)

89 ST. CLEMENT Cabernet Sauvignon Napa Valley 1981 Rel: $12.50 Cur: $24 (6/01/84) SS

82 ST. CLEMENT Cabernet Sauvignon Napa Valley 1980 Rel: $12.50 Cur: $25 (CA-3/89)

90 ST. CLEMENT Cabernet Sauvignon Napa Valley 1979 Rel: $11 Cur: $35 (CA-3/89)

88 ST. CLEMENT Cabernet Sauvignon Napa Valley 1978 Rel: $10 Cur: $40 (CA-3/89)

90 ST. CLEMENT Cabernet Sauvignon Napa Valley 1977 Rel: $10 Cur: $45 (CA-3/89)

87 ST. CLEMENT Cabernet Sauvignon Napa Valley 1975-76 Rel: $8 Cur: $50 (CA-3/89)

88 ST. FRANCIS Cabernet Sauvignon California 1985 $9 (11/30/87)

89 ST. FRANCIS Cabernet Sauvignon Sonoma County 1986 $12 (1/31/90)

90+ ST. FRANCIS Cabernet Sauvignon Sonoma Mountain 1986 $20 (4/15/88) (BT)

94 ST. FRANCIS Cabernet Sauvignon Sonoma Valley Reserve (Black Label) 1986 $20 (11/30/89)

85 ST. SUPERY Cabernet Sauvignon Napa Valley Dollarhide Ranch 1987 $13 (7/15/90)

77 SANTA BARBARA Cabernet Sauvignon Santa Ynez Valley 1987 $18 (11/15/90)

81 SANTA BARBARA Cabernet Sauvignon Santa Ynez Valley Reserve 1984 $13.50 (10/31/87)

81 SANTA BARBARA Cabernet Sauvignon Santa Ynez Valley Reserve 1974 $16 (12/15/89)

85+ SANTA CRUZ MOUNTAIN Cabernet Sauvignon Santa Cruz Mountains Bates Ranch 1989 (NR) (5/15/91) (BT)

85+ SANTA CRUZ MOUNTAIN Cabernet Sauvignon Santa Cruz Mountains Bates Ranch 1988 (NR) (4/30/90) (BT)

90+ SANTA CRUZ MOUNTAIN Cabernet Sauvignon Santa Cruz Mountains Bates Ranch 1987 (NR) (4/15/89) (BT)

93 SANTA CRUZ MOUNTAIN Cabernet Sauvignon Santa Cruz Mountains Bates Ranch 1986 (NR) (CA-3/89)

90+ SANTA CRUZ MOUNTAIN Cabernet Sauvignon Santa Cruz Mountains Bates Ranch 1986 (NR) (4/15/88) (BT)

92 SANTA CRUZ MOUNTAIN Cabernet Sauvignon Santa Cruz Mountains Bates Ranch 1985 (NA) (CA-3/89)

80+ SANTA CRUZ MOUNTAIN Cabernet Sauvignon Santa Cruz Mountains Bates Ranch 1985 (NR) (6/15/87) (BT)

87 SANTA CRUZ MOUNTAIN Cabernet Sauvignon Santa Cruz Mountains Bates Ranch 1984 Rel: $14 Cur: $14 (CA-3/89)

80 SANTA CRUZ MOUNTAIN Cabernet Sauvignon Santa Cruz Mountains Bates Ranch 1983 Rel: $12 Cur: $12 (6/15/89)

84 SANTA CRUZ MOUNTAIN Cabernet Sauvignon Santa Cruz Mountains Bates Ranch 1983 Rel: $12 Cur: $12 (CA-3/89)

72 SANTA CRUZ MOUNTAIN Cabernet Sauvignon Santa Cruz Mountains Bates Ranch 1982 Rel: $12 Cur: $15 (CA-3/89)

79 SANTA CRUZ MOUNTAIN Cabernet Sauvignon Santa Cruz Mountains Bates Ranch 1981 Rel: $12 Cur: $20 (CA-3/89)

88 SANTA CRUZ MOUNTAIN Cabernet Sauvignon Santa Cruz Mountains Bates Ranch 1981 Rel: $12 Cur: $20 (3/01/85)

86 SANTA CRUZ MOUNTAIN Cabernet Sauvignon Santa Cruz Mountains Bates Ranch 1980 Rel: $12 Cur: $27 (CA-3/89)

79 SANTA CRUZ MOUNTAIN Cabernet Sauvignon Santa Cruz Mountains Bates Ranch 1979 Rel: $12 Cur: $35 (CA-3/89)

90 SANTA CRUZ MOUNTAIN Cabernet Sauvignon Santa Cruz Mountains Bates Ranch 1978 Rel: $12 Cur: $35 (CA-3/89)

72 SANTA YNEZ VALLEY Cabernet-Merlot Santa Barbara County 1987 $13 (3/31/90)

88 V. SATTUI Cabernet Sauvignon Napa Valley Preston Vineyard 1986 Rel: $16.75 Cur: $18 (CA-3/89)

87 V. SATTUI Cabernet Sauvignon Napa Valley Preston Vineyard 1985 Rel: $15.75 Cur: $18 (CA-3/89)

86 V. SATTUI Cabernet Sauvignon Napa Valley Preston Vineyard 1984 Rel: $13.75 Cur: $20 (CA-3/89)

81 V. SATTUI Cabernet Sauvignon Napa Valley Preston Vineyard 1983 Rel: $13.75 Cur: $20 (CA-3/89)

78 V. SATTUI Cabernet Sauvignon Napa Valley Preston Vineyard Reserve 1982 Rel: $22.50 Cur: $30 (CA-3/89)

85 V. SATTUI Cabernet Sauvignon Napa Valley Preston Vineyard Reserve 1980 Rel: $30 Cur: $45 (CA-3/89)

74 SAUSAL Cabernet Sauvignon Alexander Valley 1985 $12 (7/31/89)

71 SBARBORO Cabernet Sauvignon Sonoma County 1983 $10 (11/15/87)

58 SEBASTIANI Cabernet Sauvignon North Coast Proprietor's Reserve 1979 $11 (8/01/84)

80 SEBASTIANI Cabernet Sauvignon Sonoma County Family Selection 1985 $8 (10/15/88)

86 SEBASTIANI Cabernet Sauvignon Sonoma County Reserve 1986 $13 (1/31/91)

86 SEBASTIANI Cabernet Sauvignon Sonoma County Reserve 1985 $12.50 (11/15/90)

75 SEBASTIANI Cabernet Sauvignon Sonoma Valley Eagle Vineyards 1982 $26.50 (9/15/86)

91 SEBASTIANI Cabernet Sauvignon Sonoma Valley Eagle Vineyards 1981 $25 (8/01/85)

74 SEBASTIANI Cabernet Sauvignon Sonoma Valley Reserve 1982 $11 (12/31/87)

89 SEBASTIANI ESTATES Cabernet Sauvignon Sonoma Valley Cherry Block 1985 $16.50 (3/31/90)

88 SAM J. SEBASTIANI Cabernet Sauvignon Sonoma-Napa Counties 1983 $15 (11/30/86)

85 SEGHESIO Cabernet Sauvignon Sonoma County 1987 $9 (4/30/91)

76 SEGHESIO Cabernet Sauvignon Northern Sonoma 1986 $8 (6/30/90)

84 SEGHESIO Cabernet Sauvignon Northern Sonoma 1985 $5.50 (4/15/89) BB

69 SEGHESIO Cabernet Sauvignon Northern Sonoma 1983 $6.75 (7/15/88)

77 SEGHESIO Cabernet Sauvignon Northern Sonoma 1982 $5 (4/30/87)

90+ SEQUOIA GROVE Cabernet Sauvignon Napa Valley Estate 1988 (NR) (4/30/90) (BT)

84 SEQUOIA GROVE Cabernet Sauvignon Napa Valley Estate 1986 Rel: $22 Cur: $25 (9/30/89)

90 SEQUOIA GROVE Cabernet Sauvignon Napa Valley Estate 1986 Rel: $22 Cur: $25 (CA-3/89)

92 SEQUOIA GROVE Cabernet Sauvignon Napa Valley Estate 1985 Rel: $28 Cur: $32 (CA-3/89)

92 SEQUOIA GROVE Cabernet Sauvignon Napa Valley Estate 1985 Rel: $28 Cur: $32 (8/31/88)

82 SEQUOIA GROVE Cabernet Sauvignon Napa Valley Estate 1982 Rel: $14 Cur: $22 (CA-3/89)

78 SEQUOIA GROVE Cabernet Sauvignon Napa County 1986 Rel: $16 Cur: $16 (9/30/89)

88 SEQUOIA GROVE Cabernet Sauvignon Napa County 1986 Rel: $16 Cur: $16 (CA-3/89)

86 SEQUOIA GROVE Cabernet Sauvignon Napa County 1985 Rel: $16 Cur: $16 (CA-3/89)

86 SEQUOIA GROVE Cabernet Sauvignon Napa County 1985 Rel: $16 Cur: $16 (12/15/88)

85 SEQUOIA GROVE Cabernet Sauvignon Napa Valley 1984 Rel: $12 Cur: $18 (CA-3/89)

82 SEQUOIA GROVE Cabernet Sauvignon Napa Valley 1984 Rel: $12 Cur: $18 (11/15/87)

77 SEQUOIA GROVE Cabernet Sauvignon Napa-Alexander Valleys 1983 Rel: $12.50 Cur: $18 (CA-3/89)

88 SEQUOIA GROVE Cabernet Sauvignon Napa-Alexander Valleys 1983 Rel: $12.50 Cur: $18 (2/15/87)

78 SEQUOIA GROVE Cabernet Sauvignon Napa-Alexander Valleys 1982 Rel: $12 Cur: $20 (CA-3/89)

83 SEQUOIA GROVE Cabernet Sauvignon Napa-Alexander Valleys 1982 Rel: $12 Cur: $20 (12/16/85)

84 SEQUOIA GROVE Cabernet Sauvignon Alexander Valley 1981 Rel: $12 Cur: $25 (CA-3/89)

80 SEQUOIA GROVE Cabernet Sauvignon Napa Valley 1981 Rel: $12 Cur: $25 (CA-3/89)

87 SEQUOIA GROVE Cabernet Sauvignon Alexander Valley 1981 Rel: $12 Cur: $25 (12/16/84)

87 SEQUOIA GROVE Cabernet Sauvignon Napa Valley 1981 Rel: $12 Cur: $25 (3/01/84)

85 SEQUOIA GROVE Cabernet Sauvignon Napa Valley Cask One 1980 Rel: $12 Cur: $30 (CA-3/89)

87 SEQUOIA GROVE Cabernet Sauvignon Napa Valley Cask Two 1980 Rel: $12 Cur: $30 (CA-3/89)

84 SHADOWBROOK Cabernet Sauvignon Napa Valley 1985 $9.50 (7/15/91)

90+ SHAFER Cabernet Sauvignon Napa Valley Stags Leap District 1988 $19 (4/30/90) (BT)

92 SHAFER Cabernet Sauvignon Napa Valley Stags Leap District 1987 Rel: $18 Cur: $19 (7/31/90)

93 SHAFER Cabernet Sauvignon Napa Valley Stags Leap District 1986 Rel: $16 Cur: $20 (9/30/89) SS

93 SHAFER Cabernet Sauvignon Napa Valley Stags Leap District 1986 Rel: $16 Cur: $20 (CA-3/89)

91 SHAFER Cabernet Sauvignon Napa Valley Stags Leap District 1985 Rel: $15.50 Cur: $16 (CA-3/89)

88 SHAFER Cabernet Sauvignon Napa Valley Stags Leap District 1985 Rel: $15.50 Cur: $16 (11/15/88)

91 SHAFER Cabernet Sauvignon Napa Valley Stags Leap District 1984 Rel: $14 Cur: $25 (CA-3/89)

93 SHAFER Cabernet Sauvignon Napa Valley Stags Leap District 1984 Rel: $14 Cur: $25 (12/15/87) SS

87 SHAFER Cabernet Sauvignon Napa Valley Stags Leap District 1983 Rel: $13 Cur: $13 (CA-3/89)

88 SHAFER Cabernet Sauvignon Napa Valley Stags Leap District 1982 Rel: $13 Cur: $18 (CA-3/89)

90 SHAFER Cabernet Sauvignon Napa Valley Stags Leap District 1982 Rel: $13 Cur: $18 (6/16/85)

77 SHAFER Cabernet Sauvignon Napa Valley Stags Leap District 1980 Rel: $12 Cur: $25 (CA-3/89)

73 SHAFER Cabernet Sauvignon Napa Valley Stags Leap District 1980 Rel: $12 Cur: $25 (2/15/84)

89 SHAFER Cabernet Sauvignon Napa Valley Stags Leap District 1979 Rel: $12 Cur: $35 (CA-3/89)

85 SHAFER Cabernet Sauvignon Napa Valley Stags Leap District 1978 Rel: $11 Cur: $50 (CA-3/89)

90+ SHAFER Cabernet Sauvignon Napa Valley Stags Leap District Hillside Select 1990 (NR) (5/15/91) (BT)

85+ SHAFER Cabernet Sauvignon Napa Valley Stags Leap District Hillside Select 1989 (NR) (5/15/91) (BT)

85+ SHAFER Cabernet Sauvignon Napa Valley Stags Leap District Hillside Select 1987 (NR) (4/15/89) (BT)

91 SHAFER Cabernet Sauvignon Napa Valley Stags Leap District Hillside Select 1986 $32 (3/15/91)

92 SHAFER Cabernet Sauvignon Napa Valley Stags Leap District Hillside Select 1986 $32 (CA-3/89)

85+ SHAFER Cabernet Sauvignon Napa Valley Stags Leap District Hillside Select 1986 $32 (4/15/88) (BT)

91 SHAFER Cabernet Sauvignon Napa Valley Stags Leap District Hillside Select 1985 Rel: $24.50 Cur: $28 (5/31/90) CS

93 SHAFER Cabernet Sauvignon Napa Valley Stags Leap District Hillside Select 1985 Rel: $24.50 Cur: $28 (CA-3/89)

90+ SHAFER Cabernet Sauvignon Napa Valley Stags Leap District Hillside Select 1985 Rel: $24.50 Cur: $28 (6/15/87) (BT)

89 SHAFER Cabernet Sauvignon Napa Valley Stags Leap District Hillside Select 1984 Rel: $24.50 Cur: $33 (4/30/89)

92 SHAFER Cabernet Sauvignon Napa Valley Stags Leap District Hillside Select 1984 Rel: $24.50 Cur: $33 (CA-3/89)

89 SHAFER Cabernet Sauvignon Napa Valley Stags Leap District Hillside Select 1983 Rel: $22 Cur: $24 (CA-3/89)

84 SHAFER Cabernet Sauvignon Napa Valley Stags Leap District Hillside Select 1983 Rel: $22 Cur: $24 (7/31/88)

89 SHAFER Cabernet Sauvignon Napa Valley Stags Leap District Reserve 1982 Rel: $18 Cur: $25 (CA-3/89)

80 SHENANDOAH Cabernet Sauvignon Amador County Artist Series 1987 $10 (2/28/91)

86 SHENANDOAH Cabernet Sauvignon Amador County Artist Series 1986 $12 (10/31/88)

89 SHENANDOAH Cabernet Sauvignon Amador County Artist Series 1984 $9 (8/31/87)

63 SHOWN AND SONS Cabernet Sauvignon Napa Valley Rutherford 1979 $15 (4/01/84)

86 SIERRA VISTA Cabernet Sauvignon El Dorado 1984 $9 (3/31/88)

92 SIGNORELLO Cabernet Sauvignon Napa Valley Founder's Reserve 1988 $25 (5/15/91)

93 SILVER OAK Cabernet Sauvignon Alexander Valley 1986 Rel: $26 Cur: $37 (10/31/90) SS

86 SILVER OAK Cabernet Sauvignon Alexander Valley 1985 Rel: $24 Cur: $45 (10/31/89)

95 SILVER OAK Cabernet Sauvignon Alexander Valley 1985 Rel: $24 Cur: $45 (CA-3/89)

75+ SILVER OAK Cabernet Sauvignon Alexander Valley 1985 Rel: $24 Cur: $45 (6/15/87) (BT)

89 SILVER OAK Cabernet Sauvignon Alexander Valley 1984 Rel: $22 Cur: $50 (CA-3/89)

85 SILVER OAK Cabernet Sauvignon Alexander Valley 1984 Rel: $22 Cur: $50 (12/15/88)

86 SILVER OAK Cabernet Sauvignon Alexander Valley 1983 Rel: $20 Cur: $40 (CA-3/89)

82 SILVER OAK Cabernet Sauvignon Alexander Valley 1983 Rel: $20 Cur: $40 (11/30/87)

90 SILVER OAK Cabernet Sauvignon Alexander Valley 1982 Rel: $19 Cur: $65 (CA-3/89)

90 SILVER OAK Cabernet Sauvignon Alexander Valley 1982 Rel: $19 Cur: $65 (2/15/87)

86 SILVER OAK Cabernet Sauvignon Alexander Valley 1981 Rel: $19 Cur: $65 (CA-3/89)

92 SILVER OAK Cabernet Sauvignon Alexander Valley 1981 Rel: $19 Cur: $65 (9/30/86)

88 SILVER OAK Cabernet Sauvignon Alexander Valley 1980 Rel: $18 Cur: $50 (CA-3/89)

90 SILVER OAK Cabernet Sauvignon Alexander Valley 1980 Rel: $18 Cur: $50 (3/01/85)

85 SILVER OAK Cabernet Sauvignon Alexander Valley 1979 Rel: $16 Cur: $65 (CA-3/89)

81 SILVER OAK Cabernet Sauvignon Alexander Valley 1979 Rel: $16 Cur: $65 (2/15/84)

93 SILVER OAK Cabernet Sauvignon Alexander Valley 1978 Rel: $16 Cur: $78 (CA-3/89)

91 SILVER OAK Cabernet Sauvignon Alexander Valley 1978 Rel: $16 Cur: $78 (4/30/87)

88 SILVER OAK Cabernet Sauvignon Alexander Valley 1977 Rel: $14 Cur: $75 (CA-3/89)

86 SILVER OAK Cabernet Sauvignon Alexander Valley 1976 Rel: $12 Cur: $65 (CA-3/89)

88 SILVER OAK Cabernet Sauvignon Alexander Valley 1975 Rel: $10 Cur: $98 (CA-3/89)

82 SILVER OAK Cabernet Sauvignon North Coast 1974 Rel: $8 Cur: $135 (2/15/90) (JG)

93 SILVER OAK Cabernet Sauvignon North Coast 1974 Rel: $8 Cur: $135 (CA-3/89)

81 SILVER OAK Cabernet Sauvignon North Coast 1973 Rel: $7 Cur: $130 (CA-3/89)

86 SILVER OAK Cabernet Sauvignon North Coast 1972 Rel: $6 Cur: $135 (CA-3/89)

94 SILVER OAK Cabernet Sauvignon Napa Valley 1986 Rel: $26 Cur: $40 (10/31/90) CS

88 SILVER OAK Cabernet Sauvignon Napa Valley 1985 Rel: $24 Cur: $60 (10/31/89)

85 SILVER OAK Cabernet Sauvignon Napa Valley 1985 Rel: $24 Cur: $60 (CA-3/89)

80+ SILVER OAK Cabernet Sauvignon Napa Valley 1985 Rel: $24 Cur: $60 (6/15/87) (BT)

86 SILVER OAK Cabernet Sauvignon Napa Valley 1984 Rel: $22 Cur: $55 (CA-3/89)

88 SILVER OAK Cabernet Sauvignon Napa Valley 1984 Rel: $22 Cur: $55 (12/15/88)

74 SILVER OAK Cabernet Sauvignon Napa Valley 1983 Rel: $20 Cur: $42 (CA-3/89)

87 SILVER OAK Cabernet Sauvignon Napa Valley 1983 Rel: $20 Cur: $42 (11/30/87)

88 SILVER OAK Cabernet Sauvignon Napa Valley 1982 Rel: $19 Cur: $53 (CA-3/89)

96 SILVER OAK Cabernet Sauvignon Napa Valley 1982 Rel: $19 Cur: $53 (2/15/87) CS

79 SILVER OAK Cabernet Sauvignon Napa Valley 1981 Rel: $19 Cur: $62 (CA-3/89)

75 SILVER OAK Cabernet Sauvignon Napa Valley 1981 Rel: $19 Cur: $62 (9/15/86)

73 SILVER OAK Cabernet Sauvignon Napa Valley 1980 Rel: $18 Cur: $60 (CA-3/89)

80 SILVER OAK Cabernet Sauvignon Napa Valley 1980 Rel: $18 Cur: $60 (3/01/85)

82 SILVER OAK Cabernet Sauvignon Napa Valley 1979 Rel: $18 Cur: $74 (CA-3/89)

83 SILVER OAK Cabernet Sauvignon Napa Valley 1979 Rel: $18 Cur: $74 (3/01/84)

83 SILVER OAK Cabernet Sauvignon Napa Valley Bonny's Vineyard 1985 $50 (11/15/90)

85 SILVER OAK Cabernet Sauvignon Napa Valley Bonny's Vineyard 1985 $50 (CA-3/89)

84 SILVER OAK Cabernet Sauvignon Napa Valley Bonny's Vineyard 1984 Rel: $45 Cur: $80 (10/15/89)

84 SILVER OAK Cabernet Sauvignon Napa Valley Bonny's Vineyard 1984 Rel: $45 Cur: $80 (CA-3/89)

82 SILVER OAK Cabernet Sauvignon Napa Valley Bonny's Vineyard 1983 Rel: $40 Cur: $79 (CA-3/89)

78 SILVER OAK Cabernet Sauvignon Napa Valley Bonny's Vineyard 1982 Rel: $35 Cur: $59 (CA-3/89)

66 SILVER OAK Cabernet Sauvignon Napa Valley Bonny's Vineyard 1982 Rel: $35 Cur: $59 (9/15/87)

UNITED STATES

CALIFORNIA/CABERNET SAUVIGNON & BLENDS

77 SILVER OAK Cabernet Sauvignon Napa Valley Bonny's Vineyard 1981 Rel: $35 Cur: $60 (CA-3/89)
70 SILVER OAK Cabernet Sauvignon Napa Valley Bonny's Vineyard 1980 Rel: $30 Cur: $60 (CA-3/89)
72 SILVER OAK Cabernet Sauvignon Napa Valley Bonny's Vineyard 1979 Rel: $30 Cur: $60 (CA-3/89)
81 SILVER OAK Cabernet Sauvignon Napa Valley Bonny's Vineyard 1979 Rel: $30 Cur: $60 (6/16/84)
86 SILVERADO Cabernet Sauvignon Napa Valley Stags Leap District 1988 $16 (3/31/91)
92 SILVERADO Cabernet Sauvignon Napa Valley Stags Leap District 1987 Rel: $14 Cur: $18 (4/15/90) SS
90+ SILVERADO Cabernet Sauvignon Napa Valley Stags Leap District 1987 Rel: $14 Cur: $18 (4/15/89) (BT)
94 SILVERADO Cabernet Sauvignon Napa Valley Stags Leap District 1986 Rel: $13.50 Cur: $18 (8/31/89) SS
94 SILVERADO Cabernet Sauvignon Napa Valley Stags Leap District 1986 Rel: $13.50 Cur: $18 (CA-3/89)
92 SILVERADO Cabernet Sauvignon Napa Valley Stags Leap District 1985 Rel: $12.50 Cur: $20 (CA-3/89)
91 SILVERADO Cabernet Sauvignon Napa Valley Stags Leap District 1985 Rel: $12.50 Cur: $20 (11/15/88) SS
91 SILVERADO Cabernet Sauvignon Napa Valley Stags Leap District 1984 Rel: $11.50 Cur: $22 (CA-3/89)
89 SILVERADO Cabernet Sauvignon Napa Valley Stags Leap District 1984 Rel: $11.50 Cur: $22 (11/30/87)
88 SILVERADO Cabernet Sauvignon Napa Valley Stags Leap District 1983 Rel: $11 Cur: $22 (CA-3/89)
92 SILVERADO Cabernet Sauvignon Napa Valley Stags Leap District 1983 Rel: $11 Cur: $22 (12/31/86)
88 SILVERADO Cabernet Sauvignon Napa Valley Stags Leap District 1982 Rel: $11 Cur: $22 (CA-3/89)
82 SILVERADO Cabernet Sauvignon Napa Valley Stags Leap District 1982 Rel: $11 Cur: $22 (9/30/86)
90 SILVERADO Cabernet Sauvignon Napa Valley Stags Leap District 1981 Rel: $11 Cur: $25 (CA-3/89)
91 SILVERADO Cabernet Sauvignon Napa Valley Stags Leap District 1981 Rel: $11 Cur: $25 (12/16/84)
96 SILVERADO Cabernet Sauvignon Napa Valley Stags Leap District Limited Reserve 1986 Rel: $35 Cur: $38 (12/15/90) CS
89 SIMI Cabernet Sauvignon Sonoma County 1987 $16.50 (5/15/91)
88 SIMI Cabernet Sauvignon Alexander Valley 1986 Rel: $15.50 Cur: $17 (9/30/90)
91 SIMI Cabernet Sauvignon Sonoma County 1985 Rel: $13 Cur: $18 (9/30/89)
86 SIMI Cabernet Sauvignon Sonoma County 1984 Rel: $11 Cur: $15 (10/31/88)
90 SIMI Cabernet Sauvignon Sonoma County 1982 Rel: $12 Cur: $15 (11/15/86)
79 SIMI Cabernet Sauvignon Alexander Valley 1981 Rel: $11 Cur: $11 (11/01/85)
81 SIMI Cabernet Sauvignon Alexander Valley 1980 Rel: $10 Cur: $20 (7/01/84)
91 SIMI Cabernet Sauvignon Alexander Valley 1979 Rel: $9 Cur: $28 (4/01/84) SS
85 SIMI Cabernet Sauvignon Alexander Valley 1975 Rel: $6 Cur: $32 (CA-3/89)
72 SIMI Cabernet Sauvignon Alexander Valley 1973 Rel: $6 Cur: $25 (CA-3/89)
80 SIMI Cabernet Sauvignon Alexander Valley 1972 Rel: $5 Cur: $25 (CA-3/89)
75 SIMI Cabernet Sauvignon Alexander Valley 1971 Rel: $5 Cur: $30 (CA-3/89)
73 SIMI Cabernet Sauvignon Alexander Valley 1970 Rel: $4.50 Cur: $60 (CA-3/89)
90+ SIMI Cabernet Sauvignon Alexander Valley Reserve 1987 (NR) (4/15/89) (BT)
89 SIMI Cabernet Sauvignon Alexander Valley Reserve 1986 $30 (7/31/91)
92 SIMI Cabernet Sauvignon Alexander Valley Reserve 1986 $30 (CA-3/89)
85+ SIMI Cabernet Sauvignon Alexander Valley Reserve 1986 $30 (4/15/88) (BT)
94 SIMI Cabernet Sauvignon Alexander Valley Reserve 1985 Rel: $25 Cur: $28 (8/31/90) SS
94 SIMI Cabernet Sauvignon Alexander Valley Reserve 1985 Rel: $25 Cur: $28 (CA-3/89)
92 SIMI Cabernet Sauvignon Alexander Valley Reserve 1984 Rel: $22.50 Cur: $26 (CA-3/89)
90 SIMI Cabernet Sauvignon Sonoma-Napa Counties Reserve 1982 Rel: $20 Cur: $26 (4/15/89)
88 SIMI Cabernet Sauvignon Sonoma-Napa Counties Reserve 1982 Rel: $20 Cur: $26 (CA-3/89)
79 SIMI Cabernet Sauvignon Sonoma-Napa Counties Reserve 1982 Rel: $20 Cur: $26 (2/01/86)
86 SIMI Cabernet Sauvignon Alexander Valley Reserve 1981 Rel: $25 Cur: $26 (12/15/88)
76 SIMI Cabernet Sauvignon Alexander Valley Reserve 1981 Rel: $25 Cur: $26 (2/01/86)
84 SIMI Cabernet Sauvignon Alexander Valley Reserve 1980 Rel: $20 Cur: $26 (CA-3/89)
87 SIMI Cabernet Sauvignon Alexander Valley Reserve 1980 Rel: $20 Cur: $26 (6/01/86)
87 SIMI Cabernet Sauvignon Alexander Valley Reserve 1979 Rel: $20 Cur: $36 (CA-3/89)
77 SIMI Cabernet Sauvignon Alexander Valley Reserve 1979 Rel: $20 Cur: $36 (2/01/86)
89 SIMI Cabernet Sauvignon Alexander Valley Reserve 1979 Rel: $20 Cur: $36 (9/01/85)
72 SIMI Cabernet Sauvignon Alexander Valley Reserve 1978 Rel: $17 Cur: $38 (CA-3/89)
69 SIMI Cabernet Sauvignon Alexander Valley Reserve 1978 Rel: $17 Cur: $38 (2/01/86)
70 SIMI Cabernet Sauvignon Alexander Valley Special Selection 1977 Rel: $20 Cur: $23 (CA-3/89)
85 SIMI Cabernet Sauvignon Alexander Valley Reserve 1974 Rel: $20 Cur: $61 (2/15/90) (JG)
87 SIMI Cabernet Sauvignon Alexander Valley Reserve Vintage 1974 Rel: $20 Cur: $61 (CA-3/89)
83 SIMI Cabernet Sauvignon Alexander Valley Special Reserve 1974 Rel: $20 Cur: $61 (CA-3/89)
78 SMITH & HOOK Cabernet Sauvignon Monterey 1983 $13.50 (11/15/87)
90 SMITH & HOOK Cabernet Sauvignon Monterey County 1981 $13.50 (12/16/84)
88 SMITH & HOOK Cabernet Sauvignon Napa County 1985 $12 (9/30/89)
79 SMITH & HOOK Cabernet Sauvignon Napa County 1982 $17 (6/15/87)
74 SMITH-MADRONE Cabernet Sauvignon Napa Valley 1985 Rel: $14 Cur: $15 (4/15/90)
90 SMITH-MADRONE Cabernet Sauvignon Napa Valley 1985 Rel: $14 Cur: $15 (CA-3/89)
91 SMITH-MADRONE Cabernet Sauvignon Napa Valley 1984 Rel: $14 Cur: $15 (CA-3/89)
92 SMITH-MADRONE Cabernet Sauvignon Napa Valley 1984 Rel: $14 Cur: $15 (12/31/88)

Key to Symbols

The scores reported here are the results of blind tastings conducted by our panel of senior editors. Wines that carry the initials below are results of individual tastings.

THE WINE SPECTATOR 100-POINT SCALE *95-100*—Classic, a great wine; *90-94*—Outstanding, superior character and style; *80-89*—Good to very good, a wine with special qualities; *70-79*—Average, drinkable wine that may have minor flaws; *60-69*—Below average, drinkable but not recommended; *50-59*—Poor, undrinkable, not recommended. "+"—With a score indicates a range; used primarily with barrel tastings to indicate a preliminary score.

SPECIAL DESIGNATIONS SS—Spectator Selection, CS—Cellar Selection, BB—Best Buy.

TASTER'S INITIALS (JG)—Jim Gordon, (HS)—Harvey Steiman, (JL)—James Laube, (JS)—James Suckling, (TM)—Thomas Matthews, (TR)—Terry Robards, (BT)—Barrel Tasting (these wines were tasted blind from barrel samples), (CA-date)—*California's Great Cabernets* by James Laube, (CH-date)—*California's Great Chardonnays* by James Laube, (VP-date)—*Vintage Port* by James Suckling.

DATE TASTED Dates in parentheses represent the issue in which the rating was published.

84 SMITH-MADRONE Cabernet Sauvignon Napa Valley 1983 Rel: $12.50 Cur: $15 (CA-3/89)
79 SMITH-MADRONE Cabernet Sauvignon Napa Valley 1982 Rel: $12.50 Cur: $15 (CA-3/89)
78 SMITH-MADRONE Cabernet Sauvignon Napa Valley 1981 Rel: $12.50 Cur: $15 (CA-3/89)
79 SMITH-MADRONE Cabernet Sauvignon Napa Valley 1980 Rel: $12.50 Cur: $18 (CA-3/89)
83 SMITH-MADRONE Cabernet Sauvignon Napa Valley 1980 Rel: $12.50 Cur: $18 (1/01/84)
86 SMITH-MADRONE Cabernet Sauvignon Napa Valley 1979 Rel: $14 Cur: $25 (CA-3/89)
84 SMITH-MADRONE Cabernet Sauvignon Napa Valley 1978 Rel: $14 Cur: $25 (CA-3/89)
83 SOBON ESTATE Cabernet Sauvignon Shenandoah Valley 1987 $15 (11/30/90)
80 SOLARI Cabernet Sauvignon Napa Valley Larkmead Vineyards 1985 $10 (3/15/90)
80 SOLARI Cabernet Sauvignon Napa Valley Larkmead Vineyards 1984 $12 (4/15/88)
90+ SPOTTSWOODE Cabernet Sauvignon Napa Valley 1990 (NR) (5/15/91) (BT)
90+ SPOTTSWOODE Cabernet Sauvignon Napa Valley 1989 (NR) (5/15/91) (BT)
90+ SPOTTSWOODE Cabernet Sauvignon Napa Valley 1988 (NR) (4/30/90) (BT)
96 SPOTTSWOODE Cabernet Sauvignon Napa Valley 1987 Rel: $36 Cur: $56 (9/15/90) SS
95+ SPOTTSWOODE Cabernet Sauvignon Napa Valley 1987 Rel: $36 Cur: $56 (4/15/89) (BT)
95 SPOTTSWOODE Cabernet Sauvignon Napa Valley 1986 Rel: $30 Cur: $71 (9/15/89)
95 SPOTTSWOODE Cabernet Sauvignon Napa Valley 1986 Rel: $30 Cur: $71 (CA-3/89)
90+ SPOTTSWOODE Cabernet Sauvignon Napa Valley 1986 Rel: $30 Cur: $71 (4/15/88) (BT)
95 SPOTTSWOODE Cabernet Sauvignon Napa Valley 1985 Rel: $25 Cur: $94 (CA-3/89)
95 SPOTTSWOODE Cabernet Sauvignon Napa Valley 1985 Rel: $25 Cur: $94 (11/15/88) CS
90 SPOTTSWOODE Cabernet Sauvignon Napa Valley 1984 Rel: $25 Cur: $75 (CA-3/89)
92 SPOTTSWOODE Cabernet Sauvignon Napa Valley 1984 Rel: $25 Cur: $75 (11/30/87)
89 SPOTTSWOODE Cabernet Sauvignon Napa Valley 1983 Rel: $25 Cur: $75 (CA-3/89)
81 SPOTTSWOODE Cabernet Sauvignon Napa Valley 1983 Rel: $25 Cur: $75 (11/15/86)
90 SPOTTSWOODE Cabernet Sauvignon Napa Valley 1982 Rel: $18 Cur: $110 (CA-3/89)
86 SPOTTSWOODE Cabernet Sauvignon Napa Valley 1982 Rel: $18 Cur: $110 (11/01/85)
85+ SPRING MOUNTAIN Cabernet Sauvignon Napa Valley 1988 (NR) (4/30/90) (BT)
90 SPRING MOUNTAIN Cabernet Sauvignon Napa Valley 1986 (NR) (CA-3/89)
85 SPRING MOUNTAIN Cabernet Sauvignon Napa Valley 1985 Rel: $20 Cur: $20 (10/15/89)
88 SPRING MOUNTAIN Cabernet Sauvignon Napa Valley 1985 Rel: $20 Cur: $20 (CA-3/89)
89 SPRING MOUNTAIN Cabernet Sauvignon Napa Valley 1984 Rel: $15 Cur: $22 (3/15/89)
89 SPRING MOUNTAIN Cabernet Sauvignon Napa Valley 1984 Rel: $15 Cur: $22 (CA-3/89)
79 SPRING MOUNTAIN Cabernet Sauvignon Napa Valley 1983 Rel: $15 Cur: $19 (CA-3/89)
80 SPRING MOUNTAIN Cabernet Sauvignon Napa Valley 1983 Rel: $15 Cur: $19 (9/30/87)
66 SPRING MOUNTAIN Cabernet Sauvignon Napa Valley 1982 Rel: $15 Cur: $15 (CA-3/89)
87 SPRING MOUNTAIN Cabernet Sauvignon Napa Valley 1982 Rel: $15 Cur: $15 (12/15/86)
78 SPRING MOUNTAIN Cabernet Sauvignon Napa Valley 1981 Rel: $14 Cur: $16 (CA-3/89)
86 SPRING MOUNTAIN Cabernet Sauvignon Napa Valley 1980 Rel: $13 Cur: $24 (CA-3/89)
87 SPRING MOUNTAIN Cabernet Sauvignon Napa Valley 1979 Rel: $13 Cur: $32 (CA-3/89)
83 SPRING MOUNTAIN Cabernet Sauvignon Napa Valley 1978 Rel: $12 Cur: $27 (CA-3/89)
85 SPRING MOUNTAIN Cabernet Sauvignon Napa Valley 1977 Rel: $9.50 Cur: $20 (CA-3/89)
90 STAG'S LEAP WINE CELLARS Cabernet Sauvignon Napa Valley 1988 $18 (6/15/91)
75 STAG'S LEAP WINE CELLARS Cabernet Sauvignon Napa Valley 1987 $18 (8/31/90)
82 STAG'S LEAP WINE CELLARS Cabernet Sauvignon Napa Valley 1986 $18 (6/15/89)
90 STAG'S LEAP WINE CELLARS Cabernet Sauvignon Napa Valley 1985 $16 (9/15/88)
83 STAG'S LEAP WINE CELLARS Cabernet Sauvignon Napa Valley 1984 $15 (7/15/87)
82 STAG'S LEAP WINE CELLARS Cabernet Sauvignon Napa Valley 1981 $15 (12/16/84)
90+ STAG'S LEAP WINE CELLARS Stag's Leap Vineyards Cask 23 Napa Valley Stags Leap District 1987 (NR) $65 (4/15/89) (BT)
93 STAG'S LEAP WINE CELLARS Stag's Leap Vineyards Cask 23 Napa Valley Stags Leap District 1986 Rel: $55 Cur: $73 (11/15/90)
92 STAG'S LEAP WINE CELLARS Stag's Leap Vineyards Cask 23 Napa Valley Stags Leap District 1986 Rel: $55 Cur: $73 (3/01/89)
90+ STAG'S LEAP WINE CELLARS Stag's Leap Vineyards Cask 23 Napa Valley Stags Leap District 1986 Rel: $55 Cur: $73 (4/15/88) (BT)
96 STAG'S LEAP WINE CELLARS Stag's Leap Vineyards Cask 23 Napa Valley Stags Leap District 1985 Rel: $75 Cur: $141 (11/30/89)
98 STAG'S LEAP WINE CELLARS Stag's Leap Vineyards Cask 23 Napa Valley Stags Leap District 1985 Rel: $75 Cur: $141 (3/01/89)
95+ STAG'S LEAP WINE CELLARS Stag's Leap Vineyards Cask 23 Napa Valley Stags Leap District 1985 Rel: $75 Cur: $141 (6/15/87) (BT)
93 STAG'S LEAP WINE CELLARS Cabernet Sauvignon Napa Valley Stags Leap District Stag's Leap Vineyards Cask 23 1984 Rel: $40 Cur: $89 (CA-3/89)
90 STAG'S LEAP WINE CELLARS Cabernet Sauvignon Napa Valley Stags Leap District Stag's Leap Vineyards Cask 23 1984 Rel: $40 Cur: $89 (12/31/88)
88 STAG'S LEAP WINE CELLARS Cabernet Sauvignon Napa Valley Stags Leap District Stag's Leap Vineyards Cask 23 1983 Rel: $35 Cur: $73 (CA-3/89)
82 STAG'S LEAP WINE CELLARS Cabernet Sauvignon Napa Valley Stags Leap District Stag's Leap Vineyards Cask 23 1983 Rel: $35 Cur: $73 (10/15/88)
88 STAG'S LEAP WINE CELLARS Cabernet Sauvignon Napa Valley Stags Leap District Stag's Leap Vineyards Cask 23 1979 Rel: $35 Cur: $95 (CA-3/89)
92 STAG'S LEAP WINE CELLARS Cabernet Sauvignon Napa Valley Stags Leap District Stag's Leap Vineyards Cask 23 1978 Rel: $35 Cur: $136 (CA-3/89)
91 STAG'S LEAP WINE CELLARS Cabernet Sauvignon Napa Valley Stags Leap District Stag's Leap Vineyards Cask 23 1978 Rel: $35 Cur: $136 (4/30/87)
91 STAG'S LEAP WINE CELLARS Cabernet Sauvignon Napa Valley Stags Leap District Stag's Leap Vineyards Cask 23 1977 Rel: $30 Cur: $75 (CA-3/89)
80 STAG'S LEAP WINE CELLARS Cabernet Sauvignon Napa Valley Stags Leap District Stag's Leap Vineyards Cask 23 1974 Rel: $12 Cur: $144 (2/15/90) (JG)
88 STAG'S LEAP WINE CELLARS Cabernet Sauvignon Napa Valley Stags Leap District Stag's Leap Vineyards Cask 23 1974 Rel: $12 Cur: $144 (CA-3/89)
85+ STAG'S LEAP WINE CELLARS Cabernet Sauvignon Napa Valley Stags Leap District SLV-Fay Vineyard Blend 1989 (NR) (5/15/91) (BT)
77 STAG'S LEAP WINE CELLARS Cabernet Sauvignon Napa Valley Stags Leap District SLV 1987 $28 (11/15/90)
85+ STAG'S LEAP WINE CELLARS Cabernet Sauvignon Napa Valley Stags Leap District SLV 1987 $28 (4/15/89) (BT)
91 STAG'S LEAP WINE CELLARS Cabernet Sauvignon Napa Valley Stags Leap District SLV 1986 Rel: $28 Cur: $28 (11/30/89)
89 STAG'S LEAP WINE CELLARS Cabernet Sauvignon Napa Valley Stags Leap District SLV 1986 Rel: $28 Cur: $28 (CA-3/89)
85+ STAG'S LEAP WINE CELLARS Cabernet Sauvignon Napa Valley Stags Leap District SLV 1986 Rel: $28 Cur: $28 (4/15/88) (BT)
94 STAG'S LEAP WINE CELLARS Cabernet Sauvignon Napa Valley Stags Leap District SLV 1985 Rel: $26 Cur: $38 (CA-3/89)
90 STAG'S LEAP WINE CELLARS Cabernet Sauvignon Napa Valley Stags Leap District SLV 1985 Rel: $26 Cur: $38 (10/31/88)
90+ STAG'S LEAP WINE CELLARS Cabernet Sauvignon Napa Valley Stags Leap District SLV 1985 Rel: $26 Cur: $38 (6/15/87) (BT)

92	STAG'S LEAP WINE CELLARS Cabernet Sauvignon Napa Valley Stags Leap District SLV 1984 Rel: $21 Cur: $32 (CA-3/89)
81	STAG'S LEAP WINE CELLARS Cabernet Sauvignon Napa Valley Stags Leap District SLV 1984 Rel: $21 Cur: $32 (11/30/87)
73	STAG'S LEAP WINE CELLARS Cabernet Sauvignon Napa Valley Stags Leap District Stag's Leap Vineyards 1983 Rel: $18 Cur: $33 (CA-3/89)
77	STAG'S LEAP WINE CELLARS Cabernet Sauvignon Napa Valley Stags Leap District Stag's Leap Vineyards 1983 Rel: $18 Cur: $33 (11/15/86)
75	STAG'S LEAP WINE CELLARS Cabernet Sauvignon Napa Valley Stags Leap District Stag's Leap Vineyards 1982 Rel: $16.50 Cur: $31 (CA-3/89)
69	STAG'S LEAP WINE CELLARS Cabernet Sauvignon Napa Valley Stags Leap District Stag's Leap Vineyards 1982 Rel: $16.50 Cur: $31 (10/01/85)
91	STAG'S LEAP WINE CELLARS Cabernet Sauvignon Napa Valley Stags Leap District Stag's Leap Vineyards 1981 Rel: $15 Cur: $35 (CA-3/89)
90	STAG'S LEAP WINE CELLARS Cabernet Sauvignon Napa Valley Stags Leap District Stag's Leap Vineyards 1981 Rel: $15 Cur: $35 (9/16/84) CS
68	STAG'S LEAP WINE CELLARS Cabernet Sauvignon Napa Valley Stags Leap District Stag's Leap Vineyards 1979 Rel: $15 Cur: $52 (CA-3/89)
89	STAG'S LEAP WINE CELLARS Cabernet Sauvignon Napa Valley Stags Leap District Stag's Leap Vineyards 1978 Rel: $13.50 Cur: $45 (CA-3/89)
85	STAG'S LEAP WINE CELLARS Cabernet Sauvignon Napa Valley Stags Leap District Stag's Leap Vineyards 1977 Rel: $9 Cur: $35 (CA-3/89)
90	STAG'S LEAP WINE CELLARS Cabernet Sauvignon Napa Valley Stags Leap District Stag's Leap Vineyards Lot 2 1977 Rel: $10 Cur: $61 (CA-3/89)
73	STAG'S LEAP WINE CELLARS Cabernet Sauvignon Napa Valley Stags Leap District Stag's Leap Vineyards 1976 Rel: $10 Cur: $71 (CA-3/89)
80	STAG'S LEAP WINE CELLARS Cabernet Sauvignon Napa Valley Stags Leap District Stag's Leap Vineyards Lot 2 1976 Rel: $11 Cur: $55 (CA-3/89)
74	STAG'S LEAP WINE CELLARS Cabernet Sauvignon Napa Valley Stags Leap District Stag's Leap Vineyards 1975 Rel: $8.50 Cur: $68 (CA-3/89)
83	STAG'S LEAP WINE CELLARS Cabernet Sauvignon Napa Valley Stags Leap District Stag's Leap Vineyards 1974 Rel: $8 Cur: $110 (2/15/90)
87	STAG'S LEAP WINE CELLARS Cabernet Sauvignon Napa Valley Stags Leap District Stag's Leap Vineyards 1974 Rel: $8 Cur: $110 (CA-3/89)
86	STAG'S LEAP WINE CELLARS Cabernet Sauvignon Napa Valley Stags Leap District Stag's Leap Vineyards 1973 Rel: $6 Cur: $141 (CA-3/89)
82	STAG'S LEAP WINE CELLARS Cabernet Sauvignon Napa Valley Stags Leap District Stag's Leap Vineyards 1973 Rel: $6 Cur: $141 (4/01/86)
70	STAG'S LEAP WINE CELLARS Cabernet Sauvignon Napa Valley Stags Leap District Stag's Leap Vineyards 1972 Rel: $5.50 Cur: $100 (CA-3/89)
89	STAGS' LEAP WINERY Cabernet Sauvignon Napa Valley Stags Leap District 1987 $18 (6/30/91)
89	STAGS' LEAP WINERY Cabernet Sauvignon Napa Valley Stags Leap District 1986 Rel: $17 Cur: $18 (10/31/90)
86	STAGS' LEAP WINERY Cabernet Sauvignon Napa Valley Stags Leap District 1986 Rel: $17 Cur: $18 (CA-3/89)
85	STAGS' LEAP WINERY Cabernet Sauvignon Napa Valley Stags Leap District 1985 Rel: $15 Cur: $16 (CA-3/89)
87	STAGS' LEAP WINERY Cabernet Sauvignon Napa Valley Stags Leap District 1984 Rel: $13.50 Cur: $18 (CA-3/89)
90	STAGS' LEAP WINERY Cabernet Sauvignon Napa Valley Stags Leap District 1984 Rel: $13.50 Cur: $18 (7/15/88)
80	STAGS' LEAP WINERY Cabernet Sauvignon Napa Valley Stags Leap District 1983 Rel: $12.75 Cur: $20 (CA-3/89)
71	STAGS' LEAP WINERY Cabernet Sauvignon Napa Valley Stags Leap District 1982 Rel: $12 Cur: $20 (CA-3/89)
85	STAGS' LEAP WINERY Cabernet Sauvignon Napa Valley Stags Leap District 1981 Rel: $11 Cur: $25 (CA-3/89)
86	STAGS' LEAP WINERY Cabernet Sauvignon Napa Valley Stags Leap District 1981 Rel: $11 Cur: $25 (3/01/85)
90+	STELTZNER Cabernet Sauvignon Napa Valley Stags Leap District 1990 (NR) (5/15/91) (BT)
85+	STELTZNER Cabernet Sauvignon Napa Valley Stags Leap District 1989 (NR) (5/15/91) (BT)
85+	STELTZNER Cabernet Sauvignon Napa Valley Stags Leap District 1988 (NR) (4/30/90) (BT)
82	STELTZNER Cabernet Sauvignon Napa Valley Stags Leap District 1987 $16 (11/15/90)
90+	STELTZNER Cabernet Sauvignon Napa Valley Stags Leap District 1987 $16 (4/15/89) (BT)
91	STELTZNER Cabernet Sauvignon Napa Valley Stags Leap District 1986 Rel: $16 Cur: $17 (12/31/89)
90	STELTZNER Cabernet Sauvignon Napa Valley Stags Leap District 1986 Rel: $16 Cur: $17 (CA-3/89)
80+	STELTZNER Cabernet Sauvignon Napa Valley Stags Leap District 1986 Rel: $16 Cur: $17 (4/15/88) (BT)
93	STELTZNER Cabernet Sauvignon Napa Valley Stags Leap District 1985 Rel: $16 Cur: $19 (CA-3/89)
92	STELTZNER Cabernet Sauvignon Napa Valley Stags Leap District 1985 Rel: $16 Cur: $19 (11/15/88)
90+	STELTZNER Cabernet Sauvignon Napa Valley Stags Leap District 1985 Rel: $16 Cur: $19 (6/15/87) (BT)
91	STELTZNER Cabernet Sauvignon Napa Valley Stags Leap District 1984 Rel: $15 Cur: $19 (CA-3/89)
91	STELTZNER Cabernet Sauvignon Napa Valley Stags Leap District 1984 Rel: $15 Cur: $19 (3/31/88)
90	STELTZNER Cabernet Sauvignon Napa Valley Stags Leap District 1983 Rel: $14 Cur: $18 (CA-3/89)
88	STELTZNER Cabernet Sauvignon Napa Valley Stags Leap District 1983 Rel: $14 Cur: $18 (6/30/87) (JL)
90	STELTZNER Cabernet Sauvignon Napa Valley Stags Leap District 1982 Rel: $14 Cur: $26 (CA-3/89)
93	STELTZNER Cabernet Sauvignon Napa Valley Stags Leap District 1982 Rel: $14 Cur: $26 (6/30/87) (JL)
91	STELTZNER Cabernet Sauvignon Napa Valley Stags Leap District 1982 Rel: $14 Cur: $26 (9/01/85) CS
89	STELTZNER Cabernet Sauvignon Napa Valley Stags Leap District 1981 Rel: $14 Cur: $33 (CA-3/89)
91	STELTZNER Cabernet Sauvignon Napa Valley Stags Leap District 1981 Rel: $14 Cur: $33 (6/30/87) (JL)
88	STELTZNER Cabernet Sauvignon Napa Valley Stags Leap District 1980 Rel: $14 Cur: $32 (CA-3/89)
88	STELTZNER Cabernet Sauvignon Napa Valley Stags Leap District 1980 Rel: $14 Cur: $32 (6/30/87) (JL)
89	STELTZNER Cabernet Sauvignon Napa Valley Stags Leap District 1979 Rel: $14 Cur: $42 (CA-3/89)
89	STELTZNER Cabernet Sauvignon Napa Valley Stags Leap District 1979 Rel: $14 Cur: $42 (6/30/87) (JL)
87	STELTZNER Cabernet Sauvignon Napa Valley Stags Leap District 1978 Rel: $14 Cur: $45 (CA-3/89)
87	STELTZNER Cabernet Sauvignon Napa Valley Stags Leap District 1978 Rel: $14 Cur: $45 (6/30/87) (JL)
85	STELTZNER Cabernet Sauvignon Napa Valley Stags Leap District 1977 Rel: $14 Cur: $45 (CA-3/89)
88	STELTZNER Cabernet Sauvignon Napa Valley Stags Leap District 1977 Rel: $14 Cur: $45 (6/30/87) (JL)
66	ROBERT STEMMLER Cabernet Sauvignon Sonoma County 1982 $15 (4/01/85)
74	STEPHENS Cabernet Sauvignon Napa Valley 1981 $8 (2/15/84)
85+	STERLING Cabernet Sauvignon Napa Valley 1990 (NR) (5/15/91) (BT)
80+	STERLING Cabernet Sauvignon Napa Valley 1989 (NR) (5/15/91) (BT)
90+	STERLING Cabernet Sauvignon Napa Valley 1988 $13.25 (4/30/90) (BT)
91	STERLING Cabernet Sauvignon Napa Valley 1987 Rel: $13 Cur: $13 (5/15/90)
90+	STERLING Cabernet Sauvignon Napa Valley 1987 Rel: $13 Cur: $13 (4/15/89) (BT)
91	STERLING Cabernet Sauvignon Napa Valley 1986 Rel: $14.50 Cur: $15 (3/31/89)
85+	STERLING Cabernet Sauvignon Napa Valley 1986 Rel: $14.50 Cur: $15 (4/15/88) (BT)
89	STERLING Cabernet Sauvignon Napa Valley 1985 Rel: $13 Cur: $15 (5/15/88)
81	STERLING Cabernet Sauvignon Napa Valley 1983 Rel: $12.50 Cur: $15 (2/15/87)
66	STERLING Cabernet Sauvignon Napa Valley 1982 Rel: $12.50 Cur: $15 (5/16/86)
88	STERLING Cabernet Sauvignon Napa Valley 1981 Rel: $12 Cur: $16 (8/01/85)
84	STERLING Cabernet Sauvignon Napa Valley 1980 Rel: $12.50 Cur: $25 (2/15/84)
95	STERLING Cabernet Sauvignon Napa Valley 1978 Rel: $35 Cur: $28 (6/01/86)
90	STERLING Cabernet Sauvignon Napa Valley 1974 Cur: $50 (2/15/90) (JG)
85+	STERLING Cabernet Sauvignon Napa Valley Diamond Mountain Ranch 1990 (NR) (5/15/91) (BT)
85+	STERLING Cabernet Sauvignon Napa Valley Diamond Mountain Ranch 1989 (NR) (5/15/91) (BT)
85+	STERLING Cabernet Sauvignon Napa Valley Diamond Mountain Ranch 1988 (NR) (4/30/90) (BT)
91	STERLING Cabernet Sauvignon Napa Valley Diamond Mountain Ranch 1987 $16 (11/15/90)
85+	STERLING Cabernet Sauvignon Napa Valley Diamond Mountain Ranch 1987 $16 (4/15/89) (BT)
91	STERLING Cabernet Sauvignon Napa Valley Diamond Mountain Ranch 1986 Rel: $14.50 Cur: $15 (3/15/90)
88	STERLING Cabernet Sauvignon Napa Valley Diamond Mountain Ranch 1986 Rel: $14.50 Cur: $15 (CA-3/89)
90+	STERLING Cabernet Sauvignon Napa Valley Diamond Mountain Ranch 1986 Rel: $14.50 Cur: $15 (4/15/88) (BT)
88	STERLING Cabernet Sauvignon Napa Valley Diamond Mountain Ranch 1985 Rel: $16 Cur: $18 (5/31/89)
90	STERLING Cabernet Sauvignon Napa Valley Diamond Mountain Ranch 1985 Rel: $16 Cur: $18 (CA-3/89)
85	STERLING Cabernet Sauvignon Napa Valley Diamond Mountain Ranch 1984 Rel: $15 Cur: $18 (CA-3/89)
84	STERLING Cabernet Sauvignon Napa Valley Diamond Mountain Ranch 1984 Rel: $15 Cur: $18 (2/15/88)
87	STERLING Cabernet Sauvignon Napa Valley Diamond Mountain Ranch 1983 Rel: $15 Cur: $21 (CA-3/89)
74	STERLING Cabernet Sauvignon Napa Valley Diamond Mountain Ranch 1983 Rel: $15 Cur: $21 (11/30/86)
82	STERLING Cabernet Sauvignon Napa Valley Diamond Mountain Ranch 1982 Rel: $15 Cur: $37 (CA-3/89)
94	STERLING Cabernet Sauvignon Napa Valley Diamond Mountain Ranch 1982 Rel: $15 Cur: $37 (11/16/85) CS
85+	STERLING Reserve Napa Valley 1990 (NR) (5/15/91) (BT)
90+	STERLING Reserve Napa Valley 1989 (NR) (5/15/91) (BT)
90+	STERLING Reserve Napa Valley 1988 (NR) (4/30/90) (BT)
93	STERLING Reserve Napa Valley 1987 $43 (11/15/90)
95+	STERLING Reserve Napa Valley 1987 $43 (4/15/89) (BT)
95	STERLING Reserve Napa Valley 1986 Rel: $35 Cur: $43 (3/15/90) CS
94	STERLING Reserve Napa Valley 1986 Rel: $35 Cur: $43 (CA-3/89)
90+	STERLING Reserve Napa Valley 1986 Rel: $35 Cur: $43 (4/15/88) (BT)
96	STERLING Reserve Napa Valley 1985 Rel: $30 Cur: $38 (7/15/89) SS
96	STERLING Reserve Napa Valley 1985 Rel: $30 Cur: $38 (CA-3/89)
92	STERLING Cabernet Sauvignon Napa Valley Reserve 1984 Rel: $25 Cur: $38 (3/31/89) CS
92	STERLING Cabernet Sauvignon Napa Valley Reserve 1984 Rel: $25 Cur: $38 (CA-3/89)
82	STERLING Cabernet Sauvignon Napa Valley Reserve 1983 Rel: $22.50 Cur: $30 (CA-3/89)
86	STERLING Cabernet Sauvignon Napa Valley Reserve 1983 Rel: $22.50 Cur: $30 (6/15/87)
75	STERLING Cabernet Sauvignon Napa Valley Reserve 1982 Rel: $22.50 Cur: $37 (CA-3/89)
85	STERLING Cabernet Sauvignon Napa Valley Reserve 1981 Rel: $22.50 Cur: $30 (CA-3/89)
91	STERLING Cabernet Sauvignon Napa Valley Reserve 1980 Rel: $27.50 Cur: $43 (CA-3/89)
90	STERLING Cabernet Sauvignon Napa Valley Reserve 1980 Rel: $27.50 Cur: $43 (11/01/84) CS
85	STERLING Cabernet Sauvignon Napa Valley Reserve 1979 Rel: $27.50 Cur: $45 (CA-3/89)
91	STERLING Cabernet Sauvignon Napa Valley Reserve 1979 Rel: $27.50 Cur: $45 (2/15/84)
90	STERLING Cabernet Sauvignon Napa Valley Reserve 1978 Rel: $27.50 Cur: $57 (CA-3/89)
97	STERLING Cabernet Sauvignon Napa Valley Reserve 1978 Rel: $27.50 Cur: $57 (6/01/86)
93	STERLING Cabernet Sauvignon Napa Valley Reserve 1977 Rel: $27.50 Cur: $55 (CA-3/89)
76	STERLING Cabernet Sauvignon Napa Valley Reserve 1976 Rel: $25 Cur: $44 (CA-3/89)
78	STERLING Cabernet Sauvignon Napa Valley Reserve 1975 Rel: $20 Cur: $55 (CA-3/89)
92	STERLING Cabernet Sauvignon Napa Valley Reserve 1974 Rel: $20 Cur: $87 (2/15/90) (JG)
90	STERLING Cabernet Sauvignon Napa Valley Reserve 1974 Rel: $20 Cur: $87 (CA-3/89)
89	STERLING Cabernet Sauvignon Napa Valley Reserve 1973 Rel: $10 Cur: $70 (CA-3/89)
85+	STERLING Three Palms Vineyard Napa Valley 1989 (NR) (5/15/91) (BT)
85+	STERLING Three Palms Vineyard Napa Valley 1988 (NR) (4/30/90) (BT)
87	STERLING Three Palms Vineyard Napa Valley 1987 $23 (11/15/90)
85+	STERLING Three Palms Vineyard Napa Valley 1987 $23 (4/15/89) (BT)
86	STERLING Three Palms Vineyard Napa Valley 1986 Rel: $19 Cur: $21 (12/31/89)
90+	STERLING Three Palms Vineyard Napa Valley 1986 Rel: $19 Cur: $21 (4/15/88) (BT)
93	STERLING Three Palms Vineyard Napa Valley 1985 Rel: $20 Cur: $22 (12/31/88)
76	STEVENOT Cabernet Sauvignon Calaveras County 1985 $7.50 (6/30/89)
75	STEVENOT Cabernet Sauvignon Calaveras County Grand Reserve 1984 $15 (12/31/87)
85	STONE CREEK Cabernet Sauvignon Napa Valley Limited Bottling 1986 $10 (6/15/90)
91	STONE CREEK Cabernet Sauvignon Napa Valley Special Selection 1983 $8.75 (5/31/87) BB
85+	STONEGATE Cabernet Sauvignon Napa Valley 1990 (NR) (5/15/91) (BT)

UNITED STATES

CALIFORNIA/CABERNET SAUVIGNON & BLENDS

80+ STONEGATE Cabernet Sauvignon Napa Valley 1989 (NR) (5/15/91) (BT)
86 STONEGATE Cabernet Sauvignon Napa Valley 1986 $15 (2/28/91)
79 STONEGATE Cabernet Sauvignon Napa Valley 1986 $15 (CA-3/89)
86 STONEGATE Cabernet Sauvignon Napa Valley 1985 Rel: $16 Cur: $19 (8/31/90)
75 STONEGATE Cabernet Sauvignon Napa Valley 1985 Rel: $16 Cur: $19 (4/15/90)
87 STONEGATE Cabernet Sauvignon Napa Valley 1985 Rel: $16 Cur: $19 (CA-3/89)
88 STONEGATE Cabernet Sauvignon Napa Valley 1984 Rel: $14 Cur: $14 (CA-3/89)
86 STONEGATE Cabernet Sauvignon Napa Valley 1984 Rel: $14 Cur: $14 (2/15/89)
80 STONEGATE Cabernet Sauvignon Napa Valley 1982 Rel: $12 Cur: $18 (CA-3/89)
79 STONEGATE Cabernet Sauvignon Napa Valley 1981 Rel: $12 Cur: $17 (CA-3/89)
78 STONEGATE Cabernet Sauvignon Napa Valley 1981 Rel: $12 Cur: $17 (11/15/86)
86 STONEGATE Cabernet Sauvignon Napa Valley 1980 Rel: $12 Cur: $22 (CA-3/89)
84 STONEGATE Cabernet Sauvignon Napa Valley 1979 Rel: $12 Cur: $25 (CA-3/89)
91 STONEGATE Cabernet Sauvignon Napa Valley 1978 Rel: $12 Cur: $30 (CA-3/89)
81 STONEGATE Cabernet Sauvignon Napa Valley 1977 Rel: $10 Cur: $25 (CA-3/89)
83 STRATFORD Cabernet Sauvignon California 1985 $10 (11/30/88)
86 STRATFORD Cabernet Sauvignon California 1983 $8.50 (2/15/87)
85 STRATFORD Cabernet Sauvignon Napa Valley 1987 $11.50 (4/30/90)
90 STRATFORD Cabernet Sauvignon Napa Valley Partners' Reserve 1987 $15.50 (4/30/91)
79 STREBLOW Cabernet Sauvignon Napa Valley 1987 $16 (10/15/90)
87 STREBLOW Cabernet Sauvignon Napa Valley 1986 $16 (7/31/89)
89 STREBLOW Cabernet Sauvignon Napa Valley 1985 $14.50 (6/15/88)
89 RODNEY STRONG Cabernet Sauvignon Alexander Valley Alexander's Crown Vineyard 1987 $17 (7/15/91)
87 RODNEY STRONG Cabernet Sauvignon Alexander Valley Alexander's Crown Vineyard 1985 $17 (5/31/91)
88 RODNEY STRONG Cabernet Sauvignon Alexander Valley Alexander's Crown Vineyard 1985 $15 (9/30/90)
80 RODNEY STRONG Cabernet Sauvignon Alexander Valley Alexander's Crown Vineyard 1984 $12 (4/30/89)
80 RODNEY STRONG Cabernet Sauvignon Alexander Valley Alexander's Crown Vineyard 1982 $12 (10/31/88)
77 RODNEY STRONG Cabernet Sauvignon Alexander Valley Alexander's Crown Vineyard 1981 $12 (11/30/87)
86 RODNEY STRONG Cabernet Sauvignon Alexander Valley Alexander's Crown Vineyard 1980 $11 (4/16/85)
79 RODNEY STRONG Cabernet Sauvignon Alexander Valley Alexander's Crown Vineyard 1979 $12 (4/16/84)
80 RODNEY STRONG Cabernet Sauvignon Alexander Valley Alexander's Crown Vineyard 1978 $12 (1/01/84)
85 RODNEY STRONG Cabernet Sauvignon Sonoma County 1987 $10 (6/30/91)
69 RODNEY STRONG Cabernet Sauvignon Sonoma County 1982 $7 (12/15/86)
86 RODNEY STRONG Cabernet Sauvignon Sonoma Valley 1981 $7.50 (12/16/84)
66 STUERMER Cabernet Sauvignon Lake County 1984 $15 (9/30/89)
82 SUGARLOAF RIDGE Cabernet Sauvignon Sonoma Valley 1986 $13 (3/31/90)
81 SUNNY ST. HELENA Cabernet Sauvignon Napa Valley 1985 $9 (10/31/87)
85 SUNNY ST. HELENA Cabernet Sauvignon North Coast 1988 $13 (4/30/91)
81 SUTTER HOME Cabernet Sauvignon California 1988 $5 (11/15/90) BB
77 SUTTER HOME Cabernet Sauvignon California 1987 $5.50 (6/30/89)
79 SUTTER HOME Cabernet Sauvignon California 1986 $5 (11/30/88)
80 SYLVAN SPRINGS Cabernet Sauvignon California Vintner's Reserve 1985 $5 (9/30/88) BB
78 TAFT STREET Cabernet Sauvignon California 1985 $7.50 (10/15/88)
84 TAFT STREET Cabernet Sauvignon Napa Valley 1983 $9 (1/31/87)
84 IVAN TAMAS Cabernet Sauvignon Mendocino McNab Ranch 1984 $6 (2/15/87) BB
79 IVAN TAMAS Cabernet Sauvignon North Coast 1985 $7 (12/31/87)
96 TERRACES Cabernet Sauvignon Napa Valley 1986 $23 (1/31/91)
85 TIJSSELING Cabernet Sauvignon Mendocino 1986 $8 (1/31/90) BB
90+ PHILIP TOGNI Cabernet Sauvignon Napa Valley 1990 $24 (5/15/91) (BT)
92 PHILIP TOGNI Cabernet Sauvignon Napa Valley 1988 $26 (7/15/91)
94 PHILIP TOGNI Cabernet Sauvignon Napa Valley 1987 Rel: $24 Cur: $27 (8/31/90)
89 PHILIP TOGNI Cabernet Sauvignon Napa Valley 1986 Rel: $22 Cur: $27 (7/31/89)
93 PHILIP TOGNI Cabernet Sauvignon Napa Valley 1986 Rel: $22 Cur: $27 (CA-3/89)
89 PHILIP TOGNI Cabernet Sauvignon Napa Valley 1985 Rel: $20 Cur: $25 (CA-3/89)
86 PHILIP TOGNI Cabernet Sauvignon Napa Valley 1984 Rel: $18 Cur: $35 (CA-3/89)
87 PHILIP TOGNI Cabernet Sauvignon Napa Valley 1983 Rel: $18 Cur: $50 (CA-3/89)
87 PHILIP TOGNI Cabernet Sauvignon Napa Valley Tanbark Hill Vineyard 1988 $24 (6/30/91)
83 TOYON Cabernet Sauvignon Alexander Valley 1982 $10 (11/15/86)
86 TREFETHEN Cabernet Sauvignon Napa Valley 1987 $16 (11/15/90)
84 TREFETHEN Cabernet Sauvignon Napa Valley 1986 Rel: $15.25 Cur: $17 (10/31/89)
87 TREFETHEN Cabernet Sauvignon Napa Valley 1986 Rel: $15.25 Cur: $17 (CA-3/89)
80 TREFETHEN Cabernet Sauvignon Napa Valley 1985 Rel: $15 Cur: $19 (CA-3/89)
84 TREFETHEN Cabernet Sauvignon Napa Valley 1984 Rel: $14 Cur: $16 (CA-3/89)
88 TREFETHEN Cabernet Sauvignon Napa Valley 1984 Rel: $14 Cur: $16 (5/31/88)
84 TREFETHEN Cabernet Sauvignon Napa Valley 1983 Rel: $11.75 Cur: $22 (CA-3/89)
90 TREFETHEN Cabernet Sauvignon Napa Valley 1983 Rel: $11.75 Cur: $22 (7/15/87)
58 TREFETHEN Cabernet Sauvignon Napa Valley 1982 Rel: $11 Cur: $45 (CA-3/89)
63 TREFETHEN Cabernet Sauvignon Napa Valley 1982 Rel: $11 Cur: $45 (3/16/86)
87 TREFETHEN Cabernet Sauvignon Napa Valley 1981 Rel: $11 Cur: $36 (CA-3/89)
88 TREFETHEN Cabernet Sauvignon Napa Valley 1981 Rel: $11 Cur: $36 (12/16/84) SS
68 TREFETHEN Cabernet Sauvignon Napa Valley 1980 Rel: $11 Cur: $50 (CA-3/89)
86 TREFETHEN Cabernet Sauvignon Napa Valley 1979 Rel: $11 Cur: $35 (CA-3/89)
81 TREFETHEN Cabernet Sauvignon Napa Valley 1978 Rel: $10 Cur: $45 (CA-3/89)
86 TREFETHEN Cabernet Sauvignon Napa Valley 1977 Rel: $8.50 Cur: $45 (CA-3/89)
76 TREFETHEN Cabernet Sauvignon Napa Valley 1976 Rel: $7.50 Cur: $45 (CA-3/89)

Key to Symbols

The scores reported here are the results of blind tastings conducted by our panel of senior editors. Wines that carry the initials below are results of individual tastings.

THE WINE SPECTATOR 100-POINT SCALE *95-100*—Classic, a great wine; *90-94*—Outstanding, superior character and style; *80-89*—Good to very good, a wine with special qualities; *70-79*—Average, drinkable wine that may have minor flaws; *60-69*—Below average, drinkable but not recommended; *50-59*—Poor, undrinkable, not recommended. "+"—With a score indicates a range; used primarily with barrel tastings to indicate a preliminary score.

SPECIAL DESIGNATIONS SS—Spectator Selection, CS—Cellar Selection, BB—Best Buy.

TASTER'S INITIALS (JG)—Jim Gordon, (HS)—Harvey Steiman, (JL)—James Laube, (JS)—James Suckling, (TM)—Thomas Matthews, (TR)—Terry Robards, (BT)—Barrel Tasting (these wines were tasted blind from barrel samples), (CA-date)—*California's Great Cabernets* by James Laube, (CH-date)—*California's Great Chardonnays* by James Laube, (VP-date)—*Vintage Port* by James Suckling.

DATE TASTED Dates in parentheses represent the issue in which the rating was published.

83 TREFETHEN Cabernet Sauvignon Napa Valley 1975 Rel: $7.50 Cur: $55 (CA-3/89)
84 TREFETHEN Cabernet Sauvignon Napa Valley 1974 Rel: $8 Cur: $65 (CA-3/89)
90+ TREFETHEN Cabernet Sauvignon Napa Valley Hillside Selection 1987 (NR) (4/15/89) (BT)
90 TREFETHEN Cabernet Sauvignon Napa Valley Hillside Selection 1986 (NR) (CA-3/89)
80 TREFETHEN Cabernet Sauvignon Napa Valley Hillside Selection 1985 $30 (11/15/90)
90 TREFETHEN Cabernet Sauvignon Napa Valley Hillside Selection 1985 $30 (CA-3/89)
74 TRIONE Cabernet Sauvignon Alexander Valley 1984 $10 (12/31/87)
91 TUDAL Cabernet Sauvignon Napa Valley 1986 Rel: $14.50 Cur: $20 (12/15/89)
89 TUDAL Cabernet Sauvignon Napa Valley 1986 Rel: $14.50 Cur: $20 (CA-3/89)
89 TUDAL Cabernet Sauvignon Napa Valley 1985 Rel: $14.50 Cur: $20 (CA-3/89)
91 TUDAL Cabernet Sauvignon Napa Valley 1984 Rel: $12.50 Cur: $30 (CA-3/89)
86 TUDAL Cabernet Sauvignon Napa Valley 1983 Rel: $12.50 Cur: $25 (CA-3/89)
72 TUDAL Cabernet Sauvignon Napa Valley 1982 Rel: $12 Cur: $38 (CA-3/89)
88 TUDAL Cabernet Sauvignon Napa Valley 1981 Rel: $12 Cur: $40 (CA-3/89)
85 TUDAL Cabernet Sauvignon Napa Valley 1980 Rel: $11.50 Cur: $55 (CA-3/89)
90 TUDAL Cabernet Sauvignon Napa Valley 1979 Rel: $10.75 Cur: $50 (CA-3/89)
70 TULOCAY Cabernet Sauvignon Napa Valley 1986 $12 (6/30/90)
74 TULOCAY Cabernet Sauvignon Napa Valley Egan Vineyard 1987 $16.50 (2/15/91)
82 M.G. VALLEJO Cabernet Sauvignon California 1986 $5 (6/15/90) BB
78 M.G. VALLEJO Cabernet Sauvignon California 1985 $4 (2/15/89)
67 M.G. VALLEJO Cabernet Sauvignon California 1983 $4.50 (8/31/87)
80 VANINO Cabernet Sauvignon Sonoma County 1985 $11 (9/30/88)
79 VENTANA Magnus Meritage Monterey 1986 $20 (10/31/89)
85+ VIANSA Cabernet Sauvignon Napa-Alexander Valleys 1986 (NR) (4/15/88) (BT)
77 VIANSA Cabernet Sauvignon Sonoma-Napa Counties 1986 $15 (7/31/90)
72 VIANSA Cabernet Sauvignon Sonoma-Napa Counties 1985 $13 (9/15/89)
85 VIANSA Cabernet Sauvignon Napa-Sonoma Counties 1984 $13 (7/31/88)
88 VIANSA Cabernet Sauvignon Sonoma Valley Grand Reserve 1983 $35 (10/15/88)
88 VIANSA Cabernet Sauvignon Sonoma Valley Reserve 1983 $18 (10/15/88)
85 VIANSA Obsidian Sonoma-Napa Counties 1987 $65 (7/15/91)
84 VICHON Cabernet Sauvignon Napa Valley 1988 $16 (5/15/91)
84 VICHON Cabernet Sauvignon Napa Valley 1988 $16 (11/15/90)
90+ VICHON Cabernet Sauvignon Napa Valley 1988 $16 (4/30/90) (BT)
88 VICHON Cabernet Sauvignon Napa Valley 1985 Rel: $13 Cur: $16 (CA-3/89)
91 VICHON Cabernet Sauvignon Napa Valley 1985 Rel: $13 Cur: $16 (11/15/88)
88 VICHON Cabernet Sauvignon Napa Valley 1984 Rel: $11.25 Cur: $15 (CA-3/89)
80 VICHON Cabernet Sauvignon Napa Valley 1983 Rel: $10 Cur: $14 (CA-3/89)
91 VICHON Cabernet Sauvignon Napa Valley 1983 Rel: $10 Cur: $14 (11/30/86)
76 VICHON Cabernet Sauvignon Napa Valley 1982 Rel: $13 Cur: $19 (CA-3/89)
89 VICHON Cabernet Sauvignon Napa Valley 1982 Rel: $13 Cur: $19 (7/16/86)
80 VICHON Cabernet Sauvignon Napa Valley 1981 Rel: $13 Cur: $22 (CA-3/89)
89 VICHON Cabernet Sauvignon Napa Valley 1981 Rel: $13 Cur: $22 (12/16/84)
85+ VICHON Cabernet Sauvignon Napa Valley Stags Leap District SLD 1988 $23 (4/30/90) (BT)
87 VICHON Cabernet Sauvignon Napa Valley Stags Leap District SLD 1987 Rel: $17 Cur: $21 (7/31/90)
90+ VICHON Cabernet Sauvignon Napa Valley Stags Leap District SLD 1987 Rel: $17 Cur: $21 (4/15/89) (BT)
91 VICHON Cabernet Sauvignon Napa Valley Stags Leap District SLD 1986 Rel: $21 Cur: $25 (10/31/89)
90 VICHON Cabernet Sauvignon Napa Valley Stags Leap District SLD 1986 Rel: $21 Cur: $25 (CA-3/89)
85+ VICHON Cabernet Sauvignon Napa Valley Stags Leap District SLD 1986 Rel: $21 Cur: $25 (4/15/88) (BT)
92 VICHON Cabernet Sauvignon Napa Valley Stags Leap District SLD 1985 Rel: $18 Cur: $26 (CA-3/89)
93 VICHON Cabernet Sauvignon Napa Valley Stags Leap District SLD 1985 Rel: $18 Cur: $26 (1/31/89)
85 VICHON Cabernet Sauvignon Napa Valley Stags Leap District Fay Vineyard 1984 Rel: $14 Cur: $18 (CA-3/89)
78 VICHON Cabernet Sauvignon Napa Valley Volker Eisele Vineyard 1982 Rel: $16 Cur: $19 (CA-3/89)
83 VICHON Cabernet Sauvignon Napa Valley Volker Eisele Vineyard 1980 Rel: $16 Cur: $25 (CA-3/89)
79 VICHON Cabernet Sauvignon Napa Valley Stags Leap District Fay Vineyard 1982 Rel: $14 Cur: $23 (CA-3/89)
85 VICHON Cabernet Sauvignon Napa Valley Stags Leap District Fay Vineyard 1980 Rel: $16 Cur: $25 (CA-3/89)
80+ VILLA MT. EDEN Cabernet Sauvignon Napa Valley 1988 (NR) (4/30/90) (BT)
88 VILLA MT. EDEN Cabernet Sauvignon Napa Valley 1987 $13 (2/15/91)
90+ VILLA MT. EDEN Cabernet Sauvignon Napa Valley 1987 $13 (4/15/89) (BT)
84 VILLA MT. EDEN Cabernet Sauvignon Napa Valley 1986 $13 (2/15/91)
84 VILLA MT. EDEN Cabernet Sauvignon Napa Valley 1986 $13 (CA-3/89)
80+ VILLA MT. EDEN Cabernet Sauvignon Napa Valley 1986 $13 (4/15/88) (BT)
82 VILLA MT. EDEN Cabernet Sauvignon Napa Valley 1985 Rel: $13 Cur: $13 (CA-3/89)
80 VILLA MT. EDEN Cabernet Sauvignon Napa Valley 1984 (NA) (CA-3/89)
72 VILLA MT. EDEN Cabernet Sauvignon Napa Valley 1983 Rel: $10 Cur: $10 (CA-3/89)
70 VILLA MT. EDEN Cabernet Sauvignon Napa Valley 1982 Rel: $9 Cur: $11 (CA-3/89)
71 VILLA MT. EDEN Cabernet Sauvignon Napa Valley 1982 Rel: $9 Cur: $11 (4/15/88)
62 VILLA MT. EDEN Cabernet Sauvignon Napa Valley 1980 Rel: $11.70 Cur: $14 (CA-3/89)
86 VILLA MT. EDEN Cabernet Sauvignon Napa Valley 1980 Rel: $11.70 Cur: $14 (1/01/84)
78 VILLA MT. EDEN Cabernet Sauvignon Napa Valley 1979 Rel: $12 Cur: $28 (CA-3/89)
78 VILLA MT. EDEN Cabernet Sauvignon Napa Valley 1978 Rel: $8 Cur: $42 (CA-3/89)
86 VILLA MT. EDEN Cabernet Sauvignon Napa Valley 1977 Rel: $8 Cur: $36 (CA-3/89)
70 VILLA MT. EDEN Cabernet Sauvignon Napa Valley 1976 Rel: $7 Cur: $40 (CA-3/89)
89 VILLA MT. EDEN Cabernet Sauvignon Napa Valley 1975 Rel: $7 Cur: $50 (CA-3/89)
92 VILLA MT. EDEN Cabernet Sauvignon Napa Valley 1974 Rel: $7 Cur: $85 (2/15/90) (JG)
90 VILLA MT. EDEN Cabernet Sauvignon Napa Valley 1974 Rel: $7 Cur: $85 (CA-3/89)
85+ VILLA MT. EDEN Cabernet Sauvignon Napa Valley Reserve 1988 $20 (4/30/90) (BT)
84 VILLA MT. EDEN Cabernet Sauvignon Napa Valley Reserve 1982 Rel: $16.70 Cur: $17 (CA-3/89)
85 VILLA MT. EDEN Cabernet Sauvignon Napa Valley Reserve 1981 Rel: $16.70 Cur: $20 (CA-3/89)
81 VILLA MT. EDEN Cabernet Sauvignon Napa Valley Reserve 1981 Rel: $16.70 Cur: $20 (2/01/86)
70 VILLA MT. EDEN Cabernet Sauvignon Napa Valley Reserve 1980 Rel: $20 Cur: $25 (CA-3/89)
89 VILLA MT. EDEN Cabernet Sauvignon Napa Valley Reserve 1980 Rel: $20 Cur: $25 (10/01/84)
75 VILLA MT. EDEN Cabernet Sauvignon Napa Valley Reserve 1979 Rel: $20 Cur: $30 (CA-3/89)

88 VILLA MT. EDEN Cabernet Sauvignon Napa Valley Reserve 1978 Rel: $20 Cur: $42 (CA-3/89)
79 VILLA ZAPU Cabernet Sauvignon Napa Valley 1986 $16 (10/31/89)
87 VITA NOVA Reservatum Santa Barbara County 1986 $20 (12/15/89)
84 WEIBEL Cabernet Sauvignon Mendocino County 1987 $8 (2/28/91) BB
65 WENTE BROS. Cabernet Sauvignon California 1981 $7 (12/16/85)
78 WENTE BROS. Cabernet Sauvignon Central Coast 1985 $8 (11/15/89)
86 WENTE BROS. Cabernet Sauvignon Livermore Valley Charles Wetmore Vineyard Estate Reserve 1987 $18 (4/30/91)
82 WENTE BROS. Cabernet Sauvignon Livermore Valley Estate Reserve 1986 $12 (10/15/90)
85+ WILLIAM WHEELER Cabernet Sauvignon Dry Creek Valley 1987 $14 (4/15/89) (BT)
83 WILLIAM WHEELER Cabernet Sauvignon Dry Creek Valley 1986 $12 (8/31/90)
85+ WILLIAM WHEELER Cabernet Sauvignon Dry Creek Valley 1986 $12 (4/15/88) (BT)
76 WILLIAM WHEELER Cabernet Sauvignon Dry Creek Valley 1985 $12 (7/15/89)
75 WILLIAM WHEELER Cabernet Sauvignon Dry Creek Valley 1984 $11 (4/15/88)
83 WILLIAM WHEELER Cabernet Sauvignon Dry Creek Valley Norse Vineyard Private Reserve 1985 $18 (11/15/90)
60 WILLIAM WHEELER Cabernet Sauvignon Dry Creek Valley Norse Vineyard Private Reserve 1984 $15 (7/31/89)
85 WHITE OAK Cabernet Sauvignon Alexander Valley Myers Limited Reserve 1985 $18 (7/31/89)
80 WHITE ROCK Claret Napa Valley 1986 $18 (10/31/89)
70 WHITEHALL LANE Cabernet Sauvignon California NV $7 (10/15/88)
81 WHITEHALL LANE Cabernet Sauvignon California Le Petit NV $8.50 (3/31/90)
85+ WHITEHALL LANE Cabernet Sauvignon Napa Valley 1989 (NR) (5/15/91) (BT)
84 WHITEHALL LANE Cabernet Sauvignon Napa Valley 1987 $18 (9/15/90)
90+ WHITEHALL LANE Cabernet Sauvignon Napa Valley 1987 $18 (4/15/89) (BT)
89 WHITEHALL LANE Cabernet Sauvignon Napa Valley 1986 $16 (8/31/89)
95+ WHITEHALL LANE Cabernet Sauvignon Napa Valley 1986 $16 (4/15/88) (BT)
93 WHITEHALL LANE Cabernet Sauvignon Napa Valley 1985 $16 (11/15/88)
84 WHITEHALL LANE Cabernet Sauvignon Napa Valley 1984 $14 (12/31/87)
77 WHITEHALL LANE Cabernet Sauvignon Napa Valley 1983 $14 (11/30/86)
86 WHITEHALL LANE Cabernet Sauvignon Napa Valley 1982 $12 (2/16/85)
77 WHITEHALL LANE Cabernet Sauvignon Napa Valley NV $6 (12/31/87)
95+ WHITEHALL LANE Cabernet Sauvignon Napa Valley Morisoli Vineyard 1990 (NR) (5/15/91) (BT)
90+ WHITEHALL LANE Cabernet Sauvignon Napa Valley Reserve 1987 (NR) (4/15/89) (BT)
77 WHITEHALL LANE Cabernet Sauvignon Napa Valley Reserve 1986 $30 (11/15/90)
88 WHITEHALL LANE Cabernet Sauvignon Napa Valley Reserve 1985 $30 (11/30/89)
88 WILD HORSE Cabernet Sauvignon Paso Robles 1987 $13 (4/30/91)
70 WILD HORSE Cabernet Sauvignon Paso Robles Wild Horse Vineyards 1985 $10.50 (6/30/88)
78 J. WILE & SONS Cabernet Sauvignon Napa Valley 1987 $10 (5/31/91)
78 J. WILE & SONS Cabernet Sauvignon Napa Valley 1987 $10 (3/31/91)
75 J. WILE & SONS Cabernet Sauvignon Napa Valley 1986 $7 (9/15/88)
78 J. WILE & SONS Cabernet Sauvignon Napa Valley 1985 $7 (11/15/87)
73 WILLOW CREEK Cabernet Sauvignon Napa Valley 1984 $8.50 (3/31/88)
82 WILLOW CREEK Cabernet Sauvignon Napa-Alexander Valleys 1986 $9.50 (7/31/89)
76 WOLTNER Cabernet Sauvignon North Coast 1979 $3.50 (3/16/84)
84 YORK MOUNTAIN Cabernet Sauvignon San Luis Obispo 1986 $15 (11/15/90)
83 YORK MOUNTAIN Cabernet Sauvignon San Luis Obispo 1985 $15 (12/15/89)
78 ZACA MESA Cabernet Sauvignon Santa Barbara County 1986 $9.50 (12/15/89)
79 ZACA MESA Cabernet Sauvignon Santa Barbara County 1984 $8.50 (10/31/88)
76 ZACA MESA Cabernet Sauvignon Santa Barbara County 1981 $8 (4/01/84)
80 ZACA MESA Cabernet Sauvignon Santa Barbara County Reserve 1986 $15 (12/15/88)
79 ZACA MESA Cabernet Sauvignon Santa Barbara County Reserve 1985 $15 (10/15/88)
87 ZACA MESA Cabernet Sauvignon Santa Barbara County American Reserve 1983 $13 (3/31/87)
85+ ZD Cabernet Sauvignon Napa Valley 1990 (NR) (5/15/91) (BT)
80+ ZD Cabernet Sauvignon Napa Valley 1989 (NR) (5/15/91) (BT)
86 ZD Cabernet Sauvignon Napa Valley 1988 $20 (4/30/91)
78 ZD Cabernet Sauvignon Napa Valley 1987 $16 (2/15/91)
81 ZD Cabernet Sauvignon Napa Valley 1985 $14 (5/15/89)
66 ZD Cabernet Sauvignon California 1982 $12 (7/16/86)
90 ZD Cabernet Sauvignon Napa Valley Estate Bottled 1987 $40 (1/31/91)
82 STEPHEN ZELLERBACH Cabernet Sauvignon Alexander Valley 1988 $10 (10/31/90)
86 STEPHEN ZELLERBACH Cabernet Sauvignon Alexander Valley 1984 $8 (11/30/88)
80 STEPHEN ZELLERBACH Cabernet Sauvignon Alexander Valley 1982 $6 (11/30/86)
77 STEPHEN ZELLERBACH Cabernet Sauvignon Alexander Valley 1980 $8 (4/01/85)

CHARDONNAY

84 ACACIA Chardonnay Carneros Napa Valley 1989 $16 (12/31/90)
89 ACACIA Chardonnay Carneros Napa Valley 1988 Rel: $16 Cur: $16 (1/31/90)
85 ACACIA Chardonnay Carneros Napa Valley 1988 Rel: $16 Cur: $16 (CH-1/90)
84 ACACIA Chardonnay Carneros Napa Valley 1987 Rel: $17 Cur: $17 (CH-1/90)
88 ACACIA Chardonnay Carneros Napa Valley 1987 Rel: $17 Cur: $17 (12/31/88)
87 ACACIA Chardonnay Carneros Napa Valley 1986 Rel: $15 Cur: $18 (CH-1/90)
86 ACACIA Chardonnay Carneros Napa Valley 1986 Rel: $15 Cur: $18 (12/31/87)
80 ACACIA Chardonnay Carneros Napa Valley 1985 Rel: $15 Cur: $20 (CH-1/90)
82 ACACIA Chardonnay Carneros Napa Valley 1985 Rel: $15 Cur: $20 (2/28/87)
84 ACACIA Chardonnay Carneros Napa Valley 1984 Rel: $14 Cur: $20 (CH-1/90)
93 ACACIA Chardonnay Carneros Napa Valley 1984 Rel: $14 Cur: $20 (11/16/85)
84 ACACIA Chardonnay Carneros Napa Valley 1983 Rel: $12 Cur: $19 (12/01/84)
87 ACACIA Chardonnay Carneros Napa Valley Marina Vineyard 1989 $20 (12/31/90)
90 ACACIA Chardonnay Carneros Napa Valley Marina Vineyard 1988 Rel: $20 Cur: $22 (1/31/90)
89 ACACIA Chardonnay Carneros Napa Valley Marina Vineyard 1988 Rel: $20 Cur: $22 (CH-1/90)
85 ACACIA Chardonnay Carneros Napa Valley Marina Vineyard 1987 Rel: $18 Cur: $22 (CH-1/90)
86 ACACIA Chardonnay Carneros Napa Valley Marina Vineyard 1987 Rel: $18 Cur: $22 (12/31/88)
86 ACACIA Chardonnay Carneros Napa Valley Marina Vineyard 1986 Rel: $18 Cur: $22 (CH-1/90)
84 ACACIA Chardonnay Carneros Napa Valley Marina Vineyard 1986 Rel: $18 Cur: $22 (12/31/87)
80 ACACIA Chardonnay Carneros Napa Valley Marina Vineyard 1985 Rel: $18 Cur: $22 (CH-1/90)
57 ACACIA Chardonnay Carneros Napa Valley Marina Vineyard 1985 Rel: $18 Cur: $22 (8/31/87)
86 ACACIA Chardonnay Carneros Napa Valley Marina Vineyard 1984 Rel: $16 Cur: $22 (CH-1/90)
74 ACACIA Chardonnay Carneros Napa Valley Marina Vineyard 1984 Rel: $16 Cur: $22 (11/16/85)
79 ACACIA Chardonnay Carneros Napa Valley Marina Vineyard 1983 Rel: $16 Cur: $23 (CH-1/90)
83 ACACIA Chardonnay Carneros Napa Valley Marina Vineyard 1983 Rel: $16 Cur: $23 (11/01/84)
82 ACACIA Chardonnay Carneros Napa Valley Winery Lake Vineyard 1985 Rel: $18 Cur: $25 (CH-1/90)
86 ACACIA Chardonnay Carneros Napa Valley Winery Lake Vineyard 1985 Rel: $18 Cur: $25 (1/31/87)
88 ACACIA Chardonnay Carneros Napa Valley Winery Lake Vineyard 1984 Rel: $18 Cur: $26 (CH-1/90)
84 ACACIA Chardonnay Carneros Napa Valley Winery Lake Vineyard 1984 Rel: $18 Cur: $26 (10/16/85)
87 ACACIA Chardonnay Carneros Napa Valley Winery Lake Vineyard 1983 Rel: $18 Cur: $25 (CH-1/90)
84 ACACIA Chardonnay Carneros Napa Valley Winery Lake Vineyard 1983 Rel: $18 Cur: $25 (10/16/84)
76 ACACIA Chardonnay Carneros Napa Valley Winery Lake Vineyard 1979 Rel: $16 Cur: $28 (CH-1/90)
81 ACACIA Chardonnay Napa Valley 1986 Rel: $15 Cur: $17 (CH-1/90)
82 ACACIA Chardonnay Napa Valley 1986 Rel: $15 Cur: $17 (12/31/87)
79 ACACIA Chardonnay Napa Valley 1985 Rel: $14 Cur: $16 (CH-1/90)
75 ACACIA Chardonnay Napa Valley 1985 Rel: $14 Cur: $16 (12/15/86)
89 ACACIA Chardonnay Napa Valley 1984 Rel: $12.50 Cur: $16 (CH-7/90)
75 ACACIA Chardonnay Napa Valley 1984 Rel: $12.50 Cur: $16 (CH-12/85)
80 ACACIA Chardonnay Napa Valley 1983 Rel: $12.50 Cur: $18 (CH-1/90)
85 ACACIA Chardonnay Napa Valley 1983 Rel: $12.50 Cur: $18 (10/16/84)
80 ACACIA Chardonnay Napa Valley 1982 Rel: $12 Cur: $20 (CH-1/90)
89 ADELAIDA Chardonnay Paso Robles 1988 $14 (2/15/91)
84 ADELAIDA Chardonnay Paso Robles 1987 $12.50 (12/15/89)
80 ADLER FELS Chardonnay Carneros Sangiacomo Vineyards 1989 $12.50 (4/30/91)
82 ADLER FELS Chardonnay Sonoma Valley Sobra Vista Vineyards 1989 $12 (4/15/91)
84 AHERN Chardonnay Edna Valley Paragon Vineyard 1982 $10 (2/15/84)
82 ALDERBROOK Chardonnay Dry Creek Valley 1989 $10 (3/31/91)
82 ALDERBROOK Chardonnay Dry Creek Valley 1988 $10 (2/15/90)
90 ALDERBROOK Chardonnay Dry Creek Valley 1987 $9.75 (2/15/89)
84 ALDERBROOK Chardonnay Dry Creek Valley 1986 $9.25 (4/15/88)
79 ALDERBROOK Chardonnay Dry Creek Valley 1985 $8.75 (2/15/87)
82 ALDERBROOK Chardonnay Dry Creek Valley Reserve 1988 $16 (4/15/90)
88 ALEXANDER VALLEY Chardonnay Alexander Valley 1988 $12 (6/30/90)
77 ALEXANDER VALLEY Chardonnay Alexander Valley 1987 $11 (1/31/89)
83 ALEXANDER VALLEY Chardonnay Alexander Valley 1986 $11 (4/30/88)
79 ALEXANDER VALLEY Chardonnay Alexander Valley 1985 $10.50 (5/31/87)
87 ALEXANDER VALLEY Chardonnay Alexander Valley 1983 $10 (4/01/85)
85 ALEXANDER VALLEY Chardonnay Alexander Valley 1982 $10 (3/01/84)
90 ALTAMURA Chardonnay Napa Valley 1988 (NR) (6/30/90)
90 ALTAMURA Chardonnay Napa Valley 1988 (NR) (CH-1/90)
87 ALTAMURA Chardonnay Napa Valley 1987 Rel: $16.50 Cur: $21 (6/30/90)
87 ALTAMURA Chardonnay Napa Valley 1987 Rel: $16.50 Cur: $21 (CH-1/90)
88 ALTAMURA Chardonnay Napa Valley 1986 Rel: $15 Cur: $21 (CH-1/90)
88 ALTAMURA Chardonnay Napa Valley 1986 Rel: $15 Cur: $21 (4/15/89)
91 ALTAMURA Chardonnay Napa Valley 1985 Rel: $14 Cur: $21 (CH-1/90)
91 ALTAMURA Chardonnay Napa Valley 1985 Rel: $14 Cur: $21 (2/29/88)
79 S. ANDERSON Chardonnay Napa Valley Stags Leap District 1988 $18 (12/31/90)
88 S. ANDERSON Chardonnay Napa Valley Stags Leap District 1988 $18 (CH-3/90)
85 S. ANDERSON Chardonnay Napa Valley Stags Leap District 1987 $16 (CH-6/90)
88 S. ANDERSON Chardonnay Napa Valley Stags Leap District 1987 $16 (7/15/89)
81 S. ANDERSON Chardonnay Napa Valley Stags Leap District 1986 $16 (CH-3/90)
82 S. ANDERSON Chardonnay Napa Valley Stags Leap District 1986 $16 (11/15/88)
92 S. ANDERSON Chardonnay Napa Valley Stags Leap District 1985 $14 (CH-3/90)
79 S. ANDERSON Chardonnay Napa Valley Stags Leap District 1985 $14 (8/31/87)
89 S. ANDERSON Chardonnay Napa Valley Stags Leap District 1984 $12.50 (CH-3/90)
86 S. ANDERSON Chardonnay Napa Valley Stags Leap District 1984 $12.50 (7/31/87)
86 S. ANDERSON Chardonnay Napa Valley Stags Leap District 1983 $12.50 (CH-3/90)
72 S. ANDERSON Chardonnay Napa Valley Stags Leap District 1982 $12.50 (CH-3/90)
80 S. ANDERSON Chardonnay Napa Valley Stags Leap District 1981 $12.50 (CH-3/90)
83 S. ANDERSON Chardonnay Napa Valley Stags Leap District 1980 $12.50 (CH-3/90)
89 S. ANDERSON Chardonnay Napa Valley Stags Leap District Proprietor's Reserve 1987 Rel: $20 Cur: $20 (CH-3/90)
87 S. ANDERSON Chardonnay Napa Valley Stags Leap District Proprietor's Selection 1983 Rel: $16 Cur: $40 (CH-3/90)
72 ARCIERO Chardonnay Paso Robles 1987 $9 (12/15/89)
85 ARROWOOD Chardonnay Sonoma County 1989 $19 (7/15/91)
92 ARROWOOD Chardonnay Sonoma County 1988 Rel: $18 Cur: $21 (4/30/90)
92 ARROWOOD Chardonnay Sonoma County 1988 Rel: $18 Cur: $21 (CH-4/90)
89 ARROWOOD Chardonnay Sonoma County 1987 Rel: $18 Cur: $21 (CH-4/90)
87 ARROWOOD Chardonnay Sonoma County 1987 Rel: $18 Cur: $21 (5/15/89)
89 ARROWOOD Chardonnay Sonoma County 1986 Rel: $18 Cur: $25 (CH-4/90)
87 ARROWOOD Chardonnay Sonoma County 1986 Rel: $18 Cur: $25 (5/31/88)
92 ARROWOOD Sonoma County Réserve Spéciale 1987 1.5L Rel: $50 Cur: $50 (CH-4/90)
70 DAVID ARTHUR Chardonnay Napa Valley 1985 $13 (4/15/88)
65 ASHLY Chardonnay Monterey 1986 $16.50 (10/31/88)
82 AU BON CLIMAT Chardonnay Santa Barbara County 1988 $12.50 (12/15/89)
58 AU BON CLIMAT Chardonnay Santa Barbara County 1987 $14 (3/15/89)
86 AU BON CLIMAT Chardonnay Santa Barbara County Reserve 1989 $25 (7/15/91)
91 AU BON CLIMAT Chardonnay Santa Barbara County Reserve 1988 $35 (3/15/91)
87 AU BON CLIMAT Chardonnay Santa Barbara County Reserve 1987 $20 (12/15/89)
84 AU BON CLIMAT Chardonnay Santa Barbara County Reserve 1986 $20 (6/15/88)
82 AU BON CLIMAT Chardonnay Santa Barbara County Reserve Los Alamos Vineyard 1987 $20 (12/15/89)
80 AU BON CLIMAT Chardonnay Santa Ynez Valley Benedict Vineyard 1987 $30 (12/15/89)
82 BABCOCK Chardonnay Santa Ynez Valley 1987 $12 (12/15/89)
66 BABCOCK Chardonnay Santa Ynez Valley 1986 $11 (2/15/88)
80 BABCOCK Chardonnay Santa Ynez Valley Reserve 1986 $14 (2/15/88)
90 BABCOCK Chardonnay Santa Ynez Valley Selected Barrels Reserve 1987 $20 (12/15/89)
86 BALLARD CANYON Chardonnay Santa Ynez Valley 1988 $14 (12/15/89)
79 BALLARD CANYON Chardonnay Santa Ynez Valley Dr.'s Fun Baby 1988 $10 (12/15/89)

UNITED STATES
CALIFORNIA/*CHARDONNAY*

79 BALVERNE Chardonnay Chalk Hill Deerfield Vineyard 1984 $11 (11/15/87)
57 BALVERNE Chardonnay Sonoma County Deer Hill Vineyard 1980 $12 (4/16/84)
88 BANCROFT Chardonnay Howell Mountain 1988 $14 (12/31/90)
69 BANDIERA Chardonnay Carneros 1987 $7 (12/31/88)
75 BANDIERA Chardonnay Mendocino County 1982 $6 (2/15/84)
85 BANNISTER Chardonnay Sonoma County 1989 $15 (7/15/91)
77 LAWRENCE J. BARGETTO Chardonnay California Cypress 1982 $8 (3/16/84)
79 LAWRENCE J. BARGETTO Chardonnay Central Coast Cypress 1989 $9 (7/15/91)
82 LAWRENCE J. BARGETTO Chardonnay Santa Cruz Mountains 1989 $18 (2/28/91)
78 LAWRENCE J. BARGETTO Chardonnay Santa Cruz Mountains 1988 $18 (6/30/90)
82 LAWRENCE J. BARGETTO Chardonnay Santa Cruz Mountains Miller Ranch 1987 $15 (4/15/89)
81 LAWRENCE J. BARGETTO Chardonnay Santa Maria Valley 1985 $10 (11/15/87)
75 BARON HERZOG Chardonnay Sonoma County 1989 $11 (3/31/91)
75 BARROW GREEN Chardonnay California 1988 $14.50 (7/15/91)
90 BARROW GREEN Chardonnay California 1987 $16 (11/15/89)
87 BEAUCANON Chardonnay Napa Valley 1988 $10 (7/15/91)
81 BEAULIEU Chardonnay Carneros Napa Valley Los Carneros Reserve 1989 $17 (5/31/91)
89 BEAULIEU Chardonnay Carneros Napa Valley Los Carneros Reserve 1988 Rel: $14 Cur: $14 (CH-6/90)
84 BEAULIEU Chardonnay Carneros Napa Valley Los Carneros Reserve 1988 Rel: $14 Cur: $14 (5/31/90)
87 BEAULIEU Chardonnay Carneros Napa Valley Los Carneros Reserve 1987 Rel: $14 Cur: $16 (CH-5/90)
85 BEAULIEU Chardonnay Carneros Napa Valley Los Carneros Reserve 1987 Rel: $14 Cur: $16 (4/30/89)
86 BEAULIEU Chardonnay Carneros Napa Valley Los Carneros Reserve 1986 Rel: $12 Cur: $15 (CH-6/90)
78 BEAULIEU Chardonnay Carneros Napa Valley Los Carneros Reserve 1986 Rel: $12 Cur: $15 (4/15/88)
84 BEAULIEU Chardonnay Carneros Napa Valley Los Carneros Reserve 1985 Rel: $12 Cur: $16 (CH-6/90)
85 BEAULIEU Chardonnay Carneros Napa Valley Los Carneros Reserve 1985 Rel: $12 Cur: $16 (1/31/88)
79 BEAULIEU Chardonnay Carneros Napa Valley Los Carneros Reserve 1984 Rel: $10 Cur: $16 (CH-4/90)
74 BEAULIEU Chardonnay Carneros Napa Valley Los Carneros Reserve 1983 Rel: $10 Cur: $15 (CH-4/90)
72 BEAULIEU Chardonnay Carneros Napa Valley Los Carneros Reserve 1982 Rel: $10 Cur: $16 (CH-4/90)
70 BEAULIEU Chardonnay Carneros Napa Valley Los Carneros Reserve 1981 Rel: $10 Cur: $18 (CH-4/90)
81 BEAULIEU Chardonnay Napa Valley Beaufort 1989 $11 (7/15/91)
79 BEAULIEU Chardonnay Napa Valley Beaufort 1988 $9.50 (4/30/90)
79 BEAULIEU Chardonnay Napa Valley Beaufort 1987 $12.50 (6/15/89)
85 BEAULIEU Chardonnay Napa Valley Beaufort 1986 $9 (7/15/88)
77 BEAULIEU Chardonnay Napa Valley Beaufort 1983 $10.50 (10/01/85)
70 BEAULIEU Chardonnay Napa Valley Beaufort 1979 Rel: $6 Cur: $20 (CH-4/90)
70 BEAULIEU Chardonnay Napa Valley Beaufort 1978 Rel: $6 Cur: $22 (CH-4/90)
64 BEAULIEU Chardonnay Napa Valley Beaufort 1977 Rel: $6 Cur: $22 (CH-4/90)
62 BEAULIEU Chardonnay Napa Valley Beaufort 1976 Rel: $6 Cur: $22 (CH-4/90)
61 BEAULIEU Chardonnay Napa Valley Beaufort 1975 Rel: $5 Cur: $28 (CH-4/90)
62 BEAULIEU Chardonnay Napa Valley Beaufort 1974 Rel: $5 Cur: $25 (CH-4/90)
60 BEAULIEU Chardonnay Napa Valley Beaufort 1973 Rel: $5 Cur: $30 (CH-4/90)
60 BEAULIEU Chardonnay Napa Valley Beaufort 1972 Rel: $5 Cur: $30 (CH-4/90)
58 BEAULIEU Chardonnay Napa Valley Beaufort 1971 Rel: $4 Cur: $30 (CH-4/90)
59 BEAULIEU Chardonnay Napa Valley Beaufort 1970 Rel: $4 Cur: $32 (CH-4/90)
57 BEAULIEU Chardonnay Napa Valley Beaufort 1969 Rel: $2 Cur: $35 (CH-4/90)
59 BEAULIEU Chardonnay Napa Valley Beaufort 1968 Rel: $2 Cur: $35 (CH-4/90)
75 BEAUREGARD Chardonnay Napa Valley 1987 $10 (7/15/91)
84 BELVEDERE Chardonnay Carneros 1987 $13 (4/30/89)
88 BELVEDERE Chardonnay Carneros 1986 $13 (7/15/88)
91 BELVEDERE Chardonnay Carneros Winery Lake 1983 $12 (6/01/85)
60 BELVEDERE Chardonnay Carneros Winery Lake 1982 $12 (8/01/84)
83 BELVEDERE Chardonnay Central Coast Discovery Series 1984 $4.75 (10/16/85) BB
58 BELVEDERE Chardonnay Monterey County Discovery Series 1983 $4.75 (2/01/85)
83 BELVEDERE Chardonnay North Coast Discovery Series 1984 $5 (1/01/86) BB
88 BELVEDERE Chardonnay Russian River Valley 1987 $11 (7/15/89)
85 BELVEDERE Chardonnay Russian River Valley Reserve 1989 $9 (3/31/91)
85 BELVEDERE Chardonnay Russian River Valley Reserve 1988 $9 (2/15/90)
71 BELVEDERE Chardonnay Sonoma County 1989 $6 (7/15/91)
80 BELVEDERE Chardonnay Sonoma County Bacigalupi 1986 $13 (7/15/88)
91 BELVEDERE Chardonnay Sonoma County Bacigalupi 1985 $12 (12/15/87)
73 BELVEDERE Chardonnay Sonoma County Bacigalupi 1983 $12 (11/16/85)
80 BELVEDERE Chardonnay Sonoma County Discovery Series 1989 $6 (12/31/90) BB
78 BELVEDERE Chardonnay Sonoma County Discovery Series 1987 $5.25 (7/31/88)
85 BENZIGER Chardonnay Sonoma County 1988 $10 (6/30/90)
87 BENZIGER Chardonnay Sonoma County 1987 $9.50 (7/15/89)
81 BERINGER Chardonnay Napa Valley 1989 $14 (3/15/91)
87 BERINGER Chardonnay Napa Valley 1988 $13 (4/15/90)
80 BERINGER Chardonnay Napa Valley 1987 $10 (7/15/89)
83 BERINGER Chardonnay Napa Valley 1986 $10.50 (1/31/88)
84 BERINGER Chardonnay Napa Valley 1985 $10 (4/30/87)
90 BERINGER Chardonnay Napa Valley 1984 $9 (4/15/87)

Key to Symbols

The scores reported here are the results of blind tastings conducted by our panel of senior editors. Wines that carry the initials below are results of individual tastings.

THE WINE SPECTATOR 100-POINT SCALE *95-100*—Classic, a great wine; *90-94*—Outstanding, superior character and style; *80-89*—Good to very good, a wine with special qualities; *70-79*—Average, drinkable wine that may have minor flaws; *60-69*—Below average, drinkable but not recommended; *50-59*—Poor, undrinkable, not recommended. "+"—With a score indicates a range; used primarily with barrel tastings to indicate a preliminary score.

SPECIAL DESIGNATIONS SS—Spectator Selection, CS—Cellar Selection, BB—Best Buy.

TASTER'S INITIALS (JG)—Jim Gordon, (HS)—Harvey Steiman, (JL)—James Laube, (JS)—James Suckling, (TM)—Thomas Matthews, (TR)—Terry Robards, (BT)—Barrel Tasting (these wines were tasted blind from barrel samples), (CA-date)—*California's Great Cabernets* by James Laube, (CH-date)—*California's Great Chardonnays* by James Laube, (VP-date)—*Vintage Port* by James Suckling.

DATE TASTED Dates in parentheses represent the issue in which the rating was published.

82 BERINGER Chardonnay Napa Valley 1983 $10 (9/01/85)
80 BERINGER Chardonnay Napa Valley 1982 $9.75 (4/16/84)
85 BERINGER Chardonnay Napa Valley 1981 $10 (6/01/86)
70 BERINGER Chardonnay Napa Valley Centennial Cask Selection 1974 Rel: $5 Cur: $40 (CH-4/90)
85 BERINGER Chardonnay Napa Valley Private Reserve 1989 $19 (7/15/91)
76 BERINGER Chardonnay Napa Valley Private Reserve 1988 Rel: $19 Cur: $20 (6/30/90)
87 BERINGER Chardonnay Napa Valley Private Reserve 1988 Rel: $19 Cur: $20 (CH-4/90)
79 BERINGER Chardonnay Napa Valley Private Reserve 1987 Rel: $17 Cur: $19 (CH-4/90)
67 BERINGER Chardonnay Napa Valley Private Reserve 1987 Rel: $17 Cur: $19 (5/15/89)
90 BERINGER Chardonnay Napa Valley Private Reserve 1986 Rel: $16 Cur: $22 (CH-4/90)
91 BERINGER Chardonnay Napa Valley Private Reserve 1986 Rel: $16 Cur: $22 (4/15/88)
86 BERINGER Chardonnay Napa Valley Private Reserve 1985 Rel: $15 Cur: $24 (CH-4/90)
88 BERINGER Chardonnay Napa Valley Private Reserve 1985 Rel: $15 Cur: $24 (4/15/87)
88 BERINGER Chardonnay Napa Valley Private Reserve 1984 Rel: $15 Cur: $24 (CH-4/90)
91 BERINGER Chardonnay Napa Valley Private Reserve 1984 Rel: $15 Cur: $24 (4/15/87)
76 BERINGER Chardonnay Napa Valley Private Reserve 1983 Rel: $15 Cur: $24 (CH-4/90)
89 BERINGER Chardonnay Napa Valley Private Reserve 1983 Rel: $15 Cur: $24 (4/15/87)
74 BERINGER Chardonnay Napa Valley Private Reserve 1982 Rel: $15 Cur: $22 (CH-4/90)
87 BERINGER Chardonnay Napa Valley Private Reserve 1982 Rel: $15 Cur: $22 (11/01/84)
86 BERINGER Chardonnay Napa Valley Private Reserve 1981 Rel: $15 Cur: $28 (CH-4/90)
92 BERINGER Chardonnay Napa Valley Private Reserve 1981 Rel: $15 Cur: $28 (6/01/86)
75 BERINGER Chardonnay Napa Valley Private Reserve 1980 Rel: $15 Cur: $25 (CH-4/90)
78 BERINGER Chardonnay Napa Valley Private Reserve 1979 Rel: $14 Cur: $25 (CH-4/90)
70 BERINGER Chardonnay Napa Valley Private Reserve 1978 Rel: $12 Cur: $15 (CH-4/90)
88 BERINGER Chardonnay Santa Barbara County 1974 Rel: $5 Cur: $5 (CH-4/90)
88 BLACK MOUNTAIN Chardonnay Alexander Valley Douglass Hill 1988 $10 (4/15/90)
86 BLACK MOUNTAIN Chardonnay Alexander Valley Douglass Hill 1987 $10 (12/31/88)
72 BLACK MOUNTAIN Chardonnay Alexander Valley Douglass Hill 1985 $10 (8/31/87)
88 BLACK MOUNTAIN Chardonnay Alexander Valley Gravel Bar 1987 $18 (4/15/90)
86 BLUE HERON LAKE Chardonnay Napa County 1985 $13 (8/31/87)
76 BLUE HERON LAKE Chardonnay Wild Horse Valley 1988 $13 (3/31/91)
82 BOEGER Chardonnay El Dorado 1989 $11.50 (5/31/91)
89 BOEGER Chardonnay El Dorado 1986 $10.50 (9/30/88)
86 JEAN CLAUDE BOISSET Chardonnay Napa Valley 1983 $9.50 (4/16/86)
88 BON MARCHE Chardonnay Alexander Valley 1989 $8 (3/31/91) BB
84 BONNY DOON Chardonnay California Grahm Crew 1989 $9 (9/30/90) BB
85 BONNY DOON Chardonnay Sonoma County Grahm Crew 1986 $8.50 (10/15/87)
90 BONNY DOON Chardonnay Monterey County La Reina Vineyard 1989 $14 (3/15/91)
88 BONNY DOON Chardonnay Monterey County La Reina Vineyard 1987 $15 (12/31/88)
91 BONNY DOON Chardonnay Monterey County La Reina Vineyard 1986 $13.25 (3/31/88)
73 BONNY DOON Chardonnay Monterey County La Reina Vineyard 1985 $13 (4/30/87)
79 BOUCHAINE Chardonnay Alexander Valley 1982 Rel: $14 Cur: $18 (CH-2/90)
82 BOUCHAINE Chardonnay Alexander Valley 1982 Rel: $14 Cur: $18 (11/01/84)
82 BOUCHAINE Chardonnay Carneros 1988 $15 (11/30/90)
85 BOUCHAINE Chardonnay Carneros 1988 Rel: $15 Cur: $15 (CH-6/90)
89 BOUCHAINE Chardonnay Carneros 1987 Rel: $14 Cur: $14 (8/31/90)
83 BOUCHAINE Chardonnay Carneros 1987 Rel: $14 Cur: $14 (CH-2/90)
74 BOUCHAINE Chardonnay Carneros 1987 Rel: $14 Cur: $14 (7/15/89)
88 BOUCHAINE Chardonnay Carneros 1986 Rel: $13 Cur: $13 (CH-2/90)
87 BOUCHAINE Chardonnay Carneros 1985 Rel: $15 Cur: $20 (CH-2/90)
85 BOUCHAINE Chardonnay Carneros 1984 Rel: $14 Cur: $20 (CH-2/90)
66 BOUCHAINE Chardonnay Carneros 1984 Rel: $14 Cur: $20 (CH-2/90)
86 BOUCHAINE Chardonnay Carneros 1984 Rel: $14 Cur: $20 (1/31/87)
77 BOUCHAINE Chardonnay Carneros 1983 Rel: $14 Cur: $25 (CH-2/90)
84 BOUCHAINE Chardonnay Carneros 1983 Rel: $14 Cur: $25 (9/01/85)
88 BOUCHAINE Chardonnay Carneros Estate Reserve 1988 (NR) (CH-6/90)
89 BOUCHAINE Chardonnay Carneros Estate Reserve 1987 Rel: $19 Cur: $19 (5/31/90)
86 BOUCHAINE Chardonnay Carneros Estate Reserve 1987 Rel: $19 Cur: $19 (CH-2/90)
88 BOUCHAINE Chardonnay Carneros Estate Reserve 1986 Rel: $19 Cur: $19 (CH-2/90)
88 BOUCHAINE Chardonnay Carneros Estate Reserve 1986 Rel: $19 Cur: $19 (4/15/89)
71 BOUCHAINE Chardonnay Carneros Winery Lake Vineyard 1984 Rel: $22 Cur: $22 (CH-2/90)
70 BOUCHAINE Chardonnay Carneros Winery Lake Vineyard 1984 Rel: $22 Cur: $22 (5/31/87)
91 BOUCHAINE Chardonnay Napa Valley 1986 Rel: $13 Cur: $17 (10/31/88)
82 BOUCHAINE Chardonnay Napa Valley 1985 Rel: $13 Cur: $17 (11/15/87)
80 BOUCHAINE Chardonnay Napa Valley 1984 Rel: $12.50 Cur: $15 (1/31/87)
75 BOUCHAINE Chardonnay Napa Valley 1983 Rel: $14 Cur: $25 (CH-2/90)
90 BOUCHAINE Chardonnay Napa Valley 1982 Rel: $14.50 Cur: $15 (6/16/84) SS
81 BOUCHAINE Chardonnay Napa Valley Cask 85-86 NV $7.50 (7/31/87) BB
87 BOYER Chardonnay Monterey County Ventana Vineyard 1989 $15 (7/15/91)
84 BRANDER Chardonnay Santa Ynez Valley 1987 $13 (12/15/89)
84 BRANDER Chardonnay Santa Ynez Valley Tête de Cuvée 1989 $22 (7/15/91)
79 DAVID BRUCE Chardonnay California 1984 $10 (7/16/86)
77 DAVID BRUCE Chardonnay Santa Cruz Mountains 1987 $18 (2/15/90)
69 DAVID BRUCE Chardonnay Santa Cruz Mountains 1983 $18 (9/30/86)
85 BUENA VISTA Chardonnay Carneros 1989 $11 (7/15/91)
84 BUENA VISTA Chardonnay Carneros 1989 $11 (12/31/90)
88 BUENA VISTA Chardonnay Carneros 1987 $10 (10/15/88)
83 BUENA VISTA Chardonnay Carneros 1986 $11.50 (6/30/87)
78 BUENA VISTA Chardonnay Carneros 1984 $11 (3/01/86)
83 BUENA VISTA Chardonnay Carneros Jeanette's Vineyard 1988 $26 (3/31/91)
81 BUENA VISTA Chardonnay Carneros Jeanette's Vineyard 1986 $8.50 (2/15/88)
83 BUENA VISTA Chardonnay Carneros Jeanette's Vineyard 1985 $13.25 (2/28/87)
82 BUENA VISTA Chardonnay Carneros Private Reserve 1988 $16.50 (3/31/91)
86 BUENA VISTA Chardonnay Carneros Private Reserve 1988 $16.50 (CH-6/90)
82 BUENA VISTA Chardonnay Carneros Private Reserve 1987 Rel: $16.50 Cur: $18 (CH-3/90)
82 BUENA VISTA Chardonnay Carneros Private Reserve 1987 Rel: $16.50 Cur: $18 (10/31/89)
91 BUENA VISTA Chardonnay Carneros Private Reserve 1986 Rel: $16.50 Cur: $17 (CH-3/90)
90 BUENA VISTA Chardonnay Carneros Private Reserve 1986 Rel: $16.50 Cur: $17 (12/31/88)
86 BUENA VISTA Chardonnay Carneros Private Reserve 1985 Rel: $16.50 Cur: $17 (CH-3/90)
85 BUENA VISTA Chardonnay Carneros Private Reserve 1985 Rel: $16.50 Cur: $17 (5/31/88)
75 BUENA VISTA Chardonnay Carneros Private Reserve 1984 Rel: $14.50 Cur: $16 (CH-6/90)
74 BUENA VISTA Chardonnay Carneros Private Reserve 1984 Rel: $14.50 Cur: $16 (7/31/87)
84 BUENA VISTA Chardonnay Carneros Private Reserve 1983 Rel: $14.50 Cur: $18 (CH-3/90)
70 BUENA VISTA Chardonnay Carneros Private Reserve 1982 Rel: $16.50 Cur: $17 (3/16/86)
82 BURGESS Chardonnay Napa Valley Triere Vineyard 1989 $16 (7/15/91)
90 BURGESS Chardonnay Napa Valley Triere Vineyard 1988 Rel: $16 Cur: $16 (4/30/90)
88 BURGESS Chardonnay Napa Valley Triere Vineyard 1988 Rel: $16 Cur: $16 (CH-12/89)
85 BURGESS Chardonnay Napa Valley Triere Vineyard 1987 Rel: $14.50 Cur: $15 (CH-12/89)

89 BURGESS Chardonnay Napa Valley Triere Vineyard 1987 Rel: $14.50 Cur: $15 (6/30/89)
87 BURGESS Chardonnay Napa Valley Triere Vineyard 1986 Rel: $14 Cur: $16 (CH-12/89)
88 BURGESS Chardonnay Napa Valley Triere Vineyard 1986 Rel: $14 Cur: $16 (7/15/88)
88 BURGESS Chardonnay Napa Valley Vintage Reserve 1985 Rel: $13 Cur: $16 (CH-12/89)
87 BURGESS Chardonnay Napa Valley Vintage Reserve 1985 Rel: $13 Cur: $16 (10/31/87)
79 BURGESS Chardonnay Napa Valley Vintage Reserve 1984 Rel: $13 Cur: $17 (CH-12/89)
75 BURGESS Chardonnay Napa Valley Vintage Reserve 1984 Rel: $13 Cur: $17 (9/30/86)
69 BURGESS Chardonnay Napa Valley Vintage Reserve 1983 Rel: $12 Cur: $20 (CH-12/89)
86 BURGESS Chardonnay Napa Valley Vintage Reserve 1983 Rel: $12 Cur: $20 (6/16/85)
68 BURGESS Chardonnay Napa Valley Vintage Reserve 1982 Rel: $12 Cur: $12 (CH-12/89)
75 BURGESS Chardonnay Napa Valley Vintage Reserve 1982 Rel: $12 Cur: $12 (4/01/84)
74 BURGESS Chardonnay Napa Valley 1981 Rel: $11 Cur: $16 (CH-12/89)
75 BURGESS Chardonnay Napa Valley 1980 Rel: $11 Cur: $18 (CH-12/89)
78 BURGESS Chardonnay Napa Valley 1979 Rel: $11 Cur: $18 (CH-12/89)
77 BURGESS Chardonnay Napa Valley 1978 Rel: $11 Cur: $18 (CH-12/89)
80 BURGESS Chardonnay Napa Valley 1977 Rel: $11 Cur: $23 (CH-12/89)
70 BURGESS Chardonnay Carneros Winery Lake Vineyard 1976 Rel: $10 Cur: $20 (CH-12/89)
84 BURGESS Chardonnay Carneros Winery Lake Vineyard 1975 Rel: $9 Cur: $40 (CH-12/89)
79 BURGESS Chardonnay Carneros Winery Lake Vineyard 1974 Rel: $6 Cur: $25 (CH-12/89)
85 BURGESS Chardonnay Napa Valley 1973 Rel: $6 Cur: $30 (CH-12/89)
69 BUTTERFIELD Chardonnay Napa Valley 1986 $7.50 (2/15/88)
79 DAVIS BYNUM Chardonnay Russian River Valley 1988 $10 (4/30/90)
79 DAVIS BYNUM Chardonnay Russian River Valley Limited Release 1989 $13 (4/30/91)
80 DAVIS BYNUM Chardonnay Russian River Valley Limited Release 1987 $14 (9/30/89)
82 DAVIS BYNUM Chardonnay Sonoma County Reserve Bottling 1987 $9 (7/15/89)
80 BYRON Chardonnay Santa Barbara County 1989 $13 (7/15/91)
92 BYRON Chardonnay Santa Barbara County 1988 $12 (4/30/90) SS
91 BYRON Chardonnay Santa Barbara County 1987 $11 (12/15/89)
89 BYRON Chardonnay Santa Barbara County 1987 $11 (3/31/89)
78 BYRON Chardonnay Santa Barbara County Barrel Fermented Reserve 1987 $16 (12/15/89)
86 BYRON Chardonnay Santa Barbara County Reserve 1988 $17 (11/15/90)
73 BYRON Chardonnay Santa Barbara County Reserve 1985 $13 (10/31/87)
83 CAIN Chardonnay Carneros 1989 $16 (7/15/91)
84 CAIN Chardonnay Carneros 1988 $16 (11/30/90)
86 CAIN Chardonnay Carneros 1987 $16 (12/31/89)
88 CAIN Chardonnay Carneros 1986 $16 (9/15/88)
82 CAIN Chardonnay Carneros 1985 $16 (10/31/87)
74 CAIN Chardonnay Napa-Sonoma Counties 1985 $10 (7/31/87)
83 CAIN Chardonnay Napa Valley 1987 $10 (4/30/89)
87 CAIN Chardonnay Napa Valley 1986 $10 (9/30/88)
62 CAIN Chardonnay Napa Valley 1984 $10 (10/31/86)
60 CAIN Chardonnay Napa Valley 1983 $10 (1/01/85)
79 CAKEBREAD Chardonnay Napa Valley 1989 $19.50 (7/15/91)
89 CAKEBREAD Chardonnay Napa Valley 1988 $17.50 (3/15/90)
86 CAKEBREAD Chardonnay Napa Valley 1987 $21 (6/30/89)
70 CAKEBREAD Chardonnay Napa Valley 1986 $20 (2/15/88)
88 CAKEBREAD Chardonnay Napa Valley Reserve 1986 $26 (2/15/90)
86 CALERA Chardonnay Central Coast 1988 $14 (11/30/90)
82 CALERA Chardonnay Central Coast 1987 $12 (3/15/90)
83 CALERA Chardonnay Central Coast 1986 $12 (7/31/89)
86 CALERA Chardonnay San Benito County Mount Harlan Vineyard Young Vines 1987 $22 (4/15/89)
80 CALERA Chardonnay Santa Barbara County 1985 $11.75 (7/31/87)
64 CALERA Chardonnay Santa Barbara County 1984 $11.25 (3/16/86)
83 CALERA Chardonnay Santa Barbara County Los Alamos Vineyard 1983 $10.75 (2/01/85)
72 CALLAWAY Chardonnay Temecula Calla-Lees 1989 $10 (2/28/91)
86 CALLAWAY Chardonnay Temecula Calla-Lees 1988 $10 (2/28/90)
84 CALLAWAY Chardonnay Temecula Calla-Lees 1987 $9.75 (12/31/88)
82 CALLAWAY Chardonnay Temecula Calla-Lees 1986 $9.50 (11/15/87)
86 CALLAWAY Chardonnay Temecula Calla-Lees 1985 $9.25 (3/15/87)
70 CAMBIASO Chardonnay Sonoma County 1982 $8 (4/01/84)
84 CAMBRIA Chardonnay Santa Barbara County Cambria Vineyard Sur Lees 1988 $16 (12/15/89)
86 CAMBRIA Chardonnay Santa Barbara County Reserve 1986 $25 (12/15/89)
84 CAMBRIA Chardonnay Santa Maria Valley Katherine's Vineyard 1989 $16 (12/31/90)
85 CAMBRIA Chardonnay Santa Maria Valley Reserve 1988 $25 (12/31/90)
82 CANTERBURY Chardonnay California 1989 $7.50 (7/15/91) BB
83 CANTERBURY Chardonnay California 1985 $6.50 (11/15/86) BB
82 J. CAREY Chardonnay Santa Barbara County 1989 $13 (4/30/91)
83 J. CAREY Chardonnay Santa Ynez Valley 1988 $12 (6/30/90)
85 J. CAREY Chardonnay Santa Ynez Valley 1987 $10 (12/15/89)
75 J. CAREY Chardonnay Santa Ynez Valley Adobe Canyon Vineyard 1983 $12 (6/16/84)
86 CARNEROS CREEK Chardonnay Carneros Fleur de Carneros 1989 $9 (6/30/91) BB
78 CARNEROS CREEK Chardonnay Los Carneros 1989 $13 (5/15/91)
85 CARNEROS CREEK Chardonnay Los Carneros 1988 $13 (2/15/90)
81 CARNEROS CREEK Chardonnay Los Carneros 1987 $13 (7/15/89)
87 CARNEROS CREEK Chardonnay Los Carneros 1986 $11.50 (7/15/88)
79 CARNEROS CREEK Chardonnay Los Carneros 1985 $10.50 (11/15/87)
86 CARNEROS CREEK Chardonnay Los Carneros 1984 $10.50 (4/30/87)
80 CARNEROS CREEK Chardonnay Napa Valley 1983 $11 (9/01/85)
71 CARNEROS CREEK Chardonnay Napa Valley 1982 $12 (12/16/84)
81 CARNEROS CREEK Chardonnay Napa Valley 1981 $10 (1/01/84)
79 CARNEROS CREEK Chardonnay Sonoma County 1981 $10 (1/01/84)
84 CARTLIDGE & BROWNE Chardonnay Napa Valley 1989 $9.75 (5/31/91)
81 CARTLIDGE & BROWNE Chardonnay Napa Valley 1987 $11 (4/15/90)
83 CARTLIDGE & BROWNE Chardonnay Napa Valley 1986 $10 (5/31/88)
91 CARTLIDGE & BROWNE Chardonnay Napa Valley 1985 $9.75 (3/31/87)
66 CARTLIDGE & BROWNE Chardonnay Napa Valley 1984 $11.50 (1/01/86)
78 CARTLIDGE & BROWNE Chardonnay Napa Valley 1983 $11.50 (2/16/85)
62 CASSAYRE-FORNI Chardonnay Alexander Valley 1982 $10.75 (2/15/84)
75 CASTORO Chardonnay San Luis Obispo County 1988 $8.50 (12/15/89)
83 CAYMUS Chardonnay Napa Valley 1986 $12 (8/31/88)
80 CECCHETTI SEBASTIANI Chardonnay Napa Valley 1989 $6.50 (4/30/91)
64 CECCHETTI SEBASTIANI Chardonnay Napa Valley Cask Lot 1 1987 $9.50 (4/15/89)
85 CECCHETTI SEBASTIANI Chardonnay Napa Valley Cask Lot 2 1986 $9.50 (12/15/87)
90 CHALK HILL Chardonnay Chalk Hill 1989 $14 (5/15/91) SS
76 CHALK HILL Chardonnay Napa Valley 1983 $7 (10/01/84)
68 CHALK HILL Chardonnay Sonoma County 1986 $10 (1/31/88)
82 CHALK HILL Chardonnay Sonoma County 1984 $8 (12/01/85)
79 CHALK HILL Chardonnay Sonoma County 1983 $10 (6/01/85)

85 CHALONE Chardonnay California Gavilan 1989 $12 (12/31/90)
90 CHALONE Chardonnay Chalone 1989 $25 (11/30/90)
90 CHALONE Chardonnay Chalone 1988 Rel: $22 Cur: $30 (CH-6/90)
89 CHALONE Chardonnay Chalone 1988 Rel: $22 Cur: $30 (2/28/90)
58 CHALONE Chardonnay Chalone 1987 Rel: $22 Cur: $39 (CH-1/90)
90 CHALONE Chardonnay Chalone 1987 Rel: $22 Cur: $39 (12/31/88)
94 CHALONE Chardonnay Chalone 1986 Rel: $22 Cur: $51 (CH-1/90)
80 CHALONE Chardonnay Chalone 1986 Rel: $22 Cur: $51 (12/31/87)
80 CHALONE Chardonnay Chalone 1985 Rel: $22 Cur: $95 (CH-4/90)
88 CHALONE Chardonnay Chalone 1984 Rel: $18 Cur: $56 (CH-1/90)
90 CHALONE Chardonnay Chalone 1983 Rel: $18 Cur: $60 (CH-1/90)
95 CHALONE Chardonnay Chalone 1982 Rel: $18 Cur: $61 (CH-1/90)
93 CHALONE Chardonnay Chalone 1981 Rel: $17 Cur: $68 (CH-4/90)
92 CHALONE Chardonnay Chalone 1980 Rel: $17 Cur: $58 (CH-1/90)
89 CHALONE Chardonnay Chalone 1979 Rel: $14 Cur: $69 (CH-1/90)
87 CHALONE Chardonnay Chalone Gavilan 1988 $12 (4/15/90)
89 CHALONE Chardonnay Chalone Reserve 1988 (NR) (CH-6/90)
87 CHALONE Chardonnay Chalone Reserve 1987 Rel: $35 Cur: $95 (CH-5/90)
85 CHALONE Chardonnay Chalone Reserve 1986 Rel: $28 Cur: $100 (CH-5/90)
94 CHALONE Chardonnay Chalone Reserve 1985 Rel: $28 Cur: $110 (CH-6/90)
87 CHALONE Chardonnay Chalone Reserve 1983 Rel: $25 Cur: $49 (CH-5/90)
93 CHALONE Chardonnay Chalone Reserve 1982 Rel: $25 Cur: $48 (CH-5/90)
86 CHALONE Chardonnay Chalone Reserve 1981 Rel: $20 Cur: $100 (CH-5/90)
94 CHALONE Chardonnay Chalone Reserve 1980 Rel: $18 Cur: $125 (CH-5/90)
82 CHAMISAL Chardonnay Edna Valley 1989 $14 (7/15/91)
78 CHAMISAL Chardonnay Edna Valley 1988 $14 (6/30/90)
85 CHAMISAL Chardonnay Edna Valley 1987 $14 (7/15/89)
90 CHAMISAL Chardonnay Edna Valley 1986 $13 (5/31/88)
78 CHAMISAL Chardonnay Edna Valley 1985 $10 (11/15/87)
70 CHAMISAL Chardonnay Edna Valley 1984 $10 (6/01/86)
90 CHAMISAL Chardonnay Edna Valley Special Reserve 1988 $18.50 (11/30/90)
77 CHANSA Chardonnay Santa Barbara County 1989 $10 (4/30/91)
88 CHAPPELLET Chardonnay Napa Valley 1988 $14 (5/31/91)
89 CHAPPELLET Chardonnay Napa Valley 1988 Rel: $14 Cur: $14 (CH-6/90)
82 CHAPPELLET Chardonnay Napa Valley 1987 Rel: $14 Cur: $14 (6/30/90)
87 CHAPPELLET Chardonnay Napa Valley 1987 Rel: $14 Cur: $14 (CH-3/90)
90 CHAPPELLET Chardonnay Napa Valley 1986 Rel: $14 Cur: $14 (CH-3/90)
74 CHAPPELLET Chardonnay Napa Valley 1986 Rel: $14 Cur: $14 (5/15/89)
87 CHAPPELLET Chardonnay Napa Valley 1985 Rel: $12.50 Cur: $15 (CH-3/90)
77 CHAPPELLET Chardonnay Napa Valley 1985 Rel: $12.50 Cur: $15 (7/31/88)
87 CHAPPELLET Chardonnay Napa Valley 1984 Rel: $12 Cur: $20 (CH-3/90)
79 CHAPPELLET Chardonnay Napa Valley 1983 Rel: $12 Cur: $18 (CH-3/90)
90 CHAPPELLET Chardonnay Napa Valley 1983 Rel: $12 Cur: $18 (4/16/85) (JG)
85 CHAPPELLET Chardonnay Napa Valley 1982 Rel: $12.50 Cur: $20 (CH-3/90)
91 CHAPPELLET Chardonnay Napa Valley 1982 Rel: $12.50 Cur: $20 (4/16/85) (JG)
80 CHAPPELLET Chardonnay Napa Valley 1981 Rel: $14 Cur: $22 (CH-3/90)
80 CHAPPELLET Chardonnay Napa Valley 1981 Rel: $14 Cur: $22 (4/16/85) (JG)
84 CHAPPELLET Chardonnay Napa Valley 1980 Rel: $14 Cur: $25 (CH-3/90)
85 CHAPPELLET Chardonnay Napa Valley 1980 Rel: $14 Cur: $25 (4/16/85) (JG)
79 CHAPPELLET Chardonnay Napa Valley 1979 Rel: $12 Cur: $30 (CH-3/90)
86 CHAPPELLET Chardonnay Napa Valley 1979 Rel: $12 Cur: $30 (4/16/85) (JG)
76 CHAPPELLET Chardonnay Napa Valley 1978 Rel: $11.75 Cur: $40 (CH-3/90)
87 CHAPPELLET Chardonnay Napa Valley 1978 Rel: $11.75 Cur: $40 (4/16/85) (JG)
90 CHAPPELLET Chardonnay Napa Valley 1977 Rel: $11.75 Cur: $40 (CH-6/90)
84 CHAPPELLET Chardonnay Napa Valley 1977 Rel: $11.75 Cur: $40 (4/16/85) (JG)
71 CHAPPELLET Chardonnay Napa Valley 1976 Rel: $9.75 Cur: $30 (CH-3/90)
70 CHAPPELLET Chardonnay Napa Valley 1976 Rel: $9.75 Cur: $30 (4/16/85) (JG)
82 CHAPPELLET Chardonnay Napa Valley 1975 Rel: $6.75 Cur: $40 (CH-3/90)
85 CHAPPELLET Chardonnay Napa Valley 1975 Rel: $6.75 Cur: $40 (4/16/85) (JG)
72 CHAPPELLET Chardonnay Napa Valley 1974 Rel: $6.75 Cur: $45 (CH-3/90)
83 CHAPPELLET Chardonnay Napa Valley 1974 Rel: $6.75 Cur: $45 (4/16/85) (JG)
91 CHAPPELLET Chardonnay Napa Valley 1973 Rel: $6.75 Cur: $50 (CH-3/90)
80 CHAPPELLET Chardonnay Napa Valley 1973 Rel: $6.75 Cur: $50 (4/16/85) (JG)
90 CHAPPELLET Chardonnay Napa Valley 1972 Rel: $6 Cur: $50 (4/16/85) (JG)
78 CHAPPELLET Chardonnay Napa Valley 1971 Rel: $6 Cur: $50 (4/16/85) (JG)
86 CHAPPELLET Chardonnay Napa Valley 1970 Rel: $6 Cur: $50 (4/16/85) (JG)
86 CHASE CREEK Chardonnay Napa Valley 1985 $7 (12/15/86)
77 CHASE CREEK Chardonnay Napa Valley 1984 $8.50 (11/01/85)
84 CHATEAU CHEVALIER Chardonnay California 1982 $12.50 (1/01/84)
81 CHATEAU DE BAUN Chardonnay Russian River Valley Barrel Fermented 1989 $10 (6/15/91)
75 CHATEAU DE BAUN Chardonnay Russian River Valley Barrel Fermented 1989 $10 (3/31/91)
83 CHATEAU DE LEU Chardonnay Solano County Green Valley 1989 $8 (7/15/91)
73 CHATEAU DE LEU Chardonnay Solano County Green Valley 1982 $7 (5/16/84)
76 CHATEAU JULIEN Chardonnay Monterey County Paraiso Springs Vineyard 1984 $12 (2/15/87)
85 CHATEAU LA GRANDE ROCHE Chardonnay Napa Valley 1989 $13 (11/15/90)
85 CHATEAU MONTELENA Chardonnay Alexander Valley 1988 Rel: $20 Cur: $26 (6/30/90)
91 CHATEAU MONTELENA Chardonnay Alexander Valley 1988 Rel: $20 Cur: $26 (CH-2/90)
89 CHATEAU MONTELENA Chardonnay Alexander Valley 1987 Rel: $20 Cur: $26 (CH-2/90)
90 CHATEAU MONTELENA Chardonnay Alexander Valley 1987 Rel: $20 Cur: $26 (6/30/89)
91 CHATEAU MONTELENA Chardonnay Alexander Valley 1986 Rel: $18 Cur: $26 (CH-2/90)
89 CHATEAU MONTELENA Chardonnay Alexander Valley 1986 Rel: $18 Cur: $26 (4/30/88)
91 CHATEAU MONTELENA Chardonnay Alexander Valley 1985 Rel: $16 Cur: $28 (CH-2/90)
87 CHATEAU MONTELENA Chardonnay Alexander Valley 1985 Rel: $16 Cur: $28 (6/30/87)
90 CHATEAU MONTELENA Chardonnay Alexander Valley 1984 Rel: $16 Cur: $32 (CH-2/90)
91 CHATEAU MONTELENA Chardonnay Alexander Valley 1984 Rel: $16 Cur: $32 (6/01/86)
84 CHATEAU MONTELENA Chardonnay Alexander Valley 1983 Rel: $14 Cur: $32 (CH-2/90)
85 CHATEAU MONTELENA Chardonnay Alexander Valley 1983 Rel: $14 Cur: $32 (9/16/85)
92 CHATEAU MONTELENA Chardonnay Alexander Valley 1982 Rel: $14 Cur: $36 (CH-2/90)
90 CHATEAU MONTELENA Chardonnay Alexander Valley 1982 Rel: $14 Cur: $36 (5/01/84)
91 CHATEAU MONTELENA Chardonnay Alexander Valley 1981 Rel: $14 Cur: $36 (CH-2/90)
89 CHATEAU MONTELENA Chardonnay Alexander Valley 1981 Rel: $14 Cur: $36 (4/16/84)
83 CHATEAU MONTELENA Chardonnay Napa Valley 1989 $23 (7/15/91)
86 CHATEAU MONTELENA Chardonnay Napa Valley 1988 Rel: $20 Cur: $23 (11/30/90)
88 CHATEAU MONTELENA Chardonnay Napa Valley 1988 Rel: $20 Cur: $23 (CH-7/90)
72 CHATEAU MONTELENA Chardonnay Napa Valley 1987 Rel: $20 Cur: $26 (2/15/90)
68 CHATEAU MONTELENA Chardonnay Napa Valley 1987 Rel: $20 Cur: $26 (CH-2/90)
91 CHATEAU MONTELENA Chardonnay Napa Valley 1986 Rel: $18 Cur: $26 (CH-2/90)
90 CHATEAU MONTELENA Chardonnay Napa Valley 1986 Rel: $18 Cur: $26 (12/31/88)
90 CHATEAU MONTELENA Chardonnay Napa Valley 1985 Rel: $18 Cur: $25 (CH-2/90)

UNITED STATES
CALIFORNIA/*CHARDONNAY*

78	CHATEAU MONTELENA Chardonnay Napa Valley 1985 Rel: $18 Cur: $25 (11/15/87)
88	CHATEAU MONTELENA Chardonnay Napa Valley 1984 Rel: $18 Cur: $28 (CH-2/90)
88	CHATEAU MONTELENA Chardonnay Napa Valley 1984 Rel: $18 Cur: $28 (10/31/86)
85	CHATEAU MONTELENA Chardonnay Napa Valley 1983 Rel: $16 Cur: $32 (CH-2/90)
82	CHATEAU MONTELENA Chardonnay Napa Valley 1983 Rel: $16 Cur: $32 (11/01/85)
85	CHATEAU MONTELENA Chardonnay Napa Valley 1982 Rel: $16 Cur: $32 (CH-2/90)
88	CHATEAU MONTELENA Chardonnay Napa Valley 1982 Rel: $16 Cur: $32 (10/01/84)
88	CHATEAU MONTELENA Chardonnay Napa Valley 1981 Rel: $16 Cur: $32 (CH-2/90)
79	CHATEAU MONTELENA Chardonnay Napa Valley 1980 Rel: $16 Cur: $38 (CH-2/90)
78	CHATEAU MONTELENA Chardonnay Napa Valley 1979 Rel: $16 Cur: $40 (CH-2/90)
90	CHATEAU MONTELENA Chardonnay Napa Valley 1979 Rel: $16 Cur: $40 (7/16/84)
77	CHATEAU MONTELENA Chardonnay Napa Valley 1978 Rel: $15 Cur: $45 (CH-2/90)
85	CHATEAU MONTELENA Chardonnay Napa Valley 1977 Rel: $15 Cur: $60 (CH-2/90)
77	CHATEAU MONTELENA Chardonnay Napa-Alexander Valleys 1976 Rel: $11 Cur: $50 (CH-2/90)
81	CHATEAU MONTELENA Chardonnay Napa-Alexander Valleys 1976 Rel: $11 Cur: $50 (7/16/84)
87	CHATEAU MONTELENA Chardonnay Napa Valley 1975 Rel: $9 Cur: $65 (CH-2/90)
88	CHATEAU MONTELENA Chardonnay Napa Valley 1974 Rel: $8 Cur: $70 (CH-2/90)
93	CHATEAU MONTELENA Chardonnay Napa-Alexander Valleys 1973 Rel: $6.50 Cur: $100 (CH-2/90)
95	CHATEAU MONTELENA Chardonnay Napa-Alexander Valleys 1972 Rel: $6 Cur: $110 (CH-2/90)
81	CHATEAU MONTELENA Chardonnay Napa-Alexander Valleys 1972 Rel: $6 Cur: $110 (7/16/84)
83	CHATEAU NAPA-BEAUCANON Chardonnay Napa Valley 1988 $10 (6/30/90)
85	CHATEAU NAPA-BEAUCANON Chardonnay Napa Valley 1987 $12 (1/31/89)
79	CHATEAU POTELLE Chardonnay Carneros 1988 $14 (7/15/91)
88	CHATEAU POTELLE Chardonnay Carneros 1988 $13.50 (6/30/90)
85	CHATEAU POTELLE Chardonnay Napa Valley 1987 $13 (3/31/90)
77	CHATEAU POTELLE Chardonnay Napa Valley 1986 $13 (11/15/88)
83	CHATEAU SOUVERAIN Chardonnay Sonoma County 1986 $9 (12/31/87)
74	CHATEAU SOUVERAIN Chardonnay Sonoma Valley Carneros Private Reserve 1987 $12 (4/15/89)
78	CHATEAU SOUVERAIN Chardonnay Sonoma Valley Carneros Reserve 1986 $12 (4/30/88)
90	CHATEAU ST. JEAN Chardonnay Alexander Valley Belle Terre Vineyards 1988 Rel: $16 Cur: $21 (5/31/90)
90	CHATEAU ST. JEAN Chardonnay Alexander Valley Belle Terre Vineyards 1988 Rel: $16 Cur: $21 (CH-3/90)
91	CHATEAU ST. JEAN Chardonnay Alexander Valley Belle Terre Vineyards 1987 Rel: $16 Cur: $22 (CH-3/90)
85	CHATEAU ST. JEAN Chardonnay Alexander Valley Belle Terre Vineyards 1987 Rel: $16 Cur: $22 (5/15/89)
90	CHATEAU ST. JEAN Chardonnay Alexander Valley Belle Terre Vineyards 1986 Rel: $16 Cur: $20 (CH-3/90)
92	CHATEAU ST. JEAN Chardonnay Alexander Valley Belle Terre Vineyards 1986 Rel: $16 Cur: $20 (7/15/88)
92	CHATEAU ST. JEAN Chardonnay Alexander Valley Belle Terre Vineyards 1985 Rel: $16 Cur: $25 (CH-3/90)
91	CHATEAU ST. JEAN Chardonnay Alexander Valley Belle Terre Vineyards 1985 Rel: $16 Cur: $25 (5/31/88)
85	CHATEAU ST. JEAN Chardonnay Alexander Valley Belle Terre Vineyards 1984 Rel: $16 Cur: $27 (CH-3/90)
79	CHATEAU ST. JEAN Chardonnay Alexander Valley Belle Terre Vineyards 1984 Rel: $16 Cur: $27 (6/01/86)
89	CHATEAU ST. JEAN Chardonnay Alexander Valley Belle Terre Vineyards 1983 Rel: $16.75 Cur: $30 (CH-3/90)
84	CHATEAU ST. JEAN Chardonnay Alexander Valley Belle Terre Vineyards 1983 Rel: $16.75 Cur: $30 (6/16/85)
86	CHATEAU ST. JEAN Chardonnay Alexander Valley Belle Terre Vineyards 1982 Rel: $15.50 Cur: $20 (CH-3/90)
88	CHATEAU ST. JEAN Chardonnay Alexander Valley Belle Terre Vineyards 1982 Rel: $15.50 Cur: $20 (4/16/84)
83	CHATEAU ST. JEAN Chardonnay Alexander Valley Belle Terre Vineyards 1981 Rel: $15 Cur: $18 (CH-3/90)
88	CHATEAU ST. JEAN Chardonnay Alexander Valley Belle Terre Vineyards 1981 Rel: $15 Cur: $18 (4/16/84)
88	CHATEAU ST. JEAN Chardonnay Alexander Valley Belle Terre Vineyards 1980 Rel: $15 Cur: $24 (CH-3/90)
84	CHATEAU ST. JEAN Chardonnay Alexander Valley Belle Terre Vineyards 1979 Rel: $12 Cur: $22 (CH-3/90)
73	CHATEAU ST. JEAN Chardonnay Alexander Valley Belle Terre Vineyards 1978 Rel: $14 Cur: $20 (CH-3/90)
80	CHATEAU ST. JEAN Chardonnay Alexander Valley Belle Terre Vineyards 1977 Rel: $12 Cur: $22 (CH-3/90)
77	CHATEAU ST. JEAN Chardonnay Alexander Valley Belle Terre Vineyards 1976 Rel: $7.50 Cur: $22 (CH-7/90)
88	CHATEAU ST. JEAN Chardonnay Alexander Valley Belle Terre Vineyards 1975 Rel: $7.50 Cur: $22 (CH-7/90)
74	CHATEAU ST. JEAN Chardonnay Alexander Valley Gauer Ranch 1980 Rel: $14 Cur: $18 (CH-3/90)
70	CHATEAU ST. JEAN Chardonnay Alexander Valley Gauer Ranch 1979 Rel: $14 Cur: $18 (CH-3/90)
88	CHATEAU ST. JEAN Chardonnay Alexander Valley Jimtown Ranch 1988 (NR) (CH-7/90)

87	CHATEAU ST. JEAN Chardonnay Alexander Valley Jimtown Ranch 1987 Rel: $15 Cur: $15 (CH-3/90)
86	CHATEAU ST. JEAN Chardonnay Alexander Valley Jimtown Ranch 1987 Rel: $15 Cur: $15 (7/15/89)
87	CHATEAU ST. JEAN Chardonnay Alexander Valley Jimtown Ranch 1983 Rel: $16 Cur: $20 (CH-7/90)
86	CHATEAU ST. JEAN Chardonnay Alexander Valley Jimtown Ranch 1983 Rel: $16 Cur: $20 (5/01/84)
87	CHATEAU ST. JEAN Chardonnay Alexander Valley Jimtown Ranch 1981 Rel: $14.75 Cur: $22 (CH-3/90)
77	CHATEAU ST. JEAN Chardonnay Alexander Valley Jimtown Ranch 1980 Rel: $14 Cur: $16 (CH-3/90)
88	CHATEAU ST. JEAN Chardonnay Alexander Valley Riverview Vineyards 1976 $9.50 (CH-7/90)
90	CHATEAU ST. JEAN Chardonnay Alexander Valley Robert Young Vineyards 1988 $18 (6/30/91)
91	CHATEAU ST. JEAN Chardonnay Alexander Valley Robert Young Vineyards 1988 $18 (CH-3/90)
91	CHATEAU ST. JEAN Chardonnay Alexander Valley Robert Young Vineyards 1987 Rel: $18 Cur: $25 (CH-3/90)
90	CHATEAU ST. JEAN Chardonnay Alexander Valley Robert Young Vineyards 1987 Rel: $18 Cur: $25 (6/30/89)
92	CHATEAU ST. JEAN Chardonnay Alexander Valley Robert Young Vineyards 1986 Rel: $18 Cur: $25 (CH-3/90)
89	CHATEAU ST. JEAN Chardonnay Alexander Valley Robert Young Vineyards 1986 Rel: $18 Cur: $25 (7/15/88)
91	CHATEAU ST. JEAN Chardonnay Alexander Valley Robert Young Vineyards 1985 Rel: $18 Cur: $26 (CH-3/90)
89	CHATEAU ST. JEAN Chardonnay Alexander Valley Robert Young Vineyards 1985 Rel: $18 Cur: $26 (11/30/87)
88	CHATEAU ST. JEAN Chardonnay Alexander Valley Robert Young Vineyards 1984 Rel: $20 Cur: $30 (CH-3/90)
84	CHATEAU ST. JEAN Chardonnay Alexander Valley Robert Young Vineyards 1984 Rel: $20 Cur: $30 (10/31/86)
88	CHATEAU ST. JEAN Chardonnay Alexander Valley Robert Young Vineyards 1983 Rel: $18 Cur: $33 (CH-3/90)
90	CHATEAU ST. JEAN Chardonnay Alexander Valley Robert Young Vineyards 1983 Rel: $18 Cur: $33 (9/01/85)
75	CHATEAU ST. JEAN Chardonnay Alexander Valley Robert Young Vineyards 1982 Rel: $18 Cur: $20 (CH-3/90)
88	CHATEAU ST. JEAN Chardonnay Alexander Valley Robert Young Vineyards 1982 Rel: $18 Cur: $20 (7/01/84)
86	CHATEAU ST. JEAN Chardonnay Alexander Valley Robert Young Vineyards 1981 Rel: $18 Cur: $60 (CH-3/90)
92	CHATEAU ST. JEAN Chardonnay Alexander Valley Robert Young Vineyards 1981 Rel: $18 Cur: $60 (4/16/84)
85	CHATEAU ST. JEAN Chardonnay Alexander Valley Robert Young Vineyards 1980 Rel: $18 Cur: $30 (CH-3/90)
88	CHATEAU ST. JEAN Chardonnay Alexander Valley Robert Young Vineyards 1980 Rel: $18 Cur: $30 (7/16/84)
85	CHATEAU ST. JEAN Chardonnay Alexander Valley Robert Young Vineyards 1979 Rel: $17 Cur: $34 (CH-3/90)
84	CHATEAU ST. JEAN Chardonnay Alexander Valley Robert Young Vineyards 1978 Rel: $17 Cur: $25 (CH-3/90)
87	CHATEAU ST. JEAN Chardonnay Alexander Valley Robert Young Vineyards 1978 Rel: $17 Cur: $25 (7/16/84)
68	CHATEAU ST. JEAN Chardonnay Alexander Valley Robert Young Vineyards 1977 Rel: $17 Cur: $22 (CH-3/90)
92	CHATEAU ST. JEAN Chardonnay Alexander Valley Robert Young Vineyards 1976 Rel: $8.75 Cur: $25 (CH-7/90)
90	CHATEAU ST. JEAN Chardonnay Alexander Valley Robert Young Vineyards 1976 Rel: $8.75 Cur: $25 (7/16/84)
63	CHATEAU ST. JEAN Chardonnay Alexander Valley Robert Young Vineyards 1975 Rel: $7.75 Cur: $22 (CH-7/90)
96	CHATEAU ST. JEAN Chardonnay Alexander Valley Robert Young Vineyards Reserve 1.5L 1987 (NR) (CH-7/90)
91	CHATEAU ST. JEAN Chardonnay Alexander Valley Robert Young Vineyards Reserve 1.5L 1986 (NR) (CH-7/90)
93	CHATEAU ST. JEAN Chardonnay Alexander Valley Robert Young Vineyards Reserve 1.5L 1985 Rel: $40 Cur: $40 (9/30/90)
95	CHATEAU ST. JEAN Chardonnay Alexander Valley Robert Young Vineyards Reserve 1.5L 1985 Rel: $40 Cur: $40 (CH-7/90)
87	CHATEAU ST. JEAN Chardonnay Alexander Valley Robert Young Vineyards Reserve 1.5L 1984 Rel: $40 Cur: $50 (CH-3/90)
90	CHATEAU ST. JEAN Chardonnay Alexander Valley Robert Young Vineyards Reserve 1.5L 1984 Rel: $40 Cur: $50 (5/31/88)
76	CHATEAU ST. JEAN Chardonnay Alexander Valley Robert Young Vineyards Reserve 1.5L 1982 Rel: $45 Cur: $45 (7/01/86)
89	CHATEAU ST. JEAN Chardonnay Dry Creek Valley Frank Johnson Vineyards 1986 Rel: $14 Cur: $19 (CH-7/90)
86	CHATEAU ST. JEAN Chardonnay Dry Creek Valley Frank Johnson Vineyards 1986 Rel: $14 Cur: $19 (12/31/89)
87	CHATEAU ST. JEAN Chardonnay Dry Creek Valley Frank Johnson Vineyards 1985 Rel: $14 Cur: $14 (CH-3/90)
88	CHATEAU ST. JEAN Chardonnay Dry Creek Valley Frank Johnson Vineyards 1984 Rel: $14 Cur: $20 (CH-7/90)
63	CHATEAU ST. JEAN Chardonnay Dry Creek Valley Frank Johnson Vineyards 1984 Rel: $14 Cur: $20 (12/31/86)
88	CHATEAU ST. JEAN Chardonnay Dry Creek Valley Frank Johnson Vineyards 1981 Rel: $14.75 Cur: $15 (1/01/84)
79	CHATEAU ST. JEAN Chardonnay Dry Creek Valley Frank Johnson Vineyards 1980 Rel: $14 Cur: $16 (CH-3/90)
78	CHATEAU ST. JEAN Chardonnay Dry Creek Valley Frank Johnson Vineyards 1979 Rel: $13.50 Cur: $15 (CH-3/90)
80	CHATEAU ST. JEAN Chardonnay Sonoma County 1989 $12 (6/30/91)
86	CHATEAU ST. JEAN Chardonnay Sonoma County 1988 Rel: $12 Cur: $12 (5/31/90)
83	CHATEAU ST. JEAN Chardonnay Sonoma County 1987 Rel: $12 Cur: $12 (5/15/89)
83	CHATEAU ST. JEAN Chardonnay Sonoma County 1986 Rel: $11 Cur: $11 (5/31/88)
88	CHATEAU ST. JEAN Chardonnay Sonoma County 1985 Rel: $11 Cur: $11 (4/30/87)
71	CHATEAU ST. JEAN Chardonnay Sonoma County 1984 Rel: $12 Cur: $12 (11/16/85)

86   CHATEAU ST. JEAN Chardonnay Sonoma County Bacigalupi 1975 Rel: $10 Cur: $21 (CH-7/90)

69   CHATEAU ST. JEAN Chardonnay Sonoma County Beltane Ranch 1976 Rel: $7.75 Cur: $18 (CH-7/90)

88   CHATEAU ST. JEAN Chardonnay Sonoma County Beltane Ranch 1975 Rel: $12.50 Cur: $21 (CH-7/90)

85   CHATEAU ST. JEAN Chardonnay Sonoma Valley Estate Selection 1989 $14 (7/15/91)

81   CHATEAU ST. JEAN Chardonnay Sonoma Valley Hunter Farms 1981 Rel: $14.75 Cur: $19 (CH-3/90)

67   CHATEAU ST. JEAN Chardonnay Sonoma Valley Hunter Farms 1980 Rel: $14 Cur: $17 (CH-3/90)

80   CHATEAU ST. JEAN Chardonnay Sonoma Valley Hunter Farms 1979 Rel: $14 Cur: $20 (CH-3/90)

65   CHATEAU ST. JEAN Chardonnay Sonoma Valley Hunter Farms 1978 Rel: $11.25 Cur: $18 (CH-3/90)

81   CHATEAU ST. JEAN Chardonnay Sonoma Valley Hunter Farms 1977 Rel: $10.25 Cur: $25 (CH-3/90)

81   CHATEAU ST. JEAN Chardonnay Sonoma Valley Les Pierres Vineyards 1978 Rel: $13.75 Cur: $22 (CH-3/90)

79   CHATEAU ST. JEAN Chardonnay Sonoma Valley Les Pierres Vineyards 1977 Rel: $13.75 Cur: $21 (CH-3/90)

88   CHATEAU ST. JEAN Chardonnay Sonoma Valley McCrea Vineyards 1987 Rel: $15 Cur: $15 (CH-3/90)

85   CHATEAU ST. JEAN Chardonnay Sonoma Valley McCrea Vineyards 1987 Rel: $15 Cur: $15 (7/15/89)

87   CHATEAU ST. JEAN Chardonnay Sonoma Valley McCrea Vineyards 1986 Rel: $15 Cur: $17 (CH-3/90)

86   CHATEAU ST. JEAN Chardonnay Sonoma Valley McCrea Vineyards 1985 Rel: $14.25 Cur: $17 (CH-7/90)

87   CHATEAU ST. JEAN Chardonnay Sonoma Valley McCrea Vineyards 1984 Rel: $14.25 Cur: $17 (CH-3/90)

85   CHATEAU ST. JEAN Chardonnay Sonoma Valley McCrea Vineyards 1983 Rel: $15.25 Cur: $18 (CH-7/90)

71   CHATEAU ST. JEAN Chardonnay Sonoma Valley McCrea Vineyards 1983 Rel: $15.25 Cur: $18 (1/01/86)

88   CHATEAU ST. JEAN Chardonnay Sonoma Valley McCrea Vineyards 1982 Rel: $13 Cur: $18 (CH-7/90)

75   CHATEAU ST. JEAN Chardonnay Sonoma Valley McCrea Vineyards 1981 Rel: $15 Cur: $18 (CH-3/90)

70   CHATEAU ST. JEAN Chardonnay Sonoma Valley McCrea Vineyards 1980 Rel: $15 Cur: $18 (CH-3/90)

70   CHATEAU ST. JEAN Chardonnay Sonoma Valley McCrea Vineyards 1979 Rel: $14 Cur: $18 (CH-3/90)

70   CHATEAU ST. JEAN Chardonnay Sonoma Valley McCrea Vineyards 1978 Rel: $12 Cur: $20 (CH-3/90)

85   CHATEAU ST. JEAN Chardonnay Sonoma Valley McCrea Vineyards 1977 Rel: $10.25 Cur: $25 (CH-3/90)

75   CHATEAU ST. JEAN Chardonnay Sonoma Valley McCrea Vineyards 1976 Rel: $9.25 Cur: $20 (CH-7/90)

78   CHATEAU ST. JEAN Chardonnay Sonoma Valley McCrea Vineyards 1975 Rel: $8.75 Cur: $20 (CH-7/90)

74   CHATEAU ST. JEAN Chardonnay Sonoma Valley St. Jean Vineyards 1984 Rel: $14 Cur: $14 (7/31/87)

70   CHATEAU ST. JEAN Chardonnay Sonoma Valley St. Jean Vineyards 1983 Rel: $14.75 Cur: $15 (3/16/86)

91   CHATEAU ST. JEAN Chardonnay Sonoma Valley St. Jean Vineyards 1982 Rel: $14 Cur: $14 (2/01/85)

71   CHATEAU ST. JEAN Chardonnay Sonoma Valley Wildwood Vineyards 1980 Rel: $13 Cur: $19 (CH-7/90)

65   CHATEAU ST. JEAN Chardonnay Sonoma Valley Wildwood Vineyards 1978 Rel: $12 Cur: $19 (CH-3/90)

73   CHATEAU ST. JEAN Chardonnay Sonoma Valley Wildwood Vineyards 1977 Rel: $15 Cur: $22 (CH-3/90)

82   CHATEAU ST. JEAN Chardonnay Sonoma Valley Wildwood Vineyards 1976 Rel: $10 Cur: $20 (CH-7/90)

70   CHATEAU ST. JEAN Chardonnay Sonoma Valley Wildwood Vineyards 1975 Rel: $9.50 Cur: $20 (CH-7/90)

83   CHATEAU WOLTNER Chardonnay Howell Mountain 1989 $12 (11/30/90)

82   CHATEAU WOLTNER Chardonnay Howell Mountain Estate Vineyards 1989 $16 (7/15/91)

86   CHATEAU WOLTNER Chardonnay Howell Mountain Estate Reserve 1988 Rel: $24 Cur: $24 (CH-4/90)

88   CHATEAU WOLTNER Chardonnay Howell Mountain Estate Reserve 1987 Rel: $24 Cur: $24 (CH-4/90)

77   CHATEAU WOLTNER Chardonnay Howell Mountain Estate Reserve 1987 Rel: $24 Cur: $24 (9/15/89)

91   CHATEAU WOLTNER Chardonnay Howell Mountain Estate Reserve 1986 Rel: $24 Cur: $24 (CH-4/90)

86   CHATEAU WOLTNER Chardonnay Howell Mountain St. Thomas Vineyard 1988 Rel: $36 Cur: $36 (CH-4/90)

87   CHATEAU WOLTNER Chardonnay Howell Mountain St. Thomas Vineyard 1987 Rel: $36 Cur: $36 (CH-4/90)

88   CHATEAU WOLTNER Chardonnay Howell Mountain St. Thomas Vineyard 1987 Rel: $36 Cur: $36 (9/15/89)

89   CHATEAU WOLTNER Chardonnay Howell Mountain St. Thomas Vineyard 1986 Rel: $36 Cur: $37 (CH-4/90)

68   CHATEAU WOLTNER Chardonnay Howell Mountain St. Thomas Vineyard 1985 Rel: $30 Cur: $30 (11/15/87)

86   CHATEAU WOLTNER Chardonnay Howell Mountain Titus Vineyard 1988 Rel: $54 Cur: $54 (CH-4/90)

85   CHATEAU WOLTNER Chardonnay Howell Mountain Titus Vineyard 1987 Rel: $54 Cur: $54 (CH-4/90)

80   CHATEAU WOLTNER Chardonnay Howell Mountain Titus Vineyard 1987 Rel: $54 Cur: $54 (9/15/89)

88   CHATEAU WOLTNER Chardonnay Howell Mountain Titus Vineyard 1986 Rel: $54 Cur: $54 (CH-4/90)

75   CHATEAU WOLTNER Chardonnay Howell Mountain Titus Vineyard 1985 Rel: $40 Cur: $40 (11/15/87)

79   CHATEAU WOLTNER Chardonnay Howell Mountain Woltner Estates 1985 Rel: $18 Cur: $32 (11/15/87)

74   CHESTNUT HILL Chardonnay California 1988 $8 (4/15/90)

72   CHESTNUT HILL Chardonnay Napa Valley 1984 $7.50 (4/16/86)

69   CHESTNUT HILL Chardonnay Sonoma County 1989 $7 (7/15/91)

75   CHESTNUT HILL Chardonnay Sonoma County 1986 $8 (12/31/87)

83   CHIMERE Chardonnay Edna Valley 1989 $15 (7/15/91)

72   CHIMNEY ROCK Chardonnay Napa Valley Stags Leap District 1989 $16 (7/15/91)

77   CHIMNEY ROCK Chardonnay Napa Valley Stags Leap District 1988 $15 (12/31/90)

81   CHIMNEY ROCK Chardonnay Napa Valley Stags Leap District 1987 $15 (2/15/90)

80   CHIMNEY ROCK Chardonnay Napa Valley Stags Leap District 1986 $14 (10/15/88)

78   CHRISTIAN BROTHERS Chardonnay Napa Valley 1988 $7.50 (6/30/91)

83   CHRISTIAN BROTHERS Chardonnay Napa Valley 1988 $10 (4/30/90)

69   CHRISTIAN BROTHERS Chardonnay Napa Valley 1987 $10 (11/30/89)

76   CHRISTIAN BROTHERS Chardonnay Napa Valley 1984 $8.50 (6/16/86)

88   CHRISTIAN BROTHERS Chardonnay Napa Valley Barrel Fermented 1985 $11 (7/31/87)

83   CHRISTIAN BROTHERS Chardonnay Napa Valley Private Reserve Barrel Fermented 1987 $11.50 (9/15/89)

87   CHRISTIAN BROTHERS Chardonnay Napa Valley Private Reserve Barrel Fermented 1986 $12 (12/31/88)

86   CHRISTIAN BROTHERS Chardonnay Napa Valley-Burgundy Montage Première Cuvée NV $15 (10/15/88)

78   CHRISTOPHE Chardonnay California 1989 $9 (7/15/91)

83   CHRISTOPHE Chardonnay California 1988 $7.50 (4/30/90) BB

74   CHRISTOPHE Chardonnay California 1987 $8.50 (3/31/89)

73   CHRISTOPHE Chardonnay California 1985 $6.50 (11/15/86)

84   CHRISTOPHE Chardonnay California 1984 $5.50 (12/01/85) BB

80   CHRISTOPHE Chardonnay California Reserve 1989 $12 (7/15/91)

77   CHRISTOPHE Chardonnay California Reserve 1986 $9.50 (4/15/88)

79   CINNABAR Chardonnay Santa Cruz Mountains 1989 $18 (3/31/91)

85   CLONINGER Chardonnay Monterey 1989 $15 (7/15/91)

80   CLOS DU BOIS Chardonnay Alexander Valley Barrel Fermented 1989 $11 (12/31/90)

84   CLOS DU BOIS Chardonnay Alexander Valley Barrel Fermented 1988 Rel: $11 Cur: $11 (2/15/90)

85   CLOS DU BOIS Chardonnay Alexander Valley Barrel Fermented 1988 Rel: $11 Cur: $11 (CH-2/90)

87   CLOS DU BOIS Chardonnay Alexander Valley Barrel Fermented 1987 Rel: $11 Cur: $11 (CH-2/90)

88   CLOS DU BOIS Chardonnay Alexander Valley Barrel Fermented 1987 Rel: $11 Cur: $11 (12/31/88)

80   CLOS DU BOIS Chardonnay Alexander Valley Barrel Fermented 1986 Rel: $10 Cur: $12 (CH-12/89)

80   CLOS DU BOIS Chardonnay Alexander Valley Barrel Fermented 1986 Rel: $10 Cur: $12 (10/15/87)

84   CLOS DU BOIS Chardonnay Alexander Valley Barrel Fermented 1985 Rel: $9 Cur: $12 (CH-2/90)

75   CLOS DU BOIS Chardonnay Alexander Valley Barrel Fermented 1985 Rel: $9 Cur: $12 (11/15/86)

84   CLOS DU BOIS Chardonnay Alexander Valley Barrel Fermented 1984 Rel: $8 Cur: $12 (CH-2/90)

77   CLOS DU BOIS Chardonnay Alexander Valley Barrel Fermented 1984 Rel: $8 Cur: $12 (9/16/85)

85   CLOS DU BOIS Chardonnay Alexander Valley Barrel Fermented 1982 Rel: $9 Cur: $9 (4/16/84)

92   CLOS DU BOIS Chardonnay Alexander Valley Barrel Fermented 1980 Rel: $15 Cur: $15 (4/16/84)

82   CLOS DU BOIS Chardonnay Alexander Valley Calcaire Vineyard 1989 $17 (7/15/91)

91   CLOS DU BOIS Chardonnay Alexander Valley Calcaire Vineyard 1988 Rel: $17 Cur: $20 (5/15/90)

89   CLOS DU BOIS Chardonnay Alexander Valley Calcaire Vineyard 1988 Rel: $17 Cur: $20 (CH-2/90)

88   CLOS DU BOIS Chardonnay Alexander Valley Calcaire Vineyard 1987 Rel: $20 Cur: $21 (CH-2/90)

88   CLOS DU BOIS Chardonnay Alexander Valley Calcaire Vineyard 1987 Rel: $20 Cur: $21 (1/31/89)

85   CLOS DU BOIS Chardonnay Alexander Valley Calcaire Vineyard 1986 Rel: $16 Cur: $23 (CH-2/90)

87   CLOS DU BOIS Chardonnay Alexander Valley Calcaire Vineyard 1986 Rel: $16 Cur: $23 (12/31/87)

83   CLOS DU BOIS Chardonnay Alexander Valley Calcaire Vineyard 1985 Rel: $18 Cur: $28 (CH-2/90)

87   CLOS DU BOIS Chardonnay Alexander Valley Calcaire Vineyard 1985 Rel: $18 Cur: $28 (3/15/87)

90   CLOS DU BOIS Chardonnay Alexander Valley Calcaire Vineyard 1984 Rel: $12 Cur: $30 (CH-2/90)

93   CLOS DU BOIS Chardonnay Alexander Valley Calcaire Vineyard 1984 Rel: $12 Cur: $30 (6/01/86) SS

91   CLOS DU BOIS Chardonnay Alexander Valley Calcaire Vineyard 1983 Rel: $12 Cur: $30 (CH-2/90)

94   CLOS DU BOIS Chardonnay Alexander Valley Calcaire Vineyard 1983 Rel: $12 Cur: $30 (10/16/85)

92   CLOS DU BOIS Chardonnay Alexander Valley Calcaire Vineyard 1982 Rel: $11.25 Cur: $12 (7/01/84)

82   CLOS DU BOIS Chardonnay Russian River Valley Winemaker's Reserve 1988 $24 (7/15/91)

89   CLOS DU BOIS Chardonnay Russian River Valley Winemaker's Reserve 1988 $24 (CH-5/90)

93   CLOS DU BOIS Chardonnay Alexander Valley Winemaker's Reserve 1987 Rel: $24 Cur: $24 (2/28/90)

92   CLOS DU BOIS Chardonnay Alexander Valley Winemaker's Reserve 1987 Rel: $24 Cur: $24 (CH-2/90)

89   CLOS DU BOIS Chardonnay Alexander Valley Winemaker's Reserve 1987 Rel: $24 Cur: $24 (7/15/89)

78   CLOS DU BOIS Chardonnay Alexander Valley Proprietor's Reserve 1986 Rel: $22.50 Cur: $23 (CH-5/90)

86   CLOS DU BOIS Chardonnay Alexander Valley Proprietor's Reserve 1986 Rel: $22.50 Cur: $23 (5/31/88)

85   CLOS DU BOIS Chardonnay Alexander Valley Proprietor's Reserve 1985 Rel: $22 Cur: $25 (CH-5/90)

91   CLOS DU BOIS Chardonnay Alexander Valley Proprietor's Reserve 1985 Rel: $22 Cur: $25 (6/15/87)

87   CLOS DU BOIS Chardonnay Alexander Valley Proprietor's Reserve 1984 Rel: $18 Cur: $21 (10/31/86)

UNITED STATES
CALIFORNIA/*CHARDONNAY*

70	CLOS DU BOIS Chardonnay Alexander Valley Proprietor's Reserve 1981 Rel: $15 Cur: $22 (CH-5/90)
89	CLOS DU BOIS Chardonnay Dry Creek Valley Flintwood Vineyard 1989 $17 (7/15/91)
89	CLOS DU BOIS Chardonnay Dry Creek Valley Flintwood Vineyard 1988 Rel: $18 Cur: $18 (6/30/90)
90	CLOS DU BOIS Chardonnay Dry Creek Valley Flintwood Vineyard 1988 Rel: $18 Cur: $18 (CH-2/90)
87	CLOS DU BOIS Chardonnay Dry Creek Valley Flintwood Vineyard 1987 Rel: $20 Cur: $22 (CH-2/90)
76	CLOS DU BOIS Chardonnay Dry Creek Valley Flintwood Vineyard 1987 Rel: $20 Cur: $22 (7/15/89)
88	CLOS DU BOIS Chardonnay Dry Creek Valley Flintwood Vineyard 1986 Rel: $19.50 Cur: $25 (CH-2/90)
90	CLOS DU BOIS Chardonnay Dry Creek Valley Flintwood Vineyard 1986 Rel: $19.50 Cur: $25 (12/31/87)
70	CLOS DU BOIS Chardonnay Dry Creek Valley Flintwood Vineyard 1985 Rel: $18 Cur: $32 (CH-5/90)
93	CLOS DU BOIS Chardonnay Dry Creek Valley Flintwood Vineyard 1985 Rel: $18 Cur: $32 (3/31/87)
74	CLOS DU BOIS Chardonnay Dry Creek Valley Flintwood Vineyard 1984 Rel: $11.25 Cur: $38 (CH-5/90)
92	CLOS DU BOIS Chardonnay Dry Creek Valley Flintwood Vineyard 1984 Rel: $11.25 Cur: $38 (6/01/86)
69	CLOS DU BOIS Chardonnay Dry Creek Valley Flintwood Vineyard 1983 Rel: $10.50 Cur: $37 (CH-5/90)
92	CLOS DU BOIS Chardonnay Dry Creek Valley Flintwood Vineyard 1983 Rel: $10.50 Cur: $37 (7/01/85) SS
79	CLOS DU BOIS Chardonnay Dry Creek Valley Flintwood Vineyard 1982 Rel: $11.25 Cur: $12 (7/01/84)
87	CLOS DU BOIS Chardonnay Dry Creek Valley Flintwood Vineyard 1980 Rel: $17 Cur: $32 (CH-2/90)
89	CLOS DU VAL Chardonnay Carneros Napa Valley Carneros Estate 1989 $15 (3/31/91)
83	CLOS DU VAL Chardonnay Carneros Napa Valley Carneros Estate 1988 Rel: $16 Cur: $16 (6/30/90)
88	CLOS DU VAL Chardonnay Carneros Napa Valley Carneros Estate 1988 Rel: $16 Cur: $16 (CH-6/90)
89	CLOS DU VAL Chardonnay Carneros Napa Valley Carneros Estate 1987 Rel: $13 Cur: $16 (CH-6/90)
87	CLOS DU VAL Chardonnay Napa Valley 1987 $12 (CH-6/90)
87	CLOS DU VAL Chardonnay Napa Valley 1987 $12 (6/15/89)
90	CLOS DU VAL Chardonnay Napa Valley Carneros Estate 1987 Rel: $13 Cur: $16 (6/15/89)
84	CLOS DU VAL Chardonnay Carneros Napa Valley Carneros Estate 1986 Rel: $12 Cur: $14 (CH-6/90)
87	CLOS DU VAL Chardonnay Carneros Napa Valley Carneros Estate 1986 Rel: $12 Cur: $14 (4/15/88)
87	CLOS DU VAL Chardonnay Napa Valley 1985 $11.50 (CH-6/90)
80	CLOS DU VAL Chardonnay Napa Valley 1985 $11.50 (7/31/87)
85	CLOS DU VAL Chardonnay Napa Valley 1984 $11.50 (CH-6/90)
82	CLOS DU VAL Chardonnay Napa Valley 1983 $11.50 (CH-6/90)
78	CLOS DU VAL Chardonnay Napa Valley 1981 $12.50 (CH-6/90)
80	CLOS DU VAL Chardonnay Napa Valley 1980 $12.50 (CH-6/90)
79	CLOS DU VAL Chardonnay Napa Valley Joli Val 1989 $13 (7/15/91)
86	CLOS DU VAL Chardonnay Napa Valley Joli Val 1988 $12.50 (1/31/90)
77	CLOS DU VAL Chardonnay California Gran Val 1986 $8.50 (4/15/88)
75	CLOS DU VAL Chardonnay California Gran Val 1984 $6.50 (4/16/86)
91	CLOS DU VAL Chardonnay California 1984 $11.50 (5/01/86)
79	CLOS DU VAL Chardonnay California 1983 $11.50 (2/16/85)
78	CLOS DU VAL Chardonnay California 1982 $11.50 (6/01/90)
87	CLOS PEGASE Chardonnay Alexander Valley 1985 $13 (CH-3/90)
88	CLOS PEGASE Chardonnay Alexander Valley 1985 $13 (7/15/87)
89	CLOS PEGASE Chardonnay Carneros 1988 $16.50 (CH-3/90)
90	CLOS PEGASE Chardonnay Los Carneros 1988 $16.50 (5/15/90)
90	CLOS PEGASE Chardonnay Carneros 1987 $15.50 (CH-3/90)
89	CLOS PEGASE Chardonnay Los Carneros 1987 $15.50 (2/15/90)
89	CLOS PEGASE Chardonnay Carneros 1986 $15.50 (CH-3/90)
90	CLOS PEGASE Chardonnay Los Carneros 1986 $15.50 (7/15/88)
77	CLOS PEGASE Chardonnay Napa Valley 1989 $12 (7/15/91)
86	CLOS PEGASE Chardonnay Napa Valley 1988 $12 (6/30/90)
88	CLOS PEGASE Chardonnay Napa Valley 1988 $12 (CH-3/90)
86	CLOS PEGASE Chardonnay Napa Valley 1987 $12 (CH-3/90)
82	CLOS PEGASE Chardonnay Napa Valley 1987 $12 (7/15/89)
85	CLOS PEGASE Chardonnay Napa Valley 1986 $12 (CH-3/90)
88	CLOS PEGASE Chardonnay Napa Valley 1986 $12 (3/15/88)
68	CLOS ROBERT Chardonnay Napa Valley 1985 $6 (7/31/87)
78	CLOS ROBERT Chardonnay Napa Valley Lot 3 1989 $9 (7/15/91)
82	B.R. COHN Chardonnay Sonoma Valley Olive Hill Vineyard 1988 $15 (10/31/89)
87	B.R. COHN Chardonnay Sonoma Valley Olive Hill Vineyard 1986 $12 (10/31/88)
78	B.R. COHN Chardonnay Sonoma Valley Olive Hill Vineyard 1989 $14 (5/31/91)
88	B.R. COHN Chardonnay Sonoma Valley Olive Hill Vineyard Barrel Reserve 1985 $21 (6/30/87)
81	COLBY Chardonnay Napa Valley 1986 $11 (5/31/89)
87	COLBY Chardonnay Napa Valley 1985 $10.75 (11/15/87)
81	CONCANNON Chardonnay California Selected Vineyards 1985 $10.50 (6/30/87)
88	CONCANNON Chardonnay California Selected Vineyards 1984 $9 (4/16/86)
83	CONCANNON Chardonnay Santa Clara Valley Mistral Vineyard 1988 $12 (7/15/91)
85	CONGRESS SPRINGS Chardonnay Santa Clara County Barrel Fermented 1989 $12 (7/15/91)
86	CONGRESS SPRINGS Chardonnay Santa Clara County Barrel Fermented 1988 Rel: $14 Cur: $14 (CH-4/90)
68	CONGRESS SPRINGS Chardonnay Santa Clara County Barrel Fermented 1988 Rel: $14 Cur: $14 (2/15/90)
84	CONGRESS SPRINGS Chardonnay Santa Clara County 1987 Rel: $12 Cur: $18 (CH-4/90)
79	CONGRESS SPRINGS Chardonnay Santa Clara County 1987 Rel: $12 Cur: $18 (10/31/88)
83	CONGRESS SPRINGS Chardonnay Santa Clara County 1986 Rel: $12 Cur: $18 (CH-4/90)
82	CONGRESS SPRINGS Chardonnay Santa Clara County 1986 Rel: $12 Cur: $18 (10/31/87)
87	CONGRESS SPRINGS Chardonnay Santa Clara County 1985 Rel: $12 Cur: $20 (CH-4/90)
93	CONGRESS SPRINGS Chardonnay Santa Clara County 1985 Rel: $12 Cur: $20 (10/15/86)
90	CONGRESS SPRINGS Chardonnay Santa Clara County 1984 Rel: $11 Cur: $25 (CH-4/90)
85	CONGRESS SPRINGS Chardonnay Santa Clara County Barrel Fermented 1983 Rel: $10 Cur: $25 (CH-4/90)
79	CONGRESS SPRINGS Chardonnay Santa Clara County 1982 Rel: $10 Cur: $20 (CH-4/90)
88	CONGRESS SPRINGS Chardonnay Santa Clara County San Ysidro Reserve 1989 $15 (7/15/91)
86	CONGRESS SPRINGS Chardonnay Santa Clara County San Ysidro Reserve 1988 Rel: $20 Cur: $20 (CH-4/90)
89	CONGRESS SPRINGS Chardonnay Santa Clara County San Ysidro Reserve 1988 Rel: $20 Cur: $20 (1/31/90)
90	CONGRESS SPRINGS Chardonnay Santa Clara County San Ysidro Reserve 1987 Rel: $16 Cur: $23 (CH-4/90)
90	CONGRESS SPRINGS Chardonnay Santa Clara County San Ysidro Reserve 1987 Rel: $16 Cur: $23 (11/30/88)
85	CONGRESS SPRINGS Chardonnay Santa Clara County San Ysidro Reserve 1986 Rel: $15 Cur: $22 (CH-4/90)
80	CONGRESS SPRINGS Chardonnay Santa Clara County San Ysidro Reserve 1986 Rel: $15 Cur: $22 (11/15/87)
88	CONGRESS SPRINGS Chardonnay Santa Cruz Mountains Monmartre 1988 Rel: $30 Cur: $30 (CH-4/90)
87	CONGRESS SPRINGS Chardonnay Santa Cruz Mountains Monmartre 1987 Rel: $28 Cur: $30 (CH-4/90)
87	CONGRESS SPRINGS Chardonnay Santa Cruz Mountains Monmartre 1987 Rel: $28 Cur: $30 (7/15/89)
85	CONGRESS SPRINGS Chardonnay Santa Cruz Mountains Private Reserve 1986 Rel: $20 Cur: $23 (CH-4/90)
84	CONGRESS SPRINGS Chardonnay Santa Cruz Mountains Private Reserve 1985 Rel: $16 Cur: $27 (CH-4/90)
80	CONGRESS SPRINGS Chardonnay Santa Cruz Mountains Private Reserve 1984 Rel: $16 Cur: $27 (CH-4/90)
74	CONGRESS SPRINGS Chardonnay Santa Cruz Mountains Private Reserve 1983 Rel: $15 Cur: $28 (CH-4/90)
87	CONGRESS SPRINGS Chardonnay Santa Cruz Mountains Private Reserve 1982 Rel: $15 Cur: $28 (CH-4/90)
80	CONN CREEK Chardonnay Carneros Barrel Select 1988 $13 (7/15/91)
86	CONN CREEK Chardonnay Napa Valley Barrel Select 1988 $13 (7/15/91)
88	CONN CREEK Chardonnay Napa Valley Barrel Select 1987 $12 (9/15/90)
80	CONN CREEK Chardonnay Napa Valley Barrel Select Lot No. 32 1985 $12 (2/15/88)
78	CONN CREEK Chardonnay Napa Valley Lot No. 139 1985 $12.50 (12/31/88)
83	CONN CREEK Chardonnay Napa Valley Barrel Select 1983 $14 (6/30/87)
81	CONN CREEK Chardonnay Napa Valley 1982 $12.50 (11/01/85)
84	CONN CREEK Chardonnay Napa Valley Château Maja 1984 $6.50 (4/16/86) BB
79	CONN CREEK Chardonnay North Coast Château Maja 1982 $6.50 (3/01/84)
84	CORBETT CANYON Chardonnay Central Coast 1984 $8 (3/01/86) BB
78	CORBETT CANYON Chardonnay Central Coast 1983 $8 (11/01/84)
84	CORBETT CANYON Chardonnay Central Coast Coastal Classic 1989 $7/L (7/15/91) BB
75	CORBETT CANYON Chardonnay Central Coast Coastal Classic 1988 $6.50/L (12/15/89)
79	CORBETT CANYON Chardonnay Central Coast Coastal Classic 1987 $7/L (7/15/88)
68	CORBETT CANYON Chardonnay Central Coast Coastal Classic 1986 $6.50/L (11/15/87)
78	CORBETT CANYON Chardonnay Central Coast Reserve 1988 $9.50 (7/15/91)
80	CORBETT CANYON Chardonnay Central Coast Reserve 1987 $8 (12/15/89)
66	CORBETT CANYON Chardonnay Central Coast Select 1986 $8.75 (3/15/89)
83	CORBETT CANYON Chardonnay Central Coast Select 1985 $9 (1/31/87)
67	CORBETT CANYON Chardonnay Edna Valley Winemaker's Reserve 1984 $10 (7/01/86)
76	COSENTINO Chardonnay California The Sculptor 1982 $8 (2/15/84)
81	COSENTINO Chardonnay Napa County North Coast 1989 $13 (4/15/91)
91	COSENTINO Chardonnay Napa Valley 1987 $11.50 (3/15/89)
80	COSENTINO Chardonnay Napa Valley The Sculptor 1989 $18 (7/15/91)
86	COSENTINO Chardonnay Napa Valley The Sculptor 1988 $18 (6/15/90)
84	COSENTINO Chardonnay Napa Valley The Sculptor 1987 $18 (7/15/89)
80	COSENTINO Chardonnay Napa Valley The Sculptor 1986 $17 (9/15/88)
85	COTTONWOOD CANYON Chardonnay Central Coast 1989 $14 (7/15/91)
81	CRESTON MANOR Chardonnay Central Coast 1985 $10 (11/15/87)
80	CRESTON MANOR Chardonnay San Luis Obispo County 1987 $12 (12/15/89)
82	CRICHTON HALL Chardonnay Napa Valley 1989 $16.50 (7/15/91)
82	CRICHTON HALL Chardonnay Napa Valley 1988 $16 (12/31/90)
75	CRICHTON HALL Chardonnay Napa Valley 1987 $16 (11/15/89)
87	CRONIN Chardonnay Alexander Valley Stuhlmuller Vineyard 1988 $18 (6/30/90)
84	CRONIN Chardonnay Monterey County Ventana Vineyard 1988 $18 (6/30/90)
78	CRONIN Chardonnay Napa Valley 1988 $18 (5/31/90)
85	CRONIN Chardonnay Santa Cruz Mountains 1988 $20 (4/30/91)
90	CRONIN Chardonnay Santa Cruz Mountains 1987 $18 (2/15/90)
90	CRUVINET Chardonnay California 1984 $4.50 (9/15/86)
70	CRYSTAL VALLEY Chardonnay North Coast 1986 $8.50 (11/15/87)
82	CUVAISON Chardonnay Carneros Napa Valley 1989 $14 (7/15/91)
91	CUVAISON Chardonnay Carneros Napa Valley 1988 Rel: $15 Cur: $17 (CH-4/90)
91	CUVAISON Chardonnay Carneros Napa Valley 1988 Rel: $15 Cur: $17 (2/28/90) SS
90	CUVAISON Chardonnay Napa Valley 1987 Rel: $13.50 Cur: $16 (CH-4/90)
87	CUVAISON Chardonnay Napa Valley 1987 Rel: $13.50 Cur: $16 (12/31/88)
89	CUVAISON Chardonnay Napa Valley 1986 Rel: $12.75 Cur: $18 (CH-4/90)
88	CUVAISON Chardonnay Napa Valley 1986 Rel: $12.75 Cur: $18 (12/31/87)
93	CUVAISON Chardonnay Napa Valley 1985 Rel: $12 Cur: $20 (CH-4/90)
90	CUVAISON Chardonnay Napa Valley 1985 Rel: $12 Cur: $20 (10/15/87)
82	CUVAISON Chardonnay Napa Valley 1984 Rel: $12 Cur: $20 (CH-4/90)
62	CUVAISON Chardonnay Napa Valley 1983 Rel: $12 Cur: $17 (CH-4/90)
58	CUVAISON Chardonnay Napa Valley 1983 Rel: $12 Cur: $17 (4/01/86)
61	CUVAISON Chardonnay Napa Valley 1982 Rel: $12 Cur: $17 (CH-4/90)
68	CUVAISON Chardonnay Napa Valley 1982 Rel: $12 Cur: $17 (5/16/84)

75 CUVAISON Chardonnay Napa Valley 1981 Rel: $12 Cur: $18 (CH-4/90)
87 CUVAISON Chardonnay Napa Valley 1980 Rel: $11 Cur: $26 (CH-4/90)
84 CUVAISON Chardonnay Napa Valley 1979 Rel: $10 Cur: $26 (CH-4/90)
81 CUVAISON Chardonnay Napa Valley 1978 Rel: $10 Cur: $28 (CH-4/90)
92 CUVAISON Chardonnay Carneros Napa Valley Reserve 1988 (NR) (CH-6/90)
91 CUVAISON Chardonnay Carneros Napa Valley Reserve 1987 Rel: $22 Cur: $22 (CH-7/90)
94 CUVAISON Chardonnay Carneros Napa Valley Reserve 1986 Rel: $20 Cur: $28 (CH-6/90)
90 CUVAISON Chardonnay Carneros Napa Valley Reserve 1986 Rel: $20 Cur: $28 (6/30/89)
71 CYPRESS LANE Chardonnay California 1986 $6 (12/31/87)
72 CYPRESS LANE Chardonnay California 1985 $6 (1/31/87)
87 DE LOACH Chardonnay Russian River Valley 1989 Rel: $15 Cur: $15 (3/31/91)
87 DE LOACH Chardonnay Russian River Valley 1988 Rel: $15 Cur: $15 (CH-5/90)
86 DE LOACH Chardonnay Russian River Valley 1988 Rel: $15 Cur: $15 (11/15/89)
87 DE LOACH Chardonnay Russian River Valley 1987 Rel: $15 Cur: $22 (CH-2/90)
89 DE LOACH Chardonnay Russian River Valley 1987 Rel: $15 Cur: $22 (10/31/88)
89 DE LOACH Chardonnay Russian River Valley 1986 Rel: $14 Cur: $20 (CH-2/90)
87 DE LOACH Chardonnay Russian River Valley 1986 Rel: $14 Cur: $20 (11/15/87)
90 DE LOACH Chardonnay Russian River Valley 1985 Rel: $14 Cur: $33 (CH-2/90)
88 DE LOACH Chardonnay Russian River Valley 1985 Rel: $14 Cur: $33 (12/31/86)
88 DE LOACH Chardonnay Russian River Valley 1984 Rel: $12.50 Cur: $30 (CH-2/90)
90 DE LOACH Chardonnay Russian River Valley 1984 Rel: $12.50 Cur: $30 (CH-12/85)
83 DE LOACH Chardonnay Russian River Valley 1983 Rel: $12 Cur: $22 (CH-2/90)
90 DE LOACH Chardonnay Russian River Valley 1983 Rel: $12 Cur: $22 (10/16/84)
74 DE LOACH Chardonnay Russian River Valley 1982 Rel: $12 Cur: $20 (CH-2/90)
72 DE LOACH Chardonnay Russian River Valley 1981 Rel: $10 Cur: $18 (CH-2/90)
62 DE LOACH Chardonnay Russian River Valley 1980 Rel: $10 Cur: $18 (CH-2/90)
89 DE LOACH Chardonnay Russian River Valley O.F.S. 1989 $22 (3/31/91)
87 DE LOACH Chardonnay Russian River Valley O.F.S. 1988 Rel: $22 Cur: $22 (CH-5/90)
88 DE LOACH Chardonnay Russian River Valley O.F.S. 1988 Rel: $22 Cur: $22 (2/15/90)
92 DE LOACH Chardonnay Russian River Valley O.F.S. 1987 Rel: $22 Cur: $40 (CH-5/90)
86 DE LOACH Chardonnay Russian River Valley O.F.S. 1987 Rel: $22 Cur: $40 (12/31/88)
86 DE LOACH Chardonnay Russian River Valley O.F.S. 1986 Rel: $22 Cur: $26 (CH-2/90)
89 DE LOACH Chardonnay Russian River Valley O.F.S. 1986 Rel: $22 Cur: $26 (2/29/88)
79 DE LOACH Chardonnay Russian River Valley O.F.S. 1985 Rel: $20 Cur: $47 (CH-2/90)
78 DE LOACH Chardonnay Russian River Valley O.F.S. 1985 Rel: $20 Cur: $47 (3/15/87)
90 DE LOACH Chardonnay Russian River Valley O.F.S. 1984 Rel: $20 Cur: $20 (CH-2/90)
90 DE LORIMIER Chardonnay Alexander Valley Prism 1988 $13.50 (9/30/90)
86 DE LORIMIER Chardonnay Alexander Valley Prism 1987 $13.50 (4/15/89)
86 DE MOOR Chardonnay Alexander Valley Napa Cellars Black Mountain Vineyard 1981 $11 (4/16/84)
87 DE MOOR Chardonnay Napa Valley Owners Select 1988 $14 (7/15/91)
67 DEER PARK Chardonnay Napa Valley 1989 $14 (7/15/91)
74 DEER VALLEY Chardonnay California 1989 $7 (7/15/91)
89 DEHLINGER Chardonnay Russian River Valley 1989 $13 (2/28/91)
91 DEHLINGER Chardonnay Russian River Valley 1988 Rel: $12 Cur: $12 (CH-4/90)
85 DEHLINGER Chardonnay Russian River Valley 1988 Rel: $12 Cur: $12 (2/15/90)
90 DEHLINGER Chardonnay Russian River Valley 1987 Rel: $11.50 Cur: $12 (CH-4/90)
90 DEHLINGER Chardonnay Russian River Valley 1987 Rel: $11.50 Cur: $12 (12/31/88)
87 DEHLINGER Chardonnay Russian River Valley 1986 Rel: $11 Cur: $14 (CH-4/90)
90 DEHLINGER Chardonnay Russian River Valley 1986 Rel: $11 Cur: $14 (2/29/88)
86 DEHLINGER Chardonnay Russian River Valley 1985 Rel: $10 Cur: $17 (CH-5/90)
86 DEHLINGER Chardonnay Russian River Valley 1985 Rel: $10 Cur: $17 (8/31/87)
86 DEHLINGER Chardonnay Russian River Valley 1984 Rel: $10 Cur: $14 (CH-4/90)
85 DEHLINGER Chardonnay Russian River Valley 1983 Rel: $10 Cur: $15 (CH-4/90)
55 DEHLINGER Chardonnay Russian River Valley 1982 Rel: $10 Cur: $10 (9/01/85)
87 DELICATO Chardonnay Napa Valley Barrel Fermented Golden Anniversary 1984 $10 (4/30/87)
70 DEVLIN Chardonnay Santa Cruz Mountains Meyley Vineyard 1989 $10 (7/15/91)
78 DION Chardonnay Sonoma Valley 1986 $10 (12/31/88)
88 DOLAN Chardonnay Mendocino 1987 $15 (12/31/88)
66 DOMAIN SAN MARTIN Chardonnay Central Coast 1984 $7 (4/16/86)
85 DOMAIN SAN MARTIN Chardonnay Central Coast 1983 $7 (8/01/85)
82 DOMAINE BRETON Chardonnay California 1989 $8 (2/28/91) BB
89 DOMAINE DE CLARCK Chardonnay Monterey County Première 1989 $14 (4/15/91)
83 DOMAINE LAURIER Chardonnay Sonoma County 1986 $13.50 (12/31/88)
71 DOMAINE LAURIER Chardonnay Sonoma County 1985 $13 (10/31/87)
74 DOMAINE LAURIER Chardonnay Sonoma County 1984 $13 (6/16/86)
89 DOMAINE LAURIER Chardonnay Sonoma County 1982 $13 (4/01/85)
81 DOMAINE LAURIER Chardonnay Sonoma County 1982 $13 (7/01/84)
83 DOMAINE MICHEL Chardonnay Sonoma County 1988 $16 (3/31/91)
82 DOMAINE MICHEL Chardonnay Sonoma County 1988 $16 (5/31/90)
76 DOMAINE MICHEL Chardonnay Sonoma County 1987 $16 (6/30/90)
76 DOMAINE MICHEL Chardonnay Sonoma County 1986 $16 (12/31/88)
77 DOMAINE NAPA Chardonnay Napa Valley 1989 $12.50 (7/15/91)
81 DOMAINE NAPA Chardonnay Napa Valley 1988 $12.50 (6/30/90)
80 DOMAINE NAPA Chardonnay Napa Valley 1987 $12 (7/15/89)
82 DOMAINE DE NAPA Chardonnay Napa Valley 1986 $9.50 (10/15/88)
73 DOMAINE DE NAPA Chardonnay Napa Valley Barrel Fermented 1986 $14.50 (12/31/88)
71 DOMAINE POTELLE Chardonnay California 1987 $7 (4/15/89)
80 DOMAINE POTELLE Chardonnay California 1986 $6 (4/15/88) BB
77 DOMAINE ST. GEORGE Chardonnay Sonoma County 1986 $4.50 (12/31/87)
91 DOMAINE ST. GEORGE Chardonnay Sonoma County 1984 $5 (12/16/85) BB
79 DOMAINE ST. GEORGE Chardonnay Sonoma County Select Reserve 1988 $9 (6/30/90)
86 DOMAINE ST. GEORGE Chardonnay Sonoma County Select Reserve Barrel Fermented Barrel Aged 1987 $8 (12/31/88) BB
65 DORE Chardonnay California 1985 $5 (2/15/88)
74 DORE Chardonnay California Limited Release Lot 101 1989 $8.50 (7/15/91)
85 DORE Chardonnay Santa Maria Valley Signature Selections 1984 $5 (4/16/86)
91 DRY CREEK Chardonnay Dry Creek Valley Reserve 1987 $18 (4/15/90)
86 DRY CREEK Chardonnay Dry Creek Valley Reserve 1986 $18 (11/30/89)
87 DRY CREEK Chardonnay Sonoma County 1989 $12.50 (12/31/90)
85 DRY CREEK Chardonnay Sonoma County 1988 $12.50 (5/31/90)
82 DRY CREEK Chardonnay Sonoma County 1987 $9.75 (2/15/89)
88 DRY CREEK Chardonnay Sonoma County 1986 $11 (5/31/88)
92 DRY CREEK Chardonnay Sonoma County 1985 $10 (3/15/87)
88 DRY CREEK Chardonnay Sonoma County 1984 $10 (8/31/86)
87 DRY CREEK Chardonnay Sonoma County 1983 $10 (2/16/85)
87 DRY CREEK Chardonnay Sonoma County 1982 $10 (1/01/84)
60 DRY CREEK Chardonnay Sonoma County 1978 $8 (7/16/84)
73 DRY CREEK Chardonnay Sonoma County 1976 $7 (7/16/84)
85 DRY CREEK Chardonnay Sonoma County Reserve 1988 $20 (7/15/91)
67 DRY CREEK Chardonnay Sonoma County Vintner's Reserve 1980 $14 (7/16/84)
78 DUNNEWOOD Chardonnay Napa Valley Reserve 1987 $10.50 (12/31/88)
78 DUNNEWOOD Chardonnay North Coast 1989 $7 (3/31/91)
88 DURNEY Chardonnay Carmel Valley 1988 $18 (9/30/90)
86 EBERLE Chardonnay Paso Robles 1989 $12 (7/15/91)
76 EBERLE Chardonnay Paso Robles 1988 $12 (6/30/90)
74 EBERLE Chardonnay Paso Robles 1987 $12 (6/30/90)
75 EBERLE Chardonnay Paso Robles 1987 $12 (7/15/89)
85 EBERLE Chardonnay Paso Robles 1986 $10 (12/31/88)
79 EBERLE Chardonnay Paso Robles 1982 $10 (4/16/85)
66 EDMEADES Chardonnay Anderson Valley 1982 $10 (4/16/85)
88 EDNA VALLEY Chardonnay Edna Valley 1989 $15 (12/31/90)
89 EDNA VALLEY Chardonnay Edna Valley 1988 Rel: $14.75 Cur: $16 (CH-3/90)
85 EDNA VALLEY Chardonnay Edna Valley 1988 Rel: $14.75 Cur: $16 (12/15/89)
91 EDNA VALLEY Chardonnay Edna Valley 1987 Rel: $14 Cur: $20 (CH-3/90)
91 EDNA VALLEY Chardonnay Edna Valley 1987 Rel: $14 Cur: $20 (11/30/88)
88 EDNA VALLEY Chardonnay Edna Valley 1986 Rel: $13.50 Cur: $20 (CH-3/90)
89 EDNA VALLEY Chardonnay Edna Valley 1986 Rel: $13.50 Cur: $20 (12/31/87)
85 EDNA VALLEY Chardonnay Edna Valley 1985 Rel: $13 Cur: $30 (CH-3/90)
86 EDNA VALLEY Chardonnay Edna Valley 1984 Rel: $12.50 Cur: $29 (CH-6/90)
91 EDNA VALLEY Chardonnay Edna Valley 1984 Rel: $12.50 Cur: $29 (6/16/86)
76 EDNA VALLEY Chardonnay Edna Valley 1983 Rel: $12.50 Cur: $20 (CH-3/90)
70 EDNA VALLEY Chardonnay Edna Valley 1982 Rel: $12 Cur: $32 (CH-3/90)
94 EDNA VALLEY Chardonnay Edna Valley 1981 Rel: $12 Cur: $25 (CH-3/90)
87 EDNA VALLEY Chardonnay Edna Valley 1980 Rel: $12 Cur: $44 (CH-3/90)
80 EHLERS LANE Chardonnay Napa Valley 1984 $14 (6/16/86)
78 EHLERS LANE Chardonnay Napa Valley 1983 $14 (7/01/85)
85 ELIZABETH Chardonnay Mendocino 1989 $12.50 (7/15/91)
84 ELIZABETH Chardonnay Mendocino 1988 $11.50 (7/15/91)
84 ELLISTON Chardonnay Central Coast Elliston Vineyard 1987 $18 (7/15/91)
80 ELLISTON Chardonnay Central Coast Sunol Valley Vineyard 1989 $14 (7/15/91)
83 ESTANCIA Chardonnay Alexander Valley 1988 $8 (4/30/90) BB
85 ESTANCIA Chardonnay Alexander Valley 1987 $7 (6/30/89)
84 ESTANCIA Chardonnay Alexander Valley 1986 $6.50 (1/31/88) BB
89 ESTANCIA Chardonnay Alexander Valley 1983 $7 (4/16/86)
85 ESTANCIA Chardonnay Monterey 1989 $8 (3/31/91) BB
82 ESTANCIA Chardonnay Monterey 1988 $8 (4/30/90) BB
70 ESTATE WILLIAM BACCALA Chardonnay Mendocino 1984 $11 (1/31/87)
74 ESTRELLA RIVER Chardonnay Paso Robles 1987 $8.50 (12/15/89)
82 ESTRELLA RIVER Chardonnay Paso Robles 1986 $8 (4/30/88)
65 ESTRELLA RIVER Chardonnay Paso Robles 1985 $8 (12/31/87)
70 FALCONER Chardonnay California 1989 $12 (2/28/91)
85 FALLENLEAF Chardonnay Sonoma Valley 1989 $12 (3/31/91)
89 FAR NIENTE Chardonnay Napa Valley 1989 $28 (2/28/91)
91 FAR NIENTE Chardonnay Napa Valley 1988 Rel: $26 Cur: $29 (2/15/90)
91 FAR NIENTE Chardonnay Napa Valley 1988 Rel: $26 Cur: $29 (CH-2/90)
91 FAR NIENTE Chardonnay Napa Valley 1987 Rel: $26 Cur: $30 (CH-2/90)
92 FAR NIENTE Chardonnay Napa Valley 1987 Rel: $26 Cur: $30 (12/31/88)
88 FAR NIENTE Chardonnay Napa Valley 1986 Rel: $24 Cur: $31 (CH-2/90)
75 FAR NIENTE Chardonnay Napa Valley 1986 Rel: $24 Cur: $31 (1/31/88)
90 FAR NIENTE Chardonnay Napa Valley 1985 Rel: $24 Cur: $33 (CH-2/90)
83 FAR NIENTE Chardonnay Napa Valley 1985 Rel: $24 Cur: $33 (2/28/87)
86 FAR NIENTE Chardonnay Napa Valley 1984 Rel: $22 Cur: $36 (CH-2/90)
85 FAR NIENTE Chardonnay Napa Valley 1984 Rel: $22 Cur: $36 (6/01/86)
87 FAR NIENTE Chardonnay Napa Valley 1983 Rel: $22 Cur: $38 (CH-2/90)
92 FAR NIENTE Chardonnay Napa Valley 1983 Rel: $22 Cur: $38 (4/01/85) SS
86 FAR NIENTE Chardonnay Napa Valley 1982 Rel: $18 Cur: $38 (CH-2/90)
88 FAR NIENTE Chardonnay Napa Valley 1981 Rel: $16.50 Cur: $40 (CH-2/90)
93 FAR NIENTE Chardonnay Napa Valley 1980 Rel: $16.50 Cur: $45 (CH-2/90)
92 FAR NIENTE Chardonnay Napa Valley 1979 Rel: $15 Cur: $45 (CH-2/90)
89 FAR NIENTE Chardonnay Napa Valley Estate 1983 Rel: $22 Cur: $38 (CH-2/90)
91 FAR NIENTE Chardonnay Napa Valley Estate 1982 Rel: $18 Cur: $38 (CH-2/90)
70 GARY FARRELL Chardonnay Russian River Valley Aquarius Ranch 1987 $13.50 (12/31/88)
85 GARY FARRELL Chardonnay Sonoma County 1989 $16 (7/15/91)
82 GARY FARRELL Chardonnay Sonoma County 1986 $12 (8/31/88)
80 FELTA SPRINGS Chardonnay Sonoma County 1986 $6 (6/15/88) BB
84 FELTON EMPIRE Chardonnay Monterey County 1988 $12 (4/15/90)
86 FELTON EMPIRE Chardonnay Monterey County Reserve 1988 $15 (4/15/90)
91 FERRARI-CARANO Chardonnay Alexander Valley 1989 $19.50 (6/15/91)
93 FERRARI-CARANO Chardonnay Alexander Valley 1988 Rel: $18 Cur: $18 (5/31/90) SS
93 FERRARI-CARANO Chardonnay Alexander Valley 1988 Rel: $18 Cur: $18 (CH-5/90)
94 FERRARI-CARANO Chardonnay Alexander Valley 1987 Rel: $16 Cur: $23 (CH-5/90)
94 FERRARI-CARANO Chardonnay Alexander Valley 1987 Rel: $16 Cur: $23 (5/31/89)
92 FERRARI-CARANO Chardonnay Alexander Valley 1986 Rel: $16 Cur: $28 (CH-5/90)
93 FERRARI-CARANO Chardonnay Alexander Valley 1986 Rel: $16 Cur: $28 (7/15/88)
91 FERRARI-CARANO Chardonnay Alexander Valley 1985 Rel: $14 Cur: $30 (CH-5/90)
93 FERRARI-CARANO Chardonnay Alexander Valley 1985 Rel: $14 Cur: $30 (9/15/87) SS
90 FERRARI-CARANO Chardonnay California Reserve 1988 $30 (6/15/91)
93 FERRARI-CARANO Chardonnay California Reserve 1988 Rel: $30 Cur: $30 (CH-6/90)
87 FERRARI-CARANO Chardonnay California Reserve 1987 Rel: $28 Cur: $30 (5/31/90)
89 FERRARI-CARANO Chardonnay California Reserve 1987 Rel: $28 Cur: $30 (CH-5/90)
93 FERRARI-CARANO Chardonnay California Reserve 1986 Rel: $28 Cur: $42 (CH-5/90)
92 FERRARI-CARANO Chardonnay California Reserve 1986 Rel: $28 Cur: $42 (5/31/89)
79 FETZER Chardonnay California Barrel Select 1985 $8.50 (4/30/87)
72 FETZER Chardonnay California Barrel Select 1984 $8.50 (3/01/86)
86 FETZER Chardonnay California Special Reserve 1985 $13 (11/15/87)
84 FETZER Chardonnay California Special Reserve 1984 $13 (6/01/86)
78 FETZER Chardonnay California Special Reserve 1982 $10 (4/01/84)
88 FETZER Chardonnay California Special Reserve 1981 $11 (6/01/86)
82 FETZER Chardonnay California Sundial 1989 $8 (4/30/90) BB
78 FETZER Chardonnay California Sundial 1988 $7 (5/15/89)
76 FETZER Chardonnay California Sundial 1987 $6.50 (7/31/88)
86 FETZER Chardonnay California Sundial 1986 $6.50 (9/15/87) BB
84 FETZER Chardonnay Mendocino County Barrel Select 1989 $11 (7/15/91)
82 FETZER Chardonnay Mendocino County Barrel Select 1988 $12 (3/15/90)
88 FETZER Chardonnay Mendocino County Barrel Select 1987 $10 (3/15/89)
73 FETZER Chardonnay Mendocino County Barrel Select 1986 $10 (8/31/88)
93 FETZER Chardonnay Mendocino Barrel Select 1981 $8.50 (6/01/86)
87 FETZER Chardonnay Mendocino County Reserve 1989 $18 (7/15/91)

UNITED STATES

CALIFORNIA/*CHARDONNAY*

82 FETZER Chardonnay Mendocino County Reserve 1988 $17.50 (5/31/90)
82 FETZER Chardonnay Mendocino Reserve 1987 $15 (7/15/89)
88 FETZER Chardonnay Mendocino Special Reserve 1986 $14 (12/31/88)
84 FETZER Chardonnay Mendocino County Sundial 1985 $6.50 (9/15/86) BB
86 FETZER Chardonnay Mendocino County 1984 $6.50 (4/16/86)
87 FIELD STONE Chardonnay Sonoma County 1989 $14 (3/31/91)
85 FIELD STONE Chardonnay Sonoma County 1988 $14 (4/15/91)
72 FIRESTONE Chardonnay Santa Ynez Valley 1987 $10 (12/15/89)
83 FIRESTONE Chardonnay Santa Ynez Valley 1986 $10 (12/31/88)
63 FIRESTONE Chardonnay Santa Ynez Valley 10th Anniversary 1985 $10 (4/15/88)
76 FIRESTONE Chardonnay Santa Ynez Valley 1984 $10 (5/31/87)
63 FIRESTONE Chardonnay Santa Ynez Valley 1983 $10 (3/01/86)
87 FIRESTONE Chardonnay Santa Ynez Valley Barrel Fermented 1989 $12 (4/30/91)
74 FISHER Chardonnay Napa-Sonoma Counties 1989 Rel: $12 Cur: $12 (9/30/90)
88 FISHER Chardonnay Napa-Sonoma Counties 1988 Rel: $11 Cur: $11 (9/15/89)
85 FISHER Chardonnay Sonoma-Napa Counties 1987 Rel: $11 Cur: $11 (4/15/89)
86 FISHER Chardonnay Napa-Sonoma Counties 1986 Rel: $11 Cur: $11 (7/15/88)
82 FISHER Chardonnay Napa-Sonoma Counties 1985 Rel: $11 Cur: $11 (7/15/87)
82 FISHER Chardonnay Napa-Sonoma Counties 1983 Rel: $14 Cur: $18 (CH-6/90)
87 FISHER Chardonnay Napa-Sonoma Counties 1983 Rel: $14 Cur: $18 (7/01/85)
81 FISHER Chardonnay Sonoma County 1982 Rel: $14 Cur: $22 (CH-2/90)
80 FISHER Chardonnay Sonoma County 1982 Rel: $14 Cur: $22 (6/16/84)
88 FISHER Chardonnay Sonoma County 1981 Rel: $14 Cur: $25 (CH-2/90)
85 FISHER Chardonnay Sonoma County 1980 Rel: $14 Cur: $22 (CH-2/90)
90 FISHER Chardonnay Sonoma County Coach Insignia 1988 Rel: $18 Cur: $21 (6/30/90)
87 FISHER Chardonnay Sonoma County Coach Insignia 1988 Rel: $18 Cur: $21 (CH-2/90)
84 FISHER Chardonnay Sonoma County Coach Insignia 1987 Rel: $18 Cur: $22 (CH-2/90)
84 FISHER Chardonnay Sonoma County Coach Insignia 1987 Rel: $18 Cur: $22 (1/31/90)
90 FISHER Chardonnay Sonoma County Coach Insignia 1986 Rel: $17 Cur: $20 (CH-2/90)
89 FISHER Chardonnay Sonoma County Coach Insignia 1986 Rel: $17 Cur: $20 (9/30/88)
84 FISHER Chardonnay Sonoma County Coach Insignia 1985 Rel: $16 Cur: $20 (CH-2/90)
88 FISHER Chardonnay Sonoma County Coach Insignia 1985 Rel: $16 Cur: $20 (11/15/87)
82 FISHER Chardonnay Sonoma County Coach Insignia 1984 Rel: $15 Cur: $20 (CH-2/90)
75 FISHER Chardonnay Sonoma County Coach Insignia 1984 Rel: $15 Cur: $20 (10/31/86)
79 FISHER Chardonnay Sonoma County Everyday 1984 $9 (10/16/85)
88 FISHER Chardonnay Sonoma County Whitney's Vineyard 1988 (NR) (CH-2/90)
86 FISHER Chardonnay Sonoma County Whitney's Vineyard 1987 Rel: $24 Cur: $24 (CH-2/90)
84 FISHER Chardonnay Sonoma County Whitney's Vineyard 1985 Rel: $24 Cur: $30 (CH-2/90)
90 FISHER Chardonnay Sonoma County Whitney's Vineyard 1984 Rel: $20 Cur: $30 (CH-2/90)
78 FISHER Chardonnay Sonoma County Whitney's Vineyard 1983 Rel: $20 Cur: $30 (CH-2/90)
78 FISHER Chardonnay Sonoma County Whitney's Vineyard 1982 Rel: $20 Cur: $25 (CH-6/90)
85 FISHER Chardonnay Sonoma County Whitney's Vineyard 1981 Rel: $20 Cur: $25 (CH-2/90)
92 FISHER Chardonnay Sonoma County Whitney's Vineyard 1980 Rel: $20 Cur: $30 (CH-2/90)
81 FITCH MOUNTAIN Chardonnay Napa Valley 1986 $8 (11/15/88)
87 FIVE PALMS Chardonnay Napa Valley 1985 $8 (4/30/87)
77 FLAX Chardonnay Sonoma County 1986 $14 (12/31/88)
82 FLAX Chardonnay Sonoma County 1985 $12 (10/15/87)
87 FLORA SPRINGS Chardonnay Napa Valley 1989 $15 (7/15/91)
87 FLORA SPRINGS Chardonnay Napa Valley 1988 $15 (3/15/90)
87 FLORA SPRINGS Chardonnay Napa Valley 1987 $15 (6/15/89)
77 FLORA SPRINGS Chardonnay Napa Valley 1986 $13 (7/15/88)
85 FLORA SPRINGS Chardonnay Napa Valley 1985 $15 (2/28/87)
88 FLORA SPRINGS Chardonnay Napa Valley 1984 $13.50 (10/31/86)
77 FLORA SPRINGS Chardonnay Napa Valley 1983 $13 (10/01/85)
59 FLORA SPRINGS Chardonnay Napa Valley 1982 $12 (5/16/84)
91 FLORA SPRINGS Chardonnay Napa Valley Barrel Fermented 1989 $23 (5/15/91)
91 FLORA SPRINGS Chardonnay Napa Valley Barrel Fermented 1988 Rel: $24 Cur: $24 (6/30/90)
92 FLORA SPRINGS Chardonnay Napa Valley Barrel Fermented 1988 Rel: $24 Cur: $24 (CH-4/90)
95 FLORA SPRINGS Chardonnay Napa Valley Barrel Fermented 1987 Rel: $20 Cur: $24 (CH-1/90)
93 FLORA SPRINGS Chardonnay Napa Valley Barrel Fermented 1987 Rel: $20 Cur: $24 (6/15/89)
87 FLORA SPRINGS Chardonnay Napa Valley Barrel Fermented 1986 Rel: $20 Cur: $28 (CH-1/90)
87 FLORA SPRINGS Chardonnay Napa Valley Barrel Fermented 1986 Rel: $20 Cur: $28 (7/15/88)
85 FLORA SPRINGS Chardonnay Napa Valley Barrel Fermented 1985 Rel: $18 Cur: $35 (CH-1/90)
77 FLORA SPRINGS Chardonnay Napa Valley Barrel Fermented 1985 Rel: $18 Cur: $35 (11/30/87)
88 FLORA SPRINGS Chardonnay Napa Valley Barrel Fermented 1984 Rel: $18 Cur: $28 (CH-1/90)
92 FLORA SPRINGS Chardonnay Napa Valley Barrel Fermented 1984 Rel: $18 Cur: $28 (10/31/86)
94 FLORA SPRINGS Chardonnay Napa Valley Barrel Fermented 1983 Rel: $18 Cur: $28 (CH-1/90)
70 FLORA SPRINGS Chardonnay Napa Valley Barrel Fermented 1982 Rel: $15 Cur: $15 (CH-6/88)
89 FLORA SPRINGS Chardonnay Napa Valley Special Selection 1981 Rel: $12 Cur: $25 (CH-1/90)
88 FLORA SPRINGS Chardonnay Napa Valley Special Selection 1980 Rel: $12 Cur: $25 (CH-1/90)
91 FLORA SPRINGS Chardonnay Napa Valley 1979 Rel: $9 Cur: $25 (CH-1/90)
83 THOMAS FOGARTY Chardonnay Carneros Napa Valley 1986 $15 (12/31/88)
73 THOMAS FOGARTY Chardonnay Carneros Napa Valley Winery Lake Vineyard 1985 $15 (2/15/88)
81 THOMAS FOGARTY Chardonnay Edna Valley 1987 $13.50 (12/15/89)
88 THOMAS FOGARTY Chardonnay Edna Valley Paragon Vineyards 1989 $15 (7/15/91)
88 THOMAS FOGARTY Chardonnay Monterey 1985 $15 (2/15/88)
68 THOMAS FOGARTY Chardonnay Monterey Ventana Vineyards 1986 $15 (5/31/88)
84 THOMAS FOGARTY Chardonnay Monterey Ventana Vineyards 1984 $13.50 (2/28/87)
87 THOMAS FOGARTY Chardonnay Santa Cruz Mountains 1988 $18 (7/15/91)
69 THOMAS FOGARTY Chardonnay Santa Cruz Mountains 1985 $16.50 (2/15/88)
80 FOLIE A DEUX Chardonnay Napa Valley 1989 $16 (7/15/91)
87 FOLIE A DEUX Chardonnay Napa Valley 1988 Rel: $16 Cur: $17 (CH-6/90)
85 FOLIE A DEUX Chardonnay Napa Valley 1988 Rel: $16 Cur: $17 (5/31/90)
90 FOLIE A DEUX Chardonnay Napa Valley 1987 Rel: $15 Cur: $18 (CH-6/90)
89 FOLIE A DEUX Chardonnay Napa Valley 1987 Rel: $15 Cur: $18 (5/31/89)
88 FOLIE A DEUX Chardonnay Napa Valley 1986 Rel: $15 Cur: $18 (CH-6/90)
86 FOLIE A DEUX Chardonnay Napa Valley 1986 Rel: $15 Cur: $18 (4/30/88)
88 FOLIE A DEUX Chardonnay Napa Valley 1985 Rel: $14.50 Cur: $18 (CH-6/90)
92 FOLIE A DEUX Chardonnay Napa Valley 1985 Rel: $14.50 Cur: $18 (5/31/87)
87 FOLIE A DEUX Chardonnay Napa Valley 1984 Rel: $14 Cur: $18 (CH-6/90)
84 FOLIE A DEUX Chardonnay Napa Valley 1984 Rel: $14 Cur: $18 (6/16/86)
76 FOLIE A DEUX Chardonnay Napa Valley 1983 Rel: $12 Cur: $12 (9/16/85)
78 FOLIE A DEUX Chardonnay Napa Valley 1982 Rel: $12.50 Cur: $13 (CH-7/90)
76 FOLIE A DEUX Chardonnay Napa Valley 1982 Rel: $12.50 Cur: $13 (3/01/84)
83 FOLIE A DEUX Chardonnay Napa Valley Pas de Deux 1989 $16.50 (7/15/91)
84 FOLIE A DEUX Chardonnay Napa Valley Pas de Deux 1989 $10 (12/31/90)
72 FOPPIANO Chardonnay Russian River Valley 1987 $9 (7/15/89)
75 FOPPIANO Chardonnay Sonoma County 1986 $9 (5/31/88)
78 FOPPIANO Chardonnay Sonoma County 1983 $10 (10/01/85)
83 FOREST HILL Chardonnay Napa Valley Private Reserve 1989 $24 (7/15/91)
88 FORMAN Chardonnay Napa Valley 1989 $22 (2/15/91)
92 FORMAN Chardonnay Napa Valley 1988 Rel: $20 Cur: $34 (6/30/90)
92 FORMAN Chardonnay Napa Valley 1988 Rel: $20 Cur: $34 (CH-2/90)
85 FORMAN Chardonnay Napa Valley 1988 Rel: $20 Cur: $34 (1/31/90)
89 FORMAN Chardonnay Napa Valley 1987 Rel: $18 Cur: $35 (CH-2/90)
89 FORMAN Chardonnay Napa Valley 1987 Rel: $18 Cur: $35 (12/31/88)
92 FORMAN Chardonnay Napa Valley 1986 Rel: $18 Cur: $45 (CH-2/90)
91 FORMAN Chardonnay Napa Valley 1986 Rel: $18 Cur: $45 (2/29/88)
93 FORMAN Chardonnay Napa Valley 1985 Rel: $15 Cur: $60 (CH-2/90)
91 FORMAN Chardonnay Napa Valley 1985 Rel: $15 Cur: $60 (5/31/87)
86 FORMAN Chardonnay Napa Valley 1984 Rel: $15 Cur: $45 (CH-2/90)
85 FOX MOUNTAIN Chardonnay Sonoma County Reserve 1986 $15 (4/15/91)
88 FOX MOUNTAIN Chardonnay Sonoma County Reserve 1986 $15 (6/30/89)
70 FOX MOUNTAIN Chardonnay Sonoma County Reserve 1985 $14 (12/31/88)
80 FOX MOUNTAIN Chardonnay Sonoma County Reserve 1984 $14.50 (12/31/87)
90 FOXEN Chardonnay Santa Maria Valley 1987 $18 (12/15/89)
87 FRANCISCAN Chardonnay Alexander Valley 1983 $10.50 (2/01/85)
83 FRANCISCAN Chardonnay Alexander Valley 1982 $10 (4/16/84)
84 FRANCISCAN Chardonnay Carneros Reserve 1982 Rel: $9.50 Cur: $17 (CH-4/90)
83 FRANCISCAN Chardonnay Napa Valley Oakville Estate 1989 $12 (7/15/91)
82 FRANCISCAN Chardonnay Napa Valley Oakville Estate 1988 $11 (6/30/90)
81 FRANCISCAN Chardonnay Napa Valley Oakville Estate 1987 $11 (2/15/89)
87 FRANCISCAN Chardonnay Napa Valley Oakville Estate 1986 $9.25 (5/31/88)
90 FRANCISCAN Chardonnay Napa Valley Oakville Estate 1984 $8.50 (3/15/87) BB
53 FRANCISCAN Chardonnay Napa Valley Oakville Vineyard 1983 $10 (7/01/86)
71 FRANCISCAN Chardonnay Napa Valley 1982 $9.50 (4/16/86)
84 FRANCISCAN Chardonnay Napa Valley Estate Bottled 1982 $9.50 (8/01/85)
90 FRANCISCAN Chardonnay Napa Valley Oakville Estate Cuvée Sauvage 1989 $24 (7/15/91)
94 FRANCISCAN Chardonnay Napa Valley Oakville Estate Cuvée Sauvage 1988 Rel: $20 Cur: $25 (CH-7/90)
93 FRANCISCAN Chardonnay Napa Valley Oakville Estate Cuvée Sauvage 1988 Rel: $20 Cur: $25 (6/30/90)
90 FRANCISCAN Chardonnay Napa Valley Oakville Estate Cuvée Sauvage 1987 Rel: $20 Cur: $25 (6/15/90)
91 FRANCISCAN Chardonnay Napa Valley Oakville Estate Cuvée Sauvage 1987 Rel: $20 Cur: $25 (CH-6/90)
92 FRANCISCAN Chardonnay Napa Valley Oakville Estate Reserve 1987 $15 (6/15/90)
86 FRANCISCAN Chardonnay Napa Valley Oakville Estate Reserve 1987 Rel: $20 Cur: $20 (CH-6/90)
91 FRANCISCAN Chardonnay Napa Valley Oakville Estate Reserve 1986 Rel: $14 Cur: $14 (CH-4/90)
86 FRANCISCAN Chardonnay Napa Valley Oakville Estate Reserve 1984 Rel: $12 Cur: $23 (CH-4/90)
88 FRANCISCAN Chardonnay Napa Valley Oakville Estate Reserve 1984 Rel: $10 Cur: $23 (12/15/87)
82 FRANCISCAN Chardonnay Napa Valley Oakville Estate Reserve 1983 Rel: $12 Cur: $12 (CH-4/90)
75 FREEMARK ABBEY Chardonnay Napa Valley 1989 $15 (7/15/91)
91 FREEMARK ABBEY Chardonnay Napa Valley 1988 Rel: $15 Cur: $15 (6/30/90)
89 FREEMARK ABBEY Chardonnay Napa Valley 1988 Rel: $15 Cur: $15 (CH-2/90)
84 FREEMARK ABBEY Chardonnay Napa Valley 1987 Rel: $15 Cur: $15 (CH-2/90)
86 FREEMARK ABBEY Chardonnay Napa Valley 1986 Rel: $15 Cur: $15 (CH-2/90)
77 FREEMARK ABBEY Chardonnay Napa Valley 1986 Rel: $15 Cur: $15 (3/15/89)
80 FREEMARK ABBEY Chardonnay Napa Valley 1985 Rel: $14 Cur: $25 (CH-2/90)
81 FREEMARK ABBEY Chardonnay Napa Valley 1985 Rel: $14 Cur: $25 (3/15/88)
87 FREEMARK ABBEY Chardonnay Napa Valley 1984 Rel: $14 Cur: $17 (CH-2/90)
84 FREEMARK ABBEY Chardonnay Napa Valley 1984 Rel: $14 Cur: $17 (2/28/87)
83 FREEMARK ABBEY Chardonnay Napa Valley 1983 Rel: $14 Cur: $20 (CH-2/90)
85 FREEMARK ABBEY Chardonnay Napa Valley 1983 Rel: $14 Cur: $20 (4/01/86)
72 FREEMARK ABBEY Chardonnay Napa Valley 1982 Rel: $12.75 Cur: $18 (CH-2/90)
55 FREEMARK ABBEY Chardonnay Napa Valley 1982 Rel: $12.75 Cur: $18 (3/01/85)
81 FREEMARK ABBEY Chardonnay Napa Valley 1981 Rel: $13.50 Cur: $20 (CH-2/90)
84 FREEMARK ABBEY Chardonnay Napa Valley 1980 Rel: $13.50 Cur: $38 (CH-2/90)
79 FREEMARK ABBEY Chardonnay Napa Valley 1980 Rel: $13.50 Cur: $38 (7/16/84)
76 FREEMARK ABBEY Chardonnay Napa Valley 1979 Rel: $13.25 Cur: $25 (CH-2/90)
70 FREEMARK ABBEY Chardonnay Napa Valley 1978 Rel: $10 Cur: $26 (CH-2/90)
58 FREEMARK ABBEY Chardonnay Napa Valley 1977 Rel: $10 Cur: $36 (CH-2/90)
62 FREEMARK ABBEY Chardonnay Napa Valley 1976 Rel: $9.75 Cur: $26 (CH-2/90)
82 FREEMARK ABBEY Chardonnay Napa Valley 1975 Rel: $9 Cur: $45 (CH-2/90)

Key to Symbols

The scores reported here are the results of blind tastings conducted by our panel of senior editors. Wines that carry the initials below are results of individual tastings.

THE WINE SPECTATOR 100-POINT SCALE ***95-100***—Classic, a great wine; ***90-94***—Outstanding, superior character and style; ***80-89***—Good to very good, a wine with special qualities; ***70-79***—Average, drinkable wine that may have minor flaws; ***60-69***—Below average, drinkable but not recommended; ***50-59***—Poor, undrinkable, not recommended. "+"—With a score indicates a range; used primarily with barrel tastings to indicate a preliminary score.

SPECIAL DESIGNATIONS SS—Spectator Selection, CS—Cellar Selection, BB—Best Buy.

TASTER'S INITIALS (JG)—Jim Gordon, (HS)—Harvey Steiman, (JL)—James Laube, (JS)—James Suckling, (TM)—Thomas Matthews, (TR)—Terry Robards, (BT)—Barrel Tasting (these wines were tasted blind from barrel samples), (CA-date)—*California's Great Cabernets* by James Laube, (CH-date)—*California's Great Chardonnays* by James Laube, (VP-date)—*Vintage Port* by James Suckling.

DATE TASTED Dates in parentheses represent the issue in which the rating was published.

73 FREEMARK ABBEY Chardonnay Napa Valley 1975 Rel: $9 Cur: $45 (7/16/84)
74 FREEMARK ABBEY Chardonnay Napa Valley 1974 Rel: $7.95 Cur: $42 (CH-2/90)
77 FREEMARK ABBEY Chardonnay Napa Valley 1973 Rel: $6.50 Cur: $32 (CH-2/90)
66 FREEMARK ABBEY Chardonnay Napa Valley 1973 Rel: $6.50 Cur: $32 (7/16/84)
77 FREEMARK ABBEY Chardonnay Napa Valley 1972 Rel: $6.50 Cur: $48 (CH-2/90)
70 FREEMARK ABBEY Chardonnay Napa Valley 1971 Rel: $7 Cur: $40 (CH-2/90)
55 FREEMARK ABBEY Chardonnay Napa Valley 1970 Rel: $7 Cur: $35 (CH-2/90)
60 FREEMARK ABBEY Chardonnay Napa Valley 1969 Rel: $6 Cur: $37 (CH-2/90)
73 FREEMARK ABBEY Chardonnay Napa Valley 1968 Rel: $5 Cur: $35 (CH-2/90)
84 FREEMARK ABBEY Chardonnay Napa Valley Carpy Ranch 1989 $22 (7/15/91)
84 FREEMARK ABBEY Chardonnay Napa Valley Carpy Ranch 1988 Rel: $22 Cur: $22 (4/30/90)
86 FREEMARK ABBEY Chardonnay Napa Valley Carpy Ranch 1988 Rel: $22 Cur: $22 (2/01/90)
75 FREMONT CREEK Chardonnay Mendocino County 1988 $9.50 (6/30/90)
76 FREMONT CREEK Chardonnay Mendocino-Napa Counties 1987 $9.50 (7/15/89)
87 FREMONT CREEK Chardonnay Mendocino-Napa Counties 1986 $9.50 (4/30/88)
80 J. FRITZ Chardonnay Alexander Valley Gauer Ranch 1981 $10 (4/16/84)
86 J. FRITZ Chardonnay Russian River Valley 1989 $12.50 (7/15/91)
81 J. FRITZ Chardonnay Russian River Valley 1986 $9 (2/29/88)
81 J. FRITZ Chardonnay Russian River Valley 1985 $8.50 (11/30/87)
72 J. FRITZ Chardonnay Sonoma County 1982 $9 (5/16/84)
83 FROG'S LEAP Chardonnay Carneros 1989 $16 (7/15/91)
87 FROG'S LEAP Chardonnay Carneros 1988 Rel: $16 Cur: $16 (4/30/90)
91 FROG'S LEAP Chardonnay Carneros 1988 Rel: $16 Cur: $16 (CH-3/90)
86 FROG'S LEAP Chardonnay Carneros 1987 Rel: $15 Cur: $17 (CH-3/90)
89 FROG'S LEAP Chardonnay Carneros 1987 Rel: $15 Cur: $17 (4/30/89)
87 FROG'S LEAP Chardonnay Carneros 1986 Rel: $14 Cur: $18 (CH-6/90)
82 FROG'S LEAP Chardonnay Carneros 1986 Rel: $14 Cur: $18 (6/15/88)
85 FROG'S LEAP Chardonnay Napa Valley 1988 Rel: $15 Cur: $15 (6/30/90)
87 FROG'S LEAP Chardonnay Napa Valley 1988 Rel: $15 Cur: $15 (CH-3/90)
88 FROG'S LEAP Chardonnay Napa Valley 1987 Rel: $14 Cur: $16 (CH-3/90)
90 FROG'S LEAP Chardonnay Napa Valley 1987 Rel: $14 Cur: $16 (12/31/88)
90 FROG'S LEAP Chardonnay Napa Valley 1986 Rel: $12 Cur: $18 (CH-3/90)
90 FROG'S LEAP Chardonnay Napa Valley 1986 Rel: $12 Cur: $18 (1/31/88)
84 FROG'S LEAP Chardonnay Napa Valley 1985 Rel: $12 Cur: $16 (CH-6/90)
72 FROG'S LEAP Chardonnay Napa Valley 1985 Rel: $12 Cur: $16 (3/15/87)
91 FROG'S LEAP Chardonnay Napa Valley 1984 Rel: $12 Cur: $23 (CH-3/90)
86 GAINEY Chardonnay Santa Barbara County 1989 $13 (5/31/91)
81 GAINEY Chardonnay Santa Barbara County 1988 $12.50 (2/28/91)
85 GAINEY Chardonnay Santa Barbara County 1987 $12 (12/15/89)
89 GAINEY Chardonnay Santa Barbara County Limited Selection 1987 $16 (12/15/89)
58 E.&J. GALLO Chardonnay California Limited Release NV $6 (4/16/86)
81 E.&J. GALLO Chardonnay North Coast Reserve 1989 $6.50 (7/15/91) BB
78 E.&J. GALLO Chardonnay North Coast Reserve 1987 $6 (11/30/90)
79 E.&J. GALLO Chardonnay North Coast 1985 $5 (12/31/88)
89 GAN EDEN Chardonnay Alexander Valley 1987 $9.50 (3/15/89)
87 GAN EDEN Chardonnay Sonoma County 1988 $12 (3/31/91)
88 GAN EDEN Chardonnay Sonoma County 1988 $12 (8/31/90)
76 GARLAND RANCH Chardonnay Central Coast 1989 $5 (8/31/90)
85 GAUER ESTATE Chardonnay Alexander Valley 1988 $16 (12/31/90)
84 GAUER ESTATE Chardonnay Alexander Valley 1987 $16 (11/30/90)
77 GAUER ESTATE Chardonnay Alexander Valley 1987 $16 (10/31/89)
75 GEYSER PEAK Chardonnay Alexander Valley 1982 $6.50 (4/16/84)
89 GEYSER PEAK Chardonnay Alexander Valley Barrel Fermented Estate Reserve 1989 $13 (6/15/91)
80 GEYSER PEAK Chardonnay Alexander Valley Estate Reserve 1987 $12 (6/30/89)
84 GEYSER PEAK Chardonnay Sonoma County Carneros 1985 $7 (2/28/87) BB
76 GEYSER PEAK Chardonnay Sonoma County Carneros 1984 $8 (4/16/86)
68 GEYSER PEAK Chardonnay Sonoma County Carneros 1982 $6.75 (12/16/84)
90 GIRARD Chardonnay Napa Valley 1988 $16 (11/15/90)
88 GIRARD Chardonnay Napa Valley 1988 Rel: $16 Cur: $17 (CH-6/90)
81 GIRARD Chardonnay Napa Valley 1987 Rel: $14.50 Cur: $18 (CH-3/90)
82 GIRARD Chardonnay Napa Valley 1987 Rel: $14.50 Cur: $18 (7/15/89)
92 GIRARD Chardonnay Napa Valley 1986 Rel: $13.50 Cur: $28 (CH-3/90)
93 GIRARD Chardonnay Napa Valley 1986 Rel: $13.50 Cur: $28 (8/31/88) SS
90 GIRARD Chardonnay Napa Valley 1985 Rel: $13.50 Cur: $25 (CH-3/90)
89 GIRARD Chardonnay Napa Valley 1985 Rel: $13.50 Cur: $25 (12/15/87)
80 GIRARD Chardonnay Napa Valley 1984 Rel: $13.50 Cur: $22 (CH-3/90)
82 GIRARD Chardonnay Napa Valley 1984 Rel: $13.50 Cur: $22 (2/28/87)
76 GIRARD Chardonnay Napa Valley 1983 Rel: $12.50 Cur: $22 (CH-3/90)
77 GIRARD Chardonnay Napa Valley 1983 Rel: $12.50 Cur: $22 (12/16/85)
76 GIRARD Chardonnay Napa Valley 1982 Rel: $12.50 Cur: $21 (CH-3/90)
90 GIRARD Chardonnay Napa Valley 1981 Rel: $12.50 Cur: $35 (CH-3/90)
85 GIRARD Chardonnay Napa Valley 1980 Rel: $11 Cur: $25 (CH-3/90)
91 GIRARD Chardonnay Napa Valley Reserve 1988 (NR) (CH-6/90)
90 GIRARD Chardonnay Napa Valley Reserve 1987 Rel: $25 Cur: $31 (11/15/90)
87 GIRARD Chardonnay Napa Valley Reserve 1987 Rel: $25 Cur: $31 (CH-6/90)
92 GIRARD Chardonnay Napa Valley Reserve 1986 Rel: $25 Cur: $40 (CH-3/90)
85 GIRARD Chardonnay Napa Valley Reserve 1986 Rel: $25 Cur: $40 (12/31/89)
91 GIRARD Chardonnay Napa Valley Reserve 1985 Rel: $25 Cur: $25 (CH-3/90)
78 GLEN ELLEN Chardonnay California Proprietor's Reserve 1990 $7 (7/15/91)
79 GLEN ELLEN Chardonnay California Proprietor's Reserve 1989 $6 (12/31/90)
85 GLEN ELLEN Chardonnay California Proprietor's Reserve 1984 $3.50 (10/16/85) BB
60 GLEN ELLEN Chardonnay Sonoma Valley 1984 $9 (3/16/86)
80 GLEN ELLEN Chardonnay Sonoma Valley 1983 $10 (2/01/85)
81 GOOSECROSS Chardonnay Napa Valley 1988 $14 (8/31/90)
82 GOOSECROSS Chardonnay Napa Valley 1987 $15 (1/31/90)
71 GOOSECROSS Chardonnay Napa Valley 1986 $15 (5/31/88)
90 GOOSECROSS Chardonnay Napa Valley 1985 $14 (8/31/87)
77 GOOSECROSS Chardonnay Napa Valley Reserve 1988 $18 (8/31/90)
84 GRAND CRU Chardonnay Carneros Premium Selection 1988 $13.50 (6/15/90)
74 GRAND CRU Chardonnay Carneros Premium Selection 1988 $13.50 (3/15/90)
88 GRAND CRU Chardonnay Carneros Premium Selection 1987 $12 (3/15/89)
86 GREEN & RED Chardonnay Napa Valley 1989 $14 (3/31/91)
72 GREEN & RED Chardonnay Napa Valley 1988 $12 (4/30/90)
78 GREEN & RED Chardonnay Napa Valley 1987 $11 (7/15/89)
88 GRGICH HILLS Chardonnay Napa Valley 1989 $22 (7/15/91)
89 GRGICH HILLS Chardonnay Napa Valley 1988 $22 (11/15/90)
93 GRGICH HILLS Chardonnay Napa Valley 1988 Rel: $22 Cur: $24 (CH-7/90)
90 GRGICH HILLS Chardonnay Napa Valley 1987 Rel: $22 Cur: $29 (CH-6/90)
87 GRGICH HILLS Chardonnay Napa Valley 1987 Rel: $22 Cur: $29 (7/15/89)
91 GRGICH HILLS Chardonnay Napa Valley 1986 Rel: $22 Cur: $37 (CH-3/90)
92 GRGICH HILLS Chardonnay Napa Valley 1986 Rel: $22 Cur: $37 (7/15/88)
92 GRGICH HILLS Chardonnay Napa Valley 1985 Rel: $22 Cur: $33 (CH-3/90)
87 GRGICH HILLS Chardonnay Napa Valley 1985 Rel: $22 Cur: $33 (10/15/87)
90 GRGICH HILLS Chardonnay Napa Valley 1984 Rel: $18 Cur: $33 (CH-3/90)
88 GRGICH HILLS Chardonnay Napa Valley 1984 Rel: $18 Cur: $33 (7/16/86)
92 GRGICH HILLS Chardonnay Napa Valley 1983 Rel: $17 Cur: $33 (CH-3/90)
96 GRGICH HILLS Chardonnay Napa Valley 1983 Rel: $17 Cur: $33 (10/01/85) SS
87 GRGICH HILLS Chardonnay Napa Valley 1982 Rel: $17 Cur: $44 (CH-3/90)
81 GRGICH HILLS Chardonnay Napa Valley 1982 Rel: $17 Cur: $44 (10/01/84)
88 GRGICH HILLS Chardonnay Napa Valley 1981 Rel: $17 Cur: $45 (CH-3/90)
88 GRGICH HILLS Chardonnay Napa Valley 1980 Rel: $17 Cur: $51 (CH-3/90)
95 GRGICH HILLS Chardonnay Napa Valley 1979 Rel: $16 Cur: $63 (CH-3/90)
92 GRGICH HILLS Chardonnay Napa Valley 1978 Rel: $13.75 Cur: $60 (CH-3/90)
89 GRGICH HILLS Chardonnay Sonoma County 1977 Rel: $11 Cur: $85 (CH-3/90)
85 GRGICH HILLS Chardonnay Napa Valley Hill's Cellars 1976 Rel: $8 Cur: $50 (CH-3/90)
89 GROTH Chardonnay Napa Valley 1989 $13.50 (7/15/91)
83 GROTH Chardonnay Napa Valley 1988 $13 (6/30/90)
79 GROTH Chardonnay Napa Valley 1987 $13 (7/15/89)
87 GROTH Chardonnay Napa Valley 1986 $12.50 (1/31/89)
85 GROTH Chardonnay Napa Valley 1985 $11 (2/15/88)
90 GROTH Chardonnay Napa Valley 1984 $12 (7/31/87)
82 GROTH Chardonnay Napa Valley 1982 $13 (4/16/84)
88 GUENOC Chardonnay Guenoc Valley 1989 $14 (3/31/91)
73 GUENOC Chardonnay Guenoc Valley 1987 $10 (2/15/90)
81 GUENOC Chardonnay Guenoc Valley Geneviève Magoon Vineyard Reserve 1988 $17 (12/31/90)
70 GUENOC Chardonnay Guenoc Valley Première Cuvée 1986 $17.50 (12/31/88)
88 GUENOC Chardonnay North Coast 1986 $9.75 (12/31/88)
80 GUENOC Chardonnay North Coast 1985 $9.75 (11/15/87)
83 GUENOC Chardonnay North Coast 1984 $10 (9/15/86)
78 GUNDLACH BUNDSCHU Chardonnay Sonoma Valley 1989 $12 (7/15/91)
76 GUNDLACH BUNDSCHU Chardonnay Sonoma Valley 1988 $10 (4/30/90)
79 GUNDLACH BUNDSCHU Chardonnay Sonoma Valley 1987 $11 (3/15/89)
87 GUNDLACH BUNDSCHU Chardonnay Sonoma Valley 1986 $9 (2/15/88)
80 GUNDLACH BUNDSCHU Chardonnay Sonoma Valley 1985 $10 (7/31/87)
84 GUNDLACH BUNDSCHU Chardonnay Sonoma Valley 1984 $10 (5/31/87)
76 GUNDLACH BUNDSCHU Chardonnay Sonoma Valley 1983 $9.75 (4/16/86)
83 GUNDLACH BUNDSCHU Chardonnay Sonoma Valley Jimtown Ranch 1983 $9.75 (5/01/84)
75 GUNDLACH BUNDSCHU Chardonnay Sonoma Valley Sangiacomo Ranch Special Selection 1989 $15 (7/15/91)
79 GUNDLACH BUNDSCHU Chardonnay Sonoma Valley Sangiacomo Ranch Special Selection 1988 $14 (6/30/90)
77 GUNDLACH BUNDSCHU Chardonnay Sonoma Valley Sangiacomo Ranch Special Selection 1987 $12 (7/15/89)
89 GUNDLACH BUNDSCHU Chardonnay Sonoma Valley Sangiacomo Ranch Special Selection 1986 $12 (9/30/88)
88 GUNDLACH BUNDSCHU Chardonnay Sonoma Valley Sangiacomo Ranch Special Selection 1984 $11.50 (5/31/87)
74 GUNDLACH BUNDSCHU Chardonnay Sonoma Valley Sangiacomo Ranch Special Selection 1983 $12 (12/01/85)
83 HACIENDA Chardonnay Sonoma County Clair de Lune 1988 Rel: $15 Cur: $15 (6/30/90)
85 HACIENDA Chardonnay Sonoma County Clair de Lune 1988 Rel: $15 Cur: $15 (CH-6/90)
72 HACIENDA Chardonnay Sonoma County Clair de Lune 1987 Rel: $12 Cur: $15 (CH-4/90)
73 HACIENDA Chardonnay Sonoma County Clair de Lune 1987 Rel: $12 Cur: $15 (7/15/89)
89 HACIENDA Chardonnay Sonoma County Clair de Lune 1986 Rel: $12 Cur: $18 (CH-4/90)
92 HACIENDA Chardonnay Sonoma County Clair de Lune 1986 Rel: $12 Cur: $18 (7/15/88) SS
87 HACIENDA Chardonnay Sonoma County Clair de Lune 1985 Rel: $11 Cur: $20 (CH-4/90)
91 HACIENDA Chardonnay Sonoma County Clair de Lune 1985 Rel: $11 Cur: $20 (6/30/87)
88 HACIENDA Chardonnay Sonoma County Clair de Lune 1984 Rel: $10 Cur: $18 (CH-4/90)
91 HACIENDA Chardonnay Sonoma County Clair de Lune 1984 Rel: $10 Cur: $18 (1/31/87)
83 HACIENDA Chardonnay Sonoma County Clair de Lune 1983 Rel: $10 Cur: $22 (CH-4/90)
81 HACIENDA Chardonnay Sonoma Valley Clair de Lune 1983 Rel: $10 Cur: $22 (3/16/86)
78 HACIENDA Chardonnay Sonoma County Clair de Lune 1982 Rel: $9 Cur: $20 (CH-4/90)
77 HACIENDA Chardonnay Sonoma Valley Clair de Lune 1982 Rel: $9 Cur: $20 (6/16/84)
74 HACIENDA Chardonnay Sonoma County Clair de Lune 1981 Rel: $12 Cur: $20 (CH-4/90)
80 HACIENDA Chardonnay Sonoma County Clair de Lune 1980 Rel: $10.50 Cur: $22 (CH-4/90)
86 HACIENDA Chardonnay Sonoma County Clair de Lune 1979 Rel: $9 Cur: $25 (CH-4/90)
73 HACIENDA Chardonnay Sonoma County Clair de Lune 1978 Rel: $9 Cur: $25 (CH-4/90)
76 HACIENDA Chardonnay Sonoma County Clair de Lune 1977 Rel: $8 Cur: $23 (CH-4/90)
85 HACIENDA Chardonnay Sonoma County Clair de Lune 1976 Rel: $7 Cur: $40 (CH-4/90)
80 HACIENDA Chardonnay Sonoma County Clair de Lune 1974 Rel: $5 Cur: $40 (CH-4/90)
91 HACIENDA Chardonnay Sonoma County Clair de Lune 1973 Rel: $5 Cur: $50 (CH-4/90)
85 HAGAFEN Chardonnay Napa Valley 1989 $12.50 (3/31/91)
82 HALLCREST Chardonnay California Fortuyn Cuvée 1989 $9 (4/30/91)
85 HALLCREST Chardonnay California Fortuyn Cuvée 1988 $9 (6/30/90)
88 HALLCREST Chardonnay El Dorado County Hillside Cuvée 1988 $11 (6/30/90)
91 HALLCREST Chardonnay Santa Cruz Mountains Meylay Vineyard 1989 $16.50 (4/30/91)
87 HANDLEY Chardonnay Anderson Valley 1988 $12.50 (7/15/91)
87 HANDLEY Chardonnay Dry Creek Valley 1989 $14.50 (7/15/91)
86 HANDLEY Chardonnay Dry Creek Valley 1987 $14 (7/15/89)
81 HANDLEY Chardonnay Dry Creek Valley 1986 $15 (10/31/88)
89 HANNA Chardonnay Sonoma County 1988 $13.50 (9/30/90)
73 HANNA Chardonnay Sonoma County 1987 $14.50 (7/15/89)
81 HANNA Chardonnay Sonoma County 1986 $13.50 (9/30/88)
83 HANNA Chardonnay Sonoma County 1985 $13.50 (8/31/87)
90 HANZELL Chardonnay Sonoma Valley 1988 Rel: $24 Cur: $28 (CH-5/90)
89 HANZELL Chardonnay Sonoma Valley 1987 Rel: $24 Cur: $28 (2/28/90)
90 HANZELL Chardonnay Sonoma Valley 1987 Rel: $24 Cur: $28 (CH-1/90)
87 HANZELL Chardonnay Sonoma Valley 1986 Rel: $22 Cur: $33 (CH-1/90)
90 HANZELL Chardonnay Sonoma Valley 1985 Rel: $22 Cur: $37 (CH-1/90)
84 HANZELL Chardonnay Sonoma Valley 1985 Rel: $22 Cur: $37 (3/31/88)
84 HANZELL Chardonnay Sonoma Valley 1984 Rel: $20 Cur: $49 (CH-1/90)
83 HANZELL Chardonnay Sonoma Valley 1984 Rel: $20 Cur: $49 (4/30/87)
84 HANZELL Chardonnay Sonoma Valley 1983 Rel: $20 Cur: $47 (CH-1/90)
90 HANZELL Chardonnay Sonoma Valley 1983 Rel: $20 Cur: $47 (4/16/85) (JG)
89 HANZELL Chardonnay Sonoma Valley 1982 Rel: $19 Cur: $51 (CH-1/90)
89 HANZELL Chardonnay Sonoma Valley 1982 Rel: $19 Cur: $51 (4/16/85) (JG)

UNITED STATES
CALIFORNIA/*CHARDONNAY*

86 HANZELL Chardonnay Sonoma Valley 1981 Rel: $18 Cur: $53 (CH-1/90)
78 HANZELL Chardonnay Sonoma Valley 1981 Rel: $18 Cur: $53 (4/16/85) (JG)
90 HANZELL Chardonnay Sonoma Valley 1980 Rel: $17 Cur: $60 (CH-1/90)
87 HANZELL Chardonnay Sonoma Valley 1980 Rel: $17 Cur: $60 (4/16/85) (JG)
85 HANZELL Chardonnay Sonoma Valley 1979 Rel: $16 Cur: $70 (CH-1/90)
83 HANZELL Chardonnay Sonoma Valley 1979 Rel: $16 Cur: $70 (4/16/85) (JG)
95 HANZELL Chardonnay Sonoma Valley 1978 Rel: $13 Cur: $80 (CH-1/90)
90 HANZELL Chardonnay Sonoma Valley 1978 Rel: $13 Cur: $80 (4/16/85) (JG)
88 HANZELL Chardonnay Sonoma Valley 1977 Rel: $12 Cur: $85 (CH-1/90)
80 HANZELL Chardonnay Sonoma Valley 1977 Rel: $12 Cur: $85 (4/16/85) (JG)
91 HANZELL Chardonnay Sonoma Valley 1976 Rel: $12 Cur: $90 (CH-1/90)
79 HANZELL Chardonnay Sonoma Valley 1976 Rel: $12 Cur: $90 (4/16/85) (JG)
86 HANZELL Chardonnay Sonoma Valley 1975 Rel: $10 Cur: $70 (CH-1/90)
81 HANZELL Chardonnay Sonoma Valley 1975 Rel: $10 Cur: $70 (4/16/85) (JG)
88 HANZELL Chardonnay Sonoma Valley 1974 Rel: $9 Cur: $75 (CH-1/90)
85 HANZELL Chardonnay Sonoma Valley 1973 Rel: $8 Cur: $100 (CH-1/90)
90 HANZELL Chardonnay Sonoma Valley 1972 Rel: $7 Cur: $75 (CH-1/90)
85 HANZELL Chardonnay Sonoma Valley 1971 Rel: $7 Cur: $120 (CH-1/90)
84 HANZELL Chardonnay Sonoma Valley 1970 Rel: $7 Cur: $120 (CH-1/90)
90 HANZELL Chardonnay Sonoma Valley 1969 Rel: $6 Cur: $140 (CH-1/90)
91 HANZELL Chardonnay Sonoma Valley 1968 Rel: $6 Cur: $140 (CH-1/90)
89 HANZELL Chardonnay Sonoma Valley 1967 Rel: $6 Cur: $140 (CH-1/90)
94 HANZELL Chardonnay Sonoma Valley 1966 Rel: $6 Cur: $170 (CH-1/90)
84 HANZELL Chardonnay Sonoma Valley 1965 Rel: $6 Cur: $180 (CH-1/90)
88 HANZELL Chardonnay California 1959 Rel: $4 Cur: $200 (CH-12/89)
90 HANZELL Chardonnay California 1957 Rel: $4 Cur: $240 (CH-12/89)
87 HARRISON Chardonnay Napa Valley 1989 $24 (7/15/91)
87 HAVENS Chardonnay Carneros Napa Valley 1989 $14 (7/15/91)
89 HAVENS Chardonnay Carneros Napa Valley 1988 $14 (4/30/90)
72 HAWK CREST Chardonnay California 1989 $9 (7/15/91)
74 HAWK CREST Chardonnay California 1988 $9 (12/15/89)
71 HAWK CREST Chardonnay California 1987 $7.50 (10/15/88)
67 HAWK CREST Chardonnay California 1984 $6 (4/16/86)
86 HAWK CREST Chardonnay Sonoma County 1987 $9 (7/15/89)
82 HAYWOOD Chardonnay Sonoma Valley 1986 $9.50 (10/15/88)
80 HAYWOOD Chardonnay Sonoma Valley 1982 $10 (5/16/84)
81 HAYWOOD Chardonnay Sonoma Valley Los Chamizal Vineyards 1989 $13.50 (3/31/91)
76 HAYWOOD Chardonnay Sonoma Valley Los Chamizal Vineyards 1988 $13.50 (11/30/90)
74 HAYWOOD Chardonnay Sonoma Valley Los Chamizal Vineyards 1987 $12.50 (6/30/90)
77 HAYWOOD Chardonnay Sonoma Valley Reserve 1985 $14.50 (12/31/87)
87 HEITZ Chardonnay Napa Valley 1962 Rel: $6 Cur: $125 (CH-6/90)
93 HEITZ Chardonnay Napa Valley 1961 Rel: $6 Cur: $125 (CH-6/90)
86 HESS Chardonnay Napa Valley 1989 $14.50 (7/15/91)
85 HESS Chardonnay Napa Valley 1988 Rel: $13.75 Cur: $14 (4/15/90)
88 HESS Chardonnay Napa Valley 1988 Rel: $13.75 Cur: $14 (CH-4/90)
91 HESS Chardonnay Napa Valley 1987 Rel: $13.25 Cur: $15 (CH-4/90)
90 HESS Chardonnay Napa Valley 1987 Rel: $13.25 Cur: $15 (7/15/89)
88 HESS Chardonnay Napa Valley 1986 Rel: $12.75 Cur: $16 (CH-4/90)
88 HESS Chardonnay Napa Valley 1986 Rel: $12.75 Cur: $16 (10/15/88)
86 HESS Chardonnay Napa Valley Hess Select 1989 $9.50 (12/31/90)
90 HESS Chardonnay California Hess Select 1988 $9 (11/30/89) SS
83 HIDDEN CELLARS Chardonnay Mendocino County 1989 $12 (3/31/91) (HS)
89 HIDDEN CELLARS Chardonnay Mendocino County 1987 $12 (7/15/89)
78 HIDDEN CELLARS Chardonnay Mendocino County 1986 $10.50 (5/31/88)
78 HIDDEN CELLARS Chardonnay Mendocino County Grasso Vineyard 1985 $9.75 (7/31/87)
91 HIDDEN CELLARS Chardonnay Mendocino County Reserve Barrel Fermented 1989 $16 (7/15/91)
90 WILLIAM HILL Chardonnay Napa Valley Reserve 1989 $18 (6/30/91)
90 WILLIAM HILL Chardonnay Napa Valley Reserve 1988 Rel: $18 Cur: $18 (4/30/90)
88 WILLIAM HILL Chardonnay Napa Valley Reserve 1988 Rel: $18 Cur: $18 (CH-3/90)
91 WILLIAM HILL Chardonnay Napa Valley Reserve 1987 Rel: $18 Cur: $18 (CH-3/90)
89 WILLIAM HILL Chardonnay Napa Valley Reserve 1987 Rel: $18 Cur: $18 (7/15/89)
91 WILLIAM HILL Chardonnay Napa Valley Reserve 1986 Rel: $17 Cur: $20 (CH-3/90)
79 WILLIAM HILL Chardonnay Napa Valley Reserve 1986 Rel: $17 Cur: $20 (3/31/88)
90 WILLIAM HILL Chardonnay Napa Valley Reserve 1985 Rel: $16 Cur: $24 (CH-3/90)
80 WILLIAM HILL Chardonnay Napa Valley Reserve 1985 Rel: $16 Cur: $24 (7/31/87)
88 WILLIAM HILL Chardonnay Napa Valley Reserve 1984 Rel: $20 Cur: $24 (CH-3/90)
78 WILLIAM HILL Chardonnay Napa Valley Reserve 1984 Rel: $20 Cur: $24 (7/31/87)
85 WILLIAM HILL Chardonnay Napa Valley Reserve 1983 Rel: $22 Cur: $28 (CH-3/90)
75 WILLIAM HILL Chardonnay Napa Valley Reserve 1983 Rel: $22 Cur: $28 (7/31/87)
82 WILLIAM HILL Chardonnay Napa Valley Reserve 1983 Rel: $22 Cur: $28 (3/31/87)
86 WILLIAM HILL Chardonnay Napa Valley Reserve 1982 Rel: $24 Cur: $28 (CH-3/90)
86 WILLIAM HILL Chardonnay Napa Valley Reserve 1982 Rel: $24 Cur: $28 (7/31/87)
83 WILLIAM HILL Chardonnay Napa Valley Reserve 1982 Rel: $24 Cur: $28 (11/01/84)
70 WILLIAM HILL Chardonnay Napa Valley Reserve 1980 Rel: $16 Cur: $30 (CH-3/90)
81 WILLIAM HILL Chardonnay Napa Valley Silver Label 1989 $12 (1/31/91)
85 WILLIAM HILL Chardonnay Napa Valley Silver Label 1988 $11.50 (6/30/90)
73 WILLIAM HILL Chardonnay Napa Valley Silver Label 1987 $13 (6/15/89)
80 WILLIAM HILL Chardonnay Napa Valley Silver Label 1986 $10 (4/30/88)
86 HOP KILN Chardonnay Alexander Valley Tenth Anniversary Reserve 1983 $10 (10/01/85)
83 HOUTZ Chardonnay Santa Ynez Valley 1986 $11 (12/15/89)
82 HUSCH Chardonnay Anderson Valley Special Reserve 1987 $16 (6/30/90)
88 HUSCH Chardonnay Mendocino 1988 $11 (2/28/90)
88 HUSCH Chardonnay Mendocino 1987 $10 (11/15/88)
86 HUSCH Chardonnay Mendocino 1986 $9.75 (11/30/87)
88 HUSCH Chardonnay Mendocino 1985 $9.75 (3/31/87)
88 HUSCH Chardonnay Mendocino Estate Bottled 1989 $11 (12/31/90)
87 INGLENOOK Chardonnay Napa Valley 1989 $7.50 (2/28/91) BB
80 INGLENOOK Chardonnay Napa Valley 1986 $9.50 (3/15/88)
79 INGLENOOK Chardonnay Napa Valley 1983 $9.50 (10/01/84)
88 INGLENOOK Chardonnay Napa Valley Reserve 1988 (NR) (CH-4/90)
89 INGLENOOK Chardonnay Napa Valley Reserve 1987 Rel: $14 Cur: $14 (5/31/90)
86 INGLENOOK Chardonnay Napa Valley Reserve 1987 Rel: $14 Cur: $14 (CH-4/90)
88 INGLENOOK Chardonnay Napa Valley Reserve 1986 Rel: $14.50 Cur: $15 (CH-4/90)
87 INGLENOOK Chardonnay Napa Valley Reserve 1986 Rel: $14.50 Cur: $15 (3/15/89)
78 INGLENOOK Chardonnay Napa Valley Reserve 1985 Rel: $14.50 Cur: $15 (CH-4/90)
88 INGLENOOK Chardonnay Napa Valley Reserve 1985 Rel: $14.50 Cur: $15 (4/15/88)
86 INGLENOOK Chardonnay Napa Valley Reserve 1984 Rel: $12.50 Cur: $18 (CH-4/90)
89 INGLENOOK Chardonnay Napa Valley Reserve 1984 Rel: $12.50 Cur: $18 (3/01/86)
82 INGLENOOK Chardonnay Napa Valley Reserve 1983 Rel: $16 Cur: $19 (CH-4/90)
77 INNISFREE Chardonnay Carneros 1988 $12 (5/31/90)
83 INNISFREE Chardonnay Napa Valley 1989 $11 (4/30/91)
86 INNISFREE Chardonnay Napa Valley 1988 $12 (6/15/90)
80 INNISFREE Chardonnay Napa Valley 1987 $9 (2/15/89)
80 INNISFREE Chardonnay Napa Valley 1986 $9 (12/31/87)
92 INNISFREE Chardonnay Napa Valley 1985 $9 (12/31/86)
88 INNISFREE Chardonnay Napa Valley 1984 $9 (11/16/85)
81 INNISKILLIN NAPA Chardonnay Napa Valley 1988 $14 (7/15/91)
86 IRON HORSE Chardonnay Sonoma County Green Valley 1989 $18 (3/31/91)
81 IRON HORSE Chardonnay Sonoma County Green Valley 1988 $18 (2/15/90)
76 IRON HORSE Chardonnay Sonoma County Green Valley 1987 $17 (1/31/89)
83 IRON HORSE Chardonnay Sonoma County Green Valley 1986 $12 (3/31/88)
75 IRON HORSE Chardonnay Sonoma County Green Valley 1985 $12.50 (7/31/87)
88 IRON HORSE Chardonnay Sonoma County Green Valley 1984 $12 (6/16/86)
76 IRON HORSE Chardonnay Sonoma County Green Valley 1983 $12 (11/16/85)
55 JEKEL Chardonnay Arroyo Seco 1989 $12 (7/15/91)
87 JEKEL Chardonnay Arroyo Seco 1988 $11 (4/15/90)
76 JEKEL Chardonnay Arroyo Seco 1986 $11 (4/30/89)
71 JEKEL Chardonnay Arroyo Seco 1985 $10.50 (12/31/88)
83 JEKEL Chardonnay Arroyo Seco 1984 $10.50 (5/31/87)
66 JEKEL Chardonnay Arroyo Seco 1983 $10 (4/01/86)
88 JEKEL Chardonnay Arroyo Seco 1982 $10 (1/01/84)
86 JEKEL Chardonnay Arroyo Seco 1981 $11 (6/01/86)
59 JEKEL Chardonnay Arroyo Seco Home Vineyard 1982 $10 (10/01/85)
91 JEKEL Chardonnay Arroyo Seco Home Vineyard Private Reserve 1985 $18 (4/15/89)
79 JEKEL Chardonnay Arroyo Seco Home Vineyard Private Reserve 1984 $16 (11/30/87)
93 JEKEL Chardonnay Arroyo Seco Home Vineyard Private Reserve 1982 $14 (10/01/85)
84 JEKEL Chardonnay Arroyo Seco Home Vineyard Private Reserve 1981 $15 (6/01/86)
79 JEPSON Chardonnay Mendocino 1989 $14 (7/15/91)
85 JEPSON Chardonnay Mendocino 1988 $12.50 (4/30/91)
89 JEPSON Chardonnay Mendocino 1986 $12 (11/15/88)
92 JEPSON Chardonnay Mendocino 1985 $12 (1/31/88)
80 JEPSON Chardonnay Mendocino Vintage Reserve 1986 $15 (5/31/89)
70 JOHNSON TURNBULL Chardonnay Knights Valley Teviot Springs Vineyard 1987 $12.50 (9/15/89)
88 JORDAN Chardonnay Alexander Valley 1987 $20 (6/30/90)
82 JORDAN Chardonnay Alexander Valley 1986 $20 (4/15/89)
87 JORDAN Chardonnay Alexander Valley 1985 $17 (3/15/88)
67 JORDAN Chardonnay Alexander Valley 1983 $16 (7/16/86)
85 JORDAN Chardonnay Alexander Valley 1982 $15.75 (5/16/85)
77 JORDAN Chardonnay Alexander Valley 1981 $15.75 (4/16/84)
82 JORY Chardonnay Santa Clara County San Ysidro Vineyard 1989 $17 (4/30/91)
89 JORY Chardonnay Santa Clara County San Ysidro Vineyard 1987 $16.50 (10/31/88)
73 JOULLIAN Chardonnay Carmel Valley 1989 $12 (7/15/91)
85 JUSTIN Chardonnay Paso Robles 1989 $16.50 (7/15/91)
89 JUSTIN Chardonnay Paso Robles 1988 $14 (2/15/91)
86 KALIN Chardonnay Potter Valley Cuvée BL 1988 $25 (3/31/91)
87 KALIN Chardonnay Sonoma County Cuvée DD 1988 $23 (3/31/91)
88 KALIN Chardonnay Sonoma County Cuvée LD 1988 $23 (3/15/91)
79 KALIN Chardonnay Sonoma County Cuvée LD 1987 $25 (3/15/91)
81 KALINDA Chardonnay Knights Valley 1989 $7 (7/15/91)
54 KARLY Chardonnay California 1986 $12.50 (4/15/88)
81 KARLY Chardonnay Santa Maria Valley 1985 $12 (8/31/87)
84 KEENAN Chardonnay Napa Valley 1989 $15 (7/15/91)
91 KEENAN Chardonnay Napa Valley 1988 $15 (6/30/90) SS
82 KEENAN Chardonnay Napa Valley 1987 $12.50 (6/15/89)
85 KEENAN Chardonnay Napa Valley 1986 $12 (7/15/88)
81 KEENAN Chardonnay Napa Valley 1985 $11 (7/31/87)
74 KEENAN Chardonnay Napa Valley 1983 $12.50 (9/16/85)
59 KEENAN Chardonnay Napa Valley Ann's Vineyard 1987 $13.50 (6/30/90)
77 KEENAN Chardonnay Napa Valley Ann's Vineyard 1986 $14 (4/15/89)
80 KEENAN Chardonnay Napa Valley Estate 1985 $13.50 (2/15/88)
70 KEENAN Chardonnay Napa Valley Estate 1983 $12.50 (8/31/86)
82 KENDALL-JACKSON Chardonnay Anderson Valley Dennison Vineyard 1987 Rel: $14 Cur: $14 (CH-4/90)
85 KENDALL-JACKSON Chardonnay Anderson Valley Dennison Vineyard 1985 Rel: $14 Cur: $20 (CH-4/90)
89 KENDALL-JACKSON Chardonnay Anderson Valley De Patie Vineyard 1987 Rel: $14 Cur: $14 (CH-4/90)
91 KENDALL-JACKSON Chardonnay Anderson Valley De Patie Vineyard 1987 Rel: $14 Cur: $14 (7/15/89)
85 KENDALL-JACKSON Chardonnay Anderson Valley Du Pratt Vineyard 1988 Rel: $14 Cur: $14 (CH-4/90)
90 KENDALL-JACKSON Chardonnay California Proprietor's Grand Reserve 1989 $23 (5/31/91)
87 KENDALL-JACKSON Chardonnay California The Proprietor's 1988 Rel: $24.50 Cur: $25 (CH-4/90)
88 KENDALL-JACKSON Chardonnay California The Proprietor's 1988 Rel: $24.50 Cur: $25 (2/28/90)
92 KENDALL-JACKSON Chardonnay California The Proprietor's 1987 Rel: $20 Cur: $20 (CH-4/90)
90 KENDALL-JACKSON Chardonnay California The Proprietor's 1987 Rel: $20 Cur: $20 (11/30/88)
86 KENDALL-JACKSON Chardonnay California The Proprietor's 1986 Rel: $17 Cur: $20 (CH-4/90)

Key to Symbols

The scores reported here are the results of blind tastings conducted by our panel of senior editors. Wines that carry the initials below are results of individual tastings.

THE WINE SPECTATOR 100-POINT SCALE *95-100*—Classic, a great wine; *90-94*—Outstanding, superior character and style; *80-89*—Good to very good, a wine with special qualities; *70-79*—Average, drinkable wine that may have minor flaws; *60-69*—Below average, drinkable but not recommended; *50-59*—Poor, undrinkable, not recommended. "+"—With a score indicates a range; used primarily with barrel tastings to indicate a preliminary score.

SPECIAL DESIGNATIONS SS—Spectator Selection, CS—Cellar Selection, BB—Best Buy.

TASTER'S INITIALS (JG)—Jim Gordon, (HS)—Harvey Steiman, (JL)—James Laube, (JS)—James Suckling, (TM)—Thomas Matthews, (TR)—Terry Robards, (BT)—Barrel Tasting (these wines were tasted blind from barrel samples), (CA-date)—*California's Great Cabernets* by James Laube, (CH-date)—*California's Great Chardonnays* by James Laube, (VP-date)—*Vintage Port* by James Suckling.

DATE TASTED Dates in parentheses represent the issue in which the rating was published.

79 KENDALL-JACKSON Chardonnay California The Proprieter's 1985 Rel: $18 Cur: $18 (9/15/87)
86 KENDALL-JACKSON Chardonnay California Proprietor's Reserve 1983 $13.50 (8/01/85)
84 KENDALL-JACKSON Chardonnay California Vintner's Reserve 1989 $13 (7/15/91)
89 KENDALL-JACKSON Chardonnay California Vintner's Reserve 1988 $12.50 (10/31/89)
85 KENDALL-JACKSON Chardonnay California Vintner's Reserve 1987 $12 (9/30/88)
84 KENDALL-JACKSON Chardonnay California Vintner's Reserve 1985 $9.50 (3/15/87)
59 KENDALL-JACKSON Chardonnay California Vintner's Reserve 1984 $7 (4/16/86)
66 KENDALL-JACKSON Chardonnay California Royale 1983 $11 (11/16/85)
85 KENDALL-JACKSON Chardonnay Redwood Valley Lolonis Vineyard 1988 (NR) (CH-4/90)
86 KENDALL-JACKSON Chardonnay Sonoma Valley Durell Vineyard 1989 $16 (7/15/91)
86 KENDALL-JACKSON Chardonnay Sonoma Valley Durell Vineyard 1987 Rel: $14 Cur: $14 (CH-4/90)
91 KENDALL-JACKSON Chardonnay Sonoma Valley Durell Vineyard 1986 Rel: $14 Cur: $16 (CH-6/90)
87 KENDALL-JACKSON Chardonnay Sonoma Valley Durell Vineyard 1985 Rel: $14 Cur: $20 (CH-4/90)
82 KENWOOD Chardonnay Sonoma Valley 1988 $14 (5/31/90)
86 KENWOOD Chardonnay Sonoma Valley 1987 $13 (7/15/89)
85 KENWOOD Chardonnay Sonoma Valley 1986 $12 (2/15/89)
83 KENWOOD Chardonnay Sonoma Valley Beltane Ranch 1989 $16 (7/15/91)
88 KENWOOD Chardonnay Sonoma Valley Beltane Ranch 1988 $15 (11/30/90)
89 KENWOOD Chardonnay Sonoma Valley Beltane Ranch 1988 Rel: $15 Cur: $17 (CH-7/90)
87 KENWOOD Chardonnay Sonoma Valley Beltane Ranch 1987 Rel: $15 Cur: $17 (CH-7/90)
85 KENWOOD Chardonnay Sonoma Valley Beltane Ranch 1986 Rel: $14 Cur: $18 (CH-7/90)
86 KENWOOD Chardonnay Sonoma Valley Beltane Ranch 1986 Rel: $14 Cur: $18 (5/31/88)
84 KENWOOD Chardonnay Sonoma Valley Beltane Ranch 1985 Rel: $14 Cur: $18 (CH-7/90)
87 KENWOOD Chardonnay Sonoma Valley Yulupa Vineyard 1988 Rel: $14 Cur: $14 (CH-7/90)
87 KENWOOD Chardonnay Sonoma Valley Yulupa Vineyard 1988 Rel: $14 Cur: $14 (5/31/90)
85 KENWOOD Chardonnay Sonoma Valley Yulupa Vineyard 1987 Rel: $14 Cur: $16 (CH-7/90)
82 KENWOOD Chardonnay Sonoma Valley Yulupa Vineyard 1986 Rel: $12 Cur: $17 (CH-7/90)
84 KENWOOD Chardonnay Sonoma Valley Yulupa Vineyard 1985 Rel: $12 Cur: $17 (CH-7/90)
85 KENWOOD Chardonnay Sonoma Valley Yulupa Vineyard 1985 Rel: $12 Cur: $17 (2/15/88)
85 KENWOOD Chardonnay Sonoma Valley Yulupa Vineyard 1983 Rel: $11 Cur: $18 (CH-7/90)
89 KISTLER Chardonnay Russian River Valley Dutton Ranch 1989 $24 (2/15/91)
90 KISTLER Chardonnay Russian River Valley Dutton Ranch 1988 Rel: $22 Cur: $44 (2/15/90)
92 KISTLER Chardonnay Russian River Valley Dutton Ranch 1988 Rel: $22 Cur: $44 (CH-2/90)
93 KISTLER Chardonnay Russian River Valley Dutton Ranch 1987 Rel: $18 Cur: $45 (CH-2/90)
92 KISTLER Chardonnay Russian River Valley Dutton Ranch 1987 Rel: $18 Cur: $45 (12/31/88)
90 KISTLER Chardonnay Russian River Valley Dutton Ranch 1986 Rel: $16.50 Cur: $28 (CH-2/90)
91 KISTLER Chardonnay Russian River Valley Dutton Ranch 1986 Rel: $16.50 Cur: $28 (3/15/88)
88 KISTLER Chardonnay Russian River Valley Dutton Ranch 1985 Rel: $15 Cur: $30 (CH-2/90)
89 KISTLER Chardonnay Russian River Valley Dutton Ranch 1984 Rel: $15 Cur: $30 (CH-2/90)
82 KISTLER Chardonnay Russian River Valley Dutton Ranch 1984 Rel: $15 Cur: $30 (9/30/86)
88 KISTLER Chardonnay Sonoma Mountain McCrea Vineyard 1989 Rel: $28 Cur: $29 (6/15/91)
92 KISTLER Chardonnay Sonoma Mountain McCrea Vineyard 1988 Rel: $24 Cur: $24 (4/30/90)
92 KISTLER Chardonnay Sonoma Mountain McCrea Vineyard 1988 Rel: $24 Cur: $24 (CH-2/90)
88 KISTLER Chardonnay Sonoma Valley 1989 $24 (2/15/91)
90 KISTLER Chardonnay Sonoma Valley Durell Vineyard 1989 $24 (5/15/91)
90 KISTLER Chardonnay Sonoma Valley Durell Vineyard 1988 $17 (2/28/90)
91 KISTLER Chardonnay Sonoma Valley Durell Vineyard 1988 $17 (2/01/90)
93 KISTLER Chardonnay Sonoma Valley Durell Vineyard 1987 $16 (2/01/90)
84 KISTLER Chardonnay Sonoma Valley Durell Vineyard 1987 $16 (12/31/88)
89 KISTLER Chardonnay Sonoma Valley Durell Vineyard 1986 $16 (2/01/90)
91 KISTLER Chardonnay Sonoma Valley Kistler Estate Vineyard 1989 $32 (6/15/91)
94 KISTLER Chardonnay Sonoma Valley Kistler Estate Vineyard 1988 Rel: $26 Cur: $26 (4/30/90)
95 KISTLER Chardonnay Sonoma Valley Kistler Estate Vineyard 1988 Rel: $26 Cur: $26 (2/01/90)
90 KISTLER Chardonnay Sonoma Valley Kistler Estate Vineyard 1987 Rel: $22 Cur: $55 (2/01/90)
92 KISTLER Chardonnay Sonoma Valley Kistler Estate Vineyard 1987 Rel: $22 Cur: $55 (7/15/89)
92 KISTLER Chardonnay Sonoma Valley Kistler Estate Vineyard 1986 Rel: $18 Cur: $40 (2/01/90)
74 KONOCTI Chardonnay Lake County 1989 $9.50 (4/30/91)
83 KONOCTI Chardonnay Lake County 1988 $9 (4/15/90)
73 KONOCTI Chardonnay Lake County 1987 $9 (11/15/89)
80 KONOCTI Chardonnay Lake County 1986 $8 (12/31/88)
85 KONRAD Chardonnay Mendocino County Estate 1989 $12 (7/15/91)
75 CHARLES KRUG Chardonnay Napa Valley 1989 $10 (3/31/91)
80 CHARLES KRUG Chardonnay Carneros Napa Valley 1988 $11.50 (1/31/90)
85 LA CREMA Chardonnay California 1989 $12 (7/15/91)
82 LA CREMA Chardonnay California 1988 $13.50 (6/30/90)
88 LA CREMA Chardonnay California 1987 $12 (12/31/88)
78 LA CREMA Chardonnay California 1986 $11.50 (7/15/88)
93 LA CREMA Chardonnay California 1985 $11 (2/28/87)
88 LA CREMA Chardonnay California Reserve 1989 $22 (7/15/91)
91 LA CREMA Chardonnay California Reserve 1988 Rel: $22 Cur: $22 (CH-6/90)
91 LA CREMA Chardonnay California Reserve 1988 Rel: $22 Cur: $22 (5/31/90)
83 LA CREMA Chardonnay California Reserve 1987 Rel: $22 Cur: $22 (CH-6/90)
84 LA CREMA Chardonnay California Reserve 1987 Rel: $22 Cur: $22 (5/15/89)
85 LA CREMA Chardonnay California Reserve 1986 Rel: $18 Cur: $22 (CH-6/90)
92 LA CREMA Chardonnay California Reserve 1986 Rel: $18 Cur: $22 (7/15/88)
86 LA CREMA Chardonnay California Reserve 1985 Rel: $18 Cur: $22 (CH-6/90)
92 LA CREMA Chardonnay California Reserve 1985 Rel: $18 Cur: $22 (11/15/87)
88 LA CREMA Chardonnay Monterey Ventana Vineyard 1984 Rel: $18 Cur: $24 (CH-6/90)
85 LA REINA Chardonnay Monterey County 1987 $13.50 (3/31/89)
75 LA REINA Chardonnay Monterey County 1986 $13 (12/31/88)
86 LA REINA Chardonnay Monterey 1984 $12 (2/01/86)
78 LAKESPRING Chardonnay Alexander Valley 1981 $10 (4/16/84)
88 LAKESPRING Chardonnay Napa Valley 1988 $13 (5/15/91)
72 LAKESPRING Chardonnay Napa Valley 1987 $12 (10/31/89)
90 LAKESPRING Chardonnay Napa Valley 1986 $11 (12/31/88)
71 LAKESPRING Chardonnay Napa Valley 1985 $11 (11/15/87)
70 LAKESPRING Chardonnay Napa Valley 1984 $12 (10/31/86)
73 LAMBERT BRIDGE Chardonnay Sonoma County 1985 $10 (2/15/88)
83 LAMBERT BRIDGE Chardonnay Sonoma County 1982 $13.50 (12/16/84)
76 LANDMARK Chardonnay Alexander Valley Proprietor's Grown 1982 $10 (5/01/84)
87 LANDMARK Chardonnay Sonoma County 1988 $10 (4/15/91)
71 LANDMARK Chardonnay Sonoma County 1985 $10 (2/15/88)
80 LANDMARK Chardonnay Sonoma County 1983 $9 (1/01/86)
78 LANDMARK Chardonnay Sonoma Valley 1982 $9 (5/01/84)
87 LANDMARK Chardonnay Sonoma Valley Damaris Vineyard 1989 $16 (6/30/91)
78 LANDMARK Chardonnay Sonoma Valley Two Williams Vineyard 1989 $16 (7/15/91)
79 LAURA'S Chardonnay Paso Robles 1987 $12 (12/15/89)
73 LAURA'S Chardonnay San Luis Obispo 1985 $7 (12/31/87)
88 LAURIER Chardonnay Sonoma County 1989 $16 (4/30/91)
86 LAZY CREEK Chardonnay Anderson Valley 1989 $8.50 (7/15/91)
90 LAZY CREEK Chardonnay Anderson Valley 1987 $10 (5/15/89)
83 LEEWARD Chardonnay Central Coast 1989 $11 (8/31/90)
89 LEEWARD Chardonnay Central Coast 1988 $10.50 (12/15/89)
81 LEEWARD Chardonnay Central Coast 1987 $9 (10/31/88)
86 LEEWARD Chardonnay Central Coast 1986 $8.50 (10/31/87)
78 LEEWARD Chardonnay Central Coast 1984 $8 (6/16/86)
86 LEEWARD Chardonnay Edna Valley MacGregor Vineyard 1988 $16 (4/30/90)
90 LEEWARD Chardonnay Edna Valley MacGregor Vineyard 1987 $16 (12/15/89)
85 LEEWARD Chardonnay Edna Valley MacGregor Vineyard 1986 $14 (2/29/88)
70 LEEWARD Chardonnay Edna Valley MacGregor Vineyard 1985 $14 (5/31/87)
93 LEEWARD Chardonnay Edna Valley MacGregor Vineyard 1984 $12 (6/16/86)
80 LEEWARD Chardonnay Edna Valley MacGregor Vineyard 1983 $14 (11/01/84)
74 LEEWARD Chardonnay Monterey County 1989 $14 (11/30/90)
78 LEEWARD Chardonnay Monterey County Ventana Vineyards 1983 $8 (10/16/84)
64 LEEWARD Chardonnay Santa Maria Valley Bien Nacido Vineyard 1984 $12 (12/01/85)
74 LIBERTY SCHOOL Chardonnay California Lot 11 1986 $6 (2/29/88)
77 LIBERTY SCHOOL Chardonnay California Lot 17 NV $7.50 (2/28/90)
54 LIBERTY SCHOOL Chardonnay California Lot 5 1984 $6 (10/16/85)
65 LIBERTY SCHOOL Chardonnay California Lot 7 1984 $6 (4/16/86)
80 LIBERTY SCHOOL Chardonnay California Vintner Select Series One 1989 $7.50 (2/28/91)
72 LIBERTY SCHOOL Chardonnay Napa Valley 1989 $7.50 (11/15/90)
83 LIBERTY SCHOOL Chardonnay Napa Valley Lot 15 1987 $7.50 (3/31/89) BB
88 LIMUR Chardonnay Napa Valley 1989 $19 (7/15/91)
79 LOCKWOOD Chardonnay Monterey County 1989 $14 (7/15/91)
88 LOGAN Chardonnay Monterey 1989 $12 (6/30/91)
84 LOGAN Chardonnay Monterey 1988 $12 (6/30/90)
76 J. LOHR Chardonnay California Cypress 1989 $7 (7/15/91)
90 J. LOHR Chardonnay Monterey Riverstone 1989 $12 (3/15/91) SS
90 J. LOHR Chardonnay Monterey Riverstone 1988 $12 (4/30/90)
90 J. LOHR Chardonnay Monterey Riverstone 1987 $12 (11/15/89)
78 J. LOHR Chardonnay Monterey County 1987 $10 (4/15/89)
87 J. LOHR Chardonnay Monterey County Cypress Vineyard Reserve 1986 $13.50 (12/31/88)
89 J. LOHR Chardonnay Monterey County Greenfield Vineyards 1986 $10 (4/15/88)
80 J. LOHR Chardonnay Monterey County Greenfield Vineyards 1985 $9 (6/30/87)
69 J. LOHR Chardonnay Monterey County Greenfield Vineyards 1984 $9 (4/16/86)
75 J. LOHR Chardonnay Monterey County Greenfield Vineyards 1983 $9 (7/01/85)
86 LOLONIS Chardonnay Mendocino County Lolonis Vineyards 1989 $12 (7/15/91)
74 LOLONIS Chardonnay Mendocino County Lolonis Vineyards 1984 $14 (6/30/87)
91 LOLONIS Chardonnay Mendocino County Private Reserve 1988 $19 (4/30/90)
88 LOLONIS Chardonnay Mendocino County Private Reserve Lolonis Vineyards 1989 $19 (7/15/91)
91 LONG Chardonnay Napa Valley 1989 $30 (7/15/91)
89 LONG Chardonnay Napa Valley 1988 $27.50 (5/15/91)
93 LONG Chardonnay Napa Valley 1988 Rel: $27.50 Cur: $33 (CH-4/90)
90 LONG Chardonnay Napa Valley 1987 Rel: $27.50 Cur: $35 (CH-4/90)
84 LONG Chardonnay Napa Valley 1987 Rel: $27.50 Cur: $35 (7/15/89)
92 LONG Chardonnay Napa Valley 1986 Rel: $27.50 Cur: $48 (CH-4/90)
91 LONG Chardonnay Napa Valley 1986 Rel: $27.50 Cur: $48 (12/31/88)
91 LONG Chardonnay Napa Valley 1985 Rel: $27.50 Cur: $70 (CH-4/90)
88 LONG Chardonnay Napa Valley 1984 Rel: $27.50 Cur: $70 (CH-4/90)
86 LONG Chardonnay Napa Valley 1984 Rel: $27.50 Cur: $70 (8/11/85)
87 MACROSTIE Chardonnay Carneros 1989 $14 (12/31/90)
90 MACROSTIE Chardonnay Carneros 1988 $14 (2/28/90)
89 MACROSTIE Chardonnay Carneros 1987 $14.50 (11/30/88)
83 MADDALENA Chardonnay Central Coast 1989 $8 (4/30/91) BB
80 MADDALENA Chardonnay Napa Valley 1989 $10 (7/15/91)
70 MADDALENA Chardonnay San Luis Obispo County 1982 $6 (5/16/84)
72 MADDALENA Chardonnay Santa Barbara County 1984 $5 (4/16/86)
87 MANISCHEWITZ Chardonnay Alexander Valley 1988 $7 (3/31/91)
71 MANZANITA Chardonnay Napa Valley 1984 $12.50 (10/31/86)
93 MANZANITA Chardonnay Napa Valley 1983 $12.50 (1/01/86) SS
84 MANZANITA Chardonnay Napa Valley 1982 $14 (4/01/84)
86 MANZANITA RIDGE Chardonnay Sonoma County Barrel Fermented 1989 $8 (6/30/91) BB
81 MARION Chardonnay California 1986 $5.50 (2/15/88) BB
64 MARIPOSA Chardonnay Sonoma County 1984 $5 (12/01/85)
76 MARK WEST Chardonnay Alexander Valley Wasson Vineyard 1981 $10 (4/16/84)
80 MARK WEST Chardonnay Russian River Valley 1982 $10.50 (10/16/85)
73 MARK WEST Chardonnay Russian River Valley Le Beau Vineyards 1987 $12 (6/30/90)
77 MARK WEST Chardonnay Russian River Valley Le Beau Vineyards 1986 $12 (9/15/88)
88 MARK WEST Chardonnay Russian River Valley Le Beau Vineyards Reserve 1987 $16.50 (4/15/91)
88 MARK WEST Chardonnay Russian River Valley Le Beau Vineyards Reserve 1985 $16 (10/31/87)
88 MARK WEST Chardonnay Russian River Valley Vintner's Library Selection 1980 $14 (10/01/85)
78 MARK WEST Chardonnay Sonoma Valley 1987 $8 (12/31/88)
92 MARKHAM Chardonnay Napa Valley 1989 $12 (6/15/91) SS
82 MARKHAM Chardonnay Napa Valley 1988 Rel: $12 Cur: $12 (5/31/90)
89 MARKHAM Chardonnay Napa Valley 1988 Rel: $12 Cur: $12 (CH-2/90)
87 MARKHAM Chardonnay Napa Valley 1987 Rel: $12 Cur: $14 (CH-2/90)
86 MARKHAM Chardonnay Napa Valley 1987 Rel: $12 Cur: $14 (4/30/89)
84 MARKHAM Chardonnay Napa Valley Estate 1986 Rel: $12 Cur: $15 (CH-2/90)
77 MARKHAM Chardonnay Napa Valley Estate 1986 Rel: $12 Cur: $15 (7/31/88)
86 MARKHAM Chardonnay Napa Valley Estate 1985 Rel: $12 Cur: $17 (CH-2/90)
85 MARKHAM Chardonnay Napa Valley 1984 Rel: $12 Cur: $17 (CH-2/90)
81 MARKHAM Chardonnay Napa Valley Estate 1983 Rel: $11.50 Cur: $17 (CH-2/90)
83 MARKHAM Chardonnay Napa Valley Estate 1982 Rel: $12 Cur: $17 (CH-2/90)
89 MARKHAM Chardonnay Napa Valley Estate 1982 Rel: $12 Cur: $17 (8/01/84)
81 MARTIN Chardonnay Paso Robles 1988 $10 (12/15/89)

UNITED STATES
CALIFORNIA/*CHARDONNAY*

82 MARTINELLI Chardonnay Russian River Valley 1989 $9 (7/15/91)
83 LOUIS M. MARTINI Chardonnay Los Carneros Las Amigas Vineyard Vineyard Selection 1989 $20 (7/15/91)
75 LOUIS M. MARTINI Chardonnay Napa-Sonoma Counties 1989 $9 (4/30/91)
87 LOUIS M. MARTINI Chardonnay Napa Valley Reserve 1989 $14 (12/31/90)
74 LOUIS M. MARTINI Chardonnay North Coast 1986 $9.50 (5/31/88)
70 LOUIS M. MARTINI Chardonnay North Coast 1984 $8 (4/16/86)
71 LOUIS M. MARTINI Chardonnay California 1982 $7 (3/16/84)
82 MASSON Chardonnay Monterey County 1987 $8 (11/15/88)
77 PAUL MASSON Chardonnay Monterey 1981 $8.50 (4/16/84)
91 MATANZAS CREEK Chardonnay Sonoma County 1988 Rel: $18.75 Cur: $21 (4/30/90)
89 MATANZAS CREEK Chardonnay Sonoma County 1988 Rel: $18.75 Cur: $21 (CH-2/90)
90 MATANZAS CREEK Chardonnay Sonoma County 1987 Rel: $18 Cur: $21 (CH-2/90)
87 MATANZAS CREEK Chardonnay Sonoma County 1987 Rel: $18 Cur: $21 (5/31/89)
89 MATANZAS CREEK Chardonnay Sonoma County 1986 Rel: $17.50 Cur: $24 (CH-2/90)
90 MATANZAS CREEK Chardonnay Sonoma County 1986 Rel: $17.50 Cur: $24 (5/31/88)
88 MATANZAS CREEK Chardonnay Sonoma County 1985 Rel: $16.50 Cur: $28 (CH-2/90)
87 MATANZAS CREEK Chardonnay Sonoma County 1985 Rel: $16.50 Cur: $28 (8/31/87)
89 MATANZAS CREEK Chardonnay Sonoma County 1984 Rel: $15 Cur: $28 (CH-2/90)
93 MATANZAS CREEK Chardonnay Sonoma County 1984 Rel: $15 Cur: $28 (5/16/86)
85 MATANZAS CREEK Chardonnay Sonoma County 1983 Rel: $15 Cur: $28 (CH-2/90)
88 MATANZAS CREEK Chardonnay Sonoma County 1983 Rel: $15 Cur: $28 (9/16/85)
78 MATANZAS CREEK Chardonnay Sonoma County 1982 Rel: $15 Cur: $25 (CH-2/90)
92 MATANZAS CREEK Chardonnay Sonoma County 1982 Rel: $15 Cur: $25 (7/16/84)
85 MATANZAS CREEK Chardonnay Sonoma County 1981 Rel: $15 Cur: $28 (CH-2/90)
82 MATANZAS CREEK Chardonnay Sonoma County 1980 Rel: $15 Cur: $25 (CH-2/90)
80 MATANZAS CREEK Chardonnay Napa-Sonoma Counties 1979 Rel: $14.50 Cur: $40 (CH-2/90)
79 MATANZAS CREEK Chardonnay Sonoma County 1978 Rel: $12.50 Cur: $50 (CH-2/90)
87 MATANZAS CREEK Chardonnay Sonoma Valley 1989 $19 (7/15/91)
86 MATANZAS CREEK Chardonnay Sonoma Valley Estate 1985 Rel: $18 Cur: $39 (CH-2/90)
80 MATANZAS CREEK Chardonnay Sonoma Valley Estate 1984 Rel: $18 Cur: $29 (CH-2/90)
78 MATANZAS CREEK Chardonnay Sonoma Valley Estate 1984 Rel: $18 Cur: $29 (6/01/86)
68 MATANZAS CREEK Chardonnay Sonoma Valley Estate 1983 Rel: $18 Cur: $18 (CH-2/90)
88 MATANZAS CREEK Chardonnay Sonoma Valley Estate 1982 Rel: $18 Cur: $25 (CH-2/90)
88 MATANZAS CREEK Chardonnay Sonoma Valley Estate 1982 Rel: $18 Cur: $25 (7/16/84) SS
70 MATANZAS CREEK Chardonnay Sonoma County Estate 1980 Rel: $18 Cur: $25 (CH-2/90)
86 MAYACAMAS Chardonnay Napa Valley 1988 $20 (7/15/91)
89 MAYACAMAS Chardonnay Napa Valley 1988 $20 (CH-6/90)
86 MAYACAMAS Chardonnay Napa Valley 1987 Rel: $20 Cur: $24 (9/15/90)
87 MAYACAMAS Chardonnay Napa Valley 1987 Rel: $20 Cur: $24 (CH-1/90)
87 MAYACAMAS Chardonnay Napa Valley 1986 Rel: $20 Cur: $27 (CH-3/90)
84 MAYACAMAS Chardonnay Napa Valley 1986 Rel: $20 Cur: $27 (7/15/89)
90 MAYACAMAS Chardonnay Napa Valley 1985 Rel: $20 Cur: $29 (CH-1/90)
90 MAYACAMAS Chardonnay Napa Valley 1985 Rel: $20 Cur: $29 (8/31/88)
88 MAYACAMAS Chardonnay Napa Valley 1984 Rel: $18 Cur: $28 (CH-3/90)
72 MAYACAMAS Chardonnay Napa Valley 1984 Rel: $18 Cur: $28 (7/31/87)
86 MAYACAMAS Chardonnay Napa Valley 1983 Rel: $16 Cur: $25 (CH-1/90)
91 MAYACAMAS Chardonnay Napa Valley 1983 Rel: $16 Cur: $25 (3/15/87)
85 MAYACAMAS Chardonnay Napa Valley 1982 Rel: $16 Cur: $30 (CH-1/90)
78 MAYACAMAS Chardonnay Napa Valley 1981 Rel: $16 Cur: $35 (CH-1/90)
74 MAYACAMAS Chardonnay Napa Valley 1980 Rel: $16 Cur: $35 (CH-1/90)
70 MAYACAMAS Chardonnay Napa Valley 1979 Rel: $15 Cur: $35 (CH-1/90)
75 MAYACAMAS Chardonnay Napa Valley 1978 Rel: $13 Cur: $30 (CH-1/90)
70 MAYACAMAS Chardonnay Napa Valley 1977 Rel: $12 Cur: $35 (CH-1/90)
81 MAYACAMAS Chardonnay Napa Valley 1976 Rel: $11 Cur: $45 (CH-1/90)
78 MAYACAMAS Chardonnay Napa Valley 1975 Rel: $9 Cur: $50 (CH-1/90)
70 MAYACAMAS Chardonnay Napa Valley 1974 Rel: $7.50 Cur: $50 (CH-1/90)
60 MAYACAMAS Chardonnay Napa Valley 1973 Rel: $7 Cur: $50 (CH-1/90)
59 MAYACAMAS Chardonnay Napa Valley 1972 Rel: $7 Cur: $60 (CH-1/90)
58 MAYACAMAS Chardonnay Napa Valley 1965 Rel: $2.50 Cur: $125 (CH-1/90)
92 MAYACAMAS Chardonnay Napa Valley 1964 Rel: $1.75 Cur: $200 (CH-1/90)
58 MAYACAMAS Chardonnay Napa Valley 1963 Rel: $1.75 Cur: $150 (CH-1/90)
58 MAYACAMAS Chardonnay Napa Valley 1962 Rel: $1.75 Cur: $150 (CH-1/90)
60 MAYACAMAS Chardonnay Napa Valley 1958 Rel: $1 Cur: $200 (CH-1/90)
88 MAYACAMAS Chardonnay Napa Valley 1955 Rel: $1 Cur: $330 (CH-1/90)
84 MAZZOCCO Chardonnay Alexander Valley River Lane Vineyard 1988 $16.50 (6/30/90)
88 MAZZOCCO Chardonnay Alexander Valley River Lane Vineyard 1987 $16.50 (4/15/89)
86 MAZZOCCO Chardonnay Alexander Valley River Lane Barrel Fermented 1986 $16.50 (2/15/88)
85 MAZZOCCO Chardonnay Sonoma County Barrel Fermented 1989 $11 (7/15/91)
78 MAZZOCCO Chardonnay Sonoma County Barrel Fermented 1988 $12 (11/30/89)
83 MAZZOCCO Chardonnay Sonoma County Barrel Fermented 1987 $11 (11/15/88)
85 MAZZOCCO Chardonnay Sonoma County Winemaster's Cuvée 1986 $10 (2/15/88)
72 MCDOWELL Chardonnay California 1989 $10 (7/15/91)
78 MCDOWELL Chardonnay California 1988 $8.50 (12/15/89)
86 MCDOWELL Chardonnay California 1987 $8 (7/15/89)
59 MCDOWELL Chardonnay McDowell Valley 1987 $12 (12/15/89)
76 MCDOWELL Chardonnay McDowell Valley 1986 $11 (5/31/88)
85 MCDOWELL Chardonnay McDowell Valley 1984 $11 (2/28/87)
75 MCDOWELL Chardonnay McDowell Valley Estate Reserve 1988 $13 (7/15/91)
81 MEADOW GLEN Chardonnay Sonoma County Barrel Fermented 1989 $8.50 (4/30/91)
85 MEEKER Chardonnay Dry Creek Valley 1989 $12 (7/15/91)
75 MEEKER Chardonnay Dry Creek Valley 1988 $13.50 (2/15/90)

Key to Symbols

The scores reported here are the results of blind tastings conducted by our panel of senior editors. Wines that carry the initials below are results of individual tastings.

THE WINE SPECTATOR 100-POINT SCALE *95-100*—Classic, a great wine; *90-94*—Outstanding, superior character and style; *80-89*—Good to very good, a wine with special qualities; *70-79*—Average, drinkable wine that may have minor flaws; *60-69*—Below average, drinkable but not recommended; *50-59*—Poor, undrinkable, not recommended. "+"—With a score indicates a range; used primarily with barrel tastings to indicate a preliminary score.

SPECIAL DESIGNATIONS SS—Spectator Selection, CS—Cellar Selection, BB—Best Buy.

TASTER'S INITIALS (JG)—Jim Gordon, (HS)—Harvey Steiman, (JL)—James Laube, (JS)—James Suckling, (TM)—Thomas Matthews, (TR)—Terry Robards, (BT)—Barrel Tasting (these wines were tasted blind from barrel samples), (CA-date)—*California's Great Cabernets* by James Laube, (CH-date)—*California's Great Chardonnays* by James Laube, (VP-date)—*Vintage Port* by James Suckling.

DATE TASTED Dates in parentheses represent the issue in which the rating was published.

79 MEEKER Chardonnay Dry Creek Valley 1987 $12 (2/15/89)
91 MEEKER Chardonnay Dry Creek Valley 1986 $11 (5/31/88)
79 MENDOCINO ESTATE Chardonnay Mendocino 1989 $6.50 (7/15/91)
73 MENDOCINO ESTATE Chardonnay Mendocino 1988 $6.25 (12/15/89)
65 MENDOCINO ESTATE Chardonnay Mendocino 1986 $5.50 (12/31/87)
89 MENDOCINO ESTATE Chardonnay Mendocino 1985 $5 (12/15/86) BB
82 MERIDIAN Chardonnay Edna Valley 1989 $14 (7/15/91)
80 MERIDIAN Chardonnay Edna Valley 1988 $9.75 (9/30/90)
78 MERIDIAN Chardonnay Edna Valley 1987 $12 (12/15/89)
85 MERIDIAN Chardonnay Napa Valley 1986 $12 (5/31/88)
88 MERIDIAN Chardonnay Napa Valley 1985 $11 (4/30/87)
87 MERIDIAN Chardonnay Santa Barbara County 1989 $10 (2/28/91)
89 MERIDIAN Chardonnay Santa Barbara County 1988 $10 (4/15/90)
63 MERLION Chardonnay Napa Valley 1987 $9 (12/31/90)
84 MERLION Chardonnay Napa Valley 1985 $15 (2/15/88)
89 MERRY VINTNERS Chardonnay Sonoma County 1988 $12 (1/31/91)
84 MERRY VINTNERS Chardonnay Sonoma County 1987 $12 (7/15/89)
88 MERRY VINTNERS Chardonnay Sonoma County 1984 $13.75 (6/16/86)
86 MERRY VINTNERS Chardonnay Sonoma County Reserve 1987 $15 (9/15/89)
85 MERRY VINTNERS Chardonnay Sonoma County Reserve 1986 $14.75 (11/30/88)
81 MERRY VINTNERS Chardonnay Sonoma County Reserve 1985 $15 (9/15/87)
90 MERRY VINTNERS Chardonnay Sonoma County Signature Reserve 1988 $15 (1/31/91)
85 MERRY VINTNERS Chardonnay Sonoma County Sylvan Hills Vineyard 1987 $11 (7/15/89)
85 MERRY VINTNERS Chardonnay Sonoma County Vintage Preview 1986 $9.75 (7/15/88)
83 MERRY VINTNERS Chardonnay Sonoma County Vintage Preview 1985 $9.75 (12/15/86)
91 MERRYVALE Chardonnay Napa Valley 1988 $23 (6/30/90)
93 MERRYVALE Chardonnay Napa Valley 1987 $19 (2/15/90)
72 MERRYVALE Chardonnay Napa Valley 1986 $20 (10/31/88)
90 MERRYVALE Chardonnay Napa Valley 1985 $16.50 (10/31/87)
89 MERRYVALE Chardonnay Napa Valley Starmont 1989 $16 (12/31/90)
90 MERRYVALE Chardonnay Stags Leap District 1989 $19 (12/31/90)
88 PETER MICHAEL Chardonnay Sonoma County Mon Plaisir 1989 $28 (7/15/91)
71 MICHTOM Chardonnay Alexander Valley 1983 $8 (10/16/85)
79 MILANO Chardonnay California 1985 $10 (4/15/88)
88 MILANO Chardonnay Mendocino County Sanel Valley Vineyard 1988 $18 (7/15/91)
71 MILANO Chardonnay Sonoma County Vine Hill Ranch 1985 $14 (12/31/88)
75 MILL CREEK Chardonnay Dry Creek Valley 1985 $10 (12/31/87)
64 MIRASSOU Chardonnay Monterey County 1984 $8 (12/16/85)
74 MIRASSOU Chardonnay Monterey County Fifth Generation Family Selection 1989 $9.75 (7/15/91)
77 MIRASSOU Chardonnay Monterey County Fifth Generation Family Selection 1986 $8 (11/15/87)
86 MIRASSOU Chardonnay Monterey County Fifth Generation Family Selection 1985 $8 (12/31/86)
87 MIRASSOU Chardonnay Monterey County Fifth Generation Harvest Reserve Limited Bottling 1989 $12.50 (5/15/91)
68 MIRASSOU Chardonnay Monterey County Harvest Reserve 1984 $12 (4/01/86)
74 MIRASSOU Chardonnay Monterey County Harvest Reserve 1983 $11 (1/01/85)
87 MOCERI Chardonnay Monterey County San Bernabe Vineyard 1984 $5 (7/01/86) BB
70 CK MONDAVI Chardonnay California 1986 $4.50 (8/31/87)
74 ROBERT MONDAVI Chardonnay California Woodbridge 1989 $7.25 (4/30/91)
87 ROBERT MONDAVI Chardonnay Napa Valley 1989 $16 (4/15/91)
86 ROBERT MONDAVI Chardonnay Napa Valley 1988 Rel: $16 Cur: $19 (11/30/89)
83 ROBERT MONDAVI Chardonnay Napa Valley 1987 Rel: $17 Cur: $17 (4/30/89)
88 ROBERT MONDAVI Chardonnay Napa Valley 1986 Rel: $15 Cur: $15 (7/15/88)
79 ROBERT MONDAVI Chardonnay Napa Valley 1985 Rel: $12 Cur: $15 (7/15/87)
83 ROBERT MONDAVI Chardonnay Napa Valley 1984 Rel: $10 Cur: $17 (9/15/86)
90 ROBERT MONDAVI Chardonnay Napa Valley 1983 Rel: $14 Cur: $17 (8/01/85)
82 ROBERT MONDAVI Chardonnay Napa Valley 1982 Rel: $10 Cur: $10 (8/01/84)
94 ROBERT MONDAVI Chardonnay Napa Valley 1981 Rel: $15 Cur: $15 (6/01/86)
87 ROBERT MONDAVI Chardonnay Napa Valley Barrel Fermented Reserve 1989 $28 (7/15/91)
92 ROBERT MONDAVI Chardonnay Napa Valley Reserve 1988 Rel: $26 Cur: $27 (8/31/90)
91 ROBERT MONDAVI Chardonnay Napa Valley Reserve 1988 Rel: $26 Cur: $27 (CH-6/90)
92 ROBERT MONDAVI Chardonnay Napa Valley Reserve 1987 Rel: $26 Cur: $26 (CH-6/90)
88 ROBERT MONDAVI Chardonnay Napa Valley Reserve 1987 Rel: $26 Cur: $26 (7/15/89)
89 ROBERT MONDAVI Chardonnay Napa Valley Reserve 1986 Rel: $25 Cur: $30 (CH-3/90)
88 ROBERT MONDAVI Chardonnay Napa Valley Reserve 1986 Rel: $25 Cur: $30 (2/15/89)
88 ROBERT MONDAVI Chardonnay Napa Valley Reserve 1985 Rel: $25 Cur: $30 (CH-3/90)
91 ROBERT MONDAVI Chardonnay Napa Valley Reserve 1985 Rel: $25 Cur: $30 (12/15/87)
87 ROBERT MONDAVI Chardonnay Napa Valley Reserve 1984 Rel: $22 Cur: $35 (CH-3/90)
88 ROBERT MONDAVI Chardonnay Napa Valley Reserve 1983 Rel: $20 Cur: $25 (CH-3/90)
81 ROBERT MONDAVI Chardonnay Napa Valley Reserve 1982 Rel: $20 Cur: $25 (CH-3/90)
88 ROBERT MONDAVI Chardonnay Napa Valley Reserve 1982 Rel: $20 Cur: $25 (11/01/84)
86 ROBERT MONDAVI Chardonnay Napa Valley Reserve 1981 Rel: $20 Cur: $24 (CH-3/90)
90 ROBERT MONDAVI Chardonnay Napa Valley Reserve 1981 Rel: $20 Cur: $24 (6/01/86)
69 ROBERT MONDAVI Chardonnay Napa Valley Reserve 1980 Rel: $20 Cur: $30 (CH-3/90)
79 ROBERT MONDAVI Chardonnay Napa Valley Reserve 1979 Rel: $20 Cur: $27 (CH-3/90)
69 ROBERT MONDAVI Chardonnay Napa Valley Reserve 1978 Rel: $20 Cur: $24 (CH-3/90)
68 ROBERT MONDAVI Chardonnay Napa Valley Reserve 1977 Rel: $14 Cur: $32 (CH-3/90)
78 ROBERT MONDAVI Chardonnay Napa Valley Reserve 1976 Rel: $12 Cur: $32 (CH-3/90)
75 ROBERT MONDAVI Chardonnay Napa Valley Reserve 1975 Rel: $10 Cur: $35 (CH-3/90)
83 ROBERT MONDAVI Chardonnay Napa Valley Reserve 1975 Rel: $10 Cur: $35 (7/16/84)
88 ROBERT MONDAVI Chardonnay Napa Valley Reserve 1974 Rel: $10 Cur: $45 (CH-3/90)
89 ROBERT MONDAVI Chardonnay Napa Valley Reserve 1974 Rel: $10 Cur: $45 (7/16/84)
81 MONT ST. JOHN Chardonnay Carneros Napa Valley 1987 $15 (7/15/89)
63 MONT ST. JOHN Chardonnay Carneros Napa Valley 1982 $11.50 (5/16/84)
71 MONTE VERDE Chardonnay California 1988 $9 (12/15/89)
78 MONTE VERDE Chardonnay California Proprietor's Reserve 1989 $5.50 (3/31/91)
76 MONTE VERDE Chardonnay California Proprietor's Reserve 1987 $6.50 (12/15/89)
83 MONTEREY PENINSULA Chardonnay Monterey Sleepy Hollow 1989 $12 (5/31/91)
77 MONTEREY VINEYARD Chardonnay Central Coast Classic 1989 $6 (12/31/90)
70 MONTEREY VINEYARD Chardonnay Monterey County 1985 $7 (10/15/87)
83 MONTEREY VINEYARD Chardonnay Monterey County Classic 1987 $5 (2/15/89) BB
80 MONTEREY VINEYARD Chardonnay Monterey County Limited Release 1988 $12 (2/28/91)
89 MONTEREY VINEYARD Chardonnay Monterey County Limited Release 1986 $10 (8/31/88)
89 MONTICELLO Chardonnay Napa Valley Corley Reserve 1989 $18 (7/15/91)
92 MONTICELLO Chardonnay Napa Valley Corley Reserve 1988 $17.25 (1/31/91) SS
94 MONTICELLO Chardonnay Napa Valley Corley Reserve 1988 $17.25 (CH-2/90)
86 MONTICELLO Chardonnay Napa Valley Corley Reserve 1987 Rel: $17.25 Cur: $20 (CH-6/90)

78 MONTICELLO Chardonnay Napa Valley Corley Reserve 1987 Rel: $17.25 Cur: $20 (7/15/89)
89 MONTICELLO Chardonnay Napa Valley Corley Reserve 1986 Rel: $16.50 Cur: $18 (CH-2/90)
88 MONTICELLO Chardonnay Napa Valley Corley Reserve 1986 Rel: $16.50 Cur: $18 (7/15/88)
85 MONTICELLO Chardonnay Napa Valley Corley Reserve 1985 Rel: $14 Cur: $20 (CH-2/90)
88 MONTICELLO Chardonnay Napa Valley Corley Reserve 1985 Rel: $14 Cur: $20 (7/15/87)
94 MONTICELLO Chardonnay Napa Valley Corley Reserve 1984 Rel: $12.50 Cur: $25 (CH-2/90)
89 MONTICELLO Chardonnay Napa Valley Corley Reserve 1984 Rel: $12.50 Cur: $25 (10/31/86)
80 MONTICELLO Chardonnay Napa Valley Barrel Fermented 1983 Rel: $12.50 Cur: $20 (CH-2/90)
87 MONTICELLO Chardonnay Napa Valley Barrel Fermented 1983 Rel: $12.50 Cur: $20 (12/01/85)
84 MONTICELLO Chardonnay Napa Valley Barrel Fermented 1982 Rel: $14 Cur: $20 (CH-2/90)
74 MONTICELLO Chardonnay Napa Valley Jefferson Ranch 1989 $12.50 (7/15/91)
81 MONTICELLO Chardonnay Napa Valley Jefferson Ranch 1988 Rel: $12.25 Cur: $13 (6/30/90)
90 MONTICELLO Chardonnay Napa Valley Jefferson Ranch 1988 Rel: $12.25 Cur: $13 (CH-2/90)
86 MONTICELLO Chardonnay Napa Valley Jefferson Ranch 1987 Rel: $12.25 Cur: $16 (CH-2/90)
77 MONTICELLO Chardonnay Napa Valley Jefferson Ranch 1987 Rel: $12.25 Cur: $16 (4/30/89)
86 MONTICELLO Chardonnay Napa Valley Jefferson Ranch 1986 Rel: $11 Cur: $18 (CH-2/90)
88 MONTICELLO Chardonnay Napa Valley Jefferson Ranch 1986 Rel: $11 Cur: $18 (4/15/88)
82 MONTICELLO Chardonnay Napa Valley Jefferson Ranch 1985 Rel: $11 Cur: $18 (CH-2/90)
90 MONTICELLO Chardonnay Napa Valley Jefferson Ranch 1985 Rel: $11 Cur: $18 (9/15/87)
86 MONTICELLO Chardonnay Napa Valley Jefferson Ranch 1984 Rel: $10 Cur: $18 (CH-2/90)
90 MONTICELLO Chardonnay Napa Valley Jefferson Ranch 1984 Rel: $10 Cur: $18 (9/30/86)
93 MONTICELLO Chardonnay Napa Valley Jefferson Ranch 1983 Rel: $10 Cur: $20 (CH-2/90)
74 MONTICELLO Chardonnay Napa Valley Jefferson Ranch 1983 Rel: $10 Cur: $20 (12/16/85)
82 MONTICELLO Chardonnay Napa Valley 1982 Rel: $13.50 Cur: $20 (CH-2/90)
76 MONTICELLO Chardonnay Napa Valley 1981 Rel: $12 Cur: $20 (CH-2/90)
86 MONTICELLO Chardonnay Napa Valley 1980 Rel: $12 Cur: $20 (CH-2/90)
73 MONTPELLIER Chardonnay California 1988 $7 (3/31/90)
86 MORGAN Chardonnay Edna Valley MacGregor Vineyard 1989 $16.50 (7/15/91)
84 MORGAN Chardonnay Monterey 1989 $16 (3/31/91)
89 MORGAN Chardonnay Monterey 1988 Rel: $15 Cur: $16 (CH-5/90)
88 MORGAN Chardonnay Monterey 1988 Rel: $15 Cur: $16 (2/28/90)
84 MORGAN Chardonnay Monterey 1987 Rel: $15 Cur: $16 (CH-5/90)
84 MORGAN Chardonnay Monterey 1987 Rel: $15 Cur: $16 (12/31/88)
89 MORGAN Chardonnay Monterey 1986 Rel: $14 Cur: $20 (CH-5/90)
88 MORGAN Chardonnay Monterey 1986 Rel: $14 Cur: $20 (3/15/88)
86 MORGAN Chardonnay Monterey County 1985 Rel: $14 Cur: $23 (CH-7/90)
89 MORGAN Chardonnay Monterey County 1985 Rel: $14 Cur: $23 (4/30/87)
86 MORGAN Chardonnay Monterey County 1984 Rel: $12.75 Cur: $23 (CH-5/90)
63 MORGAN Chardonnay Monterey County 1984 Rel: $12.75 Cur: $23 (2/01/86)
80 MORGAN Chardonnay Monterey County 1983 Rel: $12.50 Cur: $23 (CH-5/90)
89 MORGAN Chardonnay Monterey County 1982 Rel: $12 Cur: $28 (CH-5/90)
92 MORGAN Chardonnay Monterey Reserve 1988 Rel: $20 Cur: $20 (CH-6/90)
89 MORGAN Chardonnay Monterey Reserve 1988 Rel: $20 Cur: $20 (5/31/90)
85 MORGAN Chardonnay Monterey Reserve 1987 Rel: $19 Cur: $19 (CH-6/90)
84 MORGAN Chardonnay Monterey Reserve 1987 Rel: $19 Cur: $19 (7/15/89)
79 J.W. MORRIS Chardonnay California Private Reserve 1989 $8 (7/15/91)
66 J.W. MORRIS Chardonnay California Private Reserve 1988 $8 (5/15/90)
89 MOUNT EDEN Chardonnay Edna Valley MacGregor Vineyard 1989 $14.50 (11/30/90)
83 MOUNT EDEN Chardonnay Edna Valley MacGregor Vineyard 1988 Rel: $14 Cur: $14 (6/30/90)
88 MOUNT EDEN Chardonnay Edna Valley MacGregor Vineyard 1988 Rel: $14 Cur: $14 (CH-6/90)
94 MOUNT EDEN Chardonnay Edna Valley MEV MacGregor Vineyard 1987 Rel: $14 Cur: $20 (CH-3/90)
93 MOUNT EDEN Chardonnay Edna Valley MEV MacGregor Vineyard 1987 Rel: $14 Cur: $20 (4/30/89) SS
81 MOUNT EDEN Chardonnay Edna Valley MEV MacGregor Vineyard 1986 Rel: $13 Cur: $16 (CH-3/90)
84 MOUNT EDEN Chardonnay Edna Valley MEV MacGregor Vineyard 1986 Rel: $13 Cur: $16 (3/15/88)
87 MOUNT EDEN Chardonnay Edna Valley MEV MacGregor Vineyard 1985 Rel: $12.50 Cur: $14 (CH-3/90)
88 MOUNT EDEN Chardonnay Santa Cruz Mountains 1988 $30 (11/30/90)
88 MOUNT EDEN Chardonnay Santa Cruz Mountains 1988 $30 (CH-3/90)
90 MOUNT EDEN Chardonnay Santa Cruz Mountains 1987 Rel: $28 Cur: $44 (CH-3/90)
88 MOUNT EDEN Chardonnay Santa Cruz Mountains 1987 Rel: $28 Cur: $44 (11/15/89)
88 MOUNT EDEN Chardonnay Santa Cruz Mountains 1986 Rel: $25 Cur: $45 (CH-3/90)
87 MOUNT EDEN Chardonnay Santa Cruz Mountains 1985 Rel: $25 Cur: $67 (CH-3/90)
85 MOUNT EDEN Chardonnay Santa Cruz Mountains 1984 Rel: $23 Cur: $70 (CH-3/90)
84 MOUNT EDEN Chardonnay Santa Cruz Mountains 1983 Rel: $20 Cur: $35 (CH-3/90)
76 MOUNT EDEN Chardonnay Santa Cruz Mountains 1982 Rel: $18 Cur: $43 (CH-3/90)
89 MOUNT EDEN Chardonnay Santa Cruz Mountains 1981 Rel: $18 Cur: $60 (CH-3/90)
87 MOUNT EDEN Chardonnay Santa Cruz Mountains 1980 Rel: $30 Cur: $65 (CH-3/90)
90 MOUNT EDEN Chardonnay Santa Cruz Mountains 1979 Rel: $16 Cur: $60 (CH-3/90)
66 MOUNT EDEN Chardonnay Santa Cruz Mountains 1978 Rel: $16 Cur: $50 (CH-3/90)
85 MOUNT EDEN Chardonnay Santa Cruz Mountains 1977 Rel: $16 Cur: $70 (CH-8/90)
78 MOUNT EDEN Chardonnay Santa Cruz Mountains 1976 Rel: $16 Cur: $50 (CH-3/90)
60 MOUNT EDEN Chardonnay Santa Cruz Mountains 1975 Rel: $14 Cur: $45 (CH-3/90)
59 MOUNT EDEN Chardonnay Santa Cruz Mountains 1974 Rel: $14 Cur: $50 (CH-3/90)
82 MOUNT EDEN Chardonnay Santa Cruz Mountains 1973 Rel: $12 Cur: $55 (CH-3/90)
80 MOUNT EDEN Chardonnay Santa Cruz Mountains 1972 Rel: $20 Cur: $50 (CH-3/90)
76 MOUNT EDEN Chardonnay Monterey County 1982 Rel: $12.50 Cur: $13 (4/01/84)
83 MOUNT VEEDER Chardonnay Napa Valley 1989 $18 (4/30/91)
91 MOUNT VEEDER Chardonnay Napa Valley 1988 Rel: $15 Cur: $15 (6/30/90)
83 MOUNT VEEDER Chardonnay Napa Valley 1987 Rel: $14 Cur: $14 (6/15/89)
86 MOUNT VEEDER Chardonnay Napa County 1986 Rel: $14 Cur: $14 (2/29/88)
89 MOUNT VEEDER Chardonnay Napa County 1985 Rel: $13.50 Cur: $14 (5/31/87)
90 MOUNTAIN HOUSE Chardonnay Sonoma County 1981 $11 (2/15/84)
84 MOUNTAIN VIEW Chardonnay Monterey County 1989 $6 (4/15/91) BB
81 MOUNTAIN VIEW Chardonnay Monterey County 1988 $6.50 (4/30/90) BB
79 MOUNTAIN VIEW Chardonnay Monterey County 1987 $6 (4/30/89)
89 MOUNTAIN VIEW Chardonnay Monterey County 1985 $5 (2/15/87) BB
73 MOUNTAIN VIEW Chardonnay Napa Valley Special Selection 1982 $7.50 (4/01/84)
75 MOUNTAIN VIEW Chardonnay Sonoma County 1982 $6 (4/16/84)
70 MARION Chardonnay California 1989 $8 (7/15/91)
70 MT. MADONNA Chardonnay San Luis Obispo County 1987 $7.50 (3/31/89)
82 MURPHY-GOODE Chardonnay Alexander Valley Estate Vineyard 1989 $12 (6/30/91)
88 MURPHY-GOODE Chardonnay Alexander Valley Estate Vineyard 1988 Rel: $11.50 Cur: $12 (CH-4/90)
91 MURPHY-GOODE Chardonnay Alexander Valley Estate Vineyard 1988 Rel: $11.50 Cur: $12 (11/30/89)
87 MURPHY-GOODE Chardonnay Alexander Valley Premier Vineyard 1987 Rel: $11 Cur: $11 (CH-4/90)
82 MURPHY-GOODE Chardonnay Alexander Valley Premier Vineyard 1987 Rel: $11 Cur: $11 (1/31/89)
86 MURPHY-GOODE Chardonnay Alexander Valley Estate Vineyard 1986 Rel: $10 Cur: $12 (CH-4/90)
90 MURPHY-GOODE Chardonnay Alexander Valley Estate Vineyard 1986 Rel: $10 Cur: $12 (8/31/88)
85 MURPHY-GOODE Chardonnay Alexander Valley Estate Vineyard 1985 Rel: $9 Cur: $12 (CH-4/90)
79 MURPHY-GOODE Chardonnay Alexander Valley Estate Vineyard 1985 Rel: $9 Cur: $12 (6/30/87)
85 NAPA CELLARS Chardonnay Napa Valley 1989 $7 (4/15/91) BB
77 NAPA CREEK Chardonnay Napa Valley 1989 $13 (4/30/91)
86 NAPA CREEK Chardonnay Napa Valley 1988 $13.50 (4/15/90)
86 NAPA CREEK Chardonnay Napa Valley 1986 $12 (5/31/88)
85 NAPA RIDGE Chardonnay California 1984 $5.75 (1/31/87) BB
83 NAPA RIDGE Chardonnay Central Coast 1989 $7 (11/15/90) BB
77 NAPA RIDGE Chardonnay Central Coast 1988 $7 (6/30/90)
77 NAPA RIDGE Chardonnay North Coast 1987 $6.50 (7/15/88)
88 NAPA RIDGE Chardonnay North Coast Coastal 1989 $7 (6/30/91) BB
89 NAVARRO Chardonnay Anderson Valley 1987 $9.75 (9/30/89)
89 NAVARRO Chardonnay Anderson Valley Première Reserve 1988 $14 (12/31/90)
91 NAVARRO Chardonnay Anderson Valley Première Reserve 1988 $14 (CH-5/90)
87 NAVARRO Chardonnay Anderson Valley Première Reserve 1987 Rel: $14 Cur: $16 (CH-3/90)
84 NAVARRO Chardonnay Anderson Valley Première Reserve 1987 Rel: $14 Cur: $16 (9/30/89)
87 NAVARRO Chardonnay Anderson Valley Première Reserve 1986 Rel: $14 Cur: $18 (CH-3/90)
89 NAVARRO Chardonnay Anderson Valley Première Reserve 1986 Rel: $14 Cur: $18 (10/31/88)
89 NAVARRO Chardonnay Anderson Valley Première Reserve 1985 Rel: $12 Cur: $18 (CH-3/90)
83 NAVARRO Chardonnay Anderson Valley Première Reserve 1985 Rel: $12 Cur: $18 (11/15/87)
91 NAVARRO Chardonnay Anderson Valley Première Reserve 1984 Rel: $12 Cur: $22 (CH-3/90)
87 NAVARRO Chardonnay Mendocino 1988 $9.75 (11/30/90)
85 NAVARRO Chardonnay Mendocino Table Wine 1987 Rel: $14 Cur: $16 (9/30/89) BB
88 NAVARRO Chardonnay Mendocino 1986 $9.75 (9/30/88)
88 NAVARRO Chardonnay Mendocino 1985 $8.50 (10/31/87)
90 NEWLAN Chardonnay Napa Valley 1989 $14 (7/15/91)
91 NEWLAN Chardonnay Napa Valley 1988 $13 (6/15/90)
86 NEWLAN Chardonnay Napa Valley 1987 $13 (6/30/90)
90 NEWTON Chardonnay Napa Valley 1988 Rel: $14.50 Cur: $15 (6/30/90)
88 NEWTON Chardonnay Napa Valley 1988 Rel: $14.50 Cur: $15 (CH-3/90)
84 NEWTON Chardonnay Napa Valley 1987 Rel: $14 Cur: $14 (3/15/90)
88 NEWTON Chardonnay Napa Valley 1987 Rel: $14 Cur: $14 (CH-3/90)
85 NEWTON Chardonnay Napa Valley 1986 Rel: $14 Cur: $14 (CH-3/90)
77 NEWTON Chardonnay Napa Valley 1986 Rel: $14 Cur: $14 (7/15/88)
85 NEWTON Chardonnay Napa Valley 1985 Rel: $12.75 Cur: $19 (CH-3/90)
90 NEWTON Chardonnay Napa Valley 1985 Rel: $12.75 Cur: $19 (10/31/87)
86 NEWTON Chardonnay Napa Valley 1984 Rel: $11.50 Cur: $18 (CH-5/90)
89 NEWTON Chardonnay Napa Valley 1983 Rel: $12 Cur: $19 (CH-5/90)
82 NEWTON Chardonnay Napa Valley 1982 Rel: $16 Cur: $16 (9/01/84)
77 NEYERS Chardonnay California 1987 $14 (7/15/89)
81 NEYERS Chardonnay Carneros 1988 $17 (7/15/91)
78 NEYERS Chardonnay Napa Valley 1989 $15 (7/15/91)
79 NEYERS Chardonnay Napa Valley 1988 $15 (5/15/90)
81 NEYERS Chardonnay Napa Valley 1986 $12.50 (4/30/88)
90 NEYERS Chardonnay Napa Valley 1985 $12 (8/31/87)
85 GUSTAVE NIEBAUM Chardonnay Carneros Napa Valley Bayview Vineyard Barrel Fermented 1989 $16 (5/31/91)
91 GUSTAVE NIEBAUM Chardonnay Carneros Napa Valley Bayview Vineyard 1988 $14.50 (10/31/89)
90 GUSTAVE NIEBAUM Chardonnay Carneros Napa Valley Bayview Vineyard Special Reserve 1988 $18 (5/31/90)
82 GUSTAVE NIEBAUM Chardonnay Carneros Napa Valley Laird Vineyards 1989 $13.50 (1/31/91)
90 GUSTAVE NIEBAUM Chardonnay Carneros Napa Valley Laird Vineyards 1988 $13.50 (10/31/89)
86 GUSTAVE NIEBAUM Chardonnay Napa Valley Reference 1989 $11 (6/15/91)
71 OBESTER Chardonnay Mendocino County Barrel Fermented 1989 $13 (7/15/91)
83 OBESTER Chardonnay Mendocino County 1988 $13 (7/15/91)
80 OLIVET LANE Chardonnay Russian River Valley 1989 $12 (7/15/91)
57 OLSON Chardonnay Mendocino County 1984 $9 (4/16/86)
86 OPTIMA Chardonnay Sonoma County 1989 $25 (7/15/91)
86 PAHLMEYER Chardonnay Napa Valley Caldwell Vineyard 1989 $20 (4/30/91)
83 PARDUCCI Chardonnay Mendocino County 1989 $9.50 (7/15/91) BB
83 PARDUCCI Chardonnay Mendocino County 1988 $9.75 (4/30/90)
85 PARDUCCI Chardonnay Mendocino County 1987 $7 (10/31/88) BB
68 PARDUCCI Chardonnay Mendocino County 1986 $8 (12/31/87)
55 PARDUCCI Chardonnay Mendocino County 1984 $6 (4/16/86)
91 PARDUCCI Chardonnay Mendocino County Cellarmaster Selection 1988 $16 (6/30/90)
86 PARSONS CREEK Chardonnay Sonoma County Winemaker's Select 1988 $10 (2/28/91)
86 PATZ & HALL Chardonnay Napa Valley 1989 $25 (7/15/91)
77 PATZ & HALL Chardonnay Napa Valley 1988 $24 (6/30/90)
75 PAT PAULSEN Chardonnay Sonoma County 1983 $11 (2/16/85)
80 ROBERT PECOTA Chardonnay Alexander Valley Canepa Vineyard 1988 Rel: $16 Cur: $16 (5/15/90)
87 ROBERT PECOTA Chardonnay Alexander Valley Canepa Vineyard 1988 Rel: $16 Cur: $16 (CH-4/90)
91 ROBERT PECOTA Chardonnay Alexander Valley Canepa Vineyard 1987 Rel: $16 Cur: $20 (CH-4/90)
91 ROBERT PECOTA Chardonnay Alexander Valley Canepa Vineyard 1987 Rel: $16 Cur: $20 (12/31/88)

UNITED STATES
CALIFORNIA/*CHARDONNAY*

85 ROBERT PECOTA Chardonnay Alexander Valley Canepa Vineyard 1986 Rel: $16 Cur: $19 (CH-4/90)
77 ROBERT PECOTA Chardonnay Alexander Valley Canepa Vineyard 1986 Rel: $16 Cur: $19 (10/31/87)
89 ROBERT PECOTA Chardonnay Alexander Valley Canepa Vineyard 1985 Rel: $16 Cur: $18 (CH-7/90)
83 ROBERT PECOTA Chardonnay Alexander Valley Canepa Vineyard 1984 Rel: $14 Cur: $18 (CH-4/90)
79 ROBERT PECOTA Chardonnay Alexander Valley Canepa Vineyard 1983 Rel: $14 Cur: $18 (CH-4/90)
75 ROBERT PECOTA Chardonnay Alexander Valley Canepa Vineyard 1981 Rel: $12 Cur: $20 (CH-4/90)
89 ROBERT PECOTA Chardonnay Alexander Valley Canepa Vineyard 1980 Rel: $12 Cur: $20 (CH-4/90)
77 J. PEDRONCELLI Chardonnay Dry Creek Valley 1989 $9.50 (12/31/90)
79 J. PEDRONCELLI Chardonnay Dry Creek Valley 1988 $9 (12/15/89)
85 J. PEDRONCELLI Chardonnay Dry Creek Valley 1987 $8 (12/31/88) BB
83 J. PEDRONCELLI Chardonnay Dry Creek Valley 1986 $8 (6/15/88)
83 J. PEDRONCELLI Chardonnay Sonoma County 1985 $7.75 (7/31/87)
81 J. PEDRONCELLI Chardonnay Sonoma County 1984 $7.75 (3/01/86)
66 J. PEDRONCELLI Chardonnay Sonoma County 1983 $7.75 (6/01/85)
81 ROBERT PEPI Chardonnay Napa Valley Puncheon Fermented Reserve 1989 $20 (2/28/91)
88 ROBERT PEPI Chardonnay Napa Valley Puncheon Fermented 1988 $14 (5/31/90)
84 ROBERT PEPI Chardonnay Napa Valley 1987 $13.50 (2/15/90)
80 ROBERT PEPI Chardonnay Napa Valley 1986 $12 (10/31/88)
81 ROBERT PEPI Chardonnay Napa Valley 1985 $12 (11/15/87)
70 ROBERT PEPI Chardonnay Napa Valley 1983 $11 (3/01/86)
72 ROBERT PEPI Chardonnay Napa Valley 1982 $11 (5/01/84)
83 MARIO PERELLI-MINETTI Chardonnay Napa Valley 1989 $12.50 (4/30/91)
80 MARIO PERELLI-MINETTI Chardonnay Napa Valley 1988 $11.50 (6/30/90)
78 PERRET Chardonnay Carneros Napa Valley Perret Vineyard 1985 $14 (12/31/88)
91 PERRET Chardonnay Carneros Napa Valley Perret Vineyard 1984 $14.50 (10/15/87)
81 PERRET Chardonnay Carneros Napa Valley Perret Vineyard 1982 $14.50 (11/01/84)
84 PERRET Chardonnay Carneros Napa Valley Winery Lake Vineyard
85 JOSEPH PHELPS Chardonnay Carneros Sangiacomo Vineyard 1989 $20 (7/15/91)
89 JOSEPH PHELPS Chardonnay Carneros Sangiacomo Vineyard 1988 $16 (6/30/90)
68 JOSEPH PHELPS Chardonnay Carneros Sangiacomo Vineyard 1987 $18 (5/15/89)
93 JOSEPH PHELPS Chardonnay Carneros Sangiacomo Vineyard 1986 $16 (7/15/88)
84 JOSEPH PHELPS Chardonnay Carneros Sangiacomo Vineyard 1985 $14 (11/15/87)
79 JOSEPH PHELPS Chardonnay Carneros Sangiacomo Vineyard 1982 $14 (4/01/84)
66 JOSEPH PHELPS Chardonnay Carneros Schellville 1982 $14 (9/16/85)1985 $14.50 (12/31/88)
81 JOSEPH PHELPS Chardonnay Napa Valley 1989 $16 (7/15/91)
86 JOSEPH PHELPS Chardonnay Napa Valley 1988 $16 (6/30/90)
81 JOSEPH PHELPS Chardonnay Napa Valley 1987 $15 (3/15/89)
75 JOSEPH PHELPS Chardonnay Napa Valley 1984 $13 (6/30/87)
68 JOSEPH PHELPS Chardonnay Napa Valley 1983 $12.75 (12/15/86)
85 JOSEPH PHELPS Chardonnay Napa Valley 1982 $12.50 (4/16/85)
83 R.H. PHILLIPS Chardonnay California 1990 $8 (7/15/91) BB
83 R.H. PHILLIPS Chardonnay California 1989 $7 (4/30/91) BB
77 R.H. PHILLIPS Chardonnay California 1987 $6 (2/15/89)
67 PINE RIDGE Chardonnay Napa Valley Knollside Cuvée 1989 $16 (7/15/91)
88 PINE RIDGE Chardonnay Napa Valley Knollside Cuvée 1988 Rel: $15 Cur: $17 (CH-7/90)
85 PINE RIDGE Chardonnay Napa Valley Knollside Cuvée 1988 Rel: $15 Cur: $17 (5/15/90)
90 PINE RIDGE Chardonnay Napa Valley Knollside Cuvée 1987 Rel: $15 Cur: $17 (CH-4/90)
91 PINE RIDGE Chardonnay Napa Valley Knollside Cuvée 1987 Rel: $15 Cur: $17 (1/31/89)
88 PINE RIDGE Chardonnay Napa Valley Knollside Cuvée 1986 Rel: $14 Cur: $17 (CH-4/90)
89 PINE RIDGE Chardonnay Napa Valley Knollside Cuvée 1986 Rel: $14 Cur: $17 (3/31/88)
87 PINE RIDGE Chardonnay Napa Valley Knollside Cuvée 1985 Rel: $14 Cur: $16 (CH-4/90)
89 PINE RIDGE Chardonnay Napa Valley Knollside Cuvée 1985 Rel: $14 Cur: $16 (4/30/87)
85 PINE RIDGE Chardonnay Napa Valley Knollside Cuvée 1984 Rel: $14 Cur: $17 (CH-4/90)
88 PINE RIDGE Chardonnay Napa Valley Oak Knoll Cuvée 1983 Rel: $13 Cur: $18 (CH-4/90)
84 PINE RIDGE Chardonnay Napa Valley Oak Knoll Cuvée 1983 Rel: $13 Cur: $18 (12/16/84)
78 PINE RIDGE Chardonnay Napa Valley Oak Knoll Cuvée 1982 Rel: $13 Cur: $19 (CH-4/90)
89 PINE RIDGE Chardonnay Napa Valley Oak Knoll Cuvée 1982 Rel: $13 Cur: $19 (3/16/84) SS
84 PINE RIDGE Chardonnay Napa Valley Oak Knoll Cuvée 1981 Rel: $13 Cur: $20 (CH-4/90)
78 PINE RIDGE Chardonnay Napa Valley Stags Leap District 1988 $20 (11/30/90)
88 PINE RIDGE Chardonnay Stags Leap District 1988 Rel: $20 Cur: $20 (CH-7/90)
82 PINE RIDGE Chardonnay Napa Valley Stags Leap District 1987 Rel: $20 Cur: $23 (4/30/89)
91 PINE RIDGE Chardonnay Napa Valley Stags Leap District 1987 Rel: $20 Cur: $23 (CH-4/90)
81 PINE RIDGE Chardonnay Napa Valley Stags Leap District 1986 Rel: $19 Cur: $23 (7/15/88)
88 PINE RIDGE Chardonnay Napa Valley Stags Leap District 1986 Rel: $19 Cur: $23 (CH-4/90)
86 PINE RIDGE Chardonnay Napa Valley Stags Leap District 1985 Rel: $18 Cur: $23 (8/31/87)
85 PINE RIDGE Chardonnay Napa Valley Stags Leap District 1985 Rel: $18 Cur: $23 (CH-4/90)
86 PINE RIDGE Chardonnay Napa Valley Stags Leap District 1984 Rel: $18 Cur: $25 (6/16/86)
84 PINE RIDGE Chardonnay Napa Valley Stags Leap District 1984 Rel: $18 Cur: $25 (CH-4/90)
94 PINE RIDGE Chardonnay Napa Valley Stags Leap District 1983 Rel: $16 Cur: $25 (12/16/85) SS
86 PINE RIDGE Chardonnay Napa Valley Stags Leap District 1983 Rel: $16 Cur: $25 (CH-4/90)
82 PINE RIDGE Chardonnay Napa Valley Stags Leap District 1982 Rel: $15 Cur: $27 (12/16/84)
82 PINE RIDGE Chardonnay Napa Valley Stags Leap District 1982 Rel: $15 Cur: $27 (CH-4/90)
86 PINE RIDGE Chardonnay Napa Valley Stags Leap District 1981 Rel: $15 Cur: $31 (CH-4/90)
82 PINE RIDGE Chardonnay Napa Valley Stags Leap District 1979 Rel: $9.50 Cur: $32 (CH-4/90)
85 PLAM Chardonnay Napa Valley 1989 $16 (7/15/91)

Key to Symbols

The scores reported here are the results of blind tastings conducted by our panel of senior editors. Wines that carry the initials below are results of individual tastings.

THE WINE SPECTATOR 100-POINT SCALE ***95-100***—Classic, a great wine; ***90-94***—Outstanding, superior character and style; ***80-89***—Good to very good, a wine with special qualities; ***70-79***—Average, drinkable wine that may have minor flaws; ***60-69***—Below average, drinkable but not recommended; ***50-59***—Poor, undrinkable, not recommended. "+"—With a score indicates a range; used primarily with barrel tastings to indicate a preliminary score.

SPECIAL DESIGNATIONS SS—Spectator Selection, CS—Cellar Selection, BB—Best Buy.

TASTER'S INITIALS (JG)—Jim Gordon, (HS)—Harvey Steiman, (JL)—James Laube, (JS)—James Suckling, (TM)—Thomas Matthews, (TR)—Terry Robards, (BT)—Barrel Tasting (these wines were tasted blind from barrel samples), (CA-date)—*California's Great Cabernets* by James Laube, (CH-date)—*California's Great Chardonnays* by James Laube, (VP-date)—*Vintage Port* by James Suckling.

DATE TASTED Dates in parentheses represent the issue in which the rating was published.

85 PLAM Chardonnay Napa Valley 1988 $16 (6/30/90)
84 PLAM Chardonnay Napa Valley 1986 $18 (4/15/89)
79 PLAM Chardonnay Napa Valley 1985 $12 (7/15/88)
82 BERNARD PRADEL Chardonnay Napa Valley 1986 $9.50 (2/29/88)
89 QUAIL RIDGE Chardonnay Napa Valley 1988 $14 (2/15/90)
68 QUAIL RIDGE Chardonnay Napa Valley 1987 $15 (7/15/89)
81 QUAIL RIDGE Chardonnay Napa Valley 1986 $15 (10/31/88)
80 QUAIL RIDGE Chardonnay Napa Valley 1983 $14 (9/01/85)
85 QUAIL RIDGE Chardonnay Napa Valley 1982 $14 (5/16/84)
80 QUAIL RIDGE Chardonnay Napa Valley Winemakers' Selection 1984 $17 (12/15/87)
84 QUAIL RIDGE Chardonnay Sonoma County 1982 $9 (3/16/84)
91 QUPE Chardonnay Santa Barbara County Sierra Madre Reserve 1989 $25 (7/15/91)
81 QUPE Chardonnay Santa Barbara County Sierra Madre Reserve 1988 $12.50 (12/15/89)
85 RABBIT RIDGE Chardonnay Sonoma County 1989 $12 (4/30/91)
76 RANCHO SISQUOC Chardonnay Santa Maria Valley 1987 $10 (12/15/89)
79 KENT RASMUSSEN Chardonnay Carneros 1989 $20 (1/31/91)
90 KENT RASMUSSEN Chardonnay Carneros 1988 $19 (9/15/90)
78 KENT RASMUSSEN Chardonnay Carneros 1987 $15 (12/31/88)
87 KENT RASMUSSEN Chardonnay Carneros Napa Valley 1989 $19 (3/15/91)
65 RAVENSWOOD Chardonnay Sonoma Valley Sangiacomo 1989 $18 (7/15/91)
80 RAVENSWOOD Chardonnay Sonoma Valley Sangiacomo 1988 $18 (2/28/90)
87 RAVENSWOOD Chardonnay Sonoma Valley Sangiacomo 1987 $15 (7/15/89)
71 RAVENSWOOD Chardonnay Sonoma Valley Sangiacomo 1986 $15 (3/15/88)
91 RAVENSWOOD Chardonnay Sonoma Valley Sangiacomo 1985 $15 (3/31/87)
83 RAYMOND Chardonnay California Selection 1989 $11.50 (2/28/91)
82 RAYMOND Chardonnay California Selection 1988 $11 (10/31/89)
84 RAYMOND Chardonnay California Selection 1987 $9 (12/31/88)
82 RAYMOND Chardonnay California Selection 1986 $8.50 (11/15/87)
83 RAYMOND Chardonnay California Selection 1985 $8.50 (2/28/87)
93 RAYMOND Chardonnay California Selection 1984 $8.50 (3/01/86)
82 RAYMOND Chardonnay California Selection 1983 $8.50 (12/01/84)
80 RAYMOND Chardonnay Napa Valley 1989 $15 (7/15/91)
85 RAYMOND Chardonnay Napa Valley 1988 $15 (6/15/90)
85 RAYMOND Chardonnay Napa Valley 1987 $13 (12/31/88)
80 RAYMOND Chardonnay Napa Valley 1986 $13 (2/15/88)
92 RAYMOND Chardonnay Napa Valley 1985 $12 (9/15/87)
94 RAYMOND Chardonnay Napa Valley 1983 $12 (11/01/85)
83 RAYMOND Chardonnay Napa Valley 1982 $13 (5/16/84)
85 RAYMOND Chardonnay Napa Valley Private Reserve 1988 $22 (7/15/91)
90 RAYMOND Chardonnay Napa Valley Private Reserve 1988 Rel: $22 Cur: $22 (CH-5/90)
90 RAYMOND Chardonnay Napa Valley Private Reserve 1987 Rel: $22 Cur: $22 (5/15/90)
88 RAYMOND Chardonnay Napa Valley Private Reserve 1987 Rel: $22 Cur: $22 (CH-5/90)
87 RAYMOND Chardonnay Napa Valley Private Reserve 1986 Rel: $18 Cur: $21 (CH-5/90)
82 RAYMOND Chardonnay Napa Valley Private Reserve 1986 Rel: $18 Cur: $21 (7/15/89)
91 RAYMOND Chardonnay Napa Valley Private Reserve 1985 Rel: $18 Cur: $21 (CH-5/90)
90 RAYMOND Chardonnay Napa Valley Private Reserve 1985 Rel: $18 Cur: $21 (6/15/88)
86 RAYMOND Chardonnay Napa Valley Private Reserve 1984 Rel: $16 Cur: $16 (7/15/87)
73 RAYMOND Chardonnay Napa Valley Private Reserve 1983 Rel: $16 Cur: $16 (9/15/86)
70 RAYMOND Chardonnay Napa Valley Private Reserve 1981 Rel: $15 Cur: $25 (CH-6/90)
79 REVERE Chardonnay Napa Valley 1989 $13 (7/15/91)
84 REVERE Chardonnay Napa Valley 1988 $14 (2/28/91)
76 REVERE Chardonnay Napa Valley 1987 Rel: $14 Cur: $14 (9/15/90)
85 REVERE Chardonnay Napa Valley 1986 Rel: $15 Cur: $16 (CH-4/90)
78 REVERE Chardonnay Napa Valley 1986 Rel: $15 Cur: $16 (4/30/88)
85 REVERE Chardonnay Napa Valley 1985 Rel: $15 Cur: $20 (CH-4/90)
86 REVERE Chardonnay Napa Valley 1985 Rel: $15 Cur: $20 (5/31/87)
89 REVERE Chardonnay Napa Valley Berlenbach Vineyards 1989 $15 (7/15/91)
77 REVERE Chardonnay Napa Valley Reserve 1989 $18 (7/15/91)
93 REVERE Chardonnay Napa Valley Reserve 1988 $18 (5/15/91)
87 REVERE Chardonnay Napa Valley Reserve 1988 $18 (CH-4/90)
81 REVERE Chardonnay Napa Valley Reserve 1987 Rel: $25 Cur: $25 (9/15/90)
83 REVERE Chardonnay Napa Valley Reserve 1987 Rel: $25 Cur: $25 (CH-4/90)
87 REVERE Chardonnay Napa Valley Reserve 1986 Rel: $22 Cur: $25 (CH-4/90)
81 RIDGE Chardonnay Howell Mountain 1989 $14 (7/15/91)
85 RIDGE Chardonnay Howell Mountain 1988 $14 (7/15/91)
80 RIDGE Chardonnay Howell Mountain 1988 $15 (6/15/90)
87 RIDGE Chardonnay Howell Mountain 1987 $14 (4/30/89)
84 RIDGE Chardonnay Santa Cruz Mountains 1989 $14 (7/15/91)
89 RIDGE Chardonnay Santa Cruz Mountains 1988 $14 (7/15/91)
88 RITCHIE CREEK Chardonnay Napa Valley 1989 $15 (7/15/91)
79 RIVER OAKS Chardonnay Alexander Valley 1984 $6 (4/01/85)
77 RIVER OAKS Chardonnay Sonoma County 1985 $6 (4/16/86)
79 RIVERSIDE FARM Chardonnay California 1989 $6.75 (12/31/90)
81 ROCHE Chardonnay Carneros 1989 $13 (3/31/91)
90 ROCHE Chardonnay Carneros 1988 $11 (10/31/89)
81 ROCHIOLI Chardonnay Russian River Valley 1988 $15 (4/15/90)
83 ROCHIOLI Chardonnay Russian River Valley 1987 $14 (5/31/89)
72 ROCHIOLI Chardonnay Russian River Valley 1986 $12 (1/31/88)
86 ROMBAUER Chardonnay Napa Valley 1988 $15 (12/31/90)
88 ROMBAUER Chardonnay Napa Valley 1988 $15 (CH-6/90)
86 ROMBAUER Chardonnay Napa Valley 1987 Rel: $14.50 Cur: $15 (CH-6/90)
88 ROMBAUER Chardonnay Napa Valley 1987 Rel: $14.50 Cur: $15 (1/31/90)
85 ROMBAUER Chardonnay Napa Valley 1986 Rel: $14.50 Cur: $16 (CH-6/90)
87 ROMBAUER Chardonnay Napa Valley 1986 Rel: $14.50 Cur: $16 (10/31/88)
84 ROMBAUER Chardonnay Napa Valley 1985 Rel: $14.50 Cur: $18 (CH-6/90)
82 ROMBAUER Chardonnay Napa Valley 1985 Rel: $14.50 Cur: $18 (11/15/87)
78 ROMBAUER Chardonnay Napa Valley 1984 Rel: $14.50 Cur: $20 (CH-6/90)
87 ROMBAUER Chardonnay Napa Valley 1983 Rel: $14.50 Cur: $25 (CH-7/90)
87 ROMBAUER Chardonnay Napa Valley 1983 Rel: $14.50 Cur: $25 (6/16/85)
84 ROMBAUER Chardonnay Napa Valley 1982 Rel: $14.50 Cur: $25 (CH-6/90)
71 ROMBAUER Chardonnay Napa Valley French Vineyard 1984 $13.50 (4/01/86)
89 ROMBAUER Chardonnay Napa Valley Reserve 1988 (NR) (CH-6/90)
87 ROMBAUER Chardonnay Napa Valley Reserve 1987 Rel: $25 Cur: $25 (CH-6/90)
86 ROMBAUER Chardonnay Napa Valley Reserve 1986 Rel: $24 Cur: $24 (CH-6/90)
85 ROUDON-SMITH Chardonnay Mendocino Nelson Ranch 1986 $12 (9/15/88)
70 ROUDON-SMITH Chardonnay Santa Cruz Mountains 1985 $15 (3/31/89)
81 ROUND HILL Chardonnay California 1988 $7.50 (2/28/91) BB
83 ROUND HILL Chardonnay California House 1989 $6.50 (7/15/91) BB
77 ROUND HILL Chardonnay California House 1989 $6 (8/31/90)
83 ROUND HILL Chardonnay California House 1988 $5.50 (4/15/90) BB

79 ROUND HILL Chardonnay California House 1987 $6.25 (11/15/88)
83 ROUND HILL Chardonnay California House 1986 $5.25 (11/30/87) BB
81 ROUND HILL Chardonnay California House 1985 $5 (9/30/86) BB
79 ROUND HILL Chardonnay California House 1984 $4.75 (4/16/86)
84 ROUND HILL Chardonnay Napa Valley 1989 $9 (6/30/91)
89 ROUND HILL Chardonnay Napa Valley Reserve 1989 $11 (6/15/91)
82 ROUND HILL Chardonnay Napa Valley Reserve 1988 $11 (2/28/91)
75 ROUND HILL Chardonnay Napa Valley Reserve 1986 $9.50 (5/31/88)
82 ROUND HILL Chardonnay Napa Valley Reserve 1985 $9.50 (11/15/87)
74 ROUND HILL Chardonnay Napa Valley Van Asperen Vineyard 1988 $11 (2/28/91)
74 ROUND HILL Chardonnay Napa Valley Van Asperen Vineyard 1987 $11 (7/15/89)
72 ROUND HILL Chardonnay Napa Valley Van Asperen Reserve 1986 $11 (5/31/88)
78 ROUND HILL Chardonnay North Coast 1986 $6.75 (12/15/87)
77 RUTHERFORD ESTATE Chardonnay Napa Valley 1989 $8.50 (7/15/91)
70 RUTHERFORD ESTATE Chardonnay Napa Valley 1985 $5 (11/15/87)
90 RUTHERFORD HILL Chardonnay Napa Valley Cellar Reserve 1987 $18 (2/15/91)
87 RUTHERFORD HILL Chardonnay Napa Valley Cellar Reserve 1986 $18 (5/31/90)
87 RUTHERFORD HILL Chardonnay Napa Valley Cellar Reserve 1985 $15 (5/31/88)
83 RUTHERFORD HILL Chardonnay Napa Valley Jaeger Vineyards 1988 $13 (2/15/91)
87 RUTHERFORD HILL Chardonnay Napa Valley Jaeger Vineyards 1986 $12 (12/31/88)
80 RUTHERFORD HILL Chardonnay Napa Valley Jaeger Vineyards 1985 $11 (5/31/88)
77 RUTHERFORD HILL Chardonnay Napa Valley Jaeger Vineyards 1983 $10.75 (5/16/85)
89 RUTHERFORD HILL Chardonnay Napa Valley Jaeger Vineyards Cellar Reserve 1981 $14 (3/16/86)
57 RUTHERFORD HILL Chardonnay Napa Valley Partners Chardonnay 1984 $7 (4/16/86)
86 RUTHERFORD HILL Chardonnay Napa Valley Rutherford Knoll Special Cuvée 1987 $11 (4/30/89)
83 RUTHERFORD HILL Chardonnay Napa Valley Rutherford Knoll Special Cuvée 1986 $11 (1/31/88)
87 RUTHERFORD HILL Chardonnay Napa Valley XVS 1988 $18 (7/15/91)
83 RUTHERFORD RANCH Chardonnay Napa Valley 1987 $11 (5/15/90)
79 RUTHERFORD RANCH Chardonnay Napa Valley 1987 $11 (2/15/89)
57 RUTHERFORD RANCH Chardonnay Napa Valley 1982 $12 (5/16/84)
72 RUTHERFORD RANCH Chardonnay Napa Valley Reese Vineyard 1985 $10 (11/15/87)
54 SAGE CREEK Chardonnay Napa Valley 1982 $9 (4/16/84)
75 ST. ANDREW'S VINEYARD Chardonnay Napa Valley 1989 $14 (7/15/91)
89 ST. ANDREW'S VINEYARD Chardonnay Napa Valley 1988 $13 (12/31/90)
85 ST. ANDREW'S VINEYARD Chardonnay Napa Valley 1987 $14 (1/31/90)
90 ST. ANDREW'S VINEYARD Chardonnay Napa Valley 1986 $13 (4/30/88)
87 ST. ANDREW'S VINEYARD Chardonnay Napa Valley 1985 $13 (6/30/87)
92 ST. ANDREW'S VINEYARD Chardonnay Napa Valley 1984 $13 (1/01/86)
89 ST. ANDREW'S VINEYARD Chardonnay Napa Valley 1982 $12.50 (10/01/84)
80 ST. ANDREW'S WINERY Chardonnay Napa Valley 1989 $10 (7/15/91)
84 ST. ANDREW'S WINERY Chardonnay Napa Valley 1988 $10.50 (4/15/90)
80 ST. ANDREW'S WINERY Chardonnay Napa Valley 1987 $6.50 (7/15/88)
80 ST. ANDREW'S WINERY Chardonnay Napa Valley 1986 $8 (8/31/87)
93 ST. ANDREW'S WINERY Chardonnay Napa Valley 1985 $7.50 (11/30/86) SS
91 ST. ANDREW'S WINERY Chardonnay Napa Valley 1984 $7 (2/01/86) BB
79 ST. ANDREW'S WINERY Chardonnay Napa Valley House 1982 $7 (10/16/84)
85 ST. CLEMENT Chardonnay Carneros Abbott's Vineyard 1989 $18 (2/28/91)
91 ST. CLEMENT Chardonnay Carneros Abbott's Vineyard 1987 $17 (CH-3/90)
89 ST. CLEMENT Chardonnay Carneros Abbott's Vineyard 1987 $17 (10/31/89)
90 ST. CLEMENT Chardonnay Napa Valley 1989 $16 (5/31/91) SS
88 ST. CLEMENT Chardonnay Napa Valley 1988 Rel: $15 Cur: $16 (6/15/90)
88 ST. CLEMENT Chardonnay Napa Valley 1988 Rel: $15 Cur: $16 (CH-3/90)
86 ST. CLEMENT Chardonnay Napa Valley 1987 Rel: $15 Cur: $15 (CH-3/90)
90 ST. CLEMENT Chardonnay Napa Valley 1987 Rel: $15 Cur: $15 (9/15/89)
89 ST. CLEMENT Chardonnay Napa Valley 1986 Rel: $15 Cur: $15 (CH-3/90)
89 ST. CLEMENT Chardonnay Napa Valley 1986 Rel: $15 Cur: $15 (7/15/88)
85 ST. CLEMENT Chardonnay Napa Valley 1985 Rel: $14.50 Cur: $16 (CH-3/90)
76 ST. CLEMENT Chardonnay Napa Valley 1985 Rel: $14.50 Cur: $16 (10/15/87)
88 ST. CLEMENT Chardonnay Napa Valley 1984 Rel: $14.50 Cur: $17 (CH-3/90)
75 ST. CLEMENT Chardonnay Napa Valley 1984 Rel: $14.50 Cur: $17 (2/01/86)
76 ST. CLEMENT Chardonnay Napa Valley 1983 Rel: $14.50 Cur: $17 (CH-3/90)
73 ST. CLEMENT Chardonnay Napa Valley 1982 Rel: $14.50 Cur: $20 (CH-3/90)
75 ST. CLEMENT Chardonnay Napa Valley 1981 Rel: $13.50 Cur: $25 (CH-3/90)
83 ST. CLEMENT Chardonnay Napa Valley 1980 Rel: $12 Cur: $35 (CH-3/90)
93 ST. CLEMENT Chardonnay Napa Valley 1979 Rel: $12 Cur: $27 (CH-3/90)
70 ST. FRANCIS Chardonnay California 1989 $10 (7/15/91)
82 ST. FRANCIS Chardonnay California 1988 $10 (3/31/90)
79 ST. FRANCIS Chardonnay California 1987 $9.50 (10/15/88)
83 ST. FRANCIS Chardonnay California 1986 $9 (11/15/87)
89 ST. FRANCIS Chardonnay Sonoma Valley 1983 $10.75 (12/01/84)
84 ST. FRANCIS Chardonnay Sonoma Valley Barrel Select 1989 $15 (7/15/91)
79 ST. FRANCIS Chardonnay Sonoma Valley Barrel Select 1988 $15 (11/30/89)
82 ST. FRANCIS Chardonnay Sonoma Valley Barrel Select 1987 $14.50 (12/31/88)
91 ST. FRANCIS Chardonnay Sonoma Valley Barrel Select 1986 $12.50 (7/15/88)
69 ST. FRANCIS Chardonnay Sonoma Valley Barrel Select 1984 $12 (10/31/86)
75 ST. FRANCIS Chardonnay Sonoma Valley Poverello 1984 $6.75 (3/16/86)
87 SAINT GREGORY Chardonnay Mendocino 1989 $15 (7/15/91)
81 ST. SUPERY Chardonnay Napa Valley 1989 $12 (3/31/91)
83 ST. SUPERY Chardonnay Napa Valley St. Supéry Vineyards 1988 $11 (11/15/89)
91 SAINTSBURY Chardonnay Carneros 1989 $14 (11/15/90)
90 SAINTSBURY Chardonnay Carneros 1988 Rel: $14 Cur: $16 (3/15/90)
90 SAINTSBURY Chardonnay Carneros 1988 Rel: $14 Cur: $16 (CH-2/90)
90 SAINTSBURY Chardonnay Carneros 1987 Rel: $13 Cur: $18 (CH-2/90)
91 SAINTSBURY Chardonnay Carneros 1987 Rel: $13 Cur: $18 (11/30/88)
88 SAINTSBURY Chardonnay Carneros 1986 Rel: $12 Cur: $19 (CH-2/90)
90 SAINTSBURY Chardonnay Carneros 1986 Rel: $12 Cur: $19 (11/30/87) (JL)
90 SAINTSBURY Chardonnay Carneros 1985 Rel: $11 Cur: $19 (CH-2/90)
91 SAINTSBURY Chardonnay Carneros 1985 Rel: $11 Cur: $19 (11/30/87) (JL)
92 SAINTSBURY Chardonnay Carneros 1984 Rel: $11 Cur: $25 (CH-2/90)
93 SAINTSBURY Chardonnay Carneros 1984 Rel: $11 Cur: $25 (11/15/86)
80 SAINTSBURY Chardonnay Carneros 1983 Rel: $11 Cur: $20 (CH-2/90)
80 SAINTSBURY Chardonnay Carneros 1983 Rel: $11 Cur: $20 (11/30/87) (JL)
65 SAINTSBURY Chardonnay Sonoma County 1982 Rel: $11 Cur: $14 (CH-2/90)
86 SAINTSBURY Chardonnay Sonoma County 1982 Rel: $11 Cur: $14 (11/30/87) (JL)
87 SAINTSBURY Chardonnay Sonoma County 1981 Rel: $10 Cur: $25 (CH-2/90)
90 SAINTSBURY Chardonnay Sonoma County 1981 Rel: $10 Cur: $25 (11/30/87) (JL)
92 SAINTSBURY Chardonnay Carneros Reserve 1988 Rel: $20 Cur: $22 (5/31/90)
92 SAINTSBURY Chardonnay Carneros Reserve 1988 Rel: $20 Cur: $22 (CH-2/90)
89 SAINTSBURY Chardonnay Carneros Reserve 1987 Rel: $20 Cur: $22 (CH-2/90)
88 SAINTSBURY Chardonnay Carneros Reserve 1987 Rel: $20 Cur: $22 (7/15/89)
84 SAINTSBURY Chardonnay Carneros Reserve 1986 Rel: $20 Cur: $25 (CH-2/90)
89 SAINTSBURY Chardonnay Carneros Reserve 1986 Rel: $20 Cur: $25 (7/15/88)
75 SAN MARTIN Chardonnay San Luis Obispo County 1982 $7.50 (3/01/84)
87 SANFORD Chardonnay Santa Barbara County 1989 $16 (4/30/91)
92 SANFORD Chardonnay Santa Barbara County 1988 Rel: $16 Cur: $18 (CH-6/90)
91 SANFORD Chardonnay Santa Barbara County 1988 Rel: $16 Cur: $18 (5/15/90)
89 SANFORD Chardonnay Santa Barbara County 1988 Rel: $16 Cur: $18 (12/15/89)
92 SANFORD Chardonnay Santa Barbara County 1987 Rel: $15 Cur: $16 (CH-2/90)
90 SANFORD Chardonnay Santa Barbara County 1987 Rel: $15 Cur: $16 (11/30/88)
88 SANFORD Chardonnay Santa Barbara County 1986 Rel: $14 Cur: $16 (CH-2/90)
90 SANFORD Chardonnay Santa Barbara County 1985 Rel: $13.50 Cur: $20 (CH-2/90)
78 SANFORD Chardonnay Central Coast 1984 Rel: $12.50 Cur: $15 (CH-2/90)
88 SANFORD Chardonnay Central Coast 1983 Rel: $12 Cur: $15 (CH-2/90)
68 SANFORD Chardonnay Santa Maria Valley 1982 Rel: $12 Cur: $20 (CH-2/90)
74 SANFORD Chardonnay Santa Maria Valley 1981 Rel: $11 Cur: $20 (CH-2/90)
90 SANFORD Chardonnay Santa Barbara County Barrel Select 1989 Rel: $28 Cur: $28 (7/15/91)
94 SANFORD Chardonnay Santa Barbara County Barrel Select 1988 Rel: $25 Cur: $28 (8/31/90)
94 SANFORD Chardonnay Santa Barbara County Barrel Select 1988 Rel: $25 Cur: $28 (CH-6/90)
91 SANFORD Chardonnay Santa Barbara County Barrel Select 1987 Rel: $24 Cur: $30 (CH-2/90)
91 SANFORD Chardonnay Santa Barbara County Barrel Select 1987 Rel: $24 Cur: $30 (12/15/89)
92 SANFORD Chardonnay Santa Barbara County Barrel Select 1985 Rel: $20 Cur: $30 (CH-2/90)
92 SANFORD Chardonnay Santa Barbara County Barrel Select 1985 Rel: $20 Cur: $30 (11/30/87)
80 SANTA BARBARA Chardonnay Santa Barbara County 1989 $12 (1/31/91)
74 SANTA BARBARA Chardonnay Santa Ynez Valley 1988 $12 (4/15/90)
83 SANTA BARBARA Chardonnay Santa Ynez Valley 1987 $10 (12/15/89)
67 SANTA BARBARA Chardonnay Santa Ynez Valley 1986 $8.50 (2/29/88)
87 SANTA BARBARA Chardonnay Santa Ynez Valley Reserve 1989 $18 (5/15/91)
86 SANTA BARBARA Chardonnay Santa Ynez Valley Reserve 1988 $18 (9/30/90)
84 SANTA BARBARA Chardonnay Santa Ynez Valley Reserve 1987 $16 (12/15/89)
84 SANTA BARBARA Chardonnay Santa Ynez Valley Reserve 1986 $14 (10/15/88)
88 SANTA YNEZ VALLEY Chardonnay Santa Barbara County 1988 $13 (2/28/90)
77 SARAH'S Chardonnay Central Coast Estate 1988 $45 (5/31/91)
82 SARAH'S Chardonnay Monterey County Ventana Vineyard 1989 $22 (5/31/91)
64 SBARBORO Chardonnay Alexander Valley Gauer Ranch 1985 $10 (8/31/87)
75 SCHUG Chardonnay Carneros Beckstoffer Vineyard 1988 $15 (2/28/91)
63 SCHUG Chardonnay Carneros Napa Valley Ahollinger Vineyard 1985 $9.75 (4/30/87)
79 SCHUG Chardonnay Napa Valley Beckstoffer Vineyard 1987 $15 (5/31/90)
81 SEBASTIANI Chardonnay Sonoma County 1989 $10 (7/15/91)
79 SEBASTIANI Chardonnay Sonoma County Family Selection Reserve 1986 $10 (10/31/88)
89 SEBASTIANI Chardonnay Sonoma County Reserve 1988 $15 (6/30/91)
89 SEBASTIANI Chardonnay Sonoma County Reserve 1988 $11 (4/30/90)
71 SEBASTIANI Chardonnay Sonoma Valley 1984 $8.50 (6/16/86)
74 SEBASTIANI Chardonnay Sonoma Valley Reserve 1985 $10 (2/15/88)
74 SEBASTIANI ESTATES Chardonnay Sonoma Valley Kinneybrook 1986 $14 (3/15/88)
72 SEBASTIANI ESTATES Chardonnay Sonoma Valley Niles 1986 $17 (3/15/88)
83 SEBASTIANI ESTATES Chardonnay Sonoma County Clark Ranch 1987 $14 (6/30/90)
80 SEBASTIANI ESTATES Chardonnay Sonoma County Kinneybrook 1987 $14 (6/30/90)
90 SEBASTIANI ESTATES Chardonnay Sonoma County Wildwood Hill 1987 $14 (6/30/90)
77 SEBASTIANI ESTATES Chardonnay Sonoma County Wilson Ranch 1987 $14 (6/30/90)
83 SEBASTIANI ESTATES Chardonnay Sonoma Valley Clark Ranch 1986 $14 (3/15/88)
68 SAM J. SEBASTIANI Chardonnay Sonoma & Napa Counties 1985 $12.50 (6/30/87)
69 SEGHESIO Chardonnay California 1986 $5.50 (8/31/88)
86 SEGHESIO Chardonnay Mendocino-Sonoma Counties 1989 $9 (4/30/91)
84 SEGHESIO Chardonnay Sonoma County 1988 $12 (4/30/91)
75 SEGHESIO Chardonnay Sonoma County 1988 $8 (6/30/90)
79 SEGHESIO Chardonnay Sonoma County 1987 $7 (12/31/88)
71 SEGHESIO Chardonnay Sonoma County Reserve 1988 $12 (2/28/91)
86 SEQUOIA GROVE Chardonnay Carneros 1989 $14 (7/15/91)
86 SEQUOIA GROVE Chardonnay Carneros 1988 Rel: $14 Cur: $14 (CH-5/90)
89 SEQUOIA GROVE Chardonnay Carneros 1988 Rel: $14 Cur: $14 (4/30/90)
83 SEQUOIA GROVE Chardonnay Carneros 1987 Rel: $14 Cur: $15 (CH-5/90)
79 SEQUOIA GROVE Chardonnay Carneros 1987 Rel: $14 Cur: $15 (6/15/89)
78 SEQUOIA GROVE Chardonnay Carneros 1986 Rel: $13 Cur: $16 (CH-5/90)
79 SEQUOIA GROVE Chardonnay Carneros 1986 Rel: $13 Cur: $16 (8/31/88)
88 SEQUOIA GROVE Chardonnay Carneros 1985 Rel: $12 Cur: $16 (CH-5/90)
79 SEQUOIA GROVE Chardonnay Carneros 1985 Rel: $12 Cur: $16 (11/15/87)
87 SEQUOIA GROVE Chardonnay Napa Valley 1984 $10 (4/30/87)
85 SEQUOIA GROVE Chardonnay Napa Valley Estate 1989 $16 (7/15/91)
92 SEQUOIA GROVE Chardonnay Napa Valley Estate 1988 Rel: $16 Cur: $16 (CH-5/90)
91 SEQUOIA GROVE Chardonnay Napa Valley Estate 1988 Rel: $16 Cur: $16 (4/30/90)
88 SEQUOIA GROVE Chardonnay Napa Valley Estate 1987 Rel: $16 Cur: $16 (CH-5/90)
87 SEQUOIA GROVE Chardonnay Napa Valley Estate 1987 Rel: $12 Cur: $12 (2/15/89)
88 SEQUOIA GROVE Chardonnay Napa Valley Estate 1986 Rel: $15 Cur: $15 (CH-5/90)
90 SEQUOIA GROVE Chardonnay Napa Valley Estate 1986 Rel: $15 Cur: $15 (9/30/88)
89 SEQUOIA GROVE Chardonnay Napa Valley Estate 1985 Rel: $16 Cur: $16 (CH-5/90)
87 SEQUOIA GROVE Chardonnay Napa Valley Estate 1985 Rel: $14 Cur: $14 (11/15/87)
89 SEQUOIA GROVE Chardonnay Napa Valley Estate 1984 Rel: $14 Cur: $14 (CH-5/90)
90 SEQUOIA GROVE Chardonnay Napa Valley Estate 1984 Rel: $14 Cur: $14 (2/15/87)
87 SEQUOIA GROVE Chardonnay Napa Valley Estate 1983 Rel: $12 Cur: $12 (CH-5/90)
72 SEQUOIA GROVE Chardonnay Napa Valley Estate 1982 Rel: $12 Cur: $12 (CH-5/90)
78 SEQUOIA GROVE Chardonnay Napa Valley Estate 1982 Rel: $12 Cur: $12 (11/01/84)
88 SEQUOIA GROVE Chardonnay Napa Valley Estate 1981 Rel: $12 Cur: $12 (CH-7/90)
87 SEQUOIA GROVE Chardonnay Napa Valley Estate 1980 Rel: $10 Cur: $10 (CH-5/90)
86 SEQUOIA GROVE Chardonnay Sonoma County 1982 $10.50 (11/01/84)
76 SHADOWBROOK Chardonnay Napa Valley 1989 $9.50 (7/15/91)
84 SHAFER Chardonnay Napa Valley 1989 $15 (4/30/91)
83 SHAFER Chardonnay Napa Valley 1988 $13.50 (5/31/90)
79 SHAFER Chardonnay Napa Valley 1987 $13.50 (4/15/89)
89 SHAFER Chardonnay Napa Valley 1986 $12 (7/15/88)
67 SHAFER Chardonnay Napa Valley 1985 $11.50 (1/31/88)
66 SHAFER Chardonnay Napa Valley 1984 $12 (10/31/86)
80 SHAFER Chardonnay Napa Valley 1983 $12 (9/01/85)

UNITED STATES
CALIFORNIA/*CHARDONNAY*

79 SHAFER Chardonnay Napa Valley 1982 $11 (10/01/84)
64 SHAFER Chardonnay Napa Valley 1981 $11 (3/16/84)
85 CHARLES SHAW Chardonnay Napa Valley 1988 Rel: $11 Cur: $11 (8/31/90)
86 CHARLES SHAW Chardonnay Napa Valley 1988 Rel: $11 Cur: $11 (CH-5/90)
85 CHARLES SHAW Chardonnay Napa Valley 1987 Rel: $11 Cur: $11 (CH-5/90)
85 CHARLES SHAW Chardonnay Napa Valley 1986 Rel: $11 Cur: $11 (CH-5/90)
86 CHARLES SHAW Chardonnay Napa Valley 1986 Rel: $11 Cur: $11 (7/15/88)
87 CHARLES SHAW Chardonnay Napa Valley 1985 Rel: $12 Cur: $15 (CH-5/90)
92 CHARLES SHAW Chardonnay Napa Valley 1985 Rel: $12 Cur: $15 (7/15/87)
82 CHARLES SHAW Chardonnay Napa Valley 1984 Rel: $12 Cur: $15 (CH-5/90)
83 CHARLES SHAW Chardonnay Napa Valley 1984 Rel: $12 Cur: $15 (1/31/87)
84 CHARLES SHAW Chardonnay Napa Valley 1983 Rel: $12 Cur: $16 (CH-5/90)
85 SIGNORELLO Chardonnay Napa Valley 1989 $15 (7/15/91)
87 SIGNORELLO Chardonnay Napa Valley 1988 $14.50 (2/28/91)
78 SIGNORELLO Chardonnay Napa Valley Founder's Reserve 1989 $25 (7/15/91)
77 SIGNORELLO Chardonnay Napa Valley Founder's Reserve 1986 $13 (7/15/89)
82 SIGNORELLO Chardonnay Napa Valley Founder's Reserve 1985 $12 (2/15/88)
86 SILVERADO Chardonnay Napa Valley 1989 $14.50 (3/31/91)
88 SILVERADO Chardonnay Napa Valley 1988 Rel: $14 Cur: $15 (CH-3/90)
88 SILVERADO Chardonnay Napa Valley 1988 Rel: $14 Cur: $15 (11/30/89)
88 SILVERADO Chardonnay Napa Valley 1987 Rel: $13.50 Cur: $15 (CH-3/90)
89 SILVERADO Chardonnay Napa Valley 1987 Rel: $13.50 Cur: $15 (12/31/88)
90 SILVERADO Chardonnay Napa Valley 1986 Rel: $12 Cur: $16 (CH-3/90)
92 SILVERADO Chardonnay Napa Valley 1986 Rel: $12 Cur: $16 (4/30/88)
87 SILVERADO Chardonnay Napa Valley 1985 Rel: $11.50 Cur: $17 (CH-3/90)
88 SILVERADO Chardonnay Napa Valley 1985 Rel: $11.50 Cur: $17 (2/28/87)
81 SILVERADO Chardonnay Napa Valley 1984 Rel: $11 Cur: $18 (CH-3/90)
83 SILVERADO Chardonnay Napa Valley 1984 Rel: $11 Cur: $18 (6/16/86)
84 SILVERADO Chardonnay Napa Valley 1983 Rel: $11 Cur: $20 (CH-3/90)
90 SILVERADO Chardonnay Napa Valley 1983 Rel: $11 Cur: $20 (7/16/85)
73 SILVERADO Chardonnay Napa Valley 1982 Rel: $10 Cur: $20 (CH-3/90)
85 SILVERADO Chardonnay Napa Valley 1982 Rel: $10 Cur: $20 (3/16/84)
70 SILVERADO Chardonnay Napa Valley 1981 Rel: $10 Cur: $20 (CH-3/90)
92 SILVERADO Chardonnay Napa Valley Limited Reserve 1987 $30 (CH-7/90)
93 SILVERADO Chardonnay Napa Valley Limited Reserve 1986 $25 (11/15/90)
90 SILVERADO Chardonnay Napa Valley Limited Reserve 1986 $25 (CH-7/90)
90 SILVERADO CELLARS Chardonnay California 1988 $11 (6/30/90)
82 SILVERADO HILL CELLARS Chardonnay Napa Valley 1989 $10 (7/15/91)
73 SILVERADO HILL CELLARS Chardonnay Napa Valley Winemaker's Traditional Méthode 1988 $10 (7/15/91)
88 SIMI Chardonnay Mendocino-Sonoma-Napa Counties 1989 $15.50 (5/31/91)
87 SIMI Chardonnay Sonoma County 1988 $16 (6/15/90)
91 SIMI Chardonnay Mendocino-Sonoma-Napa Counties 1987 $14 (11/30/89)
84 SIMI Chardonnay Mendocino-Sonoma-Napa Counties 1986 $12 (2/15/89)
89 SIMI Chardonnay Mendocino-Sonoma Counties 1985 $11 (3/15/88)
77 SIMI Chardonnay Mendocino-Sonoma Counties 1984 $13 (10/31/86)
87 SIMI Chardonnay Mendocino-Sonoma Counties 1983 $12 (10/01/85)
90 SIMI Chardonnay Sonoma County 1982 $11 (10/16/84)
86 SIMI Chardonnay Mendocino County 1981 $11 (6/01/86)
90 SIMI Chardonnay Sonoma County 1981 $20 (11/01/85)
91 SIMI Chardonnay Sonoma County Reserve 1988 (NR) (CH-7/90)
92 SIMI Chardonnay Sonoma County Reserve 1987 $32 (7/15/91)
94 SIMI Chardonnay Sonoma County Reserve 1987 Rel: $32 Cur: $32 (CH-4/90)
92 SIMI Chardonnay Sonoma County Reserve 1986 Rel: $28 Cur: $33 (9/15/90)
92 SIMI Chardonnay Sonoma County Reserve 1986 Rel: $28 Cur: $33 (CH-4/90)
91 SIMI Chardonnay Sonoma County Reserve 1985 Rel: $28 Cur: $32 (CH-4/90)
89 SIMI Chardonnay Sonoma County Reserve 1984 Rel: $28 Cur: $32 (CH-4/90)
90 SIMI Chardonnay Sonoma County Reserve 1984 Rel: $28 Cur: $32 (8/31/88)
88 SIMI Chardonnay Sonoma County Reserve 1983 Rel: $22 Cur: $32 (CH-4/90)
91 SIMI Chardonnay Sonoma County Reserve 1983 Rel: $22 Cur: $32 (8/31/87)
94 SIMI Chardonnay Sonoma County Reserve 1982 Rel: $22 Cur: $60 (CH-4/90)
96 SIMI Chardonnay Sonoma County Reserve 1982 Rel: $22 Cur: $60 (5/01/86) SS
91 SIMI Chardonnay Sonoma County Reserve 1981 Rel: $20 Cur: $40 (CH-4/90)
89 SIMI Chardonnay Sonoma County Reserve 1981 Rel: $20 Cur: $40 (6/01/86)
94 SIMI Chardonnay Sonoma County Reserve 1980 Rel: $20 Cur: $40 (CH-4/90)
93 SIMI Chardonnay Mendocino County Reserve 1980 Rel: $20 Cur: $40 (4/16/84)
87 ROBERT SINSKEY Chardonnay Carneros 1988 $16 (2/28/91)
88 ROBERT SINSKEY Chardonnay Carneros Napa Valley 1987 $16 (10/31/89)
75 ROBERT SINSKEY Chardonnay Carneros Napa Valley 1986 $16.50 (7/31/88)
84 ROBERT SINSKEY Chardonnay Carneros Napa Valley Selected Cuvée 1989 $16 (7/15/91)
88 SMITH-MADRONE Chardonnay Napa Valley 1988 Rel: $13 Cur: $13 (CH-5/90)
91 SMITH-MADRONE Chardonnay Napa Valley 1987 Rel: $13 Cur: $13 (CH-5/90)
89 SMITH-MADRONE Chardonnay Napa Valley 1986 Rel: $12.50 Cur: $16 (CH-5/90)
87 SMITH-MADRONE Chardonnay Napa Valley 1985 Rel: $12.50 Cur: $16 (CH-5/90)
93 SMITH-MADRONE Chardonnay Napa Valley 1985 Rel: $12.50 Cur: $16 (6/15/87)
80 SMITH-MADRONE Chardonnay Napa Valley 1984 Rel: $12 Cur: $16 (CH-5/90)
73 SMITH-MADRONE Chardonnay Napa Valley 1984 Rel: $12 Cur: $16 (10/31/86)
71 SMITH-MADRONE Chardonnay Napa Valley 1983 Rel: $12 Cur: $15 (CH-5/90)
86 SMITH-MADRONE Chardonnay Napa Valley 1982 Rel: $12 Cur: $18 (CH-5/90)
81 SMITH-MADRONE Chardonnay Napa Valley 1981 Rel: $12 Cur: $18 (CH-5/90)
85 SMITH-MADRONE Chardonnay Napa Valley 1980 Rel: $11 Cur: $20 (CH-5/90)
92 SMITH-MADRONE Chardonnay Napa Valley 1979 Rel: $10 Cur: $28 (CH-5/90)
86 SMITH-MADRONE Chardonnay Napa Valley 1978 Rel: $10 Cur: $30 (CH-5/90)
78 SODA CANYON Chardonnay Napa Valley 8th Leaf 1986 $11 (10/15/88)

Key to Symbols

The scores reported here are the results of blind tastings conducted by our panel of senior editors. Wines that carry the initials below are results of individual tastings.

THE WINE SPECTATOR 100-POINT SCALE *95-100*—Classic, a great wine; *90-94*—Outstanding, superior character and style; *80-89*—Good to very good, a wine with special qualities; *70-79*—Average, drinkable wine that may have minor flaws; *60-69*—Below average, drinkable but not recommended; *50-59*—Poor, undrinkable, not recommended. "+"—With a score indicates a range; used primarily with barrel tastings to indicate a preliminary score.

SPECIAL DESIGNATIONS SS—Spectator Selection, CS—Cellar Selection, BB—Best Buy.

TASTER'S INITIALS (JG)—Jim Gordon, (HS)—Harvey Steiman, (JL)—James Laube, (JS)—James Suckling, (TM)—Thomas Matthews, (TR)—Terry Robards, (BT)—Barrel Tasting (these wines were tasted blind from barrel samples), (CA-date)—*California's Great Cabernets* by James Laube, (CH-date)—*California's Great Chardonnays* by James Laube, (VP-date)—*Vintage Port* by James Suckling.

DATE TASTED Dates in parentheses represent the issue in which the rating was published.

76 SOLIS Chardonnay Santa Clara County 1989 $12.50 (7/15/91)
71 SONOMA CREEK Chardonnay Carneros Barrel Fermented 1989 $10 (2/28/91)
89 SONOMA-CUTRER Chardonnay Sonoma Coast Cutrer Vineyard 1988 $17.50 (12/31/90)
92 SONOMA-CUTRER Chardonnay Sonoma Coast Cutrer Vineyard 1988 Rel: $17.50 Cur: $21 (CH-7/90)
91 SONOMA-CUTRER Chardonnay Sonoma Coast Cutrer Vineyard 1987 Rel: $17.50 Cur: $23 (CH-3/90)
68 SONOMA-CUTRER Chardonnay Sonoma Coast Cutrer Vineyard 1987 Rel: $17.50 Cur: $23 (11/30/89)
89 SONOMA-CUTRER Chardonnay Sonoma Coast Cutrer Vineyard 1986 Rel: $16 Cur: $23 (CH-3/90)
70 SONOMA-CUTRER Chardonnay Sonoma Coast Cutrer Vineyard 1986 Rel: $16 Cur: $23 (10/15/88)
87 SONOMA-CUTRER Chardonnay Russian River Valley Cutrer Vineyard 1985 Rel: $14.75 Cur: $29 (CH-3/90)
89 SONOMA-CUTRER Chardonnay Russian River Valley Cutrer Vineyard 1985 Rel: $14.75 Cur: $29 (9/15/87)
87 SONOMA-CUTRER Chardonnay Russian River Valley Cutrer Vineyard 1984 Rel: $14.25 Cur: $25 (CH-3/90)
75 SONOMA-CUTRER Chardonnay Russian River Valley Cutrer Vineyard 1984 Rel: $14.25 Cur: $25 (10/31/86)
86 SONOMA-CUTRER Chardonnay Russian River Valley Cutrer Vineyard 1983 Rel: $13.75 Cur: $25 (CH-3/90)
87 SONOMA-CUTRER Chardonnay Russian River Valley Cutrer Vineyard 1982 Rel: $13 Cur: $25 (CH-3/90)
79 SONOMA-CUTRER Chardonnay Russian River Valley Cutrer Vineyard 1982 Rel: $13 Cur: $25 (12/01/84)
91 SONOMA-CUTRER Chardonnay Russian River Valley Cutrer Vineyard 1981 Rel: $12.50 Cur: $30 (CH-3/90)
80 SONOMA-CUTRER Chardonnay Russian River Valley Cutrer Vineyard 1981 Rel: $12.50 Cur: $30 (3/01/84)
86 SONOMA-CUTRER Chardonnay Sonoma Coast Les Pierres 1989 $23 (1/31/91)
93 SONOMA-CUTRER Chardonnay Sonoma Coast Les Pierres 1988 Rel: $22.50 Cur: $23 (CH-7/90)
92 SONOMA-CUTRER Chardonnay Sonoma Coast Les Pierres 1987 Rel: $22.50 Cur: $27 (CH-3/90)
83 SONOMA-CUTRER Chardonnay Sonoma Coast Les Pierres 1987 Rel: $22.50 Cur: $27 (1/31/90)
88 SONOMA-CUTRER Chardonnay Sonoma Valley Les Pierres 1986 Rel: $19.50 Cur: $28 (CH-3/90)
86 SONOMA-CUTRER Chardonnay Sonoma Valley Les Pierres 1986 Rel: $19.50 Cur: $28 (10/15/88)
92 SONOMA-CUTRER Chardonnay Sonoma Valley Les Pierres 1985 Rel: $17.50 Cur: $30 (CH-3/90)
93 SONOMA-CUTRER Chardonnay Sonoma Valley Les Pierres 1985 Rel: $17.50 Cur: $30 (9/30/87) SS
89 SONOMA-CUTRER Chardonnay Sonoma Valley Les Pierres 1984 Rel: $16.50 Cur: $30 (CH-3/90)
86 SONOMA-CUTRER Chardonnay Sonoma Valley Les Pierres 1983 Rel: $15.50 Cur: $50 (CH-3/90)
88 SONOMA-CUTRER Chardonnay Sonoma Valley Les Pierres 1982 Rel: $15 Cur: $35 (CH-3/90)
94 SONOMA-CUTRER Chardonnay Sonoma Valley Les Pierres 1981 Rel: $14.50 Cur: $53 (CH-3/90)
82 SONOMA-CUTRER Chardonnay Sonoma Coast Russian River Ranches 1989 $14 (7/15/91)
88 SONOMA-CUTRER Chardonnay Sonoma Coast Russian River Ranches 1988 Rel: $13.25 Cur: $14 (6/30/90)
91 SONOMA-CUTRER Chardonnay Sonoma Coast Russian River Ranches 1988 Rel: $13.25 Cur: $14 (CH-3/90)
88 SONOMA-CUTRER Chardonnay Sonoma Coast Russian River Ranches 1987 Rel: $12 Cur: $16 (CH-3/90)
83 SONOMA-CUTRER Chardonnay Sonoma Coast Russian River Ranches 1987 Rel: $12 Cur: $16 (5/31/89)
86 SONOMA-CUTRER Chardonnay Russian River Valley Russian River Ranches 1986 Rel: $12 Cur: $18 (CH-3/90)
87 SONOMA-CUTRER Chardonnay Russian River Valley Russian River Ranches 1986 Rel: $12 Cur: $18 (4/30/88)
88 SONOMA-CUTRER Chardonnay Russian River Valley Russian River Ranches 1985 Rel: $11.50 Cur: $23 (CH-3/90)
93 SONOMA-CUTRER Chardonnay Russian River Valley Russian River Ranches 1985 Rel: $11.50 Cur: $23 (4/15/87)
88 SONOMA-CUTRER Chardonnay Russian River Valley Russian River Ranches 1984 Rel: $11.25 Cur: $12 (6/01/86)
85 SONOMA-CUTRER Chardonnay Russian River Valley Russian River Ranches 1983 Rel: $10.50 Cur: $25 (CH-3/90)
95 SONOMA-CUTRER Chardonnay Russian River Valley Russian River Ranches 1983 Rel: $10.50 Cur: $25 (11/16/85) SS
87 SONOMA-CUTRER Chardonnay Russian River Valley Russian River Ranches 1982 Rel: $10 Cur: $24 (CH-3/90)
92 SONOMA-CUTRER Chardonnay Russian River Valley Russian River Ranches 1982 Rel: $10 Cur: $24 (10/16/84) SS
82 SONOMA-CUTRER Chardonnay Russian River Valley Russian River Ranches 1981 Rel: $9.35 Cur: $40 (CH-3/90)
89 SONOMA-CUTRER Chardonnay Russian River Valley Estate Bottled 1981 Rel: $9.35 Cur: $40 (3/01/84)
81 SPRING MOUNTAIN Chardonnay Napa Valley 1987 $15 (11/15/89)
82 SPRING MOUNTAIN Chardonnay Napa Valley 1985 $15 (11/15/87)
58 SPRING MOUNTAIN Chardonnay Napa Valley 1984 $15 (12/31/86)
91 STAG'S LEAP WINE CELLARS Chardonnay Napa Valley Beckstoffer Ranch 1987 $19 (9/15/89)
88 STAG'S LEAP WINE CELLARS Chardonnay Napa Valley 1989 $18 (1/31/91)
87 STAG'S LEAP WINE CELLARS Chardonnay Napa Valley 1988 Rel: $18 Cur: $18 (CH-3/90)
87 STAG'S LEAP WINE CELLARS Chardonnay Napa Valley 1988 Rel: $18 Cur: $18 (2/15/90)
89 STAG'S LEAP WINE CELLARS Chardonnay Napa Valley 1987 Rel: $18 Cur: $18 (CH-3/90)
91 STAG'S LEAP WINE CELLARS Chardonnay Napa Valley 1987 Rel: $18 Cur: $18 (12/31/88)
86 STAG'S LEAP WINE CELLARS Chardonnay Napa Valley 1986 Rel: $17 Cur: $20 (CH-3/90)
91 STAG'S LEAP WINE CELLARS Chardonnay Napa Valley 1986 Rel: $17 Cur: $20 (7/15/88)
83 STAG'S LEAP WINE CELLARS Chardonnay Napa Valley 1985 Rel: $16 Cur: $25 (CH-3/90)
77 STAG'S LEAP WINE CELLARS Chardonnay Napa Valley 1984 Rel: $14 Cur: $17 (CH-6/90)
70 STAG'S LEAP WINE CELLARS Chardonnay Napa Valley 1984 Rel: $14 Cur: $17 (10/31/86)

62 STAG'S LEAP WINE CELLARS Chardonnay Napa Valley 1983 Rel: $13.50 Cur: $17 (CH-3/90)
64 STAG'S LEAP WINE CELLARS Chardonnay Napa Valley 1983 Rel: $13.50 Cur: $17 (11/16/85)
70 STAG'S LEAP WINE CELLARS Chardonnay Napa Valley 1982 Rel: $13.50 Cur: $17 (CH-3/90)
80 STAG'S LEAP WINE CELLARS Chardonnay Napa Valley 1982 Rel: $13.50 Cur: $17 (4/16/84)
79 STAG'S LEAP WINE CELLARS Chardonnay Napa Valley 1981 Rel: $13.50 Cur: $60 (CH-3/90)
78 STAG'S LEAP WINE CELLARS Chardonnay Napa Valley 1980 Rel: $10.50 Cur: $17 (CH-3/90)
59 STAG'S LEAP WINE CELLARS Chardonnay Napa Valley 1977 Rel: $8 Cur: $17 (CH-3/90)
58 STAG'S LEAP WINE CELLARS Chardonnay Napa Valley 1976 Rel: $8 Cur: $17 (CH-3/90)
82 STAG'S LEAP WINE CELLARS Chardonnay Napa Valley Haynes 1979 $12.50 (CH-3/90)
74 STAG'S LEAP WINE CELLARS Chardonnay Napa Valley Haynes 1978 $10 (CH-3/90)
67 STAG'S LEAP WINE CELLARS Chardonnay Napa Valley Haynes 1977 $9 (CH-3/90)
70 STAG'S LEAP WINE CELLARS Chardonnay Napa Valley Mirage 1982 $11.50 (CH-3/90)
90 STAG'S LEAP WINE CELLARS Chardonnay Napa Valley Reserve 1988 $28 (1/31/91)
90 STAG'S LEAP WINE CELLARS Chardonnay Napa Valley Reserve 1988 Rel: $28 Cur: $28 (CH-3/90)
88 STAG'S LEAP WINE CELLARS Chardonnay Napa Valley Reserve 1987 Rel: $28 Cur: $32 (5/31/90)
89 STAG'S LEAP WINE CELLARS Chardonnay Napa Valley Reserve 1987 Rel: $28 Cur: $32 (CH-3/90)
88 STAG'S LEAP WINE CELLARS Chardonnay Napa Valley Reserve 1986 Rel: $26 Cur: $26 (CH-6/90)
91 STAG'S LEAP WINE CELLARS Chardonnay Napa Valley Reserve 1986 Rel: $26 Cur: $26 (10/15/88)
85 STAG'S LEAP WINE CELLARS Chardonnay Napa Valley Reserve 1985 Rel: $22 Cur: $26 (CH-3/90)
86 STAG'S LEAP WINE CELLARS Chardonnay Napa Valley Reserve 1985 Rel: $22 Cur: $26 (12/15/87)
78 STAR HILL Chardonnay Napa Valley Barrel Fermented 1989 $19 (7/15/91)
84 STAR HILL Chardonnay Napa Valley Doc's Reserve Barrel Fermented 1988 $19 (6/30/90)
75 DAVID S. STARE Chardonnay Dry Creek Valley 1982 $15 (11/01/85)
82 DAVID S. STARE Chardonnay Dry Creek Valley Reserve 1985 $15 (10/15/88)
75 DAVID S. STARE Chardonnay Dry Creek Valley Reserve 1984 $15 (12/31/86)
83 STERLING Chardonnay Carneros Winery Lake 1989 $18 (7/15/91)
87 STERLING Chardonnay Carneros Winery Lake 1988 $20 (7/15/91)
91 STERLING Chardonnay Carneros Winery Lake 1988 Rel: $20 Cur: $20 (6/15/90)
90 STERLING Chardonnay Carneros Winery Lake 1988 Rel: $20 Cur: $20 (CH-4/90)
89 STERLING Chardonnay Carneros Winery Lake 1987 Rel: $20 Cur: $20 (CH-4/90)
85 STERLING Chardonnay Carneros Winery Lake 1987 Rel: $20 Cur: $20 (6/30/89)
89 STERLING Chardonnay Carneros Winery Lake 1986 Rel: $20 Cur: $23 (CH-4/90)
91 STERLING Chardonnay Carneros Winery Lake 1986 Rel: $20 Cur: $23 (7/15/88)
88 STERLING Chardonnay Napa Valley Estate 1989 $15 (4/30/91)
90 STERLING Chardonnay Napa Valley Estate 1988 Rel: $13 Cur: $19 (3/15/90)
89 STERLING Chardonnay Napa Valley Estate 1987 Rel: $14.50 Cur: $20 (4/15/89)
83 STERLING Chardonnay Napa Valley Estate 1986 Rel: $14.50 Cur: $16 (3/15/88)
69 STERLING Chardonnay Napa Valley Estate 1985 Rel: $14 Cur: $14 (7/31/87)
77 STERLING Chardonnay Napa Valley Estate 1984 Rel: $14 Cur: $14 (6/16/86)
86 STERLING Chardonnay Napa Valley Estate 1983 Rel: $14 Cur: $14 (10/01/85)
73 STERLING Chardonnay Napa Valley Estate 1982 Rel: $14 Cur: $17 (CH-4/90)
78 STERLING Chardonnay Napa Valley Estate 1982 Rel: $14 Cur: $17 (11/01/84)
71 STERLING Chardonnay Napa Valley Estate 1981 Rel: $14 Cur: $17 (CH-4/90)
70 STERLING Chardonnay Napa Valley Estate 1980 Rel: $13 Cur: $17 (CH-4/90)
73 STERLING Chardonnay Napa Valley Estate 1979 Rel: $13 Cur: $38 (CH-4/90)
70 STERLING Chardonnay Napa Valley Estate 1977 Rel: $10 Cur: $31 (CH-4/90)
59 STERLING Chardonnay Napa Valley Estate 1976 Rel: $5.25 Cur: $18 (CH-4/90)
78 STERLING Chardonnay Napa Valley Estate 1974 Rel: $4.75 Cur: $35 (CH-4/90)
85 STERLING Chardonnay Napa Valley Diamond Mountain Ranch 1988 $16 (7/15/91)
91 STERLING Chardonnay Napa Valley Diamond Mountain Ranch 1988 $16 (CH-7/90)
84 STERLING Chardonnay Napa Valley Diamond Mountain Ranch 1987 $16 (2/28/91)
88 STERLING Chardonnay Napa Valley Diamond Mountain Ranch 1987 $16 (CH-7/90)
86 STERLING Chardonnay Napa Valley Diamond Mountain Ranch 1986 Rel: $15 Cur: $15 (CH-4/90)
80 STERLING Chardonnay Napa Valley Diamond Mountain Ranch 1986 Rel: $15 Cur: $15 (6/15/89)
87 STERLING Chardonnay Napa Valley Diamond Mountain Ranch 1985 Rel: $15 Cur: $17 (CH-7/90)
73 STERLING Chardonnay Napa Valley Diamond Mountain Ranch 1985 Rel: $15 Cur: $17 (9/15/88)
86 STERLING Chardonnay Napa Valley Diamond Mountain Ranch 1984 Rel: $15 Cur: $17 (CH-4/90)
78 STERLING Chardonnay Napa Valley Diamond Mountain Ranch 1984 Rel: $15 Cur: $17 (8/31/87)
86 STERLING Chardonnay Napa Valley Diamond Mountain Ranch 1983 Rel: $15 Cur: $18 (CH-4/90)
80 STERLING Chardonnay Napa Valley Diamond Mountain Ranch 1983 Rel: $15 Cur: $18 (12/15/86)
83 STEVENOT Chardonnay California 1987 $7.50 (6/30/89)
79 STEVENOT Chardonnay California 1986 $6 (11/15/87)
86 STONE CREEK Chardonnay Alexander Valley 1989 $10 (7/15/91)
70 STONE CREEK Chardonnay Alexander Valley Special Selection 1982 $6 (2/15/84)
78 STONE CREEK Chardonnay Napa Valley Special Selection 1989 $10 (7/15/91)
68 STONE CREEK Chardonnay North Coast 1988 $7 (6/30/90)
83 STONEGATE Chardonnay Napa Valley 1988 $15 (4/15/91)
90 STONEGATE Chardonnay Napa Valley Reserve 1988 $20 (2/15/91)
86 STONEGATE Chardonnay Napa Valley Spaulding Vineyard 1983 $14 (2/15/87)
53 STONEGATE Chardonnay Napa Valley Spaulding Vineyard 1982 $14 (12/01/85)
73 STONEGATE Chardonnay Napa Valley 1988 $15 (2/15/91)
78 STONEGATE Chardonnay Napa Valley 1987 $13 (6/30/90)
89 STONEGATE Chardonnay Napa Valley 1986 $13 (12/31/88)
83 STONEGATE Chardonnay Napa Valley 1982 $10 (3/01/85)
90 STONY HILL Chardonnay Napa Valley 1988 Rel: $18 Cur: $90 (CH-6/90)
87 STONY HILL Chardonnay Napa Valley 1987 Rel: $18 Cur: $62 (CH-5/90)
87 STONY HILL Chardonnay Napa Valley 1986 Rel: $16 Cur: $68 (CH-7/90)
92 STONY HILL Chardonnay Napa Valley 1985 Rel: $16 Cur: $71 (CH-5/90)
90 STONY HILL Chardonnay Napa Valley 1984 Rel: $13 Cur: $70 (CH-5/90)
85 STONY HILL Chardonnay Napa Valley 1983 Rel: $13 Cur: $71 (CH-5/90)
85 STONY HILL Chardonnay Napa Valley 1982 Rel: $12 Cur: $66 (CH-5/90)
86 STONY HILL Chardonnay Napa Valley 1981 Rel: $12 Cur: $76 (CH-5/90)
86 STONY HILL Chardonnay Napa Valley 1980 Rel: $12 Cur: $83 (CH-5/90)
81 STONY HILL Chardonnay Napa Valley 1979 Rel: $12 Cur: $95 (CH-5/90)
85 STONY HILL Chardonnay Napa Valley 1978 Rel: $10 Cur: $101 (CH-5/90)
91 STONY HILL Chardonnay Napa Valley 1977 Rel: $9 Cur: $95 (CH-6/90)
88 STONY HILL Chardonnay Napa Valley 1976 Rel: $9 Cur: $127 (CH-6/90)
75 STONY HILL Chardonnay Napa Valley 1975 Rel: $9 Cur: $150 (CH-5/90)
73 STONY HILL Chardonnay Napa Valley 1974 Rel: $7 Cur: $112 (CH-5/90)
79 STONY HILL Chardonnay Napa Valley 1973 Rel: $7 Cur: $120 (CH-5/90)
83 STONY HILL Chardonnay Napa Valley 1972 Rel: $7 Cur: $110 (CH-5/90)
80 STONY HILL Chardonnay Napa Valley 1971 Rel: $6 Cur: $110 (CH-5/90)
92 STONY HILL Chardonnay Napa Valley 1970 Rel: $6 Cur: $175 (CH-5/90)
85 STONY HILL Chardonnay Napa Valley 1969 Rel: $5 Cur: $175 (CH-5/90)
93 STONY HILL Chardonnay Napa Valley 1968 Rel: $5 Cur: $250 (CH-5/90)
83 STONY HILL Chardonnay Napa Valley 1967 Rel: $4.50 Cur: $320 (CH-5/90)
91 STONY HILL Chardonnay Napa Valley 1966 Rel: $4.50 Cur: $300 (CH-5/90)
90 STONY HILL Chardonnay Napa Valley 1965 Rel: $4 Cur: $420 (CH-5/90)
98 STONY HILL Chardonnay Napa Valley 1964 Rel: $4 Cur: $460 (CH-5/90)
87 STONY HILL Chardonnay Napa Valley 1963 Rel: $4 Cur: $460 (CH-5/90)
96 STONY HILL Chardonnay Napa Valley 1962 Rel: $3.25 Cur: $460 (CH-5/90)
88 STONY HILL Chardonnay Napa Valley 1960 Rel: $3 Cur: $440 (CH-5/90)
81 STONY HILL Chardonnay Napa Valley SHV 1988 $18 (6/30/90)
84 STONY HILL Chardonnay Napa Valley SHV 1987 $18 (4/15/89)
76 STORRS Chardonnay Santa Cruz Mountains 1989 $11.50 (7/15/91)
86 STORRS Chardonnay Santa Cruz Mountains Gaspar Vineyard 1989 $16 (7/15/91)
83 STORRS Chardonnay Santa Cruz Mountains Meyley Vineyard 1989 $16 (7/15/91)
71 STORRS Chardonnay Santa Cruz Mountains Vanumanutagi Vineyards 1989 $14 (7/15/91)
87 STRATFORD Chardonnay California 1989 $10 (7/15/91) BB
75 STRATFORD Chardonnay California 1987 $10 (7/15/89)
89 STRATFORD Chardonnay California 1986 $9.50 (2/29/88)
80 STRATFORD Chardonnay California 1985 $9 (2/28/87)
71 STRATFORD Chardonnay California 1984 $8.50 (2/01/86)
80 STRATFORD Chardonnay California 1983 $8.50 (11/01/84)
88 STRATFORD Chardonnay California Partners' Reserve 1988 $14.50 (6/30/90)
82 STRATFORD Chardonnay California Partners' Reserve 1987 $15 (7/15/89)
76 STRATFORD Chardonnay California Partners' Reserve 1986 $14.50 (12/31/88)
68 RODNEY STRONG Chardonnay Russian River Valley River West Vineyard 1984 $10 (3/15/87)
86 RODNEY STRONG Chardonnay Sonoma County 1989 $9 (7/15/91) BB
80 RODNEY STRONG Chardonnay Sonoma County 1987 $6.50 (10/15/88)
85 RODNEY STRONG Chardonnay Sonoma County 1986 $7 (12/15/87) BB
78 RODNEY STRONG Chardonnay Sonoma County 1983 $8 (11/01/84)
79 RODNEY STRONG Chardonnay Sonoma County Chalk Hill Vineyard 1988 $12 (3/31/91)
90 RODNEY STRONG Chardonnay Sonoma County Chalk Hill Vineyard 1987 $12 (2/15/91)
72 RODNEY STRONG Chardonnay Sonoma County Chalk Hill Vineyard 1985 $10 (12/31/87)
73 RODNEY STRONG Chardonnay Sonoma County Chalk Hill Vineyard 1983 $10 (1/31/87)
79 RODNEY STRONG Chardonnay Sonoma County Chalk Hill Vineyard 1982 $9.95 (7/01/84)
78 SUNNY ST. HELENA Chardonnay California 1989 $12 (4/30/91)
65 SUNNY ST. HELENA Chardonnay Napa Valley 1986 $9 (10/31/87)
80 SUTTER HOME Chardonnay California 1989 $5 (11/15/90) BB
73 JOSEPH SWAN Chardonnay Sonoma Coast 1986 $18 (7/15/88)
77 JOSEPH SWAN Chardonnay Sonoma Coast Russian River Valley 1989 $20 (5/31/91)
84 SWANSON Chardonnay Napa Valley 1989 $15 (7/15/91)
79 SWANSON Chardonnay Napa Valley 1988 $14.50 (6/30/90)
90 SWANSON Chardonnay Napa Valley Reserve 1988 $19 (7/15/91)
68 SYLVAN SPRINGS Chardonnay California Vintner's Reserve 1986 $5 (9/30/88)
83 TAFT STREET Chardonnay Russian River Valley 1988 $12 (7/15/91)
86 TAFT STREET Chardonnay Russian River Valley 1986 $10 (12/31/88)
86 TAFT STREET Chardonnay Sonoma County 1989 $8.50 (7/15/91) BB
79 TAFT STREET Chardonnay Sonoma County 1988 $8 (1/31/90)
84 TAFT STREET Chardonnay Sonoma County 1987 $7.50 (10/15/88)
78 TAFT STREET Chardonnay Sonoma County 1986 $7 (11/15/87)
84 TALLEY Chardonnay Arroyo Grande Valley 1989 $14.50 (7/15/91)
78 TALLEY Chardonnay San Luis Obispo County 1987 $12 (12/15/89)
75 IVAN TAMAS Chardonnay Livermore Valley 1988 $7.50 (4/30/90)
77 IVAN TAMAS Chardonnay Napa Valley-Central Coast 1986 $7 (12/31/87)
86 IVAN TAMAS Chardonnay Napa Valley Reserve 1986 $15 (9/30/88)
87 TERRA Chardonnay Napa Valley 1987 $12 (7/15/91)
89 THOMAS-HSI Chardonnay Napa Valley 1988 $18 (6/30/91)
82 THOMAS-HSI Chardonnay Napa Valley 1987 $18 (6/30/90)
73 TIFFANY HILL Chardonnay Edna Valley 1989 $18 (7/15/91)
85 TIFFANY HILL Chardonnay Edna Valley 1987 $19 (3/31/89)
90 TIFFANY HILL Chardonnay Edna Valley 1986 $19 (6/15/88)
69 TIJSSELING Chardonnay Mendocino 1989 $10 (7/15/91)
70 TIJSSELING Chardonnay Mendocino 1988 $10 (2/28/90)
71 TIN PONY Chardonnay Sonoma County Green Valley 1986 $8 (9/30/88)
90 MIRIMAR TORRES Chardonnay Sonoma County Green Valley Don Miguel Vineyard 1989 $20 (5/15/91)
85 TREFETHEN Chardonnay Napa Valley 1988 $17.50 (12/31/90)
90 TREFETHEN Chardonnay Napa Valley 1988 $17.50 (CH-3/90)
88 TREFETHEN Chardonnay Napa Valley 1987 Rel: $17 Cur: $19 (CH-3/90)
81 TREFETHEN Chardonnay Napa Valley 1987 Rel: $17 Cur: $19 (11/30/89)
87 TREFETHEN Chardonnay Napa Valley 1986 Rel: $16 Cur: $22 (CH-3/90)
87 TREFETHEN Chardonnay Napa Valley 1986 Rel: $16 Cur: $22 (12/31/88)
88 TREFETHEN Chardonnay Napa Valley 1985 Rel: $16 Cur: $25 (CH-3/90)
84 TREFETHEN Chardonnay Napa Valley 1985 Rel: $16 Cur: $25 (12/31/87)
86 TREFETHEN Chardonnay Napa Valley 1984 Rel: $14.25 Cur: $28 (CH-3/90)
81 TREFETHEN Chardonnay Napa Valley 1984 Rel: $14.25 Cur: $28 (2/28/87)
77 TREFETHEN Chardonnay Napa Valley 1983 Rel: $13.75 Cur: $35 (CH-3/90)
92 TREFETHEN Chardonnay Napa Valley 1983 Rel: $13.75 Cur: $35 (12/16/85)
73 TREFETHEN Chardonnay Napa Valley 1982 Rel: $13.50 Cur: $30 (CH-3/90)
83 TREFETHEN Chardonnay Napa Valley 1981 Rel: $13 Cur: $30 (CH-3/90)
86 TREFETHEN Chardonnay Napa Valley 1980 Rel: $13 Cur: $40 (CH-3/90)
73 TREFETHEN Chardonnay Napa Valley 1979 Rel: $12 Cur: $30 (CH-3/90)
90 TREFETHEN Chardonnay Napa Valley 1978 Rel: $10 Cur: $35 (CH-3/90)
81 TREFETHEN Chardonnay Napa Valley 1977 Rel: $8.50 Cur: $35 (CH-3/90)
74 TREFETHEN Chardonnay Napa Valley 1976 Rel: $7 Cur: $40 (CH-3/90)
73 TREFETHEN Chardonnay Napa Valley 1975 Rel: $6.50 Cur: $45 (CH-3/90)

UNITED STATES
CALIFORNIA/*CHARDONNAY*

80 TREFETHEN Chardonnay Napa Valley 1974 Rel: $5.75 Cur: $50 (CH-3/90)
85 TREFETHEN Chardonnay Napa Valley 1973 Rel: $6.50 Cur: $50 (CH-3/90)
80 TULOCAY Chardonnay Napa Valley DeCelles Vineyard 1988 $14 (4/30/91)
82 ULTRAVINO Chardonnay Napa Valley 1984 $8.50 (2/15/87)
67 VALFLEUR Chardonnay Alexander Valley Jimtown Ranch 1984 $10.50 (10/31/86)
74 M.G. VALLEJO Chardonnay California 1989 $6.50 (7/15/91)
78 M.G. VALLEJO Chardonnay California 1988 $5 (4/30/90)
74 M.G. VALLEJO Chardonnay California 1987 $5 (2/15/89)
89 VEGA Chardonnay Santa Barbara County 1986 $14 (12/15/89)
76 VENTANA Chardonnay Monterey Barrel Fermented 1987 $16 (10/31/89)
79 VENTANA Chardonnay Monterey Crystal Ventana Vineyards 1986 $16 (10/31/89)
87 VENTANA Chardonnay Monterey Gold Stripe Selection 1989 $10 (7/15/91)
81 VENTANA Chardonnay Monterey Gold Stripe Selection 1988 $10 (9/30/89)
87 VENTANA Chardonnay Monterey Gold Stripe Selection 1985 $7.50 (9/15/87) BB
69 VENTANA Chardonnay Monterey Gold Stripe Selection 1984 $8 (4/16/86)
88 VENTANA Chardonnay Monterey Ventana Vineyards Gold Stripe Selection 1987 $10 (6/30/89)
85 VIANSA Chardonnay Napa-Sonoma Counties 1988 $15 (9/15/90)
84 VIANSA Chardonnay Napa-Sonoma Counties 1987 $13 (4/15/89)
87 VIANSA Chardonnay Napa-Sonoma Counties 1986 $12.50 (3/31/88)
84 VIANSA Chardonnay Napa-Sonoma Counties Reserve 1988 $18 (11/30/90)
86 VICHON Chardonnay Napa Valley Tenth Harvest 1989 $16 (3/31/91)
88 VICHON Chardonnay Napa Valley 1988 Rel: $17 Cur: $19 (CH-3/90)
89 VICHON Chardonnay Napa Valley 1988 Rel: $17 Cur: $19 (11/15/89)
87 VICHON Chardonnay Napa Valley 1987 Rel: $16 Cur: $18 (CH-3/90)
82 VICHON Chardonnay Napa Valley 1987 Rel: $16 Cur: $18 (4/15/89)
90 VICHON Chardonnay Napa Valley 1986 Rel: $15 Cur: $17 (CH-3/90)
89 VICHON Chardonnay Napa Valley 1986 Rel: $15 Cur: $17 (9/15/88)
88 VICHON Chardonnay Napa Valley 1985 Rel: $15 Cur: $17 (CH-3/90)
73 VICHON Chardonnay Napa Valley 1985 Rel: $15 Cur: $17 (8/31/87)
86 VICHON Chardonnay Napa Valley 1984 Rel: $15 Cur: $17 (CH-3/90)
70 VICHON Chardonnay Napa Valley 1984 Rel: $15 Cur: $17 (8/31/86)
71 VICHON Chardonnay Napa Valley 1983 Rel: $15 Cur: $18 (CH-3/90)
85 VICHON Chardonnay Napa Valley 1983 Rel: $15 Cur: $18 (12/16/84)
66 VICHON Chardonnay Napa Valley 1982 Rel: $15 Cur: $20 (CH-3/90)
76 VICHON Chardonnay Napa Valley 1981 Rel: $15 Cur: $25 (CH-3/90)
87 VICHON Chardonnay Napa Valley 1980 Rel: $15 Cur: $25 (CH-3/90)
79 VILLA MT. EDEN Chardonnay Carneros 1989 $12 (2/28/91)
82 VILLA MT. EDEN Chardonnay Napa Valley 1989 $12 (2/28/91)
87 VILLA MT. EDEN Chardonnay Carneros 1988 $13.50 (9/30/90)
86 VILLA MT. EDEN Chardonnay Napa Valley 1986 $12 (7/31/88)
84 VILLA MT. EDEN Chardonnay Napa Valley 1984 $9 (4/30/87)
75 VILLA MT. EDEN Chardonnay Napa Valley 1983 $10 (4/16/85)
86 VILLA ZAPU Chardonnay Napa Valley 1989 $17.50 (7/15/91)
85 VILLA ZAPU Chardonnay Napa Valley 1989 $17.50 (5/15/91)
88 VILLA ZAPU Chardonnay Napa Valley 1988 $14 (6/30/90)
73 VILLA ZAPU Chardonnay Napa Valley 1987 $14 (5/31/89)
77 VILLA ZAPU Chardonnay Napa Valley 1986 $13.75 (12/31/88)
86 VITA NOVA Chardonnay Santa Barbara County 1989 $18 (7/15/91)
91 VITA NOVA Chardonnay Santa Barbara County 1988 $13.50 (2/15/90)
82 WEIBEL Chardonnay Mendocino County 1989 $8 (3/31/91) BB
87 WEINSTOCK Chardonnay Alexander Valley 1989 $11 (3/31/91)
83 WENTE BROS. Chardonnay Central Coast Estate Grown 1989 $10.50 (7/15/91)
88 WENTE BROS. Chardonnay Livermore Valley Herman Wente Vineyard Estate Reserve 1989 $18 (4/30/91)
77 WENTE BROS. Chardonnay Central Coast Reserve Arroyo Seco Vineyards 1987 $14 (10/31/89)
80 WENTE BROS. Chardonnay Livermore Valley Reserve Herman Wente Vineyard 1986 $11 (5/31/88)
90 WENTE BROS. Chardonnay Arroyo Seco Arroyo Seco Vineyards Estate Reserve 1988 $12 (4/15/90)
84 WENTE BROS. Chardonnay Arroyo Seco Reserve Arroyo Seco Vineyard 1985 $10 (10/15/87)
79 WENTE BROS. Chardonnay Arroyo Seco Vineyard Reserve 1985 $30/1.5L (3/31/90)
90 WENTE BROS. Chardonnay Arroyo Seco Vintner Grown Reserve 1984 $9 (6/01/86)
65 WENTE BROS. Chardonnay California 1983 $7.50 (4/01/86)
75 WESTWOOD Chardonnay El Dorado 1989 $10 (7/15/91)
85 WILLIAM WHEELER Chardonnay Sonoma County 1988 $12 (6/30/90)
73 WILLIAM WHEELER Chardonnay Sonoma County 1988 $12 (5/15/90)
88 WILLIAM WHEELER Chardonnay Sonoma County 1987 $12 (7/15/89)
79 WILLIAM WHEELER Chardonnay Sonoma County 1986 $11.50 (1/31/88)
88 WILLIAM WHEELER Chardonnay Sonoma County 1984 $11 (1/31/87)
82 WILLIAM WHEELER Chardonnay Sonoma County 1983 $11 (6/01/85)
85 WHITE OAK Chardonnay Sonoma County 1989 $12 (3/31/91)
88 WHITE OAK Chardonnay Sonoma County 1988 Rel: $12 Cur: $12 (CH-5/90)
88 WHITE OAK Chardonnay Sonoma County 1988 Rel: $12 Cur: $12 (4/30/90)
85 WHITE OAK Chardonnay Sonoma County 1987 Rel: $11 Cur: $16 (CH-5/90)
81 WHITE OAK Chardonnay Sonoma County 1987 Rel: $11 Cur: $16 (6/30/89)
86 WHITE OAK Chardonnay Sonoma County 1986 Rel: $11 Cur: $16 (CH-5/90)
89 WHITE OAK Chardonnay Sonoma County 1985 Rel: $10.50 Cur: $16 (CH-5/90)
85 WHITE OAK Chardonnay Sonoma County 1985 Rel: $10.50 Cur: $16 (8/31/87)
86 WHITE OAK Chardonnay Sonoma County 1984 Rel: $10 Cur: $16 (CH-5/90)
85 WHITE OAK Chardonnay Sonoma County 1984 Rel: $10 Cur: $16 (5/01/86)
80 WHITE OAK Chardonnay Sonoma County Myers Limited Reserve 1989 $20 (3/31/91)
88 WHITE OAK Chardonnay Sonoma County Myers Limited Release 1988 Rel: $18 Cur: $20 (CH-5/90)
82 WHITE OAK Chardonnay Sonoma County Myers Limited Release 1988 Rel: $18 Cur: $20 (2/28/90)
81 WHITE OAK Chardonnay Sonoma County Myers Limited Release 1987 Rel: $18 Cur: $20 (CH-5/90)
87 WHITE OAK Chardonnay Sonoma County Myers Limited Release 1986 Rel: $16 Cur: $20 (CH-5/90)
90 WHITE OAK Chardonnay Alexander Valley Myers Limited Release 1985 Rel: $14.50 Cur: $22 (CH-5/90)
87 WHITE ROCK Chardonnay Napa Valley Barrel Fermented 1989 $16 (7/15/91)
74 WHITEHALL LANE Chardonnay Napa Valley Cerro Vista Vineyard 1982 $12 (9/01/84)
78 WHITEHALL LANE Chardonnay Napa Valley Estate Bottled 1988 $15 (6/30/90)
77 WHITEHALL LANE Chardonnay Napa Valley Le Petit 1989 $9 (2/28/91)
84 WHITEHALL LANE Chardonnay Napa Valley Le Petit 1988 $8 (4/30/90) BB
86 WILD HORSE Chardonnay Central Coast 1989 $13 (4/30/91)
90 WILD HORSE Chardonnay San Luis Obispo County 1988 $12 (4/15/90)
81 WILD HORSE Chardonnay San Luis Obispo County Wild Horse Vineyards 1987 $12 (6/15/89)
79 WILD HORSE Chardonnay San Luis Obispo County Wild Horse Vineyards 1986 $9.75 (5/31/88)
79 J. WILE & SONS Chardonnay Napa Valley 1987 $7 (2/15/89)
77 J. WILE & SONS Chardonnay Napa Valley 1986 $7 (9/15/87)
84 WILLOW CREEK Chardonnay Sonoma County 1989 $11 (9/30/90)
87 WILLOW CREEK Chardonnay Sonoma County 1988 $10 (2/28/90)
83 WINDEMERE Chardonnay Edna Valley MacGregor Vineyard 1988 $13 (4/30/91)
88 WINDEMERE Chardonnay Edna Valley MacGregor Vineyard 1987 $12 (7/15/89)
77 YORK MOUNTAIN Chardonnay San Luis Obispo 1987 $9 (12/15/89)
85 ZACA MESA Chardonnay Santa Barbara County 1989 $11 (11/15/90)
84 ZACA MESA Chardonnay Santa Barbara County 1988 $10 (2/15/90)
87 ZACA MESA Chardonnay Santa Barbara County 1987 $10 (3/31/89)
74 ZACA MESA Chardonnay Santa Barbara County 1986 $9.75 (10/15/88)
77 ZACA MESA Chardonnay Santa Barbara County 1985 $8 (10/31/87)
58 ZACA MESA Chardonnay Santa Barbara County 1983 $9.75 (4/16/86)
85 ZACA MESA Chardonnay Santa Barbara County American Reserve 1984 $13 (2/28/87)
84 ZACA MESA Chardonnay Santa Barbara County Barrel Select 1985 $9.75 (10/15/88)
86 ZACA MESA Chardonnay Santa Barbara County Reserve 1989 $16.50 (7/15/91)
87 ZACA MESA Chardonnay Santa Barbara County Reserve 1988 $15.50 (9/15/90)
80 ZACA MESA Chardonnay Santa Barbara County Reserve 1987 $15 (12/15/89)
81 ZACA MESA Chardonnay Santa Barbara County Reserve 1986 $15 (10/15/88)
87 ZD Chardonnay California 1989 $21 (2/28/91)
89 ZD Chardonnay California 1988 Rel: $20 Cur: $20 (CH-3/90)
90 ZD Chardonnay California 1988 Rel: $20 Cur: $20 (12/31/89)
85 ZD Chardonnay California 1987 Rel: $18.50 Cur: $25 (CH-3/90)
82 ZD Chardonnay California 1987 Rel: $18.50 Cur: $25 (3/15/89)
85 ZD Chardonnay California 1986 Rel: $18 Cur: $25 (CH-6/90)
89 ZD Chardonnay California 1986 Rel: $18 Cur: $25 (2/15/88)
90 ZD Chardonnay California 1985 Rel: $16 Cur: $28 (CH-3/90)
82 ZD Chardonnay California 1985 Rel: $16 Cur: $28 (3/31/87)
90 ZD Chardonnay California 1984 Rel: $15 Cur: $30 (CH-3/90)
82 ZD Chardonnay California 1984 Rel: $15 Cur: $30 (6/01/86)
74 ZD Chardonnay California 1983 Rel: $14 Cur: $25 (CH-3/90)
76 ZD Chardonnay California 1982 Rel: $14 Cur: $30 (CH-3/90)
80 ZD Chardonnay California 1982 Rel: $14 Cur: $30 (10/01/84)
87 ZD Chardonnay California 1981 Rel: $13 Cur: $28 (CH-3/90)
81 ZD Chardonnay California 1980 Rel: $13 Cur: $28 (CH-3/90)
79 STEPHEN ZELLERBACH Chardonnay Alexander Valley 1984 $6 (2/15/87)
84 STEPHEN ZELLERBACH Chardonnay Alexander Valley 1983 $9.95 (1/01/85)
75 STEPHEN ZELLERBACH Chardonnay Alexander Valley Warnecke Sonoma Vineyard 1982 $10 (4/16/84)
82 STEPHEN ZELLERBACH Chardonnay California 1987 $7 (10/15/88) BB
85 STEPHEN ZELLERBACH Chardonnay Sonoma County 1989 $8.50 (11/30/90) BB
88 STEPHEN ZELLERBACH Chardonnay Sonoma County 1988 $8 (4/15/90) BB
87 STEPHEN ZELLERBACH Chardonnay Sonoma County Reserve 1989 $13 (7/15/91)

CHENIN BLANC

75 ALEXANDER VALLEY Chenin Blanc Alexander Valley 1985 $6.50 (7/16/86)
77 ALMADEN Chenin Blanc California NV $4/1.5L (7/31/89)
84 BARON HERZOG Chenin Blanc California 1988 $4.50 (7/31/89)
84 BEAULIEU Chenin Blanc Napa Valley Chablis 1986 $5.50 (7/31/89)
83 BERINGER Chenin Blanc Napa Valley 1987 $7 (7/31/89)
87 CALLAWAY Chenin Blanc Temecula Morning Harvest 1988 $6.50 (7/31/89)
84 CALLAWAY Chenin Blanc Temecula Morning Harvest 1987 $5.50 (7/31/89)
82 CASA NUESTRA Chenin Blanc Napa Valley Dry 1987 $6.50 (7/31/89)
85 CHAPPELLET Chenin Blanc Napa Valley 1986 $7.50 (7/31/89)
84 CHRISTIAN BROTHERS Chenin Blanc Napa Valley 1987 $5 (7/31/89)
85 CHRISTIAN BROTHERS Chenin Blanc Napa Valley 1985 $5 (3/15/87)
83 R. & J. COOK Chenin Blanc Clarksburg 1988 $5.50 (7/31/89)
71 DRY CREEK Chenin Blanc Sonoma & Calaveras Counties Dry 1986 $6.25 (12/15/87)
86 DRY CREEK Chenin Blanc Yolo & Napa Counties 1988 $6.50 (7/31/89)
72 DURNEY Chenin Blanc Carmel Valley 1986 $7 (7/31/89)
88 FETZER Chenin Blanc California 1988 $6 (7/31/89)
88 FOLIE A DEUX Chenin Blanc Napa Valley 1988 $7 (7/31/89)
77 E.&J. GALLO Chenin Blanc California 1987 $3.50/1.5L (7/31/89)
83 E.&J. GALLO Chenin Blanc California Chablis Blanc NV $2.50 (7/31/89)
73 E.&J. GALLO Chenin Blanc North Coast Dry Chablis 1987 $4 (7/31/89)
82 GIRARD Chenin Blanc Napa Valley Dry 1988 $7 (7/31/89)
76 GIRARD Chenin Blanc Napa Valley Dry 1986 $6.50 (1/31/88)
79 GLEN ELLEN Chenin Blanc California Proprietor's Reserve 1988 $6 (7/31/89)
83 GRAND CRU Chenin Blanc Clarksburg Dry 1989 $6.50 (6/30/90)
82 GRAND CRU Chenin Blanc Clarksburg Dry 1986 $6.50 (12/15/87)
85 GRAND CRU Chenin Blanc Clarksburg Dry Premium Selection 1988 $7 (7/31/89)
85 GRANITE SPRINGS Chenin Blanc El Dorado 1988 $5.50 (7/31/89)
82 GUENOC Chenin Blanc Guenoc Valley 1987 $5.50 (7/31/89)
84 HACIENDA Chenin Blanc Clarksburg Dry 1988 $5.50 (7/31/89)
74 HACIENDA Chenin Blanc Clarksburg Dry 1986 $6 (6/30/87)
62 HOUTZ Chenin Blanc Santa Ynez Valley 1987 $6 (7/31/89)
86 HUSCH Chenin Blanc Mendocino 1988 $5.75 (7/31/89)
76 INGLENOOK-NAVELLE Chenin Blanc California NV $3.75/1.5L (7/31/89)
82 CHARLES KRUG Chenin Blanc Napa Valley 1987 $5.50 (7/31/89)
79 LAKESPRING Chenin Blanc Napa Valley 1985 $6 (3/15/87)

Key to Symbols

The scores reported here are the results of blind tastings conducted by our panel of senior editors. Wines that carry the initials below are results of individual tastings.

THE WINE SPECTATOR 100-POINT SCALE *95-100*—Classic, a great wine; *90-94*—Outstanding, superior character and style; *80-89*—Good to very good, a wine with special qualities; *70-79*—Average, drinkable wine that may have minor flaws; *60-69*—Below average, drinkable but not recommended; *50-59*—Poor, undrinkable, not recommended. "+"—With a score indicates a range; used primarily with barrel tastings to indicate a preliminary score.

SPECIAL DESIGNATIONS SS—Spectator Selection, CS—Cellar Selection, BB—Best Buy.

TASTER'S INITIALS (JG)—Jim Gordon, (HS)—Harvey Steiman, (JL)—James Laube, (JS)—James Suckling, (TM)—Thomas Matthews, (TR)—Terry Robards, (BT)—Barrel Tasting (these wines were tasted blind from barrel samples), (CA-date)—*California's Great Cabernets* by James Laube, (CH-date)—*California's Great Chardonnays* by James Laube, (VP-date)—*Vintage Port* by James Suckling.

DATE TASTED Dates in parentheses represent the issue in which the rating was published.

58 J. LOHR Chenin Blanc Clarksburg Pheasant's Call Vineyard 1988 $4.50 (7/31/89)
74 LOS HERMANOS Chenin Blanc California NV $4/1.5L (7/31/89)
85 MARTIN Chenin Blanc Paso Robles 1988 $6 (7/31/89)
70 LOUIS M. MARTINI Chenin Blanc Napa Valley 1987 $5 (7/31/89)
65 PAUL MASSON Chenin Blanc California 1988 $5/1.5L (7/31/89)
75 MIRASSOU Chenin Blanc Monterey 1987 $5.50 (7/31/89)
69 ROBERT MONDAVI Chenin Blanc Napa Valley 1988 $8 (6/30/90)
78 ROBERT MONDAVI Chenin Blanc Napa Valley 1987 $8 (7/31/89)
70 ROBERT MONDAVI Chenin Blanc Napa Valley 1986 $6.25 (6/30/87)
88 MONTEREY VINEYARD Chenin Blanc Monterey Classic 1988 $6.50 (7/31/89)
87 PARDUCCI Chenin Blanc Mendocino 1987 $5.75 (7/31/89)
79 PELLIGRINI Chenin Blanc Vintage White North Coast 1988 $4.50 (7/31/89)
82 R.H. PHILLIPS Chenin Blanc Yolo County Dunnigan Hills 1987 $4.50 (7/31/89)
81 PINE RIDGE Chenin Blanc Napa Valley Yountville Cuvée 1989 $7 (4/30/90)
83 PINE RIDGE Chenin Blanc Napa Valley Yountville Cuvée 1988 $7 (7/31/89)
79 PINE RIDGE Chenin Blanc Napa Valley Yountville Cuvée 1986 $6.75 (6/30/87)
82 PRESTON Chenin Blanc Dry Creek Valley 1988 $7.50 (7/31/89)
58 SAN MARTIN Chenin Blanc Monterey 1987 $6 (7/31/89)
77 SANTA BARBARA Chenin Blanc Santa Ynez Valley 1987 $7 (7/31/89)
65 SEBASTIANI Chenin Blanc California 1987 $5.25 (7/31/89)
83 SIMI Chenin Blanc Mendocino 1987 $6.50 (7/31/89)
74 SIMI Chenin Blanc Mendocino County 1986 $7 (6/30/87)
69 STEVENOT Chenin Blanc Calaveras County 1987 $5.50 (7/31/89)
79 SUNNY ST. HELENA Chenin Blanc Napa Valley 1986 $5 (12/15/87)
66 SUTTER HOME Chenin Blanc California 1988 $4 (7/31/89)
71 TAYLOR Chenin Blanc California NV $3/1.5L (7/31/89)
78 VENTANA Chenin Blanc Monterey 1988 $5.50 (7/31/89)
81 VILLA MT. EDEN Chenin Blanc Napa Valley Dry 1987 $6 (7/31/89)
83 WEIBEL Chenin Blanc Mendocino 1988 $5 (7/31/89)
84 WHITE OAK Chenin Blanc Dry Creek Valley 1988 $6.50 (7/31/89)

DESSERT

84 ARCIERO White Riesling Santa Barbara County December Late Harvest 1985 $10.50 (12/15/89)
81 AUSTIN Johannisberg Riesling Santa Barbara County Late Harvest Botrytis 1986 $8/375ml (12/15/89)
72 AUSTIN Santa Barbara County Botrytis Sierra Madre Vineyards 1985 $10/375ml (12/15/89)
89 BABCOCK Johannisberg Riesling Santa Ynez Valley Late Harvest Cluster Selected 1987 $14/375ml (12/15/89)
86 BARON HERZOG Johannisberg Riesling California 1989 $8/375ml (3/31/91)
91 BONNY DOON Muscat Canelli California Vin de Glacière 1987 $15/375ml (12/31/88)
87 BUENA VISTA White Carneros Ingrid's Vineyard Late Harvest 1989 $18 (4/30/91)
87 CHATEAU DE BAUN Symphony Sonoma County Finale 1988 $12/375ml (4/30/91)
85 CHATEAU DE BAUN Symphony Sonoma County Finale 1987 $14/375ml (4/30/89)
81 CHATEAU DE BAUN Symphony Sonoma County Finale 1986 $14/375ml (9/15/87)
92 CHATEAU ST. JEAN Gewürztraminer Alexander Valley Robert Young Vineyard Late Harvest 1983 $14/375ml (11/01/84)
91 CHATEAU ST. JEAN Gewürztraminer Alexander Valley Robert Young Vineyard Late Harvest 1982 $18/375ml (7/16/84)
86 CHATEAU ST. JEAN Johannisberg Riesling Alexander Valley Robert Young Vineyard Late Harvest 1984 $15/375ml (3/16/86)
92 CHATEAU ST. JEAN Johannisberg Riesling Alexander Valley Robert Young Vineyard Late Harvest 1983 $25/375ml (8/01/85) SS
92 CHATEAU ST. JEAN Johannisberg Riesling Alexander Valley Robert Young Vineyard Special Selection 1982 $22/375ml (9/01/84)
86 CHATEAU ST. JEAN Johannisberg Riesling Alexander Valley Select Late Harvest 1988 $20/375ml (4/30/91)
84 CHATEAU ST. JEAN Johannisberg Riesling Russian River Valley Select Late Harvest 1985 $12 (8/31/87)
85 CHATEAU ST. JEAN Sauvignon Blanc Sauvignon d'Or Sonoma County Select Late Harvest 1982 $15 (7/01/84)
86 CHATEAU ST. JEAN Sémillon d'Or Sonoma Valley St. Jean Vineyard Late Harvest 1984 $15 (11/30/86)
81 CLAIBORNE & CHURCHILL Riesling Central Coast Late Harvest 1987 $15/375ml (12/15/89)
80 CLOS DU BOIS Gewürztraminer Alexander Valley Late Harvest Individual Bunch Selection 1986 $18/375ml (8/31/87)
89 CLOS DU BOIS Johannisberg Riesling Alexander Valley Late Harvest Individual Bunch Selection 1986 $15/375ml (8/31/87)
90 CLOS DU BOIS Muscat of Alexandria Alexander Valley Fleur d'Alexandra Late Harvest 1986 $10 (5/31/88)
88 DE LOACH Gewürztraminer Russian River Valley Late Harvest 1989 $10/375ml (4/30/91)
93 DE LOACH Gewürztraminer Russian River Valley Late Harvest 1987 $10/375ml (12/31/88)
92 DE LOACH Gewürztraminer Russian River Valley Late Harvest 1984 $10 (10/01/85) BB
82 DE LORIMIER Sauvignon Blanc Alexander Valley Lace Late Harvest 1986 $11/375ml (2/29/88)
91 FETZER Johannisberg Riesling Sonoma County Reserve Late Harvest 1988 $10/375ml (3/31/91)
84 FICKLIN Port California Special Bottling No. 5 1980 $19 (4/30/91)
78 FICKLIN Tinta Port NV California $10 (4/30/91)
84 FIRESTONE Johannisberg Riesling Santa Barbara County Select Late Harvest 1989 $12/375ml (4/30/91)
79 FIRESTONE Johannisberg Riesling Santa Ynez Valley Ambassador's Vineyard Select Late Harvest 1988 $9.50/375ml (12/15/89)
89 FIRESTONE Johannisberg Riesling Santa Ynez Valley Ambassador's Vineyard Select Late Harvest 1986 $9.50/375ml (2/28/89)
88 FRANCISCAN Johannisberg Riesling Napa Valley Select Late Harvest 1983 $10/375ml (1/31/88)
92 FREEMARK ABBEY Johannisberg Riesling Napa Valley Late Harvest Edelwein Gold 1989 $22/375ml (7/15/90)
87 FREEMARK ABBEY Johannisberg Riesling Napa Valley Late Harvest Edelwein Gold 1988 $18/375ml (6/15/89)
87 FREEMARK ABBEY Johannisberg Riesling Napa Valley Late Harvest Edelwein Gold 1986 $18.50/375ml (6/15/87)
91 FREEMARK ABBEY Johannisberg Riesling Napa Valley Late Harvest Edelwein Gold 1973 (NA)/375ml (2/28/87)
85 FROG'S LEAP Sauvignon Blanc Napa Valley Late Harvest Late Leap 1986 $9.50/375ml (9/30/88)
80 GEYSER PEAK Opulence California NV $7.50 (1/31/87)
72 GRAND CRU Gewürztraminer Sonoma County Select Late Harvest 1987 $10/375ml (3/31/90)
94 HIDDEN CELLARS Riesling Mendocino Bailey Lovin Vineyard Late Harvest 1984 $10 (10/16/85)
78 INGLENOOK Gewürztraminer Napa Valley Late Harvest 1986 $9.50/375ml (5/15/88)
77 JEKEL Riesling Arroyo Seco Gravelstone Vineyard Late Harvest 1987 $13.50/375ml (2/28/89)
89 KENWOOD Johannisberg Riesling Sonoma Valley Late Harvest 1985 $10/375ml (2/28/87) BB
79 KENWOOD Johannisberg Riesling Sonoma Valley Late Harvest 1984 $8.50/375ml (9/16/85)
75 CHARLES LEFRANC Gewürztraminer San Benito County Select Late Harvest 1984 $11 (3/16/86)
79 MARK WEST Johannisberg Riesling Russian River Valley Late Harvest 1983 $10/375ml (3/16/86)
84 MAYACAMAS Zinfandel Napa Valley Late Harvest 1984 $18 (11/15/89)
86 NAVARRO Gewürztraminer Anderson Valley Late Harvest Sweet Vineyard Selection 1989 $12 (4/30/91)
93 NAVARRO Gewürztraminer Anderson Valley Late Harvest Sweet Vineyard Selection 1986 $18.50 (2/28/89)
85 NAVARRO White Riesling Anderson Valley Late Harvest Sweet Cluster Selected 1986 $25 (3/31/90)
81 NAVARRO White Riesling Cluster Selected Anderson Valley Late Harvest 1985 $10/375ml (5/15/87)
93 JOSEPH PHELPS Johannisberg Riesling Napa Valley Late Harvest 1985 $11.75 (12/15/86)
94 JOSEPH PHELPS Johannisberg Riesling Napa Valley Late Harvest 1985 $15 (8/31/86) SS
87 JOSEPH PHELPS Johannisberg Riesling Napa Valley Late Harvest 1983 $15 (9/16/84)
90 JOSEPH PHELPS Johannisberg Riesling Napa Valley Late Harvest 1982 $15 (4/16/84) CS
75 JOSEPH PHELPS Johannisberg Riesling Napa Valley Special Select Late Harvest 1983 $25 (3/16/86)
88 JOSEPH PHELPS Johannisberg Riesling Napa Valley Special Select Late Harvest 1982 $25/375ml (5/16/85)
92 JOSEPH PHELPS Johannisberg Riesling Napa Valley Special Select Late Harvest 1982 $22.50/375ml (4/16/84)
88 JOSEPH PHELPS Scheurbe Napa Valley Special Select Late Harvest 1989 $18/375ml (4/30/91)
89 JOSEPH PHELPS Sémillon Délice du Sémillon Napa Valley Late Harvest 1989 $12.50/375ml (4/30/91)
91 JOSEPH PHELPS Sémillon Délice du Sémillon Napa Valley Late Harvest 1985 $8.75/375ml (8/31/87)
61 JOSEPH PHELPS Sémillon Délice du Sémillon Napa Valley Late Harvest 1983 $15 (1/31/87)
75 BERNARD PRADEL Sauvignon Blanc Napa Valley Allais Vineyard Late Harvest Botrytis 1985 $9/375ml (5/31/88)
91 PRESTON Muscat Brûlée Dry Creek Valley Late Harvest 1987 $12/375ml (8/31/89)
87 QUADY Black Muscat California 1984 $11 (8/01/85)
85 QUADY Black Muscat California Elysium 1989 $12 (10/15/90)
90 QUADY Black Muscat California Elysium 1988 $11 (8/31/89)
82 QUADY Black Muscat California Elysium 1987 $6.50/375ml (9/30/88)
85 QUADY Black Muscat California Elysium 1985 $11 (9/15/86)
89 QUADY Orange Muscat California Essencia 1989 $12 (10/15/90)
78 QUADY Orange Muscat California Essencia 1987 $11 (8/31/89)
79 QUADY Orange Muscat California Essencia 1985 $11 (9/30/86)
88 QUADY Orange Muscat California Essencia 1984 $11 (7/01/85)
82 QUADY Port Amador County 1984 $9 (10/01/85)
75 QUADY Port Amador County Frank's Vineyard 1986 $16 (10/15/90)
68 QUADY Port Amador County Frank's Vineyard 1986 $16 (8/31/89)
65 QUADY Port Amador County Frank's Vineyard 1985 $16 (8/31/89)
81 QUADY Port Amador County Starboard 1987 $25 (3/31/91)
73 QUADY Port California 1985 $9.50 (8/31/89)
87 QUADY Port California 1984 $11 (8/01/85)
68 RANCHO SISQUOC Johannisberg Riesling Santa Maria Valley Special Select Late Harvest 1986 $18/375ml (12/15/89)
91 RAYMOND Johannisberg Riesling Napa Valley Late Harvest 1985 $8.50 (9/15/86)
66 RUTHERFORD HILL Port Napa Valley 1983 $18 (11/15/87)
88 SANTA BARBARA Johannisberg Riesling Santa Ynez Valley Late Harvest Botrytised Grapes 1986 $15/375ml (10/15/87)
74 SANTA BARBARA Zinfandel Santa Ynez Valley Late Harvest Essence 1987 $15/375ml (12/15/89)
85 STAG'S LEAP WINE CELLARS White Riesling Napa Valley Birkmyer Vineyards Late Harvest Selected Bunches 1983 $13.50/375ml (10/01/84)
90 DAVID S. STARE Sauvignon Blanc Dry Creek Valley Soleil Late Harvest Vintner's Reserve 1986 $15/375ml (6/15/89)
68 ROBERT STEMMLER Sauvignon Blanc Sonoma County Late Harvest 1985 $10/375ml (9/30/88)
87 STONEGATE Napa Valley Late Harvest 1989 $13/375ml (4/30/91)
78 VEGA Johannisberg Riesling Santa Barbara County Special Selection Late Harvest 1987 $10.50/375ml (12/15/89)
70 VENTANA White Riesling Monterey Ventana Vineyards Late Harvest Hand-Selected Clusters 1987 $14/375ml (8/31/89)
86 VICHON Sémillon Napa Valley Late Harvest Botrytis 1986 $15/375ml (12/31/88)
88 VICHON Sémillon Napa Valley Late Harvest Botrytis 1985 $15/375ml (7/15/88)
83 VILLA MT. EDEN Sauvignon Blanc Napa Valley Late Harvest 1989 $13/375ml (4/30/91)
89 VILLA MT. EDEN Sauvignon Blanc Napa Valley Late Harvest 1986 $10/375ml (5/15/88)
76 WENTE BROS. Riesling Arroyo Seco Vineyard November Late Harvest Reserve 1987 $12 (7/15/90)
95 WENTE BROS. Riesling Auslese Arroyo Seco Late Harvest 1973 (NA) (2/28/87)
91 WOODBURY Port Alexander Valley Old Vines 1981 $10 (1/01/86)

GAMAY

73 BEAULIEU Gamay Beaujolais Napa Valley 1988 $6.50 (8/31/89)
76 BEAULIEU Gamay Beaujolais Napa Valley 1987 $6.50 (9/30/88)
84 BUENA VISTA Gamay Beaujolais Carneros 1988 $7.50 (7/15/89)
82 BUENA VISTA Gamay Beaujolais Sonoma Valley Carneros 1987 $7.25 (2/29/88)
83 BUENA VISTA Gamay Beaujolais Sonoma Valley Carneros 1986 $7.25 (5/31/87)
76 DUXOUP Napa Gamay Dry Creek Valley 1988 $7.50 (2/28/90)
86 DUXOUP Napa Gamay Dry Creek Valley 1987 $7 (2/28/89) BB
83 FETZER Gamay Beaujolais Mendocino 1987 $6 (7/15/88)
74 FETZER Gamay Beaujolais Mendocino County 1988 $5 (7/15/89)
80 FETZER Gamay Beaujolais Mendocino County 1986 $4.50 (1/31/88)
62 CHARLES KRUG Gamay Beaujolais Napa Valley 1983 $4.50 (5/31/87)
78 J. LOHR Monterey Gamay Monterey County 1987 $5.50 (7/15/88)
77 J. PEDRONCELLI Gamay Beaujolais Sonoma County 1987 $4.50 (1/31/88)
87 J. PEDRONCELLI Gamay Beaujolais Sonoma County 1984 $4.50 (8/31/87) BB
85 PRESTON Gamay Beaujolais Dry Creek Valley 1988 $7 (2/15/89)
78 PRESTON Gamay Beaujolais Dry Creek Valley 1987 $6.25 (1/31/88)
88 PRESTON Gamay Beaujolais Dry Creek Valley 1986 $11 (2/15/87)
78 PRESTON Gamay Beaujolais Dry Creek Valley 1985 $5.50 (2/01/86)
78 CHARLES SHAW Gamay Beaujolais Napa Valley 1988 $6.50 (7/15/89)
77 CHARLES SHAW Gamay Beaujolais Napa Valley 1986 $6 (5/31/87)
75 WEINSTOCK Gamay Sonoma County 1989 $8 (3/31/91)

GEWÜRZTRAMINER

69 ALEXANDER VALLEY Gewürztraminer Alexander Valley 1988 $6.50 (6/30/90)

UNITED STATES
CALIFORNIA/*GEWÜRZTRAMINER*

69 ALEXANDER VALLEY Gewürztraminer Alexander Valley 1986 $6.50 (5/31/88)
55 ALEXANDER VALLEY Gewürztraminer Alexander Valley 1985 $6.50 (6/16/86)
77 ALEXANDER VALLEY Gewürztraminer Alexander Valley 1983 $6.50 (11/01/84)
73 BABCOCK Gewürztraminer Santa Ynez Valley 1987 $6.50 (2/28/89)
82 BABCOCK Gewürztraminer Santa Ynez Valley 1986 $6.50 (12/31/87)
85 BELVEDERE Gewürztraminer Los Carneros Winery Lake 1985 $7 (6/15/87)
74 BELVEDERE Gewürztraminer Los Carneros Winery Lake 1984 $7 (11/01/85)
84 BOUCHAINE Gewürztraminer Carneros 1989 $8.50 (6/15/91)
72 BUENA VISTA Gewürztraminer Sonoma Valley Carneros 1986 $7.25 (5/31/88)
63 BUENA VISTA Gewürztraminer Sonoma Valley Carneros 1984 $7 (5/16/86)
87 DAVIS BYNUM Gewürztraminer Russian River Valley McIlroy Vineyard Reserve 1987 $7 (6/15/88)
51 CALLAWAY Gewürztraminer California 1985 $5.50 (9/15/86)
83 CHATEAU ST. JEAN Gewürztraminer Alexander Valley 1985 $8 (6/16/86)
82 CHATEAU ST. JEAN Gewürztraminer Alexander Valley 1984 $8 (5/16/85)
61 CHATEAU ST. JEAN Gewürztraminer Russian River Valley Frank Johnson Vineyards 1986 $8 (9/15/87)
72 CHATEAU ST. JEAN Gewürztraminer Sonoma County 1988 $8 (1/31/90)
73 CLAIBORNE & CHURCHILL Gewürztraminer Edna Valley Dry Alsatian Style 1986 $8 (7/15/88)
76 CLOS DU BOIS Gewürztraminer Alexander Valley Early Harvest 1989 $8 (2/15/91)
77 CLOS DU BOIS Gewürztraminer Alexander Valley Early Harvest 1988 $8 (11/15/89)
85 CLOS DU BOIS Gewürztraminer Alexander Valley Early Harvest 1987 $8 (5/31/88)
77 CLOS DU BOIS Gewürztraminer Alexander Valley Early Harvest 1986 $7.50 (8/31/87)
91 CLOS DU BOIS Gewürztraminer Alexander Valley Early Harvest 1985 $7.50 (4/16/86)
87 CLOS DU BOIS Gewürztraminer Alexander Valley Early Harvest 1984 $7.50 (11/01/85)
81 DE LOACH Gewürztraminer Russian River Valley Early Harvest 1990 $8 (4/30/91)
83 DE LOACH Gewürztraminer Russian River Valley Early Harvest 1989 $7.50 (6/30/90)
83 DE LOACH Gewürztraminer Russian River Valley Early Harvest 1987 $7 (9/30/88)
74 DE LOACH Gewürztraminer Russian River Valley Early Harvest 1985 $7 (3/15/87)
86 DE LOACH Gewürztraminer Russian River Valley Early Harvest 1984 $7 (11/01/85)
75 FETZER Gewürztraminer California 1990 $6.75 (4/30/91)
79 FETZER Gewürztraminer California 1989 $6 (6/30/90)
88 FETZER Gewürztraminer California 1988 $6.50 (2/28/89) BB
84 FETZER Gewürztraminer California 1987 $6 (7/15/88) BB
82 FETZER Gewürztraminer California 1986 $4.50 (2/15/88) BB
84 FETZER Gewürztraminer California 1985 $6 (5/16/86)
69 FIELD STONE Gewürztraminer Alexander Valley 1987 $7 (2/28/89)
68 FIRESTONE Gewürztraminer Santa Ynez Valley 1984 $6.50 (8/31/86)
83 THOMAS FOGARTY Gewürztraminer Monterey Ventana Vineyards 1990 $9 (6/15/91)
67 E.&J. GALLO Gewürztraminer California Limited Release Reserve 1984 $3.50 (9/30/86)
62 GEYSER PEAK Gewürztraminer Sonoma County 1986 $5.50 (12/31/87)
76 GRAND CRU Gewürztraminer Alexander Valley 1987 $8.50 (10/31/88)
79 GRAND CRU Gewürztraminer Alexander Valley 1985 $8.50 (12/31/87)
59 GUNDLACH BUNDSCHU Gewürztraminer Sonoma Valley Rhinefarm Vineyards 1985 $12 (6/16/86)
75 HACIENDA Gewürztraminer Sonoma County 1987 $7 (10/31/88)
59 HACIENDA Gewürztraminer Sonoma County 1985 $7 (6/15/87)
70 HACIENDA Gewürztraminer Sonoma County 1984 $7 (3/01/86)
89 HANDLEY Gewürztraminer Anderson Valley 1988 $7 (1/31/90) BB
86 HANDLEY Gewürztraminer Anderson Valley 1987 $7 (2/28/89)
83 HIDDEN CELLARS Gewürztraminer Mendocino County 1987 $7 (2/28/89)
72 HOP KILN Gewürztraminer Russian River Valley 1988 $7.50 (1/31/90)
77 HOP KILN Gewürztraminer Russian River Valley 1986 $7.50 (9/15/88)
90 HOP KILN Gewürztraminer Russian River Valley 1984 $7.50 (12/01/85)
81 HUSCH Gewürztraminer Anderson Valley 1989 $8 (6/30/90)
90 HUSCH Gewürztraminer Anderson Valley 1987 $7 (9/15/88)
91 HUSCH Gewürztraminer Anderson Valley 1985 $6.25 (4/01/86)
74 INGLENOOK Gewürztraminer Napa Valley 1985 $6.50 (5/31/88)
55 KENWOOD Gewürztraminer Sonoma Valley 1984 $7.50 (9/15/86)
78 CHARLES KRUG Gewürztraminer Napa Valley 1988 $7.25 (1/31/90)
78 MARK WEST Gewürztraminer Russian River Valley 1986 $7.50 (7/15/88)
77 MARK WEST Gewürztraminer Russian River Valley 1985 $7.50 (3/15/87)
71 LOUIS M. MARTINI Gewürztraminer Russian River Valley Los Vinedos del Rio 1987 $7 (1/31/90)
76 MONTICELLO Gewürztraminer Napa Valley 1986 $7.50 (2/28/89)
81 MONTICELLO Gewürztraminer Napa Valley 1985 $7.50 (8/31/87)
70 MONTICELLO Gewürztraminer Napa Valley 1984 $7.50 (3/01/86)
86 Z MOORE Gewürztraminer Russian River Valley 1987 $8.50 (2/28/89)
89 NAVARRO Gewürztraminer Anderson Valley 1989 $8.50 (4/30/91) BB
79 NAVARRO Gewürztraminer Anderson Valley 1988 $8.50 (1/31/90)
89 NAVARRO Gewürztraminer Anderson Valley 1987 $7.50 (2/28/89)
87 NAVARRO Gewürztraminer Anderson Valley 1986 $7.50 (5/31/88)
83 NAVARRO Gewürztraminer Anderson Valley 1985 $7.50 (8/31/87)
78 PAT PAULSEN Gewürztraminer Alexander Valley 1986 $7 (12/31/87)
71 J. PEDRONCELLI Gewürztraminer Sonoma County 1987 $5.50 (2/28/89)
67 J. PEDRONCELLI Gewürztraminer Sonoma County 1986 $5.50 (9/15/88)
81 JOSEPH PHELPS Gewürztraminer Napa Valley 1988 $8.50 (6/30/90)
75 JOSEPH PHELPS Gewürztraminer Napa Valley 1984 $8 (11/01/85)
78 QUAFF Gewürztraminer Sonoma County 1990 $6.25 (4/30/91)
78 QUAFF Gewürztraminer Sonoma County 1987 $6.50 (2/28/89)
79 ROUND HILL Gewürztraminer Napa Valley 1989 $6 (2/15/91)
84 ROUND HILL Gewürztraminer Napa Valley 1988 $6.25 (1/31/90) BB
75 ROUND HILL Gewürztraminer Napa Valley 1987 $6.25 (7/15/88)
85 ROUND HILL Gewürztraminer Napa Valley 1986 $4.75 (7/31/87) BB
75 ROUND HILL Gewürztraminer Napa Valley 1985 $5.50 (6/16/86)
79 ROUND HILL Gewürztraminer Napa Valley 1984 $5 (10/16/85)
80 RUTHERFORD HILL Gewürztraminer Napa Valley 1986 $6.25 (12/31/87)
76 RUTHERFORD HILL Gewürztraminer Napa Valley 1984 $6.25 (5/16/86)
80 ST. FRANCIS Gewürztraminer Sonoma Valley 1988 $7.50 (1/31/90)
79 ST. FRANCIS Gewürztraminer Sonoma Valley 1987 $7.50 (10/31/88)
87 ST. FRANCIS Gewürztraminer Sonoma Valley 1986 $7 (1/31/88)
81 ST. FRANCIS Gewürztraminer Sonoma Valley 1984 $7 (5/16/85)
75 RODNEY STRONG Gewürztraminer Sonoma County 1987 $5.50 (2/28/89)
76 RODNEY STRONG Gewürztraminer Sonoma County 1985 $7.50 (1/31/87)
68 WENTE BROS. Gewürztraminer Arroyo Seco Vintner Grown 1986 $7.50 (9/15/87)
83 WENTE BROS. Gewürztraminer Arroyo Seco Vintner Grown 1984 $7.50 (3/01/86)
64 WENTE BROS. Gewürztraminer Arroyo Seco Arroyo Seco Vineyards Vintner Grown 1987 $9 (12/15/89)

MERLOT

83 ACACIA Merlot Napa Valley 1984 $15 (2/28/87)
85+ ALEXANDER VALLEY Merlot Alexander Valley 1990 (NR) (5/15/91) (BT)
85+ ALEXANDER VALLEY Merlot Alexander Valley 1989 (NR) (5/15/91) (BT)
88 ALEXANDER VALLEY Merlot Alexander Valley 1985 $11 (10/31/87)
65 HUNTER ASHBY Merlot Napa Valley 1982 $6.50 (12/15/87)
84 BEAUCANON Merlot Napa Valley 1988 $13 (3/31/91)
78 CHATEAU NAPA-BEAUCANON Merlot Napa Valley 1986 $13 (12/31/88)
69 BELLEROSE Merlot Sonoma County 1986 $16 (4/15/90)
73 BELLEROSE Merlot Sonoma County 1985 $16 (2/28/89)
77 BELLEROSE Merlot Sonoma County 1984 $12 (12/31/87)
87 BELVEDERE Merlot Alexander Valley Robert Young Vineyards 1986 $13 (6/30/89)
85+ BELVEDERE Merlot Alexander Valley Robert Young Vineyards 1986 $13 (4/15/88) (BT)
90 BELVEDERE Merlot Alexander Valley Robert Young Vineyards 1984 $13 (8/31/88)
70 BELVEDERE Merlot Alexander Valley Robert Young Vineyards 1983 $12 (12/31/87)
94 BELVEDERE Merlot Alexander Valley Robert Young Vineyards 1982 $12 (3/16/86)
86 BENZIGER Merlot Sonoma Valley 1987 $12 (3/31/91)
84 BENZIGER Merlot Sonoma Valley 1986 $16 (7/31/89)
90+ BERINGER Merlot Howell Mountain Bancroft Ranch 1989 (NR) (5/15/91) (BT)
90+ BERINGER Merlot Howell Mountain Bancroft Ranch 1988 (NR) (4/30/90) (BT)
91 BERINGER Merlot Howell Mountain Bancroft Ranch 1987 $29 (12/31/90)
90+ BERINGER Merlot Howell Mountain Bancroft Ranch 1987 $29 (4/15/89) (BT)
78 BOEGER Merlot El Dorado 1988 $12.50 (3/31/91)
81 BOEGER Merlot El Dorado 1987 $12.50 (7/15/90)
73 BOEGER Merlot El Dorado 1986 $12.50 (1/31/89)
82 BOEGER Merlot El Dorado 1985 $12.50 (2/15/88)
74 BOEGER Merlot El Dorado 1982 $10 (10/01/84)
84 BRAREN PAULI Merlot Alexander Valley Mauritson Vineyard 1987 $11 (3/31/91)
80+ BUENA VISTA Merlot Carneros 1987 (NR) (4/15/89) (BT)
80 BUENA VISTA Merlot Carneros 1985 $11 (6/30/88)
85+ BUENA VISTA Merlot Carneros Private Reserve 1988 (NR) (4/30/90) (BT)
84 BUENA VISTA Merlot Carneros Private Reserve 1987 $18 (3/31/91)
86 BUENA VISTA Merlot Carneros Private Reserve 1986 $16.50 (10/31/89)
85+ BUENA VISTA Merlot Carneros Private Reserve 1986 $16.50 (4/15/88) (BT)
87 BUENA VISTA Merlot Carneros Private Reserve 1984 $14.50 (2/15/88)
86 BUENA VISTA Merlot Sonoma County 1987 $11 (7/31/90)
86 CAFARO Merlot Napa Valley 1987 $18 (12/31/90)
84 CAFARO Merlot Napa Valley 1986 $18 (12/31/89)
90+ CAIN Merlot Napa Valley 1990 (NR) (5/15/91) (BT)
83 CAIN Merlot Napa Valley 1986 $14 (2/28/89)
89 CAIN Merlot Napa Valley 1984 $12 (9/30/88)
78 CAIN Merlot Napa Valley 1982 $11 (2/01/85)
88 CAPARONE Merlot Santa Maria Valley Tepusquet Vineyard 1981 $10 (3/16/84)
82 J. CAREY Merlot Santa Ynez Valley La Cuesta Vineyard 1986 $12 (12/15/89)
84 CARNEROS CREEK Merlot Napa Valley 1985 $12.50 (2/15/88)
87 CARNEROS CREEK Merlot Napa Valley 1984 $10.50 (8/31/87)
80 CARNEROS CREEK Merlot Napa Valley 1982 $9.50 (2/16/86)
84 CARNEROS CREEK Merlot Napa Valley Truchard Vineyard 1983 $10 (10/01/85)
89 CHAPPELLET Merlot Napa Valley 1987 $15 (12/31/90)
80+ CHAPPELLET Merlot Napa Valley 1987 $15 (4/15/89) (BT)
80 CHAPPELLET Merlot Napa Valley 1986 $15 (1/31/90)
78 CHAPPELLET Merlot Napa Valley 1985 $12 (12/31/88)
87 CHATEAU CHEVRE Merlot Napa Valley 1985 $16 (8/31/88)
91 CHATEAU CHEVRE Merlot Napa Valley 1984 $12.50 (10/31/87)
85 CHATEAU CHEVRE Merlot Napa Valley 1983 $12.50 (10/15/87)
84 CHATEAU CHEVRE Merlot Napa Valley 1982 $12 (10/01/85)
80 CHATEAU CHEVRE Merlot Napa Valley Reserve 1986 $25 (7/31/89)
78 CHATEAU CHEVRE Merlot Napa Valley Reserve 1984 $15 (12/15/87)
60 CHATEAU JULIEN Merlot Monterey County 1986 $10 (4/15/89)
76 CHATEAU JULIEN Merlot Santa Barbara County Bien Nacido Vineyard 1984 $12 (2/29/88)
90+ CHATEAU SOUVERAIN Merlot Alexander Valley 1990 (NR) (5/15/91) (BT)
89 CHATEAU SOUVERAIN Merlot North Coast 1981 $6.75 (10/01/85)
74 CHATEAU SOUVERAIN Merlot Sonoma County 1986 $10 (3/31/89)
86 CHATEAU SOUVERAIN Merlot Sonoma County 1984 $8.50 (7/31/87)
84 CHESTNUT HILL Merlot North Coast 1985 $8.50 (12/15/87)
80 CHRISTIAN BROTHERS Merlot Napa Valley 1985 $8 (8/31/88)
81 CLOS DU BOIS Merlot Sonoma County 1988 $15 (5/31/91)
89 CLOS DU BOIS Merlot Sonoma County 1987 $12 (4/15/90)
86 CLOS DU BOIS Merlot Sonoma County 1986 $10.75 (10/15/88)
85+ CLOS DU BOIS Merlot Sonoma County 1986 $10.75 (4/15/88) (BT)
92 CLOS DU BOIS Merlot Sonoma County 1985 Rel: $16 Cur: $16 (10/31/87) SS
87 CLOS DU BOIS Merlot Sonoma County 1984 $9 (5/16/86)
86 CLOS DU BOIS Merlot Sonoma County 1983 $9 (10/01/85)
90+ CLOS DU VAL Merlot Stags Leap District 1990 (NR) (5/15/91) (BT)
85+ CLOS DU VAL Merlot Stags Leap District 1989 (NR) (5/15/91) (BT)
89 CLOS DU VAL Merlot Stags Leap District 1988 $20 (3/31/91)
85 CLOS DU VAL Merlot Stags Leap District 1987 $17 (3/31/90)
86 CLOS DU VAL Merlot Napa Valley 1986 $16 (8/31/89)
87 CLOS DU VAL Merlot Napa Valley 1985 $15.50 (4/30/88)
88 CLOS DU VAL Merlot Napa Valley 1984 $15 (7/31/87)
92 CLOS DU VAL Merlot Napa Valley 1983 $14 (6/16/86)
80 CLOS DU VAL Merlot Napa Valley 1982 $12.50 (10/01/85)
88 CLOS DU VAL Merlot Napa Valley 1981 $13.50 (2/15/84)
84 CLOS PEGASE Merlot Napa Valley 1986 $15.50 (7/15/90)

Key to Symbols

The scores reported here are the results of blind tastings conducted by our panel of senior editors. Wines that carry the initials below are results of individual tastings.

THE WINE SPECTATOR 100-POINT SCALE *95-100*—Classic, a great wine; *90-94*—Outstanding, superior character and style; *80-89*—Good to very good, a wine with special qualities; *70-79*—Average, drinkable wine that may have minor flaws; *60-69*—Below average, drinkable but not recommended; *50-59*—Poor, undrinkable, not recommended. "+"—With a score indicates a range; used primarily with barrel tastings to indicate a preliminary score.

SPECIAL DESIGNATIONS SS—Spectator Selection, CS—Cellar Selection, BB—Best Buy.

TASTER'S INITIALS (JG)—Jim Gordon, (HS)—Harvey Steiman, (JL)—James Laube, (JS)—James Suckling, (TM)—Thomas Matthews, (TR)—Terry Robards, (BT)—Barrel Tasting (these wines were tasted blind from barrel samples), (CA-date)—*California's Great Cabernets* by James Laube, (CH-date)—*California's Great Chardonnays* by James Laube, (VP-date)—*Vintage Port* by James Suckling.

DATE TASTED Dates in parentheses represent the issue in which the rating was published.

74 CONGRESS SPRINGS Merlot Santa Clara County 1988 $14 (3/31/91)
90+ CONN CREEK Merlot Napa Valley 1988 (NR) (4/30/90) (BT)
80+ CONN CREEK Merlot Napa Valley 1987 (NR) (4/15/89) (BT)
84 CONN CREEK Merlot Napa Valley Collins Vineyard 1985 $14 (3/31/88)
87 CONN CREEK Merlot Napa Valley Collins Vineyard Barrel Select Limited Bottling 1987 $22 (12/31/90)
82 COSENTINO Merlot Napa County 1988 $18 (4/15/91)
90+ COSENTINO Merlot Napa County 1987 (NR) (4/15/89) (BT)
85 COSENTINO Merlot Napa County 1986 $14 (9/30/88)
80 COSENTINO Merlot Napa County Reserve 1987 $18 (7/31/90)
85+ COSENTINO Merlot Napa Valley 1989 (NR) (5/15/91) (BT)
86 CUVAISON Merlot Napa Valley 1988 $24 (4/15/91)
85+ CUVAISON Merlot Napa Valley 1987 (20) (4/15/89) (BT)
89 CUVAISON Merlot Napa Valley 1985 $19 (6/30/88)
90 CUVAISON Merlot Napa Valley Anniversary Release 1984 $13.50 (8/31/87)
83 DEHLINGER Merlot Sonoma County 1986 $13 (7/31/89)
85+ DEHLINGER Merlot Sonoma County 1986 $13 (4/15/88) (BT)
89 DEHLINGER Merlot Sonoma County 1985 $10.50 (4/30/88)
94 DEHLINGER Merlot Sonoma County 1984 Rel: $12 Cur: $18 (6/15/87) SS
80 DEVLIN Merlot Central Coast 1982 $8 (7/16/85)
79 DIABLO VISTA Merlot Dry Creek Valley 1981 $7.50 (5/01/84)
88 R.W. DOLAN Merlot California 1986 $8 (1/31/89)
83 DRY CREEK Merlot Dry Creek Valley 1988 $15 (3/31/91)
85+ DRY CREEK Merlot Dry Creek Valley 1986 $15 (4/15/88) (BT)
80 DRY CREEK Merlot Dry Creek Valley 1985 $7.50 (2/15/88)
78 DRY CREEK Merlot Sonoma County 1986 $15 (3/31/89)
85+ DUCKHORN Merlot Napa Valley 1990 (NR) (5/15/91) (BT)
86 DUCKHORN Merlot Napa Valley 1988 $19 (12/31/90)
91 DUCKHORN Merlot Napa Valley 1987 Rel: $18 Cur: $26 (12/31/89)
85+ DUCKHORN Merlot Napa Valley 1987 Rel: $18 Cur: $26 (4/15/89) (BT)
86 DUCKHORN Merlot Napa Valley 1986 Rel: $17 Cur: $30 (1/31/89)
90+ DUCKHORN Merlot Napa Valley 1986 Rel: $17 Cur: $30 (4/15/88) (BT)
93 DUCKHORN Merlot Napa Valley 1985 Rel: $16 Cur: $38 (12/31/87) CS
94 DUCKHORN Merlot Napa Valley 1984 Rel: $15 Cur: $40 (12/31/86) SS
94 DUCKHORN Merlot Napa Valley 1983 Rel: $15 Cur: $45 (11/01/85) CS
81 DUCKHORN Merlot Napa Valley 1982 Rel: $13 Cur: $52 (10/01/85)
92 DUCKHORN Merlot Napa Valley 1982 Rel: $13 Cur: $52 (12/16/84) SS
92 DUCKHORN Merlot Napa Valley Three Palms Vineyard 1987 Rel: $25 Cur: $50 (7/31/90)
90+ DUCKHORN Merlot Napa Valley Three Palms Vineyard 1987 Rel: $25 Cur: $50 (4/15/89) (BT)
88 DUCKHORN Merlot Napa Valley Three Palms Vineyard 1986 Rel: $20 Cur: $59 (7/31/89)
90+ DUCKHORN Merlot Napa Valley Three Palms Vineyard 1986 Rel: $20 Cur: $59 (4/15/88) (BT)
91 DUCKHORN Merlot Napa Valley Three Palms Vineyard 1985 Rel: $20 Cur: $63 (6/30/88)
89 DUCKHORN Merlot Napa Valley Three Palms Vineyard 1984 Rel: $18 Cur: $70 (7/31/87)
87 DUCKHORN Merlot Napa Valley Vine Hill Ranch 1987 $18 (7/31/90)
80 DUCKHORN Merlot Napa Valley Vine Hill Ranch 1986 $18 (7/31/89)
91 DUCKHORN Merlot Napa Valley Vine Hill Ranch 1985 $16 (6/30/88)
72 ESTATE WILLIAM BACCALA Merlot Alexander Valley 1984 $10 (2/28/87)
78 FARVIEW FARM Merlot California Templeton 1980 $6.50 (3/16/84)
83 FENESTRA Merlot Sonoma County 1986 $11 (10/15/89)
84 FERRARI-CARANO Merlot Alexander Valley 1987 $16.50 (7/31/90)
87 FERRARI-CARANO Merlot Alexander Valley 1986 $15 (6/30/89)
82 FIRESTONE Merlot Santa Ynez Valley 1988 $11 (3/31/91)
83 FIRESTONE Merlot Santa Ynez Valley 1987 $9 (12/15/89)
83 FIRESTONE Merlot Santa Ynez Valley 1986 $9 (9/30/88)
78 FIRESTONE Merlot Santa Ynez Valley 1985 $9 (4/30/88)
50 FIRESTONE Merlot Santa Ynez Valley 1981 $6.50 (5/16/86)
84 FITCH MOUNTAIN Merlot Napa Valley 1986 $9 (9/30/88)
89 FITCH MOUNTAIN Merlot Napa Valley 1985 $9 (12/15/87)
85+ FLORA SPRINGS Merlot Napa Valley 1990 (NR) (5/15/91) (BT)
85+ FLORA SPRINGS Merlot Napa Valley 1988 (NR) (4/30/90) (BT)
87 FLORA SPRINGS Merlot Napa Valley 1987 $16.50 (7/31/90)
75+ FLORA SPRINGS Merlot Napa Valley 1987 $16.50 (4/15/89) (BT)
85+ FLORA SPRINGS Merlot Napa Valley 1986 $16 (4/15/88) (BT)
82 FLORA SPRINGS Merlot Napa Valley 1985 $15 (6/30/88)
82 FOLIE A DEUX Merlot Napa Valley 1988 $18 (3/31/91)
91 FRANCISCAN Merlot Napa Valley 1981 $8.50 (10/01/85)
80+ FRANCISCAN Merlot Napa Valley Oakville Estate 1988 (NR) (4/30/90) (BT)
88 FRANCISCAN Merlot Napa Valley Oakville Estate 1987 $12.50 (6/15/90)
85+ FRANCISCAN Merlot Napa Valley Oakville Estate 1987 $12.50 (4/15/89) (BT)
80 FRANCISCAN Merlot Napa Valley Oakville Estate 1986 $12 (7/31/89)
85+ FRANCISCAN Merlot Napa Valley Oakville Estate 1986 $12 (4/15/88) (BT)
89 FRANCISCAN Merlot Napa Valley Oakville Estate 1985 $9.25 (5/31/88)
90 FRANCISCAN Merlot Napa Valley Oakville Estate 1984 Rel: $8.50 Cur: $16 (6/30/87) SS
88 FRANCISCAN Merlot Napa Valley Oakville Estate 1983 $8.50 (2/28/87)
90 FREEMARK ABBEY Merlot Napa Valley 1985 $10 (12/31/88)
82 GAINEY Merlot Santa Barbara County 1988 $13 (4/15/91)
89 GEORIS Merlot Carmel Valley 1987 $27 (3/31/91)
77 GEORIS Merlot Carmel Valley 1986 $25 (12/31/90)
83 GEORIS Merlot Carmel Valley 1985 $20 (4/15/89)
82 GEYSER PEAK Merlot Alexander Valley 1987 $8 (7/15/90)
77 GEYSER PEAK Merlot Alexander Valley 1985 $7.75 (10/15/88)
69 GEYSER PEAK Merlot Alexander Valley 1984 $7 (2/29/88)
80 GEYSER PEAK Merlot Alexander Valley 1983 $7 (12/31/86)
84 GLEN ELLEN Merlot California Proprietor's Reserve 1986 $6 (1/31/89) BB
85 GUENOC Merlot Guenoc Valley 1985 $15 (3/31/89)
80 GUENOC Merlot Lake-Napa Counties 1986 $12 (6/15/90)
81 GUNDLACH BUNDSCHU Merlot Sonoma Valley Rhinefarm Vineyards 1988 $16 (5/31/91)
85+ GUNDLACH BUNDSCHU Merlot Sonoma Valley Rhinefarm Vineyards 1988 $16 (4/30/90) (BT)
93 GUNDLACH BUNDSCHU Merlot Sonoma Valley Rhinefarm Vineyards 1987 Rel: $13 Cur: $16 (10/31/89) SS
85+ GUNDLACH BUNDSCHU Merlot Sonoma Valley Rhinefarm Vineyards 1987 $13 (4/15/89) (BT)
91 GUNDLACH BUNDSCHU Merlot Sonoma Valley Rhinefarm Vineyards 1986 $12 (12/31/88)
92 GUNDLACH BUNDSCHU Merlot Sonoma Valley Rhinefarm Vineyards 1985 Rel: $12 Cur: $20 (2/29/88) SS
88 GUNDLACH BUNDSCHU Merlot Sonoma Valley Rhinefarm Vineyards 1984 $12 (2/28/87)
92 GUNDLACH BUNDSCHU Merlot Sonoma Valley Rhinefarm Vineyards 1983 $12 (5/01/86)
88 GUNDLACH BUNDSCHU Merlot Sonoma Valley Rhinefarm Vineyards 1982 $9.25 (10/01/85)
82 HAVENS Merlot Napa Valley 1988 $14 (3/31/91)
89 HAVENS Merlot Napa Valley 1987 $14 (7/15/90)
72 HAVENS Merlot Napa Valley 1986 $13.50 (3/31/90)
75+ HAVENS Merlot Napa Valley 1986 $13.50 (4/15/88) (BT)
84 HAVENS Merlot Napa Valley 1985 $12.50 (5/31/88)
80+ HAVENS Merlot Napa Valley Reserve 1986 (NR) (4/15/88) (BT)
84 HUNTER ASHBY Merlot Napa Valley 1985 $9.75 (7/31/89)
80+ INGLENOOK Merlot Napa Valley 1987 (NR) (4/15/89) (BT)
77 INGLENOOK Merlot Napa Valley 1981 $12 (10/01/85)
67 INGLENOOK Merlot Napa Valley Limited Bottling 1982 $8.50 (5/16/86)
80 INGLENOOK Merlot Napa Valley Limited Cask Reserve Selection 1981 $12 (2/16/85)
81 INGLENOOK Merlot Napa Valley Reserve 1986 $12 (10/31/89)
91 INGLENOOK Merlot Napa Valley Reserve 1985 Rel: $10.50 Cur: $14 (10/15/88) SS
85 INGLENOOK Merlot Napa Valley Reserve 1983 $9.50 (10/15/87)
83 JAEGER Merlot Napa Valley Inglewood Vineyard 1986 $19 (3/31/91)
89 JAEGER Merlot Napa Valley Inglewood Vineyard 1985 $16 (2/15/90)
87 JAEGER Merlot Napa Valley Inglewood Vineyard 1983 $14 (2/29/88)
88 KEENAN Merlot Napa Valley 1987 Rel: $18 Cur: $20 (3/31/90)
90+ KEENAN Merlot Napa Valley 1987 Rel: $18 Cur: $20 (4/15/89) (BT)
90 KEENAN Merlot Napa Valley 1986 Rel: $18 Cur: $20 (6/30/89)
90+ KEENAN Merlot Napa Valley 1986 Rel: $18 Cur: $20 (4/15/88) (BT)
83 KEENAN Merlot Napa Valley 1985 Rel: $18 Cur: $20 (5/31/88)
94 KEENAN Merlot Napa Valley 1984 Rel: $16.50 Cur: $20 (7/31/87) CS
93 KENDALL-JACKSON Merlot Alexander Valley 1986 $16 (12/31/88)
87 KENDALL-JACKSON Merlot Sonoma County The Proprietor's 1987 $20 (12/31/90)
83 KONOCTI Merlot Lake County 1988 $9.50 (3/31/91) BB
73 KONOCTI Merlot Lake County 1987 $9.50 (12/31/90)
83 KONOCTI Merlot Lake County 1985 $8 (12/31/88)
75+ CHARLES KRUG Merlot Carneros Napa Valley 1986 (NR) (4/15/88) (BT)
85 LAKESPRING Merlot Napa Valley 1987 $14 (6/15/90)
80+ LAKESPRING Merlot Napa Valley 1987 $14 (4/15/89) (BT)
79 LAKESPRING Merlot Napa Valley 1986 $14 (3/31/89)
91 LAKESPRING Merlot Napa Valley 1985 Rel: $12 Cur: $15 (3/31/88) SS
88 LAKESPRING Merlot Napa Valley 1984 $12 (5/15/87)
87 LAKESPRING Merlot Napa Valley 1983 $11 (5/16/86)
78 LAKESPRING Merlot Napa Valley 1982 $10 (10/01/85)
69 LAMBERT BRIDGE Merlot Sonoma County 1985 $10 (12/15/87)
79 LAMBERT BRIDGE Merlot Sonoma County 1982 $11.50 (12/16/84)
88 LEEWARD Merlot Napa Valley 1985 $10 (5/15/87)
70 CHARLES LEFRANC Merlot Monterey County San Lucas Ranch 1984 $8.50 (12/15/87)
85 MARILYN MERLOT Merlot Napa Valley 1988 $12.50 (5/31/91)
85 MARILYN MERLOT Merlot Napa Valley 1986 $13 (12/31/88)
85+ MARKHAM Merlot Napa Valley 1990 (NR) (5/15/91) (BT)
90 MARKHAM Merlot Napa Valley 1988 $13.50 (4/15/91)
85+ MARKHAM Merlot Napa Valley 1988 $13.50 (4/30/90) (BT)
91 MARKHAM Merlot Napa Valley 1987 $13.50 (10/15/89)
88 MARKHAM Merlot Napa Valley 1985 $11 (4/30/88)
86 MARKHAM Merlot Napa Valley 1981 $8.75 (8/01/84)
79 LOUIS M. MARTINI Merlot North Coast 1986 $12 (10/31/89)
79 LOUIS M. MARTINI Merlot North Coast 1984 $6.75 (2/15/88)
71 LOUIS M. MARTINI Merlot North Coast 1982 $5.85 (2/16/86)
85+ LOUIS M. MARTINI Merlot Russian River Valley Los Viendos del Rio 1988 (NR) (4/30/90) (BT)
80+ LOUIS M. MARTINI Merlot Russian River Valley Los Viendos del Rio 1987 (NR) (4/15/89) (BT)
85+ LOUIS M. MARTINI Merlot Russian River Valley Los Viendos del Rio 1986 $20 (4/15/88) (BT)
79 LOUIS M. MARTINI Merlot Russian River Valley Los Vinedos del Rio 1986 $20 (3/31/90)
82 LOUIS M. MARTINI Merlot Russian River Valley Los Vinedos del Rio 1984 $12 (2/15/88)
81 LOUIS M. MARTINI Merlot Russian River Valley Los Vinedos del Rio 1981 $10 (10/01/85)
83 MASSON Merlot Monterey County Vintage Selection 1987 $8.50 (7/15/90)
92 MATANZAS CREEK Merlot Sonoma County 1987 Rel: $25 Cur: $32 (6/15/90) SS
85+ MATANZAS CREEK Merlot Sonoma County 1987 Rel: $25 Cur: $32 (4/15/89) (BT)
92 MATANZAS CREEK Merlot Sonoma County 1986 Rel: $20 Cur: $20 (6/30/89)
90+ MATANZAS CREEK Merlot Sonoma County 1986 Rel: $20 Cur: $20 (4/15/88) (BT)
88 MATANZAS CREEK Merlot Sonoma Valley 1985 Rel: $18 Cur: $40 (5/31/88)
80+ MATANZAS CREEK Merlot Sonoma Valley 1985 Rel: $18 Cur: $40 (6/15/87) (BT)
91 MATANZAS CREEK Merlot Sonoma Valley 1984 Rel: $14.50 Cur: $25 (6/30/87)
88 MATANZAS CREEK Merlot Sonoma Valley 1982 Rel: $13.50 Cur: $20 (10/01/85)
80 MATANZAS CREEK Merlot Sonoma Valley 1981 Rel: $12.50 Cur: $30 (4/16/84)
68 MILL CREEK Merlot Dry Creek Valley 1984 $8.50 (2/15/88)
80 MILL CREEK Merlot Dry Creek Valley 1983 $9 (10/01/85)
85 MILL CREEK Merlot Dry Creek Valley 1982 $8.50 (4/01/85)
84 MONTEREY PENINSULA Merlot Monterey Doctors' Reserve 1986 $16 (3/31/91)
83 MONTEREY PENINSULA Merlot Monterey Doctors' Reserve 1985 $14 (1/31/89)
74 MONTEREY PENINSULA Merlot Monterey Doctors' Reserve 1984 $12 (12/15/87)
76 MONTEREY VINEYARD Merlot Monterey County Classic 1988 $6 (12/31/90)
72 MOUNTAIN VIEW Merlot Napa County 1989 $6 (5/31/91)
90 MURPHY-GOODE Merlot Alexander Valley Premier Vineyard 1986 $14 (1/31/89)
70 NAPA CELLARS Merlot California 1989 $7 (5/31/91)
75 NAPA CREEK Merlot Napa Valley 1988 $13 (3/31/91)
83 NAPA CREEK Merlot Napa Valley 1987 $13.50 (6/15/90)
85+ NEWTON Merlot Napa Valley 1988 $11 (4/30/90) (BT)
81 NEWTON Merlot Napa Valley 1987 $17 (7/31/90)
85+ NEWTON Merlot Napa Valley 1987 $17 (4/15/89) (BT)
83 NEWTON Merlot Napa Valley 1986 $15 (12/31/88)
85+ NEWTON Merlot Napa Valley 1986 $15 (4/15/88) (BT)
93 NEWTON Merlot Napa Valley 1985 $14 (3/31/88)
90 NEWTON Merlot Napa Valley 1983 $11.50 (2/28/87)
83 NEWTON Merlot Napa Valley 1982 $12.50 (2/16/86)
83 NEWTON Merlot Napa Valley 1982 $12.50 (10/01/85)
91 NEWTON Merlot Napa Valley 1981 $12.50 (12/16/84)
85+ NEWTON Merlot Napa Valley Reserve 1987 (NR) (4/15/89) (BT)
70 PAGOR Merlot Santa Maria Valley 1984 $10.25 (4/30/88)
75 PARDUCCI Merlot Mendocino County 1983 $8 (12/15/87)
78 PARDUCCI Merlot North Coast 1988 $9.50 (4/30/91)
80 JOSEPH PHELPS Merlot Napa Valley 1987 $18 (7/31/90)
84 JOSEPH PHELPS Merlot Napa Valley 1986 $15 (6/30/88)

UNITED STATES
CALIFORNIA/*MERLOT*

85+ PINE RIDGE Merlot Napa Valley Selected Cuvée 1990 (NR) (5/15/91) (BT)
85+ PINE RIDGE Merlot Napa Valley Selected Cuvée 1988 (NR) (4/30/90) (BT)
88 PINE RIDGE Merlot Napa Valley Selected Cuvée 1987 $15 (4/15/90)
90+ PINE RIDGE Merlot Napa Valley Selected Cuvée 1987 $15 (4/15/89) (BT)
80 PINE RIDGE Merlot Napa Valley Selected Cuvée 1986 $15 (6/30/89)
85+ PINE RIDGE Merlot Napa Valley Selected Cuvée 1986 $15 (4/15/88) (BT)
91 PINE RIDGE Merlot Napa Valley Selected Cuvée 1985 Rel: $13 Cur: $18 (2/15/88) SS
80 PINE RIDGE Merlot Napa Valley Selected Cuvée 1984 $13 (5/15/87)
83 PINE RIDGE Merlot Napa Valley Selected Cuvée 1983 $13 (12/16/85)
90 PINE RIDGE Merlot Napa Valley Selected Cuvée 1982 $13 (10/01/85)
82 PINE RIDGE Merlot Napa Valley Selected Cuvée 1981 $12.50 (3/16/84)
86 QUAIL RIDGE Merlot Napa Valley 1987 $15 (6/15/90)
90 QUAIL RIDGE Merlot Napa Valley 1985 $13.50 (3/31/89)
77 RANCHO SISQUOC Merlot Santa Maria Valley 1986 $9 (12/15/89)
87 RAVENSWOOD Merlot Sonoma County 1987 $18 (1/31/90)
90+ RAVENSWOOD Merlot Sonoma County 1987 $18 (4/15/89) (BT)
80 RAVENSWOOD Merlot Sonoma County 1986 $18 (12/31/88)
90+ RAVENSWOOD Merlot Sonoma County 1986 $18 (4/15/88) (BT)
85 RAVENSWOOD Merlot Sonoma County 1984 $11 (2/28/87)
61 RAVENSWOOD Merlot Sonoma County 1983 $11 (5/16/86)
84 RAVENSWOOD Merlot Sonoma County Vintners Blend 1989 $9 (3/31/91) BB
83 RICHARDSON Merlot Carneros Sonoma Valley Gregory 1989 $14 (3/31/91)
75 RIDGE Merlot Sonoma County Bradford Mountain 1987 $17 (7/15/90)
80+ RIDGE Merlot Sonoma County Bradford Mountain 1987 $17 (4/15/89) (BT)
64 RIDGE Merlot Sonoma County Bradford Mountain 1986 $16 (7/31/89)
87 ROMBAUER Merlot Napa Valley 1987 $14 (2/15/90)
78 ROMBAUER Merlot Napa Valley 1986 $14 (7/31/89)
87 ROUND HILL Merlot Napa Valley 1984 $9 (5/15/87)
92 ROUND HILL Merlot Napa Valley 1983 $7.50 (1/31/87) SS
65 ROUND HILL Merlot Napa Valley 1982 $7.50 (2/16/86)
82 ROUND HILL Merlot Napa Valley Reserve 1986 $10.75 (12/31/88)
84 ROUND HILL Merlot Napa Valley Reserve 1985 $10 (5/31/88)
74 RUTHERFORD HILL Merlot Napa Valley 1987 $14 (3/31/91)
68 RUTHERFORD HILL Merlot Napa Valley 1986 $13 (6/15/90)
92 RUTHERFORD HILL Merlot Napa Valley 1985 $12 (1/31/89)
84 RUTHERFORD HILL Merlot Napa Valley 1984 $11 (4/30/88)
87 RUTHERFORD HILL Merlot Napa Valley 1983 $10 (8/31/87)
79 RUTHERFORD HILL Merlot Napa Valley 1982 $10.50 (5/16/86)
78 RUTHERFORD HILL Merlot Napa Valley 1981 $10 (10/01/85)
87 RUTHERFORD RANCH Merlot Napa Valley 1986 $11.75 (12/31/88)
92 RUTHERFORD RANCH Merlot Napa Valley 1985 $10.50 (4/30/88)
83 RUTHERFORD RANCH Merlot Napa Valley 1984 $9.75 (10/15/87)
85 ST. CLEMENT Merlot Napa Valley 1987 $16 (12/31/90)
74 ST. CLEMENT Merlot Napa Valley 1986 $15 (10/31/89)
91 ST. CLEMENT Merlot Napa Valley 1985 $15 (3/31/89)
81 ST. CLEMENT Merlot Napa Valley 1983 $14.50 (5/31/88)
80 ST. FRANCIS Merlot Sonoma Valley 1987 $14 (6/15/90)
85 ST. FRANCIS Merlot Sonoma Valley 1986 $14 (6/30/89)
90+ ST. FRANCIS Merlot Sonoma Valley 1986 $14 (4/15/88) (BT)
66 ST. FRANCIS Merlot Sonoma Valley 1985 $12 (10/15/88)
88 ST. FRANCIS Merlot Sonoma Valley 1984 $12 (10/31/87)
80 ST. FRANCIS Merlot Sonoma Valley 1983 $11 (7/31/87)
78 ST. FRANCIS Merlot Sonoma Valley 1982 $10.75 (10/01/85)
94 ST. FRANCIS Merlot Sonoma Valley Reserve 1986 $20 (1/31/90)
81 ST. FRANCIS Merlot Sonoma Valley Reserve 1985 $14.50 (12/31/88)
74 ST. FRANCIS Merlot Sonoma Valley Reserve 1984 $16 (2/15/88)
66 SANFORD Merlot Santa Barbara County 1984 $18 (12/31/87)
82 SANTA CRUZ MOUNTAIN Merlot California 1983 $10 (10/01/85)
90+ SANTA CRUZ MOUNTAIN Merlot Central Coast 1988 (NR) (4/30/90) (BT)
80+ SANTA CRUZ MOUNTAIN Merlot Central Coast 1987 (NR) (4/15/89) (BT)
85 SEBASTIANI Merlot Sonoma County Family Selection 1985 $7 (9/30/88)
85+ SHAFER Merlot Napa Valley 1990 (NR) (5/15/91) (BT)
83 SHAFER Merlot Napa Valley 1988 $16.50 (12/31/90)
85+ SHAFER Merlot Napa Valley 1988 $16.50 (4/30/90) (BT)
92 SHAFER Merlot Napa Valley 1987 $15 (10/15/89)
85+ SHAFER Merlot Napa Valley 1987 $15 (4/15/89) (BT)
91 SHAFER Merlot Napa Valley 1986 $13 (12/31/88)
90 SHAFER Merlot Napa Valley 1985 $12.50 (12/15/87)
87 SHAFER Merlot Napa Valley 1984 $12.50 (2/28/87)
93 SHAFER Merlot Napa Valley 1983 $10 (2/16/86)
92 SILVERADO Merlot Napa Valley 1987 $14 (4/15/90)
85+ SILVERADO Merlot Napa Valley 1987 $14 (4/15/89) (BT)
91 SILVERADO Merlot Napa Valley 1986 $12 (8/31/89)
78 SILVERADO Merlot Napa Valley 1984 $12.50 (12/15/87)
86 SILVERADO Merlot Stags Leap District 1988 $15.50 (5/31/91)
88 ROBERT SINSKEY Merlot Napa Valley 1987 $18 (3/31/91)
83 ROBERT SINSKEY Merlot Napa Valley 1986 $17 (10/15/89)
76 SMITH & HOOK Merlot Monterey Santa Lucia Highlands 1988 $15 (3/31/91)
83 SMITH & HOOK Merlot Napa County 1987 $15 (12/31/90)
75 SMITH & HOOK Merlot Napa County 1987 $15 (7/31/90)
86 SMITH & HOOK Merlot Napa County 1986 $20 (8/31/89)
86 STAG'S LEAP WINE CELLARS Merlot Napa Valley 1985 $16 (5/31/88)
78 STAG'S LEAP WINE CELLARS Merlot Napa Valley 1984 $15 (5/15/87)
78 STAG'S LEAP WINE CELLARS Merlot Napa Valley 1982 $13.50 (10/01/85)

82 STAG'S LEAP WINE CELLARS Merlot Napa Valley 1981 $13.50 (4/16/84)
84 STAGS' LEAP WINERY Merlot Napa Valley 1986 $17 (12/31/90)
83 STAGS' LEAP WINERY Merlot Napa Valley 1981 $12 (2/16/85)
85+ STELTZNER Merlot Stags Leap District 1990 (NR) (5/15/91) (BT)
90 STERLING Merlot Carneros Winery Lake 1987 $25 (12/31/90)
85+ STERLING Merlot Napa Valley 1990 (NR) (5/15/91) (BT)
83 STERLING Merlot Napa Valley 1988 $15 (4/15/91)
85+ STERLING Merlot Napa Valley 1988 $15 (4/30/90) (BT)
83 STERLING Merlot Napa Valley 1987 $13 (6/15/90)
80+ STERLING Merlot Napa Valley 1987 $13 (4/15/89) (BT)
85 STERLING Merlot Napa Valley 1986 $14 (3/31/89)
80+ STERLING Merlot Napa Valley 1986 $14 (4/15/88) (BT)
87 STERLING Merlot Napa Valley 1985 $14 (3/31/88)
93 STERLING Merlot Napa Valley 1984 $11.50 (4/30/87)
91 STERLING Merlot Napa Valley 1983 $11 (6/01/86)
83 STERLING Merlot Napa Valley 1982 $12 (10/01/85)
83 STERLING Merlot Napa Valley 1981 $11 (3/01/84)
84 STONEGATE Merlot Napa Valley 1986 $15 (4/15/90)
85+ STONEGATE Merlot Napa Valley Pershing Vineyard 1990 (NR) (5/15/91) (BT)
83 STONEGATE Merlot Napa Valley Pershing Vineyard 1987 $16.50 (3/31/91)
86 STONEGATE Merlot Napa Valley Spaulding Vineyard 1987 $16.50 (3/31/91)
84 STONEGATE Merlot Napa Valley Spaulding Vineyard 1982 $14 (2/28/87)
68 STONEGATE Merlot Napa Valley Spaulding Vineyard 1980 $12 (10/01/85)
85 STONEGATE Merlot Napa Valley Spaulding Vineyard Proprietor's Reserve 1984 $15 (12/31/88)
83 STRATFORD Merlot California 1987 $13 (10/31/89)
78 STRATFORD Merlot California 1986 $10 (1/31/89)
79 STRATFORD Merlot California 1983 $8.50 (9/30/86)
82 STRAUS Merlot Napa Valley 1988 $14 (12/31/90)
90 STRAUS Merlot Napa Valley 1987 $12 (2/15/90)
93 STRAUS Merlot Napa Valley 1986 $11 (2/28/89)
81 STRAUS Merlot Napa Valley 1985 $10 (2/15/88)
79 RODNEY STRONG Merlot Russian River Valley River West Vineyard 1985 $12 (2/28/89)
83 TAFT STREET Merlot Sonoma County 1985 $10 (5/31/88)
74 TERRA Merlot Napa Valley 1988 $12 (5/31/91)
77 M.G. VALLEJO Merlot California 1987 $7 (6/15/90)
73 M.G. VALLEJO Merlot California 1987 $7 (10/31/89)
81 VICHON Merlot Napa Valley 1988 $16 (12/31/90)
85+ VICHON Merlot Napa Valley 1988 $16 (4/30/90) (BT)
91 VICHON Merlot Napa Valley 1987 $16 (2/15/90)
80+ VICHON Merlot Napa Valley 1987 $16 (4/15/89) (BT)
90+ VICHON Merlot Napa Valley 1986 (NR) (4/15/88) (BT)
86 VICHON Merlot Napa Valley 1986 $16 (8/31/89)
73 VICHON Merlot Napa Valley 1986 $16 (6/30/89)
88 VICHON Merlot Napa Valley 1985 $14 (12/15/87)
90 VINA VISTA Merlot Alexander Valley 1985 $8 (10/31/87)
77 WILD HORSE Merlot Central Coast 1986 $11 (7/31/89)
77 WHITEHALL LANE Merlot Knights Valley 1987 $16 (7/15/90)
85+ WHITEHALL LANE Merlot Knights Valley 1987 $16 (4/15/89) (BT)
90+ WHITEHALL LANE Merlot Knights Valley 1986 (NR) (4/15/88) (BT)
87 WHITEHALL LANE Merlot Knights Valley 1984 $14 (12/31/87)
85 WHITEHALL LANE Merlot Knights Valley 1983 $12 (10/01/85)
92 WHITEHALL LANE Merlot Knights Valley 1982 Rel: $10 Cur: $19 (6/01/85) CS
72 WHITEHALL LANE Merlot Knights Valley Reserve 1986 $15 (7/31/89)
82 WHITEHALL LANE Merlot Knights Valley Summers Ranch 1988 $18 (3/31/91)
60 WOLTNER Merlot Alexander Valley Cask 465 1982 $4.75 (4/16/85)
80 YORK MOUNTAIN Merlot San Luis Obispo County 1986 $10 (12/15/89)
84 STEPHEN ZELLERBACH Merlot Alexander Valley 1982 $8.50 (10/01/85)
68 STEPHEN ZELLERBACH Merlot Alexander Valley 1980 $8.50 (5/01/84)

MUSCAT

75 ALDERBROOK Muscat Canelli Sonoma County 1989 $7.50 (7/15/90)
67 ARCIERO Muscat Canelli Paso Robles 1988 $6 (12/15/89)
72 AUSTIN Muscat Canelli Santa Barbara County 1988 $8.50 (12/15/89)
80 BENZIGER Muscat Canelli Sonoma County 1987 $10 (8/31/89)
78 CLAIBORNE & CHURCHILL Muscat Canelli California Dry Alsatian Style 1987 $8 (12/15/89)
76 EBERLE Muscat Canelli Paso Robles 1988 $7.50 (12/15/89)
76 FETZER Muscat Canelli Lake County 1985 $6 (10/31/86)
83 FOLIE A DEUX Muscat Canelli Napa Valley Muscat à Deux 1988 $7.50 (8/31/89)
83 KENDALL-JACKSON Muscat Canelli Lake County 1985 $7.50 (6/16/86)
79 MARKHAM Muscat Napa Valley Blanc 1989 $9 (7/15/90)
84 MARKHAM Muscat Napa Valley Blanc Markham Vineyard 1988 $9 (4/30/89)
93 MARKHAM Muscat Napa Valley Markham Vineyard Muscat de Frontignan 1987 $9 (5/15/88)
68 MISSION VIEW Muscat Canelli Paso Robles 1988 $7 (12/15/89)
78 ROBERT MONDAVI Muscat Napa Valley Moscato d'Oro 1988 $10 (4/30/90)
79 ROBERT MONDAVI Muscat Napa Valley Moscato d'Oro 1987 $11 (11/15/89)
83 ROBERT MONDAVI Muscat Napa Valley Moscato d'Oro 1984 $8.75 (12/31/86)
85 ROBERT PECOTA Muscato di Andrea California 1987 $9.50 (7/15/88)
89 ROBERT PECOTA Muscato di Andrea California 1986 $8.50 (8/31/87)
91 ROBERT PECOTA Muscato di Andrea California 1985 $8.50 (5/16/85)
86 ROBERT PECOTA Muscato di Andrea Napa Valley 1989 $9.25 (7/15/90)
78 PRESTON Muscat Canelli Dry Creek Valley 1987 $7 (8/31/89)

PETITE SIRAH

81 BLACK MOUNTAIN Petite Sirah Alexander Valley Bosun Crest 1985 $9 (2/15/89)
70 BOGLE Petite Sirah Clarksburg 1988 $7 (10/31/89)
73 R. & J. COOK Petite Sirah Clarksburg 1984 $6 (12/31/87)
86 R. & J. COOK Petite Sirah Clarksburg 1981 $5.50 (12/16/84)
74 FETZER Petite Syrah California Reserve 1986 $14 (8/31/90)
78 FETZER Petite Syrah Mendocino 1982 $5.50 (4/16/85)
85 FIELD STONE Petite Sirah Alexander Valley 1988 $15 (12/31/90)
84 FIELD STONE Petite Sirah Alexander Valley 1987 $15 (12/31/90)
79 FIELD STONE Petite Sirah Alexander Valley 1986 $15 (9/30/89)
83 FIELD STONE Petite Sirah Alexander Valley 1985 $11 (2/15/89)
88 FIELD STONE Petite Sirah Alexander Valley 1984 $11 (1/15/89)
69 FIELD STONE Petite Sirah Alexander Valley 1982 $8.50 (7/01/86)
86 FOPPIANO Petite Sirah Russian River Valley 1988 $8.25 (8/31/90)
83 FOPPIANO Petite Sirah Russian River Valley 1986 $8 (6/15/89)
84 FOPPIANO Petite Sirah Russian River Valley 1984 $7.50 (5/31/88)

79 FOPPIANO Petite Sirah Russian River Valley Le Grande Petite Reserve 1987 $20 (8/31/90)
78 FREEMARK ABBEY Petite Sirah Napa Valley 1980 (NA) (2/01/88)
87 FREEMARK ABBEY Petite Sirah Napa Valley 1979 (NA) (2/01/88)
80 FREEMARK ABBEY Petite Sirah Napa Valley 1978 (NA) (2/01/88)
82 FREEMARK ABBEY Petite Sirah Napa Valley 1977 (NA) (2/01/88)
77 FREEMARK ABBEY Petite Sirah Napa Valley 1976 (NA) (2/01/88)
73 FREEMARK ABBEY Petite Sirah Napa Valley 1975 (NA) (2/01/88)
80 FREEMARK ABBEY Petite Sirah Napa Valley 1974 (NA) (2/01/88)
86 FREEMARK ABBEY Petite Sirah Napa Valley 1973 (NA) (2/01/88)
76 FREEMARK ABBEY Petite Sirah Napa Valley 1972 (NA) (2/01/88)
90 FREEMARK ABBEY Petite Sirah Napa Valley 1971 (NA) (2/01/88)
81 FREEMARK ABBEY Petite Sirah Napa Valley 1969 (NA) (2/01/88)
87 FRICK Petite Sirah Monterey County 1985 $8 (2/15/89)
83 GUENOC Petite Sirah Guenoc Valley 1985 $15 (2/15/89)
77 GUENOC Petite Sirah Guenoc Valley 1984 $7 (11/15/87)
82 HOP KILN Petite Sirah Russian River Valley M. Griffin Vineyards 1987 $11 (2/28/90)
77 HOP KILN Petite Sirah Russian River Valley M. Griffin Vineyards 1985 $10.75 (3/31/88)
90 HOP KILN Petite Sirah Russian River Valley M. Griffin Vineyards 1984 $10 (2/15/87)
87 INGLENOOK Petite Sirah Napa Valley 1982 $5.50 (12/31/86) BB
86 INGLENOOK Petite Sirah Napa Valley 1981 $6 (2/01/85) BB
81 KARLY Petite Sirah Amador County Not So Petite Sirah 1988 $14 (12/31/90)
85 LOUIS M. MARTINI Petite Sirah Napa Valley 1985 $8.25 (10/31/89) BB
76 LOUIS M. MARTINI Petite Sirah Napa Valley 1983 $6 (12/31/87)
80 LOUIS M. MARTINI Petite Sirah Napa Valley 1982 $5.25 (9/15/86) BB
81 LOUIS M. MARTINI Petite Sirah Napa Valley Reserve 1986 $12 (10/31/90)
87 RIDGE Petite Sirah Napa County York Creek 1985 $9 (10/31/89)
70 RIDGE Petite Sirah Napa County York Creek 1984 $10 (1/31/88)
86 RIDGE Petite Sirah Napa County York Creek 1983 $9 (3/15/87)
90 RIDGE Petite Sirah Napa County York Creek 1981 $8.50 (10/01/84)
84 ROUDON-SMITH Petite Sirah San Luis Obispo County 1984 $8 (9/30/88)
87 STAG'S LEAP WINE CELLARS Petite Sirah Napa Valley 1987 $12 (8/31/90)
85 STAG'S LEAP WINE CELLARS Petite Sirah Napa Valley 1985 $9 (10/15/88)
73 STAG'S LEAP WINE CELLARS Petite Sirah Napa Valley 1982 $7 (12/01/85)
84 STAGS' LEAP WINERY Petite Syrah Napa Valley 1980 $10 (3/01/85)
61 WENTE BROS. Petite Sirah Livermore Valley 1981 $5 (12/01/85)

PINOT BLANC

83 AU BON CLIMAT Pinot Blanc Santa Barbara County 1990 $12.50 (7/15/91)
87 BUEHLER Pinot Blanc Napa Valley 1987 $9 (3/31/89)
84 BUEHLER Pinot Blanc Napa Valley 1986 $9 (7/15/88)
79 BUEHLER Pinot Blanc Napa Valley 1985 $8 (2/15/87)
85 BUEHLER Pinot Blanc Napa Valley 1984 $8 (2/01/86)
75 BUEHLER Pinot Blanc Napa Valley 1981 $8 (10/01/84)
84 BUEHLER Pinot Blanc Napa Valley Buehler Vineyards 1988 $9 (2/15/90)
88 CHALONE Pinot Blanc Chalone 1989 $17 (11/30/90)
88 CHALONE Pinot Blanc Chalone 1988 $17 (2/15/90)
87 CHALONE Pinot Blanc Chalone 1987 $17 (12/15/88)
89 CHATEAU ST. JEAN Pinot Blanc Alexander Valley Robert Young Vineyards 1988 $9 (5/31/91) BB
88 CHATEAU ST. JEAN Pinot Blanc Alexander Valley Robert Young Vineyards 1987 $9 (5/31/90)
85 CHATEAU ST. JEAN Pinot Blanc Alexander Valley Robert Young Vineyards 1985 $9 (12/15/89)
91 CHATEAU ST. JEAN Pinot Blanc Alexander Valley Robert Young Vineyards 1984 $9 (8/31/87)
81 CHATEAU ST. JEAN Pinot Blanc Alexander Valley Robert Young Vineyards 1983 $9 (2/01/86)
76 CHATEAU ST. JEAN Pinot Blanc Alexander Valley Robert Young Vineyards 1982 $11 (10/01/84)
84 CHATEAU ST. JEAN Pinot Blanc Sonoma County St. Jean Vineyards 1982 $10 (11/01/84)
78 CONGRESS SPRINGS Pinot Blanc Santa Clara County 1989 $9 (4/30/91)
84 CONGRESS SPRINGS Pinot Blanc Santa Clara County San Ysidro Vineyard 1988 $9.50 (8/31/89)
87 CONGRESS SPRINGS Pinot Blanc Santa Clara County San Ysidro Vineyard 1987 $9 (12/15/88)
88 CONGRESS SPRINGS Pinot Blanc Santa Cruz Mountains 1983 $9 (8/01/84)
82 ELLISTON Pinot Blanc Central Coast Sunol Valley Vineyard 1987 $10 (5/31/91)
83 JEKEL Pinot Blanc Arroyo Seco Arroyo Blanc 1985 $6 (6/15/89) BB
82 JEKEL Pinot Blanc Arroyo Seco Arroyo Blanc 1984 $6 (2/01/86)
81 JEKEL Pinot Blanc Arroyo Seco Home Vineyard 1984 $8 (3/31/89)
82 MERLION Pinot Blanc Napa Valley Coeur de Melon 1987 $9 (11/30/90)
83 MERLION Pinot Blanc Napa Valley Coeur de Melon 1986 $9.50 (1/31/88)
86 MIRASSOU Pinot Blanc Monterey County Limited Bottling Fifth Generation Harvest Reserve 1989 $12.50 (5/31/91)
70 MIRASSOU Pinot Blanc Monterey County White Burgundy 1985 $5.50 (6/30/87)
86 MONTEREY PENINSULA Pinot Blanc Arroyo Seco Cobblestone Vineyards 1986 $9 (1/31/88)
87 MONTEREY PENINSULA Pinot Blanc Monterey Doctor's Reserve 1988 $12 (4/30/91)

PINOT NOIR

89 ACACIA Pinot Noir Carneros Napa Valley 1988 $14 (2/28/91)
87 ACACIA Pinot Noir Carneros Napa Valley 1987 $13 (2/15/90)
88 ACACIA Pinot Noir Carneros Napa Valley 1986 $15 (6/15/88)
84 ACACIA Pinot Noir Carneros Napa Valley 1985 $12 (12/15/87)
95 ACACIA Pinot Noir Carneros Napa Valley 1984 $11 (12/15/86) SS
81 ACACIA Pinot Noir Carneros Napa Valley Iund Vineyard 1984 $15 (3/15/87)
77 ACACIA Pinot Noir Carneros Napa Valley Iund Vineyard 1983 $15.50 (8/31/86)
91 ACACIA Pinot Noir Carneros Napa Valley Iund Vineyard 1982 Rel: $15 Cur: $29 (7/16/84) CS
89 ACACIA Pinot Noir Carneros Napa Valley Lee Vineyard 1983 $15.50 (8/31/86)
90 ACACIA Pinot Noir Carneros Napa Valley Lee Vineyard 1982 $15 (7/16/84)
88 ACACIA Pinot Noir Carneros Napa Valley Madonna Vineyard 1986 $18 (6/15/88)
88 ACACIA Pinot Noir Carneros Napa Valley Madonna Vineyard 1985 $16 (12/15/87)
88 ACACIA Pinot Noir Carneros Napa Valley Madonna Vineyard 1984 $16 (3/15/87)
93 ACACIA Pinot Noir Carneros Napa Valley Madonna Vineyard 1983 $15.50 (8/31/86)
91 ACACIA Pinot Noir Carneros Napa Valley St. Clair Vineyard 1988 $20 (2/28/91)
89 ACACIA Pinot Noir Carneros Napa Valley St. Clair Vineyard 1987 $18 (2/15/90)
91 ACACIA Pinot Noir Carneros Napa Valley St. Clair Vineyard 1986 $18 (6/15/88)
91 ACACIA Pinot Noir Carneros Napa Valley St. Clair Vineyard 1985 $16 (12/15/87)
93 ACACIA Pinot Noir Carneros Napa Valley St. Clair Vineyard 1984 $16 (11/30/86)
95 ACACIA Pinot Noir Carneros Napa Valley St. Clair Vineyard 1983 Rel: $15 Cur: $30 (10/01/85) CS
89 ACACIA Pinot Noir Carneros Napa Valley St. Clair Vineyard 1982 $15 (7/16/84)
78 ACACIA Pinot Noir Carneros Napa Valley Winery Lake Vineyard 1983 $15 (11/16/85)
90 ACACIA Pinot Noir Carneros Napa Valley Winery Lake Vineyard 1982 $15 (7/16/84)
74 ALEXANDER VALLEY Pinot Noir Alexander Valley 1987 $9 (5/31/90)
81 ALEXANDER VALLEY Pinot Noir Alexander Valley 1985 $8 (4/15/88)
87 ALEXANDER VALLEY Pinot Noir Alexander Valley 1984 $7 (2/15/88)
75 ALEXANDER VALLEY Pinot Noir Alexander Valley 1982 $6.50 (11/01/84)
69 ALMADEN Pinot Noir San Benito County 1982 $5 (6/30/87)
70 ARIES Pinot Noir Los Carneros Cuvée Vivace 1989 $8 (4/30/91)
80 AU BON CLIMAT Pinot Noir Santa Barbara County 1988 $16 (4/30/91)
84 AU BON CLIMAT Pinot Noir Santa Barbara County 1987 $16 (12/15/89)
73 AU BON CLIMAT Pinot Noir Santa Barbara County 1985 $12 (6/15/88)
88 AU BON CLIMAT Pinot Noir Santa Ynez Valley Benedict Vineyard 1987 $30 (12/15/89)
83 AU BON CLIMAT Pinot Noir Santa Ynez Valley Rancho Vinedo Vineyard 1988 $12.50 (12/15/89)
77 AUSTIN Pinot Noir Santa Barbara County 1987 $15 (12/15/89)
78 AUSTIN Pinot Noir Santa Barbara County 1983 $25 (12/15/89)
75 AUSTIN Pinot Noir Santa Barbara County Artist Series 1988 $10 (12/15/89)
88 AUSTIN Pinot Noir Santa Barbara County Bien Nacido Vineyard 1982 $10 (3/16/85)
87 AUSTIN Pinot Noir Santa Barbara County Sierra Madre Vineyards 1982 $12 (5/01/84)
83 LAWRENCE J. BARGETTO Pinot Noir Carneros Madonna Vineyard 1985 $12.50 (9/15/88)
81 LAWRENCE J. BARGETTO Pinot Noir Santa Maria Valley 1987 $16 (2/28/91)
76 BARROW GREEN Pinot Noir California 1986 $16 (10/15/89)
77 BAY CELLARS Pinot Noir Los Carneros 1985 $15 (6/15/88)
74 BEAULIEU Pinot Noir Napa Valley Beaumont 1986 $7 (6/15/88)
78 BEAULIEU Pinot Noir Napa Valley Beaumont 1985 $6.25 (6/15/88)
85 BEAULIEU Pinot Noir Napa Valley Carneros Reserve 1989 $13 (4/30/91)
87 BEAULIEU Pinot Noir Napa Valley Carneros Reserve 1988 $9.50 (4/15/90)
90 BEAULIEU Pinot Noir Napa Valley Carneros Reserve 1987 $9.50 (12/31/88)
88 BEAULIEU Pinot Noir Napa Valley Los Carneros 1980 $10 (8/31/86)
88 BEAULIEU Pinot Noir Napa Valley Los Carneros Reserve 1986 $9.50 (9/15/88)
74 BEAULIEU Pinot Noir Napa Valley Los Carneros Reserve 1985 $9.50 (1/31/88)
73 BELVEDERE Pinot Noir Los Carneros Winery Lake 1983 $12 (12/15/87)
58 BELVEDERE Pinot Noir Los Carneros Winery Lake 1982 $12 (8/31/86)
73 BELVEDERE Pinot Noir Sonoma County Bacigalupi 1985 $12 (6/15/88)
65 BELVEDERE Pinot Noir Sonoma County Bacigalupi 1982 $12 (11/16/85)
65 BONNY DOON Pinot Noir Sonoma County 1981 $9 (3/01/84)
82 BOUCHAINE Pinot Noir Carneros 1987 $13 (10/31/90)
85 BOUCHAINE Pinot Noir Carneros Reserve 1987 $20 (10/31/90)
78 BOUCHAINE Pinot Noir Carneros Napa Valley 1988 $15 (7/31/91)
86 BOUCHAINE Pinot Noir Carneros Napa Valley 1986 $12 (5/31/89)
82 BOUCHAINE Pinot Noir Carneros Napa Valley 1985 $11.50 (12/31/88)
76 BOUCHAINE Pinot Noir Los Carneros 1985 $7.50 (6/30/87)
81 BOUCHAINE Pinot Noir Napa Valley 1982 $20 (6/30/87)
87 BOUCHAINE Pinot Noir Napa Valley Los Carneros 1982 $12.50 (7/16/85)
86 BOUCHAINE Pinot Noir Napa Valley Los Carneros Winery Lake Vineyard 1982 $15 (8/31/86)
91 BOUCHAINE Pinot Noir Napa Valley Los Carneros Winery Lake Vineyard 1982 $15 (3/01/86) CS
59 DAVID BRUCE Pinot Noir Santa Cruz Mountains 1986 $18 (3/31/90)
81 DAVID BRUCE Pinot Noir Santa Cruz Mountains 1984 $15 (6/30/87)
78 DAVID BRUCE Pinot Noir Santa Cruz Mountains 1983 $15 (8/31/86)
81 BUENA VISTA Pinot Noir Carneros 1989 $11 (7/31/91)
82 BUENA VISTA Pinot Noir Carneros 1988 $11 (12/15/90)
80 BUENA VISTA Pinot Noir Carneros Private Reserve 1987 $14 (6/30/91)
85 BUENA VISTA Pinot Noir Carneros Private Reserve 1986 $14 (3/31/90)
81 BUENA VISTA Pinot Noir Carneros Private Reserve 1984 $14.50 (2/15/88)
75 BUENA VISTA Pinot Noir Sonoma Valley Carneros 1983 $14 (8/31/86)
71 BUENA VISTA Pinot Noir Sonoma Valley Carneros 1980 $7 (4/16/84)
88 BUENA VISTA Pinot Noir Sonoma Valley Carneros Private Reserve 1981 $14 (8/31/86)
83 BYINGTON Pinot Noir California 1988 $15 (4/30/91)
74 BYINGTON Pinot Noir Napa Valley 1987 $15 (4/30/91)
61 BYINGTON Pinot Noir Napa Valley 1987 $15 (2/28/91)
82 DAVIS BYNUM Pinot Noir Russian River Valley Artist Series 1985 $15 (6/15/88)
86 DAVIS BYNUM Pinot Noir Russian River Valley Limited Release 1988 $16 (4/30/91)
83 DAVIS BYNUM Pinot Noir Russian River Valley Limited Release 1986 $14 (3/31/90)
89 DAVIS BYNUM Pinot Noir Russian River Valley Limited Release 1984 $14 (5/31/88)
71 DAVIS BYNUM Pinot Noir Russian River Valley Westside Road 1983 $10 (7/16/86)
82 DAVIS BYNUM Pinot Noir Sonoma County Reserve Bottling 1986 $9 (9/15/88)
67 DAVIS BYNUM Pinot Noir Sonoma County Reserve Bottling 1985 $7 (1/31/88)
88 BYRON Pinot Noir Santa Barbara County 1986 $12 (6/15/88)
81 BYRON Pinot Noir Santa Barbara County 1985 $12 (6/15/88)
85 BYRON Pinot Noir Santa Barbara County Reserve 1987 $16 (12/15/89)
84 BYRON Pinot Noir Santa Barbara County Reserve 1986 $12 (6/15/88)
85 BYRON Pinot Noir Santa Barbara County Sierra Madre Vineyards 1984 $12.50 (8/31/86)
82 CALERA Pinot Noir Central Coast 1987 $14 (2/15/90)
93 CALERA Pinot Noir San Benito County Jensen 1987 $30 (4/30/91)
88 CALERA Pinot Noir San Benito County Jensen 1986 $25 (5/31/89)
88 CALERA Pinot Noir San Benito County Jensen 1985 $25 (6/15/88)
80 CALERA Pinot Noir San Benito County Jensen 1983 $22 (8/31/86)
88 CALERA Pinot Noir California Jensen 1982 $23 (1/01/85)
80 CALERA Pinot Noir San Benito County Reed 1987 $35 (4/30/91)
75 CALERA Pinot Noir San Benito County Reed 1982 $23 (8/31/86)
85 CALERA Pinot Noir San Benito County Selleck 1986 $30 (3/31/90)
82 CALERA Pinot Noir Santa Barbara County Bien Nacido Vineyard 1985 $12.50 (6/15/88)
62 CALERA Pinot Noir Santa Barbara County Los Alamos Vineyard 1982 $10 (11/16/85)
88 CAMBRIA Pinot Noir Santa Maria Valley Julia's Vineyard 1988 $16 (12/15/90)
83 CARNEROS CREEK Pinot Noir Carneros 1988 $15.50 (10/31/90)
92 CARNEROS CREEK Pinot Noir Carneros 1983 $12.50 (8/31/86)
82 CARNEROS CREEK Pinot Noir Carneros Fleur de Carneros 1989 $9 (4/30/91)
85 CARNEROS CREEK Pinot Noir Carneros Fleur de Carneros 1988 $10 (2/15/90)
92 CARNEROS CREEK Pinot Noir Carneros Fleur de Carneros 1987 $9 (2/28/89) SS
89 CARNEROS CREEK Pinot Noir Carneros Signature Reserve 1988 $28 (10/31/90)
87 CARNEROS CREEK Pinot Noir Carneros Signature Reserve First Release 1987 $28 (10/31/90)
92 CARNEROS CREEK Pinot Noir Los Carneros 1986 $14.50 (12/31/88)
88 CARNEROS CREEK Pinot Noir Los Carneros 1985 $13 (4/15/88)
92 CARNEROS CREEK Pinot Noir Los Carneros 1984 $15 (3/15/87)

UNITED STATES
CALIFORNIA/*PINOT NOIR*

85 CARNEROS CREEK Pinot Noir Napa Valley Los Carneros 1987 $15 (2/15/90)
81 CARNEROS QUALITY ALLIANCE Pinot Noir Carneros 1986 $23 (7/31/89)
90 CARNEROS QUALITY ALLIANCE Pinot Noir Carneros 1985 $25 (12/31/87)
82 CASTORO Pinot Noir Central Coast 1987 $4.50 (12/15/89) BB
85 CAYMUS Pinot Noir Napa Valley 1981 $7.50 (5/01/84) BB
81 CAYMUS Pinot Noir Napa Valley 1980 $6.50 (3/16/84)
86 CAYMUS Pinot Noir Napa Valley Special Selection 1987 $14 (12/15/90)
82 CAYMUS Pinot Noir Napa Valley Special Selection 1986 $15 (12/31/89)
90 CAYMUS Pinot Noir Napa Valley Special Selection 1985 $15 (12/31/88)
79 CAYMUS Pinot Noir Napa Valley Special Selection 1984 $12.50 (2/15/88)
85 CAYMUS Pinot Noir Napa Valley Special Selection 1982 $12.50 (8/31/86)
89 CHALONE Pinot Noir Chalone 1986 $25 (12/15/90)
85 CHALONE Pinot Noir Chalone 1985 $17.50 (2/15/90)
88 CHALONE Pinot Noir Chalone 1984 $18.50 (12/15/87)
89 CHALONE Pinot Noir Chalone 1983 $18.50 (8/31/86)
66 CHALONE Pinot Noir Chalone 1982 $20 (8/31/86)
83 CHALONE Pinot Noir Chalone 1981 $18.50 (12/16/84)
71 CHALONE Pinot Noir Chalone Red Table Wine 1983 $9 (8/31/86)
92 CHALONE Pinot Noir Chalone Reserve 1981 $28 (8/31/86)
77 CHATEAU DE LEU Pinot Noir Solano County Green Valley 1985 $7 (2/28/89)
75 CHATEAU ST. JEAN Pinot Noir Sonoma Valley McCrea Vineyards 1983 $12 (9/30/87)
86 CLOS DU BOIS Pinot Noir Dry Creek Valley Proprietor's Reserve 1980 $10.75 (7/16/84)
80 CLOS DU BOIS Pinot Noir Sonoma County 1988 $12 (4/30/91)
73 CLOS DU BOIS Pinot Noir Sonoma County 1987 $12 (5/31/90)
87 CLOS DU BOIS Pinot Noir Sonoma County 1986 $11 (10/15/89)
77 CLOS DU BOIS Pinot Noir Sonoma County 1986 $11 (6/15/88)
70 CLOS DU BOIS Pinot Noir Sonoma County 1985 $10.50 (6/15/88)
86 CLOS DU BOIS Pinot Noir Sonoma County 1984 $8 (8/31/86)
70 CLOS DU BOIS Pinot Noir Sonoma County 1983 $8 (8/31/86)
60 CLOS DU BOIS Pinot Noir Sonoma County 1982 $8 (7/16/84)
84 CLOS DU VAL Pinot Noir Napa Valley 1987 $13.50 (4/30/91)
80 CLOS DU VAL Pinot Noir Napa Valley 1986 $16 (2/15/90)
80 CLOS DU VAL Pinot Noir Napa Valley 1985 $12.50 (6/15/88)
78 CLOS DU VAL Pinot Noir Napa Valley 1984 $11.50 (9/30/87)
66 CLOS DU VAL Pinot Noir Napa Valley 1983 $11.50 (8/31/86)
75 CLOS DU VAL Pinot Noir Napa Valley 1982 $10.75 (9/01/84)
84 CONGRESS SPRINGS Pinot Noir Santa Clara County 1989 $10 (4/30/91)
87 CONGRESS SPRINGS Pinot Noir Santa Clara County San Ysidro Vineyard 1988 $9 (3/31/90)
83 CORBETT CANYON Pinot Noir Central Coast Reserve 1986 $8 (12/15/89)
81 CORBETT CANYON Pinot Noir Santa Maria Valley Sierra Madre Vineyard Reserve 1985 $12 (2/15/88)
82 COSENTINO Pinot Noir Sonoma County 1989 $13 (6/30/91)
80 CRESTON MANOR Pinot Noir San Luis Obispo County Petit d'Noir 1987 $8 (8/31/88)
74 CRESTON MANOR Pinot Noir San Luis Obispo County Petit d'Noir Maceration Carbonique 1988 $8 (12/15/89)
74 CRYSTAL VALLEY Pinot Noir North Coast Reserve Edition 1986 $10.50 (6/15/88)
87 DE LOACH Pinot Noir Russian River Valley 1986 $12 (5/31/90)
72 DE LOACH Pinot Noir Russian River Valley 1985 $12 (6/15/88)
75 DE LOACH Pinot Noir Russian River Valley 1983 $10 (3/01/86)
76 DE LOACH Pinot Noir Russian River Valley 1982 $10 (8/31/86)
82 DE LOACH Pinot Noir Russian River Valley OFS 1987 $25 (10/31/90)
91 DEHLINGER Pinot Noir Russian River Valley 1987 $14 (2/15/90)
88 DEHLINGER Pinot Noir Russian River Valley 1986 $13 (5/31/89)
85 DEHLINGER Pinot Noir Russian River Valley 1985 $12 (2/15/88)
89 DEHLINGER Pinot Noir Russian River Valley 1984 $11 (6/30/87)
89 DEHLINGER Pinot Noir Russian River Valley 1983 $10 (8/31/86)
86 DEHLINGER Pinot Noir Russian River Valley 1982 $10 (10/01/85)
77 DOMAINE DE CLARCK Pinot Noir Monterey Première 1989 $15 (4/30/91)
90 DOMAINE LAURIER Pinot Noir Sonoma County Green Valley 1986 $10 (6/15/88)
63 DOMAINE LAURIER Pinot Noir Sonoma County Green Valley 1982 $10 (11/15/87)
78 DOMAINE LAURIER Pinot Noir Sonoma County Green Valley 1981 $10 (2/16/85)
79 DONNA MARIA Pinot Noir Chalk Hill 1981 $6 (9/16/84)
80 DURNEY Pinot Noir Carmel Valley 1988 $16 (4/30/91)
89 EDMEADES Pinot Noir Anderson Valley 1982 $10 (2/16/85)
76 EDNA VALLEY Pinot Noir Edna Valley 1986 $15 (12/15/89)
78 EDNA VALLEY Pinot Noir Edna Valley 1985 $15 (6/15/88)
85 EDNA VALLEY Pinot Noir Edna Valley 1984 $10 (12/15/87)
57 EDNA VALLEY Pinot Noir Edna Valley 1983 $10 (4/15/87)
80 EDNA VALLEY Pinot Noir Edna Valley 1982 $11.50 (8/31/86)
86 ETUDE Pinot Noir Napa Valley 1988 $20 (12/15/90)
83 ETUDE Pinot Noir Napa Valley 1985 $16 (6/15/88)
88 GARY FARRELL Pinot Noir Russian River Valley 1989 $16 (7/31/91)
88 GARY FARRELL Pinot Noir Russian River Valley 1988 $16 (10/31/90)
90 GARY FARRELL Pinot Noir Russian River Valley 1986 $15 (6/15/88)
62 GARY FARRELL Pinot Noir Russian River Valley 1985 $13.50 (6/15/88)
79 GARY FARRELL Pinot Noir Russian River Valley 1984 $12 (4/15/87)
88 GARY FARRELL Pinot Noir Russian River Valley 1983 $12 (8/31/86)
87 GARY FARRELL Pinot Noir Russian River Valley Allen Vineyard 1988 $25 (10/31/90)
84 GARY FARRELL Pinot Noir Sonoma County Howard Allen Vineyard 1987 $20 (2/15/90)
77 FELTON EMPIRE Pinot Noir California Tonneaux Français 1984 $12 (5/15/87)
65 FETZER Pinot Noir California Special Reserve 1980 $13 (8/31/86)
80 FETZER Pinot Noir Mendocino 1981 $5.50 (4/01/84)
87 FETZER Pinot Noir Mendocino County Reserve 1986 $17.50 (10/31/90)
87 FETZER Pinot Noir Mendocino County Reserve 1986 $17.50 (2/15/90)

78 FETZER Pinot Noir Mendocino County Special Reserve 1985 $13 (6/15/88)
77 FIRESTONE Pinot Noir Santa Ynez Valley 1986 $10 (12/15/89)
71 FIRESTONE Pinot Noir Santa Ynez Valley 1983 $9 (11/15/87)
73 FIRESTONE Pinot Noir Santa Ynez Valley 1981 $8.25 (5/16/86)
86 THOMAS FOGARTY Pinot Noir Napa Valley 1988 $15 (2/28/91)
83 THOMAS FOGARTY Pinot Noir Santa Cruz Mountains Estate 1988 $15 (2/28/91)
78 FOXEN Pinot Noir Santa Maria Valley 1987 $16 (12/15/89)
89 FRICK Pinot Noir California 1981 $12 (8/31/86)
75 FRICK Pinot Noir Santa Maria Valley 1984 $12 (2/28/89)
88 GAINEY Pinot Noir Santa Barbara County 1986 $15 (12/15/89)
82 GEYSER PEAK Pinot Noir Sonoma County Carneros 1985 $6 (6/15/88)
82 GEYSER PEAK Pinot Noir Sonoma County Carneros 1981 $5.75 (8/31/86)
87 GREENWOOD RIDGE Pinot Noir Anderson Valley 1989 $13.50 (6/30/91)
88 GUNDLACH BUNDSCHU Pinot Noir Sonoma Valley Rhinefarm Vineyards 1988 $12 (2/28/91)
89 GUNDLACH BUNDSCHU Pinot Noir Sonoma Valley Rhinefarm Vineyards 1986 $10 (6/15/88)
81 GUNDLACH BUNDSCHU Pinot Noir Sonoma Valley Rhinefarm Vineyards 1985 $10 (2/29/88)
53 GUNDLACH BUNDSCHU Pinot Noir Sonoma Valley Rhinefarm Vineyards 1984 $10 (6/30/87)
75 GUNDLACH BUNDSCHU Pinot Noir Sonoma Valley Rhinefarm Vineyards 1982 $9.25 (5/01/84)
85 HACIENDA Pinot Noir Sonoma Valley 1982 $12 (12/16/84)
78 HACIENDA Pinot Noir Sonoma Valley Estate Reserve 1987 $15 (10/31/90)
80 HACIENDA Pinot Noir Sonoma Valley Estate Reserve 1986 $15 (6/15/88)
86 HACIENDA Pinot Noir Sonoma Valley Estate Reserve 1985 $15 (6/15/88)
84 HANZELL Pinot Noir Sonoma Valley 1986 $19 (10/31/90)
82 HANZELL Pinot Noir Sonoma Valley 1985 $19 (3/31/90)
78 HANZELL Pinot Noir Sonoma Valley 1984 $17 (5/31/89)
70 HANZELL Pinot Noir Sonoma Valley 1983 $17 (4/15/88)
93 HANZELL Pinot Noir Sonoma Valley 1981 $17 (8/31/86)
72 HMR Pinot Noir Paso Robles 1979 $6.50 (2/01/85)
55 HULTGREN & SAMPERTON Pinot Noir Sonoma County 1980 $5.75 (9/01/84)
84 HUSCH Pinot Noir Anderson Valley 1988 $13 (12/15/90)
80 HUSCH Pinot Noir Anderson Valley 1987 $13 (2/15/90)
81 HUSCH Pinot Noir Anderson Valley 1986 $13 (10/15/89)
84 HUSCH Pinot Noir Anderson Valley 1985 $10 (6/15/88)
74 HUSCH Pinot Noir Anderson Valley 1983 $9 (5/31/88)
88 HUSCH Pinot Noir Anderson Valley 1982 $9 (8/31/86)
82 INGLENOOK Pinot Noir Napa Valley 1985 $9.50 (6/15/88)
64 INGLENOOK Pinot Noir Napa Valley 1982 $7.50 (12/31/86)
62 INGLENOOK Pinot Noir Napa Valley 1981 $7.50 (2/01/85)
71 INGLENOOK Pinot Noir Napa Valley 1980 $6 (3/01/84)
84 INNISFREE Pinot Noir California 1989 $11 (4/30/91)
72 IRON HORSE Pinot Noir Sonoma County Green Valley 1987 $19 (10/31/90)
76 IRON HORSE Pinot Noir Sonoma County Green Valley 1982 $10 (10/01/85)
57 JEKEL Pinot Noir Arroyo Seco Home Vineyard 1982 $9 (6/30/87)
76 JORY Pinot Noir Santa Clara County 1986 $19 (6/15/88)
80 KALIN Pinot Noir Sonoma County Cuvée DD 1986 $20 (4/30/91)
77 KENWOOD Pinot Noir Sonoma Valley Jack London Vineyard 1984 $15 (5/31/89)
85 KISTLER Pinot Noir Russian River Valley Dutton Ranch 1987 $15 (3/31/90)
89 KISTLER Pinot Noir Russian River Valley Dutton Ranch 1986 $13.50 (6/15/88)
87 CHARLES KRUG Pinot Noir Carneros 1987 $8.50 (2/28/91) BB
81 CHARLES KRUG Pinot Noir Carneros Napa Valley 1985 $8.50 (2/15/90)
75 CHARLES KRUG Pinot Noir Carneros Napa Valley 1985 $8.50 (6/15/88)
89 LA CREMA Pinot Noir California 1986 $11.75 (12/31/88)
90 LA CREMA Pinot Noir California 1985 $11 (9/30/87)
89 LA CREMA Pinot Noir California 1984 $11 (3/15/87)
85 LA CREMA Pinot Noir California Reserve 1986 $22 (5/31/89)
82 LA CREMA Pinot Noir California Reserve 1985 $17.50 (12/31/87)
74 MANISCHEWITZ Pinot Noir Russian River Valley 1989 $9 (3/31/91)
67 MARK WEST Pinot Noir Russian River Valley 1983 $10 (5/16/86)
81 MARK WEST Pinot Noir Russian River Valley Ellis Vineyard 1986 $14 (3/31/90)
84 MARK WEST Pinot Noir Russian River Valley Ellis Vineyard 1984 $10 (3/15/87)
80 MARK WEST Pinot Noir Sonoma County 1986 $8 (2/28/89)
82 LOUIS M. MARTINI Pinot Noir Carneros 1987 $7 (2/28/91) BB
85 LOUIS M. MARTINI Pinot Noir Carneros Napa Valley Las Amigas 1982 $12 (3/31/90)
85 LOUIS M. MARTINI Pinot Noir Los Carneros 1988 $8 (7/15/91) BB
85 LOUIS M. MARTINI Pinot Noir Napa Valley 1986 $8 (12/31/89) BB
68 LOUIS M. MARTINI Pinot Noir Napa Valley Las Amigas Vineyard Selection 1980 $10 (3/15/87)
82 MATANZAS CREEK Pinot Noir Sonoma County Quail Hill Ranch 1980 $9.50 (7/01/84)
74 MAYACAMAS Pinot Noir California 1981 $12 (8/31/86)
80 MAYACAMAS Pinot Noir Napa Valley 1987 $14 (4/30/91)
67 MAYACAMAS Pinot Noir Napa Valley 1986 $14 (3/31/90)
72 MAYACAMAS Pinot Noir Napa Valley 1985 $12 (6/15/88)
71 MAYACAMAS Pinot Noir Napa Valley 1984 $12 (12/31/88)
75 MCHENRY Pinot Noir Santa Cruz Mountains 1985 $13 (6/15/88)
86 MERIDIAN Pinot Noir Santa Barbara County Riverbench Vineyard 1988 $14 (2/28/91)
66 MERLION Pinot Noir Los Carneros Hyde Vineyard 1986 $13.50 (2/28/89)
71 MILL CREEK Pinot Noir Dry Creek Valley 1982 $6 (8/31/86)
78 MIRASSOU Pinot Noir Monterey Harvest Reserve 1986 $12 (4/30/91)
81 MIRASSOU Pinot Noir Monterey County Fifth Generation Family Selection 1988 $7.50 (4/30/91) BB
86 ROBERT MONDAVI Pinot Noir Napa Valley 1989 $15 (4/30/91)
89 ROBERT MONDAVI Pinot Noir Napa Valley 1988 $13 (2/15/90)
88 ROBERT MONDAVI Pinot Noir Napa Valley 1987 $12 (7/31/89)
79 ROBERT MONDAVI Pinot Noir Napa Valley 1985 $10.50 (6/15/88)
75 ROBERT MONDAVI Pinot Noir Napa Valley 1984 $8.25 (11/15/87)
79 ROBERT MONDAVI Pinot Noir Napa Valley 1983 $9.50 (8/31/86)
80 ROBERT MONDAVI Pinot Noir Napa Valley 1981 $7.50 (11/01/84)
82 ROBERT MONDAVI Pinot Noir Napa Valley Reserve 1988 $23 (10/31/90)
91 ROBERT MONDAVI Pinot Noir Napa Valley Reserve 1986 $22 (10/15/89)
92 ROBERT MONDAVI Pinot Noir Napa Valley Reserve 1985 Rel: $19 Cur: $22 (4/15/89) SS
80 ROBERT MONDAVI Pinot Noir Napa Valley Reserve 1983 $16 (11/15/87)
78 ROBERT MONDAVI Pinot Noir Napa Valley Reserve 1982 $15 (8/31/86)
86 ROBERT MONDAVI Pinot Noir Napa Valley Reserve 1981 $14 (8/31/86)
81 ROBERT MONDAVI Pinot Noir Napa Valley Reserve 1980 $13.25 (8/01/84)
81 MONT ST. JOHN Pinot Noir Carneros Napa Valley 1988 $14 (4/30/91)
76 MONT ST. JOHN Pinot Noir Carneros Napa Valley 1987 $15 (3/31/90)

82 MONT ST. JOHN Pinot Noir Carneros Napa Valley 1985 $15 (10/15/89)
73 MONT ST. JOHN Pinot Noir Carneros Napa Valley 1981 $9.75 (5/16/84)
78 MONT ST. JOHN Pinot Noir Carneros Napa Valley Madonna Vineyard 1985 $11 (6/15/88)
86 MONTEREY PENINSULA Pinot Noir Monterey Sleepy Hollow 1987 $18 (2/28/91)
84 MONTEREY VINEYARD Pinot Noir Monterey County 1987 $8.50 (3/31/90)
83 MONTEREY VINEYARD Pinot Noir Monterey County 1986 $7 (6/15/88)
80 MONTEREY VINEYARD Pinot Noir Monterey County Limited Release 1988 $9 (2/28/91)
85 MONTICELLO Pinot Noir Napa Valley 1987 $14.50 (10/15/89)
89 MONTICELLO Pinot Noir Napa Valley 1986 $12 (6/15/88)
89 MONTICELLO Pinot Noir Napa Valley 1985 $12 (12/15/87)
75 MORGAN Pinot Noir California 1988 $14 (4/30/91)
81 MORGAN Pinot Noir California 1987 $15 (7/31/89)
84 MORGAN Pinot Noir California 1986 $14 (6/15/88)
79 MOUNT EDEN Pinot Noir Santa Cruz Mountains 1987 $20 (4/15/90)
90 MOUNT EDEN Pinot Noir Santa Cruz Mountains 1985 $25 (6/15/88)
86 MOUNT EDEN Pinot Noir Santa Cruz Mountains 1984 $20 (4/15/88)
77 MOUNT EDEN Pinot Noir Santa Cruz Mountains 1983 $18 (8/31/86)
80 MOUNTAIN VIEW Pinot Noir Carneros 1986 $6 (2/28/89) BB
82 MOUNTAIN VIEW Pinot Noir Monterey & Napa Counties 1989 $6 (2/28/91) BB
72 MOUNTAIN VIEW Pinot Noir Monterey & Napa Counties 1988 $6.50 (3/31/90)
82 NAPA RIDGE Pinot Noir North Coast Coastal 1989 $7.50 (7/31/91) BB
91 NAVARRO Pinot Noir Anderson Valley 1984 $12 (1/31/88)
82 NAVARRO Pinot Noir Anderson Valley 1982 $9.75 (4/15/87)
85 NAVARRO Pinot Noir Anderson Valley Méthode à l'Ancienne 1987 $14 (4/30/91)
87 NAVARRO Pinot Noir Anderson Valley Methode à l'Ancienne 1986 $14 (3/31/90)
85 NAVARRO Pinot Noir Anderson Valley Methode à l'Ancienne 1985 $14 (2/28/89)
81 NAVARRO Pinot Noir Anderson Valley Whole Berry Fermentation 1987 $9.75 (2/28/89)
81 NEWLAN Pinot Noir Napa Valley 1987 $16 (3/31/90)
88 NEWLAN Pinot Noir Napa Valley 1985 $12 (6/15/88)
76 NEWLAN Pinot Noir Napa Valley Vieilles Vignes 1986 $19 (3/31/90)
80 NEWLAN Pinot Noir Napa Valley Vieilles Vignes 1985 $16 (6/15/88)
85 OLIVET LANE Pinot Noir Russian River Valley 1988 $9 (6/30/91) BB
87 PAGE MILL Pinot Noir Santa Barbara County Bien Nacido Vineyard 1985 $12.50 (6/15/88)
85 PAGOR Pinot Noir Santa Barbara County 1987 $10.50 (12/15/89)
85 PARDUCCI Pinot Noir Mendocino County 1988 $7.50 (4/15/90) BB
70 PARDUCCI Pinot Noir Mendocino County 1986 $7 (6/15/88)
76 PARDUCCI Pinot Noir Mendocino County 1985 $5.50 (11/15/87)
65 PARDUCCI Pinot Noir Mendocino County 1983 $6 (8/31/86)
56 PARDUCCI Pinot Noir Mendocino County 1980 $5.65 (8/01/84)
84 PARDUCCI Pinot Noir Mendocino County Cellarmaster Selection 1987 $15 (4/30/91)
84 J. PEDRONCELLI Pinot Noir Dry Creek Valley 1988 $8 (2/28/91) BB
70 J. PEDRONCELLI Pinot Noir Dry Creek Valley 1986 $7 (5/31/90)
76 J. PEDRONCELLI Pinot Noir Dry Creek Valley 1985 $7.50 (6/15/88)
67 J. PEDRONCELLI Pinot Noir Sonoma County 1983 $6 (4/15/88)
68 J. PEDRONCELLI Pinot Noir Sonoma County 1982 $5.50 (6/30/87)
84 KENT RASMUSSEN Pinot Noir Carneros 1988 $22 (10/31/90)
86 RICHARDSON Pinot Noir Sonoma Valley Los Carneros Sangiacomo 1989 $14 (4/30/91)
88 RICHARDSON Pinot Noir Sonoma Valley Los Carneros Sangiacomo 1987 $12 (10/15/89)
87 RICHARDSON Pinot Noir Sonoma Valley Los Carneros Sangiacomo 1986 $12 (6/15/88)
81 ROCHE Pinot Noir Carneros 1989 $15 (4/30/91)
89 ROCHE Pinot Noir Carneros 1988 $14 (12/31/89)
78 ROCHE Pinot Noir Carneros Unfiltered 1989 $19 (4/30/91)
85 ROCHIOLI Pinot Noir Russian River Valley 1988 $15 (10/31/90)
89 ROCHIOLI Pinot Noir Russian River Valley 1987 $15 (5/31/90)
87 ROCHIOLI Pinot Noir Russian River Valley 1986 $14.25 (10/15/89)
92 ROCHIOLI Pinot Noir Russian River Valley 1985 $12.50 (6/15/88)
84 ROCHIOLI Pinot Noir Russian River Valley 1984 $12 (11/15/87)
89 ROCHIOLI Pinot Noir Russian River Valley 1982 $12.50 (8/31/86)
77 ROLLING HILLS Pinot Noir Santa Maria Valley 1985 $6 (6/15/88)
86 ROUDON-SMITH Pinot Noir Santa Cruz Mountains 1985 $15 (6/15/88)
84 ROUDON-SMITH Pinot Noir Santa Cruz Mountains Cox Vineyard 1987 $15 (2/28/91)
74 ST. FRANCIS Pinot Noir Sonoma Valley 1986 $14 (6/15/88)
91 SAINTSBURY Pinot Noir Carneros 1988 $15 (12/15/90) SS
86 SAINTSBURY Pinot Noir Carneros 1987 $15 (7/31/89)
92 SAINTSBURY Pinot Noir Carneros 1986 $14 (6/15/88)
92 SAINTSBURY Pinot Noir Carneros 1985 $13 (11/30/87) (JL)
93 SAINTSBURY Pinot Noir Carneros 1984 $12 (12/15/86)
93 SAINTSBURY Pinot Noir Carneros 1983 $12 (12/01/85)
86 SAINTSBURY Pinot Noir Carneros 1982 $8 (11/30/87) (JL)
88 SAINTSBURY Pinot Noir Carneros Garnet 1989 $9 (12/15/90)
84 SAINTSBURY Pinot Noir Carneros Garnet 1988 $9 (3/31/90)
91 SAINTSBURY Pinot Noir Carneros Garnet 1987 $9 (12/31/88)
87 SAINTSBURY Pinot Noir Carneros Garnet 1986 $8 (12/15/87)
86 SAINTSBURY Pinot Noir Carneros Garnet 1985 $9 (3/15/87)
76 SAINTSBURY Pinot Noir Carneros Garnet 1984 $8 (8/31/86)
73 SAINTSBURY Pinot Noir Carneros Garnet 1983 Rel: NA (11/30/87) (JL)
80 SAINTSBURY Pinot Noir Carneros Rancho 1981 Rel: NA (11/30/87) (JL)
85 SANFORD Pinot Noir Central Coast 1984 $12 (5/15/87)
78 SANFORD Pinot Noir Santa Barbara County 1988 $14.50 (6/30/91)
76 SANFORD Pinot Noir Santa Barbara County 1987 $14 (2/28/91)
75 SANFORD Pinot Noir Santa Barbara County 1986 $14 (12/15/89)
74 SANFORD Pinot Noir Santa Barbara County 1985 $14 (6/15/88)
78 SANFORD Pinot Noir Santa Barbara County Barrel Select 1986 $20 (12/15/89)
75 SANFORD Pinot Noir Santa Barbara County Barrel Select 1985 $20 (6/15/88)
63 SANFORD Pinot Noir Santa Maria Valley 1982 $11 (12/01/84)
84 SANTA BARBARA Pinot Noir Santa Barbara County 1989 $11 (7/31/91)
80 SANTA BARBARA Pinot Noir Santa Barbara County 1986 $11 (6/15/88)
89 SANTA BARBARA Pinot Noir Santa Ynez Valley Reserve 1987 $20 (12/15/89)
89 SANTA CRUZ MOUNTAIN Pinot Noir Santa Cruz Mountains Jarvis Vineyard 1981 $15 (8/31/86)
62 SANTA YNEZ VALLEY Pinot Noir Santa Maria Valley 1987 $13 (3/31/90)
81 SCHUG Pinot Noir Carneros Beckstoffer Vineyard 1987 $13 (2/28/91)
87 SCHUG Pinot Noir Carneros Beckstoffer Vineyard 1986 $13 (10/31/90)
72 SEA RIDGE Pinot Noir Sonoma County 1982 $10.50 (8/31/86)
72 SEGHESIO Pinot Noir Northern Sonoma 1983 $5 (4/15/87)
84 SEGHESIO Pinot Noir Russian River Valley 1987 $8 (4/15/90)
83 SEGHESIO Pinot Noir Russian River Valley Reserve 1987 $13 (4/15/90)
84 SEGHESIO Pinot Noir Sonoma-Mendocino Counties 1984 $6.75 (5/31/88)
85 SIGNORELLO Pinot Noir Napa Valley 1988 $25 (2/28/91)
64 SIMI Pinot Noir North Coast 1981 $7 (9/16/85)
81 ROBERT SINSKEY Pinot Noir Carneros 1988 $18 (2/28/91)
86 ROBERT SINSKEY Pinot Noir Carneros Napa Valley 1987 $14 (3/31/90)
79 ROBERT SINSKEY Pinot Noir Carneros Napa Valley 1986 $12 (6/15/88)
65 SMITH-MADRONE Pinot Noir Napa Valley 1984 $10 (12/15/87)
80 SOLETERRA Pinot Noir Napa Valley Three Palms Vineyard 1982 $12 (10/16/84)
78 SOLIS Pinot Noir Santa Clara County 1988 $9 (4/30/91)
87 STAR HILL Pinot Noir Napa Valley Doc's Reserve 1987 $19 (5/31/90)
82 ROBERT STEMMLER Pinot Noir Sonoma County 1987 $19 (10/31/90)
84 ROBERT STEMMLER Pinot Noir Sonoma County 1986 $18 (6/15/88)
79 ROBERT STEMMLER Pinot Noir Sonoma County 1985 $18 (9/30/87)
90 ROBERT STEMMLER Pinot Noir Sonoma County 1984 $16 (8/31/86)
93 ROBERT STEMMLER Pinot Noir Sonoma County 1983 $15 (3/16/85) SS
87 STERLING Pinot Noir Carneros Napa Valley Winery Lake 1988 $14 (4/30/91)
86 STERLING Pinot Noir Carneros Napa Valley Winery Lake 1987 $18 (12/31/89)
89 STERLING Pinot Noir Carneros Napa Valley Winery Lake 1986 $18 (2/28/89)
83 RODNEY STRONG Pinot Noir Russian River Valley River East Vineyard 1985 $10 (2/28/91)
78 RODNEY STRONG Pinot Noir Russian River Valley River East Vineyard 1984 $8 (11/15/87)
63 RODNEY STRONG Pinot Noir Russian River Valley River East Vineyard 1981 $8.50 (8/31/86)
78 RODNEY STRONG Pinot Noir Russian River Valley River East Vineyard 1980 $10 (7/01/84)
71 SUNRISE Pinot Noir Santa Clara County San Ysidro Vineyard 1985 $12 (6/15/88)
60 SUNRISE Pinot Noir Sonoma County Green Valley Dutton Ranch Vineyard 1986 $10 (6/15/88)
82 JOSEPH SWAN Pinot Noir Sonoma Coast 1982 $17 (8/31/86)
89 JOSEPH SWAN Pinot Noir Sonoma Coast 1985 $18 (6/15/88)
79 JOSEPH SWAN Pinot Noir Sonoma Coast Russian River Valley 1988 $20 (6/30/91)
76 TAFT STREET Pinot Noir Monterey County 1982 $7.50 (5/01/84)
76 TAFT STREET Pinot Noir Santa Maria Valley 1983 $9 (4/15/87)
68 TREFETHEN Pinot Noir Napa Valley 1986 $13 (7/31/89)
74 TREFETHEN Pinot Noir Napa Valley 1985 $12 (6/15/88)
80 TREFETHEN Pinot Noir Napa Valley 1984 $9.25 (5/31/88)
83 TULOCAY Pinot Noir Napa Valley Haynes Vineyard 1985 $18 (2/28/91)
82 TULOCAY Pinot Noir Napa Valley Haynes Vineyard 1985 $18 (6/15/88)
82 VILLA MT. EDEN Pinot Noir Napa Valley 1988 $12 (2/28/91)
86 VILLA MT. EDEN Pinot Noir Napa Valley Tres Ninos Vineyard 1981 $5 (4/16/85) BB
77 WATSON Pinot Noir Santa Maria Valley Bien Nacido Vineyard 1986 $9 (12/15/89)
74 WEIBEL Pinot Noir Mendocino County 1988 $6 (2/28/91)
75 WESTWOOD Pinot Noir California 1989 $9.75 (4/30/91)
82 WHITEHALL LANE Pinot Noir Alexander Valley 1988 $13.50 (10/31/90)
88 WHITEHALL LANE Pinot Noir Napa Valley 1987 $12 (10/15/89)
82 WHITEHALL LANE Pinot Noir Napa Valley 1985 $7.50 (6/15/88)
86 WHITEHALL LANE Pinot Noir Napa Valley 1984 $7.50 (3/01/86)
90 WILD HORSE Pinot Noir Paso Robles 1987 $14 (10/15/89)
79 WILD HORSE Pinot Noir Santa Barbara County 1988 $14 (4/30/91)
82 WILD HORSE Pinot Noir Santa Barbara County 1987 $13.50 (3/31/90)
85 WILD HORSE Pinot Noir Santa Barbara County 1986 $13.50 (6/15/88)
86 WILD HORSE Pinot Noir Santa Barbara County 1985 $12.50 (6/15/88)
88 WILLIAMS SELYEM Pinot Noir Russian River Valley Allen Vineyard 1988 $25 (5/31/90)
92 WILLIAMS SELYEM Pinot Noir Russian River Valley Allen Vineyard 1987 $20 (5/31/89)
92 WILLIAMS SELYEM Pinot Noir Russian River Valley Rochioli Vineyard 1988 $40 (2/28/91)
92 WILLIAMS SELYEM Pinot Noir Sonoma Coast 1988 $18 (5/31/90)
88 WILLIAMS SELYEM Pinot Noir Sonoma Coast Summa Vineyard 1988 $25 (5/31/90)
88 WILLIAMS SELYEM Pinot Noir Sonoma County 1987 $16 (5/31/89)
91 WILLIAMS SELYEM Pinot Noir Sonoma County 1986 $16 (6/15/88)
83 WINDSOR Pinot Noir Russian River Valley Winemaster's Private Reserve 1985 $8 (6/15/88)
81 YORK MOUNTAIN Pinot Noir Central Coast 1986 $6 (6/15/88)
80 YORK MOUNTAIN Pinot Noir San Luis Obispo County 1985 $9 (6/15/88)
93 ZACA MESA Pinot Noir Santa Barbara County American Reserve 1984 $12.75 (2/15/87)
60 ZACA MESA Pinot Noir Santa Barbara County American Reserve 1983 $13 (8/31/86)
86 ZACA MESA Pinot Noir Santa Barbara County Reserve 1988 $15.50 (10/31/90)
82 ZACA MESA Pinot Noir Santa Barbara County Reserve 1987 $15 (12/15/89)
91 ZACA MESA Pinot Noir Santa Barbara County Reserve 1986 $15 (6/15/88)
59 ZACA MESA Pinot Noir Santa Ynez Valley 1981 $12 (4/01/84)
82 ZD Pinot Noir Carneros Napa Valley 1988 $17 (6/30/91)
79 ZD Pinot Noir Carneros Napa Valley 1985 $14 (7/31/89)
75 ZD Pinot Noir Napa Valley 1982 $12.50 (8/31/86)

RHÔNE-TYPE RED

87 BONNY DOON Grenache California Clos de Gilroy 1990 $8 (2/15/91) BB
88 BONNY DOON Grenache California Clos de Gilroy 1989 $7.50 (2/15/90) BB
85 BONNY DOON Grenache California Clos de Gilroy 1988 $6.75 (2/15/89) BB
87 BONNY DOON Grenache California Clos de Gilroy 1987 $6.50 (2/29/88) BB
84 BONNY DOON Grenache California Clos de Gilroy 1986 $6.50 (4/30/87)
82 BONNY DOON Grahm Crew Vin Rouge California 1989 $7.50 (10/31/90) BB
83 BONNY DOON Grahm Crew Vin Rouge California 1988 $7.50 (2/15/90)
80 BONNY DOON Grahm Crew Vin Rouge California 1985 $6.25 (9/30/87) BB
86 BONNY DOON Le Cigare Volant California 1988 $19 (12/31/90)
85 BONNY DOON Le Cigare Volant California 1987 Rel: $15 Cur: $16 (12/15/89)
92 BONNY DOON Le Cigare Volant California 1986 Rel: $13.50 Cur: $25 (11/15/88)
90 BONNY DOON Le Cigare Volant California 1985 Rel: $12.50 Cur: $25 (1/31/88)
87 BONNY DOON Le Cigare Volant California 1984 Rel: $10.50 Cur: $30 (8/31/86)
85 BONNY DOON Mourvèdre California Old Telegram 1988 $20 (12/31/90)
90 BONNY DOON Mourvèdre California Old Telegram 1986 Rel: $13.50 Cur: $40 (11/15/88)
88 BONNY DOON Syrah Santa Cruz Mountains 1988 $25 (2/15/91)
81 DAVID BRUCE Côte de Shandon Vin Rouge San Luis Obispo County 1987 $7.50 (12/31/88)
86 CHATEAU LA GRANDE ROCHE Napa Valley 1988 $13 (10/15/90)
80 CLINE Côtes d'Oakley Contra Costa County 1989 $7.50 (5/31/91)
83 CLINE Côtes d'Oakley Contra Costa County 1988 $9 (4/30/90)
91 CLINE Mourvèdre Contra Costa County 1988 $18 (4/30/90)
82 CLINE Mourvèdre Contra Costa County 1987 $18 (4/15/89)
88 CLINE Oakley Cuvée Contra Costa County 1989 $12 (5/31/91)
90 CLINE Oakley Cuvée Contra Costa County 1988 $12 (2/28/90)
78 CLINE Oakley Cuvée Contra Costa County NV $12 (4/15/89)
89 DOMAINE DE LA TERRE ROUGE Sierra Foothills 1986 $12 (4/15/89)
87 DUXOUP Syrah Dry Creek Valley 1987 $12 (4/15/89)
85 DUXOUP Syrah Dry Creek Valley 1986 $9 (4/15/89)
78 DUXOUP Syrah Sonoma County 1982 $9 (3/16/84)
79 EDMUNDS ST. JOHN Les Côtes Sauvages California 1989 $19 (7/15/91)
88 EDMUNDS ST. JOHN Les Côtes Sauvages California 1986 $13.50 (4/15/89)
87 EDMUNDS ST. JOHN Mourvèdre Napa Valley 1986 $15 (4/15/89)
81 EDMUNDS ST. JOHN Syrah California 1987 $18 (12/15/89)
91 EDMUNDS ST. JOHN Syrah Sonoma County 1986 $12 (4/15/89)

UNITED STATES

CALIFORNIA/RHÔNE-TYPE RED

82 ESTRELLA RIVER Syrah Paso Robles 1986 $8 (9/30/89)
79 ESTRELLA RIVER Syrah Paso Robles 1985 $6.50 (3/31/88)
80 ESTRELLA RIVER Syrah Paso Robles 1983 $6.50 (1/31/88) BB
82 FREY Syrah Mendocino 1986 $10 (4/15/89)
86 FRICK Grenache Napa County 1985 $7.50 (4/15/89)
90 KENDALL-JACKSON Syrah Sonoma Valley 1987 $17 (12/15/89)
92 KENDALL-JACKSON Syrah Sonoma Valley 1986 $14 (11/30/88)
80 MCDOWELL Grenache McDowell Valley 1988 $6.50 (11/15/89) BB
82 MCDOWELL Les Vieux Cépages Les Tresor McDowell Valley 1987 $14 (8/31/90)
86 MCDOWELL Les Vieux Cépages Les Tresor McDowell Valley 1986 $13 (9/30/89)
74 MCDOWELL Syrah McDowell Valley 1987 $16 (3/31/91)
80 MCDOWELL Syrah McDowell Valley 1986 $14 (8/31/90)
90 MCDOWELL Syrah McDowell Valley 1985 $12 (9/30/89)
85 MCDOWELL Syrah McDowell Valley 1985 $12 (4/15/89)
86 MCDOWELL Syrah McDowell Valley 1984 $9.50 (2/15/89)
69 MCDOWELL Syrah McDowell Valley 1983 $10 (5/31/88)
75 MCDOWELL Syrah McDowell Valley 1982 $10 (1/31/87)
90 MCDOWELL Syrah McDowell Valley 1981 $10 (12/16/84)
91 MERIDIAN Syrah Paso Robles 1988 $14 (3/31/91)
74 OJAI Red Cabernet Sauvignon Syrah California 1986 $7.50 (4/15/89)
77 OJAI Syrah California 1986 $7.50 (4/15/89)
85 JOSEPH PHELPS Vin du Mistral Rouge California 1989 $14 (7/15/91)
88 JOSEPH PHELPS Syrah Napa Valley 1986 $14 (10/31/90)
89 JOSEPH PHELPS Syrah Napa Valley 1984 $8.50 (11/15/88)
71 JOSEPH PHELPS Syrah Napa Valley 1983 $8.50 (11/15/87)
78 JOSEPH PHELPS Syrah Napa Valley 1979 $7.50 (9/16/84)
74 R.H. PHILLIPS Mourvèdre California 1988 $13/375ml (4/30/91)
80 R.H. PHILLIPS Syrah California 1987 $13 (12/31/90)
90 PRESTON Syrah-Sirah Dry Creek Valley 1986 $11 (2/15/89)
91 PRESTON Sirah-Syrah Dry Creek Valley 1985 $9.50 (1/31/88)
90 QUPE Syrah Central Coast 1988 $10.25 (12/15/89)
88 QUPE Syrah Central Coast 1987 $9 (4/15/89)
79 QUPE Syrah Central Coast 1986 $9.50 (4/15/89)
81 QUPE Syrah Santa Barbara County 1987 $20 (2/28/90)
80 SARAH'S Grenache California 1988 (NA) (4/15/89)
74 SHENANDOAH Serene Varietal Adventure Series Amador County 1989 $8 (3/31/91)
82 SIERRA VISTA Syrah El Dorado 1985 $9.75 (4/15/89)
89 SIERRA VISTA Syrah El Dorado 1983 $9 (4/15/89)
85 SOTOYOME Syrah Russian River Valley 1986 $7 (4/15/89)
77 SOTOYOME Syrah Russian River Valley 1985 $7 (4/15/89)
86 SEAN H. THACKREY Mourvèdre California 1988 $24 (9/30/90)
89 SEAN H. THACKREY Syrah Napa Valley 1988 $30 (9/30/90)
92 SEAN H. THACKREY Syrah Napa Valley 1987 $30 (9/30/89)
83 SEAN H. THACKREY Syrah Napa Valley 1986 $26 (4/15/89)
79 TRUMPETVINE Syrah California NV $5 (4/15/89)
83 WILLIAM WHEELER RS Reserve California 1988 $10 (8/31/90)

RHÔNE-TYPE WHITE

90 BONNY DOON Le Sophiste Santa Cruz Mountains 1989 $25 (1/31/91)
87 BONNY DOON Le Sophiste Santa Cruz Mountains 1987 (NR) (4/15/89)
86 CALERA Viognier San Benito County 1987 (NR) (4/15/89)
88 LA JOTA Viognier Howell Mountain 1989 $25 (1/31/91)
84 LA JOTA Viognier Howell Mountain 1987 $18 (4/15/89)
89 JOSEPH PHELPS Viognier Napa Valley 1990 $20 (6/15/91)
87 QUPE Marsanne Santa Barbara County 1988 $12.50 (12/15/89)
89 RITCHIE CREEK Viognier Napa Valley 1987 $13 (4/15/89)

RIESLING

81 ALEXANDER VALLEY Johannisberg Riesling Alexander Valley 1986 $6 (4/30/88)
83 AUSTIN White Riesling Santa Barbara County Los Alamos Vineyards 1987 $6.50 (12/15/89)
88 BABCOCK Johannisberg Riesling Santa Ynez Valley 1986 $6 (12/15/89)
74 BALLARD CANYON Johannisberg Riesling Santa Ynez Valley 1988 $7 (12/15/89)
75 BALLARD CANYON Johannisberg Riesling Santa Ynez Valley Reserve 1988 $9 (12/15/89)
75 BERINGER Johannisberg Riesling North Coast 1989 $8 (12/31/90)
77 BOEGER Johannisberg Riesling El Dorado 1987 $7 (5/31/88)
78 BUENA VISTA Johannisberg Riesling Carneros 1987 $7 (7/31/89)
79 BUENA VISTA Johannisberg Riesling Carneros 1986 $7.25 (4/30/88)
89 BUENA VISTA Johannisberg Riesling Sonoma Valley Carneros 1984 $7.75 (3/16/86)
80 CALLAWAY White Riesling California 1987 $5.50 (11/15/88)
82 CALLAWAY White Riesling Temecula 1990 $6.75 (5/15/91)
73 CALLAWAY White Riesling Temecula 1989 $6.75 (5/31/90)
84 CALLAWAY White Riesling Temecula 1988 $6.25 (7/31/89)
79 CALLAWAY White Riesling Temecula 1986 $5.50 (1/31/88)
82 CHATEAU ST. JEAN Johannisberg Riesling Sonoma County 1985 $8.50 (8/31/86)
76 CLAIBORNE & CHURCHILL Riesling Edna Valley Dry Alsatian Style 1987 $8 (12/15/89)
84 CLAIBORNE & CHURCHILL Riesling Edna Valley Dry Alsatian Style 1986 $8 (7/15/88)
87 CLOS DU BOIS Johannisberg Riesling Alexander Valley Early Harvest 1987 $8 (5/31/88)
82 CLOS DU BOIS Johannisberg Riesling Alexander Valley Early Harvest 1986 $7.50 (6/30/87)
83 CLOS DU BOIS Johannisberg Riesling Alexander Valley Early Harvest 1984 $6.50 (10/16/85)
81 CONGRESS SPRINGS Johannisberg Riesling Santa Clara County San Ysidro Vineyard 1987 $7.50 (5/31/88)
86 DRY CREEK Johannisberg Riesling Sonoma County 1988 $7 (7/31/89)
71 ESTRELLA RIVER Johannisberg Riesling Paso Robles 1988 $6 (12/15/89)
78 ESTRELLA RIVER Johannisberg Riesling Paso Robles 1986 $5.50 (12/15/87)

Key to Symbols

The scores reported here are the results of blind tastings conducted by our panel of senior editors. Wines that carry the initials below are results of individual tastings.

THE WINE SPECTATOR 100-POINT SCALE *95-100*—Classic, a great wine; *90-94*—Outstanding, superior character and style; *80-89*—Good to very good, a wine with special qualities; *70-79*—Average, drinkable wine that may have minor flaws; *60-69*—Below average, drinkable but not recommended; *50-59*—Poor, undrinkable, not recommended. "+"—With a score indicates a range; used primarily with barrel tastings to indicate a preliminary score.

SPECIAL DESIGNATIONS SS—Spectator Selection, CS—Cellar Selection, BB—Best Buy.

TASTER'S INITIALS (JG)—Jim Gordon, (HS)—Harvey Steiman, (JL)—James Laube, (JS)—James Suckling, (TM)—Thomas Matthews, (TR)—Terry Robards, (BT)—Barrel Tasting (these wines were tasted blind from barrel samples), (CA-date)—*California's Great Cabernets* by James Laube, (CH-date)—*California's Great Chardonnays* by James Laube, (VP-date)—*Vintage Port* by James Suckling.

DATE TASTED Dates in parentheses represent the issue in which the rating was published.

85 FETZER Johannisberg Riesling California 1990 $6.75 (5/15/91) BB
81 FETZER Johannisberg Riesling California 1988 $6 (7/31/89) BB
75 FETZER Johannisberg Riesling California 1987 $6 (7/15/88)
90 FETZER Johannisberg Riesling California 1985 $6 (7/01/86)
82 FIRESTONE Johannisberg Riesling Santa Barbara County Dry 1990 $9 (7/15/91)
84 FIRESTONE Johannisberg Riesling Santa Ynez Valley 1990 $7.50 (7/15/91)
84 FIRESTONE Johannisberg Riesling Santa Ynez Valley 1989 $7.50 (12/31/90)
82 FIRESTONE Johannisberg Riesling Santa Ynez Valley 1988 $7 (12/15/89)
74 FIRESTONE Johannisberg Riesling Santa Ynez Valley 1987 $6.50 (2/28/89)
88 FIRESTONE Johannisberg Riesling Santa Ynez Valley 1986 $6.50 (12/15/87) BB
83 FIRESTONE Johannisberg Riesling Santa Ynez Valley 1985 $6.50 (11/15/86)
88 FIRESTONE Johannisberg Riesling Santa Ynez Valley 1984 $6.50 (10/16/85)
77 FORTINO Johannisberg Riesling Santa Clara County 1988 $5.50 (7/31/89)
80 FRANCISCAN Johannisberg Riesling Napa Valley Oakville Estate 1985 $6.50 (5/31/88)
81 FRANCISCAN Johannisberg Riesling Napa Valley Oakville Estate 1984 $6.50 (5/15/87)
85 FREEMARK ABBEY Johannisberg Riesling Napa Valley 1990 $8 (4/30/91) BB
90 FREEMARK ABBEY Johannisberg Riesling Napa Valley 1988 $8 (8/31/89)
87 FREEMARK ABBEY Johannisberg Riesling Napa Valley 1987 $7.75 (5/31/88)
68 FREEMARK ABBEY Johannisberg Riesling Napa Valley 1986 $7.75 (6/30/87)
82 FREEMARK ABBEY Johannisberg Riesling Napa Valley 1985 $7.25 (8/31/86)
81 FREEMARK ABBEY Johannisberg Riesling Napa Valley 1984 $7 (9/01/85)
76 GAINEY Johannisberg Riesling Santa Barbara County 1989 $7.75 (9/15/90)
84 GAINEY Johannisberg Riesling Santa Barbara County 1988 $7.50 (12/15/89)
82 GAINEY Johannisberg Riesling Santa Ynez Valley 1990 $8 (6/15/91)
72 E.&J. GALLO Johannisberg Riesling California Limited Release Reserve 1984 $3.50 (9/15/86) BB
71 GEYSER PEAK Johannisberg Riesling California Soft 1989 $6 (7/31/90)
84 GEYSER PEAK Johannisberg Riesling Sonoma County Soft 1987 $5.50 (7/15/88)
70 GEYSER PEAK Johannisberg Riesling Sonoma Valley Carneros Soft 1986 $5.50 (10/31/87)
77 GREENWOOD RIDGE White Riesling Mendocino 1987 $8 (7/31/89)
90 GRGICH HILLS Johannisberg Riesling Napa Valley 1987 $7.75 (8/31/89)
58 GRGICH HILLS Johannisberg Riesling Napa Valley 1985 $7.75 (8/31/86)
81 HAGAFEN Johannisberg Riesling Napa Valley 1989 $8.75 (3/31/91)
84 HAGAFEN Johannisberg Riesling Napa Valley 1989 $8.75 (7/31/90)
74 HAGAFEN Johannisberg Riesling Napa Valley 1988 $8.75 (7/31/89)
80 HAYWOOD White Riesling Sonoma Valley 1987 $7.50 (9/30/88)
80 HAYWOOD White Riesling Sonoma Valley 1986 $7.50 (6/30/87)
73 HAYWOOD White Riesling Sonoma Valley Dry 1983 $7 (11/01/84)
85 HIDDEN CELLARS Johannisberg Riesling Potter Valley 1990 $7.50 (6/30/91) BB
83 HIDDEN CELLARS Johannisberg Riesling Potter Valley 1989 $8 (9/15/90)
77 HIDDEN CELLARS Johannisberg Riesling Potter Valley 1987 $7.50 (7/15/88)
91 HIDDEN CELLARS Johannisberg Riesling Potter Valley 1985 $7 (3/31/87)
84 INGLENOOK Johannisberg Riesling Napa Valley 1985 $6.50 (4/30/88) BB
75 JEKEL White Riesling Arroyo Seco 1987 $6.75 (2/28/89)
85 JEKEL White Riesling Arroyo Seco 1986 $6.75 (9/15/87)
85 JEKEL White Riesling Arroyo Seco 1985 $6.75 (11/15/86)
85 JEKEL White Riesling Arroyo Seco Gravelstone Vineyard Dry Styled 1987 $11.50 (2/28/89)
90 JEKEL White Riesling Arroyo Seco Gravelstone Vineyard Sweet Styled 1987 $11.50 (2/28/89)
92 JEKEL White Riesling Arroyo Seco Sweet Styled 1986 $10 (10/31/87)
85 JEKEL Johannisberg Riesling Monterey 1984 $6.75 (1/01/86)
80 KENDALL-JACKSON Johannisberg Riesling Clear Lake Vintner's Reserve 1989 $9 (12/31/90)
79 KENDALL-JACKSON Johannisberg Riesling Lake County 1985 $7.50 (8/31/86)
85 KENDALL-JACKSON Johannisberg Riesling Monterey County 1985 $7.50 (9/15/86)
89 KENWOOD Johannisberg Riesling Sonoma Valley 1987 $7.50 (9/30/88)
74 CHARLES KRUG Johannisberg Riesling Napa Valley 1986 $7 (10/31/87)
82 J. LOHR Johannisberg Riesling Monterey County Greenfield Vineyards 1989 $6.50 (12/31/90)
74 J. LOHR Johannisberg Riesling Monterey County Greenfield Vineyards 1985 $6 (9/15/86)
79 MADRONA Johannisberg Riesling El Dorado 1987 $6 (7/31/89)
74 MARION Johannisberg Riesling California 1987 $4.50 (2/28/89)
75 MARK WEST Johannisberg Riesling Russian River Valley 1986 $7 (9/15/87)
68 MARK WEST Johannisberg Riesling Russian River Valley 1985 $7 (11/30/86)
63 MIRASSOU Johannisberg Riesling Monterey County Fifth Generation Family Selection 1985 $6.50 (6/30/87)
79 MIRASSOU Riesling Monterey County Monterey Riesling 1988 $6.75 (7/31/89)
69 ROBERT MONDAVI Johannisberg Riesling Napa Valley 1989 $8.25 (5/15/91)
55 ROBERT MONDAVI Johannisberg Riesling Napa Valley 1988 $8 (9/15/90)
69 ROBERT MONDAVI Johannisberg Riesling Napa Valley Special Selection 1985 $8 (10/31/87)
83 NAVARRO White Riesling Anderson Valley 1989 $8.50 (4/30/91)
90 NAVARRO White Riesling Anderson Valley 1986 $7.50 (4/30/88)
81 J. PEDRONCELLI White Riesling Dry Creek Valley 1989 $5.50 (9/30/90) BB
87 J. PEDRONCELLI White Riesling Dry Creek Valley 1988 $5.50 (8/31/89) BB
86 JOSEPH PHELPS Johannisberg Riesling Napa Valley 1987 $8.50 (2/28/89)
81 JOSEPH PHELPS Johannisberg Riesling Napa Valley 1986 $8.50 (12/15/87)
69 JOSEPH PHELPS Johannisberg Riesling Napa Valley 1985 $8.50 (9/30/86)
89 JOSEPH PHELPS Johannisberg Riesling Napa Valley 1984 $8 (11/16/85)
85 JOSEPH PHELPS Johannisberg Riesling Napa Valley Early Harvest 1987 $8 (8/31/89)
78 RANCHO SISQUOC Johannisberg Riesling Santa Maria Valley 1988 $6.50 (12/15/89)
81 RANCHO SISQUOC Riesling Santa Maria Valley Franken Riesling Sylvaner 1988 $7 (12/15/89)
75 RAYMOND Riesling Monterey 1985 $6 (1/31/87)
79 RAYMOND Johannisberg Riesling Napa Valley 1984 $6 (11/16/85)
83 RENAISSANCE Riesling North Yuba Dry 1989 $8 (5/15/91)
80 ST. FRANCIS Johannisberg Riesling Sonoma Valley 1988 $7.50 (7/31/90)
78 ST. FRANCIS Johannisberg Riesling Sonoma Valley 1987 $7.50 (10/15/88)
87 ST. FRANCIS Johannisberg Riesling Sonoma Valley 1986 $6.50 (9/15/87)
85 ST. FRANCIS Johannisberg Riesling Sonoma Valley 1985 $6 (8/31/86) BB
76 SANTA BARBARA Johannisberg Riesling Santa Ynez Valley 1988 $7.50 (12/15/89)
84 SANTA BARBARA Johannisberg Riesling Santa Ynez Valley 1987 $7 (12/15/89)
76 SMITH-MADRONE Riesling Napa Valley 1988 $8.50 (9/15/90)
82 SMITH-MADRONE Riesling Napa Valley 1985 $7.25 (6/15/87)
75 SMITH-MADRONE Riesling Napa Valley 1985 $7.25 (11/15/86)
60 SMITH-MADRONE Riesling Napa Valley 1984 $7.25 (8/31/86)
80 SMITH-MADRONE Riesling Napa Valley 1983 $7 (11/01/84)
78 STAG'S LEAP WINE CELLARS White Riesling Napa Valley 1986 $7.50 (9/15/87)
70 STAG'S LEAP WINE CELLARS White Riesling Napa Valley Birkmyer Vineyards 1984 $7.50 (3/16/86)
88 RODNEY STRONG Johannisberg Riesling Russian River Valley Le Baron Vineyard 1983 $7.25 (7/16/84)
87 TREFETHEN White Riesling Napa Valley 1988 $8.25 (7/31/89)

80 TREFETHEN White Riesling Napa Valley 1987 $7.75 (7/15/88)
82 TREFETHEN White Riesling Napa Valley 1986 $7 (4/30/88)
85 ZACA MESA Johannisberg Riesling Santa Barbara County 1987 $6 (12/15/89) BB
72 ZACA MESA Johannisberg Riesling Santa Barbara County 1986 $5.50 (11/15/88)

SAUVIGNON BLANC

80 ADLER FELS Fumé Blanc Sonoma County 1989 $10 (4/30/91)
85 ADLER FELS Fumé Blanc Sonoma County 1986 $8.75 (10/31/87)
85 ADLER FELS Fumé Blanc Sonoma County 1984 $8.50 (10/16/85)
85 ALDERBROOK Sauvignon Blanc Dry Creek Valley 1988 $9 (3/31/90)
86 ALDERBROOK Sauvignon Blanc Dry Creek Valley 1987 $7.50 (4/15/89)
58 AMIZETTA Sauvignon Blanc Napa Valley 1986 $8 (5/31/88)
78 AUDUBON Sauvignon Blanc Pope Valley 1986 $7 (5/31/88)
65 BABCOCK Sauvignon Blanc Santa Ynez Valley 1987 $8 (12/15/89)
83 BARON HERZOG Sauvignon Blanc California 1989 $8 (3/31/91)
67 BARON HERZOG Sauvignon Blanc Sonoma County Special Reserve 1988 $10 (3/31/91)
81 BEAULIEU Sauvignon Blanc Napa Valley Dry 1989 $8.50 (4/30/91)
83 BEAULIEU Sauvignon Blanc Napa Valley Dry 1988 $8.50 (9/15/89)
82 BEAULIEU Sauvignon Blanc Napa Valley Dry 1987 $8.50 (12/31/88)
88 BEAULIEU Sauvignon Blanc Napa Valley Dry 1986 $8.50 (5/31/88)
85 BEAULIEU Sauvignon Blanc Napa Valley Dry 1985 $7 (5/15/87)
77 BELLEROSE Sauvignon Blanc Sonoma County 1985 $8.50 (2/15/87)
56 BELLEROSE Sauvignon Blanc Sonoma County Barrel Fermented 1987 $10.50 (5/15/90)
81 BELVEDERE Sauvignon Blanc Sonoma County Discovery Series 1987 $3.25 (8/31/88) BB
84 BENZIGER Fumé Blanc Sonoma County 1988 $8.50 (10/31/89)
84 BENZIGER Fumé Blanc Sonoma County 1987 $8.50 (8/31/88)
85 BERINGER Sauvignon Blanc Knights Valley 1989 $8.50 (7/31/91)
85 BERINGER Sauvignon Blanc Knights Valley 1988 $8.50 (6/30/90)
77 BERINGER Sauvignon Blanc Knights Valley 1987 $8.50 (3/15/89)
81 BERINGER Sauvignon Blanc Knights Valley 1986 $8 (5/31/88)
89 BERINGER Sauvignon Blanc Knights Valley 1985 $7.50 (4/15/87)
56 BERINGER Sauvignon Blanc Sonoma County 1983 $8 (10/16/85)
74 BERINGER Fumé Blanc Napa Valley 1988 $7.50 (8/31/90)
87 BERINGER Fumé Blanc Napa Valley 1985 $7.50 (4/15/87)
73 BOGLE Fumé Blanc California 1988 $6/1.5L (7/31/89)
84 BOUCHAINE Sauvignon Blanc Napa Valley 1984 $8.50 (2/16/86)
85 BRANDER Sauvignon Blanc Santa Ynez Valley 1987 $8 (3/15/89)
79 BRANDER Sauvignon Blanc Santa Ynez Valley 1985 $8.50 (3/15/88)
82 BRANDER Sauvignon Blanc Santa Ynez Valley Reserve 1987 $11 (12/15/89)
79 BRANDER Sauvignon Blanc Santa Ynez Valley Tête de Cuvée 1989 $9.50 (4/30/91)
86 BUENA VISTA Fumé Blanc Alexander Valley 1987 $8.50 (3/15/89)
81 BUENA VISTA Fumé Blanc Alexander Valley Wasson Vineyard 1986 $8.50 (3/15/88)
85 BUENA VISTA Sauvignon Blanc Lake County 1989 $7.50 (8/31/90)
88 BUENA VISTA Sauvignon Blanc Lake County 1988 $7.50 (9/15/89)
90 BUENA VISTA Sauvignon Blanc Lake County 1987 $7.50 (6/15/88)
91 BUENA VISTA Sauvignon Blanc Lake County 1986 $7.25 (7/15/87) SS
85 BUENA VISTA Sauvignon Blanc Lake County 1985 $7.50 (9/30/86)
84 BYRON Sauvignon Blanc Santa Barbara County 1989 $9 (4/30/91)
85 BYRON Sauvignon Blanc Santa Barbara County 1988 $8.50 (12/15/89)
83 CAIN Sauvignon Blanc Napa Valley Musqué 1989 $12 (3/15/91)
75 CAIN Sauvignon Blanc Napa-Sonoma Counties 1985 $8 (10/15/87)
70 CAKEBREAD Sauvignon Blanc Napa Valley 1987 $11 (12/31/88)
67 CAKEBREAD Sauvignon Blanc Napa Valley 1986 $10 (10/15/87)
79 CALLAWAY Sauvignon Blanc Temecula 1989 $8 (10/31/90)
68 CALLAWAY Sauvignon Blanc Temecula 1988 $8 (7/31/91)
82 CALLAWAY Sauvignon Blanc Temecula 1988 $8 (10/31/89)
78 CALLAWAY Sauvignon Blanc Temecula 1987 $8.25 (6/30/90)
71 CALLAWAY Sauvignon Blanc Temecula 1987 $8.25 (3/15/89)
76 CALLAWAY Sauvignon Blanc Temecula 1985 $7.50 (11/15/87)
70 CALLAWAY Sauvignon Blanc Temecula 1984 $7.50 (4/16/86)
75 CANTERBURY Sauvignon Blanc California 1988 $5 (10/31/89)
80 CANTERBURY Sauvignon Blanc California 1986 $4.75 (5/15/87) BB
87 J. CAREY Sauvignon Blanc Santa Ynez Valley 1988 $8 (12/15/89)
78 CASTORO Fumé Blanc San Luis Obispo County 1988 $5.25 (12/15/89)
88 CAYMUS Sauvignon Blanc Napa Valley 1989 $9 (10/31/90)
83 CAYMUS Sauvignon Blanc Napa Valley 1988 $9 (9/15/89)
84 CAYMUS Sauvignon Blanc Napa Valley 1987 $8 (7/15/88)
83 CAYMUS Sauvignon Blanc Napa Valley 1986 $7.50 (5/15/87)
84 CAYMUS Sauvignon Blanc Napa Valley 1985 $7.50 (1/31/87)
85 CHALK HILL Sauvignon Blanc Chalk Hill 1989 $8 (7/31/91)
82 CHALK HILL Sauvignon Blanc Sonoma County 1987 $7 (10/31/89)
61 CHALK HILL Sauvignon Blanc Sonoma County 1984 $7 (4/16/86)
76 CHATEAU DE LEU Sauvignon Blanc Solano County Green Valley 1985 $6 (11/15/87)
70 CHATEAU SOUVERAIN Sauvignon Blanc Alexander Valley Wasson Vineyard 1984 $8 (1/31/87)
69 CHATEAU SOUVERAIN Sauvignon Blanc Sonoma County 1986 $5 (3/15/88)
83 CHATEAU ST. JEAN Fumé Blanc Alexander Valley Robert Young Vineyards 1985 $9.50 (5/31/88)
86 CHATEAU ST. JEAN Fumé Blanc Alexander Valley Robert Young Vineyards 1984 $9.75 (4/16/86)
89 CHATEAU ST. JEAN Fumé Blanc Russian River Valley La Petite Etoile 1988 $10.50 (11/30/89)
83 CHATEAU ST. JEAN Fumé Blanc Russian River Valley La Petite Etoile 1985 $10.50 (1/31/87)
85 CHATEAU ST. JEAN Fumé Blanc Sonoma County 1989 $8 (4/30/91)
73 CHATEAU ST. JEAN Fumé Blanc Sonoma County 1988 $8 (5/15/90)
84 CHATEAU ST. JEAN Fumé Blanc Sonoma County 1986 $8 (8/31/87)
86 CHATEAU ST. JEAN Fumé Blanc Sonoma County 1985 $8 (1/31/87)
73 CHATEAU ST. JEAN Fumé Blanc Sonoma County 1984 $8.75 (10/16/85)
84 CHATEAU ST. JEAN Fumé Blanc Sonoma County La Petite Etoile 1989 $10.50 (4/30/91)
73 CHATEAU ST. JEAN Fumé Blanc Sonoma County La Petite Etoile 1984 $10.50 (11/16/85)
81 CHIMNEY ROCK Fumé Blanc Stags Leap District 1989 $11 (7/31/91)
65 CHIMNEY ROCK Fumé Blanc Napa Valley Stags Leap District 1988 $15 (5/15/90)
77 CHIMNEY ROCK Fumé Blanc Napa Valley Stags Leap District 1987 $10 (1/31/89)
80 CHIMNEY ROCK Fumé Blanc Napa Valley Stags Leap District 1986 $9 (10/15/88)
82 CHRISTOPHE Sauvignon Blanc California 1987 $7 (4/30/89) BB
86 CHRISTOPHE Sauvignon Blanc California 1986 $5 (10/31/87) BB
88 CHRISTOPHE Sauvignon Blanc California 1985 $6 (1/31/87) BB
76 CLOS DU BOIS Sauvignon Blanc Alexander Valley 1989 $8 (8/31/90)
78 CLOS DU BOIS Sauvignon Blanc Alexander Valley 1988 $11 (7/31/89)
88 CLOS DU BOIS Sauvignon Blanc Alexander Valley 1987 $8 (6/15/88)
91 CLOS DU BOIS Sauvignon Blanc Alexander Valley 1986 $7.50 (9/15/87)
71 CLOS DU BOIS Sauvignon Blanc Alexander Valley Barrel Fermented 1985 $7.50 (6/01/86)
77 CLOS DU BOIS Sauvignon Blanc Dry Creek Valley Proprietor's Reserve 1986 $10.50 (8/31/87)
73 CLOS DU BOIS Sauvignon Blanc Dry Creek Valley Proprietor's Reserve 1985 $12 (9/30/86)
87 CLOS DU VAL Sauvignon Blanc California 1985 $7.50 (2/28/87)
73 CLOS DU VAL Sauvignon Blanc Napa Valley 1986 $8 (5/31/88)
84 CLOS PEGASE Sauvignon Blanc Lake County 1987 $9.50 (5/15/90)
86 CLOS PEGASE Fumé Blanc Napa Valley 1986 $9.50 (7/15/88)
81 CLOS PEGASE Fumé Blanc Napa Valley 1986 $9.50 (11/30/87)
70 CLOS PEGASE Fumé Blanc Napa Valley 1985 $9 (8/31/87)
89 CONCANNON Sauvignon Blanc California 1983 $7 (3/01/85)
73 CONCANNON Fumé Blanc California Selected Vineyards 1987 $9.50 (4/30/91)
79 CONCANNON Sauvignon Blanc Livermore Valley 1985 $9 (8/31/87)
90 CONCANNON Sauvignon Blanc Livermore Valley 1984 $9 (4/30/87)
87 CONCANNON Sauvignon Blanc Livermore Valley Reserve 1986 $9.50 (12/31/88)
83 CONN CREEK Sauvignon Blanc Napa Valley Barrel Select 1987 $10 (4/30/89)
81 CONN CREEK Sauvignon Blanc Napa Valley Barrel Select 1986 $9.75 (3/15/88)
78 CORBETT CANYON Sauvignon Blanc Central Coast Coastal Classic 1988 $5.50/1.5L (12/15/89)
77 CORBETT CANYON Sauvignon Blanc Central Coast Reserve 1988 $6 (12/15/89)
70 CORBETT CANYON Sauvignon Blanc Central Coast Select 1985 $6 (10/31/87)
84 CORBETT CANYON Sauvignon Blanc San Luis Obispo County 1984 $6 (4/01/86) BB
72 CRESTON MANOR Sauvignon Blanc San Luis Obispo County 1987 $8.25 (12/15/89)
73 CYPRESS LANE Sauvignon Blanc California 1986 $4.50 (3/15/88)
86 DE LOACH Fumé Blanc California 1987 $9 (12/31/88)
84 DE LOACH Sauvignon Blanc Russian River Valley 1989 $9 (5/15/90)
86 DE LOACH Sauvignon Blanc Russian River Valley 1988 $9 (7/31/89)
81 DE LOACH Sauvignon Blanc Russian River Valley 1988 $9 (7/31/89)
75 DE LOACH Sauvignon Blanc Russian River Valley 1985 $8.50 (8/31/87)
51 DE LOACH Sauvignon Blanc Russian River Valley 1984 $8.50 (4/16/86)
74 DORE Fumé Blanc California 1986 $5 (3/15/88)
87 DRY CREEK Sauvignon Blanc Sonoma County 1989 $9 (12/31/90)
87 DRY CREEK Sauvignon Blanc Sonoma County 1987 $8.75 (11/15/88)
75 DRY CREEK Sauvignon Blanc Sonoma County 1986 $8.75 (8/31/87)
79 DRY CREEK Sauvignon Blanc Sonoma County 1985 $8.50 (10/15/86)
77 DRY CREEK Sauvignon Blanc Sonoma County 1984 $8.50 (4/16/86)
87 DUCKHORN Sauvignon Blanc Napa Valley 1989 $10 (12/31/90)
86 DUCKHORN Sauvignon Blanc Napa Valley 1988 $10 (2/15/90)
86 DUCKHORN Sauvignon Blanc Napa Valley 1987 $9.50 (12/31/88)
81 DUCKHORN Sauvignon Blanc Napa Valley 1986 $9.50 (12/31/87)
68 DUCKHORN Sauvignon Blanc Napa Valley 1985 $9 (1/31/87)
87 DUCKHORN Sauvignon Blanc Napa Valley 1984 $9 (12/01/85)
72 EHLERS LANE Sauvignon Blanc Napa Valley 1985 $7.50 (3/15/88)
65 EHLERS LANE Sauvignon Blanc Napa Valley 1984 $9 (6/01/86)
79 ESTANCIA Sauvignon Blanc Alexander Valley 1989 $7 (3/15/91)
82 ESTANCIA Sauvignon Blanc Alexander Valley 1988 $6 (5/15/90) BB
72 ESTANCIA Sauvignon Blanc Alexander Valley 1984 $6 (7/01/86)
89 ESTATE WILLIAM BACCALA Sauvignon Blanc Mendocino 1984 $8.50 (11/30/86)
81 ESTRELLA RIVER Sauvignon Blanc Paso Robles 1987 $6 (12/15/89)
63 GARY FARRELL Sauvignon Blanc Russian River Valley 1985 $8.50 (8/31/87)
87 FERRARI-CARANO Fumé Blanc Sonoma County 1990 $10 (7/15/91)
80 FERRARI-CARANO Fumé Blanc Sonoma County 1989 $10 (10/15/90)
88 FERRARI-CARANO Fumé Blanc Sonoma County 1988 $9 (9/15/89)
89 FERRARI-CARANO Fumé Blanc Sonoma County 1987 $9 (3/15/89)
82 FERRARI-CARANO Fumé Blanc Alexander Valley 1986 $9 (11/15/87)
76 FETZER Fumé Blanc California Valley Oaks Fumé 1989 $6.50 (12/31/90)
79 FETZER Fumé Blanc California Valley Oaks Fumé 1988 $6.50 (7/31/89)
72 FETZER Fumé Blanc California Valley Oaks Fumé 1986 $6.50 (10/15/87)
67 FETZER Fumé Blanc California Valley Oaks Fume 1985 $6.50 (9/30/86)
77 FIRESTONE Sauvignon Blanc Santa Ynez Valley 1987 $7.50 (12/15/89)
67 FLORA SPRINGS Sauvignon Blanc Napa Valley 1988 $8.50 (3/31/90)
85 FLORA SPRINGS Sauvignon Blanc Napa Valley 1986 $8.50 (8/31/88)
73 FLORA SPRINGS Sauvignon Blanc Napa Valley 1985 $8.50 (2/28/87)
68 FLORA SPRINGS Sauvignon Blanc Napa Valley 1984 $8.50 (9/30/86)
88 FLORA SPRINGS Sauvignon Blanc Napa Valley Soliloquy Special Select 1989 $20 (3/15/91)
63 FOPPIANO Sauvignon Blanc Russian River Valley 1983 $8 (11/16/85)
86 FREMONT CREEK Sauvignon Blanc Mendocino-Napa Counties 1986 $9 (5/31/88)
79 J. FRITZ Fumé Blanc Dry Creek Valley 1985 $7 (11/15/87)
87 FROG'S LEAP Sauvignon Blanc Napa Valley 1989 $9.50 (10/31/90)
76 FROG'S LEAP Sauvignon Blanc Napa Valley 1988 $9.50 (11/30/89)
87 FROG'S LEAP Sauvignon Blanc Napa Valley 1987 $9 (10/15/88)
82 GAINEY Sauvignon Blanc Santa Barbara County 1987 $8.50 (12/15/89)
77 E.&J. GALLO Sauvignon Blanc California Limited Release Reserve 1984 $3.50 (11/15/86) BB
82 E.&J. GALLO Sauvignon Blanc California Reserve 1989 $4 (7/31/91) BB
72 GAN EDEN Sauvignon Blanc Sonoma County 1988 $9 (3/31/91)
72 GEYSER PEAK Fumé Blanc Alexander Valley 1986 $6 (3/31/88)
64 GIRARD Sauvignon Blanc North Coast 1984 $8 (10/31/86)
80 GLEN ELLEN Sauvignon Blanc California Proprietor's Reserve 1990 $6 (7/31/91) BB
77 GLEN ELLEN Sauvignon Blanc California Proprietor's Reserve 1989 $5 (8/31/90)
69 GLEN ELLEN Sauvignon Blanc California Proprietor's Reserve 1987 $4.50 (8/31/88)
79 GLEN ELLEN Sauvignon Blanc California Proprietor's Reserve 1986 $4.50 (10/31/87)
82 GLEN ELLEN Fumé Blanc Sonoma County Benziger Family Selection 1986 $7 (11/15/87)
73 GLEN ELLEN Fumé Blanc Sonoma County Benziger Family Selection 1985 $7 (8/31/86)
85 GRGICH HILLS Fumé Blanc Napa Valley 1989 $11 (3/15/91)
90 GRGICH HILLS Fumé Blanc Napa Valley 1988 $10 (3/31/90)
89 GRGICH HILLS Fumé Blanc Napa Valley 1986 $10 (5/15/88)
89 GRGICH HILLS Fumé Blanc Napa Valley 1987 $10 (7/31/89)
60 GRGICH HILLS Fumé Blanc Napa Valley 1985 $9 (5/15/87)
87 GRGICH HILLS Fumé Blanc Napa Valley 1984 $9 (2/16/86)
81 GROTH Sauvignon Blanc Napa Valley 1989 $8.50 (10/31/90)
85 GROTH Sauvignon Blanc Napa Valley 1988 $8 (2/15/90)
74 GROTH Sauvignon Blanc Napa Valley 1987 $7.50 (12/31/88)
83 GROTH Sauvignon Blanc Napa Valley 1986 $7 (3/15/88)
77 GUENOC Sauvignon Blanc Guenoc Valley 1989 $10 (4/30/91)
77 GUENOC Sauvignon Blanc Lake-Napa Counties 1986 $6.75 (3/15/88)
77 GUENOC Sauvignon Blanc Lake-Napa Counties 1985 $6.75 (11/15/87)
68 HACIENDA Sauvignon Blanc Sonoma County 1984 $8 (10/16/85)
84 HANDLEY Sauvignon Blanc Dry Creek Valley 1988 $8 (8/31/90)
87 HANNA Sauvignon Blanc Sonoma County 1989 $8.50 (7/15/91)

UNITED STATES

CALIFORNIA/*SAUVIGNON BLANC*

71 HANNA Sauvignon Blanc Sonoma County 1988 $8.75 (8/31/90)
73 HANNA Sauvignon Blanc Sonoma County 1987 $8.75 (10/15/88)
84 HANNA Sauvignon Blanc Sonoma County 1986 $8.75 (11/15/87)
88 HANNA Sauvignon Blanc Sonoma County 1985 $8.75 (10/31/86)
80 HAWK CREST Sauvignon Blanc California 1989 $6 (8/31/90) BB
76 HAWK CREST Sauvignon Blanc California 1988 $6 (5/15/90)
83 HAWK CREST Sauvignon Blanc California 1987 $6 (10/31/89) BB
88 HAYWOOD Fumé Blanc Sonoma Valley 1988 $9.50 (11/30/89)
80 HAYWOOD Fumé Blanc Sonoma Valley 1987 $9.50 (5/31/88)
83 HIDDEN CELLARS Sauvignon Blanc Mendocino County Bock Vineyard 1986 $8 (8/31/88)
90 HIDDEN CELLARS Sauvignon Blanc Mendocino County White Table Wine Alchemy 1989 $18 (7/31/91)
72 HIDDEN CELLARS Sauvignon Blanc Sonoma County 1985 $8 (3/31/88)
78 LOUIS HONIG Sauvignon Blanc Napa Valley 1988 $8.75 (5/15/90)
84 LOUIS HONIG Sauvignon Blanc Napa Valley 1987 $8.75 (7/31/89)
85 LOUIS HONIG Sauvignon Blanc Napa Valley 1986 $8.25 (5/15/88)
83 LOUIS HONIG Sauvignon Blanc Napa Valley 1984 $8.25 (12/01/85)
86 HUSCH Sauvignon Blanc Mendocino La Ribera Vineyards 1987 $7.50 (10/15/88)
83 HUSCH Sauvignon Blanc Mendocino La Ribera Vineyards 1986 $7 (12/31/87)
74 INGLENOOK Sauvignon Blanc Napa Valley 1986 $7.50 (5/31/88)
83 INGLENOOK Sauvignon Blanc Napa Valley Reserve 1985 $9.50 (3/15/88)
78 INGLENOOK Sauvignon Blanc Napa Valley Reserve 1984 $9.50 (2/28/87)
82 INNISFREE Sauvignon Blanc Napa Valley 1989 $7.50 (4/30/91)
77 IRON HORSE Fumé Blanc Alexander Valley Barrel Fermented 1989 $11 (8/31/90)
84 IRON HORSE Fumé Blanc Alexander Valley Barrel Fermented 1988 $11 (11/30/89)
86 IRON HORSE Fumé Blanc Alexander Valley Barrel Fermented 1987 $10 (7/31/88)
86 IRON HORSE Fumé Blanc Alexander Valley Barrel Fermented 1986 $9.25 (8/31/87)
84 IRON HORSE Fumé Blanc Alexander Valley Proprietor Grown 1985 $8.75 (11/30/86)
66 JEPSON Sauvignon Blanc Mendocino 1987 $7 (7/31/89)
82 JEPSON Sauvignon Blanc Mendocino 1986 $7.50 (3/15/88)
80 KARLY Sauvignon Blanc Amador County 1986 $8 (3/15/88)
82 KENDALL-JACKSON Sauvignon Blanc Clear Lake 1985 $7.50 (2/15/87)
83 KENDALL-JACKSON Sauvignon Blanc Lake County Jackson Vineyard 1987 $12 (12/31/88)
90 KENDALL-JACKSON Sauvignon Blanc Lake County Vintner's Reserve 1989 $9 (10/31/90)
89 KENDALL-JACKSON Sauvignon Blanc Lake County Vintner's Reserve 1988 $9 (3/31/90)
85 KENWOOD Sauvignon Blanc Sonoma County 1988 $9 (11/30/89)
82 KENWOOD Sauvignon Blanc Sonoma County 1987 $9 (11/15/88)
88 KENWOOD Sauvignon Blanc Sonoma County 1986 $8.75 (8/31/87)
78 KENWOOD Sauvignon Blanc Sonoma County 1985 $6 (1/31/87)
88 KENWOOD Sauvignon Blanc Sonoma County 1983 $8.50 (10/16/84)
76 KONOCTI Fumé Blanc Lake County 1985 $6 (8/31/87)
85 CHARLES KRUG Sauvignon Blanc Napa Valley 1986 $7 (10/31/87)
78 LAKESPRING Sauvignon Blanc California 1986 $7.50 (5/15/88)
69 LAKESPRING Sauvignon Blanc California 1985 $7.50 (6/30/87)
79 LAKESPRING Sauvignon Blanc California 1984 $7.50 (12/01/85)
76 LAKESPRING Sauvignon Blanc Napa Valley 1988 $8.50 (11/30/89)
72 LIBERTY SCHOOL Sauvignon Blanc California Lot 6 1987 $5 (8/31/88)
70 LIBERTY SCHOOL Sauvignon Blanc Napa Valley Lot 2 1984 $5.50 (12/01/85)
81 LIBERTY SCHOOL Sauvignon Blanc Napa Valley Lot 4 1986 $5 (11/15/87) BB
78 LONG Sauvignon Blanc Napa Valley 1989 $12 (7/15/91)
87 LONG Sauvignon Blanc Sonoma County 1987 $11 (1/31/89)
87 MARKHAM Sauvignon Blanc Napa Valley 1989 $7 (10/31/90) BB
82 MARKHAM Sauvignon Blanc Napa Valley 1988 $7 (9/15/89)
86 MARKHAM Sauvignon Blanc Napa Valley 1987 $7 (4/15/89)
80 LOUIS M. MARTINI Sauvignon Blanc Napa Valley 1989 $8 (4/30/91)
85 MATANZAS CREEK Sauvignon Blanc Sonoma County 1989 $12 (7/15/91)
86 MATANZAS CREEK Sauvignon Blanc Sonoma County 1988 $12 (2/15/90)
85 MATANZAS CREEK Sauvignon Blanc Sonoma County 1987 $12 (3/15/89)
82 MATANZAS CREEK Sauvignon Blanc Sonoma County 1986 $11 (5/15/88)
70 MATANZAS CREEK Sauvignon Blanc Sonoma County 1985 $10.50 (5/15/87)
86 MATANZAS CREEK Sauvignon Blanc Sonoma County 1984 $10.50 (7/01/86)
66 MAYACAMAS Sauvignon Blanc Napa Valley 1988 $11 (8/31/90)
87 MAYACAMAS Sauvignon Blanc Napa Valley 1987 $11 (9/15/89)
86 MAYACAMAS Sauvignon Blanc Napa Valley 1985 $10 (8/31/87)
79 MCDOWELL Fumé Blanc Mendocino 1988 $7.50 (3/31/90)
72 MERIDIAN Sauvignon Blanc Napa Valley 1986 $8 (5/31/88)
80 MERRYVALE Sauvignon Blanc Napa Valley Meritage 1989 $12 (4/30/91)
80 ROBERT MONDAVI Sauvignon Blanc California Woodbridge 1989 $5 (4/30/91) BB
78 ROBERT MONDAVI Sauvignon Blanc California Woodbridge 1988 $5 (10/31/89)
81 ROBERT MONDAVI Sauvignon Blanc California White 1987 $5 (3/15/89) BB
75 ROBERT MONDAVI Sauvignon Blanc California 1986 $4 (10/15/87) BB
74 ROBERT MONDAVI Fumé Blanc Napa Valley 1988 $9.50 (5/15/90)
87 ROBERT MONDAVI Fumé Blanc Napa Valley 1987 $9.50 (7/31/89)
71 ROBERT MONDAVI Fumé Blanc Napa Valley 1986 $9.50 (7/15/88)
72 ROBERT MONDAVI Fumé Blanc Napa Valley 1985 $7.25 (2/28/87)
77 ROBERT MONDAVI Fumé Blanc Napa Valley 1984 $10 (6/01/86)
77 ROBERT MONDAVI Fumé Blanc Napa Valley Reserve 1982 $12.50 (4/16/86)
83 ROBERT MONDAVI Fumé Blanc Napa Valley To-Kalon Vineyard Reserve 1989 $15 (7/15/91)
84 ROBERT MONDAVI Fumé Blanc Napa Valley To-Kalon Vineyard Reserve 1988 $15 (8/31/90)
80 ROBERT MONDAVI Fumé Blanc Napa Valley To-Kalon Vineyard Reserve 1987 $15 (3/31/90)

Key to Symbols

The scores reported here are the results of blind tastings conducted by our panel of senior editors. Wines that carry the initials below are results of individual tastings.

THE WINE SPECTATOR 100-POINT SCALE ***95-100***—Classic, a great wine; ***90-94***—Outstanding, superior character and style; ***80-89***—Good to very good, a wine with special qualities; ***70-79***—Average, drinkable wine that may have minor flaws; ***60-69***—Below average, drinkable but not recommended; ***50-59***—Poor, undrinkable, not recommended. "+"—With a score indicates a range; used primarily with barrel tastings to indicate a preliminary score.

SPECIAL DESIGNATIONS SS—Spectator Selection, CS—Cellar Selection, BB—Best Buy.

TASTER'S INITIALS (JG)—Jim Gordon, (HS)—Harvey Steiman, (JL)—James Laube, (JS)—James Suckling, (TM)—Thomas Matthews, (TR)—Terry Robards, (BT)—Barrel Tasting (these wines were tasted blind from barrel samples), (CA-date)—*California's Great Cabernets* by James Laube, (CH-date)—*California's Great Chardonnays* by James Laube, (VP-date)—*Vintage Port* by James Suckling.

DATE TASTED Dates in parentheses represent the issue in which the rating was published.

77 ROBERT MONDAVI Fumé Blanc Napa Valley To-Kalon Vineyard Reserve 1986 $15 (7/31/89)
65 MONTEREY VINEYARD Fumé Blanc Monterey County 1984 $6 (2/28/87)
79 MONTEREY VINEYARD Sauvignon Blanc Monterey County Classic 1989 $5.50 (3/31/91)
76 MONTICELLO Sauvignon Blanc Napa Valley 1986 $7.50 (7/15/88)
75 MONTICELLO Sauvignon Blanc Napa Valley 1985 $7.50 (10/15/87)
86 MONTICELLO Sauvignon Blanc Napa Valley 1983 $7.50 (6/01/86)
83 MORGAN Sauvignon Blanc Alexander Valley 1988 $8.50 (11/30/89)
83 MORGAN Sauvignon Blanc Alexander Valley 1987 $8.50 (8/31/88)
87 MURPHY-GOODE Fumé Blanc Alexander Valley Estate Vineyard 1990 $9 (7/15/91)
89 MURPHY-GOODE Fumé Blanc Alexander Valley Estate Vineyard 1988 $8 (11/30/89)
76 MURPHY-GOODE Fumé Blanc Alexander Valley 1987 $7.50 (3/15/89)
82 MURPHY-GOODE Fumé Blanc Alexander Valley 1986 $7 (10/15/87)
88 MURPHY-GOODE Fumé Blanc Alexander Valley Estate Vineyard 1985 $8 (7/01/86)
82 NAPA RIDGE Sauvignon Blanc California 1985 $4.75 (3/31/87) BB
60 NEWTON Sauvignon Blanc Napa Valley 1985 $9.50 (9/30/87)
68 NEWTON Sauvignon Blanc Napa Valley 1984 $8 (5/15/87)
58 NEWTON Sauvignon Blanc Napa Valley 1983 $9.50 (4/16/86)
78 PARDUCCI Sauvignon Blanc Mendocino County 1988 $7.50 (5/15/90)
82 PARDUCCI Sauvignon Blanc Mendocino County 1986 $6.50 (10/15/87)
70 PARDUCCI Sauvignon Blanc Mendocino County 1984 $6 (11/01/85)
82 PARDUCCI Fumé Blanc Mendocino County Cellarmaster Selection 1988 $12 (4/30/91)
61 PAT PAULSEN Sauvignon Blanc Sonoma County 1984 $8.50 (12/01/85)
78 ROBERT PECOTA Sauvignon Blanc Napa Valley 1989 $9.25 (8/31/90)
94 ROBERT PECOTA Sauvignon Blanc Napa Valley 1985 $9.25 (10/15/86) SS
77 ROBERT PECOTA Sauvignon Blanc Napa Valley 1984 $8.50 (11/16/85)
82 ROBERT PECOTA Sauvignon Blanc Napa Valley Barrel Fermented 1986 $9.25 (10/31/87)
84 J. PEDRONCELLI Fumé Blanc Dry Creek Valley 1989 $7 (4/30/91) BB
83 J. PEDRONCELLI Fumé Blanc Dry Creek Valley 1988 $6 (9/15/89) BB
79 J. PEDRONCELLI Fumé Blanc Dry Creek Valley 1987 $6 (4/30/89)
75 J. PEDRONCELLI Fumé Blanc Dry Creek Valley 1986 $6 (11/30/87)
88 ROBERT PEPI Sauvignon Blanc Napa Valley Two-Heart Canopy 1989 $9.50 (3/31/91)
87 ROBERT PEPI Sauvignon Blanc Napa Valley Two-Heart Canopy 1988 $9.50 (2/15/90)
76 ROBERT PEPI Sauvignon Blanc Napa Valley 1987 $8.50 (11/30/89)
76 ROBERT PEPI Sauvignon Blanc Napa Valley 1986 $8.50 (5/15/88)
72 ROBERT PEPI Sauvignon Blanc Napa Valley 1985 $8.50 (12/31/87)
85 ROBERT PEPI Sauvignon Blanc Napa Valley 1984 $8 (1/31/87)
81 ROBERT PEPI Sauvignon Blanc Napa Valley 1983 $8 (2/16/86)
55 JOSEPH PHELPS Sauvignon Blanc Napa Valley 1988 $9.50 (6/30/90)
73 JOSEPH PHELPS Sauvignon Blanc Napa Valley 1987 $9 (12/31/88)
59 JOSEPH PHELPS Sauvignon Blanc Napa Valley 1986 $9 (12/31/87)
94 JOSEPH PHELPS Sauvignon Blanc Napa Valley 1984 $9 (2/01/86)
67 R.H. PHILLIPS Sauvignon Blanc Yolo County Dunnigan Hills Night Harvest 1987 $4 (3/15/89)
90 PRESTON Sauvignon Blanc Dry Creek Valley 1985 $6.75 (9/15/86)
87 PRESTON Sauvignon Blanc Dry Creek Valley Cuvée de Fumé 1990 $9.50 (7/15/91)
86 PRESTON Sauvignon Blanc Dry Creek Valley Cuvée de Fumé 1989 $8 (5/15/90)
86 PRESTON Sauvignon Blanc Dry Creek Valley Cuvée de Fumé 1988 $8 (9/15/89)
86 PRESTON Sauvignon Blanc Dry Creek Valley Cuvée de Fumé 1987 $7.25 (8/31/88)
88 PRESTON Sauvignon Blanc Dry Creek Valley Cuvée de Fumé 1986 $6.75 (8/31/87)
82 PRESTON Sauvignon Blanc Dry Creek Valley Estate Reserve 1989 $12 (12/31/90)
87 PRESTON Sauvignon Blanc Dry Creek Valley Estate Reserve 1988 $10 (11/30/89)
81 PRESTON Sauvignon Blanc Dry Creek Valley Private Reserve 1987 $9.50 (12/31/88)
89 PRESTON Sauvignon Blanc Dry Creek Valley Reserve 1986 $9.50 (10/15/87)
87 PRESTON Sauvignon Blanc Dry Creek Valley Reserve 1985 $9 (5/15/87)
92 PRESTON Sauvignon Blanc Dry Creek Valley Reserve 1984 $9 (11/01/85)
80 QUAIL RIDGE Sauvignon Blanc Napa Valley 1989 $8 (12/31/90)
85 QUAIL RIDGE Sauvignon Blanc Napa Valley 1988 $8 (11/30/89)
89 QUAIL RIDGE Sauvignon Blanc Napa Valley 1987 $7.50 (3/15/89)
83 QUIVIRA Sauvignon Blanc Dry Creek Valley 1989 $9.25 (10/31/90)
88 QUIVIRA Sauvignon Blanc Dry Creek Valley 1988 $9.50 (11/30/89)
89 QUIVIRA Sauvignon Blanc Dry Creek Valley 1987 $8.50 (10/15/88)
78 QUIVIRA Sauvignon Blanc Dry Creek Valley 1986 $8 (11/30/87)
84 QUIVIRA Sauvignon Blanc Dry Creek Valley 1985 $8 (1/31/87)
91 QUIVIRA Sauvignon Blanc Dry Creek Valley 1984 $8 (10/01/85)
80 RAYMOND Sauvignon Blanc Napa Valley 1989 $10 (4/30/91)
88 RAYMOND Sauvignon Blanc Napa Valley 1988 $8.50 (11/30/89)
85 RAYMOND Sauvignon Blanc Napa Valley 1987 $8 (1/31/89)
79 RAYMOND Sauvignon Blanc Napa Valley 1986 $7.50 (12/31/87)
87 RAYMOND Sauvignon Blanc Napa Valley 1985 $7.50 (5/15/87)
75 ROCHIOLI Sauvignon Blanc Russian River Valley 1986 $8.50 (11/30/87)
83 ROUND HILL Fumé Blanc Napa Valley House 1989 $5.75 (11/30/90) BB
81 ROUND HILL Fumé Blanc Napa Valley House 1986 $5 (1/31/88) BB
75 RUTHERFORD HILL Sauvignon Blanc Napa Valley 1987 $8 (7/31/89)
76 RUTHERFORD HILL Sauvignon Blanc Napa Valley 1986 $7 (5/31/88)
61 RUTHERFORD HILL Sauvignon Blanc Napa Valley 1985 $7 (10/15/87)
67 RUTHERFORD HILL Sauvignon Blanc Napa Valley 1984 $7.50 (12/31/86)
70 RUTHERFORD RANCH Sauvignon Blanc Napa Valley 1986 $6.75 (3/15/88)
81 ST. CLEMENT Sauvignon Blanc Napa Valley 1989 $9.50 (8/31/90)
78 ST. CLEMENT Sauvignon Blanc Napa Valley 1988 $9.50 (3/31/90)
68 ST. CLEMENT Sauvignon Blanc Napa Valley 1987 $9.50 (7/31/89)
82 ST. CLEMENT Sauvignon Blanc Napa Valley 1986 $9.50 (5/31/88)
82 ST. CLEMENT Sauvignon Blanc Napa Valley 1985 $9.50 (8/31/86)
83 ST. CLEMENT Sauvignon Blanc Napa Valley 1984 $9.50 (10/16/85)
82 ST. SUPERY Sauvignon Blanc Napa Valley Dollarhide Ranch 1989 $8 (3/15/91)
87 ST. SUPERY Sauvignon Blanc Napa Valley Dollarhide Ranch 1988 $7.50 (10/31/89)
71 ST. VRAIN Sauvignon Blanc Alexander Valley 1985 $8 (5/15/87)
65 SANFORD Sauvignon Blanc Santa Barbara County 1989 $9 (7/31/91)
85 SANFORD Sauvignon Blanc Santa Barbara County 1987 $8.50 (12/15/89)
68 SANTA BARBARA Sauvignon Blanc Santa Ynez Valley Reserve 1987 $11 (12/15/89)
72 SANTA BARBARA Sauvignon Blanc Santa Ynez Valley Valley View Vineyards 1987 $8.50 (12/15/89)
64 SEBASTIANI Sauvignon Blanc Sonoma County Reserve 1986 $9 (12/31/87)
76 SAM J. SEBASTIANI Sauvignon Blanc Sonoma-Napa Counties 1985 $10 (10/31/86)
80 SHENANDOAH Sauvignon Blanc Amador County 1986 $7 (8/31/87)
84 SHENANDOAH Sauvignon Blanc Amador County 1985 $7 (10/31/86)
78 SIGNORELLO Sauvignon Blanc Napa Valley 1987 $8.25 (4/30/89)
80 SIGNORELLO Sauvignon Blanc Napa Valley 1986 $7.25 (3/15/88)
83 SILVERADO Sauvignon Blanc Napa Valley 1989 $9 (10/31/90)
90 SILVERADO Sauvignon Blanc Napa Valley 1988 $8.50 (2/15/90) SS

86 SILVERADO Sauvignon Blanc Napa Valley 1985 $8 (2/28/87)
84 SIMI Sauvignon Blanc Sonoma County 1989 $9.50 (4/30/91)
90 SIMI Sauvignon Blanc Sonoma County 1988 $8 (10/31/90)
72 SIMI Sauvignon Blanc Sonoma County 1987 $9.50 (7/31/89)
73 SIMI Sauvignon Blanc Sonoma County 1986 $9 (10/15/88)
78 SIMI Sauvignon Blanc Sonoma County 1985 $10 (8/31/87)
76 SIMI Sauvignon Blanc Sonoma County 1984 $10.50 (10/15/86)
65 SIMI Sauvignon Blanc Sonoma County 1983 $9.50 (11/16/85)
87 SIMI Sauvignon Blanc Sonoma County 1982 $9 (4/01/84)
81 SPOTTSWOODE Sauvignon Blanc Napa Valley 1989 $11 (8/31/90)
85 SPOTTSWOODE Sauvignon Blanc Napa Valley 1985 $9 (1/31/87)
72 STAG'S LEAP WINE CELLARS Sauvignon Blanc Napa Valley 1984 $8.50 (6/01/86)
76 STAG'S LEAP WINE CELLARS Sauvignon Blanc Napa Valley Rancho Chimiles 1988 $9 (11/30/89)
80 STAG'S LEAP WINE CELLARS Sauvignon Blanc Napa Valley Rancho Chimiles 1987 $9 (1/31/89)
76 DAVID S. STARE Fumé Blanc Dry Creek Valley Reserve 1984 $11 (1/31/87)
79 STERLING Sauvignon Blanc Napa Valley 1989 $9 (3/15/91)
84 STERLING Sauvignon Blanc Napa Valley 1988 $9 (11/30/89)
73 STERLING Sauvignon Blanc Napa Valley 1987 $10 (11/15/88)
79 STERLING Sauvignon Blanc Napa Valley 1986 $9 (1/31/88)
75 STERLING Sauvignon Blanc Napa Valley 1985 $10 (11/30/86)
73 STERLING Sauvignon Blanc Napa Valley 1984 $9 (4/16/86)
87 STONEGATE Sauvignon Blanc Napa Valley 1988 $8.50 (6/30/90)
83 STRATFORD Sauvignon Blanc California 1988 $8 (5/15/90)
83 STRATFORD Sauvignon Blanc California 1986 $6.75 (11/15/87)
90 STRATFORD Sauvignon Blanc California 1985 $6.75 (11/15/86)
82 STRATFORD Sauvignon Blanc California 1984 $6.50 (12/01/85)
79 SUNNY ST. HELENA Sauvignon Blanc Napa Valley 1989 $9 (4/30/91)
62 SUNNY ST. HELENA Sauvignon Blanc Napa Valley 1986 $6 (11/15/87)
79 SUTTER HOME Sauvignon Blanc California 1989 $4.50 (4/30/91)
66 SUTTER HOME Sauvignon Blanc North Coast 1984 $4.50 (2/16/86)
77 TAFT STREET Sauvignon Blanc Napa Valley 1986 $5.50 (12/31/87)
82 PHILIP TOGNI Sauvignon Blanc Napa Valley 1989 $12.50 (7/15/91)
88 PHILIP TOGNI Sauvignon Blanc Napa Valley 1987 $10 (11/15/88)
81 M.G. VALLEJO Fumé Blanc California 1988 $5 (5/15/90) BB
78 M.G. VALLEJO Fumé Blanc California 1988 $5 (10/31/89)
82 M.G. VALLEJO Fumé Blanc California 1986 $4.50 (7/15/87) BB
81 VENTANA Sauvignon Blanc Monterey 1988 $8 (3/31/90)
85 VENTANA Sauvignon Blanc Monterey 1987 $8 (10/31/89)
87 VENTANA Sauvignon Blanc Monterey Ventana Vineyards 1986 $7.50 (11/15/87)
73 VIANSA Sauvignon Blanc Napa-Sonoma Counties 1988 $10 (10/31/90)
81 VIANSA Sauvignon Blanc Sonoma-Napa Counties 1987 $9.50 (4/30/89)
82 VIANSA Sauvignon Blanc Napa-Sonoma Counties 1986 $8.75 (5/31/88)
79 WENTE BROS. Sauvignon Blanc Livermore Valley 1983 $6.50 (2/16/86)
78 J. WILE & SONS Sauvignon Blanc Napa Valley 1986 $6 (10/31/87)
75 WILLIAM WHEELER Sauvignon Blanc Sonoma County 1986 $8 (3/15/88)
90 WILLIAM WHEELER Sauvignon Blanc Sonoma County 1985 $8 (2/28/87)
68 WHITEHALL LANE Sauvignon Blanc Napa Valley 1984 $8 (10/15/86)
72 ZACA MESA Sauvignon Blanc Central Coast 1984 $7.50 (2/15/87)
71 ZACA MESA Sauvignon Blanc Santa Barbara County 1988 $8 (12/15/89)
82 STEPHEN ZELLERBACH Sauvignon Blanc Sonoma County 1989 $5.50 (12/31/90) BB

SAUVIGNON BLENDS

89 BENZIGER A Tribute Sonoma Mountain 1988 $11.50 (12/31/90)
75 CARMENET Edna Valley 1986 $9 (12/15/88)
85 CARMENET Edna Valley 1985 $8.75 (4/15/88)
84 CARMENET Edna Valley 1983 $9 (3/16/85)
84 CARMENET Reserve Edna Valley 1988 $12 (1/31/91)
77 CARMENET Sonoma County 1987 $9.50 (3/31/90)
85 CARMENET Sonoma County 1986 $9.50 (1/31/89)
80 CARMENET Sonoma County 1985 $8.75 (12/31/87)
89 CAYMUS Conundrum California 1989 $18 (4/30/91)
83 DE LORIMIER Spectrum Alexander Valley 1988 $8.50 (9/30/90)
81 DE LORIMIER Spectrum Alexander Valley 1987 $8.50 (3/31/89)
86 DE LORIMIER Spectrum Alexander Valley 1986 $8.50 (2/29/88)
89 INGLENOOK Gravion Napa Valley 1987 $9.50 (2/28/89)
91 INGLENOOK Gravion Napa Valley 1986 $9.50 (4/30/88) SS
81 KENDALL-JACKSON Chevriot Lake County 1985 $9 (9/30/87)
89 KONOCTI Meritage Clear Lake 1988 $14 (4/30/91)
89 LYETH White Alexander Valley 1988 $12 (10/31/90)
78 LYETH White Alexander Valley 1986 $12 (9/15/89)
76 LYETH White Alexander Valley 1985 $10 (12/31/87)
76 LYETH White Alexander Valley 1983 $10 (5/01/86)
70 MERLION Chevrier Hyde Vineyards Los Carneros 1987 $10 (8/31/90)
88 MERLION Sauvrier Napa Valley 1986 $9 (9/15/88)
85 MERLION Sauvrier Napa Valley 1985 $9.50 (1/31/88)
88 GUSTAVE NIEBAUM Chevrier Herrick Vineyard Napa Valley 1988 $11.50 (12/15/89)
81 VICHON Chevrignon Napa Valley 1989 $9.75 (5/31/91)
86 VICHON Chevrignon Napa Valley 1988 $9.75 (1/31/91)
74 VICHON Chevrignon Napa Valley 1986 $9.75 (1/31/89)
70 VICHON Chevrignon Napa Valley 1985 $9.50 (8/31/87)
63 VICHON Chevrignon Napa Valley 1984 $7.50 (9/15/86)
91 VICHON Chevrignon Napa Valley 1983 $9.60 (1/01/85) SS

SÉMILLON

83 ALDERBROOK Sémillon Dry Creek Valley 1988 $9 (2/15/90)
75 ALDERBROOK Sémillon Dry Creek Valley 1985 $6.50 (4/30/88)
87 ALDERBROOK Sémillon Dry Creek Valley Rued Vineyard 1987 $7.50 (5/15/89) BB
77 J. CAREY Sémillon Santa Ynez Valley Buttonwood Farm 1987 $8 (12/15/89)
82 CLOS DU VAL Sémillon California 1987 $10 (7/15/91)
73 CLOS DU VAL Sémillon California 1986 $9 (10/31/88)
76 CLOS DU VAL Sémillon California 1985 $8.50 (8/31/87)
86 CLOS DU VAL Sémillon California 1984 $8.50 (3/01/86)
90 CLOS DU VAL Sémillon California 1983 $7.50 (3/01/85) SS
88 MERLION Sémillon Los Carneros Hyde Vineyards Chevrier 1986 $10 (9/15/88)
77 MONTICELLO Sémillon Napa Valley Chevrier Blanc 1986 $7.50 (1/31/89)
87 MONTICELLO Sémillon Napa Valley Chevrier Blanc 1984 $7.50 (1/01/86)
71 R.H. PHILLIPS Sémillon Yolo County Dunnigan Hills 1984 $6.50 (3/01/86)
76 WENTE BROS. Sémillon Livermore Valley 1983 $5 (3/01/86)

SPARKLING/BLANC DE BLANCS

81 CHATEAU ST. JEAN Brut Blanc de Blancs Sonoma County 1987 $12 (12/31/89)
88 CHATEAU ST. JEAN Brut Blanc de Blancs Sonoma County 1984 $11 (5/31/89)
88 CHATEAU ST. JEAN Brut Blanc de Blancs Sonoma County 1984 $11 (8/31/88)
76 CHATEAU ST. JEAN Brut Blanc de Blancs Sonoma County 1983 $11 (7/31/87)
79 CHATEAU ST. JEAN Brut Blanc de Blancs Sonoma County 1982 $13 (5/16/86)
82 CHATEAU ST. JEAN Brut Blanc de Blancs Sonoma County 1981 $14 (11/01/84)
86 CHATEAU ST. JEAN Brut Blanc de Blancs Sonoma County NV $12 (5/15/91)
81 ESTRELLA RIVER Blanc de Blancs Paso Robles Star Cuvée 1983 $13 (2/29/88)
89 FALCONER Brut Blanc de Blancs Russian River Valley 1984 $15 (3/15/91)
87 IRON HORSE Blanc de Blancs Sonoma County Green Valley 1986 $22 (12/31/90)
85 IRON HORSE Blanc de Blancs Sonoma County Green Valley 1985 $21 (12/31/89)
85 IRON HORSE Blanc de Blancs Sonoma County Green Valley 1985 $20 (5/31/89)
79 IRON HORSE Blanc de Blancs Sonoma County Green Valley 1984 $19 (12/31/88)
78 IRON HORSE Blanc de Blancs Sonoma County Green Valley 1982 $16.50 (5/16/86)
85 IRON HORSE Blanc de Blancs Sonoma County Green Valley Late Disgorged 1982 $24 (12/31/87)
86 IRON HORSE Blanc de Blancs Sonoma County Green Valley 1981 $18 (11/01/84)
86 JEPSON Blanc de Blancs Mendocino 1986 $16 (4/30/91)
79 KORBEL Blanc de Blancs California NV $13 (6/15/91)
73 KORBEL Blanc de Blancs California NV $14.50 (8/31/89)
64 KORBEL Blanc de Blancs California NV $14.50 (3/15/88)
73 KORBEL Blanc de Blancs California NV $14.50 (5/16/86)
69 KORBEL Blanc de Blancs California Private Reserve 1981 $34/1.5L (2/29/88)
77 HANNS KORNELL Blanc de Blancs California 1982 $14.75 (11/30/86)
91 SCHARFFENBERGER Blanc de Blancs Mendocino County 1986 $20 (3/15/91)
81 SCHARFFENBERGER Blanc de Blancs Mendocino County 1986 $18 (12/31/89)
85 SCHARFFENBERGER Blanc de Blancs Mendocino County 1985 $18 (12/31/88)
78 SCHARFFENBERGER Blanc de Blancs Mendocino County 1984 $17.50 (12/31/87)
89 SCHRAMSBERG Blanc de Blancs Napa Valley 1986 $20 (12/31/90)
84 SCHRAMSBERG Blanc de Blancs Napa Valley 1985 $20 (5/31/89)
82 SCHRAMSBERG Blanc de Blancs Napa Valley 1983 $17.50 (5/16/86)
87 SCHRAMSBERG Blanc de Blancs Napa Valley Late Disgorged 1985 $27 (6/15/91)
77 SHADOW CREEK Blanc de Blancs California 1984 $14.50 (1/31/88)
88 SHADOW CREEK Blanc de Blancs Sonoma County 1983 $15 (5/16/86)
89 SHADOW CREEK Blanc de Blancs Sonoma County 1982 $15 (10/16/85)
80 TIJSSELING Blanc de Blancs Mendocino Cuvée de Chardonnay 1985 $13 (12/31/89)

BLANC DE NOIRS

86 S. ANDERSON Blanc de Noirs Napa Valley 1987 $19 (6/15/91)
83 S. ANDERSON Blanc de Noirs Napa Valley 1986 $20 (12/31/90)
87 S. ANDERSON Blanc de Noirs Napa Valley 1985 $16 (5/31/89)
79 S. ANDERSON Blanc de Noirs Napa Valley 1984 $16 (10/15/88)
85 S. ANDERSON Blanc de Noirs Napa Valley 1983 $28 (5/31/89)
88 S. ANDERSON Blanc de Noirs Napa Valley 1983 $28 (5/31/87)
73 S. ANDERSON Brut Napa Valley Tivoli Brut Noir NV $12 (6/15/91)
84 CHANDON Blanc de Noirs Napa Valley NV $14 (5/31/89)
80 CHANDON Blanc de Noirs Napa Valley NV $27/1.5L (5/16/86)
76 CHANDON Blanc de Noirs Napa Valley NV $14 (5/16/86)
80 CHANDON Blanc de Noirs Napa-Sonoma Counties NV $15 (12/31/89)
71 CHATEAU DIANA Blanc de Noirs Monterey Special Reserve 1986 $7 (6/15/91)
68 CULBERTSON Blanc de Noir California 1983 $14 (5/16/86)
77 CULBERTSON Blanc de Noir California NV $14 (12/31/90)
83 DOMAINE MUMM Blanc de Noirs Napa Valley Cuvée Napa NV $15 (11/15/90)
79 FIRESTONE Blanc de Noirs Santa Ynez Valley 1985 $15 (12/31/88)
84 ROBERT HUNTER Brut de Noirs Sonoma Valley 1984 $15 (10/15/88)
84 ROBERT HUNTER Brut de Noirs Sonoma Valley 1983 $15 (1/31/88)
90 ROBERT HUNTER Brut de Noirs Sonoma Valley 1982 $14 (12/31/86)
87 ROBERT HUNTER Brut de Noirs Sonoma Valley 1981 $14 (12/16/84)
69 ROBERT HUNTER Brut de Noirs Sonoma Valley Later Disgorged 1981 $14 (2/01/86)
90 IRON HORSE Blanc de Noirs Sonoma County Green Valley Wedding Cuvée 1986 $19 (5/31/89)
86 IRON HORSE Blanc de Noirs Sonoma County Green Valley Wedding Cuvée 1985 $17 (12/31/88)
85 IRON HORSE Blanc de Noirs Sonoma County Green Valley Wedding Cuvée 1984 $16.50 (12/31/87)
82 IRON HORSE Blanc de Noirs Sonoma County Green Valley Wedding Cuvée 1983 $16.50 (12/31/86)
88 JORDAN Sonoma County J 1987 $22 (5/15/91)
71 KORBEL Blanc de Noirs California NV $14 (12/31/89)
87 HANNS KORNELL Blanc de Noirs California 1987 $15 (6/15/91)
69 HANNS KORNELL Blanc de Noirs California 1986 $15 (5/31/89)
71 MARK WEST Blanc de Noirs Russian River Valley 1984 $16.50 (12/31/88)
83 PAUL MASSON Blanc de Noirs Monterey Centennial Cuvée 1984 $9 (12/31/87)
69 MIRASSOU Blanc de Noirs Monterey 1983 $11 (12/31/88)
66 MIRASSOU Blanc de Noirs Monterey 1982 $10 (8/31/87)
83 PIPER SONOMA Blanc de Noirs Sonoma County 1987 $16 (6/15/91)
87 PIPER SONOMA Blanc de Noirs Sonoma County 1986 $15 (5/31/89)
88 PIPER SONOMA Blanc de Noirs Sonoma County 1983 $15 (12/31/86)
86 PIPER SONOMA Blanc de Noirs Sonoma County 1982 $15 (4/01/86)
82 SCHRAMSBERG Blanc de Noirs Napa Valley 1984 $22 (12/31/90)
90 SCHRAMSBERG Blanc de Noirs Napa Valley 1983 $21 (5/31/89)
91 SCHRAMSBERG Blanc de Noirs Napa Valley 1981 $20 (5/16/86)
87 SCHRAMSBERG Blanc de Noirs Napa Valley Late Disgorged 1983 $28 (6/15/91)
77 SEBASTIANI Blanc de Noirs Sonoma County Five Star NV $11 (4/30/90)
86 SHADOW CREEK Blanc de Noirs California 1984 $12.50 (5/31/87)
80 SHADOW CREEK Blanc de Noirs California NV $11 (6/15/91)
77 SHADOW CREEK Blanc de Noirs California NV $13 (12/31/89)
83 SHADOW CREEK Blanc de Noirs California NV $13 (5/31/89)
79 SHADOW CREEK Blanc de Noirs Sonoma County 1982 $13 (5/16/86)
78 WENTE BROS. Blanc de Noir Arroyo Seco 1983 $15 (3/31/89)

BRUT

87 S. ANDERSON Brut Napa Valley 1985 $18 (6/15/91)
82 S. ANDERSON Brut Napa Valley 1984 $18 (10/15/88)
72 S. ANDERSON Brut Napa Valley 1983 $16 (5/31/87)
81 BEAULIEU Brut Napa Valley 1982 $12 (5/31/89)
87 BEAULIEU Brut Napa Valley Champagne de Chardonnay 1982 $16 (5/31/89)
85 CHANDON Brut Napa Valley NV $28/1.5L (5/31/89)

UNITED STATES
CALIFORNIA/*SPARKLING*/BRUT

85	CHANDON Brut Napa Valley NV $14 (5/16/86)
77	CHANDON Brut Napa Valley Club Cuvée NV $17 (6/15/91)
81	CHANDON Brut Napa Valley Reserve NV $19 (12/31/89)
89	CHANDON Brut Napa Valley Reserve NV $38/1.5L (5/31/89)
87	CHANDON Brut Napa Valley Reserve NV $19 (4/15/88)
80	CHANDON Brut Napa Valley Reserve NV $38/1.5L (5/16/86)
80	CHANDON Brut Napa-Sonoma Counties NV $15 (12/31/89)
72	CHASE-LIMOGERE Brut California NV $7 (12/31/89)
84	CHATEAU DE BAUN Brut Sonoma County Symphony Romance 1988 $11 (7/15/91)
74	CHATEAU DE BAUN Brut Sonoma County Symphony Romance 1986 $12 (7/31/88)
82	CHATEAU ST. JEAN Brut Sonoma County 1987 $12 (4/30/90)
87	CHATEAU ST. JEAN Brut Sonoma County 1986 $12 (12/31/89)
86	CHATEAU ST. JEAN Brut Sonoma County 1985 $11 (12/31/88)
84	CHATEAU ST. JEAN Brut Sonoma County 1984 $11 (7/15/88)
67	CHATEAU ST. JEAN Brut Sonoma County 1983 $11 (5/31/87)
67	CHATEAU ST. JEAN Brut Sonoma County 1982 $13 (5/16/86)
81	CHATEAU ST. JEAN Brut Sonoma County 1981 $14 (11/01/84)
86	CHATEAU ST. JEAN Brut Sonoma County NV $12 (5/15/91)
80	CHATEAU ST. JEAN Brut Sonoma County Grande Cuvée 1982 $19 (6/15/91)
77	CONGRESS SPRINGS Brut Santa Clara County Brut de Pinot 1986 $8 (3/31/88)
83	CULBERTSON Brut California 1985 $14 (5/31/89)
66	CULBERTSON Brut California 1983 $14 (5/16/86)
88	DOMAINE CARNEROS Brut Carneros NV $14 (11/15/90)
91	DOMAINE MUMM Brut Carneros Winery Lake Cuvée Napa 1987 $22 (11/15/90)
87	DOMAINE MUMM Brut Carneros Winery Lake Cuvée Napa 1986 $23 (5/31/89)
89	DOMAINE MUMM Brut Napa Valley Cuvée Napa NV $14 (12/31/87)
89	DOMAINE MUMM Brut Napa Valley Cuvée Napa NV $14 (7/01/86)
82	DOMAINE MUMM Brut Napa Valley Prestige Cuvée Napa NV $15 (12/31/90)
87	DOMAINE MUMM Brut Napa Valley Prestige Cuvée Napa NV $15 (5/31/89)
88	DOMAINE MUMM Brut Napa Valley Prestige Cuvée Napa NV $14 (12/31/88)
87	DOMAINE MUMM Brut Napa Valley Reserve Cuvée Napa 1987 $22 (12/31/90)
86	DOMAINE MUMM Brut Napa Valley Reserve Cuvée Napa 1985 $21 (5/31/89)
89	DOMAINE MUMM Brut Napa Valley Reserve Cuvée Napa 1985 $21 (12/31/88)
81	GLORIA FERRER Brut Carneros Carneros Cuvée 1985 $20 (4/30/90)
86	GLORIA FERRER Brut Sonoma County NV $14 (12/31/90)
89	GLORIA FERRER Brut Sonoma County NV $14 (5/31/89)
88	GLORIA FERRER Brut Sonoma County NV $14 (1/31/88)
84	GLORIA FERRER Brut Sonoma County Royal Cuvée 1986 $16 (4/30/91)
83	GLORIA FERRER Brut Sonoma County Royal Cuvée 1985 $16 (5/31/89)
87	GLORIA FERRER Brut Sonoma County Royal Cuvée 1985 $15 (5/31/89)
89	GLORIA FERRER Brut Sonoma County Royal Cuvée 1984 $15 (4/15/88)
87	FOLIE A DEUX Brut Napa Valley Fantasie 1989 $18 (6/15/91)
81	HANDLEY Brut Anderson Valley 1984 $15 (10/15/88)
89	IRON HORSE Brut Sonoma County Green Valley 1987 $21 (11/15/90)
82	IRON HORSE Brut Sonoma County Green Valley 1986 $20 (12/31/89)
83	IRON HORSE Brut Sonoma County Green Valley 1985 $17.50 (12/31/88)
79	IRON HORSE Brut Sonoma County Green Valley 1984 $16.50 (12/31/87)
87	IRON HORSE Brut Sonoma County Green Valley 1983 $16.50 (12/31/86)
80	IRON HORSE Brut Sonoma County Green Valley 1982 $16.50 (5/16/86)
80	IRON HORSE Brut Sonoma County Green Valley Late Disgorged 1984 $23 (12/31/89)
82	JEPSON Brut Mendocino 1985 $16 (12/31/88)
83	KORBEL Brut California NV $10 (6/15/91)
78	KORBEL Brut California NV $11.50 (8/31/89)
75	KORBEL Brut California NV $11.50 (5/16/86)
79	HANNS KORNELL Brut California NV $11.50 (6/15/91)
68	HANNS KORNELL Brut California NV $11.25 (5/31/89)
70	HANNS KORNELL Brut California NV $11.25 (10/15/88)
67	LE DOMAINE Brut California NV $5 (2/28/91)
77	MAISON DEUTZ Brut San Luis Obispo County Reserve 1986 $22 (4/30/91)
89	MAISON DEUTZ Brut Santa Barbara County Cuvée NV $15 (10/31/86)
89	MAISON DEUTZ Brut Santa Barbara County Cuvée 3 NV $17 (5/31/89)
66	MIRASSOU Brut Monterey 1983 $10 (7/31/88)
78	MIRASSOU Brut Monterey 1982 $12 (9/16/85)
84	MIRASSOU Brut Monterey Cuvée 1984 $12 (6/15/91)
76	MIRASSOU Brut Monterey Reserve 1983 $15 (12/31/89)
79	MONTREAUX Brut Napa Valley 1985 $32 (12/31/90)
77	MONTREAUX Brut Napa Valley 1985 $32 (12/31/88)
79	PARSONS CREEK Brut Mendocino County Reserve NV $15 (5/31/89)
87	PIPER SONOMA Brut Sonoma County 1987 $16 (6/15/91)
82	PIPER SONOMA Brut Sonoma County 1986 $14 (5/31/89)
79	PIPER SONOMA Brut Sonoma County 1985 $14 (7/15/88)
74	PIPER SONOMA Brut Sonoma County 1983 $22/1.5L (1/31/88)
79	PIPER SONOMA Brut Sonoma County 1983 $13 (12/31/86)
62	PIPER SONOMA Brut Sonoma County 1982 $13 (5/01/86)
93	PIPER SONOMA Brut Sonoma County Reserve 1982 $20 (12/31/89)
88	PIPER SONOMA Brut Sonoma County Reserve 1982 $20 (5/31/89)
88	PIPER SONOMA Brut Sonoma County Tête de Cuvée 1983 $29 (5/31/89)
81	PIPER SONOMA Brut Sonoma County Tête de Cuvée 1981 $29 (5/16/86)
88	ROEDERER ESTATE Brut Anderson Valley NV $16 (5/31/89)
89	ROEDERER ESTATE Brut Anderson Valley NV $16 (12/31/88)
82	ST. FRANCIS Brut Sonoma Valley 1984 $9.50 (12/16/85)
84	SCHARFFENBERGER Brut Mendocino County 1983 $13 (9/30/87)
85	SCHARFFENBERGER Brut Mendocino County 1982 $12.50 (2/01/86)
85	SCHARFFENBERGER Brut Mendocino County NV $18 (6/15/91)
77	SCHARFFENBERGER Brut Mendocino County NV $14 (10/15/88)
74	SCHARFFENBERGER Brut Mendocino County NV $14 (5/16/86)
82	SCHRAMSBERG Brut Napa Valley Reserve 1983 $29 (12/31/90)
85	SCHRAMSBERG Brut Napa Valley Reserve 1982 $28 (5/31/89)
78	SCHRAMSBERG Brut Napa Valley Reserve 1981 $27 (7/31/87)
61	SCHRAMSBERG Brut Napa Valley Reserve 1980 $30 (5/16/86)
72	SEBASTIANI Brut Sonoma County Five Star NV $11 (4/30/90)
76	SHADOW CREEK Brut California NV $11 (6/15/91)
78	SHADOW CREEK Brut California NV $13 (12/31/89)
85	SHADOW CREEK Brut California NV $13 (5/31/89)
87	SHADOW CREEK Brut California Reserve Cuvée 1983 $20 (5/31/89)
76	STANFORD Brut California Governor's Cuvée NV $5 (12/31/90)
89	TIJSSELING Brut Mendocino 1986 $11.50 (12/31/89)
80	TOTT'S Brut California Reserve Cuvée NV $8 (5/31/89)
58	TOTT'S Brut California Reserve Cuvée NV $8 (12/31/88)
91	MICHEL TRIBAUT Brut Monterey County 1985 $13 (5/31/89)
84	MICHEL TRIBAUT Brut Monterey County 1984 $14 (12/31/87)
81	MICHEL TRIBAUT Brut Monterey County 1983 $14 (2/15/87)
86	VAN DER KAMP Brut Sonoma Valley 1984 $15 (5/31/89)
86	VAN DER KAMP Brut Sonoma Valley 1983 $17.50 (12/31/87)
77	WEIBEL Brut Mendocino County 1982 $13 (9/15/86)
79	WENTE BROS. Brut Arroyo Seco 1983 $10 (8/31/88)
84	WENTE BROS. Brut Arroyo Seco 1982 $8 (12/31/86)
78	WENTE BROS. Brut Arroyo Seco 1981 $8 (4/01/86)

ROSÉ

68	CHASE-LIMOGERE Brut Rosé California NV $7 (12/31/89)
83	CHATEAU DE BAUN Brut Rosé Sonoma County Symphony Rhapsody 1988 $11 (7/15/91)
88	CHATEAU DE BAUN Rosé Sonoma County Symphony Rhapsody Sec 1986 $12 (9/15/88)
80	CULBERTSON Brut Rosé California 1986 $17.50 (5/31/89)
75	HANDLEY Rosé Anderson Valley 1984 $16.75 (12/31/88)
84	IRON HORSE Brut Rosé Sonoma County Green Valley 1987 $28 (12/31/90)
83	IRON HORSE Brut Rosé Sonoma County Green Valley 1986 $23 (12/31/89)
88	IRON HORSE Brut Rosé Sonoma County Green Valley 1985 $20 (12/31/88)
78	KORBEL Brut Rosé California NV $10 (6/15/91)
82	KORBEL Brut Rosé California NV $10.50 (8/31/89)
84	J. PEDRONCELLI Brut Rosé Sonoma County 1986 $10 (7/31/89)
84	SCHARFFENBERGER Brut Rosé Mendocino County NV $18 (3/15/91)
76	SCHARFFENBERGER Brut Rosé Mendocino County NV $16 (12/31/88)
81	SCHRAMSBERG Brut Rosé Napa Valley Cuvée de Pinot 1987 $20 (12/31/90)
76	SCHRAMSBERG Brut Rosé Napa Valley Cuvée de Pinot 1986 $19 (5/31/89)
80	SCHRAMSBERG Brut Rosé Napa Valley Cuvée de Pinot 1985 $17 (4/30/88)
83	SCHRAMSBERG Brut Rosé Napa Valley Cuvée de Pinot 1984 $17 (5/31/87)
80	MICHEL TRIBAUT Rosé Monterey County 1984 $14 (12/31/87)
81	VAN DER KAMP Brut Rosé Sonoma Valley Midnight Cuvée 1987 $15 (11/15/90)
83	VAN DER KAMP Brut Rosé Sonoma Valley Midnight Cuvée 1986 $15 (5/31/89)
84	VAN DER KAMP Brut Rosé Sonoma Valley Midnight Cuvée 1985 $17.50 (12/31/87)

OTHER SPARKLING

74	ADLER FELS Sonoma County Melange à Deux 1985 $15 (10/15/87)
87	BALLATORE California NV $4 (5/01/86) BB
74	CULBERTSON California Cuvée de Frontignan Demi-Sec NV $18.50 (12/31/90)
79	CULBERTSON California Cuvée Rouge NV $14 (12/31/90)
80	CULBERTSON California Cuvée Rouge NV $12 (3/31/89)
74	CULBERTSON Natural California 1986 $18.50 (12/31/90)
81	CULBERTSON Natural California 1985 $17.50 (5/31/89)
72	CULBERTSON Natural California 1983 $16.50 (5/16/86)
89	GLORIA FERRER Natural Sonoma County Cuvée Emerald NV $11 (5/16/86)
75	KORBEL Extra Dry California NV $10 (6/15/91)
81	KORBEL Natural California NV $13 (6/15/91)
78	KORBEL Natural California NV $13 (8/31/89)
77	KORBEL Extra Dry California NV $10 (8/31/89)
73	KORBEL Sec California NV $10 (8/31/89)
77	KORBEL Natural California NV $12.50 (2/15/88)
68	KORBEL Natural California NV $12.50 (5/16/86)
73	HANNS KORNELL Extra Dry California NV $11 (5/31/89)
74	HANNS KORNELL California Sehr Trocken 1984 $14.50 (6/15/91)
83	MIRASSOU Natural Monterey Cuvée au Naturel 1984 $15 (6/15/91)
81	SCHARFFENBERGER Crémant Mendocino County Demi-Sec NV $16.50 (12/31/88)
77	SCHRAMSBERG Crémant Napa Valley Demi-Sec 1986 $20 (12/31/90)
85	SCHRAMSBERG Crémant Napa Valley Demi-Sec 1985 $19 (5/31/89)
73	STANFORD California Governor's Cuvée Extra Dry NV $5 (12/31/90)
75	TOTT'S California Reserve Cuvée Extra Dry NV $8 (2/28/89)

ZINFANDEL

88	ADELAIDA Zinfandel Paso Robles 1988 $12 (4/30/91)
78	AHERN Zinfandel Amador County 1980 $6.50 (2/15/84)
82	ALEXANDER VALLEY Zinfandel Alexander Valley 1987 $9 (3/31/90)
82	AMADOR FOOTHILL Zinfandel Fiddletown Eschen Vineyard 1986 $9 (6/15/89)
86	AMADOR FOOTHILL Zinfandel Fiddletown Eschen Vineyard 1984 $9 (10/15/88)
74	AMADOR FOOTHILL Zinfandel Fiddletown Eschen Vineyard Special Selection 1982 $9 (4/15/87)
78	ARCIERO Zinfandel Paso Robles 1985 $7.50 (12/15/89)
84	AUDUBON Zinfandel San Luis Obispo County 1983 $7 (7/15/88)
82	BALDINELLI Zinfandel Shenandoah Valley 1988 $7.75 (12/31/90)
85	BALDINELLI Zinfandel Shenandoah Valley 1987 $8 (5/15/90)
83	BALDINELLI Zinfandel Shenandoah Valley Reserve 1986 $6.75 (12/15/88) BB
86	BERINGER Zinfandel North Coast 1987 $8 (9/15/90)
87	BERINGER Zinfandel North Coast 1985 $6 (4/30/88) BB
82	BLACK MOUNTAIN Zinfandel Alexander Valley Cramer Ridge 1986 $9 (3/31/90)
80	BLACK MOUNTAIN Zinfandel Alexander Valley Cramer Ridge 1986 $9 (3/31/89)
85	BOEGER Zinfandel El Dorado Walker Vineyard 1988 $8.50 (2/15/91)
86	BOEGER Zinfandel El Dorado Walker Vineyard 1987 $8.50 (5/31/89)
73	BOEGER Zinfandel El Dorado Walker Vineyard 1986 $7 (7/31/88)
76	BOEGER Zinfandel El Dorado Walker Vineyard 1981 $6 (7/16/85)
89	BUEHLER Zinfandel Napa Valley 1987 $9.50 (5/15/90)
83	BUEHLER Zinfandel Napa Valley 1986 $8.50 (12/15/88)
89	BUEHLER Zinfandel Napa Valley 1985 $8 (12/31/87)
71	BUEHLER Zinfandel Napa Valley 1983 $6.50 (3/15/87)
91	BUEHLER Zinfandel Napa Valley 1982 $6 (3/01/85)

80 BUEHLER Zinfandel Napa Valley 1981 $6 (9/16/84)
77 BUENA VISTA Zinfandel North Coast 1984 $7.25 (4/30/88)
80 BUENA VISTA Zinfandel Sonoma County 1982 $6 (4/01/85)
80 BURGESS Zinfandel Napa Valley 1988 $12 (7/31/91)
82 BURGESS Zinfandel Napa Valley 1987 $10 (5/31/90)
82 BURGESS Zinfandel Napa Valley 1986 $9.50 (7/31/89)
87 BURGESS Zinfandel Napa Valley 1985 $9 (6/30/88)
89 BURGESS Zinfandel Napa Valley 1984 $8 (11/15/87)
81 BURGESS Zinfandel Napa Valley 1983 $7.50 (10/31/86)
85 BURGESS Zinfandel Napa Valley 1982 $6.50 (7/16/85)
81 BURGESS Zinfandel Napa Valley 1981 $6 (4/16/84)
71 CALERA Zinfandel California NV $5 (7/31/88)
81 CALERA Zinfandel Cienega Valley 1981 $7 (4/16/84)
82 CALERA Zinfandel Cienega Valley Reserve 1981 $8.50 (1/01/85)
90 CASTORO Zinfandel Paso Robles 1987 $7.50 (12/15/89)
79 CAYMUS Zinfandel California 1976 Cur: $35 (6/16/85)
83 CAYMUS Zinfandel California 1974 Cur: $45 (6/16/85)
77 CAYMUS Zinfandel California Lot 31-J 1975 Cur: $40 (6/16/85)
80 CAYMUS Zinfandel Napa Valley 1988 $9 (10/15/90)
85 CAYMUS Zinfandel Napa Valley 1987 $9.75 (10/31/89)
89 CAYMUS Zinfandel Napa Valley 1986 $9 (12/15/88)
85 CAYMUS Zinfandel Napa Valley 1985 $8 (12/31/87)
90 CAYMUS Zinfandel Napa Valley 1984 $8 (5/15/87)
79 CAYMUS Zinfandel Napa Valley 1983 $7.50 (12/31/86)
92 CAYMUS Zinfandel Napa Valley 1982 $7.50 (5/16/86)
84 CAYMUS Zinfandel Napa Valley 1981 $6.50 (12/01/84)
69 CHATEAU MONTELENA Zinfandel Napa Valley 1987 $10 (7/31/90)
80 CHATEAU MONTELENA Zinfandel Napa Valley 1986 $10 (9/15/89)
90 CHATEAU MONTELENA Zinfandel Napa Valley 1985 $10 (4/30/88)
91 CHATEAU MONTELENA Zinfandel Napa Valley John Rolleri Vineyard 1984 $10 (5/15/87)
84 CHATEAU MONTELENA Zinfandel Napa Valley 1983 $10 (5/01/86)
91 CHATEAU MONTELENA Zinfandel Napa Valley 1982 $10 (5/01/84)
80 CHATEAU MONTELENA Zinfandel Napa Valley 1981 $8 (4/16/84)
78 CHATEAU MONTELENA Zinfandel North Coast 1976 Cur: $25 (6/16/85)
90 CHATEAU MONTELENA Zinfandel Napa Valley 1973 Cur: $50 (6/16/85)
92 CHATEAU MONTELENA Zinfandel Napa-Alexander Valleys 1974 Cur: $40 (6/16/85)
82 CHATEAU SOUVERAIN Zinfandel Dry Creek Valley 1987 $9.50 (5/15/90)
81 CHATEAU SOUVERAIN Zinfandel Dry Creek Valley 1986 $5 (3/31/89) BB
85 CHATEAU SOUVERAIN Zinfandel Dry Creek Valley Bradford Mountain Vineyard 1987 $15 (5/15/90)
79 CHRISTIAN BROTHERS Zinfandel Napa Valley 1986 $5.50 (6/30/88)
86 CLINE Zinfandel Contra Costa County 1989 $9 (5/15/91)
89 CLINE Zinfandel Contra Costa County 1987 $9 (5/15/90)
87 CLINE Zinfandel Contra Costa County Reserve 1987 $12 (5/15/90)
83 CLOS DU VAL Zinfandel Stags Leap District 1987 $12.50 (5/31/90)
87 CLOS DU VAL Zinfandel Napa Valley 1986 $12 (5/31/89)
90 CLOS DU VAL Zinfandel Napa Valley 1985 $12 (4/30/88)
81 CLOS DU VAL Zinfandel Napa Valley 1984 $12 (5/31/87)
90 CLOS DU VAL Zinfandel Napa Valley 1981 $9 (5/16/84) CS
77 CLOS DU VAL Zinfandel Napa Valley 1974 Cur: $45 (6/16/85)
86 CLOS DU VAL Zinfandel Napa Valley 1973 Cur: $50 (6/16/85)
90 CLOS DU VAL Zinfandel Napa Valley 1972 Cur: $60 (6/16/85)
83 CONGRESS SPRINGS Zinfandel Santa Cruz Mountains 1987 $12 (3/15/90)
60 CONN CREEK Zinfandel Napa Valley 1979 $7.50 (3/16/84)
86 CONN CREEK Zinfandel Napa Valley Barrel Select 1986 $9 (10/15/90)
84 CONN CREEK Zinfandel Napa Valley Collins Vineyard 1983 $10 (12/15/88)
87 CORBETT CANYON Zinfandel San Luis Obispo County Select 1984 $7.50 (5/15/88)
85 CUVAISON Zinfandel Napa Valley 1986 $10 (3/15/89)
75 CUVAISON Zinfandel Napa Valley 1983 $8.50 (9/15/87)
84 DALLA VALLE Zinfandel Napa Valley 1986 $25 (2/15/91)
78 DE LOACH Zinfandel Russian River Valley 1988 $11 (9/15/90)
90 DE LOACH Zinfandel Russian River Valley 1987 $10 (9/15/89)
88 DE LOACH Zinfandel Russian River Valley 1986 $9 (10/15/88)
84 DE LOACH Zinfandel Russian River Valley 1984 $8.50 (7/31/87)
69 DE LOACH Zinfandel Russian River Valley 1983 $8 (10/15/86)
77 DE LOACH Zinfandel Russian River Valley 1982 $8 (11/01/85)
89 DE LOACH Zinfandel Russian River Valley 1981 $7.50 (6/01/85)
72 DE MOOR Zinfandel Napa Valley 1988 $10 (4/30/91)
73 DEHLINGER Zinfandel Sonoma County 1983 $8 (7/31/87)
82 DOMAINE BRETON Zinfandel Lake County 1988 $8 (2/15/91)
77 DOMAINE ST. GEORGE Zinfandel California 1989 $5 (2/15/91)
85 DRY CREEK Zinfandel Dry Creek Valley 1986 $9 (4/15/89)
86 DRY CREEK Zinfandel Dry Creek Valley Old Vines 1988 $11 (2/15/91)
87 EDMEADES Zinfandel Mendocino Ciapusci Vineyard 1981 $9 (3/01/85)
72 ESTRELLA RIVER Zinfandel Paso Robles 1987 $8 (12/15/89)
77 ESTRELLA RIVER Zinfandel San Luis Obispo County 1980 $6 (12/01/84)
91 GARY FARRELL Zinfandel Sonoma County 1985 $10 (4/30/88)
62 FARVIEW FARM Zinfandel San Luis Obispo Reserve 1980 $7 (3/16/84)
76 FETZER Zinfandel California 1989 $6.50 (11/30/90)
78 FETZER Zinfandel California 1986 $6 (9/15/88)
83 FETZER Zinfandel Lake County 1986 $6 (2/15/88) BB
81 FETZER Zinfandel Lake County 1984 $5 (4/15/87)
83 FETZER Zinfandel Lake County 1983 $4.50 (7/16/86) BB
81 FETZER Zinfandel Mendocino 1982 $5.50 (4/01/85)
78 FETZER Zinfandel Mendocino 1980 $5.50 (4/01/84)
83 FETZER Zinfandel Mendocino County Reserve 1986 $14 (7/31/90)
88 FETZER Zinfandel Mendocino County Reserve 1986 $14 (12/15/89)
77 FETZER Zinfandel Mendocino Home Vineyard 1982 $8 (11/01/84)
79 FETZER Zinfandel Mendocino Lolonis Vineyards 1982 $8 (11/01/84)
74 FETZER Zinfandel Mendocino Ricetti Vineyard Reserve 1986 $14 (7/31/90)
79 FETZER Zinfandel Mendocino Ricetti Vineyard 1985 $14 (10/15/88)
82 FETZER Zinfandel Mendocino Ricetti Vineyard 1983 $8.50 (2/16/86)
79 FETZER Zinfandel Mendocino Ricetti Vineyard 1982 $8 (10/16/84)
85 FETZER Zinfandel Mendocino Scharffenberger Vineyard 1982 $8 (10/16/84)
81 FETZER Zinfandel Mendocino Special Reserve 1985 $14 (12/15/88)
63 FETZER Zinfandel Mendocino Special Reserve 1983 $8.50 (5/01/86)
86 FOPPIANO Zinfandel Dry Creek Valley Proprietor's Reserve 1987 $12 (12/31/90)
55 FRANCISCAN Zinfandel Napa Valley 1980 $6.50 (3/16/85)
88 FRANCISCAN Zinfandel Napa Valley Oakville Estate 1989 $10 (7/31/91)
87 FRANCISCAN Zinfandel Napa Valley Oakville Estate 1988 $9 (5/31/90)
86 J FRITZ Zinfandel Dry Creek Valley 1986 $9 (3/15/89)
84 J FRITZ Zinfandel Dry Creek Valley 1984 $7 (2/15/88)
79 J FRITZ Zinfandel Dry Creek Valley 80-Year-Old Vines 1988 $10 (7/31/91)
88 FROG'S LEAP Zinfandel Napa Valley 1988 $11.50 (12/15/90)
86 FROG'S LEAP Zinfandel Napa Valley 1987 $10.50 (3/15/90)
85 FROG'S LEAP Zinfandel Napa Valley 1986 $10 (12/15/88)
79 FROG'S LEAP Zinfandel Napa Valley 1985 $9 (11/15/87)
79 GEYSER PEAK Zinfandel Alexander Valley 1984 $7.75 (7/31/88)
77 GREEN & RED Zinfandel Napa Valley 1987 $9.50 (2/15/91)
76 GREEN & RED Zinfandel Napa Valley 1986 $9 (3/15/90)
73 GREEN & RED Zinfandel Napa Valley 1985 $8.50 (6/15/89)
82 GREEN & RED Zinfandel Napa Valley 1984 $7.75 (11/15/87)
64 GREEN & RED Zinfandel Napa Valley 1983 $7.25 (7/31/87)
82 GREEN & RED Zinfandel Napa Valley 1982 $7.50 (12/16/85)
86 GREENWOOD RIDGE Zinfandel Sonoma County 1988 $11 (5/15/91)
85 GRGICH HILLS Zinfandel Alexander Valley 1986 $12 (5/15/90)
84 GRGICH HILLS Zinfandel Alexander Valley 1985 $12 (7/31/89)
90 GRGICH HILLS Zinfandel Alexander Valley 1984 $10 (3/15/87)
85 GRGICH HILLS Zinfandel Alexander Valley 1983 $10 (5/01/86)
91 GRGICH HILLS Zinfandel Alexander Valley 1982 Rel: $10 Cur: $17 (5/16/85) SS
84 GRGICH HILLS Zinfandel Sonoma County 1987 $12 (10/15/90)
86 GRGICH HILLS Zinfandel Sonoma County 1984 $11 (10/31/88)
80 GRGICH HILLS Zinfandel Sonoma County 1981 $10 (4/01/84)
76 GUENOC Zinfandel California 1988 $7.50 (9/15/90)
84 GUENOC Zinfandel Guenoc Valley 1987 $8 (5/15/90)
67 GUENOC Zinfandel Guenoc Valley 1984 $5.50 (9/15/87)
79 GUENOC Zinfandel Lake County 1985 $5.50 (3/31/89)
78 GUENOC Zinfandel Lake County 1981 $5 (5/16/84)
84 GUNDLACH BUNDSCHU Zinfandel Sonoma Valley 1989 $7.50 (7/31/91)
88 GUNDLACH BUNDSCHU Zinfandel Sonoma Valley 1988 $7 (5/31/90) BB
87 GUNDLACH BUNDSCHU Zinfandel Sonoma Valley 1987 $7.75 (3/31/89)
87 GUNDLACH BUNDSCHU Zinfandel Sonoma Valley Rhinefarm Vineyards 1989 $12 (7/31/91)
88 GUNDLACH BUNDSCHU Zinfandel Sonoma Valley Rhinefarm Vineyards 1988 $10 (12/15/90)
71 GUNDLACH BUNDSCHU Zinfandel Sonoma Valley Rhinefarm Vineyards 1987 $8.50 (9/15/89)
90 GUNDLACH BUNDSCHU Zinfandel Sonoma Valley Rhinefarm Vineyards 1986 $8 (9/15/88)
84 GUNDLACH BUNDSCHU Zinfandel Sonoma Valley Rhinefarm Vineyards 1985 $8.50 (2/29/88)
87 GUNDLACH BUNDSCHU Zinfandel Sonoma Valley Rhinefarm Vineyards 1984 $7 (4/30/87) BB
87 GUNDLACH BUNDSCHU Zinfandel Sonoma Valley Rhinefarm Vineyards 1982 $7 (2/16/86)
86 HALLCREST Zinfandel California Doe Mill Cuvée 1989 $7 (4/30/91)
89 HAYWOOD Zinfandel Sonoma Valley Los Chamizal Vineyards 1988 $12.50 (11/30/90)
89 HAYWOOD Zinfandel Sonoma Valley 1986 $11 (9/15/88)
85 HAYWOOD Zinfandel Sonoma Valley 1985 $9.50 (11/15/87)
92 HAYWOOD Zinfandel Sonoma Valley 1984 $9 (5/31/87)
85 HAYWOOD Zinfandel Sonoma Valley 1983 $8 (1/01/86)
89 HAYWOOD Zinfandel Sonoma Valley 1982 $8 (11/01/84)
86 HIDDEN CELLARS Zinfandel Mendocino Pacini Vineyard 1986 $7.50 (10/31/88)
85 HIDDEN CELLARS Zinfandel Mendocino County Pacini Vineyard 1988 $10 (12/31/90)
88 HIDDEN CELLARS Zinfandel Mendocino County Pacini Vineyard 1984 $7.50 (4/15/87)
88 HOP KILN Zinfandel Russian River Valley 1988 $12 (12/15/90)
85 HOP KILN Zinfandel Russian River Valley 1986 $10 (6/15/89)
85 HOP KILN Zinfandel Russian River Valley 1982 $8.50 (11/01/85)
80 HOP KILN Zinfandel Russian River Valley Primitivo 1985 $12 (3/15/88)
90 HOP KILN Zinfandel Russian River Valley Primitivo Reserve 1985 $12 (6/15/89)
89 HOP KILN Zinfandel Sonoma County Primitivo 1988 $14 (12/31/90)
73 INGLENOOK Zinfandel Napa Valley 1986 $8 (4/30/91)
81 INGLENOOK Zinfandel Napa Valley 1983 $7.50 (3/15/88)
79 INGLENOOK Zinfandel Napa Valley 1981 $7 (2/01/85)
81 IRON HORSE Zinfandel Alexander Valley 1982 $7 (10/16/84)
83 KARLY Zinfandel Amador County 1988 $9.50 (12/31/90)
83 KARLY Zinfandel Amador County 1987 $9.50 (3/31/90)
79 KARLY Zinfandel Amador County 1986 $9 (3/31/89)
72 KARLY Zinfandel Amador County 1985 $8.50 (12/31/87)
85 KENDALL-JACKSON Zinfandel Anderson Valley DePatie-DuPratt Vineyard 1986 $16 (12/15/89)
90 KENDALL-JACKSON Zinfandel Anderson Valley DuPratt Vineyard 1987 $20 (7/31/91)
76 KENDALL-JACKSON Zinfandel Anderson Valley DuPratt-DePatie Vineyard 1983 $10 (11/01/85)
80 KENDALL-JACKSON Zinfandel Clear Lake Vina Las Lomas Vineyard 1983 $7 (6/01/85)
88 KENDALL-JACKSON Zinfandel Mendocino 1987 $9 (3/15/90)
86 KENDALL-JACKSON Zinfandel Mendocino 1986 $9 (9/15/88)
86 KENDALL-JACKSON Zinfandel Mendocino Ciapusci Vineyard 1984 $16 (12/15/89)
82 KENWOOD Zinfandel Sonoma Valley 1988 $11 (12/31/90)
90 KENWOOD Zinfandel Sonoma Valley 1987 $11 (10/31/89)
89 KENWOOD Zinfandel Sonoma Valley 1985 $9.50 (5/15/88)
90 KENWOOD Zinfandel Sonoma Valley 1984 $8.50 (9/15/87)
88 KENWOOD Zinfandel Sonoma Valley 1983 $7.50 (11/15/86)
90 KENWOOD Zinfandel Sonoma Valley 1982 $7.50 (7/16/86)
88 KENWOOD Zinfandel Sonoma Valley Jack London Vineyard 1987 $12 (12/15/89)
83 CHARLES KRUG Zinfandel Napa Valley 1989 $6 (12/15/90) BB
83 LA JOTA Zinfandel Howell Mountain 1987 $12 (10/31/89)
89 LA JOTA Zinfandel Howell Mountain 1986 $10 (10/31/88)
85 LA JOTA Zinfandel Howell Mountain 1985 $10 (4/30/88)
88 LA JOTA Zinfandel Howell Mountain 1984 $10 (11/15/87)
89 LAMBORN FAMILY Zinfandel Howell Mountain 1988 $11 (2/15/91)
84 LAMBORN FAMILY Zinfandel Howell Mountain 1987 $10 (3/15/90)
90 LYTTON SPRINGS Zinfandel Sonoma County 1988 $12 (7/31/90)
88 LYTTON SPRINGS Zinfandel Sonoma County 1987 $12 (5/31/89)
87 LYTTON SPRINGS Zinfandel Sonoma County 1986 $10 (10/15/88)
90 LYTTON SPRINGS Zinfandel Sonoma County 1985 $8 (8/31/87)
70 LYTTON SPRINGS Zinfandel Sonoma County 1984 $8 (10/31/86)
85 LYTTON SPRINGS Zinfandel Sonoma County Valley Vista Vineyard Private Reserve 1981 $12 (1/01/85)
79 MARIETTA Zinfandel Sonoma County 1987 $8 (11/30/90)
87 MARIETTA Zinfandel Sonoma County 1985 $7.50 (12/31/87)
90 MARIETTA Zinfandel Sonoma County 1984 $7.50 (1/31/87)
73 MARIETTA Zinfandel Sonoma County 1982 $6.50 (6/16/84)

UNITED STATES

CALIFORNIA/*ZINFANDEL*

88 MARIETTA Zinfandel Sonoma County Reserve 1985 $10 (12/31/87)
83 MARK WEST Zinfandel Sonoma County Robert Rue Vineyard 1986 $14 (3/15/90)
85 MARK WEST Zinfandel Sonoma County Robert Rue Vineyard 1985 $14 (7/31/88)
78 MARTIN Zinfandel Paso Robles 1986 $8 (12/15/89)
83 MARTIN Zinfandel Paso Robles 1985 $6.50 (2/15/88)
85 MARTINELLI Zinfandel Russian River Valley 1988 $11 (4/30/91)
78 LOUIS M. MARTINI Zinfandel California 1974 Cur: $22 (6/16/85)
87 LOUIS M. MARTINI Zinfandel California 1973 Cur: $25 (6/16/85)
80 LOUIS M. MARTINI Zinfandel North Coast 1985 $6.25 (3/31/89)
84 LOUIS M. MARTINI Zinfandel North Coast 1984 $6 (2/15/88) BB
87 LOUIS M. MARTINI Zinfandel North Coast 1983 $7.75 (10/15/86)
79 LOUIS M. MARTINI Zinfandel Sonoma County 1986 $7 (10/31/89)
73 MASTANTUONO Zinfandel San Luis Obispo County Dante Dusi Vineyards Unfined & Unfiltered 1984 $18 (7/31/91)
89 MAZZOCCO Zinfandel Sonoma County Traditional Style 1988 $13 (10/15/90)
90 MAZZOCCO Zinfandel Sonoma County Traditional Style 1986 $10 (12/15/88)
80 MCDOWELL Zinfandel McDowell Valley 1988 $9.50 (12/31/90)
87 MCDOWELL Zinfandel McDowell Valley 1987 $8 (12/15/89) BB
85 MEEKER Zinfandel Dry Creek Valley 1987 $10 (3/31/90)
83 MEEKER Zinfandel Dry Creek Valley 1986 $9 (3/15/89)
90 MEEKER Zinfandel Dry Creek Valley 1985 $8 (5/15/88)
79 MENDOCINO ESTATE Zinfandel Mendocino 1985 $4.75 (2/15/88)
68 MENDOCINO ESTATE Zinfandel Mendocino 1984 $4.25 (5/31/87)
80 MILANO Zinfandel Mendocino County 1981 $6 (10/01/84)
85 MILANO Zinfandel Mendocino County Sanel Valley Vineyard 1988 $8 (4/30/91)
73 MIRASSOU Zinfandel California Dry Red Lot No. 3 NV $5 (7/31/91)
81 MIRASSOU Zinfandel California Lot No. 4 NV $5.50 (7/31/91) BB
83 MONTEREY PENINSULA Zinfandel Amador County Ferrero Ranch Doctors' Reserve 1987 $15 (5/15/91)
83 MONTEREY PENINSULA Zinfandel Amador County Ferrero Ranch Doctors' Reserve 1982 $10 (2/29/88)
75 MONTEVINA Zinfandel Amador County 1987 $7.50 (3/31/90)
75 MONTEVINA Zinfandel Shenandoah Valley Montino 1985 $5.50 (10/15/88)
75 MONTEVINA Zinfandel Shenandoah Valley Winemaker's Choice 1984 $9 (8/31/87)
78 MONTEVINA Zinfandel Shenandoah Valley Winemaker's Choice 1980 $9 (4/16/84)
86 MOUNT VEEDER Zinfandel Napa County 1982 $8.50 (3/16/85)
85 NALLE Zinfandel Dry Creek Valley 1989 $13.50 (7/31/91)
89 NALLE Zinfandel Dry Creek Valley 1988 $12.50 (7/31/90)
92 NALLE Zinfandel Dry Creek Valley 1987 $10 (5/31/89) SS
90 NALLE Zinfandel Dry Creek Valley 1986 $9 (6/30/88)
91 NALLE Zinfandel Dry Creek Valley 1985 $8 (9/15/87)
91 NALLE Zinfandel Dry Creek Valley 1984 $7.50 (10/15/86)
80 PARDUCCI Zinfandel Mendocino County 1986 $5.75 (7/15/88)
84 J. PEDRONCELLI Zinfandel Dry Creek Valley 1988 $7 (11/30/90) BB
65 J. PEDRONCELLI Zinfandel Dry Creek Valley 1987 $7 (7/31/90)
86 J. PEDRONCELLI Zinfandel Dry Creek Valley 1986 $6 (3/31/89) BB
88 J. PEDRONCELLI Zinfandel Dry Creek Valley 1984 $5.50 (7/15/88) BB
77 J. PEDRONCELLI Zinfandel Sonoma County 1983 $4.50 (9/15/87)
79 J. PEDRONCELLI Zinfandel Sonoma County 1982 $4.50 (10/31/86) BB
78 J. PEDRONCELLI Zinfandel Sonoma County 1981 $4.50 (1/01/85)
82 J. PEDRONCELLI Zinfandel Sonoma County Reserve 1981 $8 (11/15/87)
79 PESENTI Zinfandel San Luis Obispo County Family Reserve 1984 $6 (12/15/89)
74 JOSEPH PHELPS Zinfandel Alexander Valley 1985 $10 (7/31/87)
80 JOSEPH PHELPS Zinfandel Alexander Valley 1981 $6.75 (4/16/85)
85 JOSEPH PHELPS Zinfandel Alexander Valley 1980 $6.75 (7/16/84)
82 JOSEPH PHELPS Zinfandel Napa Valley 1985 $6 (12/31/86)
60 JOSEPH PHELPS Zinfandel Napa Valley 1980 $6.75 (1/01/86)
60 JOSEPH PHELPS Zinfandel Napa Valley 1979 $6.75 (4/16/84)
86 PRESTON Zinfandel Dry Creek Valley 1988 $10 (10/15/90)
83 PRESTON Zinfandel Dry Creek Valley 1987 $10 (3/15/90)
84 PRESTON Zinfandel Dry Creek Valley 1986 $8.50 (12/15/88)
91 PRESTON Zinfandel Dry Creek Valley 1985 $8.50 (11/15/87)
80 PRESTON Zinfandel Dry Creek Valley 1984 $8 (12/31/86)
84 QUIVIRA Zinfandel Dry Creek Valley 1989 $13 (7/31/91)
88 QUIVIRA Zinfandel Dry Creek Valley 1988 $12 (5/31/90)
88 QUIVIRA Zinfandel Dry Creek Valley 1987 $11 (7/31/89)
88 QUIVIRA Zinfandel Dry Creek Valley 1986 $9.75 (12/15/88)
89 QUIVIRA Zinfandel Dry Creek Valley 1986 $9.75 (12/31/87)
88 QUIVIRA Zinfandel Dry Creek Valley 1984 $7 (4/15/87)
75 QUIVIRA Zinfandel Dry Creek Valley 1983 $7 (1/01/86)
86 RABBIT RIDGE Zinfandel Russian River Valley Rabbit Ridge Ranch 1988 $8 (4/30/91)
90 A. RAFANELLI Zinfandel Dry Creek Valley 1988 $9.75 (9/15/90)
84 A. RAFANELLI Zinfandel Dry Creek Valley 1987 $9 (12/15/89)
91 A. RAFANELLI Zinfandel Dry Creek Valley 1986 $7 (9/15/88)
77 A. RAFANELLI Zinfandel Dry Creek Valley 1985 $6.25 (12/31/87)
91 A. RAFANELLI Zinfandel Dry Creek Valley 1983 $6.50 (3/01/86) BB
81 RAVENSWOOD Zinfandel Napa Valley Canard 1986 $11 (3/15/90)
85 RAVENSWOOD Zinfandel Napa Valley Canard 1985 $10 (3/15/89)
86 RAVENSWOOD Zinfandel Napa Valley Dickerson 1987 $13 (3/15/90)
88 RAVENSWOOD Zinfandel Napa Valley Dickerson 1986 $12 (12/15/88)
80 RAVENSWOOD Zinfandel Napa Valley Dickerson 1985 $10.50 (12/31/87)
80 RAVENSWOOD Zinfandel Napa Valley Vintners Blend 1985 $6.25 (5/31/87)
83 RAVENSWOOD Zinfandel North Coast Vintners Blend 1989 $7.50 (7/31/91) BB
81 RAVENSWOOD Zinfandel North Coast Vintners Blend 1988 $7.25 (10/15/90) BB

Key to Symbols

The scores reported here are the results of blind tastings conducted by our panel of senior editors. Wines that carry the initials below are results of individual tastings.

THE WINE SPECTATOR 100-POINT SCALE ***95-100***—Classic, a great wine; ***90-94***—Outstanding, superior character and style; ***80-89***—Good to very good, a wine with special qualities; ***70-79***—Average, drinkable wine that may have minor flaws; ***60-69***—Below average, drinkable but not recommended; ***50-59***—Poor, undrinkable, not recommended. "+"—With a score indicates a range; used primarily with barrel tastings to indicate a preliminary score.

SPECIAL DESIGNATIONS SS—Spectator Selection, CS—Cellar Selection, BB—Best Buy.

TASTER'S INITIALS (JG)—Jim Gordon, (HS)—Harvey Steiman, (JL)—James Laube, (JS)—James Suckling, (TM)—Thomas Matthews, (TR)—Terry Robards, (BT)—Barrel Tasting (these wines were tasted blind from barrel samples), (CA-date)—*California's Great Cabernets* by James Laube, (CH-date)—*California's Great Chardonnays* by James Laube, (VP-date)—*Vintage Port* by James Suckling.

DATE TASTED Dates in parentheses represent the issue in which the rating was published.

88 RAVENSWOOD Zinfandel Sonoma County 1987 $11 (3/15/90)
90 RAVENSWOOD Zinfandel Sonoma County 1986 $9 (12/15/88)
80 RAVENSWOOD Zinfandel Sonoma County 1985 $8.25 (12/31/87)
57 RAVENSWOOD Zinfandel Sonoma County 1983 $8 (5/01/86)
81 RAVENSWOOD Zinfandel Sonoma County Dry Creek Benchland 1981 $6.50 (4/01/84)
87 RAVENSWOOD Zinfandel Sonoma County Old Vine 1988 $11 (11/30/90)
88 RAVENSWOOD Zinfandel Sonoma County Vintners Blend 1987 $6 (6/15/89) BB
68 RAVENSWOOD Zinfandel Sonoma County Vogensen Vineyard 1981 $8 (4/16/84)
84 RAVENSWOOD Zinfandel Sonoma Valley Cooke 1987 $13 (3/15/90)
87 RAVENSWOOD Zinfandel Sonoma Valley Old Hill Vineyard 1987 $15 (3/15/90)
92 RAVENSWOOD Zinfandel Sonoma Valley Old Hill Vineyard 1986 $13 (12/15/88)
87 RAVENSWOOD Zinfandel Sonoma Valley Old Hill Vineyard 1985 $12 (12/31/87)
85 RAVENSWOOD Zinfandel Sonoma-Napa Counties Vintners Blend 1986 $5.75 (6/30/88) BB
76 RICHARDSON Zinfandel Sonoma Valley NV $9 (7/31/89)
82 RIDGE Zinfandel Howell Mountain 1988 $12 (7/31/91)
83 RIDGE Zinfandel Howell Mountain 1987 $10 (5/31/90)
73 RIDGE Zinfandel Howell Mountain 1985 $9 (5/15/88)
81 RIDGE Zinfandel Howell Mountain 1984 $9 (6/30/87)
89 RIDGE Zinfandel Howell Mountain 1983 $9 (5/01/86)
85 RIDGE Zinfandel Howell Mountain 1982 $9 (6/01/85)
82 RIDGE Zinfandel Napa County York Creek 1985 $10.50 (12/31/87)
86 RIDGE Zinfandel Napa County York Creek 1984 $10.50 (3/15/87)
91 RIDGE Zinfandel Napa County York Creek 1982 $10.50 (7/16/85) SS
89 RIDGE Zinfandel Napa County York Creek 1981 $9.50 (1/01/84)
85 RIDGE Zinfandel Paso Robles 1987 $10 (3/15/90)
81 RIDGE Zinfandel Paso Robles 1986 $7.25 (10/31/88)
90 RIDGE Zinfandel Paso Robles 1982 $8.50 (1/01/85)
88 RIDGE Zinfandel Sonoma County 1988 $8.50 (2/15/91) BB
90 RIDGE Zinfandel Sonoma County Geyserville 1988 Rel: $14 Cur: $14 (11/30/90) SS
90 RIDGE Zinfandel Sonoma County Geyserville 1987 $14 (10/31/89)
79 RIDGE Zinfandel Sonoma County Geyserville 1986 $12 (10/31/88)
83 RIDGE Zinfandel Sonoma County Geyserville 1985 $10.50 (9/15/87)
79 RIDGE Zinfandel Sonoma County Geyserville 1984 $10.50 (12/31/86)
90 RIDGE Zinfandel Sonoma County Geyserville 1982 $9.50 (9/16/84)
67 RIDGE Zinfandel Sonoma County Geyserville 1975 Cur: $33 (6/16/85)
79 RIDGE Zinfandel Sonoma County Geyserville 1974 Cur: $45 (6/16/85)
80 RIDGE Zinfandel Sonoma County Geyserville 1973 Cur: $55 (6/16/85)
82 RIDGE Zinfandel Sonoma County Lytton Springs 1988 Rel: $12 Cur: $13 (11/30/90)
91 RIDGE Zinfandel Sonoma County Lytton Springs 1987 $11 (10/31/89)
88 RIDGE Zinfandel Sonoma County Lytton Springs 1986 $10 (10/15/88)
81 RIDGE Zinfandel Sonoma County Lytton Springs 1985 $9 (9/15/87)
79 RIDGE Zinfandel Sonoma County Lytton Springs 1984 $9 (11/15/86)
77 ROSENBLUM Zinfandel Napa Valley 1987 $9 (10/31/89)
84 ROSENBLUM Zinfandel Napa Valley Hendry Vineyard Reserve 1988 $14 (4/30/91)
87 ROUDON-SMITH Zinfandel Sonoma County 1988 $12 (2/15/91)
80 ROUDON-SMITH Zinfandel Sonoma Valley Chauvet Vineyard 1985 $8.50 (3/31/89)
89 ROUND HILL Zinfandel Napa Valley 1988 $6.50 (2/15/91) BB
82 ROUND HILL Zinfandel Napa Valley 1985 $5.50 (5/15/88) BB
84 ROUND HILL Zinfandel Napa Valley 1981 $5 (4/16/84)
84 ROUND HILL Zinfandel Napa Valley Select 1987 $6 (3/31/90) BB
62 RUTHERFORD RANCH Zinfandel Napa Valley 1986 $7.75 (10/31/88)
89 RUTHERFORD RANCH Zinfandel Napa Valley 1985 $7.75 (3/15/88)
80 RUTHERFORD RANCH Zinfandel Napa Valley 1982 $6 (9/16/85)
70 SANDERLING Zinfandel Amador County 1984 $6 (5/01/86)
82 SANTA BARBARA Zinfandel Santa Ynez Valley 1987 $8.50 (12/15/89)
80 SANTA BARBARA Zinfandel Santa Ynez Valley Beaujour 1988 $7 (12/15/89)
84 SANTA YNEZ VALLEY Zinfandel Paso Robles 1987 $8 (3/31/90)
67 SANTINO Zinfandel Amador County Aged Release 1984 $7 (3/31/89)
84 SANTINO Zinfandel Fiddletown Eschen Vineyards 1983 $7.50 (4/15/87)
81 SARAFORNIA Zinfandel Napa Valley 1988 $8 (2/15/91)
78 SARAFORNIA Zinfandel Napa Valley 1987 $7 (3/15/90)
87 SAUCELITO CANYON Zinfandel San Luis Obispo County 1986 $9.50 (12/15/89)
82 SAUSAL Zinfandel Alexander Valley 1988 $8.50 (4/30/91)
83 SAUSAL Zinfandel Alexander Valley 1987 $7.75 (9/15/89)
90 SAUSAL Zinfandel Alexander Valley 1986 $6.75 (3/31/89) SS
72 SAUSAL Zinfandel Alexander Valley 1985 $6.25 (10/15/88)
78 SAUSAL Zinfandel Alexander Valley 1984 $6.75 (5/31/88)
82 SAUSAL Zinfandel Alexander Valley 1983 $5.75 (9/15/87) BB
88 SAUSAL Zinfandel Alexander Valley Private Reserve 1988 $14 (4/30/91)
86 SAUSAL Zinfandel Alexander Valley Private Reserve 1984 $10 (2/15/88)
88 SEBASTIANI Zinfandel Sonoma County Family Selection 1985 $5 (9/15/88) BB
76 SEBASTIANI Zinfandel Black Beauty Sonoma Valley Proprietor's Reserve 1980 $9 (12/16/85)
80 SEGHESIO Zinfandel Alexander Valley Reserve 1986 $9 (10/31/89)
85 SEGHESIO Zinfandel Northern Sonoma 1987 $6.50 (7/31/90) BB
80 SEGHESIO Zinfandel Northern Sonoma 1986 $6.50 (5/15/90) BB
80 SEGHESIO Zinfandel Northern Sonoma 1985 $5.50 (3/15/89) BB
76 SEGHESIO Zinfandel Northern Sonoma 1984 $5.50 (6/30/88)
73 SHAFER Zinfandel Napa Valley Last Chance 1983 $7 (2/16/86)
82 SHENANDOAH Zinfandel Amador County Classico Varietal Adventure Series 1989 $6 (4/30/91) BB
81 SHENANDOAH Zinfandel Amador County Special Reserve 1987 $8.50 (7/31/89)
86 SHENANDOAH Zinfandel Amador County Special Reserve 1986 $7.50 (7/15/88)
85 SHENANDOAH Zinfandel Amador County Special Reserve 1985 $7.50 (2/15/88)
74 SHENANDOAH Zinfandel Fiddletown Special Reserve 1983 $7 (10/15/86)
85 SHOWN AND SONS Zinfandel Napa Valley 1981 $7.50 (4/16/84)
84 SIERRA VISTA Zinfandel El Dorado Herbert Vineyards 1986 $8 (3/31/89)
73 SIERRA VISTA Zinfandel El Dorado Reeves Vineyard Special Reserve 1985 $12 (4/30/88)
60 SIMI Zinfandel Sonoma County 1982 $6.25 (5/01/86)
90 SKY Zinfandel Napa Valley 1987 $12 (10/15/90)
88 SKY Zinfandel Napa Valley 1985 $9 (10/31/88)
88 SOBON ESTATE Zinfandel Shenandoah Valley 1988 $10 (11/30/90)
72 STEVENOT Zinfandel Amador County Grand Reserve 1985 $7.50 (12/31/87)
84 STEVENOT Zinfandel Calaveras County 1986 $7.50 (7/31/89) BB
73 STEVENOT Zinfandel Calaveras County 1984 $6 (6/30/87)
75 STONY RIDGE Zinfandel Livermore Valley 1980 $7 (6/16/84)
84 STORY Zinfandel Amador County 1987 $8.50 (4/30/91)
73 STORY Zinfandel Amador County 1980 $6 (4/01/84)
79 STORY Zinfandel Amador County Shenandoah Valley Private Reserve 1984 $14 (4/30/91)
75 STORYBOOK MOUNTAIN Zinfandel Napa Valley 1988 $12.50 (12/31/90)
88 STORYBOOK MOUNTAIN Zinfandel Napa Valley 1987 $11.50 (12/15/89)

88 STORYBOOK MOUNTAIN Zinfandel Napa Valley 1986 $10.50 (12/15/88)
90 STORYBOOK MOUNTAIN Zinfandel Napa Valley 1985 $10 (12/31/87)
80 STORYBOOK MOUNTAIN Zinfandel Napa Valley 1984 $9.50 (3/15/87)
90 STORYBOOK MOUNTAIN Zinfandel Napa Valley 1983 $8.75 (4/16/86)
86 STORYBOOK MOUNTAIN Zinfandel Napa Valley 1982 $8.50 (12/01/84)
89 STORYBOOK MOUNTAIN Zinfandel Napa Valley Reserve 1987 $17.50 (12/31/90)
82 STORYBOOK MOUNTAIN Zinfandel Napa Valley Reserve 1986 $17.50 (5/15/90)
88 STORYBOOK MOUNTAIN Zinfandel Napa Valley Reserve 1985 $16.50 (5/31/89)
92 STORYBOOK MOUNTAIN Zinfandel Napa Valley Reserve 1984 $14.50 (4/30/88)
81 STORYBOOK MOUNTAIN Zinfandel Napa Valley Reserve 1983 $12.50 (7/31/87)
86 STORYBOOK MOUNTAIN Zinfandel Napa Valley Reserve 1981 $9.50 (4/16/84)
87 STORYBOOK MOUNTAIN Zinfandel Sonoma County 1986 $8.50 (10/15/88)
81 STORYBOOK MOUNTAIN Zinfandel Sonoma County 1982 $7.50 (9/16/85)
68 RODNEY STRONG Zinfandel Russian River Valley Old Vines River West Vineyard 1980 $12 (11/15/87)
71 RODNEY STRONG Zinfandel Russian River Valley Old Vines River West Vineyard 1979 $10 (3/15/87)
79 RODNEY STRONG Zinfandel Sonoma County 1986 $5.50 (3/31/89)
70 RODNEY STRONG Zinfandel Sonoma County 1982 $5.50 (12/31/87)
87 SUMMIT LAKE Zinfandel Howell Mountain 1987 $11 (2/15/91)
84 SUMMIT LAKE Zinfandel Howell Mountain 1986 $11 (3/15/90)
88 SUMMIT LAKE Zinfandel Howell Mountain 1985 $9.50 (12/15/88)
90 SUMMIT LAKE Zinfandel Howell Mountain 1984 $8.50 (4/30/88)
80 SUTTER HOME Zinfandel Amador County 1981 $6.25 (5/16/84)
86 SUTTER HOME Zinfandel Amador County 1973 Cur: $30 (6/16/85)
85 SUTTER HOME Zinfandel Amador County 1972 Cur: $25 (6/16/85)
80 SUTTER HOME Zinfandel Amador County 1970 Cur: $25 (6/16/85)
79 SUTTER HOME Zinfandel Amador County Reserve 1987 $9.50 (5/15/91)
81 SUTTER HOME Zinfandel Amador County Reserve 1985 $8.75 (11/30/90)
82 SUTTER HOME Zinfandel Amador County Reserve 1984 $9.50 (7/31/89)
79 SUTTER HOME Zinfandel Amador County Reserve 1984 $9.50 (7/31/88)
85 SUTTER HOME Zinfandel California 1989 $5 (5/15/91) BB
72 SUTTER HOME Zinfandel California 1988 $5 (3/31/91)
78 SUTTER HOME Zinfandel California 1987 $5.50 (7/31/89)
76 SUTTER HOME Zinfandel California 1986 $7 (10/15/88)
77 SUTTER HOME Zinfandel California 1984 $6 (12/31/86)
84 JOSEPH SWAN Zinfandel California 1973 Cur: $55 (6/16/85)
83 JOSEPH SWAN Zinfandel California 1969 Cur: $80 (6/16/85)
89 JOSEPH SWAN Zinfandel Sonoma Coast 1986 $12.50 (3/15/90)
82 JOSEPH SWAN Zinfandel Sonoma Coast 1985 $12 (3/15/89)
86 JOSEPH SWAN Zinfandel Sonoma Coast Ziegler Vineyard 1987 $12.50 (9/15/90)
86 JOSEPH SWAN Zinfandel Sonoma County 1987 $12.50 (7/31/90)
86 JOSEPH SWAN Zinfandel Sonoma Valley Stellwagen Vineyard 1987 $12.50 (9/15/90)
87 SYCAMORE CREEK Zinfandel California 1982 $9 (6/16/84)
89 TERRACES Zinfandel Napa Valley 1987 $12.50 (2/15/91)
87 TERRACES Zinfandel Napa Valley Hogue Vineyard 1985 $12.50 (10/31/88)
76 VALLEY OF THE MOON Zinfandel Sonoma Valley 1984 $9 (3/15/90)
78 VENDANGE Zinfandel California 1987 $5.50 (9/15/90)
90 VILLA MT. EDEN Zinfandel Napa Valley 1986 $8.50 (12/15/88)
77 WENTE BROS. Zinfandel Livermore Valley Special Selection Raboli Vineyards 1985 $10 (12/15/89)
79 WILLIAMS SELYEM Zinfandel Russian River Valley Leno Martinelli Vineyard 1985 $10 (7/31/88)
85 YORK MOUNTAIN Zinfandel San Luis Obispo County 1986 $8 (12/15/89)

OTHER CALIFORNIA RED

79 ALMADEN Premium Red California 1982 $7 (12/31/86)
79 AUDUBON Audubon Rouge California NV $4.50 (10/15/88)
80 BEAULIEU Burgundy Napa Valley 1987 $5 (1/31/91) BB
78 BEAULIEU Burgundy Napa Valley 1984 $5 (8/31/89)
79 BEAULIEU Burgundy Napa Valley 1982 $5 (10/15/88)
78 BELVEDERE Red Table Wine Sonoma County Discovery Series 1983 $3 (7/31/88)
78 BOEGER Hangtown Red California 1988 $5.25 (8/31/90)
82 BOEGER Hangtown Red California 1987 $5.25 (2/28/90) BB
73 BOEGER Hangtown Red California 1985 $5 (12/31/88)
77 BOEGER Hangtown Red California 1984 $4.75 (1/31/88)
71 BOEGER Hangtown Red California 1983 $4.50 (6/30/87)
80 CALERA Rouge de Rouge California NV $4 (1/31/87) BB
79 CHRISTOPHE Joliesse California 1987 $5 (2/28/90)
87 CLOS DU BOIS Malbec Alexander Valley L'Etranger Winemaker's Reserve 1987 $20 (1/31/91)
85 CLOS DU VAL Le Clos Napa Valley NV $5.50 (8/31/90) BB
75 R. & J. COOK Delta Red Clarksburg NV $3.50 (11/15/87)
68 DEHLINGER Young Vines Russian River Valley 1985 $9 (4/15/89)
79 DICKERSON Ruby Cabernet Napa Valley 1988 $9 (2/28/91)
76 DUNNEWOOD Reserve Red California NV $3.75 (2/28/89)
88 DUXOUP Charbono Napa Valley 1987 $9.50 (6/15/89)
78 FETZER Premium Red California 1985 $4.25 (3/15/88)
80 E.&J. GALLO Hearty Burgundy California Limited Release NV $2.75 (3/15/88) BB
77 GEYSER PEAK Red California Trione Vineyards 1987 $3.25 (2/28/90)
87 GLEN ELLEN Petite Verdot Alexander Valley Imagery Series 1988 $14.50 (7/15/91)
77 GUNDLACH BUNDSCHU Sonoma Red Sonoma Valley #2 NV $5 (11/15/89)
74 HAYWOOD Spaghetti Red California NV $6 (2/15/90)
74 HAYWOOD Spaghetti Red Sonoma County NV $4.50 (4/30/87)
74 HEITZ Ryan's Red Napa Valley NV $6 (2/28/89)
82 HEITZ Ryan's Red Napa Valley NV $6 (6/16/86) BB
83 HIDDEN CELLARS Pinot Noir Petite Syrah California Côte du Nord 1986 $7.50 (11/15/88)
85 HOP KILN Marty Griffin's Big Red Russian River Valley 1988 $7.50 (11/30/90) BB
89 HOP KILN Marty Griffin's Big Red Russian River Valley 1987 $7.50 (12/15/89) BB
85 HOP KILN Marty Griffin's Big Red Russian River Valley 1986 $6.50 (6/15/89) BB
68 HOP KILN Marty Griffin's Big Red Russian River Valley 1984 $5.75 (12/31/87)
82 INGLENOOK Charbono Napa Valley 1984 $8 (4/15/88)
79 INGLENOOK Charbono Napa Valley 1980 $8.50 (3/01/85)
77 KENWOOD Vintage Red California 1988 $5 (12/31/90)
74 KENWOOD Vintage Red California 1986 $5 (11/30/88)
77 KENWOOD Vintage Red Sonoma County 1983 $4 (5/31/88)
85 MARIETTA Old Vine Red Sonoma County Lot No. Three NV $4.50 (4/16/86) BB
77 MARIETTA Old Vine Red Sonoma County Lot No. Five NV $5 (12/31/87)
82 MARIETTA Old Vine Red Sonoma County Lot No. Seven NV $6 (11/15/89) BB
81 MARIETTA Old Vine Red Sonoma County Lot No. Eight NV $5.50 (5/31/90) BB
75 MARTIN Nebbiolo California 1987 $12 (12/15/89)
75 MARTIN Nebbiolo California 1986 $12 (12/15/89)
78 MARTIN Nebbiolo California 1982 $7 (4/01/84)
85 MARTIN Nebbiolo Paso Robles 1987 $12 (12/15/89)
83 LOUIS M. MARTINI Barbera California 1987 $6 (12/31/90) BB
80 LOUIS M. MARTINI Barbera California 1984 $7 (11/15/89)
80 LOUIS M. MARTINI Barbera Napa Valley 1981 $6 (12/31/87) BB
79 MASTANTUONO Carminello California 1988 $7 (7/15/91)
75 ROBERT MONDAVI Red California 1984 $5 (1/31/87)
82 MONTEREY PENINSULA Red California NV $6.50 (7/15/91) BB
74 MONTEREY VINEYARD Classic Red California 1982 $4.25 (6/16/86)
74 MONTEREY VINEYARD Classic Red Monterey 1984 $4.25 (11/15/87)
89 MONTEVINA Barbera Amador County 1987 $14 (5/31/91)
78 MONTEVINA Barbera Shenandoah Valley 1984 $6 (10/15/88)
70 J.W. MORRIS Red Private Reserve California 1987 $3.50 (6/30/90)
78 J.W. MORRIS Red Private Reserve California 1986 $3.50 (12/31/88)
79 J.W. MORRIS Red Private Reserve California 1984 $3 (11/15/87) BB
80 PAT PAULSEN American Gothic California 1984 $8.50 (12/31/86) BB
84 R.H. PHILLIPS Night Harvest Cuvée Rouge California NV $6 (5/31/91) BB
86 R.H. PHILLIPS Night Harvest Cuvée Rouge California NV $5 (5/15/89) BB
85 PRESTON Barbera Dry Creek Valley 1985 $8 (1/31/88)
77 PRESTON Estate Red Dry Creek Valley 1989 $5.50 (6/30/90)
82 PRESTON Estate Red Dry Creek Valley 1988 $5 (8/31/89) BB
75 RAYMOND Vintage Select Red California 1984 $4.25 (2/15/88)
69 RAYMOND Vintage Select Red California 1983 $4.25 (8/31/87)
82 RAYMOND Vintage Select Red North Coast 1982 $4.25 (4/01/86) BB
78 ROUDON-SMITH Claret Cuvée Five California NV $4.50 (3/31/89)
86 SEBASTIANI Barbera Sonoma Valley 1987 $11 (4/30/91)
78 SEGHESIO Sonoma Red Sonoma County Lot 3 NV $4 (5/31/88)
75 SEGHESIO Sonoma Red Sonoma County Lot 4 NV $5 (6/30/90)
71 STAGS' LEAP WINERY Burgundy Napa Valley 1983 $5 (9/15/87)
79 TREFETHEN Eschol Red Napa Valley NV $6 (2/15/91)
83 TREFETHEN Eshcol Red Napa Valley NV $5.25 (2/29/88) BB
80 TREFETHEN Eshcol Red Napa Valley *3 NV $6.25 (11/15/89) BB
86 TREFETHEN Eshcol Red Napa Valley Blend 184 NV $4.25 (2/01/86) BB
74 M.G. VALLEJO M.G.V. Red California NV $3 (5/31/90)
84 M.G. VALLEJO M.G.V. Red California NV $3 (3/31/88) BB
84 VERITE Bourguignon Noir Alexander Valley Cuvée Ancienne 1980 $6 (1/01/85)

OTHER CALIFORNIA WHITE

72 BEAULIEU Chablis Napa Valley 1988 $5 (12/31/90)
76 BEAULIEU Chablis Napa Valley 1986 $5 (10/31/88)
74 BELVEDERE White Table Wine Sonoma County Discovery Series 1987 $3 (7/31/88)
84 BONNY DOON Malvasia Bianca Ca' del Solo Monterey 1990 $8 (6/15/91) BB
83 BUENA VISTA Bistro Style Napa Valley 1990 $11 (7/15/91)
82 BUENA VISTA Chaarblanc Carneros 1985 $6 (5/31/88)
81 BUENA VISTA Spiceling Carneros 1985 $5 (5/31/88) BB
79 BUENA VISTA Spiceling Sonoma County 1984 $5.50 (4/16/86)
76 CALLAWAY Spring Wine Vin Blanc California 1986 $4.75 (6/15/87)
73 CARMENET Columbard Cyril Saviez Vineyard Old Vines BF Napa Valley 1986 $5 (1/31/88)
82 CHATEAU DE BAUN Château Blanc Sonoma County Reserve 1989 $5 (6/15/91) BB
78 CHATEAU DE BAUN Symphony Sonoma County 1987 $12 (5/31/90)
75 CHATEAU DE BAUN Symphony Sonoma County 1987 $12 (4/30/90)
80 CHATEAU DE BAUN Symphony Sonoma County 1987 $12 (4/30/90)
80 CHATEAU DE BAUN Symphony Sonoma Valley 1987 $8.50 (3/31/90)
70 CHATEAU DE BAUN Symphony Sonoma County 1986 $8.50 (9/15/87)
77 CHATEAU DE BAUN Symphony Sonoma County 1986 $8.50 (9/15/87)
75 CHATEAU DE BAUN Symphony Sonoma County 1986 $8.50 (9/15/87)
88 CHATEAU DE BAUN Symphony Sonoma County 1986 $10.50 (9/15/87)
80 CHATEAU ST. JEAN Vin Blanc Sonoma County 1989 $5 (2/15/91) BB
81 CHATEAU ST. JEAN Vin Blanc Sonoma County 1987 $4 (6/15/88) BB
83 CHATEAU ST. JEAN Vin Blanc Sonoma County 1986 $4 (7/15/87) BB
77 CHRISTOPHE Joliesse California 1986 $4.75 (12/31/87)
78 CHRISTOPHE Joliesse California NV $4 (6/15/89)
73 CLOS DU VAL Le Clos Napa Valley 1988 $5.50 (12/31/90)
75 FETZER Premium White California 1986 $4.25 (3/15/88)
87 GEYSER PEAK Semchard California 1989 $8 (2/15/91) BB
71 GLEN ELLEN Proprietor's Reserve White California 1987 $3.50 (7/31/88)
75 GUENOC Lillie's White Wine North Coast 1986 $5.50 (3/15/88)
82 GUNDLACH BUNDSCHU Sonoma White Wine (Chardonnay) Sonoma Valley 1987 $5 (10/31/88) BB
80 HAYWOOD Linguini White Sonoma County NV $4.50 (9/30/87) BB
88 HAYWOOD White Wine Sonoma Valley 1985 $5 (4/15/87) BB
83 HEITZ Joe's White Napa Valley NV $5 (4/30/89) BB
54 HOP KILN A Thousand Flowers Sonoma County 1984 $5 (12/01/85)
74 HUSCH La Ribera Blanc Mendocino 1986 $5 (1/31/88)
74 INGLENOOK Napa Valley 1984 $5 (7/01/86)
80 KENWOOD Vintage White California 1987 $5 (6/15/88)
83 LA CREMA Crème de Tête Select White California 1988 $5.50 (12/15/89) BB
83 LIBERTY SCHOOL Three Valley Select Series One California 1989 $4.50 (6/15/91) BB
64 J.W. MORRIS Private Reserve California 1986 $3 (1/31/88)
79 PAT PAULSEN Refrigerator White Sonoma County 1987 $6 (10/31/88)
86 PAT PAULSEN Refrigerator White Sonoma County 1986 $6 (4/30/87) BB
82 PAT PAULSEN Refrigerator White Sonoma County 1985 $6 (5/16/86) BB
69 PESENTI Grey Riesling San Luis Obispo County NV $6 (12/15/89)
83 PRESTON Estate White Dry Creek Valley 1988 $5 (9/15/89) BB
82 RABBIT RIDGE Mystique Sonoma County 1989 $7 (6/30/91) BB
76 RAYMOND Vintage Select White California 1987 $4.25 (2/28/89)
77 RAYMOND Vintage Select White California 1986 $4.25 (6/30/87)
70 SAUSAL Blanc Alexander Valley 1986 $4.75 (3/15/88)
79 SEBASTIANI La Sorella California 1988 $4 (3/31/90)
81 TREFETHEN Eschol White Napa Valley NV $6.50 (1/31/91) BB
78 TREFETHEN Eshcol White Napa Valley NV $6.25 (9/15/89)
78 TREFETHEN Eshcol White Napa Valley NV $6.25 (7/31/88)
84 TREFETHEN Eshcol White Napa Valley NV $6.25 (2/29/88) BB
84 TREFETHEN Eshcol White Napa Valley NV $6.25 (6/01/86) BB
78 M.G. VALLEJO M.G.V. White California 1986 $3 (4/15/88) BB
72 WENTE BROS. Chablis California 1984 $3.25 (6/01/86) BB
71 WENTE BROS. Le Blanc de Blanc California 1986 $5 (11/15/87)

UNITED STATES
NEW YORK/BLUSH

83   HAMPTON Blush North Fork of Long Island Sunset Blush 1987 $6 (12/15/88) (JL)
75   PALMER Blush North Fork of Long Island Pinot Noir Blanc NV $6 (12/15/88) (JL)

CABERNET FRANC

81   HARGRAVE Cabernet Franc North Fork of Long Island 1988 $14 (6/30/91)

CABERNET SAUVIGNON

86   BEDELL Cabernet Sauvignon North Fork of Long Island 1988 $15 (6/30/91)
82   BIDWELL Cabernet Sauvignon North Fork of Long Island 1988 $12 (6/30/91)
81   BIDWELL Cabernet Sauvignon North Fork of Long Island 1987 $12 (6/30/91)
76   BIDWELL Cabernet Sauvignon North Fork of Long Island 1987 $12 (6/15/90)
84   BRIDGEHAMPTON Cabernet Sauvignon Long Island 1988 $14 (6/30/91)
87   BRIDGEHAMPTON Cabernet Sauvignon Long Island 1987 $14 (6/30/91)
79   BRIDGEHAMPTON Cabernet Sauvignon Long Island 1986 $12 (12/15/88) (JL)
51   FOUR CHIMNEYS Cabernet Sauvignon New York 1984 $17 (3/16/86)
90   GRISTINA Cabernet Sauvignon North Fork of Long Island 1988 $14 (6/30/91)
87   HARGRAVE Cabernet Sauvignon North Fork of Long Island 1986 $22 (12/15/88) (JL)
82   HARGRAVE Cabernet Sauvignon North Fork of Long Island 1985 $22 (12/15/88) (JL)
86   HARGRAVE Cabernet Sauvignon North Fork of Long Island 1983 $22 (12/15/88) (JL)
70   HARGRAVE Cabernet Sauvignon North Fork of Long Island Reserve 1982 $22 (12/15/88) (JL)
78   HARGRAVE Cabernet Sauvignon North Fork of Long Island Vintner's Signature 1981 $29 (12/15/88) (JL)
79   HARGRAVE Cabernet Sauvignon North Fork of Long Island Vintner's Signature 1980 Rel: NA (12/15/88) (JL)
78   JAMESPORT Cabernet Sauvignon North Fork of Long Island North House 1987 $10 (6/30/91)
52   KNAPP Cabernet Sauvignon New York 1982 $16 (3/16/86)
78   LA REVE Cabernet Sauvignon North Fork of Long Island American Series 1986 $12 (12/15/88) (JL)
82   MATTITUCK HILLS Cabernet Sauvignon North Fork of Long Island 1987 $9 (6/30/91)
83   PALMER Cabernet Sauvignon North Fork of Long Island 1988 $13.50 (6/30/91) (TM)
82   PALMER Cabernet Sauvignon North Fork of Long Island 1986 $10 (12/15/88) (JL)
81   PECONIC BAY Cabernet Sauvignon North Fork of Long Island 1988 $13 (6/30/91)
78   PECONIC BAY Cabernet Sauvignon North Fork of Long Island 1987 $13 (6/30/91)
84   PECONIC BAY Cabernet Sauvignon North Fork of Long Island 1986 $11 (12/15/88) (JL)
78   PECONIC BAY Cabernet Sauvignon North Fork of Long Island 1985 $11 (12/15/88) (JL)
79   PETITE CHATEAU Cabernet Sauvignon North Fork of Long Island NV $10 (6/30/91)
86   PINDAR Cabernet Sauvignon North Fork of Long Island 1986 $13 (12/15/88) (JL)
71   PINDAR Cabernet Sauvignon North Fork of Long Island 1984 $9 (3/16/86)
85   PINDAR Cabernet Sauvignon North Fork of Long Island Reserve 1988 $14 (6/30/91)

CABERNET BLENDS

80   BRIDGEHAMPTON Reserve Red Grand Vineyard North Fork of Long Island 1987 $17 (6/30/91)
87   LENZ Reserve North Fork of Long Island 1986 Rel: NA (12/15/88) (JL)
85   LENZ Reserve North Fork of Long Island 1985 $14 (12/15/88) (JL)
78   LENZ Reserve North Fork of Long Island 1984 $14 (12/15/88) (JL)
83   PINDAR Mythology North Fork of Long Island 1988 $20 (6/30/91)
89   PINDAR Mythology North Fork of Long Island 1987 $20 (12/15/88) (JL)
81   PINDAR Mythology North Fork of Long Island 1987 $20 (6/30/91)
86   PINDAR Mythology North Fork of Long Island 1987 $20 (3/31/90)

CHARDONNAY

70   BANFI Chardonnay Nassau County Old Brookville 1988 $11 (6/30/91)
85   BANFI Chardonnay Nassau County Old Brookville 1987 $11.50 (12/15/90)
83   BEDELL Chardonnay North Fork of Long Island 1989 $12 (6/30/91)
88   BEDELL Chardonnay North Fork of Long Island 1987 $11 (12/15/88) (JL)
86   BEDELL Chardonnay North Fork of Long Island 1986 $9 (12/15/88) (JL)
86   BEDELL Chardonnay North Fork of Long Island 1986 $9 (12/15/88) (JL)
81   BEDELL Chardonnay North Fork of Long Island Reserve 1988 $14 (12/15/90)
89   BEDELL Chardonnay North Fork of Long Island Reserve 1986 $13 (12/15/88) (JL)
81   BIDWELL Chardonnay North Fork of Long Island 1988 $9 (6/30/91)
87   BIDWELL Chardonnay North Fork of Long Island 1986 $9 (3/31/90)
84   BRIDGEHAMPTON Chardonnay Long Island 1987 $10 (12/15/88) (JL)
87   BRIDGEHAMPTON Chardonnay Long Island 1985 $15 (12/15/88) (JL)
69   BRIDGEHAMPTON Chardonnay Long Island 1984 $9 (3/16/86)
81   BRIDGEHAMPTON Chardonnay Long Island Grand Vineyard Selection 1989 $17 (6/30/91)
91   BRIDGEHAMPTON Chardonnay Long Island Grand Vineyard Selection 1988 $18 (3/31/90)
90   BRIDGEHAMPTON Chardonnay Long Island Grand Vineyard Selection 1987 $15 (12/15/88) (JL)
80   BRIDGEHAMPTON Chardonnay Long Island Reserve 1986 $11 (12/15/88) (JL)
83   BRIDGEHAMPTON Chardonnay Long Island Reserve 1985 $15 (12/15/88) (JL)
78   BRIDGEHAMPTON Chardonnay Long Island The Hamptons Estate Reserve 1989 $14.50 (6/30/91)
76   FINGER LAKES Chardonnay Finger Lakes 1984 $9 (3/16/86)
59   FOUR CHIMNEYS Chardonnay Finger Lakes 1984 $15 (3/16/86)
73   DR. KONSTANTIN FRANK Chardonnay Finger Lakes 1980 $8 (3/16/86)
83   GLENORA Chardonnay Finger Lakes 1984 $9 (3/16/86)
90   GRISTINA Chardonnay North Fork of Long Island 1989 $13 (6/30/91)
82   HARGRAVE Chardonnay North Fork of Long Island 1988 $15 (6/30/91)
87   HARGRAVE Chardonnay North Fork of Long Island 1986 $11 (12/15/88) (JL)
92   HARGRAVE Chardonnay North Fork of Long Island 1981 $22 (12/15/88) (JL)

87   HARGRAVE Chardonnay North Fork of Long Island Collector's Series 1985 $15 (12/15/88) (JL)
80   HARGRAVE Chardonnay North Fork of Long Island Collector's Series 1981 $22 (12/15/88) (JL)
72   HERON HILL Chardonnay Finger Lakes 1984 $8 (3/16/86)
63   KNAPP Chardonnay Finger Lakes 1983 $8 (3/16/86)
89   LA REVE Chardonnay North Fork of Long Island 1986 $11 (12/15/88) (JL)
89   LA REVE Chardonnay North Fork of Long Island American Series 1986 $12 (12/15/88) (JL)
81   LENZ Chardonnay North Fork of Long Island 1989 $10 (6/30/91)
84   LENZ Chardonnay North Fork of Long Island Barrel Fermented 1989 $15 (6/30/91)
86   LENZ Chardonnay North Fork of Long Island Gold Label 1987 $13 (12/15/88) (JL)
80   LENZ Chardonnay North Fork of Long Island White Label 1987 $10 (12/15/88) (JL)
77   MATTITUCK HILLS Chardonnay North Fork of Long Island 1988 $11 (6/30/91)
48   MCGREGOR Chardonnay Finger Lakes 1984 $8 (3/16/86)
84   PALMER Chardonnay North Fork of Long Island 1989 $11.50 (6/30/91) (TM)
80   PALMER Chardonnay North Fork of Long Island 1986 $11 (12/15/88) (JL)
82   PALMER Chardonnay North Fork of Long Island Barrel Fermented 1989 $15 (6/30/91) (TM)
84   PALMER Chardonnay North Fork of Long Island Barrel Fermented 1986 $11 (12/15/88) (JL)
80   PAUMANOK Chardonnay North Fork of Long Island 1989 $10 (6/30/91)
80   PECONIC BAY Chardonnay North Fork of Long Island 1989 $11 (6/30/91)
85   PECONIC BAY Chardonnay North Fork of Long Island 1987 $11 (12/15/88) (JL)
79   PECONIC BAY Chardonnay North Fork of Long Island Reserve 1989 $15 (6/30/91)
86   PINDAR Chardonnay North Fork of Long Island 1988 $9 (6/30/91)
87   PINDAR Chardonnay North Fork of Long Island 1988 $9 (12/15/90)
88   PINDAR Chardonnay North Fork of Long Island 1986 $8 (12/15/88) (JL)
54   PINDAR Chardonnay North Fork of Long Island First Release Poetry Edition 1984 $11 (3/16/86)
84   PINDAR Chardonnay North Fork of Long Island Poetry Barrel Fermented 1986 $11 (12/15/88) (JL)
82   PINDAR Chardonnay North Fork of Long Island Reserve 1988 $12 (6/30/91)
66   PLANE'S CAYUGA Chardonnay Finger Lakes 1984 $10 (3/16/86)
61   POPLAR RIDGE Chardonnay Finger Lakes 1984 $9.50 (3/16/86)
78   PUGLIESE Chardonnay North Fork of Long Island 1988 $10 (6/30/91)
80   RIVENDELL Chardonnay New York 1989 $12 (6/30/91)
85   RIVENDELL Chardonnay New York Barrel Selection 1989 $14 (6/30/91)
86   RIVENDELL Chardonnay New York Reserve 1989 $17 (6/30/91)
87   RIVENDELL Chardonnay North Fork of Long Island Cuvée 1988 $12 (6/30/91)
79   WAGNER Chardonnay Finger Lakes 1984 $11 (3/16/86)
61   WICKHAM Chardonnay Finger Lakes 1984 $7 (3/16/86)
86   HERMANN J. WIEMER Chardonnay Finger Lakes 1984 $10 (3/16/86)

DESSERT

64   HERON HILL Dessert Finger Lakes Ingles Vineyard 1983 $6 (3/16/86)
82   HERMANN J. WIEMER Dessert Finger Lakes 1984 $9 (3/16/86)

GEWÜRZTRAMINER

82   BEDELL Gewürztraminer North Fork of Long Island 1986 $6.50 (12/15/88) (JL)
78   LENZ Gewürztraminer North Fork of Long Island 1987 $7 (12/15/88) (JL)
79   PALMER Gewürztraminer North Fork of Long Island 1987 $8 (12/15/88) (JL)
80   PINDAR Gewürztraminer North Fork of Long Island 1986 $7 (12/15/88) (JL)

LATE HARVEST

57   BALDWIN Late Harvest New York Vignoles Select 1984 $6/375ml (3/16/86)
85   BEDELL Late Harvest North Fork of Long Island 1987 $15/375ml (12/15/88) (JL)
61   FINGER LAKES Late Harvest Finger Lakes Ravat 1984 $8/375ml (3/16/86)
62   GLENORA Late Harvest Finger Lakes Ravat Blanc Select 1984 $7/375ml (3/16/86)
68   GREAT WESTERN Late Harvest Finger Lakes Vidal Blanc Laursen Farm Vineyard Special Select 1984 $5 (3/16/86)
90   PINDAR Late Harvest North Fork of Long Island Gewürztraminer 1986 $20 (12/15/88) (JL)
63   WICKHAM Late Harvest Finger Lakes Ravat Vignoles Select 1984 $6.5/375ml (3/16/86)

MERLOT

90   BEDELL Merlot North Fork of Long Island 1987 $18 (3/31/90)
88   BEDELL Merlot North Fork of Long Island 1986 $11 (12/15/88) (JL)
90   BEDELL Merlot North Fork of Long Island Reserve 1988 $14 (6/30/91)
85   BIDWELL Merlot North Fork of Long Island 1988 $11 (6/30/91)
83   BIDWELL Merlot North Fork of Long Island Reserve 1987 $16 (3/31/90)
89   BRIDGEHAMPTON Merlot Long Island 1988 $16 (6/30/91)
78   BRIDGEHAMPTON Merlot Long Island 1986 $11 (12/15/88) (JL)
79   BRIDGEHAMPTON Merlot Long Island 1985 $11 (12/15/88) (JL)
81   GRISTINA Merlot North Fork of Long Island 1988 $13 (6/30/91)
81   HARGRAVE Merlot North Fork of Long Island 1988 $17.50 (6/30/91)
85   HARGRAVE Merlot North Fork of Long Island 1985 $19 (12/15/88) (JL)
78   HARGRAVE Merlot North Fork of Long Island 1980 Rel: NA (12/15/88) (JL)
72   JAMESPORT Merlot North Fork of Long Island 1986 $9 (6/30/91)
86   LA REVE Merlot North Fork of Long Island American Series 1986 $13 (12/15/88) (JL)
80   LENZ Merlot North Fork of Long Island 1987 $12 (6/30/91)
83   LENZ Merlot North Fork of Long Island 1986 $12 (12/15/88) (JL)
84   LENZ Merlot North Fork of Long Island 1985 $11 (12/15/88) (JL)
74   LENZ Merlot North Fork of Long Island 1984 $12 (12/15/88) (JL)
86   PALMER Merlot North Fork of Long Island 1988 $13 (6/30/91) (TM)
80   PALMER Merlot North Fork of Long Island 1986 $10 (12/15/88) (JL)
78   PECONIC BAY Merlot North Fork of Long Island 1989 $13 (6/30/91)
80   PINDAR Merlot North Fork of Long Island 1987 $13 (12/15/90)
84   PINDAR Merlot North Fork of Long Island 1986 $13 (12/15/88) (JL)
83   PINDAR Merlot North Fork of Long Island Reserve 1988 $14 (6/30/91)

PINOT NOIR

75   BRIDGEHAMPTON Pinot Noir Long Island 1984 $8 (3/16/86)
75   DR. KONSTANTIN FRANK Pinot Noir Finger Lakes 1985 $15 (6/15/88)
70   MCGREGOR Pinot Noir Finger Lakes 1986 $13 (6/15/88)
67   MCGREGOR Pinot Noir Finger Lakes Reserve 1983 $14 (3/16/86)
56   PINDAR Pinot Noir North Fork of Long Island 1985 $15 (6/15/88)

RIESLING

65   BALDWIN Riesling New York Reserve 1984 $7 (3/16/86)
59   BARON HERZOG Johannisberg Riesling New York Selection 1985 $7 (3/16/86)
80   BEDELL Riesling North Fork of Long Island 1987 $7.50 (12/15/88) (JL)
78   BRIDGEHAMPTON Riesling Long Island 1987 $8 (12/15/88) (JL)
69   BRIDGEHAMPTON Riesling Long Island 1984 $7.50 (3/16/86)

Key to Symbols

The scores reported here are the results of blind tastings conducted by our panel of senior editors. Wines that carry the initials below are results of individual tastings.

THE WINE SPECTATOR 100-POINT SCALE   95-100—Classic, a great wine; **90-94**—Outstanding, superior character and style; **80-89**—Good to very good, a wine with special qualities; **70-79**—Average, drinkable wine that may have minor flaws; **60-69**—Below average, drinkable but not recommended; **50-59**—Poor, undrinkable, not recommended. "**+**"—With a score indicates a range; used primarily with barrel tastings to indicate a preliminary score.

SPECIAL DESIGNATIONS   SS—Spectator Selection, CS—Cellar Selection, BB—Best Buy.

TASTER'S INITIALS   (JG)—Jim Gordon, (HS)—Harvey Steiman, (JL)—James Laube, (JS)—James Suckling, (TM)—Thomas Matthews, (TR)—Terry Robards, (BT)—Barrel Tasting (these wines were tasted blind from barrel samples), (CA-date)—*California's Great Cabernets* by James Laube, (CH-date)—*California's Great Chardonnays* by James Laube, (VP-date)—*Vintage Port* by James Suckling.

DATE TASTED   Dates in parentheses represent the issue in which the rating was published.

57 CASCADE MOUNTAIN Riesling New York NV $7 (3/16/86)
88 FINGER LAKES Johannisberg Riesling Finger Lakes 1984 $7 (3/16/86)
56 DR. KONSTANTIN FRANK Johannisberg Riesling Finger Lakes 1982 $6 (3/16/86)
63 GLENORA Johannisberg Riesling Finger Lakes 1984 $6 (3/16/86)
55 GREAT WESTERN Johannisberg Riesling Finger Lakes Special Selection 1984 $6 (3/16/86)
91 HAZLITT 1852 Johannisberg Riesling Finger Lakes 1984 $6 (3/16/86)
68 KNAPP Johannisberg Riesling Finger Lakes 1984 $7 (3/16/86)
84 LA REVE White Riesling North Fork of Long Island 1987 $8 (12/15/88) (JL)
73 MCGREGOR Riesling Finger Lakes 1984 $7.50 (3/16/86)
76 PALMER Riesling North Fork of Long Island 1987 $7 (12/15/88) (JL)
81 PECONIC BAY Riesling North Fork of Long Island White 1987 $8 (12/15/88) (JL)
85 PINDAR Riesling North Fork of Long Island Select Berry Late Harvest 1984 $30/375ml (3/16/86)
69 PLANE'S CAYUGA Johannisberg Riesling Finger Lakes 1984 $7 (3/16/86)
68 WAGNER Johannisberg Riesling Finger Lakes 1984 $6.75 (3/16/86)
74 WICKHAM Johannisberg Riesling Finger Lakes 1984 $6 (3/16/86)
76 WIDMER Johannisberg Riesling Finger Lakes Private Reserve 1985 $7 (3/16/86)
91 HERMANN J. WIEMER Johannisberg Riesling Finger Lakes 1984 $7.50 (3/16/86)
84 WOODBURY Johannisberg Riesling New York 1984 $8 (3/16/86)

SAUVIGNON BLANC

77 BRIDGEHAMPTON Sauvignon Blanc Long Island 1986 $10 (12/15/88) (JL)
77 HARGRAVE Sauvignon Blanc North Fork of Long Island 1987 $9 (12/15/88) (JL)
83 HARGRAVE Sauvignon Blanc North Fork of Long Island 1981 $19 (12/15/88) (JL)
87 LA REVE Sauvignon Blanc North Fork of Long Island American Series 1986 $10 (12/15/88) (JL)

SEYVAL BLANC

47 BALDWIN Seyval Blanc New York Proprietor's Reserve 1983 $6 (3/16/86)
54 BENMARL Seyval Blanc Hudson River Region Estate Reserve 1984 $8 (3/16/86)
51 CLINTON Seyval Blanc Hudson River Region 1983 $8.50 (3/16/86)
58 FINGER LAKES Seyval Blanc Finger Lakes 1984 $5 (3/16/86)
51 FOUR CHIMNEYS Seyval Blanc Finger Lakes 1984 $6 (3/16/86)
89 GLENORA Seyval Blanc Finger Lakes 1984 $5 (3/16/86)
80 HERON HILL Seyval Blanc Finger Lakes Ingle Vineyard 1985 $5 (3/16/86)
55 KEDEM Seyval Blanc New York Estate Brand 1983 $5 (3/16/86)
70 WAGNER Seyval Blanc Finger Lakes Barrel Fermented 1984 $5 (3/16/86)
77 WALKER VALLEY Seyval Blanc Hudson River Region 1984 $5 (3/16/86)
72 WIDMER Seyval Blanc Finger Lakes Private Reserve 1985 $6.25 (3/16/86)
87 WOODBURY Seyval Blanc New York Proprietor's 1984 $5 (3/16/86)

SPARKLING

74 BULLY HILL Finger Lakes Brut Seyval Blanc 1988 $15 (12/31/90)
78 CASA LARGA Finger Lakes Blanc de Blancs NV $13 (12/31/90)
77 CASA LARGA Finger Lakes Brut Blanc de Blancs NV $11 (12/31/90)
80 CHATEAU FRANK Finger Lakes Brut 1985 $18 (12/31/90)
85 GLENORA Finger Lakes Blanc de Blancs 1987 $12 (12/31/90)
81 GLENORA New York Brut 1987 $12 (12/31/90)
69 GOLD SEAL New York Brut Bottle Fermented NV $7 (12/31/90)
76 GREAT WESTERN New York Blanc de Blancs NV $14 (6/30/90)
69 GREAT WESTERN New York Brut Very Dry NV $9.75 (12/31/90)
68 GREAT WESTERN New York Extra Dry NV $9.75 (12/31/90)
74 GREAT WESTERN New York Natural NV $14 (6/30/90)
71 GREAT WESTERN New York Rosé NV $9.75 (12/31/90)
72 KEDEM New York Charmat Kosher NV $6 (12/31/90)
68 LENZ North Fork of Long Island North Fork 1986 $17.50 (12/31/90)
64 MCGREGOR Finger Lakes Blanc de Blancs 1985 $15 (12/31/90)
80 PINDAR North Fork of Long Island Brut North Fork Premier Cuvée 1986 $13 (12/31/90)
86 PINDAR North Fork of Long Island Champagne NV $13 (12/15/88) (JL)
61 TAYLOR New York Brut Bottle Fermented NV $6.50 (12/31/90)
70 WOODBURY New York Blanc de Noirs 1987 $12 (12/31/90)
82 WOODBURY New York Brut Blanc de Blancs 1987 $12 (12/31/90)

OTHER NEW YORK RED

95 BALDWIN New York Landot Noir 1982 $6 (3/16/86)
68 BENMARL New York Marlboro Village Red Reserve 1982 $10 (3/16/86)
76 PLANE'S CAYUGA Finger Lakes Chancellor 1983 $5 (3/16/86)
54 POPLAR RIDGE New York Foch 1981 $7.50 (3/16/86)

OTHER NEW YORK WHITE

83 BEDELL North Fork of Long Island Cygnet NV $6 (12/15/88) (JL)
83 HAMPTON North Fork of Long Island Blanc de Mers 1987 $5 (12/15/88) (JL)
83 HARGRAVE North Fork of Long Island Pinot en Blanc 1989 $10 (6/30/91)
85 PECONIC BAY North Fork of Long Island Vin di L'Ile 1987 $8 (12/15/88) (JL)
80 PINDAR New York Pinot Meunier 1987 $25 (12/31/90)
84 RIVENDELL New York Sarabande Sur Lie 1989 $7.50 (6/30/91)

OREGON/*CHARDONNAY*

89 ADAMS Chardonnay Willamette Valley Reserve 1985 Rel: NA (9/30/87)
76 ADELSHEIM Chardonnay Oregon 1985 $12 (7/31/87)
93 ARGYLE Chardonnay Oregon Barrel Fermented 1987 $18.50 (12/15/90)
90 ARTERBERRY Chardonnay Willamette Valley 1988 $10 (1/31/91)
87 ARTERBERRY Chardonnay Willamette Valley Red Hills Vineyard 1985 Rel: NA (9/30/87)
69 BETHEL HEIGHTS Chardonnay Willamette Valley 1985 $12 (7/31/87)
84 BRIDGEVIEW Chardonnay Oregon Barrel Select 1989 $12 (3/31/91)
81 BRIDGEVIEW Chardonnay Oregon Barrel Select 1988 $12 (3/31/91)
71 CAMERON Chardonnay Willamette Valley Reserve 1985 $16.50 (7/31/87)
75 ELK COVE Chardonnay Willamette Valley 1988 $12 (3/31/91)
70 ELK COVE Chardonnay Willamette Valley 1986 $12 (5/31/88)
78 ELK COVE Chardonnay Willamette Valley 1985 $9.75 (7/31/87)
90 EYRIE Chardonnay Willamette Valley Yamhill County 1985 $12.50 (7/31/87)
86 GIRARDET Chardonnay Oregon 1986 Rel: NA (9/30/87)
84 HENRY Chardonnay Umpqua Valley 1985 Rel: NA (9/30/87)
77 MONTINORE Chardonnay Washington County 1988 $11 (3/31/91)
69 OAK KNOLL Chardonnay Oregon 1985 $12 (7/31/87)
83 OAK KNOLL Chardonnay Willamette Valley 1988 $11 (3/31/91)
85 PONZI Chardonnay Willamette Valley 1985 $10.50 (7/31/87)
69 REX HILL Chardonnay Willamette Valley 1985 $15 (5/31/88)
87 SOKOL BLOSSER Chardonnay Yamhill County Redland 1988 $12 (3/31/91)
71 SOKOL BLOSSER Chardonnay Yamhill County Reserve 1985 $15 (7/31/87)
86 TUALATIN Chardonnay Willamette Valley Barrel Fermented 1988 $14 (3/31/91)
91 TUALATIN Chardonnay Willamette Valley Barrel Fermented Private Reserve 1988 $20 (3/31/91)
92 TUALATIN Chardonnay Willamette Valley Private Reserve 1985 Rel: NA (9/30/87)
64 VALLEY VIEW Chardonnay Oregon 1986 $6 (5/31/88)
84 VALLEY VIEW Chardonnay Oregon 1985 $15 (2/15/87)
81 VALLEY VIEW Chardonnay Oregon Barrel Select 1988 $12 (3/31/91)
91 VERITAS Chardonnay Oregon 1985 Rel: NA (9/30/87)
83 VERITAS Chardonnay Willamette Valley 1988 $12 (3/31/91)
79 YAMHILL VALLEY Chardonnay Oregon 1985 $12.50 (7/31/87)
84 YAMHILL VALLEY Chardonnay Willamette Valley 1988 $12 (3/31/91)
83 YAMHILL VALLEY Chardonnay Willamette Valley 1988 $12 (12/15/90)

PINOT NOIR

89 ADAMS Pinot Noir Yamhill County 1985 $25 (2/15/90)
89 ADAMS Pinot Noir Yamhill County 1985 $25 (6/15/87)
91 PETER F. ADAMS Pinot Noir Yamhill County 1983 Rel: NA (2/15/90)
72 ADELSHEIM Pinot Noir Oregon 1987 $13 (2/15/90)
75 ADELSHEIM Pinot Noir Oregon 1985 $25 (2/15/90)
87 ADELSHEIM Pinot Noir Polk County 1986 $15 (6/15/88)
70 ADELSHEIM Pinot Noir Polk County The Eola Hills 1987 $16 (2/15/90)
89 ADELSHEIM Pinot Noir Willamette Valley 1988 $13 (4/15/91)
88 ADELSHEIM Pinot Noir Yamhill County 1985 $16 (6/15/87)
70 ADELSHEIM Pinot Noir Yamhill County 1983 $40 (2/15/90)
73 ADELSHEIM Pinot Noir Yamhill County Elizabeth's Reserve 1987 $19 (2/15/90)
75 AIRLIE Pinot Noir Willamette Valley 1987 $9 (2/15/90)
80 ALPINE Pinot Noir Willamette Valley Vintage Select 1985 $17 (6/15/87)
82 AMITY Pinot Noir Oregon 1988 $10 (5/31/91)
73 AMITY Pinot Noir Oregon 1983 $30 (2/15/90)
85 AMITY Pinot Noir Oregon 1983 $30 (8/31/86)
84 AMITY Pinot Noir Gamay Noir Oregon 1988 $9 (2/15/90)
80 AMITY Pinot Noir Oregon Winemaker's Reserve 1985 Rel: NA (2/15/90)
75 AMITY Pinot Noir Oregon Winemaker's Reserve 1983 $30 (2/15/90)
81 AMITY Pinot Noir Willamette Valley 1987 $15 (2/15/90)
74 AMITY Pinot Noir Willamette Valley 1986 $12.50 (2/15/90)
85 AMITY Pinot Noir Willamette Valley 1985 $25 (2/15/90)
87 AMITY Pinot Noir Willamette Valley 1985 $25 (6/15/88)
77 AMITY Pinot Noir Willamette Valley 1982 $9.50 (3/01/86)
79 AMITY Pinot Noir Willamette Valley Estate 1987 $25 (2/15/90)
79 AMITY Pinot Noir Willamette Valley Estate 1985 $25 (2/15/90)
76 AMITY Pinot Noir Willamette Valley Estate Bottled 1983 $30 (2/15/90)
83 AMITY Pinot Noir Willamette Valley Winemaker's Reserve 1987 $30 (2/15/90)
68 ANKENY Pinot Noir Willamette Valley Estate Bottled 1986 $9 (6/15/88)
79 ARTERBERRY Pinot Noir Willamette Valley Winemaker's Reserve 1988 $14 (1/31/91)
70 ARTERBERRY Pinot Noir Yamhill County Red Hills Vineyard Winemaker's Reserve 1986 $14.75 (6/15/88)
95 ARTERBERRY Pinot Noir Yamhill County Red Hills Vineyard Winemaker's Reserve 1985 $16 (6/15/87)
86 ARTERBERRY Pinot Noir Yamhill County Red Hills Vineyard Winemaker's Reserve 1983 $16 (2/15/90)
90 ARTERBERRY Pinot Noir Yamhill County Weber Vineyards Winemaker's Reserve 1987 $14 (2/15/90)
80 AUTUMN WIND Pinot Noir Willamette Valley 1988 $12 (4/15/91)
83 AUTUMN WIND Pinot Noir Willamette Valley 1987 $15 (2/15/90)
85 BAY CELLARS Pinot Noir Willamette Valley 1985 $18 (6/15/88)
86 BETHEL HEIGHTS Pinot Noir Willamette Valley 1987 $12 (2/15/90)
86 BETHEL HEIGHTS Pinot Noir Willamette Valley 1986 $15 (6/15/88)
79 BETHEL HEIGHTS Pinot Noir Willamette Valley 1985 $15 (2/15/90)
78 BETHEL HEIGHTS Pinot Noir Willamette Valley 1985 $15 (6/15/87)
87 BETHEL HEIGHTS Pinot Noir Willamette Valley Estate Grown 1988 $15 (4/15/91)
86 BETHEL HEIGHTS Pinot Noir Willamette Valley Estate Grown Reserve 1988 $18 (4/15/91)
86 BETHEL HEIGHTS Pinot Noir Willamette Valley.Unfiltered 1985 $12 (2/15/90)
90 BONNY DOON Pinot Noir Oregon Bethel Heights Vineyard 1985 $18 (6/15/88)
88 BONNY DOON Pinot Noir Oregon Temperance Hill Vineyard 1985 $18 (6/15/88)
79 BRIDGEVIEW Pinot Noir Oregon 1986 $8 (2/15/90)
88 BRIDGEVIEW Pinot Noir Oregon Estate Bottled 1988 $8 (2/15/90)
87 BRIDGEVIEW Pinot Noir Oregon Estate Bottled 1986 $8 (6/15/88)
80 BRIDGEVIEW Pinot Noir Oregon Special Reserve 1987 $12 (2/15/90)
89 BRIDGEVIEW Pinot Noir Oregon Winemaker's Reserve 1987 $15 (2/15/90)
76 BROADLEY Pinot Noir Oregon 1987 $8 (2/15/90)
88 BROADLEY Pinot Noir Oregon Reserve 1987 $12 (2/15/90)
73 BROADLEY Pinot Noir Oregon Reserve 1986 $11.50 (6/15/88)
88 CALLAHAN RIDGE Pinot Noir Oregon Elkton Vineyards 1987 $8 (2/15/90)
81 CAMERON Pinot Noir Willamette Valley 1987 $14 (2/15/90)
86 CAMERON Pinot Noir Willamette Valley 1986 $15 (6/15/88)
82 CAMERON Pinot Noir Willamette Valley 1985 $14 (2/15/90)
91 CAMERON Pinot Noir Willamette Valley 1985 $14 (6/15/87)
80 CAMERON Pinot Noir Willamette Valley Reserve 1986 $18 (2/15/90)
63 CAMERON Pinot Noir Willamette Valley Reserve 1985 $25 (2/15/90)
86 CAMERON Pinot Noir Willamette Valley Vintage Reserve 1987 $18 (2/15/90)
55 CHATEAU BENOIT Pinot Noir Oregon 1986 $15 (6/15/88)
55 CHATEAU BENOIT Pinot Noir Oregon 1985 $14 (6/15/88)
83 COOPER MOUNTAIN Pinot Noir Willamette Valley 1988 $13 (4/15/91) (JL)
87 COOPER MOUNTAIN Pinot Noir Willamette Valley 1987 $13 (2/15/90)
83 COOPER MOUNTAIN Pinot Noir Willamette Valley Reserve 1988 $20 (4/15/91)
89 DOMAINE DROUHIN Pinot Noir Oregon 1988 $32 (5/31/91)
78 ELK COVE Pinot Noir Willamette Valley 1988 $15 (1/31/91)
81 ELK COVE Pinot Noir Willamette Valley Dundee Hills Vineyard 1987 $15 (2/15/90)
78 ELK COVE Pinot Noir Willamette Valley Dundee Hills Vineyard 1986 $15 (6/15/88)
85 ELK COVE Pinot Noir Willamette Valley Dundee Hills Vineyard 1985 $15 (6/15/87)
78 ELK COVE Pinot Noir Willamette Valley Estate Bottled 1987 $15 (2/15/90)
65 ELK COVE Pinot Noir Willamette Valley Estate Bottled 1986 $15 (2/15/90)
87 ELK COVE Pinot Noir Willamette Valley Estate Bottled 1986 $15 (6/15/88)
85 ELK COVE Pinot Noir Willamette Valley Reserve 1987 $15 (12/15/90)
79 ELK COVE Pinot Noir Willamette Valley Reserve 1985 $15 (2/15/90)
79 ELK COVE Pinot Noir Willamette Valley Reserve 1983 $20 (2/15/90)
81 ELK COVE Pinot Noir Willamette Valley Reserve 1983 $20 (8/31/86)
80 ELK COVE Pinot Noir Willamette Valley Wind Hills Vineyard 1988 $18 (1/31/91)
75 ELK COVE Pinot Noir Willamette Valley Wind Hills Vineyard 1987 $15 (2/15/90)

UNITED STATES
OREGON/*PINOT NOIR*

85 ELK COVE Pinot Noir Willamette Valley Wind Hills Vineyard 1986 $15 (6/15/88)
91 ELK COVE Pinot Noir Willamette Valley Wind Hills Vineyard 1985 $15 (6/15/87)
71 ELLENDALE Pinot Noir Willamette Valley Estate Bottled 1986 $12 (6/15/88)
78 ELLENDALE Pinot Noir Willamette Valley Estate Bottled 1985 $15 (6/15/88)
76 EOLA HILLS Pinot Noir Oregon 1987 $12 (2/15/90)
77 EOLA HILLS Pinot Noir Oregon 1986 $15 (2/15/90)
81 EOLA HILLS Pinot Noir Oregon 1986 $15 (6/15/88)
68 EVESHAM WOOD Pinot Noir Willamette Valley 1986 $12 (2/15/90)
84 EVESHAM WOOD Pinot Noir Willamette Valley 1986 $12 (6/15/88)
80 EYRIE Pinot Noir Willamette Valley 1987 $20 (2/15/90)
83 EYRIE Pinot Noir Willamette Valley 1986 $19.50 (6/15/88)
91 EYRIE Pinot Noir Willamette Valley 1985 $25 (2/15/90)
87 EYRIE Pinot Noir Willamette Valley 1985 $25 (6/15/88)
84 EYRIE Pinot Noir Willamette Valley 1984 $15 (8/31/86)
87 EYRIE Pinot Noir Willamette Valley 1983 $30 (2/15/90)
94 EYRIE Pinot Noir Willamette Valley 1983 $20 (8/31/86)
86 EYRIE Pinot Noir Willamette Valley Reserve 1987 $25 (2/15/90)
89 FORGERON Pinot Noir Oregon 1985 $19 (2/15/90)
76 FORGERON Pinot Noir Oregon Vinters Reserve 1987 $12 (2/15/90)
67 GIRARD Pinot Noir Oregon 1987 $12 (2/15/90)
75 GIRARDET Pinot Noir Umpqua Valley 1987 $12 (2/15/90)
81 HENRY Pinot Noir Umpqua Valley 1986 $10 (4/15/91)
85 HENRY Pinot Noir Umpqua Valley 1985 $15 (2/15/90)
80 HENRY Pinot Noir Umpqua Valley 1985 $15 (6/15/88)
78 HIDDEN SPRINGS Pinot Noir Oregon 1985 $12 (6/15/88)
86 HONEYWOOD Pinot Noir Willamette Valley 1986 $9 (6/15/88)
82 KNUDSEN ERATH Pinot Noir Willamette Valley 1988 $11 (5/31/91)
65 KNUDSEN ERATH Pinot Noir Willamette Valley 1987 $11 (2/15/90)
64 KNUDSEN ERATH Pinot Noir Willamette Valley 1986 $10 (2/15/90)
71 KNUDSEN ERATH Pinot Noir Willamette Valley 1986 $10 (6/15/88)
81 KNUDSEN ERATH Pinot Noir Willamette Valley NV $6 (6/16/86) BB
89 KNUDSEN ERATH Pinot Noir Willamette Valley Leland Vineyards Reserve 1987 $24 (2/15/90)
87 KNUDSEN ERATH Pinot Noir Willamette Valley Vintage Select 1986 $15 (6/15/88)
90 KNUDSEN ERATH Pinot Noir Willamette Valley Vintage Select 1985 Rel: NA (9/30/87)
75 KNUDSEN ERATH Pinot Noir Yamhill County Vintage Select 1985 $20 (2/15/90)
93 KNUDSEN ERATH Pinot Noir Yamhill County Vintage Select 1985 $20 (6/15/87)
81 KNUDSEN ERATH Pinot Noir Yamhill County Vintage Select 1983 $35 (2/15/90)
94 KNUDSEN ERATH Pinot Noir Yamhill County Vintage Select 1983 $35 (8/31/86)
94 KNUDSEN ERATH Pinot Noir Yamhill County Vintage Select 1983 $35 (7/01/86) SS
90 MCKINLAY Pinot Noir Willamette Valley 1988 $13 (4/15/91)
88 MONTINORE Pinot Noir Washington County 1988 $13.50 (4/15/91)
81 MONTINORE Pinot Noir Washington County 1987 $12.50 (2/15/90)
78 OAK KNOLL Pinot Noir Oregon Vintage Select 1983 $20 (2/15/90)
77 OAK KNOLL Pinot Noir Oregon Vintage Select 1982 $25 (2/15/90)
81 OAK KNOLL Pinot Noir Willamette Valley 1988 $11 (4/15/91)
65 OAK KNOLL Pinot Noir Willamette Valley 1985 $10 (6/15/87)
81 OAK KNOLL Pinot Noir Willamette Valley Vintage Select 1988 $18 (5/31/91)
77 OAK KNOLL Pinot Noir Willamette Valley Vintage Select 1987 $17.50 (2/15/90)
59 OAK KNOLL Pinot Noir Willamette Valley Vintage Select 1985 $17.50 (2/15/90)
70 OAK KNOLL Pinot Noir Willamette Valley Vintage Select 1985 $17.50 (6/15/87)
75 PANTHER CREEK Pinot Noir Willamette Valley 1988 $15 (4/15/91)
74 PANTHER CREEK Pinot Noir Willamette Valley 1987 $17 (4/15/90)
69 PANTHER CREEK Pinot Noir Willamette Valley Oak Grove Vineyard Abbey Ridge Vineyard 1986 $15 (6/15/88)
58 PANTHER CREEK Pinot Noir Willamette Valley Oak Knoll and Freedom Hill Vineyards 1987 $17 (2/15/90)
73 PELLIER Pinot Noir Willamette Valley 1985 $8 (6/15/88)
76 PONZI Pinot Noir Willamette Valley 1988 $16 (5/31/91)
88 PONZI Pinot Noir Willamette Valley 1987 $15 (2/15/90)
84 PONZI Pinot Noir Willamette Valley 1985 $20 (2/15/90)
90 PONZI Pinot Noir Willamette Valley 1985 $20 (6/15/87)
86 PONZI Pinot Noir Willamette Valley Reserve 1988 $25 (4/15/91)
91 PONZI Pinot Noir Willamette Valley Reserve 1987 $20 (2/15/90)
81 PONZI Pinot Noir Willamette Valley Reserve 1986 $15 (6/15/88)
81 REX HILL Pinot Noir Oregon 1985 $15 (2/15/90)
77 REX HILL Pinot Noir Oregon 1985 $15 (6/15/88)
84 REX HILL Pinot Noir Oregon Archibald Vineyards 1985 $30 (2/15/90)
78 REX HILL Pinot Noir Oregon Archibald Vineyards 1985 $30 (6/15/88)
74 REX HILL Pinot Noir Oregon Dundee Hills Vineyards 1985 $25 (2/15/90)
72 REX HILL Pinot Noir Oregon Dundee Hills Vineyards 1985 $25 (6/15/88)
77 REX HILL Pinot Noir Oregon Dundee Hills Vineyards 1983 $35 (2/15/90)
86 REX HILL Pinot Noir Oregon Dundee Hills Vineyards 1983 $35 (8/31/86)
66 REX HILL Pinot Noir Oregon Maresh Vineyards 1985 $40 (2/15/90)
79 REX HILL Pinot Noir Oregon Maresh Vineyards 1985 $40 (6/15/88)
64 REX HILL Pinot Noir Oregon Maresh Vineyards 1983 $40 (2/15/90)
77 REX HILL Pinot Noir Oregon Medici Vineyard 1985 $28 (2/15/90)
76 REX HILL Pinot Noir Oregon Medici Vineyard 1985 $28 (6/15/88)
79 REX HILL Pinot Noir Oregon Wirtz Vineyards 1985 $18 (6/15/88)
88 REX HILL Pinot Noir Willamette Valley 1988 $18 (4/15/91)
79 REX HILL Pinot Noir Willamette Valley 1985 $15 (6/15/88)
70 SCHWARZENBERG Pinot Noir Oregon 1987 $13.50 (2/15/90)
75 SILVER FALLS Pinot Noir Willamette Valley 1987 $10 (2/15/90)
80 SISKIYOU Pinot Noir Oregon Estate 1987 $13 (2/15/90)

Key to Symbols

The scores reported here are the results of blind tastings conducted by our panel of senior editors. Wines that carry the initials below are results of individual tastings.

THE WINE SPECTATOR 100-POINT SCALE ***95-100***—Classic, a great wine; ***90-94***—Outstanding, superior character and style; ***80-89***—Good to very good, a wine with special qualities; ***70-79***—Average, drinkable wine that may have minor flaws; ***60-69***—Below average, drinkable but not recommended; ***50-59***—Poor, undrinkable, not recommended. "+"—With a score indicates a range; used primarily with barrel tastings to indicate a preliminary score.

SPECIAL DESIGNATIONS SS—Spectator Selection, CS—Cellar Selection, BB—Best Buy.

TASTER'S INITIALS (JG)—Jim Gordon, (HS)—Harvey Steiman, (JL)—James Laube, (JS)—James Suckling, (TM)—Thomas Matthews, (TR)—Terry Robards, (BT)—Barrel Tasting (these wines were tasted blind from barrel samples), (CA-date)—*California's Great Cabernets* by James Laube, (CH-date)—*California's Great Chardonnays* by James Laube, (VP-date)—*Vintage Port* by James Suckling.

DATE TASTED Dates in parentheses represent the issue in which the rating was published.

92 SOKOL BLOSSER Pinot Noir Willamette Valley Red Hills Vineyard 1985 Rel: NA (9/30/87)
59 SOKOL BLOSSER Pinot Noir Yamhill County 1986 $10 (6/15/88)
63 SOKOL BLOSSER Pinot Noir Yamhill County 1982 $8.95 (2/16/85)
79 SOKOL BLOSSER Pinot Noir Yamhill County Hyland Vineyards 1986 $15 (6/15/88)
86 SOKOL BLOSSER Pinot Noir Yamhill County Hyland Vineyards 1985 $15 (6/15/87)
82 SOKOL BLOSSER Pinot Noir Yamhill County Hyland Vineyards 1983 $14 (8/31/86)
86 SOKOL BLOSSER Pinot Noir Yamhill County Hyland Vineyards Reserve 1985 $18 (6/15/88)
67 SOKOL BLOSSER Pinot Noir Yamhill County Hyland Vineyards Reserve 1983 $30 (2/15/90)
77 SOKOL BLOSSER Pinot Noir Yamhill County Red Hills 1986 $15 (6/15/88)
80 SOKOL BLOSSER Pinot Noir Yamhill County Red Hills 1985 $15 (6/15/87)
74 SOKOL BLOSSER Pinot Noir Yamhill County Red Hills Reserve 1985 $30 (2/15/90)
82 SOKOL BLOSSER Pinot Noir Yamhill County Red Hills Reserve 1985 $30 (6/15/88)
82 SOKOL BLOSSER Pinot Noir Yamhill County Redland 1988 $13 (4/15/91)
66 SOKOL BLOSSER Pinot Noir Yamhill County Redland 1987 $13 (2/15/90)
76 ST. JOSEF'S WEINKELLER Pinot Noir Oregon 1987 $8 (4/15/91)
89 ST. JOSEF'S WEINKELLER Pinot Noir Oregon 1985 $16 (2/15/90)
79 ST. JOSEF'S WEINKELLER Pinot Noir Oregon 1985 $16 (6/15/88)
84 STATON HILLS Pinot Noir Oregon 1987 $13 (4/15/91)
75 STATON HILLS Pinot Noir Oregon 1987 $13 (2/15/90)
64 STATON HILLS Pinot Noir Oregon 1986 $13 (2/15/90)
64 TUALATIN Pinot Noir Willamette Valley 1983 $10 (8/31/86)
79 TUALATIN Pinot Noir Willamette Valley Estate Bottled 1987 $14 (2/15/90)
85 TUALATIN Pinot Noir Willamette Valley Estate Bottled 1986 $13.50 (6/15/88)
84 TUALATIN Pinot Noir Willamette Valley Private Reserve 1985 $14 (2/15/90)
89 TUALATIN Pinot Noir Willamette Valley Private Reserve 1985 $14 (6/15/87)
73 VALLEY VIEW Pinot Noir Oregon 1982 $8.50 (3/01/86)
76 VALLEY VIEW Pinot Noir Oregon 1980 $7.50 (9/16/84)
88 VERITAS Pinot Noir Oregon 1985 $15 (6/15/87)
87 VERITAS Pinot Noir Willamette Valley 1988 $15 (5/31/91)
77 VERITAS Pinot Noir Willamette Valley 1987 $15 (2/15/90)
93 WASSON BROS Pinot Noir Oregon 1985 Rel: NA (9/30/87)
86 YAMHILL VALLEY Pinot Noir Oregon 1985 $16 (6/15/87)
92 YAMHILL VALLEY Pinot Noir Oregon 1983 $17 (8/31/86)
76 YAMHILL VALLEY Pinot Noir Willamette Valley 1988 $12 (1/31/91)
87 YAMHILL VALLEY Pinot Noir Willamette Valley 1983 $35 (2/15/90)

OTHER OREGON RED

80 ELK COVE Cabernet Sauvignon Commander's Cabernet Willamette Valley Dundee Hills Vineyard 1987 $15 (3/31/91)
87 ST. JOSEF'S WEINKELLER Cabernet Sauvignon Oregon 1985 $15 (3/31/91)
78 VALLEY VIEW Merlot Oregon 1983 $10 (5/31/88)
74 VALLEY VIEW Rogue Red Oregon NV $3.75 (2/15/88)

OTHER OREGON WHITE

82 ARGYLE Brut Oregon Cuvée Limited 1987 $18.50 (12/31/90)
60 ELK COVE Gewürztraminer Willamette Valley 1986 $6.75 (7/15/88)
69 FORGERON Chenin Blanc Oregon 1987 $7.50 (7/31/89)
81 KNUDSEN ERATH Gewürztraminer Willamette Valley Dry 1989 $7 (6/30/91)
84 MONTINORE White Riesling Yamhill County Late Harvest 1989 $7 (3/31/91)
83 MONTINORE White Riesling Oregon Ultra Late Harvest 1987 $22/375ml (3/31/91)
80 TUALATIN White Riesling Willamette Valley 1989 $6.50 (6/30/91)
89 TUALATIN White Riesling Willamette Valley 1988 $6 (7/31/89) BB
85 YAMHILL VALLEY Pinot Gris Willamette Valley 1990 $10 (6/30/91)

WASHINGTON/*BLUSH*

75 CHATEAU STE. MICHELLE Blush Columbia Valley Blush Riesling 1988 $5 (10/15/89)
64 COLUMBIA CREST Blush Columbia Valley Vineyard Reserve 1986 $5 (10/15/89)
82 HOGUE Blush Washington 1988 $6 (10/15/89)
80 PONTIN DEL ROZA Blush Yakima Valley Roza Sunset 1988 $6 (10/15/89)
59 SADDLE MOUNTAIN Blush Columbia Valley Blush White Riesling 1988 $5 (10/15/89)

CABERNET SAUVIGNON & BLENDS

80 ARBOR CREST Cabernet Sauvignon Columbia Valley Bacchus Vineyard 1985 $11 (10/15/89)
77 ARBOR CREST Cabernet Sauvignon Columbia Valley Bacchus Vineyard 1983 $12.50 (12/15/87)
85 CHATEAU STE. MICHELLE Cabernet Sauvignon Benton County Cold Creek Vineyards Château Reserve 1980 $21 (10/15/89)
75 CHATEAU STE. MICHELLE Cabernet Sauvignon Benton County Cold Creek Vineyards Château Reserve 1980 $20 (12/15/86)
88 CHATEAU STE. MICHELLE Cabernet Sauvignon Columbia Valley 1986 $12 (9/30/90)
85 CHATEAU STE. MICHELLE Cabernet Sauvignon Columbia Valley Twentieth Vintage 1987 $12 (9/30/90)
85 CHATEAU STE. MICHELLE Cabernet Sauvignon Washington 1985 $11.50 (10/15/89)
89 CHATEAU STE. MICHELLE Cabernet Sauvignon Washington 1984 $11 (12/31/88)
81 CHATEAU STE. MICHELLE Cabernet Sauvignon Washington 1983 $10 (11/15/87)
65 CHATEAU STE. MICHELLE Cabernet Sauvignon Washington 1980 $9 (3/01/85)
83 CHATEAU STE. MICHELLE Cabernet Sauvignon Washington Cold Creek Vineyard Limited Bottling 1985 $19 (12/15/90)
82 CHATEAU STE. MICHELLE Cabernet Sauvignon Washington Cold Creek Vineyard Limited Bottling 1985 $16 (10/15/89)
90 CHATEAU STE. MICHELLE Cabernet Sauvignon Washington River Ridge Vineyard Limited Bottling 1985 $17 (11/30/90)
88 CHATEAU STE. MICHELLE Cabernet Sauvignon Washington River Ridge Vineyard Limited Bottling 1985 $16 (10/15/89)
86 COLUMBIA Cabernet Sauvignon Columbia Valley 1988 $10 (3/31/91)
87 COLUMBIA Cabernet Sauvignon Columbia Valley 1987 $9.50 (6/15/90)
85 COLUMBIA Cabernet Sauvignon Columbia Valley 1986 $10 (10/15/89)
79 COLUMBIA Cabernet Sauvignon Columbia Valley 1985 $9.50 (7/15/88)
85 COLUMBIA Cabernet Sauvignon Columbia Valley David Lake Sagemoor Vineyards 1986 $16 (5/15/91)
85 COLUMBIA Cabernet Sauvignon Columbia Valley Sagemoor Vineyards 1985 $15 (10/15/89)
86 COLUMBIA Cabernet Sauvignon Washington Bacchus Vineyard 1981 $12 (8/01/84)
76 COLUMBIA Cabernet Sauvignon Yakima Valley 1981 $8 (8/01/84)
91 COLUMBIA Cabernet Sauvignon Yakima Valley Otis Vineyard 1985 $15 (10/15/89)
83 COLUMBIA Cabernet Sauvignon Yakima Valley Otis Vineyard 1981 $13 (8/01/84)
82 COLUMBIA Cabernet Sauvignon Yakima Valley Red Willow Vineyard 1985 $15 (10/15/89)
84 COLUMBIA Cabernet Sauvignon Yakima Valley Red Willow Vineyard 1981 $35 (10/15/89)
88 COLUMBIA CREST Cabernet Sauvignon Columbia Valley 1986 $8 (1/31/91) BB
88 COLUMBIA CREST Cabernet Sauvignon Columbia Valley 1986 $8 (12/15/90)

81 COLUMBIA CREST Cabernet Sauvignon Columbia Valley 1985 $8 (10/15/89)
78 COLUMBIA CREST Cabernet Sauvignon Columbia Valley 1985 $8 (7/31/89)
79 COLUMBIA CREST Cabernet Sauvignon Columbia Valley 1984 $7.50 (7/15/88)
80 COVEY RUN Cabernet Sauvignon Yakima Valley 1986 $10 (10/15/89)
82 FRENCH CREEK Cabernet Sauvignon Washington 1985 $8 (10/15/88)
88 HOGUE Cabernet Sauvignon Washington Reserve 1987 $19 (3/31/91)
81 HOGUE Cabernet Sauvignon Washington Reserve 1985 $18 (10/15/89)
89 KIONA Cabernet Sauvignon Yakima Valley Estate Bottled 1986 $14 (10/15/89)
80 LATAH CREEK Cabernet Sauvignon Washington 1986 $13 (10/15/88)
83 LATAH CREEK Cabernet Sauvignon Washington Limited Bottling 1987 $13 (10/15/89)
83 LATAH CREEK Cabernet Sauvignon Washington Limited Bottling 1987 $13 (7/31/89)
81 LEONETTI Cabernet Sauvignon Columbia Valley 1986 $20 (10/15/89)
85 LEONETTI Cabernet Sauvignon Walla Walla Valley Seven Hills Vineyard 1985 $22 (10/15/89)
91 LEONETTI Cabernet Sauvignon Washington 1987 $22 (6/15/90)
84 LEONETTI Cabernet Sauvignon Washington Reserve 1985 $40 (6/15/91)
81 MERCER RANCH Cabernet Sauvignon Columbia Valley Mercer Ranch Vineyard Block 1 1985 $13 (10/15/89)
84 PRESTON WINE CELLARS Cabernet Sauvignon Washington 1982 $8 (5/31/88)
85 PRESTON WINE CELLARS Cabernet Sauvignon Washington Oak Aged 1989 $10 (5/15/91)
62 PRESTON WINE CELLARS Cabernet Sauvignon Washington Preston Vineyard Selected Reserve 1987 $13.50 (10/15/89)
78 QUARRY LAKE Cabernet Sauvignon Washington 1986 $10 (10/15/89)
74 QUILCEDA CREEK Cabernet Sauvignon Washington 1985 $16.50 (10/15/89)
77 STE. CHAPELLE Cabernet Sauvignon Washington 1983 $9 (4/30/88)
80 STE. CHAPELLE Cabernet Sauvignon Washington 1981 $9 (5/15/87)
81 STE. CHAPELLE Cabernet Sauvignon Washington Collectors' Series 1981 $18 (10/15/89)
90 SNOQUALMIE Cabernet Sauvignon Columbia Valley 1987 $10 (9/30/90)
86 STATON HILLS Cabernet Sauvignon Washington 1987 $13 (3/31/91)
80 STATON HILLS Cabernet Sauvignon Washington 1986 $12 (10/15/89)
83 STATON HILLS Cabernet Sauvignon Washington Estate Bottled 1986 $20 (3/31/91)
80 PAUL THOMAS Cabernet Sauvignon Washington 1989 $11 (12/31/90)
84 PAUL THOMAS Cabernet Sauvignon Washington 1986 $14 (9/30/90)
88 PAUL THOMAS Cabernet Sauvignon Washington 1985 $20 (10/15/89)
88 PAUL THOMAS Cabernet Sauvignon Washington 1985 $20 (7/31/89)
95 WOODWARD CANYON Cabernet Sauvignon Columbia Valley 1987 $18.50 (12/31/90)
93 WOODWARD CANYON Cabernet Sauvignon Columbia Valley 1986 $18.50 (10/15/89)
89 WOODWARD CANYON Charbonneau Walla Walla County 1987 $20 (12/31/90)

CHARDONNAY

85 ARBOR CREST Chardonnay Columbia Valley 1988 $9.50 (3/31/90)
84 ARBOR CREST Chardonnay Columbia Valley 1987 $9.25 (10/15/89)
78 ARBOR CREST Chardonnay Columbia Valley 1984 $9.25 (7/31/87)
69 ARBOR CREST Chardonnay Washington Sagemoore Vineyards 1983 $10 (11/01/85)
85 ARBOR CREST Chardonnay Washington Sagemoore Vineyards 1982 $14 (1/01/85)
84 CHATEAU STE. MICHELLE Chardonnay Columbia Valley 1988 $10 (9/30/90)
81 CHATEAU STE. MICHELLE Chardonnay Washington 1987 $10 (10/15/89)
67 CHATEAU STE. MICHELLE Chardonnay Washington 1984 $10 (7/31/87)
73 CHATEAU STE. MICHELLE Chardonnay Washington 1982 $9 (4/16/86)
87 CHATEAU STE. MICHELLE Chardonnay Washington Cold Creek Vineyard Limited Bottling 1987 $13 (10/15/89)
82 CHATEAU STE. MICHELLE Chardonnay Washington Cold Creek Vineyard Limited Bottling 1986 $13 (12/31/88)
81 CHATEAU STE. MICHELLE Chardonnay Washington River Ridge Vineyard Château Reserve 1983 $18 (7/31/87)
85 CHATEAU STE. MICHELLE Chardonnay Washington River Ridge Vineyard Limited Bottling 1987 $13 (10/15/89)
82 CHINOOK Chardonnay Washington 1987 $11 (10/15/89)
78 COLUMBIA Chardonnay Columbia Valley 1989 $7 (5/31/91)
79 COLUMBIA Chardonnay Columbia Valley 1988 $8.50 (9/30/90)
89 COLUMBIA Chardonnay Columbia Valley Sagemoor Vineyards Barrel Fermented The Woodburne Collection 1989 $10 (3/31/91)
79 COLUMBIA Chardonnay Washington 1985 $8 (7/31/87)
80 COLUMBIA Chardonnay Washington Jolona Vineyard 1982 $12 (9/01/84)
80 COLUMBIA Chardonnay Yakima Valley Brookside Vineyards 1987 $15 (10/15/89)
46 COLUMBIA Chardonnay Yakima Valley Wyckoff Vineyard 1983 $8.50 (4/16/86)
86 COLUMBIA CREST Chardonnay Columbia Valley 1989 $7 (9/30/90) BB
80 COLUMBIA CREST Chardonnay Columbia Valley 1987 $7 (12/31/88)
79 COLUMBIA CREST Chardonnay Columbia Valley 1986 $8 (12/31/87)
86 COLUMBIA CREST Chardonnay Columbia Valley Barrel Select 1989 $15 (5/31/91)
77 COLUMBIA CREST Chardonnay Columbia Valley Vintage Select 1987 $7 (10/15/89)
86 COVEY RUN Chardonnay Yakima Valley 1989 $10 (3/31/91)
82 COVEY RUN Chardonnay Yakima Valley 1987 $9 (10/15/89)
89 COVEY RUN Chardonnay Yakima Valley Reserve 1989 $15 (7/15/91)
80 HOGUE Chardonnay Washington 1988 $8 (6/15/90)
83 HOGUE Chardonnay Washington 1987 $8 (10/15/89)
81 HOGUE Chardonnay Washington 1986 $8 (12/31/87)
86 HOGUE Chardonnay Washington Reserve 1989 $13 (5/31/91)
88 HOGUE Chardonnay Yakima Valley Reserve 1987 $10 (10/15/89)
91 KIONA Chardonnay Yakima Valley Barrel Fermented 1987 $10 (10/15/89)
82 LATAH CREEK Chardonnay Washington 1987 $9 (10/15/89)
70 LATAH CREEK Chardonnay Washington 1986 $8.50 (12/31/87)
80 LATAH CREEK Chardonnay Washington Feather 1988 $6 (10/15/89)
91 PRESTON WINE CELLARS Chardonnay Washington Barrel Fermented 1989 $12 (5/31/91)
82 PRESTON WINE CELLARS Chardonnay Washington Preston Vineyard Hand Harvested 1987 $10 (10/15/89)
74 QUARRY LAKE Chardonnay Washington 1987 $10 (10/15/89)
88 SILVER LAKE Chardonnay Columbia Valley Reserve 1989 $16 (5/31/91)
83 SNOQUALMIE Chardonnay Columbia Valley 1987 $8 (10/15/89)
85 SNOQUALMIE Chardonnay Columbia Valley Reserve 1987 $13 (10/15/89)
53 SNOQUALMIE Chardonnay Yakima Valley 1984 $9 (4/16/86)
70 SNOQUALMIE Chardonnay Yakima Valley Early Release 1984 $7 (4/16/86)
82 STATON HILLS Chardonnay Washington 1989 $10 (7/15/91)
79 STATON HILLS Chardonnay Washington 1988 $10 (5/31/91)
81 STATON HILLS Chardonnay Washington 1987 $10 (10/15/89)
85 STEWART Chardonnay Columbia Valley 1988 $10 (3/31/91)
78 STEWART Chardonnay Columbia Valley Reserve 1988 $17 (5/31/91)
90 STEWART Chardonnay Columbia Valley Reserve 1987 $15 (3/31/90)
89 PAUL THOMAS Chardonnay Washington 1988 $11 (10/15/89)
81 PAUL THOMAS Chardonnay Washington 1987 $10 (10/15/89)
85 PAUL THOMAS Chardonnay Washington Private Reserve 1987 $18 (10/15/89)

81 WOODWARD CANYON Chardonnay Columbia Valley 1987 $18 (10/15/89)
85 WOODWARD CANYON Chardonnay Washington 1986 $16 (4/30/88)
81 WOODWARD CANYON Chardonnay Washington 1984 $21 (5/15/87)

CHENIN BLANC

78 BOOKWALTER Chenin Blanc Washington Joseph Roberts Vineyards 1988 $6 (10/15/89)
75 CASCADE MOUNTAIN Chenin Blanc Washington Vouvray 1987 $5.25 (10/15/89)
88 CHATEAU STE. MICHELLE Chenin Blanc Columbia Valley 1988 $6 (7/31/89)
80 CHATEAU STE. MICHELLE Chenin Blanc Washington 1987 $6 (10/15/89)
84 CHATEAU STE. MICHELLE Chenin Blanc Washington 1986 $4 (7/31/89)
82 CHATEAU STE. MICHELLE Chenin Blanc Washington 1985 $5 (1/31/87)
77 COLUMBIA CREST Chenin Blanc Columbia Valley 1986 $5.25 (10/15/89)
74 HOGUE Chenin Blanc Washington 1988 $6 (10/15/89)
76 KIONA Chenin Blanc Yakima Valley Estate Bottled 1988 $5.75 (10/15/89)
68 LAKESIDE Chenin Blanc Washington NV $6 (7/31/89)
83 QUARRY LAKE Chenin Blanc Washington 1987 $5.50 (10/15/89)
76 SADDLE MOUNTAIN Chenin Blanc Columbia Valley 1988 $5 (10/15/89)
71 SALISHAN Chenin Blanc Washington Dry 1988 $6.25 (10/15/89)
80 SNOQUALMIE Chenin Blanc Columbia Valley 1988 $6.50 (10/15/89)
68 SNOQUALMIE Chenin Blanc Columbia Valley 1988 $6.50 (7/31/89)
84 PAUL THOMAS Chenin Blanc Washington 1988 $7 (10/15/89)
81 WORDEN Chenin Blanc Washington 1988 $6 (10/15/89)

DESSERT

58 ARBOR CREST Dessert Washington Dionysius Vineyard 1982 $6/375ml (4/16/84)
71 BAINBRIDGE ISLAND Dessert Washington Siegerrebe Botrytis Affected 1987 $15/375ml (10/15/89)
78 BOOKWALTER Dessert Washington 1987 $5.5/375ml (10/15/89)
91 CHATEAU STE. MICHELLE Dessert Yakima Valley Château Reserve Hand-Selected Cluster 1985 $22 (7/31/89)
85 COLUMBIA Dessert Columbia Valley Cellarmaster's Reserve 1988 $7 (10/15/89) BB
87 COVEY RUN Dessert Yakima Valley Ice Wine 1987 $24/375ml (10/15/89)
83 COVEY RUN Dessert Yakima Valley Mahre Vineyards Botrytis 1986 $7 (10/15/89)
82 HINZERLING Dessert Yakima Valley Selected Cluster Die 1985 $12/375ml (10/15/89)
79 HOGUE Dessert Yakima Valley Markin Vineyard 1987 $7.50 (10/15/89)
87 HYATT Dessert Yakima Valley 1987 $8 (10/15/89)
75 KIONA Dessert Yakima Valley Ice Wine 1989 $15/375ml (6/15/91)
80 PRESTON WINE CELLARS Dessert Washington Ice Wine 1986 $38 (10/15/89)
85 SILVER LAKE Dessert Columbia Valley Ice Wine 1989 $25/375ml (6/15/91)
84 SNOQUALMIE Dessert Columbia Valley 1988 $7 (10/15/89)
83 STEWART Dessert Columbia Valley 1987 $8/375ml (7/31/89)
80 STEWART Dessert Columbia Valley Select 1986 $6.5/375ml (10/15/89)
85 THURSTON WOLFE Dessert Washington Black Muscat 1987 $9 (10/15/89)
83 THURSTON WOLFE Dessert Washington Sweet Rebecca 1987 $9 (10/15/89)

GEWÜRZTRAMINER

79 CHATEAU STE. MICHELLE Gewürztraminer Columbia Valley 1988 $6.50 (10/15/89)
74 COLUMBIA Gewürztraminer Washington 1985 $6 (5/15/87)
81 COLUMBIA CREST Gewürztraminer Columbia Valley 1987 $6 (10/15/89)
80 COLUMBIA CREST Gewürztraminer Columbia Valley 1986 $6 (12/15/87)
76 COVEY RUN Gewürztraminer Yakima Valley 1989 $7 (6/15/91)
77 COVEY RUN Gewürztraminer Yakima Valley 1988 $5.50 (10/15/89)
85 HOODSPORT Gewürztraminer Washington 1988 $6 (10/15/89) BB
79 SNOQUALMIE Gewürztraminer Columbia Valley 1988 $6 (10/15/89)
69 STEWART Gewürztraminer Yakima Valley 1988 $5.50 (10/15/89)

MERLOT

83 ARBOR CREST Merlot Columbia Valley 1987 $8 (10/15/89)
75 ARBOR CREST Merlot Columbia Valley Bacchus Vineyard 1985 $8 (7/31/87)
83 ARBOR CREST Merlot Columbia Valley Bacchus Vineyard Cameo Reserve 1985 $10 (12/15/87)
85 ARBOR CREST Merlot Columbia Valley Cameo Reserve 1987 $11 (6/15/90)
82 ARBOR CREST Merlot Washington Bacchus Vineyard 1982 $8.25 (11/01/84)
84 CHATEAU STE. MICHELLE Merlot Columbia Valley 1987 $12 (9/30/90)
84 CHATEAU STE. MICHELLE Merlot Columbia Valley 1986 $12 (9/30/90)
89 CHATEAU STE. MICHELLE Merlot Columbia Valley River Ridge Vineyard 1985 $17.50 (9/30/90)
80 CHATEAU STE. MICHELLE Merlot Washington 1983 $10 (12/31/88)
87 CHATEAU STE. MICHELLE Merlot Washington River Ridge Vineyard 1985 $14 (10/15/89)
87 CHATEAU STE. MICHELLE Merlot Washington River Ridge Vineyard Château Reserve 1983 $15 (12/31/88)
83 CHINOOK Merlot Washington 1986 $12.50 (10/15/89)
81 COLUMBIA Merlot Columbia Valley 1988 $10 (3/31/91)
84 COLUMBIA Merlot Columbia Valley 1986 $10 (10/15/89)
86 COLUMBIA Merlot Columbia Valley 1985 $9.50 (5/31/88)
75 COLUMBIA Merlot Washington 1984 $9 (5/15/87)
87 COLUMBIA Merlot Washington 1981 $25 (10/15/89)
78 COLUMBIA Merlot Washington 1981 $25 (8/01/84)
82 COLUMBIA Merlot Yakima Valley Red Willow Vineyard Milestone David Lake 1988 $16 (3/31/91)
80 COLUMBIA Merlot Yakima Valley Red Willow Vineyard Milestone 1987 $15 (10/15/89)
86 COLUMBIA CREST Merlot Columbia Valley 1987 $8 (9/30/90) BB
85 COLUMBIA CREST Merlot Columbia Valley 1985 $8 (10/15/89)
80 COLUMBIA CREST Merlot Columbia Valley 1985 $8 (7/31/89)
78 COLUMBIA CREST Merlot Columbia Valley 1984 $7.50 (5/31/88)
84 COLUMBIA CREST Merlot Columbia Valley Barrel Select 1987 $15 (5/31/91)
87 COVEY RUN Merlot Yakima Valley 1988 $10 (10/15/89)
82 COVEY RUN Merlot Yakima Valley 1986 $9 (10/15/89)
85 COVEY RUN Merlot Yakima Valley 1985 $9 (4/15/89)
82 COVEY RUN Merlot Yakima Valley 1984 $8.50 (11/15/87)
83 FRENCH CREEK Merlot Washington 1985 $11.50 (12/31/88)
76 HAVILAND Merlot Washington 1982 $8 (10/01/84)
82 HOGUE Merlot Washington 1986 $12 (10/15/89)
85 HOGUE Merlot Washington 1986 $12 (4/15/89)
80 HOGUE Merlot Washington 1985 $12 (11/15/87)
89 HOGUE Merlot Washington Reserve 1987 $19 (3/31/91)
84 KIONA Merlot Columbia Valley 1988 $12 (5/31/91)
89 LATAH CREEK Merlot Washington 1986 $10 (5/31/88)
90 LATAH CREEK Merlot Washington Limited Bottling 1987 $10 (10/15/89)
88 LEONETTI Merlot Columbia Valley 1987 $16 (10/15/89)

UNITED STATES
WASHINGTON/MERLOT

93   LEONETTI Merlot Washington 1989 $18 (5/31/91)
90   LEONETTI Merlot Washington 1988 $17 (4/15/90)
81   QUARRY LAKE Merlot Washington 1986 $10 (10/15/89)
73   STE. CHAPELLE Merlot Washington 1987 $10 (9/30/90)
81   STE. CHAPELLE Merlot Washington Dionysus Vineyard 1986 $12 (5/31/88)
91   SNOQUALMIE Merlot Columbia Valley Reserve 1987 $12 (9/30/90)
76   STATON HILLS Merlot Washington 1987 $12 (10/15/89)
86   STONE CREEK Merlot Columbia Valley 1989 $7 (5/31/91) BB
78   STONE CREEK Merlot Columbia Valley 1988 $6 (9/30/90)
89   PAUL THOMAS Merlot Washington 1987 $16 (9/30/90)

RIESLING

88   ARBOR CREST Johannisberg Riesling Washington 1984 $6.50 (9/01/85)
80   ARBOR CREST Johannisberg Riesling Washington Stewart's Sunnyside Vineyard Select Late Harvest 1982 $7.15 (3/16/84)
88   BARNARD GRIFFIN Johannisberg Riesling Columbia Valley 1987 $6.50 (10/15/89) BB
66   BLACKWOOD CANYON White Riesling Columbia Valley Claar Vineyard Dry 1987 $9 (10/15/89)
74   BONAIR Johannisberg Riesling Yakima Valley 1987 $5.50 (10/15/89)
75   CASCADE CREST Johannisberg Riesling Yakima Valley 1987 $6 (10/15/89)
85   CHATEAU STE. MICHELLE Johannisberg Riesling Columbia Valley 1988 $6.50 (10/15/89)
85   CHATEAU STE. MICHELLE Riesling Columbia Valley Dry River Ridge Vineyard 1990 $7 (6/15/91) BB
78   CHATEAU STE. MICHELLE White Riesling Columbia Valley Sweet Select 1988 $7 (10/15/89)
82   CHATEAU STE. MICHELLE Johannisberg Riesling Washington 1987 $6 (4/15/89)
75   CHATEAU STE. MICHELLE Johannisberg Riesling Washington 1986 $5.50 (11/15/87)
74   CHATEAU STE. MICHELLE Riesling Washington Reserve Hahn Hill Vineyards Hand-Selected 1984 $14 (12/15/87)
73   COLUMBIA Johannisberg Riesling Columbia Valley Cellarmaster's Reserve 1987 $7 (5/31/88)
87   COLUMBIA Johannisberg Riesling Washington 1986 $6 (5/15/87)
70   COLUMBIA CREST Johannisberg Riesling Columbia Valley 1986 $6 (10/15/89)
80   COLUMBIA CREST Johannisberg Riesling Columbia Valley 1986 $6 (11/15/87)
79   COVEY RUN Johannisberg Riesling Washington 1988 $5.50 (10/15/89)
88   COVEY RUN Johannisberg Riesling Yakima Valley 1989 $7 (8/31/90) BB
84   COVEY RUN Johannisberg Riesling Yakima Valley 1986 $6 (11/15/87)
78   FACELLI Johannisberg Riesling Washington Dry 1988 $7.50 (10/15/89)
76   HAVILAND Riesling Washington 1983 $6 (10/01/84)
83   HOGUE Johannisberg Riesling Washington 1986 $6 (11/15/87)
80   HOGUE Riesling Washington Dry Schwartzman Vineyard Reserve 1989 $8.50 (6/15/91)
90   HOGUE Johannisberg Riesling Yakima Valley 1988 $6 (10/15/89) BB
60   HOGUE Johannisberg Riesling Yakima Valley 1985 $6 (5/15/87)
83   HOGUE Johannisberg Riesling Yakima Valley Classic 1987 $5.50 (7/15/88)
80   HOGUE Johannisberg Riesling Yakima Valley Dry Schwartzman Vineyard 1988 $6.50 (10/15/89)
84   HOGUE Johannisberg Riesling Yakima Valley Dry Schwartzman Vineyard 1988 $6.50 (10/15/89)
80   HOGUE Johannisberg Riesling Yakima Valley Dry Schwartzman Vineyard 1988 $6.50 (7/31/89)
79   HOGUE Riesling Yakima Valley Markin Vineyard 1984 $7 (1/01/86)
87   HOODSPORT Johannisberg Riesling Washington 1988 $6 (10/15/89) BB
74   KIONA White Riesling Columbia Valley 1988 $6 (10/15/89)
81   F.W. LANGGUTH Johannisberg Riesling Columbia Valley 1986 $6 (7/15/88)
87   F.W. LANGGUTH Johannisberg Riesling Columbia Valley Select Harvest 1983 $8 (10/01/84)
88   F.W. LANGGUTH Johannisberg Riesling Washington Anders Gyving Vineyard 1983 $7 (10/16/84)
82   LATAH CREEK Johannisberg Riesling Washington 1987 $5.50 (4/15/89) BB
83   LATAH CREEK Johannisberg Riesling Washington 1986 $5.50 (11/15/87)
65   NEUHARTH Johannisberg Riesling Washington 1987 $8.75 (10/15/89)
71   PRESTON WINE CELLARS Johannisberg Riesling Washington Preston Vineyard Hand Harvested 1987 $5.75 (10/15/89)
79   SALISHAN White Riesling Washington Dry 1988 $5 (10/15/89)
87   SILVER LAKE Riesling Columbia Valley Dry 1989 $6 (6/15/91) BB
80   SNOQUALMIE Johannisberg Riesling Columbia Valley 1988 $6 (10/15/89)
81   SNOQUALMIE Johannisberg Riesling Columbia Valley RS 1.9% 1988 $6 (10/15/89)
75   SNOQUALMIE Johannisberg Riesling Washington 1986 $6 (7/15/88)
68   STEWART White Riesling Columbia Valley 1988 $15/375ml (10/15/89)
72   STEWART White Riesling Columbia Valley 1988 $6.50 (10/15/89)
80   STEWART White Riesling Columbia Valley 1987 $6 (4/15/89)
85   PAUL THOMAS Johannisberg Riesling Washington 1988 $7 (10/15/89)
85   PAUL THOMAS Riesling Washington Dry 1988 $7 (10/15/89)
77   PAUL THOMAS Riesling Washington Dry 1987 $7 (7/31/89)
68   WHITE HERON Johannisberg Riesling Washington 1987 $5 (7/31/89)
85   WORDEN Johannisberg Riesling Washington Charbonneau Vineyards 1988 $6 (10/15/89)
85   WORDEN Johannisberg Riesling Washington Charbonneau Vineyards 1988 $6 (7/31/89)

SAUVIGNON BLANC

78   ARBOR CREST Sauvignon Blanc Columbia Valley 1986 $7.50 (11/15/87)
87   ARBOR CREST Sauvignon Blanc Columbia Valley 1985 $7.50 (8/31/86)
85   ARBOR CREST Sauvignon Blanc Columbia Valley Wahluke Slope 1987 $7.50 (10/15/89)
95   ARBOR CREST Sauvignon Blanc Washington 1984 $7.50 (11/16/85)
75   BARNARD GRIFFIN Washington Barrel Fermented 1987 $9 (10/15/89)
78   CHATEAU STE. MICHELLE Sauvignon Blanc Columbia Valley 1988 $7 (12/31/90)
89   CHINOOK Sauvignon Blanc Washington 1987 $8.25 (10/15/89)

82   COLUMBIA CREST Sauvignon Blanc Columbia Valley 1986 $7 (10/15/89)
80   COVEY RUN Washington 1988 $8 (10/15/89)
88   HOGUE Washington 1988 $8 (10/15/89)
78   PRESTON Washington Oak Aged 1989 $7 (7/15/91)
68   QUARRY LAKE Sauvignon Blanc Washington 1987 $7.50 (10/15/89)
86   SADDLE MOUNTAIN Columbia Valley 1988 $5 (10/15/89) BB
88   SNOQUALMIE Columbia Valley 1987 $7 (10/15/89) BB
71   STATON HILLS Sauvignon Blanc Washington 1987 $8 (10/15/89)
78   STEWART Sauvignon Blanc Yakima Valley 1988 $8 (10/15/89)
76   TAGARIS Washington 1988 $8 (10/15/89)
85   PAUL THOMAS Sauvignon Blanc Washington 1987 $9 (10/15/89)
85   WATERBROOK Sauvignon Blanc Washington 1987 $9 (10/15/89)
73   WORDEN Washington 1987 $7 (10/15/89)

SÉMILLON

83   BLACKWOOD CANYON Sémillon Yakima Valley Barrel Fermented 1987 $9 (10/15/89)
87   CASCADE CREST Sémillon Yakima Valley Blanc 1987 $5.50 (10/15/89) BB
84   COLUMBIA Sémillon Columbia Valley 1988 $6 (10/15/89) BB
78   COLUMBIA CREST Sémillon Columbia Valley 1986 $5.75 (10/15/89)
82   FACELLI Sémillon Washington 1988 $8 (10/15/89)
72   HOGUE Sémillon Washington Reserve 1986 $8 (10/15/89)
79   LATAH CREEK Sémillon Washington 1986 $6 (10/15/89)
67   PORTTEUS Sémillon Yakima Valley 1987 $7 (10/15/89)
74   SNOQUALMIE Sémillon Columbia Valley 1988 $6 (10/15/89)

SPARKLING

85   DOMAINE STE. MICHELLE Columbia Valley Blanc de Blanc 1986 $15 (12/31/90)
86   DOMAINE STE. MICHELLE Columbia Valley Blanc de Noir 1985 $20 (12/31/90)
78   DOMAINE STE. MICHELLE Columbia Valley Brut NV $13 (12/31/90)
78   DOMAINE STE. MICHELLE Columbia Valley Brut NV $13 (10/15/89)
82   HOGUE Yakima Valley Brut NV $12 (10/15/89)
77   STATON HILLS Washington Blanc de Noir NV $16 (10/15/89)
80   STE. CHAPELLE Washington Brut Chardonnay Champagne NV $9 (3/15/88)
76   STE. CHAPELLE Washington Sec Johannisberg Riesling Champagne NV $7 (3/15/88)

OTHER WASHINGTON RED

83   CAVATAPPI Washington Nebbiolo Maddalena Red Willow Vineyards 1988 $19 (6/15/91)
83   COLUMBIA Pinot Noir Washington Barrel-Fermented The Woodburne Collection 1987 $10 (3/31/91)
88   COLUMBIA Pinot Noir Washington The Woodburne Collection 1987 $10 (3/31/91)
71   COLUMBIA Pinot Noir Washington Yakima County 1981 $7 (9/01/84)
90   COLUMBIA Syrah Yakima Valley Red Willow Vineyard 1988 $25 (5/15/91)

OTHER WASHINGTON WHITE

84   BAINBRIDGE ISLAND Washington 1987 $6 (10/15/89)
77   BAINBRIDGE ISLAND Washington Dry 1987 $6 (10/15/89)
73   COLUMBIA CREST Columbia Valley Sémillon-Chardonnay 1989 $7 (7/15/91)
81   LATAH CREEK Muscat Washington 1987 $6 (10/15/89)
63   MOUNT BAKER Washington 1988 $6 (10/15/89)

OTHER UNITED STATES/AMERICAN

82   BEL ARBORS Cabernet Sauvignon American Founder's Selection NV $5 (10/15/89) BB
81   BEL ARBORS Chardonnay American Founder's Selection NV $5 (10/31/89) BB
72   BEL ARBORS Merlot American Founder's Selection American Grown NV $5 (6/15/90)
81   BEL ARBORS Sauvignon Blanc American Founder's Selection NV $5 (10/15/89) BB
75   COOK'S Brut American Imperial Grand Reserve Extremely Dry NV $6 (12/31/87)
72   COOK'S Sparkling Rosé Blush NV $4 (10/15/88)
77   GOLD SEAL Blanc de Blanc American Charles Fournier Special Selection NV $10 (6/30/90)
82   GRAYSON White Zinfandel American NV $4 (6/15/89)
70   GREAT WESTERN Blanc de Noirs American NV $14 (3/31/90)
83   PRINCE MICHEL Red Le Ducq Lot 87 NV $50 (6/30/90)

IDAHO

83   STE. CHAPELLE Chardonnay Idaho 1988 $10 (12/15/90)
74   STE. CHAPELLE Chardonnay Idaho 1986 $10 (4/30/88)
62   STE. CHAPELLE Chardonnay Idaho Canyon 1985 $7 (4/30/88)
83   STE. CHAPELLE Chardonnay Idaho Reserve 1988 $15 (3/31/91)
83   STE. CHAPELLE Chardonnay Idaho Symms Family Vineyard 1983 $10 (10/01/85)
83   STE. CHAPELLE Chardonnay Idaho Symms Family Vineyard 1982 $10 (4/16/86)
87   STE. CHAPELLE Chardonnay Idaho Symms Family Vineyard 1982 $10 (1/01/85)
79   STE. CHAPELLE Johannisberg Riesling Late Harvest Idaho Botrytis 1986 $15 (2/15/88)
81   STE. CHAPELLE Johannisberg Riesling Idaho 1989 $6 (12/15/90) BB
88   STE. CHAPELLE Johannisberg Riesling Idaho 1988 $6 (7/31/89) BB
79   STE. CHAPELLE Johannisberg Riesling Idaho 1987 $6 (10/15/88)
81   STE. CHAPELLE Riesling Idaho Special Harvest Winery Block 1986 $10 (7/31/87)

NEW ENGLAND

77   CROSSWOODS Chardonnay Southeastern New England 1986 $15 (10/31/89)

NEW MEXICO

80   ANDERSON VALLEY Cabernet Sauvignon New Mexico 1986 $11 (7/31/89)
79   ANDERSON VALLEY Chardonnay New Mexico Barrel Fermented 1987 $8.50 (4/15/89)
70   ANDERSON VALLEY Chardonnay New Mexico Barrel Fermented 1986 $7 (3/15/88)
79   ANDERSON VALLEY Sauvignon Blanc New Mexico 1987 $7 (4/15/89)
77   DOMAINE CHEURLIN Brut New Mexico NV $12 (9/15/87)
80   DOMAINE CHEURLIN Extra Dry New Mexico NV $12 (9/15/87)
80   GRUET Brut Blanc de Noirs New Mexico NV $13 (3/31/90)
79   GRUET Brut New Mexico NV $13 (3/31/90)

TEXAS

78   FALL CREEK Cabernet Sauvignon Texas 1988 $13 (7/15/91)
83   FALL CREEK Sauvignon Blanc Texas 1989 $8.50 (7/15/91)
73   FALL CREEK Carnelian Llano County 1988 $13 (7/15/91)
82   LLANO ESTACADO Chenin Blanc Texas 1988 $6.50 (7/31/89)
86   MESSINA HOF Chenin Blanc Brazos Valley 1988 $7 (7/31/89)
79   MOYER Brut Natural Texas NV $11 (7/31/89)

VIRGINIA

87   PRINCE MICHEL Chardonnay Virginia Barrel Select 1988 $15 (6/30/90)
83   PRINCE MICHEL Virginia Le Ducq Lot 87 NV $50 (6/30/90)

SECTION C: WINES LISTED BY COUNTRY/TYPE/VINTAGE/SCORE

AUSTRALIA

CABERNET SAUVIGNON

1988

89 ROSEMOUNT Cabernet Sauvignon Coonawarra Show Reserve 1988 $16 (5/31/91)
87 CHATEAU TAHBILK Cabernet Sauvignon Goulburn Valley 1988 $12 (3/31/91)
86 CHATEAU REYNELLA Cabernet Sauvignon Coonawarra 1988 $8.50 (4/30/91)
86 MITCHELTON Cabernet Sauvignon Goulburn Valley 1988 $13 (4/15/91)
86 MARK SWANN Cabernet Sauvignon South Australia Proprietor's Reserve 1988 $5.50 (2/28/91) BB
83 HARDY'S Cabernet Sauvignon South Australia The Hardy Collection 1988 $10 (2/15/91)
83 ORLANDO Cabernet Sauvignon South Eastern Australia Jacob's Creek 1988 $7 (7/15/91) BB
82 SEPPELT Cabernet Sauvignon South Eastern Australia Reserve Bin 1988 $9 (7/15/91)
81 SEPPELT Cabernet Sauvignon Padthaway Black Label 1988 $12 (3/31/91)
78 HOUGHTON Cabernet Sauvignon Frankland River Wildflower Ridge 1988 $9 (7/15/91)
76 ROSEMOUNT Cabernet Sauvignon Hunter Valley 1988 $10 (1/31/90)

1987

89 CHATEAU TAHBILK Cabernet Sauvignon Goulburn Valley 1987 $11 (7/31/90)
88 ROSEMOUNT Cabernet Sauvignon Coonawarra Show Reserve 1987 $15 (2/28/91)
85 BLACK OPAL Cabernet Sauvignon South Eastern Australia 1987 $8 (2/28/90) BB
85 ORLANDO Cabernet Sauvignon South Eastern Australia Jacob's Creek 1987 $7 (7/31/90) BB
84 CAPE MENTELLE Cabernet Sauvignon Western Australia 1987 $18.50 (3/31/91)
84 COLDSTREAM HILLS Cabernet Sauvignon Lilydale 1987 $20 (1/31/90)
84 MARK SWANN Cabernet Sauvignon Coonawarra 1987 $7 (2/28/91) BB
83 BAROSSA VALLEY Cabernet Sauvignon South Australia 1987 $11 (1/31/90)
83 BROWN BROTHERS Cabernet Sauvignon Victoria Family Reserve 1987 $11.50 (9/15/90)
83 PENFOLDS Cabernet Sauvignon South Australia Bin 707 1987 $38 (5/31/91)
83 ROSEMOUNT Cabernet Sauvignon Hunter Valley 1987 $10 (7/31/89)
82 BROWN BROTHERS Cabernet Sauvignon Victoria Family Selection 1987 $9.50 (7/15/90)
81 HARDY'S Cabernet Sauvignon Coonawarra 1987 $10.50 (7/15/90)
81 MONTROSE Cabernet Sauvignon Mudgee 1987 $10 (2/28/91)
81 MARK SWANN Cabernet Sauvignon South Australia Proprietor's Reserve 1987 $5.50 (7/31/89) BB
80 PETER LEHMANN Cabernet Sauvignon Barossa Valley 1987 $8 (3/31/91)
78 ORLANDO Cabernet Sauvignon Coonawarra St.-Hugo 1987 $15 (5/31/91)
77 SEPPELT Cabernet Sauvignon South Eastern Australia Murray River 1987 $5 (4/15/88)

1986

93 ROSEMOUNT Cabernet Sauvignon Hunter Valley 1986 $11 (1/31/89) SS
91 HENSCHKE Cabernet Sauvignon Barossa Valley Cyril Henschke 1986 $23 (9/15/89)
90 MILDARA Cabernet Sauvignon Coonawarra 1986 $10 (1/31/89)
90 PENFOLDS Cabernet Sauvignon South Australia Bin 707 1986 $28 (9/30/89)
89 REDBANK Cabernet Sauvignon South Eastern Australia Redbank Cabernet 1986 $54 (1/31/90)
88 CHATEAU TAHBILK Cabernet Sauvignon Goulburn Valley 1986 $10 (3/31/89)
88 ROSEMOUNT Cabernet Sauvignon Coonawarra Kirri Billi Vineyard 1986 $19.50 (10/31/90)
88 SEAVIEW Cabernet Sauvignon South Australia 1986 $10 (7/31/90)
87 ORLANDO Cabernet Sauvignon South Eastern Australia Jacob's Creek 1986 $7 (5/15/89) BB
86 MONTROSE Cabernet Sauvignon Mudgee 1986 $8 (7/31/89)
85 PETER LEHMANN Cabernet Sauvignon Barossa Valley 1986 $9 (1/31/90)
85 ROO'S LEAP Cabernet Sauvignon McLaren Vale Limited Edition 1986 $9.50 (1/31/90)
83 CASSEGRAIN Cabernet Sauvignon Pokolbin 1986 $18 (3/31/91)
83 LINDEMANS Cabernet Sauvignon Coonawarra 1986 $14 (10/31/90)
81 ORLANDO Cabernet Sauvignon Coonawarra St.-Hugo 1986 $8 (2/28/91)
80 MILDARA Cabernet Sauvignon Murray River Valley 1986 $8 (1/31/89)
79 HARDY'S Cabernet Sauvignon Keppoch 1986 $7.50 (7/15/90)
78 MARK SWANN Cabernet Sauvignon South Australia Proprietor's Reserve 1986 $5 (10/31/88)
76 HARDY'S Cabernet Sauvignon McLaren Vale The Hardy Collection No. Eight 1986 $10.50 (1/31/89)
74 REDBANK Cabernet Sauvignon South Eastern Australia Long Paddock 1986 $13 (1/31/90)
73 LONGLEAT Cabernet Sauvignon Goulburn Valley Revi Resco 1986 $9 (9/30/89)
73 MITCHELTON Cabernet Sauvignon Goulburn Valley 1986 $13 (1/31/90)

1985

90 HENSCHKE Cabernet Sauvignon Barossa Valley Cyril Henschke 1985 $21 (1/31/89)
90 ORLANDO Cabernet Sauvignon Coonawarra St.-Hugo 1985 $15 (4/30/89)
89 MILDARA Cabernet Sauvignon Coonawarra 1985 $8 (4/15/88) BB
89 ROO'S LEAP Cabernet Sauvignon McLaren Vale 1985 $10 (11/30/88)
88 MARK SWANN Cabernet Sauvignon Coonawarra 1985 $7 (10/31/88) BB
86 LINDEMANS Cabernet Sauvignon Coonawarra 1985 $14 (4/30/89)
85 MILDARA Cabernet Sauvignon McLaren Vale Private Reserve 1985 $13 (1/31/89)
85 ROSEMOUNT Cabernet Sauvignon Hunter Valley 1985 $9 (1/31/88)
84 KOALA RIDGE Cabernet Sauvignon Barossa Valley 1985 $9 (1/31/89)
82 ROSEMOUNT Cabernet Sauvignon Coonawarra Show Reserve 1985 $14 (1/31/89)
81 BLACK OPAL Cabernet Sauvignon Hunter Valley 1985 $8 (7/15/88) BB
81 HARDY'S Cabernet Sauvignon Keppoch Bird Series 1985 $6 (9/30/88) BB
80 HARDY'S Cabernet Sauvignon Keppoch 1985 $7.25 (10/31/88)
80 LINDEMANS Cabernet Sauvignon Coonawarra St.-George Vineyard 1985 $21 (4/30/89)
80 MONTROSE Cabernet Sauvignon Mudgee Special Reserve 1985 $16 (1/31/90)
79 LINDEMANS Cabernet Sauvignon South Australia Bin 45 1985 $6 (1/31/88)
79 SALTRAM Cabernet Sauvignon Hazelwood 1985 $8.50 (7/31/89)
76 BERRI Cabernet Sauvignon Barossa Valley 1985 $7 (4/30/88)
76 BROWN BROTHERS Cabernet Sauvignon Victoria Family Selection 1985 $7.50 (5/15/89)
75 HARDY'S Cabernet Sauvignon McLaren Vale Captain's Selection 1985 $4.50 (7/15/88)
74 REDBANK Cabernet Sauvignon South Eastern Australia Long Paddock 1985 $7 (7/15/91)
64 SEPPELT Cabernet Sauvignon South Eastern Australia Black Label 1985 $11 (4/30/88)

1984

94 HENSCHKE Cabernet Sauvignon Barossa Valley Cyril Henschke 1984 $18.50 (12/15/87)
91 PETALUMA Cabernet Sauvignon Coonawarra 1984 $18 (5/31/87)
88 LINDEMANS Cabernet Sauvignon Coonawarra St.-George Vineyard 1984 $15 (1/31/88)
88 MONTROSE Cabernet Sauvignon Mudgee 1984 $10 (4/30/88)
88 TYRRELL'S Cabernet Sauvignon Hunter Valley Classic 1984 $7 (9/15/90) BB
86 BROWN BROTHERS Cabernet Sauvignon Victoria St.-George Vineyard 1984 $8 (5/31/87)
86 ROSEMOUNT Cabernet Sauvignon Coonawarra Show Reserve 1984 $13.50 (2/28/87)
85 TALTARNI Cabernet Sauvignon Victoria 1984 $9.25 (11/15/87)
84 LINDEMANS Cabernet Sauvignon Coonawarra 1984 $12 (2/15/88)
84 ROUGE HOMME Cabernet Sauvignon Coonawarra 1984 $12 (2/15/88)
84 ST.-HUBERTS Cabernet Sauvignon Yarra Valley 1984 $13 (11/15/87)
84 WIRRA WIRRA Cabernet Sauvignon McLaren Vale 1984 $14 (1/31/88)
81 CHATEAU TAHBILK Cabernet Sauvignon Goulburn Valley 1984 $7.50 (11/15/87)
80 CHATEAU REYNELLA Cabernet Sauvignon Coonawarra 1984 $7.50 (4/30/88)
79 CLYDE PARK Cabernet Sauvignon Geelong 1984 $15 (3/15/88)
79 HUNGERFORD HILL Cabernet Sauvignon Coonawarra 1984 $11 (3/15/88)
78 WOLF BLASS Cabernet Sauvignon South Australia Yellow Label 1984 $10 (4/30/89)
78 ROSEMOUNT Cabernet Sauvignon Hunter Valley 1984 $9.50 (4/30/87)
77 MILDARA Cabernet Sauvignon Coonawarra 1984 $6.50 (4/30/87)
77 MARK SWANN Cabernet Sauvignon Coonawarra 1984 $8 (8/31/87)
75 HILL-SMITH Cabernet Sauvignon Barossa Valley 1984 $9.50 (8/31/87)
73 GRANTS Cabernet Sauvignon Barossa Valley 1984 $8 (11/15/87)
73 YARRA YERING Cabernet Sauvignon Coldstream Dry Red Wine No. 1 1984 $14 (5/31/88)
68 VIRGIN HILLS Cabernet Sauvignon Bendigo 1984 $17 (4/30/88)

1983

87 TYRRELL'S Cabernet Sauvignon Hunter Valley Premier Selection 1983 $8 (4/30/88) BB
86 WOLF BLASS Cabernet Sauvignon South Australia Yellow Label 1983 $9 (12/15/87)
86 LEEUWIN Cabernet Sauvignon Margaret River 1983 $18 (5/31/88)
82 WYNDHAM Cabernet Sauvignon Hunter Valley Bin 444 1983 $6.50 (7/15/88) BB
81 PETER LEHMANN Cabernet Sauvignon Barossa Valley 1983 $9 (7/01/87)
76 WOLF BLASS Cabernet Sauvignon South Australia President's Selection 1983 $13.50 (4/30/88)
76 DENMAN Cabernet Sauvignon Hunter Valley 1983 $5 (11/15/87)

1982

90 WYNNS Cabernet Sauvignon Coonawarra 1982 $15 (11/30/88)
89 BLUE PYRENEES Cabernet Sauvignon Australia 1982 $20 (5/31/87)
84 TALTARNI Cabernet Sauvignon Victoria 1982 $9.25 (4/30/87)
83 LEASINGHAM Cabernet Sauvignon Australia Bin 49 Winemakers Selection 1982 $7.25 (11/15/87)
79 LINDEMANS Cabernet Sauvignon Coonawarra 1982 $8 (9/30/86)
78 SEPPELT Cabernet Sauvignon South Eastern Australia Black Label 1982 $12.50 (4/01/86)
78 MARK SWANN Cabernet Sauvignon Coonawarra 1982 $7.50 (3/16/84)

1981

90 PENFOLDS Cabernet Sauvignon South Australia Bin 707 1981 $18 (7/01/87)
82 HILL-SMITH Cabernet Sauvignon Barossa Valley 1981 $9.50 (7/16/86)
80 TALTARNI Cabernet Sauvignon Victoria 1981 $7.50 (5/16/85)

1980

84 CHATEAU REYNELLA Cabernet Sauvignon Coonawarra 1980 $15 (5/31/87)
81 TALTARNI Cabernet Sauvignon Victoria 1980 $6.75 (3/01/84)

1979

79 LEEUWIN Cabernet Sauvignon Margaret River 1979 $20 (9/15/89)

NV

88 LINDEMANS Cabernet Sauvignon Coonawarra St.-George Vineyard NV $15 (5/31/87)

CABERNET BLENDS

1990

84 ROSEMOUNT Shiraz Cabernet Sauvignon South Eastern Australia 1990 $7 (7/15/91) BB

1989

81 ROSEMOUNT Cabernet Shiraz South Eastern Australia 1989 $6 (7/31/90) BB

1988

84 TYRRELL'S Cabernet Merlot Australia Old Winery 1988 $7.50 (3/31/91) BB
75 JOHNSTONE Cabernet Shiraz Hunter Valley 1988 $6.50 (7/15/91)
73 OXFORD LANDING Cabernet Sauvignon Shiraz South Australia 1988 $7 (9/15/90)

1987

91 WYNDHAM Cabernet Shiraz Hunter Valley 1987 $7 (1/31/90) BB
88 PENFOLDS Cabernet Shiraz South Australia Bin 389 1987 $14 (2/28/91)
86 MITCHELTON Cabernet Shiraz Merlot Victoria 1987 $9 (1/31/90)
86 PENFOLDS Cabernet Sauvignon Shiraz South Australia Koonunga Hill 1987 $7.50 (2/28/91) BB
84 SEAVIEW Cabernet Shiraz South Australia 1987 $8 (7/31/90)
79 TYRRELL'S Cabernet Sauvignon Merlot Hunter Valley 1987 $7 (9/15/90)

1986

88 TYRRELL'S Cabernet Sauvignon Merlot Hunter Valley 1986 $8 (1/31/90) BB
87 PETALUMA Cabernet Sauvignon Merlot Coonawarra 1986 $25 (5/31/91)
87 WYNDHAM Cabernet Shiraz Hunter Valley 1986 $6.50 (12/31/88) BB
86 REDBANK Cabernet Blend South Eastern Australia Sally's Paddock 1986 $32 (1/31/90)
84 LINDEMANS Shiraz Cabernet Coonawarra Limestone Ridge Vineyard 1986 $24 (7/31/90)
83 GOVERNOR PHILLIP Cabernet Sauvignon Shiraz Barossa Valley 1986 $6 (7/31/89) BB
83 PENFOLDS Cabernet Shiraz South Australia Bin 389 1986 $15 (1/31/90)
82 SEPPELT Cabernet Shiraz South Eastern Australia 1986 $8 (1/31/90)
80 BERRI Shiraz Cabernet South Australia Vintage Selection 1986 $9.50 (3/15/88)
80 MILDARA Cabernet Merlot Murray River Valley 1986 $7.50 (3/31/89)
78 PETER LEHMANN Cabernet Blend Barossa Valley 1986 $8 (2/28/91)
78 LINDEMANS Cabernet Blend Coonawarra Pyrus 1986 $24 (7/31/90)
78 PENFOLDS Cabernet Sauvignon Shiraz South Australia Koonunga Hill 1986 $7.50 (5/15/89)

1985

89 BERRI Cabernet Shiraz Australia 1985 $10 (7/01/87)
89 WIRRA WIRRA Cabernet Shiraz Merlot McLaren Vale Church Block 1985 $11 (3/15/88)
88 HOUGHTON Cabernet Shiraz McLaren Vale Wildflower Ridge 1985 $9 (12/31/88)
87 CULLENS Cabernet Merlot Margaret River 1985 $15 (11/15/87)
87 LINDEMANS Cabernet Blend Coonawarra Pyrus 1985 $20 (5/31/88)
87 WYNDHAM Cabernet Shiraz Hunter Valley 1985 $6.50 (3/15/88) BB
86 BAROSSA VALLEY Shiraz Cabernet Sauvignon Barossa Valley 1985 $8 (9/30/89) BB
86 PENFOLDS Cabernet Shiraz South Australia Bin 389 1985 $14 (12/31/88)
84 TYRRELL'S Cabernet Merlot Hunter Valley 1985 $9 (7/31/89)
83 PETER LEHMANN Shiraz Cabernet Sauvignon Barossa Valley 1985 $7 (1/31/90)
80 HUNGERFORD HILL Cabernet Merlot Hunter Valley 1985 $10 (2/28/90)
80 HUNGERFORD HILL Cabernet Merlot Hunter Valley 1985 $10 (2/28/90) (JL)
80 JUD'S HILL Cabernet Sauvignon Merlot Australia 1985 $13 (4/30/88)
80 LAKE'S FOLLY Cabernet Hunter Valley 1985 $15.50 (3/31/89)
80 MILDARA Cabernet Sauvignon Merlot Coonawarra 1985 $5.50 (1/31/88) BB
79 HENSCHKE Cabernet Blend Barossa Valley Keyneton Estate 1985 $11.50 (3/31/89)
78 MITCHELTON Cabernet Sauvignon Merlot Australia Print Label 1985 $17 (1/31/90)

AUSTRALIA
CABERNET BLENDS

78   STANLEY Shiraz Cabernet Sauvignon Coonawarra Private Reserve 1985 $4 (12/15/87)
72   HOLLICK Cabernet Merlot Coonawarra 1985 $16 (5/31/88)
68   LINDEMANS Shiraz Cabernet Coonawarra Limestone Ridge Vineyard 1985 $21 (7/31/89)
67   YALUMBA Cabernet Shiraz Coonawarra 1985 $6.50 (9/30/89)

1984

92   PETALUMA Cabernet Merlot Coonawarra 1984 $18 (5/31/87)
89   KRONDORF Cabernet Sauvignon Franc McLaren Vale 1984 $9 (4/15/87) BB
89   PENFOLDS Cabernet Shiraz South Australia Koonunga Hill 1984 $7 (7/01/87)
89   SALTRAM Cabernet Sauvignon Shiraz Barossa Valley 1984 $12 (1/31/90)
87   LINDEMANS Cabernet Shiraz Coonawarra Limestone Ridge 1984 $15 (7/01/87)
86   ELDERTON Cabernet Sauvignon Merlot Barossa Valley 1984 $11 (4/30/88)
85   HENSCHKE Cabernet Blend Barossa Valley Keyneton Estate 1984 $12 (2/15/88)
84   LEASINGHAM Cabernet Malbec Australia Bin 56 Winemakers Selection 1984 $7.25 (11/15/87)
82   MILDARA Cabernet Sauvignon Merlot Coonawarra 1984 $5 (6/15/87) BB
82   TYRRELL'S Cabernet Sauvignon Merlot Hunter Valley 1984 $9 (7/15/88)
81   LEASINGHAM Shiraz Cabernet Malbec Australia Hutt Creek Claret 1984 $4 (9/30/87) BB
79   WYNNS Cabernet Hermitage Coonawarra 1984 $10 (12/31/88)
78   YALUMBA Cabernet Sauvignon Shiraz Coonawarra 1984 $6 (1/31/88)
76   HARDY'S Cabernet Malbec Reynella McLaren Vale Hardy Collection No. 9 1984 $6.50 (7/15/88)

1983

91   PENFOLDS Cabernet Shiraz South Australia Bin 389 1983 $15 (7/01/87)
87   WOLF BLASS Cabernet Shiraz Australia Yellow Label 1983 $3 (7/01/87)
87   BROWN BROTHERS Shiraz Mondeuse Cabernet Sauvignon Australia 1983 $10 (7/01/87)
84   TYRRELL'S Cabernet Merlot New South Wales Victoria 1983 $8 (3/15/88)
79   LEASINGHAM Cabernet Shiraz Australia Bin 68 1983 $5.25 (11/15/87)
77   WOLF BLASS Cabernet Merlot South Australia Black Label 1983 $25 (4/30/89)

1982

89   PETALUMA Cabernet Shiraz Coonawarra 1982 $16 (7/01/87)
88   WOLF BLASS Cabernet Shiraz Clare Barossa Valleys Black Label 1982 $25 (4/15/88)
70   LINDEMANS Shiraz Cabernet Coonawarra Limestone Ridge Lindemans Classic 1982 $38 (7/31/90)

1981

90   WOLF BLASS Cabernet Shiraz Langhorne Creek 1981 $18 (7/01/87)

1980

89   WOLF BLASS Cabernet Shiraz Australia Black Label 1980 $18 (7/01/87)

CHARDONNAY

1990

88   ROSEMOUNT Chardonnay Hunter Valley Matured in Oak Casks 1990 $9 (5/15/91)
85   LINDEMANS Chardonnay South Eastern Australia Bin 65 1990 $7 (2/28/91) BB
85   OXFORD LANDING Chardonnay South Australia 1990 $7 (2/28/91) BB
84   ORLANDO Chardonnay South Eastern Australia Jacob's Creek 1990 $7 (5/15/91) BB

1989

92   ROSEMOUNT Chardonnay Hunter Valley Show Reserve 1989 $16 (5/31/91)
90   MOUNTADAM Chardonnay Eden Valley 1989 $25 (3/31/91)
89   CASSEGRAIN Chardonnay Hastings Valley Fromenteau Vineyard 1989 $25 (3/31/91)
89   SEPPELT Chardonnay Barooga Padthaway Black Label 1989 $14 (3/31/91)
88   SEPPELT Chardonnay South Eastern Australia Reserve Bin 1989 $10 (7/31/90)
87   CASSEGRAIN Chardonnay South Eastern Australia 1989 $14.50 (3/31/91)
86   PIPERS BROOK Chardonnay Tasmania 1989 $25 (3/31/91)
85   KOALA RIDGE Chardonnay Barossa Valley 1989 $9 (5/31/91)
85   LINDEMANS Chardonnay South Eastern Australia Bin 65 1989 $6 (4/30/90) BB
85   MONTROSE Chardonnay Mudgee 1989 $10 (2/28/91)
85   WYNDHAM Chardonnay Hunter Valley 1989 $11.50 (5/15/91)
84   MITCHELTON Chardonnay Goulburn Valley Wood Matured Reserve 1989 $15 (3/31/91)
84   ROTHBURY Chardonnay Hunter Valley Brokenback Vineyard 1989 $9 (10/15/90)
84   TYRRELL'S Chardonnay Hunter Valley 1989 $7 (10/15/90) BB
83   LEASINGHAM Chardonnay Clare Valley Domaine 1989 $8.50 (10/15/90)
83   MONTROSE Chardonnay South Eastern Australia Bin 747 1989 $8 (2/28/91) BB
83   RICHMOND GROVE Chardonnay Hunter Valley French Cask 1989 $7 (5/15/91) BB
82   OXFORD LANDING Chardonnay South Australia 1989 $7 (10/15/90) BB
80   CAPE MENTELLE Chardonnay Margaret River 1989 $20 (3/31/91)
80   MITCHELTON Chardonnay Victoria 1989 $8 (4/15/91)
80   ROSEMOUNT Chardonnay Hunter Valley Matured in Oak Casks 1989 $9 (4/30/90)
79   MARK SWANN Chardonnay Barossa Valley 1989 $7 (2/28/91)
78   MARK SWANN Chardonnay Victoria Proprietor's Reserve 1989 $7 (5/31/91)
76   ORLANDO Chardonnay South Eastern Australia Jacob's Creek 1989 $7 (6/15/90)
75   MILDARA Chardonnay Barossa Valley 1989 $7.50 (2/28/91)
70   TYRRELL'S Chardonnay Hunter Valley Vat 47 Pinot Chardonnay 1989 $13 (10/15/90)

1988

92   TARRA WARRA Chardonnay Yarra Glen 1988 $25 (12/31/90)
90   MITCHELTON Chardonnay Goulburn Valley Reserve 1988 $14 (3/15/90)
89   ROTHBURY Chardonnay Hunter Valley Brokenback Vineyard 1988 $10 (3/15/89)

87   LINDEMANS Chardonnay South Eastern Australia Bin 65 1988 $6 (5/15/89) BB
86   PIPERS BROOK Chardonnay Tasmania 1988 $25 (3/31/91)
85   CHATEAU REYNELLA Chardonnay McLaren Vale 1988 $9 (7/31/90)
85   ROSEMOUNT Chardonnay Hunter Valley Show Reserve 1988 $16 (3/15/90)
85   ROTHBURY Chardonnay Hunter Valley Reserve 1988 $18.50 (10/15/90)
84   MONTROSE Chardonnay Mudgee 1988 $9 (6/15/90)
83   PENFOLDS Chardonnay South Australia 1988 $9.50 (1/31/90)
83   WYNDHAM Chardonnay Hunter Valley Bin 222 1988 $7 (1/31/90)
82   HARDY'S Chardonnay Sunraysia 1988 $7 (7/31/90) BB
82   ROSEMOUNT Chardonnay Hunter Valley Matured in Oak Casks 1988 $10 (3/15/90)
81   BAROSSA VALLEY Chardonnay South Australia 1988 $11 (3/15/90)
81   PETER LEHMANN Chardonnay Barossa Valley 1988 $11 (7/31/89)
81   LINDEMANS Chardonnay Padthaway 1988 $15 (7/31/89)
80   BROWN BROTHERS Chardonnay King Valley Family Selection 1988 $11.50 (7/15/90)
80   HARDY'S Chardonnay Padthaway Clare Valley The Hardy Collection 1988 $10.50 (7/15/90)
80   ORLANDO Chardonnay South Eastern Australia Jacob's Creek 1988 $7 (1/31/90)
79   MITCHELTON Chardonnay Victoria 1988 $10 (3/15/90)
77   TYRRELL'S Chardonnay Hunter Valley Vat 47 Pinot Chardonnay 1988 $16 (7/31/89)
71   SEAVIEW Chardonnay South Australia 1988 $10 (7/15/90)
68   TYRRELL'S Chardonnay Hunter Valley 1988 $9 (7/31/89)

1987

92   ROSEMOUNT Chardonnay Hunter Valley Show Reserve 1987 $16.50 (2/15/89)
91   BROWN BROTHERS Chardonnay King Valley Family Reserve 1987 $15.50 (7/15/90) SS
89   ROTHBURY Chardonnay Hunter Valley Reserve 1987 $19 (2/15/89)
88   MILDARA Chardonnay Barossa Valley 1987 $12 (12/31/88)
88   PETALUMA Chardonnay Australia 1987 $21 (5/31/91)
88   RIDDOCH Chardonnay Victoria 1987 $9 (10/15/90)
88   ROO'S LEAP Chardonnay Hunter Valley Barrel Fermented 1987 $10 (2/15/89)
88   ROTHBURY Chardonnay Hunter Valley Brokenback Vineyard 1987 $7.50 (2/15/88)
87   COLDSTREAM HILLS Chardonnay Lilydale Three Vineyards Blend 1987 $20 (1/31/90)
87   COLDSTREAM HILLS Chardonnay Lilydale Yarra Ridge Vineyard 1987 $19 (10/15/90)
87   ROSEMOUNT Chardonnay Hunter Valley Matured in Oak Casks 1987 $10.50 (3/15/89)
85   BLACK OPAL Chardonnay Hunter Valley 1987 $9 (7/31/89)
85   YALUMBA Chardonnay Barossa Valley 1987 $8 (3/15/89)
84   BROWN BROTHERS Chardonnay King Valley 1987 $11 (7/31/89)
84   WYNNS Chardonnay Coonawarra 1987 $16 (12/31/88)
83   HEGGIES Chardonnay Barossa Valley 1987 $14 (1/31/90)
83   LINDEMANS Chardonnay Victoria Bin 65 1987 $6 (2/15/88) BB
83   ORLANDO Chardonnay South Eastern Australia Jacob's Creek 1987 $6.50 (3/15/89) BB
82   WOLF BLASS Chardonnay South Australia Premiére Release 1987 $9 (4/15/89)
82   CHATEAU REYNELLA Chardonnay McLaren Vale 1987 $11.50 (12/31/88)
82   SALTRAM Chardonnay Hazelwood 1987 $8.50 (7/31/89)
82   SALTRAM Chardonnay McLaren Vale Hunter Valley Mamre Brook 1987 $12 (7/31/89)
80   KOALA RIDGE Chardonnay Barossa Valley 1987 $7 (3/15/90)
80   PENFOLDS Chardonnay South Australia 1987 $8 (2/15/89)
80   ROSEMOUNT Chardonnay Hunter Valley Giants Creek Vineyard 1987 $20 (3/15/89)
80   SEPPELT Chardonnay South Eastern Australia Reserve Bin 1987 $9 (5/31/88)
79   MILDARA Chardonnay Merbian Church Hill 1987 $5.50 (2/15/88)
79   SEPPELT Chardonnay Barooga Padthaway Black Label Great Western Vineyards 1987 $15 (7/31/89)
79   MARK SWANN Chardonnay South Australia Proprietor's Reserve 1987 $5 (2/15/89)
78   MONTROSE Chardonnay Mudgee 1987 $8 (7/31/89)
78   WOODLEY Chardonnay South Eastern Australia Queen Adelaide 1987 $8 (5/31/88)
75   HARDY'S Chardonnay South Eastern Australia Bird Series 1987 $6 (5/31/88)
74   BALGOWNIE Chardonnay Coonawarra Series One Premier Cuvée 1987 $6.50 (9/30/88)
73   PEACOCK HILL Chardonnay Hunter Valley 1987 $11 (5/31/88)
72   LEO BURNING Chardonnay South Australia 1987 $7 (5/31/88)
72   HARDY'S Chardonnay Padthaway Hardy Collection No. 1 1987 $7 (5/31/88)
71   WYNDHAM Chardonnay Hunter Valley 1987 $7.75 (1/31/90)
70   MILDARA Chardonnay Murray River Valley 1987 $8 (2/15/89)
69   HARDY'S Chardonnay Padthaway Hardy Collection No. 1 1987 $11.50 (2/15/89)
69   HARDY'S Chardonnay South Eastern Australia 1987 $7.50 (7/15/90)
69   HOUGHTON Chardonnay Western Australia Gold Reserve 1987 $10 (10/31/90)

1986

91   MONTROSE Chardonnay Australia Show Reserve 1986 $14 (5/31/87)
91   ROSEMOUNT Chardonnay Hunter Valley Roxburgh 1986 $25 (5/31/87)
90   CLYDE PARK Chardonnay Geelong 1986 $15 (2/15/88)
90   PETALUMA Chardonnay Australia 1986 $18 (5/31/87)
90   ROSEMOUNT Chardonnay Hunter Valley Show Reserve 1986 $16 (12/31/87)
90   ROTHBURY Chardonnay Hunter Valley Brokenback Vineyard 1986 $9.50 (5/31/87)
89   BERRI Chardonnay Barossa Valley 1986 $12 (5/31/87)
89   BERRI Chardonnay South Australia Vintage Selection 1986 $7.75 (2/15/88)
88   EVANS FAMILY Chardonnay Hunter Valley Vintage Selection 1986 $14 (2/15/88)
87   KRONDORF Chardonnay Barossa Valley 1986 $8 (3/31/87) BB
87   LINDEMANS Chardonnay Padthaway 1986 $12 (12/31/87)
87   MONTROSE Chardonnay Mudgee Stoney Creek Vineyard Special Reserve 1986 $13 (3/15/90)
87   ROSEMOUNT Chardonnay Hunter Valley Matured in Oak Casks 1986 $9 (5/31/88)
87   SEPPELT Chardonnay South Eastern Australia Reserve Bin 1986 $8 (2/15/88)
86   HOLLICK Chardonnay Coonawarra 1986 $16 (5/15/88)
86   HUNGERFORD HILL Chardonnay Hunter Valley 1986 $12 (2/15/88)
85   TYRRELL'S Chardonnay Hunter Valley Vat 47 Pinot Chardonnay 1986 $12 (5/15/88)
84   KOALA RIDGE Chardonnay Barossa Valley 1986 $8 (2/15/89)
83   ROTHBURY Chardonnay Hunter Valley Reserve 1986 $15 (2/15/88)
82   MILDARA Chardonnay Merbian Church Hill 1986 $5 (6/15/87) BB
82   TYRRELL'S Chardonnay Hunter Valley 1986 $7.50 (5/15/88)
81   WOLF BLASS Chardonnay South Australia Premiére Release 1986 $10 (5/15/88)
81   MONTROSE Chardonnay Mudgee 1986 $10 (2/15/88)
80   ANDREW GARRETT Chardonnay South Australia 1986 $9.75 (12/31/87)
79   BLACK OPAL Chardonnay Hunter Valley 1986 $8 (12/31/87)
78   YALUMBA Chardonnay Eden Valley 1986 $7 (12/31/87)
77   GRANTS Chardonnay McLaren Vale 1986 $8 (12/15/87)
77   MOUNTADAM Chardonnay Eden Valley High Eden Ridge 1986 $17 (5/15/88)
73   HILL-SMITH Chardonnay Barossa Valley 1986 $8 (11/15/87)
72   COLDSTREAM HILLS Chardonnay Lilydale Three Vineyards Blend 1986 $18 (5/31/88)
69   RIDDOCH Chardonnay Victoria 1986 $9 (5/31/88)
68   COLDSTREAM HILLS Chardonnay Lilydale Yarra Ridge Vineyard 1986 $18 (5/31/88)
68   ORLANDO Chardonnay McLaren Vale St.-Hugo 1986 $15 (7/31/90)

1985

92 ROTHBURY Chardonnay Hunter Valley Reserve 1985 $25 (5/31/87)
91 ORLANDO Chardonnay McLaren Vale St.-Hugo 1985 $15 (7/31/89)
89 CHATEAU REYNELLA Chardonnay McLaren Vale 1985 $7 (5/15/88) BB
88 ROSEMOUNT Chardonnay Hunter Valley Roxburgh 1985 $25 (8/31/87)
88 ROSEMOUNT Chardonnay Hunter Valley Show Reserve 1985 $15 (4/15/87)
87 BLACK OPAL Chardonnay Hunter Valley 1985 $8 (5/15/87) BB
85 BROWN BROTHERS Chardonnay Victoria Estate Selection 1985 $8 (8/31/87)
85 KRONDORF Chardonnay Australia 1985 $13 (4/15/87)
84 MILDARA Chardonnay Coonawarra 1985 $7.50 (4/15/87)
83 CULLENS Chardonnay Western Australia Margaret River 1985 $18 (11/15/87)
83 ROSEMOUNT Chardonnay Hunter Valley Matured in Oak Casks 1985 $10 (4/15/87)
81 LINDEMANS Chardonnay Padthaway 1985 $9 (2/28/87)
80 DENMAN Chardonnay Hunter Valley Private Bin 1985 $6 (12/31/87)
78 EVANS FAMILY Chardonnay Hunter Valley 1985 $13 (4/15/87)
77 LINDEMANS Chardonnay South Australia Bin 65 1985 $6 (2/28/87)
74 SEPPELT Chardonnay South Eastern Australia Reserve Bin 1985 $8 (9/30/86)
72 HILL-SMITH Chardonnay Barossa Valley 1985 $9.50 (5/15/87)
69 HEGGIES Chardonnay Barossa Valley 1985 $13 (12/15/87)
66 ST.-HUBERTS Chardonnay Yarra Valley 1985 $13.25 (12/31/87)
64 WIRRA WIRRA Chardonnay McLaren Vale David Paxton's Hillstowe Vineyard 1985 $14 (12/31/87)

1984

89 MONTROSE Chardonnay Mudgee Special Reserve 1984 $15 (5/15/87)
84 SEPPELT Chardonnay South Eastern Australia Reserve Bin 1984 $8.50 (2/01/86)
69 ROTHBURY Chardonnay Hunter Valley 1984 $8 (7/01/86)

1983

84 LEEUWIN Chardonnay Margaret River Second Release 1983 $24 (5/31/88)
81 MARK SWANN Chardonnay McLaren Vale 1983 $11 (9/16/84)

NV

86 BROWN BROTHERS Chardonnay Australia Family Reserve NV $9 (5/31/87)
86 HARDY'S Chardonnay Australia NV $10 (5/31/87)

DESSERT

1988

83 PETER LEHMANN Sémillon Late Harvest Barossa Valley Botrytis Sauternes 1988 $6/375ml (4/15/91) BB
83 LINDEMANS Sémillon Late Harvest Padthaway Botrytis Griffith 1988 $12/375ml (7/31/90)

1987

91 LINDEMANS Sémillon Late Harvest Padthaway Botrytis Griffith 1987 $12/375ml (10/31/89)
89 PETER LEHMANN Sémillon Late Harvest Barossa Valley Botrytis Sauternes 1987 $8/375ml (10/31/89)
88 PENFOLDS Rhine Riesling Late Harvest South Australia 1987 $5.50/375ml (3/15/89) BB
84 BROWN BROTHERS Port Victoria Family Selection 1987 $12.50 (7/31/90)
84 PENFOLDS Sémillon Late Harvest South Australia 1987 $6.50/375ml (3/15/89)
73 BROWN BROTHERS Muscat of Alexandria Victoria Lexia Family Selection 1987 $8.50 (7/31/90)
71 PEWSEY VALE Rhine Riesling Late Harvest Barossa Valley Botrytis Individual Vineyard Selection 1987 $9/375ml (10/31/89)

1986

92 HEGGIES Rhine Riesling Late Harvest Barossa Valley Botrytis Affected 1986 $8/375ml (2/15/88)
90 PEWSEY VALE Rhine Riesling Late Harvest Barossa Valley Botrytis 1986 $8/375ml (2/15/88)
84 HILL-SMITH Sémillon Late Harvest Barossa Valley Autumn Harvest Botrytis Affected 1986 $10/375ml (3/15/89)
77 BROWN BROTHERS Muscat of Alexandria Victoria Lexia 1986 $8 (5/15/89)

1985

88 HILL-SMITH Sémillon Late Harvest Barossa Valley Autumn Harvest Botrytis 1985 $8/375ml (2/15/88)

1984

89 PETER LEHMANN Sémillon Late Harvest Barossa Valley Botrytis Sauternes 1984 $15 (7/01/87)
83 YALUMBA Sémillon Late Harvest Barossa Valley Botrytis Affected 1984 $5.50/375ml (3/15/89)

1983

84 HILL-SMITH Sémillon Late Harvest Barossa Valley Autumn Harvest Botrytis 1983 $8/375ml (8/31/86)

1982

72 HARDY'S Port Australia 1982 $15 (7/31/90)

1980

78 MARK SWANN Port Australia Vintage 1980 $10 (4/16/84)

1978

70 SEPPELT Port McLaren Flat Barossa 1978 $15 (2/15/88)

NV

95 SEPPELT Tawny Port Australia Old Trafford NV $15 (3/15/89)
95 YALUMBA Port Barossa Valley Galway Pipe NV $10.50 (1/31/87)
92 CAMPBELLS Muscat Rutherglen Old NV $15 (7/01/87)
92 MORRIS Tokay Australia Show Reserve NV $15 (7/01/87)
92 SEPPELT Port Barossa Valley Para Port Bin 109 NV $25 (2/15/88)
92 MARK SWANN Dessert Rutherglen Gold Vintner's Select NV $10/375ml (12/31/88)
91 CAMPBELLS Tokay Rutherglen Old NV $15 (7/01/87)
91 ROSEWOOD Muscat Australia Liqueur NV $50 (7/01/87)
91 ROSEWOOD Muscat Rutherglen Special Liqueur NV $30 (7/01/87)
91 YALUMBA Port Barossa Valley Galway Pipe NV $18 (4/15/91)
91 YALUMBA Muscat Rutherglen Museum Show Reserve NV $10/375ml (4/15/91)
90 ROSEWOOD Muscat Rutherglen Old Liqueur NV $40 (7/01/87)

90 YALUMBA Tawny Port South Australia Clocktower NV $6 (5/31/87) BB
84 LINDEMANS Tawny Port Australia Macquarie Very Special Wood Matured NV $11 (7/31/90)
84 YALUMBA Tawny Port South Australia Clocktower NV $8.50 (4/15/91) BB
83 HARDY'S Tawny Port Australia Tall Ships NV $11 (7/31/90)
79 SEPPELT Port Barossa Valley Para Port No. 110 NV $25 (3/15/89)
78 SEPPELT Tawny Port Barossa Valley Mount Rufus NV $12 (2/15/88)

PINOT NOIR

1988

86 MOUNTADAM Pinot Noir Eden Valley 1988 $25 (3/31/91)
86 ROO'S LEAP Pinot Noir McLaren Vale 1988 $8 (2/28/91)
86 TARRA WARRA Pinot Noir Yarra Glen 1988 $25 (12/31/90)
68 TYRRELL'S Pinot Noir Hunter River 1988 $14 (1/31/90)

1987

84 ROSEMOUNT Pinot Noir Hunter Valley Giants Creek Vineyard 1987 $20 (2/28/90)

1986

81 TERRACE VALE Pinot Noir Hunter Valley 1986 $9.25 (3/15/88)
74 HUNGERFORD HILL Pinot Noir Hunter Valley 1986 $12 (2/28/90)
74 HUNGERFORD HILL Pinot Noir Hunter Valley 1986 $12 (2/28/90)
73 BANNOCKBURN Pinot Noir Geelong 1986 $26 (1/31/90)
73 LINDEMANS Pinot Noir Padthaway 1986 $12 (9/15/89)

1985

87 TYRRELL'S Pinot Noir Hunter River 1985 $10 (7/01/87)
84 ROSEMOUNT Pinot Noir Hunter Valley 1985 $9.50 (4/30/87)
80 ST.-HUBERTS Pinot Noir Yarra Valley 1985 $11.50 (11/15/87)
74 BANNOCKBURN Pinot Noir Geelong 1985 $16.50 (3/15/88)

1984

82 LINDEMANS Pinot Noir Padthaway 1984 $12 (2/15/88)
70 HUNGERFORD HILL Pinot Noir Hunter Valley 1984 $11 (3/15/88)

1983

89 ROTHBURY Pinot Noir Hunter Valley Director's Reserve 1983 $15 (7/01/87)
87 ROTHBURY Pinot Noir Hunter Valley 1983 $10 (7/01/87)
83 BROWN BROTHERS Pinot Noir Victoria 1983 $9 (7/01/87)
76 TOLLEY'S Pinot Noir Barossa Valley Selected Harvest 1983 $5 (11/15/87)

NV

80 ROSEMOUNT Pinot Noir Hunter Valley NV $9 (7/01/87)

SAUVIGNON BLANC

1989

76 TALTARNI Sauvignon Blanc Victoria 1989 $10 (10/31/90)

1988

89 TALTARNI Sauvignon Blanc Victoria 1988 $15 (9/15/89)

1987

77 WOLF BLASS Sauvignon Blanc South Australia 1987 $9 (2/15/88)
75 MILDARA Fumé Blanc Victoria 1987 $5.50 (2/15/88)
71 BERRI Fumé Blanc South Australia Vintage Selection 1987 $6.50 (3/15/88)
68 KOALA RIDGE Sauvignon Blanc Barossa Valley 1987 $8 (10/31/89)

1986

85 ROSEMOUNT Fumé Blanc Australia 1986 $7 (5/31/87)
84 HARDY'S Fumé Blanc Padthaway Hardy Collection No. 6 1986 $6 (9/30/88) BB
84 HILL-SMITH Fumé Blanc Barossa Valley 1986 $6.25 (7/15/87) BB
78 YALUMBA Sauvignon Blanc Barossa Valley Fumé Style 1986 $6 (2/15/88)
76 MILDARA Fumé Blanc Coonawarra 1986 $5 (5/15/87)
67 LINDEMANS Sauvignon Blanc Victoria Bin 95 1986 $6 (2/15/88)

1985

87 BROWN BROTHERS Sauvignon Blanc Victoria Estate Selection 1985 $7.50 (8/31/87)
82 LINDEMANS Sauvignon Blanc South Australia Bin 95 1985 $5 (2/15/87) BB
80 DE BORTOLI Sauvignon Blanc Australia Riverina 1985 $6 (2/28/87)
78 MONTROSE Fumé Blanc Mudgee 1985 $7.50 (5/15/87)
77 HARDY'S Fumé Blanc South Australia Captain's Selection 1985 $4.50 (9/30/88)
72 KATNOOK Sauvignon Blanc Coonawarra 1985 $9.50 (5/15/87)
69 LINDEMANS Sauvignon Blanc Padthaway 1985 $12 (2/15/88)

NV

83 MARK SWANN Sauvignon Blanc Australia Proprietor's Reserve NV $4.50 (8/31/87) BB

SÉMILLON

1988

80 TYRRELL'S Sémillon Hunter Valley Classic 1988 $7 (4/15/91)

1987

84 ROSEMOUNT Sémillon Hunter Valley Wood Matured 1987 $9 (10/31/89)

1986

87 ROTHBURY Sémillon Hunter Valley 1986 $7 (5/31/87)
86 LINDEMANS Sémillon Hunter Valley 1986 $11 (5/31/87)
86 WYNDHAM Sémillon Hunter Valley Bin 777 1986 $6.50 (5/31/88) BB
80 HENSCHKE Sémillon Barossa Valley Matured in French Oak 1986 $12 (2/15/88)
80 MONTROSE Sémillon Mudgee 1986 $8 (5/31/88)
77 ROTHBURY Sémillon Hunter Valley Brokenback Vineyard 1986 $8 (12/15/87)
77 YARRA YERING Sémillon Coldstream 1986 $17 (5/31/88)
72 ROSEMOUNT Sémillon Hunter Valley Wood Matured 1986 $8 (12/15/87)

AUSTRALIA
SÉMILLON

1985
84   TYRRELL'S Sémillon Hunter Valley 1985 $7 (5/31/87)
70   DENMAN Sémillon Hunter Valley Bin 3 1985 $5 (12/15/87)

1984
86   ROTHBURY Sémillon Hunter Valley 1984 $10 (5/31/87)
71   PETER LEHMANN Sémillon Barossa Valley 1984 $5 (5/15/87)
64   LINDEMANS Sémillon South Australia Bin 77 1984 $5 (8/31/86)

1983
85   TOLLEY'S Sémillon Barossa Valley Wood Aged Selected Harvest 1983 $5 (12/31/87)

1982
62   MARK SWANN Sémillon Australia Dry 1982 $5.50 (3/16/84)

SÉMILLON BLENDS

1990
84   ROSEMOUNT Sémillon-Chardonnay South Eastern Australia 1990 $7 (5/31/91) BB
82   COLDRIDGE Sémillon Chardonnay Victoria 1990 $6 (4/15/91) BB

1989
86   PENFOLDS Sémillon Chardonnay Koonunga Hill South Australia 1989 $6 (9/15/90) BB

1988
81   LINDEMANS Sémillon Chardonnay Bin 77 South Eastern Australia 1988 $6 (4/15/91) BB
78   ROSEMOUNT Sémillon-Chardonnay South Eastern Australia 1988 $6 (6/15/90) BB

1987
82   ROSEMOUNT Sémillon Chardonnay Hunter Valley 1987 $9 (7/31/89)
79   YALUMBA Sémillon Chardonnay Eden Valley 1987 $7.50 (4/15/89)
78   LINDEMANS Sémillon Chardonnay Bin 77 New South Wales 1987 $6 (5/31/88)

1986
86   HARDY'S Sauvignon Blanc Sémillon Australia 1986 $7 (5/31/87)
73   YALUMBA Sémillon Chardonnay Eden Valley 1986 $6 (2/15/88)
70   HILL-SMITH Sémillon Chenin Blanc Varietal White Barossa Valley 1986 $4 (12/15/87)
69   CHATEAU TAHBILK Sémillon Sauvignon Blanc Goulburn Valley 1986 $8.25 (2/15/88)

1985
87   ROSEMOUNT Sémillon Chardonnay Hunter Valley 1985 $9.50 (2/28/87)

NV
87   ROTHBURY Chardonnay Sémillon Hunter Valley NV $9 (5/31/87)

SHIRAZ

1989
91   ROSEMOUNT Shiraz Hunter Valley 1989 $8 (2/15/91) SS

1988
90   ROSEMOUNT Shiraz Hunter Valley 1988 $8 (1/31/90) SS
88   CAPE MENTELLE Shiraz Margaret River 1988 $15 (2/28/91)
86   MITCHELTON Shiraz Goulburn Valley 1988 $8 (3/15/91) BB
80   HUNGERFORD HILL Shiraz Hunter Valley 1988 $10 (2/28/90)
78   MONTROSE Shiraz Mudgee 1988 $9 (3/15/91)

1987
87   CASSEGRAIN Shiraz Pokolbin Leonard Select Vineyard 1987 $20 (3/15/91)
87   CHATEAU TAHBILK Shiraz Goulburn Valley 1987 $11 (3/15/91)
87   HARDY'S Shiraz McLaren Vale 1987 $7.50 (7/15/90) BB
87   ROSEMOUNT Shiraz Hunter Valley 1987 $9 (7/31/89)
86   HENSCHKE Shiraz Australia Keyneton Mount Edelstone 1987 $16.50 (5/31/91)
85   ROTHBURY Shiraz Hunter Valley Herlstone Vineyard 1987 $9.50 (5/31/91)
84   PETER LEHMANN Shiraz Barossa Valley 1987 $8 (4/15/91) BB
84   LINDEMANS Shiraz South Eastern Australia Bin 50 1987 $5.50 (7/15/90) BB
81   LINDEMANS Shiraz Hunter Valley 1987 $10 (2/15/91)

1986
92   ROSEMOUNT Shiraz Hunter Valley 1986 $9 (4/15/89)
90   HENSCHKE Shiraz Barossa Valley Mount Edelstone 1986 $17 (10/31/89)
89   HARDY'S Shiraz McLaren Vale 1986 $7.50 (12/31/88) BB
89   MILDARA Shiraz Coonawarra 1986 $9 (12/31/88)
88   CHATEAU TAHBILK Shiraz Victoria 1986 $10 (3/31/89)
87   HENSCHKE Shiraz Barossa Valley Hill of Grace 1986 $26 (9/30/89)
86   HILL-SMITH Shiraz Barossa Valley 1986 $9 (2/28/91) BB
85   BROWN BROTHERS Shiraz Victoria Family Selection 1986 $8 (7/15/90)
85   WYNDHAM Shiraz Hunter Valley Bin 555 1986 $7 (1/31/90) BB
84   TALTARNI Shiraz Victoria 1986 $10 (10/31/90)
84   TYRRELL'S Shiraz Hunter Valley Classic 1986 $8 (1/31/90) BB
83   LINDEMANS Shiraz Barossa Valley 1986 $12 (5/15/89)

78   LINDEMANS Shiraz South Australia Bin 50 1986 $5.50 (5/15/89)
76   ROTHBURY Shiraz Hunter Valley Herlstone Vineyard 1986 $10.50 (7/31/89)
73   TERRACE VALE Shiraz Hunter Valley Bin 6 1986 $9.50 (3/15/88)

1985
91   TALTARNI Shiraz Victoria 1985 $10 (11/30/88) SS
88   HOUGHTON Shiraz McLaren Vale Wildflower Ridge 1985 $9 (12/31/88)
87   PENFOLDS Shiraz South Australia Magill Estate Vineyard 1985 $45 (7/31/89)
85   BERRI Shiraz Barossa Valley 1985 $9.25 (2/15/88)
84   PETER LEHMANN Shiraz Barossa Valley Dry Red 1985 $7.25 (7/31/89) BB
83   BROWN BROTHERS Shiraz Victoria 1985 $7 (5/15/89) BB
81   HENSCHKE Shiraz Barossa Valley Mount Edelstone 1985 $14.50 (3/31/89)
80   ROSEMOUNT Shiraz Hunter Valley 1985 $8 (2/15/88)
78   ROTHBURY Shiraz Hunter Valley Herlstone Vineyard 1985 $10.50 (3/31/89)

1984
90   HENSCHKE Shiraz Barossa Valley Mount Edelstone 1984 $14 (2/15/88)
90   ROTHBURY Shiraz Hunter Valley Herlstone Vineyard 1984 $9.50 (5/15/87)
87   MONTROSE Shiraz Mudgee 1984 $10 (7/01/87)
87   SEPPELT Shiraz South Eastern Australia Black Label 1984 $12 (12/31/88)
83   ROSEMOUNT Shiraz Hunter Valley 1984 $7.50 (4/30/87)
82   HILL-SMITH Shiraz Barossa Valley 1984 $6.25 (5/15/87)
81   BANNOCKBURN Shiraz Geelong 1984 $13 (10/31/89)
81   SALTRAM Shiraz Hazelwood 1984 $8.50 (7/31/89)
79   HARDY'S Shiraz McLaren Vale Padthaway Bird Series 1984 $5.50 (7/15/88)
77   CHATEAU TAHBILK Shiraz Goulburn Valley 1984 $6 (11/15/87)
75   TALTARNI Shiraz Victoria 1984 $9.25 (2/15/88)

1983
92   BROWN BROTHERS Shiraz Australia 1983 $9 (7/01/87)
92   PENFOLDS Shiraz South Australia Grange Hermitage Bin 95 1983 $80 (3/15/91)
86   MONTROSE Shiraz Mudgee 1983 $7 (3/15/88)
81   PETER LEHMANN Shiraz Barossa Valley 1983 $7 (7/01/87)
79   PETER LEHMANN Shiraz Barossa Valley Dry Red 1983 $5 (4/30/87)
74   SEPPELT Shiraz South Eastern Australia Black Label 1983 $10 (2/15/88)

1982
96   PENFOLDS Shiraz South Australia Grange Hermitage Bin 95 1982 Rel: $60 Cur: $68 (9/30/89) CS
86   TALTARNI Shiraz Victoria 1982 $9.25 (4/30/87)
80   ANDREW GARRETT Shiraz South Australia Clarendon Estate 1982 $8.75 (11/15/87)
79   LEASINGHAM Shiraz Australia Bin 61 1982 $4.25 (12/15/87)
75   TYRRELL'S Shiraz Hunter Valley 1982 $7 (7/15/88)

1981
93   PENFOLDS Shiraz South Australia Grange Hermitage Bin 95 1981 Rel: $49 Cur: $62 (12/31/88) CS

1980
89   PENFOLDS Shiraz South Australia Grange Hermitage Bin 95 1980 Cur: $98 (10/29/87) (JL)
80   MARK SWANN Shiraz Eden Valley 1980 $6.50 (3/16/84)
77   TALTARNI Shiraz Victoria 1980 $6.75 (3/16/84)
73   LINDEMANS Shiraz Hunter Valley Bin 5910 Lindemans Classic 1980 $30 (7/31/90)

1970
89   LINDEMANS Shiraz Hunter Valley Bin 4110 Lindemans Classic 1970 $60 (9/15/89)

1967
95   PENFOLDS Shiraz South Australia Grange Hermitage Bin 95 1967 Cur: $67 (10/29/87) (JL)

1966
92   PENFOLDS Shiraz South Australia Grange Hermitage Bin 95 1966 Cur: $100 (10/29/87) (JL)

1965
96   LINDEMANS Shiraz Hunter Valley Bin 3110 Lindemans Classic 1965 $95 (9/15/89)

SPARKLING

1985
87   LASSETER Brut Australia 1985 $17 (10/31/89)
85   SEPPELT Brut Australia Fleur de Lys 1985 $18 (12/31/88)

1984
84   YALUMBA Brut de Brut Australia 1984 $8.25 (3/15/88)

1983
82   TYRRELL'S Brut Pinot Noir Hunter Valley 1983 $19 (9/30/88)

NV
84   LASSETER Brut Australia NV $10 (12/31/88)
84   YALUMBA Brut Rosé South Australia Angas NV $9 (12/31/90)
82   SEPPELT Brut South Eastern Australia Imperial NV $10 (1/31/90)
78   ANGAS Brut Rosé Australia NV $8 (12/31/87)
78   YALUMBA Brut South Australia Angas NV $9 (12/31/90)
76   ANGAS Brut Australia NV $8 (12/31/87)

OTHER AUSTRALIA RED

1988
83   ROSEMOUNT Dry Red Diamond Reserve Hunter Valley 1988 $6.50 (2/28/90) BB
83   ROSEMOUNT Dry Red Diamond Reserve Hunter Valley 1988 $6.50 (9/15/87) BB (JL)
78   HARDY'S Premium Classic Dry Red South Australia 1988 $5.25 (7/31/90) BB

1986
86   ROSEMOUNT Dry Red Diamond Reserve Hunter Valley 1986 $6.50 (9/15/87) BB
85   WYNDHAM Merlot Hunter Valley 1986 $8 (1/31/90) BB
79   TYRRELL'S Long Flat Red Hunter Valley 1986 $6 (1/31/90)
75   HARDY'S Premium Classic Dry Red McLaren Vale 1986 $6 (5/15/89)

Key to Symbols

The scores reported here are the results of blind tastings conducted by our panel of senior editors. Wines that carry the initials below are results of individual tastings.

THE WINE SPECTATOR 100-POINT SCALE   *95-100*—Classic, a great wine; *90-94*—Outstanding, superior character and style; *80-89*—Good to very good, a wine with special qualities; *70-79*—Average, drinkable wine that may have minor flaws; *60-69*—Below average, drinkable but not recommended; *50-59*—Poor, undrinkable, not recommended. "+"—With a score indicates a range; used primarily with barrel tastings to indicate a preliminary score.

SPECIAL DESIGNATIONS   SS—Spectator Selection, CS—Cellar Selection, BB—Best Buy.

TASTER'S INITIALS   (JG)—Jim Gordon, (HS)—Harvey Steiman, (JL)—James Laube, (JS)—James Suckling, (TM)—Thomas Matthews, (TR)—Terry Robards, (BT)—Barrel Tasting (these wines were tasted blind from barrel samples), (CA-date)—*California's Great Cabernets* by James Laube, (CH-date)—*California's Great Chardonnays* by James Laube, (VP-date)—*Vintage Port* by James Suckling.

DATE TASTED   Dates in parentheses represent the issue in which the rating was published.

1985

81   TYRRELL'S Long Flat Red Hunter Valley 1985 $5.25 (7/31/89) BB
80   KOALA RIDGE Hermitage Barossa Valley 1985 $9 (1/31/90)
75   HILL-SMITH Varietal Red Barossa Valley 1985 $4 (1/31/88)

1984

90   ROTHBURY Hermitage Hunter Valley 1984 $10 (7/01/87)
83   TYRRELL'S Long Flat Red Hunter Valley 1984 $6 (9/30/88) BB
71   KOALA RIDGE Hermitage Barossa Valley 1984 $8.50 (8/31/87)

1983

90   ROTHBURY Hermitage Hunter Valley 1983 $15 (7/01/87)
79   TYRRELL'S Long Flat Red Hunter Valley 1983 $6 (4/15/88)

1982

84   TYRRELL'S Hermitage Hunter River 1982 $8 (7/01/87)

NV

82   GOVERNOR PHILLIP Classic Australian Red Australia NV $5 (7/31/89) BB

OTHER AUSTRALIA WHITE

1990

76   PEWSEY VALE Rhine Riesling Adelaide Hills Individual Vineyard Selection 1990 $9.50 (7/15/91)

1989

86   TYRRELL'S Long Flat White Hunter Valley 1989 $5 (10/31/90) BB
80   CHATEAU TAHBILK Marsanne Goulburn Valley 1989 $10 (7/15/91)

1988

79   HARDY'S Premium Classic Dry White South Australia 1988 $5.25 (6/15/90) BB
79   HARDY'S Premium Classic Dry White South Australia 1988 $6 (5/15/89)

1987

79   PEWSEY VALE Rhine Riesling Barossa Valley Individual Vineyard Selection 1987 $5.50 (3/15/89)
75   BERRI Columbard Chardonnay Vintage Selection South Australia 1987 $6.50 (3/15/88)
68   ROSEMOUNT Diamond Reserve Dry White Hunter Valley 1987 $6.50 (7/31/89)

1986

86   PETALUMA Rhine Riesling Australia 1986 $8 (5/31/87)
84   PEWSEY VALE Rhine Riesling Barossa Valley Individual Vineyard Selection 1986 $6 (2/15/88)
83   ROSEMOUNT Dry White Diamond Reserve Hunter Valley 1986 $6.50 (9/15/87) BB
80   TYRRELL'S Long Flat White Hunter Valley 1986 $6 (3/15/88) BB

1985

75   CHATEAU TAHBILK Marsanne Goulburn Valley 1985 $6 (2/15/88)

1984

78   HILL-SMITH Sémillon Chenin Blanc Varietal White Barossa Valley 1984 $4 (11/15/86) BB

NV

90   HARDY'S Rhine Riesling Australia NV $7 (5/31/87)
84   TYRRELL'S Long Flat White Hunter Valley NV $4 (5/31/87)

CHILE
CABERNET SAUVIGNON

1990

73   SAN JOSE DE SANTIAGO Cabernet Sauvignon Colchagua Valley 1990 $3 (6/15/91)

1989

82   MIGUEL TORRES Cabernet Sauvignon Curicó 1989 $7 (6/15/91) BB

1988

87   MIGUEL TORRES Cabernet Sauvignon Curicó 1988 $4.50 (9/15/90) BB
86   SANTA MONICA Cabernet Sauvignon Rancagua 1988 $6 (3/15/90) BB
84   CANEPA Cabernet Sauvignon Maipo Valley Reserva 1988 $6.50 (6/15/90) BB
84   SANTA RITA Cabernet Sauvignon Maipo Valley Reserva 1988 $9.75 (6/15/91)
84   VALLE DE SAN FERNANDO Cabernet Sauvignon San Fernando Valley 1988 $6 (9/15/90) BB
83   UNDURRAGA Cabernet Sauvignon Maipo Valley 1988 $5.25 (9/15/90) BB
82   LOS VASCOS Cabernet Sauvignon Colchagua 1988 $7 (6/15/91) BB
81   VINA DEL MAR Cabernet Sauvignon Curicó Selección Especial 35 1988 $6 (6/15/91) BB
79   LA PLAYA Cabernet Sauvignon Maipo Valley 1988 $5 (6/15/91)
77   ALAMEDA Cabernet Sauvignon Maipo Valley 1988 $7 (6/15/91)
73   MONTES Cabernet Sauvignon Curicó Valley 1988 $4.50 (2/15/90)
69   LOS PUMAS Cabernet Sauvignon Curicó Valley 1988 $4 (9/15/90)

1987

87   UNDURRAGA Cabernet Sauvignon Maipo Valley 1987 $5.25 (2/15/90) BB
86   CALITERRA Cabernet Sauvignon Maipo 1987 $6 (9/15/90) BB
86   LOS VASCOS Cabernet Sauvignon Colchagua 1987 $5 (9/15/90) BB
85   CONCHA Y TORO Cabernet Sauvignon Maipo Puente Alto Vineyard Private Reserve Don Melchor 1987 $13 (6/30/90)
85   SANTA RITA Cabernet Sauvignon Maipo Valley Reserva 1987 $11.50 (9/15/90)
84   MONTES Cabernet Sauvignon Curicó Valley 1987 $7 (2/15/90) BB
84   MONTES Cabernet Sauvignon Curicó Valley Special Selection 1987 $12 (9/15/90)
83   VINA DEL MAR Cabernet Sauvignon Curicó Selección Especial 35 1987 $6 (9/15/90) BB
82   ERRAZURIZ PANQUEHUE Cabernet Sauvignon Aconcagua 1987 $9 (9/15/90)
82   SANTA RITA Cabernet Sauvignon Maipo Valley Medalla Real 1987 $12 (6/15/91)
78   CARTA VIEJA Cabernet Sauvignon Maule Valley 1987 $6 (6/15/91)
78   SAN MARTIN Cabernet Sauvignon Maipo Valley International Series 1987 $4.50 (6/15/90) BB
78   SANTA RITA Cabernet Sauvignon Maipo Valley 120 Medalla Real 1987 $11 (6/15/90)
71   COUSINO-MACUL Cabernet Sauvignon Maipo 1987 $6 (9/15/90)

1986

87   SANTA RITA Cabernet Sauvignon Maipo Valley Reserva 1986 $6.25 (5/15/89) BB
85   CALITERRA Cabernet Sauvignon Maipo 1986 $6 (7/31/89) BB
85   VINA SAN PEDRO Cabernet Sauvignon Lontue Gato de Oro 1986 $4.50 (2/15/90) BB
83   SANTA RITA Cabernet Sauvignon Maipo Valley 120 1986 $5 (5/15/89) BB
83   UNDURRAGA Cabernet Sauvignon Maipo Valley Reserve Selection 1986 $8 (6/15/91) BB
80   VINA DEL MAR Cabernet Sauvignon Lontue Selección Especial 17 1986 $6 (2/15/90) BB
78   SANTA CAROLINA Cabernet Sauvignon Maipo Valley Santa Rosa Vineyard 1986 $4 (4/30/88)
78   SANTA RITA Cabernet Sauvignon Maipo Valley Medalla Real 1986 $5 (3/15/90)
75   CANEPA Cabernet Sauvignon Maipo Valley 1986 $6 (6/15/90)
75   CARTA VIEJA Cabernet Sauvignon Maule Valley 1986 $4 (6/15/90)
75   CARTA VIEJA Cabernet Sauvignon Maule Valley Antiqua Selection 1986 $8 (6/15/91)
74   LA PLAYA Cabernet Sauvignon Maipo Valley 1986 $4.50 (3/15/90)
72   COUSINO-MACUL Cabernet Sauvignon Maipo 1986 $8 (9/15/90)

1985

86   VINA DEL MAR Cabernet Sauvignon Lontue 1985 $6 (4/30/88) BB
85   UNDURRAGA Cabernet Sauvignon Maipo Valley Reserve Selection 1985 $7.75 (3/15/90) BB
84   LOS VASCOS Cabernet Sauvignon Colchagua 1985 $5 (11/15/87)
82   ERRAZURIZ PANQUEHUE Cabernet Sauvignon Aconcagua 1985 $5.50 (9/15/88)
80   VINA SAN PEDRO Cabernet Sauvignon Lontue Gato Negro 1985 $4.50 (11/15/88) BB
80   WALNUT CREST Cabernet Sauvignon Maipo 1985 $4 (6/30/90) BB
79   VALLE DE SAN FERNANDO Cabernet Sauvignon San Fernando 1985 $7 (7/31/89)
78   UNDURRAGA Cabernet Sauvignon Maipo Valley Santa Ana 1985 $5 (11/15/87)
75   CANEPA Cabernet Sauvignon Maipo 1985 $4 (11/15/87)
75   CONCHA Y TORO Cabernet Sauvignon Maipo Valley 1985 $5 (3/15/90)
75   SANTA RITA Cabernet Sauvignon Maipo Valley Medalla Real 1985 $8 (3/31/88)
75   ST. MORILLON Cabernet Sauvignon Lontue 1985 $4 (9/15/90)
73   MIGUEL TORRES Cabernet Sauvignon Curicó 1985 $5 (3/31/88)
69   CONCHA Y TORO Cabernet Sauvignon Maipo 1985 $5 (9/15/90)
68   CARTA VIEJA Cabernet Sauvignon Maule Valley 1985 $3 (7/31/89)

1984

89   CONCHA Y TORO Cabernet Sauvignon Maipo 1984 $5.50 (4/30/88) BB
88   LOS VASCOS Cabernet Sauvignon Colchagua 1984 $4.50 (4/30/88) BB
87   ERRAZURIZ PANQUEHUE Cabernet Sauvignon Aconcagua Antigua Reserva Don Maximiano 1984 $7.50 (9/15/88) BB
87   SANTA RITA Cabernet Sauvignon Maipo Valley 120 Medalla Real 1984 $9 (7/15/87)
86   COUSINO-MACUL Cabernet Sauvignon Maipo 1984 $5.50 (2/15/89) BB
85   CONCHA Y TORO Cabernet Sauvignon Maipo Reserva Special Casillero del Diablo 1984 $7 (11/15/87)
85   SANTA RITA Cabernet Sauvignon Maipo Valley 120 Medalla Real 1984 $9 (11/15/87)
83   VALLE DE SAN FERNANDO Cabernet Sauvignon San Fernando Gran Reserva 1984 $6 (7/31/89) BB
83   VINA SAN PEDRO Cabernet Sauvignon Lontue Gato Negro 1984 $4.50 (5/15/88) BB

81   VALDIVIESO Cabernet Sauvignon Maipo Valley 1984 $7 (9/15/90)
81   VALLE DE SAN FERNANDO Cabernet Sauvignon San Fernando Gran Reserva 1984 $6 (9/15/90) BB
79   MIGUEL TORRES Cabernet Sauvignon Curicó 1984 $4.50 (1/31/87)
77   COUSINO-MACUL Cabernet Sauvignon Maipo Antiguas Reservas 1984 $9 (9/15/90)
77   ALEJANDRO HERNANDEZ MUNOZ Cabernet Sauvignon Maipo Cabernet Vina Portal del Alto Gran Vino 1984 $3.50 (3/15/90)

1983

85   COUSINO-MACUL Cabernet Sauvignon Maipo 1983 $6 (5/15/88) BB
82   ALEJANDRO HERNANDEZ MUNOZ Cabernet Sauvignon Maipo Vina Portal del Alto Gran Reserva Tinto 1983 $4 (9/15/90) BB
77   VALLE DE SAN FERNANDO Cabernet Sauvignon San Fernando 1983 $4 (11/15/88)
76   CANEPA Cabernet Sauvignon Maipo Valley Finisismo 1983 $9 (6/30/90)
76   VINA SAN PEDRO Cabernet Sauvignon Lontue Gato Negro 1983 $4.50 (3/15/87)
75   CONCHA Y TORO Cabernet Sauvignon Maipo Valley Puente Alto Vineyard Special Reserve 1983 $8 (9/15/90)
65   CONCHA Y TORO Cabernet Sauvignon Maipo Valley Puente Alto Vineyard Special Reserve 1983 $8 (2/15/90)
60   CHATEAU ANDREW Cabernet Sauvignon Colchagua 1983 $6 (12/01/85)

1982

81   VALLE DE SAN FERNANDO Cabernet Sauvignon San Fernando Gran Reserva 1982 $6 (11/15/88) BB
78   VINA SAN PEDRO Cabernet Sauvignon Lontue Castillo de Molina 1982 $7.50 (2/15/89)
76   SANTA CAROLINA Cabernet Sauvignon Maipo Valley Estrella de Oro 1982 $8 (3/15/90)

1981

83   VINA SAN PEDRO Cabernet Sauvignon Lontue Castillo de Molina 1981 $7.50 (11/15/87) BB
80   CONCHA Y TORO Cabernet Sauvignon Maipo Special Reserve 1981 $6.75 (4/30/88)
80   COUSINO-MACUL Cabernet Sauvignon Maipo Antiguas Reservas 1981 $9 (2/15/89)

1980

80   COUSINO-MACUL Cabernet Sauvignon Maipo Antiguas Reservas 1980 $8 (5/15/88)
68   ERRAZURIZ PANQUEHUE Cabernet Sauvignon Aconcagua Antigua Reserva Don Maximiano 1980 $6 (11/15/87)

1979

81   VINA SAN PEDRO Cabernet Sauvignon Lontue Castillo de Molina 1979 $7.50 (3/15/87)

NV

86   VINTERRA Cabernet Sauvignon Maipo-Napa Valleys NV $7 (2/15/90) BB
80   LIBERTY SCHOOL Cabernet Sauvignon Lontue NV $6 (9/15/88) BB

CHARDONNAY

1990

82   SANTA RITA Chardonnay Maipo Valley Medalla Real 1990 $11.50 (6/15/91)
78   CALITERRA Chardonnay Curicó 1990 $6 (6/15/91)

1989

83   ERRAZURIZ PANQUEHUE Chardonnay Maule Reserva 1989 $7 (9/15/90) BB
79   CALITERRA Chardonnay Curicó 1989 $7 (9/15/90)
78   SANTA RITA Chardonnay Maipo Valley Reserva 1989 $9.50 (6/30/90)
76   COUSINO-MACUL Chardonnay Maipo 1989 $7 (9/15/90)
75   MIGUEL TORRES Chardonnay Curicó 1989 $7.50 (3/31/90)
72   CANEPA Chardonnay Maipo Valley 1989 $6.50 (6/30/90)

1988

82   COUSINO-MACUL Chardonnay Maipo Reserva 1988 $7.75 (4/30/90) BB
81   SAN MARTIN Chardonnay Maipo Valley International Series 1988 $4.50 (4/30/90) BB
74   WALNUT CREST Chardonnay Maipo 1988 $4 (4/30/90)
70   SANTA MONICA Chardonnay Rancagua 1988 $6 (3/31/90)

1987

85   COUSINO-MACUL Chardonnay Maipo 1987 $6 (3/31/90) BB
79   SANTA RITA Chardonnay Maipo Valley Reserva 1987 $7.50 (3/31/90)
73   VINA SAN PEDRO Chardonnay Lontue Gato de Oro Gran Reserva 1987 $7 (5/15/88)
70   LIBERTY SCHOOL Chardonnay Maule 1987 $6 (9/15/88)
67   CONCHA Y TORO Chardonnay Maipo Valley 1987 $5 (4/30/90)

1986

86   SANTA RITA Chardonnay Maipo Valley Medalla Real 1986 $8 (3/31/88)
82   COUSINO-MACUL Chardonnay Maipo 1986 $6 (5/15/88)
81   CANEPA Chardonnay Maipo 1986 $4 (11/15/87)
81   VINA SAN PEDRO Chardonnay Lontue Gato de Oro 1986 $7.50 (2/28/87) BB
80   SANTA CAROLINA Chardonnay Maipo Valley Los Toros Vineyard 1986 $4 (3/31/88) BB
75   COUSINO-MACUL Chardonnay Maipo 1986 $5 (11/15/87)
74   ERRAZURIZ PANQUEHUE Chardonnay Aconcagua 1986 $5 (11/15/87)

1983

65   CONCHA Y TORO Chardonnay Maipo 1983 $5 (11/15/87)

NV

84   VINTERRA Chardonnay Maipo-Napa Valleys NV $7 (3/31/90) BB
71   SANTA CAROLINA Chardonnay Maipo Valley Valle del Maipo NV $5 (3/31/90)

MERLOT

1989

80   SANTA RITA Merlot Maipo Valley 120 1989 $7 (6/15/91) BB
80   VINA DEL MAR Merlot Curicó Selección Especial 12 1989 $6 (6/15/91) BB
79   MONTES Merlot Curicó Valley 1989 $7 (9/15/90)

1988

84   VINA SAN PEDRO Merlot Lontue Valley 1988 $5 (12/31/90) BB
82   VINA DEL MAR Merlot Curicó Selección Especial 12 1988 $6 (9/15/90) BB
80   VINA DEL MAR Merlot Lontue 1988 $6 (7/31/89) BB

79 CANEPA Merlot Maipo Valley 1988 $6 (6/30/90) BB
68 LA PLAYA Merlot Maipo Valley 1988 $5 (6/15/91)

1987

85 WALNUT CREST Merlot Rapel 1987 $4 (6/30/90) BB
81 VINA SAN PEDRO Merlot Lontue Gato de Oro 1987 $6 (2/15/89) BB
77 ROBERT ALLISON Merlot Maipo Valley 1987 $5 (6/30/90)
75 LA PLAYA Merlot Maipo Valley 1987 $4.50 (3/15/90)

1986

76 CONCHA Y TORO Merlot Rapel 1986 $4.50 (3/15/90)

SAUVIGNON BLANC

1989

75 UNDURRAGA Sauvignon Blanc Maipo Valley 1989 $5.25 (3/31/90)

1988

87 ERRAZURIZ PANQUEHUE Sauvignon Blanc Maule 1988 $5.50 (9/15/88) BB
85 SANTA MONICA Sauvignon Blanc Rancagua 1988 $6 (3/31/90) BB
83 LOS VASCOS Sauvignon Blanc Colchagua 1988 $4.75 (3/31/90) BB

1987

84 VINA SAN PEDRO Sauvignon Blanc Lontue Gato Blanco 1987 $5 (11/15/87)
82 LIBERTY SCHOOL Sauvignon Blanc Maule 1987 $5 (9/15/88) BB
82 MIGUEL TORRES Sauvignon Blanc Curicó 1987 $4.50 (3/15/88) BB
79 LOS VASCOS Sauvignon Blanc Colchagua 1987 $4 (11/15/87)
76 VINA SAN PEDRO Fumé Blanc Lontue Gran Reserva 1987 $6.25 (9/15/88)
69 VALLE DE SAN FERNANDO Sauvignon Blanc San Fernando 1987 $4 (9/15/88)

1986

86 VINA SAN PEDRO Fumé Blanc Lontue 1986 $6 (11/15/87)
75 VINA SAN PEDRO Sauvignon Blanc Lontue Gato Blanco 1986 $4.50 (9/15/88)
70 CANEPA Sauvignon Blanc Maipo 1986 $4 (11/15/87)
70 VILLA RICA Sauvignon Blanc Aconcagua 1986 $5 (11/15/87)

1985

83 SANTA RITA Sauvignon Blanc Maipo 120 Tres Medallas 1985 $7 (11/15/87)
77 VINA SAN PEDRO Sauvignon Blanc Lontue Gato Blanco 1985 $4.50 (4/30/88)
74 MIGUEL TORRES Sauvignon Blanc Curicó 1985 $4 (10/31/87)
74 MIGUEL TORRES Sauvignon Blanc Curicó District 1985 $4 (10/31/87)
71 SANTA RITA Sauvignon Blanc Maipo Medalla Real 1985 $4.50 (3/15/88)

1984

70 VINA SAN PEDRO Sauvignon Blanc Lontue Gato Blanco 1984 $4.25 (3/15/87)
68 VINA SAN PEDRO Sauvignon Blanc Lontue San Pedro 1984 $7 (2/28/87)

NV

77 SANTA RITA Sauvignon Blanc Maipo Valley 120 Tres Medallas NV $5 (7/15/87)

OTHER CHILE RED

1986

80 CONCHA Y TORO Cabernet Sauvignon Merlot Rapel 1986 $4.25 (9/15/90) BB

1984

74 CANEPA Cabernet Sauvignon Malbec Maipo 1984 $4 (3/15/88)
74 ALEJANDRO HERNANDEZ MUNOZ Pinot Noir Maipo Vina Portal del Alto Gran Vino 1984 $3.50 (3/15/90)

1983

78 MIGUEL TORRES Santa Digna 1983 (NA) (2/16/86)

1979

69 SANTA CAROLINA Reserva de Familia 1979 $9 (11/15/87)

OTHER CHILE WHITE

1988

81 SANTA MONICA Sémillon Rancagua Seaborne 1988 $5 (3/31/90) BB

1985

76 MIGUEL TORRES Santa Digna 1985 (NA) (2/16/86)

1984

48 CHATEAU ANDREW Chevrier Colchagua 1984 $5.25 (5/16/86)

FRANCE
ALSACE/*GEWÜRZTRAMINER*

1989

97   TRIMBACH Gewürztraminer Alsace Sélection de Grains Nobles Hors Choix 1989 (NA) (11/15/91)
97   TRIMBACH Gewürztraminer Alsace Vendange Tardive 1989 (NA) (11/15/90)
96   LEON BEYER Gewürztraminer Alsace Sélection de Grains Nobles 1989 (NA) (11/15/90)
96   HUGEL Gewürztraminer Alsace Sélection de Grains Nobles ''S'' 1989 (NA) (11/15/90)
94   DOPFF AU MOULIN Gewürztraminer Alsace Sélection de Grains Nobles 1989 (NA) (11/15/90)
93   DOMAINE LUCIEN ALBRECHT Gewürztraminer Alsace Sélection de Grains Nobles 1989 (NA) (11/15/90)
93   KUENTZ-BAS Gewürztraminer Alsace Eichberg 1989 (NA) (11/15/90)
92   TRIMBACH Gewürztraminer Alsace Réserve 1989 (NA) (11/15/90)
91   LEON BEYER Gewürztraminer Alsace Comtes d'Eguisheim 1989 (NA) (11/15/90)
91   HUGEL Gewürztraminer Alsace Sélection de Grains Nobles 'T' 1989 (NA) (11/15/90)
90   LEON BEYER Gewürztraminer Alsace 1989 (NA) (11/15/90)
90   HUGEL Gewürztraminer Alsace Vendange Tardive 1989 (NA) (11/15/90)
90   JOSMEYER Gewürztraminer Alsace Hengst 1989 (NA) (11/15/90)
90   DOMAINE OSTERTAG Gewürztraminer Alsace Vignoble d'Epfig 1989 $14 (11/15/90)
90   DOMAINES SCHLUMBERGER Gewürztraminer Alsace Kessler 1989 (NA) (11/15/90)
89   HUGEL Gewürztraminer Alsace Sélection de Grains Nobles 'R' 1989 (NA) (11/15/90)
88   BOTT FRERES Gewürztraminer Alsace Reserve Personnelle 1989 $17 (6/30/91)
88   JOSMEYER Gewürztraminer Alsace Vendange Tardive 1989 (NA) (11/15/90)
88   PIERRE SPARR Gewürztraminer Alsace Brand 1989 (NA) (11/15/90)
87   BOTT FRERES Gewürztraminer Alsace Cuvée Exceptionnelle 1989 $13.50 (6/30/91)
87   DOPFF AU MOULIN Gewürztraminer Alsace Réserve 1989 (NA) (11/15/90)
87   PIERRE SPARR Gewürztraminer Alsace Sélection de Grains Nobles Cuvée Centenaire Mambo 1989 (NA) (11/15/90)
87   DOMAINE WEINBACH Gewürztraminer Alsace Sélection de Grains Nobles Clos des Capucins Quintes 1989 $275 (11/15/90)
86   KUENTZ-BAS Gewürztraminer Alsace 1989 (NA) (11/15/90)
86   KUENTZ-BAS Gewürztraminer Alsace Vendange Tardive Eichberg 1989 (NA) (11/15/90)
86   TRIMBACH Gewürztraminer Alsace 1989 (NA) (11/15/90)
86   ALSACE WILLM Gewürztraminer Alsace Sélection de Grains Nobles 1989 (NA) (11/15/90)
85   DOMAINE LUCIEN ALBRECHT Gewürztraminer Alsace Vendange Tardive 1989 (NA) (11/15/90)
85   HUGEL Gewürztraminer Alsace 1989 (NA) (11/15/90)
85   JOSMEYER Gewürztraminer Alsace Sélection de Grains Nobles 1989 (NA) (11/15/90)
85   GUSTAVE LORENTZ Gewürztraminer Alsace 1989 (NA) (11/15/90)
85   GUSTAVE LORENTZ Gewürztraminer Alsace Altenberg 1989 (NA) (11/15/90)
85   TRIMBACH Gewürztraminer Alsace Carte d'Or 1989 (NA) (11/15/90)
84   KUENTZ-BAS Gewürztraminer Alsace Réserve Personnelle 1989 (NA) (11/15/90)
84   MURE Gewürztraminer Alsace Zinnkoepflé 1989 (NA) (11/15/90)
84   DOMAINE ZIND HUMBRECHT Gewürztraminer Alsace Herrenweg Turckheim 1989 $25 (11/15/90)
83   JOSMEYER Gewürztraminer Alsace Cuvée des Folastries 1989 $16 (11/15/90)
83   MARC KREYDENWEISS Gewürztraminer Alsace Vendange Tardive Kritt 1989 (NA) (11/15/90)
83   ALSACE WILLM Gewürztraminer Alsace Clos Gaensbroennel Kirchberg de Barr 1989 (NA) (11/15/90)
83   DOMAINE ZIND HUMBRECHT Gewürztraminer Alsace Clos Windsbuhl 1989 $36 (11/15/90)
82   DOPFF AU MOULIN Gewürztraminer Alsace 1989 (NA) (11/15/90)
81   DOPFF AU MOULIN Gewürztraminer Alsace Vendange Tardive 1989 (NA) (11/15/90)
81   DOPFF & IRION Gewürztraminer Alsace 1989 (NA) (11/15/90)
80   DOPFF & IRION Gewürztraminer Alsace Cuvée René Dopff 1989 (NA) (11/15/90)
80   DOMAINE WEINBACH Gewürztraminer Alsace Clos des Capucins Cuvée Laurence (Cask 17) 1989 $50 (11/15/90)
80   ALSACE WILLM Gewürztraminer Alsace Vendange Tardive Gaensbroennel 1989 (NA) (11/15/90)
79   MARC KREYDENWEISS Gewürztraminer Alsace Kritt 1989 $19 (11/15/90)
79   GUSTAVE LORENTZ Gewürztraminer Alsace Réserve 1989 (NA) (11/15/90)
79   DOMAINES SCHLUMBERGER Gewürztraminer Alsace Sélection de Grains Nobles 1989 (NA) (11/15/90)
79   PIERRE SPARR Gewürztraminer Alsace 1989 (NA) (11/15/90)
79   DOMAINE WEINBACH Gewürztraminer Alsace Clos des Capucins (Cask 21) 1989 (NA) (11/15/90)
79   DOMAINE WEINBACH Gewürztraminer Alsace Clos des Capucins Cuvée Laurence (Cask 8) 1989 $50 (11/15/90)
78   DOMAINES SCHLUMBERGER Gewürztraminer Alsace Kitterlé 1989 (NA) (11/15/90)
75   LEON BEYER Gewürztraminer Alsace Vendange Tardive 1989 (NA) (11/15/90)
73   DOMAINES SCHLUMBERGER Gewürztraminer Alsace 1989 (NA) (11/15/90)
69   ALSACE WILLM Gewürztraminer Alsace 1989 (NA) (11/15/90)
68   PIERRE SPARR Gewürztraminer Alsace Vendange Tardive Mambourg Cuvée Centenaire 1989 (NA) (11/15/90)

1988

92   DOMAINE WEINBACH Gewürztraminer Alsace Vendange Tardive 1988 $67.50 (10/15/89)
91   GUSTAVE LORENTZ Gewürztraminer Alsace Sélection de Grains Nobles 1988 (NA) (10/15/89)
90   DOPFF AU MOULIN Gewürztraminer Alsace Vendange Tardive 1988 (NA) (10/15/89)
89   LEON BEYER Gewürztraminer Alsace Cuvée des Comtes d'Eguisheim 1988 $25 (10/15/89)
89   GUSTAVE LORENTZ Gewürztraminer Alsace 1988 (NA) (10/15/89)
87   TRIMBACH Gewürztraminer Alsace Vendange Tardive 1988 (NA) (10/15/89)
86   MARC KREYDENWEISS Gewürztraminer Alsace Kritt 1988 $19 (10/15/89)
86   DOMAINE OSTERTAG Gewürztraminer Alsace 1988 (NA) (10/15/89)

85   LEON BEYER Gewürztraminer Alsace 1988 $11.50 (10/15/89)
85   DOMAINE WEINBACH Gewürztraminer Alsace Cuvée Théo 1988 (NA) (10/15/89)
85   DOMAINE ZIND HUMBRECHT Gewürztraminer Alsace Vendnage Tardive Rangen 1988 (NA) (10/15/89)
84   DOPFF AU MOULIN Gewürztraminer Alsace 1988 (NA) (10/15/89)
84   KUENTZ-BAS Gewürztraminer Alsace Cuvée Tradition 1988 (NA) (10/15/89)
84   DOMAINE WEINBACH Gewürztraminer Alsace Clos des Capucins Réserve Personnelle Théo Faller 1988 $21 (6/30/91)
83   HUGEL Gewürztraminer Alsace 1988 $14.25 (10/15/89)
83   TRIMBACH Gewürztraminer Alsace 1988 $8.50 (10/15/89)
83   DOMAINE WEINBACH Gewürztraminer Alsace Cuvée Laurence 1988 $34 (10/15/89)
83   DOMAINE ZIND HUMBRECHT Gewürztraminer Alsace 1988 (NA) (10/15/89)
82   DOPFF AU MOULIN Gewürztraminer Alsace Brand 1988 (NA) (10/15/89)
82   DOPFF & IRION Gewürztraminer Alsace 1988 $11 (10/15/89)
80   CUVEE LEON Gewürztraminer Alsace 1988 $11 (3/31/91)
78   DOMAINES SCHLUMBERGER Gewürztraminer Alsace 1988 (NA) (10/15/89)
78   DOMAINES SCHLUMBERGER Gewürztraminer Alsace Sélection de Grains Nobles 1988 (NA) (10/15/89)
63   BOTT FRERES Gewürztraminer Alsace Vendange Tardive 1988 $40 (7/31/91)

1986

87   HUGEL Gewürztraminer Alsace 1986 $11 (7/15/88)
86   GUSTAVE LORENTZ Gewürztraminer Alsace 1986 $11 (7/31/89)
84   SALZMANN Gewürztraminer Alsace Cuvée Réservee 1986 $14 (7/15/88)
84   DOMAINE ZIND HUMBRECHT Gewürztraminer Alsace 1986 $10 (7/15/88)
83   TRIMBACH Gewürztraminer Alsace 1986 $12 (7/15/88)
78   J. BECKER Gewürztraminer Alsace 1986 $13 (7/15/88)
76   J. BECKER Gewürztraminer Alsace Frohen 1986 $16.50 (7/15/88)
75   MURE Gewürztraminer Alsace 1986 $7.50 (7/15/88)
74   DOMAINE OSTERTAG Gewürztraminer Alsace Vignoble de Nothalten 1986 $14 (7/15/88)

1985

94   DOMAINE ZIND HUMBRECHT Gewürztraminer Alsace Guebershwihr Vendange Tardive 1985 $40 (9/15/87)
91   ALSACE WILLM Gewürztraminer Alsace 1985 $11 (7/15/88)
91   DOMAINE ZIND HUMBRECHT Gewürztraminer Alsace Hengst 1985 $29 (9/15/87)
90   HUGEL Gewürztraminer Alsace 1985 $12.25 (8/31/87)
90   SALZMANN Gewürztraminer Alsace 1985 $16 (6/15/87)
90   DOMAINES SCHLUMBERGER Gewürztraminer Alsace Fleur de Guebwiller 1985 $14.50 (7/15/88)
89   DOMAINE WEINBACH Gewürztraminer Alsace Clos des Capucins 1985 $21 (7/15/88)
88   DOMAINE ZIND HUMBRECHT Gewürztraminer Alsace Herrenweg Turckheim 1985 $14 (7/31/87)
87   ROLLY GASSMAN Gewürztraminer Alsace Brandhurst 1985 $17 (7/15/88)
83   DOPFF & IRION Gewürztraminer Alsace Les Socières Château de Riquewihr 1985 $34 (3/15/87)
83   PIERRE SPARR Gewürztraminer Alsace Cuvée Centenaire Mambourg 1985 $17.50 (7/15/88)
81   DOPFF AU MOULIN Gewürztraminer Alsace 1985 $10.50 (7/15/88)
81   DOMAINE ZIND HUMBRECHT Gewürztraminer Alsace Goldert Vendnage Tardive 1985 $40 (9/15/87)
80   DOMAINE WEINBACH Gewürztraminer Alsace Clos des Capucins Personnelle 1985 $16 (7/15/88)
70   MURE Gewürztraminer Alsace Clos St.-Landelin Vorbourg 1985 $12 (6/15/87)
68   LOUIS SIPP Gewürztraminer Alsace 1985 $9 (7/15/88)
64   MURE Gewürztraminer Alsace 1985 $7 (6/15/87)
60   DOPFF & IRION Gewürztraminer Alsace Les Sorcières Château de Riquewihr 1985 $13 (3/15/87)
58   DOPFF & IRION Gewürztraminer Alsace 1985 $9 (3/15/87)

1983

95   HUGEL Gewürztraminer Alsace Sélection de Grains Nobles 1983 (NA) (4/30/87) (JS)
95   HUGEL Gewürztraminer Alsace Vendange Tardive 1983 (NA) (4/30/87) (JS)
87   DOMAINES SCHLUMBERGER Gewürztraminer Alsace Fleur de Guebwiller 1983 $11.50 (8/31/87)
85   HUGEL Gewürztraminer Alsace Réserve Personnelle 1983 $19 (10/15/87)
82   TRIMBACH Gewürztraminer Alsace 1983 $7 (9/01/85)
76   DOPFF & IRION Gewürztraminer Alsace Vendange Tardives 1983 $26 (3/15/87)
59   RENE SCHMIDT Gewürztraminer Alsace Cuvée Particulière Réserve 1983 $9 (6/01/86)

1981

93   HUGEL Gewürztraminer Alsace Sélection de Grains Nobles 1981 (NA) (4/30/87) (JS)

1976

90   HUGEL Gewürztraminer Alsace Sélection de Grains Nobles 1976 (NA) (4/30/87) (JS)
88   HUGEL Gewürztraminer Alsace Vendange Tardive 1976 (NA) (4/30/87) (JS)

1966

75   HUGEL Gewürztraminer Alsace Vendange Tardive 1966 (NA) (4/30/87) (JS)

1961

98   HUGEL Gewürztraminer Alsace Sélection de Grains Nobles 1961 (NA) (4/30/87) (JS)

PINOT BLANC

1989

89   JOSMEYER Pinot Blanc Alsace Pinot Auxerrois ''H'' Vieilles Vignes 1989 (NA) (11/15/90)
88   DOMAINE WEINBACH Pinot Blanc Alsace 1989 (NA) (11/15/90)
86   HUGEL Pinot Blanc Alsace 1989 (NA) (11/15/90)
86   MARC KREYDENWEISS Pinot Blanc Alsace Kritt Klevner 1989 $17 (11/15/90)
86   TRIMBACH Pinot Blanc Alsace 1989 (NA) (11/15/90)
86   TRIMBACH Pinot Blanc Alsace Sélection 1989 (NA) (11/15/90)
85   JOSMEYER Pinot Blanc Alsace Les Lutins 1989 $15 (11/15/90)
84   DOPFF & IRION Pinot Blanc Alsace 1989 (NA) (11/15/90)
83   MARC KREYDENWEISS Pinot Blanc Alsace Kritt 1989 $14 (11/15/90)
83   GUSTAVE LORENTZ Pinot Blanc Alsace 1989 $11 (11/15/90)
83   ALSACE WILLM Pinot Blanc Alsace 1989 (NA) (11/15/90)
81   DOMAINE OSTERTAG Pinot Blanc Alsace Barriques 1989 $14 (7/31/91)
78   LEON BEYER Pinot Blanc Alsace 1989 (NA) (11/15/90)
76   DOMAINE ZIND HUMBRECHT Pinot Blanc Alsace 1989 (NA) (11/15/90)
75   DOMAINE LUCIEN ALBRECHT Pinot Blanc Alsace 1989 $7 (11/15/90)
73   KUENTZ-BAS Pinot Blanc Alsace 1989 (NA) (11/15/90)

1988

87   MARC KREYDENWEISS Pinot Blanc Alsace Kritt 1988 $13 (10/15/89)
87   TRIMBACH Pinot Blanc Alsace 1988 $8 (11/15/90) BB
87   DOMAINE ZIND HUMBRECHT Pinot Blanc Alsace 1988 (NA) (10/15/89)
84   KUENTZ-BAS Pinot Blanc Alsace Cuvée Tradition 1988 (NA) (10/15/89)
84   DOMAINES SCHLUMBERGER Pinot Blanc Alsace 1988 (NA) (10/15/89)
83   HUGEL Pinot Blanc Alsace 1988 $9 (10/15/89)
83   CUVEE LEON Pinot Blanc Alsace Pinot Blanc 1988 $10 (3/31/91)
83   TRIMBACH Pinot Blanc Alsace 1988 $7 (10/15/89)
82   DOPFF & IRION Pinot Blanc Alsace Cuvée René Dopff 1988 (NA) (10/15/89)
80   DOMAINE WEINBACH Pinot Blanc Alsace Clos des Capucins 1988 (NA) (10/15/89)
79   LEON BEYER Pinot Blanc Alsace Blanc de Blancs 1988 $8.75 (10/15/89)
79   GUSTAVE LORENTZ Pinot Blanc Alsace 1988 $12 (10/15/89)
74   DOMAINE WEINBACH Pinot Blanc Alsace Clos des Capucins Réserve Particulière 1988 $19 (10/15/89)

1987

84   LEON BEYER Pinot Blanc Alsace de Blancs 1987 $9 (7/31/89)

1986

86   TRIMBACH Pinot Blanc Alsace 1986 $9 (7/15/88)
83   DOMAINES SCHLUMBERGER Pinot Blanc Alsace 1986 $8.75 (7/15/88)
81   J. BECKER Pinot Blanc Alsace 1986 $9.50 (7/15/88)
78   GUSTAVE LORENTZ Pinot Blanc Alsace Réserve 1986 $7 (7/31/89)
71   HUGEL Pinot Blanc Alsace Cuvée les Amours 1986 $7.75 (7/15/88)

1985

82   DOPFF & IRION Pinot Blanc Alsace de Blancs 1985 $7 (2/28/87)
78   ALSACE WILLM Pinot Blanc Alsace Cordon d'Alsace 1985 $7.75 (7/15/88)
75   HUGEL Pinot Blanc Alsace Cuvée les Amours 1985 $9 (5/31/87)

1983

82   DOMAINES SCHLUMBERGER Pinot Blanc Alsace 1983 $8 (6/15/87)

1982

80   HUGEL Pinot Blanc Alsace Cuvée les Amours 1982 $6 (10/16/84)

RIESLING

1989

97   TRIMBACH Riesling Alsace Vendange Tardive Clos Ste.-Hune Hors Choix 1989 (NA) (11/15/90)
96   TRIMBACH Riesling Alsace Vendange Tardive Clos Ste.-Hune 1989 (NA) (11/15/90)
96   DOMAINE WEINBACH Riesling Alsace Sélection de Grains Nobles Clos des Capucins 1989 (NA) (11/15/90)
95   DOPFF AU MOULIN Riesling Alsace Sélection de Grains Nobles 1989 (NA) (11/15/90)
95   TRIMBACH Riesling Alsace Vendange Tardive Cuvée Frédéric Emile 1989 (NA) (11/15/90)
92   LEON BEYER Riesling Alsace Cuvée Particulière 1989 (NA) (11/15/90)
92   TRIMBACH Riesling Alsace Cuvée Frédéric Emile 1989 (NA) (11/15/90)
90   HUGEL Riesling Alsace Jubilée Réserve Personnelle 1989 (NA) (11/15/90)
90   HUGEL Riesling Alsace Vendange Tardive 1989 (NA) (11/15/90)
90   JOSMEYER Riesling Alsace Hengst 1989 (NA) (11/15/90)
90   TRIMBACH Riesling Alsace Réserve 1989 (NA) (11/15/90)
90   TRIMBACH Riesling Alsace Sélection de Grains Nobles Frédéric Emile 1989 (NA) (11/15/90)
89   MURE Riesling Alsace Sélection de Grains Nobles Clos St.-Landelin Vorbour 1989 (NA) (11/15/90)
89   DOMAINES SCHLUMBERGER Riesling Alsace Kitterlé 1989 (NA) (11/15/90)
89   DOMAINE ZIND HUMBRECHT Riesling Alsace Herrenweg 1989 $24 (11/15/90)
88   GUSTAVE LORENTZ Riesling Alsace Altenberg 1989 (NA) (11/15/90)
88   DOMAINE OSTERTAG Riesling Alsace Muenchberg 1989 $33 (7/31/91)
88   DOMAINE WEINBACH Riesling Alsace Clos des Capucins Cuvée Théo 1989 $31 (11/15/90)
87   DOMAINE LUCIEN ALBRECHT Riesling Alsace Sélection de Grains Nobles Pfingstberg 1989 (NA) (11/15/90)
87   HUGEL Riesling Alsace 1989 (NA) (11/15/90)
87   MURE Riesling Alsace Clos St.-Landelin Vorburg 1989 (NA) (11/15/90)
87   DOMAINE OSTERTAG Riesling Alsace Fronholz 1989 (NA) (7/31/91)
87   DOMAINE OSTERTAG Riesling Alsace Vignoble d'Epfig 1989 $14 (7/31/91)
87   DOMAINE ZIND HUMBRECHT Riesling Alsace Vendange Tardive Brand 1989 (NA) (11/15/90)
86   DOPFF AU MOULIN Riesling Alsace Vendange Tardive 1989 (NA) (11/15/90)
86   HUGEL Riesling Alsace Cuvée Tradition 1989 (NA) (11/15/90)
86   JOSMEYER Riesling Alsace La Kottabe 1989 (NA) (11/15/90)
86   DOMAINES SCHLUMBERGER Riesling Alsace 1989 (NA) (11/15/90)
86   PIERRE SPARR Riesling Alsace Schlossberg Cuvée Réserve 1989 (NA) (11/15/90)
86   TRIMBACH Riesling Alsace 1989 (NA) (11/15/90)
86   DOMAINE WEINBACH Riesling Alsace Clos des Capucins Réserve Personnelle 1989 $23 (11/15/90)
86   DOMAINE ZIND HUMBRECHT Riesling Alsace Clos St.-Urbain Rangen 1989 $45 (11/15/90)
85   DOMAINE OSTERTAG Riesling Alsace en Barriques Heissenberg 1989 $24 (7/31/91)
85   ALSACE WILLM Riesling Alsace 1989 (NA) (11/15/90)
84   LEON BEYER Riesling Alsace 1989 (NA) (11/15/90)
84   MARC KREYDENWEISS Riesling Alsace Weibelsberg 1989 (NA) (11/15/90)
84   DOMAINE WEINBACH Riesling Alsace Clos des Capucins Schlossberg 1989 $31 (11/15/90)
83   MARC KREYDENWEISS Riesling Alsace Andlau 1989 $18 (11/15/90)
83   KUENTZ-BAS Riesling Alsace Pfersigberg 1989 (NA) (11/15/90)
82   MARC KREYDENWEISS Riesling Alsace Kastelberg 1989 (NA) (11/15/90)
82   ALSACE WILLM Riesling Alsace Kirchberg de Barr 1989 (NA) (11/15/90)
81   BOTT FRERES Riesling Alsace Cuvée Exceptionnelle 1989 $13 (7/31/91)
81   DOPFF & IRION Riesling Alsace 1989 (NA) (11/15/90)
81   DOPFF & IRION Riesling Alsace Schoenenbourg 1989 (NA) (11/15/90)
81   DOMAINE WEINBACH Riesling Alsace Clos des Capucins Réserve Personnelle Théo Faller 1989 $23 (7/31/91)
80   LEON BEYER Riesling Alsace Sélection de Grains Nobles 1989 (NA) (11/15/90)
80   DOPFF AU MOULIN Riesling Alsace 1989 (NA) (11/15/90)
80   DOPFF & IRION Riesling Alsace Les Murailles Château de Riquewihr 1989 (NA) (11/15/90)
80   DOMAINE WEINBACH Riesling Alsace Clos des Capucins Cuvée Ste.-Catherine 1989 $43 (11/15/90)
80   ALSACE WILLM Riesling Alsace Cuvée Emile Willm 1989 (NA) (11/15/90)

79   LEON BEYER Riesling Alsace Vendange Tardive 1989 (NA) (11/15/90)
79   DOPFF AU MOULIN Riesling Alsace Propre Récolte 1989 (NA) (11/15/90)
79   MARC KREYDENWEISS Riesling Alsace Vendange Tardive Weibelsberg 1989 (NA) (11/15/90)
79   KUENTZ-BAS Riesling Alsace Réserve Personelle 1989 (NA) (11/15/90)
79   PIERRE SPARR Riesling Alsace Altenbourg Cuvée Centenaire 1989 (NA) (11/15/90)
78   DOPFF AU MOULIN Riesling Alsace Schoenenbourg 1989 (NA) (11/15/90)
78   MURE Riesling Alsace Vendange Tardive Clos St.-Landelin Vorbourg 1989 (NA) (11/15/90)
75   GUSTAVE LORENTZ Riesling Alsace Réserve 1989 (NA) (11/15/90)
74   GUSTAVE LORENTZ Riesling Alsace 1989 $15 (11/15/90)
69   KUENTZ-BAS Riesling Alsace 1989 (NA) (11/15/90)

1988

95   MARC KREYDENWEISS Riesling Alsace Sélection de Grains Nobles Weibelsberg 1988 (NA) (10/15/89)
91   TRIMBACH Riesling Alsace Cuvée Frédéric Emile 1988 $15 (10/15/89)
90   MARC KREYDENWEISS Riesling Alsace Vendange Tardive Kastelberg 1988 $26 (10/15/89)
90   DOMAINES SCHLUMBERGER Riesling Alsace Kitterlé 1988 $14 (10/15/89)
89   HUGEL Riesling Alsace Cuvée Tradition 1988 (NA) (10/15/89)
89   DOMAINE OSTERTAG Riesling Alsace 1988 (NA) (10/15/89)
87   LEON BEYER Riesling Alsace Sélection de Grains Nobles 1988 $25 (10/15/89)
87   DOPFF & IRION Riesling Alsace Vendange Tardive 1988 (NA) (10/15/89)
87   HUGEL Riesling Alsace 1988 $12.50 (10/15/89)
87   DOMAINE WEINBACH Riesling Alsace Cuvée Ste.-Catherine 1988 $30 (10/15/89)
87   DOMAINE ZIND HUMBRECHT Riesling Alsace 1988 (NA) (10/15/89)
86   MARC KREYDENWEISS Riesling Alsace 1988 $15.50 (10/15/89)
86   TRIMBACH Riesling Alsace 1988 $7.50 (10/15/89)
86   DOMAINE ZIND HUMBRECHT Riesling Alsace Rangen 1988 (NA) (10/15/89)
85   DOPFF & IRION Riesling Alsace Cuvée René Dopff 1988 $9.25 (10/15/89)
85   GUSTAVE LORENTZ Riesling Alsace 1988 $15 (10/15/89)
85   DOMAINES SCHLUMBERGER Riesling Alsace 1988 (NA) (10/15/89)
84   DOPFF AU MOULIN Riesling Alsace 1988 (NA) (10/15/89)
84   MARC KREYDENWEISS Riesling Alsace Grand Cru Weibelsberg 1988 $23 (10/15/89)
84   KUENTZ-BAS Riesling Alsace Cuvée Tradition 1988 (NA) (10/15/89)
84   KUENTZ-BAS Riesling Alsace Réserve Personelle 1988 (NA) (10/15/89)
84   GUSTAVE LORENTZ Riesling Alsace Altenberg de Bergheim 1988 (NA) (10/15/89)
83   DOPFF AU MOULIN Riesling Alsace Vendange Tardive 1988 (NA) (10/15/89)
82   DOMAINES SCHLUMBERGER Riesling Alsace Saering 1988 (NA) (10/15/89)
81   DOMAINE OSTERTAG Riesling Alsace Muenchberg 1988 (NA) (10/15/89)
80   LEON BEYER Riesling Alsace 1988 $10.50 (10/15/89)
80   DOMAINE WEINBACH Riesling Alsace Cuvée Théo 1988 (NA) (10/15/89)
79   DOPFF & IRION Riesling Alsace Les Murailles 1988 (NA) (10/15/89)
78   DOMAINE WEINBACH Riesling Alsace Clos des Capucins Réserve Personnelle Théo Faller 1988 $18 (7/31/91)

1987

76   LEON BEYER Riesling Alsace Réserve 1987 $13 (7/31/89)
71   WOLFBERGER Riesling Alsace 1987 $8 (7/31/89)

1986

91   TRIMBACH Riesling Alsace Clos Ste.-Hune 1986 (NA) (5/15/89) (JS)
80   DOMAINE ZIND HUMBRECHT Riesling Alsace 1986 $12.50 (7/15/88)
79   GUSTAVE LORENTZ Riesling Alsace Réserve 1986 $9.50 (7/31/89)
79   TRIMBACH Riesling Alsace 1986 $10 (7/15/88)
77   J. BECKER Riesling Alsace 1986 $11 (7/15/88)
76   DOMAINE FERNAND GRESSER Riesling Alsace Andlau 1986 $15 (7/15/88)
74   DOMAINES SCHLUMBERGER Riesling Alsace des Princes Abbes 1986 $10.50 (7/15/88)

1985

90   TRIMBACH Riesling Alsace Clos Ste.-Hune 1985 (NA) (5/15/89) (JS)
86   DOMAINE ZIND HUMBRECHT Riesling Alsace Clos St.-Urbain 1985 $26 (9/15/87)
85   DOMAINE ZIND HUMBRECHT Riesling Alsace Vendange Tardive 1985 $19 (9/15/87)
84   DOPFF & IRION Riesling Alsace 1985 $8 (4/30/87)
82   DOMAINE WEINBACH Riesling Alsace Schlossberg Clos des Capucins 1985 $18 (7/15/88)
80   HUGEL Riesling Alsace 1985 $10.50 (10/15/87)
79   DOPFF & IRION Riesling Alsace Les Murailles Château de Riquewihr 1985 $12 (3/15/87)
79   DOPFF & IRION Riesling Alsace Les Sorcières Château de Riquewihr 1985 $12 (3/15/87)
79   DOMAINES SCHLUMBERGER Riesling Alsace Saering 1985 $14.50 (7/15/88)
76   DOMAINE OSTERTAG Riesling Alsace 1985 $10 (7/15/88)
75   ALSACE WILLM Riesling Alsace 1985 $10 (7/15/88)
70   DOMAINE ZIND HUMBRECHT Riesling Alsace Réserve 1985 $11 (7/31/87)
69   MURE Riesling Alsace Clos St.-Landelin Vorbourg 1985 $11.50 (5/31/87)

1983

95   TRIMBACH Riesling Alsace Clos Ste.-Hune 1983 (NA) (5/15/89) (JS)
88   HUGEL Riesling Alsace Vendange Tardive 1983 (NA) (4/30/87) (JS)
84   DOPFF & IRION Riesling Alsace Vendange Tardives 1983 $23 (3/15/87)
62   RENE SCHMIDT Riesling Alsace Schoenenberg Cuvée Particulière Réserve 1983 $9 (4/01/86)

1982

85   TRIMBACH Riesling Alsace Clos Ste.-Hune 1982 $24 (5/15/89) (JS)
74   TRIMBACH Riesling Alsace 1982 $6.50 (1/01/85)

1981

91   TRIMBACH Riesling Alsace Clos Ste.-Hune 1981 (NA) (5/15/89) (JS)
80   HUGEL Riesling Alsace Vendange Tardive 1981 (NA) (4/30/87) (JS)

1979

87   TRIMBACH Riesling Alsace Clos Ste.-Hune 1979 (NA) (5/15/89) (JS)

1976

98   HUGEL Riesling Alsace Sélection de Grains Nobles 1976 (NA) (4/30/87) (JS)
92   HUGEL Riesling Alsace Vendange Tardive 1976 (NA) (4/30/87) (JS)
91   TRIMBACH Riesling Alsace Clos Ste.-Hune 1976 (NA) (5/15/89) (JS)

1975

95   TRIMBACH Riesling Alsace Clos Ste.-Hune 1975 (NA) (5/15/89) (JS)

1973

82   TRIMBACH Riesling Alsace Clos Ste.-Hune 1973 (NA) (5/15/89) (JS)

FRANCE
ALSACE/RIESLING

1971
94   TRIMBACH Riesling Alsace Clos Ste.-Hune 1971 (NA) (5/15/89) (JS)

1967
85   TRIMBACH Riesling Alsace Clos Ste.-Hune 1967 (NA) (5/15/89) (JS)

1966
94   TRIMBACH Riesling Alsace Clos Ste.-Hune 1966 (NA) (5/15/89) (JS)

1961
95   HUGEL Riesling Alsace Vendange Tardive 1961 (NA) (4/30/87) (JS)

TOKAY PINOT GRIS

1989
99   TRIMBACH Tokay Pinot Gris Alsace Sélection de Grains Nobles Hors Choix 1989 (NA) (11/15/90)
95   DOMAINE WEINBACH Tokay Pinot Gris Alsace Sélection de Grains Nobles Clos des Capucins 1989 (NA) (11/15/90)
94   HUGEL Tokay Pinot Gris Alsace Sélection de Grains Nobles 1989 (NA) (11/15/90)
93   LEON BEYER Tokay Pinot Gris Alsace Sélection de Grains Nobles 1989 (NA) (11/15/90)
91   DOMAINE ZIND HUMBRECHT Tokay Pinot Gris Alsace Vendange Tardive Clos Windsbuhl 1989 (NA) (11/15/90)
90   HUGEL Tokay Pinot Gris Alsace Vendange Tardive 1989 (NA) (11/15/90)
90   MARC KREYDENWEISS Tokay Pinot Gris Alsace Sélection de Grains Nobles Moenchberg 1989 (NA) (11/15/90)
90   KUENTZ-BAS Tokay Pinot Gris Alsace Sélection de Grains Nobles Cuvée Jeremy 1989 (NA) (11/15/90)
90   MURE Tokay Pinot Gris Alsace Vendange Tardive Clos St.-Landelin Vorbourg 1989 (NA) (11/15/90)
90   TRIMBACH Tokay Pinot Gris Alsace Sélection de Grains Nobles Réserve 1989 (NA) (11/15/90)
90   DOMAINE WEINBACH Tokay Pinot Gris Alsace Clos des Capucins Cuvée Ste.-Catherine 1989 $43 (11/15/90)
90   ALSACE WILLM Tokay Pinot Gris Alsace Sélection de Grains Nobles 1989 (NA) (11/15/90)
89   PIERRE SPARR Tokay Pinot Gris Alsace Prestige Tête de Cuvée 1989 (NA) (11/15/90)
88   DOMAINE LUCIEN ALBRECHT Tokay Pinot Gris Alsace Vendange Tardive 1989 (NA) (11/15/90)
88   MARC KREYDENWEISS Tokay Pinot Gris Alsace Vendange Tardive Grand Cru Moenchberg 1989 (11/15/90)
88   PIERRE SPARR Tokay Pinot Gris Alsace Carte d'Or 1989 (NA) (11/15/90)
87   DOPFF AU MOULIN Tokay Pinot Gris Alsace Sélection de Grains Nobles 1989 (NA) (11/15/90)
87   DOPFF & IRION Tokay Pinot Gris Alsace Les Maquisards 1989 (NA) (11/15/90)
87   ALSACE WILLM Tokay Pinot Gris Alsace 1989 (NA) (11/15/90)
86   JOSMEYER Tokay Pinot Gris Alsace 1989 (NA) (11/15/90)
86   JOSMEYER Tokay Pinot Gris Alsace Sélection de Grains Nobles Hengst 1989 (NA) (11/15/90)
86   KUENTZ-BAS Tokay Pinot Gris Alsace Cuvée Tradition 1989 (NA) (11/15/90)
86   GUSTAVE LORENTZ Tokay Pinot Gris Alsace Sélection de Grains Nobles 1989 (NA) (11/15/90)
86   MURE Tokay Pinot Gris Alsace Sélection de Grains Nobles Clos St.-Landelin Vorbour 1989 (NA) (11/15/90)
86   DOMAINE WEINBACH Tokay Pinot Gris Alsace Vendange Tardive Clos des Capucins 1989 (NA) (11/15/90)
85   DOPFF & IRION Tokay Pinot Gris Alsace Cuvée René Dopff 1989 (NA) (11/15/90)
85   TRIMBACH Tokay Pinot Gris Alsace Réserve Tradition 1989 (NA) (11/15/90)
85   DOMAINE ZIND HUMBRECHT Tokay Pinot Gris Alsace Sélection de Grains Nobles Clos St.-Urbain Rangen 1989 (NA) (11/15/90)
84   LEON BEYER Tokay Pinot Gris Alsace Réserve 1989 (NA) (11/15/90)
82   GUSTAVE LORENTZ Tokay Pinot Gris Alsace 1989 $15 (11/15/90)
82   GUSTAVE LORENTZ Tokay Pinot Gris Alsace Réserve 1989 (NA) (11/15/90)
82   MURE Tokay Pinot Gris Alsace Clos St.-Landelin Vorbourg 1989 (NA) (11/15/90)
81   KUENTZ-BAS Tokay Pinot Gris Alsace Réserve Personele 1989 (NA) (11/15/90)
80   DOMAINE LUCIEN ALBRECHT Tokay Pinot Gris Alsace Pfingstberg 1989 (NA) (11/15/90)
80   DOMAINE LUCIEN ALBRECHT Tokay Pinot Gris Alsace Réserve du Domaine 1989 (NA) (11/15/90)
78   DOMAINES SCHLUMBERGER Tokay Pinot Gris Alsace Vendange Tardive 1989 (NA) (11/15/90)
78   PIERRE SPARR Tokay Pinot Gris Alsace Vendange Tardive Cuvée Centenaire 1989 (NA) (11/15/90)
77   LEON BEYER Tokay Pinot Gris Alsace Vendange Tardive 1989 (NA) (11/15/90)

1988
90   DOMAINE ZIND HUMBRECHT Tokay Pinot Gris Alsace Clos Jebsal 1988 (NA) (10/15/89)
87   DOPFF AU MOULIN Tokay Pinot Gris Alsace Sélection de Grains Nobles 1988 (NA) (10/15/89)
87   GUSTAVE LORENTZ Tokay Pinot Gris Alsace 1988 $14 (10/15/89)
86   DOPFF AU MOULIN Tokay Pinot Gris Alsace 1988 (NA) (10/15/89)
86   HUGEL Tokay Pinot Gris Alsace Tradition 1988 (NA) (10/15/89)
86   MARC KREYDENWEISS Tokay Pinot Gris Alsace 1988 $23 (10/15/89)
86   KUENTZ-BAS Tokay Pinot Gris Alsace Réserve Personele 1988 (NA) (10/15/89)
86   TRIMBACH Tokay Pinot Gris Alsace Réserve Tradition 1988 (NA) (10/15/89)
84   DOMAINE OSTERTAG Tokay Pinot Gris Alsace Moenchberg 1988 $28 (10/15/89)
83   GUSTAVE LORENTZ Tokay Pinot Gris Alsace Altenberg de Bergheim 1988 (NA) (10/15/89)

83   TRIMBACH Tokay Pinot Gris Alsace 1988 $9 (10/15/89)
82   DOMAINE ZIND HUMBRECHT Tokay Pinot Gris Alsace 1988 (NA) (10/15/89)
81   KUENTZ-BAS Tokay Pinot Gris Alsace Cuvée Tradition 1988 (NA) (10/15/89)
81   DOMAINES SCHLUMBERGER Tokay Pinot Gris Alsace 1988 (NA) (10/15/89)
79   DOPFF & IRION Tokay Pinot Gris Alsace Cuvée René Dopff 1988 $10 (10/15/89)
79   DOMAINE WEINBACH Tokay Pinot Gris Alsace Clos des Capucins Cuvée Ste.-Catherine Théo Falle 1988 $35 (7/31/91)
78   LEON BEYER Tokay Pinot Gris Alsace Cuvée Particulière 1988 $12 (10/15/89)

1986
86   DOMAINE ZIND HUMBRECHT Tokay Pinot Gris Alsace Clos St.-Urbain Rangen de Thann 1986 $35 (7/15/88)
85   DOMAINE ZIND HUMBRECHT Tokay Pinot Gris Alsace Vieille Vigne 1986 $15 (7/15/88)

1985
74   MURE Tokay Pinot Gris Alsace Clos St.-Landelin Vorbourg 1985 $11.50 (5/31/87)

1983
86   HUGEL Tokay Pinot Gris Alsace Vendange Tardive 1983 (NA) (4/30/87) (JS)

1976
87   HUGEL Tokay Pinot Gris Alsace Sélection de Grains Nobles 1976 (NA) (4/30/87) (JS)
80   HUGEL Tokay Pinot Gris Alsace Vendange Tardive 1976 (NA) (4/30/87) (JS)

OTHER ALSACE

1989
84   DOMAINE OSTERTAG Pinot Gris Alsace Barriques 1989 $24 (7/31/91)
81   TRIMBACH Sylvaner Alsace Sélection 1989 (NA) (11/15/90)
80   BOTT FRERES Tokay d'Alsace Alsace Cuvée Exceptionnelle 1989 $13.50 (7/31/91)
77   DOMAINE OSTERTAG Sylvaner Alsace Vieilles Vignes 1989 $12 (7/31/91)

1988
78   DOMAINE WEINBACH Muscat Alsace Clos des Capucins Théo Faller 1988 $23 (7/31/91)

1986
80   DOMAINE ZIND HUMBRECHT Sylvaner Alsace 1986 $7.50 (7/15/88)
78   TRIMBACH Pinot Gris Alsace 1986 $12.50 (7/15/88)
74   DOMAINE ZIND HUMBRECHT Pinot d'Alsace Alsace 1986 $9 (7/15/88)

1985
80   SALZMANN Tokay d'Alsace Alsace Schlossberg 1985 $12.25 (5/31/87)
78   TRIMBACH Sylvaner Alsace 1985 $8 (7/15/88)
76   DOPFF & IRION Pinot Gris Alsace Les Maquisards Château de Riquewihr 1985 $12 (2/28/87)
73   HUGEL Sylvaner Alsace 1985 $7.25 (7/15/88)
72   DOMAINE OSTERTAG Sylvaner Alsace 1985 $8.75 (7/15/88)

1983
87   LEON BEYER Pinot Gris Alsace Sélection de Grains Nobles 1983 $48/H (7/31/89)
68   KLUG Muscat Alsace 1983 $4.75 (12/16/85)
49   KLUG Pinot d'Alsace Alsace 1983 $4.50 (12/01/85)

1982
88   TRIMBACH Pinot Gris Alsace Réserve 1982 $7 (1/01/85)

BEAUJOLAIS

1989
87   GEORGES DUBOEUF Beaujolais-Villages 1989 $8 (11/15/90) BB
86   GEORGES DUBOEUF Beaujolais 1989 $7 (11/15/90) BB
86   GERARD GELIN Beaujolais-Villages Domaine des Nugues 1989 $8 (11/15/90) BB
82   NICOLAS Beaujolais-Villages 1989 $8 (11/15/90) BB
79   LOUIS JADOT Beaujolais Jadot 1989 $6 (11/15/90)

1988
93   GEORGES DUBOEUF Moulin-à-Vent New Barrel Aged 1988 $12.25 (5/31/89) (TM)
92   TRENEL & FILS Morgon Côte de Py 1988 $17 (5/31/89) (TM)
91   MOMMESSIN Moulin-à-Vent Domaine de Champ de Cour 1988 $12.50 (5/31/89) (TM)
91   DOMAINE DE LA ROCHELLE Moulin-à-Vent 1988 $10 (5/31/89) (TM)
90   GEORGES DUBOEUF Morgon Jean Descombes 1988 $11.25 (5/31/89) (TM)
90   TRENEL & FILS Moulin-à-Vent La Rochelle 1988 $17 (5/31/89) (TM)
89   GEORGES DUBOEUF Fleurie 1988 $14.50 (5/31/89) (TM)
89   GEORGES DUBOEUF Brouilly Château de Nervers 1988 $11 (5/31/89) (TM)
89   PIERRE FERRAUD & FILS Chénas Cuvée Jean-Michel 1988 $10 (5/31/89) (TM)
89   PIERRE FERRAUD & FILS Morgon Domaine de l'Eveque 1988 $16 (5/31/89) (TM)
88   PHILIPPE ANTOINE Moulin-à-Vent 1988 $11.50 (5/31/89) (TM)
88   MOMMESSIN Morgon Domaine de Lathevalle 1988 $10 (5/31/89) (TM)
88   DOMAINE DE PETIT-CHENE Moulin-à-Vent 1988 $10 (5/31/89) (TM)
88   THORIN Moulin-à-Vent Château des Jacques 1988 $16 (5/31/89) (TM)
87   GEORGES DUBOEUF Morgon 1988 $10.75 (5/31/89) (TM)
87   GEORGES DUBOEUF Moulin-à-Vent 1988 $12.25 (5/31/89) (TM)
87   PIERRE FERRAUD & FILS Fleurie 1988 $15 (5/31/89) (TM)
87   DOMAINE JEAN GAUDET Morgon 1988 $10 (5/31/89) (TM)
87   MOMMESSIN Fleurie 1988 $13.50 (5/31/89) (TM)
87   TRENEL & FILS St.-Amour 1988 $15 (5/31/89) (TM)
86   PIERRE FERRAUD & FILS Fleurie Château de Grand Pre 1988 $16 (5/31/89) (TM)
86   MOMMESSIN Morgon 1988 $10 (5/31/89) (TM)
86   TRENEL & FILS Chénas 1988 $14 (5/31/89) (TM)
86   TRENEL & FILS Fleurie 1988 $14 (5/31/89) (TM)
85   PHILIPPE ANTOINE Juliénas 1988 $11.50 (5/31/89) (TM)
85   GEORGES DUBOEUF Chénas 1988 $10 (5/31/89) (TM)
85   PIERRE FERRAUD & FILS St.-Amour 1988 $12 (5/31/89) (TM)
85   MOMMESSIN Régnié 1988 $10.50 (5/31/89) (TM)
84   PHILIPPE ANTOINE Fleurie 1988 $11.50 (5/31/89) (TM)
84   BARTON & GUESTIER Moulin-à-Vent 1988 $13 (5/31/89) (TM)
84   GEORGES DUBOEUF Chiroubles 1988 $11 (5/31/89) (TM)
84   PIERRE FERRAUD & FILS Brouilly Domaine Rolland 1988 $16 (5/31/89) (TM)
84   DOMAINE DE L'INSTITUT PASTEUR Côte-de-Brouilly 1988 $10 (5/31/89) (TM)
84   MOMMESSIN St.-Amour Domaine de Monreve 1988 $12 (5/31/89) (TM)
83   GEORGES DUBOEUF Brouilly 1988 $11 (5/31/89) (TM)

83 GEORGES DUBOEUF Beaujolais-Villages 1988 $8 (5/31/89) (TM)
83 GEORGES DUBOEUF Régnié 1988 $8 (5/31/89) (TM)
83 PIERRE FERRAUD & FILS Côte-de-Brouilly 1988 $16 (5/31/89) (TM)
83 PIERRE FERRAUD & FILS Moulin-à-Vent 1988 $16 (5/31/89) (TM)
83 MOMMESSIN Chiroubles Château de Raosset 1988 $11.25 (5/31/89) (TM)
83 TRENEL & FILS Chiroubles 1988 $12 (5/31/89) (TM)
83 TRENEL & FILS Régnié 1988 $12 (5/31/89) (TM)
82 PHILIPPE ANTOINE Brouilly 1988 $11.50 (5/31/89) (TM)
82 BARTON & GUESTIER Brouilly 1988 $11 (5/31/89) (TM)
82 DOMAINE ST.-CHARLES Beaujolais-Villages Château du Bluizard 1988 $8 (11/15/90) BB
81 PHILIPPE ANTOINE Régnié 1988 $11.50 (5/31/89) (TM)
81 PIERRE FERRAUD & FILS Régnié 1988 $10 (5/31/89) (TM)
81 PIERRE FERRAUD & FILS Beaujolais-Villages Cuvée Ensorceleuse 1988 $10 (5/31/89) (TM)
81 MOMMESSIN Brouilly Château de Briante 1988 $11.50 (5/31/89) (TM)
81 MOMMESSIN Juliénas Domaine de la Conseillere 1988 $10.50 (5/31/89) (TM)
79 PIERRE FERRAUD & FILS Chiroubles Domaine de la Chapelle du Bois 1988 $12 (5/31/89) (TM)
79 THORIN Beaujolais-Villages 1988 $7 (5/31/89) (TM)
78 MOMMESSIN Beaujolais-Villages Château de Montmelas 1988 $9.50 (5/31/89) (TM)
78 CHATEAU DES RAVATYS Brouilly 1988 $10 (5/31/89) (TM)
78 TRENEL & FILS Beaujolais-Villages 1988 $9 (5/31/89) (TM)
77 PHILIPPE ANTOINE Beaujolais-Villages 1988 $5.50 (5/31/89) (TM)
77 BARTON & GUESTIER Beaujolais-Villages 1988 $9 (5/31/89) (TM)
77 JEAN CLAUDE BOISSET Beaujolais 1988 $6.75 (11/15/90)
76 JEAN CLAUDE BOISSET Beaujolais-Villages 1988 $7.50 (11/15/90)
76 DOMAINE DU MONT VERRIER Beaujolais-Villages 1988 $10 (5/31/89) (TM)
75 BARTON & GUESTIER Beaujolais-Villages St.-Louis 1988 $7.50 (5/31/89) (TM)
75 ANTONIN RODET Beaujolais-Villages Rodet 1988 $8 (11/15/90)
73 PIERRE FERRAUD & FILS Juliénas 1988 $12 (5/31/89) (TM)

1987

83 LOUIS JADOT Moulin-à-Vent 1987 $10.50 (7/15/88)
83 PELLERIN Brouilly 1987 $8.50 (4/15/89)
81 LOUIS JADOT Brouilly 1987 $8.50 (7/15/88)
80 LOUIS JADOT Juliénas 1987 $8.50 (7/15/88)
79 LOUIS JADOT Fleurie 1987 $11 (7/15/88)
79 JAFFELIN Beaujolais-Villages Domaine de Riberolles 1987 $7 (4/15/89)

1986

92 GEORGES DUBOEUF Moulin-à-Vent 1986 $10 (7/31/87) SS
90 GEORGES DUBOEUF Brouilly 1986 $9 (7/31/87)
90 GEORGES DUBOEUF Côte-de-Brouilly 1986 $9 (7/31/87)
88 GEORGES DUBOEUF Morgon 1986 $9 (7/31/87)
87 GEORGES DUBOEUF Chiroubles 1986 $9.50 (7/31/87)
87 GEORGES DUBOEUF Fleurie 1986 $10 (7/31/87)
87 GEORGES DUBOEUF St.-Amour 1986 $9.50 (7/31/87)
85 GEORGES DUBOEUF Chénas 1986 $8.50 (7/31/87)
84 GEORGES DUBOEUF Juliénas 1986 $9 (7/31/87)
83 ROGER VERGE Juliénas 1986 $9.25 (12/31/87)
79 ROGER VERGE Moulin-à-Vent 1986 $12 (12/31/87)
76 ROGER VERGE Fleurie 1986 $9.25 (12/31/87)
75 PHILIPPE ANTOINE Beaujolais-Villages 1986 $6.50 (3/15/88)
74 SYLVAIN FESSY Morgon Cuvée André Gauthier 1986 $7 (12/31/87)
71 SYLVAIN FESSY Juliénas Cuvée Michel Tête 1986 $7 (12/31/87)

1985

89 JAFFELIN Moulin-à-Vent 1985 $9.75 (12/15/86)
87 GEORGES DUBOEUF Morgon 1985 $10 (12/15/86)
87 GEORGES DUBOEUF Moulin-à-Vent 1985 $10 (12/15/86)
87 SYLVAIN FESSY Brouilly Domaine de Chavannes 1985 $8 (12/15/86)
86 SYLVAIN FESSY Juliénas Cuvée Michel Tête 1985 $8.50 (12/15/86)
85 JAFFELIN Fleurie 1985 $9.75 (12/15/86)
85 PAUL JANIN Moulin-à-Vent 1985 $12.75 (10/31/87)
83 GEORGES DUBOEUF St.-Amour 1985 $8 (12/15/86)
82 GEORGES DUBOEUF Brouilly 1985 $9 (12/15/86)
81 GEORGES DUBOEUF Chénas 1985 $9 (12/15/86)
81 MOILLARD Fleurie Grumage 1985 $8 (12/15/86)
81 ROMANECHE-THORINS Moulin-à-Vent Château des Jacques 1985 $10 (3/15/88)
78 GEORGES DUBOEUF Chiroubles 1985 $9 (12/15/86)
76 SYLVAIN FESSY Morgon Cuvée André Gauthier 1985 $8.50 (12/15/86)
72 SYLVAIN FESSY Côte-de-Brouilly Domaine de Chavannes 1985 $8 (12/15/86)
69 GEORGES DUBOEUF Fleurie 1985 $10 (12/15/86)
55 ALIGNE Moulin-à-Vent 1985 $12 (3/15/87)

1984

81 BICHOT Brouilly 1984 $7 (2/01/86)
75 LOUIS CHAMPAGNON Chénas 1984 $7 (5/01/86)
74 CHARLES MONCAUT Fleurie 1984 $6.75 (12/01/85)
68 LOUIS CHAMPAGNON Moulin-à-Vent 1984 $7.25 (5/01/86)

1983

85 DOMAINE DE ROBERT Fleurie 1983 $8 (12/16/85)
83 PAUL JANIN Moulin-à-Vent 1983 $9 (11/01/85)
68 LOUIS JADOT Fleurie 1983 $9 (11/01/85)

BORDEAUX RED/*BORDEAUX*

1989

84   CHATEAU GOFFRETEAU Bordeaux Rouge 1989 $8 (5/15/91) BB
82   LA CAVE TROISGROS Bordeaux Rouge 1989 $9.50 (5/15/91)
80+ CHATEAU BONNET Bordeaux 1989 (NR) (4/30/91) (BT)
79   CHATEAU LAGRAVE PARAN Bordeaux 1989 $8 (2/28/91)
74   CHATEAU TALMONT Bordeaux 1989 $8 (2/28/91)
75+ CHATEAU LAMARTINE Bordeaux 1989 (NR) (4/30/91) (BT)

1988

84   BARTON & GUESTIER Bordeaux Merlot 1988 $6 (2/15/90) BB
82   CHATEAU LAGRAVE PARAN Bordeaux 1988 $6 (7/15/90) BB

81 MOUTON-CADET Bordeaux 1988 $9 (4/30/91) BB
79 ARMAND ROUX Bordeaux Verdillac 1988 $6.25 (7/15/90) BB
78 CHATEAU BONNET Bordeaux Reserve 1988 $11 (7/15/91)
78 MARQUIS DES TOURS Bordeaux 1988 $5 (2/28/91)
77 CHATEAU BONNET Bordeaux 1988 $7.50 (4/30/91)
73 BARTON & GUESTIER Bordeaux Cabernet Sauvignon 1988 $6 (2/15/90)

1987

80 CHATEAU LAGRAVE PARAN Bordeaux 1987 $7 (5/15/90) BB
79 CHATEAU BONNET Bordeaux 1987 $7 (4/15/90)
79 CHATEAU DAVRIL Bordeaux 1987 $5 (9/30/89)
79 MOUTON-CADET Bordeaux 1987 $7.50 (4/15/90)
78 CHATEAU DU CHALET Bordeaux 1987 $6 (4/15/90)
77 DOMAINE SAINTE-ANNE Bordeaux 1987 $5 (5/15/90)

1986

81 MOUTON-CADET Bordeaux 1986 $7.25 (2/15/89) BB
80 CHEVALIER DUCLA Bordeaux 1986 $5.50 (5/15/89) BB
79 CHATEAU FAURIE-PASCAUD Bordeaux 1986 $5 (6/30/88)
79 CHATEAU LAURETAN Bordeaux 1986 $5 (5/15/89)
78 ST.-JOVIAN Bordeaux Cabernet Sauvignon 1986 $4.50 (7/31/88)
77 LA COUR PAVILLON Bordeaux 1986 $7.25 (2/28/91)
77 CHATEAU L'ESPERANCE Bordeaux 1986 $7 (9/30/89)
76 ST.-JOVIAN Bordeaux Merlot 1986 $5 (5/15/89)
74 CHARTRON LA FLEUR Bordeaux 1986 $4.50 (5/15/89)
73 CHATEAU BONNET Bordeaux 1986 $6 (5/15/89)
73 CHATEAU DU MOULIN DE PEYRONIN Bordeaux 1986 $10 (3/31/90)
72 YVON MAU Bordeaux Officiel du Bicentenaire de la Revolution Française 1986 $4.50 (6/30/89)
70 CHATEAU LES ALOUETTES Bordeaux Kosher 1986 $10 (3/31/90)
70 CHATEAU MAROTTE Bordeaux 1986 $3.50 (4/30/88)
68 YVON MAU Bordeaux Officiel du Bicentenaire de la Revolution Française 1986 $4.50 (5/15/89)

1985

84 MAITRE D'ESTOURNEL Bordeaux 1985 $7.25 (5/31/88)
80 LE BORDEAUX PRESTIGE Bordeaux 1985 $9.50 (9/30/88)
80 MOUTON-CADET Bordeaux 1985 $6.50 (5/15/88) BB
78 DOMAINE DE CHEVAL BLANC Bordeaux 1985 $5 (5/15/88)
77 CHEVALIER VEDRINES Bordeaux 1985 $6 (6/30/88)
75 CHATEAU BRIOT Bordeaux 1985 $4 (5/15/87)
75 CHATEAU LES CONFRERIES Bordeaux 1985 $3.50 (2/15/88)
75 ST.-JOVIAN Bordeaux 1985 $4.50 (5/15/88)
74 LA COMBE DES DAMES Bordeaux 1985 $6.50 (3/15/88)
72 CHATEAU RAUZAN DESPAGNE Bordeaux 1985 $5.75 (2/15/88)
67 LA COUR PAVILLON Bordeaux 1985 $6.75 (7/15/88)

1983

81 BEAU MAYNE Bordeaux 1983 $5 (3/31/87) BB
75 MICHEL LYNCH Bordeaux 1983 $6.75 (10/15/87)
72 CHATEAU BONNET Bordeaux 1983 $4.75 (5/01/86)
68 LA COUR PAVILLON Bordeaux 1983 $7 (8/31/87)
53 CHATEAU BOIS-VERT Bordeaux 1983 $3.75 (11/16/85)

1982

79 LES DOUELLES Bordeaux 1982 $3 (10/01/85) BB
77 PONTALLIER JOHNSON Bordeaux Merlot 1982 $8 (10/15/87)
73 CHATEAU BONNET Bordeaux 1982 $4.50 (4/16/85)
73 CHATEAU ST.-SULPICE Bordeaux 1982 $6 (5/15/87)

BORDEAUX SUPÉRIEUR

1989

82 CHATEAU ROC MIGNON D'ADRIEN Bordeaux Supérieur 1989 $6 (2/28/91) BB
79 CHATEAU LA TERRASSE Bordeaux Supérieur 1989 $8 (3/31/91)

1988

84 CHATEAU VIEUX GABRIAN Bordeaux Supérieur 1988 $11 (4/30/91)
82 CHATEAU DE LA GRAVE Bordeaux Supérieur 1988 $8 (7/15/90) BB
82 CHATEAU LAGARENNE Bordeaux Supérieur 1988 $8 (7/31/90) BB
81 CHATEAU GOFFRETEAU Bordeaux Supérieur 1988 $6 (2/28/91) BB
80 ST.-JOVIAN Bordeaux Supérieur Premium 1988 $5.50 (7/31/91) BB
79 BEAUCLAIRE Bordeaux Supérieur 1988 $6 (12/31/90)
75 PIERRE JEAN Bordeaux Supérieur 1988 $8 (7/31/91)
65 CHATEAU JONQUEYRES Bordeaux Supérieur Cuvée Vieilles Vignes 1988 $12 (3/31/91)

1987

76 CHATEAU HAUT MALLET Bordeaux Supérieur 1987 $7.50 (4/15/90)

1986

82 CHATEAU GOFFRETEAU Bordeaux Supérieur 1986 $6 (6/15/89) BB
81 CHATEAU LA CROIX ST.-JEAN Bordeaux Supérieur 1986 $6 (11/30/88) BB
81 CHATEAU LESCALLE Bordeaux Supérieur 1986 $6 (6/30/89)
81 CHATEAU DE PARENCHERE Bordeaux Supérieur 1986 $9 (6/30/89)
80 CHATEAU BRASSAC Bordeaux Supérieur 1986 $5.50 (8/31/88) BB
78 CHATEAU CANDELAY Bordeaux Supérieur 1986 $6 (6/15/89)
78 CHATEAU DE SOURS Bordeaux Supérieur 1986 $7 (9/30/89)
77 CHATEAU LES GRANDS JAYS Bordeaux Supérieur 1986 $6 (5/15/89)
77 CHATEAU TOUR DE BELLEGARDE Bordeaux Supérieur 1986 $4.75 (5/15/89)
76 CHATEAU LA CROIX DE GIRON Bordeaux Supérieur 1986 $5.25 (5/15/89)
76 CHATEAU LA TERRASSE Bordeaux Supérieur 1986 $8 (6/30/89)

1985

81 CHATEAU LANDEREAU Bordeaux Supérieur 1985 $6.75 (2/15/88) BB
78 CHATEAU LA TERRASSE Bordeaux Supérieur 1985 $6 (11/15/87)
71 CHATEAU LES CHARMILLES Bordeaux Supérieur 1985 $8 (2/15/88)
71 CHATEAU HAUT-COLAS NOUET Bordeaux Supérieur 1985 $4 (11/15/87)
70 CHATEAU BELLERIVE Bordeaux Supérieur 1985 $7 (11/15/87)
70 CHATEAU JALOUSIE-BEAULIEU Bordeaux Supérieur 1985 $7 (12/31/88)

FRANCE
BORDEAUX RED/CÔTES DE FRANCS

1984

76   CHATEAU LAMARTINE Bordeaux Supérieur 1984 $9 (5/15/87)

1983

83   CHATEAU REYNIER Bordeaux Supérieur 1983 $3.50 (10/16/85) BB

1982

74   G. MICHELOT Bordeaux Supérieur 1982 $5 (1/01/86) BB
74   CHATEAU LA TERRASSE Bordeaux Supérieur 1982 $4.50 (11/16/85)
72   CHATEAU BELLERIVE Bordeaux Supérieur 1982 $8 (12/16/85)
71   CHATEAU DE LUCAT Bordeaux Supérieur 1982 $4 (10/01/85)

CÔTES DE FRANCS

1989

80+   CHATEAU PUYGUERAUD Côtes de Francs 1989 (NR) (4/30/90) (BT)
75+   CHATEAU FRANCS Côtes de Francs 1989 (NR) (4/30/90) (BT)

1988

80+   CHATEAU LA CLAVERIE Côtes de Francs 1988 $18 (8/31/90) (BT)
80+   CHATEAU FRANCS Côtes de Francs 1988 (NR) (8/31/90) (BT)
80+   CHATEAU PUYGUERAUD Côtes de Francs 1988 $15 (8/31/90) (BT)
80+   CHATEAU PUYGUERAUD Côtes de Francs 1988 $15 (6/30/89) (BT)
70+   CHATEAU LA CLAVERIE Côtes de Francs 1988 $18 (6/30/89) (BT)
70+   CHATEAU FRANCS Côtes de Francs 1988 (NR) (6/30/89) (BT)
70+   CHATEAU LA PRADE Côtes de Francs 1988 (NR) (6/30/89) (BT)

1986

84   CHATEAU PUYGUERAUD Côtes de Francs 1986 Rel: $12 Cur: $12 (6/15/89)
73   LAURIOL Côtes de Francs 1986 $8 (6/15/89)

1985

83   CHATEAU PUYGUERAUD Côtes de Francs 1985 Rel: $9 Cur: $9 (6/30/88)
78   LAURIOL Côtes de Francs 1985 $6.50 (6/30/88)

1983

82   CHATEAU PUYGUERAUD Côtes de Francs 1983 Rel: $7.50 Cur: $8 (10/16/85)

FRONSAC/CANON-FRONSAC

1990

80+   CHATEAU CANON (FRONSAC) Canon-Fronsac 1990 (NR) (4/30/91) (BT)
80+   CHATEAU CANON MOUEIX Canon-Fronsac 1990 (NR) (4/30/91) (BT)
80+   CHATEAU DE LA DAUPHINE Fronsac 1990 (NR) (4/30/91) (BT)
80+   CHATEAU MAZERIS Canon-Fronsac 1990 (NR) (4/30/91) (BT)
75+   CHATEAU CANON DE BREM Canon-Fronsac 1990 (NR) (4/30/91) (BT)

1989

85+   CHATEAU FONTENIL Fronsac 1989 (NR) (4/30/91) (BT)
85+   CHATEAU MAZERIS Canon-Fronsac 1989 (NR) (4/30/91) (BT)
85+   CHATEAU MAZERIS Canon-Fronsac 1989 (NR) (4/30/90) (BT)
80+   CHATEAU CANON (FRONSAC) Canon-Fronsac 1989 (NR) (4/30/91) (BT)
80+   CHATEAU CANON (FRONSAC) Canon-Fronsac 1989 (NR) (4/30/90) (BT)
80+   CHATEAU CANON DE BREM Canon-Fronsac 1989 (NR) (4/30/91) (BT)
80+   CHATEAU CANON DE BREM Canon-Fronsac 1989 (NR) (4/30/90) (BT)
80+   CHATEAU CANON MOUEIX Canon-Fronsac 1989 (NR) (4/30/90) (BT)
80+   CHATEAU DE CARLES Fronsac 1989 (NR) (4/30/91) (BT)
80+   CHATEAU DE LA DAUPHINE Fronsac 1989 (NR) (4/30/91) (BT)
80+   CHATEAU DE LA DAUPHINE Fronsac 1989 (NR) (4/30/90) (BT)
75+   CHATEAU LA VIEILLE CURE Fronsac 1989 (NR) (4/30/91) (BT)
70+   CHATEAU CANON MOUEIX Canon-Fronsac 1989 (NR) (4/30/91) (BT)

1988

85+   CHATEAU CANON MOUEIX Canon-Fronsac 1988 $16 (8/31/90) (BT)
80+   CHATEAU CANON DE BREM Canon-Fronsac 1988 $13 (6/30/89) (BT)
80+   CHATEAU DE LA DAUPHINE Fronsac 1988 (NR) (8/31/90) (BT)
75+   CHATEAU DE LA DAUPHINE Fronsac 1988 (NR) (6/30/89) (BT)
75+   CHATEAU MAZERIS Canon-Fronsac 1988 $18 (6/30/89) (BT)

1987

82   CHATEAU LA VIEILLE CURE Fronsac 1987 $14 (5/15/90)
80+   CHATEAU CANON DE BREM Canon-Fronsac 1987 $14 (6/30/89) (BT)
75+   CHATEAU CANON MOUEIX Canon-Fronsac 1987 $14 (6/30/89) (BT)
75+   CHATEAU CANON MOUEIX Canon-Fronsac 1987 $14 (6/30/88) (BT)
75+   CHATEAU DE LA DAUPHINE Fronsac 1987 $17 (6/30/89) (BT)
75+   CHATEAU DE LA DAUPHINE Fronsac 1987 $17 (6/30/88) (BT)
75+   CHATEAU MAZERIS Canon-Fronsac 1987 $12.50 (6/30/89) (BT)
70+   CHATEAU MAZERIS Canon-Fronsac 1987 $12.50 (6/30/88) (BT)

1986

81   CHATEAU LA VALADE Fronsac 1986 $5.25 (5/15/89) BB
81   CHATEAU LA VIEILLE CURE Fronsac 1986 $15 (5/15/91)
80+   CHATEAU CANON MOUEIX Canon-Fronsac 1986 $15 (6/30/88) (BT)
80+   CHATEAU CANON MOUEIX Canon-Fronsac 1986 $15 (5/15/87) (BT)

80+   CHATEAU MAZERIS Canon-Fronsac 1986 $12.50 (6/30/88) (BT)
78   CHATEAU MOULIN HAUT-LAROQUE Fronsac 1986 $11 (11/15/89)
76   CHATEAU FONTENIL Fronsac 1986 $14 (2/15/90)
75+   CHATEAU DE LA DAUPHINE Fronsac 1986 $20 (6/30/88) (BT)
70+   CHATEAU CANON DE BREM Canon-Fronsac 1986 $15 (5/15/87) (BT)
70+   CHATEAU DE LA DAUPHINE Fronsac 1986 $20 (5/15/87) (BT)
70+   CHATEAU FONTENIL Fronsac 1986 $14 (5/15/87) (BT)
70+   CHATEAU MAZERIS Canon-Fronsac 1986 $12.50 (5/15/87) (BT)

1985

88   CHATEAU LA VIEILLE CURE Fronsac 1985 $15 (12/31/88)
87   CHATEAU FONTENIL Fronsac 1985 $14 (9/30/88)
84   CHATEAU DE LA DAUPHINE Fronsac 1985 $20 (9/30/88)
83   A. MOUEIX Fronsac 1985 $9.50 (9/30/88)
80+   CHATEAU CANON DE BREM Canon-Fronsac 1985 (NR) (5/15/87) (BT)
80+   CHATEAU CANON MOUEIX Canon-Fronsac 1985 $15 (5/15/87) (BT)
80+   CHATEAU DE LA DAUPHINE Fronsac 1985 $20 (5/15/87) (BT)
80+   CHATEAU MAZERIS Canon-Fronsac 1985 $12.50 (5/15/87) (BT)
70+   CHATEAU CANON DE BREM Canon-Fronsac 1985 (NR) (4/16/86) (BT)
60+   CHATEAU DE LA DAUPHINE Fronsac 1985 $20 (4/16/86) (BT)

GRAVES/PESSAC-LÉOGNAN

1990

95+   CHATEAU DE FIEUZAL Pessac-Léognan 1990 (NR) (4/30/91) (BT)
95+   CHATEAU HAUT-BRION Pessac-Léognan 1990 (NR) (4/30/91) (BT)
95+   CHATEAU LA MISSION-HAUT-BRION Pessac-Léognan 1990 (NR) (4/30/91) (BT)
95+   CHATEAU PAPE-CLEMENT Pessac-Léognan 1990 (NR) (4/30/91) (BT)
90+   CHATEAU BOUSCAUT Pessac-Léognan 1990 (NR) (4/30/91) (BT)
90+   CHATEAU CARBONNIEUX Pessac-Léognan 1990 (NR) (4/30/91) (BT)
90+   DOMAINE DE CHEVALIER Pessac-Léognan 1990 (NR) (4/30/91) (BT)
90+   CHATEAU LA LOUVIERE Pessac-Léognan 1990 (NR) (4/30/91) (BT)
90+   CHATEAU OLIVIER Pessac-Léognan 1990 (NR) (4/30/91) (BT)
85+   CHATEAU HAUT-BAILLY Pessac-Léognan 1990 (NR) (4/30/91) (BT)
85+   CHATEAU SMITH-HAUT-LAFITE Pessac-Léognan 1990 (NR) (4/30/91) (BT)

1989

95+   CHATEAU DE FIEUZAL Pessac-Léognan 1989 (NR) (4/30/90) (BT)
95+   CHATEAU HAUT-BRION Pessac-Léognan 1989 (NR) (4/30/91) (BT)
95+   CHATEAU HAUT-BRION Pessac-Léognan 1989 (NR) (4/30/90) (BT)
95+   CHATEAU LA MISSION-HAUT-BRION Pessac-Léognan 1989 (NR) (4/30/91) (BT)
95+   CHATEAU LA MISSION-HAUT-BRION Pessac-Léognan 1989 (NR) (4/30/90) (BT)
95+   CHATEAU PAPE-CLEMENT Pessac-Léognan 1989 (NR) (4/30/91) (BT)
90+   CHATEAU BAHANS-HAUT-BRION Pessac-Léognan 1989 (NR) (4/30/91) (BT)
90+   CHATEAU BARET Pessac-Léognan 1989 (NR) (4/30/91) (BT)
90+   CHATEAU BOUSCAUT Pessac-Léognan 1989 (NR) (4/30/91) (BT)
90+   DOMAINE DE CHEVALIER Pessac-Léognan 1989 (NR) (4/30/91) (BT)
90+   DOMAINE DE CHEVALIER Pessac-Léognan 1989 (NR) (4/30/90) (BT)
90+   CHATEAU LA LOUVIERE Pessac-Léognan 1989 (NR) (4/30/91) (BT)
90+   CHATEAU LA LOUVIERE Pessac-Léognan 1989 (NR) (4/30/90) (BT)
90+   CHATEAU OLIVIER Pessac-Léognan 1989 (NR) (4/30/91) (BT)
90+   CHATEAU OLIVIER Pessac-Léognan 1989 (NR) (4/30/90) (BT)
85+   CHATEAU BARET Pessac-Léognan 1989 (NR) (4/30/90) (BT)
85+   CHATEAU CARBONNIEUX Pessac-Léognan 1989 (NR) (4/30/90) (BT)
85+   CHATEAU DE CRUZEAU Pessac-Léognan 1989 (NR) (4/30/91) (BT)
85+   CHATEAU DE FRANCE Pessac-Léognan 1989 (NR) (4/30/91) (BT)
85+   CHATEAU HAUT-BERGEY Pessac-Léognan 1989 (NR) (4/30/91) (BT)
85+   CHATEAU LARRIVET-HAUT-BRION Pessac-Léognan 1989 (NR) (4/30/91) (BT)
85+   CHATEAU PAPE-CLEMENT Pessac-Léognan 1989 (NR) (4/30/90) (BT)
85+   CHATEAU DE ROCHEMORIN Pessac-Léognan 1989 (NR) (4/30/91) (BT)
85+   CHATEAU SMITH-HAUT-LAFITE Pessac-Léognan 1989 (NR) (4/30/91) (BT)
85+   CHATEAU SMITH-HAUT-LAFITE Pessac-Léognan 1989 (NR) (4/30/90) (BT)
85+   CHATEAU LA TOUR-HAUT-BRION Pessac-Léognan 1989 (NR) (4/30/91) (BT)
85+   CHATEAU LA TOUR-MARTILLAC Pessac-Léognan 1989 (NR) (4/30/91) (BT)
80+   CHATEAU CARBONNIEUX Pessac-Léognan 1989 (NR) (4/30/91) (BT)
80+   CHATEAU HAUT-BAILLY Pessac-Léognan 1989 (NR) (4/30/90) (BT)
80+   CHATEAU MALARTIC-LAGRAVIERE Pessac-Léognan 1989 (NR) (4/30/90) (BT)

1988

98   CHATEAU HAUT-BRION Pessac-Léognan 1988 $95 (4/30/91)
95+   CHATEAU DE FIEUZAL Pessac-Léognan 1988 $32 (8/31/90) (BT)
95+   CHATEAU HAUT-BRION Pessac-Léognan 1988 $95 (8/31/90) (BT)
95+   CHATEAU HAUT-BRION Pessac-Léognan 1988 $95 (6/30/89) (BT)
95+   CHATEAU LA MISSION-HAUT-BRION Pessac-Léognan 1988 $90 (8/31/90) (BT)
95+   CHATEAU LA MISSION-HAUT-BRION Pessac-Léognan 1988 $90 (6/30/89) (BT)
95+   CHATEAU PAPE-CLEMENT Pessac-Léognan 1988 $40 (6/30/89) (BT)
94   CHATEAU HAUT-BAILLY Pessac-Léognan 1988 $30 (4/30/91)
94   CHATEAU LARRIVET-HAUT-BRION Pessac-Léognan 1988 $25 (4/30/91)
93   CHATEAU PAPE-CLEMENT Pessac-Léognan 1988 $40 (12/31/90)
92   CHATEAU DE FRANCE Pessac-Léognan 1988 $18 (2/28/91) SS
91   DOMAINE DE CHEVALIER Pessac-Léognan 1988 $37 (7/15/91)
91   CHATEAU DE FIEUZAL Pessac-Léognan 1988 $32 (4/30/91)
91   CHATEAU OLIVIER Pessac-Léognan 1988 $23 (2/15/91)
91   CHATEAU LA TOUR-HAUT-BRION Pessac-Léognan 1988 $37 (6/15/91) CS
90+   DOMAINE DE CHEVALIER Pessac-Léognan 1988 $37 (6/30/89) (BT)
90+   CHATEAU DE FIEUZAL Pessac-Léognan 1988 $32 (6/30/89) (BT)
90+   CHATEAU HAUT-BAILLY Pessac-Léognan 1988 $30 (8/31/90) (BT)
90+   CHATEAU OLIVIER Pessac-Léognan 1988 $23 (8/31/90) (BT)
88   CHATEAU LA TOUR-MARTILLAC Pessac-Léognan 1988 $24 (2/28/91)
87   CHATEAU LE BONNAT Graves 1988 $18 (12/31/90)
87   CHATEAU BOUSCAUT Pessac-Léognan 1988 $20 (4/30/91)
87   CHATEAU DE CRUZEAU Pessac-Léognan 1988 $14 (2/28/91)
87   CHATEAU LA MISSION-HAUT-BRION Pessac-Léognan 1988 $90 (4/30/91)
86   CHATEAU CARBONNIEUX Pessac-Léognan 1988 $20 (2/28/91)
85+   CHATEAU LA LOUVIERE Pessac-Léognan 1988 $20 (8/31/90) (BT)
85+   CHATEAU MALARTIC-LAGRAVIERE Pessac-Léognan 1988 $20 (6/30/89) (BT)
85+   CHATEAU LA TOUR-HAUT-BRION Pessac-Léognan 1988 $37 (8/31/90) (BT)
85+   CHATEAU LA TOUR-MARTILLAC Pessac-Léognan 1988 $24 (8/31/90) (BT)
84   CHATEAU MALARTIC-LAGRAVIERE Pessac-Léognan 1988 $20 (7/15/91)
80+   CHATEAU BAHANS-HAUT-BRION Pessac-Léognan 1988 $20 (8/31/90) (BT)

80+ CHATEAU BAHANS-HAUT-BRION Pessac-Léognan 1988 $20 (6/30/89) (BT)
80+ CHATEAU BROWN Pessac-Léognan 1988 $17 (6/30/89) (BT)
80+ CHATEAU CARBONNIEUX Pessac-Léognan 1988 $20 (8/31/90) (BT)
80+ CHATEAU CARBONNIEUX Pessac-Léognan 1988 $20 (6/30/89) (BT)
80+ CHATEAU DE FRANCE Pessac-Léognan 1988 $18 (6/30/89) (BT)
80+ CHATEAU HAUT-BERGEY Pessac-Léognan 1988 $12 (6/30/89) (BT)
80+ CHATEAU LA LOUVIERE Pessac-Léognan 1988 $20 (6/30/89) (BT)
80+ CHATEAU SMITH-HAUT-LAFITE Pessac-Léognan 1988 $15 (6/30/89) (BT)
80+ CHATEAU LA TOUR-HAUT-BRION Pessac-Léognan 1988 $37 (6/30/89) (BT)
80+ CHATEAU LA TOUR-MARTILLAC Pessac-Léognan 1988 $24 (6/30/89) (BT)
76 CHATEAU MERIC Graves 1988 $17 (4/30/91)
75+ CHATEAU BOUSCAUT Pessac-Léognan 1988 $20 (6/30/89) (BT)
75+ CHATEAU CARMES-HAUT-BRION Pessac-Léognan 1988 $22 (6/30/89) (BT)
75+ CHATEAU LA GARDE Pessac-Léognan 1988 $15 (6/30/89) (BT)
75+ CHATEAU LES HAUTS DE SMITH Pessac-Léognan 1988 (NR) (6/30/89) (BT)
75+ CHATEAU OLIVIER Pessac-Léognan 1988 $23 (6/30/89) (BT)
75+ CHATEAU PIQUE-CAILLOU Pessac-Léognan 1988 (NR) (6/30/89) (BT)
75+ CHATEAU DE ROCHEMORIN Pessac-Léognan 1988 (NR) (6/30/89) (BT)
70+ CHATEAU BARET Pessac-Léognan 1988 $15 (6/30/89) (BT)
70+ CHATEAU LARRIVET-HAUT-BRION Pessac-Léognan 1988 $25 (6/30/89) (BT)
60+ CHATEAU LE PAPE Pessac-Léognan 1988 (NR) (6/30/89) (BT)

1987

90 CHATEAU HAUT-BRION Pessac-Léognan 1987 Rel: $70 Cur: $70 (10/15/90)
89 CHATEAU LA MISSION-HAUT-BRION Pessac-Léognan 1987 Rel: $39 Cur: $41 (5/15/90)
87 CHATEAU LA TOUR-HAUT-BRION Pessac-Léognan 1987 Rel: $22 Cur: $22 (5/15/90)
85+ CHATEAU DE FIEUZAL Pessac-Léognan 1987 Rel: $18 Cur: $18 (6/30/89) (BT)
85+ CHATEAU HAUT-BRION Pessac-Léognan 1987 Rel: $70 Cur: $70 (6/30/89) (BT)
85+ CHATEAU HAUT-BRION Pessac-Léognan 1987 Rel: $70 Cur: $70 (6/30/88) (BT)
85+ CHATEAU HAUT-BAILLY Pessac-Léognan 1987 Rel: $20 Cur: $20 (6/30/88) (BT)
85+ CHATEAU LA MISSION-HAUT-BRION Pessac-Léognan 1987 Rel: $39 Cur: $41 (6/30/89) (BT)
85+ CHATEAU LA MISSION-HAUT-BRION Pessac-Léognan 1987 Rel: $39 Cur: $41 (6/30/88) (BT)
85+ CHATEAU PAPE-CLEMENT Pessac-Léognan 1987 Rel: $24 Cur: $25 (6/30/88) (BT)
84 CHATEAU PAPE-CLEMENT Pessac-Léognan 1987 Rel: $24 Cur: $25 (5/15/90)
84 CHATEAU SMITH-HAUT-LAFITE Pessac-Léognan 1987 Rel: $15 Cur: $15 (5/15/90)
83 CHATEAU LE BONNAT Graves 1987 $12 (4/15/90)
81 CHATEAU DE FIEUZAL Pessac-Léognan 1987 Rel: $18 Cur: $18 (5/15/90)
80 CHATEAU CARBONNIEUX Pessac-Léognan 1987 $15 (5/15/90)
80+ CHATEAU BOUSCAUT Pessac-Léognan 1987 Rel: $10 Cur: $10 (6/30/89) (BT)
80+ CHATEAU BOUSCAUT Pessac-Léognan 1987 Rel: $10 Cur: $10 (6/30/88) (BT)
80+ CHATEAU CARBONNIEUX Pessac-Léognan 1987 $15 (6/30/89) (BT)
80+ CHATEAU CARBONNIEUX Pessac-Léognan 1987 $15 (6/30/88) (BT)
80+ DOMAINE DE CHEVALIER Pessac-Léognan 1987 Rel: $29 Cur: $29 (6/30/89) (BT)
80+ DOMAINE DE CHEVALIER Pessac-Léognan 1987 Rel: $29 Cur: $29 (6/30/88) (BT)
80+ CHATEAU DE FIEUZAL Pessac-Léognan 1987 Rel: $18 Cur: $18 (6/30/88) (BT)
80+ CHATEAU DE FRANCE Pessac-Léognan 1987 $15 (6/30/89) (BT)
80+ CHATEAU LA LOUVIERE Pessac-Léognan 1987 Rel: $20 Cur: $20 (6/30/89) (BT)
80+ CHATEAU LA LOUVIERE Pessac-Léognan 1987 Rel: $20 Cur: $20 (6/30/88) (BT)
80+ CHATEAU MALARTIC-LAGRAVIERE Pessac-Léognan 1987 Rel: $18 Cur: $18 (6/30/89) (BT)
80+ CHATEAU OLIVIER Pessac-Léognan 1987 Rel: $20 Cur: $24 (6/30/89) (BT)
80+ CHATEAU OLIVIER Pessac-Léognan 1987 Rel: $20 Cur: $24 (6/30/88) (BT)
80+ CHATEAU PAPE-CLEMENT Pessac-Léognan 1987 Rel: $24 Cur: $25 (6/30/89) (BT)
80+ CHATEAU SMITH-HAUT-LAFITE Pessac-Léognan 1987 Rel: $15 Cur: $15 (6/30/89) (BT)
80+ CHATEAU LA TOUR-HAUT-BRION Pessac-Léognan 1987 Rel: $22 Cur: $22 (6/30/89) (BT)
80+ CHATEAU LA TOUR-HAUT-BRION Pessac-Léognan 1987 Rel: $22 Cur: $22 (6/30/88) (BT)
78 CHATEAU MAGNEAU Graves 1987 $12 (5/15/90)
75+ CHATEAU BAHANS-HAUT-BRION Pessac-Léognan 1987 $19 (6/30/89) (BT)
75+ CHATEAU BARET Pessac-Léognan 1987 $14 (6/30/89) (BT)
75+ CHATEAU BROWN Pessac-Léognan 1987 $15 (6/30/89) (BT)
75+ CHATEAU CARMES-HAUT-BRION Pessac-Léognan 1987 Rel: $20 Cur: $20 (6/30/89) (BT)
75+ CHATEAU CARMES-HAUT-BRION Pessac-Léognan 1987 Rel: $20 Cur: $20 (6/30/88) (BT)
75+ CHATEAU DE CRUZEAU Pessac-Léognan 1987 $12 (6/30/89) (BT)
75+ CHATEAU LARRIVET-HAUT-BRION Pessac-Léognan 1987 $17 (6/30/89) (BT)
75+ CHATEAU LARRIVET-HAUT-BRION Pessac-Léognan 1987 $17 (6/30/88) (BT)
75+ CHATEAU LE PAPE Pessac-Léognan 1987 (NR) (6/30/89) (BT)
75+ CHATEAU DE ROCHEMORIN Pessac-Léognan 1987 (NR) (6/30/89) (BT)
75+ CHATEAU LE SARTRE Pessac-Léognan 1987 (NR) (6/30/89) (BT)
75+ CHATEAU LA TOUR-MARTILLAC Pessac-Léognan 1987 $15 (6/30/88) (BT)
70+ CHATEAU DE FRANCE Pessac-Léognan 1987 $15 (6/30/88) (BT)
70+ CHATEAU LA GARDE Pessac-Léognan 1987 $13 (6/30/89) (BT)
70+ CHATEAU LES HAUTS DE SMITH Pessac-Léognan 1987 (NR) (6/30/89) (BT)
70+ CHATEAU PIQUE-CAILLOU Pessac-Léognan 1987 (NR) (6/30/89) (BT)
70+ CHATEAU PIQUE-CAILLOU Pessac-Léognan 1987 (NR) (6/30/88) (BT)
70+ CHATEAU LA TOUR-LEOGNAN Pessac-Léognan 1987 $10 (6/30/89) (BT)
65+ CHATEAU CHENE VERT Pessac-Léognan 1987 (NR) (6/30/89) (BT)
65+ CHATEAU HAUT-BERGEY Pessac-Léognan 1987 $10 (6/30/89) (BT)

1986

95+ CHATEAU HAUT-BRION Pessac-Léognan 1986 Rel: $88 Cur: $88 (6/30/88) (BT)
94 CHATEAU LA MISSION-HAUT-BRION Pessac-Léognan 1986 Rel: $50 Cur: $60 (6/15/89)
92 CHATEAU HAUT-BRION Pessac-Léognan 1986 Rel: $88 Cur: $88 (6/30/89)
92 CHATEAU PAPE-CLEMENT Pessac-Léognan 1986 Rel: $36 Cur: $36 (6/30/89)
91 CHATEAU HAUT-BAILLY Pessac-Léognan 1986 Rel: $23 Cur: $28 (6/15/89)
91 CHATEAU LA LOUVIERE Pessac-Léognan 1986 Rel: $15 Cur: $25 (6/15/89)
90 CHATEAU DE FIEUZAL Pessac-Léognan 1986 Rel: $21 Cur: $23 (6/30/89)
90 CHATEAU MALARTIC-LAGRAVIERE Pessac-Léognan 1986 Rel: $18 Cur: $23 (6/15/89)
90 CHATEAU LA TOUR-MARTILLAC Pessac-Léognan 1986 $15 (2/15/90)
90+ DOMAINE DE CHEVALIER Pessac-Léognan 1986 Rel: $33 Cur: $38 (6/30/88) (BT)
90+ DOMAINE DE CHEVALIER Pessac-Léognan 1986 Rel: $33 Cur: $38 (5/15/87) (BT)
90+ CHATEAU DE FIEUZAL Pessac-Léognan 1986 Rel: $21 Cur: $23 (6/30/88) (BT)
90+ CHATEAU DE FRANCE Pessac-Léognan 1986 $15 (5/15/87) (BT)
90+ CHATEAU HAUT-BRION Pessac-Léognan 1986 Rel: $88 Cur: $88 (5/15/87) (BT)
90+ CHATEAU HAUT-BAILLY Pessac-Léognan 1986 Rel: $23 Cur: $28 (6/30/88) (BT)
90+ CHATEAU HAUT-BAILLY Pessac-Léognan 1986 Rel: $23 Cur: $28 (5/15/87) (BT)
90+ CHATEAU LA MISSION-HAUT-BRION Pessac-Léognan 1986 Rel: $50 Cur: $60 (6/30/88) (BT)
90+ CHATEAU LA MISSION-HAUT-BRION Pessac-Léognan 1986 Rel: $50 Cur: $60 (5/15/87) (BT)
90+ CHATEAU PAPE-CLEMENT Pessac-Léognan 1986 Rel: $36 Cur: $36 (6/30/88) (BT)
89 DOMAINE DE CHEVALIER Pessac-Léognan 1986 Rel: $33 Cur: $38 (6/15/89)
87 CHATEAU CARBONNIEUX Pessac-Léognan 1986 $18 (9/15/89)
87 CHATEAU DE CRUZEAU Pessac-Léognan 1986 $10 (6/30/89)
86 CHATEAU BAHANS-HAUT-BRION Pessac-Léognan 1986 $22 (9/15/89)
85 CHATEAU LA TOUR-LEOGNAN Pessac-Léognan 1986 $11 (2/15/89)
85+ CHATEAU CARBONNIEUX Pessac-Léognan 1986 $18 (6/30/88) (BT)
85+ CHATEAU LA LOUVIERE Pessac-Léognan 1986 Rel: $15 Cur: $25 (6/30/88) (BT)
85+ CHATEAU OLIVIER Pessac-Léognan 1986 Rel: $16 Cur: $19 (6/30/88) (BT)
85+ CHATEAU SMITH-HAUT-LAFITE Pessac-Léognan 1986 Rel: $15 Cur: $15 (6/30/88) (BT)
85+ CHATEAU LA TOUR-HAUT-BRION Pessac-Léognan 1986 Cur: $34 (6/30/88) (BT)
84 CHATEAU DE ROCHEMORIN Pessac-Léognan 1986 Rel: $10 Cur: $10 (6/15/89)
83 CHATEAU RAHOUL Graves 1986 $18 (12/31/90)
82 CHATEAU LARRIVET-HAUT-BRION Pessac-Léognan 1986 $17 (6/15/89)
81 CHATEAU HAUT-GARDERE Pessac-Léognan 1986 $11 (9/30/89)
80 DOMAINE DE GRAND MAISON Pessac-Léognan 1986 $8.50 (4/15/90)
80+ CHATEAU BAHANS-HAUT-BRION Pessac-Léognan 1986 $22 (6/30/88) (BT)
80+ CHATEAU BAHANS-HAUT-BRION Pessac-Léognan 1986 $22 (5/15/87) (BT)
80+ CHATEAU BROWN Pessac-Léognan 1986 $19 (5/15/87) (BT)
80+ CHATEAU CARMES-HAUT-BRION Pessac-Léognan 1986 Rel: $26 Cur: $26 (6/30/88) (BT)
80+ CHATEAU DE FRANCE Pessac-Léognan 1986 $15 (6/30/88) (BT)
80+ CHATEAU HAUT-BERGEY Pessac-Léognan 1986 $12 (6/30/88) (BT)
80+ CHATEAU HAUT-BERGEY Pessac-Léognan 1986 $12 (5/15/87) (BT)
80+ CHATEAU HAUT-GARDERE Pessac-Léognan 1986 $11 (5/15/87) (BT)
80+ CHATEAU LARRIVET-HAUT-BRION Pessac-Léognan 1986 $17 (6/30/88) (BT)
80+ CHATEAU LARRIVET-HAUT-BRION Pessac-Léognan 1986 $17 (5/15/87) (BT)
80+ CHATEAU LA LOUVIERE Pessac-Léognan 1986 Rel: $15 Cur: $25 (5/15/87) (BT)
80+ CHATEAU MALARTIC-LAGRAVIERE Pessac-Léognan 1986 Rel: $18 Cur: $23 (6/30/88) (BT)
80+ CHATEAU PAPE-CLEMENT Pessac-Léognan 1986 Rel: $36 Cur: $36 (5/15/87) (BT)
80+ CHATEAU PIQUE-CAILLOU Pessac-Léognan 1986 (NR) (6/30/88) (BT)
80+ CHATEAU RAHOUL Graves 1986 $18 (5/15/87) (BT)
80+ CHATEAU LA TOUR-HAUT-BRION Pessac-Léognan 1986 Cur: $34 (5/15/87) (BT)
80+ CHATEAU LA TOUR-MARTILLAC Pessac-Léognan 1986 $15 (6/30/88) (BT)
80+ CHATEAU LA TOUR-MARTILLAC Pessac-Léognan 1986 $15 (5/15/87) (BT)
78 CHATEAU BOUSCAUT Pessac-Léognan 1986 Rel: $9 Cur: $12 (2/15/89)
70+ CHATEAU BARET Pessac-Léognan 1986 $16 (5/15/87) (BT)
70+ CHATEAU DE FIEUZAL Pessac-Léognan 1986 Rel: $21 Cur: $23 (5/15/87) (BT)
70+ CHATEAU LA GARDE Pessac-Léognan 1986 $14 (5/15/87) (BT)
70+ CHATEAU MALARTIC-LAGRAVIERE Pessac-Léognan 1986 Rel: $18 Cur: $23 (5/15/87) (BT)
70+ CHATEAU DE ROCHEMORIN Pessac-Léognan 1986 Rel: $10 Cur: $10 (5/15/87) (BT)
70+ CHATEAU SMITH-HAUT-LAFITE Pessac-Léognan 1986 Rel: $15 Cur: $15 (5/15/87) (BT)
60+ CHATEAU PIQUE-CAILLOU Pessac-Léognan 1986 (NR) (5/15/87) (BT)

1985

96 CHATEAU HAUT-BRION Graves 1985 Rel: $70 Cur: $84 (4/30/88)
95 CHATEAU LA MISSION-HAUT-BRION Graves 1985 Rel: $70 Cur: $73 (4/30/88)
93 CHATEAU OLIVIER Graves 1985 Rel: $15 Cur: $24 (2/15/89) SS
92 DOMAINE DE CHEVALIER Graves 1985 Rel: $43 Cur: $56 (9/30/88) CS
90 CHATEAU BOUSCAUT Graves 1985 Rel: $15 Cur: $15 (12/31/88)
90 CHATEAU DE FIEUZAL Graves 1985 Rel: $24 Cur: $24 (6/15/88)
90+ DOMAINE DE CHEVALIER Graves 1985 Rel: $43 Cur: $56 (5/15/87) (BT)
90+ CHATEAU HAUT-BRION Graves 1985 Rel: $70 Cur: $84 (5/15/87) (BT)
90+ CHATEAU HAUT-BRION Graves 1985 Rel: $70 Cur: $84 (4/16/86) (BT)
90+ CHATEAU MALARTIC-LAGRAVIERE Graves 1985 Rel: $22.50 Cur: $23 (5/15/87) (BT)
90+ CHATEAU LA MISSION-HAUT-BRION Graves 1985 Rel: $70 Cur: $73 (5/15/87) (BT)
90+ CHATEAU LA MISSION-HAUT-BRION Graves 1985 Rel: $70 Cur: $73 (4/16/86) (BT)
89 CHATEAU HAUT-BAILLY Graves 1985 Rel: $28 Cur: $28 (6/15/88)
89 CHATEAU SMITH-HAUT-LAFITE Graves 1985 Rel: $15 Cur: $23 (11/30/88)
87 CHATEAU CARBONNIEUX Graves 1985 $16 (11/30/88)
87 CHATEAU LA LOUVIERE Graves 1985 Rel: $16 Cur: $16 (6/30/88)
87 CHATEAU LA TOUR-MARTILLAC Graves 1985 $19.50 (8/31/88)
86 CHATEAU LA TOUR-HAUT-BRION Graves 1985 Rel: $42 Cur: $42 (2/15/89)
85 CHATEAU DE CRUZEAU Graves 1985 $9 (6/15/88) BB
85 CHATEAU RESPIDE-MEDEVILLE Graves 1985 $12.50 (2/29/88)
85 CHATEAU DE ROCHEMORIN Graves 1985 Rel: $9 Cur: $9 (6/15/88)
84 CHATEAU BONNET Graves 1985 $5.50 (4/15/88) BB
83 CHATEAU PAPE-CLEMENT Graves 1985 Rel: $44 Cur: $47 (6/30/88)
80+ CHATEAU BAHANS-HAUT-BRION Graves 1985 $20 (5/15/87) (BT)
80+ CHATEAU BOUSCAUT Graves 1985 Rel: $15 Cur: $15 (5/15/87) (BT)
80+ CHATEAU DE FIEUZAL Graves 1985 Rel: $24 Cur: $24 (5/15/87) (BT)
80+ CHATEAU HAUT-BAILLY Graves 1985 Rel: $28 Cur: $28 (5/15/87) (BT)
80+ CHATEAU PAPE-CLEMENT Graves 1985 Rel: $44 Cur: $47 (5/15/87) (BT)
80+ CHATEAU LA TOUR-HAUT-BRION Graves 1985 Rel: $42 Cur: $42 (5/15/87) (BT)
77 CHATEAU HAUT-GARDERE Graves 1985 $15 (7/31/88)
70+ CHATEAU LA TOUR-HAUT-BRION Graves 1985 Rel: $42 Cur: $42 (4/16/86) (BT)

1984

90 DOMAINE DE CHEVALIER Graves 1984 Rel: $20 Cur: $34 (8/31/87)
89 CHATEAU LA MISSION-HAUT-BRION Graves 1984 Rel: $55 Cur: $55 (5/01/89)
87 CHATEAU HAUT-BAILLY Graves 1984 Rel: $15 Cur: $19 (6/15/87)
80 CHATEAU HAUT-BRION Graves 1984 Rel: $36 Cur: $53 (7/31/87)

1983

95 CHATEAU HAUT-BRION Graves 1983 Rel: $86.50 Cur: $87 (9/30/86) SS
92 CHATEAU OLIVIER Graves 1983 Rel: $15 Cur: $20 (5/01/89)
90 CHATEAU LA MISSION-HAUT-BRION Graves 1983 Rel: $63 Cur: $63 (4/16/86)
90 CHATEAU LA TOUR-HAUT-BRION Graves 1983 Rel: $25 Cur: $33 (3/15/87)
89 CHATEAU PAPE-CLEMENT Graves 1983 Rel: $20 Cur: $30 (3/31/87)
86 CHATEAU HAUT-BAILLY Graves 1983 Rel: $21 Cur: $21 (4/16/86)
78 CHATEAU LA LOUVIERE Graves 1983 Rel: $11 Cur: $16 (11/30/86)

1982

96 CHATEAU LA MISSION-HAUT-BRION Graves 1982 Cur: $85 (5/01/85)
94 CHATEAU LA LOUVIERE Graves 1982 Rel: $11.50 Cur: $25 (10/16/85) SS

FRANCE
BORDEAUX RED/*GRAVES*/*PESSAC-LÉOGNAN*

92   CHATEAU HAUT-BRION Graves 1982 Rel: $60 Cur: $117 (7/01/85)
89   CHATEAU OLIVIER Graves 1982 Rel: $17.50 Cur: $26 (3/15/87)
84   CHATEAU DE CRUZEAU Graves 1982 $7 (12/16/85)
84   CHATEAU PAPE-CLEMENT Graves 1982 Rel: $24 Cur: $31 (2/01/85)
81   CHATEAU DE FIEUZAL Graves 1982 Rel: $12 Cur: $22 (5/01/85)
81   CHATEAU DE FIEUZAL Graves 1982 Rel: $12 Cur: $22 (2/01/85)

1981

92   CHATEAU HAUT-BRION Graves 1981 Rel: $56 Cur: $65 (5/01/89)
91   CHATEAU LA MISSION-HAUT-BRION Graves 1981 Cur: $56 (5/01/85)
87   CHATEAU HAUT-BAILLY Graves 1981 Rel: $13.50 Cur: $21 (6/01/84)
86   CHATEAU BOUSCAUT Graves 1981 Rel: $12.50 Cur: $13 (5/01/84)
86   CHATEAU OLIVIER Graves 1981 Rel: $14 Cur: $14 (10/16/85)
79   CHATEAU SMITH-HAUT-LAFITE Graves 1981 Rel: $12.50 Cur: $13 (6/01/84)
77   CHATEAU PAPE-CLEMENT Graves 1981 Rel: $17.50 Cur: $19 (6/01/84)
75   CHATEAU FERRANDE Graves 1981 $7.50 (3/16/85)

1980

81   CHATEAU LA MISSION-HAUT-BRION Graves 1980 Cur: $40 (5/01/85)

1979

94   CHATEAU HAUT-BRION Graves 1979 Cur: $88 (10/15/89) (JS)
89   CHATEAU LA MISSION-HAUT-BRION Graves 1979 Rel: $48 Cur: $70 (10/15/89) (JS)
89   CHATEAU LA MISSION-HAUT-BRION Graves 1979 Rel: $48 Cur: $70 (5/01/85)
87   DOMAINE DE CHEVALIER Graves 1979 Cur: $40 (10/15/89) (JS)
86   CHATEAU LA TOUR-HAUT-BRION Graves 1979 Cur: $30 (10/15/89) (JS)
84   CHATEAU HAUT-BAILLY Graves 1979 Cur: $23 (10/15/89) (JS)
84   CHATEAU PAPE-CLEMENT Graves 1979 Cur: $22 (10/15/89) (JS)
83   CHATEAU DE FIEUZAL Graves 1979 Cur: $25 (10/15/89) (JS)
69   CHATEAU SMITH-HAUT-LAFITE Graves 1979 Cur: $20 (10/15/89) (JS)

1978

88   CHATEAU LA MISSION-HAUT-BRION Graves 1978 Cur: $120 (5/01/85)

1970

67   CHATEAU HAUT-BRION Graves 1970 Cur: $150 (4/01/86)

1962

90   CHATEAU PAPE-CLEMENT Graves 1962 Cur: $120 (11/30/87) (JS)
85   CHATEAU LA TOUR-HAUT-BRION Graves 1962 Cur: $40 (11/30/87) (JS)
70   CHATEAU HAUT-BRION Graves 1962 Cur: $157 (11/30/87) (JS)
68   CHATEAU LA MISSION-HAUT-BRION Graves 1962 Cur: $157 (11/30/87) (JS)

1961

92   CHATEAU LA MISSION-HAUT-BRION Graves 1961 Cur: $450 (3/16/86) (JL)
84   CHATEAU HAUT-BRION Graves 1961 Cur: $434 (3/16/86) (JL)
77   CHATEAU PAPE-CLEMENT Graves 1961 Cur: $160 (3/16/86) (JL)
76   DOMAINE DE CHEVALIER Graves 1961 Cur: $150 (3/16/86) (JL)

1959

97   DOMAINE DE CHEVALIER Graves 1959 Cur: $100 (10/15/90) (JS)
85   CHATEAU LA MISSION-HAUT-BRION Graves 1959 Cur: $390 (10/15/90) (JS)
80   CHATEAU PAPE-CLEMENT Graves 1959 Cur: $125 (10/15/90) (JS)

1945

99   CHATEAU HAUT-BRION Graves 1945 Cur: $857 (3/16/86) (JL)
94   CHATEAU HAUT-BAILLY Graves 1945 Cur: $200 (3/16/86) (JL)
70   CHATEAU LA MISSION-HAUT-BRION Graves 1945 Cur: $681 (3/16/86) (JL)
67   CHATEAU LA TOUR-HAUT-BRION Graves 1945 Cur: $513 (3/16/86) (JL)
59   DOMAINE DE CHEVALIER Graves 1945 Cur: $180 (3/16/86) (JL)

HAUT-MÉDOC

1990

85+   CHATEAU CITRAN Haut-Médoc 1990 (NR) (4/30/91) (BT)
85+   CHATEAU COUFRAN Haut-Médoc 1990 (NR) (4/30/91) (BT)
85+   CHATEAU SOCIANDO-MALLET Haut-Médoc 1990 (NR) (4/30/91) (BT)
85+   CHATEAU SOUDARS Haut-Médoc 1990 (NR) (4/30/91) (BT)
85+   CHATEAU VERDIGNAN Haut-Médoc 1990 (NR) (4/30/91) (BT)
80+   CHATEAU CANTEMERLE Haut-Médoc 1990 (NR) (4/30/91) (BT)
80+   CHATEAU LANESSAN Haut-Médoc 1990 (NR) (4/30/91) (BT)
80+   CHATEAU MALESCASSE Haut-Médoc 1990 (NR) (4/30/91) (BT)
75+   CHATEAU LAROSE-TRINTAUDON Haut-Médoc 1990 (NR) (4/30/91) (BT)
75+   CHATEAU LA TOUR CARNET Haut-Médoc 1990 (NR) (4/30/91) (BT)

1989

90+   CHATEAU CANTEMERLE Haut-Médoc 1989 (NR) (4/30/91) (BT)
90+   CHATEAU CANTEMERLE Haut-Médoc 1989 (NR) (4/30/90) (BT)
90+   CHATEAU CITRAN Haut-Médoc 1989 (NR) (4/30/91) (BT)
90+   CHATEAU CITRAN Haut-Médoc 1989 (NR) (4/30/90) (BT)
90+   CHATEAU LIVERSAN Haut-Médoc 1989 (NR) (4/30/91) (BT)
90+   CHATEAU SOCIANDO-MALLET Haut-Médoc 1989 (NR) (4/30/91) (BT)
85+   CHATEAU ARNAULD Haut-Médoc 1989 (NR) (4/30/91) (BT)
85+   CHATEAU BEAUMONT Haut-Médoc 1989 (NR) (4/30/91) (BT)
85+   CHATEAU COUFRAN Haut-Médoc 1989 (NR) (4/30/91) (BT)

85+   CHATEAU LA LAGUNE Haut-Médoc 1989 (NR) (4/30/90) (BT)
85+   CHATEAU LANESSAN Haut-Médoc 1989 (NR) (4/30/90) (BT)
85+   CHATEAU RAMAGE LA BATISSE Haut-Médoc 1989 (NR) (4/30/91) (BT)
85+   CHATEAU SENEJAC Haut-Médoc 1989 (NR) (4/30/91) (BT)
85+   CHATEAU SOCIANDO-MALLET Haut-Médoc 1989 (NR) (4/30/90) (BT)
80+   CHATEAU D'AGASSAC Haut-Médoc 1989 (NR) (4/30/91) (BT)
80+   CHATEAU DE CAMENSAC Haut-Médoc 1989 (NR) (4/30/90) (BT)
80+   CHATEAU CARONNE STE.-GEMME Haut-Médoc 1989 (NR) (4/30/91) (BT)
80+   CHATEAU COUFRAN Haut-Médoc 1989 (NR) (4/30/91) (BT)
80+   CHATEAU HANTEILLAN Haut-Médoc 1989 (NR) (4/30/91) (BT)
80+   CHATEAU LAROSE-TRINTAUDON Haut-Médoc 1989 (NR) (4/30/90) (BT)
80+   CHATEAU MALESCASSE Haut-Médoc 1989 (NR) (4/30/91) (BT)
80+   CHATEAU SOUDARS Haut-Médoc 1989 (NR) (4/30/90) (BT)
80+   CHATEAU VERDIGNAN Haut-Médoc 1989 (NR) (4/30/90) (BT)
75+   CHATEAU LANESSAN Haut-Médoc 1989 (NR) (4/30/91) (BT)
75+   CHATEAU LAROSE-TRINTAUDON Haut-Médoc 1989 (NR) (4/30/91) (BT)
75+   CHATEAU SOUDARS Haut-Médoc 1989 (NR) (4/30/91) (BT)
75+   CHATEAU VERDIGNAN Haut-Médoc 1989 (NR) (4/30/91) (BT)
70+   CHATEAU MALESCASSE Haut-Médoc 1989 (NR) (4/30/90) (BT)

1988

91   CHATEAU CITRAN Haut-Médoc 1988 $15 (4/30/91)
91   CHATEAU LA LAGUNE Haut-Médoc 1988 $24 (4/30/91)
90+   CHATEAU CITRAN Haut-Médoc 1988 $15 (8/31/90) (BT)
90+   CHATEAU CITRAN Haut-Médoc 1988 $15 (6/30/89) (BT)
90+   CHATEAU LA LAGUNE Haut-Médoc 1988 $24 (8/31/90) (BT)
90+   CHATEAU LA LAGUNE Haut-Médoc 1988 $24 (6/30/89) (BT)
88   CHATEAU SOUDARS Haut-Médoc 1988 $15 (4/30/91)
88   CHATEAU TOUR DU HAUT-MOULIN Haut-Médoc 1988 $20 (4/30/91)
87   CHATEAU LIVERSAN Haut-Médoc 1988 $14 (7/31/91)
87   CHATEAU SOCIANDO-MALLET Haut-Médoc 1988 $26 (3/31/91)
86   CHATEAU DE LAMARQUE Haut-Médoc 1988 $20 (4/30/91)
86   CHATEAU VERDIGNAN Haut-Médoc 1988 $15 (4/30/91)
85   CHATEAU BEL AIR Haut-Médoc 1988 $15 (4/30/91)
85   CHATEAU CANTEMERLE Haut-Médoc 1988 $25 (3/15/91)
85+   CHATEAU COUFRAN Haut-Médoc 1988 $15 (8/31/90) (BT)
85+   CHATEAU DE LAMARQUE Haut-Médoc 1988 $20 (8/31/90) (BT)
85+   CHATEAU LANESSAN Haut-Médoc 1988 $25 (8/31/90) (BT)
85+   CHATEAU MALESCASSE Haut-Médoc 1988 $14 (6/30/89) (BT)
85+   CHATEAU SOCIANDO-MALLET Haut-Médoc 1988 $26 (8/31/90) (BT)
85+   CHATEAU SOCIANDO-MALLET Haut-Médoc 1988 $26 (6/30/89) (BT)
85+   CHATEAU LA TOUR CARNET Haut-Médoc 1988 $23 (8/31/90) (BT)
84   CHATEAU ARNAULD Haut-Médoc 1988 $15 (4/30/91)
84   CHATEAU COUFRAN Haut-Médoc 1988 $15 (4/30/91)
84   CHATEAU LAROSE-TRINTAUDON Haut-Médoc 1988 $12 (4/30/91)
82   CHATEAU BEAUMONT Haut-Médoc 1988 $15 (7/15/91)
82   CHATEAU SEGUR Haut-Médoc 1988 $15 (12/31/90)
80   CHATEAU LANESSAN Haut-Médoc 1988 $25 (7/31/91)
80+   CHATEAU ARNAULD Haut-Médoc 1988 $15 (6/30/89) (BT)
80+   CHATEAU DE CAMENSAC Haut-Médoc 1988 $16 (6/30/89) (BT)
80+   CHATEAU COUFRAN Haut-Médoc 1988 $15 (6/30/89) (BT)
80+   CHATEAU LAMOTHE-BERGERON Haut-Médoc 1988 $15 (6/30/89) (BT)
80+   CHATEAU LANESSAN Haut-Médoc 1988 $25 (6/30/89) (BT)
80+   CHATEAU LAROSE-TRINTAUDON Haut-Médoc 1988 $12 (6/30/89) (BT)
80+   CHATEAU MAGNOL Haut-Médoc 1988 (NR) (6/30/89) (BT)
79   CHATEAU BELGRAVE Haut-Médoc 1988 $28 (7/31/91)
78   CHATEAU SENEJAC Haut-Médoc 1988 $11.50 (4/30/91)
80+   CHATEAU SENEJAC Haut-Médoc 1988 $11.50 (6/30/89) (BT)
80+   CHATEAU SOUDARS Haut-Médoc 1988 $15 (8/31/90) (BT)
80+   CHATEAU VERDIGNAN Haut-Médoc 1988 $15 (8/31/90) (BT)
80+   CHATEAU VILLEGEORGE Haut-Médoc 1988 $15 (6/30/89) (BT)
76   CHATEAU FOURNAS-BERNADOTTE Haut-Médoc 1988 $18 (6/15/91)
75+   CHATEAU BEAUMONT Haut-Médoc 1988 $15 (6/30/89) (BT)
75+   CHATEAU BELGRAVE Haut-Médoc 1988 $28 (6/30/89) (BT)
75+   CHATEAU CANTEMERLE Haut-Médoc 1988 $25 (6/30/89) (BT)
75+   CHATEAU CARONNE STE.-GEMME Haut-Médoc 1988 (NR) (6/30/89) (BT)
75+   CHATEAU HANTEILLAN Haut-Médoc 1988 $17 (6/30/89) (BT)
75+   CHATEAU LACHESNAYE Haut-Médoc 1988 $24 (6/30/89) (BT)
75+   CHATEAU DE LAMARQUE Haut-Médoc 1988 $20 (6/30/89) (BT)
75+   CHATEAU LIVERSAN Haut-Médoc 1988 $14 (6/30/89) (BT)
75+   CHATEAU VERDIGNAN Haut-Médoc 1988 $15 (6/30/89) (BT)
70+   CHATEAU D'ARSAC Haut-Médoc 1988 $7 (6/30/89) (BT)
70+   CHATEAU CLEMENT-PICHON Haut-Médoc 1988 $15 (6/30/89) (BT)
70+   CHATEAU LA FLEUR BECADE Haut-Médoc 1988 (NR) (6/30/89) (BT)
70+   CHATEAU FONTESTEAU Haut-Médoc 1988 (NR) (6/30/89) (BT)
70+   CHATEAU FOURNAS-BERNADOTTE Haut-Médoc 1988 $18 (6/30/89) (BT)
70+   CHATEAU SOUDARS Haut-Médoc 1988 $15 (6/30/89) (BT)
60+   CHATEAU PROCHE PONTET Haut-Médoc 1988 (NR) (6/30/89) (BT)
55   CHATEAU DE CAMENSAC Haut-Médoc 1988 $16 (7/15/91)

1987

89   CHATEAU LA LAGUNE Haut-Médoc 1987 Rel: $20 Cur: $20 (5/15/90)
88   CHATEAU SOCIANDO-MALLET Haut-Médoc 1987 Rel: $15 Cur: $15 (5/15/90)
87   CHATEAU CANTEMERLE Haut-Médoc 1987 Rel: $21 Cur: $21 • (5/15/90)
86   CHATEAU SOCIANDO-MALLET Haut-Médoc 1987 Rel: $15 Cur: $15 (11/30/89) (JS)
85+   CHATEAU CANTEMERLE Haut-Médoc 1987 Rel: $21 Cur: $21 (6/30/88) (BT)
85+   CHATEAU LA LAGUNE Haut-Médoc 1987 Rel: $20 Cur: $20 (6/30/88) (BT)
83   CHATEAU TOUR-DU-MIRAIL Haut-Médoc 1987 Rel: $10 Cur: $10 (11/30/89) (JS)
82   CHATEAU RAMAGE LA BATISSE Haut-Médoc 1987 Rel: $12 Cur: $12 (11/30/89) (JS)
81   CHATEAU CISSAC Haut-Médoc 1987 Rel: $14 Cur: $14 (11/30/89) (JS)
81   CHATEAU COUFRAN Haut-Médoc 1987 Rel: $12 Cur: $12 (11/30/89) (JS)
80   CHATEAU TOUR DU HAUT-MOULIN Haut-Médoc 1987 Rel: $15 Cur: $15 (11/30/89) (JS)
80+   CHATEAU CANTEMERLE Haut-Médoc 1987 Rel: $21 Cur: $21 (6/30/89) (BT)
80+   CHATEAU CITRAN Haut-Médoc 1987 Rel: $14 Cur: $14 (6/30/88) (BT)
80+   CHATEAU COUFRAN Haut-Médoc 1987 Rel: $12 Cur: $12 (6/30/89) (BT)
80+   CHATEAU COUFRAN Haut-Médoc 1987 Rel: $12 Cur: $12 (6/30/88) (BT)
79   CHATEAU ARNAULD Haut-Médoc 1987 Rel: $13 Cur: $13 (11/30/89) (JS)
78   CHATEAU VERDIGNAN Haut-Médoc 1987 Rel: $15 Cur: $15 (11/30/89) (JS)
77   CHATEAU SOUDARS Haut-Médoc 1987 $12 (11/30/89) (JS)
76   CHATEAU LA TONNELLE Haut-Médoc 1987 (NR) (11/30/89) (JS)

75 CHATEAU HANTEILLAN Haut-Médoc 1987 Rel: $13 Cur: $13 (11/30/89) (JS)
75 BARONS EDMOND & BENJAMIN ROTHSCHILD Haut-Médoc 1987 $24 (3/31/91)
75+ CHATEAU ARNAULD Haut-Médoc 1987 Rel: $13 Cur: $13 (6/30/89) (BT)
75+ CHATEAU BEAUMONT Haut-Médoc 1987 $13 (6/30/89) (BT)
75+ CHATEAU BEAUMONT Haut-Médoc 1987 $13 (6/30/88) (BT)
75+ CHATEAU DE CAMENSAC Haut-Médoc 1987 Rel: $12 Cur: $12 (6/30/89) (BT)
75+ CHATEAU DE CAMENSAC Haut-Médoc 1987 Rel: $12 Cur: $12 (6/30/88) (BT)
75+ CHATEAU CARONNE STE.-GEMME Haut-Médoc 1987 (NR) (6/30/89) (BT)
75+ CHATEAU CITRAN Haut-Médoc 1987 Rel: $14 Cur: $14 (6/30/89) (BT)
75+ CHATEAU HANTEILLAN Haut-Médoc 1987 Rel: $13 Cur: $13 (6/30/89) (BT)
75+ CHATEAU LACHESNAYE Haut-Médoc 1987 $19 (6/30/89) (BT)
75+ CHATEAU DE LAMARQUE Haut-Médoc 1987 Rel: $10 Cur: $10 (6/30/89) (BT)
75+ CHATEAU LAROSE-TRINTAUDON Haut-Médoc 1987 Rel: $9 Cur: $9 (6/30/89) (BT)
75+ CHATEAU LAROSE-TRINTAUDON Haut-Médoc 1987 Rel: $9 Cur: $9 (6/30/88) (BT)
75+ CHATEAU LIVERSAN Haut-Médoc 1987 Rel: $13 Cur: $13 (6/30/89) (BT)
75+ CHATEAU MAGNOL Haut-Médoc 1987 (NR) (6/30/89) (BT)
75+ CHATEAU MALESCASSE Haut-Médoc 1987 Rel: $9 Cur: $9 (6/30/89) (BT)
75+ CHATEAU MALESCASSE Haut-Médoc 1987 Rel: $9 Cur: $9 (6/30/88) (BT)
75+ CHATEAU VILLEGEORGE Haut-Médoc 1987 Rel: $12 Cur: $12 (6/30/89) (BT)
74 CHATEAU DE LAMARQUE Haut-Médoc 1987 Rel: $10 Cur: $10 (11/30/89) (JS)
74 CHATEAU LAMOTHE-CISSAC Haut-Médoc 1987 $10 (11/30/89) (JS)
74 CHATEAU LESTAGE-SIMON Haut-Médoc 1987 Rel: $13 Cur: $13 (11/30/89) (JS)
74 CHATEAU MALESCASSE Haut-Médoc 1987 Rel: $9 Cur: $9 (11/30/89) (JS)
74 CHATEAU MOULIN-ROUGE Haut-Médoc 1987 Rel: $12 Cur: $12 (11/30/89) (JS)
74 CHATEAU TOUR-DU-ROC Haut-Médoc 1987 Rel: $10 Cur: $10 (11/30/89) (JS)
73 CHATEAU CLEMENT-PICHON Haut-Médoc 1987 $14 (11/30/89) (JS)
73 CHATEAU LANDAT Haut-Médoc 1987 $7 (11/30/89) (JS)
71 CHATEAU LAROSE-TRINTAUDON Haut-Médoc 1987 Rel: $9 Cur: $9 (11/30/89) (JS)
70+ CHATEAU D'ARSAC Haut-Médoc 1987 $6 (6/30/89) (BT)
70+ CHATEAU FONTESTEAU Haut-Médoc 1987 (NR) (6/30/89) (BT)
70+ CHATEAU DE LAMARQUE Haut-Médoc 1987 Rel: $10 Cur: $10 (6/30/88) (BT)
70+ CHATEAU LAMOTHE-BERGERON Haut-Médoc 1987 Rel: $10 Cur: $10 (6/30/89) (BT)
70+ CHATEAU LANESSAN Haut-Médoc 1987 Rel: $14 Cur: $14 (6/30/89) (BT)
70+ CHATEAU LANESSAN Haut-Médoc 1987 Rel: $14 Cur: $14 (6/30/88) (BT)
70+ CHATEAU SENEJAC Haut-Médoc 1987 Rel: $9 Cur: $9 (6/30/89) (BT)
70+ CHATEAU SOCIANDO-MALLET Haut-Médoc 1987 Rel: $15 Cur: $15 (6/30/89) (BT)
70+ CHATEAU SOUDARS Haut-Médoc 1987 $12 (6/30/89) (BT)
65+ CHATEAU FOURNAS-BERNADOTTE Haut-Médoc 1987 $13 (6/30/89) (BT)
65+ CHATEAU VERDIGNAN Haut-Médoc 1987 Rel: $15 Cur: $15 (6/30/89) (BT)

1986

94 CHATEAU SOCIANDO-MALLET Haut-Médoc 1986 Rel: $25 Cur: $25 (11/30/89) (JS)
90 CHATEAU TOUR DU HAUT-MOULIN Haut-Médoc 1986 Rel: $16 Cur: $16 (11/30/89) (JS)
90+ CHATEAU CANTEMERLE Haut-Médoc 1986 Rel: $30 Cur: $30 (5/15/87) (BT)
89 CHATEAU CANTEMERLE Haut-Médoc 1986 Rel: $30 Cur: $30 (6/30/89)
89 CHATEAU LA LAGUNE Haut-Médoc 1986 Rel: $22 Cur: $26 (6/30/89)
88 CHATEAU BEL-AIR Haut-Médoc 1986 $9 (11/15/89) BB
88 CHATEAU MALESCASSE Haut-Médoc 1986 Rel: $9 Cur: $9 (11/30/89) (JS)
87 CHATEAU MOULIN-ROUGE Haut-Médoc 1986 Rel: $14 Cur: $14 (11/30/89) (JS)
85 CHATEAU CLEMENT-PICHON Haut-Médoc 1986 $11 (11/30/89) (JS)
85 CHATEAU COUFRAN Haut-Médoc 1986 Rel: $13 Cur: $15 (6/30/89)
85 CHATEAU LAROSE-TRINTAUDON Haut-Médoc 1986 Rel: $10 Cur: $10 (11/15/89) (JS)
85 CHATEAU LESTAGE-SIMON Haut-Médoc 1986 Rel: $13 Cur: $13 (11/30/89) (JS)
85 CHATEAU MALESCASSE Haut-Médoc 1986 Rel: $9 Cur: $9 (6/30/89)
85+ CHATEAU CANTEMERLE Haut-Médoc 1986 Rel: $30 Cur: $30 (6/30/88) (BT)
84 CHATEAU BEAUMONT Haut-Médoc 1986 $9 (6/30/89)
84 CHATEAU SOCIANDO-MALLET Haut-Médoc 1986 Rel: $25 Cur: $25 (6/30/89)
84 CHATEAU TOUR DU HAUT-MOULIN Haut-Médoc 1986 Rel: $16 Cur: $16 (6/30/89)
83 CHATEAU DE CAMENSAC Haut-Médoc 1986 Rel: $14 Cur: $14 (6/30/89)
83 CHATEAU VERDIGNAN Haut-Médoc 1986 Rel: $15 Cur: $15 (6/30/89)
82 CHATEAU ARNAULD Haut-Médoc 1986 Cur: $18 (11/30/89) (JS)
82 CHATEAU COUFRAN Haut-Médoc 1986 Rel: $13 Cur: $15 (11/30/89) (JS)
82 CHATEAU RAMAGE LA BATISSE Haut-Médoc 1986 Rel: $14 Cur: $14 (11/30/89) (JS)
81 CHATEAU BELGRAVE Haut-Médoc 1986 Rel: $16 Cur: $16 (3/31/90)
81 CHATEAU HANTEILLAN Haut-Médoc 1986 Rel: $15 Cur: $15 (11/30/89) (JS)
80+ CHATEAU BEAUMONT Haut-Médoc 1986 $9 (6/30/88) (BT)
80+ CHATEAU DE CAMENSAC Haut-Médoc 1986 Rel: $14 Cur: $14 (5/15/87) (BT)
80+ CHATEAU COUFRAN Haut-Médoc 1986 Rel: $13 Cur: $15 (6/30/88) (BT)
80+ CHATEAU DE LAMARQUE Haut-Médoc 1986 Rel: $12 Cur: $12 (6/30/88) (BT)
80+ CHATEAU LANESSAN Haut-Médoc 1986 Rel: $16 Cur: $16 (6/30/88) (BT)
80+ CHATEAU MALESCASSE Haut-Médoc 1986 Rel: $9 Cur: $9 (6/30/88) (BT)
80+ CHATEAU LA TOUR CARNET Haut-Médoc 1986 Rel: $22 Cur: $22 (5/15/87) (BT)
79 CHATEAU CISSAC Haut-Médoc 1986 Rel: $20 Cur: $20 (11/30/89) (JS)
79 CHATEAU SOUDARS Haut-Médoc 1986 $13 (11/30/89) (JS)
79 CHATEAU TOUR-DU-MIRAIL Haut-Médoc 1986 Rel: $12 Cur: $12 (11/30/89) (JS)
78 CHATEAU CANTELAUDE Haut-Médoc 1986 $17 (6/30/89)
78 CHATEAU BARREYRES Haut-Médoc 1986 $8.25 (6/30/89)
78 CHATEAU LAROSE-TRINTAUDON Haut-Médoc 1986 Rel: $10 Cur: $10 (11/30/89) (JS)
76 CHATEAU CLEMENT-PICHON Haut-Médoc 1986 $11 (9/30/89)
76 BARONS EDMOND & BENJAMIN ROTHSCHILD Haut-Médoc 1986 $48 (3/31/91)
76 CHATEAU TOUR-DU-ROC Haut-Médoc 1986 Rel: $11 Cur: $11 (11/30/89) (JS)
76 CHATEAU VERDIGNAN Haut-Médoc 1986 Rel: $15 Cur: $15 (11/30/89) (JS)
75 CHATEAU DE LAMARQUE Haut-Médoc 1986 Rel: $12 Cur: $12 (11/30/89) (JS)
70 CHATEAU LA TONNELLE Haut-Médoc 1986 $11 (11/30/89) (JS)
70+ CHATEAU BEAUMONT Haut-Médoc 1986 $9 (5/15/87) (BT)
70+ CHATEAU DE LAMARQUE Haut-Médoc 1986 Rel: $12 Cur: $12 (5/15/87) (BT)
70+ CHATEAU LAROSE-TRINTAUDON Haut-Médoc 1986 Rel: $10 Cur: $10 (5/15/87) (BT)
70+ CHATEAU MALESCASSE Haut-Médoc 1986 Rel: $9 Cur: $9 (5/15/87) (BT)
70+ CHATEAU VILLEGEORGE Haut-Médoc 1986 Rel: $13 Cur: $13 (5/15/87) (BT)
69 CHATEAU LAMOTHE-CISSAC Haut-Médoc 1986 $12 (11/30/89) (JS)
67 CHATEAU TOUR-DU-ROC Haut-Médoc 1986 Rel: $11 Cur: $11 (9/30/89)

1985

90 CHATEAU LIVERSAN Haut-Médoc 1985 Rel: $16 Cur: $18 (4/30/88)
90+ CHATEAU DE CAMENSAC Haut-Médoc 1985 Rel: $16 Cur: $18 (5/15/87) (BT)
90+ CHATEAU LA TOUR CARNET Haut-Médoc 1985 Rel: $22 Cur: $22 (5/15/87) (BT)
89 CHATEAU LA LAGUNE Haut-Médoc 1985 Rel: $22 Cur: $27 (5/15/88)
88 CHATEAU CANTEMERLE Haut-Médoc 1985 Rel: $30 Cur: $30 (8/31/88)
87 CHATEAU LANESSAN Haut-Médoc 1985 Rel: $16.50 Cur: $17 (4/30/88)
85 CHATEAU COUFRAN Haut-Médoc 1985 Rel: $11 Cur: $15 (6/30/88)

85 CHATEAU PICHON Haut-Médoc 1985 $13 (8/31/88)
85 CHATEAU SOCIANDO-MALLET Haut-Médoc 1985 Rel: $17 Cur: $21 (4/30/88)
84 CHATEAU LAROSE-TRINTAUDON Haut-Médoc 1985 Rel: $8.50 Cur: $9 (11/30/88) BB
84 CHATEAU TOUR DU HAUT-MOULIN Haut-Médoc 1985 Rel: $15 Cur: $15 (2/15/89)
82 CHATEAU ARNAULD Haut-Médoc 1985 Rel: $15 Cur: $15 (2/15/88)
82 CHATEAU LA BATISSE Haut-Médoc 1985 $10 (6/30/88)
81 CHATEAU VERDIGNAN Haut-Médoc 1985 Rel: $13 Cur: $14 (2/15/88)
80 CHATEAU BEL-AIR Haut-Médoc 1985 $5 (3/15/88) BB
80+ CHATEAU VILLEGEORGE Haut-Médoc 1985 Rel: $13 Cur: $13 (5/15/87) (BT)
79 CHATEAU CISSAC Haut-Médoc 1985 Rel: $16 Cur: $16 (7/31/88)
77 CHATEAU LA TONNELLE Haut-Médoc 1985 $10 (2/15/89)
75 CHATEAU D'ARSAC Haut-Médoc 1985 $5.75 (2/15/89)
74 CHATEAU BEAUMONT Haut-Médoc 1985 $8.50 (4/30/88)
71 CHATEAU LA TOUR CARNET Haut-Médoc 1985 Rel: $22 Cur: $22 (12/31/88)

1984

86 CHATEAU LA LAGUNE Haut-Médoc 1984 Rel: $13.50 Cur: $21 (3/31/87)
85 CHATEAU CANTEMERLE Haut-Médoc 1984 Rel: $17 Cur: $17 (6/15/87)
84 CHATEAU SOCIANDO-MALLET Haut-Médoc 1984 Rel: $11 Cur: $17 (3/31/87)

1983

85 CHATEAU LA LAGUNE Haut-Médoc 1983 Rel: $20 Cur: $28 (4/16/86)
83 CHATEAU BEL-AIR Haut-Médoc 1983 $6 (12/31/86)
83 CHATEAU MOULIN-ROUGE Haut-Médoc 1983 Rel: $10 Cur: $10 (7/31/87)
82 CHATEAU CITRAN Haut-Médoc 1983 Rel: $10 Cur: $11 (4/01/86)
77 CHATEAU MAGNOL Haut-Médoc 1983 $9.50 (7/31/87)
77 CHATEAU SOCIANDO-MALLET Haut-Médoc 1983 Rel: $15 Cur: $18 (4/16/86)
75 CHATEAU ARNAULD Haut-Médoc 1983 Rel: $8 Cur: $15 (1/01/86)
73 CHATEAU LAROSE-TRINTAUDON Haut-Médoc 1983 Rel: $7 Cur: $13 (10/15/86)
69 CHATEAU LA TOUR CARNET Haut-Médoc 1983 Rel: $13 Cur: $13 (2/29/88)
69 CHATEAU VERDIGNAN Haut-Médoc 1983 Rel: $8 Cur: $17 (4/01/86)
63 CHATEAU GRAND MOULIN Haut-Médoc 1983 $6.75 (4/16/86)
60 LES CLOCHERS DU HAUT-MEDOC Haut-Médoc 1983 $7 (6/15/87)

1982

97 CHATEAU LA LAGUNE Haut-Médoc 1982 Rel: $28 Cur: $43 (5/01/89)
92 CHATEAU CANTEMERLE Haut-Médoc 1982 Rel: $30 Cur: $30 (5/01/89)
92 CHATEAU SOCIANDO-MALLET Haut-Médoc 1982 Cur: $37 (11/30/89) (JS)
84 CHATEAU LESTAGE-SIMON Haut-Médoc 1982 Rel: $10 Cur: $14 (11/30/89) (JS)
84 CHATEAU TOUR DU HAUT-MOULIN Haut-Médoc 1982 Cur: $17 (11/30/89) (JS)
84 CHATEAU TOUR-DU-ROC Haut-Médoc 1982 Rel: $9 Cur: $12 (11/30/89) (JS)
83 CHATEAU COUFRAN Haut-Médoc 1982 Rel: $9 Cur: $15 (11/30/89) (JS)
83 CHATEAU VERDIGNAN Haut-Médoc 1982 Rel: $7.50 Cur: $15 (2/16/85) BB
82 CHATEAU MALESCASSE Haut-Médoc 1982 Rel: $7 Cur: $10 (11/30/89) (JS)
81 CHATEAU CISSAC Haut-Médoc 1982 Cur: $24 (11/30/89) (JS)
81 CHATEAU HANTEILLAN Haut-Médoc 1982 Cur: $12 (11/30/89) (JS)
81 CHATEAU LAROSE-TRINTAUDON Haut-Médoc 1982 Rel: $6 Cur: $11 (2/16/86) BB
80 CHATEAU MOULIN-ROUGE Haut-Médoc 1982 Rel: $9 Cur: $13 (11/30/89) (JS)
79 CHATEAU DE LAMARQUE Haut-Médoc 1982 Rel: $9 Cur: $14 (11/30/89) (JS)
79 CHATEAU LAROSE-TRINTAUDON Haut-Médoc 1982 Rel: $6 Cur: $11 (11/30/89) (JS)
79 CHATEAU TOUR-DU-MIRAIL Haut-Médoc 1982 Rel: $9 Cur: $9 (11/30/89) (JS)
78 CHATEAU CITRAN Haut-Médoc 1982 Rel: $6 Cur: $11 (4/01/85)
77 CHATEAU LANDAY Haut-Médoc 1982 $6.75 (2/16/85)
76 CHATEAU VERDIGNAN Haut-Médoc 1982 Rel: $7.50 Cur: $15 (11/30/89) (JS)
75 CHATEAU SEGUR Haut-Médoc 1982 $6 (4/16/85)
71 CHATEAU ARNAULD Haut-Médoc 1982 Cur: $17 (11/30/89) (JS)
68 CHATEAU RAMAGE LA BATISSE Haut-Médoc 1982 Rel: $11 Cur: $11 (11/30/89) (JS)

1981

82 CHATEAU LA LAGUNE Haut-Médoc 1981 Rel: $25 Cur: $31 (5/01/89)
77 CHATEAU DE MALLERET Haut-Médoc 1981 $5.99 (3/01/85)
72 CHATEAU BEL-AIR Haut-Médoc 1981 $6 (5/01/84)
72 CHATEAU LABAT Haut-Médoc 1981 $7 (4/01/85)
72 CHATEAU LANDAY Haut-Médoc 1981 $6.50 (2/16/85)
70 CHATEAU CANTEMERLE Haut-Médoc 1981 Rel: $13.50 Cur: $17 (5/01/84)
69 CHATEAU MAGNOL Haut-Médoc 1981 $8.75 (8/31/87)

1979

86 CHATEAU LA LAGUNE Haut-Médoc 1979 Cur: $29 (10/15/89) (JS)
82 CHATEAU DE CAMENSAC Haut-Médoc 1979 Cur: $22 (10/15/89) (JS)
78 CHATEAU CANTEMERLE Haut-Médoc 1979 Cur: $20 (10/15/89) (JS)
76 CHATEAU LAROSE-TRINTAUDON Haut-Médoc 1979 Rel: $5 Cur: $15 (10/15/89) (JS)

1962

90 CHATEAU CANTEMERLE Haut-Médoc 1962 Cur: $101 (11/30/87) (JS)
80 CHATEAU LA LAGUNE Haut-Médoc 1962 Cur: $65 (11/30/87) (JS)

1961

78 CHATEAU CANTEMERLE Haut-Médoc 1961 Cur: $151 (3/16/86) (JL)

1945

92 CHATEAU CANTEMERLE Haut-Médoc 1945 Cur: $300 (3/16/86) (JL)
88 CHATEAU LA TOUR CARNET Haut-Médoc 1945 Cur: $130 (3/16/86) (JL)
87 CHATEAU LA LAGUNE Haut-Médoc 1945 Cur: $200 (3/16/86) (JL)

LISTRAC

1990

85+ CHATEAU FOURCAS-HOSTEN Listrac 1990 (NR) (4/30/91) (BT)

1989

85+ CHATEAU FONREAUD Listrac 1989 (NR) (4/30/91) (BT)
85+ CHATEAU FOURCAS-DUPRE Listrac 1989 (NR) (4/30/91) (BT)
85+ CHATEAU FOURCAS-HOSTEN Listrac 1989 (NR) (4/30/91) (BT)
75+ CHATEAU FOURCAS-HOSTEN Listrac 1989 (NR) (4/30/90) (BT)

1988

83 CHATEAU FOURCAS-DUPRE Listrac 1988 $22 (4/30/91)
83 CHATEAU FOURCAS-LOUBANEY Listrac 1988 $17 (2/28/91)
82 CHATEAU FONREAUD Listrac 1988 $15 (4/30/91)

FRANCE
BORDEAUX RED/LISTRAC

82   CHATEAU FOURCAS-HOSTEN Listrac 1988 $13.50 (7/15/91)
81   CHATEAU CLARKE Listrac 1988 $18 (4/30/91)
80+   CHATEAU CLARKE Listrac 1988 $18 (6/30/89) (BT)
80+   CHATEAU FOURCAS-HOSTEN Listrac 1988 $13.50 (8/31/90) (BT)
70+   CHATEAU FONREAUD Listrac 1988 $15 (6/30/89) (BT)
70+   CHATEAU FOURCAS-DUPRE Listrac 1988 $22 (6/30/89) (BT)
70+   CHATEAU FOURCAS-HOSTEN Listrac 1988 $13.50 (6/30/89) (BT)

1987

79   CHATEAU DUCLUZEAU Listrac 1987 $7 (11/30/89) (JS)
75+   CHATEAU CLARKE Listrac 1987 $15 (6/30/89) (BT)
75+   CHATEAU FOURCAS-DUPRE Listrac 1987 Rel: $15 Cur: $15 (6/30/89) (BT)
75+   CHATEAU FOURCAS-DUPRE Listrac 1987 Rel: $15 Cur: $15 (6/30/88) (BT)
70+   CHATEAU FOURCAS-HOSTEN Listrac 1987 Rel: $11 Cur: $11 (6/30/89) (BT)
70+   CHATEAU FOURCAS-HOSTEN Listrac 1987 Rel: $11 Cur: $11 (6/30/88) (BT)
65+   CHATEAU FONREAUD Listrac 1987 $10 (6/30/89) (BT)
65+   CHATEAU FONREAUD Listrac 1987 $10 (6/30/88) (BT)

1986

90   CHATEAU CLARKE Listrac 1986 $17 (11/15/89)
83   CHATEAU DUCLUZEAU Listrac 1986 $11 (11/30/89) (JS)
79   CHATEAU FOURCAS-HOSTEN Listrac 1986 Rel: $13.50 Cur: $14 (11/15/89)
75+   CHATEAU FOURCAS-DUPRE Listrac 1986 Rel: $15 Cur: $15 (6/30/88) (BT)
75+   CHATEAU FOURCAS-HOSTEN Listrac 1986 Rel: $13.50 Cur: $14 (6/30/88) (BT)
70+   CHATEAU CLARKE Listrac 1986 $17 (5/15/87) (BT)
70+   CHATEAU FONREAUD Listrac 1986 $10 (6/30/88) (BT)
70+   CHATEAU FOURCAS-HOSTEN Listrac 1986 Rel: $13.50 Cur: $14 (5/15/87) (BT)
60+   CHATEAU FOURCAS-DUPRE Listrac 1986 Rel: $15 Cur: $15 (5/15/87) (BT)

1983

89   CHATEAU FOURCAS-DUPRE Listrac 1983 Rel: $9 Cur: $15 (10/31/86)
83   CHATEAU FOURCAS-HOSTEN Listrac 1983 Rel: $11 Cur: $16 (10/15/86)

1982

80   CHATEAU DUCLUZEAU Listrac 1982 Cur: $12 (11/30/89) (JS)
68   CHATEAU CLARKE Listrac 1982 $13 (10/15/86)

MARGAUX

1990

95+   CHATEAU CANTENAC-BROWN Margaux 1990 (NR) (4/30/91) (BT)
95+   CHATEAU MARGAUX Margaux 1990 (NR) (4/30/91) (BT)
90+   CHATEAU CANUET Margaux 1990 (NR) (4/30/91) (BT)
90+   CHATEAU D'ISSAN Margaux 1990 (NR) (4/30/91) (BT)
90+   CHATEAU MONBRISON Margaux 1990 (NR) (4/30/91) (BT)
90+   CHATEAU PALMER Margaux 1990 (NR) (4/30/91) (BT)
85+   CHATEAU D'ANGLUDET Margaux 1990 (NR) (4/30/91) (BT)
85+   CHATEAU GISCOURS Margaux 1990 (NR) (4/30/91) (BT)
85+   CHATEAU KIRWAN Margaux 1990 (NR) (4/30/91) (BT)
85+   CHATEAU LABEGORCE-ZEDE Margaux 1990 (NR) (4/30/91) (BT)
85+   PAVILLON ROUGE DU CHATEAU MARGAUX Margaux 1990 (NR) (4/30/91) (BT)
85+   CHATEAU PRIEURE-LICHINE Margaux 1990 (NR) (4/30/91) (BT)
85+   CHATEAU RAUSAN-SEGLA Margaux 1990 (NR) (4/30/91) (BT)
85+   CHATEAU SIRAN Margaux 1990 (NR) (4/30/91) (BT)
85+   CHATEAU DU TERTRE Margaux 1990 (NR) (4/30/91) (BT)
80+   CHATEAU RAUZAN-GASSIES Margaux 1990 (NR) (4/30/91) (BT)

1989

95+   CHATEAU LABEGORCE-ZEDE Margaux 1989 (NR) (4/30/91) (BT)
95+   CHATEAU MARGAUX Margaux 1989 (NR) (4/30/91) (BT)
95+   CHATEAU MARGAUX Margaux 1989 (NR) (4/30/90) (BT)
90+   CHATEAU D'ANGLUDET Margaux 1989 (NR) (4/30/90) (BT)
90+   CHATEAU CANTENAC-BROWN Margaux 1989 (NR) (4/30/91) (BT)
90+   CHATEAU CANUET Margaux 1989 (NR) (4/30/91) (BT)
90+   CHATEAU LA GURGUE Margaux 1989 (NR) (4/30/90) (BT)
90+   CHATEAU MONBRISON Margaux 1989 (NR) (4/30/91) (BT)
90+   CHATEAU MONBRISON Margaux 1989 (NR) (4/30/90) (BT)
90+   CHATEAU PALMER Margaux 1989 (NR) (4/30/91) (BT)
90+   CHATEAU PALMER Margaux 1989 (NR) (4/30/90) (BT)
90+   CHATEAU RAUSAN-SEGLA Margaux 1989 (NR) (4/30/91) (BT)
90+   CHATEAU RAUSAN-SEGLA Margaux 1989 (NR) (4/30/90) (BT)
90+   CHATEAU SIRAN Margaux 1989 (NR) (4/30/91) (BT)
90+   CHATEAU SIRAN Margaux 1989 (NR) (4/30/90) (BT)
85+   CHATEAU DAUZAC Margaux 1989 (NR) (4/30/91) (BT)
85+   CHATEAU GISCOURS Margaux 1989 (NR) (4/30/91) (BT)
85+   CHATEAU GISCOURS Margaux 1989 (NR) (4/30/90) (BT)
85+   CHATEAU D'ISSAN Margaux 1989 (NR) (4/30/91) (BT)
85+   CHATEAU LABEGORCE-ZEDE Margaux 1989 (NR) (4/30/90) (BT)
85+   CHATEAU MALESCOT-ST.-EXUPERY Margaux 1989 (NR) (4/30/90) (BT)
85+   CHATEAU PRIEURE-LICHINE Margaux 1989 (NR) (4/30/91) (BT)
85+   CHATEAU PRIEURE-LICHINE Margaux 1989 (NR) (4/30/90) (BT)
85+   CHATEAU DU TERTRE Margaux 1989 (NR) (4/30/91) (BT)
85+   CHATEAU DU TERTRE Margaux 1989 (NR) (4/30/90) (BT)
80+   CHATEAU DAUZAC Margaux 1989 (NR) (4/30/90) (BT)
80+   CHATEAU D'ISSAN Margaux 1989 (NR) (4/30/90) (BT)

80+   CHATEAU LASCOMBES Margaux 1989 (NR) (4/30/90) (BT)
80+   CHATEAU RAUZAN-GASSIES Margaux 1989 (NR) (4/30/91) (BT)
80+   CHATEAU LA TOUR-DE-MONS Margaux 1989 (NR) (4/30/91) (BT)
75+   CHATEAU CANUET Margaux 1989 (NR) (4/30/91) (BT)
75+   CHATEAU KIRWAN Margaux 1989 (NR) (4/30/91) (BT)
70+   CHATEAU CANTENAC-BROWN Margaux 1989 (NR) (4/30/90) (BT)
70+   CHATEAU KIRWAN Margaux 1989 (NR) (4/30/90) (BT)

1988

97   CHATEAU MARGAUX Margaux 1988 $75 (3/31/91) CS
96   CHATEAU PALMER Margaux 1988 $65 (2/28/91) CS
95+   CHATEAU MARGAUX Margaux 1988 $75 (8/31/90) (BT)
95+   CHATEAU MARGAUX Margaux 1988 $75 (6/30/89) (BT)
92   CHATEAU MARQUIS DE TERME Margaux 1988 $23 (4/30/91)
92   CHATEAU MONBRISON Margaux 1988 $20 (2/28/91)
92   CHATEAU RAUSAN-SEGLA Margaux 1988 $40 (3/15/91)
90   CHATEAU DAUZAC Margaux 1988 $20 (6/30/91)
90   CHATEAU LA GURGUE Margaux 1988 $29 (4/30/91)
90   CHATEAU PRIEURE-LICHINE Margaux 1988 $30 (4/30/91)
89   CHATEAU CANTENAC-BROWN Margaux 1988 $25 (4/30/91)
90+   CHATEAU CANTENAC-BROWN Margaux 1988 $25 (8/31/90) (BT)
90+   CHATEAU D'ISSAN Margaux 1988 $30 (8/31/90) (BT)
90+   CHATEAU MONBRISON Margaux 1988 $20 (8/31/90) (BT)
90+   CHATEAU PALMER Margaux 1988 $65 (8/31/90) (BT)
90+   CHATEAU PALMER Margaux 1988 $65 (6/30/89) (BT)
90+   CHATEAU PRIEURE-LICHINE Margaux 1988 $30 (8/31/90) (BT)
90+   CHATEAU DU TERTRE Margaux 1988 $40 (6/30/89) (BT)
89   CHATEAU GISCOURS Margaux 1988 $30 (4/30/91)
89   CHATEAU MALESCOT-ST.-EXUPERY Margaux 1988 $23 (4/30/91)
88   CHATEAU D'ISSAN Margaux 1988 $30 (4/30/91)
88   PAVILLON ROUGE DU CHATEAU MARGAUX Margaux 1988 $30 (4/30/91)
88   CHATEAU SIRAN Margaux 1988 $19 (6/30/91)
87   CHATEAU KIRWAN Margaux 1988 $28 (4/30/91)
86   CHATEAU DE LA DAME Margaux 1988 $15 (2/15/91)
86   CHATEAU DU TERTRE Margaux 1988 $40 (6/30/91)
85   CHATEAU D'ANGLUDET Margaux 1988 $22 (2/28/91)
85+   CHATEAU D'ANGLUDET Margaux 1988 $22 (8/31/90) (BT)
85+   CHATEAU D'ANGLUDET Margaux 1988 $22 (6/30/89) (BT)
85+   CHATEAU BOYD-CANTENAC Margaux 1988 $20 (6/30/89) (BT)
85+   CHATEAU CANUET Margaux 1988 $15 (8/31/90) (BT)
85+   CHATEAU LASCOMBES Margaux 1988 $25 (6/30/89) (BT)
85+   CHATEAU MALESCOT-ST.-EXUPERY Margaux 1988 $23 (6/30/89) (BT)
85+   CHATEAU MONBRISON Margaux 1988 $20 (6/30/89) (BT)
85+   CHATEAU POUGET Margaux 1988 $18 (6/30/89) (BT)
85+   CHATEAU RAUSAN-SEGLA Margaux 1988 $40 (6/30/89) (BT)
85+   CHATEAU SIRAN Margaux 1988 $19 (8/31/90) (BT)
83   CHATEAU LABEGORCE-ZEDE Margaux 1988 $20 (4/30/91)
80+   CHATEAU BRANE-CANTENAC Margaux 1988 $42 (6/30/89) (BT)
80+   CHATEAU CANTENAC-BROWN Margaux 1988 $25 (6/30/89) (BT)
80+   CHATEAU DESMIRAIL Margaux 1988 $25 (6/30/89) (BT)
80+   CHATEAU GISCOURS Margaux 1988 $30 (6/30/89) (BT)
80+   CHATEAU D'ISSAN Margaux 1988 $30 (6/30/89) (BT)
80+   CHATEAU MARQUIS DE TERME Margaux 1988 $23 (6/30/89) (BT)
80+   CHATEAU PRIEURE-LICHINE Margaux 1988 $30 (6/30/89) (BT)
75+   CHATEAU DAUZAC Margaux 1988 $20 (6/30/89) (BT)
75+   CHATEAU DURFORT-VIVENS Margaux 1988 $40 (6/30/89) (BT)
75+   CHATEAU LA GURGUE Margaux 1988 $29 (8/31/90) (BT)
75+   CHATEAU LA GURGUE Margaux 1988 $29 (6/30/89) (BT)
75+   CHATEAU KIRWAN Margaux 1988 $28 (6/30/89) (BT)
75+   CHATEAU LAMOUROUX Margaux 1988 (NR) (6/30/89) (BT)
75+   CHATEAU MARQUIS-D'ALESME-BECKER Margaux 1988 $20 (6/30/89) (BT)
75+   CHATEAU MARSAC-SEGUINEAU Margaux 1988 (NR) (6/30/89) (BT)
75+   CHATEAU SEGONNES Margaux 1988 $18 (6/30/89) (BT)
75+   CHATEAU SIRAN Margaux 1988 $19 (6/30/89) (BT)

1987

87   CHATEAU MARGAUX Margaux 1987 Rel: $55 Cur: $55 (5/15/90)
86   CHATEAU MONBRISON Margaux 1987 Rel: $20 Cur: $20 (11/30/89) (JS)
85   CHATEAU MONBRISON Margaux 1987 Rel: $20 Cur: $20 (5/15/90)
85+   CHATEAU D'ISSAN Margaux 1987 Rel: $20 Cur: $20 (6/30/88) (BT)
85+   CHATEAU LASCOMBES Margaux 1987 Rel: $24 Cur: $24 (6/30/88) (BT)
85+   CHATEAU MARGAUX Margaux 1987 Rel: $55 Cur: $55 (6/30/89) (BT)
85+   CHATEAU MARGAUX Margaux 1987 Rel: $55 Cur: $55 (6/30/88) (BT)
85+   CHATEAU PALMER Margaux 1987 Rel: $28 Cur: $29 (6/30/89) (BT)
85+   CHATEAU PALMER Margaux 1987 Rel: $28 Cur: $29 (6/30/88) (BT)
84   CHATEAU D'ANGLUDET Margaux 1987 Rel: $13 Cur: $14 (11/30/89) (JS)
84   CHATEAU LABEGORCE-ZEDE Margaux 1987 Rel: $16 Cur: $16 (11/30/89) (JS)
84   CHATEAU PALMER Margaux 1987 Rel: $28 Cur: $29 (5/15/90)
82   CHATEAU LA GURGUE Margaux 1987 Rel: $13 Cur: $13 (11/30/89) (JS)
81   CHATEAU LA GURGUE Margaux 1987 Rel: $13 Cur: $13 (5/15/90)
80+   CHATEAU BRANE-CANTENAC Margaux 1987 Rel: $25 Cur: $25 (6/30/89) (BT)
80+   CHATEAU BRANE-CANTENAC Margaux 1987 Rel: $25 Cur: $25 (6/30/88) (BT)
80+   CHATEAU CANTENAC-BROWN Margaux 1987 Rel: $18 Cur: $22 (6/30/88) (BT)
80+   CHATEAU GISCOURS Margaux 1987 Rel: $20 Cur: $20 (6/30/88) (BT)
80+   CHATEAU LA GURGUE Margaux 1987 Rel: $13 Cur: $13 (6/30/89) (BT)
80+   CHATEAU KIRWAN Margaux 1987 Rel: $22 Cur: $22 (6/30/88) (BT)
80+   CHATEAU LASCOMBES Margaux 1987 Rel: $24 Cur: $24 (6/30/89) (BT)
80+   CHATEAU MONBRISON Margaux 1987 Rel: $20 Cur: $20 (6/30/89) (BT)
80+   CHATEAU MONBRISON Margaux 1987 Rel: $20 Cur: $20 (6/30/88) (BT)
80+   CHATEAU PRIEURE-LICHINE Margaux 1987 Rel: $13.50 Cur: $17 (6/30/88) (BT)
79   CHATEAU CANUET Margaux 1987 $12.50 (11/30/89) (JS)
79   PAVILLON ROUGE DU CHATEAU MARGAUX Margaux 1987 Rel: $19 Cur: $21 (5/15/90)
78   CHATEAU D'ANGLUDET Margaux 1987 Rel: $13 Cur: $14 (5/15/90)
78   CHATEAU CANTENAC-BROWN Margaux 1987 Rel: $18 Cur: $22 (2/15/90)
78   CHATEAU PRIEURE-LICHINE Margaux 1987 Rel: $13.50 Cur: $17 (2/15/90)
77   CHATEAU LABEGORCE Margaux 1987 $30 (3/31/91)
76   CHATEAU D'ISSAN Margaux 1987 Rel: $20 Cur: $20 (5/15/90)
75+   CHATEAU D'ANGLUDET Margaux 1987 Rel: $13 Cur: $14 (6/30/89) (BT)
75+   CHATEAU D'ANGLUDET Margaux 1987 Rel: $13 Cur: $14 (6/30/88) (BT)
75+   CHATEAU BOYD-CANTENAC Margaux 1987 Rel: $15 Cur: $15 (6/30/89) (BT)

75+ CHATEAU DURFORT-VIVENS Margaux 1987 Rel: $24 Cur: $24 (6/30/89) (BT)
75+ CHATEAU DURFORT-VIVENS Margaux 1987 Rel: $24 Cur: $24 (6/30/88) (BT)
75+ CHATEAU GISCOURS Margaux 1987 Rel: $20 Cur: $20 (6/30/89) (BT)
75+ CHATEAU D'ISSAN Margaux 1987 Rel: $20 Cur: $20 (6/30/89) (BT)
75+ CHATEAU MARQUIS DE TERME Margaux 1987 Rel: $20 Cur: $20 (6/30/89) (BT)
75+ CHATEAU SIRAN Margaux 1987 $14 (6/30/89) (BT)
74 CHATEAU CANUET Margaux 1987 $12.50 (5/15/90)
70+ CHATEAU CANTENAC-BROWN Margaux 1987 Rel: $18 Cur: $22 (6/30/89) (BT)
70+ CHATEAU DAUZAC Margaux 1987 Rel: $15 Cur: $15 (6/30/89) (BT)
70+ CHATEAU DAUZAC Margaux 1987 Rel: $15 Cur: $15 (6/30/88) (BT)
70+ CHATEAU DESMIRAIL Margaux 1987 Rel: $18 Cur: $18 (6/30/89) (BT)
70+ CHATEAU KIRWAN Margaux 1987 Rel: $22 Cur: $22 (6/30/89) (BT)
70+ CHATEAU LAMOUROUX Margaux 1987 (NR) (6/30/89) (BT)
70+ CHATEAU MALESCOT-ST.-EXUPERY Margaux 1987 Rel: $20 Cur: $20 (6/30/89) (BT)
70+ CHATEAU MARQUIS-D'ALESME-BECKER Margaux 1987 Rel: $15 Cur: $15 (6/30/89) (BT)
70+ CHATEAU POUGET Margaux 1987 Rel: $15 Cur: $15 (6/30/89) (BT)
70+ CHATEAU PRIEURE-LICHINE Margaux 1987 Rel: $13.50 Cur: $17 (6/30/89) (BT)
70+ CHATEAU RAUZAN-GASSIES Margaux 1987 Rel: $20 Cur: $20 (6/30/88) (BT)
70+ CHATEAU SEGONNES Margaux 1987 Rel: $15 Cur: $15 (6/30/89) (BT)
70+ CHATEAU DU TERTRE Margaux 1987 Rel: $18 Cur: $18 (6/30/89) (BT)
70+ CHATEAU DU TERTRE Margaux 1987 Rel: $18 Cur: $18 (6/30/88) (BT)
65+ CHATEAU MARSAC-SEGUINEAU Margaux 1987 Rel: $10 Cur: $10 (6/30/89) (BT)

1986

98 CHATEAU MARGAUX Margaux 1986 Rel: $80 Cur: $100 (12/15/89) (JS)
98 CHATEAU MARGAUX Margaux 1986 Rel: $80 Cur: $100 (6/15/89) CS
95+ CHATEAU MARGAUX Margaux 1986 Rel: $80 Cur: $100 (6/30/88) (BT)
94 CHATEAU PALMER Margaux 1986 Rel: $40 Cur: $53 (6/15/89)
92 CHATEAU MONBRISON Margaux 1986 Rel: $20 Cur: $20 (11/30/89) (JS)
92 CHATEAU PRIEURE-LICHINE Margaux 1986 Rel: $21 Cur: $23 (6/15/89)
91 CHATEAU D'ANGLUDET Margaux 1986 Rel: $17 Cur: $25 (6/15/89)
91 CHATEAU LABEGORCE-ZEDE Margaux 1986 Rel: $18 Cur: $22 (11/30/89) (JS)
90 CHATEAU D'ANGLUDET Margaux 1986 Rel: $17 Cur: $25 (11/30/89) (JS)
90 CHATEAU DESMIRAIL Margaux 1986 Rel: $22 Cur: $22 (6/30/89)
90 CHATEAU DURFORT-VIVENS Margaux 1986 Rel: $25 Cur: $25 (6/15/89)
90 CHATEAU LA TOUR-DE-MONS Margaux 1986 Rel: $19 Cur: $19 (11/30/89) (JS)
90 CHATEAU LA TOUR-DE-MONS Margaux 1986 Rel: $19 Cur: $19 (6/15/89)
90+ CHATEAU D'ANGLUDET Margaux 1986 Rel: $17 Cur: $25 (6/30/88) (BT)
90+ CHATEAU BRANE-CANTENAC Margaux 1986 Rel: $26 Cur: $30 (6/30/88) (BT)
90+ CHATEAU GISCOURS Margaux 1986 Rel: $30 Cur: $30 (6/30/88) (BT)
90+ CHATEAU D'ISSAN Margaux 1986 Rel: $22 Cur: $23 (6/30/88) (BT)
90+ CHATEAU MARGAUX Margaux 1986 Rel: $80 Cur: $100 (5/15/87) (BT)
90+ CHATEAU PRIEURE-LICHINE Margaux 1986 Rel: $21 Cur: $23 (5/15/87) (BT)
89 CHATEAU DU TERTRE Margaux 1986 Rel: $22 Cur: $22 (6/15/89)
88 CHATEAU CANUET Margaux 1986 $15 (11/30/89) (JS)
88 CHATEAU MALESCOT-ST.-EXUPERY Margaux 1986 Rel: $26 Cur: $29 (6/15/89)
88 CHATEAU RAUZAN-GASSIES Margaux 1986 Rel: $24 Cur: $25 (6/30/89)
87 CHATEAU BRANE-CANTENAC Margaux 1986 Rel: $26 Cur: $30 (6/15/89)
87 CHATEAU LABEGORCE-ZEDE Margaux 1986 Rel: $18 Cur: $22 (6/15/89)
87 CHATEAU RAUSAN-SEGLA Margaux 1986 Rel: $28 Cur: $38 (9/15/89)
86 CHATEAU LA GURGUE Margaux 1986 Rel: $22 Cur: $23 (6/15/89)
86 CHATEAU LABEGORCE Margaux 1986 $15 (2/15/90)
85 CHATEAU LA GURGUE Margaux 1986 Rel: $22 Cur: $23 (11/30/89) (JS)
85+ CHATEAU CANTENAC-BROWN Margaux 1986 Rel: $24 Cur: $27 (6/30/88) (BT)
85+ CHATEAU DURFORT-VIVENS Margaux 1986 Rel: $25 Cur: $25 (6/30/88) (BT)
85+ CHATEAU KIRWAN Margaux 1986 Rel: $25 Cur: $25 (6/30/88) (BT)
85+ CHATEAU MONBRISON Margaux 1986 Rel: $20 Cur: $20 (6/30/88) (BT)
85+ CHATEAU PRIEURE-LICHINE Margaux 1986 Rel: $21 Cur: $23 (6/30/88) (BT)
85+ CHATEAU RAUSAN-SEGLA Margaux 1986 Rel: $28 Cur: $38 (6/30/88) (BT)
84 PAVILLON ROUGE DU CHATEAU MARGAUX Margaux 1986 Rel: $24 Cur: $30 (6/30/89)
83 CHATEAU GISCOURS Margaux 1986 Rel: $30 Cur: $30 (6/15/89)
83 CHATEAU D'ISSAN Margaux 1986 Rel: $22 Cur: $23 (6/15/89)
82 CHATEAU KIRWAN Margaux 1986 Rel: $25 Cur: $25 (6/30/89)
80+ CHATEAU BOYD-CANTENAC Margaux 1986 Rel: $15 Cur: $15 (5/15/87) (BT)
80+ CHATEAU BRANE-CANTENAC Margaux 1986 Rel: $26 Cur: $30 (5/15/87) (BT)
80+ CHATEAU DURFORT-VIVENS Margaux 1986 Rel: $25 Cur: $25 (5/15/87) (BT)
80+ CHATEAU LASCOMBES Margaux 1986 Cur: $24 (6/30/88) (BT)
80+ CHATEAU RAUSAN-SEGLA Margaux 1986 Rel: $28 Cur: $38 (5/15/87) (BT)
80+ CHATEAU DU TERTRE Margaux 1986 Rel: $22 Cur: $22 (6/30/88) (BT)
80+ CHATEAU DU TERTRE Margaux 1986 Rel: $22 Cur: $22 (5/15/87) (BT)
79 CHATEAU MARQUIS DE TERME Margaux 1986 Rel: $23 Cur: $25 (6/30/89)
78 CHATEAU RICHETERRE Margaux 1986 $12.50 (2/15/89)
70+ CHATEAU D'ANGLUDET Margaux 1986 Rel: $17 Cur: $25 (5/15/87) (BT)
70+ CHATEAU DAUZAC Margaux 1986 Cur: $20 (6/30/88) (BT)
70+ CHATEAU DAUZAC Margaux 1986 Cur: $20 (5/15/87) (BT)
70+ CHATEAU DESMIRAIL Margaux 1986 Rel: $22 Cur: $22 (5/15/87) (BT)
70+ CHATEAU GISCOURS Margaux 1986 Rel: $30 Cur: $30 (5/15/87) (BT)
70+ CHATEAU D'ISSAN Margaux 1986 Rel: $22 Cur: $23 (5/15/87) (BT)
70+ CHATEAU KIRWAN Margaux 1986 Rel: $25 Cur: $25 (5/15/87) (BT)
70+ CHATEAU LASCOMBES Margaux 1986 Cur: $24 (5/15/87) (BT)
70+ CHATEAU POUGET Margaux 1986 Rel: $16 Cur: $16 (5/15/87) (BT)
70+ CHATEAU RAUZAN-GASSIES Margaux 1986 Rel: $24 Cur: $25 (6/30/88) (BT)

1985

99 CHATEAU MARGAUX Margaux 1985 Rel: $76 Cur: $92 (4/30/88)
97 CHATEAU MARGAUX Margaux 1985 Rel: $76 Cur: $92 (12/15/89) (JS)
93 PAVILLON ROUGE DU CHATEAU MARGAUX Margaux 1985 Rel: $23 Cur: $26 (4/15/88) SS
93 CHATEAU DU TERTRE Margaux 1985 Rel: $14 Cur: $23 (6/30/88) SS
92 CHATEAU RAUSAN-SEGLA Margaux 1985 Rel: $24 Cur: $24 (5/31/88)
90 CHATEAU D'ANGLUDET Margaux 1985 Rel: $17 Cur: $21 (4/15/88)
90 CHATEAU BOYD-CANTENAC Margaux 1985 Rel: $22 Cur: $22 (4/15/88)
90 CHATEAU LA GURGUE Margaux 1985 Rel: $17 Cur: $17 (2/15/88)
90 CHATEAU KIRWAN Margaux 1985 Rel: $29 Cur: $33 (2/15/89)
90 CHATEAU PALMER Margaux 1985 Rel: $40 Cur: $55 (4/15/88)
90 CHATEAU SIRAN Margaux 1985 $15.50 (9/30/88)
90+ CHATEAU BRANE-CANTENAC Margaux 1985 Rel: $24 Cur: $31 (5/15/87) (BT)
90+ CHATEAU KIRWAN Margaux 1985 Rel: $29 Cur: $33 (5/15/87) (BT)
90+ CHATEAU MARGAUX Margaux 1985 Rel: $76 Cur: $92 (5/15/87) (BT)
89 CHATEAU BRANE-CANTENAC Margaux 1985 Rel: $24 Cur: $31 (6/30/88)
88 CHATEAU D'ISSAN Margaux 1985 Rel: $23 Cur: $27 (4/15/88)
87 CHATEAU DAUZAC Margaux 1985 Rel: $21 Cur: $21 (9/30/88)
87 CHATEAU MALESCOT-ST.-EXUPERY Margaux 1985 Rel: $24 Cur: $24 (9/30/88)
86 CHATEAU GISCOURS Margaux 1985 Rel: $35 Cur: $35 (9/30/88)
84 CHATEAU LABEGORCE-ZEDE Margaux 1985 Rel: $13 Cur: $13 (2/29/88)
84 CHATEAU MARQUIS-D'ALESME-BECKER Margaux 1985 Rel: $19 Cur: $30 (6/30/88)
82 CHATEAU HAUT-BRETON-LARIGAUDIERE Margaux 1985 $16.50 (2/15/88)
82 CHATEAU PRIEURE-LICHINE Margaux 1985 Rel: $24 Cur: $24 (2/15/88)
80+ CHATEAU D'ANGLUDET Margaux 1985 Rel: $17 Cur: $21 (5/15/87) (BT)
80+ CHATEAU DAUZAC Margaux 1985 Rel: $21 Cur: $21 (5/15/87) (BT)
80+ CHATEAU DESMIRAIL Margaux 1985 Rel: $20 Cur: $20 (5/15/87) (BT)
80+ CHATEAU DURFORT-VIVENS Margaux 1985 Rel: $20 Cur: $20 (5/15/87) (BT)
80+ CHATEAU GISCOURS Margaux 1985 Rel: $35 Cur: $35 (4/16/86) (BT)
80+ CHATEAU LASCOMBES Margaux 1985 Rel: $20 Cur: $20 (5/15/87) (BT)
80+ CHATEAU PRIEURE-LICHINE Margaux 1985 Rel: $24 Cur: $24 (5/15/87) (BT)
80+ CHATEAU RAUSAN-SEGLA Margaux 1985 Rel: $24 Cur: $24 (5/15/87) (BT)
80+ CHATEAU DU TERTRE Margaux 1985 Rel: $14 Cur: $23 (5/15/87) (BT)
79 CHATEAU DE CLAIREFONT Margaux 1985 $9.25 (4/30/88)
75 BARTON & GUESTIER Margaux 1985 $12 (4/30/88)
70+ CHATEAU BOYD-CANTENAC Margaux 1985 Rel: $22 Cur: $22 (5/15/87) (BT)
70+ CHATEAU GISCOURS Margaux 1985 Rel: $35 Cur: $35 (5/15/87) (BT)
70+ CHATEAU POUGET Margaux 1985 Rel: $14 Cur: $17 (5/15/87) (BT)
70+ CHATEAU PRIEURE-LICHINE Margaux 1985 Rel: $24 Cur: $24 (4/16/86) (BT)
60+ CHATEAU D'ISSAN Margaux 1985 Rel: $23 Cur: $27 (5/15/87) (BT)

1984

93 CHATEAU MARGAUX Margaux 1984 Rel: $35 Cur: $62 (2/28/87) CS
91 CHATEAU MARGAUX Margaux 1984 Rel: $35 Cur: $62 (7/15/87) (HS)
86 CHATEAU D'ISSAN Margaux 1984 Rel: $10 Cur: $19 (3/31/87)
85 CHATEAU CANTENAC-BROWN Margaux 1984 Rel: $19 Cur: $19 (5/15/87)
84 CHATEAU PALMER Margaux 1984 Rel: $41 Cur: $41 (10/15/87)
80 CHATEAU PRIEURE-LICHINE Margaux 1984 Rel: $14 Cur: $15 (11/30/86)
78 CHATEAU MONBRISON Margaux 1984 Rel: $15 Cur: $15 (5/15/87)
69 CHATEAU MARQUIS-D'ALESME-BECKER Margaux 1984 Rel: $16.50 Cur: $17 (6/15/87)

1983

99 CHATEAU MARGAUX Margaux 1983 Rel: $70 Cur: $100 (4/16/86) SS
96 CHATEAU PRIEURE-LICHINE Margaux 1983 Rel: $18 Cur: $26 (4/16/86)
94 CHATEAU BRANE-CANTENAC Margaux 1983 Rel: $19 Cur: $30 (4/16/86)
93 CHATEAU D'ANGLUDET Margaux 1983 Rel: $17.50 Cur: $23 (10/15/86)
92 CHATEAU MARGAUX Margaux 1983 Rel: $70 Cur: $100 (12/15/89) (JS)
91 CHATEAU D'ISSAN Margaux 1983 Rel: $24 Cur: $28 (4/16/86)
91 CHATEAU DU TERTRE Margaux 1983 Rel: $14.25 Cur: $30 (7/16/86)
90 CHATEAU LA GURGUE Margaux 1983 Rel: $9.75 Cur: $10 (1/01/86)
90 CHATEAU PALMER Margaux 1983 Rel: $45 Cur: $77 (7/16/86) CS
88 CHATEAU LABEGORCE-ZEDE Margaux 1983 Rel: $15 Cur: $15 (10/15/86)
86 CHATEAU BOYD-CANTENAC Margaux 1983 Rel: $19 Cur: $19 (4/16/86)
86 CHATEAU KIRWAN Margaux 1983 Rel: $16 Cur: $22 (7/16/86)
86 CHATEAU POUGET Margaux 1983 Rel: $11.25 Cur: $19 (2/15/87)
84 CHATEAU LASCOMBES Margaux 1983 Rel: $32 Cur: $32 (2/15/88)
84 CHATEAU MARQUIS-D'ALESME-BECKER Margaux 1983 Rel: $15 Cur: $15 (12/31/86)
82 CHATEAU MALESCOT-ST.-EXUPERY Margaux 1983 Rel: $16 Cur: $22 (9/30/86)
80 PAVILLON ROUGE DU CHATEAU MARGAUX Margaux 1983 Rel: $25 Cur: $26 (6/30/87)
78 CHATEAU GISCOURS Margaux 1983 Cur: $26 (5/01/89)
68 CHATEAU MARSAC-SEGUINEAU Margaux 1983 Rel: $9 Cur: $9 (9/30/86)

1982

98 CHATEAU MARGAUX Margaux 1982 Rel: $60 Cur: $138 (12/15/89) (JS)
96 CHATEAU MARGAUX Margaux 1982 Rel: $60 Cur: $138 (6/16/85) CS
95 CHATEAU D'ANGLUDET Margaux 1982 Rel: $15 Cur: $27 (12/01/85) CS
95 CHATEAU PALMER Margaux 1982 Cur: $65 (5/01/85)
91 CHATEAU BOYD-CANTENAC Margaux 1982 Rel: $14.75 Cur: $25 (5/01/85)
91 CHATEAU CANTENAC-BROWN Margaux 1982 Rel: $12 Cur: $18 (5/01/85)
90 CHATEAU D'ANGLUDET Margaux 1982 Rel: $15 Cur: $27 (11/30/89) (JS)
90 CHATEAU MONBRISON Margaux 1982 Rel: $14 Cur: $20 (11/30/89) (JS)
90 CHATEAU LA TOUR-DE-MONS Margaux 1982 Cur: $16 (11/30/89) (JS)
89 CHATEAU PRIEURE-LICHINE Margaux 1982 Rel: $15 Cur: $27 (5/01/85)
88 CHATEAU BRANE-CANTENAC Margaux 1982 Rel: $22 Cur: $30 (5/01/85)
88 CHATEAU GISCOURS Margaux 1982 Rel: $26 Cur: $34 (12/01/85)
87 CHATEAU LABEGORCE-ZEDE Margaux 1982 Cur: $18 (11/30/89) (JS)
85 CHATEAU LA GURGUE Margaux 1982 Cur: $24 (11/30/89) (JS)
85 PAVILLON ROUGE DU CHATEAU MARGAUX Margaux 1982 Cur: $28 (7/15/87) (HS)

1981

97 CHATEAU MARGAUX Margaux 1981 Cur: $94 (7/15/87) (HS)
91 CHATEAU CANTENAC-BROWN Margaux 1981 Rel: $12 Cur: $12 (3/01/85)
90 CHATEAU PALMER Margaux 1981 Rel: $24.50 Cur: $50 (5/01/85)
90 CHATEAU RAUSAN-SEGLA Margaux 1981 Rel: $16 Cur: $23 (5/01/84)
87 CHATEAU MALESCOT-ST.-EXUPERY Margaux 1981 Rel: $13 Cur: $22 (5/01/89)
87 PAVILLON ROUGE DU CHATEAU MARGAUX Margaux 1981 Cur: $25 (7/15/87) (HS)
86 CHATEAU PALMER Margaux 1981 Rel: $24.50 Cur: $50 (5/15/84)
86 CHATEAU PRIEURE-LICHINE Margaux 1981 Rel: $12 Cur: $24 (11/01/84)
86 CHATEAU RAUSAN-SEGLA Margaux 1981 Rel: $16 Cur: $23 (10/16/84)
85 CHATEAU LASCOMBES Margaux 1981 Rel: $19 Cur: $31 (5/16/85)
82 CHATEAU GISCOURS Margaux 1981 Rel: $12.50 Cur: $40 (6/01/84)

1980

90 CHATEAU MARGAUX Margaux 1980 Rel: $30 Cur: $66 (5/01/84) CS
86 CHATEAU PALMER Margaux 1980 Cur: $23 (5/01/85)
80 CHATEAU GISCOURS Margaux 1980 Cur: $23 (2/16/84)
80 CHATEAU MARGAUX Margaux 1980 Rel: $30 Cur: $66 (7/15/87) (HS)
76 PAVILLON ROUGE DU CHATEAU MARGAUX Margaux 1980 Cur: $20 (7/15/87) (HS)

1979

94 CHATEAU MARGAUX Margaux 1979 Cur: $118 (7/15/87) (HS)
93 CHATEAU MARGAUX Margaux 1979 Cur: $118 (10/15/89) (JS)
91 CHATEAU MARGAUX Margaux 1979 Cur: $118 (12/15/89) (JS)
90 CHATEAU PALMER Margaux 1979 Cur: $67 (10/15/89) (JS)
88 CHATEAU GISCOURS Margaux 1979 Cur: $34 (2/16/84)
87 CHATEAU GISCOURS Margaux 1979 Cur: $34 (10/15/89) (JS)
87 CHATEAU PALMER Margaux 1979 Cur: $67 (5/01/85)

FRANCE
BORDEAUX RED/*MARGAUX*

84   CHATEAU LASCOMBES Margaux 1979 Cur: $15 (10/15/89) (JS)
80   CHATEAU BRANE-CANTENAC Margaux 1979 Cur: $21 (10/15/89) (JS)
78   PAVILLON ROUGE DU CHATEAU MARGAUX Margaux 1979 Cur: $34 (7/15/87) (HS)
69   CHATEAU RAUSAN-SEGLA Margaux 1979 Cur: $28 (10/15/89) (JS)

1978
92   CHATEAU MARGAUX Margaux 1978 Cur: $175 (12/15/89) (JS)
92   CHATEAU MARGAUX Margaux 1978 Cur: $175 (7/15/87) (HS)
87   CHATEAU GISCOURS Margaux 1978 Cur: $59 (2/16/84)
81   CHATEAU PALMER Margaux 1978 Rel: $35 Cur: $91 (5/01/85)
     CHATEAU PALMER Margaux 1978 Rel: $35 Cur: $91 (11/01/83) CS

1977
75   CHATEAU MARGAUX Margaux 1977 Cur: $34 (7/15/87) (HS)

1976
83   CHATEAU GISCOURS Margaux 1976 Cur: $45 (2/16/84)
81   CHATEAU MARGAUX Margaux 1976 Cur: $90 (7/15/87) (HS)

1975
88   CHATEAU MARGAUX Margaux 1975 Cur: $119 (7/15/87) (HS)

1971
77   CHATEAU MARGAUX Margaux 1971 Cur: $76 (7/15/87) (HS)

1970
81   CHATEAU GISCOURS Margaux 1970 Cur: $73 (2/16/84)
70   CHATEAU MARGAUX Margaux 1970 Cur: $144 (7/15/87) (HS)

1967
84   CHATEAU MARGAUX Margaux 1967 Cur: $58 (7/15/87) (HS)

1966
90   CHATEAU MARGAUX Margaux 1966 Cur: $161 (7/15/87) (HS)

1964
89   CHATEAU GISCOURS Margaux 1964 Cur: $116/1.5L (2/16/84)
86   CHATEAU MARGAUX Margaux 1964 Cur: $115 (7/15/87) (HS)

1962
86   CHATEAU MARGAUX Margaux 1962 Cur: $376/1.5L (12/15/89) (JS)
85   CHATEAU MARGAUX Margaux 1962 Cur: $179 (7/15/87) (HS)
80   CHATEAU PALMER Margaux 1962 Cur: $150 (11/30/87) (JS)
68   CHATEAU GISCOURS Margaux 1962 Cur: $33 (11/30/87) (JS)
65   CHATEAU MALESCOT-ST.-EXUPERY Margaux 1962 Cur: $80 (11/30/87) (JS)
60   CHATEAU BRANE-CANTENAC Margaux 1962 Cur: $65 (11/30/87) (JS)

1961
98   CHATEAU MARGAUX Margaux 1961 Cur: $1,050/1.5L (12/15/89) (JS)
94   CHATEAU MARGAUX Margaux 1961 Cur: $500 (7/15/87) (HS)
93   CHATEAU PALMER Margaux 1961 Cur: $479 (3/16/86) (JL)
78   CHATEAU GISCOURS Margaux 1961 Cur: $100 (3/16/86) (JL)
66   CHATEAU MALESCOT-ST.-EXUPERY Margaux 1961 Cur: $135 (3/16/86) (JL)
65   CHATEAU BOYD-CANTENAC Margaux 1961 Cur: $100 (3/16/86) (JL)
64   CHATEAU BRANE-CANTENAC Margaux 1961 Cur: $135 (3/16/86) (JL)
63   CHATEAU RAUSAN-SEGLA Margaux 1961 Cur: $146 (3/16/86) (JL)

1959
98   CHATEAU PALMER Margaux 1959 Cur: $247 (10/15/90) (JS)
95   CHATEAU MARGAUX Margaux 1959 Cur: $377 (12/15/89) (JS)
95   CHATEAU MARGAUX Margaux 1959 Cur: $377 (7/15/87) (HS)
93   CHATEAU MARGAUX Margaux 1959 Cur: $377 (10/15/90) (JS)
89   CHATEAU CANTENAC-BROWN Margaux 1959 Cur: $100 (10/15/90) (JS)
87   CHATEAU MALESCOT-ST.-EXUPERY Margaux 1959 Cur: $150 (10/15/90) (JS)
80   CHATEAU PRIEURE-LICHINE Margaux 1959 Cur: $50 (10/15/90) (JS)
73   CHATEAU RAUZAN-GASSIES Margaux 1959 Cur: $93 (10/15/90) (JS)

1957
90   CHATEAU MARGAUX Margaux 1957 Cur: $200 (7/15/87) (HS)

1955
79   CHATEAU MARGAUX Margaux 1955 Cur: $233 (7/15/87) (HS)

1953
94   CHATEAU MARGAUX Margaux 1953 Cur: $846/1.5L (7/15/87) (HS)
90   CHATEAU MARGAUX Margaux 1953 Cur: $403 (7/15/87) (HS)
84   CHATEAU MARGAUX Margaux 1953 Cur: $403 (12/15/89) (JS)

1952
85   CHATEAU MARGAUX Margaux 1952 Cur: $483/1.5L (7/15/87) (HS)

1950
89   CHATEAU MARGAUX Margaux 1950 Cur: $586/1.5L (7/15/87) (HS)

1949
95   CHATEAU MARGAUX Margaux 1949 Cur: $207 (7/15/87) (HS)

1947
96   CHATEAU MARGAUX Margaux 1947 Cur: $358 (7/15/87) (HS)

1945
91   CHATEAU RAUZAN-GASSIES Margaux 1945 Cur: $300 (3/16/86) (JL)
90   CHATEAU MARGAUX Margaux 1945 Cur: $793 (3/16/86) (JL)
90   CHATEAU PALMER Margaux 1945 Cur: $400 (3/16/86) (JL)
89   CHATEAU LA TOUR-DE-MONS Margaux 1945 Cur: $200 (3/16/86) (JL)
88   CHATEAU KIRWAN Margaux 1945 Cur: $150 (3/16/86) (JL)
87   CHATEAU BRANE-CANTENAC Margaux 1945 Cur: $200 (3/16/86) (JL)
81   CHATEAU MALESCOT-ST.-EXUPERY Margaux 1945 Cur: $200 (3/16/86) (JL)
75   CHATEAU CANTENAC-BROWN Margaux 1945 Cur: $150 (3/16/86) (JL)
73   CHATEAU RAUSAN-SEGLA Margaux 1945 Cur: $150 (3/16/86) (JL)

1943
78   CHATEAU MARGAUX Margaux 1943 Cur: $320 (7/15/87) (HS)

1937
82   CHATEAU MARGAUX Margaux 1937 Cur: $340 (7/15/87) (HS)

1934
88   CHATEAU MARGAUX Margaux 1934 Cur: $272 (7/15/87) (HS)

1929
83   CHATEAU MARGAUX Margaux 1929 Cur: $750 (7/15/87) (HS)

1928
84   CHATEAU MARGAUX Margaux 1928 Cur: $1,724/1.5L (7/15/87) (HS)
73   CHATEAU MARGAUX Margaux 1928 Cur: $821 (7/15/87) (HS)

1926
77   CHATEAU MARGAUX Margaux 1926 Cur: $300 (7/15/87) (HS)

1924
73   CHATEAU MARGAUX Margaux 1924 Cur: $380 (7/15/87) (HS)

1923
81   CHATEAU MARGAUX Margaux 1923 Cur: $327 (7/15/87) (HS)

1920
79   CHATEAU MARGAUX Margaux 1920 Cur: $415 (7/15/87) (HS)

1918
80   CHATEAU MARGAUX Margaux 1918 Cur: $500 (7/15/87) (HS)

1917
62   CHATEAU MARGAUX Margaux 1917 Cur: $300 (7/15/87) (HS)

1916
63   PAVILLON ROUGE DU CHATEAU MARGAUX Margaux 1916 (NA) (7/15/87) (HS)

1909
65   CHATEAU MARGAUX Margaux 1909 Cur: $475 (7/15/87) (HS)

1908
85   CHATEAU MARGAUX Margaux 1908 Cur: $525 (7/15/87) (HS)

1905
64   CHATEAU MARGAUX Margaux 1905 Cur: $800 (7/15/87) (HS)

1900
93   CHATEAU MARGAUX Margaux 1900 Cur: $2,000 (7/15/87) (HS)

1899
94   CHATEAU MARGAUX Margaux 1899 Cur: $1,700 (7/15/87) (HS)

1898
75   CHATEAU MARGAUX Margaux 1898 Cur: $2,062 (7/15/87) (HS)

1893
95   CHATEAU MARGAUX Margaux 1893 Cur: $2,000 (7/15/87) (HS)

1892
80   CHATEAU MARGAUX Margaux 1892 Cur: $750 (7/15/87) (HS)

1887
81   CHATEAU MARGAUX Margaux 1887 Cur: $757 (7/15/87) (HS)

1875
100 CHATEAU MARGAUX Margaux 1875 $15,000/3L (12/15/88) (JS)

1870
89   CHATEAU MARGAUX Margaux 1870 Cur: $3,300 (7/15/87) (HS)

1868
69   CHATEAU MARGAUX Margaux 1868 Cur: $2,000 (7/15/87) (HS)

1865
97   CHATEAU MARGAUX Margaux 1865 Cur: $5,000 (7/15/87) (HS)

1864
98   CHATEAU MARGAUX Margaux 1864 Cur: $3,500 (7/15/87) (HS)

1848
95   CHATEAU MARGAUX Margaux 1848 Cur: $10,000 (7/15/87) (HS)

1847
96   CHATEAU MARGAUX Margaux 1847 Cur: $52,500/1.5L (7/15/87) (HS)

Key to Symbols

The scores reported here are the results of blind tastings conducted by our panel of senior editors. Wines that carry the initials below are results of individual tastings.

THE WINE SPECTATOR 100-POINT SCALE   95-100—Classic, a great wine; *90-94*—Outstanding, superior character and style; *80-89*—Good to very good, a wine with special qualities; *70-79*—Average, drinkable wine that may have minor flaws; *60-69*—Below average, drinkable but not recommended; *50-59*—Poor, undrinkable, not recommended. "*+*"—With a score indicates a range; used primarily with barrel tastings to indicate a preliminary score.

SPECIAL DESIGNATIONS   SS—Spectator Selection, CS—Cellar Selection, BB—Best Buy.

TASTER'S INITIALS   (JG)—Jim Gordon, (HS)—Harvey Steiman, (JL)—James Laube, (JS)—James Suckling, (TM)—Thomas Matthews, (TR)—Terry Robards, (BT)—Barrel Tasting, (CA-date)—*California's Great Cabernets* by James Laube, (CH-date)—*California's Great Chardonnays* by James Laube, (VP-date)—*Vintage Port* by James Suckling.

DATE TASTED   Dates in parentheses represent the issue in which the rating was published.

1791

97   CHATEAU MARGAUX Margaux 1791 (NA) (7/15/87) (HS)

1771

99   CHATEAU MARGAUX Margaux 1771 (NA) (7/15/87) (HS)

MÉDOC

1990

80+ CHATEAU GREYSAC Médoc 1990 (NR) (4/30/91) (BT)

1989

85+ CHATEAU GREYSAC Médoc 1989 (NR) (4/30/91) (BT)
85+ CHATEAU LOUDENNE Médoc 1989 (NR) (4/30/91) (BT)
85+ CHATEAU PLAGNAC Médoc 1989 (NR) (4/30/91) (BT)
80+ CHATEAU LA CARDONNE Médoc 1989 (NR) (4/30/91) (BT)
80+ CHATEAU LA TOUR-HAUT-CAUSSAN Médoc 1989 (NR) (4/30/91) (BT)
75+ CHATEAU GREYSAC Médoc 1989 (NR) (4/30/90) (BT)
75+ CHATEAU LA TOUR DE BY Médoc 1989 (NR) (4/30/91) (BT)

1988

87   CHATEAU GREYSAC Médoc 1988 $15 (4/30/91)
86   CHATEAU LA TOUR DE BY Médoc 1988 $12.50 (6/15/91)
84   CHATEAU LE BOSCQ Médoc 1988 $20 (4/30/91)
84   CHATEAU LES ORMES-SORBET Médoc 1988 $20 (4/30/91)
80   CHATEAU PATACHE D'AUX Médoc 1988 $10 (4/30/91)
80+ CHATEAU LA TOUR-HAUT-CAUSSAN Médoc 1988 $12.50 (6/30/89) (BT)
79   CHATEAU PLAGNAC Médoc 1988 $8.50 (4/30/91)
79   CHATEAU LA TOUR-HAUT-CAUSSAN Médoc 1988 $12.50 (7/15/91)
75+ CHATEAU LA CROIX LANDON Médoc 1988 (NR) (6/30/89) (BT)
75+ CHATEAU GREYSAC Médoc 1988 $15 (6/30/89) (BT)
75+ CHATEAU LES ORMES-SORBET Médoc 1988 $20 (6/30/89) (BT)
75+ CHATEAU LA TOUR DE BY Médoc 1988 $12.50 (6/30/89) (BT)

1987

80   CHATEAU LA TOUR-HAUT-CAUSSAN Médoc 1987 Rel: $11 Cur: $11 (11/30/89) (JS)
80+ CHATEAU LA TOUR-HAUT-CAUSSAN Médoc 1987 Rel: $11 Cur: $11 (6/30/89) (BT)
79   CHATEAU LA TOUR DE BY Médoc 1987 Rel: $10 Cur: $10 (11/30/89) (JS)
77   CHATEAU PLAGNAC Médoc 1987 $8 (11/30/89) (JS)
75   CHATEAU LOUDENNE Médoc 1987 Rel: $10 Cur: $10 (11/30/89) (JS)
75+ CHATEAU GREYSAC Médoc 1987 Rel: $9 Cur: $9 (6/30/89) (BT)
75+ CHATEAU LES ORMES-SORBET Médoc 1987 Rel: $14 Cur: $14 (6/30/89) (BT)
72   CHATEAU POTENSAC Médoc 1987 Rel: $9.50 Cur: $12 (5/15/90)
70+ CHATEAU LA CARDONNE Médoc 1987 Rel: $10 Cur: $10 (6/30/88) (BT)
70+ CHATEAU POTENSAC Médoc 1987 Rel: $9.50 Cur: $12 (6/30/88) (BT)
70+ CHATEAU LA TOUR DE BY Médoc 1987 Rel: $10 Cur: $10 (6/30/89) (BT)
70+ CHATEAU LA TOUR DE BY Médoc 1987 Rel: $10 Cur: $10 (6/30/88) (BT)

1986

88   CHATEAU LA TOUR-HAUT-CAUSSAN Médoc 1986 Rel: $14 Cur: $14 (11/30/89) (JS)
86   CHATEAU POTENSAC Médoc 1986 Rel: $15 Cur: $15 (11/30/89) (JS)
85   CHATEAU GREYSAC Médoc 1986 Rel: $10 Cur: $10 (11/30/89) (JS)
84   CHATEAU LA CARDONNE Médoc 1986 Rel: $10 Cur: $10 (2/15/90)
84   CHATEAU LA TOUR DE BY Médoc 1986 Rel: $12 Cur: $12 (2/15/89)
82   CHATEAU PLAGNAC Médoc 1986 $9 (11/30/89) (JS)
80   CHATEAU LA TOUR DE BY Médoc 1986 Rel: $12 Cur: $12 (11/30/89) (JS)
80+ CHATEAU POTENSAC Médoc 1986 Rel: $15 Cur: $15 (6/30/88) (BT)
80+ CHATEAU LA TOUR DE BY Médoc 1986 Rel: $12 Cur: $12 (6/30/88) (BT)
79   CHATEAU BELLERIVE Médoc 1986 $4.50 (2/15/89)
79   CHATEAU PLAGNAC Médoc 1986 $9 (6/30/89)
75   CHATEAU LE BOSCQ Médoc 1986 $10 (6/30/89)
74   CHATEAU LOUDENNE Médoc 1986 Rel: $12 Cur: $12 (11/30/89) (JS)
75+ CHATEAU LA CARDONNE Médoc 1986 Rel: $10 Cur: $10 (6/30/88) (BT)
70+ CHATEAU PLAGNAC Médoc 1986 $9 (5/15/87) (BT)
70+ CHATEAU POTENSAC Médoc 1986 Rel: $15 Cur: $15 (5/15/87) (BT)
60+ CHATEAU GREYSAC Médoc 1986 Rel: $10 Cur: $10 (5/15/87) (BT)

1985

83   CHATEAU LA CARDONNE Médoc 1985 Rel: $9 Cur: $9 (12/31/88)
83   CHATEAU LA TOUR-ST.-BONNET Médoc 1985 $9 (6/30/88)
82   CHATEAU ST.-CHRISTOPHE Médoc 1985 $6.50 (7/31/88) BB
80+ CHATEAU POTENSAC Médoc 1985 Rel: $11 Cur: $16 (5/15/87) (BT)
79   CHATEAU ST.-BONNET Médoc 1985 $9 (4/15/88)
77   CHATEAU GREYSAC Médoc 1985 Rel: $9 Cur: $9 (12/31/88)
77   CHATEAU ST.-BONNET Médoc 1985 $9 (2/15/88)
75   CHATEAU LOUDENNE Médoc 1985 Rel: $13.50 Cur: $14 (11/30/88)
72   ALFRED SCHYLER Médoc 1985 $8.50 (6/30/88)
70   CHATEAU ST.-SEVE Médoc 1985 $6 (11/15/87)
68   CHATEAU PLAGNAC Médoc 1985 $9 (8/31/88)

1984

80   CHATEAU LA TOUR-HAUT-CAUSSAN Médoc 1984 Rel: $10 Cur: $10 (2/15/88)

1983

79   CHATEAU LA CARDONNE Médoc 1983 Rel: $7 Cur: $7 (10/15/86)
78   CHATEAU LA TOUR DE BY Médoc 1983 Rel: $7 Cur: $7 (10/16/85)
75   CHATEAU POTENSAC Médoc 1983 Rel: $9 Cur: $15 (10/15/86)
70   CHATEAU LE BOSCQ Médoc 1983 $8 (1/01/86)
65   CHATEAU GREYSAC Médoc 1983 Rel: $8.50 Cur: $9 (7/31/87)
63   CHATEAU ROQUEGRAVE Médoc 1983 $6 (4/01/86)

1982

86   CHATEAU LA TOUR DE BY Médoc 1982 Rel: $5.50 Cur: $10 (2/01/85) BB
83   CHATEAU PATACHE D'AUX Médoc 1982 Rel: $5 Cur: $18 (5/01/85)
83   CHATEAU LA TOUR-HAUT-CAUSSAN Médoc 1982 Cur: $10 (11/30/89) (JS)
80   CHATEAU GREYSAC Médoc 1982 Rel: $8 Cur: $10 (11/30/89) (JS)
80   CHATEAU LA TOUR DE BY Médoc 1982 Rel: $5.50 Cur: $10 (11/30/89) (JS)
76   CHATEAU LE BOSCQ Médoc 1982 $6 (10/01/85) BB
74   CHATEAU LOUDENNE Médoc 1982 Rel: $10 Cur: $12 (11/30/89) (JS)

1981

84   CHATEAU LOUDENNE Médoc 1981 Rel: $10.75 Cur: $11 (9/01/84)
77   CHATEAU GREYSAC Médoc 1981 Rel: $8 Cur: $8 (6/01/84)

MOULIS

1990

85+ CHATEAU CHASSE-SPLEEN Moulis 1990 (NR) (4/30/91) (BT)
85+ CHATEAU POUJEAUX Moulis 1990 (NR) (4/30/91) (BT)

1989

90+ CHATEAU CHASSE-SPLEEN Moulis 1989 (NR) (4/30/91) (BT)
90+ CHATEAU CHASSE-SPLEEN Moulis 1989 (NR) (4/30/90) (BT)
90+ CHATEAU POUJEAUX Moulis 1989 (NR) (4/30/91) (BT)
85+ CHATEAU POUJEAUX Moulis 1989 (NR) (4/30/90) (BT)

1988

89   CHATEAU CHASSE-SPLEEN Moulis 1988 $26 (3/31/91)
88   CHATEAU POUJEAUX Moulis 1988 $15 (2/28/91)
85+ CHATEAU CHASSE-SPLEEN Moulis 1988 $26 (8/31/90) (BT)
85+ CHATEAU CHASSE-SPLEEN Moulis 1988 $26 (6/30/89) (BT)
82   CHATEAU MAUCAILLOU Moulis 1988 $14 (7/31/91)
81   CHATEAU LA MOULINE Moulis 1988 $20 (2/15/91)
80+ CHATEAU BRILLETTE Moulis 1988 $15 (6/30/89) (BT)
80+ CHATEAU MAUCAILLOU Moulis 1988 $14 (6/30/89) (BT)
80+ CHATEAU POUJEAUX Moulis 1988 $15 (6/30/89) (BT)

1987

85+ CHATEAU CHASSE-SPLEEN Moulis 1987 Rel: $15 Cur: $16 (6/30/88) (BT)
82   CHATEAU CHASSE-SPLEEN Moulis 1987 Rel: $15 Cur: $16 (11/30/89) (JS)
81   CHATEAU POUJEAUX Moulis 1987 Rel: $15 Cur: $15 (11/30/89) (JS)
78   CHATEAU CHASSE-SPLEEN Moulis 1987 Rel: $15 Cur: $16 (2/15/90)
80+ CHATEAU CHASSE-SPLEEN Moulis 1987 Rel: $15 Cur: $16 (6/30/89) (BT)
80+ CHATEAU MAUCAILLOU Moulis 1987 Rel: $14 Cur: $14 (6/30/88) (BT)
80+ CHATEAU POUJEAUX Moulis 1987 Rel: $15 Cur: $15 (6/30/89) (BT)
80+ CHATEAU POUJEAUX Moulis 1987 Rel: $15 Cur: $15 (6/30/88) (BT)
74   CHATEAU POUJEAUX Moulis 1987 Rel: $15 Cur: $15 (5/15/90)
75+ CHATEAU BRILLETTE Moulis 1987 $15 (6/30/89) (BT)
72   CHATEAU BRILLETTE Moulis 1987 $15 (11/30/89) (JS)
71   CHATEAU DUPLESSIS-FABRE Moulis 1987 $7 (11/30/89) (JS)
70+ CHATEAU MAUCAILLOU Moulis 1987 $14 (6/30/89) (BT)

1986

90   CHATEAU CHASSE-SPLEEN Moulis 1986 Rel: $26 Cur: $26 (11/30/89) (JS)
90+ CHATEAU CHASSE-SPLEEN Moulis 1986 Rel: $26 Cur: $26 (6/30/88) (BT)
88   CHATEAU POUJEAUX Moulis 1986 Rel: $22 Cur: $22 (11/30/89) (JS)
85   CHATEAU CHASSE-SPLEEN Moulis 1986 Rel: $26 Cur: $26 (6/30/89)
85+ CHATEAU MAUCAILLOU Moulis 1986 Rel: $18 Cur: $18 (6/30/88) (BT)
85+ CHATEAU POUJEAUX Moulis 1986 Rel: $22 Cur: $22 (6/30/88) (BT)
83   CHATEAU POUJEAUX Moulis 1986 Rel: $22 Cur: $22 (6/30/89)
78   CHATEAU BRILLETTE Moulis 1986 $14 (11/30/89) (JS)
78   CHATEAU BRILLETTE Moulis 1986 $14 (6/30/89)
74   CHATEAU DUPLESSIS-FABRE Moulis 1986 $7 (11/30/89) (JS)
70+ CHATEAU POUJEAUX Moulis 1986 Rel: $22 Cur: $22 (5/15/87) (BT)

1985

88   CHATEAU MAUCAILLOU Moulis 1985 Rel: $18 Cur: $18 (8/31/88)
87   CHATEAU POUJEAUX Moulis 1985 Rel: $18.50 Cur: $19 (9/30/88)
86   CHATEAU CHASSE-SPLEEN Moulis 1985 Rel: $22 Cur: $28 (5/15/88)

1984

74   CHATEAU CHASSE-SPLEEN Moulis 1984 Rel: $13 Cur: $15 (6/15/87)

1983

87   CHATEAU CHASSE-SPLEEN Moulis 1983 Rel: $16.50 Cur: $23 (4/16/86)
87   CHATEAU MAUCAILLOU Moulis 1983 Rel: $16 Cur: $16 (3/15/87)
79   CHATEAU POUJEAUX Moulis 1983 Rel: $13 Cur: $19 (10/31/86)

1982

90   CHATEAU CHASSE-SPLEEN Moulis 1982 Rel: $14.75 Cur: $36 (11/30/89) (JS)
90   CHATEAU CHASSE-SPLEEN Moulis 1982 Rel: $14.75 Cur: $36 (2/16/85)
90   CHATEAU MAUCAILLOU Moulis 1982 Rel: $15 Cur: $25 (11/30/89) (JS)
90   CHATEAU MAUCAILLOU Moulis 1982 Rel: $15 Cur: $25 (4/16/86)
88   CHATEAU POUJEAUX Moulis 1982 Cur: $23 (11/30/89) (JS)
85   CHATEAU BRILLETTE Moulis 1982 Cur: $18 (11/30/89) (JS)
79   CHATEAU DUPLESSIS-FABRE Moulis 1982 Cur: $10 (11/30/89) (JS)

1981

88   CHATEAU MAUCAILLOU Moulis 1981 Rel: $12 Cur: $14 (10/01/85)

PAUILLAC

1990

95+ CHATEAU LAFITE-ROTHSCHILD Pauillac 1990 (NR) (4/30/91) (BT)
95+ CHATEAU LATOUR Pauillac 1990 (NR) (4/30/91) (BT)
95+ CHATEAU MOUTON-ROTHSCHILD Pauillac 1990 (NR) (4/30/91) (BT)
95+ CHATEAU PICHON-BARON Pauillac 1990 (NR) (4/30/91) (BT)
90+ CHATEAU CLERC-MILON Pauillac 1990 (NR) (4/30/91) (BT)
90+ CHATEAU HAUT-BATAILLEY Pauillac 1990 (NR) (4/30/91) (BT)
90+ CHATEAU LYNCH-BAGES Pauillac 1990 (NR) (4/30/91) (BT)
90+ CHATEAU PIBRAN Pauillac 1990 (NR) (4/30/91) (BT)
90+ LES TOURELLS DE LONGUEVILLE Pauillac 1990 (NR) (4/30/91) (BT)
85+ CHATEAU BATAILLEY Pauillac 1990 (NR) (4/30/91) (BT)
85+ CHATEAU CROIZET-BAGES Pauillac 1990 (NR) (4/30/91) (BT)
85+ CHATEAU DUHART-MILON Pauillac 1990 (NR) (4/30/91) (BT)
85+ CHATEAU HAUT-BAGES-AVEROUS Pauillac 1990 (NR) (4/30/91) (BT)
85+ CHATEAU LYNCH-MOUSSAS Pauillac 1990 (NR) (4/30/91) (BT)
85+ CHATEAU MOUTON-BARONNE-PHILIPPE Pauillac 1990 (NR) (4/30/91) (BT)
85+ CHATEAU PICHON-LALANDE Pauillac 1990 (NR) (4/30/91) (BT)
80+ CARRUADES DE LAFITE Pauillac 1990 (NR) (4/30/91) (BT)

FRANCE
BORDEAUX RED/*PAUILLAC*

80+ LES FORTS DE LATOUR Pauillac 1990 (NR) (4/30/91) (BT)
80+ CHATEAU PONTET-CANET Pauillac 1990 (NR) (4/30/91) (BT)

1989

95+ CHATEAU HAUT-BATAILLEY Pauillac 1989 (NR) (4/30/90) (BT)
95+ CHATEAU LAFITE-ROTHSCHILD Pauillac 1989 (NR) (4/30/91) (BT)
95+ CHATEAU LAFITE-ROTHSCHILD Pauillac 1989 (NR) (4/30/90) (BT)
95+ CHATEAU LATOUR Pauillac 1989 (NR) (4/30/91) (BT)
95+ CHATEAU LYNCH-BAGES Pauillac 1989 (NR) (4/30/91) (BT)
95+ CHATEAU LYNCH-BAGES Pauillac 1989 (NR) (4/30/90) (BT)
95+ CHATEAU MOUTON-ROTHSCHILD Pauillac 1989 (NR) (4/30/91) (BT)
95+ CHATEAU MOUTON-ROTHSCHILD Pauillac 1989 (NR) (4/30/90) (BT)
95+ CHATEAU PIBRAN Pauillac 1989 (NR) (4/30/91) (BT)
95+ CHATEAU PICHON-BARON Pauillac 1989 (NR) (4/30/90) (BT)
90+ CHATEAU CLERC-MILON Pauillac 1989 (NR) (4/30/90) (BT)
90+ CHATEAU DUHART-MILON Pauillac 1989 (NR) (4/30/91) (BT)
90+ CHATEAU DUHART-MILON Pauillac 1989 (NR) (4/30/90) (BT)
90+ CHATEAU GRAND-PUY-LACOSTE Pauillac 1989 (NR) (4/30/91) (BT)
90+ CHATEAU HAUT-BAGES-AVEROUS Pauillac 1989 (NR) (4/30/90) (BT)
90+ CHATEAU HAUT-BAGES-LIBERAL Pauillac 1989 (NR) (4/30/90) (BT)
90+ CHATEAU LATOUR Pauillac 1989 (NR) (4/30/90) (BT)
90+ CHATEAU MOUTON-BARONNE-PHILIPPE Pauillac 1989 (NR) (4/30/91) (BT)
90+ CHATEAU MOUTON-BARONNE-PHILIPPE Pauillac 1989 (NR) (4/30/90) (BT)
90+ CHATEAU PIBRAN Pauillac 1989 (NR) (4/30/90) (BT)
90+ CHATEAU PICHON-BARON Pauillac 1989 (NR) (4/30/91) (BT)
90+ CHATEAU PICHON-LALANDE Pauillac 1989 (NR) (4/30/91) (BT)
90+ CHATEAU PICHON-LALANDE Pauillac 1989 (NR) (4/30/90) (BT)
90+ CHATEAU PONTET-CANET Pauillac 1989 (NR) (4/30/91) (BT)
90+ LES TOURELLS DE LONGUEVILLE Pauillac 1989 (NR) (4/30/91) (BT)
90+ LES TOURELLS DE LONGUEVILLE Pauillac 1989 (NR) (4/30/90) (BT)
85+ CHATEAU BATAILLEY Pauillac 1989 (NR) (4/30/91) (BT)
85+ CHATEAU BATAILLEY Pauillac 1989 (NR) (4/30/90) (BT)
85+ CARRUADES DE LAFITE Pauillac 1989 (NR) (4/30/91) (BT)
85+ CARRUADES DE LAFITE Pauillac 1989 (NR) (4/30/90) (BT)
85+ CHATEAU CLERC-MILON Pauillac 1989 (NR) (4/30/91) (BT)
85+ LES FORTS DE LATOUR Pauillac 1989 (NR) (4/30/91) (BT)
85+ CHATEAU GRAND-PUY-LACOSTE Pauillac 1989 (NR) (4/30/90) (BT)
85+ CHATEAU HAUT-BAGES-AVEROUS Pauillac 1989 (NR) (4/30/91) (BT)
85+ CHATEAU HAUT-BAGES-MONPELOU Pauillac 1989 (NR) (4/30/90) (BT)
85+ CHATEAU HAUT-BATAILLEY Pauillac 1989 (NR) (4/30/91) (BT)
85+ CHATEAU LYNCH-MOUSSAS Pauillac 1989 (NR) (4/30/91) (BT)
80+ CHATEAU CROIZET-BAGES Pauillac 1989 (NR) (4/30/91) (BT)
80+ MOULIN DE DUHART Pauillac 1989 (NR) (4/30/90) (BT)

1988

100 CHATEAU MOUTON-ROTHSCHILD Pauillac 1988 $105 (4/30/91)
96   CHATEAU LAFITE-ROTHSCHILD Pauillac 1988 $100 (4/30/91) CS
95   CHATEAU LYNCH-BAGES Pauillac 1988 $35 (3/15/91) CS
95   CHATEAU PICHON-BARON Pauillac 1988 $30 (3/31/91) SS
95+ CHATEAU LAFITE-ROTHSCHILD Pauillac 1988 $100 (8/31/90) (BT)
95+ CHATEAU LAFITE-ROTHSCHILD Pauillac 1988 $100 (6/30/89) (BT)
95+ CHATEAU MOUTON-ROTHSCHILD Pauillac 1988 $105 (8/31/90) (BT)
95+ CHATEAU MOUTON-ROTHSCHILD Pauillac 1988 $105 (6/30/89) (BT)
95+ CHATEAU PICHON-BARON Pauillac 1988 $30 (8/31/90) (BT)
94   CHATEAU CLERC-MILON Pauillac 1988 $26 (4/30/91) SS
93   CHATEAU HAUT-BAGES-AVEROUS Pauillac 1988 $23 (4/30/91)
93   CHATEAU LATOUR Pauillac 1988 $90 (4/30/91)
91   CHATEAU PICHON-LALANDE Pauillac 1988 $50 (4/30/91)
90   CHATEAU BATAILLEY Pauillac 1988 $23 (4/30/91)
90   CHATEAU GRAND-PUY-LACOSTE Pauillac 1988 $33 (4/30/91)
90   CHATEAU MOUTON-BARONNE-PHILIPPE Pauillac 1988 $25 (4/30/91)
90+ CHATEAU CLERC-MILON Pauillac 1988 $26 (8/31/90) (BT)
90+ CHATEAU LATOUR Pauillac 1988 $90 (8/31/90) (BT)
90+ CHATEAU LATOUR Pauillac 1988 $90 (6/30/89) (BT)
90+ CHATEAU LYNCH-BAGES Pauillac 1988 $35 (8/31/90) (BT)
90+ CHATEAU LYNCH-BAGES Pauillac 1988 $35 (6/30/89) (BT)
90+ CHATEAU PICHON-LALANDE Pauillac 1988 $50 (8/31/90) (BT)
89   CHATEAU GRAND-PUY-DUCASSE Pauillac 1988 $21 (4/30/91)
89   CHATEAU LACOSTE-BORIE Pauillac 1988 $19 (4/30/91)
88   CHATEAU HAUT-BAGES-LIBERAL Pauillac 1988 $17.50 (3/15/91)
88   RESERVE DE LA COMTESSE Pauillac 1988 $23 (3/15/91)
85+ CHATEAU BATAILLEY Pauillac 1988 $23 (6/30/89) (BT)
85+ CHATEAU CLERC-MILON Pauillac 1988 $26 (6/30/89) (BT)
85+ CHATEAU DUHART-MILON Pauillac 1988 $20 (8/31/90) (BT)
85+ CHATEAU GRAND-PUY-LACOSTE Pauillac 1988 $33 (8/31/90) (BT)
85+ CHATEAU GRAND-PUY-LACOSTE Pauillac 1988 $33 (6/30/89) (BT)
85+ CHATEAU HAUT-BAGES-AVEROUS Pauillac 1988 $23 (8/31/90) (BT)
85+ CHATEAU HAUT-BATAILLEY Pauillac 1988 $26 (6/30/89) (BT)
85+ CHATEAU MOUTON-BARONNE-PHILIPPE Pauillac 1988 $25 (8/31/90) (BT)
85+ CHATEAU PIBRAN Pauillac 1988 $27 (8/31/90) (BT)
85+ CHATEAU PIBRAN Pauillac 1988 $27 (6/30/89) (BT)
85+ CHATEAU PICHON-BARON Pauillac 1988 $30 (6/30/89) (BT)
85+ CHATEAU PICHON-LALANDE Pauillac 1988 $50 (6/30/89) (BT)
85+ LES TOURELLES DE LONGUEVILLE Pauillac 1988 $25 (8/31/90) (BT)

80+ CHATEAU BERNADOTTE Pauillac 1988 $20 (6/30/89) (BT)
80+ CARRUADES DE LAFITE Pauillac 1988 $19 (8/31/90) (BT)
80+ CHATEAU DUHART-MILON Pauillac 1988 $20 (6/30/89) (BT)
80+ CHATEAU GRAND-PUY-DUCASSE Pauillac 1988 $21 (6/30/89) (BT)
80+ CHATEAU HAUT-BAGES-AVEROUS Pauillac 1988 $23 (6/30/89) (BT)
80+ CHATEAU HAUT-BAGES-LIBERAL Pauillac 1988 $17.50 (6/30/89) (BT)
80+ CHATEAU LYNCH-MOUSSAS Pauillac 1988 $25 (6/30/89) (BT)
80+ CHATEAU MOUTON-BARONNE-PHILIPPE Pauillac 1988 $25 (6/30/89) (BT)
80+ CHATEAU PEDESCLAUX Pauillac 1988 $20 (6/30/89) (BT)
80+ CHATEAU PONTET-CANET Pauillac 1988 (NR) (6/30/89) (BT)
80+ LES TOURELLS DE LONGUEVILLE Pauillac 1988 $25 (6/30/89) (BT)
75+ CHATEAU FONBADET Pauillac 1988 $16 (6/30/89) (BT)
70+ CHATEAU HAUT-BAGES-LIBERAL Pauillac 1988 $17.50 (8/31/90) (BT)

1987

90+ CHATEAU MOUTON-ROTHSCHILD Pauillac 1987 Rel: $56 Cur: $69 (6/30/89) (BT)
90+ CHATEAU MOUTON-ROTHSCHILD Pauillac 1987 Rel: $56 Cur: $69 (6/30/88) (BT)
89   CHATEAU MOUTON-ROTHSCHILD Pauillac 1987 Rel: $56 Cur: $69 (5/15/90)
88   CHATEAU PICHON-BARON Pauillac 1987 Rel: $20 Cur: $41 (10/15/90)
87   CHATEAU LYNCH-BAGES Pauillac 1987 Rel: $27 Cur: $27 (10/31/89) (JS)
87   CHATEAU PICHON-LALANDE Pauillac 1987 Rel: $30 Cur: $30 (2/15/90)
86   CHATEAU HAUT-BATAILLEY Pauillac 1987 Rel: $17 Cur: $17 (5/15/90)
86   CHATEAU LYNCH-BAGES Pauillac 1987 Rel: $27 Cur: $27 (2/15/90)
85   CHATEAU HAUT-BAGES-AVEROUS Pauillac 1987 Rel: $15 Cur: $15 (11/30/89) (JS)
85   CHATEAU LAFITE-ROTHSCHILD Pauillac 1987 Rel: $60 Cur: $60 (5/15/90)
85   CHATEAU PIBRAN Pauillac 1987 Rel: $20 Cur: $20 (11/30/89) (JS)
85+ CHATEAU LAFITE-ROTHSCHILD Pauillac 1987 Rel: $60 Cur: $60 (6/30/89) (BT)
85+ CHATEAU LAFITE-ROTHSCHILD Pauillac 1987 Rel: $60 Cur: $60 (6/30/88) (BT)
85+ CHATEAU LATOUR Pauillac 1987 Rel: $60 Cur: $60 (6/30/89) (BT)
85+ CHATEAU LATOUR Pauillac 1987 Rel: $60 Cur: $60 (6/30/88) (BT)
85+ CHATEAU PICHON-BARON Pauillac 1987 Rel: $20 Cur: $41 (6/30/89) (BT)
85+ CHATEAU PICHON-BARON Pauillac 1987 Rel: $20 Cur: $41 (6/30/88) (BT)
85+ CHATEAU PICHON-LALANDE Pauillac 1987 Rel: $30 Cur: $30 (6/30/89) (BT)
85+ CHATEAU PICHON-LALANDE Pauillac 1987 Rel: $30 Cur: $30 (6/30/88) (BT)
82   RESERVE DE LA COMTESSE Pauillac 1987 Rel: $14 Cur: $16 (5/15/90)
81   DOMAINES BARONS DE ROTHSCHILD Pauillac Réserve Spéciale 1987 $12 (12/31/90)
80   CHATEAU LATOUR Pauillac 1987 Rel: $60 Cur: $60 (10/15/90)
80+ CHATEAU CLERC-MILON Pauillac 1987 Cur: $19 (6/30/89) (BT)
80+ CHATEAU CLERC-MILON Pauillac 1987 Cur: $19 (6/30/88) (BT)
80+ CHATEAU DUHART-MILON Pauillac 1987 Rel: $22 Cur: $22 (6/30/89) (BT)
80+ CHATEAU DUHART-MILON Pauillac 1987 Rel: $22 Cur: $22 (6/30/88) (BT)
80+ CHATEAU GRAND-PUY-LACOSTE Pauillac 1987 Rel: $22 Cur: $22 (6/30/88) (BT)
80+ CHATEAU HAUT-BATAILLEY Pauillac 1987 Rel: $17 Cur: $17 (6/30/88) (BT)
80+ CHATEAU LYNCH-BAGES Pauillac 1987 Rel: $27 Cur: $27 (6/30/89) (BT)
80+ CHATEAU LYNCH-BAGES Pauillac 1987 Rel: $27 Cur: $27 (6/30/88) (BT)
80+ CHATEAU MOUTON-BARONNE-PHILIPPE Pauillac 1987 Rel: $16 Cur: $16 (6/30/89) (BT)
80+ CHATEAU MOUTON-BARONNE-PHILIPPE Pauillac 1987 Rel: $16 Cur: $16 (6/30/88) (BT)
80+ CHATEAU PIBRAN Pauillac 1987 Rel: $20 Cur: $20 (6/30/89) (BT)
79   CHATEAU BERNADOTTE Pauillac 1987 $20 (11/30/89) (JS)
79   CHATEAU DUHART-MILON Pauillac 1987 Rel: $22 Cur: $22 (5/15/90)
77   CHATEAU GRAND-PUY-LACOSTE Pauillac 1987 Rel: $22 Cur: $22 (5/15/90)
75+ CHATEAU BATAILLEY Pauillac 1987 Rel: $18 Cur: $18 (6/30/89) (BT)
75+ CHATEAU BATAILLEY Pauillac 1987 Rel: $18 Cur: $18 (6/30/88) (BT)
75+ CHATEAU BERNADOTTE Pauillac 1987 (NR) (6/30/89) (BT)
75+ CARRUADES DE LAFITE Pauillac 1987 Cur: $19 (6/30/89) (BT)
75+ CHATEAU FONBADET Pauillac 1987 $15 (6/30/89) (BT)
75+ LES FORTS DE LATOUR Pauillac 1987 (NR) (6/30/89) (BT)
75+ CHATEAU GRAND-PUY-DUCASSE Pauillac 1987 Rel: $18 Cur: $18 (6/30/89) (BT)
75+ CHATEAU HAUT-BAGES-AVEROUS Pauillac 1987 Rel: $15 Cur: $15 (6/30/89) (BT)
75+ CHATEAU HAUT-BAGES-AVEROUS Pauillac 1987 Rel: $15 Cur: $15 (6/30/88) (BT)
75+ CHATEAU HAUT-BAGES-LIBERAL Pauillac 1987 Rel: $14 Cur: $14 (6/30/89) (BT)
75+ CHATEAU HAUT-BAGES-LIBERAL Pauillac 1987 Rel: $14 Cur: $14 (6/30/88) (BT)
75+ CHATEAU PIBRAN Pauillac 1987 Rel: $20 Cur: $20 (6/30/88) (BT)
75+ CHATEAU PONTET-CANET Pauillac 1987 Cur: $14 (6/30/89) (BT)
75+ CHATEAU PONTET-CANET Pauillac 1987 Cur: $14 (6/30/88) (BT)
75+ LES TOURELLS DE LONGUEVILLE Pauillac 1987 $17 (6/30/89) (BT)
70+ CHATEAU LYNCH-MOUSSAS Pauillac 1987 Rel: $17 Cur: $17 (6/30/89) (BT)
70+ MOULIN DE DUHART Pauillac 1987 (NR) (6/30/89) (BT)
65+ CHATEAU LYNCH-MOUSSAS Pauillac 1987 Rel: $17 Cur: $17 (6/30/88) (BT)
60+ CHATEAU CROIZET-BAGES Pauillac 1987 Rel: $15 Cur: $15 (6/30/88) (BT)

1986

98   CHATEAU MOUTON-ROTHSCHILD Pauillac 1986 Rel: $102 Cur: $114 (5/31/89) CS
97   CHATEAU CLERC-MILON Pauillac 1986 Rel: $23 Cur: $32 (5/31/89)
97   CHATEAU MOUTON-ROTHSCHILD Pauillac 1986 Rel: $102 Cur: $114 (5/15/91) (PM)
97   CHATEAU PICHON-BARON Pauillac 1986 Rel: $31 Cur: $58 (5/31/89)
97   CHATEAU PICHON-LALANDE Pauillac 1986 Rel: $50 Cur: $57 (5/31/89)
96   CHATEAU LAFITE-ROTHSCHILD Pauillac 1986 Rel: $102 Cur: $102 (3/31/89) (JS)
95   CHATEAU LAFITE-ROTHSCHILD Pauillac 1986 Rel: $102 Cur: $102 (5/31/89)
94   CHATEAU LYNCH-BAGES Pauillac 1986 Rel: $37 Cur: $37 (10/31/89) (JS)
93   CHATEAU LATOUR Pauillac 1986 Rel: $90 Cur: $90 (3/31/89) (HS)
93   CHATEAU LATOUR Pauillac 1986 Rel: $90 Cur: $90 (5/31/89)
93   CHATEAU LYNCH-BAGES Pauillac 1986 Rel: $37 Cur: $37 (5/31/89)
93   CHATEAU MOUTON-BARONNE-PHILIPPE Pauillac 1986 Rel: $23 Cur: $23 (5/31/89)
92   CHATEAU BERNADOTTE Pauillac 1986 $20 (11/30/89) (JS)
91   CHATEAU HAUT-BAGES-LIBERAL Pauillac 1986 Rel: $17 Cur: $22 (5/31/89)
90   CHATEAU DUHART-MILON Pauillac 1986 Rel: $30 Cur: $30 (5/31/89)
90   CHATEAU HAUT-BAGES-AVEROUS Pauillac 1986 Rel: $15 Cur: $19 (11/30/89) (JS)
90   RESERVE DE LA COMTESSE Pauillac 1986 Rel: $20 Cur: $25 (5/31/89)
90+ CHATEAU CLERC-MILON Pauillac 1986 Rel: $23 Cur: $32 (6/30/88) (BT)
90+ CHATEAU DUHART-MILON Pauillac 1986 Rel: $30 Cur: $30 (6/30/88) (BT)
90+ CHATEAU LAFITE-ROTHSCHILD Pauillac 1986 Rel: $102 Cur: $102 (6/30/88) (BT)
90+ CHATEAU LAFITE-ROTHSCHILD Pauillac 1986 Rel: $102 Cur: $102 (5/15/87) (BT)
90+ CHATEAU LATOUR Pauillac 1986 Rel: $90 Cur: $90 (6/30/88) (BT)
90+ CHATEAU LATOUR Pauillac 1986 Rel: $90 Cur: $90 (5/15/87) (BT)
90+ CHATEAU LYNCH-BAGES Pauillac 1986 Rel: $37 Cur: $37 (6/30/88) (BT)
90+ CHATEAU MOUTON-ROTHSCHILD Pauillac 1986 Rel: $102 Cur: $114 (6/30/88) (BT)
90+ CHATEAU MOUTON-ROTHSCHILD Pauillac 1986 Rel: $102 Cur: $114 (5/15/87) (BT)

90+ CHATEAU PICHON-LALANDE Pauillac 1986 Rel: $50 Cur: $57 (6/30/88) (BT)
90+ CHATEAU PICHON-LALANDE Pauillac 1986 Rel: $50 Cur: $57 (5/15/87) (BT)
89 CHATEAU PONTET-CANET Pauillac 1986 Rel: $21 Cur: $21 (5/31/89)
88 CHATEAU GRAND-PUY-LACOSTE Pauillac 1986 Rel: $25 Cur: $27 (5/31/89)
88 CHATEAU PIBRAN Pauillac 1986 Rel: $18 Cur: $18 (11/30/89) (JS)
86 CHATEAU LYNCH-MOUSSAS Pauillac 1986 Rel: $18 Cur: $18 (6/30/89)
85 CHATEAU GRAND-PUY-DUCASSE Pauillac 1986 Rel: $22 Cur: $24 (6/30/89)
85 CHATEAU HAUT-BAGES-AVEROUS Pauillac 1986 Rel: $15 Cur: $19 (5/31/89)
85 CHATEAU HAUT-BATAILLEY Pauillac 1986 Rel: $23 Cur: $23 (5/31/89)
85+ CHATEAU GRAND-PUY-LACOSTE Pauillac 1986 Rel: $25 Cur: $27 (6/30/88) (BT)
85+ CHATEAU MOUTON-BARONNE-PHILIPPE Pauillac 1986 Rel: $23 Cur: $23 (6/30/88) (BT)
85+ CHATEAU PICHON-BARON Pauillac 1986 Rel: $31 Cur: $58 (6/30/88) (BT)
84 CHATEAU LACOSTE-BORIE Pauillac 1986 $15 (6/30/89)
80+ CHATEAU BATAILLEY Pauillac 1986 Cur: $36 (6/30/88) (BT)
80+ CHATEAU CLERC-MILON Pauillac 1986 Rel: $23 Cur: $32 (5/15/87) (BT)
80+ CHATEAU GRAND-PUY-LACOSTE Pauillac 1986 Rel: $25 Cur: $27 (5/15/87) (BT)
80+ CHATEAU HAUT-BAGES-AVEROUS Pauillac 1986 Rel: $15 Cur: $19 (6/30/88) (BT)
80+ CHATEAU HAUT-BAGES-LIBERAL Pauillac 1986 Rel: $17 Cur: $22 (6/30/88) (BT)
80+ CHATEAU HAUT-BATAILLEY Pauillac 1986 Rel: $23 Cur: $23 (5/15/87) (BT)
80+ CHATEAU LYNCH-BAGES Pauillac 1986 Rel: $37 Cur: $37 (5/15/87) (BT)
80+ CHATEAU PONTET-CANET Pauillac 1986 Rel: $21 Cur: $21 (6/30/88) (BT)
79 CHATEAU PEDESCLAUX Pauillac 1986 Rel: $18 Cur: $18 (2/15/90)
78 CHATEAU CROIZET-BAGES Pauillac 1986 Rel: $15 Cur: $15 (6/30/89)
75+ CHATEAU LYNCH-MOUSSAS Pauillac 1986 Rel: $18 Cur: $18 (6/30/88) (BT)
70+ CARRUADES DE LAFITE Pauillac 1986 Cur: $30 (5/15/87) (BT)
70+ LES FORTS DE LATOUR Pauillac 1986 (NR) (5/15/87) (BT)
70+ CHATEAU HAUT-BAGES-AVEROUS Pauillac 1986 Rel: $15 Cur: $19 (5/15/87) (BT)
70+ CHATEAU MOUTON-BARONNE-PHILIPPE Pauillac 1986 Rel: $23 Cur: $23 (5/15/87) (BT)
70+ CHATEAU PONTET-CANET Pauillac 1986 Rel: $21 Cur: $21 (5/15/87) (BT)
65+ CHATEAU CROIZET-BAGES Pauillac 1986 Rel: $15 Cur: $15 6/30/88) (BT)
60+ CHATEAU DUHART-MILON Pauillac 1986 Rel: $30 Cur: $30 (5/15/87) (BT)
60+ CHATEAU LACOSTE-BORIE Pauillac 1986 $15 (5/15/87) (BT)

1985

97 CHATEAU LAFITE-ROTHSCHILD Pauillac 1985 Rel: $80 Cur: $99 (5/31/88) CS
97 CHATEAU LATOUR Pauillac 1985 Rel: $82 Cur: $95 (4/30/88)
97 CHATEAU LYNCH-BAGES Pauillac 1985 Rel: $37 Cur: $45 (4/30/88) CS
96 CHATEAU LATOUR Pauillac 1985 Rel: $82 Cur: $95 (3/31/90) (HS)
95 CHATEAU PICHON-LALANDE Pauillac 1985 Rel: $40 Cur: $53 (2/29/88) CS
94 CHATEAU LAFITE-ROTHSCHILD Pauillac 1985 Rel: $80 Cur: $99 (3/31/89) (JS)
94 CHATEAU MOUTON-ROTHSCHILD Pauillac 1985 Rel: $90 Cur: $90 (4/30/88)
94 CHATEAU PICHON-BARON Pauillac 1985 Rel: $32 Cur: $36 (4/30/88)
93 CHATEAU LYNCH-BAGES Pauillac 1985 Rel: $37 Cur: $45 (10/31/89) (JS)
91 CHATEAU CLERC-MILON Pauillac 1985 Rel: $18.50 Cur: $24 (5/15/88)
91 CHATEAU GRAND-PUY-LACOSTE Pauillac 1985 Rel: $23 Cur: $30 (6/30/88)
91 CHATEAU MOUTON-BARONNE-PHILIPPE Pauillac 1985 Rel: $18 Cur: $26 (5/15/88) SS
90 CHATEAU GRAND-PUY-DUCASSE Pauillac 1985 Rel: $19 Cur: $20 (2/29/88)
90+ CHATEAU CLERC-MILON Pauillac 1985 Rel: $18.50 Cur: $24 (4/16/86) (BT)
90+ CHATEAU LAFITE-ROTHSCHILD Pauillac 1985 Rel: $80 Cur: $99 (5/15/87) (BT)
90+ CHATEAU LATOUR Pauillac 1985 Rel: $82 Cur: $95 (5/15/87) (BT)
90+ CHATEAU LYNCH-BAGES Pauillac 1985 Rel: $37 Cur: $45 (5/15/87) (BT)
90+ CHATEAU MOUTON-ROTHSCHILD Pauillac 1985 Rel: $90 Cur: $90 (5/15/87) (BT)
90+ CHATEAU MOUTON-ROTHSCHILD Pauillac 1985 Rel: $90 Cur: $90 (4/16/86) (BT)
90+ CHATEAU PICHON-LALANDE Pauillac 1985 Rel: $40 Cur: $53 (5/15/87) (BT)
90+ CHATEAU PICHON-LALANDE Pauillac 1985 Rel: $40 Cur: $53 (4/16/86) (BT)
89 CHATEAU BERNADOTTE Pauillac 1985 $19 (3/31/88)
88 CHATEAU HAUT-BAGES-LIBERAL Pauillac 1985 Rel: $16 Cur: $23 (4/30/88)
87 CHATEAU DUHART-MILON Pauillac 1985 Rel: $34 Cur: $34 (6/30/88)
82 CHATEAU HAUT-BAGES-AVEROUS Pauillac 1985 Rel: $17 Cur: $17 (4/30/88)
81 CHATEAU HAUT-BATAILLEY Pauillac 1985 Rel: $17 Cur: $21 (11/30/88)
80+ CHATEAU CLERC-MILON Pauillac 1985 Rel: $18.50 Cur: $24 (5/15/87) (BT)
80+ CHATEAU DUHART-MILON Pauillac 1985 Rel: $34 Cur: $34 (5/15/87) (BT)
80+ LES FORTS DE LATOUR Pauillac 1985 Rel: $40 Cur: $40 (5/15/87) (BT)
80+ CHATEAU GRAND-PUY-LACOSTE Pauillac 1985 Rel: $23 Cur: $30 (4/16/86) (BT)
80+ CHATEAU HAUT-BATAILLEY Pauillac 1985 Rel: $17 Cur: $21 (5/15/87) (BT)
80+ CHATEAU LYNCH-BAGES Pauillac 1985 Rel: $37 Cur: $45 (4/16/86) (BT)
80+ CHATEAU PONTET-CANET Pauillac 1985 Cur: $20 (5/15/87) (BT)
70+ CHATEAU HAUT-BAGES-AVEROUS Pauillac 1985 Rel: $17 Cur: $17 (5/15/87) (BT)
70+ CHATEAU HAUT-BATAILLEY Pauillac 1985 Rel: $17 Cur: $21 (4/16/86) (BT)
70+ CHATEAU MOUTON-BARONNE-PHILIPPE Pauillac 1985 Rel: $18 Cur: $26 (5/15/87) (BT)
70+ CHATEAU MOUTON-BARONNE-PHILIPPE Pauillac 1985 Rel: $18 Cur: $26 (4/16/86) (BT)
60+ CHATEAU HAUT-BAGES-AVEROUS Pauillac 1985 Rel: $17 Cur: $17 (4/16/86) (BT)

1984

94 CHATEAU PICHON-LALANDE Pauillac 1984 Rel: $27 Cur: $34 (1/31/87) CS
93 CHATEAU LAFITE-ROTHSCHILD Pauillac 1984 Rel: $51 Cur: $68 (3/31/87)
92 CHATEAU LATOUR Pauillac 1984 Rel: $40 Cur: $61 (3/31/87)
92 CHATEAU MOUTON-ROTHSCHILD Pauillac 1984 Rel: $40 Cur: $63 (3/31/87)
90 CHATEAU LYNCH-BAGES Pauillac 1984 Rel: $19 Cur: $27 (3/31/87)
87 CHATEAU LAFITE-ROTHSCHILD Pauillac 1984 Rel: $51 Cur: $68 (5/01/89)
87 CHATEAU LYNCH-BAGES Pauillac 1984 Rel: $19 Cur: $27 (10/31/89) (JS)
83 CHATEAU GRAND-PUY-LACOSTE Pauillac 1984 Rel: $24.50 Cur: $25 (10/15/87)
78 CHATEAU CLERC-MILON Pauillac 1984 Rel: $18 Cur: $18 (6/15/87)
78 CHATEAU PICHON-BARON Pauillac 1984 Rel: $23 Cur: $24 (9/30/88)
67 CHATEAU HAUT-BAGES-LIBERAL Pauillac 1984 Rel: $19 Cur: $19 (6/15/87)
64 CHATEAU MOUTON-BARONNE-PHILIPPE Pauillac 1984 Rel: $17.50 Cur: $18 (6/15/87)

1983

97 CHATEAU LATOUR Pauillac 1983 Rel: $72 Cur: $85 (3/01/86)
97 CHATEAU PICHON-LALANDE Pauillac 1983 Rel: $44 Cur: $53 (3/01/86) SS
96 CHATEAU MOUTON-ROTHSCHILD Pauillac 1983 Rel: $57 Cur: $86 (3/01/86)
94 CHATEAU LAFITE-ROTHSCHILD Pauillac 1983 Rel: $60 Cur: $94 (12/15/88) (TR)
94 CHATEAU PICHON-BARON Pauillac 1983 Rel: $18 Cur: $35 (3/01/86)
93 CHATEAU LATOUR Pauillac 1983 Rel: $72 Cur: $85 (3/31/90) (HS)
91 CHATEAU CLERC-MILON Pauillac 1983 Rel: $16.50 Cur: $18 (4/01/86)
90 CHATEAU BERNADOTTE Pauillac 1983 $14.50 (2/15/87)

90 CHATEAU LAFITE-ROTHSCHILD Pauillac 1983 Rel: $60 Cur: $94 (3/31/89) (JS)
90 CHATEAU LYNCH-BAGES Pauillac 1983 Rel: $25 Cur: $45 (3/01/86)
88 CHATEAU LYNCH-BAGES Pauillac 1983 Rel: $25 Cur: $45 (10/31/89) (JS)
88 MOULIN DES CARRUADES Pauillac 1983 $14 (10/31/86)
88 CHATEAU MOUTON-BARONNE-PHILIPPE Pauillac 1983 Rel: $16.50 Cur: $17 (3/01/86)
85 LES FORTS DE LATOUR Pauillac 1983 Rel: $32 Cur: $32 (10/15/90)
84 CHATEAU LAFITE-ROTHSCHILD Pauillac 1983 Rel: $60 Cur: $94 (5/01/89)
82 RESERVE DE LA COMTESSE Pauillac 1983 Rel: $18 Cur: $21 (3/01/86)
75 CHATEAU LACOSTE-BORIE Pauillac 1983 $7.50 (6/15/87)
67 CHATEAU HAUT-BAGES-LIBERAL Pauillac 1983 Rel: $18 Cur: $18 (5/01/86)

1982

99 CHATEAU LATOUR Pauillac 1982 Cur: $150 (3/31/90) (HS)
97 CHATEAU LATOUR Pauillac 1982 Cur: $150 (5/01/89)
95 CHATEAU LAFITE-ROTHSCHILD Pauillac 1982 Rel: $120 Cur: $172 (3/31/89) (JS)
94 CHATEAU LYNCH-BAGES Pauillac 1982 Rel: $27.50 Cur: $54 (3/01/85) CS
94 CHATEAU PICHON-LALANDE Pauillac 1982 Rel: $29 Cur: $89 (2/01/85) SS
93 CHATEAU MOUTON-ROTHSCHILD Pauillac 1982 Cur: $176 (5/15/91) (PM)
91 CHATEAU LAFITE-ROTHSCHILD Pauillac 1982 Rel: $120 Cur: $172 (5/01/89)
90 CHATEAU LYNCH-BAGES Pauillac 1982 Rel: $27.50 Cur: $54 (10/31/89) (JS)
90 CHATEAU PIBRAN Pauillac 1982 Cur: $15 (11/30/89) (JS)
89 CHATEAU HAUT-BAGES-AVEROUS Pauillac 1982 Cur: $25 (11/30/89) (JS)
86 CHATEAU CLERC-MILON Pauillac 1982 Rel: $15 Cur: $27 (4/01/85)
86 CHATEAU FONBADET Pauillac 1982 $16 (8/01/85)
86 LES FORTS DE LATOUR Pauillac 1982 Rel: $55 Cur: $55 (10/15/90)
86 CHATEAU MOUTON-BARONNE-PHILIPPE Pauillac 1982 Rel: $15 Cur: $27 (4/01/85)
85 CHATEAU MOUTON-ROTHSCHILD Pauillac 1982 Cur: $176 (6/16/86) (TR)
78 CHATEAU PICHON-BARON Pauillac 1982 Rel: $12.50 Cur: $37 (9/30/88)

1981

93 CHATEAU PICHON-LALANDE Pauillac 1981 Rel: $21 Cur: $56 (5/01/85)
92 CHATEAU LATOUR Pauillac 1981 Cur: $81 (5/01/89)
92 CHATEAU LYNCH-BAGES Pauillac 1981 Rel: $15.50 Cur: $37 (6/01/84)
90 CHATEAU LAFITE-ROTHSCHILD Pauillac 1981 Rel: $75 Cur: $131 (5/01/89)
90 CHATEAU LATOUR Pauillac 1981 Cur: $81 (3/31/90) (HS)
90 CHATEAU LYNCH-BAGES Pauillac 1981 Rel: $15.50 Cur: $37 (10/31/89) (JS)
86 CHATEAU MOUTON-ROTHSCHILD Pauillac 1981 Rel: $40 Cur: $84 (6/16/86) (TR)
84 CHATEAU PICHON-BARON Pauillac 1981 Rel: $13.50 Cur: $33 (9/30/88)
81 CHATEAU MOUTON-BARONNE-PHILIPPE Pauillac 1981 Rel: $12 Cur: $15 (6/01/84)

1980

92 CHATEAU PICHON-LALANDE Pauillac 1980 Rel: $14 Cur: $36 (5/01/85)
90 CHATEAU PICHON-LALANDE Pauillac 1980 Rel: $14 Cur: $36 (3/01/84) CS
88 CHATEAU LYNCH-BAGES Pauillac 1980 Cur: $24 (10/31/89) (JS)
81 CHATEAU LAFITE-ROTHSCHILD Pauillac 1980 Rel: $52 (12/15/88) (TR)
79 CHATEAU PICHON-BARON Pauillac 1980 Cur: $17 (9/30/88)
67 CHATEAU MOUTON-ROTHSCHILD Pauillac 1980 Cur: $85 (6/16/86) (TR)

1979

96 CHATEAU MOUTON-ROTHSCHILD Pauillac 1979 Cur: $91 (10/15/89) (JS)
92 CHATEAU LAFITE-ROTHSCHILD Pauillac 1979 Cur: $116 (10/15/89) (JS)
91 CHATEAU LYNCH-BAGES Pauillac 1979 Cur: $40 (10/15/89) (JS)
90 CHATEAU LATOUR Pauillac 1979 Cur: $92 (3/31/90) (HS)
90 CHATEAU PICHON-LALANDE Pauillac 1979 Cur: $64 (5/01/85)
88 CHATEAU GRAND-PUY-LACOSTE Pauillac 1979 Cur: $33 (10/15/89) (JS)
88 CHATEAU LAFITE-ROTHSCHILD Pauillac 1979 Cur: $116 (12/15/88) (TR)
88 CHATEAU PICHON-BARON Pauillac 1979 Cur: $29 (10/15/89) (JS)
87 LES FORTS DE LATOUR Pauillac 1979 Cur: $35 (10/15/89) (JS)
87 CHATEAU LYNCH-BAGES Pauillac 1979 Cur: $40 (10/31/89) (JS)
86 CHATEAU DUHART-MILON Pauillac 1979 Cur: $26 (10/15/89) (JS)
85 CHATEAU MOUTON-ROTHSCHILD Pauillac 1979 Cur: $91 (6/16/86) (TR)
84 CHATEAU HAUT-BAGES-AVEROUS Pauillac 1979 Cur: $18 (10/15/89) (JS)
84 CHATEAU LATOUR Pauillac 1979 Cur: $92 (10/15/89) (JS)
84 CHATEAU PICHON-BARON Pauillac 1979 Cur: $29 (9/30/88)
82 CHATEAU HAUT-BATAILLEY Pauillac 1979 Cur: $28 (10/15/89) (JS)

1978

94 CHATEAU LATOUR Pauillac 1978 Cur: $139 (3/31/90) (HS)
92 CHATEAU LAFITE-ROTHSCHILD Pauillac 1978 Cur: $161 (12/15/88) (TR)
92 CHATEAU LYNCH-BAGES Pauillac 1978 Cur: $52 (10/31/89) (JS)
92 CHATEAU MOUTON-ROTHSCHILD Pauillac 1978 Cur: $127 (5/15/91) (PM)
91 CHATEAU PICHON-LALANDE Pauillac 1978 Cur: $89 (5/01/85)
88 CHATEAU MOUTON-ROTHSCHILD Pauillac 1978 Cur: $127 (6/16/86) (TR)
80 CHATEAU PICHON-BARON Pauillac 1978 Cur: $39 (9/30/88)

1977

78 CHATEAU LYNCH-BAGES Pauillac 1977 Cur: $25 (10/31/89) (JS)
76 CHATEAU LAFITE-ROTHSCHILD Pauillac 1977 Cur: $47 (12/15/88) (TR)
76 CHATEAU PICHON-BARON Pauillac 1977 Cur: $13 (9/30/88)
68 CHATEAU MOUTON-ROTHSCHILD Pauillac 1977 Cur: $82 (6/16/86) (TR)

1976

92 CHATEAU LAFITE-ROTHSCHILD Pauillac 1976 Cur: $160 (3/31/89) (JS)
87 CHATEAU LATOUR Pauillac 1976 Cur: $92 (3/31/90) (HS)
86 CHATEAU LAFITE-ROTHSCHILD Pauillac 1976 Cur: $160 (12/15/88) (TR)
85 CHATEAU MOUTON-ROTHSCHILD Pauillac 1976 Cur: $96 (6/16/86) (TR)
73 CHATEAU PICHON-BARON Pauillac 1976 Cur: $20 (9/30/88)
70 CHATEAU LYNCH-BAGES Pauillac 1976 Cur: $55 (10/31/89) (JS)

1975

93 CHATEAU LATOUR Pauillac 1975 Cur: $149 (3/31/90) (HS)
90 CHATEAU LYNCH-BAGES Pauillac 1975 Cur: $70 (10/31/89) (JS)
89 CHATEAU MOUTON-ROTHSCHILD Pauillac 1975 Cur: $153 (5/15/91) (PM)
88 CHATEAU LAFITE-ROTHSCHILD Pauillac 1975 Cur: $190 (12/15/88) (TR)
86 CHATEAU MOUTON-ROTHSCHILD Pauillac 1975 Cur: $153 (6/16/86) (TR)
74 CHATEAU PICHON-BARON Pauillac 1975 Cur: $59 (9/30/88)

1974

78 CHATEAU PICHON-BARON Pauillac 1974 Cur: $20 (9/30/88)
75 CHATEAU LAFITE-ROTHSCHILD Pauillac 1974 Cur: $56 (12/15/88) (TR)

FRANCE
BORDEAUX RED/PAUILLAC

67   CHATEAU MOUTON-ROTHSCHILD Pauillac 1974 Cur: $145 (6/16/86) (TR)

1973

82   CHATEAU LYNCH-BAGES Pauillac 1973 Cur: $30 (10/31/89) (JS)
80   CHATEAU LAFITE-ROTHSCHILD Pauillac 1973 Cur: $54 (12/15/88) (TR)
78   CHATEAU PICHON-BARON Pauillac 1973 Cur: $13 (9/30/88)
75   CHATEAU MOUTON-ROTHSCHILD Pauillac 1973 Cur: $119 (6/16/86) (TR)

1972

78   CHATEAU LAFITE-ROTHSCHILD Pauillac 1972 Cur: $58 (12/15/88) (TR)
68   CHATEAU PICHON-BARON Pauillac 1972 Cur: $13 (9/30/88)
55   CHATEAU MOUTON-ROTHSCHILD Pauillac 1972 Cur: $138 (6/16/86) (TR)

1971

87   CHATEAU LAFITE-ROTHSCHILD Pauillac 1971 Cur: $109 (12/15/88) (TR)
84   CHATEAU LATOUR Pauillac 1971 Cur: $127 (3/31/90) (HS)
78   CHATEAU MOUTON-ROTHSCHILD Pauillac 1971 Cur: $102 (6/16/86) (TR)
71   CHATEAU PICHON-BARON Pauillac 1971 Cur: $31 (9/30/88)
67   CHATEAU LYNCH-BAGES Pauillac 1971 Cur: $28 (10/31/89) (JS)

1970

97   CHATEAU LATOUR Pauillac 1970 Cur: $197 (3/31/90) (HS)
91   CHATEAU LAFITE-ROTHSCHILD Pauillac 1970 Cur: $187 (12/15/88) (TR)
90   CHATEAU LYNCH-BAGES Pauillac 1970 Cur: $115 (10/31/89) (JS)
85   CHATEAU MOUTON-ROTHSCHILD Pauillac 1970 Cur: $195 (6/16/86) (TR)
84   CHATEAU MOUTON-ROTHSCHILD Pauillac 1970 Cur: $195 (5/15/91) (PM)
83   CHATEAU PICHON-BARON Pauillac 1970 Cur: $69 (9/30/88)

1969

83   CHATEAU LAFITE-ROTHSCHILD Pauillac 1969 Cur: $32 (12/15/88) (TR)
78   CHATEAU MOUTON-ROTHSCHILD Pauillac 1969 Cur: $269 (6/16/86) (TR)
78   CHATEAU PICHON-BARON Pauillac 1969 Cur: $21 (9/30/88)

1968

71   CHATEAU LAFITE-ROTHSCHILD Pauillac 1968 Cur: $35 (12/15/88) (TR)
64   CHATEAU MOUTON-ROTHSCHILD Pauillac 1968 Cur: $476 (6/16/86) (TR)

1967

87   CHATEAU MOUTON-ROTHSCHILD Pauillac 1967 Cur: $100 (6/16/86) (TR)
85   CHATEAU LAFITE-ROTHSCHILD Pauillac 1967 Cur: $79 (12/15/88) (TR)
82   CARRUADES DE LAFITE Pauillac 1967 Cur: $37 (11/30/87)
80   CHATEAU PICHON-BARON Pauillac 1967 Cur: $46 (9/30/88)
79   CHATEAU LATOUR Pauillac 1967 Cur: $100 (3/31/90) (HS)
79   CHATEAU LYNCH-BAGES Pauillac 1967 Cur: $55 (10/31/89) (JS)

1966

93   CHATEAU LAFITE-ROTHSCHILD Pauillac 1966 Cur: $192 (12/15/88) (TR)
93   CHATEAU LATOUR Pauillac 1966 Cur: $222 (3/31/90) (HS)
90   CHATEAU LYNCH-BAGES Pauillac 1966 Cur: $125 (10/31/89) (JS)
88   CHATEAU MOUTON-ROTHSCHILD Pauillac 1966 Cur: $224 (5/15/91) (PM)
86   CHATEAU MOUTON-ROTHSCHILD Pauillac 1966 Cur: $224 (6/16/86) (TR)
80   CHATEAU PICHON-BARON Pauillac 1966 Cur: $59 (9/30/88)

1965

76   CHATEAU LAFITE-ROTHSCHILD Pauillac 1965 Cur: $45 (12/15/88) (TR)
74   CHATEAU LATOUR Pauillac 1965 Cur: $135 (3/31/90) (HS)
61   CHATEAU MOUTON-ROTHSCHILD Pauillac 1965 Cur: $836 (6/16/86) (TR)

1964

88   CHATEAU LATOUR Pauillac 1964 Cur: $378/1.5L (3/31/90) (HS)
88   CHATEAU PICHON-BARON Pauillac 1964 Cur: $63 (9/30/88)
86   CHATEAU LATOUR Pauillac 1964 Cur: $180 (3/31/90) (HS)
84   CHATEAU LAFITE-ROTHSCHILD Pauillac 1964 Cur: $96 (12/15/88) (TR)
84   CHATEAU MOUTON-ROTHSCHILD Pauillac 1964 Cur: $124 (6/16/86) (TR)
81   CARRUADES DE LAFITE Pauillac 1964 Cur: $45 (11/30/87)
76   CHATEAU LYNCH-BAGES Pauillac 1964 Cur: $90 (10/31/89) (JS)

1963

78   CHATEAU LAFITE-ROTHSCHILD Pauillac 1963 Cur: $286 (12/15/88) (TR)
77   CHATEAU LATOUR Pauillac 1963 Cur: $135 (3/31/90) (HS)
77   CHATEAU MOUTON-ROTHSCHILD Pauillac 1963 Cur: $1,157 (6/16/86) (TR)

1962

98   CHATEAU LATOUR Pauillac 1962 Cur: $250 (11/30/87) (JS)
98   CHATEAU MOUTON-ROTHSCHILD Pauillac 1962 Cur: $273 (11/30/87) (JS)
94   CHATEAU LYNCH-BAGES Pauillac 1962 Cur: $124 (10/31/89) (JS)
93   CHATEAU MOUTON-ROTHSCHILD Pauillac 1962 Cur: $273 (5/15/91) (PM)
92   CHATEAU LATOUR Pauillac 1962 Cur: $525/1.5L (3/31/90) (HS)
88   CHATEAU PICHON-BARON Pauillac 1962 Cur: $85 (9/30/88)
87   CHATEAU LAFITE-ROTHSCHILD Pauillac 1962 Cur: $205 (12/15/88) (TR)
85   CHATEAU PICHON-LALANDE Pauillac 1962 Cur: $125 (11/30/87) (JS)
83   CHATEAU CROIZET-BAGES Pauillac 1962 Cur: $60 (11/30/87) (JS)
80   CHATEAU LYNCH-BAGES Pauillac 1962 Cur: $124 (11/30/87) (JS)
75   CARRUADES DE LAFITE Pauillac 1962 Cur: $76 (11/30/87) (JS)

1961

99   CHATEAU LATOUR Pauillac 1961 Cur: $635 (3/31/90) (HS)
97   CHATEAU LATOUR Pauillac 1961 Cur: $635 (3/16/86) (JL)
96   CHATEAU GRAND-PUY-LACOSTE Pauillac 1961 Cur: $181 (3/16/86) (JL)
96   CHATEAU LYNCH-BAGES Pauillac 1961 Cur: $225 (3/16/86) (JL)
94   CHATEAU LAFITE-ROTHSCHILD Pauillac 1961 Cur: $572 (12/15/88) (TR)
94   CHATEAU MOUTON-ROTHSCHILD Pauillac 1961 Cur: $646 (6/16/86) (TR)
91   CHATEAU HAUT-BATAILLEY Pauillac 1961 Cur: $95 (3/16/86) (JL)
90   CHATEAU MOUTON-ROTHSCHILD Pauillac 1961 Cur: $646 (5/15/91) (PM)
86   CHATEAU LYNCH-BAGES Pauillac 1961 Cur: $225 (10/31/89) (JS)
84   CHATEAU BATAILLEY Pauillac 1961 Cur: $127 (3/16/86) (JL)
84   CHATEAU PICHON-BARON Pauillac 1961 Cur: $164 (9/30/88)
79   CHATEAU PICHON-LALANDE Pauillac 1961 Cur: $225 (3/16/86) (JL)
66   CHATEAU PONTET-CANET Pauillac 1961 Cur: $95 (3/16/86) (JL)
62   CHATEAU MOUTON-BARONNE-PHILIPPE Pauillac 1961 Cur: $125 (3/16/86) (JL)

1960

88   CHATEAU LATOUR Pauillac 1960 Cur: $275 (3/31/90) (HS)
86   CHATEAU LAFITE-ROTHSCHILD Pauillac 1960 Cur: $90 (12/15/88) (TR)
84   CHATEAU MOUTON-ROTHSCHILD Pauillac 1960 Cur: $536 (6/16/86) (TR)
81   CHATEAU PICHON-BARON Pauillac 1960 Cur: $50 (9/30/88)
76   CHATEAU LYNCH-BAGES Pauillac 1960 Cur: $55 (10/31/89) (JS)

1959

99   CHATEAU MOUTON-ROTHSCHILD Pauillac 1959 Cur: $456 (10/15/90) (JS)
98   CHATEAU LATOUR Pauillac 1959 Cur: $446 (10/15/90) (JS)
98   CHATEAU MOUTON-ROTHSCHILD Pauillac 1959 Cur: $456 (5/15/91) (PM)
97   CHATEAU PICHON-LALANDE Pauillac 1959 Cur: $175 (10/15/90) (JS)
95   CHATEAU LAFITE-ROTHSCHILD Pauillac 1959 Cur: $550 (12/15/88) (TR)
95   CHATEAU LATOUR Pauillac 1959 Cur: $446 (3/31/90) (HS)
95   CHATEAU LATOUR Pauillac 1959 Cur: $937/1.5L (3/31/90) (HS)
95   CHATEAU LYNCH-BAGES Pauillac 1959 Cur: $195 (10/15/90) (JS)
95   CHATEAU LYNCH-BAGES Pauillac 1959 Cur: $195 (10/31/89) (JS)
94   CHATEAU PICHON-BARON Pauillac 1959 Cur: $174 (10/15/90) (JS)
90   CHATEAU LAFITE-ROTHSCHILD Pauillac 1959 Cur: $550 (10/15/90) (JS)
88   CARRUADES DE LAFITE Pauillac 1959 Cur: $100 (11/30/87)
88   CHATEAU MOUTON-ROTHSCHILD Pauillac 1959 Cur: $456 (6/16/86) (TR)
88   CHATEAU PICHON-BARON Pauillac 1959 Cur: $174 (9/30/88)
86   CHATEAU LYNCH-MOUSSAS Pauillac 1959 Cur: $101 (10/15/90) (JS)
85   CHATEAU HAUT-BAGES-LIBERAL Pauillac Belgian Bottled 1959 Cur: $55 (10/15/90) (JS)
84   CARRUADES DE LAFITE Pauillac 1959 (NA) (10/15/90) (JS)

1958

89   CHATEAU LAFITE-ROTHSCHILD Pauillac 1958 Cur: $105 (12/15/88) (TR)
81   CHATEAU LATOUR Pauillac 1958 Cur: $140 (3/31/90) (HS)
79   CHATEAU LYNCH-BAGES Pauillac 1958 Cur: $60 (10/31/89) (JS)
79   CHATEAU PICHON-BARON Pauillac 1958 Cur: $95 (9/30/88)
68   CHATEAU MOUTON-ROTHSCHILD Pauillac 1958 Cur: $761 (6/16/86) (TR)

1957

88   CHATEAU LYNCH-BAGES Pauillac 1957 Cur: $95 (10/31/89) (JS)
86   CHATEAU LAFITE-ROTHSCHILD Pauillac 1957 Cur: $125 (12/15/88) (TR)
86   CHATEAU MOUTON-ROTHSCHILD Pauillac 1957 Cur: $444 (6/16/86) (TR)
76   CHATEAU PICHON-BARON Pauillac 1957 Cur: $110 (9/30/88)

1956

86   CHATEAU LAFITE-ROTHSCHILD Pauillac 1956 Cur: $250 (12/15/88) (TR)
85   CHATEAU MOUTON-ROTHSCHILD Pauillac 1956 Cur: $2,421 (6/16/86) (TR)
62   CHATEAU LATOUR Pauillac 1956 Cur: $248 (3/31/90) (HS)

1955

95   CHATEAU MOUTON-ROTHSCHILD Pauillac 1955 Cur: $430 (5/15/91) (PM)
92   CHATEAU LYNCH-BAGES Pauillac 1955 Cur: $245 (10/31/89) (JS)
92   CHATEAU MOUTON-ROTHSCHILD Pauillac 1955 Cur: $430 (6/16/86) (TR)
90   CHATEAU LATOUR Pauillac 1955 Cur: $315 (3/31/90) (HS)
84   CHATEAU LAFITE-ROTHSCHILD Pauillac 1955 Cur: $324 (12/15/88) (TR)
81   CHATEAU PICHON-BARON Pauillac 1955 Cur: $122 (9/30/88)

1954

84   CHATEAU LAFITE-ROTHSCHILD Pauillac 1954 Cur: $290 (12/15/88) (TR)
81   CHATEAU MOUTON-ROTHSCHILD Pauillac 1954 Cur: $4,000 (6/16/86) (TR)
80   CHATEAU PICHON-BARON Pauillac 1954 Cur: $95 (9/30/88)
74   CHATEAU LYNCH-BAGES Pauillac 1954 Cur: $75 (10/31/89) (JS)

1953

94   CHATEAU MOUTON-ROTHSCHILD Pauillac 1953 Cur: $675 (5/15/91) (PM)
87   CHATEAU LAFITE-ROTHSCHILD Pauillac 1953 Cur: $457 (12/15/88) (TR)
80   CHATEAU LATOUR Pauillac 1953 Cur: $279 (3/31/90) (HS)
80   CHATEAU PICHON-BARON Pauillac 1953 Cur: $200 (9/30/88)
77   CHATEAU LYNCH-BAGES Pauillac 1953 Cur: $313 (10/31/89) (JS)

1952

91   CHATEAU LATOUR Pauillac 1952 Cur: $260 (3/31/90) (HS)
90   CHATEAU MOUTON-ROTHSCHILD Pauillac 1952 Cur: $400 (6/16/86) (TR)
84   CHATEAU LAFITE-ROTHSCHILD Pauillac 1952 Cur: $193 (12/15/88) (TR)
84   CHATEAU PICHON-BARON Pauillac 1952 Cur: $105 (9/30/88)
83   CHATEAU LYNCH-BAGES Pauillac 1952 Cur: $100 (10/31/89) (JS)

1951

84   CHATEAU MOUTON-ROTHSCHILD Pauillac 1951 Cur: $1,850 (6/16/86) (TR)
83   CHATEAU LAFITE-ROTHSCHILD Pauillac 1951 Cur: $150 (12/15/88) (TR)

1950

84   CHATEAU LAFITE-ROTHSCHILD Pauillac 1950 Cur: $297 (12/15/88) (TR)
83   CHATEAU MOUTON-ROTHSCHILD Pauillac 1950 Cur: $869 (6/16/86) (TR)
83   CHATEAU PICHON-BARON Pauillac 1950 Cur: $150 (9/30/88)
79   CHATEAU LATOUR Pauillac 1950 Cur: $334 (3/31/90) (HS)

1949

94   CHATEAU LATOUR Pauillac 1949 Cur: $517 (3/31/90) (HS)

Key to Symbols

The scores reported here are the results of blind tastings conducted by our panel of senior editors. Wines that carry the initials below are results of individual tastings.

THE WINE SPECTATOR 100-POINT SCALE 95-100—Classic, a great wine; *90-94*—Outstanding, superior character and style; *80-89*—Good to very good, a wine with special qualities; *70-79*—Average, drinkable wine that may have minor flaws; *60-69*—Below average, drinkable but not recommended; *50-59*—Poor, undrinkable, not recommended. *''+''*—With a score indicates a range; used primarily with barrel tastings to indicate a preliminary score.

SPECIAL DESIGNATIONS SS—Spectator Selection, CS—Cellar Selection, BB—Best Buy.

TASTER'S INITIALS (JG)—Jim Gordon, (HS)—Harvey Steiman, (JL)—James Laube, (JS)—James Suckling, (TM)—Thomas Matthews, (TR)—Terry Robards, (BT)—Barrel Tasting (these wines were tasted blind from barrel samples), (CA-date)—*California's Great Cabernets* by James Laube, (CH-date)—*California's Great Chardonnays* by James Laube, (VP-date)—*Vintage Port* by James Suckling.

DATE TASTED Dates in parentheses represent the issue in which the rating was published.

94   CHATEAU MOUTON-ROTHSCHILD Pauillac 1949 Cur: $1,156 (6/16/86) (TR)
88   CHATEAU LAFITE-ROTHSCHILD Pauillac 1949 Cur: $478 (12/15/88) (TR)
87   CHATEAU MOUTON-ROTHSCHILD Pauillac 1949 Cur: $1,156 (5/15/91) (PM)
87   CHATEAU PICHON-BARON Pauillac 1949 Cur: $175 (9/30/88)
84   CHATEAU LYNCH-BAGES Pauillac 1949 Cur: $175 (10/31/89) (JS)

1948

87   CHATEAU MOUTON-ROTHSCHILD Pauillac 1948 Cur: $1,900 (6/16/86) (TR)
84   CHATEAU LAFITE-ROTHSCHILD Pauillac 1948 Cur: $600 (12/15/88) (TR)
84   CHATEAU LATOUR Pauillac 1948 Cur: $383 (3/31/90) (HS)

1947

95   CHATEAU MOUTON-ROTHSCHILD Pauillac 1947 Cur: $1,310 (6/16/86) (TR)
91   CHATEAU LATOUR Pauillac 1947 Cur: $392 (3/31/90) (HS)
90   CHATEAU LYNCH-BAGES Pauillac 1947 Cur: $350 (10/31/89) (JS)
86   CHATEAU LAFITE-ROTHSCHILD Pauillac 1947 Cur: $406 (12/15/88) (TR)
80   CHATEAU PICHON-BARON Pauillac 1947 Cur: $200 (9/30/88)
75   CHATEAU MOUTON-ROTHSCHILD Pauillac 1947 Cur: $1,310 (5/15/91) (PM)

1946

90   CHATEAU LAFITE-ROTHSCHILD Pauillac 1946 Cur: $450 (12/15/88) (TR)
77   CHATEAU MOUTON-ROTHSCHILD Pauillac 1946 Cur: $5,719 (6/16/86) (TR)

1945

100 CHATEAU MOUTON-ROTHSCHILD Pauillac 1945 Cur: $1,850 (5/15/91) (PM)
98   CHATEAU LATOUR Pauillac 1945 Cur: $1,150 (3/31/90) (HS)
98   CHATEAU LATOUR Pauillac 1945 Cur: $1,150 (3/16/86) (JL)
95   CHATEAU MOUTON-ROTHSCHILD Pauillac 1945 Cur: $1,850 (3/16/86) (JL)
92   CHATEAU LAFITE-ROTHSCHILD Pauillac 1945 Cur: $849 (3/16/86) (JL)
87   CHATEAU BATAILLEY Pauillac 1945 Cur: $300 (3/16/86) (JL)
80   CHATEAU GRAND-PUY-LACOSTE Pauillac 1945 Cur: $375 (3/16/86) (JL)
80   CHATEAU LYNCH-BAGES Pauillac (Bottled in Denmark) 1945 Cur: $350 (10/31/89) (JS)
80   CHATEAU MOUTON-BARONNE-PHILIPPE Pauillac 1945 Cur: $390 (3/16/86) (JL)
80   CHATEAU PICHON-LALANDE Pauillac 1945 Cur: $400 (3/16/86) (JL)
75   CHATEAU PICHON-BARON Pauillac 1945 Cur: $367 (9/30/88)
65   CHATEAU LYNCH-BAGES Pauillac 1945 Cur: $350 (3/16/86) (JL)
60   CHATEAU PONTET-CANET Pauillac 1945 Cur: $250 (3/16/86) (JL)

1944

86   CHATEAU MOUTON-ROTHSCHILD Pauillac 1944 Cur: $950 (6/16/86) (TR)
70   CHATEAU LATOUR Pauillac 1944 Cur: $330 (3/31/90) (HS)

1943

80   CHATEAU LAFITE-ROTHSCHILD Pauillac 1943 Cur: $320 (12/15/88) (TR)
78   CHATEAU MOUTON-ROTHSCHILD Pauillac 1943 Cur: $477 (6/16/86) (TR)
67   CHATEAU LATOUR Pauillac 1943 Cur: $238 (3/31/90) (HS)

1942

80   CHATEAU LAFITE-ROTHSCHILD Pauillac 1942 Cur: $317 (12/15/88) (TR)
59   CHATEAU LATOUR Pauillac 1942 Cur: $330 (3/31/90) (HS)

1941

78   CHATEAU LAFITE-ROTHSCHILD Pauillac 1941 Cur: $500 (12/15/88) (TR)

1940

77   CHATEAU LAFITE-ROTHSCHILD Pauillac 1940 Cur: $695 (12/15/88) (TR)
77   CHATEAU MOUTON-ROTHSCHILD Pauillac 1940 Cur: $525 (6/16/86) (TR)
64   CHATEAU LATOUR Pauillac 1940 Cur: $368 (3/31/90) (HS)

1939

78   CHATEAU LAFITE-ROTHSCHILD Pauillac 1939 Cur: $320 (12/15/88) (TR)
55   CHATEAU MOUTON-ROTHSCHILD Pauillac 1939 Cur: $500 (6/16/86) (TR)

1938

76   CHATEAU LAFITE-ROTHSCHILD Pauillac 1938 Cur: $225 (12/15/88) (TR)
73   CHATEAU MOUTON-ROTHSCHILD Pauillac 1938 Cur: $500 (6/16/86) (TR)

1937

95   CHATEAU MOUTON-ROTHSCHILD Pauillac 1937 Cur: $438 (12/15/88) (JS)
91   CHATEAU MOUTON-ROTHSCHILD Pauillac 1937 Cur: $438 (5/15/91) (PM)
89   CHATEAU LATOUR Pauillac 1937 Cur: $355 (3/31/90) (HS)
80   CHATEAU LAFITE-ROTHSCHILD Pauillac 1937 Cur: $250 (12/15/88) (TR)
77   CARRUADES DE LAFITE Pauillac 1937 Cur: $125 (11/30/87)

1936

75   CHATEAU LATOUR Pauillac 1936 Cur: $396 (3/31/90) (HS)
63   CHATEAU MOUTON-ROTHSCHILD Pauillac 1936 Cur: $246 (6/16/86) (TR)

1934

90   CHATEAU MOUTON-ROTHSCHILD Pauillac 1934 Cur: $450 (5/15/91) (PM)
87   CHATEAU LAFITE-ROTHSCHILD Pauillac 1934 Cur: $355 (12/15/88) (TR)
84   CARRUADES DE LAFITE Pauillac 1934 Cur: $145 (11/30/87)
83   CHATEAU LATOUR Pauillac 1934 Cur: $333 (3/31/90) (HS)

1933

79   CHATEAU LAFITE-ROTHSCHILD Pauillac 1933 Cur: $200 (12/15/88) (TR)
78   CHATEAU MOUTON-ROTHSCHILD Pauillac 1933 Cur: $421/375ml (6/16/86) (TR)

1931

76   CHATEAU LAFITE-ROTHSCHILD Pauillac 1931 Cur: $550 (12/15/88) (TR)

1929

95   CHATEAU LATOUR Pauillac 1929 Cur: $2,310/1.5L (3/31/90) (HS)
88   CHATEAU LAFITE-ROTHSCHILD Pauillac 1929 Cur: $857 (12/15/88) (TR)
86   CHATEAU MOUTON-ROTHSCHILD Pauillac 1929 Cur: $800 (6/16/86) (TR)
75   CHATEAU MOUTON-ROTHSCHILD Pauillac 1929 Cur: $800 (5/15/91) (PM)

1928

91   CHATEAU LATOUR Pauillac 1928 Cur: $2,310/1.5L (3/31/90) (HS)
89   CHATEAU MOUTON-ROTHSCHILD Pauillac 1928 Cur: $950 (5/15/91) (PM)

83   CHATEAU LAFITE-ROTHSCHILD Pauillac 1928 Cur: $699 (12/15/88) (TR)

1926

87   CHATEAU LATOUR Pauillac 1926 Cur: $773 (3/31/90) (HS)
65   CHATEAU MOUTON-ROTHSCHILD Pauillac 1926 Cur: $800 (6/16/86) (TR)

1925

74   CHATEAU LAFITE-ROTHSCHILD Pauillac 1925 Cur: $193 (12/15/88) (TR)
40   CHATEAU MOUTON-ROTHSCHILD Pauillac 1925 Cur: $1,100 (6/16/86) (TR)

1924

91   CHATEAU LATOUR Pauillac 1924 Cur: $750 (3/31/90) (HS)
79   CHATEAU LAFITE-ROTHSCHILD Pauillac 1924 Cur: $528 (12/15/88) (TR)
69   CHATEAU MOUTON-ROTHSCHILD Pauillac 1924 Cur: $1,910 (6/16/86) (TR)

1923

84   CHATEAU LAFITE-ROTHSCHILD Pauillac 1923 Cur: $292 (12/15/88) (TR)

1921

84   CHATEAU MOUTON-ROTHSCHILD Pauillac 1921 Cur: $500 (6/16/86) (TR)
80   CHATEAU MOUTON-ROTHSCHILD Pauillac 1921 Cur: $500 (5/15/91) (PM)
77   CHATEAU LAFITE-ROTHSCHILD Pauillac 1921 Cur: $500 (12/15/88) (TR)

1920

75   CHATEAU LAFITE-ROTHSCHILD Pauillac 1920 Cur: $575 (12/15/88) (TR)
75   CHATEAU MOUTON-ROTHSCHILD Pauillac 1920 Cur: $700 (6/16/86) (TR)
50   CHATEAU LATOUR Pauillac 1920 Cur: $524 (3/31/90) (HS)

1919

79   CHATEAU MOUTON-ROTHSCHILD Pauillac 1919 Cur: $600 (5/15/91) (PM)
77   CHATEAU LAFITE-ROTHSCHILD Pauillac 1919 Cur: $738 (12/15/88) (TR)

1918

83   CHATEAU MOUTON-ROTHSCHILD Pauillac 1918 Cur: $1,637 (5/15/91) (PM)
79   CHATEAU LAFITE-ROTHSCHILD Pauillac 1918 Cur: $575 (12/15/88) (TR)
75   CHATEAU LATOUR Pauillac 1918 Cur: $575 (3/31/90) (HS)

1916

83   CHATEAU LAFITE-ROTHSCHILD Pauillac 1916 Cur: $450 (12/15/88) (TR)
67   CHATEAU MOUTON-ROTHSCHILD Pauillac 1916 Cur: $413 (6/16/86) (TR)

1914

75   CHATEAU LAFITE-ROTHSCHILD Pauillac 1914 Cur: $559 (12/15/88) (TR)
65   CHATEAU MOUTON-ROTHSCHILD Pauillac 1914 Cur: $400 (6/16/86) (TR)

1913

77   CHATEAU LAFITE-ROTHSCHILD Pauillac 1913 Cur: $500 (12/15/88) (TR)

1912

76   CHATEAU LAFITE-ROTHSCHILD Pauillac 1912 Cur: $520 (12/15/88) (TR)
62   CHATEAU MOUTON-ROTHSCHILD Pauillac 1912 Cur: $400 (6/16/86) (TR)

1911

81   CHATEAU LAFITE-ROTHSCHILD Pauillac 1911 Cur: $394 (12/15/88) (TR)

1910

77   CHATEAU LAFITE-ROTHSCHILD Pauillac 1910 Cur: $569 (12/15/88) (TR)
76   CHATEAU MOUTON-ROTHSCHILD Pauillac 1910 Cur: $400 (5/15/91) (PM)

1909

65   CHATEAU LAFITE-ROTHSCHILD Pauillac 1909 Cur: $700 (6/16/86) (TR)

1908

50   CHATEAU MOUTON-ROTHSCHILD Pauillac 1908 Cur: $700 (6/16/86) (TR)

1907

79   CHATEAU LAFITE-ROTHSCHILD Pauillac 1907 Cur: $700 (12/15/88) (TR)
50   CHATEAU MOUTON-ROTHSCHILD Pauillac 1907 Cur: $600 (6/16/86) (TR)

1906

78   CHATEAU LAFITE-ROTHSCHILD Pauillac 1906 Cur: $350 (12/15/88) (TR)
66   CHATEAU MOUTON-ROTHSCHILD Pauillac 1906 Cur: $800 (6/16/86) (TR)

1905

88   CHATEAU MOUTON-ROTHSCHILD Pauillac 1905 Cur: $963 (5/15/91) (PM)
82   CHATEAU LAFITE-ROTHSCHILD Pauillac 1905 Cur: $413 (12/15/88) (TR)

1904

80   CHATEAU LAFITE-ROTHSCHILD Pauillac 1904 Cur: $660 (12/15/88) (TR)

1902

80   CARRUADES DE LAFITE Pauillac 1902 Cur: $275 (11/30/87)
79   CHATEAU LAFITE-ROTHSCHILD Pauillac 1902 Cur: $504 (12/15/88) (TR)

1900

90   CHATEAU LATOUR Pauillac 1900 Cur: $2,000 (3/31/90) (HS)
90   CHATEAU MOUTON-ROTHSCHILD Pauillac 1900 Cur: $1,800 (5/15/91) (PM)

1899

94   CHATEAU LATOUR Pauillac 1899 Cur: $1,900 (3/31/90) (HS)
82   CHATEAU MOUTON-ROTHSCHILD Pauillac 1899 Cur: $1,900 (6/16/86) (TR)
78   CHATEAU LAFITE-ROTHSCHILD Pauillac 1899 Cur: $1,957 (12/15/88) (TR)
50   CHATEAU LATOUR Pauillac 1899 Cur: $3,990/1.5L (3/31/90) (HS)

1898

79   CHATEAU LAFITE-ROTHSCHILD Pauillac 1898 Cur: $750 (12/15/88) (TR)

1897

81   CHATEAU LAFITE-ROTHSCHILD Pauillac 1897 Cur: $1,155 (12/15/88) (TR)

FRANCE
BORDEAUX RED/PAUILLAC

1896
79   CHATEAU LAFITE-ROTHSCHILD Pauillac 1896 Cur: $1,200 (12/15/88) (TR)

1895
89   CHATEAU LAFITE-ROTHSCHILD Pauillac 1895 Cur: $2,050 (12/15/88) (TR)

1894
75   CHATEAU LAFITE-ROTHSCHILD Pauillac 1894 Cur: $1,000 (12/15/88) (TR)

1893
84   CHATEAU LAFITE-ROTHSCHILD Pauillac 1893 Cur: $1,200 (12/15/88) (TR)
67   CHATEAU LATOUR Pauillac 1893 Cur: $4,500 (3/31/90) (HS)

1892
85   CHATEAU LAFITE-ROTHSCHILD Pauillac 1892 Cur: $1,300 (12/15/88) (TR)
63   CHATEAU LATOUR Pauillac 1892 Cur: $1,200 (3/31/90) (HS)

1891
84   CHATEAU LAFITE-ROTHSCHILD Pauillac 1891 Cur: $1,100 (12/15/88) (TR)

1890
83   CHATEAU LAFITE-ROTHSCHILD Pauillac 1890 Cur: $1,100 (12/15/88) (TR)

1889
85   CHATEAU LAFITE-ROTHSCHILD Pauillac 1889 Cur: $750 (12/15/88) (TR)

1888
82   CHATEAU LAFITE-ROTHSCHILD Pauillac 1888 Cur: $900 (12/15/88) (TR)
60   CHATEAU MOUTON-ROTHSCHILD Pauillac 1888 Cur: $1,100 (6/16/86) (TR)

1886
88   CHATEAU LAFITE-ROTHSCHILD Pauillac 1886 Cur: $1,100 (12/15/88) (TR)
60   CHATEAU MOUTON-ROTHSCHILD Pauillac 1886 Cur: $1,200 (6/16/86) (TR)

1882
82   CHATEAU LAFITE-ROTHSCHILD Pauillac 1882 Cur: $800 (12/15/88) (TR)

1881
85   CHATEAU LAFITE-ROTHSCHILD Pauillac 1881 Cur: $715 (12/15/88) (TR)
74   CHATEAU MOUTON-ROTHSCHILD Pauillac 1881 Cur: $1,375 (6/16/86) (TR)

1880
82   CHATEAU LAFITE-ROTHSCHILD Pauillac 1880 Cur: $1,500 (12/15/88) (TR)

1879
83   CHATEAU LAFITE-ROTHSCHILD Pauillac 1879 Cur: $2,800 (12/15/88) (TR)

1878
99   CHATEAU MOUTON-ROTHSCHILD Pauillac 1878 Cur: $3,200 (5/15/91) (PM)
83   CHATEAU LAFITE-ROTHSCHILD Pauillac 1878 Cur: $2,475 (12/15/88) (TR)

1877
88   CHATEAU LAFITE-ROTHSCHILD Pauillac 1877 Cur: $2,500 (12/15/88) (TR)

1876
84   CHATEAU LAFITE-ROTHSCHILD Pauillac 1876 Cur: $1,307 (12/15/88) (TR)

1875
97   CHATEAU LAFITE-ROTHSCHILD Pauillac 1875 Cur: $8,400/1.5L (12/15/88) (TR)
95   CHATEAU LATOUR Pauillac 1875 Cur: $3,780/1.5L (12/15/88)
91   CHATEAU LAFITE-ROTHSCHILD Pauillac 1875 Cur: $4,000 (12/15/88) (TR)
77   CHATEAU LATOUR Pauillac 1875 Cur: $1,800 (3/31/90) (HS)

1874
97   CHATEAU LATOUR Pauillac 1874 Cur: $3,213 (3/31/90) (HS)
95   CHATEAU MOUTON-ROTHSCHILD Pauillac 1874 Cur: $2,500 (5/15/91) (PM)
84   CHATEAU LAFITE-ROTHSCHILD Pauillac 1874 Cur: $1,599 (12/15/88) (TR)
73   CHATEAU MOUTON-ROTHSCHILD Pauillac 1874 Cur: $2,500 (6/16/86) (TR)

1870
95   CHATEAU LAFITE-ROTHSCHILD Pauillac 1870 Cur: $6,375 (12/15/88) (TR)
94   CHATEAU LATOUR Pauillac 1870 Cur: $4,000 (3/31/90) (HS)
87   CHATEAU MOUTON-ROTHSCHILD Pauillac 1870 Cur: $3,500 (5/15/91) (PM)
78   CHATEAU MOUTON-ROTHSCHILD Pauillac 1870 Cur: $3,500 (6/16/86) (TR)

1869
82   CHATEAU LAFITE-ROTHSCHILD Pauillac 1869 Cur: $2,407 (12/15/88) (TR)
40   CHATEAU MOUTON-ROTHSCHILD Pauillac 1869 Cur: $1,700 (6/16/86) (TR)

1868
86   CHATEAU LAFITE-ROTHSCHILD Pauillac 1868 Cur: $1,788 (12/15/88) (TR)

1867
40   CHATEAU MOUTON-ROTHSCHILD Pauillac 1867 Cur: $2,100 (6/16/86) (TR)

1865
94   CHATEAU LATOUR Pauillac 1865 Cur: $14,700/1.5L (3/31/90) (HS)
84   CHATEAU LAFITE-ROTHSCHILD Pauillac 1865 Cur: $3,771 (12/15/88) (TR)

1864
84   CHATEAU LAFITE-ROTHSCHILD Pauillac 1864 Cur: $4,675 (12/15/88) (TR)
59   CHATEAU LATOUR Pauillac 1864 $10,000/1.5L (3/31/90) (HS)

1858
96   CHATEAU LAFITE-ROTHSCHILD Pauillac 1858 Cur: $3,225 (12/15/88) (TR)

1848
92   CHATEAU LAFITE-ROTHSCHILD Pauillac 1848 Cur: $10,000 (12/15/88) (TR)

1847
93   CHATEAU LATOUR Pauillac 1847 (NA)/1.5L (3/31/90) (HS)

1846
83   CHATEAU LAFITE-ROTHSCHILD Pauillac 1846 Cur: $9,625 (12/15/88) (TR)

1844
84   CHATEAU LAFITE-ROTHSCHILD Pauillac 1844 Cur: $5,638 (12/15/88) (TR)

1832
82   CHATEAU LAFITE-ROTHSCHILD Pauillac 1832 Cur: $9,000 (12/15/88) (TR)

1806
83   CHATEAU LAFITE-ROTHSCHILD Pauillac 1806 (NA) (12/15/88) (TR)

NV
85   DOMAINES BARONS DE ROTHSCHILD Pauillac Réserve Spéciale NV $12 (2/15/90)

POMEROL

1990
95+ CHATEAU PETRUS Pomerol 1990 (NR) (4/30/91) (BT)
95+ CHATEAU TROTANOY Pomerol 1990 (NR) (4/30/91) (BT)
90+ CHATEAU CLINET Pomerol 1990 (NR) (4/30/91) (BT)
90+ CLOS L'EGLISE Pomerol 1990 (NR) (4/30/91) (BT)
90+ CHATEAU LA CONSEILLANTE Pomerol 1990 (NR) (4/30/91) (BT)
90+ CHATEAU LA CROIX Pomerol 1990 (NR) (4/30/91) (BT)
90+ DOMAINE DE L'EGLISE Pomerol 1990 (NR) (4/30/91) (BT)
90+ CHATEAU L'EVANGILE Pomerol 1990 (NR) (4/30/91) (BT)
90+ CHATEAU LA FLEUR-PETRUS Pomerol 1990 (NR) (4/30/91) (BT)
90+ CHATEAU LA FLEUR DE GAY Pomerol 1990 (NR) (4/30/91) (BT)
90+ CHATEAU LE GAY Pomerol 1990 (NR) (4/30/91) (BT)
90+ CHATEAU GAZIN Pomerol 1990 (NR) (4/30/91) (BT)
90+ CHATEAU LA GRAVE TRIGANT DE BOISSET Pomerol 1990 (NR) (4/30/91) (BT)
90+ CHATEAU LAGRANGE Pomerol 1990 (NR) (4/30/91) (BT)
90+ CHATEAU LATOUR A POMEROL Pomerol 1990 (NR) (4/30/91) (BT)
90+ CHATEAU PETIT-VILLAGE Pomerol 1990 (NR) (4/30/91) (BT)
90+ CHATEAU ROUGET Pomerol 1990 (NR) (4/30/91) (BT)
85+ CHATEAU LE BON-PASTEUR Pomerol 1990 (NR) (4/30/91) (BT)
85+ CHATEAU BOURGNEUF-VAYRON Pomerol 1990 (NR) (4/30/91) (BT)
85+ CHATEAU CERTAN DE MAY Pomerol 1990 (NR) (4/30/91) (BT)
85+ CHATEAU PLINCE Pomerol 1990 (NR) (4/30/91) (BT)
80+ CHATEAU LA CROIX DE GAY Pomerol 1990 (NR) (4/30/91) (BT)
75+ CHATEAU DE SALES Pomerol 1990 (NR) (4/30/91) (BT)

1989
95+ CHATEAU CLINET Pomerol 1989 (NR) (4/30/90) (BT)
95+ CLOS L'EGLISE Pomerol 1989 (NR) (4/30/91) (BT)
95+ CHATEAU LA FLEUR-PETRUS Pomerol 1989 (NR) (4/30/91) (BT)
95+ CHATEAU LA FLEUR DE GAY Pomerol 1989 (NR) (4/30/91) (BT)
95+ CHATEAU LA FLEUR DE GAY Pomerol 1989 (NR) (4/30/90) (BT)
95+ CHATEAU LE GAY Pomerol 1989 (NR) (4/30/91) (BT)
95+ CHATEAU LAFLEUR Pomerol 1989 (NR) (4/30/91) (BT)
95+ CHATEAU PETRUS Pomerol 1989 (NR) (4/30/91) (BT)
95+ CHATEAU PETRUS Pomerol 1989 (NR) (4/30/90) (BT)
95+ CHATEAU LE PIN Pomerol 1989 (NR) (4/30/90) (BT)
95+ CHATEAU LA POINTE Pomerol 1989 (NR) (4/30/91) (BT)
95+ CHATEAU TROTANOY Pomerol 1989 (NR) (4/30/91) (BT)
90+ CHATEAU CERTAN DE MAY Pomerol 1989 (NR) (4/30/91) (BT)
90+ CHATEAU CLINET Pomerol 1989 (NR) (4/30/91) (BT)
90+ CHATEAU LA CROIX Pomerol 1989 (NR) (4/30/91) (BT)
90+ CHATEAU LA CROIX DU CASSE Pomerol 1989 (NR) (4/30/91) (BT)
90+ DOMAINE DE L'EGLISE Pomerol 1989 (NR) (4/30/90) (BT)
90+ CHATEAU FEYTIT-CLINET Pomerol 1989 (NR) (4/30/91) (BT)
90+ CHATEAU LE GAY Pomerol 1989 (NR) (4/30/90) (BT)
90+ CHATEAU GAZIN Pomerol 1989 (NR) (4/30/91) (BT)
90+ CHATEAU GAZIN Pomerol 1989 (NR) (4/30/90) (BT)
90+ CHATEAU LA GRAVE TRIGANT DE BOISSET Pomerol 1989 (NR) (4/30/91) (BT)
90+ CHATEAU LAFLEUR Pomerol 1989 (NR) (4/30/90) (BT)
90+ CHATEAU LATOUR A POMEROL Pomerol 1989 (NR) (4/30/91) (BT)
90+ CHATEAU MAZEYRES Pomerol 1989 (NR) (4/30/91) (BT)
90+ CHATEAU MOULINET Pomerol 1989 (NR) (4/30/91) (BT)
90+ CHATEAU PRIEURS DE LA COMMANDERIE Pomerol 1989 (NR) (4/30/91) (BT)
90+ CHATEAU DE SALES Pomerol 1989 (NR) (4/30/91) (BT)
90+ CHATEAU TAILLEFER Pomerol 1989 (NR) (4/30/91) (BT)
90+ CHATEAU TROTANOY Pomerol 1989 (NR) (4/30/90) (BT)
85+ CHATEAU LE BON-PASTEUR Pomerol 1989 (NR) (4/30/91) (BT)
85+ CHATEAU LE BON-PASTEUR Pomerol 1989 (NR) (4/30/90) (BT)
85+ CHATEAU BONALGUE Pomerol 1989 (NR) (4/30/91) (BT)
85+ CHATEAU BOURGNEUF-VAYRON Pomerol 1989 (NR) (4/30/90) (BT)
85+ CHATEAU LA CABANNE Pomerol 1989 (NR) (4/30/91) (BT)
85+ CLOS DU CLOCHER Pomerol 1989 (NR) (4/30/91) (BT)
85+ CHATEAU LA CONSEILLANTE Pomerol 1989 (NR) (4/30/91) (BT)
85+ CHATEAU LA FLEUR-PETRUS Pomerol 1989 (NR) (4/30/90) (BT)
85+ CHATEAU HAUT-MAILLET Pomerol 1989 (NR) (4/30/91) (BT)

85+ CHATEAU LAGRANGE Pomerol 1989 (NR) (4/30/91) (BT)
85+ CHATEAU LAGRANGE Pomerol 1989 (NR) (4/30/90) (BT)
85+ CHATEAU MONTVIEL Pomerol 1989 (NR) (4/30/91) (BT)
85+ CHATEAU PETIT-VILLAGE Pomerol 1989 (NR) (4/30/91) (BT)
85+ CHATEAU PETIT-VILLAGE Pomerol 1989 (NR) (4/30/90) (BT)
85+ CHATEAU LA POINTE Pomerol 1989 (NR) (4/30/90) (BT)
85+ CHATEAU ROUGET Pomerol 1989 (NR) (4/30/91) (BT)
85+ CHATEAU ROUGET Pomerol 1989 (NR) (4/30/90) (BT)
85+ CHATEAU DE SALES Pomerol 1989 (NR) (4/30/90) (BT)
80+ CHATEAU BOURGNEUF-VAYRON Pomerol 1989 (NR) (4/30/91) (BT)
80+ CLOS L'EGLISE Pomerol 1989 (NR) (4/30/90) (BT)
80+ CHATEAU LA GRAVE TRIGANT DE BOISSET Pomerol 1989 (NR) (4/30/90) (BT)
80+ CHATEAU LATOUR A POMEROL Pomerol 1989 (NR) (4/30/90) (BT)
80+ CHATEAU PLINCE Pomerol 1989 (NR) (4/30/91) (BT)
80+ CHATEAU PLINCE Pomerol 1989 (NR) (4/30/90) (BT)

1988

95 CHATEAU LE PIN Pomerol 1988 $65 (6/30/91) CS
95+ CHATEAU CLINET Pomerol 1988 $31 (8/31/90) (BT)
95+ CHATEAU LA FLEUR DE GAY Pomerol 1988 $57 (6/30/89) (BT)
95+ CHATEAU LAFLEUR Pomerol 1988 (NR) (6/30/89) (BT)
95+ CHATEAU LATOUR A POMEROL Pomerol 1988 $55 (6/30/89) (BT)
95+ CHATEAU PETRUS Pomerol 1988 $221 (8/31/90) (BT)
95+ CHATEAU PETRUS Pomerol 1988 $221 (6/30/89) (BT)
95+ CHATEAU TROTANOY Pomerol 1988 $48 (8/31/90) (BT)
94 CHATEAU LA FLEUR DE GAY Pomerol 1988 $57 (6/30/91)
92 CHATEAU CLINET Pomerol 1988 $31 (2/28/91)
91 CHATEAU L'EGLISE-CLINET Pomerol 1988 $47 (12/31/90)
91 CHATEAU TAILHAS Pomerol 1988 $20 (4/30/91)
91 VIEUX CHATEAU CERTAN Pomerol 1988 $60 (3/31/91)
90 CHATEAU BEAUREGARD Pomerol 1988 $36 (7/31/91)
90 CHATEAU BOURGNEUF-VAYRON Pomerol 1988 $19 (6/30/91)
90 CHATEAU CERTAN DE MAY Pomerol 1988 $66 (6/30/91)
90 CHATEAU LA CONSEILLANTE Pomerol 1988 $56 (3/31/91)
90+ CHATEAU LE BON-PASTEUR Pomerol 1988 $23 (8/31/90) (BT)
90+ CHATEAU LE BON-PASTEUR Pomerol 1988 $23 (6/30/89) (BT)
90+ CHATEAU CERTAN DE MAY Pomerol 1988 $66 (6/30/89) (BT)
90+ CHATEAU LA FLEUR DE GAY Pomerol 1988 $57 (8/31/90) (BT)
90+ CHATEAU LE GAY Pomerol 1988 $30 (8/31/90) (BT)
90+ CHATEAU LE GAY Pomerol 1988 $30 (6/30/89) (BT)
90+ CHATEAU GAZIN Pomerol 1988 $30 (8/31/90) (BT)
90+ CHATEAU GAZIN Pomerol 1988 $30 (6/30/89) (BT)
90+ CHATEAU LA GRAVE TRIGANT DE BOISSET Pomerol 1988 $24 (8/31/90) (BT)
90+ CHATEAU LAFLEUR Pomerol 1988 (NR) (8/31/90) (BT)
90+ CHATEAU PETIT-VILLAGE Pomerol 1988 $26 (8/31/90) (BT)
90+ CHATEAU LE PIN Pomerol 1988 $65 (6/30/89) (BT)
90+ CHATEAU TROTANOY Pomerol 1988 $48 (6/30/89) (BT)
89 CHATEAU CERTAN-GIRAUD Pomerol 1988 $23 (2/28/91)
89 CHATEAU LA CROIX DE GAY Pomerol 1988 $26 (6/30/91)
88 CLOS RENE Pomerol 1988 $24 (4/30/91)
88 CHATEAU MOULINET Pomerol 1988 $17 (7/31/91)
87 CHATEAU L'EVANGILE Pomerol 1988 $38 (6/30/91)
87 CHATEAU GAZIN Pomerol 1988 $30 (6/30/91)
87 CHATEAU TAILLEFER Pomerol 1988 $22 (6/30/91)
85 CHATEAU LE BON-PASTEUR Pomerol 1988 $23 (2/28/91)
85 CHATEAU L'ENCLOS Pomerol 1988 $17 (3/15/91)
85+ CHATEAU BONALGUE Pomerol 1988 (NR) (6/30/89) (BT)
85+ CHATEAU BOURGNEUF-VAYRON Pomerol 1988 $19 (6/30/89) (BT)
85+ CHATEAU CLINET Pomerol 1988 $31 (6/30/89) (BT)
85+ CHATEAU LA CONSEILLANTE Pomerol 1988 $56 (6/30/89) (BT)
85+ CHATEAU LA CROIX DE GAY Pomerol 1988 $26 (8/31/90) (BT)
85+ CHATEAU LA CROIX DE GAY Pomerol 1988 $26 (6/30/89) (BT)
85+ CHATEAU LA CROIX DU CASSE Pomerol 1988 $20 (6/30/89) (BT)
85+ CHATEAU LA FLEUR-PETRUS Pomerol 1988 $63 (6/30/89) (BT)
85+ CHATEAU LA GRAVE TRIGANT DE BOISSET Pomerol 1988 $24 (6/30/89) (BT)
85+ CHATEAU LAGRANGE Pomerol 1988 $25 (6/30/89) (BT)
85+ CHATEAU PETIT-VILLAGE Pomerol 1988 $26 (6/30/89) (BT)
85+ VIEUX CHATEAU CERTAN Pomerol 1988 $60 (8/31/90) (BT)
83 CLOS L'EGLISE Pomerol 1988 $24 (6/30/91)
83 CHATEAU LE GAY Pomerol 1988 $30 (4/30/91)
83 CHATEAU LA POINTE Pomerol 1988 $35 (7/31/91)
82 CHATEAU LA CROIX Pomerol 1988 $19 (7/31/91)
80+ CHATEAU CERTAN-GIRAUD Pomerol 1988 $23 (6/30/89) (BT)
80+ CLOS DU CLOCHER Pomerol 1988 $22 (6/30/89) (BT)
80+ CLOS L'EGLISE Pomerol 1988 $24 (6/30/89) (BT)
80+ CLOS RENE Pomerol 1988 $24 (6/30/89) (BT)
80+ CHATEAU L'EVANGILE Pomerol 1988 $38 (6/30/89) (BT)
80+ CHATEAU MOULINET Pomerol 1988 $17 (6/30/89) (BT)
80+ CHATEAU LA POINTE Pomerol 1988 $35 (6/30/89) (BT)
70+ CHATEAU LA CROIX Pomerol 1988 $19 (6/30/89) (BT)
70+ CHATEAU DE SALES Pomerol 1988 (NR) (6/30/89) (BT)
70+ CHATEAU TAILLEFER Pomerol 1988 $22 (6/30/89) (BT)

1987

90+ CHATEAU CLINET Pomerol 1987 Rel: $25 Cur: $25 (6/30/89) (BT)
88 CHATEAU TROTANOY Pomerol 1987 Rel: $45 Cur: $45 (10/15/88) (JS)
86 CHATEAU LA CONSEILLANTE Pomerol 1987 Rel: $35 Cur: $35 (5/15/90)
85 CHATEAU PETRUS Pomerol 1987 Rel: $175 Cur: $175 (2/15/91) (JS)
85+ CHATEAU LE BON-PASTEUR Pomerol 1987 Rel: $22 Cur: $22 (6/30/89) (BT)
85+ CHATEAU CERTAN DE MAY Pomerol 1987 Rel: $50 Cur: $50 (6/30/89) (BT)
85+ CHATEAU CLINET Pomerol 1987 Rel: $25 Cur: $25 (6/30/88) (BT)
85+ CHATEAU LA CONSEILLANTE Pomerol 1987 Rel: $35 Cur: $35 (6/30/88) (BT)
85+ CHATEAU LA CROIX DE GAY Pomerol 1987 Rel: $20 Cur: $20 (6/30/88) (BT)
85+ CHATEAU LA FLEUR DE GAY Pomerol 1987 Rel: $38 Cur: $38 (6/30/89) (BT)
85+ CHATEAU LA FLEUR DE GAY Pomerol 1987 Rel: $38 Cur: $38 (6/30/88) (BT)
85+ CHATEAU PETIT-VILLAGE Pomerol 1987 Rel: $22 Cur: $22 (6/30/88) (BT)
85+ CHATEAU PETRUS Pomerol 1987 Rel: $175 Cur: $175 (6/30/89) (BT)
85+ CHATEAU PETRUS Pomerol 1987 Rel: $175 Cur: $175 (6/30/88) (BT)
85+ CHATEAU LE PIN Pomerol 1987 Rel: $45 Cur: $53 (6/30/89) (BT)
85+ CHATEAU TROTANOY Pomerol 1987 Rel: $45 Cur: $45 (6/30/89) (BT)
85+ CHATEAU TROTANOY Pomerol 1987 Rel: $45 Cur: $45 (6/30/88) (BT)
85+ VIEUX CHATEAU CERTAN Pomerol 1987 Rel: $30 Cur: $30 (6/30/89) (BT)
85+ VIEUX CHATEAU CERTAN Pomerol 1987 Rel: $30 Cur: $30 (6/30/88) (BT)
84 CHATEAU PETRUS Pomerol 1987 Rel: $175 Cur: $175 (10/15/90)
84 VIEUX CHATEAU CERTAN Pomerol 1987 Rel: $30 Cur: $30 (5/15/90)
83 CHATEAU L'EGLISE-CLINET Pomerol 1987 Rel: $22 Cur: $23 (2/15/90)
81 CHATEAU LE BON-PASTEUR Pomerol 1987 Rel: $22 Cur: $22 (5/15/90)
80+ CHATEAU LE BON-PASTEUR Pomerol 1987 Rel: $22 Cur: $22 (6/30/88) (BT)
80+ CHATEAU BONALGUE Pomerol 1987 Rel: $18 Cur: $18 (6/30/89) (BT)
80+ CHATEAU LA CABANNE Pomerol 1987 Rel: $20 Cur: $20 (6/30/89) (BT)
80+ CLOS DU CLOCHER Pomerol 1987 Rel: $18 Cur: $18 (6/30/89) (BT)
80+ CHATEAU LA CONSEILLANTE Pomerol 1987 Rel: $35 Cur: $35 (6/30/89) (BT)
80+ CHATEAU LA CROIX DE GAY Pomerol 1987 Rel: $20 Cur: $20 (6/30/89) (BT)
80+ CHATEAU L'ENCLOS Pomerol 1987 Rel: $15 Cur: $15 (6/30/89) (BT)
80+ CHATEAU L'EVANGILE Pomerol 1987 Rel: $25 Cur: $31 (6/30/89) (BT)
80+ CHATEAU L'EVANGILE Pomerol 1987 Rel: $25 Cur: $31 (6/30/88) (BT)
80+ CHATEAU LA FLEUR-PETRUS Pomerol 1987 Rel: $36 Cur: $36 (6/30/89) (BT)
80+ CHATEAU GAZIN Pomerol 1987 Rel: $22 Cur: $22 (6/30/89) (BT)
80+ CHATEAU LA GRAVE TRIGANT DE BOISSET Pomerol 1987 Rel: $21 Cur: $21 (6/30/89) (BT)
80+ CHATEAU LA GRAVE TRIGANT DE BOISSET Pomerol 1987 Rel: $21 Cur: $21 (6/30/88) (BT)
80+ CHATEAU LATOUR A POMEROL Pomerol 1987 Rel: $35 Cur: $35 (6/30/89) (BT)
80+ CHATEAU MONTVIEL Pomerol 1987 Rel: $20 Cur: $20 (6/30/89) (BT)
80+ CHATEAU PETIT-VILLAGE Pomerol 1987 Rel: $22 Cur: $22 (6/30/89) (BT)
75+ CHATEAU BONALGUE Pomerol 1987 Rel: $18 Cur: $18 (6/30/88) (BT)
75+ CHATEAU BOURGNEUF-VAYRON Pomerol 1987 Rel: $13 Cur: $13 (6/30/89) (BT)
75+ CHATEAU BOURGNEUF-VAYRON Pomerol 1987 Rel: $13 Cur: $13 (6/30/88) (BT)
75+ CHATEAU LA CABANNE Pomerol 1987 Rel: $20 Cur: $20 (6/30/88) (BT)
75+ CHATEAU CERTAN-GIRAUD Pomerol 1987 Rel: $18 Cur: $18 (6/30/89) (BT)
75+ CLOS L'EGLISE Pomerol 1987 Rel: $20 Cur: $20 (6/30/89) (BT)
75+ CLOS RENE Pomerol 1987 Rel: $20 Cur: $20 (6/30/89) (BT)
75+ CHATEAU LA CROIX Pomerol 1987 Rel: $15 Cur: $15 (6/30/89) (BT)
75+ CHATEAU LA CROIX Pomerol 1987 Rel: $15 Cur: $15 (6/30/88) (BT)
75+ CHATEAU LA CROIX DU CASSE Pomerol 1987 Rel: $17 Cur: $17 (6/30/88) (BT)
75+ CHATEAU MONTVIEL Pomerol 1987 Rel: $20 Cur: $20 (6/30/88) (BT)
75+ CHATEAU MOULINET Pomerol 1987 Rel: $15 Cur: $15 (6/30/89) (BT)
75+ CHATEAU MOULINET Pomerol 1987 Rel: $15 Cur: $15 (6/30/88) (BT)
75+ CHATEAU NENIN Pomerol 1987 Rel: $20 Cur: $20 (6/30/88) (BT)
75+ CHATEAU PLINCE Pomerol 1987 Rel: $16 Cur: $21 (6/30/89) (BT)
75+ CHATEAU TAILLEFER Pomerol 1987 Rel: $18 Cur: $18 (6/30/89) (BT)
70+ CLOS DU CLOCHER Pomerol 1987 Rel: $18 Cur: $18 (6/30/88) (BT)
70+ CHATEAU GOMBAUDE-GUILLOT Pomerol 1987 Rel: $17 Cur: $17 (6/30/89) (BT)
70+ CHATEAU LA POINTE Pomerol 1987 Rel: $21 Cur: $21 (6/30/88) (BT)
70+ CHATEAU PRIEURS DE LA COMMANDERIE Pomerol 1987 (NR) (6/30/88) (BT)
70+ CHATEAU TAILLEFER Pomerol 1987 Rel: $18 Cur: $18 (6/30/88) (BT)

1986

96 CHATEAU PETRUS Pomerol 1986 Rel: $200 Cur: $285 (2/15/91) (JS)
95 CHATEAU LA FLEUR DE GAY Pomerol 1986 Rel: $43 Cur: $48 (10/31/89) CS
95 CHATEAU PETRUS Pomerol 1986 Rel: $200 Cur: $285 (11/15/89)
95 CHATEAU LE PIN Pomerol 1986 Rel: $55 Cur: $105 (6/15/89)
95+ CHATEAU PETRUS Pomerol 1986 Rel: $200 Cur: $285 (6/30/88) (BT)
95+ VIEUX CHATEAU CERTAN Pomerol 1986 Rel: $40 Cur: $54 (6/30/88) (BT)
94 CLOS RENE Pomerol 1986 Rel: $19 Cur: $25 (6/15/89) SS
93 CHATEAU CERTAN DE MAY Pomerol 1986 Rel: $53 Cur: $70 (9/15/89)
93 CHATEAU LA CONSEILLANTE Pomerol 1986 Rel: $40 Cur: $54 (6/15/89)
93 CHATEAU LA FLEUR-PETRUS Pomerol 1986 Rel: $52 Cur: $52 (2/15/90) CS
93 VIEUX CHATEAU CERTAN Pomerol 1986 Rel: $40 Cur: $54 (6/15/89)
92 CHATEAU LE BON-PASTEUR Pomerol 1986 Rel: $22 Cur: $25 (6/15/89)
92 CHATEAU L'ENCLOS Pomerol 1986 Rel: $20 Cur: $20 (6/15/89)
91 CHATEAU L'EGLISE-CLINET Pomerol 1986 Rel: $29 Cur: $45 (6/15/89)
90 CHATEAU LAFLEUR Pomerol 1986 Rel: $100 Cur: $138 (10/31/89)
90 CHATEAU LA POINTE Pomerol 1986 Rel: $21 Cur: $21 (6/15/89)
90+ CHATEAU LE BON-PASTEUR Pomerol 1986 Rel: $22 Cur: $25 (6/30/88) (BT)
90+ CHATEAU CERTAN DE MAY Pomerol 1986 Rel: $53 Cur: $70 (5/15/87) (BT)
90+ CHATEAU CLINET Pomerol 1986 Rel: $25 Cur: $27 (6/30/88) (BT)
90+ CHATEAU CLINET Pomerol 1986 Rel: $25 Cur: $27 (5/15/87) (BT)
90+ CLOS L'EGLISE Pomerol 1986 Rel: $28 Cur: $28 (5/15/87) (BT)
90+ CHATEAU LA CONSEILLANTE Pomerol 1986 Rel: $40 Cur: $54 (6/30/88) (BT)
90+ CHATEAU LA CROIX DE GAY Pomerol 1986 Rel: $20 Cur: $22 (6/30/88) (BT)
90+ CHATEAU L'EVANGILE Pomerol 1986 Rel: $62 Cur: $62 (6/30/88) (BT)
90+ CHATEAU LA FLEUR DE GAY Pomerol 1986 Rel: $43 Cur: $48 (6/30/88) (BT)
90+ CHATEAU LA GRAVE TRIGANT DE BOISSET Pomerol 1986 Rel: $35 Cur: $35 (5/15/87) (BT)
90+ CHATEAU LATOUR A POMEROL Pomerol 1986 Cur: $39 (5/15/87) (BT)
90+ CHATEAU PETIT-VILLAGE Pomerol 1986 Rel: $24 Cur: $25 (6/30/88) (BT)
90+ CHATEAU PETRUS Pomerol 1986 Rel: $200 Cur: $285 (5/15/87) (BT)
90+ CHATEAU TROTANOY Pomerol 1986 Rel: $68 Cur: $68 (6/30/88) (BT)
90+ CHATEAU TROTANOY Pomerol 1986 Rel: $68 Cur: $68 (5/15/87) (BT)
90+ VIEUX CHATEAU CERTAN Pomerol 1986 Rel: $40 Cur: $54 (5/15/87) (BT)
89 CHATEAU LA GRAVE TRIGANT DE BOISSET Pomerol 1986 Rel: $35 Cur: $35 (3/31/90)
88 CHATEAU L'EVANGILE Pomerol 1986 Rel: $62 Cur: $62 (9/15/89)
87 CHATEAU BEAUREGARD Pomerol 1986 Rel: $22 Cur: $24 (6/15/89)
86 CHATEAU CERTAN-GIRAUD Pomerol 1986 Rel: $22 Cur: $22 (6/30/89)
86 CLOS L'EGLISE Pomerol 1986 Rel: $28 Cur: $28 (2/15/90)
86 CHATEAU DE SALES Pomerol 1986 Rel: $20 Cur: $20 (6/30/89)
85+ CHATEAU BONALGUE Pomerol 1986 Cur: $26 (6/30/88) (BT)
85+ CHATEAU LA CABANNE Pomerol 1986 (NR) (6/30/88) (BT)
85+ CHATEAU LA GRAVE TRIGANT DE BOISSET Pomerol 1986 Rel: $35 Cur: $35 (6/30/88) (BT)
84 CHATEAU NENIN Pomerol 1986 Rel: $22 Cur: $22 (6/30/89)
83 CHATEAU TROTANOY Pomerol 1986 Rel: $68 Cur: $68 (10/31/89)
80+ CHATEAU LE BON-PASTEUR Pomerol 1986 Rel: $22 Cur: $25 (5/15/87) (BT)
80+ CHATEAU BOURGNEUF-VAYRON Pomerol 1986 Rel: $22 Cur: $25 (6/30/88) (BT)
80+ CLOS DU CLOCHER Pomerol 1986 Rel: $20 Cur: $20 (6/30/88) (BT)
80+ CHATEAU LA CROIX Pomerol 1986 Rel: $25 Cur: $25 (6/30/88) (BT)
80+ CHATEAU LA CROIX DE GAY Pomerol 1986 Rel: $20 Cur: $22 (5/15/87) (BT)
80+ CHATEAU GAZIN Pomerol 1986 Rel: $21 Cur: $23 (5/15/87) (BT)
80+ CHATEAU MONTVIEL Pomerol 1986 Rel: $29 Cur: $29 (6/30/88) (BT)

FRANCE
BORDEAUX RED/*POMEROL*

80+ CHATEAU MOULINET Pomerol 1986 Rel: $15 Cur: $15 (6/30/88) (BT)
80+ CHATEAU PETIT-VILLAGE Pomerol 1986 Rel: $24 Cur: $25 (5/15/87) (BT)
80+ CHATEAU TAILLEFER Pomerol 1986 Rel: $20 Cur: $20 (6/30/88) (BT)
78   CHATEAU CLINET Pomerol 1986 Rel: $25 Cur: $27 (9/15/89)
78   LA PETITE EGLISE Pomerol 1986 Rel: $15 Cur: $15 (9/15/89)
75+ CHATEAU NENIN Pomerol 1986 Rel: $22 Cur: $22 (6/30/88) (BT)
75+ CHATEAU LA POINTE Pomerol 1986 Rel: $21 Cur: $21 (6/30/88) (BT)
75+ CHATEAU PRIEURS DE LA COMMANDERIE Pomerol 1986 (NR) (6/30/88) (BT)
73   LA PETITE EGLISE Pomerol 1986 Rel: $15 Cur: $15 (6/30/89)
70+ CHATEAU BOURGNEUF-VAYRON Pomerol 1986 Rel: $22 Cur: $25 (5/15/87) (BT)
70+ CHATEAU LA CABANNE Pomerol 1986 (NR) (5/15/87) (BT)
70+ CHATEAU MAZEYRES Pomerol 1986 (NR) (6/30/88) (BT)

1985
98   CHATEAU PETRUS Pomerol 1985 Rel: $160 Cur: $350 (5/31/88)
97   CHATEAU PETRUS Pomerol 1985 Rel: $160 Cur: $350 (2/15/91) (JS)
95   CHATEAU LAFLEUR Pomerol 1985 Cur: $135 (5/01/89)
93   CHATEAU LA CONSEILLANTE Pomerol 1985 Rel: $50 Cur: $63 (2/29/88)
93   CHATEAU LA CROIX Pomerol 1985 Rel: $25 Cur: $25 (5/15/88)
93   CHATEAU L'EGLISE-CLINET Pomerol 1985 Rel: $30 Cur: $57 (2/29/88)
93   CHATEAU PRIEURS DE LA COMMANDERIE Pomerol 1985 Rel: $27 Cur: $27 (9/30/88)
93   CHATEAU TROTANOY Pomerol 1985 Rel: $70 Cur: $85 (4/30/88)
92   CHATEAU LE BON-PASTEUR Pomerol 1985 Rel: $20 Cur: $49 (5/15/88)
92   CLOS RENE Pomerol 1985 Rel: $17 Cur: $20 (3/15/88)
92   CHATEAU L'EVANGILE Pomerol 1985 Rel: $55 Cur: $73 (2/29/88)
91   CHATEAU CLINET Pomerol 1985 Rel: $34 Cur: $34 (4/30/88)
91   CHATEAU LA CROIX DE GAY Pomerol 1985 Rel: $33 Cur: $33 (3/15/88) CS
90   CHATEAU GAZIN Pomerol 1985 Rel: $21 Cur: $28 (9/30/88)
90   VIEUX CHATEAU CERTAN Pomerol 1985 Rel: $38 Cur: $56 (6/30/88)
90+ CHATEAU BOURGNEUF-VAYRON Pomerol 1985 Rel: $28 Cur: $28 (5/15/87) (BT)
90+ CHATEAU CERTAN DE MAY Pomerol 1985 Rel: $70 Cur: $85 (5/15/87) (BT)
90+ CHATEAU LA FLEUR-PETRUS Pomerol 1985 Rel: $50 Cur: $54 (4/16/86) (BT)
90+ CHATEAU LATOUR A POMEROL Pomerol 1985 Rel: $61 (5/15/87) (BT)
90+ CHATEAU PETRUS Pomerol 1985 Rel: $160 Cur: $350 (5/15/87) (BT)
90+ CHATEAU TROTANOY Pomerol 1985 Rel: $70 Cur: $85 (5/15/87) (BT)
88   CLOS DU CLOCHER Pomerol 1985 Rel: $17 Cur: $20 (2/29/88)
88   CHATEAU FEYTIT-CLINET Pomerol 1985 Rel: $30 Cur: $30 (4/30/88)
87   CHATEAU DE SALES Pomerol 1985 Rel: $14 Cur: $18 (6/30/88)
86   CHATEAU BOURGNEUF-VAYRON Pomerol 1985 Rel: $28 Cur: $28 (11/30/88)
86   CHATEAU CERTAN DE MAY Pomerol 1985 Rel: $70 Cur: $85 (4/30/88)
86   CHATEAU LA FLEUR-PETRUS Pomerol 1985 Rel: $50 Cur: $54 (6/30/88)
85   CHATEAU CERTAN-GIRAUD Pomerol 1985 Rel: $25 Cur: $25 (4/30/88)
82   CHATEAU LA CROIX DU CASSE Pomerol 1985 Rel: $25 Cur: $25 (5/15/88)
81   CHATEAU TAILLEFER Pomerol 1985 Rel: $19 Cur: $19 (6/30/88)
80+ CHATEAU LE BON-PASTEUR Pomerol 1985 Rel: $20 Cur: $49 (5/15/87) (BT)
80+ CHATEAU LA CABANNE Pomerol 1985 (NR) (5/15/87) (BT)
80+ CHATEAU CLINET Pomerol 1985 Rel: $34 Cur: $34 (5/15/87) (BT)
80+ CLOS L'EGLISE Pomerol 1985 Rel: $21 Cur: $25 (5/15/87) (BT)
80+ CHATEAU LA CROIX DE GAY Pomerol 1985 Rel: $33 Cur: $33 (5/15/87) (BT)
80+ CHATEAU LA GRAVE TRIGANT DE BOISSET Pomerol 1985 Cur: $29 (5/15/87) (BT)
80+ CHATEAU LAGRANGE Pomerol 1985 Cur: $22 (4/16/86) (BT)
70+ CHATEAU BOURGNEUF-VAYRON Pomerol 1985 Rel: $28 Cur: $28 (4/16/86) (BT)
70+ CLOS RENE Pomerol 1985 Rel: $17 Cur: $20 (4/16/86) (BT)
70+ CHATEAU LA CONSEILLANTE Pomerol 1985 Rel: $50 Cur: $63 (4/16/86) (BT)
70+ CHATEAU L'EGLISE-CLINET Pomerol 1985 Rel: $30 Cur: $57 (4/16/86) (BT)
70+ CHATEAU GAZIN Pomerol 1985 Rel: $21 Cur: $28 (5/15/87) (BT)
70+ CHATEAU PLINCE Pomerol 1985 Rel: $17 Cur: $17 (5/15/87) (BT)
60+ CHATEAU LE BON-PASTEUR Pomerol 1985 Rel: $20 Cur: $49 (4/16/86) (BT)
60+ CHATEAU LE GAY Pomerol 1985 Cur: $26 (4/16/86) (BT)
56   CHATEAU LA MADELEINE Pomerol 1985 $10 (3/15/88)
50+ CHATEAU LA POINTE Pomerol 1985 Rel: $16 Cur: $16 (4/16/86) (BT)

1984
93   CHATEAU LA CONSEILLANTE Pomerol 1984 Rel: $26 Cur: $38 (3/31/87)
90   CHATEAU PETRUS Pomerol 1984 Rel: $125 Cur: $187 (9/15/87)
86   CHATEAU LE BON-PASTEUR Pomerol 1984 Rel: $12.50 Cur: $23 (6/15/87)
83   CHATEAU L'ENCLOS Pomerol 1984 Rel: $16 Cur: $20 (3/31/87)
83   CHATEAU PETRUS Pomerol 1984 Rel: $125 Cur: $187 (2/15/91) (JS)
79   CHATEAU L'EVANGILE Pomerol 1984 Rel: $31 Cur: $75 (2/15/87)

1983
94   CHATEAU LA CROIX DE GAY Pomerol 1983 Rel: $16 Cur: $23 (7/01/86) CS
94   CHATEAU PETRUS Pomerol 1983 Rel: $125 Cur: $285 (2/15/87)
92   CHATEAU L'EVANGILE Pomerol 1983 Rel: $42 Cur: $51 (3/16/86)
91   CLOS RENE Pomerol 1983 Rel: $17 Cur: $23 (3/16/86)
91   CHATEAU PETRUS Pomerol 1983 Rel: $125 Cur: $285 (2/15/91) (JS)
88   CHATEAU L'EGLISE-CLINET Pomerol 1983 Rel: $19 Cur: $24 (3/16/86)
88   CHATEAU TROTANOY Pomerol 1983 Cur: $58 (10/15/88) (JS)
86   CHATEAU LE BON-PASTEUR Pomerol 1983 Rel: $22.50 Cur: $35 (6/16/86)
84   CHATEAU LA CONSEILLANTE Pomerol 1983 Rel: $33 Cur: $40 (11/15/86)
84   CHATEAU LA CROIX Pomerol 1983 Rel: $14 Cur: $19 (11/30/86)
83   VIEUX CHATEAU CERTAN Pomerol 1983 Rel: $33 Cur: $36 (3/16/86)
79   CHATEAU PRIEURS DE LA COMMANDERIE Pomerol 1983 Rel: $25 Cur: $25 (9/30/86)
77   CHATEAU LA LOUBIERE Pomerol 1983 Rel: $15 Cur: $15 (6/16/86)
70   CHATEAU FEYTIT-CLINET Pomerol 1983 Rel: $13 Cur: $17 (7/16/86)

1982
96   CHATEAU LA CONSEILLANTE Pomerol 1982 Rel: $29.50 Cur: $70 (5/15/89) (TR)
96   CHATEAU PETRUS Pomerol 1982 Cur: $530 (2/15/91) (JS)
95   CHATEAU LE PIN Pomerol 1982 Cur: $217 (5/15/89) (TR)
95   CHATEAU TROTANOY Pomerol 1982 Cur: $162 (10/15/88) (JS)
94   CHATEAU LAFLEUR Pomerol 1982 Cur: $237 (5/15/89) (TR)
93   CHATEAU LA CONSEILLANTE Pomerol 1982 Rel: $29.50 Cur: $70 (2/16/85)
93   CHATEAU L'EVANGILE Pomerol 1982 Rel: $55 Cur: $85 (5/15/89) (TR)
93   CHATEAU PETRUS Pomerol 1982 Cur: $530 (5/01/89)
92   CHATEAU CERTAN DE MAY Pomerol 1982 Cur: $114 (5/15/89) (TR)
92   CHATEAU L'EGLISE-CLINET Pomerol 1982 Rel: $18 Cur: $27 (5/01/85)
92   CHATEAU LATOUR A POMEROL Pomerol 1982 Cur: $81 (5/15/89) (TR)
92   CHATEAU PETIT-VILLAGE Pomerol 1982 Cur: $48 (5/15/89) (TR)
92   CHATEAU PETRUS Pomerol 1982 Cur: $530 (5/15/89) (TR)
92   CHATEAU PLINCE Pomerol 1982 Cur: $25 (5/15/89) (TR)
91   CHATEAU LE BON-PASTEUR Pomerol 1982 Cur: $50 (5/15/89) (TR)
91   CHATEAU LA CROIX DE GAY Pomerol 1982 Rel: $16.25 Cur: $17 (5/15/89) (TR)
91   CHATEAU FEYTIT-CLINET Pomerol 1982 Rel: $14.75 Cur: $20 (5/15/89) (TR)
91   CHATEAU LA GRAVE TRIGANT DE BOISSET Pomerol 1982 Cur: $40 (5/15/89) (TR)
91   CHATEAU LAFLEUR Pomerol 1982 Cur: $237 (5/01/89)
90   CHATEAU CERTAN-GIRAUD Pomerol 1982 Cur: $37 (5/15/89) (TR)
90   CHATEAU L'EVANGILE Pomerol 1982 Rel: $55 Cur: $85 (5/01/89)
90   CHATEAU TROTANOY Pomerol 1982 Cur: $162 (5/15/89) (TR)
89   CHATEAU BEAUREGARD Pomerol 1982 Rel: $16 Cur: $21 (5/15/89) (TR)
89   CHATEAU LA CROIX Pomerol 1982 Rel: $23 Cur: $23 (5/15/89) (TR)
89   CHATEAU LE GAY Pomerol 1982 Cur: $40 (5/15/89) (TR)
89   CHATEAU NENIN Pomerol 1982 Cur: $30 (5/15/89) (TR)
89   VIEUX CHATEAU CERTAN Pomerol 1982 Rel: $29 Cur: $59 (5/15/89) (TR)
88   CLOS L'EGLISE Pomerol 1982 Cur: $27 (5/15/89) (TR)
88   CHATEAU LA FLEUR-PETRUS Pomerol 1982 Cur: $85 (5/15/89) (TR)
88   CHATEAU LA FLEUR DE GAY Pomerol 1982 Cur: $45 (5/15/89) (TR)
88   CHATEAU GAZIN Pomerol 1982 Cur: $30 (5/15/89) (TR)
88   CHATEAU LA LOUBIERE Pomerol 1982 Rel: $13 Cur: $13 (5/15/89) (TR)
88   CHATEAU DE SALES Pomerol 1982 Cur: $23 (5/15/89) (TR)
88   CHATEAU LA VIOLETTE Pomerol 1982 Cur: $25 (5/15/89) (TR)
87   CLOS RENE Pomerol 1982 Cur: $24 (5/15/89) (TR)
87   CHATEAU L'EGLISE-CLINET Pomerol 1982 Rel: $18 Cur: $27 (5/15/89) (TR)
87   CHATEAU FEYTIT-CLINET Pomerol 1982 Rel: $14.75 Cur: $20 (3/16/85)
87   CHATEAU MOULINET Pomerol 1982 Rel: $9.75 Cur: $10 (5/15/89) (TR)
86   CHATEAU LA CROIX Pomerol 1982 Rel: $23 Cur: $23 (5/01/89)
86   CHATEAU L'ENCLOS Pomerol 1982 Rel: $20 Cur: $25 (5/15/89) (TR)
86   CHATEAU MOULINET Pomerol 1982 Rel: $9.75 Cur: $10 (4/01/85)
86   CHATEAU ROUGET Pomerol 1982 Cur: $19 (5/15/89) (TR)
85   CHATEAU LA POINTE Pomerol 1982 Cur: $22 (5/15/89) (TR)
85   CHATEAU LA ROSE FIGEAC Pomerol 1982 Cur: $25 (5/15/89) (TR)
85   CHATEAU TAILLEFER Pomerol 1982 (NA) (5/15/89) (TR)
85   VIEUX CHATEAU CERTAN Pomerol 1982 Rel: $29 Cur: $59 (2/16/85)
84   CHATEAU ENCLOS-HAUT-MAZEYRES Pomerol 1982 (NA) (5/15/89) (TR)
84   CHATEAU LAGRANGE Pomerol 1982 Cur: $30 (5/15/89) (TR)
83   CHATEAU BOURGNEUF-VAYRON Pomerol 1982 Cur: $23 (5/15/89) (TR)
83   CLOS DES LITANIES Pomerol 1982 (NA) (5/15/89) (TR)
83   CLOS DU CLOCHER Pomerol 1982 Cur: $33 (5/15/89) (TR)
83   CHATEAU GOMBAUDE-GUILLOT Pomerol 1982 Cur: $28 (5/15/89) (TR)
83   CHATEAU HERMITAGE Pomerol 1982 (NA) (5/15/89) (TR)
83   CHATEAU LAFLEUR DU ROY Pomerol 1982 (NA) (5/15/89) (TR)
82   CHATEAU TAILHAS Pomerol 1982 Rel: $15 Cur: $15 (5/15/89) (TR)
82   CHATEAU VIEUX-FERRAND Pomerol 1982 (NA) (5/15/89) (TR)
80   CHATEAU LA CROIX-TOULIFAUT Pomerol 1982 (NA) (5/15/89) (TR)
78   CHATEAU CLINET Pomerol 1982 Cur: $38 (5/15/89) (TR)

1981
95   CHATEAU TROTANOY Pomerol 1981 Cur: $61 (10/15/88) (JS)
90   CHATEAU PETRUS Pomerol 1981 Cur: $310 (2/15/91) (JS)
80   CHATEAU LAFLEUR Pomerol 1981 Rel: $22 Cur: $110 (6/01/84)
72   CHATEAU LA CROIX Pomerol 1981 Rel: $13.75 Cur: $14 (5/01/89)

1980
86   CHATEAU PETRUS Pomerol 1980 Cur: $185 (2/15/91) (JS)
83   CHATEAU TROTANOY Pomerol 1980 Cur: $42 (10/15/88) (JS)

1979
96   CHATEAU LAFLEUR Pomerol 1979 Cur: $175 (10/15/89) (JS)
93   CHATEAU PETRUS Pomerol 1979 Cur: $325 (10/15/89) (JS)
91   CHATEAU LE BON-PASTEUR Pomerol 1979 Cur: $28 (10/15/89) (JS)
90   CHATEAU CERTAN DE MAY Pomerol 1979 Cur: $65 (10/15/89) (JS)
90   CHATEAU LA GRAVE TRIGANT DE BOISSET Pomerol 1979 Cur: $25 (10/15/89) (JS)
90   CHATEAU PETRUS Pomerol 1979 Cur: $325 (2/15/91) (JS)
88   CHATEAU TROTANOY Pomerol 1979 Cur: $65 (10/15/89) (JS)
87   VIEUX CHATEAU CERTAN Pomerol 1979 Cur: $48 (10/15/89) (JS)
79   CHATEAU LA VIOLETTE Pomerol 1979 Cur: $25 (10/15/89) (JS)
60   CHATEAU LA CROIX Pomerol 1979 Rel: $11 Cur: $22 (4/01/84)

1978
89   CHATEAU PETRUS Pomerol 1978 Cur: $380 (2/15/91) (JS)
83   CHATEAU TROTANOY Pomerol 1978 Cur: $70 (10/15/88) (JS)

1976
86   CHATEAU PETRUS Pomerol 1976 Cur: $290 (2/15/91) (JS)
86   CHATEAU TROTANOY Pomerol 1976 Cur: $83 (10/15/88) (JS)

1975
93   CHATEAU PETRUS Pomerol 1975 Cur: $495 (2/15/91) (JS)
84   CHATEAU TROTANOY Pomerol 1975 Cur: $138 (10/15/88) (JS)

1973
78   CHATEAU PETRUS Pomerol 1973 Cur: $240 (2/15/91) (JS)

1971
94   CHATEAU PETRUS Pomerol 1971 Cur: $475 (2/15/91) (JS)
90   CHATEAU TROTANOY Pomerol 1971 Cur: $180 (10/15/88) (JS)

1970

95   CHATEAU TROTANOY Pomerol 1970 Cur: $176 (10/15/88) (JS)
92   CHATEAU PETRUS Pomerol 1970 Cur: $550 (2/15/91) (JS)

1968

79   CHATEAU PETRUS Pomerol 1968 Cur: $200 (2/15/91) (JS)

1967

87   CHATEAU PETRUS Pomerol 1967 Cur: $310 (2/15/91) (JS)
84   CHATEAU TROTANOY Pomerol 1967 Cur: $62 (10/15/88) (JS)

1966

93   CHATEAU PETRUS Pomerol 1966 Cur: $500 (2/15/91) (JS)
92   CHATEAU TROTANOY Pomerol 1966 Cur: $144 (10/15/88) (JS)

1964

94   CHATEAU PETRUS Pomerol 1964 Cur: $575 (2/15/91) (JS)

1962

94   CHATEAU PETRUS Pomerol 1962 Cur: $565 (2/15/91) (JS)
90   CHATEAU PETRUS Pomerol 1962 Cur: $565 (11/30/87) (JS)
88   CHATEAU TROTANOY Pomerol 1962 Cur: $139 (10/15/88) (JS)
80   CHATEAU LA POINTE Pomerol 1962 Cur: $35 (11/30/87) (JS)
60   CLOS RENE Pomerol 1962 Cur: $35 (11/30/87) (JS)
60   CHATEAU LA CONSEILLANTE Pomerol 1962 Cur: $55 (11/30/87) (JS)
60   VIEUX CHATEAU CERTAN Pomerol 1962 Cur: $65 (11/30/87) (JS)

1961

100   CHATEAU PETRUS Pomerol 1961 Cur: $2,000 (2/15/91) (JS)
96   CHATEAU TROTANOY Pomerol 1961 Cur: $550 (10/15/88) (JS)
94   CHATEAU LATOUR A POMEROL Pomerol 1961 Cur: $1,100 (3/16/86) (JL)
92   CHATEAU PETRUS Pomerol 1961 Cur: $2,000 (3/16/86) (JL)
90   VIEUX CHATEAU CERTAN Pomerol 1961 Cur: $229 (3/16/86) (JL)
83   CHATEAU GAZIN Pomerol 1961 Cur: $120 (3/16/86) (JL)
77   CHATEAU L'EVANGILE Pomerol 1961 Cur: $253 (3/16/86) (JL)
63   CLOS L'EGLISE Pomerol 1961 Cur: $75 (3/16/86) (JL)

1959

97   CHATEAU PETRUS Pomerol 1959 Cur: $925 (10/15/90) (JS)
96   CHATEAU PETRUS Pomerol 1959 Cur: $925 (2/15/91) (JS)
96   CHATEAU PETRUS Pomerol 1959 Cur: $925 (12/15/88)
92   CHATEAU LA FLEUR-PETRUS Pomerol (Bottled in England) 1959 Cur: $150 (10/15/90) (JS)
92   CHATEAU TROTANOY Pomerol 1959 Cur: $192 (10/15/88) (JS)
91   VIEUX CHATEAU CERTAN Pomerol 1959 Cur: $120 (10/15/90) (JS)
90   CHATEAU LATOUR A POMEROL Pomerol 1959 Cur: $575 (10/15/90) (JS)
90   CHATEAU TROTANOY Pomerol 1959 Cur: $192 (10/15/90) (JS)
88   CLOS RENE Pomerol 1959 Cur: $50 (10/15/90) (JS)
88   CHATEAU LA CONSEILLANTE Pomerol 1959 Cur: $150 (10/15/90) (JS)
88   CHATEAU NENIN Pomerol 1959 Cur: $96 (10/15/90) (JS)
86   CHATEAU PETIT-VILLAGE Pomerol 1959 Cur: $80 (10/15/90) (JS)

1958

85   CHATEAU PETRUS Pomerol 1958 Cur: $460 (2/15/91) (JS)

1955

94   CHATEAU TROTANOY Pomerol 1955 Cur: $192 (10/15/88) (JS)
91   CHATEAU PETRUS Pomerol 1955 Cur: $575 (2/15/91) (JS)

1953

92   CHATEAU PETRUS Pomerol 1953 Cur: $780 (2/15/91) (JS)
86   CHATEAU TROTANOY Pomerol 1953 Cur: $300 (10/15/88) (JS)

1952

89   CHATEAU PETRUS Pomerol 1952 Cur: $565 (2/15/91) (JS)
83   CHATEAU TROTANOY Pomerol 1952 Cur: $138 (10/15/88) (JS)

1950

99   CHATEAU PETRUS Pomerol 1950 Cur: $850 (2/15/91) (JS)

1949

98   CHATEAU PETRUS Pomerol 1949 Cur: $1,200 (2/15/91) (JS)

1948

91   CHATEAU PETRUS Pomerol 1948 Cur: $1,200 (2/15/91) (JS)

1947

97   CHATEAU PETRUS Pomerol 1947 Cur: $1,700 (2/15/91) (JS)
80   CHATEAU TROTANOY Pomerol 1947 Cur: $550 (10/15/88) (JS)

1945

100   CHATEAU PETRUS Pomerol 1945 Cur: $2,700 (2/15/91) (JS)
98   CHATEAU TROTANOY Pomerol 1945 Cur: $500 (10/15/88) (JS)
87   CLOS L'EGLISE Pomerol 1945 Cur: $225 (3/16/86) (JL)
84   CHATEAU PETRUS Pomerol 1945 Cur: $2,700 (3/16/86) (JL)
79   CLOS RENE Pomerol 1945 Cur: $100 (3/16/86) (JL)
78   CHATEAU L'ENCLOS Pomerol 1945 Cur: $100 (3/16/86) (JL)
78   CHATEAU LA POINTE Pomerol 1945 Cur: $250 (3/16/86) (JL)
74   CHATEAU NENIN Pomerol 1945 Cur: $250 (3/16/86) (JL)
70   CHATEAU LA CROIX DE GAY Pomerol 1945 Cur: $362 (3/16/86) (JL)
64   CHATEAU LAFLEUR Pomerol 1945 Cur: $400 (3/16/86) (JL)
63   CHATEAU LA FLEUR-PETRUS Pomerol 1945 Cur: $300 (3/16/86) (JL)
58   CHATEAU LAFLEUR-GAZIN Pomerol 1945 (NA) (3/16/86) (JL)
50   VIEUX CHATEAU CERTAN Pomerol 1945 Cur: $893 (3/16/86) (JL)

1934

60   CHATEAU TROTANOY Pomerol 1934 Cur: $350 (10/15/88) (JS)

1928

95   CHATEAU TROTANOY Pomerol 1928 Cur: $600 (10/15/88) (JS)

1924

89   CHATEAU TROTANOY Pomerol 1924 Cur: $650 (10/15/88) (JS)

St.-Emilion

1990

95+   CHATEAU BEAUSEJOUR-DUFFAU-LAGARROSSE St.-Emilion 1990 (NR) (4/30/91) (BT)
95+   CHATEAU LAFLEUR-ST.-EMILION St.-Emilion 1990 (NR) (4/30/91) (BT)
90+   CHATEAU AUSONE St.-Emilion 1990 (NR) (4/30/91) (BT)
90+   CHATEAU CANON St.-Emilion 1990 (NR) (4/30/91) (BT)
90+   CHATEAU CANON-LA-GAFFELIERE St.-Emilion 1990 (NR) (4/30/91) (BT)
90+   CHATEAU CHEVAL BLANC St.-Emilion 1990 (NR) (4/30/91) (BT)
90+   CHATEAU LA DOMINIQUE St.-Emilion 1990 (NR) (4/30/91) (BT)
90+   CHATEAU MAGDELAINE St.-Emilion 1990 (NR) (4/30/91) (BT)
90+   CHATEAU PAVIE St.-Emilion 1990 (NR) (4/30/91) (BT)
90+   CHATEAU PAVIE-DECESSE St.-Emilion 1990 (NR) (4/30/91) (BT)
90+   CHATEAU TROPLONG-MONDOT St.-Emilion 1990 (NR) (4/30/91) (BT)
90+   CHATEAU TROTTEVIEILLE St.-Emilion 1990 (NR) (4/30/91) (BT)
85+   CHATEAU L'ANGELUS St.-Emilion 1990 (NR) (4/30/91) (BT)
85+   CHATEAU BELAIR St.-Emilion 1990 (NR) (4/30/91) (BT)
85+   CLOS FOURTET St.-Emilion 1990 (NR) (4/30/91) (BT)
85+   CHATEAU FIGEAC St.-Emilion 1990 (NR) (4/30/91) (BT)
85+   CHATEAU DE FRANC-MAYNE St.-Emilion 1990 (NR) (4/30/91) (BT)
85+   CHATEAU LARMANDE St.-Emilion 1990 (NR) (4/30/91) (BT)
85+   CHATEAU PUY-BLANQUET St.-Emilion 1990 (NR) (4/30/91) (BT)
80+   CHATEAU BALESTARD LA TONNELLE St.-Emilion 1990 (NR) (4/30/91) (BT)
80+   CHATEAU FONROQUE St.-Emilion 1990 (NR) (4/30/91) (BT)
80+   CHATEAU MOULIN DU CADET St.-Emilion 1990 (NR) (4/30/91) (BT)
60+   CHATEAU LA GAFFELIERE St.-Emilion 1990 (NR) (4/30/91) (BT)

1989

95+   CHATEAU AUSONE St.-Emilion 1989 (NR) (4/30/91) (BT)
95+   CHATEAU CANON-LA-GAFFELIERE St.-Emilion 1989 (NR) (4/30/91) (BT)
95+   CHATEAU CHEVAL BLANC St.-Emilion 1989 (NR) (4/30/91) (BT)
95+   CHATEAU CHEVAL BLANC St.-Emilion 1989 (NR) (4/30/90) (BT)
95+   CHATEAU CLOS DES JACOBINS St.-Emilion 1989 (NR) (4/30/90) (BT)
95+   CHATEAU FIGEAC St.-Emilion 1989 (NR) (4/30/91) (BT)
95+   CHATEAU FIGEAC St.-Emilion 1989 (NR) (4/30/90) (BT)
95+   CHATEAU LARMANDE St.-Emilion 1989 (NR) (4/30/91) (BT)
90+   CHATEAU AUSONE St.-Emilion 1989 (NR) (4/30/90) (BT)
90+   CHATEAU BEAUSEJOUR-DUFFAU-LAGARROSSE St.-Emilion 1989 (NR) (4/30/91) (BT)
90+   CHATEAU BELAIR St.-Emilion 1989 (NR) (4/30/91) (BT)
90+   CHATEAU CANON St.-Emilion 1989 (NR) (4/30/91) (BT)
90+   CLOS FOURTET St.-Emilion 1989 (NR) (4/30/91) (BT)
90+   CHATEAU LA DOMINIQUE St.-Emilion 1989 (NR) (4/30/91) (BT)
90+   CHATEAU DE FRANC-MAYNE St.-Emilion 1989 (NR) (4/30/90) (BT)
90+   CHATEAU LA GAFFELIERE St.-Emilion 1989 (NR) (4/30/91) (BT)
90+   CHATEAU HAUT-CORBIN St.-Emilion 1989 (NR) (4/30/90) (BT)
90+   CHATEAU LARMANDE St.-Emilion 1989 (NR) (4/30/91) (BT)
90+   CHATEAU TROPLONG-MONDOT St.-Emilion 1989 (NR) (4/30/91) (BT)
90+   CHATEAU TROPLONG-MONDOT St.-Emilion 1989 (NR) (4/30/90) (BT)
90+   CHATEAU TROTTEVIEILLE St.-Emilion 1989 (NR) (4/30/91) (BT)
90+   CHATEAU VILLEMAURINE St.-Emilion 1989 (NR) (4/30/91) (BT)
85+   CHATEAU L'ANGELUS St.-Emilion 1989 (NR) (4/30/91) (BT)
85+   CHATEAU BALESTARD LA TONNELLE St.-Emilion 1989 (NR) (4/30/91) (BT)
85+   CHATEAU BELAIR St.-Emilion 1989 (NR) (4/30/90) (BT)
85+   CHATEAU CANON-LA-GAFFELIERE St.-Emilion 1989 (NR) (4/30/91) (BT)
85+   CHATEAU CAP DE MOURLIN St.-Emilion 1989 (NR) (4/30/91) (BT)
85+   CLOS FOURTET St.-Emilion 1989 (NR) (4/30/90) (BT)
85+   CLOS LARCIS St.-Emilion 1989 (NR) (4/30/91) (BT)
85+   CHATEAU CLOS ST.-MARTIN St.-Emilion 1989 (NR) (4/30/91) (BT)
85+   CHATEAU DASSAULT St.-Emilion 1989 (NR) (4/30/91) (BT)
85+   CHATEAU FONPLEGADE St.-Emilion 1989 (NR) (4/30/91) (BT)
85+   CHATEAU FONROQUE St.-Emilion 1989 (NR) (4/30/91) (BT)
85+   CHATEAU FONROQUE St.-Emilion 1989 (NR) (4/30/90) (BT)
85+   CHATEAU HAUT-SARPE St.-Emilion 1989 (NR) (4/30/91) (BT)
85+   CHATEAU LAFLEUR-ST.-EMILION St.-Emilion 1989 (NR) (4/30/91) (BT)
85+   CHATEAU MAGDELAINE St.-Emilion 1989 (NR) (4/30/91) (BT)
85+   CHATEAU MOULIN DU CADET St.-Emilion 1989 (NR) (4/30/91) (BT)
85+   CHATEAU PAVIE St.-Emilion 1989 (NR) (4/30/91) (BT)
85+   CHATEAU PAVIE-DECESSE St.-Emilion 1989 (NR) (4/30/91) (BT)
85+   CHATEAU PUY-BLANQUET St.-Emilion 1989 (NR) (4/30/91) (BT)
85+   CHATEAU LA SERRE St.-Emilion 1989 (NR) (4/30/91) (BT)
85+   CHATEAU LA TOUR-DU-PIN-FIGEAC St.-Emilion 1989 (NR) (4/30/91) (BT)
85+   CHATEAU LA TOUR-FIGEAC St.-Emilion 1989 (NR) (4/30/91) (BT)
85+   CHATEAU TROTTEVIEILLE St.-Emilion 1989 (NR) (4/30/91) (BT)
80+   CHATEAU BERGAT St.-Emilion 1989 (NR) (4/30/90) (BT)
80+   CHATEAU CADET-PIOLA St.-Emilion 1989 (NR) (4/30/91) (BT)
80+   CLOS DE L'ORATOIRE St.-Emilion 1989 (NR) (4/30/91) (BT)
80+   CHATEAU LA CLUSIERE St.-Emilion 1989 (NR) (4/30/91) (BT)
80+   CHATEAU FAURIE-DE-SOUCHARD St.-Emilion 1989 (NR) (4/30/91) (BT)
80+   CHATEAU DE FRANC-MAYNE St.-Emilion 1989 (NR) (4/30/91) (BT)
80+   CHATEAU MAGDELAINE St.-Emilion 1989 (NR) (4/30/90) (BT)
80+   CHATEAU PUY-BLANQUET St.-Emilion 1989 (NR) (4/30/90) (BT)
80+   CHATEAU DU ROCHER-BELLEVUE-FIGEAC St.-Emilion 1989 (NR) (4/30/90) (BT)
75+   CHATEAU BEAUSEJOUR-DUFFAU-LAGARROSSE St.-Emilion 1989 (NR) (4/30/90) (BT)
75+   CHATEAU FLEUR-POURRET St.-Emilion 1989 (NR) (4/30/90) (BT)
75+   CHATEAU GUADET-ST.-JULIEN St.-Emilion 1989 (NR) (4/30/91) (BT)
75+   CHATEAU LAFLEUR-ST.-EMILION St.-Emilion 1989 (NR) (4/30/90) (BT)
75+   CHATEAU PETIT-FIGEAC St.-Emilion 1989 (NR) (4/30/90) (BT)
75+   CHATEAU PETIT-FAURIE-DE-SOUTARD St.-Emilion 1989 (NR) (4/30/91) (BT)
70+   CHATEAU LA GAFFELIERE St.-Emilion 1989 (NR) (4/30/90) (BT)
70+   CHATEAU LAFLEUR-POURRET St.-Emilion 1989 (NR) (4/30/91) (BT)
70+   CHATEAU PETIT-FIGEAC St.-Emilion 1989 (NR) (4/30/91) (BT)

1988

95+   CHATEAU AUSONE St.-Emilion 1988 $76 (8/31/90) (BT)
95+   CHATEAU AUSONE St.-Emilion 1988 $76 (6/30/89) (BT)
94   CHATEAU L'ARROSEE St.-Emilion 1988 $34 (3/15/91)
94   CHATEAU PAVIE-DECESSE St.-Emilion 1988 $27 (3/31/91)

FRANCE
BORDEAUX RED/ST.-EMILION

93   CHATEAU L'ANGELUS St.-Emilion 1988 $41 (3/31/91)
93   CHATEAU CHEVAL BLANC St.-Emilion 1988 $105 (12/31/90) CS
93   CHATEAU FIGEAC St.-Emilion 1988 $45 (6/30/91)
91   CHATEAU BALESTARD LA TONNELLE St.-Emilion 1988 $25 (4/30/91)
91   CHATEAU FRANC BIGAROUX St.-Emilion 1988 $24 (7/31/91)
91   CHATEAU TRIMOULET St.-Emilion 1988 $16 (6/15/91)
90   CHATEAU CANON St.-Emilion 1988 $40 (6/30/91)
90   CHATEAU CLOS DES JACOBINS St.-Emilion 1988 $26 (4/15/91)
90   CHATEAU DU TERTRE St.-Emilion 1988 $40 (6/15/91)
90   CHATEAU TERTRE-ROTEBOEUF St.-Emilion 1988 $40 (6/15/91)
90+   CHATEAU BEAUSEJOUR-DUFFAU-LAGARROSSE St.-Emilion 1988 $32 (8/31/90) (BT)
90+   CHATEAU CANON St.-Emilion 1988 $40 (6/30/89) (BT)
90+   CHATEAU CHEVAL BLANC St.-Emilion 1988 $105 (8/31/90) (BT)
90+   CHATEAU CHEVAL BLANC St.-Emilion 1988 $105 (6/30/89) (BT)
90+   CLOS FOURTET St.-Emilion 1988 $20 (6/30/89) (BT)
90+   CHATEAU CLOS ST.-MARTIN St.-Emilion 1988 (NR) (6/30/89) (BT)
90+   CHATEAU FONROQUE St.-Emilion 1988 $18 (8/31/90) (BT)
89   CHATEAU CADET-PIOLA St.-Emilion 1988 $20 (7/15/91)
89   CHATEAU GRAND-MAYNE St.-Emilion 1988 $20 (4/30/91)
89   CHATEAU PAVIE St.-Emilion 1988 $46 (3/31/91)
87   CHATEAU BEAU-SEJOUR BECOT St.-Emilion 1988 $21 (6/30/91)
87   CHATEAU BEAUSEJOUR-DUFFAU-LAGARROSSE St.-Emilion 1988 $32 (4/30/91)
87   CHATEAU GRAND-MAYNE St.-Emilion 1988 $20 (7/15/91)
87   CHATEAU DU ROCHER-BELLEVUE-FIGEAC St.-Emilion 1988 $13.50 (4/30/91)
86   CHATEAU CANON-LA-GAFFELIERE St.-Emilion 1988 $30 (6/30/91)
86   CHATEAU LA DOMINIQUE St.-Emilion 1988 $25 (6/30/91)
86   CHATEAU GRAND-PONTET St.-Emilion 1988 $21 (7/15/91)
86   CHATEAU LARMANDE St.-Emilion 1988 $23 (4/30/91)
85   CHATEAU CORMEIL-FIGEAC St.-Emilion 1988 $20 (4/30/91)
85   CHATEAU FONPLEGADE St.-Emilion 1988 $18 (6/30/91)
85   PIERRE JEAN St.-Emilion 1988 $10 (6/30/91) BB
85   CHATEAU TERTRE-DAUGAY St.-Emilion 1988 $20 (4/30/91)
85   CHATEAU TROPLONG-MONDOT St.-Emilion 1988 $21 (7/15/91)
85   CHATEAU TROTTEVIEILLE St.-Emilion 1988 $20 (4/30/91)
85+   CHATEAU BEAUSEJOUR-DUFFAU-LAGARROSSE St.-Emilion 1988 $32 (6/30/89) (BT)
85+   CHATEAU BELAIR St.-Emilion 1988 $28 (6/30/89) (BT)
85+   CHATEAU CANON St.-Emilion 1988 $40 (8/31/90) (BT)
85+   CHATEAU CANON-LA-GAFFELIERE St.-Emilion 1988 $30 (8/31/90) (BT)
85+   CHATEAU CANON-LA-GAFFELIERE St.-Emilion 1988 $30 (6/30/89) (BT)
85+   CLOS FOURTET St.-Emilion 1988 $20 (8/31/90) (BT)
85+   CHATEAU FIGEAC St.-Emilion 1988 $45 (8/31/90) (BT)
85+   CHATEAU FIGEAC St.-Emilion 1988 $45 (6/30/89) (BT)
85+   CHATEAU DE FRANC-MAYNE St.-Emilion 1988 $15 (8/31/90) (BT)
85+   CHATEAU LARMANDE St.-Emilion 1988 $23 (8/31/90) (BT)
85+   CHATEAU MAGDELAINE St.-Emilion 1988 $50 (8/31/90) (BT)
85+   CHATEAU PETIT-FIGEAC St.-Emilion 1988 $17 (8/31/90) (BT)
84   CHATEAU CAP DE MOURLIN St.-Emilion 1988 $20 (4/30/91)
84   CHATEAU CHAUVIN St.-Emilion 1988 $20 (6/30/91)
84   CHATEAU LA GAFFELIERE St.-Emilion 1988 $36 (4/30/91)
83   CHATEAU DASSAULT St.-Emilion 1988 $16 (7/15/91)
83   CHATEAU DE FRANC-MAYNE St.-Emilion 1988 $15 (7/15/91)
83   CHATEAU HAUT-SARPE St.-Emilion 1988 $16 (6/30/91)
82   CHATEAU LARCIS-DUCASSE St.-Emilion 1988 $20 (4/30/91)
82   CHATEAU PETIT-FAURIE-DE-SOUTARD St.-Emilion 1988 $20 (4/30/91)
81   COUVENT DES JACOBINS St.-Emilion 1988 $28 (3/31/91)
81   CHATEAU DESTIEUX St.-Emilion 1988 $19 (6/30/91)
80   CHATEAU LA SERRE St.-Emilion 1988 $18 (6/15/91)
80+   CHATEAU L'ANGELUS St.-Emilion 1988 $41 (6/30/89) (BT)
80+   CHATEAU BALESTARD LA TONNELLE St.-Emilion 1988 $25 (6/30/89) (BT)
80+   CHATEAU BELAIR St.-Emilion 1988 $28 (8/31/90) (BT)
80+   CHATEAU CAP DE MOURLIN St.-Emilion 1988 $20 (6/30/89) (BT)
80+   CHATEAU FONROQUE St.-Emilion 1988 $18 (6/30/89) (BT)
80+   CHATEAU LA GAFFELIERE St.-Emilion 1988 $36 (6/30/89) (BT)
80+   CHATEAU HAUT-SARPE St.-Emilion 1988 $16 (6/30/89) (BT)
80+   CHATEAU LARMANDE St.-Emilion 1988 $23 (6/30/89) (BT)
80+   CHATEAU MOULIN DU CADET St.-Emilion 1988 (NR) (6/30/89) (BT)
80+   CHATEAU PAVIE St.-Emilion 1988 $46 (6/30/89) (BT)
80+   CHATEAU LA SERRE St.-Emilion 1988 $18 (6/30/89) (BT)
80+   CHATEAU LA TOUR-DU-PIN-FIGEAC St.-Emilion 1988 $24 (6/30/89) (BT)
80+   CHATEAU TROPLONG-MONDOT St.-Emilion 1988 $21 (8/31/90) (BT)
80+   CHATEAU TROPLONG-MONDOT St.-Emilion 1988 $21 (6/30/89) (BT)
80+   CHATEAU TROTTEVIEILLE St.-Emilion 1988 $20 (6/30/89) (BT)
79   CHATEAU TERTRE-ROTEBOEUF St.-Emilion 1988 $40 (3/31/91)
78   CHATEAU JACQUES-BLANC St.-Emilion Cuvée du Maitre 1988 $23 (4/30/91)
77   CHATEAU LA TOUR-DU-PIN-FIGEAC St.-Emilion 1988 $24 (7/15/91)
75+   CHATEAU CADET-PIOLA St.-Emilion 1988 $20 (6/30/89) (BT)
75+   CLOS DE L'ORATOIRE St.-Emilion 1988 (NR) (6/30/89) (BT)
75+   CHATEAU LA DOMINIQUE St.-Emilion 1988 $25 (6/30/89) (BT)
75+   CHATEAU FAURIE-DE-SOUCHARD St.-Emilion 1988 $22 (6/30/89) (BT)
75+   CHATEAU FLEUR-POURRET St.-Emilion 1988 (NR) (8/31/90) (BT)
75+   CHATEAU FONPLEGADE St.-Emilion 1988 $18 (6/30/89) (BT)
75+   CHATEAU GUADET-ST.-JULIEN St.-Emilion 1988 (NR) (6/30/89) (BT)
75+   CHATEAU LARCIS-DUCASSE St.-Emilion 1988 $20 (6/30/89) (BT)
75+   CHATEAU MAGDELAINE St.-Emilion 1988 $50 (6/30/89) (BT)

75+   CHATEAU PAVIE-DECESSE St.-Emilion 1988 $27 (6/30/89) (BT)
75+   CHATEAU PUY-BLANQUET St.-Emilion 1988 $15 (6/30/89) (BT)
72   CHATEAU CORBIN-MICHOTTE St.-Emilion 1988 $15 (7/15/91)
70+   CHATEAU PETIT-FAURIE-DE-SOUTARD St.-Emilion 1988 $20 (6/30/89) (BT)
70+   CHATEAU LA TOUR-FIGEAC St.-Emilion 1988 $17 (6/30/89) (BT)
65+   CHATEAU LA CLUSIERE St.-Emilion 1988 $20 (6/30/89) (BT)
65+   CHATEAU DASSAULT St.-Emilion 1988 $16 (6/30/89) (BT)

1987

90+   CHATEAU CANON St.-Emilion 1987 Rel: $32 Cur: $32 (6/30/88) (BT)
89   LE PETIT CHEVAL St.-Emilion 1987 $35 (3/31/91)
87   CHATEAU CHEVAL BLANC St.-Emilion 1987 Rel: $57 Cur: $57 (5/15/90)
85   CHATEAU L'ANGELUS St.-Emilion 1987 Rel: $30 Cur: $30 (5/15/90)
85+   CHATEAU AUSONE St.-Emilion 1987 Rel: $55 Cur: $55 (6/30/89) (BT)
85+   CHATEAU AUSONE St.-Emilion 1987 Rel: $55 Cur: $55 (6/30/88) (BT)
85+   CHATEAU BEAUSEJOUR-DUFFAU-LAGARROSSE St.-Emilion 1987 Rel: $20 Cur: $20 (6/30/89) (BT)
85+   CHATEAU BELAIR St.-Emilion 1987 Rel: $25 Cur: $25 (6/30/89) (BT)
85+   CHATEAU CANON St.-Emilion 1987 Rel: $32 Cur: $32 (6/30/89) (BT)
85+   CHATEAU PAVIE St.-Emilion 1987 Rel: $30 Cur: $31 (6/30/89) (BT)
84   CHATEAU FIGEAC St.-Emilion 1987 Rel: $35 Cur: $35 (5/15/90)
83   CHATEAU TERTRE-ROTEBOEUF St.-Emilion 1987 Rel: $15 Cur: $23 (2/15/90)
82   CHATEAU L'ARROSEE St.-Emilion 1987 Rel: $25 Cur: $25 (5/15/90)
82   CHATEAU CHEVAL BLANC St.-Emilion 1987 Rel: $57 Cur: $57 (2/15/91) (JS)
82   CHATEAU PAVIE St.-Emilion 1987 Rel: $30 Cur: $31 (5/15/90)
81   CHATEAU DU BEAU-VALLON St.-Emilion 1987 $10 (5/15/90)
81   CHATEAU CHEVAL BLANC St.-Emilion 1987 Rel: $57 Cur: $57 (3/31/90)
80+   CHATEAU L'ANGELUS St.-Emilion 1987 Rel: $30 Cur: $30 (6/30/89) (BT)
80+   CHATEAU BELAIR St.-Emilion 1987 Rel: $25 Cur: $25 (6/30/88) (BT)
80+   CHATEAU CHEVAL BLANC St.-Emilion 1987 Rel: $57 Cur: $57 (6/30/89) (BT)
80+   CHATEAU CHEVAL BLANC St.-Emilion 1987 Rel: $57 Cur: $57 (6/30/88) (BT)
80+   CLOS FOURTET St.-Emilion 1987 Rel: $20 Cur: $20 (6/30/89) (BT)
80+   CHATEAU CLOS ST.-MARTIN St.-Emilion 1987 (NR) (6/30/89) (BT)
80+   CHATEAU LA DOMINIQUE St.-Emilion 1987 Rel: $20 Cur: $20 (6/30/89) (BT)
80+   CHATEAU FIGEAC St.-Emilion 1987 Rel: $35 Cur: $35 (6/30/89) (BT)
80+   CHATEAU FIGEAC St.-Emilion 1987 Rel: $35 Cur: $35 (6/30/88) (BT)
80+   CHATEAU LARMANDE St.-Emilion 1987 Rel: $17 Cur: $17 (6/30/89) (BT)
80+   CHATEAU MAGDELAINE St.-Emilion 1987 Rel: $32 Cur: $32 (6/30/89) (BT)
80+   CHATEAU MAGDELAINE St.-Emilion 1987 Cur: $32 (6/30/88) (BT)
80+   CHATEAU PAVIE St.-Emilion 1987 Rel: $30 Cur: $31 (6/30/88) (BT)
80+   CHATEAU LA TOUR-DU-PIN-FIGEAC St.-Emilion 1987 Rel: $17 Cur: $17 (6/30/89) (BT)
80+   CHATEAU TROPLONG-MONDOT St.-Emilion 1987 Rel: $16 Cur: $16 (6/30/89) (BT)
80+   CHATEAU TROPLONG-MONDOT St.-Emilion 1987 Rel: $16 Cur: $16 (6/30/88) (BT)
80+   CHATEAU TROTTEVIEILLE St.-Emilion 1987 Rel: $15 Cur: $15 (6/30/89) (BT)
79   CHATEAU CANON St.-Emilion 1987 Rel: $32 Cur: $32 (5/15/90)
77   CLOS J. KANON St.-Emilion 1987 $10 (5/15/90)
75+   CHATEAU L'ANGELUS St.-Emilion 1987 Rel: $30 Cur: $30 (6/30/88) (BT)
75+   CHATEAU BALESTARD LA TONNELLE St.-Emilion 1987 Rel: $20 Cur: $20 (6/30/89) (BT)
75+   CHATEAU BALESTARD LA TONNELLE St.-Emilion 1987 Rel: $20 Cur: $20 (6/30/88) (BT)
75+   CHATEAU CANON-LA-GAFFELIERE St.-Emilion 1987 Cur: $15 (6/30/88) (BT)
75+   CHATEAU CAP DE MOURLIN St.-Emilion 1987 Rel: $15 Cur: $15 (6/30/88) (BT)
75+   CLOS DE L'ORATOIRE St.-Emilion 1987 (NR) (6/30/89) (BT)
75+   CHATEAU DASSAULT St.-Emilion 1987 Rel: $14 Cur: $14 (6/30/89) (BT)
75+   CHATEAU FLEUR-POURRET St.-Emilion 1987 (NR) (6/30/88) (BT)
75+   CHATEAU FONROQUE St.-Emilion 1987 Rel: $15 Cur: $15 (6/30/89) (BT)
75+   CHATEAU FONROQUE St.-Emilion 1987 Rel: $15 Cur: $15 (6/30/88) (BT)
75+   CHATEAU DE FRANC-MAYNE St.-Emilion 1987 (NR) (6/30/88) (BT)
75+   CHATEAU LA GAFFELIERE St.-Emilion 1987 Rel: $20 Cur: $20 (6/30/89) (BT)
75+   CHATEAU HAUT-SARPE St.-Emilion 1987 Rel: $14 Cur: $14 (6/30/89) (BT)
75+   CHATEAU LARCIS-DUCASSE St.-Emilion 1987 Rel: $17 Cur: $17 (6/30/89) (BT)
75+   CHATEAU LARMANDE St.-Emilion 1987 Rel: $17 Cur: $17 (6/30/88) (BT)
75+   CHATEAU MOULIN DU CADET St.-Emilion 1987 (NR) (6/30/89) (BT)
75+   CHATEAU PAVIE-DECESSE St.-Emilion 1987 Rel: $21 Cur: $21 (6/30/89) (BT)
75+   CHATEAU PAVIE-DECESSE St.-Emilion 1987 Rel: $21 Cur: $21 (6/30/88) (BT)
75+   CHATEAU PETIT-FAURIE-DE-SOUTARD St.-Emilion 1987 Rel: $15 Cur: $15 (6/30/89) (BT)
75+   CHATEAU PUY-BLANQUET St.-Emilion 1987 Rel: $14 Cur: $14 (6/30/88) (BT)
75+   CHATEAU LA SERRE St.-Emilion 1987 Rel: $15 Cur: $15 (6/30/89) (BT)
75+   CHATEAU LA TOUR-FIGEAC St.-Emilion 1987 Rel: $14 Cur: $14 (6/30/89) (BT)
75+   CHATEAU VILLEMAURINE St.-Emilion 1987 (NR) (6/30/88) (BT)
73   CHATEAU CLOS DES JACOBINS St.-Emilion 1987 Rel: $23.50 Cur: $24 (5/15/90)
70+   CHATEAU CADET-PIOLA St.-Emilion 1987 Rel: $16 Cur: $16 (6/30/89) (BT)
70+   CHATEAU CANON-LA-GAFFELIERE St.-Emilion 1987 Cur: $15 (6/30/89) (BT)
70+   CHATEAU CAP DE MOURLIN St.-Emilion 1987 Rel: $15 Cur: $15 (6/30/89) (BT)
70+   CHATEAU FAURIE-DE-SOUCHARD St.-Emilion 1987 $19 (6/30/89) (BT)
70+   CHATEAU FONPLEGADE St.-Emilion 1987 Rel: $15 Cur: $15 (6/30/89) (BT)
70+   CHATEAU FONPLEGADE St.-Emilion 1987 Rel: $15 Cur: $15 (6/30/88) (BT)
70+   CHATEAU GUADET-ST.-JULIEN St.-Emilion 1987 (NR) (6/30/89) (BT)
70+   CHATEAU LARCIS-DUCASSE St.-Emilion 1987 Rel: $17 Cur: $17 (6/30/88) (BT)

1986

98   CHATEAU CHEVAL BLANC St.-Emilion 1986 Rel: $80 Cur: $85 (6/30/89) CS
95   CHATEAU CANON St.-Emilion 1986 Rel: $45 Cur: $45 (5/15/89) (TM)
95   CHATEAU LA DOMINIQUE St.-Emilion 1986 Rel: $29 Cur: $29 (6/30/89)
95+   CHATEAU CANON St.-Emilion 1986 Rel: $45 Cur: $45 (6/30/88) (BT)
95+   CHATEAU CHEVAL BLANC St.-Emilion 1986 Rel: $80 Cur: $85 (6/30/88) (BT)
94   CHATEAU L'ANGELUS St.-Emilion 1986 Rel: $26 Cur: $30 (6/30/89)
94   CHATEAU CLOS DES JACOBINS St.-Emilion 1986 Rel: $34 Cur: $34 (6/30/89)
94   CHATEAU MAGDELAINE St.-Emilion 1986 Rel: $48 Cur: $48 (2/15/90)
93   CHATEAU CANON St.-Emilion 1986 Rel: $45 Cur: $45 (6/30/89)
93   CHATEAU CHEVAL BLANC St.-Emilion 1986 Rel: $80 Cur: $85 (2/15/91) (JS)
93   CHATEAU PAVIE St.-Emilion 1986 Rel: $35 Cur: $35 (6/30/89)
93   CHATEAU PAVIE-DECESSE St.-Emilion 1986 Rel: $33 Cur: $33 (6/30/89)
91   CHATEAU BEAUSEJOUR-DUFFAU-LAGARROSSE St.-Emilion 1986 Rel: $27 Cur: $29 (6/30/89)
91   CHATEAU CANON-LA-GAFFELIERE St.-Emilion 1986 Rel: $21 Cur: $28 (6/30/89)
91   CLOS J. KANON St.-Emilion 1986 $17 (11/15/89)
91   CHATEAU LARMANDE St.-Emilion 1986 Rel: $19 Cur: $26 (6/30/89)

90 CHATEAU TERTRE-ROTEBOEUF St.-Emilion 1986 Rel: $25 Cur: $34 (6/30/89)
90+ CHATEAU AUSONE St.-Emilion 1986 Rel: $90 Cur: $98 (6/30/88) (BT)
90+ CHATEAU AUSONE St.-Emilion 1986 Rel: $90 Cur: $98 (5/15/87) (BT)
90+ CHATEAU CANON-LA-GAFFELIERE St.-Emilion 1986 Rel: $21 Cur: $28 (5/15/87) (BT)
90+ CHATEAU FIGEAC St.-Emilion 1986 Rel: $45 Cur: $45 (6/30/88) (BT)
90+ CHATEAU MAGDELAINE St.-Emilion 1986 Rel: $48 Cur: $48 (6/30/88) (BT)
90+ CHATEAU MAGDELAINE St.-Emilion 1986 Rel: $48 Cur: $48 (5/15/87) (BT)
89 CHATEAU FIGEAC St.-Emilion 1986 Rel: $45 Cur: $45 (6/30/89)
88 CHATEAU CORBIN St.-Emilion 1986 $15 (6/30/89)
88 CHATEAU TROPLONG-MONDOT St.-Emilion 1986 Rel: $20 Cur: $23 (6/30/89)
87 CHATEAU L'ARROSEE St.-Emilion 1986 Rel: $31 Cur: $37 (2/15/89)
87 CHATEAU CAP DE MOURLIN St.-Emilion 1986 Rel: $18 Cur: $18 (6/30/89)
87 CHATEAU GRAND-MAYNE St.-Emilion 1986 $16 (6/30/89)
86 CHATEAU CANON St.-Emilion 1986 Rel: $45 Cur: $45 (3/31/90)
86 CHATEAU FOMBRAUGE St.-Emilion 1986 Rel: $19 Cur: $19 (6/30/89)
85 CHATEAU AUSONE St.-Emilion 1986 Rel: $90 Cur: $98 (6/30/89)
85+ CHATEAU BELAIR St.-Emilion 1986 Rel: $26 Cur: $35 (6/30/88) (BT)
85+ CHATEAU PAVIE St.-Emilion 1986 Rel: $35 Cur: $35 (6/30/88) (BT)
85+ CHATEAU PAVIE-DECESSE St.-Emilion 1986 Rel: $33 Cur: $33 (6/30/88) (BT)
85+ CHATEAU TROPLONG-MONDOT St.-Emilion 1986 Rel: $20 Cur: $23 (6/30/88) (BT)
84 CHATEAU DU BEAU-VALLON St.-Emilion 1986 $10 (9/30/89)
84 CHATEAU DU CAUZE St.-Emilion 1986 $15 (6/30/89)
82 CHATEAU BELAIR St.-Emilion 1986 Rel: $26 Cur: $35 (3/31/90)
82 CLOS LABARDE St.-Emilion 1986 $15 (6/30/89)
82 CHATEAU LA FLEUR St.-Emilion 1986 $13.50 (2/15/90)
80 CLOS FOURTET St.-Emilion 1986 Rel: $29 Cur: $35 (6/30/89)
80 CHATEAU PETIT-FAURIE-DE-SOUTARD St.-Emilion 1986 Rel: $15 Cur: $15 (6/30/89)
80+ CHATEAU L'ANGELUS St.-Emilion 1986 Rel: $26 Cur: $30 (6/30/88) (BT)
80+ CHATEAU L'ANGELUS St.-Emilion 1986 Rel: $26 Cur: $30 (5/15/87) (BT)
80+ CHATEAU BALESTARD LA TONNELLE St.-Emilion 1986 Rel: $22 Cur: $22 (6/30/88) (BT)
80+ CHATEAU BELAIR St.-Emilion 1986 Rel: $26 Cur: $35 (5/15/87) (BT)
80+ CHATEAU CANON-LA-GAFFELIERE St.-Emilion 1986 Rel: $21 Cur: $28 (6/30/88) (BT)
80+ CHATEAU CAP DE MOURLIN St.-Emilion 1986 Rel: $18 Cur: $18 (6/30/88) (BT)
80+ CHATEAU CLOS DES JACOBINS St.-Emilion 1986 Rel: $34 Cur: $34 (5/15/87) (BT)
80+ CHATEAU FONPLEGADE St.-Emilion 1986 Rel: $15 Cur: $15 (6/30/88) (BT)
80+ CHATEAU FONROQUE St.-Emilion 1986 Cur: $19 (6/30/88) (BT)
80+ CHATEAU FONROQUE St.-Emilion 1986 Cur: $19 (5/15/87) (BT)
80+ CHATEAU LA GAFFELIERE St.-Emilion 1986 Cur: $22 (5/15/87) (BT)
80+ CHATEAU LARCIS-DUCASSE St.-Emilion 1986 Rel: $20 Cur: $25 (6/30/88) (BT)
80+ CHATEAU LARMANDE St.-Emilion 1986 Rel: $19 Cur: $26 (6/30/88) (BT)
80+ CHATEAU LARMANDE St.-Emilion 1986 Rel: $19 Cur: $26 (5/15/87) (BT)
80+ CHATEAU PUY-BLANQUET St.-Emilion 1986 Rel: $16 Cur: $16 (6/30/88) (BT)
80+ CHATEAU DU ROCHER-BELLEVUE-FIGEAC St.-Emilion 1986 Rel: $12 Cur: $16 (5/15/87) (BT)
80+ CHATEAU TROPLONG-MONDOT St.-Emilion 1986 Rel: $20 Cur: $23 (5/15/87) (BT)
80+ CHATEAU VILLEMAURINE St.-Emilion 1986 (NR) (6/30/88) (BT)
79 CHATEAU BEAU-SEJOUR BECOT St.-Emilion 1986 Rel: $22 Cur: $22 (7/31/89)
79 CHATEAU ROLAND St.-Emilion 1986 $11.25 (6/30/89)
75 CHATEAU CHAUVIN St.-Emilion 1986 $15 (6/30/89)
75 CHATEAU CORMEIL-FIGEAC St.-Emilion 1986 $12 (6/30/89)
72 CHATEAU GRAND-BARRAIL-LAMARZELLE-FIGEAC St.-Emilion 1986 Rel: $15 Cur: $15 (6/30/89)
70+ CHATEAU FONPLEGADE St.-Emilion 1986 Rel: $15 Cur: $15 (5/15/87) (BT)
70+ CHATEAU HAUT-CORBIN St.-Emilion 1986 Rel: $14 Cur: $14 (5/15/87) (BT)
70+ CHATEAU LE JURAT St.-Emilion 1986 (NR) (5/15/87) (BT)
70+ CHATEAU PUY-BLANQUET St.-Emilion 1986 Rel: $16 Cur: $16 (5/15/87) (BT)
65+ CHATEAU DE FRANC-MAYNE St.-Emilion 1986 Rel: $16 Cur: $16 (6/30/88) (BT)

1985

98 CHATEAU CHEVAL BLANC St.-Emilion 1985 Rel: $80 Cur: $91 (2/15/91) (JS)
95 CHATEAU FIGEAC St.-Emilion 1985 Rel: $37 Cur: $53 (5/15/88)
94 CHATEAU L'ANGELUS St.-Emilion 1985 Rel: $26 Cur: $34 (3/31/88) CS
94 CHATEAU AUSONE St.-Emilion 1985 Rel: $100 Cur: $121 (11/30/87) (TR)
94 CHATEAU CHEVAL BLANC St.-Emilion 1985 Rel: $80 Cur: $91 (2/29/88)
93 CHATEAU LARMANDE St.-Emilion 1985 Rel: $23 Cur: $23 (5/15/88)
92 CHATEAU PAVIE St.-Emilion 1985 Rel: $38 Cur: $38 (5/15/88)
91 CHATEAU CANON St.-Emilion 1985 Rel: $34 Cur: $47 (5/15/89) (TM)
91 CHATEAU LA SERRE St.-Emilion 1985 Rel: $15 Cur: $15 (5/15/88)
90 CHATEAU CANON St.-Emilion 1985 Rel: $34 Cur: $47 (3/31/88)
90 CHATEAU MAGDELAINE St.-Emilion 1985 Rel: $40 Cur: $41 (6/30/88)
90+ CHATEAU AUSONE St.-Emilion 1985 Rel: $100 Cur: $121 (5/15/87) (BT)
90+ CHATEAU AUSONE St.-Emilion 1985 Rel: $100 Cur: $121 (4/16/86) (BT)
90+ CHATEAU CANON-LA-GAFFELIERE St.-Emilion 1985 Rel: $20 Cur: $37 (5/15/87) (BT)
90+ CHATEAU MAGDELAINE St.-Emilion 1985 Rel: $40 Cur: $41 (5/15/87) (BT)
89 CHATEAU CLOS DES JACOBINS St.-Emilion 1985 Rel: $31 Cur: $31 (9/30/88)
89 CHATEAU PAVIE-DECESSE St.-Emilion 1985 Rel: $27 Cur: $27 (3/31/88)
89 CHATEAU DE ROUFFLIAC St.-Emilion 1985 $15 (9/30/88)
89 CHATEAU TERTRE-ROTEBOEUF St.-Emilion 1985 Rel: $23 Cur: $25 (6/30/88)
88 CHATEAU TROPLONG-MONDOT St.-Emilion 1985 Rel: $21 Cur: $21 (6/30/88)
87 CHATEAU AUSONE St.-Emilion 1985 Rel: $100 Cur: $121 (5/31/88)
87 CHATEAU LA CLOTTE St.-Emilion 1985 $27 (5/15/88)
87 CHATEAU FOMBRAUGE St.-Emilion 1985 Rel: $15 Cur: $17 (5/15/88)
86 CHATEAU CORBIN St.-Emilion 1985 $15 (5/31/88)
85 CHATEAU L'ARROSEE St.-Emilion 1985 Rel: $24 Cur: $40 (2/29/88)
85 BARON PHILIPPE DE ROTHSCHILD St.-Emilion 1985 $10.50 (9/30/88)
85 CHATEAU SOUTARD St.-Emilion 1985 Rel: $20 Cur: $20 (5/15/88)
84 COUVENT DES JACOBINS St.-Emilion 1985 Rel: $27 Cur: $27 (3/31/88)
84 CHATEAU DESTIEUX St.-Emilion 1985 $14 (3/31/88)
84 CHATEAU FUMET-PEYROUTAS St.-Emilion 1985 $7.25 (7/31/88) BB
84 CHATEAU LEYDET-FIGEAC St.-Emilion 1985 $18 (9/30/88)
83 CHATEAU LA DOMINIQUE St.-Emilion 1985 Rel: $30 Cur: $32 (3/31/88)
82 CHATEAU DU BEAU-VALLON St.-Emilion 1985 $8.50 (9/30/88)
82 CHATEAU TOUR-BALADOZ St.-Emilion 1985 $11.50 (2/29/88)
80+ CHATEAU BELAIR St.-Emilion 1985 Cur: $33 (4/16/86) (BT)
80+ CHATEAU CAP DE MOURLIN St.-Emilion 1985 Rel: $15 Cur: $15 (5/15/87) (BT)
80+ CHATEAU FIGEAC St.-Emilion 1985 Rel: $37 Cur: $53 (5/15/87) (BT)
80+ CHATEAU FONROQUE St.-Emilion 1985 Cur: $23 (5/15/87) (BT)
80+ CHATEAU LA GAFFELIERE St.-Emilion 1985 Cur: $35 (5/15/87) (BT)
80+ CHATEAU TERTRE-DAUGAY St.-Emilion 1985 Rel: $15 Cur: $18 (5/15/87) (BT)
79 CHATEAU TOUR-GRAND-FAURIE St.-Emilion 1985 $9.75 (2/15/89)
70+ CHATEAU CANON St.-Emilion 1985 Rel: $34 Cur: $47 (4/16/86) (BT)
70+ CHATEAU FONPLEGADE St.-Emilion 1985 Rel: $15 Cur: $15 (5/15/87) (BT)
70+ CHATEAU FONROQUE St.-Emilion 1985 Cur: $23 (4/16/86) (BT)
60+ CHATEAU PUY-BLANQUET St.-Emilion 1985 Rel: $13 Cur: $13 (4/16/86) (BT)

1984

91 CHATEAU CHEVAL BLANC St.-Emilion 1984 Rel: $69 Cur: $69 (3/31/87)
88 CHATEAU CHEVAL BLANC St.-Emilion 1984 Rel: $69 Cur: $69 (5/15/87)
85 CHATEAU CHEVAL BLANC St.-Emilion 1984 Rel: $69 Cur: $69 (2/15/91) (HS)
83 CHATEAU CLOS DES JACOBINS St.-Emilion 1984 Rel: $20 Cur: $20 (5/15/87)
83 CHATEAU FIGEAC St.-Emilion 1984 Rel: $26 Cur: $30 (3/31/87)
78 CHATEAU CHEVAL BLANC St.-Emilion 1984 Rel: $69 Cur: $69 (2/15/91) (JS)

1983

96 CHATEAU AUSONE St.-Emilion 1983 Cur: $123 (11/30/87) (TR)
96 CHATEAU CHEVAL BLANC St.-Emilion 1983 Rel: $63 Cur: $80 (2/15/91) (JS)
95 COUVENT DES JACOBINS St.-Emilion 1983 Rel: $18 Cur: $27 (3/16/86)
92 CHATEAU L'ANGELUS St.-Emilion 1983 Rel: $22 Cur: $24 (3/16/86)
92 CHATEAU PAVIE St.-Emilion 1983 Rel: $23 Cur: $27 (3/16/86)
92 CHATEAU PAVIE-DECESSE St.-Emilion 1983 Rel: $17 Cur: $17 (3/16/86)
90 CHATEAU BERLIQUET St.-Emilion 1983 $12 (12/31/86)
88 CHATEAU CANON St.-Emilion 1983 Rel: $31 Cur: $42 (5/15/89) (TM)
88 CHATEAU LA DOMINIQUE St.-Emilion 1983 Rel: $18 Cur: $29 (5/16/86)
87 CHATEAU L'ARROSEE St.-Emilion 1983 Rel: $20 Cur: $33 (5/16/86)
87 CHATEAU JEAN FAURE St.-Emilion 1983 $17 (3/31/87)
87 CHATEAU LARMANDE St.-Emilion 1983 Rel: $13 Cur: $16 (3/16/86)
87 CHATEAU MAUVINON St.-Emilion 1983 $10 (11/30/86)
85 CHATEAU CHEVAL BLANC St.-Emilion 1983 Rel: $63 Cur: $80 (3/16/86)
81 CHATEAU TERTRE-ROTEBOEUF St.-Emilion 1983 Rel: $11.50 Cur: $20 (5/16/86)
79 CHATEAU LA COMMANDERIE St.-Emilion 1983 $10.50 (1/01/86)
77 CHATEAU FIGEAC St.-Emilion 1983 Rel: $37 Cur: $43 (5/16/86)
76 CHATEAU PUY-BLANQUET St.-Emilion 1983 Rel: $9.50 Cur: $10 (12/31/86)
73 CHATEAU CANON St.-Emilion 1983 Rel: $31 Cur: $42 (3/16/86)
73 CHATEAU DU ROCHER St.-Emilion 1983 $11 (5/15/87)
68 CHATEAU LA CLOTTE St.-Emilion 1983 $12 (5/16/86)
64 CHATEAU LAROQUE St.-Emilion 1983 $12.50 (2/15/88)

1982

97 CHATEAU CHEVAL BLANC St.-Emilion 1982 Rel: $69 Cur: $143 (2/15/91) (JS)
96 CHATEAU CHEVAL BLANC St.-Emilion 1982 Rel: $69 Cur: $143 (5/15/89) (TR)
96 CHATEAU CHEVAL BLANC St.-Emilion 1982 Rel: $69 Cur: $143 (5/01/85)
96 CHATEAU CHEVAL BLANC St.-Emilion 1982 Rel: $69 Cur: $143 (2/16/85) CS
95 CHATEAU MAGDELAINE St.-Emilion 1982 Cur: $53 (5/15/89) (TR)
94 CHATEAU CANON St.-Emilion 1982 Cur: $60 (5/15/89) (TR)
93 CHATEAU AUSONE St.-Emilion 1982 Cur: $167 (5/15/89) (TR)
92 CHATEAU FIGEAC St.-Emilion 1982 Cur: $54 (5/15/89) (TR)
92 CHATEAU FIGEAC St.-Emilion 1982 Cur: $54 (5/01/85)
91 CHATEAU L'ARROSEE St.-Emilion 1982 Cur: $40 (5/15/89) (TR)
91 CHATEAU CANON St.-Emilion 1982 Cur: $60 (5/15/89) (TM)
91 CHATEAU LARMANDE St.-Emilion 1982 Cur: $13 (5/15/89) (TR)
90 CHATEAU BEAUSEJOUR-DUFFAU-LAGARROSSE St.-Emilion 1982 Cur: $30 (5/15/89) (TR)
90 CHATEAU BELAIR St.-Emilion 1982 Cur: $26 (5/15/89) (TR)
90 CHATEAU DASSAULT St.-Emilion 1982 Cur: $20 (5/15/89) (TR)
90 CHATEAU PAVIE St.-Emilion 1982 Rel: $23.50 Cur: $37 (3/16/85)
89 CHATEAU PAVIE St.-Emilion 1982 Rel: $23.50 Cur: $37 (5/15/89) (TR)
89 CHATEAU PAVIE-DECESSE St.-Emilion 1982 Cur: $30 (5/15/89) (TR)
89 CHATEAU PAVIE MACQUIN St.-Emilion 1982 (NA) (5/15/89) (TR)
89 CHATEAU LA TOUR-FIGEAC St.-Emilion 1982 Cur: $22 (5/15/89) (TR)
88 CHATEAU L'ANGELUS St.-Emilion 1982 Rel: $20.50 Cur: $32 (5/15/89) (TR)
88 CHATEAU CADET-PIOLA St.-Emilion 1982 Cur: $23 (5/15/89) (TR)
88 CLOS FOURTET St.-Emilion 1982 Rel: $20 Cur: $29 (6/01/85)
88 CHATEAU LA CLUSIERE St.-Emilion 1982 Cur: $20 (5/15/89) (TR)
88 CHATEAU LA GAFFELIERE St.-Emilion 1982 Cur: $25 (5/15/89) (TR)
88 CHATEAU RIPEAU St.-Emilion 1982 Cur: $18 (5/15/89) (TR)
88 CHATEAU LA TOUR-DU-PIN-FIGEAC St.-Emilion 1982 Cur: $26 (5/15/89) (TR)
87 CLOS FOURTET St.-Emilion 1982 Rel: $20 Cur: $29 (5/15/89) (TR)
87 CHATEAU HAUT-SARPE St.-Emilion 1982 Cur: $20 (5/15/89) (TR)
87 CHATEAU TROTTEVIEILLE St.-Emilion 1982 Cur: $35 (5/15/89) (TR)
87 CHATEAU YON-FIGEAC St.-Emilion 1982 (NA) (5/15/89) (TR)
86 CHATEAU CAP DE MOURLIN (JACQUES) St.-Emilion 1982 (NA) (5/15/89) (TR)
85 CHATEAU L'ANGELUS St.-Emilion 1982 Rel: $20.50 Cur: $32 (3/16/85)
85 CHATEAU BEAU-SEJOUR BECOT St.-Emilion 1982 Cur: $25 (5/15/89) (TR)
85 CHATEAU JEAN FAURE St.-Emilion 1982 $14 (11/16/85)
85 CHATEAU GRAND-BARRAIL-LAMARZELLE-FIGEAC St.-Emilion 1982 (NA) (5/15/89) (TR)
85 CHATEAU LARCIS-DUCASSE St.-Emilion 1982 Cur: $25 (5/15/89) (TR)
85 CHATEAU TERTRE-ROTEBOEUF St.-Emilion 1982 Rel: $10 Cur: $17 (9/16/85)
84 CHATEAU AUSONE St.-Emilion 1982 Cur: $167 (11/30/87) (TR)
84 CHATEAU CURE-BON-LA-MADELAINE St.-Emilion 1982 Cur: $30 (5/15/89) (TR)
84 CHATEAU SOUTARD St.-Emilion 1982 Cur: $30 (5/15/89) (TR)
83 CHATEAU BALESTARD LA TONNELLE St.-Emilion 1982 Cur: $25 (5/15/89) (TR)
83 CHATEAU CLOS DES JACOBINS St.-Emilion 1982 Cur: $38 (5/15/89) (TR)
83 CHATEAU CLOS LA MADELAINE St.-Emilion 1982 (NA) (5/15/89) (TR)
83 CHATEAU CROQUE-MICHOTTE St.-Emilion 1982 Cur: $24 (5/15/89) (TR)
83 CHATEAU GRAND-PONTET St.-Emilion 1982 Cur: $26 (5/15/89) (TR)
83 CHATEAU VIEUX SARPE St.-Emilion 1982 (NA) (5/15/89) (TR)
83 CHATEAU VILLEMAURINE St.-Emilion 1982 (NA) (5/15/89) (TR)
82 CHATEAU LA TOUR-DU-PIN-FIGEAC-BELIEVIER St.-Emilion 1982 (NA) (5/15/89) (TR)
81 CHATEAU CAP DE MOURLIN (JEAN) St.-Emilion 1982 (NA) (5/15/89) (TR)
81 CHATEAU GRANDES-MURAILLES St.-Emilion 1982 (NA) (5/15/89) (TR)
81 CHATEAU LA TOUR DU PIN St.-Emilion 1982 $12 (5/01/85)
81 CHATEAU TRIMOULET St.-Emilion 1982 (NA) (5/15/89) (TR)
80 CHATEAU MATRAS St.-Emilion 1982 (NA) (5/15/89) (TR)
80 VIEUX CHATEAU GUIBEAU St.-Emilion 1982 $8 (9/16/85)
79 CHATEAU CARTEYRON St.-Emilion 1982 $7.25 (9/01/85)
79 CHATEAU DURAND-LAPLAGNE St.-Emilion 1982 $7.50 (9/16/85)
78 CLOS DE L'ORATOIRE St.-Emilion 1982 (NA) (5/15/89) (TR)
78 CHATEAU LE COUVENT St.-Emilion 1982 $13 (6/16/86)

FRANCE
BORDEAUX RED/St.-Emilion

78   CHATEAU FONROQUE St.-Emilion 1982 Cur: $17 (5/15/89) (TR)
77   CHATEAU FONPLEGADE St.-Emilion 1982 Cur: $25 (5/15/89) (TR)
75   CHATEAU VILLADIERE St.-Emilion 1982 $8 (9/01/85)

1981
90   CHATEAU AUSONE St.-Emilion 1981 Cur: $88 (11/30/87) (TR)
90   CHATEAU CHEVAL BLANC St.-Emilion 1981 Rel: $46 Cur: $78 (2/15/91) (JS)
88   CHATEAU CHEVAL BLANC St.-Emilion 1981 Rel: $46 Cur: $78 (5/01/89)
86   CHATEAU FIGEAC St.-Emilion 1981 Cur: $34 (5/01/85)
84   CHATEAU PAVIE St.-Emilion 1981 Rel: $15.50 Cur: $21 (6/01/84)
82   CHATEAU CANON St.-Emilion 1981 Cur: $31 (5/15/89) (TM)
81   CHATEAU CLOS DES JACOBINS St.-Emilion 1981 Rel: $16 Cur: $31 (6/01/84)
78   A. MOUEIX St.-Emilion 1981 $7.50 (9/01/85)
76   CHATEAU LARMANDE St.-Emilion 1981 Rel: $10.50 Cur: $11 (8/01/84)
73   CHATEAU HAUT-CADET St.-Emilion 1981 $6.50 (4/01/85)

1980
90   CHATEAU FIGEAC St.-Emilion 1980 Cur: $30 (5/01/85)
86   CHATEAU AUSONE St.-Emilion 1980 Cur: $29 (11/30/87) (TR)
84   CHATEAU CHEVAL BLANC St.-Emilion 1980 Cur: $48 (2/15/91) (JS)
80   CHATEAU CANON St.-Emilion 1980 Cur: $19 (5/15/89) (TM)

1979
94   CHATEAU AUSONE St.-Emilion 1979 Cur: $83 (11/30/87) (TR)
92   CHATEAU AUSONE St.-Emilion 1979 Cur: $83 (10/15/89) (JS)
89   CHATEAU CANON St.-Emilion 1979 Cur: $40 (5/15/89) (TM)
89   CHATEAU MAGDELAINE St.-Emilion 1979 Cur: $40 (10/15/89) (JS)
88   CHATEAU CHEVAL BLANC St.-Emilion 1979 Cur: $76 (2/15/91) (JS)
86   CHATEAU PAVIE St.-Emilion 1979 Cur: $34 (10/15/89) (JS)
85   CHATEAU CHEVAL BLANC St.-Emilion 1979 Cur: $76 (10/15/89) (JS)
82   CHATEAU L'ANGELUS St.-Emilion 1979 Cur: $22 (10/15/89) (JS)
82   CHATEAU FIGEAC St.-Emilion 1979 Cur: $38 (10/15/89) (JS)
81   CHATEAU LA DOMINIQUE St.-Emilion 1979 Cur: $27 (10/15/89) (JS)
81   CHATEAU LA GAFFELIERE St.-Emilion 1979 Cur: $43 (10/15/89) (JS)
80   CHATEAU FIGEAC St.-Emilion 1979 Cur: $38 (5/01/85)
78   CHATEAU HAUT-SARPE St.-Emilion 1979 Rel: $11 Cur: $11 (4/01/84)

1978
94   CHATEAU CHEVAL BLANC St.-Emilion 1978 Cur: $120 (2/15/91) (JS)
93   CHATEAU AUSONE St.-Emilion 1978 Cur: $71 (11/30/87) (TR)
84   CHATEAU CANON St.-Emilion 1978 Cur: $59 (5/15/89) (TM)
83   CHATEAU FIGEAC St.-Emilion 1978 Cur: $51 (5/01/85)

1977
83   CHATEAU AUSONE St.-Emilion 1977 Cur: $29 (11/30/87) (TR)
74   CHATEAU CHEVAL BLANC St.-Emilion 1977 Cur: $38 (2/15/91) (JS)

1976
89   CHATEAU AUSONE St.-Emilion 1976 Cur: $117 (11/30/87) (TR)
88   CHATEAU CHEVAL BLANC St.-Emilion 1976 Cur: $80 (2/15/91) (JS)

1975
91   CHATEAU CHEVAL BLANC St.-Emilion 1975 Cur: $140 (2/15/91) (JS)
84   CHATEAU CANON St.-Emilion 1975 Cur: $38 (5/15/89) (TM)

1974
83   CHATEAU CHEVAL BLANC St.-Emilion 1974 Cur: $43 (2/15/91) (JS)
76   CHATEAU AUSONE St.-Emilion 1974 Cur: $28 (11/30/87) (TR)

1973
83   CHATEAU CHEVAL BLANC St.-Emilion 1973 Cur: $60 (2/15/91) (JS)
77   CHATEAU AUSONE St.-Emilion 1973 Cur: $35 (11/30/87) (TR)

1972
82   CHATEAU CHEVAL BLANC St.-Emilion 1972 Cur: $40 (2/15/91) (JS)
75   CHATEAU AUSONE St.-Emilion 1972 Cur: $30 (11/30/87) (TR)

1971
89   CHATEAU CHEVAL BLANC St.-Emilion 1971 Cur: $130 (2/15/91) (JS)
85   CHATEAU CANON St.-Emilion 1971 Cur: $53 (5/15/89) (TM)
83   CHATEAU AUSONE St.-Emilion 1971 Cur: $118 (11/30/87) (TR)

1970
93   CHATEAU CANON St.-Emilion 1970 Cur: $60 (5/15/89) (TM)
88   CHATEAU CHEVAL BLANC St.-Emilion 1970 Cur: $165 (2/15/91) (JS)
82   CHATEAU AUSONE St.-Emilion 1970 Cur: $125 (11/30/87) (TR)

1969
76   CHATEAU AUSONE St.-Emilion 1969 Cur: $27 (11/30/87) (TR)
75   CHATEAU CHEVAL BLANC St.-Emilion 1969 Cur: $68 (2/15/91) (JS)

1967
85   CHATEAU CHEVAL BLANC St.-Emilion 1967 Cur: $102 (2/15/91) (JS)
79   CHATEAU AUSONE St.-Emilion 1967 Cur: $68 (11/30/87) (TR)

1966
91   CHATEAU CANON St.-Emilion 1966 Cur: $69 (5/15/89) (TM)
87   CHATEAU CHEVAL BLANC St.-Emilion 1966 Cur: $140 (2/15/91) (JS)
85   CHATEAU AUSONE St.-Emilion 1966 Cur: $162 (11/30/87) (TR)

1964
94   CHATEAU CHEVAL BLANC St.-Emilion 1964 Cur: $220 (2/15/91) (HS)
89   CHATEAU CANON St.-Emilion 1964 Cur: $60 (5/15/89) (TM)
85   CHATEAU CHEVAL BLANC St.-Emilion 1964 Cur: $220 (2/15/91) (JS)
78   CHATEAU AUSONE St.-Emilion 1964 Cur: $87 (11/30/87) (TR)

1962
93   CHATEAU CANON St.-Emilion 1962 Cur: $100 (5/15/89) (TM)
90   CHATEAU FIGEAC St.-Emilion 1962 Cur: $66 (11/30/87) (JS)
88   CHATEAU LA GAFFELIERE St.-Emilion 1962 Cur: $60 (10/30/87) (JS)
85   CHATEAU AUSONE St.-Emilion 1962 Cur: $130 (11/30/87) (JS)
85   CHATEAU CHEVAL BLANC St.-Emilion 1962 Cur: $150 (2/15/91) (JS)
75   CHATEAU CHEVAL BLANC St.-Emilion 1962 Cur: $150 (11/30/87) (JS)
75   CHATEAU TROTTEVIEILLE St.-Emilion 1962 Cur: $30 (11/30/87) (JS)
68   CHATEAU L'ANGELUS St.-Emilion 1962 Cur: $45 (11/30/87) (JS)

1961
96   CHATEAU CHEVAL BLANC St.-Emilion 1961 Cur: $420 (2/15/91) (JS)
88   CHATEAU CANON St.-Emilion 1961 Cur: $100 (5/15/89) (TM)
86   CHATEAU MAGDELAINE St.-Emilion 1961 Cur: $250 (3/16/86) (JL)
84   CHATEAU FIGEAC St.-Emilion 1961 Cur: $176 (3/16/86) (JL)
82   CHATEAU AUSONE St.-Emilion 1961 Cur: $302 (11/30/87) (TR)
78   CHATEAU CHEVAL BLANC St.-Emilion 1961 Cur: $420 (3/16/86) (JL)
76   CHATEAU LA GAFFELIERE St.-Emilion 1961 Cur: $125 (3/16/86) (JL)
75   CHATEAU BELAIR St.-Emilion 1961 Cur: $113 (3/16/86) (JL)
66   CLOS FOURTET St.-Emilion 1961 Cur: $106 (3/16/86) (JL)
62   CHATEAU PAVIE St.-Emilion 1961 Cur: $125 (3/16/86) (JL)

1960
81   CHATEAU CHEVAL BLANC St.-Emilion 1960 Cur: $150 (2/15/91) (JS)

1959
96   CHATEAU CHEVAL BLANC St.-Emilion 1959 Cur: $335 (10/15/90) (JS)
95   CHATEAU CANON St.-Emilion 1959 Cur: $125 (5/15/89) (TM)
90   CHATEAU CHEVAL BLANC St.-Emilion 1959 Cur: $335 (2/15/91) (JS)
89   CHATEAU MAGDELAINE St.-Emilion 1959 Cur: $150 (10/15/90) (JS)
82   CHATEAU LA GAFFELIERE St.-Emilion 1959 Cur: $95 (10/15/90) (JS)
79   CHATEAU AUSONE St.-Emilion 1959 Cur: $275 (10/15/90) (JS)
76   CHATEAU AUSONE St.-Emilion 1959 Cur: $275 (11/30/87) (TR)

1958
86   CHATEAU CHEVAL BLANC St.-Emilion 1958 Cur: $180 (2/15/91) (JS)
79   CHATEAU AUSONE St.-Emilion 1958 Cur: $95 (11/30/87) (TR)

1957
74   CHATEAU AUSONE St.-Emilion 1957 Cur: $200 (11/30/87) (TR)

1956
86   CHATEAU AUSONE St.-Emilion 1956 Cur: $175 (11/30/87) (TR)

1955
94   CHATEAU CHEVAL BLANC St.-Emilion 1955 Cur: $200 (2/15/91) (JS)
91   CHATEAU AUSONE St.-Emilion 1955 Cur: $275 (11/30/87) (TR)
88   CHATEAU CANON St.-Emilion 1955 Cur: $110 (5/15/89) (TM)

1954
87   CHATEAU AUSONE St.-Emilion 1954 Cur: $180 (11/30/87) (TR)

1953
88   CHATEAU CANON St.-Emilion 1953 Cur: $125 (5/15/89) (TM)
87   CHATEAU CHEVAL BLANC St.-Emilion 1953 Cur: $390 (2/15/91) (JS)
78   CHATEAU AUSONE St.-Emilion 1953 Cur: $253 (11/30/87) (TR)

1952
91   CHATEAU CHEVAL BLANC St.-Emilion 1952 Cur: $268 (2/15/91) (JS)
85   CHATEAU AUSONE St.-Emilion 1952 Cur: $180 (11/30/87) (TR)

1951
76   CHATEAU CHEVAL BLANC St.-Emilion 1951 Cur: $150 (2/15/91) (JS)

1950
95   CHATEAU CHEVAL BLANC St.-Emilion 1950 Cur: $275 (2/15/91) (HS)
89   CHATEAU CHEVAL BLANC St.-Emilion 1950 Cur: $275 (2/15/91) (JS)
78   CHATEAU AUSONE St.-Emilion 1950 Cur: $217 (11/30/87) (TR)

1949
93   CHATEAU CHEVAL BLANC St.-Emilion 1949 Cur: $565 (2/15/91) (HS)
91   CHATEAU AUSONE St.-Emilion 1949 Cur: $265 (11/30/87) (TR)
84   CHATEAU CHEVAL BLANC St.-Emilion 1949 Cur: $565 (2/15/91) (JS)

1948
97   CHATEAU CHEVAL BLANC St.-Emilion 1948 Cur: $300 (2/15/91) (JS)

1947
100   CHATEAU CHEVAL BLANC St.-Emilion 1947 Cur: $1,225 (2/15/91) (JS)
91   CHATEAU CANON St.-Emilion 1947 Cur: $250 (5/15/89) (TM)
83   CHATEAU AUSONE St.-Emilion 1947 Cur: $275 (11/30/87) (TR)

1946
87   CHATEAU CHEVAL BLANC St.-Emilion 1946 Cur: $340 (2/15/91) (JS)

1945
95   CHATEAU CHEVAL BLANC St.-Emilion 1945 Cur: $590 (3/16/86) (JL)
85   CHATEAU LA GAFFELIERE St.-Emilion 1945 Cur: $140 (3/16/86) (JL)
75   CHATEAU AUSONE St.-Emilion 1945 Cur: $320 (3/16/86) (JL)

Key to Symbols

The scores reported here are the results of blind tastings conducted by our panel of senior editors. Wines that carry the initials below are results of individual tastings.

THE WINE SPECTATOR 100-POINT SCALE   95-100—Classic, a great wine; **90-94**—Outstanding, superior character and style; **80-89**—Good to very good, a wine with special qualities; **70-79**—Average, drinkable wine that may have minor flaws; **60-69**—Below average, drinkable but not recommended; **50-59**—Poor, undrinkable, not recommended. "**+**"—With a score indicates a range; used primarily with barrel tastings to indicate a preliminary score.

SPECIAL DESIGNATIONS   SS—Spectator Selection, CS—Cellar Selection, BB—Best Buy.

TASTER'S INITIALS   (JG)—Jim Gordon, (HS)—Harvey Steiman, (JL)—James Laube, (JS)—James Suckling, (TM)—Thomas Matthews, (TR)—Terry Robards, (BT)—Barrel Tasting (these wines were tasted blind from barrel samples), (CA-date)—*California's Great Cabernets* by James Laube, (CH-date)—*California's Great Chardonnays* by James Laube, (VP-date)—*Vintage Port* by James Suckling.

DATE TASTED   Dates in parentheses represent the issue in which the rating was published.

70   CHATEAU GRAND-CORBIN-DESPAGNE St.-Emilion 1945 Cur: $100 (3/16/86) (JL)
68   CLOS FOURTET St.-Emilion 1945 Cur: $175 (3/16/86) (JL)

1943
85   CHATEAU CHEVAL BLANC St.-Emilion 1943 Cur: $185 (2/15/91) (JS)
84   CHATEAU AUSONE St.-Emilion 1943 Cur: $350 (11/30/87) (TR)

1942
81   CHATEAU AUSONE St.-Emilion 1942 Cur: $250 (11/30/87) (TR)

1941
71   CHATEAU CHEVAL BLANC St.-Emilion 1941 Cur: $175 (2/15/91) (JS)

1940
83   CHATEAU CHEVAL BLANC St.-Emilion 1940 Cur: $500 (2/15/91) (JS)

1938
75   CHATEAU CHEVAL BLANC St.-Emilion 1938 Cur: $150 (2/15/91) (JS)

1937
93   CHATEAU CHEVAL BLANC St.-Emilion 1937 Cur: $400 (2/15/91) (JS)
83   CHATEAU AUSONE St.-Emilion 1937 Cur: $200 (11/30/87) (TR)

1936
82   CHATEAU AUSONE St.-Emilion 1936 Cur: $300 (11/30/87) (TR)
81   CHATEAU CHEVAL BLANC St.-Emilion 1936 Cur: $275 (2/15/91) (JS)

1934
93   CHATEAU CHEVAL BLANC St.-Emilion 1934 Cur: $325 (2/15/91) (JS)

1933
88   CHATEAU CHEVAL BLANC St.-Emilion 1933 Cur: $275 (2/15/91) (JS)

1931
72   CHATEAU CHEVAL BLANC St.-Emilion 1931 Cur: $225 (2/15/91) (JS)

1930
82   CHATEAU CHEVAL BLANC St.-Emilion 1930 Cur: $275 (2/15/91) (JS)

1929
90   CHATEAU CHEVAL BLANC St.-Emilion 1929 Cur: $450 (2/15/91) (JS)
83   CHATEAU AUSONE St.-Emilion 1929 Cur: $290 (11/30/87) (TR)

1928
92   CHATEAU CHEVAL BLANC St.-Emilion 1928 Cur: $475 (2/15/91) (JS)
83   CHATEAU AUSONE St.-Emilion 1928 Cur: $330 (11/30/87) (TR)

1926
85   CHATEAU CHEVAL BLANC St.-Emilion 1926 Cur: $400 (2/15/91) (JS)
82   CHATEAU AUSONE St.-Emilion 1926 Cur: $249 (11/30/87) (TR)

1925
75   CHATEAU AUSONE St.-Emilion 1925 Cur: $200 (11/30/87) (TR)

1924
95   CHATEAU AUSONE St.-Emilion 1924 Cur: $225 (11/30/87) (TR)
69   CHATEAU CHEVAL BLANC St.-Emilion 1924 Cur: $450 (2/15/91) (JS)

1923
76   CHATEAU AUSONE St.-Emilion 1923 Cur: $200 (11/30/87) (TR)
65   CHATEAU CHEVAL BLANC St.-Emilion 1923 Cur: $200 (2/15/91) (JS)

1921
100 CHATEAU CHEVAL BLANC St.-Emilion 1921 Cur: $500 (2/15/91) (JS)
94   CHATEAU AUSONE St.-Emilion 1921 Cur: $250 (11/30/87) (TR)

1919
70   CHATEAU CHEVAL BLANC St.-Emilion 1919 Cur: $500 (2/15/91) (JS)

1918
87   CHATEAU AUSONE St.-Emilion 1918 Cur: $475 (11/30/87) (TR)

1917
70   CHATEAU CHEVAL BLANC St.-Emilion 1917 Cur: $500 (2/15/91) (JS)

1916
86   CHATEAU AUSONE St.-Emilion 1916 Cur: $475 (11/30/87) (TR)
71   CHATEAU CHEVAL BLANC St.-Emilion 1916 Cur: $500 (2/15/91) (JS)

1915
72   CHATEAU CHEVAL BLANC St.-Emilion 1915 Cur: $500 (2/15/91) (JS)

1914
79   CHATEAU AUSONE St.-Emilion 1914 Cur: $375 (11/30/87) (TR)

1913
81   CHATEAU AUSONE St.-Emilion 1913 Cur: $375 (11/30/87) (TR)

1912
79   CHATEAU AUSONE St.-Emilion 1912 Cur: $375 (11/30/87) (TR)

1908
71   CHATEAU CHEVAL BLANC St.-Emilion 1908 Cur: $500 (2/15/91) (JS)

1905
82   CHATEAU AUSONE St.-Emilion 1905 Cur: $600 (11/30/87) (TR)
70   CHATEAU CHEVAL BLANC St.-Emilion 1905 Cur: $600 (2/15/91) (JS)

1902
83   CHATEAU AUSONE St.-Emilion 1902 Cur: $500 (11/30/87) (TR)

1900
78   CHATEAU AUSONE St.-Emilion 1900 Cur: $1,000 (11/30/87) (TR)

1899
90   CHATEAU CHEVAL BLANC St.-Emilion 1899 Cur: $1,200 (2/15/91) (JS)
77   CHATEAU AUSONE St.-Emilion 1899 Cur: $1,500 (11/30/87) (TR)

1894
85   CHATEAU AUSONE St.-Emilion 1894 Cur: $800 (11/30/87) (TR)

1879
93   CHATEAU AUSONE St.-Emilion 1879 Cur: $700 (11/30/87) (TR)

1877
92   CHATEAU AUSONE St.-Emilion 1877 Cur: $2,200 (11/30/87) (TR)

ST.-EMILION SATELLITES

1990
80+ CHATEAU ST.-ANDRE CORBIN St.-Georges-St.-Emilion 1990 (NR) (4/30/91) (BT)

1989
80+ CHATEAU ST.-ANDRE CORBIN St.-Georges-St.-Emilion 1989 (NR) (4/30/91) (BT)
75+ CHATEAU ST.-ANDRE CORBIN St.-Georges-St.-Emilion 1989 (NR) (4/30/90) (BT)

1988
80+ CHATEAU ST.-ANDRE CORBIN St.-Georges-St.-Emilion 1988 (NR) (6/30/89) (BT)

1987
75+ CHATEAU ST.-ANDRE CORBIN St.-Georges-St.-Emilion 1987 (NR) (6/30/89) (BT)

1986
87   CHATEAU ST.-GEORGES St.-Georges-St.-Emilion 1986 $14 (7/15/90)
81   CHATEAU TOUR CALON Montagne-St.-Emilion 1986 $10 (9/30/89)
77   CHATEAU ST.-ANDRE CORBIN St.-Georges-St.-Emilion 1986 Rel: $22 Cur: 22 (3/31/90)
71   CHATEAU DU CHEVALIER Montagne-St.-Emilion 1986 $19 (3/31/91)
70+ CHATEAU ST.-ANDRE CORBIN St.-Georges-St.-Emilion 1986 Rel: $22 Cur: 22 (5/15/87) (BT)

1985
87   CHATEAU ST.-GEORGES St.-Georges-St.-Emilion 1985 $11 (7/31/89)
80   CHATEAU MAISON-BLANCHE Montagne-St.-Emilion 1985 $13 (2/15/89)
80+ CHATEAU ST.-ANDRE CORBIN St.-Georges-St.-Emilion 1985 (NR) (5/15/87) (BT)
78   CHATEAU MAISON-NEUVE Montagne-St.-Emilion 1985 $7 (3/15/88)

1983
75   CHATEAU FAIZEAU Montagne-St.-Emilion 1983 $9 (11/15/87)

1982
73   CHATEAU DE LUSSAC Lussac-St.-Emilion 1982 $6.75 (5/01/84)
64   CHATEAU LE MAYNE Puisseguin-St.-Emilion 1982 $7.50 (12/01/85)

ST.-ESTÈPHE

1990
95+ CHATEAU HAUT-MARBUZET St.-Estèphe 1990 (NR) (4/30/91) (BT)
95+ CHATEAU LES ORMES DE PEZ St.-Estèphe 1990 (NR) (4/30/91) (BT)
90+ CHATEAU BEAU-SITE St.-Estèphe 1990 (NR) (4/30/91) (BT)
90+ CHATEAU CHAMBERT-MARBUZET St.-Estèphe 1990 (NR) (4/30/91) (BT)
90+ CHATEAU COS D'ESTOURNEL St.-Estèphe 1990 (NR) (4/30/91) (BT)
90+ CHATEAU MONTROSE St.-Estèphe 1990 (NR) (4/30/91) (BT)
85+ CHATEAU CALON-SEGUR St.-Estèphe 1990 (NR) (4/30/91) (BT)
85+ CHATEAU COS-LABORY St.-Estèphe 1990 (NR) (4/30/91) (BT)
85+ CHATEAU LAFON-ROCHET St.-Estèphe 1990 (NR) (4/30/91) (BT)
85+ CHATEAU PHELAN-SEGUR St.-Estèphe 1990 (NR) (4/30/91) (BT)
80+ CHATEAU MEYNEY St.-Estèphe 1990 (NR) (4/30/91) (BT)

1989
95+ CHATEAU COS D'ESTOURNEL St.-Estèphe 1989 (NR) (4/30/91) (BT)
95+ CHATEAU COS D'ESTOURNEL St.-Estèphe 1989 (NR) (4/30/90) (BT)
90+ CHATEAU BEAU-SITE St.-Estèphe 1989 (NR) (4/30/91) (BT)
90+ CHATEAU BEAU-SITE St.-Estèphe 1989 (NR) (4/30/90) (BT)
90+ CHATEAU CAPBERN-GASQUETON St.-Estèphe 1989 (NR) (4/30/91) (BT)
90+ CHATEAU COS-LABORY St.-Estèphe 1989 (NR) (4/30/91) (BT)
90+ CHATEAU COS-LABORY St.-Estèphe 1989 (NR) (4/30/90) (BT)
90+ CHATEAU HAUT-MARBUZET St.-Estèphe 1989 (NR) (4/30/91) (BT)
90+ CHATEAU HAUT-MARBUZET St.-Estèphe 1989 (NR) (4/30/90) (BT)
90+ CHATEAU LAFON-ROCHET St.-Estèphe 1989 (NR) (4/30/91) (BT)
90+ CHATEAU LAFON-ROCHET St.-Estèphe 1989 (NR) (4/30/90) (BT)
90+ CHATEAU MEYNEY St.-Estèphe 1989 (NR) (4/30/91) (BT)
90+ CHATEAU MEYNEY St.-Estèphe 1989 (NR) (4/30/90) (BT)
90+ CHATEAU MONTROSE St.-Estèphe 1989 (NR) (4/30/91) (BT)
90+ CHATEAU MONTROSE St.-Estèphe 1989 (NR) (4/30/90) (BT)
90+ CHATEAU LES ORMES DE PEZ St.-Estèphe 1989 (NR) (4/30/91) (BT)
90+ CHATEAU TRONQUOY-LALANDE St.-Estèphe 1989 (NR) (4/30/90) (BT)
85+ CHATEAU CALON-SEGUR St.-Estèphe 1989 (NR) (4/30/91) (BT)
85+ CHATEAU CHAMBERT-MARBUZET St.-Estèphe 1989 (NR) (4/30/91) (BT)
85+ CHATEAU LILIAN-LADOUYS St.-Estèphe 1989 (NR) (4/30/91) (BT)
85+ CHATEAU LES ORMES DE PEZ St.-Estèphe 1989 (NR) (4/30/90) (BT)
85+ CHATEAU PHELAN-SEGUR St.-Estèphe 1989 (NR) (4/30/91) (BT)
80+ CHATEAU CALON-SEGUR St.-Estèphe 1989 (NR) (4/30/90) (BT)
80+ CHATEAU CHAMBERT-MARBUZET St.-Estèphe 1989 (NR) (4/30/90) (BT)

1988
95   CHATEAU COS D'ESTOURNEL St.-Estèphe 1988 $30 (7/15/91) CS
95+ CHATEAU COS D'ESTOURNEL St.-Estèphe 1988 $30 (8/31/90) (BT)
95+ CHATEAU COS D'ESTOURNEL St.-Estèphe 1988 $30 (6/30/89) (BT)
95+ CHATEAU MONTROSE St.-Estèphe 1988 $41 (6/30/89) (BT)
92   CHATEAU DE MARBUZET St.-Estèphe 1988 $15 (7/15/91) SS
91   CHATEAU HAUT-MARBUZET St.-Estèphe 1988 $25 (12/31/90) SS

FRANCE
BORDEAUX RED/ST.-ESTÈPHE

90+ CHATEAU HAUT-MARBUZET St.-Estèphe 1988 $25 (6/30/89) (BT)
88 CHATEAU MEYNEY St.-Estèphe 1988 $17 (3/15/91)
88 CHATEAU LES ORMES DE PEZ St.-Estèphe 1988 $21 (4/30/91)
87 CHATEAU MONTROSE St.-Estèphe 1988 $41 (3/31/91)
87 CHATEAU PHELAN-SEGUR St.-Estèphe 1988 $20 (7/15/91)
85 CHATEAU CALON-SEGUR St.-Estèphe 1988 $30 (7/15/91)
85 CHATEAU COS-LABORY St.-Estèphe 1988 $20 (4/30/91)
85+ CHATEAU COS-LABORY St.-Estèphe 1988 $20 (8/31/90) (BT)
85+ CHATEAU COS-LABORY St.-Estèphe 1988 $20 (6/30/89) (BT)
85+ CHATEAU HAUT-MARBUZET St.-Estèphe 1988 $25 (8/31/90) (BT)
85+ CHATEAU LAFON-ROCHET St.-Estèphe 1988 $17 (6/30/89) (BT)
85+ CHATEAU DE MARBUZET St.-Estèphe 1988 $15 (6/30/89) (BT)
84 CHATEAU TRONQUOY-LALANDE St.-Estèphe 1988 $14 (7/15/91)
83 CHATEAU DE PEZ St.-Estèphe 1988 $19 (6/15/91)
80+ CHATEAU BEAU-SITE St.-Estèphe 1988 $14 (6/30/89) (BT)
80+ CHATEAU CALON-SEGUR St.-Estèphe 1988 $30 (6/30/89) (BT)
80+ CHATEAU MEYNEY St.-Estèphe 1988 $17 (6/30/89) (BT)
80+ CHATEAU MONTROSE St.-Estèphe 1988 $41 (8/31/90) (BT)
80+ CHATEAU LES ORMES DE PEZ St.-Estèphe 1988 $21 (6/30/89) (BT)
80+ CHATEAU PHELAN-SEGUR St.-Estèphe 1988 $20 (8/31/90) (BT)
80+ CHATEAU PHELAN-SEGUR St.-Estèphe 1988 $20 (6/30/89) (BT)
80+ CHATEAU TRONQUOY-LALANDE St.-Estèphe 1988 $14 (6/30/89) (BT)
75+ CHATEAU CAPBERN-GASQUETON St.-Estèphe 1988 (NR) (6/30/89) (BT)
75+ CHATEAU CHAMBERT-MARBUZET St.-Estèphe 1988 $26 (8/31/90) (BT)
75+ CHATEAU LA COMMANDERIE St.-Estèphe 1988 (NR) (6/30/89) (BT)

1987

87 CHATEAU MEYNEY St.-Estèphe 1987 Rel: $14 Cur: $14 (5/15/90)
86 CHATEAU LES ORMES DE PEZ St.-Estèphe 1987 Rel: $15 Cur: $15 (11/30/89) (JS)
85 CHATEAU HAUT-MARBUZET St.-Estèphe 1987 Rel: $20 Cur: $20 (5/15/90)
85+ CHATEAU COS D'ESTOURNEL St.-Estèphe 1987 Rel: $30 Cur: $30 (6/30/89) (BT)
85+ CHATEAU COS D'ESTOURNEL St.-Estèphe 1987 Rel: $30 Cur: $30 (6/30/88) (BT)
84 CHATEAU TRONQUOY-LALANDE St.-Estèphe 1987 Rel: $13 Cur: $13 (11/30/89) (JS)
83 CHATEAU COS D'ESTOURNEL St.-Estèphe 1987 Rel: $30 Cur: $30 (5/15/90) (HS)
83 CHATEAU MEYNEY St.-Estèphe 1987 Rel: $14 Cur: $14 (11/30/89) (JS)
83 CHATEAU LES ORMES DE PEZ St.-Estèphe 1987 Rel: $15 Cur: $15 (5/15/90)
82 CHATEAU HAUT-MARBUZET St.-Estèphe 1987 Rel: $20 Cur: $20 (11/30/89) (JS)
82 CHATEAU PHELAN-SEGUR St.-Estèphe 1987 Rel: $16 Cur: $16 (11/30/89) (JS)
81 CHATEAU BEAU-SITE St.-Estèphe 1987 Rel: $12 Cur: $12 (11/30/89) (JS)
81 CHATEAU COS D'ESTOURNEL St.-Estèphe 1987 Rel: $30 Cur: $30 (5/15/90)
80 CHATEAU DE MARBUZET St.-Estèphe 1987 Rel: $14 Cur: $14 (11/30/89) (JS)
80 CHATEAU MONTROSE St.-Estèphe 1987 Rel: $17 Cur: $18 (2/15/90)
80+ CHATEAU CALON-SEGUR St.-Estèphe 1987 Rel: $25 Cur: $25 (6/30/88) (BT)
80+ CHATEAU LAFON-ROCHET St.-Estèphe 1987 Cur: $13 (6/30/89) (BT)
80+ CHATEAU LAFON-ROCHET St.-Estèphe 1987 Cur: $13 (6/30/88) (BT)
80+ CHATEAU MONTROSE St.-Estèphe 1987 Rel: $17 Cur: $18 (6/30/89) (BT)
79 CHATEAU CHAMBERT-MARBUZET St.-Estèphe 1987 Rel: $18 Cur: $18 (11/30/89) (JS)
79 CHATEAU LE CROCK St.-Estèphe 1987 $16 (11/30/89) (JS)
75+ CHATEAU BEAU-SITE St.-Estèphe 1987 Rel: $12 Cur: $12 (6/30/89) (BT)
75+ CHATEAU CALON-SEGUR St.-Estèphe 1987 Rel: $25 Cur: $25 (6/30/89) (BT)
75+ CHATEAU HAUT-MARBUZET St.-Estèphe 1987 Rel: $20 Cur: $20 (6/30/89) (BT)
75+ CHATEAU MEYNEY St.-Estèphe 1987 Rel: $14 Cur: $14 (6/30/89) (BT)
75+ CHATEAU LES ORMES DE PEZ St.-Estèphe 1987 Rel: $15 Cur: $15 (6/30/89) (BT)
75+ CHATEAU LES ORMES DE PEZ St.-Estèphe 1987 Rel: $15 Cur: $15 (6/30/88) (BT)
75+ CHATEAU PHELAN-SEGUR St.-Estèphe 1987 Rel: $16 Cur: $16 (6/30/89) (BT)
75+ CHATEAU TRONQUOY-LALANDE St.-Estèphe 1987 Rel: $13 Cur: $13 (6/30/89) (BT)
70+ CHATEAU DE MARBUZET St.-Estèphe 1987 Rel: $14 Cur: $14 (6/30/89) (BT)
70+ CHATEAU DE MARBUZET St.-Estèphe 1987 Rel: $14 Cur: $14 (6/30/88) (BT)
65+ CHATEAU COS-LABORY St.-Estèphe 1987 Rel: $15 Cur: $15 (6/30/88) (BT)

1986

96 CHATEAU MONTROSE St.-Estèphe 1986 Rel: $31 Cur: $31 (5/15/89) SS
93 CHATEAU COS D'ESTOURNEL St.-Estèphe 1986 Rel: $40 Cur: $45 (5/31/89)
93 CHATEAU HAUT-MARBUZET St.-Estèphe 1986 Rel: $30 Cur: $30 (5/31/89)
92 CHATEAU COS D'ESTOURNEL St.-Estèphe 1986 Rel: $40 Cur: $45 (5/15/90) (HS)
92 CHATEAU LE CROCK St.-Estèphe 1986 $18 (11/30/89) (JS)
92 CHATEAU HAUT-MARBUZET St.-Estèphe 1986 Rel: $30 Cur: $30 (11/30/89) (JS)
92 CHATEAU DE MARBUZET St.-Estèphe 1986 Rel: $15 Cur: $16 (6/30/89)
92 CHATEAU TRONQUOY-LALANDE St.-Estèphe 1986 Rel: $15 Cur: $16 (11/30/89) (JS)
90 CHATEAU MEYNEY St.-Estèphe 1986 Rel: $19 Cur: $19 (6/30/89)
90 CHATEAU LES ORMES DE PEZ St.-Estèphe 1986 Rel: $21 Cur: $21 (5/31/89)
90 CHATEAU DE PEZ St.-Estèphe 1986 Rel: $17 Cur: $17 (6/30/89)
90+ CHATEAU COS D'ESTOURNEL St.-Estèphe 1986 Rel: $40 Cur: $45 (6/30/88) (BT)
90+ CHATEAU COS D'ESTOURNEL St.-Estèphe 1986 Rel: $40 Cur: $45 (5/15/87) (BT)
90+ CHATEAU MONTROSE St.-Estèphe 1986 Rel: $31 Cur: $31 (6/30/88) (BT)
90+ CHATEAU MONTROSE St.-Estèphe 1986 Rel: $31 Cur: $31 (5/15/87) (BT)
89 CHATEAU CHAMBERT-MARBUZET St.-Estèphe 1986 Rel: $25 Cur: $28 (11/30/89) (JS)
88 CHATEAU LE CROCK St.-Estèphe 1986 $18 (6/30/89)
88 CHATEAU MEYNEY St.-Estèphe 1986 Rel: $19 Cur: $19 (11/30/89) (JS)
87 CHATEAU LES ORMES DE PEZ St.-Estèphe 1986 Rel: $21 Cur: $21 (11/30/89) (JS)
86 CHATEAU BEAU-SITE St.-Estèphe 1986 Rel: $15 Cur: $15 (11/30/89) (JS)
86 CHATEAU CALON-SEGUR St.-Estèphe 1986 Rel: $32 Cur: $32 (5/31/89)
86 CHATEAU DE MARBUZET St.-Estèphe 1986 Rel: $15 Cur: $16 (11/30/89) (JS)
86 CHATEAU PHELAN-SEGUR St.-Estèphe 1986 Rel: $19 Cur: $19 (11/30/89) (JS)
85+ CHATEAU CALON-SEGUR St.-Estèphe 1986 Rel: $32 Cur: $32 (6/30/88) (BT)
85+ CHATEAU LAFON-ROCHET St.-Estèphe 1986 Cur: $18 (6/30/88) (BT)
85+ CHATEAU LES ORMES DE PEZ St.-Estèphe 1986 Rel: $21 Cur: $21 (6/30/88) (BT)
82 CHATEAU LES HAUTS DE BRAME St.-Estèphe 1986 $18.50 (10/31/89)
81 CHATEAU CHAMBERT-MARBUZET St.-Estèphe 1986 Rel: $25 Cur: $28 (5/31/89)
80 CHATEAU LES HAUTS DE BRAME St.-Estèphe 1986 $22 (3/31/91)
80+ CHATEAU CALON-SEGUR St.-Estèphe 1986 Rel: $32 Cur: $32 (5/15/87) (BT)
80+ CHATEAU LAFON-ROCHET St.-Estèphe 1986 Cur: $18 (5/15/87) (BT)
80+ CHATEAU DE MARBUZET St.-Estèphe 1986 Rel: $15 Cur: $16 (5/15/87) (BT)
80+ CHATEAU PHELAN-SEGUR St.-Estèphe 1986 Rel: $19 Cur: $19 (5/15/87) (BT)
77 CHATEAU PHELAN-SEGUR St.-Estèphe 1986 Rel: $19 Cur: $19 (6/30/89)
76 CHATEAU CAPBERN-GASQUETON St.-Estèphe 1986 Rel: $20 Cur: $20 (11/30/89) (JS)
75+ CHATEAU COS-LABORY St.-Estèphe 1986 Rel: $16 Cur: $16 (6/30/88) (BT)
70+ CHATEAU MEYNEY St.-Estèphe 1986 Rel: $19 Cur: $19 (5/15/87) (BT)
70+ CHATEAU LES ORMES DE PEZ St.-Estèphe 1986 Rel: $21 Cur: $21 (5/15/87) (BT)

1985

95 CHATEAU COS D'ESTOURNEL St.-Estèphe 1985 Rel: $33 Cur: $51 (5/15/90) (HS)
92 CHATEAU COS D'ESTOURNEL St.-Estèphe 1985 Rel: $33 Cur: $51 (4/30/88)
92 CHATEAU MEYNEY St.-Estèphe 1985 Rel: $16 Cur: $17 (8/31/88)
91 CHATEAU HAUT-MARBUZET St.-Estèphe 1985 Rel: $25 Cur: $47 (6/30/88)
90 CHATEAU MONTROSE St.-Estèphe 1985 Rel: $33 Cur: $33 (4/30/88)
90 CHATEAU DE PEZ St.-Estèphe 1985 Rel: $15 Cur: $22 (6/30/88)
90+ CHATEAU COS D'ESTOURNEL St.-Estèphe 1985 Rel: $33 Cur: $51 (5/15/87) (BT)
90+ CHATEAU MONTROSE St.-Estèphe 1985 Rel: $33 Cur: $33 (5/15/87) (BT)
89 CHATEAU LES ORMES DE PEZ St.-Estèphe 1985 Rel: $16 Cur: $18 (4/30/88)
88 CHATEAU CALON-SEGUR St.-Estèphe 1985 Rel: $30 Cur: $30 (5/31/88)
87 CHATEAU CHAMBERT-MARBUZET St.-Estèphe 1985 Rel: $28 Cur: $31 (6/30/88)
87 CHATEAU COS-LABORY St.-Estèphe 1985 Rel: $16 Cur: $17 (4/30/88)
87 CHATEAU DE MARBUZET St.-Estèphe 1985 Rel: $11.50 Cur: $21 (6/30/88)
85 CHATEAU CAPBERN-GASQUETON St.-Estèphe 1985 Rel: $18 Cur: $18 (8/31/88)
80+ CHATEAU CALON-SEGUR St.-Estèphe 1985 Rel: $30 Cur: $30 (5/15/87) (BT)
80+ CHATEAU DE MARBUZET St.-Estèphe 1985 Rel: $11.50 Cur: $21 (5/15/87) (BT)
80+ CHATEAU MONTROSE St.-Estèphe 1985 Rel: $33 Cur: $33 (4/16/86) (BT)
80+ CHATEAU LES ORMES DE PEZ St.-Estèphe 1985 Rel: $16 Cur: $18 (5/15/87) (BT)
79 CHATEAU LE CROCK St.-Estèphe 1985 $16.50 (2/15/88)
70+ CHATEAU LAFON-ROCHET St.-Estèphe 1985 Cur: $16 (5/15/87) (BT)
50+ CHATEAU LES ORMES DE PEZ St.-Estèphe 1985 Rel: $16 Cur: $18 (4/16/86) (BT)

1984

93 CHATEAU COS D'ESTOURNEL St.-Estèphe 1984 Rel: $29 Cur: $29 (3/31/87)
88 CHATEAU MONTROSE St.-Estèphe 1984 Rel: $14 Cur: $25 (3/31/87)
81 CHATEAU COS D'ESTOURNEL St.-Estèphe 1984 Rel: $29 Cur: $29 (5/15/90) (HS)
79 CHATEAU MEYNEY St.-Estèphe 1984 Rel: $10 Cur: $11 (5/15/87)
73 CHATEAU COS-LABORY St.-Estèphe 1984 Rel: $12 Cur: $12 (6/15/87)

1983

95 CHATEAU COS D'ESTOURNEL St.-Estèphe 1983 Rel: $29 Cur: $54 (5/16/86) SS
92 CHATEAU MEYNEY St.-Estèphe 1983 Rel: $11 Cur: $18 (10/15/86)
91 CHATEAU DE MARBUZET St.-Estèphe 1983 Rel: $9 Cur: $22 (10/15/86)
87 CHATEAU MONTROSE St.-Estèphe 1983 Rel: $18.50 Cur: $46 (5/16/86)
86 CHATEAU COS-LABORY St.-Estèphe 1983 Rel: $9.50 Cur: $17 (5/16/86)
86 CHATEAU LES ORMES DE PEZ St.-Estèphe 1983 Rel: $17 Cur: $17 (10/15/86)
85 CHATEAU COS D'ESTOURNEL St.-Estèphe 1983 Rel: $29 Cur: $54 (5/15/90) (HS)
83 CHATEAU CALON-SEGUR St.-Estèphe 1983 Rel: $16.50 Cur: $26 (10/31/86)
81 CHATEAU LE CROCK St.-Estèphe 1983 $9.50 (12/16/85)
77 CHATEAU CHAMBERT-MARBUZET St.-Estèphe 1983 Rel: $15 Cur: $15 (9/30/86)
66 CHATEAU CAPBERN-GASQUETON St.-Estèphe 1983 Rel: $19 Cur: $19 (2/15/88)

1982

93 CHATEAU COS D'ESTOURNEL St.-Estèphe 1982 Rel: $23 Cur: $77 (7/16/85) CS
92 CHATEAU COS D'ESTOURNEL St.-Estèphe 1982 Rel: $23 Cur: $77 (5/15/90) (HS)
92 CHATEAU HAUT-MARBUZET St.-Estèphe 1982 Cur: $57 (11/30/89) (JS)
92 CHATEAU MONTROSE St.-Estèphe 1982 Rel: $18 Cur: $39 (5/01/85)
91 CHATEAU CAPBERN-GASQUETON St.-Estèphe 1982 Rel: $11 Cur: $28 (9/16/85)
90 CHATEAU DE PEZ St.-Estèphe 1982 Rel: $12 Cur: $21 (4/01/86)
88 CHATEAU CHAMBERT-MARBUZET St.-Estèphe 1982 Cur: $30 (11/30/89) (JS)
88 CHATEAU PHELAN-SEGUR St.-Estèphe 1982 Cur: $25 (11/30/89) (JS)
87 CHATEAU LES ORMES DE PEZ St.-Estèphe 1982 Cur: $23 (11/30/89) (JS)
86 CHATEAU BEAU-SITE St.-Estèphe 1982 Cur: $15 (11/30/89) (JS)
86 CHATEAU DE MARBUZET St.-Estèphe 1982 Cur: $22 (11/30/89) (JS)
86 CHATEAU MEYNEY St.-Estèphe 1982 Cur: $22 (11/30/89) (JS)
86 CHATEAU TRONQUOY-LALANDE St.-Estèphe 1982 Cur: $18 (11/30/89) (JS)
83 CHATEAU CAPBERN-GASQUETON St.-Estèphe 1982 Rel: $11 Cur: $28 (11/30/89) (JS)
81 CHATEAU HAUT-COUTELIN St.-Estèphe 1982 $12.50 (2/15/88)
80 CHATEAU LE CROCK St.-Estèphe 1982 Cur: $20 (11/30/89) (JS)

1981

90 CHATEAU MONTROSE St.-Estèphe 1981 Rel: $14 Cur: $29 (12/01/84)
89 CHATEAU COS D'ESTOURNEL St.-Estèphe 1981 Rel: $23.50 Cur: $41 (6/01/84)
87 CHATEAU COS D'ESTOURNEL St.-Estèphe 1981 Rel: $23.50 Cur: $41 (5/15/90) (HS)
74 CHATEAU LAFFITTE-CARCASSET St.-Estèphe 1981 $7 (3/16/85)

1980

83 CHATEAU COS D'ESTOURNEL St.-Estèphe 1980 Cur: $38 (5/15/90) (HS)

1979

92 CHATEAU COS D'ESTOURNEL St.-Estèphe 1979 Cur: $47 (5/15/90) (HS)
87 CHATEAU COS D'ESTOURNEL St.-Estèphe 1979 Cur: $47 (10/15/89) (JS)
87 CHATEAU MEYNEY St.-Estèphe 1979 Cur: $18 (10/15/89) (JS)
85 CHATEAU HAUT-MARBUZET St.-Estèphe 1979 Cur: $30 (10/15/89) (JS)
81 CHATEAU MONTROSE St.-Estèphe 1979 Cur: $32 (10/15/89) (JS)

1978

93 CHATEAU COS D'ESTOURNEL St.-Estèphe 1978 Cur: $53 (5/15/90) (HS)

1977

85 CHATEAU COS D'ESTOURNEL St.-Estèphe 1977 Cur: $30 (5/15/90) (HS)

Key to Symbols

The scores reported here are the results of blind tastings conducted by our panel of senior editors. Wines that carry the initials below are results of individual tastings.

THE WINE SPECTATOR 100-POINT SCALE *95-100*—Classic, a great wine; *90-94*—Outstanding, superior character and style; *80-89*—Good to very good, a wine with special qualities; *70-79*—Average, drinkable wine that may have minor flaws; *60-69*—Below average, drinkable but not recommended; *50-59*—Poor, undrinkable, not recommended. "+"—With a score indicates a range; used primarily with barrel tastings to indicate a preliminary score.

SPECIAL DESIGNATIONS SS—Spectator Selection, CS—Cellar Selection, BB—Best Buy.

TASTER'S INITIALS (JG)—Jim Gordon, (HS)—Harvey Steiman, (JL)—James Laube, (JS)—James Suckling, (TM)—Thomas Matthews, (TR)—Terry Robards, (BT)—Barrel Tasting (these wines were tasted blind from barrel samples), (CA-date)—*California's Great Cabernets* by James Laube, (CH-date)—*California's Great Chardonnays* by James Laube, (VP-date)—*Vintage Port* by James Suckling.

DATE TASTED Dates in parentheses represent the issue in which the rating was published.

1976

84   CHATEAU COS D'ESTOURNEL St.-Estèphe 1976 Cur: $46 (5/15/90) (HS)

1975

88   CHATEAU COS D'ESTOURNEL St.-Estèphe 1975 Cur: $61 (5/15/90) (HS)

1973

82   CHATEAU COS D'ESTOURNEL St.-Estèphe 1973 Cur: $31 (5/15/90) (HS)

1971

91   CHATEAU COS D'ESTOURNEL St.-Estèphe 1971 Cur: $50 (5/15/90) (HS)

1970

89   CHATEAU COS D'ESTOURNEL St.-Estèphe 1970 Cur: $92 (5/15/90) (HS)
80   CHATEAU MONTROSE St.-Estèphe 1970 Cur: $92 (4/01/86)

1969

58   CHATEAU COS D'ESTOURNEL St.-Estèphe 1969 Cur: $18 (5/15/90) (HS)

1967

82   CHATEAU COS D'ESTOURNEL St.-Estèphe 1967 Cur: $34 (5/15/90) (HS)

1966

74   CHATEAU COS D'ESTOURNEL St.-Estèphe 1966 Cur: $100 (5/15/90) (HS)

1964

84   CHATEAU COS D'ESTOURNEL St.-Estèphe 1964 Cur: $75 (5/15/90) (HS)

1962

90   CHATEAU MONTROSE St.-Estèphe 1962 Cur: $100 (11/30/87) (JS)
85   CHATEAU COS D'ESTOURNEL St.-Estèphe 1962 Cur: $124 (11/30/87) (JS)
79   CHATEAU COS D'ESTOURNEL St.-Estèphe 1962 Cur: $124 (5/15/90) (HS)
70   CHATEAU CALON-SEGUR St.-Estèphe 1962 Cur: $69 (11/30/87) (JS)
70   CHATEAU HAUT-MARBUZET St.-Estèphe 1962 Cur: $50 (11/30/87) (JS)

1961

87   CHATEAU COS D'ESTOURNEL St.-Estèphe 1961 Cur: $217 (5/15/90) (HS)
87   CHATEAU MONTROSE St.-Estèphe 1961 Cur: $230 (3/16/86) (JL)
84   CHATEAU CALON-SEGUR St.-Estèphe 1961 Cur: $134 (3/16/86) (JL)
67   CHATEAU PHELAN-SEGUR St.-Estèphe 1961 Cur: $43 (3/16/86) (JL)
58   CHATEAU LAFON-ROCHET St.-Estèphe 1961 Cur: $80 (3/16/86) (JL)

1960

79   CHATEAU COS D'ESTOURNEL St.-Estèphe 1960 Cur: $85 (5/15/90) (HS)

1959

90   CHATEAU COS D'ESTOURNEL St.-Estèphe 1959 Cur: $215 (10/15/90) (JS)
90   CHATEAU MONTROSE St.-Estèphe 1959 Cur: $131 (10/15/90) (JS)
83   CHATEAU COS D'ESTOURNEL St.-Estèphe 1959 Cur: $215 (5/15/90) (HS)
83   CHATEAU HAUT-MARBUZET St.-Estèphe (Bottled in England) 1959 Cur: $60 (10/15/90) (JS)
82   CHATEAU CALON-SEGUR St.-Estèphe 1959 Cur: $162 (10/15/90) (JS)

1958

89   CHATEAU COS D'ESTOURNEL St.-Estèphe 1958 Cur: $95 (5/15/90) (HS)

1956

79   CHATEAU COS D'ESTOURNEL St.-Estèphe 1956 Cur: $60 (5/15/90) (HS)

1955

90   CHATEAU COS D'ESTOURNEL St.-Estèphe 1955 Cur: $137 (5/15/90) (HS)

1954

81   CHATEAU COS D'ESTOURNEL St.-Estèphe 1954 Cur: $80 (5/15/90) (HS)

1953

91   CHATEAU COS D'ESTOURNEL St.-Estèphe 1953 Cur: $262 (5/15/90) (HS)

1952

95   CHATEAU COS D'ESTOURNEL St.-Estèphe 1952 Cur: $120 (5/15/90) (HS)

1950

86   CHATEAU COS D'ESTOURNEL St.-Estèphe 1950 Cur: $100 (5/15/90) (HS)

1949

80   CHATEAU COS D'ESTOURNEL St.-Estèphe 1949 Cur: $195 (5/15/90) (HS)

1947

91   CHATEAU COS D'ESTOURNEL St.-Estèphe 1947 Cur: $300 (5/15/90) (HS)

1945

94   CHATEAU CALON-SEGUR St.-Estèphe 1945 Cur: $309 (3/16/86) (JL)
88   CHATEAU MONTROSE St.-Estèphe 1945 Cur: $300 (3/16/86) (JL)
87   CHATEAU COS D'ESTOURNEL St.-Estèphe 1945 Cur: $360 (3/16/86) (JL)
77   CHATEAU COS D'ESTOURNEL St.-Estèphe 1945 Cur: $360 (5/15/90) (HS)
75   CHATEAU LAFON-ROCHET St.-Estèphe 1945 Cur: $100 (3/16/86) (JL)

1943

85   CHATEAU COS D'ESTOURNEL St.-Estèphe 1943 Cur: $220 (5/15/90) (HS)

1942

78   CHATEAU COS D'ESTOURNEL St.-Estèphe 1942 Cur: $110 (5/15/90) (HS)

1937

64   CHATEAU COS D'ESTOURNEL St.-Estèphe 1937 Cur: $260 (5/15/90) (HS)

1934

88   CHATEAU COS D'ESTOURNEL St.-Estèphe 1934 Cur: $175 (5/15/90) (HS)

1929

92   CHATEAU COS D'ESTOURNEL St.-Estèphe 1929 Cur: $575 (5/15/90) (HS)

1928

90   CHATEAU COS D'ESTOURNEL St.-Estèphe 1928 Cur: $454 (5/15/90) (HS)

1926

77   CHATEAU COS D'ESTOURNEL St.-Estèphe 1926 Cur: $300 (5/15/90) (HS)

1924

82   CHATEAU COS D'ESTOURNEL St.-Estèphe 1924 Cur: $300 (5/15/90) (HS)

1921

65   CHATEAU COS D'ESTOURNEL St.-Estèphe 1921 Cur: $200 (5/15/90) (HS)

1920

93   CHATEAU COS D'ESTOURNEL St.-Estèphe 1920 Cur: $350 (5/15/90) (HS)

1917

73   CHATEAU COS D'ESTOURNEL St.-Estèphe 1917 Cur: $250 (5/15/90) (HS)

1905

65   CHATEAU COS D'ESTOURNEL St.-Estèphe 1905 Cur: $250 (5/15/90) (HS)

1904

63   CHATEAU COS D'ESTOURNEL St.-Estèphe 1904 Cur: $210 (5/15/90) (HS)

1899

87   CHATEAU COS D'ESTOURNEL St.-Estèphe 1899 Cur: $940 (5/15/90) (HS)

1898

72   CHATEAU COS D'ESTOURNEL St.-Estèphe 1898 Cur: $500 (5/15/90) (HS)

1890

69   CHATEAU COS D'ESTOURNEL St.-Estèphe 1890 Cur: $330 (5/15/90) (HS)

1870

90   CHATEAU COS D'ESTOURNEL St.-Estèphe 1870 Cur: $1,238 (5/15/90) (HS)

1869

82   CHATEAU COS D'ESTOURNEL St.-Estèphe 1869 Cur: $1,200 (5/15/90) (HS)

St.-Julien

1990

95+   CHATEAU DUCRU-BEAUCAILLOU St.-Julien 1990 (NR) (4/30/91) (BT)
95+   CHATEAU LEOVILLE-BARTON St.-Julien 1990 (NR) (4/30/91) (BT)
95+   CHATEAU LEOVILLE-POYFERRE St.-Julien 1990 (NR) (4/30/91) (BT)
90+   CHATEAU GRUAUD-LAROSE St.-Julien 1990 (NR) (4/30/91) (BT)
90+   CHATEAU LAGRANGE St.-Julien 1990 (NR) (4/30/91) (BT)
90+   CHATEAU LANGOA-BARTON St.-Julien 1990 (NR) (4/30/91) (BT)
90+   CHATEAU TALBOT St.-Julien 1990 (NR) (4/30/91) (BT)
85+   CHATEAU BEYCHEVELLE St.-Julien 1990 (NR) (4/30/91) (BT)
85+   CHATEAU GLORIA St.-Julien 1990 (NR) (4/30/91) (BT)
85+   CHATEAU ST.-PIERRE St.-Julien 1990 (NR) (4/30/91) (BT)
80+   CHATEAU BRANAIRE-DUCRU St.-Julien 1990 (NR) (4/30/91) (BT)

1989

95+   CHATEAU LEOVILLE-BARTON St.-Julien 1989 (NR) (4/30/90) (BT)
95+   CHATEAU TALBOT St.-Julien 1989 (NR) (4/30/90) (BT)
90+   CHATEAU BRANAIRE-DUCRU St.-Julien 1989 (NR) (4/30/90) (BT)
90+   CHATEAU DUCRU-BEAUCAILLOU St.-Julien 1989 (NR) (4/30/91) (BT)
90+   CHATEAU DUCRU-BEAUCAILLOU St.-Julien 1989 (NR) (4/30/90) (BT)
90+   CHATEAU GLORIA St.-Julien 1989 (NR) (4/30/90) (BT)
90+   CHATEAU GRUAUD-LAROSE St.-Julien 1989 (NR) (4/30/91) (BT)
90+   CHATEAU LAGRANGE St.-Julien 1989 (NR) (4/30/91) (BT)
90+   CHATEAU LANGOA-BARTON St.-Julien 1989 (NR) (4/30/91) (BT)
90+   CHATEAU LEOVILLE-BARTON St.-Julien 1989 (NR) (4/30/91) (BT)
90+   CHATEAU LEOVILLE-POYFERRE St.-Julien 1989 (NR) (4/30/91) (BT)
90+   CHATEAU ST.-PIERRE St.-Julien 1989 (NR) (4/30/91) (BT)
90+   CHATEAU ST.-PIERRE St.-Julien 1989 (NR) (4/30/90) (BT)
90+   CHATEAU TALBOT St.-Julien 1989 (NR) (4/30/91) (BT)
85+   CHATEAU BEYCHEVELLE St.-Julien 1989 (NR) (4/30/91) (BT)
85+   CHATEAU BEYCHEVELLE St.-Julien 1989 (NR) (4/30/90) (BT)
85+   CHATEAU BRANAIRE-DUCRU St.-Julien 1989 (NR) (4/30/91) (BT)
85+   LES FIEFS DE LAGRANGE St.-Julien 1989 (NR) (4/30/91) (BT)
85+   CHATEAU GLORIA St.-Julien 1989 (NR) (4/30/91) (BT)
85+   CHATEAU GRUAUD-LAROSE St.-Julien 1989 (NR) (4/30/90) (BT)
85+   CHATEAU LALANDE-BORIE St.-Julien 1989 (NR) (4/30/91) (BT)
85+   CHATEAU LANGOA-BARTON St.-Julien 1989 (NR) (4/30/90) (BT)
85+   CHATEAU LEOVILLE-POYFERRE St.-Julien 1989 (NR) (4/30/90) (BT)
85+   CHATEAU TERREY-GROS-CAILLOUX St.-Julien 1989 (NR) (4/30/91) (BT)
80+   CHATEAU DU GLANA St.-Julien 1989 (NR) (4/30/91) (BT)
80+   LADY LANGOA St.-Julien 1989 (NR) (4/30/91) (BT)

1988

96   CHATEAU LAGRANGE St.-Julien 1988 $26 (4/30/91)
95+   CHATEAU BEYCHEVELLE St.-Julien 1988 $40 (6/30/89) (BT)
93   CHATEAU BEYCHEVELLE St.-Julien 1988 $40 (4/30/91)
92   CHATEAU DUCRU-BEAUCAILLOU St.-Julien 1988 $48 (4/30/91)
92   LES FIEFS DE LAGRANGE St.-Julien 1988 $17 (4/30/91)
91   CHATEAU LEOVILLE-BARTON St.-Julien 1988 $20 (3/31/91)
90   CHATEAU GLORIA St.-Julien 1988 $23 (3/31/91)
90   CHATEAU TALBOT St.-Julien 1988 $25 (3/15/91)
90+   CHATEAU BRANAIRE-DUCRU St.-Julien 1988 $16 (6/30/89) (BT)
90+   CHATEAU DUCRU-BEAUCAILLOU St.-Julien 1988 $48 (8/31/90) (BT)
90+   CHATEAU GRUAUD-LAROSE St.-Julien 1988 Rel: $31 Cur: $31 (8/31/90) (BT)
90+   CHATEAU ST.-PIERRE St.-Julien 1988 $32 (8/31/90) (BT)
90+   CHATEAU TALBOT St.-Julien 1988 $25 (6/30/89) (BT)

FRANCE
BORDEAUX RED/*ST.-JULIEN*

89 CHATEAU GRUAUD-LAROSE St.-Julien 1988 Rel: $31 Cur: $31 (2/28/91) (TR)
87 CHATEAU LALANDE-BORIE St.-Julien 1988 $17 (4/30/91)
86 CHATEAU LANGOA-BARTON St.-Julien 1988 $25 (7/15/91)
85 CHATEAU ST.-PIERRE St.-Julien 1988 $32 (4/30/91)
85+ CHATEAU BRANAIRE-DUCRU St.-Julien 1988 $16 (8/31/90) (BT)
85+ CHATEAU DUCRU-BEAUCAILLOU St.-Julien 1988 $48 (6/30/89) (BT)
85+ CHATEAU GLORIA St.-Julien 1988 $23 (8/31/90) (BT)
85+ CHATEAU GRUAUD-LAROSE St.-Julien 1988 $31 (6/30/89) (BT)
85+ CHATEAU LANGOA-BARTON St.-Julien 1988 $25 (8/31/90) (BT)
85+ CHATEAU LEOVILLE-BARTON St.-Julien 1988 $20 (8/31/90) (BT)
85+ CHATEAU LEOVILLE-BARTON St.-Julien 1988 $20 (6/30/89) (BT)
85+ CHATEAU LEOVILLE-POYFERRE St.-Julien 1988 $23 (6/30/89) (BT)
85+ CHATEAU ST.-PIERRE St.-Julien 1988 $32 (6/30/89) (BT)
84 CHATEAU GRUAUD-LAROSE St.-Julien 1988 $31 (3/31/91)
81 CHATEAU LEOVILLE-POYFERRE St.-Julien 1988 $23 (7/15/91)
80+ CHATEAU GLORIA St.-Julien 1988 $23 (6/30/89) (BT)
80+ CHATEAU LANGOA-BARTON St.-Julien 1988 $25 (6/30/89) (BT)
80+ CHATEAU LEOVILLE-POYFERRE St.-Julien 1988 $23 (8/31/90) (BT)
80+ CHATEAU TERREY-GROS-CAILLOUX St.-Julien 1988 $14 (6/30/89) (BT)
75+ CHATEAU DU GLANA St.-Julien 1988 (NR) (6/30/89) (BT)

1987

89 CHATEAU ST.-PIERRE St.-Julien 1987 Rel: $17.50 Cur: $18 (5/15/90)
86 CHATEAU DUCRU-BEAUCAILLOU St.-Julien 1987 Rel: $35 Cur: $35 (5/15/90)
86 CHATEAU LEOVILLE-POYFERRE St.-Julien 1987 Rel: $24 Cur: $24 (5/15/90)
85 CHATEAU TALBOT St.-Julien 1987 Rel: $23.50 Cur: $24 (5/15/90)
85 CHATEAU TERREY-GROS-CAILLOUX St.-Julien 1987 $12 (11/30/89) (JS)
85+ CHATEAU BEYCHEVELLE St.-Julien 1987 Rel: $28 Cur: $28 (6/30/89) (BT)
85+ CHATEAU GRUAUD-LAROSE St.-Julien 1987 Rel: $22 Cur: $22 (6/30/89) (BT)
85+ CHATEAU LEOVILLE-LAS CASES St.-Julien 1987 Cur: $32 (6/30/88) (BT)
85+ CHATEAU LEOVILLE-POYFERRE St.-Julien 1987 Rel: $24 Cur: $24 (6/30/89) (BT)
85+ CHATEAU LEOVILLE-POYFERRE St.-Julien 1987 Rel: $24 Cur: $24 (6/30/88) (BT)
84 CHATEAU GLORIA St.-Julien 1987 Rel: $14.50 Cur: $15 (11/30/89) (JS)
84 CHATEAU LEOVILLE-LAS CASES St.-Julien 1987 Cur: $32 (2/15/90) (PM)
83 CHATEAU GRUAUD-LAROSE St.-Julien 1987 Rel: $22 Cur: $22 (2/28/91) (TR)
81 CHATEAU DU GLANA St.-Julien 1987 (NR) (11/30/89) (JS)
81 CHATEAU LALANDE-BORIE St.-Julien 1987 Rel: $15 Cur: $15 (11/30/89) (JS)
80 CHATEAU GLORIA St.-Julien 1987 Rel: $14.50 Cur: $15 (5/15/90)
80 CHATEAU LEOVILLE-BARTON St.-Julien 1987 Rel: $20 Cur: $20 (5/15/90)
80+ CHATEAU BEYCHEVELLE St.-Julien 1987 Rel: $28 Cur: $28 (6/30/88) (BT)
80+ CHATEAU BRANAIRE-DUCRU St.-Julien 1987 Rel: $15 Cur: $15 (6/30/89) (BT)
80+ CLOS DU MARQUIS St.-Julien 1987 Rel: $12 Cur: $14 (6/30/88) (BT)
80+ CHATEAU DUCRU-BEAUCAILLOU St.-Julien 1987 Rel: $35 Cur: $35 (6/30/88) (BT)
80+ CHATEAU GLORIA St.-Julien 1987 Rel: $14.50 Cur: $15 (6/30/89) (BT)
80+ CHATEAU GRUAUD-LAROSE St.-Julien 1987 Rel: $22 Cur: $22 (6/30/88) (BT)
80+ CHATEAU LANGOA-BARTON St.-Julien 1987 Rel: $17 Cur: $17 (6/30/88) (BT)
80+ CHATEAU LEOVILLE-BARTON St.-Julien 1987 Rel: $20 Cur: $20 (6/30/89) (BT)
80+ CHATEAU ST.-PIERRE St.-Julien 1987 Rel: $17.50 Cur: $18 (6/30/89) (BT)
80+ CHATEAU TALBOT St.-Julien 1987 Rel: $23.50 Cur: $24 (6/30/89) (BT)
80+ CHATEAU TALBOT St.-Julien 1987 Rel: $23.50 Cur: $24 (6/30/88) (BT)
79 CHATEAU BEYCHEVELLE St.-Julien 1987 Rel: $28 Cur: $28 (5/15/90)
79 CLOS DU MARQUIS St.-Julien 1987 Rel: $12 Cur: $14 (5/15/90)
79 CHATEAU MOULIN-RICHE St.-Julien 1987 Rel: $18 Cur: $18 (11/30/89) (JS)
78 CHATEAU GRUAUD-LAROSE St.-Julien 1987 Rel: $22 Cur: $22 (5/15/90)
75+ CHATEAU DU GLANA St.-Julien 1987 (NR) (6/30/89) (BT)
75+ CHATEAU LAGRANGE St.-Julien 1987 Rel: $25 Cur: $25 (6/30/88) (BT)
75+ CHATEAU LANGOA-BARTON St.-Julien 1987 Rel: $17 Cur: $17 (6/30/89) (BT)
75+ CHATEAU TERREY-GROS-CAILLOUX St.-Julien 1987 $12 (6/30/89) (BT)
70+ LES FIEFS DE LAGRANGE St.-Julien 1987 Rel: $14 Cur: $14 (6/30/88) (BT)
65+ CHATEAU BRANAIRE-DUCRU St.-Julien 1987 Rel: $15 Cur: $15 (6/30/88) (BT)

1986

96 CHATEAU LEOVILLE-LAS CASES St.-Julien 1986 Rel: $44 Cur: $61 (2/15/90) (PM)
96 CHATEAU LEOVILLE-LAS CASES St.-Julien 1986 Rel: $44 Cur: $61 (9/15/89) CS
93 CHATEAU BEYCHEVELLE St.-Julien 1986 Rel: $37 Cur: $37 (5/31/89)
93 CHATEAU GRUAUD-LAROSE St.-Julien 1986 Rel: $34 Cur: $34 (5/31/89)
92 CHATEAU ST.-PIERRE St.-Julien 1986 Rel: $17 Cur: $21 (9/15/89) SS
91 CHATEAU DUCRU-BEAUCAILLOU St.-Julien 1986 Rel: $52 Cur: $52 (6/30/89)
91 CHATEAU LALANDE-BORIE St.-Julien 1986 Rel: $17 Cur: $17 (11/30/89) (JS)
91 CHATEAU TALBOT St.-Julien 1986 Rel: $32 Cur: $32 (5/31/89)
90 CHATEAU LEOVILLE-BARTON St.-Julien 1986 Rel: $24 Cur: $28 (5/31/89)
90+ CHATEAU BEYCHEVELLE St.-Julien 1986 Rel: $37 Cur: $37 (5/15/87) (BT)
90+ CHATEAU BRANAIRE-DUCRU St.-Julien 1986 Rel: $16 Cur: $20 (5/15/87) (BT)
90+ CHATEAU DUCRU-BEAUCAILLOU St.-Julien 1986 Rel: $52 Cur: $52 (6/30/88) (BT)
90+ CHATEAU DUCRU-BEAUCAILLOU St.-Julien 1986 Rel: $52 Cur: $52 (5/15/87) (BT)
90+ CHATEAU GRUAUD-LAROSE St.-Julien 1986 Rel: $34 Cur: $34 (5/15/87) (BT)
90+ CHATEAU LEOVILLE-BARTON St.-Julien 1986 Rel: $24 Cur: $28 (6/30/88) (BT)
90+ CHATEAU LEOVILLE-BARTON St.-Julien 1986 Rel: $24 Cur: $28 (5/15/87) (BT)
90+ CHATEAU LEOVILLE-LAS CASES St.-Julien 1986 Rel: $44 Cur: $61 (6/30/88) (BT)
89 CHATEAU GLORIA St.-Julien 1986 Rel: $18 Cur: $18 (11/30/89) (JS)
89 CHATEAU GLORIA St.-Julien 1986 Rel: $18 Cur: $18 (5/31/89)
89 CHATEAU GRUAUD-LAROSE St.-Julien 1986 Rel: $34 Cur: $34 (2/28/91) (TR)
88 CHATEAU MOULIN-RICHE St.-Julien 1986 Rel: $20 Cur: $20 (11/30/89) (JS)
87 CHATEAU TERREY-GROS-CAILLOUX St.-Julien 1986 $12 (11/30/89) (JS)
86 CHATEAU LAGRANGE St.-Julien 1986 Rel: $20 Cur: $28 (2/15/90)
86 CHATEAU LEOVILLE-POYFERRE St.-Julien 1986 Rel: $24 Cur: $27 (5/31/89)
85+ CHATEAU BRANAIRE-DUCRU St.-Julien 1986 Rel: $16 Cur: $20 (6/30/88) (BT)
85+ CLOS DU MARQUIS St.-Julien 1986 Rel: $17 Cur: $20 (6/30/88) (BT)
85+ CHATEAU GRUAUD-LAROSE St.-Julien 1986 Rel: $34 Cur: $34 (6/30/88) (BT)
85+ CHATEAU LAGRANGE St.-Julien 1986 Rel: $20 Cur: $28 (6/30/88) (BT)
85+ CHATEAU LANGOA-BARTON St.-Julien 1986 Rel: $22 Cur: $25 (6/30/88) (BT)
85+ CHATEAU LEOVILLE-POYFERRE St.-Julien 1986 Rel: $24 Cur: $27 (6/30/88) (BT)
85+ CHATEAU TALBOT St.-Julien 1986 Rel: $32 Cur: $32 (6/30/88) (BT)
84 CLOS DU MARQUIS St.-Julien 1986 Rel: $17 Cur: $20 (9/15/89)
84 CHATEAU DU GLANA St.-Julien 1986 $17 (11/30/89) (JS)
84 CHATEAU LALANDE-BORIE St.-Julien 1986 Rel: $17 Cur: $17 (11/15/89)
80+ CLOS DU MARQUIS St.-Julien 1986 Rel: $17 Cur: $20 (5/15/87) (BT)
80+ LES FIEFS DE LAGRANGE St.-Julien 1986 Rel: $17 Cur: $17 (6/30/88) (BT)
80+ CHATEAU TALBOT St.-Julien 1986 Rel: $32 Cur: $32 (5/15/87) (BT)
70+ CHATEAU LALANDE-BORIE St.-Julien 1986 Rel: $17 Cur: $17 (5/15/87) (BT)
70+ CHATEAU LANGOA-BARTON St.-Julien 1986 Rel: $22 Cur: $25 (5/15/87) (BT)

1985

95 CHATEAU BEYCHEVELLE St.-Julien 1985 Rel: $35 Cur: $39 (8/31/88) CS
95 CHATEAU DUCRU-BEAUCAILLOU St.-Julien 1985 Rel: $50 Cur: $51 (6/15/88)
94 CHATEAU LEOVILLE-LAS CASES St.-Julien 1985 Rel: $45 Cur: $55 (2/15/90) (PM)
93 CHATEAU GRUAUD-LAROSE St.-Julien 1985 Rel: $31 Cur: $33 (2/28/91) (TR)
92 CHATEAU LEOVILLE-BARTON St.-Julien 1985 Rel: $24 Cur: $31 (4/15/88)
92 CHATEAU LEOVILLE-POYFERRE St.-Julien 1985 Rel: $19 Cur: $27 (4/30/88)
91 CHATEAU LANGOA-BARTON St.-Julien 1985 Rel: $20 Cur: $22 (6/15/88)
90 CHATEAU GRUAUD-LAROSE St.-Julien 1985 Rel: $31 Cur: $33 (4/30/88)
90 CHATEAU LEOVILLE-LAS CASES St.-Julien 1985 Rel: $45 Cur: $55 (8/31/88)
90+ CHATEAU BEYCHEVELLE St.-Julien 1985 Rel: $35 Cur: $39 (4/16/86) (BT)
90+ CHATEAU DUCRU-BEAUCAILLOU St.-Julien 1985 Rel: $50 Cur: $51 (5/15/87) (BT)
90+ CHATEAU DUCRU-BEAUCAILLOU St.-Julien 1985 Rel: $50 Cur: $51 (4/16/86) (BT)
90+ CHATEAU LEOVILLE-LAS CASES St.-Julien 1985 Rel: $45 Cur: $55 (5/15/87) (BT)
89 CHATEAU BRANAIRE-DUCRU St.-Julien 1985 Rel: $25 Cur: $25 (6/30/88)
89 CHATEAU GLORIA St.-Julien 1985 Rel: $14 Cur: $20 (4/15/88)
87 CHATEAU TALBOT St.-Julien 1985 Rel: $26 Cur: $26 (4/30/88)
84 CLOS DU MARQUIS St.-Julien 1985 Rel: $14 Cur: $20 (9/30/88)
83 BARTON & GUESTIER St.-Julien 1985 $12.50 (2/15/88)
83 CHATEAU LAGRANGE St.-Julien 1985 Rel: $23 Cur: $27 (9/30/88)
83 CHATEAU MOULIN-RICHE St.-Julien 1985 Rel: $20 Cur: $20 (6/15/88)
80+ CLOS DU MARQUIS St.-Julien 1985 Rel: $14 Cur: $20 (5/15/87) (BT)
80+ CHATEAU LAGRANGE St.-Julien 1985 Rel: $23 Cur: $27 (5/15/87) (BT)
80+ CHATEAU LEOVILLE-BARTON St.-Julien 1985 Rel: $24 Cur: $31 (4/16/86) (BT)
70+ LES FIEFS DE LAGRANGE St.-Julien 1985 Rel: $17 Cur: $18 (5/15/87) (BT)
70+ CHATEAU LANGOA-BARTON St.-Julien 1985 Rel: $20 Cur: $22 (4/16/86) (BT)
70+ CHATEAU LEOVILLE-POYFERRE St.-Julien 1985 Rel: $19 Cur: $27 (4/16/86) (BT)
70+ CHATEAU ST.-PIERRE St.-Julien 1985 Cur: $21 (4/16/86) (BT)
60+ CHATEAU GLORIA St.-Julien 1985 Rel: $14 Cur: $20 (4/16/86) (BT)

1984

88 CHATEAU GRUAUD-LAROSE St.-Julien 1984 Rel: $21.50 Cur: $23 (5/15/87)
87 CHATEAU DUCRU-BEAUCAILLOU St.-Julien 1984 Rel: $24 Cur: $31 (8/31/87)
87 CHATEAU GLORIA St.-Julien 1984 Rel: $8 Cur: $14 (3/15/87) BB
85 CHATEAU LEOVILLE-POYFERRE St.-Julien 1984 Rel: $24.50 Cur: $25 (10/15/87)
83 CHATEAU GRUAUD-LAROSE St.-Julien 1984 Rel: $21.50 Cur: $23 (2/28/91) (TR)
82 CHATEAU LEOVILLE-LAS CASES St.-Julien 1984 Rel: $33 Cur: $33 (2/15/90) (PM)
80 CHATEAU TALBOT St.-Julien 1984 Rel: $19 Cur: $20 (5/15/87)
78 CHATEAU BEYCHEVELLE St.-Julien 1984 Rel: $32 Cur: $32 (5/15/87)
78 CHATEAU LEOVILLE-LAS CASES St.-Julien 1984 Rel: $33 Cur: $33 (10/15/87)

1983

92 CHATEAU LEOVILLE-BARTON St.-Julien 1983 Rel: $24 Cur: $26 (3/01/86)
90 CHATEAU DUCRU-BEAUCAILLOU St.-Julien 1983 Rel: $27 Cur: $42 (6/16/86)
89 CHATEAU TALBOT St.-Julien 1983 Rel: $22 Cur: $26 (9/30/86)
88 CHATEAU BEYCHEVELLE St.-Julien 1983 Rel: $25 Cur: $30 (3/01/86)
88 CHATEAU BRANAIRE-DUCRU St.-Julien 1983 Rel: $24 Cur: $24 (3/01/86)
88 CHATEAU GRUAUD-LAROSE St.-Julien 1983 Rel: $19 Cur: $32 (7/16/86)
85 LES FIEFS DE LAGRANGE St.-Julien 1983 Rel: $10 Cur: $13 (5/01/86)
85 CHATEAU GRUAUD-LAROSE St.-Julien 1983 Rel: $19 Cur: $32 (2/28/91) (TR)
85 CHATEAU LEOVILLE-LAS CASES St.-Julien 1983 Rel: $26 Cur: $44 (2/15/90) (PM)
84 CHATEAU LEOVILLE-LAS CASES St.-Julien 1983 Rel: $26 Cur: $44 (3/31/87)
83 CHATEAU GLORIA St.-Julien 1983 Rel: $10 Cur: $18 (10/15/86)
83 CHATEAU LEOVILLE-POYFERRE St.-Julien 1983 Rel: $20 Cur: $25 (3/01/86)
76 CHATEAU DU MOULIN DE LA BRIDAN St.-Julien 1983 $11.25 (4/01/86)

1982

98 CHATEAU LEOVILLE-LAS CASES St.-Julien 1982 Rel: $59 Cur: $93 (2/15/90) (PM)
93 CHATEAU LEOVILLE-LAS CASES St.-Julien 1982 Rel: $59 Cur: $93 (5/01/89)
93 CHATEAU ST.-PIERRE St.-Julien 1982 Rel: $15 Cur: $23 (12/16/85) CS
92 CHATEAU DUCRU-BEAUCAILLOU St.-Julien 1982 Rel: $28 Cur: $76 (5/01/85)
92 CHATEAU LALANDE-BORIE St.-Julien 1982 Rel: $15 Cur: $17 (11/30/89) (JS)
90 CHATEAU GRUAUD-LAROSE St.-Julien 1982 Rel: $40 Cur: $51 (5/01/89)
90 CHATEAU MOULIN-RICHE St.-Julien 1982 Cur: $22 (11/30/89) (JS)
89 CHATEAU BEYCHEVELLE St.-Julien 1982 Rel: $35 Cur: $44 (12/31/89) (TM)
89 CHATEAU GRUAUD-LAROSE St.-Julien 1982 Rel: $40 Cur: $51 (2/28/91) (TR)
89 CHATEAU LEOVILLE-POYFERRE St.-Julien 1982 Rel: $20 Cur: $43 (6/01/85)
88 CHATEAU TALBOT St.-Julien 1982 Rel: $26 Cur: $34 (5/01/89)
85 CHATEAU DU GLANA St.-Julien 1982 Cur: $12 (11/30/89) (JS)
83 CHATEAU GLORIA St.-Julien 1982 Rel: $14.75 Cur: $29 (11/30/89) (JS)
81 CHATEAU GLORIA St.-Julien 1982 Rel: $14.75 Cur: $29 (2/16/85)
76 CHATEAU LALANDE-BORIE St.-Julien 1982 Rel: $15 Cur: $17 (10/15/86)

1981

93 CHATEAU DUCRU-BEAUCAILLOU St.-Julien 1981 Rel: $25 Cur: $49 (5/01/85)
91 CHATEAU LEOVILLE-LAS CASES St.-Julien 1981 Rel: $23.50 Cur: $50 (6/01/84)
90 CHATEAU GRUAUD-LAROSE St.-Julien 1981 Rel: $18.50 Cur: $35 (2/28/91) (TR)
88 CHATEAU LEOVILLE-POYFERRE St.-Julien 1981 Rel: $12.50 Cur: $25 (6/01/84)
87 CHATEAU GRUAUD-LAROSE St.-Julien 1981 Rel: $18.50 Cur: $35 (6/01/84)
86 CHATEAU LEOVILLE-LAS CASES St.-Julien 1981 Rel: $23.50 Cur: $50 (2/15/90) (PM)
83 CHATEAU TALBOT St.-Julien 1981 Rel: $17 Cur: $30 (6/01/84)
82 CHATEAU GLORIA St.-Julien 1981 Rel: $10 Cur: $22 (6/01/84)

Key to Symbols

The scores reported here are the results of blind tastings conducted by our panel of senior editors. Wines that carry the initials below are results of individual tastings.

THE WINE SPECTATOR 100-POINT SCALE ***95-100***—Classic, a great wine; ***90-94***—Outstanding, superior character and style; ***80-89***—Good to very good, a wine with special qualities; ***70-79***—Average, drinkable wine that may have minor flaws; ***60-69***—Below average, drinkable but not recommended; ***50-59***—Poor, undrinkable, not recommended. "+"—With a score indicates a range; used primarily with barrel tastings to indicate a preliminary score.

SPECIAL DESIGNATIONS SS—Spectator Selection, CS—Cellar Selection, BB—Best Buy.

TASTER'S INITIALS (JG)—Jim Gordon, (HS)—Harvey Steiman, (JL)—James Laube, (JS)—James Suckling, (TM)—Thomas Matthews, (TR)—Terry Robards, (BT)—Barrel Tasting (these wines were tasted blind from barrel samples), (CA-date)—*California's Great Cabernets* by James Laube, (CH-date)—*California's Great Chardonnays* by James Laube, (VP-date)—*Vintage Port* by James Suckling.

DATE TASTED Dates in parentheses represent the issue in which the rating was published.

81   CHATEAU BEYCHEVELLE St.-Julien 1981 Rel: $17.50 Cur: $27 (5/01/84)

1980

88   CHATEAU DUCRU-BEAUCAILLOU St.-Julien 1980 Rel: $13.50 Cur: $23 (5/01/84) CS
84   CHATEAU LEOVILLE-LAS CASES St.-Julien 1980 Cur: $71/1.5L (2/15/90) (PM)
83   CHATEAU GRUAUD-LAROSE St.-Julien 1980 Cur: $25 (2/28/91) (TR)

1979

95   CHATEAU LEOVILLE-LAS CASES St.-Julien 1979 Cur: $51 (10/15/89) (JS)
92   CHATEAU BEYCHEVELLE St.-Julien 1979 Cur: $38 (10/15/89) (JS)
90   CHATEAU LEOVILLE-LAS CASES St.-Julien 1979 Cur: $51 (2/15/90) (PM)
89   CHATEAU GRUAUD-LAROSE St.-Julien 1979 Cur: $30 (2/28/91) (TR)
87   CHATEAU DUCRU-BEAUCAILLOU St.-Julien 1979 Cur: $48 (10/15/89) (JS)
84   CHATEAU ST.-PIERRE St.-Julien 1979 Cur: $24 (10/15/89) (JS)
84   CHATEAU TALBOT St.-Julien 1979 Cur: $26 (10/15/89) (JS)
83   CHATEAU GLORIA St.-Julien 1979 Cur: $18 (10/15/89) (JS)
83   CHATEAU GRUAUD-LAROSE St.-Julien 1979 Cur: $30 (10/15/89) (JS)
81   CHATEAU DUCRU-BEAUCAILLOU St.-Julien 1979 Cur: $48 (5/01/85)

1978

94   CHATEAU LEOVILLE-LAS CASES St.-Julien 1978 Cur: $73 (2/15/90) (PM)
91   CHATEAU DUCRU-BEAUCAILLOU St.-Julien 1978 Cur: $75 (5/01/85)
91   CHATEAU GRUAUD-LAROSE St.-Julien 1978 Cur: $43 (2/28/91) (TR)
86   CHATEAU BEYCHEVELLE St.-Julien 1978 Cur: $41 (12/31/89) (TM)

1977

71   CHATEAU GRUAUD-LAROSE St.-Julien 1977 Cur: $33 (2/28/91) (TR)

1976

85   CHATEAU GRUAUD-LAROSE St.-Julien 1976 Cur: $34 (2/28/91) (TR)

1975

89   CHATEAU GRUAUD-LAROSE St.-Julien 1975 Cur: $52 (2/28/91) (TR)

1974

65   CHATEAU GRUAUD-LAROSE St.-Julien 1974 Cur: $28 (2/28/91) (TR)
63   CHATEAU GRUAUD-LAROSE St.-Julien 1974 Cur: $28 (2/28/91) (TR)

1973

76   CHATEAU GRUAUD-LAROSE St.-Julien 1973 Cur: $28 (2/28/91) (TR)

1971

85   CHATEAU BEYCHEVELLE St.-Julien 1971 Cur: $50 (12/31/89) (TM)
85   CHATEAU GRUAUD-LAROSE St.-Julien 1971 Cur: $31 (2/28/91) (TR)
76   CHATEAU LEOVILLE-LAS CASES St.-Julien 1971 Cur: $66 (4/01/86)

1970

89   CHATEAU GRUAUD-LAROSE St.-Julien 1970 Cur: $74 (2/28/91) (TR)
89   CHATEAU LEOVILLE-LAS CASES St.-Julien 1970 Cur: $89 (2/15/90) (PM)

1969

50   CHATEAU GRUAUD-LAROSE St.-Julien 1969 Cur: $15 (2/28/91) (TR)

1968

65   CHATEAU GRUAUD-LAROSE St.-Julien 1968 Cur: $15 (2/28/91) (TR)

1967

83   CHATEAU BEYCHEVELLE St.-Julien 1967 Cur: $36 (12/31/89) (TM)
78   CHATEAU GRUAUD-LAROSE St.-Julien 1967 Cur: $33 (2/28/91) (TR)

1966

87   CHATEAU GRUAUD-LAROSE St.-Julien 1966 Cur: $115 (2/28/91) (TR)

1964

88   CHATEAU GRUAUD-LAROSE St.-Julien 1964 Cur: $70 (2/28/91) (TR)

1962

95   CHATEAU BEYCHEVELLE St.-Julien 1962 Cur: $89 (11/30/87) (JS)
94   CHATEAU GRUAUD-LAROSE St.-Julien 1962 Cur: $95 (2/28/91) (TR)
88   CHATEAU GRUAUD-LAROSE St.-Julien 1962 Cur: $95 (11/30/87) (JS)
85   CHATEAU LEOVILLE-LAS CASES St.-Julien 1962 Cur: $92 (11/30/87) (JS)
80   CHATEAU DUCRU-BEAUCAILLOU St.-Julien 1962 Cur: $120 (11/30/87) (JS)
70   CHATEAU LEOVILLE-BARTON St.-Julien 1962 Cur: $80 (11/30/87) (JS)
68   CHATEAU ST.-PIERRE St.-Julien 1962 Cur: $55 (11/30/87) (JS)
55   CHATEAU TALBOT St.-Julien 1962 Cur: $63 (11/30/87) (JS)

1961

95   CHATEAU GRUAUD-LAROSE St.-Julien 1961 Cur: $243 (2/28/91) (TR)
94   CHATEAU DUCRU-BEAUCAILLOU St.-Julien 1961 Cur: $314 (3/16/86) (JL)
88   CHATEAU LEOVILLE-LAS CASES St.-Julien 1961 Cur: $245 (3/16/86) (JL)
86   CHATEAU GRUAUD-LAROSE St.-Julien 1961 Cur: $243 (3/16/86) (JL)
79   CHATEAU BRANAIRE-DUCRU St.-Julien 1961 Cur: $114 (3/16/86) (JL)
77   CHATEAU LEOVILLE-POYFERRE St.-Julien 1961 Cur: $125 (3/16/86) (JL)
76   CHATEAU LEOVILLE-BARTON St.-Julien 1961 Cur: $125 (3/16/86) (JL)
68   CHATEAU BEYCHEVELLE St.-Julien 1961 Cur: $158 (3/16/86) (JL)
67   CHATEAU LAGRANGE St.-Julien 1961 Cur: $90 (3/16/86) (JL)
63   CHATEAU LANGOA-BARTON St.-Julien 1961 Cur: $113 (3/16/86) (JL)

1959

96   CHATEAU LEOVILLE-LAS CASES St.-Julien 1959 Cur: $208 (10/15/90) (JS)
90   CHATEAU DUCRU-BEAUCAILLOU St.-Julien 1959 Cur: $250 (10/15/90) (JS)
86   CHATEAU BRANAIRE-DUCRU St.-Julien 1959 Cur: $127 (10/15/90) (JS)
86   CHATEAU TALBOT St.-Julien 1959 Cur: $110 (10/15/90) (JS)
85   CHATEAU GRUAUD-LAROSE St.-Julien 1959 Cur: $145 (2/28/91) (TR)
85   CHATEAU LEOVILLE-BARTON St.-Julien 1959 Cur: $125 (10/15/90) (JS)
80   CHATEAU BEYCHEVELLE St.-Julien 1959 Cur: $155 (10/15/90) (JS)

1957

78   CHATEAU GRUAUD-LAROSE St.-Julien 1957 Cur: $65 (2/28/91) (TR)

1955

87   CHATEAU GRUAUD-LAROSE St.-Julien 1955 Cur: $150 (2/28/91) (TR)

1953

88   CHATEAU GRUAUD-LAROSE St.-Julien 1953 Cur: $150 (2/28/91) (TR)

1952

85   CHATEAU GRUAUD-LAROSE St.-Julien 1952 Cur: $157 (2/28/91) (TR)

1950

83   CHATEAU GRUAUD-LAROSE St.-Julien 1950 Cur: $250 (2/28/91) (TR)

1949

85   CHATEAU GRUAUD-LAROSE St.-Julien 1949 Cur: $255 (2/28/91) (TR)

1948

92   CHATEAU BEYCHEVELLE St.-Julien 1948 Cur: $175 (12/31/89) (TM)

1947

88   CHATEAU GRUAUD-LAROSE St.-Julien 1947 Cur: $285 (2/28/91) (TR)

1945

96   CHATEAU GRUAUD-LAROSE St.-Julien 1945 Cur: $375 (2/28/91) (TR)
88   CHATEAU BEYCHEVELLE St.-Julien 1945 Cur: $413 (3/16/86) (JL)
86   CHATEAU GRUAUD-LAROSE St.-Julien 1945 Cur: $375 (3/16/86) (JL)
81   CHATEAU TALBOT St.-Julien 1945 Cur: $310 (3/16/86) (JL)
80   CHATEAU LEOVILLE-POYFERRE St.-Julien 1945 Cur: $206 (3/16/86) (JL)
79   CHATEAU DUCRU-BEAUCAILLOU St.-Julien 1945 Cur: $463 (3/16/86) (JL)
75   CHATEAU LEOVILLE-LAS CASES St.-Julien 1945 Cur: $454 (3/16/86) (JL)
73   CHATEAU LEOVILLE-BARTON St.-Julien 1945 Cur: $333 (3/16/86) (JL)
71   CHATEAU LANGOA-BARTON St.-Julien 1945 Cur: $250 (3/16/86) (JL)
67   CHATEAU BRANAIRE-DUCRU St.-Julien 1945 Cur: $175 (3/16/86) (JL)

1943

83   CHATEAU GRUAUD-LAROSE St.-Julien 1943 Cur: $200 (2/28/91) (TR)

1937

87   CHATEAU GRUAUD-LAROSE St.-Julien 1937 Cur: $150 (2/28/91) (TR)

1934

83   CHATEAU GRUAUD-LAROSE St.-Julien 1934 Cur: $150 (2/28/91) (TR)

1929

95   CHATEAU BEYCHEVELLE St.-Julien 1929 Cur: $500 (12/31/89) (TM)
85   CHATEAU GRUAUD-LAROSE St.-Julien 1929 Cur: $550 (2/28/91) (TR)

1928

94   CHATEAU GRUAUD-LAROSE St.-Julien 1928 Cur: $500 (2/28/91) (TR)

1926

95   CHATEAU GRUAUD-LAROSE St.-Julien 1926 Cur: $250 (2/28/91) (TR)

1924

89   CHATEAU GRUAUD-LAROSE St.-Julien 1924 Cur: $250 (2/28/91) (TR)

1921

87   CHATEAU GRUAUD-LAROSE St.-Julien 1921 Cur: $250 (2/28/91) (TR)

1920

85   CHATEAU GRUAUD-LAROSE St.-Julien 1920 Cur: $300 (2/28/91) (TR)

1918

78   CHATEAU GRUAUD-LAROSE St.-Julien 1918 Cur: $300 (2/28/91) (TR)

1907

72   CHATEAU GRUAUD-LAROSE St.-Julien 1907 Cur: $255 (2/28/91) (TR)

1906

85   CHATEAU GRUAUD-LAROSE St.-Julien 1906 Cur: $300 (2/28/91) (TR)

1899

83   CHATEAU GRUAUD-LAROSE St.-Julien 1899 Cur: $600 (2/28/91) (TR)

1893

78   CHATEAU GRUAUD-LAROSE St.-Julien 1893 Cur: $500 (2/28/91) (TR)

1887

71   CHATEAU GRUAUD-LAROSE St.-Julien 1887 Cur: $400 (2/28/91) (TR)

1878

83   CHATEAU GRUAUD-LAROSE St.-Julien 1878 Cur: $500 (2/28/91) (TR)

1870

87   CHATEAU GRUAUD-LAROSE St.-Julien 1870 Cur: $2,300 (2/28/91) (TR)

1865

65   CHATEAU GRUAUD-LAROSE St.-Julien 1865 Cur: $1,800 (2/28/91) (TR)

1844

85   CHATEAU GRUAUD-LAROSE St.-Julien 1844 (NA) (2/28/91) (TR)

1834

83   CHATEAU GRUAUD-LAROSE St.-Julien 1834 (NA) (2/28/91) (TR)

1819

89   CHATEAU GRUAUD-LAROSE St.-Julien 1819 (NA) (2/28/91) (TR)

FRANCE
BORDEAUX RED/OTHER BORDEAUX RED

1989

85   CHATEAU PLAISANCE Premières Côtes de Blaye Cuvée Spéciale 1989 $9 (2/28/91) BB
80   CHATEAU PEYRAUD Premières Côtes de Blaye 1989 $8 (3/31/91)
80+ CHATEAU SIAURAC Lalande-de-Pomerol 1989 (NR) (4/30/91) (BT)
78   CHATEAU PERENNE Premières Côtes de Blaye 1989 $9 (3/31/91)
70+ CHATEAU SIAURAC Lalande-de-Pomerol 1989 (NR) (4/30/90) (BT)

1988

85   CHATEAU BERTINERIE Premières Côtes de Blaye 1988 $10 (7/15/90)
83   CHATEAU PITRAY Côtes de Castillon 1988 $7 (2/28/91) BB
81   CHATEAU HAUT-RIAN Premières Côtes de Bordeaux 1988 $7 (5/15/90) BB
78   CHATEAU GRAND-CLARET Premières Côtes de Bordeaux 1988 $7 (7/31/91)
76   CHATEAU DE LA MEULIERE Premières Côtes de Bordeaux 1988 $9 (2/28/91)
75+ CHATEAU SIAURAC Lalande-de-Pomerol 1988 $20 (6/30/89) (BT)

1987

75+ CHATEAU SIAURAC Lalande-de-Pomerol 1987 Rel: $17 Cur: $17 (6/30/89) (BT)

1986

82   CHATEAU PERENNE Premières Côtes de Blaye 1986 $7 (6/30/89)
81   CHATEAU PITRAY Côtes de Castillon 1986 $6 (9/30/89) BB
81   CHATEAU SAUVAGE Premières Côtes de Bordeaux 1986 $9 (4/15/90)
80   CHATEAU BEAUSEJOUR Côtes de Castillon 1986 $5 (6/15/89) BB
79   CHATEAU LA CROIX DE MILLORIT Côtes de Bourg 1986 $9/375ml (5/15/91)
79   CHATEAU SEGONZAC Premières Côtes de Blaye 1986 $9.75 (6/30/89)
77   CHATEAU LA PIERRIERE Côtes de Castillon 1986 $6 (12/31/88)
76   CHATEAU CAYLA Premières Côtes de Bordeaux 1986 $7 (6/30/89)

1985

88   CHATEAU GRAND-ORMEAU Lalande-de-Pomerol 1985 $16 (5/31/88)
85   CHATEAU DE BEL-AIR Lalande-de-Pomerol 1985 $18 (9/30/88)
85   CHATEAU SEGONZAC Premières Côtes de Blaye 1985 $9 (2/15/88)
81   CHATEAU MAYNE-DAVID Côtes de Castillon 1985 $6 (2/28/87) BB
80   CHATEAU PERENNE Premières Côtes de Blaye 1985 $7 (2/15/88)
76   CHATEAU DE BELCIER Côtes de Castillon 1985 $5 (6/30/88)
76   CHATEAU CLAIRAC Premières Côtes de Blaye 1985 $4.50 (4/15/88)
76   CHATEAU GRAND-CHEMIN Côtes de Bourg 1985 $8 (6/15/89)
75   CHATEAU DUPLESSY Premières Côtes de Bordeaux 1985 $6 (5/31/88)
74   CHATEAU LA GROLET Côtes de Bourg 1985 $7 (2/15/88)
73   CHATEAU CAYLA Premières Côtes de Bordeaux 1985 $4 (5/31/88)
72   CHATEAU LEZONGARS Premières Côtes de Bordeaux 1985 $7 (11/15/87)
72   DOMAINE LA TUQUE BEL-AIR Côtes de Castillon 1985 $8.50 (9/30/88)
71   CHATEAU DE PRIEURE Premières Côtes de Bordeaux 1985 $4.50 (5/31/88)
69   CHATEAU LA GROLET Côtes de Bourg 1985 $7 (5/15/88)

1983

79   CHATEAU LEON Côtes de Bordeaux 1983 $5.50 (11/15/86)

1982

79   CHATEAU PERENNE Premières Côtes de Blaye 1982 $5 (11/16/85) BB
79   CHATEAU PERENNE Premières Côtes de Blaye 1982 $5 (5/01/85)
78   CHATEAU CHANGROLLE Lalande-de-Pomerol 1982 $6 (12/16/84)
70   CHATEAU DE LA GRAVE Côtes de Bourg 1982 $5.25 (2/16/85)

1981

74   CHATEAU DE LA GRAVE Côtes de Bourg 1981 $4.99 (2/16/85)

BORDEAUX WHITE/GRAVES-PESSAC-LÉOGNAN

1989

90   CHATEAU DE CRUZEAU Pessac-Léognan 1989 $16 (6/15/91)
90   CHATEAU DE ROCHEMORIN Pessac-Léognan 1989 $17 (6/15/91)
89   CHATEAU COUHINS-LURTON Pessac-Léognan 1989 $25 (7/31/91)
88   CHATEAU LE SARTRE Pessac-Léognan 1989 $13.50 (3/31/91)
86   CHATEAU LA TOUR-MARTILLAC Pessac-Léognan 1989 $28 (2/28/91)
81   CHATEAU CARBONNIEUX Pessac-Léognan 1989 $22 (2/28/91)

1988

95+ CHATEAU DE FIEUZAL Pessac-Léognan 1988 $45 (6/30/89) (BT)
95+ CHATEAU HAUT-BRION Pessac-Léognan 1988 $84 (6/30/89) (BT)
95+ CHATEAU LAVILLE-HAUT-BRION Pessac-Léognan 1988 $64 (6/30/89) (BT)
90+ DOMAINE DE CHEVALIER Pessac-Léognan 1988 (NR) (6/30/89) (BT)
90+ CHATEAU LA TOUR-MARTILLAC Pessac-Léognan 1988 $30 (6/30/89) (BT)
87   CHATEAU HAUT-BRION Pessac-Léognan 1988 $84 (12/15/90)
85   CHATEAU LAVILLE-HAUT-BRION Pessac-Léognan 1988 $64 (12/15/90)
85+ CHATEAU COUHINS-LURTON Pessac-Léognan 1988 $28 (6/30/89) (BT)
85+ CHATEAU LA GARDE Pessac-Léognan 1988 $15 (6/30/89) (BT)
85+ CHATEAU LA LOUVIERE Pessac-Léognan 1988 $15 (6/30/89) (BT)
85+ CHATEAU MALARTIC-LAGRAVIERE Pessac-Léognan 1988 $31 (6/30/89) (BT)
84   CHATEAU LE BONNAT Graves 1988 $17 (3/31/90)
84   CHATEAU RAHOUL Graves 1988 $20 (3/31/91)
83   CHATEAU COUHINS-LURTON Pessac-Léognan 1988 $28 (5/31/90)
83   CHATEAU LA LOUVIERE Pessac-Léognan 1988 $15 (5/31/90)

83   CHATEAU LA LOUVIERE Pessac-Léognan 1988 $15 (5/15/90)
82   CHATEAU DE CRUZEAU Pessac-Léognan 1988 $13 (5/31/90)
82   CHATEAU OLIVIER Pessac-Léognan 1988 $23 (3/31/91)
82   CHATEAU DE ROCHEMORIN Pessac-Léognan 1988 Rel: $15 Cur: $15 (5/31/90)
80+ CHATEAU BARET Pessac-Léognan 1988 $19 (6/30/89) (BT)
80+ CHATEAU BOUSCAUT Pessac-Léognan 1988 $15 (6/30/89) (BT)
80+ CHATEAU CARBONNIEUX Pessac-Léognan 1988 $20 (6/30/89) (BT)
80+ CHATEAU DE CRUZEAU Pessac-Léognan 1988 $13 (6/30/89) (BT)
80+ CHATEAU OLIVIER Pessac-Léognan 1988 $23 (6/30/89) (BT)
80+ CHATEAU DE ROCHEMORIN Pessac-Léognan 1988 Rel: $15 Cur: $15 (6/30/89) (BT)
80+ CHATEAU LE SARTRE Pessac-Léognan 1988 $12 (6/30/89) (BT)
80+ CHATEAU SMITH-HAUT-LAFITE Pessac-Léognan 1988 (NR) (6/30/89) (BT)
80+ CHATEAU LA TOUR-LEOGNAN Pessac-Léognan 1988 (NR) (6/30/89) (BT)
79   CHATEAU MALARTIC-LAGRAVIERE Pessac-Léognan 1988 $31 (7/31/91)

1987

95+ DOMAINE DE CHEVALIER Pessac-Léognan 1987 Rel: $49 Cur: $49 (6/30/89) (BT)
95+ CHATEAU HAUT-BRION Pessac-Léognan 1987 $70 (6/30/89) (BT)
95+ CHATEAU LAVILLE-HAUT-BRION Pessac-Léognan 1987 $50 (6/30/89) (BT)
93   CHATEAU LA TOUR-MARTILLAC Pessac-Léognan 1987 $15 (1/31/90)
90+ DOMAINE DE CHEVALIER Pessac-Léognan 1987 Rel: $49 Cur: $49 (7/15/88) (BT)
90+ CHATEAU COUHINS-LURTON Pessac-Léognan 1987 $25 (6/30/89) (BT)
90+ CHATEAU DE FIEUZAL Pessac-Léognan 1987 $40 (6/30/89) (BT)
90+ CHATEAU HAUT-BRION Pessac-Léognan 1987 $70 (7/15/88) (BT)
90+ CHATEAU LAVILLE-HAUT-BRION Pessac-Léognan 1987 $50 (7/15/88) (BT)
90+ CHATEAU MALARTIC-LAGRAVIERE Pessac-Léognan 1987 $30 (6/30/89) (BT)
85   CHATEAU LAVILLE-HAUT-BRION Pessac-Léognan 1987 $50 (1/31/90)
85   CHATEAU LA LOUVIERE Pessac-Léognan 1987 $15 (7/31/89)
85+ CHATEAU BOUSCAUT Pessac-Léognan 1987 $13 (6/30/89) (BT)
85+ CHATEAU DE FIEUZAL Pessac-Léognan 1987 $40 (6/30/89) (BT)
85+ CHATEAU LA LOUVIERE Pessac-Léognan 1987 $15 (6/30/89) (BT)
85+ CHATEAU LA LOUVIERE Pessac-Léognan 1987 $15 (7/15/88) (BT)
85+ CHATEAU DE ROCHEMORIN Pessac-Léognan 1987 Rel: $9 Cur: $9 (6/30/89) (BT)
85+ CHATEAU SMITH-HAUT-LAFITE Pessac-Léognan 1987 $17 (6/30/89) (BT)
85+ CHATEAU LA TOUR-MARTILLAC Pessac-Léognan 1987 $15 (6/30/89) (BT)
82   CHATEAU DE CRUZEAU Pessac-Léognan 1987 $9 (7/31/89)
80   CHATEAU DE ROCHEMORIN Pessac-Léognan 1987 Rel: $9 Cur: $9 (7/31/89)
80+ CHATEAU CARBONNIEUX Pessac-Léognan 1987 $15 (6/30/89) (BT)
80+ CHATEAU CARBONNIEUX Pessac-Léognan 1987 $15 (7/15/88) (BT)
80+ CHATEAU DE CRUZEAU Pessac-Léognan 1987 $9 (6/30/89) (BT)
80+ CHATEAU LA GARDE Pessac-Léognan 1987 $13 (6/30/89) (BT)
80+ CHATEAU LARRIVET-HAUT-BRION Pessac-Léognan 1987 (NR) (7/15/88) (BT)
80+ CHATEAU SMITH-HAUT-LAFITE Pessac-Léognan 1987 $17 (7/15/88) (BT)
80+ CHATEAU LA TOUR-MARTILLAC Pessac-Léognan 1987 $15 (7/15/88) (BT)
78   CHATEAU HAUT-BRION Pessac-Léognan 1987 $70 (1/31/90)
75+ CHATEAU BARET Pessac-Léognan 1987 $15 (6/30/89) (BT)
75+ CHATEAU OLIVIER Pessac-Léognan 1987 $20 (6/30/89) (BT)
75+ CHATEAU OLIVIER Pessac-Léognan 1987 $20 (7/15/88) (BT)

1986

88   CHATEAU COUHINS-LURTON Pessac-Léognan 1986 $22.50 (8/31/88)
88   CHATEAU OLIVIER Pessac-Léognan 1986 $16 (3/31/89)
87   CHATEAU LA LOUVIERE Pessac-Léognan 1986 $20 (8/31/88)
86   CHATEAU DE ROCHEMORIN Pessac-Léognan 1986 Rel: $10 Cur: $10 (8/31/88)
82   CHATEAU DE CRUZEAU Pessac-Léognan 1986 $8 (4/30/88)
77   CHATEAU CHERCHY Graves 1986 $6.50 (5/31/88)

1985

90   CHATEAU DE FIEUZAL Graves 1985 $39 (11/15/87)
90+ DOMAINE DE CHEVALIER Graves 1985 Cur: $85 (5/15/87) (BT)
90+ CHATEAU HAUT-BRION Graves 1985 $81 (5/15/87) (BT)
90+ CHATEAU LAVILLE-HAUT-BRION Graves 1985 $66 (5/15/87) (BT)
84   CHATEAU MALARTIC-LAGRAVIERE Graves 1985 $22.50 (11/15/87)
81   CHATEAU CARBONNIEUX Graves 1985 $13 (3/31/87)
80   CHATEAU CHERCHY Graves 1985 $5 (6/30/87) BB
79   CHATEAU HAUT-BRION Graves 1985 $81 (11/15/87)
70   CHATEAU DOMS Graves 1985 $7 (4/30/87)

1984

84   CHATEAU RESPIDE-MEDEVILLE Graves 1984 $7.50 (7/16/86)
80   CHATEAU PIRON Graves 1984 $7.50 (7/16/86)
74   CHATEAU LE MERLE Graves 1984 $6 (12/01/85)
73   CHATEAU OLIVIER Graves 1984 $15 (3/31/87)
57   CHATEAU DU GRAND-ABORD Graves 1984 $4 (6/01/86)

1983

88   CHATEAU LA LOUVIERE Graves 1983 $9.75 (9/16/85)
86   DOMAINE DE CHEVALIER Graves 1983 Rel: $65 Cur: $66 (11/15/87)
86   CHATEAU LAVILLE-HAUT-BRION Graves 1983 $57 (11/15/87)
78   CHATEAU DU MAYNE Graves 1983 $6 (9/16/85)
78   CHATEAU R Graves Dry 1983 $6 (2/01/85)
74   CHATEAU COUHINS-LURTON Graves 1983 $11.50 (7/16/86)
73   CHATEAU PIRON Graves 1983 $6.50 (5/16/85)
56   CHATEAU COUHINS-LURTON Graves 1983 $11.50 (12/16/85)

1982

81   CHATEAU CARBONNIEUX Graves 1982 $11.50 (2/15/84)
71   CHATEAU PIRON Graves 1982 $6.75 (3/01/84)

1974

80   LES PLANTIERS DU HAUT-BRION Graves 1974 $24 (3/31/89)

OTHER BORDEAUX WHITE

1990

85   CHATEAU BONNET Entre-Deux-Mers 1990 $9 (7/31/91) BB
84   CHATEAU DUCLA Entre-Deux-Mers 1990 $7 (6/15/91) BB
81   PIERRE JEAN Bordeaux Blanc de Blancs 1990 $7 (6/15/91) BB
76   ST.-JOVIAN Bordeaux Premium 1990 $5.50 (6/15/91)
75   LA CAVE TROISGROS Bordeaux Blanc 1990 $9 (6/15/91)

75	PIERRE DOURTHE Bordeaux Sémillon 1990 $4 (6/15/91)
70	CHATEAU COTES DES CHARIS Bordeaux Sauvignon Blanc Sec 1990 $10 (6/15/91)

1989

84	ALPHA Bordeaux 1989 $16 (2/28/91)
84	CHATEAU BONNET Entre-Deux-Mers Oak Aged 1989 $13 (6/15/91)
78	LA COUR PAVILLON Bordeaux Sec 1989 $7.25 (3/31/91)
78	LE SEC DE LA TOUR-BLANCHE Bordeaux Sauvignon 1989 $9 (3/31/91)
76	CHATEAU CHEVAL BLANC Bordeaux 1989 $5 (7/31/91)

1988

84	CHATEAU BONNET Entre-Deux-Mers 1988 $7 (5/15/89) BB
80	CHATEAU BONNET Entre-Deux-Mers 1988 $7 (5/31/90)
78	BARTON & GUESTIER Bordeaux Sauvignon Blanc 1988 $6 (3/31/90)
77	YVON MAU Bordeaux Officiel du Bicentenaire de la Revolution Française 1988 $4.50 (7/31/89)
72	CHATEAU LE GORRE Bordeaux Blanc Sec 1988 $9 (3/31/90)
71	CHATEAU BALLUE-MONDON Bordeaux Sauvignon Blanc Sec 1988 $8 (3/31/90)

1987

83	PIERRE DOURTHE Bordeaux 1987 $10 (9/30/88)
83	MAITRE D'ESTOURNEL Bordeaux 1987 $7 (8/31/88) BB
81	CHATEAU DUCLA Entre-Deux-Mers 1987 $5 (9/30/88) BB
79	CHATEAU BONNET Entre-Deux-Mers 1987 $6 (8/31/88)
78	CHATEAU LARROQUE Bordeaux Sec 1987 $5 (3/31/89)
70	MOUTON-CADET Bordeaux Blanc 1987 $7.25 (7/31/89)
69	ST.-JOVIAN Bordeaux Sauvignon Blanc 1987 $4 (8/31/88)

1986

79	CHATEAU BONNET Entre-Deux-Mers 1986 $4.50 (4/30/88)
78	CHATEAU LAURETAN Bordeaux 1986 $5.50 (8/31/88)
78	VALMAISON Bordeaux 1986 $4 (11/15/87) BB
77	CHEVALIER VEDRINES Bordeaux Sauvignon Blanc 1986 $6 (5/31/88)
77	MICHEL LYNCH Bordeaux 1986 $6 (10/15/87)
76	CHATEAU LE REY Bordeaux 1986 $4 (9/30/88)
75	MOUTON-CADET Bordeaux 1986 $5.50 (5/31/88)
73	CHATEAU MAROTTE Bordeaux 1986 $3.50 (3/31/88)
72	CHATEAU LOUDENNE Bordeaux 1986 $12 (3/31/89)
71	LA COUR PAVILLON Bordeaux Sec 1986 $7 (3/31/88)
70	ALEXIS LICHINE Bordeaux Blanc 1986 $4.50 (3/31/89)

1985

84	MAITRE D'ESTOURNEL Bordeaux 1985 $5 (12/31/86) BB
80	BEAU MAYNE Bordeaux 1985 $5 (4/30/87)
79	CHATEAU LARROQUE Bordeaux 1985 $3.75 (10/15/87) BB
78	CHATEAU THIEULEY Bordeaux 1985 $4 (5/31/88)
75	CHATEAU TALBOT Bordeaux 1985 $9 (4/30/87)
73	CHATEAU LOUDENNE Bordeaux 1985 $10.50 (7/15/87)
71	CHATEAU LAMOTHE Bordeaux 1985 $5 (10/15/87)

1984

86	A. MOUEIX Bordeaux 1984 $2.50 (4/16/86) BB
85	CHATEAU LARROQUE Bordeaux 1984 $3.75 (12/15/86) BB
75	AUGEY Bordeaux 1984 $4.50 (10/15/86)
69	CHATEAU NICOT Haut-Benauge 1984 $4 (11/16/85)
63	LA COUR PAVILLON Bordeaux Sec 1984 $7 (7/15/87)
62	CHATEAU REYNIER Entre-Deux-Mers 1984 $3.25 (12/16/85)

1983

86	PAVILLON BLANC DU CHATEAU MARGAUX Bordeaux 1983 Cur: $44 (7/15/87) (HS)
54	M. DE MALLE Bordeaux 1983 $6.25 (7/01/86)

1979

91	PAVILLON BLANC DU CHATEAU MARGAUX Bordeaux 1979 Rel: $49 Cur: $49 (7/15/87) (HS)

1978

80	PAVILLON BLANC DU CHATEAU MARGAUX Bordeaux 1978 Cur: $50 (7/15/87) (HS)

1961

84	PAVILLON BLANC DU CHATEAU MARGAUX Bordeaux 1961 Cur: $122 (7/15/87) (HS)

1928

86	PAVILLON BLANC DU CHATEAU MARGAUX Bordeaux 1928 Cur: $300 (7/15/87) (HS)

1926

92	PAVILLON BLANC DU CHATEAU MARGAUX Bordeaux 1926 Cur: $300 (7/15/87) (HS)

NV

77	CHATEAU TAREY DU CASTEL Bordeaux NV $3.25 (5/31/88)

BURGUNDY RED/*CÔTE DE BEAUNE*/ALOXE-CORTON

1989

95+	BOUCHARD PERE & FILS Corton Le Corton Domaines du Château de Beaune 1989 $77 (7/15/90) (BT)
90+	DOMAINE DU CLOS FRANTIN Corton 1989 (NR) (7/15/90) (BT)
90+	FAIVELEY Corton Clos des Cortons 1989 (NR) (7/15/90) (BT)
90+	LOUIS JADOT Corton Pougets 1989 (NR) (7/15/90) (BT)
85+	DUBREUIL-FONTAINE Corton Bressandes 1989 (NR) (7/15/90) (BT)

1988

93	LOUIS JADOT Corton Pougets 1988 $61 (3/31/91)
92	MAISON AMBROISE Corton Le Rognet 1988 $43 (11/30/90)
92	JOSEPH DROUHIN Corton Bressandes 1988 $60 (11/15/90)
91	BOUCHARD PERE & FILS Corton Le Corton Domaines du Château de Beaune 1988 $77 (3/31/91)
90	FAIVELEY Corton Clos des Cortons 1988 $120 (3/31/91)

90+	BOUCHARD PERE & FILS Corton Le Corton Domaines du Château de Beaune 1988 $77 (7/15/90) (BT)
90+	F. CHAUVENET Corton Bressandes 1988 $58 (7/15/90) (BT)
90+	MOMMESSIN Corton Bressandes 1988 $30 (7/15/90) (BT)
90+	TOLLOT-BEAUT Corton Bressandes 1988 $55 (7/15/90) (BT)
89	DOMAINE CHANDON DE BRIAILLES Corton Bressandes 1988 $75 (2/28/91)
85+	JOSEPH DROUHIN Corton 1988 $64 (7/15/90) (BT)
85+	TOLLOT-BEAUT Aloxe-Corton 1988 $35 (7/15/90) (BT)
80+	LOUIS JADOT Corton Pougets 1988 $61 (7/15/90) (BT)
80+	TOLLOT-BEAUT Corton 1988 $55 (7/15/90) (BT)
75+	DOMAINE DU CLOS FRANTIN Corton 1988 $52 (7/15/90) (BT)
75+	JOSEPH DROUHIN Aloxe-Corton 1988 $37 (7/15/90) (BT)
75+	DUBREUIL-FONTAINE Aloxe-Corton 1988 (NR) (7/15/90) (BT)

1987

92	FAIVELEY Corton Clos des Cortons 1987 $50 (3/31/90)
92	PRINCE FLORENT DE MERODE Corton Bressandes 1987 $42 (3/31/91)
92	PRINCE FLORENT DE MERODE Corton Renardes 1987 $36 (3/31/90)
90	MAISON AMBROISE Corton Le Rognet 1987 $38 (3/31/90)
90	EDMOND CORNU Corton Les Bressandes 1987 $53 (12/31/90)
88	PRINCE FLORENT DE MERODE Corton Maréchaudes 1987 $36 (8/31/90)
87	LOUIS JADOT Corton Pougets 1987 $39 (6/15/90)
87	PRINCE FLORENT DE MERODE Aloxe-Corton 1987 $30 (2/28/91)
87	PRINCE FLORENT DE MERODE Corton Clos du Roi 1987 $44 (3/31/90)
85	DUBREUIL-FONTAINE Corton Clos du Roi 1987 $34 (12/31/90)
83	EDMOND CORNU Aloxe-Corton Les Moutottes 1987 $35 (12/31/90)

1986

90	CHANSON PERE & FILS Corton 1986 $30 (4/30/89)
90	JOSEPH DROUHIN Corton Bressandes 1986 $45 (4/30/89)
89	DOMAINE MEO-CAMUZET Corton 1986 $50 (10/31/88)
88	DOMAINE CHANDON DE BRIAILLES Corton Bressandes 1986 $43 (2/28/90)
88	OLIVIER LEFLAIVE FRERES Corton Bressandes 1986 $45 (7/31/88)
87	F. CHAUVENET Corton 1986 $50 (7/31/88)
87	JAFFELIN Corton 1986 $45 (12/31/88)
87	TOLLOT-BEAUT Corton 1986 $45 (8/31/89)
86	LOUIS JADOT Corton Pougets 1986 $42 (4/30/89)
86	LOUIS JADOT Corton Pougets 1986 $42 (7/31/88)
85	BOUCHARD PERE & FILS Corton Le Corton Domaines du Château de Beaune 1986 $47 (7/31/88)
85	DOMAINE CHANDON DE BRIAILLES Corton Clos du Roi 1986 $47 (2/28/90)
84	PRINCE FLORENT DE MERODE Corton Bressandes 1986 $38 (8/31/89)
83	JOSEPH DROUHIN Aloxe-Corton 1986 $25 (4/30/89)
82	PRINCE FLORENT DE MERODE Corton Maréchaudes 1986 $33 (8/31/89)
80	PRINCE FLORENT DE MERODE Corton Clos du Roi 1986 $49 (8/31/89)
78	PIERRE BITOUZET Aloxe-Corton Valozières 1986 $18.50 (8/31/90)
76	PRINCE FLORENT DE MERODE Corton Renardes 1986 $38 (8/31/89)

1985

97	F. CHAUVENET Corton Hospices de Beaune Docteur-Peste 1985 $133 (7/15/88)
97	TOLLOT-BEAUT Corton 1985 $49 (3/15/88)
96	F. CHAUVENET Corton 1985 $53 (7/31/87)
93	PRINCE FLORENT DE MERODE Corton Bressandes 1985 $52 (2/15/88)
92	CAPTAIN-GAGNEROT Corton Les Renardes 1985 $70 (12/31/88)
92	JOSEPH DROUHIN Corton 1985 $48 (11/15/87)
92	MOILLARD Corton Clos des Vergennes 1985 $36 (5/31/87)
92	GASTON & PIERRE RAVAUT Corton Hautes-Mourottes 1985 $46 (7/31/88)
91	BONNEAU DU MARTRAY Corton 1985 $62 (10/15/88)
91	MOMMESSIN Corton 1985 $28 (2/15/88)
90	PIERRE ANDRE Corton Pougets 1985 $45 (7/15/88)
90	JOSEPH DROUHIN Aloxe-Corton 1985 $23 (11/15/87)
90	DUBREUIL-FONTAINE Corton Clos du Roi 1985 $49 (7/15/88)
90	LOUIS LATOUR Corton Domaine Latour 1985 $38 (3/15/88)
89	LOUIS JADOT Corton Pougets 1985 $47 (3/15/88)
89	LOUIS LATOUR Corton Château Corton Grancey 1985 $46 (3/15/88)
89	LOUIS LATOUR Corton Clos de la Vigne au Saint 1985 $43 (3/15/88)
89	TOLLOT-BEAUT Aloxe-Corton 1985 $35 (3/15/88)
88	PIERRE ANDRE Corton Clos du Roi 1985 $45 (7/15/88)
88	GASTON & PIERRE RAVAUT Aloxe-Corton 1985 $35 (7/31/88)
87	JEANNE-MARIE DE CHAMPS Corton Hospices de Beaune Cuvée Charlotte-Dumay 1985 $76 (10/15/88)
86	DUBREUIL-FONTAINE Corton Bressandes 1985 $50 (1/31/89)
86	DOMAINE LEQUIN-ROUSSOT Corton Les Languettes 1985 $39 (7/15/88)
84	LUPE-CHOLET Aloxe-Corton 1985 $18 (3/15/88)
84	CHARLES VIENOT Corton Maréchaude 1985 $57 (7/15/88)
81	PRINCE FLORENT DE MERODE Corton Maréchaudes 1985 $49 (3/15/88)
80	MACHARD DE GRAMONT Aloxe-Corton Les Morais 1985 $34 (7/15/88)
79	FAIVELEY Corton Clos des Cortons 1985 $80 (3/15/88)
76	LOUIS LATOUR Aloxe-Corton Les Chaillots 1985 $37 (4/15/88)

1984

87	MOILLARD Corton Clos du Roi 1984 $24 (5/31/87)

1983

91	JAFFELIN Corton 1983 $33 (4/01/86) CS
88	MOILLARD Corton Clos des Vergennes 1983 $19 (10/01/85)
85	CHEVALIER PERE & FILS Aloxe-Corton 1983 $19 (9/15/86)
84	DOMAINE CHANDON DE BRIAILLES Aloxe-Corton 1983 $25 (9/15/86)
83	BOUCHARD PERE & FILS Corton Le Corton Domaines du Château de Beaune 1983 $37 (9/15/86)
68	BICHOT Aloxe-Corton 1983 $18 (11/30/86)

1982

87	ADRIEN BELLAND Corton Grèves 1982 $16.50 (9/01/85)
86	DUBREUIL-FONTAINE Corton Clos du Roi 1982 $25 (9/16/85)
85	DUBREUIL-FONTAINE Corton Bressandes 1982 $24 (10/16/85)

1959

89	LOUIS LATOUR Corton Château Corton Grancey 1959 Cur: $130 (8/31/90) (TR)

FRANCE
BURGUNDY RED/CÔTE DE BEAUNE/ALOXE-CORTON

1955
85   LOUIS LATOUR Aloxe-Corton 1955 (NA) (8/31/90) (TR)

1953
91   LOUIS LATOUR Corton Château Corton Grancey 1953 Cur: $195 (8/31/90) (TR)

1952
92   DR. BAROLET Aloxe-Corton Villamont 1952 Cur: $75 (8/31/90) (TR)

1947
85   LOUIS LATOUR Corton Château Corton Grancey 1947 Cur: $96 (8/31/90) (TR)

1945
86   DOUDET-NAUDIN Corton Renardes 1945 (NA) (8/31/90) (TR)

BEAUNE

1989
95+   BOUCHARD PERE & FILS Beaune Grèves Vigne de l'Enfant Jésus 1989 $59 (7/15/90) (BT)
95+   LOUIS JADOT Beaune Clos des Ursules 1989 (NR) (7/15/90) (BT)
90+   JAFFELIN Beaune Les Champimonts 1989 (NR) (7/15/90) (BT)
90+   DOMAINE PIERRE LABET Beaune Coucherias 1989 (NR) (7/15/90) (BT)
90+   MOMMESSIN Beaune Les Epenottes 1989 (NR) (7/15/90) (BT)
85+   BOUCHARD PERE & FILS Beaune Clos de la Mousse Domaines du Château de Beaune 1989 $36 (7/15/90) (BT)
85+   JOSEPH DROUHIN Beaune Clos des Mouches 1989 $62 (7/15/90) (BT)
85+   JACQUES GERMAIN Beaune Cent Vignes 1989 (NR) (7/15/90) (BT)
85+   JACQUES GERMAIN Beaune Les Boucherottes 1989 (NR) (7/15/90) (BT)
85+   JACQUES GERMAIN Beaune Les Crâs 1989 (NR) (7/15/90) (BT)
85+   JACQUES GERMAIN Beaune Vigne-Franches 1989 (NR) (7/15/90) (BT)
85+   LOUIS JADOT Beaune Boucherottes 1989 (NR) (7/15/90) (BT)
85+   LOUIS JADOT Beaune Clos des Coucereaux 1989 (NR) (7/15/90) (BT)
85+   LOUIS JADOT Beaune Les Chouacheux 1989 (NR) (7/15/90) (BT)
80+   BOUCHARD PERE & FILS Beaune Marconnets Domaines du Château de Beaune 1989 $41 (7/15/90) (BT)
80+   JACQUES GERMAIN Beaune Les Teurons 1989 (NR) (7/15/90) (BT)
80+   LOUIS JADOT Beaune Bressandes 1989 (NR) (7/15/90) (BT)

1988
92   LOUIS JADOT Beaune Boucherottes 1988 $33 (3/31/91)
91   BOUCHARD PERE & FILS Beaune Grèves Vigne de l'Enfant Jésus 1988 $59 (4/30/91)
91   LOUIS JADOT Beaune Clos des Ursules 1988 $40 (3/31/91)
91   ALBERT MOROT Beaune Cent-Vignes 1988 $30 (4/30/91)
90   JACQUES GERMAIN Beaune Les Teurons 1988 $42 (2/15/91)
90   LOUIS JADOT Beaune Clos des Coucereaux 1988 $33 (3/31/91)
90   REMOISSENET Beaune Grèves 1988 $30 (11/30/90)
90+   JACQUES GERMAIN Beaune Cent Vignes 1988 (NR) (7/15/90) (BT)
90+   JACQUES GERMAIN Beaune Les Crâs 1988 (NR) (7/15/90) (BT)
90+   JACQUES GERMAIN Beaune Vignes Franches 1988 (NR) (7/15/90) (BT)
90+   LOUIS JADOT Beaune Clos des Coucereaux 1988 $33 (7/15/90) (BT)
90+   LOUIS JADOT Beaune Les Chouacheux 1988 $25 (7/15/90) (BT)
88   JEAN-MARC BOILLOT Beaune Montremenots 1988 $37 (5/15/91)
88   DOMAINE JEAN CHARTRON Beaune Hospices de Beaune Cuvée Cyrot-Chaudron 1988 $40 (2/15/91)
88   JOSEPH DROUHIN Beaune Clos des Mouches 1988 $50 (2/15/91)
88   POTHIER-RIEUSSET Beaune Boucherottes 1988 $35 (11/30/90)
87   ALBERT MOROT Beaune Bressandes 1988 $30 (3/31/91)
86   JEAN GARAUDET Beaune Clos des Mouches 1988 $40 (11/15/90)
86   ALBERT MOROT Beaune Grèves 1988 $32 (7/15/91)
86   PAUL PERNOT Beaune Teurons 1988 $33 (3/31/91)
86   TOLLOT-BEAUT Beaune Clos du Roi 1988 $53 (2/28/91)
85   DOMAINE MARC MOREY Beaune Les Paules 1988 $24 (8/31/90)
85+   F. CHAUVENET Beaune Grèves 1988 $25 (7/15/90) (BT)
85+   JACQUES GERMAIN Beaune Les Teurons 1988 $42 (7/15/90) (BT)
85+   LOUIS JADOT Beaune Boucherottes 1988 $33 (7/15/90) (BT)
85+   LOUIS JADOT Beaune Clos des Ursules 1988 $40 (7/15/90) (BT)
85+   TOLLOT-BEAUT Beaune Clos du Roi 1988 $53 (7/15/90) (BT)
85+   TOLLOT-BEAUT Beaune Grèves 1988 $35 (7/15/90) (BT)
84   CHANSON PERE & FILS Beaune Clos des Fèves 1988 $35 (8/31/90)
82   BICHOT Beaune 1988 $15 (8/31/90)
82   DOMAINE PRIEUR-BRUNET Beaune Clos du Roy 1988 $30 (12/31/90)
80   ALBERT MOROT Beaune Teurons 1988 $33 (7/15/91)
80+   BOUCHARD PERE & FILS Beaune Grèves Vigne de l'Enfant Jésus 1988 $59 (7/15/90) (BT)
80+   JOSEPH DROUHIN Beaune Clos des Mouches 1988 $54 (7/15/90) (BT)
80+   LOUIS JADOT Beaune Bressandes 1988 $26 (7/15/90) (BT)
75+   JAFFELIN Beaune Les Champimonts 1988 $30 (7/15/90) (BT)
71   DOMAINE ALETH GIRARDIN Beaune Clos des Mouches 1988 $36 (7/15/91)
70+   BOUCHARD PERE & FILS Beaune Teurons Domaines du Château de Beaune 1988 $36 (7/15/90) (BT)
70+   F. CHAUVENET Beaune Theurons 1988 $25 (7/15/90) (BT)

1987
88   PIERRE BOUREE FILS Beaune Epenottes 1987 $35 (6/15/90)
88   PARIGOT PERE & FILS Beaune Grèves 1987 $26 (2/28/90)

1987 (cont.)
87   A.R. CHOPPIN Beaune Teurons 1987 $30 (2/28/90)
85   CHANSON PERE & FILS Beaune Clos des Fèves 1987 $23 (7/31/89)
83   A.R. CHOPPIN Beaune Toussaints 1987 $30 (2/28/90)
83   JOSEPH DROUHIN Beaune Clos des Mouches 1987 $47 (6/15/90)
81   LOUIS JADOT Beaune Clos des Ursules 1987 $27 (6/15/90)

1986
94   JOSEPH DROUHIN Beaune Clos des Mouches 1986 $38 (11/15/87)
90   F. CHAUVENET Beaune Grèves 1986 $25 (7/31/88)
90   LOUIS JADOT Beaune Bressandes 1986 $24 (5/31/89)
89   LUPE-CHOLET Beaune Avaux 1986 (NA) (7/31/88)
88   LOUIS JADOT Beaune Clos des Ursules 1986 Rel: $27 Cur: $32 (3/15/89) (JS)
88   POTHIER-RIEUSSET Beaune Boucherottes 1986 $19 (5/31/89)
86   DOMAINE MUSSY Beaune Epenottes 1986 $28 (5/31/89)
86   DOMAINE MUSSY Beaune Montremenots 1986 $28 (5/31/89)
85   LOUIS JADOT Beaune Les Chouacheux 1986 $24 (5/31/89)
85   JAFFELIN Beaune Hospices de Beaune Cuvée Clos des Avaux 1986 $65 (12/31/88)
83   BOUCHARD PERE & FILS Beaune Marconnets Domaines du Château de Beaune 1986 $24 (7/31/88)
82   BOUCHARD PERE & FILS Beaune Grèves Vigne de l'Enfant Jésus 1986 Rel: $47 Cur: $49 (7/31/88)
82   F. CHAUVENET Beaune Clos des Mouches 1986 $27 (12/31/88)
82   F. CHAUVENET Beaune Clos des Mouches 1986 $27 (7/31/88)
81   BOUCHARD PERE & FILS Beaune Teurons Domaines du Château de Beaune 1986 $32 (7/31/88)
81   CHANSON PERE & FILS Beaune Clos des Marconnets 1986 $20 (5/31/89)
80   BICHOT Beaune Bressandes 1986 $24 (7/31/88)
80   MOILLARD Beaune Grèves Domaine Thomas-Moillard 1986 $14 (12/31/88)
79   F. CHAUVENET Beaune Grèves 1986 $25 (12/31/88)
78   BOUCHARD PERE & FILS Beaune Clos de la Mousse Domaines du Château de Beaune 1986 $33 (7/31/88)
77   JAFFELIN Beaune du Châpitre 1986 $18 (12/31/88)
70   JACQUES GERMAIN Beaune Les Teurons 1986 $33 (7/31/88)
69   DOMAINE JEAN GUITTON Beaune Les Sizies 1986 $19 (5/31/89)

1985
95   LOUIS JADOT Beaune Clos des Ursules 1985 Rel: $30 Cur: $30 (3/15/88) SS
92   CHANSON PERE & FILS Beaune Clos des Fèves 1985 $25 (1/31/89)
92   LOUIS JADOT Beaune Hospices de Beaune Cuvée Nicolas-Rolin 1985 $85 (3/15/88)
91   BOUCHARD PERE & FILS Beaune Grèves Vigne de l'Enfant Jésus 1985 $61 (1/31/89)
91   LOUIS JADOT Beaune Boucherottes 1985 $30 (3/15/88)
91   LOUIS JADOT Beaune Clos des Coucereaux 1985 $30 (3/15/88)
91   LOUIS JADOT Beaune Clos des Ursules 1985 Rel: $30 Cur: $30 (3/15/89) (JS)
91   LOUIS JADOT Beaune Les Chouacheux 1985 $30 (3/15/88)
90   A.R. CHOPPIN Beaune Bressandes 1985 $32 (9/30/87)
90   LOUIS JADOT Beaune Hospices de Beaune Cuvée Dames-Hospitalier 1985 $85 (3/15/88)
90   LOUIS LATOUR Beaune Vignes Franches 1985 $31 (3/15/88)
89   BOUCHARD PERE & FILS Beaune Marconnets Domaines du Château de Beaune 1985 $35 (1/31/89)
89   MACHARD DE GRAMONT Beaune Les Chouacheux 1985 $34 (5/31/88)
89   MOILLARD Beaune Grèves 1985 $25 (3/15/87)
89   DOMAINE RENE MONNIER Beaune Cent Vignes 1985 $25 (10/31/87)
88   F. CHAUVENET Beaune Theurons 1985 $23 (7/31/87)
87   A.R. CHOPPIN Beaune Teurons 1985 $32 (10/31/87)
87   LOUIS JADOT Beaune Bressandes 1985 $30 (3/15/88)
87   CHATEAU DE MEURSAULT Beaune Cent-Vignes 1985 $31 (2/28/90)
86   FAIVELEY Beaune Champs-Pimont 1985 $36 (3/15/88)
85   BOUCHARD PERE & FILS Beaune Teurons Domaines du Château de Beaune 1985 $35 (1/31/89)
85   DOMAINE DUCHET Beaune Cent-Vignes 1985 $27 (3/15/88)
84   DOMAINE MARC MOREY Beaune Les Paules 1985 $15 (12/31/88)
81   A.R. CHOPPIN Beaune Cent Vignes 1985 $32 (10/31/87)
81   DOMAINE HENRI CLERC & FILS Beaune Chaume Gaufriot 1985 $29 (11/15/88)
79   A.R. CHOPPIN Beaune Grèves 1985 $32 (9/30/87)

1984
87   MOILLARD Beaune Grèves 1984 $11.50 (2/15/87)

1983
93   LOUIS JADOT Beaune Clos des Ursules 1983 Cur: $25 (3/15/89) (JS)
85   BOUCHARD PERE & FILS Beaune Grèves Vigne de l'Enfant Jésus 1983 $30 (9/15/86)
71   BOUCHARD PERE & FILS Beaune Teurons Domaines du Château de Beaune 1983 $21.2: (9/15/86)
68   JAFFELIN Beaune Les Champimonts 1983 $17.50 (9/15/86)
68   MOILLARD Beaune 1983 $10 (10/16/85)

1980
91   F. CHAUVENET Beaune Hospices de Beaune Rosseau-Deslandes 1980 $36 (6/16/86)
83   LOUIS JADOT Beaune Clos des Ursules 1980 Cur: $26 (3/15/89) (JS)

1978
89   LOUIS JADOT Beaune Clos des Ursules 1978 Cur: $47 (3/15/89) (JS)

1976
85   LOUIS JADOT Beaune Clos des Ursules 1976 Cur: $40 (3/15/89) (JS)

1973
86   LOUIS JADOT Beaune Clos des Ursules 1973 (NA) (3/15/89) (JS)

1971
78   LOUIS JADOT Beaune Clos des Ursules 1971 Cur: $60 (3/15/89) (JS)

1969
90   LOUIS JADOT Beaune Clos des Ursules 1969 Cur: $120 (3/15/89) (JS)

1966
90   LOUIS JADOT Beaune Clos des Ursules 1966 Cur: $130 (3/15/89) (JS)

1964
86   LOUIS JADOT Beaune Clos des Ursules 1964 (NA) (3/15/89) (JS)

Key to Symbols

The scores reported here are the results of blind tastings conducted by our panel of senior editors. Wines that carry the initials below are results of individual tastings.

THE WINE SPECTATOR 100-POINT SCALE 95-100—Classic, a great wine; 90-94—Outstanding, superior character and style; 80-89—Good to very good, a wine with special qualities; 70-79—Average, drinkable wine that may have minor flaws; 60-69—Below average, drinkable but not recommended; 50-59—Poor, undrinkable, not recommended. "+"—With a score indicates a range; used primarily with barrel tastings to indicate a preliminary score.

SPECIAL DESIGNATIONS SS—Spectator Selection, CS—Cellar Selection, BB—Best Buy.

TASTER'S INITIALS (JG)—Jim Gordon, (HS)—Harvey Steiman, (JL)—James Laube, (JS)—James Suckling, (TM)—Thomas Matthews, (TR)—Terry Robards, (BT)—Barrel Tasting (these wines were tasted blind from barrel samples), (CA-date)—California's Great Cabernets by James Laube, (CH-date)—California's Great Chardonnays by James Laube, (VP-date)—Vintage Port by James Suckling.

DATE TASTED Dates in parentheses represent the issue in which the rating was published.

1962
79 LOUIS JADOT Beaune Clos des Ursules 1962 (NA) (3/15/89) (JS)

1961
88 LOUIS JADOT Beaune Clos des Ursules 1961 (NA) (3/15/89) (JS)

1959
98 LOUIS JADOT Beaune Clos des Ursules 1959 (NA) (3/15/89) (JS)
80 JOSEPH DROUHIN Beaune Grèves 1959 Cur: $90 (8/31/90) (TR)

1957
89 LOUIS JADOT Beaune Clos des Ursules 1957 (NA) (3/15/89) (JS)

1954
81 LOUIS JADOT Beaune Clos des Ursules 1954 (NA) (3/15/89) (JS)

1952
87 LOUIS JADOT Beaune Clos des Ursules 1952 (NA) (3/15/89) (JS)

1949
86 LOUIS JADOT Beaune Clos des Ursules 1949 (NA) (3/15/89) (JS)

1947
95 LOUIS JADOT Beaune Clos des Ursules 1947 (NA) (3/15/89) (JS)
87 LIGER-BELAIR Beaune Les Avaux 1947 (NA) (8/31/90) (TR)

1945
90 LEON VOILLAND Beaune Clos du Roy 1945 (NA) (8/31/90) (TR)
84 LOUIS JADOT Beaune Clos des Ursules 1945 (NA) (3/15/89) (JS)

1937
92 LOUIS JADOT Beaune Clos des Ursules 1937 (NA) (3/15/89) (JS)

1933
80 LOUIS JADOT Beaune Clos des Ursules 1933 (NA) (3/15/89) (JS)

1928
97 LOUIS JADOT Beaune Clos des Ursules 1928 (NA) (3/15/89) (JS)

1926
88 LOUIS JADOT Beaune Clos des Ursules 1926 (NA) (3/15/89) (JS)

1923
78 LOUIS JADOT Beaune Clos des Ursules 1923 (NA) (3/15/89) (JS)

1919
90 LOUIS JADOT Beaune Clos des Ursules 1919 (NA) (3/15/89) (JS)

1915
95 LOUIS JADOT Beaune Clos des Ursules 1915 (NA) (3/15/89) (JS)

1911
81 LOUIS JADOT Beaune Clos des Ursules 1911 (NA) (3/15/89) (JS)

1906
92 LOUIS JADOT Beaune Clos des Ursules 1906 (NA) (3/15/89) (JS)

1904
88 LOUIS JADOT Beaune Clos des Ursules 1904 (NA) (3/15/89) (JS)

1895
80 LOUIS JADOT Beaune Clos des Ursules 1895 (NA) (3/15/89) (JS)

1887
90 LOUIS JADOT Beaune Clos des Ursules 1887 (NA) (3/15/89) (JS)

CHASSAGNE-MONTRACHET

1989
80+ LOUIS JADOT Chassagne-Montrachet Domaine Duc de Magenta 1989 (NR) (7/15/90) (BT)
80+ JAFFELIN Chassagne-Montrachet 1989 (NR) (7/15/90) (BT)
80+ OLIVIER LEFLAIVE FRERES Chassagne-Montrachet 1989 (NR) (7/15/90) (BT)
75+ MOMMESSIN Chassagne-Montrachet 1989 (NR) (7/15/90) (BT)

1988
86 JEAN-NOEL GAGNARD Chassagne-Montrachet Morgeot 1988 $20 (12/31/90)
85 BOUCHARD PERE & FILS Chassagne-Montrachet 1988 $22 (4/30/91)
85 LOUIS JADOT Chassagne-Montrachet Morgeot Domaine du Duc de Magenta Clos de la Chapelle 1988 $20 (3/31/91)
83 DOMAINE PRIEUR-BRUNET Chassagne-Montrachet Morgeot 1988 $17 (11/15/90)
80+ LOUIS JADOT Chassagne-Montrachet Domaine Duc de Magenta 1988 $18 (7/15/90) (BT)
80+ JAFFELIN Chassagne-Montrachet 1988 $20 (7/15/90) (BT)

1987
75 BERNARD MOREY Chassagne-Montrachet 1987 $20 (10/31/89)

1986
89 OLIVIER LEFLAIVE FRERES Chassagne-Montrachet 1986 $26 (2/29/88)
84 PAUL PILLOT Chassagne-Montrachet Clos St.-Jean 1986 $23 (2/28/90)
77 LOUIS JADOT Chassagne-Montrachet Duc de Magenta Morgeot Clos de la Chapelle 1986 $17.50 (10/31/89)
61 BERNARD MOREAU Chassagne-Montrachet Morgeot La Cardeuse 1986 $15.50 (12/31/88)

1985
89 CHATEAU DE LA MALTROYE Chassagne-Montrachet Clos St.-Jean 1985 $19 (10/15/88)
88 HENRI MEURGEY Chassagne-Montrachet Clos de la Boudriotte 1985 $40 (10/31/88)
86 JEAN-CHARLES FORNEROT Chassagne-Montrachet La Maltroie 1985 $19 (7/31/88)
86 DOMAINE LEQUIN-ROUSSOT Chassagne-Montrachet Morgeot 1985 $24 (5/31/88)
86 CHATEAU DE LA MALTROYE Chassagne-Montrachet Boudriottes 1985 $17 (10/15/88)
86 PAUL PILLOT Chassagne-Montrachet Clos St.-Jean 1985 $24 (11/15/88)

85 FONTAINE-GAGNARD Chassagne-Montrachet 1985 $15.50 (12/31/88)
84 MOILLARD Chassagne-Montrachet Morgeot 1985 $15 (5/31/87)
83 JEAN-CHARLES FORNEROT Chassagne-Montrachet Les Champs Gain 1985 $19 (7/31/89)
83 LOUIS JADOT Chassagne-Montrachet Duc de Magenta Morgeot Clos de la Chapelle 1985 $19 (4/15/88)
83 OLIVIER LEFLAIVE FRERES Chassagne-Montrachet 1985 $32 (10/31/88)
79 JEAN-NOEL GAGNARD Chassagne-Montrachet Morgeot 1985 $18 (11/30/87)

1983
86 DOMAINE ROUX PERE & FILS Chassagne-Montrachet Clos St.-Jean 1983 $13 (9/16/85)
65 CHATEAU DE LA MALTROYE Chassagne-Montrachet Clos St.-Jean 1983 $12.50 (11/16/85)

PERNAND-VERGELESSES

1989
82 DOMAINE DELARCHE Pernand-Vergelesses 1989 $15/375ml (4/30/91)
80+ LOUIS JADOT Pernand-Vergelesses 1989 (NR) (7/15/90) (BT)
70+ DUBREUIL-FONTAINE Pernand-Vergelesses Ile des Vergelesses 1989 (NR) (7/15/90) (BT)

1988
86 LOUIS JADOT Pernand-Vergelesses Clos de la Croix de Pierre 1988 $16.50 (3/31/91)
85 CHANSON PERE & FILS Pernand-Vergelesses Les Vergelesses 1988 $24 (8/31/90)
83 DOMAINE CHANDON DE BRIAILLES Pernand-Vergelesses Ile des Vergelesses 1988 $35 (2/28/91)
80+ LOUIS JADOT Pernand-Vergelesses 1988 $16 (7/15/90) (BT)
79 DOMAINE RAPET Pernand-Vergelesses 1988 $31 (2/28/91)

1987
79 LOUIS JADOT Pernand-Vergelesses Clos de la Croix de Pierre 1987 $15 (11/15/90)

1986
85 LOUIS JADOT Pernand-Vergelesses Clos de la Croix de Pierre 1986 $17 (7/31/89)

1985
91 JOSEPH DROUHIN Pernand-Vergelesses 1985 $17 (11/15/87)
89 DOMAINE DELARCHE Pernand-Vergelesses Ile des Vergelesses 1985 $23 (10/15/88)
85 LOUIS JADOT Pernand-Vergelesses 1985 $18 (4/15/88)
83 LOUIS JADOT Pernand-Vergelesses Clos de la Croix de Pierre 1985 $18 (4/15/88)

1982
78 DUBREUIL-FONTAINE Pernand-Vergelesses Ile des Vergelesses 1982 $18 (10/16/85)

POMMARD

1989
80+ BOUCHARD PERE & FILS Pommard 1989 $38 (7/15/90) (BT)
80+ JOSEPH DROUHIN Pommard 1989 $46 (7/15/90) (BT)
80+ JOSEPH DROUHIN Pommard Epenots 1989 $60 (7/15/90) (BT)
80+ OLIVIER LEFLAIVE FRERES Pommard 1989 (NR) (7/15/90) (BT)
70+ MAURICE CHENU Pommard 1989 (NR) (7/15/90) (BT)

1988
90 COMTE ARMAND Pommard Clos des Epeneaux 1988 $46 (2/28/91)
90 BOUCHARD PERE & FILS Pommard 1988 $37 (4/30/91)
90 JEAN GARAUDET Pommard Les Charmots 1988 $46 (11/15/90)
90+ BOUCHARD PERE & FILS Pommard Premier Cru Domaines du Château de Beaune 1988 $53 (7/15/90) (BT)
89 BOUCHARD PERE & FILS Pommard Premier Cru Domaines du Château de Beaune 1988 $53 (3/31/91)
88 JEAN GARAUDET Pommard 1988 $37 (11/15/90)
88 LEROY Pommard Les Vignots 1988 $84 (4/30/91)
88 DOMAINE CHANTAL LESCURE Pommard Les Bertins 1988 $40 (11/30/90)
87 BICHOT Pommard 1988 $25 (8/31/90)
87 CHARTRON & TREBUCHET Pommard Les Epenots 1988 $45 (2/28/91)
87 DOMAINE ALETH GIRARDIN Pommard Charmots 1988 $44 (7/15/91)
86 LOUIS JADOT Pommard Grands Epenots 1988 $38 (3/31/91)
85+ F. CHAUVENET Pommard Chanlins 1988 $55 (7/15/90) (BT)
85+ JOSEPH DROUHIN Pommard 1988 $40 (7/15/90) (BT)
85+ JOSEPH DROUHIN Pommard Epenots 1988 $55 (7/15/90) (BT)
83 LOUIS JADOT Pommard 1988 $36 (3/31/91)
83 CHATEAU DE PULIGNY-MONTRACHET Pommard 1988 $34 (8/31/90)
80+ BICHOT Pommard Rugiens 1988 $40 (7/15/90) (BT)
80+ LOUIS JADOT Pommard Grands Epenots 1988 $38 (7/15/90) (BT)
77 JEAN-MARC BOILLOT Pommard Saucilles 1988 $47 (5/15/91)
75+ MAURICE CHENU Pommard 1988 (NR) (7/15/90) (BT)
75+ OLIVIER LEFLAIVE FRERES Pommard 1988 $31 (7/15/90) (BT)

1987
88 JEAN GARAUDET Pommard 1987 $25 (9/15/89)
88 JEAN GARAUDET Pommard Les Charmots 1987 $30 (9/15/89)
87 PARIGOT PERE & FILS Pommard Les Charmots 1987 $28 (7/31/89)
81 COMTE ARMAND Pommard Clos des Epeneaux 1987 $41 (8/31/90)
79 ROGER CAILLOT Pommard 1987 $35 (9/15/89)
79 DOMAINE COSTE-CAUMARTIN Pommard Les Fremiers 1987 $26 (11/15/90)
78 JEAN MICHELOT Pommard 1987 $33 (8/31/90)
76 DOMAINE COSTE-CAUMARTIN Pommard 1987 $21 (11/15/90)
76 PRINCE FLORENT DE MERODE Pommard Clos de la Platière 1987 $36 (8/31/90)
63 DOMAINE JEAN-MARC BOULEY Pommard Les Rugiens 1987 $34 (11/15/90)

1986
90 F. CHAUVENET Pommard Les Chanlins 1986 $40 (7/31/88)
87 BOUCHARD PERE & FILS Pommard Premier Cru Domaines du Château de Beaune 1986 $41 (7/31/88)
87 JOSEPH DROUHIN Pommard 1986 $27 (4/30/89)
87 POTHIER-RIEUSSET Pommard Clos de Verger 1986 $33 (9/15/89)
86 PRINCE FLORENT DE MERODE Pommard Clos de la Platière 1986 $35 (7/31/89)
86 DOMAINE MUSSY Pommard Premier Cru 1986 $35 (4/30/89)
83 JOSEPH DROUHIN Pommard Epenots 1986 $40 (7/31/88)
79 BICHOT Pommard 1986 $20 (9/15/89)
79 JAFFELIN Pommard 1986 $26 (4/30/89)
78 DOMAINE JEAN PASCAL Pommard La Chanière 1986 $30 (10/15/88)

FRANCE
BURGUNDY RED/CÔTE DE BEAUNE/POMMARD

76   POTHIER-RIEUSSET Pommard 1986 $25 (9/15/89)
75   THORIN Pommard 1986 $24 (2/28/90)
72   POTHIER-RIEUSSET Pommard Rugiens 1986 $35 (9/15/89)
70   LA POUSSE D'OR Pommard Les Jarollières 1986 $45 (4/30/89)
66   DOMAINE MUSSY Pommard 1986 $32 (4/30/89)

1985

95   F. CHAUVENET Pommard Epenots 1985 $48 (7/31/87)
95   JOSEPH DROUHIN Pommard Epenots 1985 $41 (11/15/87)
94   PRINCE FLORENT DE MERODE Pommard Clos de la Platière 1985 $45 (3/15/88)
93   JOSEPH DROUHIN Pommard 1985 $33 (11/15/87)
93   PARIGOT PERE & FILS Pommard Les Charmots 1985 $24 (6/15/87) CS
92   DOMAINE JEAN-MARC BOULEY Pommard Les Rugiens 1985 $30 (10/31/88)
92   DOMAINE DE COURCEL Pommard Rugiens 1985 $40 (4/30/88)
92   MOILLARD Pommard Clos des Epeneaux 1985 $40 (6/30/88) CS
91   COMTE ARMAND Pommard Clos des Epeneaux 1985 $44 (3/15/88)
91   BICHOT Pommard Hospices de Beaune Cuvée Cyrot-Chaudron 1985 $60 (10/31/88)
91   LOUIS JADOT Pommard Chaponnières 1985 $39 (3/15/88)
89   DOMAINE DE COURCEL Pommard Clos des Epeneaux 1985 $37 (4/30/88)
89   JAFFELIN Pommard 1985 $38 (3/15/88)
89   LOUIS LATOUR Pommard Epenots 1985 $46 (3/15/88)
89   DOMAINE RENE MONNIER Pommard Les Vignots 1985 $30 (11/15/88)
88   DOMAINE F. BUFFET Pommard Rugiens 1985 $40 (10/15/88)
87   MICHELOT Pommard 1985 $29 (4/30/88)
87   LA POUSSE D'OR Pommard Les Jarollières 1985 $39 (3/15/88)
86   DOMAINE MUSSY Pommard 1985 $35 (10/15/88)
85   MOILLARD Pommard Rugiens 1985 $40 (6/30/88)
81   BARTON & GUESTIER Pommard 1985 $21 (11/30/87)
81   CHARLES VIENOT Pommard 1985 $33 (4/30/88)
79   LABOURE-ROI Pommard Les Bertins 1985 $29 (3/15/88)
78   JEAN CLAUDE BOISSET Pommard 1985 $28 (4/30/88)
76   JEAN CLAUDE BOISSET Pommard Rugiens 1985 $33 (3/15/88)

1984

71   PRINCE FLORENT DE MERODE Pommard Clos de la Platière 1984 $23 (2/15/88)

1983

86   LUPE-CHOLET Pommard Les Boucherottes 1983 $19 (6/16/86)
83   BICHOT Pommard 1983 $19 (9/15/86)
81   JAFFELIN Pommard 1983 $19 (9/15/86)
78   MICHELOT Pommard 1983 $21 (6/16/86)
74   BOUCHARD PERE & FILS Pommard 1983 $23 (9/15/86)

1982

91   F. CHAUVENET Pommard Hospices de Beaune Cuvée Dames-de-la-Charite 1982 $36 (2/01/85) CS
83   DOMAINE PARENT Pommard 1982 $18 (11/01/85)
82   ROBERT MAX Pommard 1982 $15.50 (12/16/84)
81   DOMAINE RENE MONNIER Pommard Les Vignots 1982 $16.50 (7/01/85)

1981

83   JOSEPH DROUHIN Pommard 1981 $27.75 (9/01/84)

1979

88   CHATEAU DE POMMARD Pommard 1979 $33 (9/01/85)

1959

94   DOMAINE PARENT Pommard Les Epenots 1959 (NA) (8/31/90) (TR)

SANTENAY

1989

80+   LOUIS JADOT Santenay Clos de Malte 1989 (NR) (7/15/90) (BT)
80+   MOMMESSIN Santenay Grand Clos Rousseau 1989 (NR) (7/15/90) (BT)

1988

86   JESSIAUME PERE & FILS Santenay Gravières 1988 $21 (3/31/91)
84   JEAN-NOEL GAGNARD Santenay Clos de Tavannes 1988 $25 (11/15/90)
80   DOMAINE PRIEUR-BRUNET Santenay Maladière 1988 $20 (11/15/90)
75+   MOMMESSIN Santenay Grand Clos Rousseau 1988 $23 (7/15/90) (BT)
70+   BICHOT Santenay Clos Rousseau 1988 $20 (7/15/90) (BT)

1987

87   DOMAINE JEAN GIRARDIN Santenay Clos Rousseau Château de la Charrière 1987 $25 (2/28/91)
87   BERNARD MOREY Santenay Grand Clos Rousseau 1987 $24 (10/15/89)
83   DOMAINE JEAN GIRARDIN Santenay Comme Château de la Charrière 1987 $25 (2/28/91)
78   ADRIEN BELLAND Santenay Comme 1987 $22 (11/15/90)
76   DOMAINE LEQUIN-ROUSSOT Santenay 1987 $15 (11/15/90)

1986

81   OLIVIER LEFLAIVE FRERES Santenay 1986 $17 (7/31/88)
80   DOMAINE JEAN GIRARDIN Santenay Comme Château de la Charrière 1986 $23 (10/15/89)
78   BICHOT Santenay 1986 $12 (10/15/89)
78   LA POUSSE D'OR Santenay Clos Tavannes 1986 $27 (6/15/89)

1985

88   PIERRE BOUREE FILS Santenay Gravières 1985 $30 (5/31/88)
88   LOUIS CLAIR Santenay Gravières Domaine de L'Abbaye 1985 $16.50 (10/15/87)
88   JOSEPH DROUHIN Santenay 1985 $17 (11/15/87)
87   PROSPER MAUFOUX Santenay Les Gravières 1985 $18 (10/15/88)
85   DOMAINE LEQUIN-ROUSSOT Santenay La Comme 1985 $24 (5/31/88)
85   PROSPER MAUFOUX Santenay Les Gravières 1985 $18 (10/15/89)
84   F. CHAUVENET Santenay 1985 $18 (7/31/87)
84   JAFFELIN Santenay La Maladière 1985 $22 (3/15/88)
83   DOMAINE ROUX PERE & FILS Santenay 1985 $21 (10/31/87)
78   DOMAINE LEQUIN-ROUSSOT Santenay 1985 $18 (5/31/88)
67   LA POUSSE D'OR Santenay Clos Tavannes 1985 $22 (3/15/88)
66   BICHOT Santenay Les Gravières 1985 $15 (3/15/88)

1982

91   ADRIEN BELLAND Santenay Comme 1982 $12 (8/01/85) CS

SAVIGNY-LÈS-BEAUNE

1989

80+   BOUCHARD PERE & FILS Savigny-lès-Beaune Les Lavières Domaines du Château de Beaune 1989 $29 (7/15/90) (BT)
80+   JOSEPH DROUHIN Savigny-lès-Beaune 1989 $25 (7/15/90) (BT)
80+   DUBREUIL-FONTAINE Savigny-lès-Beaune Les Vergelesses 1989 (NR) (7/15/90) (BT)
75+   MAURICE CHENU Savigny-lès-Beaune 1989 (NR) (7/15/90) (BT)

1988

86   DOMAINE CHANDON DE BRIAILLES Savigny-lès-Beaune Les Lavières 1988 $31 (2/28/91)
86   ALBERT MOROT Savigny-lès-Beaune Vergelesses La Bataillère 1988 $26 (3/31/91)
85+   TOLLOT-BEAUT Savigny-lès-Beaune Lavières 1988 $28 (7/15/90) (BT)
83   BOUCHARD PERE & FILS Savigny-lès-Beaune Les Lavières Domaines du Château de Beaune 1988 $29 (4/30/91)
83   VALENTIN BOUCHOTTE Savigny-lès-Beaune Hauts-Jarrons 1988 $31 (2/28/91)
80   HENRI DE VILLAMONT Savigny-lès-Beaune Le Village 1988 $18 (3/31/91)
80+   BICHOT Savigny-lès-Beaune 1988 $17 (7/15/90) (BT)
80+   JOSEPH DROUHIN Savigny-lès-Beaune 1988 $22 (7/15/90) (BT)
75+   BOUCHARD PERE & FILS Savigny-lès-Beaune Les Lavières Domaines du Château de Beaune 1988 $29 (7/15/90) (BT)
75+   MAURICE CHENU Savigny-lès-Beaune 1988 (NR) (7/15/90) (BT)
75+   DUBREUIL-FONTAINE Savigny-lès-Beaune Les Vergelesses 1988 (NR) (7/15/90) (BT)

1987

80   MAURICE ECARD Savigny-lès-Beaune Les Serpentières 1987 $17 (10/15/89)
79   A.R. CHOPPIN Savigny-lès-Beaune Vergelesses 1987 $32 (2/28/90)

1986

87   PIERRE BITOUZET Savigny-lès-Beaune Lavières 1986 $14.50 (3/31/90)
84   JEAN-MARC PAVELOT Savigny-lès-Beaune 1986 $17.50 (10/15/89)
81   BICHOT Savigny-lès-Beaune 1986 $10 (10/15/89)
78   BOUCHARD PERE & FILS Savigny-lès-Beaune Les Lavières Domaines du Château de Beaune 1986 $25 (7/31/88)

1985

91   JOSEPH DROUHIN Savigny-lès-Beaune 1985 $21 (11/15/87) SS
89   MACHARD DE GRAMONT Savigny-lès-Beaune Les Guettes 1985 $25 (7/31/88)
89   JEAN-MARC PAVELOT Savigny-lès-Beaune Les Guettes 1985 $20 (2/15/88)
88   DUBREUIL-FONTAINE Savigny-lès-Beaune Les Vergelesses 1985 $24 (1/31/89)
87   A.R. CHOPPIN Savigny-lès-Beaune Vergelesses 1985 $25 (10/31/87)
85   PIERRE ANDRE Savigny-lès-Beaune Clos des Guettes 1985 $19.50 (7/31/88)
83   LUPE-CHOLET Savigny-lès-Beaune Les Serpentières 1985 $17 (3/15/88)
80   BRUNO CLAIR Savigny-lès-Beaune La Dominode 1985 $24 (3/15/88)
80   MOMMESSIN Savigny-lès-Beaune 1985 $16.50 (7/31/88)
67   PIERRE BITOUZET Savigny-lès-Beaune Lavières 1985 $19 (3/15/88)

1981

79   JOSEPH DROUHIN Savigny-lès-Beaune 1981 $15.75 (9/01/84)

VOLNAY

1989

85+   BOUCHARD PERE & FILS Volnay Caillerets Ancienne Cuvée Carnot Château de Beaun 1989 $50 (7/15/90) (BT)
85+   BOUCHARD PERE & FILS Volnay Taillepieds Domaines du Château de Beaune 1989 $50 (7/15/90) (BT)
85+   OLIVIER LEFLAIVE FRERES Volnay Clos de la Barre 1989 (NR) (7/15/90) (BT)
80+   JOSEPH DROUHIN Volnay 1989 $43 (7/15/90) (BT)
80+   JAFFELIN Volnay 1989 (NR) (7/15/90) (BT)

1988

92   ROSSIGNOL-FEVRIER Volnay 1988 $32 (3/31/91)
90   DOMAINE MICHEL LAFARGE Volnay Clos des Chênes 1988 $65 (7/15/91)
90   DOMAINE MICHEL LAFARGE Volnay Clos du Château des Ducs 1988 $65 (7/15/91)
90+   BOUCHARD PERE & FILS Volnay Taillepieds Domaines du Château de Beaune 1988 $50 (7/15/90) (BT)
89   JACQUES THEVENOT-MACHAL Volnay-Santenots 1988 $36 (11/15/90)
88   BOUCHARD PERE & FILS Volnay Taillepieds Domaines du Château de Beaune 1988 $50 (3/31/91)
88   CHATEAU DES HERBEUX Volnay Santenots 1988 $36 (11/30/90)
87   BOUCHARD PERE & FILS Volnay Caillerets Ancienne Cuvée Carnot Domaines du Chât 1988 $47 (3/31/91)
87   DOMAINE MICHEL LAFARGE Volnay Premier Cru 1988 $44 (7/15/91)
87   CHATEAU DE MEURSAULT Volnay Clos des Chênes 1988 $47 (7/15/91)
86   DOMAINE ROUX PERE & FILS Volnay en Champans 1988 $35 (3/31/90)
85   PIERRE BOILLOT Volnay-Santenots 1988 $37 (8/31/90)
85   JOSEPH DROUHIN Volnay Clos des Chênes 1988 $45 (2/15/91)
85   DOMAINE PRIEUR-BRUNET Volnay-Santenots 1988 $35 (11/30/90)
85+   JAFFELIN Volnay 1988 $31 (7/15/90) (BT)
85+   OLIVIER LEFLAIVE FRERES Volnay Clos de la Barre 1988 $40 (7/15/90) (BT)
85+   MOMMESSIN Volnay Le Clos des Chênes 1988 $38 (7/15/90) (BT)

Key to Symbols

The scores reported here are the results of blind tastings conducted by our panel of senior editors. Wines that carry the initials below are results of individual tastings.

THE WINE SPECTATOR 100-POINT SCALE   95-100—Classic, a great wine; **90-94**—Outstanding, superior character and style; **80-89**—Good to very good, a wine with special qualities; **70-79**—Average, drinkable wine that may have minor flaws; **60-69**—Below average, drinkable but not recommended; **50-59**—Poor, undrinkable, not recommended. "**+**"—With a score indicates a range; used primarily with barrel tastings to indicate a preliminary score.

SPECIAL DESIGNATIONS   SS—Spectator Selection, CS—Cellar Selection, BB—Best Buy.

TASTER'S INITIALS   (JG)—Jim Gordon, (HS)—Harvey Steiman, (JL)—James Laube, (JS)—James Suckling, (TM)—Thomas Matthews, (TR)—Terry Robards, (BT)—Barrel Tasting (these wines were tasted blind from barrel samples), (CA-date)—*California's Great Cabernets* by James Laube, (CH-date)—*California's Great Chardonnays* by James Laube, (VP-date)—*Vintage Port* by James Suckling.

DATE TASTED   Dates in parentheses represent the issue in which the rating was published.

84   BICHOT Volnay 1988 $25 (8/31/90)
80+ BICHOT Volnay 1988 $25 (7/15/90) (BT)
80+ JOSEPH DROUHIN Volnay 1988 $36 (7/15/90) (BT)

1987

86   PIERRE BOILLOT Volnay-Santenots 1987 $37 (6/15/90)
85   JOSEPH DROUHIN Volnay Clos des Chênes 1987 $30 (6/15/90)
82   LA POUSSE D'OR Volnay Les Caillerets Clos des 60 Ouvrées 1987 $29 (6/15/90)
80   BITOUZET-PRIEUR Volnay Clos des Chênes 1987 $36 (12/31/90)
78   OLIVIER LEFLAIVE FRERES Volnay 1987 $27 (8/31/90)

1986

91   LUPE-CHOLET Volnay Hospices de Beaune Cuvée Blondeau 1986 (NA) (7/31/88)
89   OLIVIER LEFLAIVE FRERES Volnay Clos de la Barre 1986 $28 (7/31/88)
86   JAFFELIN Volnay 1986 $27 (4/30/89)
85   POTHIER-EMONIN Volnay 1986 $24 (4/30/89)
84   BICHOT Volnay Premier Cru 1986 $25 (7/31/88)
83   BOUCHARD PERE & FILS Volnay Caillerets Ancienne Cuvée Carnot Château de Beaun 1986 $34 (7/31/88)
83   LA POUSSE D'OR Volnay Les Caillerets Clos des 60 Ouvrées 1986 $41 (4/30/89)
80   JOSEPH DROUHIN Volnay Clos des Chênes 1986 $31 (4/30/89)
77   BICHOT Volnay-Santenots 1986 $22 (10/31/89)
75   LA POUSSE D'OR Volnay Clos de la Bousse d'Or 1986 $46 (4/30/89)

1985

93   POTHIER-RIEUSSET Volnay 1985 $21 (2/15/88)
92   DOMAINE ROUX PERE & FILS Volnay en Champans 1985 $25 (3/15/87)
91   BITOUZET-PRIEUR Volnay Pitures 1985 $36 (7/31/88)
91   DOMAINE F. BUFFET Volnay Champans 1985 $35 (10/15/88)
91   DOMAINE F. BUFFET Volnay Clos de la Rougeotte 1985 $35 (10/15/88)
91   MOMMESSIN Volnay Hospices de Beaune Cuvée General-Muteau 1985 $80 (3/15/88)
90   DOMAINE JEAN-MARC BOULEY Volnay Caillerets 1985 $27 (10/15/88)
90   LA POUSSE D'OR Volnay Les Caillerets 1985 $35 (3/15/88)
89   MOILLARD Volnay Clos des Chênes 1985 $32 (7/15/88)
88   BICHOT Volnay Hospices de Beaune Cuvée Blondeau 1985 $53 (4/30/89)
88   BOUCHARD PERE & FILS Volnay Frémiets Clos de la Rougeotte Domaines du Château 1985 $35 (1/31/89)
88   JOSEPH DROUHIN Volnay 1985 $29 (11/15/87)
88   JAFFELIN Volnay 1985 $30 (3/15/88)
87   BOUCHARD PERE & FILS Volnay Caillerets Ancienne Cuvée Carnot Château de Beaun 1985 $44 (1/31/89)
87   DOMAINE JEAN-MARC BOULEY Volnay Clos des Chênes 1985 $27 (10/15/88)
87   REMY GAUTHIER Volnay Santenots 1985 $27 (3/15/88)
87   MONTHELIE-DOUHAIRET Volnay Champans 1985 $25 (7/15/88)
86   DOMAINE LUCIEN BOILLOT Volnay Les Angles 1985 $33 (7/15/88)
86   JEAN CLAUDE BOISSET Volnay Clos des Chênes 1985 $28 (4/15/88)
86   LA POUSSE D'OR Volnay Les Caillerets Clos des 60 Ouvrées 1985 $39 (3/15/88)
80   MARQUIS D'ANGERVILLE Volnay Clos des Ducs 1985 $35 (3/15/88)

1983

92   JAFFELIN Volnay 1983 $17 (10/16/85)
75   MOILLARD Volnay Clos des Chênes 1983 $15 (12/01/85)
68   BICHOT Volnay 1983 $18 (9/15/86)

1982

92   BICHOT Volnay Hospices de Beaune Cuvée Blondeau 1982 $26 (8/01/84) SS

1959

91   ARMAND ROUX Volnay Hospices de Beaune Général Muteau 1959 Cur: $115 (8/31/90) (TR)

1953

86   PIERRE LATOUR Volnay Caillerets 1953 (NA) (8/31/90) (TR)

1952

90   PIERRE LATOUR Volnay Caillerets 1952 (NA) (8/31/90) (TR)

OTHER COTE DE BEAUNE RED

1989

85+ DOMAINE JEAN CHARTRON Puligny-Montrachet Clos du Caillerets 1989 (NR) (7/15/90) (BT)
85+ MAURICE CHENU Côte de Beaune-Villages 1989 (NR) (7/15/90) (BT)
80+ JAFFELIN Monthélie 1989 (NR) (7/15/90) (BT)
75+ LOUIS JADOT Côte de Beaune-Villages 1989 (NR) (7/15/90) (BT)

1988

88   JEAN GARAUDET Monthélie 1988 $23 (11/15/90)
88   JAYER-GILLES Bourgogne Hautes Côtes de Beaune 1988 $26 (5/15/91)
88   TOLLOT-BEAUT Chorey-lès-Beaune 1988 $25 (12/31/90)
85   LEROY Auxey-Duresses Les Clous 1988 $52 (5/15/91)
85+ DOMAINE JEAN CHARTRON Puligny-Montrachet Clos du Caillerets 1988 (NR) (7/15/90) (BT)
83   MOILLARD Bourgogne Hautes Côtes de Beaune Les Alouettes 1988 $15 (7/15/91)
80+ MAURICE CHENU Côte de Beaune-Villages 1988 (NR) (7/15/90) (BT)
80+ JAFFELIN Monthélie 1988 $21 (7/15/90) (BT)
79   CHARTRON & TREBUCHET Côte de Beaune-Villages 1988 $16 (2/28/91)
79   DOMAINE RENE MANUEL Meursault Clos de La Baronne 1988 $18 (3/31/91)
77   CHATEAU DE PULIGNY-MONTRACHET Monthélie 1988 $16 (11/15/90)
75+ LOUIS JADOT Côte de Beaune-Villages 1988 $13.50 (7/15/90) (BT)

1987

87   J.-F. COCHE-DURY Auxey-Duresses 1987 $30 (2/28/90)
84   PRUNIER Auxey-Duresses Clos du Val 1987 $25 (11/15/89)
83   DOMAINE PONNELLE Côte de Beaune Les Pierres Blanches 1987 $14 (3/31/91)
80   J.-F. COCHE-DURY Meursault 1987 $30 (2/28/90)
78   EDMOND CORNU Ladoix 1987 $18 (2/28/91)
77   PRINCE FLORENT DE MERODE Ladoix Les Chaillots 1987 $18 (11/15/90)
73   M & G Côte de Beaune-Villages 1987 $20 (3/31/91)

1986

80   JACQUES GERMAIN Chorey-lès-Beaune Château de Chorey-lès-Beaune 1986 $16 (7/31/89)

79   JAFFELIN Monthélie 1986 $15 (6/15/89)
78   JOSEPH DROUHIN Côte de Beaune-Villages 1986 $12.50 (6/15/89)
78   LOUIS JADOT Côte de Beaune-Villages 1986 $15 (6/15/89)
75   JACQUES GERMAIN Chorey-lès-Beaune Château de Chorey-lès-Beaune 1986 $16 (7/31/88)
74   PRINCE FLORENT DE MERODE Ladoix Les Chaillots 1986 $17.50 (8/31/89)

1985

88   GASTON & PIERRE RAVAUT Ladoix Les Corvées 1985 $26 (7/31/88)
86   BICHOT Monthélie Hospices de Beaune Cuvée Lebelin 1985 $52 (10/15/87)
85   JOSEPH DROUHIN Côte de Beaune-Villages 1985 $13.50 (11/15/87)
85   MOMMESSIN Côte de Beaune-Villages 1985 $13 (2/15/88)
84   F. CHAUVENET Côte de Beaune-Villages 1985 $16 (7/31/87)
84   MACHARD DE GRAMONT Chorey-lès-Beaune Les Beaumonts 1985 $22 (7/31/88)
83   TOLLOT-BEAUT Chorey-Côte-de-Beaune 1985 $18 (4/15/88)
82   JEAN-CHARLES FORNEROT St.-Aubin Les Perrières 1985 $15 (7/31/89)
81   F. CHAUVENET Puligny-Montrachet 1985 $16 (6/15/87)
81   MONTHELIE-DOUHAIRET Monthélie 1985 $16 (6/30/88)
79   LOUIS JADOT Côte de Beaune-Villages 1985 $16.50 (4/15/88)

1983

82   BOUCHARD PERE & FILS Côte de Beaune-Villages Clos des Topes Bizot 1983 $21.25 (9/15/86)
76   DOMAINE DU MOULIN AUX MOINES Auxey-Duresses 1983 $10 (3/15/87)
69   LUPE-CHOLET Monthélie 1983 $9 (9/15/86)
63   DOMAINE JEAN MORETEAUX Côte de Beaune-Villages 1983 $8.50 (3/16/86)

1982

88   BOUCHARD PERE & FILS Côte de Beaune-Villages 1982 $18.50 (5/16/84) SS
86   JEAN CLAUDE BOISSET Côte de Beaune-Villages 1982 $5 (7/01/85) BB

CÔTE DE NUITS/CHAMBOLLE-MUSIGNY

1989

85+ BOUCHARD PERE & FILS Chambolle-Musigny 1989 (NR) (7/15/90) (BT)
85+ LOUIS JADOT Musigny Le Musigny 1989 (NR) (7/15/90) (BT)
75+ DOMAINE DUJAC Bonnes Mares 1989 (NR) (7/15/90) (BT)

1988

93   DROUHIN-LAROZE Bonnes Mares 1988 $81 (12/31/90)
93   DOMAINE ROBERT GROFFIER Chambolle-Musigny Amoureuses 1988 $66 (11/15/90)
93   COMTE DE VOGUE Musigny Cuvée Vieilles Vignes 1988 $134 (12/31/90)
92   DOMAINE PONSOT Chambolle-Musigny Les Charmes 1988 $58 (4/30/91)
91   DOMAINE CECI Chambolle-Musigny Aux Echanges 1988 $33 (7/15/91)
90   DOMAINE ROBERT GROFFIER Bonnes Mares 1988 $80 (11/15/90)
90   COMTE DE VOGUE Musigny Cuvée Vieilles Vignes 1988 $134 (2/28/91)
90+ DOMAINE DUJAC Bonnes Mares 1988 $86 (7/15/90) (BT)
90+ LUPE-CHOLET Bonnes Mares 1988 (NR) (7/15/90) (BT)
90+ MOMMESSIN Chambolle-Musigny Les Charmes 1988 $42 (7/15/90) (BT)
90+ DOMAINE DANIEL RION Chambolle-Musigny Les Beaux Bruns 1988 $37 (7/15/90) (BT)
89   DOMAINE ROBERT GROFFIER Chambolle-Musigny Les Sentiers 1988 $45 (11/15/90)
89   JACQUES-FREDERIC MUGNIER Chambolle-Musigny Les Fuées 1988 $60 (5/15/91)
89   DOMAINE G. ROUMIER Chambolle-Musigny 1988 $30 (7/15/91)
89   COMTE DE VOGUE Bonnes Mares 1988 $93 (3/31/91)
89   COMTE DE VOGUE Chambolle-Musigny Les Amoureuses 1988 $93 (2/28/91)
88   GHISLAINE BARTHOD Chambolle-Musigny 1988 $50 (3/15/91)
88   LOUIS JADOT Bonnes Mares 1988 $65 (3/15/91)
88   JAFFELIN Chambolle-Musigny 1988 $32 (12/31/90)
87   GHISLAINE BARTHOD Chambolle-Musigny Les Crâs 1988 $45 (2/28/91)
87   GUY CASTAGNIER Bonnes Mares 1988 $67 (7/15/91)
87   JOSEPH DROUHIN Chambolle-Musigny Les Amoureuses 1988 $76 (12/31/90)
87   DOMAINE DANIEL RION Chambolle-Musigny Les Beaux Bruns 1988 $37 (1/31/91)
86   LABOURE-ROI Chambolle-Musigny 1988 $35 (2/28/91)
86   GEORGES MUGNERET Chambolle-Musigny Les Feusselottes 1988 $54 (11/15/90)
86   JACQUES-FREDERIC MUGNIER Chambolle-Musigny 1988 $48 (5/15/91)
86   JACQUES-FREDERIC MUGNIER Chambolle-Musigny Les Amoureuses 1988 $80 (5/15/91)
86   DOMAINE B. SERVEAU Chambolle-Musigny Les Chabiots 1988 $39 (2/28/91)
85+ JOSEPH DROUHIN Chambolle-Musigny 1988 $38 (7/15/90) (BT)
85+ LOUIS JADOT Musigny Le Musigny 1988 $82 (7/15/90) (BT)
84   REMOISSENET Bonnes Mares 1988 $80 (12/31/90)
84   DOMAINE B. SERVEAU Chambolle-Musigny Les Amoureuses 1988 $66 (2/28/91)
83   GHISLAINE BARTHOD Chambolle-Musigny Les Beaux-Bruns 1988 $45 (2/28/91)
83   CHATEAU DES HERBEUX Musigny 1988 $75 (12/31/90)
83   HENRI DE VILLAMONT Chambolle-Musigny 1988 $39 (2/15/91)
81   GHISLAINE BARTHOD Chambolle-Musigny Les Véroilles 1988 $45 (2/28/91)
79   DOMAINE B. SERVEAU Chambolle-Musigny Les Sentiers 1988 $39 (2/28/91)
78   VOLPATO-COSTAILLE Chambolle-Musigny 1988 $34 (2/28/91)
73   HAEGELEN-JAYER Chambolle-Musigny 1988 $39 (5/15/91)

1987

93   DOMAINE DUJAC Chambolle-Musigny Les Gruenchers 1987 $47 (3/31/90)
92   GEORGES LIGNIER Bonnes Mares 1987 $75 (3/31/90)
92   GEORGES MUGNERET Chambolle-Musigny Les Feusselottes 1987 $41 (10/15/89)
91   DOMAINE DUJAC Bonnes Mares 1987 $62 (3/31/90)
91   LOUIS JADOT Bonnes Mares 1987 $52 (6/15/90)
89   DOMAINE BERTHEAU Bonnes Mares 1987 $55 (6/15/90)
89   DROUHIN-LAROZE Bonnes Mares 1987 $38 (3/31/90)
89   DOMAINE ROBERT GROFFIER Bonnes Mares 1987 $67 (7/31/89)
88   OLIVIER LEFLAIVE FRERES Bonnes Mares 1987 $50 (9/30/90)
87   DOMAINE ROBERT GROFFIER Chambolle-Musigny Les Sentiers 1987 $37 (8/31/89)
87   COMTE DE VOGUE Bonnes Mares 1987 $69 (7/15/90)
87   COMTE DE VOGUE Chambolle-Musigny Les Amoureuses 1987 $74 (3/31/90)
87   COMTE DE VOGUE Musigny Cuvée Vieilles Vignes 1987 $100 (3/31/90)
86   DOMAINE ROBERT GROFFIER Chambolle-Musigny Amoureuses 1987 $51 (8/31/89)
85   JEAN GRIVOT Chambolle-Musigny La Combe d'Orvaux 1987 $47 (6/15/90)
84   DOMAINE BERTHEAU Chambolle-Musigny Les Amoureuses 1987 $50 (6/15/90)
82   PIERRE BOURÉE FILS Chambolle-Musigny 1987 $44 (6/15/90)
82   PIERRE BOUREE FILS Chambolle-Musigny Charmes 1987 $56 (6/15/90)
81   DOMAINE BERTHEAU Chambolle-Musigny Les Charmes 1987 $35 (6/15/90)
80   DOMAINE BERTHEAU Chambolle-Musigny 1987 $25 (6/15/90)
78   DOMAINE B. SERVEAU Chambolle-Musigny Les Chabiots 1987 $30 (6/15/90)

FRANCE
BURGUNDY RED/CÔTE DE NUITS/CHAMBOLLE-MUSIGNY

77   GEORGES LIGNIER Chambolle-Musigny 1987 $32 (6/15/90)
72   DOMAINE CECI Chambolle-Musigny Les Echanges 1987 $20 (3/31/90)

1986

91   GUY CASTAGNIER Bonnes Mares 1986 $50 (4/15/89)
90   DOMAINE ROBERT GROFFIER Chambolle-Musigny Les Sentiers 1986 $36 (2/28/89)
90   GEORGES MUGNERET Chambolle-Musigny Les Feusselottes 1986 $45 (11/15/88)
90   DOMAINE DANIEL RION Chambolle-Musigny Les Beaux Bruns 1986 $39 (7/31/88)
89   LOUIS JADOT Bonnes Mares 1986 $57 (4/15/89)
89   GEORGES MUGNERET Chambolle-Musigny Les Feusselottes 1986 $45 (7/31/88)
88   JOSEPH DROUHIN Chambolle-Musigny 1986 $27 (7/31/88)
86   MOILLARD Bonnes Mares Domaine Thomas-Moillard 1986 $45 (11/15/88)
86   DOMAINE DANIEL RION Chambolle-Musigny Les Beaux Bruns 1986 $39 (4/15/89)
85   DOMAINE DUJAC Bonnes Mares 1986 $60 (4/15/89)
85   CLAUDE MARCHAND Chambolle-Musigny 1986 $32 (7/15/89)
84   GUY CASTAGNIER Chambolle-Musigny 1986 $31 (7/15/89)
84   DOMAINE ROBERT GROFFIER Chambolle-Musigny Amoureuses 1986 $50 (2/28/89)
83   LOUIS JADOT Bonnes Mares 1986 $57 (7/31/88)
82   DOMAINE DUJAC Bonnes Mares 1986 $60 (7/31/88)
82   HERVE ROUMIER Chambolle-Musigny 1986 $29 (8/31/89)
81   LUPE-CHOLET Chambolle-Musigny 1986 $20 (7/31/88)
78   MICHEL CLERGET Chambolle-Musigny 1986 $23 (8/31/89)
78   LOUIS JADOT Chambolle-Musigny 1986 $30 (7/15/89)
77   LOUIS JADOT Musigny Le Musigny 1986 $70 (4/15/89)
76   MICHEL CLERGET Chambolle-Musigny Les Charmes 1986 $33 (8/31/89)
76   DOMAINE DUJAC Chambolle-Musigny Les Gruenchers 1986 $48 (7/31/88)
73   BOUCHARD PERE & FILS Chambolle-Musigny 1986 $29 (7/31/88)

1985

95   LOUIS JADOT Bonnes Mares 1985 Rel: $48 Cur: $78 (3/15/88)
94   DOMAINE PONSOT Chambolle-Musigny Les Charmes 1985 $75 (6/15/88)
93   JOSEPH DROUHIN Chambolle-Musigny 1985 $33 (11/15/87)
92   COMTE DE VOGUE Musigny Cuvée Vieilles Vignes 1985 $125 (3/31/88)
91   PIERRE BOUREE FILS Bonnes Mares 1985 $85 (5/31/88)
91   DOMAINE DES CHEZEAUX Chambolle-Musigny Les Charmes 1985 $75 (6/15/88)
91   LOUIS JADOT Chambolle-Musigny 1985 $33 (5/15/88)
91   DOMAINE B. SERVEAU Chambolle-Musigny Les Amoureuses 1985 $75 (6/15/88)
90   DOMAINE B. SERVEAU Chambolle-Musigny Les Chabiots 1985 $39 (6/15/88)
89   FAIVELEY Chambolle-Musigny 1985 $45 (5/15/88)
89   HERVE ROUMIER Chambolle-Musigny Les Amoureuses 1985 $65 (3/31/88)
88   G. BARTHOD-NOELLAT Chambolle-Musigny Les Crâs 1985 $37 (7/31/88)
88   LOUIS JADOT Musigny Le Musigny 1985 $74 (3/31/88)
88   DOMAINE DANIEL RION Chambolle-Musigny Les Beaux Bruns 1985 $33 (3/31/88)
87   DOMAINE G. ROUMIER Chambolle-Musigny 1985 $26 (2/15/88)
83   MICHEL CLERGET Chambolle-Musigny Les Charmes 1985 $56 (5/15/88)
82   REMOISSENET Bonnes Mares 1985 $88 (3/15/88)
74   DOMAINE DUJAC Chambolle-Musigny Les Gruenchers 1985 $43 (3/31/88)
73   MICHEL CLERGET Chambolle-Musigny 1985 $38 (5/15/88)

1984

92   MOILLARD Bonnes Mares 1984 $35 (5/31/87)
92   MOILLARD Musigny 1984 $38 (5/31/87)
91   DOMAINE B. SERVEAU Chambolle-Musigny Les Chabiots 1984 $23 (4/15/87)
89   MOILLARD Chambolle-Musigny 1984 $15 (11/30/86)
82   G. BARTHOD-NOELLAT Chambolle-Musigny Charmes 1984 $27 (10/31/87)

1983

91   ARLAUD Bonnes Mares 1983 $30 (12/01/85)
81   JAFFELIN Chambolle-Musigny 1983 $21 (3/16/86)

1982

83   F. CHAUVENET Chambolle-Musigny Les Charmes 1982 $33 (4/30/87)

1981

88   FAIVELEY Chambolle-Musigny 1981 $24 (5/01/86)

1979

88   COMTE DE VOGUE Bonnes Mares 1979 Cur: $48 (11/16/84) (HS)
87   COMTE DE VOGUE Musigny Vieilles Vignes 1979 Cur: $114 (11/16/84) (HS)

1976

90   COMTE DE VOGUE Bonnes Mares 1976 Cur: $68 (11/16/84) (HS)
86   COMTE DE VOGUE Musigny Vieilles Vignes 1976 Cur: $119 (11/16/84) (HS)

1972

80   COMTE DE VOGUE Musigny Vieilles Vignes 1972 Cur: $122 (11/16/84) (HS)
79   COMTE DE VOGUE Bonnes Mares 1972 Cur: $125 (11/16/84) (HS)

1971

90   COMTE DE VOGUE Musigny Vieilles Vignes 1971 Cur: $235 (11/16/84) (HS)
88   COMTE DE VOGUE Bonnes Mares 1971 Cur: $164 (11/16/84) (HS)
86   COMTE DE VOGUE Chambolle-Musigny Les Amoureuses 1971 Cur: $85 (11/16/84) (HS)

1970

78   COMTE DE VOGUE Chambolle-Musigny Les Amoureuses 1970 Cur: $55 (11/16/84) (HS)

1969

65   COMTE DE VOGUE Musigny Vieilles Vignes 1969 Cur: $220 (11/16/84) (HS)

1966

92   COMTE DE VOGUE Musigny Vieilles Vignes 1966 Cur: $210 (11/16/84) (HS)

1962

90   COMTE DE VOGUE Musigny Vieilles Vignes 1962 Cur: $567/1.5L (11/16/84) (HS)

1961

93   COMTE DE VOGUE Musigny Vieilles Vignes 1961 Cur: $343 (11/16/84) (HS)

1959

89   COMTE DE VOGUE Musigny Vieilles Vignes 1959 Cur: $432 (11/16/84) (HS)
87   COMTE DE VOGUE Bonnes Mares Avery Bottling 1959 Cur: $179 (11/16/84) (HS)
83   COMTE DE VOGUE Bonnes Mares 1959 Cur: $179 (11/16/84) (HS)
75   NICOLAS Bonnes Mares 1959 (NA) (8/31/90) (TR)

1957

95   COMTE DE VOGUE Musigny Vieilles Vignes 1957 Cur: $255 (8/31/90) (TR)
80   COMTE DE VOGUE Musigny Vieilles Vignes 1957 Cur: $255 (11/16/84) (HS)

1955

91   COMTE DE VOGUE Bonnes Mares 1955 Cur: $285 (11/16/84) (HS)
65   JOSEPH DROUHIN Chambolle-Musigny Les Amoureuses 1955 Cur: $250 (8/31/90) (TR)

1953

81   COMTE DE VOGUE Musigny 1953 Cur: $200 (11/16/84) (HS)

1952

85   COMTE DE VOGUE Musigny 1952 Cur: $200 (11/16/84) (HS)

1949

98   COMTE DE VOGUE Musigny 1949 Cur: $600 (11/16/84) (HS)
92   FAIVELEY Musigny Le Musigny 1949 Cur: $250 (8/31/90) (TR)
90   COMTE DE VOGUE Bonnes Mares 1949 Cur: $1260/1.5L (11/16/84) (HS)

1945

96   COMTE DE VOGUE Musigny 1945 Cur: $1350/1.5L (11/16/84) (HS)

1937

93   COMTE DE VOGUE Musigny 1937 Cur: $650 (11/16/84) (HS)

1934

95   COMTE DE VOGUE Musigny 1934 Cur: $600 (11/16/84) (HS)
82   COMTE DE VOGUE Bonnes Mares Grivolet 1934 Cur: $400 (11/16/84) (HS)

FIXIN

1988

75+   MOMMESSIN Fixin 1988 $19 (7/15/90) (BT)

1986

85   MOILLARD Fixin Clos de la Perrière 1986 $18 (2/28/89)
84   MONGEARD-MUGNERET Fixin 1986 $19 (10/15/89)

1985

90   JEHAN JOLIET Fixin Clos de la Perrière 1985 $25 (7/31/88)
82   GELIN & MOLIN Fixin Clos du Châpitre Domaine Marion 1985 $25 (5/01/88)
79   MOILLARD Fixin Clos d'Entre Deux Velles 1985 $16 (5/31/87)
76   PIERRE GELIN Fixin Clos Napolèon 1985 $25 (4/30/88)
71   CLEMANCEY FRERES Fixin Les-Hervelets 1985 $21 (4/30/88)

1984

78   MOILLARD Fixin Clos d'Entre Deux Velles 1984 $11 (11/30/86)

1983

78   MOILLARD Fixin Clos de la Perrière 1983 $12 (10/16/85)

1959

94   PIERRE PONNELLE Fixin Hervelets 1959 (NA) (8/31/90) (TR)

GEVREY-CHAMBERTIN

1989

95+   JOSEPH DROUHIN Griotte-Chambertin 1989 $95 (7/15/90) (BT)
90+   BOUCHARD PERE & FILS Chambertin 1989 (NR) (7/15/90) (BT)
90+   JOSEPH DROUHIN Charmes-Chambertin 1989 $85 (7/15/90) (BT)
90+   DOMAINE DUJAC Charmes-Chambertin 1989 (NR) (7/15/90) (BT)
90+   LOUIS JADOT Chambertin Clos de Bèze 1989 (NR) (7/15/90) (BT)
85+   LOUIS JADOT Chapelle-Chambertin 1989 (NR) (7/15/90) (BT)
85+   LOUIS JADOT Gevrey-Chambertin Clos St.-Jacques 1989 (NR) (7/15/90) (BT)
80+   DOMAINE DU CLOS FRANTIN Gevrey-Chambertin 1989 (NR) (7/15/90) (BT)
80+   MOMMESSIN Gevrey-Chambertin Estournelles St.-Jacques 1989 (NR) (7/15/90) (BT)
75+   OLIVIER LEFLAIVE FRERES Gevrey-Chambertin 1989 (NR) (7/15/90) (BT)

1988

96   LOUIS JADOT Chambertin Clos de Bèze 1988 $97 (3/15/91)
95   ARMAND ROUSSEAU Chambertin Clos de Bèze 1988 $188 (5/15/91)
95+   FAIVELEY Chambertin Clos de Bèze 1988 $114 (7/15/90) (BT)
94   JOSEPH DROUHIN Chambertin 1988 $112 (2/15/91)
94   LOUIS JADOT Griotte-Chambertin 1988 $75 (3/15/91)
93   GUY CASTAGNIER Latricières-Chambertin 1988 $63 (7/15/91)
93   JOSEPH DROUHIN Charmes-Chambertin 1988 $65 (11/15/90)
93   LOUIS JADOT Chapelle-Chambertin 1988 $75 (3/15/91)
93   ARMAND ROUSSEAU Chambertin 1988 $201 (5/15/91)
92   DROUHIN-LAROZE Chambertin Clos de Bèze 1988 $88 (12/31/90)
92   GEORGES MUGNERET Ruchottes-Chambertin 1988 $80 (11/15/90)
92   SERAFIN PERE & FILS Gevrey-Chambertin 1988 $35 (3/31/91)
92   SERAFIN PERE & FILS Gevrey-Chambertin Le Fonteny 1988 $50 (5/15/91)

Key to Symbols

The scores reported here are the results of blind tastings conducted by our panel of senior editors. Wines that carry the initials below are results of individual tastings.

THE WINE SPECTATOR 100-POINT SCALE   95-100—Classic, a great wine; *90-94*—Outstanding, superior character and style; *80-89*—Good to very good, a wine with special qualities; *70-79*—Average, drinkable wine that may have minor flaws; *60-69*—Below average, drinkable but not recommended; *50-59*—Poor, undrinkable, not recommended. "*+*"—With a score indicates a range; used primarily with barrel tastings to indicate a preliminary score.

SPECIAL DESIGNATIONS   SS—Spectator Selection, CS—Cellar Selection, BB—Best Buy.

TASTER'S INITIALS   (JG)—Jim Gordon, (HS)—Harvey Steiman, (JL)—James Laube, (JS)—James Suckling, (TM)—Thomas Matthews, (TR)—Terry Robards, (BT)—Barrel Tasting (these wines were tasted blind from barrel samples), (CA-date)—*California's Great Cabernets* by James Laube, (CH-date)—*California's Great Chardonnays* by James Laube, (VP-date)—*Vintage Port* by James Suckling.

DATE TASTED   Dates in parentheses represent the issue in which the rating was published.

92 LOUIS TRAPET Chambertin 1988 $111 (7/15/91)
91 GUY CASTAGNIER Mazis-Chambertin 1988 $63 (7/15/91)
91 JOSEPH DROUHIN Griotte-Chambertin 1988 $81 (11/15/90)
91 DROUHIN-LAROZE Latricières-Chambertin 1988 $68 (12/31/90)
91 LOUIS JADOT Gevrey-Chambertin Estournelles St.-Jacques 1988 $50 (3/15/91)
91 LOUIS JADOT Ruchottes-Chambertin 1988 $75 (3/15/91)
91 CHARLES MORTET Gevrey-Chambertin Clos Prieur 1988 $41 (2/15/91)
91 DOMAINE PONSOT Latricières-Chambertin 1988 $150 (5/15/91)
91 SERAFIN PERE & FILS Gevrey-Chambertin Les Cazetiers 1988 $53 (5/15/91)
90 DOMAINE DES CHEZEAUX Griotte-Chambertin 1988 $110 (5/15/91)
90 BERNARD HERESZTYN Gevrey-Chambertin Les Goulots 1988 $44 (7/15/91)
90+ F. CHAUVENET Charmes-Chambertin 1988 $78 (7/15/90) (BT)
90+ JOSEPH DROUHIN Griotte-Chambertin 1988 $81 (7/15/90) (BT)
90+ DOMAINE DUJAC Charmes-Chambertin 1988 $66 (7/15/90) (BT)
90+ LOUIS JADOT Chambertin Clos de Bèze 1988 $97 (7/15/90) (BT)
90+ JAFFELIN Charmes-Chambertin 1988 $68 (7/15/90) (BT)
89 DOMAINE PIERRE AMIOT Gevrey-Chambertin Les Combottes 1988 $64 (3/15/91)
89 BOUCHARD PERE & FILS Chambertin Clos de Bèze 1988 $82 (4/30/91)
89 PIERRE BOUREE FILS Charmes-Chambertin 1988 $75 (3/31/91)
89 FAIVELEY Gevrey-Chambertin Les Cazetiers 1988 $57 (3/31/91)
89 CHARLES MORTET Gevrey-Chambertin 1988 $35 (2/15/91)
89 DOMAINE PONSOT Griotte-Chambertin 1988 $150 (5/15/91)
89 LOUIS TRAPET Chambertin Cuvée Vieilles Vignes 1988 $133 (7/15/91)
89 LOUIS TRAPET Chapelle-Chambertin 1988 $84 (7/15/91)
88 ALAIN BURGUET Gevrey-Chambertin Vieilles Vignes 1988 $45 (12/31/90)
88 DROUHIN-LAROZE Chapelle-Chambertin 1988 $68 (12/31/90)
88 DROUHIN-LAROZE Gevrey-Chambertin Clos Prieur 1988 $44 (12/31/90)
88 LOUIS JADOT Gevrey-Chambertin Clos St.-Jacques 1988 $52 (3/15/91)
87 DOMAINE DU CLOS FRANTIN Gevrey-Chambertin 1988 $37 (7/15/90)
87 JOSEPH DROUHIN Latricières-Chambertin 1988 $72 (2/15/91)
87 CHATEAU DES HERBEUX Chambertin 1988 $75 (12/31/90)
87 CHARLES MORTET Gevrey-Chambertin Les Champeaux 1988 $46 (3/15/91)
86 DOMAINE DUJAC Gevrey-Chambertin Aux Combottes 1988 $54 (3/31/91)
86 DOMAINE MAUME Charmes-Chambertin 1988 $60 (7/15/91)
85 DOMAINE DUJAC Charmes-Chambertin 1988 $66 (3/31/91)
85 G. VACHET-ROUSSEAU Gevrey-Chambertin 1988 $30 (12/31/90)
85+ LOUIS JADOT Chapelle-Chambertin 1988 $75 (7/15/90) (BT)
85+ LOUIS JADOT Gevrey-Chambertin Clos St.-Jacques 1988 $52 (7/15/90) (BT)
84 DOMAINE MICHEL ESMONIN Gevrey-Chambertin Estournelles St.-Jacques 1988 $40 (3/31/91)
84 LOUIS TRAPET Latricières-Chambertin 1988 $84 (7/15/91)
82 STANISLAS HERESZTYN Gevrey-Chambertin Les Champonnets 1988 $37 (12/31/90)
82 PHILIPPE LECLERC Gevrey-Chambertin La Combe aux Moines 1988 $80 (7/15/91)
82 PHILIPPE LECLERC Gevrey-Chambertin Les Cazetiers 1988 $80 (7/15/91)
81 LABOURE-ROI Gevrey-Chambertin 1988 $35 (12/31/90)
81 LOUIS TRAPET Gevrey-Chambertin 1988 $40 (7/15/91)
80 DROUHIN-LAROZE Gevrey-Chambertin Lavaux-St.-Jacques 1988 $44 (12/31/90)
80 PHILIPPE NADDEF Gevrey-Chambertin 1988 $25 (7/15/91)
80+ LOUIS JADOT Gevrey-Chambertin Estournelles St.-Jacques 1988 $50 (7/15/90) (BT)
80+ OLIVIER LEFLAIVE FRERES Gevrey-Chambertin 1988 $35 (7/15/90) (BT)
79 CHARLOPIN-PARIZOT Gevrey-Chambertin Cuvée Vieilles Vignes 1988 $31 (12/31/90)
75+ JOSEPH DROUHIN Gevrey-Chambertin 1988 $41 (7/15/90) (BT)
74 PHILIPPE LECLERC Gevrey-Chambertin Les Platières 1988 $45 (7/15/91)
72 DOMAINE ROY PERE & FILS Gevrey-Chambertin Vieilles Vignes 1988 $30 (12/31/90)
70+ F. CHAUVENET Gevrey-Chambertin Lavaux St.-Jacques 1988 $48 (7/15/90) (BT)
70+ F. CHAUVENET Gevrey-Chambertin Petite Chapelle 1988 $40 (7/15/90) (BT)
69 PHILIPPE NADDEF Mazis-Chambertin 1988 $60 (7/15/91)
68 DOMAINE ROY PERE & FILS Gevrey-Chambertin Clos Prieur 1988 $35 (12/31/90)

1987

93 DOMAINE GEOFFROY Gevrey-Chambertin Clos Prieur 1987 $29 (3/31/90)
93 GEORGES MUGNERET Ruchottes-Chambertin 1987 $56 (10/15/89)
92 DOMAINE GEOFFROY Mazis-Chambertin 1987 $48 (3/31/90)
92 LOUIS JADOT Mazis-Chambertin 1987 $50 (5/31/90)
91 SERAFIN PERE & FILS Gevrey-Chambertin Vieilles Vignes 1987 $35 (3/31/90)
91 LOUIS TRAPET Chambertin 1987 $75 (5/31/90)
90 PIERRE BOUREE FILS Chambertin 1987 $100 (5/31/90)
90 DROUHIN-LAROZE Chambertin Clos de Bèze 1987 $40 (3/31/90)
90 PHILIPPE NADDEF Gevrey-Chambertin Les Champeaux 1987 $28 (3/31/90)
89 LOUIS JADOT Chambertin Clos de Bèze 1987 $65 (7/15/90)
89 PHILIPPE NADDEF Mazis-Chambertin 1987 $50 (3/31/90)
88 DOMAINE PIERRE AMIOT Gevrey-Chambertin Les Combottes 1987 $42 (12/15/89)
88 DROUHIN-LAROZE Latricières-Chambertin 1987 $36 (3/31/90)
88 DOMAINE ROBERT GROFFIER Chambertin Clos de Bèze 1987 $45 (7/31/89)
88 PHILIPPE NADDEF Gevrey-Chambertin Les Cazetiers 1987 $35 (3/31/90)
88 LOUIS TRAPET Latricières-Chambertin 1987 $62 (5/31/90)
87 PIERRE BOUREE FILS Charmes-Chambertin 1987 $66 (5/31/90)
87 DOMAINE MICHEL ESMONIN Gevrey-Chambertin Clos-St.-Jacques 1987 $44 (3/31/90)
87 GEORGES LIGNIER Gevrey-Chambertin Les Combottes 1987 $34 (5/31/90)
87 CHARLES MORTET Chambertin 1987 $69 (3/31/90)
86 PIERRE BOUREE FILS Gevrey-Chambertin Clos St.-Jacques 1987 $56 (5/31/90)
86 CHARLES MORTET Gevrey-Chambertin 1987 $28 (3/31/90)
86 PHILIPPE NADDEF Gevrey-Chambertin 1987 $19 (3/31/90)
85 DOMAINE LUCIEN BOILLOT Gevrey-Chambertin Les Cherbaudes 1987 $25 (5/31/90)
85 PHILIPPE LECLERC Gevrey-Chambertin Les Cazetiers 1987 $63 (5/31/90)
84 GEORGES LIGNIER Gevrey-Chambertin 1987 $29 (5/31/90)
83 FAIVELEY Chambertin Clos de Bèze 1987 $70 (3/31/90)
83 STANISLAS HERESZTYN Gevrey-Chambertin 1987 $25 (3/31/90)
83 CHARLES MORTET Gevrey-Chambertin Clos Prieur 1987 $32 (3/31/90)
82 DOMAINE DU CLOS FRANTIN Gevrey-Chambertin 1987 $20 (3/31/90)
82 DOMAINE JEAN-PHILIPPE MARCHAND Gevrey-Chambertin Les Combottes 1987 $30 (7/15/90)
81 PHILIPPE LECLERC Gevrey-Chambertin Les Platières 1987 $35 (5/31/90)
81 CLAUDE MARCHAND Gevrey-Chambertin 1987 $22 (7/15/90)
81 CHARLES MORTET Gevrey-Chambertin Les Champeaux 1987 $36 (3/31/90)
80 PIERRE BOUREE FILS Gevrey-Chambertin Les Cazetiers 1987 $66 (5/31/90)
80 DOMAINE DUJAC Gevrey-Chambertin Aux Combottes 1987 $42 (5/31/90)
80 LOUIS JADOT Griotte-Chambertin 1987 $50 (7/15/90)
80 DOMAINE MAUME Gevrey-Chambertin en Pallud 1987 $36 (3/31/90)
79 LOUIS TRAPET Chapelle-Chambertin Réserve Jean Trapet 1987 $62 (3/15/91)
77 DOMAINE MAUME Gevrey-Chambertin 1987 $25 (3/31/90)
76 PHILIPPE LECLERC Gevrey-Chambertin Combe aux Moines 1987 $68 (5/31/90)
76 DOMAINE JEAN-PHILIPPE MARCHAND Charmes-Chambertin 1987 $60 (12/31/90)
74 DOMAINE MAUME Mazis-Chambertin 1987 $56 (3/31/90)
74 LOUIS TRAPET Gevrey-Chambertin 1987 $30 (7/15/90)
73 M & G Gevrey-Chambertin 1987 $40 (3/31/91)
69 PHILIPPE ROSSIGNOL Gevrey-Chambertin 1987 $23 (5/31/90)
66 MOILLARD Gevrey-Chambertin 1987 $20 (3/31/90)

1986

92 JOSEPH DROUHIN Griotte-Chambertin 1986 $81 (7/31/88)
92 CLAUDE MARCHAND Charmes-Chambertin 1986 $50 (7/15/89)
91 JOSEPH DROUHIN Charmes-Chambertin 1986 $56 (2/28/89) CS
91 JOSEPH DROUHIN Charmes-Chambertin 1986 $56 (7/31/88)
91 CHARLES MORTET Chambertin 1986 $62 (2/28/89)
91 GEORGES MUGNERET Ruchottes-Chambertin 1986 $55 (11/15/88)
90 F. CHAUVENET Charmes-Chambertin 1986 $65 (7/31/88)
90 DOMAINE DU CLOS FRANTIN Chambertin 1986 $63 (2/28/89)
90 JOSEPH DROUHIN Chambertin 1986 $80 (2/28/89)
90 LOUIS JADOT Chambertin Clos de Bèze 1986 $63 (7/15/89)
90 GEORGES MUGNERET Ruchottes-Chambertin 1986 Rel: $55 Cur: $55 (7/31/88)
89 F. CHAUVENET Gevrey-Chambertin Estournel St.-Jacques 1986 $35 (7/31/88)
89 DOMAINE GEOFFROY Gevrey-Chambertin Clos Prieur 1986 $29 (7/15/89)
89 LOUIS JADOT Gevrey-Chambertin Clos St.-Jacques 1986 $44 (7/31/88)
89 JAFFELIN Chambertin Le Chambertin 1986 $65 (12/31/88)
89 CLAUDE MARCHAND Gevrey-Chambertin 1986 $28 (7/15/89)
88 DOMAINE BACHELET Gevrey-Chambertin Vieilles Vignes 1986 $24 (7/15/89)
88 DOMAINE DU CLOS FRANTIN Chambertin 1986 $63 (7/31/88)
88 FAIVELEY Chambertin Clos de Bèze 1986 $66 (7/15/89)
88 OLIVIER LEFLAIVE FRERES Charmes-Chambertin 1986 $50 (7/31/88)
87 DOMAINE BACHELET Charmes-Chambertin Vieilles Vignes 1986 $43 (7/15/89)
87 LOUIS JADOT Gevrey-Chambertin Estournelles St.-Jacques 1986 $40 (7/15/89)
87 CHARLES MORTET Gevrey-Chambertin 1986 $24 (2/28/89)
86 F. CHAUVENET Gevrey-Chambertin Lavaux St.-Jacques 1986 $35 (7/31/88)
86 R. HERESZTYN-BAILLY Gevrey-Chambertin 1986 $20 (7/15/89)
86 CHARLES MORTET Gevrey-Chambertin Les Champeaux 1986 $33 (2/28/89)
86 ANTONIN RODET Gevrey-Chambertin 1986 $25 (7/15/90)
85 F. CHAUVENET Gevrey-Chambertin Clos St.-Jacques 1986 $35 (7/31/88)
85 DOMAINE DUJAC Charmes-Chambertin 1986 $50 (7/31/88)
85 DOMAINE GEOFFROY Gevrey-Chambertin Les Champeaux 1986 $36 (7/15/89)
85 DOMAINE ROBERT GROFFIER Gevrey-Chambertin 1986 $27 (2/28/89)
85 JAFFELIN Gevrey-Chambertin 1986 $49 (2/28/89)
84 ALAIN BURGUET Gevrey-Chambertin Vieilles Vignes 1986 $33 (7/15/89)
84 LOUIS JADOT Gevrey-Chambertin Clos St.-Jacques 1986 $44 (7/15/89)
84 CHARLES MORTET Gevrey-Chambertin Clos Prieur 1986 $30 (2/28/89)
83 DOMAINE BACHELET Gevrey-Chambertin Les Corbeaux Vieilles Vignes 1986 $30 (7/15/89)
83 JOSEPH DROUHIN Gevrey-Chambertin 1986 $27 (2/28/89)
82 R. HERESZTYN-BAILLY Gevrey-Chambertin Les Goulots 1986 $28 (10/15/89)
81 BOUCHARD PERE & FILS Chambertin 1986 $78 (7/31/88)
79 DOMAINE GEOFFROY Gevrey-Chambertin Les Escorvées 1986 $26 (7/15/89)
77 LOUIS JADOT Gevrey-Chambertin 1986 $25 (7/15/89)
77 JAFFELIN Charmes-Chambertin 1986 $45 (12/31/88)
76 DOMAINE MARCHAND-GRILLOT Gevrey-Chambertin Petite Chapelle 1986 $30 (10/15/89)

1985

97 F. CHAUVENET Charmes-Chambertin 1985 $72 (7/31/87)
97 ARMAND ROUSSEAU Chambertin 1985 $100 (3/15/88)
96 FAIVELEY Chambertin Clos de Bèze 1985 $105 (3/15/88)
95 JOSEPH DROUHIN Chambertin 1985 $75 (11/15/87)
95 JOSEPH DROUHIN Griotte-Chambertin 1985 $68 (11/15/87)
95 DOMAINE DUJAC Charmes-Chambertin 1985 $100 (3/15/88)
95 LOUIS LATOUR Chambertin Cuvée Héritiers Latour 1985 $76 (3/15/88)
94 LOUIS JADOT Gevrey-Chambertin Clos St.-Jacques 1985 $45 (3/31/88)
94 MOILLARD Charmes-Chambertin 1985 $55 (5/31/88)
94 PHILIPPE NADDEF Gevrey-Chambertin 1985 $25 (4/15/88)
94 DOMAINE TORTOCHOT Chambertin 1985 $90 (12/31/88)
93 PIERRE GELIN Gevrey-Chambertin 1985 $25 (4/15/88)
92 PIERRE BOUREE FILS Chambertin 1985 $113 (5/31/88)
92 DROUHIN-LAROZE Chambertin Clos de Bèze 1985 $70 (10/15/88)
92 FAIVELEY Gevrey-Chambertin Les Cazetiers 1985 $53 (3/31/88)
92 FAIVELEY Mazis-Chambertin 1985 $81 (3/15/88)
92 PHILIPPE LECLERC Gevrey-Chambertin Combe aux Moines 1985 $70 (10/15/88)
92 CHARLES MORTET Gevrey-Chambertin Clos Prieur 1985 $29 (7/31/88)
92 GEORGES MUGNERET Ruchottes-Chambertin 1985 $63 (2/15/88)
92 ARMAND ROUSSEAU Gevrey-Chambertin Clos St.-Jacques 1985 $80 (10/15/88)
91 PIERRE BOUREE FILS Gevrey-Chambertin Cazetiers 1985 $67 (5/31/88)
91 DOMAINE DES CHEZEAUX Griotte-Chambertin 1985 $100 (6/15/88)
91 JOSEPH DROUHIN Gevrey-Chambertin 1985 $33 (11/15/87)
91 REMOISSENET Chambertin 1985 $100 (3/15/88)
90 DROUHIN-LAROZE Mazis-Chambertin 1985 $47 (10/15/88)
90 FAIVELEY Gevrey-Chambertin 1985 $38 (4/15/88)
90 PIERRE GELIN Mazis-Chambertin 1985 $25 (3/15/88)
90 LOUIS JADOT Chapelle-Chambertin 1985 $54 (3/15/88)
90 PHILIPPE LECLERC Gevrey-Chambertin Les Platières 1985 $38 (10/15/88)
90 MOMMESSIN Gevrey-Chambertin 1985 $25 (2/15/88)
90 CHARLES MORTET Chambertin 1985 $64 (6/15/88)
89 BARTON & GUESTIER Gevrey-Chambertin 1985 $21 (4/30/88)
89 JOSEPH DROUHIN Charmes-Chambertin 1985 $60 (11/15/87)
89 LOUIS JADOT Chambertin Clos de Bèze 1985 $66 (3/15/88)
89 PHILIPPE LECLERC Gevrey-Chambertin Les Cazetiers 1985 $64 (10/15/88)
88 PIERRE BOUREE FILS Charmes-Chambertin 1985 $68 (5/31/88)
88 F. CHAUVENET Gevrey-Chambertin Charreux 1985 $33 (10/15/87)
88 FAIVELEY Latricières-Chambertin 1985 $77 (3/15/88)
88 HENRI MAGNIEN Gevrey-Chambertin Les Cazetiers 1985 $35 (10/15/87)
88 LOUIS TRAPET Chambertin 1985 $80 (3/15/88)
87 DOMAINE CLAUDINE DESCHAMPS Gevrey-Chambertin Bel-Air 1985 $28 (3/31/88)
87 CHARLES VIENOT Gevrey-Chambertin 1985 $32 (4/30/88)
86 LOUIS JADOT Gevrey-Chambertin Estournelles St.-Jacques 1985 $41 (3/31/88)

FRANCE
BURGUNDY RED/COTE DE NUITS/GEVREY-CHAMBERTIN

86	ARMAND ROUSSEAU Charmes-Chambertin 1985 $63 (10/15/88)
85	PIERRE BOUREE FILS Gevrey-Chambertin Clos de la Justice 1985 $51 (5/31/88)
85	LOUIS LATOUR Charmes-Chambertin 1985 $50 (3/15/88)
85	ARMAND ROUSSEAU Mazis-Chambertin Mazy-Chambertin 1985 $61 (10/15/88)
84	PIERRE GELIN Chambertin Clos de Bèze 1985 $77 (3/15/88)
84	LOUIS TRAPET Chapelle-Chambertin 1985 $64 (3/15/88)
83	MOMMESSIN Charmes-Chambertin 1985 $45 (2/15/88)
82	DOMAINE RENE LECLERC Gevrey-Chambertin Combes aux Moines 1985 $55 (10/31/88)
81	HENRI MAGNIEN Gevrey-Chambertin 1985 $25 (10/15/87)
80	HENRI MAGNIEN Gevrey-Chambertin Premier Cru 1985 $29 (10/15/87)
80	PHILIPPE NADDEF Gevrey-Chambertin Les Champeaux 1985 $29 (3/31/88)
79	PHILIPPE LECLERC Gevrey-Chambertin Les Champeaux 1985 $55 (10/31/88)
79	LOUIS TRAPET Gevrey-Chambertin 1985 $40 (5/31/88)
77	LOUIS LATOUR Gevrey-Chambertin 1985 $36 (10/15/88)
66	LEONARD DE ST.-AUBIN Gevrey-Chambertin 1985 $25 (11/30/87)
64	CHARLOPIN-PARIZOT Gevrey-Chambertin 1985 $22 (11/30/87)

1984

90	PHILIPPE LECLERC Gevrey-Chambertin 1984 $26 (7/15/87)
83	PHILIPPE LECLERC Gevrey-Chambertin Les Cazetiers 1984 $38 (8/31/87)
83	GEORGES MUGNERET Ruchottes-Chambertin 1984 $34 (3/15/87)
82	PHILIPPE LECLERC Gevrey-Chambertin Combe aux Moines 1984 $42 (8/31/87)
80	MOILLARD Chambertin Clos de Bèze 1984 $42 (5/31/87)
76	MOILLARD Chambertin 1984 $42 (5/31/87)

1983

93	JAFFELIN Chambertin Le Chambertin 1983 $48 (4/16/86)
93	MOILLARD Chambertin Clos de Bèze 1983 $37 (9/16/85) CS
88	F. CHAUVENET Charmes-Chambertin 1983 $24 (9/15/86)
77	JAFFELIN Gevrey-Chambertin 1983 $17 (10/01/85)
72	F. CHAUVENET Mazis-Chambertin 1983 $27 (6/30/87)
72	HENRI MAGNIEN Gevrey-Chambertin Les Cazetiers 1983 $17.50 (12/16/85)
68	HENRI MAGNIEN Gevrey-Chambertin 1983 $13 (2/01/86)
64	G. VACHET-ROUSSEAU Gevrey-Chambertin 1983 $16 (5/01/86)
59	LUPE-CHOLET Gevrey-Chambertin Lavaux St.-Jacques 1983 $27 (11/30/86)
58	BICHOT Gevrey-Chambertin 1983 $13 (2/01/86)

1982

92	GEORGES MUGNERET Ruchottes-Chambertin 1982 $26 (9/01/85) SS
92	ANTONIN RODET Gevrey-Chambertin Lavaux St.-Jacques 1982 $35 (6/30/87)
89	HENRI MAGNIEN Gevrey-Chambertin 1982 $12 (7/01/85)
80	BOUCHARD PERE & FILS Gevrey-Chambertin 1982 $18 (6/16/84)
80	PIERRE GELIN Gevrey-Chambertin 1982 $18.75 (3/16/85)
80	HENRI MAGNIEN Gevrey-Chambertin Les Cazetiers 1982 $16 (5/01/84)
74	JEAN CLAUDE BOISSET Gevrey-Chambertin 1982 $9 (6/01/85)
68	PHILIPPE LECLERC Gevrey-Chambertin Les Cazetiers 1982 $21 (11/16/85)

1980

91	BEAULT-FORGEOT Mazis-Chambertin Hospice de Beaune Cuvée Madeleine-Collignon 1980 $56 (7/01/84)

1959

98	PIERRE BOUREE FILS Latricières-Chambertin 1959 Cur: $150 (8/31/90) (TR)
84	BOUCHARD AINE Chambertin Clos de Bèze 1959 Cur: $90 (8/31/90) (TR)

1947

94	FORTNUM & MASON Charmes-Chambertin Bottled in England 1947 (NA) (8/31/90) (TR)

1945

96	LEBEGUE-BICHOT Chambertin Clos de Bèze 1945 Cur: $305 (8/31/90) (TR)

MOREY-ST.-DENIS

1989

90+	JOSEPH DROUHIN Clos de la Roche 1989 $81 (7/15/90) (BT)
90+	OLIVIER LEFLAIVE FRERES Morey-St.-Denis 1989 (NR) (7/15/90) (BT)
85+	DOMAINE DUJAC Clos de la Roche Clos la Roche 1989 (NR) (7/15/90) (BT)
85+	JAFFELIN Morey-St.-Denis Les Ruchots 1989 (NR) (7/15/90) (BT)
80+	MOMMESSIN Clos de Tart 1989 (NR) (7/15/90) (BT)

1988

95+	MOMMESSIN Clos de Tart 1988 $112 (7/15/90) (BT)
93	JOSEPH DROUHIN Clos de la Roche 1988 $73 (2/15/91)
92	JOSEPH DROUHIN Morey-St.-Denis Monts-Luisants 1988 $38 (2/28/91)
91	PIERRE BOUREE FILS Clos de la Roche 1988 $85 (3/31/91)
91	GUY CASTAGNIER Clos de la Roche 1988 $63 (7/15/91)
91	MOILLARD Morey-St.-Denis Monts Luisants 1988 $30 (12/15/90)
91	ARMAND ROUSSEAU Clos de la Roche 1988 $75 (5/15/91)
91	DOMAINE FABIEN & LOUIS SAIER Clos des Lambrays 1988 $75 (3/31/91)
90	DOMAINE DUJAC Clos de la Roche Clos la Roche 1988 $75 (3/31/91)
90+	OLIVIER LEFLAIVE FRERES Clos de la Roche 1988 $60 (7/15/90) (BT)
89	GUY CASTAGNIER Clos St.-Denis 1988 $63 (7/15/91)
89	DOMAINE PONSOT Clos de la Roche Cuvée William 1988 $150 (5/15/91)
88	DOMAINE PONSOT Clos de la Roche Cuvée Vieilles Vignes 1988 $185 (5/15/91)
88	DOMAINE B. SERVEAU Morey-St.-Denis Les Sorbets 1988 $35 (2/28/91)

86	DOMAINE PIERRE AMIOT Clos de la Roche 1988 $75 (3/15/91)
85	DOMAINE PONSOT Clos St.-Denis Cuvée Vieilles Vignes 1988 $165 (7/15/91)
85	DOMAINE PONSOT Morey-St.-Denis Monts-Luisants 1988 $40 (4/30/91)
85+	F. CHAUVENET Clos St.-Denis 1988 $48 (7/15/90) (BT)
85+	JOSEPH DROUHIN Clos de la Roche 1988 $73 (7/15/90) (BT)
85+	DOMAINE DUJAC Clos de la Roche Clos la Roche 1988 $75 (7/15/90) (BT)
83	DOMAINE G. ROUMIER Morey-St.-Denis Clos de la Bussière 1988 $30 (7/15/91)
80	DOMAINE PIERRE AMIOT Morey-St.-Denis Les Ruchots 1988 $57 (2/28/91)
80+	JAFFELIN Morey-St.-Denis Les Ruchots 1988 $31 (7/15/90) (BT)

1987

90	GEORGES LIGNIER Clos de la Roche 1987 $55 (3/31/90)
89	GEORGES LIGNIER Clos St.-Denis 1987 $49 (5/15/90)
88	GEORGES LIGNIER Morey-St.-Denis Clos des Ormes 1987 $32 (5/15/90)
86	DOMAINE PIERRE AMIOT Clos de la Roche 1987 $49 (12/15/89)
86	DOMAINE DUJAC Clos de la Roche Clos la Roche 1987 $53 (3/31/90)
85	PIERRE BOUREE FILS Clos de la Roche 1987 $86 (6/15/90)
85	DOMAINE DUJAC Clos St.-Denis 1987 $58 (3/31/90)
83	DOMAINE B. SERVEAU Morey-St.-Denis Les Sorbets 1987 $30 (5/15/90)
82	GEORGES LIGNIER Morey-St.-Denis 1987 $25 (5/15/90)
80	CLAUDE MARCHAND Morey-St.-Denis 1987 $30 (9/30/90)
74	PIERRE BOUREE FILS Morey-St.-Denis 1987 $35 (5/15/90)
69	CLAUDE MARCHAND Morey-St.-Denis Clos des Ormes 1987 $30 (9/30/90)

1986

90	F. CHAUVENET Clos St.-Denis 1986 $50 (2/28/89)
89	DOMAINE DUJAC Clos St.-Denis 1986 $56 (7/31/88)
88	F. CHAUVENET Clos St.-Denis 1986 $50 (7/31/88)
85	JOSEPH DROUHIN Clos de la Roche 1986 $53 (7/31/88)
85	CLAUDE MARCHAND Morey-St.-Denis Clos des Ormes 1986 $33 (7/15/89)
84	GUY CASTAGNIER Clos St.-Denis 1986 $43 (7/15/89)
83	JOSEPH DROUHIN Clos de la Roche 1986 $53 (7/15/89)
82	FAIVELEY Clos de la Roche 1986 $55 (7/15/89)
79	DOMAINE DUJAC Clos de la Roche Clos la Roche 1986 $56 (7/31/88)
75	GUY CASTAGNIER Clos de la Roche 1986 $43 (7/15/89)
66	GUY CASTAGNIER Morey-St.-Denis 1986 $28 (7/15/89)

1985

97	JOSEPH DROUHIN Clos de la Roche 1985 $60 (11/15/87)
95	DOMAINE DUJAC Clos de la Roche Clos la Roche 1985 $85 (3/15/88)
94	F. CHAUVENET Clos St.-Denis 1985 $67 (7/31/87)
92	DOMAINE G. ROUMIER Morey-St.-Denis Clos de la Bussière 1985 $27 (4/30/88)
91	DOMAINE DUJAC Clos St.-Denis 1985 $89 (3/15/88)
91	GEORGES LIGNIER Clos St.-Denis 1985 $54 (3/15/88)
91	MOMMESSIN Clos de Tart 1985 $95 (2/15/88)
91	REMOISSENET Clos de la Roche 1985 $72 (3/15/88)
90	DOMAINE PONSOT Clos de la Roche Cuvée Vieilles Vignes 1985 $200 (6/15/88)
88	DOMAINE B. SERVEAU Morey-St.-Denis Les Sorbets 1985 $39 (6/15/88)
87	MOILLARD Morey-St.-Denis Monts Luisants 1985 $21.50 (5/31/87)
86	GEORGES LIGNIER Morey-St.-Denis Clos des Ormes 1985 $28 (3/15/88)
85	GEORGES LIGNIER Clos de la Roche 1985 $63 (3/15/88)
82	GEORGES LIGNIER Morey-St.-Denis 1985 $23 (3/15/88)
78	FAIVELEY Clos de la Roche 1985 $88 (3/15/88)
78	DOMAINE FABIEN & LOUIS SAIER Clos des Lambrays Domaine des Lambrays 1985 $55 (2/15/88)
73	BRUNO CLAIR Morey-St.-Denis 1985 $20 (5/15/88)

1984

87	DOMAINE B. SERVEAU Morey-St.-Denis Les Sorbets 1984 $22.50 (3/15/87)
73	DOMAINE PONSOT Clos de la Roche 1984 $29 (2/15/88)

1982

93	DOMAINE PIERRE AMIOT Clos de la Roche 1982 $27.50 (6/16/85) SS
88	DOMAINE PIERRE AMIOT Morey-St.-Denis Aux Charmes 1982 $18 (7/01/85)

1950

78	MOMMESSIN Clos de Tart 1950 Cur: $125 (8/31/90) (TR)

NUITS-ST.-GEORGES

1989

90+	DOMAINE DANIEL RION Nuits-St.-Georges Les Vignes Rondes 1989 (NR) (7/15/90) (BT)
85+	DOMAINE DANIEL RION Nuits-St.-Georges Grandes Vignes 1989 (NR) (7/15/90) (BT)
85+	BOUCHARD PERE & FILS Nuits-St.-Georges Clos St.-Marc 1989 $57 (7/15/90) (BT)
85+	JOSEPH DROUHIN Nuits-St.-Georges 1989 $43 (7/15/90) (BT)
85+	DOMAINE HENRI GOUGES Nuits-St.-Georges Les St.-Georges 1989 (NR) (7/15/90) (BT)
85+	LUPE-CHOLET Nuits-St.-Georges Château Gris 1989 (NR) (7/15/90) (BT)
80+	DOMAINE DU CLOS FRANTIN Nuits-St.-Georges 1989 (NR) (7/15/90) (BT)
80+	DOMAINE HENRI GOUGES Nuits-St.-Georges Clos des Porrets-St.-Georges 1989 (NR) (7/15/90) (BT)
80+	LOUIS JADOT Nuits-St.-Georges 1989 (NR) (7/15/90) (BT)
80+	LOUIS JADOT Nuits-St.-Georges Clos des Corvées 1989 (NR) (7/15/90) (BT)
80+	MOMMESSIN Nuits-St.-Georges Les Vaucrains 1989 (NR) (7/15/90) (BT)
75+	DOMAINE HENRI GOUGES Nuits-St.-Georges Les Pruliers 1989 (NR) (7/15/90) (BT)
70+	FAIVELEY Nuits-St.-Georges Clos de la Maréchale 1989 (NR) (7/15/90) (BT)

1988

95+	DOMAINE DANIEL RION Nuits-St.-Georges Les Vignes Rondes 1988 $54 (7/15/90) (BT)
93	BERTRAND AMBROISE Nuits-St.-Georges En Rue de Chaux 1988 $40 (5/15/91)
93	LEROY Nuits-St.-Georges Aux Boudots 1988 $230 (4/30/91)
93	DOMAINE DANIEL RION Nuits-St.-Georges Les Lavières 1988 $33 (2/15/91)
92	DOMAINE MEO-CAMUZET Nuits-St.-Georges Aux Boudots 1988 $80 (11/30/90)
92	DOMAINE DANIEL RION Nuits-St.-Georges Les Vignes Rondes 1988 $54 (1/31/91)
91	A. CHOPIN Nuits-St.-Georges Aux Murgers 1988 $28 (7/15/90)
91	DOMAINE MEO-CAMUZET Nuits-St.-Georges 1988 $50 (11/30/90)
91	DOMAINE MEO-CAMUZET Nuits-St.-Georges Aux Murgers 1988 $80 (11/30/90)
91	ALAIN MICHELOT Nuits-St.-Georges 1988 $39 (7/15/91)
91	DOMAINE DANIEL RION Nuits-St.-Georges Les Argillières 1988 $54 (1/31/91)
91	DOMAINE DANIEL RION Nuits-St.-Georges Hauts Pruliers 1988 $54 (1/31/91)
90	JEANNE-MARIE DE CHAMPS Nuits-St.-Georges Les Terres Blanches 1988 $39 (7/15/91)
90	ALAIN MICHELOT Nuits-St.-Georges Les Chaignots 1988 $56 (5/15/91)

90+ LUPE-CHOLET Nuits-St.-Georges Château Gris 1988 $50 (7/15/90) (BT)
90+ DOMAINE DANIEL RION Nuits-St.-Georges Hauts Pruliers 1988 $54 (7/15/90) (BT)
90+ FAIVELEY Nuits-St.-Georges Les Porets St.-Georges 1988 $54 (7/15/90) (BT)
89 JEANNE-MARIE DE CHAMPS Nuits-St.-Georges Les Didiers Hospices de Nuits Cuvée Jacques Duret 1988 $49 (9/30/90)
89 JEAN GRIVOT Nuits-St.-Georges Les Pruliers 1988 $53 (4/30/91)
89 HAEGELEN-JAYER Nuits-St.-Georges Les Damodes 1988 $39 (5/15/91)
89 LOUIS JADOT Nuits-St.-Georges Clos des Corvées 1988 $49 (2/28/91)
89 LEROY Nuits-St.-Georges Aux Allots 1988 $84 (4/30/91)
89 ALAIN MICHELOT Nuits-St.-Georges Les Richemone 1988 $54 (5/15/91)
89 MOILLARD Nuits-St.-Georges Les Thorey 1988 $50 (12/31/90)
88 LOUIS JADOT Nuits-St.-Georges Les Boudots 1988 $49 (2/28/91)
88 BERTRAND MACHARD DE GRAMONT Nuits-St.-Georges Les Hauts Pruliers 1988 $37 (7/15/91)
87 DOMAINE DE L'ARLOT Nuits-St.-Georges Clos de L'Arlot 1988 $43 (3/31/91)
87 JEAN GRIVOT Nuits-St.-Georges Les Boudots 1988 $54 (4/30/91)
87 LAROCHE Nuits-St.-Georges 1988 $28 (11/15/90)
87 ALAIN MICHELOT Nuits-St.-Georges Les Vaucrains 1988 $56 (5/15/91)
85 DOMAINE DE L'ARLOT Nuits-St.-Georges Clos des Forets St.-Georges 1988 $53 (3/31/91)
85 FAIVELEY Nuits-St.-Georges Les Damodes 1988 $52 (3/31/91)
85+ LOUIS JADOT Nuits-St.-Georges Clos des Corvées 1988 $49 (7/15/90) (BT)
85+ DOMAINE DANIEL RION Nuits-St.-Georges Grandes Vignes 1988 (NR) (7/15/90) (BT)
84 DOMAINE B. SERVEAU Nuits-St.-Georges Chaines Carteaux 1988 $39 (3/31/91)
83 JEANNE-MARIE DE CHAMPS Nuits-St.-Georges Les Didiers Hospices de Nuits Cuvée Cabet 1988 $49 (9/30/90)
83 ALAIN MICHELOT Nuits-St.-Georges Les Cailles 1988 $54 (5/15/91)
83 ALAIN MICHELOT Nuits-St.-Georges Les Porets-St.-Georges 1988 $56 (5/15/91)
82 LEROY Nuits-St.-Georges Aux Lavières 1988 $84 (4/30/91)
81 JEAN GROS Nuits-St.-Georges 1988 $42 (2/28/91)
80 GEORGES MUGNERET Nuits-St.-Georges Les Chaignots 1988 $47 (11/15/90)
80+ F. CHAUVENET Nuits-St.-Georges Les Chaignots 1988 $38 (7/15/90) (BT)
80+ DOMAINE DU CLOS FRANTIN Nuits-St.-Georges 1988 $37 (7/15/90) (BT)
80+ DOMAINE HENRI GOUGES Nuits-St.-Georges Clos des Porrets-St.-Georges 1988 $50 (7/15/90) (BT)
80+ DOMAINE DANIEL RION Nuits-St.-Georges Clos des Argillières 1988 $54 (7/15/90) (BT)
76 FAIVELEY Nuits-St.-Georges Clos de la Maréchale 1988 $50 (3/15/91)
76 GERARD MUGNERET Nuits-St.-Georges Les Boudots 1988 $48 (2/28/91)
75+ BOUCHARD PERE & FILS Nuits-St.-Georges Clos St.-Marc 1988 $52 (7/15/90) (BT)
75+ DOMAINE HENRI GOUGES Nuits-St.-Georges Les St.-Georges 1988 $54 (7/15/90) (BT)
75+ LOUIS JADOT Nuits-St.-Georges 1988 $27 (7/15/90) (BT)

1987

95 DOMAINE DANIEL RION Nuits-St.-Georges Les Vignes Rondes 1987 $35 (4/30/90)
93 DOMAINE MEO-CAMUZET Nuits-St.-Georges Aux Murgers 1987 $56 (12/15/89)
92 DOMAINE DANIEL RION Nuits-St.-Georges Clos des Argillières 1987 $30 (4/30/90)
91 DOMAINE DANIEL RION Nuits-St.-Georges Hauts Pruliers 1987 $35 (4/30/90)
88 DOMAINE LUCIEN BOILLOT Nuits-St.-Georges Les Pruliers 1987 $25 (7/15/90)
88 JEAN GRIVOT Nuits-St.-Georges Les Roncières 1987 $55 (7/15/90)
88 DOMAINE MEO-CAMUZET Nuits-St.-Georges Aux Boudots 1987 $56 (12/15/89)
88 MOILLARD Nuits-St.-Georges Clos de Thorey Domaine Thomas-Moillard 1987 $27 (12/15/89)
88 GERARD MUGNERET Nuits-St.-Georges Les Boudots 1987 $40 (7/15/90)
87 DENIS CHEVILLON Nuits-St.-Georges Les Chaignots 1987 $33 (7/15/90)
87 GEORGES MUGNERET Nuits-St.-Georges Les Chaignots 1987 $41 (10/15/89)
87 DOMAINE DANIEL RION Nuits-St.-Georges Les Lavières 1987 $21 (4/30/90)
86 DOMAINE MEO-CAMUZET Nuits-St.-Georges 1987 $42 (12/15/89)
86 EMMANUEL ROUGET Nuits-St.-Georges 1987 $32 (3/31/90)
85 A. CHOPIN Nuits-St.-Georges Aux Murgers 1987 $26 (12/15/89)
85 BERTRAND MACHARD DE GRAMONT Nuits-St.-Georges Les Hauts Pruliers 1987 $32 (4/30/90)
84 DENIS CHEVILLON Nuits-St.-Georges Les Pruliers 1987 $38 (7/15/90)
84 LOUIS JADOT Nuits-St.-Georges Clos des Corvées 1987 $35 (4/30/90)
84 LUPE-CHOLET Nuits-St.-Georges Château Gris 1987 $38 (3/31/90)
83 DOMAINE DE L'ARLOT Nuits-St.-Georges Clos des Forets St.-Georges 1987 $43 (3/31/90)
82 BERTRAND MACHARD DE GRAMONT Nuits-St.-Georges Les Allots 1987 $30 (7/15/90)
81 JEAN GRIVOT Nuits-St.-Georges Les Charmois 1987 $47 (7/15/90)
81 MONGEARD-MUGNERET Nuits-St.-Georges Les Boudots 1987 $32 (4/30/90)
79 RION PERE & FILS Nuits-St.-Georges Les Murgers 1987 $31 (3/31/90)
71 JEAN GRIVOT Nuits-St.-Georges Les Pruliers 1987 $55 (7/15/90)

1986

92 DOMAINE MEO-CAMUZET Nuits-St.-Georges Aux Boudots 1986 $46 (11/15/88)
92 DOMAINE DANIEL RION Nuits-St.-Georges Hauts Pruliers 1986 $45 (7/31/88)
91 LUPE-CHOLET Nuits-St.-Georges Les Vignes Rondex Hospice de Nuits 1986 (NA) (7/31/88)
91 DOMAINE MEO-CAMUZET Nuits-St.-Georges Aux Murgers 1986 Rel: $48 Cur: $48 (7/31/88)
91 DOMAINE DANIEL RION Nuits-St.-Georges Hauts Pruliers 1986 $45 (4/30/89)
90 DOMAINE HENRI GOUGES Nuits-St.-Georges Les Chaignots 1986 $40 (7/31/88)
90 DOMAINE MEO-CAMUZET Nuits-St.-Georges 1986 $32 (11/15/88)
90 DOMAINE MEO-CAMUZET Nuits-St.-Georges Aux Murgers 1986 $48 (11/15/88)
90 DOMAINE DANIEL RION Nuits-St.-Georges Clos des Argillières 1986 $47 (4/30/89)
89 GEORGES MUGNERET Nuits-St.-Georges Les Chaignots 1986 $40 (11/15/88)
89 DOMAINE DANIEL RION Nuits-St.-Georges Clos des Argillières 1986 Rel: $47 Cur: $47 (7/31/88)
88 ALAIN MICHELOT Nuits-St.-Georges Les Vaucrains 1986 $30 (12/15/89)
88 DOMAINE DANIEL RION Nuits-St.-Georges Les Vignes Rondes 1986 $43 (4/30/89)
88 DOMAINE DANIEL RION Nuits-St.-Georges Les Vignes Rondes 1986 $43 (7/31/88)
87 F. CHAUVENET Nuits-St.-Georges Les Chaignots 1986 $40 (7/31/88)
86 JOSEPH DROUHIN Nuits-St.-Georges 1986 $25 (4/30/89)
86 LUPE-CHOLET Nuits-St.-Georges Château Gris 1986 $33 (7/31/88)
85 BICHOT Nuits-St.-Georges Les Vignerondes Hospices de Nuits Cuvée Richard de Bligny 1986 $40 (2/28/89)
85 JOSEPH DROUHIN Nuits-St.-Georges Les Roncières 1986 $38 (4/30/89)
85 LOUIS JADOT Nuits-St.-Georges Les Boudots 1986 $38 (4/30/89)
85 DOMAINE DANIEL RION Nuits-St.-Georges 1986 $31 (4/30/89)
84 DOMAINE HENRI GOUGES Nuits-St.-Georges 1986 $30 (7/31/88)
83 LOUIS JADOT Nuits-St.-Georges Clos des Corvées 1986 $37 (4/30/89)
82 DOMAINE DU CLOS FRANTIN Nuits-St.-Georges 1986 $20 (11/15/88)
81 ALAIN MICHELOT Nuits-St.-Georges Les Champs-Perdrix 1986 $30 (12/15/89)

80 BICHOT Nuits-St.-Georges Les Maladières Hospices de Nuits Cuvée Grangier 1986 $33 (3/31/90)
80 JAFFELIN Nuits-St.-Georges 1986 $28 (2/28/89)
78 A. CHOPIN Nuits-St.-Georges Aux Murgers 1986 $29 (10/15/88)
78 2MOILLARD Nuits-St.-Georges Clos de Thorey Domaine Thomas-Moillard 1986 $28 (11/15/88)
77 BICHOT Nuits-St.-Georges Les Boudots Hospices de Nuits Cuvée Mesny de Boissea 1986 $36 (3/31/90)
77 CATHIARD-MOLINIER Nuits-St.-Georges Les Meurgers 1986 $22.50 (2/28/89)
77 BERTRAND MACHARD DE GRAMONT Nuits-St.-Georges Les Hauts Pruliers 1986 $22 (12/15/89)
75 BICHOT Nuits-St.-Georges Les Maladières Hospices de Nuits 1986 $33 (2/28/89)
74 ROBERT CHEVILLON Nuits-St.-Georges 1986 $37 (12/15/89)

1985

96 JEANNE-MARIE DE CHAMPS Nuits-St.-Georges Les Didiers Hospices de Nuits Cuvée Cabet 1985 $53 (3/15/88)
96 LOUIS JADOT Nuits-St.-Georges Clos des Corvées 1985 $44 (3/15/88)
94 DOMAINE DANIEL RION Nuits-St.-Georges Clos des Argillières 1985 $44 (3/15/88)
93 PIERRE BOUREE FILS Nuits-St.-Georges Les Vaucrains 1985 $68 (5/31/88)
93 JOSEPH DROUHIN Nuits-St.-Georges Les Roncières 1985 $38 (11/15/87)
92 JOSEPH DROUHIN Nuits-St.-Georges 1985 $29 (11/15/87)
91 LOUIS JADOT Nuits-St.-Georges 1985 $30 (4/15/88)
91 DOMAINE DANIEL RION Nuits-St.-Georges Les Vignes Rondes 1985 $40 (3/15/88)
90 FAIVELEY Nuits-St.-Georges 1985 $40 (3/15/88)
90 MACHARD DE GRAMONT Nuits-St.-Georges Les Hauts Pruliers 1985 $36 (2/15/88)
90 DOMAINE MEO-CAMUZET Nuits-St.-Georges Aux Murgers 1985 $50 (4/15/88)
89 MACHARD DE GRAMONT Nuits-St.-Georges En la Perrière Noblot 1985 $41 (5/31/88)
89 MOILLARD Nuits-St.-Georges Clos de Thorey 1985 $38 (5/31/87)
88 JEAN CHAUVENET Nuits-St.-Georges Les Bousselots 1985 $49 (5/31/88)
88 J. JAYER Nuits-St.-Georges Les Lavières 1985 $38 (3/15/88)
88 LUPE-CHOLET Nuits-St.-Georges Château Gris 1985 $39 (2/15/88)
88 DOMAINE DANIEL RION Nuits-St.-Georges Hauts Pruliers 1985 $43 (3/15/88)
87 BOUCHARD PERE & FILS Nuits-St.-Georges Clos-St.-Marc 1985 $53 (2/28/89)
87 REMOISSENET Nuits-St.-Georges Aux Argillats 1985 $34 (10/15/88)
86 MACHARD DE GRAMONT Nuits-St.-Georges Les Allots 1985 $35 (5/31/88)
86 DOMAINE B. SERVEAU Nuits-St.-Georges Chaines Carteaux 1985 $39 (6/15/88)
85 DOMAINE BERTAGNA Nuits-St.-Georges Aux Murgers 1985 $41 (2/28/89)
85 ROBERT CHEVILLON Nuits-St.-Georges 1985 $40 (4/30/88)
85 FAIVELEY Nuits-St.-Georges Clos de la Maréchale 1985 $51 (3/15/88)
85 JEAN GROS Nuits-St.-Georges 1985 $36 (7/31/88)
85 DOMAINE DANIEL RION Nuits-St.-Georges 1985 $28 (3/15/88)
84 F. CHAUVENET Nuits-St.-Georges Les Plateaux 1985 $34 (7/31/87)
84 CHEVALIER DE BEAUBASSIN Nuits-St.-Georges 1985 $31 (4/30/88)
84 MACHARD DE GRAMONT Nuits-St.-Georges Les Hauts Poirets 1985 $41 (6/15/88)
81 HENRI & GILLES REMORIQUET Nuits-St.-Georges Rue de Chaux 1985 $21.50 (7/31/88)
80 F. CHAUVENET Nuits-St.-Georges Les Perrières 1985 $48 (7/31/87)
79 JEAN CLAUDE BOISSET Nuits-St.-Georges 1985 $25 (4/30/88)
78 MACHARD DE GRAMONT Nuits-St.-Georges Les Vallerots 1985 $47 (5/31/88)
76 FAIVELEY Nuits-St.-Georges Les Porets St.-Georges 1985 $47 (3/15/88)
75 LOUIS JADOT Nuits-St.-Georges Les Boudots 1985 $42 (3/15/88)
75 DOMAINE LEQUIN-ROUSSOT Nuits-St.-Georges 1985 $39 (4/15/88)
71 LEONARD DE ST.-AUBIN Nuits-St.-Georges 1985 $25 (11/30/87)
68 DOMAINE HENRI GOUGES Nuits-St.-Georges Les St.-Georges 1985 $45 (2/15/88)

1984

90 CHARLES MONCAUT Nuits-St.-Georges Les Argillières 1984 $32 (6/15/87)
89 GEORGES MUGNERET Nuits-St.-Georges Les Chaignots 1984 $26 (3/15/87)
84 MOILLARD Nuits-St.-Georges Clos de Thorey 1984 $24.50 (5/31/87)
78 MONGEARD-MUGNERET Nuits-St.-Georges Les Boudots 1984 $23 (2/15/88)

1983

84 MOILLARD Nuits-St.-Georges Clos de Thorey 1983 $19 (9/16/85)
83 DOMAINE DU CLOS FRANTIN Nuits-St.-Georges 1983 $18 (2/01/86)
77 LUPE-CHOLET Nuits-St.-Georges Château Gris 1983 $24 (6/16/86)
74 BOUCHARD PERE & FILS Nuits-St.-Georges Clos-St.-Marc 1983 $33 (9/15/86)
72 JAFFELIN Nuits-St.-Georges 1983 $18.50 (9/15/86)
68 BOUCHARD PERE & FILS Nuits-St.-Georges 1983 $21.25 (9/15/86)

1982

90 ALAIN MICHELOT Nuits-St.-Georges Les Cailles 1982 $19.50 (7/16/85)
86 ALAIN MICHELOT Nuits-St.-Georges 1982 $17 (5/01/84)
84 FAIVELEY Nuits-St.-Georges Clos de la Maréchale 1982 $20 (5/01/86)
84 GILLES REMORIQUET Nuits-St.-Georges 1982 $18.50 (7/16/85)
78 F. CHAUVENET Nuits-St.-Georges Les Plateaux 1982 $16 (1/01/85)

1981

83 BEAULT-FORGEOT Nuits-St.-Georges Les Plateaux 1981 $17 (7/01/84)

1959

87 BOUCHARD PERE & FILS Nuits-St.-Georges Les Cailles 1959 Cur: $90 (8/31/90) (TR)

1943

91 JULES BELIN Nuits-St.-Georges Les St.-Georges 1943 (NA) (8/31/90) (TR)

VOSNE-ROMANÉE

1989

90+ BOUCHARD PERE & FILS Echézeaux 1989 (NR) (7/15/90) (BT)
90+ BOUCHARD PERE & FILS La Romanée Château de Vosne-Romanée 1989 (NR) (7/15/90) (BT)
90+ JOSEPH DROUHIN Grands Echézeaux 1989 $120 (7/15/90) (BT)
85+ BOUCHARD PERE & FILS Vosne-Romanée Aux Reignots Château de Vosne-Romanée 1989 (NR) (7/15/90) (BT)
85+ DOMAINE DU CLOS FRANTIN Vosne-Romanée Les Malconsorts 1989 (NR) (7/15/90) (BT)
80+ DOMAINE DU CLOS FRANTIN Echézeaux 1989 (NR) (7/15/90) (BT)
80+ JOSEPH DROUHIN Vosne-Romanée Les Beaumonts 1989 (NR) (7/15/90) (BT)
80+ MOMMESSIN Echézeaux 1989 (NR) (7/15/90) (BT)
70+ DOMAINE DU CLOS FRANTIN Vosne-Romanée 1989 (NR) (7/15/90) (BT)

FRANCE
BURGUNDY RED/CÔTE DE NUITS/VOSNE-ROMANÉE

1988

98   JEAN GROS Richebourg 1988 $190 (2/28/91)
98   ROMANEE-CONTI La Tâche 1988 $450 (4/30/91)
98   ROMANEE-CONTI Romanée-Conti 1988 $600 (4/30/91)
97   A.-F. GROS Richebourg 1988 $190 (2/15/91)
97   ROMANEE-CONTI Romanée-St.-Vivant 1988 $360 (4/30/91)
96   LEROY Richebourg 1988 $325 (4/30/91)
96   DOMAINE MEO-CAMUZET Richebourg 1988 $253 (11/30/90)
96   EMMANUEL ROUGET Echézeaux 1988 $81 (11/15/90)
95   LEROY Romanée-St.-Vivant 1988 $325 (4/30/91)
95+ DOMAINE DU CLOS FRANTIN Echézeaux 1988 $56 (7/15/90) (BT)
94   DOMAINE GROS FRERE & SOEUR Grands Echézeaux 1988 $110 (3/15/91)
94   JEAN GROS Vosne-Romanée Clos des Réas 1988 $50 (2/28/91)
94   DOMAINE MEO-CAMUZET Vosne-Romanée Au Cros-Parantoux 1988 $84 (11/30/90)
94   ROMANEE-CONTI Richebourg 1988 $400 (4/30/91)
93   JOSEPH DROUHIN Echézeaux 1988 $60 (11/15/90)
93   LEROY Vosne-Romanée Les Beaux Monts 1988 $180 (4/30/91)
93   DOMAINE DANIEL RION Vosne-Romanée Les Chaumes 1988 $54 (1/31/91)
92   RENE ENGEL Echézeaux 1988 $56 (3/31/91)
92   DOMAINE DANIEL RION Vosne-Romanée Beaux-Monts 1988 $53 (2/15/91)
92   ROMANEE-CONTI Echézeaux 1988 $225 (4/30/91)
92   ROMANEE-CONTI Grands Echézeaux 1988 $315 (4/30/91)
91   ROBERT ARNOUX Romanée-St.-Vivant 1988 $250 (11/15/90)
91   DOMAINE GROS FRERE & SOEUR Richebourg 1988 $192 (2/28/91)
91   A.-F. GROS Echézeaux 1988 $84 (2/15/91)
91   J. JAYER Echézeaux 1988 $100 (3/15/91)
90   JOSEPH DROUHIN Vosne-Romanée Les Suchots 1988 $57 (2/28/91)
90   DOMAINE DUJAC Echézeaux 1988 $70 (3/31/91)
90   JEAN GROS Vosne-Romanée 1988 $38 (2/28/91)
90+ BOUCHARD PERE & FILS La Romanée Chateau de Vosne-Romanée 1988 $238 (7/15/90) (BT)
90+ F. CHAUVENET Echézeaux 1988 $50 (7/15/90) (BT)
90+ DOMAINE DANIEL RION Vosne-Romanée Les Chaumes 1988 $54 (7/15/90) (BT)
89   RENE ENGEL Vosne-Romanée Les Brûlées 1988 $45 (2/28/91)
89   DOMAINE GROS FRERE & SOEUR Vosne-Romanée 1988 $46 (3/31/91)
89   BERTRAND MACHARD DE GRAMONT Vosne-Romanée Les Réas 1988 $32 (7/15/91)
89   DOMAINE MEO-CAMUZET Vosne-Romanée Aux Brûlées 1988 $84 (11/30/90)
89   MUGNERET-GIBOURG Echézeaux 1988 $70 (11/15/90)
88   DOMAINE MEO-CAMUZET Vosne-Romanée Les Chaumes 1988 $60 (11/30/90)
88   MOILLARD Vosne-Romanée Malconsorts Domaine Thomas-Moillard 1988 $50 (3/31/91)
88   MONGEARD-MUGNERET Echézeaux Vieille Vigne 1988 $61 (2/15/91)
87   BICHOT Vosne-Romanée Les Beaux Monts 1988 $34 (7/15/90)
87   CHANSON PERE & FILS Vosne-Romanée Suchots 1988 $55 (9/30/90)
87   DOMAINE MEO-CAMUZET Vosne-Romanée 1988 $50 (12/31/90)
86   ROBERT ARNOUX Vosne-Romanée Les Suchots 1988 $76 (2/28/91)
86   GERARD MUGNERET Vosne-Romanée 1988 $37 (2/28/91)
85+ DOMAINE DU CLOS FRANTIN Vosne-Romanée Les Malconsorts 1988 $58 (7/15/90) (BT)
85+ DOMAINE DANIEL RION Vosne-Romanée Beaux-Monts 1988 $53 (7/15/90) (BT)
84   GERARD MUGNERET Vosne-Romanée Les Suchots 1988 $57 (2/28/91)
81   RENE ENGEL Vosne-Romanée 1988 $30 (7/15/90)
80   ROBERT ARNOUX Vosne-Romanée Les Chaumes 1988 $62 (2/28/91)
80   JOSEPH DROUHIN Vosne-Romanée Les Beaumonts 1988 $56 (3/31/91)
80+ DOMAINE DANIEL RION Vosne-Romanée Beaux-Monts 1988 $53 (7/15/90) (BT)
75+ JOSEPH DROUHIN Vosne-Romanée Les Suchots 1988 $64 (7/15/90) (BT)
71   A.-F. GROS Vosne-Romanée aux Réas 1988 $41 (2/28/91)
70+ BOUCHARD PERE & FILS Vosne-Romanée Aux Reignots Château de Vosne-Romanée 1988 $50 (7/15/90) (BT)
64   MUGNERET-GIBOURG Vosne-Romanée 1988 $34 (12/31/90)
60   ROBERT ARNOUX Vosne-Romanée Les Chaumes 1988 $62 (12/31/90)
60   ROBERT ARNOUX Vosne-Romanée Les Suchots 1988 $76 (12/31/90)

1987

96   DOMAINE MEO-CAMUZET Richebourg 1987 $165 (12/15/89)
95   JEAN GROS Richebourg 1987 Rel: $99 Cur: $170 (3/31/91)
95   DOMAINE MEO-CAMUZET Vosne-Romanée Au Cros-Parantoux 1987 $63 (12/15/89)
95   DOMAINE MEO-CAMUZET Vosne-Romanée Aux Brûlées 1987 $63 (12/15/89)
93   JEAN GROS Vosne-Romanée Clos des Réas 1987 $37 (4/30/90)
93   MUGNERET-GIBOURG Echézeaux 1987 $50 (10/15/89)
93   ROMANEE-CONTI Richebourg 1987 $190 (9/30/90)
93   ROMANEE-CONTI Echézeaux 1987 $98 (9/30/90)
92   ROMANEE-CONTI La Tâche 1987 $225 (9/30/90)
91   DOMAINE FRANCOIS LAMARCHE Vosne-Romanée La Grande Rue 1987 $68 (9/30/90)
91   MOILLARD Vosne-Romanée Malconsorts Domaine Thomas-Moillard 1987 $30 (8/31/90)
91   EMMANUEL ROUGET Vosne-Romanée 1987 $32 (3/31/90)
90   DOMAINE MEO-CAMUZET Vosne-Romanée 1987 $35 (12/15/89)
90   MUGNERET-GIBOURG Vosne-Romanée 1987 $30 (10/15/89)
89   JEAN GROS Vosne-Romanée 1987 $32 (4/30/90)
89   DOMAINE DANIEL RION Vosne-Romanée 1987 $21 (4/30/90)
89   ROMANEE-CONTI Grands Echézeaux 1987 $145 (9/30/90)
89   ROMANEE-CONTI Romanée-Conti 1987 $350 (9/30/90)
89   ROMANEE-CONTI Romanée-St.-Vivant 1987 $175 (9/30/90)
88   DOMAINE DU CLOS FRANTIN Vosne-Romanée Les Malconsorts 1987 $30 (7/15/90)
88   DOMAINE DANIEL RION Vosne-Romanée Les Chaumes 1987 $35 (4/30/90)
88   EMMANUEL ROUGET Echézeaux 1987 $55 (3/31/90)

87   DOMAINE FRANCOIS LAMARCHE Echézeaux 1987 $48 (9/30/90)
86   DOMAINE DU CLOS FRANTIN Grands Echézeaux 1987 $56 (7/15/90)
86   MONGEARD-MUGNERET Echézeaux Vieille Vigne 1987 $42 (5/15/90)
85   MONGEARD-MUGNERET Grands Echézeaux 1987 $65 (5/15/90)
82   DOMAINE DUJAC Echézeaux 1987 $56 (5/15/90)
82   MONGEARD-MUGNERET Vosne-Romanée Les Suchots 1987 $35 (6/15/90)
82   GERARD MUGNERET Vosne-Romanée Les Suchots 1987 $42 (7/15/90)
80   FAIVELEY Echézeaux 1987 $53 (3/31/90)
79   GERARD MUGNERET Vosne-Romanée 1987 $32 (7/15/90)
74   MONGEARD-MUGNERET Vosne-Romanée Les Petits Monts 1987 $35 (4/30/90)
71   ALAIN GUYARD Vosne-Romanée Aux Réas 1987 $29 (7/15/90)
68   PIERRE BOUREE FILS Vosne-Romanée 1987 $44 (7/15/90)
62   MONGEARD-MUGNERET Vosne-Romanée Les Orveaux 1987 $35 (7/15/90)

1986

98   ROMANEE-CONTI La Tâche 1986 Rel: $250 Cur: $250 (8/31/89) CS
98   ROMANEE-CONTI Romanée-St.-Vivant 1986 Rel: $195 Cur: $195 (8/31/89)
97   DOMAINE MEO-CAMUZET Richebourg 1986 $160 (7/31/88)
95   DOMAINE DANIEL RION Vosne-Romanée Les Chaumes 1986 $47 (7/31/88)
95   ROMANEE-CONTI Romanée-Conti 1986 $400 (8/31/89)
94   ROMANEE-CONTI Grands Echézeaux 1986 $160 (8/31/89)
94   ROMANEE-CONTI Richebourg 1986 $230 (8/31/89)
93   DOMAINE MEO-CAMUZET Vosne-Romanée Au Cros-Parantoux 1986 $60 (7/31/88)
93   DOMAINE DANIEL RION Vosne-Romanée Les Chaumes 1986 Rel: $47 Cur: $54 (4/30/89) CS
92   JOSEPH DROUHIN Echézeaux 1986 $60 (7/31/88)
92   MONGEARD-MUGNERET Grands Echézeaux 1986 $73 (8/31/89)
92   ROMANEE-CONTI Echézeaux 1986 $110 (8/31/89)
91   BOUCHARD PERE & FILS La Romanée Château de Vosne-Romanée 1986 $200 (7/31/88)
91   DOMAINE DU CLOS FRANTIN Echézeaux 1986 $30 (7/31/88)
91   DOMAINE DANIEL RION Vosne-Romanée Beaux-Monts 1986 $43 (4/30/89)
90   DOMAINE DU CLOS FRANTIN Echézeaux 1986 $30 (11/30/88)
90   DOMAINE DU CLOS FRANTIN Vosne-Romanée Les Malconsorts 1986 Rel: $30 Cur: $35 (7/31/88)
90   JEAN GROS Vosne-Romanée Clos des Réas 1986 $36 (2/28/89)
90   DOMAINE MEO-CAMUZET Richebourg 1986 $160 (10/31/88)
90   MONGEARD-MUGNERET Echézeaux Vieille Vigne 1986 $44 (8/31/89)
89   BOUCHARD PERE & FILS Vosne-Romanée Aux Reignots Château de Vosne-Romanée 1986 $50 (7/31/88)
89   DOMAINE DU CLOS FRANTIN Vosne-Romanée 1986 $19 (7/31/88)
89   DOMAINE DUJAC Echézeaux 1986 $52 (4/30/89)
89   EMMANUEL ROUGET Vosne-Romanée Les Beaumonts 1986 $40 (12/31/88)
88   DOMAINE DU CLOS FRANTIN Richebourg 1986 $100 (8/31/89)
88   DOMAINE MEO-CAMUZET Vosne-Romanée 1986 $30 (10/31/88)
88   MOILLARD Vosne-Romanée Malconsorts Domaine Thomas-Moillard 1986 $29 (10/31/88)
88   DOMAINE DANIEL RION Vosne-Romanée Beaux-Monts 1986 Rel: $43 Cur: $43 (7/31/88)
87   DOMAINE DU CLOS FRANTIN Grands Echézeaux 1986 $60 (2/28/89)
87   MUGNERET-GIBOURG Echézeaux 1986 $55 (7/31/88)
87   DOMAINE DANIEL RION Vosne-Romanée 1986 $31 (4/30/89)
87   EMMANUEL ROUGET Echézeaux 1986 $55 (12/31/88)
86   DOMAINE DU CLOS FRANTIN Grands Echézeaux 1986 $60 (7/31/88)
86   JAFFELIN Echézeaux 1986 $45 (12/31/88)
86   DOMAINE DANIEL RION Vosne-Romanée 1986 $31 (7/31/88)
85   MICHEL CLERGET Echézeaux 1986 $31 (8/31/89)
84   MUGNERET-GIBOURG Vosne-Romanée 1986 $33 (7/31/88)
83   DOMAINE MEO-CAMUZET Vosne-Romanée Les Chaumes 1986 $38 (12/31/88)
83   DOMAINE MEO-CAMUZET Vosne-Romanée Les Chaumes 1986 $38 (7/31/88)
83   MUGNERET-GIBOURG Echézeaux 1986 $55 (11/30/88)
82   MONGEARD-MUGNERET Vosne-Romanée Les Orveaux 1986 $34 (8/31/89)
81   MUGNERET-GIBOURG Vosne-Romanée 1986 $33 (12/31/88)
80   DOMAINE DU CLOS FRANTIN Vosne-Romanée 1986 $19 (12/31/88)
79   DOMAINE DU CLOS FRANTIN Vosne-Romanée Les Malconsorts 1986 $30 (10/31/88)
79   JAFFELIN Vosne-Romanée 1986 $30 (2/28/89)
79   MONGEARD-MUGNERET Vosne-Romanée 1986 $26 (8/31/89)
78   RENE ENGEL Echézeaux 1986 $38 (11/30/88)
75   RENE ENGEL Vosne-Romanée 1986 $29 (2/28/89)
71   GEORGES CLERGET Vosne-Romanée Les Violettes 1986 $23 (8/31/89)
71   RENE ENGEL Grands Echézeaux 1986 $50 (11/30/88)
68   RENE ENGEL Vosne-Romanée Les Brûlées 1986 $32 (10/31/88)
61   A. PERNIN-ROSSIN Vosne-Romanée 1986 $31 (2/28/89)

1985

100 ROMANEE-CONTI Richebourg 1985 Rel: $210 Cur: $310 (2/29/88)
99   ROMANEE-CONTI Romanée-Conti 1985 Rel: $375 Cur: $1078 (1/31/90) (JS)
98   LOUIS LATOUR Romanée-St.-Vivant Les Quatre Journaux 1985 Rel: $99 Cur: $110 (3/15/88)
98   ROMANEE-CONTI La Tâche 1985 Rel: $225 Cur: $302 (2/29/88)
97   DOMAINE MEO-CAMUZET Richebourg 1985 Rel: $150 Cur: $235 (3/31/88)
96   DOMAINE DU CLOS FRANTIN Echézeaux 1985 $37 (9/15/87)
96   ROMANEE-CONTI Echézeaux 1985 $95 (2/29/88)
96   ROMANEE-CONTI Romanée-Conti 1985 $375 (2/29/88)
95   DOMAINE DU CLOS FRANTIN Vosne-Romanée Les Malconsorts 1985 $40 (9/30/87)
95   MOILLARD Vosne-Romanée Malconsorts Domaine Thomas-Moillard 1985 $47 (7/31/88)
95   DOMAINE DANIEL RION Vosne-Romanée Beaux-Monts 1985 Rel: $38 Cur: $55 (2/29/88)
94   JOSEPH DROUHIN Vosne-Romanée Les Suchots 1985 $42 (11/15/87)
94   MOILLARD Echézeaux 1985 $47 (4/15/88)
94   ROMANEE-CONTI Grands Echézeaux 1985 $140 (2/29/88)
93   JOSEPH DROUHIN Grands Echézeaux 1985 $75 (11/15/87)
93   JOSEPH DROUHIN Vosne-Romanée Les Beaumonts 1985 $42 (11/15/87)
93   MUGNERET-GIBOURG Echézeaux 1985 $57 (2/29/88)
92   F. CHAUVENET Vosne-Romanée Les Suchots 1985 $46 (7/31/87)
92   DOMAINE MEO-CAMUZET Vosne-Romanée Les Chaumes 1985 $80 (3/31/88)
92   MONGEARD-MUGNERET Richebourg 1985 $123 (3/15/88)
91   DOMAINE DU CLOS FRANTIN Vosne-Romanée 1985 $29 (10/15/87)
91   DOMAINE FRANCOIS LAMARCHE Vosne-Romanée Suchots 1985 $36 (10/15/88)
91   B. MUGNERET-GOUACHON Echézeaux 1985 $29 (12/31/88)
91   REMOISSENET Richebourg 1985 $138 (3/15/88)
91   REMOISSENET Vosne-Romanée Les Suchots 1985 $75 (3/15/88)
90   ROBERT ARNOUX Vosne-Romanée Les Suchots 1985 $52 (7/31/88)

90   BOUCHARD PERE & FILS Vosne-Romanée Aux Reignots Château de Vosne-Romanée 1985 $51 (2/28/89)
90   RENE ENGEL Echézeaux 1985 $32 (10/15/87)
90   MOILLARD Vosne-Romanée Malconsorts 1985 $21 (12/15/86)
90   RENE MUGNERET Vosne-Romanée 1985 $27 (4/30/88)
89   F. CHAUVENET Echézeaux 1985 $47 (7/31/87)
89   FAIVELEY Echézeaux 1985 $74 (3/31/88)
89   DOMAINE FRANCOIS LAMARCHE Vosne-Romanée La Grande Rue 1985 $60 (10/15/88)
88   ROMANEE-CONTI Romanée-St.-Vivant 1985 $175 (2/29/88)
87   JEAN GRIVOT Vosne-Romanée 1985 $31 (4/30/88)
87   JEAN GROS Vosne-Romanée Clos des Réas 1985 $55 (7/31/88)
87   LOUIS LATOUR Echézeaux 1985 $49 (3/15/88)
86   RENE ENGEL Grands Echézeaux 1985 $43 (10/15/87)
86   LOUIS JADOT Vosne-Romanée 1985 $33 (3/31/88)
86   LOUIS LATOUR Vosne-Romanée Beaumonts 1985 $36 (3/15/88)
85   RENE ENGEL Vosne-Romanée Les Brûlées 1985 $28 (10/15/87)
85   MUGNERET-GIBOURG Vosne-Romanée 1985 $33 (2/29/88)
84   DOMAINE FRANCOIS LAMARCHE Vosne-Romanée Malconsorts 1985 $44 (10/15/88)
82   DOMAINE BERTAGNA Vosne-Romanée Les Beaux Monts Bas 1985 $35 (10/15/88)
82   MICHEL CLERGET Echézeaux 1985 $51 (7/31/88)
82   MONGEARD-MUGNERET Vosne-Romanée Les Orveaux 1985 $32 (3/15/88)
80   J. JAYER Vosne-Romanée Les Rouges 1985 $44 (3/15/88)
78   DOMAINE DANIEL RION Vosne-Romanée 1985 $28 (2/29/88)
77   RENE ENGEL Vosne-Romanée 1985 $24 (10/15/87)
75   REMOISSENET Echézeaux 1985 $73 (3/15/88)
71   DOMAINE GROS FRERE & SOEUR Grands Echézeaux 1985 $75 (3/31/88)
70   DOMAINE GROS FRERE & SOEUR Vosne-Romanée 1985 $35 (4/15/88)

1984

96   MOILLARD Echézeaux 1984 $21.50 (11/15/86) SS
96   ROMANEE-CONTI Romanée-St.-Vivant 1984 $70 (2/28/87)
95   MOILLARD Vosne-Romanée Malconsorts 1984 $24 (12/15/86) CS
95   ROMANEE-CONTI La Tâche 1984 $105 (2/28/87)
94   ROMANEE-CONTI Romanée-Conti 1984 Cur: $637 (1/31/90) (JS)
91   ROMANEE-CONTI Richebourg 1984 $102 (2/28/87)
90   MOILLARD Grands Echézeaux 1984 $39 (5/31/87)
90   ROMANEE-CONTI Echézeaux 1984 $52 (2/28/87)
88   ROMANEE-CONTI Grands Echézeaux 1984 $64 (2/28/87)
87   MOILLARD Romanée-St.-Vivant 1984 $42 (5/31/87)
85   MUGNERET-GIBOURG Echézeaux 1984 $32 (3/15/87)
80   MOILLARD Vosne-Romanée Malconsorts 1984 $24 (5/31/87)
68   MONGEARD-MUGNERET Echézeaux 1984 $28 (2/15/88)
68   MONGEARD-MUGNERET Vosne-Romanée Les Orveaux 1984 $18 (2/15/88)

1983

90   JAFFELIN Echézeaux 1983 $30 (5/01/86)
78   RENE ENGEL Vosne-Romanée Les Brûlées 1983 $22 (3/16/86)
78   ROMANEE-CONTI Romanée-Conti 1983 Rel: $250 Cur: $746 (1/31/90) (JS)
73   RENE MUGNERET Vosne-Romanée 1983 $16 (11/16/85)
67   RENE ENGEL Vosne-Romanée 1983 $19.50 (2/16/86)
66   ROMANEE-CONTI Romanée-St.-Vivant 1983 $125 (11/30/86)
65   ROMANEE-CONTI Romanée-Conti 1983 $250 (11/30/86)
64   ROMANEE-CONTI Grands Echézeaux 1983 $100 (11/30/86)
63   DOMAINE DANIEL RION Vosne-Romanée 1983 $19 (2/01/86)
63   ROMANEE-CONTI Echézeaux 1983 $75 (11/30/86)
62   CHARLES MONCAUT Vosne-Romanée Cuvée Particulière 1983 $16 (9/15/86)
61   ROMANEE-CONTI La Tâche 1983 $150 (11/30/86)
52   ROMANEE-CONTI Richebourg 1983 $150 (11/30/86)

1982

94   HENRI JAYER Echézeaux 1982 $41 (6/16/86) CS
86   RENE MUGNERET Vosne-Romanée 1982 $17 (7/16/85)
85   ROMANEE-CONTI Romanée-Conti 1982 Cur: $442 (1/31/90) (JS)
58   JAYER-GILLES Echézeaux 1982 $23 (11/01/85)

1981

68   FAIVELEY Echézeaux 1981 $40 (5/01/86)

1979

90   ROMANEE-CONTI Romanée-Conti 1979 Cur: $781 (1/31/90) (JS)
86   MOMMESSIN Echézeaux 1979 $18.50 (2/16/86)

1978

95   ROMANEE-CONTI Romanée-Conti 1978 Cur: $1470 (1/31/90) (JS)

1975

82   ROMANEE-CONTI Romanée-Conti 1975 Cur: $776 (1/31/90) (JS)

1964

98   ROMANEE-CONTI Romanée-Conti 1964 Cur: $1150 (1/31/90) (JS)

1963

50   ROMANEE-CONTI Romanée-Conti 1963 Cur: $1200 (1/31/90) (JS)

1959

94   ARMAND ROUX Echézeaux 1959 Cur: $110 (8/31/90) (TR)
91   ARMAND ROUX Richebourg 1959 Cur: $130 (8/31/90) (TR)
68   ROMANEE-CONTI Romanée-Conti 1959 Cur: $1810 (1/31/90) (JS)

1954

88   ROMANEE-CONTI Richebourg 1954 Cur: $175 (8/31/90) (TR)

1953

94   LOUIS LATOUR Romanée-St.-Vivant Les Quatre Journaux 1953 Cur: $225 (8/31/90) (TR)
93   ROMANEE-CONTI Romanée-Conti 1953 Cur: $2064 (1/31/90) (JS)

1952

97   ROMANEE-CONTI Echézeaux 1952 Cur: $96 (8/31/90) (TR)

1949

95   REMOISSENET Vosne-Romanée Clos de Réas 1949 Cur: $138 (8/31/90) (TR)

1947

65   ROMANEE-CONTI Richebourg 1947 Cur: $750 (8/31/90) (TR)

1942

93   ROMANEE-CONTI Grands Echézeaux 1942 Cur: $230 (8/31/90) (TR)

1937

94   ROMANEE-CONTI Romanée-Conti 1937 Cur: $1,950 (12/15/88)
50   ROMANEE-CONTI Romanée-Conti 1937 Cur: $1,950 (1/31/90) (JS)

1935

50   ROMANEE-CONTI Romanée-Conti 1935 Cur: $600 (1/31/90) (JS)

1934

66   ROMANEE-CONTI Romanée-Conti 1934 Cur: $2,057 (1/31/90) (JS)

1929

50   ROMANEE-CONTI Romanée-Conti 1929 Cur: $2,332 (1/31/90) (JS)

VOUGEOT

1989

85+ FAIVELEY Clos de Vougeot 1989 (NR) (7/15/90) (BT)
85+ LOUIS JADOT Clos Vougeot 1989 (NR) (7/15/90) (BT)
85+ J. LABET & N. DECHELETTE Clos Vougeot Château de la Tour 1989 (NR) (7/15/90) (BT)

1988

93   DOMAINE CECI Clos de Vougeot 1988 $48 (7/15/91)
92   CHOPIN-GROFFIER Vougeot 1988 $32 (5/15/91)
92   DOMAINE GROS FRERE & SOEUR Clos Vougeot Musigni 1988 $95 (3/31/91)
92   DOMAINE MEO-CAMUZET Clos de Vougeot 1988 $95 (11/30/90)
92   DOMAINE DANIEL RION Clos Vougeot 1988 $75 (1/31/91)
91   RENE ENGEL Clos Vougeot 1988 $75 (3/15/91)
91   J. LABET & N. DECHELETTE Clos Vougeot Château de la Tour 1988 $50 (11/30/90)
90   JOSEPH DROUHIN Clos de Vougeot 1988 $85 (2/15/91)
90+ FAIVELEY Clos de Vougeot 1988 $92 (7/15/90) (BT)
90+ J. LABET & N. DECHELETTE Clos Vougeot Château de la Tour 1988 $50 (7/15/90) (BT)
89   DROUHIN-LAROZE Clos de Vougeot 1988 $81 (12/31/90)
89   LEROY Clos de Vougeot 1988 $260 (4/30/91)
87   CHOPIN-GROFFIER Clos Vougeot 1988 $70 (5/15/91)
86   CHATEAU DES HERBEUX Clos Vougeot 1988 $65 (11/30/90)
85   JEAN GRIVOT Clos de Vougeot 1988 $70 (4/30/91)
85+ JOSEPH DROUHIN Clos de Vougeot 1988 $93 (7/15/90) (BT)
84   GEORGES MUGNERET Clos de Vougeot 1988 $90 (11/15/90)
80+ LOUIS JADOT Clos Vougeot 1988 $52 (7/15/90) (BT)
78   ROBERT ARNOUX Clos Vougeot 1988 $70 (3/15/91)
73   HAEGELEN-JAYER Clos de Vougeot 1988 $69 (5/15/91)
75+ DOMAINE DANIEL RION Clos Vougeot 1988 $75 (7/15/90) (BT)

1987

91   GEORGES MUGNERET Clos Vougeot 1987 $68 (10/15/89)
86   DOMAINE FRANCOIS LAMARCHE Clos de Vougeot 1987 $55 (9/30/90)
86   RION PERE & FILS Clos Vougeot 1987 $48 (11/15/90)
85   DOMAINE DU CLOS FRANTIN Clos de Vougeot 1987 $56 (7/15/90)
84   J. LABET & N. DECHELETTE Clos Vougeot Château de la Tour 1987 $50 (2/15/91)
82   DOMAINE CECI Clos de Vougeot 1987 $40 (3/31/91)
81   MONGEARD-MUGNERET Clos de Vougeot 1987 $53 (5/15/90)
79   DROUHIN-LAROZE Clos de Vougeot 1987 $38 (3/31/90)
70   JEAN TARDY Clos de Vougeot 1987 $49 (3/31/90)

1986

91   DOMAINE MEO-CAMUZET Clos de Vougeot 1986 $55 (11/30/88)
90   DOMAINE DU CLOS FRANTIN Clos de Vougeot 1986 $37 (7/31/88)
90   GEORGES MUGNERET Clos Vougeot 1986 $73 (11/30/88)
90   GEORGES MUGNERET Clos Vougeot 1986 $73 (7/31/88)
90   DOMAINE DANIEL RION Clos Vougeot 1986 $70 (4/15/89)
87   F. CHAUVENET Clos de Vougeot 1986 $57 (7/31/88)
87   DOMAINE DU CLOS FRANTIN Clos de Vougeot 1986 $37 (11/30/88)
87   LOUIS JADOT Clos Vougeot 1986 $50 (4/15/89)
87   MONGEARD-MUGNERET Clos de Vougeot 1986 $56 (7/31/89)
86   JOSEPH DROUHIN Clos de Vougeot 1986 $55 (4/15/89)
86   JOSEPH DROUHIN Clos de Vougeot 1986 $55 (7/31/88)
85   DOMAINE DANIEL RION Clos Vougeot 1986 $70 (7/31/88)
84   CHARLES MORTET Clos Vougeot 1986 $43 (4/15/89)
81   RENE ENGEL Clos Vougeot 1986 $50 (11/30/88)
79   F. CHAUVENET Clos de Vougeot 1986 $57 (12/31/88)
77   JAFFELIN Clos de Vougeot 1986 $45 (12/31/88)

1985

96   JAFFELIN Clos de Vougeot 1985 $49 (6/15/88)
94   JOSEPH DROUHIN Clos de Vougeot 1985 $57 (11/15/87)
93   DOMAINE MEO-CAMUZET Clos de Vougeot 1985 $65 (3/31/88)
90   HAEGELEN-JAYER Clos Vougeot 1985 $64 (4/15/88)
90   J. LABET & N. DECHELETTE Clos Vougeot Château de la Tour 1985 $53 (6/15/88)
90   DOMAINE FRANCOIS LAMARCHE Clos de Vougeot 1985 $48 (10/15/88)
88   DROUHIN-LAROZE Clos de Vougeot 1985 $60 (10/15/88)
87   DOMAINE BERTAGNA Vougeot Clos de la Perrière 1985 $40 (4/15/89)
86   CAPTAIN-GAGNEROT Clos Vougeot 1985 $67 (12/31/88)
85   DOMAINE BERTAGNA Vougeot Les Crâs 1985 $30 (3/31/88)
85   RENE ENGEL Clos Vougeot 1985 $43 (10/15/87)
82   LOUIS JADOT Clos Vougeot 1985 $53 (3/31/88)
81   JEAN GRIVOT Clos de Vougeot 1985 $62 (4/30/88)
75   DOMAINE GROS FRERE & SOEUR Clos de Vougeot Musigny 1985 $70 (3/31/88)

1984

90   MOILLARD Clos de Vougeot 1984 $32 (5/31/87)

FRANCE
BURGUNDY RED/CÔTE DE NUITS/VOUGEOT

1983
95   MOILLARD Clos de Vougeot 1983 $26 (10/16/85) CS
80   RENE ENGEL Clos Vougeot 1983 $30 (2/16/86)
49   HENRI REBOURSEAU Clos de Vougeot 1983 $25 (11/16/85)

1979
66   J. LABET & N. DECHELETTE Clos Vougeot Château de la Tour 1979 $40 (9/01/84)

1959
85   BOUCHARD PERE & FILS Clos de Vougeot 1959 Cur: $120 (8/31/90) (TR)

1942
84   THOMAS BASSOT Clos de Vougeot 1942 (NA) (8/31/90) (TR)

OTHER CÔTE DE NUITS RED

1988
83   DOMAINE SIRUGUE Côte de Nuits-Villages Clos de la Belle Marguerite 1988 $16 (3/31/91)
82   CHATEAU DE PULIGNY-MONTRACHET Côte de Nuits-Villages 1988 $17 (3/31/91)
80   DOMAINE DE L'ARLOT Côte de Nuits-Villages Clos du Châpeau 1988 $21 (3/31/91)
80   A.-F. GROS Bourgogne Hautes Côtes de Nuits 1988 $22 (3/31/91)

1987
82   MAISON AMBROISE Côte de Nuits-Villages 1987 $15 (2/28/90)
78   MICHEL GROS Hautes Côtes de Nuits 1987 $14 (2/28/90)
78   LOUIS TRAPET Marsannay 1987 $17 (3/31/91)

1986
81   DOMAINE DANIEL RION Côte de Nuits-Villages 1986 $15 (7/31/88)
77   LOUIS JADOT Marsannay 1986 $11.50 (6/15/89)

1985
89   PHILIPPE ROSSIGNOL Côte de Nuits-Villages 1985 $24 (7/31/88)
86   JOSEPH DROUHIN Côte de Nuits-Villages 1985 $19.50 (11/15/87)
85   MOMMESSIN Côte de Nuits-Villages 1985 $17 (7/31/88)
83   A. CHOPIN Côte de Nuits-Villages 1985 $9 (10/31/87) BB

1983
78   JEAN CLAUDE BOISSET Côte de Nuits-Villages 1983 $13 (2/01/86)
76   MOILLARD Hautes Côtes de Nuits 1983 $6.50 (11/01/85)

CHALONNAISE

1988
84   FAIVELEY Mercurey Clos du Roy 1988 $22 (3/31/91)
84   DOMAINE JOBLOT Givry Clos du Cellier aux Moines 1988 $19 (12/31/90)
83   REMOISSENET Mercurey Clos Fortoul 1988 $17 (3/31/91)
82   DUVERNAY Rully Les Cloux 1988 $18 (12/31/90)
81   FAIVELEY Mercurey Domaine de la Croix Jacquelet 1988 $17.50 (3/31/91)
78   CHANSON PERE & FILS Givry 1988 $13 (12/31/90)
68   REMOISSENET Givry du Domaine Thénard 1988 $19 (3/31/91)
67   DOMAINE FABIEN & LOUIS SAIER Mercurey Les Chenelots 1988 $17 (4/30/91)

1987
68   MICHEL BRIDAY Rully Champ Clou 1987 $16 (12/31/90)

1986
83   FAIVELEY Rully 1986 $17.50 (6/15/89)
77   JAFFELIN Rully 1986 $13 (6/15/89)

1985
85   CHARLES VIENOT Mercurey 1985 $12.50 (4/30/88)
83   JOSEPH DROUHIN Mercurey 1985 $17 (11/15/87)
83   DOMAINE FABIEN & LOUIS SAIER Mercurey Les Champs Martins 1985 $20 (3/31/88)
81   FAIVELEY Mercurey Clos du Roy 1985 $23 (4/30/88)
77   REMOISSENET Givry du Domaine Thénard 1985 $18 (4/30/88)
75   FAIVELEY Mercurey Clos des Myglands 1985 $20 (4/30/88)
70   JEAN CHOFFLET Givry 1985 $12 (11/15/87)

1983
56   DOMAINE DU CHATEAU DE MERCEY Mercurey 1983 $10.25 (5/01/86)

1981
68   FAIVELEY Mercurey Clos des Myglands 1981 $11 (6/16/86)

OTHER BURGUNDY RED

1989
85   JOSEPH DROUHIN Bourgogne Pinot Noir Laforet 1989 $9 (4/30/91) BB
84   DOMAINE MEO-CAMUZET Bourgogne Passetoutgrains 1989 $17 (7/15/91)
78   HENRI DE VILLAMONT Bourgogne Pinot Noir 1989 $11 (3/31/91)
75+   CHARTRON & TREBUCHET Bourgogne 1989 (NR) (7/15/90) (BT)
70+   LOUIS JADOT Bourgogne 1989 (NR) (7/15/90) (BT)

1988
87   LEROY Bourgogne Leroy D'Auvenay 1988 $14.50 (4/30/91)
84   JOSEPH DROUHIN Bourgogne Pinot Noir Laforet 1988 $10 (3/31/91) BB
83   LABOURE-ROI Bourgogne 1988 $12 (3/31/91)
83   LUPE-CHOLET Bourgogne Pinot Noir Comte de Lupé 1988 $9 (2/28/90) BB
82   GHISLAINE BARTHOD Bourgogne 1988 $20 (3/31/91)
80   DOMAINE RAPET Bourgogne en Bully 1988 $18.50 (3/31/91)
75+   DOMAINE JEAN CHARTRON Bourgogne Pinot Noir L'Orme 1988 (NR) (7/15/90) (BT)
73   JEAN-CLAUDE VOLPATO Bourgogne Passetoutgrain 1988 $12.50 (3/31/91)
70+   LOUIS JADOT Bourgogne Pinot Noir 1988 (NR) (7/15/90) (BT)
68   CHATEAU DE DRACY Bourgogne Pinot Noir 1988 $8 (2/28/90)

1987
79   J.-F. COCHE-DURY Bourgogne Pinot Noir 1987 $25 (2/28/90)
78   JOSEPH DROUHIN Bourgogne Pinot Noir Laforet 1987 $8.75 (6/15/89)
78   LUPE-CHOLET Bourgogne Hautes Côtes de Beaune 1987 $10 (4/15/90)

1986
81   MOILLARD Bourgogne Hautes Côtes de Nuits Les Hameaux 1986 $11 (12/31/88)
79   CHARLES MORTET Bourgogne 1986 $15 (6/15/89)
79   POTHIER-RIEUSSET Bourgogne Rouge 1986 $10 (6/15/89)
78   LUPE-CHOLET Bourgogne Clos de la Roche 1986 $10 (7/31/88)
77   BICHOT Bourgogne Croix St.-Louis 1986 $6 (10/31/88)
76   CHATEAU DE DRACY Bourgogne 1986 $6.50 (12/31/88)

1985
84   JEAN-LUC JOILLOT Bourgogne Tastevinage 1985 $14.50 (6/30/88)
83   POTHIER-RIEUSSET Bourgogne Rouge 1985 $7.50 (6/30/88) BB
81   BICHOT Bourgogne Le Bourgogne Bichot Pinot Noir 1985 $8 (11/15/87)
81   MACHARD DE GRAMONT Bourgogne Pinot Noir Domaine de la Vierge Romaine 1985 $13 (6/30/88)
80   F. CHAUVENET Bourgogne Pinot Noir Château Marguerite de Bourgogne 1985 $10 (6/30/88)
79   LUPE-CHOLET Bourgogne Clos de Lupé 1985 $15 (3/31/88)
78   JOSEPH DROUHIN Bourgogne Pinot Noir Laforet 1985 $8.50 (11/15/87)
78   LOUIS JADOT Bourgogne Pinot Noir Jadot 1985 $11 (4/30/88)
78   MOILLARD Bourgogne Pinot Noir 1985 $7 (3/31/88)
78   CHARLES VIENOT Bourgogne 1985 $9 (6/15/89)
77   DOMAINE JEAN MORETEAUX Bourgogne Pinot Noir Les Clous 1985 $9 (11/15/87)
76   HENRI BOILLOT Bourgogne 1985 $13 (12/31/88)
76   DOMAINE B. SERVEAU Bourgogne Rouge 1985 $13 (11/15/87)
75   CAVE DES VIGNERONS DE BUXY Bourgogne Pinot Noir Grande Réserve 1985 $7 (6/30/88)
73   LEROY Bourgogne d'Auvenay 1985 $12 (3/31/88)

1983
78   LIONEL J. BRUCK Bourgogne St.-Vincent Pinot Noir 1983 $10 (2/15/87)
75   CHARLES VIENOT Bourgogne 1983 $6.50 (12/16/85)
73   CAVE DES VIGNERONS DE BUXY Bourgogne Pinot Noir Grande Réserve 1983 $5 (2/01/86)
71   JOSEPH DROUHIN Bourgogne Pinot Noir Laforet 1983 $7.50 (11/01/85)
61   MOMMESSIN Bourgogne Pinot Noir 1983 $5 12/16/86)

1982
52   CHARLES VIENOT Bourgogne 1982 $6 (11/01/85)

1979
75   FAIVELEY Bourgogne Cuvée Joseph Faiveley 1979 $8 (4/16/86) BB

BURGUNDY WHITE/CÔTE DE BEAUNE/ALOXE-CORTON

1989
91   JOSEPH DROUHIN Corton-Charlemagne 1989 Rel: $92 Cur: $92 (2/28/91)
85   CHARTRON & TREBUCHET Corton-Charlemagne 1989 $105 (2/28/91)

1988
95   CHARTRON & TREBUCHET Corton-Charlemagne 1988 $70 (2/28/90)
95   LOUIS LATOUR Corton-Charlemagne 1988 Rel: $85 Cur: $86 (10/15/90)
94   MARIUS DELARCHE PERE & FILS Corton-Charlemagne 1988 $60 (7/31/90)
93   LOUIS JADOT Corton-Charlemagne 1988 Rel: $98 Cur: $98 (4/30/91)
91   PIERRE BITOUZET Corton-Charlemagne 1988 $75 (12/31/90)
90   LABOURE-ROI Corton-Charlemagne 1988 $50 (10/15/90)
84   DOMAINE CHANDON DE BRIAILLES Corton 1988 $88 (2/28/91)
71   DOMAINE DU CLOS FRANTIN Corton-Charlemagne 1988 $66 (4/30/91)

1987
92   PIERRE BITOUZET Corton-Charlemagne 1987 $68 (11/15/89)
91   CHARTRON & TREBUCHET Corton-Charlemagne 1987 $79 (3/31/89)
90   JOSEPH DROUHIN Corton-Charlemagne 1987 Rel: $90 Cur: $90 (3/31/89)
90   A. LIGERET Corton-Charlemagne 1987 $83 (10/15/90)
88   J.-F. COCHE-DURY Corton-Charlemagne 1987 $122 (2/28/90)
84   MICHEL JUILLOT Corton-Charlemagne 1987 $77 (2/28/90)

1986
95   PIERRE BITOUZET Corton-Charlemagne 1986 $72 (9/30/88)
95   CHARTRON & TREBUCHET Corton-Charlemagne 1986 $92 (5/31/88)
92   LOUIS JADOT Corton-Charlemagne 1986 Rel: $92 Cur: $92 (5/31/89)
90   JOSEPH DROUHIN Corton-Charlemagne 1986 Rel: $98 Cur: $98 (12/15/88)
90   MOILLARD Corton-Charlemagne 1986 $70 (5/31/88)
89   JEAN-CLAUDE BELLAND Corton-Charlemagne 1986 $58 (3/31/89)
88   BONNEAU DU MARTRAY Corton-Charlemagne 1986 Rel: $60 Cur: $66 (2/28/90)
87   DOMAINE DU CLOS FRANTIN Corton-Charlemagne 1986 $55 (3/31/89)
85   DOMAINE DELARCHE Corton-Charlemagne 1986 $65 (9/30/88)
83   OLIVIER LEFLAIVE FRERES Corton-Charlemagne 1986 $67 (7/31/90)
82   REMOISSENET Corton-Charlemagne Diamond Jubilee 1986 $82 (12/15/88)

1985
96   F. CHAUVENET Corton-Charlemagne 1985 $70 (4/30/87)
96   F. CHAUVENET Corton-Charlemagne Hospices de Beaune Cuvée François de Salins 1985 $140 (7/31/87)

96	LOUIS LATOUR Corton-Charlemagne 1985 Rel: $88 Cur: $95 (11/15/87)
94	JOSEPH DROUHIN Corton-Charlemagne 1985 Rel: $78 Cur: $78 (4/30/87)
92	REINE PEDAUQUE Corton-Charlemagne 1985 $60 (11/15/89)
90	REMOISSENET Corton-Charlemagne Diamond Jubilee 1985 $100 (3/15/88)
87	BICHOT Corton-Charlemagne 1985 $63 (3/15/88)
84	BONNEAU DU MARTRAY Corton-Charlemagne 1985 Rel: $65 Cur: $69 (5/31/88)

1984

90	MOILLARD Corton-Charlemagne 1984 $51 (5/31/87)
86	JAFFELIN Corton-Charlemagne 1984 $60 (5/01/86)

1983

92	MOILLARD Corton-Charlemagne 1983 $34 (10/01/85)

1982

95	F. CHAUVENET Corton Vergennes Hospices de Beaune Cuvée Paul Chanson 1982 $83 (8/01/85)
82	LOUIS LATOUR Corton-Charlemagne 1982 Rel: $65 Cur: $79 (12/01/85)
73	REINE PEDAUQUE Corton-Charlemagne 1982 $33 (8/01/85)

CHASSAGNE-MONTRACHET

1989

94	CHARTRON & TREBUCHET Chassagne-Montrachet Les Morgeots 1989 $54 (2/15/91)
90	JOSEPH DROUHIN Chassagne-Montrachet Marquis de Laguiche 1989 $58 (2/15/91)
90	LAROCHE Chassagne-Montrachet 1989 $45 (2/28/91)
89	DOMAINE ROUX PERE & FILS Chassagne-Montrachet 1989 $45 (2/28/91)
88	BOUCHARD PERE & FILS Chassagne-Montrachet 1989 $17 (4/30/91)
88	CHARTRON & TREBUCHET Chassagne-Montrachet 1989 $46 (2/15/91)
88	DOMAINE ROUX PERE & FILS Chassagne-Montrachet Morgeot 1989 $55 (2/28/91)
87	CHATEAU DE LA MALTROYE Chassagne-Montrachet Morgeot Vigne Blanche 1989 $40 (2/28/91)
86	CHATEAU DE LA MALTROYE Chassagne-Montrachet Grandes Ruchottes 1989 $40 (2/28/91)

1988

96	CHARTRON & TREBUCHET Chassagne-Montrachet Les Morgeots 1988 $34 (2/28/90)
92	DOMAINE RAMONET Chassagne-Montrachet Morgeot 1988 $59 (2/28/91)
91	CHARTRON & TREBUCHET Chassagne-Montrachet 1988 $26 (2/28/90)
91	JEAN-NOEL GAGNARD Chassagne-Montrachet Première Cru 1988 $50 (10/15/90)
91	FERNAND PILLOT Chassagne-Montrachet Morgeot 1988 $35 (5/15/90)
91	DOMAINE ETIENNE SAUZET Chassagne-Montrachet 1988 $38 (2/15/91)
90	MICHEL COLIN-DELEGER Chassagne-Montrachet Les Chaumées 1988 $48 (2/28/91)
90	MICHEL COLIN-DELEGER Chassagne-Montrachet Les Remilly 1988 $30 (5/15/90)
90	LAROCHE Chassagne-Montrachet Première Cru 1988 $39 (2/15/91)
90	LEROY Chassagne-Montrachet Les Ruchottes 1988 $116 (4/30/91)
90	FERNAND PILLOT Chassagne-Montrachet Grandes Ruchottes 1988 $43 (5/15/90)
89	LOUIS JADOT Chassagne-Montrachet Morgeot Clos de la Chapelle Domaine du Duc de Magenta 1988 $43 (4/30/91)
88	MICHEL COLIN-DELEGER Chassagne-Montrachet Les Vergers 1988 $48 (5/15/90)
88	JEAN PILLOT Chassagne-Montrachet Les Caillerets 1988 $39 (2/28/91)
88	DOMAINE ROUX PERE & FILS Chassagne-Montrachet 1988 $35 (2/28/90)
87	JOSEPH DROUHIN Chassagne-Montrachet 1988 $39 (3/31/90)
87	FERNAND PILLOT Chassagne-Montrachet Les Vergers 1988 $35 (5/15/90)
86	AMIOT-BONFILS Chassagne-Montrachet Les Champgains 1988 $27 (3/31/90)
86	JEAN CLAUDE BOISSET Chassagne-Montrachet 1988 $28 (2/15/91)
86	MICHEL COLIN-DELEGER Chassagne-Montrachet 1988 $40 (2/28/91)
86	LEROY Chassagne-Montrachet Les Chenevottes 1988 $116 (4/30/91)
86	DOMAINE PONAVOY Chassagne-Montrachet 1988 $40 (2/15/91)
86	DOMAINE RAMONET Chassagne-Montrachet 1988 $43 (2/28/91)
86	DOMAINE ROUX PERE & FILS Chassagne-Montrachet Morgeot 1988 $39 (2/28/90)
84	A. LIGERET Chassagne-Montrachet Réserve Antonin Toursier 1988 $45 (2/15/91)
83	MADAME FRANCOIS COLIN Chassagne-Montrachet Clos Devant 1988 $26 (5/15/90)
83	HENRI GERMAIN Chassagne-Montrachet Morgeot 1988 $43 (4/30/91)
83	LAROCHE Chassagne-Montrachet 1988 $33 (2/15/91)
82	BICHOT Chassagne-Montrachet Morgeot-Vignes-Blanches 1988 $40 (2/15/91)
80	BACHELET-RAMONET Chassagne-Montrachet 1988 $37 (4/30/91)
80	JEAN-NOEL GAGNARD Chassagne-Montrachet Morgeot 1988 $54 (11/15/90)
78	HENRI GERMAIN Chassagne-Montrachet Morgeot 1988 $43 (2/15/91)
70	AMIOT-BONFILS Chassagne-Montrachet Les Caillerets 1988 $27 (5/15/90)

1987

91	PAUL PILLOT Chassagne-Montrachet La Romanée 1987 $48 (2/28/90)
91	PAUL PILLOT Chassagne-Montrachet Les Grandes Ruchottes 1987 $38 (2/28/90)
90	CHARTRON & TREBUCHET Chassagne-Montrachet Les Morgeots 1987 $40 (3/15/89)
90	MICHEL COLIN-DELEGER Chassagne-Montrachet Les Vergers 1987 $42 (11/15/89)
88	MICHEL COLIN-DELEGER Chassagne-Montrachet Morgeot 1987 $43 (5/31/89)
88	BERNARD MOREY Chassagne-Montrachet Morgeot 1987 $42 (5/31/89)
87	BACHELET-RAMONET Chassagne-Montrachet 1987 $36 (11/15/89)
87	BACHELET-RAMONET Chassagne-Montrachet Caillerets 1987 $35 (5/15/90)
86	AMIOT-PONSOT Chassagne-Montrachet Les Champ Gain 1987 $42 (5/31/89)
86	DOMAINE RAMONET Chassagne-Montrachet Les Ruchottes 1987 $52 (2/28/90)
84	JOSEPH DROUHIN Chassagne-Montrachet Marquis de Laguiche 1987 Rel: $48 Cur: $61 (3/15/89)
83	JAFFELIN Chassagne-Montrachet 1987 $30 (3/15/89)
82	JOSEPH DROUHIN Chassagne-Montrachet 1987 $39 (3/15/89)
79	DOMAINE RAMONET Chassagne-Montrachet Morgeot 1987 $49 (2/28/90)
79	DOMAINE ROUX PERE & FILS Chassagne-Montrachet Morgeot 1987 $43 (5/31/89)
74	MOILLARD Chassagne-Montrachet La Romanée 1987 $31 (11/15/89)
73	LUPE-CHOLET Chassagne-Montrachet Morgeot Vignes Blanches 1987 $45 (11/15/89)
71	PROSPER MAUFOUX Chassagne-Montrachet Les Chenevottes 1987 $37 (2/28/91)

1986

94	DOMAINE MARC MOREY Chassagne-Montrachet Morgeot 1986 $37 (9/30/88)
93	F. CHAUVENET Chassagne-Montrachet Morgeot 1986 $45 (5/31/88)
93	MICHEL COLIN-DELEGER Chassagne-Montrachet Les Remilly 1986 $38 (10/31/88)
92	LOUIS LATOUR Chassagne-Montrachet Première Cru 1986 $43 (2/29/88)
91	JOSEPH DROUHIN Chassagne-Montrachet Marquis de Laguiche 1986 Rel: $43 Cur: $43 (5/31/88)
91	LOUIS JADOT Chassagne-Montrachet 1986 $32 (5/31/89)

91	BERNARD MOREAU Chassagne-Montrachet Grandes Ruchottes 1986 $38 (9/30/88)
91	BERNARD MOREY Chassagne-Montrachet Les Baudines 1986 $41 (2/29/88)
91	BERNARD MOREY Chassagne-Montrachet Les Embrazées 1986 $40 (12/15/88)
91	DOMAINE MARC MOREY Chassagne-Montrachet Virondot 1986 $42 (12/15/88)
91	PAUL PILLOT Chassagne-Montrachet Les Grandes Ruchottes 1986 $30 (11/15/88)
91	DOMAINE ROUX PERE & FILS Chassagne-Montrachet Morgeot 1986 $36 (2/29/88)
90	BICHOT Chassagne-Montrachet La Romanée 1986 $32 (4/30/88)
90	LOUIS LATOUR Chassagne-Montrachet 1986 $38 (9/30/88)
90	CHATEAU DE LA MALTROYE Chassagne-Montrachet Morgeot Vigne Blanche 1986 $29 (9/30/88)
90	JEAN-MARC MOREY Chassagne-Montrachet Les Chaumées 1986 $38 (12/15/88)
90	DOMAINE ROUX PERE & FILS Chassagne-Montrachet 1986 $34 (2/29/88)
89	GEORGES DELEGER Chassagne-Montrachet 1986 $82 (12/15/88)
89	JEAN-NOEL GAGNARD Chassagne-Montrachet Morgeot 1986 $54 (11/15/88)
88	MOILLARD Chassagne-Montrachet La Romanée 1986 $40 (4/30/88)
88	BERNARD MOREY Chassagne-Montrachet Les Baudines 1986 $41 (12/15/88)
88	BERNARD MOREY Chassagne-Montrachet Morgeot 1986 $35 (12/15/88)
88	JEAN-MARC MOREY Chassagne-Montrachet Champs-Gains 1986 $38 (12/15/88)
87	F. CHAUVENET Chassagne-Montrachet Clos St.-Marc 1986 $38 (6/30/88)
87	LOUIS LATOUR Chassagne-Montrachet 1986 $38 (2/29/88)
86	HENRI GERMAIN Chassagne-Montrachet Morgeot 1986 $39 (3/15/89)
86	CHATEAU DE LA MALTROYE Chassagne-Montrachet Morgeot-Fairendes 1986 $26 (9/30/88)
86	JEAN-MARC MOREY Chassagne-Montrachet Les Chênevottes 1986 $34 (12/15/88)
85	LOUIS JADOT Chassagne-Montrachet Morgeot Clos de la Chapelle Domaine de la Duc de Magent 1986 $41 (5/31/89)
85	OLIVIER LEFLAIVE FRERES Chassagne-Montrachet Les Baudines 1986 $38 (10/15/90)
85	LUPE-CHOLET Chassagne-Montrachet La Romanée 1986 $26 (2/29/88)
85	JEAN-MARC MOREY Chassagne-Montrachet Les Caillerets 1986 $39 (12/15/88)
84	JOSEPH DROUHIN Chassagne-Montrachet 1986 $35 (6/30/88)
83	JEAN-NOEL GAGNARD Chassagne-Montrachet 1986 $36 (3/15/89)
83	DOMAINE MARC MOREY Chassagne-Montrachet 1986 $34 (9/30/88)
81	HENRI DE VILLAMONT Chassagne-Montrachet Les Vergers 1986 $29 (12/15/88)
77	PHILIPPE BOUZEREAU Chassagne-Montrachet Les Meix Goudard 1986 $29 (11/15/88)
76	LEONARD DE ST.-AUBIN Chassagne-Montrachet 1986 $25 (12/31/87)
74	JEAN-NOEL GAGNARD Chassagne-Montrachet Première Cru 1986 $47 (12/15/88)
74	CHATEAU DE LA MALTROYE Chassagne-Montrachet Maltroie-Crets 1986 $27 (10/31/88)

1985

96	F. CHAUVENET Chassagne-Montrachet 1985 Rel: $35 Cur: $43 (3/15/87) SS
96	F. CHAUVENET Chassagne-Montrachet Morgeot 1985 Rel: $37 Cur: $52 (5/15/87) CS
94	FERNAND COFFINET Chassagne-Montrachet 1985 $25 (5/15/87)
94	JEAN-NOEL GAGNARD Chassagne-Montrachet Les Caillerets 1985 $45 (9/15/87)
93	HUBERT BOUZEREAU Chassagne-Montrachet 1985 $35 (8/31/87)
93	JOSEPH DROUHIN Chassagne-Montrachet Marquis de Laguiche 1985 Rel: $40 Cur: $40 (2/29/88)
92	BACHELET-RAMONET Chassagne-Montrachet Caillerets 1985 $41 (11/15/87)
92	JEAN-NOEL GAGNARD Chassagne-Montrachet 1985 $40 (9/15/87)
91	BACHELET-RAMONET Chassagne-Montrachet Caillerets 1985 $41 (2/29/88)
91	F. CHAUVENET Chassagne-Montrachet Clos St.-Marc 1985 $43 (6/15/87)
91	LOUIS JADOT Chassagne-Montrachet 1985 $32 (2/29/88)
91	LABOURE-ROI Chassagne-Montrachet 1985 $31.50 (8/31/87)
90	REMOISSENET Chassagne-Montrachet Les Caillerets 1985 $63 (2/29/88)
89	JEAN GERMAIN Chassagne-Montrachet 1985 $35 (9/15/87)
89	LOUIS JADOT Chassagne-Montrachet Morgeot Clos de la Chapelle Domaine du Duc de Magenta 1985 $38 (2/29/88)
89	PROSPER MAUFOUX Chassagne-Montrachet 1985 $31 (4/30/88)
88	BLAIN-GAGNARD Chassagne-Montrachet Caillerets 1985 $45 (5/31/88)
88	LOUIS LATOUR Chassagne-Montrachet 1985 $33 (2/29/88)
88	PAUL PILLOT Chassagne-Montrachet Les Grandes Ruchottes 1985 $30 (10/31/87)
88	DOMAINE ROUX PERE & FILS Chassagne-Montrachet 1985 $32 (2/28/87)
86	JEAN-NOEL GAGNARD Chassagne-Montrachet Morgeot 1985 $45 (9/15/87)
86	DOMAINE ROUX PERE & FILS Chassagne-Montrachet 1985 $32 (8/31/87)
85	LOUIS LATOUR Chassagne-Montrachet 1985 $33 (6/15/87)
85	FERNAND PILLOT Chassagne-Montrachet Les Vergers 1985 $28 (5/31/89)
84	PAUL PILLOT Chassagne-Montrachet Les Caillerets 1985 $30 (10/31/87)
83	CORON PERE Chassagne-Montrachet 1985 $20 (8/31/87)
75	JEAN-MARC MOREY Chassagne-Montrachet Champs-Gains 1985 $30 (10/31/87)
71	C. BERGERET Chassagne-Montrachet Morgeot 1985 $35 (8/31/87)
71	FONTAINE-GAGNARD Chassagne-Montrachet Morgeot 1985 $45 (5/31/88)
69	C. BERGERET Chassagne-Montrachet 1985 $31 (8/31/87)

1984

96	JEAN-NOEL GAGNARD Chassagne-Montrachet 1984 $32 (4/30/87)
88	LOUIS JADOT Chassagne-Montrachet Morgeot 1984 $38 (2/29/88)
81	LOUIS JADOT Chassagne-Montrachet 1984 $30 (2/29/88)
78	LOUIS LATOUR Chassagne-Montrachet 1984 $33 (2/29/88)

1983

93	JEAN GERMAIN Chassagne-Montrachet 1983 $18 (9/01/85)
91	JOSEPH DROUHIN Chassagne-Montrachet Marquis de Laguiche 1983 Rel: $35 Cur: $35 (2/29/88)
91	JAFFELIN Chassagne-Montrachet Les Caillerets 1983 $20 (6/01/85)
89	LOUIS JADOT Chassagne-Montrachet 1983 $28 (2/29/88)
88	CHATEAU DE LA MALTROYE Chassagne-Montrachet Morgeot Vigne Blanche 1983 $17 (6/16/85)
87	JEAN-NOEL GAGNARD Chassagne-Montrachet 1983 $25 (10/01/85)
86	LOUIS JADOT Chassagne-Montrachet Morgeot 1983 $34 (2/29/88)
80	CHATEAU DE LA MALTROYE Chassagne-Montrachet Clos de la Maltroye 1983 $21 (6/01/86)
79	CHATEAU DE LA MALTROYE Chassagne-Montrachet Morgeot-Fairendes 1983 $19 (11/16/85)

1982

88	LOUIS LATOUR Chassagne-Montrachet 1982 $33 (2/29/88)
87	JOSEPH DROUHIN Chassagne-Montrachet 1982 $21.75 (10/01/84)
86	F. CHAUVENET Chassagne-Montrachet 1982 $13 (3/16/85)
86	BERNARD MOREY Chassagne-Montrachet 1982 $11.25 (3/01/85)
80	BOUCHARD PERE & FILS Chassagne-Montrachet 1982 $17.50 (7/01/84)

FRANCE
BURGUNDY WHITE/*COTE DE BEAUNE*/CHASSAGNE-MONTRACHET

1981

58   ANTONIN RODET Chassagne-Montrachet 1981 $14 (12/01/84)

MEURSAULT

1989

93   MICHEL BOUZEREAU Meursault Genevrières 1989 $46 (5/31/91)
91   CHARTRON & TREBUCHET Meursault Les Charmes 1989 $57 (2/28/91)
91   CHATEAU DE PULIGNY-MONTRACHET Meursault Les Perrières 1989 $57 (2/28/91)
90   MICHEL BOUZEREAU Meursault Les Grands Charrons 1989 $33 (5/31/91)
90   CHATEAU DE PULIGNY-MONTRACHET Meursault Les Poruzots 1989 $55 (2/28/91)
88   CHARTRON & TREBUCHET Meursault 1989 $41 (2/28/91)
87   MICHEL BOUZEREAU Meursault Les Tessons 1989 $35 (5/31/91)
84   JOSEPH DROUHIN Meursault Perrières 1989 $60 (2/28/91)
83   BOUCHARD PERE & FILS Meursault 1989 $37 (4/30/91)
82   CHATEAU DE PULIGNY-MONTRACHET Meursault 1989 $42 (2/28/91)

1988

93   MICHEL BOUZEREAU Meursault Genevrières 1988 $37 (7/15/90)
93   MICHELOT-BUISSON Meursault Genevrières 1988 $55 (2/28/91)
92   BICHOT Meursault Charmes 1988 $40 (7/15/90)
92   CHATEAU DES HERBEUX Meursault Perrières 1988 $42 (7/15/90)
91   MICHEL BOUZEREAU Meursault Les Grands Charrons 1988 $25 (8/31/90)
91   HENRI GERMAIN Meursault 1988 $35 (2/28/91)
91   DOMAINE GUY ROULOT Meursault Les Tessons Clos de Mon Plaisir 1988 $35 (5/15/90)
90   PIERRE BOILLOT Meursault Charmes 1988 $47 (8/31/90)
90   MICHEL BOUZEREAU Meursault Les Tessons 1988 $28 (8/31/90)
90   LOUIS JADOT Meursault Perrières 1988 $57 (4/30/91)
89   JOSEPH DROUHIN Meursault 1988 $34 (3/31/90)
89   HENRI GERMAIN Meursault Charmes 1988 $42 (5/15/90)
89   LEROY Meursault Perrières 1988 $150 (4/30/91)
89   DOMAINE PRIEUR-BRUNET Meursault Chevalières 1988 $30 (2/28/91)
88   JOSEPH DROUHIN Meursault Perrières 1988 $48 (3/31/90)
88   JEAN MICHELOT Meursault 1988 $33 (5/15/90)
87   PIERRE BOILLOT Meursault 1988 $37 (8/31/90)
87   LABOURE-ROI Meursault 1988 $35 (8/31/90)
87   LEROY Meursault Les Narvaux 1988 $100 (4/30/91)
87   DOMAINE GUY ROULOT Meursault Les Meix Chavaux 1988 $33 (5/15/90)
86   DOMAINE RENE MANUEL Meursault Clos des Bouches Chères 1988 $50 (8/31/90)
85   BICHOT Meursault Poruzot 1988 $36 (7/15/90)
85   DOMAINE PRIEUR-BRUNET Meursault Charmes 1988 $35 (8/31/90)
84   C. MICHELOT Meursault Charmes 1988 $55 (2/28/91)
83   JEAN CLAUDE BOISSET Meursault 1988 $28 (5/31/91)
83   A. LIGERET Meursault Les Narvaux 1988 $45 (10/15/90)
83   MESTRE-MICHELOT Meursault Sous la Velle 1988 $40 (2/28/91)
82   LAROCHE Meursault 1988 $28 (8/31/90)
81   JEAN CLAUDE BOISSET Meursault 1988 $27 (5/15/90)
79   CHATEAU DE PULIGNY-MONTRACHET Meursault Les Poruzots 1988 $52 (7/15/90)
69   LUPE-CHOLET Meursault Charmes 1988 $40 (2/28/90)

1987

91   CHARTRON & TREBUCHET Meursault Genevrières Hospices de Beaune Cuvée Baudot 1987 $87 (3/15/89)
91   J.-F. COCHE-DURY Meursault Les Chevalières 1987 $36 (2/28/90)
91   PIERRE MOREY Meursault Genevrières 1987 $41 (11/15/89)
90   J.-F. COCHE-DURY Meursault Les Rougeots 1987 $33 (2/28/90)
90   J.-F. COCHE-DURY Meursault Perrières 1987 $50 (2/28/90)
87   BITOUZET-PRIEUR Meursault Charmes 1987 $41 (2/28/91)
87   BITOUZET-PRIEUR Meursault Clos du Cromin 1987 $34 (8/31/90)
87   PIERRE MOREY Meursault Charmes 1987 $41 (2/28/90)
86   BITOUZET-PRIEUR Meursault 1987 $28 (7/15/90)
86   J.-F. COCHE-DURY Meursault 1987 $33 (2/28/90)
86   PROSPER MAUFOUX Meursault 1987 $27 (5/15/90)
85   FRANCOIS JOBARD Meursault Blagny 1987 $37 (7/15/90)
84   THORIN Meursault 1987 $25 (12/15/89)
83   PHILIPPE BOUZEREAU Meursault Poruzot 1987 $36 (11/15/89)
83   JAFFELIN Meursault 1987 $25 (3/15/89)
82   C. MICHELOT Meursault Grands Charrons 1987 $41 (8/31/90)
81   DOMAINE JOSEPH MATROT Meursault 1987 $30 (5/15/90)
81   MICHELOT-BUISSON Meursault 1987 $37 (8/31/90)
81   JACQUES THEVENOT-MACHAL Meursault Poruzot 1987 $38 (7/31/89)
80   PHILIPPE BOUZEREAU Meursault Genevrières 1987 $37 (7/15/90)
80   JOSEPH DROUHIN Meursault Perrières 1987 $44 (4/30/89)
80   FRANCOIS JOBARD Meursault Charmes 1987 $34 (8/31/90)
79   PIERRE BOILLOT Meursault Charmes 1987 $44 (8/31/90)
79   MESTRE-MICHELOT Meursault Charmes 1987 $50 (8/31/90)
78   C. MICHELOT Meursault Les Tillets 1987 $32 (8/31/90)
78   MICHELOT-BUISSON Meursault 1987 $50 (8/31/90)
77   R. BALLOT-MILLOT & FILS Meursault Charmes 1987 $34 (8/31/90)
76   FRANCOIS JOBARD Meursault 1987 $25 (7/15/90)
76   FRANCOIS JOBARD Meursault Poruzot 1987 $40 (7/15/90)
75   BICHOT Meursault 1987 $24 (9/30/89)
75   PHILIPPE BOUZEREAU Meursault Charmes 1987 $37 (11/15/89)
75   FRANCOIS JOBARD Meursault Genevrières 1987 $34 (8/31/90)

75   M & G Meursault Les Forges 1987 $42 (3/31/91)
74   MOILLARD Meursault Charmes 1987 $33 (9/30/89)
73   DOMAINE JOSEPH MATROT Meursault 1987 $30 (7/31/89)
63   MOILLARD Meursault 1987 $24 (11/15/89)

1986

94   CHATEAU DE MEURSAULT Meursault 1986 Rel: $55 Cur: $55 (7/31/91)
92   BICHOT Meursault Hospices de Beaune Cuvée Goureau 1986 $55 (2/15/88)
92   F. CHAUVENET Meursault Les Poruzots 1986 $40 (4/30/88)
92   PIERRE MOREY Meursault Perrières 1986 $47 (12/15/88)
91   G. MICHELOT Meursault Clos du Cromin 1986 $39 (3/15/89)
91   REMOISSENET Meursault Genevrières 1986 $49 (12/15/88)
90   JEAN MICHELOT Meursault 1986 $27 (12/15/88)
90   PIERRE MOREY Meursault Les Tessons 1986 $35 (12/15/88)
90   DOMAINE PRIEUR-BRUNET Meursault Charmes 1986 $30 (4/30/89)
90   DOMAINE ROUGEOT-LATOUR Meursault Charmes 1986 $38 (6/30/88)
89   DOMAINE LAROCHE Meursault Poruzot 1986 $27 (10/31/88)
89   LUPE-CHOLET Meursault Hospices de Beaune Cuvée Goureau 1986 $45 (2/15/88)
89   DOMAINE RENE MONNIER Meursault Le Limozin 1986 $32 (12/15/88)
89   DOMAINE RENE MONNIER Meursault Les Chevalires 1986 $34 (10/15/88)
89   PIERRE MOREY Meursault Charmes 1986 $47 (12/15/88)
88   JOSEPH DROUHIN Meursault Perrières 1986 $41 (5/31/88)
88   HENRI GERMAIN Meursault 1986 $27 (4/30/89)
88   MOILLARD Meursault Clos du Cromin 1986 $28 (10/15/88)
88   MICHEL POUHIN-SEURRE Meursault Le Limosin 1986 $25 (2/15/88)
87   CHARTRON & TREBUCHET Meursault Charmes 1986 $45 (5/31/88)
86   F. CHAUVENET Meursault Les Perrières 1986 $40 (4/30/88)
86   HENRI GERMAIN Meursault Charmes 1986 $39 (4/30/89)
86   LABOURE-ROI Meursault 1986 $28 (4/30/88)
86   MESTRE-MICHELOT Meursault Le Limozin 1986 $39 (3/15/89)
86   JACQUES THEVENOT-MACHAL Meursault Poruzot 1986 $38 (3/15/88)
85   F. CHAUVENET Meursault Les Genevrières 1986 $40 (4/30/88)
85   MICHELOT-BUISSON Meursault Charmes 1986 $50 (3/15/89)
84   GUY BOCARD Meursault Limozin 1986 $28 (10/15/88)
83   BOUCHARD PERE & FILS Meursault Clos des Corvées de Citeaux 1986 $26 (3/15/89)
83   JOSEPH DROUHIN Meursault 1986 $29 (5/31/88)
82   BICHOT Meursault Charmes 1986 $37 (3/15/88)
82   FRANCOIS JOBARD Meursault 1986 $30 (9/30/89)
82   LAROCHE Meursault Perrières 1986 $20 (10/31/88)
82   MOILLARD Meursault Poruzots 1986 $37 (5/31/88)
81   PHILIPPE BOUZEREAU Meursault Les Narvaux 1986 $31 (3/15/89)
80   LUPE-CHOLET Meursault 1986 $26 (2/15/88)
77   BOUCHARD PERE & FILS Meursault Genevrières Domaines du Château de Beaune 1986 $44 (3/15/89)
77   F. CHAUVENET Meursault Les Boucheres 1986 $40 (6/30/88)
77   NOIROT-CARRIERE Meursault Perrières 1986 $39 (2/28/90)
74   MOILLARD Meursault Charmes 1986 $37 (5/31/88)
72   MICHELOT-BUISSON Meursault Genevrières 1986 $50 (3/15/89)
71   HENRI DE VILLAMONT Meursault Les Genevrières 1986 $29 (12/15/88)
69   GUY BOCARD Meursault Les Grands Charrons 1986 $27 (10/15/88)
69   DOMAINE ROUGEOT-LATOUR Meursault Les Pellans 1986 $25 (10/15/88)
68   REMOISSENET Meursault Charmes 1986 $49 (12/15/88)
65   DOMAINE JOSEPH MATROT Meursault Les Chevalières 1986 $36 (12/15/88)
65   REMOISSENET Meursault Cuvée Maurice Chevalier 1986 $35 (3/15/89)

1985

95   CHATEAU DE MEURSAULT Meursault 1985 Rel: $50 Cur: $50 (12/31/87)
95   MOILLARD Meursault Charmes 1985 $30 (11/30/86)
93   BICHOT Meursault Charmes 1985 $30 (2/15/88)
93   DOMAINE RENE MANUEL Meursault Clos des Bouches Chères 1985 $39 (8/31/87)
93   MICHELOT-BUISSON Meursault Le Limozin 1985 $37 (8/31/87)
91   GUY BOCARD Meursault Charmes 1985 $32 (9/30/87)
91   F. CHAUVENET Meursault Hospices de Beaune Cuvée Jehan-Humblot 1985 $90 (7/31/87)
89   REMOISSENET Meursault Genevrières 1985 $60 (3/15/88)
88   R. BALLOT-MILLOT & FILS Meursault Les Criots 1985 $34 (4/30/88)
88   HUBERT BOUZEREAU Meursault Limozin 1985 $27 (8/31/87)
88   PATRIARCHE Meursault Réserve St.-Anne 1985 $23 (9/30/89)
87   JOSEPH DROUHIN Meursault Perrières 1985 $40 (4/30/87)
87   DOMAINE RENE MONNIER Meursault Charmes 1985 $39 (12/15/88)
87   ROLAND THEVENIN Meursault Les Casse Têtes 1985 $20 (4/30/87)
86   F. CHAUVENET Meursault Charmes Hospices de Beaune Cuvée de Bahèzre-de-Lanlay 1985 $141 (3/15/89)
86   LOUIS LATOUR Meursault 1985 $25 (11/15/87)
85   GUY BOCARD Meursault Limozin 1985 $28 (4/30/87)
85   DOMAINE RENE MANUEL Meursault Poruzot 1985 $37 (8/31/87)
84   F. CHAUVENET Meursault Les Casse Têtes 1985 $32 (8/31/87)
82   DOMAINE ROUX PERE & FILS Meursault 1985 $27.50 (2/28/87)
81   CHEVALIER DE BEAUBASSIN Meursault 1985 $24 (4/30/88)
75   PIERRE MATROT Meursault 1985 $27.50 (12/31/87)
75   REMOISSENET Meursault Cuvée Maurice Chevalier 1985 $42 (3/15/88)
73   HUBERT BOUZEREAU Meursault Les Narvaux 1985 $25 (4/30/87)
73   FRANCOIS JOBARD Meursault Poruzot 1985 $28 (11/15/87)
70   HUBERT BOUZEREAU Meursault Les Tessons 1985 $25 (5/31/88)
70   LABOURE-ROI Meursault 1985 $32 (11/15/86)
64   CORON PERE Meursault 1985 $18 (8/31/87)

1984

90   ALBERT GRIVAULT Meursault Clos des Perrières 1984 $50 (8/31/87)
90   LUPE-CHOLET Meursault 1984 $20 (10/31/86)
83   LOUIS LATOUR Meursault 1984 $28 (4/30/87)
80   OLIVIER LEFLAIVE FRERES Meursault 1984 $22 (7/16/86)
71   F. CHAUVENET Meursault Les Casse Têtes 1984 $19 (7/16/86)
64   MAZILLY PERE Meursault 1984 $17.50 (4/30/87)

1983

88   F. CHAUVENET Meursault Genevrières Hospices de Beaune Cuvée Baudot 1983 $55 (11/01/85)
86   JAFFELIN Meursault 1983 $16.50 (6/01/85)
83   LOUIS LATOUR Meursault Première Cru 1983 $24 (11/16/85)
76   PIERRE MOREY Meursault Les Tessons 1983 $17.25 (10/16/85)

75   BOUCHARD PERE & FILS Meursault 1983 $20 (4/30/87)
66   CHARLES MONCAUT Meursault 1983 $16 (6/01/86)
60   BOYER-MARTENOT Meursault Les Narvaux 1983 $15 (2/16/86)

1982

92   F. CHAUVENET Meursault Hospices de Beaune Cuvée Loppin 1982 Rel: $33 Cur: $65 (1/01/85) CS
82   F. CHAUVENET Meursault Les Casse Têtes 1982 $11 (3/01/85)
45   LOUIS LATOUR Meursault Blagny Château de Blagny 1982 Rel: $65 Cur: $79 (12/01/85)

1959

86   DENIS CHEVILLON Meursault Charmes 1959 (NA) (8/31/90) (TR)

1947

90   VINCENT VIAL Meursault 1947 (NA) (8/31/90) (TR)

MONTRACHET

1989

94   DOMAINE JEAN CHARTRON Chevalier-Montrachet 1989 Rel: $125 Cur: $125 (2/28/91)
93   PAUL PERNOT Bâtard-Montrachet 1989 $160 (2/28/91)
92   CHARTRON & TREBUCHET Bâtard-Montrachet 1989 $120 (2/28/91)

1988

97   DOMAINE JEAN CHARTRON Chevalier-Montrachet 1988 Rel: $95 Cur: $106 (2/28/90)
96   DOMAINE RAMONET Montrachet 1988 Rel: $590 Cur: $590 (2/28/91)
95   CHARTRON & TREBUCHET Bâtard-Montrachet 1988 $90 (2/28/90)
95   JOSEPH DROUHIN Montrachet Marquis de Laguiche 1988 Rel: $180 Cur: $250 (2/28/91)
95   DOMAINE RAMONET Bâtard-Montrachet 1988 Rel: $190 Cur: $190 (2/28/91)
94   ROMANEE-CONTI Montrachet 1988 Rel: $600 Cur: $613 (4/30/91)
94   DOMAINE ETIENNE SAUZET Bâtard-Montrachet 1988 $92 (12/31/90)
93   LOUIS LATOUR Montrachet 1988 Rel: $200 Cur: $200 (10/15/90)
93   DOMAINE ETIENNE SAUZET Bâtard-Montrachet 1988 $92 (2/28/91)
93   DOMAINE BARON THENARD Montrachet 1988 Rel: $180 Cur: $180 (12/31/90)
92   LOUIS JADOT Chevalier-Montrachet Les Demoiselles 1988 Rel: $127 Cur: $127 (5/31/91)
90   AMIOT-BONFILS Montrachet 1988 $135 (2/28/90)
90   CHATEAU DES HERBEUX Chevalier-Montrachet 1988 $100 (7/31/90)
87   DOMAINE PRIEUR-BRUNET Bâtard-Montrachet 1988 $75 (7/31/90)
78   CHATEAU DES HERBEUX Montrachet 1988 $165 (7/31/90)

1987

95   JOSEPH DROUHIN Montrachet Marquis de Laguiche 1987 Rel: $180 Cur: $209 (10/15/90)
94   DOMAINE LEFLAIVE Chevalier-Montrachet 1987 Rel: $99 Cur: $103 (12/31/90)
94   ROMANEE-CONTI Montrachet 1987 Rel: $525 Cur: $525 (12/31/90)
93   CHARTRON & TREBUCHET Montrachet Le Montrachet 1987 $240 (2/28/89)
92   DOMAINE JEAN CHARTRON Chevalier-Montrachet 1987 Rel: $100 Cur: $100 (2/28/89)
92   CHARTRON & TREBUCHET Bâtard-Montrachet 1987 $100 (3/31/89)
90   JOSEPH DROUHIN Bâtard-Montrachet 1987 Rel: $98 Cur: $98 (3/31/89)
89   LOUIS LATOUR Bâtard-Montrachet 1987 Rel: $82 Cur: $83 (2/28/90)
87   DOMAINE RAMONET Bâtard-Montrachet 1987 Rel: $119 Cur: $119 (2/28/90)
85   DOMAINE LEQUIN-ROUSSOT Bâtard-Montrachet 1987 $79 (7/31/90)
83   DOMAINE LEFLAIVE Bienvenues-Bâtard-Montrachet 1987 Rel: $79 Cur: $86 (12/31/90)

1986

97   JOSEPH DROUHIN Montrachet Marquis de Laguiche 1986 Rel: $200 Cur: $244 (10/31/88) CS
95   DOMAINE JEAN CHARTRON Chevalier-Montrachet 1986 Rel: $125 Cur: $125 (5/31/88)
95   JEAN-NOEL GAGNARD Bâtard-Montrachet 1986 $93 (12/31/88)
95   LOUIS LATOUR Montrachet 1986 Rel: $125 Cur: $179 (10/31/88)
95   REMOISSENET Bienvenues-Bâtard-Montrachet 1986 $100 (11/15/88)
94   JOSEPH DROUHIN Bâtard-Montrachet 1986 Rel: $113 Cur: $113 (12/31/88)
94   LOUIS LATOUR Chevalier-Montrachet Les Demoiselles 1986 Rel: $150 Cur: $150 (10/31/88)
94   MOILLARD Bâtard-Montrachet 1986 $70 (5/31/88)
93   LOUIS JADOT Bâtard-Montrachet 1986 $99 (5/31/89)
92   JOSEPH DROUHIN Bâtard-Montrachet 1986 Rel: $113 Cur: $113 (2/29/88)
92   DOMAINE JACQUES PRIEUR Montrachet 1986 $165 (2/28/89)
91   BOUCHARD PERE & FILS Chevalier-Montrachet Domaines du Château de Beaune 1986 Rel: $92 Cur: $92 (2/29/88)
91   REMOISSENET Montrachet Le Montrachet du Domaine Thénard 1986 Rel: $125 Cur: $166 (2/29/88)
90   DOMAINE HENRI CLERC & FILS Bâtard-Montrachet 1986 $104 (3/31/89)
90   DOMAINE HENRI CLERC & FILS Bienvenues-Bâtard-Montrachet 1986 $69 (2/29/88)
90   DOMAINE ETIENNE SAUZET Bâtard-Montrachet 1986 $85 (2/29/88)
87   LAROCHE Criots-Bâtard-Montrachet 1986 $63 (10/31/88)
85   REMOISSENET Montrachet Le Montrachet du Domaine Thénard 1986 Rel: $125 Cur: $166 (12/31/88)
82   REMOISSENET Bienvenues-Bâtard-Montrachet 1986 $87 (2/29/88)
81   REMOISSENET Bâtard-Montrachet 1986 $87 (2/29/88)
68   BOUCHARD PERE & FILS Chevalier-Montrachet Domaines du Château de Beaune 1986 Rel: $92 Cur: $92 (2/28/89)

1985

100   JOSEPH DROUHIN Montrachet Marquis de Laguiche 1985 Rel: $142 Cur: $265 (2/29/88)
96   ROMANEE-CONTI Montrachet 1985 Cur: $638 (2/28/87) (HS)
95   JOSEPH DROUHIN Bâtard-Montrachet 1985 Rel: $95 Cur: $95 (2/29/88)
94   LOUIS JADOT Bâtard-Montrachet 1985 $88 (2/29/88)
94   LOUIS JADOT Chevalier-Montrachet Les Demoiselles 1985 Rel: $150 Cur: $166 (2/29/88)
93   ROGER CAILLOT Bâtard-Montrachet 1985 $90 (5/31/88)
93   LOUIS LATOUR Bâtard-Montrachet 1985 Rel: $93 Cur: $93 (11/15/87)
91   DOMAINE JEAN CHARTRON Chevalier-Montrachet 1985 Rel: $75 Cur: $75 (10/31/87)
91   REMOISSENET Montrachet Le Montrachet du Domaine Thénard 1985 Cur: $155 (2/29/88)
84   JOSEPH DROUHIN Chevalier-Montrachet 1985 $100 (4/30/87)

1984

93   ROMANEE-CONTI Montrachet 1984 Cur: $453 (2/28/87) (HS)
92   JOSEPH DROUHIN Bâtard-Montrachet 1984 Rel: $65 Cur: $65 (2/29/88)
92   LOUIS JADOT Chevalier-Montrachet Les Demoiselles 1984 Rel: $95 Cur: $95 (2/29/88)
84   JAFFELIN Bâtard-Montrachet 1984 $77 (6/01/86)

1983

97   DOMAINE LEFLAIVE Chevalier-Montrachet 1983 Cur: $150 (2/29/88)
95   ROMANEE-CONTI Montrachet 1983 Cur: $726 (2/28/87) (HS)
92   LOUIS JADOT Bâtard-Montrachet 1983 $80 (2/29/88)
90   BICHOT Bâtard-Montrachet 1983 $60 (2/29/88)

1982

93   ROMANEE-CONTI Montrachet 1982 Cur: $596 (2/28/87) (HS)

1981

91   ROMANEE-CONTI Montrachet 1981 Cur: $473 (2/28/87) (HS)

1980

88   ROMANEE-CONTI Montrachet 1980 Cur: $400 (2/28/87) (HS)

1979

97   JOSEPH DROUHIN Montrachet Marquis de Laguiche 1979 Cur: $250 (2/29/88)
95   DOMAINE LEFLAIVE Bienvenues-Bâtard-Montrachet 1979 Cur: $137 (2/29/88)
93   BACHELET-RAMONET Bienvenues-Bâtard-Montrachet 1979 (NA) (2/29/88)
89   ROMANEE-CONTI Montrachet 1979 Cur: $600 (2/28/87) (HS)
88   LOUIS LATOUR Montrachet 1979 Cur: $200 (2/29/88)

1978

98   ROMANEE-CONTI Montrachet 1978 Cur: $635 (2/28/87) (HS)

1977

90   ROMANEE-CONTI Montrachet 1977 Cur: $217 (2/28/87) (HS)

1976

94   ROMANEE-CONTI Montrachet 1976 Cur: $505 (2/28/87) (HS)

1975

89   ROMANEE-CONTI Montrachet 1975 Cur: $425 (2/28/87) (HS)

1974

87   ROMANEE-CONTI Montrachet 1974 Cur: $425 (2/28/87) (HS)

1973

99   ROMANEE-CONTI Montrachet 1973 Cur: $499 (2/28/87) (HS)
98   LOUIS JADOT Montrachet 1973 Cur: $300 (2/29/88)

1972

92   ROMANEE-CONTI Montrachet 1972 Cur: $575 (2/28/87) (HS)

1971

94   ROMANEE-CONTI Montrachet 1971 Cur: $750 (2/28/87) (HS)

1970

86   ROMANEE-CONTI Montrachet 1970 Cur: $675 (2/28/87) (HS)

1969

88   ROMANEE-CONTI Montrachet 1969 Cur: $985 (2/28/87) (HS)

1968

85   ROMANEE-CONTI Montrachet 1968 Cur: $825 (2/28/87) (HS)

1967

85   ROMANEE-CONTI Montrachet 1967 Cur: $1,275 (2/28/87) (HS)

1966

95   ROMANEE-CONTI Montrachet 1966 Cur: $800 (2/28/87) (HS)

1964

82   ROMANEE-CONTI Montrachet 1964 Cur: $650 (2/28/87) (HS)

PULIGNY-MONTRACHET

1989

91   MICHEL BOUZEREAU Puligny-Montrachet Les Champs-Gains 1989 $42 (5/31/91)
90   JOSEPH DROUHIN Puligny-Montrachet Les Pucelles 1989 $68 (2/28/91)
89   DOMAINE JEAN CHARTRON Puligny-Montrachet Clos du Cailleret 1989 $79 (2/28/91)
89   PAUL PERNOT Puligny-Montrachet Folatières 1989 $70 (2/28/91)
88   DOMAINE JEAN CHARTRON Puligny-Montrachet Clos de la Pucelle 1989 $69 (2/28/91)
88   DOMAINE JEAN CHARTRON Puligny-Montrachet Les Folatières 1989 $62 (2/28/91)
84   JAFFELIN Puligny-Montrachet 1989 $42 (5/31/91)
83   DOMAINE ROUX PERE & FILS Puligny-Montrachet Champs-Gains 1989 $55 (2/28/91)
80   LAROCHE Puligny-Montrachet 1989 $47 (2/28/91)
80   PAUL PERNOT Puligny-Montrachet 1989 $52 (2/28/91)
76   JEAN PILLOT Puligny-Montrachet 1989 $42 (4/30/91)
74   CHATEAU DE PULIGNY-MONTRACHET Puligny-Montrachet 1989 $66 (2/28/91)

1988

94   DOMAINE JEAN CHARTRON Puligny-Montrachet Les Folatières 1988 $38 (3/15/90)
93   PAUL PERNOT Puligny-Montrachet Folatières 1988 $74 (12/31/90)
93   DOMAINE ETIENNE SAUZET Puligny-Montrachet Les Combettes 1988 $56 (12/31/90)
92   A. LIGERET Puligny-Montrachet Les Referts 1988 $51 (12/31/90)
92   DOMAINE ROUX PERE & FILS Puligny-Montrachet Champs-Gains 1988 $40 (3/15/90)
92   DOMAINE ETIENNE SAUZET Puligny-Montrachet Les Referts 1988 $47 (12/31/90)
91   CHARTRON & TREBUCHET Puligny-Montrachet Les Garennes 1988 $38 (3/15/90)
91   LOUIS JADOT Puligny-Montrachet Clos de la Garenne Domaine du duc de Magenta 1988 $52 (4/30/91)
91   DOMAINE ETIENNE SAUZET Puligny-Montrachet Champ Canet 1988 $50 (12/31/90)
90   MICHEL BOUZEREAU Puligny-Montrachet Les Champs-Gains 1988 $32 (7/31/90)
90   CHARTRON & TREBUCHET Puligny-Montrachet 1988 $30 (3/15/90)
90   PROSPER MAUFOUX Puligny-Montrachet 1988 $31 (4/30/90)
90   PAUL PERNOT Puligny-Montrachet Les Pucelles 1988 $74 (12/31/90)
90   DOMAINE ETIENNE SAUZET Puligny-Montrachet Les Perrières 1988 $70 (2/28/91)
89   CHARTRON & TREBUCHET Puligny-Montrachet Les Referts 1988 $35 (3/15/90)
89   MADAME FRANCOIS COLIN Puligny-Montrachet Les Demoiselles 1988 $47 (6/30/90)
88   LOUIS CARILLON Puligny-Montrachet Les Perrières 1988 $39 (2/28/91)

FRANCE
BURGUNDY WHITE/*CÔTE DE BEAUNE*/PULIGNY-MONTRACHET

88 JACQUES THEVENOT-MACHAL Puligny-Montrachet Les Folatières au Chaniot 1988 $40 (12/31/90)
87 AMIOT-BONFILS Puligny-Montrachet Les Demoiselles 1988 $33 (3/15/90)
87 LOUIS JADOT Puligny-Montrachet 1988 $36 (5/31/91)
85 LOUIS CARILLON Puligny-Montrachet 1988 $36 (2/28/91)
85 DOMAINE JEAN CHARTRON Puligny-Montrachet Clos de la Pucelle 1988 $40 (3/15/90)
84 DOMAINE LAROCHE Puligny-Montrachet Folatières 1988 $39 (6/30/90)
83 DOMAINE MAROSLAVAC Puligny-Montrachet Clos du Vieux Château 1988 $40 (7/31/90)
81 JEAN CLAUDE BOISSET Puligny-Montrachet 1988 $29 (6/30/90)
78 JOSEPH DROUHIN Puligny-Montrachet 1988 $39 (3/15/90)
76 BICHOT Puligny-Montrachet Les Chalumeaux 1988 $39 (6/30/90)
73 ROGER CAILLOT Puligny-Montrachet Les Folatières 1988 $40 (6/30/90)
72 PAUL PERNOT Puligny-Montrachet 1988 $40 (2/28/91)
71 CHANSON PERE & FILS Puligny-Montrachet 1988 $44 (10/15/90)

1987

93 OLIVIER LEFLAIVE FRERES Puligny-Montrachet 1987 $33 (6/30/90)
90 CHARTRON & TREBUCHET Puligny-Montrachet Les Garennes 1987 $40 (2/28/89)
88 DOMAINE JEAN CHARTRON Puligny-Montrachet Les Folatières 1987 $45 (2/28/89)
87 JOSEPH DROUHIN Puligny-Montrachet 1987 $38 (4/15/89)
87 THORIN Puligny-Montrachet 1987 $32 (11/15/89)
83 DOMAINE ROUX PERE & FILS Puligny-Montrachet La Garenne 1987 $44 (4/15/89)
82 LOUIS CARILLON Puligny-Montrachet 1987 $36 (9/30/89)
82 LUPE-CHOLET Puligny-Montrachet Les Chalumeaux 1987 $46 (11/15/89)
82 J. RIGER-BRISET Puligny-Montrachet 1987 $35 (3/15/90)
81 DOMAINE JEAN CHARTRON Puligny-Montrachet Clos de la Pucelle 1987 $45 (2/28/89)
81 JOSEPH DROUHIN Puligny-Montrachet Clos de la Garenne 1987 $44 (4/15/89)
80 C. MICHELOT Puligny-Montrachet 1987 $41 (6/30/90)
79 CHARTRON & TREBUCHET Puligny-Montrachet Les Referts 1987 $40 (2/28/89)
79 DOMAINE HENRI CLERC & FILS Puligny-Montrachet Les Folatières 1987 $41 (7/31/89)
79 CHARLES VIENOT Puligny-Montrachet Champs Gain 1987 $38 (7/31/89)
78 JOSEPH DROUHIN Puligny-Montrachet Les Folatières 1987 $44 (4/15/89)
78 JACQUES THEVENOT-MACHAL Puligny-Montrachet Les Folatières au Chaniot 1987 $43 (4/15/89)
77 BICHOT Puligny-Montrachet 1987 $28 (9/30/89)
75 DOMAINE HENRI CLERC & FILS Puligny-Montrachet Les Combettes 1987 $41 (7/31/89)
70 JEAN CLAUDE BOISSET Puligny-Montrachet 1987 $33 (7/31/89)

1986

94 DOMAINE JEAN CHARTRON Puligny-Montrachet Clos de la Pucelle 1986 $50 (5/31/88)
93 CHARTRON & TREBUCHET Puligny-Montrachet Les Garennes 1986 $49 (5/31/88)
93 DOMAINE HENRI CLERC & FILS Puligny-Montrachet Les Folatières 1986 $44 (11/15/88)
93 JOSEPH DROUHIN Puligny-Montrachet Les Folatières 1986 $40 (2/29/88)
93 OLIVIER LEFLAIVE FRERES Puligny-Montrachet Les Chalumeaux 1986 $36 (4/15/89)
93 OLIVIER LEFLAIVE FRERES Puligny-Montrachet Les Pucelles 1986 $65 (9/30/88)
93 DOMAINE JEAN PASCAL Puligny-Montrachet Hameau de Blagny 1986 $40 (6/15/88)
93 DOMAINE ETIENNE SAUZET Puligny-Montrachet Les Combettes 1986 $50 (4/30/88)
93 DOMAINE ETIENNE SAUZET Puligny-Montrachet Les Truffières 1986 $45 (2/29/88)
92 JEAN-MARC BOILLOT Puligny-Montrachet Les Pucelles 1986 $43 (9/30/88)
92 DOMAINE LAROCHE Puligny-Montrachet Château de Puligny-Montrachet 1986 $60 (9/30/88)
92 REMOISSENET Puligny-Montrachet Les Combettes 1986 $57 (11/15/88)
92 DOMAINE ROUX PERE & FILS Puligny-Montrachet Les Enseignères 1986 $36 (2/29/88)
92 DOMAINE ETIENNE SAUZET Puligny-Montrachet 1986 $40 (4/30/88)
91 CHARTRON & TREBUCHET Puligny-Montrachet Les Referts 1986 $46 (5/31/88)
91 GERARD CHAVY Puligny-Montrachet Les Pucelles 1986 $30 (12/15/88)
91 JOSEPH DROUHIN Puligny-Montrachet Les Folatières 1986 $40 (5/31/88)
91 LOUIS JADOT Puligny-Montrachet Clos de la Garenne Domaine du duc de Magenta 1986 $57 (5/31/89)
91 OLIVIER LEFLAIVE FRERES Puligny-Montrachet Les Folatières 1986 $36 (2/29/88)
91 DOMAINE JEAN PASCAL Puligny-Montrachet Les Chalumeaux 1986 $40 (6/15/88)
91 DOMAINE ETIENNE SAUZET Puligny-Montrachet Champ Canet 1986 $48 (4/30/88)
90 BOUCHARD PERE & FILS Puligny-Montrachet Les Folatières 1986 $33 (2/28/89)
90 DOMAINE JEAN CHARTRON Puligny-Montrachet Les Folatières 1986 $50 (2/28/88)
90 CHARTRON & TREBUCHET Puligny-Montrachet Les Garennes 1986 $49 (2/29/88)
90 JOSEPH DROUHIN Puligny-Montrachet Les Pucelles 1986 $50 (2/29/88)
90 OLIVIER LEFLAIVE FRERES Puligny-Montrachet 1986 $29 (2/29/88)
90 OLIVIER LEFLAIVE FRERES Puligny-Montrachet Les Combettes 1986 $46 (2/29/88)
90 DOMAINE ETIENNE SAUZET Puligny-Montrachet Champ Canet 1986 $50 (2/29/88)
89 JOSEPH DROUHIN Puligny-Montrachet Clos de la Garenne 1986 $40 (6/15/88)
89 CHATEAU DES HERBEUX Puligny-Montrachet Les Combettes 1986 $21 (2/28/89)
89 PAUL PERNOT Puligny-Montrachet Folatières 1986 $50 (2/28/89)
89 DOMAINE ROUX PERE & FILS Puligny-Montrachet La Garenne 1986 $37.50 (12/31/87)
88 DOMAINE JEAN CHARTRON Puligny-Montrachet Les Folatières 1986 $50 (5/31/88)
88 JOSEPH DROUHIN Puligny-Montrachet 1986 $34 (2/29/88)
88 OLIVIER LEFLAIVE FRERES Puligny-Montrachet 1986 $30 (7/31/89)
88 PIERRE MATROT Puligny-Montrachet Les Combettes 1986 $37 (12/15/88)
88 MOILLARD Puligny-Montrachet 1986 $33 (5/31/88)
88 DOMAINE ETIENNE SAUZET Puligny-Montrachet 1986 $40 (2/29/88)
87 BOUCHARD PERE & FILS Puligny-Montrachet 1986 $31 (2/28/89)
87 LOUIS LATOUR Puligny-Montrachet 1986 $41 (2/29/88)
87 OLIVIER LEFLAIVE FRERES Puligny-Montrachet Les Champs-Gains 1986 $36 (2/29/88)
87 DOMAINE ETIENNE SAUZET Puligny-Montrachet Les Referts 1986 $45 (2/29/88)
87 LEONARD DE ST.-AUBIN Puligny-Montrachet 1986 $25 (11/15/87)

86 PHILIPPE BOUZEREAU Puligny-Montrachet Les Champs-Gains 1986 $38 (11/15/88)
85 JAFFELIN Puligny-Montrachet Champ Canet 1986 $40 (12/15/88)
85 REMOISSENET Puligny-Montrachet Les Folatières 1986 $50 (11/15/88)
85 HENRI DE VILLAMONT Puligny-Montrachet Les Folatières 1986 $30 (12/15/88)
82 LOUIS LATOUR Puligny-Montrachet 1986 $41 (9/30/88)
82 JACQUES THEVENOT-MACHAL Puligny-Montrachet Les Charmes 1986 $35 (2/29/88)
81 DOMAINE RENE MONNIER Puligny-Montrachet Les Folatières 1986 $44 (11/15/88)
81 CHATEAU DE PULIGNY-MONTRACHET Puligny-Montrachet 1986 $60 (2/29/88)
81 JACQUES THEVENOT-MACHAL Puligny-Montrachet Les Folatières au Chaniot 1986 $38 (2/29/88)
75 HENRI BOILLOT Puligny-Montrachet Clos de la Moushere 1986 $36 (9/30/88)
68 PROSPER MAUFOUX Puligny-Montrachet 1986 $36 (5/31/89)

1985

94 PHILIPPE BOUZEREAU Puligny-Montrachet Les Champs-Gains 1985 $34 (4/15/87)
93 LOUIS JADOT Puligny-Montrachet Les Combettes 1985 $45 (2/29/88)
93 DOMAINE ETIENNE SAUZET Puligny-Montrachet Les Perrières 1985 $39 (10/15/87)
92 JOSEPH DROUHIN Puligny-Montrachet Les Pucelles 1985 $50 (4/30/87)
92 LOUIS JADOT Puligny-Montrachet Clos de la Garenne Domaine du duc de Magenta 1985 $50 (2/29/88)
92 JAFFELIN Puligny-Montrachet 1985 $33 (4/15/87)
92 DOMAINE LEFLAIVE Puligny-Montrachet Les Pucelles 1985 Cur: $75 (2/29/88)
92 DOMAINE JEAN PASCAL Puligny-Montrachet Les Champ Gains 1985 $31 (9/15/87)
92 DOMAINE ROUX PERE & FILS Puligny-Montrachet La Garenne 1985 $30 (4/15/87)
91 DOMAINE LEFLAIVE Puligny-Montrachet Les Folatières 1985 Cur: $52 (2/29/88)
91 DOMAINE ETIENNE SAUZET Puligny-Montrachet Les Truffières 1985 $42 (2/29/88)
90 LOUIS JADOT Puligny-Montrachet 1985 $33 (2/29/88)
90 DOMAINE LEFLAIVE Puligny-Montrachet Clavoillon 1985 Cur: $64 (2/29/88)
90 PATRIARCHE Puligny-Montrachet 1985 $30 (9/30/89)
90 DOMAINE ETIENNE SAUZET Puligny-Montrachet Champ Canet 1985 $37 (10/15/87)
90 DOMAINE ETIENNE SAUZET Puligny-Montrachet Les Combettes 1985 $50 (2/29/88)
89 ADRIEN BELLAND Puligny-Montrachet 1985 $35 (9/15/87)
89 LOUIS LATOUR Puligny-Montrachet 1985 $30 (2/29/88)
88 MICHEL BOUZEREAU Puligny-Montrachet 1985 $30 (5/31/88)
88 JOSEPH DROUHIN Puligny-Montrachet Les Folatières 1985 $35 (2/29/88)
88 LOUIS LATOUR Puligny-Montrachet 1985 $37 (4/15/87)
88 DOMAINE LEFLAIVE Puligny-Montrachet 1985 $40 (2/29/88)
88 DOMAINE ROUX PERE & FILS Puligny-Montrachet Les Enseignères 1985 $34 (9/15/87)
85 BOUCHARD PERE & FILS Puligny-Montrachet Les Folatières 1985 $33 (2/29/88)
83 LOUIS JADOT Puligny-Montrachet 1985 $33 (2/29/88)
82 GERARD CHAVY Puligny-Montrachet 1985 $27.50 (12/31/87)
81 LABOURE-ROI Puligny-Montrachet 1985 $23 (11/15/86)
79 CHATEAU DE PULIGNY-MONTRACHET Puligny-Montrachet 1985 $55 (2/29/88)
79 REMOISSENET Puligny-Montrachet Les Folatières 1985 $56 (2/29/88)
74 DOMAINE JEAN CHARTRON Puligny-Montrachet Clos de la Pucelle 1985 $39 (11/15/87)
73 MACHARD DE GRAMONT Puligny-Montrachet Les Houillères 1985 $47 (5/31/88)
66 F. CHAUVENET Puligny-Montrachet Reuchaux 1985 $35 (2/28/87)

1984

89 LOUIS JADOT Puligny-Montrachet 1984 $30 (2/29/88)
89 LOUIS JADOT Puligny-Montrachet Les Combettes 1984 $37 (2/29/88)
88 F. CHAUVENET Puligny-Montrachet Champs-Gain 1984 $40 (4/30/87)
83 JOSEPH DROUHIN Puligny-Montrachet 1984 $27 (2/29/88)
83 OLIVIER LEFLAIVE FRERES Puligny-Montrachet 1984 $25 (6/01/86)
75 ADRIEN BELLAND Puligny-Montrachet 1984 $27.25 (1/31/87)
69 GERARD CHAVY Puligny-Montrachet 1984 $22 (11/15/87)
63 CHARLES VIENOT Puligny-Montrachet 1984 $30.50 (2/28/87)

1983

96 JEAN GERMAIN Puligny-Montrachet Les Champs-Gains 1983 $27 (3/01/86)
92 JAFFELIN Puligny-Montrachet 1983 $20.75 (2/01/86)
90 JEAN GERMAIN Puligny-Montrachet 1983 $12 (9/01/85)
90 JAFFELIN Puligny-Montrachet Les Folatières 1983 $20 (6/16/85)
90 LOUIS LATOUR Puligny-Montrachet 1983 $35 (2/29/88)
88 ADRIEN BELLAND Puligny-Montrachet 1983 $20 (9/16/85)
87 LOUIS JADOT Puligny-Montrachet Les Combettes 1983 $34 (2/29/88)
66 LOUIS JADOT Puligny-Montrachet 1983 $25 (2/29/88)

1982

94 DOMAINE LEFLAIVE Puligny-Montrachet Les Pucelles 1982 Cur: $72 (2/29/88)
88 F. CHAUVENET Puligny-Montrachet Champs-Gain 1982 $17 (3/16/85)
87 BOUCHARD PERE & FILS Puligny-Montrachet 1982 $17.95 (6/16/84)
86 LOUIS LATOUR Puligny-Montrachet Les Folatières 1982 $38 (2/29/88)
85 F. CHAUVENET Puligny-Montrachet Reuchaux 1982 $20 (9/16/85)
84 BERNARD THEVENOT Puligny-Montrachet 1982 $15 (10/16/84)

1979

95 DOMAINE LEFLAIVE Puligny-Montrachet Les Pucelles 1979 Cur: $100 (2/29/88)

OTHER CÔTE DE BEAUNE WHITE

1989

88 JAFFELIN Santenay Les Gravières 1989 $25 (5/31/91)
87 JOSEPH DROUHIN Auxey-Duresses 1989 $22 (2/28/91)
86 CHARTRON & TREBUCHET St.-Aubin La Chatenière 1989 $24 (2/28/91)
86 JOSEPH DROUHIN Pernand-Vergelesses 1989 $23 (2/28/91)
85 CHARTRON & TREBUCHET St.-Romain 1989 $20 (2/28/91)
85 DOMAINE ROUX PERE & FILS St.-Aubin La Pucelle 1989 $26 (2/28/91)
82 CHATEAU DE PULIGNY-MONTRACHET Monthélie Chardonnay 1989 $26 (2/28/91)
78 MOILLARD Bourgogne Hautes Côtes de Beaune Les Alouettes 1989 $15 (6/15/91)

1988

90 JOSEPH DROUHIN Beaune Clos des Mouches 1988 Rel: $64 Cur: $64 (7/31/90)
88 LOUIS JADOT Auxey-Duresses Domaine du Duc de Magenta 1988 $23 (4/30/91)
87 CHARTRON & TREBUCHET Santenay Sous la Fée 1988 $18 (3/15/90)
85 CHARTRON & TREBUCHET St.-Aubin La Chatenière 1988 $18 (3/15/90)
85 LOUIS JADOT Pernand-Vergelesses 1988 $21 (4/30/91)
85 DOMAINE ROUX PERE & FILS St.-Aubin La Pucelle 1988 $18.50 (3/15/90)
84 JAYER-GILLES Bourgogne Hautes Côtes de Beaune 1988 $22 (6/15/91)
83 CHARTRON & TREBUCHET Pernand-Vergelesses 1988 $18 (3/15/90)

83   LUPE-CHOLET Pernand-Vergelesses 1988 $15 (3/15/90)
80   LOUIS JADOT Savigny-lès-Beaune Blanc 1988 $24 (4/30/91)
80   LUPE-CHOLET Bourgogne Hautes Côtes de Beaune 1988 $10 (4/30/90)
75   PROSPER MAUFOUX Auxey-Duresses 1988 $18 (4/30/91)
73   JAYER-GILLES Bourgogne Hautes Côtes de Beaune 1988 $22 (2/28/91)
72   CHANSON PERE & FILS Pernand-Vergelesses Les Caradeux 1988 $25 (8/31/90)
68   DOMAINE PONNELLE Côte de Beaune Les Pierres Blanches 1988 $18 (2/28/91)

1987

83   CHARTRON & TREBUCHET Beaune 1987 $30 (2/28/89)
83   CHARTRON & TREBUCHET St.-Aubin La Chatenière 1987 $20 (4/15/89)
81   JOSEPH DROUHIN Beaune Clos des Mouches 1987 Rel: $48 Cur: $53 (4/30/89)
81   JOSEPH DROUHIN St.-Aubin 1987 $21 (4/15/89)
79   CHARTRON & TREBUCHET Santenay Sous la Fée 1987 $23 (4/30/89)

1986

87   JOSEPH DROUHIN Beaune Clos des Mouches 1986 Rel: $56 Cur: $56 (12/15/88)
84   PRUNIER Auxey-Duresses 1986 $25 (11/15/89)
82   JOSEPH DROUHIN St.-Aubin 1986 $20 (10/15/88)
81   BOUCHARD PERE & FILS Beaune Clos St.-Landry Domaines du Château de Beaune 1986 $33 (2/28/89)
79   CHANSON PERE & FILS Pernand-Vergelesses 1986 $16 (7/31/89)

1985

84   JAFFELIN St.-Aubin 1985 $13 (3/31/87)
79   JAFFELIN Auxey-Duresses 1985 $13 (3/31/87)
78   LUPE-CHOLET Savigny-lès-Beaune 1985 $10 (11/15/86)
75   JEAN LAFOUGE Auxey-Duresses 1985 $18.50 (6/15/87)
73   DUBREUIL-FONTAINE Pernand-Vergelesses Ile des Vergelesses 1985 $22 (2/28/89)

1984

78   CHARLES VIENOT St.-Aubin 1984 $13 (3/31/87)
77   JEAN GERMAIN St.-Romain Clos le Château 1984 $14.50 (7/16/86)
69   ROLAND THEVENIN Auxey-Duresses Chanterelle 1984 $10 (3/31/87)

1983

83   JEAN GERMAIN St.-Romain Clos Sous le Château 1983 $12 (9/16/85)
79   JAFFELIN Auxey-Duresses 1983 $11 (11/01/85)

CHALLONAISE

1989

86   JOSEPH DROUHIN Rully 1989 $17.50 (2/28/91)
81   OLIVIER LEFLAIVE FRERES Rully Premier Cru 1989 $20 (7/31/91)
78   CHARTRON & TREBUCHET Rully La Chaume 1989 $18 (4/30/91)

1988

88   CHARTRON & TREBUCHET Rully La Chaume 1988 $14 (3/15/90)
87   DUVERNAY Mercurey La Chiquette 1988 $17 (4/30/91)
86   FAIVELEY Mercurey Clos Rochette 1988 $22 (4/30/91)
86   JAFFELIN Rully Barrel Fermented 1988 $13 (3/15/90)
83   ALAIN ROY-THEVENIN Montagny Château de la Saule 1988 $12 (8/31/90)
83   DOMAINE FABIEN & LOUIS SAIER Mercurey Blanc Les Chenelots 1988 $17 (4/30/91)
80   LUPE-CHOLET Rully Marissou 1988 $16 (3/15/90)
79   JEAN-MARC BOILLOT Montagny Premier Cru 1988 $22 (8/31/90)

1987

82   JAFFELIN Rully Blanc 1987 $13 (3/15/89)
81   JOSEPH DROUHIN Rully 1987 $15 (4/30/89)
80   OLIVIER LEFLAIVE FRERES Montagny Premier Cru 1987 $15.50 (8/31/90)
74   CHARTRON & TREBUCHET Rully La Chaume 1987 $15 (4/30/89)

1986

88   JOSEPH DROUHIN Rully 1986 $14 (6/15/88)
87   JAFFELIN Rully Blanc 1986 $12 (2/15/88)
83   JOSEPH DROUHIN Montagny 1986 $15 (6/15/88)
83   JEAN VACHET Montagny Les Coeres 1986 $16 (1/31/89)
69   CHARTRON & TREBUCHET Mercurey 1986 $20 (5/31/88)

1985

88   JAFFELIN Rully Blanc 1985 $11 (3/31/87)
85   CHATEAU DE CHAMIREY Mercurey 1985 $13.50 (1/31/87)
65   ANTONIN RODET Montagny Les Chagnots 1985 $10 (11/15/86)

1984

56   PROSPER MAUFOUX Montagny 1984 $11 (3/31/87)
50   BICHOT Rully 1984 $8 (6/01/86)

1983

74   FAIVELEY Rully 1983 $10.25 (8/31/86)
62   FAIVELEY Mercurey Blanc Clos de la Rochette 1983 $14 (3/31/87)

MÂCONNAIS/MÂCON

1989

84   GEORGES DUBOEUF Mâcon-Lugny Fête des Fleurs 1989 $9 (10/31/90)
83   BICHOT Mâcon-Villages 1989 $9 (7/15/90)
82   DOMAINE DU VIEUX ST.-SORLIN Mâcon-La Roche Vineuse 1989 $13.50 (2/28/91)
81   GEORGES DUBOEUF Mâcon-Villages 1989 $8.50 (10/31/90)
81   ROBERT SARRAU Mâcon-Villages 1989 $8 (10/31/90)
80   LABOURE-ROI Mâcon-Villages 1989 $10 (4/30/91)
78   DOMAINE TALMARD Mâcon-Chardonnay 1989 $10 (10/31/90)
77   MOILLARD Mâcon-Villages Domaine de Montbellet 1989 $10.50 (4/30/91)
76   DOMAINE DES ROCHES Mâcon-Igé 1989 $9 (10/31/90)
71   LES ACACIAS Mâcon-Villages Cave de Viré 1989 $11 (2/28/91)

1988

86   DOMAINE DU VIEUX ST.-SORLIN Mâcon-La Roche Vineuse Eleve en futs de Chêne 1988 $11 (7/15/90)
84   LOUIS JADOT Mâcon-Villages La Fontaine 1988 $9 (9/15/89)
84   MAURICE JOSSERAND Mâcon-Péronne Domaine du Mortier 1988 $8 (12/31/90) BB

84   JEAN-CLAUDE THEVENET Mâcon-Pierreclos 1988 $6.25 (7/15/90) BB
82   PROSPER MAUFOUX Mâcon-Villages 1988 $10.50 (7/15/90)
81   BARTON & GUESTIER Mâcon-Villages 1988 $9 (9/30/89)
81   CAVE DE CHARDONNAY Mâcon-Chardonnay Chardonnay de Chardonnay 1988 $9 (7/15/90) BB
80   DOMAINE EMILIAN GILLET Mâcon-Clessé Quintaine 1988 $17 (8/31/90)
80   DOMAINE TALMARD Mâcon-Chardonnay 1988 $9 (7/15/90)
79   GEORGES DUBOEUF Mâcon-Villages 1988 $8 (9/30/89)
79   LAROCHE Mâcon-Villages 1988 $8.50 (7/15/90)
79   J.J. VINCENT Mâcon-Villages 1988 $7 (10/31/90)
78   M & G Mâcon-Villages 1988 $14 (3/31/91)
77   GEORGES DUBOEUF Mâcon-Villages La Coupe Perration 1988 $8 (9/30/89)
76   LES ACACIAS Mâcon-Viré Vieilles Vignes 1988 $9 (8/31/90)
76   JEAN CLAUDE BOISSET Mâcon-Blanc-Villages 1988 $9 (12/31/90)
76   REINE PEDAUQUE Mâcon-Villages Coupées 1988 $9.50 (9/30/89)

1987

84   DOMAINE DES ROCHES Mâcon-Igé 1987 $7 (5/15/89) BB
82   BICHOT Mâcon-Villages 1987 $6 (1/31/89) BB
80   F. CHAUVENET Mâcon-Villages Les Jumelles 1987 $7 (10/31/88)
79   GEORGES DUBOEUF Mâcon-Villages 1987 $7 (6/30/88)
77   J.J. VINCENT Mâcon-Villages Pièce d'Or 1987 $7 (5/15/89)
76   JEAN CLAUDE BOISSET Mâcon-Blanc-Villages 1987 $8.50 (9/15/89)
74   PIERRE JANNY Mâcon-Villages Domaine du Prieuré 1987 $7 (1/31/89)
74   THORIN Mâcon-Villages 1987 $8.50 (1/31/89)

1986

84   MANCIAT-PONCET Mâcon-Charnay Domaine des Crays 1986 $11.50 (4/15/88)
84   CAVE DE PRISSE Mâcon-Prissé Les Clochettes 1986 $8.50 (1/31/89)
81   LE GRAND CHENEAU Mâcon-Viré 1986 $6.50 (6/30/88) BB
79   F. CHAUVENET Mâcon-Villages Les Jumelles 1986 $8 (10/31/87)
79   LES GIRAUDIERES Mâcon-Villages 1986 $7.25 (10/31/87)
79   LABOURE-ROI Mâcon-Lugny 1986 $9 (4/15/88)
77   PIERRE JANNY Mâcon-Villages Domaine du Prieuré 1986 $6.50 (2/15/88)
76   CHEVALIER DE BEAUBASSIN Mâcon-Blanc-Villages 1986 $9 (4/15/88)
75   RAOUL CLERGET Mâcon-Villages 1986 $5.75 (10/15/88)
73   GEORGES DUBOEUF Mâcon-Villages 1986 $7 (7/31/88)
72   JOSEPH DROUHIN Mâcon-Villages 1986 $8.75 (6/15/88)
71   SYLVAIN FESSY Mâcon-Clessé Les Jumelles 1986 $7.50 (2/15/88)
69   PHILIPPE ANTOINE Mâcon-Villages 1986 $8 (4/15/88)
69   GEORGES BLANC Mâcon-Clessé 1986 $8 (3/15/88)
67   JEAN CLAUDE BOISSET Mâcon-Blanc-Villages 1986 $7.75 (10/31/87)

1985

92   MANCIAT-PONCET Mâcon-Charnay Domaine des Crays 1985 $9.50 (12/15/86)
84   CAVE DE LUGNY Mâcon-Lugny Les Charmes Pinot Chardonnay 1985 $7.50 (3/31/87)
83   GEORGES DUBOEUF Mâcon-Villages 1985 $8.50 (3/31/87)
80   PROSPER MAUFOUX Mâcon-Viré Château de Viré 1985 $11 (4/30/88)
78   F. CHAUVENET Mâcon-Villages Les Jumelles 1985 $8 (3/31/87)
78   CORON PERE Mâcon-Villages Blanc 1985 $8 (3/31/87)
78   LE GRAND CHENEAU Mâcon-Viré Chardonnay 1985 $6 (3/31/87)
76   LACHARME Mâcon-La Roche Vineuse 1985 $9 (9/15/86)
76   LOUIS LATOUR Mâcon-Villages Chameroy 1985 $11 (3/31/87)
75   VIGNERONS Mâcon-Villages Pinot Chardonnay 1985 $7.50 (3/31/87)
71   LOUIS JADOT Mâcon-Villages La Fontaine 1985 $7.50 (3/31/87)
71   JAFFELIN Mâcon-Villages 1985 $9.25 (3/31/87)
70   ALEXIS LICHINE Mâcon-Villages Pinot Chardonnay 1985 $6.75 (3/31/87)
65   MOMMESSIN Mâcon-Villages Le Beau Champ 1985 $6.75 (3/31/87)
60   DOMAINE TALMARD Mâcon-Chardonnay 1985 $6 (3/31/87)
55   LUPE-CHOLET Mâcon-Villages Les Roches 1985 $6.75 (9/15/86)

1984

90   DOMAINE TALMARD Mâcon-Chardonnay 1984 $6 (11/01/85) BB
84   LOUIS-RENE SAVIN Mâcon-Villages 1984 $8 (3/31/87)
83   J.J. VINCENT Mâcon-Villages 1984 $7 (2/16/86)
81   MOMMESSIN Mâcon Chardonnay 1984 $5 (12/16/85) BB
77   PROSPER MAUFOUX Mâcon-Villages 1984 $9.25 (3/31/87)
75   ARTISAN CRU Mâcon-Villages 1984 $7 (9/15/86)
75   JEAN CLAUDE BOISSET Mâcon-Blanc-Villages 1984 $7.75 (11/15/86)
72   CORON PERE Mâcon-Fuissé St.-Jacques 1984 $8.50 (3/31/87)
71   BOUCHARD PERE & FILS Mâcon-Villages Le Chamville 1984 $8.50 (3/31/87)
63   LES ACACIAS Mâcon-Villages 1984 $5.25 (11/16/85)
63   PROSPER MAUFOUX Mâcon-Viré Château de Viré 1984 $9.25 (3/31/87)
62   LES CHAZELLES Mâcon-Villages 1984 $8.25 (9/15/86)

1983

65   MOREAU Mâcon-Vinzelles Chardonnay Réserve La Couronne 1983 $9.50 (5/01/86)

POUILLY

1990

83   JAFFELIN Pouilly-Fuissé 1990 $18 (7/31/91)

1989

91   ROGER SAUMAIZE Pouilly-Fuissé Clos de la Roche 1989 $28 (7/31/91)
89   ROGER SAUMAIZE Pouilly-Fuissé Les Ronchevats 1989 $31 (7/31/91)
87   LOUIS JADOT Pouilly-Fuissé Cuvée Réserve Spéciale 1989 $21 (7/31/91)
86   GEORGES DUBOEUF Pouilly-Fuissé 1989 $15 (7/31/91)
85   BOUCHARD PERE & FILS Pouilly-Fuissé 1989 $25 (4/30/91)
79   J.J. VINCENT Pouilly-Fuissé 1989 $15 (4/30/91)

1988

90   J.J. VINCENT Pouilly-Fuissé 1988 $15 (10/31/90)
89   THIERRY GUERIN Pouilly-Fuissé Clos de France 1988 $23 (7/31/90)
89   LABOURE-ROI Pouilly-Fuissé 1988 $18 (10/31/90)
86   ANDRE BESSON Pouilly-Fuissé Domaine de Pouilly 1988 $15 (7/31/90)
86   LOUIS CURVEUX Pouilly-Fuissé Les Menestrières 1988 $23 (7/31/90)
85   LOUIS JADOT Pouilly-Fuissé 1988 $16 (9/30/89)
84   GEORGES DUBOEUF Pouilly-Fuissé 1988 $12 (9/30/89)
76   REINE PEDAUQUE Pouilly-Fuissé Griselles 1988 $16 (9/30/89)
73   BICHOT Pouilly-Fuissé 1988 $13 (12/31/90)

FRANCE
BURGUNDY WHITE/MÂCONNAIS/POUILLY

70   A. LIGERET Pouilly-Fuissé 1988 $21 (2/15/91)
59   BICHOT Pouilly-Fuissé 1988 $13 (8/31/90)

1987

84   BICHOT Pouilly-Fuissé 1987 $10 (4/30/89)
83   JOSEPH DROUHIN Pouilly-Fuissé 1987 $18 (4/30/89)
81   GEORGES DUBOEUF Pouilly-Fuissé 1987 $12 (6/15/88)
78   F. CHAUVENET Pouilly-Fuissé Clos de France 1987 $13 (4/30/89)
77   M. VINCENT Pouilly-Fuissé Château Fuissé 1987 $27 (11/30/90)
75   PELLERIN Pouilly-Fuissé 1987 $12 (4/30/89)
75   CHARLES VIENOT Pouilly-Fuissé 1987 $13.50 (4/30/89)
70   LUPE-CHOLET Pouilly-Fuissé 1987 $12.50 (4/30/89)

1986

90   JEAN CLAUDE BOISSET Pouilly-Fuissé 1986 $10 (9/30/87)
90   ROGER LASSARAT Pouilly-Fuissé Clos de France 1986 $26 (4/30/88)
89   M. VINCENT Pouilly-Fuissé Château Fuissé 1986 $29 (10/31/90)
86   SYLVAIN FESSY Pouilly-Fuissé Cuvée Gilles Guérrin 1986 $12 (12/31/87)
82   GEORGES DUBOEUF Pouilly-Fuissé 1986 $14 (7/31/87)
82   J.A. FERRET Pouilly-Fuissé Les Perrières Cuvée Spèciale 1986 $30 (7/31/90)
82   HENRY FESSY Pouilly-Fuissé 1986 $10 (10/15/88)
79   PHILIPPE ANTOINE Pouilly-Fuissé 1986 $15 (4/30/88)
79   BICHOT Pouilly-Fuissé 1986 $11 (3/15/88)
79   F. CHAUVENET Pouilly-Fuissé Clos de France 1986 $14 (10/15/87)
79   ROGER VERGE Pouilly-Fuissé 1986 $15 (3/15/88)
76   JOSEPH DROUHIN Pouilly-Fuissé 1986 $17.50 (6/30/88)
67   RAOUL CLERGET Pouilly-Fuissé 1986 $10 (10/15/88)

1985

92   LABOURE-ROI Pouilly-Fuissé 1985 $18 (3/31/87)
90   LOUIS JADOT Pouilly-Fuissé 1985 $19.25 (3/31/87)
90   DOMAINE LAPIERRE Pouilly-Fuissé 1985 $13.50 (3/31/87)
89   JAFFELIN Pouilly-Fuissé 1985 $18.50 (4/15/87)
88   ROGER LASSARAT Pouilly-Fuissé Clos de France 1985 $23 (12/31/87)
88   MANCIAT-PONCET Pouilly-Fuissé La Roche 1985 $20 (2/15/88)
87   BOUCHARD AINE Pouilly-Fuissé Réserve 1985 $17.50 (3/31/87)
85   BICHOT Pouilly-Fuissé 1985 $16 (3/31/87)
84   ROLAND THEVENIN Pouilly-Fuissé Les Moulins 1985 $19 (3/31/87)
81   THIERRY GUERIN Pouilly-Fuissé 1985 $18.50 (3/31/87)
80   BICHOT Pouilly-Fuissé 1985 $16 (8/31/86)
80   GEORGES DUBOEUF Pouilly-Fuissé 1985 $14.50 (3/31/87)
80   ANTONIN RODET Pouilly-Fuissé Rodet 1985 $19 (10/15/87)
77   JEAN CLAUDE BOISSET Pouilly-Fuissé 1985 $16.50 (3/31/87)
70   CHARLES VIENOT Pouilly-Vinzelles 1985 $16 (3/31/87)
62   CHARLES MONCAUT Pouilly-Fuissé 1985 $18 (6/15/87)

1984

89   JAFFELIN Pouilly-Fuissé 1984 $18.50 (3/31/87)
87   BOUCHARD PERE & FILS Pouilly-Fuissé 1984 $20 (3/31/87)
84   DOMAINE DELACOUR Pouilly-Fuissé 1984 $18 (3/31/87)
80   CHARLES VIENOT Pouilly-Fuissé 1984 $19 (3/31/87)
79   BOUCHARD PERE & FILS Pouilly-Vinzelles 1984 $12.50 (3/31/87)
78   PROSPER MAUFOUX Pouilly-Fuissé 1984 $16.50 (3/31/87)
71   J.J. VINCENT Pouilly-Fuissé 1984 $17 (2/16/86)
68   LOUIS LATOUR Pouilly-Fuissé Latour 1984 $25 (4/30/87)
64   LUPE-CHOLET Pouilly-Fuissé 1984 $19.25 (8/31/86)

1983

78   CHATEAU DE BEAUREGARD Pouilly-Fuissé 1983 $14.50 (3/16/85)
55   CHATEAU DE LAYE Pouilly-Vinzelles 1983 $8 (12/01/85)

1982

76   F. CHAUVENET Pouilly-Fuissé 1982 $8.50 (3/01/84)

ST.-VÉRAN

1989

85   JOSEPH DROUHIN St.-Véran 1989 $15.50 (2/28/91)
85   GEORGES DUBOEUF St.-Véran 1989 $10 (10/31/90)
80   JAFFELIN St.-Véran 1989 $14 (7/31/91)
79   THIERRY GUERIN St.-Véran 1989 $9 (3/31/91)
68   JEAN CLAUDE BOISSET St.-Véran 1989 $12 (7/31/91)

1988

85   J.J. VINCENT St.-Véran 1988 $10 (10/31/90)
82   GEORGES DUBOEUF St.-Véran 1988 $9 (9/30/89)
82   PROSPER MAUFOUX St.-Véran 1988 $12 (7/31/90)
81   JEAN CLAUDE BOISSET St.-Véran 1988 $9.50 (7/31/90)
81   LAROCHE St.-Véran 1988 $10 (7/31/90)
80   GEORGES DUBOEUF St.-Véran Coupe Louis Dailly 1988 $9 (9/30/89)
77   ROGER LASSARAT St.-Véran Cuvée Prestige 1988 $15 (8/31/90)
75   ANCIEN DOMAINE DU CHAPITRE DE MACON St.-Véran Les Colombière 1988 $12 (8/31/90)

1987

80   GEORGES DUBOEUF St.-Véran Coupe Louis Dailly 1987 $9 (10/15/88)
80   THIERRY GUERIN St.-Véran La Côte Rôtie 1987 $8.50 (4/30/89)
77   GEORGES DUBOEUF St.-Véran 1987 $9 (10/15/88)

1986

83   PHILIPPE ANTOINE St.-Véran 1986 $10 (4/30/88)
79   GEORGES DUBOEUF St.-Véran 1986 $9 (7/31/87)
79   THIERRY GUERIN St.-Véran La Côte Rôtie 1986 $11.50 (10/15/88)
75   SYLVAIN FESSY St.-Véran Cuvée Prissé 1986 $8 (2/15/88)
73   ROGER LASSARAT St.-Véran La Côte Rôtie 1986 $13 (4/30/88)
72   GEORGES BLANC St.-Véran 1986 $10 (12/31/87)

1985

92   CAVE DE PRISSE St.-Véran Les Blanchettes 1985 $10 (3/31/87)
88   JAFFELIN St.-Véran 1985 $9.25 (3/31/87)
87   GEORGES DUBOEUF St.-Véran 1985 $10 (3/31/87)
87   J.J. VINCENT St.-Véran 1985 $12 (3/31/87)
81   F. CHAUVENET St.-Véran 1985 $12 (3/31/87)
76   MOMMESSIN St.-Véran Domaine de l'Evèque 1985 $10.50 (3/31/87)
75   CHARLES MONCAUT St.-Véran 1985 $10.25 (6/15/87)
72   THIERRY GUERIN St.-Véran La Côte Rôtie 1985 $10 (3/31/87)
67   PROSPER MAUFOUX St.-Véran 1985 $12 (3/31/87)

1984

81   LOUIS JADOT St.-Véran 1984 $9 (3/31/87)
68   JEAN CLAUDE BOISSET St.-Véran 1984 $10 (3/31/87)

1983

82   VIGNERONS St.-Véran 1983 $7 (10/16/85) BB
62   F. CHAUVENET St.-Véran 1983 $6 (12/16/85)

OTHER BURGUNDY WHITE

1990

81   JAFFELIN Bourgogne Chardonnay 1990 $9 (7/31/91) BB

1989

83   PAUL PERNOT Bourgogne Chardonnay Champerrier 1989 $16 (4/30/91)
83   CHATEAU DE PULIGNY-MONTRACHET Côte de Nuits-Villages 1989 $27 (2/28/91)
82   JOSEPH DROUHIN Bourgogne Chardonnay Laforet 1989 $9 (4/30/91) BB
78   CHARTRON & TREBUCHET Bourgogne Chardonnay 1989 $10 (2/28/91)
78   PROSPER MAUFOUX Bourgogne Aligoté 1989 $12 (7/31/91)
73   DOMAINE B. SERVEAU Bourgogne Chardonnay 1989 $16 (4/30/91)

1988

87   DOMAINE PONSOT Morey-St.-Denis Monts-Luisants 1988 $50 (5/31/91)
85   JAFFELIN Bourgogne Blanc 1988 $9 (3/31/90)
84   DOMAINE DE L'ARLOT Nuits-St.-Georges Clos de L'Arlot 1988 $27/375ml (4/30/91)
84   LUPE-CHOLET Bourgogne Chardonnay Comtesse de Lupé 1988 $9 (4/30/90) BB
84   JEAN MICHELOT Bourgogne Aligoté 1988 $11.50 (7/31/90)
84   MOREAU Bourgogne Chardonnay 1988 $8 (4/30/91) BB
83   CHARTRON & TREBUCHET Bourgogne Blanc Hommage à Victor Hugo 1988 $10 (3/31/90)
83   CHATEAU DE MEURSAULT Bourgogne Chardonnay Clos du Château 1988 $23 (4/30/91)
81   LOUIS JADOT Bourgogne Chardonnay 1988 $9.50 (9/30/89)
81   CHATEAU DE PULIGNY-MONTRACHET Bourgogne Clos du Château 1988 $19 (7/31/90)
79   JOSEPH DROUHIN Bourgogne Chardonnay Laforet 1988 $8.75 (9/30/89)
76   BICHOT Le Bourgogne Bichot 1988 $8 (4/30/90)
76   LEROY Bourgogne d'Auvenay 1988 $14.50 (4/30/91)
76   DOMAINE JOSEPH MATROT Bourgogne Chardonnay 1988 $15.50 (4/30/91)
74   FAIVELEY Bourgogne Chardonnay 1988 $14 (7/31/90)
72   THEVENOT-LE-BRUN Bourgogne Aligoté 1988 $11.50 (7/31/90)

1987

83   CALVET Bourgogne Chardonnay Première 1987 $10 (4/30/89)
80   LUPE-CHOLET Bourgogne Chardonnay Comtesse de Lupé 1987 $8.25 (3/15/89) BB
80   DOMAINE JOSEPH MATROT Bourgogne Chardonnay 1987 $16 (9/15/89)
79   BICHOT Bourgogne Le Bourgogne Bichot 1987 $8 (5/15/89)
79   OLIVIER LEFLAIVE FRERES Bourgogne Les Sétilles 1987 $8.50 (3/31/90)
78   CHARTRON & TREBUCHET Bourgogne Blanc Hommage à Victor Hugo 1987 $13 (3/15/89)
78   DOMAINE JOSEPH MATROT Bourgogne Chardonnay 1987 $16 (4/15/90)
76   JAFFELIN Bourgogne Chardonnay du Châpitre 1987 $9.50 (3/15/89)
75   PIERRE BOILLOT Bourgogne Aligoté 1987 $13 (7/31/90)

1986

84   LEROY Bourgogne d'Auvenay 1986 $17 (9/15/89)
81   JOSEPH DROUHIN Bourgogne Chardonnay Laforet 1986 $8.50 (1/31/88)
80   DOMAINE DUJAC Morey-St.-Denis Vin Gris de Pinot Noir 1986 $13 (4/15/89)
80   DOMAINE LAROCHE Bourgogne Clos du Château 1986 $16 (1/31/89)
80   DOMAINE ROUGEOT-LATOUR Bourgogne Chardonnay Clos des Six Ouvrées 1986 $15 (10/15/88)
78   LOUIS JADOT Bourgogne Chardonnay 1986 $10 (10/15/88)
78   MOILLARD Hautes Côtes de Nuits 1986 $12 (1/31/89)
74   LOUIS JADOT Bourgogne Chardonnay 1986 $10 (2/15/88)
70   CHARTRON & TREBUCHET Bourgogne Blanc Hommage à Victor Hugo 1986 $13 (5/31/88)
65   A. & P. DE VILLAINE Bourgogne Les Clous Bouzeron 1986 $16 (1/31/89)

1985

87   OLIVIER LEFLAIVE FRERES Bourgogne Les Sétilles 1985 $12 (3/31/87)
85   JOSEPH DROUHIN Bourgogne Chardonnay Laforet 1985 $8.25 (3/31/87)
84   JOSEPH DROUHIN Bourgogne Chardonnay Laforet 1985 $8.25 (8/31/86) BB
82   CHATEAU DE MEURSAULT Bourgogne Chardonnay Clos du Château 1985 $20 (3/31/90)
80   JAFFELIN Bourgogne Chardonnay du Châpitre 1985 $9.50 (3/31/87)
79   LOUIS LATOUR Bourgogne Chardonnay Latour 1985 $11 (3/31/87)
79   DOMAINE LATOUR GIRAUD Bourgogne Chardonnay 1985 $11 (3/31/87)
76   ROLAND THEVENIN Bourgogne Chardonnay Réserve Roland Thévenin 1985 $8 (3/31/87)
74   PIERRE MOREY Bourgogne Aligoté 1985 $9.75 (2/15/88)
72   CHATEAU MARGUERITE DE BOURGOGNE Bourgogne Chardonnay 1985 $14 (6/30/87)
71   FAIVELEY Bourgogne Chardonnay Cuvée Joseph Faiveley 1985 $13.50 (3/31/87)

---

71 DOMAINE DU CHATEAU DE MERCEY Bourgogne Blanc Côtes de Beaune 1985 $8.50 (3/31/87)
70 CHARTRON & TREBUCHET Bourgogne Aligoté Les Equinces 1985 $9 (4/30/87)
65 LOUIS JADOT Bourgogne Chardonnay 1985 $9 (3/31/87)

1984

79 LIONEL J. BRUCK Bourgogne St.-Vincent Pinot Chardonnay 1984 $10 (3/31/87)
68 DOMAINE HENRI CLERC & FILS Bourgogne Blanc 1984 $10 (3/31/87)

1983

79 LEROY Bourgogne d'Auvenay 1983 $14.50 (12/31/87)
74 JAFFELIN Bourgogne Chardonnay du Châpitre 1983 $6.25 (1/01/85)
64 MOREAU Bourgogne Chardonnay 1983 $6.50 (6/01/86)
61 JOSEPH DROUHIN Bourgogne Chardonnay Laforet 1983 $7.50 (6/01/86)
61 FAIVELEY Bourgogne Chardonnay Cuvée Joseph Faiveley 1983 $7.50 (5/01/86)

CHABLIS

1989

92 DOMAINE AUFFRAY Chablis Les Clos 1989 $50 (1/31/91)
89 JOSEPH DROUHIN Chablis Vaudésir 1989 $54 (2/28/91)
88 DOMAINE AUFFRAY Chablis Vaillons 1989 $27 (1/31/91)
88 DOMAINE LAROCHE Chablis Les Blanchots Vieilles Vignes 1989 $72 (1/31/91)
87 DOMAINE LAROCHE Chablis Cuvée Première 1989 $25 (1/31/91)
87 DOMAINE LAROCHE Chablis Les Blanchots 1989 $57 (1/31/91)
87 MOREAU Chablis Vaillon 1989 $20 (2/28/91)
86 DOMAINE AUFFRAY Chablis Champs Royaux 1989 $19 (1/31/91)
86 JEAN-MARC BROCARD Chablis Domaine Ste.-Claire 1989 $13 (1/31/91)
86 JOSEPH DROUHIN Chablis Montmains 1989 $23 (2/28/91)
86 DOMAINE LAROCHE Chablis Les Vaillons 1989 $33 (1/31/91)
82 DOMAINE LAROCHE Chablis St.-Martin 1989 $21 (2/28/91)
81 MOILLARD Chablis 1989 $26 (2/28/91)
74 DOMAINE AUFFRAY Chablis Montée de Tonnerre 1989 $25 (2/28/91)

1988

93 DOMAINE AUFFRAY Chablis Vaillons 1988 $20 (12/15/89)
92 DOMAINE AUFFRAY Chablis Les Clos 1988 $38 (3/31/90)
92 DOMAINE DAUVISSAT-CAMUS Chablis Les Clos 1988 $41 (7/31/90)
92 DOMAINE LONG DEPAQUIT Chablis Moutonne 1988 $47 (7/31/90)
91 DOMAINE DAUVISSAT-CAMUS Chablis Vaillons 1988 $25 (7/15/90)
90 DOMAINE LAROCHE Chablis St.-Martin 1988 $15 (12/15/89)
90 DOMAINE LONG DEPAQUIT Chablis Les Clos 1988 $42 (7/15/90)
89 LAURENT TRIBUT Chablis Beauroy 1988 $17 (7/15/90)
88 DOMAINE LAROCHE Chablis Les Fourchaumes 1988 $23 (12/15/89)
88 DOMAINE LAROCHE Chablis Les Vaillons 1988 $22 (12/15/89)
88 DOMAINE LONG DEPAQUIT Chablis Les Blanchots 1988 $38 (1/31/91)
88 MOREAU Chablis Domaine de Bieville 1988 $15 (2/28/91)
87 DOMAINE AUFFRAY Chablis Montée de Tonnerre 1988 $21 (3/31/90)
87 JOSEPH DROUHIN Chablis Vaudésir 1988 $38 (3/31/90)
87 DOMAINE LAROCHE Chablis 1988 $15.50 (7/31/90)
87 DOMAINE LAROCHE Chablis Les Vaudevey 1988 $24 (7/31/90)
87 DOMAINE LONG DEPAQUIT Chablis Les Vaillons 1988 $20 (7/31/90)
87 DOMAINE LONG DEPAQUIT Chablis Les Vaudésirs 1988 $40 (7/31/90)
87 LAURENT TRIBUT Chablis 1988 $17 (7/31/90)
86 DOMAINE DAUVISSAT-CAMUS Chablis Les Preuses 1988 $41 (7/31/90)
86 DOMAINE LAROCHE Chablis Les Blanchots Vieilles Vignes 1988 $58 (7/31/90)
86 LOUIS MICHEL & FILS Chablis Montée de Tonnerre 1988 $26 (7/31/90)
85 YVONNE FEBVRE Chablis Blanchot 1988 $23 (1/31/91)
85 DOMAINE LAROCHE Chablis 1988 $15.50 (3/31/90)
84 BICHOT Chablis 1988 $17 (3/31/90)
84 DOMAINE LAROCHE Chablis Les Montmains 1988 $25 (7/31/90)
84 DOMAINE TRIBAUT-DAUVISSAT Chablis 1988 $18 (1/31/91)
83 DOMAINE LAROCHE Chablis Laroche Cuvée Première 1988 $16 (12/15/89)
83 DOMAINE LAROCHE Chablis Les Clos 1988 $49 (12/15/89)
82 BICHOT Chablis Les Vaillons 1988 $17 (12/15/89)
82 LUPE-CHOLET Chablis Château de Viviers 1988 $15 (3/31/90)
81 DOMAINE DE LA MALADIERE Chablis 1988 $13 (2/28/91)
80 DOMAINE AUFFRAY Chablis Valmur 1988 $32 (12/15/89)
80 LAROCHE Chablis Fourchaume 1988 $23 (7/31/90)
79 DOMAINE AUFFRAY Chablis Champs Royaux 1988 $12 (3/31/90)
79 DOMAINE SEGUINOT Chablis 1988 $16 (2/28/91)
77 LOUIS MICHEL & FILS Chablis 1988 $16.50 (7/15/90)
76 CHATEAU DE MALIGNY Chablis 1988 $15 (7/31/90)
74 DOMAINE DAUVISSAT-CAMUS Chablis La Forest 1988 $25 (7/31/90)
72 JOSEPH DROUHIN Chablis 1988 $18 (3/31/90)
71 CHATEAU DE MALIGNY Chablis Fourchaume 1988 $22 (7/31/90)
70 LABOURE-ROI Chablis Fourchaumes 1988 $22 (7/31/90)

1987

97 RENE DAUVISSAT Chablis Preuses 1987 $43 (3/31/89)
95 RENE DAUVISSAT Chablis Les Clos 1987 $40 (3/31/89)
95 DOMAINE LAROCHE Chablis Blanchots 1987 $40 (3/31/89)
95 MOREAU Chablis Clos des Hospices 1987 (NA) (3/31/89)
94 DOMAINE LAROCHE Chablis Blanchots Vieille Vignes 1987 $50 (3/31/89)
93 JEAN-PAUL DROIN Chablis Les Clos 1987 $38 (3/31/89)
93 DOMAINE LAROCHE Chablis Fourchaume Vieille Vignes 1987 $45 (3/31/89)
92 RENE DAUVISSAT Chablis La Foret 1987 $25 (3/31/89)
92 RENE DAUVISSAT Chablis Vaillons 1987 $24 (3/31/89)
92 MOREAU Chablis Les Clos 1987 $38 (3/31/89)
92 FRANCOIS RAVENEAU Chablis Blanchot 1987 $40 (3/31/90)
92 JEAN-MARIE RAVENEAU Chablis Valmur 1987 $40 (3/31/90)
91 JEAN DAUVISSAT Chablis Vaillons 1987 $22 (1/31/91)
91 JEAN-PAUL DROIN Chablis Vaillons 1987 $24 (3/31/89)
91 JOSEPH DROUHIN Chablis Les Roncières 1987 $23 (3/31/89)
91 MOREAU Chablis Vaillons 1987 (NA) (3/31/89)
91 MOREAU Chablis Valmur 1987 (NA) (3/31/89)
91 ALBERT PIC & FILS Chablis Les Clos 1987 $40 (3/31/89)
91 THORIN Chablis Fourchaume 1987 $24 (10/15/89)
90 RENE DAUVISSAT Chablis Séchet 1987 $24 (3/31/89)
90 JEAN-PAUL DROIN Chablis Montée de Tonnerre 1987 $24 (3/31/89)
90 JEAN-PAUL DROIN Chablis Vaudésir 1987 $38 (3/31/89)
90 JEAN DURUP Chablis Vaudevey 1987 (NA) (3/31/89)
90 DOMAINE LAROCHE Chablis Fourchaume 1987 $26 (3/31/89)
90 DOMAINE LAROCHE Chablis Les Clos 1987 $50 (3/31/89)
90 DOMAINE LONG DEPAQUIT Chablis Les Preuses 1987 $30 (3/31/89)
90 MOREAU Chablis Fourchaume 1987 $24 (3/31/89)
90 MOREAU Chablis Preuses 1987 (NA) (3/31/89)
90 MOREAU Chablis Vaudésir 1987 (NA) (3/31/89)
90 FRANCOIS RAVENEAU Chablis Clos 1987 $50 (3/31/90)
90 FRANCOIS RAVENEAU Chablis Montée de Tonnerre 1987 $35 (3/31/90)
90 JEAN-MARIE RAVENEAU Chablis Chapelot 1987 $25 (3/31/90)
89 JEAN-PAUL DROIN Chablis Montains 1987 $24 (3/31/89)
89 JOSEPH DROUHIN Chablis Les Suchots 1987 $20 (3/31/89)
89 LOUIS MICHEL & FILS Chablis Vaudésir 1987 $31 (7/15/90)
89 MOREAU Chablis Bougros 1987 (NA) (3/31/89)
89 MOREAU Chablis Les Clos Clos des Hospices 1987 $60 (2/28/91)
89 ALBERT PIC & FILS Chablis Grenouilles 1987 $40 (3/31/89)
89 ALBERT PIC & FILS Chablis Vaudésir 1987 $40 (3/31/89)
89 A. REGNARD & FILS Chablis Fourchaume 1987 $22 (3/31/89)
89 CHARLES VIENOT Chablis Vauignot 1987 $20 (3/31/89)
88 RENE DAUVISSAT Chablis Tribaut 1987 $24 (3/31/89)
88 DOMAINE DAUVISSAT-CAMUS Chablis Les Clos 1987 $37 (10/15/89)
88 JEAN DURUP Chablis Fourchaume 1987 (NA) (3/31/89)
88 DOMAINE LONG DEPAQUIT Chablis Les Blanchots 1987 $29 (3/31/89)
88 MOREAU Chablis Vaudevey 1987 (NA) (3/31/89)
88 BARON PATRICK Chablis Valmur 1987 $30 (3/31/89)
88 JEAN-MARIE RAVENEAU Chablis Vaillons 1987 $25 (3/31/90)
88 A. REGNARD & FILS Chablis Vaillons 1987 $20 (3/31/89)
87 LA CHABLISIENNE Chablis Grande Cuvée 1987 (NA) (3/31/89)
87 DOMAINE DAUVISSAT-CAMUS Chablis Les Preuses 1987 $37 (10/15/89)
87 JEAN-PAUL DROIN Chablis Fourchaume 1987 $24 (3/31/89)
87 JOSEPH DROUHIN Chablis Premier Cru 1987 $20 (3/31/89)
87 DOMAINE LAROCHE Chablis Vaillons 1987 $25 (3/31/89)
87 LOUIS MICHEL & FILS Chablis Montée de Tonnerre 1987 $20 (7/15/90)
87 MOREAU Chablis Montmains 1987 (NA) (3/31/89)
87 ALBERT PIC & FILS Chablis Blanchots 1987 $40 (3/31/89)
86 JEAN-PAUL DROIN Chablis Valmur 1987 $38 (3/31/89)
86 JEAN DURUP Chablis 1987 (NA) (3/31/89)
86 DOMAINE LONG DEPAQUIT Chablis Les Vaillons 1987 $15 (12/31/88)
86 DOMAINE LONG DEPAQUIT Chablis Vaudésirs 1987 $30 (3/31/89)
86 MOILLARD Chablis 1987 $17 (10/15/89)
86 MOREAU Chablis Les Clos Clos des Hospices 1987 $52 (10/15/89)
86 BARON PATRICK Chablis Clos 1987 $30 (3/31/89)
86 ALBERT PIC & FILS Chablis Valmur 1987 $40 (3/31/89)
85 BICHOT Chablis 1987 $11 (3/31/89)
85 LA CHABLISIENNE Chablis Fourchaume 1987 $18 (3/31/89)
85 JOSEPH DROUHIN Chablis 1987 $20 (3/31/89)
85 DOMAINE LAROCHE Chablis Vaudevey 1987 $23 (3/31/89)
85 DOMAINE LONG DEPAQUIT Chablis Les Lys 1987 $15 (12/31/88)
85 DOMAINE LONG DEPAQUIT Chablis Moutonne 1987 $36 (3/31/89)
85 MOREAU Chablis Côte de Lechet 1987 $11 (3/31/89)
85 BARON PATRICK Chablis 1987 $22 (3/31/89)
85 ALBERT PIC & FILS Chablis Bougros 1987 $38 (3/31/89)
85 A. REGNARD & FILS Chablis Mont de Milieu 1987 $20 (3/31/89)
84 JOSEPH DROUHIN Chablis 1987 $14 (3/31/89)
84 MOREAU Chablis Les Clos 1987 $38 (2/28/91)
84 MOREAU Chablis Voucoupin 1987 (NA) (3/31/89)
84 ALBERT PIC & FILS Chablis Preuses 1987 $38 (3/31/89)
84 A. REGNARD & FILS Chablis Montmains 1987 $20 (3/31/89)
83 DOMAINE DAUVISSAT-CAMUS Chablis La Forest 1987 $22 (10/15/89)
83 JOSEPH DROUHIN Chablis Montmains 1987 $22 (3/31/89)
83 DOMAINE LONG DEPAQUIT Chablis 1987 $12 (3/31/89)
83 MOREAU Chablis 1987 (NA) (3/31/89)
83 A. REGNARD & FILS Chablis Montée de Tonnerre 1987 $20 (3/31/89)
82 LA CHABLISIENNE Chablis 1987 $13 (3/31/89)
82 JEAN-PAUL DROIN Chablis Grenouilles 1987 $40 (3/31/89)
82 DOMAINE LAROCHE Chablis St.-Martin 1987 $17 (3/31/89)
82 BARON PATRICK Chablis 1987 $17 (3/31/89)
82 ALBERT PIC & FILS Chablis 1987 $16 (3/31/89)
81 JEAN-PAUL DROIN Chablis Vosgros 1987 $24 (3/31/89)
81 JOSEPH DROUHIN Chablis 1987 $14 (3/31/89)
80 JEAN-PAUL DROIN Chablis 1987 (NA) (3/31/89)
80 LOUIS MICHEL & FILS Chablis Montmain 1987 $20 (7/15/90)
78 DOMAINE DAUVISSAT-CAMUS Chablis Vaillons 1987 $22 (10/15/89)
77 LA CHABLISIENNE Petit Chablis 1987 (NA) (3/31/89)
74 DOMAINE LAROCHE Chablis 1987 $26 (3/31/91)
68 DOMAINE TRIBAUT-DAUVISSAT Chablis 1987 $15 (10/15/89)

1986

96 MOREAU Chablis Les Clos 1986 $36 (3/31/89)
95 DOMAINE DAUVISSAT-CAMUS Chablis Les Clos 1986 $40 (9/15/88)
95 JOSEPH DROUHIN Chablis Les Clos 1986 $31 (3/31/89)
95 MOREAU Chablis Preuses 1986 (NA) (3/31/89)
94 DOMAINE DAUVISSAT-CAMUS Chablis Les Preuses 1986 $40 (9/15/88)
93 ALBERT PIC & FILS Chablis Valmur 1986 $40 (3/31/89)
93 FRANCOIS RAVENEAU Chablis Valmur 1986 $35 (3/31/89)
92 JOSEPH DROUHIN Chablis Vaudésir 1986 $34 (3/31/89)
92 JOSEPH DROUHIN Chablis Vaudésir 1986 $34 (5/15/88)
92 MOREAU Chablis Vaillons 1986 $21 (3/31/89)
92 ALBERT PIC & FILS Chablis Grenouilles 1986 $40 (3/31/89)
92 ALBERT PIC & FILS Chablis Les Clos 1986 $40 (3/31/89)
91 RENE DAUVISSAT Chablis Premier Cru La Forêt 1986 $25 (3/31/89)
91 MOREAU Chablis Les Clos 1986 $36 (5/15/88)
91 MOREAU Chablis Vaudésir 1986 $36 (3/31/89)
91 BARON PATRICK Chablis Valmur 1986 $30 (3/31/89)
91 ALBERT PIC & FILS Chablis Vaudésir 1986 $40 (3/31/89)
90 LA CHABLISIENNE Chablis Grande Cuvée 1986 (NA) (3/31/89)
90 LA CHABLISIENNE Chablis Vaudésir 1986 (NA) (3/31/89)
90 JEAN-PAUL DROIN Chablis Montée de Tonnerre 1986 $21 (5/15/88)

FRANCE
CHABLIS

90   DOMAINE LONG DEPAQUIT Chablis Les Clos 1986 $32 (3/31/88)
90   MOREAU Chablis Beauroy 1986 (NA) (3/31/89)
90   MOREAU Chablis Mont de Milieu 1986 $30 (3/31/89)
90   MOREAU Chablis Valmur 1986 $38 (2/28/91)
90   A. REGNARD & FILS Chablis Fourchaume 1986 $22 (3/31/89)
90   A. REGNARD & FILS Chablis Montée de Tonnerre 1986 $21 (3/31/89)
89   DOMAINE LAROCHE Chablis Les Clos 1986 $50 (12/31/88)
89   MOREAU Chablis Bougros 1986 (NA) (3/31/89)
89   BARON PATRICK Chablis Clos 1986 $30 (3/31/89)
88   DOMAINE AUFFRAY Chablis Champs Royaux 1986 $17 (9/15/88)
88   DOMAINE AUFFRAY Chablis Les Preuses 1986 $36 (9/15/88)
88   LA CHABLISIENNE Chablis Grenouilles 1986 (NA) (3/31/89)
88   LA CHABLISIENNE Chablis Les Clos 1986 (NA) (3/31/89)
88   LAROCHE Chablis 1986 $12 (5/15/88)
88   DOMAINE LONG DEPAQUIT Chablis Moutonne 1986 $35 (3/31/88)
88   MOREAU Chablis Montmains 1986 $21 (3/31/89)
88   ALBERT PIC & FILS Chablis Les Preuses 1986 $37 (9/15/88)
88   JACQUES TREMBLAY Chablis Fourchaume 1986 (NA) (3/31/89)
87   JEAN-PAUL DROIN Chablis Les Clos 1986 $32 (5/15/88)
87   JOSEPH DROUHIN Chablis Bougros 1986 $33 (5/15/88)
87   DOMAINE LONG DEPAQUIT Chablis Les Blanchots 1986 $28 (3/31/88)
87   MOREAU Chablis Montmain 1986 $21 (2/28/91)
87   MOREAU Chablis Valmur 1986 $38 (3/31/89)
87   MOREAU Chablis Vaudevey 1986 (NA) (3/31/89)
87   ALBERT PIC & FILS Chablis Blanchots 1986 $40 (3/31/89)
87   ALBERT PIC & FILS Chablis Preuses 1986 $38 (3/31/89)
87   A. REGNARD & FILS Chablis Vaillons 1986 $20 (3/31/89)
87   ANDRE VANNIER Chablis Les Preuses 1986 $33 (5/15/88)
86   LA CHABLISIENNE Chablis Montée de Tonnerre 1986 (NA) (3/31/89)
86   DOMAINE LAROCHE Chablis Les Fourchaumes 1986 $29 (5/15/88)
86   DOMAINE LAROCHE Chablis Les Vaillons 1986 $29 (12/31/88)
86   DOMAINE LAROCHE Chablis St.-Martin 1986 $16 (12/31/88)
86   MOREAU Chablis Voucoupin 1986 (NA) (3/31/89)
86   A. REGNARD & FILS Chablis Vaillons 1986 $20 (9/15/88)
86   THORIN Chablis Fourchaume 1986 $23 (2/15/89)
85   DOMAINE AUFFRAY Chablis Fourchaume 1986 $24 (9/15/88)
85   JEAN DAUVISSAT Chablis Vaillons Vieilles Vignes 1986 $24 (7/15/90)
85   DOMAINE DAUVISSAT-CAMUS Chablis La Forest 1986 $25 (9/15/88)
85   JEAN-PAUL DROIN Chablis Fourchaume 1986 $17 (7/15/88)
85   JOSEPH DROUHIN Chablis Premier Cru 1986 $19.50 (5/15/88)
85   DOMAINE LONG DEPAQUIT Chablis Les Vaudésirs 1986 $28 (3/31/88)
85   CHATEAU DE MALIGNY Chablis Fourchaume 1986 $18 (3/31/89)
85   MOREAU Chablis 1986 (NA) (3/31/89)
85   MOREAU Chablis Côte de Lechet 1986 $11 (3/31/89)
85   BARON PATRICK Chablis 1986 $22 (3/31/89)
85   ALBERT PIC & FILS Chablis Bougros 1986 $38 (3/31/89)
85   A. REGNARD & FILS Chablis Mont de Milieu 1986 $20 (3/31/89)
84   LA CHABLISIENNE Chablis Beauroy 1986 (NA) (3/31/89)
84   DOMAINE DAUVISSAT-CAMUS Chablis Vaillons 1986 $24.50 (9/15/88)
84   BARON PATRICK Chablis 1986 $17 (3/31/89)
84   ALBERT PIC & FILS Chablis Les Clos 1986 $40 (9/15/88)
83   JOSEPH DROUHIN Chablis 1986 $14 (5/15/88)
83   ALBERT PIC & FILS Chablis 1986 $16 (3/31/89)
83   ALBERT PIC & FILS Chablis Vaudésir 1986 $40 (9/15/88)
83   A. REGNARD & FILS Chablis Fourchaume 1986 $22 (9/15/88)
83   GUY ROBIN Chablis Vaudésir 1986 $37 (2/28/91)
82   JEAN DAUVISSAT Chablis Les Preuses 1986 $30 (7/15/90)
82   JEAN DAUVISSAT Chablis Vaillons 1986 $19 (7/15/90)
82   DOMAINE LAROCHE Chablis Les Vaillons 1986 $29 (9/15/88)
81   MOREAU Chablis Fourchaume 1986 $21 (3/31/89)
79   PATRIARCHE Chablis Cuvée des Quatre Vents 1986 $13 (10/15/89)
79   ALBERT PIC & FILS Chablis 1986 $16 (9/15/88)
78   MOREAU Chablis Les Clos Clos des Hospices 1986 $35 (10/15/88)
78   ALBERT PIC & FILS Chablis Valmur 1986 $40 (10/15/88)
78   A. REGNARD & FILS Chablis Mont de Milieu 1986 $20 (10/15/88)
77   ALBERT PIC & FILS Chablis Bougros 1986 $38 (9/15/88)
76   SIMONNET-FEBVRE Chablis Vaillons 1986 $17 (5/15/88)
75   DOMAINE AUFFRAY Chablis Montée de Tonnerre 1986 $24 (10/15/88)
75   ROLAND LAVANTUREUX Chablis Petit 1986 $11 (5/15/88)
71   DOMAINE LONG DEPAQUIT Chablis 1986 $15 (5/15/88)
70   DOMAINE AUFFRAY Chablis Les Clos 1986 $36 (10/15/88)
70   A. REGNARD & FILS Chablis Montée de Tonnerre 1986 $21 (10/15/88)
70   A. REGNARD & FILS Chablis Montmains 1986 $20 (9/15/88)
68   ROLAND LAVANTUREUX Chablis 1986 $16 (1/31/89)
68   SIMONNET-FEBVRE Chablis 1986 $12 (5/15/88)
67   DOMAINE LONG DEPAQUIT Chablis Vaucopins 1986 $18 (5/15/88)
66   DOMAINE AUFFRAY Chablis 1986 $12.95 (11/15/87)
62   ANDRE VANNIER Chablis Les Clos 1986 $32 (9/15/88)
55   SIMONNET-FEBVRE Chablis Les Clos 1986 $29 (7/15/88)

1985

90   DOMAINE ANTOINE CHAPUIS Chablis Montée de Tonnerre 1985 $21 (8/31/87)
89   CHATEAU GRENOUILLES Chablis Grenouille 1985 $34 (8/31/87)

---

89   MOILLARD Chablis Vaillons 1985 $16 (5/31/87)
88   DOMAINE DAUVISSAT-CAMUS Chablis Vaillons 1985 $28 (11/15/87)
88   DOMAINE DE L'EGLANTIERE Chablis 1985 $14.25 (1/31/87)
88   DOMAINE LONG DEPAQUIT Chablis Les Clos 1985 $32 (8/31/87)
88   ANTONIN RODET Chablis Montmains 1985 $20 (4/15/87)
87   DOMAINE LONG DEPAQUIT Chablis Moutonne 1985 $35 (11/15/87)
86   DOMAINE LAROCHE Chablis Les Bouguerots 1985 $33 (6/15/87)
86   DOMAINE LONG DEPAQUIT Chablis Les Vaudésirs 1985 $30 (6/30/87)
84   MOREAU Chablis Domaine de Bieville 1985 $13.50 (4/15/87)
83   BOUCHARD PERE & FILS Chablis 1985 $15 (10/15/87)
83   DOMAINE LAROCHE Chablis St.-Martin 1985 $16 (6/30/87)
80   DOMAINE LAROCHE Chablis Les Vaudevey 1985 $19 (6/15/87)
80   ROLAND LAVANTUREUX Chablis 1985 $17 (5/15/88)
80   DOMAINE LONG DEPAQUIT Chablis 1985 $14 (11/15/87)
80   DOMAINE LONG DEPAQUIT Chablis 1985 $14 (11/15/86)
80   DOMAINE LONG DEPAQUIT Chablis Les Vaillons 1985 $21 (6/30/87)
79   DOMAINE MICHEL ROBIN Chablis Vaillons 1985 $21.50 (8/31/87)
75   JEAN CLAUDE BOISSET Chablis 1985 $14 (1/31/87)
74   DOMAINE DAUVISSAT-CAMUS Chablis La Forest 1985 $28 (11/15/87)
74   DOMAINE MICHEL ROBIN Chablis Blanchots 1985 $34 (8/31/87)
72   J BILLAUD-SIMON Chablis Montée de Tonnerre 1985 $19.50 (9/30/87)
68   MOILLARD Chablis 1985 $14 (5/31/87)
67   M. DEOLIVEIRA Chablis Les Clos 1985 $34 (8/31/87)

1984

93   DOMAINE LAROCHE Chablis Les Blanchots 1984 $27.25 (2/28/87)
92   DOMAINE AUFFRAY Chablis Les Preuses 1984 $30 (4/15/87)
91   DOMAINE LONG DEPAQUIT Chablis Les Vaudésirs 1984 $20 (10/15/86) CS
90   PHILIPPE TESTUT Chablis 1984 $12.50 (4/15/87)
85   DOMAINE LAROCHE Chablis Les Fourchaumes 1984 $18 (1/31/87)
79   DOMAINE LAROCHE Chablis Les Beauroys 1984 $19 (10/31/87)
76   DOMAINE LONG DEPAQUIT Chablis Les Blanchots 1984 $20 (9/15/86)
75   DOMAINE LAROCHE Chablis Les Vaudevey 1984 $17 (1/31/87)
73   YVONNE FEBVRE Chablis Montée de Tonnerre 1984 $14.75 (1/31/87)
72   CHATEAU DE VIVIERS Chablis 1984 $11.75 (7/16/86)
67   DOMAINE LONG DEPAQUIT Chablis Les Beugnons 1984 $12 (7/16/86)
65   BICHOT Chablis 1984 $9 (2/16/86)

1983

91   DOMAINE LAROCHE Chablis 1983 $13 (11/15/86)
90   ANDRE VANNIER Chablis Les Preuses 1983 $17.50 (3/01/85)
87   DOMAINE LONG DEPAQUIT Chablis Moutonne 1983 $20 (12/16/85)
86   JAFFELIN Chablis Fourchaume 1983 $14.50 (10/16/85)
79   A. REGNARD & FILS Chablis Fourchaume 1983 $11 (11/01/84)
77   DOMAINE LAROCHE Chablis Les Vaudevey 1983 $15 (12/01/85)
66   DOMAINE LAROCHE Chablis Les Vaillons 1983 $15 (2/16/86)
63   ANDRE VANNIER Chablis Les Clos 1983 $17.50 (3/16/85)
62   MOREAU Chablis 1983 $9.50 (12/01/85)

1982

85   JEAN CLAUDE BOISSET Chablis Grenouilles 1982 $15 (6/16/85)
82   F. CHAUVENET Chablis Montmains 1982 $10 (7/01/85)

1979

87   BARON PATRICK Chablis 1979 $12.75 (6/16/84)

CHAMPAGNE/BLANC DE BLANCS

1985

92   TAITTINGER Brut Blanc de Blancs Champagne Comtes de Champagne 1985 (NA) (12/31/90)
90   AYALA Brut Blanc de Blancs Champagne 1985 $57 (12/31/90)
87   PHILIPPONNAT Brut Blanc de Blancs Champagne Grand Blanc 1985 $40 (12/31/90)
83   BONNAIRE Brut Blanc de Blancs Champagne Cramant 1985 $42 (12/31/89)
83   DEUTZ Brut Blanc de Blancs Champagne 1985 $42 (12/31/90)
82   AYALA Brut Blanc de Blancs Champagne 1985 $57 (12/31/89)

1983

94   BRUNO PAILLARD Brut Blanc de Blancs Champagne 1983 $40 (5/31/87)
93   TAITTINGER Brut Blanc de Blancs Champagne Comtes de Champagne 1983 $92 (12/31/90)
90   BILLECART-SALMON Brut Blanc de Blancs Champagne 1983 $50 (5/15/88)
90   DE CASTELLANE Brut Blanc de Blancs Champagne Brut Chardonnay 1983 (NA) (12/31/90)
89   H. GERMAINE Blanc de Blancs Champagne Crémant 1983 $24 (12/31/90)
88   BILLECART-SALMON Brut Blanc de Blancs Champagne 1983 $50 (12/31/89)
87   BONNAIRE Brut Blanc de Blancs Champagne Cramant 1983 $38 (2/29/88)
87   DOM RUINART Brut Blanc de Blancs Champagne 1983 Rel: $60 Cur: $60 (12/31/90)
83   LOUIS ROEDERER Brut Blanc de Blancs Champagne 1983 $45 (12/31/90)
82   TAILLEVENT Brut Blanc de Blancs Champagne 1983 $33 (12/31/89)

1982

95   TAITTINGER Brut Blanc de Blancs Champagne Comtes de Champagne 1982 Rel: $83 Cur: $83 (12/31/89)
94   DOM RUINART Brut Blanc de Blancs Champagne 1982 Rel: $61 Cur: $70 (12/31/89) CS
91   BEAUMET Brut Blanc de Blancs Champagne Cuvée Malakoff 1982 $41 (12/31/90)
91   POL ROGER Brut Blanc de Blancs Champagne Blanc de Chardonnay 1982 $50 (12/31/90)
90   A. CHARBAUT Brut Blanc de Blancs Champagne 1982 $43 (4/15/90)
90   DEUTZ Brut Blanc de Blancs Champagne 1982 $39 (5/31/87)
90   POL ROGER Brut Blanc de Blancs Champagne Blanc de Chardonnay 1982 $50 (12/31/88)
90   DOM RUINART Brut Blanc de Blancs Champagne 1982 $61 (12/31/90)
90   SALON Brut Blanc de Blancs Champagne Le Mesnil 1982 $119 (12/31/90)
89   SALON Brut Blanc de Blancs Champagne Le Mesnil 1982 $119 (12/31/89)
87   A. CHARBAUT Brut Blanc de Blancs Champagne Certificate 1982 Rel: $82 Cur: $82 (12/31/89)
86   BILLECART-SALMON Brut Blanc de Blancs Champagne 1982 $43 (5/31/87)
86   GEORGE GOULET Blanc de Blancs Champagne Crémant 1982 $30 (7/31/88)
85   AYALA Brut Blanc de Blancs Champagne 1982 $29 (4/15/88)
85   BEAUMET Brut Blanc de Blancs Champagne Cuvée Malakoff 1982 $41 (4/15/90)
85   R & L LEGRAS Brut Blanc de Blancs Champagne Présidence 1982 $29 (5/31/87)
84   DELAMOTTE Blanc de Blancs Champagne 1982 $28 (4/15/88)
84   KRUG Brut Blanc de Blancs Champagne Clos du Mesnil 1982 Rel: $120 Cur: $195 (12/31/90)
77   H. GERMAINE Blanc de Blancs Crémant Champagne 1982 $53 (5/31/87)

1981

93 TAITTINGER Brut Blanc de Blancs Champagne Comtes de Champagne 1981 Rel: $69 Cur: $72 (4/15/88)
90 DOM RUINART Brut Blanc de Blancs Champagne 1981 Rel: $61 Cur: $67 (12/31/89)
87 KRUG Brut Blanc de Blancs Champagne Clos du Mesnil 1981 Rel: $120 Cur: $162 (12/31/90)
87 KRUG Brut Blanc de Blancs Champagne Clos du Mesnil 1981 Rel: $120 Cur: $162 (12/31/89)
84 DE CASTELLANE Brut Blanc de Blancs Champagne 1981 $33 (4/15/88)
78 CHARLES HEIDSIECK Brut Blanc de Blancs Champagne Brut de Chardonnay 1981 $30 (5/31/87)

1980

92 PHILIPPONNAT Brut Blanc de Blancs Champagne 1980 $26 (5/31/87)
91 DE CASTELLANE Brut Blanc de Blancs Champagne 1980 $22 (5/31/87)
89 PHILIPPONNAT Brut Blanc de Blancs Champagne Cuvée Première 1980 $39 (12/31/88)
80 KRUG Brut Blanc de Blancs Champagne Clos du Mesnil 1980 Rel: $100 Cur: $160 (5/31/87)

1979

96 A. CHARBAUT Brut Blanc de Blancs Champagne 1979 $34 (5/31/87)
94 LOUIS ROEDERER Brut Blanc de Blancs Champagne 1979 $39 (5/31/87)
93 SALON Brut Blanc de Blancs Champagne Le Mesnil 1979 Disgorged Summer 1988 $119 (12/31/89)
92 A. CHARBAUT Brut Blanc de Blancs Champagne Certificate 1979 Rel: $80 Cur: $80 (7/15/88)
92 SALON Brut Blanc de Blancs Champagne Le Mesnil 1979 $119 (12/31/88)
92 TAITTINGER Brut Blanc de Blancs Champagne Comtes de Champagne 1979 Rel: $65 Cur: $65 (5/31/87)
91 DOM RUINART Brut Blanc de Blancs Champagne 1979 Rel: $39 Cur: $52 (10/31/86)
89 BEAUMET Brut Blanc de Blancs Champagne Cuvée Malakoff 1979 $30 (5/31/87)
87 MARIE STUART Brut Blanc de Blancs Champagne 1979 $25 (12/31/87)
86 BONNAIRE Brut Blanc de Blancs Champagne Cramant 1979 $40 (5/31/87)
84 POL ROGER Brut Blanc de Blancs Champagne Blanc de Chardonnay 1979 $41 (12/31/90)
72 POL ROGER Brut Blanc de Blancs Champagne Blanc de Chardonnay 1979 $35 (5/31/87)

1978

87 DOM RUINART Brut Blanc de Blancs Champagne 1978 Rel: $40 Cur: $50 (5/16/86)

1976

97 A. CHARBAUT Brut Blanc de Blancs Champagne Certificate 1976 Rel: $63 Cur: $63 (2/01/86) SS
91 SALON Brut Blanc de Blancs Champagne Le Mesnil 1976 $225/1.5L (12/31/88)
89 SALON Brut Blanc de Blancs Champagne Le Mesnil 1976 Rel: $71 Cur: $105 (5/31/87)
87 A. CHARBAUT Brut Blanc de Blancs Champagne Certificate 1976 Rel: $63 Cur: $63 (5/31/87)
85 R & L LEGRAS Brut Blanc de Blancs Champagne Cuvée St.-Vincent 1976 $33 (5/31/87)
84 DOM RUINART Brut Blanc de Blancs Champagne 1976 Rel: $30 Cur: $45 (10/01/84)
83 TAITTINGER Brut Blanc de Blancs Champagne Comtes de Champagne 1976 Rel: $66 Cur: $126 (5/16/86)

1975

70 BRUNO PAILLARD Brut Blanc de Blancs Champagne 1975 $42 (5/31/87)

NV

92 GUY LARMANDIER Brut Blanc de Blancs Champagne Cramant NV $26.50 (5/31/87)
91 G.H. MUMM Brut Blanc de Blancs Champagne Mumm de Cramant NV $43 (12/31/90)
90 BONNAIRE Brut Blanc de Blancs Champagne Cramant NV $30 (12/31/89)
90 BONNAIRE Brut Blanc de Blancs Champagne Cramant NV $30 (5/31/87)
90 ELLNER Brut Blanc de Blancs Champagne NV $32 (7/31/89)
89 JACQUESSON Blanc de Blancs Champagne NV $40 (12/31/90)
89 LECHERE Brut Blanc de Blancs Champagne NV $25 (12/31/87)
88 JOSEPH PERRIER Brut Blanc de Blancs Champagne Cuvée Royale NV $37 (12/31/90)
88 BATISTE PERTOIS Brut Blanc de Blancs Champagne Cramant Cuvée de Réserve NV $24 (12/31/89)
86 BEAUMET Brut Blanc de Blancs Champagne NV $25 (5/31/87)
86 A. CHARBAUT Brut Blanc de Blancs Champagne NV $32 (12/31/88)
86 ANDRE DRAPPIER Brut Blanc de Blancs Champagne Signature NV $23 (2/01/86)
86 DUVAL-LEROY Brut Blanc de Blancs Champagne NV (NA) (12/31/90)
86 LECHERE Brut Blanc de Blancs Champagne Cuvée Orient Express NV $45 (12/31/90)
86 MARQUIS DE SADE Brut Blanc de Blancs Champagne Grand Cru NV $41 (12/31/90)
86 G.H. MUMM Brut Blanc de Blancs Champagne Mumm de Cramant NV $43 (1/31/89)
86 JOSEPH PERRIER Brut Blanc de Blancs Champagne Cuvée Royale NV $34 (5/31/87)
86 DE VENOGE Brut Blanc de Blancs Champagne NV $38 (12/31/89)
85 BEAUMET Brut Blanc de Blancs Champagne NV $30 (12/31/90)
85 BRICOUT Brut Blanc de Blancs Champagne NV $21 (12/31/87)
85 HENRIOT Brut Blanc de Blancs Champagne de Chardonnay NV (NA) (12/31/90)
85 JACQUART Brut Blanc de Blancs Champagne NV $25 (12/31/90)
85 JACQUESSON Blanc de Blancs Champagne NV $25 (5/31/87)
85 BRUNO PAILLARD Blanc de Blancs Crémant Champagne NV $36 (12/31/90)
85 MARIE STUART Brut NV $22 (12/31/87)
84 CHARLES HEIDSIECK Brut Blanc de Blancs Champagne NV (NA) (12/31/90)
83 A. CHARBAUT Brut Blanc de Blancs Champagne NV $40 (12/31/90)
81 DE CASTELLANE Brut Blanc de Blancs Champagne Brut Chardonnay NV $26 (12/31/90)
81 LECHERE Brut Blanc de Blancs Champagne Première Cru NV $30 (5/31/87)
80 JOSEPH PERRIER Brut Blanc de Blancs Champagne Cuvée Royale NV $31 (12/31/89)
79 DELAMOTTE Blanc de Blancs Champagne NV $24 (12/31/87)
77 JEAN-MARIE Brut Blanc de Blancs Champagne NV (NA) (12/31/90)
76 ANDRE DRAPPIER Brut Blanc de Blancs Champagne NV $30 (5/31/87)
75 R & L LEGRAS Brut Blanc de Blancs Champagne NV $24 (5/31/87)
75 BRUNO PAILLARD Blanc de Blancs Crémant Champagne NV $25 (5/31/87)
74 BEAUMET Brut Blanc de Blancs Champagne NV $25 (12/31/88)
74 GEORGE GOULET Brut Blanc de Blancs Champagne Cuvée G NV $26 (7/31/88)
74 OUDINOT Brut Blanc de Blancs Champagne NV $25 (12/31/90)
85 BARANCOURT Brut Blanc de Blancs Champagne Cramant Grand Cru NV $30 (12/31/90)
71 BARANCOURT Brut Blanc de Blancs Champagne Cramant NV $20 (5/31/87)
65 BRICOUT Brut Blanc de Blancs Champagne NV $21 (12/31/86)

BRUT

1986

87 MOET & CHANDON Brut Champagne Impérial 1986 Rel: $40 Cur: $40 (12/31/90)

1985

96 BOLLINGER Brut Champagne Grand Année 1985 $45 (12/31/90)

94 A. CHARBAUT Brut Champagne 1985 $49 (12/31/90)
93 CHARLES HEIDSIECK Brut Champagne 1985 $50 (12/31/90)
93 LANSON Brut Champagne 1985 $37 (12/31/90)
91 VEUVE CLICQUOT Brut Champagne La Grande Dame 1985 Rel: $72 Cur: $82 (12/31/90)
90 BARANCOURT Champagne Cuvée de Fondateurs 1985 (NA) (12/31/90)
90 HEIDSIECK MONOPOLE Brut Champagne Dry Monopole 1985 (NA) (12/31/90)
90 OUDINOT Brut Champagne 1985 $28 (12/31/90)
90 BRUNO PAILLARD Brut Champagne 1985 $40 (12/31/90)
89 AYALA Brut Champagne 1985 $57 (12/31/90)
89 GOSSET Brut Champagne Grande Millésime 1985 $72 (4/30/91)
89 TAITTINGER Brut Champagne 1985 (NA) (12/31/90)
88 MARQUIS DE SADE Brut Champagne Private Reserve 1985 $50 (12/31/90)
88 PIPER-HEIDSIECK Brut Champagne 1985 (NA) (12/31/90)
87 LAURENT-PERRIER Brut Champagne 1985 $40 (12/31/90)
87 MOET & CHANDON Brut Champagne Impérial 1985 Rel: $57 Cur: $127 (12/31/90)
87 POMMERY Brut Champagne 1985 $40 (12/31/90)
86 DEUTZ Brut Champagne George Mathieu Réserve 1985 $46 (12/31/90)
86 MOET & CHANDON Brut Champagne Impérial 1985 Rel: $57 Cur: $127 (12/31/89)
86 G.H. MUMM Brut Champagne Cordon Rouge 1985 $34 (12/31/90)
86 G.H. MUMM Brut Champagne René Lalou 1985 $58 (12/31/90)
86 PERRIER-JOUET Brut Champagne Fleur de Champagne 1985 $75 (12/31/90)
86 POL ROGER Brut Champagne Réserve 1985 $35 (12/31/90)
86 DE VENOGE Brut Champagne 1985 $38 (12/31/90)
85 BRICOUT Brut Champagne Elegance de Bricout 1985 (NA) (12/31/90)
85 GOSSET Brut Champagne Grande Millésime 1985 Rel: $72 Cur: $90 (12/31/90)
85 PHILIPPONNAT Brut Champagne Clos des Goisses 1985 (NA) (12/31/90)
85 LOUIS ROEDERER Brut Champagne 1985 $50 (12/31/90)
84 AYALA Brut Champagne Grand Cuvée 1985 $57 (12/31/89)
84 DE CASTELLANE Brut Champagne 1985 $27 (12/31/90)
84 DUVAL-LEROY Champagne Cuvée des Roys 1985 (NA) (12/31/90)
84 JACQUESSON Brut Champagne Perfection 1985 (NA) (12/31/90)
83 DEUTZ Brut Champagne 1985 $40 (12/31/90)
82 JOSEPH PERRIER Brut Champagne 1985 $37 (12/31/90)
82 JOSEPH PERRIER Brut Champagne Cuvée Royale 1985 $37 (12/31/90)
81 BRICOUT Brut Champagne 1985 (NA) (12/31/90)
80 PIPER-HEIDSIECK Champagne Rare 1985 (NA) (12/31/90)
75 JEAN-MARIE Brut Champagne 1985 (NA) (12/31/90)

1983

92 VEUVE CLICQUOT Brut Champagne La Grande Dame 1983 Rel: $79 Cur: $79 (12/31/89)
90 BRICOUT Brut Champagne Carte d'Or Prestige 1983 $25 (12/31/88)
90 VEUVE CLICQUOT Brut Champagne Gold Label 1983 $42 (12/31/90)
90 CHARLES HEIDSIECK Brut Champagne 1983 $41 (3/31/91)
90 LOUIS ROEDERER Brut Champagne Cristal 1983 Rel: $120 Cur: $120 (12/31/88)
89 BILLECART-SALMON Brut Champagne 1983 $47 (12/31/89)
89 COMTE AUDOIN DE DAMPIERRE Brut Champagne Grande Année 1983 $32 (12/31/90)
89 TAITTINGER Brut Champagne Collection Vieira da Silva 1983 Rel: $95 Cur: $95 (12/31/89)
88 JACQUART Brut Champagne 1983 $43 (4/15/90)
88 PERRIER-JOUET Brut Champagne Fleur de Champagne 1983 $65 (12/31/89)
88 LOUIS ROEDERER Brut Champagne Cristal 1983 Rel: $120 Cur: $120 (12/31/89)
87 BOLLINGER Brut Champagne Grand Année 1983 $43 (12/31/88)
87 CHARLES HEIDSIECK Brut Champagne Millésime 1983 $38 (12/31/89)
86 BOLLINGER Brut Champagne Grand Année 1983 $43 (12/31/89)
86 VEUVE CLICQUOT Brut Champagne La Grande Dame 1983 Rel: $79 Cur: $79 (7/31/89)
85 LANSON Brut Champagne 1983 $30 (12/31/90)
84 TAITTINGER Brut Champagne 1983 Rel: $35 Cur: $37 (12/31/89)
83 LECLERC-BRIANT Brut Champagne Spécial Club 1983 $35 (12/31/89)
83 MOET & CHANDON Brut Champagne Impérial 1983 Rel: $40 Cur: $43 (12/31/88)
80 AYALA Brut Champagne 1983 $30 (12/31/89)
80 CANARD-DUCHENE Brut Champagne Patrimoine 1983 $42 (12/31/89)
78 BRICOUT Brut Champagne Carte d'Or Prestige 1983 $25 (12/31/87)
75 BRICOUT Brut Champagne Carte d'Or Prestige 1983 $25 (12/31/89)
69 MOET & CHANDON Brut Champagne Impérial 1983 Rel: $40 Cur: $43 (12/31/89)

1982

93 BOLLINGER Brut Champagne Grand Année 1982 $30 (7/15/88)
93 VEUVE CLICQUOT Brut Champagne 1982 Rel: $32 Cur: $41 (5/31/87) SS
93 CHARLES HEIDSIECK Brut Champagne 1982 $33 (12/31/88) SS
93 LAURENT-PERRIER Brut Champagne 1982 $36 (12/31/88)
93 DOM PERIGNON Brut Champagne 1982 Rel: $75 Cur: $84 (10/15/88)
93 JOSEPH PERRIER Brut Champagne Cuvée Josephine 1982 $100 (12/31/88)
93 POMMERY Brut Champagne 1982 $24 (2/15/88)
93 LOUIS ROEDERER Brut Champagne 1982 $45 (12/31/88)
92 KRUG Brut Champagne 1982 Rel: $135 Cur: $135 (12/31/89)
92 LANSON Brut Champagne 1982 $27 (10/15/88)
92 LAURENT-PERRIER Brut Champagne Cuvée Grand Siècle 1982 $70 (12/31/88)
92 LOUIS ROEDERER Brut Champagne Cristal 1982 Rel: $106 Cur: $119 (9/30/87)
92 POL ROGER Brut Champagne Cuvée Sir Winston Churchill 1982 $63 (4/15/90)
91 ELLNER Brut Champagne 1982 $38 (7/31/89)
90 HENRI ABELE Brut Champagne Grande Marque Impériale 1982 $29 (7/31/87)
90 BRICOUT Brut Champagne Elegance de Bricout 1982 $50 (12/31/88)
90 DEUTZ Brut Champagne Cuvée William Deutz 1982 Rel: $61 Cur: $72 (12/31/88)
90 GOSSET Brut Champagne Grande Millésime 1982 $60 (12/31/90)
90 GEORGE GOULET Brut Champagne 1982 $30 (7/31/88)
90 HEIDSIECK MONOPOLE Brut Champagne Diamant Rosé 1982 Rel: $55 Cur: $55 (11/30/87)
90 JACQUART Brut Champagne 1982 $39 (12/31/88)
90 JACQUART Brut Champagne La Cuvée Renommée 1982 $64 (12/31/88)
90 G.H. MUMM Brut Champagne René Lalou 1982 Rel: $55 Cur: $61 (9/30/88)
90 TAITTINGER Brut Champagne Collection Masson 1982 Rel: $96 Cur: $96 (12/31/88)
89 PAUL BARA Brut Champagne 1982 $34 (12/31/88)
89 DEUTZ Brut Champagne George Mathieu 1982 $40 (12/31/89)
89 HEIDSIECK MONOPOLE Brut Champagne Diamant Bleu 1982 Rel: $40 Cur: $62 (11/30/87)
89 JOSEPH PERRIER Brut Champagne Cuvée Royale 1982 $35 (12/31/90)
89 PIPER-HEIDSIECK Brut Champagne Sauvage 1982 $30 (12/31/89)
89 TAITTINGER Brut Champagne Millésime 1982 Rel: $38 Cur: $38 (12/31/88)
88 DE CASTELLANE Brut Champagne Cuvée Florens de Castellane 1982 $59 (12/31/90)
88 HEIDSIECK MONOPOLE Brut Champagne Dry Monopole 1982 $37.50 (12/31/88)
88 PERRIER-JOUET Brut Champagne Fleur de Champagne 1982 $65 (12/31/88)
87 AYALA Brut Champagne Grand Cuvée 1982 $52 (4/15/88)
87 DEUTZ Brut Champagne Cuvée Georges Mathieu 1982 $34 (10/15/88)

FRANCE
CHAMPAGNE/BRUT

87   GEORGE GOULET Brut Champagne Cuvée du Centenaire 1982 $47 (7/31/88)
86   AYALA Brut Champagne 1982 $27 (4/15/88)
86   PIPER-HEIDSIECK Brut Champagne 1982 $32 (12/31/88)
85   VEUVE CLICQUOT Brut Champagne Gold Label 1982 $37 (12/31/88)
85   DEUTZ Brut Champagne Cuvée William Deutz 1982 Rel: $61 Cur: $72 (12/31/89)
85   GOSSET Brut Champagne Grande Millésime 1982 Rel: $60 Cur: $64 (12/31/88)
85   G.H. MUMM Brut Champagne Cordon Rouge 1982 $37 (12/31/88)
84   MOET & CHANDON Brut Champagne Impérial 1982 Rel: $33 Cur: $39 (4/15/88)
84   PHILIPPONNAT Brut Champagne Clos des Goisses 1982 $89 (12/31/88)
84   PHILIPPONNAT Brut Champagne Grand Blanc 1982 $38 (12/31/88)
82   JOSEPH PERRIER Brut Champagne Cuvée Josephine 1982 $100 (12/31/89)
82   POL ROGER Brut Champagne Extra Cuvée de Réserve 1982 $30 (12/31/90)

1981

92   TAITTINGER Brut Champagne Collection Arman 1981 Rel: $80 Cur: $85 (5/31/87) CS
91   KRUG Brut Champagne 1981 Rel: $85 Cur: $102 (12/31/88)
91   LOUIS ROEDERER Brut Champagne Cristal 1981 Rel: $85 Cur: $100 (5/16/86)
89   LANSON Champagne 225th Anniversary Cuvée 1981 $43 (10/15/88)
89   MARQUIS DE SADE Brut Champagne Private Reserve 1981 $56 (12/31/90)
87   DE CASTELLANE Champagne Cuvée Commodore 1981 $50 (4/15/88)

1980

95   LANSON Champagne 225th Anniversary Spécial Cuvée 1980 $43 (11/30/86)
94   DOM PERIGNON Brut Champagne 1980 Rel: $60 Cur: $94 (9/15/86) SS
91   MOET & CHANDON Brut Champagne Impérial 1980 Rel: $30 Cur: $58 (3/16/85)

1979

96   VEUVE CLICQUOT Brut Champagne La Grande Dame 1979 Rel: $61 Cur: $74 (5/16/86)
96   GOSSET Brut Champagne Grande Millésime 1979 Rel: $45 Cur: $84 (7/15/87)
95   G.H. MUMM Brut Champagne René Lalou 1979 Rel: $56 Cur: $68 (5/16/86)
94   BOLLINGER Brut Champagne Extra RD 1979 Rel: $79 Cur: $87 (12/31/89)
93   HEIDSIECK MONOPOLE Brut Champagne Diamant Bleu 1979 Rel: $39 Cur: $39 (5/16/86)
93   JACQUESSON Brut Champagne Signature 1979 $34 (7/31/87)
93   G.H. MUMM Brut Champagne Cordon Rouge 1979 $24 (2/16/86)
93   PERRIER-JOUET Brut Champagne Fleur de Champagne 1979 $50 (2/01/86)
92   ALFRED GRATIEN Brut Champagne 1979 $28 (9/16/85)
90   DEUTZ Brut Champagne Cuvée William Deutz 1979 Rel: $35 Cur: $47 (7/16/85)
90   LAURENT-PERRIER Brut Champagne Cuvée Grand Siècle 1979 $45 (2/15/88)
90   POL ROGER Brut Champagne 1979 $23 (9/01/85)
89   PIPER-HEIDSIECK Champagne Rare 1979 $65 (3/15/87)
88   VEUVE CLICQUOT Brut Champagne 1979 Rel: $50 Cur: $75 (12/16/85)
87   JOSEPH PERRIER Brut Champagne 1979 $22 (10/01/85)
85   LECLERC-BRIANT Brut Champagne 1979 $31 (3/15/88)
74   A. CHARBAUT Brut Champagne 1979 $23 (2/01/86)

1978

88   DOM PERIGNON Brut Champagne 1978 Rel: $61 Cur: $120 (5/16/86)

1976

93   KRUG Brut Champagne 1976 Rel: $70 Cur: $123 (5/16/86)
88   BOLLINGER Brut Champagne Extra RD 1976 Rel: $59 Cur: $73 (4/15/88)
88   PIPER-HEIDSIECK Champagne Rare 1976 $66 (8/01/85)

1975

89   BOLLINGER Brut Champagne Extra RD 1975 Rel: $64 Cur: $93 (5/16/86)

1955

90   PERRIER-JOUET Brut Champagne 1955 (NA)/1.5L (10/15/87) (JS)

1947

85   PERRIER-JOUET Brut Champagne 1947 (NA)/1.5L (10/15/87) (JS)

1928

97   PERRIER-JOUET Brut Champagne 1928 (NA) (10/15/87) (JS)

1914

55   PERRIER-JOUET Brut Champagne 1914 (NA) (10/15/87) (JS)

1911

95   PERRIER-JOUET Brut Champagne 1911 (NA) (10/15/87) (JS)

1900

97   PERRIER-JOUET Brut Champagne 1900 (NA) (10/15/87) (JS)

1893

80   PERRIER-JOUET Brut Champagne 1893 (NA) (10/15/87) (JS)

1825

95   PERRIER-JOUET Brut Champagne 1825 (NA) (10/15/87) (JS)

NV

94   KRUG Brut Champagne Grande Cuvée NV $88 (12/31/87)
93   ALFRED GRATIEN Brut Champagne NV $23 (11/01/85)
92   BOLLINGER Brut Champagne Spécial Cuvée NV $25 (12/31/87) SS

Key to Symbols

The scores reported here are the results of blind tastings conducted by our panel of senior editors. Wines that carry the initials below are results of individual tastings.

THE WINE SPECTATOR 100-POINT SCALE 95-100—Classic, a great wine; 90-94—Outstanding, superior character and style; 80-89—Good to very good, a wine with special qualities; 70-79—Average, drinkable wine that may have minor flaws; 60-69—Below average, drinkable but not recommended; 50-59—Poor, undrinkable, not recommended. "+"—With a score indicates a range; used primarily with barrel tastings to indicate a preliminary score.

SPECIAL DESIGNATIONS SS—Spectator Selection, CS—Cellar Selection, BB—Best Buy.

TASTER'S INITIALS (JG)—Jim Gordon, (HS)—Harvey Steiman, (JL)—James Laube, (JS)—James Suckling, (TM)—Thomas Matthews, (TR)—Terry Robards, (BT)—Barrel Tasting (these wines were tasted blind from barrel samples), (CA-date)—California's Great Cabernets by James Laube, (CH-date)—California's Great Chardonnays by James Laube, (VP-date)—Vintage Port by James Suckling.

DATE TASTED Dates in parentheses represent the issue in which the rating was published.

92   GOSSET Brut Champagne Grande Réserve NV $39 (12/31/87)
92   LANSON Brut Champagne Black Label Cuvée NV $29 (1/31/87)
92   JOSEPH PERRIER Brut Champagne NV $19 (11/16/85)
92   POL ROGER Brut Champagne Réserve NV $30 (12/31/88)
91   BILLECART-SALMON Brut Champagne NV $30 (12/31/87)
91   VEUVE CLICQUOT Brut Champagne NV $27 (12/31/87)
91   KRUG Brut Champagne Grande Cuvée NV $88 (12/31/89)
91   PERRIER-JOUET Brut Champagne Grand Brut NV $25 (12/31/87)
91   TAILLEVENT Brut Champagne Grande Réserve NV $23 (12/31/89)
90   GOSSET Brut Champagne Grande Réserve NV $39 (12/31/90)
90   GOSSET Brut Champagne Réserve NV $34 (12/31/90)
90   LAURENT-PERRIER Brut Champagne NV $23 (12/31/87)
90   JOSEPH PERRIER Brut Champagne Cuvée Royale NV $30 (1/31/89)
89   CANARD-DUCHENE Brut Champagne Patrimoine NV $35 (12/31/89)
89   CATTIER Brut Champagne Clos du Moulin NV $37 (12/31/89)
89   DEUTZ Brut Champagne 150 Anniversaire NV $50 (12/31/88)
89   DEUTZ Brut Champagne Cuvée Lallier Gold Lack NV $25 (12/31/88)
89   PIPER-HEIDSIECK Brut Champagne Cuvée NV $22 (12/31/89)
89   POL ROGER Brut Champagne NV $24 (12/31/87)
89   TAITTINGER Brut Champagne NV $26 (12/31/87)
88   JACQUESSON Brut Champagne Perfection NV $24 (12/31/88)
88   LANSON Brut Champagne Black Label Cuvée NV $29 (12/31/88)
88   JOSEPH PERRIER Brut Champagne Cuvée Royale NV $30 (12/31/90)
87   ELLNER Brut Champagne Réserve NV $30 (7/31/89)
86   SERGE FAUST Brut Champagne Cuvée de Réserve à Vandières NV $33 (12/31/90)
86   HEIDSIECK MONOPOLE Brut Champagne Dry Monopole NV $35 (12/31/88)
86   HENRIOT Brut Champagne NV $21 (7/01/86)
85   CANARD-DUCHENE Brut Champagne Cuvée Bicentenaire NV $39 (12/31/89)
85   CANARD-DUCHENE Brut Champagne Cuvée Spéciale de Charles VII NV $75 (12/31/89)
85   CHARLES HEIDSIECK Brut Champagne Réserve NV $25 (12/31/88)
85   LAURENT-PERRIER Brut Champagne L.P. NV $15 (12/31/90)
85   TAITTINGER Brut Champagne La Française NV $27 (12/31/89)
84   BEAUMET Brut Champagne NV $22 (12/31/89)
84   MOET & CHANDON Brut Champagne Impérial NV Rel: $25.50 Cur: $26 (5/16/86)
84   PERRIER-JOUET Brut Champagne Grand Brut NV $22 (12/31/89)
84   MARIE STUART Brut Champagne Cuvée de la Reine NV $26 (12/31/87)
83   AYALA Brut Champagne NV $23 (4/15/88)
83   GEORGE GOULET Brut Champagne NV $21 (7/31/88)
83   JACQUART Brut Champagne NV $24 (12/31/88)
83   JOSEPH PERRIER Brut Champagne Cuvée Royale NV $30 (4/15/90)
83   TAITTINGER Brut Champagne La Française NV $27 (7/15/88)
82   BRICOUT Brut Champagne Carte Noire Réserve NV $20 (12/31/88)
82   CATTIER Brut Champagne NV $17 (12/31/89)
82   PHILIPPONNAT Brut Champagne Royale Réserve NV $24 (12/31/88)
82   LOUIS ROEDERER Brut Champagne NV $25 (5/16/86)
82   MARIE STUART Brut Champagne NV $22 (12/31/87)
81   DEUTZ Brut Champagne NV $28 (12/31/89)
81   G.H. MUMM Brut Champagne Cordon Rouge NV $25 (12/31/87)
80   DE CASTELLANE Brut Champagne NV $24 (4/15/88)
80   DEUTZ Brut Champagne Cuvée Lallier Gold Lack NV $33 (12/31/90)
80   LECLERC-BRIANT Brut Champagne Réserve NV $23 (3/15/88)
79   HENRI ABELE Brut Champagne Le Sourire de Reims NV $24 (7/31/87)
79   BRICOUT Brut Champagne Carte Noire Réserve NV $20 (7/31/87)
79   LANSON Brut Champagne Black Label NV $21 (12/31/88)
79   POMMERY Brut Champagne NV $23 (12/31/87)
78   AYALA Brut Champagne Extra Quality NV $28 (12/31/87)
78   DELAMOTTE Brut Champagne NV $20 (12/31/87)
78   GOSSET Brut Champagne Réserve NV $34 (12/31/88)
78   PIPER-HEIDSIECK Brut Champagne Extra NV $26 (12/31/87)
78   POMMERY Brut Champagne NV $23 (5/16/86)
78   LOUIS ROEDERER Brut Champagne Premier NV $27 (12/31/87)
78   JULIEN TARIN Brut Champagne NV $25 (2/15/87)
77   A. CHARBAUT Brut Champagne NV $24 (12/31/88)
73   NICHOLAS FEUILLATTE Brut Champagne Réserve Particulière NV $17 (12/31/87)
73   LAURENT-PERRIER Brut Champagne Ultra Cuvée Sans Dosage NV $27 (1/31/88)
73   TAITTINGER Brut Champagne Réserve NV $24 (5/16/86)
70   HENRIOT Brut Champagne Cuvée du Soleil NV $27 (12/31/87)
69   BRICOUT Brut Champagne Carte d'Or Prestige NV $19 (12/31/86)

ROSÉ

1985

88   DEUTZ Brut Rosé Champagne 1985 $46 (12/31/90)
88   DEUTZ Brut Rosé Champagne 1985 $46 (12/31/89)
88   PERRIER-JOUET Brut Rosé Champagne Fleur de Champagne 1985 Rel: $70 Cur: $79 (12/31/89)
87   G.H. MUMM Brut Rosé Champagne Cordon Rosé 1985 $35 (12/31/89)

1983

90   BEAUMET Brut Rosé Champagne 1983 $30 (12/31/89)
89   BOLLINGER Brut Rosé Champagne Grand Année 1983 $50 (12/31/89)
89   CHARLES HEIDSIECK Brut Rosé Champagne 1983 $49 (3/31/91)
88   MOET & CHANDON Brut Rosé Champagne Impérial 1983 Rel: $40 Cur: $43 (12/31/89)
88   OUDINOT Brut Rosé Champagne 1983 $25 (12/31/89)
86   VEUVE CLICQUOT Brut Rosé Champagne 1983 $47 (12/31/89)
86   G.H. MUMM Brut Rosé Champagne Cordon Rosé 1983 $30 (7/31/89)
84   BOLLINGER Brut Rosé Champagne Grand Année 1983 $50 (12/31/88)
81   G.H. MUMM Brut Rosé Champagne Cordon Rosé 1983 $30 (12/31/89)
75   HEIDSIECK MONOPOLE Brut Rosé Champagne 1983 $40 (12/31/89)

1982

92   TAITTINGER Brut Rosé Champagne Comtes de Champagne 1982 Rel: $100 Cur: $100 (12/31/89)
91   CHARLES HEIDSIECK Brut Rosé Champagne 1982 $40 (12/31/88)
91   LAURENT-PERRIER Brut Rosé Champagne Grand Siècle Cuvée Alexandra 1982 $125 (12/31/89)
90   MOET & CHANDON Brut Rosé Champagne Impérial 1982 $36 (4/15/88)
89   PERRIER-JOUET Brut Rosé Champagne Fleur de Champagne 1982 Rel: $57 Cur: $64 (11/15/87)
88   A. CHARBAUT Brut Rosé Champagne Certificate 1982 $82 (12/31/89)

88 GOSSET Brut Rosé Champagne 1982 $75 (12/31/88)
88 JACQUART Brut Rosé Champagne La Cuvée Renommée 1982 $74 (12/31/88)
88 LANSON Brut Rosé Champagne 1982 $35 (12/31/88)
86 DEUTZ Brut Rosé Champagne 1982 $35 (12/31/87)
85 GEORGE GOULET Brut Rosé Champagne 1982 $31 (7/15/88)
84 HEIDSIECK MONOPOLE Brut Rosé Champagne 1982 $43 (12/31/88)
84 PIPER-HEIDSIECK Brut Rosé Champagne 1982 $38 (12/31/88)
83 G.H. MUMM Brut Rosé Champagne Cordon Rosé 1982 (12/31/88)
80 BOLLINGER Brut Rosé Champagne Grand Année 1982 $35 (7/15/88)
80 POL ROGER Rosé Champagne 1982 $34 (12/31/88)

1981

93 HENRIOT Brut Rosé Champagne 1981 $28 (7/01/86)
72 ANDRE DRAPPIER Brut Rosé Champagne Val des Demoiselles 1981 $23 (12/16/85)
67 DEUTZ Brut Rosé Champagne 1981 $27 (12/16/85)

1979

94 BOLLINGER Brut Rosé Champagne Grand Année 1979 $40 (12/16/85)
92 DOM RUINART Brut Rosé Champagne 1979 Rel: $55 Cur: $55 (9/30/88)
89 A. CHARBAUT Brut Rosé Champagne Certificate 1979 $80 (7/15/88)
89 VEUVE CLICQUOT Brut Rosé Champagne 1979 $35 (7/16/86)
88 POL ROGER Rosé Champagne 1979 $28 (12/16/85)
79 BEAUMET Brut Rosé Champagne 1979 $16.50 (12/16/85)
72 HEIDSIECK MONOPOLE Brut Rosé Champagne 1979 $27 (12/16/85)
69 LOUIS ROEDERER Brut Rosé Champagne Cristal 1979 $87 (12/16/85)

1978

91 DOM RUINART Brut Rosé Champagne 1978 Rel: $40 Cur: $40 (9/30/86)
90 DOM PERIGNON Brut Rosé Champagne 1978 Rel: $89 Cur: $199 (10/15/86)
90 PERRIER-JOUET Brut Rosé Champagne Fleur de Champagne 1978 Rel: $55 Cur: $55 (12/16/85)
82 VEUVE CLICQUOT Brut Rosé Champagne 1978 $60 (12/16/85)
70 MOET & CHANDON Brut Rosé Champagne Impérial 1978 $55 (12/16/85)

1976

90 TAITTINGER Brut Rosé Champagne Comtes de Champagne 1976 Rel: $70 Cur: $85 (12/16/85)
61 CHARLES HEIDSIECK Brut Rosé Champagne 1976 $25 (12/16/85)
61 DOM RUINART Brut Rosé Champagne 1976 Rel: $35 Cur: $60 (12/16/85)

1975

93 DOM PERIGNON Brut Rosé Champagne 1975 Rel: $85 Cur: $85 (12/16/85)
67 POL ROGER Rosé Champagne 1975 $33 (12/16/85)

NV

96 KRUG Brut Rosé Champagne NV $115 (12/16/85)
95 GOSSET Brut Rosé Champagne NV $37 (12/16/85)
93 KRUG Brut Rosé Champagne NV $115 (12/31/89)
92 LAURENT-PERRIER Brut Rosé Champagne Cuvée NV $28 (3/15/88)
91 DELAMOTTE Rosé Champagne Spécial NV $28 (12/31/87)
90 BRICOUT Brut Rosé Champagne NV $28 (12/31/88)
90 JACQUART Brut Rosé Champagne NV $38 (12/31/88)
89 DE CASTELLANE Brut Rosé Champagne NV $31 (4/15/88)
89 DIEBOLT-VALLOIS Brut Rosé Champagne Cramant NV $21 (10/31/87)
89 MICHEL GONET Brut Rosé Champagne NV $21 (12/16/85)
89 PHILIPPONNAT Brut Rosé Champagne Royale Réserve NV $38 (12/31/88)
88 DE CASTELLANE Brut Rosé Champagne NV $31 (12/31/90)
88 DE VENOGE Rosé Champagne Crémant NV $26 (12/31/88)
86 A. CHARBAUT Brut Rosé Champagne NV $32 (12/31/88)
86 JOSEPH PERRIER Brut Rosé Champagne Cuvée Royale NV $40 (12/31/90)
86 POMMERY Brut Rosé Champagne NV $27 (12/16/85)
85 AYALA Brut Rosé Champagne NV $26 (4/15/88)
85 GOSSET Brut Rosé Champagne NV $37 (12/31/90)
85 JOSEPH PERRIER Brut Rosé Champagne Cuvée Royale NV $40 (12/31/89)
84 JACQUESSON Brut Rosé Champagne Perfection NV $27 (12/31/88)
84 GUY LARMANDIER Brut Rosé Champagne NV $20 (12/31/89)
84 LECLERC-BRIANT Brut Rosé Champagne NV $28 (3/15/88)
82 TAILLEVENT Brut Rosé Champagne Phantom of the Opera NV $32 (12/31/89)
81 BRICOUT Brut Rosé Champagne NV $28 (12/31/87)
81 ALFRED GRATIEN Rosé Champagne NV $24 (10/01/85)
80 AYALA Brut Rosé Champagne Extra Quality NV $20 (5/31/87)
80 BILLECART-SALMON Brut Rosé Champagne NV $28 (12/16/85)
80 MARIE STUART Brut Rosé Champagne NV $23 (12/31/87)
79 LOUIS ROEDERER Brut Rosé Champagne NV $37 (12/16/85)
77 HENRI ABELE Brut Rosé Champagne NV $29 (7/31/87)
73 LANSON Brut Rosé Champagne NV $24 (12/31/86)
72 PHILIPPONNAT Brut Rosé Champagne NV $26 (12/16/85)
53 GEORGES VESSELLE Brut Rosé Champagne de Noirs NV $30 (12/16/85)

OTHER CHAMPAGNE

1985

90 BEAUMET Brut Blanc de Noirs Champagne 1985 $30 (12/31/90)

1983

89 BEAUMET Brut Blanc de Noirs Champagne 1983 $30 (12/31/89)

NV

90 G.H. MUMM Extra Dry Champagne NV $26 (1/31/89)
89 JACQUART Extra Dry Champagne NV $23 (12/31/88)
87 A. CHARBAUT Extra Dry Champagne NV $22 (12/31/88)
86 HEIDSIECK MONOPOLE Extra Dry Champagne NV $35 (12/31/88)
86 LANSON Extra Dry Champagne Ivory Label NV $19 (12/31/88)
85 G.H. MUMM Extra Dry Champagne Cordon Vert NV $23 (4/15/90)
74 MARIE STUART Extra Dry Champagne NV $19 (12/31/87)
70 LANSON Extra Dry Champagne White Label NV $19 (12/31/88)

LOIRE RED

1987

86 DOMAINE DESSERRE Chinon 1987 $9 (12/31/88)
85 DOMAINE HENRY PELLE Menetou-Salon Morogues 1987 $11 (7/15/89)
82 GILBERT DELAGOUTTIERE St.-Nicolas de Bourgueil 1987 $9 (12/31/88)

1986

89 CHARLES JOGUET Chinon Cuvée du Clos de la Dioterie 1986 $21 (12/31/88)
86 CLOS DE L'ABBAYE Bourgueil 1986 $16 (8/31/89)
82 CHARLES JOGUET Chinon Cuvée des Varennes du Grand Clos 1986 $15 (4/30/88)
79 HAUT POITOU Haut Poitou Cabernet 1986 $6 (10/31/88)
78 DOMAINE MORIN HER Chinon 1986 $7.50 (12/31/88)
72 COULY-DUTHEIL Chinon Les Gravières d'Amador Abbe de Turpennay 1986 $10 (4/30/88)

1985

87 COULY-DUTHEIL Saumur Champigny La Vigneronne 1985 $10 (2/15/87)
86 COULY-DUTHEIL Chinon Les Gravières d'Amador Abbe de Turpennay 1985 $9.25 (2/28/87)
83 PIERRE CHAINIER SELECTION Chinon 1985 $7.75 (9/30/88)
83 DOMAINE DU GRAND CLOS Bourgueil 1985 $9 (9/30/87)
78 PIERRE CHAINIER SELECTION Bourgueil 1985 $7.75 (9/30/88)
71 JOEL & CLARRISE TALUAU St.-Nicolas de Bourgueil 1985 $12 (4/15/88)

1981

86 COULY-DUTHEIL Chinon Domaine de Versailles 1981 $12.25 (3/15/87)

LOIRE WHITE/*MUSCADET DE SÈVRE & MAINE*

1990

84 CHATEAU DE LA RAGOTIERE Muscadet de Sèvre & Maine Sur Lie 1990 $14.50 (6/15/91)

1989

88 DOMAINE DE LA QUILLA Muscadet de Sèvre & Maine Sur Lie 1989 $7 (11/30/90) BB
74 DOMAINE DE L'ALOUETTE Muscadet de Sèvre & Maine Sur Lie 1989 $7 (11/30/90)

1988

85 LOUIS METAIREAU Muscadet de Sèvre & Maine Sur Lie Carte Noire 1988 $8 (11/30/90) BB
84 CLOS DE BEAUREGARD Muscadet de Sèvre & Maine Sur Lie 1988 $6.75 (4/15/90) BB
78 CHATEAU DE LA RAGOTIERE Muscadet de Sèvre & Maine Sur Lie 1988 $10 (4/15/90)
77 ANDRE-MICHEL BREGEON Muscadet de Sèvre & Maine Sur Lie 1988 $6.75 (11/15/90)

1987

81 LOUIS METAIREAU Muscadet de Sèvre & Maine Sur Lie Cuvée One 1987 $11 (7/15/89)
77 LES FRERES COUILLAUD Muscadet de Sèvre & Maine Château de la Ragotière Sur Lie 1987 $10 (7/15/89)

1986

82 DOMAINE DE LA POMMERAYE Muscadet de Sèvre & Maine Sur Lie 1986 $6 (12/31/88) BB
80 LOUIS METAIREAU Muscadet de Sèvre & Maine Sur Lie Carte Noire 1986 $8.75 (2/28/89)
78 LES FRERES COUILLAUD Muscadet de Sèvre & Maine Château de la Ragotière 1986 $9.75 (4/15/88)

1985

88 CHATEAU DE LA MERCREDIERE Muscadet de Sèvre & Maine Sur Lie 1985 $6 (9/30/86) BB
83 CLOS DES BOURGUIGNONS Muscadet de Sèvre & Maine Sur Lie 1985 $5 (6/15/87) BB
83 LOUIS METAIREAU Muscadet de Sèvre & Maine Sur Lie Carte Noire 1985 $8.25 (10/31/87)
76 CHATEAU DU CLERAY Muscadet de Sèvre & Maine Sur Lie 1985 $7 (5/15/87)
68 CHATEAU DE LA MOUCHETIERE Muscadet de Sèvre & Maine 1985 $5 (10/15/86)

1984

80 LOUIS METAIREAU Muscadet de Sèvre & Maine Grand Mouton Sur Lie 1984 $8.50 (11/15/87)

1983

89 LOUIS METAIREAU Muscadet de Sèvre & Maine Sur Lie Cuvée One 1983 $9.75 (5/01/84)
85 LOUIS METAIREAU Muscadet de Sèvre & Maine Sur Lie Carte Noire 1983 $6.50 (4/16/85) BB

POUILLY-FUMÉ

1989

90 DOMAINE J.-M. MASSON-BLONDELET Pouilly-Fumé Les Bascoins 1989 $20 (3/31/91)
87 JEAN-CLAUDE CHATELAIN Pouilly-Fumé Domaine des Chailloux 1989 $18 (3/31/91)
86 DE LADOUCETTE Pouilly-Fumé 1989 $22 (4/30/91)
85 DOMAINE DENIS GAUDRY Pouilly-Fumé Côteaux du Petit Boisgibault 1989 $15 (3/31/91)
84 DOMAINE J.-M. MASSON-BLONDELET Pouilly-Fumé Les Angelots 1989 $20 (3/31/91)

1988

88 PAUL FIGEAT Pouilly-Fumé 1988 $14 (4/15/90)
88 DE LADOUCETTE Pouilly-Fumé Baron de L 1988 $49 (5/31/91)
87 JEAN-CLAUDE CHATELAIN Pouilly-Fumé Domaine des Chailloux 1988 $17.50 (9/15/90)
84 JEAN-CLAUDE GUYOT Pouilly-Fumé Les Loges 1988 $11 (3/31/91)
82 DE LADOUCETTE Pouilly-Fumé La Ladoucette 1988 $18 (9/15/90)

1987

88 PASCAL JOLIVET Pouilly-Fumé Cuvée Pascal Jolivet 1987 $29 (9/15/90)
86 F. TINEL-BLONDELET Pouilly-Fumé L'Arret Buffatte 1987 $14.50 (2/28/89)
78 F. TINEL-BLONDELET Pouilly-Fumé 1987 $12.50 (2/28/89)

1986

77 DOMAINE DENIS GAUDRY Pouilly-Fumé Côteaux du Petit Boisgibault 1986 $14 (5/31/88)

1985

90 DE LADOUCETTE Pouilly-Fumé Baron de L 1985 $40 (7/15/89)

FRANCE
LOIRE WHITE/*POUILLY-FUMÉ*

1984
91   DE LADOUCETTE Pouilly-Fumé 1984 $10.50 (3/31/87)

1983
81   PHILIPPE CHASE Pouilly-Fumé 1983 $11.50 (10/15/86)

SANCERRE
1989
88   COMTE LAFOND Sancerre 1989 $21 (4/30/91)
86   CHERRIER PERE Sancerre Domaine des Chasseignes 1989 $16 (3/31/91)
86   PAUL COTAT Sancerre Chavignol La Grande Côte 1989 $25 (2/28/91)
85   PAUL COTAT Sancerre Chavignol Les Culs de Beaujeu 1989 $22 (2/28/91)
82   PAUL COTAT Sancerre Chavignol Réserve des Monts Damnés 1989 $19 (2/28/91)
82   JEAN PAUL PICARD Sancerre 1989 $14.50 (4/30/91)

1988
85   PAUL COTAT Sancerre Chavignol La Grande Côte 1988 $18 (4/15/90)
85   DOMAINE JEAN-MAX ROGER Sancerre Le Chêne Marchand 1988 $17.50 (9/15/90)
84   COMPTE LAFOND Sancerre Omina Pro Petri Sede 1988 $16 (11/15/90)
84   PASCAL JOLIVET Sancerre 1988 $15.50 (9/15/90)
82   PASCAL JOLIVET Sancerre Domaine du Colombier 1988 $18 (9/15/90)
77   PAUL COTAT Sancerre Chavignol Les Culs de Beaujeu 1988 $15 (4/15/90)
76   DOMAINE LAPORTE Sancerre Domaine du Rochoy 1988 $16 (4/15/90)
76   PROSPER MAUFOUX Sancerre 1988 $15 (4/15/90)
75   ETIENNE HENRI Sancerre 1988 $35 (2/28/91)

1987
88   HIPPOLYTE REVERDY Sancerre Les Perriers 1987 $13 (2/28/89)
85   DOMAINE LAPORTE Sancerre Domaine du Rochoy 1987 $13.50 (2/28/89)
68   DOMAINE ALPHONSE MELLOT Sancerre 1987 $16 (3/31/91)

1986
85   HIPPOLYTE REVERDY Sancerre Les Perriers 1986 $10 (12/15/87)
85   REVERDY-DUCROUX Sancerre Clos les Perriers 1986 $10 (2/15/88)
83   CHERRIER PERE Sancerre Domaine des Chasseignes 1986 $12.50 (5/31/88)
80   CHEVALIER DE BEAUBASSIN Sancerre 1986 $12.50 (5/31/88)
71   JEAN VATAN Sancerre Les Perriers 1986 $10 (2/15/88)

1985
91   PAUL COTAT Sancerre Chavignol La Grande Côte 1985 $13 (3/15/87)
89   PAUL COTAT Sancerre Chavignol Les Culs de Beaujeu 1985 $12.25 (2/15/87)
76   LA BOURGEOISE Sancerre Chavignol 1985 $13 (10/31/87)
76   DOMAINE DU NOZAY Sancerre 1985 $10.25 (6/15/87)
72   PAUL COTAT Sancerre Chavignol Réserve des Monts Damnes 1985 $13 (2/15/87)
71   MICHEL NATHAN Sancerre Domaine des Grandes Pierres 1985 $12.50 (9/30/87)

1984
83   LUCIEN CROCHET Sancerre Clos Chêne Marchand 1984 $11.25 (3/01/86)

1983
79   GITTON PERE Sancerre Les Romains 1983 $8 (3/01/86)
75   GITTON PERE Sancerre de la Vigne du Larrey 1983 $9.50 (3/01/86)

SAVENNIÈRES
1989
91   N. JOLY Savennières Clos de la Coulée de Serrant 1989 $33 (11/30/90)

1988
85   DOMAINE DES BAUMARD Savennières Clos du Papillon 1988 $9.50 (4/15/90)
78   DOMAINE DES BAUMARD Savennières 1988 $8.75 (4/15/90)

1987
86   A. JOLY Savennières Clos de la Coulée de Serrant 1987 $36 (2/15/89) (TM)

1986
87   A. JOLY Savennières Clos de la Coulée de Serrant 1986 $38 (7/15/89)
84   PIERRE & YVES SOULEZ Savennières Clos du Papillon 1986 $15 (2/28/89)
83   PIERRE & YVES SOULEZ Savennières Château de Chamboureau 1986 $12 (2/28/89)
77   PIERRE & YVES SOULEZ Savennières Roche aux Moines Château de Chamboureau 1986 $18.50 (2/28/89)

1985
80   PIERRE & YVES SOULEZ Savennières Clos du Papillon 1985 $12 (9/30/87)

1982
87   A. JOLY Savennières Clos de la Coulée de Serrant 1982 (NA) (2/15/89) (TM)

1976
93   A. JOLY Savennières Clos de la Coulée de Serrant 1976 (NA) (2/15/89) (TM)

OTHER LOIRE WHITE
1989
90   DOMAINE LE PEU DE LA MORIETTE Vouvray 1989 $12 (4/30/91)
88   DOMAINE DU CLOS NAUDIN Vouvray Demi-Sec 1989 $19.50 (3/31/91)
83   DOMAINE DU CLOS NAUDIN Vouvray Sec 1989 $17.50 (3/31/91)
77   ROBERT MICHELE Vouvray Les Trois Fils 1989 $9 (4/30/91)

1988
87   MARC BREDIF Vouvray 1988 $11 (4/30/91)
84   PIERRE & YVES SOULEZ Quarts de Chaume L'Amandier 1988 $28 (11/30/90)
82   DOMAINE DES BAUMARD Quarts de Chaume 1988 $20 (4/15/90)
81   DOMAINE DES BAUMARD Côteaux du Layon Clos de Ste.-Catherine 1988 $10.50 (4/15/90)

1987
84   DOMAINE CHAVET Menetou-Salon 1987 $9.50 (7/15/89)
79   HAUT POITOU Haut Poitou Chardonnay 1987 $6 (12/31/88)
75   LANGLOIS-CHATEAU Vin de Pays du Jardin de la France Chardonnay 1987 $7 (10/15/88)
72   LANGLOIS-CHATEAU Saumur 1987 $6 (12/31/88)
69   DOMAINE LE PEU DE LA MORIETTE Vouvray 1987 $10 (2/28/89)

1985
77   COULY-DUTHEIL Touraine Sauvignon 1985 $8 (3/15/87)

RHÔNE RED/*CHÂTEAUNEUF-DU-PAPE*
1989
92   DOMAINE DE MARCOUX Châteauneuf-du-Pape Vieilles Vignes 1989 $24 (7/15/91)
91   PAUL JABOULET AINE Châteauneuf-du-Pape Les Cédres 1989 $23 (7/15/91)

1988
90   E. GUIGAL Châteauneuf-du-Pape 1988 $20 (11/30/90)
88   CHATEAU DE BEAUCASTEL Châteauneuf-du-Pape 1988 $28 (3/31/91)
88   DOMAINE FONT DE MICHELLE Châteauneuf-du-Pape 1988 $18 (9/30/90)
88   DOMAINE ROGER SABON & FILS Châteauneuf-du-Pape 1988 $20 (9/30/90)
87   LES CAVES ST.-PIERRE Châteauneuf-du-Pape Clefs des Prelats 1988 $13 (1/31/91)
87   CHATEAU ST.-ANDRE Châteauneuf-du-Pape 1988 $16 (11/30/90)
86   DOMAINE DU CAILLOU Châteauneuf-du-Pape 1988 $22 (3/31/91)
86   CLOS DES PAPES Châteauneuf-du-Pape 1988 $19 (9/30/90)
86   CHATEAU RAYAS Châteauneuf-du-Pape Réserve 1988 $71 (3/31/91)
86   CHATEAU SIMIAN Châteauneuf-du-Pape 1988 $20 (7/15/91)
85   DOMAINE DU HAUT DES TERRES BLANCHES Châteauneuf-du-Pape 1988 $16 (7/15/91)
85   DOMAINE ROGER SABON & FILS Châteauneuf-du-Pape Cuvée Prestige 1988 $23 (9/30/90)
84   PIERRE ANDRE Châteauneuf-du-Pape 1988 $23 (3/31/91)
84   BICHOT Châteauneuf-du-Pape 1988 $13 (9/30/90)
82   CHATEAU CABRIERES Châteauneuf-du-Pape 1988 $17 (11/30/90)
82   DOMAINE CHANTE PERDRIX Châteauneuf-du-Pape 1988 $17 (5/31/91)
82   CLOS DU MONT-OLIVET Châteauneuf-du-Pape 1988 $18.50 (1/31/91)
82   DOMAINE LOU FREJAU Châteauneuf-du-Pape 1988 $17 (3/31/91)
81   DOMAINE DU VIEUX TELEGRAPHE Châteauneuf-du-Pape 1988 $20 (3/31/91)
80   DOMAINE ROGER SABON & FILS Châteauneuf-du-Pape Cuvée Réserve 1988 $20 (9/30/90)
79   DELAS Châteauneuf-du-Pape Cuvée de Haute Pierre 1988 $17 (11/30/90)

1987
86   CHATEAU DE BEAUCASTEL Châteauneuf-du-Pape 1987 $17 (9/30/89)
83   CHATEAU DE BEAUCASTEL Châteauneuf-du-Pape 1987 $17 (11/30/89) (HS)
83   DOMAINE DE MONPERTUIS Châteauneuf-du-Pape 1987 $14 (6/30/90)
82   BICHOT Châteauneuf-du-Pape 1987 $10 (3/15/90)
81   DOMAINE DU VIEUX TELEGRAPHE Châteauneuf-du-Pape 1987 $17 (9/30/90)

1986
91   LE VIEUX DONJON Châteauneuf-du-Pape 1986 $15.50 (11/30/88)
91   DOMAINE DU VIEUX TELEGRAPHE Châteauneuf-du-Pape 1986 $17 (11/30/88) CS
89   CHATEAU DE BEAUCASTEL Châteauneuf-du-Pape 1986 $25 (10/15/88)
89   LES CAILLOUX Châteauneuf-du-Pape Sélection Reflets 1986 $14 (5/31/89)
89   DOMAINE DU VIEUX LAZARET Châteauneuf-du-Pape 1986 $13.50 (1/31/89)
88   CHATEAU DE BEAUCASTEL Châteauneuf-du-Pape 1986 $25 (11/30/89) (HS)
88   CHATEAU RAYAS Châteauneuf-du-Pape Réserve 1986 $48 (12/15/89)
87   DOMAINE LOU FREJAU Châteauneuf-du-Pape 1986 $15.50 (1/31/89)
87   E. GUIGAL Châteauneuf-du-Pape 1986 $19 (3/15/90)
87   PIGNAN Châteauneuf-du-Pape Réserve 1986 $22 (9/30/90)
87   THORIN Châteauneuf-du-Pape 1986 $13 (11/30/88)
86   BICHOT Châteauneuf-du-Pape 1986 $9 (11/30/88)
86   CUVEE DU BELVEDERE Châteauneuf-du-Pape Le Boucou 1986 $16 (1/31/89)
85   CHATEAU DES FINES ROCHES Châteauneuf-du-Pape 1986 $14 (9/30/90)
85   DU PELOUX Châteauneuf-du-Pape 1986 $12 (4/15/89)
82   HENRI BONNEAU Châteauneuf-du-Pape Réserve des Celestins 1986 $19.50 (5/31/89)
80   JEAN CLAUDE BOISSET Châteauneuf-du-Pape 1986 $12 (11/30/88)
77   DOMAINE ALAIN GRANGEON Châteauneuf-du-Pape 1986 $16 (1/31/89)
73   DOMAINE DE MONPERTUIS Châteauneuf-du-Pape 1986 $18 (9/30/89)

1985
95   PIGNAN Châteauneuf-du-Pape Réserve 1985 $14 (8/31/87) SS
93   CUVEE DU BELVEDERE Châteauneuf-du-Pape Le Boucou 1985 $18 (2/15/88)
93   CHATEAU RAYAS Châteauneuf-du-Pape Réserve 1985 $41 (7/31/88)
91   DELAS Châteauneuf-du-Pape 1985 $17 (10/31/87)
90   CHATEAU DE BEAUCASTEL Châteauneuf-du-Pape 1985 Rel: $16 Cur: $24 (11/30/89) (HS)
90   CHATEAU DE LA ROQUETTE Châteauneuf-du-Pape 1985 $13 (7/31/88) SS
90   DOMAINE DU VIEUX TELEGRAPHE Châteauneuf-du-Pape 1985 Rel: $17 Cur: $21 (11/30/87)
89   CHATEAU DE BEAUCASTEL Châteauneuf-du-Pape 1985 Rel: $16 Cur: $24 (9/30/87)
89   M. CHAPOUTIER Châteauneuf-du-Pape La Bernardine 1985 $25 (3/15/90)
88   CHATEAU MONT-REDON Châteauneuf-du-Pape 1985 $11.50 (10/15/88)
87   CLOS DE L'ORATOIRE DES PAPES Châteauneuf-du-Pape 1985 $10 (7/31/88)
87   CHATEAU DE LA GARDINE Châteauneuf-du-Pape 1985 $15 (12/31/87)
87   E. GUIGAL Châteauneuf-du-Pape 1985 $18 (10/15/88)
86   BICHOT Châteauneuf-du-Pape 1985 $12 (11/15/87)
86   DOMAINE FONT DE MICHELLE Châteauneuf-du-Pape 1985 $13.50 (10/31/87)
86   CHATEAU MAUCOIL Châteauneuf-du-Pape Réserve Suzeraine 1985 $12.50 (11/15/87)

85 JACQUES CORTENAY Châteauneuf-du-Pape 1985 $8 (9/30/87) BB
85 DOMAINE DES SENECHAUX Châteauneuf-du-Pape 1985 $17 (10/15/88)
85 DOMAINE DU VIEUX LAZARET Châteauneuf-du-Pape 1985 $12 (11/15/87)
82 BOSQUET DES PAPES Châteauneuf-du-Pape 1985 $18 (1/31/89)
82 BOUCHARD PERE & FILS Châteauneuf-du-Pape 1985 $11.50 (9/30/87)
80 CHATEAU DES FINES ROCHES Châteauneuf-du-Pape 1985 $12 (10/31/87)
79 DOMAINE DE BEAURENARD Châteauneuf-du-Pape 1985 $16 (10/31/87)
79 LE VIEUX DONJON Châteauneuf-du-Pape 1985 $16 (2/15/88)
74 CLOS DU MONT-OLIVET Châteauneuf-du-Pape 1985 $15 (7/31/88)
71 DOMAINE FRANCOIS LAGET Châteauneuf-du-Pape 1985 $14 (9/30/87)

1984

92 CHATEAU MONT-REDON Châteauneuf-du-Pape 1984 $10.50 (9/30/87)
91 BOSQUET DES PAPES Châteauneuf-du-Pape 1984 $17 (11/15/87)
89 CHATEAU DE BEAUCASTEL Châteauneuf-du-Pape 1984 $12.50 (11/30/89) (HS)
89 CHATEAU DES FINES ROCHES Châteauneuf-du-Pape 1984 $12 (9/30/87)
89 DOMAINE DU VIEUX TELEGRAPHE Châteauneuf-du-Pape 1984 Rel: $12.50 Cur: $13 (9/30/87)
88 PERE ANSELME Châteauneuf-du-Pape La Fiole 1984 $12 (10/31/87)
82 CHATEAU DE BEAUCASTEL Châteauneuf-du-Pape 1984 $12.50 (9/30/87)
79 LE VIEUX DONJON Châteauneuf-du-Pape 1984 $14 (10/31/87)
78 DOMAINE DURIEU Châteauneuf-du-Pape 1984 $13 (11/15/87)
78 CHATEAU DE LA GARDINE Châteauneuf-du-Pape 1984 $15 (12/31/87)
76 HENRI BOIRON Châteauneuf-du-Pape Les Relagnes 1984 $12.75 (11/15/87)
76 DOMAINE FRANCOIS LAGET Châteauneuf-du-Pape 1984 $14 (12/31/87)
74 PERE ANSELME Châteauneuf-du-Pape La Fiole Grand Cuvée 1984 $13 (10/31/87)
72 CHATEAU DE VAUDIEU Châteauneuf-du-Pape 1984 $12.50 (11/15/87)

1983

92 PERE ANSELME Châteauneuf-du-Pape 1983 $12.50 (9/30/87)
92 CHATEAU RAYAS Châteauneuf-du-Pape Réserve 1983 Rel: $30 Cur: $43 (8/31/86)
89 M. CHAPOUTIER Châteauneuf-du-Pape La Bernardine 1983 $15 (9/30/87)
89 DOMAINE FRANCOIS LAGET Châteauneuf-du-Pape 1983 $12 (9/30/87)
88 DOMAINE DU HAUT DES TERRES BLANCHES Châteauneuf-du-Pape Réserve du Vatican 1983 $12 (9/30/87)
87 CHATEAU DE BEAUCASTEL Châteauneuf-du-Pape 1983 Rel: $17.50 Cur: $28 (9/30/87)
87 CHATEAU FORTIA Châteauneuf-du-Pape 1983 Rel: $13.50 Cur: $24 (12/31/87)
87 CHATEAU DE LA GARDINE Châteauneuf-du-Pape 1983 $12 (9/30/87)
87 E. GUIGAL Châteauneuf-du-Pape 1983 $18 (11/30/87)
85 CHATEAU DE BEAUCASTEL Châteauneuf-du-Pape 1983 Rel: $17.50 Cur: $28 (11/30/89) (HS)
83 CLOS DU MONT-OLIVET Châteauneuf-du-Pape 1983 $13.50 (1/31/87)
82 PAUL JABOULET AINE Châteauneuf-du-Pape 1983 $10 (9/30/87)
81 BOURGOGNE ST.-VINCENT Châteauneuf-du-Pape 1983 $8.50 (7/16/85)
81 M. CHAPOUTIER Châteauneuf-du-Pape La Bernardine 1983 $15 (6/01/86)
79 HENRI BOIRON Châteauneuf-du-Pape 1983 $11 (8/31/86)
78 DOMAINE JEAN DEYDIER & FILS Châteauneuf-du-Pape Les Clefs d'Or 1983 $16 (10/31/87)
77 DOMAINE DU VIEUX TELEGRAPHE Châteauneuf-du-Pape 1983 Rel: $17 Cur: $31 (9/30/87)
74 BARTON & GUESTIER Châteauneuf-du-Pape 1983 $11 (9/30/87)
62 DOMAINE DU BOIS DAUPHIN Châteauneuf-du-Pape 1983 $12 (11/15/87)
62 CUVEE DU BELVEDERE Châteauneuf-du-Pape Le Boucou 1983 $16 (11/15/87)
58 LANCON PERE & FILS Châteauneuf-du-Pape Domaine de la Solitude 1983 $14 (12/31/87)

1982

92 CHATEAU DE BEAUCASTEL Châteauneuf-du-Pape 1982 Cur: $30 (11/30/89) (HS)
91 CLOS DU MONT-OLIVET Châteauneuf-du-Pape 1982 $12 (3/16/86)
85 DOMAINE DE BEAURENARD Châteauneuf-du-Pape 1982 $9 (4/01/85) BB
75 LOUIS MOUSSET Châteauneuf-du-Pape 1982 $6 (12/16/84)

1981

88 CHATEAU DE BEAUCASTEL Châteauneuf-du-Pape 1981 Cur: $39 (11/30/89) (HS)
87 DOMAINE LUCIEN BARROT Châteauneuf-du-Pape 1981 $16 (9/30/87)

1980

87 PIGNAN Châteauneuf-du-Pape Réserve 1980 $12.75 (10/15/86)
83 CHATEAU DE BEAUCASTEL Châteauneuf-du-Pape 1980 Cur: $32 (11/30/89) (HS)

1978

67 DOMAINE DE LA VIEILLE JULIENNE Châteauneuf-du-Pape 1978 $20 (11/15/87)

1972

73 DOMAINE DE LA VIEILLE JULIENNE Châteauneuf-du-Pape 1972 $20 (11/15/87)

NV

86 PERE ANSELME Châteauneuf-du-Pape La Fiole du Pape NV $14 (9/30/89)
82 PERE ANSELME Châteauneuf-du-Pape La Fiole du Pape Uno Bono Fiolo NV $13 (1/31/88)

CORNAS

1988

85 J. VIDAL-FLEURY Cornas 1988 $20 (1/31/91)
83 JEAN LIONNET Cornas Cuvée Rochepertuis 1988 $28 (1/31/91)

1987

90 JEAN LIONNET Cornas 1987 $23 (3/31/90)
88 NOEL VERSET Cornas 1987 $23 (3/31/90)
84 JEAN-LUC COLOMBO Cornas Les Ruchets 1987 $50 (1/31/91)

1986

89 MARCEL JUGE Cornas 1986 $23 (1/31/89)
89 CAVE DE TAIN L'HERMITAGE Cornas Michel Courtial 1986 $11 (7/31/89)
88 A. CLAPE Cornas 1986 $22 (1/31/89)
87 MARCEL JUGE Cornas Cuvée S C 1986 $30 (6/15/89)
87 JEAN LIONNET Cornas 1986 $23 (1/31/89)
86 NOEL VERSET Cornas 1986 $25 (1/31/89)
85 MARCEL JUGE Cornas Cuvée C 1986 $25 (6/15/89)
83 MARCEL JUGE Cornas 1986 $23 (11/30/90)

1985

81 GUY DE BARJAC Cornas 1985 $17 (10/15/88)

1984

78 A. CLAPE Cornas 1984 $12.50 (8/31/87)

CÔTE-RÔTIE

1989

86 M. CHAPOUTIER Côte-Rôtie 1989 $30 (7/31/91)

1988

90 PIERRE GAILLARD Côte-Rôtie Côte Brune et Blonde 1988 $30 (11/30/90)
89 JASMIN Côte-Rôtie 1988 $32 (12/31/90)
88 J. VIDAL-FLEURY Côte-Rôtie Côtes Brune et Blonde 1988 $30 (10/15/90)
87 BERNARD BURGAUD Côte-Rôtie 1988 $40 (3/31/91)
87 GEORGES DUBOEUF Côte-Rôtie Domaine de la Rousse 1988 $18 (7/31/91)
84 PIERRE BARGE Côte-Rôtie 1988 $42 (7/31/91)
78 GUY BERNARD Côte-Rôtie 1988 $30 (10/15/90)
70 FRANCOIS GERARD Côte-Rôtie 1988 $36 (7/31/91)

1987

95 E. GUIGAL Côte-Rôtie La Turque 1987 $145 (7/31/91)
93 E. GUIGAL Côte-Rôtie La Landonne 1987 $125 (7/31/91) CS
92 E. GUIGAL Côte-Rôtie La Mouline 1987 $115 (7/31/91)
90 E. GUIGAL Côte-Rôtie Côtes Brune et Blonde 1987 $25 (1/31/91)
90 JASMIN Côte-Rôtie 1987 $30 (6/30/90)
87 BERNARD GUY Côte-Rôtie 1987 $25 (8/31/89)
86 R. ROSTAING Côte-Rôtie Côte Blonde 1987 $40 (6/30/90)
85 BERNARD BURGAUD Côte-Rôtie 1987 $29 (2/28/90)
84 LES CAVES ST.-PIERRE Côte-Rôtie Marquis de Tournelles 1987 $23 (1/31/91)
82 PIERRE GAILLARD Côte-Rôtie Côte Brune et Blonde 1987 $24 (8/31/89)
77 FRANCOIS GERARD Côte-Rôtie 1987 $30 (10/15/90)
73 GENTAZ-DERVIEUX Côte-Rôtie Côte Brune Cuvée Réserve 1987 $40 (6/30/90)

1986

95 E. GUIGAL Côte-Rôtie La Turque 1986 Rel: $99 Cur: $340 (10/15/90) CS
93 BERNARD BURGAUD Côte-Rôtie 1986 $31 (1/31/89)
93 E. GUIGAL Côte-Rôtie La Mouline 1986 Rel: $99 Cur: $135 (10/15/90)
91 E. GUIGAL Côte-Rôtie La Landonne 1986 Rel: $99 Cur: $140 (10/15/90)
90 E. GUIGAL Côte-Rôtie Côtes Brune et Blonde 1986 $28 (2/28/90)
89 BERNARD GUY Côte-Rôtie 1986 $29 (9/30/88)
86 PIERRE GAILLARD Côte-Rôtie Côte Brune et Blonde 1986 $25 (11/30/88)
85 GILBERT CLUSEL Côte-Rôtie La Vialliere 1986 $23 (4/15/89)

1985

98 E. GUIGAL Côte-Rôtie La Mouline 1985 Cur: $370 (3/15/90) (HS)
98 E. GUIGAL Côte-Rôtie La Turque 1985 Cur: $660 (3/15/90) (HS)
93 PAUL JABOULET AINE Côte-Rôtie Les Jumelles 1985 Rel: $35 Cur: $35 (9/30/88)
92 E. GUIGAL Côte-Rôtie Côtes Brune et Blonde 1985 Rel: $30 Cur: $34 (1/31/89)
91 E. GUIGAL Côte-Rôtie Côtes Brune et Blonde 1985 Rel: $30 Cur: $34 (3/15/90) (HS)
90 E. GUIGAL Côte-Rôtie La Landonne 1985 Cur: $370 (3/15/90) (HS)
90 J. VIDAL-FLEURY Côte-Rôtie Côtes Brune et Blonde 1985 Rel: $25 Cur: $25 (3/15/90) (HS)
88 JOSEPH JAMET Côte-Rôtie 1985 $33 (4/15/89)
88 ANDRE PASSAT Côte-Rôtie 1985 $25 (10/15/87)
75 L. DE VALLOUIT Côte-Rôtie 1985 $20 (10/15/87)

1984

90 BERNARD BURGAUD Côte-Rôtie 1984 $22 (10/15/87)
86 E. GUIGAL Côte-Rôtie La Landonne 1984 Cur: $111 (3/15/90) (HS)
83 E. GUIGAL Côte-Rôtie Côtes Brune et Blonde 1984 Rel: $25 Cur: $27 (11/30/87)
73 J. VIDAL-FLEURY Côte-Rôtie Côte Blonde La Chatillonne 1984 $26 (10/31/87)

1983

94 E. GUIGAL Côte-Rôtie Côtes Brune et Blonde 1983 Rel: $21 Cur: $34 (3/15/90) (HS)
94 E. GUIGAL Côte-Rôtie La Landonne 1983 Cur: $310 (3/15/90) (HS)
94 E. GUIGAL Côte-Rôtie La Mouline 1983 Cur: $310 (3/15/90) (HS)
92 BERNARD BURGAUD Côte-Rôtie 1983 $18 (5/01/86)
92 E. GUIGAL Côte-Rôtie Côtes Brune et Blonde 1983 Rel: $21 Cur: $34 (4/30/87) CS

1982

92 E. GUIGAL Côte-Rôtie La Mouline 1982 Cur: $210 (3/15/90) (HS)
90 E. GUIGAL Côte-Rôtie La Landonne 1982 Cur: $210 (3/15/90) (HS)
89 E. GUIGAL Côte-Rôtie Côtes Brune et Blonde 1982 Cur: $40 (3/15/90) (HS)
68 PERE ANSELME Côte-Rôtie Tête de Cuvée 1982 $13 (10/15/87)

1981

90 E. GUIGAL Côte-Rôtie La Mouline 1981 Cur: $151 (3/15/90) (HS)
82 E. GUIGAL Côte-Rôtie La Landonne 1981 Cur: $156 (3/15/90) (HS)

1980

89 E. GUIGAL Côte-Rôtie Côtes Brune et Blonde 1980 Rel: $13 Cur: $32 (9/16/84)
84 E. GUIGAL Côte-Rôtie La Landonne 1980 Cur: $170 (3/15/90) (HS)

1979

91 E. GUIGAL Côte-Rôtie La Landonne 1979 Cur: $260 (3/15/90) (HS)
85 E. GUIGAL Côte-Rôtie La Mouline 1979 Cur: $260 (3/15/90) (HS)

1978

96 E. GUIGAL Côte-Rôtie La Mouline 1978 Cur: $430 (3/15/90) (HS)
95 E. GUIGAL Côte-Rôtie Côtes Brune et Blonde 1978 Cur: $78 (3/15/90) (HS)
95 E. GUIGAL Côte-Rôtie La Landonne 1978 Cur: $410 (3/15/90) (HS)

1977

75 E. GUIGAL Côte-Rôtie La Mouline 1977 Cur: $263 (3/15/90) (HS)

1976

88 E. GUIGAL Côte-Rôtie Côtes Brune et Blonde 1976 Cur: $65 (3/15/90) (HS)
87 E. GUIGAL Côte-Rôtie La Mouline 1976 Cur: $330 (3/15/90) (HS)

FRANCE
RHÔNE RED/CÔTE-RÔTIE

1975
75   E. GUIGAL Côte-Rôtie La Mouline 1975 Cur: $225 (3/15/90) (HS)

1974
89   E. GUIGAL Côte-Rôtie La Mouline 1974 Cur: $300 (3/15/90) (HS)

1973
84   E. GUIGAL Côte-Rôtie La Mouline 1973 Cur: $242 (3/15/90) (HS)

1971
88   E. GUIGAL Côte-Rôtie La Mouline 1971 Cur: $300 (3/15/90) (HS)

1970
74   E. GUIGAL Côte-Rôtie La Mouline 1970 Cur: $300 (3/15/90) (HS)

1969
93   E. GUIGAL Côte-Rôtie Côtes Brune et Blonde 1969 Cur: $100 (3/15/90) (HS)
90   E. GUIGAL Côte-Rôtie La Mouline 1969 Cur: $900 (3/15/90) (HS)

1968
82   E. GUIGAL Côte-Rôtie La Mouline 1968 Cur: $300 (3/15/90) (HS)

1967
86   E. GUIGAL Côte-Rôtie La Mouline 1967 Cur: $510 (3/15/90) (HS)

1966
88   E. GUIGAL Côte-Rôtie Côtes Brune et Blonde 1966 Cur: $145 (3/15/90) (HS)
88   E. GUIGAL Côte-Rôtie La Mouline 1966 Cur: $760 (3/15/90) (HS)

1964
92   E. GUIGAL Côte-Rôtie Côtes Brune et Blonde 1964 Cur: $100 (3/15/90) (HS)

1962
89   E. GUIGAL Côte-Rôtie Côtes Brune et Blonde 1962 Cur: $100 (3/15/90) (HS)

1961
82   E. GUIGAL Côte-Rôtie Côtes Brune et Blonde 1961 Cur: $100 (3/15/90) (HS)

1945
85   J. VIDAL-FLEURY Côte-Rôtie Côtes Brune et Blonde 1945 Cur: $175 (3/15/90) (HS)

1934
85   J. VIDAL-FLEURY Côte-Rôtie Côtes Brune et Blonde 1934 Cur: $300 (3/15/90) (HS)

CÔTES DU RHÔNE

1989
87   LA VIEILLE FERME Côtes du Rhône Réserve 1989 $9 (3/15/91) BB
85   MOILLARD Côtes du Rhône Les Violettes 1989 $7.50 (5/31/91) BB
84   PROSPER MAUFOUX Côtes du Rhône 1989 $9 (5/31/91)
83   CHATEAU DU BOIS DE LA GARDE Côtes du Rhône 1989 $8 (5/31/91)
82   BOUCHARD PERE & FILS Côtes du Rhône 1989 $8.50 (7/15/91) BB
80   GEORGES DUBOEUF Côtes du Rhône 1989 $6 (10/15/90) BB
80   PAR E. REYNAUD Côtes du Rhône Château des Tours 1989 $12 (3/15/91)

1988
86   DOMAINE BRUSSET Côtes du Rhône-Villages Côteaux des Trabers 1988 $7.75 (12/15/90) BB
86   LA VIEILLE FERME Côtes du Rhône Réserve 1988 $8 (12/31/89) BB
85   J. VIDAL-FLEURY Côtes du Rhône 1988 $9 (12/15/90)
84   LES CAVES ST.-PIERRE Côtes du Rhône-Villages Les Lissandres 1988 $7.25 (12/15/90) BB
84   DELAS Côtes du Rhône St.-Esprit 1988 $6.75 (12/15/90) BB
84   DOMAINE DE LA GUICHARDE Côtes du Rhône 1988 $7 (3/15/91) BB
84   PAUL JABOULET AINE Côtes du Rhône Parallele 45 1988 $6.50 (12/15/89) BB
84   MOILLARD Côtes du Rhône Les Violettes 1988 $6 (8/31/89) BB
84   LA VIEILLE FERME Côtes du Rhône Réserve 1988 $8 (12/15/90) BB
82   CHATEAU DU BOIS DE LA GARDE Côtes du Rhône 1988 $7 (10/31/90) BB
81   CAVE DES COTEAUX CAIRANNE Côtes du Rhône-Villages 1988 $6.50 (2/28/90) BB
81   E. GUIGAL Côtes du Rhône 1988 $11.50 (7/15/91)
81   ARMAND ROUX Côtes du Rhône La Berberine 1988 $7.50 (10/31/90) BB
80   ABEL CLEMENT Côtes du Rhône 1988 $6 (2/28/90) BB
79   G. BAROUX Côtes du Rhône Château de Bourdines 1988 $8 (12/15/90)
79   PROSPER MAUFOUX Côtes du Rhône 1988 $6.50 (6/30/90)
79   DOMAINE ROGER SABON & FILS Côtes du Rhône 1988 $11 (10/31/90)
78   DOMAINE DURIEU Côtes du Rhône-Villages 1988 $6 (3/15/91)
78   SERRE DE LAUZIERE Côtes du Rhône-Villages 1988 $7 (10/31/90)
76   CAVE DES COTEAUX CAIRANNE Côtes du Rhône-Villages Cairanne 1988 $6.25 (6/30/90)
75   DOMAINE ST.-GAYAN Côtes du Rhône 1988 $6 (10/31/90)
74   J.Y. MULTIER Côtes du Rhône Cépage Syrah 1988 $10 (12/15/90)
68   DOMAINE DE LA MORDOREE Côtes du Rhône 1988 $5.50 (2/28/90)

1987
81   DOMAINE LES GOUBERT Côtes du Rhône-Villages Beaumes de Venise 1987 $9 (7/31/89)

80   DOMAINE STE.-ANNE Côtes du Rhône-Villages Cuvée Notre-Dame des Cellettes 1987 $7.50 (1/31/89)
80   LA VIEILLE FERME Côtes du Rhône Réserve 1987 $6.50 (6/15/89) BB
78   JEAN CLAUDE BOISSET Côtes du Rhône 1987 $4.50 (7/31/89)
78   DOMAINE DES RICHARDS Côtes du Rhône-Villages 1987 $4 (1/31/89)
77   DOMAINE MICHEL BERNARD Côtes du Rhône Domaine de la Serrière 1987 $7 (3/15/91)
77   CAVE DES COTEAUX CAIRANNE Côtes du Rhône Le Château à Cairanne 1987 $7 (12/15/89)
77   CHATEAU D'ORSAN Côtes du Rhône 1987 $4 (11/15/88)
76   CRU DE COUDELET Côtes du Rhône 1987 $12 (12/15/89)
75   DOMAINE LES AUSSELONS Côtes du Rhône Vinsobres 1987 $8 (6/30/90)
74   PROSPER MAUFOUX Côtes du Rhône 1987 $6.25 (6/15/89)
73   CHATEAU D'AIGUEVILLE Côtes du Rhône 1987 $5 (1/31/89)
72   BICHOT Côtes du Rhône 1987 $3.50 (11/15/88)
67   THORIN Côtes du Rhône L'Escalou 1987 $6 (1/31/89)

1986
87   M. CHAPOUTIER Côtes du Rhône Cuvée de Belleruche 1986 $12 (12/15/89)
86   CAVE DES COTEAUX CAIRANNE Côtes du Rhône 1986 $7.25 (7/31/88)
84   CRU DE COUDELET Côtes du Rhône 1986 $15 (9/30/88)
84   E. GUIGAL Côtes du Rhône 1986 $9 (2/28/90)
82   CAVE DES COTEAUX CAIRANNE Côtes du Rhône Le Château à Cairanne 1986 $6 (7/31/88) BB
82   DOMAINE DES CEDRES Côtes du Rhône Pons Dominique 1986 $10 (3/31/90)
82   MOMMESSIN Côtes du Rhône 1986 $4.75 (4/30/88) BB
82   DOMAINE LA SOUMADE Côtes du Rhône-Villages Rasteau 1986 $11 (2/28/90)
81   CHATEAU D'ORSAN Côtes du Rhône 1986 $4 (2/29/88) BB
80   LAURENT CHARLES BROTTE Côtes du Rhône-Villages Seguret 1986 $6 (9/30/89) BB
80   CHATEAU DU TRIGNON Côtes du Rhône-Villages Rasteau 1986 $9 (12/15/90)
79   JEAN LIONNET Côtes du Rhône Cépage Syrah 1986 $10 (9/30/88)
79   VIGNOBLE DE LA JASSE Côtes du Rhône 1986 $8 (12/15/89)
78   DOMAINE LES GOUBERT Côtes du Rhône 1986 $6.75 (3/31/88)
78   DU PELOUX Côtes du Rhône-Villages 1986 $5.50 (5/15/89)
75   DU PELOUX Côtes du Rhône 1986 $4.50 (5/15/89)
73   JEAN CLAUDE BOISSET Côtes du Rhône 1986 $4 (10/31/87)
73   DOMAINE LOU FREJAU Côtes du Rhône 1986 $8 (5/31/89)
72   PERE ANSELME Côtes du Rhône-Villages Seguret 1986 $5.25 (5/15/89)
68   BOKOBSA Côtes du Rhône Cuvée du Centenaire 1986 $6.50 (2/28/90)
61   DOMAINE BRUSSET Côtes du Rhône-Villages Cairanne Côteaux des Trabers 1986 $7 (6/15/89)

1985
89   CHARLES ROUX Côtes du Rhône-Villages Rasteau 1985 $10 (2/28/90)
88   J. VIDAL-FLEURY Côtes du Rhône 1985 $7.50 (10/31/87) BB
87   CHATEAU DE FONSALETTE Côtes du Rhône Réserve 1985 $15.50 (9/30/88)
85   CAVE DES COTEAUX CAIRANNE Côtes du Rhône Domaine le Château 1985 $6.25 (8/31/87) BB
85   CRU DE COUDELET Côtes du Rhône 1985 $12 (4/30/88)
85   E. GUIGAL Côtes du Rhône 1985 $8 (9/30/88)
85   MOILLARD Côtes du Rhône Les Violettes 1985 $4.50 (11/15/86) BB
85   LA VIEILLE FERME Côtes du Rhône Réserve 1985 $7 (11/15/88) BB
83   KERMIT LYNCH Côtes du Rhône 1985 $9 (1/31/89)
81   DOMAINE RABASSE CHARAVIN Côtes du Rhône 1985 $6 (8/31/87) BB
80   DELAS Côtes du Rhône St.-Esprit 1985 $5.50 (12/15/87) BB
80   DOMAINE LES GOUBERT Côtes du Rhône-Villages Beaumes de Venise 1985 $9.25 (4/30/88)
79   CAVE DES VIGNERONS A CHUSCLAN Côtes du Rhône Prieure St.-Julien 1985 $4.25 (12/31/87) BB
79   CHATEAU D'ORSAN Côtes du Rhône 1985 $6.75 (12/15/87)
78   ABEL CLEMENT Côtes du Rhône 1985 $5 (1/31/87) BB
77   JEAN CLAUDE BOISSET Côtes du Rhône 1985 $3.75 (11/30/86) BB
77   PATRIARCHE Côtes du Rhône-Villages Cuvée Leblanc-Vatel 1985 $5.50 (8/31/89)
76   DOMAINE LES GOUBERT Côtes du Rhône-Villages Sablet 1985 $8.25 (4/30/88)
75   PERE ANSELME Côtes du Rhône-Villages Marescal 1985 $5.25 (12/31/87)
75   BICHOT Côtes du Rhône 1985 $5.75 (12/15/87)
75   DOMAINE ST.-GAYAN Côtes du Rhône 1985 $6 (4/30/88)
74   ALIGNE Côtes du Rhône 1985 $6 (2/28/87)
74   CHATEAU LA BORIE Côtes du Rhône Cuvée de Prestige 1985 $6 (7/15/87)
73   PAUL JABOULET AINE Côtes du Rhône Parallele 45 1985 $6.50 (4/30/88)

1984
84   E. GUIGAL Côtes du Rhône 1984 $7 (12/15/87) BB
72   DOMAINE DE L'AMEILLAUD Côtes du Rhône 1984 $4.50 (6/01/86)
68   CHATEAU D'AIGUEVILLE Côtes du Rhône 1984 $4.50 (10/15/87)

1983
87   CHATEAU LA BORIE Côtes du Rhône Cuvée de Prestige 1983 $4 (3/16/85) BB
84   DOMAINE DE LA RENJARDIERE Côtes du Rhône 1983 $4.50 (3/16/86) BB
81   LOUIS MOUSSET Côtes du Rhône 1983 $2.50 (12/16/84) BB

1982
85   E. GUIGAL Côtes du Rhône 1982 $6 (5/01/86) BB
84   LA RAMILLADE Côtes du Rhône 1982 $5 (11/01/85) BB
69   DOMAINE LA SOUMADE Côtes du Rhône-Villages Rasteau Cuvée Réserve 1982 $5.50 (10/31/87)

1981
86   E. GUIGAL Côtes du Rhône 1981 $5 (5/01/84) BB

1980
85   E. GUIGAL Côtes du Rhône 1980 $4.50 (5/01/84) BB

CROZES-HERMITAGE

1989
90   PAUL JABOULET AINE Crozes-Hermitage Domaine de Thalabert 1989 $18 (7/15/91)
89   CHATEAU CURSON Crozes-Hermitage 1989 $17 (7/15/91)
88   ALAIN GRAILLOT Crozes-Hermitage 1989 $13.50 (3/31/91)

1988
86   J. VIDAL-FLEURY Crozes-Hermitage 1988 $13.50 (12/31/90)

Key to Symbols

The scores reported here are the results of blind tastings conducted by our panel of senior editors. Wines that carry the initials below are results of individual tastings.

THE WINE SPECTATOR 100-POINT SCALE   95-100—Classic, a great wine; **90-94**—Outstanding, superior character and style; **80-89**—Good to very good, a wine with special qualities; **70-79**—Average, drinkable wine that may have minor flaws; **60-69**—Below average, drinkable but not recommended; **50-59**—Poor, undrinkable, not recommended. "**+**"—With a score indicates a range; used primarily with barrel tastings to indicate a preliminary score.

SPECIAL DESIGNATIONS   SS—Spectator Selection, **CS**—Cellar Selection, **BB**—Best Buy.

TASTER'S INITIALS   (JG)—Jim Gordon, **(HS)**—Harvey Steiman, **(JL)**—James Laube, **(JS)**—James Suckling, **(TM)**—Thomas Matthews, **(TR)**—Terry Robards, **(BT)**—Barrel Tasting (these wines were tasted blind from barrel samples), **(CA-**date)—*California's Great Cabernets* by James Laube, **(CH-**date)—*California's Great Chardonnays* by James Laube, **(VP-**date)—*Vintage Port* by James Suckling.

DATE TASTED Dates in parentheses represent the issue in which the rating was published.

85 GEORGES DUBOEUF Crozes-Hermitage 1988 $9 (1/31/91)
85 FERRATON PERE Crozes-Hermitage La Matinière 1988 $14 (6/30/90)
83 PAUL JABOULET AINE Crozes-Hermitage Domaine de Thalabert 1988 $13 (10/15/90)
78 BERNARD CHAVE Crozes-Hermitage 1988 $14 (2/15/91)
70 WILLI'S WINE BAR Crozes-Hermitage Cuvée Anniversaire 1980-1990 1988 $11 (3/31/91)

1987

83 PAUL JABOULET AINE Crozes-Hermitage Domaine de Thalabert 1987 $10 (3/31/90)
83 LUPE-CHOLET Crozes-Hermitage 1987 $8 (3/31/90) BB

1986

88 ALAIN GRAILLOT Crozes-Hermitage 1986 $9.75 (4/15/89)
88 PAUL JABOULET AINE Crozes-Hermitage Domaine de Thalabert 1986 Rel: $13.50 Cur: $16 (9/30/88)
84 DESMEURE Crozes-Hermitage Domaine des Remizières Cuvée Particulaire 1986 $8 (5/31/89) BB
80 PERE ANSELME Crozes-Hermitage 1986 $7.75 (7/31/89)
78 J. VIDAL-FLEURY Crozes-Hermitage 1986 $10 (5/31/88)
77 CAVE DE TAIN L'HERMITAGE Crozes-Hermitage Michel Courtial 1986 $6 (5/15/89)

1985

92 J. VIDAL-FLEURY Crozes-Hermitage 1985 Rel: $11 Cur: $13 (10/31/87) CS
86 BERNARD CHAVE Crozes-Hermitage 1985 $12.25 (11/30/88)
85 PAUL JABOULET AINE Crozes-Hermitage Domaine de Thalabert 1985 Rel: $13.50 Cur: $30 (9/30/88)
78 DELAS Crozes-Hermitage 1985 $7.50 (12/15/87)

1983

84 PERE ANSELME Crozes-Hermitage 1983 $7.50 (10/15/87) BB

GIGONDAS

1989

84 PAUL JABOULET AINE Gigondas 1989 $18 (7/15/91)

1988

90 DANIEL BRUSSET Gigondas Les Hauts de Montmirail 1988 $16.50 (9/30/90)
85 E. GUIGAL Gigondas 1988 $13 (3/31/91)
79 GEORGES DUBOEUF Gigondas 1988 $10 (9/30/90)

1986

92 DOMAINE LES GOUBERT Gigondas Cuvée Florence 1986 $24 (4/30/88)
92 DOMAINE RASPAIL-AY Gigondas 1986 $15 (1/31/89)
90 DOMAINE DU GOUR DE CHAULE Gigondas 1986 $13 (9/15/90)
87 E. GUIGAL Gigondas 1986 $15 (11/30/90)
81 DOMAINE LES GOUBERT Gigondas 1986 $13 (3/15/90)

1985

93 MICHEL FARAUD Gigondas Domaine du Cayron 1985 $15.75 (11/30/88)
91 E. GUIGAL Gigondas 1985 Rel: $12.50 Cur: $15 (9/30/88) SS
89 DOMAINE LES GOUBERT Gigondas 1985 $11.50 (4/30/88)
86 DOMAINE DE FONT-SANE Gigondas 1985 $13 (1/31/89)
86 J. VIDAL-FLEURY Gigondas 1985 $13 (10/31/87)
78 CHATEAU DE MONTMIRAIL Gigondas Cuvée de Beauchamp 1985 $14 (9/30/88)
65 PROSPER MAUFOUX Gigondas 1985 $11 (4/30/88)

1984

86 E. GUIGAL Gigondas 1984 Rel: $13 Cur: $15 (11/30/87)
86 DOMAINE LES PALLIERES Gigondas 1984 $14 (9/30/89)

1983

91 E. GUIGAL Gigondas 1983 Rel: $12.50 Cur: $25 (7/31/87)
90 CHATEAU DE MONTMIRAIL Gigondas Cuvée de Beauchamp 1983 $11 (11/30/86)
88 DOMAINE LES GOUBERT Gigondas 1983 $15 (1/31/89)
75 LOUIS MOUSSET Gigondas 1983 $6 (12/01/84)

1982

89 DOMAINE LES PALLIERES Gigondas 1982 $11 (5/31/87)

1981

90 DOMAINE LES PALLIERES Gigondas 1981 $10.25 (3/15/87)

HERMITAGE

1988

92 PAUL JABOULET AINE Hermitage La Chapelle 1988 $40 (3/31/91)
88 LES CAVES ST.-PIERRE Hermitage Tertre des Carmes 1988 $23 (12/31/90)

1987

89 J.L. CHAVE Hermitage 1987 Rel: $48 Cur: $48 (6/30/90)
86 E. GUIGAL Hermitage 1987 $29 (1/31/91)

1986

92 E. GUIGAL Hermitage 1986 Rel: $32 Cur: $32 (2/28/90) CS
91 PAUL JABOULET AINE Hermitage La Chapelle 1986 $35 (9/30/88)
89 PAUL JABOULET AINE Hermitage La Chapelle 1986 $35 (11/15/89) (JS)
89 CAVE DE TAIN L'HERMITAGE Hermitage Michel Courtial 1986 $15 (3/31/90)
86 BERNARD CHAVE Hermitage 1986 $32 (11/30/88)
82 CAVE DE TAIN L'HERMITAGE Hermitage 1986 $15.50 (7/15/89)
68 DESMEURE Hermitage Domaine des Remizières 1986 $19 (4/15/89)

1985

93 PAUL JABOULET AINE Hermitage La Chapelle 1985 $50 (11/15/89) (JS)
92 E. GUIGAL Hermitage 1985 Rel: $33 Cur: $33 (4/15/89) CS
90 PAUL JABOULET AINE Hermitage La Chapelle 1985 $50 (12/31/87)
89 J. VIDAL-FLEURY Hermitage 1985 $22.50 (10/31/87)
87 H. SORREL Hermitage 1985 $29 (7/31/88)

1984

89 J.L. CHAVE Hermitage 1984 Rel: $25 Cur: $25 (8/31/87)
80 PAUL JABOULET AINE Hermitage La Chapelle 1984 Cur: $17 (11/15/89) (JS)

1983

94 PAUL JABOULET AINE Hermitage La Chapelle 1983 Cur: $63 (11/15/89) (JS)
88 DOMAINE DE L'HERMITE Hermitage 1983 $9.50 (5/01/86)
87 E. GUIGAL Hermitage 1983 Rel: $21 Cur: $29 (4/30/87)
84 H. SORREL Hermitage Le Greal 1983 $19.50 (5/01/86)
83 M. CHAPOUTIER Hermitage M. de la Sizeranne 1983 $19 (5/01/86)
79 L. DE VALLOUIT Hermitage 1983 $12 (5/01/86)

1982

93 PAUL JABOULET AINE Hermitage La Chapelle 1982 Rel: $17.50 Cur: $50 (11/01/84) CS
91 E. GUIGAL Hermitage 1982 Rel: $18 Cur: $29 (5/01/86)
89 PAUL JABOULET AINE Hermitage La Chapelle 1982 Rel: $17.50 Cur: $50 (11/15/89) (JS)

1981

88 M. CHAPOUTIER Hermitage M. de la Sizeranne 1981 $10 (11/01/84)
83 PAUL JABOULET AINE Hermitage La Chapelle 1981 Cur: $30 (11/15/89) (JS)

1980

91 E. GUIGAL Hermitage 1980 Rel: $13 Cur: $37 (9/01/84) CS
84 DOMAINE DE L'HERMITE Hermitage 1980 $12.25 (5/01/86)
83 J.L. CHAVE Hermitage 1980 Rel: $25 Cur: $37 (5/01/86)
79 PAUL JABOULET AINE Hermitage La Chapelle 1980 Cur: $28 (11/15/89) (JS)
74 H. SORREL Hermitage Le Meal 1980 $25 (5/01/86)

1979

86 PAUL JABOULET AINE Hermitage La Chapelle 1979 Cur: $50 (11/15/89) (JS)

1978

98 PAUL JABOULET AINE Hermitage La Chapelle 1978 Cur: $181 (11/15/89) (JS)
91 E. GUIGAL Hermitage 1978 Cur: $71 (3/15/90) (HS)

1976

87 PAUL JABOULET AINE Hermitage La Chapelle 1976 Cur: $142 (11/15/89) (JS)
80 E. GUIGAL Hermitage 1976 Cur: $75 (3/15/90) (HS)

1975

81 PAUL JABOULET AINE Hermitage La Chapelle 1975 Cur: $35 (11/15/89) (JS)

1974

85 PAUL JABOULET AINE Hermitage La Chapelle 1974 Cur: $128 (11/15/89) (JS)

1973

89 PAUL JABOULET AINE Hermitage La Chapelle 1973 Cur: $58 (11/15/89) (JS)

1972

90 PAUL JABOULET AINE Hermitage La Chapelle 1972 Cur: $135 (11/15/89) (JS)

1971

86 PAUL JABOULET AINE Hermitage La Chapelle 1971 Cur: $175 (10/29/87)
85 PAUL JABOULET AINE Hermitage La Chapelle 1971 Cur: $175 (11/15/89) (JS)

1970

93 PAUL JABOULET AINE Hermitage La Chapelle 1970 Cur: $215 (11/15/89) (JS)

1969

95 PAUL JABOULET AINE Hermitage La Chapelle 1969 Cur: $195 (10/29/87)
92 PAUL JABOULET AINE Hermitage La Chapelle 1969 Cur: $195 (11/15/89) (JS)
84 E. GUIGAL Hermitage 1969 Cur: $100 (3/15/90) (HS)

1967

83 PAUL JABOULET AINE Hermitage La Chapelle 1967 Cur: $65 (11/15/89) (JS)

1966

95 PAUL JABOULET AINE Hermitage La Chapelle 1966 Cur: $175 (11/15/89) (JS)
90 E. GUIGAL Hermitage 1966 Cur: $100 (3/15/90) (HS)

1964

93 E. GUIGAL Hermitage 1964 Cur: $100 (3/15/90) (HS)
93 PAUL JABOULET AINE Hermitage La Chapelle 1964 Cur: $320 (11/15/89) (JS)

1962

91 PAUL JABOULET AINE Hermitage La Chapelle 1962 Cur: $150 (11/15/89) (JS)

1961

100 PAUL JABOULET AINE Hermitage La Chapelle 1961 Cur: $587 (11/15/89) (JS)

1959

77 PAUL JABOULET AINE Hermitage La Chapelle 1959 Cur: $500 (11/15/89) (JS)

1955

88 PAUL JABOULET AINE Hermitage La Chapelle 1955 Cur: $320 (11/15/89) (JS)

1953

90 PAUL JABOULET AINE Hermitage La Chapelle 1953 Cur: $550 (11/15/89) (JS)

1952

77 PAUL JABOULET AINE Hermitage La Chapelle 1952 Cur: $450 (11/15/89) (JS)

1949

77 PAUL JABOULET AINE Hermitage La Chapelle 1949 Cur: $800 (11/15/89) (JS)

1945

80 J. VIDAL-FLEURY Hermitage 1945 Cur: $175 (3/15/90) (HS)

1944

93 PAUL JABOULET AINE Hermitage La Chapelle 1944 Cur: $800 (11/15/89) (JS)

1937

91 J. VIDAL-FLEURY Hermitage 1937 Cur: $135 (3/15/90) (HS)
50 PAUL JABOULET AINE Hermitage La Chapelle 1937 Cur: $850 (11/15/89) (JS)

FRANCE
RHÔNE RED/HERMITAGE

NV
88   M. CHAPOUTIER Hermitage Le Pavillon NV $60 (1/31/89)
83   M. CHAPOUTIER Hermitage M. de la Sizeranne Grande Cuvée NV $14 (5/01/86)

OTHER RHÔNE RED

1989
79   LA BOUVERIE Costières de Nimes 1989 $6 (7/15/91)

1988
89   J. VIDAL-FLEURY Vacqueyras 1988 $13.50 (12/15/90)
87   PIERRE GAILLARD St.-Joseph Clos de Cuminaille 1988 $15 (12/31/90)
84   DOMAINE DES LONES Côteaux du Tricastin 1988 $11 (5/31/91)
84   J. VIDAL-FLEURY St.-Joseph 1988 $14 (1/31/91)
82   DOMAINE ST.-SAUVEUR Côtes du Ventoux 1988 $5.50 (9/30/89) BB
82   CHATEAU VAL JOANIS Côtes du Lubéron 1988 $7 (6/30/90) BB
78   DOMAINE DES LONES Côteaux du Tricastin 1988 $7.50 (10/15/90)
78   L. DE VALLOUIT Vin de Pays des Collines Rhodanienn Les Sables 1988 $4.75 (6/30/90) BB
78   LA VIEILLE FERME Côtes du Ventoux 1988 $8 (6/30/90)
76   GEORGES DUBOEUF St.-Joseph 1988 $11 (11/30/90)
75   JEAN CLAUDE BOISSET Côtes du Ventoux 1988 $4 (10/15/90)

1987
87   PIERRE GAILLARD St.-Joseph Clos de Cuminaille 1987 $14 (3/15/90)
81   LA VIEILLE FERME Côtes du Ventoux 1987 $5.75 (6/15/89) BB
80   CUILLERON St.-Joseph Cuvée de la Côte 1987 $16 (11/30/90)

1986
88   DOMAINE DE LA MORDOREE Lirac 1986 $11 (9/30/88)
88   CHATEAU DES ROQUES Vacqueyras Cuvée de Noe 1986 $7.50 (12/15/89) BB
83   LA VIEILLE FERME Côtes du Ventoux 1986 $6 (10/15/88) BB
82   DOMAINE DES LONES Côteaux du Tricastin 1986 $7.25 (10/15/88)
79   CAVE DE TAIN L'HERMITAGE St.-Joseph Michel Courtial 1986 $8 (7/31/89)

1985
86   PAUL JABOULET AINE St.-Joseph Le Grand Pompée 1985 $11.25 (10/15/88)
83   DOMAINE LE COUROULU Vacqueyras 1985 $8 (1/31/89) BB
83   CHATEAU DE MILLE Côtes du Lubéron 1985 $8.50 (12/15/88)

1983
83   DOMAINE LE CLOS DES CAZAUX Vacqueyras Cuvée des Templiers 1983 $11 (1/31/87)
76   CUILLERON St.-Joseph 1983 $12.50 (2/16/86)

RHÔNE WHITE/CHÂTEAUNEUF-DU-PAPE

1988
87   CHATEAU DE BEAUCASTEL Châteauneuf-du-Pape Roussanne Vieille Vigne 1988 $46 (12/31/90)
87   DOMAINE DE MONPERTUIS Châteauneuf-du-Pape 1988 $29 (3/31/91)
80   DOMAINE DE MONPERTUIS Châteauneuf-du-Pape 1988 $22 (11/30/90)

1987
79   CHATEAU MONT-REDON Châteauneuf-du-Pape 1987 $20 (10/31/89)
74   LAURENT CHARLES BROTTE Châteauneuf-du-Pape 1987 $14 (10/31/89)

1986
85   CHATEAU RAYAS Châteauneuf-du-Pape Réserve 1986 $44 (3/15/89)
84   CHATEAU DE BEAUCASTEL Châteauneuf-du-Pape 1986 $29 (2/29/88)
81   DOMAINE DU VIEUX LAZARET Châteauneuf-du-Pape 1986 $14.50 (3/15/89)
77   DOMAINE DU VIEUX TELEGRAPHE Châteauneuf-du-Pape 1986 $15 (11/15/87)
74   DOMAINE JEAN DEYDIER & FILS Châteauneuf-du-Pape Les Clefs D'Or 1986 $17 (11/15/87)

1985
82   CHATEAU DE BEAUCASTEL Châteauneuf-du-Pape 1985 $27 (11/15/87)
81   DOMAINE FONT DE MICHELLE Châteauneuf-du-Pape 1985 $15 (11/15/87)
73   DELAS Châteauneuf-du-Pape 1985 $18 (11/15/87)

1984
84   PIERRE ANDRE Châteauneuf-du-Pape 1984 $16.50 (10/01/85)

OTHER RHÔNE WHITE

1989
83   E. GUIGAL Côtes du Rhône 1989 $10 (3/31/91)
80   E. GUIGAL Tavel 1989 $15 (3/31/91)
80   LA VIEILLE FERME Côtes du Lubéron 1989 $7 (4/30/91) BB
79   LA BOUVERIE Costières de Nimes 1989 $6 (7/15/91)
67   PROSPER MAUFOUX Côtes du Rhône 1989 $8 (3/31/91)

1988
91   CUILLERON Condrieu 1988 $34 (12/31/90)
87   E. GUIGAL Hermitage 1988 $23 (3/31/91)

1988
85   LA VIEILLE FERME Côtes du Rhône Réserve 1988 $8 (10/31/89)
83   E. GUIGAL Côtes du Rhône 1988 $9 (3/15/90)
81   CUILLERON St.-Joseph Blanc 1988 $17 (12/31/90)
81   GEORGES VERNAY Condrieu 1988 $40 (10/31/89)
78   LA VIEILLE FERME Côtes du Lubéron 1988 $6.50 (3/15/90)
76   JEAN CLAUDE BOISSET Côtes du Rhône 1988 $4.50 (10/31/89)
68   CHATEAU DES ROQUES Côtes du Rhône-Villages Cuvée Bethleem 1988 $7.50 (3/31/90)

1987
89   E. GUIGAL Condrieu Viognier 1987 Rel: $48 Cur: $48 (3/15/89)
87   DEZORMEAUX Condrieu Viognier Côteaux du Colombier 1987 $37 (3/15/89)
86   CHATEAU MONT-REDON Côtes du Rhône 1987 $8 (10/31/89) BB
85   GEORGES VERNAY Condrieu 1987 $36 (3/15/89)
81   PROSPER MAUFOUX Côtes du Rhône 1987 $6 (7/15/89)
77   DOMAINE DE LA CAVALE Côtes du Lubéron 1987 $7 (2/15/89)
77   GEORGES VERNAY Condrieu Côteau de Vernon 1987 $43 (10/31/89)
70   PAUL JABOULET AINE Crozes-Hermitage Moute Blanche 1987 $11.50 (10/15/88)

1986
88   E. GUIGAL Hermitage 1986 Rel: $27 Cur: $27 (3/15/90) (HS)
87   PIERRE GAILLARD Côtes du Rhône Viognier Clos de Cuminaille 1986 $25 (3/15/89)
87   CHATEAU GRILLET Château-Grillet 1986 Rel: $75 Cur: $75 (3/15/89)
84   CAVE DE TAIN L'HERMITAGE Crozes-Hermitage Michel Courtial 1986 $8.50 (3/15/90)
83   M. CHAPOUTIER Hermitage Spécial Cuvée 180th Anniversary 1986 $24 (12/31/90)
80   CHATEAU DE FONSALETTE Côtes du Rhône 1986 $18.50 (3/15/89)
80   CHATEAU GRILLET Château-Grillet 1986 $75 (11/30/90)
71   LA VIEILLE FERME Côtes du Lubéron 1986 $6 (4/15/88)
70   JEAN CLAUDE BOISSET Côtes du Rhône 1986 $4.50 (11/15/87)
68   DOMAINE LES GOUBERT Côtes du Rhône-Villages Sablet 1986 $7 (3/31/88)

1985
81   VINCENT L. DARNAT Côtes du Rhône Blanc 1985 $5.50 (2/29/88) BB
81   CHATEAU DE SEGRIES Lirac 1985 $10 (12/15/89)
80   M. CHAPOUTIER Hermitage Chante Alouette 1985 $23 (3/15/90)
76   E. GUIGAL Hermitage 1985 Rel: $23 Cur: $23 (12/15/87)

1984
83   H. SORREL Hermitage Les Rocoules 1984 $20 (5/01/86)

1983
81   J.L. CHAVE Hermitage 1983 Rel: $20 Cur: $48 (5/01/86)
78   PAUL JABOULET AINE Hermitage Le Chevalier de Sterimberg 1983 $11 (5/01/86)
70   M. CHAPOUTIER Hermitage Chante Alouette 1983 $16 (5/01/86)

1981
64   E. GUIGAL Hermitage 1981 Rel: $15 Cur: $15 (5/01/86)

SAUTERNES

1989
95+   CHATEAU BASTOR-LAMONTAGNE Sauternes 1989 (NR) (6/15/90) (BT)
95+   CHATEAU CAILLOU Barsac 1989 (NR) (6/15/90) (BT)
95+   CHATEAU COUTET Barsac 1989 (NR) (6/15/90) (BT)
95+   CHATEAU LAFAURIE-PEYRAGUEY Sauternes 1989 (NR) (6/15/90) (BT)
90+   CHATEAU D'ARMAJAN-DES-ORMES Sauternes 1989 (NR) (6/15/90) (BT)
90+   CHATEAU BROUSTET Barsac 1989 (NR) (6/15/90) (BT)
90+   CHATEAU CLIMENS Barsac 1989 (NR) (6/15/90) (BT)
90+   CHATEAU DOISY-DUBROCA Barsac 1989 (NR) (6/15/90) (BT)
90+   CHATEAU DOISY-VEDRINES Sauternes 1989 (NR) (6/15/90) (BT)
90+   CHATEAU GRAVES Barsac 1989 (NR) (6/15/90) (BT)
90+   CHATEAU HAUT-BERGERON Sauternes 1989 (NR) (6/15/90) (BT)
90+   CHATEAU RIEUSSEC Sauternes 1989 (NR) (6/15/90) (BT)
90+   CHATEAU SIGALAS RABAUD Sauternes 1989 (NR) (6/15/90) (BT)
90+   CHATEAU SUDUIRAUT Sauternes 1989 (NR) (6/15/90) (BT)
85+   DOMAINE DE BARJUNEAU-CHAUVIN Sauternes 1989 (NR) (6/15/90) (BT)
85+   CHATEAU CAMERON Sauternes 1989 (NR) (6/15/90) (BT)
85+   CHATEAU CANTEGRIL Barsac 1989 (NR) (6/15/90) (BT)
85+   CHATEAU DOISY-DAENE Sauternes 1989 (NR) (6/15/90) (BT)
85+   CHATEAU FILHOT Sauternes 1989 (NR) (6/15/90) (BT)
85+   CHATEAU GUIRAUD Sauternes 1989 (NR) (6/15/90) (BT)
85+   CHATEAU HAUT-BOMMES Sauternes 1989 (NR) (6/15/90) (BT)
85+   CHATEAU LES JUSTICES Sauternes 1989 (NR) (6/15/90) (BT)
85+   CHATEAU LAMOTHE GUIGNARD Sauternes 1989 (NR) (6/15/90) (BT)
85+   CHATEAU LAMOTHE-DESPUJOLS Sauternes 1989 (NR) (6/15/90) (BT)
85+   CHATEAU LIOT Barsac 1989 (NR) (6/15/90) (BT)
85+   CHATEAU DE MALLE Sauternes 1989 (NR) (6/15/90) (BT)
85+   CHATEAU NAIRAC Barsac 1989 (NR) (6/15/90) (BT)
85+   CHATEAU PIADA Sauternes 1989 (NR) (6/15/90) (BT)
85+   CHATEAU PIOT-DAVID Barsac 1989 (NR) (6/15/90) (BT)
85+   CHATEAU RABAUD-PROMIS Sauternes 1989 (NR) (6/15/90) (BT)
85+   CHATEAU ROUMIEU-LACOSTE Barsac 1989 (NR) (6/15/90) (BT)
85+   CHATEAU ST.-MARC Barsac 1989 (NR) (6/15/90) (BT)
85+   CHATEAU SUAU Barsac 1989 (NR) (6/15/90) (BT)
85+   CHATEAU LA TOUR BLANCHE Sauternes 1989 (NR) (6/15/90) (BT)
80+   CHATEAU BECHEREAU Sauternes 1989 (NR) (6/15/90) (BT)
80+   CHATEAU CLOS HAUT-PEYRAGUEY Sauternes 1989 (NR) (6/15/90) (BT)
80+   CHATEAU DE RAYNE VIGNEAU Sauternes 1989 (NR) (6/15/90) (BT)
80+   CHATEAU ROMER DU HAYOT Sauternes 1989 (NR) (6/15/90) (BT)
75+   CHATEAU D'ARCHE-PUGNEAU Sauternes 1989 (NR) (6/15/90) (BT)
75+   CHATEAU MONT-JOYE Barsac 1989 (NR) (6/15/90) (BT)
70+   CHATEAU PROST Barsac 1989 (NR) (6/15/90) (BT)
60+   CHATEAU DUDON Barsac 1989 (NR) (6/15/90) (BT)

1988
95+   CHATEAU LES JUSTICES Sauternes 1988 $28 (6/15/90) (BT)
95+   CHATEAU RABAUD-PROMIS Sauternes 1988 $35 (6/15/90) (BT)
95+   CHATEAU RIEUSSEC Sauternes 1988 Rel: $50 Cur: $50 (6/15/90) (BT)
90+   CHATEAU D'ARCHE Sauternes 1988 Rel: $20 Cur: $28 (6/15/90) (BT)
90+   CHATEAU CLIMENS Barsac 1988 Rel: $48 Cur: $48 (6/15/90) (BT)
90+   CHATEAU COUTET Barsac 1988 Rel: $47 Cur: $47 (6/15/90) (BT)

Key to Symbols

The scores reported here are the results of blind tastings conducted by our panel of senior editors. Wines that carry the initials below are results of individual tastings.

THE WINE SPECTATOR 100-POINT SCALE   95-100—Classic, a great wine; **90-94**—Outstanding, superior character and style; **80-89**—Good to very good, a wine with special qualities; **70-79**—Average, drinkable wine that may have minor flaws; **60-69**—Below average, drinkable but not recommended; **50-59**—Poor, undrinkable, not recommended. "+"—With a score indicates a range; used primarily with barrel tastings to indicate a preliminary score.

SPECIAL DESIGNATIONS   SS—Spectator Selection, CS—Cellar Selection, BB—Best Buy.

TASTER'S INITIALS   (JG)—Jim Gordon, (HS)—Harvey Steiman, (JL)—James Laube, (JS)—James Suckling, (TM)—Thomas Matthews, (TR)—Terry Robards, (BT)—Barrel Tasting (these wines were tasted blind from barrel samples), (CA-date)—*California's Great Cabernets* by James Laube, (CH-date)—*California's Great Chardonnays* by James Laube, (VP-date)—*Vintage Port* by James Suckling.

DATE TASTED   Dates in parentheses represent the issue in which the rating was published.

90+ CHATEAU DOISY-VEDRINES Sauternes 1988 Rel: $31 Cur: $31 (6/15/90) (BT)
90+ CHATEAU HAUT-BERGERON Sauternes 1988 Rel: $31 (6/15/90) (BT)
90+ CHATEAU LAFAURIE-PEYRAGUEY Sauternes 1988 Rel: $35 Cur: $35 (6/15/90) (BT)
90+ CHATEAU PIADA Sauternes 1988 (NR) (6/15/90) (BT)
87   CHATEAU D'ARCHE Sauternes 1988 $20/375ml (4/30/91)
87   CHATEAU LES JUSTICES Sauternes 1988 $28 (2/15/91)
85   CHATEAU LAFAURIE-PEYRAGUEY Sauternes 1988 $35 (4/30/91)
85+ CHATEAU BASTOR-LAMONTAGNE Sauternes 1988 $18 (6/15/90) (BT)
85+ CHATEAU CAILLOU Barsac 1988 Rel: $37 Cur: $37 (6/15/90) (BT)
85+ CHATEAU CAMERON Sauternes 1988 (NR) (6/15/90) (BT)
85+ CHATEAU CLOS HAUT-PEYRAGUEY Sauternes 1988 $26 (6/15/90) (BT)
85+ CHATEAU DOISY-DAENE Sauternes 1988 Rel: $34 Cur: $34 (6/15/90) (BT)
85+ CHATEAU DOISY-DUBROCA Barsac 1988 Rel: $30 Cur: $30 (6/15/90) (BT)
85+ CHATEAU FARLURET Barsac 1988 (NR) (6/15/90) (BT)
85+ CHATEAU FILHOT Sauternes 1988 Rel: $25 Cur: $25 (6/15/90) (BT)
85+ CHATEAU GUIRAUD Sauternes 1988 Rel: $38 Cur: $38 (6/15/90) (BT)
85+ CHATEAU HAUT-CLAVERIE Sauternes 1988 (NR) (6/15/90) (BT)
85+ CHATEAU LAMOTHE GUIGNARD Sauternes 1988 $35 (6/15/90) (BT)
85+ CHATEAU DE MALLE Sauternes 1988 (NR) (6/15/90) (BT)
85+ CHATEAU NAIRAC Barsac 1988 $30 (6/15/90) (BT)
85+ CHATEAU DE RAYNE VIGNEAU Sauternes 1988 Rel: $31 (6/15/90) (BT)
85+ CHATEAU ROMER DU HAYOT Sauternes 1988 $17 (6/15/90) (BT)
85+ CHATEAU SUDUIRAUT Sauternes 1988 Rel: $45 Cur: $45 (6/15/90) (BT)
85+ CHATEAU LA TOUR BLANCHE Sauternes 1988 $29 (6/15/90) (BT)
84   CHATEAU LAMOTHE Sauternes 1988 $16/375ml (3/31/91)
83   CHATEAU BROUSTET Barsac 1988 $19/375ml (3/31/91)
82   CHATEAU BASTOR-LAMONTAGNE Sauternes 1988 $18 (2/15/91)
80+ CHATEAU BROUSTET Barsac 1988 $19 (6/15/90) (BT)
80+ CHATEAU DE LA CHARTREUSE Sauternes 1988 (NR) (6/15/90) (BT)
80+ CHATEAU LANGE Sauternes 1988 (NR) (6/15/90) (BT)
80+ CHATEAU LIOT Barsac 1988 $25 (6/15/90) (BT)
80+ CHATEAU MENOTA Barsac 1988 (NR) (6/15/90) (BT)
80+ DOMAINE DE MONTEILS Sauternes 1988 (NR) (6/15/90) (BT)
80+ CHATEAU ROLLAND Barsac 1988 (NR) (6/15/90) (BT)
80+ CHATEAU SUAU Barsac 1988 (NR) (6/15/90) (BT)
75+ CHATEAU D'ARCHE-PUGNEAU Sauternes 1988 (NR) (6/15/90) (BT)
75+ CHATEAU HAUT-BOMMES Sauternes 1988 (NR) (6/15/90) (BT)
72   CHATEAU ROMER DU HAYOT Sauternes 1988 $17/375ml (4/30/91)
70+ CHATEAU BOUYOT Barsac 1988 (NR) (6/15/90) (BT)

1987

89   CHATEAU RIEUSSEC Sauternes 1987 Rel: $31 Cur: $31 (6/15/90)
87   CHATEAU LAFAURIE-PEYRAGUEY Sauternes 1987 Rel: $27 Cur: $27 (6/15/90)
86   CHATEAU PIADA Sauternes 1987 $35 (3/31/91)
85   CHATEAU D'ARCHE Sauternes 1987 (NA) (6/15/90)
85   CHATEAU CAILLOU Barsac 1987 (NA) (6/15/90)
84   CHATEAU LAMOTHE-DESPUJOLS Sauternes 1987 (NA) (6/15/90)
83   CHATEAU CLOS HAUT-PEYRAGUEY Sauternes 1987 (NA) (6/15/90)
83   CHATEAU RABAUD-PROMIS Sauternes 1987 (NA) (6/15/90)
82   CHATEAU CAMERON Sauternes 1987 (NA) (6/15/90)
82   CHATEAU LA TOUR BLANCHE Sauternes 1987 (NA) (6/15/90)
81   CHATEAU HAUT-BERGERON Sauternes 1987 (NA) (6/15/90)
81   CHATEAU DE MALLE Sauternes 1987 (NA) (6/15/90)
81   CHATEAU NAIRAC Barsac 1987 $31 (6/15/90)
80   CHATEAU COUTET Barsac 1987 (NA) (6/15/90)
79   CHATEAU LA VIOLETTE Sauternes 1987 (NA) (6/15/90)
78   CHATEAU LANGE Sauternes 1987 (NA) (6/15/90)
78   CHATEAU MENOTA Barsac 1987 (NA) (6/15/90)
77   CHATEAU DE LA CHARTREUSE Sauternes 1987 (NA) (6/15/90)
77   CHATEAU LAMOTHE GUIGNARD Sauternes 1987 (NA) (6/15/90)
77   CHATEAU DE RAYNE VIGNEAU Sauternes 1987 (NA) (6/15/90)
77   CHATEAU ROLLAND Barsac 1987 (NA) (6/15/90)
76   CHATEAU PIADA Sauternes 1987 (NA) (6/15/90)
75   CHATEAU LES JUSTICES Sauternes 1987 (NA) (6/15/90)
74   DOMAINE DE BARJUNEAU-CHAUVIN Sauternes 1987 (NA) (6/15/90)
74   CHATEAU BOUYOT Barsac 1987 (NA) (6/15/90)
74   CHATEAU HAUT-BOMMES Sauternes 1987 (NA) (6/15/90)
72   CHATEAU D'ARMAJAN-DES-ORMES Sauternes 1987 (NA) (6/15/90)
72   CHATEAU GUIRAUD Sauternes 1987 (NA) (6/15/90)
72   CHATEAU GUIRAUD Sauternes Le Dauphin 1987 Rel: $11 Cur: $11 (12/31/89)
72   DOMAINE DE MONTEILS Sauternes 1987 (NA) (6/15/90)
71   CHATEAU D'ARCHE-PUGNEAU Sauternes 1987 (NA) (6/15/90)
69   CHATEAU ST.-MARC Barsac 1987 (NA) (6/15/90)
68   CHATEAU FILHOT Sauternes 1987 Rel: $19 Cur: $19 (6/15/90)
67   CHATEAU BASTOR-LAMONTAGNE Sauternes 1987 (NA) (6/15/90)
63   CHATEAU MONT-JOYE Barsac 1987 (NA) (6/15/90)

1986

95+ CHATEAU FILHOT Sauternes 1986 Rel: $19 Cur: $24 (6/30/88) (BT)
95+ CHATEAU RABAUD-PROMIS Sauternes 1986 $28 (6/30/88) (BT)
90+ CHATEAU D'ARCHE Sauternes 1986 Rel: $32 Cur: $32 (6/30/88) (BT)
90+ CHATEAU GUIRAUD Sauternes 1986 Rel: $48 Cur: $48 (6/30/88) (BT)
89   CHATEAU GUIRAUD Sauternes 1986 Rel: $48 Cur: $48 (12/31/89)
87   CHATEAU LIOT Barsac 1986 $22 (12/31/89)
87   CHATEAU D'YQUEM Sauternes 1986 $310 (2/28/91)
86   CHATEAU DOISY-VEDRINES Sauternes 1986 Rel: $19 Cur: $19 (12/31/89)
86   CHATEAU LAFAURIE-PEYRAGUEY Sauternes 1986 Rel: $27 Cur: $35 (12/31/89)
86   CHATEAU DE RAYNE VIGNEAU Sauternes 1986 Rel: $49 Cur: $49 (12/31/89)
85   CHATEAU D'ARCHE Sauternes 1986 Rel: $32 Cur: $32 (12/31/89)
85   CHATEAU LES JUSTICES Sauternes 1986 $16 (12/31/89)
85   CHATEAU LAMOTHE Sauternes 1986 $29 (12/31/89)
85   CHATEAU SUDUIRAUT Sauternes 1986 Rel: $35 Cur: $35 (12/31/89)
85+ CHATEAU CLIMENS Barsac 1986 Rel: $48 Cur: $48 (6/30/88) (BT)
85+ CHATEAU LAFAURIE-PEYRAGUEY Sauternes 1986 Rel: $27 Cur: $35 (6/30/88) (BT)
85+ CHATEAU DE MALLE Sauternes 1986 (NR) (6/30/88) (BT)
85+ CHATEAU NAIRAC Barsac 1986 $31 (6/30/88) (BT)
85+ CHATEAU ROMER DU HAYOT Sauternes 1986 $22 (6/30/88) (BT)
85+ CHATEAU SUAU Sauternes 1986 (NR) (6/30/88) (BT)
85+ CHATEAU LA TOUR BLANCHE Sauternes 1986 $26 (6/30/88) (BT)
84   CHATEAU CLIMENS Barsac 1986 Rel: $48 Cur: $48 (12/31/89)

83   CHATEAU FILHOT Sauternes 1986 Rel: $19 Cur: $24 (12/31/89)
80   CHATEAU SUDUIRAUT Sauternes 1986 Cur: $50 (12/31/89)
80+ CHATEAU CLOS HAUT-PEYRAGUEY Sauternes 1986 $23 (6/30/88) (BT)
80+ CHATEAU COUTET Barsac 1986 Cur: $30 (6/30/88) (BT)
80+ CHATEAU DOISY-VEDRINES Sauternes 1986 Rel: $19 Cur: $19 (6/30/88) (BT)
80+ CHATEAU LAMOTHE Sauternes 1986 $29 (6/30/88) (BT)
80+ CHATEAU DE RAYNE VIGNEAU Sauternes 1986 Rel: $49 Cur: $49 (6/30/88) (BT)
79   CHATEAU LA TOUR BLANCHE Sauternes 1986 $26 (12/31/89)
78   CHATEAU PASCAUD-VILLEFRANCHE Sauternes 1986 $24 (12/31/89)
78   CHATEAU ROMER DU HAYOT Sauternes 1986 $22 (12/31/89)
77   CHATEAU NAIRAC Barsac 1986 $31 (12/31/89)
77   CHATEAU SIGALAS RABAUD Sauternes 1986 Rel: $42 Cur: $42 (12/31/89)
75+ CHATEAU BROUSTET Barsac 1986 (NR) (6/30/88) (BT)
75+ CHATEAU CAILLOU Barsac 1986 Rel: $30 Cur: $30 (6/30/88) (BT)
75+ CHATEAU LAMOTHE GUIGNARD Sauternes 1986 $30 (6/30/88) (BT)
68   CHATEAU DOISY-DAENE Sauternes 1986 Rel: $35 Cur: $35 (12/31/89)

1985

94   CHATEAU D'YQUEM Sauternes 1985 Rel: $225 Cur: $225 (3/31/90)
92   CHATEAU LAFAURIE-PEYRAGUEY Sauternes 1985 Rel: $32 Cur: $35 (9/30/88)
86   CHATEAU RIEUSSEC Sauternes 1985 Cur: $38 (5/31/88)
85   CHATEAU LA TOUR BLANCHE Sauternes 1985 $25 (7/15/88)
84   CHATEAU LIOT Barsac 1985 $9.25 (5/31/88)
82   CHATEAU BASTOR-LAMONTAGNE Sauternes 1985 $20 (5/31/88)
82   CHATEAU SIGALAS RABAUD Sauternes 1985 Rel: $41 Cur: $41 (7/15/88)
81   DOMAINE DE CAPLANE Sauternes 1985 $11 (9/30/88)
81   CHATEAU SUDUIRAUT Sauternes 1985 Cur: $32 (11/30/88) (JS)
75   BARTON & GUESTIER Sauternes 1985 $12 (5/31/88)
73   CHATEAU DOISY-DAENE Sauternes 1985 Rel: $24 Cur: $24 (5/31/88)

1984

96   CHATEAU D'YQUEM Sauternes 1984 Rel: $149 Cur: $151 (3/31/90)
81   CHATEAU SUDUIRAUT Sauternes 1984 Cur: $22 (11/30/88) (JS)

1983

97   CHATEAU D'YQUEM Sauternes 1983 Rel: $180 Cur: $229 (1/31/88)
95   CHATEAU CLIMENS Barsac 1983 Rel: $50 Cur: $50 (1/31/88) CS
95   CHATEAU D'YQUEM Sauternes 1983 Rel: $180 Cur: $229 (10/15/87) CS
94   CHATEAU RIEUSSEC Sauternes 1983 Rel: $52 Cur: $57 (1/31/88)
93   CHATEAU D'ARCHE Sauternes 1983 Rel: $23 Cur: $43 (1/31/88)
93   CHATEAU RAYMOND-LAFON Sauternes 1983 Rel: $38 Cur: $60 (1/31/88)
93   CHATEAU RIEUSSEC Sauternes 1983 Rel: $52 Cur: $57 (3/16/86) CS
92   CHATEAU NAIRAC Barsac 1983 $15 (4/15/87)
91   CHATEAU LAFAURIE-PEYRAGUEY Sauternes 1983 Rel: $24 Cur: $40 (1/31/88)
90   CHATEAU DE LA CHARTREUSE Sauternes 1983 $10 (1/31/88)
90   CHATEAU RABAUD-PROMIS Sauternes 1983 $54 (1/31/88)
88   CHATEAU SIGALAS RABAUD Sauternes 1983 Rel: $24 Cur: $29 (1/31/88)
87   CHATEAU DOISY-DAENE Sauternes 1983 Rel: $21 Cur: $31 (1/31/88)
87   CHATEAU LA TOUR BLANCHE Sauternes 1983 $32 (1/31/88)
86   CHATEAU COUTET Barsac 1983 Rel: $30 Cur: $35 (1/31/88)
86   CHATEAU FILHOT Sauternes 1983 Rel: $21 Cur: $35 (1/31/88)
85   CHATEAU SUDUIRAUT Sauternes 1983 Rel: $30 Cur: $38 (11/30/88) (JS)
82   CHATEAU BASTOR-LAMONTAGNE Sauternes 1983 $20 (1/31/88)
82   CHATEAU SUDUIRAUT Sauternes 1983 Rel: $30 Cur: $38 (1/31/88)
77   CHATEAU DE RAYNE VIGNEAU Sauternes 1983 Rel: $17 Cur: $20 (1/31/88)
76   CHATEAU CAILLOU Barsac 1983 Rel: $22 Cur: $22 (1/31/88)
76   CHATEAU GUIRAUD Sauternes 1983 Rel: $30 Cur: $41 (1/31/88)
73   CHATEAU DOISY-VEDRINES Sauternes 1983 Rel: $18 Cur: $24 (1/31/88)
72   CHATEAU ROMER DU HAYOT Sauternes 1983 $19 (1/31/88)
70   CHATEAU PIADA Barsac 1983 $11 (1/31/88)
67   CHATEAU LES JUSTICES Sauternes 1983 $15 (1/31/88)
67   CHATEAU ROMER DU HAYOT Sauternes 1983 $19 (10/15/86)
65   CHATEAU PASCAUD-VILLEFRANCHE Sauternes 1983 $10 (1/31/88)
62   CHATEAU GUIRAUD Sauternes 1983 Rel: $30 Cur: $41 (4/30/87)
62   CHATEAU PAJOT Sauternes 1983 $8 (1/31/88)
56   CHATEAU LIOT Barsac 1983 $11.25 (4/01/86)

1982

90   CHATEAU SUDUIRAUT Sauternes Cuvée Madame 1982 (NA) (11/30/88) (JS)
86   CHATEAU RIEUSSEC Sauternes 1982 Rel: $6.50 Cur: $45/375ml (2/01/85)
83   CHATEAU SUDUIRAUT Sauternes 1982 Cur: $43 (11/30/88) (JS)
82   CHATEAU ROMER DU HAYOT Sauternes 1982 $13 (10/16/85)

1981

90   CHATEAU RIEUSSEC Sauternes 1981 Rel: $14.50 Cur: $32 (12/01/84)
84   CHATEAU DE MALLE Sauternes Comte de Bournazel 1981 $13 (8/31/86)

1980

80   CHATEAU FILHOT Sauternes 1980 Rel: $11.50 Cur: $25 (5/01/84)

1979

92   CHATEAU SUDUIRAUT Sauternes 1979 Rel: $19 Cur: $40 (2/16/84) CS
86   CHATEAU SUDUIRAUT Sauternes 1979 Rel: $19 Cur: $40 (11/30/88) (JS)

1978

78   CHATEAU SUDUIRAUT Sauternes 1978 Cur: $42 (11/30/88) (JS)

1976

94   CHATEAU D'YQUEM Sauternes 1976 Cur: $290 (12/15/88)
77   CHATEAU SUDUIRAUT Sauternes 1976 Cur: $79 (11/30/88) (JS)

1975

84   CHATEAU SUDUIRAUT Sauternes 1975 Cur: $51 (11/30/88) (JS)

1972

77   CHATEAU SUDUIRAUT Sauternes 1972 Cur: $25 (11/30/88) (JS)

1970

81   CHATEAU SUDUIRAUT Sauternes 1970 Cur: $56 (11/30/88) (JS)

FRANCE
SAUTERNES

1969
88   CHATEAU SUDUIRAUT Sauternes 1969 Cur: $70 (11/30/88) (JS)

1959
93   CHATEAU SUDUIRAUT Sauternes 1959 Cur: $200 (11/30/88) (JS)

1937
93   CHATEAU D'YQUEM Sauternes 1937 Cur: $1,030/1.5L (12/15/88)

1928
90   CHATEAU SUDUIRAUT Sauternes 1928 Cur: $500 (11/30/88) (JS)

OTHER FRANCE DESSERT

1989
89   DOMAINE DU CLOS NAUDIN Vouvray Moelleux Réserve 1989 $54 (3/31/91)
87   DOMAINE DE LA MELOTERIE Vouvray Demi-Sec 1989 $9 (6/15/91)
83   DOMAINE DU CLOS NAUDIN Vouvray Moelleux 1989 $34 (4/30/91)
80   DOMAINE LE PEU DE LA MORIETTE Vouvray Moelleux Cuvée Exceptionelle 1989 $19 (6/15/91)

1988
86   DOMAINE DE DURBAN Muscat de Beaumes-de-Venise 1988 $15 (3/31/91)
82   DOMAINE DU MAS BLANC Collioure Cuvée Cosprons Levants 1988 $21 (3/31/91)
81   M & G Vouvray Moelleux 1988 $10 (3/31/91)
80   DOMAINE ST.-SAUVEUR Muscat de Beaumes-de-Venise Vin Doux Naturel 1988 $17 (3/31/91)
76   CHATEAU LE BARRADIS Monbazillac 1988 $20 (7/15/91)

1986
84   PAUL JABOULET AINE Muscat de Beaumes-de-Venise Vin Doux Naturel 1986 $17 (10/15/88)
80   CHATEAU DE RICAUD Loupiac 1986 $17/375ml (12/31/89)

1985
78   CHATEAU LAURETTE Ste.-Croix-de-Mont 1985 $8.50 (9/30/88)
75   MARC BREDIF Vouvray Vin Moelleux Nectar 1985 $9/375ml (6/15/91)

1982
82   DOMAINE DU MAS BLANC Banyuls Vieilles Vignes 1982 $27 (2/28/91)
80   DOMAINE DU MAS BLANC Banyuls Vendanges Tardives 1982 $26 (2/28/91)

1976
85   DOMAINE DU MAS BLANC Banyuls Vieilles Vignes 1976 $40 (2/28/91)

NV
88   PROSPER MAUFOUX Muscat de Beaumes-de-Venise NV $16 (8/31/89)
82   LEYRAT Pineau des Charentes Grande Réserve Sélection Robert Hass NV $23 (3/31/91)

OTHER FRANCE RED

1989
82   CHATEAU LA DECELLE Côteaux du Tricastin 1989 $7.50 (7/15/91) BB
78   PAR E. REYNAUD Vin de Pays de Vaucluse Domaine des Tours 1989 $8 (3/31/91)
74   GUY CHEVALIER Vin de Pays de l'Aude Le Texas 1989 $9 (7/15/91)

1988
85   CELLIER DE LA DONA Côtes du Roussillon-Villages 1988 $8.50 (10/15/90) BB
81   CHANTOVENT Cabernet Sauvignon Vin de Pays d'Oc Prestige 1988 $6 (3/15/90) BB
81   ROGER MARES Cabernet-Syrah Mas des Bressades 1988 $10.50 (10/31/90)
80   CHANTEFLEUR Cabernet Sauvignon Vin de Pays de l'Ardèche 1988 $6 (5/31/90) BB
80   CHATEAU LES OLLIEUX Corbières 1988 $5.25 (11/30/90) BB
79   VIGNERONS ARDECHOIS Vin de Pays des Côteaux de l'Ardeche 1988 $4.50 (4/30/90) BB
79   MAS DE GOURGONNIER Côteaux des Baux en Provence Les Baux de Provence 1988 $8.50 (4/30/91)
78   DOMAINE LA ROSIERE Côteaux des Baronnies Syrah 1988 $6.50 (2/28/90)
78   CLOS DE VILLEMAJOU Corbières 1988 $6 (4/30/90)
77   CHATEAU CAPENDU Corbières Cuvée Elevée en Futs Grande Réserve 1988 $6 (5/31/90)
77   DOMAINE DONA BAISSAS Côtes du Roussillon-Villages 1988 $7 (10/15/90)
77   CHATEAU MILLEGRAND Minervois 1988 $5 (4/30/90)
77   DOMAINE PERRIERE Vin de Pays de l'Aude Les Amandiers 1988 $4.50 (4/15/90)
76   DOMAINE DU PUGET Merlot Vin de Pays de l'Aude 1988 $4 (6/30/90)
75   CHANTEFLEUR Merlot Vin de Pays d'Oc 1988 $6 (5/31/90)
75   DOMAINE RICHEAUME Cabernet Sauvignon Côtes de Provence 1988 $15 (10/31/90)
74   DOMAINE DE SAULT Corbières 1988 $5 (6/30/90)
73   CHANTOVENT Merlot Vin de Pays d'Oc Prestige 1988 $6 (3/15/90)
73   DOMAINE RICHEAUME Côtes de Provence Syrah 1988 $15 (10/31/90)
70   FORTANT Cabernet Sauvignon Vin de Pays d'Oc 1988 $6 (4/30/90)
70   FORTANT Merlot Vin de Pays d'Oc 1988 $6 (5/31/91)
69   CHATEAU CANET Minervois Cuvée Elevée en Futs Grande Réserve 1988 $6 (5/31/90)
67   HERZOG Cabernet Sauvignon Vin de Pays d'Oc 1988 $6 (3/15/90)
67   CHATEAU DE PARAZA Minervois Cuvée Spéciale 1988 $7 (5/31/91)
63   CHATEAU LA PALME Côtes du Frontonnais 1988 $7 (7/31/91)

1987
88   DOMAINE TEMPIER Bandol Cuvée Spéciale Cabassaou 1987 $23 (10/31/90)
86   DOMAINE TEMPIER Bandol Cuvée Spéciale La Migoua 1987 $22 (10/31/90)
85   MAS DE DAUMAS GASSAC Vin de Pays de l'Herault 1987 $23 (10/31/89)
83   DANIEL BESSIERE Côteaux du Languedoc 1987 $5 (9/30/89) BB
83   LA ROGUE Bandol 1987 $10.50 (11/30/90)
82   DOMAINE TEMPIER Bandol Cuvée Spéciale La Tourtine 1987 $22 (10/31/90)
80   CHATEAUX DE MOUJAN Côteaux du Languedoc 1987 $4 (8/31/89)
79   DANIEL BESSIERE St.-Chinian 1987 $6 (8/31/89)
78   CHANTOVENT Cabernet Sauvignon Vin de Pays d'Oc Prestige 1987 $5 (10/31/89)
78   LAJOLIE Cabernet Sauvignon Vin de Pays d'Oc 1987 $6 (10/31/88)
78   MOCERI Merlot Vin de Pays de l'Aude 1987 $4 (6/30/90)
78   DOMAINES OTT Côtes de Provence Société Civile des Domaines Ott Frères 1987 $22 (5/31/91)
78   CHATEAU PECH DE JAMMES Cahors 1987 $9 (6/30/90)
78   DOMAINE DE TREVALLON Côteaux d'Aix en Provence Les Baux 1987 $18 (3/31/90)
77   MARILYN MERLOT Merlot Vin de Pays de l'Aude 1987 $6 (3/15/90)
77   MOCERI Cabernet Sauvignon Vin de Pays de l'Aude 1987 $4 (6/30/90) BB
77   PLACE D'ARGENT Merlot Vin de Pays de l'Aude 1987 $5 (4/30/90)
76   TROUBADOUR Merlot Vin de Pays de l'Aude 1987 $5 (8/31/90)
75   DOMAINE DU CEDRE Cahors Le Prestige 1987 $14 (3/15/90)
75   CHATEAU DE PIBARNON Bandol 1987 $17 (3/15/90)
73   DANIEL BESSIERE Faugères 1987 $6 (9/15/89)
72   DOMAINES GAVOTY Côtes de Provence Cuvée Clarendon 1987 $8.50 (3/31/90)

1986
87   DOMAINE DE TREVALLON Côteaux d'Aix en Provence Les Baux 1986 $21 (4/15/89)
85   CHATEAU DE BEAUREGARD Côteaux du Languedoc 1986 $3.75 (5/31/88) BB
83   CHATEAU PRADEAUX Bandol 1986 $17.50 (10/31/90)
82   DOMAINE DE LA BOUSQUETTE St.-Chinian 1986 $8 (3/31/90)
81   DANIEL BESSIERE Minervois 1986 $6 (9/15/89) BB
81   MAS DE DAUMAS GASSAC Vin de Pays de l'Herault 1986 $25 (12/15/88)
80   CHATEAU VANNIERES Côtes de Provence La Provence de Vannières 1986 $15 (8/31/89)
79   CHANTOVENT Cabernet Sauvignon Vin de Pays d'Oc Prestige 1986 $6.50 (5/15/89)
79   CHATEAU DE PADERE Buzet 1986 $5.75 (12/15/88)
77   CHATEAU ETANG DES COLOMBES Corbières Cuvée du Bicentenaire 1986 $9 (3/31/91)
77   DOMAINE DE FONTSAINTE Corbières Réserve la Demoiselle 1986 $7 (8/31/89)
76   DOMAINE DES JOUGLA St.-Chinian 1986 $6.75 (5/15/89)
76   CHATEAU DE PARAZA Minervois Cuvée Spéciale 1986 $6 (10/15/88)
74   CHATEAU DE LA TUILERIE Costières du Gard 1986 $4.75 (6/30/88)
72   CHATEAU FABAS Minervois 1986 $5.50 (9/15/89)
69   CHANTOVENT Merlot Vin de Pays d'Oc Prestige 1986 $6.50 (5/15/89)
67   CHATEAU VANNIERES Bandol 1986 $15 (9/15/89)
60   DOMAINE SARDA-MALET Côtes du Roussillon 1986 $7.50 (10/15/90)

1985
82   CLOS TRIGUEDINA Cahors Prince Probus 1985 $17 (2/28/91)
82   CHATEAU DE TIREGAND Pécharmant 1985 $8 (10/31/88)
82   DOMAINE DE TREVALLON Côteaux d'Aix en Provence Les Baux 1985 $13 (2/29/88)
81   CHATEAU DU CAYROU Cahors 1985 $8.75 (12/31/88)
80   DOMAINE DU CEDRE Cahors Le Prestige 1985 $9 (12/31/88)
80   CHATEAU DE PARAZA Minervois 1985 $6.25 (2/29/88)
80   PLACE D'ARGENT Merlot Vin de Pays de l'Aude 1985 $5.50 (12/15/88) BB
79   LES PRODUCTEURS DU MONT TAUCH Fitou 1985 $6 (4/15/89)
79   CHATEAU MONTUS Madiran 1985 $10 (4/15/89)
79   CHATEAU DE PIBARNON Bandol 1985 $17.25 (10/15/88)
78   GILBERT ALQUIER Faugères 1985 $7 (9/30/87)
78   PLACE D'ARGENT Cabernet Sauvignon Vin de Pays de l'Aude 1985 $5.50 (4/15/89)
77   DOMAINE D'ORMESSON Vin de Pays d'Oc 1985 $4 (4/15/89)
77   CHATEAU DE LA TUILERIE Costières du Gard 1985 $6 (2/15/87) BB
73   CHATEAU ETANG DES COLOMBES Corbières Cuvée du Bicentenaire 1985 $6 (4/15/88)
72   CHATEAU BELLEVUE LA FORET Côtes du Frontonnais 1985 $6 (11/15/87)
72   DOMAINE DU MEUNIER Côtes de Gascogne 1985 $5 (5/31/88)
71   CHATEAU TRINITE VALROSE Ile de Patires 1985 $6 (11/15/87)
71   CLOS DE VILLEMAJOU Corbières 1985 $7.50 (5/31/90)

1984
83   DOMAINE DE FONTSAINTE Corbières Rouge Réserve la Demoiselle 1984 $8 (10/31/87)
82   MAS DE GOURGONNIER Côteaux des Baux en Provence Côteaux d'Aix 1984 $5.50 (3/15/87) BB
79   DOMAINE TEMPIER Bandol 1984 $15 (12/15/87)
75   ST.-FLORANT Cabernet Sauvignon 1984 $5 (2/28/87)
70   CHATEAU DE PIBARNON Bandol 1984 (NA) (8/31/86)

1983
80   CLOS TRIGUEDINA Cahors 1983 $11 (2/28/91)
80   CHATEAU LES MUTS Côtes de Bergerac 1983 $6.50 (11/15/86)
80   CHATEAU VANNIERES Bandol 1983 (NA) (8/31/86) (JS)
79   CLOS TRIGUEDINA Cahors Prince Probus 1983 $14.25 (12/31/88)
78   DOMAINE TEMPIER Bandol 1983 $16 (8/31/87)
77   CHATEAU PECH DE JAMMES Cahors 1983 $9.50 (10/15/88)
76   CHATEAU PETIT CHOLET 1983 $3.25 (4/16/85)
70   MAS DE GOURGONNIER Côteaux des Baux en Provence 1983 $3.75 (12/16/85)
68   CHATEAU L'OREE DU BOIS 1983 $4 (5/01/86)
67   DOMAINES LAFRAN-VEYROLLES Bandol 1983 (NA) (8/31/86)
65   MAS DE LA ROUVIERE Bandol 1983 (NA) (8/31/86)

1982
79   CHATEAU L'OREE DU BOIS 1982 $4 (3/16/85)
76   CHATEAU DE CHARRON 1982 $5 (7/01/85)
75   CHATEAU DE PIBARNON Bandol 1982 $9.75 (10/01/85)
73   MAS DE LA ROUVIERE Bandol 1982 (NA) (8/31/86)
60   DOMAINE DE TERREBRUNE Bandol 1982 (NA) (8/31/86)

1981
89   CHATEAU VIGNELAURE Côteaux d'Aix en Provence 1981 $10 (10/01/84)
73   DOMAINE TEMPIER Bandol 1981 (NA) (8/31/86)
68   DOMAINE DE LA VIVONNE Bandol 1981 (NA) (8/31/86)
58   CHATEAU PRADEAUX Bandol Réserve 1981 (NA) (8/31/86) (JS)

1979

80 MAS DE LA ROUVIERE Bandol 1979 (NA) (8/31/86)

NV

88 HERZOG Cabernet Sauvignon Vin de Pays d'Oc NV $7 (3/31/91) BB
85 LA SABONITE Vin de Table Français NV $5.50 (9/30/88) BB
81 MOILLARD Moillard Rouge NV $4.50 (5/31/88) BB
79 CHEVALIER DE BEAUBASSIN Cuvée Montgolfier NV $4 (3/31/88)
79 RAOUL CLERGET Prestige de Raoul Clerget NV $3 (7/15/88)
79 CLOS STE. NICOLE Merlot French-California Cuvée NV $5 (10/31/89)
78 PERE ANSELME Merlot Vin de Pays des Côteaux d'Enserune NV $5.50 (7/15/89)
77 CLOS STE. NICOLE Cabernet Sauvignon French-California Cuvée NV $5 (10/31/89)
75 BICHOT Vin Rouge NV $3 (8/31/89)
75 JEAN CORDIER Vin de Table Rouge Français NV $3 (12/31/90)
75 HERZOG Merlot Vin de Pays d'Oc NV $7 (3/31/91)
72 BOUCHARD AINE Merlot Vin de Pays de l'Aude NV $5 (6/30/90)
72 ST.-CESAIRE Vin de Pays des Bouches du Rhône NV $4.25 (6/30/90)
68 BICHOT Vin Rouge NV $3 (2/16/86)
66 JEAN CORDIER Rouge NV $3 (12/15/88)

OTHER FRANCE SPARKLING

1988

83 DARGENT Brut Blanc de Blancs Côtes du Jura Chardonnay 1988 $10.50 (6/15/90)

1986

82 MONMOUSSIN Brut Touraine Etoile 1986 $13 (12/31/90)
81 LAURENS Blanc de Blancs Blanquette de Limoux Clos des Demoiselles 1986 $11 (12/31/90)
80 JEAN PHILIPPE Brut Blanquette de Limoux 1986 $10.25 (6/15/90)
79 CHARBAUT FRERES Brut Blanc de Blancs Crémant de Bourgogne 1986 $11.50 (12/31/90)
79 CHARBAUT FRERES Brut Rosé Crémant de Bourgogne 1986 $11.50 (12/31/90)
78 DOMAINE ROBERT Brut Blanc de Blancs Blanquette de Limoux 1986 $8.75 (6/15/90)

1985

87 BOUVET Brut Saumur Saphir 1985 $14 (10/15/88)
85 SILVER CLOUD Brut Blanc de Blancs Blanquette de Limoux 1985 $9 (4/15/90)
84 BOUVET Brut Saumur Saphir 1985 $14 (6/15/90)
81 MONMOUSSIN Extra Dry Vouvray 1985 $13 (12/31/90)
57 KRITER Blanc de Blancs Brut de Brut 1985 $9 (6/15/90)

1984

86 DARGENT Brut Rosé Côtes du Jura 1984 $10 (3/31/88)
82 DARGENT Brut Blanc de Blancs Côtes du Jura 1984 $10 (3/31/88)

1983

83 KRITER Brut Blanc de Blancs Extra Leger 1983 $6 (5/31/87) BB
79 MONMOUSSIN Brut Touraine Monmousseau 1983 $11 (2/15/88)
77 DOMAINE ROBERT Brut Blanc de Blancs Blanquette de Limoux 1983 $8 (1/31/88)
70 COMTE DE BAILLY Brut Crémant de Bourgogne 1983 $8 (10/15/86)
69 MONMOUSSIN Brut Vouvray Cuvée du Centenaire 1983 $11 (1/31/88)
57 KRITER Brut Blanc de Blancs Imperial 1983 $12 (6/15/90)

1982

84 CHATEAU DE POCE Brut Crémant de Loire 1982 $12 (7/31/88)

NV

88 CHARLES DE FERE Brut Tradition NV $12 (6/15/90)
87 VARICHON & CLERC Brut Blanc de Blancs NV $7 (12/31/89) BB
86 BOUVET Sparkling Rubis NV $12 (9/30/88)
86 LANGLOIS-CHATEAU Rosé Saumur Crémant NV $10.50 (7/15/88)
85 BOUVET Brut Saumur Signature NV $11.50 (10/15/88)
85 BOUVET Brut Rosé Excellence NV $12 (10/15/88)
84 DOMAINE DU BICHERON Blanc de Blancs Crémant de Bourgogne NV $12 (3/31/90)
84 LANGLOIS-CHATEAU Brut Crémant de Loire NV $10.50 (7/15/88)
84 DOMAINE DE MARTINOLES Brut Blanquette de Limoux NV $8 (4/15/90) BB
83 GEORGES BLANC Sparkling Blanc de Blanc NV $9 (12/31/87)
83 GRATIEN Brut Saumur NV $9.25 (6/15/90)
83 KRITER Demi-Sec Délicatesse NV $12 (6/15/90)
83 ALSACE WILLM Brut Crémant d'Alsace NV $10.50 (4/15/90)
83 WOLFBERGER Sparkling Crémant d'Alsace NV $12 (7/31/89)
82 GRANDIN Brut Ingrandes-Sur-Loire NV $10 (6/15/90)
82 VARICHON & CLERC Demi-Sec NV $7 (1/31/90) BB
81 MAISTRE BLANQUETIER Brut Blanquette de Limoux Le Berceau NV $9 (4/15/90)
81 BOUVET Brut Saumur Ladubay Tresor NV $44 (10/15/88)
81 DE JESSY Extra Dry NV $9 (6/15/90)
81 CHATEAU DE POCE Brut Touraine Crémant de Blancs NV $10.75 (10/15/88)
80 BOUVET Brut Rosé NV $10 (6/15/90)
80 BOUVET Brut Rosé Excellence NV $12 (6/15/90)
80 LE CARDINALE Brut NV $5.25 (6/15/90) BB
80 JEAN PHILIPPE Brut Blanquette de Limoux NV $9.75 (1/31/88)
79 BRUMMELL Blanc de Blancs Carte Noir NV $7.25 (6/15/90)
79 BERNARD DELMAS Brut Blanquette de Limoux NV $14 (3/31/90)
79 MURE Brut Crémant d'Alsace Réserve NV $7 (6/15/90)
78 LES ACACIAS Brut Crémant de Bourgogne Cépage Chardonnay NV $11 (6/15/90)
78 VEUVE AMIOT Brut Saumur Cuvée Haute Tradition NV $13 (3/31/90)
77 CHARLES DE FERE Brut Blanc de Blancs Réserve NV $10 (6/15/90)
76 GRAND IMPERIAL Brut NV $4.50 (6/15/90)
75 BOUVET Brut Saumur Signature NV $11.50 (6/15/90)
74 PAUL CHAMBLAIN Brut Blanc de Blancs NV $6.75 (6/15/90)
74 GRATIEN Sparkling Saumur Rouge NV $12 (7/15/88)
74 PHILIPPE HERARD Brut Blanc de Blancs NV $9.50 (6/15/90)
72 BOUVET Sparkling Rubis NV $12 (6/15/90)
71 KRITER Brut Rosé NV $9 (6/15/90)
71 KRITER Demi-Sec NV $9 (6/15/90)
70 BLANQUETTE DE LIMOUX Brut Blanc de Blancs Blanquette de Limoux Cuvée Réserve NV $9 (5/31/87)
70 BARON CHAGALE Brut Blanc de Blancs NV $6 (6/15/90)
70 CHARLES DE FERE Brut Rosé NV $10 (6/15/90)

---

65 MURE Sparkling Crémant d'Alsace Réserve NV $11.50 (5/31/87)
63 LA FOLIE Brut Blanc de Blancs Réserve NV $5.50 (6/15/90)
61 AUBEL Brut Blanc de Blancs NV $6 (6/01/86)

OTHER FRANCE WHITE

1989

86 DOMAINE DU TARIQUET Vin de Pays des Côtes de Gascogne 1989 $5.75 (11/15/90) BB
82 DOMAINE ST. MARTIN DE LA GARRIGUE Chardonnay Vin de Pays des Côteaux de Bessilles 1989 $12 (4/30/91)
80 GEORGES DUBOEUF Chardonnay Vin de Pays d'Oc 1989 $6.50 (11/15/90) BB
80 DOMAINE DE POUY Vin de Pays des Côtes de Gascogne Cépage Ugni Blanc 1989 $5 (11/30/90) BB
76 HERZOG Chardonnay Vin de Pays d'Oc 1989 $9 (3/31/91)
75 BOUCHARD PERE & FILS Chardonnay Vin de Pays d'Oc Première 1989 $9 (4/30/91)
69 FORTANT Chardonnay Vin de Pays d'Oc 1989 $6 (5/31/91)

1988

80 DOMAINE DES JOUGLA Limoux 1988 $8 (3/31/90)
79 CHANTEFLEUR Chardonnay Vin de Pays d'Oc 1988 $6 (4/30/90)
75 DOMAINE AUFFRAY Chardonnay Vin de Pays de l'Yonne 1988 $8 (4/15/90)
74 DOMAINE DE PETIT ROUBIE Sauvignon Blanc Côteaux du Languedoc Picpoul de Pinet 1988 $7 (3/31/90)

1987

77 BICHOT Côtes de Duras 1987 $4 (5/15/89)
74 BOUCHARD AINE Chardonnay Vin de Pays de l'Aude 1987 $6.50 (9/30/88)
74 DOMAINE DU MONTMARIN Vin de Pays des Côtes de Thongue Cépage Marsanne 1987 $5 (2/15/89)
73 LAROCHE Chardonnay 1987 $7 (3/31/88)
73 LAROCHE Chardonnay Vin de Pays l'Ile de Beaute 1987 $7 (10/31/89)
68 LES PRODUCTEURS DU MONT TAUCH Corbières 1987 $5 (2/15/89)

1986

80 LABOURE-ROI Chardonnay Vin de Pays d'Oc 1986 $7 (3/31/88) BB
75 BICHOT Côtes de Duras 1986 $3.50 (12/31/88)
72 LOUIS LATOUR Chardonnay Vin de Pays des Côteaux de l'Ardeche 1986 $8.50 (12/31/88)
70 PHILIPPE ANTOINE Chardonnay 1986 $5 (3/31/88)
70 LAROCHE Chardonnay 1986 $7 (8/31/87)
68 CHEVALIER DE BEAUBASSIN Chardonnay Vin de Pays d'Oc 1986 $4.75 (4/15/88)
64 GEORGES DUBOEUF Chardonnay Vin de Pays d'Oc 1986 $5 (7/31/87)

1985

73 CHATEAU DE LA TUILERIE Costières du Gard 1985 $4.50 (1/31/87)
65 ST.-FLORANT Chardonnay 1985 $5 (2/15/87)

1984

75 CLOS STE. MAGDELEINE Cassis 1984 $12 (11/15/87)

1983

46 CHATEAU DE FONTBLANCHE Cassis E. Bodin 1983 $6.50 (11/16/85)

NV

85 MAS DE DAUMAS GASSAC Vin de Pays de l'Herault NV $37 (3/31/90)
75 CHEVALIER DE BEAUBASSIN Cuvée Montgolfier NV $3.75 (5/31/88)
75 MOREAU Moreau Blanc NV $4 (3/31/87)
73 DOMAINE DE FONTSAINTE Corbières Gris de Gris NV $7 (10/31/87)
72 JEAN CORDIER Vin de Table Blanc Français NV $3 (12/31/90)

GERMANY

RIESLING/*MOSEL-SAAR-RUWER*

1989

100 EGON MULLER Trockenbeerenauslese Mosel-Saar-Ruwer Scharzhofberger 1989 (NA) (12/15/90) (JS)

99 C. VON SCHUBERT Beerenauslese Mosel-Saar-Ruwer Maximin Grunhauser Abtsberg 1989 (NA) (12/15/90)

97 EGON MULLER Auslese Mosel-Saar-Ruwer Scharzhofberger Gold Cap 1989 $385 (12/15/90) (JS)

97 EGON MULLER Eiswein Mosel-Saar-Ruwer Scharzhofberger 1989 (NA) (12/15/90) (JS)

97 SELBACH-OSTER Trockenbeerenauslese Mosel-Saar-Ruwer Zeltingen-Rachtiger Sonnenuhr 1989 $100/375ml (12/15/90)

96 C. VON SCHUBERT Trockenbeerenauslese Mosel-Saar-Ruwer Maximin Grunhauser Herrenberg 1989 (NA) (12/15/90)

96 ZILLIKEN Eiswein Mosel-Saar-Ruwer Saarburger Rausch 1989 (NA) (12/15/90)

95 EGON MULLER Beerenauslese Mosel-Saar-Ruwer Scharzhofberger 1989 (NA) (12/15/90) (JS)

95 EGON MULLER Trockenbeerenauslese Mosel-Saar-Ruwer Le Gallais Wiltingener Braune Kupp 1989 (NA) (12/15/90) (JS)

95 JOH. JOS. PRUM Beerenauslese Mosel-Saar-Ruwer Wehlener Sonnenuhr 1989 (NA) (12/15/90) (JS)

95 C. VON SCHUBERT Auslese Mosel-Saar-Ruwer Maximin Grunhauser Abtsberg (cask 96) 1989 (NA) (12/15/90)

95 ZILLIKEN Auslese Mosel-Saar-Ruwer Saarburger Rausch Long Gold Cap 1989 $64 (12/15/90)

95+ BERT SIMON Trockenbeerenauslese Mosel-Saar-Ruwer Serriger Würtzberg 1989 $96/375ml (12/15/90) (BT)

94 KESSELSTATT Beerenauslese Mosel-Saar-Ruwer Scharzhofberger 1989 $220 (12/15/90)

94 KESSELSTATT Trockenbeerenauslese Mosel-Saar-Ruwer Scharzhofberger 1989 $150 (12/15/90)

94 EGON MULLER Spätlese Mosel-Saar-Ruwer Scharzhofberger 1989 $31 (12/15/90) (JS)

94 JOH. JOS. PRUM Auslese Mosel-Saar-Ruwer Wehlener Sonnenuhr Long Gold Cap 1989 $249 (12/15/90) (JS)

93 EGON MULLER Auslese Mosel-Saar-Ruwer Scharzhofberger 1989 (NA) (12/15/90) (JS)

93 BERT SIMON Beerenauslese Mosel-Saar-Ruwer Serriger Würtzberg 1989 $53/375ml (12/15/90)

93 VON HOVEL Beerenauslese Mosel-Saar-Ruwer Oberemmeler Hütte 1989 $88/375ml (12/15/90)

92 FRITZ HAAG Auslese Mosel-Saar-Ruwer Brauneberger Juffer-Sonnenuhr Long Gold Cap 1989 $150 (12/15/90) (JS)

92 KESSELSTATT Auslese Mosel-Saar-Ruwer Oberemmeler Karlsberg 1989 $32 (12/15/90)

92 KESSELSTATT Auslese Mosel-Saar-Ruwer Scharzhofberger Gold Cap 1989 $48 (12/15/90)

92 JOH. JOS. PRUM Auslese Mosel-Saar-Ruwer Wehlener Sonnenuhr 1989 $35 (12/15/90) (JS)

92 MAX FERD. RICHTER Trockenbeerenauslese Mosel-Saar-Ruwer Mülheimer Sonnenlay 1989 $100/375ml (12/15/90)

92 VON HOVEL Auslese Mosel-Saar-Ruwer Oberemmeler Hütte Gold Cap 1989 $45/375ml (12/15/90)

91 EGON MULLER Beerenauslese Mosel-Saar-Ruwer Le Gallais Wiltingener Braune Kupp 1989 (NA) (12/15/90) (JS)

91 PETER NICOLAY Trockenbeerenauslese Mosel-Saar-Ruwer Urziger Würzgarten 1989 $325 (12/15/90) (JS)

91 JOH. JOS. PRUM Kabinett Mosel-Saar-Ruwer Wehlener Sonnenuhr 1989 $21 (12/15/90) (JS)

91 JOH. JOS. PRUM Spätlese Mosel-Saar-Ruwer Wehlener Sonnenuhr 1989 $29 (12/15/90) (JS)

91 SELBACH-OSTER Beerenauslese Mosel-Saar-Ruwer Zeltingen-Rachtiger Sonnenuhr 1989 $56/375ml (12/15/90)

91 DR. H. THANISCH (MULLER-BURGGRAEFF) Beerenauslese Mosel-Saar-Ruwer Bernkasteler Doctor 1989 $240 (12/15/90) (JS)

91 C. VON SCHUBERT Auslese Mosel-Saar-Ruwer Maximin Grunhauser Herrenberg (cask 93) 1989 $80 (12/15/90)

90 FRIEDRICH-WILHELM-GYMNASIUM Beerenauslese Mosel-Saar-Ruwer Graacher Himmelreich 1989 $150 (12/15/90) (JS)

90 FRITZ HAAG Auslese Mosel-Saar-Ruwer Brauneberger Juffer-Sonnenuhr Gold Cap 1989 $150 (12/15/90) (JS)

90 KESSELSTATT Spätlese Mosel-Saar-Ruwer Scharzhofberger 1989 $13 (12/15/90)

90 LINGENFELDER Spätlese Mosel-Saar-Ruwer Grosskarlbacher Burgweg Scheurebe 1989 $14 (12/15/90) (JS)

90 STAATLICHEN WEINBAUDOMANEN Auslese Mosel-Saar-Ruwer Schlossböckelheimer Kupfergrube 1989 $19 (12/15/90)

90 STAATLICHEN WEINBAUDOMANEN Spätlese Mosel-Saar-Ruwer Schlossböckelheimer Kupfergrube 1989 (NA) (12/15/90)

90 VON HOVEL Spätlese Mosel-Saar-Ruwer Oberemmeler Hütte 1989 $16 (12/15/90)

90 C. VON SCHUBERT Auslese Mosel-Saar-Ruwer Maximin Grunhauser Abtsberg (cask 98) 1989 $45 (12/15/90)

90 C. VON SCHUBERT Auslese Mosel-Saar-Ruwer Maximin Grunhauser Abtsberg (cask 133) 1989 $70 (12/15/90)

90 C. VON SCHUBERT Kabinett Mosel-Saar-Ruwer Maximin Grunhauser Abtsberg 1989 $20 (12/15/90)

90 C. VON SCHUBERT Spätlese Mosel-Saar-Ruwer Maximin Grunhauser Abtsberg 1989 $28 (12/15/90)

89 EGON MULLER Auslese Mosel-Saar-Ruwer Le Gallais Wiltingener Braune Kupp 1989 (NA) (12/15/90) (JS)

89 PETER NICOLAY Auslese Mosel-Saar-Ruwer Urziger Goldwingert 1989 $30 (12/15/90) (JS)

88 LINGENFELDER Auslese Mosel-Saar-Ruwer Grosskarlbacher Burgweg Scheurebe 1989 $20/375ml (12/15/90) (JS)

88 LINGENFELDER Beerenauslese Mosel-Saar-Ruwer Grosskarlbacher Burgweg Scheurebe 1989 $65/375ml (12/15/90) (JS)

88 STAATLICHEN WEINBAUDOMANEN Trockenbeerenauslese Mosel-Saar-Ruwer Schlossböckelheimer Kupfergrube 1989 $150 (12/15/90)

88 DR. H. THANISCH (MULLER-BURGGRAEFF) Eiswein Mosel-Saar-Ruwer Bernkasteler Doctor 1989 $190 (12/15/90) (JS)

88 ZILLIKEN Auslese Mosel-Saar-Ruwer Saarburger Rausch 1989 $35 (12/15/90)

Key to Symbols

The scores reported here are the results of blind tastings conducted by our panel of senior editors. Wines that carry the initials below are results of individual tastings.

THE WINE SPECTATOR 100-POINT SCALE ***95-100***—Classic, a great wine; ***90-94***—Outstanding, superior character and style; ***80-89***—Good to very good, a wine with special qualities; ***70-79***—Average, drinkable wine that may have minor flaws; ***60-69***—Below average, drinkable but not recommended; ***50-59***—Poor, undrinkable, not recommended. "+"—With a score indicates a range; used primarily with barrel tastings to indicate a preliminary score.

SPECIAL DESIGNATIONS SS—Spectator Selection, CS—Cellar Selection, BB—Best Buy.

TASTER'S INITIALS (JG)—Jim Gordon, (HS)—Harvey Steiman, (JL)—James Laube, (JS)—James Suckling, (TM)—Thomas Matthews, (TR)—Terry Robards, (BT)—Barrel Tasting (these wines were tasted blind from barrel samples), (CA-date)—*California's Great Cabernets* by James Laube, (CH-date)—*California's Great Chardonnays* by James Laube, (VP-date)—*Vintage Port* by James Suckling.

DATE TASTED Dates in parentheses represent the issue in which the rating was published.

87 WEGELER DEINHARD Spätlese Mosel-Saar-Ruwer Wehlener Sonnenuhr 1989 $17 (12/15/90) (JS)

87 KESSELSTATT Auslese Mosel-Saar-Ruwer Scharzhofberger 1989 $25 (12/15/90)

87 KESSELSTATT Kabinett Mosel-Saar-Ruwer Josephshöfer 1989 $8.50 (12/15/90)

87 MAX FERD. RICHTER Auslese Mosel-Saar-Ruwer Mülheimer Helenenkloster 1989 $20 (12/15/90)

87 SELBACH-OSTER Spätlese Mosel-Saar-Ruwer Bernkasteler Badstube 1989 $11.50 (12/15/90)

87 BERT SIMON Kabinett Mosel-Saar-Ruwer Eitelsbacher Marienholz 1989 $13 (12/15/90)

87 BERT SIMON Spätlese Mosel-Saar-Ruwer Serriger Würtzberg 1989 $15 (12/15/90)

87 DR. H. THANISCH (MULLER-BURGGRAEFF) Kabinett Mosel-Saar-Ruwer Lieserer Niederberg-Heldenberg 1989 $14 (12/15/90) (JS)

87 VON HOVEL Eiswein Mosel-Saar-Ruwer Oberemmeler Hütte 1989 $147/375ml (12/15/90)

86 WEGELER DEINHARD Kabinett Mosel-Saar-Ruwer Wehlener Sonnenuhr 1989 $13.50 (12/15/90) (JS)

86 FRITZ HAAG Spätlese Mosel-Saar-Ruwer Brauneberger Juffer-Sonnenuhr 1989 $27 (12/15/90) (JS)

86 KESSELSTATT Auslese Mosel-Saar-Ruwer Josephshöfer 1989 $39 (12/15/90)

86 KESSELSTATT Spätlese Mosel-Saar-Ruwer Piesporter Goldtröpfchen 1989 $15 (12/15/90)

86 EGON MULLER Kabinett Mosel-Saar-Ruwer Scharzhofberger 1989 $25 (12/15/90) (JS)

86 DR. PAULY-BERGWEILER Beerenauslese Mosel-Saar-Ruwer Bernkasteler Badstube 1989 $60 (12/15/90) (JS)

86 SELBACH-OSTER Spätlese Mosel-Saar-Ruwer Zeltingen-Rachtiger Himmelreich 1989 $11.50 (12/15/90)

86 BERT SIMON Auslese Mosel-Saar-Ruwer Patheiger Kaseler Kehrnagel Long Gold Cap 1989 $24/375ml (12/15/90)

86 BERT SIMON Auslese Mosel-Saar-Ruwer Serriger Würtzberg Gold Cap 1989 $31 (12/15/90)

86 VON HOVEL Auslese Mosel-Saar-Ruwer Oberemmeler Hütte 1989 $27 (12/15/90)

86 VON HOVEL Kabinett Mosel-Saar-Ruwer Scharzhofberger 1989 $12 (12/15/90)

86 C. VON SCHUBERT Auslese Mosel-Saar-Ruwer Maximin Grunhauser Herrenberg 1989 $40 (12/15/90)

85 WEGELER DEINHARD Auslese Mosel-Saar-Ruwer Bernkasteler Graben 1989 $22 (12/15/90) (JS)

85 FRITZ HAAG Kabinett Mosel-Saar-Ruwer Brauneberger Juffer-Sonnenuhr 1989 $18 (12/15/90) (JS)

85 KESSELSTATT Spätlese Mosel-Saar-Ruwer Bernkastler Lay 1989 $13 (12/15/90)

85 EGON MULLER Spätlese Mosel-Saar-Ruwer Le Gallais Wiltingener Braune Kupp 1989 $29 (12/15/90) (JS)

85 MAX FERD. RICHTER Kabinett Mosel-Saar-Ruwer Graacher Himmelreich 1989 $11 (12/15/90)

85 MAX FERD. RICHTER Kabinett Mosel-Saar-Ruwer Wehlener Sonnenuhr 1989 $11 (12/15/90)

85 SELBACH-OSTER Spätlese Mosel-Saar-Ruwer Zeltingen-Rachtiger Sonnenuhr 1989 $18 (12/15/90)

85 BERT SIMON Auslese Mosel-Saar-Ruwer Serringer Herrenberg 1989 $21 (12/15/90)

85 BERT SIMON Kabinett Mosel-Saar-Ruwer Serringer Herrenberg 1989 $11.50 (12/15/90)

85 BERT SIMON Spätlese Mosel-Saar-Ruwer Kastel-Staadt Maximiner Prälat 1989 $13 (12/15/90)

85 STAATLICHEN WEINBAUDOMANEN Qualitätswein Mosel-Saar-Ruwer Schlossböckelheimer Kupfergrube 1989 $9 (12/15/90)

85 DR. H. THANISCH (MULLER-BURGGRAEFF) Auslese Mosel-Saar-Ruwer Brauneberger Juffer-Sonnenuhr 1989 $25 (12/15/90) (JS)

85 C. VON SCHUBERT Auslese Mosel-Saar-Ruwer Maximin Grunhauser Abtsberg 1989 $40 (12/15/90)

85 ZILLIKEN Kabinett Mosel-Saar-Ruwer Saarburger Rausch (AP12) 1989 $14 (12/15/90)

85 ZILLIKEN Spätlese Mosel-Saar-Ruwer Saarburger Rausch 1989 $19 (12/15/90)

84 FRIEDRICH-WILHELM-GYMNASIUM Kabinett Mosel-Saar-Ruwer Graacher Himmelreich 1989 $10 (12/15/90) (JS)

84 KESSELSTATT Kabinett Mosel-Saar-Ruwer Scharzhofberger 1989 $11 (12/15/90)

84 KESSELSTATT Spätlese Mosel-Saar-Ruwer Josephshöfer 1989 $14 (12/15/90)

84 DR. PAULY-BERGWEILER Kabinett Mosel-Saar-Ruwer Wehlener Sonnenuhr 1989 $18 (12/15/90) (JS)

84 MAX FERD. RICHTER Kabinett Mosel-Saar-Ruwer Brauneberger Juffer 1989 $11 (12/15/90)

84 MAX FERD. RICHTER Spätlese Mosel-Saar-Ruwer Brauneberger Juffer 1989 $13 (12/15/90)

84 SELBACH-OSTER Kabinett Mosel-Saar-Ruwer Bernkasteler Badstube 1989 $10 (12/15/90)

84 SELBACH-OSTER Spätlese Mosel-Saar-Ruwer Bernkasteler Badstube 1989 $11.50 (12/15/90)

84 BERT SIMON Auslese Mosel-Saar-Ruwer Kaseler Gold Cap 1989 $32 (12/15/90)

84 BERT SIMON Kabinett Mosel-Saar-Ruwer Serriger Würtzberg 1989 $13 (12/15/90)

84 ZILLIKEN Spätlese Mosel-Saar-Ruwer Saarburger Rausch (AP6) 1989 $19 (12/15/90)

83 WEGELER DEINHARD Kabinett Mosel-Saar-Ruwer Bernkasteler Badstube 1989 $10.50 (12/15/90) (JS)

83 WEGELER DEINHARD Spätlese Mosel-Saar-Ruwer Graacher Himmelreich 1989 $17 (12/15/90) (JS)

83 FRIEDRICH-WILHELM-GYMNASIUM Spätlese Mosel-Saar-Ruwer Falkensteiner Hofberg 1989 (NA) (12/15/90) (JS)

83 KESSELSTATT Qualitätswein Mosel-Saar-Ruwer Josephshöfer 1989 $7 (12/15/90)

83 PETER NICOLAY Auslese Mosel-Saar-Ruwer Urziger Würzgarten 1989 $30 (12/15/90) (JS)

83 DR. PAULY-BERGWEILER Beerenauslese Mosel-Saar-Ruwer Wehlener Sonnenuhr 1989 $70 (12/15/90) (JS)

83 MAX FERD. RICHTER Qualitätswein Halbtrocken Mosel-Saar-Ruwer Dr. Richter 1989 $8 (12/15/90)

82 FRIEDRICH-WILHELM-GYMNASIUM Auslese Mosel-Saar-Ruwer Mehringer Blattenberg 1989 (NA) (12/15/90) (JS)

82 FRIEDRICH-WILHELM-GYMNASIUM Auslese Mosel-Saar-Ruwer Trittenheimer Apotheke 1989 $19 (12/15/90) (JS)

82 KESSELSTATT Qualitätswein Mosel-Saar-Ruwer Berkastler Badstube 1989 $8 (12/15/90)

82 KESSELSTATT Spätlese Mosel-Saar-Ruwer Ockfener Bockstein 1989 $16 (12/15/90)

82 MAX FERD. RICHTER Eiswein Mosel-Saar-Ruwer Mülheimer Helenenkloster 1989 $50/375ml (12/15/90)

82 VON HOVEL Spätlese Mosel-Saar-Ruwer Scharzhofberger 1989 $16 (12/15/90)

81 WEGELER DEINHARD Spätlese Mosel-Saar-Ruwer Bernkasteler Graben 1989 $17 (12/15/90) (JS)

81 FRITZ HAAG Auslese Mosel-Saar-Ruwer Brauneberger Juffer-Sonnenuhr 1989 $150 (12/15/90) (JS)

81 DR. PAULY-BERGWEILER Eiswein Mosel-Saar-Ruwer Graacher Himmelreich 1989 $100 (12/15/90) (JS)

81 MAX FERD. RICHTER Spätlese Mosel-Saar-Ruwer Wehlener Sonnenuhr 1989 $13 (12/15/90)

81 SELBACH-OSTER Kabinett Mosel-Saar-Ruwer Wehlener Sonnenuhr 1989 $10 (12/15/90)

81 SELBACH-OSTER Spätlese Mosel-Saar-Ruwer Wehlener Sonnenuhr 1989 $10 (12/15/90)

81 DR. H. THANISCH (MULLER-BURGGRAEFF) Kabinett Mosel-Saar-Ruwer Bernkastler Lay 1989 $13.50 (12/15/90) (JS)

81 DR. H. THANISCH (MULLER-BURGGRAEFF) Spätlese Mosel-Saar-Ruwer Lieserer Niederberg-Helden 1989 $15 (12/15/90) (JS)

81 ZILLIKEN Kabinett Mosel-Saar-Ruwer Ockfener Bockstein 1989 $14 (12/15/90)

80 FRIEDRICH-WILHELM-GYMNASIUM Spätlese Mosel-Saar-Ruwer Oberemmeler Rosenberg 1989 (NA) (12/15/90) (JS)
80 DR. PAULY-BERGWEILER Auslese Mosel-Saar-Ruwer Bernkasteler Alte Badstube am Doctorberg 1989 $45 (12/15/90) (JS)
80 DR. PAULY-BERGWEILER Spätlese Mosel-Saar-Ruwer Bernkasteler Alte Badstube am Doctorberg 1989 $30 (12/15/90) (JS)
80 MAX FERD. RICHTER Auslese Mosel-Saar-Ruwer Brauneberger Juffer 1989 $17 (12/15/90)
80 MAX FERD. RICHTER Auslese Mosel-Saar-Ruwer Veldenzer Elisenberg 1989 $16 (12/15/90)
80 VON HOVEL Kabinett Mosel-Saar-Ruwer Oberemmeler Hütte 1989 $12 (12/15/90)
80 C. VON SCHUBERT Qualitätswein Mosel-Saar-Ruwer Maximin Grunhauser Herrenberg 1989 $13 (12/15/90)
79 BERT SIMON Kabinett Halbtrocken Mosel-Saar-Ruwer Mertesdorfer Herrenberg 1989 $13 (12/15/90)
79 DR. H. THANISCH (MULLER-BURGGRAEFF) Kabinett Mosel-Saar-Ruwer Graacher Himmelreich 1989 $14 (12/15/90) (JS)
79 ZILLIKEN Spätlese Mosel-Saar-Ruwer Ockfener Bockstein 1989 $18 (12/15/90)
78 BERT SIMON Spätlese Mosel-Saar-Ruwer Patheiger Kaseler Kehrnagel 1989 $15 (12/15/90)
78 DR. H. THANISCH (MULLER-BURGGRAEFF) Spätlese Mosel-Saar-Ruwer Brauneberger Juffer-Sonnenuhr 1989 $19 (12/15/90) (JS)
78 C. VON SCHUBERT Kabinett Mosel-Saar-Ruwer Brüderberg 1989 $9.50 (12/15/90)
77 KESSELSTATT Kabinett Mosel-Saar-Ruwer Graacher Himmelreich 1989 $10 (12/15/90)
77 ZILLIKEN Kabinett Mosel-Saar-Ruwer Saarburger Rausch (AP5) 1989 $14 (12/15/90)
74 DR. H. THANISCH (MULLER-BURGGRAEFF) Kabinett Halbtrocken Mosel-Saar-Ruwer Bernkasteler Doctor 1989 (NA) (12/15/90) (JS)
71 DR. H. THANISCH (MULLER-BURGGRAEFF) Spätlese Mosel-Saar-Ruwer Bernkasteler Doctor 1989 (NA) (12/15/90) (JS)

1988

99 EGON MULLER Beerenauslese Mosel-Saar-Ruwer Scharzhofberger 1988 $70 (9/30/89) (JS)
98 JOH. JOS. PRUM Auslese Mosel-Saar-Ruwer Wehlener Sonnenuhr Gold Cap 1988 $80 (9/30/89)
98 JOH. JOS. PRUM Spätlese Mosel-Saar-Ruwer Wehlener Sonnenuhr (Cask 2) 1988 $24 (9/30/89)
97 JOH. JOS. PRUM Spätlese Mosel-Saar-Ruwer Wehlener Sonnenuhr (Cask 1) 1988 $20 (9/30/89) (JS)
97 ZILLIKEN Eiswein Mosel-Saar-Ruwer Saarburger Rausch 1988 (NA) (9/30/89) (JS)
96 IMMICH-BATTERIEBERG Auslese Mosel-Saar-Ruwer 1988 (NA) (9/30/89) (JS)
96 IMMICH-BATTERIEBERG Spätlese Mosel-Saar-Ruwer Enkircher Batterieberg 1988 (NA) (9/30/89) (JS)
96 C. VON SCHUBERT Spätlese Mosel-Saar-Ruwer Maximin Grunhauser Abtsberg 1988 $18 (9/30/89)
95 FRIEDRICH-WILHELM-GYMNASIUM Auslese Mosel-Saar-Ruwer Mehringer Goldkupp 1988 $30 (9/30/89) (JS)
95 TYRELL Spätlese Mosel-Saar-Ruwer Karthäuserhofberg (AP10) 1988 (NA) (9/30/89) (JS)
95 C. VON SCHUBERT Auslese Mosel-Saar-Ruwer Maximin Grunhauser Herrenberg (AP153) 1988 $30 (9/30/89) (JS)
95 ZILLIKEN Spätlese Mosel-Saar-Ruwer Saarburger Rausch 1988 $17 (9/30/89)
94 DR. FISCHER Auslese Mosel-Saar-Ruwer Wawerner Herrenberg 1988 (NA) (9/30/89) (JS)
94 KESSELSTATT Spätlese Mosel-Saar-Ruwer Kaseler Nies'chen 1988 $20 (9/30/89) (JS)
94 S.A. PRUM Auslese Mosel-Saar-Ruwer Graacher Himmelreich 1988 $25 (9/30/89) (JS)
94 MAX FERD. RICHTER Spätlese Mosel-Saar-Ruwer Brauneberger Juffer-Sonnenuhr 1988 (NA) (9/30/89) (JS)
94 MAX FERD. RICHTER Spätlese Mosel-Saar-Ruwer Veldenzer Elisenberg 1988 (NA) (9/30/89) (JS)
93 SELBACH-OSTER Spätlese Mosel-Saar-Ruwer Zeltinger Sonnenuhr 1988 $12.50 (9/30/89) (JS)
93 DR. LOOSEN ST. JOHANNISHOF Auslese Mosel-Saar-Ruwer Wehlener Sonnenuhr Gold Cap 1988 (NA) (9/30/89) (JS)
92 JOH. JOS. CHRISTOFFEL Auslese Mosel-Saar-Ruwer Erdener Treppchen 1988 (NA) (9/30/89) (JS)
92 REINHOLD HAART Spätlese Mosel-Saar-Ruwer Piesporter Goldtröpfchen 1988 (NA) (9/30/89) (JS)
92 EGON MULLER Eiswein Mosel-Saar-Ruwer Scharzhofberger 1988 (NA) (9/30/89) (JS)
92 EGON MULLER Kabinett Mosel-Saar-Ruwer Scharzhofberger 1988 $13 (9/30/89) (JS)
92 THANISCH (KNABBEN-SPIER) Auslese Mosel-Saar-Ruwer Bernkasteler Lay 1988 (NA) (9/30/89) (JS)
91 REINHOLD HAART Spätlese Mosel-Saar-Ruwer Piesporter Goldtröpfchen (AP6) 1988 (NA) (9/30/89) (JS)
91 MILZ Auslese Mosel-Saar-Ruwer Drhoner Hofberger 1988 (NA) (9/30/89) (JS)
91 SELBACH-OSTER Auslese Mosel-Saar-Ruwer Zeltinger Sonnenuhr (AP5) 1988 $22 (9/30/89) (JS)
90 BISCHOFLICHE WEINGUTER Auslese Mosel-Saar-Ruwer Kassler Neis'chen 1988 (NA) (9/30/89) (JS)
90 HERIBERT KERPEN Spätlese Mosel-Saar-Ruwer Wehlener Sonnenuhr 1988 $12 (9/30/89) (JS)
90 KESSELSTATT Kabinett Mosel-Saar-Ruwer Josephshöfer 1988 $14 (9/30/89)
90 MONCHHOF Kabinett Mosel-Saar-Ruwer Urziger Würzgarten 1988 $15 (9/30/89)
90 JOH. JOS. PRUM Auslese Mosel-Saar-Ruwer Wehlener Sonnenuhr 1988 $33 (9/30/89) (JS)
90 SCHLOSS SAARSTEIN (EBERT) Kabinett Mosel-Saar-Ruwer Serriger Schloss Saarsteiner (AP15) 1988 (NA) (9/30/89) (JS)
90 BERT SIMON Spätlese Mosel-Saar-Ruwer Serriger Würtzberg 1988 (NA) (9/30/89) (JS)
90 DR. LOOSEN ST. JOHANNISHOF Auslese Mosel-Saar-Ruwer Erdener Prälat Gold Cap 1988 (NA) (9/30/89) (JS)
90 DR. LOOSEN ST. JOHANNISHOF Spätlese Mosel-Saar-Ruwer Erdener Prälat 1988 (NA) (9/30/89) (JS)
90 THANISCH (KNABBEN-SPIER) Spätlese Mosel-Saar-Ruwer Bernkasteler Doctor 1988 $15 (9/30/89) (JS)
90 DR. H. THANISCH (MULLER-BURGGRAEFF) Auslese Mosel-Saar-Ruwer Bernkasteler Doctor 1988 (NA) (9/30/89) (JS)
90 VEREINIGTE HOSPITIEN Auslese Mosel-Saar-Ruwer Piesporter Schubertslay 1988 (NA) (9/30/89) (JS)
90 VEREINIGTE HOSPITIEN Auslese Mosel-Saar-Ruwer Wehlener Sonnenuhr 1988 (NA) (9/30/89) (JS)
90 VON HOVEL Kabinett Mosel-Saar-Ruwer Scharzhofberger 1988 $12 (9/30/89) (JS)
89 JOH. JOS. CHRISTOFFEL Auslese Mosel-Saar-Ruwer Erdener Treppchen 1988 (NA) (9/30/89) (JS)
89 THANISCH (KNABBEN-SPIER) Spätlese Mosel-Saar-Ruwer Bernkasteler Lay 1988 $12 (9/30/89) (JS)
89 VON HOVEL Spätlese Mosel-Saar-Ruwer Oberemmeler Hütte 1988 $15 (9/30/89) (JS)
89 C. VON SCHUBERT Kabinett Mosel-Saar-Ruwer Maximin Grunhauser Herrenberg 1988 $10 (9/30/89) (JS)
88 WEGELER DEINHARD Spätlese Mosel-Saar-Ruwer Wehlener Sonnenuhr 1988 $15 (9/30/89) (JS)
88 REINHOLD HAART Auslese Mosel-Saar-Ruwer Piesporter Goldtröpfchen 1988 (NA) (9/30/89) (JS)
88 REINHOLD HAART Kabinett Mosel-Saar-Ruwer Piesporter Goldtröpfchen 1988 (NA) (9/30/89)
88 DR. HEIDEMANNS-BERGWEILER Spätlese Mosel-Saar-Ruwer Wehlener Sonnenuhr 1988 (NA) (9/30/89) (JS)
88 S.A. PRUM Spätlese Mosel-Saar-Ruwer Bernkasteler Graben 1988 $17.50 (9/30/89) (JS)
88 MAX FERD. RICHTER Spätlese Mosel-Saar-Ruwer Wehlener Sonnenuhr 1988 (NA) (9/30/89) (JS)
88 SCHLOSS SAARSTEIN (EBERT) Auslese Mosel-Saar-Ruwer Serriger Schloss Saarsteiner Gold Cup 1988 $25 (9/30/89) (JS)
87 MAX FERD. RICHTER Auslese Mosel-Saar-Ruwer Brauneberger Juffer-Sonnenuhr 1988 (NA) (9/30/89) (JS)
87 WILLI SCHAEFER Spätlese Mosel-Saar-Ruwer Wehlener Sonnenuhr 1988 $10 (9/30/89) (JS)
87 BERT SIMON Auslese Mosel-Saar-Ruwer Serriger Würtzberg 1988 (NA) (9/30/89) (JS)
86 FRITZ HAAG Auslese Mosel-Saar-Ruwer Brauneberger Juffer-Sonnenuhr 1988 (NA) (9/30/89) (JS)
86 FRITZ HAAG Spätlese Mosel-Saar-Ruwer Brauneberger Juffer-Sonnenuhr 1988 (NA) (9/30/89) (JS)
86 MONCHHOF Spätlese Mosel-Saar-Ruwer Erdener Treppchen 1988 (NA) (9/30/89) (JS)
86 DR. PAULY-BERGWEILER Spätlese Mosel-Saar-Ruwer Bernkasteler Lay 1988 (NA) (9/30/89) (JS)
86 STUDERT-PRUM Auslese Mosel-Saar-Ruwer Wehlener Sonnenuhr 1988 (NA) (9/30/89) (JS)
86 DR. H. THANISCH (MULLER-BURGGRAEFF) Kabinett Mosel-Saar-Ruwer Lieserer Niederberg-Heldenberg 1988 (NA) (9/30/89)
86 TYRELL Spätlese Mosel-Saar-Ruwer Karthäuserhofberg 1988 (NA) (9/30/89) (JS)
86 DR. WEINS-PRUM Auslese Mosel-Saar-Ruwer Erdener Prälat 1988 (NA) (9/30/89) (JS)
86 WELLER-LEHNERT Auslese Mosel-Saar-Ruwer Piesporter Goldtröpfchen 1988 (NA) (9/30/89) (JS)
85 BISCHOFLICHE WEINGUTER Spätlese Mosel-Saar-Ruwer Trittenheimer Apotheke 1988 (NA) (9/30/89) (JS)
85 JOH. JOS. CHRISTOFFEL Spätlese Mosel-Saar-Ruwer Urziger Würzgarten 1988 (NA) (9/30/89) (JS)
85 WEGELER DEINHARD Auslese Mosel-Saar-Ruwer Wehlener Sonnenuhr 1988 $17.50 (9/30/89) (JS)
85 DR. FISCHER Kabinett Mosel-Saar-Ruwer Ockfener Bockstein 1988 $13 (9/30/89) (JS)
85 FRITZ HAAG Auslese Mosel-Saar-Ruwer Brauneberger Juffer-Sonnenuhr (AP16) 1988 (NA) (9/30/89) (JS)
85 DR. HEIDEMANNS-BERGWEILER Spätlese Mosel-Saar-Ruwer Bernkasteler Badstube 1988 (NA) (9/30/89) (JS)
85 PETER NICOLAY Kabinett Mosel-Saar-Ruwer Urziger Goldwinger 1988 (NA) (9/30/89)
85 S.A. PRUM Auslese Mosel-Saar-Ruwer Wehlener Sonnenuhr 1988 $25 (9/30/89) (JS)
85 SCHLOSS SAARSTEIN (EBERT) Spätlese Mosel-Saar-Ruwer Serriger Schloss Saarsteiner 1988 (NA) (9/30/89) (JS)
85 DR. H. THANISCH (MULLER-BURGGRAEFF) Auslese Mosel-Saar-Ruwer Brauneberger Juffer-Sonnenuhr 1988 (NA) (9/30/89) (JS)
85 TYRELL Kabinett Mosel-Saar-Ruwer Karthäuserhofberg (AP3) 1988 (NA) (9/30/89) (JS)
85 TYRELL Kabinett Mosel-Saar-Ruwer Karthäuserhofberg (AP9) 1988 (NA) (9/30/89) (JS)
85 TYRELL Spätlese Mosel-Saar-Ruwer Karthäuserhofberg (AP8) 1988 (NA) (9/30/89) (JS)
84 BISCHOFLICHE WEINGUTER Spätlese Mosel-Saar-Ruwer Ayler Kupp 1988 (NA) (9/30/89) (JS)
84 JOH. JOS. CHRISTOFFEL Spätlese Mosel-Saar-Ruwer Erdener Treppchen 1988 $10 (9/30/89) (JS)
84 WEGELER DEINHARD Spätlese Mosel-Saar-Ruwer Bernkasteler Graben 1988 $14.50 (9/30/89) (JS)
84 HERIBERT KERPEN Auslese Mosel-Saar-Ruwer Wehlener Sonnenuhr (AP12) 1988 $15 (9/30/89) (JS)
84 KESSELSTATT Kabinett Mosel-Saar-Ruwer Piesporter Goldtröpfchen 1988 (NA) (9/30/89)
84 MONCHHOF Spätlese Mosel-Saar-Ruwer Urziger Würzgarten 1988 (NA) (9/30/89) (JS)
84 SELBACH-OSTER Spätlese Mosel-Saar-Ruwer Wehlener Klosterberg 1988 $11 (9/30/89) (JS)
84 BERT SIMON Qualitätswein Mosel-Saar-Ruwer 1988 $6 (9/30/89) (JS)
84 DR. LOOSEN ST. JOHANNISHOF Kabinett Mosel-Saar-Ruwer Wehlener Sonnenuhr 1988 (NA) (9/30/89)
84 DR. WEINS-PRUM Kabinett Mosel-Saar-Ruwer Wehlener Sonnenuhr 1988 (NA) (9/30/89)
84 DR. WEINS-PRUM Spätlese Mosel-Saar-Ruwer Wehlener Sonnenuhr 1988 (NA) (9/30/89) (JS)
83 DR. FISCHER Spätlese Mosel-Saar-Ruwer Ockfener Bockstein 1988 $15 (9/30/89) (JS)
83 FRITZ HAAG Kabinett Mosel-Saar-Ruwer Brauneberger Juffer-Sonnenuhr 1988 (NA) (9/30/89)
83 MILZ Spätlese Mosel-Saar-Ruwer Piesporter Hofberg 1988 (NA) (9/30/89) (JS)
83 MILZ Spätlese Mosel-Saar-Ruwer Trittenheimer Altärchen 1988 (NA) (9/30/89) (JS)
83 MONCHHOF Spätlese Mosel-Saar-Ruwer Wehlener Klosterberg 1988 (NA) (9/30/89) (JS)
83 S.A. PRUM Spätlese Mosel-Saar-Ruwer Wehlener Sonnenuhr 1988 $18 (9/30/89) (JS)
83 SCHLOSS SAARSTEIN (EBERT) Kabinett Mosel-Saar-Ruwer Serriger Schloss Saarsteiner (AP10) 1988 (NA) (9/30/89) (JS)
83 VEREINIGTE HOSPITIEN Spätlese Mosel-Saar-Ruwer Wiltinger Hölle 1988 (NA) (9/30/89) (JS)
82 BERT SIMON Kabinett Mosel-Saar-Ruwer Serriger Würtzberg 1988 (NA) (9/30/89) (JS)
82 THANISCH (KNABBEN-SPIER) Auslese Mosel-Saar-Ruwer Bernkasteler Badstube 1988 $25 (9/30/89) (JS)
82 DR. WEINS-PRUM Spätlese Mosel-Saar-Ruwer Urziger Würzgarten 1988 (NA) (9/30/89) (JS)
81 DR. FISCHER Qualitätswein Mosel-Saar-Ruwer Ockfener Bockstein 1988 $6 (9/30/89) (JS)
81 FRIEDRICH-WILHELM-GYMNASIUM Auslese Mosel-Saar-Ruwer Graacher Himmelreich 1988 (NA) (9/30/89) (JS)
81 DR. HEIDEMANNS-BERGWEILER Auslese Mosel-Saar-Ruwer Bernkasteler Alte Badstube am Doctorberg 1988 (NA) (9/30/89)
81 S.A. PRUM Kabinett Mosel-Saar-Ruwer Graacher Himmelreich 1988 (NA) (9/30/89)
81 S.A. PRUM Spätlese Mosel-Saar-Ruwer Graacher Himmelreich 1988 $18 (9/30/89) (JS)
81 WILLI SCHAEFER Kabinett Mosel-Saar-Ruwer Graacher Himmelreich 1988 $8 (9/30/89)
81 SELBACH-OSTER Kabinett Mosel-Saar-Ruwer Zeltinger Himmelreich 1988 $8.50 (9/30/89)
81 VON HOVEL Auslese Mosel-Saar-Ruwer Oberemmeler Hütte Gold Cap 1988 (NA) (9/30/89) (JS)
80 DR. PAULY-BERGWEILER Auslese Mosel-Saar-Ruwer Graacher Himmelreich 1988 (NA) (9/30/89) (JS)
80 WILLI SCHAEFER Auslese Mosel-Saar-Ruwer Graacher Domprobst 1988 $13 (9/30/89) (JS)
80 WILLI SCHAEFER Spätlese Mosel-Saar-Ruwer Graacher Domprobst 1988 $10 (9/30/89) (JS)

GERMANY
RIESLING/MOSEL-SAAR-RUWER

80 C. VON SCHUBERT Qualitätswein Mosel-Saar-Ruwer Maximin Grunhauser Abtsberg 1988 $10 (9/30/89) (JS)
79 WEGELER DEINHARD Kabinett Mosel-Saar-Ruwer Bernkasteler Badstube 1988 $9 (9/30/89)
79 DR. HEIDEMANNS-BERGWEILER Auslese Mosel-Saar-Ruwer Graacher Himmelreich 1988 (NA) (9/30/89) (JS)
79 VEREINIGTE HOSPITIEN Kabinett Mosel-Saar-Ruwer Serriger Schloss Saarfelser Schloss-berger 1988 (NA) (9/30/89) (JS)
79 ZILLIKEN Kabinett Mosel-Saar-Ruwer Saarburger Rausch (AP7) 1988 $9 (9/30/89) (JS)
78 BISCHOFLICHE WEINGUTER Auslese Mosel-Saar-Ruwer Drhoner Hofberger 1988 (NA) (9/30/89) (JS)
78 MILZ Auslese Mosel-Saar-Ruwer Trittenheimer Felsenkopf 1988 (NA) (9/30/89) (JS)
78 ZILLIKEN Kabinett Mosel-Saar-Ruwer Saarburger Rausch (AP5) 1988 $9 (9/30/89) (JS)
76 DR. PAULY-BERGWEILER Kabinett Mosel-Saar-Ruwer Bernkasteler Alte Badstube am Doctorberg 1988 (NA) (9/30/89)
70 DR. H. THANISCH (MULLER-BURGGRAEFF) Spätlese Mosel-Saar-Ruwer Lieserer Niederberg-Helden 1988 (NA) (9/30/89) (JS)

1987

88 DR. MEYER Qualitätswein Mosel-Saar-Ruwer Piesporter Michelsberg 1987 $4 (10/15/88) BB
87 C. VON SCHUBERT Qualitätswein Mosel-Saar-Ruwer Maximin Grunhauser Abtsberg 1987 $13 (4/30/89)
85 GOLDENER OKTOBER Qualitätswein Mosel-Saar-Ruwer Piesporter Michelsberg 1987 $7 (1l/30/88)
85 SICHEL White Novum 1987 $7.50 (10/15/88)
82 G. VON SCHUBERT Kabinett Mosel-Saar-Ruwer Maximin Grunhauser Herrenberg 1987 $12 (4/30/89)
81 ZACH. BERGWEILER PRUM-ERBEN Qualitätswein Mosel-Saar-Ruwer Bernkasteler Badstube Dr. Heidemanns Bergweiler 1987 $11 (4/30/89)
78 J & H SELBACH Bernkasteler Badstube Dr. Heidemanns Bergweiler Mosel-Saar-Ruwer Hochgewächs 1987 $7 (10/15/88)

1986

92 JOH. JOS. PRUM Spätlese Mosel-Saar-Ruwer Wehlener Sonnenuhr 1986 (NA) (4/15/89)
91 WEGELER DEINHARD Spätlese Mosel-Saar-Ruwer Bernkasteler Doctor 1986 (NA) (4/15/89)
91 FRITZ HAAG Spätlese Mosel-Saar-Ruwer Brauneberger Juffer-Sonnenuhr 1986 (NA) (4/15/89)
90 PETER NICOLAY Kabinett Mosel-Saar-Ruwer Urziger Würzgarten 1986 $10 (11/30/87)
88 WEGELER DEINHARD Spätlese Mosel-Saar-Ruwer Wehlener Sonnenuhr 1986 (NA) (4/15/89)
88 DR. H. THANISCH (MULLER-BURGGRAEFF) Spätlese Mosel-Saar-Ruwer Bernkasteler Kurfurstlay 1986 $12 (11/30/87)
86 PETER NICOLAY Spätlese Mosel-Saar-Ruwer Urziger Goldwingert 1986 (NA) (4/15/89)
86 DR. PAULY-BERGWEILER Spätlese Mosel-Saar-Ruwer Bernkasteler Alte Badstube am Doctorberg 1986 $24 (10/15/88)
86 DR. PAULY-BERGWEILER Spätlese Mosel-Saar-Ruwer Wehlener Sonnenuhr 1986 $13 (11/30/87)
86 SELBACH-OSTER Kabinett Mosel-Saar-Ruwer Wehlener Klosterberg 1986 $8 (11/30/88)
85 DR. HEIDEMANNS-BERGWEILER Spätlese Mosel-Saar-Ruwer Bernkasteler Doctor 1986 (NA) (4/15/89)
85 DR. LOOSEN ST. JOHANNISHOF Spätlese Mosel-Saar-Ruwer Erdener Prälat 1986 (NA) (4/15/89)
84 LEONARD KREUSCH Kabinett Mosel-Saar-Ruwer Bereich Bernkastel 1986 $6 (11/30/88)
84 LEONARD KREUSCH Kabinett Mosel-Saar-Ruwer Zeltinger Himmelreich 1986 $5.75 (11/30/88)
84 DR. H. THANISCH (MULLER-BURGGRAEFF) Kabinett Mosel-Saar-Ruwer Bernkasteler Doctor 1986 $29 (11/30/87)
83 J. LAUERBURG Spätlese Mosel-Saar-Ruwer Bernkasteler Doctor 1986 (NA) (4/15/89)
83 RUDOLF MULLER Spätlese Mosel-Saar-Ruwer Wehlener Sonnenuhr 1986 $8.25 (11/30/87)
83 PETER NICOLAY Auslese Mosel-Saar-Ruwer Erdener Prälat 1986 $21 (1/31/88)
82 DR. PAULY-BERGWEILER Spätlese Mosel-Saar-Ruwer Bernkasteler Alte Badstube am Doctorberg 1986 $24 (4/15/89)
82 DR. LOOSEN ST. JOHANNISHOF Spätlese Mosel-Saar-Ruwer Bernkasteler Doctor 1986 (NA) (4/15/89)
81 SELBACH-OSTER Bernkasteler Doctor Mosel-Saar-Ruwer Hochgewächs Graacher Himmel-reich 1986 $6 (10/15/88)
80 RUDOLF MULLER Spätlese Mosel-Saar-Ruwer Piesporter Treppchen 1986 $8.25 (11/30/87)
79 THANISCH (KNABBEN-SPIER) Spätlese Mosel-Saar-Ruwer Bernkasteler Doctor 1986 (NA) (4/15/89)
78 RUDOLF MULLER Kabinett Mosel-Saar-Ruwer Piesporter Treppchen 1986 $6.75 (1/31/88)
77 PETER NICOLAY Kabinett Mosel-Saar-Ruwer Erdener Treppchen Artist 1986 $40/1.5L (9/15/88)
76 RUDOLF MULLER Kabinett Mosel-Saar-Ruwer Reiler Mullay-Hofberg 1986 $7.25 (1/31/88)
76 SELBACH-OSTER Eiswein Mosel-Saar-Ruwer Zeltinger Himmelreich 1986 $40/375ml (4/30/89)
74 GEBERT Qualitätswein Mosel-Saar-Ruwer Ockfener Bockstein 1986 $6 (11/30/87)
72 DR. H. THANISCH (MULLER-BURGGRAEFF) Kabinett Mosel-Saar-Ruwer Bernkasteler Badstube 1986 $11 (11/30/87)
64 DR. H. THANISCH (MULLER-BURGGRAEFF) Spätlese Mosel-Saar-Ruwer Bernkasteler Doctor 1986 (NA) (4/15/89)

1985

97 FRITZ HAAG Spätlese Mosel-Saar-Ruwer Brauneberger Juffer-Sonnenuhr 1985 (NA) (4/15/89) (JS)
94 PETER NICOLAY Eiswein Mosel-Saar-Ruwer Urziger Würzgarten 1985 $66 (11/30/87)
92 RUDOLF MULLER Spätlese Mosel-Saar-Ruwer Wehlener Sonnenuhr 1985 $7.50 (3/31/87)

92 DR. LOOSEN ST. JOHANNISHOF Auslese Mosel-Saar-Ruwer Erdener Prälat 1985 $20 (11/15/86)
91 DR. PAULY-BERGWEILER Auslese Mosel-Saar-Ruwer Bernkasteler Alte Badstube am Doctorberg 1985 $30 (1/31/88)
91 JOH. JOS. PRUM Spätlese Mosel-Saar-Ruwer Graacher Himmelreich 1985 $15.50 (4/15/89)
90 RUDOLF MULLER Kabinett Mosel-Saar-Ruwer Piesporter Goldtröpfchen 1985 $9.50 (4/15/87)
90 DR. PAULY-BERGWEILER Spätlese Mosel-Saar-Ruwer Bernkasteler Badstube 1985 $10 (9/30/86)
90 JOH. JOS. PRUM Auslese Mosel-Saar-Ruwer Wehlener Sonnenuhr 1985 $20 (5/31/87)
90 SELBACH-OSTER Spätlese Mosel-Saar-Ruwer Bernkasteler Badstube 1985 $9.50 (9/15/88)
89 J & H SELBACH Spätlese Mosel-Saar-Ruwer Piesporter Goldtröpfchen 1985 $14 (9/15/88)
88 DR. FISCHER Spätlese Mosel-Saar-Ruwer Ockfener Bockstein 1985 $13 (5/15/87)
88 JOH. JOS. PRUM Spätlese Mosel-Saar-Ruwer Wehlener Sonnenuhr 1985 (NA) (4/15/89)
88 DR. H. THANISCH (MULLER-BURGGRAEFF) Spätlese Mosel-Saar-Ruwer Bernkasteler Badstube 1985 $11.25 (4/15/87)
87 DR. PAULY-BERGWEILER Eiswein Mosel-Saar-Ruwer Bernkasteler Badstube 1985 $100 (9/15/88)
86 BISCHOFLICHES PRIESTERSEMINAR Auslese Mosel-Saar-Ruwer Erdener Treppchen 1985 $14 (11/30/87)
86 DR. PAULY-BERGWEILER Spätlese Mosel-Saar-Ruwer Bernkasteler Alte Badstube am Doctorberg 1985 (NA) (4/15/89)
86 J & H SELBACH Kabinett Mosel-Saar-Ruwer Zeltinger Himmelreich 1985 $7.50 (10/15/88)
86 PETER NICOLAY Kabinett Mosel-Saar-Ruwer Urziger Würzgarten 1985 $7 (11/15/86)
85 DR. PAULY-BERGWEILER Auslese Mosel-Saar-Ruwer Bernkasteler Lay 1985 $14 (1/31/87)
85 DR. LOOSEN ST. JOHANNISHOF Spätlese Mosel-Saar-Ruwer Erdener Treppchen 1985 $11 (1/31/87)
85 THANISCH (KNABBEN-SPIER) Spätlese Mosel-Saar-Ruwer Graacher Himmelreich 1985 (NA) (4/15/89)
84 WEGELER DEINHARD Spätlese Mosel-Saar-Ruwer Wehlener Sonnenuhr 1985 (NA) (4/15/89)
84 RUDOLF MULLER Qualitätswein Mosel-Saar-Ruwer Scharzhofberger 1985 $6.50 (5/15/87)
84 PETER NICOLAY Spätlese Mosel-Saar-Ruwer Urziger Goldwingert 1985 (NA) (4/15/89)
83 JOSEFINENGRUND LEIWEN Auslese Mosel-Saar-Ruwer Leiwener Laurentiuslay 1985 $11 (1/31/87)
83 RUDOLF MULLER Kabinett Mosel-Saar-Ruwer Ockfener Bockstein 1985 $7 (4/15/87)
83 SELBACH-OSTER Eiswein Mosel-Saar-Ruwer Zeltinger Himmelreich 1985 $35/375ml (4/30/89)
82 GEBERT Qualitätswein Mosel-Saar-Ruwer Ockfener Bockstein 1985 $6.50 (5/15/87)
82 J. LAUERBURG Spätlese Mosel-Saar-Ruwer Bernkasteler Doctor 1985 (NA) (4/15/89)
82 JOSEFINENGRUND LEIWEN Kabinett Mosel-Saar-Ruwer Leiwener Klostergarten 1985 $6 (1/31/87)
82 DR. PAULY-BERGWEILER Kabinett Mosel-Saar-Ruwer Graacher Himmelreich 1985 $8 (11/15/86)
82 SELBACH-OSTER Spätlese Mosel-Saar-Ruwer Graacher Himmelreich 1985 $8 (9/15/88)
82 THANISCH (KNABBEN-SPIER) Spätlese Mosel-Saar-Ruwer Bernkasteler Lay 1985 (NA) (4/15/89)
81 DR. LOOSEN ST. JOHANNISHOF Kabinett Mosel-Saar-Ruwer Wehlener Sonnenuhr 1985 $8 (1/31/87)
80 SELBACH-OSTER Spätlese Mosel-Saar-Ruwer Graacher Himmelreich 1985 $10 (10/15/88)
80 DR. H. THANISCH (MULLER-BURGGRAEFF) Spätlese Mosel-Saar-Ruwer Bernkasteler Kurfurstlay 1985 $9.50 (4/15/87)
80 VON HOVEL Kabinett Mosel-Saar-Ruwer Oberemmeler Hütte 1985 $8 (10/15/87)
79 RUDOLF MULLER Kabinett Mosel-Saar-Ruwer Piesporter Treppchen 1985 $6 (4/15/87)
79 PETER NICOLAY Auslese Mosel-Saar-Ruwer Urziger Goldwingert 1985 $10 (1/31/87)
78 REINHOLD HAART Spätlese Mosel-Saar-Ruwer Piesporter Goldtröpfchen 1985 (NA) (4/15/89)
78 J. LAUERBURG Spätlese Mosel-Saar-Ruwer Bernkasteler Lay 1985 (NA) (4/15/89)
78 ZILLIKEN Spätlese Mosel-Saar-Ruwer Saarburger Rausch 1985 $9.25 (5/15/87)
77 JOH. JOS. PRUM Spätlese Mosel-Saar-Ruwer Graacher Himmelreich 1985 $15.50 (5/15/87)
77 DR. H. THANISCH (MULLER-BURGGRAEFF) Spätlese Mosel-Saar-Ruwer Bernkasteler Doctor 1985 (NA) (4/15/89)
76 JOH. JOS. PRUM Kabinett Mosel-Saar-Ruwer Wehlener Sonnenuhr 1985 $11.50 (4/15/89)
74 RUDOLF MULLER Spätlese Mosel-Saar-Ruwer Scharzhofberger 1985 $8 (4/15/87)
74 DR. F. PRUM Spätlese Mosel-Saar-Ruwer Graacher Domprobst 1985 $12 (10/15/87)
73 WEGELER DEINHARD Kabinett Mosel-Saar-Ruwer Wehlener Sonnenuhr 1985 (10/15/87)
72 DR. H. THANISCH (MULLER-BURGGRAEFF) Spätlese Mosel-Saar-Ruwer Bernkasteler Kurfurstlay 1985 $9.50 (4/15/89)
70 FRITZ HAAG Kabinett Mosel-Saar-Ruwer Brauneberger Juffer-Sonnenuhr 1985 $9 (6/30/87)
68 HAVEMEYER Spätlese Mosel-Saar-Ruwer Piesporter Goldtröpfchen 1985 $17 (11/30/87)
68 PETER NICOLAY Spätlese Mosel-Saar-Ruwer Erdener Treppchen 1985 $8 (11/15/86)

1983

91 JOH. JOS. PRUM Kabinett Mosel-Saar-Ruwer Wehlener Klosterberg 1983 $9 (11/16/84) SS
91 JOH. JOS. PRUM Spätlese Mosel-Saar-Ruwer Wehlener Sonnenuhr 1983 $13 (5/01/85) SS
90 DR. FISCHER Auslese Mosel-Saar-Ruwer Ockfener Bockstein 1983 $12 (3/16/85)
90 KESSELSTATT Eiswein Mosel-Saar-Ruwer Oberemmeler Karlsberg 1983 $150 (4/30/89)
90 RUDOLF MULLER Kabinett Mosel-Saar-Ruwer Piesporter Goldtröpfchen 1983 $7.50 (6/16/85)
87 DR. PAULY-BERGWEILER Eiswein Mosel-Saar-Ruwer Graacher Himmelreich 1983 $90 (9/16/85)
87 JOH. JOS. PRUM Kabinett Mosel-Saar-Ruwer Wehlener Nonnenberg 1983 $9 (5/01/85)
87 DR. LOOSEN ST. JOHANNISHOF Spätlese Mosel-Saar-Ruwer Erdener Treppchen 1983 $9 (3/01/85)
86 BAUM Eiswein Mosel-Saar-Ruwer Ockenheimer St. Rochuskapelle 1983 $24.50 (10/01/84)
86 BISCHOFLICHE WEINGUTER Auslese Mosel-Saar-Ruwer Kassler Neis'chen 1983 $10.50 (4/01/85)
86 WOLFGANG ZAHN Spätlese Mosel-Saar-Ruwer Piesporter Goldtröpfchen 1983 $10 (5/16/85)
85 BAUM Spätlese Mosel-Saar-Ruwer Piesporter Goldtropchen 1983 $11 (10/01/84)
85 DR. LOOSEN ST. JOHANNISHOF Kabinett Mosel-Saar-Ruwer Erdener Treppchen 1983 $7 (3/16/85)
84 J & H SELBACH Spätlese Mosel-Saar-Ruwer Brauneberger Mandelgraben 1983 $4.50 (11/16/84) BB
82 DR. PAULY-BERGWEILER Auslese Mosel-Saar-Ruwer Wehlener Sonnenuhr 1983 $15.50 (9/01/85)
80 STAATLICHEN WEINBAUDOMANEN Spätlese Mosel-Saar-Ruwer Serriger Vogelsang 1983 $7 (11/01/84)
80 H. THAPRICH Spätlese Mosel-Saar-Ruwer Bernkasteler Badstube 1983 $8.50 (4/01/85)
79 BAUM Qualitätswein Mosel-Saar-Ruwer Piesporter Michelsberg 1983 $4 (4/01/84)

79	BISCHOFLICHE WEINGUTER Kabinett Mosel-Saar-Ruwer Trittenheimer Apotheke 1983 $8 (5/01/85)
79	KARL JOSTOCK-THUL Kabinett Mosel-Saar-Ruwer Piesporter Treppchen 1983 $4.75 (11/01/84)
78	DR. PAULY-BERGWEILER Spätlese Mosel-Saar-Ruwer Bernkasteler Badstube 1983 $9.50 (10/01/85)
78	DR. LOOSEN ST. JOHANNISHOF Kabinett Mosel-Saar-Ruwer Bernkasteler Badstube 1983 $6.50 (4/01/85)
78	DR. LOOSEN ST. JOHANNISHOF Kabinett Mosel-Saar-Ruwer Wehlener Sonnenuhr 1983 $6 (4/01/85)
78	H. THAPRICH Spätlese Mosel-Saar-Ruwer Bernkasteler Lay 1983 $8.25 (3/16/85)
77	BAUM Spätlese Mosel-Saar-Ruwer Weingartener Trappenberg 1983 $5 (10/01/84)
76	BISCHOFLICHE WEINGUTER Spätlese Mosel-Saar-Ruwer Kaseler Nies'chen 1983 $8.50 (5/01/85)
72	RUDOLF MULLER Spätlese Mosel-Saar-Ruwer Ockfener Bockstein 1983 $9.25 (5/15/87)
70	DR. PAULY-BERGWEILER Spätlese Mosel-Saar-Ruwer Brauneberger Juffer 1983 $9.50 (10/01/85)
50	JOH. JOS. PRUM Spätlese Mosel-Saar-Ruwer Bernkasteler Badstube 1983 $11 (11/16/85)

1982

74	DR. ZENZEN Spätlese Mosel-Saar-Ruwer Valwiger Herrenberg 1982 $12 (2/01/86)

1981

70	DR. ZENZEN Kabinett Mosel-Saar-Ruwer Erdener Treppchen 1981 $8 (4/01/86)

1976

90	DR. ZENZEN Beerenauslese Mosel-Saar-Ruwer Erdener Treppchen 1976 $90 (2/01/86)

NAHE

1989

91	HANS CRUSIUS & SOHN Auslese Nahe Schlossböckelheimer Felsenberg Gold Capsule 1989 $35 (12/15/90)
91	STAATLICHEN WEINBAUDOMANEN Beerenauslese Nahe Münsterer Pittersberg 1989 $41 (12/15/90)
88	HANS CRUSIUS & SOHN Auslese Nahe Traisener Rotenfels 1989 $24 (12/15/90)
87	STAATLICHEN WEINBAUDOMANEN Beerenauslese Nahe Niederhausener Hermannsberg 1989 $65 (12/15/90)
86	STAATLICHEN WEINBAUDOMANEN Auslese Nahe Münsterer Dautenpflänzer 1989 $14 (12/15/90)
86	STAATLICHEN WEINBAUDOMANEN Auslese Nahe Niederhausener Hermannshöhle 1989 $25 (12/15/90)
86	STAATLICHEN WEINBAUDOMANEN Spätlese Nahe Niederhausener Kertz 1989 $14 (12/15/90)
85	HANS CRUSIUS & SOHN Kabinett Nahe Traisener Rotenfels 1989 $14 (12/15/90)
82	HANS CRUSIUS & SOHN Qualitätswein Halbtrocken Nahe 1989 $11 (12/15/90)
80	STAATLICHEN WEINBAUDOMANEN Kabinett Nahe Niederhausener Steinberg 1989 $9 (12/15/90)
78	HANS CRUSIUS & SOHN Spätlese Nahe Traisener Rotenfels 1989 $17 (12/15/90)
78	STAATLICHEN WEINBAUDOMANEN Kabinett Nahe Altenbamberger Rothenberg 1989 $10 (12/15/90)

RHEINGAU

1989

99	LANGWERTH VON SIMMERN Trockenbeerenauslese Rheingau Erbacher Marcobrunn 1989 (NA) (12/15/90)
98	DR. WEIL Beerenauslese Rheingau 1989 (NA) (12/15/90)
94	LANGWERTH VON SIMMERN Auslese Rheingau Hattenheimer Mannberg 1989 $50 (12/15/90)
93	SCHLOSS SCHONBORN Spätlese Rheingau Erbacher Marcobrunn 1989 (NA) (12/15/90)
93	DR. WEIL Trockenbeerenauslese Rheingau 1989 (NA) (12/15/90)
92	SCHLOSS REINHARTSHAUSEN Auslese Rheingau Erbacher Siegelsberg 1989 (NA) (12/15/90)
92	SCHLOSS SCHONBORN Kabinett Rheingau Winkeler Gutenberg 1989 (NA) (12/15/90)
91	LANGWERTH VON SIMMERN Auslese Rheingau Hattenheimer Nussbrunnen 1989 $57 (12/15/90)
91	SCHLOSS SCHONBORN Spätlese Rheingau Hattenheimer Pfaffenberg 1989 (NA) (12/15/90)
91	DR. WEIL Spätlese Halbtrocken Rheingau 1989 (NA) (12/15/90)
90	SCHLOSS SCHONBORN Auslese Rheingau Rüdeshemier Berg Schlossberg 1989 (NA) (12/15/90)
90	SCHLOSS SCHONBORN Spätlese Rheingau Hattenheimer Nussbrunnen 1989 (NA) (12/15/90)
89	SCHLOSS REINHARTSHAUSEN Spätlese Rheingau Erbacher Siegelsberg 1989 (NA) (12/15/90)
88	LANGWERTH VON SIMMERN Kabinett Rheingau Hattenheimer Nussbrunnen 1989 $13.50 (12/15/90)
88	DOMDECHANT WERNER'SCHES Auslese Rheingau Hochheimer 1989 (NA) (12/15/90)
88	DOMDECHANT WERNER'SCHES Kabinett Rheingau Hochheimer Domdechaney 1989 (NA) (12/15/90)
87	LANGWERTH VON SIMMERN Spätlese Rheingau Erbacher Marcobrunn 1989 $25 (12/15/90)
87	LANGWERTH VON SIMMERN Spätlese Rheingau Rauenthaler Baiken 1989 $25 (12/15/90)
87	SCHLOSS SCHONBORN Auslese Rheingau Hattenheimer Nussbrunnen 1989 (NA) (12/15/90)
87	SCHLOSS SCHONBORN Spätlese Halbtrocken Rheingau Hochheimer Kirchenstück 1989 (NA) (12/15/90)
86	SCHLOSS JOHANNISBERGER Kabinett Rheingau 1989 (NA) (12/15/90)
86	SCHLOSS REINHARTSHAUSEN Qualitätswein Rheingau Erbacher Schlossberg 1989 (NA) (12/15/90)
86	SCHLOSS SCHONBORN Spätlese Rheingau 1989 (NA) (12/15/90)
86	DOMDECHANT WERNER'SCHES Kabinett Rheingau Hochheimer Hölle (AP989) 1989 (NA) (12/15/90)
85	SCHLOSS GROENESTEYN Auslese Rheingau Rüdesheimer Berg Rottland 1989 $40 (12/15/90)
84	SCHLOSS JOHANNISBERGER Qualitätswein Rheingau 1989 (NA) (12/15/90)
84	LANGWERTH VON SIMMERN Kabinett Rheingau Hattenheimer Mannberg 1989 $25 (12/15/90)
84	LANGWERTH VON SIMMERN Spätlese Rheingau Hattenheimer Nussbrunnen 1989 $25 (12/15/90)
84	SCHLOSS SCHONBORN Spätlese Rheingau Hochheimer Kirchenstück 1989 (NA) (12/15/90)

84	DOMDECHANT WERNER'SCHES Kabinett Halbtrocken Rheingau Hochheimer Stein 1989 (NA) (12/15/90)
84	DOMDECHANT WERNER'SCHES Trockenbeerenauslese Rheingau Hochheimer 1989 (NA) (12/15/90)
83	SCHLOSS GROENESTEYN Kabinett Rheingau Kiedricher Gräfenberg 1989 $12 (12/15/90)
83	SCHLOSS GROENESTEYN Spätlese Rheingau Kiedricher Sandgrub 1989 $16 (12/15/90)
83	LANGWERTH VON SIMMERN Kabinett Rheingau Erbacher Marcobrunn 1989 $16 (12/15/90)
83	SCHLOSS SCHONBORN Kabinett Rheingau Johannisberger Klaus 1989 $10 (12/15/90)
83	DR. WEIL Auslese Rheingau Kiedricher Gräfenberg 1989 (NA) (12/15/90)
83	DR. WEIL Kabinett Rheingau Kiedricher Gräfenberg 1989 (NA) (12/15/90)
83	DOMDECHANT WERNER'SCHES Kabinett Rheingau Hochheimer Hölle (AP1,490) 1989 (NA) (12/15/90)
83	DOMDECHANT WERNER'SCHES Spätlese Rheingau Hochheimer Domdechaney 1989 $16 (12/15/90)
81	SCHLOSS GROENESTEYN Kabinett Rheingau Kiedricher Sandgrub 1989 $12 (12/15/90)
80	SCHLOSS GROENESTEYN Spätlese Rheingau Rüdesheimer Berg Rottland 1989 $15 (12/15/90)
80	LANGWERTH VON SIMMERN Kabinett Rheingau Eltviller Sonnerberg 1989 $11 (12/15/90)
79	DOMDECHANT WERNER'SCHES Beerenauslese Rheingau Hochheimer 1989 (NA) (12/15/90)
79	DOMDECHANT WERNER'SCHES Kabinett Rheingau Hochheimer Domdechaney 1989 (NA) (12/15/90)
78	SCHLOSS GROENESTEYN Spätlese Rheingau Kiedricher Gräfenberg 1989 $16 (12/15/90)
78	DR. WEIL Spätlese Rheingau 1989 (NA) (12/15/90)
77	DOMDECHANT WERNER'SCHES Qualitätswein Rheingau Hochheimer 1989 (NA) (12/15/90)

1988

93	DOMDECHANT WERNER'SCHES Spätlese Rheingau Hochheimer Domdechaney 1988 $12.50 (9/30/89) (JS)
93	DOMDECHANT WERNER'SCHES Spätlese Halbtrocken Rheingau Hochheimer Hölle 1988 $12.50 (9/30/89) (JS)
92	GEHEIMRAT ASCHROTT Spätlese Halbtrocken Rheingau Hochheimer Hölle 1988 (NA) (9/30/89) (JS)
92	WEGELER DEINHARD Kabinett Halbtrocken Rheingau Winkeler Hasensprung Charta 1988 $15 (9/30/89) (JS)
91	SCHLOSS GROENESTEYN Kabinett Rheingau Kiedricher Gräfenberg 1988 (NA) (9/30/89) (JS)
90	LANGWERTH VON SIMMERN Spätlese Rheingau Rauenthaler Baiken 1988 (NA) (9/30/89) (JS)
89	WEGELER DEINHARD Spätlese Rheingau Mittelheimer St. Nikolaus 1988 (NA) (9/30/89) (JS)
89	SCHLOSS GROENESTEYN Kabinett Rheingau Kiedricher Sandgrub 1988 (NA) (9/30/89) (JS)
89	LANDGRAF VON HESSEN Spätlese Rheingau Eltville Sonnenberg 1988 (NA) (9/30/89) (JS)
89	BALTHASAR RESS Kabinett Halbtrocken Rheingau Geisenheimer Kläuserweg Charta 1988 $9.50 (9/30/89) (JS)
89	BALTHASAR RESS Spätlese Halbtrocken Rheingau Rüdesheimer Berg Rottland 1988 $14 (9/30/89) (JS)
89	SCHLOSS SCHONBORN Spätlese Halbtrocken Rheingau Hochheimer Hölle 1988 (NA) (9/30/89) (JS)
89	STAATSWEINGUTER Spätlese Rheingau Eltville Rauenthaler Baiken 1988 $25 (9/30/89) (JS)
88	WEGELER DEINHARD Kabinett Rheingau Rüdesheimer Berg Rottland 1988 (NA) (9/30/89) (JS)
88	SCHLOSS SCHONBORN Spätlese Halbtrocken Rheingau Rüdesheimer Bischofsberg 1988 (NA) (9/30/89) (JS)
88	STAATSWEINGUTER Kabinett Halbtrocken Rheingau Eltville Hochheimer Kirchenstück 1988 $8 (9/30/89) (JS)
87	GEHEIMRAT ASCHROTT Kabinett Rheingau Hochheimer Stielweg 1988 (NA) (9/30/89) (JS)
87	FREIHERR ZU KNYPHAUSEN Kabinett Rheingau Erbacher Steinmorgen 1988 (NA) (9/30/89) (JS)
87	DOMDECHANT WERNER'SCHES Kabinett Rheingau Hochheimer Hölle 1988 $10.50 (9/30/89) (JS)
87	DOMDECHANT WERNER'SCHES Kabinett Halbtrocken Rheingau Werner Hochheimer Stein 1988 $10.50 (9/30/89) (JS)
86	FREIHERR ZU KNYPHAUSEN Kabinett Halbtrocken Rheingau Erbacher Steinmorgen 1988 (NA) (9/30/89) (JS)
86	SCHLOSS SCHONBORN Spätlese Rheingau Hattenheimer Nussbrunnen 1988 $21 (9/30/89) (JS)
85	GEHEIMRAT ASCHROTT Spätlese Rheingau Hochheimer Hölle 1988 (NA) (9/30/89) (JS)
85	GEORG BREUER Qualitätswein Rheingau Rüdesheimer Berg Roseneck Charta 1988 $14 (9/30/89) (JS)
85	GEORG BREUER Qualitätswein Rheingau Rüdesheimer Berg Rottland Charta 1988 $14 (9/30/89) (JS)
85	FURST VON METTERNICH Kabinett Halbtrocken Rheingau Schloss Johannisberg 1988 $15 (9/30/89) (JS)
84	FREIHERR ZU KNYPHAUSEN Kabinett Rheingau Kiedricher Sandgrub 1988 (NA) (9/30/89) (JS)
84	LANGWERTH VON SIMMERN Spätlese Rheingau Hattenheimer Nussbrunnen 1988 (NA) (9/30/89) (JS)
84	BALTHASAR RESS Spätlese Rheingau Rüdesheimer Berg Schlossberg 1988 $13.50 (9/30/89) (JS)
84	DR. WEIL Kabinett Halbtrocken Rheingau Kiedricher Wasseros Charta 1988 (NA) (9/30/89) (JS)
84	DR. WEIL Spätlese Rheingau Kiedricher Gräfenberg 1988 (NA) (9/30/89) (JS)
83	GEORG BREUER Kabinett Halbtrocken Rheingau Rüdesheimer Berg Schlossberg Charta 1988 $22.40 (9/30/89) (JS)
82	GEORG BREUER Kabinett Halbtrocken Rheingau Rüdesheimer Bischofsberg Charta 1988 $16 (9/30/89) (JS)
82	FREIHERR ZU KNYPHAUSEN Kabinett Halbtrocken Rheingau Erbacher Marcobrunn Charta 1988 (NA) (9/30/89) (JS)
82	SCHLOSS GROENESTEYN Kabinett Rheingau Rüdesheimer Klosterlay 1988 (NA) (9/30/89) (JS)
81	GEORG BREUER Qualitätswein Rheingau Charta 1988 $14 (9/30/89) (JS)
81	WEGELER DEINHARD Spätlese Rheingau Rüdesheimer Berg Rottland 1988 (NA) (9/30/89) (JS)
81	LANDGRAF VON HESSEN Kabinett Rheingau Johannisberger Klaus 1988 (NA) (9/30/89) (JS)
81	SCHLOSS SCHONBORN Kabinett Halbtrocken Rheingau Geisenheimer Schlossberg 1988 (NA) (9/30/89) (JS)
80	LANDGRAF VON HESSEN Kabinett Rheingau Prinz von Hessen 1988 (NA) (9/30/89) (JS)

GERMANY
RIESLING/*RHEINGAU*

80   LANDGRAF VON HESSEN Kabinett Halbtrocken Rheingau Winkeler Jesuitengarten 1988 (NA) (9/30/89) (JS)
80   LANGWERTH VON SIMMERN Kabinett Rheingau Kiedricher Sandgrub 1988 (NA) (9/30/89) (JS)
79   GEHEIMRAT ASCHROTT Kabinett Rheingau Hochheimer Kirchenstück 1988 (NA) (9/30/89) (JS)
79   STAATSWEINGUTER Kabinett Rheingau Eltville Rauenthaler Baiken 1988 $7.50 (9/30/89) (JS)
78   BALTHASAR RESS Kabinett Halbtrocken Rheingau Hattenheimer Nussbrunnen Charta 1988 $9.50 (9/30/89) (JS)
78   STAATSWEINGUTER Kabinett Rheingau Eltville Rauenthaler Gehrn 1988 $8 (9/30/89) (JS)
75   FURST VON METTERNICH Qualitätswein Rheingau Schloss Johannisberg 1988 $15 (9/30/89) (JS)
74   SCHLOSS GROENESTEYN Kabinett Rheingau Rüdesheimer Berg Rottland 1988 (NA) (9/30/89) (JS)

1986
67   JAKOB DEMMER Rüdesheimer Berg Rottland Rheingau Dry 1986 $4 (11/30/88)

1985
89   SCHLOSS VOLLRADS Qualitätswein Rheingau Grungold 1985 $8.50 (5/15/87)
83   LANGWERTH VON SIMMERN Kabinett Rheingau Hattenheimer Mannberg 1985 $8.50 (1/31/87)
81   SCHLOSS SCHONBORN Kabinett Rheingau Bereich Johannisberg 1985 $10.50 (1/31/88)
78   SCHLOSS GROENESTEYN Kabinett Rheingau Rüdesheimer Berg Rottland 1985 $9 (10/15/87)
78   SCHLOSS VOLLRADS Kabinett Rheingau Blaugold 1985 $11.50 (5/15/87)

1983
90   SCHLOSS JOHANNISBERGER Spätlese Rheingau Grunlack 1983 $20 (8/01/85)
88   SCHLOSS JOHANNISBERGER Kabinett Rheingau Rotlack 1983 $12 (8/01/85)
86   SCHLOSS GROENESTEYN Kabinett Rheingau Rüdesheimer Berg Rottland 1983 $5.75 (1/01/85) BB
81   MADRIGAL Qualitätswein Rheingau Bereich Johannisberg 1983 $5.50 (10/01/84)
80   SCHLOSS VOLLRADS Kabinett Rheingau 1983 $8 (3/01/85)
76   LANGWERTH VON SIMMERN Spätlese Rheingau Hattenheimer Nussbrunnen 1983 $12 (4/01/85)
59   DOMAINE CLEMENS Qualitätswein Rheingau Bereich Johannisberg 1983 $6 (9/01/85)

1982
74   DOMAINE CLEMENS Qualitätswein Rheingau Bereich Johannisberg 1982 $6 (9/16/84)

1981
91   FURST VON METTERNICH Bereich Johannisberg Rheingau Extra Trocken 1981 $13 (4/01/84)

1937
95   SCHLOSS REINHARTSHAUSEN Trockenbeerenauslese Rheingau Erbacher Markobrunn 1937 (NA) (12/15/88)

RHEINHESSEN

1989
91   LOUIS GUNTRUM Auslese Rheinhessen Oppenheimer Schützenhütte 1989 (NA) (12/15/90)
90   HEYL ZU HERRNSHEIM Trockenbeerenauslese Rheinhessen Niersteiner Olberg 1989 $50 (12/15/90)
88   BALBACH Spätlese Rheinhessen Niersteiner Rehbach 1989 (NA) (12/15/90) (JS)
88   HEYL ZU HERRNSHEIM Auslese Rheinhessen Niersteiner Olberg 1989 $25 (12/15/90)
86   LOUIS GUNTRUM Beerenauslese Rheinhessen Niersteiner Pettenthal 1989 (NA) (12/15/90)
86   LOUIS GUNTRUM Kabinett Trocken Rheinhessen Classic Niersteiner Olberg 1989 (NA) (12/15/90)
86   LOUIS GUNTRUM Kabinett Trocken Rheinhessen Classic Oppenheimer Sackträger 1989 (NA) (12/15/90)
86   HEYL ZU HERRNSHEIM Spätlese Rheinhessen Niersteiner Brudersberg 1989 $15 (12/15/90)
85   BALBACH Spätlese Rheinhessen Niersteiner Pettenthal 1989 (NA) (12/15/90) (JS)
85   LOUIS GUNTRUM Trockenbeerenauslese Rheinhessen Oppenheimer Sackträger 1989 (NA) (12/15/90)
85   HEYL ZU HERRNSHEIM Kabinett Rheinhessen Niersteiner Olberg 1989 $12 (12/15/90)
85   HEYL ZU HERRNSHEIM Kabinett Rheinhessen Niersteiner Pettenthal 1989 $11 (12/15/90)
84   BALBACH Auslese Rheinhessen Niersteiner Pettenthal 1989 (NA) (12/15/90) (JS)
84   BALBACH Beerenauslese Rheinhessen Niersteiner Pettenthal 1989 (NA) (12/15/90) (JS)
84   BALBACH Spätlese Rheinhessen Niersteiner Hipping 1989 (NA) (12/15/90) (JS)
84   LOUIS GUNTRUM Auslese Trocken Rheinhessen Niersteiner Pettenthal 1989 (NA) (12/15/90)
84   LOUIS GUNTRUM Kabinett Rheinhessen Niersteiner Bergkirche 1989 (NA) (12/15/90)
84   HEYL ZU HERRNSHEIM Spätlese Rheinhessen Niersteiner Olberg 1989 $15 (12/15/90)
84   HEYL ZU HERRNSHEIM Spätlese Rheinhessen Niersteiner Pettenthal 1989 $15 (12/15/90)
82   LOUIS GUNTRUM Spätlese Trocken Rheinhessen Niersteiner Pettenthal 1989 (NA) (12/15/90)
81   BALBACH Spätlese Rheinhessen Niersteiner Spiegelberg 1989 (NA) (12/15/90) (JS)
80   BALBACH Auslese Rheinhessen Niersteiner Hipping 1989 (NA) (12/15/90) (JS)
79   LOUIS GUNTRUM Spätlese Trocken Rheinhessen Oppenheimer Kreuz 1989 (NA) (12/15/90)
74   LOUIS GUNTRUM Spätlese Rheinhessen Oppenheimer Herrenberg 1989 (NA) (12/15/90)
69   BALBACH Kabinett Rheinhessen 1989 (NA) (12/15/90) (JS)

1988
95   HEYL ZU HERRNSHEIM Spätlese Halbtrocken Rheinhessen Niersteiner Pettenthal 1988 (NA) (9/30/89) (JS)
91   LOUIS GUNTRUM Spätlese Rheinhessen Heiligenbaum 1988 (NA) (9/30/89) (JS)
91   HEYL ZU HERRNSHEIM Kabinett Halbtrocken Rheinhessen Niersteiner Pettenthal 1988 (NA) (9/30/89) (JS)
90   HEYL ZU HERRNSHEIM Kabinett Rheinhessen Niersteiner Olberg 1988 (NA) (9/30/89) (JS)
89   HEYL ZU HERRNSHEIM Spätlese Rheinhessen Niersteiner Olberg 1988 (NA) (9/30/89) (JS)
88   BALBACH Spätlese Rheinhessen Niersteiner Rehbach 1988 $12 (9/30/89) (JS)
88   LOUIS GUNTRUM Kabinett Halbtrocken Rheinhessen Oppenheimer Herrenberg 1988 (NA) (9/30/89) (JS)
86   BALBACH Spätlese Rheinhessen Niersteiner Pettenthal 1988 $12 (9/30/89) (JS)
85   BALBACH Spätlese Rheinhessen Niersteiner Hipping 1988 $12 (9/30/89) (JS)
82   BALBACH Kabinett Rheinhessen Niersteiner Rehbach 1988 $9 (9/30/89) (JS)

1987
81   DR. MEYER Kabinett Rheinhessen Bereich Nierstein 1987 $4 (10/15/88) BB
81   DR. MEYER White Rheinhessen Liebfraumilch 1987 $3 (11/30/88) BB
81   RUDOLF MULLER White Rheinhessen Liebfraumilch Mariengold 1987 $4 (11/30/88) BB
75   DR. MEYER Qualitätswein Rheinhessen Zeller Schwarze Katz 1987 $4 (11/30/88)

1986
85   REINHOLD SENFTER Kabinett Rheinhessen Niersteiner Oelberg 1986 $8.25 (1/31/88)
82   DR. MEYER Spätlese Rheinhessen Mainzer Domherr 1986 $5 (11/30/88) BB
64   RUDOLF MULLER Kabinett Rheinhessen Niersteiner Spiegelberg 1986 $5.75 (11/30/87)

1985
82   BAUM Kabinett Rheinhessen Mainzer Domherr 1985 $5 (10/15/86) BB
79   BALBACH Auslese Rheinhessen Niersteiner Pettenthal 1985 $16.25 (1/31/87)
61   BALBACH Spätlese Rheinhessen Niersteiner Pettenthal 1985 $10 (1/31/87)
60   BALBACH Kabinett Rheinhessen Niersteiner Klostergarten 1985 $8 (1/31/87)

1984
76   BAUM Qualitätswein Rheinhessen Niersteiner Gutes Domtal 1984 $4.50 (5/16/85)

1983
83   BALBACH Spätlese Rheinhessen Niersteiner Pattenthal 1983 $9 (4/16/85)
80   BALBACH Kabinett Rheinhessen Niersteiner Bildstock 1983 $7 (3/01/85)
51   KURFURSTENHOF Spätlese Rheinhessen Bornheimer Adelberg 1983 $4.50 (12/01/85)

RHEINPFALZ

1989
96   LINGENFELDER Trockenbeerenauslese Rheinpfalz Freinsheimer Goldberg 1989 $100/375ml (12/15/90) (JS)
95   DR. BURKLIN-WOLF Auslese Rheinpfalz Wachenheimer Gerümpel 1989 $34 (12/15/90)
95   DR. BURKLIN-WOLF Beerenauslese Rheinpfalz Wachenheimer Gerümpel 1989 (NA) (12/15/90)
95   DR. BURKLIN-WOLF Trockenbeerenauslese Rheinpfalz Wachenheimer Luginsland 1989 $165 (12/15/90)
94   DR. BURKLIN-WOLF Auslese Rheinpfalz Forster Pechstein 1989 $25 (12/15/90)
93   DR. BURKLIN-WOLF Beerenauslese Rheinpfalz Wachenheimer Rechbächel 1989 $95/375ml (12/15/90)
93   WEGELER DEINHARD Trockenbeerenauslese Rheinpfalz Deidesheimer Herrgottsacker 1989 (NA) (12/15/90) (JS)
92   LINGENFELDER Trockenbeerenauslese Rheinpfalz Grosskarlbacher Osterberg 1989 $85/375ml (12/15/90) (JS)
90   DR. BURKLIN-WOLF Spätlese Rheinpfalz Forster Jusuitgarten 1989 $18 (12/15/90)
90   LINGENFELDER Spätlese Rheinpfalz Freinsheimer Goldberg 1989 $15 (12/15/90) (JS)
90   PFEFFINGEN Spätlese Rheinpfalz Ungsteiner Herrenberg 1989 $16 (12/15/90)
89   BASSERMANN-JORDAN Kabinett Rheinpfalz Deidesheimer 1989 $9 (12/15/90)
88   LINGENFELDER Spätlese Trocken Rheinpfalz Freinsheimer Goldberg 1989 $15 (12/15/90) (JS)
87   BASSERMANN-JORDAN Auslese Rheinpfalz Deidesheimer Hohenmorgen 1989 (NA) (12/15/90)
87   DR. BURKLIN-WOLF Kabinett Rheinpfalz Ruppertsberger Hoheburg 1989 (NA) (12/15/90)
87   WEGELER DEINHARD Spätlese Rheinpfalz Deidesheimer Herrgottsacker 1989 $13 (12/15/90) (JS)
86   BASSERMANN-JORDAN Kabinett Rheinpfalz Deddesheimer Hohenmorgen 1989 $10 (12/15/90)
85   DR. BURKLIN-WOLF Spätlese Rheinpfalz Wachenheimer Gerümpel 1989 $15 (12/15/90)
85   WEGELER DEINHARD Auslese Rheinpfalz Deidesheimer Herrgottsacker 1989 $17 (12/15/90) (JS)
85   PFEFFINGEN Auslese Rheinpfalz Ungsteiner Herrenberg 1989 $25 (12/15/90)
85   PFEFFINGEN Auslese Rheinpfalz Ungsteiner Weilberg 1989 $25 (12/15/90)
85   PFEFFINGEN Auslese Trocken Rheinpfalz Ungsteiner Herrenberg Scheurebe 1989 $25 (12/15/90)
85   PFEFFINGEN Spätlese Halbtrocken Rheinpfalz Ungsteiner Herrenberg 1989 $16 (12/15/90)
84   DR. BURKLIN-WOLF Spätlese Rheinpfalz Deidesheimer Hohenmorgen 1989 $14 (12/15/90)
84   PFEFFINGEN Spätlese Halbtrocken Rheinpfalz Ungsteiner Herrenberg Scheurebe 1989 $16 (12/15/90)
84   PFEFFINGEN Spätlese Trocken Rheinpfalz Ungsteiner Weilberg 1989 $16 (12/15/90)
83   DR. BURKLIN-WOLF Kabinett Rheinpfalz Wachenheimer Gerümpel 1989 $9 (12/15/90)
82   WEGELER DEINHARD Kabinett Rheinpfalz Deidesheimer Herrgottsacker 1989 $10 (12/15/90) (JS)
81   PFEFFINGEN Kabinett Rheinpfalz Ungsteiner Hönigsäckel 1989 $16 (12/15/90)
81   PFEFFINGEN Spätlese Rheinpfalz Ungsteiner Herrenberg Scheurebe 1989 $16 (12/15/90)
80   DR. BURKLIN-WOLF Spätlese Trocken Rheinpfalz Geheimrat Dr. Albert Bürklin-Wolf 1989 (NA) (12/15/90)
78   DR. BURKLIN-WOLF Kabinett Rheinpfalz Wachenheimer Rechbächel 1989 (NA) (12/15/90)

1988
94   MESSMER BURRWEILER Spätlese Trocken Rheinpfalz Schlossgarten 1988 $10 (9/30/89) (JS)
94   PFEFFINGEN Spätlese Rheinpfalz Ungsteiner Herrenberg 1988 $16 (9/30/89) (JS)
92   MULLER-CATOIR Kabinett Halbtrocken Rheinpfalz Haardter Bürgergarten 1988 $9 (9/30/89)
92   MULLER-CATOIR Spätlese Trocken Rheinpfalz Mussbacher Eselshaut 1988 $14 (9/30/89) (JS)

92   PFEFFINGEN Kabinett Halbtrocken Rheinpfalz Ungsteiner Hönigsäckel 1988 (NA) (9/30/89)
      (JS)

92   SICHEL Beerenauslese Rheinpfalz Deidesheimer Hofstuck 1988 $9.75/375ml (3/15/90)

91   LINGENFELDER Spätlese Trocken Rheinpfalz Freinsheimer Goldberg 1988 $12 (9/30/89)
      (JS)

90   MESSMER BURRWEILER Kabinett Rheinpfalz Schlossgarten 1988 (NA) (9/30/89) (JS)

90   PFEFFINGEN Spätlese Halbtrocken Rheinpfalz Ungsteiner Herrenberg 1988 $16 (9/30/89)
      (JS)

89   LINGENFELDER Spätlese Rheinpfalz Freinsheimer Goldberg 1988 $12 (9/30/89) (JS)

88   DR. BURKLIN-WOLF Spätlese Trocken Rheinpfalz Wachenheimer Gerümpel 1988 $10
      (9/30/89) (JS)

88   PFEFFINGEN Kabinett Rheinpfalz Ungsteiner Hönigsäckel 1988 $15 (9/30/89) (JS)

87   DR. BURKLIN-WOLF Beerenauslese Rheinpfalz Wachenheimer Goldbächel 1988 $30
      (9/30/89) (JS)

87   MESSMER BURRWEILER Kabinett Halbtrocken Rheinpfalz Schlossgarten 1988 $8 (9/30/89)
      (JS)

87   MESSMER BURRWEILER Spätlese Rheinpfalz Schäwer 1988 $9 (9/30/89) (JS)

86   WEGELER DEINHARD Spätlese Rheinpfalz Forster Ungeheuer 1988 $12 (9/30/89) (JS)

85   DR. BURKLIN-WOLF Kabinett Halbtrocken Rheinpfalz 1988 $8 (9/30/89) (JS)

85   WEGELER DEINHARD Spätlese Trocken Rheinpfalz Deidesheimer Herrgottsacker 1988
      (NA) (9/30/89) (JS)

84   WEGELER DEINHARD Spätlese Rheinpfalz Deidesheimer Herrgottsacker 1988 $11 (9/30/89)
      (JS)

82   K. NECKERAUER Spätlese Trocken Rheinpfalz Weisenheimer Hahnen 1988 $8 (9/30/89) (JS)

81   K. NECKERAUER Spätlese Trocken Rheinpfalz Weisenheimer Altenberg 1988 $8 (9/30/89)
      (JS)

79   DR. BURKLIN-WOLF Trockenbeerenauslese Rheinpfalz Ruppertsberger Linsenbusch 1988
      $9 (9/30/89) (JS)

72   K. NECKERAUER Kabinett Halbtrocken Rheinpfalz Weisenheimer Hasenzeile 1988 $7
      (9/30/89) (JS)

1986

88   JAKOB DEMMER Spätlese Rheinpfalz Weingartener Trappenberg 1986 $5 (11/30/88) BB

1985

61   DR. BURKLIN-WOLF Kabinett Rheinpfalz Deidesheimer Hohenmorgen 1985 $6.25 (6/30/87)

1983

74   BASSERMANN-JORDAN Kabinett Rheinpfalz Deddesheimer Herrgottsaker 1983 $7
      (3/16/85)

SPARKLING

1986

84   RUDOLF MULLER Sparkling Mosel-Saar-Ruwer Mosel-Riesling Sekt 1986 $7.50 (10/15/88)

1985

72   DR. H. THANISCH Sparkling Mosel-Saar-Ruwer Brut 1985 $12.50 (1/31/88)

NV

81   DEINHARD Sparkling Riesling Lila Imperial NV $7 (8/31/89) BB
72   HENKELL Sparkling Trocken Feinertrockner Sekt NV $10 (10/15/88)
66   RUDOLF MULLER Sparkling Splendid Sektkellerei Gold NV $6.25 (6/30/87)

ITALY
DESSERT

1989
85   BENI DI BATASIOLO Moscato d'Asti 1989 $14 (7/15/91)
81   JERMANN Moscato Rosa del FVG Vigna Bellina 1989 $26 (3/15/91)

1988
91   MACULAN Torcolato 1988 $35 (4/15/91)
73   ABBAZIA DI ROSAZZO Ronco della Abbazia 1988 $11/375ml (7/15/91)

1987
87   MARCO DE BARTOLI Moscato di Pantelleria 1987 $16 (3/31/90)
85   JERMANN Moscato Rosa del FVG Vigna Bellina 1987 $20 (9/15/88)
76   RUSSIZ SUPERIORE Verduzzo 1987 (NA) (9/15/88)

1986
83   ABBAZIA DI ROSAZZO Colli Orientali del Friuli Verduzzo 1986 $22 (10/15/88)

1985
87   MARCO DE BARTOLI Marsala Superiore Vigna La Miccia 1985 $16 (3/31/90)
84   MACULAN Torcolato 1985 $15/375ml (3/31/89)
79   LUNGAROTTI Vin Santo 1985 $7/375ml (3/15/91)
78   CASTELLO DI GABBIANO Vin Santo 1985 $20 (3/15/91)

1984
89   I SELVATICI Vin Santo 1984 $16/375ml (4/30/91)
88   CASTELLARE DI CASTELLINA Vin Santo 1984 $28/375ml (9/30/90)
85   CARLO HAUNER Malvasia delle Lipari 1984 $15/375ml (12/31/88)

1983
83   CASTELCOSA Picolit 1983 (NA) (9/15/88)
83   MONTE VERTINE M 1983 $20 (2/15/87)
82   MACULAN Torcolato 1983 $29 (11/15/87)
81   LUNGAROTTI Vin Santo 1983 $9.50 (3/15/89)

1982
96   MARTINI DI CIGALA San Giusto a Rentennano Vin Santo 1982 $18/375ml (12/31/88)
92   CASTELLO DI MONTEGROSSI Vin Santo 1982 $19/375ml (3/31/90)

1981
89   MARTINI DI CIGALA San Giusto a Rentennano Vin Santo 1981 $25 (12/31/87)
87   FRESCOBALDI Pomino Tenuta di Pomino Vin Santo 1981 $20 (10/15/88)
68   CAPEZZANA Vin Santo di Carmignano 1981 $16 (10/31/86)

1977
92   AVIGNONESI Vin Santo 1977 $18 (10/01/85)
85   BARONE RICASOLI Vin Santo Brolio 1977 $13 (3/31/90)

NV
93   ISOLE E OLENA Vin Santo NV $17/375ml (3/31/90)
89   MONTE VERTINE Vin Santo NV $20 (2/15/87)

PIEDMONT RED/BARBARESCO DOCG

1987
89   CERETTO Barbaresco Bricco Asili Bricco Asili 1987 $40 (4/30/91)
89   CERETTO Barbaresco Bricco Asili Faset 1987 $31 (7/15/91)
89   MOCCAGATTA Barbaresco Bric Balin 1987 $28 (7/15/91)
86   CERETTO Barbaresco Asij 1987 $22 (7/15/91)
86   MOCCAGATTA Barbaresco Vigneto Basarin 1987 $23 (7/15/91)
79   CASTELLO DI NEIVE Barbaresco Vigneto Santo Stefano 1987 $20 (12/31/90)

1986
93   GAJA Barbaresco Sori Tildin 1986 Rel: $94 Cur: $109 (1/31/90)
92   GAJA Barbaresco 1986 $47 (1/31/90) CS
91   GAJA Barbaresco Sori San Lorenzo 1986 Rel: $89 Cur: $106 (1/31/90)
90   MARCHESI DI GRESY Barbaresco Gaiun Martinenga 1986 Rel: $64 Cur: $96 (9/15/90)
90   PRODUTTORI DEL BARBARESCO Barbaresco 1986 $12 (10/31/90)
89   GIUSEPPE CORTESE Barbaresco Rabajà 1986 $19 (9/15/90)
89   GAJA Barbaresco Costa Russi 1986 Rel: $85 Cur: $126 (1/31/90)
88   MARCHESI DI GRESY Barbaresco Martinenga 1986 Rel: $56 Cur: $84 (9/15/90)
87   LA CA'NOVA Barbaresco 1986 $14.50 (10/31/90)
87   GIACOSA FRATELLI Barbaresco 1986 $17 (7/15/91)
87   VIETTI Barbaresco Della Località Rabajà 1986 $18 (10/31/90)
86   FRATELLI CIGLIUTI Barbaresco Serraboella 1986 $20 (8/31/90)
86   PRUNOTTO Barbaresco Montestefano 1986 $37 (12/31/90)
86   ALFREDO & GIOVANNI ROAGNA Barbaresco 1986 $26 (7/15/91)
85   CERETTO Barbaresco Bricco Asili Bricco Asili 1986 Rel: $35 Cur: $41 (4/15/90)
82   VALFIERI Barbaresco 1986 $12 (9/15/90)
72   GIACOSA FRATELLI Barbaresco Suri Secondine 1986 $11.50 (10/31/90)

1985
98   GAJA Barbaresco Sori Tildin 1985 Rel: $94 Cur: $125 (9/15/89) (HS)
97   GAJA Barbaresco Sori Tildin 1985 Rel: $94 Cur: $125 (12/15/88)
96   GAJA Barbaresco Costa Russi 1985 Rel: $83 Cur: $100 (12/15/88)
96   GAJA Barbaresco Sori San Lorenzo 1985 Rel: $88 Cur: $102 (12/15/88)
95   GAJA Barbaresco 1985 Rel: $45 Cur: $58 (9/15/89) (HS)

95   GAJA Barbaresco 1985 Rel: $45 Cur: $58 (12/15/88) CS
95   MARCHESI DI GRESY Barbaresco Gaiun Martinenga 1985 Rel: $55 Cur: $73 (1/31/89) CS
92   CA'ROME Barbaresco Maria di Brun 1985 $37 (1/31/90)
92   MARCHESI DI GRESY Barbaresco Camp Gros Martinenga 1985 Rel: $58 Cur: $73 (1/31/89)
92   PRODUTTORI DEL BARBARESCO Barbaresco Asili Riserva 1985 $27 (10/31/90)
90   CAVALOTTO Barbaresco Vigna San Giuseppe Riserva 1985 $22 (2/28/91)
90   CERETTO Barbaresco Bricco Asili Bricco Asili 1985 Rel: $35 Cur: $39 (9/15/88) (HS)
90   MARCHESI DI GRESY Barbaresco Martinenga 1985 Rel: $39 Cur: $57 (1/31/89)
89   CERETTO Barbaresco Bricco Asili Bricco Asili 1985 Rel: $35 Cur: $39 (8/31/89)
89   ALFREDO & GIOVANNI ROAGNA Barbaresco 1985 $37 (2/28/89)
88   CA'ROME Barbaresco 1985 $28 (1/31/90)
88   ELIA PASQUERO Barbaresco Sori' Paitin 1985 $14 (3/31/90)
87   CERETTO Barbaresco Bricco Asili Faset 1985 $31 (1/31/90)
87   PRUNOTTO Barbaresco Montestefano 1985 $29 (3/31/90)
87   FRANCESCO RINALDI & FIGLI Barbaresco 1985 $23 (9/15/90)
86   PRODUTTORI DEL BARBARESCO Barbaresco Ovello Riserva 1985 $25 (10/31/90)
86   TRAVERSA Barbaresco Sori Ciabot 1985 $23 (9/15/90)
85   GIUSEPPE MASCARELLO & FIGLIO Barbaresco Marcarini 1985 $29.50 (8/31/89)
84   CERETTO Barbaresco Bricco Asili Faset 1985 $31 (9/15/88) (HS)
84   BRUNO GIACOSA Barbaresco 1985 $42 (8/31/89)
82   PRODUTTORI DEL BARBARESCO Barbaresco Montestefano Riserva 1985 $25 (10/31/90)
81   VIETTI Barbaresco 1985 $28 (7/31/89)
70   VALFIERI Barbaresco 1985 $8.25 (7/31/89)
64   CERETTO Barbaresco Asij 1985 $15 (1/31/90)

1984
84   MARCHESI DI GRESY Barbaresco Martinenga 1984 Rel: $20 Cur: $36 (9/15/88) (HS)
80   CERETTO Barbaresco Bricco Asili Bricco Asili 1984 Rel: $15 Cur: $19 (9/15/88) (HS)
80   PRODUTTORI DEL BARBARESCO Barbaresco 1984 $12 (9/15/88) (HS)

1983
93   GAJA Barbaresco 1983 Rel: $35 Cur: $53 (9/15/89) (HS)
90   GAJA Barbaresco 1983 Rel: $35 Cur: $53 (7/31/89)
90   GAJA Barbaresco Sori San Lorenzo 1983 Cur: $99 (9/15/88) (HS)
88   GAJA Barbaresco Sori Tildin 1983 Cur: $97 (9/15/89) (HS)
88   BRUNO GIACOSA Barbaresco 1983 $24 (7/31/87)
88   MARCHESI DI GRESY Barbaresco Camp Gros Martinenga 1983 Rel: $30 Cur: $85 (9/15/88) (HS)
87   MARCHESI DI GRESY Barbaresco Martinenga 1983 Rel: $20 Cur: $68 (9/15/88) (HS)
85   PRODUTTORI DEL BARBARESCO Barbaresco 1983 $12 (9/15/88) (HS)
84   MARCHESI DI GRESY Barbaresco Gaiun Martinenga 1983 Rel: $30 Cur: $83 (9/15/88) (HS)
80   FONTANAFREDDA Barbaresco 1983 $11.50 (9/15/88) (HS)
79   BERSANO Barbaresco 1983 $7.75 (1/31/89)
79   GIUSEPPE CORTESE Barbaresco Spéciale 1983 $13 (8/31/89)
79   FRANCESCO RINALDI & FIGLI Barbaresco 1983 $16 (1/31/89)
75   GIUSEPPE CORTESE Barbaresco Vigna in Rabata 1983 $18 (1/31/90)

1982
94   GAJA Barbaresco Sori Tildin 1982 Cur: $140 (9/15/89) (HS)
93   GAJA Barbaresco 1982 Cur: $103 (9/15/89) (HS)
92   BRUNO GIACOSA Barbaresco Santo Stefano 1982 $57 (9/15/88)
91   GAJA Barbaresco Costa Russi 1982 Cur: $93 (9/15/88) (HS)
91   PRODUTTORI DEL BARBARESCO Barbaresco Paje 1982 $22 (9/15/88) (HS)
91   PRODUTTORI DEL BARBARESCO Barbaresco Pora 1982 $18 (9/15/88) (HS)
90   BRUNO GIACOSA Barbaresco Santo Stefano di Neive Riserva 1982 $60 (9/15/88) (HS)
89   MARCHESI DI GRESY Barbaresco Camp Gros Martinenga 1982 Rel: $26 Cur: $75 (9/15/88) (HS)
89   PRODUTTORI DEL BARBARESCO Barbaresco Asili Riserva 1982 $22 (9/15/88) (HS)
89   PRODUTTORI DEL BARBARESCO Barbaresco Moccagatta 1982 $22 (9/15/88) (HS)
89   PRODUTTORI DEL BARBARESCO Barbaresco Rabajà 1982 $22 (9/15/88) (HS)
88   PRODUTTORI DEL BARBARESCO Barbaresco Montestefano 1982 $18 (9/15/88) (HS)
87   CERETTO Barbaresco Bricco Asili Bricco Asili 1982 Rel: $19 Cur: $54 (9/15/88) (HS)
87   MARCHESI DI GRESY Barbaresco Gaiun Martinenga 1982 Rel: $26 Cur: $75 (9/15/88) (HS)
87   PRODUTTORI DEL BARBARESCO Barbaresco 1982 $12 (9/15/88) (HS)
87   PRODUTTORI DEL BARBARESCO Barbaresco Rio Sordo 1982 $22 (9/15/88) (HS)
86   MARCHESI DI GRESY Barbaresco Martinenga 1982 Rel: $20 Cur: $68 (9/15/88) (HS)
86   CASTELLO DI NEIVE Barbaresco Vigneto Santo Stefano 1982 $27 (9/15/88) (HS)
86   PRODUTTORI DEL BARBARESCO Barbaresco Ovello 1982 $22 (9/15/88) (HS)
85   GIUSEPPE CORTESE Barbaresco 1982 $19 (12/15/88)
85   PRODUTTORI DEL BARBARESCO Barbaresco Montefico 1982 $22 (9/15/88) (HS)
84   ODDERO Barbaresco 1982 $15 (9/15/88)
84   VIETTI Barbaresco 1982 $15 (7/31/87)
83   BAVA Barbaresco 1982 $23 (4/30/91)
81   FONTANAFREDDA Barbaresco 1982 (NA) (9/15/88) (HS)
81   PRUNOTTO Barbaresco Rabajà Riserva 1982 $19 (7/31/87)
77   LE TERRE FORTI Barbaresco 1982 $19 (9/15/90)

1981
90   GAJA Barbaresco 1981 Cur: $110 (9/15/89) (HS)
87   GAJA Barbaresco Sori Tildin 1981 Cur: $150 (9/15/89) (HS)
84   SCARPA Barbaresco 1981 $20 (9/15/88) (HS)
72   GIUSEPPE CORTESE Barbaresco Vigna in Rabata 1981 $12 (8/31/89)
63   DE FORVILLE Barbaresco 1981 $14 (2/16/86)
58   CERETTO Barbaresco 1981 $9.50 (5/16/86)

1980
88   GAJA Barbaresco 1980 Rel: $14 Cur: $75 (7/01/85)
68   PIO CESARE Barbaresco Riserva 1980 $15.50 (12/16/85)

1979
91   PRODUTTORI DEL BARBARESCO Barbaresco Pora 1979 $24 (9/15/88) (HS)
90   PRODUTTORI DEL BARBARESCO Barbaresco 1979 (NA) (9/15/88) (HS)
90   SCARPA Barbaresco 1979 $20 (9/15/88) (HS)
89   GAJA Barbaresco 1979 Cur: $130 (9/15/89) (HS)
89   GAJA Barbaresco Sori Tildin 1979 Cur: $225 (9/15/89) (HS)
87   MARCHESI DI GRESY Barbaresco Camp Gros Martinenga 1979 Cur: $40 (9/15/88) (HS)
81   MARCHESI DI GRESY Barbaresco Martinenga 1979 Cur: $30 (9/15/88) (HS)
79   LE COLLINE Barbaresco Riserva Spéciale 1979 $15 (7/31/87)

1978

93   GAJA Barbaresco 1978 Cur: $130 (9/15/89) (HS)
92   PRODUTTORI DEL BARBARESCO Barbaresco Montefico 1978 $30 (9/15/88) (HS)
90   CERETTO Barbaresco Bricco Asili Bricco Asili 1978 Cur: $75 (3/01/86) (JS)
90   GAJA Barbaresco Sori Tildin 1978 Cur: $220 (9/15/89) (HS)
90   SCARPA Barbaresco 1978 $27 (9/15/88) (HS)
89   MARCHESI DI GRESY Barbaresco Martinenga 1978 Cur: $40 (9/15/88) (HS)
86   FONTANAFREDDA Barbaresco 1978 (NA) (9/15/88) (HS)
83   SCARPA Barbaresco I Tetti di Neive 1978 $27 (3/15/87)

1976

91   GAJA Barbaresco 1976 Cur: $130 (9/15/89) (HS)
89   CERETTO Barbaresco Bricco Asili Bricco Asili 1976 (NA) (9/15/88) (HS)

1975

76   BERSANO Barbaresco 1975 (NA) (9/15/88) (HS)

1974

90   CERETTO Barbaresco Bricco Asili Bricco Asili 1974 (NA) (3/01/86) (JS)
89   GAJA Barbaresco 1974 Cur: $145 (9/15/89) (HS)
89   SCARPA Barbaresco 1974 (NA) (9/15/88) (HS)

1973

88   GAJA Barbaresco Sori Tildin 1973 Cur: $156 (9/15/89) (HS)

1971

91   GAJA Barbaresco Sori Tildin 1971 Cur: $200 (9/15/89) (HS)
86   GAJA Barbaresco 1971 Cur: $156 (9/15/89) (HS)
78   BERSANO Barbaresco 1971 (NA) (9/15/88) (HS)

1970

78   GAJA Barbaresco Sori Tildin 1970 Cur: $220 (9/15/89) (HS)

1967

83   GAJA Barbaresco 1967 Cur: $170 (9/15/89) (HS)

1964

87   GAJA Barbaresco 1964 Cur: $195 (9/15/89) (HS)
85   BERSANO Barbaresco 1964 (NA) (9/15/88) (HS)

1961

92   GAJA Barbaresco 1961 Cur: $270 (9/15/89) (HS)

BARBERA DOC

1989

91   ELIO ALTARE Barbera d'Alba 1989 $13 (3/15/91)
89   FRATELLI CIGLIUTI Barbera d'Alba Serraboella 1989 $13.50 (3/15/91)
89   MOCCAGATTA Barbera d'Alba 1989 $14 (3/15/91)
88   NEGRO Barbera d'Alba Nicolon 1989 $11.50 (3/15/91)
86   CONTERNO FANTINO Barbera d'Alba Vignota 1989 $20 (3/15/91)
86   GIUSEPPE CORTESE Barbera d'Alba 1989 $11 (7/15/91)
85   VIETTI Barbera d'Alba Scarrone 1989 $13 (3/15/91)

1988

90   MARCARINI Barbera d'Alba Ciabot Camerano 1988 $18 (3/15/91)
90   ROCCHE COSTAMAGNA Barbera d'Alba 1988 $11.50 (3/15/91)
88   BENI DI BATASIOLO Barbera d'Alba 1988 $10.50 (4/15/91)
88   LUIGI COPPO Barbera d'Asti Camp du Rouss 1988 $21 (3/15/91)
86   GIUSEPPE CORTESE Barbera d'Alba 1988 $9 (3/15/91)
85   PARUSSO Barbera d'Alba 1988 $12 (3/15/91)
84   ELIO ALTARE Barbera d'Alba 1988 $10 (3/31/90)
84   CLERICO Barbera d'Alba 1988 $12 (3/15/91)
84   RICCARDO FENOCCHIO Barbera d'Alba Pianpolvere Soprano 1988 $10 (3/15/91)
83   CASTELLO DI NEIVE Barbera d'Alba Vigneto Messoirano 1988 $11 (7/15/91)
83   ELIA PASQUERO Barbera d'Alba Sori'Paitin 1988 $8 (3/15/91)
79   VIETTI Barbera d'Alba Pianromualdo 1988 $15 (3/15/91)
78   MARCHESI DI BAROLO Barbera del Monferrato Le Lune 1988 $6 (7/15/91)

1987

92   ELIO ALTARE Barbera d'Alba 1987 $11.50 (8/31/89)
90   LUIGI COPPO Barbera d'Asti Pomorosso 1987 $41 (3/15/91)
89   CASETTA Barbera d'Alba Vigna Lazaretto 1987 $9 (3/15/91) BB
88   GAJA Barbera d'Alba Vignarey 1987 $35 (4/15/91)
87   FRANCESCO RINALDI & FIGLI Barbera d'Alba 1987 $10 (3/15/91)
86   VIETTI Barbera d'Alba Della Località Scarrone 1987 $11 (8/31/89)
85   CLERICO Barbera d'Alba 1987 $8 (8/31/89)
85   GIUSEPPE MASCARELLO & FIGLIO Barbera d'Alba Superiore Ginestra 1987 $11 (3/15/91)
85   PRUNOTTO Barbera d'Alba 1987 $9.50 (3/31/90)
83   GIUSEPPE MASCARELLO & FIGLIO Barbera d'Alba Superiore Santo Stefano di Perno 1987 $13 (9/15/90)
83   MIRAFIORE Barbera d'Alba 1987 $12.50 (4/15/91)
81   PIO CESARE Barbera d'Alba 1987 $12.50 (4/15/91)
81   PRUNOTTO Barbera d'Alba Pian Romualdo 1987 $14.50 (9/15/90)
80   BERSANO Barbera d'Asti 1987 $9 (3/15/91)
80   GIUSEPPE MASCARELLO & FIGLIO Barbera d'Alba Fasana 1987 $10 (3/15/91)
75   RICCARDO FENOCCHIO Barbera d'Alba Pianpolvere Soprano 1987 $10 (3/15/91)
74   FATTORIA MASSARA Barbera d'Alba 1987 $7.75 (9/15/90)
73   BRUNO GIACOSA Barbera d'Alba Altavilla d'Alba 1987 $12.50 (3/15/91)
69   CASTELLO DI NEIVE Barbera d'Alba Vigneto Messoirano 1987 $11 (4/15/91)
69   VALFIERI Barbera d'Alba 1987 $7 (9/15/90)

1986

88   GAJA Barbera d'Alba Vignarey 1986 $27.50 (3/15/91)
88   FRANCESCO RINALDI & FIGLI Barbera d'Alba 1986 $9 (2/15/89)
87   LUIGI COPPO Barbera d'Asti Camp du Rouss 1986 $19 (3/31/90)
86   MICHELE CHIARLO Barbera d'Asti Superiore 1986 $18 (3/15/91)
86   GIACOSA FRATELLI Barbera d'Alba Maria Gioana 1986 $22 (3/15/91)
84   LUIGI COPPO Barbera d'Asti Pomorosso 1986 $41 (3/15/91)

83   RICCARDO FENOCCHIO Barbera d'Alba Pianpolvere Soprano 1986 $8.50 (3/15/89)
77   BRUNO GIACOSA Barbera d'Alba Altavilla d'Alba 1986 $12.50 (3/15/91)
76   LIVIO PAVESE Barbera d'Asti Superiore 1986 $9 (3/15/91)

1985

88   SCARPA Barbera d'Asti 1985 $12 (8/31/89)
87   BAVA Barbera d'Asti 1985 $13 (3/15/91)
86   RICCARDO FENOCCHIO Barbera d'Alba Pianpolvere Soprano 1985 $15 (3/15/91)
85   GIUSEPPE MASCARELLO & FIGLIO Barbera d'Alba Fasana 1985 $9 (11/30/87)
84   CLERICO Barbera d'Alba 1985 $8.25 (11/30/87)
83   G.D. VAJRA Barbera d'Alba Bricco delle Viole Riserva 1985 $22 (7/31/89)
82   MARCHESI DI BAROLO Barbera del Monferrato 1985 $5 (9/15/87) BB
81   PRUNOTTO Barbera d'Alba 1985 $8 (7/15/88)
78   LUIGI CALDI Barbera d'Asti 1985 $7 (7/31/89)
78   PIO CESARE Barbera d'Alba 1985 $11.50 (11/15/88)
77   ODDERO Barbera d'Alba 1985 $9 (7/15/88)

1984

82   GAJA Barbera d'Alba Vignarey 1984 $13.50 (2/15/87)

1983

89   PRUNOTTO Barbera d'Alba 1983 $6 (7/15/87) BB

BAROLO DOCG

1986

91   CERETTO Barolo Bricco Rocche Prapò 1986 $50 (2/28/91)
89   CERETTO Barolo Bricco Rocche Bricco Rocche 1986 $119 (4/30/91)
89   LUCIANO SANDRONE Barolo Cannubi Boschis 1986 $34 (12/31/90)
88   GIUSEPPE MASCARELLO & FIGLIO Barolo Monprivato Falletto 1986 $47 (7/15/90)
87   MAURO MOLINO Barolo Vigna Conca 1986 $29 (2/28/91)
83   PARUSSO Barolo Mariondino 1986 $23 (4/30/91)
83   FRANCESCO RINALDI & FIGLI Barolo 1986 $22 (7/15/91)
80   CERETTO Barolo Bricco Rocche Brunate 1986 $40 (4/30/91)

1985

94   CERETTO Barolo Bricco Rocche Bricco Rocche 1985 Rel: $56 Cur: $103 (9/15/88) (HS)
94   GIUSEPPE MASCARELLO & FIGLIO Barolo Santo Stefano di Perno 1985 $35 (10/15/90)
93   GIUSEPPE MASCARELLO & FIGLIO Barolo Belvedere 1985 $35 (6/15/90) CS
92   ELIO ALTARE Barolo 1985 $24 (1/31/90)
92   CERETTO Barolo Bricco Rocche Brunate 1985 $41 (1/31/90)
92   CLERICO Barolo Ciabot Mentin Ginestra 1985 Rel: $27 Cur: $40 (4/15/90) CS
92   PRUNOTTO Barolo Bussia 1985 $38 (9/15/90)
92   LUCIANO SANDRONE Barolo Cannubi Boschis 1985 $30 (1/31/90)
91   CERETTO Barolo Bricco Rocche Prapò 1985 $50 (9/15/88) (HS)
91   PIO CESARE Barolo Ornato Riserva 1985 $48 (5/15/91)
91   G.D. VAJRA Barolo Fossati Vineyard 1985 $34 (12/31/90)
90   ALDO CONTERNO Barolo Bricco Bussia Vigna Cicala 1985 $40 (6/15/90)
90   MARCARINI Barolo Brunate 1985 $35 (3/31/90)
90   SCARPA Barolo 1985 (NA) (9/15/88) (HS)
90   PAOLO SCAVINO Barolo Brico dell Fiasco 1985 $39 (6/15/90)
90   SEBASTE Barolo 1985 (NA) (9/15/88) (HS)
90   VALFIERI Barolo 1985 $13.50 (10/15/90)
89   AZELIA Barolo Bricco Fiasco 1985 $30 (9/15/90)
89   CA'ROME Barolo 1985 $35 (10/15/90)
89   CERETTO Barolo Bricco Rocche Brunate 1985 $41 (9/15/88) (HS)
89   PIO CESARE Barolo 1985 $38 (5/15/91)
89   MICHELE CHIARLO Barolo Granduca 1985 $20 (2/28/91)
89   FRANCESCO RINALDI & FIGLI Barolo La Brunata 1985 $24 (7/15/91)
88   MARCHESI DI BAROLO Barolo Cannubi 1985 $29 (10/15/90)
88   MARCHESI DI BAROLO Barolo Valletta 1985 $29 (10/15/90)
88   PAOLO SCAVINO Barolo 1985 $21 (10/15/90)
87   BEL COLLE Barolo Vigna Monvigliero 1985 $20 (10/15/90)
87   MICHELE CHIARLO Barolo Rocche di Castiglione Riserva 1985 $44 (2/28/91)
87   ALDO CONTERNO Barolo Bussia Soprana 1985 $40 (9/15/90)
87   GIACOMO CONTERNO Barolo 1985 $23 (4/15/90)
87   VOERZIO Barolo 1985 $18 (1/31/90)
86   CARRETTA Barolo Poderi Cannubi 1985 $22 (10/15/90)
86   CERETTO Barolo Bricco Rocche Bricco Rocche 1985 Rel: $56 Cur: $103 (3/31/90)
86   BRUNO GIACOSA Barolo Collina Rionda di Serralunga 1985 $50 (4/30/91)
86   MARCHESI DI BAROLO Barolo Coste di Rosé 1985 $29 (10/15/90)
86   GIUSEPPE MASCARELLO & FIGLIO Barolo Monprivato 1985 $53 (6/15/90)
86   FRANCESCO RINALDI & FIGLI Barolo La Brunata 1985 $24 (6/15/90)
85   MARCHESI DI BAROLO Barolo Brunate 1985 $29 (10/15/90)
85   PRUNOTTO Barolo Cannubi 1985 $32 (3/31/90)
85   RENATO RATTI Barolo 1985 $23 (9/15/90)
84   BENI DI BATASIOLO Barolo 1985 $14.50 (3/31/90)
84   ALDO CONTERNO Barolo Bricco Bussia Vigna Colonnello 1985 $40 (6/15/90)
84   PARUSSO Barolo 1985 $27 (4/30/91)
83   BAVA Barolo 1985 $19 (4/30/91)
82   CERETTO Barolo Zonchera 1985 $16 (6/15/90)
82   MAURO MOLINO Barolo Vigna Conca 1985 $25 (3/31/90)
82   PRUNOTTO Barolo 1985 $31 (3/31/90)
82   RENATO RATTI Barolo Marcenasco 1985 $37 (10/15/90)
81   AZELIA Barolo Bricco Fiasco 1985 $30 (7/15/91)
81   MICHELE CHIARLO Barolo Vigna Rionda di Serralunga Riserva 1985 $39 (2/28/91)
80   FATTORIA MASSARA Barolo 1985 $20 (6/15/90)
79   BERSANO Barolo 1985 $10 (10/15/90)
78   CERETTO Barolo Bricco Rocche Prapò 1985 $50 (3/31/90)
78   FRANCESCO RINALDI & FIGLI Barolo Cannubbio 1985 $25 (6/15/90)
74   PAOLO SCAVINO Barolo Cannubi 1985 $30 (1/31/90)
72   ROCCHE COSTAMAGNA Barolo Rocche di la Morra 1985 $25 (2/28/91)
63   GIUSEPPE MASCARELLO & FIGLIO Barolo Santo Stefano di Perno 1985 $35 (9/15/90)

1984

88   PAOLO CORDERO DI MONTEZEMOLO Barolo Monfalletto 1984 (NA) (9/15/88) (HS)
85   CLERICO Barolo 1984 $13 (8/31/88)
85   SEBASTE Barolo 1984 (NA) (9/15/88) (HS)
84   SEBASTE Barolo Bussia Riserva 1984 $17 (7/31/89)
83   CERETTO Barolo Zonchera 1984 $16 (9/15/88) (HS)

ITALY
PIEDMONT RED/BAROLO DOCG

82 LUCIANO SANDRONE Barolo 1984 $13.50 (8/31/88)
62 RICCARDO FENOCCHIO Barolo Pianpolvere Soprano 1984 $15 (7/31/89)

1983

90 LUCIANO SANDRONE Barolo 1983 $20 (12/15/87)
89 MARCARINI Barolo Brunate 1983 $23 (9/15/88) (HS)
88 PIO CESARE Barolo 1983 Cur: $33 (9/15/88) (HS)
88 CLERICO Barolo Ciabot Mentin Ginestra 1983 $19 (12/15/87)
88 GIACOMO CONTERNO Barolo 1983 $23 (9/15/88) (HS)
88 BARTOLO MASCARELLO Barolo 1983 $27 (5/31/88)
88 PRUNOTTO Barolo Bussia 1983 $23 (9/15/88) (HS)
88 VOERZIO Barolo 1983 $15 (9/15/88) (HS)
87 MICHELE CHIARLO Barolo Vigna Rionda di Serralunga Riserva 1983 $36 (2/28/91)
87 PAOLO CORDERO DI MONTEZEMOLO Barolo Monfalletto 1983 $17 (9/15/88) (HS)
87 MARCARINI Barolo La Serra 1983 $17 (9/15/88) (HS)
87 RENATO RATTI Barolo 1983 $20 (10/15/88)
86 CERETTO Barolo Bricco Rocche Prapò 1983 $31 (7/31/89)
86 PAOLO CORDERO DI MONTEZEMOLO Barolo Enrico VI 1983 $20 (9/15/88) (HS)
86 GIUSEPPE MASCARELLO & FIGLIO Barolo Monprivato 1983 $28 (9/15/88) (HS)
86 RENATO RATTI Barolo Rocche Marcenasco 1983 $30 (1/31/89)
86 GIOVANNI & BATTISTA RINALDI Barolo 1983 (NA) (9/15/88) (HS)
86 SEBASTE Barolo 1983 (NA) (9/15/88) (HS)
85 CERETTO Barolo Bricco Rocche Brunate 1983 Rel: $27 Cur: $37 (7/31/89)
85 ALDO CONTERNO Barolo Bussia Soprana 1983 $25 (9/15/88) (HS)
85 PAOLO CORDERO DI MONTEZEMOLO Barolo Monfalletto 1983 $17 (2/28/89)
85 BRUNO GIACOSA Barolo Villero di Castiglione 1983 $29 (1/31/89)
85 ODDERO Barolo 1983 $15 (9/15/88) (HS)
85 PRUNOTTO Barolo Cannubi 1983 (NA) (9/15/88) (HS)
85 PAOLO SCAVINO Barolo 1983 (NA) (9/15/88) (HS)
84 FRANCESCO RINALDI & FIGLI Barolo 1983 $20 (9/15/88) (HS)
83 FONTANAFREDDA Barolo 1983 $16 (9/15/88) (HS)
81 BERSANO Barolo 1983 $9 (11/15/88)
80 GIUSEPPE MASCARELLO & FIGLIO Barolo Monprivato Falletto 1983 $23 (7/31/89)
78 MICHELE CHIARLO Barolo Rocche di Castiglione Riserva 1983 $30 (2/28/91)
77 GIUSEPPE MASCARELLO & FIGLIO Barolo Villero 1983 $17 (10/15/88)
75 CONTRATTO Barolo 1983 $10 (3/31/90)

1982

94 LUCIANO SANDRONE Barolo 1982 $15 (6/30/87)
93 ALDO CONTERNO Barolo Granbussia 1982 (NA) (9/15/88) (HS)
93 RENATO RATTI Barolo 1982 Rel: $17 Cur: $28 (6/30/87) CS
92 AZELIA Barolo Bricco Punta 1982 $23 (11/15/88)
92 EREDI VIRGINIA FERRERO Barolo S. Rocco 1982 $22 (7/15/88)
92 COLLI MONFORTESI Barolo 1982 $15 (4/30/87) SS
92 ODDERO Barolo 1982 $14 (9/15/88) (HS)
91 CEREQUIO Barolo 1982 $18.50 (11/15/88)
91 CERETTO Barolo Bricco Rocche Bricco Rocche 1982 Cur: $100 (9/15/88) (HS)
91 PIO CESARE Barolo 1982 Cur: $36 (9/15/88) (HS)
91 MARCARINI Barolo La Serra 1982 $18 (9/15/88) (HS)
91 PRUNOTTO Barolo Bussia 1982 $25 (9/15/88) (HS)
91 SEBASTE Barolo 1982 (NA) (9/15/88) (HS)
91 G.D. VAJRA Barolo 1982 $14 (3/15/87)
91 G.D. VAJRA Barolo Bricco delle Viole 1982 $19 (8/31/88)
91 VOERZIO Barolo La Serra di La Morra 1982 $12 (7/31/87)
90 CERETTO Barolo Zonchera 1982 $16 (6/30/87)
90 GIACOMO CONTERNO Barolo 1982 $25 (9/15/88) (HS)
90 FONTANAFREDDA Barolo Lazarito 1982 $42 (9/15/88) (HS)
90 FONTANAFREDDA Barolo Vigna la Rosa 1982 Rel: $40 Cur: $45 (2/15/88) CS
90 BRUNO GIACOSA Barolo Rocche 1982 $41 (9/15/88)
90 MARCARINI Barolo Brunate 1982 $18 (9/15/88) (HS)
90 RENATO RATTI Barolo Marcenasco 1982 Rel: $23 Cur: $37 (6/30/87)
90 SEBASTE Barolo Bussia Riserva 1982 $15 (11/15/87)
90 VIETTI Barolo Rocche 1982 Rel: $45 Cur: $60 (9/15/88) (HS)
90 VOERZIO Barolo 1982 $12 (9/15/88) (HS)
89 MICHELE CHIARLO Barolo Vigna Rionda di Serralunga Riserva 1982 $32 (1/31/90)
89 FONTANAFREDDA Barolo Vigna La Rosa 1982 Rel: $40 Cur: $45 (9/15/88) (HS)
89 MARCHESI DI BAROLO Barolo Brunate 1982 $13.50 (2/15/89)
89 GIUSEPPE MASCARELLO & FIGLIO Barolo Monprivato 1982 $22 (9/15/88) (HS)
89 VIETTI Barolo Bussia 1982 $20 (9/15/87)
89 VIETTI Barolo Villero Riserva 1982 $45 (9/15/88) (HS)
88 ELIO ALTARE Barolo 1982 $13 (6/30/87)
88 PAOLO CORDERO DI MONTEZEMOLO Barolo Enrico VI 1982 $25 (9/15/88) (HS)
88 SCARPA Barolo 1982 (NA) (9/15/88) (HS)
88 PAOLO SCAVINO Barolo 1982 (NA) (9/15/88) (HS)
87 ELIO ALTARE Barolo Vigneto Arborina 1982 $15 (9/15/87)
87 MARCHESI DI BAROLO Barolo Riserva 1982 $13.50 (2/15/89)
87 GIUSEPPE MASCARELLO & FIGLIO Barolo Dardi 1982 $18 (9/15/87)
86 PIO CESARE Barolo Riserva 1982 $31 (11/15/88)
86 ALDO CONTERNO Barolo Bricco Bussia Vigna Cicala 1982 $20 (9/15/87)
85 BEL COLLE Barolo Riserva 1982 $15 (3/31/90)
85 ALDO CONTERNO Barolo Bussia Soprana 1982 Rel: $17.50 Cur: $33 (9/15/87)
85 FONTANAFREDDA Barolo San Pietro 1982 $42 (9/15/88) (HS)
85 VIETTI Barolo Rocche 1982 Rel: $45 Cur: $60 (7/31/89)
84 CONTERNO FANTINO Barolo Sori' Ginestra Riserva 1982 $24 (1/31/90)

84 FONTANAFREDDA Barolo 1982 $16 (9/15/88) (HS)
84 GIOVANNI & BATTISTA RINALDI Barolo 1982 (NA) (9/15/88) (HS)
83 FRANCESCO RINALDI & FIGLI Barolo 1982 Rel: $16 Cur: $50 (9/15/88) (HS)
83 AURELIO SETTIMO Barolo Vigna Rocche 1982 $19 (5/31/88)
81 LUIGI EINAUDI Barolo 1982 $22.50 (6/30/87)
81 GIUSEPPE MASCARELLO & FIGLIO Barolo 1982 $28 (6/30/87)
80 BRUNO GIACOSA Barolo Le Rocche di Castiglione Falletto 1982 $38 (7/31/89)
79 BENI DI BATASIOLO Barolo Riserva 1982 $17 (3/31/90)
79 FRANCO-FIORINA Barolo 1982 $22 (5/31/88)
79 FRANCESCO RINALDI & FIGLI Barolo Riserva Brunata 1982 $27 (6/30/87)
75 PRUNOTTO Barolo Cannubi 1982 $25 (9/15/88) (HS)
75 FRANCESCO RINALDI & FIGLI Barolo Cannubbio 1982 $16 (10/31/87)
74 RICCARDO FENOCCHIO Barolo Pianpolvere Soprano 1982 $26 (7/31/89)
72 BRUNO GIACOSA Barolo Riserva 1982 $65 (1/31/90)

1981

88 PAOLO CORDERO DI MONTEZEMOLO Barolo Enrico VI 1981 Cur: $25 (9/15/88) (HS)
88 RENATO RATTI Barolo Marcenasco Rocche 1981 $19 (6/30/87)
87 PIO CESARE Barolo 1981 Cur: $25 (9/15/88) (HS)
84 GIUSEPPE MASCARELLO & FIGLIO Barolo Monprivato 1981 Cur: $23 (9/15/88) (HS)
84 RENATO RATTI Barolo Marcenasco 1981 $14.50 (6/30/87)

1980

96 CERETTO Barolo Zonchera 1980 Rel: $9.50 Cur: $17 (2/16/86) SS
91 PAOLO CORDERO DI MONTEZEMOLO Barolo 1980 Rel: $16.50 Cur: $20 (12/15/87) CS
91 PAOLO CORDERO DI MONTEZEMOLO Barolo Monfalletto 1980 $10.75 (1/31/87)
90 CERETTO Barolo Bricco Rocche Rocche 1980 Cur: $60 (3/01/86) (JS)
89 MARCARINI Barolo La Serra 1980 $9.50 (4/16/86)
87 VIETTI Barolo Rocche 1980 Cur: $30 (9/15/88) (HS)
86 CLERICO Barolo Vigna Bricotto della Bussia 1980 $8.25 (9/01/85) BB
86 ALDO CONTERNO Barolo Bussia Soprana 1980 Cur: $35 (9/15/88) (HS)
85 PAOLO CORDERO DI MONTEZEMOLO Barolo Enrico VI 1980 (NA) (9/15/88) (HS)
83 RENATO RATTI Barolo 1980 $10 (2/15/87)
80 CEREQUIO Barolo Riserva 1980 $13 (7/31/89)
78 BRUNO GIACOSA Barolo 1980 $19 (9/15/87)
78 PRUNOTTO Barolo Ginestra di Monforte d'Alba Riserva 1980 $13.50 (6/30/87)
76 GIUSEPPE MASCARELLO & FIGLIO Barolo Monprivato 1980 Cur: $23 (9/15/88) (HS)
73 ODDERO Barolo 1980 $7 (5/16/86)
73 AURELIO SETTIMO Barolo Vigna Rocche 1980 $17 (5/31/88)
72 PIO CESARE Barolo Riserva 1980 $18.50 (2/15/87)
65 PRUNOTTO Barolo Riserva 1980 $12.50 (6/30/87)
62 CARRETTA Barolo Poderi Cannubi 1980 $14 (9/15/87)

1979

89 RENATO RATTI Barolo 1979 Rel: $8.50 Cur: $9 (1/01/86)
88 MARCARINI Barolo Brunate 1979 Cur: $29 (9/15/88) (HS)
86 CERETTO Barolo Bricco Rocche Brunate 1979 Cur: $42 (3/01/86) (JS)
85 SEBASTE Barolo 1979 (NA) (9/15/88) (HS)
83 GIUSEPPE MASCARELLO & FIGLIO Barolo Monprivato 1979 Cur: $28 (9/15/88) (HS)
82 PAOLO CORDERO DI MONTEZEMOLO Barolo Monfalletto 1979 Cur: $33 (9/15/88) (HS)
79 VIETTI Barolo Rocche 1979 (NA) (9/15/88) (HS)
76 CONTRATTO Barolo 1979 $9 (9/30/86)
69 CEREQUIO Barolo 1979 $13 (7/31/89)
67 EREDI VIRGINIA FERRERO Barolo S. Rocco Riserva 1979 $19 (7/31/89)
67 AURELIO SETTIMO Barolo Vigna Rocche 1979 $25 (5/31/88)

1978

95 CERETTO Barolo Bricco Rocche Prapò 1978 Cur: $95 (3/01/86) (JS)
92 ALDO CONTERNO Barolo Bussia Soprana 1978 Cur: $64 (9/15/88) (HS)
92 VIETTI Barolo Rocche 1978 Cur: $60 (9/15/88) (HS)
91 GIUSEPPE MASCARELLO & FIGLIO Barolo 1978 $19.50 (9/16/84)
90 LIVIO PAVESE Barolo Riserva Spéciale 1978 $12 (9/16/84)
89 PIO CESARE Barolo Riserva 1978 Rel: $19 Cur: $28 (10/01/84) SS
89 FRANCESCO RINALDI & FIGLI Barolo 1978 Rel: $12 Cur: $69 (9/16/84)
89 SCARPA Barolo 1978 $27 (9/15/88) (HS)
88 BRUNO GIACOSA Barolo 1978 $31 (9/16/84)
86 CERETTO Barolo Bricco Rocche Brunate 1978 Cur: $92 (9/15/88) (HS)
86 CONTRATTO Barolo del Centenario Riserva 1978 $18 (5/16/86)
86 MARCHESI DI BAROLO Barolo Riserva 1978 $20 (2/28/89)
86 GIUSEPPE MASCARELLO & FIGLIO Barolo Monprivato 1978 Cur: $42 (9/15/88) (HS)
86 PRUNOTTO Barolo Bussia 1978 Cur: $50 (9/15/88) (HS)
85 PIO CESARE Barolo 1978 Cur: $28 (9/15/88) (HS)
84 PAOLO CORDERO DI MONTEZEMOLO Barolo Monfalletto 1978 (NA) (9/15/88) (HS)
84 VIETTI Barolo 1978 $12 (9/16/84)
83 GIACOMO CONTERNO Barolo Riserva Spéciale 1978 (NA) (9/15/88) (HS)
81 SCARPA Barolo Le Coste di Monforte 1978 $27 (3/15/87)
80 FONTANAFREDDA Barolo 1978 $12.75 (2/15/84)
80 MARCARINI Barolo Brunate 1978 Cur: $44 (9/15/88) (HS)
79 MARCARINI Barolo La Serra 1978 $18 (9/16/84)
78 PRUNOTTO Barolo Cannubi 1978 (NA) (9/15/88) (HS)
73 VILLADORIA Barolo Riserva Spéciale 1978 $14 (8/31/86)

1977

69 PAOLO CORDERO DI MONTEZEMOLO Barolo Monfalletto 1977 (NA) (9/15/88) (HS)

1976

82 CERETTO Barolo Bricco Rocche Prapò 1976 $70 (9/15/88) (HS)

1975

77 PAOLO CORDERO DI MONTEZEMOLO Barolo Monfalletto 1975 (NA) (9/15/88) (HS)

1974

91 GIUSEPPE MASCARELLO & FIGLIO Barolo Monprivato 1974 Cur: $90 (9/15/88) (HS)
90 ALDO CONTERNO Barolo Bussia Soprana 1974 Cur: $60 (9/15/88) (HS)
80 PRUNOTTO Barolo Bussia 1974 Cur: $65 (9/15/88) (HS)
79 BERSANO Barolo 1974 (NA) (9/15/88) (HS)
77 PIO CESARE Barolo 1974 Cur: $40 (9/15/88) (HS)

1973

65 PAOLO CORDERO DI MONTEZEMOLO Barolo Monfalletto 1973 (NA) (9/15/88) (HS)

1971

90   PRUNOTTO Barolo Bussia 1971 Cur: $75 (9/15/88) (HS)
89   MARCARINI Barolo Brunate 1971 Cur: $60 (9/15/88) (HS)
88   CERETTO Barolo Bricco Rocche Prapò 1971 $100 (10/30/87)
87   ALDO CONTERNO Barolo Bussia Soprana 1971 Cur: $50 (9/15/88) (HS)
86   VIETTI Barolo Rocche 1971 Cur: $70 (9/15/88) (HS)
85   CERETTO Barolo Cannubi 1971 (NA) (3/01/86) (JS)
85   PAOLO CORDERO DI MONTEZEMOLO Barolo Monfalletto 1971 (NA) (9/15/88) (HS)
81   GIUSEPPE MASCARELLO & FIGLIO Barolo Monprivato 1971 Cur: $73 (9/15/88) (HS)
80   PIO CESARE Barolo 1971 Cur: $38 (9/15/88) (HS)
77   BERSANO Barolo 1971 (NA) (9/15/88) (HS)

1970

88   GIACOMO CONTERNO Barolo Riserva Spéciale 1970 (NA) (9/15/88) (HS)
80   GIUSEPPE MASCARELLO & FIGLIO Barolo Monprivato 1970 Cur: $60 (9/15/88) (HS)

1967

90   CERETTO Barolo Bricco Rocche Brunate 1967 (NA) (10/20/87)
82   PRUNOTTO Barolo Bussia 1967 Cur: $49 (9/15/88) (HS)

1964

96   MARCARINI Barolo Brunate 1964 (NA) (9/15/88) (HS)
80   BERSANO Barolo 1964 (NA) (9/15/88) (HS)
80   PRUNOTTO Barolo Bussia 1964 Cur: $85 (9/15/88) (HS)

1961

93   VIETTI Barolo Rocche 1961 Cur: $100 (9/15/88) (HS)
91   PRUNOTTO Barolo Bussia 1961 Cur: $110 (9/15/88) (HS)

DOLCETTO DOC

1989

89   MARCARINI Dolcetto d'Alba Boschi di Berri 1989 $23 (4/30/91)
88   BRUNO GIACOSA Dolcetto d'Alba 1989 $12 (2/28/91)
88   MARCHESI DI BAROLO Dolcetto d'Alba Madonna di Como 1989 $9 (12/31/90) BB
87   CHIONETTI Dolcetto di Dogliani Briccolero 1989 $15.50 (4/30/91)
87   MAURO MOLINO Dolcetto d'Alba 1989 $14 (2/28/91)
87   LUCIANO SANDRONE Dolcetto d'Alba 1989 $12 (7/15/91)
85   GIUSEPPE MASCARELLO & FIGLIO Dolcetto d'Alba Gagliassi 1989 $13 (7/15/91)
85   VIETTI Dolcetto d'Alba Bussia 1989 $12 (2/28/91)
84   MARCARINI Dolcetto d'Alba Fontanazza 1989 $13.50 (4/30/91)
83   GIUSEPPE CORTESE Dolcetto d'Alba 1989 $9.75 (12/31/90)
83   FRANCO-FIORINA Dolcetto d'Alba 1989 $13 (4/30/91)
83   ROCCHE COSTAMAGNA Dolcetto d'Alba 1989 $12 (4/30/91)
82   BENI DI BATASIOLO Dolcetto d'Alba 1989 $12 (7/15/91)
81   ELIO ALTARE Dolcetto d'Alba 1989 $12 (7/15/91)
81   LUIGI COPPO Dolcetto d'Alba 1989 $10.50 (7/15/91)
81   DE FORVILLE Dolcetto d'Alba Vigneto Loreto 1989 $12 (2/28/91)
80   CASTELLO DI NEIVE Dolcetto d'Alba Vigneto Basarin 1989 $12 (2/28/91)
80   FRANCESCO RINALDI & FIGLI Dolcetto d'Alba 1989 $12 (7/15/91)
79   ABBAZIA DI VALLE CHIARA Dolcetto d'Ovada 1989 $13 (7/15/91)
79   AZELIA Dolcetto d'Alba Bricco dell'Oriolo 1989 $9.25 (7/15/91)
79   CERETTO Dolcetto d'Alba Rossana 1989 $16 (4/30/91)
78   ODDERO Dolcetto d'Alba 1989 $8.75 (4/30/91)
76   EILO GRASSO Dolcetto d'Alba Gavarini Vigna dei Grassi 1989 $18 (7/15/91)

1988

87   MARCARINI Dolcetto d'Alba Fontanazza 1988 $11 (3/31/90)
87   VIETTI Dolcetto d'Alba della Località Disa 1988 $12 (9/15/90)
87   VOERZIO Dolcetto d'Alba Priavino 1988 $11 (12/31/90)
86   MARCARINI Dolcetto d'Alba Boschi di Berri 1988 $17 (3/31/90)
86   FRANCESCO RINALDI & FIGLI Dolcetto d'Alba Roussot 1988 $10 (9/15/90)
85   BENI DI BATASIOLO Dolcetto d'Alba 1988 $10.50 (12/31/90)
84   CASCINA BORDINO Dolcetto d'Alba 1988 $9.50 (3/31/90)
82   ELIO ALTARE Dolcetto d'Alba 1988 $10 (3/31/90)
82   GIUSEPPE MASCARELLO & FIGLIO Dolcetto d'Alba Bricco Ravera 1988 $10 (9/15/90)
82   MAURO MOLINO Dolcetto d'Alba 1988 $12 (3/31/90)
81   VALFIERI Dolcetto d'Alba 1988 $8.50 (12/31/90)
78   GIUSEPPE CORTESE Dolcetto d'Alba 1988 $8 (3/31/90)
78   FRANCESCO RINALDI & FIGLI Dolcetto d'Alba Roussot 1988 $10 (7/15/91)

1987

90   ELIO ALTARE Dolcetto d'Alba 1987 $9 (2/28/89)
89   MARCARINI Dolcetto d'Alba Boschi di Berri 1987 $13 (3/15/89)
88   GIUSEPPE MASCARELLO & FIGLIO Dolcetto d'Alba Bricco Falletto 1987 $9 (3/15/89)
87   CLERICO Dolcetto d'Alba 1987 $7.50 (8/31/88)
87   MARCHESI DI BAROLO Dolcetto d'Alba Madonna di Como 1987 $8 (2/15/89)
86   CERETTO Dolcetto d'Alba Rossana 1987 $12 (3/15/89)
86   FRANCESCO RINALDI & FIGLI Dolcetto d'Alba Roussot Alto 1987 $9 (3/31/90)
85   AZELIA Dolcetto d'Alba 1987 $7 (3/15/89)
84   ALDO CONTERNO Dolcetto d'Alba 1987 $12 (9/15/90)
83   CAVALOTTO Dolcetto d'Alba Mallera 1987 $9 (3/15/89)
82   GIUSEPPE MASCARELLO & FIGLIO Dolcetto d'Alba Gagliassi Monforte 1987 $9 (3/15/89)
80   GIUSEPPE MASCARELLO & FIGLIO Dolcetto d'Alba Gagliassi 1987 $10 (3/31/90)
80   CASTELLO DI NEIVE Dolcetto d'Alba Vigneto Basarin 1987 $11 (3/15/89)
78   MARCARINI Dolcetto d'Alba Fontanazza 1987 $9.75 (3/15/89)
78   ODDERO Dolcetto d'Alba 1987 $9.50 (3/15/89)
78   VALFIERI Dolcetto d'Alba 1987 $5.75 (3/15/89)
76   FRANCO-FIORINA Dolcetto d'Alba 1987 $8.75 (7/31/89)
65   VILLADORIA Dolcetto d'Alba 1987 $6 (3/15/89)

1986

85   ODDERO Dolcetto d'Alba 1986 $9.50 (3/15/89)
83   ODDERO Dolcetto d'Alba 1986 $9.50 (8/31/89)
81   MARCHESI DI GRESY Dolcetto d'Alba Monte Aribaldo 1986 $8 (10/31/88)
80   BEL COLLE Dolcetto d'Alba 1986 $7.50 (4/15/88)
80   CLERICO Dolcetto d'Alba 1986 $7.75 (12/31/87)
80   LUCIANO SANDRONE Dolcetto d'Alba 1986 $8.75 (12/31/87)
78   AZELIA Dolcetto d'Alba Cascina Nuova 1986 $8.50 (12/31/87)

73   CASTELLO DI NEIVE Dolcetto d'Alba Vigneto Valtorta 1986 $12 (3/15/89)
73   CASTELLO DI NEIVE Dolcetto d'Alba Vigneto Valtorta 1986 $12 (8/31/88)

1985

90   RENATO RATTI Dolcetto d'Alba Vigna Colombe 1985 $9.25 (2/28/87)
88   PRUNOTTO Dolcetto d'Alba Gagliassi di Monforte Riserva 1985 $11.50 (3/15/89)
87   LUCIANO SANDRONE Dolcetto d'Alba 1985 $6.50 (7/31/87) BB
84   PRUNOTTO Dolcetto d'Alba 1985 $10 (3/15/89)
82   MARCARINI Dolcetto d'Alba Fontanazza 1985 $7.50 (2/15/87)
80   GIUSEPPE MASCARELLO & FIGLIO Dolcetto d'Alba Venora 1985 $7 (12/31/87)
77   CERETTO Dolcetto d'Alba Vigna 1985 $11 (3/15/89)
77   ALDO CONTERNO Dolcetto d'Alba 1985 $10 (5/15/87)
77   BRUNO GIACOSA Dolcetto d'Alba Plinet di Trezzo Tinella 1985 $8 (12/31/87)
74   CERETTO Dolcetto d'Alba Rossana 1985 $8.75 (12/31/87)
74   VIETTI Dolcetto d'Alba Disa 1985 $7 (9/15/87)
71   PIO CESARE Dolcetto d'Alba 1985 $10 (10/31/86)

1984

88   PIO CESARE Dolcetto d'Alba 1984 $7.50 (11/16/85)
82   ELVIO COGNO Dolcetto d'Alba 1984 $5.50 (2/16/86)
68   CLERICO Dolcetto d'Alba 1984 $4 (9/15/87)

1983

58   LUIGI EINAUDI Dolcetto di Dogliani 1983 $7 (9/30/86)

VINO DA TAVOLA

1989

86   MAURO MOLINO Nebbiolo delle Langhe 1989 $14 (2/28/91)
85   ELIO ALTARE 1989 $11.50 (7/15/91)
85   ROCCHE COSTAMAGNA Roccardo Nebbiolo delle Langhe 1989 $13 (4/30/91)
84   MARCARINI Lasarin Nebbiolo delle Langhe 1989 $9.50 (4/30/91)
83   EILO GRASSO Gavarini 1989 $20 (7/15/91)

1988

92   GIACOMO BOLOGNA Barbera Bricco della Bigotta 1988 $40 (3/15/91)
91   GIACOMO BOLOGNA Bricco dell' Uccellone Barbera 1988 $45 (3/15/91)
91   CONTERNO FANTINO Monprá 1988 $27 (3/15/91)
90   CLERICO Arte 1988 $26 (2/28/91)
88   VALLANA Barbera del Piemonte 1988 $8 (3/15/91)
83   TRAVAGLINI Spanna 1988 $10 (7/15/91)
82   PRODUTTORI DEL BARBARESCO Nebbioio delle Langhe 1988 $9 (2/28/91)
80   GIUSEPPE CORTESE Vigna in Rabajà 1988 $12.50 (2/28/91)
80   LUIGI & ITALO NERVI Spanna 1988 $9 (7/15/91)

1987

88   GIACOMO BOLOGNA Barbera Bricco della Bigotta 1987 $34 (3/15/91)
88   GIACOMO BOLOGNA Bricco dell' Uccellone Barbera 1987 $45 (3/15/91)

1986

89   GIACOMO BOLOGNA Bricco dell' Uccellone Barbera 1986 $38 (3/15/91)
89   CASAL THAULERO Abbazia di Propezzano 1986 $19 (7/15/91)
88   BERSANO Castellengo 1986 $16 (4/15/91)
88   GIACOMO BOLOGNA Barbera Bricco della Bigotta 1986 $34 (3/15/91)
87   DESSILANI Barbera del Piemonte 1986 $7 (3/15/91) BB
80   MICHELE CHIARLO Barilot 1986 $27 (2/28/91)

1988

84   MARCARINI Nebbiolo delle Langhe 1988 $10 (3/31/90)
84   MAURO MOLINO Nebbiolo delle Langhe 1988 $12 (3/31/90)
81   ELIO ALTARE Nebbiolo delle Langhe 1988 $10 (3/31/90)
80   VALLANA Barbera 1988 $7 (3/31/90)

1987

89   ELIO ALTARE Nebbiolo Vigna Larigi 1987 $28 (5/31/90)
87   LUIGI COPPO Mondaccione 1987 $13.50 (3/31/90)
85   ELIO ALTARE Nebbiolo delle Langhe 1987 $9 (7/31/89)
85   VIETTI Fioretto 1987 $17 (6/15/90)
84   ELIO ALTARE Nebbiolo Vigna Arborina 1987 $32 (9/15/90)
78   CLERICO Arte 1987 $22 (1/31/90)

1986

94   GAJA Cabernet Sauvignon Darmagi 1986 Rel: $76 Cur: $76 (1/31/90)
90   ELIO ALTARE Nebbiolo Vigna Arborina 1986 $20 (2/28/89)
90   VALLANA Barbera 1986 $6 (2/15/89) BB
89   SEBASTE Bricco Viole 1986 $16 (1/31/89)
88   CLERICO Arte 1986 $22 (2/15/89)
82   MARCHESI DI GRESY Nebbiolo Martinenga 1986 $11 (10/15/88)

1985

94   GAJA Cabernet Sauvignon Darmagi 1985 Rel: $70 Cur: $70 (3/15/89) CS
91   CLERICO Arte 1985 $22 (1/31/88)
91   SEBASTE Bricco Viole 1985 $13 (10/31/87)
88   GIACOMO BOLOGNA Bricco dell' Uccellone Barbera 1985 $33 (8/31/89)
85   ALDO CONTERNO Nebbiolo delle Langhe Bussia Conca Tre Pile 1985 $13 (11/15/88)
79   BRICCO DEL DRAGO Vigna 'd le Mace 1985 $22 (1/31/89)
79   DESSILANI Caramino Riserva 1985 $13 (9/15/90)

1984

61   CASCINACASTLE'T Passum 1984 $25 (12/31/88)

1983

91   GAJA Cabernet Sauvignon Darmagi 1983 Rel: $51 Cur: $68 (7/15/88)
88   PIO CESARE Nebbiolo 1983 $8 (2/16/86)
84   ALDO CONTERNO Nebbiolo Il Favot Monforte Bussia 1983 $12.50 (5/31/90)
82   PIO CESARE Ornato 1983 $15.50 (3/31/88)
70   LUIGI EINAUDI Nebbiolo delle Langhe 1983 $8 (7/01/86)

1982

84   BRICCO DEL DRAGO Vigna 'd le Mace 1982 $14 (11/30/87)

ITALY
PIEDMONT RED/*VINO DA TAVOLA*

65   ACCOMASSO Nebbiolo delle Langhe 1982 $14 (7/31/89)

NV

83   ALDO CONTERNO Nebbiolo Il Favot Monforte Bussia NV $10 (5/31/90)
82   ALFREDO & GIOVANNI ROAGNA Opera Prima Imbottigliato il 15 Novembre 1986 NV $17 (12/31/87)
76   ALFREDO & GIOVANNI ROAGNA Opera Prima IV NV $23 (7/31/89)

OTHER PIEDMONT RED DOC

1989

78   FRANCO-FIORINA Freisa delle Langhe 1989 $16 (7/15/91)

1988

85   CANTINA DELLA PORTA ROSSA Diano d'Alba Vigna Bruni 1988 $25 (2/15/91)
81   CERETTO Nebbiolo d'Alba Lantasco 1988 $18 (4/30/91)
75   GIUSEPPE MASCARELLO & FIGLIO Grignolino del Monferrato Casalese Besso 1988 $9.50 (1/31/90)

1987

84   GIACOMO BOLOGNA Brachetto d'Acqui 1987 $16 (3/31/90)
78   MARCHISIO Roero Vigneti Mongalletto 1987 $10 (3/31/90)

1986

85   GIUSEPPE MASCARELLO & FIGLIO Nebbiolo d'Alba San Rocco 1986 $15 (9/15/90)
82   PRUNOTTO Roero 1986 $10 (6/30/88)

1985

88   PRUNOTTO Roero 1985 $9 (7/31/87)
87   GAJA Nebbiolo d'Alba Vignaveja 1985 $30 (2/15/89)
80   FRANCO-FIORINA Nebbiolo d'Alba 1985 $9.25 (8/31/88)
72   GIUSEPPE POGGIO Bricco Trionzo 1985 $10 (3/15/89)

1983

94   GAJA Nebbiolo d'Alba Vignaveja 1983 $16 (2/15/87) SS
81   RENATO RATTI Nebbiolo d'Alba 1983 $7 (6/16/86) BB
77   LUIGI & ITALO NERVI Gattinara Vigneto Valferana 1983 $15 (5/31/90)
76   VALLANA Gattinara 1983 $10 (1/31/90)
69   VIETTI Nebbiolo d'Alba San Michele 1983 $7 (9/15/87)
68   LUIGI & ITALO NERVI Gattinara Vigneto Molsino 1983 $15 (5/31/90)
63   LUIGI & ITALO NERVI Gattinara 1983 $11 (5/31/90)
62   PRUNOTTO Nebbiolo d'Alba 1983 $8 (7/15/87)

1982

69   LUIGI CALDI Gattinara 1982 $12 (1/31/90)

1980

63   TRAVAGLINI Gattinara 1980 $8.75 (12/16/85)

1976

74   LE COLLINE Gattinara Monsecco 1976 $13.50 (8/31/87)

PIEDMONT WHITE/*VINO DA TAVOLA*

1989

83   FRANCO-FIORINA Chardonnay 1989 $21 (3/31/91)
82   BENI DI BATASIOLO Chardonnay delle Langhe Vigneto Morino 1989 $27 (7/15/91)
82   CERETTO Arneis Blange' 1989 $19 (7/15/91)
79   BENI DI BATASIOLO Chardonnay delle Langhe 1989 $14 (7/15/91)
70   FRANCO-FIORINA Freisa delle Langhe 1989 $15.50 (4/15/91)
76   BOLLA Chardonnay 1989 $6 (4/30/90)
75   DE FORVILLE Chardonnay 1989 $12 (2/15/91)

1988

87   BENI DI BATASIOLO Chardonnay Vigneto Morino 1988 $25 (12/31/90)
86   GAJA Chardonnay Gaia-Rey 1988 $68 (12/31/90)
85   GAJA Chardonnay Rossj-Bass 1988 $45 (3/31/90)
82   BOLLA Chardonnay 1988 $6 (9/15/89) (JS)
75   FRANCO-FIORINA Favorita delle Langhe 1988 $12 (4/30/90)
74   MOCCAGATTA Chardonnay Vigneto Buschet 1988 (NA) (9/15/89)

1987

95   GAJA Chardonnay Gaia-Rey 1987 Rel: $43 Cur: $43 (9/15/89)
92   PIO CESARE Chardonnay 1987 $29 (9/15/89)
89   ALFREDO & GIOVANNI ROAGNA Chardonnay 1987 $20 (9/15/89)
88   GAJA Chardonnay Gaia-Rey 1987 Rel: $43 Cur: $43 (3/31/89)
85   MARCHESI DI GRESY Chardonnay 1987 $37 (9/15/89) (HS)
75   MOCCAGATTA Chardonnay Bric Buschet 1987 (NA) (9/15/89)

1986

90   PIO CESARE Chardonnay 1986 $29 (10/15/88)
90   GAJA Chardonnay Gaia-Rey 1986 Rel: $37 Cur: $37 (6/30/88)
88   PIO CESARE Chardonnay 1986 $29 (9/15/89)
74   SEBASTE Arneis 1986 $11.50 (11/15/87)
72   CASTELLO DI NEIVE Arneis Delle Langhe 1986 $18 (10/15/88)

1985

98   GAJA Chardonnay Gaia-Rey 1985 Rel: $45 Cur: $65 (9/15/89)

WHITE DOC

1989

84   MICHELE CHIARLO Gavi Granduca 1989 $12 (1/31/91)
83   VILLA BANFI Gavi Principessa 1989 $12 (12/31/90)
83   VALFIERI Gavi Villa Montersino Vigneti Borghero 1989 $16 (7/15/91)
78   BAVA Gavi 1989 $13 (7/15/91)
77   CORTE VECCHIA Bianco di Custoza 1989 $7 (7/15/91)
77   GIACOSA FRATELLI Roero Arneis 1989 $17 (7/15/91)
71   GIACOSA FRATELLI Gavi 1989 $14 (7/15/91)

1987

86   VILLA BANFI Gavi Principessa 1987 $12 (12/31/88)
83   LA BATTISTINA Gavi 1987 $18 (4/30/90)
81   BOLLA Gavi di Gavi 1987 $8 (10/15/89)
79   VALFIERI Gavi 1987 $5.75 (7/31/89)

1986

86   PIO CESARE Cortese di Gavi 1986 $15 (10/15/88)
80   VILLA BANFI Gavi Principessa 1986 $11 (3/31/88)
80   LA SCOLCA Gavi La Scolca 1986 $23 (6/30/88)
75   BOLLA Gavi di Gavi 1986 $8.50 (10/15/88)
75   LA SCOLCA Gavi Villa Scolca 1986 $14 (6/30/88)

1985

85   PIO CESARE Cortese di Gavi 1985 $13 (11/30/86)
82   VILLA BANFI Gavi Principessa 1985 $10 (10/15/86)
82   NEIRANO Gavi 1985 $5 (10/15/86)
80   LA BATTISTINA Gavi Bricco Battistina 1985 $24 (12/31/88)

1984

70   CONTRATTO Gavi 1984 $8 (10/15/86)
61   FONTANAFREDDA Gavi 1984 $6.75 (4/16/86)

1983

85   VILLA BANFI Gavi Principessa 1983 $10 (4/16/85)

SPARKLING

1989

75   ZONIN 1989 $7 (7/15/91)

1987

80   CASCINETTA Moscato d'Asti 1987 $9 (12/31/90)

1986

83   FOSS MARAI Prosecco di Valdobbiadene 1986 $7 (12/31/88) BB

1985

88   FERRARI Brut Perle' 1985 $30 (12/31/90)
86   FRESCOBALDI Brut 1985 $12 (12/31/90)
81   VILLA BANFI Brut 1985 $15.50 (6/30/90)

1984

90   VILLA BANFI Brut 1984 $14 (3/31/88)
84   GIROLAMO DORIGO Cuvée Pinot pas Dose Montsclapade 1984 $22 (3/31/88)

1983

78   CINZANO Pas Dose 1983 $30 (12/31/86)

1982

91   VENEGAZZU Brut di Venegazzu 1982 $12 (12/15/86)
88   VILLA BANFI Brut 1982 $13 (12/31/86)
86   GIULIO FERRARI Riserva del Fondatore 1982 $50 (12/31/90)
84   BELLAVISTA Brut Franciacorta Gran Cuvée 1982 $27 (12/31/86)
83   LA VERSA Brut Metodo Classico 1982 (NA) (12/31/86)
75   CARPENE MALVOLTI Brut 1982 $14 (12/31/86)

1981

97   FERRARI Brut de Brut 1981 $22 (12/31/86)
84   FERRARI Brut de Brut 1981 $22 (5/31/87)
80   GUIDO BERLUCCHI Brut Cuvée Impériale 1981 $14.50 (12/31/86)
78   CONTE BALDUINO Brut Extra Riccadonna 1981 $13.50 (12/31/86)
68   RICCADONNA Riserva Privata 1981 $12.50 (12/31/86)
64   CONTRATTO Brut Classico Riserva Dégorgement Spring 1985 1981 $19 (12/31/86)

NV

92   MONTE ROSSA Franciacorta Non Docato NV (NA) (12/31/86)
90   FERRARI Brut de Brut NV $16 (12/31/86)
90   MONTE ROSSA Brut Franciacorta NV (NA) (12/31/86)
88   CA' DEL BOSCO Brut Franciacorta NV $25 (10/15/88)
88   FERRARI Brut NV $20 (12/31/90)
87   CA' DEL BOSCO Franciacorta Dosage Zero NV $25 (12/31/86)
86   FONTANAFREDDA Asti Spumante The Royal Preserves NV $10.50 (1/31/88)
86   GANCIA Brut NV $11 (12/31/89) BB
85   GANCIA Gran Cuvée NV $10.50 (12/31/86)
85   GANCIA dei Gancia NV $10 (12/31/86)
84   BERA Moscato d'Asti NV $14 (7/15/91)
84   CINZANO Dry Pinot Nature NV $7 (2/16/86) BB
84   CINZANO Pinot Nature NV $7 (12/31/86)
84   GANCIA Asti Spumante NV $12.50 (8/31/90)
84   FOSS MARAI Brut NV $8 (3/15/89) BB
83   BERA Asti Spumante NV $15 (7/15/91)
83   CINZANO Sauvignon Blanc Dry NV $7 (12/31/86)
83   CINZANO Sauvignon Blanc Dry NV $7 (3/16/86) BB
83   EQUIPE 5 Brut Riserva NV $20 (12/31/86)

82   BELLAVISTA Brut Cuvée NV $17.50 (12/31/86)
82   CA' DEL BOSCO Franciacorta Crémant NV $29 (10/15/88)
82   CONTRATTO Brut Classico Dégorgement Winter 1989 NV $10 (6/15/90)
82   FAZI-BATTAGLIA Brut NV $10 (12/31/86)
82   GANCIA Brut NV $11 (12/31/90)
82   GANCIA Crémant Gran Riserva NV $15 (12/31/86)
82   GANCIA Brut Extra NV $6.25 (12/31/86)
82   LUNGAROTTI Brut NV $23 (3/15/89)
81   GUIDO BERLUCCHI Cuvée Impériale NV $12.50 (9/15/89)
81   BONARDI Moscato d'Asti NV $12 (3/31/90)
80   GUIDO BERLUCCHI Brut Cuvée Impériale NV $13 (12/31/86)
80   GANCIA Pinot di Pinot NV $12 (12/31/86)
79   BRENTA D'ORO Asti Spumante Vezza d'Alba NV $7 (5/31/87)
78   CINZANO Chardonnay Dry NV $7 (12/31/86)
78   CINZANO Chardonnay Dry NV $7 (2/01/86)
78   EQUIPE 5 Brut NV $15 (12/31/86)
78   FOSS MARAI Prosecco di Valdobbiadene NV $11 (12/31/90)
77   CELLA Asti Spumante NV $7.50 (1/31/88)
76   BONARDI Asti Spumante NV $9.75 (2/15/87)
75   GUIDO BERLUCCHI Cuvée Impériale Pas Dose NV $13 (12/31/86)
75   BURATI Asti Spumante NV $6.50 (3/15/89)
75   CONTRATTO Asti Spumante Fermentazione Naturale NV $8 (10/31/86)
75   GANCIA Brut NV $11 (12/31/86)
75   RICCADONNA Presidente Extra Seco NV $5.75 (12/31/86)
72   MARTINI & ROSSI Brut Riserva Montelera NV $15 (12/31/90)
68   ANTINORI Nature NV $18 (12/31/86)
68   FONTANAFREDDA Contessa Rosa NV $5.75 (12/31/86)
62   MARTINI & ROSSI Brut Montelera Riserva NV $12.50 (12/31/86)
60   CONTRATTO Classico Reserve for England Dégorgement Spring 1985 NV $15 (12/31/86)

TUSCANY RED/*BRUNELLO DI MONTALCINO DOCG*

1985

95   POGGIO ANTICO Brunello di Montalcino 1985 $36 (11/30/90) CS
93   PODERE IL POGGIOLO Brunello di Montalcino 1985 $34 (11/30/90)
92   VILLA BANFI Brunello di Montalcino 1985 $30 (10/15/90)
91   ALTESINO Brunello di Montalcino Vigna Altesino 1985 $32 (9/30/90)
91   VILLA NICOLA Brunello di Montalcino 1985 $32 (11/30/90)
91   IL PODERUCCIO Brunello di Montalcino I Due Cipressi 1985 $22 (4/15/91)
90   VAL DI SUGA Brunello di Montalcino Vigna del Lago 1985 $52 (7/15/91)
89   SOLDERA Brunello di Montalcino 1985 $90 (7/15/91)
88   CAPARZO Brunello di Montalcino La Casa 1985 $53 (7/15/91)
88   COL D'ORCIA Brunello di Montalcino 1985 $23 (11/30/90)
88   VAL DI SUGA Brunello di Montalcino 1985 $23 (9/30/90)
85   SAN FELICE Brunello di Montalcino Campogiovanni 1985 $24 (9/30/90)
83   CAPARZO Brunello di Montalcino 1985 $34 (7/15/91)
83   PERTIMALI Brunello di Montalcino Riserva 1985 $41 (11/30/90)
83   POGGIO SALVI Brunello di Montalcino 1985 $30 (11/30/90)
80   GEOGRAFICO Brunello di Montalcino 1985 $30 (7/15/91)
78   LA TORRE Brunello di Montalcino 1985 $30 (4/15/91)

1984

91   CIACCI PICCOLOMINI D'ARAGONA Brunello di Montalcino 1984 $25 (6/15/90)

1983

91   BIONDI-SANTI Brunello di Montalcino Il Greppo 1983 $66 (11/30/89)
88   CONTI D'ATTIMIS Brunello di Montalcino Ferrante 1983 $35 (9/30/90)
86   ALTESINO Brunello di Montalcino Riserva 1983 $29 (11/30/89)
86   S. CARLO Brunello di Montalcino 1983 $23 (6/15/90)
84   ALTESINO Brunello di Montalcino Vigna Altesino 1983 $26 (1/31/90)
73   LISINI Brunello di Montalcino 1983 $22 (7/31/89)
63   ALTESINO Brunello di Montalcino Vigna Altesino 1983 $26 (9/30/89)

1982

98   BIONDI-SANTI Brunello di Montalcino Riserva 1982 Rel: $80 Cur: $98 (9/15/86)
95   CAPARZO Brunello di Montalcino 1982 Cur: $31 (9/15/86)
95   IL POGGIONE Brunello di Montalcino 1982 $30 (9/15/86)
94   BIONDI-SANTI Brunello di Montalcino Riserva 1982 Rel: $80 Cur: $98 (10/15/88) CS
92   BIONDI-SANTI Brunello di Montalcino Il Greppo 1982 $45 (10/15/88)
92   BIONDI-SANTI Brunello di Montalcino Il Greppo 1982 $45 (9/15/86)
92   POGGIO ANTICO Brunello di Montalcino 1982 $25 (11/30/89)
92   SAN FELICE Brunello di Montalcino Campogiovanni 1982 Rel: $22 Cur: $22 (7/31/88) CS
90   GREPPONE MAZZI Brunello di Montalcino 1982 (NA) (9/15/86)
90   PIAN DI CONTE Brunello di Montalcino 1982 (NA) (9/15/86)
89   VILLA BANFI Brunello di Montalcino 1982 Rel: $28 Cur: $38 (12/15/87)
89   COL D'ORCIA Brunello di Montalcino Poggio al Vento Riserva 1982 $40 (4/15/91)
89   DEI ROSETI Brunello di Montalcino 1982 $20 (7/31/89)
89   VAL DI SUGA Brunello di Montalcino Riserva 1982 $20 (11/30/89)
87   MASTROIANNI Brunello di Montalcino 1982 $17.50 (6/15/90)
85   ALTESINO Brunello di Montalcino 1982 $22 (9/15/86)
84   IL CASELLO Brunello di Montalcino 1982 $18 (7/31/88)
84   LISINI Brunello di Montalcino 1982 $25 (1/31/89)
83   EMILIO COSTANTI Brunello di Montalcino 1982 $32 (9/15/86)
81   EMILIO COSTANTI Brunello di Montalcino 1982 $32 (7/31/88)
80   FATTORIA DEI BARBI Brunello di Montalcino 1982 $20 (9/15/86)
78   FATTORIA DEI BARBI Brunello di Montalcino 1982 $20 (3/15/89)
78   IL POGGIONE Brunello di Montalcino 1982 $30 (7/31/88)
77   PERTIMALI Brunello di Montalcino 1982 $25 (1/31/88)
67   CAPARZO Brunello di Montalcino La Casa 1982 $50 (11/30/89)
64   FATTORIA DEI BARBI Brunello di Montalcino Vigna del Fiore 1982 Rel: $23 Cur: $23 (3/15/89)
56   LA CHIESA DI S. RESTITUTA Brunello di Montalcino 1982 $23 (3/15/89)

1981

93   BIONDI-SANTI Brunello di Montalcino Il Greppo 1981 Rel: $40 Cur: $53 (9/15/86)
93   IL POGGIONE Brunello di Montalcino 1981 $28 (9/15/86)
92   VILLA BANFI Brunello di Montalcino 1981 Rel: $23 Cur: $32 (3/31/87) CS
90   CAPARZO Brunello di Montalcino 1981 Rel: $18 Cur: $18 (9/15/86)
89   COL D'ORCIA Brunello di Montalcino Riserva 1981 $22.50 (7/31/88)
88   PIAN DI CONTE Brunello di Montalcino 1981 (NA) (9/15/86)

88   POGGIO SALVI Brunello di Montalcino 1981 $20 (10/15/88)
85   FATTORIA DEI BARBI Brunello di Montalcino 1981 Rel: $20 Cur: $24 (9/15/86)
85   POGGIO SALVI Brunello di Montalcino Riserva 1981 $35 (11/30/90)
84   IL CASELLO Brunello di Montalcino 1981 $15 (10/31/87)
83   CAPARZO Brunello di Montalcino La Casa 1981 $50 (6/15/90)
81   FATTORIA DEI BARBI Brunello di Montalcino Blue Label 1981 $20 (1/31/91)
80   ALTESINO Brunello di Montalcino 1981 $22 (9/15/86)
80   IL CASELLO Brunello di Montalcino 1981 $15 (9/15/86)
80   EMILIO COSTANTI Brunello di Montalcino 1981 $20 (9/15/86)
75   VILLA NICOLA Brunello di Montalcino Riserva 1981 $14 (9/15/88)
70   CAPARZO Brunello di Montalcino Riserva 1981 $23 (6/15/90)
70   COL D'ORCIA Brunello di Montalcino 1981 $22.50 (9/15/86)
70   GREPPONE MAZZI Brunello di Montalcino 1981 (NA) (9/15/86)

1980

91   ALTESINO Brunello di Montalcino 1980 $18 (9/15/86)
90   VILLA BANFI Brunello di Montalcino 1980 Rel: $20 Cur: $33 (9/15/86)
89   EMILIO COSTANTI Brunello di Montalcino 1980 $17 (9/15/86)
88   BIONDI-SANTI Brunello di Montalcino Il Greppo 1980 $40 (9/15/86)
88   CAPARZO Brunello di Montalcino 1980 $23 (9/15/86)
72   CAMIGLIANO Brunello di Montalcino 1980 $8.50 (9/15/86)

1979

94   COL D'ORCIA Brunello di Montalcino 1979 $15.50 (9/15/86) CS
93   CASTIGLIONE DEL BOSCO Brunello di Montalcino 1979 $14 (4/30/87)
90   VILLA BANFI Brunello di Montalcino 1979 Rel: $18 Cur: $35 (4/16/85) SS
89   CAPARZO Brunello di Montalcino La Casa 1979 $27 (9/15/86)
88   DEI ROSETI Brunello di Montalcino 1979 $10 (8/31/86)
88   POGGIO SALVI Brunello di Montalcino 1979 $15 (3/15/87)
82   ALTESINO Brunello di Montalcino 1979 $20 (9/15/86)
79   IL POGGIONE Brunello di Montalcino Riserva 1979 $35 (9/15/86)
77   ARGIANO Brunello di Montalcino 1979 $11.25 (9/15/86)
72   MASTROIANNI Brunello di Montalcino 1979 $17.50 (9/15/86)
72   POGGIO ANTICO Brunello di Montalcino 1979 $12.50 (9/15/86)
69   LA PODERINA Brunello di Montalcino 1979 $12.50 (2/16/86)

1978

92   IL POGGIONE Brunello di Montalcino Riserva 1978 Rel: $35 Cur: $47 (7/01/84) SS
70   BIONDI-SANTI Brunello di Montalcino Il Greppo 1978 $45 (9/15/86)
68   ARGIANO Brunello di Montalcino Riserva 1978 $12.50 (9/15/86)
67   VAL DI SUGA Brunello di Montalcino Riserva 1978 $13.50 (3/15/87)
65   COL D'ORCIA Brunello di Montalcino Riserva 1978 $18.50 (9/15/86)
    FATTORIA DEI BARBI Brunello di Montalcino 1978 Rel: $11 Cur: $30 (10/01/84) CS

1977

86   FATTORIA DEI BARBI Brunello di Montalcino Riserva 1977 $20 (9/15/86)
85   CAMIGLIANO Brunello di Montalcino Riserva 1977 $11 (8/01/85)
67   ARGIANO Brunello di Montalcino Riserva 1977 $12.50 (9/15/86)

1975

78   LISINI Brunello di Montalcino 1975 Rel: $30 Cur: $30 (9/15/86)

CHIANTI DOCG

1989

85   VILLA CILNIA Chianti Colli Aretini 1989 $10 (4/30/91)
83   BARONE RICASOLI Chianti 1989 $7 (4/15/91) BB
80   VIGNE TOSCANE Chianti Terre Toscane 1989 $5 (11/30/90) BB
76   PLACIDO Chianti 1989 $6 (7/15/91)
70   FRESCOBALDI Chianti 1989 $5.50 (4/15/91)

1988

91   DIEVOLE Chianti Classico Dieulele 1988 $22 (4/15/91)
90   FRESCOBALDI Chianti Rufina Castello di Nipozzano Riserva 1988 (NA) (11/30/89) (BT) (HS)
89   VILLA CILNIA Chianti Colli Aretini 1988 $10 (4/15/91)
89   ISOLE E OLENA Chianti Classico 1988 $9 (11/30/90) BB
89   RIECINE Chianti Classico 1988 $22 (4/30/91)
88   TENUTA FARNETA Chianti di Collalto 1988 $6 (12/15/90) BB
88   TALOSA Chianti Colli Senesi 1988 $8 (11/30/90) BB
88   VIGNAMAGGIO Chianti Classico Barrel 1988 (NA) (11/30/89) (HS)
87   FATTORIA DI AMA Chianti Classico Castello di Ama 1988 $18.50 (4/15/91)
87   FRESCOBALDI Chianti Rufina Montesodi 1988 (NA) (11/30/89) (BT) (HS)
87   LE MASSE Chianti Classico 1988 $12.50 (4/30/91)
87   SAN LEONINO Chianti Classico 1988 $10 (12/15/90)
86   FATTORIA DI FELSINA Chianti Classico 1988 $13 (11/30/89) (BT) (HS)
86   FATTORIA LA QUERCE Chianti Classico 1988 $9 (11/30/89) (BT) (HS)
85   CASTELLO DI FONTERUTOLI Chianti Classico 1988 $14 (11/30/90)
85   CASTELLO DI FONTERUTOLI Chianti Classico 1988 $14 (11/30/89) (BT) (HS)
85   FRESCOBALDI Chianti 1988 $5 (11/30/89) BB
83   VILLA CAFAGGIO Chianti Classico 1988 $10 (11/30/90)
83   FATTORIA MONTELLORI Chianti Putto 1988 $6 (11/30/90)
82   BADIA A COLTIBUONO Chianti Cetamura 1988 $7 (12/15/90) BB
82   CASTELLARE DI CASTELLINA Chianti Classico 1988 $12.50 (11/30/90)
82   DIEVOLE Chianti Classico Vigna Campi Nuovi 1988 $15 (4/15/91)
81   LILLIANO Chianti Classico 1988 $10 (11/30/90)
78   CONTI D'ATTIMIS Chianti Classico Odorico 1988 $10 (11/30/90)
77   CARATELLO Chianti Classico 1988 $9 (12/15/90)

1987

90   CASTELLO DI FONTERUTOLI Chianti Classico 1987 $11 (11/30/89)
90   FONTODI Chianti Classico 1987 $11 (11/30/89) (HS)
89   ROCCA DELLE MACIE Chianti Classico Riserva di Fizzano 1987 (NA) (11/30/89) (HS)
89   VISTARENNI Chianti Classico 1987 $10 (10/15/89)
88   ANTINORI Chianti Classico Tenute Antinori 1987 (NA) (11/30/89) (HS)
88   ISOLE E OLENA Chianti Classico 1987 Rel: $9 Cur: $12 (9/15/89)
88+ RUFFINO Chianti Classico Nozzole Vigneto La Forra 1987 (NA) (11/30/89) (BT) (HS)
87   FATTORIA DI AMA Chianti Classico 1987 $9 (11/30/89) (HS)
86   VILLA CAFAGGIO Chianti Classico 1987 $9 (9/15/89)
86   LILLIANO Chianti Classico 1987 $8.50 (11/30/89)

ITALY
TUSCANY RED/CHIANTI DOCG

86   A. SARDELLI Chianti Classico Bartenura 1987 $7 (10/15/89) BB
86+   VIGNAMAGGIO Chianti Classico Riserva 1987 (NA) (11/30/89) (BT) (HS)
85   BADIA A COLTIBUONO Chianti Classico 1987 $8 (11/30/89) (HS)
85   VILLA BANFI Chianti 1987 $7.50/1.5L (11/30/89) BB
85   PODERE IL PALAZZINO Chianti Classico 1987 $9 (11/30/89) (HS)
85   CASTELLO DI VOLPAIA Chianti Classico 1987 $16 (11/30/89) (HS)
84   DIEVOLE Chianti Classico Vigna Campi Nuovi 1987 $10 (11/30/90)
84   CASTELLO DEI RAMPOLLA Chianti Classico 1987 $15 (4/15/91)
83   ANTINORI Chianti Classico Pèppoli 1987 $17.50 (5/15/90)
83   DIEVOLE Chianti Classico Villa Dievole 1987 $8 (12/15/90)
83   FATTORIA DI FELSINA Chianti Classico 1987 $10 (11/30/89) (HS)
83   FATTORIA DI FELSINA Chianti Classico Berardenga 1987 $8 (5/15/90)
83   VITTORIO INNOCENTI Chianti 1987 $7 (5/15/90) BB
83   RIECINE Chianti Classico 1987 $20 (4/30/91)
83   RUFFINO Chianti Classico 1987 $7 (4/30/90) BB
82   CONTI D'ATTIMIS Chianti Classico Ermanno 1987 $11 (9/15/90)
82   ROCCA DELLE MACIE Chianti Classico 1987 (NA) (11/30/89) (HS)
81   CASTELLARE DI CASTELLINA Chianti Classico 1987 $11 (11/30/89)
81   FONTODI Chianti Classico 1987 $11 (11/30/89)
81   CASTELLO DI GABBIANO Chianti Classico 1987 $7 (11/30/89)
80   MELINI Chianti Classico 1987 $7 (4/30/90)
80   FATTORIA LA QUERCE Chianti Classico 1987 $7 (11/30/89) (HS)
80   VILLA SANTINA Chianti 1987 $5 (11/30/89) BB
79   BARONE RICASOLI Chianti Classico Ricasoli 1987 $6 (11/30/89) (HS)
79   BARONE RICASOLI Chianti Classico San Ripolo 1987 $10 (4/15/91)
78   B. ARRIGONI Chianti Putto 1987 $4.50 (11/30/89)
78   VITICCIO Chianti Classico 1987 $9 (4/30/90)
76   VILLA CILNIA Chianti Colli Aretini 1987 $8.25 (10/15/89)
76   COLI Chianti 1987 $6 (11/30/89)
76   FATTORIA DI LUCIGNANO Chianti Colli Fiorentini 1987 $6 (6/30/89)
75   FRESCOBALDI Chianti 1987 $4.50 (5/15/89)
75   SACCARDI Chianti Classico 1987 $10 (5/15/90)
74   FATTORIA DEL CERRO Chianti Colli Senesi 1987 $5 (7/31/89)
74   MARTINI DI CIGALA Chianti Classico San Giusto a Rentennano 1987 $9 (3/31/90)
70   A. SARDELLI Chianti Classico Bartenura 1987 $9 (3/31/91)
68   LANCIOLA II Chianti Colli Fiorentini 1987 $7.75 (5/15/89)
67   PODERE IL PALAZZINO Chianti Classico 1987 $12 (3/31/90)

1986

90   FATTORIA DI AMA Chianti Classico Castello di Ama Vigneto Bellavista 1986 $36 (11/30/89) (HS)
90   ANTINORI Chianti Classico Pèppoli 1986 $17 (7/15/89)
90   CASTELLO DI VOLPAIA Chianti Classico 1986 $10 (11/30/89) (HS)
89   VILLA CAFAGGIO Chianti Classico 1986 $9 (3/31/90)
89   CASTELLO DI MONTEGROSSI Chianti Classico 1986 $8 (7/15/89)
88   CASTELLO DI FONTERUTOLI Chianti Classico Ser Lapo Riserva 1986 $25 (11/30/90)
88   VITICCIO Chianti Classico 1986 $8 (3/31/89) BB
87   FATTORIA DI AMA Chianti Classico Castello di Ama 1986 $8 (1/31/89)
87   FATTORIA DI AMA Chianti Classico Castello di Ama Vigneto La Casuccia 1986 $40 (11/30/89) (HS)
87   VILLA CILNIA Chianti Colli Aretini 1986 $9 (5/31/89) BB
86   CASTELLO DI CACCHIANO Chianti Classico 1986 $8 (5/15/90)
86   CASTELLO DI CACCHIANO Chianti Classico 1986 $8 (11/30/89)
86   VILLA CAFAGGIO Chianti Classico Riserva 1986 $18 (12/15/90)
86   CASTELLARE DI CASTELLINA Chianti Classico Riserva 1986 $11 (11/30/89) (HS)
86   CECCHI Chianti Classico 1986 $7 (7/15/89)
86   ISOLE E OLENA Chianti Classico 1986 Rel: $7.50 Cur: $8 (7/31/88)
86   PODERE IL PALAZZINO Chianti Classico 1986 $9 (11/30/89) (HS)
86   PODERE IL PALAZZINO Chianti Classico 1986 $9 (1/31/89)
85   CASTELLO D'ALBOLA Chianti Classico 1986 $7.50 (11/30/89)
85   BRUGNANO Chianti Colli Fiorentini 1986 $5 (1/31/89) BB
85   CASTELLO DI FONTERUTOLI Chianti Classico 1986 $11 (1/31/89)
85   MONSANTO Chianti Classico Riserva 1986 $15 (4/15/91)
85   VECCHIE TERRE DI MONTEFILI Chianti Classico 1986 $14 (4/30/90)
85   RUFFINO Chianti Classico Aziano 1986 $5 (5/31/89) BB
85   VIGNAMAGGIO Chianti Classico 1986 $12 (5/15/90)
85+   VIGNAMAGGIO Chianti Classico Riserva 1986 (NA) (11/30/89) (BT) (HS)
84   FATTORIA DI AMA Chianti Classico Castello di Ama Vigneto San Lorenzo 1986 $36 (11/30/89) (HS)
84   BARONE RICASOLI Chianti Ricasoli 1986 $5.50 (5/15/89) BB
84   BARONE RICASOLI Chianti Classico Brolio 1986 $8 (11/30/89)
83   MELINI Chianti Classico 1986 $6 (10/31/88) BB
83   VIGNAMAGGIO Chianti Classico 1986 $12 (11/30/89) (HS)
82   CASTELLARE DI CASTELLINA Chianti Classico 1986 $11 (10/15/89)
82   FRESCOBALDI Chianti Rufina Castello di Nipozzano Riserva 1986 $11 (9/15/90)
82   CASTELLO DI GABBIANO Chianti Classico 1986 $7.75 (5/31/89) BB
82   CASTELLO DI GABBIANO Chianti Classico 1986 $7.75 (9/15/88)
82   SELVAPIANA Chianti Classico 1986 $5 (11/30/89) (HS)
81   FATTORIA LA QUERCE Chianti Classico 1986 $7 (11/30/89) (HS)
80   CECCHI Chianti 1986 $5 (1/31/89)
80   ROCCA DELLE MACIE Chianti Classico 1986 (NA) (11/30/89) (HS)
79   CASTELL'IN VILLA Chianti Classico 1986 $13 (9/15/90)
79   VILLA MARCIALLA Chianti Colli Fiorentini 1986 $6 (10/15/89)
79   MARTINI DI CIGALA Chianti Classico San Giusto a Rentennano 1986 $8 (1/31/89)

78   BOSCARELLI Chianti Colli Senesi 1986 $8 (1/31/89)
78   FATTORIA DI FELSINA Chianti Classico 1986 $7.50 (11/30/89) (HS)
78   PASOLINI Chianti 1986 $6.50 (12/15/90)
78   VISTARENNI Chianti Classico 1986 $18 (7/31/89)
77   VITTORIO INNOCENTI Chianti 1986 $7 (3/31/90)
77   BARONE RICASOLI Chianti Classico Brolio 1986 $8 (11/30/90)
75   FRESCOBALDI Chianti 1986 $3.50 (12/15/87)
75   CASTELLO DI VOLPAIA Chianti Classico 1986 $10 (3/31/89)
74   FONTODI Chianti Classico 1986 $9 (1/31/89)
72   FATTORIA DI FELSINA Chianti Classico Berardenga 1986 $7.50 (12/15/88)
70   LILLIANO Chianti Classico 1986 $7.75 (5/15/89)
68   CARATELLO Chianti Classico 1986 $6.75 (1/31/89)
68   FATTORIA LA QUERCE Chianti Classico Caratello 1986 $6.75 (11/30/89) (HS)

1985

95   FATTORIA DI FELSINA Chianti Classico Berardenga Vigneto Rancia Riserva 1985 $23 (11/30/89) (BT) (HS)
94   FATTORIA DI AMA Chianti Classico Castello di Ama Vigneto Bellavista 1985 $30 (7/31/89)
93   FATTORIA DI FELSINA Chianti Classico Berardenga Vigneto Rancia Riserva 1985 $23 (4/30/90) CS
93   PODERE IL PALAZZINO Chianti Classico 1985 $11 (11/30/87) SS
93   PODERE IL PALAZZINO Chianti Classico Riserva 1985 $11 (11/30/89) (HS)
92   ANTINORI Chianti Classico Pèppoli 1985 $16 (5/31/88)
92   ANTINORI Chianti Classico Tenute Antinori 1985 $21 (11/30/89) (HS)
92   FONTODI Chianti Classico Riserva Vigna del Sorbo 1985 $18 (11/30/89) (HS)
92   LE MASSE Chianti Classico 1985 $12 (7/15/89)
91   FATTORIA DI AMA Chianti Classico Castello di Ama Vigneto La Casuccia 1985 $35 (7/31/89)
91   CELLOLE Chianti Classico Riserva 1985 $13 (11/30/89)
91   MARTINI DI CIGALA Chianti Classico San Giusto a Rentennano Riserva 1985 $17 (11/30/89)
91   CASTELLO DI FONTERUTOLI Chianti Classico Ser Lapo Riserva 1985 $18 (11/30/89)
91   FATTORIA LA QUERCE Chianti Classico Riserva 1985 $16 (11/30/89)
91   SELVAPIANA Chianti Rufina Bucerchiale Riserva 1985 $15 (11/30/89) (HS)
91   SELVAPIANA Chianti Rufina Vigneto Bucerchiale Riserva 1985 $19 (9/15/90)
90   ANTINORI Chianti Classico Santa Cristina 1985 $6 (10/31/88) BB
90   FRESCOBALDI Chianti Rufina Montesodi 1985 Cur: $32 (11/30/89) (HS)
90   LAMBOLE DI LAMBOLE Chianti Classico Vigneto di Campolungo 1985 $20 (4/30/90)
90   LE MASSE Chianti Classico Riserva 1985 $18 (9/15/90)
90   CASTELLO DEI RAMPOLLA Chianti Classico 1985 $8 (9/15/88)
90   RUFFINO Chianti Classico Nozzole Vigneto La Forra 1985 (NA) (11/30/89) (HS)
90   RUFFINO Chianti Classico Riserva Ducale 1985 $13 (5/15/90)
90   VIGNAMAGGIO Chianti Classico Riserva 1985 $17 (5/15/90)
90   CASTELLO DI VOLPAIA Chianti Classico 1985 $10 (6/30/89) SS
89   ANTINORI Chianti Classico Riserva 1985 $9 (10/15/89)
89   FATTORIA DI FELSINA Chianti Classico Berardenga Riserva 1985 $11 (11/30/89) (BT) (HS)
89   ISOLE E OLENA Chianti Classico 1985 Rel: $7.50 Cur: $14 (5/31/88) BB
89   LILLIANO Chianti Classico Riserva 1985 $14 (11/30/89)
89   MONSANTO Chianti Classico Riserva 1985 $10 (11/30/89) (HS)
89   SACCARDI Chianti Classico 1985 $6 (11/30/87) BB
89   SAN FELICE Chianti Classico Il Grigio Riserva 1985 $10 (11/30/89) (HS)
89   SAN FELICE Chianti Classico Poggio Rosso Riserva 1985 (NA) (11/30/89) (HS)
89   SELVAPIANA Chianti Classico Riserva 1985 $11 (11/30/89) (HS)
89   VIGNAMAGGIO Chianti Classico Riserva 1985 $17 (11/30/89) (HS)
88   VILLA CAFAGGIO Chianti Classico Riserva 1985 $13 (9/15/89)
88   CASTELLO DI FONTERUTOLI Chianti Classico 1985 $11 (11/30/89) (HS)
88   FRESCOBALDI Chianti Rufina Castello di Nipozzano Riserva 1985 $11 (11/30/89)
88   ROCCA DELLE MACIE Chianti Classico Riserva di Fizzano 1985 (NA) (11/30/89) (HS)
88   CASTELLO DI VOLPAIA Chianti Classico Riserva 1985 $13 (11/30/89) (HS)
87   CASTELLO DI CACCHIANO Chianti Classico 1985 $10 (10/31/88)
87   MARTINI DI CIGALA Chianti Classico San Giusto a Rentennano 1985 $8 (11/30/87)
87   MELINI Chianti Classico Riserva Vigneti la Selvanella 1985 $7 (11/30/89) BB
87   BARONE RICASOLI Chianti Classico Brolio 1985 $7 (10/31/88) BB
86   FATTORIA DI AMA Chianti Classico Castello di Ama Vigneto San Lorenzo 1985 $32 (11/30/89) (HS)
86   BADIA A COLTIBUONO Chianti Classico Riserva 1985 Cur: $18 (11/30/89) (HS)
86   VILLA BANFI Chianti Classico Riserva 1985 $9 (5/15/90)
86   CASTELL'IN VILLA Chianti Classico 1985 $11.50 (6/30/89)
86   CASTELLARE DI CASTELLINA Chianti Classico Riserva 1985 $16 (11/30/89)
86   FATTORIA DI FELSINA Chianti Classico Berardenga Riserva 1985 $11 (5/15/90)
86   CASTELLO DI MONTEGROSSI Chianti Classico 1985 $7.25 (9/15/88)
86   SAN FELICE Chianti Classico Il Grigio Riserva 1985 $10 (9/15/90)
86   VIGNAMAGGIO Chianti Classico 1985 $11 (8/31/88)
85   FEDERICO BONFIO Chianti Le Portine Riserva 1985 $9.50 (3/31/90)
85   FEDERICO BONFIO Chianti Proprietor's Reserve 1985 $15 (3/31/90)
85   CASTELLARE DI CASTELLINA Chianti Classico 1985 $11 (3/31/88)
85   FONTODI Chianti Classico Riserva 1985 $12 (11/30/89)
85   FRESCOBALDI Chianti Rufina Castello di Nipozzano Riserva 1985 $11 (11/30/89) (HS)
85   BARONE RICASOLI Chianti Classico Brolio 1985 $7 (11/30/89) (HS)
85   RUFFINO Chianti Classico Riserva Ducale 1985 $13 (11/30/89) (HS)
85   VITICCIO Chianti Classico Riserva 1985 $11 (11/30/89)
84   VILLA CAFAGGIO Chianti Classico 1985 $8 (5/31/88)
84   CONTI D'ATTIMIS Chianti Classico Ermanno Riserva 1985 $13 (9/15/90)
83   POGGIARELLO Chianti Classico De Rham I Riservati 4 1985 $6 (10/31/88) BB
83   FATTORIA LA QUERCE Chianti 1985 $9.50 (11/30/87)
82   MELINI Chianti Classico 1985 $5 (7/31/88) BB
81   CASTELLO DEI RAMPOLLA Chianti Classico Riserva 1985 $16 (4/30/90)
81   BARONE RICASOLI Chianti Classico Brolio Riserva 1985 $12 (9/15/90)
80   CASTELLO DI CACCHIANO Chianti Classico Millennio Riserva 1985 $18 (9/15/90)
80   MONSANTO Chianti Classico Riserva Il Poggio Vineyard 1985 $25 (3/31/90)
80   RUFFINO Chianti Classico Aziano 1985 $9 (8/31/88)
79   PODERE IL PALAZZINO Chianti Classico Riserva 1985 $22 (3/31/90)
79   PASOLINI Chianti 1985 $5 (9/15/88)
78   CASTELLO DI MONTEGROSSI Chianti Classico 1985 $7.25 (2/15/88)
78   CASTELLO DI SAN POLO IN ROSSO Chianti Classico Riserva 1985 $14 (11/30/89)
78   CASTELLO DI VOLPAIA Chianti Classico Riserva 1985 $13 (3/31/90)
77   CAMIGLIANO Chianti Colli Senesi 1985 $3.50 (12/15/87)
76   CASTELLO D'ALBOLA Chianti Classico Riserva 1985 $12 (11/30/89)
76   FEDERICO BONFIO Chianti Le Poggiolo Riserva 1985 $10.50 (3/31/90)
76   PAGLIARESE Chianti Classico 1985 $6 (3/31/88)
74   LILLIANO Chianti Classico 1985 $6 (10/31/87)

72   CASTELLO DI GABBIANO Chianti Classico 1985 $7 (2/15/88)
67   FATTORIA DI FOGNANO Chianti Colli Senesi 1985 $6.50 (5/15/89)
67   CASTELLO DI SAN POLO IN ROSSO Chianti Classico 1985 $10 (11/30/89)

1984

78   RUFFINO Chianti Classico 1984 $5 (11/30/86)
77   VILLA BROTINI Chianti Classico Villa Brotini 1984 $5.75 (12/31/87)
74   VITICCIO Chianti Classico 1984 $5.75 (11/15/87)
73   BARONE RICASOLI Chianti Classico Brolio 1984 $4 (9/15/87)
72   BOSCARELLI Chianti Colli Senesi 1984 $6 (9/15/87)
72   VILLA SANTINA Chianti Classico 1984 $5 (11/15/87)

1983

91   VILLA CAFAGGIO Chianti Classico 1983 $10.50 (9/15/87)
91   FATTORIA DI FELSINA Chianti Classico Berardenga Vigneto Rancia Riserva 1983 $17 (12/15/88)
90   FATTORIA DI AMA Chianti Classico Castello di Ama Vigneto Bellavista 1983 Rel: $25 Cur: $25 (12/15/87)
90   ANTINORI Chianti Classico Tenute Antinori 1983 $16 (11/30/89) (HS)
89   FRESCOBALDI Chianti Rufina Castello di Nipozzano Riserva 1983 Rel: $10 Cur: $11 (11/30/89) (HS)
88   CASTELLO DI FONTERUTOLI Chianti Classico Riserva 1983 $15 (11/30/89) (HS)
88   CASTELLO DI FONTERUTOLI Chianti Classico Ser Lapo Riserva 1983 $15 (1/31/89)
88   VIGNAMAGGIO Chianti Classico Riserva 1983 $15 (7/31/88)
88   CASTELLO DI VOLPAIA Chianti Classico 1983 (NA) (9/15/87) (HS)
87   CASTELL'IN VILLA Chianti Classico 1983 $7 (9/15/87)
87   FATTORIA DI FELSINA Chianti Classico Berardenga Riserva 1983 $12 (11/30/89) (HS)
87   FATTORIA DI FELSINA Chianti Classico Berardenga Vigneto Rancia Riserva 1983 $17 (12/15/88)
87   FONTODI Chianti Classico Riserva 1983 $8.75 (9/15/87)
87   MARTINI DI CIGALA Chianti Classico San Giusto a Rentennano Riserva 1983 $11 (11/15/87)
87   SACCARDI Chianti Classico Riserva 1983 $12 (5/15/90)
87   SAN FELICE Chianti Classico Poggio Rosso Riserva 1983 (NA) (11/30/89) (HS)
87   CASTELLO DI VOLPAIA Chianti Classico Riserva 1983 $11.50 (5/31/89)
86   MONSANTO Chianti Classico Il Poggio Vineyard Riserva 1983 $23 (11/30/89) (HS)
86   SELVAPIANA Chianti Classico Riserva 1983 $10 (11/30/89) (HS)
85   CASTELLO DI GABBIANO Chianti Classico 1983 $6 (5/31/87) BB
85   ISOLE E OLENA Chianti Classico 1983 Rel: $5 Cur: $9 (12/15/86) BB
85   BARONE RICASOLI Chianti Classico Brolio Riserva del Barone 1983 $11 (11/30/89) (HS)
85   SAN FELICE Chianti Classico Il Grigio Riserva 1983 $12 (11/30/89) (HS)
85   VIGNAMAGGIO Chianti Classico Riserva 1983 $15 (5/15/90)
84   CASTELLO DEI RAMPOLLA Chianti Classico 1983 $7 (7/31/87) BB
84   RUFFINO Chianti Classico Riserva Ducale 1983 $17 (11/30/89) (HS)
84   VILLA CERNA Chianti Classico Riserva 1983 $8.25 (3/31/89) BB
83   CAPEZZANA Chianti Montalbano 1983 $6 (9/15/86) BB
83   FRESCOBALDI Chianti Rufina Castello di Nipozzano Riserva 1983 $10 (10/31/88)
83   BARONE RICASOLI Chianti Classico Brolio Riserva 1983 $10 (3/31/89) BB
83   BARONE RICASOLI Chianti Classico Ricasoli Riserva 1983 $8 (11/30/89) (HS)
82   CAMIGLIANO Chianti Colli Senesi 1983 $2.75 (5/16/85) BB
80   VILLA CAFAGGIO Chianti Classico Riserva 1983 $10 (5/31/88)
80   MARTINI DI CIGALA Chianti Classico San Giusto a Rentennano 1983 $6.25 (9/15/87)
80   PODERE IL PALAZZINO Chianti Classico Riserva 1983 $21 (11/15/87)
80   BARONE RICASOLI Chianti Classico Brolio Riserva 1983 $10 (5/15/90)
80   VITICCIO Chianti Classico Riserva 1983 $12 (11/30/89)
79   ANTINORI Chianti Classico Riserva Villa Antinori 1983 $9.25 (3/31/89)
79   SACCARDI Chianti Classico Riserva 1983 $12 (3/31/89)
78   BADIA A COLTIBUONO Chianti Classico Riserva 1983 $15 (11/30/89) (HS)
78   PODERE IL PALAZZINO Chianti Classico 1983 $5 (9/16/85)
77   VITICCIO Chianti Classico Viticcio Riserva 1983 $8 (11/15/87)
73   CASTELLO DI CACCHIANO Chianti Classico 1983 $6 (9/15/87)
70   CARATELLO Chianti Classico 1983 $4 (8/31/86)
70   FATTORIA LA QUERCE Chianti Classico Caratello 1983 $4 (11/30/89) (HS)

1982

93   MONSANTO Chianti Classico Il Poggio Vineyard Riserva 1982 $23 (11/30/89) (HS)
90   ANTINORI Chianti Classico Riserva Marchese Antinori 1982 $16 (5/31/89)
90   SAN FELICE Chianti Classico Il Grigio Riserva 1982 $11 (5/31/88)
88   BADIA A COLTIBUONO Chianti Classico Riserva 1982 $13 (7/31/88)
88   MONSANTO Chianti Classico Riserva Il Poggio Vineyard 1982 $23 (6/30/89)
87   ANTINORI Chianti Classico Riserva 1982 $10 (9/15/87)
87   FONTODI Chianti Classico Riserva 1982 $7.50 (9/15/87)
87   ROCCA DELLE MACIE Chianti Classico Riserva di Fizzano 1982 $15.50 (3/31/89)
87   SELVAPIANA Chianti Classico Riserva 1982 $10 (11/30/89) (HS)
86   CASTELL'IN VILLA Chianti Classico Riserva 1982 $18 (11/30/90)
86   FRESCOBALDI Chianti Rufina Montesodi 1982 Rel: $28 Cur: $31 (12/15/88)
85   CARATELLO Chianti Classico 1982 $3.50 (3/01/86) BB
85   CASTELVECCHI Chianti Classico Riserva 1982 $13 (5/15/90)
85   VIGNETI LA SELVANELLA Chianti Classico Riserva 1982 $6 (6/30/88) BB
84   CASTELLO DI GABBIANO Chianti Classico Riserva 1982 $10.50 (7/31/88)
84   SAN FELICE Chianti Classico Poggio Rosso Riserva 1982 $15 (11/30/89) (HS)
84   VITICCIO Chianti Classico Viticcio Riserva 1982 $8.75 (11/15/87)
84   CASTELLO DI VOLPAIA Chianti Classico Riserva 1982 $11 (9/15/87) (HS)
83   VILLA BANFI Chianti Classico Riserva 1982 $7 (12/15/87)
81   CASA FRANCESCO Chianti Classico 1982 $6 (11/30/89)
81   SAN FELICE Chianti Classico Poggio Rosso Riserva 1982 $15 (9/15/90)
80   RUFFINO Chianti Classico Riserva Ducale 1982 $20 (5/31/89)
79   FEDERICO BONFIO Chianti Le Portine Riserva 1982 $9 (11/15/87)
79   CASTELLO DI GABBIANO Chianti Classico Riserva Gold Label 1982 $21 (11/30/89)
78   CASTELLO DI TIZZANO Chianti Classico Riserva 1982 $18 (7/15/89)
73   FEDERICO BONFIO Chianti Il Poggiolo Riserva 1982 $7 (11/15/87)
72   MONSANTO Chianti Classico Riserva 1982 $10 (2/15/88)
71   BORGIANNI Chianti Classico 1982 $3.50 (4/01/85)
68   CASTELLO DI GABBIANO Chianti Classico 1982 $6.25 (1/01/86)
66   VILLA CAFAGGIO Chianti Classico 1982 $4 (10/16/85)
64   CASTELLO DEI RAMPOLLA Chianti Classico 1982 $6 (10/16/85)

1981

87   SAN FELICE Chianti Classico Poggio Rosso Riserva 1981 $15 (8/31/88)
86   CASTELLO DI VOLPAIA Chianti Classico Riserva 1981 (NA) (9/15/87) (HS)
82   MONSANTO Chianti Classico Il Poggio Vineyard Riserva 1981 $17 (11/30/89) (HS)

82   PAGLIARESE Chianti Classico Boscardini Riserva 1981 $9.25 (5/31/88)
81   CASTELLO DI GABBIANO Chianti Classico Riserva Gold Label 1981 $18 (2/15/88)
81   SACCARDI Chianti Classico Riserva 1981 $9 (11/30/87)
80   VILLA BANFI Chianti Classico Riserva 1981 $7 (8/31/86)
72   NOZZOLE Chianti Classico Riserva 1981 $7 (10/31/87)
69   PODERE IL PALAZZINO Chianti Classico Riserva 1981 $6.25 (4/16/86)
67   MONSANTO Chianti Classico Riserva 1981 $10 (12/15/87)
66   RUFFINO Chianti Classico Riserva Ducale 1981 $9 (10/31/86)

1980

90   ANTINORI Chianti Classico Riserva Marchese Antinori 1980 $16 (9/15/87)
85   PAGLIARESE Chianti Classico Boscardini Riserva 1980 $9.50 (3/15/87)

1979

93   MONSANTO Chianti Classico Riserva Il Poggio Vineyard 1979 $16 (9/15/87)
83   MONSANTO Chianti Classico Riserva 1979 $9.50 (11/01/84)
80   RUFFINO Chianti Classico Riserva Ducale 1979 Rel: $16 Cur: $23 (9/16/85)
70   RUFFINO Chianti Classico Riserva Ducale 1979 Rel: $16 Cur: $23 (9/30/86)

1978

90   BARONE RICASOLI Chianti Classico Brolio Riserva del Barone 1978 $10.50 (6/01/85)
82   RUFFINO Chianti Classico Riserva Ducale 1978 Cur: $55 (11/30/89) (HS)
78   VITICCIO Chianti Classico Viticcio Riserva 1978 $12.50 (11/30/87)
73   SAN FELICE Chianti Classico Poggio Rosso Riserva 1978 $14 (3/15/87)
71   LUIANO Chianti Classico Riserva 1978 $6 (8/31/86)

1977

89   RUFFINO Chianti Classico Riserva Ducale 1977 Cur: $39 (9/16/85) (JS)
81   CASTELLO DI VOLPAIA Chianti Classico Riserva 1977 (NA) (9/15/87) (HS)

1975

86   RUFFINO Chianti Classico Riserva Ducale 1975 Cur: $57 (9/16/85) (JS)
71   VITICCIO Chianti Classico Viticcio Riserva 1975 $13.50 (11/15/87)

1971

85   RUFFINO Chianti Classico Riserva Ducale 1971 Cur: $61 (9/16/85) (JS)

1970

85   CASTELLO DI VOLPAIA Chianti Classico Riserva 1970 (NA) (9/15/87) (HS)

1962

68   RUFFINO Chianti Classico Riserva Ducale 1962 Cur: $75 (9/16/85) (JS)

1958

82   RUFFINO Chianti Classico Riserva Ducale 1958 Cur: $144 (9/16/85) (JS)

ROSSO DI MONTALCINO

1988

89   VILLA NICOLA Rosso di Montalcino 1988 $15 (1/31/91)
87   DEI ROSETI Rosso di Montalcino 1988 $13 (1/31/91)
87   VAL DI SUGA Rosso di Montalcino 1988 $10 (4/30/91)
84   COL D'ORCIA Rosso di Montalcino 1988 $9 (4/30/91)
83   IL PODERUCCIO Rosso di Montalcino I Due Cipressi 1988 $9.50 (4/30/91)
82   CASTIGLIONE DEL BOSCO Rosso di Montalcino 1988 $11 (7/15/91)
82   CIACCI PICCOLOMINI D'ARAGONA Rosso di Montalcino 1988 $16 (4/30/91)
81   CAPARZO Rosso di Montalcino 1988 $14 (4/30/91)
79   LISINI Rosso di Montalcino 1988 $14 (4/30/91)
73   ALTESINO Rosso di Montalcino 1988 $14.50 (7/15/91)

1987

85   VILLA BANFI Rosso di Montalcino Centine 1987 $8 (6/15/90) BB
84   MASTROIANNI Rosso di Montalcino 1987 $10 (6/15/90)
84   PERTIMALI Rosso di Montalcino 1987 $12.50 (1/31/91)
84   PERTIMALI Rosso di Montalcino 1987 $12.50 (11/30/89)
79   MASTROIANNI Rosso di Montalcino 1987 $10 (7/15/91)
68   SAN FILIPPO Rosso di Montalcino 1987 $11 (4/30/91)

1986

87   VILLA BANFI Rosso di Montalcino Centine 1986 $7 (11/30/89) BB
86   CAPARZO Rosso di Montalcino 1986 $10 (9/30/89)
83   LA CHIESA DI S. RESTITUTA Rosso di Montalcino 1986 $9.50 (5/31/88)
82   S. CARLO Rosso di Montalcino 1986 $10 (7/15/89)
81   VAL DI SUGA Rosso di Montalcino 1986 $9 (11/30/89)
80   ALTESINO Rosso di Montalcino 1986 $10 (7/15/89)
78   CAPRILI Rosso di Montalcino 1986 $10 (1/31/89)

1985

88   VILLA BANFI Rosso di Montalcino Centine 1985 $7 (11/30/87) BB
85   IL POGGIONE Rosso di Montalcino 1985 $17 (3/31/88)
80   COL D'ORCIA Rosso di Montalcino 1985 $7.50 (6/30/88)
79   DEI ROSETI Rosso di Montalcino 1985 $9 (9/15/88)
78   DEI ROSETI Rosso di Montalcino 1985 $9 (7/15/89)

1984

83   BIONDI-SANTI Rosso di Montalcino Il Greppo 1984 $23 (8/31/88)
82   BIONDI-SANTI Rosso di Montalcino Il Greppo 1984 $23 (1/31/90)

1983

89   VILLA BANFI Rosso di Montalcino Centine 1983 $7 (4/30/87) BB
87   LA PODERINA Rosso di Montalcino 1983 $6.50 (12/01/85) BB
76   COL D'ORCIA Rosso di Montalcino 1983 $6 (6/30/87)

VINO NOBILE DI MONTEPULCIANO DOCG

1987

84   POLIZIANO Vino Nobile di Montepulciano 1987 $12 (3/15/91)
82   CECCHI Vino Nobile di Montepulciano 1987 $9 (11/30/90)
75   CONTI D'ATTIMIS Vino Nobile di Montepulciano Varnero 1987 $14 (9/15/90)

1986

87   CANTINE BAIOCCHI Vino Nobile di Montepulciano 1986 $15 (3/15/91)

ITALY
TUSCANY RED/*VINO NOBILE DI MONTEPULCIANO DOCG*

85   GEOGRAFICO Vino Nobile di Montepulciano Vigneti alla Cerraia 1986 $14.50 (7/15/91)
84   TALOSA Vino Nobile di Montepulciano Riserva 1986 $15 (7/15/91)
80   TENUTA TREROSE Vino Nobile di Montepulciano 1986 $16 (7/15/91)

1985

90   TENUTA TREROSE Vino Nobile di Montepulciano 1985 $11 (11/15/88)
89   POLIZIANO Vino Nobile di Montepulciano 1985 $13 (9/15/88)
86   AVIGNONESI Vino Nobile di Montepulciano 1985 $12 (2/15/88)
86   FASSATI Vino Nobile di Montepulciano Riserva 1985 $22 (11/30/89)
85   CANTINE BAIOCCHI Vino Nobile di Montepulciano Riserva 1985 $10 (11/30/89)
85   DEI Vino Nobile di Montepulciano Riserva 1985 $13 (4/15/90)
85   TENUTA TREROSE Vino Nobile di Montepulciano Riserva 1985 $19 (7/15/91)
82   MELINI Vino Nobile di Montepulciano 1985 $10 (4/15/90)
81   BIGI Vino Nobile di Montepulciano 1985 $11.50 (11/30/90)
81   CANTINA GATTAVECCHI Vino Nobile di Montepulciano Riserva 1985 $11 (11/30/89)
77   VITTORIO INNOCENTI Vino Nobile di Montepulciano 1985 $10 (3/31/90)
76   BOSCARELLI Vino Nobile di Montepulciano Riserva 1985 $15 (6/15/90)
68   BINDELLA Vino Nobile di Montepulciano Riserva 1985 $27 (10/31/90)

1983

86   E. CASASLTE Vino Nobile di Montepulciano 1983 $9 (11/30/87)
85   FATTORIA DI FOGNANO Vino Nobile di Montepulciano Riserva Talosa 1983 $7 (5/15/89) BB
77   CECCHI Vino Nobile di Montepulciano 1983 $9 (5/15/89)
74   MELINI Vino Nobile di Montepulciano Riserva 1983 $7.50 (6/30/88)

1982

77   BIGI Vino Nobile di Montepulciano Riserva 1982 $9 (1/31/88)
72   TALOSA Vino Nobile di Montepulciano Riserva 1982 $8.50 (4/15/88)

1981

86   AVIGNONESI Vino Nobile di Montepulciano 1981 $7.25 (10/01/85)
76   FATTORIA DI FOGNANO Vino Nobile di Montepulciano Riserva Talosa 1981 $8.50 (5/15/89)
71   BOSCARELLI Vino Nobile di Montepulciano 1981 $10 (7/01/86)
70   BOSCARELLI Vino Nobile di Montepulciano Riserva 1981 $11 (10/31/86)

1980

86   SANGUINETO Vino Nobile di Montepulciano Riserva 1980 $9 (10/31/86)
85   AVIGNONESI Vino Nobile di Montepulciano 1980 $6.75 (7/01/85)
84   BIGI Vino Nobile di Montepulciano Riserva 1980 $8 (9/01/85)

1978

73   FASSATI Vino Nobile di Montepulciano Riserva 1978 $8.50 (7/01/86)

VINO DA TAVOLA

1989

82   ISOLE E OLENA Antiche Tenute 1989 $6 (10/31/90) BB
80   ANTINORI Santa Cristina 1989 $7 (7/15/91)

1988

95   PODERE IL PALAZZINO Grosso Sanese 1988 (NA) (11/30/89) (HS)
93   FRESCOBALDI Mormoreto Predicato di Biturica 1988 (NA) (11/30/89) (HS)
88   PODERE IL PALAZZINO Grosso Sanese 1988 $29 (3/15/91)
86   CASTELLO DI GABBIANO Merlot 1988 $55 (7/15/91)
85   ANTINORI Santa Cristina 1988 $6.50 (1/31/91) BB
84   CASTELLO D'ALBOLA Acciaiolo 1988 $50 (4/15/91)
83   ISOLE E OLENA Antiche Tenute 1988 $6 (9/15/89) BB
80   FATTORIA DEI BARBI Brusco dei Barbi 1988 $9.50 (10/31/90)
80   VITTORIO INNOCENTI Acerone 1988 $13 (7/15/91)

1987

92   VIGNAMAGGIO Gherardino 1987 (NA) (11/30/89) (HS)
91   MONTE VERTINE Riserva 1987 $30 (3/15/91)
90   MONTE VERTINE Le Pergole Torte 1987 $41 (1/31/91)
90   PODERE IL PALAZZINO Grosso Sanese 1987 $25 (11/30/89) (HS)
90   ROCCA DELLE MACIE Ser Gioveto 1987 (NA) (11/30/89) (HS)
89   ORNELLAIA 1987 $46 (11/30/90)
89   CASTELLO DI VOLPAIA Balifico 1987 (NA) (11/30/89) (HS)
87   CASTELLARE DI CASTELLARE Coniale di Castellare 1987 $31 (10/31/90)
87   MONTE VERTINE Il Sodaccio 1987 $32 (1/31/91)
86   AVIGNONESI Grifi 1987 $21 (4/15/91)
86   CASTELLARE DI CASTELLINA I Sodi di San Niccolo 1987 $32 (4/15/91)
85   DEI ROSETI Belconvento 1987 $24 (3/15/91)
82   RIECINE La Gioia di Riecine 1987 $45 (4/30/91)
82   SASSICAIA 1987 $45 (3/15/91)
81   ANTINORI Santa Cristina 1987 $6 (4/30/89) BB
81   ISOLE E OLENA Antiche Tenute 1987 $4.50 (1/31/89) BB
78   CAPEZZANA Barco Reale 1987 $11.50 (7/15/91)

1986

95   SASSICAIA 1986 $50 (12/15/89)
94   CASTELLARE DI CASTELLINA I Sodi di San Niccolo 1986 $25 (11/30/89)

Key to Symbols

The scores reported here are the results of blind tastings conducted by our panel of senior editors. Wines that carry the initials below are results of individual tastings.

THE WINE SPECTATOR 100-POINT SCALE **95-100**—Classic, a great wine; **90-94**—Outstanding, superior character and style; **80-89**—Good to very good, a wine with special qualities; **70-79**—Average, drinkable wine that may have minor flaws; **60-69**—Below average, drinkable but not recommended; **50-59**—Poor, undrinkable, not recommended. "**+**"—With a score indicates a range; used primarily with barrel tastings to indicate a preliminary score.

SPECIAL DESIGNATIONS SS—Spectator Selection, CS—Cellar Selection, BB—Best Buy.

TASTER'S INITIALS (JG)—Jim Gordon, (HS)—Harvey Steiman, (JL)—James Laube, (JS)—James Suckling, (TM)—Thomas Matthews, (TR)—Terry Robards, (BT)—Barrel Tasting (these wines were tasted blind from barrel samples), (CA-date)—*California's Great Cabernets* by James Laube, (CH-date)—*California's Great Chardonnays* by James Laube, (VP-date)—*Vintage Port* by James Suckling.

DATE TASTED Dates in parentheses represent the issue in which the rating was published.

---

93   ORNELLAIA 1986 Rel: $25 Cur: $41 (12/15/89) CS
92   VITICCIO Prunaio 1986 $19 (3/31/90) SS
91   VIGNAMAGGIO Gherardino 1986 (NA) (11/30/89) (HS)
90   VILLA CILNIA Le Vignacce 1986 $19 (11/30/89)
90   FONTODI Flaccianello 1986 $29 (11/30/89) (HS)
90   CASTELLO DI GABBIANO R & R 1986 $38 (1/31/91)
90   MONTE VERTINE Il Sodaccio 1986 $30 (9/30/89)
90   MONTE VERTINE Le Pergole Torte 1986 $36 (9/30/89)
90   VISTARENNI Codirosso 1986 $22 (11/30/89)
88   MARTINI DI CIGALA San Giusto a Rentennano Percarlo 1986 $24 (11/30/89)
88   FONTODI Flaccianello 1986 Rel: $29 Cur: $31 (9/30/89)
87   FATTORIA DI AMA Vigna l'Apparita Merlot 1986 (NA) (11/30/89) (HS)
87   CASTELLO DI FONTERUTOLI Concerto di Fonterutoli 1986 $35 (3/15/91)
87   PODERE IL PALAZZINO Grosso Sanese 1986 $22 (2/15/89)
86   AVIGNONESI Grifi 1986 Rel: $18 Cur: $24 (1/31/89)
86   VILLA CILNIA Vocato 1986 $10.50 (5/15/89)
86   ISOLE E OLENA Cepparello 1986 $20 (9/30/89)
86   MONTE VERTINE Riserva 1986 $26 (9/30/89)
86   CASTELLO DI VOLPAIA Coltassala 1986 (NA) (11/30/89) (HS)
85   ALTESINO Alte d'Altesi 1986 $32 (7/15/89)
85   CASTELLO DI CACCHIANO RF 1986 $16.50 (6/15/90)
85   FATTORIA LA QUERCE Querciolaia 1986 (NA) (11/30/89) (HS)
84   ROCCA DELLE MACIE Gioveto 1986 $15 (2/15/89)
84   ROCCA DELLE MACIE Ser Gioveto 1986 $15 (11/30/89) (HS)
83   TERRICCI Antiche Terre de'Ricci 1986 $23 (5/15/90)
83   CASTELLO DI VOLPAIA Balifico 1986 $19 (4/30/89)
82   FATTORIA DI AMA Colline di Ama 1986 $9 (11/15/87)
82   S. FABIANO CALCINAIA Cerviolo 1986 $18.50 (3/31/90)
81   BADIA A COLTIBUONO Coltibuono Rosso 1986 $6.75 (7/31/88)
79   FATTORIA DEI BARBI Brusco dei Barbi 1986 $9 (4/30/89)
79   TOSCOLO Red Tuscan Table Wine 1986 $4.25 (1/31/89)
78   ISOLE E OLENA Antiche Tenute 1986 $5 (11/15/88)
76   CASTELLO DEI RAMPOLLA Sammarco 1986 $46 (3/15/91)
70   MARSILIO FICINO Poggio Il Pino 1986 $6 (7/31/89)
68   TERUZZI & PUTHOD Vigna Peperino 1986 $11 (1/31/90)

1985

96   CASTELLARE DI CASTELLINA I Sodi di San Niccolo 1985 $25 (5/31/88)
94   PODERE IL PALAZZINO Grosso Sanese 1985 $13 (12/15/87)
93   CASTELLO DI GABBIANO Ania 1985 $30 (1/31/90)
93   FATTORIA LA QUERCE La Corte 1985 $20 (11/30/89)
92   FATTORIA DI AMA Vigna l'Apparita Merlot 1985 (NA) (11/30/89) (HS)
92   ANTINORI Solàia 1985 Rel: $62 Cur: $96 (12/15/89)
92   BOSCARELLI 1985 $30 (2/15/89)
92   MARTINI DI CIGALA San Giusto a Rentennano Percarlo 1985 $25 (2/15/89)
92   SASSICAIA 1985 Rel: $48 Cur: $84 (5/15/89) CS
92   TERUZZI & PUTHOD Vigna Peperino 1985 $10.50 (10/31/88)
91   CASTELLO DI CACCHIANO RF 1985 $15.50 (8/31/88)
91   CAPEZZANA Ghiaie della Furba 1985 $20 (1/31/90)
91   FATTORIA DI FELSINA Fontalloro 1985 $24 (9/15/88)
91   FONTODI Flaccianello 1985 Rel: $23 Cur: $33 (1/31/89)
91   CASTELLO DI GABBIANO R & R 1985 $30 (3/31/90)
91   MONSANTO Tinscvil 1985 $22 (11/30/89) (HS)
91   MONTE VERTINE Il Sodaccio 1985 $25 (3/15/89)
91   SAN FELICE Vigorello 1985 $18 (11/30/89) (HS)
91   TERRICCI Antiche Terre de'Ricci 1985 $22.50 (3/15/89)
91   VIGNAMAGGIO Gherardino 1985 (NA) (11/30/89) (HS)
91   VINATIERRI Rosso 1985 (NA) (9/15/87) (HS)
91   CASTELLO DI VOLPAIA Balifico 1985 $21 (11/30/89) (HS)
90   CASTELLO DEI RAMPOLLA Sammarco 1985 (NA) (11/30/89) (HS)
90   RUFFINO Cabreo Il Borgo Predicato di Biturica 1985 $21 (9/30/89)
89   MONTE VERTINE Sangioveto 1985 $17 (8/31/88)
89   SAN FELICE Predicato di Biturica 1985 $25 (11/30/89) (HS)
89   SAN FELICE Vigorello 1985 $18 (9/15/90)
88   VILLA CILNIA Le Vignacce 1985 $20 (7/15/89)
88   MONSANTO Tinscvil 1985 $22 (9/15/90)
88   MONTE VERTINE Le Pergole Torte 1985 $33 (4/30/89)
88   ROCCA DELLE MACIE Ser Gioveto 1985 $15 (11/30/89) (HS)
88   VITICCIO Prunaio 1985 $18 (4/30/89)
88   CASTELLO DI VOLPAIA Coltassala 1985 $19 (11/30/89) (HS)
87   ANTINORI Tignanello 1985 $30 (4/15/90)
87   ISOLE E OLENA Cepparello 1985 $15 (11/15/88)
87   SAN FELICE Predicato di Biturica 1985 $25 (9/15/90)
86   FATTORIA LE CORTI Masso Tondo 1985 $20 (4/30/89)
86   LILLIANO Anagallis 1985 $34 (3/31/90)
86   DEI ROSETI Belconvento 1985 $23 (7/15/89)
85   AVIGNONESI Grifi 1985 Rel: $16.50 Cur: $27 (2/15/88)
85   BADIA A COLTIBUONO Sangioveto 1985 (NA) (11/30/89) (HS)
85   FATTORIA DEI BARBI Brusco dei Barbi 1985 $9 (10/15/88)
85   CASTELLO DI MONTE ANTICO 1985 $6.75 (6/30/88)
85   FATTORIA LA QUERCE Querciolaia 1985 $30 (2/15/89)
84   FATTORIA BAGGIOLINO Poggio Brandi 1985 $19 (9/15/89)
84   CASTELLO DI FONTERUTOLI Concerto di Fonterutoli 1985 $25 (2/15/89)
82   ALTESINO Palazzo Altesi 1985 $23 (10/31/90)
80   VILLA CAFAGGIO Solàtio Basilica 1985 $22 (9/30/89)
79   VILLA CAFAGGIO San Martino 1985 $20 (9/30/89)
78   VITTORIO INNOCENTI Acerone 1985 $9 (9/15/89)
77   CAPARZO Ca' del Pazzo 1985 $28 (5/15/90)
76   AMBRA Barco Reale 1985 $7 (4/15/88)
75   CASTELLO DI VOLPAIA Coltassala 1985 $19 (4/30/89)

1984

89   VILLA BANFI Cabernet Sauvignon Tavernelle 1984 $18 (1/31/88)
85   SASSICAIA 1984 $57 (3/15/89)

1983

95   FONTODI Flaccianello 1983 $19 (7/15/87)
93   BADIA A COLTIBUONO Sangioveto 1983 $20 (9/15/87) (HS)
93   MONTE VERTINE Il Sodaccio 1983 $19.50 (2/15/87)
91   AVIGNONESI Grifi 1983 Rel: $12 Cur: $22 (6/01/86)

90   MONTE VERTINE Le Pergole Torte 1983 $24.50 (2/15/87)
90   SAN FELICE Vigorello 1983 (NA) (11/30/89) (HS)
88   ALTESINO Palazzo Altesi 1983 $17.50 (2/15/88)
88   ANTINORI Tignanello 1983 $25 (12/15/89)
88   FRESCOBALDI Mormoreto Predicato di Biturica 1983 $34 (2/15/89)
88   CASTELLO DEI RAMPOLLA Sammarco 1983 $28 (9/15/88)
87   CASTELLARE DI CASTELLINA I Sodi di San Niccolo 1983 $18 (5/31/88)
87   MONSANTO Cabernet Sauvignon Nemo 1983 $28 (9/15/90)
87   SAN FELICE Predicato di Biturica 1983 (NA) (11/30/89) (HS)
86   CASTELLO DI FONTERUTOLI Concerto di Fonterutoli 1983 $15 (11/30/89) (HS)
86   FRESCOBALDI Mormoreto Predicato di Biturica 1983 $27 (1/31/88)
86   CASTELLO DI VOLPAIA Coltassala 1983 $22 (9/15/88)
85   BOSCARELLI 1983 $29 (6/30/88)
85   MONTE VERTINE 1983 $15 (2/15/87)
84   BADIA A COLTIBUONO Sangioveto 1983 $20 (11/30/89) (HS)
84   VINATIERRI Rosso 1983 $14 (9/15/87) (HS)
83   CASTELLO DI GABBIANO Ania 1983 $25 (7/15/87)
83   FATTORIA LA QUERCE La Corte 1983 $17 (11/30/89) (HS)
77   MARTINI DI CIGALA San Giusto a Rentennano Percarlo 1983 $13 (9/15/87)
75   CECCHI Spargolo Predicato di Cardisco 1983 $25 (3/15/91)

1982

92   SAN FELICE Predicato di Biturica 1982 Rel: $19 Cur: $19 (1/31/88) SS
91   ANTINORI Tignanello 1982 $37 (7/15/87) CS
90   MONTE VERTINE Le Pergole Torte 1982 $16.50 (7/16/86)
89   CASTELLARE DI CASTELLINA I Sodi di San Niccolo 1982 (NA) (9/15/87) (HS)
88   VILLA BANFI Cabernet Sauvignon Tavernelle 1982 $15 (8/01/85)
87   AVIGNONESI Grifi 1982 $10 (6/16/85)
87   BADIA A COLTIBUONO Sangioveto 1982 $21 (11/30/89) (HS)
87   SAN FELICE Vigorello 1982 $15 (11/30/89) (HS)
87   CASTELLO DI VOLPAIA Coltassala 1982 (NA) (9/15/87) (HS)
84   MONTE VERTINE Riserva 1982 $18 (2/15/87)
84   SAN FELICE Vigorello 1982 $15 (8/31/88)
84   SASSICAIA 1982 Rel: $45 Cur: $110 (7/31/87)
83   BADIA A COLTIBUONO Sangioveto 1982 $21 (9/15/88)
82   CASTELLO DI MONTE ANTICO 1982 $3.75 (4/01/86) BB
81   ANTINORI Solàia 1982 $62 (7/31/87)
68   CECCHI Spargolo Predicato di Cardisco 1982 $12 (9/30/89)

1981

90   MONTE VERTINE Riserva 1981 $15 (8/31/86)
90   CASTELLO DI VOLPAIA Coltassala 1981 (NA) (9/15/87) (HS)
87   BADIA A COLTIBUONO Sangioveto 1981 $21 (9/15/87) (HS)
87   CASTELLARE DI CASTELLINA I Sodi di San Niccolo 1981 (NA) (9/15/87) (HS)
87   MONTE VERTINE Le Pergole Torte 1981 $11.25 (7/16/85)
84   SAN FELICE Vigorello 1981 $13 (1/31/88)
79   EMILIO COSTANTI Vermiglio 1981 $7.50 (10/31/86)

1980

95   SAN FELICE Vigorello 1980 Rel: $12 Cur: $12 (2/28/87) SS

OTHER TUSCANY RED DOC

1989

83   AVIGNONESI Rosso di Montepulciano 1989 $12 (4/30/91)

1986

87   FRESCOBALDI Pomino Tenuta di Pomino 1986 Rel: $14 Cur: $14 (1/31/90)
86   LE PUPILLE Morellino di Scansano Riserva 1986 $16 (6/30/91)
81   CAPEZZANA Carmignano 1986 $15 (7/15/91)
81   IL COLLE Rosso delle Colline Lucchesi 1986 $7.50 (3/31/90)
80   AMBRA Carmignano 1986 $12.50 (5/15/89)

1985

93   FRESCOBALDI Pomino Tenuta di Pomino 1985 Rel: $12 Cur: $16 (9/15/88) SS
83   AMBRA Carmignano 1985 $10.50 (4/15/88)
83   CAPEZZANA Carmignano Riserva 1985 $25 (7/15/91)
80   VILLA IL POGGIOLO Carmignano Riserva 1985 $16 (5/15/90)

1984

79   AMBRA Carmignano 1984 $8.75 (12/31/87)

1983

88   AMBRA Carmignano 1983 $9 (7/16/86) BB

1982

87   MORBELLI Carema 1982 $21 (11/30/89)

TUSCANY WHITE/*VINO DA TAVOLA*

1989

90   CASTELLO D'ALBOLA Chardonnay 1989 $50 (2/15/91)
87   COL D'ORCIA Ghiaie Bianche 1989 $12 (12/31/90)
87   ISOLE E OLENA Chardonnay Collezione de Marchi 1989 $23 (7/15/91)
80   VILLA CILNIA Poggio Garbato 1989 $9.25 (7/15/91)
79   ANTINORI Galestro 1989 $7 (12/31/90)
74   PLACIDO 1989 $6 (7/15/91)

1988

87   AVIGNONESI Sauvignon Blanc Il Vignola 1988 $20 (10/15/89)
87   ISOLE E OLENA Chardonnay Collezione de Marchi 1988 $16 (9/15/89)
86   VILLA BANFI Chardonnay Fontanelle 1988 $11 (12/31/90)
86   FATTORIA DI FELSINA Berardenga I Sistri 1988 $24 (3/31/90)
86   NOZZOLE Chardonnay Vigneto Le Bruniche 1988 $9.25 (3/31/90)
85   ANTINORI Bianco Toscano 1988 $6.50 (10/15/89) BB
84   CAPEZZANA Chardonnay 1988 $14 (9/15/89)
84   NOZZOLE Chardonnay Vigneto Le Bruniche 1988 $10 (9/15/89)
83   CASTELLO DI GABBIANO Chardonnay Ariella 1988 $23 (1/31/91)
82   FATTORIA DI AMA Chardonnay Colline di Ama 1988 $17 (9/15/89)
79   CASTELLARE DI CASTELLINA Canonico di Castellare 1988 $18 (12/31/90)

78   VILLA BANFI Chardonnay Centine 1988 $8 (4/30/90)
73   ISOLE E OLENA Chardonnay Collezione de Marchi 1988 $17 (3/31/90)

1987

90   AVIGNONESI Chardonnay Il Marzocco 1987 $18 (9/15/89)
88   FONTODI Meriggio 1987 $17 (12/31/88)
87   CASTELLO DI GABBIANO Chardonnay Ariella 1987 $23 (3/31/90)
84   VILLA BANFI Chardonnay Centine 1987 $8 (3/31/89)
83   AVIGNONESI Terre di Cortona 1987 $18 (3/31/89)
82   FATTORIA DI AMA Chardonnay Colline di Ama 1987 $17 (9/15/89)
82   AVIGNONESI Chardonnay Il Marzocco 1987 $18 (3/31/90)
82   CAPEZZANA Chardonnay 1987 $14 (9/15/89)
82   FONTODI Meriggio 1987 $17 (3/31/90)
80   VILLA BANFI Chardonnay Fontanelle 1987 $16.50 (9/15/89)
79   S. FABIANO CALCINAIA Cerviolo 1987 $18.50 (3/31/90)
79   TOSCOLO Tuscan Table Wine 1987 $4.25 (12/31/88)
78   CASTELLO DI GABBIANO Bianco del Castello 1987 $8 (12/31/90)
78   RUFFINO Libaio 1987 $8.50 (9/15/89)
75   VILLA BANFI Pinot Grigio San Angelo 1987 $12 (11/15/88)
74   ANTINORI Galestro 1987 $6 (10/15/88)

1986

92   AVIGNONESI Chardonnay Il Marzocco 1986 $16 (2/15/88)
90   RUFFINO Cabreo Vigneto la Pietra 1986 $18 (9/15/89)
88   FATTORIA DI AMA Chardonnay Colline di Ama 1986 $17 (11/15/87)
87   AVIGNONESI Terre di Cortona 1986 $9.50 (2/15/88)
87   VILLA BANFI Chardonnay Fontanelle 1986 $16.50 (10/15/88)
86   VILLA BANFI Chardonnay Fontanelle 1986 $16.50 (9/15/89)
81   VILLA BANFI Chardonnay Centine 1986 $7 (12/31/87)
79   FATTORIA DI AMA Chardonnay Colline di Ama 1986 $17 (9/15/89)
79   RUFFINO Libaio 1986 $8 (11/15/87)
77   VILLA BANFI Pinot Grigio San Angelo 1986 $10 (12/15/87)
65   ANTINORI Galestro 1986 $6 (11/15/87)

1985

83   RUFFINO Cabreo Vigneto la Pietra 1985 $18 (9/15/89)
82   RUFFINO Cabreo La Pietra Predicato del Muschio 1985 $17 (10/15/88)
78   FRESCOBALDI Vergena Predicato del Selvante 1985 $25 (11/15/88)
77   ANTINORI Galestro 1985 $4 (4/30/87)
69   CASTELLO DI GABBIANO Chardonnay Ariella 1985 $25 (8/31/87)

1984

84   VILLA BANFI Chardonnay Fontanelle 1984 $10 (1/31/87)
72   CAPEZZANA Chardonnay 1984 $11 (10/15/86)

1983

90   RUFFINO Cabreo la Pietra Predicato del Muschio 1983 $17 (3/31/87)

NV

68   FRESCOBALDI Bianco NV $3.50 (12/15/87)

WHITE DOC

1989

84   TERUZZI & PUTHOD Vernaccia di San Gimignano Terre di Tufo 1989 $20 (12/31/90)
82   BARONE RICASOLI Vernaccia di San Gimignano 1989 $9 (4/15/91)
78   MELINI Vernaccia di San Gimignano Lydia 1989 $8 (7/15/91)
78   SAN QUIRICO Vernaccia di San Gimignano 1989 $8.50 (7/15/91)
75   TONI PAOLA Vernaccia di San Gimignano Ambra delle Torri 1989 $9.75 (7/15/91)

1988

81   ANGELO DEL TUFO Vernaccia di San Gimignano 1988 $7.50 (4/30/90)

1987

88   TERUZZI & PUTHOD Vernaccia di San Gimignano Terre di Tufo 1987 $11.50 (10/15/88)
82   CECCHI Vernaccia di San Gimignano 1987 $6 (5/15/89) BB
77   SALVUCCI Vernaccia di San Gimignano 1987 $5.50 (5/15/89)

1986

87   TERUZZI & PUTHOD Vernaccia di San Gimignano Riserva 1986 $7.50 (11/15/88) BB
85   FRESCOBALDI Pomino Tenuta di Pomino Il Benefizio 1986 $20 (3/31/90)

1985

79   FRESCOBALDI Pomino Tenuta di Pomino Il Benefizio 1985 $18.50 (10/15/88)
71   RICCARDO FALCHINI Vernaccia di San Gimignano 1985 $5 (4/30/87)

1983

63   FRESCOBALDI Pomino Tenuta di Pomino Il Benefizio 1983 $15 (6/30/87)
61   ZONIN Vernaccia di San Gimignano 1983 $5 (4/16/86)

1982

62   IL CIPRESSINO Vernaccia di San Gimignano 1982 $5 (8/31/87)

OTHER ITALY NORTH RED/*CABERNET DOC*

1988

84   LIVIO FELLUGA Cabernet Franc Collio 1988 $15 (6/30/91)
76   ENO-FRIULIA Cabernet Sauvignon Collio 1988 $12 (7/15/91)

1987

84   TIEFENBRUNNER Cabernet Alto Adige 1987 $9 (3/31/89)

1986

83   RUSSIZ SUPERIORE Cabernet Franc Collio 1986 $15 (9/15/88) (TM)
75   LIVIO FELLUGA Cabernet Franc Collio 1986 $14 (9/15/88) (TM)

1985

85   PLOZNER Cabernet Sauvignon Grave del Friuli 1985 $6 (9/15/88) (TM)
80   FANTINEL Cabernet Sauvignon Grave del Friuli 1985 $7 (7/31/87)

ITALY
OTHER ITALY NORTH RED/*CABERNET DOC*

1984
85   COLLAVINI Cabernet Sauvignon Grave del Friuli 1984 $8 (4/15/90) BB

1983
80   PLOZNER Cabernet Sauvignon Grave del Friuli Bollini 1983 $6 (9/15/88) (TM)
73   BOLLINI Cabernet Sauvignon Grave del Friuli 1983 $6.25 (7/31/87)

1982
87   SANTA MARGHERITA Cabernet Sauvignon Pramaggiore 1982 $5.50 (12/01/85) BB

RECIOTO DELLA VALPOLICELLA DOC

1985
86   ANSELMI Recioto della Valpolicella 1985 $19 (6/30/91)
83   BOLLA Recioto della Valpolicella Amarone 1985 $16 (10/31/88)
83   SANTI Recioto della Valpolicella 1985 $20 (6/30/91)

1983
90   LUIGI RIGHETTI Recioto della Valpolicella Amarone Capitel de' Roari 1983 $16 (2/15/89)
85   MASI Recioto della Valpolicella Amarone Campolongo 1983 $26 (4/15/88)
70   REMO FARINA Recioto della Valpolicella Amarone Classico 1983 $12.50 (3/31/90)

1982
79   SARTORI Recioto della Valpolicella Amarone Classico Superiore 1982 $11 (11/15/88)

1981
84   MASI Recioto della Valpolicella Amarone Classico 1981 $15 (10/31/88)
81   ZENATO Recioto della Valpolicella Amarone Classico 1981 $11 (3/15/89)
62   SCAMPERLE Recioto della Valpolicella Amarone Classico 1981 $11 (8/01/85)

1980
88   MASI Recioto della Valpolicella Amarone Mazzano 1980 $26 (10/31/88)
85   ALLEGRINI Recioto della Valpolicella Classico Amarone Superiore 1980 $13 (12/31/87)

1979
80   LA COLOMBAIA Recioto della Valpolicella Amarone 1979 $12 (7/01/86)

1978
77   SCAMPERLE Recioto della Valpolicella Amarone Classico 1978 $9.50 (9/01/84)

VALPOLICELLA DOC

1988
82   GUERRIERI RIZZARDI Valpolicella Poiega Classico 1988 $9 (12/15/89)

1987
79   GUERRIERI RIZZARDI Valpolicella Classico Superiore 1987 $6.50 (3/31/90)
78   MASI Valpolicella Classico Superiore 1987 $7.25 (12/31/90)

1986
78   BOLLA Valpolicella Vigneti di Jago Classico 1986 $12 (12/31/90)
71   BOLLA Valpolicella 1986 $6 (12/15/89)

1985
81   BOSCAINI Valpolicella Classico Superiore Marano 1985 $6 (9/15/88) BB
80   SARTORI Valpolicella Classico Superiore 1985 $4.75 (11/15/88) BB
77   BOLLA Valpolicella 1985 $5.50 (10/31/88)
76   MASI Valpolicella Classico Superiore 1985 $5 (5/31/88)

1983
78   ALLEGRINI Valpolicella Classico Superiore Palazzo della Torre 1983 $7 (12/31/87)
71   MASI Valpolicella Classico Serego Alighieri 1983 $9.50 (5/15/87)

VINO DA TAVOLA

1988
80   VIGNALTA Merlot 1988 $18 (4/15/91)

1987
92   CA' DEL BOSCO Maurizio Zanella 1987 $40 (4/15/90)
88   CA' DEL BOSCO Maurizio Zanella 1987 $40 (12/31/90)
87   ABBAZIA DI ROSAZZO Ronco dei Roseti 1987 $35 (7/15/91)
85   ABBAZIA DI ROSAZZO Pignolo 1987 $36 (6/30/91)
82   CA' DEL BOSCO Pinot Noir Pinero 1987 $69 (6/15/90)
82   PIGHIN Blended Red 1987 (NA) (9/15/88) (TM)
81   LIVON Schioppettino 1987 $18 (4/15/90)

1986
92   BELLAVISTA Solesine 1986 $30 (5/15/89)
88   BOLLA Creso Rosso 1986 $25 (4/15/90)
86   ANTONUTTI Poggio Alto 1986 $15 (4/15/90)
85   ABBAZIA DI ROSAZZO Ronco dei Roseti 1986 $22 (3/15/89)
80   RONCO DEL GNEMIZ Rosso 1986 $15 (3/31/89)
74   FARALTA Rosso del Friuli-Venezia Giulia 1986 $12.50 (4/15/90)
71   MACULAN Palazzotto 1986 $19 (3/31/89)

1985
92   CA' DEL BOSCO Maurizio Zanella 1985 Rel: $38 Cur: $38 (9/15/88)
91   VENEGAZZU Della Casa 1985 $25 (3/31/90)
86   ABBAZIA DI ROSAZZO Pignolo 1985 $22 (9/15/88) (TM)
85   BARONE FINI Cabernet Sauvignon Cabernello 1985 $9.75 (4/15/88)
84   FRANCESCO GRAVNER Rujno 1985 (NA) (9/15/88) (TM)
84   VALLE SELEZIONE ARALDICA L'Araldo Collina Friulana 1985 $20 (5/15/91)
82   CASTELCOSA Refosco 1985 (NA) (9/15/88) (TM)
77   MASI Campo Fiorin 1985 $11.50 (9/15/90)

1984
86   BERTANI Catullo 1984 $9 (2/15/89)

1983
87   ABBAZIA DI ROSAZZO Ronco dei Roseti 1983 $20 (9/15/88) (TM)
86   VENEGAZZU Della Casa 1983 $25 (2/15/89)
84   RONCHI DI CIALLA Schioppettino di Cialla 1983 $25 (3/31/89)
84   TEDESCHI Capitel San Rocco 1983 $11 (2/15/89)
81   BERTANI Catullo 1983 $9 (6/30/88)
81   MASI Campo Fiorin 1983 $7.50 (5/15/89) BB

1982
82   VENEGAZZU Della Casa 1982 $15 (7/15/87)

1981
88   MASI Campo Fiorin 1981 $8 (4/15/88) BB

1980
72   VENEGAZZU Della Casa 1980 $10 (2/15/87)
84   MASO CANTANGHEL Pinot Nero Altesino Riserva 1988 $33 (2/15/91)
76   BARONE FINI Cabernet Sauvignon Cabernello 1988 $10 (7/15/91)

OTHER RED DOC

1989
82   TENUTA MAZZOLINO Oltrepò Pavese Barbera 1989 $10 (4/15/91)
78   ZENATO Bardolino Classico Superiore 1989 $7.75 (7/15/91)

1988
84   LIVIO FELLUGA Merlot Collio 1988 $16 (7/15/91)
82   ENO-FRIULIA Merlot Collio 1988 $12 (4/30/91)
82   MASI Bardolino Classico Superiore 1988 $9 (5/15/91) BB
81   TENUTA IL BOSCO Pinot Nero Oltrepò Pavese 1988 $9.50 (6/30/91)
81   CASA GIRELLI Pinot Nero Trentino i Mesi 1988 $10 (2/15/91)

1987
84   BORGO CONVENTI Merlot Collio 1987 $15 (3/31/89)
77   CA' DEL BOSCO Franciacorta 1987 $16 (12/31/90)

1986
92   MACULAN Breganze Cabernet Fratta 1986 $29 (3/31/89)
85   MACULAN Breganze Rosso Brentino 1986 $9.50 (3/31/89)
82   GIOVANNI DRI Refosco Colli Orientali del Friuli 1986 $11 (9/15/89)
80   RUSSIZ SUPERIORE Merlot Collio 1986 $14 (9/15/88) (TM)
80   SARTORI Merlot Grave del Friuli 1986 $6.25 (11/15/88)
79   TORRESELLA Merlot Lison-Pramaggiore 1986 $5.75 (10/31/88)
75   JOSEF BRIGL Santa Maddalena 1986 $6.75 (10/15/88)

1985
83   CA' DEL BOSCO Franciacorta 1985 $11 (9/15/88)
83   FANTINEL Merlot Grave del Friuli 1985 $7 (7/31/87)
82   BOSCAINI Bardolino Classico Superiore Le Canne 1985 $6 (7/31/88) BB
80   GIROLAMO DORIGO Merlot Colli Orientali del Friuli Montsclapade 1985 $10 (4/15/88)
77   MASI Bardolino Classico 1985 $5 (5/31/88)
70   GIROLAMO DORIGO Pinot Nero Colli Orientali del Friuli Montsclapade 1985 $10 (4/15/88)
68   SARTORI Bardolino Classico Superiore 1985 $4.75 (11/15/88)

1984
80   MASI Bardolino Classico 1984 $5 (5/15/87) BB

1983
79   RONCHI DI CIALLA Refosco Colli Orientali del Friuli dal Peduncolo Rosso di Cialla 1983 $23 (3/31/89)
64   PLOZNER Merlot Grave del Friuli 1983 $5.50 (7/01/86)

1982
74   BOLLA Bardolino 1982 $5.50 (10/31/88)

OTHER ITALY NORTH WHITE/*CHARDONNAY DOC*

1989
84   COLTERENZIO Chardonnay Alto Adige 1989 $8 (1/31/91) BB
84   VENICA Chardonnay Dolegna del Collio 1989 $17 (1/31/91)
82   TIEFENBRUNNER Chardonnay Alto Adige 1989 $10 (7/15/91)
81   CASA GIRELLI Chardonnay Trentino i Mesi 1989 $8 (2/15/91) BB
77   JOSEF BRIGL Chardonnay Alto Adige 1989 $10 (7/15/91)
76   CA'VESCOVO Chardonnay Aqueileia 1989 $8 (7/15/91)
75   SANTA MARGHERITA Chardonnay Alto Adige 1989 $13 (12/31/90)

1988
88   ALOIS LAGEDER Chardonnay Alto Adige Buchhoiz 1988 $13 (9/15/89)
85   BOLLINI Chardonnay Trentino di Mezzocorona 1988 $7 (9/15/89)
85   MALPAGA Chardonnay Trentino 1988 $8 (9/15/89)
85   PIGHIN Chardonnay Grave del Friuli 1988 $8 (9/15/89)
85   ZENI Chardonnay Trentino 1988 $12 (9/15/89)
84   CAVIT Chardonnay Trentino 1988 $6 (9/15/89)
84   KETTMEIR Chardonnay Alto Adige 1988 $11 (9/15/89)
83   HOSTATTER Chardonnay Alto Adige 1988 (NA) (9/15/89)
82   LIVON Chardonnay Grave del Friuli Vigneto Medeuzza 1988 $14 (12/31/90)

---

80   PIGHIN Chardonnay Grave del Friuli Pighin di Capriva 1988 $9.25 (9/15/89)
78   PLOZNER Chardonnay Grave del Friuli 1988 $6 (9/15/89)

1987

84   BOLLINI Chardonnay Trentino di Mezzocorona 1987 $7.25 (9/15/89)
84   POJER E SANDRI Chardonnay Trentino 1987 $8 (9/15/89)
80   ISTITUTO AGRARIO PROVINCIALE Chardonnay Trentino 1987 $10 (9/15/89)
79   MASI Chardonnay Trentino Rosabel 1987 (NA) (9/15/89)
75   MALPAGA Chardonnay Trentino 1987 $8 (9/15/89)
70   SARTORI Chardonnay Grave del Friuli 1987 $6.25 (11/15/88)

1986

85   CA' DEL BOSCO Chardonnay Franciacorta 1986 $38 (9/15/89)
85   PLOZNER Chardonnay Grave del Friuli Riserva 1986 $6 (9/15/88)
82   ALOIS LAGEDER Chardonnay Alto Adige Loewengang 1986 $19 (9/15/89)
81   PLOZNER Chardonnay Grave del Friuli 1986 $8 (9/15/88)
78   SAN MICHELE Chardonnay Alto Adige 1986 $8.50 (10/15/88)
75   CANTINE MEZZACORONA Chardonnay Trentino 1986 $6 (12/31/87)
65   JOSEF BRIGL Chardonnay Alto Adige 1986 $8 (10/15/88)
60   CASTEL SAN VALENTINO Chardonnay Alto Adige Egart 1986 $6.25 (12/15/87)

1985

90   ALOIS LAGEDER Chardonnay Alto Adige Loewengang 1985 $19 (9/15/89)
86   CA' DEL BOSCO Chardonnay Franciacorta 1985 $38 (10/15/88)
82   POJER E SANDRI Chardonnay Trentino 1985 $7.50 (9/15/89)
71   SANTA MARGHERITA Chardonnay Alto Adige 1985 $8.50 (11/15/87)

1984

79   SANTA MARGHERITA Chardonnay Alto Adige 1984 $6.50 (12/16/85)

1983

58   CONSORZIO VITICOLTORI ALTO ADIGE Chardonnay Alto Adige 1983 $4 (11/01/85)

1982

80   ISTITUTO AGRARIO PROVINCIALE Chardonnay Trentino 1982 $10.50 (9/15/89)

CHARDONNAY VINO DA TAVOLA

1989

89   MASO CANTANGHEL Chardonnay Altesino Vigna Piccola 1989 $25 (1/31/91)
88   RONCO DEL GNEMIZ Chardonnay 1989 $27 (7/15/91)
84   PUIATTI Chardonnay 1989 $17 (3/31/91)
84   VIGNE DAL LEON Chardonnay Tullio Zamò 1989 $27 (7/15/91)
80   ENO-FRIULIA Chardonnay 1989 $12 (3/31/91)
80   JERMANN Chardonnay 1989 $17.50 (3/31/91)
78   TORRE ROSAZZA Chardonnay 1989 $15 (2/15/91)

1988

87   BORTOLUZZI Chardonnay 1988 $11 (9/15/89)
86   LA CASTELLADA Chardonnay 1988 $14 (3/31/90)
86   JERMANN Chardonnay Dreams 1988 $40 (4/30/90)
84   MARIN RONCO FORNAZ Chardonnay 1988 (NA) (9/15/89)
83   CA'RONESCA Chardonnay 1988 $11 (9/15/88)
83   TORRESELLA Chardonnay 1988 $6 (9/15/89)
82   MARCO FELLUGA Chardonnay 1988 $9 (9/15/89)
82   FOSSI Chardonnay dell' Alto Adige 1988 $11.50 (7/15/91)
81   TORRE ROSAZZA Chardonnay 1988 (NA) (9/15/89)
80   GUERRIERI RIZZARDI Chardonnay 1988 (NA) (9/15/89)
80   VIGNALTA Chardonnay Selezione Vendemmia 1988 $18 (2/15/91)
79   LA CADALORA Chardonnay della Vallagarina 1988 $11.25 (9/15/89)
77   VENEGAZZU Chardonnay 1988 $8.50 (9/15/89)

1987

90   MACULAN Chardonnay 1987 $22 (9/15/89)
90   RONCO DEL GNEMIZ Chardonnay 1987 $18 (9/15/89)
89   MACULAN Chardonnay Ferrata 1987 $240/3L (9/15/89)
85   JERMANN Chardonnay 1987 $15 (9/15/89)
84   LA CADALORA Chardonnay della Vallagarina 1987 $8.25 (3/31/89)
83   BELLAVISTA Chardonnay Uccellanda 1987 $30 (9/15/89)
83   STELIO GALLO Chardonnay 1987 (NA) (9/15/89)
82   CASTELCOSA Chardonnay 1987 $12.50 (9/15/89)
82   VOLPE PASINI Chardonnay 1987 (NA) (9/15/89)
80   MARCO FELLUGA Chardonnay 1987 $9 (9/15/89)
80   JERMANN Chardonnay 1987 $15 (9/15/88)
79   TENUTA VILLANOVA Chardonnay 1987 $7 (11/15/88)
76   PIGHIN Chardonnay 1987 $8.50 (9/15/88)
72   BORTOLUZZI Chardonnay 1987 $11 (5/15/89)

1986

92   BELLAVISTA Chardonnay Uccellanda 1986 $30 (9/15/89)
90   FRANCESCO GRAVNER Chardonnay di Oslavia 1986 (NA) (9/15/88)
87   MACULAN Chardonnay 1986 $18 (9/15/89)
85   CASTELCOSA Chardonnay 1986 $9.50 (9/15/89)
83   CASTELCOSA Chardonnay Pra di Pradis 1986 $13 (9/15/89)
82   ABBAZIA DI ROSAZZO Chardonnay 1986 $12 (4/15/88)
81   STELIO GALLO Chardonnay 1986 (NA) (9/15/89)
80   RONCO DEL GNEMIZ Chardonnay 1986 $12.50 (4/15/88)
79   JERMANN Chardonnay 1986 $12 (10/15/88)
79   TORRESELLA Chardonnay 1986 $5.75 (3/31/89)
73   FRANCESCO PECORARI Chardonnay Vigna di S. Lorenzo 1986 $10 (12/15/87)

1985

91   JERMANN Chardonnay 1985 $12 (9/15/89)
87   MACULAN Chardonnay 1985 $22 (9/15/89)
61   FANTINEL Chardonnay 1985 $7 (6/30/87)

1984

87   MACULAN Chardonnay 1984 $25 (9/15/89)

1983

51   POJER E SANDRI Chardonnay di Faedo 1983 $6.50 (6/16/86)

NV

92   JERMANN Chardonnay Dreams NV $34 (3/31/90)

PINOT GRIGIO DOC

1989

85   PUIATTI Pinot Grigio Collio 1989 $17 (3/31/91)
83   TIEFENBRUNNER Pinot Grigio Alto Adige 1989 $10 (6/30/91)
81   CA'RONESCA Pinot Grigio Colli Orientali del Friuli 1989 $19 (3/31/91)
80   ENO-FRIULIA Pinot Grigio Collio 1989 $12 (3/31/91)
79   COLTERENZIO Pinot Grigio Alto Adige 1989 $10 (3/31/91)
79   SUBIDA DI MONTE Pinot Grigio Collio 1989 $10.50 (7/15/91)
78   LIVIO FELLUGA Pinot Grigio Colli Orientali del Friuli 1989 $18 (3/31/91)

1987

82   PIGHIN Pinot Grigio Grave del Friuli 1987 $9 (9/15/88)
77   ABBAZIA DI ROSAZZO Pinot Grigio Colli Orientali del Friuli 1987 $15 (9/15/88)
77   LIVIO FELLUGA Pinot Grigio Colli Orientali del Friuli 1987 $15 (9/15/88)
74   CA'RONESCA Pinot Grigio Collio 1987 $14.50 (9/15/88)

1986

82   BOLLINI Pinot Grigio Valdadige 1986 $6.50 (3/31/88) BB
80   ABBAZIA DI ROSAZZO Pinot Grigio Colli Orientali del Friuli 1986 $12 (4/15/88)
78   BOLLA Pinot Grigio Alto Adige 1986 $8.50 (10/15/88)
78   BARONE FINI Pinot Grigio Valdadige 1986 $6 (3/31/88)
78   RONCO DEL GNEMIZ Pinot Grigio Colli Orientali del Friuli 1986 $12.50 (4/15/88)
76   CANTINE MEZZACORONA Pinot Grigio Trentino 1986 $10 (3/31/88)
75   SAN MICHELE Pinot Grigio Alto Adige 1986 $9 (10/15/88)
75   CASTEL SAN VALENTINO Pinot Grigio Alto Adige di Magre 1986 $6.50 (12/15/87)
74   CANTINE MEZZACORONA Pinot Grigio Trentino 1986 $10 (12/31/87)

1985

80   CASTEL SAN VALENTINO Pinot Grigio Alto Adige di Magre 1985 $6.25 (11/15/87)
77   SANTA MARGHERITA Pinot Grigio Alto Adige 1985 $12 (2/28/87)
74   FANTINEL Pinot Grigio Grave del Friuli 1985 $7 (6/30/87)
73   LA COLOMBAIA Pinot Grigio Valdadige 1985 $7 (4/30/87)
73   STEVERJAN Pinot Grigio Collio 1985 $9.50 (2/28/87)
69   BOLLINI Pinot Grigio Valdadige 1985 $6.25 (4/30/87)

1984

86   BOLLINI Pinot Grigio Valdadige 1984 $5.50 (2/01/86) BB
78   PLOZNER Pinot Grigio Grave del Friuli 1984 $4.50 (11/16/85) BB
70   SANTA MARGHERITA Pinot Grigio Alto Adige 1984 $9 (4/16/86)

SAUVIGNON BLANC DOC

1989

87   SUBIDA DI MONTE Sauvignon Collio 1989 $11 (7/15/91)
84   CA'RONESCA Sauvignon Colli Orientali del Friuli del Podere 1989 $19 (4/15/91)
83   ABBAZIA DI ROSAZZO Sauvignon Colli Orientali del Friuli 1989 $19 (7/15/91)
83   LA VIARTE Sauvignon Colli Orientali del Friuli 1989 $19.50 (7/15/91)

1987

85   CA'RONESCA Sauvignon Colli Orientali del Friuli del Podere 1987 $15 (9/15/88)
85   CA'RONESCA Sauvignon Blanc Collio 1987 (NA) (9/15/88)
83   ABBAZIA DI ROSAZZO Sauvignon Colli Orientali del Friuli 1987 $15 (9/15/88)
83   RUSSIZ SUPERIORE Sauvignon Blanc Collio 1987 (NA) (9/15/88)
81   PIGHIN Sauvignon Blanc Collio 1987 $12.50 (9/15/88)
80   LIVIO FELLUGA Sauvignon Blanc Colli Orientali del Friuli 1987 $15 (9/15/88)

1986

86   FRANCESCO GRAVNER Sauvignon Blanc Collio 1986 (NA) (9/15/88)
83   ABBAZIA DI ROSAZZO Sauvignon Colli Orientali del Friuli 1986 $12 (4/15/88)

1984

65   CA'BOLANI Sauvignon Aquileia 1984 $5.25 (6/16/86)

TOCAI FRIULANO DOC

1989

82   VENICA Tocai Friulano Collio 1989 $15 (2/15/91)
81   LIVIO FELLUGA Tocai Friulano Colli Orientali del Friuli 1989 $15.50 (4/15/91)
77   VIGNE DAL LEON Tocai Friulano Colli Orientali del Friuli 1989 $18.50 (7/15/91)

1988

82   LIVON Tocai Friulano Collio Vigneto di Ruttars 1988 $15 (12/31/90)

1987

88   CA'RONESCA Tocai Friulano Collio 1987 (NA) (9/15/88)
85   LE DUE TERRE Tocai Friulano Colli Orientali del Friuli 1987 $10 (9/15/88)
85   SCHIOPETTO Tocai Friulano Collio 1987 (NA) (9/15/88)
82   LIVIO FELLUGA Tocai Friulano Colli Orientali del Friuli 1987 $13 (9/15/88)
80   ABBAZIA DI ROSAZZO Tocai Friulano Colli Orientali del Friuli 1987 $14 (9/15/88)

1986

78   DORO PRINCIC Tocai Friulano Collio 1986 $11 (4/15/88)
75   RONCO DEL GNEMIZ Tocai Friulano Colli Orientali del Friuli 1986 $11 (4/15/88)
72   FRANCESCO PECORARI Tocai Friulano Collio Vigna di S. Lorenzo 1986 $9 (12/15/87)

OTHER VINO DA TAVOLA

1989

89   ABBAZIA DI ROSAZZO Ronco delle Acacie 1989 $36 (7/15/91)
88   JERMANN Vintage Tunina 1989 $35 (4/15/91)
87   JERMANN Pinot Bianco 1989 $17.50 (4/15/91)
84   ABBAZIA DI ROSAZZO Ronco di Corte 1989 $27 (7/15/91)
84   JERMANN Sauvignon 1989 $17.50 (4/15/91)
84   JERMANN Vinnae da Vinnaioli 1989 $17.50 (4/15/91)

ITALY
OTHER ITALY NORTH WHITE/OTHER VINO DA TAVOLA

84   MACULAN Dindarello 1989 $24 (7/15/91)
82   JERMANN Pinot Grigio 1989 $17.50 (3/31/91)
82   RONCO DEL GNEMIZ Müller Thurgau 1989 $18.50 (7/15/91)
74   MONTEVINO Pinot Grigio del Veneto 1989 $6.50 (7/15/91)

1988

73   SANTA MARGHERITA Cuvée Margherita del Veneto Orientale 1988 $11 (12/31/90)

1987

88   JERMANN Traminer 1987 (NA) (9/15/88)
86   ABBAZIA DI ROSAZZO Ronco delle Acacie 1987 (NA) (9/15/88)
86   BERTANI Catullo 1987 $8 (3/31/89)
83   MACULAN Prato di Canzio 1987 $17 (10/15/89)
82   FRANCESCO GRAVNER Vinograd Breg 1987 (NA) (9/15/88)
80   RUSSIZ SUPERIORE Roncuz 1987 (NA) (9/15/88)
79   JERMANN Vinnae 1987 (NA) (9/15/88)
78   JERMANN Pinot Grigio 1987 $15 (9/15/88)
78   MASI Masianco 1987 $6.75 (5/15/89)

1986

88   JERMANN Vintage Tunina 1986 $26 (9/15/88)
85   LIVIO FELLUGA Terre Alta 1986 $15 (9/15/88)
79   JERMANN Pinot Bianco 1986 $10 (10/15/88)
79   MASI Masianco 1986 $6.75 (10/15/88)
79   DORO PRINCIC Riesling 1986 $11 (4/15/88)

1985

91   ABBAZIA DI ROSAZZO Ronco delle Acacie 1985 (NA) (9/15/88)
84   STELIO GALLO Sauvignon Blanc 1985 (NA) (9/15/88)
82   CONTE CE CUCCANEA Collavini 1985 (NA) (9/15/88)
62   MASI Masianco 1985 $6 (4/30/87)

1984

86   SANTA MARGHERITA Luna del Feldi di Rovere 1984 $12.50 (1/01/86)

NV

81   FRANCO FURLAN Tai di Castelcosa NV $16 (4/30/90)

OTHER WHITE DOC

1989

85   PUIATTI Pinot Bianco Collio 1989 $17 (4/15/91)
82   BOSCAINI Soave Classico Monteleone 1989 $8 (6/30/91) BB
81   ANSELMI Soave Classico Superiore 1989 $8 (7/15/91)
81   BOLLA Soave Classico Vigneti di Castellaro 1989 $12 (12/31/90)
80   ZENATO Bianco di Custoza Sole del Benaco 1989 $9 (6/30/91)
78   FOSS MARAI Prosecco di Valdobbiadene 1989 $7.50 (12/31/90)
78   DORO PRINCIC Pinot Bianco Collio 1989 $14 (7/15/91)
76   ANSELMI Soave Classico Capitel Foscarino 1989 $20 (7/15/91)

1988

85   LA VIARTE Colli Orientali del Friuli Ribolla 1988 $18 (12/31/90)
78   CA' DEL BOSCO Franciacorta 1988 $16.50 (4/30/90)

1987

85   MACULAN Breganze Bianco Breganze di Breganze 1987 $7.50 (5/15/89) BB
84   CA'RONESCA Pinot Bianco Collio 1987 (NA) (9/15/88)
84   RUSSIZ SUPERIORE Pinot Bianco Collio 1987 (NA) (9/15/88)
79   FRANCESCO GRAVNER Ribolla Gialla Collio 1987 (NA) (9/15/88)
77   FRANCESCO GRAVNER Riesling Collio Italico 1987 (NA) (9/15/88)

1986

86   SCHIOPETTO Pinot Bianco Collio 1986 (NA) (9/15/88)
85   CA' DEL BOSCO Franciacorta 1986 $13 (10/15/88)
79   ABBAZIA DI ROSAZZO Ribolla Gialla Colli Orientali del Friuli 1986 $12 (4/15/88)
77   CASTEL SAN VALENTINO Pinot Bianco Alto Adige Tenuta Schulthaus 1986 $6.25 (12/15/87)
74   DORO PRINCIC Pinot Bianco Collio 1986 $11 (4/15/88)

1985

78   CAMPAGNOLA Soave Classico 1985 $3.25 (4/15/87) BB
74   PIEROPAN Soave Classico 1985 $7.25 (4/30/87)
70   MASI Soave Classico Col Baraca 1985 $8 (4/30/87)

1984

62   MASI Soave Classico Col Baraca 1984 $7.50 (4/16/86)

OTHER ITALY RED/RED DOC

1989

89   MASTROBERARDINO Lacryma Christi del Vesuvio 1989 $14 (7/15/91)
83   LUNGAROTTI Torgiano Torre di Giano 1989 $11 (7/15/91)
81   CASAL RONCHER Montepulciano d'Abruzzo 1989 $6 (6/30/91) BB
75   UMANI RONCHI Montepulciano d'Abruzzo 1989 $5 (2/15/91)

1988

84   DR. COSIMO TAURINO Salice Salentino Rosato 1988 $7.25 (3/15/91) BB
83   ANTONIO & ELIO MONTI Montepulciano d'Abruzzo 1988 $6.25 (2/15/91) BB
80   CASAL THAULERO Montepulciano d'Abruzzo 1988 $5 (5/31/90) BB
80   ZONIN Montepulciano d'Abruzzo 1988 $6 (6/30/91) BB
78   BARONE CORNACCHIA Montepulciano d'Abruzzo 1988 $5 (12/31/90)

1987

85   FATTORIA PARADISO Sangiovese di Romagna Riserva Superiore Vigna delle Lepri 1987 $16 (7/15/91)
84   DR. COSIMO TAURINO Salice Salentino Rosato 1987 $6.50 (12/31/89) BB
83   LUNGAROTTI Torgiano Rubesco 1987 $11 (5/15/91)
80   CAMILLO MONTORI Montepulciano d'Abruzzo 1987 $8 (3/31/90)
78   ZONIN Montepulciano d'Abruzzo 1987 $4.50 (3/31/90)

1986

87   MASTROBERARDINO Taurasi 1986 $18 (7/15/91)

1985

85   DR. COSIMO TAURINO Salice Salentino Riserva 1985 $8 (2/15/91) BB
84   ADANTI Montefalco d'Arquata 1985 $7.75 (7/31/88)
84   MASTROBERARDINO Taurasi Riserva 1985 $21.50 (6/30/91)
84   CASTELLO DI SALLE Montepulciano d'Abruzzo 1985 $15 (6/15/90) BB
83   RIVERA Castel del Monte Il Falcone Riserva 1985 $16.50 (12/31/90)
83   SASSO Aglianico del Vulture 1985 $11 (3/15/89)
79   CITRA Montepulciano d'Abruzzo 1985 $4.50 (7/31/87)
74   LUNGAROTTI Torgiano Rubesco 1985 $11 (9/15/89)
70   D'ANGELO Aglianico del Vulture 1985 $18 (9/15/89)
70   ARPA CLASSICA Sangiovese di Romagna 1985 $4 (12/31/87)

1984

74   BRUNO NICODEMI Montepulciano d'Abruzzo Dei Colli Venia 1984 $5.50 (11/15/87)

1983

86   CASAL THAULERO Montepulciano d'Abruzzo 1983 $6.50 (6/30/87) BB
81   DR. COSIMO TAURINO Salice Salentino Rosso Riserva 1983 $6.50 (12/15/89) BB
81   ZONIN Montepulciano d'Abruzzo 1983 $4 (5/16/86) BB
77   ADANTI Montefalco Sagrantino d'Arquata 1983 $12.25 (10/15/88)

1982

84   CONSORZIO VITICOLTORI DEL VULTURE Aglianico del Vulture 1982 $6 (9/15/88) BB
82   DR. COSIMO TAURINO Salice Salentino 1982 $6 (3/31/89) BB
75   MASTROBERARDINO Taurasi 1982 $13 (7/15/87)

1981

85   DR. COSIMO TAURINO Brindisi Patriglione 1981 $14 (12/31/90)
81   DR. COSIMO TAURINO Salice Salentino Riserva 1981 $6 (3/31/88) BB
78   MASTROBERARDINO Taurasi Riserva 1981 Rel: $21 Cur: $21 (2/15/89)

1980

84   LUNGAROTTI Torgiano Rubesco Monticchio Riserva 1980 $27 (7/15/91)
84   DR. COSIMO TAURINO Salice Salentino Riserva 1980 $5 (12/15/87) BB
75   MASTROBERARDINO Taurasi Riserva 1980 Rel: $15 Cur: $15 (9/15/89)

1979

82   DR. COSIMO TAURINO Brindisi Patriglione Riserva 1979 $12 (3/31/89)
80   VALENTINI Montepulciano d'Abruzzo 1979 $28 (2/15/89)
77   LUNGAROTTI Torgiano Rubesco 1979 $8.50 (1/01/86)
65   CITRA Montepulciano d'Abruzzo Rubino 1979 $5.75 (7/31/87)

1978

82   LUNGAROTTI Torgiano Rubesco Monticchio Riserva 1978 $23 (9/15/89)

1977

93   STRUZZIERO Taurasi Riserva 1977 Rel: $22.50 Cur: $24 (8/31/86) CS
92   MASTROBERARDINO Taurasi Riserva 1977 Rel: $28 Cur: $51 (10/16/84) CS

VINO DA TAVOLA

1989

87   MASTROBERARDINO Avellanio 1989 $10.50 (7/15/91)

1987

84   GIROLAMO DORIGO Montsclapade 1987 $25 (2/15/91)
77   REGALEALI Rosso 1987 $11 (12/15/89)
73   SOLICHIATA Torrepalino 1987 $5.75 (4/15/90)

1986

83   PAOLA DI MAURO Vigna del Vassalle 1986 $12 (3/31/90)
82   TORRE GAIA Il Dugentino 1986 $5 (9/15/88)
80   PAOLA DI MAURO Colle Picchioni 1986 $15 (3/31/90)

1985

92   A. BERTELLI I Fossaretti 1985 $34 (12/31/90)
74   RIGALEALI Conte Tasca d'Almerita 1985 $7.25 (4/15/88)
72   MIRAFIORE Z 1985 $4 (1/31/87)
71   CORVO Rosso 1985 $5.75 (9/15/88)
70   VALLANIA Terre Rosse 1985 $9 (3/31/90)

1984

92   CORVO Duca di Salaparuta Duca Enrico 1984 $27 (9/15/89)
84   REGALEALI Rosso del Conte 1984 $19 (7/31/89)

1983

85   LUNGAROTTI Cabernet Sauvignon 1983 $18 (5/15/91)
80   FATTORIA PARADISO Barbarossa 1983 $13.50 (3/15/89)
76   VILLA MATILDE Falerno 1983 $5 (5/15/87)

1982

77   LUNGAROTTI San Giorgio 1982 $34 (7/15/91)

1981

86   DR. COSIMO TAURINO Notarpanaro 1981 $9 (5/15/91)

1979

79   LUNGAROTTI Cabernet Sauvignon 1979 $11 (2/15/87)
75   LUNGAROTTI San Giorgio 1979 $18 (3/15/87)

1978

84   LUNGAROTTI San Giorgio 1978 $18.50 (4/16/85)
80   DR. COSIMO TAURINO Notarpanaro 1978 $8 (3/31/89)

1975

78   DR. COSIMO TAURINO Notarpanaro 1975 $8 (4/15/88)

OTHER ITALY WHITE/*VINO DA TAVOLA*

1990

80   SETTESOLI Bianco Feudo dei Fiori 1990 $9 (6/30/91)
79   SETTESOLI Bianco 1990 $7 (7/15/91)

1989

86   ANTINORI Castello della Sala Borro della Sala 1989 $11.50 (1/31/91)
84   MASTROBERARDINO Plinius D'Irpinia Bianco 1989 $17 (7/15/91)
82   REGALEALI Nozze d'Oro 1989 $20 (7/15/91)
81   CARLO HAUNER Salina Bianco 1989 $11.50 (7/15/91)
81   LUNGAROTTI Pinot Grigio 1989 $11 (3/31/91)
79   FATTORIA PARADISO Pagadebit di Romagna Secco Vigna Dello Spungone 1989 $13 (7/15/91)
79   PRATOSCURO 1989 $18 (12/31/90)
77   LUNGAROTTI Chardonnay 1989 $11 (3/31/91)

1988

89   ANTINORI Castello della Sala Cervaro della Sala 1988 $21 (1/31/91)
84   TORREBIANCO Chardonnay 1988 $12.50 (9/15/88)
83   FATTORIA PARADISO Chardonnay Emilia-Romagna 1988 $10 (9/15/89)
82   LUNGAROTTI Chardonnay 1988 $10 (9/15/89)

1987

84   TORREBIANCO Chardonnay 1987 $12.50 (9/15/88)
83   ANTINORI Castello della Sala Cervaro della Sala 1987 $20 (4/30/90)
83   LUNGAROTTI Chardonnay 1987 $10.50 (9/15/89)
81   CORVO Duca di Salaparuta Bianca di Valguarnera 1987 $34 (12/31/90)
78   TORREBIANCO Chardonnay 1987 $12.50 (12/31/90)
77   ANTINORI Castello della Sala Borro della Sala 1987 $10 (10/15/89)
76   FOLONARI Chardonnay 1987 $5 (9/15/89)

1986

76   ANTINORI Castello della Sala Cervaro della Sala 1986 $6 (12/31/87)
73   ADANTI Arquata de Bevagna 1986 $6.50 (10/15/88)

1985

90   ANTINORI Castello della Sala Cervaro della Sala 1985 $18 (12/15/87)
87   LUNGAROTTI Chardonnay I Palazzi 1985 $16 (9/15/89)
75   VILLA MATILDE Falerno 1985 $5 (2/28/87)

1984

71   CORVO Blanco 1984 $5 (11/01/85)

1983

79   FABIO BERIN Berin 1983 $9.75 (10/15/86)
68   LUNGAROTTI Chardonnay I Palazzi 1983 $16 (2/28/87)

WHITE DOC

1989

89   COLLE DEI BARDELLINI Vermentino Riviera Ligure di Ponent Vigna ''U Munte'' 1989 $18 (1/31/91)
84   MASTROBERARDINO Fiano di Avellino Vignadora 1989 $30 (7/15/91)
83   VILLA BIANCHI Verdicchio dei Castelli di Jesi Classico 1989 $7 (6/30/91) BB
83   VASELLI Orvieto Classico Torre Sant' Andrea 1989 $11 (12/31/90)
81   FATTORIA PARADISO Albana di Romagna Secco Vigna Dell'Olivo 1989 $13 (7/15/91)
81   BARONE RICASOLI Orvieto Classico Secco 1989 $8 (4/15/91) BB
80   ANTINORI Orvieto Classico Campogrande Secco 1989 $7.25 (7/15/91)
77   FALESCO Est! Est!! Est!!! di Montefiascone Poggio dei Gelsi 1989 $12 (7/15/91)
77   ZENATO Lugana San Benedetto 1989 $9.25 (7/15/91)
76   MASTROBERARDINO Lacryma Christi del Vesuvio 1989 $13 (7/15/91)
76   VASELLI Orvieto Classico Torre Sant' Andrea 1989 $14 (7/15/91)
75   VASELLI Orvieto Classico Secco 1989 $7.75 (7/15/91)

1988

79   MASTROBERARDINO Fiano di Avellino Apianum Vigna d'Oro 1988 $25 (4/30/90)
73   BUCCI Verdicchio dei Castelli di Jesi Classico 1988 $14 (12/31/90)

1987

89   MASTROBERARDINO Lacryma Christi del Vesuvio 1987 $9 (3/31/89)
78   ANTINORI Orvieto Classico 1987 $5 (5/15/89)
78   RUFFINO Orvieto Classico 1987 $6.25 (5/15/89)

1986

79   MASTROBERARDINO Greco di Tufo Vignadangelo 1986 $15 (10/15/89)
78   MASTROBERARDINO Fiano di Avellino Vignadora 1986 $22.50 (10/15/89)

1985

86   MASTROBERARDINO Greco di Tufo Vignadangelo 1985 $13.50 (5/31/87)
83   MASTROBERARDINO Fiano di Avellino Vignadora 1985 $25 (5/31/87)
82   RUFFINO Orvieto Classico 1985 $5 (10/31/86) BB
72   ANTINORI Orvieto Classico 1985 $5 (4/30/87)
72   MACHIAVELLI Orvieto Classico 1985 $4 (4/30/87)

1984

91   STRUZZIERO Greco di Tufo 1984 $7.50 (9/15/86)
82   FONTANA CANDIDA Frascati Superiore 1984 $5 (1/01/86) BB
80   VALENTINI Trebbiano d'Abruzzo 1984 $20 (3/31/89)
78   COTTI Orvieto Classico 1984 $5.50 (1/01/86)
74   CASTELLUCCI Verdicchio dei Castelli di Jesi 1984 $4 (6/16/86)
71   VASELLI Orvieto Classico Secco 1984 $4.50 (7/01/86)
63   VILLA SIMONE Frascati Superiore 1984 $6.50 (6/16/86)

1979

90   MASTROBERARDINO Lacryma Christi del Vesuvio 1979 $6.25 (1/01/84) SS

PORTUGAL
VINTAGE PORT

1988

93   GRAHAM Vintage Port Malvedos 1988 Rel: $26 Cur: $27 (1/31/91)
78   QUINTA DE LA ROSA Vintage Port 1988 (NR) (VP-5/90)

1987

94   QUINTA DO NOVAL Vintage Port Nacional 1987 (NR) (VP-1/90)
93   TAYLOR FLADGATE Vintage Port Quinta de Vargellas 1987 (NR) (VP-2/90)
91   GRAHAM Vintage Port Malvedos 1987 (NR) (VP-2/90)
91   NIEPOORT Vintage Port 1987 Rel: $27 Cur: $27 (VP-11/89)
90   FONSECA Vintage Port Guimaraens 1987 (NR) (VP-2/90)
89   QUINTA DO NOVAL Vintage Port 1987 (NR) (VP-1/90)
88   FERREIRA Vintage Port 1987 (NR) (VP-11/89)
88   OFFLEY Vintage Port Boa Vista 1987 (NR) (VP-1/90)
87   DELAFORCE Vintage Port Quinta da Corte 1987 (NR) (VP-2/90)
86   DOW Vintage Port Quinta do Bomfim 1987 (NR) (VP-2/90)
86   KOPKE Vintage Port 1987 Rel: $24 Cur: $24 (VP-1/90)
86   QUINTA DA EIRA VELHA Vintage Port 1987 (NR) (VP-5/90)
86   ROZES Vintage Port 1987 (NR) (VP-6/90)
86   WARRE Vintage Port Quinta da Cavadinha 1987 (NR) (VP-2/90)
84   CALEM Vintage Port Quinta do Foz 1987 Rel: $28 Cur: $28 (VP-6/90)
84   MARTINEZ Vintage Port 1987 (NR) (VP-5/90)
84   OFFLEY Vintage Port 1987 (NR) (VP-1/90)
83   CHURCHILL Vintage Port Agua Alta 1987 Rel: $37 Cur: $37 (4/15/91)
83   CHURCHILL Vintage Port Agua Alta 1987 Rel: $37 Cur: $37 (VP-5/90)
83   QUINTA DE VAL FIGUERIA Vintage Port 1987 (NR) (VP-2/90)
82   FONSECA Vintage Port Quinta do Panascal 1987 (NR) (VP-2/90)
81   BARROS Vintage Port 1987 Rel: $28 Cur: $28 (VP-1/90)
81   QUINTA DA ROMANEIRA Vintage Port 1987 (NR) (VP-1/90)
80   C. DA SILVA Vintage Port Presidential 1987 (NR) (VP-2/90)
80   QUINTA DO CRASTO Vintage Port 1987 (NR) (VP-1/90)
80   ROYAL OPORTO Vintage Port 1987 Rel: $12 Cur: $14 (VP-11/89)
79   CROFT Vintage Port Quinta da Roeda 1987 (NR) (VP-2/90)

1986

88   TAYLOR FLADGATE Vintage Port Quinta de Vargellas 1986 (NR) (VP-2/90)
86   FONSECA Vintage Port Guimaraens 1986 (NR) (VP-2/90)
85   GRAHAM Vintage Port Malvedos 1986 Rel: $35 Cur: $35 (VP-2/90)
85   WARRE Vintage Port Quinta da Cavadinha 1986 (NR) (VP-2/90)
84   GRAHAM Vintage Port Malvedos 1986 Rel: $35 Cur: $35/375ml (3/31/90)
82   DOW Vintage Port Quinta do Bomfim 1986 (NR) (VP-2/90)
79   FONSECA Vintage Port Quinta do Panascal 1986 (NR) (VP-2/90)
78   CHURCHILL Vintage Port Fojo 1986 (NR) (VP-2/90)

1985

96   GRAHAM Vintage Port 1985 Rel: $31 Cur: $47 (VP-6/90)
95   FONSECA Vintage Port 1985 Rel: $32 Cur: $40 (VP-6/90)
95   QUINTA DO NOVAL Vintage Port Nacional 1985 Cur: $200 (VP-11/89)
93   BURMESTER Vintage Port 1985 Rel: $25 Cur: $25 (VP-1/90)
93   COCKBURN Vintage Port 1985 Rel: $33 Cur: $46 (10/31/88)
93   WARRE Vintage Port 1985 Rel: $28 Cur: $38 (10/31/88)
92   CROFT Vintage Port 1985 Rel: $30 Cur: $42 (10/31/88)
92   FERREIRA Vintage Port 1985 Rel: $20 Cur: $28 (10/31/88)
92   GRAHAM Vintage Port 1985 Rel: $31 Cur: $47 (10/31/88)
92   NIEPOORT Vintage Port 1985 Rel: $25 Cur: $33 (VP-6/90)
91   DOW Vintage Port 1985 Rel: $30 Cur: $37 (9/30/87)
91   FONSECA Vintage Port 1985 Rel: $32 Cur: $40 (9/30/87)
91   GRAHAM Vintage Port 1985 Rel: $31 Cur: $47 (9/30/87) CS
91   QUINTA DO NOVAL Vintage Port 1985 Rel: $22 Cur: $35 (10/31/88)
91   TAYLOR FLADGATE Vintage Port 1985 Rel: $32 Cur: $53 (10/31/88)
91   WARRE Vintage Port 1985 Rel: $28 Cur: $38 (VP-6/90)
90   COCKBURN Vintage Port 1985 Rel: $33 Cur: $46 (VP-6/90)
90   KOPKE Vintage Port 1985 Rel: $18 Cur: $21 (VP-1/90)
90   TAYLOR FLADGATE Vintage Port 1985 Rel: $32 Cur: $53 (VP-6/90)
89   DOW Vintage Port 1985 Rel: $30 Cur: $37 (VP-6/90)
89   MARTINEZ Vintage Port 1985 Rel: $21 Cur: $29 (VP-6/90)
89   NIEPOORT Vintage Port 1985 Rel: $25 Cur: $33 (1/31/88)
89   OFFLEY Vintage Port Boa Vista 1985 Rel: $22 Cur: $31 (VP-6/90)
89   SMITH WOODHOUSE Vintage Port 1985 Rel: $22 Cur: $34 (VP-6/90)
88   CALEM Vintage Port 1985 Rel: $25 Cur: $38 (VP-6/90)
88   ROCHA Vintage Port 1985 $32 (4/15/91)
87   BURMESTER Vintage Port 1985 Rel: $25 Cur: $25 (12/31/88)
87   FERREIRA Vintage Port 1985 Rel: $20 Cur: $28 (VP-11/89)
87   MARTINEZ Vintage Port 1985 Rel: $21 Cur: $29 (9/30/87)
87   QUARLES HARRIS Vintage Port 1985 Rel: $21 Cur: $30 (9/30/87)
87   SMITH WOODHOUSE Vintage Port 1985 Rel: $22 Cur: $34 (9/30/87)
87   VAN ZELLER Vintage Port Quinta do Roriz 1985 (NR) (VP-7/90)
86   QUINTA DO NOVAL Vintage Port 1985 Rel: $22 Cur: $35 (VP-6/90)
85   GOULD CAMPBELL Vintage Port 1985 Rel: $23 Cur: $33 (VP-6/90)
85   MORGAN Vintage Port 1985 (NR) (VP-2/90)
85   OFFLEY Vintage Port Boa Vista 1985 Rel: $22 Cur: $31 (9/30/87)
85   POCAS JUNIOR Vintage Port 1985 Rel: $17 Cur: $19 (VP-2/90)
85   QUARLES HARRIS Vintage Port 1985 Rel: $21 Cur: $30 (VP-6/90)
85   RAMOS-PINTO Vintage Port 1985 Rel: $21 Cur: $32 (VP-11/89)
84   CALEM Vintage Port 1985 Rel: $25 Cur: $38 (9/30/87)
84   CHURCHILL Vintage Port 1985 Rel: $22 Cur: $39 (9/30/87)

84   HOOPER Vintage Port 1985 Rel: $15 Cur: $20 (9/30/87)
84   REBELLO-VALENTE Vintage Port 1985 Rel: $23 Cur: $42 (9/30/87)
83   SANDEMAN Vintage Port 1985 Rel: $22 Cur: $33 (VP-6/90)
81   CHURCHILL Vintage Port 1985 Rel: $22 Cur: $39 (VP-2/90)
81   CROFT Vintage Port 1985 Rel: $30 Cur: $42 (VP-6/90)
81   DELAFORCE Vintage Port 1985 Rel: $24 Cur: $41 (VP-6/90)
81   GOULD CAMPBELL Vintage Port 1985 Rel: $23 Cur: $33 (9/30/87)
81   REBELLO-VALENTE Vintage Port 1985 Rel: $23 Cur: $42 (VP-6/90)
81   ROZES Vintage Port 1985 Rel: $16 Cur: $21 (VP-5/90)
81   WIESE & KROHN Vintage Port 1985 Rel: $21 Cur: $32 (VP-1/90)
80   BARROS Vintage Port 1985 Rel: $24 Cur: $29 (VP-1/90)
80   HOOPER Vintage Port 1985 Rel: $15 Cur: $20 (VP-6/90)
80   SANDEMAN Vintage Port 1985 Rel: $22 Cur: $33 (9/30/87)
80   VAN ZELLER Vintage Port 1985 (NR) (VP-1/90)
78   C. DA SILVA Vintage Port Presidential 1985 Rel: $30 Cur: $30 (VP-2/90)
78   FONSECA Vintage Port Quinta do Panascal 1985 (NR) (VP-2/90)
78   QUINTA DA ROMANEIRA Vintage Port 1985 Rel: $29 Cur: $29 (VP-1/90)
76   MESSIAS Vintage Port 1985 Rel: $12 Cur: $16 (9/30/87)
76   OSBORNE Vintage Port 1985 Rel: $20 Cur: $26 (VP-2/89)
76   QUINTA DO INFANTADO Vintage Port 1985 Rel: $33 Cur: $33 (VP-7/90)
72   FEIST Vintage Port 1985 Rel: $20 Cur: $25 (VP-1/90)
72   FEUERHEERD Vintage Port 1985 (NR) (VP-1/90)
71   QUINTA DO CRASTO Vintage Port 1985 Rel: $24 Cur: $24 (VP-1/90)
71   ROYAL OPORTO Vintage Port 1985 Rel: $12 Cur: $17 (VP-6/90)
70   BORGES Vintage Port 1985 Rel: $15 Cur: $15 (VP-5/90)
70   VIEIRA DE SOUSA Vintage Port 1985 (NR) (VP-1/90)
69   A. PINTOS DOS SANTOS Vintage Port 1985 (NR) (VP-1/90)
67   MESSIAS Vintage Port 1985 Rel: $12 Cur: $16 (VP-2/90)

1984

87   TAYLOR FLADGATE Vintage Port Quinta de Vargellas 1984 (NR) (VP-2/90)
86   DOW Vintage Port Quinta do Bomfim 1984 (NR) (VP-2/90)
86   WIESE & KROHN Vintage Port 1984 Rel: $13 Cur: $20 (VP-1/90)
85   FONSECA Vintage Port Guimaraens 1984 (NR) (VP-2/90)
84   BURMESTER Vintage Port 1984 (NA) (VP-1/90)
84   DELAFORCE Vintage Port Quinta da Corte 1984 (NR) (VP-2/90)
83   GRAHAM Vintage Port Malvedos 1984 (NR) (VP-2/90)
81   WARRE Vintage Port Quinta da Cavadinha 1984 (NR) (VP-2/90)
79   CHURCHILL Vintage Port Fojo 1984 (NA) (VP-2/90)
78   MESSIAS Vintage Port 1984 Rel: $11 Cur: $15 (VP-2/90)
70   FONSECA Vintage Port Quinta do Panascal 1984 (NR) (VP-2/90)
65   ROYAL OPORTO Vintage Port 1984 Rel: $11 Cur: $16 (VP-11/89)

1983

97   COCKBURN Vintage Port 1983 Rel: $22 Cur: $45 (VP-6/90)
97   TAYLOR FLADGATE Vintage Port 1983 Rel: $25 Cur: $45 (3/31/87)
95   GRAHAM Vintage Port 1983 Rel: $30 Cur: $43 (10/31/88)
95   SMITH WOODHOUSE Vintage Port 1983 Rel: $22 Cur: $33 (3/31/87)
94   DOW Vintage Port 1983 Rel: $20 Cur: $36 (VP-6/90)
94   WARRE Vintage Port 1983 Rel: $28 Cur: $43 (12/31/86) CS
93   GRAHAM Vintage Port 1983 Rel: $30 Cur: $43 (VP-6/90)
92   COCKBURN Vintage Port 1983 Rel: $22 Cur: $45 (8/31/87) CS
92   SMITH WOODHOUSE Vintage Port 1983 Rel: $22 Cur: $33 (VP-6/90)
91   COCKBURN Vintage Port 1983 Rel: $22 Cur: $45 (10/31/88)
91   FERREIRA Vintage Port Quinta do Seixo 1983 Rel: $14 Cur: $26 (VP-11/89)
91   FERREIRA Vintage Port Quinta do Seixo 1983 Rel: $14 Cur: $26 (3/31/87)
91   OFFLEY Vintage Port Boa Vista 1983 Rel: $22 Cur: $28 (VP-1/90)
90   FONSECA Vintage Port 1983 Rel: $24 Cur: $40 (VP-6/90)
90   GOULD CAMPBELL Vintage Port 1983 Rel: $22 Cur: $34 (VP-6/90)
90   QUARLES HARRIS Vintage Port 1983 Rel: $18 Cur: $33 (3/31/87)
89   FONSECA Vintage Port 1983 Rel: $24 Cur: $40 (10/31/88)
89   FONSECA Vintage Port 1983 Rel: $24 Cur: $40 (3/31/87)
89   QUARLES HARRIS Vintage Port 1983 Rel: $18 Cur: $33 (VP-2/90)
89   RAMOS-PINTO Vintage Port 1983 Rel: $17 Cur: $32 (VP-11/89)
89   TAYLOR FLADGATE Vintage Port 1983 Rel: $25 Cur: $45 (VP-6/90)
88   DOW Vintage Port 1983 Rel: $20 Cur: $36 (10/31/88)
88   GOULD CAMPBELL Vintage Port 1983 Rel: $22 Cur: $34 (3/31/87)
88   TAYLOR FLADGATE Vintage Port 1983 Rel: $25 Cur: $45 (10/31/88)
88   WARRE Vintage Port 1983 Rel: $28 Cur: $43 (VP-6/90)
87   FERREIRA Vintage Port Quinta do Seixo 1983 Rel: $14 Cur: $26 (10/31/88)
85   CROFT Vintage Port Quinta da Roeda 1983 Rel: $22 Cur: $22 (VP-2/90)
85   KOPKE Vintage Port 1983 Rel: $18 Cur: $23 (VP-1/90)
84   CALEM Vintage Port 1983 Rel: $18 Cur: $40 (VP-6/90)
84   NIEPOORT Vintage Port 1983 Rel: $14 Cur: $33 (VP-6/90)
84   VAN ZELLER Vintage Port 1983 Rel: $22 Cur: $36 (VP-1/90)
84   VAN ZELLER Vintage Port Quinta do Roriz 1983 $22 (VP-7/90)
84   WARRE Vintage Port 1983 Rel: $28 Cur: $43 (10/31/88)
79   FONSECA Vintage Port Quinta do Panascal 1983 (NR) (VP-2/90)
78   REBELLO-VALENTE Vintage Port 1983 Rel: $23 Cur: $36 (VP-6/90)
77   MESSIAS Vintage Port Quinta do Cachão 1983 Rel: $8 Cur: $11 (VP-2/90)
76   BARROS Vintage Port 1983 Rel: $8 Cur: $33 (VP-1/90)
76   ROYAL OPORTO Vintage Port 1983 Rel: $9 Cur: $15 (VP-6/90)
70   BORGES Vintage Port 1983 Rel: $12 Cur: $29 (VP-5/90)
69   CHURCHILL Vintage Port Agua Alta 1983 Rel: $22 Cur: $41 (VP-7/90)
60   HOOPER Vintage Port 1983 Cur: $16 (VP-3/90)

1982

93   NIEPOORT Vintage Port 1982 Rel: $13 Cur: $39 (3/31/87)
90   GRAHAM Vintage Port Malvedos 1982 (NR) (VP-2/90)
90   NIEPOORT Vintage Port 1982 Rel: $13 Cur: $39 (VP-6/90)
90   QUINTA DO NOVAL Vintage Port Nacional 1982 Cur: $190 (11/01/85) (JS)
86   CHAMPALIMAUD Vintage Port 1982 Rel: $20 Cur: $20 (VP-2/90)
86   QUINTA DO NOVAL Vintage Port Nacional 1982 Cur: $190 (VP-11/89)
86   WARRE Vintage Port Quinta da Cavadinha 1982 (NR) (VP-2/90)
85   FERREIRA Vintage Port 1982 Rel: $14 Cur: $32 (10/31/88)
85   QUINTA DO NOVAL Vintage Port 1982 Rel: $23 Cur: $36 (10/31/88)
85   SANDEMAN Vintage Port 1982 Rel: $19 Cur: $36 (10/31/88)
85   WIESE & KROHN Vintage Port 1982 Rel: $13 Cur: $32 (12/31/88)
84   OFFLEY Vintage Port Boa Vista 1982 Rel: $18 Cur: $23 (VP-6/90)
83   KOPKE Vintage Port 1982 Rel: $16 Cur: $26 (VP-1/90)

83 WIESE & KROHN Vintage Port 1982 Rel: $13 Cur: $32 (VP-1/90)
82 CALEM Vintage Port Quinta do Foz 1982 Rel: $16 Cur: $37 (VP-6/90)
82 CROFT Vintage Port 1982 Rel: $22 Cur: $41 (10/31/88)
82 DOW Vintage Port Quinta do Bomfim 1982 (NR) (VP-2/90)
82 FONSECA Vintage Port Guimaraens 1982 (NR) (VP-2/90)
82 MARTINEZ Vintage Port 1982 Rel: $17 Cur: $28 (VP-6/90)
82 SANDEMAN Vintage Port 1982 Rel: $19 Cur: $36 (VP-6/90)
81 FERREIRA Vintage Port 1982 Rel: $14 Cur: $32 (VP-11/89)
81 QUINTA DA EIRA VELHA Vintage Port 1982 (NR) (VP-3/90)
81 TAYLOR FLADGATE Vintage Port Quinta de Vargellas 1982 (NR) (VP-2/90)
79 BORGES Vintage Port 1982 Rel: $12 Cur: $30 (VP-5/90)
79 RAMOS-PINTO Vintage Port 1982 Rel: $12 Cur: $31 (VP-11/89)
78 CHURCHILL Vintage Port 1982 (NA) (VP-6/90)
78 FEIST Vintage Port 1982 (NA) (VP-1/90)
78 QUINTA DO NOVAL Vintage Port 1982 Rel: $23 Cur: $36 (VP-6/90)
75 ROZES Vintage Port 1982 (NR) (VP-6/90)
72 MESSIAS Vintage Port 1982 Rel: $7 Cur: $13 (VP-2/90)
72 OSBORNE Vintage Port 1982 Rel: $13 Cur: $26 (VP-1/90)
70 A. PINTOS DOS SANTOS Vintage Port 1982 (NR) (VP-1/90)
70 QUINTA DO INFANTADO Vintage Port 1982 Rel: $35 Cur: $35 (VP-7/90)
69 CROFT Vintage Port 1982 Rel: $22 Cur: $41 (VP-4/90)
69 DELAFORCE Vintage Port 1982 Rel: $20 Cur: $27 (VP-6/90)
68 HOOPER Vintage Port 1982 Cur: $18 (VP-5/90)
60 ROYAL OPORTO Vintage Port 1982 Rel: $9 Cur: $19 (VP-6/90)

1980

92 WARRE Vintage Port 1980 Rel: $16 Cur: $36 (10/01/84) CS
90 DOW Vintage Port 1980 Rel: $15 Cur: $39 (VP-6/90)
90 GRAHAM Vintage Port 1980 Rel: $18 Cur: $42 (VP-6/90)
90 OFFLEY Vintage Port Boa Vista 1980 Rel: $14 Cur: $30 (VP-6/90)
90 SMITH WOODHOUSE Vintage Port 1980 Rel: $15 Cur: $33 (VP-6/90)
90 WARRE Vintage Port 1980 Rel: $16 Cur: $36 (10/31/88)
89 DOW Vintage Port 1980 Rel: $15 Cur: $39 (10/31/88)
88 BURMESTER Vintage Port 1980 Rel: $18 Cur: $33 (VP-1/90)
88 GRAHAM Vintage Port 1980 Rel: $18 Cur: $42 (4/16/85) CS
88 TAYLOR FLADGATE Vintage Port 1980 Rel: $21 Cur: $41 (VP-6/90)
88 WARRE Vintage Port 1980 Rel: $16 Cur: $36 (VP-6/90)
87 GRAHAM Vintage Port 1980 Rel: $18 Cur: $42 (10/31/88)
87 NIEPOORT Vintage Port 1980 Rel: $12 Cur: $35 (VP-6/90)
86 GOULD CAMPBELL Vintage Port 1980 Rel: $15 Cur: $44 (VP-2/90)
86 SANDEMAN Vintage Port 1980 Rel: $19 Cur: $46 (10/31/88)
85 FONSECA Vintage Port 1980 Rel: $22 Cur: $40 (3/31/87) (JS)
85 SANDEMAN Vintage Port 1980 Rel: $19 Cur: $46 (VP-6/90)
85 TAYLOR FLADGATE Vintage Port 1980 Rel: $21 Cur: $41 (10/31/88)
84 FERREIRA Vintage Port 1980 Rel: $13 Cur: $21 (10/31/88)
84 SMITH WOODHOUSE Vintage Port 1980 Rel: $15 Cur: $33 (5/01/84)
83 QUARLES HARRIS Vintage Port 1980 Rel: $13 Cur: $29 (VP-2/90)
81 DELAFORCE Vintage Port Quinta da Corte 1980 (NA) (VP-2/90)
80 FERREIRA Vintage Port 1980 Rel: $13 Cur: $21 (VP-1/90)
80 QUINTA DO NOVAL Vintage Port Nacional 1980 Cur: $280 (VP-2/90)
80 REBELLO-VALENTE Vintage Port 1980 Rel: $16 Cur: $50 (VP-2/90)
78 CALEM Vintage Port 1980 Rel: $14 Cur: $38 (VP-6/90)
76 FEUERHEERD Vintage Port 1980 (NA) (VP-1/90)
75 CROFT Vintage Port Quinta da Roeda 1980 Rel: $25 Cur: $30 (VP-2/90)
74 FONSECA Vintage Port 1980 Rel: $22 Cur: $40 (VP-6/90)
74 RAMOS-PINTO Vintage Port 1980 Rel: $11 Cur: $25 (VP-11/89)
71 KOPKE Vintage Port 1980 Rel: $16 Cur: $31 (VP-1/90)
70 BORGES Vintage Port 1980 Rel: $11 Cur: $23 (VP-5/90)
70 A. PINTOS DOS SANTOS Vintage Port 1980 (NA) (VP-1/90)
70 VIEIRA DE SOUSA Vintage Port 1980 (NA) (VP-1/90)
67 HOOPER Vintage Port 1980 Cur: $22 (VP-5/90)
60 ROYAL OPORTO Vintage Port 1980 Rel: $8 Cur: $20 (VP-6/90)

1979

82 WARRE Vintage Port Quinta da Cavadinha 1979 Rel: $25 Cur: $25 (7/31/90)
82 WARRE Vintage Port Quinta da Cavadinha 1979 Rel: $25 Cur: $25 (2/90)
81 DOW Vintage Port Quinta do Bomfim 1979 Rel: $28 Cur: $28 (VP-2/90)
74 GRAHAM Vintage Port Malvedos 1979 (NA) (VP-2/90)
69 HUTCHESON Vintage Port 1979 Cur: $40 (VP-1/90)
69 KOPKE Vintage Port 1979 (NA) (VP-1/90)
65 BORGES Vintage Port 1979 Rel: $11 Cur: $22 (VP-5/90)

1978

91 QUINTA DO NOVAL Vintage Port Nacional 1978 Cur: $242 (11/01/85) (JS)
90 WARRE Vintage Port Quinta da Cavadinha 1978 Rel: $28 Cur: $28 (11/30/88)
89 FERREIRA Vintage Port 1978 Rel: $11 Cur: $28 (VP-11/89)
88 DOW Vintage Port Quinta do Bomfim 1978 Rel: $27 Cur: $30 (11/30/88)
85 DOW Vintage Port Quinta do Bomfim 1978 Rel: $27 Cur: $30 (VP-2/90)
85 QUINTA DA EIRA VELHA Vintage Port 1978 Rel: $22 Cur: $30 (VP-3/90)
85 TAYLOR FLADGATE Vintage Port Quinta de Vargellas 1978 Rel: $29 Cur: $34 (VP-2/90)
84 WIESE & KROHN Vintage Port 1978 Rel: $11 Cur: $37 (VP-1/90)
83 CROFT Vintage Port Quinta da Roeda 1978 Rel: $22 Cur: $29 (VP-2/90)
83 WARRE Vintage Port Quinta da Cavadinha 1978 Rel: $28 Cur: $28 (VP-2/90)
82 GRAHAM Vintage Port Malvedos 1978 Rel: $30 Cur: $34 (VP-2/90)
81 GRAHAM Vintage Port Malvedos 1978 Rel: $30 Cur: $34 (11/30/88)
81 NIEPOORT Vintage Port 1978 Rel: $11 Cur: $32 (VP-11/89)
80 DELAFORCE Vintage Port Quinta da Corte 1978 Rel: $24 Cur: $24 (VP-2/90)
80 FONSECA Vintage Port Guimaraens 1978 Rel: $32 Cur: $35 (VP-2/90)
78 FEIST Vintage Port 1978 (NA) (VP-1/90)
78 QUINTA DO NOVAL Vintage Port 1978 Rel: $18 Cur: $39 (10/31/88)
77 C. DA SILVA Vintage Port Presidential 1978 Cur: $37 (VP-2/90)
77 QUINTA DO NOVAL Vintage Port Nacional 1978 Cur: $242 (VP-11/89)
75 BARROS Vintage Port 1978 Rel: $7 Cur: $30 (VP-1/90)
75 QUINTA DO INFANTADO Vintage Port 1978 (NA) (VP-7/90)
74 VIEIRA DE SOUSA Vintage Port 1978 (NA) (VP-1/90)
72 QUINTA DO NOVAL Vintage Port 1978 Rel: $18 Cur: $39 (VP-11/89)
70 KOPKE Vintage Port 1978 Cur: $29 (VP-1/90)
70 QUINTA DO CRASTO Vintage Port 1978 (NA) (VP-1/90)
68 ROYAL OPORTO Vintage Port 1978 Rel: $8 Cur: $24 (VP-11/89)

1977

100 FONSECA Vintage Port 1977 Rel: $16 Cur: $70 (VP-4/90)
98 TAYLOR FLADGATE Vintage Port 1977 Rel: $17 Cur: $75 (VP-4/90)
94 DOW Vintage Port 1977 Rel: $12 Cur: $61 (VP-4/90)
94 GRAHAM Vintage Port 1977 Rel: $15 Cur: $66 (10/31/88)
93 CROFT Vintage Port 1977 Rel: $14 Cur: $63 (10/31/88)
93 GOULD CAMPBELL Vintage Port 1977 Rel: $11 Cur: $50 (VP-2/90)
92 DOW Vintage Port 1977 Rel: $12 Cur: $61 (10/31/88)
92 TAYLOR FLADGATE Vintage Port 1977 Rel: $17 Cur: $75 (10/31/88)
92 WARRE Vintage Port 1977 Rel: $15 Cur: $61 (VP-4/90)
91 FONSECA Vintage Port 1977 Rel: $16 Cur: $70 (10/31/88)
91 GRAHAM Vintage Port 1977 Rel: $15 Cur: $66 (3/16/84) CS
90 FERREIRA Vintage Port 1977 Rel: $11 Cur: $51 (10/31/88)
90 GRAHAM Vintage Port 1977 Rel: $15 Cur: $66 (VP-4/90)
89 NIEPOORT Vintage Port 1977 Rel: $11 Cur: $50 (VP-4/90)
89 QUARLES HARRIS Vintage Port 1977 Rel: $11 Cur: $43 (VP-2/90)
89 REBELLO-VALENTE Vintage Port 1977 Rel: $12 Cur: $47 (VP-2/90)
89 SMITH WOODHOUSE Vintage Port 1977 Rel: $11 Cur: $50 (VP-2/90)
89 WARRE Vintage Port 1977 Rel: $15 Cur: $61 (10/31/88)
88 OFFLEY Vintage Port Boa Vista 1977 Rel: $11 Cur: $49 (VP-1/90)
88 SANDEMAN Vintage Port 1977 Rel: $15 Cur: $74 (10/31/88)
86 FERREIRA Vintage Port 1977 Rel: $11 Cur: $51 (VP-11/89)
85 CROFT Vintage Port 1977 Rel: $14 Cur: $63 (VP-4/90)
85 SANDEMAN Vintage Port 1977 Rel: $15 Cur: $74 (VP-6/90)
82 BURMESTER Vintage Port 1977 Rel: $11 Cur: $37 (VP-1/90)
82 DIEZ HERMANOS Vintage Port 1977 (NA) (VP-4/90)
81 ROCHA Vintage Port 1977 $19 (4/30/91)
80 DELAFORCE Vintage Port 1977 Rel: $11 Cur: $62 (VP-2/90)
78 MORGAN Vintage Port 1977 (NR) (VP-1/90)
78 QUINTA DO NOVAL Vintage Port 1977 Cur: $50 (10/31/88)
74 ROYAL OPORTO Vintage Port 1977 Rel: $8 Cur: $30 (VP-11/89)
72 C. DA SILVA Vintage Port Presidential 1977 Cur: $39 (VP-2/90)
69 CALEM Vintage Port 1977 Rel: $11 Cur: $66 (VP-11/89)
69 FEUERHEERD Vintage Port 1977 Cur: $17 (VP-1/90)
68 KOPKE Vintage Port 1977 (NA) (VP-1/90)
60 MESSIAS Vintage Port Quinta do Cachão 1977 Rel: $7 Cur: $20 (VP-2/90)

1976

89 FONSECA Vintage Port Guimaraens 1976 Rel: $32 Cur: $38 (VP-2/90)
81 TAYLOR FLADGATE Vintage Port Quinta de Vargellas 1976 Rel: $29 Cur: $42 (VP-2/90)
74 GRAHAM Vintage Port Malvedos 1976 Rel: $17 Cur: $31 (VP-2/90)

1975

88 QUINTA DO NOVAL Vintage Port Nacional 1975 Cur: $285 (11/01/85) (JS)
86 CALEM Vintage Port 1975 Cur: $50 (VP-2/90)
86 QUINTA DO NOVAL Vintage Port Nacional 1975 Cur: $285 (VP-11/89)
84 FERREIRA Vintage Port 1975 Cur: $41 (10/31/88)
82 KOPKE Vintage Port 1975 Cur: $28 (VP-1/90)
81 FERREIRA Vintage Port 1975 Cur: $41 (VP-11/89)
81 FONSECA Vintage Port 1975 Cur: $50 (10/31/88)
81 QUINTA DO NOVAL Vintage Port 1975 Cur: $60 (VP-11/89)
81 TAYLOR FLADGATE Vintage Port 1975 Cur: $47 (10/31/88)
80 CROFT Vintage Port 1975 Cur: $45 (10/31/88)
80 DOW Vintage Port 1975 Cur: $46 (VP-4/89)
80 SMITH WOODHOUSE Vintage Port 1975 Cur: $40 (VP-2/90)
80 WIESE & KROHN Vintage Port 1975 Cur: $49 (VP-1/90)
79 FONSECA Vintage Port 1975 Cur: $50 (VP-8/88)
79 NIEPOORT Vintage Port 1975 Cur: $37 (VP-11/89)
79 QUINTA DO NOVAL Vintage Port 1975 Cur: $60 (10/31/88)
78 GRAHAM Vintage Port 1975 Cur: $49 (VP-2/89)
78 GRAHAM Vintage Port 1975 Cur: $49 (10/31/88)
78 SANDEMAN Vintage Port 1975 Cur: $49 (VP-3/90)
78 TAYLOR FLADGATE Vintage Port 1975 Cur: $47 (VP-12/89)
77 COCKBURN Vintage Port 1975 Cur: $47 (VP-1/90)
76 CROFT Vintage Port 1975 Cur: $45 (VP-8/88)
76 DELAFORCE Vintage Port 1975 Cur: $43 (VP-2/90)
76 GOULD CAMPBELL Vintage Port 1975 Cur: $33 (VP-2/90)
75 COCKBURN Vintage Port 1975 Cur: $47 (10/31/88)
75 DOW Vintage Port 1975 Cur: $46 (10/31/88)
75 MARTINEZ Vintage Port 1975 Cur: $40 (VP-2/90)
75 OFFLEY Vintage Port Boa Vista 1975 Cur: $27 (VP-2/89)
75 REBELLO-VALENTE Vintage Port 1975 Cur: $53 (VP-2/90)
75 SANDEMAN Vintage Port 1975 Cur: $49 (10/31/88)
75 WARRE Vintage Port 1975 Cur: $43 (VP-8/88)
74 POCAS JUNIOR Vintage Port 1975 Cur: $42 (VP-2/90)
74 VASCONCELLOS Vintage Port Butler & Nephew 1975 Cur: $37 (VP-7/90)
74 WARRE Vintage Port 1975 Cur: $43 (10/31/88)
73 QUARLES HARRIS Vintage Port 1975 Cur: $38 (VP-4/90)

1974

85 TAYLOR FLADGATE Vintage Port Quinta de Vargellas 1974 Rel: $27 Cur: $41 (3/31/87) (JS)
84 FONSECA Vintage Port Guimaraens 1974 Cur: $40 (VP-1/90)
78 TAYLOR FLADGATE Vintage Port Quinta de Vargellas 1974 Rel: $27 Cur: $41 (VP-2/90)
74 BARROS Vintage Port 1974 Cur: $40 (VP-1/90)
74 KOPKE Vintage Port 1974 (NA) (VP-1/90)

1972

84 TAYLOR FLADGATE Vintage Port Quinta de Vargellas 1972 Cur: $48 (VP-2/90)
83 REBELLO-VALENTE Vintage Port 1972 Cur: $53 (VP-1/90)
79 DOW Vintage Port 1972 Cur: $39 (VP-1/90)
79 OFFLEY Vintage Port Boa Vista 1972 Cur: $30 (VP-2/89)
76 QUINTA DE LA ROSA Vintage Port 1972 (NA) (VP-10/89)
75 FONSECA Vintage Port Guimaraens 1972 Cur: $43 (VP-2/90)

1970

98 QUINTA DO NOVAL Vintage Port Nacional 1970 Cur: $370 (VP-11/89)
98 TAYLOR FLADGATE Vintage Port 1970 Cur: $81 (VP-12/89)
96 FONSECA Vintage Port 1970 Cur: $76 (VP-12/89)
94 DOW Vintage Port 1970 Cur: $73 (VP-12/89)

PORTUGAL
VINTAGE PORT

94	FONSECA Vintage Port 1970 Cur: $76 (10/31/88)
94	GRAHAM Vintage Port 1970 Cur: $83 (VP-12/89)
93	NIEPOORT Vintage Port 1970 Cur: $55 (VP-1/90)
92	REBELLO-VALENTE Vintage Port 1970 Cur: $50 (VP-2/90)
91	GRAHAM Vintage Port 1970 Cur: $83 (10/31/88)
90	CROFT Vintage Port 1970 Cur: $76 (10/31/88)
90	DOW Vintage Port 1970 Cur: $73 (10/31/88)
89	CROFT Vintage Port 1970 Cur: $76 (VP-12/89)
89	DELAFORCE Vintage Port 1970 Cur: $57 (VP-2/90)
89	MARTINEZ Vintage Port 1970 Cur: $60 (VP-2/90)
89	QUARLES HARRIS Vintage Port 1970 Cur: $52 (VP-2/90)
89	QUINTA DO NOVAL Vintage Port 1970 Cur: $71 (VP-11/89)
89	QUINTA DO NOVAL Vintage Port Nacional 1970 Cur: $370 (11/01/85) (JS)
89	TAYLOR FLADGATE Vintage Port 1970 Cur: $81 (10/31/88)
89	WARRE Vintage Port 1970 Cur: $74 (10/31/88)
88	GOULD CAMPBELL Vintage Port 1970 Cur: $54 (VP-2/90)
88	MORGAN Vintage Port 1970 (NR) (VP-2/90)
88	WARRE Vintage Port 1970 Cur: $74 (VP-12/89)
87	COCKBURN Vintage Port 1970 Cur: $78 (10/31/88)
87	MESSIAS Vintage Port Quinta do Cachão 1970 Cur: $55 (VP-2/90)
87	QUINTA DO NOVAL Vintage Port 1970 Cur: $71 (10/31/88)
86	BURMESTER Vintage Port 1970 Cur: $55 (VP-1/90)
86	COCKBURN Vintage Port 1970 Cur: $78 (VP-12/89)
86	FERREIRA Vintage Port 1970 Cur: $45 (VP-4/89)
86	SMITH WOODHOUSE Vintage Port 1970 Cur: $58 (VP-2/90)
86	VAN ZELLER Vintage Port Quinta do Roriz 1970 (NA) (VP-7/90)
84	POCAS JUNIOR Vintage Port 1970 Cur: $52 (VP-2/90)
83	SANDEMAN Vintage Port 1970 Cur: $74 (VP-3/90)
82	BARROS Vintage Port 1970 Cur: $60 (VP-1/90)
82	KOPKE Vintage Port 1970 Cur: $41 (VP-1/90)
82	SANDEMAN Vintage Port 1970 Cur: $74 (10/31/88)
81	OFFLEY Vintage Port Boa Vista 1970 Cur: $60 (VP-2/89)
81	RAMOS-PINTO Vintage Port 1970 Cur: $100 (VP-11/89)
81	VASCONCELLOS Vintage Port Gonzalez Byass 1970 Cur: $50 (VP-6/90)
80	CALEM Vintage Port 1970 Cur: $50 (VP-11/89)
80	FEUERHEERD Vintage Port 1970 Cur: $45 (VP-1/90)
79	HUTCHESON Vintage Port 1970 Cur: $50 (VP-1/90)
77	OSBORNE Vintage Port 1970 Cur: $50 (VP-1/90)
76	VASCONCELLOS Vintage Port Butler & Nephew 1970 Cur: $50 (VP-7/90)
75	C. DA SILVA Vintage Port Presidential 1970 Cur: $46 (VP-2/90)
75	ROYAL OPORTO Vintage Port 1970 Cur: $36 (VP-11/89)
74	WIESE & KROHN Vintage Port 1970 Cur: $75 (VP-1/90)
71	VIEIRA DE SOUSA Vintage Port 1970 (NA) (VP-1/90)
70	A. PINTOS DOS SANTOS Vintage Port 1970 (NA) (VP-1/90)
59	BORGES Vintage Port 1970 Cur: $86 (VP-5/90)

1969
85	TAYLOR FLADGATE Vintage Port Quinta de Vargellas 1969 Cur: $50 (VP-2/90)

1968
84	FONSECA Vintage Port Guimaraens 1968 Cur: $51 (VP-2/90)
82	TAYLOR FLADGATE Vintage Port Quinta de Vargellas 1968 Cur: $61 (VP-2/90)
80	TAYLOR FLADGATE Vintage Port Quinta de Vargellas 1968 Cur: $61 (3/31/87) (JS)
70	GRAHAM Vintage Port Malvedos 1968 Cur: $50 (VP-2/90)

1967
95	QUINTA DO NOVAL Vintage Port Nacional 1967 Cur: $380 (VP-11/89)
93	MARTINEZ Vintage Port 1967 Cur: $56 (VP-2/90)
91	REBELLO-VALENTE Vintage Port 1967 Cur: $77 (VP-2/90)
90	FONSECA Vintage Port Guimaraens 1967 Cur: $56 (VP-2/90)
90	SANDEMAN Vintage Port 1967 Cur: $58 (VP-3/90)
89	SANDEMAN Vintage Port 1967 Cur: $58 (10/31/88)
88	QUINTA DO NOVAL Vintage Port 1967 Cur: $52 (VP-12/89)
88	QUINTA DO NOVAL Vintage Port 1967 Cur: $52 (10/31/88)
88	QUINTA DO NOVAL Vintage Port Nacional 1967 Cur: $380 (11/01/85) (JS)
87	COCKBURN Vintage Port 1967 Cur: $74 (10/31/88)
85	COCKBURN Vintage Port 1967 Cur: $74 (VP-12/89)
85	CROFT Vintage Port Quinta da Roeda 1967 Cur: $60 (VP-1/90)
82	TAYLOR FLADGATE Vintage Port Quinta de Vargellas 1967 Cur: $66 (VP-2/90)
78	FONSECA Vintage Port Guimaraens 1967 Cur: $56 (3/31/87) (JS)
75	WIESE & KROHN Vintage Port 1967 Cur: $65 (VP-1/90)
72	ROYAL OPORTO Vintage Port 1967 Cur: $30 (VP-11/89)

1966
98	QUINTA DO NOVAL Vintage Port Nacional 1966 Cur: $310 (VP-11/89)
97	FONSECA Vintage Port 1966 Cur: $84 (VP-2/90)
94	DOW Vintage Port 1966 Cur: $90 (VP-12/89)
94	GRAHAM Vintage Port 1966 Cur: $88 (10/31/88)
93	GRAHAM Vintage Port 1966 Cur: $88 (VP-12/89)
93	SANDEMAN Vintage Port 1966 Cur: $89 (10/31/88)
93	WARRE Vintage Port 1966 Cur: $85 (10/31/88)
92	SANDEMAN Vintage Port 1966 Cur: $89 (VP-3/90)
91	COCKBURN Vintage Port 1966 (NA) (10/31/88)
91	QUINTA DO NOVAL Vintage Port 1966 Cur: $87 (VP-12/89)

91	WARRE Vintage Port 1966 Cur: $85 (VP-6/89)
90	CROFT Vintage Port 1966 Cur: $83 (VP-12/89)
90	DOW Vintage Port 1966 Cur: $90 (10/31/88)
90	OFFLEY Vintage Port Boa Vista 1966 Cur: $70 (VP-2/89)
90	QUINTA DO NOVAL Vintage Port 1966 Cur: $87 (10/31/88)
90	SANDEMAN Vintage Port 1966 Cur: $89 (7/15/90) (JS)
89	NIEPOORT Vintage Port 1966 Cur: $70 (VP-11/89)
89	QUINTA DO NOVAL Vintage Port Nacional 1966 Cur: $310 (11/01/85) (JS)
89	TAYLOR FLADGATE Vintage Port 1966 Cur: $95 (VP-12/89)
88	TAYLOR FLADGATE Vintage Port 1966 Cur: $95 (10/31/88)
87	FERREIRA Vintage Port 1966 Cur: $81 (10/31/88)
87	FONSECA Vintage Port 1966 Cur: $84 (10/31/88)
85	DELAFORCE Vintage Port 1966 Cur: $65 (VP-2/90)
85	FERREIRA Vintage Port 1966 Cur: $81 (VP-11/89)
84	CROFT Vintage Port 1966 Cur: $83 (10/31/88)
84	GOULD CAMPBELL Vintage Port 1966 Cur: $70 (VP-2/90)
84	MESSIAS Vintage Port Quinta do Cachão 1966 Cur: $30 (VP-2/90)
83	SMITH WOODHOUSE Vintage Port 1966 Cur: $88 (VP-2/90)
82	CALEM Vintage Port 1966 Cur: $65 (VP-11/89)
82	QUINTA DE LA ROSA Vintage Port 1966 (NA) (VP-10/89)
82	REBELLO-VALENTE Vintage Port 1966 Cur: $70 (VP-2/90)
81	KOPKE Vintage Port 1966 Cur: $65 (VP-1/90)
80	MORGAN Vintage Port 1966 (NR) (VP-2/90)
74	QUARLES HARRIS Vintage Port 1966 Cur: $78 (VP-2/90)

1965
89	FONSECA Vintage Port Guimaraens 1965 Cur: $64 (VP-2/90)
87	DOW Vintage Port Quinta do Bomfim 1965 (NA) (VP-6/90)
85	WIESE & KROHN Vintage Port 1965 Cur: $100 (VP-1/90)
80	TAYLOR FLADGATE Vintage Port Quinta de Vargellas 1965 Cur: $60 (VP-2/90)
79	GRAHAM Vintage Port Malvedos 1965 Cur: $58 (VP-2/90)

1964
90	FONSECA Vintage Port Guimaraens 1964 Cur: $60 (VP-2/90)
84	QUINTA DO NOVAL Vintage Port Nacional 1964 Cur: $350 (VP-11/89)
82	GRAHAM Vintage Port Malvedos 1964 Cur: $54 (VP-2/90)
75	TAYLOR FLADGATE Vintage Port Quinta de Vargellas 1964 Cur: $50 (VP-7/90)

1963
100	QUINTA DO NOVAL Vintage Port Nacional 1963 Cur: $750 (VP-11/89)
98	FONSECA Vintage Port 1963 Cur: $162 (VP-12/89)
97	FONSECA Vintage Port 1963 Cur: $162 (10/31/88)
97	GRAHAM Vintage Port 1963 Cur: $159 (VP-12/89)
97	TAYLOR FLADGATE Vintage Port 1963 Cur: $159 (VP-12/89)
97	WARRE Vintage Port 1963 Cur: $132 (10/31/88)
96	SANDEMAN Vintage Port 1963 Cur: $112 (7/15/90) (JS)
96	SANDEMAN Vintage Port 1963 Cur: $112 (VP-3/90)
95	QUINTA DO NOVAL Vintage Port Nacional 1963 Cur: $750 (11/01/85) (JS)
95	SANDEMAN Vintage Port 1963 Cur: $112 (10/31/88)
93	DELAFORCE Vintage Port 1963 Cur: $100 (VP-2/90)
92	DOW Vintage Port 1963 Cur: $132 (VP-2/90)
92	GRAHAM Vintage Port 1963 Cur: $159 (10/31/88)
92	WARRE Vintage Port 1963 Cur: $132 (VP-12/89)
91	COCKBURN Vintage Port 1963 Cur: $110 (10/31/88)
91	CROFT Vintage Port 1963 Cur: $122 (VP-12/89)
90	DOW Vintage Port 1963 Cur: $132 (10/31/88)
90	FERREIRA Vintage Port 1963 Cur: $110 (10/31/88)
90	NIEPOORT Vintage Port 1963 Cur: $90 (VP-11/89)
90	TAYLOR FLADGATE Vintage Port 1963 Cur: $159 (10/31/88)
89	QUINTA DO NOVAL Vintage Port 1963 Cur: $123 (10/31/88)
89	SMITH WOODHOUSE Vintage Port 1963 Cur: $110 (VP-2/90)
88	COCKBURN Vintage Port 1963 Cur: $110 (VP-12/89)
87	VASCONCELLOS Vintage Port Gonzalez Byass 1963 Cur: $82 (VP-7/90)
87	WIESE & KROHN Vintage Port 1963 Cur: $145 (VP-1/90)
86	CROFT Vintage Port 1963 Cur: $122 (10/31/88)
86	MORGAN Vintage Port 1963 (NR) (VP-2/90)
85	FERREIRA Vintage Port 1963 Cur: $110 (VP-8/88)
85	QUARLES HARRIS Vintage Port 1963 Cur: $110 (VP-2/90)
85	QUINTA DE LA ROSA Vintage Port 1963 (NA) (VP-10/89)
85	REBELLO-VALENTE Vintage Port 1963 Cur: $92 (VP-2/90)
84	QUINTA DO NOVAL Vintage Port 1963 Cur: $123 (VP-12/89)
83	BURMESTER Vintage Port 1963 Cur: $131 (VP-1/90)
83	RAMOS-PINTO Vintage Port 1963 Cur: $80 (VP-11/89)
82	CALEM Vintage Port 1963 Cur: $85 (VP-12/89)
82	MARTINEZ Vintage Port 1963 Cur: $95 (VP-2/90)
82	POCAS JUNIOR Vintage Port 1963 Cur: $100 (VP-2/90)
80	OFFLEY Vintage Port Boa Vista 1963 Cur: $110 (VP-2/89)
73	ROYAL OPORTO Vintage Port 1963 Cur: $55 (VP-11/89)
71	MESSIAS Vintage Port 1963 Cur: $40 (VP-2/90)

1962
89	GRAHAM Vintage Port Malvedos 1962 Cur: $65 (VP-2/90)
88	FONSECA Vintage Port Guimaraens 1962 Cur: $70 (VP-2/90)
86	QUINTA DO NOVAL Vintage Port Nacional 1962 Cur: $350 (VP-11/89)

1961
87	GRAHAM Vintage Port Malvedos 1961 Cur: $65 (VP-2/90)
85	FONSECA Vintage Port Guimaraens 1961 Cur: $70 (VP-2/90)
85	WIESE & KROHN Vintage Port 1961 Cur: $125 (VP-1/90)
68	TAYLOR FLADGATE Vintage Port Quinta de Vargellas 1961 Cur: $45 (VP-2/90)

1960
94	DOW Vintage Port 1960 Cur: $89 (10/31/88)
90	CROFT Vintage Port 1960 Cur: $93 (VP-9/89)
90	CROFT Vintage Port 1960 Cur: $93 (10/31/88)
90	WARRE Vintage Port 1960 Cur: $91 (10/31/88)
89	WIESE & KROHN Vintage Port 1960 Cur: $115 (VP-1/90)
88	DOW Vintage Port 1960 Cur: $89 (VP-2/90)
88	GRAHAM Vintage Port 1960 Cur: $102 (10/31/88)
88	QUINTA DE LA ROSA Vintage Port 1960 (NA) (VP-10/89)

Key to Symbols

The scores reported here are the results of blind tastings conducted by our panel of senior editors. Wines that carry the initials below are results of individual tastings.

THE WINE SPECTATOR 100-POINT SCALE   95-100—Classic, a great wine; *90-94*—Outstanding, superior character and style; *80-89*—Good to very good, a wine with special qualities; *70-79*—Average, drinkable wine that may have minor flaws; *60-69*—Below average, drinkable but not recommended; *50-59*—Poor, undrinkable, not recommended. "*+*"—With a score indicates a range; used primarily with barrel tastings to indicate a preliminary score.

SPECIAL DESIGNATIONS SS—Spectator Selection, CS—Cellar Selection, BB—Best Buy.

TASTER'S INITIALS (JG)—Jim Gordon, (HS)—Harvey Steiman, (JL)—James Laube, (JS)—James Suckling, (TM)—Thomas Matthews, (TR)—Terry Robards, (BT)—Barrel Tasting (these wines were tasted blind from barrel samples), (CA-date)—*California's Great Cabernets* by James Laube, (CH-date)—*California's Great Chardonnays* by James Laube, (VP-date)—*Vintage Port* by James Suckling.

DATE TASTED Dates in parentheses represent the issue in which the rating was published.

88   QUINTA DO NOVAL Vintage Port Nacional 1960 Cur: $350 (11/01/85) (JS)
87   KOPKE Vintage Port 1960 Cur: $65 (VP-1/90)
87   QUINTA DO NOVAL Vintage Port 1960 Cur: $84 (10/31/88)
86   FERREIRA Vintage Port 1960 Cur: $95 (10/31/88)
85   REBELLO-VALENTE Vintage Port 1960 Cur: $55 (VP-11/88)
84   GRAHAM Vintage Port 1960 Cur: $102 (VP-8/88)
84   QUINTA DO NOVAL Vintage Port Nacional 1960 Cur: $350 (VP-11/89)
84   TAYLOR FLADGATE Vintage Port 1960 Cur: $100 (10/31/88)
83   VAN ZELLER Vintage Port Quinta do Roriz 1960 (NA) (VP-7/90)
82   COCKBURN Vintage Port 1960 Cur: $98 (10/31/88)
82   OSBORNE Vintage Port 1960 Cur: $60 (VP-1/90)
82   POCAS JUNIOR Vintage Port 1960 Cur: $80 (VP-2/90)
82   QUINTA DO NOVAL Vintage Port 1960 Cur: $84 (VP-11/89)
82   WARRE Vintage Port 1960 Cur: $91 (VP-8/88)
81   FONSECA Vintage Port 1960 Cur: $95 (10/31/88)
80   COCKBURN Vintage Port 1960 Cur: $98 (VP-8/88)
80   FERREIRA Vintage Port 1960 Cur: $95 (VP-8/88)
80   FONSECA Vintage Port 1960 Cur: $95 (VP-8/88)
80   SANDEMAN Vintage Port 1960 Cur: $80 (10/31/88)
80   TAYLOR FLADGATE Vintage Port 1960 Cur: $100 (VP-8/88)
79   SANDEMAN Vintage Port 1960 Cur: $80 (7/15/90) (JS)
79   SANDEMAN Vintage Port 1960 Cur: $80 (VP-3/90)
78   OFFLEY Vintage Port Boa Vista 1960 Cur: $60 (VP-2/89)

1958

88   FONSECA Vintage Port Guimaraens 1958 Cur: $90 (VP-2/90)
87   WIESE & KROHN Vintage Port 1958 Cur: $180 (VP-1/90)
84   COCKBURN Vintage Port 1958 (NA) (VP-11/89)
82   QUINTA DO NOVAL Vintage Port 1958 Cur: $100 (VP-11/89)
82   SANDEMAN Vintage Port 1958 Cur: $75 (VP-3/90)
81   WARRE Vintage Port 1958 Cur: $99 (VP-11/89)
79   GRAHAM Vintage Port Malvedos 1958 Cur: $65 (VP-2/90)
79   QUINTA DO CRASTO Vintage Port 1958 (NA) (VP-8/90)
68   TAYLOR FLADGATE Vintage Port Quinta de Vargellas 1958 Cur: $50 (VP-2/90)

1957

85   SANDEMAN Vintage Port 1957 (NA) (VP-10/88)
84   GRAHAM Vintage Port Malvedos 1957 Cur: $70 (VP-2/90)

1955

98   NIEPOORT Vintage Port 1955 Cur: $175 (VP-8/90)
96   FONSECA Vintage Port 1955 Cur: $214 (VP-8/88)
94   GRAHAM Vintage Port 1955 Cur: $210 (VP-11/89)
94   SANDEMAN Vintage Port 1955 Cur: $159 (VP-3/90)
91   DOW Vintage Port 1955 Cur: $219 (VP-4/90)
90   COCKBURN Vintage Port 1955 Cur: $155 (VP-11/89)
88   QUINTA DO NOVAL Vintage Port 1955 Cur: $156 (VP-8/90)
88   TAYLOR FLADGATE Vintage Port 1955 Cur: $206 (VP-11/89)
86   MARTINEZ Vintage Port 1955 Cur: $120 (VP-11/89)
86   WARRE Vintage Port 1955 Cur: $191 (VP-11/89)
85   FERREIRA Vintage Port 1955 Cur: $119 (VP-11/89)
84   CROFT Vintage Port 1955 Cur: $184 (VP-11/89)

1954

91   GRAHAM Vintage Port 1954 Cur: $187 (VP-2/90)

1952

85   GRAHAM Vintage Port Malvedos 1952 Cur: $125 (VP-11/89)

1950

90   QUINTA DO NOVAL Vintage Port Nacional 1950 Cur: $850 (VP-11/89)
87   SANDEMAN Vintage Port 1950 Cur: $170 (VP-3/90)
86   DOW Vintage Port 1950 Cur: $110 (VP-11/89)
85   QUINTA DO NOVAL Vintage Port 1950 Cur: $240 (VP-11/89)
79   FERREIRA Vintage Port 1950 Cur: $90 (VP-11/89)
77   CROFT Vintage Port 1950 Cur: $170 (VP-4/90)
76   COCKBURN Vintage Port 1950 Cur: $100 (VP-11/89)

1948

100   FONSECA Vintage Port 1948 Cur: $340 (VP-11/89)
99   TAYLOR FLADGATE Vintage Port 1948 Cur: $330 (VP-11/89)
95   GRAHAM Vintage Port 1948 Cur: $290 (VP-11/89)

1947

93   QUINTA DO NOVAL Vintage Port 1947 Cur: $280 (VP-11/89)
90   COCKBURN Vintage Port 1947 Cur: $191 (VP-11/89)
90   SANDEMAN Vintage Port 1947 Cur: $196 (VP-3/90)
88   DOW Vintage Port 1947 Cur: $249 (VP-11/89)
88   WARRE Vintage Port 1947 Cur: $237 (VP-11/89)

1945

99   CROFT Vintage Port 1945 Cur: $380 (VP-11/89)
97   NIEPOORT Vintage Port 1945 Cur: $250 (VP-2/90)
97   TAYLOR FLADGATE Vintage Port 1945 Cur: $680 (VP-11/89)
95   GRAHAM Vintage Port 1945 Cur: $510 (VP-11/89)
95   SANDEMAN Vintage Port 1945 Cur: $350 (VP-3/90)
92   QUINTA DO NOVAL Vintage Port 1945 Cur: $310 (VP-11/89)
92   REBELLO-VALENTE Vintage Port 1945 Cur: $245 (VP-5/90)
91   FONSECA Vintage Port 1945 Cur: $660 (VP-11/89)
89   DOW Vintage Port 1945 Cur: $440 (VP-11/89)
87   WARRE Vintage Port 1945 Cur: $360 (VP-11/89)
81   FERREIRA Vintage Port 1945 Cur: $225 (VP-11/89)

1942

93   NIEPOORT Vintage Port 1942 Cur: $240 (VP-4/90)
89   GRAHAM Vintage Port 1942 Cur: $420 (VP-4/90)
88   SANDEMAN Vintage Port 1942 Cur: $210 (VP-3/90)
86   QUINTA DO NOVAL Vintage Port 1942 Cur: $200 (VP-4/90)
78   TAYLOR FLADGATE Vintage Port 1942 Cur: $275 (VP-4/90)
75   REBELLO-VALENTE Vintage Port 1942 Cur: $140 (VP-2/85)

1941

50   QUINTA DO NOVAL Vintage Port 1941 Cur: $70 (VP-9/85)

1938

79   TAYLOR FLADGATE Vintage Port 1938 Cur: $265 (VP-4/90)
71   QUINTA DO NOVAL Vintage Port 1938 Cur: $110 (VP-9/85)

1935

94   GRAHAM Vintage Port 1935 Cur: $400 (VP-4/90)
93   CROFT Vintage Port 1935 Cur: $320 (VP-2/90)
93   FERREIRA Vintage Port 1935 Cur: $200 (VP-2/90)
92   COCKBURN Vintage Port 1935 Cur: $330 (VP-2/90)
92   SANDEMAN Vintage Port 1935 Cur: $460 (VP-3/90)
90   QUINTA DA ROMANEIRA Vintage Port 1935 (NA) (VP-2/90)
88   TAYLOR FLADGATE Vintage Port 1935 Cur: $390 (VP-2/90)
79   DOW Vintage Port 1935 Cur: $300 (VP-6/90)

1934

98   QUINTA DO NOVAL Vintage Port 1934 Cur: $310 (VP-2/90)
94   SANDEMAN Vintage Port 1934 Cur: $300 (VP-3/90)
91   FONSECA Vintage Port 1934 Cur: $330 (VP-2/90)
87   WARRE Vintage Port 1934 Cur: $285 (VP-2/90)
84   DOW Vintage Port 1934 Cur: $350 (VP-6/90)

1931

100   QUINTA DO NOVAL Vintage Port Nacional 1931 Cur: $3,700 (VP-11/89)
99   QUINTA DO NOVAL Vintage Port 1931 Cur: $1,000 (VP-11/89)
89   COCKBURN Vintage Port 1931 (NA) (VP-1/90)

1927

100   FONSECA Vintage Port 1927 Cur: $430 (VP-12/89)
97   NIEPOORT Vintage Port 1927 Cur: $260 (VP-4/90)
95   TAYLOR FLADGATE Vintage Port 1927 Cur: $440 (VP-12/89)
94   GRAHAM Vintage Port 1927 Cur: $570 (VP-2/90)
93   QUINTA DO NOVAL Vintage Port 1927 Cur: $450 (VP-12/89)
93   WARRE Vintage Port 1927 Cur: $400 (VP-12/89)
92   SANDEMAN Vintage Port 1927 Cur: $400 (VP-3/90)
91   COCKBURN Vintage Port 1927 Cur: $340 (VP-12/89)
87   CROFT Vintage Port 1927 Cur: $460 (VP-12/89)
87   DOW Vintage Port 1927 Cur: $480 (VP-4/90)
87   QUINTA DE LA ROSA Vintage Port Feuerheerd Quinta de la Rosa 1927 (NA) (VP-12/89)

1920

78   SANDEMAN Vintage Port 1920 Cur: $300 (VP-3/90)

1917

88   SANDEMAN Vintage Port 1917 Cur: $300 (VP-3/90)

1912

91   COCKBURN Vintage Port 1912 Cur: $350 (VP-10/87)

1911

82   SANDEMAN Vintage Port 1911 Cur: $282 (VP-6/90)

1908

89   COCKBURN Vintage Port 1908 Cur: $400 (VP-10/87)
75   SANDEMAN Vintage Port 1908 Cur: $320 (VP-3/90)

1904

88   SANDEMAN Vintage Port 1904 Cur: $420 (VP-3/90)
75   COCKBURN Vintage Port 1904 Cur: $390 (VP-10/87)

1900

79   WARRE Vintage Port 1900 Cur: $430 (VP-11/89)

1896

82   COCKBURN Vintage Port 1896 Cur: $400 (VP-2/90)
81   SANDEMAN Vintage Port 1896 Cur: $600 (VP-3/90)

1887

74   SANDEMAN Vintage Port 1887 Cur: $600 (VP-3/90)

1871

98   ROYAL OPORTO Vintage Port 1871 (NA) (VP-11/89)

1870

98   SANDEMAN Vintage Port 1870 Cur: $700 (VP-3/90)

OTHER PORT

1940

96   QUARLES HARRIS Ruby Port Club 1940 $70 (1/31/88)

NV

96   BARROS Tawny Port 20 Year Old NV $35 (2/28/90) (JS)
95   BURMESTER Tawny Port 20 Year Old NV $40 (2/28/90) (JS)
93   MARTINEZ Tawny Port 20 Year Old Directors NV $25 (2/28/90) (JS)
90   FONSECA Tawny Port 20 Year Old Duque de Bragança 20 Year Old Port Bin 27 NV $40 (2/28/90) (JS)
89   DELAFORCE Fine Ruby Port NV $8.50 (3/31/88)
89   DOW Tawny Port 20 Year Old NV $10 (3/31/88)
89   OFFLEY Ruby Port Boa Vista Special Reserve NV $35 (2/28/90) (JS)
89   POCAS JUNIOR Tawny Port 20 Year Old NV $35 (2/28/90) (JS)
88   FONSECA Tawny Port 20 Year Old Duque de Bragança 20 Year Old Port Bin 27 NV $16 (3/31/88)
88   KOPKE Tawny Port 20 Year Old NV $30 (2/28/90) (JS)
88   WIESE & KROHN Tawny Port 20 Year Old NV $33 (2/28/90) (JS)
87   FERREIRA Tawny Port 20 Year Old Duque de Bragança 20 Year Old Port NV $30 (3/31/87)
87   SANDEMAN Fine Ruby Port NV $29 (2/28/90) (JS)

PORTUGAL
OTHER PORT

86   COCKBURN Fine Ruby Port NV $35 (2/28/90) (JS)
86   DELAFORCE Fine Ruby Port NV $9 (4/16/85)
86   SANDEMAN Fine Ruby Port NV $12.50 (3/31/88)
85   COCKBURN Fine Ruby Port NV $10 (3/31/88)
85   COCKBURN Fine Ruby Port NV $8 (3/31/88)
85   TAYLOR FLADGATE Fine Ruby Port Oporto Portugal Bicentennial Special Club NV $38 (2/28/90) (JS)
85   WARRE Fine Ruby Port Oporto Portugal Bicentennial Special Club 10 Year Old Sir William NV $24 (4/15/91)
84   GRAHAM Fine Ruby Port NV $36 (2/28/90) (JS)
84   RAMOS-PINTO Ruby Port NV $39 (2/28/90) (JS)
84   TAYLOR FLADGATE Fine Ruby Port Oporto Portugal Bicentennial Special Club NV $12.95 (2/16/85)
84   WARRE Fine Ruby Port Oporto Portugal Bicentennial Special Club 10 Year Old Sir William NV $38 (2/28/90) (JS)
84   WARRE Fine Ruby Port Oporto Portugal Bicentennial Special Club 10 Year Old Sir William NV $8.25 (3/31/88)
83   CALEM Tawny Port 20 Años NV $35 (4/15/90) (JS)
83   CHURCHILL Tawny Port 20 Años Finest Vintage Character NV $18.50 (4/15/91)
83   FERREIRA Tawny Port 20 Year Old Duque de Bragança 20 Year Old Port NV $7 (3/31/88)
83   WARRE Fine Ruby Port Oporto Portugal Bicentennial Special Club 10 Year Old Sir William NV $20 (4/30/91)
82   DOW Tawny Port 20 Year Old NV $23 (2/28/90) (JS)
82   QUINTA DO NOVAL Tawny Port 20 Year Old NV $32 (2/28/90) (JS)
82   WARRE Fine Ruby Port Oporto Portugal Bicentennial Special Club 10 Year Old Sir William NV $11.50 (1/31/87)
81   ROBERTSON Fine Ruby Port NV $33 (2/28/90) (JS)
80   FERREIRA Tawny Port 20 Year Old Duque de Bragança 20 Year Old Port NV $38 (2/28/90) (JS)
80   GRAHAM Fine Ruby Port NV $15/375ml (3/31/88)
79   NIEPOORT Ruby Port NV $7 (3/31/88)
79   RAMOS-PINTO Ruby Port NV $8.75 (3/31/88)
79   SMITH WOODHOUSE Fine Ruby Port Oporto Portugal Bicentennial NV $9.50 (6/01/85)
78   HOOPER Tawny Port 20 Year Old NV $35 (2/28/90) (JS)
78   C. PINTO Ruby Port Boa Vista Special Reserve Vinho do Porto Consolador NV $7.50 (3/31/88)
78   SANDEMAN Fine Ruby Port NV $8.25 (3/31/88)
78   TAYLOR FLADGATE Fine Ruby Port Oporto Portugal Bicentennial Special Club NV $8 (3/31/88)
77   AVERY Club NV $9.50 (3/31/88)
77   ROBERTSON Fine Ruby Port NV $9.75 (3/31/88)
77   ROYAL OPORTO Ruby Port NV $25 (2/28/90) (JS)
76   CROFT Tawny Port 20 Year Old NV $38 (2/28/90) (JS)
76   SANDEMAN Fine Ruby Port NV $13 (1/01/85)
75   OFFLEY Ruby Port Boa Vista Special Reserve NV $9.75 (3/31/88)
74   GRAHAM Fine Ruby Port NV $7 (3/31/88)
74   SMITH WOODHOUSE Fine Ruby Port Oporto Portugal Bicentennial NV $8 (3/31/88)
72   KOPKE Tawny Port 20 Year Old NV $6.50 (3/31/88)
72   QUARLES HARRIS Ruby Port Club NV $7.50 (3/31/88)
68   ROYAL OPORTO Ruby Port NV $7.25 (3/31/88)

OTHER PORTUGAL

1989

84   QUINTA DO CARDO Castelo Rodrigo 1989 $7 (12/31/90) BB

1987

84   JOSE MARIA DA FONSECA Periquita 1987 $5.75 (12/31/90) BB
81   QUINTA DO COTTO Grande Escolha 1987 $18 (12/31/90)
77   CAVES ALIANCA Reserva 1987 $5 (7/15/91)
74   QUINTA DO COTTO Vinho Tinto 1987 $9 (4/30/91)

1986

82   JOSE MARIA DA FONSECA Tinto Velho Requengos de Monsarax Colheita 1986 $9.75 (12/31/90)

1984

83   JOSE MARIA DA FONSECA Pasmados 1984 $7.25 (4/30/91) BB
78   CAVES ALIANCA Garrafeira 1984 $8 (7/15/91)
76   ESTEVA 1984 $5 (12/15/87)
74   CAVES ALIANCA Vinho Tinto 1984 $8 (7/15/91)

1982

88   JOSE MARIA DA FONSECA Garrafeira RA 1982 $13.50 (12/31/90)
84   CAVES ALIANCA Garrafeira 1982 $9 (7/15/91)

NV

83   JOSE MARIA DA FONSECA Garrafeira CO 1982 $13.50 (12/31/90)
65   CORADO Vinho Verde White Periquita NV $4.50 (9/30/86)

Key to Symbols

The scores reported here are the results of blind tastings conducted by our panel of senior editors. Wines that carry the initials below are results of individual tastings.

THE WINE SPECTATOR 100-POINT SCALE   *95-100*—Classic, a great wine; *90-94*—Outstanding, superior character and style; *80-89*—Good to very good, a wine with special qualities; *70-79*—Average, drinkable wine that may have minor flaws; *60-69*—Below average, drinkable but not recommended; *50-59*—Poor, undrinkable, not recommended. "+"—With a score indicates a range; used primarily with barrel tastings to indicate a preliminary score.

SPECIAL DESIGNATIONS   SS—Spectator Selection, CS—Cellar Selection, BB—Best Buy.

TASTER'S INITIALS   (JG)—Jim Gordon, (HS)—Harvey Steiman, (JL)—James Laube, (JS)—James Suckling, (TM)—Thomas Matthews, (TR)—Terry Robards, (BT)—Barrel Tasting (these wines were tasted blind from barrel samples), (CA-date)—*California's Great Cabernets* by James Laube, (CH-date)—*California's Great Chardonnays* by James Laube, (VP-date)—*Vintage Port* by James Suckling.

DATE TASTED   Dates in parentheses represent the issue in which the rating was published.

SPAIN
SPAIN RED/*NAVARRA*

1989
83   BODEGAS PRINCIPE DE VIANA Cabernet Sauvignon Navarra 1989 $8 (3/31/91) BB
82   BODEGAS MUGA-VILLFRANCA Navarra Mendiani 1989 $4 (6/15/91) BB

1988
85   BODEGAS BRANAVIEJA Navarra Pleno 1988 $6 (12/15/90) BB

1986
73   OCHOA Navarra 1986 $5.50 (4/15/89)

1985
77   SENORIO DE SARRIA Navarra 1985 $5 (7/31/89)

1984
86   LAS CAMPANAS Navarra 1984 $6 (3/31/90) BB
83   SENORIO DE SARRIA Navarra 1984 $5 (2/28/90) BB
82   OCHOA Navarra Crianza 1984 $7.50 (4/15/89)

1982
77   VINA MAGANA Navarra 1982 $16 (11/15/87)
77   VINICOLA NAVARRA Navarra Las Campanas Tino Tinto 1982 $5 (1/31/88)
73   BODEGAS MAGANA Navarra 1982 $14 (3/31/90)

1981
65   SENORIO DE SARRIA Navarra Gran Reserva 1981 $11 (3/31/90)

1980
85   OCHOA Navarra Reserva 1980 $10.50 (4/15/89)

1978
81   BODEGAS IRACHE Navarra Castillo Irache Reserva 1978 $12 (3/31/90)

1976
80   VINICOLA NAVARRA Navarra Castillo de Tiebas Reserva 1976 $7 (1/31/88)

NV
78   FINO ALAIZ Navarra NV $4 (10/31/88)

PENEDÈS

1989
82   TORRES Merlot Penedès Viña Las Torres 1989 $13 (10/15/90)

1988
83   MONT-MARCAL Penedès Tinto 1988 $8 (3/31/91)
83   TORRES Merlot Penedès Viña Las Torres 1988 $10 (3/31/90)
82   TORRES Penedès Sangre de Toro 1988 $6.50 (3/31/91) BB
81   TORRES Penedès Coronas 1988 $7 (6/15/91) BB
79   TORRES Penedès Más Borras 1988 $18 (10/15/90)

1987
82   TORRES Penedès Sangre de Toro 1987 $5.25 (11/30/89) BB
80   TORRES Penedès Coronas 1987 $6.50 (10/15/90) BB
78   GRAN CAUS Penedès Can Ràfols dels Caus 1987 $11 (10/15/90)

1986
86   TORRES Penedès Gran Coronas Reserva 1986 $12 (11/30/89)
83   TORRES Penedès Gran Sangre de Toro Reserva 1986 $10 (10/15/90)
80   TORRES Penedès Sangre de Toro 1986 $4.75 (12/15/88) BB
78   TORRES Penedès Coronas 1986 $6.25 (11/30/89)
77   GRAN CAUS Cabernet Sauvignon-Cabernet Franc-Merlot Penedès 1986 $12 (4/30/89)
76   VALLFORMOSA Penedès Vall Fort 1986 $7 (5/31/91)

1985
89   TORRES Penedès Gran Coronas 1985 $11 (11/30/88)
87   TORRES Penedès Gran Sangre de Toro Reserva 1985 $9 (11/30/89)
86   TORRES Penedès Coronas 1985 $5.50 (11/30/88) BB
85   TORRES Penedès Gran Coronas Más la Plana Reserva 1985 Rel: $32 Cur: $32 (10/15/90)
81   TORRES Penedès Sangre de Toro 1985 $5.50 (6/15/88) BB
77   GRAN CAUS Cabernet Sauvignon-Cabernet Franc-Merlot Penedès 1985 $11.75 (10/15/88)
77   TORRES Penedès Gran Coronas Reserva 1985 $12 (3/31/90)

1984
84   VALLFORMOSA Penedès Vall Fort 1984 $7 (3/31/91) BB
78   TORRES Penedès Gran Sangre de Toro 1984 $9 (9/15/88)
77   JEAN LEON Cabernet Sauvignon Penedès 1984 $12 (3/31/91)
76   TORRES Penedès Viña Magdala 1984 $11 (7/31/89)
68   GRAN CAUS Penedès 1984 $12 (9/15/88)

1983
91   TORRES Penedès Gran Sangre de Toro Reserva 1983 $9.50 (6/15/88) SS
85   JEAN LEON Cabernet Sauvignon Penedès 1983 $8.50 (3/31/90)
85   TORRES Penedès Gran Coronas Más la Plana Reserva 1983 Rel: $26 Cur: $26 (3/31/90)
84   TORRES Penedès Coronas 1983 $4.50 (6/30/87)
82   TORRES Penedès Gran Coronas Black Label Reserva 1983 Rel: $26 Cur: $26 (11/30/88)
79   TORRES Penedès Sangre de Toro 1983 $4 (6/15/87)
74   TORRES Penedès Viña Magdala 1983 $9.50 (6/15/88)

1982
88   TORRES Penedès Gran Coronas Black Label Reserva 1982 Rel: $27 Cur: $29 (2/16/86)
85   TORRES Penedès Gran Coronas Black Label Reserva 1982 Rel: $27 Cur: $29 (6/15/88)
83   TORRES Penedès Sangre de Toro 1982 (NA) (2/16/86) (JS)
77   RENE BARBIER Penedès 1982 $3 (1/31/87)
76   TORRES Penedès Coronas 1982 $4.50 (2/16/86) (JS)

1981
83   TORRES Penedès Gran Coronas Black Label Reserva 1981 Rel: $18 Cur: $23 (10/15/87)
80   TORRES Penedès Gran Sangre de Toro Reserva 1981 $5.50 (6/15/87)
74   RENE BARBIER Cabernet Sauvignon Penedès 1981 $5 (3/31/90)
69   RENE BARBIER Cabernet Sauvignon Penedès 1981 $5 (1/31/87)

1980
84   VALLFORMOSA Penedès Vall Reserva Tinto Propia 1980 $10 (3/31/91)

1979
79   TORRES Penedès Gran Sangre de Toro 1979 $9 (2/16/86) (JS)
75   TORRES Penedès Gran Coronas 1979 $9 (2/16/86) (JS)
72   TORRES Penedès Viña Magdala 1979 (NA) (2/16/86) (JS)

1978
85   TORRES Penedès Gran Coronas Black Label Reserva 1978 Cur: $65 (2/16/86)
77   RENE BARBIER Penedès Reserva 1978 $4.50 (3/31/90)
73   RENE BARBIER Penedès Reserva 1978 $4.50 (1/31/87)
66   JEAN LEON Cabernet Sauvignon Penedès 1978 $6.50 (4/16/84)

RIBERA DEL DUERO

1989
85   VINA MAYOR Ribera del Duero Tinto 1989 $7 (3/31/91) BB

1988
82   BODEGA HNOS. PEREZ PASCUAS Ribera del Duero Viña Pedrosa 1988 $16.50 (5/31/91)

1987
84   PESQUERA Ribera del Duero 1987 $17 (9/30/90)
82   BODEGAS MAURO Ribera del Duero 1987 $17 (10/15/90)
81   BODEGAS BALBAS Ribera del Duero 1987 $14 (9/30/90)
77   BODEGA HNOS. PEREZ PASCUAS Ribera del Duero Viña Pedrosa 1987 $15 (9/30/90)

1986
92   PESQUERA Ribera del Duero Reserva 1986 $26 (9/30/90)
91   PESQUERA Ribera del Duero 1986 $26 (4/30/89)
91   PESQUERA Ribera del Duero Reserva 1986 $26 (3/31/90) (TM)
90   BODEGAS VEGA SICILIA Ribera del Duero Valbuena 3 Años 1986 $47 (12/15/90)
88   BODEGA HNOS. PEREZ PASCUAS Ribera del Duero Viña Pedrosa 1986 $14 (3/31/90)
87   BODEGAS BALBAS Ribera del Duero 1986 $15 (7/31/89)
82   BODEGA HNOS. PEREZ PASCUAS Ribera del Duero Viña Pedrosa 1986 $14 (7/31/89)
81   SENORIO DE NAVA Ribera del Duero 1986 $8 (11/15/89)
76   BODEGAS MAURO Ribera del Duero 1986 $17 (3/31/90)
60   BODEGAS ISMAEL ARROYO Ribera del Duero Mesoñeros de Castilla 1986 $6 (4/30/88)

1985
92   BODEGAS VEGA SICILIA Ribera del Duero Valbuena 3 Años 1985 $40 (3/31/90) CS
89   PESQUERA Ribera del Duero 1985 $16 (4/30/88)
89   PESQUERA Ribera del Duero Reserva 1985 $16 (3/31/90) (TM)
88   BODEGAS MAURO Ribera del Duero 1985 $15 (3/31/90)
87   PENALBA Ribera del Duero Crianza 1985 $9 (2/28/90)
83   BODEGAS BALBAS Ribera del Duero 1985 $13 (9/15/88)
83   BODEGA HNOS. PEREZ PASCUAS Ribera del Duero Viña Pedrosa 1985 $16 (9/15/88)
75   BODEGAS BALBAS Ribera del Duero Reserva 1985 (NA) (3/31/90) (TM)

1984
90   BODEGAS VEGA SICILIA Ribera del Duero Valbuena 5 Años 1984 $49 (3/31/90)
89   PESQUERA Ribera del Duero 1984 $14 (11/15/87) (JL)
86   PESQUERA Ribera del Duero 1984 $14 (10/15/87)
85   BODEGAS MAURO Ribera del Duero 1984 $16 (9/15/88)
79   BODEGAS VEGA SICILIA Ribera del Duero Valbuena 3 Años 1984 $28 (4/30/89)
78   BODEGAS MAURO Ribera del Duero 1984 (NA) (3/31/90) (TM)

1983
94   PESQUERA Ribera del Duero 1983 $12 (11/15/87) (JL)
93   PESQUERA Ribera del Duero 1983 $12 (12/31/86)
88   BODEGAS VEGA SICILIA Ribera del Duero Valbuena 3 Años 1983 $22.50 (10/15/88)
86   PENALBA Ribera del Duero 1983 $12 (2/28/90)
82   BODEGAS MAURO Ribera del Duero 1983 $15 (10/15/87)

1982
94   PESQUERA Ribera del Duero Janus Reserva Especial 1982 Rel: $75 Cur: $75 (9/15/88)
92   PESQUERA Ribera del Duero Janus Reserva Especial 1982 Rel: $75 Cur: $75 (3/31/90)
91   BODEGAS VEGA SICILIA Ribera del Duero Valbuena 5 Años 1982 $37 (3/31/90)
91   BODEGAS VEGA SICILIA Ribera del Duero Valbuena 5 Años 1982 $36 (10/15/88)
90   BODEGAS VEGA SICILIA Ribera del Duero Valbuena 1982 $25 (10/15/88)
89   PESQUERA Ribera del Duero 1982 (NA) (11/15/87) (JL)
70   PENALBA Ribera del Duero Reserva 1982 (NA) (3/31/90) (TM)

1980
73   PENALBA Ribera del Duero Gran Reserva 1980 (NA) (3/31/90) (TM)

1979
95   BODEGAS VEGA SICILIA Ribera del Duero Unico 1979 Rel: $75 Cur: $80 (3/31/90)
90   PESQUERA Ribera del Duero 1979 (NA) (11/15/87) (JL)

1978
89   PESQUERA Ribera del Duero 1978 (NA) (11/15/87) (JL)

1976
91   BODEGAS VEGA SICILIA Ribera del Duero Unico 1976 Rel: $60 Cur: $83 (4/30/89)

1975
88   PESQUERA Ribera del Duero 1975 (NA) (11/15/87) (JL)

1973
90   BODEGAS VEGA SICILIA Ribera del Duero Unico 1973 Cur: $82 (3/31/90) (TM)

1962
89   BODEGAS VEGA SICILIA Ribera del Duero Unico 1962 Rel: $106 Cur: $113 (3/31/90)

NV
79   BODEGAS VEGA SICILIA Ribera del Duero Unico Reserva Especial NV $156 (3/31/90)

SPAIN
SPAIN RED/*RIOJA*

1989

83   BODEGAS MARTINEZ BUJANDA Rioja Valdemar Vino Tinto 1989 $7 (6/30/90) BB
77   BODEGAS MUERZA Rioja Rioja Vega 1989 $7 (3/31/91)

1988

78   CODICE Rioja 1988 $6 (6/15/91)
77   VINA BERCEO Rioja 1988 $5 (11/15/89)
70   VINA BERCEO Rioja 1988 $5 (9/30/90)

1987

86   VINA BERCEO Rioja 1987 $5 (4/15/89) BB
84   BODEGAS BERBERANA Rioja Carta de Plata 1987 $7.50 (12/15/90) BB
83   BODEGAS OLARRA Rioja Añares 1987 $6.50 (3/31/90) BB
83   BODEGAS PALACIO Rioja Cosme Palacio y Hermanos 1987 (NA) (3/31/90) (TM)
81   BODEGAS CAMPO VIEJO Rioja 1987 $6.50 (9/30/90) BB
80   ARTADI Rioja Alavesa 1987 $6 (4/30/88)
80   GRAN CONDAL Rioja 1987 $6.50 (3/31/90)
75   BODEGAS RIOJANAS Rioja Canchales 1987 $4 (3/15/90)

1986

88   BODEGAS BERBERANA Rioja Carta de Plata 1986 $6 (5/15/89) BB
88   BODEGAS PALACIO Rioja Cosme Palacio y Hermanos 1986 $9 (2/28/89)
87   VINA BERCEO Rioja Crianza 1986 $7 (9/30/90) BB
87   REMELLURI Rioja 1986 $11 (12/15/90)
82   MARQUES DE CACERES Rioja 1986 $9 (5/31/91)
82   CUNE Rioja Clarete 1986 $7 (2/28/90) BB
81   MARQUES DE ARIENZO Rioja 1986 $8 (3/31/90) (TM)
81   BODEGAS BERBERANA Rioja Carta de Oro 1986 $8 (3/31/90)
81   CUNE Rioja Viña Real 1986 $8 (3/31/90)
81   BODEGAS MUGA Rioja Crianza 1986 $12 (5/31/91)
80   BODEGAS MARTINEZ BUJANDA Rioja Conde de Valdemar 1986 $7 (6/30/90) BB
80   BODEGAS PALACIO Rioja Glorioso 1986 $8 (3/31/90) (TM)
78   BODEGAS ONDARRE Rioja Tidon 1986 $4.50 (12/15/88)
77   VINADRIAN Rioja Tinto 1986 $3.75 (10/15/88)
75   BODEGAS MUERZA Rioja Rioja Vega Crianza 1986 $10 (3/31/91)
70   VINA BERCEO Rioja Crianza 1986 $7 (11/15/89)
66   BODEGAS MONTECILLO Rioja Viña Cumbrero 1986 $5 (3/31/90)

1985

90   BODEGAS BERBERANA Rioja Reserva 1985 $10 (2/28/90)
89   BODEGAS BERBERANA Rioja Carta de Plata 1985 $6 (10/31/88) BB
89   BODEGAS MARTINEZ BUJANDA Rioja Conde de Valdemar 1985 $7 (12/15/88) BB
88   CUNE Rioja 1985 $17 (3/31/90) (TM)
88   CUNE Rioja Contino Reserva 1985 $14 (12/15/90)
88   REMELLURI Rioja 1985 $10 (3/31/90) (TM)
87   MARQUES DE MURRIETA Rioja 1985 $17 (2/28/90)
85   BODEGAS BRETON Rioja Lorinon Crianza 1985 $9 (3/31/90)
85   BODEGAS CAMPO VIEJO Rioja Viña Alcorta 1985 $10 (9/30/90)
85   CUNE Rioja Clarete 1985 $6 (4/15/89) BB
85   CUNE Rioja Reserva 1985 $8.50 (3/31/90)
85   CUNE Rioja Viña Real Crianza 1985 $7 (3/31/90) (TM)
85   BODEGAS PALACIO Rioja Glorioso 1985 $7 (2/28/89) BB
85   LA RIOJA ALTA Rioja Viña Alberdi 1985 $8 (3/15/90) BB
84   MARQUES DE ARIENZO Rioja 1985 $8 (7/31/89) BB
83   BODEGAS CAMPO VIEJO Rioja 1985 $6.50 (3/15/90) BB
83   CONDE DE VALDEMAR Rioja Reserva 1985 $9 (11/15/89)
83   FAUSTINO V Rioja 1985 $7.50 (10/15/88)
83   BODEGAS MUGA Rioja Crianza 1985 (NA) (3/31/90) (TM)
82   MARQUES DE CACERES Rioja 1985 $9.50 (12/15/88)
82   BODEGAS CAMPO VIEJO Rioja Reserva 1985 $9 (9/30/90)
82   BODEGAS OLARRA Rioja Añares 1985 $6 (2/28/89) BB
81   BODEGAS EL COTO Rioja 1985 $5 (3/31/90) BB
81   BODEGAS PALACIOS REMONDO Rioja Herencia 1985 (NA) (3/31/90) (TM)
80   MARQUES DE CACERES Rioja 1985 $9.50 (3/31/90)
80   BODEGAS MONTECILLO Rioja Viña Cumbrero 1985 $5 (11/15/88) BB
80   FREDERICO PATERNINA Rioja Banda Azul 1985 $5 (3/15/90) BB
79   BODEGAS CORRAL Rioja Don Jacobo 1985 $8 (3/31/90)
79   LA RIOJA ALTA Rioja Viña Ardanza 1985 $15 (3/31/90)
78   MARQUES DE ARIENZO Rioja 1985 $7.50 (3/15/90)
78   BODEGAS BERBERANA Rioja Carta de Oro 1985 $6 (7/31/89)
76   VINA BERCEO Rioja Reserva 1985 $10 (3/31/90)
67   BODEGAS EL COTO Rioja Crianza 1985 $5.50 (3/31/90)
62   MARQUES DE RISCAL Rioja Reserva 1985 $9.50 (3/31/90)
59   BODEGAS MONTECILLO Rioja Viña Cumbrero 1985 $5 (3/31/90)

1984

84   CUNE Rioja Contino Reserva 1984 $12 (3/31/90)
82   BODEGAS CAMPO VIEJO Rioja 1984 $5.25 (1/31/88) BB
82   BODEGAS MUGA Rioja 1984 $8.50 (4/30/89)
81   BODEGAS EL COTO Rioja 1984 $7 (3/31/90) BB
80   CUNE Rioja Clarete 1984 $6 (10/15/88) BB
80   BODEGAS ONDARRE Rioja Ondarre 1984 $5 (11/15/88) BB

78   MARQUES DEL PUERTO Rioja 1984 $7 (2/28/90)
77   REMELLURI Rioja 1984 $9 (3/31/90) (TM)
76   VINA BERCEO Rioja Tinto Crianza 1984 $5.75 (10/15/88)
70   R. LOPEZ DE HEREDIA Rioja Cubillo 1984 $5.50 (3/31/90)
70   BODEGAS OLARRA Rioja Cerro Añon 1984 $4.50 (12/01/85)
69   BODEGAS MONTECILLO Rioja Viña Cumbrero 1984 $4 (11/30/87)
68   MARQUES DE RISCAL Rioja 1984 $9 (11/15/88)
58   MARQUES DE RISCAL Rioja 1984 $9 (3/31/90)

1983

87   BODEGAS BERBERANA Rioja Berberana Reserva 1983 $7 (4/30/89) BB
87   BODEGAS OLARRA Rioja Tinto 1983 $5 (9/30/86) BB
86   BODEGAS BERBERANA Rioja Reserva 1983 $9 (11/15/89)
84   MARQUES DE ARIENZO Rioja Reserva 1983 $12 (5/31/91)
84   MARQUES DE ARIENZO Rioja Reserva 1983 $13 (3/31/90) (TM)
84   MARQUES DE MURRIETA Rioja Reserva 1983 $13 (3/31/90)
83   BODEGAS RIOJANAS Rioja Monte Real Reserva 1983 $7.50 (3/31/90) BB
81   MARQUES DE ARIENZO Rioja 1983 $5 (6/30/88) BB
79   BODEGAS BILBAINAS Rioja Viña Pomal 1983 $8 (6/30/90)
79   R. LOPEZ DE HEREDIA Rioja Tondonia Reserva 1983 $5.50 (3/31/90)
78   R. LOPEZ DE HEREDIA Rioja Bosconia Reserva 1983 $5.50 (3/31/90)
77   REMELLURI Rioja 1983 $11.50 (3/31/90)
76   BODEGAS OLARRA Rioja Añares 1983 $6.50 (2/28/90)
76   LA RIOJA ALTA Rioja Viña Ardanza Reserva 1983 $21 (12/15/90)
73   BODEGAS OLARRA Rioja Añares Reserva 1983 $12 (2/28/90)
69   VINA BERCEO Rioja Reserva 1983 $10 (11/15/89)
68   BODEGAS RIOJANAS Rioja Viña Albina 1983 $7.50 (3/31/90)
61   BODEGAS OLARRA Rioja Cerro Añon Reserva 1983 $10.50 (3/31/90)

1982

90   BODEGAS PALACIOS REMONDO Rioja 1982 (NA) (11/15/87) (JL)
89   BODEGAS MONTECILLO Rioja Viña Cumbrero 1982 $4 (12/31/86) BB
87   MARQUES DE CACERES Rioja 1982 $7.50 (11/15/87) (JL)
87   BODEGAS CAMPO VIEJO Rioja Viña Alcorta Reserva 1982 (NA) (11/15/87) (JL)
86   BODEGAS EL COTO Rioja Gran Reserva 1982 (NA) (11/15/87) (JL)
86   BODEGAS OLARRA Rioja 1982 (NA) (11/15/87) (JL)
85   GURPEGUI Rioja Viña Berceo Reserva 1982 (NA) (11/15/87) (JL)
84   R. LOPEZ DE HEREDIA Rioja Bosconia Reserva 1982 $5.50 (11/15/87) (JL)
84   NUESTRA SENORA DE LA ANTIGUA Rioja 1982 (NA) (11/15/87) (JL)
84   REMELLURI Rioja Alavesa Labastida 1982 $8 (9/30/86)
84   LA RIOJA ALTA Rioja Viña Ardanza Reserva 1982 $15 (3/31/90)
84   MARQUES DE RISCAL Rioja 1982 $7 (11/15/87) (JL)
83   CUNE Rioja Clarete 1982 $4.50 (6/01/85)
82   BODEGAS BERBERANA Rioja Reserva 1982 $10 (12/15/88)
82   BODEGAS BERONIA Rioja Reserva 1982 $12 (3/31/90) (TM)
82   REMELLURI Rioja 1982 $12 (3/31/90) (TM)
81   CUNE Rioja Contino Reserva 1982 $12 (4/30/89)
80   BODEGAS RIOJANAS Rioja Viña Albina Gran Reserva 1982 $10 (11/15/87) (JL)
79   BODEGAS MARTINEZ BUJANDA Rioja Conde de Valdemar Reserva 1982 (NA) (11/15/87) (JL)
79   BODEGAS CORRAL Rioja Don Jacobo 1982 $7 (11/15/87) (JL)
79   GRAN CONDAL Rioja Gran Reserva 1982 $10 (11/15/87) (JL)
79   BODEGAS MONTECILLO Rioja Viña Cumbrero 1982 $4 (11/15/87) (JL)
79   BODEGAS PALACIO Rioja Glorioso Reserva 1982 $18 (3/31/90) (TM)
78   MARQUES DEL PUERTO Rioja 1982 $6 (11/15/87) (JL)
77   BODEGAS MUGA Rioja 1982 $7 (11/15/87) (JL)
76   VINA BERCEO Rioja Tinto Reserva 1982 $8.50 (10/15/88)
76   LA RIOJA ALTA Rioja Viña Ardanza Reserva 1982 $15 (3/31/90) (TM)
74   MARQUES DE RISCAL Rioja 1982 $7 (6/15/87)
70   R. LOPEZ DE HEREDIA Rioja Bosconia 1982 $6 (12/31/87)

1981

88   ANARES Rioja Reserva 1981 $8 (9/30/86)
88   MARQUES DE CACERES Rioja 1981 $5.50 (11/01/85) BB
88   CUNE Rioja Viña Real Gran Reserva 1981 $17 (3/31/90)
88   FAUSTINO I Rioja Gran Reserva 1981 $12 (10/31/88)
86   BODEGAS CORRAL Rioja Don Jacobo Reserva 1981 $10.50 (3/31/90)
86   CUNE Rioja Imperial Gran Reserva 1981 $21 (3/31/90)
86   BODEGAS MONTECILLO Rioja Viña Monty Gran Reserva 1981 $9.25 (7/31/89)
84   BODEGAS OLARRA Rioja Añares Gran Reserva 1981 $16 (3/31/90)
84   BODEGAS ONDARRE Rioja Reserva 1981 $7 (12/15/88) BB
83   MARQUES DE ARIENZO Rioja Gran Reserva 1981 $18 (5/31/91)
83   MARQUES DE ARIENZO Rioja Reserva 1981 $12 (7/31/89)
83   BODEGAS PALACIO Rioja Glorioso Reserva 1981 $10 (2/28/89)
81   BODEGAS EL COTO Rioja Coto de Imaz Reserva 1981 $9 (3/31/90)
80   GRAN CONDAL Rioja Gran Reserva 1981 $8 (11/30/87)
80   BODEGAS MUGA Rioja Prado Enea Reserva 1981 $20 (4/30/89)
79   BODEGAS MUGA Rioja Prado Enea Gran Reserva 1981 (NA) (3/31/90) (TM)
78   BODEGAS CAMPO VIEJO Rioja Reserva 1981 $7.25 (11/15/88)
78   R. LOPEZ DE HEREDIA Rioja Tondonia 1981 $6 (12/31/87)
78   BODEGAS MONTECILLO Rioja Viña Monty Gran Reserva 1981 $5 (11/15/88)
78   BODEGAS OLARRA Rioja Cerro Añon Reserva 1981 $8 (9/30/86)
76   BODEGAS CAMPO VIEJO Rioja Viña Alcorta 1981 $7.25 (10/31/88)
75   BODEGAS PALACIO Rioja Glorioso Gran Reserva 1981 (NA) (3/31/90) (TM)
74   BODEGAS OLARRA Rioja Cerro Añon Gran Reserva 1981 $13.50 (3/31/90)
73   MONTE VELAZ Rioja 1981 $4 (10/15/87)
73   BODEGAS MONTECILLO Rioja Viña Cumbrero 1981 $4 (6/01/86) BB
69   MARQUES DE CACERES Rioja Reserva 1981 $20 (3/31/90)
64   BODEGAS CAMPO VIEJO Rioja Viña Alcorta (Tempranillo) 1981 $7 (3/31/90)

1980

87   BODEGAS OLARRA Rioja Tinto 1980 $4.50 (3/16/85) BB
83   CUNE Rioja Contino Reserva 1980 $10.75 (1/31/87)
83   MARQUES DE MURRIETA Rioja Reserva 1980 $27 (3/31/90)
82   BODEGAS BERBERANA Rioja Gran Reserva 1980 $9 (10/31/88)
82   GRAN CONDAL Rioja Reserva 1980 $7 (11/30/87) BB
79   BODEGAS MONTECILLO Rioja Viña Monty Gran Reserva 1980 $7 (11/30/87)
77   VINA BERCEO Rioja Tinto Reserva 1980 $8.50 (10/15/88)
76   MARQUES DE ARIENZO Rioja Reserva 1980 $8 (6/30/88)
75   CUNE Rioja Viña Real 1980 $5.50 (6/01/85)

75   BODEGAS OLARRA Rioja Cerro Añon 1980 $4.50 (4/01/85)

1978

89   MARQUES DE MURRIETA Rioja Gran Reserva 1978 $29 (3/31/90)
88   BODEGAS BILBAINAS Rioja Viña Pomal Gran Reserva 1978 $20 (3/31/90)
88   BODEGAS PALACIO Rioja Glorioso Gran Reserva 1978 $15 (2/28/89)
85   BODEGAS MONTECILLO Rioja Especial Gran Reserva 1978 $30 (3/31/90)
85   MARQUES DEL PUERTO Rioja Gran Reserva 1978 $20 (3/31/90)
83   BODEGAS CAMPO VIEJO Rioja Gran Reserva 1978 $13.50 (9/30/90)
83   BODEGAS OLARRA Rioja Cerro Añon Reserva 1978 $8 (3/01/85)
82   BODEGAS OLARRA Rioja Reserva 1978 $7.50 (3/16/85)
81   BODEGAS MONTECILLO Rioja Viña Monty 1978 $7 (9/30/86)
79   BODEGAS MUGA Rioja Prado Enea Reserva 1978 $18 (3/31/90)
78   MARQUES DE ARIENZO Rioja Gran Reserva 1978 $18 (3/31/90) (TM)
78   BODEGAS CAMPO VIEJO Rioja Gran Reserva 1978 $13.50 (11/15/88)
78   CUNE Rioja 1978 $5.50 (6/16/85)
76   PRIVILEGIO DEL RAY SANCHO Rioja 1978 $3 (4/01/84)
70   CUNE Rioja Imperial Gran Reserva 1978 $15 (3/31/90)
65   LA RIOJA ALTA Rioja Viña Ardanza Reserva 1978 $6 (9/30/86)

1976

90   LA RIOJA ALTA Rioja Reserva 904 Gran Reserva 1976 Cur: $26 (3/31/90) (TM)
88   BODEGAS DOMECQ Rioja Gran Reserva 1976 $19 (11/15/89)
84   BODEGAS MUGA Rioja Prado Enea Gran Reserva 1976 (NA) (3/31/90) (TM)
83   R. LOPEZ DE HEREDIA Rioja Tondonia Gran Reserva 1976 $14 (3/31/90)
77   BODEGAS MUGA Rioja Gran Reserva 1976 (NA) (3/31/90) (TM)
72   MARQUES DE ARIENZO Rioja Gran Reserva 1976 $18 (3/31/90)
72   R. LOPEZ DE HEREDIA Rioja Bosconia Gran Reserva 1976 $14 (3/31/90)
70   MARQUES DE ARIENZO Rioja Gran Reserva 1976 $18 (11/15/87)
70   BODEGAS MONTECILLO Rioja Viña Monty 1976 $6 (5/16/86)

1975

87   MARQUES DE MURRIETA Rioja Gran Reserva 1975 $33 (3/31/90)
87   MARQUIS DE VILLAMAGNA Rioja Gran Reserva 1975 $19 (10/31/88)
85   BODEGAS MONTECILLO Rioja Gran Reserva 1975 $29 (12/15/88)
84   CUNE Rioja Imperial Gran Reserva 1975 $24 (3/31/90)
67   MARQUES DE CACERES Rioja Reserva 1975 $9.50 (12/01/85)

1973

85   CUNE Rioja Imperial Gran Reserva 1973 (NA) (3/31/90) (TM)
84   LA RIOJA ALTA Rioja Reserva 904 Gran Reserva 1973 $10 (9/30/86)
83   LA RIOJA ALTA Rioja Reserva 890 Gran Reserva 1973 Cur: $54 (3/31/90) (TM)
80   R. LOPEZ DE HEREDIA Rioja Bosconia Gran Reserva 1973 $14 (3/31/90)
79   R. LOPEZ DE HEREDIA Rioja Tondonia Gran Reserva 1973 $15 (12/31/87)
75   R. LOPEZ DE HEREDIA Rioja Bosconia Gran Reserva 1973 $15 (12/31/87)

1968

92   MARQUES DE MURRIETA Rioja Castillo Ygay Gran Reserva 1968 Rel: $85 Cur: $98 (3/31/90)

1952

94   MARQUES DE MURRIETA Rioja Castillo Ygay Gran Reserva 1952 $150 (3/31/90)

OTHER SPAIN RED

1989

81   VEGA DE MORIZ Valdepeñas Cencibel 1989 $5.50 (6/15/91) BB

1988

81   MONTESIERRA Somontano 1988 $6 (3/31/90)
78   MONTESIERRA Somontano 1988 $6 (5/15/89)

1987

84   RAIMAT Costers del Segre Abadia 1987 $9 (3/31/90)
81   PADORNINA El Bierzo 1987 $8 (3/31/90)
81   BODEGA SAN VALERO Cariñena Don Mendo Tinto Especial 1987 $5 (11/30/89) BB
80   MONTESIERRA Somontano 1987 $5.50 (9/15/88)
80   TAJA Jumilla 1987 $6 (3/31/90) BB

1986

91   LAR DE BARROS Tierra de Barros Tinto Reserva 1986 $8 (10/15/90) SS
82   COLEGIATA Toro Tinto 1986 $5 (11/30/89) BB
81   RAIMAT Cabernet Sauvignon Costers del Segre 1986 $10 (3/31/90)
79   FARINA Tinto Crianzano Tierra del Vino 1986 $7 (11/30/89)
77   COLEGIATA Toro Gran Colegiata Tinto de Crianza 1986 $7 (11/30/89)
77   MONTESIERRA Somontano 1986 $5 (11/15/87)

1985

88   COLEGIATA Toro Tinto 1985 $5 (11/30/89) BB
86   MARQUES DE GRINON Tinto do Toledo 1985 $12 (2/28/90)
85   J. DIAZ Madrid 1985 $5.75 (3/31/90) BB
85   BODEGAS PORTO Toro Tinto de Crianza Gran Colegiata 1985 $5 (12/31/87)
85   VINOS DE LEON Tinto Palacio de Leon 1985 $4.50 (11/15/89) BB
84   BODEGAS PORTO Toro Tinto Colegiata 1985 $4 (12/31/87) BB
82   CASA DE LA VINA Valdepeñas Cencibel 1985 $6.50 (3/31/90)
80   BODEGAS JAIME CARRERAS Valencia 1985 $4 (3/31/90) BB
75   CASTILLO JUMILLA Jumilla 1985 $5 (7/31/89)
74   PADORNINA El Bierzo 1985 $7 (6/30/90)
72   J. DIAZ Madrid Tinto de Madrid 1985 $6 (6/30/88)
70   BODEGAS PIQUERAS Almansa Castillo de Almansa Vino de Crianza 1985 $7.50 (4/30/91)

1983

88   BODEGAS PIQUERAS Almansa Castillo de Almansa Vino de Crianza 1983 $6.50 (7/31/89) BB
82   BODEGAS C. AUGUSTO EGLI Utiel-Requena Casa lo Alto 1983 $9 (7/31/89)
80   RENE BARBIER Red Table Wine 1983 $3 (3/31/90) BB
77   LAR DE BARROS Tierra de Barros Tinto Reserva 1983 $7.50 (10/15/87)
74   CASTILLO DE ALMANSA Almansa Crianza 1983 $7 (3/31/90)
74   BODEGAS PIQUERAS Almansa Castello de Almansa 1983 $7 (3/31/90)

1982

90   LAR DE LARES Tierra de Barros Gran Reserva 1982 $14 (6/15/91)
87   ESTOLA La Mancha Reserva 1982 $6 (11/15/89) BB
87   LAR DE BARROS Tierra de Barros Tinto Reserva 1982 $5.50 (5/15/87) BB
85   MONTE DUCAY Cariñena Gran Reserva 1982 $8 (11/30/89)
84   BODEGAS INVIOSA Tierra de Barros Lar de Lares Gran Reserva 1982 $12 (3/31/90)
83   MARQUES DE CARO Valencia Vinedos del Valle de Albaida Reserva Garnacha Tintorera 1982 $6.50 (12/15/88) BB
83   BODEGAS PIQUERAS Almansa Castello de Almansa 1983 $6 (10/31/88) BB
78   BODEGAS PORTO Toro Tinto de Crianza Gran Colegiata 1982 $5.50 (11/30/87)

1978

82   MONTE DUCAY Cariñena Vinedos Propios Tinto Gran Reserva 1978 $8.50 (10/31/88)

SPAIN WHITE/*PENEDÈS*

1990

84   TORRES Penedès Viña Esmeralda 1990 $10.50 (7/15/91)
81   TORRES Penedès Fransola (Green Label) 1990 $16 (7/15/91)

1989

93   TORRES Penedès Milmanda 1989 $40 (12/15/90)
84   TORRES Penedès Viña Esmeralda 1989 $9 (3/31/90)
80   TORRES Penedès Gran Viña Sol 1989 $10 (12/15/90)
73   TORRES Penedès Viña Sol 1989 $7 (7/15/91)

1988

88   JEAN LEON Chardonnay Penedès 1988 $34 (1/31/91)
83   TORRES Penedès Gran Viña Sol 1988 $14 (3/31/90)
80   TORRES Penedès Milmanda 1988 $35 (3/31/90)
79   TORRES Penedès Fransola 1988 $14.50 (3/31/90)
75   BALADA Penedès Macabeo Gran Blanc 1988 $8 (3/31/90)
72   TORRES Penedès Viña Sol 1988 $5.25 (3/31/90)

1987

94   TORRES Penedès Milmanda 1987 $35 (12/15/88)
86   TORRES Penedès Fransola Reserva 1987 $12.50 (12/15/88)
81   GRAN CAUS Chardonnay Penedès Chenin Blanc Xarel-lo 1987 $10 (5/15/89)
81   TORRES Penedès Gran Viña Sol 1987 $8 (12/15/88)
74   TORRES Penedès Viña Esmeralda 1987 $8.50 (6/15/88)

1986

87   TORRES Penedès Gran Viña Sol Green Label 1986 $14 (10/15/88)

1985

83   TORRES Penedès Gran Viña Sol 1985 $5 (4/30/87) BB
75   TORRES Penedès Viña Esmeralda 1985 $7.50 (2/16/86) (JS)
74   TORRES Penedès San Valentin 1985 (NA) (2/16/86) (JS)

1984

80   TORRES Penedès Gran Viña Sol 1984 $5 (2/16/86)
78   TORRES Penedès Gran Viña Sol Green Label 1984 $12 (2/16/86)
78   TORRES Penedès Viña Sol 1984 $4.50 (2/16/86) (JS)
75   TORRES Penedès Gran Viña Sol Reserva 1984 $12 (11/15/87)

NV

81   NAVERAN Penedès NV $9 (12/31/88)

RIOJA

1989

80   BODEGAS MONTECILLO Rioja Viña Cumbrero 1989 $6 (7/15/91) BB

1988

82   BODEGAS OLARRA Rioja Añares Blanco Seco 1988 $7 (3/31/90) BB
78   MARQUES DE CACERES Rioja 1988 $7.50 (3/31/90)
72   BODEGAS MONTECILLO Rioja Viña Cumbrero 1988 $5 (3/31/90)

1987

83   MARQUES DE CACERES Rioja 1987 $6.75 (12/15/88)
69   FREDERICO PATERNINA Rioja Banda Dorada 1987 $5 (3/31/90)

1986

76   FAUSTINO V Rioja 1986 $7.50 (11/30/88)
75   BODEGAS ONDARRE Rioja Ondarre 1986 $5 (11/30/88)
70   BODEGAS MONTECILLO Rioja Viña Cumbrero 1986 $4 (2/15/88)

1985

88   MARQUES DE MURRIETA Rioja 1985 $14 (3/31/90)
76   BODEGAS MONTECILLO Rioja Viña Cumbrero 1985 $4 (10/15/86) BB

1984

85   MARQUES DE MURRIETA Rioja 1984 $13 (3/31/90)
79   CUNE Rioja Blanco 1984 $6.75 (2/15/88)
68   BODEGAS MONTECILLO Rioja Viña Cumbrero 1984 $4 (5/01/86)
62   R. LOPEZ DE HEREDIA Rioja Tondonia 1984 $6 (2/15/88)
59   MARQUES DE CACERES Rioja 1984 $4.25 (5/16/86)

1978

91   MARQUES DE MURRIETA Rioja Gran Reserva 1978 $29 (3/31/90)

OTHER SPAIN WHITE

1990

85   MORGADIO ALBARINO Rias Baixas 1990 $22 (7/15/91)
84   CARBALLO DO REI CONDADO Rias Baixas 1990 $14 (7/15/91)

1989

82   RAIMAT Chardonnay Costers del Segre 1989 $10 (12/15/90)

SPAIN
SPAIN WHITE/OTHER SPAIN WHITE

80   MARQUES DE ALLELLA Alella 1989 $17 (12/15/90)
77   HIJOS DE ANTONIO BARCELO Rueda Vino Blanco Santorcal 1989 $6 (7/15/91)

1988

81   MARQUES DE RISCAL Sauvignon Blanc Rueda 1988 $7.50 (3/31/90)
77   ANGEL RODRIGUEZ VIDAL Rueda Martinsancho Verdejo 1988 $9 (3/31/90)

1987

85   MARQUES DE RISCAL Sauvignon Blanc Rueda 1987 $7.25 (12/15/88)
70   MARQUES DE RISCAL Rueda 1987 $5 (10/15/88)

SPARKLING

1988

84   CODORNIU Brut Blanc de Blancs Cava 1988 $9 (12/31/90) BB
78   CODORNIU Brut Cava Anna de Codorniu 1988 $8 (12/31/90)
74   XIPELLA Blanc de Blancs Conca de Barbera 1988 $6 (3/31/90)

1987

75   CODORNIU Brut Cava Anna de Codorniu 1987 $7 (8/31/90)

1986

84   CODORNIU Brut Cava Chardonnay 1986 $12 (7/31/89)
82   CODORNIU Brut Cava Clasico 1986 $6 (5/15/89) BB
79   LEMBEY Brut Cava Pedro Domecq 1986 $7.25 (7/15/90)
77   CODORNIU Brut Blanc de Blancs Cava 1986 $8 (7/31/89)

1985

85   LEMBEY Sparkling Cava Première Cuvée 1985 $12 (7/15/91)
81   FREIXENET Brut Nature Cava 1985 $10 (12/31/90)
79   CODORNIU Brut Cava 1985 $7.25 (5/31/88)
76   CODORNIU Brut Cava Anna de Codorniu 1985 $6.50 (7/31/89)
74   LEMBEY Brut Cava 1985 $6.50 (5/31/88)
73   CASTELLBLANCH Brut Cava Zero 1985 $6 (12/31/88)
72   CODORNIU Extra Dry Cava 1985 $7.25 (5/31/88)

1984

85   FERRET Brut Nature Cava Rosat 1984 $15 (5/31/88)
78   FERRET Brut Nature Cava 1984 $14 (5/31/88)
75   FREIXENET Brut Nature Cava 1984 $8.50 (5/31/88)
73   CODORNIU Brut Cava Anna de Codorniu 1984 $7.50 (5/31/88)
72   CODORNIU Blanc de Blancs Cava 1984 $9.25 (5/31/88)
70   LEMBEY Brut Cava 1984 $6.50 (5/31/88)

1983

79   JUVE Y CAMPS Brut Cava Natural Reserva de la Familia 1983 $10 (5/31/88)
78   SEGURA VIUDAS Brut Cava 1983 $7 (5/31/88)
73   CODORNIU Brut Cava Gran Reserve 1983 $14 (5/31/88)
55   CODORNIU Brut Cava Clasico 1983 $6 (4/01/86)

1982

81   CASTELLBLANCH Brut Cava Zero 1982 $6 (5/31/88)
72   LEMBEY Brut Cava 1982 $6 (12/16/85) BB

1981

87   SEGURA VIUDAS Brut Cava 1981 $7 (11/30/86) BB
80   JUVE Y CAMPS Brut Cava Natural Reserva de la Familia 1981 $10 (7/16/86)
69   PAUL CHENEAU Brut Cava Vintage Cuvée Spéciale 1981 $9 (5/31/88)

NV

87   VALLFORMOSA Brut Nature Cava NV $11 (10/15/88)
86   MONT-MARCAL Brut Cava Gran Reserva NV $13 (5/31/88)
85   FREIXENET Brut Cava Carta Nevada NV $7 (5/31/88)
84   FREIXENET Semi-Seco Cava Carta Nevada NV $7 (5/31/88)
83   CAVAS HILL Blanc de Blancs Cava Reserva Oro Seco NV $8 (5/31/88)
83   ROVELLATS Brut Cava Imperial NV $13 (12/31/90)
82   FREIXENET Brut Rosé Cava NV $7 (5/31/88)
82   VALLFORMOSA Brut Penedès NV $7.50 (4/30/88)
82   XENIUS Sparkling Cava NV $7.50 (7/15/90) BB
81   MONT-MARCAL Brut Cava Tradición NV $7 (5/31/88)
81   BODEGAS ONDARRE Brut Rioja Ondarre NV $11 (12/31/88)
81   SEGURA VIUDAS Brut Cava Reserva Heredad NV $12 (5/31/88)
80   VALLFORMOSA Brut Cava NV $10 (12/31/90) BB
79   CADIZ Brut Cava Reserva NV $7 (5/31/88)
79   MARQUES DE MONISTROL Brut Blanc de Blancs Cava NV $7.25 (5/31/88)
79   VALLFORMOSA Brut Nature Cava NV $11 (12/31/90)
79   VALLFORMOSA Brut Cava NV $10 (10/15/88)
78   CASTELLBLANCH Brut Cava Extra NV $5.25 (5/31/88)
78   FERRET Brut Nature Cava NV $11.50 (9/30/87)
78   FREIXENET Brut Cava Carta Nevada NV $7 (12/31/90)
78   FREIXENET Brut Cava Cordon Negro NV $7.75 (12/31/90)
78   MONT-MARCAL Brut Cava NV $8 (7/15/90)
78   ROVELLATS Brut Nature Cava Gran Reserva NV $17 (12/31/90)
77   FREIXENET Blanc de Blancs Cava Extra Dry Seco NV $6.25 (5/31/88)

75   PAUL CHENEAU Brut Blanc de Blancs Cava NV $7.25 (5/31/88)
74   FREIXENET Brut Cava Cordon Negro NV $7.75 (5/31/88)
74   JUVE Y CAMPS Brut Cava Grand Cru NV $12.50 (5/31/88)
74   SEGURA VIUDAS Brut Cava Reserva NV $6.50 (10/15/86) BB
73   SEGURA VIUDAS Brut Cava Reserva Heredad NV $12 (12/31/86)
72   SEGURA VIUDAS Brut Cava Reserva NV $6.50 (5/31/88)
71   FREIXENET Semi-Seco Cava Carta Nevada NV $7 (12/31/90)
70   DUBOSC Brut Cava NV $8 (4/30/88)
70   SEGURA VIUDAS Brut Blanc de Blancs Cava NV $6.75 (5/31/88)
67   FERRET Brut Cava NV $11 (9/30/87)

OTHER INTERNATIONAL
ARGENTINA

1990

83   FINCA FLICHMAN Chardonnay Mendoza Proprietor's Private Reserve 1990 $6 (4/30/91) BB
79   FINCA FLICHMAN White Mendoza Selection Flichman 1990 $4.50 (7/15/91)
78   FINCA FLICHMAN Chardonnay Mendoza Caballero de la Cepa 1990 $8 (7/15/91)
76   FINCA FLICHMAN White Mendoza 1990 $4 (7/15/91)

1989

78   TRAPICHE Chardonnay Mendoza Reserve 1989 $5.50 (9/15/90)

1988

84   FINCA FLICHMAN Red Mendoza Argenta 1988 $4 (3/15/91) BB
79   FINCA FLICHMAN Red Mendoza Selection 1988 $4.50 (3/15/91) BB
79   PASCUAL TOSO Cabernet Sauvignon Mendoza 1988 $7 (3/15/91)
74   TRAPICHE Malbec Mendoza Vintner's Selection Oak Cask Reserve 1988 $8 (7/15/91)
66   FINCA FLICHMAN Mendoza Merlot Proprietor's Private Reserve 1988 $6 (3/15/91)

1987

83   TRAPICHE Malbec Mendoza Reserve 1987 $5 (9/15/90) BB
81   FINCA FLICHMAN Cabernet Sauvignon Mendoza Proprietor's Private Reserve 1987 $6 (3/15/91) BB
77   VALENTIN BIANCHI Cabernet Sauvignon Mendoza Elsa's Vineyard 1987 $7 (7/15/91)

1986

77   TRAPICHE Cabernet Sauvignon Mendoza Reserve 1986 $5.50 (9/15/90)

1985

76   VALENTIN BIANCHI Malbec Mendoza Elsa's Vineyard 1985 $6 (7/15/91)
69   TRAPICHE Cabernet Sauvignon Mendoza Vintner's Selection Oak Cask Reserve 1986 $8 (7/15/91)
68   FINCA FLICHMAN Cabernet Sauvignon Mendoza Caballero de la Cepa 1985 $8 (3/15/91)

1982

81   TRAPICHE Cabernet Sauvignon Mendoza 1982 $4 (2/15/89) BB
76   FOND DE CAVE Cabernet Sauvignon Mendoza 1982 $7 (2/15/89)

1981

79   NAVARRO CORREAS Cabernet Sauvignon Mendoza 1981 $8.50 (2/15/89)

AUSTRIA

1985

77   STEGENDORF Burgenland Kabinett 1985 $5 (8/31/87)

BRAZIL

1987

78   MARCUS JAMES White Zinfandel Aurora Valley 1987 $4 (6/15/89)

BULGARIA

1987

79   BALKAN CREST Chardonnay Shoumen Khan Krum Vineyards Reserve 1987 $6 (7/15/91)

1985

58   BALKAN CREST Cabernet Sauvignon Stara Zagora Oriahovitza Vineyards Reserve 1985 $6 (7/15/91)

GREECE

1981

78   ODYSSEY North Greece Cava Premium Dry 1981 $3.50 (12/15/87)

ISRAEL

1989

84   YARDEN Chardonnay Galil 1989 $10 (3/31/91)
79   YARDEN Sauvignon Blanc Galil 1989 $9 (3/31/91)
77   YARDEN Mt. Hermon White Galil 1989 $6 (3/31/91)
72   CARMEL Chenin Blanc Galil 1989 $6 (3/31/91)
70   YARDEN Mt. Hermon Red Galil 1989 $7 (3/31/91)

1988

77   YARDEN Merlot Galil Special Reserve 1988 $14 (3/31/91)
75   GAMLA Late Harvest Sauvignon Blanc Galil 1988 $14 (3/31/91)
75   GAMLA Sauvignon Blanc Galil 1988 $9 (3/31/91)
74   GAMLA Sauvignon Blanc Galil Special Reserve 1988 $10 (3/31/91)
72   GOLAN Sauvignon Blanc Galil 1988 $8 (3/31/91)
66   GAMLA Chardonnay Galil Special Reserve 1988 $11 (3/31/91)

1987

75   GAMLA Cabernet Sauvignon Galil 1987 $9.50 (3/31/91)

1986

85   GOLAN Cabernet Sauvignon Galil 1986 $11 (3/31/91)
83   GAMLA Cabernet Sauvignon Galil Special Reserve 1986 $12 (3/31/91)
79   YARDEN Cabernet Sauvignon Galil 1986 $14 (6/30/90)
79   YARDEN Merlot Galil Special Reserve 1986 $12 (6/30/90)
78   CARMEL Cabernet Sauvignon Samson 1986 $7.50 (3/31/91)

1985

82   YARDEN Cabernet Sauvignon Galil 1985 $14 (6/30/90)

1981

69   CARMEL Cabernet Sauvignon Israel Galil 1981 $7 (6/30/87)

LEBANON

1983

86   CHATEAU MUSAR Lebanon 1983 $17 (7/15/91)

1982

87   CHATEAU MUSAR Lebanon 1982 $15 (7/15/91)

1981

84   CHATEAU MUSAR Lebanon 1981 $18 (7/15/91)

1980

91   CHATEAU MUSAR Lebanon 1980 Rel: $11 Cur: $18 (7/31/88)

MADEIRA

NV

78   BLANDYS Rainwater NV $6.99 (6/01/85)

MEXICO

1987

82   SAN MARTIN Petite Sirah Baja California International Series 1987 $4 (8/31/90) BB
73   PINSON Chardonnay 1987 $4.50 (6/30/90)

NEW ZEALAND

1990

83   MORTON Chardonnay Hawke's Bay 1990 $10 (7/15/91)

1989

91   KUMEU RIVER Chardonnay Kumeu 1989 $27 (12/31/90)
88   BABICH Chardonnay Hawke's Bay Irongate 1989 $17 (3/31/91)
86   STONELEIGH Chardonnay Marlborough 1989 $11 (7/15/91)
82   LONGRIDGE Chardonnay Hawke's Bay 1989 $10 (7/15/91)
74   BABICH Cabernet Sauvignon Hawke's Bay 1989 $10 (7/15/91)

1988

82   HOUSE OF NOBILO Pinotage Huapai Valley (Pinot Noir Clone) 1988 $15 (7/15/91)
78   MORTON Chardonnay Hawke's Bay Winemaker's Selection 1988 $13 (7/15/91)

1987

93   KUMEU RIVER Chardonnay Kumeu 1987 $29 (3/31/89)
87   KUMEU RIVER Merlot Cabernet Kumeu 1987 $18 (12/31/90)
82   MORTON Sauvignon Blanc Hawke's Bay Winemaker's Selection 1987 $9 (2/15/88)

1986

92   CORBANS Chardonnay Marlborough 1986 $10 (5/15/88)
90   MORTON Chardonnay Hawke's Bay Winemaker's Selection 1986 $12 (2/15/88)
90   MORTON Chardonnay New Zealand Winery Reserve 1986 $38 (5/15/88)
87   CORBANS Sauvignon Blanc Marlborough 1986 $10 (5/15/88)
87   HUNTER'S Chardonnay Marlborough 1986 $13 (2/15/88)
86   BABICH Chardonnay Henderson Valley 1986 $10 (5/15/88)
84   BABICH Sauvignon Blanc Hawke's Bay 1986 $11 (5/15/88)
80   HUNTER'S Müller-Thurgau Marlborough 1986 $6.50 (4/30/87)
78   NAUTILUS Sauvignon Blanc Hawke's Bay 1986 $11.50 (2/15/88)
74   VILLA MARIA Cabernet Sauvignon Auckland Reserve 1986 $30 (7/15/88)
71   HUNTER'S Sauvignon Blanc Marlborough 1986 $8.50 (2/15/88)

1985

88   HUNTER'S Chardonnay Marlborough 1985 $9.25 (3/15/87)
73   GOLDWATER ESTATE Cabernet Merlot Franc Waiheke Island 1985 $27 (7/15/88)

ROMANIA

NV

55   PREMIAT Brut Transylvania Méthode Champenoise NV $6 (6/01/86)

YUGOSLAVIA

1987

70   LE SABLE Pinot Noir Oplenac 1987 $4.50 (3/31/91)

1986

64   LE SABLE Cabernet Sauvignon Primorska Region 1986 $4.50 (3/31/91)

1985

81   CANTERBURY Cabernet Sauvignon Yugoslavia Istria 1985 $5.50 (9/30/89) BB
77   AVIA Cabernet Sauvignon Yugoslavia Primorska Region 1985 $3 (3/31/89)
75   AVIA Merlot Yugoslavia Primorska Hrvatska-Istria 1985 $3 (3/31/89)

UNITED STATES
CALIFORNIA/*BLUSH*

1990

87   JOSEPH PHELPS Grenache Rosé California Vin du Mistral 1990 $9 (6/15/91) BB
84   BONNY DOON Vin Gris de Cigare California 1990 $7 (7/15/91) BB
82   MCDOWELL Grenache Rosé McDowell Valley Les Vieux Cépages 1990 $7.50 (6/15/91) BB
77   DE LOACH White Zinfandel Russian River Valley 1990 $7.50 (3/31/91)
77   SUTTER HOME White Zinfandel California 1990 $5.50 (3/31/91)

1989

84   JOSEPH PHELPS Grenache Rosé California Vin du Mistral 1989 $9 (11/30/90)
84   STEVENOT White Zinfandel Amador County 1989 $5 (12/31/90) BB
82   MCDOWELL Grenache Rosé McDowell Valley Les Vieux Cépages 1989 $6.50 (10/31/90) BB
80   GLEN ELLEN White Zinfandel California Proprietor's Reserve 1989 $5 (12/31/90)
79   BARON HERZOG White Zinfandel California 1989 $7 (3/31/91)
78   BONNY DOON Vin Gris de Cigare California 1989 $7.50 (10/31/90)
77   MANISCHEWITZ White Zinfandel Sonoma County 1989 $6 (3/31/91)
75   WEINSTOCK White Zinfandel Sonoma County 1989 $8 (3/31/91)
74   HAGAFEN Pinot Noir Blanc California 1989 $6 (3/31/91)
68   SUTTER HOME White Zinfandel California 1989 $4.50 (12/31/90)

1988

89   BONNY DOON Vin Gris de Cigare California 1988 $6.75 (7/31/89) BB
88   BUEHLER White Zinfandel Napa Valley 1988 $6 (6/15/89)
88   HOP KILN White Zinfandel Russian River Valley 1988 $6.75 (6/15/89)
87   J. PEDRONCELLI White Zinfandel Sonoma County 1988 $6 (6/15/89)
87   SANTINO White Zinfandel Amador County 1988 $5 (6/15/89)
86   CRESTON MANOR White Zinfandel San Luis Obispo 1988 $7 (6/15/89)
86   KENWOOD White Zinfandel Sonoma Valley 1988 $6.75 (6/15/89)
85   FETZER White Zinfandel California 1988 $7 (6/15/89)
85   CK MONDAVI White Zinfandel California 1988 $5.25 (6/15/89)
85   IVAN TAMAS White Zinfandel Mendocino 1988 $5.75 (6/15/89)
84   GLEN ELLEN White Zinfandel California Proprietor's Reserve 1988 $5.75 (6/15/89)
84   SEGHESIO White Zinfandel Northern Sonoma 1988 $5.50 (6/15/89)
84   WILLIAM WHEELER White Zinfandel Sonoma County Young Vines 1988 $6 (6/15/89)
83   BEL ARBRES White Zinfandel California 1988 $5.25 (6/15/89)
82   DE LOACH White Zinfandel Russian River Valley 1988 $7.50 (6/15/89)
81   LOUIS M. MARTINI White Zinfandel Napa Valley 1988 $5.50 (6/15/89)
81   SHENANDOAH White Zinfandel Amador County 1988 $6 (6/15/89)
81   SIMI Rosé of Cabernet Sauvignon Sonoma County 1988 $7 (11/15/89)
80   BARON HERZOG White Zinfandel California 1988 $6 (6/15/89)
80   ROBERT MONDAVI White Zinfandel California 1988 $5.50 (6/15/89)
80   RIVERSIDE FARM White Zinfandel California 1988 $5.25 (6/15/89)
79   BLOSSOM HILL White Zinfandel California 1988 $7/1.5L (6/15/89)
79   E.&J. GALLO White Zinfandel California 1988 $5 (6/15/89)
78   BELVEDERE White Zinfandel California Discovery Series 1988 $4 (6/15/89)
77   CHATEAU SOUVERAIN White Zinfandel California 1988 $5.75 (6/15/89)
77   CHRISTIAN BROTHERS White Zinfandel Napa Valley 1988 $5.50 (6/15/89)
77   SUTTER HOME White Zinfandel California 1988 $5.25 (6/15/89)
76   KARLY White Zinfandel Amador County 1988 $7 (6/15/89)
76   MADRONA White Zinfandel El Dorado 1988 $5.25 (6/15/89)
75   MIRASSOU White Zinfandel California 1988 $6.50 (6/15/89)
75   NAPA RIDGE White Zinfandel Lodi 1988 $6 (6/15/89)
74   BANDIERA White Zinfandel California 1988 $5.25 (6/15/89)
74   PAUL MASSON White Zinfandel California 1988 $7/1.5L (6/15/89)
73   DELICATO White Zinfandel California 1988-$5.25 (6/15/89)
73   GRAND CRU White Zinfandel California 1988 $5 (6/15/89)
73   J.W. MORRIS White Zinfandel California 1988 $5 (6/15/89)
72   WILLIAM BATES White Zinfandel California 1988 $4 (6/15/89)
72   BERINGER White Zinfandel North Coast 1988 $7.50 (6/15/89)
72   CHARLES KRUG White Zinfandel North Coast 1988 $6 (6/15/89)
70   SAUSAL White Zinfandel Alexander Valley 1988 $6 (6/15/89)
69   SEBASTIANI White Zinfandel California 1988 $5 (6/15/89)
67   CASTORO White Zinfandel San Luis Obispo 1988 $6 (6/15/89)
65   BOEGER White Zinfandel El Dorado 1988 $7.50 (6/15/89)
65   AUGUST SEBASTIANI White Zinfandel California 1988 $7.50/1.5L (6/15/89)
65   WEIBEL White Zinfandel Mendocino 1988 $5 (6/15/89)
61   LOS HERMANOS White Zinfandel California 1988 $8/1.5L (6/15/89)

1987

84   BONNY DOON Vin Gris de Cigare California 1987 $6.50 (4/15/89)
80   FENESTRA White Zinfandel Livermore Valley 1987 $5 (6/15/89)
75   GARLAND RANCH White Zinfandel Monterey 1987 $6 (6/15/89)
72   E.&J. GALLO White Grenache California 1987 $3.50 (4/15/89)
69   BRUTOCAO White Zinfandel Mendocino 1987 $7 (6/15/89)
68   NORTH COAST CELLARS White Zinfandel North Coast 1987 $6 (6/15/89)
66   REDWOOD VALLEY White Zinfandel California 1987 $6/1.5L (6/15/89)

1986

84   BEL ARBRES White Merlot California 1986 $5 (3/31/87)
83   WILLIAM WHEELER White Zinfandel Sonoma County Young Vines 1986 $5.50 (3/31/87)
82   BUENA VISTA Pinot Noir Blanc Carneros 1986 $4.75 (10/31/87) BB
82   J. PEDRONCELLI White Zinfandel Sonoma County 1986 $4.50 (3/31/87)
82   SHENANDOAH White Zinfandel Amador County 1986 $5 (3/31/87)
80   KENWOOD White Zinfandel Sonoma Valley 1986 $5.75 (3/31/87)
80   ROBERT MONDAVI Rosé California 1986 $5 (3/31/87)
80   VENTANA White Zinfandel Monterey Primrose Ventana Vineyards 1986 $5 (10/31/87)

78   ROBERT MONDAVI Zinfandel Rosé California 1986 $4 (10/31/87)
78   ST. FRANCIS Pinot Noir Blanc Sonoma Valley 1986 $5.50 (10/31/87)
73   DE LOACH White Zinfandel Russian River Valley 1986 $6 (3/31/87)
70   BANDIERA White Zinfandel North Coast 1986 $4 (3/31/87)
70   LA CREMA Pinot Noir Blanc California Vin Gris 1986 $8 (10/31/87)
70   CHARLES SHAW Gamay Blanc Napa Valley 1986 $4.50 (3/31/87)
70   SUTTER HOME White Zinfandel California 1986 $4.75 (3/31/87)
68   CHRISTIAN BROTHERS White Zinfandel Napa Valley 1986 $5 (3/31/87)
65   BUEHLER White Zinfandel Napa Valley 1986 $5.50 (3/31/87)

1985

86   STERLING Cabernet Blanc Napa Valley 1985 $6.25 (4/01/86)
85   BUEHLER White Zinfandel Napa Valley 1985 $8 (2/16/86)
85   BUENA VISTA Pinot Noir Blanc Carneros Steelhead Run 1985 $5.50 (7/01/86) BB
83   J. PEDRONCELLI White Zinfandel Sonoma County 1985 $4.50 (2/16/86) BB
81   DE LOACH White Zinfandel Russian River Valley 1985 $5.50 (4/16/86)
81   SIMI Rosé of Cabernet Sauvignon Sonoma County 1985 $7 (7/16/86)
80   J. PEDRONCELLI Blush Sonoma County 1985 $3.50 (7/16/86)
80   ZACA MESA White Zinfandel Santa Barbara County 1985 $5.50 (3/31/87)
74   ROBERT MONDAVI Zinfandel Rosé California 1985 $3.75 (9/30/86)
73   GLEN ELLEN White Zinfandel California Proprietor's Reserve 1985 $4 (2/16/86)
70   BELVEDERE White Zinfandel California Discovery Series 1985 $3.25 (2/16/86)
69   ROBERT MONDAVI White Zinfandel California 1985 $5.75 (6/16/86)
67   DOMAINE SAN MARTIN White Zinfandel Central Coast 1985 $4 (3/31/87)
63   MONTEVINA White Zinfandel Shenandoah Valley 1985 $5 (2/16/86)
62   SUTTER HOME White Zinfandel California 1985 $4.50 (2/16/86)
61   CHARLES LEFRANC White Zinfandel California 1985 $5 (5/01/86)

1984

74   FIRESTONE Rosé of Cabernet Sauvignon Santa Ynez Valley 1984 $4.50 (2/01/86)

NV

69   INGLENOOK-NAVELLE White Zinfandel California NV $7.50/1.5L (6/15/89)

CABERNET FRANC

1988

88   WHITEHALL LANE Cabernet Franc Napa Valley 1988 $18.50 (11/15/90)
84   DEHLINGER Cabernet Franc Russian River Valley 1988 $13 (4/30/91)
83   KONOCTI Cabernet Franc Lake County 1988 $9.50 (2/28/91)
77   SEBASTIANI ESTATES Cabernet Franc California 1988 $8.50 (7/15/91)
76   AUSTIN Cabernet Franc Santa Barbara County 1988 $12 (11/15/90)

1987

89   GUNDLACH BUNDSCHU Cabernet Franc Sonoma Valley Rhinefarm Vineyards 1987 $12 (9/15/90)
85+   COSENTINO Cabernet Franc Napa County 1987 $12.50 (4/15/89) (BT)
85+   IRON HORSE Cabernet Franc Alexander Valley 1987 (NR) (4/15/89) (BT)
82   NELSON ESTATE Cabernet Franc Sonoma County 1987 $16 (4/30/91)
79   NEYERS Cabernet Franc Napa Valley 1987 $16 (11/15/90)
75   COSENTINO Cabernet Franc Napa County 1987 $12.50 (9/30/89)

1986

92   COSENTINO Cabernet Franc North Coast 1986 $14 (7/31/88)
90+   COSENTINO Cabernet Franc North Coast 1986 $14 (4/15/88) (BT)
88   CONGRESS SPRINGS Cabernet Franc Santa Cruz Mountains 1986 $18 (7/31/89)
81   LA JOTA Cabernet Franc Howell Mountain 1986 $25 (10/15/89)

1985

85   CHATEAU CHEVRE Cabernet Franc Napa Valley 1985 $16 (7/31/88)
70   GUENOC Cabernet Franc Lake County 1985 $15 (2/15/89)

CABERNET SAUVIGNON & BLENDS

1990

95+   PAHLMEYER Caldwell Vineyard Napa Valley 1990 (NR) (5/15/91) (BT)
95+   WHITEHALL LANE Cabernet Sauvignon Napa Valley Morisoli Vineyard 1990 (NR) (5/15/91) (BT)
90+   ALEXANDER VALLEY Cabernet Sauvignon Alexander Valley 1990 (NR) (5/15/91) (BT)
90+   S. ANDERSON Cabernet Sauvignon Napa Valley Stags Leap District Richard Chambers Vineyard 1990 (NR) (5/15/91) (BT)
90+   CAIN Five Napa Valley 1990 (NR) (5/15/91) (BT)
90+   CORISON Cabernet Sauvignon Napa Valley 1990 (NR) (5/15/91) (BT)
90+   DUNN Cabernet Sauvignon Howell Mountain 1990 (NR) (5/15/91) (BT)
90+   DUNN Cabernet Sauvignon Napa Valley 1990 (NR) (5/15/91) (BT)
90+   FISHER Cabernet Sauvignon Sonoma County Coach Insignia 1990 (NR) (5/15/91) (BT)
90+   FLORA SPRINGS Cabernet Sauvignon Napa Valley 1990 (NR) (5/15/91) (BT)
90+   FLORA SPRINGS Trilogy Napa Valley 1990 (NR) (5/15/91) (BT)
90+   GIRARD Cabernet Sauvignon Napa Valley 1990 (NR) (5/15/91) (BT)
90+   GIRARD Cabernet Sauvignon Napa Valley Reserve 1990 (NR) (5/15/91) (BT)
90+   GRACE FAMILY Cabernet Sauvignon Napa Valley 1990 (NR) (5/15/91) (BT)
90+   GROTH Cabernet Sauvignon Napa Valley 1990 (NR) (5/15/91) (BT)
90+   JOHNSON TURNBULL Cabernet Sauvignon Napa Valley Vineyard Selection 67 1990 (NR) (5/15/91) (BT)
90+   LA JOTA Cabernet Sauvignon Howell Mountain 1990 (NR) (5/15/91) (BT)
90+   JUDD'S HILL Cabernet Sauvignon Napa Valley 1990 (NR) (5/15/91) (BT)
90+   LAUREL GLEN Cabernet Sauvignon Sonoma Mountain 1990 (NR) (5/15/91) (BT)
90+   LIVINGSTON Cabernet Sauvignon Napa Valley Moffett Vineyard 1990 (NR) (5/15/91) (BT)
90+   LONG Cabernet Sauvignon Napa Valley 1990 (NR) (5/15/91) (BT)
90+   MERRYVALE Profile Napa Valley 1990 (NR) (5/15/91) (BT)
90+   ROBERT MONDAVI Cabernet Sauvignon Napa Valley 1990 (NR) (5/15/91) (BT)
90+   ROBERT MONDAVI Cabernet Sauvignon Napa Valley Reserve 1990 (NR) (5/15/91) (BT)
90+   ROBERT PECOTA Cabernet Sauvignon Napa Valley Kara's Vineyard 1990 (NR) (5/15/91) (BT)
90+   JOSEPH PHELPS Cabernet Sauvignon Napa Valley Backus Vineyard 1990 (NR) (5/15/91) (BT)
90+   JOSEPH PHELPS Insignia Napa Valley 1990 (NR) (5/15/91) (BT)
90+   RIDGE Cabernet Sauvignon Santa Cruz Mountains Monte Bello 1990 (NR) (5/15/91) (BT)
90+   SHAFER Cabernet Sauvignon Napa Valley Stags Leap District Hillside Select 1990 (NR) (5/15/91) (BT)
90+   SPOTTSWOODE Cabernet Sauvignon Napa Valley 1990 (NR) (5/15/91) (BT)

90+ STELTZNER Cabernet Sauvignon Napa Valley Stags Leap District 1990 (NR) (5/15/91) (BT)
90+ PHILIP TOGNI Cabernet Sauvignon Napa Valley 1990 $24 (5/15/91) (BT)
85+ BEAULIEU Cabernet Sauvignon Napa Valley Georges de Latour Private Reserve 1990 (NR) (5/15/91) (BT)
85+ BEAULIEU Cabernet Sauvignon Napa Valley Rutherford 1990 (NR) (5/15/91) (BT)
85+ CHATEAU SOUVERAIN Cabernet Sauvignon Alexander Valley 1990 (NR) (5/15/91) (BT)
85+ B.R. COHN Cabernet Sauvignon Sonoma Valley Olive Hill Vineyard 1990 (NR) (5/15/91) (BT)
85+ DIAMOND CREEK Cabernet Sauvignon Napa Valley Gravelly Meadow 1990 (NR) (5/15/91) (BT)
85+ DIAMOND CREEK Cabernet Sauvignon Napa Valley Red Rock Terrace 1990 (NR) (5/15/91) (BT)
85+ DIAMOND CREEK Cabernet Sauvignon Napa Valley Volcanic Hill 1990 (NR) (5/15/91) (BT)
85+ HESS Cabernet Sauvignon Napa Valley 1990 (NR) (5/15/91) (BT)
85+ LIVINGSTON Cabernet Sauvignon Napa Valley Stanley's Selection 1990 (NR) (5/15/91) (BT)
85+ MARKHAM Cabernet Sauvignon Napa Valley 1990 (NR) (5/15/91) (BT)
85+ MONTICELLO Cabernet Sauvignon Napa Valley Corley Reserve 1990 (NR) (5/15/91) (BT)
85+ JOSEPH PHELPS Cabernet Sauvignon Napa Valley 1990 (NR) (5/15/91) (BT)
85+ PINE RIDGE Cabernet Sauvignon Napa Valley Rutherford Cuvée 1990 (NR) (5/15/91) (BT)
85+ PINE RIDGE Cabernet Sauvignon Napa Valley Stags Leap District Pine Ridge Stags Leap Vineyard 1990 (NR) (5/15/91) (BT)
85+ STERLING Cabernet Sauvignon Napa Valley 1990 (NR) (5/15/91) (BT)
85+ STERLING Cabernet Sauvignon Napa Valley Diamond Mountain Ranch 1990 (NR) (5/15/91) (BT)
85+ STERLING Reserve Napa Valley 1990 (NR) (5/15/91) (BT)
85+ STONEGATE Cabernet Sauvignon Napa Valley 1990 (NR) (5/15/91) (BT)
85+ ZD Cabernet Sauvignon Napa Valley 1990 (NR) (5/15/91) (BT)
80+ WILLIAM HILL Cabernet Sauvignon Napa Valley Reserve 1990 (NR) (5/15/91) (BT)
80+ PINE RIDGE Cabernet Sauvignon Napa Valley Andrus Reserve 1990 (NR) (5/15/91) (BT)

1989

90+ S. ANDERSON Cabernet Sauvignon Napa Valley Stags Leap District Richard Chambers Vineyard 1989 (NR) (5/15/91) (BT)
90+ CAIN Five Napa Valley 1989 (NR) (5/15/91) (BT)
90+ CHATEAU SOUVERAIN Cabernet Sauvignon Alexander Valley 1989 (NR) (5/15/91) (BT)
90+ DIAMOND CREEK Cabernet Sauvignon Napa Valley Volcanic Hill 1989 (NR) (5/15/91) (BT)
90+ DUNN Cabernet Sauvignon Howell Mountain 1989 (NR) (5/15/91) (BT)
90+ FLORA SPRINGS Trilogy Napa Valley 1989 (NR) (5/15/91) (BT)
90+ GIRARD Cabernet Sauvignon Napa Valley Reserve 1989 (NR) (5/15/91) (BT)
90+ GROTH Cabernet Sauvignon Napa Valley 1989 (NR) (5/15/91) (BT)
90+ HESS Cabernet Sauvignon Napa Valley 1989 (NR) (5/15/91) (BT)
90+ JUDD'S HILL Cabernet Sauvignon Napa Valley 1989 (NR) (5/15/91) (BT)
90+ LA JOTA Cabernet Sauvignon Howell Mountain 1989 (NR) (5/15/91) (BT)
90+ LAUREL GLEN Cabernet Sauvignon Sonoma Mountain 1989 (NR) (5/15/91) (BT)
90+ LONG Cabernet Sauvignon Napa Valley 1989 (NR) (5/15/91) (BT)
90+ ROBERT MONDAVI Cabernet Sauvignon Napa Valley Reserve 1989 (NR) (5/15/91) (BT)
90+ MONTICELLO Cabernet Sauvignon Napa Valley Corley Reserve 1989 (NR) (5/15/91) (BT)
90+ ROBERT PECOTA Cabernet Sauvignon Napa Valley Kara's Vineyard 1989 (NR) (5/15/91) (BT)
90+ JOSEPH PHELPS Cabernet Sauvignon Napa Valley Backus Vineyard 1989 (NR) (5/15/91) (BT)
90+ JOSEPH PHELPS Cabernet Sauvignon Napa Valley Eisele Vineyard 1989 (NR) (5/15/91) (BT)
90+ PINE RIDGE Cabernet Sauvignon Napa Valley Rutherford Cuvée 1989 (NR) (5/15/91) (BT)
90+ SPOTTSWOODE Cabernet Sauvignon Napa Valley 1989 (NR) (5/15/91) (BT)
90+ STERLING Reserve Napa Valley 1989 (NR) (5/15/91) (BT)
87 BON MARCHE Cabernet Sauvignon Alexander Valley 1989 $8 (2/28/91) BB
85+ MERRYVALE Profile Napa Valley 1989 (NR) (5/15/91) (BT)
85+ ALEXANDER VALLEY Cabernet Sauvignon Alexander Valley 1989 (NR) (5/15/91) (BT)
85+ BEAULIEU Cabernet Sauvignon Napa Valley Georges de Latour Private Reserve 1989 (NR) (5/15/91) (BT)
85+ BEAULIEU Cabernet Sauvignon Napa Valley Rutherford 1989 (NR) (5/15/91) (BT)
85+ BERINGER Cabernet Sauvignon Knights Valley 1989 (NR) (5/15/91) (BT)
85+ BERINGER Cabernet Sauvignon Napa Valley Private Reserve 1989 (NR) (5/15/91) (BT)
85+ BERINGER Cabernet Sauvignon Napa Valley Chabot Vineyard 1989 (NR) (5/15/91) (BT)
85+ CARMENET Sonoma Valley 1989 (NR) (5/15/91) (BT)
85+ CLOS DU VAL Cabernet Sauvignon Napa Valley Stags Leap District 1989 (NR) (5/15/91) (BT)
85+ B.R. COHN Cabernet Sauvignon Sonoma Valley Olive Hill Vineyard 1989 (NR) (5/15/91) (BT)
85+ CORISON Cabernet Sauvignon Napa Valley 1989 (NR) (5/15/91) (BT)
85+ COSENTINO Cabernet Sauvignon North Coast 1989 (NR) (5/15/91) (BT)
85+ COSENTINO The Poet California 1989 (NR) (5/15/91) (BT)
85+ DIAMOND CREEK Cabernet Sauvignon Napa Valley Gravelly Meadow 1989 (NR) (5/15/91) (BT)
85+ DIAMOND CREEK Cabernet Sauvignon Napa Valley Red Rock Terrace 1989 (NR) (5/15/91) (BT)
85+ DOMAINE MICHEL Cabernet Sauvignon Sonoma County 1989 $15 (5/15/91) (BT)
85+ DOMAINE MICHEL Cabernet Sauvignon Sonoma County Reserve 1989 $20 (5/15/91) (BT)
85+ DUNN Cabernet Sauvignon Napa Valley 1989 (NR) (5/15/91) (BT)
85+ FISHER Cabernet Sauvignon Sonoma County Coach Insignia 1989 (NR) (5/15/91) (BT)
85+ FLORA SPRINGS Cabernet Sauvignon Napa Valley 1989 (NR) (5/15/91) (BT)
85+ GIRARD Cabernet Sauvignon Napa Valley 1989 (NR) (5/15/91) (BT)
85+ GRACE FAMILY Cabernet Sauvignon Napa Valley 1989 (NR) (5/15/91) (BT)
85+ WILLIAM HILL Cabernet Sauvignon Napa Valley Reserve 1989 (NR) (5/15/91) (BT)
85+ JOHNSON TURNBULL Cabernet Sauvignon Napa Valley Vineyard Selection 67 1989 (NR) (5/15/91) (BT)
85+ LIVINGSTON Cabernet Sauvignon Napa Valley Moffett Vineyard 1989 (NR) (5/15/91) (BT)
85+ LIVINGSTON Cabernet Sauvignon Napa Valley Stanley's Selection 1989 (NR) (5/15/91) (BT)
85+ MARKHAM Cabernet Sauvignon Napa Valley 1989 (NR) (5/15/91) (BT)
85+ LOUIS M. MARTINI Cabernet Sauvignon Sonoma Valley Monte Rosso 1989 (NR) (5/15/91) (BT)
85+ NIEBAUM-COPPOLA Rubicon Napa Valley 1989 (NR) (5/15/91) (BT)
85+ PAHLMEYER Caldwell Vineyard Napa Valley 1989 (NR) (5/15/91) (BT)
85+ JOSEPH PHELPS Cabernet Sauvignon Napa Valley 1989 (NR) (5/15/91) (BT)
85+ JOSEPH PHELPS Insignia Napa Valley 1989 (NR) (5/15/91) (BT)
85+ PINE RIDGE Cabernet Sauvignon Napa Valley Diamond Mountain 1989 (NR) (5/15/91) (BT)
85+ SANTA CRUZ MOUNTAIN Cabernet Sauvignon Santa Cruz Mountains Bates Ranch 1989 (NR) (5/15/91) (BT)
85+ SHAFER Cabernet Sauvignon Napa Valley Stags Leap District Hillside Select 1989 (NR) (5/15/91) (BT)
85+ STAG'S LEAP WINE CELLARS Cabernet Sauvignon Napa Valley Stags Leap District SLV-Fay Vineyard Blend 1989 (NR) (5/15/91) (BT)
85+ STELTZNER Cabernet Sauvignon Napa Valley Stags Leap District 1989 (NR) (5/15/91) (BT)
85+ STERLING Cabernet Sauvignon Napa Valley Diamond Mountain Ranch 1989 (NR) (5/15/91) (BT)
85+ STERLING Three Palms Vineyard Napa Valley 1989 (NR) (5/15/91) (BT)
85+ WHITEHALL LANE Cabernet Sauvignon Napa Valley 1989 (NR) (5/15/91) (BT)
83 OCTOPUS MOUNTAIN Cabernet Sauvignon Anderson Valley Dennison Vineyards 1989 $12.50 (7/31/91)
82 R.H. PHILLIPS Cabernet Sauvignon California 1989 $8 (7/31/91) BB
80 MURPHY-GOODE Cabernet Sauvignon Alexander Valley Goode-Ready The Second Cabernet 1989 $10 (6/15/91)
80+ PINE RIDGE Cabernet Sauvignon Napa Valley Stags Leap District Pine Ridge Stags Leap Vineyard 1989 (NR) (5/15/91) (BT)
80+ RAVENSWOOD Pickberry Vineyards Sonoma Mountain 1989 (NR) (5/15/91) (BT)
80+ STERLING Cabernet Sauvignon Napa Valley 1989 (NR) (5/15/91) (BT)
80+ STONEGATE Cabernet Sauvignon Napa Valley 1989 (NR) (5/15/91) (BT)
80+ ZD Cabernet Sauvignon Napa Valley 1989 (NR) (5/15/91) (BT)
73 BARON HERZOG Cabernet Sauvignon Sonoma County 1989 $11 (3/31/91)

1988

95+ BERINGER Cabernet Sauvignon Napa Valley Private Reserve 1988 (NR) (4/30/90) (BT)
95+ DUNN Cabernet Sauvignon Howell Mountain 1988 (NR) (4/30/91) (BT)
92 GRACE FAMILY Cabernet Sauvignon Napa Valley 1988 $63 (6/30/91)
92 SIGNORELLO Cabernet Sauvignon Napa Valley Founder's Reserve 1988 $25 (5/15/91)
92 PHILIP TOGNI Cabernet Sauvignon Napa Valley 1988 $26 (7/15/91)
91 ROBERT MONDAVI Cabernet Sauvignon Napa Valley Reserve 1988 $45 (5/31/91) CS
90 LAUREL GLEN Cabernet Sauvignon Sonoma Mountain 1988 $30 (5/15/91) CS
90 STAG'S LEAP WINE CELLARS Cabernet Sauvignon Napa Valley 1988 $18 (6/15/91)
90+ ALEXANDER VALLEY Cabernet Sauvignon Alexander Valley 1988 $12 (4/30/90) (BT)
90+ BERINGER Cabernet Sauvignon Knights Valley 1988 (NR) (4/30/90) (BT)
90+ BERINGER Cabernet Sauvignon Napa Valley Chabot Vineyard 1988 (NR) (4/30/90) (BT)
90+ CARMENET Sonoma Valley 1988 (NR) (4/30/90) (BT)
90+ DIAMOND CREEK Cabernet Sauvignon Napa Valley Gravelly Meadow 1988 $40 (4/30/90) (BT)
90+ DIAMOND CREEK Cabernet Sauvignon Napa Valley Red Rock Terrace 1988 $40 (4/30/91) (BT)
90+ DIAMOND CREEK Cabernet Sauvignon Napa Valley Volcanic Hill 1988 $40 (4/30/91) (BT)
90+ DUNN Cabernet Sauvignon Napa Valley 1988 (NR) (4/30/91) (BT)
90+ FAR NIENTE Cabernet Sauvignon Napa Valley 1988 (NR) (4/30/90) (BT)
90+ FLORA SPRINGS Cabernet Sauvignon Napa Valley 1988 (NR) (4/30/90) (BT)
90+ FLORA SPRINGS Trilogy Napa Valley 1988 $30 (4/30/90) (BT)
90+ FRANCISCAN Meritige Napa Valley 1988 (NR) (4/30/90) (BT)
90+ GRACE FAMILY Cabernet Sauvignon Napa Valley 1988 $63 (4/30/90) (BT)
90+ GROTH Cabernet Sauvignon Napa Valley 1988 (NR) (4/30/90) (BT)
90+ GUNDLACH BUNDSCHU Cabernet Sauvignon Sonoma Valley Rhinefarm Vineyards 1988 (NR) (4/30/90) (BT)
90+ HESS Cabernet Sauvignon Napa Valley 1988 (NR) (4/30/90) (BT)
90+ LA JOTA Cabernet Sauvignon Howell Mountain 1988 $28 (4/30/90) (BT)
90+ LAUREL GLEN Cabernet Sauvignon Sonoma Mountain 1988 $30 (4/30/90) (BT)
90+ LIVINGSTON Cabernet Sauvignon Napa Valley Moffett Vineyard 1988 $30 (4/30/90) (BT)
90+ ROBERT MONDAVI Cabernet Sauvignon Napa Valley Reserve 1988 $45 (4/30/90) (BT)
90+ PRESTON Cabernet Sauvignon Dry Creek Valley 1988 $15 (4/30/90) (BT)
90+ RAYMOND Cabernet Sauvignon Napa Valley Private Reserve 1988 (NR) (4/30/90) (BT)
90+ SEQUOIA GROVE Cabernet Sauvignon Napa Valley Estate 1988 (NR) (4/30/90) (BT)
90+ SHAFER Cabernet Sauvignon Napa Valley Stags Leap District 1988 $19 (4/30/90) (BT)
90+ SPOTTSWOODE Cabernet Sauvignon Napa Valley 1988 (NR) (4/30/90) (BT)
90+ STERLING Cabernet Sauvignon Napa Valley 1988 $13.25 (4/30/90) (BT)
90+ STERLING Reserve Napa Valley 1988 (NR) (4/30/90) (BT)
90+ VICHON Cabernet Sauvignon Napa Valley 1988 $16 (4/30/90) (BT)
89 B.R. COHN Cabernet Sauvignon Sonoma Valley Olive Hill Vineyard 1988 $25 (5/15/91)
89 DIAMOND CREEK Cabernet Sauvignon Napa Valley Red Rock Terrace 1988 $40 (11/15/90)
89 NEWTON Claret Napa Valley 1988 $11 (3/15/91)
89 RAVENSWOOD Cabernet Sauvignon Sonoma Valley 1988 $14 (3/15/91)
88 COSENTINO Cabernet Sauvignon North Coast 1988 $15 (5/31/91)
88 DIAMOND CREEK Cabernet Sauvignon Napa Valley Volcanic Hill 1988 $40 (11/15/90)
88 FROG'S LEAP Cabernet Sauvignon Napa Valley 1988 $17 (12/15/90)
88 HAGAFEN Cabernet Sauvignon Napa Valley 1988 $20 (3/31/91)
87 CHALK HILL Cabernet Sauvignon Chalk Hill 1988 $12 (6/15/91)
87 DIAMOND CREEK Cabernet Sauvignon Napa Valley Gravelly Meadow 1988 $40 (11/15/90)
87 KATHRYN KENNEDY Lateral California 1988 $14.50 (10/15/90)
87 MOUNT EDEN Cabernet Sauvignon Santa Cruz Mountains Lathweisen Ridge 1988 $12 (4/30/91)
87 PHILIP TOGNI Cabernet Sauvignon Napa Valley Tanbark Hill Vineyard 1988 $24 (6/30/91)
86 BEAULIEU Cabernet Sauvignon Napa Valley Rutherford 1988 $11 (7/15/91)
86 HUSCH Cabernet Sauvignon Mendocino La Ribera Vineyards 1988 $12 (6/30/91)
86 MERRYVALE Cabernet Sauvignon Napa Valley 1988 $18 (7/15/91)
86 SILVERADO Cabernet Sauvignon Napa Valley Stags Leap District 1988 $16 (3/31/91)
86 ZD Cabernet Sauvignon Napa Valley 1988 $20 (4/30/91)
85 COSENTINO The Poet California 1988 $27 (5/31/91)
85 DUCKHORN Cabernet Sauvignon Napa Valley 1988 $20 (7/31/91)
85 LAUREL GLEN Terra Rosa Napa Valley 1988 $12 (11/15/90)
85 SUNNY ST. HELENA Cabernet Sauvignon North Coast 1988 $13 (4/30/91)
85+ BUENA VISTA Cabernet Sauvignon Carneros 1988 $13 (4/30/90) (BT)
85+ FISHER Cabernet Sauvignon Sonoma County Coach Insignia 1988 (NR) (4/30/91) (BT)
85+ FRANCISCAN Cabernet Sauvignon Napa Valley Oakville Estate 1988 (NR) (4/30/90) (BT)
85+ GIRARD Cabernet Sauvignon Napa Valley 1988 (NR) (4/30/90) (BT)
85+ GIRARD Cabernet Sauvignon Napa Valley Reserve 1988 (NR) (4/30/90) (BT)
85+ HAYWOOD Cabernet Sauvignon Sonoma Valley 1988 (NR) (4/30/90) (BT)
85+ JOHNSON TURNBULL Cabernet Sauvignon Napa Valley 1988 (NR) (4/30/90) (BT)
85+ JOHNSON TURNBULL Cabernet Sauvignon Napa Valley Vineyard Selection 67 1988 (NR) (4/30/90) (BT)
85+ JORDAN Cabernet Sauvignon Alexander Valley 1988 (NR) (4/30/90) (BT)
85+ LYETH Red Alexander Valley 1988 (NR) (4/30/90) (BT)
85+ MARKHAM Cabernet Sauvignon Napa Valley 1988 (NR) (4/30/90) (BT)
85+ MERRYVALE Profile Napa Valley 1988 (NR) (4/30/90) (BT)
85+ MOUNT EDEN Cabernet Sauvignon Santa Cruz Mountains 1988 (NR) (4/30/90) (BT)
85+ NEWTON Cabernet Sauvignon Napa Valley 1988 (NR) (4/30/90) (BT)
85+ NIEBAUM-COPPOLA Rubicon Napa Valley 1988 (NR) (4/30/90) (BT)
85+ PAHLMEYER Caldwell Vineyard Napa Valley 1988 $30 (4/30/90) (BT)
85+ ROBERT PEPI Cabernet Sauvignon Napa Valley Vine Hill Ranch 1988 (NR) (4/30/90) (BT)
85+ RAYMOND Cabernet Sauvignon Napa Valley 1988 (NR) (4/30/90) (BT)
85+ RIDGE Cabernet Sauvignon Santa Cruz Mountains Monte Bello 1988 (NR) (4/30/90) (BT)

UNITED STATES
CALIFORNIA/*CABERNET SAUVIGNON & BLENDS*

85+ SANTA CRUZ MOUNTAIN Cabernet Sauvignon Santa Cruz Mountains Bates Ranch 1988 (NR) (4/30/90) (BT)
85+ SPRING MOUNTAIN Cabernet Sauvignon Napa Valley 1988 (NR) (4/30/90) (BT)
85+ STELTZNER Cabernet Sauvignon Napa Valley Stags Leap District 1988 (NR) (4/30/90) (BT)
85+ STERLING Cabernet Sauvignon Napa Valley Diamond Mountain Ranch 1988 (NR) (4/30/90) (BT)
85+ STERLING Three Palms Vineyard Napa Valley 1988 (NR) (4/30/90) (BT)
85+ VICHON Cabernet Sauvignon Napa Valley Stags Leap District SLD 1988 $23 (4/30/90) (BT)
85+ VILLA MT. EDEN Cabernet Sauvignon Napa Valley Reseve 1988 $20 (4/30/90) (BT)
84 FIRESTONE Cabernet Sauvignon Santa Ynez Valley Reserve 1988 $18 (2/28/91)
84 INNISFREE Cabernet Sauvignon Napa Valley 1988 $11 (4/30/91)
84 VICHON Cabernet Sauvignon Napa Valley 1988 $16 (5/15/91)
84 VICHON Cabernet Sauvignon Napa Valley 1988 $16 (11/15/90)
83 CHRISTOPHE Cabernet Sauvignon California 1988 $9 (3/31/91)
83 DOMAINE ST. GEORGE Cabernet Sauvignon Sonoma County 1988 $6 (11/15/90) BB
83 LAUREL GLEN Cabernet Sauvignon Sonoma County Counterpoint 1988 $13 (7/15/91)
83 MONTPELLIER Cabernet Sauvignon California 1988 $7 (7/31/91) BB
82 CLOS DU VAL Cabernet Sauvignon Napa Valley Joli Val 1988 $13 (7/31/91)
82 PELLEGRINI FAMILY Cabernet Sauvignon Alexander Valley Cloverdale Ranch Estate Cuvée 1988 $12 (6/15/91)
82 RAVENSWOOD Pickberry Vineyards Sonoma Mountain 1988 $27 (4/30/91)
82 STEPHEN ZELLERBACH Cabernet Sauvignon Alexander Valley 1988 $10 (10/31/90)
81 DRY CREEK Cabernet Sauvignon Sonoma County 1988 $14 (5/31/91)
81 ESTANCIA Cabernet Sauvignon Alexander Valley 1988 $9 (5/31/91)
81 FETZER Cabernet Sauvignon California 1988 $8 (1/31/91) BB
81 LOUIS M. MARTINI Cabernet Sauvignon Sonoma County 1988 $9 (4/30/91) BB
81 ROBERT MONDAVI Cabernet Sauvignon California Woodbridge 1988 $6 (2/28/91) BB
81 SUTTER HOME Cabernet Sauvignon California 1988 $5 (11/15/90) BB
80 MOUNTAIN VIEW Cabernet Sauvignon North Coast 1988 $6 (4/30/91) BB
80+ BUEHLER Cabernet Sauvignon Napa Valley 1988 (NR) (4/30/90) (BT)
80+ CHIMNEY ROCK Cabernet Sauvignon Napa Valley Stags Leap District 1988 (NR) (4/30/90) (BT)
80+ EBERLE Cabernet Sauvignon Paso Robles 1988 (NR) (4/30/91) (BT)
80+ IRON HORSE Cabernets Alexander Valley 1988 (NR) (4/30/90) (BT)
80+ LOUIS M. MARTINI Cabernet Sauvignon Sonoma Valley Monte Rosso 1988 (NR) (4/30/90) (BT)
80+ PINE RIDGE Cabernet Sauvignon Napa Valley Andrus Reserve 1988 (NR) (4/30/90) (BT)
80+ PINE RIDGE Cabernet Sauvignon Napa Valley Diamond Mountain 1988 (NR) (4/30/90) (BT)
80+ PINE RIDGE Cabernet Sauvignon Napa Valley Rutherford Cuvée 1988 (NR) (4/30/90) (BT)
80+ PINE RIDGE Cabernet Sauvignon Napa Valley Stags Leap District Pine Ridge Stags Leap Vineyard 1988 (NR) (4/30/90) (BT)
80+ VILLA MT. EDEN Cabernet Sauvignon Napa Valley 1988 (NR) (4/30/90) (BT)
79 BEAULIEU Cabernet Sauvignon Napa Valley Beau Tour 1988 $7 (9/30/90)
77 CLOS DU BOIS Cabernet Sauvignon Alexander Valley 1988 $14 (7/15/91)
77 MONTEVINA Cabernet Sauvignon California 1988 $8.50 (2/15/90)
76 MONTPELLIER Cabernet Sauvignon California 1988 $7 (10/31/89)
70 FREEMARK ABBEY Cabernet Sauvignon Napa Valley 1988 $15 (12/31/90)

1987

97 GRACE FAMILY Cabernet Sauvignon Napa Valley 1987 Rel: $56 Cur: $200 (6/30/90)
97 OPUS ONE Napa Valley 1987 Rel: $68 Cur: $69 (11/15/90) CS
96 SPOTTSWOODE Cabernet Sauvignon Napa Valley 1987 Rel: $36 Cur: $56 (9/15/90) SS
95 DIAMOND CREEK Cabernet Sauvignon Napa Valley Volcanic Hill 1987 Rel: $40 Cur: $41 (12/15/89)
95 DUCKHORN Cabernet Sauvignon Napa Valley 1987 Rel: $20 Cur: $27 (6/30/90) CS
95 WILLIAM HILL Cabernet Sauvignon Napa Valley Reserve 1987 Rel: $24 Cur: $25 (11/15/90) SS
95 LA JOTA Cabernet Sauvignon Howell Mountain 1987 Rel: $25 Cur: $28 (7/31/90) SS
95+ BERINGER Cabernet Sauvignon Napa Valley Private Reserve 1987 (NR) (4/15/89) (BT)
95+ GRACE FAMILY Cabernet Sauvignon Napa Valley 1987 Rel: $56 Cur: $200 (4/15/89) (BT)
95+ GRGICH HILLS Cabernet Sauvignon Napa Valley 1987 (NR) (4/15/89) (BT)
95+ KEENAN Cabernet Sauvignon Napa Valley 1987 Rel: $18 Cur: $19 (4/15/89) (BT)
95+ SPOTTSWOODE Cabernet Sauvignon Napa Valley 1987 Rel: $36 Cur: $56 (4/15/89) (BT)
95+ STERLING Reserve Napa Valley 1987 Rel: $43 Cur: $43 (4/15/89) (BT)
94 DIAMOND CREEK Cabernet Sauvignon Napa Valley Red Rock Terrace 1987 Rel: $40 Cur: $42 (12/15/89)
94 DUNN Cabernet Sauvignon Howell Mountain 1987 $36 (4/15/91)
94 FROG'S LEAP Cabernet Sauvignon Napa Valley 1987 Rel: $15 Cur: $20 (12/31/89) SS
94 HESS Cabernet Sauvignon Napa Valley 1987 $17 (4/15/91) SS
94 LAUREL GLEN Cabernet Sauvignon Sonoma Mountain Counterpoint 1987 $13 (10/31/89)
94 LIVINGSTON Cabernet Sauvignon Napa Valley Moffett Vineyard 1987 $24 (11/15/90)
94 PHILIP TOGNI Cabernet Sauvignon Napa Valley 1987 Rel: $24 Cur: $27 (8/31/90)
93 BENZIGER Cabernet Sauvignon Sonoma County 1987 $10 (9/30/90) SS
93 CAYMUS Cabernet Sauvignon Napa Valley 1987 Rel: $16 Cur: $19 (9/15/90)
93 DUNN Cabernet Sauvignon Napa Valley 1987 $33 (11/15/90)
93 FORMAN Cabernet Sauvignon Napa Valley 1987 Rel: $26 Cur: $44 (9/30/90)
93 LOUIS M. MARTINI Cabernet Sauvignon Sonoma Valley Monte Rosso 1987 Rel: $20 Cur: $23 (11/15/90)
93 MAZZOCCO Cabernet Sauvignon Alexander Valley Claret Style 1987 $20 (8/31/90)
93 STERLING Reserve Napa Valley 1987 $43 (11/15/90)
92 CAIN Cabernet Sauvignon Napa Valley Estate 1987 $25 (10/15/90)
92 CHATEAU ST. JEAN Cabernet Sauvignon Alexander Valley 1987 $16 (6/30/91) SS
92 CLOS DU VAL Cabernet Sauvignon Napa Valley Stags Leap District 1987 $17 (6/30/91)

92 B.R. COHN Cabernet Sauvignon Sonoma Valley Olive Hill Vineyard 1987 Rel: $25 Cur: $27 (6/30/90)
92 CORISON Cabernet Sauvignon Napa Valley 1987 $20 (11/15/90)
92 CUVAISON Cabernet Sauvignon Napa Valley 1987 Rel: $17.50 Cur: $19 (10/31/90)
92 FOLIE A DEUX Cabernet Sauvignon Napa Valley 1987 $18 (11/15/90)
92 GUENOC Cabernet Sauvignon Napa Valley Beckstoffer Reserve 1987 $24 (6/30/91)
92 KENWOOD Cabernet Sauvignon Sonoma Valley Jack London Vineyard 1987 $18 (1/31/91)
92 MORGAN Cabernet Sauvignon Carmel Valley 1987 $16 (9/30/90)
92 OPTIMA Cabernet Sauvignon Sonoma County 1987 $22 (12/15/90)
92 SHAFER Cabernet Sauvignon Napa Valley Stags Leap District 1987 Rel: $18 Cur: $19 (7/31/90)
92 SILVERADO Cabernet Sauvignon Napa Valley Stags Leap District 1987 Rel: $14 Cur: $18 (4/15/90) SS
91 VINCENT ARROYO Cabernet Sauvignon Napa Valley 1987 $12 (11/15/90)
91 CAIN Five Napa Valley 1987 $30 (4/30/91)
91 DIAMOND CREEK Cabernet Sauvignon Napa Valley Lake 1987 $100 (11/15/90)
91 EDMUNDS ST. JOHN Les Fleurs du Chaparral Napa Valley 1987 $15 (8/31/90)
91 FLORA SPRINGS Cabernet Sauvignon Napa Valley Cellar Select 1987 $25 (11/15/90)
91 HACIENDA Antares Sonoma County 1987 $28 (11/15/90)
91 OAKFORD Cabernet Sauvignon Napa Valley 1987 $25 (11/15/90)
91 PAHLMEYER Caldwell Vineyard Napa Valley 1987 $28 (11/15/90)
91 A. RAFANELLI Cabernet Sauvignon Dry Creek Valley 1987 $12 (8/31/90)
91 STERLING Cabernet Sauvignon Napa Valley 1987 Rel: $13 Cur: $13 (5/15/90)
91 STERLING Cabernet Sauvignon Napa Valley Diamond Mountain Ranch 1987 $16 (11/15/90)
90 BERINGER Cabernet Sauvignon Knights Valley 1987 $15.50 (11/15/90)
90 CAKEBREAD Cabernet Sauvignon Napa Valley 1987 Rel: $18 Cur: $18 (10/15/90)
90 CHIMNEY ROCK Cabernet Sauvignon Napa Valley Stags Leap District 1987 $18 (7/31/91) SS
90 CLOS DU BOIS Marlstone Vineyard Alexander Valley 1987 $20 (7/31/91)
90 DIAMOND CREEK Cabernet Sauvignon Napa Valley Gravelly Meadow 1987 Rel: $40 Cur: $43 (12/15/89)
90 FLORA SPRINGS Trilogy Napa Valley 1987 $35 (5/15/91)
90 GAN EDEN Cabernet Sauvignon Alexander Valley 1987 $18 (3/31/91)
90 GEYSER PEAK Réserve Alexandre Alexander Valley 1987 $18 (6/15/91)
90 HUSCH Cabernet Sauvignon Mendocino La Ribera Vineyards 1987 $12 (11/15/90)
90 JUSTIN Reserve Paso Robles 1987 $20 (2/15/91)
90 KENWOOD Cabernet Sauvignon Sonoma Valley 1987 $15 (7/15/91)
90 LAUREL GLEN Cabernet Sauvignon Sonoma Mountain 1987 Rel: $22 Cur: $25 (9/15/90)
90 ROBERT MONDAVI Cabernet Sauvignon Napa Valley Reserve 1987 Rel: $43 Cur: $47 (8/31/90)
90 MONTICELLO Cabernet Sauvignon Napa Valley Corley Reserve 1987 $25 (11/15/90)
90 MONTICELLO Cabernet Sauvignon Napa Valley Jefferson Cuvée 1987 $14 (9/30/90)
90 ROBERT PECOTA Cabernet Sauvignon Napa Valley Kara's Vineyard 1987 Rel: $16 Cur: $17 (10/15/90)
90 ROBERT PEPI Cabernet Sauvignon Napa Valley Vine Hill Ranch 1987 $20 (4/30/91)
90 STRATFORD Cabernet Sauvignon Napa Valley Partners' Reserve 1987 $15.50 (4/30/91)
90 ZD Cabernet Sauvignon Napa Valley Estate Bottled 1987 $40 (1/31/91)
90+ BEAULIEU Cabernet Sauvignon Napa Valley Georges de Latour Private Reserve 1987 $35 (4/15/89) (BT)
90+ BERINGER Cabernet Sauvignon Napa Valley Chabot Vineyard 1987 (NR) (4/15/89) (BT)
90+ BUEHLER Cabernet Sauvignon Napa Valley 1987 Rel: $16 Cur: $19 (4/15/89) (BT)
90+ CARMENET Sonoma Valley 1987 Rel: $20 Cur: $20 (4/15/89) (BT)
90+ CAYMUS Cabernet Sauvignon Napa Valley 1987 Rel: $16 Cur: $19 (4/15/89) (BT)
90+ CHATEAU MONTELENA Cabernet Sauvignon Napa Valley 1987 (NR) (4/15/89) (BT)
90+ CHRISTIAN BROTHERS Cabernet Sauvignon Napa Valley 1987 (NR) (4/15/89) (BT)
90+ CONN CREEK Cabernet Sauvignon Napa Valley Barrel Select 1987 Rel: $17 Cur: $17 (4/15/89) (BT)
90+ CONN CREEK Cabernet Sauvignon Napa Valley Barrel Select Private Reserve 1987 (NR) (4/15/89) (BT)
90+ COSENTINO Cabernet Sauvignon North Coast 1987 $16 (4/15/89) (BT)
90+ COSENTINO The Poet California 1987 $25 (4/15/89) (BT)
90+ DIAMOND CREEK Cabernet Sauvignon Napa Valley Gravelly Meadow 1987 Rel: $40 Cur: $43 (4/15/89) (BT)
90+ DIAMOND CREEK Cabernet Sauvignon Napa Valley Red Rock Terrace 1987 Rel: $40 Cur: $42 (4/15/89) (BT)
90+ DOMINUS Napa Valley 1987 (NR) (4/15/89) (BT)
90+ DRY CREEK Meritage Dry Creek Valley 1987 $24 (4/15/89) (BT)
90+ DUNN Cabernet Sauvignon Howell Mountain 1987 Rel: $36 Cur: $58 (4/15/89) (BT)
90+ DUNN Cabernet Sauvignon Napa Valley 1987 Rel: $33 Cur: $43 (4/15/89) (BT)
90+ FAR NIENTE Cabernet Sauvignon Napa Valley 1987 Rel: $33 Cur: $34 (4/15/89) (BT)
90+ FLORA SPRINGS Cabernet Sauvignon Napa Valley Cellar Select 1987 Rel: $25 Cur: $26 (4/15/89) (BT)
90+ GIRARD Cabernet Sauvignon Napa Valley 1987 Rel: $16 Cur: $18 (4/15/89) (BT)
90+ GIRARD Cabernet Sauvignon Napa Valley Reserve 1987 (NR) (4/15/89) (BT)
90+ GROTH Cabernet Sauvignon Napa Valley 1987 Rel: $20 Cur: $21 (4/15/89) (BT)
90+ HESS Cabernet Sauvignon Napa Valley 1987 Rel: $17 Cur: $17 (4/15/89) (BT)
90+ WILLIAM HILL Cabernet Sauvignon Napa Valley Reserve 1987 Rel: $24 Cur: $25 (4/15/89) (BT)
90+ INGLENOOK Cabernet Sauvignon Napa Valley Reserve Cask 1987 (NR) (4/15/89) (BT)
90+ IRON HORSE Cabernets Alexander Valley 1987 Rel: $18.50 Cur: $18 (4/15/89) (BT)
90+ JOHNSON TURNBULL Cabernet Sauvignon Napa Valley Vineyard Selection 67 1987 Rel: $22 Cur: $26 (4/15/89) (BT)
90+ LA JOTA Cabernet Sauvignon Howell Mountain 1987 Rel: $25 Cur: $28 (4/15/89) (BT)
90+ LAUREL GLEN Cabernet Sauvignon Sonoma Mountain 1987 Rel: $22 Cur: $25 (4/15/89) (BT)
90+ LIVINGSTON Cabernet Sauvignon Napa Valley Moffett Vineyard 1987 Rel: $24 Cur: $26 (4/15/89) (BT)
90+ LOUIS M. MARTINI Cabernet Sauvignon Sonoma Valley Monte Rosso 1987 Rel: $20 Cur: $23 (4/15/89) (BT)
90+ ROBERT MONDAVI Cabernet Sauvignon Napa Valley Reserve 1987 Rel: $43 Cur: $47 (4/15/89) (BT)
90+ NEWTON Cabernet Sauvignon Napa Valley 1987 (NR) (4/15/89) (BT)
90+ PINE RIDGE Cabernet Sauvignon Napa Valley Rutherford Cuvée 1987 Rel: $16.50 Cur: $17 (4/15/89) (BT)
90+ KENT RASMUSSEN Cabernet Sauvignon Napa Valley 1987 $20 (4/15/87) (BT)
90+ RAVENSWOOD Cabernet Sauvignon Sonoma Valley 1987 Rel: $11 Cur: $13 (4/15/89) (BT)
90+ SANTA CRUZ MOUNTAIN Cabernet Sauvignon Santa Cruz Mountains Bates Ranch 1987 (NR) (4/15/89) (BT)
90+ SILVERADO Cabernet Sauvignon Napa Valley Stags Leap District 1987 Rel: $14 Cur: $18 (4/15/89) (BT)
90+ SIMI Cabernet Sauvignon Alexander Valley Reserve 1987 (NR) (4/15/89) (BT)

90+ STAG'S LEAP WINE CELLARS Stag's Leap Vineyards Cask 23 Napa Valley Stags Leap District 1987 Cur: $65 (4/15/89) (BT)
90+ STELTZNER Cabernet Sauvignon Napa Valley Stags Leap District 1987 Rel: $16 Cur: $18 (4/15/89) (BT)
90+ STERLING Cabernet Sauvignon Napa Valley 1987 Rel: $13 Cur: $13 (4/15/89) (BT)
90+ TREFETHEN Cabernet Sauvignon Napa Valley Hillside Selection 1987 (NR) (4/15/89) (BT)
90+ VICHON Cabernet Sauvignon Napa Valley Stags Leap District SLD 1987 Rel: $17 Cur: $21 (4/15/89) (BT)
90+ VILLA MT. EDEN Cabernet Sauvignon Napa Valley 1987 (NR) (4/15/89) (BT)
90+ WHITEHALL LANE Cabernet Sauvignon Napa Valley 1987 $18 (4/15/89) (BT)
90+ WHITEHALL LANE Cabernet Sauvignon Napa Valley Reserve 1987 (NR) (4/15/89) (BT)
89 ABREU Cabernet Sauvignon Napa Valley Madrona Ranch 1987 $25 (7/31/91)
89 ADELAIDA Cabernet Sauvignon Paso Robles 1987 $14 (2/28/91)
89 CARMENET Sonoma Valley 1987 Rel: $20 Cur: $20 (11/15/90)
89 CRONIN Cabernet Sauvignon Merlot Robinson Vineyard Napa Valley 1987 $17 (2/28/91)
89 FRANCISCAN Cabernet Sauvignon Napa Valley Oakville Estate 1987 $12 (2/15/91)
89 GEYSER PEAK Cabernet Sauvignon Alexander Valley Estate Reserve 1987 $14 (6/15/91)
89 GUENOC Cabernet Sauvignon Lake County 1987 $12 (7/15/91)
89 JOHNSON TURNBULL Cabernet Sauvignon Napa Valley Vineyard Selection 67 1987 $22 (6/30/91)
89 KATHRYN KENNEDY Cabernet Sauvignon Santa Cruz Mountains 1987 $45 (1/31/91)
89 MURPHY-GOODE Cabernet Sauvignon Alexander Valley 1987 $16.50 (5/31/90)
89 NALLE Cabernet Sauvignon Dry Creek Valley 1987 $18 (1/31/91)
89 SIMI Cabernet Sauvignon Sonoma County 1987 $16.50 (5/15/91)
89 STAGS' LEAP WINERY Cabernet Sauvignon Napa Valley Stags Leap District 1987 $18 (6/30/91)
89 RODNEY STRONG Cabernet Sauvignon Alexander Valley Alexander's Crown Vineyard 1987 $17 (7/15/91)
88 DEHLINGER Cabernet Sauvignon Russian River Valley 1987 $13 (2/28/91)
88 ESTANCIA Meritage Alexander Valley 1987 $12 (1/31/91)
88 FAR NIENTE Cabernet Sauvignon Napa Valley 1987 $33 (11/15/90)
88 GEYSER PEAK Cabernet Sauvignon Sonoma County 1987 $8.50 (11/30/90) BB
88 GUENOC Langtry Meritage Lake-Napa Counties 1987 $35 (4/15/91)
88 HAGAFEN Cabernet Sauvignon Napa Valley 1987 $20 (4/30/90)
88 KENWOOD Cabernet Sauvignon Sonoma Valley Artist Series 1987 $35 (11/15/90)
88 LYTTON SPRINGS Cabernet Sauvignon Mendocino County Private Reserve 1987 $18 (9/15/90)
88 JOSEPH PHELPS Cabernet Sauvignon Napa Valley Backus Vineyard 1987 $30 (7/15/91)
88 PRESTON Cabernet Sauvignon Dry Creek Valley 1987 Rel: $14 Cur: $14 (10/31/90)
88 RIDGE Cabernet Sauvignon Santa Cruz Mountains Monte Bello 1987 $45 (11/15/90)
88 VILLA MT. EDEN Cabernet Sauvignon Napa Valley 1987 $13 (2/15/91)
88 WILD HORSE Cabernet Sauvignon Paso Robles 1987 $13 (4/30/91)
87 ALEXANDER VALLEY Cabernet Sauvignon Alexander Valley 1987 Rel: $12 Cur: $13 (5/31/90)
87 ARROWOOD Cabernet Sauvignon Sonoma County 1987 $22 (11/15/90)
87 CHATEAU SOUVERAIN Cabernet Sauvignon Alexander Valley 1987 $9.50 (11/15/90)
87 CONN CREEK Cabernet Sauvignon Napa Valley Barrel Select 1987 $17 (7/15/91)
87 GARY FARRELL Cabernet Sauvignon Sonoma County 1987 $16 (10/31/90)
87 FRANCISCAN Meritage Napa Valley 1987 $17 (4/30/91)
87 HUSCH Cabernet Sauvignon Mendocino North Field Select 1987 $16 (11/15/90)
87 KLEIN Cabernet Sauvignon Santa Cruz Mountains 1987 $19 (10/15/90)
87 MARIETTA Cabernet Sauvignon Sonoma County 1987 $10 (2/28/91)
87 LOUIS M. MARTINI Cabernet Sauvignon Napa Valley Reserve 1987 $14 (10/15/90)
87 ROBERT MONDAVI Cabernet Sauvignon Napa Valley 1987 Rel: $20 Cur: $21 (5/31/90)
87 PEJU Cabernet Sauvignon Napa Valley HB Vineyard 1987 $20 (11/15/90)
87 QUIVIRA Cabernet Sauvignon Dry Creek Valley 1987 $15 (11/15/90)
87 STERLING Three Palms Vineyard Napa Valley 1987 $23 (11/15/90)
87 VICHON Cabernet Sauvignon Napa Valley Stags Leap District SLD 1987 Rel: $17 Cur: $21 (7/31/90)
86 CLOS DU BOIS Cabernet Sauvignon Alexander Valley 1987 $11 (2/15/90)
86 COSENTINO Cabernet Sauvignon North Coast Reserve 1987 $28 (2/28/91)
86 FREEMARK ABBEY Cabernet Sauvignon Napa Valley 1987 $16 (7/31/91)
86 GIRARD Cabernet Sauvignon Napa Valley 1987 $16 (11/15/90)
86 IRON HORSE Cabernets Alexander Valley 1987 $18.50 (3/15/91)
86 KEENAN Cabernet Sauvignon Napa Valley 1987 Rel: $18 Cur: $19 (5/31/90)
86 LAUREL GLEN Terra Rosa Napa Valley 1987 $14 (7/31/90)
86 J. LOHR Cabernet Sauvignon Paso Robles Seven Oaks 1987 $12 (4/30/91)
86 BERNARD PRADEL Cabernet Sauvignon Napa Valley 1987 $20 (10/15/90)
86 ROLLING HILLS Cabernet Sauvignon California 1987 $7 (12/15/89) BB
86 TREFETHEN Cabernet Sauvignon Napa Valley 1987 $16 (11/15/90)
86 WENTE BROS. Cabernet Sauvignon Livermore Valley Charles Wetmore Vineyard Estate Reserve 1987 $18 (4/30/91)
85 BEAULIEU Cabernet Sauvignon Napa Valley Rutherford 1987 $10 (12/15/90)
85 BENZIGER Cabernet Sauvignon Sonoma Valley Estate Bottled 1987 $12 (11/15/90)
85 BENZIGER A Tribute Sonoma Mountain 1987 $20 (12/31/90)
85 BOEGER Cabernet Sauvignon El Dorado 1987 $11 (3/15/91)
85 BUEHLER Cabernet Sauvignon Napa Valley 1987 Rel: $16 Cur: $19 (7/31/90)
85 COSENTINO The Poet California 1987 $25 (9/15/90)
85 DE LOACH Cabernet Sauvignon Russian River Valley O.F.S. 1987 $22 (10/15/90)
85 ETUDE Cabernet Sauvignon Napa Valley 1987 $24 (10/31/90)
85 FIELD STONE Cabernet Sauvignon Alexander Valley 1987 $14 (2/28/91)
85 FISHER Cabernet Sauvignon Sonoma-Napa Counties Coach Insignia 1987 Rel: $20 Cur: $22 (9/30/90)
85 GUNDLACH BUNDSCHU Cabernet Sauvignon Sonoma Valley Rhinefarm Vineyards 1987 Rel: $15 Cur: $15 (5/15/91)
85 WILLIAM HILL Cabernet Sauvignon Napa Valley Silver Label 1987 $14 (11/15/90)
85 KONOCTI Meritage Red Clear Lake 1987 $17 (4/15/91)
85 MOUNT EDEN Cabernet Sauvignon Santa Cruz Mountains Young Vine Cuvée 1987 $12 (4/15/90)
85 MOUNT VEEDER Cabernet Sauvignon Napa Valley 1987 $20 (4/30/91)
85 J. PEDRONCELLI Cabernet Sauvignon Dry Creek Valley 1987 $8.50 (11/15/90) BB
85 ST. SUPERY Cabernet Sauvignon Napa Valley Dollarhide Ranch 1987 $13 (7/15/90)
85 SEGHESIO Cabernet Sauvignon Sonoma County 1987 $9 (4/30/91)
85 STRATFORD Cabernet Sauvignon Napa Valley 1987 $11.50 (4/30/90)
85 RODNEY STRONG Cabernet Sauvignon Sonoma County 1987 $10 (6/30/91)
85 VIANSA Obsidian Sonoma-Napa Counties 1987 $65 (7/15/91)
85+ ARROWOOD Cabernet Sauvignon Sonoma County 1987 Rel: $22 Cur: $24 (4/15/89) (BT)
85+ CHAPPELLET Cabernet Sauvignon Napa Valley 1987 (NR) (4/15/89) (BT)
85+ CHIMNEY ROCK Cabernet Sauvignon Napa Valley Stags Leap District 1987 Rel: $18 Cur: $19 (4/15/89) (BT)
85+ DIAMOND CREEK Cabernet Sauvignon Napa Valley Volcanic Hill 1987 Rel: $40 Cur: $41 (4/15/89) (BT)
85+ DRY CREEK Cabernet Sauvignon Sonoma County 1987 $12.50 (4/15/89) (BT)
85+ DUCKHORN Cabernet Sauvignon Napa Valley 1987 Rel: $20 Cur: $27 (4/15/89) (BT)
85+ FETZER Cabernet Sauvignon Mendocino Special Reserve 1987 (NR) (4/15/89) (BT)
85+ FISHER Cabernet Sauvignon Sonoma County Cosch Insignia 1987 Rel: $20 Cur: $22 (4/15/89) (BT)
85+ FRANCISCAN Cabernet Sauvignon Napa Valley Oakville Estate 1987 $12 (4/15/89) (BT)
85+ FRANCISCAN Meritige Napa Valley 1987 Rel: $17 Cur: $18 (4/15/89) (BT)
85+ GUNDLACH BUNDSCHU Cabernet Sauvignon Sonoma Valley Rhinefarm Vineyards 1987 (NR) (4/15/89) (BT)
85+ INGLENOOK Niebaum Claret Napa Valley 1987 (NR) (4/15/89) (BT)
85+ MONTICELLO Cabernet Sauvignon Napa Valley Corley Reserve 1987 Rel: $25 Cur: $26 (4/15/89) (BT)
85+ MONTICELLO Cabernet Sauvignon Napa Valley Jefferson Cuvée 1987 $14 (4/15/89) (BT)
85+ MOUNT EDEN Cabernet Sauvignon Santa Cruz Mountains 1987 Rel: $28 Cur: $29 (4/15/89) (BT)
85+ NEYERS Cabernet Sauvignon Napa Valley 1987 (NR) (4/15/89) (BT)
85+ ROBERT PECOTA Cabernet Sauvignon Napa Valley Kara's Vineyard 1987 Rel: $16 Cur: $17 (4/15/89) (BT)
85+ JOSEPH PHELPS Cabernet Sauvignon Napa Valley Backus Vineyard 1987 Rel: $30 Cur: $31 (4/15/89) (BT)
85+ PINE RIDGE Cabernet Sauvignon Napa Valley Andrus Reserve 1987 (NR) (4/15/89) (BT)
85+ PINE RIDGE Cabernet Sauvignon Napa Valley Diamond Mountain 1987 Rel: $35 Cur: $37 (4/15/89) (BT)
85+ PINE RIDGE Cabernet Sauvignon Napa Valley Stags Leap District Pine Ridge Stags Leap Vineyard 1987 (NR) (4/15/89) (BT)
85+ SHAFER Cabernet Sauvignon Napa Valley Stags Leap District Hillside Select 1987 (NR) (4/15/89) (BT)
85+ STAG'S LEAP WINE CELLARS Cabernet Sauvignon Napa Valley Stags Leap District SLV 1987 Rel: $28 Cur: $29 (4/15/89) (BT)
85+ STERLING Cabernet Sauvignon Napa Valley Diamond Mountain Ranch 1987 (NR) (4/15/89) (BT)
85+ STERLING Three Palms Vineyard Napa Valley 1987 Rel: $23 Cur: $24 (4/15/89) (BT)
85+ WILLIAM WHEELER Cabernet Sauvignon Dry Creek Valley 1987 (NR) (4/15/89) (BT)
84 BRAREN PAULI Cabernet Sauvignon Mendocino 1987 $8.50 (3/31/91) BB
84 CAFARO Cabernet Sauvignon Napa Valley 1987 $20 (11/15/90)
84 CINNABAR Cabernet Sauvignon Santa Cruz Mountains 1987 $18 (3/31/91)
84 DOMAINE MICHEL Cabernet Sauvignon Sonoma County 1987 $19.50 (3/31/91)
84 DRY CREEK Cabernet Sauvignon Sonoma County 1987 $12.50 (4/15/90)
84 DRY CREEK Meritage Dry Creek Valley 1987 $24 (7/31/91)
84 FERRARI-CARANO Cabernet Sauvignon Alexander Valley 1987 $17.50 (7/15/91)
84 FLORA SPRINGS Trilogy Napa Valley 1987 $35 (1/31/91)
84 LEEWARD Cabernet Sauvignon Alexander Valley 1987 $13 (11/15/90)
84 J. LOHR Cabernet Sauvignon California 1987 $7 (2/15/90) BB
84 PESENTI Cabernet Sauvignon San Luis Obispo County Family Reserve 1987 $8 (12/15/89)
84 PINE RIDGE Cabernet Sauvignon Napa Valley Diamond Mountain 1987 $35 (11/15/90)
84 RAVENSWOOD Cabernet Sauvignon Sonoma Valley 1987 Rel: $11 Cur: $13 (5/31/90)
84 WEIBEL Cabernet Sauvignon Mendocino County 1987 $8 (2/28/91) BB
84 WHITEHALL LANE Cabernet Sauvignon Napa Valley 1987 $18 (9/15/90)
83 BUENA VISTA Cabernet Sauvignon Carneros 1987 $13 (10/15/90)
83 CHATEAU SOUVERAIN Cabernet Sauvignon Alexander Valley Private Reserve 1987 $15 (5/15/91)
83 CONCANNON Cabernet Sauvignon Livermore Valley Reserve 1987 $16 (7/15/91)
83 KISTLER Cabernet Sauvignon Sonoma Valley Kistler Estate Vineyard 1987 $25 (2/28/91)
83 MONTEREY VINEYARD Cabernet Sauvignon Monterey County Classic 1987 $6 (1/31/91) BB
83 J.W. MORRIS Cabernet Sauvignon California Private Reserve 1987 $8 (3/31/90)
83 MARIO PERELLI-MINETTI Cabernet Sauvignon Napa Valley 1987 $12 (4/30/91)
83 RAYMOND Cabernet Sauvignon Napa Valley 1987 $17 (2/28/91)
83 RUTHERFORD RANCH Cabernet Sauvignon Napa Valley 1987 $13 (4/30/91)
83 SOBON ESTATE Cabernet Sauvignon Shenandoah Valley 1987 $15 (11/30/90)
82 FIRESTONE Cabernet Sauvignon Santa Ynez Valley 1987 $11 (5/31/90)
82 GAINEY Cabernet Sauvignon Santa Barbara County 1987 $13 (11/15/90)
82 STELTZNER Cabernet Sauvignon Napa Valley Stags Leap District 1987 $16 (11/15/90)
81 BEAULIEU Cabernet Sauvignon Napa Valley Beau Tour 1987 $8 (5/31/89) BB
81 J. CAREY Cabernet Sauvignon Santa Ynez Valley La Cuesta Vineyard Reserve 1987 $16 (5/31/91)
81 GAN EDEN Cabernet Sauvignon Alexander Valley 1987 $18 (11/15/90)
81 GROTH Cabernet Sauvignon Napa Valley 1987 Rel: $20 Cur: $21 (10/31/90)
81 JOULLIAN Cabernet Sauvignon Carmel Valley 1987 $14 (7/31/91)
81 LA VIEILLE MONTAGNE Cabernet Sauvignon Napa Valley 1987 $14 (6/15/91)
80 CHESTNUT HILL Cabernet Sauvignon Sonoma County 1987 $9 (3/31/90)
80 COSENTINO Cabernet Sauvignon North Coast 1987 $16 (6/30/90)
80 ESTANCIA Cabernet Sauvignon Alexander Valley 1987 $7 (7/15/90) BB
80 HANNA Cabernet Sauvignon Sonoma County 1987 $16 (8/31/90)
80 JOHNSON TURNBULL Cabernet Sauvignon Napa Valley 1987 $16 (11/15/90)
80 MONTE VERDE Cabernet Sauvignon California Proprietor's Reserve 1987 $6.50/1.5L (12/15/89)
80 PARDUCCI Cabernet Sauvignon North Coast 1987 $9.50 (4/30/91)
80 PINE RIDGE Cabernet Sauvignon Napa Valley Rutherford Cuvée 1987 $16.50 (11/15/90)
80 SHENANDOAH Cabernet Sauvignon Amador County Artist Series 1987 $10 (2/28/91)
80+ BUENA VISTA Cabernet Sauvignon Carneros 1987 $13 (4/15/89) (BT)
80+ CLOS DU VAL Cabernet Sauvignon Napa Valley Stags Leap District 1987 Rel: $17 Cur: $17 (4/15/89) (BT)
80+ HAYWOOD Cabernet Sauvignon Sonoma Valley Los Chamizal Vineyards 1987 $16 (4/15/87) (BT)
80+ LAKESPRING Cabernet Sauvignon Napa Valley 1987 $14 (4/15/89) (BT)
80+ RIDGE Cabernet Sauvignon Santa Cruz Mountains Monte Bello 1987 Rel: $45 Cur: $52 (4/15/89) (BT)
79 DAVIS BYNUM Cabernet Sauvignon Sonoma County 1987 $10.50 (11/15/90)
79 GLEN ELLEN Cabernet Sauvignon California Proprietor's Reserve 1987 $6 (1/31/91)
79 HAWK CREST Cabernet Sauvignon North Coast 1987 $8 (3/31/90)
79 STREBLOW Cabernet Sauvignon Napa Valley 1987 $16 (10/15/90)
78 MCDOWELL Cabernet Sauvignon California 1987 $9 (11/15/90)
78 POPPY HILL Cabernet Sauvignon California 1987 $7.50 (5/31/91)
78 J. WILE & SONS Cabernet Sauvignon Napa Valley 1987 $10 (5/31/91)
78 J. WILE & SONS Cabernet Sauvignon Napa Valley 1987 $10 (3/31/91)
78 ZD Cabernet Sauvignon Napa Valley 1987 $16 (2/15/91)
77 SANTA BARBARA Cabernet Sauvignon Santa Ynez Valley Reserve 1987 $18 (11/15/90)

UNITED STATES

CALIFORNIA/CABERNET SAUVIGNON & BLENDS

77 STAG'S LEAP WINE CELLARS Cabernet Sauvignon Napa Valley Stags Leap District SLV 1987 $28 (11/15/90)
77 SUTTER HOME Cabernet Sauvignon California 1987 $5.50 (6/30/89)
75 BELVEDERE Cabernet Sauvignon Sonoma County Discovery Series 1987 $6 (6/15/90)
75 JOSEPH PHELPS Cabernet Sauvignon Napa Valley 1987 $14.50 (7/15/91)
75 STAG'S LEAP WINE CELLARS Cabernet Sauvignon Napa Valley 1987 $18 (8/31/90)
75+ JOSEPH PHELPS Cabernet Sauvignon Napa Valley Eisele Vineyard 1987 Rel: $40 Cur: $41 (4/15/89) (BT)
74 ROBERT MONDAVI Cabernet Sauvignon California Woodbridge 1987 $6 (9/15/89)
74 NAPA RIDGE Cabernet Sauvignon North Coast 1987 $7 (11/15/90)
74 TULOCAY Cabernet Sauvignon Napa Valley Egan Vineyard 1987 $16.50 (2/15/91)
72 SANTA YNEZ VALLEY Cabernet-Merlot Santa Barbara County 1987 $13 (3/31/90)
65 MOUNT EDEN Cabernet Sauvignon Santa Cruz Mountains 1987 $28 (4/30/91)

1986

98 CAYMUS Cabernet Sauvignon Napa Valley Special Selection 1986 $50 (1/31/91) CS
98 CAYMUS Cabernet Sauvignon Napa Valley Special Selection 1986 $50 (CA-3/89)
96 BERINGER Cabernet Sauvignon Napa Valley Private Reserve 1986 Rel: $35 Cur: $39 (CA-3/89)
96 DIAMOND CREEK Cabernet Sauvignon Napa Valley Red Rock Terrace 1986 Rel: $30 Cur: $46 (CA-3/89)
96 DIAMOND CREEK Cabernet Sauvignon Napa Valley Volcanic Hill 1986 Rel: $30 Cur: $52 (CA-3/89)
96 JOSEPH PHELPS Insignia Napa Valley 1986 Rel: $40 Cur: $40 (CA-3/89)
96 SILVERADO Cabernet Sauvignon Napa Valley Stags Leap District Limited Reserve 1986 Rel: $35 Cur: $38 (12/15/90) CS
96 TERRACES Cabernet Sauvignon Napa Valley 1986 $23 (1/31/91)
95 BERINGER Cabernet Sauvignon Napa Valley Private Reserve 1986 Rel: $35 Cur: $39 (9/15/90) CS
95 DUNN Cabernet Sauvignon Howell Mountain 1986 Rel: $30 Cur: $91 (7/31/90) CS
95 DUNN Cabernet Sauvignon Napa Valley 1986 Rel: $27 Cur: $55 (10/15/89) CS
95 HEITZ Cabernet Sauvignon Napa Valley Martha's Vineyard 1986 $60 (4/15/91) CS
95 WILLIAM HILL Cabernet Sauvignon Napa Valley Reserve 1986 Rel: $24.50 Cur: $25 (CA-3/89)
95 JOHNSON TURNBULL Cabernet Sauvignon Napa Valley Vineyard Selection 82 1986 Rel: $14.50 Cur: $25 (8/31/89)
95 JOHNSON TURNBULL Cabernet Sauvignon Napa Valley Vineyard Selection 82 1986 Rel: $14.50 Cur: $25 (CA-3/89)
95 KENWOOD Cabernet Sauvignon Sonoma Valley Artist Series 1986 Rel: $30 Cur: $31 (11/30/89) CS
95 ROBERT MONDAVI Cabernet Sauvignon Napa Valley Reserve 1986 Rel: $35 Cur: $39 (11/15/89)
95 ROBERT MONDAVI Cabernet Sauvignon Napa Valley Reserve 1986 Rel: $35 Cur: $39 (CA-3/89)
95 OPUS ONE Napa Valley 1986 Rel: $55 Cur: $60 (11/30/89)
95 OPUS ONE Napa Valley 1986 Rel: $55 Cur: $60 (CA-3/89)
95 JOSEPH PHELPS Cabernet Sauvignon Napa Valley Eisele Vineyard 1986 Rel: $40 Cur: $41 (CA-3/89)
95 SPOTTSWOODE Cabernet Sauvignon Napa Valley 1986 Rel: $30 Cur: $71 (9/15/89)
95 SPOTTSWOODE Cabernet Sauvignon Napa Valley 1986 Rel: $30 Cur: $71 (CA-3/89)
95 STERLING Reserve Napa Valley 1986 Rel: $35 Cur: $43 (3/15/90) CS
95+ BERINGER Cabernet Sauvignon Napa Valley Private Reserve 1986 Rel: $35 Cur: $39 (4/15/88) (BT)
95+ WILLIAM HILL Cabernet Sauvignon Napa Valley Reserve 1986 Rel: $24.50 Cur: $25 (4/15/88) (BT)
95+ JOHNSON TURNBULL Cabernet Sauvignon Napa Valley 1986 Rel: $14.50 Cur: $25 (4/15/88) (BT)
95+ WHITEHALL LANE Cabernet Sauvignon Napa Valley 1986 $16 (4/15/88) (BT)
94 CAYMUS Cabernet Sauvignon Napa Valley 1986 Rel: $22 Cur: $29 (3/15/90) SS
94 B.R. COHN Cabernet Sauvignon Sonoma Valley Olive Hill Vineyard 1986 Rel: $18 Cur: $27 (5/31/89)
94 B.R. COHN Cabernet Sauvignon Sonoma Valley Olive Hill Vineyard 1986 Rel: $18 Cur: $27 (CA-3/89)
94 CUVAISON Cabernet Sauvignon Napa Valley 1986 Rel: $15 Cur: $20 (7/15/89)
94 DIAMOND CREEK Cabernet Sauvignon Napa Valley Gravelly Meadow 1986 Rel: $30 Cur: $48 (CA-3/89)
94 DUCKHORN Cabernet Sauvignon Napa Valley 1986 Rel: $18 Cur: $24 (7/31/89) SS
94 DUCKHORN Cabernet Sauvignon Napa Valley 1986 Rel: $18 Cur: $24 (CA-3/89)
94 DUNN Cabernet Sauvignon Howell Mountain 1986 Rel: $30 Cur: $91 (CA-3/89)
94 FLORA SPRINGS Trilogy Napa Valley 1986 Rel: $33 Cur: $33 (2/15/90)
94 FROG'S LEAP Cabernet Sauvignon Napa Valley 1986 Rel: $14 Cur: $20 (CA-3/89)
94 FROG'S LEAP Cabernet Sauvignon Napa Valley 1986 Rel: $14 Cur: $20 (12/31/88)
94 KEENAN Cabernet Sauvignon Napa Valley 1986 Rel: $16.50 Cur: $17 (CA-3/89)
94 KENWOOD Cabernet Sauvignon Sonoma Valley Artist Series 1986 Rel: $30 Cur: $31 (CA-3/89)
94 ST. FRANCIS Cabernet Sauvignon Sonoma Valley Reserve (Black Label) 1986 $20 (11/30/89)
94 SILVER OAK Cabernet Sauvignon Napa Valley 1986 Rel: $26 Cur: $40 (10/31/90) CS
94 SILVERADO Cabernet Sauvignon Napa Valley Stags Leap District 1986 Rel: $13.50 Cur: $18 (8/31/89) SS
94 SILVERADO Cabernet Sauvignon Napa Valley Stags Leap District 1986 Rel: $13.50 Cur: $18 (CA-3/89)
94 STERLING Reserve Napa Valley 1986 Rel: $35 Cur: $43 (CA-3/89)
93 BEAULIEU Cabernet Sauvignon Napa Valley Georges de Latour Private Reserve 1986 Rel: $31 Cur: $39 (3/31/91) (JL)

Key to Symbols

The scores reported here are the results of blind tastings conducted by our panel of senior editors. Wines that carry the initials below are results of individual tastings.

THE WINE SPECTATOR 100-POINT SCALE *95-100*—Classic, a great wine; *90-94*—Outstanding, superior character and style; *80-89*—Good to very good, a wine with special qualities; *70-79*—Average, drinkable wine that may have minor flaws; *60-69*—Below average, drinkable but not recommended; *50-59*—Poor, undrinkable, not recommended. "+"—With a score indicates a range; used primarily with barrel tastings to indicate a preliminary score.

SPECIAL DESIGNATIONS SS—Spectator Selection, CS—Cellar Selection, BB—Best Buy.

TASTER'S INITIALS (JG)—Jim Gordon, (HS)—Harvey Steiman, (JL)—James Laube, (JS)—James Suckling, (TM)—Thomas Matthews, (TR)—Terry Robards, (BT)—Barrel Tasting (these wines were tasted blind from barrel samples), (CA-date)—*California's Great Cabernets* by James Laube, (CH-date)—*California's Great Chardonnays* by James Laube, (VP-date)—*Vintage Port* by James Suckling.

DATE TASTED Dates in parentheses represent the issue in which the rating was published.

93 BEAULIEU Cabernet Sauvignon Napa Valley Georges de Latour Private Reserve 1986 Rel: $31 Cur: $39 (CA-3/89)
93 BERINGER Cabernet Sauvignon Napa Valley Chabot Vineyard 1986 (NR) (CA-3/89)
93 BUENA VISTA Cabernet Sauvignon Carneros Private Reserve 1986 Rel: $25 Cur: $28 (10/15/90)
93 BUENA VISTA Cabernet Sauvignon Carneros Private Reserve 1986 Rel: $25 Cur: $28 (CA-3/89)
93 CAFARO Cabernet Sauvignon Napa Valley 1986 $18 (11/15/89)
93 CARMENET Sonoma Valley 1986 Rel: $20 Cur: $21 (3/01/89)
93 CHATEAU MONTELENA Cabernet Sauvignon Napa Valley 1986 Rel: $25 Cur: $30 (10/15/90)
93 CHATEAU MONTELENA Cabernet Sauvignon Napa Valley 1986 Rel: $25 Cur: $30 (CA-3/89)
93 CINNABAR Cabernet Sauvignon Santa Cruz Mountains 1986 $15 (11/15/89)
93 CUVAISON Cabernet Sauvignon Napa Valley 1986 Rel: $15 Cur: $20 (CA-3/89)
93 DIAMOND CREEK Cabernet Sauvignon Napa Valley Red Rock Terrace 1986 Rel: $30 Cur: $46 (12/31/88)
93 DOMINUS Napa Valley 1986 $45 (3/01/89)
93 DUNN Cabernet Sauvignon Napa Valley 1986 Rel: $27 Cur: $55 (CA-3/89)
93 FORMAN Cabernet Sauvignon Napa Valley 1986 Rel: $20 Cur: $48 (6/15/89)
93 FORMAN Cabernet Sauvignon Napa Valley 1986 Rel: $20 Cur: $48 (CA-3/89)
93 GRACE FAMILY Cabernet Sauvignon Napa Valley 1986 Rel: $40 Cur: $245 (CA-3/89)
93 GROTH Cabernet Sauvignon Napa Valley Reserve 1986 Rel: $40 Cur: $41 (CA-3/89)
93 HESS Cabernet Sauvignon Napa Valley Reserve 1986 Rel: $33 Cur: $45 (9/15/90)
93 HESS Cabernet Sauvignon Napa Valley Reserve 1986 Rel: $33 Cur: $45 (CA-3/89)
93 KEENAN Cabernet Sauvignon Napa Valley 1986 Rel: $16.50 Cur: $17 (8/31/89)
93 ROBERT MONDAVI Cabernet Sauvignon Napa Valley 1986 Rel: $18 Cur: $22 (7/31/89)
93 MOUNT VEEDER Meritage Napa Valley 1986 (NR) (CA-3/89)
93 GUSTAVE NIEBAUM Cabernet Sauvignon Napa Valley Tench Vineyard 1986 $16 (10/15/89)
93 JOSEPH PHELPS Cabernet Sauvignon Napa Valley Backus Vineyard 1986 Rel: $22 Cur: $35 (CA-3/89)
93 JOSEPH PHELPS Insignia Napa Valley 1986 Rel: $40 Cur: $40 (8/31/90) CS
93 SANTA CRUZ MOUNTAIN Cabernet Sauvignon Santa Cruz Mountains Bates Ranch 1986 (NR) (CA-3/89)
93 SHAFER Cabernet Sauvignon Napa Valley Stags Leap District 1986 Rel: $16 Cur: $20 (9/30/89) SS
93 SHAFER Cabernet Sauvignon Napa Valley Stags Leap District 1986 Rel: $16 Cur: $20 (CA-3/89)
93 SILVER OAK Cabernet Sauvignon Alexander Valley 1986 Rel: $26 Cur: $37 (10/31/90) SS
93 STAG'S LEAP WINE CELLARS Stag's Leap Vineyards Cask 23 Napa Valley Stags Leap District 1986 Rel: $55 Cur: $73 (11/15/90)
93 PHILIP TOGNI Cabernet Sauvignon Napa Valley 1986 Rel: $22 Cur: $27 (CA-3/89)
92 ARROWOOD Cabernet Sauvignon Sonoma County 1986 Rel: $20 Cur: $24 (10/15/89)
92 CAYMUS Cabernet Sauvignon Napa Valley 1986 Rel: $22 Cur: $29 (CA-3/89)
92 CHAPPELLET Cabernet Sauvignon Napa Valley Reserve 1986 Rel: $18 Cur: $20 (CA-3/89)
92 CLOS DU VAL Cabernet Sauvignon Napa Valley Stags Leap District 1986 Rel: $17.50 Cur: $18 (CA-3/89)
92 ETUDE Cabernet Sauvignon Napa Valley 1986 $20 (9/30/89)
92 GROTH Cabernet Sauvignon Napa Valley 1986 Rel: $18 Cur: $25 (11/15/89)
92 GROTH Cabernet Sauvignon Napa Valley 1986 Rel: $18 Cur: $25 (CA-3/89)
92 HAYWOOD Cabernet Sauvignon Sonoma Valley 1986 Rel: $16 Cur: $16 (11/15/89)
92 INGLENOOK Cabernet Sauvignon Napa Valley Reserve Cask 1986 (NR) (CA-3/89)
92 INGLENOOK Reunion Napa Valley 1986 (NR) (CA-3/89)
92 LA JOTA Cabernet Sauvignon Howell Mountain 1986 Rel: $21 Cur: $27 (CA-3/89)
92 MONTICELLO Cabernet Sauvignon Napa Valley Corley Reserve 1986 Rel: $24 Cur: $24 (3/15/90)
92 NIEBAUM-COPPOLA Rubicon Napa Valley 1986 (NR) (CA-3/89)
92 PEJU Cabernet Sauvignon Napa Valley HB Vineyard 1986 $20 (11/15/89)
92 PINE RIDGE Cabernet Sauvignon Napa Valley Andrus Reserve 1986 Rel: $40 Cur: $40 (CA-3/89)
92 PINE RIDGE Cabernet Sauvignon Napa Valley Diamond Mountain 1986 Rel: $30 Cur: $30 (11/30/89)
92 PLAM Cabernet Sauvignon Napa Valley 1986 $24 (9/15/89)
92 SHAFER Cabernet Sauvignon Napa Valley Stags Leap District Hillside Select 1986 Rel: $32 Cur: $33 (CA-3/89)
92 SIMI Cabernet Sauvignon Alexander Valley Reserve 1986 (NR) (CA-3/89)
92 STAG'S LEAP WINE CELLARS Stag's Leap Vineyards Cask 23 Napa Valley Stags Leap District 1986 Rel: $55 Cur: $73 (3/01/89)
91 BUEHLER Cabernet Sauvignon Napa Valley 1986 Rel: $15 Cur: $15 (CA-3/89)
91 BUENA VISTA Cabernet Sauvignon Carneros 1986 $11 (10/15/89)
91 BURGESS Cabernet Sauvignon Napa Valley Vintage Selection 1986 Rel: $20 Cur: $22 (CA-3/89)
91 CAIN Five Napa Valley 1986 $30 (2/15/90)
91 CARMENET Sonoma Valley 1986 Rel: $20 Cur: $21 (7/31/89)
91 CLOS DU VAL Cabernet Sauvignon Napa Valley Stags Leap District 1986 Rel: $17.50 Cur: $18 (5/31/90)
91 CLOS DU VAL Cabernet Sauvignon Napa Valley Joli Val 1986 Rel: $12.50 Cur: $13 (CA-3/89)
91 CONN CREEK Cabernet Sauvignon Napa Valley Barrel Select Private Reserve 1986 $37 (12/15/90)
91 DIAMOND CREEK Cabernet Sauvignon Napa Valley Gravelly Meadow 1986 Rel: $30 Cur: $48 (12/31/88)
91 DIAMOND CREEK Cabernet Sauvignon Napa Valley Volcanic Hill 1986 Rel: $30 Cur: $52 (12/31/88)
91 DOMINUS Napa Valley 1986 $45 (2/28/91)
91 FAR NIENTE Cabernet Sauvignon Napa Valley 1986 Rel: $30 Cur: $30 (9/30/89)
91 FAR NIENTE Cabernet Sauvignon Napa Valley 1986 Rel: $30 Cur: $30 (CA-3/89)
91 GIRARD Cabernet Sauvignon Napa Valley Reserve 1986 Rel: $25 Cur: $51 (CA-3/89)
91 GRGICH HILLS Cabernet Sauvignon Napa Valley 1986 $20 (CA-3/89)
91 GROTH Cabernet Sauvignon Napa Valley Reserve 1986 $40 (4/30/91)
91 HACIENDA Antares Sonoma County 1986 $28 (7/31/89)
91 HAYWOOD Cabernet Sauvignon Sonoma Valley 1986 Rel: $16 Cur: $16 (CA-3/89)
91 HESS Cabernet Sauvignon Napa Valley 1986 Rel: $14 Cur: $17 (CA-3/89)
91 WILLIAM HILL Cabernet Sauvignon Napa Valley Reserve 1986 Rel: $24.50 Cur: $25 (11/15/89)
91 KENDALL-JACKSON Cabernet Sauvignon California Cardinale 1986 $65 (11/15/90)
91 KISTLER Cabernet Sauvignon Sonoma Valley Kistler Estate Vineyard 1986 Rel: $20 Cur: $30 (CA-3/89)
91 MARKHAM Cabernet Sauvignon Napa Valley 1986 Rel: $13 Cur: $15 (CA-3/89)
91 NEWTON Cabernet Sauvignon Napa Valley 1986 Rel: $16 Cur: $18 (5/31/90)

91 NEWTON Cabernet Sauvignon Napa Valley 1986 Rel: $16 Cur: $18 (CA-3/89)
91 OPTIMA Cabernet Sauvignon Sonoma County 1986 $22 (2/15/90)
91 PINE RIDGE Cabernet Sauvignon Napa Valley Diamond Mountain 1986 Rel: $30 Cur: $30 (CA-3/89)
91 PINE RIDGE Cabernet Sauvignon Napa Valley Stags Leap District Pine Ridge Stags Leap Vineyard 1986 Cur: $29 (CA-3/89)
91 A. RAFANELLI Cabernet Sauvignon Dry Creek Valley 1986 $9.50 (9/30/89)
91 SHAFER Cabernet Sauvignon Napa Valley Stags Leap District Hillside Select 1986 $32 (3/15/91)
91 STAG'S LEAP WINE CELLARS Cabernet Sauvignon Napa Valley Stags Leap District SLV 1986 Rel: $28 Cur: $28 (11/30/89)
91 STELTZNER Cabernet Sauvignon Napa Valley Stags Leap District 1986 Rel: $16 Cur: $17 (12/31/89)
91 STERLING Cabernet Sauvignon Napa Valley 1986 Rel: $14.50 Cur: $15 (3/31/89)
91 STERLING Cabernet Sauvignon Napa Valley Diamond Mountain Ranch 1986 Rel: $14.50 Cur: $15 (3/15/90)
91 TUDAL Cabernet Sauvignon Napa Valley 1986 Rel: $14.50 Cur: $20 (12/15/89)
91 VICHON Cabernet Sauvignon Napa Valley Stags Leap District SLD 1986 Rel: $21 Cur: $25 (10/31/89)
90 BUENA VISTA Cabernet Sauvignon Sonoma County 1986 $11 (11/15/89)
90 CAKEBREAD Cabernet Sauvignon Napa Valley 1986 Rel: $18 Cur: $18 (8/31/89)
90 CAYMUS Cabernet Sauvignon Napa Valley Cuvée 1986 $15 (8/31/89)
90 CHATEAU ST. JEAN Cabernet Sauvignon Alexander Valley 1986 Rel: $19 Cur: $20 (10/15/89)
90 COSENTINO Cabernet Sauvignon North Coast Reserve 1986 $18 (5/15/90)
90 DEHLINGER Cabernet Sauvignon Russian River Valley 1986 $13 (3/15/90)
90 FETZER Cabernet Sauvignon Mendocino Barrel Select 1986 $11 (4/15/90)
90 FISHER Cabernet Sauvignon Sonoma County Coach Insignia 1986 Rel: $20 Cur: $21 (CA-3/89)
90 FREEMARK ABBEY Cabernet Sauvignon Napa Valley Bosché 1986 Rel: $24 Cur: $25 (CA-3/89)
90 HANZELL Cabernet Sauvignon Sonoma Valley 1986 Rel: $22 Cur: $27 (10/31/90)
90 HESS Cabernet Sauvignon Napa Valley 1986 Rel: $14 Cur: $17 (11/15/89)
90 IRON HORSE Cabernets Alexander Valley 1986 Rel: $17.50 Cur: $18 (4/15/90)
90 KENWOOD Cabernet Sauvignon Sonoma Valley Jack London Vineyard 1986 Rel: $18 Cur: $18 (9/15/89)
90 LIVINGSTON Cabernet Sauvignon Napa Valley Moffett Vineyard 1986 Rel: $24 Cur: $28 (CA-3/89)
90 MORGAN Cabernet Sauvignon Carmel Valley 1986 $16 (9/15/89)
90 MURPHY-GOODE Cabernet Sauvignon Alexander Valley Premier Vineyard 1986 $16 (11/15/89)
90 PINE RIDGE Cabernet Sauvignon Napa Valley Rutherford Cuvée 1986 Rel: $16 Cur: $17 (5/31/90)
90 PINE RIDGE Cabernet Sauvignon Napa Valley Rutherford Cuvée 1986 Rel: $16 Cur: $17 (CA-3/89)
90 RAYMOND Cabernet Sauvignon Napa Valley 1986 Rel: $16 Cur: $17 (5/31/90)
90 ST. CLEMENT Cabernet Sauvignon Napa Valley 1986 Rel: $18 Cur: $18 (9/30/90)
90 SEQUOIA GROVE Cabernet Sauvignon Napa Valley Estate 1986 Rel: $22 Cur: $25 (CA-3/89)
90 SPRING MOUNTAIN Cabernet Sauvignon Napa Valley 1986 (NR) (CA-3/89)
90 STELTZNER Cabernet Sauvignon Napa Valley Stags Leap District 1986 Rel: $16 Cur: $17 (CA-3/89)
90 TREFETHEN Cabernet Sauvignon Napa Valley Hillside Selection 1986 (NR) (CA-3/89)
90 VICHON Cabernet Sauvignon Napa Valley Stags Leap District SLD 1986 Rel: $21 Cur: $25 (CA-3/89)
90+ ARROWOOD Cabernet Sauvignon Sonoma County 1986 Rel: $20 Cur: $24 (4/15/88) (BT)
90+ CARMENET Sonoma Valley 1986 Rel: $20 Cur: $21 (4/15/88) (BT)
90+ CHATEAU MONTELENA Cabernet Sauvignon Napa Valley 1986 Rel: $25 Cur: $30 (4/15/88) (BT)
90+ CUVAISON Cabernet Sauvignon Napa Valley 1986 Rel: $15 Cur: $20 (4/15/88) (BT)
90+ DEHLINGER Cabernet Sauvignon Russian River Valley 1986 (NR) (4/15/88) (BT)
90+ DIAMOND CREEK Cabernet Sauvignon Napa Valley Volcanic Hill 1986 Rel: $30 Cur: $52 (4/15/88) (BT)
90+ DUNN Cabernet Sauvignon Howell Mountain 1986 Rel: $30 Cur: $91 (4/15/88) (BT)
90+ DUNN Cabernet Sauvignon Napa Valley 1986 Rel: $27 Cur: $55 (4/15/88) (BT)
90+ GIRARD Cabernet Sauvignon Napa Valley Reserve 1986 Rel: $25 Cur: $51 (4/15/88) (BT)
90+ GRACE FAMILY Cabernet Sauvignon Napa Valley 1986 Rel: $40 Cur: $245 (4/15/88) (BT)
90+ HAYWOOD Cabernet Sauvignon Sonoma Valley 1986 Rel: $16 Cur: $16 (4/15/88) (BT)
90+ INGLENOOK Cabernet Sauvignon Napa Valley Reserve Cask 1986 (NR) (4/15/88) (BT)
90+ KEENAN Cabernet Sauvignon Napa Valley 1986 Rel: $16.50 Cur: $17 (4/15/88) (BT)
90+ LA JOTA Cabernet Sauvignon Howell Mountain 1986 Rel: $21 Cur: $27 (4/15/88) (BT)
90+ LAUREL GLEN Cabernet Sauvignon Sonoma Mountain 1986 Rel: $20 Cur: $27 (4/15/88) (BT)
90+ ROBERT MONDAVI Cabernet Sauvignon Napa Valley Reserve 1986 Rel: $35 Cur: $39 (4/15/88) (BT)
90+ NEWTON Cabernet Sauvignon Napa Valley 1986 Rel: $16 Cur: $18 (4/15/88) (BT)
90+ J. PEDRONCELLI Cabernet Sauvignon Dry Creek Valley 1986 $7 (4/15/88) (BT)
90+ JOSEPH PHELPS Cabernet Sauvignon Napa Valley Backus Vineyard 1986 Rel: $22 Cur: $35 (4/15/88) (BT)
90+ JOSEPH PHELPS Cabernet Sauvignon Napa Valley Eisele Vineyard 1986 Rel: $40 Cur: $41 (4/15/88) (BT)
90+ PINE RIDGE Cabernet Sauvignon Napa Valley Diamond Mountain 1986 Rel: $30 Cur: $30 (4/15/88) (BT)
90+ ST. FRANCIS Cabernet Sauvignon Sonoma Mountain 1986 (NR) (4/15/88) (BT)
90+ SANTA CRUZ MOUNTAIN Cabernet Sauvignon Santa Cruz Mountains Bates Ranch 1986 (NR) (4/15/88) (BT)
90+ SPOTTSWOODE Cabernet Sauvignon Napa Valley 1986 Rel: $30 Cur: $71 (4/15/88) (BT)
90+ STAG'S LEAP WINE CELLARS Stag's Leap Vineyards Cask 23 Napa Valley Stags Leap District 1986 Rel: $55 Cur: $73 (4/15/88) (BT)
90+ STERLING Cabernet Sauvignon Napa Valley Diamond Mountain Ranch 1986 (NR) (4/15/88) (BT)
90+ STERLING Reserve Napa Valley 1986 Rel: $35 Cur: $43 (4/15/88) (BT)
90+ STERLING Three Palms Vineyard Napa Valley 1986 Rel: $19 Cur: $21 (4/15/88) (BT)
89 ALEXANDER VALLEY Cabernet Sauvignon Alexander Valley 1986 Rel: $11.50 Cur: $12 (12/31/88)
89 BEAULIEU Cabernet Sauvignon Napa Valley Georges de Latour Private Reserve 1986 $31 (11/15/90)
89 BUENA VISTA Cabernet Sauvignon Carneros Private Reserve 1986 $25 (3/15/91)
89 CAKEBREAD Cabernet Sauvignon Napa Valley 1986 Rel: $18 Cur: $18 (CA-3/89)
89 GAINEY Cabernet Sauvignon Santa Barbara County Limited Selection 1986 $15 (12/15/89)
89 GEYSER PEAK Réserve Alexandre Alexander Valley 1986 $20 (9/30/90)
89 GIRARD Cabernet Sauvignon Napa Valley 1986 Rel: $16 Cur: $17 (11/15/89)
89 GUNDLACH BUNDSCHU Cabernet Sauvignon Sonoma Valley Rhinefarm Vineyards 1986 Rel: $12 Cur: $12 (3/01/89)
89 HEITZ Cabernet Sauvignon Napa Valley Bella Oaks Vineyard 1986 $21.50 (4/15/91)
89 KLEIN Cabernet Sauvignon Santa Cruz Mountains 1986 $22 (9/30/89)
89 LAUREL GLEN Cabernet Sauvignon Sonoma Mountain 1986 Rel: $20 Cur: $27 (CA-3/89)
89 MERRYVALE Red Table Wine Napa Valley 1986 Rel: $25 Cur: $25 (CA-3/89)
89 MONTICELLO Cabernet Sauvignon Napa Valley Jefferson Cuvée 1986 $14 (4/15/89)
89 NEWLAN Cabernet Sauvignon Napa Valley 1986 $15 (4/30/91)
89 PAHLMEYER Caldwell Vineyard Napa Valley 1986 $25 (11/15/89)
89 QUAIL RIDGE Cabernet Sauvignon Napa Valley 1986 $15 (11/15/90)
89 RAVENSWOOD Pickberry Vineyards Sonoma Mountain 1986 Rel: $25 Cur: $28 (CA-3/89)
89 ROMBAUER Le Meilleur du Chai Napa Valley 1986 Rel: $35 Cur: $16 (CA-3/89)
89 ST. FRANCIS Cabernet Sauvignon Sonoma County 1986 $12 (1/31/90)
89 SIMI Cabernet Sauvignon Alexander Valley Reserve 1986 $30 (7/31/91)
89 STAG'S LEAP WINE CELLARS Cabernet Sauvignon Napa Valley Stags Leap District SLV 1986 Rel: $28 Cur: $28 (CA-3/89)
89 STAGS' LEAP WINERY Cabernet Sauvignon Napa Valley Stags Leap District 1986 Rel: $17 Cur: $18 (10/31/90)
89 PHILIP TOGNI Cabernet Sauvignon Napa Valley 1986 Rel: $22 Cur: $27 (7/31/89)
89 TUDAL Cabernet Sauvignon Napa Valley 1986 Rel: $14.50 Cur: $20 (CA-3/89)
89 WHITEHALL LANE Cabernet Sauvignon Napa Valley 1986 $16 (8/31/89)
88 ALEXANDER VALLEY Cabernet Sauvignon Alexander Valley 1986 Rel: $11.50 Cur: $12 (CA-3/89)
88 BURGESS Cabernet Sauvignon Napa Valley Vintage Selection 1986 Rel: $20 Cur: $22 (7/15/90)
88 CHATEAU CHEVRE Chev Reserve Napa Valley 1986 $25 (7/31/89)
88 CHRISTIAN BROTHERS Cabernet Sauvignon Napa Valley 1986 $9.50 (11/15/90)
88 CLOS PEGASE Cabernet Sauvignon Napa Valley 1986 $16.50 (9/30/90)
88 CRONIN Cabernet Sauvignon Merlot Shaw-Cronin Cuvée San Mateo County 1986 $15 (2/28/91)
88 CRONIN Cabernet Sauvignon Merlot Robinson Vineyard Napa Valley 1986 $16 (2/15/90)
88 DRY CREEK Cabernet Sauvignon Sonoma County 1986 $11 (3/31/89)
88 HEITZ Cabernet Sauvignon Napa Valley 1986 $18 (4/15/91)
88 IRON HORSE Cabernets Alexander Valley 1986 Rel: $17.50 Cur: $18 (CA-3/89)
88 JORDAN Cabernet Sauvignon Alexander Valley 1986 $22 (11/15/90)
88 JORDAN Cabernet Sauvignon Alexander Valley 1986 $22 (CA-3/89)
88 LAKESPRING Cabernet Sauvignon Napa Valley 1986 Rel: $14 Cur: $18 (CA-3/89)
88 LIVINGSTON Cabernet Sauvignon Napa Valley Moffett Vineyard 1986 Rel: $24 Cur: $28 (11/30/89)
88 LYETH Red Alexander Valley 1986 $23 (11/15/90)
88 MONTICELLO Cabernet Sauvignon Napa Valley Corley Reserve 1986 Rel: $24 Cur: $24 (CA-3/89)
88 ROBERT PECOTA Cabernet Sauvignon Napa Valley Kara's Vineyard 1986 Rel: $16 Cur: $16 (CA-3/89)
88 ROBERT PEPI Cabernet Sauvignon Napa Valley Vine Hill Ranch 1986 Rel: $18 Cur: $24 (10/31/90)
88 PRESTON Cabernet Sauvignon Dry Creek Valley 1986 Rel: $11 Cur: $15 (CA-3/89)
88 RAVENSWOOD Cabernet Sauvignon Sonoma County 1986 Rel: $12 Cur: $16 (12/31/88)
88 RIDGE Cabernet Sauvignon Napa County York Creek 1986 $18 (CA-3/89)
88 ROMBAUER Cabernet Sauvignon Napa Valley 1986 Rel: $15 Cur: $16 (4/15/90)
88 RUTHERFORD HILL Cabernet Sauvignon Napa Valley XVS 1986 (NR) (CA-3/89)
88 V. SATTUI Cabernet Sauvignon Napa Valley Preston Vineyard 1986 Rel: $16.75 Cur: $18 (CA-3/89)
88 SEQUOIA GROVE Cabernet Sauvignon Napa County 1986 Rel: $16 Cur: $16 (CA-3/89)
88 SIMI Cabernet Sauvignon Alexander Valley 1986 Rel: $15.50 Cur: $17 (9/30/90)
88 STERLING Cabernet Sauvignon Napa Valley Diamond Mountain Ranch 1986 Rel: $14.50 Cur: $15 (CA-3/89)
87 BUENA VISTA L'Année Carneros 1986 $35 (2/28/91)
87 CHIMNEY ROCK Cabernet Sauvignon Napa Valley Stags Leap District 1986 Rel: $15 Cur: $17 (9/30/89)
87 CLOS DU BOIS Cabernet Sauvignon Alexander Valley Briarcrest Vineyard 1986 Rel: $17 Cur: $18 (8/31/90)
87 CLOS DU VAL Cabernet Sauvignon Napa Valley Joli Val 1986 Rel: $12.50 Cur: $13 (12/15/89)
87 CONN CREEK Cabernet Sauvignon Napa Valley Barrel Select 1986 Rel: $15 Cur: $16 (CA-3/89)
87 FISHER Cabernet Sauvignon Sonoma County Coach Insignia 1986 Rel: $20 Cur: $21 (1/31/90)
87 GIRARD Cabernet Sauvignon Napa Valley Reserve 1986 $25 (11/15/90)
87 GUNDLACH BUNDSCHU Cabernet Sauvignon Sonoma Valley 1986 $9.50 (11/15/89)
87 HANNA Cabernet Sauvignon Sonoma County 1986 $16 (7/31/89)
87 JOHNSON TURNBULL Cabernet Sauvignon Napa Valley Vineyard Selection 67 1986 Rel: $20 Cur: $30 (CA-3/89)
87 CHARLES KRUG Cabernet Sauvignon Napa Valley 1986 $10.50 (2/28/91)
87 CHARLES KRUG Cabernet Sauvignon Napa Valley Vintage Select 1986 (NR) (CA-3/89)
87 LAUREL GLEN Cabernet Sauvignon Sonoma Mountain 1986 Rel: $20 Cur: $27 (5/15/89)
87 MARKHAM Cabernet Sauvignon Napa Valley 1986 $13 (4/30/91)
87 MONT ST. JOHN Cabernet Sauvignon Napa Valley 1986 $14 (4/30/91)
87 MOUNT VEEDER Cabernet Sauvignon Napa Valley 1986 Rel: $18 Cur: $22 (CA-3/89)
87 PRESTON Cabernet Sauvignon Dry Creek Valley 1986 Rel: $11 Cur: $15 (3/15/90)
87 ST. ANDREW'S WINERY Cabernet Sauvignon Napa Valley 1986 $14.50 (4/30/90)
87 ST. CLEMENT Cabernet Sauvignon Napa Valley 1986 Rel: $18 Cur: $18 (CA-3/89)
87 STREBLOW Cabernet Sauvignon Napa Valley 1986 $16 (7/31/89)
87 TREFETHEN Cabernet Sauvignon Napa Valley 1986 Rel: $15.25 Cur: $17 (CA-3/89)
87 VITA NOVA Reservatum Santa Barbara County 1986 $20 (12/15/89)
86 CHIMNEY ROCK Cabernet Sauvignon Napa Valley Stags Leap District 1986 Rel: $15 Cur: $17 (CA-3/89)
86 CLOS DU BOIS Cabernet Sauvignon Alexander Valley 1986 $12 (5/31/89)
86 COSENTINO The Poet California 1986 $22 (7/31/89)
86 CUTLER Cabernet Sauvignon Sonoma Valley Batto Ranch 1986 $17 (11/15/90)
86 GAN EDEN Cabernet Sauvignon Alexander Valley 1986 $15 (2/15/89)
86 JOHNSON TURNBULL Cabernet Sauvignon Napa Valley Vineyard Selection 67 1986 Rel: $20 Cur: $30 (4/15/90)
86 KENWOOD Cabernet Sauvignon Sonoma Valley 1986 $15 (9/30/89)
86 LONG Cabernet Sauvignon Napa Valley 1986 Rel: $40 Cur: $45 (CA-3/89)
86 LOUIS M. MARTINI Cabernet Sauvignon Sonoma Valley Monte Rosso 1986 Rel: $20 Cur: $22 (CA-3/89)
86 MAYACAMAS Cabernet Sauvignon Napa Valley 1986 $25 (CA-3/89)
86 MERRYVALE Red Table Wine Napa Valley 1986 Rel: $25 Cur: $25 (10/15/90)

UNITED STATES
CALIFORNIA/CABERNET SAUVIGNON & BLENDS

86 ROBERT PECOTA Cabernet Sauvignon Napa Valley Kara's Vineyard 1986 Rel: $16 Cur: $16 (9/15/89)
86 RAVENSWOOD Cabernet Sauvignon Sonoma County 1986 Rel: $12 Cur: $16 (CA-3/89)
86 RAYMOND Cabernet Sauvignon Napa Valley Private Reserve 1986 Rel: $26 Cur: $26 (CA-3/89)
86 ROMBAUER Cabernet Sauvignon Napa Valley 1986 Rel: $15 Cur: $16 (CA-3/89)
86 SEBASTIANI Cabernet Sauvignon Sonoma County Reserve 1986 $13 (1/31/91)
86 SHENANDOAH Cabernet Sauvignon Amador County Artist Series 1986 $12 (10/31/88)
86 STAGS' LEAP WINERY Cabernet Sauvignon Napa Valley Stags Leap District 1986 Rel: $17 Cur: $18 (CA-3/89)
86 STERLING Three Palms Vineyard Napa Valley 1986 Rel: $19 Cur: $21 (12/31/89)
86 STONEGATE Cabernet Sauvignon Napa Valley 1986 $15 (2/28/91)
85 BANDIERA Cabernet Sauvignon Napa Valley 1986 $6.50 (10/31/89) BB
85 BEAULIEU Cabernet Sauvignon Napa Valley Rutherford 1986 Rel: $11.25 Cur: $12 (9/15/89)
85 BUEHLER Cabernet Sauvignon Napa Valley 1986 Rel: $15 Cur: $15 (4/30/89)
85 CAIN Cabernet Sauvignon Napa Valley 1986 $16 (8/31/90)
85 CHATEAU NAPA-BEAUCANON Cabernet Sauvignon Napa Valley 1986 $15 (12/31/88)
85 CHATEAU SOUVERAIN Cabernet Sauvignon Alexander Valley 1986 $8.50 (11/15/89) BB
85 CLOS DU BOIS Marlstone Vineyard Alexander Valley 1986 Rel: $20 Cur: $21 (8/31/90)
85 CUTLER Satyre Sonoma Valley 1986 $20 (2/28/91)
85 DALLA VALLE Cabernet Sauvignon Napa Valley 1986 $20 (6/30/90)
85 EBERLE Cabernet Sauvignon Paso Robles 1986 Rel: $12 Cur: $12 (11/15/89)
85 EBERLE Cabernet Sauvignon Paso Robles 1986 Rel: $12 Cur: $12 (CA-3/89)
85 ESTANCIA Cabernet Sauvignon Alexander Valley 1986 $8 (4/15/89) BB
85 FIELD STONE Cabernet Sauvignon Alexander Valley Hoot Owl Reserve 1986 $20 (12/15/90)
85 FLORA SPRINGS Cabernet Sauvignon Napa Valley 1986 Rel: $15 Cur: $16 (3/15/90)
85 FLORA SPRINGS Trilogy Napa Valley 1986 Rel: $33 Cur: $33 (CA-3/89)
85 FOLIE A DEUX Cabernet Sauvignon Napa Valley 1986 $16.50 (4/15/90)
85 FREMONT CREEK Cabernet Sauvignon Mendocino-Napa Counties 1986 $8 (4/30/91) BB
85 GEYSER PEAK Cabernet Sauvignon Alexander Valley Estate Reserve 1986 $15 (9/30/90)
85 GRAND CRU Cabernet Sauvignon Alexander Valley Collector's Reserve 1986 $22 (5/15/90)
85 INGLENOOK Cabernet Sauvignon Napa Valley 1986 $7.50 (2/28/91) BB
85 KENDALL-JACKSON Cabernet Sauvignon California The Proprietor's 1986 $24 (3/15/90)
85 KENDALL-JACKSON Cabernet Sauvignon California Vintner's Reserve 1986 $11 (12/31/88)
85 LA JOTA Cabernet Sauvignon Howell Mountain 1986 Rel: $21 Cur: $27 (10/15/89)
85 MOUNT EDEN Cabernet Sauvignon Santa Cruz Mountains 1986 Rel: $28 Cur: $28 (CA-3/89)
85 RIDGE Cabernet Sauvignon Santa Cruz Mountains Monte Bello 1986 Rel: $35 Cur: $45 (CA-3/89)
85 STONE CREEK Cabernet Sauvignon Napa Valley Limited Bottling 1986 $10 (6/15/90)
85 TIJSSELING Cabernet Sauvignon Mendocino 1986 $8 (1/31/90) BB
85+ ALEXANDER VALLEY Cabernet Sauvignon Alexander Valley 1986 Rel: $11.50 Cur: $12 (4/15/88) (BT)
85+ BELVEDERE Cabernet Sauvignon Alexander Valley Robert Young Vineyards 1986 (NR) (4/15/88) (BT)
85+ BELVEDERE Cabernet Sauvignon Napa Valley York Creek 1986 (NR) (4/15/88) (BT)
85+ BERINGER Cabernet Sauvignon Napa Valley Chabot Vineyard 1986 (NR) (4/15/88) (BT)
85+ BUENA VISTA Cabernet Sauvignon Carneros 1986 $11 (4/15/88) (BT)
85+ BUENA VISTA Cabernet Sauvignon Carneros Private Reserve 1986 Rel: $25 Cur: $28 (4/15/88) (BT)
85+ BURGESS Cabernet Sauvignon Napa Valley Vintage Selection 1986 Rel: $20 Cur: $22 (4/15/88) (BT)
85+ CAYMUS Cabernet Sauvignon Napa Valley 1986 Rel: $22 Cur: $29 (4/15/88) (BT)
85+ CHATEAU ST. JEAN Cabernet Sauvignon Alexander Valley 1986 Rel: $19 Cur: $20 (4/15/88) (BT)
85+ CHRISTIAN BROTHERS Cabernet Sauvignon Napa Valley 1986 $9.50 (4/15/88) (BT)
85+ CLOS DU BOIS Cabernet Sauvignon Alexander Valley 1986 $12 (4/15/88) (BT)
85+ CONN CREEK Cabernet Sauvignon Napa Valley Barrel Select 1986 Rel: $15 Cur: $16 (4/15/88) (BT)
85+ DIAMOND CREEK Cabernet Sauvignon Napa Valley Red Rock Terrace 1986 Rel: $30 Cur: $46 (4/15/88) (BT)
85+ ETUDE Cabernet Sauvignon Napa Valley 1986 $20 (4/15/88) (BT)
85+ FETZER Cabernet Sauvignon California 1986 (NR) (4/15/88) (BT)
85+ FIRESTONE Cabernet Sauvignon Santa Ynez Valley 1986 $10 (4/15/88) (BT)
85+ FISHER Cabernet Sauvignon Sonoma County Coach Insignia 1986 Rel: $20 Cur: $21 (4/15/88) (BT)
85+ FLORA SPRINGS Cabernet Sauvignon Napa Valley 1986 Rel: $15 Cur: $16 (4/15/88) (BT)
85+ FORMAN Cabernet Sauvignon Napa Valley 1986 Rel: $20 Cur: $48 (4/15/88) (BT)
85+ GEYSER PEAK Cabernet Sauvignon Alexander Valley 1986 (NR) (4/15/88) (BT)
85+ GRGICH HILLS Cabernet Sauvignon Napa Valley 1986 $20 (4/15/88) (BT)
85+ GROTH Cabernet Sauvignon Napa Valley 1986 Rel: $18 Cur: $25 (4/15/88) (BT)
85+ WILLIAM HILL Cabernet Sauvignon Napa Valley Silver Label 1986 $13 (4/15/88) (BT)
85+ CHARLES KRUG Cabernet Sauvignon Napa Valley Slinsen Ranch 1986 (NR) (4/15/88) (BT)
85+ LOUIS M. MARTINI Cabernet Sauvignon Sonoma Valley Monte Rosso 1986 Rel: $20 Cur: $22 (4/15/88) (BT)
85+ MOUNT VEEDER Cabernet Sauvignon Napa Valley 1986 Rel: $18 Cur: $22 (4/15/88) (BT)
85+ MOUNT VEEDER Meritage Napa Valley 1986 (NR) (4/15/88) (BT)
85+ NEYERS Cabernet Sauvignon Napa Valley 1986 (NR) (4/15/88) (BT)
85+ PAHLMEYER Caldwell Vineyard Napa Valley 1986 $25 (4/15/88) (BT)
85+ ROBERT PECOTA Cabernet Sauvignon Napa Valley Kara's Vineyard 1986 Rel: $16 Cur: $16 (4/15/88) (BT)
85+ ROBERT PEPI Cabernet Sauvignon Napa Valley Vine Hill Ranch 1986 Rel: $18 Cur: $24 (4/15/88) (BT)
85+ JOSEPH PHELPS Cabernet Sauvignon Napa Valley 1986 Rel: $15 Cur: $18 (4/15/88) (BT)
85+ JOSEPH PHELPS Insignia Napa Valley 1986 Rel: $40 Cur: $40 (4/15/88) (BT)

Key to Symbols

The scores reported here are the results of blind tastings conducted by our panel of senior editors. Wines that carry the initials below are results of individual tastings.

THE WINE SPECTATOR 100-POINT SCALE *95-100*—Classic, a great wine; *90-94*—Outstanding, superior character and style; *80-89*—Good to very good, a wine with special qualities; *70-79*—Average, drinkable wine that may have minor flaws; *60-69*—Below average, drinkable but not recommended; *50-59*—Poor, undrinkable, not recommended. "+"—With a score indicates a range; used primarily with barrel tastings to indicate a preliminary score.

SPECIAL DESIGNATIONS SS—Spectator Selection, CS—Cellar Selection, BB—Best Buy.

TASTER'S INITIALS (JG)—Jim Gordon, (HS)—Harvey Steiman, (JL)—James Laube, (JS)—James Suckling, (TM)—Thomas Matthews, (TR)—Terry Robards, (BT)—Barrel Tasting (these wines were tasted blind from barrel samples), (CA-date)—*California's Great Cabernets* by James Laube, (CH-date)—*California's Great Chardonnays* by James Laube, (VP-date)—*Vintage Port* by James Suckling.

DATE TASTED Dates in parentheses represent the issue in which the rating was published.

85+ PINE RIDGE Cabernet Sauvignon Napa Valley Rutherford Cuvée 1986 Rel: $16 Cur: $17 (4/15/88) (BT)
85+ RAVENSWOOD Pickberry Vineyards Sonoma Mountain 1986 Rel: $25 Cur: $28 (4/15/88) (BT)
85+ RIDGE Cabernet Sauvignon Santa Cruz Mountains Monte Bello 1986 Rel: $35 Cur: $45 (4/15/88) (BT)
85+ SHAFER Cabernet Sauvignon Napa Valley Stags Leap District Hillside Select 1986 Rel: $32 Cur: $33 (4/15/88) (BT)
85+ SIMI Cabernet Sauvignon Alexander Valley Reserve 1986 (NR) (4/15/88) (BT)
85+ STAG'S LEAP WINE CELLARS Cabernet Sauvignon Napa Valley Stags Leap District SLV 1986 Rel: $28 Cur: $28 (4/15/88) (BT)
85+ STERLING Cabernet Sauvignon Napa Valley 1986 Rel: $14.50 Cur: $15 (4/15/88) (BT)
85+ VIANSA Cabernet Sauvignon Napa-Alexander Valleys 1986 (NR) (4/15/88) (BT)
85+ VICHON Cabernet Sauvignon Napa Valley Stags Leap District SLD 1986 Rel: $21 Cur: $25 (4/15/88) (BT)
85+ WILLIAM WHEELER Cabernet Sauvignon Dry Creek Valley 1986 $12 (4/15/88) (BT)
84 DAVIS BYNUM Cabernet Sauvignon Sonoma County 1986 $10 (11/15/89)
84 CHATEAU POTELLE Cabernet Sauvignon Alexander Valley 1986 $14.50 (10/31/90)
84 DE LORIMIER Mosaic Alexander Valley 1986 $16 (10/31/89)
84 FRANCISCAN Cabernet Sauvignon Napa Valley Oakville Estate 1986 $11 (7/15/90)
84 HUSCH Cabernet Sauvignon Mendocino 1986 $12 (2/15/90)
84 KISTLER Cabernet Sauvignon Sonoma Valley Kistler Estate Vineyard 1986 Rel: $20 Cur: $30 (9/30/89)
84 LA VIEILLE MONTAGNE Cabernet Sauvignon Napa Valley 1986 $14 (6/30/90)
84 J. LOHR Cabernet Sauvignon California 1986 $6.50 (4/15/89) BB
84 PAUL MASSON Cabernet Sauvignon California Vintner's Selection 1986 $6 (6/30/89)
84 MERLION Cabernet Sauvignon Napa Valley 1986 $16.50 (11/15/90)
84 ROMBAUER Le Meilleur du Chai Napa Valley 1986 $35 (5/15/91)
84 SEQUOIA GROVE Cabernet Sauvignon Napa Valley Estate 1986 Rel: $22 Cur: $25 (9/30/89)
84 TREFETHEN Cabernet Sauvignon Napa Valley 1986 Rel: $15.25 Cur: $17 (10/31/89)
84 VILLA MT. EDEN Cabernet Sauvignon Napa Valley 1986 $13 (2/15/91)
84 VILLA MT. EDEN Cabernet Sauvignon Napa Valley 1986 $13 (CA-3/89)
84 YORK MOUNTAIN Cabernet Sauvignon San Luis Obispo 1986 $15 (11/15/90)
83 BARON HERZOG Cabernet Sauvignon Sonoma County Special Reserve 1986 $14 (11/15/89)
83 BEAULIEU Cabernet Sauvignon Napa Valley Beau Tour 1986 $7 (10/31/88)
83 BELLEROSE Cuvée Bellerose Sonoma County 1986 $18 (1/31/90)
83 CECCHETTI SEBASTIANI Cabernet Sauvignon Alexander Valley 1986 $8.50 (4/15/89)
83 FREEMARK ABBEY Cabernet Sauvignon Napa Valley 1986 $15 (11/15/90)
83 JEKEL Cabernet Sauvignon Arroyo Seco 1986 $13 (11/15/90)
83 LOLONIS Cabernet Sauvignon Mendocino County Private Reserve 1986 $15 (5/15/90)
83 MIRASSOU Cabernet Sauvignon California Fifth Generation Family Selection 1986 $9.75 (5/31/91)
83 MONTEREY VINEYARD Cabernet Sauvignon Monterey County Limited Release 1986 $10 (11/15/89)
83 MOUNT EDEN Cabernet Sauvignon Santa Cruz Mountains 1986 Rel: $28 Cur: $28 (8/31/90)
83 MOUNT VEEDER Cabernet Sauvignon Napa Valley 1986 $18 (11/15/90)
83 J. PEDRONCELLI Cabernet Sauvignon Dry Creek Valley 1986 $7 (9/15/89) BB
83 JOSEPH PHELPS Cabernet Sauvignon Napa Valley Backus Vineyard 1986 Rel: $22 Cur: $35 (1/31/90)
83 RENAISSANCE Cabernet Sauvignon North Yuba 1986 $15 (7/15/91)
83 WILLIAM WHEELER Cabernet Sauvignon Dry Creek Valley 1986 $12 (8/31/90)
82 BENZIGER Cabernet Sauvignon Sonoma County 1986 $10 (7/31/89)
82 DUNNEWOOD Cabernet Sauvignon Napa Valley Napa Reserve 1986 $10.50 (6/15/90)
82 GLEN ELLEN Cabernet Sauvignon California Proprietor's Reserve 1986 $4.50 (7/15/88) BB
82 HAWK CREST Cabernet Sauvignon North Coast 1986 $7.50 (10/15/88) BB
82 BERNARD PRADEL Cabernet Sauvignon Napa Valley 1986 $12 (1/31/90)
82 RIDGE Cabernet Sauvignon Santa Cruz Mountains Monte Bello 1986 Rel: $35 Cur: $45 (9/15/89)
82 ROUND HILL Cabernet Sauvignon Napa Valley 1986 $8 (10/15/88)
82 STAG'S LEAP WINE CELLARS Cabernet Sauvignon Napa Valley 1986 $18 (6/15/89)
82 SUGARLOAF RIDGE Cabernet Sauvignon Sonoma Valley 1986 $13 (3/31/90)
82 M.G. VALLEJO Cabernet Sauvignon California 1986 $5 (6/15/90) BB
82 WENTE BROS. Cabernet Sauvignon Livermore Valley Estate Reserve 1986 $12 (10/15/90)
82 WILLOW CREEK Cabernet Sauvignon Napa-Alexander Valleys 1986 $9.50 (7/31/89)
81 FIRESTONE Cabernet Sauvignon Santa Ynez Valley 1986 $10 (12/15/89)
81 KATHRYN KENNEDY Cabernet Sauvignon Santa Cruz Mountains 1986 $30 (3/15/90)
81 ROUDON-SMITH Cabernet Sauvignon Santa Cruz Mountains 1986 $12 (3/15/91)
80 ARCIERO Cabernet Sauvignon Paso Robles 1986 $9 (11/15/90)
80 CASTORO Cabernet Sauvignon Paso Robles Hope Farms 1986 $8.50 (12/15/89)
80 CORBETT CANYON Cabernet Sauvignon Central Coast Coastal Classic 1986 $6.50/L (12/15/89)
80 DRY CREEK Meritage Dry Creek Valley 1986 $22 (9/15/90)
80 FERRARI-CARANO Cabernet Sauvignon Alexander Valley 1986 $17.50 (9/15/90)
80 KONOCTI Cabernet Sauvignon Lake County 1986 $9 (4/30/90)
80 LOUIS M. MARTINI Cabernet Sauvignon North Coast 1986 $9.25 (9/15/89)
80 ROBERT MONDAVI Cabernet Sauvignon California Cabernet 1986 $5.50 (12/15/88) BB
80 PINE RIDGE Cabernet Sauvignon Napa Valley Andrus Reserve 1986 Rel: $40 Cur: $40 (5/15/90)
80 ROUND HILL Cabernet Sauvignon Napa Valley Reserve 1986 $9 (6/30/90)
80 WHITE ROCK Claret Napa Valley 1986 $18 (10/31/89)
80 ZACA MESA Cabernet Sauvignon Santa Barbara County Reserve 1986 $15 (12/15/88)
80+ BUEHLER Cabernet Sauvignon Napa Valley 1986 Rel: $15 Cur: $15 (4/15/88) (BT)
80+ CHAPPELLET Cabernet Sauvignon Napa Valley Reserve 1986 Rel: $18 Cur: $20 (4/15/88) (BT)
80+ CONN CREEK Cabernet Sauvignon Napa Valley Barrel Select Private Reserve 1986 Rel: $37 Cur: $38 (4/15/88) (BT)
80+ DRY CREEK Cabernet Sauvignon Sonoma County 1986 $11 (4/15/88) (BT)
80+ EBERLE Cabernet Sauvignon Paso Robles 1986 Rel: $12 Cur: $12 (4/15/88) (BT)
80+ FRANCISCAN Cabernet Sauvignon Napa Valley Oakville Estate 1986 (NR) (4/15/88) (BT)
80+ IRON HORSE Cabernets Alexander Valley 1986 Rel: $17.50 Cur: $18 (4/15/88) (BT)
80+ PINE RIDGE Cabernet Sauvignon Napa Valley Stags Leap District Pine Ridge Stags Leap Vineyard 1986 Rel: $29 Cur: $29 (4/15/88) (BT)
80+ PRESTON Cabernet Sauvignon Dry Creek Valley 1986 Rel: $11 Cur: $15 (4/15/88) (BT)
80+ ST. ANDREW'S WINERY Cabernet Sauvignon Napa Valley 1986 (NR) (4/15/88) (BT)
80+ STELTZNER Cabernet Sauvignon Napa Valley Stags Leap District 1986 Rel: $16 Cur: $17 (4/15/88) (BT)
80+ VILLA MT. EDEN Cabernet Sauvignon Napa Valley 1986 (NR) (4/15/88) (BT)
79 ARCIERO Cabernet Sauvignon Paso Robles 1986 $9 (12/31/89)
79 DOMAINE ST. GEORGE Cabernet Sauvignon Russian River Valley Select Reserve 1986 $9 (5/31/90)

79 FOPPIANO Cabernet Sauvignon Sonoma County 1986 $9 (11/15/90)
79 FRANCISCAN Meritage Napa Valley 1986 Rel: $15 Cur: $18 (7/31/90)
79 GRAND CRU Cabernet Sauvignon Sonoma County Premium Selection 1986 $12 (4/30/90)
79 LEEWARD Cabernet Sauvignon Alexander Valley 1986 $12 (10/15/89)
79 MASSON Cabernet Sauvignon Monterey County Vintage Selection 1986 $9 (11/15/89)
79 MOUNTAIN VIEW Cabernet Sauvignon Mendocino County 1986 $6.50 (3/31/90)
79 PARDUCCI Cabernet Merlot Cellarmaster Selection Mendocino County 1986 $15 (4/30/91)
79 STONEGATE Cabernet Sauvignon Napa Valley 1986 Rel: $15 Cur: $18 (CA-3/89)
79 SUTTER HOME Cabernet Sauvignon California 1986 $5 (11/30/88)
79 VENTANA Magnus Meritage Monterey 1986 $20 (10/31/89)
79 VILLA ZAPU Cabernet Sauvignon Napa Valley 1986 $16 (10/31/89)
78 BENZIGER Cabernet Sauvignon Sonoma Valley 1986 $17 (4/30/90)
78 CHRISTOPHE Cabernet Sauvignon Napa Valley Reserve 1986 $12 (11/15/90)
78 DE MOOR Cabernet Sauvignon Napa Valley Owners Select 1986 $16 (2/28/91)
78 GUENOC Cabernet Sauvignon Lake County 1986 $12.50 (4/30/91)
78 MAZZOCCO Cabernet Sauvignon Alexander Valley Claret Style 1986 $20 (7/31/89)
78 RAVENSWOOD Pickberry Vineyards Sonoma Mountain 1986 Rel: $25 Cur: $28 (2/15/89)
78 SEQUOIA GROVE Cabernet Sauvignon Napa County 1986 Rel: $16 Cur: $16 (9/30/89)
78 ZACA MESA Cabernet Sauvignon Santa Barbara County 1986 $9.50 (12/15/89)
77 FLORA SPRINGS Cabernet Sauvignon Napa Valley 1986 Rel: $15 Cur: $16 (CA-3/89)
77 MADDALENA Cabernet Sauvignon Alexander Valley Reserve 1986 $10 (3/31/90)
77 JOSEPH PHELPS Cabernet Sauvignon Napa Valley Eisele Vineyard 1986 Rel: $40 Cur: $41 (8/31/90)
77 VIANSA Cabernet Sauvignon Sonoma-Napa Counties 1986 $15 (7/31/90)
77 WHITEHALL LANE Cabernet Sauvignon Napa Valley Reserve 1986 $30 (11/15/90)
76 FREEMARK ABBEY Cabernet Sauvignon Napa Valley Bosché 1986 Rel: $24 Cur: $25 (7/31/90)
76 FREMONT CREEK Cabernet Sauvignon Mendocino-Napa Counties 1986 $8 (11/15/89)
76 MONTEREY VINEYARD Cabernet Sauvignon Monterey County Classic +1986 $5.50 (10/31/89)
76 SEGHESIO Cabernet Sauvignon Northern Sonoma 1986 $8 (6/30/90)
75 DOMAINE MICHEL Cabernet Sauvignon Sonoma County 1986 $19 (6/30/90)
75 PARSONS CREEK Cabernet Sauvignon Sonoma County 1986 $13 (11/15/89)
75 J. WILE & SONS Cabernet Sauvignon Napa Valley 1986 $7 (9/15/88)
75+ BELVEDERE Cabernet Sauvignon Sonoma County Bradford Mountain 1986 (NR) (4/15/88) (BT)
75+ COSENTINO Cabernet Sauvignon North Coast 1986 $13 (4/15/88) (BT)
75+ MONTICELLO Cabernet Sauvignon Napa Valley Corley Reserve 1986 Rel: $24 Cur: $24 (4/15/88) (BT)
75+ RUTHERFORD HILL Cabernet Sauvignon Napa Valley 1986 Rel: $14 Cur: $15 (4/15/88) (BT)
74 AUSTIN A Genoux Santa Barbara County 1986 $15 (12/15/89)
74 BARON HERZOG Cabernet Sauvignon Sonoma County Special Reserve 1986 $16 (3/31/91)
74 INGLENOOK Niebaum Claret Napa Valley 1986 $12.50 (6/30/91)
74 KENDALL-JACKSON Cabernet Sauvignon Lake County 1986 $7.75 (7/31/88)
73 DUNNEWOOD Cabernet Sauvignon California 1986 $7 (6/15/90)
73 INNISFREE Cabernet Sauvignon Napa Valley 1986 $10.50 (6/30/90)
73 RANCHO SISQUOC Cabernet Sauvignon Santa Maria Valley 1986 $10 (12/15/89)
72 MEEKER Cabernet Sauvignon Dry Creek Valley 1986 $18.50 (2/15/90)
72 MISSION VIEW Cabernet Sauvignon Paso Robles 1986 $12 (12/15/89)
70 GARLAND RANCH Cabernet Sauvignon Central Coast 1986 $6.75 (10/31/89)
70 MCDOWELL Cabernet Sauvignon McDowell Valley 1986 $8 (4/30/90)
70 TULOCAY Cabernet Sauvignon Napa Valley 1986 $12 (6/30/90)
69 HOP KILN Cabernet Sauvignon Dry Creek Valley 1986 $12 (6/15/89)
68 RIDGE Cabernet Sauvignon Santa Cruz Mountains 1986 $15 (10/31/89)
68 RUTHERFORD HILL Cabernet Sauvignon Napa Valley 1986 $14 (2/28/91)
60 MIRASSOU Cabernet Sauvignon Monterey County Fifth Generation Harvest Reserve 1986 $12.50 (7/31/91)
55 CONN CREEK Cabernet Sauvignon Napa Valley Barrel Select 1986 $15 (2/28/91)

1985

99 CAYMUS Cabernet Sauvignon Napa Valley Special Selection 1985 Rel: $50 Cur: $127 (4/30/90)
99 CAYMUS Cabernet Sauvignon Napa Valley Special Selection 1985 Rel: $50 Cur: $127 (CA-3/89)
98 HEITZ Cabernet Sauvignon Napa Valley Martha's Vineyard 1985 Rel: $60 Cur: $118 (4/30/90)
98 HEITZ Cabernet Sauvignon Napa Valley Martha's Vineyard 1985 Rel: $60 Cur: $118 (CA-3/89)
98 STAG'S LEAP WINE CELLARS Stag's Leap Vineyards Cask 23 Napa Valley Stags Leap District 1985 Rel: $75 Cur: $141 (3/01/89)
97 KENDALL-JACKSON Cabernet Sauvignon California Cardinale 1985 $45 (11/15/89)
96 BERINGER Cabernet Sauvignon Napa Valley Private Reserve 1985 Rel: $30 Cur: $42 (CA-3/89)
96 HESS Cabernet Sauvignon Napa Valley 1985 Rel: $13 Cur: $40 (CA-3/89)
96 STAG'S LEAP WINE CELLARS Stag's Leap Vineyards Cask 23 Napa Valley Stags Leap District 1985 Rel: $75 Cur: $141 (11/30/89)
96 STERLING Reserve Napa Valley 1985 Rel: $30 Cur: $38 (7/15/89) SS
96 STERLING Reserve Napa Valley 1985 Rel: $30 Cur: $38 (CA-3/89)
95 BEAULIEU Cabernet Sauvignon Napa Valley Georges de Latour Private Reserve 1985 Rel: $25 Cur: $29 (3/31/91) (JL)
95 BEAULIEU Cabernet Sauvignon Napa Valley Georges de Latour Private Reserve 1985 Rel: $25 Cur: $29 (CA-3/89)
95 BERINGER Cabernet Sauvignon Napa Valley Private Reserve 1985 Rel: $30 Cur: $42 (12/15/89) SS
95 CHATEAU MONTELENA Cabernet Sauvignon Napa Valley 1985 Rel: $25 Cur: $44 (CA-3/89)
95 DOMINUS Napa Valley 1985 Rel: $45 Cur: $50 (3/01/89)
95 GRACE FAMILY Cabernet Sauvignon Napa Valley 1985 Rel: $50 Cur: $250 (CA-3/89)
95 GROTH Cabernet Sauvignon Napa Valley Reserve 1985 Rel: $30 Cur: $166 (4/15/90)
95 INGLENOOK Cabernet Sauvignon Napa Valley Reserve Cask 1985 Rel: $16 Cur: $19 (CA-3/89)
95 KENDALL-JACKSON Cabernet Sauvignon California Proprietor's Reserve 1985 $20 (12/15/88)
95 ROBERT MONDAVI Cabernet Sauvignon Napa Valley Reserve 1985 Rel: $40 Cur: $43 (11/15/89) SS
95 ROBERT MONDAVI Cabernet Sauvignon Napa Valley Reserve 1985 Rel: $40 Cur: $43 (CA-3/89)
95 OPUS ONE Napa Valley 1985 Rel: $55 Cur: $69 (6/15/89)
95 OPUS ONE Napa Valley 1985 Rel: $55 Cur: $69 (CA-3/89)
95 RIDGE Cabernet Sauvignon Santa Cruz Mountains Monte Bello 1985 Rel: $40 Cur: $89 (CA-3/89)
95 RIDGE Cabernet Sauvignon Santa Cruz Mountains Monte Bello 1985 Rel: $40 Cur: $89 (7/15/88) CS
95 SILVER OAK Cabernet Sauvignon Alexander Valley 1985 Rel: $24 Cur: $45 (CA-3/89)
95 SPOTTSWOODE Cabernet Sauvignon Napa Valley 1985 Rel: $25 Cur: $94 (CA-3/89)
95 SPOTTSWOODE Cabernet Sauvignon Napa Valley 1985 Rel: $25 Cur: $94 (11/15/88) CS
95+ BERINGER Cabernet Sauvignon Napa Valley Private Reserve 1985 Rel: $30 Cur: $42 (6/15/87) (BT)
95+ STAG'S LEAP WINE CELLARS Stag's Leap Vineyards Cask 23 Napa Valley Stags Leap District 1985 Rel: $75 Cur: $141 (6/15/87) (BT)
94 ARROWOOD Cabernet Sauvignon Sonoma County 1985 Rel: $19 Cur: $25 (12/15/88)
94 BUENA VISTA Cabernet Sauvignon Carneros Private Reserve 1985 Rel: $18 Cur: $23 (10/15/89) SS
94 CLOS DU VAL Reserve Napa Valley Stags Leap District 1985 $45 (11/15/90)
94 CLOS DU VAL Reserve Napa Valley Stags Leap District 1985 $45 (CA-3/89)
94 B.R. COHN Cabernet Sauvignon Sonoma Valley Olive Hill Vineyard 1985 Rel: $16 Cur: $35 (CA-3/89)
94 B.R. COHN Cabernet Sauvignon Sonoma Valley Olive Hill Vineyard 1985 Rel: $16 Cur: $35 (11/15/88)
94 DUNN Cabernet Sauvignon Napa Valley 1985 Rel: $20 Cur: $64 (CA-3/89)
94 DUNN Cabernet Sauvignon Napa Valley 1985 Rel: $20 Cur: $64 (9/15/88) CS
94 WILLIAM HILL Cabernet Sauvignon Napa Valley Reserve 1985 Rel: $22.50 Cur: $27 (CA-3/89)
94 INGLENOOK Reunion Napa Valley 1985 Rel: $35 Cur: $36 (CA-3/89)
94 ROBERT MONDAVI Cabernet Sauvignon Napa Valley 1985 Rel: $15 Cur: $20 (12/15/88) SS
94 JOSEPH PHELPS Cabernet Sauvignon Napa Valley Eisele Vineyard 1985 Rel: $40 Cur: $43 (CA-3/89)
94 PINE RIDGE Cabernet Sauvignon Napa Valley Stags Leap District Pine Ridge Stags Leap Vineyard 1985 Rel: $26 Cur: $26 (CA-3/89)
94 SIMI Cabernet Sauvignon Alexander Valley Reserve 1985 Rel: $25 Cur: $28 (8/31/90) SS
94 SIMI Cabernet Sauvignon Alexander Valley Reserve 1985 Rel: $25 Cur: $28 (CA-3/89)
94 STAG'S LEAP WINE CELLARS Cabernet Sauvignon Napa Valley Stags Leap District SLV 1985 Rel: $26 Cur: $38 (CA-3/89)
93 BUEHLER Cabernet Sauvignon Napa Valley 1985 Rel: $14 Cur: $16 (CA-3/89)
93 BUENA VISTA Cabernet Sauvignon Carneros Private Reserve 1985 Rel: $18 Cur: $23 (CA-3/89)
93 BURGESS Cabernet Sauvignon Napa Valley Vintage Selection 1985 Rel: $18 Cur: $23 (CA-3/89)
93 CLOS DU VAL Cabernet Sauvignon Napa Valley Stags Leap District 1985 Rel: $16 Cur: $25 (CA-3/89)
93 DIAMOND CREEK Cabernet Sauvignon Napa Valley Red Rock Terrace 1985 Rel: $30 Cur: $51 (CA-3/89)
93 DIAMOND CREEK Cabernet Sauvignon Napa Valley Volcanic Hill 1985 Rel: $30 Cur: $50 (CA-3/89)
93 FORMAN Cabernet Sauvignon Napa Valley 1985 Rel: $18 Cur: $68 (CA-3/89)
93 FREEMARK ABBEY Cabernet Sauvignon Napa Valley Bosché 1985 Rel: $24 Cur: $24 (CA-3/89)
93 GRACE FAMILY Cabernet Sauvignon Napa Valley 1985 Rel: $50 Cur: $250 (12/15/88)
93 GROTH Cabernet Sauvignon Napa Valley 1985 Rel: $16 Cur: $32 (11/15/88)
93 GROTH Cabernet Sauvignon Napa Valley Reserve 1985 Rel: $30 Cur: $166 (CA-3/89)
93 KATHRYN KENNEDY Cabernet Sauvignon Santa Cruz Mountains 1985 $25 (12/15/88)
93 KISTLER Cabernet Sauvignon Sonoma Valley Kistler Estate Vineyard 1985 Rel: $16 Cur: $30 (CA-3/89)
93 LAUREL GLEN Cabernet Sauvignon Sonoma Mountain 1985 Rel: $18 Cur: $39 (CA-3/89)
93 MARKHAM Cabernet Sauvignon Napa Valley 1985 Rel: $13 Cur: $16 (CA-3/89)
93 OPTIMA Cabernet Sauvignon Sonoma County 1985 $18.50 (12/15/88)
93 JOSEPH PHELPS Insignia Napa Valley 1985 Rel: $40 Cur: $46 (7/31/89) CS
93 PINE RIDGE Cabernet Sauvignon Napa Valley Rutherford Cuvée 1985 Rel: $16 Cur: $19 (CA-3/89)
93 ST. CLEMENT Cabernet Sauvignon Napa Valley 1985 Rel: $17 Cur: $19 (CA-3/89)
93 SHAFER Cabernet Sauvignon Napa Valley Stags Leap District Hillside Select 1985 Rel: $24.50 Cur: $28 (CA-3/89)
93 STELTZNER Cabernet Sauvignon Napa Valley Stags Leap District 1985 Rel: $16 Cur: $19 (CA-3/89)
93 STERLING Three Palms Vineyard Napa Valley 1985 Rel: $20 Cur: $22 (12/31/88)
93 VICHON Cabernet Sauvignon Napa Valley Stags Leap District SLD 1985 Rel: $18 Cur: $26 (1/31/89)
93 WHITEHALL LANE Cabernet Sauvignon Napa Valley 1985 $16 (11/15/88)
92 ALEXANDER VALLEY Cabernet Sauvignon Alexander Valley 1985 Rel: $11 Cur: $15 (11/15/87)
92 BURGESS Cabernet Sauvignon Napa Valley Vintage Selection 1985 Rel: $18 Cur: $23 (7/15/89)
92 CAYMUS Cabernet Sauvignon Napa Valley 1985 Rel: $18 Cur: $38 (CA-3/89)
92 CAYMUS Cabernet Sauvignon Napa Valley Cuvée 1985 $12 (7/15/88)
92 CHATEAU MONTELENA Cabernet Sauvignon Napa Valley 1985 Rel: $25 Cur: $44 (11/15/89) CS
92 CLOS DU VAL Reserve Napa Valley Stags Leap District 1985 Rel: $45 Cur: $47 (11/15/89)
92 DIAMOND CREEK Cabernet Sauvignon Napa Valley Gravelly Meadow 1985 Rel: $30 Cur: $56 (CA-3/89)
92 DUCKHORN Cabernet Sauvignon Napa Valley 1985 Rel: $17.50 Cur: $38 (CA-3/89)
92 ETUDE Cabernet Sauvignon California 1985 Rel: $16 Cur: $16 (12/15/88)
92 FAR NIENTE Cabernet Sauvignon Napa Valley 1985 Rel: $28 Cur: $28 (CA-3/89)
92 FORMAN Cabernet Sauvignon Napa Valley 1985 Rel: $18 Cur: $68 (6/15/88)
92 GRGICH HILLS Cabernet Sauvignon Napa Valley 1985 Rel: $20 Cur: $23 (CA-3/89)
92 HEITZ Cabernet Sauvignon Napa Valley Bella Oaks Vineyard 1985 Rel: $25 Cur: $32 (5/15/90) CS
92 HEITZ Cabernet Sauvignon Napa Valley Bella Oaks Vineyard 1985 Rel: $25 Cur: $32 (CA-3/89)
92 WILLIAM HILL Cabernet Sauvignon Napa Valley Reserve 1985 Rel: $22.50 Cur: $27 (11/15/88)
92 KISTLER Cabernet Sauvignon Sonoma Valley Kistler Estate Vineyard 1985 Rel: $16 Cur: $30 (5/31/88)
92 LAKESPRING Cabernet Sauvignon Napa Valley 1985 Rel: $12 Cur: $12 (7/15/88)
92 LONG Cabernet Sauvignon Napa Valley 1985 Rel: $36 Cur: $50 (CA-3/89)
92 LYETH Red Alexander Valley 1985 Rel: $22 Cur: $22 (CA-3/89)
92 MAYACAMAS Cabernet Sauvignon Napa Valley 1985 Rel: $25 Cur: $30 (1/31/90)
92 MAYACAMAS Cabernet Sauvignon Napa Valley 1985 Rel: $25 Cur: $30 (CA-3/89)
92 MONTICELLO Cabernet Sauvignon Napa Valley Corley Reserve 1985 Rel: $22.50 Cur: $30 (7/31/89)

UNITED STATES
CALIFORNIA/*CABERNET SAUVIGNON & BLENDS*

92 PINE RIDGE Cabernet Sauvignon Napa Valley Andrus Reserve Cuvée Duet 1985 Rel: $40 Cur: $45 (CA-3/89)
92 RIDGE Cabernet Sauvignon Napa County York Creek 1985 Rel: $16 Cur: $18 (CA-3/89)
92 RUTHERFORD RANCH Cabernet Sauvignon Napa Valley 1985 Rel: $11 Cur: $11 (5/15/90) SS
92 SANTA CRUZ MOUNTAIN Cabernet Sauvignon Santa Cruz Mountains Bates Ranch 1985 (NA) (CA-3/89)
92 SEQUOIA GROVE Cabernet Sauvignon Napa Valley Estate 1985 Rel: $28 Cur: $32 (CA-3/89)
92 SEQUOIA GROVE Cabernet Sauvignon Napa Valley Estate 1985 Rel: $28 Cur: $32 (8/31/88)
92 SILVERADO Cabernet Sauvignon Napa Valley Stags Leap District 1985 Rel: $12.50 Cur: $20 (CA-3/89)
92 STELTZNER Cabernet Sauvignon Napa Valley Stags Leap District 1985 Rel: $16 Cur: $19 (11/15/88)
92 VICHON Cabernet Sauvignon Napa Valley Stags Leap District SLD 1985 Rel: $18 Cur: $26 (CA-3/89)
91 BEAULIEU Cabernet Sauvignon Napa Valley Georges de Latour Private Reserve 1985 Rel: $25 Cur: $29 (12/31/89)
91 BERINGER Cabernet Sauvignon Napa Valley Chabot Vineyard 1985 Rel: $30 Cur: $30 (CA-3/89)
91 CARMENET Sonoma Valley 1985 Rel: $18.50 Cur: $23 (CA-3/89)
91 CARMENET Sonoma Valley 1985 Rel: $18.50 Cur: $23 (12/31/88)
91 CONN CREEK Cabernet Sauvignon Napa Valley Barrel Select Private Reserve 1985 Rel: $30 Cur: $34 (9/15/90)
91 CUTLER Cabernet Sauvignon Sonoma Valley Batto Ranch 1985 $20 (7/31/89)
91 CUVAISON Cabernet Sauvignon Napa Valley 1985 Rel: $14 Cur: $20 (3/31/89)
91 DIAMOND CREEK Cabernet Sauvignon Napa Valley Red Rock Terrace 1985 Rel: $30 Cur: $51 (11/30/87)
91 DRY CREEK Cabernet Sauvignon Sonoma County 1985 Rel: $11 Cur: $16 (5/31/88) SS
91 DUCKHORN Cabernet Sauvignon Napa Valley 1985 Rel: $17.50 Cur: $38 (6/15/88) CS
91 FISHER Cabernet Sauvignon Sonoma County Coach Insignia 1985 Rel: $18 Cur: $20 (9/15/88)
91 GROTH Cabernet Sauvignon Napa Valley 1985 Rel: $16 Cur: $32 (CA-3/89)
91 GUNDLACH BUNDSCHU Cabernet Sauvignon Sonoma Valley Rhinefarm Vineyards 1985 Rel: $9 Cur: $12 (3/01/89)
91 HAYWOOD Cabernet Sauvignon Sonoma Valley 1985 Rel: $14.50 Cur: $17 (3/15/88)
91 HESS Cabernet Sauvignon Napa Valley 1985 Rel: $13 Cur: $40 (11/15/88)
91 INGLENOOK Reunion Napa Valley 1985 Rel: $35 Cur: $36 (7/15/89)
91 KENWOOD Cabernet Sauvignon Sonoma Valley 1985 $14.50 (2/15/89)
91 KENWOOD Cabernet Sauvignon Sonoma Valley Artist Series 1985 Rel: $30 Cur: $31 (CA-3/89)
91 KENWOOD Cabernet Sauvignon Sonoma Valley Artist Series 1985 Rel: $30 Cur: $31 (2/15/89)
91 LA JOTA Cabernet Sauvignon Howell Mountain 1985 Rel: $18 Cur: $36 (11/15/88)
91 LAUREL GLEN Cabernet Sauvignon Sonoma Mountain 1985 Rel: $18 Cur: $39 (4/30/88)
91 MARKHAM Cabernet Sauvignon Napa Valley 1985 Rel: $13 Cur: $16 (4/15/90)
91 MERRYVALE Red Table Wine Napa Valley 1985 Rel: $24 Cur: $24 (CA-3/89)
91 NIEBAUM-COPPOLA Rubicon Napa Valley 1985 Rel: $28 Cur: $28 (CA-3/89)
91 JOSEPH PHELPS Cabernet Sauvignon Napa Valley Backus Vineyard 1985 Rel: $27.50 Cur: $32 (12/31/88)
91 PLAM Cabernet Sauvignon Napa Valley 1985 $24 (6/30/88)
91 BERNARD PRADEL Cabernet Sauvignon Napa Valley 1985 $12 (4/30/89)
91 RAYMOND Cabernet Sauvignon Napa Valley Private Reserve 1985 Rel: $24 Cur: $25 (7/15/90) CS
91 SHAFER Cabernet Sauvignon Napa Valley Stags Leap District Hillside Select 1985 Rel: $24.50 Cur: $28 (5/31/90) CS
91 SHAFER Cabernet Sauvignon Napa Valley Stags Leap District 1985 Rel: $15.50 Cur: $16 (CA-3/89)
91 SILVERADO Cabernet Sauvignon Napa Valley Stags Leap District 1985 Rel: $12.50 Cur: $20 (11/15/88) SS
91 SIMI Cabernet Sauvignon Sonoma County 1985 Rel: $13 Cur: $18 (9/30/89)
91 VICHON Cabernet Sauvignon Napa Valley 1985 Rel: $13 Cur: $16 (11/15/88)
90 CAKEBREAD Cabernet Sauvignon Napa Valley 1985 Rel: $17 Cur: $19 (4/15/88)
90 CARNEROS CREEK Cabernet Sauvignon Los Carneros 1985 $15 (10/31/89)
90 CAYMUS Cabernet Sauvignon Napa Valley 1985 Rel: $18 Cur: $38 (11/15/88)
90 CHRISTIAN BROTHERS Cabernet Sauvignon Napa Valley 1985 $8 (6/15/88)
90 CLOS DU VAL Cabernet Sauvignon Napa Valley Stags Leap District 1985 Rel: $16 Cur: $25 (6/15/89)
90 CONN CREEK Cabernet Sauvignon Napa Valley Barrel Select 1985 Rel: $15 Cur: $18 (9/15/90)
90 CUVAISON Cabernet Sauvignon Napa Valley 1985 Rel: $14 Cur: $20 (CA-3/89)
90 FAR NIENTE Cabernet Sauvignon Napa Valley 1985 Rel: $28 Cur: $28 (12/31/88)
90 FISHER Cabernet Sauvignon Sonoma County Coach Insignia 1985 Rel: $18 Cur: $20 (CA-3/89)
90 FLORA SPRINGS Cabernet Sauvignon Napa Valley 1985 Rel: $15 Cur: $18 (7/31/89)
90 FRANCISCAN Meritage Napa Valley 1985 Rel: $20 Cur: $20 (3/31/90)
90 FREEMARK ABBEY Cabernet Sauvignon Napa Valley Bosché 1985 Rel: $24 Cur: $24 (7/31/89)
90 GRGICH HILLS Cabernet Sauvignon Napa Valley 1985 Rel: $20 Cur: $23 (10/31/90)
90 WILLIAM HILL Cabernet Sauvignon Napa Valley Silver Label 1985 $12 (4/30/88)
90 INGLENOOK Cabernet Sauvignon Napa Valley Reserve Cask 1985 $16 (2/15/91) CS
90 ROBERT PEPI Cabernet Sauvignon Napa Valley Vine Hill Ranch 1985 Rel: $18 Cur: $23 (CA-3/89)
90 JOSEPH PHELPS Cabernet Sauvignon Napa Valley Backus Vineyard 1985 Rel: $27.50 Cur: $32 (CA-3/89)
90 ROMBAUER Le Meilleur du Chai Napa Valley 1985 Rel: $37.50 Cur: $42 (10/31/89)

Key to Symbols

The scores reported here are the results of blind tastings conducted by our panel of senior editors. Wines that carry the initials below are results of individual tastings.

THE WINE SPECTATOR 100-POINT SCALE *95-100*—Classic, a great wine; *90-94*—Outstanding, superior character and style; *80-89*—Good to very good, a wine with special qualities; *70-79*—Average, drinkable wine that may have minor flaws; *60-69*—Below average, drinkable but not recommended; *50-59*—Poor, undrinkable, not recommended. "+"—With a score indicates a range; used primarily with barrel tastings to indicate a preliminary score.

SPECIAL DESIGNATIONS SS—Spectator Selection, CS—Cellar Selection, BB—Best Buy.

TASTER'S INITIALS (JG)—Jim Gordon, (HS)—Harvey Steiman, (JL)—James Laube, (JS)—James Suckling, (TM)—Thomas Matthews, (TR)—Terry Robards, (BT)—Barrel Tasting (these wines were tasted blind from barrel samples), (CA-date)—*California's Great Cabernets* by James Laube, (CH-date)—*California's Great Chardonnays* by James Laube, (VP-date)—*Vintage Port* by James Suckling.

DATE TASTED Dates in parentheses represent the issue in which the rating was published.

90 ROMBAUER Le Meilleur du Chai Napa Valley 1985 Rel: $37.50 Cur: $42 (CA-3/89)
90 ST. CLEMENT Cabernet Sauvignon Napa Valley 1985 Rel: $17 Cur: $19 (3/15/90)
90 SMITH-MADRONE Cabernet Sauvignon Napa Valley 1985 Rel: $14 Cur: $15 (CA-3/89)
90 STAG'S LEAP WINE CELLARS Cabernet Sauvignon Napa Valley 1985 $16 (9/15/88)
90 STAG'S LEAP WINE CELLARS Cabernet Sauvignon Napa Valley Stags Leap District SLV 1985 Rel: $26 Cur: $38 (10/31/88)
90 STERLING Cabernet Sauvignon Napa Valley Diamond Mountain Ranch 1985 Rel: $16 Cur: $18 (CA-3/89)
90 TREFETHEN Cabernet Sauvignon Napa Valley Hillside Selection 1985 Rel: $30 Cur: $30 (CA-3/89)
90+ CARMENET Sonoma Valley 1985 Rel: $18.50 Cur: $23 (6/15/87) (BT)
90+ CAYMUS Cabernet Sauvignon Napa Valley 1985 Rel: $18 Cur: $38 (6/15/87) (BT)
90+ CHATEAU MONTELENA Cabernet Sauvignon Napa Valley 1985 Rel: $25 Cur: $44 (6/15/87) (BT)
90+ CONN CREEK Cabernet Sauvignon Napa Valley Reserve 1985 Rel: $30 Cur: $34 (6/15/87) (BT)
90+ DOMINUS Napa Valley 1985 Rel: $45 Cur: $50 (6/15/87) (BT)
90+ FAR NIENTE Cabernet Sauvignon Napa Valley 1985 Rel: $28 Cur: $28 (6/15/87) (BT)
90+ GROTH Cabernet Sauvignon Napa Valley 1985 Rel: $16 Cur: $32 (6/15/87) (BT)
90+ WILLIAM HILL Cabernet Sauvignon Napa Valley Reserve 1985 Rel: $22.50 Cur: $27 (6/15/87) (BT)
90+ INGLENOOK Cabernet Sauvignon Napa Valley Reserve Cask 1985 Rel: $16 Cur: $19 (6/15/87) (BT)
90+ LAUREL GLEN Cabernet Sauvignon Sonoma Mountain 1985 Rel: $18 Cur: $39 (6/15/87) (BT)
90+ LIVINGSTON Cabernet Sauvignon Napa Valley Moffett Vineyard 1985 Rel: $18 Cur: $30 (6/15/87) (BT)
90+ ROBERT MONDAVI Cabernet Sauvignon Napa Valley Reserve 1985 Rel: $40 Cur: $43 (6/15/87) (BT)
90+ NEYERS Cabernet Sauvignon Napa Valley 1985 $14 (6/15/87) (BT)
90+ JOSEPH PHELPS Cabernet Sauvignon Napa Valley Backus Vineyard 1985 Rel: $27.50 Cur: $32 (6/15/87) (BT)
90+ PINE RIDGE Cabernet Sauvignon Napa Valley Andrus Reserve Cuvée Duet 1985 Rel: $40 Cur: $45 (6/15/87) (BT)
90+ PINE RIDGE Cabernet Sauvignon Napa Valley Rutherford Cuvée 1985 Rel: $16 Cur: $19 (6/15/87) (BT)
90+ PINE RIDGE Cabernet Sauvignon Napa Valley Stags Leap District Pine Ridge Stags Leap Vineyard 1985 Rel: $26 Cur: $26 (6/15/87) (BT)
90+ RIDGE Cabernet Sauvignon Santa Cruz Mountains Monte Bello 1985 Rel: $40 Cur: $89 (6/15/87) (BT)
90+ ST. CLEMENT Cabernet Sauvignon Napa Valley 1985 Rel: $17 Cur: $19 (6/15/87) (BT)
90+ SHAFER Cabernet Sauvignon Napa Valley Stags Leap District Hillside Select 1985 Rel: $24.50 Cur: $28 (6/15/87) (BT)
90+ STAG'S LEAP WINE CELLARS Cabernet Sauvignon Napa Valley Stags Leap District SLV 1985 Rel: $26 Cur: $38 (6/15/87) (BT)
90+ STELTZNER Cabernet Sauvignon Napa Valley Stags Leap District 1985 Rel: $16 Cur: $19 (6/15/87) (BT)
89 BUEHLER Cabernet Sauvignon Napa Valley 1985 Rel: $14 Cur: $16 (4/30/88)
89 DIAMOND CREEK Cabernet Sauvignon Napa Valley Gravelly Meadow 1985 Rel: $30 Cur: $56 (11/30/87)
89 DIAMOND CREEK Cabernet Sauvignon Napa Valley Three Vineyard Blend 1985 Rel: $50 Cur: $100 (CA-3/89)
89 DRY CREEK Meritage Dry Creek Valley 1985 $22 (11/15/89)
89 DUNN Cabernet Sauvignon Howell Mountain 1985 Rel: $30 Cur: $112 (CA-3/89)
89 EBERLE Cabernet Sauvignon Paso Robles 1985 Rel: $12 Cur: $17 (CA-3/89)
89 FRANCISCAN Meritage Napa Valley 1985 Rel: $20 Cur: $20 (CA-3/89)
89 GIRARD Cabernet Sauvignon Napa Valley Reserve 1985 Rel: $25 Cur: $41 (CA-3/89)
89 HAYWOOD Cabernet Sauvignon Sonoma Valley 1985 Rel: $14.50 Cur: $17 (CA-3/89)
89 KENWOOD Cabernet Sauvignon Sonoma Valley Jack London Vineyard 1985 Rel: $18 Cur: $19 (10/15/88)
89 KONOCTI Cabernet Sauvignon Lake County 1985 $7.50 (11/15/89) BB
89 J. LOHR Cabernet Sauvignon Napa Valley Carol's Vineyard Reserve 1985 $14.50 (12/15/88)
89 NEWTON Cabernet Sauvignon Napa Valley 1985 Rel: $15.25 Cur: $18 (CA-3/89)
89 NEWTON Cabernet Sauvignon Napa Valley 1985 Rel: $15.25 Cur: $18 (1/31/89)
89 GUSTAVE NIEBAUM Cabernet Sauvignon Napa Valley Reference 1985 $13.50 (10/31/89)
89 ROBERT PECOTA Cabernet Sauvignon Napa Valley Kara's Vineyard 1985 Rel: $16 Cur: $20 (12/15/88)
89 PRESTON Cabernet Sauvignon Dry Creek Valley 1985 Rel: $11 Cur: $15 (CA-3/89)
89 RUTHERFORD HILL Cabernet Sauvignon Napa Valley XVS 1985 Rel: $25 Cur: $27 (CA-3/89)
89 ST. ANDREW'S WINERY Cabernet Sauvignon Napa Valley 1985 $10.50 (5/15/88)
89 SEBASTIANI ESTATES Cabernet Sauvignon Sonoma Valley Cherry Block 1985 $16.50 (3/31/90)
89 STERLING Cabernet Sauvignon Napa Valley 1985 Rel: $13 Cur: $15 (5/15/88)
89 STREBLOW Cabernet Sauvignon Napa Valley 1985 $14.50 (6/15/88)
89 PHILIP TOGNI Cabernet Sauvignon Napa Valley 1985 Rel: $20 Cur: $25 (CA-3/89)
89 TUDAL Cabernet Sauvignon Napa Valley 1985 Rel: $14.50 Cur: $20 (CA-3/89)
88 ALEXANDER VALLEY Cabernet Sauvignon Alexander Valley 1985 Rel: $11 Cur: $15 (CA-3/89)
88 CHAPPELLET Cabernet Sauvignon Napa Valley Reserve 1985 Rel: $20 Cur: $21 (CA-3/89)
88 CHIMNEY ROCK Cabernet Sauvignon Napa Valley Stags Leap District 1985 Rel: $15 Cur: $19 (10/31/88)
88 CLOS DU BOIS Marlstone Vineyard Alexander Valley 1985 Rel: $19.50 Cur: $23 (CA-3/89)
88 CLOS DU VAL Cabernet Sauvignon Napa Valley Gran Val 1985 $8.50 (5/31/88)
88 DIAMOND CREEK Cabernet Sauvignon Napa Valley Volcanic Hill 1985 Rel: $30 Cur: $50 (11/30/87)
88 DUNN Cabernet Sauvignon Howell Mountain 1985 Rel: $30 Cur: $112 (4/15/89)
88 FLORA SPRINGS Cabernet Sauvignon Napa Valley 1985 Rel: $15 Cur: $18 (CA-3/89)
88 FLORA SPRINGS Trilogy Napa Valley 1985 Rel: $30 Cur: $43 (CA-3/89)
88 FRANCISCAN Cabernet Sauvignon Napa Valley Library Selection 1985 Rel: $17.50 Cur: $20 (CA-3/89)
88 FRANCISCAN Cabernet Sauvignon Napa Valley Oakville Estate Reserve 1985 Rel: $17.50 Cur: $20 (5/31/90)
88 FREEMARK ABBEY Cabernet Sauvignon Napa Valley Sycamore Vineyards 1985 $25 (10/31/89)
88 GEYSER PEAK Réserve Alexandre Alexander Valley 1985 $19 (9/30/89)
88 GIRARD Cabernet Sauvignon Napa Valley 1985 Rel: $15 Cur: $18 (9/15/88)
88 IRON HORSE Cabernets Alexander Valley 1985 Rel: $16 Cur: $17 (12/31/88)
88 JOHNSON TURNBULL Cabernet Sauvignon Napa Valley 1985 Rel: $14.50 Cur: $18 (7/15/88)

88 JORDAN Cabernet Sauvignon Alexander Valley 1985 Rel: $19.50 Cur: $25 (9/15/89)
88 LA JOTA Cabernet Sauvignon Howell Mountain 1985 Rel: $18 Cur: $36 (CA-3/89)
88 LAKESPRING Cabernet Sauvignon Napa Valley 1985 Rel: $12 Cur: $12 (CA-3/89)
88 J. LOHR Cabernet Sauvignon Napa Valley Carol's Vineyard Reserve Lot 2 1985 $17.50 (9/30/90)
88 MONTICELLO Cabernet Sauvignon Napa Valley Corley Reserve 1985 Rel: $22.50 Cur: $30 (CA-3/89)
88 PINE RIDGE Cabernet Sauvignon Napa Valley Rutherford Cuvée 1985 Rel: $16 Cur: $19 (2/15/89)
88 RAYMOND Cabernet Sauvignon Napa Valley Private Reserve 1985 Rel: $24 Cur: $25 (CA-3/89)
88 RUTHERFORD HILL Cabernet Sauvignon Napa Valley XVS 1985 Rel: $25 Cur: $27 (4/30/89)
88 ST. FRANCIS Cabernet Sauvignon California 1985 $9 (11/30/87)
88 SHAFER Cabernet Sauvignon Napa Valley Stags Leap District 1985 Rel: $15.50 Cur: $16 (11/15/88)
88 SILVER OAK Cabernet Sauvignon Napa Valley 1985 Rel: $24 Cur: $60 (10/31/89)
88 SMITH & HOOK Cabernet Sauvignon Napa County 1985 $12 (9/30/89)
88 SPRING MOUNTAIN Cabernet Sauvignon Napa Valley 1985 Rel: $20 Cur: $20 (CA-3/89)
88 STERLING Cabernet Sauvignon Napa Valley Diamond Mountain Ranch 1985 Rel: $16 Cur: $18 (5/31/89)
88 RODNEY STRONG Cabernet Sauvignon Alexander Valley Alexander's Crown Vineyard 1985 $15 (9/30/90)
88 VICHON Cabernet Sauvignon Napa Valley 1985 Rel: $13 Cur: $16 (CA-3/89)
88 WHITEHALL LANE Cabernet Sauvignon Napa Valley Reserve 1985 $30 (11/30/89)
87 BERINGER Cabernet Sauvignon Knights Valley 1985 $12 (5/31/88)
87 BLACK MOUNTAIN Cabernet Sauvignon Alexander Valley Fat Cat 1985 $18 (4/30/90)
87 CAIN Five Napa Valley 1985 $26 (6/15/89)
87 CHATEAU SOUVERAIN Cabernet Sauvignon Sonoma County 1985 $8 (11/30/88)
87 CHIMNEY ROCK Cabernet Sauvignon Napa Valley Stags Leap District 1985 Rel: $15 Cur: $19 (CA-3/89)
87 CLOS DU BOIS Cabernet Sauvignon Alexander Valley 1985 $10.50 (4/15/88)
87 CONCANNON Cabernet Sauvignon Livermore Valley Reserve 1985 $13.50 (2/15/89)
87 CONN CREEK Cabernet Sauvignon Napa Valley Barrel Select Private Reserve 1985 Rel: $30 Cur: $34 (CA-3/89)
87 ESTANCIA Cabernet Sauvignon Alexander Valley 1985 $6.50 (6/15/88) BB
87 FETZER Cabernet Sauvignon California Reserve 1985 $17 (11/15/89)
87 FIELD STONE Cabernet Sauvignon Alexander Valley Hoot Owl Creek Vineyards 1985 $20 (3/31/89)
87 FLORA SPRINGS Trilogy Napa Valley 1985 Rel: $30 Cur: $43 (2/15/89)
87 FRANCISCAN Cabernet Sauvignon Napa Valley Oakville Estate Reserve 1985 Rel: $17.50 Cur: $20 (CA-3/89)
87 GUENOC Cabernet Sauvignon Guenoc Valley Premier Cuvée 1985 $17.50 (12/15/88)
87 IRON HORSE Cabernets Alexander Valley 1985 Rel: $16 Cur: $17 (CA-3/89)
87 MERRYVALE Red Table Wine Napa Valley 1985 Rel: $24 Cur: $24 (11/15/88)
87 MONTICELLO Cabernet Sauvignon Napa Valley Jefferson Cuvée 1985 $12 (2/29/88)
87 MOUNT VEEDER Cabernet Sauvignon Napa Valley 1985 Rel: $18 Cur: $23 (CA-3/89)
87 NAVARRO Cabernet Sauvignon Mendocino 1985 $14 (11/15/90)
87 NEWLAN Cabernet Sauvignon Napa Valley 1985 $15 (3/31/90)
87 NIEBAUM-COPPOLA Rubicon Napa Valley 1985 $28 (11/15/90)
87 RIDGE Cabernet Sauvignon Santa Cruz Mountains Jimsomare 1985 $16 (2/15/89)
87 V SATTUI Cabernet Sauvignon Napa Valley Preston Vineyard 1985 Rel: $15.75 Cur: $18 (CA-3/89)
87 STONEGATE Cabernet Sauvignon Napa Valley 1985 Rel: $16 Cur: $19 (CA-3/89)
87 RODNEY STRONG Cabernet Sauvignon Alexander Valley Alexander's Crown Vineyard 1985 $17 (5/31/91)
86 CHATEAU ST. JEAN Cabernet Sauvignon Alexander Valley 1985 Rel: $19 Cur: $23 (11/15/88)
86 CLOS DU BOIS Cabernet Sauvignon Alexander Valley Briarcrest Vineyard 1985 Rel: $16 Cur: $20 (6/15/89)
86 CLOS PEGASE Cabernet Sauvignon Napa Valley 1985 $17 (5/31/88)
86 FETZER Cabernet Sauvignon Sonoma County Reserve 1985 $24 (8/31/90)
86 FRANCISCAN Cabernet Sauvignon Napa Valley Oakville Estate 1985 $11 (5/15/89)
86 GIRARD Cabernet Sauvignon Napa Valley Reserve 1985 Rel: $25 Cur: $41 (2/15/90)
86 GLEN ELLEN Cabernet Sauvignon Sonoma Valley Imagery Series 1985 $12.50 (2/15/89)
86 HANNA Cabernet Sauvignon Sonoma Valley 1985 $14 (6/30/88)
86 INNISFREE Cabernet Sauvignon Napa Valley 1985 $9 (3/15/89)
86 KEENAN Cabernet Sauvignon Napa Valley 1985 Rel: $15 Cur: $21 (CA-3/89)
86 LIVINGSTON Cabernet Sauvignon Napa Valley Moffett Vineyard 1985 Rel: $18 Cur: $30 (CA-3/89)
86 LYETH Red Alexander Valley 1985 Rel: $22 Cur: $22 (5/31/89)
86 MOUNT EDEN Cabernet Sauvignon Santa Cruz Mountains 1985 Rel: $28 Cur: $29 (CA-3/89)
86 ROBERT PECOTA Cabernet Sauvignon Napa Valley Kara's Vineyard 1985 Rel: $16 Cur: $20 (CA-3/89)
86 PRESTON Cabernet Sauvignon Dry Creek Valley 1985 Rel: $11 Cur: $15 (9/30/88)
86 ROUND HILL Cabernet Sauvignon Napa Valley Reserve 1985 $10.50 (5/31/88)
86 SEBASTIANI Cabernet Sauvignon Sonoma County Reserve 1985 $12.50 (11/15/90)
86 SEQUOIA GROVE Cabernet Sauvignon Napa County 1985 Rel: $16 Cur: $16 (CA-3/89)
86 SEQUOIA GROVE Cabernet Sauvignon Napa County 1985 Rel: $16 Cur: $16 (12/15/88)
86 SILVER OAK Cabernet Sauvignon Alexander Valley 1985 Rel: $24 Cur: $45 (10/31/89)
86 STONEGATE Cabernet Sauvignon Napa Valley 1985 Rel: $16 Cur: $19 (8/31/90)
85 BEAULIEU Cabernet Sauvignon Napa Valley Rutherford 1985 Rel: $9.50 Cur: $10 (6/15/88)
85 CAKEBREAD Cabernet Sauvignon Napa Valley Rutherford Reserve 1985 $40 (CA-3/89)
85 CONN CREEK Cabernet Sauvignon Napa Valley Barrel Select 1985 Rel: $15 Cur: $18 (CA-3/89)
85 CRUVINET Cabernet Sauvignon Alexander Valley 1985 $7 (9/15/88) BB
85 FETZER Cabernet Sauvignon Mendocino Barrel Select 1985 $10 (12/15/88)
85 FROG'S LEAP Cabernet Sauvignon Napa Valley 1985 Rel: $12 Cur: $18 (CA-3/89)
85 JORDAN Cabernet Sauvignon Alexander Valley 1985 Rel: $19.50 Cur: $25 (CA-3/89)
85 LIVINGSTON Cabernet Sauvignon Napa Valley Moffett Vineyard 1985 Rel: $18 Cur: $30 (10/15/88)
85 MERLION Cabernet Sauvignon Napa Valley 1985 $13.50 (8/31/88)
85 J. PEDRONCELLI Cabernet Sauvignon Dry Creek Valley Reserve 1985 $14 (3/31/90)
85 ROBERT PEPI Cabernet Sauvignon Napa Valley Vine Hill Ranch 1985 Rel: $18 Cur: $23 (7/31/90)
85 RAVENSWOOD Cabernet Sauvignon Sonoma County 1985 Rel: $12 Cur: $17 (CA-3/89)
85 ROMBAUER Cabernet Sauvignon Napa Valley 1985 Rel: $14.75 Cur: $17 (4/30/89)
85 ROMBAUER Cabernet Sauvignon Napa Valley 1985 Rel: $14.75 Cur: $17 (CA-3/89)
85 SILVER OAK Cabernet Sauvignon Napa Valley 1985 Rel: $24 Cur: $60 (CA-3/89)
85 SILVER OAK Cabernet Sauvignon Napa Valley Bonny's Vineyard 1985 Rel: $50 Cur: $125 (CA-3/89)
85 SPRING MOUNTAIN Cabernet Sauvignon Napa Valley 1985 Rel: $20 Cur: $20 (10/15/89)
85 STAGS' LEAP WINERY Cabernet Sauvignon Napa Valley Stags Leap District 1985 Rel: $15 Cur: $16 (CA-3/89)
85 WHITE OAK Cabernet Sauvignon Alexander Valley Myers Limited Reserve 1985 $18 (7/31/89)
85+ BEAULIEU Cabernet Sauvignon Napa Valley Georges de Latour Private Reserve 1985 Rel: $25 Cur: $29 (6/15/87) (BT)
85+ BERINGER Cabernet Sauvignon Knights Valley 1985 (NR) (6/15/87) (BT)
85+ BURGESS Cabernet Sauvignon Napa Valley Vintage Selection 1985 Rel: $18 Cur: $23 (6/15/87) (BT)
85+ DIAMOND CREEK Cabernet Sauvignon Napa Valley Red Rock Terrace 1985 Rel: $30 Cur: $51 (6/15/87) (BT)
85+ DUNN Cabernet Sauvignon Howell Mountain 1985 Rel: $30 Cur: $112 (6/15/87) (BT)
85+ FLORA SPRINGS Cabernet Sauvignon Napa Valley 1985 Rel: $15 Cur: $18 (6/15/87) (BT)
85+ GIRARD Cabernet Sauvignon Napa Valley 1985 Rel: $15 Cur: $18 (6/15/87) (BT)
85+ GRACE FAMILY Cabernet Sauvignon Napa Valley 1985 Rel: $50 Cur: $250 (6/15/87) (BT)
85+ HAYWOOD Cabernet Sauvignon Sonoma Valley 1985 Rel: $14.50 Cur: $17 (6/15/87) (BT)
85+ LA JOTA Cabernet Sauvignon Howell Mountain 1985 Rel: $18 Cur: $36 (6/15/87) (BT)
85+ MONTICELLO Cabernet Sauvignon Napa Valley Jefferson Cuvée 1985 $12 (6/15/87) (BT)
85+ MOUNT VEEDER Cabernet Sauvignon Napa Valley 1985 Rel: $18 Cur: $23 (6/15/87) (BT)
85+ JOSEPH PHELPS Cabernet Sauvignon Napa Valley Eisele Vineyard 1985 Rel: $40 Cur: $43 (6/15/87) (BT)
84 BUENA VISTA Cabernet Sauvignon Carneros 1985 $10 (11/15/88)
84 CAKEBREAD Cabernet Sauvignon Napa Valley 1985 Rel: $17 Cur: $19 (CA-3/89)
84 CHAPPELLET Cabernet Sauvignon Napa Valley Reserve 1985 Rel: $20 Cur: $21 (2/15/90)
84 COSENTINO Cabernet Sauvignon North Coast 1985 $10.50 (9/15/88)
84 DOMINUS Napa Valley 1985 Rel: $45 Cur: $50 (2/15/90)
84 FIELD STONE Cabernet Sauvignon Alexander Valley Turkey Hill Vineyard 1985 $18 (2/28/91)
84 GUENOC Cabernet Sauvignon Guenoc Valley Premier Cuvée 1985 $17.50 (10/15/90)
84 HUSCH Cabernet Sauvignon Mendocino La Ribera Cabernet 1985 $5 (11/30/87) BB
84 CHARLES KRUG Cabernet Sauvignon Napa Valley Vintage Select 1985 (NA) (CA-3/89)
84 JOSEPH PHELPS Cabernet Sauvignon Napa Valley 1985 Rel: $14 Cur: $19 (5/15/89)
84 RAYMOND Cabernet Sauvignon Napa Valley 1985 Rel: $15 Cur: $16 (12/15/89)
84 SEGHESIO Cabernet Sauvignon Northern Sonoma 1985 $5.50 (4/15/89) BB
84 SHADOWBROOK Cabernet Sauvignon Napa Valley 1985 $9.50 (7/15/91)
83 BEAULIEU Cabernet Sauvignon Napa Valley Beau Tour 1985 $7 (6/15/88)
83 BENZIGER Cabernet Sauvignon Sonoma Valley 1985 $16 (12/15/88)
83 J. CAREY Cabernet Sauvignon Santa Ynez Valley 1985 $10 (11/15/89)
83 HACIENDA Cabernet Sauvignon Sonoma County 1985 $15 (9/30/90)
83 INGLENOOK Cabernet Sauvignon Napa Valley 1985 $9.50 (3/31/89)
83 JOHNSON TURNBULL Cabernet Sauvignon Napa Valley 1985 Rel: $14.50 Cur: $18 (CA-3/89)
83 KALIN Cabernet Sauvignon Sonoma County Reserve 1985 $23 (4/15/91)
83 LEEWARD Cabernet Sauvignon Alexander Valley 1985 $12 (10/31/87)
83 MARIETTA Cabernet Sauvignon Sonoma County 1985 $10 (6/30/90)
83 NEYERS Cabernet Sauvignon Napa Valley 1985 $14 (7/15/89)
83 PINE RIDGE Cabernet Sauvignon Napa Valley Andrus Reserve Cuvée Duet 1985 Rel: $40 Cur: $45 (10/15/88)
83 RAVENSWOOD Cabernet Sauvignon Sonoma County 1985 Rel: $12 Cur: $17 (5/31/88)
83 SILVER OAK Cabernet Sauvignon Napa Valley Bonny's Vineyard 1985 $50 (11/15/90)
83 STRATFORD Cabernet Sauvignon California 1985 $10 (11/30/88)
83 WILLIAM WHEELER Cabernet Sauvignon Dry Creek Valley Norse Vineyard Private Reserve 1985 $18 (11/15/90)
83 YORK MOUNTAIN Cabernet Sauvignon San Luis Obispo 1985 $15 (12/15/89)
82 BELLEROSE Cuvée Bellerose Sonoma County 1985 $16 (12/15/88)
82 CLOS DU BOIS Cabernet Sauvignon Alexander Valley Briarcrest Vineyard 1985 Rel: $16 Cur: $20 (CA-3/89)
82 EBERLE Cabernet Sauvignon Paso Robles 1985 Rel: $12 Cur: $17 (2/15/89)
82 FETZER Cabernet Sauvignon Lake County 1985 $6.50 (8/31/87) BB
82 FROG'S LEAP Cabernet Sauvignon Napa Valley 1985 Rel: $12 Cur: $18 (12/31/87)
82 INGLENOOK Niebaum Claret Napa Valley 1985 $12 (3/15/89)
82 QUAIL RIDGE Cabernet Sauvignon Napa Valley 1985 $15 (7/31/89)
82 RUTHERFORD HILL Cabernet Sauvignon Napa Valley 1985 Rel: $14 Cur: $16 (4/30/90)
82 VILLA MT. EDEN Cabernet Sauvignon Napa Valley 1985 Rel: $13 Cur: $13 (CA-3/89)
81 BELVEDERE Cabernet Sauvignon Alexander Valley Robert Young Vineyard Gifts of the Land 1985 $16 (1/31/91)
81 CAIN Cabernet Sauvignon Napa Valley 1985 $16 (4/15/89)
81 CLOS DU BOIS Marlstone Vineyard Alexander Valley 1985 Rel: $19.50 Cur: $23 (6/15/89)
81 COSENTINO Cabernet Sauvignon North Coast Reserve 1985 $18 (4/30/89)
81 DOMAINE DE NAPA Cabernet Sauvignon Napa Valley 1985 $12 (12/15/88)
81 GRAND CRU Cabernet Sauvignon Alexander Valley Collector's Reserve 1985 $18 (7/15/89)
81 MIRASSOU Cabernet Sauvignon Napa Valley Fifth Generation Harvest Reserve 1985 $12 (11/15/89)
81 MOUNT EDEN Cabernet Sauvignon Santa Cruz Mountains 1985 Rel: $28 Cur: $29 (11/15/89)
81 JOSEPH PHELPS Cabernet Sauvignon Napa Valley Eisele Vineyard 1985 Rel: $40 Cur: $43 (5/31/89)
81 SUNNY ST. HELENA Cabernet Sauvignon Napa Valley 1985 $9 (10/31/87)
81 ZD Cabernet Sauvignon Napa Valley 1985 $14 (5/15/89)
80 BELVEDERE Cabernet Sauvignon Alexander Valley Robert Young Vineyard Gifts of the Land 1985 $15 (11/30/89)
80 HEITZ Cabernet Sauvignon Napa Valley 1985 Rel: $18 Cur: $21 (5/15/90)
80 LA FERRONNIERE Cabernet Sauvignon Napa Valley 1985 $14 (1/31/90)
80 LOUIS M. MARTINI Cabernet Sauvignon Sonoma Valley Monte Rosso 1985 Rel: $22 Cur: $23 (CA-3/89)
80 MILANO Cabernet Sauvignon Mendocino County Sanel Valley Vineyard 1985 $18 (9/30/89)
80 R.H. PHILLIPS Cabernet Sauvignon California 1985 $6 (11/30/88)
80 SEBASTIANI Cabernet Sauvignon Sonoma County Family Selection 1985 $8 (10/15/88)
80 SOLARI Cabernet Sauvignon Napa Valley Larkmead Vineyards 1985 $10 (3/15/90)
80 SYLVAN SPRINGS Cabernet Sauvignon California Vintner's Reserve 1985 $5 (9/30/88) BB
80 TREFETHEN Cabernet Sauvignon Napa Valley 1985 Rel: $15 Cur: $19 (CA-3/89)
80 TREFETHEN Cabernet Sauvignon Napa Valley Hillside Selection 1985 $30 (11/15/90)
80 VANINO Cabernet Sauvignon Sonoma County 1985 $11 (9/30/88)
80+ BEAULIEU Cabernet Sauvignon Napa Valley Rutherford 1985 (NR) (6/15/87) (BT)
80+ CAYMUS Cabernet Sauvignon Napa Valley Cuvée 1985 $12 (6/15/87) (BT)
80+ DIAMOND CREEK Cabernet Sauvignon Napa Valley Gravelly Meadow 1985 Rel: $30 Cur: $56 (6/15/87) (BT)
80+ DIAMOND CREEK Cabernet Sauvignon Napa Valley Volcanic Hill 1985 $30 (6/15/87) (BT)

UNITED STATES
CALIFORNIA/CABERNET SAUVIGNON & BLENDS

80+ FISHER Cabernet Sauvignon Sonoma County Coach Insignia 1985 Rel: $18 Cur: $20 (6/15/87) (BT)

80+ FREEMARK ABBEY Cabernet Sauvignon Napa Valley Bosché 1985 Rel: $24 Cur: $24 (6/15/87) (BT)

80+ JOHNSON TURNBULL Cabernet Sauvignon Napa Valley 1985 Rel: $14.50 Cur: $18 (6/15/87) (BT)

80+ KENWOOD Cabernet Sauvignon Sonoma Valley Jack London Vineyard 1985 Rel: $18 Cur: $19 (6/15/87) (BT)

80+ LONG Cabernet Sauvignon Napa Valley 1985 Rel: $36 Cur: $50 (6/15/87) (BT)

80+ LYETH Red Alexander Valley 1985 Rel: $22 Cur: $22 (6/15/87) (BT)

80+ RAYMOND Cabernet Sauvignon Napa Valley 1985 Rel: $16 (6/15/87) (BT)

80+ RUTHERFORD HILL Cabernet Sauvignon Napa Valley 1985 Rel: $14 Cur: $16 (6/15/87) (BT)

80+ SANTA CRUZ MOUNTAIN Cabernet Sauvignon Santa Cruz Mountains Bates Ranch 1985 (NR) (6/15/87) (BT)

80+ SILVER OAK Cabernet Sauvignon Napa Valley 1985 Rel: $24 Cur: $60 (6/15/87) (BT)

79 LAWRENCE J. BARGETTO Cabernet Sauvignon Sonoma County Cypress 1985 $8.50 (11/15/89)

79 CORBETT CANYON Cabernet Sauvignon Santa Barbara-San Luis Obispo Cos Select 1985 $10 (5/31/88)

79 COSENTINO The Poet California 1985 $18 (8/31/88)

79 DE MOOR Cabernet Sauvignon Napa Valley 1985 Rel: $14 Cur: $14 (CA-3/89)

79 FREEMARK ABBEY Cabernet Sauvignon Napa Valley 1985 Rel: $15 Cur: $15 (10/31/89)

79 GRAND CRU Cabernet Sauvignon Sonoma County Premium Selection 1985 $9 (6/15/89)

79 KEENAN Cabernet Sauvignon Napa Valley 1985 Rel: $15 Cur: $21 (3/31/89)

79 J. PEDRONCELLI Cabernet Sauvignon Dry Creek Valley 1985 $7 (10/15/88)

79 IVAN TAMAS Cabernet Sauvignon North Coast 1985 $7 (12/31/87)

79 ZACA MESA Cabernet Sauvignon Santa Barbara County Reserve 1985 $15 (10/15/88)

78 FREMONT CREEK Cabernet Sauvignon Mendocino-Napa Counties 1985 $9.50 (3/31/88)

78 GUNDLACH BUNDSCHU Cabernet Sauvignon Sonoma Valley Rhinefarm Vineyards 1985 Rel: $9 Cur: $12 (3/31/89)

78 MADDALENA Cabernet Sauvignon Alexander Valley Reserve 1985 $11 (6/30/89)

78 MASSON Cabernet Sauvignon Monterey County Vintage Selection 1985 $8 (9/15/88)

78 RICHARD MICHAELS Cabernet Sauvignon California 1985 $10 (9/30/88)

78 ROBERT MONDAVI Cabernet Sauvignon California Cabernet 1985 $4.25 (10/31/87) BB

78 PAT PAULSEN Cabernet Sauvignon Sonoma County 1985 $11 (12/31/87)

78 A. RAFANELLI Cabernet Sauvignon Dry Creek Valley 1985 $8 (9/15/88)

78 RICHARDSON Cabernet Sauvignon Sonoma Valley 1985 $12 (11/30/88)

78 TAFT STREET Cabernet Sauvignon California 1985 $7.50 (10/15/88)

78 M.G. VALLEJO Cabernet Sauvignon California 1985 $4 (2/15/89)

78 WENTE BROS. Cabernet Sauvignon Central Coast 1985 $8 (11/15/89)

78 J. WILE & SONS Cabernet Sauvignon Napa Valley 1985 $7 (11/15/87)

77 ARCIERO Cabernet Sauvignon Paso Robles 1985 $6 (12/31/87)

77 AUDUBON Cabernet Sauvignon Napa Valley 1985 $11 (6/15/88)

77 BOEGER Cabernet Sauvignon El Dorado 1985 $11 (2/15/89)

77 CHESTNUT HILL Cabernet Sauvignon Sonoma County 1985 $7.75 (10/15/88)

77 GEYSER PEAK Cabernet Sauvignon Alexander Valley Estate Reserve 1985 $15 (5/15/89)

77 CHARLES KRUG Cabernet Sauvignon Napa Valley 1985 $10.50 (1/31/90)

77 MOUNTAIN VIEW Cabernet Sauvignon Mendocino County 1985 $6 (2/15/89)

77 PESENTI Cabernet Sauvignon San Luis Obispo County Family Reserve 1985 $13 (12/15/89)

76 BYRON Cabernet Sauvignon Central Coast 1985 $14 (12/15/89)

76 LOUIS M. MARTINI Cabernet Sauvignon North Coast 1985 $8.25 (10/31/88)

76 MEEKER Cabernet Sauvignon Dry Creek Valley 1985 $18 (4/30/89)

76 PARSONS CREEK Cabernet Sauvignon Sonoma County 1985 $13 (6/30/89)

76 STEVENOT Cabernet Sauvignon Calaveras County 1985 $7.50 (6/30/89)

76 WILLIAM WHEELER Cabernet Sauvignon Dry Creek Valley 1985 $12 (7/15/89)

75 CRESTON MANOR Cabernet Sauvignon Central Coast Winemaker's Selection 1985 $16.50 (12/15/89)

75 FOX MOUNTAIN Cabernet Sauvignon Russian River Valley Reserve 1985 $19 (9/15/89)

75 HAWK CREST Cabernet Sauvignon North Coast 1985 $6.50 (7/31/88)

75 HOP KILN Cabernet Sauvignon Dry Creek Valley 1985 $10 (10/15/88)

75 MONTEREY VINEYARD Cabernet Sauvignon Monterey County Limited Release 1985 $10 (8/31/88)

75 ROMBAUER Cabernet Sauvignon Napa Valley 1985 Rel: $14.75 Cur: $17 (2/15/89)

75 STONEGATE Cabernet Sauvignon Napa Valley 1985 Rel: $16 Cur: $19 (4/15/90)

75+ FREEMARK ABBEY Cabernet Sauvignon Napa Valley 1985 Rel: $15 Cur: $15 (6/15/87) (BT)

75+ FREEMARK ABBEY Cabernet Sauvignon Napa Valley Sycamore Vineyards 1985 $25 (6/15/87) (BT)

75+ MONTICELLO Cabernet Sauvignon Napa Valley Corley Reserve 1985 Rel: $22.50 Cur: $30 (6/15/87) (BT)

75+ SILVER OAK Cabernet Sauvignon Alexander Valley 1985 Rel: $24 Cur: $45 (6/15/87) (BT)

74 CHRISTOPHE Cabernet Sauvignon Napa Valley Reserve 1985 $12.50 (11/15/89)

74 DEHLINGER Cabernet Sauvignon Russian River Valley 1985 $13 (5/31/89)

74 FITCH MOUNTAIN Cabernet Sauvignon Napa Valley 1985 $9 (4/15/89)

74 MADDALENA Cabernet Sauvignon Sonoma County 1985 $6 (5/31/88)

74 J.W. MORRIS Cabernet Sauvignon Alexander Valley 1985 $8 (2/15/89)

74 SAUSAL Cabernet Sauvignon Alexander Valley 1985 $12 (7/31/89)

74 SMITH-MADRONE Cabernet Sauvignon Napa Valley 1985 Rel: $14 Cur: $15 (4/15/90)

73 MONTEREY VINEYARD Cabernet Sauvignon Monterey-Sonoma-San Luis Obispo Co. Classic 1985 $5 (2/15/89)

72 DEER VALLEY Cabernet Sauvignon Monterey 1985 $5.50 (12/31/87)

72 FIRESTONE Cabernet Sauvignon Santa Ynez Valley 1985 $9.50 (8/31/88)

72 RIVERSIDE FARM Cabernet Sauvignon California 1985 $4.50 (5/31/88)

72 VIANSA Cabernet Sauvignon Sonoma-Napa Counties 1985 $13 (9/15/89)

71 FOPPIANO Cabernet Sauvignon Russian River Valley 1985 $9 (6/30/89)

71 LAURA'S Cabernet Sauvignon Paso Robles 1985 $12 (12/15/89)

70 AMIZETTA Cabernet Sauvignon Napa Valley 1985 $16 (5/31/88)

70 CHAPPELLET Cabernet Sauvignon Napa Valley Reserve 1985 Rel: $20 Cur: $21 (5/31/89)

70 FIELD STONE Cabernet Sauvignon Alexander Valley Home Ranch Vineyard 1985 $14 (4/15/89)

70 THOMAS FOGARTY Cabernet Sauvignon Napa Valley 1985 $15 (7/15/91)

70 WILD HORSE Cabernet Sauvignon Paso Robles Wild Horse Vineyards 1985 $10.50 (6/30/88)

68 CRESTON MANOR Cabernet Sauvignon San Luis Obispo County 1985 $12 (12/15/89)

67 ESTRELLA RIVER Cabernet Sauvignon Paso Robles 1985 $9 (11/15/89)

67 FIRESTONE Cabernet Sauvignon Santa Ynez Valley Vintage Reserve 1985 $25 (12/15/89)

66 DELICATO Cabernet Sauvignon California 1985 $6 (6/30/88)

64 RIDGE Cabernet Sauvignon Santa Cruz Mountains 1985 $12 (6/15/89)

63 HOUTZ Cabernet Sauvignon Santa Ynez Valley 1985 $8 (12/15/89)

62 MARION Cabernet Sauvignon California 1985 $5.50 (12/31/87)

61 MENDOCINO ESTATE Cabernet Sauvignon Mendocino 1985 $5.50 (2/15/88)

57 J FRITZ Cabernet Sauvignon Alexander Valley 1985 $10 (12/31/88)

1984

98 CAYMUS Cabernet Sauvignon Napa Valley Special Selection 1984 Rel: $35 Cur: $118 (7/15/89) CS

98 CAYMUS Cabernet Sauvignon Napa Valley Special Selection 1984 Rel: $35 Cur: $118 (CA-3/89)

97 DUNN Cabernet Sauvignon Howell Mountain 1984 Rel: $25 Cur: $128 (CA-3/89)

97 HEITZ Cabernet Sauvignon Napa Valley Martha's Vineyard 1984 Rel: $40 Cur: $77 (3/15/89) SS

97 HEITZ Cabernet Sauvignon Napa Valley Martha's Vineyard 1984 Rel: $40 Cur: $77 (CA-3/89)

97 RIDGE Cabernet Sauvignon Santa Cruz Mountains Monte Bello 1984 Rel: $35 Cur: $80 (CA-3/89)

96 DIAMOND CREEK Cabernet Sauvignon Napa Valley Red Rock Terrace 1984 Rel: $25 Cur: $65 (CA-3/89)

95 DIAMOND CREEK Cabernet Sauvignon Napa Valley Red Rock Terrace 1984 Rel: $25 Cur: $65 (9/30/86) CS

95 FROG'S LEAP Cabernet Sauvignon Napa Valley 1984 Rel: $10 Cur: $25 (3/31/87) SS

95 RIDGE Cabernet Sauvignon Santa Cruz Mountains Monte Bello 1984 Rel: $35 Cur: $80 (9/15/87) CS

94 BERINGER Cabernet Sauvignon Napa Valley Private Reserve 1984 Rel: $25 Cur: $38 (CA-3/89)

94 BERINGER Cabernet Sauvignon Napa Valley Private Reserve 1984 Rel: $25 Cur: $38 (2/15/89) CS

94 BUENA VISTA Cabernet Sauvignon Carneros 1984 $10 (8/31/87)

94 CHATEAU MONTELENA Cabernet Sauvignon Napa Valley 1984 Rel: $20 Cur: $39 (CA-3/89)

94 CHATEAU MONTELENA Cabernet Sauvignon Napa Valley 1984 Rel: $20 Cur: $39 (10/15/88)

94 CONN CREEK Cabernet Sauvignon Napa Valley Collins Vineyard Private Reserve 1984 Rel: $23 Cur: $30 (3/31/89)

94 DIAMOND CREEK Cabernet Sauvignon Napa Valley Gravelly Meadow 1984 Rel: $25 Cur: $65 (CA-3/89)

94 DIAMOND CREEK Cabernet Sauvignon Napa Valley Volcanic Hill 1984 Rel: $25 Cur: $62 (CA-3/89)

94 DIAMOND CREEK Cabernet Sauvignon Napa Valley Volcanic Hill 1984 Rel: $25 Cur: $62 (11/15/86)

94 GRGICH HILLS Cabernet Sauvignon Napa Valley 1984 Rel: $17 Cur: $24 (CA-3/89)

94 GROTH Cabernet Sauvignon Napa Valley Reserve 1984 Rel: $25 Cur: $90 (CA-3/89)

94 KEENAN Cabernet Sauvignon Napa Valley 1984 Rel: $13.50 Cur: $30 (10/15/87) SS

94 OPUS ONE Napa Valley 1984 Rel: $50 Cur: $70 (CA-3/89)

94 OPUS ONE Napa Valley 1984 Rel: $50 Cur: $70 (5/31/88)

94 ROMBAUER Le Meilleur du Chai Napa Valley 1984 Rel: $32.50 Cur: $47 (3/31/89)

93 ALEXANDER VALLEY Cabernet Sauvignon Alexander Valley 1984 Rel: $10.50 Cur: $18 (5/15/87) SS

93 BURGESS Cabernet Sauvignon Napa Valley Vintage Selection 1984 Rel: $17 Cur: $25 (CA-3/89)

93 CARMENET Sonoma Valley 1984 Rel: $16 Cur: $30 (5/31/87)

93 B.R. COHN Cabernet Sauvignon Sonoma Valley Olive Hill Vineyard 1984 Rel: $15 Cur: $35 (CA-3/89)

93 DIAMOND CREEK Cabernet Sauvignon Napa Valley Gravelly Meadow 1984 Rel: $25 Cur: $65 (11/15/86)

93 DUNN Cabernet Sauvignon Howell Mountain 1984 Rel: $25 Cur: $128 (3/31/88)

93 DUNN Cabernet Sauvignon Napa Valley 1984 Rel: $18 Cur: $65 (CA-3/89)

93 GIRARD Cabernet Sauvignon Napa Valley Reserve 1984 Rel: $25 Cur: $45 (12/15/88)

93 HAYWOOD Cabernet Sauvignon Sonoma Valley 1984 Rel: $12.50 Cur: $20 (10/31/87)

93 HESS Cabernet Sauvignon Napa Valley Reserve 1984 Rel: $22 Cur: $110 (CA-3/89)

93 KENWOOD Cabernet Sauvignon Sonoma Valley Artist Series 1984 Rel: $30 Cur: $35 (CA-3/89)

93 KENWOOD Cabernet Sauvignon Sonoma Valley Artist Series 1984 Rel: $30 Cur: $35 (11/30/87)

93 PINE RIDGE Cabernet Sauvignon Napa Valley Andrus Reserve 1984 Rel: $37 Cur: $40 (CA-3/89)

93 PINE RIDGE Cabernet Sauvignon Napa Valley Stags Leap District Pine Ridge Stags Leap Vineyard 1984 Rel: $25 Cur: $39 (CA-3/89)

93 SHAFER Cabernet Sauvignon Napa Valley Stags Leap District 1984 Rel: $14 Cur: $25 (12/15/87) SS

93 STAG'S LEAP WINE CELLARS Cabernet Sauvignon Napa Valley Stags Leap District Stag's Leap Vineyards Cask 23 1984 Rel: $40 Cur: $89 (CA-3/89)

92 ALEXANDER VALLEY Cabernet Sauvignon Alexander Valley 1984 Rel: $10.50 Cur: $18 (CA-3/89)

92 BEAULIEU Cabernet Sauvignon Napa Valley Georges de Latour Private Reserve 1984 Rel: $25 Cur: $28 (3/31/91) (JL)

92 BUEHLER Cabernet Sauvignon Napa Valley 1984 Rel: $13 Cur: $23 (5/31/87)

92 BURGESS Cabernet Sauvignon Napa Valley Vintage Selection 1984 Rel: $17 Cur: $25 (7/31/88)

92 CARMENET Sonoma Valley 1984 Rel: $16 Cur: $30 (CA-3/89)

92 CLOS DU VAL Cabernet Sauvignon Napa Valley Stags Leap District 1984 Rel: $15 Cur: $17 (CA-3/89)

92 DIAMOND CREEK Cabernet Sauvignon Napa Valley Lake 1984 Rel: $50 Cur: $250 (CA-3/89)

92 DUCKHORN Cabernet Sauvignon Napa Valley 1984 Rel: $17 Cur: $32 (CA-3/89)

92 FAR NIENTE Cabernet Sauvignon Napa Valley 1984 Rel: $25 Cur: $30 (CA-3/89)

92 FAR NIENTE Cabernet Sauvignon Napa Valley 1984 Rel: $25 Cur: $30 (10/15/87)

92 FORMAN Cabernet Sauvignon Napa Valley 1984 Rel: $18 Cur: $71 (CA-3/89)
92 FORMAN Cabernet Sauvignon Napa Valley 1984 Rel: $18 Cur: $71 (4/30/87)
92 FROG'S LEAP Cabernet Sauvignon Napa Valley 1984 Rel: $10 Cur: $25 (CA-3/89)
92 GIRARD Cabernet Sauvignon Napa Valley Reserve 1984 Rel: $25 Cur: $45 (CA-3/89)
92 GRACE FAMILY Cabernet Sauvignon Napa Valley 1984 Rel: $38 Cur: $285 (CA-3/89)
92 GROTH Cabernet Sauvignon Napa Valley 1984 Rel: $14 Cur: $39 (CA-3/89)
92 HESS Cabernet Sauvignon Napa Valley Reserve 1984 Rel: $22 Cur: $110 (11/15/88)
92 INGLENOOK Cabernet Sauvignon Napa Valley Reserve Cask 1984 Rel: $22 Cur: $17 (CA-3/89)
92 INGLENOOK Reunion Napa Valley 1984 Rel: $35 Cur: $35 (CA-3/89)
92 KEENAN Cabernet Sauvignon Napa Valley 1984 Rel: $13.50 Cur: $30 (CA-3/89)
92 LAKESPRING Cabernet Sauvignon Napa Valley Reserve Selection 1984 Rel: $15 Cur: $21 (CA-3/89)
92 LAKESPRING Cabernet Sauvignon Napa Valley Reserve Selection 1984 Rel: $15 Cur: $21 (10/31/88) SS
92 ROBERT MONDAVI Cabernet Sauvignon Napa Valley Reserve 1984 Rel: $37 Cur: $38 (CA-3/89)
92 SHAFER Cabernet Sauvignon Napa Valley Stags Leap District Hillside Select 1984 Rel: $24.50 Cur: $33 (CA-3/89)
92 SIMI Cabernet Sauvignon Alexander Valley Reserve 1984 Rel: $22.50 Cur: $26 (CA-3/89)
92 SMITH-MADRONE Cabernet Sauvignon Napa Valley 1984 Rel: $14 Cur: $15 (12/31/88)
92 SPOTTSWOODE Cabernet Sauvignon Napa Valley 1984 Rel: $25 Cur: $75 (11/30/87)
92 STAG'S LEAP WINE CELLARS Cabernet Sauvignon Napa Valley Stags Leap District SLV 1984 Rel: $21 Cur: $32 (CA-3/89)
92 STERLING Cabernet Sauvignon Napa Valley Reserve 1984 Rel: $25 Cur: $38 (3/31/89) CS
92 STERLING Cabernet Sauvignon Napa Valley Reserve 1984 Rel: $25 Cur: $38 (CA-3/89)
91 BEAULIEU Cabernet Sauvignon Napa Valley Georges de Latour Private Reserve 1984 Rel: $25 Cur: $28 (CA-3/89)
91 BEAULIEU Cabernet Sauvignon Napa Valley Georges de Latour Private Reserve 1984 Rel: $25 Cur: $28 (12/31/88)
91 CAYMUS Cabernet Sauvignon Napa Valley 1984 Rel: $16 Cur: $42 (CA-3/89)
91 FREEMARK ABBEY Cabernet Sauvignon Napa Valley Sycamore Vineyards 1984 $20 (12/15/88)
91 WILLIAM HILL Cabernet Sauvignon Napa Valley Reserve 1984 Rel: $18.25 Cur: $26 (CA-3/89)
91 WILLIAM HILL Cabernet Sauvignon Napa Valley Reserve 1984 Rel: $18.25 Cur: $26 (4/15/88) CS
91 KENWOOD Cabernet Sauvignon Sonoma Valley Jack London Vineyard 1984 Rel: $16 Cur: $21 (11/30/87)
91 LYETH Red Alexander Valley 1984 Rel: $18 Cur: $26 (3/15/88)
91 MARKHAM Cabernet Sauvignon Napa Valley 1984 Rel: $12 Cur: $18 (CA-3/89)
91 MONTICELLO Cabernet Sauvignon Napa Valley Corley Reserve 1984 Rel: $18.50 Cur: $28 (CA-3/89)
91 NEWTON Cabernet Sauvignon Napa Valley 1984 Rel: $13.50 Cur: $22 (9/30/87)
91 ROBERT PECOTA Cabernet Sauvignon Napa Valley Kara's Vineyard 1984 Rel: $14 Cur: $20 (10/15/87)
91 JOSEPH PHELPS Cabernet Sauvignon Napa Valley 1984 Rel: $14 Cur: $25 (10/31/88)
91 JOSEPH PHELPS Insignia Napa Valley 1984 Rel: $30 Cur: $35 (11/15/88)
91 PINE RIDGE Cabernet Sauvignon Napa Valley Stags Leap District Pine Ridge Stags Leap Vineyard 1984 Rel: $25 Cur: $39 (2/15/88)
91 PRESTON Cabernet Sauvignon Dry Creek Valley 1984 Rel: $11 Cur: $15 (10/15/87)
91 SHAFER Cabernet Sauvignon Napa Valley Stags Leap District 1984 Rel: $14 Cur: $25 (CA-3/89)
91 SILVERADO Cabernet Sauvignon Napa Valley Stags Leap District 1984 Rel: $11.50 Cur: $22 (CA-3/89)
91 SMITH-MADRONE Cabernet Sauvignon Napa Valley 1984 Rel: $14 Cur: $15 (CA-3/89)
91 STELTZNER Cabernet Sauvignon Napa Valley Stags Leap District 1984 Rel: $15 Cur: $19 (CA-3/89)
91 STELTZNER Cabernet Sauvignon Napa Valley Stags Leap District 1984 Rel: $15 Cur: $19 (3/31/88)
91 TUDAL Cabernet Sauvignon Napa Valley 1984 Rel: $12.50 Cur: $30 (CA-3/89)
90 BUENA VISTA Cabernet Sauvignon Carneros Private Reserve 1984 Rel: $18 Cur: $18 (CA-3/89)
90 CAYMUS Cabernet Sauvignon Napa Valley 1984 Rel: $16 Cur: $42 (12/31/87)
90 CLOS DU BOIS Cabernet Sauvignon Alexander Valley Briarcrest Vineyard 1984 Rel: $16 Cur: $24 (7/15/88)
90 DOMINUS Napa Valley 1984 Rel: $40 Cur: $55 (3/01/89)
90 DOMINUS Napa Valley 1984 Rel: $40 Cur: $55 (5/15/88) CS
90 DUNN Cabernet Sauvignon Napa Valley 1984 Rel: $18 Cur: $65 (11/30/87)
90 FISHER Cabernet Sauvignon Sonoma County Coach Insignia 1984 Rel: $18 Cur: $25 (11/15/87)
90 GRACE FAMILY Cabernet Sauvignon Napa Valley 1984 Rel: $38 Cur: $285 (4/15/88)
90 INGLENOOK Cabernet Sauvignon Napa Valley Reserve Cask 1984 Rel: $22 Cur: $17 (7/31/90)
90 JOHNSON TURNBULL Cabernet Sauvignon Napa Valley 1984 Rel: $14.50 Cur: $23 (CA-3/89)
90 LYETH Red Alexander Valley 1984 Rel: $18 Cur: $26 (CA-3/89)
90 MAYACAMAS Cabernet Sauvignon Napa Valley 1984 Rel: $20 Cur: $26 (CA-3/89)
90 MERRYVALE Red Table Wine Napa Valley 1984 Rel: $24 Cur: $28 (10/31/87)
90 ROBERT MONDAVI Cabernet Sauvignon Napa Valley Reserve 1984 Rel: $37 Cur: $38 (12/31/88)
90 MONTICELLO Cabernet Sauvignon Napa Valley Corley Reserve 1984 Rel: $18.50 Cur: $28 (11/30/87)
90 MONTICELLO Cabernet Sauvignon Napa Valley Jefferson Cuvée 1984 $11 (11/30/87)
90 MOUNT EDEN Cabernet Sauvignon Santa Cruz Mountains 1984 Rel: $22 Cur: $26 (10/31/88)
90 OPTIMA Cabernet Sauvignon Sonoma County 1984 $16.50 (2/29/88)
90 PINE RIDGE Cabernet Sauvignon Napa Valley Andrus Reserve 1984 Rel: $37 Cur: $40 (6/30/88)
90 PINE RIDGE Cabernet Sauvignon Napa Valley Rutherford Cuvée 1984 Rel: $14 Cur: $29 (CA-3/89)
90 RAYMOND Cabernet Sauvignon Napa Valley 1984 Rel: $13 Cur: $17 (2/15/89)
90 ROMBAUER Le Meilleur du Chai Napa Valley 1984 Rel: $32.50 Cur: $47 (CA-3/89)
90 ST. CLEMENT Cabernet Sauvignon Napa Valley 1984 Rel: $15 Cur: $17 (10/15/88)
90 SPOTTSWOODE Cabernet Sauvignon Napa Valley 1984 Rel: $25 Cur: $75 (CA-3/89)
90 STAG'S LEAP WINE CELLARS Cabernet Sauvignon Napa Valley Stags Leap District Stag's Leap Vineyards Cask 23 1984 Rel: $40 Cur: $89 (12/31/88)
90 STAGS' LEAP WINERY Cabernet Sauvignon Napa Valley Stags Leap District 1984 Rel: $13.50 Cur: $18 (7/15/88)
89 CAKEBREAD Cabernet Sauvignon Napa Valley 1984 Rel: $16 Cur: $25 (CA-3/89)
89 CLOS DU BOIS Marlstone Vineyard Alexander Valley 1984 Rel: $19.50 Cur: $27 (CA-3/89)
89 B.R. COHN Cabernet Sauvignon Sonoma Valley Olive Hill Vineyard 1984 Rel: $15 Cur: $35 (6/30/88)
89 B.R. COHN Cabernet Sauvignon Sonoma Valley Olive Hill Vineyard 1984 Rel: $15 Cur: $35 (6/30/88)
89 CUVAISON Cabernet Sauvignon Napa Valley 1984 Rel: $14 Cur: $18 (CA-3/89)
89 DANIEL Cabernet Sauvignon Napa Valley 1984 $21 (7/15/88)
89 DE LOACH Cabernet Sauvignon Dry Creek Valley 1984 $11 (12/15/87)
89 DE MOOR Cabernet Sauvignon Napa Valley 1984 Rel: $14 Cur: $16 (8/31/88)
89 DIAMOND CREEK Cabernet Sauvignon Napa Valley Three Vineyard Blend 1984 Rel: $50 Cur: $100 (CA-3/89)
89 FISHER Cabernet Sauvignon Sonoma County Coach Insignia 1984 Rel: $18 Cur: $25 (CA-3/89)
89 GEYSER PEAK Réserve Alexandre Alexander Valley 1984 $19 (8/31/88)
89 HEITZ Cabernet Sauvignon Napa Valley 1984 Rel: $15 Cur: $18 (1/31/90) (JL)
89 LAUREL GLEN Cabernet Sauvignon Sonoma Mountain 1984 Rel: $15 Cur: $45 (CA-3/89)
89 LOUIS M. MARTINI Cabernet Sauvignon Sonoma Valley Monte Rosso 1984 Rel: $22 Cur: $23 (CA-3/89)
89 JOSEPH PHELPS Insignia Napa Valley 1984 Rel: $30 Cur: $35 (CA-3/89)
89 RAYMOND Cabernet Sauvignon Napa Valley Private Reserve 1984 Rel: $20 Cur: $22 (CA-3/89)
89 ST. CLEMENT Cabernet Sauvignon Napa Valley 1984 Rel: $15 Cur: $17 (CA-3/89)
89 SHAFER Cabernet Sauvignon Napa Valley Stags Leap District Hillside Select 1984 Rel: $24.50 Cur: $33 (4/30/89)
89 SHENANDOAH Cabernet Sauvignon Amador County Artist Series 1984 $9 (8/31/87)
89 SILVER OAK Cabernet Sauvignon Alexander Valley 1984 Rel: $22 Cur: $50 (CA-3/89)
89 SILVERADO Cabernet Sauvignon Napa Valley Stags Leap District 1984 Rel: $11.50 Cur: $22 (11/30/87)
89 SPRING MOUNTAIN Cabernet Sauvignon Napa Valley 1984 Rel: $15 Cur: $22 (3/15/89)
89 SPRING MOUNTAIN Cabernet Sauvignon Napa Valley 1984 Rel: $15 Cur: $22 (CA-3/89)
88 BELVEDERE Cabernet Sauvignon Alexander Valley Robert Young Vineyards 1984 $13 (7/15/88)
88 BUENA VISTA L'Année Carneros 1984 $32/1.5L (2/15/88)
88 CAYMUS Cabernet Sauvignon Napa Valley Cuvée 1984 $12 (8/31/87)
88 CHAPPELLET Cabernet Sauvignon Napa Valley 1984 Rel: $18 Cur: $23 (7/31/88)
88 CONN CREEK Cabernet Sauvignon Napa Valley Collins Vineyard Private Reserve 1984 Rel: $23 Cur: $30 (CA-3/89)
88 DE MOOR Cabernet Sauvignon Napa Valley 1984 Rel: $14 Cur: $16 (CA-3/89)
88 DOLAN Cabernet Sauvignon Mendocino 1984 $12 (5/31/88)
88 DRY CREEK David S. Stare Vintner's Reserve Sonoma County 1984 $18 (5/31/88)
88 FIELD STONE Cabernet Sauvignon Alexander Valley Turkey Hill Vineyard 1984 $16 (12/31/88)
88 FOLIE A DEUX Cabernet Sauvignon Napa Valley 1984 $14.50 (5/31/88)
88 FREEMARK ABBEY Cabernet Sauvignon Napa Valley Bosché 1984 Rel: $20 Cur: $25 (CA-3/89)
88 GIRARD Cabernet Sauvignon Napa Valley 1984 Rel: $11 Cur: $12 (11/30/87)
88 HAYWOOD Cabernet Sauvignon Sonoma Valley 1984 Rel: $12.50 Cur: $20 (CA-3/89)
88 HIDDEN CELLARS Cabernet Sauvignon Mendocino County Mountanos Vineyard 1984 $12 (8/31/88)
88 LA JOTA Cabernet Sauvignon Howell Mountain 1984 Rel: $15 Cur: $32 (CA-3/89)
88 LONG Cabernet Sauvignon Napa Valley 1984 Rel: $32 Cur: $48 (CA-3/89)
88 LONG Cabernet Sauvignon Napa Valley 1984 Rel: $32 Cur: $48 (12/15/88)
88 MOUNT VEEDER Cabernet Sauvignon Napa Valley 1984 Rel: $14 Cur: $18 (CA-3/89)
88 JOSEPH PHELPS Cabernet Sauvignon Napa Valley Backus Vineyard 1984 Rel: $20 Cur: $39 (12/31/87)
88 JOSEPH PHELPS Cabernet Sauvignon Napa Valley Eisele Vineyard 1984 Rel: $35 Cur: $39 (3/15/88)
88 BERNARD PRADEL Cabernet Sauvignon Napa Valley 1984 $11 (2/29/88)
88 QUAIL RIDGE Cabernet Sauvignon Napa Valley 1984 $15 (3/31/89)
88 RIDGE Cabernet Sauvignon Napa County York Creek 1984 Rel: $14 Cur: $16 (CA-3/89)
88 ROUND HILL Cabernet Sauvignon Napa Valley Reserve 1984 $10 (10/31/87)
88 RUTHERFORD HILL Cabernet Sauvignon Napa Valley 1984 Rel: $12.50 Cur: $15 (CA-3/89)
88 RUTHERFORD HILL Cabernet Sauvignon Napa Valley 1984 Rel: $12.50 Cur: $15 (8/31/88)
88 SILVER OAK Cabernet Sauvignon Napa Valley 1984 Rel: $22 Cur: $55 (12/15/88)
88 STONEGATE Cabernet Sauvignon Napa Valley 1984 Rel: $14 Cur: $14 (CA-3/89)
88 TREFETHEN Cabernet Sauvignon Napa Valley 1984 Rel: $14 Cur: $16 (5/31/88)
88 VICHON Cabernet Sauvignon Napa Valley 1984 Rel: $11.25 Cur: $15 (CA-3/89)
87 BERINGER Cabernet Sauvignon Napa Valley Chabot Vineyard 1984 Rel: $30 Cur: $32 (CA-3/89)
87 BUEHLER Cabernet Sauvignon Napa Valley 1984 Rel: $13 Cur: $23 (CA-3/89)
87 CAKEBREAD Cabernet Sauvignon Napa Valley 1984 Rel: $16 Cur: $25 (9/30/87)
87 CHAPPELLET Cabernet Sauvignon Napa Valley Reserve 1984 Rel: $18 Cur: $23 (CA-3/89)
87 CHIMNEY ROCK Cabernet Sauvignon Napa Valley Stags Leap District 1984 Rel: $15 Cur: $18 (4/30/88)
87 CHRISTIAN BROTHERS Cabernet Sauvignon Napa Valley 1984 $7 (10/15/87) BB
87 CLOS DU BOIS Cabernet Sauvignon Alexander Valley 1984 $10 (6/15/87)
87 CLOS DU BOIS Cabernet Sauvignon Alexander Valley Briarcrest Vineyard 1984 Rel: $16 Cur: $24 (CA-3/89)
87 DOMAINE PHILIPPE Cabernet Sauvignon Napa Valley Select Cuvée 1984 $6.50 (5/15/88) BB
87 DUCKHORN Cabernet Sauvignon Napa Valley 1984 Rel: $17 Cur: $32 (6/15/87)
87 FIVE PALMS Cabernet Sauvignon Napa Valley 1984 $6 (3/31/87) BB
87 FRANCISCAN Cabernet Sauvignon Napa Valley Private Reserve 1984 Rel: $9 Cur: $15 (CA-3/89)
87 GRGICH HILLS Cabernet Sauvignon Napa Valley 1984 Rel: $17 Cur: $24 (4/30/89)
87 HACIENDA Cabernet Sauvignon Sonoma Valley Estate Reserve 1984 $18 (5/31/91)
87 INGLENOOK Reunion Napa Valley 1984 Rel: $35 Cur: $35 (10/15/88)
87 CHARLES KRUG Cabernet Sauvignon Napa Valley Vintage Select 1984 Rel: $20 Cur: $24 (6/30/90)
87 CHARLES KRUG Cabernet Sauvignon Napa Valley Vintage Select 1984 Rel: $20 Cur: $24 (CA-3/89)
87 LAUREL GLEN Cabernet Sauvignon Sonoma Mountain 1984 Rel: $15 Cur: $45 (4/30/87)
87 LIVINGSTON Cabernet Sauvignon Napa Valley Moffett Vineyard 1984 Rel: $18 Cur: $29 (CA-3/89)
87 MARKHAM Cabernet Sauvignon Napa Valley 1984 Rel: $12 Cur: $18 (10/31/88)
87 NEWTON Cabernet Sauvignon Napa Valley 1984 Rel: $13.50 Cur: $22 (CA-3/89)
87 ROBERT PEPI Cabernet Sauvignon Napa Valley Vine Hill Ranch 1984 Rel: $16 Cur: $21 (CA-3/89)
87 JOSEPH PHELPS Cabernet Sauvignon Napa Valley Eisele Vineyard 1984 Rel: $35 Cur: $39 (CA-3/89)

UNITED STATES

CALIFORNIA/*CABERNET SAUVIGNON & BLENDS*

87 PINE RIDGE Cabernet Sauvignon Napa Valley Rutherford Cuvée 1984 Rel: $14 Cur: $29 (8/31/87)
87 PRESTON Cabernet Sauvignon Dry Creek Valley 1984 Rel: $11 Cur: $15 (CA-3/89)
87 RAYMOND Cabernet Sauvignon Napa Valley Private Reserve 1984 Rel: $20 Cur: $22 (7/15/89)
87 SANTA CRUZ MOUNTAIN Cabernet Sauvignon Santa Cruz Mountains Bates Ranch 1984 Rel: $14 Cur: $14 (CA-3/89)
87 STAGS' LEAP WINERY Cabernet Sauvignon Napa Valley Stags Leap District 1984 Rel: $13.50 Cur: $18 (CA-3/89)
86 CLOS DU VAL Cabernet Sauvignon Napa Valley Stags Leap District 1984 Rel: $15 Cur: $17 (4/15/88)
86 CONN CREEK Cabernet Sauvignon Napa Valley Barrel Select Lot 79 1984 Rel: $13 Cur: $20 (CA-3/89)
86 CONN CREEK Cabernet Sauvignon Napa Valley Barrel Select Lot 79 1984 Rel: $13 Cur: $20 (12/31/88)
86 DOMAINE MICHEL Cabernet Sauvignon Sonoma County 1984 $19 (9/15/87)
86 EBERLE Cabernet Sauvignon Paso Robles 1984 Rel: $12 Cur: $17 (CA-3/89)
86 GROTH Cabernet Sauvignon Napa Valley 1984 Rel: $14 Cur: $39 (2/15/88)
86 HEITZ Cabernet Sauvignon Napa Valley 1984 Rel: $15 Cur: $18 (5/15/89)
86 HEITZ Cabernet Sauvignon Napa Valley Bella Oaks Vineyard 1984 Rel: $25 Cur: $32 (5/15/89)
86 HEITZ Cabernet Sauvignon Napa Valley Bella Oaks Vineyard 1984 Rel: $25 Cur: $32 (CA-3/89)
86 IRON HORSE Cabernet Sauvignon Alexander Valley 1984 Rel: $14 Cur: $16 (CA-3/89)
86 JORDAN Cabernet Sauvignon Alexander Valley 1984 Rel: $19 Cur: $39 (CA-3/89)
86 JORDAN Cabernet Sauvignon Alexander Valley 1984 Rel: $19 Cur: $39 (7/15/88)
86 LIVINGSTON Cabernet Sauvignon Napa Valley Moffett Vineyard 1984 Rel: $18 Cur: $29 (11/15/87)
86 MERRYVALE Red Table Wine Napa Valley 1984 Rel: $24 Cur: $28 (CA-3/89)
86 MONTEVINA Cabernet Sauvignon Shenandoah Valley Limited Release 1984 $7.50 (8/31/88) BB
86 JOSEPH PHELPS Cabernet Sauvignon Napa Valley Backus Vineyard 1984 Rel: $20 Cur: $39 (CA-3/89)
86 V. SATTUI Cabernet Sauvignon Napa Valley Preston Vineyard 1984 Rel: $13.75 Cur: $20 (CA-3/89)
86 SIERRA VISTA Cabernet Sauvignon El Dorado 1984 $9 (3/31/88)
86 SILVER OAK Cabernet Sauvignon Napa Valley 1984 Rel: $22 Cur: $55 (CA-3/89)
86 SIMI Cabernet Sauvignon Sonoma County 1984 Rel: $11 Cur: $15 (10/31/88)
86 STONEGATE Cabernet Sauvignon Napa Valley 1984 Rel: $14 Cur: $14 (2/15/89)
86 PHILIP TOGNI Cabernet Sauvignon Napa Valley 1984 Rel: $18 Cur: $35 (CA-3/89)
86 STEPHEN ZELLERBACH Cabernet Sauvignon Alexander Valley 1984 $8 (11/30/88)
85 BERINGER Cabernet Sauvignon Napa Valley Chabot Vineyard 1984 Rel: $30 Cur: $32 (9/15/90)
85 CAKEBREAD Cabernet Sauvignon Napa Valley Rutherford Reserve 1984 Rel: $35 Cur: $38 (2/15/90)
85 CLOS DU BOIS Marlstone Vineyard Alexander Valley 1984 Rel: $19.50 Cur: $27 (5/15/88)
85 CLOS DU VAL Cabernet Sauvignon Napa Valley Gran Val 1984 $8.50 (2/15/87) BB
85 DRY CREEK Cabernet Sauvignon Sonoma County 1984 $10 (5/15/87)
85 DUNNEWOOD Cabernet Sauvignon Napa Valley Reserve 1984 $10.50 (12/31/88)
85 FETZER Cabernet Sauvignon Mendocino Special Reserve 1984 $14 (12/31/88)
85 FLORA SPRINGS Cabernet Sauvignon Napa Valley 1984 Rel: $13 Cur: $18 (CA-3/89)
85 FOX MOUNTAIN Cabernet Sauvignon Russian River Valley Reserve 1984 $18 (3/15/89)
85 GUNDLACH BUNDSCHU Cabernet Sauvignon Sonoma Valley Rhinefarm Vineyards 1984 Rel: $9 Cur: $12 (3/01/89)
85 LOUIS M. MARTINI Cabernet Sauvignon North Coast Special Selection 1984 (NA) (CA-3/89)
85 NIEBAUM-COPPOLA Rubicon Napa Valley 1984 (NR) (CA-3/89)
85 ROBERT PECOTA Cabernet Sauvignon Napa Valley Kara's Vineyard 1984 Rel: $14 Cur: $20 (CA-3/89)
85 RUTHERFORD RANCH Cabernet Sauvignon Napa Valley 1984 Rel: $12.50 Cur: $13 (5/31/89)
85 SEQUOIA GROVE Cabernet Sauvignon Napa Valley 1984 Rel: $12 Cur: $18 (CA-3/89)
85 SILVER OAK Cabernet Sauvignon Alexander Valley 1984 Rel: $22 Cur: $50 (12/15/88)
85 STERLING Cabernet Sauvignon Napa Valley Diamond Mountain Ranch 1984 Rel: $15 Cur: $18 (CA-3/89)
85 VIANSA Cabernet Sauvignon Napa-Sonoma Counties 1984 $13 (7/31/88)
85 VICHON Cabernet Sauvignon Napa Valley Stags Leap District Fay Vineyard 1984 Rel: $14 Cur: $18 (CA-3/89)
84 FLORA SPRINGS Trilogy Napa Valley 1984 Rel: $30 Cur: $32 (CA-3/89)
84 FRANCISCAN Cabernet Sauvignon Napa Valley Oakville Estate 1984 $9.50 (9/15/88)
84 FREEMARK ABBEY Cabernet Sauvignon Napa Valley 1984 Rel: $14 Cur: $14 (2/15/89)
84 GARLAND RANCH Cabernet Sauvignon Monterey County 1984 $6.75 (8/31/88) BB
84 GROTH Cabernet Sauvignon Napa Valley Reserve 1984 Rel: $25 Cur: $90 (4/15/89)
84 GUNDLACH BUNDSCHU Cabernet Sauvignon Sonoma Valley Rhinefarm Vineyards 1984 Rel: $9 Cur: $12 (9/30/88)
84 KENDALL-JACKSON Cardinale California 1984 $12 (7/31/87)
84 LA JOTA Cabernet Sauvignon Howell Mountain 1984 Rel: $15 Cur: $32 (11/15/87)
84 MOUNT EDEN Cabernet Sauvignon Santa Cruz Mountains 1984 Rel: $22 Cur: $26 (CA-3/89)
84 ROMBAUER Cabernet Sauvignon Napa Valley 1984 Rel: $13.50 Cur: $21 (CA-3/89)
84 ROUND HILL Cabernet Sauvignon Napa Valley 1984 $8.50 (5/31/88)
84 SILVER OAK Cabernet Sauvignon Napa Valley Bonny's Vineyard 1984 Rel: $45 Cur: $80 (10/15/89)
84 SILVER OAK Cabernet Sauvignon Napa Valley Bonny's Vineyard 1984 Rel: $45 Cur: $80 (CA-3/89)
84 STERLING Cabernet Sauvignon Napa Valley Diamond Mountain Ranch 1984 Rel: $15 Cur: $18 (2/15/88)
84 IVAN TAMAS Cabernet Sauvignon Mendocino McNab Ranch 1984 $6 (2/15/87) BB
84 TREFETHEN Cabernet Sauvignon Napa Valley 1984 Rel: $14 Cur: $16 (CA-3/89)
84 WHITEHALL LANE Cabernet Sauvignon Napa Valley 1984 $14 (12/31/87)
83 CHATEAU POTELLE Cabernet Sauvignon Alexander Valley 1984 $13 (12/31/88)
83 CHATEAU SOUVERAIN Cabernet Sauvignon Sonoma County 1984 $8.50 (8/31/87)
83 KENWOOD Cabernet Sauvignon Sonoma Valley 1984 $12 (5/31/88)
83 MOUNT VEEDER Cabernet Sauvignon Napa Valley 1984 Rel: $14 Cur: $18 (11/15/88)
83 STAG'S LEAP WINE CELLARS Cabernet Sauvignon Napa Valley 1984 $15 (7/15/87)
82 CHATEAU DIANA Cabernet Sauvignon Central Coast Limited Edition 1984 $6 (11/30/88) BB
82 CHIMNEY ROCK Cabernet Sauvignon Napa Valley Stags Leap District 1984 Rel: $15 Cur: $18 (CA-3/89)
82 CORBETT CANYON Cabernet Sauvignon Central Coast Select 1984 $8 (2/15/87)
82 FETZER Cabernet Sauvignon Mendocino Barrel Select 1984 $9 (11/30/87)
82 FIELD STONE Cabernet Sauvignon Alexander Valley Hoot Owl Creek Vineyards 1984 $14 (10/15/88)
82 GLEN ELLEN Cabernet Sauvignon Sonoma Valley Benziger Family Selection 1984 $14 (10/15/87)
82 J. LOHR Cabernet Sauvignon California 1984 $5 (11/30/86) BB
82 MADDALENA Cabernet Sauvignon Sonoma County Vintner's Reserve 1984 $9 (3/31/87)
82 SEQUOIA GROVE Cabernet Sauvignon Napa Valley 1984 Rel: $12 Cur: $18 (11/15/87)
81 BOEGER Cabernet Sauvignon El Dorado 1984 $10.50 (5/31/88)
81 KENDALL-JACKSON Cabernet Sauvignon Lake County 1984 $7.50 (11/15/87) BB
81 MONTEREY PENINSULA Cabernet Sauvignon Monterey Doctors' Reserve 1984 $16 (2/28/91)
81 SANTA BARBARA Cabernet Sauvignon Santa Ynez Valley Reserve 1984 $13.50 (10/31/87)
81 STAG'S LEAP WINE CELLARS Cabernet Sauvignon Napa Valley Stags Leap District SLV 1984 Rel: $21 Cur: $32 (11/30/87)
80 FREEMARK ABBEY Cabernet Sauvignon Napa Valley Bosché 1984 Rel: $20 Cur: $25 (4/30/88)
80 LAMBERT BRIDGE Cabernet Sauvignon Sonoma County 1984 $10 (4/15/87)
80 CHARLES LEFRANC Cabernet Sauvignon Napa County 1984 $12 (10/15/87)
80 MAYACAMAS Cabernet Sauvignon Napa Valley 1984 Rel: $20 Cur: $26 (4/15/89)
80 ROBERT MONDAVI Cabernet Sauvignon Napa Valley 1984 Rel: $13 Cur: $34 (12/31/87)
80 ROBERT PEPI Cabernet Sauvignon Napa Valley Vine Hill Ranch 1984 Rel: $16 Cur: $21 (8/31/89)
80 RAVENSWOOD Cabernet Sauvignon Sonoma County 1984 Rel: $12 Cur: $25 (CA-3/89)
80 ROMBAUER Cabernet Sauvignon Napa Valley 1984 Rel: $13.50 Cur: $21 (2/15/88)
80 SOLARI Cabernet Sauvignon Napa Valley Larkmead Vineyards 1984 $12 (4/15/88)
80 RODNEY STRONG Cabernet Sauvignon Alexander Valley Alexander's Crown Vineyard 1984 $12 (4/30/89)
80 VILLA MT. EDEN Cabernet Sauvignon Napa Valley 1984 (NA) (CA-3/89)
79 CAIN Cabernet Sauvignon Napa Valley 1984 $14 (5/31/88)
79 ESTANCIA Cabernet Sauvignon Alexander Valley 1984 $6.50 (12/31/87)
79 GUNDLACH BUNDSCHU Cabernet Sauvignon Sonoma Valley Batto Ranch 1984 Rel: $14 Cur: $16 (CA-3/89)
79 ZACA MESA Cabernet Sauvignon Santa Barbara County 1984 $8.50 (10/31/88)
78 BEAULIEU Cabernet Sauvignon Napa Valley Rutherford 1984 Rel: $9.50 Cur: $10 (8/31/87)
78 COSENTINO Cabernet Sauvignon North Coast Reserve Edition 1984 $14 (3/31/88)
78 MARIETTA Cabernet Sauvignon Sonoma County 1984 $10 (12/31/87)
78 MEEKER Cabernet Sauvignon Dry Creek Valley 1984 $18 (6/15/88)
78 MENDOCINO ESTATE Cabernet Sauvignon Mendocino 1984 $4.75 (6/15/87)
78 RIDGE Cabernet Sauvignon Napa County York Creek 1984 Rel: $14 Cur: $16 (2/15/87)
78 ROUDON-SMITH Cabernet Sauvignon Santa Cruz Mountains 1984 $12 (6/30/88)
77 BELLEROSE Cuvée Bellerose Sonoma County 1984 $14 (11/15/87)
77 FOPPIANO Cabernet Sauvignon Russian River Valley 1984 $8.50 (4/30/88)
77 GEYSER PEAK Cabernet Sauvignon Alexander Valley 1984 $7.50 (3/15/88)
77 HOP KILN Cabernet Sauvignon Alexander Valley 1984 $10 (3/31/88)
76 DEHLINGER Cabernet Sauvignon Russian River Valley 1984 $12 (2/15/88)
76 HAWK CREST Cabernet Sauvignon North Coast 1984 $7 (10/15/87)
76 KONOCTI Cabernet Sauvignon Lake County 1984 $7.50 (2/15/89)
75 ACACIA Cabernet Sauvignon Napa Valley 1984 $15 (12/15/86)
75 CRYSTAL VALLEY Cabernet Sauvignon North Coast Reserve Edition 1984 $14 (10/15/87)
75 GRAND CRU Cabernet Sauvignon Sonoma County 1984 $8.50 (12/31/87)
75 JADE MOUNTAIN Cabernet Sauvignon Alexander Valley Icaria Creek Vineyard deCarteret 1984 $8.75 (6/30/88)
75 MICHAEL'S Cabernet Sauvignon Napa Valley Summit Vineyard Reserve 1984 $15 (3/31/88)
75 NEYERS Cabernet Sauvignon Napa Valley 1984 $12.50 (4/30/88)
75 RIVER OAKS Cabernet Sauvignon North Coast 1984 $6 (10/15/87)
75 STEVENOT Cabernet Sauvignon Calaveras County Grand Reserve 1984 $15 (12/31/87)
75 WILLIAM WHEELER Cabernet Sauvignon Dry Creek Valley 1984 $11 (4/15/88)
74 FETZER Cabernet Sauvignon Lake County 1984 $8 (5/15/87)
74 PARDUCCI Cabernet Sauvignon Mendocino County 1984 $8.50 (7/31/88)
74 TRIONE Cabernet Sauvignon Alexander Valley 1984 $10 (12/31/87)
73 FLORA SPRINGS Trilogy Napa Valley 1984 Rel: $30 Cur: $32 (2/29/88)
73 HUSCH Cabernet Sauvignon Mendocino La Ribera Vineyards 1984 $10 (12/31/87)
73 JOHNSON TURNBULL Cabernet Sauvignon Napa Valley 1984 Rel: $14.50 Cur: $23 (7/31/87)
73 WILLOW CREEK Cabernet Sauvignon Napa Valley 1984 $8.50 (3/31/88)
72 JEAN CLAUDE BOISSET Cabernet Sauvignon Napa Valley 1984 $7 (12/31/87)
72 J. CAREY Cabernet Sauvignon Santa Ynez Valley 1984 $9 (3/31/88)
72 FIRESTONE Cabernet Sauvignon Santa Ynez Valley 1984 $9.50 (3/31/88)
72 RUTHERFORD ESTATE Cabernet Sauvignon Napa Valley 1984 $5 (11/15/87)
71 DAVIS BYNUM Cabernet Sauvignon Napa Valley Reserve Bottling 1984 $7 (12/15/87)
71 CLOS ROBERT Cabernet Sauvignon Napa Valley Proprietor's Reserve 1984 $7 (12/31/87)
71 CRESTON MANOR Cabernet Sauvignon Central Coast Winemaker's Selection 1984 $16 (12/15/87)
71 FLORA SPRINGS Cabernet Sauvignon Napa Valley 1984 Rel: $13 Cur: $18 (7/31/88)
70 PAT PAULSEN Cabernet Sauvignon Alexander Valley 1984 $11 (4/30/87)
69 RIDGE Cabernet Sauvignon Santa Cruz Mountains Jimsomare 1984 $16 (10/31/87)
68 INNISFREE Cabernet Sauvignon Napa Valley 1984 $9 (12/15/87)
66 STUERMER Cabernet Sauvignon Lake County 1984 $15 (9/30/89)
64 DORE Cabernet Sauvignon California 1984 $5 (12/31/87)
64 RIDGE Cabernet Sauvignon Santa Cruz Mountains 1984 $12 (6/15/87)
63 JEKEL Cabernet Sauvignon Monterey 1984 $12 (7/31/89)
60 WILLIAM WHEELER Cabernet Sauvignon Dry Creek Valley Norse Vineyard Private Reserve 1984 $15 (7/31/89)

Key to Symbols

The scores reported here are the results of blind tastings conducted by our panel of senior editors. Wines that carry the initials below are results of individual tastings.

THE WINE SPECTATOR 100-POINT SCALE ***95-100***—Classic, a great wine; ***90-94***—Outstanding, superior character and style; ***80-89***—Good to very good, a wine with special qualities; ***70-79***—Average, drinkable wine that may have minor flaws; ***60-69***—Below average, drinkable but not recommended; ***50-59***—Poor, undrinkable, not recommended. "+"—With a score indicates a range; used primarily with barrel tastings to indicate a preliminary score.

SPECIAL DESIGNATIONS SS—Spectator Selection, CS—Cellar Selection, BB—Best Buy.

TASTER'S INITIALS (JG)—Jim Gordon, (HS)—Harvey Steiman, (JL)—James Laube, (JS)—James Suckling, (TM)—Thomas Matthews, (TR)—Terry Robards, (BT)—Barrel Tasting (these wines were tasted blind from barrel samples), (CA-date)—*California's Great Cabernets* by James Laube, (CH-date)—*California's Great Chardonnays* by James Laube, (VP-date)—*Vintage Port* by James Suckling.

DATE TASTED Dates in parentheses represent the issue in which the rating was published.

1983

96	NEWTON Cabernet Sauvignon Napa Valley 1983 Rel: $12.50 Cur: $36 (4/15/87) SS
95	DUNN Cabernet Sauvignon Howell Mountain 1983 Rel: $18 Cur: $116 (5/15/87)
95	DUNN Cabernet Sauvignon Napa Valley 1983 Rel: $15 Cur: $85 (CA-3/89)
95	DUNN Cabernet Sauvignon Napa Valley 1983 Rel: $15 Cur: $85 (10/31/86) SS
95	INGLENOOK Reunion Napa Valley 1983 Rel: $33 Cur: $38 (11/30/87) CS
94	CAYMUS Cabernet Sauvignon Napa Valley 1983 Rel: $15 Cur: $42 (11/30/86) CS
94	MERRYVALE Red Table Wine Napa Valley 1983 Rel: $18 Cur: $28 (2/15/87)
94	ROBERT MONDAVI Cabernet Sauvignon Napa Valley 1983 Rel: $12 Cur: $26 (4/15/87)
93	BUEHLER Cabernet Sauvignon Napa Valley 1983 Rel: $12 Cur: $23 (7/16/86) SS
93	CAKEBREAD Cabernet Sauvignon Napa Valley 1983 Rel: $16 Cur: $25 (11/30/86)
93	CHATEAU MONTELENA Cabernet Sauvignon Napa Valley 1983 Rel: $18 Cur: $28 (11/15/87) CS
93	DIAMOND CREEK Cabernet Sauvignon Napa Valley Gravelly Meadow 1983 Rel: $20 Cur: $40 (2/01/86) CS
93	FAR NIENTE Cabernet Sauvignon Napa Valley 1983 Rel: $25 Cur: $32 (6/16/86)
93	INGLENOOK Reunion Napa Valley 1983 Rel: $33 Cur: $38 (CA-3/89)
92	CHATEAU MONTELENA Cabernet Sauvignon Napa Valley 1983 Rel: $18 Cur: $28 (CA-3/89)
92	DUNN Cabernet Sauvignon Howell Mountain 1983 Rel: $18 Cur: $116 (CA-3/89)
92	GROTH Cabernet Sauvignon Napa Valley Reserve 1983 Rel: $25 Cur: $90 (CA-3/89)
92	GROTH Cabernet Sauvignon Napa Valley Reserve 1983 Rel: $25 Cur: $90 (12/15/88)
92	KENWOOD Cabernet Sauvignon Sonoma Valley Artist Series 1983 Rel: $30 Cur: $38 (11/15/86) CS
92	NEWTON Cabernet Sauvignon Napa Valley 1983 Rel: $12.50 Cur: $36 (CA-3/89)
92	ROUND HILL Cabernet Sauvignon Napa Valley Reserve 1983 $9.50 (12/15/86)
92	SILVERADO Cabernet Sauvignon Napa Valley Stags Leap District 1983 Rel: $11 Cur: $22 (12/31/86)
91	BUEHLER Cabernet Sauvignon Napa Valley 1983 Rel: $12 Cur: $23 (CA-3/89)
91	CAYMUS Cabernet Sauvignon Napa Valley Special Selection 1983 Rel: $35 Cur: $115 (CA-3/89)
91	CHESTNUT HILL Cabernet Sauvignon Napa Valley 1983 $7 (10/31/86) BB
91	GLEN ELLEN Cabernet Sauvignon Sonoma Valley Benziger Family Selection 1983 $9.75 (5/15/87)
91	GRACE FAMILY Cabernet Sauvignon Napa Valley 1983 Rel: $38 Cur: $330 (CA-3/89)
91	LYETH Red Alexander Valley 1983 Rel: $17 Cur: $23 (6/30/87)
91	ROBERT MONDAVI Cabernet Sauvignon Napa Valley Reserve 1983 Rel: $30 Cur: $36 (11/30/87)
91	RAYMOND Cabernet Sauvignon Napa Valley Private Reserve 1983 Rel: $18 Cur: $25 (6/30/88)
91	ST. CLEMENT Cabernet Sauvignon Napa Valley 1983 Rel: $14.50 Cur: $17 (CA-3/89)
91	STONE CREEK Cabernet Sauvignon Napa Valley Special Selection 1983 $8.75 (5/31/87) BB
91	VICHON Cabernet Sauvignon Napa Valley 1983 Rel: $10 Cur: $14 (11/30/86)
90	ALEXANDER VALLEY Cabernet Sauvignon Alexander Valley 1983 Rel: $10.50 Cur: $18 (CA-3/89)
90	BERINGER Cabernet Sauvignon Napa Valley Private Reserve 1983 Rel: $19 Cur: $33 (4/15/87)
90	BUENA VISTA Cabernet Sauvignon Carneros Private Reserve 1983 Rel: $18 Cur: $25 (2/15/88)
90	CAYMUS Cabernet Sauvignon Napa Valley Special Selection 1983 Rel: $35 Cur: $115 (5/31/88)
90	FORMAN Cabernet Sauvignon Napa Valley 1983 Rel: $15.50 Cur: $70 (CA-3/89)
90	GRGICH HILLS Cabernet Sauvignon Napa Valley 1983 Rel: $17 Cur: $26 (4/30/88)
90	HEITZ Cabernet Sauvignon Napa Valley Bella Oaks Vineyard 1983 Rel: $15 Cur: $27 (4/30/88)
90	HEITZ Cabernet Sauvignon Napa Valley Martha's Vineyard 1983 Rel: $32.50 Cur: $53 (4/30/88)
90	LA JOTA Cabernet Sauvignon Howell Mountain 1983 Rel: $15 Cur: $30 (3/31/87)
90	MARKHAM Cabernet Sauvignon Napa Valley 1983 Rel: $13 Cur: $15 (7/31/89)
90	MAYACAMAS Cabernet Sauvignon Napa Valley 1983 Rel: $20 Cur: $26 (CA-3/89)
90	ROMBAUER Le Meilleur du Chai Napa Valley 1983 Rel: $30 Cur: $45 (CA-3/89)
90	STELTZNER Cabernet Sauvignon Napa Valley Stags Leap District 1983 Rel: $14 Cur: $18 (CA-3/89)
90	TREFETHEN Cabernet Sauvignon Napa Valley 1983 Rel: $11.75 Cur: $22 (7/15/87)
89	BERINGER Cabernet Sauvignon Napa Valley Private Reserve 1983 Rel: $19 Cur: $33 (CA-3/89)
89	CRYSTAL VALLEY Cabernet Sauvignon North Coast 1983 $8.50 (8/31/86) BB
89	DIAMOND CREEK Cabernet Sauvignon Napa Valley Gravelly Meadow 1983 Rel: $20 Cur: $40 (CA-3/89)
89	DIAMOND CREEK Cabernet Sauvignon Napa Valley Red Rock Terrace 1983 Rel: $20 Cur: $37 (2/01/86)
89	DIAMOND CREEK Cabernet Sauvignon Napa Valley Volcanic Hill 1983 Rel: $20 Cur: $35 (CA-3/89)
89	DUCKHORN Cabernet Sauvignon Napa Valley 1983 Rel: $16 Cur: $44 (7/01/86)
89	GUENOC Cabernet Sauvignon Lake County 1983 $9.75 (9/30/86)
89	HEITZ Cabernet Sauvignon Napa Valley Martha's Vineyard 1983 Rel: $32.50 Cur: $53 (CA-3/89)
89	HESS Cabernet Sauvignon Napa Valley Reserve 1983 Rel: $22 Cur: $98 (9/15/88)
89	WILLIAM HILL Cabernet Sauvignon Napa Valley Gold Label 1983 Rel: $18.25 Cur: $25 (8/31/87)
89	INGLENOOK Cabernet Sauvignon Napa Valley Reserve Cask 1983 Rel: $15.50 Cur: $19 (CA-3/89)
89	MARKHAM Cabernet Sauvignon Napa Valley 1983 Rel: $13 Cur: $15 (CA-3/89)
89	OPUS ONE Napa Valley 1983 Rel: $50 Cur: $66 (CA-3/89)
89	ROBERT PEPI Cabernet Sauvignon Napa Valley Vine Hill Ranch 1983 Rel: $16 Cur: $21 (5/31/88)
89	JOSEPH PHELPS Insignia Napa Valley 1983 Rel: $25 Cur: $35 (CA-3/89)
89	RAYMOND Cabernet Sauvignon Napa Valley 1983 Rel: $13 Cur: $20 (2/15/88)
89	ST. CLEMENT Cabernet Sauvignon Napa Valley 1983 Rel: $14.50 Cur: $17 (6/01/86)
89	SHAFER Cabernet Sauvignon Napa Valley Stags Leap District Hillside Select 1983 Rel: $22 Cur: $24 (CA-3/89)
89	SPOTTSWOODE Cabernet Sauvignon Napa Valley 1983 Rel: $25 Cur: $75 (CA-3/89)
88	BELVEDERE Cabernet Sauvignon Alexander Valley Robert Young Vineyards 1983 $12 (5/15/87)
88	CAKEBREAD Cabernet Sauvignon Napa Valley Rutherford Reserve 1983 Rel: $35 Cur: $35 (CA-3/89)
88	CLOS DU BOIS Marlstone Vineyard Alexander Valley 1983 Rel: $20 Cur: $25 (9/15/87)
88	CONN CREEK Cabernet Sauvignon Napa Valley Barrel Select 1983 Rel: $13 Cur: $15 (12/31/88)
88	DIAMOND CREEK Cabernet Sauvignon Napa Valley Red Rock Terrace 1983 Rel: $20 Cur: $37 (CA-3/89)
88	DUCKHORN Cabernet Sauvignon Napa Valley 1983 Rel: $16 Cur: $44 (CA-3/89)
88	GRGICH HILLS Cabernet Sauvignon Napa Valley 1983 Rel: $17 Cur: $26 (CA-3/89)
88	GROTH Cabernet Sauvignon Napa Valley 1983 Rel: $13 Cur: $22 (CA-3/89)
88	HESS Cabernet Sauvignon Napa Valley Reserve 1983 Rel: $22 Cur: $98 (CA-3/89)
88	INGLENOOK Cabernet Sauvignon Napa Valley Reserve Cask 1983 Rel: $15.50 Cur: $19 (9/15/87)
88	INGLENOOK Niebaum Claret Napa Valley 1983 $12 (11/30/87)
88	JOHNSON TURNBULL Cabernet Sauvignon Napa Valley 1983 Rel: $12.50 Cur: $18 (CA-3/89)
88	MERRYVALE Red Table Wine Napa Valley 1983 Rel: $18 Cur: $28 (CA-3/89)
88	MONTICELLO Cabernet Sauvignon Napa Valley Corley Reserve 1983 Rel: $24 Cur: $26 (CA-3/89)
89	OPUS ONE Napa Valley 1983 Rel: $50 Cur: $66 (6/15/87)
88	JOSEPH PHELPS Insignia Napa Valley 1983 Rel: $25 Cur: $35 (10/30/87)
88	PINE RIDGE Cabernet Sauvignon Napa Valley Andrus Reserve 1983 Rel: $35 Cur: $40 (CA-3/89)
88	SAM J. SEBASTIANI Cabernet Sauvignon Sonoma-Napa Counties 1983 $15 (11/30/86)
88	SEQUOIA GROVE Cabernet Sauvignon Napa-Alexander Valleys 1983 Rel: $12.50 Cur: $18 (2/15/87)
88	SILVERADO Cabernet Sauvignon Napa Valley Stags Leap District 1983 Rel: $11 Cur: $22 (CA-3/89)
88	STAG'S LEAP WINE CELLARS Cabernet Sauvignon Napa Valley Stags Leap District Stag's Leap Vineyards Cask 23 1983 Rel: $35 Cur: $73 (CA-3/89)
88	STELTZNER Cabernet Sauvignon Napa Valley Stags Leap District 1983 Rel: $14 Cur: $18 (6/30/87) (JL)
88	VIANSA Cabernet Sauvignon Sonoma Valley Grand Reserve 1983 $35 (10/15/88)
88	VIANSA Cabernet Sauvignon Sonoma Valley Reserve 1983 $18 (10/15/88)
87	ALEXANDER VALLEY Cabernet Sauvignon Alexander Valley 1983 Rel: $10.50 Cur: $18 (1/01/86)
87	BUENA VISTA Cabernet Sauvignon Carneros Private Reserve 1983 Rel: $18 Cur: $25 (CA-3/89)
87	BURGESS Cabernet Sauvignon Napa Valley Vintage Selection 1983 Rel: $17 Cur: $21 (CA-3/89)
87	CAYMUS Cabernet Sauvignon Napa Valley 1983 Rel: $15 Cur: $42 (CA-3/89)
87	CONN CREEK Cabernet Sauvignon Napa Valley Collins Vineyard Proprietor's Special Selection 1983 Cur: $70 (CA-3/89)
87	DIAMOND CREEK Cabernet Sauvignon Napa Valley Volcanic Hill 1983 Rel: $20 Cur: $35 (2/01/86)
87	DOMINUS Napa Valley 1983 Rel: $43 Cur: $50 (3/01/89)
87	FAR NIENTE Cabernet Sauvignon Napa Valley 1983 Rel: $25 Cur: $32 (CA-3/89)
87	GEYSER PEAK Cabernet Sauvignon Alexander Valley 1983 $7 (3/15/87) BB
87	GIRARD Cabernet Sauvignon Napa Valley Reserve 1983 Rel: $18 Cur: $25 (CA-3/89)
87	KEENAN Cabernet Sauvignon Napa Valley 1983 Rel: $11 Cur: $18 (CA-3/89)
87	KEENAN Cabernet Sauvignon Napa Valley 1983 Rel: $11 Cur: $18 (2/15/87)
87	KENWOOD Cabernet Sauvignon Sonoma Valley Artist Series 1983 Rel: $30 Cur: $38 (CA-3/89)
87	SHAFER Cabernet Sauvignon Napa Valley Stags Leap District 1983 Rel: $13 Cur: $13 (CA-3/89)
87	SILVER OAK Cabernet Sauvignon Napa Valley 1983 Rel: $20 Cur: $42 (11/30/87)
87	STERLING Cabernet Sauvignon Napa Valley Diamond Mountain Ranch 1983 Rel: $15 Cur: $21 (CA-3/89)
87	PHILIP TOGNI Cabernet Sauvignon Napa Valley 1983 Rel: $18 Cur: $50 (CA-3/89)
87	ZACA MESA Cabernet Sauvignon Santa Barbara County American Reserve 1983 $13 (3/31/87)
86	BALDINELLI Cabernet Sauvignon Shenandoah Valley 1983 $7.75 (11/30/88)
86	BALVERNE Cabernet Sauvignon Chalk Hill Laurel Vineyard 1983 $13 (2/15/89)
86	CLOS DU VAL Cabernet Sauvignon Napa Valley Stags Leap District 1983 Rel: $15 Cur: $18 (CA-3/89)
86	DE MOOR Cabernet Sauvignon Napa Valley 1983 Rel: $12 Cur: $16 (CA-3/89)
86	DOLAN Cabernet Sauvignon Mendocino 1983 $12 (2/29/88)
86	DOMINUS Napa Valley 1983 Rel: $43 Cur: $50 (4/15/89)
86	DURNEY Cabernet Sauvignon Carmel Valley Private Reserve 1983 $20 (4/30/91)
86	FREEMARK ABBEY Cabernet Sauvignon Napa Valley Bosché 1983 Rel: $18 Cur: $38 (CA-3/89)
86	GIRARD Cabernet Sauvignon Napa Valley Reserve 1983 Rel: $18 Cur: $25 (12/15/87)
86	HACIENDA Cabernet Sauvignon Sonoma Valley 1983 $11 (5/31/88)
86	HEITZ Cabernet Sauvignon Napa Valley Bella Oaks Vineyard 1983 Rel: $15 Cur: $27 (CA-3/89)
86	JOHNSON TURNBULL Cabernet Sauvignon Napa Valley 1983 Rel: $12.50 Cur: $18 (9/15/86)
86	KENWOOD Cabernet Sauvignon Sonoma Valley Jack London Vineyard 1983 Rel: $15 Cur: $21 (2/15/87)
86	LOUIS M. MARTINI Cabernet Sauvignon Sonoma Valley Monte Rosso 1983 Rel: $22 Cur: $22 (CA-3/89)
86	JOSEPH PHELPS Cabernet Sauvignon Napa Valley Eisele Vineyard 1983 Rel: $25 Cur: $36 (CA-3/89)
86	PRESTON Cabernet Sauvignon Dry Creek Valley 1983 Rel: $11 Cur: $15 (CA-3/89)
86	PRESTON Cabernet Sauvignon Dry Creek Valley 1983 Rel: $11 Cur: $15 (7/16/86)
86	SILVER OAK Cabernet Sauvignon Alexander Valley 1983 Rel: $20 Cur: $40 (CA-3/89)
86	STERLING Cabernet Sauvignon Napa Valley Reserve 1983 Rel: $22.50 Cur: $30 (6/15/87)
86	STRATFORD Cabernet Sauvignon California 1983 $8.50 (2/15/87)
86	TUDAL Cabernet Sauvignon Napa Valley 1983 Rel: $12.50 Cur: $25 (CA-3/89)
85	BERINGER Cabernet Sauvignon Napa Valley Chabot Vineyard 1983 Rel: $27 Cur: $33 (CA-3/89)
85	BURGESS Cabernet Sauvignon Napa Valley Vintage Selection 1983 Rel: $17 Cur: $21 (10/15/87)
85	CARMENET Sonoma Valley 1983 Rel: $18 Cur: $23 (CA-3/89)
85	DE LOACH Cabernet Sauvignon Dry Creek Valley 1983 $11 (9/30/86)
85	DEHLINGER Cabernet Sauvignon Russian River Valley 1983 $11 (6/15/87)
85	FRANCISCAN Cabernet Sauvignon Napa Valley Private Reserve 1983 Rel: $8.50 Cur: $15 (CA-3/89)
85	FROG'S LEAP Cabernet Sauvignon Napa Valley 1983 Rel: $10 Cur: $20 (5/16/86)
85	GRACE FAMILY Cabernet Sauvignon Napa Valley 1983 Rel: $38 Cur: $330 (6/15/87)
85	GROTH Cabernet Sauvignon Napa Valley 1983 Rel: $13 Cur: $22 (8/31/86)
85	HEITZ Cabernet Sauvignon Napa Valley 1983 Rel: $13 Cur: $18 (1/31/90) (JL)
85	WILLIAM HILL Cabernet Sauvignon Napa Valley Gold Label 1983 Rel: $18.25 Cur: $25 (CA-3/89)
85	KENWOOD Cabernet Sauvignon Sonoma Valley 1983 $10 (2/15/88)

UNITED STATES

CALIFORNIA/*CABERNET SAUVIGNON & BLENDS*

85 LAKESPRING Cabernet Sauvignon Napa Valley 1983 Rel: $11 Cur: $13 (CA-3/89)

85 JOSEPH PHELPS Cabernet Sauvignon Napa Valley Backus Vineyard 1983 Rel: $16.50 Cur: $28 (CA-3/89)

85 JOSEPH PHELPS Cabernet Sauvignon Napa Valley Backus Vineyard 1983 Rel: $16.50 Cur: $28 (6/15/87)

85 PINE RIDGE Cabernet Sauvignon Napa Valley Stags Leap District Pine Ridge Stags Leap Vineyard 1983 Rel: $20 Cur: $27 (CA-3/89)

84 CARMENET Sonoma Valley 1983 Rel: $18 Cur: $23 (9/30/86)

84 EBERLE Cabernet Sauvignon Paso Robles 1983 Rel: $10 Cur: $18 (CA-3/89)

84 HESS Cabernet Sauvignon Napa Valley 1983 Rel: $13 Cur: $18 (CA-3/89)

84 KONOCTI Cabernet Sauvignon Lake County 1983 $6 (6/15/87) BB

84 LA JOTA Cabernet Sauvignon Howell Mountain 1983 Rel: $15 Cur: $30 (CA-3/89)

84 MOUNT VEEDER Cabernet Sauvignon Napa Valley 1983 Rel: $14 Cur: $22 (CA-3/89)

84 PAT PAULSEN Cabernet Sauvignon Alexander Valley 1983 $11 (7/01/86)

84 JOSEPH PHELPS Cabernet Sauvignon Napa Valley 1983 Rel: $13 Cur: $14 (8/31/87)

84 PINE RIDGE Cabernet Sauvignon Napa Valley Rutherford Cuvée 1983 Rel: $14 Cur: $18 (CA-3/89)

84 RAYMOND Cabernet Sauvignon Napa Valley Private Reserve 1983 Rel: $18 Cur: $25 (CA-3/89)

84 RIDGE Cabernet Sauvignon Santa Cruz Mountains 1983 Rel: $12 Cur: $15 (CA-3/89)

84 SANTA CRUZ MOUNTAIN Cabernet Sauvignon Santa Cruz Mountains Bates Ranch 1983 Rel: $12 Cur: $12 (CA-3/89)

84 SHAFER Cabernet Sauvignon Napa Valley Stags Leap District Hillside Select 1983 Rel: $22 Cur: $24 (7/31/88)

84 SMITH-MADRONE Cabernet Sauvignon Napa Valley 1983 Rel: $12.50 Cur: $15 (CA-3/89)

84 TAFT STREET Cabernet Sauvignon Napa Valley 1983 $9 (1/31/87)

84 TREFETHEN Cabernet Sauvignon Napa Valley 1983 Rel: $11.75 Cur: $22 (CA-3/89)

83 BERINGER Cabernet Sauvignon Knights Valley 1983 $9 (4/15/87)

83 J. CAREY Cabernet Sauvignon Santa Ynez Valley La Cuesta Vineyard 1983 $9.50 (12/15/89)

83 CARNEROS CREEK Cabernet Sauvignon Napa Valley Reserve 1983 $13.50 (10/15/88)

83 FETZER Cabernet Sauvignon Lake County 1983 $5.50 (5/01/86)

83 LOUIS M. MARTINI Cabernet Sauvignon Sonoma Valley Monte Rosso Los Niños 1983 Rel: $25 Cur: $25 (CA-3/89)

83 ROBERT MONDAVI Cabernet Sauvignon Napa Valley Reserve 1983 Rel: $30 Cur: $36 (CA-3/89)

83 RIDGE Cabernet Sauvignon Howell Mountain 1983 $12 (3/16/86)

83 RUTHERFORD HILL Cabernet Sauvignon Napa Valley 1983 Rel: $12.50 Cur: $16 (CA-3/89)

83 RUTHERFORD HILL Cabernet Sauvignon Napa Valley 1983 Rel: $12.50 Cur: $16 (9/15/87)

83 RUTHERFORD RANCH Cabernet Sauvignon Napa Valley 1983 Rel: $10.25 Cur: $11 (12/31/87)

82 BEAULIEU Cabernet Sauvignon Napa Valley Georges de Latour Private Reserve 1983 Rel: $24 Cur: $28 (3/31/91) (JL)

82 BEAULIEU Cabernet Sauvignon Napa Valley Georges de Latour Private Reserve 1983 Rel: $24 Cur: $28 (CA-3/89)

82 BOEGER Cabernet Sauvignon El Dorado 1983 $10 (8/31/87)

82 CHRISTOPHE Cabernet Sauvignon Napa Valley Reserve 1983 $9.50 (3/31/88)

82 CONN CREEK Cabernet Sauvignon Napa Valley Barrel Select 1983 Rel: $13 Cur: $15 (CA-3/89)

82 HESS Cabernet Sauvignon Napa Valley 1983 Rel: $13 Cur: $18 (11/15/87)

82 INNISFREE Cabernet Sauvignon Napa Valley 1983 $9 (11/15/86)

82 IRON HORSE Cabernet Sauvignon Alexander Valley 1983 Rel: $12 Cur: $16 (CA-3/89)

82 KENDALL-JACKSON Cardinale California 1983 $9 (10/16/85)

82 CHARLES KRUG Cabernet Sauvignon Napa Valley Vintage Select 1983 Cur: $26 (CA-3/89)

82 SILVER OAK Cabernet Sauvignon Alexander Valley 1983 Rel: $20 Cur: $40 (11/30/87)

82 SILVER OAK Cabernet Sauvignon Napa Valley Bonny's Vineyard 1983 Rel: $40 Cur: $79 (CA-3/89)

82 STAG'S LEAP WINE CELLARS Cabernet Sauvignon Napa Valley Stags Leap District Stag's Leap Vineyards Cask 23 1983 Rel: $35 Cur: $73 (10/15/88)

82 STERLING Cabernet Sauvignon Napa Valley Reserve 1983 Rel: $22.50 Cur: $30 (CA-3/89)

81 JORDAN Cabernet Sauvignon Alexander Valley 1983 Rel: $18 Cur: $32 (7/15/87)

81 CHARLES KRUG Cabernet Sauvignon Napa Valley Vintage Select 1983 Rel: $20 Cur: $26 (6/30/90)

81 PINE RIDGE Cabernet Sauvignon Napa Valley Rutherford Cuvée 1983 Rel: $14 Cur: $18 (4/30/87)

81 V. SATTUI Cabernet Sauvignon Napa Valley Preston Vineyard 1983 Rel: $13.75 Cur: $20 (CA-3/89)

81 SPOTTSWOODE Cabernet Sauvignon Napa Valley 1983 Rel: $25 Cur: $75 (11/15/86)

81 STERLING Cabernet Sauvignon Napa Valley 1983 Rel: $12.50 Cur: $15 (2/15/87)

80 BEAULIEU Cabernet Sauvignon Napa Valley Rutherford 1983 Rel: $6.50 Cur: $12 (6/15/87)

80 CORBETT CANYON Cabernet Sauvignon Central Coast 1983 $7 (5/16/86) BB

80 ESTRELLA RIVER Cabernet Sauvignon Paso Robles 1983 $8 (4/15/88)

80 FREEMARK ABBEY Cabernet Sauvignon Napa Valley Bosché 1983 Rel: $18 Cur: $38 (6/15/87)

80 FROG'S LEAP Cabernet Sauvignon Napa Valley 1983 Rel: $10 Cur: $20 (CA-3/89)

80 GEYSER PEAK Réserve Alexandre Alexander Valley 1983 $15 (4/30/87)

80 HEITZ Cabernet Sauvignon Napa Valley 1983 Rel: $13 Cur: $18 (4/30/88)

80 INGLENOOK Cabernet Sauvignon Napa Valley 1983 $9.50 (3/15/88)

80 LAURA'S Cabernet Sauvignon Paso Robles 1983 $8.50 (12/31/87)

80 MAYACAMAS Cabernet Sauvignon Napa Valley 1983 Rel: $20 Cur: $26 (9/15/88)

80 ROBERT PEPI Cabernet Sauvignon Napa Valley Vine Hill Ranch 1983 Rel: $16 Cur: $21 (CA-3/89)

80 SANTA CRUZ MOUNTAIN Cabernet Sauvignon Santa Cruz Mountains Bates Ranch 1983 Rel: $12 Cur: $12 (6/15/89)

80 SPRING MOUNTAIN Cabernet Sauvignon Napa Valley 1983 Rel: $15 Cur: $19 (9/30/87)

80 STAGS' LEAP WINERY Cabernet Sauvignon Napa Valley Stags Leap District 1983 Rel: $12.75 Cur: $20 (CA-3/89)

80 VICHON Cabernet Sauvignon Napa Valley 1983 Rel: $10 Cur: $14 (CA-3/89)

79 BELVEDERE Cabernet Sauvignon Napa Valley York Creek Vineyard 1983 $12 (12/31/87)

79 DAVID BRUCE Cabernet Sauvignon California Vintner's Select 1983 $12.50 (9/30/86)

79 DANIEL Cabernet Sauvignon Napa Valley 1983 $20 (4/30/89)

79 EBERLE Cabernet Sauvignon Paso Robles 1983 Rel: $10 Cur: $18 (6/15/87)

79 EHLERS LANE Cabernet Sauvignon Napa Valley 1983 $12 (6/15/87)

79 FLORA SPRINGS Cabernet Sauvignon Napa Valley 1983 Rel: $13 Cur: $15 (12/15/86)

79 MOUNT EDEN Cabernet Sauvignon Santa Cruz Mountains 1983 Rel: $20 Cur: $21 (CA-3/89)

79 NEYERS Cabernet Sauvignon Napa Valley 1983 $12 (8/31/87)

79 PINE RIDGE Cabernet Sauvignon Napa Valley Stags Leap District Pine Ridge Stags Leap Vineyard 1983 Rel: $20 Cur: $27 (7/15/87)

79 SPRING MOUNTAIN Cabernet Sauvignon Napa Valley 1983 Rel: $15 Cur: $19 (CA-3/89)

78 CHALK HILL Cabernet Sauvignon Sonoma County 1983 $10 (11/15/86)

78 FELTA SPRINGS Cabernet Sauvignon Sonoma County 1983 $5 (3/31/87)

78 JORDAN Cabernet Sauvignon Alexander Valley 1983 Rel: $18 Cur: $32 (CA-3/89)

78 KISTLER Cabernet Sauvignon Napa Valley Veeder Hills Vineyard 1983 Rel: $13.50 Cur: $25 (CA-3/89)

78 LONG Cabernet Sauvignon Napa Valley 1983 Rel: $32 Cur: $40 (CA-3/89)

78 LYETH Red Alexander Valley 1983 Rel: $17 Cur: $23 (CA-3/89)

78 MONT ST. JOHN Cabernet Sauvignon Napa Valley 1983 $15 (7/31/89)

78 RIDGE Cabernet Sauvignon Santa Cruz Mountains Jimsomare 1983 $10 (11/30/86)

78 SMITH & HOOK Cabernet Sauvignon Monterey 1983 $13.50 (11/15/87)

77 BEAULIEU Cabernet Sauvignon Napa Valley Georges de Latour Private Reserve 1983 Rel: $24 Cur: $28 (5/31/88)

77 BUENA VISTA Cabernet Sauvignon Carneros 1983 $9.75 (6/15/87)

77 CAKEBREAD Cabernet Sauvignon Napa Valley 1983 Rel: $16 Cur: $25 (CA-3/89)

77 CHAPPELLET Cabernet Sauvignon Napa Valley 1983 Rel: $12 Cur: $16 (CA-3/89)

77 CLOS DU VAL Cabernet Sauvignon Napa Valley Stags Leap District 1983 Rel: $15 Cur: $18 (9/15/87)

77 CONCANNON Cabernet Sauvignon Livermore Valley 1983 $11.50 (6/15/87)

77 FIRESTONE Cabernet Sauvignon Santa Ynez Valley 1983 $9 (6/15/87)

77 GUNDLACH BUNDSCHU Cabernet Sauvignon Sonoma Valley Batto Ranch 1983 Rel: $14 Cur: $15 (CA-3/89)

77 HAYWOOD Cabernet Sauvignon Sonoma Valley 1983 Rel: $12.50 Cur: $20 (CA-3/89)

77 HAYWOOD Cabernet Sauvignon Sonoma Valley 1983 Rel: $12.50 Cur: $20 (5/15/87)

77 LAKESPRING Cabernet Sauvignon Napa Valley 1983 Rel: $11 Cur: $13 (12/15/86)

77 MONTICELLO Cabernet Sauvignon Napa Valley Jefferson Cuvée 1983 $10 (11/30/86)

77 RIVERSIDE FARM Cabernet Sauvignon North Coast 1983 $3.75 (9/15/86)

77 SEQUOIA GROVE Cabernet Sauvignon Napa-Alexander Valleys 1983 Rel: $12.50 Cur: $18 (CA-3/89)

77 STAG'S LEAP WINE CELLARS Cabernet Sauvignon Napa Valley Stags Leap District Stag's Leap Vineyards 1983 Rel: $18 Cur: $33 (11/15/86)

77 WHITEHALL LANE Cabernet Sauvignon Napa Valley 1983 $14 (11/30/86)

76 CECCHETTI SEBASTIANI Cabernet Sauvignon Sonoma County 1983 $12.50 (9/30/86)

76 MCDOWELL Cabernet Sauvignon McDowell Valley 1983 $11 (4/15/88)

76 JOSEPH PHELPS Cabernet Sauvignon Napa Valley Eisele Vineyard 1983 Rel: $25 Cur: $36 (8/31/87)

76 RAVENSWOOD Cabernet Sauvignon Sonoma County 1983 Rel: $9.50 Cur: $19 (CA-3/89)

75 ADELAIDA Cabernet Sauvignon Paso Robles 1983 $12 (12/15/89)

75 CAIN Cabernet Sauvignon Napa Valley 1983 $14 (8/31/87)

75 CUVAISON Cabernet Sauvignon Napa Valley 1983 Rel: $12 Cur: $15 (CA-3/89)

75 FRANCISCAN Cabernet Sauvignon Napa Valley Oakville Estate 1983 $9 (4/30/87)

75 MATANZAS CREEK Cabernet Sauvignon Sonoma Valley 1983 $14 (7/16/86)

75 MOUNT VEEDER Cabernet Sauvignon Napa Valley 1983 Rel: $14 Cur: $22 (10/31/87)

75 J. PEDRONCELLI Cabernet Sauvignon Dry Creek Valley 1983 $6.50 (8/31/87)

75 RIVER OAKS Cabernet Sauvignon Sonoma County 1983 $6 (12/15/86)

74 ALMADEN Cabernet Sauvignon Monterey County Vintage Classic Selection 1983 $5 (10/15/87)

74 BELLEROSE Cuvée Bellerose Sonoma County 1983 $12 (1/31/87)

74 CLOS DU BOIS Cabernet Sauvignon Alexander Valley Briarcrest Vineyard 1983 Rel: $12 Cur: $28 (CA-3/89)

74 DRY CREEK David S. Stare Vintner's Selection Dry Creek Valley 1983 $15 (12/31/86)

74 FIELD STONE Cabernet Sauvignon Alexander Valley 1983 $11 (10/15/88)

74 GUNDLACH BUNDSCHU Cabernet Sauvignon Sonoma Valley Batto Ranch 1983 $14 (2/15/88)

74 SILVER OAK Cabernet Sauvignon Napa Valley 1983 Rel: $20 Cur: $42 (CA-3/89)

74 STERLING Cabernet Sauvignon Napa Valley Diamond Mountain Ranch 1983 Rel: $15 Cur: $21 (11/30/86)

73 FISHER Cabernet Sauvignon Sonoma County 1983 $12.50 (6/15/87)

73 GUNDLACH BUNDSCHU Cabernet Sauvignon Sonoma Valley Rhinefarm Vineyards 1983 Rel: $9 Cur: $14 (3/01/89)

73 RIDGE Cabernet Sauvignon Napa County York Creek 1983 Rel: $12 Cur: $16 (CA-3/89)

73 ROMBAUER Cabernet Sauvignon Napa Valley 1983 Rel: $13.50 Cur: $19 (CA-3/89)

73 ROMBAUER Cabernet Sauvignon Napa Valley 1983 Rel: $13.50 Cur: $19 (9/15/87)

73 STAG'S LEAP WINE CELLARS Cabernet Sauvignon Napa Valley Stags Leap District Stag's Leap Vineyards 1983 Rel: $18 Cur: $33 (CA-3/89)

72 DELICATO Cabernet Sauvignon Carneros Napa Valley 1983 $10 (6/15/87)

72 LONG Cabernet Sauvignon Napa Valley 1983 Rel: $32 Cur: $40 (8/31/87)

72 VILLA MT. EDEN Cabernet Sauvignon Napa Valley 1983 Rel: $10 Cur: $10 (CA-3/89)

71 GIRARD Cabernet Sauvignon Napa Valley 1983 Rel: $12 Cur: $13 (12/15/86)

71 SBARBORO Cabernet Sauvignon Sonoma County 1983 $10 (11/15/87)

70 CLOS DU BOIS Marlstone Vineyard Alexander Valley 1983 Rel: $20 Cur: $25 (CA-3/89)

70 FETZER Cabernet Sauvignon California Barrel Select 1983 $8 (6/15/87)

69 KENDALL-JACKSON Cabernet Sauvignon Lake County 1983 $7 (5/01/86)

69 LOUIS M. MARTINI Cabernet Sauvignon North Coast 1983 $7 (3/31/87)

69 SEGHESIO Cabernet Sauvignon Northern Sonoma 1983 $6.75 (7/15/88)

68 FREEMARK ABBEY Cabernet Sauvignon Napa Valley 1983 Rel: $12 Cur: $12 (2/15/88)

68 GRAND CRU Cabernet Sauvignon Sonoma County 1983 $8.50 (11/16/85)

67 JEKEL Cabernet Sauvignon Monterey 1983 $8 (2/15/89)

67 MIRASSOU Cabernet Sauvignon Napa Valley Fifth Generation Harvest Reserve 1983 $12 (12/15/86)

67 M.G. VALLEJO Cabernet Sauvignon California 1983 $4.50 (8/31/87)

65 ESTRELLA RIVER Cabernet Sauvignon Paso Robles Founders Epic Collection 1983 $12 (12/15/89)

65 CK MONDAVI Cabernet Sauvignon Napa Valley 1983 $4.50 (10/15/87)

62 CARNEROS CREEK Cabernet Sauvignon Napa Valley 1983 $10.50 (8/31/87)

61 KISTLER Cabernet Sauvignon Napa Valley Veeder Hills Vineyard 1983 Rel: $13.50 Cur: $25 (1/31/87)

Key to Symbols

The scores reported here are the results of blind tastings conducted by our panel of senior editors. Wines that carry the initials below are results of individual tastings.

THE WINE SPECTATOR 100-POINT SCALE ***95-100***—Classic, a great wine; ***90-94***—Outstanding, superior character and style; ***80-89***—Good to very good, a wine with special qualities; ***70-79***—Average, drinkable wine that may have minor flaws; ***60-69***—Below average, drinkable but not recommended; ***50-59***—Poor, undrinkable, not recommended. "+"—With a score indicates a range; used primarily with barrel tastings to indicate a preliminary score.

SPECIAL DESIGNATIONS SS—Spectator Selection, CS—Cellar Selection, BB—Best Buy.

TASTER'S INITIALS (JG)—Jim Gordon, (HS)—Harvey Steiman, (JL)—James Laube, (JS)—James Suckling, (TM)—Thomas Matthews, (TR)—Terry Robards, (BT)—Barrel Tasting (these wines were tasted blind from barrel samples), (CA-date)—*California's Great Cabernets* by James Laube, (CH-date)—*California's Great Chardonnays* by James Laube, (VP-date)—*Vintage Port* by James Suckling.

DATE TASTED Dates in parentheses represent the issue in which the rating was published.

59   LAUREL GLEN Cabernet Sauvignon Sonoma Mountain 1983 Rel: $11 Cur: $12 (CA-3/89)

1982

97   DUNN Cabernet Sauvignon Napa Valley 1982 Rel: $13 Cur: $95 (11/01/85) SS
96   SILVER OAK Cabernet Sauvignon Napa Valley 1982 Rel: $19 Cur: $53 (2/15/87) CS
95   BELVEDERE Cabernet Sauvignon Alexander Valley Robert Young Vineyards 1982 $12 (12/01/85) SS
95   DUNN Cabernet Sauvignon Howell Mountain 1982 Rel: $15 Cur: $160 (CA-3/89)
95   ROBERT MONDAVI Cabernet Sauvignon Napa Valley Reserve 1982 Rel: $30 Cur: $39 (2/15/87)
95   RAVENSWOOD Cabernet Sauvignon Sonoma County 1982 Rel: $11 Cur: $18 (4/01/86) SS
94   BERINGER Cabernet Sauvignon Napa Valley Private Reserve 1982 Rel: $19 Cur: $43 (4/15/87)
94   CAYMUS Cabernet Sauvignon Napa Valley 1982 Rel: $14 Cur: $43 (4/01/86)
94   CAYMUS Cabernet Sauvignon Napa Valley 1982 Rel: $14 Cur: $43 (2/01/85)
94   DUNN Cabernet Sauvignon Napa Valley 1982 Rel: $13 Cur: $95 (CA-3/89)
94   HEITZ Cabernet Sauvignon Napa Valley Martha's Vineyard 1982 Rel: $30 Cur: $65 (4/15/87) CS
94   WILLIAM HILL Cabernet Sauvignon Napa Valley Gold Label 1982 Rel: $18 Cur: $32 (6/16/86) SS
94   LAKESPRING Cabernet Sauvignon Napa Valley Vintage Selection 1982 Rel: $14 Cur: $24 (12/15/86)
94   STERLING Cabernet Sauvignon Napa Valley Diamond Mountain Ranch 1982 Rel: $15 Cur: $37 (11/16/85) CS
93   BEAULIEU Cabernet Sauvignon Napa Valley Georges de Latour Private Reserve 1982 Rel: $24 Cur: $39 (3/15/87) CS
93   CARMENET Sonoma Valley 1982 Rel: $16 Cur: $31 (10/16/85)
93   FREEMARK ABBEY Cabernet Sauvignon Napa Valley Bosché 1982 Rel: $15 Cur: $41 (5/16/86) CS
93   INGLENOOK Cabernet Sauvignon Napa Valley Reserve Cask 1982 Rel: $22 Cur: $28 (2/15/87)
93   OPUS ONE Napa Valley 1982 Rel: $50 Cur: $83 (5/01/86) CS
93   STELTZNER Cabernet Sauvignon Napa Valley Stags Leap District 1982 Rel: $14 Cur: $26 (6/30/87) (JL)
92   ALEXANDER VALLEY Cabernet Sauvignon Alexander Valley 1982 Rel: $10 Cur: $16 (11/01/84) SS
92   BERINGER Cabernet Sauvignon Napa Valley Private Reserve 1982 Rel: $19 Cur: $43 (CA-3/89)
92   CAYMUS Cabernet Sauvignon Napa Valley Special Selection 1982 Rel: $35 Cur: $100 (CA-3/89)
92   CHATEAU MONTELENA Cabernet Sauvignon Napa Valley 1982 Rel: $16 Cur: $41 (CA-3/89)
92   DIAMOND CREEK Cabernet Sauvignon Napa Valley Volcanic Hill 1982 Rel: $20 Cur: $68 (12/16/84) CS
92   GRGICH HILLS Cabernet Sauvignon Napa Valley 1982 Rel: $17 Cur: $29 (4/15/87)
92   MARKHAM Cabernet Sauvignon Napa Valley 1982 Rel: $13 Cur: $18 (11/15/87)
92   ROBERT MONDAVI Cabernet Sauvignon Napa Valley Reserve 1982 Rel: $30 Cur: $39 (2/01/85)
92   MONTICELLO Cabernet Sauvignon Napa Valley Corley Reserve 1982 Rel: $15 Cur: $32 (12/16/85)
92   JOSEPH PHELPS Insignia Napa Valley 1982 Rel: $25 Cur: $35 (10/30/87)
92   ST. CLEMENT Cabernet Sauvignon Napa Valley 1982 Rel: $13.50 Cur: $20 (3/16/85) CS
91   CLOS DU BOIS Cabernet Sauvignon Alexander Valley Briarcrest Vineyard 1982 Rel: $12 Cur: $35 (7/31/87)
91   CLOS DU VAL Cabernet Sauvignon Napa Valley Stags Leap District 1982 Rel: $13.25 Cur: $24 (7/01/86)
91   DIAMOND CREEK Cabernet Sauvignon Napa Valley Gravelly Meadow 1982 Rel: $20 Cur: $58 (12/16/84)
91   HEITZ Cabernet Sauvignon Napa Valley Bella Oaks Vineyard 1982 Rel: $16 Cur: $31 (4/30/87)
91   INGLENOOK Cabernet Sauvignon Napa Valley Reserve Cask 1982 Rel: $22 Cur: $28 (CA-3/89)
91   KEENAN Cabernet Sauvignon Napa Valley 1982 Rel: $10 Cur: $24 (1/01/86)
91   MONTICELLO Cabernet Sauvignon Napa Valley Jefferson Cuvée 1982 $10 (2/01/86)
91   PINE RIDGE Cabernet Sauvignon Napa Valley Stags Leap District Pine Ridge Stags Leap Vineyard 1982 Rel: $20 Cur: $34 (10/31/86) CS
91   RAYMOND Cabernet Sauvignon Napa Valley 1982 Rel: $12 Cur: $16 (11/15/86)
91   ROMBAUER Cabernet Sauvignon Napa Valley 1982 Rel: $12 Cur: $33 (2/16/86)
91   ST. CLEMENT Cabernet Sauvignon Napa Valley 1982 Rel: $13.50 Cur: $20 (CA-3/89)
91   STELTZNER Cabernet Sauvignon Napa Valley Stags Leap District 1982 Rel: $14 Cur: $26 (9/01/85) CS
90   ALEXANDER VALLEY Cabernet Sauvignon Alexander Valley 1982 Rel: $10 Cur: $16 (CA-3/89)
90   BEAULIEU Cabernet Sauvignon Napa Valley Georges de Latour Private Reserve 1982 Rel: $24 Cur: $39 (3/31/91) (JL)
90   BERINGER Cabernet Sauvignon Knights Valley 1982 $9 (4/15/87)
90   CAYMUS Cabernet Sauvignon Napa Valley 1982 Rel: $14 Cur: $43 (CA-3/89)
90   CAYMUS Cabernet Sauvignon Napa Valley Special Selection 1982 Rel: $35 Cur: $100 (11/30/87)
90   CLOS DU VAL Reserve Napa Valley Stags Leap District 1982 Rel: $28 Cur: $37 (CA-3/89)
90   CUVAISON Cabernet Sauvignon Napa Valley 1982 Rel: $11 Cur: $18 (10/15/87)
90   DUCKHORN Cabernet Sauvignon Napa Valley 1982 Rel: $15 Cur: $53 (CA-3/89)
90   WILLIAM HILL Cabernet Sauvignon Napa Valley Gold Label 1982 Rel: $18 Cur: $32 (CA-3/89)
90   MARKHAM Cabernet Sauvignon Napa Valley 1982 Rel: $13 Cur: $18 (CA-3/89)
90   ROBERT MONDAVI Cabernet Sauvignon Napa Valley 1982 Rel: $11 Cur: $20 (7/01/85)
90   MONTICELLO Cabernet Sauvignon Napa Valley Corley Reserve 1982 Rel: $15 Cur: $32 (CA-3/89)
90   OPUS ONE Napa Valley 1982 Rel: $50 Cur: $83 (CA-3/89)
90   PINE RIDGE Cabernet Sauvignon Napa Valley Rutherford Cuvée 1982 Rel: $13 Cur: $24 (CA-3/89)
90   PINE RIDGE Cabernet Sauvignon Napa Valley Stags Leap District Pine Ridge Stags Leap Vineyard 1982 Rel: $20 Cur: $34 (CA-3/89)
90   SHAFER Cabernet Sauvignon Napa Valley Stags Leap District 1982 Rel: $13 Cur: $18 (6/16/85)
90   SILVER OAK Cabernet Sauvignon Alexander Valley 1982 Rel: $19 Cur: $65 (CA-3/89)
90   SILVER OAK Cabernet Sauvignon Alexander Valley 1982 Rel: $19 Cur: $65 (2/15/87)
90   SIMI Cabernet Sauvignon Sonoma County 1982 Rel: $12 Cur: $15 (11/15/86)
90   SIMI Cabernet Sauvignon Sonoma-Napa Counties Reserve 1982 Rel: $20 Cur: $26 (4/15/89)
90   SPOTTSWOODE Cabernet Sauvignon Napa Valley 1982 Rel: $18 Cur: $110 (CA-3/89)

90   STELTZNER Cabernet Sauvignon Napa Valley Stags Leap District 1982 Rel: $14 Cur: $26 (CA-3/89)
89   BERINGER Cabernet Sauvignon Napa Valley Chabot Vineyard 1982 Rel: $25 Cur: $40 (CA-3/89)
89   COLONY Cabernet Sauvignon Sonoma County 1982 $7 (3/16/86) BB
89   DIAMOND CREEK Cabernet Sauvignon Napa Valley Gravelly Meadow 1982 Rel: $20 Cur: $58 (CA-3/89)
89   DIAMOND CREEK Cabernet Sauvignon Napa Valley Volcanic Hill 1982 Rel: $20 Cur: $68 (CA-3/89)
89   GIRARD Cabernet Sauvignon Napa Valley 1982 Rel: $12.50 Cur: $30 (2/16/86)
89   GRACE FAMILY Cabernet Sauvignon Napa Valley 1982 Rel: $31 Cur: $249 (CA-3/89)
89   GUNDLACH BUNDSCHU Cabernet Sauvignon Sonoma Valley Batto Ranch 1982 $12 (6/16/85)
89   KENWOOD Cabernet Sauvignon Sonoma Valley Artist Series 1982 Rel: $25 Cur: $42 (11/01/85)
89   MCDOWELL Cabernet Sauvignon McDowell Valley 1982 $11 (12/15/86)
89   NIEBAUM-COPPOLA Rubicon Napa Valley 1982 Rel: $40 Cur: $40 (CA-3/89)
89   SHAFER Cabernet Sauvignon Napa Valley Stags Leap District Reserve 1982 Rel: $18 Cur: $25 (CA-3/89)
89   VICHON Cabernet Sauvignon Napa Valley 1982 Rel: $13 Cur: $19 (7/16/86)
88   BALVERNE Cabernet Sauvignon Sonoma County 1982 $12 (8/31/88)
88   BEAULIEU Cabernet Sauvignon Napa Valley Georges de Latour Private Reserve 1982 Rel: $24 Cur: $39 (CA-3/89)
88   BUEHLER Cabernet Sauvignon Napa Valley 1982 Rel: $12 Cur: $30 (CA-3/89)
88   BURGESS Cabernet Sauvignon Napa Valley Vintage Selection 1982 Rel: $16 Cur: $23 (CA-3/89)
88   CLOS DU BOIS Cabernet Sauvignon Dry Creek Valley Proprietor's Reserve 1982 $19 (9/15/87)
88   CLOS DU VAL Cabernet Sauvignon Napa Valley Stags Leap District 1982 Rel: $13.25 Cur: $24 (CA-3/89)
88   CLOS DU VAL Cabernet Sauvignon Napa Valley Stags Leap District 1982 Rel: $13.25 Cur: $24 (2/01/85)
88   CLOS DU VAL Cabernet Sauvignon Napa Valley Gran Val 1982 $7.50 (4/16/84)
88   CLOS DU VAL Reserve Napa Valley Stags Leap District 1982 Rel: $28 Cur: $37 (11/15/87)
88   DE MOOR Cabernet Sauvignon Napa Valley Owners Select 1982 Rel: $12 Cur: $19 (CA-3/89)
88   FISHER Cabernet Sauvignon Sonoma County 1982 $12.50 (11/01/85)
88   FREEMARK ABBEY Cabernet Sauvignon Napa Valley Bosché 1982 Rel: $15 Cur: $41 (CA-3/89)
88   GROTH Cabernet Sauvignon Napa Valley 1982 Rel: $13 Cur: $35 (CA-3/89)
88   HEITZ Cabernet Sauvignon Napa Valley Martha's Vineyard 1982 Rel: $30 Cur: $65 (CA-3/89)
88   KEENAN Cabernet Sauvignon Napa Valley 1982 Rel: $10 Cur: $24 (CA-3/89)
88   LAKESPRING Cabernet Sauvignon Napa Valley Vintage Selection 1982 Rel: $14 Cur: $24 (CA-3/89)
88   MATANZAS CREEK Cabernet Sauvignon Sonoma Valley 1982 $14 (8/01/85)
88   NIEBAUM-COPPOLA Rubicon Napa Valley 1982 Rel: $40 Cur: $40 (10/15/89)
88   ROBERT PEPI Cabernet Sauvignon Napa Valley Vine Hill Ranch 1982 Rel: $14 Cur: $17 (CA-3/89)
88   RAYMOND Cabernet Sauvignon Napa Valley Private Reserve 1982 Rel: $16 Cur: $27 (6/15/87)
88   RIDGE Cabernet Sauvignon Howell Mountain 1982 $12 (6/01/85)
88   ROUND HILL Cabernet Sauvignon Napa Valley 1982 $9 (5/16/86)
88   RUTHERFORD HILL Cabernet Sauvignon Napa Valley 1982 Rel: $12.50 Cur: $23 (11/15/86)
88   SHAFER Cabernet Sauvignon Napa Valley Stags Leap District 1982 Rel: $13 Cur: $18 (CA-3/89)
88   SILVER OAK Cabernet Sauvignon Napa Valley 1982 Rel: $19 Cur: $53 (CA-3/89)
88   SILVERADO Cabernet Sauvignon Napa Valley Stags Leap District 1982 Rel: $11 Cur: $22 (CA-3/89)
88   SIMI Cabernet Sauvignon Sonoma-Napa Counties Reserve 1982 Rel: $20 Cur: $26 (CA-3/89)
87   BUENA VISTA Cabernet Sauvignon Carneros Private Reserve 1982 Rel: $18 Cur: $30 (2/15/87)
87   CARMENET Sonoma Valley 1982 Rel: $16 Cur: $31 (CA-3/89)
87   DIAMOND CREEK Cabernet Sauvignon Napa Valley Red Rock Terrace 1982 Rel: $20 Cur: $66 (CA-3/89)
87   EBERLE Cabernet Sauvignon Paso Robles 1982 Rel: $10 Cur: $24 (9/30/86)
87   ESTANCIA Cabernet Sauvignon Alexander Valley 1982 $6 (4/15/87) BB
87   FROG'S LEAP Cabernet Sauvignon Napa Valley 1982 Rel: $9 Cur: $25 (CA-3/89)
87   GIRARD Cabernet Sauvignon Napa Valley 1982 Rel: $12.50 Cur: $30 (CA-3/89)
87   GRGICH HILLS Cabernet Sauvignon Napa Valley 1982 Rel: $17 Cur: $29 (CA-3/89)
87   KENWOOD Cabernet Sauvignon Sonoma Valley Artist Series 1982 Rel: $25 Cur: $42 (CA-3/89)
87   MENDOCINO ESTATE Cabernet Sauvignon Mendocino 1982 $4.25 (10/15/86) BB
87   PRESTON Cabernet Sauvignon Dry Creek Valley 1982 Rel: $11 Cur: $18 (CA-3/89)
87   SPRING MOUNTAIN Cabernet Sauvignon Napa Valley 1982 Rel: $15 Cur: $15 (12/15/86)
86   CAKEBREAD Cabernet Sauvignon Napa Valley 1982 Rel: $16 Cur: $28 (CA-3/89)
86   CLOS DU BOIS Marlstone Vineyard Alexander Valley 1982 Rel: $16 Cur: $26 (9/30/86)
86   DE MOOR Cabernet Sauvignon Napa Valley 1982 Rel: $12 Cur: $18 (CA-3/89)
86   DIAMOND CREEK Cabernet Sauvignon Napa Valley Red Rock Terrace 1982 Rel: $20 Cur: $66 (1/01/85)
86   DUCKHORN Cabernet Sauvignon Napa Valley 1982 Rel: $15 Cur: $53 (5/16/85)
86   HACIENDA Cabernet Sauvignon Sonoma Valley Selected Reserve 1982 $18 (3/31/87)
86   JOHNSON TURNBULL Cabernet Sauvignon Napa Valley 1982 Rel: $12.50 Cur: $20 (10/16/85)
86   KISTLER Cabernet Sauvignon Napa Valley Veeder Hills Vineyard 1982 Rel: $12 Cur: $26 (CA-3/89)
86   LYETH Red Alexander Valley 1982 Rel: $16 Cur: $35 (6/16/86)
86   PINE RIDGE Cabernet Sauvignon Napa Valley Rutherford Cuvée 1982 Rel: $13 Cur: $24 (10/01/85)
86   QUAIL RIDGE Cabernet Sauvignon Napa Valley 1982 $13 (9/16/85)
86   SPOTTSWOODE Cabernet Sauvignon Napa Valley 1982 Rel: $18 Cur: $110 (11/01/85)
86   WHITEHALL LANE Cabernet Sauvignon Napa Valley 1982 $12 (2/16/85)
85   BUENA VISTA Cabernet Sauvignon Carneros 1982 $11 (9/16/85)
85   BUENA VISTA Cabernet Sauvignon Carneros Private Reserve 1982 Rel: $18 Cur: $30 (CA-3/89)
85   CHRISTOPHE Cabernet Sauvignon California 1982 $4.50 (12/16/85) BB
85   CONN CREEK Cabernet Sauvignon Napa Valley Barrel Select 1982 Rel: $12 Cur: $20 (CA-3/89)
85   CONN CREEK Cabernet Sauvignon Napa Valley Collins Vineyard Proprietor's Special Selection 1982 Cur: $70 (CA-3/89)
85   ESTRELLA RIVER Cabernet Sauvignon Paso Robles 1982 $10 (6/15/87)
85   GLEN ELLEN Cabernet Sauvignon Sonoma Valley Glen Ellen Estate 1982 $9.75 (2/01/85)

UNITED STATES
CALIFORNIA/CABERNET SAUVIGNON & BLENDS

85 HEITZ Cabernet Sauvignon Napa Valley Bella Oaks Vineyard 1982 Rel: $16 Cur: $31 (CA-3/89)
85 LAUREL GLEN Cabernet Sauvignon Sonoma Mountain 1982 Rel: $12.50 Cur: $35 (CA-3/89)
85 LYETH Red Alexander Valley 1982 Rel: $16 Cur: $35 (CA-3/89)
85 LOUIS M. MARTINI Cabernet Sauvignon Sonoma Valley Monte Rosso 1982 Rel: $22 Cur: $22 (CA-3/89)
85 PAT PAULSEN Cabernet Sauvignon Alexander Valley 1982 $10 (3/01/85) BB
85 ROBERT PECOTA Cabernet Sauvignon Napa Valley 1982 Rel: $12 Cur: $20 (CA-3/89)
85 JOSEPH PHELPS Cabernet Sauvignon Napa Valley Eisele Vineyard 1982 Rel: $30 Cur: $39 (CA-3/89)
85 JOSEPH PHELPS Insignia Napa Valley 1982 Rel: $25 Cur: $35 (CA-3/89)
85 RAYMOND Cabernet Sauvignon Napa Valley Private Reserve 1982 Rel: $16 Cur: $27 (CA-3/89)
84 ALEXANDER VALLEY Cabernet Sauvignon Alexander Valley 1982 Rel: $10 Cur: $16 (2/01/85)
84 DIAMOND CREEK Cabernet Sauvignon Napa Valley Gravelly Meadow Special Selection 1982 Rel: $20 Cur: $40 (CA-3/89)
84 FAR NIENTE Cabernet Sauvignon Napa Valley 1982 Rel: $25 Cur: $35 (9/16/85)
84 FREEMARK ABBEY Cabernet Sauvignon Napa Valley 1982 Rel: $12 Cur: $12 (2/15/87)
84 GROTH Cabernet Sauvignon Napa Valley 1982 Rel: $13 Cur: $35 (11/01/84)
84 JORDAN Cabernet Sauvignon Alexander Valley 1982 Rel: $18 Cur: $39 (2/01/86)
84 JORDAN Cabernet Sauvignon Alexander Valley 1982 Rel: $18 Cur: $39 (2/01/85)
84 LA JOTA Cabernet Sauvignon Howell Mountain 1982 Rel: $13.50 Cur: $28 (CA-3/89)
84 ROBERT PEPI Cabernet Sauvignon Napa Valley Vine Hill Ranch 1982 Rel: $14 Cur: $17 (3/31/87)
84 JOSEPH PHELPS Cabernet Sauvignon Napa Valley Eisele Vineyard 1982 Rel: $30 Cur: $39 (12/15/86)
84 PRESTON Cabernet Sauvignon Dry Creek Valley 1982 Rel: $11 Cur: $18 (7/01/85)
84 RAVENSWOOD Cabernet Sauvignon Sonoma County 1982 Rel: $11 Cur: $18 (CA-3/89)
84 RUTHERFORD RANCH Cabernet Sauvignon Napa Valley 1982 Rel: $9 Cur: $9 (6/15/87)
84 VILLA MT. EDEN Cabernet Sauvignon Napa Valley Reserve 1982 Rel: $16.70 Cur: $17 (CA-3/89)
83 BRUTOCAO Cabernet Sauvignon Mendocino 1982 $9 (11/30/88)
83 IRON HORSE Cabernet Sauvignon Alexander Valley 1982 Rel: $12 Cur: $18 (CA-3/89)
83 LAUREL GLEN Cabernet Sauvignon Sonoma Mountain 1982 Rel: $12.50 Cur: $35 (6/01/86)
83 MILANO Cabernet Sauvignon Mendocino County Sanel Valley Vineyard 1982 $12.50 (12/15/87)
83 MONTEREY PENINSULA Cabernet Sauvignon Monterey Doctors' Reserve Lot II 1982 $14 (6/15/87)
83 ROMBAUER Cabernet Sauvignon Napa Valley 1982 Rel: $12 Cur: $33 (CA-3/89)
83 RUTHERFORD HILL Cabernet Sauvignon Napa Valley 1982 Rel: $12.50 Cur: $23 (CA-3/89)
83 SEQUOIA GROVE Cabernet Sauvignon Napa-Alexander Valleys 1982 Rel: $12 Cur: $20 (12/16/85)
83 TOYON Cabernet Sauvignon Alexander Valley 1982 $10 (11/15/86)
82 CUVAISON Cabernet Sauvignon Napa Valley 1982 Rel: $11 Cur: $18 (CA-3/89)
82 DOMAINE LAURIER Cabernet Sauvignon Sonoma County Green Valley 1982 $12 (2/16/85)
82 FAR NIENTE Cabernet Sauvignon Napa Valley 1982 Rel: $25 Cur: $35 (CA-3/89)
82 E.&J. GALLO Cabernet Sauvignon Northern Sonoma Reserve 1982 $6 (5/31/91) BB
82 JOHNSON TURNBULL Cabernet Sauvignon Napa Valley 1982 Rel: $12.50 Cur: $20 (CA-3/89)
82 LOUIS M. MARTINI Cabernet Sauvignon Sonoma Valley Monte Rosso Los Niños 1982 Rel: $25 Cur: $25 (CA-3/89)
82 MIRASSOU Cabernet Sauvignon Napa Valley Harvest Reserve 1982 $12 (4/16/86)
82 MIRASSOU Cabernet Sauvignon North Coast 1982 $7 (10/16/85) BB
82 ROBERT MONDAVI Cabernet Sauvignon Napa Valley Reserve 1982 Rel: $30 Cur: $39 (CA-3/89)
82 MONT ST. JOHN Cabernet Sauvignon Napa Valley 1982 $15 (3/15/89)
82 JOSEPH PHELPS Cabernet Sauvignon Napa Valley 1982 Rel: $12 Cur: $17 (12/15/86)
82 RIVER OAKS Cabernet Sauvignon Sonoma County 1982 $6 (4/01/85) BB
82 SEQUOIA GROVE Cabernet Sauvignon Napa Valley Estate 1982 Rel: $14 Cur: $22 (CA-3/89)
82 SILVERADO Cabernet Sauvignon Napa Valley Stags Leap District 1982 Rel: $11 Cur: $22 (9/30/86)
82 STERLING Cabernet Sauvignon Napa Valley Diamond Mountain Ranch 1982 Rel: $15 Cur: $37 (CA-3/89)
81 BEAULIEU Cabernet Sauvignon Napa Valley Rutherford 1982 Rel: $8.50 Cur: $14 (4/16/86)
81 BURGESS Cabernet Sauvignon Napa Valley Vintage Selection 1982 Rel: $16 Cur: $23 (10/15/86)
81 DRY CREEK Cabernet Sauvignon Sonoma County 1982 $9.50 (2/01/85)
81 MILL CREEK Cabernet Sauvignon Dry Creek Valley 1982 $9.50 (12/31/87)
80 BELVEDERE Cabernet Sauvignon Lake County Discovery Series 1982 $4 (4/01/85) BB
80 CHAPPELLET Cabernet Sauvignon Napa Valley 1982 Rel: $9.25 Cur: $16 (CA-3/89)
80 DIAMOND CREEK Cabernet Sauvignon Napa Valley Red Rock Terrace Special Selection 1982 Rel: $20 Cur: $35 (CA-3/89)
80 HEITZ Cabernet Sauvignon Napa Valley 1982 Rel: $13.50 Cur: $21 (1/31/90) (JL)
80 INNISFREE Cabernet Sauvignon Napa Valley 1982 $9 (12/16/85)
80 STONEGATE Cabernet Sauvignon Napa Valley 1982 Rel: $12 Cur: $18 (CA-3/89)
80 RODNEY STRONG Cabernet Sauvignon Alexander Valley Alexander's Crown Vineyard 1982 $12 (10/31/88)
80 STEPHEN ZELLERBACH Cabernet Sauvignon Alexander Valley 1982 $6 (11/30/86)
79 CHATEAU MONTELENA Cabernet Sauvignon Napa Valley 1982 Rel: $16 Cur: $41 (10/15/86)
79 CLOS DU BOIS Marlstone Vineyard Alexander Valley 1982 Rel: $16 Cur: $26 (CA-3/89)
79 DIAMOND CREEK Cabernet Sauvignon Napa Valley Volcanic Hill Special Selection 1982 Rel: $20 Cur: $35 (CA-3/89)

Key to Symbols

The scores reported here are the results of blind tastings conducted by our panel of senior editors. Wines that carry the initials below are results of individual tastings.

THE WINE SPECTATOR 100-POINT SCALE *95-100*—Classic, a great wine; *90-94*—Outstanding, superior character and style; *80-89*—Good to very good, a wine with special qualities; *70-79*—Average, drinkable wine that may have minor flaws; *60-69*—Below average, drinkable but not recommended; *50-59*—Poor, undrinkable, not recommended. "+"—With a score indicates a range; used primarily with barrel tastings to indicate a preliminary score.

SPECIAL DESIGNATIONS SS—Spectator Selection, CS—Cellar Selection, BB—Best Buy.

TASTER'S INITIALS (JG)—Jim Gordon, (HS)—Harvey Steiman, (JL)—James Laube, (JS)—James Suckling, (TM)—Thomas Matthews, (TR)—Terry Robards, (BT)—Barrel Tasting (these wines were tasted blind from barrel samples), (CA-date)—*California's Great Cabernets* by James Laube, (CH-date)—*California's Great Chardonnays* by James Laube, (VP-date)—*Vintage Port* by James Suckling.

DATE TASTED Dates in parentheses represent the issue in which the rating was published.

79 HAYWOOD Cabernet Sauvignon Sonoma Valley 1982 Rel: $11 Cur: $20 (CA-3/89)
79 CHARLES KRUG Cabernet Sauvignon Napa Valley 1982 $7 (10/31/87)
79 LLORDS & ELWOOD Cabernet Sauvignon Napa Valley 1982 $8 (12/15/87)
79 SIMI Cabernet Sauvignon Sonoma-Napa Counties Reserve 1982 Rel: $20 Cur: $26 (2/01/86)
79 SMITH & HOOK Cabernet Sauvignon Napa County 1982 $17 (6/15/87)
79 SMITH-MADRONE Cabernet Sauvignon Napa Valley 1982 Rel: $12.50 Cur: $15 (CA-3/89)
79 VICHON Cabernet Sauvignon Napa Valley Stags Leap District Fay Vineyard 1982 Rel: $14 Cur: $23 (CA-3/89)
78 CAIN Cabernet Sauvignon Napa Valley 1982 $11 (9/30/86)
78 FETZER Cabernet Sauvignon Lake County 1982 $5.50 (5/16/84)
78 FIELD STONE Cabernet Sauvignon Alexander Valley Turkey Hill Vineyard 1982 $12 (3/16/86)
78 FLORA SPRINGS Cabernet Sauvignon Napa Valley 1982 Rel: $9 Cur: $9 (10/15/86)
78 KONOCTI Cabernet Sauvignon Lake County 1982 $7 (11/15/86)
78 V. SATTUI Cabernet Sauvignon Napa Valley Preston Vineyard Reserve 1982 Rel: $22.50 Cur: $30 (CA-3/89)
78 SEQUOIA GROVE Cabernet Sauvignon Napa-Alexander Valleys 1982 Rel: $12 Cur: $20 (CA-3/89)
78 SILVER OAK Cabernet Sauvignon Napa Valley Bonny's Vineyard 1982 Rel: $35 Cur: $59 (CA-3/89)
78 VICHON Cabernet Sauvignon Napa Valley Volker Eisele Vineyard 1982 Rel: $16 Cur: $19 (CA-3/89)
77 FOX MOUNTAIN Cabernet Sauvignon Russian River Valley Reserve 1982 $18 (12/31/87)
77 MAYACAMAS Cabernet Sauvignon Napa Valley 1982 Rel: $20 Cur: $27 (CA-3/89)
77 MAYACAMAS Cabernet Sauvignon Napa Valley 1982 Rel: $20 Cur: $27 (3/31/87)
77 SEGHESIO Cabernet Sauvignon Northern Sonoma 1982 $5 (4/30/87)
76 HANZELL Cabernet Sauvignon Sonoma Valley 1982 Rel: $20 Cur: $30 (3/31/87)
76 VICHON Cabernet Sauvignon Napa Valley 1982 Rel: $13 Cur: $19 (CA-3/89)
75 RIDGE Cabernet Sauvignon Santa Cruz Mountains Monte Bello 1982 Rel: $18 Cur: $26 (CA-3/89)
75 RIDGE Cabernet Sauvignon Santa Cruz Mountains Monte Bello 1982 Rel: $18 Cur: $26 (11/30/86)
75 SEBASTIANI Cabernet Sauvignon Sonoma Valley Eagle Vineyards 1982 $26.50 (9/15/86)
75 STAG'S LEAP WINE CELLARS Cabernet Sauvignon Napa Valley Stags Leap District Stag's Leap Vineyards 1982 Rel: $16.50 Cur: $31 (CA-3/89)
75 STERLING Cabernet Sauvignon Napa Valley Reserve 1982 Rel: $22.50 Cur: $37 (CA-3/89)
74 HEITZ Cabernet Sauvignon Napa Valley 1982 Rel: $13.50 Cur: $21 (6/15/87)
74 MONTEREY PENINSULA Cabernet Sauvignon Monterey County 1982 $11 (3/31/87)
74 SEBASTIANI Cabernet Sauvignon Sonoma Valley Reserve 1982 $11 (12/31/87)
73 DEHLINGER Cabernet Sauvignon Russian River Valley 1982 $11 (8/31/86)
73 FETZER Cabernet Sauvignon Mendocino Barrel Select 1982 $7 (2/01/85)
73 JORDAN Cabernet Sauvignon Alexander Valley 1982 Rel: $18 Cur: $39 (CA-3/89)
73 J. PEDRONCELLI Cabernet Sauvignon Dry Creek Valley Reserve 1982 $13 (10/15/89)
73 RIDGE Cabernet Sauvignon Napa County York Creek 1982 Rel: $12 Cur: $16 (CA-3/89)
72 BELVEDERE Cabernet Sauvignon Napa Valley York Creek Vineyard 1982 $12 (9/15/86)
72 EBERLE Cabernet Sauvignon Paso Robles 1982 Rel: $10 Cur: $24 (CA-3/89)
72 NAPA RIDGE Cabernet Sauvignon North Coast 1982 $5.75 (3/31/87)
72 SANTA CRUZ MOUNTAIN Cabernet Sauvignon Santa Cruz Mountains Bates Ranch 1982 Rel: $12 Cur: $15 (CA-3/89)
72 TUDAL Cabernet Sauvignon Napa Valley 1982 Rel: $12 Cur: $38 (CA-3/89)
71 BELVEDERE Cabernet Sauvignon Napa Valley Discovery Series 1982 $4 (2/16/86)
71 CARNEROS CREEK Cabernet Sauvignon Napa Valley 1982 $11 (2/16/86)
71 EBERLE Cabernet Sauvignon Paso Robles Reserve 1982 Rel: $25 Cur: $30 (CA-3/89)
71 GUNDLACH BUNDSCHU Cabernet Sauvignon Sonoma Valley Rhinefarm Vineyards Reserve 1982 Rel: $20 Cur: $21 (9/15/87)
71 JEKEL Cabernet Sauvignon Monterey 1982 $11 (1/31/87)
71 STAGS' LEAP WINERY Cabernet Sauvignon Napa Valley Stags Leap District 1982 Rel: $12 Cur: $20 (CA-3/89)
71 VILLA MT. EDEN Cabernet Sauvignon Napa Valley 1982 Rel: $9 Cur: $11 (4/15/88)
70 CAKEBREAD Cabernet Sauvignon Napa Valley 1982 Rel: $16 Cur: $28 (7/16/86)
70 CARNEROS CREEK Cabernet Sauvignon Napa Valley Fay Vineyard 1982 $13.50 (5/15/87)
70 GRAND CRU Cabernet Sauvignon Alexander Valley Collector's Reserve 1982 $15 (9/30/87)
70 GUNDLACH BUNDSCHU Cabernet Sauvignon Sonoma Valley Batto Ranch 1982 Rel: $12 Cur: $18 (CA-3/89)
70 MOUNT EDEN Cabernet Sauvignon Santa Cruz Mountains 1982 Rel: $18 Cur: $20 (CA-3/89)
70 VILLA MT. EDEN Cabernet Sauvignon Napa Valley 1982 Rel: $9 Cur: $11 (CA-3/89)
69 JEKEL Cabernet Sauvignon Monterey Home Vineyard Private Reserve 1982 Rel: $20 Cur: $20 (2/01/86)
69 STAG'S LEAP WINE CELLARS Cabernet Sauvignon Napa Valley Stags Leap District Stag's Leap Vineyards 1982 Rel: $16.50 Cur: $31 (10/01/85)
69 RODNEY STRONG Cabernet Sauvignon Sonoma County 1982 $7 (12/15/86)
68 GEYSER PEAK Cabernet Sauvignon Alexander Valley 1982 $7 (9/15/86)
68 MILL CREEK Cabernet Sauvignon Dry Creek Valley 1982 $9.50 (6/15/88)
68 MOUNT VEEDER Cabernet Sauvignon Napa Valley 1982 Rel: $12.50 Cur: $17 (CA-3/89)
66 CHALK HILL Cabernet Sauvignon Sonoma County 1982 $9 (11/01/85)
66 CLOS DU BOIS Cabernet Sauvignon Alexander Valley Briarcrest Vineyard 1982 Rel: $12 Cur: $35 (CA-3/89)
66 NEWTON Cabernet Sauvignon Napa Valley 1982 Rel: $12.50 Cur: $21 (CA-3/89)
66 SILVER OAK Cabernet Sauvignon Napa Valley Bonny's Vineyard 1982 Rel: $35 Cur: $59 (9/15/87)
66 SPRING MOUNTAIN Cabernet Sauvignon Napa Valley 1982 Rel: $15 Cur: $15 (CA-3/89)
66 ROBERT STEMMLER Cabernet Sauvignon Sonoma County 1982 $15 (4/01/85)
66 STERLING Cabernet Sauvignon Napa Valley 1982 Rel: $12.50 Cur: $15 (5/16/86)
66 ZD Cabernet Sauvignon California 1982 $12 (7/16/86)
65 GUNDLACH BUNDSCHU Cabernet Sauvignon Sonoma Valley Rhinefarm Vineyards 1982 Rel: $9 Cur: $13 (3/01/89)
64 BEAULIEU Cabernet Sauvignon Napa Valley Beau Tour 1982 $7.50 (10/15/86)
64 MOUNT VEEDER Cabernet Sauvignon Napa Valley 1982 Rel: $12.50 Cur: $17 (6/15/87)
63 HACIENDA Cabernet Sauvignon Sonoma Valley 1982 $11 (9/01/85)
63 TREFETHEN Cabernet Sauvignon Napa Valley 1982 Rel: $11 Cur: $45 (3/16/86)
58 TREFETHEN Cabernet Sauvignon Napa Valley 1982 Rel: $11 Cur: $45 (CA-3/89)

1981

96 CLOS DU BOIS Marlstone Vineyard Alexander Valley 1981 Rel: $15 Cur: $32 (3/16/86)
95 DE MOOR Cabernet Sauvignon Napa Valley Napa Cellars 1981 Rel: $12 Cur: $25 (4/16/86)
94 CAYMUS Cabernet Sauvignon Napa Valley Special Selection 1981 Rel: $35 Cur: $115 (11/30/86)
94 ROBERT MONDAVI Cabernet Sauvignon Napa Valley Reserve 1981 Rel: $30 Cur: $34 (2/16/86) CS
94 OPUS ONE Napa Valley 1981 Rel: $50 Cur: $91 (5/16/85) CS

93 BERINGER Cabernet Sauvignon Napa Valley Private Reserve 1981 Rel: $18 Cur: $30 (4/15/87)
93 BERINGER Cabernet Sauvignon Napa Valley Private Reserve Lemmon-Chabot Vineyard 1981 Rel: $23 Cur: $42 (4/15/87)
93 CAYMUS Cabernet Sauvignon Napa Valley 1981 Rel: $14 Cur: $55 (2/01/86)
93 CAYMUS Cabernet Sauvignon Napa Valley 1981 Rel: $14 Cur: $55 (2/01/85)
93 CAYMUS Cabernet Sauvignon Napa Valley Special Selection 1981 Rel: $35 Cur: $115 (CA-3/89)
93 DUNN Cabernet Sauvignon Howell Mountain 1981 Rel: $14 Cur: $157 (12/16/84)
93 INGLENOOK Cabernet Sauvignon Napa Valley Reserve Cask 1981 Rel: $15.50 Cur: $22 (CA-3/89)
93 LAUREL GLEN Cabernet Sauvignon Sonoma Mountain 1981 Rel: $12.50 Cur: $42 (2/16/85) SS
93 ROBERT PEPI Cabernet Sauvignon Napa Valley Vine Hill Ranch 1981 Rel: $14 Cur: $20 (1/01/86) CS
93 PINE RIDGE Cabernet Sauvignon Napa Valley Rutherford Cuvée 1981 Rel: $13 Cur: $28 (12/16/84)
92 BERINGER Cabernet Sauvignon Napa Valley Private Reserve 1981 Rel: $18 Cur: $30 (6/01/86) CS
92 DIAMOND CREEK Cabernet Sauvignon Napa Valley Volcanic Hill 1981 Rel: $20 Cur: $49 (CA-3/89)
92 INGLENOOK Cabernet Sauvignon Napa Valley Reserve Cask 1981 Rel: $15.50 Cur: $22 (10/15/86)
92 IRON HORSE Cabernet Sauvignon Alexander Valley 1981 Rel: $12 Cur: $16 (12/16/84)
92 LAUREL GLEN Cabernet Sauvignon Sonoma Mountain 1981 Rel: $12.50 Cur: $42 (CA-3/89)
92 JOSEPH PHELPS Insignia Napa Valley 1981 Rel: $25 Cur: $47 (CA-3/89)
92 PINE RIDGE Cabernet Sauvignon Napa Valley Stags Leap District Pine Ridge Stags Leap Vineyard 1981 Rel: $20 Cur: $50 (CA-3/89)
92 RAYMOND Cabernet Sauvignon Napa Valley Private Reserve 1981 Rel: $16 Cur: $35 (8/31/86)
92 RIDGE Cabernet Sauvignon Santa Cruz Mountains Monte Bello 1981 Rel: $25 Cur: $65 (CA-3/89)
92 SILVER OAK Cabernet Sauvignon Alexander Valley 1981 Rel: $19 Cur: $65 (9/30/86)
91 BERINGER Cabernet Sauvignon Napa Valley Private Reserve 1981 Rel: $18 Cur: $30 (CA-3/89)
91 CLOS DU BOIS Cabernet Sauvignon Alexander Valley 1981 $9 (3/01/86)
91 DIAMOND CREEK Cabernet Sauvignon Napa Valley Red Rock Terrace 1981 Rel: $20 Cur: $55 (CA-3/89)
91 HEITZ Cabernet Sauvignon Napa Valley Martha's Vineyard 1981 Rel: $30 Cur: $61 (4/16/86) CS
91 MAYACAMAS Cabernet Sauvignon Napa Valley 1981 Rel: $18 Cur: $27 (CA-3/89)
91 NEWTON Cabernet Sauvignon Napa Valley 1981 Rel: $12.50 Cur: $21 (12/16/84)
91 JOSEPH PHELPS Cabernet Sauvignon Napa Valley Backus Vineyard 1981 Rel: $15 Cur: $50 (CA-3/89)
91 SEBASTIANI Cabernet Sauvignon Sonoma Valley Eagle Vineyards 1981 $25 (8/01/85)
91 SILVERADO Cabernet Sauvignon Napa Valley Stags Leap District 1981 Rel: $11 Cur: $25 (12/16/84)
91 STAG'S LEAP WINE CELLARS Cabernet Sauvignon Napa Valley Stags Leap District Stag's Leap Vineyards 1981 Rel: $15 Cur: $35 (CA-3/89)
91 STELTZNER Cabernet Sauvignon Napa Valley Stags Leap District 1981 Rel: $14 Cur: $33 (6/30/87) (JL)
90 BUENA VISTA Cabernet Sauvignon Carneros 1981 $11 (12/16/84)
90 DIAMOND CREEK Cabernet Sauvignon Napa Valley Three Vineyard Blend 1981 Rel: $20 Cur: $100 (CA-3/89)
90 DUNN Cabernet Sauvignon Howell Mountain 1981 Rel: $14 Cur: $157 (CA-3/89)
90 GUNDLACH BUNDSCHU Cabernet Sauvignon Sonoma Valley Rhinefarm Vineyards Reserve 1981 Rel: $20 Cur: $26 (3/01/89)
90 HEITZ Cabernet Sauvignon Napa Valley Bella Oaks Vineyard 1981 Rel: $16 Cur: $50 (CA-3/89)
90 JORDAN Cabernet Sauvignon Alexander Valley 1981 Rel: $17 Cur: $44 (5/01/85) CS
90 CHARLES KRUG Cabernet Sauvignon Napa Valley Vintage Select 1981 Rel: $20 Cur: $24 (9/30/90)
90 LOUIS M. MARTINI Cabernet Sauvignon Sonoma Valley Monte Rosso 1981 Rel: $25 Cur: $25 (12/15/86)
90 ROBERT MONDAVI Cabernet Sauvignon Napa Valley 1981 Rel: $11 Cur: $27 (12/16/84)
90 JOSEPH PHELPS Cabernet Sauvignon Napa Valley Backus Vineyard 1981 Rel: $15 Cur: $50 (4/16/85)
90 JOSEPH PHELPS Insignia Napa Valley 1981 Rel: $25 Cur: $47 (10/30/87)
90 RUTHERFORD HILL Cabernet Sauvignon Napa Valley 1981 Rel: $11.50 Cur: $19 (6/01/86)
90 SILVERADO Cabernet Sauvignon Napa Valley Stags Leap District 1981 Rel: $11 Cur: $25 (CA-3/89)
90 SMITH & HOOK Cabernet Sauvignon Monterey County 1981 $13.50 (12/16/84)
90 STAG'S LEAP WINE CELLARS Cabernet Sauvignon Napa Valley Stags Leap District Stag's Leap Vineyards 1981 Rel: $15 Cur: $35 (9/16/84) CS
89 ALEXANDER VALLEY Cabernet Sauvignon Alexander Valley 1981 Rel: $9 Cur: $18 (2/01/86)
89 ALEXANDER VALLEY Cabernet Sauvignon Alexander Valley 1981 Rel: $9 Cur: $18 (2/01/85)
89 BUENA VISTA Cabernet Sauvignon Carneros 1981 $11 (2/16/85)
89 CLOS DU VAL Cabernet Sauvignon Napa Valley Stags Leap District 1981 Rel: $12.50 Cur: $18 (2/01/86)
89 CLOS DU VAL Cabernet Sauvignon Napa Valley Stags Leap District 1981 Rel: $12.50 Cur: $18 (2/01/85)
89 CUVAISON Cabernet Sauvignon Napa Valley 1981 Rel: $11 Cur: $18 (11/30/86)
89 DIAMOND CREEK Cabernet Sauvignon Napa Valley Gravelly Meadow 1981 Rel: $20 Cur: $58 (CA-3/89)
89 FIRESTONE Cabernet Sauvignon Santa Ynez Valley 1981 $8 (3/01/85)
89 FREEMARK ABBEY Cabernet Sauvignon Napa Valley Bosché 1981 Rel: $14 Cur: $36 (7/01/85)
89 GIRARD Cabernet Sauvignon Napa Valley 1981 Rel: $12.50 Cur: $20 (8/01/85)
89 HEITZ Cabernet Sauvignon Napa Valley Martha's Vineyard 1981 Rel: $30 Cur: $61 (CA-3/89)
89 JORDAN Cabernet Sauvignon Alexander Valley 1981 Rel: $17 Cur: $44 (2/01/86)
89 JORDAN Cabernet Sauvignon Alexander Valley 1981 Rel: $17 Cur: $44 (2/01/85)
89 KENWOOD Cabernet Sauvignon Sonoma Valley Artist Series 1981 Rel: $25 Cur: $55 (CA-3/89)
89 KENWOOD Cabernet Sauvignon Sonoma Valley Artist Series 1981 Rel: $25 Cur: $55 (9/16/84) SS
89 ROBERT MONDAVI Cabernet Sauvignon Napa Valley Reserve 1981 Rel: $30 Cur: $34 (2/01/85)
89 NIEBAUM-COPPOLA Rubicon Napa Valley 1981 Rel: $35 Cur: $35 (11/15/88)
89 JOSEPH PHELPS Cabernet Sauvignon Napa Valley Eisele Vineyard 1981 Rel: $30 Cur: $44 (CA-3/89)
89 RIDGE Cabernet Sauvignon Napa County York Creek 1981 Rel: $12 Cur: $20 (12/16/84)
89 RIDGE Cabernet Sauvignon Santa Cruz Mountains Monte Bello 1981 Rel: $25 Cur: $65 (8/01/85)
89 ST. CLEMENT Cabernet Sauvignon Napa Valley 1981 Rel: $12.50 Cur: $24 (6/01/84) SS
89 STELTZNER Cabernet Sauvignon Napa Valley Stags Leap District 1981 Rel: $14 Cur: $33 (CA-3/89)
89 VICHON Cabernet Sauvignon Napa Valley 1981 Rel: $13 Cur: $22 (12/16/84)
88 ADELAIDA Cabernet Sauvignon Paso Robles 1981 $7.25 (3/01/84)
88 BUENA VISTA Cabernet Sauvignon Carneros Private Reserve Special Selection 1981 Rel: $18 Cur: $30 (7/01/86)
88 BURGESS Cabernet Sauvignon Napa Valley Vintage Selection 1981 Rel: $16 Cur: $25 (CA-3/89)
88 CAKEBREAD Cabernet Sauvignon Napa Valley 1981 Rel: $16 Cur: $30 (CA-3/89)
88 CAYMUS Cabernet Sauvignon Napa Valley 1981 Rel: $14 Cur: $55 (CA-3/89)
88 CLOS DU BOIS Cabernet Sauvignon Alexander Valley Briarcrest Vineyard 1981 Rel: $12 Cur: $37 (CA-3/89)
88 ESTRELLA RIVER Cabernet Sauvignon Paso Robles 1981 $9 (5/01/85)
88 GRACE FAMILY Cabernet Sauvignon Napa Valley 1981 Rel: $28 Cur: $300 (CA-3/89)
88 GUNDLACH BUNDSCHU Cabernet Sauvignon Sonoma Valley Batto Ranch 1981 Rel: $10 Cur: $18 (CA-3/89)
88 GUNDLACH BUNDSCHU Cabernet Sauvignon Sonoma Valley Rhinefarm Vineyards Reserve 1981 Rel: $20 Cur: $26 (11/30/86)
88 WILLIAM HILL Cabernet Sauvignon Napa Valley Gold Label 1981 Rel: $16.25 Cur: $28 (12/15/84)
88 OPUS ONE Napa Valley 1981 Rel: $50 Cur: $91 (CA-3/89)
88 PINE RIDGE Cabernet Sauvignon Napa Valley Rutherford Cuvée 1981 Rel: $13 Cur: $28 (CA-3/89)
88 PINE RIDGE Cabernet Sauvignon Napa Valley Stags Leap District Stags Leap Cuvée 1981 Rel: $20 Cur: $50 (2/01/85)
88 ROMBAUER Cabernet Sauvignon Napa Valley 1981 Rel: $12 Cur: $24 (12/16/84)
88 SANTA CRUZ MOUNTAIN Cabernet Sauvignon Santa Cruz Mountains Bates Ranch 1981 Rel: $12 Cur: $20 (3/01/85)
88 STERLING Cabernet Sauvignon Napa Valley 1981 Rel: $12 Cur: $16 (8/01/85)
88 TREFETHEN Cabernet Sauvignon Napa Valley 1981 Rel: $11 Cur: $36 (12/16/84) SS
88 TUDAL Cabernet Sauvignon Napa Valley 1981 Rel: $12 Cur: $40 (CA-3/89)
87 ALEXANDER VALLEY Cabernet Sauvignon Alexander Valley 1981 Rel: $9 Cur: $18 (CA-3/89)
87 BEAULIEU Cabernet Sauvignon Napa Valley Georges de Latour Private Reserve 1981 Rel: $24 Cur: $36 (CA-3/89)
87 BERINGER Cabernet Sauvignon Napa Valley Chabot Vineyard 1981 Rel: $23 Cur: $42 (CA-3/89)
87 BURGESS Cabernet Sauvignon Napa Valley Vintage Selection 1981 Rel: $16 Cur: $25 (9/16/85)
87 DEHLINGER Cabernet Sauvignon Sonoma County 1981 $9 (5/16/85)
87 DUCKHORN Cabernet Sauvignon Napa Valley 1981 Rel: $15 Cur: $68 (CA-3/89)
87 EBERLE Cabernet Sauvignon Paso Robles 1981 Rel: $10 Cur: $24 (4/16/85)
87 JOHNSON TURNBULL Cabernet Sauvignon Napa Valley 1981 Rel: $12 Cur: $26 (CA-3/89)
87 KISTLER Cabernet Sauvignon Napa Valley Veeder Hills-Veeder Peak 1981 Rel: $12 Cur: $32 (CA-3/89)
87 LAKESPRING Cabernet Sauvignon Napa Valley 1981 Rel: $11 Cur: $20 (9/16/84)
87 NIEBAUM-COPPOLA Rubicon Napa Valley 1981 Rel: $35 Cur: $35 (CA-3/89)
87 RAYMOND Cabernet Sauvignon Napa Valley Private Reserve 1981 Rel: $16 Cur: $35 (CA-3/89)
87 RIDGE Cabernet Sauvignon Santa Cruz Mountains Jimsomare-Monte Bello 1981 $12 (1/01/85)
87 SEQUOIA GROVE Cabernet Sauvignon Alexander Valley 1981 Rel: $12 Cur: $25 (12/16/84)
87 SEQUOIA GROVE Cabernet Sauvignon Napa Valley 1981 Rel: $12 Cur: $25 (3/01/84)
87 TREFETHEN Cabernet Sauvignon Napa Valley 1981 Rel: $11 Cur: $36 (CA-3/89)
86 BEAULIEU Cabernet Sauvignon Napa Valley Georges de Latour Private Reserve 1981 Rel: $24 Cur: $36 (3/31/91) (JL)
86 BERINGER Cabernet Sauvignon Knights Valley 1981 $9 (10/01/85)
86 BUENA VISTA Cabernet Sauvignon Carneros Private Reserve Special Selection 1981 Rel: $18 Cur: $30 (CA-3/89)
86 CONN CREEK Cabernet Sauvignon Napa Valley Collins Vineyard Proprietor's Special Selection 1981 Cur: $70 (CA-3/89)
86 DE MOOR Cabernet Sauvignon Napa Valley Napa Cellars 1981 Rel: $12 Cur: $25 (CA-3/89)
86 FETZER Cabernet Sauvignon Mendocino County 1981 $7 (12/16/84)
86 FREEMARK ABBEY Cabernet Sauvignon Napa Valley Bosché 1981 Rel: $14 Cur: $36 (CA-3/89)
86 GIRARD Cabernet Sauvignon Napa Valley 1981 Rel: $12.50 Cur: $20 (CA-3/89)
86 GRGICH HILLS Cabernet Sauvignon Napa Valley 1981 Rel: $17 Cur: $35 (CA-3/89)
86 HEITZ Cabernet Sauvignon Napa Valley 1981 Rel: $13.25 Cur: $25 (1/31/90) (JL)
86 LAKESPRING Cabernet Sauvignon Napa Valley 1981 Rel: $11 Cur: $20 (CA-3/89)
86 MARKHAM Cabernet Sauvignon Napa Valley 1981 Rel: $13 Cur: $20 (CA-3/89)
86 MOUNT EDEN Cabernet Sauvignon Santa Cruz Mountains 1981 Rel: $18 Cur: $25 (CA-3/89)
86 ROBERT PEPI Cabernet Sauvignon Napa Valley Vine Hill Ranch 1981 Rel: $14 Cur: $20 (CA-3/89)
86 JOSEPH PHELPS Cabernet Sauvignon Napa Valley 1981 Rel: $11 Cur: $24 (9/01/85)
86 ROUND HILL Cabernet Sauvignon Napa Valley 1981 $9 (3/16/85)
86 SILVER OAK Cabernet Sauvignon Alexander Valley 1981 Rel: $19 Cur: $65 (CA-3/89)
86 SIMI Cabernet Sauvignon Alexander Valley Reserve 1981 Rel: $25 Cur: $26 (12/15/88)
86 STAGS' LEAP WINERY Cabernet Sauvignon Napa Valley Stags Leap District 1981 Rel: $11 Cur: $25 (3/01/85)
86 RODNEY STRONG Cabernet Sauvignon Sonoma Valley 1981 $7.50 (12/16/84)
85 BUEHLER Cabernet Sauvignon Napa Valley 1981 Rel: $11 Cur: $20 (CA-3/89)
85 CLOS DU BOIS Marlstone Vineyard Alexander Valley 1981 Rel: $15 Cur: $32 (CA-3/89)
85 CONN CREEK Cabernet Sauvignon Napa Valley 1981 Rel: $14 Cur: $18 (CA-3/89)
85 CONN CREEK Cabernet Sauvignon Napa Valley 1981 Rel: $14 Cur: $18 (12/16/84)
85 EBERLE Cabernet Sauvignon Paso Robles 1981 Rel: $10 Cur: $24 (CA-3/89)
85 FISHER Cabernet Sauvignon Sonoma County 1981 $12 (12/01/84)
85 GUNDLACH BUNDSCHU Cabernet Sauvignon Sonoma Valley 1981 $7 (5/16/85)
85 HAYWOOD Cabernet Sauvignon Sonoma Valley 1981 Rel: $11 Cur: $20 (CA-3/89)
85 WILLIAM HILL Cabernet Sauvignon Napa Valley Gold Label 1981 Rel: $16.25 Cur: $28 (CA-3/89)
85 LOUIS M. MARTINI Cabernet Sauvignon Sonoma Valley Monte Rosso Los Niños 1981 Rel: $25 Cur: $25 (CA-3/89)
85 RAYMOND Cabernet Sauvignon Napa Valley 1981 Rel: $11 Cur: $17 (CA-3/89)
85 RUTHERFORD HILL Cabernet Sauvignon Napa Valley 1981 Rel: $11.50 Cur: $19 (CA-3/89)
85 ST. CLEMENT Cabernet Sauvignon Napa Valley 1981 Rel: $12.50 Cur: $24 (CA-3/89)

UNITED STATES

CALIFORNIA/*CABERNET SAUVIGNON & BLENDS*

85 STAGS' LEAP WINERY Cabernet Sauvignon Napa Valley Stags Leap District 1981 Rel: $11 Cur: $25 (CA-3/89)
85 STERLING Cabernet Sauvignon Napa Valley Reserve 1981 Rel: $22.50 Cur: $30 (CA-3/89)
85 VILLA MT. EDEN Cabernet Sauvignon Napa Valley Reserve 1981 Rel: $16.70 Cur: $20 (CA-3/89)
84 GUNDLACH BUNDSCHU Cabernet Sauvignon Sonoma Valley 1981 $7 (3/01/89)
84 HAWK CREST Cabernet Sauvignon Mendocino 1981 $5 (3/16/85) BB
84 HAYWOOD Cabernet Sauvignon Sonoma Valley 1981 Rel: $11 Cur: $20 (9/01/84)
84 JORDAN Cabernet Sauvignon Alexander Valley 1981 Rel: $17 Cur: $44 (CA-3/89)
84 KEENAN Cabernet Sauvignon Napa Valley 1981 Rel: $13.50 Cur: $22 (CA-3/89)
84 MATANZAS CREEK Cabernet Sauvignon Sonoma Valley 1981 $16 (4/16/84)
84 SEQUOIA GROVE Cabernet Sauvignon Alexander Valley 1981 Rel: $12 Cur: $25 (CA-3/89)
83 CHALK HILL Cabernet Sauvignon Sonoma County 1981 $8 (4/01/84)
83 DEVLIN Cabernet Sauvignon Sonoma County 1981 $6 (8/01/85)
83 GEYSER PEAK Cabernet Sauvignon Sonoma County 1981 $7 (6/16/85)
83 LOUIS M. MARTINI Cabernet Sauvignon North Coast 1981 $6.50 (3/01/85)
83 ROBERT MONDAVI Cabernet Sauvignon Napa Valley Reserve 1981 Rel: $30 Cur: $34 (CA-3/89)
83 NEWTON Cabernet Sauvignon Napa Valley 1981 Rel: $12.50 Cur: $21 (CA-3/89)
83 RIDGE Cabernet Sauvignon Santa Barbara County Tepusquet Vineyard 1981 $9 (4/16/84)
82 CLOS DU VAL Cabernet Sauvignon Napa Valley Stags Leap District 1981 Rel: $12.50 Cur: $18 (CA-3/89)
82 CONCANNON Cabernet Sauvignon Livermore Valley 1981 $12 (12/16/84)
82 DURNEY Cabernet Sauvignon Carmel Valley 1981 $12.50 (9/01/84)
82 FLORA SPRINGS Cabernet Sauvignon Napa Valley 1981 Rel: $12 Cur: $12 (12/16/84)
82 CHARLES KRUG Cabernet Sauvignon Napa Valley Vintage Select 1981 Cur: $24 (CA-3/89)
82 ROMBAUER Cabernet Sauvignon Napa Valley 1981 Rel: $12 Cur: $24 (CA-3/89)
82 STAG'S LEAP WINE CELLARS Cabernet Sauvignon Napa Valley 1981 $15 (12/16/84)
81 BEAULIEU Cabernet Sauvignon Napa Valley Rutherford 1981 Rel: $9 Cur: $20 (5/16/85)
81 CHAPPELLET Cabernet Sauvignon Napa Valley 1981 Rel: $11 Cur: $23 (12/16/84)
81 FOPPIANO Cabernet Sauvignon Russian River Valley 1981 $7.75 (4/16/85)
81 MOUNT EDEN Cabernet Sauvignon Santa Cruz Mountains 1981 Rel: $18 Cur: $25 (11/01/84)
81 MOUNT VEEDER Cabernet Sauvignon Napa Valley 1981 Rel: $12.50 Cur: $25 (7/16/86)
81 VILLA MT. EDEN Cabernet Sauvignon Napa Valley Reserve 1981 Rel: $16.70 Cur: $20 (2/01/86)
80 ALMADEN Cabernet Sauvignon Monterey County 1981 $5.85 (7/01/84)
80 BEAULIEU Cabernet Sauvignon Napa Valley Georges de Latour Private Reserve 1981 Rel: $24 Cur: $36 (8/31/86)
80 JEAN CLAUDE BOISSET Cabernet Sauvignon Napa Valley 1981 $9 (5/01/85)
80 CAPARONE Cabernet Sauvignon Santa Maria Valley Tepusquet Vineyard 1981 $10 (3/16/84)
80 CHATEAU MONTELENA Cabernet Sauvignon Napa Valley 1981 Rel: $16 Cur: $37 (CA-3/89)
80 DE LOACH Cabernet Sauvignon Dry Creek Valley 1981 $11 (4/01/85)
80 EBERLE Cabernet Sauvignon Paso Robles Reserve 1981 Rel: $25 Cur: $35 (CA-3/89)
80 J. PEDRONCELLI Cabernet Sauvignon Dry Creek Valley 1981 $6 (12/01/84) BB
80 SEQUOIA GROVE Cabernet Sauvignon Napa Valley 1981 Rel: $12 Cur: $25 (CA-3/89)
80 VICHON Cabernet Sauvignon Napa Valley 1981 Rel: $13 Cur: $22 (CA-3/89)
79 CHAPPELLET Cabernet Sauvignon Napa Valley 1981 Rel: $11 Cur: $23 (CA-3/89)
79 FOX MOUNTAIN Cabernet Sauvignon Russian River Valley Reserve 1981 $16 (12/15/86)
79 FREEMARK ABBEY Cabernet Sauvignon Napa Valley 1981 Rel: $10.50 Cur: $11 (10/01/85)
79 HEITZ Cabernet Sauvignon Napa Valley Bella Oaks Vineyard 1981 Rel: $16 Cur: $50 (4/16/86)
79 IRON HORSE Cabernet Sauvignon Alexander Valley 1981 Rel: $12 Cur: $16 (CA-3/89)
79 SANTA CRUZ MOUNTAIN Cabernet Sauvignon Santa Cruz Mountains Bates Ranch 1981 Rel: $12 Cur: $20 (CA-3/89)
79 SILVER OAK Cabernet Sauvignon Napa Valley 1981 Rel: $19 Cur: $62 (CA-3/89)
79 SIMI Cabernet Sauvignon Alexander Valley 1981 Rel: $11 Cur: $11 (11/01/85)
79 STONEGATE Cabernet Sauvignon Napa Valley 1981 Rel: $12 Cur: $17 (CA-3/89)
78 GUENOC Cabernet Sauvignon Lake County 1981 $8.50 (12/16/84)
78 MARIETTA Cabernet Sauvignon Sonoma County 1981 $9 (6/16/84)
78 MCDOWELL Cabernet Sauvignon McDowell Valley 1981 $11 (12/16/84)
78 PAT PAULSEN Cabernet Sauvignon Sonoma County 1981 $8 (1/01/84)
78 JOSEPH PHELPS Cabernet Sauvignon Napa Valley Eisele Vineyard 1981 Rel: $30 Cur: $44 (11/16/85)
78 SMITH-MADRONE Cabernet Sauvignon Napa Valley 1981 Rel: $12.50 Cur: $15 (CA-3/89)
78 SPRING MOUNTAIN Cabernet Sauvignon Napa Valley 1981 Rel: $14 Cur: $16 (CA-3/89)
78 STONEGATE Cabernet Sauvignon Napa Valley 1981 Rel: $12 Cur: $17 (11/15/86)
77 CARNEROS CREEK Cabernet Sauvignon Napa Valley 1981 $12 (12/16/84)
77 LYETH Red Alexander Valley 1981 Rel: $15 Cur: $31 (CA-3/89)
77 MOUNT VEEDER Cabernet Sauvignon Napa Valley 1981 Rel: $12.50 Cur: $25 (CA-3/89)
77 RAYMOND Cabernet Sauvignon Napa Valley 1981 Rel: $11 Cur: $17 (5/01/85)
77 SILVER OAK Cabernet Sauvignon Napa Valley Bonny's Vineyard 1981 Rel: $35 Cur: $60 (CA-3/89)
77 RODNEY STRONG Cabernet Sauvignon Alexander Valley Alexander's Crown Vineyard 1981 $12 (11/30/87)
76 J. CAREY Cabernet Sauvignon Santa Ynez Valley Alamo Pintado Vineyard 1981 $9.50 (6/16/84)
76 DOMAINE SAN MARTIN Cabernet Sauvignon Central Coast 1981 $7.75 (10/01/85)
76 JEKEL Cabernet Sauvignon Monterey Home Vineyard Private Reserve 1981 Rel: $20 Cur: $18 (2/01/86)
76 JOHNSON TURNBULL Cabernet Sauvignon Napa Valley 1981 Rel: $12 Cur: $26 (4/16/84)
76 CHARLES LEFRANC Cabernet Sauvignon Monterey County 1981 $8.50 (9/16/85)
76 RIDGE Cabernet Sauvignon Napa County York Creek 1981 Rel: $12 Cur: $20 (CA-3/89)
76 RIVER OAKS Cabernet Sauvignon Sonoma County 1981 $6 (7/01/84)

Key to Symbols

The scores reported here are the results of blind tastings conducted by our panel of senior editors. Wines that carry the initials below are results of individual tastings.

THE WINE SPECTATOR 100-POINT SCALE ***95-100***—Classic, a great wine; ***90-94***—Outstanding, superior character and style; ***80-89***—Good to very good, a wine with special qualities; ***70-79***—Average, drinkable wine that may have minor flaws; ***60-69***—Below average, drinkable but not recommended; ***50-59***—Poor, undrinkable, not recommended. "+"—With a score indicates a range; used primarily with barrel tastings to indicate a preliminary score.

SPECIAL DESIGNATIONS SS—Spectator Selection, CS—Cellar Selection, BB—Best Buy.

TASTER'S INITIALS (JG)—Jim Gordon, (HS)—Harvey Steiman, (JL)—James Laube, (JS)—James Suckling, (TM)—Thomas Matthews, (TR)—Terry Robards, (BT)—Barrel Tasting (these wines were tasted blind from barrel samples), (CA-date)—*California's Great Cabernets* by James Laube, (CH-date)—*California's Great Chardonnays* by James Laube, (VP-date)—*Vintage Port* by James Suckling.

DATE TASTED Dates in parentheses represent the issue in which the rating was published.

76 SIMI Cabernet Sauvignon Alexander Valley Reserve 1981 Rel: $25 Cur: $26 (2/01/86)
76 ZACA MESA Cabernet Sauvignon Santa Barbara County 1981 $8 (4/01/84)
75 E.&J. GALLO Cabernet Sauvignon Limited Release 1981 $5 (12/31/88)
75 HEITZ Cabernet Sauvignon Napa Valley 1981 Rel: $13.25 Cur: $25 (5/16/86)
75 LAMBERT BRIDGE Cabernet Sauvignon Sonoma County 1981 $12 (1/01/85)
75 SILVER OAK Cabernet Sauvignon Napa Valley 1981 Rel: $19 Cur: $62 (9/15/86)
74 CUVAISON Cabernet Sauvignon Napa Valley 1981 Rel: $11 Cur: $18 (CA-3/89)
74 MONTICELLO Cabernet Sauvignon Napa Valley 1981 $13.50 (7/16/84)
74 STEPHENS Cabernet Sauvignon Napa Valley 1981 $8 (2/15/84)
73 PARDUCCI Cabernet Sauvignon Mendocino County 1981 $6.50 (2/01/86)
72 CHATEAU ST. JEAN Cabernet Sauvignon Sonoma County 1981 Rel: $15 Cur: $20 (11/30/86)
65 HAWK CREST Cabernet Sauvignon North Coast 1981 $5 (2/01/86)
65 WENTE BROS. Cabernet Sauvignon California 1981 $7 (12/16/85)
63 RIDGE Cabernet Sauvignon Napa County 1981 $12 (2/15/84)
60 CAMBIASO Cabernet Sauvignon Dry Creek Valley 1981 $4.75 (6/16/84)

1980

96 CAYMUS Cabernet Sauvignon Napa Valley Special Selection 1980 Rel: $30 Cur: $128 (3/16/86) SS
96 PINE RIDGE Cabernet Sauvignon Napa Valley Andrus Reserve 1980 Rel: $30 Cur: $60 (CA-3/89)
94 CAYMUS Cabernet Sauvignon Napa Valley 1980 Rel: $12.50 Cur: $53 (2/01/86)
94 CAYMUS Cabernet Sauvignon Napa Valley 1980 Rel: $12.50 Cur: $53 (2/01/85)
93 BEAULIEU Cabernet Sauvignon Napa Valley Georges de Latour Private Reserve 1980 Rel: $24 Cur: $48 (3/31/91) (JL)
93 BEAULIEU Cabernet Sauvignon Napa Valley Georges de Latour Private Reserve 1980 Rel: $24 Cur: $48 (CA-3/89)
93 BEAULIEU Cabernet Sauvignon Napa Valley Georges de Latour Private Reserve 1980 Rel: $24 Cur: $48 (9/16/85) SS
93 BERINGER Cabernet Sauvignon Napa Valley Private Reserve Lemmon-Chabot Vineyard 1980 Rel: $20 Cur: $42 (8/01/84) CS
93 CONN CREEK Cabernet Sauvignon Napa Valley Collins Vineyard Proprietor's Special Selection 1980 Cur: $70 (CA-3/89)
93 HEITZ Cabernet Sauvignon Napa Valley Bella Oaks Vineyard 1980 Rel: $20 Cur: $51 (CA-3/89)
93 HEITZ Cabernet Sauvignon Napa Valley Martha's Vineyard 1980 Rel: $30 Cur: $65 (7/01/85) CS
93 OPUS ONE Napa Valley 1980 Rel: $50 Cur: $134 (CA-3/89)
93 PINE RIDGE Cabernet Sauvignon Napa Valley Andrus Reserve 1980 Rel: $30 Cur: $60 (12/01/84) CS
92 CAYMUS Cabernet Sauvignon Napa Valley Special Selection 1980 Rel: $30 Cur: $128 (CA-3/89)
92 DIAMOND CREEK Cabernet Sauvignon Napa Valley Gravelly Meadow 1980 Rel: $20 Cur: $66 (CA-3/89)
92 DUNN Cabernet Sauvignon Howell Mountain 1980 Rel: $13 Cur: $172 (CA-3/89)
92 GIRARD Cabernet Sauvignon Napa Valley 1980 Rel: $11 Cur: $25 (CA-3/89)
92 GRACE FAMILY Cabernet Sauvignon Napa Valley 1980 Rel: $25 Cur: $350 (CA-3/89)
92 MAYACAMAS Cabernet Sauvignon Napa Valley 1980 Rel: $18 Cur: $38 (CA-3/89)
92 NIEBAUM-COPPOLA Rubicon Napa Valley 1980 Rel: $30 Cur: $35 (10/15/87)
92 OPUS ONE Napa Valley 1980 Rel: $50 Cur: $134 (7/16/85)
92 RUTHERFORD HILL Cabernet Sauvignon Napa Valley Cask Lot 2 Limited Edition 1980 Rel: $11.50 Cur: $21 (7/31/87)
91 CHAPPELLET Cabernet Sauvignon Napa Valley 1980 Rel: $18 Cur: $29 (CA-3/89)
91 DUCKHORN Cabernet Sauvignon Napa Valley 1980 Rel: $14 Cur: $69 (CA-3/89)
91 LONG Cabernet Sauvignon Napa Valley 1980 Rel: $32 Cur: $50 (CA-3/89)
91 ROBERT MONDAVI Cabernet Sauvignon Napa Valley Reserve 1980 Rel: $30 Cur: $37 (2/01/86)
91 ROBERT MONDAVI Cabernet Sauvignon Napa Valley Reserve 1980 Rel: $30 Cur: $37 (2/01/85)
91 OPUS ONE Napa Valley 1980 Rel: $50 Cur: $134 (4/01/84) CS
91 PINE RIDGE Cabernet Sauvignon Napa Valley Rutherford District 1980 Rel: $12 Cur: $37 (CA-3/89)
91 STERLING Cabernet Sauvignon Napa Valley Reserve 1980 Rel: $27.50 Cur: $43 (CA-3/89)
90 BURGESS Cabernet Sauvignon Napa Valley Vintage Selection 1980 Rel: $16 Cur: $39 (5/01/84) SS
90 CAYMUS Cabernet Sauvignon Napa Valley 1980 Rel: $12.50 Cur: $53 (CA-3/89)
90 DIAMOND CREEK Cabernet Sauvignon Napa Valley Volcanic Hill 1980 Rel: $20 Cur: $75 (CA-3/89)
90 GRGICH HILLS Cabernet Sauvignon Napa-Sonoma Counties 1980 Rel: $16 Cur: $33 (CA-3/89)
90 HEITZ Cabernet Sauvignon Napa Valley Bella Oaks Vineyard 1980 Rel: $20 Cur: $51 (7/16/85)
90 JOSEPH PHELPS Insignia Napa Valley 1980 Rel: $25 Cur: $52 (CA-3/89)
90 JOSEPH PHELPS Insignia Napa Valley 1980 Rel: $25 Cur: $52 (10/30/87)
90 JOSEPH PHELPS Insignia Napa Valley 1980 Rel: $25 Cur: $52 (7/01/84) CS
90 SILVER OAK Cabernet Sauvignon Alexander Valley 1980 Rel: $18 Cur: $50 (3/01/85)
90 STERLING Cabernet Sauvignon Napa Valley Reserve 1980 Rel: $27.50 Cur: $43 (11/01/84) CS
89 BERINGER Cabernet Sauvignon Napa Valley Private Reserve Lemmon-Chabot Vineyard 1980 Rel: $20 Cur: $42 (CA-3/89)
89 HEITZ Cabernet Sauvignon Napa Valley Martha's Vineyard 1980 Rel: $30 Cur: $65 (CA-3/89)
89 INGLENOOK Cabernet Sauvignon Napa Valley Cask 1980 Rel: $15.50 Cur: $22 (9/16/84)
89 MARKHAM Cabernet Sauvignon Napa Valley 1980 Rel: $13 Cur: $26 (CA-3/89)
89 JOSEPH PHELPS Cabernet Sauvignon Napa Valley 1980 Rel: $10.75 Cur: $31 (7/01/84)
89 VILLA MT. EDEN Cabernet Sauvignon Napa Valley Reserve 1980 Rel: $20 Cur: $25 (10/01/84)
88 BEAULIEU Cabernet Sauvignon Napa Valley Rutherford 1980 Rel: $9 Cur: $30 (6/01/85) (JL)
88 BERINGER Cabernet Sauvignon Knights Valley 1980 $8 (2/15/84)
88 BERINGER Cabernet Sauvignon Napa Valley Private Reserve State Lane Vineyard 1980 Rel: $15 Cur: $40 (8/01/84)
88 BURGESS Cabernet Sauvignon Napa Valley Vintage Selection 1980 Rel: $16 Cur: $39 (CA-3/89)
88 CLOS DU VAL Cabernet Sauvignon Napa Valley Stags Leap District 1980 Rel: $12.50 Cur: $28 (CA-3/89)
88 CONN CREEK Cabernet Sauvignon Napa Valley 1980 Rel: $13 Cur: $28 (CA-3/89)
88 FREEMARK ABBEY Cabernet Sauvignon Napa Valley Bosché 1980 Rel: $14.50 Cur: $38 (CA-3/89)
88 HEITZ Cabernet Sauvignon Napa Valley 1980 Rel: $12 Cur: $24 (1/31/90) (JL)
88 INGLENOOK Cabernet Sauvignon Napa Valley Cask 1980 Rel: $15.50 Cur: $22 (CA-3/89)
88 LAKESPRING Cabernet Sauvignon Napa Valley 1980 Rel: $10 Cur: $21 (CA-3/89)

88 RIDGE Cabernet Sauvignon Napa County York Creek 1980 Rel: $12 Cur: $30 (CA-3/89)
88 RUTHERFORD HILL Cabernet Sauvignon Napa Valley Cask Lot 2 Limited Edition 1980 Rel: $11.50 Cur: $21 (CA-3/89)
88 SILVER OAK Cabernet Sauvignon Alexander Valley 1980 Rel: $18 Cur: $50 (CA-3/89)
88 STELTZNER Cabernet Sauvignon Napa Valley Stags Leap District 1980 Rel: $14 Cur: $32 (CA-3/89)
88 STELTZNER Cabernet Sauvignon Napa Valley Stags Leap District 1980 Rel: $14 Cur: $32 (6/30/87) (JL)
87 DUNN Cabernet Sauvignon Howell Mountain 1980 Rel: $13 Cur: $172 (3/16/84)
87 WILLIAM HILL Cabernet Sauvignon Napa Valley Gold Label 1980 Rel: $18.25 Cur: $32 (CA-3/89)
87 INGLENOOK Cabernet Sauvignon Napa Valley 1980 $8 (2/15/84)
87 JOHNSON TURNBULL Cabernet Sauvignon Napa Valley 1980 Rel: $12 Cur: $29 (CA-3/89)
87 MOUNT VEEDER Cabernet Sauvignon Napa Valley Bernstein Vineyards 1980 Rel: $13.50 Cur: $30 (CA-3/89)
87 NIEBAUM-COPPOLA Rubicon Napa Valley 1980 Rel: $30 Cur: $35 (CA-3/89)
87 SEQUOIA GROVE Cabernet Sauvignon Napa Valley Cask Two 1980 Rel: $12 Cur: $30 (CA-3/89)
87 SIMI Cabernet Sauvignon Alexander Valley Reserve 1980 Rel: $20 Cur: $26 (6/01/86)
86 CHATEAU MONTELENA Cabernet Sauvignon Napa Valley 1980 Rel: $16 Cur: $54 (CA-3/89)
86 CONN CREEK Cabernet Sauvignon Napa Valley 1980 Rel: $13 Cur: $28 (2/15/84)
86 DIAMOND CREEK Cabernet Sauvignon Napa Valley Red Rock Terrace 1980 Rel: $20 Cur: $57 (CA-3/89)
86 FRANCISCAN Cabernet Sauvignon Alexander Valley 1980 $7.50 (10/16/84)
86 HAYWOOD Cabernet Sauvignon Sonoma Valley 1980 Rel: $9.75 Cur: $12 (CA-3/89)
86 IRON HORSE Cabernet Sauvignon Alexander Valley 1980 Rel: $12 Cur: $20 (CA-3/89)
86 ROMBAUER Cabernet Sauvignon Napa Valley 1980 Rel: $10 Cur: $25 (CA-3/89)
86 SANTA CRUZ MOUNTAIN Cabernet Sauvignon Santa Cruz Mountains Bates Ranch 1980 Rel: $12 Cur: $27 (CA-3/89)
86 SPRING MOUNTAIN Cabernet Sauvignon Napa Valley 1980 Rel: $13 Cur: $24 (CA-3/89)
86 STONEGATE Cabernet Sauvignon Napa Valley 1980 Rel: $12 Cur: $22 (CA-3/89)
86 RODNEY STRONG Cabernet Sauvignon Alexander Valley Alexander's Crown Vineyard 1980 $11 (4/16/85)
86 VILLA MT. EDEN Cabernet Sauvignon Napa Valley 1980 Rel: $11.70 Cur: $14 (1/01/84)
85 BERINGER Cabernet Sauvignon Napa Valley Private Reserve State Lane Vineyard 1980 Rel: $15 Cur: $40 (CA-3/89)
85 CUVAISON Cabernet Sauvignon Napa Valley 1980 Rel: $11 Cur: $18 (2/16/85)
85 FLORA SPRINGS Cabernet Sauvignon Napa Valley 1980 Rel: $12 Cur: $28 (CA-3/89)
85 GRAND CRU Cabernet Sauvignon Alexander Valley Collector's Reserve 1980 $14.50 (11/01/84)
85 KEENAN Cabernet Sauvignon Napa Valley 1980 Rel: $13.50 Cur: $40 (1/01/84)
85 KISTLER Cabernet Sauvignon Napa Valley Veeder Hills-Veeder Peak 1980 Rel: $16 Cur: $45 (CA-3/89)
85 MOUNT EDEN Cabernet Sauvignon Santa Cruz Mountains 1980 Rel: $30 Cur: $35 (CA-3/89)
85 MOUNT VEEDER Cabernet Sauvignon Napa Valley Bernstein Vineyards 1980 Rel: $13.50 Cur: $30 (5/16/84)
85 RAYMOND Cabernet Sauvignon Napa Valley Private Reserve 1980 Cur: $34 (CA-3/89)
85 V. SATTUI Cabernet Sauvignon Napa Valley Preston Vineyard Reserve 1980 Rel: $30 Cur: $45 (CA-3/89)
85 SEQUOIA GROVE Cabernet Sauvignon Napa Valley Cask One 1980 Rel: $12 Cur: $30 (CA-3/89)
85 TUDAL Cabernet Sauvignon Napa Valley 1980 Rel: $11.50 Cur: $55 (CA-3/89)
85 VICHON Cabernet Sauvignon Napa Valley Stags Leap District Fay Vineyard 1980 Rel: $16 Cur: $25 (CA-3/89)
84 BUENA VISTA Cabernet Sauvignon Carneros Special Selection 1980 Rel: $18 Cur: $30 (CA-3/89)
84 CAKEBREAD Cabernet Sauvignon Napa Valley 1980 Rel: $14 Cur: $30 (CA-3/89)
84 FREEMARK ABBEY Cabernet Sauvignon Napa Valley Bosché 1980 Rel: $14.50 Cur: $38 (2/01/86)
84 FREEMARK ABBEY Cabernet Sauvignon Napa Valley Bosché 1980 Rel: $14.50 Cur: $38 (2/01/85)
84 FREEMARK ABBEY Cabernet Sauvignon Napa Valley 1980 Rel: $14.50 Cur: $22 (5/16/84)
84 KISTLER Cabernet Sauvignon Sonoma Valley Glen Ellen Vineyard 1980 Rel: $16 Cur: $45 (CA-3/89)
84 LOUIS M. MARTINI Cabernet Sauvignon North Coast Special Selection 1980 Rel: $12 Cur: $15 (CA-3/89)
84 SIMI Cabernet Sauvignon Alexander Valley Reserve 1980 Rel: $20 Cur: $26 (CA-3/89)
84 STERLING Cabernet Sauvignon Napa Valley 1980 Rel: $12.50 Cur: $25 (2/15/84)
83 ALEXANDER VALLEY Cabernet Sauvignon Alexander Valley 1980 Rel: $9 Cur: $16 (CA-3/89)
83 CHATEAU MONTELENA Cabernet Sauvignon Napa Valley 1980 Rel: $16 Cur: $54 (10/01/84)
83 CHATEAU SOUVERAIN Cabernet Sauvignon North Coast Vintage Selection 1980 $13 (9/16/85)
83 CLOS DU VAL Cabernet Sauvignon Napa Valley Stags Leap District 1980 Rel: $12.50 Cur: $28 (2/01/86)
83 CLOS DU VAL Cabernet Sauvignon Napa Valley Stags Leap District 1980 Rel: $12.50 Cur: $28 (2/01/85)
83 SMITH-MADRONE Cabernet Sauvignon Napa Valley 1980 Rel: $12.50 Cur: $18 (1/01/84)
83 VICHON Cabernet Sauvignon Napa Valley Volker Eisele Vineyard 1980 Rel: $16 Cur: $25 (CA-3/89)
82 BUEHLER Cabernet Sauvignon Napa Valley 1980 Rel: $10 Cur: $25 (CA-3/89)
82 CHATEAU CHEVALIER Cabernet Sauvignon Napa Valley 1980 $11.25 (1/01/84)
82 CHATEAU ST. JEAN Cabernet Sauvignon Sonoma Valley Wildwood Vineyards 1980 Rel: $17 Cur: $18 (9/01/85)
82 HEITZ Cabernet Sauvignon Napa Valley 1980 Rel: $12 Cur: $24 (6/01/85)
82 JORDAN Cabernet Sauvignon Alexander Valley 1980 Rel: $17 Cur: $46 (2/01/86)
82 JORDAN Cabernet Sauvignon Alexander Valley 1980 Rel: $17 Cur: $46 (2/01/85)
82 RAYMOND Cabernet Sauvignon Napa Valley 1980 Rel: $12 Cur: $19 (CA-3/89)
82 RUTHERFORD HILL Cabernet Sauvignon Napa Valley 1980 Rel: $11.50 Cur: $21 (CA-3/89)
82 RUTHERFORD HILL Cabernet Sauvignon Napa Valley 1980 Rel: $11.50 Cur: $21 (10/16/84)
82 ST. CLEMENT Cabernet Sauvignon Napa Valley 1980 Rel: $12.50 Cur: $25 (CA-3/89)
81 CLOS DU BOIS Cabernet Sauvignon Sonoma County 1980 $9 (7/01/84)
81 RAYMOND Cabernet Sauvignon Napa Valley 1980 Rel: $12 Cur: $19 (1/01/84)
81 ROUND HILL Cabernet Sauvignon Napa Valley 1980 $7.50 (4/16/84)
81 SIMI Cabernet Sauvignon Alexander Valley 1980 Rel: $10 Cur: $20 (7/01/84)
80 ALEXANDER VALLEY Cabernet Sauvignon Alexander Valley 1980 Rel: $9 Cur: $16 (2/01/86)

80 ALEXANDER VALLEY Cabernet Sauvignon Alexander Valley 1980 Rel: $9 Cur: $16 (2/01/85)
80 CLOS DU BOIS Cabernet Sauvignon Alexander Valley Briarcrest Vineyard 1980 Rel: $12 Cur: $32 (CA-3/89)
80 DE MOOR Cabernet Sauvignon Napa Valley Napa Cellars 1980 Rel: $12 Cur: $20 (CA-3/89)
80 GUNDLACH BUNDSCHU Cabernet Sauvignon Sonoma Valley Batto Ranch 1980 Rel: $8 Cur: $20 (CA-3/89)
80 JORDAN Cabernet Sauvignon Alexander Valley 1980 Rel: $17 Cur: $46 (CA-3/89)
80 KEENAN Cabernet Sauvignon Napa Valley 1980 Rel: $13.50 Cur: $40 (CA-3/89)
80 KENWOOD Cabernet Sauvignon Sonoma Valley Artist Series 1980 Rel: $20 Cur: $55 (CA-3/89)
80 KENWOOD Cabernet Sauvignon Sonoma Valley Jack London Vineyard 1980 Rel: $12.50 Cur: $15 (5/16/84)
80 RIDGE Cabernet Sauvignon Santa Cruz Mountains Monte Bello 1980 Rel: $30 Cur: $45 (CA-3/89)
80 SILVER OAK Cabernet Sauvignon Napa Valley 1980 Rel: $18 Cur: $60 (3/01/85)
79 BELLEROSE Cuvée Bellerose Sonoma County 1980 $10.50 (11/01/84)
79 CHARLES KRUG Cabernet Sauvignon Napa Valley Vintage Select 1980 Rel: $15 Cur: $23 (CA-3/89)
79 ROBERT MONDAVI Cabernet Sauvignon Napa Valley Reserve 1980 Rel: $30 Cur: $37 (CA-3/89)
79 PARDUCCI Cabernet Sauvignon Mendocino County 1980 $6.25 (2/01/86)
79 RAVENSWOOD Cabernet Sauvignon Sonoma County 1980 Rel: $10.50 Cur: $16 (CA-3/89)
79 SMITH-MADRONE Cabernet Sauvignon Napa Valley 1980 Rel: $12.50 Cur: $18 (CA-3/89)
78 DRY CREEK Cabernet Sauvignon Sonoma County 1980 $9.50 (4/16/84)
78 DRY CREEK Cabernet Sauvignon Sonoma County Special Reserve 1980 $13 (5/01/86)
78 EBERLE Cabernet Sauvignon Paso Robles 1980 Rel: $10 Cur: $24 (CA-3/89)
78 E.&J. GALLO Cabernet Sauvignon California Limited Release Reserve 1980 $8 (11/15/86)
78 HAYWOOD Cabernet Sauvignon Sonoma Valley 1980 Rel: $9.75 Cur: $12 (2/15/84)
78 LOUIS M. MARTINI Cabernet Sauvignon North Coast Special Selection 1980 Rel: $12 Cur: $15 (12/15/86)
77 CLOS DU BOIS Marlstone Vineyard Alexander Valley 1980 Rel: $15 Cur: $29 (CA-3/89)
77 CUVAISON Cabernet Sauvignon Napa Valley 1980 Rel: $11 Cur: $18 (CA-3/89)
77 ESTRELLA RIVER Cabernet Sauvignon San Luis Obispo County 1980 $10 (3/16/85)
77 SHAFER Cabernet Sauvignon Napa Valley Stags Leap District 1980 Rel: $12 Cur: $25 (CA-3/89)
77 STEPHEN ZELLERBACH Cabernet Sauvignon Alexander Valley 1980 $8 (4/01/85)
76 BOEGER Cabernet Sauvignon El Dorado 1980 $8.50 (4/16/84)
75 MONT ST. JOHN Cabernet Sauvignon Napa Valley Private Reserve 1980 Rel: $11.50 (5/16/84)
75 NAPA SUN Cabernet Sauvignon Napa Valley 1980 $5.99 (3/16/84)
74 ADLER FELS Cabernet Sauvignon Napa Valley 1980 $10 (10/01/84)
73 SHAFER Cabernet Sauvignon Napa Valley Stags Leap District 1980 Rel: $12 Cur: $25 (2/15/84)
73 SILVER OAK Cabernet Sauvignon Napa Valley 1980 Rel: $18 Cur: $60 (CA-3/89)
70 RIDGE Cabernet Sauvignon Santa Cruz Mountains Monte Bello 1980 Rel: $30 Cur: $45 (4/01/85)
70 SILVER OAK Cabernet Sauvignon Napa Valley Bonny's Vineyard 1980 Rel: $30 Cur: $60 (CA-3/89)
70 VILLA MT. EDEN Cabernet Sauvignon Napa Valley Reserve 1980 Rel: $20 Cur: $25 (CA-3/89)
68 TREFETHEN Cabernet Sauvignon Napa Valley 1980 Rel: $11 Cur: $50 (CA-3/89)
66 CLOS DU BOIS Cabernet Sauvignon Alexander Valley Briarcrest Vineyard 1980 Rel: $12 Cur: $32 (4/16/86)
63 JEKEL Cabernet Sauvignon Arroyo Seco Home Vineyard 1980 $25 (2/01/86)
62 MOUNTAIN VIEW Cabernet Sauvignon North Coast 1980 $5 (4/16/84)
62 VILLA MT. EDEN Cabernet Sauvignon Napa Valley 1980 Rel: $11.70 Cur: $14 (CA-3/89)
58 CHRISTIAN BROTHERS Cabernet Sauvignon Napa Valley 1980 $6.75 (10/01/85)
57 GEYSER PEAK Cabernet Sauvignon Alexander Valley 1980 $6.50 (1/01/85)
55 NEWTON Cabernet Sauvignon Napa Valley 1980 Rel: $12 Cur: $30 (CA-3/89)

1979

97 CAYMUS Cabernet Sauvignon Napa Valley Special Selection 1979 Rel: $30 Cur: $165 (CA-3/89)
95 DIAMOND CREEK Cabernet Sauvignon Napa Valley Volcanic Hill First Pick 1979 Rel: $15 Cur: $90 (CA-3/89)
95 MAYACAMAS Cabernet Sauvignon Napa Valley 1979 Rel: $18 Cur: $44 (CA-3/89)
94 HEITZ Cabernet Sauvignon Napa Valley Martha's Vineyard 1979 Rel: $25 Cur: $71 (2/15/84) SS
93 BEAULIEU Cabernet Sauvignon Napa Valley Georges de Latour Private Reserve 1979 Rel: $21 Cur: $53 (3/01/84) SS
93 CAYMUS Cabernet Sauvignon Napa Valley Special Selection 1979 Rel: $30 Cur: $165 (6/01/85) SS
93 CLOS DU VAL Cabernet Sauvignon Napa Valley Stags Leap District 1979 Rel: $12.50 Cur: $40 (2/01/86)
93 CLOS DU VAL Cabernet Sauvignon Napa Valley Stags Leap District 1979 Rel: $12.50 Cur: $40 (2/01/85)
93 FREEMARK ABBEY Cabernet Sauvignon Napa Valley Bosché 1979 Rel: $12 Cur: $34 (CA-3/89)
93 HEITZ Cabernet Sauvignon Napa Valley Martha's Vineyard 1979 Rel: $25 Cur: $71 (CA-3/89)
93 WILLIAM HILL Cabernet Sauvignon Napa Valley Gold Label 1979 Rel: $18 Cur: $45 (CA-3/89)
92 BUENA VISTA Cabernet Sauvignon Carneros Special Selection 1979 Rel: $18 Cur: $35 (CA-3/89)
92 CAYMUS Cabernet Sauvignon Napa Valley 1979 Rel: $12 Cur: $55 (CA-3/89)
92 CLOS DU VAL Cabernet Sauvignon Napa Valley Stags Leap District Reserve 1979 Rel: $25 Cur: $55 (CA-3/89)
92 DIAMOND CREEK Cabernet Sauvignon Napa Valley Red Rock Terrace 1979 Rel: $15 Cur: $90 (CA-3/89)
92 GRACE FAMILY Cabernet Sauvignon Napa Valley 1979 Rel: $20 Cur: $400 (CA-3/89)
92 ROBERT MONDAVI Cabernet Sauvignon Napa Valley Reserve 1979 Rel: $25 Cur: $46 (CA-3/89)
92 MOUNT VEEDER Cabernet Sauvignon Napa Valley Bernstein Vineyards 1979 Rel: $13.50 Cur: $43 (CA-3/89)
92 JOSEPH PHELPS Cabernet Sauvignon Napa Valley Eisele Vineyard 1979 Rel: $30 Cur: $54 (CA-3/89)
91 CLOS DU VAL Cabernet Sauvignon Napa Valley Stags Leap District Reserve 1979 Rel: $25 Cur: $55 (9/01/84) SS
91 DIAMOND CREEK Cabernet Sauvignon Napa Valley Gravelly Meadow 1979 Rel: $15 Cur: $94 (CA-3/89)
91 DUNN Cabernet Sauvignon Howell Mountain 1979 Rel: $12.50 Cur: $225 (CA-3/89)

UNITED STATES
CALIFORNIA/CABERNET SAUVIGNON & BLENDS

91   IRON HORSE Cabernet Sauvignon Alexander Valley 1979 Rel: $12 Cur: $25 (CA-3/89)
91   KENWOOD Cabernet Sauvignon Sonoma Valley Artist Series 1979 Rel: $20 Cur: $70 (CA-3/89)
91   SIMI Cabernet Sauvignon Alexander Valley 1979 Rel: $9 Cur: $28 (4/01/84) SS
91   STERLING Cabernet Sauvignon Napa Valley Reserve 1979 Rel: $27.50 Cur: $45 (2/15/84)
90   BEAULIEU Cabernet Sauvignon Napa Valley Georges de Latour Private Reserve 1979 Rel: $21 Cur: $53 (CA-3/89)
90   CAYMUS Cabernet Sauvignon Napa Valley 1979 Rel: $12 Cur: $55 (2/01/86)
90   CAYMUS Cabernet Sauvignon Napa Valley 1979 Rel: $12 Cur: $55 (2/01/85)
90   CLOS DU VAL Cabernet Sauvignon Napa Valley Stags Leap District 1979 Rel: $12.50 Cur: $40 (CA-3/89)
90   LONG Cabernet Sauvignon Napa Valley 1979 Rel: $32 Cur: $59 (CA-3/89)
90   ROBERT MONDAVI Cabernet Sauvignon Napa Valley Reserve 1979 Rel: $25 Cur: $46 (2/01/86)
90   ROBERT MONDAVI Cabernet Sauvignon Napa Valley Reserve 1979 Rel: $25 Cur: $46 (2/01/85)
90   OPUS ONE Napa Valley 1979 Rel: $50 Cur: $194 (CA-3/89)
90   OPUS ONE Napa Valley 1979 Rel: $50 Cur: $194 (7/16/85)
90   JOSEPH PHELPS Insignia Napa Valley 1979 Rel: $25 Cur: $55 (CA-3/89)
90   ST. CLEMENT Cabernet Sauvignon Napa Valley 1979 Rel: $11 Cur: $35 (CA-3/89)
90   TUDAL Cabernet Sauvignon Napa Valley 1979 Rel: $10.75 Cur: $50 (CA-3/89)
89   BEAULIEU Cabernet Sauvignon Napa Valley Rutherford 1979 Rel: $9 Cur: $25 (6/01/85) (JL)
89   BERINGER Cabernet Sauvignon Napa Valley Private Reserve State Lane Vineyard 1979 Rel: $15 Cur: $42 (CA-3/89)
89   FREEMARK ABBEY Cabernet Sauvignon Napa Valley 1979 Rel: $10.50 Cur: $25 (1/01/84)
89   SHAFER Cabernet Sauvignon Napa Valley Stags Leap District 1979 Rel: $12 Cur: $35 (CA-3/89)
89   SIMI Cabernet Sauvignon Alexander Valley Reserve 1979 Rel: $20 Cur: $36 (9/01/85)
89   STELTZNER Cabernet Sauvignon Napa Valley Stags Leap District 1979 Rel: $14 Cur: $42 (CA-3/89)
89   STELTZNER Cabernet Sauvignon Napa Valley Stags Leap District 1979 Rel: $14 Cur: $42 (6/30/87) (JL)
88   CHATEAU MONTELENA Cabernet Sauvignon Alexander Valley Sonoma 1979 Rel: $14 Cur: $45 (CA-3/89)
88   MARKHAM Cabernet Sauvignon Napa Valley 1979 Rel: $13 Cur: $31 (CA-3/89)
88   RIDGE Cabernet Sauvignon Napa County York Creek 1979 Rel: $12 Cur: $30 (CA-3/89)
88   STAG'S LEAP WINE CELLARS Cabernet Sauvignon Napa Valley Stags Leap District Stag's Leap Vineyards Cask 23 1979 Rel: $35 Cur: $95 (CA-3/89)
87   BEAULIEU Cabernet Sauvignon Napa Valley Georges de Latour Private Reserve 1979 Rel: $21 Cur: $53 (3/31/91) (JL)
87   BURGESS Cabernet Sauvignon Napa Valley Vintage Selection 1979 Rel: $16 Cur: $35 (CA-3/89)
87   CHATEAU MONTELENA Cabernet Sauvignon Napa Valley 1979 Rel: $16 Cur: $45 (CA-3/89)
87   RUTHERFORD HILL Cabernet Sauvignon Napa Valley 1979 Rel: $11.50 Cur: $22 (CA-3/89)
87   SIMI Cabernet Sauvignon Alexander Valley Reserve 1979 Rel: $20 Cur: $36 (CA-3/89)
87   SPRING MOUNTAIN Cabernet Sauvignon Napa Valley 1979 Rel: $13 Cur: $32 (CA-3/89)
86   ALEXANDER VALLEY Cabernet Sauvignon Alexander Valley 1979 Rel: $7 Cur: $18 (CA-3/89)
86   FREEMARK ABBEY Cabernet Sauvignon Napa Valley Bosché 1979 Rel: $12 Cur: $34 (2/01/86)
86   HEITZ Cabernet Sauvignon Napa Valley 1979 Rel: $11.25 Cur: $45 (1/31/90) (JL)
86   JOSEPH PHELPS Cabernet Sauvignon Napa Valley Eisele Vineyard 1979 Rel: $30 Cur: $54 (2/16/84) (HS)
86   SMITH-MADRONE Cabernet Sauvignon Napa Valley 1979 Rel: $14 Cur: $25 (CA-3/89)
86   TREFETHEN Cabernet Sauvignon Napa Valley 1979 Rel: $11 Cur: $35 (CA-3/89)
85   DE MOOR Cabernet Sauvignon Napa Valley Napa Cellars 1979 Rel: $10 Cur: $25 (CA-3/89)
85   JOHNSON TURNBULL Cabernet Sauvignon Napa Valley 1979 Rel: $10.50 Cur: $29 (CA-3/89)
85   ROBERT MONDAVI Cabernet Sauvignon Napa Valley 1979 Cur: $25 (7/16/85) (JL)
85   NEWTON Cabernet Sauvignon Napa Valley 1979 Rel: $12 Cur: $30 (CA-3/89)
85   PINE RIDGE Cabernet Sauvignon Napa Valley Rutherford District 1979 Rel: $9 Cur: $45 (CA-3/89)
85   RAYMOND Cabernet Sauvignon Napa Valley 1979 Rel: $12 Cur: $20 (CA-3/89)
85   SILVER OAK Cabernet Sauvignon Alexander Valley 1979 Rel: $16 Cur: $65 (CA-3/89)
85   STERLING Cabernet Sauvignon Napa Valley Reserve 1979 Rel: $27.50 Cur: $45 (CA-3/89)
84   ALEXANDER VALLEY Cabernet Sauvignon Alexander Valley 1979 Rel: $7 Cur: $18 (2/01/86)
84   ALEXANDER VALLEY Cabernet Sauvignon Alexander Valley 1979 Rel: $7 Cur: $18 (2/01/85)
84   ESTRELLA RIVER Cabernet Sauvignon San Luis Obispo County 1979 $6 (3/01/84) BB
84   LOUIS M. MARTINI Cabernet Sauvignon Sonoma Valley Monte Rosso Lot 2 1979 Rel: $10 Cur: $19 (CA-3/89)
84   STONEGATE Cabernet Sauvignon Napa Valley 1979 Rel: $12 Cur: $25 (CA-3/89)
83   SILVER OAK Cabernet Sauvignon Napa Valley 1979 Rel: $18 Cur: $74 (3/01/84)
82   CAKEBREAD Cabernet Sauvignon Napa Valley 1979 Rel: $13 Cur: $30 (CA-3/89)
82   DIAMOND CREEK Cabernet Sauvignon Napa Valley Volcanic Hill Second Pick 1979 Rel: $15 Cur: $45 (CA-3/89)
82   EBERLE Cabernet Sauvignon San Luis Obispo 1979 Rel: $10 Cur: $25 (CA-3/89)
82   CHARLES KRUG Cabernet Sauvignon Napa Valley Vintage Select 1979 Rel: $12.50 Cur: $20 (CA-3/89)
82   SILVER OAK Cabernet Sauvignon Napa Valley 1979 Rel: $18 Cur: $74 (CA-3/89)
81   HEITZ Cabernet Sauvignon Napa Valley 1979 Rel: $11.25 Cur: $45 (2/16/84) (HS)
81   JORDAN Cabernet Sauvignon Alexander Valley 1979 Rel: $16 Cur: $57 (2/01/86)

81   JORDAN Cabernet Sauvignon Alexander Valley 1979 Rel: $16 Cur: $57 (2/01/85)
81   NIEBAUM-COPPOLA Rubicon Napa Valley 1979 Rel: $25 Cur: $40 (2/28/87) (JG)
81   JOSEPH PHELPS Insignia Napa Valley 1979 Rel: $25 Cur: $55 (10/30/87)
81   SILVER OAK Cabernet Sauvignon Alexander Valley 1979 Rel: $16 Cur: $65 (2/15/84)
81   SILVER OAK Cabernet Sauvignon Napa Valley Bonny's Vineyard 1979 Rel: $30 Cur: $60 (6/16/84)
80   GUNDLACH BUNDSCHU Cabernet Sauvignon Sonoma Valley Batto Ranch 1979 Rel: $8 Cur: $22 (CA-3/89)
79   CHAPPELLET Cabernet Sauvignon Napa Valley 1979 Rel: $13 Cur: $29 (CA-3/89)
79   FRANCISCAN Cabernet Sauvignon Napa Valley 1979 Rel: $8.50 Cur: $18 (CA-3/89)
79   JORDAN Cabernet Sauvignon Alexander Valley 1979 Rel: $16 Cur: $57 (CA-3/89)
79   SANTA CRUZ MOUNTAIN Cabernet Sauvignon Santa Cruz Mountains Bates Ranch 1979 Rel: $12 Cur: $35 (CA-3/89)
79   RODNEY STRONG Cabernet Sauvignon Alexander Valley Alexander's Crown Vineyard 1979 $12 (4/16/84)
78   VILLA MT. EDEN Cabernet Sauvignon Napa Valley 1979 Rel: $12 Cur: $28 (CA-3/89)
77   CONN CREEK Cabernet Sauvignon Napa Valley 1979 Rel: $13 Cur: $25 (CA-3/89)
77   INGLENOOK Cabernet Sauvignon Napa Valley Cask 1979 Rel: $10.75 Cur: $23 (CA-3/89)
77   JEKEL Cabernet Sauvignon Monterey Home Vineyard Private Reserve 1979 $18 (2/01/86)
77   SIMI Cabernet Sauvignon Alexander Valley Reserve 1979 Rel: $20 Cur: $36 (2/01/86)
76   CHATEAU ST. JEAN Cabernet Sauvignon Sonoma Valley Wildwood Vineyards 1979 Rel: $17 Cur: $18 (7/01/84)
76   WOLTNER Cabernet Sauvignon North Coast 1979 $3.50 (3/16/84)
75   CLOS DU BOIS Marlstone Vineyard Alexander Valley 1979 Rel: $16 Cur: $30 (CA-3/89)
75   CUVAISON Cabernet Sauvignon Napa Valley 1979 Rel: $11 Cur: $20 (CA-3/89)
75   NIEBAUM-COPPOLA Rubicon Napa Valley 1979 Rel: $25 Cur: $40 (CA-3/89)
75   VILLA MT. EDEN Cabernet Sauvignon Napa Valley Reserve 1979 Rel: $20 Cur: $30 (CA-3/89)
74   KEENAN Cabernet Sauvignon Napa Valley 1979 Rel: $12 Cur: $38 (CA-3/89)
73   FIRESTONE Cabernet Sauvignon Santa Ynez Valley Vintage Reserve 1979 $12 (3/16/86)
72   SILVER OAK Cabernet Sauvignon Napa Valley Bonny's Vineyard 1979 Rel: $30 Cur: $60 (CA-3/89)
69   MOUNT EDEN Cabernet Sauvignon Santa Cruz Mountains 1979 Rel: $25 Cur: $45 (CA-3/89)
69   PARDUCCI Cabernet Sauvignon Mendocino County 1979 $8 (2/01/86)
68   STAG'S LEAP WINE CELLARS Cabernet Sauvignon Napa Valley Stags Leap District Stag's Leap Vineyards 1979 Rel: $15 Cur: $52 (CA-3/89)
63   SHOWN AND SONS Cabernet Sauvignon Napa Valley Rutherford 1979 $15 (4/01/84)
59   RAVENSWOOD Cabernet Sauvignon California 1979 Rel: $8 Cur: $8 (CA-3/89)
58   SEBASTIANI Cabernet Sauvignon North Coast Proprietor's Reserve 1979 $11 (8/01/84)

1978

99   DIAMOND CREEK Cabernet Sauvignon Napa Valley Lake 1978 Rel: $25 Cur: $350 (CA-3/89)
98   CAYMUS Cabernet Sauvignon Napa Valley Special Selection 1978 Rel: $30 Cur: $225 (4/30/87)
97   CAYMUS Cabernet Sauvignon Napa Valley Special Selection 1978 Rel: $30 Cur: $225 (CA-3/89)
97   ROBERT MONDAVI Cabernet Sauvignon Napa Valley Reserve 1978 Rel: $40 Cur: $70 (6/01/86)
97   JOSEPH PHELPS Cabernet Sauvignon Napa Valley Eisele Vineyard 1978 Rel: $30 Cur: $90 (CA-3/89)
97   STERLING Cabernet Sauvignon Napa Valley Reserve 1978 Rel: $27.50 Cur: $57 (6/01/86)
96   BUENA VISTA Cabernet Sauvignon Carneros Special Selection 1978 Rel: $18 Cur: $35 (6/01/86)
96   JOSEPH PHELPS Cabernet Sauvignon Napa Valley Eisele Vineyard 1978 Rel: $30 Cur: $90 (4/30/87)
95   CAYMUS Cabernet Sauvignon Napa Valley Special Selection 1978 Rel: $30 Cur: $225 (6/16/84) CS
95   DIAMOND CREEK Cabernet Sauvignon Napa Valley Volcanic Hill 1978 Rel: $12.50 Cur: $90 (CA-3/89)
95   WILLIAM HILL Cabernet Sauvignon Napa Valley Gold Label 1978 Rel: $16.25 Cur: $46 (CA-3/89)
95   WILLIAM HILL Cabernet Sauvignon Napa Valley Gold Label 1978 Rel: $16.25 Cur: $46 (4/30/87)
95   STERLING Cabernet Sauvignon Napa Valley 1978 Cur: $28 (6/01/86)
94   BUENA VISTA Cabernet Sauvignon Sonoma Valley 1978 $12 (6/01/86)
94   CLOS DU VAL Cabernet Sauvignon Napa Valley Stags Leap District Reserve 1978 Rel: $30 Cur: $50 (CA-3/89)
94   KENWOOD Cabernet Sauvignon Sonoma Valley Artist Series 1978 Rel: $20 Cur: $95 (4/30/87)
94   MAYACAMAS Cabernet Sauvignon Napa Valley 1978 Rel: $18 Cur: $60 (CA-3/89)
93   BURGESS Cabernet Sauvignon Napa Valley Vintage Selection 1978 Rel: $14 Cur: $34 (CA-3/89)
93   CHATEAU MONTELENA Cabernet Sauvignon Napa Valley 1978 Rel: $16 Cur: $79 (CA-3/89)
93   DIAMOND CREEK Cabernet Sauvignon Napa Valley Gravelly Meadow 1978 Rel: $12.50 Cur: $95 (CA-3/89)
93   FREEMARK ABBEY Cabernet Sauvignon Napa Valley Bosché 1978 Rel: $12.50 Cur: $50 (CA-3/89)
93   SILVER OAK Cabernet Sauvignon Alexander Valley 1978 Rel: $16 Cur: $78 (CA-3/89)
92   BEAULIEU Cabernet Sauvignon Napa Valley Georges de Latour Private Reserve 1978 Rel: $19 Cur: $57 (4/30/87)
92   BERINGER Cabernet Sauvignon Napa Valley Private Reserve Lemmon Ranch Vineyard 1978 Rel: $15 Cur: $36 (CA-3/89)
92   BERINGER Cabernet Sauvignon Napa Valley Private Reserve Lemmon Ranch Vineyard 1978 Rel: $15 Cur: $36 (4/30/87)
92   BERINGER Cabernet Sauvignon Napa Valley Private Reserve Lemmon Ranch Vineyard 1978 Rel: $15 Cur: $36 (4/30/87)
92   CLOS DU VAL Cabernet Sauvignon Napa Valley Stags Leap District 1978 Rel: $12 Cur: $36 (CA-3/89)
92   CONN CREEK Cabernet Sauvignon Napa Valley Lot 2 1978 Rel: $12 Cur: $35 (CA-3/89)
92   DIAMOND CREEK Cabernet Sauvignon Napa Valley Red Rock Terrace 1978 Rel: $12.50 Cur: $104 (CA-3/89)
92   DUCKHORN Cabernet Sauvignon Napa Valley 1978 Rel: $10.50 Cur: $85 (CA-3/89)
92   FREEMARK ABBEY Cabernet Sauvignon Napa Valley Bosché 1978 Rel: $12.50 Cur: $50 (4/30/87)
92   ROBERT MONDAVI Cabernet Sauvignon Napa Valley Reserve 1978 Rel: $40 Cur: $70 (CA-3/89)
92   STAG'S LEAP WINE CELLARS Cabernet Sauvignon Napa Valley Stags Leap District Stag's Leap Vineyards Cask 23 1978 Rel: $35 Cur: $136 (CA-3/89)

91   BEAULIEU Cabernet Sauvignon Napa Valley Georges de Latour Private Reserve 1978 Rel: $19 Cur: $57 (CA-3/89)
91   CAYMUS Cabernet Sauvignon Napa Valley 1978 Rel: $12 Cur: $60 (2/01/85)
91   HEITZ Cabernet Sauvignon Napa Valley Martha's Vineyard 1978 Rel: $22 Cur: $110 (CA-3/89)
91   HEITZ Cabernet Sauvignon Napa Valley Martha's Vineyard 1978 Rel: $22 Cur: $110 (2/16/84) (HS)
91   RIDGE Cabernet Sauvignon Santa Cruz Mountains Monte Bello 1978 Rel: $30 Cur: $94 (CA-3/89)
91   SILVER OAK Cabernet Sauvignon Alexander Valley 1978 Rel: $16 Cur: $78 (4/30/87)
91   STAG'S LEAP WINE CELLARS Cabernet Sauvignon Napa Valley Stags Leap District Stag's Leap Vineyards Cask 23 1978 Rel: $35 Cur: $136 (4/30/87)
91   STONEGATE Cabernet Sauvignon Napa Valley 1978 Rel: $12 Cur: $30 (CA-3/89)
90   BEAULIEU Cabernet Sauvignon Napa Valley Georges de Latour Private Reserve 1978 Rel: $19 Cur: $57 (3/31/91) (JL)
90   BUENA VISTA Cabernet Sauvignon Carneros Special Selection 1978 Rel: $18 Cur: $35 (CA-3/89)
90   CLOS DU VAL Cabernet Sauvignon Napa Valley Stags Leap District 1978 Rel: $12 Cur: $36 (6/01/86)
90   HEITZ Cabernet Sauvignon Napa Valley 1978 Rel: $11 Cur: $30 (1/31/90) (JL)
90   HEITZ Cabernet Sauvignon Napa Valley Bella Oaks Vineyard 1978 Rel: $15 Cur: $60 (2/16/84) (HS)
90   INGLENOOK Cabernet Sauvignon Napa Valley Cask 1978 Rel: $9.25 Cur: $25 (4/30/87)
90   KENWOOD Cabernet Sauvignon Sonoma Valley Artist Series 1978 Rel: $20 Cur: $95 (CA-3/89)
90   PINE RIDGE Cabernet Sauvignon Napa Valley Rutherford District 1978 Rel: $7.50 Cur: $50 (4/30/87)
90   SANTA CRUZ MOUNTAIN Cabernet Sauvignon Santa Cruz Mountains Bates Ranch 1978 Rel: $12 Cur: $35 (CA-3/89)
90   STERLING Cabernet Sauvignon Napa Valley Reserve 1978 Rel: $27.50 Cur: $57 (CA-3/89)
89   DE MOOR Cabernet Sauvignon Napa Valley Napa Cellars 1978 Rel: $10 Cur: $28 (CA-3/89)
89   HEITZ Cabernet Sauvignon Napa Valley Bella Oaks Vineyard 1978 Rel: $15 Cur: $60 (CA-3/89)
89   JORDAN Cabernet Sauvignon Alexander Valley 1978 Rel: $16 Cur: $61 (4/30/87)
89   MOUNT VEEDER Cabernet Sauvignon Napa Valley Bernstein Vineyards 1978 Rel: $12.75 Cur: $40 (CA-3/89)
89   JOSEPH PHELPS Cabernet Sauvignon Napa Valley Backus Vineyard 1978 Rel: $16.50 Cur: $55 (CA-3/89)
89   PINE RIDGE Cabernet Sauvignon Napa Valley Rutherford District 1978 Rel: $7.50 Cur: $50 (CA-3/89)
89   STAG'S LEAP WINE CELLARS Cabernet Sauvignon Napa Valley Stags Leap District Stag's Leap Vineyards 1978 Rel: $13.50 Cur: $45 (CA-3/89)
88   ALEXANDER VALLEY Cabernet Sauvignon Alexander Valley 1978 Rel: $6.50 Cur: $20 (2/01/86)
88   ALEXANDER VALLEY Cabernet Sauvignon Alexander Valley 1978 Rel: $6.50 Cur: $20 (2/01/85)
88   CHAPPELLET Cabernet Sauvignon Napa Valley 1978 Rel: $13 Cur: $36 (CA-3/89)
88   DIAMOND CREEK Cabernet Sauvignon Napa Valley Gravelly Meadow 1978 Rel: $12.50 Cur: $95 (4/30/87)
88   ROBERT MONDAVI Cabernet Sauvignon Napa Valley 1978 Cur: $38 (6/01/86)
88   MOUNT EDEN Cabernet Sauvignon Santa Cruz Mountains 1978 Rel: $25 Cur: $55 (CA-3/89)
88   NIEBAUM-COPPOLA Rubicon Napa Valley 1978 Rel: $25 Cur: $25 (CA-3/89)
88   ST. CLEMENT Cabernet Sauvignon Napa Valley 1978 Rel: $10 Cur: $40 (CA-3/89)
88   VILLA MT. EDEN Cabernet Sauvignon Napa Valley Reserve 1978 Rel: $20 Cur: $42 (CA-3/89)
87   BUEHLER Cabernet Sauvignon Napa Valley 1978 Rel: $10 Cur: $35 (CA-3/89)
87   CAYMUS Cabernet Sauvignon Napa Valley 1978 Rel: $12 Cur: $60 (CA-3/89)
87   CHATEAU MONTELENA Cabernet Sauvignon Napa Valley 1978 Rel: $16 Cur: $79 (4/30/87)
87   CHATEAU MONTELENA Cabernet Sauvignon Alexander Valley Sonoma 1978 Rel: $12 Cur: $68 (CA-3/89)
87   JOSEPH PHELPS Insignia Napa Valley 1978 Rel: $25 Cur: $86 (CA-3/89)
87   JOSEPH PHELPS Insignia Napa Valley 1978 Rel: $25 Cur: $86 (10/30/87)
87   RIDGE Cabernet Sauvignon Napa County York Creek 1978 Rel: $12 Cur: $35 (CA-3/89)
87   STELTZNER Cabernet Sauvignon Napa Valley Stags Leap District 1978 Rel: $14 Cur: $45 (CA-3/89)
87   STELTZNER Cabernet Sauvignon Napa Valley Stags Leap District 1978 Rel: $14 Cur: $45 (6/30/87) (JL)
86   CAKEBREAD Cabernet Sauvignon Napa Valley Lot 2 1978 Rel: $12 Cur: $50 (CA-3/89)
86   CONN CREEK Cabernet Sauvignon Napa Valley Lot 1 1978 Rel: $12 Cur: $35 (CA-3/89)
86   CONN CREEK Cabernet Sauvignon Napa Valley Lot 1 1978 Rel: $12 Cur: $35 (4/30/87)
86   GRACE FAMILY Cabernet Sauvignon Napa Valley 1978 Rel: $20 Cur: $500 (CA-3/89)
86   INGLENOOK Cabernet Sauvignon Napa Valley Cask 1978 Rel: $9.25 Cur: $25 (CA-3/89)
86   LOUIS M. MARTINI Cabernet Sauvignon California Special Selection 1978 Rel: $9 Cur: $29 (CA-3/89)
86   MOUNT VEEDER Cabernet Sauvignon Napa Valley Sidehill Ranch 1978 Rel: $13.50 Cur: $40 (CA-3/89)
85   CAKEBREAD Cabernet Sauvignon Napa Valley 1978 Rel: $12 Cur: $35 (CA-3/89)
85   CLOS DU VAL Cabernet Sauvignon Napa Valley Stags Leap District Reserve 1978 Rel: $30 Cur: $50 (4/30/87)
85   MARKHAM Cabernet Sauvignon Napa Valley 1978 Rel: $13 Cur: $35 (CA-3/89)
85   NIEBAUM-COPPOLA Rubicon Napa Valley 1978 Rel: $25 Cur: $25 (2/28/87) (JG)
85   SHAFER Cabernet Sauvignon Napa Valley Stags Leap District 1978 Rel: $11 Cur: $50 (CA-3/89)
84   CLOS DU VAL Cabernet Sauvignon Napa Valley Stags Leap District 1978 Rel: $12 Cur: $36 (2/01/85)
84   SMITH-MADRONE Cabernet Sauvignon Napa Valley 1978 Rel: $14 Cur: $25 (CA-3/89)
83   ROBERT MONDAVI Cabernet Sauvignon Napa Valley Reserve 1978 Rel: $40 Cur: $70 (2/01/85)
83   RAVENSWOOD Cabernet Sauvignon Sonoma Valley Olive Hill 1978 Rel: $10.50 Cur: $24 (CA-3/89)
83   SPRING MOUNTAIN Cabernet Sauvignon Napa Valley 1978 Rel: $12 Cur: $27 (CA-3/89)
82   RAYMOND Cabernet Sauvignon Napa Valley 1978 Rel: $10 Cur: $30 (CA-3/89)
82   RUTHERFORD HILL Cabernet Sauvignon Napa Valley 1978 Rel: $12 Cur: $25 (CA-3/89)
81   JORDAN Cabernet Sauvignon Alexander Valley 1978 Rel: $16 Cur: $61 (CA-3/89)
81   RAVENSWOOD Cabernet Sauvignon California 1978 Rel: $10 Cur: $20 (CA-3/89)
81   TREFETHEN Cabernet Sauvignon Napa Valley 1978 Rel: $10 Cur: $45 (CA-3/89)
80   ALEXANDER VALLEY Cabernet Sauvignon Alexander Valley 1978 Rel: $6.50 Cur: $20 (CA-3/89)

80   FREEMARK ABBEY Cabernet Sauvignon Napa Valley Bosché 1978 Rel: $12.50 Cur: $50 (2/01/85)
80   HEITZ Cabernet Sauvignon Napa Valley Fay Vineyard 1978 Rel: $12.75 Cur: $32 (2/16/84) (HS)
80   IRON HORSE Cabernet Sauvignon Alexander Valley 1978 Rel: $12 Cur: $25 (CA-3/89)
80   RODNEY STRONG Cabernet Sauvignon Alexander Valley Alexander's Crown Vineyard 1978 $12 (1/01/84)
78   FRANCISCAN Cabernet Sauvignon Napa Valley Reserve 1978 Rel: $15 Cur: $23 (CA-3/89)
78   JORDAN Cabernet Sauvignon Alexander Valley 1978 Rel: $16 Cur: $61 (2/01/85)
78   CHARLES KRUG Cabernet Sauvignon Napa Valley Vintage Select 1978 Rel: $11 Cur: $22 (CA-3/89)
78   VILLA MT. EDEN Cabernet Sauvignon Napa Valley 1978 Rel: $8 Cur: $42 (CA-3/89)
75   MAYACAMAS Cabernet Sauvignon Napa Valley 1978 Rel: $18 Cur: $60 (4/30/87)
75   PARDUCCI Cabernet Sauvignon Mendocino County 1978 $5.50 (2/01/86)
75   PARDUCCI Cabernet Merlot Cellarmaster Selection Mendocino County 1978 $12 (2/01/86)
74   KEENAN Cabernet Sauvignon Napa Valley 1978 Rel: $12 Cur: $40 (CA-3/89)
72   CLOS DU BOIS Marlstone Vineyard Alexander Valley 1978 Rel: $16 Cur: $30 (CA-3/89)
72   CUVAISON Cabernet Sauvignon Napa Valley 1978 Rel: $10 Cur: $30 (CA-3/89)
72   SIMI Cabernet Sauvignon Alexander Valley Reserve 1978 Rel: $17 Cur: $38 (CA-3/89)
70   JEKEL Cabernet Sauvignon Monterey Home Vineyard Private Reserve 1978 $16 (2/01/86)
69   SIMI Cabernet Sauvignon Alexander Valley Reserve 1978 Rel: $17 Cur: $38 (2/01/86)
65   CUVAISON Cabernet Sauvignon Napa Valley 1978 Rel: $10 Cur: $30 (5/16/84)

1977

94   CHATEAU MONTELENA Cabernet Sauvignon Napa Valley 1977 Rel: $12 Cur: $70 (CA-3/89)
94   RIDGE Cabernet Sauvignon Santa Cruz Mountains Monte Bello 1977 Rel: $40 Cur: $100 (CA-3/89)
93   NIEBAUM-COPPOLA Rubicon Napa Valley 1977 (NR) (2/28/87) (JG)
93   STERLING Cabernet Sauvignon Napa Valley Reserve 1977 Rel: $27.50 Cur: $55 (CA-3/89)
92   BURGESS Cabernet Sauvignon Napa Valley Vintage Selection 1977 Rel: $12 Cur: $45 (CA-3/89)
92   INGLENOOK Cabernet Sauvignon Napa Valley Cask 1977 Rel: $8.75 Cur: $25 (6/01/85) (JL)
92   MAYACAMAS Cabernet Sauvignon Napa Valley 1977 Rel: $15 Cur: $60 (CA-3/89)
91   CHATEAU MONTELENA Cabernet Sauvignon Alexander Valley Sonoma 1977 Rel: $12 Cur: $65 (CA-3/89)
91   HEITZ Cabernet Sauvignon Napa Valley Bella Oaks Vineyard 1977 Rel: $30 Cur: $66 (CA-3/89)
91   ROBERT MONDAVI Cabernet Sauvignon Napa Valley Reserve 1977 Rel: $35 Cur: $45 (7/16/85) (JL)
91   MOUNT EDEN Cabernet Sauvignon Santa Cruz Mountains 1977 Rel: $20 Cur: $54 (CA-3/89)
91   JOSEPH PHELPS Insignia Napa Valley 1977 Rel: $25 Cur: $75 (CA-3/89)
91   JOSEPH PHELPS Insignia Napa Valley 1977 Rel: $25 Cur: $75 (10/30/87)
91   STAG'S LEAP WINE CELLARS Cabernet Sauvignon Napa Valley Stags Leap District Stag's Leap Vineyards Cask 23 1977 Rel: $30 Cur: $75 (CA-3/89)
90   CONN CREEK Cabernet Sauvignon Napa Valley 1977 Rel: $12 Cur: $40 (CA-3/89)
90   HEITZ Cabernet Sauvignon Napa Valley Martha's Vineyard 1977 Rel: $30 Cur: $75 (1/31/90) (JL)
90   HEITZ Cabernet Sauvignon Napa Valley Martha's Vineyard 1977 Rel: $30 Cur: $75 (CA-3/89)
90   ST. CLEMENT Cabernet Sauvignon Napa Valley 1977 Rel: $10 Cur: $45 (CA-3/89)
90   STAG'S LEAP WINE CELLARS Cabernet Sauvignon Napa Valley Stags Leap District Stag's Leap Vineyards Lot 2 1977 Rel: $10 Cur: $61 (CA-3/89)
89   CLOS DU VAL Cabernet Sauvignon Napa Valley Stags Leap District 1977 Rel: $10 Cur: $40 (CA-3/89)
89   DIAMOND CREEK Cabernet Sauvignon Napa Valley Gravelly Meadow 1977 Rel: $10 Cur: $80 (CA-3/89)
89   GUNDLACH BUNDSCHU Cabernet Sauvignon Sonoma Valley Batto Ranch 1977 Rel: $8 Cur: $24 (CA-3/89)
89   HEITZ Cabernet Sauvignon Napa Valley Bella Oaks Vineyard 1977 Rel: $30 Cur: $66 (2/16/84) (HS)
89   ROBERT MONDAVI Cabernet Sauvignon Napa Valley 1977 Cur: $30 (7/16/85) (JL)
88   BERINGER Cabernet Sauvignon Napa Valley Private Reserve Lemmon Ranch Vineyard 1977 Rel: $12 Cur: $75 (CA-3/89)
88   DIAMOND CREEK Cabernet Sauvignon Napa Valley Red Rock Terrace First Pick 1977 Rel: $10 Cur: $72 (CA-3/89)
88   FREEMARK ABBEY Cabernet Sauvignon Napa Valley Bosché 1977 Rel: $12.50 Cur: $31 (CA-3/89)
88   HEITZ Cabernet Sauvignon Napa Valley Martha's Vineyard 1977 Rel: $30 Cur: $75 (2/16/84) (HS)
88   MOUNT VEEDER Cabernet Sauvignon Napa Valley Niebaum-Coppola 1977 Rel: $9.75 Cur: $60 (CA-3/89)
88   RIDGE Cabernet Sauvignon Napa County York Creek 1977 Rel: $12 Cur: $35 (CA-3/89)
88   SILVER OAK Cabernet Sauvignon Alexander Valley 1977 Rel: $14 Cur: $75 (CA-3/89)
88   STELTZNER Cabernet Sauvignon Napa Valley Stags Leap District 1977 Rel: $14 Cur: $45 (6/30/87) (JL)
87   CLOS DU VAL Cabernet Sauvignon Napa Valley Stags Leap District Reserve 1977 Rel: $20 Cur: $53 (CA-3/89)
86   JOSEPH PHELPS Cabernet Sauvignon Napa Valley Backus Vineyard 1977 Rel: $15 Cur: $63 (CA-3/89)
86   TREFETHEN Cabernet Sauvignon Napa Valley 1977 Rel: $8.50 Cur: $45 (CA-3/89)
86   VILLA MT. EDEN Cabernet Sauvignon Napa Valley 1977 Rel: $8 Cur: $36 (CA-3/89)
85   MOUNT VEEDER Cabernet Sauvignon Napa Valley Bernstein Vineyards 1977 Rel: $11 Cur: $50 (CA-3/89)
85   SPRING MOUNTAIN Cabernet Sauvignon Napa Valley 1977 Rel: $9.50 Cur: $20 (CA-3/89)
85   STAG'S LEAP WINE CELLARS Cabernet Sauvignon Napa Valley Stags Leap District Stag's Leap Vineyards 1977 Rel: $9 Cur: $35 (CA-3/89)
85   STELTZNER Cabernet Sauvignon Napa Valley Stags Leap District 1977 Rel: $14 Cur: $45 (CA-3/89)
84   DIAMOND CREEK Cabernet Sauvignon Napa Valley Volcanic Hill 1977 Rel: $10 Cur: $66 (CA-3/89)
84   INGLENOOK Cabernet Sauvignon Napa Valley Cask 1977 Rel: $8.75 Cur: $25 (CA-3/89)
84   ROBERT MONDAVI Cabernet Sauvignon Napa Valley Reserve 1977 Rel: $35 Cur: $45 (CA-3/89)
84   RAYMOND Cabernet Sauvignon Napa Valley 1977 Rel: $8.50 Cur: $27 (CA-3/89)
83   HEITZ Cabernet Sauvignon Napa Valley 1977 Rel: $11 Cur: $48 (1/31/90) (JL)
82   CHAPPELLET Cabernet Sauvignon Napa Valley 1977 Rel: $12 Cur: $33 (CA-3/89)
82   KENWOOD Cabernet Sauvignon Sonoma Valley Artist Series 1977 Rel: $15 Cur: $175 (CA-3/89)
82   JOSEPH PHELPS Cabernet Sauvignon Napa Valley Eisele Vineyard 1977 Rel: $25 Cur: $56 (CA-3/89)

UNITED STATES
CALIFORNIA/CABERNET SAUVIGNON & BLENDS

82   RAVENSWOOD Cabernet Sauvignon El Dorado County Madrona Vineyards 1977 Rel: $8.50 Cur: $9 (CA-3/89)
81   STONEGATE Cabernet Sauvignon Napa Valley 1977 Rel: $10 Cur: $25 (CA-3/89)
79   BEAULIEU Cabernet Sauvignon Napa Valley Georges de Latour Private Reserve 1977 Rel: $16 Cur: $46 (3/31/91) (JL)
79   BEAULIEU Cabernet Sauvignon Napa Valley Georges de Latour Private Reserve 1977 Rel: $16 Cur: $46 (CA-3/89)
79   CUVAISON Cabernet Sauvignon Napa Valley 1977 Rel: $10 Cur: $30 (CA-3/89)
78   HEITZ Cabernet Sauvignon Napa Valley Fay Vineyard 1977 Rel: $17.50 Cur: $32 (2/16/84) (HS)
77   CAYMUS Cabernet Sauvignon Napa Valley 1977 Rel: $10 Cur: $41 (CA-3/89)
77   FIRESTONE Cabernet Sauvignon Santa Ynez Valley Special Release 1977 $9.50 (4/16/85)
77   JORDAN Cabernet Sauvignon Alexander Valley 1977 Rel: $14 Cur: $70 (CA-3/89)
75   DIAMOND CREEK Cabernet Sauvignon Napa Valley Red Rock Terrace Second Pick 1977 Rel: $10 Cur: $45 (CA-3/89)
74   CHARLES KRUG Cabernet Sauvignon Napa Valley Vintage Select 1977 Rel: $10 Cur: $22 (CA-3/89)
73   HEITZ Cabernet Sauvignon Napa Valley 1977 Rel: $11 Cur: $48 (2/16/84) (HS)
72   BUENA VISTA Cabernet Sauvignon Sonoma Valley Cask 34 1977 Rel: $12 Cur: $40 (CA-3/89)
72   RUTHERFORD HILL Cabernet Sauvignon Napa Valley 1977 Rel: $10 Cur: $18 (CA-3/89)
70   LOUIS M. MARTINI Cabernet Sauvignon California Special Selection 1977 Rel: $9 Cur: $20 (CA-3/89)
70   SIMI Cabernet Sauvignon Alexander Valley Special Selection 1977 Rel: $20 Cur: $23 (CA-3/89)
69   KEENAN Cabernet Sauvignon Napa Valley 1977 Rel: $12 Cur: $40 (CA-3/89)

1976

94   HEITZ Cabernet Sauvignon Napa Valley Martha's Vineyard 1976 Rel: $30 Cur: $86 (2/16/84) (HS)
93   JOSEPH PHELPS Insignia Napa Valley 1976 Rel: $20 Cur: $120 (CA-3/89)
92   HEITZ Cabernet Sauvignon Napa Valley Bella Oaks Vineyard 1976 Rel: $30 Cur: $62 (2/16/84) (HS)
90   BEAULIEU Cabernet Sauvignon Napa Valley Georges de Latour Private Reserve 1976 Rel: $19 Cur: $60 (6/01/85) (JL)
90   CAYMUS Cabernet Sauvignon Napa Valley Special Selection 1976 Rel: $35 Cur: $220 (CA-3/89)
90   CHATEAU MONTELENA Cabernet Sauvignon North Coast 1976 Rel: $10 Cur: $75 (CA-3/89)
90   ROBERT MONDAVI Cabernet Sauvignon Napa Valley Reserve 1976 Rel: $25 Cur: $55 (7/16/85) (JL)
88   BEAULIEU Cabernet Sauvignon Napa Valley Georges de Latour Private Reserve 1976 Rel: $19 Cur: $60 (3/31/91) (JL)
87   BURGESS Cabernet Sauvignon Napa Valley Vintage Selection 1976 Rel: $12 Cur: $40 (CA-3/89)
87   DIAMOND CREEK Cabernet Sauvignon Napa Valley Volcanic Hill 1976 Rel: $9 Cur: $90 (CA-3/89)
86   BEAULIEU Cabernet Sauvignon Napa Valley Georges de Latour Private Reserve 1976 Rel: $19 Cur: $60 (CA-3/89)
86   CONN CREEK Cabernet Sauvignon Napa Valley 1976 Rel: $12 Cur: $45 (CA-3/89)
86   LOUIS M. MARTINI Cabernet Sauvignon California Special Selection 1976 Rel: $9 Cur: $32 (CA-3/89)
86   SILVER OAK Cabernet Sauvignon Alexander Valley 1976 Rel: $12 Cur: $65 (CA-3/89)
85   CAYMUS Cabernet Sauvignon Napa Valley 1976 Rel: $10 Cur: $63 (CA-3/89)
85   DIAMOND CREEK Cabernet Sauvignon Napa Valley Gravelly Meadow 1976 Rel: $9 Cur: $90 (CA-3/89)
85   DIAMOND CREEK Cabernet Sauvignon Napa Valley Red Rock Terrace 1976 Rel: $9 Cur: $95 (CA-3/89)
85   FREEMARK ABBEY Cabernet Sauvignon Napa Valley Bosché 1976 Rel: $12.50 Cur: $45 (CA-3/89)
85   HEITZ Cabernet Sauvignon Napa Valley Bella Oaks Vineyard 1976 Rel: $30 Cur: $62 (CA-3/89)
85   HEITZ Cabernet Sauvignon Napa Valley Martha's Vineyard 1976 Rel: $30 Cur: $86 (CA-3/89)
85   JOSEPH PHELPS Insignia Napa Valley 1976 Rel: $20 Cur: $120 (10/30/87)
84   MAYACAMAS Cabernet Sauvignon Napa Valley 1976 Rel: $15 Cur: $50 (CA-3/89)
84   ROBERT MONDAVI Cabernet Sauvignon Napa Valley 1976 Cur: $43 (7/16/85) (JL)
84   ROBERT MONDAVI Cabernet Sauvignon Napa Valley Reserve 1976 Rel: $25 Cur: $55 (CA-3/89)
83   MOUNT EDEN Cabernet Sauvignon Santa Cruz Mountains 1976 Rel: $20 Cur: $68 (CA-3/89)
83   RIDGE Cabernet Sauvignon Santa Cruz Mountains Monte Bello 1976 Rel: $15 Cur: $65 (CA-3/89)
82   CLOS DU VAL Cabernet Sauvignon Napa Valley 1976 Rel: $9 Cur: $55 (CA-3/89)
80   STAG'S LEAP WINE CELLARS Cabernet Sauvignon Napa Valley Stags Leap District Stag's Leap Vineyards Lot 2 1976 Rel: $11 Cur: $55 (CA-3/89)
79   CUVAISON Cabernet Sauvignon Napa Valley 1976 Rel: $10 Cur: $30 (CA-3/89)
79   JORDAN Cabernet Sauvignon Alexander Valley 1976 Rel: $10 Cur: $76 (CA-3/89)
78   RAYMOND Cabernet Sauvignon Napa Valley 1976 Rel: $6 Cur: $35 (CA-3/89)
77   KENWOOD Cabernet Sauvignon Sonoma County Artist Series 1976 Rel: $10 Cur: $160 (CA-3/89)
77   MOUNT VEEDER Cabernet Sauvignon Napa Valley Bernstein Vineyards 1976 Rel: $11 Cur: $35 (CA-3/89)
76   CHAPPELLET Cabernet Sauvignon Napa Valley 1976 Rel: $12 Cur: $41 (CA-3/89)
76   STERLING Cabernet Sauvignon Napa Valley Reserve 1976 Rel: $25 Cur: $44 (CA-3/89)
76   TREFETHEN Cabernet Sauvignon Napa Valley 1976 Rel: $7.50 Cur: $45 (CA-3/89)

Key to Symbols

The scores reported here are the results of blind tastings conducted by our panel of senior editors. Wines that carry the initials below are results of individual tastings.

THE WINE SPECTATOR 100-POINT SCALE 95-100—Classic, a great wine; 90-94—Outstanding, superior character and style; 80-89—Good to very good, a wine with special qualities; 70-79—Average, drinkable wine that may have minor flaws; 60-69—Below average, drinkable but not recommended; 50-59—Poor, undrinkable, not recommended. "+"—With a score indicates a range; used primarily with barrel tastings to indicate a preliminary score.

SPECIAL DESIGNATIONS SS—Spectator Selection, CS—Cellar Selection, BB—Best Buy.

TASTER'S INITIALS (JG)—Jim Gordon, (HS)—Harvey Steiman, (JL)—James Laube, (JS)—James Suckling, (TM)—Thomas Matthews, (TR)—Terry Robards, (BT)—Barrel Tasting (these wines were tasted blind from barrel samples), (CA-date)—California's Great Cabernets by James Laube, (CH-date)—California's Great Chardonnays by James Laube, (VP-date)—Vintage Port by James Suckling.

DATE TASTED Dates in parentheses represent the issue in which the rating was published.

---

73   RUTHERFORD HILL Cabernet Sauvignon Napa Valley 1976 Rel: $9 Cur: $17 (CA-3/89)
73   STAG'S LEAP WINE CELLARS Cabernet Sauvignon Napa Valley Stags Leap District Stag's Leap Vineyards 1976 Rel: $10 Cur: $71 (CA-3/89)
72   INGLENOOK Cabernet Sauvignon Napa Valley Cask 1976 Rel: $8.75 Cur: $19 (CA-3/89)
70   VILLA MT. EDEN Cabernet Sauvignon Napa Valley 1976 Rel: $7 Cur: $40 (CA-3/89)
68   RIDGE Cabernet Sauvignon Napa County York Creek 1976 Rel: $10 Cur: $36 (CA-3/89)
66   BUENA VISTA Cabernet Sauvignon Sonoma Valley 1976 $12 (CA-3/89)
60   ALEXANDER VALLEY Cabernet Sauvignon Alexander Valley 1976 Rel: $5.50 Cur: $18 (CA-3/89)

1975-1976

87   ST. CLEMENT Cabernet Sauvignon Napa Valley 1975-76 Rel: $8 Cur: $50 (CA-3/89)

1975

97   JOSEPH PHELPS Cabernet Sauvignon Napa Valley Eisele Vineyard 1975 Rel: $15 Cur: $162 (CA-3/89)
93   DIAMOND CREEK Cabernet Sauvignon Napa Valley Volcanic Hill 1975 Rel: $7.50 Cur: $80 (CA-3/89)
92   CAYMUS Cabernet Sauvignon Napa Valley Special Selection 1975 Rel: $22 Cur: $250 (CA-3/89)
92   HEITZ Cabernet Sauvignon Napa Valley Martha's Vineyard 1975 Rel: $25 Cur: $100 (CA-3/89)
91   JOSEPH PHELPS Insignia Napa Valley 1975 Rel: $15 Cur: $113 (10/30/87)
90   FREEMARK ABBEY Cabernet Sauvignon Napa Valley Bosché 1975 Rel: $10 Cur: $57 (CA-3/89)
90   HEITZ Cabernet Sauvignon Napa Valley Martha's Vineyard 1975 Rel: $25 Cur: $100 (2/16/84) (HS)
90   MOUNT EDEN Cabernet Sauvignon Santa Cruz Mountains 1975 Rel: $20 Cur: $70 (CA-3/89)
89   CAYMUS Cabernet Sauvignon Napa Valley 1975 Rel: $8.50 Cur: $87 (CA-3/89)
89   CLOS DU VAL Cabernet Sauvignon Napa Valley Stags Leap District 1975 Rel: $9 Cur: $65 (CA-3/89)
89   MAYACAMAS Cabernet Sauvignon Napa Valley 1975 Rel: $12 Cur: $64 (CA-3/89)
89   ROBERT MONDAVI Cabernet Sauvignon Napa Valley Reserve 1975 Rel: $30 Cur: $65 (7/16/85) (JL)
89   VILLA MT. EDEN Cabernet Sauvignon Napa Valley 1975 Rel: $7 Cur: $50 (CA-3/89)
88   BURGESS Cabernet Sauvignon Napa Valley Vintage Selection 1975 Rel: $9 Cur: $45 (CA-3/89)
88   CUVAISON Cabernet Sauvignon Napa Valley Philip Togni Signature 1975 Rel: $40 Cur: $60 (CA-3/89)
88   DIAMOND CREEK Cabernet Sauvignon Napa Valley Red Rock Terrace 1975 Rel: $7.50 Cur: $88 (CA-3/89)
88   RIDGE Cabernet Sauvignon Santa Cruz Mountains Monte Bello 1975 Rel: $10 Cur: $95 (CA-3/89)
88   SILVER OAK Cabernet Sauvignon Alexander Valley 1975 Rel: $10 Cur: $98 (CA-3/89)
87   RIDGE Cabernet Sauvignon Napa County York Creek 1975 Rel: $10 Cur: $53 (CA-3/89)
86   CHATEAU MONTELENA Cabernet Sauvignon North Coast 1975 Rel: $9 Cur: $100 (CA-3/89)
86   ROBERT MONDAVI Cabernet Sauvignon Napa Valley Reserve 1975 Rel: $30 Cur: $65 (CA-3/89)
85   DIAMOND CREEK Cabernet Sauvignon Napa Valley Gravelly Meadow 1975 Rel: $7.50 Cur: $80 (CA-3/89)
85   JOSEPH PHELPS Insignia Napa Valley 1975 Rel: $15 Cur: $113 (CA-3/89)
85   SIMI Cabernet Sauvignon Alexander Valley 1975 Rel: $6 Cur: $32 (CA-3/89)
83   BEAULIEU Cabernet Sauvignon Napa Valley Georges de Latour Private Reserve 1975 Rel: $16 Cur: $57 (3/31/91) (JL)
83   MOUNT VEEDER Cabernet Sauvignon Napa Valley Bernstein Vineyards 1975 Rel: $11 Cur: $35 (CA-3/89)
83   TREFETHEN Cabernet Sauvignon Napa Valley 1975 Rel: $7.50 Cur: $55 (CA-3/89)
82   FRANCISCAN Cabernet Sauvignon Napa Valley Reserve 1975 Rel: $12 Cur: $32 (CA-3/89)
79   BEAULIEU Cabernet Sauvignon Napa Valley Georges de Latour Private Reserve 1975 Rel: $16 Cur: $57 (CA-3/89)
79   CUVAISON Cabernet Sauvignon Napa Valley 1975 Rel: $10 Cur: $33 (CA-3/89)
79   ROBERT MONDAVI Cabernet Sauvignon Napa Valley 1975 Cur: $38 (7/16/85) (JL)
78   CHAPPELLET Cabernet Sauvignon Napa Valley 1975 Rel: $10 Cur: $45 (CA-3/89)
78   STERLING Cabernet Sauvignon Napa Valley Reserve 1975 Rel: $20 Cur: $55 (CA-3/89)
75   ALEXANDER VALLEY Cabernet Sauvignon Alexander Valley 1975 Rel: $5.50 Cur: $20 (CA-3/89)
74   STAG'S LEAP WINE CELLARS Cabernet Sauvignon Napa Valley Stags Leap District Stag's Leap Vineyards 1975 Rel: $8.50 Cur: $68 (CA-3/89)
73   KENWOOD Cabernet Sauvignon Sonoma County Artist Series 1975 Rel: $6.50 Cur: $500 (CA-3/89)
69   RUTHERFORD HILL Cabernet Sauvignon Napa Valley 1975 Rel: $9 Cur: $18 (CA-3/89)
64   BUENA VISTA Cabernet Sauvignon Sonoma Valley 1975 $12 (CA-3/89)

1974

99   HEITZ Cabernet Sauvignon Napa Valley Martha's Vineyard 1974 Rel: $25 Cur: $235 (CA-3/89)
97   MAYACAMAS Cabernet Sauvignon Napa Valley 1974 Rel: $9.50 Cur: $115 (2/15/90) (JG)
96   DIAMOND CREEK Cabernet Sauvignon Napa Valley Gravelly Meadow 1974 Rel: $7.50 Cur: $140 (2/15/90) (JG)
95   DIAMOND CREEK Cabernet Sauvignon Napa Valley Volcanic Hill 1974 Rel: $7.50 Cur: $135 (2/15/90) (JG)
95   MAYACAMAS Cabernet Sauvignon Napa Valley 1974 Rel: $9.50 Cur: $115 (CA-3/89)
94   CONN CREEK Cabernet Sauvignon Napa Valley 1974 Rel: $9 Cur: $198 (CA-3/89)
94   HEITZ Cabernet Sauvignon Napa Valley Martha's Vineyard 1974 Rel: $25 Cur: $235 (2/15/90) (JG)
94   INGLENOOK Cabernet Sauvignon Napa Valley Cask 1974 Rel: $9 Cur: $46 (6/01/85) (JL)
94   ROBERT MONDAVI Cabernet Sauvignon Napa Valley Reserve 1974 Rel: $30 Cur: $96 (7/16/85) (JL)
93   JOSEPH PHELPS Insignia Napa Valley 1974 Rel: $12 Cur: $200 (10/30/87)
93   RIDGE Cabernet Sauvignon Santa Cruz Mountains Monte Bello 1974 Rel: $12 Cur: $155 (CA-3/89)
93   SILVER OAK Cabernet Sauvignon North Coast 1974 Rel: $8 Cur: $135 (CA-3/89)
92   ROBERT MONDAVI Cabernet Sauvignon Napa Valley Reserve 1974 Rel: $30 Cur: $96 (2/15/90) (JG)
92   ROBERT MONDAVI Cabernet Sauvignon Napa Valley Reserve 1974 Rel: $30 Cur: $96 (CA-3/89)
92   RIDGE Cabernet Sauvignon Santa Cruz Mountains Monte Bello 1974 Rel: $12 Cur: $155 (2/15/90) (JG)
92   STERLING Cabernet Sauvignon Napa Valley Reserve 1974 Rel: $20 Cur: $87 (2/15/90) (JG)

92 VILLA MT. EDEN Cabernet Sauvignon Napa Valley 1974 Rel: $7 Cur: $85 (2/15/90) (JG)
91 BEAULIEU Cabernet Sauvignon Napa Valley Georges de Latour Private Reserve 1974 Rel: $12 Cur: $81 (6/01/85) (JL)
91 CAYMUS Cabernet Sauvignon Napa Valley 1974 Rel: $7 Cur: $110 (2/15/90) (JG)
91 CLOS DU VAL Cabernet Sauvignon Napa Valley Stags Leap District 1974 Rel: $7.50 Cur: $75 (CA-3/89)
91 FREEMARK ABBEY Cabernet Sauvignon Napa Valley Bosché 1974 Rel: $7.75 Cur: $76 (CA-3/89)
91 CHARLES KRUG Cabernet Sauvignon Napa Valley Vintage Select Lot F-1 1974 Rel: $9 Cur: $50 (6/01/85) (JL)
90 CHATEAU MONTELENA Cabernet Sauvignon Napa Valley 1974 Rel: $9 Cur: $100 (2/15/90) (JG)
90 CHATEAU MONTELENA Cabernet Sauvignon Napa Valley 1974 Rel: $9 Cur: $100 (CA-3/89)
90 CONN CREEK Cabernet Sauvignon Napa Valley 1974 Rel: $9 Cur: $198 (2/15/90) (JG)
90 ROBERT MONDAVI Cabernet Sauvignon Napa Valley 1974 Cur: $50 (7/16/85) (JL)
90 JOSEPH PHELPS Insignia Napa Valley 1974 Rel: $12 Cur: $200 (CA-3/89)
90 STERLING Cabernet Sauvignon Napa Valley 1974 Cur: $50 (2/15/90) (JG)
90 STERLING Cabernet Sauvignon Napa Valley Reserve 1974 Rel: $20 Cur: $87 (CA-3/89)
90 VILLA MT. EDEN Cabernet Sauvignon Napa Valley 1974 Rel: $7 Cur: $85 (CA-3/89)
89 MOUNT VEEDER Cabernet Sauvignon Napa Valley 1974 Rel: $8 Cur: $65 (2/15/90) (JG)
88 DIAMOND CREEK Cabernet Sauvignon Napa Valley Gravelly Meadow 1974 Rel: $7.50 Cur: $140 (CA-3/89)
88 CHARLES KRUG Cabernet Sauvignon Napa Valley Vintage Select Lot F-1 1974 Rel: $9 Cur: $50 (CA-3/89)
88 LOUIS M. MARTINI Cabernet Sauvignon California Special Selection 1974 Rel: $10 Cur: $41 (6/01/85) (JL)
88 STAG'S LEAP WINE CELLARS Cabernet Sauvignon Napa Valley Stags Leap District Stag's Leap Vineyards Cask 23 1974 Rel: $12 Cur: $144 (CA-3/89)
87 BEAULIEU Cabernet Sauvignon Napa Valley Georges de Latour Private Reserve 1974 Rel: $12 Cur: $81 (2/15/90) (JG)
87 CAYMUS Cabernet Sauvignon Napa Valley 1974 Rel: $7 Cur: $110 (CA-3/89)
87 CHATEAU MONTELENA Cabernet Sauvignon Alexander Valley Sonoma 1974 Rel: $9 Cur: $100 (CA-3/89)
87 DIAMOND CREEK Cabernet Sauvignon Napa Valley Volcanic Hill 1974 Rel: $7.50 Cur: $135 (CA-3/89)
87 CHARLES KRUG Cabernet Sauvignon Napa Valley Vintage Select 1974 Rel: $9 Cur: $50 (2/15/90) (JG)
87 MOUNT EDEN Cabernet Sauvignon Santa Cruz Mountains 1974 Rel: $20 Cur: $120 (2/15/90) (JG)
87 MOUNT EDEN Cabernet Sauvignon Santa Cruz Mountains 1974 Rel: $20 Cur: $120 (CA-3/89)
87 RIDGE Cabernet Sauvignon Napa County York Creek 1974 Rel: $6.75 Cur: $54 (CA-3/89)
87 SIMI Cabernet Sauvignon Alexander Valley Reserve Vintage 1974 Rel: $20 Cur: $61 (CA-3/89)
87 STAG'S LEAP WINE CELLARS Cabernet Sauvignon Napa Valley Stags Leap District Stag's Leap Vineyards 1974 Rel: $8 Cur: $110 (CA-3/89)
86 BURGESS Cabernet Sauvignon Napa Valley Vintage Selection 1974 Rel: $9 Cur: $70 (CA-3/89)
86 INGLENOOK Cabernet Sauvignon Napa Valley Cask 1974 Rel: $9 Cur: $46 (CA-3/89)
86 CHARLES KRUG Cabernet Sauvignon Napa Valley Vintage Select 1974 Rel: $9 Cur: $50 (6/01/85) (JL)
85 SIMI Cabernet Sauvignon Alexander Valley Reserve 1974 Rel: $20 Cur: $61 (2/15/90) (JG)
84 CHATEAU SOUVERAIN Cabernet Sauvignon Sonoma County Vintage Selection 1974 Cur: $50 (2/15/90) (JG)
84 TREFETHEN Cabernet Sauvignon Napa Valley 1974 Rel: $8 Cur: $65 (CA-3/89)
83 SIMI Cabernet Sauvignon Alexander Valley Special Reserve 1974 Rel: $20 Cur: $61 (CA-3/89)
83 STAG'S LEAP WINE CELLARS Cabernet Sauvignon Napa Valley Stags Leap District Stag's Leap Vineyards 1974 Rel: $8 Cur: $110 (2/15/90)
82 SILVER OAK Cabernet Sauvignon North Coast 1974 Rel: $8 Cur: $135 (2/15/90) (JG)
81 SANTA BARBARA Cabernet Sauvignon Santa Ynez Valley Reserve 1974 $16 (12/15/89)
80 MOUNT VEEDER Cabernet Sauvignon Napa Valley 1974 Rel: $8 Cur: $65 (CA-3/89)
80 STAG'S LEAP WINE CELLARS Cabernet Sauvignon Napa Valley Stags Leap District Stag's Leap Vineyards Cask 23 1974 Rel: $12 Cur: $144 (2/15/90) (JG)
79 BEAULIEU Cabernet Sauvignon Napa Valley Georges de Latour Private Reserve 1974 Rel: $12 Cur: $81 (3/31/91) (JL)
79 BEAULIEU Cabernet Sauvignon Napa Valley Georges de Latour Private Reserve 1974 Rel: $12 Cur: $81 (CA-3/89)
79 INGLENOOK Cabernet Sauvignon Napa Valley Cask A8 1974 Rel: $9 Cur: $46 (2/15/90) (JG)
79 ROBERT MONDAVI Cabernet Sauvignon Napa Valley 1974 Cur: $50 (2/15/90) (JG)
78 CHAPPELLET Cabernet Sauvignon Napa Valley 1974 Rel: $7.50 Cur: $66 (2/15/90) (JG)
78 RAYMOND Cabernet Sauvignon Napa Valley 1974 Rel: $5.50 Cur: $60 (CA-3/89)
77 LOUIS M. MARTINI Cabernet Sauvignon California Special Selection 1974 Rel: $10 Cur: $41 (CA-3/89)
74 CLOS DU BOIS Cabernet Sauvignon Sonoma County Dry Creek 1974 Cur: $40 (2/15/90) (JG)
70 CHAPPELLET Cabernet Sauvignon Napa Valley 1974 Rel: $7.50 Cur: $66 (CA-3/89)
68 BUENA VISTA Cabernet Sauvignon Sonoma Valley Cask 25 1974 Rel: $12 Cur: $40 (CA-3/89)

1973

93 CAYMUS Cabernet Sauvignon Napa Valley 1973 Rel: $6 Cur: $126 (CA-3/89)
92 CONN CREEK Cabernet Sauvignon Napa Valley Stags Leap District 1973 Rel: $9 Cur: $70 (CA-3/89)
92 HEITZ Cabernet Sauvignon Napa Valley Martha's Vineyard 1973 Rel: $11 Cur: $120 (CA-3/89)
91 ROBERT MONDAVI Cabernet Sauvignon Napa Valley Reserve 1973 Rel: $12 Cur: $80 (7/16/85) (JL)
91 MOUNT EDEN Cabernet Sauvignon Santa Cruz Mountains 1973 Rel: $14 Cur: $120 (CA-3/89)
90 CLOS DU VAL Cabernet Sauvignon Napa Valley Stags Leap District Reserve 1973 Rel: $10 Cur: $100 (CA-3/89)
90 MOUNT VEEDER Cabernet Sauvignon Napa Valley 1973 Rel: $8 Cur: $70 (CA-3/89)
89 STERLING Cabernet Sauvignon Napa Valley Reserve 1973 Rel: $10 Cur: $70 (CA-3/89)
88 FREEMARK ABBEY Cabernet Sauvignon Napa Valley Bosché 1973 Rel: $8 Cur: $70 (CA-3/89)
87 CHATEAU MONTELENA Cabernet Sauvignon Alexander Valley Sonoma 1973 Rel: $8 Cur: $100 (CA-3/89)
87 MAYACAMAS Cabernet Sauvignon Napa Valley 1973 Rel: $9 Cur: $90 (CA-3/89)
87 RIDGE Cabernet Sauvignon Santa Cruz Mountains Monte Bello 1973 Rel: $10 Cur: $110 (CA-3/89)

86 CLOS DU VAL Cabernet Sauvignon Napa Valley Stags Leap District 1973 Rel: $6 Cur: $75 (CA-3/89)
86 ROBERT MONDAVI Cabernet Sauvignon Napa Valley 1973 Cur: $35 (7/16/85) (JL)
86 STAG'S LEAP WINE CELLARS Cabernet Sauvignon Napa Valley Stags Leap District Stag's Leap Vineyards 1973 Rel: $6 Cur: $141 (CA-3/89)
82 ROBERT MONDAVI Cabernet Sauvignon Napa Valley Reserve 1973 Rel: $12 Cur: $80 (CA-3/89)
82 STAG'S LEAP WINE CELLARS Cabernet Sauvignon Napa Valley Stags Leap District Stag's Leap Vineyards 1973 Rel: $6 Cur: $141 (4/01/86)
81 SILVER OAK Cabernet Sauvignon North Coast 1973 Rel: $7 Cur: $130 (CA-3/89)
80 DIAMOND CREEK Cabernet Sauvignon Napa Valley Volcanic Hill 1973 Rel: $7.50 Cur: $200 (CA-3/89)
79 BEAULIEU Cabernet Sauvignon Napa Valley Georges de Latour Private Reserve 1973 Rel: $9 Cur: $55 (CA-3/89)
78 HEITZ Cabernet Sauvignon Napa Valley 1973 Cur: $38 (1/31/90) (JL)
75 BEAULIEU Cabernet Sauvignon Napa Valley Georges de Latour Private Reserve 1973 Rel: $9 Cur: $55 (3/31/91) (JL)
73 CHARLES KRUG Cabernet Sauvignon Napa Valley Vintage Select 1973 Rel: $9 Cur: $40 (CA-3/89)
72 SIMI Cabernet Sauvignon Alexander Valley 1973 Rel: $6 Cur: $25 (CA-3/89)
69 CHAPPELLET Cabernet Sauvignon Napa Valley 1973 Rel: $7.50 Cur: $68 (CA-3/89)
67 INGLENOOK Cabernet Sauvignon Napa Valley Cask 1973 Rel: $8 Cur: $39 (CA-3/89)

1972

90 CLOS DU VAL Cabernet Sauvignon Napa Valley Stags Leap District 1972 Rel: $6 Cur: $75 (CA-3/89)
86 CAYMUS Cabernet Sauvignon Napa Valley 1972 Rel: $4.50 Cur: $110 (CA-3/89)
86 SILVER OAK Cabernet Sauvignon North Coast 1972 Rel: $6 Cur: $135 (CA-3/89)
85 DIAMOND CREEK Cabernet Sauvignon Napa Valley Volcanic Hill 1972 Rel: $7.50 Cur: $200 (CA-3/89)
84 MOUNT EDEN Cabernet Sauvignon Santa Cruz Mountains 1972 Rel: $20 Cur: $60 (CA-3/89)
84 RIDGE Cabernet Sauvignon Santa Cruz Mountains Monte Bello 1972 Rel: $10 Cur: $100 (CA-3/89)
82 MAYACAMAS Cabernet Sauvignon Napa Valley 1972 Rel: $8 Cur: $70 (CA-3/89)
81 CLOS DU VAL Cabernet Sauvignon Napa Valley Stags Leap District 1972 Rel: $6 Cur: $75 (4/01/86)
80 FREEMARK ABBEY Cabernet Sauvignon Napa Valley Bosché 1972 Rel: $6 Cur: $30 (CA-3/89)
80 ROBERT MONDAVI Cabernet Sauvignon Napa Valley 1972 Rel: $6 Cur: $45 (7/16/85) (JL)
80 SIMI Cabernet Sauvignon Alexander Valley 1972 Rel: $5 Cur: $25 (CA-3/89)
79 HEITZ Cabernet Sauvignon Napa Valley Martha's Vineyard 1972 Rel: $12.75 Cur: $114 (CA-3/89)
77 CHARLES KRUG Cabernet Sauvignon Napa Valley Vintage Select 1972 Rel: $9 Cur: $45 (CA-3/89)
75 ROBERT MONDAVI Cabernet Sauvignon Napa Valley 1972 Rel: $6 Cur: $45 (CA-3/89)
74 DIAMOND CREEK Cabernet Sauvignon Napa Valley Red Rock Terrace 1972 Rel: $7.50 Cur: $200 (CA-3/89)
73 BEAULIEU Cabernet Sauvignon Napa Valley Georges de Latour Private Reserve 1972 Rel: $6 Cur: $45 (CA-3/89)
71 BEAULIEU Cabernet Sauvignon Napa Valley Georges de Latour Private Reserve 1972 Rel: $6 Cur: $45 (3/31/91) (JL)
70 STAG'S LEAP WINE CELLARS Cabernet Sauvignon Napa Valley Stags Leap District Stag's Leap Vineyards 1972 Rel: $5.50 Cur: $100 (CA-3/89)
67 CHAPPELLET Cabernet Sauvignon Napa Valley 1972 Rel: $6.50 Cur: $41 (CA-3/89)
67 INGLENOOK Cabernet Sauvignon Napa Valley Cask 1972 Rel: $7 Cur: $44 (CA-3/89)
63 LOUIS M. MARTINI Cabernet Sauvignon California Special Selection 1972 Rel: $5 Cur: $50 (CA-3/89)

1971

93 ROBERT MONDAVI Cabernet Sauvignon Napa Valley Reserve 1971 Rel: $12 Cur: $130 (CA-3/89)
90 ROBERT MONDAVI Cabernet Sauvignon Napa Valley Reserve 1971 Rel: $12 Cur: $130 (7/16/85) (JL)
87 MAYACAMAS Cabernet Sauvignon Napa Valley 1971 Rel: $8 Cur: $75 (4/01/86)
87 ROBERT MONDAVI Cabernet Sauvignon Napa Valley 1971 Rel: $6 Cur: $43 (7/16/85) (JL)
86 FREEMARK ABBEY Cabernet Sauvignon Napa Valley Bosché 1971 Rel: $6.75 Cur: $50 (CA-3/89)
85 MAYACAMAS Cabernet Sauvignon Napa Valley 1971 Rel: $8 Cur: $75 (CA-3/89)
85 RIDGE Cabernet Sauvignon Santa Cruz Mountains Monte Bello 1971 Rel: $10 Cur: $164 (CA-3/89)
85 RIDGE Cabernet Sauvignon Santa Cruz Mountains Monte Bello 1971 Rel: $10 Cur: $164 (4/01/86)
79 BEAULIEU Cabernet Sauvignon Napa Valley Georges de Latour Private Reserve 1971 Rel: $8 Cur: $60 (3/31/91) (JL)
79 CHARLES KRUG Cabernet Sauvignon Napa Valley Vintage Select 1971 Rel: $7.50 Cur: $42 (CA-3/89)
75 SIMI Cabernet Sauvignon Alexander Valley 1971 Rel: $5 Cur: $30 (CA-3/89)
73 INGLENOOK Cabernet Sauvignon Napa Valley Cask 1971 Rel: $6.50 Cur: $50 (CA-3/89)
67 BEAULIEU Cabernet Sauvignon Napa Valley Georges de Latour Private Reserve 1971 Rel: $8 Cur: $60 (CA-3/89)
65 CHAPPELLET Cabernet Sauvignon Napa Valley 1971 Rel: $7.50 Cur: $80 (CA-3/89)

1970

98 HEITZ Cabernet Sauvignon Napa Valley Martha's Vineyard 1970 Rel: $12.75 Cur: $275 (CA-3/89)
96 MAYACAMAS Cabernet Sauvignon Napa Valley 1970 Rel: $8 Cur: $130 (CA-3/89)
96 RIDGE Cabernet Sauvignon Santa Cruz Mountains Monte Bello 1970 Rel: $10 Cur: $197 (CA-3/89)
95 BEAULIEU Cabernet Sauvignon Napa Valley Georges de Latour Private Reserve 1970 Rel: $8 Cur: $130 (CA-3/89)
95 BEAULIEU Cabernet Sauvignon Napa Valley Georges de Latour Private Reserve 1970 Rel: $8 Cur: $130 (6/01/85) (JL)
93 BEAULIEU Cabernet Sauvignon Napa Valley Georges de Latour Private Reserve 1970 Rel: $8 Cur: $130 (3/31/91) (JL)
93 CHAPPELLET Cabernet Sauvignon Napa Valley 1970 Rel: $7.50 Cur: $95 (CA-3/89)
93 ROBERT MONDAVI Cabernet Sauvignon Napa Valley Unfiltered 1970 Rel: $12 Cur: $105 (7/16/85) (JL)
93 ROBERT MONDAVI Cabernet Sauvignon Napa Valley Unfined 1970 Rel: $12 Cur: $105 (7/16/85) (JL)

UNITED STATES
CALIFORNIA/CABERNET SAUVIGNON & BLENDS

91 FREEMARK ABBEY Cabernet Sauvignon Napa Valley Bosché 1970 Rel: $8.75 Cur: $117 (CA-3/89)
90 BEAULIEU Cabernet Sauvignon Napa Valley Rutherford 1970 Cur: $67 (6/01/85) (JL)
90 INGLENOOK Cabernet Sauvignon Napa Valley Cask 1970 Rel: $6.50 Cur: $75 (6/01/85) (JL)
89 ROBERT MONDAVI Cabernet Sauvignon Napa Valley Unfined 1970 Rel: $12 Cur: $105 (CA-3/89)
88 LOUIS M. MARTINI Cabernet Sauvignon California Special Selection 1970 Rel: $8 Cur: $60 (CA-3/89)
85 INGLENOOK Cabernet Sauvignon Napa Valley Cask 1970 Rel: $6.50 Cur: $75 (CA-3/89)
75 CHARLES KRUG Cabernet Sauvignon Napa Valley Vintage Select 1970 Rel: $7.50 Cur: $60 (CA-3/89)
74 HEITZ Cabernet Sauvignon Napa Valley 1970 Cur: $78 (1/31/90) (JL)
73 SIMI Cabernet Sauvignon Alexander Valley 1970 Rel: $4.50 Cur: $60 (CA-3/89)

1969

93 HEITZ Cabernet Sauvignon Napa Valley Martha's Vineyard 1969 Rel: $12.75 Cur: $275 (CA-3/89)
92 BEAULIEU Cabernet Sauvignon Napa Valley Georges de Latour Private Reserve 1969 Rel: $6.50 Cur: $100 (3/31/91) (JL)
92 ROBERT MONDAVI Cabernet Sauvignon Napa Valley Unfined 1969 Rel: $12 Cur: $140 (7/16/85) (JL)
92 RIDGE Cabernet Sauvignon Santa Cruz Mountains Monte Bello 1969 Rel: $7.50 Cur: $200 (CA-3/89)
90 BEAULIEU Cabernet Sauvignon Napa Valley Georges de Latour Private Reserve 1969 Rel: $6.50 Cur: $100 (CA-3/89)
89 MAYACAMAS Cabernet Sauvignon California 1969 Rel: $6.50 Cur: $108 (CA-3/89)
87 CHAPPELLET Cabernet Sauvignon Napa Valley 1969 Rel: $10 Cur: $125 (CA-3/89)
86 ROBERT MONDAVI Cabernet Sauvignon Napa Valley 1969 Cur: $86 (7/16/85) (JL)
86 ROBERT MONDAVI Cabernet Sauvignon Napa Valley Unfined 1969 Rel: $12 Cur: $140 (CA-3/89)
85 CHARLES KRUG Cabernet Sauvignon Napa Valley Vintage Select 1969 Rel: $6.50 Cur: $55 (6/01/85) (JL)
81 CHARLES KRUG Cabernet Sauvignon Napa Valley Vintage Select 1969 Rel: $6.50 Cur: $55 (CA-3/89)
80 INGLENOOK Cabernet Sauvignon Napa Valley Cask 1969 Rel: $6.50 Cur: $80 (CA-3/89)
68 FREEMARK ABBEY Cabernet Sauvignon Napa Valley 1969 Cur: $57 (4/01/86)

1968

99 HEITZ Cabernet Sauvignon Napa Valley Martha's Vineyard 1968 Rel: $9.50 Cur: $390 (CA-3/89)
93 BEAULIEU Cabernet Sauvignon Napa Valley Georges de Latour Private Reserve 1968 Rel: $6 Cur: $153 (6/01/85) (JL)
92 BEAULIEU Cabernet Sauvignon Napa Valley Georges de Latour Private Reserve 1968 Rel: $6 Cur: $153 (3/31/91) (JL)
91 BEAULIEU Cabernet Sauvignon Napa Valley Georges de Latour Private Reserve 1968 Rel: $6 Cur: $153 (CA-3/89)
90 LOUIS M. MARTINI Cabernet Sauvignon California Special Selection 1968 Rel: $6 Cur: $75 (CA-3/89)
90 LOUIS M. MARTINI Cabernet Sauvignon California Special Selection 1968 Rel: $6 Cur: $75 (6/01/85) (JL)
88 CHAPPELLET Cabernet Sauvignon Napa Valley 1968 Rel: $5.50 Cur: $100 (CA-3/89)
88 CHARLES KRUG Cabernet Sauvignon Napa Valley Vintage Select 1968 Rel: $6.50 Cur: $90 (6/01/85) (JL)
88 MAYACAMAS Cabernet Sauvignon California 1968 Rel: $4.50 Cur: $125 (CA-3/89)
87 RIDGE Cabernet Sauvignon Santa Cruz Mountains Monte Bello 1968 Rel: $7.50 Cur: $200 (CA-3/89)
85 INGLENOOK Cabernet Sauvignon Napa Valley Cask 1968 Rel: $6 Cur: $90 (CA-3/89)
83 ROBERT MONDAVI Cabernet Sauvignon Napa Valley Unfined 1968 Rel: $8.50 Cur: $135 (CA-3/89)
80 CHARLES KRUG Cabernet Sauvignon Napa Valley Vintage Select 1968 Rel: $6.50 Cur: $90 (CA-3/89)

1967

86 HEITZ Cabernet Sauvignon Napa Valley Martha's Vineyard 1967 Rel: $7.50 Cur: $300 (CA-3/89)
85 BEAULIEU Cabernet Sauvignon Napa Valley Georges de Latour Private Reserve 1967 Rel: $5.25 Cur: $110 (CA-3/89)
84 ROBERT MONDAVI Cabernet Sauvignon Napa Valley 1967 Rel: $5 Cur: $100 (CA-3/89)
83 ROBERT MONDAVI Cabernet Sauvignon Napa Valley 1967 Rel: $5 Cur: $100/1.5L (7/16/85) (JL)
82 BEAULIEU Cabernet Sauvignon Napa Valley Georges de Latour Private Reserve 1967 Rel: $5.25 Cur: $110 (3/31/91) (JL)
73 INGLENOOK Cabernet Sauvignon Napa Valley Cask 1967 Rel: $6 Cur: $84 (CA-3/89)
65 MAYACAMAS Cabernet Sauvignon California 1967 Rel: $4 Cur: $125 (CA-3/89)

1966

92 HEITZ Cabernet Sauvignon Napa Valley Martha's Vineyard 1966 Rel: $8 Cur: $470 (CA-3/89)
91 BEAULIEU Cabernet Sauvignon Napa Valley Georges de Latour Private Reserve 1966 Rel: $5.25 Cur: $145 (6/01/85) (JL)
87 BEAULIEU Cabernet Sauvignon Napa Valley Georges de Latour Private Reserve 1966 Rel: $5.25 Cur: $145 (3/31/91) (JL)
87 BEAULIEU Cabernet Sauvignon Napa Valley Georges de Latour Private Reserve 1966 Rel: $5.25 Cur: $145 (CA-3/89)

87 CHARLES KRUG Cabernet Sauvignon Napa Valley Vintage Select 1966 Rel: $6 Cur: $88 (6/01/85) (JL)
87 LOUIS M. MARTINI Cabernet Sauvignon California Special Selection 1966 Rel: $6 Cur: $150 (CA-3/89)
84 INGLENOOK Cabernet Sauvignon Napa Valley Cask 1966 Rel: $5.75 Cur: $114 (6/01/85) (JL)
80 ROBERT MONDAVI Cabernet Sauvignon Napa Valley 1966 Rel: $5 Cur: $165 (CA-3/89)
79 ROBERT MONDAVI Cabernet Sauvignon Napa Valley 1966 Rel: $5 Cur: $165/1.5L (7/16/85) (JL)
78 ROBERT MONDAVI Cabernet Sauvignon Napa Valley 1966 Rel: $5 Cur: $165 (7/16/85) (JL)
75 MAYACAMAS Cabernet Sauvignon California 1966 Rel: $3.50 Cur: $125 (CA-3/89)
73 INGLENOOK Cabernet Sauvignon Napa Valley Cask 1966 Rel: $5.75 Cur: $114 (CA-3/89)

1965

90 CHARLES KRUG Cabernet Sauvignon Napa Valley Vintage Select 1965 Rel: $5 Cur: $86 (6/01/85) (JL)
87 CHARLES KRUG Cabernet Sauvignon Napa Valley Vintage Select 1965 Rel: $5 Cur: $86 (CA-3/89)
86 RIDGE Cabernet Sauvignon Santa Cruz Mountains Monte Bello 1965 Rel: $6.50 Cur: $275 (CA-3/89)
85 BEAULIEU Cabernet Sauvignon Napa Valley Georges de Latour Private Reserve 1965 Rel: $5.25 Cur: $130 (CA-3/89)
77 BEAULIEU Cabernet Sauvignon Napa Valley Georges de Latour Private Reserve 1965 Rel: $5.25 Cur: $130 (3/31/91) (JL)
74 CHARLES KRUG Cabernet Sauvignon Napa Valley 1965 Cur: $35 (7/16/85) (JL)
65 MAYACAMAS Cabernet Sauvignon California 1965 Rel: $2.75 Cur: $200 (CA-3/89)

1964

90 RIDGE Cabernet Sauvignon Santa Cruz Mountains Monte Bello 1964 Rel: $6.50 Cur: $310 (CA-3/89)
86 CHARLES KRUG Cabernet Sauvignon Napa Valley Vintage Select 1964 Rel: $4 Cur: $75 (CA-3/89)
86 CHARLES KRUG Cabernet Sauvignon Napa Valley Vintage Select 1964 Rel: $4 Cur: $75 (7/16/85) (JL)
86 LOUIS M. MARTINI Cabernet Sauvignon California Special Selection 1964 Rel: $6 Cur: $100 (6/01/85) (JL)
85 LOUIS M. MARTINI Cabernet Sauvignon California Special Selection 1964 Rel: $6 Cur: $100 (CA-3/89)
84 BEAULIEU Cabernet Sauvignon Napa Valley Georges de Latour Private Reserve 1964 Rel: $4.25 Cur: $145 (CA-3/89)
72 BEAULIEU Cabernet Sauvignon Napa Valley Georges de Latour Private Reserve 1964 Rel: $4.25 Cur: $145 (3/31/91) (JL)

1963

79 CHARLES KRUG Cabernet Sauvignon Napa Valley Vintage Select 1963 Rel: $3.50 Cur: $77 (7/16/85) (JL)
74 BEAULIEU Cabernet Sauvignon Napa Valley Georges de Latour Private Reserve 1963 Rel: $3.50 Cur: $120 (3/31/91) (JL)
74 CHARLES KRUG Cabernet Sauvignon Napa Valley Vintage Select 1963 Rel: $3.50 Cur: $77 (CA-3/89)
70 BEAULIEU Cabernet Sauvignon Napa Valley Georges de Latour Private Reserve 1963 Rel: $3.50 Cur: $120 (CA-3/89)
70 RIDGE Cabernet Sauvignon Santa Cruz Mountains Monte Bello 1963 Rel: $5 Cur: $490 (CA-3/89)
69 MAYACAMAS Cabernet Sauvignon California 1963 Rel: $2 Cur: $150 (CA-3/89)

1962

84 CHARLES KRUG Cabernet Sauvignon Napa Valley 1962 Cur: $60 (7/16/85) (JL)
78 CHARLES KRUG Cabernet Sauvignon Napa Valley Vintage Select 1962 Rel: $3.50 Cur: $113 (CA-3/89)
78 CHARLES KRUG Cabernet Sauvignon Napa Valley Vintage Select 1962 Rel: $3.50 Cur: $113 (7/16/85) (JL)
75 BEAULIEU Cabernet Sauvignon Napa Valley Georges de Latour Private Reserve 1962 Rel: $3.50 Cur: $125 (3/31/91) (JL)
73 BEAULIEU Cabernet Sauvignon Napa Valley Georges de Latour Private Reserve 1962 Rel: $3.50 Cur: $125 (CA-3/89)
73 LOUIS M. MARTINI Cabernet Sauvignon California Private Reserve 1962 Rel: $3.50 Cur: $80 (CA-3/89)
68 MAYACAMAS Cabernet Sauvignon California 1962 Rel: $2 Cur: $150 (CA-3/89)

1961

89 CHARLES KRUG Cabernet Sauvignon Napa Valley Vintage Select 1961 Rel: $3.50 Cur: $140 (CA-3/89)
88 CHARLES KRUG Cabernet Sauvignon Napa Valley Vintage Select 1961 Rel: $3.50 Cur: $140 (7/16/85) (JL)
84 CHARLES KRUG Cabernet Sauvignon Napa Valley 1961 Cur: $105 (7/16/85) (JL)
80 LOUIS M. MARTINI Cabernet Sauvignon California Special Selection 1961 Rel: $4 Cur: $160 (CA-3/89)
78 BEAULIEU Cabernet Sauvignon Napa Valley Georges de Latour Private Reserve 1961 Rel: $3.50 Cur: $205 (CA-3/89)
77 BEAULIEU Cabernet Sauvignon Napa Valley Georges de Latour Private Reserve 1961 Rel: $3.50 Cur: $205 (3/31/91) (JL)

1960

89 INGLENOOK Cabernet Sauvignon Napa Valley 1960 Cur: $135 (6/01/85) (JL)
89 CHARLES KRUG Cabernet Sauvignon Napa Valley Vintage Select 1960 Rel: $2.25 Cur: $70 (7/16/85) (JL)
85 BEAULIEU Cabernet Sauvignon Napa Valley Georges de Latour Private Reserve 1960 Rel: $3.50 Cur: $150 (3/31/91) (JL)
80 INGLENOOK Cabernet Sauvignon Napa Valley Cask 1960 Rel: $2.75 Cur: $140 (CA-3/89)
79 CHARLES KRUG Cabernet Sauvignon Napa Valley Vintage Select 1960 Rel: $2.25 Cur: $70 (CA-3/89)

1959

89 BEAULIEU Cabernet Sauvignon Napa Valley Georges de Latour Private Reserve 1959 Rel: $3.50 Cur: $340 (3/31/91) (JL)
89 BEAULIEU Cabernet Sauvignon Napa Valley Georges de Latour Private Reserve 1959 Rel: $3.50 Cur: $340 (CA-3/89)
87 LOUIS M. MARTINI Cabernet Sauvignon California Special Selection 1959 Rel: $4.50 Cur: $140 (CA-3/89)

Key to Symbols

The scores reported here are the results of blind tastings conducted by our panel of senior editors. Wines that carry the initials below are results of individual tastings.

THE WINE SPECTATOR 100-POINT SCALE   95-100—Classic, a great wine; *90-94*—Outstanding, superior character and style; *80-89*—Good to very good, a wine with special qualities; *70-79*—Average, drinkable wine that may have minor flaws; *60-69*—Below average, drinkable but not recommended; *50-59*—Poor, undrinkable, not recommended. "+"—With a score indicates a range; used primarily with barrel tastings to indicate a preliminary score.

SPECIAL DESIGNATIONS SS—Spectator Selection, CS—Cellar Selection, BB—Best Buy.

TASTER'S INITIALS (JG)—Jim Gordon, (HS)—Harvey Steiman, (JL)—James Laube, (JS)—James Suckling, (TM)—Thomas Matthews, (TR)—Terry Robards, (BT)—Barrel Tasting (these wines were tasted blind from barrel samples), (CA-date)—*California's Great Cabernets* by James Laube, (CH-date)—*California's Great Chardonnays* by James Laube, (VP-date)—*Vintage Port* by James Suckling.

DATE TASTED Dates in parentheses represent the issue in which the rating was published.

85 CHARLES KRUG Cabernet Sauvignon Napa Valley Vintage Select 1959 Rel: $2.25 Cur: $140 (CA-3/89)

78 CHARLES KRUG Cabernet Sauvignon Napa Valley Vintage Select 1959 Rel: $2.25 Cur: $140 (7/16/85) (JL)

1958

97 BEAULIEU Cabernet Sauvignon Napa Valley Georges de Latour Private Reserve 1958 Rel: $3 Cur: $490 (3/31/91) (JL)

96 BEAULIEU Cabernet Sauvignon Napa Valley Georges de Latour Private Reserve 1958 Rel: $3 Cur: $490 (CA-3/89)

94 INGLENOOK Cabernet Sauvignon Napa Valley Cask 1958 Rel: $2.50 Cur: $250 (CA-3/89)

91 CHARLES KRUG Cabernet Sauvignon Napa Valley Vintage Select 1958 Rel: $2 Cur: $310 (7/16/85) (JL)

88 INGLENOOK Cabernet Sauvignon Napa Valley 1958 Cur: $140 (6/01/85) (JL)

88 CHARLES KRUG Cabernet Sauvignon Napa Valley Vintage Select 1958 Rel: $2 Cur: $310 (CA-3/89)

88 LOUIS M. MARTINI Cabernet Sauvignon California Special Selection 1958 Rel: $4.50 Cur: $200 (CA-3/89)

86 BEAULIEU Cabernet Sauvignon Napa Valley Georges de Latour Private Reserve 1958 Rel: $3 Cur: $490 (2/28/87) (JL)

79 INGLENOOK Cabernet Sauvignon Napa Valley Cask F-11 1958 Rel: $2.50 Cur: $250 (2/28/87)

1957

92 LOUIS M. MARTINI Cabernet Sauvignon California Special Selection 1957 Rel: $3.50 Cur: $175 (6/01/85) (JL)

91 LOUIS M. MARTINI Cabernet Sauvignon California Special Selection 1957 Rel: $3.50 Cur: $175 (CA-3/89)

81 CHARLES KRUG Cabernet Sauvignon Napa Valley Vintage Select 1957 Rel: $2 Cur: $275 (7/16/85) (JL)

69 BEAULIEU Cabernet Sauvignon Napa Valley Georges de Latour Private Reserve 1957 Rel: $2.50 Cur: $235 (3/31/91) (JL)

1956

90 CHARLES KRUG Cabernet Sauvignon Napa Valley Vintage Select 1956 Rel: $1.40 Cur: $425 (CA-3/89)

88 BEAULIEU Cabernet Sauvignon Napa Valley Georges de Latour Private Reserve 1956 Rel: $2.50 Cur: $600 (3/31/91) (JL)

88 BEAULIEU Cabernet Sauvignon Napa Valley Georges de Latour Private Reserve 1956 Rel: $2.50 Cur: $600 (CA-3/89)

85 CHARLES KRUG Cabernet Sauvignon Napa Valley Vintage Select 1956 Rel: $1.40 Cur: $425 (7/16/85) (JL)

77 LOUIS M. MARTINI Cabernet Sauvignon California Private Reserve 1956 Rel: $2.50 Cur: $80 (CA-3/89)

1955

93 INGLENOOK Cabernet Sauvignon Napa Valley Cask 1955 Rel: $1.85 Cur: $400 (CA-3/89)

93 INGLENOOK Cabernet Sauvignon Napa Valley Cask 1955 Rel: $1.85 Cur: $400 (6/01/85) (JL)

89 LOUIS M. MARTINI Cabernet Sauvignon California Special Selection 1955 Rel: $2.50 Cur: $190 (6/01/85) (JL)

87 LOUIS M. MARTINI Cabernet Sauvignon California Special Selection 1955 Rel: $2.50 Cur: $190 (CA-3/89)

85 BEAULIEU Cabernet Sauvignon Napa Valley Georges de Latour Private Reserve 1955 Rel: $2.50 Cur: $550 (3/31/91) (JL)

1954

86 BEAULIEU Cabernet Sauvignon Napa Valley Georges de Latour Private Reserve 1954 Rel: $2.50 Cur: $330 (3/31/91) (JL)

1953

91 BEAULIEU Cabernet Sauvignon Napa Valley Georges de Latour Private Reserve 1953 Rel: $2.50 Cur: $600 (3/31/91) (JL)

1952

93 LOUIS M. MARTINI Cabernet Sauvignon California Special Selection 1952 Rel: $2.50 Cur: $350 (CA-3/89)

93 LOUIS M. MARTINI Cabernet Sauvignon California Private Reserve 1952 Rel: $2.50 Cur: $350 (2/28/87) (HS)

92 CHARLES KRUG Cabernet Sauvignon Napa Valley Vintage Select 1952 Rel: $1.26 Cur: $525 (CA-3/89)

91 BEAULIEU Cabernet Sauvignon Napa Valley Georges de Latour Private Reserve 1952 Rel: $2.50 Cur: $600 (3/31/91) (JL)

90 CHARLES KRUG Cabernet Sauvignon Napa Valley Vintage Select 1952 Rel: $1.26 Cur: $525 (7/16/85) (JL)

86 CHARLES KRUG Cabernet Sauvignon Napa Valley 1952 Cur: $250 (7/16/85) (JL)

1951

98 BEAULIEU Cabernet Sauvignon Napa Valley Georges de Latour Private Reserve 1951 Rel: $1.82 Cur: $1,000 (2/28/87) (JL)

92 BEAULIEU Cabernet Sauvignon Napa Valley Georges de Latour Private Reserve 1951 Rel: $1.82 Cur: $1,000 (3/31/91) (JL)

90 BEAULIEU Cabernet Sauvignon Napa Valley Georges de Latour Private Reserve 1951 Rel: $1.82 Cur: $1,000 (CA-3/89)

90 LOUIS M. MARTINI Cabernet Sauvignon California Special Selection 1951 Rel: $2 Cur: $282 (2/28/87) (HS)

88 CHARLES KRUG Cabernet Sauvignon Napa Valley Vintage Select 1951 Rel: $1.25 Cur: $450 (7/16/85) (JL)

87 LOUIS M. MARTINI Cabernet Sauvignon California Special Selection 1951 Rel: $2 Cur: $282 (CA-3/89)

85 CHARLES KRUG Cabernet Sauvignon Napa Valley Vintage Select 1951 Rel: $1.25 Cur: $450 (CA-3/89)

80 CHARLES KRUG Cabernet Sauvignon Napa Valley 1951 Cur: $250 (7/16/85) (JL)

1950

88 BEAULIEU Cabernet Sauvignon Napa Valley Georges de Latour Private Reserve 1950 Rel: $1.82 Cur: $800 (3/31/91) (JL)

82 CHARLES KRUG Cabernet Sauvignon Napa Valley Vintage Select 1950 Rel: $1.25 Cur: $500 (7/16/85) (JL)

79 CHARLES KRUG Cabernet Sauvignon Napa Valley Vintage Select 1950 Rel: $1.25 Cur: $500 (CA-3/89)

1949

92 INGLENOOK Cabernet Sauvignon Napa Valley Cask 1949 Rel: $1.49 Cur: $750 (CA-3/89)

88 BEAULIEU Cabernet Sauvignon Napa Valley Georges de Latour Private Reserve 1949 Rel: $1.82 Cur: $950 (3/31/91) (JL)

1948

85 BEAULIEU Cabernet Sauvignon Napa Valley Georges de Latour Private Reserve 1948 Rel: $1.82 Cur: $1,040 (CA-3/89)

79 BEAULIEU Cabernet Sauvignon Napa Valley Georges de Latour Private Reserve 1948 Rel: $1.82 Cur: $1,040 (3/31/91) (JL)

1947

93 BEAULIEU Cabernet Sauvignon Napa Valley Georges de Latour Private Reserve 1947 Rel: $1.82 Cur: $1,350 (CA-3/89)

90 LOUIS M. MARTINI Cabernet Sauvignon California Special Selection 1947 Rel: $1.50 Cur: $700 (CA-3/89)

89 BEAULIEU Cabernet Sauvignon Napa Valley Georges de Latour Private Reserve 1947 Rel: $1.82 Cur: $1,350 (3/31/91) (JL)

89 CHARLES KRUG Cabernet Sauvignon Napa Valley 1947 Cur: $300 (7/16/85) (JL)

1946

90 CHARLES KRUG Cabernet Sauvignon Napa Valley Vintage Select 1946 Rel: $1 Cur: $750 (7/16/85) (JL)

88 BEAULIEU Cabernet Sauvignon Napa Valley Georges de Latour Private Reserve 1946 Rel: $1.47 Cur: $1,000 (CA-3/89)

88 CHARLES KRUG Cabernet Sauvignon Napa Valley Vintage Select 1946 Rel: $1 Cur: $750 (CA-3/89)

87 BEAULIEU Cabernet Sauvignon Napa Valley Georges de Latour Private Reserve 1946 Rel: $1.47 Cur: $1,000 (3/31/91) (JL)

87 INGLENOOK Cabernet Sauvignon Napa Valley 1946 Rel: $1.49 Cur: $900 (CA-3/89)

1945

75 LOUIS M. MARTINI Cabernet Sauvignon California Special Selection 1945 Rel: $1.50 Cur: $400 (CA-3/89)

75 LOUIS M. MARTINI Cabernet Sauvignon California Special Selection 1945 Rel: $1.50 Cur: $400 (6/01/85) (JL)

70 BEAULIEU Cabernet Sauvignon Napa Valley Georges de Latour Private Reserve 1945 Rel: $1.47 Cur: $700 (3/31/91) (JL)

1944

95 CHARLES KRUG Cabernet Sauvignon Napa Valley 1944 Rel: $0.95 Cur: $420 (7/16/85)

88 CHARLES KRUG Cabernet Sauvignon Napa Valley 1944 Rel: $0.95 Cur: $420 (CA-3/89)

87 BEAULIEU Cabernet Sauvignon Napa Valley Georges de Latour Private Reserve 1944 Rel: $1.47 Cur: $680 (CA-3/89)

75 BEAULIEU Cabernet Sauvignon Napa Valley Georges de Latour Private Reserve 1944 Rel: $1.47 Cur: $680 (3/31/91) (JL)

1943

91 INGLENOOK Cabernet Sauvignon Napa Valley 1943 Rel: $1.49 Cur: $970 (CA-3/89)

87 BEAULIEU Cabernet Sauvignon Napa Valley Georges de Latour Private Reserve 1943 Rel: $1.45 Cur: $500 (3/31/91) (JL)

77 LOUIS M. MARTINI Cabernet Sauvignon California Private Reserve Villa del Rey 1943 Rel: $1.50 Cur: $400 (6/01/85) (JL)

70 LOUIS M. MARTINI Cabernet Sauvignon California Private Reserve Villa del Rey 1943 Rel: $1.50 Cur: $400 (CA-3/89)

1942

87 BEAULIEU Cabernet Sauvignon Napa Valley Georges de Latour Private Reserve 1942 Rel: $1.45 Cur: $1,300 (CA-3/89)

85 BEAULIEU Cabernet Sauvignon Napa Valley Georges de Latour Private Reserve 1942 Rel: $1.45 Cur: $1,300 (3/31/91) (JL)

1941

100 INGLENOOK Cabernet Sauvignon Napa Valley 1941 Rel: $1.49 Cur: $1,790 (CA-3/89)

95 INGLENOOK Cabernet Sauvignon Napa Valley 1941 Rel: $1.49 Cur: $1,790 (6/01/85) (JL)

89 BEAULIEU Cabernet Sauvignon Napa Valley Georges de Latour Private Reserve 1941 Rel: $1.45 Cur: $1,200 (3/31/91) (JL)

85 BEAULIEU Cabernet Sauvignon Napa Valley Georges de Latour Private Reserve 1941 Rel: $1.45 Cur: $1,200 (CA-3/89)

1940

89 BEAULIEU Cabernet Sauvignon Napa Valley Georges de Latour Private Reserve 1940 Rel: $1.45 Cur: $1,200 (3/31/91) (JL)

1939

91 BEAULIEU Cabernet Sauvignon Napa Valley Georges de Latour Private Reserve 1939 Rel: $1.45 Cur: $1,500 (3/31/91) (JL)

90 LOUIS M. MARTINI Cabernet Sauvignon California Special Reserve 1939 Rel: $1.25 Cur: $1,000 (CA-3/89)

90 LOUIS M. MARTINI Cabernet Sauvignon California Special Reserve 1939 Rel: $1.25 Cur: $1,000 (6/01/85) (JL)

82 BEAULIEU Cabernet Sauvignon Napa Valley Georges de Latour Private Reserve 1939 Rel: $1.45 Cur: $1,500 (CA-3/89)

1936

86 BEAULIEU Cabernet Sauvignon Napa Valley Georges de Latour Private Reserve 1936 Rel: $1.45 Cur: $1,500 (3/31/91) (JL)

1933

95 INGLENOOK Cabernet Sauvignon Napa Valley 1933 Rel: $1.30 Cur: $1,600 (CA-3/89)

1897

87 INGLENOOK Cabernet Sauvignon California Claret-Medoc Type 1897 (NA) (CA-3/89)

NV

90 HEITZ Cabernet Sauvignon Napa Valley Z-91 NV (NA) (1/31/90) (JL)

UNITED STATES
CALIFORNIA/*CABERNET SAUVIGNON & BLENDS*

89 LAUREL GLEN Cabernet Sauvignon Sonoma Mountain Counterpoint Cuvée 85-86 NV $11 (5/31/88)
84 CHRISTIAN BROTHERS Montage Premier Cuvée Bordeaux-Napa Valley NV $15 (10/15/88)
83 R.H. PHILLIPS Cabernet Sauvignon California Night Harvest NV $4 (11/30/88) BB
81 LIBERTY SCHOOL Cabernet Sauvignon California Lot 18 NV $7.50 (4/30/89) BB
81 WHITEHALL LANE Cabernet Sauvignon California Le Petit NV $8.50 (3/31/90)
79 ROUND HILL Cabernet Sauvignon California Lot 7 NV $6 (10/31/90)
79 ROUND HILL Cabernet Sauvignon California House Lot 8 NV $6.25 (7/31/91)
78 ROUND HILL Cabernet Sauvignon California House Lot 7 NV $6.25 (2/15/89)
77 LIBERTY SCHOOL Cabernet Sauvignon California Lot 19 NV $7.50 (11/15/89)
77 WHITEHALL LANE Cabernet Sauvignon Napa Valley NV $6 (12/31/87)
76 ROUND HILL Cabernet Sauvignon California House Lot 5 NV $5 (9/30/86) BB
75 HEITZ Cabernet Sauvignon Napa Valley MZ-1 NV (NA) (1/31/90) (JL)
73 LIBERTY SCHOOL Cabernet Sauvignon California Lot 17 NV $6 (2/29/88)
73 MENDOCINO VINEYARDS Cabernet Sauvignon Mendocino County NV $6 (4/15/89)
72 ROUND HILL Cabernet Sauvignon California House Lot 6 NV $5 (10/15/87)
70 WHITEHALL LANE Cabernet Sauvignon California NV $7 (10/15/88)
68 HEITZ Cabernet Sauvignon Napa Valley NV (NA) (1/31/90) (JL)
64 LIBERTY SCHOOL Cabernet Sauvignon Alexander Valley Lot 13 NV $6 (1/01/86)

CHARDONNAY

1990

83 R.H. PHILLIPS Chardonnay California 1990 $8 (7/15/91) BB
78 GLEN ELLEN Chardonnay California Proprietor's Reserve 1990 $7 (7/15/91)

1989

92 MARKHAM Chardonnay Napa Valley 1989 $12 (6/15/91) SS
91 FERRARI-CARANO Chardonnay Alexander Valley 1989 $19.50 (6/15/91)
91 FLORA SPRINGS Chardonnay Napa Valley Barrel Fermented 1989 $23 (5/15/91)
91 HALLCREST Chardonnay Santa Cruz Mountains Meylay Vineyard 1989 $16.50 (4/30/91)
91 HIDDEN CELLARS Chardonnay Mendocino County Reserve Barrel Fermented 1989 $16 (7/15/91)
91 KISTLER Chardonnay Sonoma Valley Kistler Estate Vineyard 1989 $32 (6/15/91)
91 LONG Chardonnay Napa Valley 1989 $30 (7/15/91)
91 QUPE Chardonnay Santa Barbara County Sierra Madre Reserve 1989 $25 (7/15/91)
91 SAINTSBURY Chardonnay Carneros 1989 $14 (11/15/90)
90 BONNY DOON Chardonnay Monterey County La Reina Vineyard 1989 $14 (3/15/91)
90 CHALK HILL Chardonnay Chalk Hill 1989 $14 (5/15/91) SS
90 CHALONE Chardonnay Chalone 1989 $25 (11/30/90)
90 FRANCISCAN Chardonnay Napa Valley Oakville Estate Cuvée Sauvage 1989 $24 (7/15/91)
90 WILLIAM HILL Chardonnay Napa Valley Reserve 1989 $18 (6/30/91)
90 KENDALL-JACKSON Chardonnay California Proprietor's Grand Reserve 1989 $23 (5/31/91)
90 KISTLER Chardonnay Sonoma Valley Durell Vineyard 1989 $24 (5/15/91)
90 J. LOHR Chardonnay Monterey Riverstone 1989 $12 (3/15/91) SS
90 MERRYVALE Chardonnay Stags Leap District 1989 $19 (12/31/90)
90 NEWLAN Chardonnay Napa Valley 1989 $14 (7/15/91)
90 ST. CLEMENT Chardonnay Napa Valley 1989 $16 (5/31/91) SS
90 SANFORD Chardonnay Santa Barbara County Barrel Select 1989 Rel: $28 Cur: $28 (7/15/91)
90 MIRIMAR TORRES Chardonnay Sonoma County Green Valley Don Miguel Vineyard 1989 $20 (5/15/91)
89 CLOS DU BOIS Chardonnay Dry Creek Valley Flintwood Vineyards 1989 $17 (7/15/91)
89 CLOS DU VAL Chardonnay Carneros Napa Valley Carneros Estate 1989 $15 (3/31/91)
89 DE LOACH Chardonnay Russian River Valley O.F.S. 1989 $22 (3/31/91)
89 DEHLINGER Chardonnay Russian River Valley 1989 $13 (2/28/91)
89 DOMAINE DE CLARCK Chardonnay Monterey County Première 1989 $14 (4/15/91)
89 FAR NIENTE Chardonnay Napa Valley 1989 $28 (2/28/91)
89 GEYSER PEAK Chardonnay Alexander Valley Barrel Fermented Estate Reserve 1989 $13 (6/15/91)
89 GROTH Chardonnay Napa Valley 1989 $13.50 (7/15/91)
89 KISTLER Chardonnay Russian River Valley Dutton Ranch 1989 $24 (2/15/91)
89 MERRYVALE Chardonnay Napa Valley Starmont 1989 $16 (12/31/90)
89 MONTICELLO Chardonnay Napa Valley Corley Reserve 1989 $18 (7/15/91)
89 MOUNT EDEN Chardonnay Edna Valley MacGregor Vineyard 1989 $14.50 (11/30/90)
89 REVERE Chardonnay Napa Valley Berlenbach Vineyards 1989 $15 (7/15/91)
89 ROUND HILL Chardonnay Napa Valley Reserve 1989 $11 (6/15/91)
88 BON MARCHE Chardonnay Alexander Valley 1989 $8 (3/31/91) BB
88 CONGRESS SPRINGS Chardonnay Santa Clara County San Ysidro Reserve 1989 $15 (7/15/91)
88 EDNA VALLEY Chardonnay Edna Valley 1989 $15 (12/31/90)
88 THOMAS FOGARTY Chardonnay Edna Valley Paragon Vineyards 1989 $15 (7/15/91)
88 FORMAN Chardonnay Napa Valley 1989 $22 (2/15/91)
88 GRGICH HILLS Chardonnay Napa Valley 1989 $22 (7/15/91)
88 GUENOC Chardonnay Guenoc Valley 1989 $14 (3/31/91)
88 HUSCH Chardonnay Mendocino Estate Bottled 1989 $11 (12/31/90)
88 KISTLER Chardonnay Sonoma Mountain McCrea Vineyard 1989 Rel: $28 Cur: $29 (6/15/91)
88 KISTLER Chardonnay Sonoma Valley 1989 $24 (2/15/91)
88 LA CREMA Chardonnay California Reserve 1989 $22 (7/15/91)
88 LAURIER Chardonnay Sonoma County 1989 $16 (4/30/91)
88 LIMUR Chardonnay Napa Valley 1989 $19 (7/15/91)
88 LOGAN Chardonnay Monterey 1989 $12 (6/30/91)
88 LOLONIS Chardonnay Mendocino County Private Reserve Lolonis Vineyards 1989 $19 (7/15/91)
88 PETER MICHAEL Chardonnay Sonoma County Mon Plaisir 1989 $28 (7/15/91)
88 NAPA RIDGE Chardonnay North Coast Coastal 1989 $7 (6/30/91) BB
88 RITCHIE CREEK Chardonnay Napa Valley 1989 $15 (7/15/91)
88 SIMI Chardonnay Mendocino-Sonoma-Napa Counties 1989 $15.50 (5/31/91)
88 STAG'S LEAP WINE CELLARS Chardonnay Napa Valley 1989 $18 (1/31/91)
88 STERLING Chardonnay Napa Valley 1989 $15 (4/30/91)
88 WENTE BROS. Chardonnay Livermore Valley Herman Wente Vineyard Estate Reserve 1989 $18 (4/30/91)
87 ACACIA Chardonnay Carneros Napa Valley Marina Vineyard 1989 $20 (12/31/90)
87 BOYER Chardonnay Monterey County Ventana Vineyard 1989 $15 (7/15/91)
87 DE LOACH Chardonnay Russian River Valley 1989 Rel: $15 Cur: $15 (3/31/91)
87 DRY CREEK Chardonnay Sonoma County 1989 $12.50 (12/31/90)
87 FETZER Chardonnay Mendocino County Reserve 1989 $18 (7/15/91)
87 FIELD STONE Chardonnay Sonoma County 1989 $14 (3/31/91)
87 FIRESTONE Chardonnay Santa Ynez Valley Barrel Fermented 1989 $12 (4/30/91)
87 FLORA SPRINGS Chardonnay Napa Valley 1989 $15 (7/15/91)
87 HANDLEY Chardonnay Dry Creek Valley 1989 $14.50 (7/15/91)
87 HARRISON Chardonnay Napa Valley 1989 $24 (7/15/91)
87 HAVENS Chardonnay Carneros Napa Valley 1989 $14 (7/15/91)
87 INGLENOOK Chardonnay Napa Valley 1989 $7.50 (2/28/91) BB
87 LANDMARK Chardonnay Sonoma Valley Damaris Vineyard 1989 $16 (6/30/91)
87 MACROSTIE Chardonnay Carneros 1989 $14 (12/31/90)
87 LOUIS M. MARTINI Chardonnay Napa Valley Reserve 1989 $14 (12/31/90)
87 MATANZAS CREEK Chardonnay Sonoma Valley 1989 $19 (7/15/91)
87 MERIDIAN Chardonnay Santa Barbara County 1989 $10 (2/28/91)
87 MIRASSOU Chardonnay Monterey County Fifth Generation Harvest Reserve Limited Bottling 1989 $12.50 (5/15/91)
87 ROBERT MONDAVI Chardonnay Napa Valley 1989 $16 (4/15/91)
87 ROBERT MONDAVI Chardonnay Napa Valley Barrel Fermented Reserve 1989 $28 (7/15/91)
87 KENT RASMUSSEN Chardonnay Carneros Napa Valley 1989 $19 (3/15/91)
87 SAINT GREGORY Chardonnay Mendocino 1989 $15 (7/15/91)
87 SANFORD Chardonnay Santa Barbara County 1989 $16 (4/30/91)
87 SANTA BARBARA Chardonnay Santa Ynez Valley Reserve 1989 $18 (5/15/91)
87 STRATFORD Chardonnay California 1989 $10 (7/15/91) BB
87 VENTANA Chardonnay Monterey Gold Stripe Selection 1989 $10 (7/15/91)
87 WEINSTOCK Chardonnay Alexander Valley 1989 $11 (3/31/91)
87 WHITE ROCK Chardonnay Napa Valley Barrel Fermented 1989 $16 (7/15/91)
87 ZD Chardonnay California 1989 $21 (2/28/91)
87 STEPHEN ZELLERBACH Chardonnay Sonoma County Reserve 1989 $13 (7/15/91)
86 AU BON CLIMAT Chardonnay Santa Barbara County Reserve 1989 $25 (7/15/91)
86 CARNEROS CREEK Chardonnay Carneros Fleur de Carneros 1989 $9 (6/30/91) BB
86 EBERLE Chardonnay Paso Robles 1989 $12 (7/15/91)
86 J FRITZ Chardonnay Russian River Valley 1989 $12.50 (7/15/91)
86 GAINEY Chardonnay Santa Barbara County 1989 $13 (5/31/91)
86 GREEN & RED Chardonnay Napa Valley 1989 $14 (3/31/91)
86 HESS Chardonnay Napa Valley 1989 $14.50 (7/15/91)
86 HESS Chardonnay Napa Valley Hess Select 1989 $9.50 (12/31/90)
86 IRON HORSE Chardonnay Sonoma County Green Valley 1989 $18 (3/31/91)
86 KENDALL-JACKSON Chardonnay Sonoma Valley Durell Vineyard 1989 $16 (7/15/91)
86 LAZY CREEK Chardonnay Anderson Valley 1989 $8.50 (7/15/91)
86 LOLONIS Chardonnay Mendocino County Lolonis Vineyards 1989 $12 (7/15/91)
86 MANZANITA RIDGE Chardonnay Sonoma County Barrel Fermented 1989 $8 (6/30/91) BB
86 MORGAN Chardonnay Edna Valley MacGregor Vineyard 1989 $16.50 (7/15/91)
86 GUSTAVE NIEBAUM Chardonnay Napa Valley Reference 1989 $11 (6/15/91)
86 OPTIMA Chardonnay Sonoma County 1989 $25 (7/15/91)
86 PAHLMEYER Chardonnay Napa Valley Caldwell Vineyard 1989 $20 (4/30/91)
86 PATZ & HALL Chardonnay Napa Valley 1989 $25 (7/15/91)
86 SEGHESIO Chardonnay Mendocino-Sonoma Counties 1989 $9 (4/30/91)
86 SEQUOIA GROVE Chardonnay Carneros 1989 $14 (7/15/91)
86 SILVERADO Chardonnay Napa Valley 1989 $14.50 (3/31/91)
86 SONOMA-CUTRER Chardonnay Sonoma Coast Les Pierres 1989 $23 (1/31/91)
86 STONE CREEK Chardonnay Alexander Valley 1989 $10 (7/15/91)
86 STORRS Chardonnay Santa Cruz Mountains Gaspar Vineyard 1989 $16 (7/15/91)
86 RODNEY STRONG Chardonnay Sonoma County 1989 $9 (7/15/91) BB
86 TAFT STREET Chardonnay Sonoma County 1989 $8.50 (7/15/91) BB
86 VICHON Chardonnay Napa Valley Tenth Harvest 1989 $16 (3/31/91)
86 VILLA ZAPU Chardonnay Napa Valley 1989 $17.50 (7/15/91)
86 VITA NOVA Chardonnay Santa Barbara County 1989 $18 (7/15/91)
86 WILD HORSE Chardonnay Central Coast 1989 $13 (4/30/91)
86 ZACA MESA Chardonnay Santa Barbara County Reserve 1989 $16.50 (7/15/91)
85 ARROWOOD Chardonnay Sonoma County 1989 $19 (7/15/91)
85 BANNISTER Chardonnay Sonoma County 1989 $15 (7/15/91)
85 BELVEDERE Chardonnay Russian River Valley Reserve 1989 $9 (3/31/91)
85 BERINGER Chardonnay Napa Valley Private Reserve 1989 $19 (7/15/91)
85 BUENA VISTA Chardonnay Carneros 1989 $11 (7/15/91)
85 CHALONE Chardonnay California Gavilan 1989 $12 (12/31/90)
85 CHATEAU LA GRANDE ROCHE Chardonnay Napa Valley 1989 $13 (11/15/90)
85 CHATEAU ST. JEAN Chardonnay Sonoma Valley Estate Selection 1989 $14 (7/15/91)
85 CLONINGER Chardonnay Monterey 1989 $15 (7/15/91)
85 CONGRESS SPRINGS Chardonnay Santa Clara County Barrel Fermented 1989 $12 (7/15/91)
85 COTTONWOOD CANYON Chardonnay Central Coast 1989 $14 (7/15/91)
85 ELIZABETH Chardonnay Mendocino 1989 $12.50 (7/15/91)
85 ESTANCIA Chardonnay Monterey 1989 $8 (3/31/91) BB
85 FALLENLEAF Chardonnay Sonoma Valley 1989 $12 (3/31/91)
85 GARY FARRELL Chardonnay Sonoma County 1989 $16 (7/15/91)
85 HAGAFEN Chardonnay Napa Valley 1989 $12.50 (3/31/91)
85 JUSTIN Chardonnay Paso Robles 1989 $16.50 (7/15/91)
85 KONRAD Chardonnay Mendocino County Estate 1989 $12 (7/15/91)
85 LA CREMA Chardonnay California 1989 $12 (7/15/91)
85 MAZZOCCO Chardonnay Sonoma County Barrel Fermented 1989 $11 (7/15/91)
85 MEEKER Chardonnay Dry Creek Valley 1989 $12 (7/15/91)
85 NAPA CELLARS Chardonnay Napa Valley 1989 $7 (4/15/91) BB
85 GUSTAVE NIEBAUM Chardonnay Carneros Napa Valley Bayview Vineyard Barrel Fermented 1989 $16 (5/31/91)
85 JOSEPH PHELPS Chardonnay Carneros Sangiacomo Vineyard 1989 $20 (7/15/91)
85 PLAM Chardonnay Napa Valley 1989 $16 (7/15/91)
85 RABBIT RIDGE Chardonnay Sonoma County 1989 $12 (4/30/91)
85 ST. CLEMENT Chardonnay Carneros Abbott's Vineyard 1989 $18 (2/28/91)
85 SEQUOIA GROVE Chardonnay Napa Valley Estate 1989 $16 (7/15/91)
85 SIGNORELLO Chardonnay Napa Valley 1989 $15 (7/15/91)
85 VILLA ZAPU Chardonnay Napa Valley 1989 $17.50 (5/15/91)

Key to Symbols

The scores reported here are the results of blind tastings conducted by our panel of senior editors. Wines that carry the initials below are results of individual tastings.

THE WINE SPECTATOR 100-POINT SCALE *95-100*—Classic, a great wine; *90-94*—Outstanding, superior character and style; *80-89*—Good to very good, a wine with special qualities; *70-79*—Average, drinkable wine that may have minor flaws; *60-69*—Below average, drinkable but not recommended; *50-59*—Poor, undrinkable, not recommended. "+"—With a score indicates a range; used primarily with barrel tastings to indicate a preliminary score.

SPECIAL DESIGNATIONS SS—Spectator Selection, CS—Cellar Selection, BB—Best Buy.

TASTER'S INITIALS (JG)—Jim Gordon, (HS)—Harvey Steiman, (JL)—James Laube, (JS)—James Suckling, (TM)—Thomas Matthews, (TR)—Terry Robards, (BT)—Barrel Tasting (these wines were tasted blind from barrel samples), (CA-date)—*California's Great Cabernets* by James Laube, (CH-date)—*California's Great Chardonnays* by James Laube, (VP-date)—*Vintage Port* by James Suckling.

DATE TASTED Dates in parentheses represent the issue in which the rating was published.

85 WHITE OAK Chardonnay Sonoma County 1989 $12 (3/31/91)
85 ZACA MESA Chardonnay Santa Barbara County 1989 $11 (11/15/90)
85 STEPHEN ZELLERBACH Chardonnay Sonoma County 1989 $8.50 (11/30/90) BB
84 ACACIA Chardonnay Carneros Napa Valley 1989 $16 (12/31/90)
84 BONNY DOON Chardonnay California Grahm Crew 1989 $9 (9/30/90) BB
84 BRANDER Chardonnay Santa Ynez Valley Tête de Cuvée 1989 $22 (7/15/91)
84 BUENA VISTA Chardonnay Carneros 1989 $11 (12/31/90)
84 CAMBRIA Chardonnay Santa Maria Valley Katherine's Vineyard 1989 $16 (12/31/90)
84 CARTLIDGE & BROWNE Chardonnay Napa Valley 1989 $9.75 (5/31/91)
84 CORBETT CANYON Chardonnay Central Coast Coastal Classic 1989 $7/L (7/15/91) BB
84 FETZER Chardonnay Mendocino County Barrel Select 1989 $11 (7/15/91)
84 FOLIE A DEUX Chardonnay Napa Valley Pas de Deux 1989 $10 (12/31/90)
84 FREEMARK ABBEY Chardonnay Napa Valley Carpy Ranch 1989 $22 (7/15/91)
84 KEENAN Chardonnay Napa Valley 1989 $15 (7/15/91)
84 KENDALL-JACKSON Chardonnay California Vintner's Reserve 1989 $13 (7/15/91)
84 MORGAN Chardonnay Monterey 1989 $16 (3/31/91)
84 MOUNTAIN VIEW Chardonnay Monterey County 1989 $6 (4/15/91) BB
84 RIDGE Chardonnay Santa Cruz Mountains 1989 $14 (7/15/91)
84 ROUND HILL Chardonnay Napa Valley 1989 $9 (6/30/91)
84 ST. FRANCIS Chardonnay Sonoma Valley Barrel Select 1989 $15 (7/15/91)
84 SHAFER Chardonnay Napa Valley 1989 $15 (4/30/91)
84 ROBERT SINSKEY Chardonnay Carneros Napa Valley Selected Cuvée 1989 $16 (7/15/91)
84 SWANSON Chardonnay Napa Valley 1989 $15 (7/15/91)
84 TALLEY Chardonnay Arroyo Grande Valley 1989 $14.50 (7/15/91)
84 WILLOW CREEK Chardonnay Sonoma County 1989 $11 (9/30/90)
83 CAIN Chardonnay Carneros 1989 $16 (7/15/91)
83 CHATEAU DE LEU Chardonnay Solano County Green Valley 1989 $8 (7/15/91)
83 CHATEAU MONTELENA Chardonnay Napa Valley 1989 $23 (7/15/91)
83 CHATEAU WOLTNER Chardonnay Howell Mountain 1989 $12 (11/30/90)
83 CHIMERE Chardonnay Edna Valley 1989 $15 (7/15/91)
83 FOLIE A DEUX Chardonnay Napa Valley Pas de Deux 1989 $16.50 (7/15/91)
83 FOREST HILL Chardonnay Napa Valley Private Reserve 1989 $24 (7/15/91)
83 FRANCISCAN Chardonnay Napa Valley Oakville Estate 1989 $12 (7/15/91)
83 FROG'S LEAP Chardonnay Carneros 1989 $16 (7/15/91)
83 HIDDEN CELLARS Chardonnay Mendocino County 1989 $12 (3/31/91) (HS)
83 INNISFREE Chardonnay Napa Valley 1989 $11 (4/30/91)
83 KENWOOD Chardonnay Sonoma Valley Beltane Ranch 1989 $16 (7/15/91)
83 LEEWARD Chardonnay Central Coast 1989 $11 (8/31/90)
83 MADDALENA Chardonnay Central Coast 1989 $8 (4/30/91) BB
83 LOUIS M. MARTINI Chardonnay Los Carneros Las Amigas Vineyard Vineyard Selection 1989 $20 (7/15/91)
83 MONTEREY PENINSULA Chardonnay Monterey Sleepy Hollow 1989 $12 (5/31/91)
83 MOUNT VEEDER Chardonnay Napa Valley 1989 $18 (4/30/91)
83 NAPA RIDGE Chardonnay Central Coast 1989 $7 (11/15/90) BB
83 PARDUCCI Chardonnay Mendocino County 1989 $9.50 (7/15/91) BB
83 MARIO PERELLI-MINETTI Chardonnay Napa Valley 1989 $12.50 (4/30/91)
83 R.H. PHILLIPS Chardonnay California 1989 $7 (4/30/91) BB
83 RAYMOND Chardonnay California Selection 1989 $11.50 (2/28/91)
83 ROUND HILL Chardonnay California House 1989 $6.50 (7/15/91) BB
83 STERLING Chardonnay Carneros Winery Lake 1989 $18 (7/15/91)
83 STORRS Chardonnay Santa Cruz Mountains Meyley Vineyard 1989 $16 (7/15/91)
83 WENTE BROS. Chardonnay Central Coast Estate Grown 1989 $10.50 (7/15/91)
82 ADLER FELS Chardonnay Sonoma Valley Sobra Vista Vineyards 1989 $12 (4/15/91)
82 ALDERBROOK Chardonnay Dry Creek Valley 1989 $10 (3/31/91)
82 LAWRENCE J. BARGETTO Chardonnay Santa Cruz Mountains 1989 $18 (2/28/91)
82 BOEGER Chardonnay El Dorado 1989 $11.50 (5/31/91)
82 BURGESS Chardonnay Napa Valley Triere Vineyard 1989 $16 (7/15/91)
82 CANTERBURY Chardonnay California 1989 $7.50 (7/15/91) BB
82 J. CAREY Chardonnay Santa Barbara County 1989 $13 (4/30/91)
82 CHAMISAL Chardonnay Edna Valley 1989 $14 (7/15/91)
82 CHATEAU WOLTNER Chardonnay Howell Mountain Estate Vineyards 1989 $16 (7/15/91)
82 CLOS DU BOIS Chardonnay Alexander Valley Calcaire Vineyard 1989 $17 (7/15/91)
82 CRICHTON HALL Chardonnay Napa Valley 1989 $16.50 (7/15/91)
82 CUVAISON Chardonnay Carneros Napa Valley 1989 $14 (7/15/91)
82 DOMAINE BRETON Chardonnay California 1989 $8 (2/28/91) BB
82 FETZER Chardonnay California Sundial 1989 $8 (4/30/90) BB
82 HALLCREST Chardonnay California Fortuyn Cuvée 1989 $9 (4/30/91)
82 JORY Chardonnay Santa Clara County San Ysidro Vineyard 1989 $17 (4/30/91)
82 MARTINELLI Chardonnay Russian River Valley 1989 $9 (7/15/91)
82 MERIDIAN Chardonnay Edna Valley 1989 $14 (7/15/91)
82 MURPHY-GOODE Chardonnay Alexander Valley Estate Vineyard 1989 $12 (6/30/91)
82 GUSTAVE NIEBAUM Chardonnay Carneros Napa Valley Laird Vineyards 1989 $13.50 (1/31/91)
82 SARAH'S Chardonnay Monterey County Ventana Vineyard 1989 $22 (5/31/91)
82 SILVERADO HILL CELLARS Chardonnay Napa Valley 1989 $10 (7/15/91)
82 SONOMA-CUTRER Chardonnay Sonoma Coast Russian River Ranches 1989 $14 (7/15/91)
82 VILLA MT. EDEN Chardonnay Napa Valley 1989 $12 (2/28/91)
82 WEIBEL Chardonnay Mendocino County 1989 $8 (3/31/91) BB
81 BEAULIEU Chardonnay Carneros Napa Valley Carneros Reserve 1989 $17 (5/31/91)
81 BEAULIEU Chardonnay Napa Valley Beaufort 1989 $11 (7/15/91)
81 BERINGER Chardonnay Napa Valley 1989 $14 (3/15/91)
81 CHATEAU DE BAUN Chardonnay Russian River Valley Barrel Fermented 1989 $10 (6/15/91)
81 COSENTINO Chardonnay Napa County 1989 $13 (4/15/91)
81 E.&J. GALLO Chardonnay North Coast Reserve 1989 $6.50 (7/15/91) BB
81 HAYWOOD Chardonnay Sonoma Valley Los Chamizal Vineyards 1989 $13.50 (3/31/91)
81 WILLIAM HILL Chardonnay Napa Valley Silver Label 1989 $12 (1/31/91)
81 KALINDA Chardonnay Knights Valley 1989 $7 (7/15/91)
81 MEADOW GLEN Chardonnay Sonoma County Barrel Fermented 1989 $8.50 (4/30/91)
81 ROBERT PEPI Chardonnay Napa Valley Puncheon Fermented Reserve 1989 $20 (2/28/91)
81 JOSEPH PHELPS Chardonnay Napa Valley 1989 $16 (7/15/91)
81 RIDGE Chardonnay Howell Mountain 1989 $14 (7/15/91)
81 ROCHE Chardonnay Carneros 1989 $13 (3/31/91)
81 ST. SUPERY Chardonnay Napa Valley 1989 $12 (3/31/91)
81 SEBASTIANI Chardonnay Sonoma County 1989 $10 (7/15/91)
80 ADLER FELS Chardonnay Carneros Sangiacomo Vineyards 1989 $12.50 (4/30/91)
80 BELVEDERE Chardonnay Sonoma County Discovery Series 1989 $6 (12/31/90) BB
80 BYRON Chardonnay Santa Barbara County 1989 $13 (7/15/91)
80 CECCHETTI SEBASTIANI Chardonnay Napa Valley 1989 $6.50 (4/30/91)
80 CHATEAU ST. JEAN Chardonnay Sonoma County 1989 $12 (6/30/91)
80 CHRISTOPHE Chardonnay California Reserve 1989 $12 (7/15/91)

80 CLOS DU BOIS Chardonnay Alexander Valley Barrel Fermented 1989 $11 (12/31/90)
80 COSENTINO Chardonnay Napa Valley The Sculptor 1989 $18 (7/15/91)
80 ELLISTON Chardonnay Central Coast Sunol Valley Vineyard 1989 $14 (7/15/91)
80 FOLIE A DEUX Chardonnay Napa Valley 1989 $16 (7/15/91)
80 LIBERTY SCHOOL Chardonnay California Vintner Select Series One 1989 $7.50 (2/28/91)
80 MADDALENA Chardonnay Napa Valley 1989 $10 (7/15/91)
80 OLIVET LANE Chardonnay Russian River Valley 1989 $12 (7/15/91)
80 RAYMOND Chardonnay Napa Valley 1989 $15 (7/15/91)
80 ST. ANDREW'S WINERY Chardonnay Napa Valley 1989 $10 (7/15/91)
80 SANTA BARBARA Chardonnay Santa Barbara County 1989 $12 (1/31/91)
80 SUTTER HOME Chardonnay California 1989 $5 (11/15/90) BB
80 WHITE OAK Chardonnay Sonoma County Myers Limited Reserve 1989 $20 (3/31/91)
79 LAWRENCE J. BARGETTO Chardonnay Central Coast Cypress 1989 $9 (7/15/91)
79 DAVIS BYNUM Chardonnay Russian River Valley Limited Release 1989 $13 (4/30/91)
79 CAKEBREAD Chardonnay Napa Valley 1989 $19.50 (7/15/91)
79 CINNABAR Chardonnay Santa Cruz Mountains 1989 $18 (3/31/91)
79 CLOS DU VAL Chardonnay Napa Valley Joli Val 1989 $13 (7/15/91)
79 GLEN ELLEN Chardonnay California Proprietor's Reserve 1989 $6 (12/31/90)
79 JEPSON Chardonnay Mendocino 1989 $14 (7/15/91)
79 LOCKWOOD Chardonnay Monterey County 1989 $14 (7/15/91)
79 MENDOCINO ESTATE Chardonnay Mendocino 1989 $6.50 (7/15/91)
79 J.W. MORRIS Chardonnay California Private Reserve 1989 $8 (7/15/91)
79 KENT RASMUSSEN Chardonnay Carneros 1989 $20 (1/31/91)
79 REVERE Chardonnay Napa Valley 1989 $13 (7/15/91)
79 RIVERSIDE FARM Chardonnay California 1989 $6.75 (12/31/90)
79 VILLA MT. EDEN Chardonnay Carneros 1989 $12 (2/28/91)
78 CARNEROS CREEK Chardonnay Los Carneros 1989 $13 (5/15/91)
78 CHRISTOPHE Chardonnay California 1989 $9 (7/15/91)
78 CLOS ROBERT Chardonnay Napa Valley Lot 3 1989 $9 (7/15/91)
78 B.R. COHN Chardonnay Sonoma Valley Olive Hill Vineyard 1989 $14 (5/31/91)
78 DUNNEWOOD Chardonnay North Coast 1989 $7 (3/31/91)
78 GUNDLACH BUNDSCHU Chardonnay Sonoma Valley 1989 $12 (7/15/91)
78 LANDMARK Chardonnay Sonoma Valley Two Williams Vineyard 1989 $16 (7/15/91)
78 MONTE VERDE Chardonnay California Proprietor's Reserve 1989 $5.50 (3/31/91)
78 NEYERS Chardonnay Napa Valley 1989 $15 (7/15/91)
78 SIGNORELLO Chardonnay Napa Valley Founder's Reserve 1989 $25 (7/15/91)
78 STAR HILL Chardonnay Napa Valley Barrel Fermented 1989 $19 (7/15/91)
78 STONE CREEK Chardonnay Napa Valley Special Selection 1989 $10 (7/15/91)
78 SUNNY ST. HELENA Chardonnay California 1989 $12 (4/30/91)
77 CHANSA Chardonnay Santa Barbara County 1989 $10 (4/30/91)
77 CLOS PEGASE Chardonnay Napa Valley 1989 $12 (7/15/91)
77 DOMAINE NAPA Chardonnay Napa Valley 1989 $12.50 (7/15/91)
77 MONTEREY VINEYARD Chardonnay Central Coast Classic 1989 $6 (12/31/90)
77 NAPA CREEK Chardonnay Napa Valley 1989 $13 (4/30/91)
77 J. PEDRONCELLI Chardonnay Dry Creek Valley 1989 $9.50 (12/31/90)
77 REVERE Chardonnay Napa Valley Reserve 1989 $18 (7/15/91)
77 ROUND HILL Chardonnay California House 1989 $6 (8/31/90)
77 RUTHERFORD ESTATE Chardonnay Napa Valley 1989 $8.50 (7/15/91)
77 JOSEPH SWAN Chardonnay Sonoma Coast Russian River Valley 1989 $20 (5/31/91)
77 WHITEHALL LANE Chardonnay Napa Valley Le Petit 1989 $9 (2/28/91)
76 GARLAND RANCH Chardonnay Central Coast 1989 $5 (8/31/90)
76 J. LOHR Chardonnay California Cypress 1989 $7 (7/15/91)
76 SHADOWBROOK Chardonnay Napa Valley 1989 $9.50 (7/15/91)
76 SOLIS Chardonnay Santa Clara County 1989 $12.50 (7/15/91)
76 STORRS Chardonnay Santa Cruz Mountains 1989 $11.50 (7/15/91)
75 BARON HERZOG Chardonnay Sonoma County 1989 $11 (3/31/91)
75 CHATEAU DE BAUN Chardonnay Russian River Valley Barrel Fermented 1989 $10 (3/31/91)
75 FREEMARK ABBEY Chardonnay Napa Valley 1989 $15 (7/15/91)
75 GUNDLACH BUNDSCHU Chardonnay Sonoma Valley Sangiacomo Ranch Special Selection 1989 $15 (7/15/91)
75 CHARLES KRUG Chardonnay Napa Valley 1989 $10 (3/31/91)
75 LOUIS M. MARTINI Chardonnay Napa-Sonoma Counties 1989 $9 (4/30/91)
75 ST. ANDREW'S VINEYARD Chardonnay Napa Valley 1989 $14 (7/15/91)
75 WESTWOOD Chardonnay El Dorado 1989 $10 (7/15/91)
74 DEER VALLEY Chardonnay California 1989 $7 (7/15/91)
74 DORE Chardonnay California Limited Release Lot 101 1989 $8.50 (7/15/91)
74 FISHER Chardonnay Napa-Sonoma Counties 1989 Rel: $12 Cur: $12 (9/30/90)
74 KONOCTI Chardonnay Lake County 1989 $9.50 (4/30/91)
74 LEEWARD Chardonnay Monterey County 1989 $14 (11/30/90)
74 MIRASSOU Chardonnay Monterey County Fifth Generation Family Selection 1989 $9.75 (7/15/91)
74 ROBERT MONDAVI Chardonnay California Woodbridge 1989 $7.25 (4/30/91)
74 MONTICELLO Chardonnay Napa Valley Jefferson Ranch 1989 $12.50 (7/15/91)
74 M.G. VALLEJO Chardonnay California 1989 $6.50 (7/15/91)
73 JOULLIAN Chardonnay Carmel Valley 1989 $12 (7/15/91)
73 TIFFANY HILL Chardonnay Edna Valley 1989 $18 (7/15/91)
72 CALLAWAY Chardonnay Temecula Calla-Lees 1989 $10 (2/28/91)
72 CHIMNEY ROCK Chardonnay Napa Valley Stags Leap District 1989 $16 (7/15/91)
72 HAWK CREST Chardonnay California 1989 $9 (7/15/91)
72 LIBERTY SCHOOL Chardonnay Napa Valley 1989 $7.50 (11/15/90)
72 MCDOWELL Chardonnay California 1989 $10 (7/15/91)
71 BELVEDERE Chardonnay Sonoma County 1989 $6 (7/15/91)
71 OBESTER Chardonnay Mendocino County Barrel Fermented 1989 $13 (7/15/91)
71 SONOMA CREEK Chardonnay Carneros Barrel Fermented 1989 $10 (2/28/91)
71 STORRS Chardonnay Santa Cruz Mountains Vanumanutagi Vineyards 1989 $14 (7/15/91)
70 DEVLIN Chardonnay Santa Cruz Mountains Meyley Vineyard 1989 $10 (7/15/91)
70 FALCONER Chardonnay California 1989 $12 (2/28/91)
70 MARION Chardonnay California 1989 $8 (7/15/91)
70 ST. FRANCIS Chardonnay California 1989 $10 (7/15/91)
69 CHESTNUT HILL Chardonnay Sonoma County 1989 $7 (7/15/91)
69 TIJSSELING Chardonnay Mendocino 1989 $10 (7/15/91)
67 DEER PARK Chardonnay Napa Valley 1989 $14 (7/15/91)
67 PINE RIDGE Chardonnay Napa Valley Knollside Cuvée 1989 $16 (7/15/91)
65 RAVENSWOOD Chardonnay Sonoma Valley Sangiacomo 1989 $18 (7/15/91)
55 JEKEL Chardonnay Arroyo Seco 1989 $12 (7/15/91)

1988

95 KISTLER Chardonnay Sonoma Valley Kistler Estate Vineyard 1988 Rel: $26 Cur: $26 (2/01/90)

UNITED STATES

CALIFORNIA/*CHARDONNAY*

94 FRANCISCAN Chardonnay Napa Valley Oakville Estate Cuvée Sauvage 1988 Rel: $20 Cur: $25 (CH-7/90)
94 KISTLER Chardonnay Sonoma Valley Kistler Estate Vineyard 1988 Rel: $26 Cur: $26 (4/30/90)
94 MONTICELLO Chardonnay Napa Valley Corley Reserve 1988 Rel: $17.25 Cur: $18 (CH-2/90)
94 SANFORD Chardonnay Santa Barbara County Barrel Select 1988 Rel: $25 Cur: $28 (8/31/90)
94 SANFORD Chardonnay Santa Barbara County Barrel Select 1988 Rel: $25 Cur: $28 (CH-6/90)
93 FERRARI-CARANO Chardonnay Alexander Valley 1988 Rel: $18 Cur: $18 (5/31/90) SS
93 FERRARI-CARANO Chardonnay Alexander Valley 1988 Rel: $18 Cur: $18 (CH-5/90)
93 FERRARI-CARANO Chardonnay California Reserve 1988 Rel: $30 Cur: $30 (CH-6/90)
93 FRANCISCAN Chardonnay Napa Valley Oakville Estate Cuvée Sauvage 1988 Rel: $20 Cur: $25 (6/30/90)
93 GRGICH HILLS Chardonnay Napa Valley 1988 Rel: $22 Cur: $24 (CH-7/90)
93 LONG Chardonnay Napa Valley 1988 Rel: $27.50 Cur: $33 (CH-4/90)
93 REVERE Chardonnay Napa Valley Reserve 1988 $18 (5/15/91)
93 SONOMA-CUTRER Chardonnay Sonoma Coast Les Pierres 1988 Rel: $22.50 Cur: $23 (CH-7/90)
92 ARROWOOD Chardonnay Sonoma County 1988 Rel: $18 Cur: $21 (4/30/90)
92 ARROWOOD Chardonnay Sonoma County 1988 Rel: $18 Cur: $21 (CH-4/90)
92 ARROWOOD Chardonnay Sonoma County Réserve Spéciale 1.5L 1988 $50/1.5L (CH-4/90)
92 BYRON Chardonnay Santa Barbara County 1988 $12 (4/30/90) SS
92 CUVAISON Chardonnay Carneros Napa Valley Reserve 1988 (NR) (CH-6/90)
92 FLORA SPRINGS Chardonnay Napa Valley Barrel Fermented 1988 Rel: $24 Cur: $24 (CH-4/90)
92 FORMAN Chardonnay Napa Valley 1988 Rel: $20 Cur: $34 (6/30/90)
92 FORMAN Chardonnay Napa Valley 1988 Rel: $20 Cur: $34 (CH-2/90)
92 JUSTIN Chardonnay Paso Robles 1988 $14 (2/15/91)
92 KISTLER Chardonnay Russian River Valley Dutton Ranch 1988 Rel: $22 Cur: $44 (CH-2/90)
92 KISTLER Chardonnay Sonoma Mountain McCrea Vineyard 1988 Rel: $24 Cur: $24 (4/30/90)
92 KISTLER Chardonnay Sonoma Mountain McCrea Vineyard 1988 Rel: $24 Cur: $24 (CH-2/90)
92 ROBERT MONDAVI Chardonnay Napa Valley Reserve 1988 Rel: $26 Cur: $27 (8/31/90)
92 MONTICELLO Chardonnay Napa Valley Corley Reserve 1988 $17.25 (1/31/91) SS
92 MORGAN Chardonnay Monterey Reserve 1988 Rel: $20 Cur: $20 (CH-6/90)
92 SAINTSBURY Chardonnay Carneros Reserve 1988 Rel: $20 Cur: $22 (5/31/90)
92 SAINTSBURY Chardonnay Carneros Reserve 1988 Rel: $20 Cur: $22 (CH-2/90)
92 SANFORD Chardonnay Santa Barbara County 1988 Rel: $16 Cur: $18 (CH-6/90)
92 SEQUOIA GROVE Chardonnay Napa Valley Estate 1988 Rel: $16 Cur: $16 (CH-5/90)
92 SONOMA-CUTRER Chardonnay Sonoma Coast Cutrer Vineyard 1988 Rel: $17.50 Cur: $21 (CH-7/90)
91 AU BON CLIMAT Chardonnay Santa Barbara County Reserve 1988 $35 (3/15/91)
91 CHATEAU MONTELENA Chardonnay Alexander Valley 1988 Rel: $20 Cur: $26 (CH-2/90)
91 CHATEAU ST. JEAN Chardonnay Alexander Valley Robert Young Vineyards 1988 Rel: $18 Cur: $23 (CH-3/90)
91 CLOS DU BOIS Chardonnay Alexander Valley Calcaire Vineyard 1988 Rel: $17 Cur: $20 (5/15/90)
91 CUVAISON Chardonnay Carneros Napa Valley 1988 Rel: $15 Cur: $17 (CH-4/90)
91 CUVAISON Chardonnay Carneros Napa Valley 1988 Rel: $15 Cur: $17 (2/28/90) SS
91 DEHLINGER Chardonnay Russian River Valley 1988 Rel: $12 Cur: $12 (CH-4/90)
91 FAR NIENTE Chardonnay Napa Valley 1988 Rel: $26 Cur: $29 (2/15/90)
91 FAR NIENTE Chardonnay Napa Valley 1988 Rel: $26 Cur: $29 (CH-2/90)
91 FLORA SPRINGS Chardonnay Napa Valley Barrel Fermented 1988 Rel: $24 Cur: $24 (6/30/90)
91 FREEMARK ABBEY Chardonnay Napa Valley 1988 Rel: $15 Cur: $15 (6/30/90)
91 FROG'S LEAP Chardonnay Carneros 1988 Rel: $16 Cur: $16 (CH-3/90)
91 GIRARD Chardonnay Napa Valley Reserve 1988 (NR) (CH-6/90)
91 KEENAN Chardonnay Napa Valley 1988 $15 (6/30/90) SS
91 KISTLER Chardonnay Sonoma Valley Durell Vineyard 1988 $17 (2/01/90)
91 LA CREMA Chardonnay California Reserve 1988 Rel: $22 Cur: $22 (CH-6/90)
91 LA CREMA Chardonnay California Reserve 1988 Rel: $22 Cur: $22 (5/31/90)
91 LOLONIS Chardonnay Mendocino County Private Reserve 1988 $19 (4/30/90)
91 MATANZAS CREEK Chardonnay Sonoma County 1988 Rel: $18.75 Cur: $21 (4/30/90)
91 MERRYVALE Chardonnay Napa Valley 1988 $23 (6/30/90)
91 ROBERT MONDAVI Chardonnay Napa Valley Reserve 1988 Rel: $26 Cur: $27 (CH-6/90)
91 MOUNT VEEDER Chardonnay Napa Valley 1988 Rel: $15 Cur: $15 (6/30/90)
91 MURPHY-GOODE Chardonnay Alexander Valley Estate Vineyard 1988 Rel: $11.50 Cur: $12 (11/30/89)
91 NAVARRO Chardonnay Anderson Valley Première Reserve 1988 Rel: $14 Cur: $16 (CH-5/90)
91 NEWLAN Chardonnay Napa Valley 1988 $13 (6/15/90)
91 GUSTAVE NIEBAUM Chardonnay Carneros Napa Valley Bayview Vineyard 1988 $14.50 (10/31/89)
91 PARDUCCI Chardonnay Mendocino County Cellarmaster Selection 1988 $16 (6/30/90)
91 SANFORD Chardonnay Santa Barbara County 1988 Rel: $16 Cur: $18 (5/15/90)
91 SEQUOIA GROVE Chardonnay Napa Valley Estate 1988 Rel: $16 Cur: $16 (4/30/90)
91 SIMI Chardonnay Sonoma County Reserve 1988 (NR) (CH-7/90)
91 SONOMA-CUTRER Chardonnay Sonoma Coast Russian River Ranches 1988 Rel: $13.25 Cur: $14 (CH-3/90)
91 STERLING Chardonnay Napa Valley Diamond Mountain Ranch 1988 Rel: $16 Cur: $16 (CH-7/90)
91 STERLING Chardonnay Carneros Winery Lake 1988 Rel: $20 Cur: $20 (6/15/90)
91 VITA NOVA Chardonnay Santa Barbara County 1988 $13.50 (2/15/90)
90 ACACIA Chardonnay Carneros Napa Valley Marina Vineyard 1988 Rel: $20 Cur: $22 (1/31/90)
90 ALTAMURA Chardonnay Napa Valley 1988 (NR) (6/30/90)

Key to Symbols

The scores reported here are the results of blind tastings conducted by our panel of senior editors. Wines that carry the initials below are results of individual tastings.

THE WINE SPECTATOR 100-POINT SCALE ***95-100***—Classic, a great wine; ***90-94***—Outstanding, superior character and style; ***80-89***—Good to very good, a wine with special qualities; ***70-79***—Average, drinkable wine that may have minor flaws; ***60-69***—Below average, drinkable but not recommended; ***50-59***—Poor, undrinkable, not recommended. "+"—With a score indicates a range; used primarily with barrel tastings to indicate a preliminary score.

SPECIAL DESIGNATIONS SS—Spectator Selection, CS—Cellar Selection, BB—Best Buy.

TASTER'S INITIALS (JG)—Jim Gordon, (HS)—Harvey Steiman, (JL)—James Laube, (JS)—James Suckling, (TM)—Thomas Matthews, (TR)—Terry Robards, (BT)—Barrel Tasting (these wines were tasted blind from barrel samples), (CA-date)—*California's Great Cabernets* by James Laube, (CH-date)—*California's Great Chardonnays* by James Laube, (VP-date)—*Vintage Port* by James Suckling.

DATE TASTED Dates in parentheses represent the issue in which the rating was published.

90 ALTAMURA Chardonnay Napa Valley 1988 (NR) (CH-1/90)
90 BURGESS Chardonnay Napa Valley Triere Vineyard 1988 Rel: $16 Cur: $16 (4/30/90)
90 CHALONE Chardonnay Chalone 1988 Rel: $22 Cur: $30 (CH-6/90)
90 CHAMISAL Chardonnay Edna Valley Special Reserve 1988 $18.50 (11/30/90)
90 CHATEAU ST. JEAN Chardonnay Alexander Valley Belle Terre Vineyards 1988 Rel: $16 Cur: $21 (5/31/90)
90 CHATEAU ST. JEAN Chardonnay Alexander Valley Belle Terre Vineyards 1988 Rel: $16 Cur: $21 (CH-3/90)
90 CHATEAU ST. JEAN Chardonnay Alexander Valley Robert Young Vineyards 1988 $18 (6/30/91)
90 CLOS DU BOIS Chardonnay Dry Creek Valley Flintwood Vineyard 1988 Rel: $18 Cur: $18 (CH-2/90)
90 CLOS PEGASE Chardonnay Carneros 1988 $16.50 (5/15/90)
90 DE LORIMIER Chardonnay Alexander Valley Prism 1988 $13.50 (9/30/90)
90 FERRARI-CARANO Chardonnay California Reserve 1988 $30 (6/15/91)
90 FISHER Chardonnay Sonoma County Coach Insignia 1988 Rel: $18 Cur: $21 (6/30/90)
90 GIRARD Chardonnay Napa Valley 1988 $16 (11/15/90)
90 HANZELL Chardonnay Sonoma Valley 1988 Rel: $24 Cur: $28 (CH-5/90)
90 HESS Chardonnay California Hess Select 1988 $9 (11/30/89) SS
90 WILLIAM HILL Chardonnay Napa Valley Reserve 1988 Rel: $18 Cur: $18 (4/30/90)
90 KISTLER Chardonnay Russian River Valley Dutton Ranch 1988 Rel: $22 Cur: $44 (2/15/90)
90 KISTLER Chardonnay Sonoma Valley Durell Vineyard 1988 $17 (2/28/90)
90 J. LOHR Chardonnay Monterey Riverstone 1988 $12 (4/30/90)
90 MACROSTIE Chardonnay Carneros 1988 $14 (2/28/90)
90 MERRY VINTNERS Chardonnay Sonoma County Signature Reserve 1988 $15 (1/31/91)
90 MONTICELLO Chardonnay Napa Valley Jefferson Ranch 1988 Rel: $12.25 Cur: $13 (CH-2/90)
90 NEWTON Chardonnay Napa Valley 1988 Rel: $14.50 Cur: $15 (6/30/90)
90 GUSTAVE NIEBAUM Chardonnay Carneros Napa Valley Bayview Vineyard Special Reserve 1988 $18 (5/31/90)
90 GUSTAVE NIEBAUM Chardonnay Carneros Napa Valley Laird Vineyards 1988 $13.50 (10/31/89)
90 KENT RASMUSSEN Chardonnay Carneros 1988 $19 (9/15/90)
90 RAYMOND Chardonnay Napa Valley Private Reserve 1988 Rel: $22 Cur: $22 (CH-5/90)
90 ROCHE Chardonnay Carneros 1988 $11 (10/31/89)
90 SAINTSBURY Chardonnay Carneros 1988 Rel: $14 Cur: $16 (3/15/90)
90 SAINTSBURY Chardonnay Carneros 1988 Rel: $14 Cur: $16 (CH-2/90)
90 SILVERADO CELLARS Chardonnay California 1988 $11 (6/30/90)
90 STAG'S LEAP WINE CELLARS Chardonnay Napa Valley Reserve 1988 $28 (1/31/91)
90 STAG'S LEAP WINE CELLARS Chardonnay Napa Valley Reserve 1988 Rel: $28 Cur: $28 (CH-3/90)
90 STERLING Chardonnay Napa Valley 1988 Rel: $13 Cur: $19 (3/15/90)
90 STERLING Chardonnay Carneros Winery Lake 1988 Rel: $20 Cur: $20 (CH-4/90)
90 STONEGATE Chardonnay Napa Valley Reserve 1988 $20 (2/15/91)
90 STONY HILL Chardonnay Napa Valley 1988 Rel: $18 Cur: $90 (CH-6/90)
90 SWANSON Chardonnay Napa Valley Reserve 1988 $19 (7/15/91)
90 TREFETHEN Chardonnay Napa Valley 1988 Rel: $17.50 Cur: $19 (CH-3/90)
90 WENTE BROS. Chardonnay Arroyo Seco Arroyo Seco Vineyards Estate Reserve 1988 $12 (4/15/90)
90 WILD HORSE Chardonnay San Luis Obispo County 1988 $12 (4/15/90)
90 ZD Chardonnay California 1988 Rel: $20 Cur: $20 (12/31/89)
89 ACACIA Chardonnay Carneros Napa Valley 1988 Rel: $16 Cur: $16 (1/31/90)
89 ACACIA Chardonnay Carneros Napa Valley Marina Vineyard 1988 Rel: $20 Cur: $22 (CH-1/90)
89 ADELAIDA Chardonnay Paso Robles 1988 $14 (2/15/91)
89 BEAULIEU Chardonnay Carneros Napa Valley Carneros Reserve 1988 Rel: $14 Cur: $14 (CH-6/90)
89 CAKEBREAD Chardonnay Napa Valley 1988 $17.50 (3/15/90)
89 CHALONE Chardonnay Chalone 1988 Rel: $22 Cur: $30 (2/28/90)
89 CHALONE Chardonnay Chalone Reserve 1988 (NR) (CH-6/90)
89 CHAPPELLET Chardonnay Napa Valley 1988 Rel: $14 Cur: $14 (CH-6/90)
89 CLOS DU BOIS Chardonnay Alexander Valley Calcaire Vineyard 1988 Rel: $17 Cur: $20 (CH-2/90)
89 CLOS DU BOIS Chardonnay Russian River Valley Winemaker's Reserve 1988 Rel: $24 Cur: $24 (CH-5/90)
89 CLOS DU BOIS Chardonnay Dry Creek Valley Flintwood Vineyard 1988 Rel: $18 Cur: $18 (6/30/90)
89 CLOS PEGASE Chardonnay Carneros 1988 $16.50 (CH-3/90)
89 CONGRESS SPRINGS Chardonnay Santa Clara County San Ysidro Reserve 1988 Rel: $20 Cur: $20 (1/31/90)
89 EDNA VALLEY Chardonnay Edna Valley 1988 Rel: $14.75 Cur: $16 (CH-3/90)
89 FREEMARK ABBEY Chardonnay Napa Valley 1988 Rel: $15 Cur: $15 (CH-2/90)
89 GRGICH HILLS Chardonnay Napa Valley 1988 $22 (11/15/90)
89 HANNA Chardonnay Sonoma County 1988 $13.50 (9/30/90)
89 HAVENS Chardonnay Carneros Napa Valley 1988 $14 (4/30/90)
89 KENDALL-JACKSON Chardonnay California Vintner's Reserve 1988 $12.50 (10/31/89)
89 KENWOOD Chardonnay Sonoma Valley Beltane Ranch 1988 Rel: $15 Cur: $17 (CH-7/90)
89 LEEWARD Chardonnay Central Coast 1988 $10.50 (12/15/89)
89 LONG Chardonnay Napa Valley 1988 $27.50 (5/15/91)
89 MARKHAM Chardonnay Napa Valley 1988 Rel: $12 Cur: $12 (CH-2/90)
89 MATANZAS CREEK Chardonnay Sonoma County 1988 Rel: $18.75 Cur: $21 (CH-2/90)
89 MAYACAMAS Chardonnay Napa Valley 1988 Rel: $20 Cur: $20 (CH-6/90)
89 MERIDIAN Chardonnay Santa Barbara County 1988 $10 (4/15/90)
89 MERRY VINTNERS Chardonnay Sonoma County 1988 $12 (1/31/91)
89 MORGAN Chardonnay Monterey 1988 Rel: $15 Cur: $16 (CH-5/90)
89 MORGAN Chardonnay Monterey Reserve 1988 Rel: $20 Cur: $20 (5/31/90)
89 NAVARRO Chardonnay Anderson Valley Première Reserve 1988 $14 (12/31/90)
89 JOSEPH PHELPS Chardonnay Carneros Sangiacomo Vineyard 1988 $16 (6/30/90)
89 QUAIL RIDGE Chardonnay Napa Valley 1988 $14 (2/15/90)
89 RIDGE Chardonnay Santa Cruz Mountains 1988 $14 (7/15/91)
89 ROMBAUER Chardonnay Napa Valley Reserve 1988 (NR) (CH-6/90)
89 ST. ANDREW'S VINEYARD Chardonnay Napa Valley 1988 $13 (12/31/90)
89 SANFORD Chardonnay Santa Barbara County 1988 Rel: $16 Cur: $18 (12/15/89)
89 SEBASTIANI Chardonnay Sonoma County Reserve 1988 $15 (6/30/91)
89 SEBASTIANI Chardonnay Sonoma County Reserve 1988 $11 (4/30/90)
89 SEQUOIA GROVE Chardonnay Carneros 1988 Rel: $14 Cur: $14 (4/30/90)
89 SONOMA-CUTRER Chardonnay Sonoma Coast Cutrer Vineyard 1988 $17.50 (12/31/90)
89 THOMAS-HSI Chardonnay Napa Valley 1988 $18 (6/30/91)
89 VICHON Chardonnay Napa Valley 1988 Rel: $17 Cur: $19 (11/15/89)
89 ZD Chardonnay California 1988 Rel: $20 Cur: $20 (CH-3/90)

88 ALEXANDER VALLEY Chardonnay Alexander Valley 1988 $12 (6/30/90)
88 S. ANDERSON Chardonnay Napa Valley Stags Leap District 1988 $18 (CH-3/90)
88 BANCROFT Chardonnay Howell Mountain 1988 $14 (12/31/90)
88 BLACK MOUNTAIN Chardonnay Alexander Valley Douglass Hill 1988 $10 (4/15/90)
88 BOUCHAINE Chardonnay Carneros Estate Reserve 1988 (NR) (CH-6/90)
88 BURGESS Chardonnay Napa Valley Triere Vineyard 1988 Rel: $16 Cur: $16 (CH-12/89)
88 CHAPPELLET Chardonnay Napa Valley 1988 $14 (5/31/91)
88 CHATEAU MONTELENA Chardonnay Napa Valley 1988 Rel: $20 Cur: $23 (CH-7/90)
88 CHATEAU POTELLE Chardonnay Carneros 1988 $13.50 (6/30/90)
88 CHATEAU ST. JEAN Chardonnay Alexander Valley Jimtown Ranch 1988 (NR) (CH-7/90)
88 CLOS DU VAL Chardonnay Carneros Napa Valley Carneros Estate 1988 Rel: $16 Cur: $16 (CH-6/90)
88 CLOS PEGASE Chardonnay Napa Valley 1988 $12 (CH-3/90)
88 CONGRESS SPRINGS Chardonnay Santa Cruz Mountains Monmartre 1988 Rel: $30 Cur: $30 (CH-4/90)
88 DE LOACH Chardonnay Russian River Valley O.F.S. 1988 Rel: $22 Cur: $22 (2/15/90)
88 DURNEY Chardonnay Carmel Valley 1988 $18 (9/30/90)
88 FISHER Chardonnay Napa-Sonoma Counties 1988 Rel: $11 Cur: $11 (9/15/89)
88 FISHER Chardonnay Sonoma County Whitney's Vineyard 1988 (NR) (CH-2/90)
88 GAN EDEN Chardonnay Sonoma County 1988 $12 (8/31/90)
88 GIRARD Chardonnay Napa Valley 1988 Rel: $16 Cur: $17 (CH-6/90)
88 HALLCREST Chardonnay El Dorado County Hillside Cuvée 1988 $11 (6/30/90)
88 HESS Chardonnay Napa Valley 1988 Rel: $13.75 Cur: $14 (CH-4/90)
88 WILLIAM HILL Chardonnay Napa Valley Reserve 1988 Rel: $18 Cur: $18 (CH-3/90)
88 HUSCH Chardonnay Mendocino 1988 $11 (2/28/90)
88 INGLENOOK Chardonnay Napa Valley Reserve 1988 (NR) (CH-4/90)
88 KALIN Chardonnay Sonoma County Cuvée LD 1988 $23 (3/15/91)
88 KENDALL-JACKSON Chardonnay California The Proprietor's 1988 Rel: $24.50 Cur: $25 (2/28/90)
88 KENWOOD Chardonnay Sonoma Valley Beltane Ranch 1988 $15 (11/30/90)
88 LAKESPRING Chardonnay Napa Valley 1988 $13 (5/15/91)
88 MILANO Chardonnay Mendocino County Sanel Valley Vineyard 1988 $18 (7/15/91)
88 MORGAN Chardonnay Monterey 1988 Rel: $15 Cur: $16 (2/28/90)
88 MOUNT EDEN Chardonnay Santa Cruz Mountains 1988 $30 (11/30/90)
88 MOUNT EDEN Chardonnay Santa Cruz Mountains 1988 Rel: $30 Cur: $40 (CH-3/90)
88 MOUNT EDEN Chardonnay Edna Valley MacGregor Vineyard 1988 Rel: $14 Cur: $14 (CH-6/90)
88 MURPHY-GOODE Chardonnay Alexander Valley Estate Vineyard 1988 Rel: $11.50 Cur: $12 (CH-4/90)
88 NEWTON Chardonnay Napa Valley 1988 Rel: $14.50 Cur: $15 (CH-3/90)
88 ROBERT PEPI Chardonnay Napa Valley Puncheon Fermented 1988 $14 (5/31/90)
88 PINE RIDGE Chardonnay Napa Valley Knollside Cuvée 1988 Rel: $15 Cur: $17 (CH-7/90)
88 PINE RIDGE Chardonnay Napa Valley Stags Leap District 1988 Rel: $20 Cur: $20 (CH-7/90)
88 ROMBAUER Chardonnay Napa Valley 1988 Rel: $15 Cur: $15 (CH-6/90)
88 ST. CLEMENT Chardonnay Napa Valley 1988 Rel: $15 Cur: $16 (6/15/90)
88 ST. CLEMENT Chardonnay Napa Valley 1988 Rel: $15 Cur: $16 (CH-3/90)
88 SANTA YNEZ VALLEY Chardonnay Santa Barbara County 1988 $13 (2/28/90)
88 SILVERADO Chardonnay Napa Valley 1988 Rel: $14 Cur: $15 (CH-3/90)
88 SILVERADO Chardonnay Napa Valley 1988 Rel: $14 Cur: $15 (11/30/89)
88 SMITH-MADRONE Chardonnay Napa Valley 1988 Rel: $13 Cur: $13 (CH-5/90)
88 SONOMA-CUTRER Chardonnay Russian River Valley Russian River Ranches 1988 Rel: $13.25 Cur: $14 (6/30/90)
88 STRATFORD Chardonnay California Partners Reserve 1988 $14.50 (6/30/90)
88 VICHON Chardonnay Napa Valley 1988 Rel: $17 Cur: $19 (CH-3/90)
88 VILLA ZAPU Chardonnay Napa Valley 1988 $14 (6/30/90)
88 WHITE OAK Chardonnay Sonoma County 1988 Rel: $12 Cur: $12 (CH-5/90)
88 WHITE OAK Chardonnay Sonoma County 1988 Rel: $12 Cur: $12 (4/30/90)
88 WHITE OAK Chardonnay Sonoma County Myers Limited Release 1988 Rel: $18 Cur: $20 (CH-5/90)
88 STEPHEN ZELLERBACH Chardonnay Sonoma County 1988 $8 (4/15/90) BB
87 BEAUCANON Chardonnay Napa Valley 1988 $10 (7/15/91)
87 BERINGER Chardonnay Napa Valley 1988 $13 (4/15/90)
87 BERINGER Chardonnay Napa Valley Private Reserve 1988 Rel: $19 Cur: $20 (CH-4/90)
87 CHALONE Chardonnay Chalone Gavilan 1988 $12 (4/15/90)
87 CRONIN Chardonnay Alexander Valley Stuhlmuller Vineyard 1988 $18 (6/30/90)
87 DE LOACH Chardonnay Russian River Valley 1988 Rel: $15 Cur: $15 (CH-5/90)
87 DE LOACH Chardonnay Russian River Valley O.F.S. 1988 Rel: $22 Cur: $22 (CH-5/90)
87 DE MOOR Chardonnay Napa Valley Owners Select 1988 $14 (7/15/91)
87 FISHER Chardonnay Sonoma County Coach Insignia 1988 Rel: $18 Cur: $21 (CH-2/90)
87 FLORA SPRINGS Chardonnay Napa Valley 1988 $15 (3/15/90)
87 THOMAS FOGARTY Chardonnay Santa Cruz Mountains 1988 $18 (7/15/91)
87 FOLIE A DEUX Chardonnay Napa Valley 1988 Rel: $16 Cur: $17 (CH-6/90)
87 FROG'S LEAP Chardonnay Carneros 1988 Rel: $16 Cur: $16 (4/30/90)
87 FROG'S LEAP Chardonnay Napa Valley 1988 Rel: $15 Cur: $15 (CH-3/90)
87 GAN EDEN Chardonnay Sonoma County 1988 $12 (3/31/91)
87 HANDLEY Chardonnay Anderson Valley 1988 $12.50 (7/15/91)
87 JEKEL Chardonnay Arroyo Seco 1988 $11 (4/15/90)
87 KALIN Chardonnay Sonoma County Cuvée DD 1988 $23 (3/31/91)
87 KENDALL-JACKSON Chardonnay California The Proprietor's 1988 Rel: $24.50 Cur: $25 (CH-4/90)
87 KENWOOD Chardonnay Sonoma Valley Yulupa Vineyard 1988 Rel: $14 Cur: $14 (CH-7/90)
87 KENWOOD Chardonnay Sonoma Valley Yulupa Vineyard 1988 Rel: $14 Cur: $14 (5/31/90)
87 LANDMARK Chardonnay Sonoma County 1988 $10 (4/15/91)
87 MANISCHEWITZ Chardonnay Alexander Valley 1988 $7 (3/31/91)
87 NAVARRO Chardonnay Mendocino 1988 $9.75 (11/30/90)
87 ROBERT PECOTA Chardonnay Alexander Valley Canepa Vineyard 1988 Rel: $16 Cur: $16 (CH-4/90)
87 REVERE Chardonnay Napa Valley Reserve 1988 Rel: $18 Cur: $18 (CH-4/90)
87 RUTHERFORD HILL Chardonnay Napa Valley XVS 1988 $18 (7/15/91)
87 SIGNORELLO Chardonnay Napa Valley 1988 $14.50 (2/28/91)
87 SIMI Chardonnay Sonoma County 1988 $16 (6/15/90)
87 ROBERT SINSKEY Chardonnay Carneros 1988 $16 (2/28/91)
87 STAG'S LEAP WINE CELLARS Chardonnay Napa Valley 1988 Rel: $18 Cur: $18 (CH-3/90)
87 STAG'S LEAP WINE CELLARS Chardonnay Napa Valley 1988 Rel: $18 Cur: $18 (2/15/90)
87 STERLING Chardonnay Carneros Winery Lake 1988 $20 (7/15/91)
87 VILLA MT. EDEN Chardonnay Carneros 1988 $13.50 (9/30/90)
87 WILLOW CREEK Chardonnay Sonoma County 1988 $10 (2/28/90)
87 ZACA MESA Chardonnay Santa Barbara County Reserve 1988 $15.50 (9/15/90)
86 BALLARD CANYON Chardonnay Santa Ynez Valley 1988 $14 (12/15/89)
86 BUENA VISTA Chardonnay Carneros Private Reserve 1988 Rel: $16.50 Cur: $17 (CH-6/90)
86 BYRON Chardonnay Santa Barbara County Reserve 1988 $17 (11/15/90)
86 CALERA Chardonnay Central Coast 1988 $14 (11/30/90)
86 CALLAWAY Chardonnay Temecula Calla-Lees 1988 $10 (2/28/90)
86 CHATEAU MONTELENA Chardonnay Napa Valley 1988 $20 (11/30/90)
86 CHATEAU ST. JEAN Chardonnay Sonoma County 1988 Rel: $12 Cur: $12 (5/31/90)
86 CHATEAU WOLTNER Chardonnay Howell Mountain Estate Reserve 1988 Rel: $24 Cur: $24 (CH-4/90)
86 CHATEAU WOLTNER Chardonnay Howell Mountain St. Thomas Vineyard 1988 Rel: $36 Cur: $36 (CH-4/90)
86 CHATEAU WOLTNER Chardonnay Howell Mountain Titus Vineyard 1988 Rel: $54 Cur: $54 (CH-4/90)
86 CLOS DU VAL Chardonnay Napa Valley Joli Val 1988 $12.50 (1/31/90)
86 CLOS PEGASE Chardonnay Napa Valley 1988 $12 (6/30/90)
86 CONGRESS SPRINGS Chardonnay Santa Clara County Barrel Fermented 1988 Rel: $14 Cur: $14 (CH-4/90)
86 CONGRESS SPRINGS Chardonnay Santa Clara County San Ysidro Reserve 1988 Rel: $20 Cur: $20 (CH-4/90)
86 CONN CREEK Chardonnay Napa Valley Barrel Select 1988 $13 (7/15/91)
86 COSENTINO Chardonnay Napa Valley The Sculptor 1988 $18 (6/15/90)
86 DE LOACH Chardonnay Russian River Valley 1988 Rel: $15 Cur: $15 (11/15/89)
86 FELTON EMPIRE Chardonnay Monterey County Reserve 1988 $15 (4/15/90)
86 FREEMARK ABBEY Chardonnay Napa Valley Carpy Ranch 1988 Rel: $22 Cur: $22 (2/01/90)
86 INNISFREE Chardonnay Napa Valley 1988 $12 (6/15/90)
86 KALIN Chardonnay Potter Valley Cuvée BL 1988 $25 (3/31/91)
86 LEEWARD Chardonnay Edna Valley MacGregor Vineyard 1988 $16 (4/30/90)
86 MAYACAMAS Chardonnay Napa Valley 1988 $20 (7/15/91)
86 ROBERT MONDAVI Chardonnay Napa Valley 1988 Rel: $16 Cur: $19 (11/30/89)
86 NAPA CREEK Chardonnay Napa Valley 1988 $13.50 (4/15/90)
86 PARSONS CREEK Chardonnay Sonoma County Winemaker's Select 1988 $10 (2/28/91)
86 JOSEPH PHELPS Chardonnay Napa Valley 1988 $16 (6/30/90)
86 ROMBAUER Chardonnay Napa Valley 1988 $15 (12/31/90)
86 SANTA BARBARA Chardonnay Santa Ynez Valley Reserve 1988 $18 (9/30/90)
86 SEQUOIA GROVE Chardonnay Carneros 1988 Rel: $14 Cur: $14 (CH-5/90)
86 CHARLES SHAW Chardonnay Napa Valley 1988 Rel: $11 Cur: $11 (CH-5/90)
85 ACACIA Chardonnay Carneros Napa Valley 1988 Rel: $16 Cur: $16 (CH-1/90)
85 BELVEDERE Chardonnay Russian River Valley Reserve 1988 $9 (2/15/90)
85 BENZIGER Chardonnay Sonoma County 1988 $10 (6/30/90)
85 BOUCHAINE Chardonnay Carneros 1988 Rel: $15 Cur: $15 (CH-6/90)
85 CAMBRIA Chardonnay Santa Maria Valley Reserve 1988 $25 (12/31/90)
85 CARNEROS CREEK Chardonnay Los Carneros 1988 $13 (2/15/90)
85 CHATEAU MONTELENA Chardonnay Alexander Valley 1988 Rel: $20 Cur: $26 (6/30/90)
85 CLOS DU BOIS Chardonnay Alexander Valley Barrel Fermented 1988 Rel: $11 Cur: $11 (CH-2/90)
85 CRONIN Chardonnay Santa Cruz Mountains 1988 $20 (4/30/91)
85 DEHLINGER Chardonnay Russian River Valley 1988 Rel: $12 Cur: $12 (2/15/90)
85 DRY CREEK Chardonnay Sonoma County 1988 $12.50 (5/31/90)
85 DRY CREEK Chardonnay Sonoma County Reserve 1988 $20 (7/15/91)
85 EDNA VALLEY Chardonnay Edna Valley 1988 Rel: $14.75 Cur: $16 (12/15/89)
85 FIELD STONE Chardonnay Sonoma County 1988 $14 (4/15/91)
85 FOLIE A DEUX Chardonnay Napa Valley 1988 Rel: $16 Cur: $17 (5/31/90)
85 FORMAN Chardonnay Napa Valley 1988 Rel: $20 Cur: $34 (1/31/90)
85 FROG'S LEAP Chardonnay Napa Valley 1988 Rel: $15 Cur: $15 (6/30/90)
85 GAUER ESTATE Chardonnay Alexander Valley 1988 $16 (12/31/90)
85 HACIENDA Chardonnay Sonoma County Clair de Lune 1988 Rel: $15 Cur: $15 (CH-6/90)
85 HALLCREST Chardonnay California Fortuyn Cuvée 1988 $9 (6/30/90)
85 HESS Chardonnay Napa Valley 1988 Rel: $13.75 Cur: $14 (4/15/90)
85 WILLIAM HILL Chardonnay Napa Valley Silver Label 1988 $11.50 (6/30/90)
85 JEPSON Chardonnay Mendocino 1988 $12.50 (4/30/91)
85 KENDALL-JACKSON Chardonnay Anderson Valley Du Pratt Vineyard 1988 Rel: $14 Cur: $14 (CH-4/90)
85 KENDALL-JACKSON Chardonnay Redwood Valley Lolonis Vineyard 1988 (NR) (CH-4/90)
85 PINE RIDGE Chardonnay Napa Valley Knollside Cuvée 1988 Rel: $15 Cur: $17 (5/15/90)
85 PLAM Chardonnay Napa Valley 1988 $16 (6/30/90)
85 RAYMOND Chardonnay Napa Valley 1988 Rel: $15 Cur: $15 (6/15/90)
85 RAYMOND Chardonnay Napa Valley Private Reserve 1988 $22 (7/15/91)
85 RIDGE Chardonnay Howell Mountain 1988 $14 (7/15/91)
85 CHARLES SHAW Chardonnay Napa Valley 1988 Rel: $11 Cur: $11 (8/31/90)
85 STERLING Chardonnay Napa Valley Diamond Mountain Ranch 1988 $16 (7/15/91)
85 TREFETHEN Chardonnay Napa Valley 1988 $17.50 (12/31/90)
85 VIANSA Chardonnay Napa-Sonoma Counties 1988 $15 (9/15/90)
85 WILLIAM WHEELER Chardonnay Sonoma County 1988 $12 (6/30/90)
84 BEAULIEU Chardonnay Carneros Napa Valley Los Carneros Reserve 1988 Rel: $14 Cur: $14 (5/31/90)
84 CAIN Chardonnay Carneros 1988 $16 (11/30/90)
84 CAMBRIA Chardonnay Santa Barbara County Cambria Vineyard Sur Lees 1988 $16 (12/15/89)
84 CLOS DU BOIS Chardonnay Alexander Valley Barrel Fermented 1988 Rel: $11 Cur: $11 (2/15/90)
84 CRONIN Chardonnay Monterey County Ventana Vineyard 1988 $18 (6/30/90)
84 ELIZABETH Chardonnay Mendocino 1988 $11.50 (7/15/91)
84 FELTON EMPIRE Chardonnay Monterey County 1988 $12 (4/15/90)
84 FREEMARK ABBEY Chardonnay Napa Valley Carpy Ranch 1988 Rel: $22 Cur: $22 (4/30/90)
84 GRAND CRU Chardonnay Carneros Premium Selection 1988 $13.50 (6/15/90)
84 LOGAN Chardonnay Monterey 1988 $12 (6/30/90)
84 MAZZOCCO Chardonnay Alexander Valley River Lane Vineyard 1988 $16.50 (6/30/90)
84 REVERE Chardonnay Napa Valley 1988 $14 (2/28/91)
84 ST. ANDREW'S WINERY Chardonnay Napa Valley 1988 $10.50 (4/15/90)
84 SEGHESIO Chardonnay Sonoma County 1988 $12 (4/30/91)
84 STAR HILL Chardonnay Napa Valley Doc's Reserve Barrel Fermented 1988 $19 (6/30/90)
84 VIANSA Chardonnay Napa-Sonoma Counties Reserve 1988 $18 (11/30/90)
84 WHITEHALL LANE Chardonnay Napa Valley Le Petit 1988 $8 (4/30/90) BB
84 ZACA MESA Chardonnay Santa Barbara County 1988 $10 (2/15/90)
83 BUENA VISTA Chardonnay Carneros Jeanette's Vineyard 1988 $26 (3/31/91)
83 J. CAREY Chardonnay Santa Ynez Valley 1988 $12 (6/30/90)
83 CHATEAU NAPA-BEAUCANON Chardonnay Napa Valley 1988 $10 (6/30/90)
83 CHRISTIAN BROTHERS Chardonnay Napa Valley 1988 $10 (4/30/90)
83 CHRISTOPHE Chardonnay California 1988 $7.50 (4/30/90) BB

UNITED STATES
CALIFORNIA/*CHARDONNAY*

83 CLOS DU VAL Chardonnay Carneros Napa Valley Carneros Estate 1988 Rel: $16 Cur: $16 (6/30/90)
83 CONCANNON Chardonnay Santa Clara Valley Mistral Vineyard 1988 $12 (7/15/91)
83 DOMAINE MICHEL Chardonnay Sonoma County 1988 $16 (3/31/91)
83 ESTANCIA Chardonnay Alexander Valley 1988 $8 (4/30/90) BB
83 GROTH Chardonnay Napa Valley 1988 $13 (6/30/90)
83 HACIENDA Chardonnay Sonoma County Clair de Lune 1988 Rel: $15 Cur: $15 (6/30/90)
83 KONOCTI Chardonnay Lake County 1988 $9 (4/15/90)
83 MOUNT EDEN Chardonnay Edna Valley MacGregor Vineyard 1988 Rel: $14 Cur: $14 (6/30/90)
83 OBESTER Chardonnay Mendocino County 1988 $13 (7/15/91)
83 PARDUCCI Chardonnay Mendocino County 1988 $9.75 (4/30/90)
83 ROUND HILL Chardonnay California House 1988 $5.50 (4/15/90) BB
83 RUTHERFORD HILL Chardonnay Napa Valley Jaeger Vineyards 1988 $13 (2/15/91)
83 ST. SUPERY Chardonnay Napa Valley St.-Supery Vineyards 1988 $11 (11/15/89)
83 SHAFER Chardonnay Napa Valley 1988 $13.50 (5/31/90)
83 STONEGATE Chardonnay Napa Valley 1988 $15 (4/15/91)
83 TAFT STREET Chardonnay Russian River Valley 1988 $12 (7/15/91)
83 WINDEMERE Chardonnay Edna Valley MacGregor Vineyard 1988 $13 (4/30/91)
82 ALDERBROOK Chardonnay Dry Creek Valley 1988 $10 (2/15/90)
82 ALDERBROOK Chardonnay Dry Creek Valley Reserve 1988 $16 (4/15/90)
82 AU BON CLIMAT Chardonnay Santa Barbara County 1988 $12.50 (12/15/89)
82 BOUCHAINE Chardonnay Carneros 1988 $15 (11/30/90)
82 BUENA VISTA Chardonnay Carneros Private Reserve 1988 $16.50 (3/31/91)
82 CLOS DU BOIS Chardonnay Russian River Valley Winemaker's Reserve 1988 $24 (7/15/91)
82 B.R. COHN Chardonnay Sonoma Valley Olive Hill Vineyard 1988 $15 (10/31/89)
82 CRICHTON HALL Chardonnay Napa Valley 1988 $16 (12/31/90)
82 DOMAINE MICHEL Chardonnay Sonoma County 1988 $16 (5/31/90)
82 ESTANCIA Chardonnay Monterey 1988 $8 (4/30/90) BB
82 FETZER Chardonnay Mendocino County Barrel Select 1988 $12 (3/15/90)
82 FETZER Chardonnay Mendocino County Reserve 1988 $17.50 (5/31/90)
82 FRANCISCAN Chardonnay Napa Valley Oakville Estate 1988 $11 (6/30/90)
82 KENWOOD Chardonnay Sonoma Valley 1988 $14 (5/31/90)
82 LA CREMA Chardonnay California 1988 $13.50 (6/30/90)
82 MARKHAM Chardonnay Napa Valley 1988 Rel: $12 Cur: $12 (5/31/90)
82 RAYMOND Chardonnay California Selection 1988 $11 (10/31/89)
82 ROUND HILL Chardonnay Napa Valley Reserve 1988 $11 (2/28/91)
82 ST. FRANCIS Chardonnay California 1988 $10 (3/31/90)
82 WHITE OAK Chardonnay Sonoma County Myers Limited Release 1988 Rel: $18 Cur: $20 (2/28/90)
81 DOMAINE NAPA Chardonnay Napa Valley 1988 $12.50 (6/30/90)
81 GAINEY Chardonnay Santa Barbara County 1988 $12.50 (2/28/91)
81 GOOSECROSS Chardonnay Napa Valley 1988 $14 (8/31/90)
81 GUENOC Chardonnay Guenoc Valley Genevieve Magoon Vineyard Reserve 1988 $17 (12/31/90)
81 INNISKILLIN NAPA Chardonnay Napa Valley 1988 $14 (7/15/91)
81 IRON HORSE Chardonnay Sonoma County Green Valley 1988 $18 (2/15/90)
81 MARTIN Chardonnay Paso Robles 1988 $10 (12/15/89)
81 MONTICELLO Chardonnay Napa Valley Jefferson Ranch 1988 Rel: $12.25 Cur: $13 (6/30/90)
81 MOUNTAIN VIEW Chardonnay Monterey County 1988 $6.50 (4/30/90) BB
81 NEYERS Chardonnay Carneros 1988 $17 (7/15/91)
81 QUPE Chardonnay Santa Barbara County Sierra Madre Reserve 1988 $12.50 (12/15/89)
81 ROCHIOLI Chardonnay Russian River Valley 1988 $15 (4/15/90)
81 ROUND HILL Chardonnay California 1988 $7.50 (2/28/91) BB
81 STONY HILL Chardonnay Napa Valley SHV 1988 Rel: $18 Cur: $90 (6/30/90)
81 VENTANA Chardonnay Monterey Gold Stripe Selection 1988 $10 (9/30/89)
80 CONN CREEK Chardonnay Carneros Barrel Select 1988 $13 (7/15/91)
80 CHARLES KRUG Chardonnay Carneros Napa Valley 1988 $11.50 (1/31/90)
80 MERIDIAN Chardonnay Edna Valley 1988 $9.75 (9/30/90)
80 MONTEREY VINEYARD Chardonnay Monterey County Limited Release 1988 $12 (2/28/91)
80 ROBERT PECOTA Chardonnay Alexander Valley Canepa Vineyard 1988 Rel: $16 Cur: $16 (5/15/90)
80 MARIO PERELLI-MINETTI Chardonnay Napa Valley 1988 $11.50 (6/30/90)
80 RAVENSWOOD Chardonnay Sonoma Valley Sangiacomo 1988 $18 (2/28/90)
80 RIDGE Chardonnay Howell Mountain 1988 $15 (6/15/90)
80 TULOCAY Chardonnay Napa Valley DeCelles Vineyard 1988 $14 (4/30/91)
79 S. ANDERSON Chardonnay Napa Valley Stags Leap District 1988 $18 (12/31/90)
79 BALLARD CANYON Chardonnay Santa Ynez Valley Dr.'s Fun Baby 1988 $10 (12/15/89)
79 BEAULIEU Chardonnay Napa Valley Beaufort 1988 Rel: $9.50 Cur: $10 (4/30/90)
79 DAVIS BYNUM Chardonnay Russian River Valley 1988 $10 (4/30/90)
79 CHATEAU POTELLE Chardonnay Carneros 1988 $14 (7/15/91)
79 DOMAINE ST. GEORGE Chardonnay Sonoma County Select Reserve 1988 $9 (6/30/90)
79 GUNDLACH BUNDSCHU Chardonnay Sonoma Valley Sangiacomo Ranch Special Selection 1988 $14 (6/30/90)
79 NEYERS Chardonnay Napa Valley 1988 $15 (5/15/90)
79 J. PEDRONCELLI Chardonnay Dry Creek Valley 1988 $9 (12/15/89)
79 ST. FRANCIS Chardonnay Sonoma Valley Barrel Select 1988 $15 (11/30/89)
79 RODNEY STRONG Chardonnay Sonoma County Chalk Hill Vineyard 1988 $12 (3/31/91)
79 SWANSON Chardonnay Napa Valley 1988 $14.50 (6/30/90)
79 TAFT STREET Chardonnay Sonoma County 1988 $8 (1/31/90)
78 LAWRENCE J. BARGETTO Chardonnay Santa Cruz Mountains 1988 $18 (6/30/90)
78 CHAMISAL Chardonnay Edna Valley 1988 $14 (6/30/90)
78 CHRISTIAN BROTHERS Chardonnay Napa Valley 1988 $7.50 (6/30/91)

Key to Symbols

The scores reported here are the results of blind tastings conducted by our panel of senior editors. Wines that carry the initials below are results of individual tastings.

THE WINE SPECTATOR 100-POINT SCALE *95-100*—Classic, a great wine; *90-94*—Outstanding, superior character and style; *80-89*—Good to very good, a wine with special qualities; *70-79*—Average, drinkable wine that may have minor flaws; *60-69*—Below average, drinkable but not recommended; *50-59*—Poor, undrinkable, not recommended. "+"—With a score indicates a range; used primarily with barrel tastings to indicate a preliminary score.

SPECIAL DESIGNATIONS SS—Spectator Selection, CS—Cellar Selection, BB—Best Buy.

TASTER'S INITIALS (JG)—Jim Gordon, (HS)—Harvey Steiman, (JL)—James Laube, (JS)—James Suckling, (TM)—Thomas Matthews, (TR)—Terry Robards, (BT)—Barrel Tasting (these wines were tasted blind from barrel samples), (CA-date)—*California's Great Cabernets* by James Laube, (CH-date)—*California's Great Chardonnays* by James Laube, (VP-date)—*Vintage Port* by James Suckling.

DATE TASTED Dates in parentheses represent the issue in which the rating was published.

78 CORBETT CANYON Chardonnay Central Coast Reserve 1988 $9.50 (7/15/91)
78 CRONIN Chardonnay Napa Valley 1988 $18 (5/31/90)
78 FETZER Chardonnay California Sundial 1988 $7 (5/15/89)
78 MAZZOCCO Chardonnay Sonoma County Barrel Fermented 1988 $12 (11/30/89)
78 MCDOWELL Chardonnay California 1988 $8.50 (12/15/89)
78 PINE RIDGE Chardonnay Napa Valley Stags Leap District Stags Leap District 1988 $20 (11/30/90)
78 M.G. VALLEJO Chardonnay California 1988 $5 (4/30/90)
78 WHITEHALL LANE Chardonnay Napa Valley Estate Bottled 1988 $15 (6/30/90)
77 CHIMNEY ROCK Chardonnay Napa Valley Stags Leap District 1988 $15 (12/31/90)
77 GOOSECROSS Chardonnay Napa Valley Reserve 1988 $18 (8/31/90)
77 INNISFREE Chardonnay Carneros 1988 $12 (5/31/90)
77 NAPA RIDGE Chardonnay Central Coast 1988 $7 (6/30/90)
77 PATZ & HALL Chardonnay Napa Valley 1988 $24 (6/30/90)
77 SARAH'S Chardonnay Central Coast Estate 1988 $45 (5/31/91)
76 BERINGER Chardonnay Napa Valley Private Reserve 1988 Rel: $19 Cur: $20 (6/30/90)
76 BLUE HERON LAKE Chardonnay Wild Horse Valley 1988 $13 (3/31/91)
76 EBERLE Chardonnay Paso Robles 1988 $12 (6/30/90)
76 GUNDLACH BUNDSCHU Chardonnay Sonoma Valley 1988 $10 (4/30/90)
76 HAYWOOD Chardonnay Sonoma Valley Los Chamizal Vineyards 1988 $13.50 (11/30/90)
75 BARROW GREEN Chardonnay California 1988 $14.50 (7/15/91)
75 CASTORO Chardonnay San Luis Obispo County 1988 $8.50 (12/15/89)
75 CORBETT CANYON Chardonnay Central Coast Coastal Classic 1988 $6.50/L (12/15/89)
75 FREMONT CREEK Chardonnay Mendocino County 1988 $9.50 (6/30/90)
75 MCDOWELL Chardonnay McDowell Valley Estate Reserve 1988 $13 (7/15/91)
75 MEEKER Chardonnay Dry Creek Valley 1988 $13.50 (2/15/90)
75 SCHUG Chardonnay Carneros Beckstoffer Vineyard 1988 $15 (2/28/91)
75 SEGHESIO Chardonnay Sonoma County 1988 $8 (6/30/90)
75 IVAN TAMAS Chardonnay Livermore Valley 1988 $7.50 (4/30/90)
74 CHESTNUT HILL Chardonnay California 1988 $8 (4/15/90)
74 GRAND CRU Chardonnay Carneros Premium Selection 1988 $13.50 (3/15/90)
74 HAWK CREST Chardonnay California 1988 $9 (12/15/89)
74 ROUND HILL Chardonnay Napa Valley Van Asperen Vineyard 1988 $11 (2/28/91)
74 SANTA BARBARA Chardonnay Santa Ynez Valley 1988 $12 (4/15/90)
73 MENDOCINO ESTATE Chardonnay Mendocino 1988 $6.25 (12/15/89)
73 MONTPELLIER Chardonnay California 1988 $7 (3/31/90)
73 SILVERADO HILL CELLARS Chardonnay Napa Valley Winemaker's Traditional Méthode 1988 $10 (7/15/91)
73 STONEGATE Chardonnay Napa Valley 1988 $15 (2/15/91)
73 WILLIAM WHEELER Chardonnay Sonoma County 1988 $12 (5/15/90)
72 GREEN & RED Chardonnay Napa Valley 1988 $12 (4/30/90)
71 MONTE VERDE Chardonnay California 1988 $9 (12/15/89)
71 SEGHESIO Chardonnay Sonoma County Reserve 1988 $12 (2/28/91)
70 TIJSSELING Chardonnay Mendocino 1988 $10 (2/28/90)
68 CONGRESS SPRINGS Chardonnay Santa Clara County Barrel Fermented 1988 Rel: $14 Cur: $14 (2/15/90)
68 STONE CREEK Chardonnay North Coast 1988 $7 (6/30/90)
66 J.W. MORRIS Chardonnay California Private Reserve 1988 $8 (5/15/90)

1987

96 CHATEAU ST. JEAN Chardonnay Alexander Valley Robert Young Vineyards Reserve 1.5L 1987 (NR) (CH-7/90)
95 FLORA SPRINGS Chardonnay Napa Valley Barrel Fermented 1987 Rel: $20 Cur: $24 (CH-1/90)
94 FERRARI-CARANO Chardonnay Alexander Valley 1987 Rel: $16 Cur: $23 (CH-5/90)
94 FERRARI-CARANO Chardonnay Alexander Valley 1987 Rel: $16 Cur: $23 (5/31/89)
94 MOUNT EDEN Chardonnay Edna Valley MEV MacGregor Vineyard 1987 Rel: $14 Cur: $20 (CH-3/90)
94 SIMI Chardonnay Sonoma County Reserve 1987 Rel: $32 Cur: $32 (CH-4/90)
93 CLOS DU BOIS Chardonnay Alexander Valley Winemaker's Reserve 1987 Rel: $24 Cur: $24 (2/28/90)
93 FLORA SPRINGS Chardonnay Napa Valley Barrel Fermented 1987 Rel: $20 Cur: $24 (6/15/89)
93 KISTLER Chardonnay Russian River Valley Dutton Ranch 1987 Rel: $18 Cur: $45 (CH-2/90)
93 KISTLER Chardonnay Sonoma Valley Durell Vineyard 1987 $16 (2/01/90)
93 MERRYVALE Chardonnay Napa Valley 1987 $19 (2/15/90)
93 MOUNT EDEN Chardonnay Edna Valley MEV MacGregor Vineyard 1987 Rel: $14 Cur: $20 (4/30/89) SS
92 CLOS DU BOIS Chardonnay Alexander Valley Winemaker's Reserve 1987 Rel: $24 Cur: $24 (CH-2/90)
92 DE LOACH Chardonnay Russian River Valley O.F.S. 1987 Rel: $22 Cur: $40 (CH-5/90)
92 FAR NIENTE Chardonnay Napa Valley 1987 Rel: $26 Cur: $30 (12/31/88)
92 FRANCISCAN Chardonnay Napa Valley Oakville Estate Reserve 1987 $15 (6/15/90)
92 KENDALL-JACKSON Chardonnay California The Proprietor's 1987 Rel: $20 Cur: $20 (CH-4/90)
92 KISTLER Chardonnay Russian River Valley Dutton Ranch 1987 Rel: $18 Cur: $45 (12/31/88)
92 KISTLER Chardonnay Sonoma Valley Kistler Estate Vineyard 1987 Rel: $22 Cur: $55 (7/15/89)
92 ROBERT MONDAVI Chardonnay Napa Valley Reserve 1987 Rel: $26 Cur: $26 (CH-6/90)
92 SANFORD Chardonnay Santa Barbara County 1987 Rel: $15 Cur: $16 (CH-2/90)
92 SILVERADO Chardonnay Napa Valley Limited Reserve 1987 Rel: $30 Cur: $30 (CH-7/90)
92 SIMI Chardonnay Sonoma County Reserve 1987 $32 (7/15/91)
92 SONOMA-CUTRER Chardonnay Sonoma Coast Les Pierres 1987 Rel: $22.50 Cur: $27 (CH-3/90)
91 BYRON Chardonnay Santa Barbara County 1987 $11 (12/15/89)
91 CHATEAU ST. JEAN Chardonnay Alexander Valley Belle Terre Vineyards 1987 Rel: $16 Cur: $22 (CH-3/90)
91 CHATEAU ST. JEAN Chardonnay Alexander Valley Robert Young Vineyards 1987 Rel: $18 Cur: $25 (CH-3/90)
91 COSENTINO Chardonnay Napa Valley 1987 $11.50 (3/15/89)
91 CUVAISON Chardonnay Carneros Napa Valley Reserve 1987 Rel: $22 Cur: $22 (CH-7/90)
91 DRY CREEK Chardonnay Dry Creek Valley Reserve 1987 $18 (4/15/90)
91 EDNA VALLEY Chardonnay Edna Valley 1987 Rel: $14 Cur: $20 (CH-3/90)
91 EDNA VALLEY Chardonnay Edna Valley 1987 Rel: $14 Cur: $20 (11/30/88)
91 FAR NIENTE Chardonnay Napa Valley 1987 Rel: $26 Cur: $30 (CH-2/90)
91 FRANCISCAN Chardonnay Napa Valley Oakville Estate Cuvée Sauvage 1987 Rel: $20 Cur: $25 (CH-6/90)
91 HESS Chardonnay Napa Valley 1987 Rel: $13.25 Cur: $15 (CH-4/90)
91 WILLIAM HILL Chardonnay Napa Valley Reserve 1987 Rel: $18 Cur: $18 (CH-3/90)

91 KENDALL-JACKSON Chardonnay Anderson Valley De Patie Vineyard 1987 Rel: $14 Cur: $14 (7/15/89)
91 ROBERT PECOTA Chardonnay Alexander Valley Canepa Vineyard 1987 Rel: $16 Cur: $20 (CH-4/90)
91 ROBERT PECOTA Chardonnay Alexander Valley Canepa Vineyard 1987 Rel: $16 Cur: $20 (12/31/88)
91 PINE RIDGE Chardonnay Napa Valley Knollside Cuvée 1987 Rel: $15 Cur: $17 (1/31/89)
91 PINE RIDGE Chardonnay Napa Valley Stags Leap District 1987 Rel: $20 Cur: $23 (CH-4/90)
91 ST. CLEMENT Chardonnay Carneros Abbott's Vineyard 1987 $17 (CH-3/90)
91 SAINTSBURY Chardonnay Carneros 1987 Rel: $13 Cur: $18 (11/30/88)
91 SANFORD Chardonnay Santa Barbara County Barrel Select 1987 Rel: $24 Cur: $30 (CH-2/90)
91 SANFORD Chardonnay Santa Barbara County Barrel Select 1987 Rel: $24 Cur: $30 (12/15/89)
91 SIMI Chardonnay Mendocino-Sonoma-Napa Counties 1987 $14 (11/30/89)
91 SMITH-MADRONE Chardonnay Napa Valley 1987 Rel: $13 Cur: $13 (CH-5/90)
91 SONOMA-CUTRER Chardonnay Sonoma Coast Cutrer Vineyard 1987 Rel: $17.50 Cur: $23 (CH-3/90)
91 STAG'S LEAP WINE CELLARS Chardonnay Napa Valley Beckstoffer Ranch 1987 $19 (9/15/89)
91 STAG'S LEAP WINE CELLARS Chardonnay Napa Valley 1987 Rel: $18 Cur: $18 (12/31/88)
90 ALDERBROOK Chardonnay Dry Creek Valley 1987 $9.75 (2/15/89)
90 BABCOCK Chardonnay Santa Ynez Valley Selected Barrels Reserve 1987 $20 (12/15/89)
90 BARROW GREEN Chardonnay California 1987 $16 (11/15/89)
90 CHALONE Chardonnay Chalone 1987 Rel: $22 Cur: $39 (12/31/88)
90 CHATEAU MONTELENA Chardonnay Alexander Valley 1987 Rel: $20 Cur: $26 (6/30/89)
90 CHATEAU ST. JEAN Chardonnay Alexander Valley Robert Young Vineyards 1987 Rel: $18 Cur: $25 (6/30/89)
90 CLOS DU VAL Chardonnay Napa Valley Carneros Estate 1987 Rel: $13 Cur: $16 (6/15/89)
90 CLOS PEGASE Chardonnay Carneros 1987 $15.50 (CH-3/90)
90 CONGRESS SPRINGS Chardonnay Santa Clara County San Ysidro Reserve 1987 Rel: $16 Cur: $23 (CH-4/90)
90 CONGRESS SPRINGS Chardonnay Santa Clara County San Ysidro Reserve 1987 Rel: $16 Cur: $23 (11/30/88)
90 CRONIN Chardonnay Santa Cruz Mountains 1987 $18 (2/15/90)
90 CUVAISON Chardonnay Napa Valley 1987 Rel: $13.50 Cur: $16 (CH-4/90)
90 DEHLINGER Chardonnay Russian River Valley 1987 Rel: $11.50 Cur: $12 (CH-4/90)
90 DEHLINGER Chardonnay Russian River Valley 1987 Rel: $11.50 Cur: $12 (12/31/88)
90 FOLIE A DEUX Chardonnay Napa Valley 1987 Rel: $15 Cur: $18 (CH-6/90)
90 FOXEN Chardonnay Santa Maria Valley 1987 $18 (12/15/89)
90 FRANCISCAN Chardonnay Napa Valley Oakville Estate Cuvée Sauvage 1987 Rel: $20 Cur: $25 (6/15/90)
90 FROG'S LEAP Chardonnay Napa Valley 1987 Rel: $14 Cur: $16 (12/31/88)
90 GIRARD Chardonnay Napa Valley Reserve 1987 Rel: $25 Cur: $31 (11/15/90)
90 GRGICH HILLS Chardonnay Napa Valley 1987 Rel: $22 Cur: $29 (CH-6/90)
90 HANZELL Chardonnay Sonoma Valley 1987 Rel: $24 Cur: $28 (CH-1/90)
90 HESS Chardonnay Napa Valley 1987 Rel: $13.25 Cur: $15 (7/15/89)
90 KENDALL-JACKSON Chardonnay California The Proprietor's 1987 Rel: $20 Cur: $20 (11/30/88)
90 KISTLER Chardonnay Sonoma Valley Kistler Estate Vineyard 1987 Rel: $22 Cur: $55 (2/01/90)
90 LAZY CREEK Chardonnay Anderson Valley 1987 $10 (5/15/89)
90 LEEWARD Chardonnay Edna Valley MacGregor Vineyard 1987 $16 (12/15/89)
90 J. LOHR Chardonnay Monterey Riverstone 1987 $12 (11/15/89)
90 LONG Chardonnay Napa Valley 1987 Rel: $27.50 Cur: $35 (CH-4/90)
90 MATANZAS CREEK Chardonnay Sonoma County 1987 Rel: $18 Cur: $21 (CH-2/90)
90 MOUNT EDEN Chardonnay Santa Cruz Mountains 1987 Rel: $28 Cur: $44 (CH-3/90)
90 PINE RIDGE Chardonnay Napa Valley Knollside Cuvée 1987 Rel: $15 Cur: $17 (CH-4/90)
90 RAYMOND Chardonnay Napa Valley Private Reserve 1987 Rel: $22 Cur: $22 (5/15/90)
90 RUTHERFORD HILL Chardonnay Napa Valley Cellar Reserve 1987 $18 (2/15/91)
90 ST. CLEMENT Chardonnay Napa Valley 1987 Rel: $15 Cur: $15 (9/15/89)
90 SAINTSBURY Chardonnay Carneros 1987 Rel: $13 Cur: $18 (CH-2/90)
90 SANFORD Chardonnay Santa Barbara County 1987 Rel: $15 Cur: $16 (11/30/88)
90 SEBASTIANI ESTATES Chardonnay Sonoma County Wildwood Hill 1987 $14 (6/30/90)
90 RODNEY STRONG Chardonnay Sonoma County Chalk Hill Vineyard 1987 $12 (2/15/91)
89 S. ANDERSON Chardonnay Napa Valley Stags Leap District Proprietor's Reserve 1987 Rel: $20 Cur: $20 (CH-3/90)
89 ARROWOOD Chardonnay Sonoma County 1987 Rel: $18 Cur: $21 (CH-4/90)
89 BOUCHAINE Chardonnay Carneros 1987 Rel: $14 Cur: $14 (8/31/90)
89 BOUCHAINE Chardonnay Carneros Estate Reserve 1987 Rel: $19 Cur: $19 (5/31/90)
89 BURGESS Chardonnay Napa Valley Triere Vineyard 1987 Rel: $14.50 Cur: $15 (6/30/89)
89 BYRON Chardonnay Santa Barbara County 1987 $11 (3/31/89)
89 CHATEAU MONTELENA Chardonnay Alexander Valley 1987 Rel: $20 Cur: $26 (CH-2/90)
89 CLOS DU BOIS Chardonnay Alexander Valley Winemaker's Reserve 1987 Rel: $24 Cur: $24 (7/15/89)
89 CLOS DU VAL Chardonnay Carneros Napa Valley Carneros Estate 1987 Rel: $13 Cur: $16 (CH-6/90)
89 CLOS PEGASE Chardonnay Carneros 1987 $15.50 (2/15/90)
89 DE LOACH Chardonnay Russian River Valley 1987 Rel: $15 Cur: $22 (10/31/88)
89 FERRARI-CARANO Chardonnay California Reserve 1987 Rel: $28 Cur: $30 (CH-5/90)
89 FOLIE A DEUX Chardonnay Napa Valley 1987 Rel: $15 Cur: $18 (5/31/89)
89 FORMAN Chardonnay Napa Valley 1987 Rel: $18 Cur: $35 (CH-2/90)
89 FORMAN Chardonnay Napa Valley 1987 Rel: $18 Cur: $35 (12/31/88)
89 FROG'S LEAP Chardonnay Carneros 1987 Rel: $15 Cur: $17 (4/30/89)
89 GAINEY Chardonnay Santa Barbara County Limited Selection 1987 $16 (12/15/89)
89 GAN EDEN Chardonnay Alexander Valley 1987 $9.50 (3/15/89)
89 HANZELL Chardonnay Sonoma Valley 1987 Rel: $24 Cur: $28 (2/28/90)
89 HIDDEN CELLARS Chardonnay Mendocino County 1987 $12 (7/15/89)
89 WILLIAM HILL Chardonnay Napa Valley Reserve 1987 Rel: $18 Cur: $18 (7/15/89)
89 INGLENOOK Chardonnay Napa Valley Reserve 1987 Rel: $14 Cur: $14 (5/31/90)
89 JORY Chardonnay Santa Clara County San Ysidro Vineyard 1987 $16.50 (10/31/88)
89 KENDALL-JACKSON Chardonnay Anderson Valley De Patie Vineyard 1987 Rel: $14 Cur: $14 (CH-4/90)
89 MACROSTIE Chardonnay Carneros 1987 $14.50 (11/30/88)
89 NAVARRO Chardonnay Anderson Valley 1987 $9.75 (9/30/89)
89 ST. CLEMENT Chardonnay Carneros Abbott's Vineyard 1987 $17 (10/31/89)
89 SAINTSBURY Chardonnay Carneros Reserve 1987 Rel: $20 Cur: $22 (CH-2/90)
89 SILVERADO Chardonnay Napa Valley 1987 Rel: $13.50 Cur: $15 (12/31/88)
89 STAG'S LEAP WINE CELLARS Chardonnay Napa Valley 1987 Rel: $18 Cur: $18 (CH-3/90)
89 STAG'S LEAP WINE CELLARS Chardonnay Napa Valley Reserve 1987 Rel: $28 Cur: $32 (CH-3/90)
89 STERLING Chardonnay Napa Valley 1987 Rel: $14.50 Cur: $20 (4/15/89)
89 STERLING Chardonnay Carneros Winery Lake 1987 Rel: $20 Cur: $20 (CH-4/90)
88 ACACIA Chardonnay Carneros Napa Valley 1987 Rel: $17 Cur: $17 (12/31/88)
88 S. ANDERSON Chardonnay Napa Valley Stags Leap District 1987 $16 (7/15/89)
88 BELVEDERE Chardonnay Russian River Valley 1987 $11 (7/15/89)
88 BLACK MOUNTAIN Chardonnay Alexander Valley Gravel Bar 1987 $18 (4/15/90)
88 BONNY DOON Chardonnay Monterey County La Reina Vineyard 1987 $15 (12/31/88)
88 BUENA VISTA Chardonnay Carneros 1987 $10 (10/15/88)
88 CHATEAU ST. JEAN Chardonnay Sonoma Valley McCrea Vineyards 1987 Rel: $15 Cur: $15 (CH-3/90)
88 CHATEAU WOLTNER Chardonnay Howell Mountain Estate Reserve 1987 Rel: $24 Cur: $24 (CH-4/90)
88 CHATEAU WOLTNER Chardonnay Howell Mountain St. Thomas Vineyard 1987 Rel: $36 Cur: $36 (9/15/89)
88 CLOS DU BOIS Chardonnay Alexander Valley Barrel Fermented 1987 Rel: $11 Cur: $11 (12/31/88)
88 CLOS DU BOIS Chardonnay Alexander Valley Calcaire Vineyard 1987 Rel: $20 Cur: $21 (CH-2/90)
88 CLOS DU BOIS Chardonnay Alexander Valley Calcaire Vineyard 1987 Rel: $20 Cur: $21 (1/31/89)
88 CONN CREEK Chardonnay Napa Valley Barrel Select 1987 $12 (9/15/90)
88 DOLAN Chardonnay Mendocino 1987 $15 (12/31/88)
88 FETZER Chardonnay Mendocino County Barrel Select 1987 $10 (3/15/89)
88 FROG'S LEAP Chardonnay Napa Valley 1987 Rel: $14 Cur: $16 (CH-3/90)
88 GRAND CRU Chardonnay Carneros Premium Selection 1987 $12 (3/15/89)
88 HUSCH Chardonnay Mendocino 1987 $10 (11/15/88)
88 JORDAN Chardonnay Alexander Valley 1987 $20 (6/30/90)
88 LA CREMA Chardonnay California 1987 $12 (12/31/88)
88 MARK WEST Chardonnay Russian River Valley Le Beau Vineyards Reserve 1987 $16.50 (4/15/91)
88 MAZZOCCO Chardonnay Alexander Valley River Lane Vineyard 1987 $16.50 (4/15/89)
88 ROBERT MONDAVI Chardonnay Napa Valley Reserve 1987 Rel: $26 Cur: $26 (7/15/89)
88 MOUNT EDEN Chardonnay Santa Cruz Mountains 1987 Rel: $28 Cur: $44 (11/15/89)
88 NEWTON Chardonnay Napa Valley 1987 Rel: $14 Cur: $14 (CH-3/90)
88 RAYMOND Chardonnay Napa Valley Private Reserve 1987 Rel: $22 Cur: $22 (CH-5/90)
88 ROMBAUER Chardonnay Napa Valley 1987 Rel: $14.50 Cur: $15 (1/31/90)
88 SAINTSBURY Chardonnay Carneros Reserve 1987 Rel: $20 Cur: $22 (7/15/89)
88 SEQUOIA GROVE Chardonnay Napa Valley Estate 1987 Rel: $16 Cur: $16 (CH-5/90)
88 SILVERADO Chardonnay Napa Valley 1987 Rel: $13.50 Cur: $15 (CH-3/90)
88 ROBERT SINSKEY Chardonnay Carneros Napa Valley 1987 $16 (10/31/89)
88 SONOMA-CUTRER Chardonnay Sonoma Coast Russian River Ranches 1987 Rel: $12 Cur: $16 (CH-3/90)
88 STAG'S LEAP WINE CELLARS Chardonnay Napa Valley Reserve 1987 Rel: $28 Cur: $32 (5/31/90)
88 STERLING Chardonnay Napa Valley Diamond Mountain Ranch 1987 Rel: $16 Cur: $16 (CH-7/90)
88 TREFETHEN Chardonnay Napa Valley 1987 Rel: $16.75 Cur: $19 (CH-3/90)
88 VENTANA Chardonnay Monterey Ventana Vineyards Gold Stripe Selection 1987 $10 (6/30/89)
88 WILLIAM WHEELER Chardonnay Sonoma County 1987 $12 (7/15/89)
88 WINDEMERE Chardonnay Edna Valley MacGregor Vineyard 1987 $12 (7/15/89)
87 ALTAMURA Chardonnay Napa Valley 1987 Rel: $16.50 Cur: $21 (6/30/90)
87 ALTAMURA Chardonnay Napa Valley 1987 Rel: $16.50 Cur: $21 (CH-1/90)
87 ARROWOOD Chardonnay Sonoma County 1987 Rel: $18 Cur: $21 (5/15/89)
87 AU BON CLIMAT Chardonnay Santa Barbara County Reserve 1987 $20 (12/15/89)
87 BEAULIEU Chardonnay Carneros Napa Valley Los Carneros Reserve 1987 Rel: $14 Cur: $16 (CH-5/90)
87 BENZIGER Chardonnay Sonoma County 1987 $9.50 (7/15/89)
87 CHALONE Chardonnay Chalone Reserve 1987 Rel: $35 Cur: $95 (CH-5/90)
87 CHAPPELLET Chardonnay Napa Valley 1987 Rel: $14 Cur: $14 (CH-3/90)
87 CHATEAU ST. JEAN Chardonnay Alexander Valley Jimtown Ranch 1987 Rel: $15 Cur: $15 (CH-3/90)
87 CHATEAU WOLTNER Chardonnay Howell Mountain St. Thomas Vineyard 1987 Rel: $36 Cur: $36 (CH-4/90)
87 CLOS DU BOIS Chardonnay Alexander Valley Barrel Fermented 1987 Rel: $11 Cur: $11 (CH-2/90)
87 CLOS DU BOIS Chardonnay Dry Creek Valley Flintwood Vineyard 1987 Rel: $20 Cur: $22 (CH-2/90)
87 CLOS DU VAL Chardonnay Napa Valley 1987 $12 (CH-6/90)
87 CLOS DU VAL Chardonnay Napa Valley 1987 $12 (6/15/89)
87 CONGRESS SPRINGS Chardonnay Santa Cruz Mountains Monmartre 1987 Rel: $28 Cur: $30 (CH-4/90)
87 CONGRESS SPRINGS Chardonnay Santa Cruz Mountains Monmartre 1987 Rel: $28 Cur: $30 (7/15/89)
87 CUVAISON Chardonnay Napa Valley 1987 Rel: $13.50 Cur: $16 (12/31/88)
87 DE LOACH Chardonnay Russian River Valley 1987 Rel: $15 Cur: $22 (CH-2/90)
87 FERRARI-CARANO Chardonnay California Reserve 1987 Rel: $28 Cur: $30 (5/31/90)
87 FLORA SPRINGS Chardonnay Napa Valley 1987 $15 (6/15/89)
87 GIRARD Chardonnay Napa Valley Reserve 1987 Rel: $25 Cur: $31 (CH-6/90)
87 GRGICH HILLS Chardonnay Napa Valley 1987 Rel: $22 Cur: $29 (7/15/89)
87 KENWOOD Chardonnay Sonoma Valley Beltane Ranch 1987 Rel: $15 Cur: $17 (CH-7/90)
87 MARKHAM Chardonnay Napa Valley 1987 Rel: $12 Cur: $14 (CH-2/90)
87 MATANZAS CREEK Chardonnay Sonoma County 1987 Rel: $18 Cur: $21 (5/31/89)
87 MAYACAMAS Chardonnay Napa Valley 1987 Rel: $20 Cur: $24 (CH-1/90)
87 MURPHY-GOODE Chardonnay Alexander Valley Premier Vineyard 1987 Rel: $11 Cur: $11 (CH-4/90)
87 NAVARRO Chardonnay Anderson Valley Première Reserve 1987 Rel: $14 Cur: $16 (CH-3/90)
87 RAVENSWOOD Chardonnay Sonoma Valley Sangiacomo 1987 $15 (7/15/89)
87 RIDGE Chardonnay Howell Mountain 1987 $14 (4/30/89)
87 ROMBAUER Chardonnay Napa Valley Reserve 1987 Rel: $25 Cur: $25 (CH-6/90)
87 SEQUOIA GROVE Chardonnay Napa Valley Estate 1987 Rel: $12 Cur: $12 (2/15/89)
87 STONY HILL Chardonnay Napa Valley 1987 Rel: $18 Cur: $62 (CH-5/90)
87 TERRA Chardonnay Napa Valley 1987 $12 (7/15/91)
87 VICHON Chardonnay Napa Valley 1987 Rel: $16 Cur: $18 (CH-3/90)
87 ZACA MESA Chardonnay Santa Barbara County 1987 $10 (3/31/89)
86 ACACIA Chardonnay Carneros Napa Valley Marina Vineyard 1987 Rel: $18 Cur: $22 (12/31/88)
86 BLACK MOUNTAIN Chardonnay Alexander Valley Douglass Hill 1987 $10 (12/31/88)
86 BOUCHAINE Chardonnay Carneros Estate Reserve 1987 Rel: $19 Cur: $19 (CH-2/90)
86 CAIN Chardonnay Carneros 1987 $16 (12/31/89)
86 CAKEBREAD Chardonnay Napa Valley 1987 $21 (6/30/89)

UNITED STATES
CALIFORNIA/*CHARDONNAY*

86 CALERA Chardonnay San Benito County Mount Harlan Vineyard Young Vines 1987 $22 (4/15/89)
86 CHATEAU ST. JEAN Chardonnay Alexander Valley Jimtown Ranch 1987 Rel: $15 Cur: $15 (7/15/89)
86 CLOS PEGASE Chardonnay Napa Valley 1987 $12 (CH-3/90)
86 DE LOACH Chardonnay Russian River Valley O.F.S. 1987 Rel: $22 Cur: $40 (12/31/88)
86 DE LORIMIER Chardonnay Alexander Valley Prism 1987 $13.50 (4/15/89)
86 DOMAINE ST. GEORGE Chardonnay Sonoma County Select Reserve Barrel Fermented Barrel Aged 1987 $8 (12/31/88) BB
86 FISHER Chardonnay Sonoma County Whitney's Vineyard 1987 Rel: $24 Cur: $24 (CH-2/90)
86 FRANCISCAN Chardonnay Napa Valley Oakville Estate Reserve 1987 Rel: $20 Cur: $20 (CH-6/90)
86 FROG'S LEAP Chardonnay Carneros 1987 Rel: $15 Cur: $17 (CH-3/90)
86 HANDLEY Chardonnay Dry Creek Valley 1987 $14 (7/15/89)
86 HAWK CREST Chardonnay Sonoma County 1987 $9 (7/15/89)
86 INGLENOOK Chardonnay Napa Valley Reserve 1987 Rel: $14 Cur: $14 (CH-4/90)
86 KENDALL-JACKSON Chardonnay Sonoma Valley Durell Vineyard 1987 Rel: $14 Cur: $14 (CH-4/90)
86 KENWOOD Chardonnay Sonoma Valley 1987 $13 (7/15/89)
86 MARKHAM Chardonnay Napa Valley 1987 Rel: $12 Cur: $14 (4/30/89)
86 MAYACAMAS Chardonnay Napa Valley 1987 Rel: $20 Cur: $24 (9/15/90)
86 MCDOWELL Chardonnay California 1987 $8 (7/15/89)
86 MERRY VINTNERS Chardonnay Sonoma County Reserve 1987 $15 (9/15/89)
86 MONTICELLO Chardonnay Napa Valley Corley Reserve 1987 Rel: $17.25 Cur: $20 (CH-6/90)
86 MONTICELLO Chardonnay Napa Valley Jefferson Ranch 1987 Rel: $12.25 Cur: $16 (CH-2/90)
86 NEWLAN Chardonnay Napa Valley 1987 $13 (6/30/90)
86 ROMBAUER Chardonnay Napa Valley 1987 Rel: $14.50 Cur: $15 (CH-6/90)
86 RUTHERFORD HILL Chardonnay Napa Valley Rutherford Knoll Special Cuvée 1987 $11 (4/30/89)
86 ST. CLEMENT Chardonnay Napa Valley 1987 Rel: $15 Cur: $15 (CH-3/90)
85 ACACIA Chardonnay Carneros Napa Valley Marina Vineyard 1987 Rel: $18 Cur: $22 (CH-1/90)
85 S. ANDERSON Chardonnay Napa Valley Stags Leap District 1987 $16 (CH-6/90)
85 BEAULIEU Chardonnay Carneros Napa Valley Los Carneros Reserve 1987 Rel: $14 Cur: $16 (4/30/89)
85 BURGESS Chardonnay Napa Valley Triere Vineyard 1987 Rel: $14.50 Cur: $15 (CH-12/89)
85 J. CAREY Chardonnay Santa Ynez Valley 1987 $10 (12/15/89)
85 CHAMISAL Chardonnay Edna Valley 1987 $14 (7/15/89)
85 CHATEAU NAPA-BEAUCANON Chardonnay Napa Valley 1987 $12 (1/31/89)
85 CHATEAU POTELLE Chardonnay Napa Valley 1987 $13 (3/31/90)
85 CHATEAU ST. JEAN Chardonnay Alexander Valley Belle Terre Vineyards 1987 Rel: $16 Cur: $22 (5/15/89)
85 CHATEAU ST. JEAN Chardonnay Sonoma Valley McCrea Vineyards 1987 Rel: $15 Cur: $15 (7/15/89)
85 CHATEAU WOLTNER Chardonnay Howell Mountain Titus Vineyard 1987 Rel: $54 Cur: $54 (CH-4/90)
85 ESTANCIA Chardonnay Alexander Valley 1987 $7 (6/30/89)
85 FISHER Chardonnay Sonoma-Napa Counties 1987 Rel: $11 Cur: $11 (4/15/89)
85 GAINEY Chardonnay Santa Barbara County 1987 $12 (12/15/89)
85 KENDALL-JACKSON Chardonnay California Vintner's Reserve 1987 $12 (9/30/88)
85 KENWOOD Chardonnay Sonoma Valley Yulupa Vineyard 1987 Rel: $14 Cur: $16 (CH-7/90)
85 LA REINA Chardonnay Monterey County 1987 $13.50 (3/31/89)
85 MERRY VINTNERS Chardonnay Sonoma County Sylvan Hills Vineyard 1987 $11 (7/15/89)
85 MORGAN Chardonnay Monterey Reserve 1987 Rel: $19 Cur: $19 (CH-6/90)
85 NAVARRO Chardonnay Mendocino Table Wine 1987 Rel: $14 Cur: $16 (9/30/89) BB
85 PARDUCCI Chardonnay Mendocino County 1987 $7 (10/31/88) BB
85 J. PEDRONCELLI Chardonnay Dry Creek Valley 1987 $8 (12/31/88) BB
85 RAYMOND Chardonnay Napa Valley 1987 Rel: $13 Cur: $13 (12/31/88)
85 CHARLES SHAW Chardonnay Napa Valley 1987 Rel: $11 Cur: $11 (CH-5/90)
85 ST. ANDREW'S VINEYARD Chardonnay Napa Valley 1987 $14 (1/31/90)
85 STERLING Chardonnay Carneros Winery Lake 1987 Rel: $20 Cur: $20 (6/30/89)
85 TIFFANY HILL Chardonnay Edna Valley 1987 $19 (3/31/89)
85 WHITE OAK Chardonnay Sonoma County 1987 Rel: $11 Cur: $16 (CH-5/90)
85 ZD Chardonnay California 1987 Rel: $18.50 Cur: $25 (CH-3/90)
84 ACACIA Chardonnay Carneros Napa Valley 1987 Rel: $17 Cur: $17 (CH-1/90)
84 ADELAIDA Chardonnay Paso Robles 1987 $12.50 (12/15/89)
84 BELVEDERE Chardonnay Carneros 1987 $13 (4/30/89)
84 BRANDER Chardonnay Santa Ynez Valley 1987 $13 (12/15/89)
84 CALLAWAY Chardonnay Temecula Calla-Lees 1987 $9.75 (12/31/88)
84 CONGRESS SPRINGS Chardonnay Santa Clara County 1987 Rel: $12 Cur: $18 (CH-4/90)
84 COSENTINO Chardonnay Napa Valley The Sculptor 1987 $18 (7/15/89)
84 ELLISTON Chardonnay Central Coast Elliston Vineyard 1987 $18 (7/15/91)
84 FISHER Chardonnay Sonoma County Coach Insignia 1987 Rel: $18 Cur: $22 (CH-2/90)
84 FISHER Chardonnay Sonoma County Coach Insignia 1987 Rel: $18 Cur: $22 (1/31/90)
84 FREEMARK ABBEY Chardonnay Napa Valley 1987 Rel: $15 Cur: $15 (CH-2/90)
84 GAUER ESTATE Chardonnay Alexander Valley 1987 $16 (11/30/90)
84 KISTLER Chardonnay Sonoma Valley Durell Vineyard 1987 $16 (12/31/88)
84 LA CREMA Chardonnay California Reserve 1987 Rel: $22 Cur: $22 (5/15/89)
84 LONG Chardonnay Napa Valley 1987 Rel: $27.50 Cur: $35 (7/15/89)
84 MERRY VINTNERS Chardonnay Sonoma County 1987 $12 (7/15/89)
84 MORGAN Chardonnay Monterey 1987 Rel: $15 Cur: $16 (CH-5/90)
84 MORGAN Chardonnay Monterey 1987 Rel: $15 Cur: $16 (12/31/88)
84 MORGAN Chardonnay Monterey Reserve 1987 Rel: $19 Cur: $19 (7/15/89)
84 NAVARRO Chardonnay Anderson Valley Première Reserve 1987 Rel: $14 Cur: $16 (9/30/89)
84 NEWTON Chardonnay Napa Valley 1987 Rel: $14 Cur: $14 (3/15/90)
84 ROBERT PEPI Chardonnay Napa Valley 1987 $13.50 (2/15/90)
84 RAYMOND Chardonnay California Selection 1987 $9 (12/31/88)
84 SANTA BARBARA Chardonnay Santa Ynez Valley Reserve 1987 $16 (12/15/89)
84 STERLING Chardonnay Napa Valley Diamond Mountain Ranch 1987 $16 (2/28/91)
84 STONY HILL Chardonnay Napa Valley SHV 1987 Rel: $18 Cur: $62 (4/15/89)
84 TAFT STREET Chardonnay Sonoma County 1987 $7.50 (10/15/88)
84 VIANSA Chardonnay Napa-Sonoma Counties 1987 $13 (4/15/89)
83 BOUCHAINE Chardonnay Carneros 1987 Rel: $14 Cur: $14 (CH-2/90)
83 CAIN Chardonnay Napa Valley 1987 $10 (4/30/89)
83 CHATEAU ST. JEAN Chardonnay Sonoma County 1987 Rel: $12 Cur: $12 (5/15/89)
83 CHRISTIAN BROTHERS Chardonnay Napa Valley Private Reserve Barrel Fermented 1987 $11.50 (9/15/89)
83 LA CREMA Chardonnay California Reserve 1987 Rel: $22 Cur: $22 (CH-6/90)
83 LIBERTY SCHOOL Chardonnay Napa Valley Lot 15 1987 $7.50 (3/31/89) BB
83 MAZZOCCO Chardonnay Sonoma County Barrel Fermented 1987 $11 (11/15/88)
83 ROBERT MONDAVI Chardonnay Napa Valley 1987 Rel: $17 Cur: $17 (4/30/89)
83 MONTEREY VINEYARD Chardonnay Monterey County Classic 1987 $5 (2/15/89) BB
83 MOUNT VEEDER Chardonnay Napa Valley 1987 Rel: $14 Cur: $14 (6/15/89)
83 REVERE Chardonnay Napa Valley Reserve 1987 Rel: $25 Cur: $25 (CH-4/90)
83 ROCHIOLI Chardonnay Russian River Valley 1987 $14 (5/31/89)
83 RUTHERFORD RANCH Chardonnay Napa Valley 1987 $11 (5/15/90)
83 SANTA BARBARA Chardonnay Santa Ynez Valley 1987 $10 (12/15/89)
83 SEBASTIANI ESTATES Chardonnay Sonoma County Clark Ranch 1987 $14 (6/30/90)
83 SEQUOIA GROVE Chardonnay Carneros 1987 Rel: $14 Cur: $15 (CH-5/90)
83 SONOMA-CUTRER Chardonnay Sonoma Coast Les Pierres 1987 Rel: $22.50 Cur: $27 (1/31/90)
83 SONOMA-CUTRER Chardonnay Sonoma Coast Russian River Ranches 1987 Rel: $12 Cur: $16 (5/31/89)
83 STEVENOT Chardonnay California 1987 $7.50 (6/30/89)
82 AU BON CLIMAT Chardonnay Santa Barbara County Reserve Los Alamos Vineyard 1987 $20 (12/15/89)
82 BABCOCK Chardonnay Santa Ynez Valley 1987 $12 (12/15/89)
82 LAWRENCE J. BARGETTO Chardonnay Santa Cruz Mountains Miller Ranch 1987 $15 (4/15/89)
82 BUENA VISTA Chardonnay Carneros Private Reserve 1987 Rel: $16.50 Cur: $18 (CH-3/90)
82 BUENA VISTA Chardonnay Carneros Private Reserve 1987 Rel: $16.50 Cur: $18 (10/31/89)
82 DAVIS BYNUM Chardonnay Sonoma County Reserve Bottling 1987 $9 (7/15/89)
82 CALERA Chardonnay Central Coast 1987 $12 (3/15/90)
82 CHAPPELLET Chardonnay Napa Valley 1987 Rel: $14 Cur: $14 (6/30/90)
82 CLOS PEGASE Chardonnay Napa Valley 1987 $12 (7/15/89)
82 DRY CREEK Chardonnay Sonoma County 1987 $9.75 (2/15/89)
82 FETZER Chardonnay Mendocino Reserve 1987 $15 (7/15/89)
82 GIRARD Chardonnay Napa Valley 1987 Rel: $14.50 Cur: $18 (7/15/89)
82 GOOSECROSS Chardonnay Napa Valley 1987 $15 (1/31/90)
82 HUSCH Chardonnay Anderson Valley Special Reserve 1987 $16 (6/30/90)
82 KEENAN Chardonnay Napa Valley 1987 $12.50 (6/15/89)
82 KENDALL-JACKSON Chardonnay Anderson Valley Dennison Vineyard 1987 Rel: $14 Cur: $14 (CH-4/90)
82 MASSON Chardonnay Monterey County 1987 $8 (11/15/88)
82 MURPHY-GOODE Chardonnay Alexander Valley Premier Vineyard 1987 Rel: $11 Cur: $11 (1/31/89)
82 PINE RIDGE Chardonnay Napa Valley Stags Leap District 1987 Rel: $20 Cur: $23 (4/30/89)
82 ST. FRANCIS Chardonnay Sonoma Valley Barrel Select 1987 $14.50 (12/31/88)
82 STRATFORD Chardonnay California Partners' Reserve 1987 $15 (7/15/89)
82 THOMAS-HSI Chardonnay Napa Valley 1987 $18 (6/30/90)
82 VICHON Chardonnay Napa Valley 1987 Rel: $16 Cur: $18 (4/15/89)
82 ZD Chardonnay California 1987 Rel: $18.50 Cur: $25 (3/15/89)
82 STEPHEN ZELLERBACH Chardonnay California 1987 $7 (10/15/88) BB
81 CARNEROS CREEK Chardonnay Los Carneros 1987 $13 (7/15/89)
81 CARTLIDGE & BROWNE Chardonnay Napa Valley 1987 $11 (4/15/90)
81 CHIMNEY ROCK Chardonnay Napa Valley Stags Leap District 1987 $15 (2/15/90)
81 THOMAS FOGARTY Chardonnay Edna Valley 1987 $13.50 (12/15/89)
81 FRANCISCAN Chardonnay Napa Valley Oakville Estate 1987 $11 (2/15/89)
81 GIRARD Chardonnay Napa Valley 1987 Rel: $14.50 Cur: $18 (CH-3/90)
81 LEEWARD Chardonnay Central Coast 1987 $9 (10/31/88)
81 MONT ST. JOHN Chardonnay Carneros Napa Valley 1987 $15 (7/15/89)
81 JOSEPH PHELPS Chardonnay Napa Valley 1987 $15 (3/15/89)
81 REVERE Chardonnay Napa Valley Reserve 1987 Rel: $25 Cur: $25 (9/15/90)
81 SPRING MOUNTAIN Chardonnay Napa Valley 1987 $15 (11/15/89)
81 TREFETHEN Chardonnay Napa Valley 1987 Rel: $16.75 Cur: $19 (11/30/89)
81 WHITE OAK Chardonnay Sonoma County 1987 Rel: $11 Cur: $16 (6/30/89)
81 WHITE OAK Chardonnay Sonoma County Myers Limited Release 1987 Rel: $18 Cur: $20 (CH-5/90)
81 WILD HORSE Chardonnay San Luis Obispo County Wild Horse Vineyards 1987 $12 (6/15/89)
80 AU BON CLIMAT Chardonnay Santa Ynez Valley Benedict Vineyard 1987 $30 (12/15/89)
80 BERINGER Chardonnay Napa Valley 1987 $10 (7/15/89)
80 DAVIS BYNUM Chardonnay Russian River Valley Limited Release 1987 $14 (9/30/89)
80 CHATEAU WOLTNER Chardonnay Howell Mountain Titus Vineyard 1987 Rel: $54 Cur: $54 (9/15/89)
80 CORBETT CANYON Chardonnay Central Coast Reserve 1987 $8 (12/15/89)
80 CRESTON MANOR Chardonnay San Luis Obispo County 1987 $12 (12/15/89)
80 DOMAINE NAPA Chardonnay Napa Valley 1987 $12 (7/15/89)
80 GEYSER PEAK Chardonnay Alexander Valley Estate Reserve 1987 $12 (6/30/89)
80 INNISFREE Chardonnay Napa Valley 1987 $9 (2/15/89)
80 ST. ANDREW'S WINERY Chardonnay Napa Valley 1987 $6.50 (7/15/88)
80 SEBASTIANI ESTATES Chardonnay Sonoma County Kinneybrook 1987 $14 (6/30/90)
80 RODNEY STRONG Chardonnay Sonoma County 1987 $6.50 (10/15/88)
80 ZACA MESA Chardonnay Santa Barbara County Reserve 1987 $15 (12/15/89)
79 BEAULIEU Chardonnay Napa Valley Beaufort 1987 Rel: $12.50 Cur: $13 (6/15/89)
79 BERINGER Chardonnay Napa Valley Private Reserve 1987 Rel: $17 Cur: $19 (CH-4/90)
79 CONGRESS SPRINGS Chardonnay Santa Clara County 1987 Rel: $12 Cur: $18 (10/31/88)
79 CORBETT CANYON Chardonnay Central Coast Coastal Classic 1987 $7/L (7/15/88)
79 GROTH Chardonnay Napa Valley 1987 $13 (7/15/89)
79 GUNDLACH BUNDSCHU Chardonnay Sonoma Valley 1987 $11 (3/15/89)
79 KALIN Chardonnay Sonoma County Cuvée LD 1987 $25 (3/15/91)
79 LAURA'S Chardonnay Paso Robles 1987 $12 (12/15/89)
79 MEEKER Chardonnay Dry Creek Valley 1987 $12 (2/15/89)

Key to Symbols

The scores reported here are the results of blind tastings conducted by our panel of senior editors. Wines that carry the initials below are results of individual tastings.

THE WINE SPECTATOR 100-POINT SCALE ***95-100***—Classic, a great wine; ***90-94***—Outstanding, superior character and style; ***80-89***—Good to very good, a wine with special qualities; ***70-79***—Average, drinkable wine that may have minor flaws; ***60-69***—Below average, drinkable but not recommended; ***50-59***—Poor, undrinkable, not recommended. "+"—With a score indicates a range; used primarily with barrel tastings to indicate a preliminary score.

SPECIAL DESIGNATIONS SS—Spectator Selection, CS—Cellar Selection, BB—Best Buy.

TASTER'S INITIALS (JG)—Jim Gordon, (HS)—Harvey Steiman, (JL)—James Laube, (JS)—James Suckling, (TM)—Thomas Matthews, (TR)—Terry Robards, (BT)—Barrel Tasting (these wines were tasted blind from barrel samples), (CA-date)—*California's Great Cabernets* by James Laube, (CH-date)—*California's Great Chardonnays* by James Laube, (VP-date)—*Vintage Port* by James Suckling.

DATE TASTED Dates in parentheses represent the issue in which the rating was published.

79 MOUNTAIN VIEW Chardonnay Monterey County 1987 $6 (4/30/89)
79 ROUND HILL Chardonnay California House 1987 $6.25 (11/15/88)
79 RUTHERFORD RANCH Chardonnay Napa Valley 1987 $11 (2/15/89)
79 ST. FRANCIS Chardonnay California 1987 $9.50 (10/15/88)
79 SCHUG Chardonnay Napa Valley Beckstoffer Vineyard 1987 $15 (5/31/90)
79 SEGHESIO Chardonnay Sonoma County 1987 $7 (12/31/88)
79 SEQUOIA GROVE Chardonnay Carneros 1987 Rel: $14 Cur: $15 (6/15/89)
79 SHAFER Chardonnay Napa Valley 1987 $13.50 (4/15/89)
79 J. WILE & SONS Chardonnay Napa Valley 1987 $7 (2/15/89)
78 BELVEDERE Chardonnay Sonoma County Discovery Series 1987 $5.25 (7/31/88)
78 BYRON Chardonnay Santa Barbara County Barrel Fermented Reserve 1987 $16 (12/15/89)
78 DUNNEWOOD Chardonnay Napa Valley Reserve 1987 $10.50 (12/31/88)
78 E.&J. GALLO Chardonnay North Coast Reserve 1987 $6 (11/30/90)
78 GREEN & RED Chardonnay Napa Valley 1987 $11 (7/15/89)
78 J. LOHR Chardonnay Monterey County 1987 $10 (4/15/89)
78 MARK WEST Chardonnay Sonoma Valley 1987 $8 (12/31/88)
78 MERIDIAN Chardonnay Edna Valley 1987 $12 (12/15/89)
78 MONTICELLO Chardonnay Napa Valley Corley Reserve 1987 Rel: $17.25 Cur: $20 (7/15/89)
78 STONEGATE Chardonnay Napa Valley 1987 $13 (6/30/90)
78 TALLEY Chardonnay San Luis Obispo County 1987 $12 (12/15/89)
77 ALEXANDER VALLEY Chardonnay Alexander Valley 1987 $11 (1/31/89)
77 DAVID BRUCE Chardonnay Santa Cruz Mountains 1987 $18 (2/15/90)
77 CHATEAU WOLTNER Chardonnay Howell Mountain Estate Reserve 1987 Rel: $24 Cur: $24 (9/15/89)
77 GAUER ESTATE Chardonnay Alexander Valley 1987 $16 (10/31/89)
77 GUNDLACH BUNDSCHU Chardonnay Sonoma Valley Sangiacomo Ranch Special Selection 1987 $12 (7/15/89)
77 MONTICELLO Chardonnay Napa Valley Jefferson Ranch 1987 Rel: $12.25 Cur: $16 (4/30/89)
77 NAPA RIDGE Chardonnay North Coast 1987 $6.50 (7/15/88)
77 NEYERS Chardonnay California 1987 $14 (7/15/89)
77 R.H. PHILLIPS Chardonnay California 1987 $6 (2/15/89)
77 SEBASTIANI ESTATES Chardonnay Sonoma County Wilson Ranch 1987 $14 (6/30/90)
77 WENTE BROS. Chardonnay Central Coast Reserve Arroyo Seco Vineyards 1987 $14 (10/31/89)
77 YORK MOUNTAIN Chardonnay San Luis Obispo 1987 $9 (12/15/89)
76 CLOS DU BOIS Chardonnay Dry Creek Valley Flintwood Vineyard 1987 Rel: $20 Cur: $22 (7/15/89)
76 DOMAINE MICHEL Chardonnay Sonoma County 1987 $16 (6/30/90)
76 FETZER Chardonnay California Sundial 1987 $6.50 (7/31/88)
76 FREMONT CREEK Chardonnay Mendocino-Napa Counties 1987 $9.50 (7/15/89)
76 IRON HORSE Chardonnay Sonoma County Green Valley 1987 $17 (1/31/89)
76 MONTE VERDE Chardonnay California Proprietor's Reserve 1987 $6.50 (12/15/89)
76 RANCHO SISQUOC Chardonnay Santa Maria Valley 1987 $10 (12/15/89)
76 REVERE Chardonnay Napa Valley 1987 Rel: $14 Cur: $14 (9/15/90)
76 VENTANA Chardonnay Monterey Barrel Fermented 1987 $16 (10/31/89)
75 BEAUREGARD Chardonnay Napa Valley 1987 $10 (7/15/91)
75 CRICHTON HALL Chardonnay Napa Valley 1987 $16 (11/15/89)
75 EBERLE Chardonnay Paso Robles 1987 $12 (7/15/89)
75 STRATFORD Chardonnay California 1987 $10 (7/15/89)
74 BOUCHAINE Chardonnay Carneros 1987 Rel: $14 Cur: $14 (7/15/89)
74 CHATEAU SOUVERAIN Chardonnay Sonoma Valley Carneros Private Reserve 1987 $12 (4/15/89)
74 CHRISTOPHE Chardonnay California 1987 $8.50 (3/31/89)
74 EBERLE Chardonnay Paso Robles 1987 $12 (6/30/90)
74 ESTRELLA RIVER Chardonnay Paso Robles 1987 $8.50 (12/15/89)
74 HAYWOOD Chardonnay Sonoma Valley Los Chamizal Vineyards 1987 $12.50 (6/30/90)
74 ROUND HILL Chardonnay Napa Valley Van Asperen Vineyard 1987 $11 (7/15/89)
74 M.G. VALLEJO Chardonnay California 1987 $5 (2/15/89)
73 GUENOC Chardonnay Guenoc Valley 1987 $10 (2/15/90)
73 HACIENDA Chardonnay Sonoma County Clair de Lune 1987 Rel: $12 Cur: $15 (7/15/89)
73 HANNA Chardonnay Sonoma County 1987 $14.50 (7/15/89)
73 WILLIAM HILL Chardonnay Napa Valley Silver Label 1987 $13 (6/15/89)
73 KONOCTI Chardonnay Lake County 1987 $9 (11/15/89)
73 MARK WEST Chardonnay Russian River Valley Le Beau Vineyards 1987 $12 (6/30/90)
73 VILLA ZAPU Chardonnay Napa Valley 1987 $14 (5/31/89)
72 ARCIERO Chardonnay Paso Robles 1987 $9 (12/15/89)
72 CHATEAU MONTELENA Chardonnay Napa Valley 1987 Rel: $20 Cur: $26 (2/15/90)
72 FIRESTONE Chardonnay Santa Ynez Valley 1987 $10 (12/15/89)
72 FOPPIANO Chardonnay Russian River Valley 1987 $9 (7/15/89)
72 HACIENDA Chardonnay Sonoma County Clair de Lune 1987 Rel: $12 Cur: $15 (CH-4/90)
72 LAKESPRING Chardonnay Napa Valley 1987 $12 (10/31/89)
71 DOMAINE POTELLE Chardonnay California 1987 $7 (4/15/89)
71 HAWK CREST Chardonnay California 1987 $7.50 (10/15/88)
70 GARY FARRELL Chardonnay Russian River Valley Aquarius Ranch 1987 $13.50 (12/31/88)
70 JOHNSON TURNBULL Chardonnay Knights Valley Teviot Springs Vineyard 1987 $12.50 (9/15/89)
70 MT. MADONNA Chardonnay San Luis Obispo County 1987 $7.50 (3/31/89)
69 BANDIERA Chardonnay Carneros 1987 $7 (12/31/88)
69 CHRISTIAN BROTHERS Chardonnay Napa Valley 1987 $10 (11/30/89)
68 CHATEAU MONTELENA Chardonnay Napa Valley 1987 Rel: $20 Cur: $26 (CH-2/90)
68 JOSEPH PHELPS Chardonnay Carneros Sangiacomo Vineyard 1987 $18 (5/15/89)
68 QUAIL RIDGE Chardonnay Napa Valley 1987 $15 (7/15/89)
68 SONOMA-CUTRER Chardonnay Sonoma Coast Cutrer Vineyard 1987 Rel: $17.50 Cur: $23 (11/30/89)
67 BERINGER Chardonnay Napa Valley Private Reserve 1987 Rel: $17 Cur: $19 (5/15/89)
64 CECCHETTI SEBASTIANI Chardonnay Napa Valley Cask Lot 1 1987 $9.50 (4/15/89)
63 MERLION Chardonnay Napa Valley 1987 $9 (12/31/90)
59 KEENAN Chardonnay Napa Valley Ann's Vineyard 1987 $13.50 (6/30/90)
59 MCDOWELL Chardonnay McDowell Valley 1987 $12 (12/15/89)
58 AU BON CLIMAT Chardonnay Santa Barbara County 1987 $14 (3/15/89)
58 CHALONE Chardonnay Chalone 1987 Rel: $22 Cur: $39 (CH-1/90)

1986

94 CHALONE Chardonnay Chalone 1986 Rel: $22 Cur: $51 (CH-1/90)
94 CUVAISON Chardonnay Carneros Napa Valley Reserve 1986 Rel: $20 Cur: $28 (CH-6/90)
93 FERRARI-CARANO Chardonnay Alexander Valley 1986 Rel: $16 Cur: $28 (7/15/88)
93 FERRARI-CARANO Chardonnay California Reserve 1986 Rel: $28 Cur: $42 (CH-5/90)
93 GIRARD Chardonnay Napa Valley 1986 Rel: $13.50 Cur: $28 (8/31/88) SS
93 JOSEPH PHELPS Chardonnay Carneros Sangiacomo Vineyard 1986 $16 (7/15/88)

93 SILVERADO Chardonnay Napa Valley Limited Reserve 1986 $25 (11/15/90)
92 CHATEAU ST. JEAN Chardonnay Alexander Valley Belle Terre Vineyards 1986 Rel: $16 Cur: $20 (7/15/88)
92 CHATEAU ST. JEAN Chardonnay Alexander Valley Robert Young Vineyards 1986 Rel: $18 Cur: $25 (CH-3/90)
92 FERRARI-CARANO Chardonnay Alexander Valley 1986 Rel: $16 Cur: $28 (CH-5/90)
92 FERRARI-CARANO Chardonnay California Reserve 1986 Rel: $28 Cur: $42 (5/31/89)
92 FORMAN Chardonnay Napa Valley 1986 Rel: $18 Cur: $45 (CH-2/90)
92 GIRARD Chardonnay Napa Valley 1986 Rel: $13.50 Cur: $28 (CH-3/90)
92 GIRARD Chardonnay Napa Valley Reserve 1986 Rel: $25 Cur: $40 (CH-3/90)
92 GRGICH HILLS Chardonnay Napa Valley 1986 Rel: $22 Cur: $37 (7/15/88)
92 HACIENDA Chardonnay Sonoma County Clair de Lune 1986 Rel: $12 Cur: $18 (7/15/88) SS
92 KISTLER Chardonnay Sonoma Valley Kistler Estate Vineyard 1986 Rel: $18 Cur: $40 (2/01/90)
92 LA CREMA Chardonnay California Reserve 1986 Rel: $18 Cur: $22 (7/15/88)
92 LONG Chardonnay Napa Valley 1986 Rel: $27.50 Cur: $48 (CH-4/90)
92 SILVERADO Chardonnay Napa Valley 1986 Rel: $12 Cur: $16 (4/30/88)
92 SIMI Chardonnay Sonoma County Reserve 1986 Rel: $28 Cur: $33 (9/15/90)
92 SIMI Chardonnay Sonoma County Reserve 1986 Rel: $28 Cur: $33 (CH-4/90)
91 BERINGER Chardonnay Napa Valley Private Reserve 1986 Rel: $16 Cur: $22 (4/15/88)
91 BONNY DOON Chardonnay Monterey County La Reina Vineyard 1986 $13.25 (3/31/88)
91 BOUCHAINE Chardonnay Napa Valley 1986 Rel: $13 Cur: $17 (10/31/88)
91 BUENA VISTA Chardonnay Carneros Private Reserve 1986 Rel: $16.50 Cur: $17 (CH-3/90)
91 CHATEAU MONTELENA Chardonnay Alexander Valley 1986 Rel: $18 Cur: $26 (CH-2/90)
91 CHATEAU MONTELENA Chardonnay Napa Valley 1986 Rel: $18 Cur: $26 (CH-2/90)
91 CHATEAU ST. JEAN Chardonnay Alexander Valley Robert Young Vineyards Reserve 1.5L 1986 (NA) (CH-7/90)
91 CHATEAU WOLTNER Chardonnay Howell Mountain Estate Reserve 1986 Rel: $24 Cur: $24 (CH-4/90)
91 FORMAN Chardonnay Napa Valley 1986 Rel: $18 Cur: $45 (2/29/88)
91 FRANCISCAN Chardonnay Napa Valley Oakville Estate Reserve 1986 Rel: $14 Cur: $14 (CH-4/90)
91 GRGICH HILLS Chardonnay Napa Valley 1986 Rel: $22 Cur: $37 (CH-3/90)
91 WILLIAM HILL Chardonnay Napa Valley Reserve 1986 Rel: $17 Cur: $20 (CH-3/90)
91 KENDALL-JACKSON Chardonnay Sonoma Valley Durell Vineyard 1986 Rel: $14 Cur: $16 (CH-6/90)
91 KISTLER Chardonnay Russian River Valley Dutton Ranch 1986 Rel: $16.50 Cur: $28 (3/15/88)
91 LONG Chardonnay Napa Valley 1986 Rel: $27.50 Cur: $48 (12/31/88)
91 MEEKER Chardonnay Dry Creek Valley 1986 $11 (5/31/88)
91 ST. FRANCIS Chardonnay Sonoma Valley Barrel Select 1986 $12.50 (7/15/88)
91 STAG'S LEAP WINE CELLARS Chardonnay Napa Valley 1986 Rel: $17 Cur: $20 (7/15/88)
91 STAG'S LEAP WINE CELLARS Chardonnay Napa Valley Reserve 1986 Rel: $26 Cur: $26 (10/15/88)
91 STERLING Chardonnay Carneros Winery Lake 1986 Rel: $20 Cur: $23 (7/15/88)
90 BERINGER Chardonnay Napa Valley Private Reserve 1986 Rel: $16 Cur: $22 (CH-4/90)
90 BUENA VISTA Chardonnay Carneros Private Reserve 1986 Rel: $16.50 Cur: $17 (12/31/88)
90 CHAMISAL Chardonnay Edna Valley 1986 $13 (5/31/88)
90 CHAPPELLET Chardonnay Napa Valley 1986 Rel: $14 Cur: $14 (CH-3/90)
90 CHATEAU MONTELENA Chardonnay Napa Valley 1986 Rel: $18 Cur: $26 (12/31/88)
90 CHATEAU ST. JEAN Chardonnay Alexander Valley Belle Terre Vineyards 1986 Rel: $16 Cur: $20 (CH-3/90)
90 CLOS DU BOIS Chardonnay Dry Creek Valley Flintwood Vineyard 1986 Rel: $19.50 Cur: $25 (12/31/87)
90 CLOS PEGASE Chardonnay Carneros 1986 $15.50 (7/15/88)
90 CUVAISON Chardonnay Carneros Napa Valley Reserve 1986 Rel: $20 Cur: $28 (6/30/89)
90 DEHLINGER Chardonnay Russian River Valley 1986 Rel: $11 Cur: $14 (2/29/88)
90 FISHER Chardonnay Sonoma County Coach Insignia 1986 Rel: $17 Cur: $20 (CH-2/90)
90 FROG'S LEAP Chardonnay Napa Valley 1986 Rel: $12 Cur: $18 (CH-3/90)
90 FROG'S LEAP Chardonnay Napa Valley 1986 Rel: $12 Cur: $18 (1/31/88)
90 KISTLER Chardonnay Russian River Valley Dutton Ranch 1986 Rel: $16.50 Cur: $28 (CH-2/90)
90 LAKESPRING Chardonnay Napa Valley 1986 $11 (12/31/88)
90 MATANZAS CREEK Chardonnay Sonoma County 1986 Rel: $17.50 Cur: $24 (5/31/88)
90 MURPHY-GOODE Chardonnay Alexander Valley Estate Vineyard 1986 Rel: $10 Cur: $12 (8/31/88)
90 ST. ANDREW'S VINEYARD Chardonnay Napa Valley 1986 $13 (4/30/88)
90 SAINTSBURY Chardonnay Carneros 1986 Rel: $12 Cur: $19 (11/30/87) (JL)
90 SEQUOIA GROVE Chardonnay Napa Valley Estate 1986 Rel: $15 Cur: $15 (9/30/88)
90 SILVERADO Chardonnay Napa Valley 1986 Rel: $12 Cur: $16 (CH-3/90)
90 SILVERADO Chardonnay Napa Valley Limited Reserve 1986 Rel: $25 Cur: $25 (CH-7/90)
90 TIFFANY HILL Chardonnay Edna Valley 1986 $19 (6/15/88)
90 VICHON Chardonnay Napa Valley 1986 Rel: $15 Cur: $17 (CH-3/90)
89 ARROWOOD Chardonnay Sonoma County 1986 Rel: $18 Cur: $25 (CH-4/90)
89 BOEGER Chardonnay El Dorado 1986 $10.50 (9/30/88)
89 CHATEAU MONTELENA Chardonnay Alexander Valley 1986 Rel: $18 Cur: $26 (4/30/88)
89 CHATEAU ST. JEAN Chardonnay Alexander Valley Robert Young Vineyards 1986 Rel: $18 Cur: $25 (7/15/88)
89 CHATEAU ST. JEAN Chardonnay Dry Creek Valley Frank Johnson Vineyards 1986 Rel: $14 Cur: $19 (CH-7/90)
89 CHATEAU WOLTNER Chardonnay Howell Mountain St. Thomas Vineyard 1986 Rel: $36 Cur: $37 (CH-4/90)
89 CLOS PEGASE Chardonnay Carneros 1986 $15.50 (CH-3/90)
89 CUVAISON Chardonnay Napa Valley 1986 Rel: $12.75 Cur: $18 (CH-4/90)
89 DE LOACH Chardonnay Russian River Valley 1986 Rel: $14 Cur: $20 (CH-2/90)
89 DE LOACH Chardonnay Russian River Valley O.F.S. 1986 Rel: $22 Cur: $26 (2/29/88)
89 EDNA VALLEY Chardonnay Edna Valley 1986 Rel: $13.50 Cur: $20 (12/31/87)
89 FISHER Chardonnay Sonoma County Coach Insignia 1986 Rel: $17 Cur: $20 (9/30/88)
89 GUNDLACH BUNDSCHU Chardonnay Sonoma Valley Sangiacomo Ranch Special Selection 1986 $12 (9/30/88)
89 HACIENDA Chardonnay Sonoma County Clair de Lune 1986 Rel: $12 Cur: $18 (CH-4/90)
89 JEPSON Chardonnay Mendocino 1986 $12 (11/15/88)
89 KISTLER Chardonnay Sonoma Valley Durell Vineyard 1986 $16 (2/01/90)
89 J. LOHR Chardonnay Monterey County Greenfield Vineyards 1986 $10 (4/15/88)
89 MATANZAS CREEK Chardonnay Sonoma County 1986 Rel: $17.50 Cur: $24 (CH-2/90)
89 ROBERT MONDAVI Chardonnay Napa Valley Reserve 1986 Rel: $25 Cur: $30 (CH-3/90)
89 MONTEREY VINEYARD Chardonnay Monterey County Limited Release 1986 $10 (8/31/88)
89 MONTICELLO Chardonnay Napa Valley Corley Reserve 1986 Rel: $16.50 Cur: $18 (CH-2/90)
89 MORGAN Chardonnay Monterey 1986 Rel: $14 Cur: $20 (CH-5/90)

UNITED STATES
CALIFORNIA/*CHARDONNAY*

89 NAVARRO Chardonnay Anderson Valley Première Reserve 1986 Rel: $14 Cur: $18 (10/31/88)
89 PINE RIDGE Chardonnay Napa Valley Knollside Cuvée 1986 Rel: $14 Cur: $17 (3/31/88)
89 ST. CLEMENT Chardonnay Napa Valley 1986 Rel: $15 Cur: $15 (CH-3/90)
89 ST. CLEMENT Chardonnay Napa Valley 1986 Rel: $15 Cur: $15 (7/15/88)
89 SAINTSBURY Chardonnay Carneros Reserve 1986 Rel: $20 Cur: $25 (7/15/88)
89 SHAFER Chardonnay Napa Valley 1986 $12 (7/15/88)
89 SMITH-MADRONE Chardonnay Napa Valley 1986 Rel: $12.50 Cur: $16 (CH-5/90)
89 SONOMA-CUTRER Chardonnay Russian River Valley Cutrer Vineyard 1986 Rel: $16 Cur: $23 (CH-3/90)
89 STERLING Chardonnay Carneros Winery Lake 1986 Rel: $20 Cur: $23 (CH-4/90)
89 STONEGATE Chardonnay Napa Valley 1986 $13 (12/31/88)
89 STRATFORD Chardonnay California 1986 $9.50 (2/29/88)
89 VEGA Chardonnay Santa Barbara County 1986 $14 (12/15/89)
89 VICHON Chardonnay Napa Valley 1986 Rel: $15 Cur: $17 (9/15/88)
89 ZD Chardonnay California 1986 Rel: $18 Cur: $25 (2/15/88)
88 ALTAMURA Chardonnay Napa Valley 1986 Rel: $15 Cur: $21 (CH-1/90)
88 ALTAMURA Chardonnay Napa Valley 1986 Rel: $15 Cur: $21 (4/15/89)
88 BELVEDERE Chardonnay Carneros 1986 $13 (7/15/88)
88 BOUCHAINE Chardonnay Carneros 1986 Rel: $13 Cur: $13 (CH-2/90)
88 BOUCHAINE Chardonnay Carneros Estate Reserve 1986 Rel: $19 Cur: $19 (CH-2/90)
88 BOUCHAINE Chardonnay Carneros Estate Reserve 1986 Rel: $19 Cur: $19 (4/15/89)
88 BURGESS Chardonnay Napa Valley Triere Vineyard 1986 Rel: $14 Cur: $16 (7/15/88)
88 CAIN Chardonnay Carneros 1986 $16 (9/15/88)
88 CAKEBREAD Chardonnay Napa Valley Reserve 1986 $26 (2/15/90)
88 CHATEAU WOLTNER Chardonnay Howell Mountain Titus Vineyard 1986 Rel: $54 Cur: $54 (CH-4/90)
88 CLOS DU BOIS Chardonnay Dry Creek Valley Flintwood Vineyard 1986 Rel: $19.50 Cur: $25 (CH-2/90)
88 CLOS PEGASE Chardonnay Napa Valley 1986 $12 (3/15/88)
88 CUVAISON Chardonnay Napa Valley 1986 Rel: $12.75 Cur: $18 (12/31/87)
88 DRY CREEK Chardonnay Sonoma County 1986 $11 (5/31/88)
88 EDNA VALLEY Chardonnay Edna Valley 1986 Rel: $13.50 Cur: $20 (CH-3/90)
88 FAR NIENTE Chardonnay Napa Valley 1986 Rel: $24 Cur: $31 (CH-2/90)
88 FETZER Chardonnay Mendocino Special Reserve 1986 $14 (12/31/88)
88 FOLIE A DEUX Chardonnay Napa Valley 1986 Rel: $15 Cur: $18 (CH-6/90)
88 FOX MOUNTAIN Chardonnay Sonoma County Reserve 1986 $15 (6/30/89)
88 GUENOC Chardonnay North Coast 1986 $9.75 (12/31/88)
88 HESS Chardonnay Napa Valley 1986 Rel: $12.75 Cur: $16 (CH-4/90)
88 HESS Chardonnay Napa Valley 1986 Rel: $12.75 Cur: $16 (10/15/88)
88 INGLENOOK Chardonnay Napa Valley Reserve 1986 Rel: $14.50 Cur: $15 (CH-4/90)
88 ROBERT MONDAVI Chardonnay Napa Valley 1986 Rel: $15 Cur: $15 (7/15/88)
88 ROBERT MONDAVI Chardonnay Napa Valley Reserve 1986 Rel: $25 Cur: $30 (2/15/89)
88 MONTICELLO Chardonnay Napa Valley Corley Reserve 1986 Rel: $16.50 Cur: $18 (7/15/88)
88 MONTICELLO Chardonnay Napa Valley Jefferson Ranch 1986 Rel: $11 Cur: $18 (4/15/88)
88 MORGAN Chardonnay Monterey 1986 Rel: $14 Cur: $20 (3/15/88)
88 MOUNT EDEN Chardonnay Santa Cruz Mountains 1986 Rel: $25 Cur: $45 (CH-3/90)
88 NAVARRO Chardonnay Mendocino 1986 $9.75 (9/30/88)
88 PINE RIDGE Chardonnay Napa Valley Knollside Cuvée 1986 Rel: $14 Cur: $17 (CH-4/90)
88 PINE RIDGE Chardonnay Napa Valley Stags Leap District 1986 Rel: $19 Cur: $23 (CH-4/90)
88 SAINTSBURY Chardonnay Carneros 1986 Rel: $12 Cur: $19 (CH-2/90)
88 SANFORD Chardonnay Santa Barbara County 1986 Rel: $14 Cur: $16 (CH-2/90)
88 SEBASTIANI ESTATES Chardonnay Sonoma Valley Clark Ranch 1986 $14 (3/15/88)
88 SEQUOIA GROVE Chardonnay Napa Valley Estate 1986 Rel: $15 Cur: $15 (CH-5/90)
88 SONOMA-CUTRER Chardonnay Sonoma Valley Les Pierres 1986 Rel: $19.50 Cur: $28 (CH-3/90)
88 STAG'S LEAP WINE CELLARS Chardonnay Napa Valley Reserve 1986 Rel: $26 Cur: $26 (CH-6/90)
87 ACACIA Chardonnay Carneros Napa Valley 1986 Rel: $15 Cur: $18 (CH-1/90)
87 ARROWOOD Chardonnay Sonoma County 1986 Rel: $18 Cur: $25 (5/31/88)
87 BURGESS Chardonnay Napa Valley Triere Vineyard 1986 Rel: $14 Cur: $16 (CH-12/89)
87 CAIN Chardonnay Napa Valley 1986 $10 (9/30/88)
87 CARNEROS CREEK Chardonnay Los Carneros 1986 $11.50 (7/15/88)
87 CHATEAU ST. JEAN Chardonnay Sonoma Valley McCrea Vineyards 1986 Rel: $15 Cur: $17 (CH-3/90)
87 CHRISTIAN BROTHERS Chardonnay Napa Valley Private Reserve Barrel Fermented 1986 $12 (12/31/88)
87 CLOS DU BOIS Chardonnay Alexander Valley Calcaire Vineyard 1986 Rel: $16 Cur: $23 (12/31/87)
87 CLOS DU VAL Chardonnay Carneros Napa Valley Carneros Estate 1986 Rel: $12 Cur: $14 (4/15/88)
87 B.R. COHN Chardonnay Sonoma Valley Olive Hill Vineyard 1986 $12 (10/31/88)
87 DE LOACH Chardonnay Russian River Valley 1986 Rel: $14 Cur: $20 (11/15/87)
87 DEHLINGER Chardonnay Russian River Valley 1986 Rel: $11 Cur: $14 (CH-4/90)
87 FLORA SPRINGS Chardonnay Napa Valley Barrel Fermented 1986 Rel: $20 Cur: $28 (CH-1/90)
87 FLORA SPRINGS Chardonnay Napa Valley Barrel Fermented 1986 Rel: $20 Cur: $28 (7/15/88)
87 FRANCISCAN Chardonnay Napa Valley Oakville Estate 1986 $9.25 (5/31/88)
87 FREMONT CREEK Chardonnay Mendocino-Napa Counties 1986 $9.50 (4/30/88)
87 FROG'S LEAP Chardonnay Carneros 1986 Rel: $14 Cur: $18 (CH-6/90)
87 GROTH Chardonnay Napa Valley 1986 $12.50 (1/31/89)
87 GUNDLACH BUNDSCHU Chardonnay Sonoma Valley 1986 $9 (2/15/88)
87 HANZELL Chardonnay Sonoma Valley 1986 Rel: $22 Cur: $33 (CH-1/90)
87 INGLENOOK Chardonnay Napa Valley Reserve 1986 Rel: $14.50 Cur: $15 (3/15/89)

Key to Symbols

The scores reported here are the results of blind tastings conducted by our panel of senior editors. Wines that carry the initials below are results of individual tastings.

THE WINE SPECTATOR 100-POINT SCALE ***95-100***—Classic, a great wine; ***90-94***—Outstanding, superior character and style; ***80-89***—Good to very good, a wine with special qualities; ***70-79***—Average, drinkable wine that may have minor flaws; ***60-69***—Below average, drinkable but not recommended; ***50-59***—Poor, undrinkable, not recommended. "+"—With a score indicates a range; used primarily with barrel tastings to indicate a preliminary score.

SPECIAL DESIGNATIONS SS—Spectator Selection, CS—Cellar Selection, BB—Best Buy.

TASTER'S INITIALS (JG)—Jim Gordon, (HS)—Harvey Steiman, (JL)—James Laube, (JS)—James Suckling, (TM)—Thomas Matthews, (TR)—Terry Robards, (BT)—Barrel Tasting (these wines were tasted blind from barrel samples), (CA-date)—*California's Great Cabernets* by James Laube, (CH-date)—*California's Great Chardonnays* by James Laube, (VP-date)—*Vintage Port* by James Suckling.

DATE TASTED Dates in parentheses represent the issue in which the rating was published.

87 J. LOHR Chardonnay Monterey County Cypress Vineyard Reserve 1986 $13.50 (12/31/88)
87 MAYACAMAS Chardonnay Napa Valley 1986 Rel: $20 Cur: $27 (CH-3/90)
87 NAVARRO Chardonnay Anderson Valley Première Reserve 1986 Rel: $14 Cur: $18 (CH-3/90)
87 RAYMOND Chardonnay Napa Valley Private Reserve 1986 Rel: $18 Cur: $21 (CH-5/90)
87 REVERE Chardonnay Napa Valley Reserve 1986 Rel: $22 Cur: $25 (CH-4/90)
87 ROMBAUER Chardonnay Napa Valley 1986 Rel: $14.50 Cur: $16 (10/31/88)
87 RUTHERFORD HILL Chardonnay Napa Valley Jaeger Vineyards 1986 $12 (12/31/88)
87 RUTHERFORD HILL Chardonnay Napa Valley Cellar Reserve 1986 $18 (5/31/90)
87 SONOMA-CUTRER Chardonnay Russian River Valley Russian River Ranches 1986 Rel: $12 Cur: $18 (4/30/88)
87 STONY HILL Chardonnay Napa Valley 1986 Rel: $16 Cur: $68 (CH-7/90)
87 TREFETHEN Chardonnay Napa Valley 1986 Rel: $16.25 Cur: $22 (CH-3/90)
87 TREFETHEN Chardonnay Napa Valley 1986 Rel: $16.25 Cur: $22 (12/31/88)
87 VIANSA Chardonnay Napa-Sonoma Counties 1986 $12.50 (3/31/88)
87 WHITE OAK Chardonnay Sonoma County Myers Limited Release 1986 Rel: $16 Cur: $20 (CH-5/90)
86 ACACIA Chardonnay Carneros Napa Valley 1986 Rel: $15 Cur: $18 (12/31/87)
86 ACACIA Chardonnay Carneros Napa Valley Marina Vineyard 1986 Rel: $18 Cur: $22 (CH-1/90)
86 BEAULIEU Chardonnay Carneros Napa Valley Los Carneros Reserve 1986 Rel: $12 Cur: $15 (CH-6/90)
86 CAMBRIA Chardonnay Santa Barbara County Reserve 1986 $25 (12/15/89)
86 CHATEAU ST. JEAN Chardonnay Dry Creek Valley Frank Johnson Vineyards 1986 Rel: $14 Cur: $19 (12/31/89)
86 CLOS DU BOIS Chardonnay Alexander Valley Proprietor's Reserve 1986 Rel: $22.50 Cur: $23 (5/31/88)
86 DE LOACH Chardonnay Russian River Valley O.F.S. 1986 Rel: $22 Cur: $26 (CH-2/90)
86 DRY CREEK Chardonnay Dry Creek Valley Reserve 1986 $18 (11/30/89)
86 FETZER Chardonnay California Sundial 1986 $6.50 (9/15/87) BB
86 FISHER Chardonnay Napa-Sonoma Counties 1986 Rel: $11 Cur: $11 (7/15/88)
86 FOLIE A DEUX Chardonnay Napa Valley 1986 Rel: $15 Cur: $18 (4/30/88)
86 FREEMARK ABBEY Chardonnay Napa Valley 1986 Rel: $15 Cur: $15 (CH-2/90)
86 HUSCH Chardonnay Mendocino 1986 $9.75 (11/30/87)
86 KENDALL-JACKSON Chardonnay California The Proprietor's 1986 Rel: $17 Cur: $20 (CH-4/90)
86 KENWOOD Chardonnay Sonoma Valley Beltane Ranch 1986 Rel: $14 Cur: $18 (5/31/88)
86 LEEWARD Chardonnay Central Coast 1986 $8.50 (10/31/87)
86 MAZZOCCO Chardonnay Alexander Valley River Lane Barrel Fermented 1986 $16.50 (2/15/88)
86 MONTICELLO Chardonnay Napa Valley Jefferson Ranch 1986 Rel: $11 Cur: $18 (CH-2/90)
86 MOUNT VEEDER Chardonnay Napa County 1986 Rel: $14 Cur: $14 (2/29/88)
86 MURPHY-GOODE Chardonnay Alexander Valley Estate Vineyard 1986 Rel: $10 Cur: $12 (CH-4/90)
86 NAPA CREEK Chardonnay Napa Valley 1986 $12 (5/31/88)
86 ROMBAUER Chardonnay Napa Valley Reserve 1986 Rel: $24 Cur: $24 (CH-6/90)
86 CHARLES SHAW Chardonnay Napa Valley 1986 Rel: $11 Cur: $11 (7/15/88)
86 SONOMA-CUTRER Chardonnay Sonoma Valley Les Pierres Vineyard 1986 Rel: $19.50 Cur: $28 (10/15/88)
86 SONOMA-CUTRER Chardonnay Russian River Valley Russian River Ranches 1986 Rel: $12 Cur: $18 (CH-3/90)
86 STAG'S LEAP WINE CELLARS Chardonnay Napa Valley 1986 Rel: $17 Cur: $20 (CH-3/90)
86 STERLING Chardonnay Napa Valley Diamond Mountain Ranch 1986 Rel: $15 Cur: $15 (CH-4/90)
86 TAFT STREET Chardonnay Russian River Valley 1986 $10 (12/31/88)
86 IVAN TAMAS Chardonnay Napa Valley Reserve 1986 $15 (9/30/88)
86 VILLA MT. EDEN Chardonnay Napa Valley 1986 $12 (7/31/88)
86 WHITE OAK Chardonnay Sonoma County 1986 Rel: $11 Cur: $16 (CH-5/90)
85 BEAULIEU Chardonnay Napa Valley Beaufort 1986 Rel: $9 Cur: $9 (7/15/88)
85 BONNY DOON Chardonnay Sonoma County Grahm Crew 1986 $8.50 (10/15/87)
85 CECCHETTI SEBASTIANI Chardonnay Napa Valley Cask Lot 2 1986 $9.50 (12/15/87)
85 CHALONE Chardonnay Chalone Reserve 1986 Rel: $28 Cur: $100 (CH-5/90)
85 CLOS DU BOIS Chardonnay Alexander Valley Calcaire Vineyard 1986 Rel: $16 Cur: $23 (CH-2/90)
85 CLOS PEGASE Chardonnay Napa Valley 1986 $12 (CH-3/90)
85 CONGRESS SPRINGS Chardonnay Santa Cruz Mountains Private Reserve 1986 Rel: $20 Cur: $23 (CH-4/90)
85 CONGRESS SPRINGS Chardonnay Santa Clara County San Ysidro Reserve 1986 Rel: $15 Cur: $22 (CH-4/90)
85 EBERLE Chardonnay Paso Robles 1986 $10 (12/31/88)
85 FOX MOUNTAIN Chardonnay Sonoma County Reserve 1986 $15 (4/15/91)
85 GIRARD Chardonnay Napa Valley Reserve 1986 Rel: $25 Cur: $40 (12/31/89)
85 KEENAN Chardonnay Napa Valley 1986 $12 (7/15/88)
85 KENWOOD Chardonnay Sonoma Valley 1986 $12 (2/15/89)
85 KENWOOD Chardonnay Sonoma Valley Beltane Ranch 1986 Rel: $14 Cur: $18 (CH-7/90)
85 LA CREMA Chardonnay California Reserve 1986 Rel: $18 Cur: $22 (CH-6/90)
85 LEEWARD Chardonnay Edna Valley MacGregor Vineyard 1986 $14 (2/29/88)
85 MAZZOCCO Chardonnay Sonoma County Winemaster's Cuvée 1986 $10 (2/15/88)
85 MERIDIAN Chardonnay Napa Valley 1986 $12 (5/31/88)
85 MERRY VINTNERS Chardonnay Sonoma County Reserve 1986 $14.75 (11/30/88)
85 MERRY VINTNERS Chardonnay Sonoma County Vintage Preview 1986 $9.75 (7/15/88)
85 NEWTON Chardonnay Napa Valley 1986 Rel: $14 Cur: $14 (CH-3/90)
85 ROBERT PECOTA Chardonnay Alexander Valley Canepa Vineyard 1986 Rel: $16 Cur: $19 (CH-4/90)
85 REVERE Chardonnay Napa Valley 1986 Rel: $15 Cur: $16 (CH-4/90)
85 ROMBAUER Chardonnay Napa Valley 1986 Rel: $14.50 Cur: $16 (CH-6/90)
85 ROUDON-SMITH Chardonnay Mendocino Nelson Ranch 1986 $12 (9/15/88)
85 CHARLES SHAW Chardonnay Napa Valley 1986 Rel: $11 Cur: $11 (CH-5/90)
85 RODNEY STRONG Chardonnay Sonoma County 1986 $7 (12/15/87) BB
85 ZD Chardonnay California 1986 Rel: $18 Cur: $25 (CH-6/90)
84 ACACIA Chardonnay Carneros Napa Valley Marina Vineyard 1986 Rel: $18 Cur: $22 (12/31/87)
84 ALDERBROOK Chardonnay Dry Creek Valley 1986 $9.25 (4/15/88)
84 AU BON CLIMAT Chardonnay Santa Barbara County Reserve 1986 $20 (6/15/88)
84 CLOS DU VAL Chardonnay Carneros Napa Valley Carneros Estate 1986 Rel: $12 Cur: $14 (CH-6/90)
84 ESTANCIA Chardonnay Alexander Valley 1986 $6.50 (1/31/88) BB
84 MARKHAM Chardonnay Napa Valley Estate 1986 Rel: $12 Cur: $15 (CH-2/90)
84 MAYACAMAS Chardonnay Napa Valley 1986 Rel: $20 Cur: $27 (7/15/89)
84 MOUNT EDEN Chardonnay Edna Valley MEV MacGregor Vineyard 1986 Rel: $13 Cur: $16 (3/15/88)

84 PLAM Chardonnay Napa Valley 1986 $18 (4/15/89)
84 SAINTSBURY Chardonnay Carneros Reserve 1986 Rel: $20 Cur: $25 (CH-2/90)
84 SANTA BARBARA Chardonnay Santa Ynez Valley Reserve 1986 $14 (10/15/88)
84 SIMI Chardonnay Mendocino-Sonoma-Napa Counties 1986 $12 (2/15/89)
83 ALEXANDER VALLEY Chardonnay Alexander Valley 1986 $11 (4/30/88)
83 BERINGER Chardonnay Napa Valley 1986 $10.50 (1/31/88)
83 BUENA VISTA Chardonnay Carneros 1986 $11.50 (6/30/87)
83 CALERA Chardonnay Central Coast 1986 $12 (7/31/89)
83 CARTLIDGE & BROWNE Chardonnay Napa Valley 1986 $10 (5/31/88)
83 CAYMUS Chardonnay Napa Valley 1986 $12 (8/31/88)
83 CHATEAU SOUVERAIN Chardonnay Sonoma County 1986 $9 (12/31/87)
83 CHATEAU ST. JEAN Chardonnay Sonoma County 1986 Rel: $11 Cur: $11 (5/31/88)
83 CONGRESS SPRINGS Chardonnay Santa Clara County 1986 Rel: $12 Cur: $18 (CH-4/90)
83 DOMAINE LAURIER Chardonnay Sonoma County 1986 $13.50 (12/31/88)
83 FIRESTONE Chardonnay Santa Ynez Valley 1986 $10 (12/31/88)
83 THOMAS FOGARTY Chardonnay Carneros Napa Valley 1986 $15 (12/31/88)
83 HOUTZ Chardonnay Santa Ynez Valley 1986 $11 (12/15/89)
83 IRON HORSE Chardonnay Sonoma County Green Valley 1986 $12 (3/31/88)
83 J. PEDRONCELLI Chardonnay Dry Creek Valley 1986 $8 (6/15/88)
83 ROUND HILL Chardonnay California House 1986 $5.25 (11/30/87) BB
83 RUTHERFORD HILL Chardonnay Napa Valley Rutherford Knoll Special Cuvée 1986 $11 (1/31/88)
83 ST. FRANCIS Chardonnay California 1986 $9 (11/15/87)
83 STERLING Chardonnay Napa Valley 1986 Rel: $14.50 Cur: $16 (3/15/88)
82 ACACIA Chardonnay Napa Valley 1986 Rel: $15 Cur: $17 (12/31/87)
82 S. ANDERSON Chardonnay Napa Valley Stags Leap District 1986 $16 (11/15/88)
82 CALLAWAY Chardonnay Temecula Calla-Lees 1986 $9.50 (11/15/87)
82 CONGRESS SPRINGS Chardonnay Santa Clara County 1986 Rel: $12 Cur: $18 (10/31/87)
82 DOMAINE DE NAPA Chardonnay Napa Valley 1986 $9.50 (10/15/88)
82 ESTRELLA RIVER Chardonnay Paso Robles 1986 $8 (4/30/88)
82 GARY FARRELL Chardonnay Sonoma County 1986 $12 (8/31/88)
82 FROG'S LEAP Chardonnay Carneros 1986 Rel: $14 Cur: $18 (6/15/88)
82 HAYWOOD Chardonnay Sonoma Valley 1986 $9.50 (10/15/88)
82 JORDAN Chardonnay Alexander Valley 1986 $20 (4/15/89)
82 KENWOOD Chardonnay Sonoma Valley Yulupa Vineyard 1986 Rel: $12 Cur: $17 (CH-7/90)
82 BERNARD PRADEL Chardonnay Napa Valley 1986 $9.50 (2/29/88)
82 RAYMOND Chardonnay California Selection 1986 $8.50 (11/15/87)
82 RAYMOND Chardonnay Napa Valley Private Reserve 1986 Rel: $18 Cur: $21 (7/15/89)
82 SEBASTIANI ESTATES Chardonnay Sonoma Valley Niles 1986 $17 (3/15/88)
81 ACACIA Chardonnay Napa Valley 1986 Rel: $15 Cur: $17 (CH-1/90)
81 S. ANDERSON Chardonnay Napa Valley Stags Leap District 1986 $16 (CH-3/90)
81 BUENA VISTA Chardonnay Carneros Jeanette's Vineyard 1986 $8.50 (2/15/88)
81 COLBY Chardonnay Napa Valley 1986 $11 (5/31/89)
81 FITCH MOUNTAIN Chardonnay Napa Valley 1986 $8 (11/15/88)
81 J FRITZ Chardonnay Russian River Valley 1986 $9 (2/29/88)
81 HANDLEY Chardonnay Dry Creek Valley 1986 $15 (10/31/88)
81 HANNA Chardonnay Sonoma County 1986 $13.50 (9/30/88)
81 MARION Chardonnay California 1986 $5.50 (2/15/88) BB
81 MOUNT EDEN Chardonnay Edna Valley MEV MacGregor Vineyard 1986 Rel: $13 Cur: $16 (CH-3/90)
81 NEYERS Chardonnay Napa Valley 1986 $12.50 (4/30/88)
81 PINE RIDGE Chardonnay Napa Valley Stags Leap District 1986 Rel: $19 Cur: $23 (7/15/88)
81 QUAIL RIDGE Chardonnay Napa Valley 1986 $15 (10/31/88)
81 ZACA MESA Chardonnay Santa Barbara County Reserve 1986 $15 (10/15/88)
80 BABCOCK Chardonnay Santa Ynez Valley Reserve 1986 $14 (2/15/88)
80 BELVEDERE Chardonnay Sonoma County Bacigalupi 1986 $13 (7/15/88)
80 CHALONE Chardonnay Chalone 1986 Rel: $22 Cur: $51 (12/31/87)
80 CHIMNEY ROCK Chardonnay Napa Valley Stags Leap District 1986 $14 (10/15/88)
80 CLOS DU BOIS Chardonnay Alexander Valley Barrel Fermented 1986 Rel: $10 Cur: $12 (CH-12/89)
80 CLOS DU BOIS Chardonnay Alexander Valley Barrel Fermented 1986 Rel: $10 Cur: $12 (10/15/87)
80 CONGRESS SPRINGS Chardonnay Santa Clara County San Ysidro Reserve 1986 Rel: $15 Cur: $22 (11/15/87)
80 COSENTINO Chardonnay Napa Valley The Sculptor 1986 $17 (9/15/88)
80 DOMAINE POTELLE Chardonnay California 1986 $6 (4/15/88) BB
80 FELTA SPRINGS Chardonnay Sonoma County 1986 $6 (6/15/88) BB
80 WILLIAM HILL Chardonnay Napa Valley Silver Label 1986 $10 (4/30/88)
80 INGLENOOK Chardonnay Napa Valley 1986 $9.50 (3/15/88)
80 INNISFREE Chardonnay Napa Valley 1986 $9 (12/31/87)
80 JEPSON Chardonnay Mendocino Vintage Reserve 1986 $15 (5/31/89)
80 KONOCTI Chardonnay Lake County 1986 $8 (12/31/88)
80 ROBERT PEPI Chardonnay Napa Valley 1986 $12 (10/31/88)
80 RAYMOND Chardonnay Napa Valley 1986 Rel: $13 Cur: $13 (2/15/88)
80 ST. ANDREW'S WINERY Chardonnay Napa Valley 1986 $8 (8/31/87)
80 STERLING Chardonnay Napa Valley Diamond Mountain Ranch 1986 Rel: $15 Cur: $15 (6/15/89)
80 WENTE BROS. Chardonnay Livermore Valley Reserve Herman Wente Vineyard 1986 $11 (5/31/88)
79 WILLIAM HILL Chardonnay Napa Valley Reserve 1986 Rel: $17 Cur: $20 (3/31/88)
79 SEBASTIANI Chardonnay Sonoma County Family Selection Reserve 1986 $10 (10/31/88)
79 SEQUOIA GROVE Chardonnay Carneros 1986 Rel: $13 Cur: $16 (8/31/88)
79 STEVENOT Chardonnay California 1986 $6 (11/15/87)
79 VENTANA Chardonnay Monterey Crystal Ventana Vineyards 1986 $16 (10/31/89)
79 WILLIAM WHEELER Chardonnay Sonoma County 1986 $11.50 (1/31/88)
79 WILD HORSE Chardonnay San Luis Obispo County Wild Horse Vineyards 1986 $9.75 (5/31/88)
78 BEAULIEU Chardonnay Carneros Napa Valley Los Carneros Reserve 1986 Rel: $12 Cur: $15 (4/15/88)
78 CHATEAU SOUVERAIN Chardonnay Sonoma Valley Carneros Reserve 1986 $12 (4/30/88)
78 CLOS DU BOIS Chardonnay Alexander Valley Proprietor's Reserve 1986 Rel: $22.50 Cur: $23 (CH-5/90)
78 DION Chardonnay Sonoma Valley 1986 $10 (12/31/88)
78 HIDDEN CELLARS Chardonnay Mendocino County 1986 $10.50 (5/31/88)
78 LA CREMA Chardonnay California 1986 $11.50 (7/15/88)
78 REVERE Chardonnay Napa Valley 1986 Rel: $15 Cur: $16 (4/30/88)
78 ROUND HILL Chardonnay North Coast 1986 $6.75 (12/15/87)
78 SEQUOIA GROVE Chardonnay Carneros 1986 Rel: $13 Cur: $16 (CH-5/90)
78 SODA CANYON Chardonnay Napa Valley 8th Leaf 1986 $11 (10/15/88)
78 TAFT STREET Chardonnay Sonoma County 1986 $7 (11/15/87)
77 CHATEAU POTELLE Chardonnay Napa Valley 1986 $13 (11/15/88)
77 CHRISTOPHE Chardonnay California Reserve 1986 $9.50 (4/15/88)
77 CLOS DU VAL Chardonnay California Gran Val 1986 $8.50 (4/15/88)
77 DOMAINE ST. GEORGE Chardonnay Sonoma County 1986 $4.50 (12/31/87)
77 FLAX Chardonnay Sonoma County 1986 $14 (12/31/88)
77 FLORA SPRINGS Chardonnay Napa Valley 1986 $13 (7/15/88)
77 FREEMARK ABBEY Chardonnay Napa Valley 1986 Rel: $15 Cur: $15 (3/15/89)
77 KEENAN Chardonnay Napa Valley Ann's Vineyard 1986 $14 (4/15/89)
77 MARK WEST Chardonnay Russian River Valley Le Beau Vineyards 1986 $12 (9/15/88)
77 MARKHAM Chardonnay Napa Valley Estate 1986 Rel: $12 Cur: $15 (7/31/88)
77 MIRASSOU Chardonnay Monterey County Fifth Generation Family Selection 1986 $8 (11/15/87)
77 NEWTON Chardonnay Napa Valley 1986 Rel: $14 Cur: $14 (7/15/88)
77 ROBERT PECOTA Chardonnay Alexander Valley Canepa Vineyard 1986 Rel: $16 Cur: $19 (10/31/87)
77 SIGNORELLO Chardonnay Napa Valley Founder's Reserve 1986 $13 (7/15/89)
77 IVAN TAMAS Chardonnay Napa Valley-Central Coast 1986 $7 (12/31/87)
77 VILLA ZAPU Chardonnay Napa Valley 1986 $13.75 (12/31/88)
77 J. WILE & SONS Chardonnay Napa Valley 1986 $7 (9/15/87)
76 DOMAINE MICHEL Chardonnay Sonoma County 1986 $16 (12/31/88)
76 JEKEL Chardonnay Arroyo Seco 1986 $11 (4/30/89)
76 MCDOWELL Chardonnay McDowell Valley 1986 $11 (5/31/88)
76 STRATFORD Chardonnay California Partners' Reserve 1986 $14.50 (12/31/88)
75 CHESTNUT HILL Chardonnay Sonoma County 1986 $8 (12/31/87)
75 FAR NIENTE Chardonnay Napa Valley 1986 Rel: $24 Cur: $31 (1/31/88)
75 FOPPIANO Chardonnay Sonoma County 1986 $9 (5/31/88)
75 LA REINA Chardonnay Monterey County 1986 $13 (12/31/88)
75 ROUND HILL Chardonnay Napa Valley Reserve 1986 $9.50 (5/31/88)
75 ROBERT SINSKEY Chardonnay Carneros Napa Valley 1986 $16.50 (7/31/88)
74 CHAPPELLET Chardonnay Napa Valley 1986 Rel: $14 Cur: $14 (5/15/89)
74 LIBERTY SCHOOL Chardonnay California Lot 11 1986 $6 (2/29/88)
74 LOUIS M. MARTINI Chardonnay North Coast 1986 $9.50 (5/31/88)
74 SEBASTIANI ESTATES Chardonnay Sonoma Valley Kinneybrook 1986 $14 (3/15/88)
74 ZACA MESA Chardonnay Santa Barbara County 1986 $9.75 (10/15/88)
73 DOMAINE DE NAPA Chardonnay Napa Valley Barrel Fermented 1986 $14.50 (12/31/88)
73 FETZER Chardonnay Mendocino County Barrel Select 1986 $10 (8/31/88)
73 JOSEPH SWAN Chardonnay Sonoma Coast 1986 $18 (7/15/88)
72 MERRYVALE Chardonnay Napa Valley 1986 $20 (10/31/88)
72 ROCHIOLI Chardonnay Russian River Valley 1986 $12 (1/31/88)
72 ROUND HILL Chardonnay Napa Valley Van Asperen Reserve 1986 $11 (5/31/88)
71 CYPRESS LANE Chardonnay California 1986 $6 (12/31/87)
71 GOOSECROSS Chardonnay Napa Valley 1986 $15 (5/31/88)
71 RAVENSWOOD Chardonnay Sonoma Valley Sangiacomo 1986 $15 (3/15/88)
71 TIN PONY Chardonnay Sonoma County Green Valley 1986 $8 (9/30/88)
70 CAKEBREAD Chardonnay Napa Valley 1986 $20 (2/15/88)
70 CRYSTAL VALLEY Chardonnay North Coast 1986 $8.50 (11/15/87)
70 GUENOC Chardonnay Guenoc Valley Premier Cuvée 1986 $17.50 (12/31/88)
70 CK MONDAVI Chardonnay California 1986 $4.50 (8/31/87)
70 SONOMA-CUTRER Chardonnay Sonoma Coast Cutrer Vineyard 1986 Rel: $16 Cur: $23 (10/15/88)
69 BUTTERFIELD Chardonnay Napa Valley 1986 $7.50 (2/15/88)
69 SEGHESIO Chardonnay California 1986 $5.50 (8/31/88)
68 CHALK HILL Chardonnay Sonoma County 1986 $10 (1/31/88)
68 CORBETT CANYON Chardonnay Central Coast Coastal Classic 1986 $6.50/L (11/15/87)
68 THOMAS FOGARTY Chardonnay Monterey Ventana Vineyards 1986 $15 (5/31/88)
68 PARDUCCI Chardonnay Mendocino County 1986 $8 (12/31/87)
68 SYLVAN SPRINGS Chardonnay California Vintner's Reserve 1986 $5 (9/30/88)
67 SANTA BARBARA Chardonnay Santa Ynez Valley 1986 $8.50 (2/29/88)
66 BABCOCK Chardonnay Santa Ynez Valley 1986 $11 (2/15/88)
66 CORBETT CANYON Chardonnay Central Coast Select 1986 $8.75 (3/15/89)
65 ASHLY Chardonnay Monterey 1986 $16.50 (10/31/88)
65 MENDOCINO ESTATE Chardonnay Mendocino 1986 $5.50 (12/31/87)
65 SUNNY ST. HELENA Chardonnay Napa Valley 1986 $9 (10/31/87)
54 KARLY Chardonnay California 1986 $12.50 (4/15/88)

1985

95 CHATEAU ST. JEAN Chardonnay Alexander Valley Robert Young Vineyards Reserve 1.5L 1985 Rel: $40 Cur: $40 (CH-7/90)
94 CHALONE Chardonnay Chalone Reserve 1985 Rel: $28 Cur: $110 (CH-6/90)
93 CHATEAU ST. JEAN Chardonnay Alexander Valley Robert Young Vineyards Reserve 1.5L 1985 Rel: $40 Cur: $40/1.5L (9/30/90)
93 CLOS DU BOIS Chardonnay Dry Creek Valley Flintwood Vineyard 1985 Rel: $18 Cur: $32 (3/31/87)
93 CONGRESS SPRINGS Chardonnay Santa Clara County 1985 Rel: $12 Cur: $20 (10/15/86)
93 CUVAISON Chardonnay Napa Valley 1985 Rel: $12 Cur: $20 (CH-4/90)
93 FERRARI-CARANO Chardonnay Alexander Valley 1985 Rel: $14 Cur: $30 (9/15/87) SS
93 FORMAN Chardonnay Napa Valley 1985 Rel: $15 Cur: $60 (CH-2/90)
93 LA CREMA Chardonnay California 1985 $11 (2/28/87)
93 ST. ANDREW'S WINERY Chardonnay Napa Valley 1985 $7.50 (11/30/86) SS
93 SMITH-MADRONE Chardonnay Napa Valley 1985 Rel: $12.50 Cur: $16 (6/15/87)
93 SONOMA-CUTRER Chardonnay Sonoma Valley Les Pierres 1985 Rel: $17.50 Cur: $30 (9/30/87) SS
93 SONOMA-CUTRER Chardonnay Russian River Valley Russian River Ranches 1985 Rel: $11.50 Cur: $25 (4/15/87)
92 S. ANDERSON Chardonnay Napa Valley Stags Leap District 1985 $14 (CH-3/90)
92 CHATEAU ST. JEAN Chardonnay Alexander Valley Belle Terre Vineyards 1985 Rel: $16 Cur: $25 (CH-3/90)
92 DRY CREEK Chardonnay Sonoma County 1985 $10 (3/15/87)
92 FOLIE A DEUX Chardonnay Napa Valley 1985 Rel: $14.50 Cur: $18 (5/31/87)
92 GRGICH HILLS Chardonnay Napa Valley 1985 Rel: $22 Cur: $33 (CH-3/90)
92 INNISFREE Chardonnay Napa Valley 1985 $9 (12/31/86)
92 JEPSON Chardonnay Mendocino 1985 $12 (1/31/88)
92 LA CREMA Chardonnay California Reserve 1985 Rel: $18 Cur: $22 (11/15/87)
92 RAYMOND Chardonnay Napa Valley 1985 Rel: $12 Cur: $12 (9/15/87)
92 SANFORD Chardonnay Santa Barbara County Barrel Select 1985 Rel: $20 Cur: $30 (CH-2/90)
92 SANFORD Chardonnay Santa Barbara County Barrel Select 1985 Rel: $20 Cur: $30 (11/30/87)
92 CHARLES SHAW Chardonnay Napa Valley 1985 Rel: $12 Cur: $15 (7/15/87)
92 SONOMA-CUTRER Chardonnay Sonoma Valley Les Pierres 1985 Rel: $17.50 Cur: $30 (CH-3/90)
92 STONY HILL Chardonnay Napa Valley 1985 Rel: $16 Cur: $71 (CH-5/90)

UNITED STATES

CALIFORNIA/*CHARDONNAY*

91 ALTAMURA Chardonnay Napa Valley 1985 Rel: $14 Cur: $21 (CH-1/90)

91 ALTAMURA Chardonnay Napa Valley 1985 Rel: $14 Cur: $21 (2/29/88)

91 BELVEDERE Chardonnay Sonoma County Bacigalupi 1985 $12 (12/15/87)

91 CARTLIDGE & BROWNE Chardonnay Napa Valley 1985 $9.75 (3/31/87)

91 CHATEAU MONTELENA Chardonnay Alexander Valley 1985 Rel: $16 Cur: $28 (CH-2/90)

91 CHATEAU ST. JEAN Chardonnay Alexander Valley Belle Terre Vineyards 1985 Rel: $16 Cur: $25 (5/31/88)

91 CHATEAU ST. JEAN Chardonnay Alexander Valley Robert Young Vineyards 1985 Rel: $18 Cur: $26 (CH-3/90)

91 CLOS DU BOIS Chardonnay Alexander Valley Proprietor's Reserve 1985 Rel: $22 Cur: $25 (6/15/87)

91 FERRARI-CARANO Chardonnay Alexander Valley 1985 Rel: $14 Cur: $30 (CH-5/90)

91 FORMAN Chardonnay Napa Valley 1985 Rel: $15 Cur: $60 (5/31/87)

91 GIRARD Chardonnay Napa Valley Reserve 1985 Rel: $25 Cur: $25 (CH-3/90)

91 HACIENDA Chardonnay Sonoma County Clair de Lune 1985 Rel: $11 Cur: $20 (6/30/87)

91 JEKEL Chardonnay Arroyo Seco Home Vineyard Private Reserve 1985 $18 (4/15/89)

91 LONG Chardonnay Napa Valley 1985 Rel: $27.50 Cur: $70 (CH-4/90)

91 ROBERT MONDAVI Chardonnay Napa Valley Reserve 1985 Rel: $25 Cur: $30 (12/15/87)

91 RAVENSWOOD Chardonnay Sonoma Valley Sangiacomo 1985 $15 (3/31/87)

91 RAYMOND Chardonnay Napa Valley Private Reserve 1985 Rel: $18 Cur: $21 (CH-5/90)

91 SAINTSBURY Chardonnay Carneros 1985 Rel: $11 Cur: $19 (11/30/87) (JL)

91 SIMI Chardonnay Sonoma County Reserve 1985 Rel: $28 Cur: $32 (CH-4/90)

90 CHATEAU MONTELENA Chardonnay Napa Valley 1985 Rel: $18 Cur: $25 (CH-2/90)

90 CUVAISON Chardonnay Napa Valley 1985 Rel: $12 Cur: $20 (10/15/87)

90 DE LOACH Chardonnay Russian River Valley 1985 Rel: $14 Cur: $33 (CH-2/90)

90 FAR NIENTE Chardonnay Napa Valley 1985 Rel: $24 Cur: $33 (CH-2/90)

90 GIRARD Chardonnay Napa Valley 1985 Rel: $13.50 Cur: $25 (CH-3/90)

90 GOOSECROSS Chardonnay Napa Valley 1985 $14 (8/31/87)

90 HANZELL Chardonnay Sonoma Valley 1985 Rel: $22 Cur: $37 (CH-1/90)

90 WILLIAM HILL Chardonnay Napa Valley Reserve 1985 Rel: $16 Cur: $24 (CH-3/90)

90 MAYACAMAS Chardonnay Napa Valley 1985 Rel: $20 Cur: $29 (CH-1/90)

90 MAYACAMAS Chardonnay Napa Valley 1985 Rel: $20 Cur: $29 (8/31/88)

90 MERRYVALE Chardonnay Napa Valley 1985 $16.50 (10/31/87)

90 MONTICELLO Chardonnay Napa Valley Jefferson Ranch 1985 Rel: $11 Cur: $18 (9/15/87)

90 NEWTON Chardonnay Napa Valley 1985 Rel: $12.75 Cur: $19 (10/31/87)

90 NEYERS Chardonnay Napa Valley 1985 $12 (8/31/87)

90 RAYMOND Chardonnay Napa Valley Private Reserve 1985 Rel: $18 Cur: $21 (6/15/88)

90 SAINTSBURY Chardonnay Carneros 1985 Rel: $11 Cur: $19 (CH-2/90)

90 SANFORD Chardonnay Santa Barbara County 1985 Rel: $13.50 Cur: $20 (CH-2/90)

90 WHITE OAK Chardonnay Alexander Valley Myers Limited Release 1985 Rel: $14.50 Cur: $22 (CH-5/90)

90 ZD Chardonnay California 1985 Rel: $16 Cur: $28 (CH-3/90)

89 CHATEAU ST. JEAN Chardonnay Alexander Valley Robert Young Vineyards 1985 Rel: $18 Cur: $26 (11/30/87)

89 GIRARD Chardonnay Napa Valley 1985 Rel: $13.50 Cur: $25 (12/15/87)

89 MENDOCINO ESTATE Chardonnay Mendocino 1985 $5 (12/15/86) BB

89 MORGAN Chardonnay Monterey County 1985 Rel: $14 Cur: $23 (4/30/87)

89 MOUNT VEEDER Chardonnay Napa County 1985 Rel: $13.50 Cur: $14 (5/31/87)

89 MOUNTAIN VIEW Chardonnay Monterey County 1985 $5 (2/15/87) BB

89 NAVARRO Chardonnay Anderson Valley Première Reserve 1985 Rel: $12 Cur: $18 (CH-3/90)

89 ROBERT PECOTA Chardonnay Alexander Valley Canepa Vineyard 1985 Rel: $16 Cur: $18 (CH-7/90)

89 PINE RIDGE Chardonnay Napa Valley Knollside Cuvée 1985 Rel: $14 Cur: $16 (4/30/87)

89 SEQUOIA GROVE Chardonnay Napa Valley Estate 1985 Rel: $16 Cur: $16 (CH-5/90)

89 SIMI Chardonnay Mendocino-Sonoma Counties 1985 $11 (3/15/88)

89 SONOMA-CUTRER Chardonnay Russian River Valley Cutrer Vineyard 1985 Rel: $14.75 Cur: $29 (9/15/87)

89 WHITE OAK Chardonnay Sonoma County 1985 Rel: $10.50 Cur: $16 (CH-5/90)

88 BERINGER Chardonnay Napa Valley Private Reserve 1985 Rel: $15 Cur: $24 (4/15/87)

88 BURGESS Chardonnay Napa Valley Vintage Reserve 1985 Rel: $13 Cur: $16 (CH-12/89)

88 CHATEAU ST. JEAN Chardonnay Sonoma County 1985 Rel: $11 Cur: $11 (4/30/87)

88 CHRISTIAN BROTHERS Chardonnay Napa Valley Barrel Fermented 1985 $11 (7/31/87)

88 CLOS PEGASE Chardonnay Alexander Valley 1985 $13 (7/15/87)

88 B.R. COHN Chardonnay Sonoma Valley Olive Hill Vineyard Barrel Reserve 1985 $21 (6/30/87)

88 DE LOACH Chardonnay Russian River Valley 1985 Rel: $14 Cur: $33 (12/31/86)

88 FISHER Chardonnay Sonoma County Coach Insignia 1985 Rel: $16 Cur: $20 (11/15/87)

88 THOMAS FOGARTY Chardonnay Monterey 1985 $15 (2/15/88)

88 FOLIE A DEUX Chardonnay Napa Valley 1985 Rel: $14.50 Cur: $18 (CH-6/90)

88 HUSCH Chardonnay Mendocino 1985 $9.75 (3/31/87)

88 INGLENOOK Chardonnay Napa Valley Reserve 1985 Rel: $14.50 Cur: $15 (4/15/88)

88 KISTLER Chardonnay Russian River Valley Dutton Ranch 1985 Rel: $15 Cur: $30 (CH-2/90)

88 MARK WEST Chardonnay Russian River Valley Le Beau Vineyards Reserve 1985 $16 (10/31/87)

88 MATANZAS CREEK Chardonnay Sonoma County 1985 Rel: $16.50 Cur: $28 (CH-2/90)

88 MERIDIAN Chardonnay Napa Valley 1985 $11 (4/30/87)

88 ROBERT MONDAVI Chardonnay Napa Valley Reserve 1985 Rel: $25 Cur: $30 (CH-3/90)

88 MONTICELLO Chardonnay Napa Valley Corley Reserve 1985 Rel: $14 Cur: $20 (7/15/87)

88 NAVARRO Chardonnay Mendocino 1985 $8.50 (10/31/87)

88 SEQUOIA GROVE Chardonnay Carneros 1985 Rel: $12 Cur: $16 (CH-5/90)

88 SILVERADO Chardonnay Napa Valley 1985 Rel: $11.50 Cur: $17 (2/28/87)

88 SONOMA-CUTRER Chardonnay Russian River Valley Russian River Ranches 1985 Rel: $11.50 Cur: $25 (CH-3/90)

88 TREFETHEN Chardonnay Napa Valley 1985 Rel: $15.25 Cur: $25 (CH-3/90)

Key to Symbols

The scores reported here are the results of blind tastings conducted by our panel of senior editors. Wines that carry the initials below are results of individual tastings.

THE WINE SPECTATOR 100-POINT SCALE ***95-100***—Classic, a great wine; ***90-94***—Outstanding, superior character and style; ***80-89***—Good to very good, a wine with special qualities; ***70-79***—Average, drinkable wine that may have minor flaws; ***60-69***—Below average, drinkable but not recommended; ***50-59***—Poor, undrinkable, not recommended. "+"—With a score indicates a range; used primarily with barrel tastings to indicate a preliminary score.

SPECIAL DESIGNATIONS SS—Spectator Selection, CS—Cellar Selection, BB—Best Buy.

TASTER'S INITIALS (JG)—Jim Gordon, (HS)—Harvey Steiman, (JL)—James Laube, (JS)—James Suckling, (TM)—Thomas Matthews, (TR)—Terry Robards, (BT)—Barrel Tasting (these wines were tasted blind from barrel samples), (CA-date)—*California's Great Cabernets* by James Laube, (CH-date)—*California's Great Chardonnays* by James Laube, (VP-date)—*Vintage Port* by James Suckling.

DATE TASTED Dates in parentheses represent the issue in which the rating was published.

88 VICHON Chardonnay Napa Valley 1985 Rel: $15 Cur: $17 (CH-3/90)

87 BOUCHAINE Chardonnay Carneros 1985 Rel: $15 Cur: $20 (CH-2/90)

87 BOUCHAINE Chardonnay Carneros 1985 Rel: $15 Cur: $20 (CH-2/90)

87 BURGESS Chardonnay Napa Valley Vintage Reserve 1985 Rel: $13 Cur: $16 (10/31/87)

87 CHAPPELLET Chardonnay Napa Valley 1985 Rel: $12.50 Cur: $15 (CH-3/90)

87 CHATEAU MONTELENA Chardonnay Alexander Valley 1985 Rel: $16 Cur: $28 (6/30/87)

87 CHATEAU ST. JEAN Chardonnay Dry Creek Valley Frank Johnson Vineyards 1985 Rel: $14 Cur: $14 (CH-3/90)

87 CLOS DU BOIS Chardonnay Alexander Valley Calcaire Vineyard 1985 Rel: $18 Cur: $28 (3/15/87)

87 CLOS DU VAL Chardonnay Napa Valley 1985 $11.50 (CH-6/90)

87 CLOS PEGASE Chardonnay Alexander Valley 1985 $13 (CH-3/90)

87 COLBY Chardonnay Napa Valley 1985 $10.75 (11/15/87)

87 CONGRESS SPRINGS Chardonnay Santa Clara County 1985 Rel: $12 Cur: $20 (CH-4/90)

87 FIVE PALMS Chardonnay Napa Valley 1985 $8 (4/30/87)

87 GRGICH HILLS Chardonnay Napa Valley 1985 Rel: $22 Cur: $33 (10/15/87)

87 HACIENDA Chardonnay Sonoma County Clair de Lune 1985 Rel: $11 Cur: $20 (CH-4/90)

87 JORDAN Chardonnay Alexander Valley 1985 $17 (3/15/88)

87 KENDALL-JACKSON Chardonnay Sonoma Valley Durell Vineyard 1985 Rel: $14 Cur: $20 (CH-4/90)

87 MATANZAS CREEK Chardonnay Sonoma County 1985 Rel: $16.50 Cur: $28 (8/31/87)

87 MOUNT EDEN Chardonnay Santa Cruz Mountains 1985 Rel: $25 Cur: $67 (CH-3/90)

87 MOUNT EDEN Chardonnay Edna Valley MEV MacGregor Vineyard 1985 Rel: $12.50 Cur: $14 (CH-3/90)

87 PINE RIDGE Chardonnay Napa Valley Knollside Cuvée 1985 Rel: $14 Cur: $16 (CH-4/90)

87 RUTHERFORD HILL Chardonnay Napa Valley Cellar Reserve 1985 $15 (5/31/88)

87 ST. ANDREW'S VINEYARD Chardonnay Napa Valley 1985 $13 (6/30/87)

87 SEQUOIA GROVE Chardonnay Napa Valley Estate 1985 Rel: $14 Cur: $14 (11/15/87)

87 CHARLES SHAW Chardonnay Napa Valley 1985 Rel: $12 Cur: $15 (CH-5/90)

87 SILVERADO Chardonnay Napa Valley 1985 Rel: $11.50 Cur: $17 (CH-3/90)

87 SMITH-MADRONE Chardonnay Napa Valley 1985 Rel: $12.50 Cur: $16 (CH-5/90)

87 SONOMA-CUTRER Chardonnay Russian River Valley Cutrer Vineyard 1985 Rel: $14.75 Cur: $29 (CH-3/90)

87 STERLING Chardonnay Napa Valley Diamond Mountain Ranch 1985 Rel: $15 Cur: $17 (CH-7/90)

87 VENTANA Chardonnay Monterey Gold Stripe Selection 1985 $7.50 (9/15/87) BB

86 ACACIA Chardonnay Carneros Napa Valley Winery Lake Vineyard 1985 Rel: $18 Cur: $25 (1/31/87)

86 BERINGER Chardonnay Napa Valley Private Reserve 1985 Rel: $15 Cur: $24 (CH-4/90)

86 BLUE HERON LAKE Chardonnay Napa County 1985 $13 (8/31/87)

86 BUENA VISTA Chardonnay Carneros Private Reserve 1985 Rel: $16.50 Cur: $17 (CH-3/90)

86 CALLAWAY Chardonnay Temecula Calla-Lees 1985 $9.25 (3/15/87)

86 CHASE CREEK Chardonnay Napa Valley 1985 $7 (12/15/86)

86 CHATEAU ST. JEAN Chardonnay Sonoma Valley McCrea Vineyards 1985 Rel: $14.25 Cur: $17 (CH-7/90)

86 DEHLINGER Chardonnay Russian River Valley 1985 Rel: $10 Cur: $17 (CH-5/90)

86 DEHLINGER Chardonnay Russian River Valley 1985 Rel: $10 Cur: $17 (8/31/87)

86 FETZER Chardonnay California Special Reserve 1985 $13 (11/15/87)

86 LA CREMA Chardonnay California Reserve 1985 Rel: $18 Cur: $22 (CH-6/90)

86 MARKHAM Chardonnay Napa Valley Estate 1985 Rel: $12 Cur: $17 (CH-2/90)

86 MATANZAS CREEK Chardonnay Sonoma Valley Estate 1985 Rel: $18 Cur: $39 (CH-2/90)

86 MIRASSOU Chardonnay Monterey County Fifth Generation Family Selection 1985 $8 (12/31/86)

86 MORGAN Chardonnay Monterey County 1985 Rel: $14 Cur: $23 (CH-7/90)

86 PINE RIDGE Chardonnay Napa Valley Stags Leap District 1985 Rel: $18 Cur: $23 (8/31/87)

86 REVERE Chardonnay Napa Valley 1985 Rel: $15 Cur: $20 (5/31/87)

86 STAG'S LEAP WINE CELLARS Chardonnay Napa Valley Reserve 1985 Rel: $22 Cur: $26 (12/15/87)

85 BEAULIEU Chardonnay Carneros Napa Valley Los Carneros Reserve 1985 Rel: $12 Cur: $16 (1/31/88)

85 BUENA VISTA Chardonnay Carneros Private Reserve 1985 Rel: $16.50 Cur: $17 (5/31/88)

85 CLOS DU BOIS Chardonnay Alexander Valley Proprietor's Reserve 1985 Rel: $22 Cur: $25 (CH-5/90)

85 EDNA VALLEY Chardonnay Edna Valley 1985 Rel: $13 Cur: $30 (CH-3/90)

85 FLORA SPRINGS Chardonnay Napa Valley 1985 $15 (2/28/87)

85 FLORA SPRINGS Chardonnay Napa Valley Barrel Fermented 1985 Rel: $18 Cur: $35 (CH-1/90)

85 GROTH Chardonnay Napa Valley 1985 $11 (2/15/88)

85 KENDALL-JACKSON Chardonnay Anderson Valley Dennison Vineyard 1985 Rel: $14 Cur: $20 (CH-4/90)

85 KENWOOD Chardonnay Sonoma Valley Yulupa Vineyard 1985 Rel: $12 Cur: $17 (2/15/88)

85 MONTICELLO Chardonnay Napa Valley Corley Reserve 1985 Rel: $14 Cur: $20 (CH-2/90)

85 MURPHY-GOODE Chardonnay Alexander Valley Estate Vineyard 1985 Rel: $9 Cur: $12 (CH-4/90)

85 NEWTON Chardonnay Napa Valley 1985 Rel: $12.75 Cur: $19 (CH-3/90)

85 PINE RIDGE Chardonnay Napa Valley Stags Leap District 1985 Rel: $18 Cur: $23 (CH-4/90)

85 REVERE Chardonnay Napa Valley 1985 Rel: $15 Cur: $20 (CH-4/90)

85 ST. CLEMENT Chardonnay Napa Valley 1985 Rel: $14.50 Cur: $16 (CH-3/90)

85 STAG'S LEAP WINE CELLARS Chardonnay Napa Valley Reserve 1985 Rel: $22 Cur: $26 (CH-3/90)

85 WHITE OAK Chardonnay Sonoma County 1985 Rel: $10.50 Cur: $16 (8/31/87)

84 BEAULIEU Chardonnay Carneros Napa Valley Los Carneros Reserve 1985 Rel: $12 Cur: $16 (CH-6/90)

84 BERINGER Chardonnay Napa Valley 1985 $10 (4/30/87)

84 CLOS DU BOIS Chardonnay Alexander Valley Barrel Fermented 1985 Rel: $9 Cur: $12 (CH-2/90)

84 CONGRESS SPRINGS Chardonnay Santa Cruz Mountains Private Reserve 1985 Rel: $16 Cur: $27 (CH-4/90)

84 FETZER Chardonnay Mendocino County Sundial 1985 $6.50 (9/15/86) BB

84 FISHER Chardonnay Sonoma County Coach Insignia 1985 Rel: $16 Cur: $20 (CH-2/90)

84 FISHER Chardonnay Sonoma County Whitney's Vineyard 1985 Rel: $24 Cur: $30 (CH-2/90)

84 FROG'S LEAP Chardonnay Napa Valley 1985 Rel: $12 Cur: $16 (CH-6/90)

84 GEYSER PEAK Chardonnay Sonoma County Carneros 1985 $7 (2/28/87) BB

84 HANZELL Chardonnay Sonoma Valley 1985 Rel: $22 Cur: $37 (3/31/88)

84 KENDALL-JACKSON Chardonnay California Vintner's Reserve 1985 $9.50 (3/15/87)

84 KENWOOD Chardonnay Sonoma Valley Beltane Ranch 1985 Rel: $14 Cur: $18 (CH-7/90)

84 KENWOOD Chardonnay Sonoma Valley Yulupa Vineyard 1985 Rel: $12 Cur: $17 (CH-7/90)

84 MERLION Chardonnay Napa Valley 1985 $15 (2/15/88)

84 PERRET Chardonnay Carneros Napa Valley Winery Lake Vineyard 1985 $14.50 (12/31/88)

84 JOSEPH PHELPS Chardonnay Carneros Sangiacomo Vineyard 1985 $14 (11/15/87)

84 ROMBAUER Chardonnay Napa Valley 1985 Rel: $14.50 Cur: $18 (CH-6/90)
84 TREFETHEN Chardonnay Napa Valley 1985 Rel: $15.25 Cur: $25 (12/31/87)
84 WENTE BROS. Chardonnay Arroyo Seco Reserve Arroyo Seco Vineyard 1985 $10 (10/15/87)
84 ZACA MESA Chardonnay Santa Barbara County Barrel Select 1985 $9.75 (10/15/88)
83 BUENA VISTA Chardonnay Carneros Jeanette's Vineyard 1985 $13.25 (2/28/87)
83 CANTERBURY Chardonnay California 1985 $6.50 (11/15/86) BB
83 CLOS DU BOIS Chardonnay Alexander Valley Calcaire Vineyard 1985 Rel: $18 Cur: $28 (CH-2/90)
83 CORBETT CANYON Chardonnay Central Coast Select 1985 $9 (1/31/87)
83 FAR NIENTE Chardonnay Napa Valley 1985 Rel: $24 Cur: $33 (2/28/87)
83 HANNA Chardonnay Sonoma County 1985 $13.50 (8/31/87)
83 MERRY VINTNERS Chardonnay Sonoma County Vintage Preview 1985 $9.75 (12/15/86)
83 NAVARRO Chardonnay Anderson Valley Première Reserve 1985 Rel: $12 Cur: $18 (11/15/87)
83 J. PEDRONCELLI Chardonnay Sonoma County 1985 $7.75 (7/31/87)
83 RAYMOND Chardonnay California Selection 1985 $8.50 (2/28/87)
83 STAG'S LEAP WINE CELLARS Chardonnay Napa Valley 1985 Rel: $16 Cur: $25 (CH-3/90)
82 ACACIA Chardonnay Carneros Napa Valley 1985 Rel: $15 Cur: $20 (2/28/87)
82 ACACIA Chardonnay Carneros Napa Valley Winery Lake Vineyard 1985 Rel: $18 Cur: $25 (CH-1/90)
82 BOUCHAINE Chardonnay Napa Valley 1985 Rel: $13 Cur: $17 (11/15/87)
82 CAIN Chardonnay Carneros 1985 $16 (10/31/87)
82 FISHER Chardonnay Napa-Sonoma Counties 1985 Rel: $11 Cur: $11 (7/15/87)
82 FLAX Chardonnay Sonoma County 1985 $12 (10/15/87)
82 MONTICELLO Chardonnay Napa Valley Jefferson Ranch 1985 Rel: $11 Cur: $18 (CH-2/90)
82 ROMBAUER Chardonnay Napa Valley 1985 Rel: $14.50 Cur: $18 (11/15/87)
82 ROUND HILL Chardonnay Napa Valley Reserve 1985 $9.50 (11/15/87)
82 SIGNORELLO Chardonnay Napa Valley Founder's Reserve 1985 $12 (2/15/88)
82 SPRING MOUNTAIN Chardonnay Napa Valley 1985 $15 (11/15/87)
82 DAVID S. STARE Chardonnay Dry Creek Valley Reserve 1985 $15 (10/15/88)
82 ZD Chardonnay California 1985 Rel: $16 Cur: $28 (3/31/87)
81 LAWRENCE J. BARGETTO Chardonnay Santa Maria Valley 1985 $10 (11/15/87)
81 CONCANNON Chardonnay California Selected Vineyards 1985 $10.50 (6/30/87)
81 CRESTON MANOR Chardonnay Central Coast 1985 $10 (11/15/87)
81 FREEMARK ABBEY Chardonnay Napa Valley 1985 Rel: $14 Cur: $25 (3/15/88)
81 J FRITZ Chardonnay Russian River Valley 1985 $8.50 (11/30/87)
81 KARLY Chardonnay Santa Maria Valley 1985 $12 (8/31/87)
81 KEENAN Chardonnay Napa Valley 1985 $11 (7/31/87)
81 MERRY VINTNERS Chardonnay Sonoma County Reserve 1985 $15 (9/15/87)
81 ROBERT PEPI Chardonnay Napa Valley 1985 $12 (11/15/87)
81 ROUND HILL Chardonnay California House 1985 $5 (9/30/86) BB
80 ACACIA Chardonnay Carneros Napa Valley 1985 Rel: $15 Cur: $20 (CH-1/90)
80 ACACIA Chardonnay Carneros Napa Valley Marina Vineyard 1985 Rel: $18 Cur: $22 (CH-1/90)
80 CALERA Chardonnay Santa Barbara County 1985 $11.75 (7/31/87)
80 CHALONE Chardonnay Chalone 1985 Rel: $22 Cur: $95 (CH-4/90)
80 CLOS DU VAL Chardonnay Napa Valley 1985 $11.50 (7/31/87)
80 CONN CREEK Chardonnay Napa Valley Barrel Select Lot No. 32 1985 $12 (2/15/88)
80 FREEMARK ABBEY Chardonnay Napa Valley 1985 Rel: $14 Cur: $25 (CH-2/90)
80 GUENOC Chardonnay North Coast 1985 $9.75 (11/15/87)
80 GUNDLACH BUNDSCHU Chardonnay Sonoma Valley 1985 $10 (7/31/87)
80 WILLIAM HILL Chardonnay Napa Valley Reserve 1985 Rel: $16 Cur: $24 (7/31/87)
80 KEENAN Chardonnay Napa Valley Estate 1985 $13.50 (2/15/88)
80 J. LOHR Chardonnay Monterey County Greenfield Vineyards 1985 $9 (6/30/87)
80 RUTHERFORD HILL Chardonnay Napa Valley Jaeger Vineyards 1985 $11 (5/31/88)
80 STRATFORD Chardonnay California 1985 $9 (2/28/87)
79 ACACIA Chardonnay Napa Valley 1985 Rel: $14 Cur: $16 (CH-1/90)
79 ALDERBROOK Chardonnay Dry Creek Valley 1985 $8.75 (2/15/87)
79 ALEXANDER VALLEY Chardonnay Alexander Valley 1985 $10.50 (5/31/87)
79 S. ANDERSON Chardonnay Napa Valley Stags Leap District 1985 $14 (8/31/87)
79 CARNEROS CREEK Chardonnay Los Carneros 1985 $10.50 (11/15/87)
79 CHATEAU WOLTNER Chardonnay Howell Mountain Woltner Estates 1985 Rel: $18 Cur: $32 (11/15/87)
79 DE LOACH Chardonnay Russian River Valley O.F.S. 1985 Rel: $20 Cur: $47 (CH-2/90)
79 FETZER Chardonnay California Barrel Select 1985 $8.50 (4/30/87)
79 E.&J. GALLO Chardonnay North Coast 1985 $5 (12/31/88)
79 KENDALL-JACKSON Chardonnay California The Proprieter's 1985 Rel: $18 Cur: $18 (9/15/87)
79 MILANO Chardonnay California 1985 $10 (4/15/88)
79 ROBERT MONDAVI Chardonnay Napa Valley 1985 Rel: $12 Cur: $15 (7/15/87)
79 MURPHY-GOODE Chardonnay Alexander Valley Estate Vineyard 1985 Rel: $9 Cur: $12 (6/30/87)
79 PLAM Chardonnay Napa Valley 1985 $12 (7/15/88)
79 SEQUOIA GROVE Chardonnay Carneros 1985 Rel: $12 Cur: $16 (11/15/87)
79 WENTE BROS. Chardonnay Arroyo Seco Vineyard Reserve 1985 $30/1.5L (3/31/90)
78 CHAMISAL Chardonnay Edna Valley 1985 $10 (11/15/87)
78 CHATEAU MONTELENA Chardonnay Napa Valley 1985 Rel: $18 Cur: $25 (11/15/87)
78 CONN CREEK Chardonnay Napa Valley Lot No. 139 1985 $12.50 (12/31/88)
78 DE LOACH Chardonnay Russian River Valley O.F.S. 1985 Rel: $20 Cur: $47 (3/15/87)
78 HIDDEN CELLARS Chardonnay Mendocino County Grasso Vineyard 1985 $9.75 (7/31/87)
78 INGLENOOK Chardonnay Napa Valley Reserve 1985 Rel: $14.50 Cur: $15 (CH-4/90)
78 PERRET Chardonnay Carneros Napa Valley Perret Vineyard 1985 $14 (12/31/88)
77 CHAPPELLET Chardonnay Napa Valley 1985 Rel: $12.50 Cur: $15 (7/31/88)
77 FLORA SPRINGS Chardonnay Napa Valley Barrel Fermented 1985 Rel: $18 Cur: $35 (11/30/87)
77 HAYWOOD Chardonnay Sonoma Valley Reserve 1985 $14.50 (12/31/87)
77 RIVER OAKS Chardonnay Sonoma County 1985 $6 (4/16/86)
77 ZACA MESA Chardonnay Santa Barbara County 1985 $8 (10/31/87)
76 ST. CLEMENT Chardonnay Napa Valley 1985 Rel: $14.50 Cur: $16 (10/15/87)
75 ACACIA Chardonnay Napa Valley 1985 Rel: $14 Cur: $16 (12/15/86)
75 CHATEAU WOLTNER Chardonnay Howell Mountain Titus Vineyard 1985 Rel: $40 Cur: $40 (11/15/87)
75 CLOS DU BOIS Chardonnay Alexander Valley Barrel Fermented 1985 Rel: $9 Cur: $12 (11/15/86)
75 IRON HORSE Chardonnay Sonoma County Green Valley 1985 $12.50 (7/31/87)
75 MILL CREEK Chardonnay Dry Creek Valley 1985 $10 (12/31/87)
74 CAIN Chardonnay Napa-Sonoma Counties 1985 $10 (7/31/87)
74 SEBASTIANI Chardonnay Sonoma Valley Reserve 1985 $10 (2/15/88)
73 BONNY DOON Chardonnay Monterey County La Reina Vineyard 1985 $13 (4/30/87)
73 BYRON Chardonnay Santa Barbara County Reserve 1985 $13 (10/31/87)
73 CHRISTOPHE Chardonnay California 1985 $6.50 (11/15/86)
73 THOMAS FOGARTY Chardonnay Carneros Napa Valley Winery Lake Vineyard 1985 $15 (2/15/88)
73 LAMBERT BRIDGE Chardonnay Sonoma County 1985 $10 (2/15/88)
73 LAURA'S Chardonnay San Luis Obispo 1985 $7 (12/31/87)
73 STERLING Chardonnay Napa Valley Diamond Mountain Ranch 1985 Rel: $15 Cur: $17 (9/15/88)
73 VICHON Chardonnay Napa Valley 1985 Rel: $15 Cur: $17 (8/31/87)
72 BLACK MOUNTAIN Chardonnay Alexander Valley Douglass Hill 1985 $10 (8/31/87)
72 CYPRESS LANE Chardonnay California 1985 $6 (1/31/87)
72 FROG'S LEAP Chardonnay Napa Valley 1985 Rel: $12 Cur: $16 (3/15/87)
72 RUTHERFORD RANCH Chardonnay Napa Valley Reese Vineyard 1985 $10 (11/15/87)
72 RODNEY STRONG Chardonnay Sonoma County Chalk Hill Vineyard 1985 $10 (12/31/87)
71 DOMAINE LAURIER Chardonnay Sonoma County 1985 $13 (10/31/87)
71 JEKEL Chardonnay Arroyo Seco 1985 $10.50 (12/31/88)
71 LAKESPRING Chardonnay Napa Valley 1985 $11 (11/15/87)
71 LANDMARK Chardonnay Sonoma County 1985 $10 (2/15/88)
71 MILANO Chardonnay Sonoma County Vine Hill Ranch 1985 $14 (12/31/88)
70 DAVID ARTHUR Chardonnay Napa Valley 1985 $13 (4/15/88)
70 CLOS DU BOIS Chardonnay Dry Creek Valley Flintwood Vineyard 1985 Rel: $18 Cur: $32 (CH-5/90)
70 FOX MOUNTAIN Chardonnay Sonoma County Reserve 1985 $14 (12/31/88)
70 LEEWARD Chardonnay Edna Valley MacGregor Vineyard 1985 $14 (5/31/87)
70 MONTEREY VINEYARD Chardonnay Monterey County 1985 $7 (10/15/87)
70 ROUDON-SMITH Chardonnay Santa Cruz Mountains 1985 $15 (3/31/89)
70 RUTHERFORD ESTATE Chardonnay Napa Valley 1985 $5 (11/15/87)
69 THOMAS FOGARTY Chardonnay Santa Cruz Mountains 1985 $16.50 (2/15/88)
69 STERLING Chardonnay Napa Valley 1985 Rel: $14 Cur: $14 (7/31/87)
68 CHATEAU WOLTNER Chardonnay Howell Mountain St. Thomas Vineyard 1985 Rel: $30 Cur: $30 (11/15/87)
68 CLOS ROBERT Chardonnay Napa Valley 1985 $6 (7/31/87)
68 SAM J. SEBASTIANI Chardonnay Sonoma-Napa Counties 1985 $12.50 (6/30/87)
67 SHAFER Chardonnay Napa Valley 1985 $11.50 (1/31/88)
65 DORE Chardonnay California 1985 $5 (2/15/88)
65 ESTRELLA RIVER Chardonnay Paso Robles 1985 $8 (12/31/87)
64 SBARBORO Chardonnay Alexander Valley Gauer Ranch 1985 $10 (8/31/87)
63 FIRESTONE Chardonnay Santa Ynez Valley 10th Anniversary 1985 $10 (4/15/88)
63 SCHUG Chardonnay Carneros Napa Valley Ahollinger Vineyard 1985 $9.75 (4/30/87)
57 ACACIA Chardonnay Carneros Napa Valley Marina Vineyard 1985 Rel: $18 Cur: $22 (8/31/87)

1984

94 MONTICELLO Chardonnay Napa Valley Corley Reserve 1984 Rel: $12.50 Cur: $25 (CH-2/90)
93 ACACIA Chardonnay Carneros Napa Valley 1984 Rel: $14 Cur: $20 (11/16/85)
93 CLOS DU BOIS Chardonnay Alexander Valley Calcaire Vineyard 1984 Rel: $12 Cur: $30 (6/01/86) SS
93 LEEWARD Chardonnay Edna Valley MacGregor Vineyard 1984 $12 (6/16/86)
93 MATANZAS CREEK Chardonnay Sonoma County 1984 Rel: $15 Cur: $28 (5/16/86)
93 RAYMOND Chardonnay California Selection 1984 $8.50 (3/01/86)
93 SAINTSBURY Chardonnay Carneros 1984 Rel: $11 Cur: $25 (11/15/86)
92 CLOS DU BOIS Chardonnay Dry Creek Valley Flintwood Vineyard 1984 Rel: $11.25 Cur: $38 (6/01/86)
92 FLORA SPRINGS Chardonnay Napa Valley Barrel Fermented 1984 Rel: $18 Cur: $28 (10/31/86)
92 ST. ANDREW'S VINEYARD Chardonnay Napa Valley 1984 $13 (1/01/86)
92 SAINTSBURY Chardonnay Carneros 1984 Rel: $11 Cur: $25 (CH-2/90)
91 BERINGER Chardonnay Napa Valley Private Reserve 1984 Rel: $15 Cur: $24 (4/15/87)
91 CHATEAU MONTELENA Chardonnay Alexander Valley 1984 Rel: $16 Cur: $32 (6/01/86)
91 CLOS DU VAL Chardonnay California 1984 $11.50 (5/01/86)
91 DOMAINE ST. GEORGE Chardonnay Sonoma County 1984 $5 (12/16/85) BB
91 EDNA VALLEY Chardonnay Edna Valley 1984 Rel: $12.50 Cur: $29 (6/16/86)
91 FROG'S LEAP Chardonnay Napa Valley 1984 Rel: $12 Cur: $23 (CH-3/90)
91 HACIENDA Chardonnay Sonoma County Clair de Lune 1984 Rel: $10 Cur: $18 (1/31/87)
91 NAVARRO Chardonnay Anderson Valley Première Reserve 1984 Rel: $12 Cur: $22 (CH-3/90)
91 PERRET Chardonnay Carneros Napa Valley Perret Vineyard 1984 $14.50 (10/15/87)
91 ST. ANDREW'S WINERY Chardonnay Napa Valley 1984 $7 (2/01/86) BB
90 BERINGER Chardonnay Napa Valley 1984 $9 (4/15/87)
90 CHATEAU MONTELENA Chardonnay Alexander Valley 1984 Rel: $16 Cur: $32 (CH-2/90)
90 CHATEAU ST. JEAN Chardonnay Alexander Valley Robert Young Vineyards Reserve 1984 1.5L Rel: $40 Cur: $50 (5/31/88)
90 CLOS DU BOIS Chardonnay Alexander Valley Calcaire Vineyard 1984 Rel: $12 Cur: $30 (CH-2/90)
90 CONGRESS SPRINGS Chardonnay Santa Clara County 1984 Rel: $11 Cur: $25 (CH-4/90)
90 CRUVINET Chardonnay California 1984 $4.50 (9/15/86)
90 DE LOACH Chardonnay Russian River Valley 1984 Rel: $12.50 Cur: $30 (CH-12/85)
90 DE LOACH Chardonnay Russian River Valley O.F.S. 1984 Rel: $20 Cur: $20 (CH-2/90)
90 FISHER Chardonnay Sonoma County Whitney's Vineyard 1984 Rel: $20 Cur: $30 (CH-2/90)
90 FRANCISCAN Chardonnay Napa Valley Oakville Estate 1984 $8.50 (3/15/87) BB
90 GRGICH HILLS Chardonnay Napa Valley 1984 Rel: $18 Cur: $33 (CH-3/90)
90 GROTH Chardonnay Napa Valley 1984 $12 (7/31/87)
90 MONTICELLO Chardonnay Napa Valley Jefferson Ranch 1984 Rel: $10 Cur: $18 (9/30/86)
90 SEQUOIA GROVE Chardonnay Napa Valley Estate 1984 Rel: $14 Cur: $14 (2/15/87)
90 SIMI Chardonnay Sonoma County Reserve 1984 Rel: $28 Cur: $32 (8/31/88)
90 STONY HILL Chardonnay Napa Valley 1984 Rel: $13 Cur: $70 (CH-5/90)
90 WENTE BROS. Chardonnay Arroyo Seco Vintner Grown Reserve 1984 $9 (6/01/86)
90 ZD Chardonnay California 1984 Rel: $15 Cur: $30 (CH-3/90)
89 ACACIA Chardonnay Napa Valley 1984 Rel: $12.50 Cur: $16 (CH-7/90)
89 S. ANDERSON Chardonnay Napa Valley Stags Leap District 1984 $12.50 (CH-3/90)
89 INGLENOOK Chardonnay Napa Valley Reserve 1984 Rel: $12.50 Cur: $18 (3/01/86)
89 KISTLER Chardonnay Russian River Valley Dutton Ranch 1984 Rel: $15 Cur: $30 (CH-2/90)
89 MATANZAS CREEK Chardonnay Sonoma County 1984 Rel: $15 Cur: $28 (CH-2/90)
89 MONTICELLO Chardonnay Napa Valley Corley Reserve 1984 Rel: $12.50 Cur: $25 (10/31/86)
89 SEQUOIA GROVE Chardonnay Napa Valley Estate 1984 Rel: $14 Cur: $14 (CH-5/90)
89 SIMI Chardonnay Sonoma County Reserve 1984 Rel: $28 Cur: $32 (CH-4/90)
89 SONOMA-CUTRER Chardonnay Sonoma Valley Les Pierres 1984 Rel: $16.50 Cur: $30 (CH-3/90)
88 ACACIA Chardonnay Carneros Napa Valley Winery Lake Vineyard 1984 Rel: $18 Cur: $26 (CH-1/90)
88 BERINGER Chardonnay Napa Valley Private Reserve 1984 Rel: $15 Cur: $24 (CH-4/90)

UNITED STATES

CALIFORNIA/*CHARDONNAY*

88 CHALONE Chardonnay Chalone 1984 Rel: $18 Cur: $56 (CH-1/90)
88 CHATEAU MONTELENA Chardonnay Napa Valley 1984 Rel: $18 Cur: $28 (CH-2/90)
88 CHATEAU MONTELENA Chardonnay Napa Valley 1984 Rel: $18 Cur: $28 (10/31/86)
88 CHATEAU ST. JEAN Chardonnay Alexander Valley Robert Young Vineyards 1984 Rel: $20 Cur: $30 (CH-3/90)
88 CHATEAU ST. JEAN Chardonnay Dry Creek Valley Frank Johnson Vineyards 1984 Rel: $14 Cur: $20 (CH-7/90)
88 CONCANNON Chardonnay California Selected Vineyards 1984 $9 (4/16/86)
88 DE LOACH Chardonnay Russian River Valley 1984 Rel: $12.50 Cur: $30 (CH-2/90)
88 DRY CREEK Chardonnay Sonoma County 1984 $10 (8/31/86)
88 FLORA SPRINGS Chardonnay Napa Valley 1984 $13.50 (10/31/86)
88 FLORA SPRINGS Chardonnay Napa Valley Barrel Fermented 1984 Rel: $18 Cur: $28 (CH-1/90)
88 FRANCISCAN Chardonnay Napa Valley Oakville Estate Reserve 1984 Rel: $10 Cur: $23 (12/15/87)
88 GRGICH HILLS Chardonnay Napa Valley 1984 Rel: $18 Cur: $33 (7/16/86)
88 GUNDLACH BUNDSCHU Chardonnay Sonoma Valley Sangiacomo Ranch Special Selection 1984 $11.50 (5/31/87)
88 HACIENDA Chardonnay Sonoma County Clair de Lune 1984 Rel: $10 Cur: $18 (CH-4/90)
88 WILLIAM HILL Chardonnay Napa Valley Reserve 1984 Rel: $20 Cur: $24 (CH-3/90)
88 INNISFREE Chardonnay Napa Valley 1984 $9 (11/16/85)
88 IRON HORSE Chardonnay Sonoma County Green Valley 1984 $12 (6/16/86)
88 LA CREMA Chardonnay Monterey Ventana Vineyard 1984 Rel: $18 Cur: $24 (CH-6/90)
88 LONG Chardonnay Napa Valley 1984 Rel: $27.50 Cur: $70 (CH-4/90)
88 MAYACAMAS Chardonnay Napa Valley 1984 Rel: $18 Cur: $28 (CH-3/90)
88 MERRY VINTNERS Chardonnay Sonoma County 1984 $13.75 (6/16/86)
88 ST. CLEMENT Chardonnay Napa Valley 1984 Rel: $14.50 Cur: $17 (CH-3/90)
88 SONOMA-CUTRER Chardonnay Russian River Valley Russian River Ranches 1984 Rel: $11.25 Cur: $12 (6/01/86)
88 WILLIAM WHEELER Chardonnay Sonoma County 1984 $11 (1/31/87)
87 CHAPPELLET Chardonnay Napa Valley 1984 Rel: $12 Cur: $20 (CH-3/90)
87 CHATEAU ST. JEAN Chardonnay Alexander Valley Robert Young Vineyards Reserve 1.5L 1984 Rel: $40 Cur: $50 (CH-3/90)
87 CHATEAU ST. JEAN Chardonnay Sonoma Valley McCrea Vineyards 1984 Rel: $14.25 Cur: $17 (CH-3/90)
87 CLOS DU BOIS Chardonnay Alexander Valley Proprietor's Reserve 1984 Rel: $18 Cur: $21 (10/31/86)
87 DELICATO Chardonnay Napa Valley Barrel Fermented Golden Anniversary 1984 $10 (4/30/87)
87 FOLIE A DEUX Chardonnay Napa Valley 1984 Rel: $14 Cur: $18 (CH-6/90)
87 FREEMARK ABBEY Chardonnay Napa Valley 1984 Rel: $14 Cur: $17 (CH-2/90)
87 MOCERI Chardonnay Monterey County San Bernabe Vineyard 1984 $5 (7/01/86) BB
87 ROBERT MONDAVI Chardonnay Napa Valley Reserve 1984 Rel: $22 Cur: $35 (CH-3/90)
87 SEQUOIA GROVE Chardonnay Napa Valley 1984 $10 (4/30/87)
87 SONOMA-CUTRER Chardonnay Russian River Valley Cutrer Vineyard 1984 Rel: $14.25 Cur: $25 (CH-3/90)
86 ACACIA Chardonnay Carneros Napa Valley Marina Vineyard 1984 Rel: $16 Cur: $22 (CH-1/90)
86 S. ANDERSON Chardonnay Napa Valley Stags Leap District 1984 $12.50 (7/31/87)
86 BOUCHAINE Chardonnay Carneros 1984 Rel: $14 Cur: $20 (1/31/87)
86 CARNEROS CREEK Chardonnay Los Carneros 1984 $10.50 (4/30/87)
86 DEHLINGER Chardonnay Russian River Valley 1984 Rel: $10 Cur: $14 (CH-4/90)
86 EDNA VALLEY Chardonnay Edna Valley 1984 Rel: $12.50 Cur: $29 (CH-6/90)
86 FAR NIENTE Chardonnay Napa Valley 1984 Rel: $22 Cur: $36 (CH-2/90)
86 FETZER Chardonnay Mendocino County 1984 $6.50 (4/16/86)
86 FORMAN Chardonnay Napa Valley 1984 Rel: $15 Cur: $45 (CH-2/90)
86 FRANCISCAN Chardonnay Napa Valley Oakville Estate Reserve 1984 Rel: $12 Cur: $23 (CH-4/90)
86 INGLENOOK Chardonnay Napa Valley Reserve 1984 Rel: $12.50 Cur: $18 (CH-4/90)
86 LA REINA Chardonnay Monterey 1984 $12 (2/01/86)
86 MONTICELLO Chardonnay Napa Valley Jefferson Ranch 1984 Rel: $10 Cur: $18 (CH-2/90)
86 MORGAN Chardonnay Monterey County 1984 Rel: $12.75 Cur: $23 (CH-5/90)
86 NEWTON Chardonnay Napa Valley 1984 Rel: $11.50 Cur: $18 (CH-5/90)
86 PINE RIDGE Chardonnay Napa Valley Stags Leap District 1984 Rel: $18 Cur: $25 (6/16/86)
86 RAYMOND Chardonnay Napa Valley Private Reserve 1984 Rel: $16 Cur: $16 (7/15/87)
86 STERLING Chardonnay Napa Valley Diamond Mountain Ranch 1984 Rel: $15 Cur: $17 (CH-4/90)
86 TREFETHEN Chardonnay Napa Valley 1984 Rel: $14.25 Cur: $28 (CH-3/90)
86 VICHON Chardonnay Napa Valley 1984 Rel: $15 Cur: $17 (CH-3/90)
86 WHITE OAK Chardonnay Sonoma County 1984 Rel: $10 Cur: $16 (CH-5/90)
85 BOUCHAINE Chardonnay Carneros 1984 Rel: $14 Cur: $20 (CH-2/90)
85 CHATEAU ST. JEAN Chardonnay Alexander Valley Belle Terre Vineyards 1984 Rel: $16 Cur: $27 (CH-3/90)
85 CLOS DU VAL Chardonnay Napa Valley 1984 $11.50 (CH-6/90)
85 DORE Chardonnay Santa Maria Valley Signature Selections 1984 $5 (4/16/86)
85 FAR NIENTE Chardonnay Napa Valley 1984 Rel: $22 Cur: $36 (6/01/86)
85 GLEN ELLEN Chardonnay California Proprietor's Reserve 1984 $3.50 (10/16/85) BB
85 MARKHAM Chardonnay Napa Valley 1984 Rel: $12 Cur: $17 (CH-2/90)
85 MCDOWELL Chardonnay McDowell Valley 1984 $11 (2/28/87)
85 MOUNT EDEN Chardonnay Santa Cruz Mountains 1984 Rel: $23 Cur: $70 (CH-3/90)
85 NAPA RIDGE Chardonnay California 1984 $5.75 (1/31/87) BB
85 PINE RIDGE Chardonnay Napa Valley Knollside Cuvée 1984 Rel: $14 Cur: $17 (CH-4/90)
85 WHITE OAK Chardonnay Sonoma County 1984 Rel: $10 Cur: $16 (5/01/86)
85 ZACA MESA Chardonnay Santa Barbara County American Reserve 1984 $13 (2/28/87)

Key to Symbols

The scores reported here are the results of blind tastings conducted by our panel of senior editors. Wines that carry the initials below are results of individual tastings.

THE WINE SPECTATOR 100-POINT SCALE ***95-100***—Classic, a great wine; ***90-94***—Outstanding, superior character and style; ***80-89***—Good to very good, a wine with special qualities; ***70-79***—Average, drinkable wine that may have minor flaws; ***60-69***—Below average, drinkable but not recommended; ***50-59***—Poor, undrinkable, not recommended. "+"—With a score indicates a range; used primarily with barrel tastings to indicate a preliminary score.

SPECIAL DESIGNATIONS SS—Spectator Selection, CS—Cellar Selection, BB—Best Buy.

TASTER'S INITIALS (JG)—Jim Gordon, (HS)—Harvey Steiman, (JL)—James Laube, (JS)—James Suckling, (TM)—Thomas Matthews, (TR)—Terry Robards, (BT)—Barrel Tasting (these wines were tasted blind from barrel samples), (CA-date)—*California's Great Cabernets* by James Laube, (CH-date)—*California's Great Chardonnays* by James Laube, (VP-date)—*Vintage Port* by James Suckling.

DATE TASTED Dates in parentheses represent the issue in which the rating was published.

84 ACACIA Chardonnay Carneros Napa Valley 1984 Rel: $14 Cur: $20 (CH-1/90)
84 ACACIA Chardonnay Carneros Napa Valley Winery Lake Vineyard 1984 Rel: $18 Cur: $26 (10/16/85)
84 CHATEAU ST. JEAN Chardonnay Alexander Valley Robert Young Vineyards 1984 Rel: $20 Cur: $30 (10/31/86)
84 CHRISTOPHE Chardonnay California 1984 $5.50 (12/01/85) BB
84 CLOS DU BOIS Chardonnay Alexander Valley Barrel Fermented 1984 Rel: $8 Cur: $12 (CH-2/90)
84 CONN CREEK Chardonnay Napa Valley Château Maja 1984 $6.50 (4/16/86) BB
84 CORBETT CANYON Chardonnay Central Coast 1984 $8 (3/01/86) BB
84 FETZER Chardonnay California Special Reserve 1984 $13 (6/01/86)
84 THOMAS FOGARTY Chardonnay Monterey Ventana Vineyards 1984 $13.50 (2/28/87)
84 FOLIE A DEUX Chardonnay Napa Valley 1984 Rel: $14 Cur: $18 (6/16/86)
84 FREEMARK ABBEY Chardonnay Napa Valley 1984 Rel: $14 Cur: $17 (2/28/87)
84 GUNDLACH BUNDSCHU Chardonnay Sonoma Valley 1984 $10 (5/31/87)
84 HANZELL Chardonnay Sonoma Valley 1984 Rel: $20 Cur: $49 (CH-1/90)
84 PINE RIDGE Chardonnay Napa Valley Stags Leap District 1984 Rel: $18 Cur: $25 (CH-4/90)
84 VILLA MT. EDEN Chardonnay Napa Valley 1984 $9 (4/30/87)
83 BELVEDERE Chardonnay Central Coast Discovery Series 1984 $4.75 (10/16/85) BB
83 BELVEDERE Chardonnay North Coast Discovery Series 1984 $5 (1/01/86) BB
83 GUENOC Chardonnay North Coast 1984 $10 (9/15/86)
83 HANZELL Chardonnay Sonoma Valley 1984 Rel: $20 Cur: $49 (4/30/87)
83 JEKEL Chardonnay Arroyo Seco 1984 $10.50 (5/31/87)
83 ROBERT MONDAVI Chardonnay Napa Valley 1984 Rel: $10 Cur: $17 (9/15/86)
83 ROBERT PECOTA Chardonnay Alexander Valley Canepa Vineyard 1984 Rel: $14 Cur: $18 (CH-4/90)
83 CHARLES SHAW Chardonnay Napa Valley 1984 Rel: $12 Cur: $15 (1/31/87)
83 SILVERADO Chardonnay Napa Valley 1984 Rel: $11 Cur: $18 (6/16/86)
82 CHALK HILL Chardonnay Sonoma County 1984 $8 (12/01/85)
82 CUVAISON Chardonnay Napa Valley 1984 Rel: $12 Cur: $20 (CH-4/90)
82 FISHER Chardonnay Sonoma County Coach Insignia 1984 Rel: $15 Cur: $20 (CH-2/90)
82 GIRARD Chardonnay Napa Valley 1984 Rel: $13.50 Cur: $22 (2/28/87)
82 KISTLER Chardonnay Russian River Valley Dutton Ranch 1984 Rel: $15 Cur: $30 (9/30/86)
82 CHARLES SHAW Chardonnay Napa Valley 1984 Rel: $12 Cur: $15 (CH-5/90)
82 ULTRAVINO Chardonnay Napa Valley 1984 $8.50 (2/15/87)
82 ZD Chardonnay California 1984 Rel: $15 Cur: $30 (6/01/86)
81 J. PEDRONCELLI Chardonnay Sonoma County 1984 $7.75 (3/01/86)
81 SILVERADO Chardonnay Napa Valley 1984 Rel: $11 Cur: $18 (CH-3/90)
81 TREFETHEN Chardonnay Napa Valley 1984 Rel: $14.25 Cur: $28 (2/28/87)
80 BOUCHAINE Chardonnay Napa Valley 1984 Rel: $12.50 Cur: $15 (1/31/87)
80 CONGRESS SPRINGS Chardonnay Santa Cruz Mountains Private Reserve 1984 Rel: $16 Cur: $27 (CH-4/90)
80 EHLERS LANE Chardonnay Napa Valley 1984 $14 (6/16/86)
80 FOX MOUNTAIN Chardonnay Sonoma County Reserve 1984 $14.50 (12/31/87)
80 GIRARD Chardonnay Napa Valley 1984 Rel: $13.50 Cur: $22 (CH-3/90)
80 MATANZAS CREEK Chardonnay Sonoma Valley Estate 1984 Rel: $18 Cur: $29 (CH-2/90)
80 QUAIL RIDGE Chardonnay Napa Valley Winemakers' Selection 1984 $17 (12/15/87)
80 SMITH-MADRONE Chardonnay Napa Valley 1984 Rel: $12 Cur: $16 (CH-5/90)
79 BALVERNE Chardonnay Chalk Hill Deerfield Vineyard 1984 $11 (11/15/87)
79 BEAULIEU Chardonnay Carneros Napa Valley Los Carneros Reserve 1984 Rel: $10 Cur: $16 (CH-4/90)
79 DAVID BRUCE Chardonnay California 1984 $10 (7/16/86)
79 BURGESS Chardonnay Napa Valley Vintage Reserve 1984 Rel: $13 Cur: $17 (CH-12/89)
79 CHATEAU ST. JEAN Chardonnay Alexander Valley Belle Terre Vineyards 1984 Rel: $16 Cur: $27 (6/01/86)
79 FISHER Chardonnay Sonoma County Everyday 1984 $9 (10/16/85)
79 JEKEL Chardonnay Arroyo Seco Home Vineyard Private Reserve 1984 $16 (11/30/87)
79 RIVER OAKS Chardonnay Alexander Valley 1984 $6 (4/01/85)
79 ROUND HILL Chardonnay California House 1984 $4.75 (4/16/86)
79 STEPHEN ZELLERBACH Chardonnay Alexander Valley 1984 $6 (2/15/87)
78 BUENA VISTA Chardonnay Carneros 1984 $11 (3/01/86)
78 WILLIAM HILL Chardonnay Napa Valley Reserve 1984 Rel: $20 Cur: $24 (7/31/87)
78 LEEWARD Chardonnay Central Coast 1984 $8 (6/16/86)
78 MATANZAS CREEK Chardonnay Sonoma Valley Estate 1984 Rel: $18 Cur: $29 (6/01/86)
78 ROMBAUER Chardonnay Napa Valley 1984 Rel: $14.50 Cur: $20 (CH-6/90)
78 SANFORD Chardonnay Central Coast 1984 Rel: $12.50 Cur: $15 (CH-2/90)
78 STERLING Chardonnay Napa Valley Diamond Mountain Ranch 1984 Rel: $15 Cur: $17 (8/31/87)
77 CHASE CREEK Chardonnay Napa Valley 1984 $8.50 (11/01/85)
77 CLOS DU BOIS Chardonnay Alexander Valley Barrel Fermented 1984 Rel: $8 Cur: $12 (9/16/85)
77 SIMI Chardonnay Mendocino-Sonoma Counties 1984 $13 (10/31/86)
77 STAG'S LEAP WINE CELLARS Chardonnay Napa Valley 1984 Rel: $14 Cur: $17 (CH-6/90)
77 STERLING Chardonnay Napa Valley 1984 Rel: $14 Cur: $14 (6/16/86)
76 CHATEAU JULIEN Chardonnay Monterey County Paraiso Springs Vineyard 1984 $12 (2/15/87)
76 CHRISTIAN BROTHERS Chardonnay Napa Valley 1984 $8.50 (6/16/86)
76 FIRESTONE Chardonnay Santa Ynez Valley 1984 $10 (5/31/87)
76 GEYSER PEAK Chardonnay Sonoma County Carneros 1984 $8 (4/16/86)
75 ACACIA Chardonnay Napa Valley 1984 Rel: $12.50 Cur: $16 (CH-12/85)
75 BUENA VISTA Chardonnay Carneros Private Reserve 1984 Rel: $14.50 Cur: $16 (CH-6/90)
75 BURGESS Chardonnay Napa Valley Vintage Reserve 1984 Rel: $13 Cur: $17 (9/30/86)
75 CLOS DU VAL Chardonnay California Gran Val 1984 $6.50 (4/16/86)
75 FISHER Chardonnay Sonoma County Coach Insignia 1984 Rel: $15 Cur: $20 (10/31/86)
75 JOSEPH PHELPS Chardonnay Napa Valley 1984 $13 (6/30/87)
75 ST. CLEMENT Chardonnay Napa Valley 1984 Rel: $14.50 Cur: $17 (2/01/86)
75 ST. FRANCIS Chardonnay Sonoma Valley Poverello 1984 $6.75 (3/16/86)
75 SONOMA-CUTRER Chardonnay Russian River Valley Cutrer Vineyard 1984 Rel: $14.25 Cur: $25 (10/31/86)
75 DAVID S. STARE Chardonnay Dry Creek Valley Reserve 1984 $15 (12/31/86)
74 ACACIA Chardonnay Carneros Napa Valley Marina Vineyard 1984 Rel: $16 Cur: $22 (11/16/85)
74 BUENA VISTA Chardonnay Carneros Private Reserve 1984 Rel: $14.50 Cur: $16 (7/31/87)
74 CHATEAU ST. JEAN Chardonnay Sonoma Valley St. Jean Vineyards 1984 Rel: $14 Cur: $14 (7/31/87)
74 CLOS DU BOIS Chardonnay Dry Creek Valley Flintwood Vineyard 1984 Rel: $11.25 Cur: $38 (CH-5/90)
74 DOMAINE LAURIER Chardonnay Sonoma County 1984 $13 (6/16/86)
74 LOLONIS Chardonnay Mendocino County Lolonis Vineyards 1984 $14 (6/30/87)
73 SMITH-MADRONE Chardonnay Napa Valley 1984 Rel: $12 Cur: $16 (10/31/86)

72   CHESTNUT HILL Chardonnay Napa Valley 1984 $7.50 (4/16/86)
72   FETZER Chardonnay California Barrel Select 1984 $8.50 (3/01/86)
72   MADDALENA Chardonnay Santa Barbara County 1984 $5 (4/16/86)
72   MAYACAMAS Chardonnay Napa Valley 1984 Rel: $18 Cur: $28 (7/31/87)
71   BOUCHAINE Chardonnay Carneros Winery Lake Vineyard 1984 Rel: $22 Cur: $22 (CH-2/90)
71   CHATEAU ST. JEAN Chardonnay Sonoma County 1984 Rel: $12 Cur: $12 (11/16/85)
71   MANZANITA Chardonnay Napa Valley 1984 $12.50 (10/31/86)
71   ROMBAUER Chardonnay Napa Valley French Vineyard 1984 $13.50 (4/01/86)
71   SEBASTIANI Chardonnay Sonoma Valley 1984 $8.50 (6/16/86)
71   STRATFORD Chardonnay California 1984 $8.50 (2/01/86)
70   ESTATE WILLIAM BACCALA Chardonnay Mendocino 1984 $11 (1/31/87)
70   BOUCHAINE Chardonnay Carneros Winery Lake Vineyard 1984 Rel: $22 Cur: $22 (5/31/87)
70   CHAMISAL Chardonnay Edna Valley 1984 $10 (6/01/86)
70   LAKESPRING Chardonnay Napa Valley 1984 $12 (10/31/86)
70   LOUIS M. MARTINI Chardonnay North Coast 1984 $8 (4/16/86)
70   STAG'S LEAP WINE CELLARS Chardonnay Napa Valley 1984 Rel: $14 Cur: $17 (10/31/86)
70   VICHON Chardonnay Napa Valley 1984 Rel: $15 Cur: $17 (8/31/86)
69   J. LOHR Chardonnay Monterey County Greenfield Vineyards 1984 $9 (4/16/86)
69   ST. FRANCIS Chardonnay Sonoma Valley Barrel Select 1984 $12 (10/31/86)
69   VENTANA Chardonnay Monterey Gold Stripe Selection 1984 $8 (4/16/86)
68   MIRASSOU Chardonnay Monterey County Harvest Reserve 1984 $12 (4/01/86)
68   RODNEY STRONG Chardonnay Russian River Valley River West Vineyard 1984 $10 (3/15/87)
67   CORBETT CANYON Chardonnay Edna Valley Winemaker's Reserve 1984 $10 (7/01/86)
67   HAWK CREST Chardonnay California 1984 $6 (4/16/86)
67   VALFLEUR Chardonnay Alexander Valley Jimtown Ranch 1984 $10.50 (10/31/86)
66   BOUCHAINE Chardonnay Carneros 1984 Rel: $14 Cur: $20 (CH-2/90)
66   CARTLIDGE & BROWNE Chardonnay Napa Valley 1984 $11.50 (1/01/86)
66   DOMAINE SAN MARTIN Chardonnay Central Coast 1984 $7 (4/16/86)
66   SHAFER Chardonnay Napa Valley 1984 $12 (10/31/86)
65   LIBERTY SCHOOL Chardonnay California Lot 7 1984 $6 (4/16/86)
64   CALERA Chardonnay Santa Barbara County 1984 $11.25 (3/16/86)
64   LEEWARD Chardonnay Santa Maria Valley Bien Nacido Vineyard 1984 $12 (12/01/85)
64   MARIPOSA Chardonnay Sonoma County 1984 $5 (12/01/85)
64   MIRASSOU Chardonnay Monterey County 1984 $8 (12/16/85)
63   CHATEAU ST. JEAN Chardonnay Dry Creek Valley Frank Johnson Vineyards 1984 Rel: $14 Cur: $20 (12/31/86)
63   MORGAN Chardonnay Monterey County 1984 Rel: $12.75 Cur: $23 (2/01/86)
62   CAIN Chardonnay Napa Valley 1984 $10 (10/31/86)
60   GLEN ELLEN Chardonnay Sonoma Valley 1984 $9 (3/16/86)
59   KENDALL-JACKSON Chardonnay California Vintner's Reserve 1984 $7 (4/16/86)
58   SPRING MOUNTAIN Chardonnay Napa Valley 1984 $15 (12/31/86)
57   OLSON Chardonnay Mendocino County 1984 $9 (4/16/86)
57   RUTHERFORD HILL Chardonnay Napa Valley Partners Chardonnay 1984 $7 (4/16/86)
55   PARDUCCI Chardonnay Mendocino County 1984 $6 (4/16/86)
54   LIBERTY SCHOOL Chardonnay California Lot 5 1984 $6 (10/16/85)

1983

96   GRGICH HILLS Chardonnay Napa Valley 1983 Rel: $17 Cur: $33 (10/01/85) SS
95   SONOMA-CUTRER Chardonnay Russian River Valley Russian River Ranches 1983 Rel: $10.50 Cur: $25 (11/16/85) SS
94   CLOS DU BOIS Chardonnay Alexander Valley Calcaire Vineyard 1983 Rel: $12 Cur: $30 (10/16/85)
94   FLORA SPRINGS Chardonnay Napa Valley Barrel Fermented 1983 Rel: $18 Cur: $28 (CH-1/90)
94   PINE RIDGE Chardonnay Napa Valley Stags Leap District 1983 Rel: $16 Cur: $25 (12/16/85) SS
94   RAYMOND Chardonnay Napa Valley 1983 Rel: $12 Cur: $12 (11/01/85)
93   MANZANITA Chardonnay Napa Valley 1983 $12.50 (1/01/86) SS
93   MONTICELLO Chardonnay Napa Valley Jefferson Ranch 1983 Rel: $10 Cur: $20 (CH-2/90)
92   CLOS DU BOIS Chardonnay Dry Creek Valley Flintwood Vineyard 1983 Rel: $10.50 Cur: $37 (7/01/85) SS
92   FAR NIENTE Chardonnay Napa Valley 1983 Rel: $22 Cur: $38 (4/01/85) SS
92   GRGICH HILLS Chardonnay Napa Valley 1983 Rel: $17 Cur: $33 (CH-3/90)
92   TREFETHEN Chardonnay Napa Valley 1983 Rel: $13.75 Cur: $35 (12/16/85)
91   BELVEDERE Chardonnay Carneros Winery Lake 1983 $12 (6/01/85)
91   CLOS DU BOIS Chardonnay Alexander Valley Calcaire Vineyard 1983 Rel: $12 Cur: $30 (CH-2/90)
91   MAYACAMAS Chardonnay Napa Valley 1983 Rel: $16 Cur: $25 (3/15/87)
91   SIMI Chardonnay Sonoma County Reserve 1983 Rel: $22 Cur: $32 (8/31/87)
90   CHALONE Chardonnay Chalone 1983 Rel: $18 Cur: $60 (CH-1/90)
90   CHAPPELLET Chardonnay Napa Valley 1983 Rel: $12 Cur: $18 (4/16/85) (JG)
90   CHATEAU ST. JEAN Chardonnay Alexander Valley Robert Young Vineyards 1983 Rel: $18 Cur: $33 (9/01/85)
90   DE LOACH Chardonnay Russian River Valley 1983 Rel: $12 Cur: $22 (10/16/84)
90   HANZELL Chardonnay Sonoma Valley 1983 Rel: $20 Cur: $47 (4/16/85) (JG)
90   ROBERT MONDAVI Chardonnay Napa Valley 1983 Rel: $14 Cur: $17 (8/01/85)
90   SILVERADO Chardonnay Napa Valley 1983 Rel: $11 Cur: $20 (7/16/85)
89   BERINGER Chardonnay Napa Valley Private Reserve 1983 Rel: $15 Cur: $24 (4/15/87)
89   CHATEAU ST. JEAN Chardonnay Alexander Valley Belle Terre Vineyards 1983 Rel: $16.75 Cur: $30 (CH-3/90)
89   ESTANCIA Chardonnay Alexander Valley 1983 $7 (4/16/86)
89   FAR NIENTE Chardonnay Napa Valley Estate 1983 Rel: $22 Cur: $38 (CH-2/90)
89   NEWTON Chardonnay Napa Valley 1983 Rel: $12 Cur: $19 (CH-5/90)
89   ST. FRANCIS Chardonnay Sonoma Valley 1983 $10.75 (12/01/84)
88   CHATEAU ST. JEAN Chardonnay Alexander Valley Robert Young Vineyards 1983 Rel: $18 Cur: $33 (CH-3/90)
88   MATANZAS CREEK Chardonnay Sonoma County 1983 Rel: $15 Cur: $28 (9/16/85)
88   ROBERT MONDAVI Chardonnay Napa Valley Reserve 1983 Rel: $20 Cur: $25 (CH-3/90)
88   PINE RIDGE Chardonnay Napa Valley Oak Knoll Cuvée 1983 Rel: $13 Cur: $18 (CH-4/90)
88   SANFORD Chardonnay Central Coast 1983 Rel: $12 Cur: $15 (CH-2/90)
88   SIMI Chardonnay Sonoma County Reserve 1983 Rel: $22 Cur: $32 (CH-4/90)
87   ACACIA Chardonnay Carneros Napa Valley Winery Lake Vineyard 1983 Rel: $18 Cur: $25 (CH-1/90)
87   ALEXANDER VALLEY Chardonnay Alexander Valley 1983 $10 (4/01/85)
87   S. ANDERSON Chardonnay Napa Valley Stags Leap District Proprietor's Selection 1983 Rel: $16 Cur: $40 (CH-3/90)
87   CHALONE Chardonnay Chalone Reserve 1983 Rel: $25 Cur: $49 (CH-5/90)

87   CHATEAU ST. JEAN Chardonnay Alexander Valley Jimtown Ranch 1983 Rel: $16 Cur: $20 (CH-7/90)
87   DRY CREEK Chardonnay Sonoma County 1983 $10 (2/16/85)
87   FAR NIENTE Chardonnay Napa Valley 1983 Rel: $22 Cur: $38 (CH-2/90)
87   FISHER Chardonnay Napa-Sonoma Counties 1983 Rel: $14 Cur: $18 (7/01/85)
87   FRANCISCAN Chardonnay Alexander Valley 1983 $10.50 (2/01/85)
87   MONTICELLO Chardonnay Napa Valley Barrel Fermented 1983 Rel: $12.50 Cur: $20 (12/01/85)
87   ROMBAUER Chardonnay Napa Valley 1983 Rel: $14.50 Cur: $25 (CH-7/90)
87   ROMBAUER Chardonnay Napa Valley 1983 Rel: $14.50 Cur: $25 (6/16/85)
87   SEQUOIA GROVE Chardonnay Napa Valley Estate 1983 Rel: $12 Cur: $12 (CH-5/90)
87   SIMI Chardonnay Mendocino-Sonoma Counties 1983 $12 (10/01/85)
86   S. ANDERSON Chardonnay Napa Valley Stags Leap District 1983 $12.50 (CH-3/90)
86   JEAN CLAUDE BOISSET Chardonnay Napa Valley 1983 $9.50 (4/16/86)
86   BURGESS Chardonnay Napa Valley Vintage Reserve 1983 Rel: $12 Cur: $20 (6/16/85)
86   CHATEAU ST. JEAN Chardonnay Alexander Valley Jimtown Ranch 1983 Rel: $16 Cur: $20 (5/01/85)
86   HOP KILN Chardonnay Alexander Valley Tenth Anniversary Reserve 1983 $10 (10/01/85)
86   KENDALL-JACKSON Chardonnay California Proprietor's Reserve 1983 $13.50 (8/01/85)
86   MAYACAMAS Chardonnay Napa Valley 1983 Rel: $16 Cur: $25 (CH-1/90)
86   PINE RIDGE Chardonnay Napa Valley Stags Leap District 1983 Rel: $16 Cur: $25 (CH-4/90)
86   SONOMA-CUTRER Chardonnay Russian River Valley Cutrer Vineyard 1983 Rel: $13.75 Cur: $25 (CH-3/90)
86   SONOMA-CUTRER Chardonnay Sonoma Valley Les Pierres 1983 Rel: $15.50 Cur: $50 (CH-3/90)
86   STERLING Chardonnay Napa Valley 1983 Rel: $14 Cur: $14 (10/01/85)
86   STERLING Chardonnay Napa Valley Diamond Mountain Ranch 1983 Rel: $15 Cur: $18 (CH-4/90)
86   STONEGATE Chardonnay Napa Valley Spaulding Vineyard 1983 $14 (2/15/87)
85   ACACIA Chardonnay Napa Valley 1983 Rel: $12.50 Cur: $18 (10/16/84)
85   CHATEAU MONTELENA Chardonnay Alexander Valley 1983 Rel: $14 Cur: $32 (9/16/85)
85   CHATEAU MONTELENA Chardonnay Napa Valley 1983 Rel: $16 Cur: $32 (CH-2/90)
85   CHATEAU ST. JEAN Chardonnay Sonoma Valley McCrea Vineyards 1983 Rel: $15.25 Cur: $18 (CH-7/90)
85   CONGRESS SPRINGS Chardonnay Santa Clara County Barrel Fermented 1983 Rel: $10 Cur: $25 (CH-4/90)
85   DEHLINGER Chardonnay Russian River Valley 1983 Rel: $10 Cur: $15 (CH-4/90)
85   DOMAINE SAN MARTIN Chardonnay Central Coast 1983 $7 (8/01/85)
85   FREEMARK ABBEY Chardonnay Napa Valley 1983 Rel: $14 Cur: $20 (CH-2/90)
85   FREEMARK ABBEY Chardonnay Napa Valley 1983 Rel: $14 Cur: $20 (4/01/86)
85   WILLIAM HILL Chardonnay Napa Valley Reserve 1983 Rel: $22 Cur: $28 (CH-3/90)
85   KENWOOD Chardonnay Sonoma Valley Yulupa Vineyard 1983 Rel: $11 Cur: $18 (CH-7/90)
85   MATANZAS CREEK Chardonnay Sonoma County 1983 Rel: $15 Cur: $28 (CH-2/90)
85   SONOMA-CUTRER Chardonnay Russian River Valley Russian River Ranches 1983 Rel: $10.50 Cur: $25 (CH-3/90)
85   STONY HILL Chardonnay Napa Valley 1983 Rel: $13 Cur: $78 (CH-5/90)
85   VICHON Chardonnay Napa Valley 1983 Rel: $15 Cur: $18 (12/16/84)
84   ACACIA Chardonnay Carneros Napa Valley 1983 Rel: $12 Cur: $19 (12/01/84)
84   ACACIA Chardonnay Carneros Napa Valley Winery Lake Vineyard 1983 Rel: $18 Cur: $25 (10/16/84)
84   BOUCHAINE Chardonnay Carneros 1983 Rel: $14 Cur: $25 (9/01/85)
84   BUENA VISTA Chardonnay Carneros Private Reserve 1983 Rel: $14.50 Cur: $18 (CH-3/90)
84   CHATEAU MONTELENA Chardonnay Alexander Valley 1983 Rel: $14 Cur: $32 (CH-2/90)
84   CHATEAU ST. JEAN Chardonnay Alexander Valley Belle Terre Vineyards 1983 Rel: $16.75 Cur: $30 (6/16/85)
84   HANZELL Chardonnay Sonoma Valley 1983 Rel: $20 Cur: $47 (CH-1/90)
84   MOUNT EDEN Chardonnay Santa Cruz Mountains 1983 Rel: $20 Cur: $35 (CH-3/90)
84   PINE RIDGE Chardonnay Napa Valley Oak Knoll Cuvée 1983 Rel: $13 Cur: $18 (12/16/84)
84   CHARLES SHAW Chardonnay Napa Valley 1983 Rel: $12 Cur: $16 (CH-5/90)
84   SILVERADO Chardonnay Napa Valley 1983 Rel: $11 Cur: $20 (CH-3/90)
84   STEPHEN ZELLERBACH Chardonnay Alexander Valley 1983 $9.95 (1/01/85)
83   ACACIA Chardonnay Carneros Napa Valley Marina Vineyard 1983 Rel: $16 Cur: $23 (11/01/84)
83   CALERA Chardonnay Santa Barbara County Los Alamos Vineyard 1983 $10.75 (2/01/85)
83   CONN CREEK Chardonnay Napa Valley Barrel Select 1983 $14 (6/30/87)
83   DE LOACH Chardonnay Russian River Valley 1983 Rel: $12 Cur: $22 (CH-2/90)
83   GUNDLACH BUNDSCHU Chardonnay Sonoma Valley 1983 $9.75 (5/01/85)
83   HACIENDA Chardonnay Sonoma County Clair de Lune 1983 Rel: $10 Cur: $22 (CH-4/90)
82   BERINGER Chardonnay Napa Valley 1983 $10 (9/01/85)
82   CHATEAU MONTELENA Chardonnay Napa Valley 1983 Rel: $16 Cur: $32 (11/01/85)
82   CLOS DU VAL Chardonnay Napa Valley 1983 $11.50 (CH-6/90)
82   FISHER Chardonnay Napa-Sonoma Counties 1983 Rel: $14 Cur: $18 (CH-6/90)
82   FRANCISCAN Chardonnay Napa Valley Oakville Estate Reserve 1983 Rel: $12 Cur: $12 (CH-4/90)
82   WILLIAM HILL Chardonnay Napa Valley Reserve 1983 Rel: $22 Cur: $28 (3/31/87)
82   INGLENOOK Chardonnay Napa Valley Reserve 1983 Rel: $16 Cur: $19 (CH-4/90)
82   RAYMOND Chardonnay California Selection 1983 $8.50 (12/01/84)
82   WILLIAM WHEELER Chardonnay Sonoma County 1983 $11 (6/01/85)
81   HACIENDA Chardonnay Sonoma Valley Clair de Lune 1983 Rel: $10 Cur: $22 (3/16/86)
81   MARKHAM Chardonnay Napa Valley Estate 1983 Rel: $11.50 Cur: $17 (CH-2/90)
80   ACACIA Chardonnay Napa Valley 1983 Rel: $12.50 Cur: $18 (CH-1/90)
80   CARNEROS CREEK Chardonnay Napa Valley 1983 $11 (9/01/85)
80   GLEN ELLEN Chardonnay Sonoma Valley 1983 $10 (2/01/85)
80   LANDMARK Chardonnay Sonoma County 1983 $9 (1/01/86)
80   LEEWARD Chardonnay Edna Valley MacGregor Vineyard 1983 $14 (11/01/84)
80   MONTICELLO Chardonnay Napa Valley Barrel Fermented 1983 Rel: $12.50 Cur: $20 (CH-2/90)
80   MORGAN Chardonnay Monterey County 1983 Rel: $12.50 Cur: $23 (CH-5/90)
80   QUAIL RIDGE Chardonnay Napa Valley 1983 $14 (9/01/85)
80   SAINTSBURY Chardonnay Carneros 1983 Rel: $11 Cur: $20 (CH-2/90)
80   SAINTSBURY Chardonnay Carneros 1983 Rel: $11 Cur: $20 (11/30/87) (JL)
80   SHAFER Chardonnay Napa Valley 1983 $12 (9/01/85)
80   STERLING Chardonnay Napa Valley Diamond Mountain Ranch 1983 Rel: $15 Cur: $18 (12/15/86)
80   STRATFORD Chardonnay California 1983 $8.50 (11/01/84)
79   ACACIA Chardonnay Carneros Napa Valley Marina Vineyard 1983 Rel: $16 Cur: $23 (CH-1/90)
79   CHALK HILL Chardonnay Sonoma County 1983 $10 (6/01/85)
79   CHAPPELLET Chardonnay Napa Valley 1983 Rel: $12 Cur: $18 (CH-3/90)
79   CLOS DU VAL Chardonnay California 1983 $11.50 (2/16/85)

UNITED STATES
CALIFORNIA/*CHARDONNAY*

79 INGLENOOK Chardonnay Napa Valley 1983 $9.50 (10/01/84)
79 ROBERT PECOTA Chardonnay Alexander Valley Canepa Vineyard 1983 Rel: $14 Cur: $18 (CH-4/90)
78 CARTLIDGE & BROWNE Chardonnay Napa Valley 1983 $11.50 (2/16/85)
78 CORBETT CANYON Chardonnay Central Coast 1983 $8 (11/01/84)
78 EHLERS LANE Chardonnay Napa Valley 1983 $14 (7/01/85)
78 FISHER Chardonnay Sonoma County Whitney's Vineyard 1983 Rel: $20 Cur: $30 (CH-2/90)
78 FOPPIANO Chardonnay Sonoma County 1983 $10 (10/01/85)
78 LEEWARD Chardonnay Monterey County Ventana Vineyards 1983 $8 (10/16/84)
78 RODNEY STRONG Chardonnay Sonoma County 1983 $8 (11/01/84)
77 BEAULIEU Chardonnay Napa Valley Beaufort 1983 Rel: $10.50 Cur: $11 (10/01/85)
77 BOUCHAINE Chardonnay Carneros 1983 Rel: $14 Cur: $25 (CH-2/90)
77 FLORA SPRINGS Chardonnay Napa Valley 1983 $13 (10/01/85)
77 GIRARD Chardonnay Napa Valley 1983 Rel: $12.50 Cur: $22 (12/16/85)
77 RUTHERFORD HILL Chardonnay Napa Valley Jaeger Vineyards 1983 $10.75 (5/16/85)
77 TREFETHEN Chardonnay Napa Valley 1983 Rel: $13.75 Cur: $35 (CH-3/90)
76 BERINGER Chardonnay Napa Valley Private Reserve 1983 Rel: $15 Cur: $24 (CH-4/90)
76 CHALK HILL Chardonnay Napa Valley 1983 $7 (10/01/84)
76 EDNA VALLEY Chardonnay Edna Valley 1983 Rel: $12.50 Cur: $20 (CH-3/90)
76 FOLIE A DEUX Chardonnay Napa Valley 1983 Rel: $12 Cur: $12 (9/16/85)
76 GIRARD Chardonnay Napa Valley 1983 Rel: $12.50 Cur: $22 (CH-3/90)
76 GUNDLACH BUNDSCHU Chardonnay Sonoma Valley 1983 $9.75 (4/16/86)
76 IRON HORSE Chardonnay Sonoma County Green Valley 1983 $12 (11/16/85)
76 ST. CLEMENT Chardonnay Napa Valley 1983 Rel: $14.50 Cur: $17 (CH-3/90)
75 BOUCHAINE Chardonnay Carneros 1983 Rel: $14 Cur: $25 (CH-2/90)
75 J. CAREY Chardonnay Santa Ynez Valley Adobe Canyon Vineyard 1983 $12 (6/16/84)
75 WILLIAM HILL Chardonnay Napa Valley Reserve 1983 Rel: $22 Cur: $28 (7/31/87)
75 J. LOHR Chardonnay Monterey County Greenfield Vineyards 1983 $9 (7/01/85)
75 PAT PAULSEN Chardonnay Sonoma County 1983 $11 (2/16/85)
75 VILLA MT. EDEN Chardonnay Napa Valley 1983 $10 (4/16/85)
74 BEAULIEU Chardonnay Carneros Napa Valley Los Carneros Reserve 1983 Rel: $10 Cur: $15 (CH-4/90)
74 CONGRESS SPRINGS Chardonnay Santa Cruz Mountains Private Reserve 1983 Rel: $15 Cur: $28 (CH-4/90)
74 GUNDLACH BUNDSCHU Chardonnay Sonoma Valley Sangiacomo Ranch Special Selection 1983 $12 (12/01/85)
74 KEENAN Chardonnay Napa Valley 1983 $12.50 (9/16/85)
74 MIRASSOU Chardonnay Monterey County Harvest Reserve 1983 $11 (1/01/85)
74 MONTICELLO Chardonnay Napa Valley Jefferson Ranch 1983 Rel: $10 Cur: $20 (12/16/85)
74 ZD Chardonnay California 1983 Rel: $14 Cur: $25 (CH-3/90)
73 BELVEDERE Chardonnay Sonoma County Bacigalupi 1983 $12 (11/16/85)
73 RAYMOND Chardonnay Napa Valley Private Reserve 1983 Rel: $16 Cur: $16 (9/15/86)
73 RODNEY STRONG Chardonnay Sonoma County Chalk Hill Vineyard 1983 $10 (1/31/87)
71 CHATEAU ST. JEAN Chardonnay Sonoma Valley McCrea Vineyards 1983 Rel: $15.25 Cur: $18 (1/01/86)
71 MICHTOM Chardonnay Alexander Valley 1983 $8 (10/16/85)
71 SMITH-MADRONE Chardonnay Napa Valley 1983 Rel: $12 Cur: $15 (CH-5/90)
71 VICHON Chardonnay Napa Valley 1983 Rel: $15 Cur: $18 (CH-3/90)
70 CHATEAU ST. JEAN Chardonnay Sonoma Valley St. Jean Vineyards 1983 Rel: $14.75 Cur: $15 (3/16/86)
70 KEENAN Chardonnay Napa Valley Estate 1983 $12.50 (8/31/86)
70 ROBERT PEPI Chardonnay Napa Valley 1983 $11 (3/01/86)
69 DAVID BRUCE Chardonnay Santa Cruz Mountains 1983 $18 (9/30/86)
69 BURGESS Chardonnay Napa Valley Vintage Reserve 1983 Rel: $12 Cur: $20 (CH-12/89)
69 CLOS DU BOIS Chardonnay Dry Creek Valley Flintwood Vineyard 1983 Rel: $10.50 Cur: $37 (CH-5/90)
68 MATANZAS CREEK Chardonnay Sonoma Valley Estate 1983 Rel: $18 Cur: $18 (CH-2/90)
68 JOSEPH PHELPS Chardonnay Napa Valley 1983 $12.75 (12/15/86)
67 JORDAN Chardonnay Alexander Valley 1983 $16 (7/16/86)
66 JEKEL Chardonnay Arroyo Seco 1983 $10 (4/01/86)
66 KENDALL-JACKSON Chardonnay California Royale 1983 $11 (11/16/85)
66 J. PEDRONCELLI Chardonnay Sonoma County 1983 $7.75 (6/01/85)
65 WENTE BROS. Chardonnay California 1983 $7.50 (4/01/86)
64 STAG'S LEAP WINE CELLARS Chardonnay Napa Valley 1983 Rel: $13.50 Cur: $17 (11/16/85)
63 FIRESTONE Chardonnay Santa Ynez Valley 1983 $10 (3/01/86)
62 CUVAISON Chardonnay Napa Valley 1983 Rel: $12 Cur: $17 (CH-4/90)
62 STAG'S LEAP WINE CELLARS Chardonnay Napa Valley 1983 Rel: $13.50 Cur: $17 (CH-3/90)
60 CAIN Chardonnay Napa Valley 1983 $10 (1/01/85)
58 BELVEDERE Chardonnay Monterey County Discovery Series 1983 $4.75 (2/01/85)
58 CUVAISON Chardonnay Napa Valley 1983 Rel: $12 Cur: $17 (4/01/86)
58 ZACA MESA Chardonnay Santa Barbara County 1983 $9.75 (4/16/86)
53 FRANCISCAN Chardonnay Napa Valley Oakville Vineyard 1983 $10 (7/01/86)

1982

96 SIMI Chardonnay Sonoma County Reserve 1982 Rel: $22 Cur: $60 (5/01/86) SS
95 CHALONE Chardonnay Chalone 1982 Rel: $18 Cur: $61 (CH-1/90)
94 SIMI Chardonnay Sonoma County Reserve 1982 Rel: $22 Cur: $60 (CH-4/90)
93 CHALONE Chardonnay Chalone Reserve 1982 Rel: $25 Cur: $48 (CH-5/90)
93 JEKEL Chardonnay Arroyo Seco Home Vineyard Private Reserve 1982 $14 (10/01/85)
92 CHATEAU MONTELENA Chardonnay Alexander Valley 1982 Rel: $14 Cur: $36 (CH-2/90)
92 CLOS DU BOIS Chardonnay Alexander Valley Calcaire Vineyard 1982 Rel: $11.25 Cur: $12 (7/01/84)
92 MATANZAS CREEK Chardonnay Sonoma County 1982 Rel: $15 Cur: $25 (7/16/84)
92 SONOMA-CUTRER Chardonnay Russian River Valley Russian River Ranches 1982 Rel: $10 Cur: $24 (10/16/84) SS
91 CHAPPELLET Chardonnay Napa Valley 1982 Rel: $12.50 Cur: $20 (4/16/85) (JG)
91 CHATEAU ST. JEAN Chardonnay Sonoma Valley St. Jean Vineyards 1982 Rel: $14 Cur: $14 (2/01/85)
91 FAR NIENTE Chardonnay Napa Valley Estate 1982 Rel: $18 Cur: $38 (CH-2/90)
90 BOUCHAINE Chardonnay Napa Valley 1982 Rel: $14.50 Cur: $15 (6/16/84) SS
90 CHATEAU MONTELENA Chardonnay Alexander Valley 1982 Rel: $14 Cur: $36 (5/01/84)
90 SIMI Chardonnay Sonoma County 1982 $11 (10/16/84)
89 DOMAINE LAURIER Chardonnay Sonoma County 1982 $13 (4/01/85)
89 HANZELL Chardonnay Sonoma Valley 1982 Rel: $19 Cur: $51 (CH-1/90)
89 HANZELL Chardonnay Sonoma Valley 1982 Rel: $19 Cur: $51 (4/16/85) (JG)
89 MARKHAM Chardonnay Napa Valley Estate 1982 Rel: $12 Cur: $17 (8/01/84)
89 MORGAN Chardonnay Monterey County 1982 Rel: $12 Cur: $28 (CH-5/90)
89 PINE RIDGE Chardonnay Napa Valley Oak Knoll Cuvée 1982 Rel: $13 Cur: $19 (3/16/84) SS
89 ST. ANDREW'S VINEYARD Chardonnay Napa Valley 1982 $12.50 (10/01/84)
88 CHATEAU MONTELENA Chardonnay Napa Valley 1982 Rel: $16 Cur: $32 (10/01/84)
88 CHATEAU ST. JEAN Chardonnay Alexander Valley Belle Terre Vineyards 1982 Rel: $15.50 Cur: $20 (4/16/84)
88 CHATEAU ST. JEAN Chardonnay Alexander Valley Robert Young Vineyards 1982 Rel: $18 Cur: $20 (7/01/84)
88 CHATEAU ST. JEAN Chardonnay Sonoma Valley McCrea Vineyards 1982 Rel: $13 Cur: $18 (CH-7/90)
88 JEKEL Chardonnay Arroyo Seco 1982 $10 (1/01/84)
88 MATANZAS CREEK Chardonnay Sonoma Valley Estate 1982 Rel: $18 Cur: $25 (CH-2/90)
88 MATANZAS CREEK Chardonnay Sonoma Valley Estate 1982 Rel: $18 Cur: $25 (7/16/84) SS
88 ROBERT MONDAVI Chardonnay Napa Valley Reserve 1982 Rel: $20 Cur: $25 (11/01/84)
88 SONOMA-CUTRER Chardonnay Sonoma Valley Les Pierres 1982 Rel: $15 Cur: $35 (CH-3/90)
87 BERINGER Chardonnay Napa Valley Private Reserve 1982 Rel: $15 Cur: $22 (11/01/84)
87 CONGRESS SPRINGS Chardonnay Santa Cruz Mountains Private Reserve 1982 Rel: $15 Cur: $28 (CH-4/90)
87 DRY CREEK Chardonnay Sonoma County 1982 $10 (1/01/84)
87 GRGICH HILLS Chardonnay Napa Valley 1982 Rel: $17 Cur: $44 (CH-3/90)
87 SONOMA-CUTRER Chardonnay Russian River Valley Cutrer Vineyard 1982 Rel: $13 Cur: $25 (CH-3/90)
87 SONOMA-CUTRER Chardonnay Russian River Valley Russian River Ranches 1982 Rel: $10 Cur: $24 (CH-3/90)
86 CHATEAU ST. JEAN Chardonnay Alexander Valley Belle Terre Vineyards 1982 Rel: $15.50 Cur: $20 (CH-3/90)
86 FAR NIENTE Chardonnay Napa Valley 1982 Rel: $18 Cur: $38 (CH-2/90)
86 WILLIAM HILL Chardonnay Napa Valley Reserve 1982 Rel: $24 Cur: $28 (CH-3/90)
86 WILLIAM HILL Chardonnay Napa Valley Reserve 1982 Rel: $24 Cur: $28 (7/31/87)
86 SAINTSBURY Chardonnay Sonoma County 1982 Rel: $11 Cur: $14 (11/30/87) (JL)
86 SEQUOIA GROVE Chardonnay Sonoma County 1982 $10.50 (11/01/84)
86 SMITH-MADRONE Chardonnay Napa Valley 1982 Rel: $12 Cur: $18 (CH-5/90)
85 ALEXANDER VALLEY Chardonnay Alexander Valley 1982 $10 (3/01/84)
85 CHAPPELLET Chardonnay Napa Valley 1982 Rel: $12.50 Cur: $20 (CH-3/90)
85 CHATEAU MONTELENA Chardonnay Napa Valley 1982 Rel: $16 Cur: $32 (CH-2/90)
85 CLOS DU BOIS Chardonnay Alexander Valley Barrel Fermented 1982 Rel: $9 Cur: $9 (4/16/84)
85 JORDAN Chardonnay Alexander Valley 1982 $15.75 (5/16/85)
85 MAYACAMAS Chardonnay Napa Valley 1982 Rel: $16 Cur: $30 (CH-1/90)
85 JOSEPH PHELPS Chardonnay Napa Valley 1982 $12.50 (4/16/85)
85 QUAIL RIDGE Chardonnay Napa Valley 1982 $14 (5/16/84)
85 SILVERADO Chardonnay Napa Valley 1982 Rel: $10 Cur: $20 (3/16/84)
85 STONY HILL Chardonnay Napa Valley 1982 Rel: $12 Cur: $66 (CH-5/90)
84 AHERN Chardonnay Edna Valley Paragon Vineyard 1982 $10 (2/15/84)
84 CHATEAU CHEVALIER Chardonnay California 1982 $12.50 (1/01/84)
84 FRANCISCAN Chardonnay Carneros Reserve 1982 Rel: $9.50 Cur: $17 (CH-4/90)
84 FRANCISCAN Chardonnay Napa Valley Estate Bottled 1982 $9.50 (8/01/85)
84 MANZANITA Chardonnay Napa Valley 1982 $14 (4/01/84)
84 MONTICELLO Chardonnay Napa Valley Barrel Fermented 1982 Rel: $14 Cur: $20 (CH-2/90)
84 QUAIL RIDGE Chardonnay Sonoma County 1982 $9 (3/16/84)
84 ROMBAUER Chardonnay Napa Valley 1982 Rel: $14.50 Cur: $25 (CH-6/90)
83 FRANCISCAN Chardonnay Alexander Valley 1982 $10 (4/16/84)
83 WILLIAM HILL Chardonnay Napa Valley Reserve 1982 Rel: $24 Cur: $28 (11/01/84)
83 LAMBERT BRIDGE Chardonnay Sonoma County 1982 $13.50 (12/16/84)
83 MARKHAM Chardonnay Napa Valley Estate 1982 Rel: $12 Cur: $17 (CH-2/90)
83 RAYMOND Chardonnay Napa Valley 1982 Rel: $13 Cur: $15 (5/16/84)
83 STONEGATE Chardonnay Napa Valley 1982 $10 (3/01/85)
82 BOUCHAINE Chardonnay Alexander Valley 1982 $14 (11/01/84)
82 GROTH Chardonnay Napa Valley 1982 $13 (4/16/84)
82 ROBERT MONDAVI Chardonnay Napa Valley 1982 Rel: $10 Cur: $10 (8/01/84)
82 MONTICELLO Chardonnay Napa Valley 1982 Rel: $13.50 Cur: $20 (CH-2/90)
82 NEWTON Chardonnay Napa Valley 1982 Rel: $16 Cur: $16 (9/01/84)
82 PINE RIDGE Chardonnay Napa Valley Stags Leap District Stag's Leap Cuvée 1982 Rel: $15 Cur: $27 (12/16/84)
82 PINE RIDGE Chardonnay Napa Valley Stags Leap District Stags Leap Vineyard 1982 Rel: $15 Cur: $27 (CH-4/90)
81 CONN CREEK Chardonnay Napa Valley 1982 $12.50 (11/01/85)
81 DOMAINE LAURIER Chardonnay Sonoma County 1982 $13 (7/01/84)
81 FISHER Chardonnay Sonoma County 1982 Rel: $14 Cur: $22 (CH-2/90)
81 GRGICH HILLS Chardonnay Napa Valley 1982 Rel: $17 Cur: $44 (10/01/84)
81 ROBERT MONDAVI Chardonnay Napa Valley Reserve 1982 Rel: $20 Cur: $25 (CH-3/90)
81 PERRET Chardonnay Carneros Napa Valley Perret Vineyard 1982 $14.50 (11/01/84)
80 ACACIA Chardonnay Napa Valley 1982 Rel: $12 Cur: $20 (CH-1/90)
80 BERINGER Chardonnay Napa Valley 1982 $9.75 (4/16/84)
80 FISHER Chardonnay Sonoma County 1982 Rel: $14 Cur: $22 (6/16/84)
80 HAYWOOD Chardonnay Sonoma Valley 1982 $10 (5/16/84)
80 MARK WEST Chardonnay Russian River Valley 1982 $10.50 (10/16/85)
80 STAG'S LEAP WINE CELLARS Chardonnay Napa Valley 1982 Rel: $13.50 Cur: $17 (4/16/84)
80 ZD Chardonnay California 1982 Rel: $14 Cur: $30 (10/01/84)
79 BOUCHAINE Chardonnay Alexander Valley 1982 Rel: $14 Cur: $14 (CH-2/90)
79 CLOS DU BOIS Chardonnay Dry Creek Valley Flintwood Vineyard 1982 Rel: $11.25 Cur: $12 (7/01/84)
79 CONGRESS SPRINGS Chardonnay Santa Clara County 1982 Rel: $10 Cur: $20 (CH-4/90)
79 CONN CREEK Chardonnay North Coast Château Maja 1982 $6.50 (3/01/84)
79 EBERLE Chardonnay Paso Robles 1982 $10 (4/16/85)
79 JOSEPH PHELPS Chardonnay Carneros Sangiacomo Vineyard 1982 $14 (4/01/84)
79 ST. ANDREW'S WINERY Chardonnay Napa Valley House 1982 $7 (10/16/84)

Key to Symbols

The scores reported here are the results of blind tastings conducted by our panel of senior editors. Wines that carry the initials below are results of individual tastings.

THE WINE SPECTATOR 100-POINT SCALE ***95-100***—Classic, a great wine; ***90-94***—Outstanding, superior character and style; ***80-89***—Good to very good, a wine with special qualities; ***70-79***—Average, drinkable wine that may have minor flaws; ***60-69***—Below average, drinkable but not recommended; ***50-59***—Poor, undrinkable, not recommended. "+"—With a score indicates a range; used primarily with barrel tastings to indicate a preliminary score.

SPECIAL DESIGNATIONS SS—Spectator Selection, CS—Cellar Selection, BB—Best Buy.

TASTER'S INITIALS (JG)—Jim Gordon, (HS)—Harvey Steiman, (JL)—James Laube, (JS)—James Suckling, (TM)—Thomas Matthews, (TR)—Terry Robards, (BT)—Barrel Tasting (these wines were tasted blind from barrel samples), (CA-date)—*California's Great Cabernets* by James Laube, (CH-date)—*California's Great Chardonnays* by James Laube, (VP-date)—*Vintage Port* by James Suckling.

DATE TASTED Dates in parentheses represent the issue in which the rating was published.

79 SHAFER Chardonnay Napa Valley 1982 $11 (10/01/84)
79 SONOMA-CUTRER Chardonnay Russian River Valley Cutrer Vineyard 1982 Rel: $13 Cur: $25 (12/01/84)
79 RODNEY STRONG Chardonnay Sonoma County Chalk Hill Vineyard 1982 $9.95 (7/01/84)
78 CLOS DU VAL Chardonnay California 1982 $11.50 (6/01/90)
78 FETZER Chardonnay California Special Reserve 1982 $10 (4/01/84)
78 FISHER Chardonnay Sonoma County Whitney's Vineyard 1982 Rel: $20 Cur: $25 (CH-6/90)
78 FOLIE A DEUX Chardonnay Napa Valley 1982 Rel: $12.50 Cur: $13 (CH-7/90)
78 HACIENDA Chardonnay Sonoma County Clair de Lune 1982 Rel: $9 Cur: $20 (CH-4/90)
78 LANDMARK Chardonnay Sonoma Valley 1982 $9 (5/01/84)
78 MATANZAS CREEK Chardonnay Sonoma County 1982 Rel: $15 Cur: $25 (CH-2/90)
78 PINE RIDGE Chardonnay Napa Valley Oak Knoll Cuvée 1982 Rel: $13 Cur: $19 (CH-4/90)
78 SEQUOIA GROVE Chardonnay Napa Valley Estate 1982 Rel: $12 Cur: $12 (11/01/84)
78 STERLING Chardonnay Napa Valley 1982 Rel: $14 Cur: $17 (11/01/84)
77 LAWRENCE J. BARGETTO Chardonnay California Cypress 1982 $8 (3/16/84)
77 HACIENDA Chardonnay Sonoma Valley Clair de Lune 1982 Rel: $9 Cur: $20 (6/16/84)
76 CHATEAU ST. JEAN Chardonnay Alexander Valley Robert Young Vineyards Reserve 1982 1.5L Rel: $45 Cur: $45 (7/01/86)
76 COSENTINO Chardonnay California The Sculptor 1982 $8 (2/15/84)
76 FOLIE A DEUX Chardonnay Napa Valley 1982 Rel: $12.50 Cur: $13 (3/01/84)
76 GIRARD Chardonnay Napa Valley 1982 Rel: $12.50 Cur: $21 (CH-3/90)
76 LANDMARK Chardonnay Alexander Valley Proprietor's Grown 1982 $10 (5/01/84)
76 MOUNT EDEN Chardonnay Santa Cruz Mountains 1982 Rel: $18 Cur: $43 (CH-3/90)
76 MOUNT EDEN Chardonnay Monterey County 1982 Rel: $12.50 Cur: $13 (4/01/84)
76 ZD Chardonnay California 1982 Rel: $14 Cur: $30 (CH-3/90)
75 BANDIERA Chardonnay Mendocino County 1982 $6 (2/15/84)
75 BURGESS Chardonnay Napa Valley Vintage Reserve 1982 Rel: $12 Cur: $12 (4/01/84)
75 CHATEAU ST. JEAN Chardonnay Alexander Valley Robert Young Vineyards 1982 Rel: $18 Cur: $20 (CH-3/90)
75 GEYSER PEAK Chardonnay Alexander Valley 1982 $6.50 (4/16/84)
75 MOUNTAIN VIEW Chardonnay Sonoma County 1982 $6 (4/16/84)
75 SAN MARTIN Chardonnay San Luis Obispo County 1982 $7.50 (3/01/84)
75 DAVID S. STARE Chardonnay Dry Creek Valley 1982 $15 (11/01/85)
75 STEPHEN ZELLERBACH Chardonnay Alexander Valley Warnecke Sonoma Vineyard 1982 $10 (4/16/84)
74 BERINGER Chardonnay Napa Valley Private Reserve 1982 Rel: $15 Cur: $22 (CH-4/90)
74 DE LOACH Chardonnay Russian River Valley 1982 Rel: $12 Cur: $20 (CH-2/90)
74 WHITEHALL LANE Chardonnay Napa Valley Cerro Vista Vineyard 1982 $12 (9/01/84)
73 CHATEAU DE LEU Chardonnay Solano County Green Valley 1982 $7 (5/16/84)
73 MOUNTAIN VIEW Chardonnay Napa Valley Special Selection 1982 $7.50 (4/01/84)
73 ST. CLEMENT Chardonnay Napa Valley 1982 Rel: $14.50 Cur: $20 (CH-3/90)
73 SILVERADO Chardonnay Napa Valley 1982 Rel: $10 Cur: $20 (CH-3/90)
73 STERLING Chardonnay Napa Valley Estate 1982 Rel: $14 Cur: $17 (CH-4/90)
73 TREFETHEN Chardonnay Napa Valley 1982 Rel: $13.50 Cur: $30 (CH-3/90)
72 S. ANDERSON Chardonnay Napa Valley Stags Leap District 1982 $12.50 (CH-3/90)
72 BEAULIEU Chardonnay Carneros Napa Valley Los Carneros Reserve 1982 Rel: $10 Cur: $16 (CH-4/90)
72 FREEMARK ABBEY Chardonnay Napa Valley 1982 Rel: $12.75 Cur: $18 (CH-2/90)
72 J FRITZ Chardonnay Sonoma County 1982 $9 (5/16/84)
72 ROBERT PEPI Chardonnay Napa Valley 1982 $11 (5/01/84)
72 SEQUOIA GROVE Chardonnay Napa Valley Estate 1982 Rel: $12 Cur: $12 (CH-5/90)
71 CARNEROS CREEK Chardonnay Napa Valley 1982 $12 (12/16/84)
71 FRANCISCAN Chardonnay Napa Valley 1982 $9.50 (4/16/86)
71 LOUIS M. MARTINI Chardonnay California 1982 $7 (3/16/84)
70 BUENA VISTA Chardonnay Carneros Private Reserve 1982 Rel: $16.50 Cur: $17 (3/16/86)
70 CAMBIASO Chardonnay Sonoma County 1982 $8 (4/01/84)
70 EDNA VALLEY Chardonnay Edna Valley 1982 Rel: $12 Cur: $32 (CH-3/90)
70 FLORA SPRINGS Chardonnay Napa Valley Barrel Fermented 1982 Rel: $15 Cur: $15 (CH-6/88)
70 MADDALENA Chardonnay San Luis Obispo County 1982 $6 (5/16/84)
70 STAG'S LEAP WINE CELLARS Chardonnay Napa Valley 1982 Rel: $13.50 Cur: $17 (CH-3/90)
70 STAG'S LEAP WINE CELLARS Chardonnay Napa Valley Mirage 1982 $11.50 (CH-3/90)
70 STONE CREEK Chardonnay Alexander Valley Special Selection 1982 $6 (2/15/84)
68 BURGESS Chardonnay Napa Valley Vintage Reserve 1982 Rel: $12 Cur: $12 (CH-12/89)
68 CUVAISON Chardonnay Napa Valley 1982 Rel: $12 Cur: $17 (5/16/84)
68 GEYSER PEAK Chardonnay Sonoma County Carneros 1982 $6.75 (12/16/84)
68 SANFORD Chardonnay Santa Maria Valley 1982 Rel: $12 Cur: $20 (CH-2/90)
66 EDMEADES Chardonnay Anderson Valley 1982 $10 (4/16/85)
66 JOSEPH PHELPS Chardonnay Carneros Schellville 1982 $14 (9/16/85)
66 VICHON Chardonnay Napa Valley 1982 Rel: $15 Cur: $20 (CH-3/90)
65 SAINTSBURY Chardonnay Sonoma County 1982 Rel: $11 Cur: $14 (CH-2/90)
63 MONT ST. JOHN Chardonnay Carneros Napa Valley 1982 $11.50 (5/16/84)
62 CASSAYRE-FORNI Chardonnay Alexander Valley 1982 $10.75 (2/15/84)
61 CUVAISON Chardonnay Napa Valley 1982 Rel: $12 Cur: $17 (CH-4/90)
60 BELVEDERE Chardonnay Carneros Winery Lake 1982 $12 (8/01/84)
59 FLORA SPRINGS Chardonnay Napa Valley 1982 $12 (5/16/84)
59 JEKEL Chardonnay Arroyo Seco Home Vineyard 1982 $10 (10/01/85)
57 RUTHERFORD RANCH Chardonnay Napa Valley 1982 $12 (5/16/84)
55 DEHLINGER Chardonnay Russian River Valley 1982 Rel: $10 Cur: $10 (9/01/85)
55 FREEMARK ABBEY Chardonnay Napa Valley 1982 Rel: $12.75 Cur: $18 (3/01/85)
54 SAGE CREEK Chardonnay Napa Valley 1982 $9 (4/16/84)
53 STONEGATE Chardonnay Napa Valley Spaulding Vineyard 1982 $14 (12/01/85)

1981

94 EDNA VALLEY Chardonnay Edna Valley 1981 Rel: $12 Cur: $25 (CH-3/90)
94 ROBERT MONDAVI Chardonnay Napa Valley 1981 Rel: $15 Cur: $15 (6/01/86)
94 SONOMA-CUTRER Chardonnay Sonoma Valley Les Pierres 1981 Rel: $14.50 Cur: $53 (CH-3/90)
93 CHALONE Chardonnay Chalone 1981 Rel: $17 Cur: $68 (CH-4/90)
93 FETZER Chardonnay Mendocino Barrel Select 1981 $8.50 (6/01/86)
92 BERINGER Chardonnay Napa Valley Private Reserve 1981 Rel: $15 Cur: $28 (6/01/86)
92 CHATEAU ST. JEAN Chardonnay Alexander Valley Robert Young Vineyards 1981 Rel: $18 Cur: $60 (4/16/84)
91 CHATEAU MONTELENA Chardonnay Alexander Valley 1981 Rel: $14 Cur: $36 (CH-2/90)
91 SIMI Chardonnay Sonoma County Reserve 1981 Rel: $20 Cur: $40 (CH-4/90)
91 SONOMA-CUTRER Chardonnay Russian River Valley Cutrer Vineyard 1981 Rel: $12.50 Cur: $30 (CH-3/90)
90 GIRARD Chardonnay Napa Valley 1981 Rel: $12.50 Cur: $35 (CH-3/90)
90 ROBERT MONDAVI Chardonnay Napa Valley Reserve 1981 Rel: $20 Cur: $24 (6/01/86)
90 MOUNTAIN HOUSE Chardonnay Sonoma County 1981 $11 (2/15/84)
90 SAINTSBURY Chardonnay Sonoma County 1981 Rel: $10 Cur: $25 (11/30/87) (JL)
90 SIMI Chardonnay Sonoma County 1981 $20 (11/01/85)
89 CHATEAU MONTELENA Chardonnay Alexander Valley 1981 Rel: $14 Cur: $36 (4/16/84)
89 FLORA SPRINGS Chardonnay Napa Valley Special Selection 1981 Rel: $12 Cur: $25 (CH-1/90)
89 MOUNT EDEN Chardonnay Santa Cruz Mountains 1981 Rel: $18 Cur: $60 (CH-3/90)
89 RUTHERFORD HILL Chardonnay Napa Valley Jaeger Vineyards Cellar Reserve 1981 $14 (3/16/86)
89 SIMI Chardonnay Sonoma County Reserve 1981 Rel: $20 Cur: $40 (6/01/86)
89 SONOMA-CUTRER Chardonnay Russian River Valley Estate Bottled 1981 Rel: $9.35 Cur: $40 (3/01/84)
88 CHATEAU MONTELENA Chardonnay Napa Valley 1981 Rel: $16 Cur: $32 (CH-2/90)
88 CHATEAU ST. JEAN Chardonnay Alexander Valley Belle Terre Vineyards 1981 Rel: $15 Cur: $18 (4/16/84)
88 CHATEAU ST. JEAN Chardonnay Dry Creek Valley Frank Johnson Vineyards 1981 Rel: $14.75 Cur: $15 (1/01/84)
88 FAR NIENTE Chardonnay Napa Valley 1981 Rel: $16.50 Cur: $40 (CH-2/90)
88 FETZER Chardonnay California Special Reserve 1981 $11 (6/01/86)
88 FISHER Chardonnay Sonoma County 1981 Rel: $14 Cur: $25 (CH-2/90)
88 GRGICH HILLS Chardonnay Napa Valley 1981 Rel: $17 Cur: $45 (CH-3/90)
88 SEQUOIA GROVE Chardonnay Napa Valley Estate 1981 Rel: $12 Cur: $12 (CH-7/90)
87 CHATEAU ST. JEAN Chardonnay Alexander Valley Jimtown Ranch 1981 Rel: $14.75 Cur: $22 (CH-3/90)
87 SAINTSBURY Chardonnay Sonoma County 1981 Rel: $10 Cur: $25 (CH-2/90)
87 ZD Chardonnay California 1981 Rel: $13 Cur: $28 (CH-3/90)
86 BERINGER Chardonnay Napa Valley Private Reserve 1981 Rel: $15 Cur: $28 (CH-4/90)
86 CHALONE Chardonnay Chalone Reserve 1981 Rel: $20 Cur: $100 (CH-5/90)
86 CHATEAU ST. JEAN Chardonnay Alexander Valley Robert Young Vineyards 1981 Rel: $18 Cur: $60 (CH-3/90)
86 DE MOOR Chardonnay Alexander Valley Napa Cellars Black Mountain Vineyard 1981 $11 (4/16/84)
86 HANZELL Chardonnay Sonoma Valley 1981 Rel: $18 Cur: $53 (CH-1/90)
86 JEKEL Chardonnay Arroyo Seco 1981 $11 (6/01/86)
86 ROBERT MONDAVI Chardonnay Napa Valley Reserve 1981 Rel: $20 Cur: $24 (CH-3/90)
86 PINE RIDGE Chardonnay Napa Valley Stags Leap District 1981 Rel: $15 Cur: $31 (CH-4/90)
86 SIMI Chardonnay Mendocino County 1981 $11 (6/01/86)
86 STONY HILL Chardonnay Napa Valley 1981 Rel: $12 Cur: $76 (CH-5/90)
85 BERINGER Chardonnay Napa Valley 1981 $10 (6/01/86)
85 FISHER Chardonnay Sonoma County Whitney's Vineyard 1981 Rel: $20 Cur: $25 (CH-2/90)
85 MATANZAS CREEK Chardonnay Sonoma County 1981 Rel: $15 Cur: $28 (CH-2/90)
84 JEKEL Chardonnay Arroyo Seco Home Vineyard Private Reserve 1981 $15 (6/01/86)
84 PINE RIDGE Chardonnay Napa Valley Oak Knoll Cuvée 1981 Rel: $13 Cur: $20 (CH-4/90)
83 CHATEAU ST. JEAN Chardonnay Alexander Valley Belle Terre Vineyards 1981 Rel: $15 Cur: $18 (CH-3/90)
83 TREFETHEN Chardonnay Napa Valley 1981 Rel: $13 Cur: $30 (CH-3/90)
82 SONOMA-CUTRER Chardonnay Russian River Valley Russian River Ranches 1981 Rel: $9.35 Cur: $40 (CH-3/90)
81 CARNEROS CREEK Chardonnay Napa Valley 1981 $10 (1/01/84)
81 CHATEAU ST. JEAN Chardonnay Sonoma Valley Hunter Farms 1981 Rel: $14.75 Cur: $19 (CH-3/90)
81 FREEMARK ABBEY Chardonnay Napa Valley 1981 Rel: $13.50 Cur: $20 (CH-2/90)
81 SMITH-MADRONE Chardonnay Napa Valley 1981 Rel: $12 Cur: $18 (CH-5/90)
80 S. ANDERSON Chardonnay Napa Valley Stags Leap District 1981 $12.50 (CH-3/90)
80 CHAPPELLET Chardonnay Napa Valley 1981 Rel: $14 Cur: $22 (CH-3/90)
80 CHAPPELLET Chardonnay Napa Valley 1981 Rel: $14 Cur: $22 (4/16/85) (JG)
80 J FRITZ Chardonnay Alexander Valley Gauer Ranch 1981 $10 (4/16/84)
80 SONOMA-CUTRER Chardonnay Russian River Valley Cutrer Vineyard 1981 Rel: $12.50 Cur: $30 (3/01/84)
79 CARNEROS CREEK Chardonnay Sonoma County 1981 $10 (1/01/84)
79 STAG'S LEAP WINE CELLARS Chardonnay Napa Valley 1981 Rel: $13.50 Cur: $60 (CH-3/90)
78 CLOS DU VAL Chardonnay Napa Valley 1981 $12.50 (CH-6/90)
78 HANZELL Chardonnay Sonoma Valley 1981 Rel: $18 Cur: $53 (4/16/85) (JG)
78 LAKESPRING Chardonnay Alexander Valley 1981 $10 (4/16/84)
78 MAYACAMAS Chardonnay Napa Valley 1981 Rel: $16 Cur: $35 (CH-1/90)
77 JORDAN Chardonnay Alexander Valley 1981 $15.75 (4/16/84)
77 PAUL MASSON Chardonnay Monterey 1981 $8.50 (4/16/84)
76 MARK WEST Chardonnay Alexander Valley Wasson Vineyard 1981 $10 (4/16/84)
76 MONTICELLO Chardonnay Napa Valley 1981 Rel: $12 Cur: $20 (CH-2/90)
76 VICHON Chardonnay Napa Valley 1981 Rel: $15 Cur: $25 (CH-3/90)
75 CHATEAU ST. JEAN Chardonnay Sonoma Valley McCrea Vineyards 1981 Rel: $15 Cur: $18 (CH-3/90)
75 CUVAISON Chardonnay Napa Valley 1981 Rel: $12 Cur: $18 (CH-4/90)
75 ROBERT PECOTA Chardonnay Alexander Valley Canepa Vineyard 1981 Rel: $12 Cur: $20 (CH-4/90)
75 ST. CLEMENT Chardonnay Napa Valley 1981 Rel: $13.50 Cur: $25 (CH-3/90)
74 BURGESS Chardonnay Napa Valley 1981 Rel: $11 Cur: $16 (CH-12/89)
74 HACIENDA Chardonnay Sonoma County Clair de Lune 1981 Rel: $12 Cur: $20 (CH-4/90)
74 SANFORD Chardonnay Santa Maria Valley 1981 Rel: $11 Cur: $20 (CH-2/90)
72 DE LOACH Chardonnay Russian River Valley 1981 Rel: $10 Cur: $18 (CH-2/90)
71 STERLING Chardonnay Napa Valley Estate 1981 Rel: $14 Cur: $17 (CH-4/90)
70 BEAULIEU Chardonnay Carneros Napa Valley Los Carneros Reserve 1981 Rel: $10 Cur: $18 (CH-4/90)
70 CLOS DU BOIS Chardonnay Alexander Valley Proprietor's Reserve 1981 Rel: $15 Cur: $22 (CH-5/90)
70 RAYMOND Chardonnay Napa Valley Private Reserve 1981 Rel: $15 Cur: $25 (CH-6/90)
70 SILVERADO Chardonnay Napa Valley 1981 Rel: $10 Cur: $20 (CH-3/90)
64 SHAFER Chardonnay Napa Valley 1981 $11 (3/16/84)

1980

94 CHALONE Chardonnay Chalone Reserve 1980 Rel: $18 Cur: $125 (CH-5/90)
94 SIMI Chardonnay Sonoma County Reserve 1980 Rel: $20 Cur: $40 (CH-4/90)
93 FAR NIENTE Chardonnay Napa Valley 1980 Rel: $16.50 Cur: $45 (CH-2/90)
93 SIMI Chardonnay Mendocino County Reserve 1980 Rel: $20 Cur: $40 (4/16/84)
92 CHALONE Chardonnay Chalone 1980 Rel: $17 Cur: $58 (CH-1/90)
92 CLOS DU BOIS Chardonnay Alexander Valley Barrel Fermented 1980 Rel: $15 Cur: $15 (4/16/84)
92 FISHER Chardonnay Sonoma County Whitney's Vineyard 1980 Rel: $20 Cur: $30 (CH-2/90)
90 HANZELL Chardonnay Sonoma Valley 1980 Rel: $17 Cur: $60 (CH-1/90)
89 ROBERT PECOTA Chardonnay Alexander Valley Canepa Vineyard 1980 Rel: $12 Cur: $20 (CH-4/90)
88 CHATEAU ST. JEAN Chardonnay Alexander Valley Belle Terre Vineyards 1980 Rel: $15 Cur: $24 (CH-3/90)

UNITED STATES
CALIFORNIA/CHARDONNAY

88   CHATEAU ST. JEAN Chardonnay Alexander Valley Robert Young Vineyards 1980 Rel: $18 Cur: $30 (7/16/84)
88   FLORA SPRINGS Chardonnay Napa Valley Special Selection 1980 Rel: $12 Cur: $25 (CH-1/90)
88   GRGICH HILLS Chardonnay Napa Valley 1980 Rel: $17 Cur: $51 (CH-3/90)
88   MARK WEST Chardonnay Russian River Valley Vintner's Library Selection 1980 $14 (10/01/85)
87   CLOS DU BOIS Chardonnay Dry Creek Valley Flintwood Vineyard 1980 Rel: $17 Cur: $32 (CH-2/90)
87   CUVAISON Chardonnay Napa Valley 1980 Rel: $11 Cur: $26 (CH-4/90)
87   EDNA VALLEY Chardonnay Edna Valley 1980 Rel: $12 Cur: $44 (CH-3/90)
87   HANZELL Chardonnay Sonoma Valley 1980 Rel: $17 Cur: $60 (4/16/85) (JG)
87   MOUNT EDEN Chardonnay Santa Cruz Mountains 1980 Rel: $30 Cur: $65 (CH-3/90)
87   SEQUOIA GROVE Chardonnay Napa Valley Estate 1980 Rel: $10 Cur: $10 (CH-5/90)
87   VICHON Chardonnay Napa Valley 1980 Rel: $15 Cur: $25 (CH-3/90)
86   MONTICELLO Chardonnay Napa Valley 1980 Rel: $12 Cur: $20 (CH-2/90)
86   STONY HILL Chardonnay Napa Valley 1980 Rel: $12 Cur: $83 (CH-5/90)
86   TREFETHEN Chardonnay Napa Valley 1980 Rel: $13 Cur: $40 (CH-3/90)
85   CHAPPELLET Chardonnay Napa Valley 1980 Rel: $14 Cur: $25 (4/16/85) (JG)
85   CHATEAU ST. JEAN Chardonnay Alexander Valley Robert Young Vineyards 1980 Rel: $18 Cur: $30 (CH-3/90)
85   FISHER Chardonnay Sonoma County 1980 Rel: $14 Cur: $22 (CH-2/90)
85   GIRARD Chardonnay Napa Valley 1980 Rel: $11 Cur: $25 (CH-3/90)
85   SMITH-MADRONE Chardonnay Napa Valley 1980 Rel: $11 Cur: $20 (CH-5/90)
84   CHAPPELLET Chardonnay Napa Valley 1980 Rel: $14 Cur: $25 (CH-3/90)
84   FREEMARK ABBEY Chardonnay Napa Valley 1980 Rel: $13.50 Cur: $38 (CH-2/90)
83   S. ANDERSON Chardonnay Napa Valley Stags Leap District 1980 $12.50 (CH-3/90)
83   ST. CLEMENT Chardonnay Napa Valley 1980 Rel: $12 Cur: $35 (CH-3/90)
82   MATANZAS CREEK Chardonnay Sonoma County 1980 Rel: $15 Cur: $25 (CH-2/90)
81   ZD Chardonnay California 1980 Rel: $13 Cur: $28 (CH-3/90)
80   CLOS DU VAL Chardonnay Napa Valley 1980 $12.50 (CH-6/90)
80   HACIENDA Chardonnay Sonoma County Clair de Lune 1980 Rel: $10.50 Cur: $22 (CH-4/90)
79   CHATEAU MONTELENA Chardonnay Napa Valley 1980 Rel: $16 Cur: $38 (CH-2/90)
79   CHATEAU ST. JEAN Chardonnay Dry Creek Valley Frank Johnson Vineyards 1980 Rel: $14 Cur: $16 (CH-3/90)
79   FREEMARK ABBEY Chardonnay Napa Valley 1980 Rel: $13.50 Cur: $38 (7/16/84)
78   STAG'S LEAP WINE CELLARS Chardonnay Napa Valley 1980 Rel: $10.50 Cur: $17 (CH-3/90)
77   CHATEAU ST. JEAN Chardonnay Alexander Valley Jimtown Ranch 1980 Rel: $14 Cur: $16 (CH-3/90)
75   BERINGER Chardonnay Napa Valley Private Reserve 1980 Rel: $15 Cur: $25 (CH-4/90)
75   BURGESS Chardonnay Napa Valley 1980 Rel: $11 Cur: $18 (CH-12/89)
74   CHATEAU ST. JEAN Chardonnay Alexander Valley Gauer Ranch 1980 Rel: $14 Cur: $18 (CH-3/90)
74   MAYACAMAS Chardonnay Napa Valley 1980 Rel: $16 Cur: $35 (CH-1/90)
71   CHATEAU ST. JEAN Chardonnay Sonoma Valley Wildwood Vineyards 1980 Rel: $13 Cur: $19 (CH-7/90)
70   CHATEAU ST. JEAN Chardonnay Sonoma Valley McCrea Vineyards 1980 Rel: $15 Cur: $18 (CH-3/90)
70   WILLIAM HILL Chardonnay Napa Valley Reserve 1980 Rel: $16 Cur: $30 (CH-3/90)
70   MATANZAS CREEK Chardonnay Sonoma County Estate 1980 Rel: $18 Cur: $25 (CH-2/90)
70   STERLING Chardonnay Napa Valley Estate 1980 Rel: $13 Cur: $17 (CH-4/90)
69   ROBERT MONDAVI Chardonnay Napa Valley Reserve 1980 Rel: $20 Cur: $30 (CH-3/90)
67   CHATEAU ST. JEAN Chardonnay Sonoma Valley Hunter Farms 1980 Rel: $14 Cur: $17 (CH-3/90)
67   DRY CREEK Chardonnay Sonoma County Vintners Reserve 1980 $14 (7/16/84)
62   DE LOACH Chardonnay Russian River Valley 1980 Rel: $10 Cur: $18 (CH-2/90)
57   BALVERNE Chardonnay Sonoma County Deer Hill Vineyard 1980 $12 (4/16/84)

1979

95   GRGICH HILLS Chardonnay Napa Valley 1979 Rel: $16 Cur: $63 (CH-3/90)
93   ST. CLEMENT Chardonnay Napa Valley 1979 Rel: $12 Cur: $27 (CH-3/90)
92   FAR NIENTE Chardonnay Napa Valley 1979 Rel: $15 Cur: $45 (CH-2/90)
92   SMITH-MADRONE Chardonnay Napa Valley 1979 Rel: $10 Cur: $28 (CH-5/90)
91   FLORA SPRINGS Chardonnay Napa Valley 1979 Rel: $9 Cur: $25 (CH-1/90)
90   CHATEAU MONTELENA Chardonnay Napa Valley 1979 Rel: $16 Cur: $40 (7/16/84)
90   MOUNT EDEN Chardonnay Santa Cruz Mountains 1979 Rel: $16 Cur: $60 (CH-3/90)
89   CHALONE Chardonnay Chalone 1979 Rel: $14 Cur: $69 (CH-1/90)
86   CHAPPELLET Chardonnay Napa Valley 1979 Rel: $12 Cur: $30 (4/16/85) (JG)
86   HACIENDA Chardonnay Sonoma County Clair de Lune 1979 Rel: $9 Cur: $25 (CH-4/90)
85   CHATEAU ST. JEAN Chardonnay Alexander Valley Robert Young Vineyards 1979 Rel: $17 Cur: $34 (CH-3/90)
85   HANZELL Chardonnay Sonoma Valley 1979 Rel: $16 Cur: $70 (CH-1/90)
84   CHATEAU ST. JEAN Chardonnay Alexander Valley Belle Terre Vineyards 1979 Rel: $12 Cur: $22 (CH-3/90)
84   CUVAISON Chardonnay Napa Valley 1979 Rel: $10 Cur: $26 (CH-4/90)
83   HANZELL Chardonnay Sonoma Valley 1979 Rel: $16 Cur: $70 (4/16/85) (JG)
82   PINE RIDGE Chardonnay Napa Valley Stags Leap District 1979 Rel: $9.50 Cur: $32 (CH-4/90)
82   STAG'S LEAP WINE CELLARS Chardonnay Napa Valley Haynes 1979 $12.50 (CH-3/90)
81   STONY HILL Chardonnay Napa Valley 1979 Rel: $12 Cur: $95 (CH-5/90)
80   CHATEAU ST. JEAN Chardonnay Sonoma Valley Hunter Farms 1979 Rel: $14 Cur: $20 (CH-3/90)
80   MATANZAS CREEK Chardonnay Napa-Sonoma Counties 1979 Rel: $14.50 Cur: $40 (CH-2/90)
79   CHAPPELLET Chardonnay Napa Valley 1979 Rel: $12 Cur: $30 (CH-3/90)
79   ROBERT MONDAVI Chardonnay Napa Valley Reserve 1979 Rel: $20 Cur: $27 (CH-3/90)
78   BERINGER Chardonnay Napa Valley Private Reserve 1979 Rel: $14 Cur: $25 (CH-4/90)
78   BURGESS Chardonnay Napa Valley 1979 Rel: $11 Cur: $18 (CH-12/89)

78   CHATEAU MONTELENA Chardonnay Napa Valley 1979 Rel: $16 Cur: $40 (CH-2/90)
78   CHATEAU ST. JEAN Chardonnay Dry Creek Valley Frank Johnson Vineyards 1979 Rel: $13.50 Cur: $15 (CH-3/90)
76   ACACIA Chardonnay Carneros Napa Valley Winery Lake Vineyard 1979 Rel: $16 Cur: $28 (CH-1/90)
76   FREEMARK ABBEY Chardonnay Napa Valley 1979 Rel: $13.25 Cur: $25 (CH-2/90)
73   STERLING Chardonnay Napa Valley Estate 1979 Rel: $13 Cur: $38 (CH-4/90)
73   TREFETHEN Chardonnay Napa Valley 1979 Rel: $12 Cur: $30 (CH-3/90)
70   BEAULIEU Chardonnay Napa Valley Beaufort 1979 Rel: $6 Cur: $20 (CH-4/90)
70   CHATEAU ST. JEAN Chardonnay Alexander Valley Gauer Ranch 1979 Rel: $14 Cur: $18 (CH-3/90)
70   CHATEAU ST. JEAN Chardonnay Sonoma Valley McCrea Vineyards 1979 Rel: $14 Cur: $18 (CH-3/90)
70   MAYACAMAS Chardonnay Napa Valley 1979 Rel: $15 Cur: $35 (CH-1/90)

1978

95   HANZELL Chardonnay Sonoma Valley 1978 Rel: $13 Cur: $80 (CH-1/90)
92   GRGICH HILLS Chardonnay Napa Valley 1978 Rel: $13.75 Cur: $60 (CH-3/90)
90   HANZELL Chardonnay Sonoma Valley 1978 Rel: $13 Cur: $80 (4/16/85) (JG)
90   TREFETHEN Chardonnay Napa Valley 1978 Rel: $10 Cur: $35 (CH-3/90)
87   CHAPPELLET Chardonnay Napa Valley 1978 Rel: $11.75 Cur: $40 (4/16/85) (JG)
87   CHATEAU ST. JEAN Chardonnay Alexander Valley Robert Young Vineyards 1978 Rel: $17 Cur: $25 (7/16/84)
86   SMITH-MADRONE Chardonnay Napa Valley 1978 Rel: $10 Cur: $30 (CH-5/90)
85   STONY HILL Chardonnay Napa Valley 1978 Rel: $10 Cur: $101 (CH-5/90)
84   CHATEAU ST. JEAN Chardonnay Alexander Valley Robert Young Vineyards 1978 Rel: $17 Cur: $25 (CH-3/90)
81   CHATEAU ST. JEAN Chardonnay Sonoma Valley Les Pierres Vineyards 1978 Rel: $13.75 Cur: $22 (CH-3/90)
81   CUVAISON Chardonnay Napa Valley 1978 Rel: $10 Cur: $28 (CH-4/90)
79   MATANZAS CREEK Chardonnay Sonoma County 1978 Rel: $12.50 Cur: $50 (CH-2/90)
77   BURGESS Chardonnay Napa Valley 1978 Rel: $11 Cur: $18 (CH-12/89)
77   CHATEAU MONTELENA Chardonnay Napa Valley 1978 Rel: $15 Cur: $45 (CH-2/90)
76   CHAPPELLET Chardonnay Napa Valley 1978 Rel: $11.75 Cur: $40 (CH-3/90)
75   MAYACAMAS Chardonnay Napa Valley 1978 Rel: $13 Cur: $30 (CH-1/90)
74   STAG'S LEAP WINE CELLARS Chardonnay Napa Valley Haynes 1978 $10 (CH-3/90)
73   CHATEAU ST. JEAN Chardonnay Alexander Valley Belle Terre Vineyards 1978 Rel: $14 Cur: $20 (CH-3/90)
73   HACIENDA Chardonnay Sonoma County Clair de Lune 1978 Rel: $9 Cur: $25 (CH-4/90)
70   BEAULIEU Chardonnay Napa Valley Beaufort 1978 Rel: $6 Cur: $22 (CH-4/90)
70   BERINGER Chardonnay Napa Valley Private Reserve 1978 Rel: $12 Cur: $15 (CH-4/90)
70   CHATEAU ST. JEAN Chardonnay Sonoma Valley McCrea Vineyards 1978 Rel: $12 Cur: $20 (CH-3/90)
70   FREEMARK ABBEY Chardonnay Napa Valley 1978 Rel: $10 Cur: $26 (CH-2/90)
69   ROBERT MONDAVI Chardonnay Napa Valley Reserve 1978 Rel: $20 Cur: $24 (CH-3/90)
66   MOUNT EDEN Chardonnay Santa Cruz Mountains 1978 Rel: $14 Cur: $50 (CH-3/90)
65   CHATEAU ST. JEAN Chardonnay Sonoma Valley Hunter Farms 1978 Rel: $11.25 Cur: $18 (CH-3/90)
65   CHATEAU ST. JEAN Chardonnay Sonoma Valley Wildwood Vineyards 1978 Rel: $12 Cur: $19 (CH-3/90)
60   DRY CREEK Chardonnay Sonoma County 1978 $8 (7/16/84)

1977

91   STONY HILL Chardonnay Napa Valley 1977 Rel: $9 Cur: $95 (CH-6/90)
90   CHAPPELLET Chardonnay Napa Valley 1977 Rel: $11.75 Cur: $40 (CH-6/90)
89   GRGICH HILLS Chardonnay Sonoma County 1977 Rel: $11 Cur: $85 (CH-3/90)
88   HANZELL Chardonnay Sonoma Valley 1977 Rel: $12 Cur: $85 (CH-1/90)
85   CHATEAU MONTELENA Chardonnay Napa Valley 1977 Rel: $15 Cur: $60 (CH-2/90)
85   CHATEAU ST. JEAN Chardonnay Sonoma Valley McCrea Vineyards 1977 Rel: $10.25 Cur: $25 (CH-3/90)
85   MOUNT EDEN Chardonnay Santa Cruz Mountains 1977 Rel: $16 Cur: $70 (CH-8/90)
84   CHAPPELLET Chardonnay Napa Valley 1977 Rel: $11.75 Cur: $40 (4/16/85) (JG)
81   CHATEAU ST. JEAN Chardonnay Sonoma Valley Hunter Farms 1977 Rel: $10.25 Cur: $25 (CH-3/90)
81   TREFETHEN Chardonnay Napa Valley 1977 Rel: $8.50 Cur: $35 (CH-3/90)
80   BURGESS Chardonnay Napa Valley 1977 Rel: $11 Cur: $23 (CH-12/89)
80   CHATEAU ST. JEAN Chardonnay Alexander Valley Belle Terre Vineyards 1977 Rel: $12 Cur: $22 (CH-3/90)
80   HANZELL Chardonnay Sonoma Valley 1977 Rel: $12 Cur: $85 (4/16/85) (JG)
79   CHATEAU ST. JEAN Chardonnay Sonoma Valley Les Pierres Vineyards 1977 Rel: $13.75 Cur: $21 (CH-3/90)
76   HACIENDA Chardonnay Sonoma County Clair de Lune 1977 Rel: $8 Cur: $23 (CH-4/90)
73   CHATEAU ST. JEAN Chardonnay Sonoma Valley Wildwood Vineyards 1977 Rel: $15 Cur: $22 (CH-3/90)
70   MAYACAMAS Chardonnay Napa Valley 1977 Rel: $12 Cur: $35 (CH-1/90)
70   STERLING Chardonnay Napa Valley Estate 1977 Rel: $10 Cur: $31 (CH-4/90)
68   CHATEAU ST. JEAN Chardonnay Alexander Valley Robert Young Vineyards 1977 Rel: $17 Cur: $22 (CH-3/90)
68   ROBERT MONDAVI Chardonnay Napa Valley Reserve 1977 Rel: $14 Cur: $32 (CH-3/90)
67   STAG'S LEAP WINE CELLARS Chardonnay Napa Valley Haynes 1977 $9 (CH-3/90)
64   BEAULIEU Chardonnay Napa Valley Beaufort 1977 Rel: $6 Cur: $22 (CH-4/90)
59   STAG'S LEAP WINE CELLARS Chardonnay Napa Valley 1977 Rel: $8 Cur: $17 (CH-3/90)
58   FREEMARK ABBEY Chardonnay Napa Valley 1977 Rel: $10 Cur: $36 (CH-2/90)

1976

92   CHATEAU ST. JEAN Chardonnay Alexander Valley Robert Young Vineyards 1976 Rel: $8.75 Cur: $25 (CH-7/90)
91   HANZELL Chardonnay Sonoma Valley 1976 Rel: $12 Cur: $90 (CH-1/90)
90   CHATEAU ST. JEAN Chardonnay Alexander Valley Robert Young Vineyards 1976 Rel: $8.75 Cur: $25 (7/16/84)
88   CHATEAU ST. JEAN Chardonnay Alexander Valley Riverview Vineyards 1976 $9.50 (CH-7/90)
88   STONY HILL Chardonnay Napa Valley 1976 Rel: $9 Cur: $127 (CH-6/90)
85   GRGICH HILLS Chardonnay Napa Valley Hill's Cellars 1976 Rel: $8 Cur: $50 (CH-3/90)
85   HACIENDA Chardonnay Sonoma County Clair de Lune 1976 Rel: $7 Cur: $40 (CH-4/90)
82   CHATEAU ST. JEAN Chardonnay Sonoma Valley Wildwood Vineyards 1976 Rel: $10 Cur: $20 (CH-7/90)
81   CHATEAU MONTELENA Chardonnay Napa-Alexander Valleys 1976 Rel: $11 Cur: $50 (7/16/84)
81   MAYACAMAS Chardonnay Napa Valley 1976 Rel: $11 Cur: $45 (CH-1/90)

79 HANZELL Chardonnay Sonoma Valley 1976 Rel: $12 Cur: $90 (4/16/85) (JG)
78 ROBERT MONDAVI Chardonnay Napa Valley Reserve 1976 Rel: $12 Cur: $32 (CH-3/90)
78 MOUNT EDEN Chardonnay Santa Cruz Mountains 1976 Rel: $16 Cur: $50 (CH-3/90)
77 CHATEAU MONTELENA Chardonnay Napa-Alexander Valleys 1976 Rel: $11 Cur: $50 (CH-2/90)
77 CHATEAU ST. JEAN Chardonnay Alexander Valley Belle Terre Vineyards 1976 Rel: $7.50 Cur: $22 (CH-7/90)
75 CHATEAU ST. JEAN Chardonnay Sonoma Valley McCrea Vineyards 1976 Rel: $9.25 Cur: $20 (CH-7/90)
74 TREFETHEN Chardonnay Napa Valley 1976 Rel: $7 Cur: $40 (CH-3/90)
73 DRY CREEK Chardonnay Sonoma County 1976 $7 (7/16/84)
71 CHAPPELLET Chardonnay Napa Valley 1976 Rel: $9.75 Cur: $30 (CH-3/90)
70 BURGESS Chardonnay Carneros Winery Lake Vineyard 1976 Rel: $10 Cur: $20 (CH-12/89)
70 CHAPPELLET Chardonnay Napa Valley 1976 Rel: $9.75 Cur: $30 (4/16/85) (JG)
69 CHATEAU ST. JEAN Chardonnay Sonoma County Beltane Ranch 1976 Rel: $7.75 Cur: $18 (CH-7/90)
62 BEAULIEU Chardonnay Napa Valley Beaufort 1976 Rel: $6 Cur: $22 (CH-4/90)
62 FREEMARK ABBEY Chardonnay Napa Valley 1976 Rel: $9.75 Cur: $26 (CH-2/90)
59 STERLING Chardonnay Napa Valley Estate 1976 Rel: $5.25 Cur: $18 (CH-4/90)
58 STAG'S LEAP WINE CELLARS Chardonnay Napa Valley 1976 Rel: $8 Cur: $17 (CH-3/90)

1975

88 CHATEAU ST. JEAN Chardonnay Alexander Valley Belle Terre Vineyards 1975 Rel: $7.50 Cur: $22 (CH-7/90)
88 CHATEAU ST. JEAN Chardonnay Sonoma County Beltane Ranch 1975 Rel: $12.50 Cur: $21 (CH-7/90)
87 CHATEAU MONTELENA Chardonnay Napa Valley 1975 Rel: $9 Cur: $65 (CH-2/90)
86 CHATEAU ST. JEAN Chardonnay Sonoma County Bacigalupi 1975 Rel: $10 Cur: $21 (CH-7/90)
86 HANZELL Chardonnay Sonoma Valley 1975 Rel: $10 Cur: $70 (CH-1/90)
85 CHAPPELLET Chardonnay Napa Valley 1975 Rel: $6.75 Cur: $40 (4/16/85) (JG)
84 BURGESS Chardonnay Carneros Winery Lake Vineyard 1975 Rel: $9 Cur: $40 (CH-12/89)
83 ROBERT MONDAVI Chardonnay Napa Valley Reserve 1975 Rel: $10 Cur: $35 (7/16/84)
82 CHAPPELLET Chardonnay Napa Valley 1975 Rel: $6.75 Cur: $40 (CH-3/90)
82 FREEMARK ABBEY Chardonnay Napa Valley 1975 Rel: $9 Cur: $45 (CH-2/90)
81 HANZELL Chardonnay Sonoma Valley 1975 Rel: $10 Cur: $70 (4/16/85) (JG)
78 CHATEAU ST. JEAN Chardonnay Sonoma Valley McCrea Vineyards 1975 Rel: $8.75 Cur: $20 (CH-7/90)
78 MAYACAMAS Chardonnay Napa Valley 1975 Rel: $9 Cur: $50 (CH-1/90)
75 ROBERT MONDAVI Chardonnay Napa Valley Reserve 1975 Rel: $10 Cur: $35 (CH-3/90)
75 STONY HILL Chardonnay Napa Valley 1975 Rel: $9 Cur: $150 (CH-5/90)
73 FREEMARK ABBEY Chardonnay Napa Valley 1975 Rel: $9 Cur: $45 (7/16/84)
73 TREFETHEN Chardonnay Napa Valley 1975 Rel: $6.50 Cur: $45 (CH-3/90)
70 CHATEAU ST. JEAN Chardonnay Sonoma Valley Wildwood Vineyards 1975 Rel: $9.50 Cur: $20 (CH-7/90)
63 CHATEAU ST. JEAN Chardonnay Alexander Valley Robert Young Vineyards 1975 Rel: $7.75 Cur: $22 (CH-7/90)
61 BEAULIEU Chardonnay Napa Valley Beaufort 1975 Rel: $5 Cur: $28 (CH-4/90)
60 MOUNT EDEN Chardonnay Santa Cruz Mountains 1975 Rel: $14 Cur: $45 (CH-3/90)

1974

89 ROBERT MONDAVI Chardonnay Napa Valley Reserve 1974 Rel: $10 Cur: $45 (7/16/84)
88 BERINGER Chardonnay Santa Barbara County 1974 Rel: $5 Cur: $5 (CH-4/90)
88 CHATEAU MONTELENA Chardonnay Napa Valley 1974 Rel: $8 Cur: $70 (CH-2/90)
88 HANZELL Chardonnay Sonoma Valley 1974 Rel: $9 Cur: $75 (CH-1/90)
88 ROBERT MONDAVI Chardonnay Napa Valley Reserve 1974 Rel: $10 Cur: $45 (CH-3/90)
83 CHAPPELLET Chardonnay Napa Valley 1974 Rel: $6.75 Cur: $45 (4/16/85) (JG)
80 HACIENDA Chardonnay Sonoma County Clair de Lune 1974 Rel: $5 Cur: $40 (CH-4/90)
80 TREFETHEN Chardonnay Napa Valley 1974 Rel: $5.75 Cur: $50 (CH-3/90)
79 BURGESS Chardonnay Carneros Winery Lake Vineyard 1974 Rel: $6 Cur: $25 (CH-12/89)
78 STERLING Chardonnay Napa Valley Estate 1974 Rel: $4.75 Cur: $35 (CH-4/90)
74 FREEMARK ABBEY Chardonnay Napa Valley 1974 Rel: $7.95 Cur: $42 (CH-2/90)
73 STONY HILL Chardonnay Napa Valley 1974 Rel: $7 Cur: $112 (CH-5/90)
72 CHAPPELLET Chardonnay Napa Valley 1974 Rel: $6.75 Cur: $45 (CH-3/90)
70 BERINGER Chardonnay Napa Valley Centennial Cask Selection 1974 Rel: $5 Cur: $40 (CH-4/90)
70 MAYACAMAS Chardonnay Napa Valley 1974 Rel: $7.50 Cur: $50 (CH-1/90)
62 BEAULIEU Chardonnay Napa Valley Beaufort 1974 Rel: $5 Cur: $25 (CH-4/90)
59 MOUNT EDEN Chardonnay Santa Cruz Mountains 1974 Rel: $14 Cur: $50 (CH-3/90)

1973

93 CHATEAU MONTELENA Chardonnay Napa-Alexander Valleys 1973 Rel: $6.50 Cur: $100 (CH-2/90)
91 CHAPPELLET Chardonnay Napa Valley 1973 Rel: $6.75 Cur: $50 (CH-3/90)
91 HACIENDA Chardonnay Sonoma County Clair de Lune 1973 Rel: $5 Cur: $50 (CH-4/90)
85 BURGESS Chardonnay Napa Valley 1973 Rel: $6 Cur: $30 (CH-12/89)
85 HANZELL Chardonnay Sonoma Valley 1973 Rel: $8 Cur: $100 (CH-1/90)
85 TREFETHEN Chardonnay Napa Valley 1973 Rel: $6.50 Cur: $50 (CH-3/90)
82 MOUNT EDEN Chardonnay Santa Cruz Mountains 1973 Rel: $12 Cur: $55 (CH-3/90)
80 CHAPPELLET Chardonnay Napa Valley 1973 Rel: $6.75 Cur: $50 (4/16/85) (JG)
79 STONY HILL Chardonnay Napa Valley 1973 Rel: $7 Cur: $120 (CH-5/90)
77 FREEMARK ABBEY Chardonnay Napa Valley 1973 Rel: $6.50 Cur: $32 (CH-2/90)
66 FREEMARK ABBEY Chardonnay Napa Valley 1973 Rel: $6.50 Cur: $32 (7/16/84)
60 BEAULIEU Chardonnay Napa Valley Beaufort 1973 Rel: $5 Cur: $30 (CH-4/90)
60 MAYACAMAS Chardonnay Napa Valley 1973 Rel: $7 Cur: $50 (CH-1/90)

1972

95 CHATEAU MONTELENA Chardonnay Napa-Alexander Valleys 1972 Rel: $6 Cur: $110 (CH-2/90)
90 CHAPPELLET Chardonnay Napa Valley 1972 Rel: $6 Cur: $50 (4/16/85) (JG)
90 HANZELL Chardonnay Sonoma Valley 1972 Rel: $7 Cur: $75 (CH-1/90)
83 STONY HILL Chardonnay Napa Valley 1972 Rel: $7 Cur: $110 (CH-5/90)
81 CHATEAU MONTELENA Chardonnay Napa-Alexander Valleys 1972 Rel: $6 Cur: $110 (7/16/84)
80 MOUNT EDEN Chardonnay Santa Cruz Mountains 1972 Rel: $20 Cur: $50 (CH-3/90)
77 FREEMARK ABBEY Chardonnay Napa Valley 1972 Rel: $6.50 Cur: $48 (CH-2/90)
60 BEAULIEU Chardonnay Napa Valley Beaufort 1972 Rel: $5 Cur: $30 (CH-4/90)
59 MAYACAMAS Chardonnay Napa Valley 1972 Rel: $7 Cur: $60 (CH-1/90)

1971

85 HANZELL Chardonnay Sonoma Valley 1971 Rel: $7 Cur: $120 (CH-1/90)
80 STONY HILL Chardonnay Napa Valley 1971 Rel: $6 Cur: $110 (CH-5/90)
78 CHAPPELLET Chardonnay Napa Valley 1971 Rel: $6 Cur: $50 (4/16/85) (JG)
70 FREEMARK ABBEY Chardonnay Napa Valley 1971 Rel: $7 Cur: $40 (CH-2/90)
58 BEAULIEU Chardonnay Napa Valley Beaufort 1971 Rel: $4 Cur: $30 (CH-4/90)

1970

92 STONY HILL Chardonnay Napa Valley 1970 Rel: $6 Cur: $175 (CH-5/90)
86 CHAPPELLET Chardonnay Napa Valley 1970 Rel: $6 Cur: $50 (4/16/85) (JG)
84 HANZELL Chardonnay Sonoma Valley 1970 Rel: $7 Cur: $120 (CH-1/90)
59 BEAULIEU Chardonnay Napa Valley Beaufort 1970 Rel: $4 Cur: $32 (CH-4/90)
55 FREEMARK ABBEY Chardonnay Napa Valley 1970 Rel: $7 Cur: $35 (CH-2/90)

1969

90 HANZELL Chardonnay Sonoma Valley 1969 Rel: $6 Cur: $140 (CH-1/90)
85 STONY HILL Chardonnay Napa Valley 1969 Rel: $5 Cur: $175 (CH-5/90)
60 FREEMARK ABBEY Chardonnay Napa Valley 1969 Rel: $6 Cur: $37 (CH-2/90)
57 BEAULIEU Chardonnay Napa Valley Beaufort 1969 Rel: $2 Cur: $35 (CH-4/90)

1968

93 STONY HILL Chardonnay Napa Valley 1968 Rel: $5 Cur: $250 (CH-5/90)
91 HANZELL Chardonnay Sonoma Valley 1968 Rel: $6 Cur: $140 (CH-1/90)
73 FREEMARK ABBEY Chardonnay Napa Valley 1968 Rel: $5 Cur: $35 (CH-2/90)
59 BEAULIEU Chardonnay Napa Valley Beaufort 1968 Rel: $2 Cur: $35 (CH-4/90)

1967

89 HANZELL Chardonnay Sonoma Valley 1967 Rel: $6 Cur: $140 (CH-1/90)
83 STONY HILL Chardonnay Napa Valley 1967 Rel: $4.50 Cur: $320 (CH-5/90)

1966

94 HANZELL Chardonnay Sonoma Valley 1966 Rel: $6 Cur: $170 (CH-1/90)
91 STONY HILL Chardonnay Napa Valley 1966 Rel: $4.50 Cur: $300 (CH-5/90)

1965

90 STONY HILL Chardonnay Napa Valley 1965 Rel: $4 Cur: $420 (CH-5/90)
84 HANZELL Chardonnay Sonoma Valley 1965 Rel: $6 Cur: $180 (CH-1/90)
58 MAYACAMAS Chardonnay Napa Valley 1965 Rel: $2.50 Cur: $125 (CH-1/90)

1964

98 STONY HILL Chardonnay Napa Valley 1964 Rel: $4 Cur: $460 (CH-5/90)
92 MAYACAMAS Chardonnay Napa Valley 1964 Rel: $1.75 Cur: $200 (CH-1/90)

1963

87 STONY HILL Chardonnay Napa Valley 1963 Rel: $4 Cur: $460 (CH-5/90)
58 MAYACAMAS Chardonnay Napa Valley 1963 Rel: $1.75 Cur: $150 (CH-1/90)

1962

96 STONY HILL Chardonnay Napa Valley 1962 Rel: $3.25 Cur: $460 (CH-5/90)
87 HEITZ Chardonnay Napa Valley 1962 Rel: $6 Cur: $125 (CH-6/90)
58 MAYACAMAS Chardonnay Napa Valley 1962 Rel: $1.75 Cur: $150 (CH-1/90)

1961

93 HEITZ Chardonnay Napa Valley 1961 Rel: $6 Cur: $125 (CH-6/90)

1960

88 STONY HILL Chardonnay Napa Valley 1960 Rel: $3 Cur: $440 (CH-5/90)

1959

88 HANZELL Chardonnay California 1959 Rel: $4 Cur: $200 (CH-12/89)

1958

60 MAYACAMAS Chardonnay Napa Valley 1958 Rel: $1 Cur: $200 (CH-1/90)

1957

90 HANZELL Chardonnay California 1957 Rel: $4 Cur: $240 (CH-12/89)

1955

88 MAYACAMAS Chardonnay Napa Valley 1955 Rel: $1 Cur: $330 (CH-1/90)

NV

86 CHRISTIAN BROTHERS Chardonnay Napa Valley-Burgundy Montage Premier Cuvée NV $15 (10/15/88)
81 BOUCHAINE Chardonnay Napa Valley Cask 85-86 NV $7.50 (7/31/87) BB
77 LIBERTY SCHOOL Chardonnay California Lot 17 NV $7.50 (2/28/90)
58 E.&J. GALLO Chardonnay California Limited Release NV $6 (4/16/86)

CHENIN BLANC

1989

83 GRAND CRU Chenin Blanc Clarksburg Dry 1989 $6.50 (6/30/90)
81 PINE RIDGE Chenin Blanc Napa Valley Yountville Cuvée 1989 $7 (4/30/90)

1988

88 FETZER Chenin Blanc California 1988 $6 (7/31/89)
88 FOLIE A DEUX Chenin Blanc Napa Valley 1988 $7 (7/31/89)
88 MONTEREY VINEYARD Chenin Blanc Monterey Classic 1988 $6.50 (7/31/89)
87 CALLAWAY Chenin Blanc Temecula Morning Harvest 1988 $6.50 (7/31/89)
86 DRY CREEK Chenin Blanc Yolo-Napa Counties 1988 $6.50 (7/31/89)
86 HUSCH Chenin Blanc Mendocino 1988 $5.75 (7/31/89)
85 GRAND CRU Chenin Blanc Clarksburg Dry Premium Selection 1988 $7 (7/31/89)
85 GRANITE SPRINGS Chenin Blanc El Dorado 1988 $5.50 (7/31/89)
85 MARTIN Chenin Blanc Paso Robles 1988 $6 (7/31/89)
84 BARON HERZOG Chenin Blanc California 1988 $4.50 (7/31/89)
84 HACIENDA Chenin Blanc Clarksburg Dry 1988 $5.50 (7/31/89)
84 WHITE OAK Chenin Blanc Dry Creek Valley 1988 $6.50 (7/31/89)
83 R.&J. COOK Chenin Blanc Clarksburg 1988 $5.50 (7/31/89)
83 PINE RIDGE Chenin Blanc Napa Valley Yountville Cuvée 1988 $7 (7/31/89)
83 WEIBEL Chenin Blanc Mendocino 1988 $5 (7/31/89)

UNITED STATES
CALIFORNIA/CHENIN BLANC

82   GIRARD Chenin Blanc Napa Valley Dry 1988 $7 (7/31/89)
82   PRESTON Chenin Blanc Dry Creek Valley 1988 $7.50 (7/31/89)
79   GLEN ELLEN Chenin Blanc California Proprietor's Reserve 1988 $6 (7/31/89)
79   PELLIGRINI Chenin Blanc North Coast Vintage White 1988 $4.50 (7/31/89)
78   VENTANA Chenin Blanc Monterey 1988 $5.50 (7/31/89)
69   ROBERT MONDAVI Chenin Blanc Napa Valley 1988 $8 (6/30/90)
66   SUTTER HOME Chenin Blanc California 1988 $4 (7/31/89)
65   PAUL MASSON Chenin Blanc California 1988 $5/1.5L (7/31/89)
58   J. LOHR Chenin Blanc Clarksburg Pheasant's Call Vineyard 1988 $4.50 (7/31/89)

1987

87   PARDUCCI Chenin Blanc Mendocino 1987 $5.75 (7/31/89)
84   CALLAWAY Chenin Blanc Temecula Morning Harvest 1987 $5.50 (7/31/89)
84   CHRISTIAN BROTHERS Chenin Blanc Napa Valley 1987 $5 (7/31/89)
83   BERINGER Chenin Blanc Napa Valley 1987 $7 (7/31/89)
83   SIMI Chenin Blanc Mendocino 1987 $6.50 (7/31/89)
82   CASA NUESTRA Chenin Blanc Napa Valley Dry 1987 $6.50 (7/31/89)
82   GUENOC Chenin Blanc Guenoc Valley 1987 $5.50 (7/31/89)
82   CHARLES KRUG Chenin Blanc Napa Valley 1987 $5.50 (7/31/89)
82   R.H. PHILLIPS Chenin Blanc Yolo County Dunnigan Hills 1987 $4.50 (7/31/89)
81   VILLA MT. EDEN Chenin Blanc Napa Valley Dry 1987 $6 (7/31/89)
78   ROBERT MONDAVI Chenin Blanc Napa Valley 1987 $8 (7/31/89)
77   E.&J. GALLO Chenin Blanc California 1987 $3.50/1.5L (7/31/89)
77   SANTA BARBARA Chenin Blanc Santa Ynez Valley 1987 $7 (7/31/89)
75   MIRASSOU Chenin Blanc Monterey 1987 $5.50 (7/31/89)
73   E.&J. GALLO Chenin Blanc North Coast Dry Chablis 1987 $4 (7/31/89)
70   LOUIS M. MARTINI Chenin Blanc Napa Valley 1987 $5 (7/31/89)
69   STEVENOT Chenin Blanc Calaveras County 1987 $5.50 (7/31/89)
65   SEBASTIANI Chenin Blanc California 1987 $5.25 (7/31/89)
62   HOUTZ Chenin Blanc Santa Ynez Valley 1987 $6 (7/31/89)
58   SAN MARTIN Chenin Blanc Monterey 1987 $6 (7/31/89)

1986

85   CHAPPELLET Chenin Blanc Napa Valley 1986 $7.50 (7/31/89)
84   BEAULIEU Chenin Blanc Napa Valley Chablis 1986 $5.50 (7/31/89)
82   GRAND CRU Chenin Blanc Clarksburg Dry 1986 $6.50 (12/15/87)
79   PINE RIDGE Chenin Blanc Napa Valley Yountville Cuvée 1986 $6.75 (6/30/87)
79   SUNNY ST. HELENA Chenin Blanc Napa Valley 1986 $5 (12/15/87)
76   GIRARD Chenin Blanc Napa Valley Dry 1986 $6.50 (1/31/88)
74   HACIENDA Chenin Blanc Clarksburg Dry 1986 $6 (6/30/87)
74   SIMI Chenin Blanc Mendocino County 1986 $7 (6/30/87)
72   DURNEY Chenin Blanc Carmel Valley 1986 $7 (7/31/89)
71   DRY CREEK Chenin Blanc Sonoma-Calaveras Counties Dry 1986 $6.25 (12/15/87)
70   ROBERT MONDAVI Chenin Blanc Napa Valley 1986 $6.25 (6/30/87)

1985

85   CHRISTIAN BROTHERS Chenin Blanc Napa Valley 1985 $5 (3/15/87)
79   LAKESPRING Chenin Blanc Napa Valley 1985 $6 (3/15/87)
75   ALEXANDER VALLEY Chenin Blanc Alexander Valley 1985 $6.50 (7/16/86)

NV

83   E.&J. GALLO Chenin Blanc California Chablis Blanc NV $2.50 (7/31/89)
77   ALMADEN Chenin Blanc California NV $4/1.5L (7/31/89)
76   INGLENOOK-NAVELLE Chenin Blanc California NV $3.75/1.5L (7/31/89)
74   LOS HERMANOS Chenin Blanc California NV $4/1.5L (7/31/89)
71   TAYLOR Chenin Blanc California NV $3/1.5L (7/31/89)

DESSERT

1989

92   FREEMARK ABBEY Johannisberg Riesling Late Harvest Napa Valley Edelwein Gold 1989 $22/375ml (7/15/90)
89   JOSEPH PHELPS Sémillon Late Harvest Napa Valley Délice du Sémillon 1989 $12.50/375ml (4/30/91)
89   QUADY Orange Muscat California Essensia 1989 $12 (10/15/90)
88   DE LOACH Gewürztraminer Late Harvest Russian River Valley 1989 $10/375ml (4/30/91)
88   JOSEPH PHELPS Scheurbe Late Harvest Napa Valley Scheurebe Special Select 1989 $18/375ml (4/30/91)
87   BUENA VISTA Late Harvest Carneros Ingrid's Vineyard Late Harvest White 1989 $18 (4/30/91)
87   STONEGATE Late Harvest Napa Valley Late Harvest 1989 $13/375ml (4/30/91)
86   BARON HERZOG Johannisberg Riesling Late Harvest California 1989 $8/375ml (3/31/91)
86   NAVARRO Gewürztraminer Late Harvest Anderson Valley Sweet Vineyard Selection 1989 $12 (4/30/91)
85   QUADY Black Muscat California Elysium 1989 $12 (10/15/90)
84   FIRESTONE Johannisberg Riesling Late Harvest Santa Barbara County Selected Harvest 1989 $12/375ml (4/30/91)
83   VILLA MT. EDEN Sauvignon Blanc Late Harvest Napa Valley 1989 $13/375ml (4/30/91)

1988

91   FETZER Johannisberg Riesling Late Harvest Sonoma County Reserve 1988 $10/375ml (3/31/91)
90   QUADY Black Muscat California Elysium 1988 $11 (8/31/89)

87   CHATEAU DE BAUN Symphony Late Harvest Sonoma County Finale 1988 $12/375ml (4/30/91)
87   FREEMARK ABBEY Johannisberg Riesling Late Harvest Napa Valley Edelwein Gold 1988 $18/375ml (6/15/89)
86   CHATEAU ST. JEAN Johannisberg Riesling Late Harvest Alexander Valley Select Late Harvest 1988 $20/375ml (4/30/91)
79   FIRESTONE Johannisberg Riesling Late Harvest Santa Ynez Valley Ambassador's Vineyard Select Harvest 1988 $9.50/375ml (12/15/89)

1987

93   DE LOACH Gewürztraminer Late Harvest Russian River Valley 1987 $10/375ml (12/31/88)
91   BONNY DOON Muscat Canelli Late Harvest California Vin de Glacière 1987 $15/375ml (12/31/88)
91   PRESTON Muscat Brûlée Late Harvest Dry Creek Valley 1987 $12/375ml (8/31/89)
89   BABCOCK Johannisberg Riesling Late Harvest Santa Ynez Valley Cluster Selected 1987 $14/375ml (12/15/89)
85   CHATEAU DE BAUN Symphony Late Harvest Sonoma County Finale 1987 $14/375ml (4/30/91)
82   QUADY Black Muscat California Elysium 1987 $6.50/375ml (9/30/88)
81   CLAIBORNE & CHURCHILL Riesling Late Harvest Central Coast 1987 $15/375ml (12/15/89)
81   QUADY Dessert Amador County Starboard 1987 $25 (3/31/91)
78   QUADY Orange Muscat California Essensia 1987 $11 (8/31/89)
78   VEGA Johannisberg Riesling Late Harvest Santa Barbara County Special Selection 1987 $10.50/375ml (12/15/89)
77   JEKEL Riesling Late Harvest Arroyo Seco Gravelstone Vineyard 1987 $13.50/375ml (2/28/89)
76   WENTE BROS. Riesling Late Harvest Arroyo Seco November Harvest Reserve Arroyo Seco Vineyard 1987 $12 (7/15/90)
74   SANTA BARBARA Zinfandel Late Harvest Santa Ynez Valley Essence 1987 $15/375ml (12/15/89)
72   GRAND CRU Gewürztraminer Late Harvest Sonoma County Select 1987 $10/375ml (3/31/90)
70   VENTANA White Riesling Late Harvest Monterey Ventana Vineyards Hand-Selected Clusters 1987 $14/375ml (8/31/89)

1986

93   NAVARRO Gewürztraminer Late Harvest Anderson Valley Vineyard Selection 1986 $18.50 (2/28/91)
90   CLOS DU BOIS Muscat of Alexandria Late Harvest Alexander Valley Fleur d'Alexandra 1986 $10 (5/31/88)
90   DAVID S. STARE Sauvignon Blanc Late Harvest Dry Creek Valley Soleil Vintner's Reserve 1986 $15/375ml (6/15/89)
89   CLOS DU BOIS Johannisberg Riesling Late Harvest Alexander Valley Individual Bunch Selection 1986 $15/375ml (8/31/87)
89   FIRESTONE Johannisberg Riesling Late Harvest Santa Ynez Valley Ambassador's Vineyard Selected 1986 $9.50/375ml (2/28/89)
89   VILLA MT. EDEN Sauvignon Blanc Late Harvest Napa Valley 1986 $10/375ml (5/15/88)
88   SANTA BARBARA Johannisberg Riesling Late Harvest Santa Ynez Valley Botrytised Grapes 1986 $15/375ml (10/15/87)
87   FREEMARK ABBEY Johannisberg Riesling Late Harvest Napa Valley Edelwein Gold 1986 $18.50/375ml (6/15/87)
86   VICHON Sémillon Late Harvest Napa Valley Botrytis 1986 $15/375ml (12/31/88)
85   FROG'S LEAP Sauvignon Blanc Late Harvest Napa Valley Sauvignon Blanc Late Leap 1986 $9.50/375ml (9/30/88)
85   NAVARRO White Riesling Late Harvest Anderson Valley Sweet Cluster Selected 1986 $25 (3/31/90)
82   DE LORIMIER Sauvignon Blanc Late Harvest Alexander Valley Lace 1986 $11/375ml (2/29/88)
81   AUSTIN Johannisberg Riesling Late Harvest Santa Barbara County Botrytis 1986 $8/375ml (12/15/89)
81   CHATEAU DE BAUN Symphony Late Harvest Sonoma County Finale 1986 $14/375ml (9/15/87)
80   CLOS DU BOIS Gewürztraminer Late Harvest Alexander Valley Individual Bunch Selected 1986 $18/375ml (8/31/87)
78   INGLENOOK Gewürztraminer Late Harvest Napa Valley 1986 $9.50/375ml (5/15/88)
75   QUADY Port Amador County Frank's Vineyard 1986 $16 (10/15/90)
68   QUADY Port Amador County Frank's Vineyard 1986 $16 (8/31/89)
68   RANCHO SISQUOC Johannisberg Riesling Late Harvest Santa Maria Valley Special Select 1986 $18/375ml (12/15/89)

1985

94   JOSEPH PHELPS Scheurbe Late Harvest Napa Valley 1985 $15 (8/31/86) SS
93   JOSEPH PHELPS Johannisberg Riesling Late Harvest Napa Valley 1985 $11.75 (12/15/86)
91   JOSEPH PHELPS Sémillon Late Harvest Napa Valley Délice du Sémillon 1985 $8.75/375ml (8/31/87)
91   RAYMOND Johannisberg Riesling Late Harvest Napa Valley 1985 $8.50 (9/15/86)
89   KENWOOD Johannisberg Riesling Late Harvest Sonoma Valley 1985 $10/375ml (2/28/87) BB
88   VICHON Sémillon Late Harvest Napa Valley Botrytis 1985 $15/375ml (7/15/88)
85   QUADY Black Muscat California Elysium 1985 $11 (9/15/86)
84   ARCIERO White Riesling Late Harvest Santa Barbara County December Harvest 1985 $10.50 (12/15/89)
84   CHATEAU ST. JEAN Johannisberg Riesling Late Harvest Russian River Valley Select 1985 $12 (8/31/87)
81   NAVARRO White Riesling Late Harvest Anderson Valley Cluster Selected 1985 $10/375ml (5/15/87)
79   QUADY Orange Muscat California Essensia 1985 $11 (9/30/86)
75   BERNARD PRADEL Sauvignon Blanc Late Harvest Napa Valley Allais Vineyard Botrytis 1985 $9/375ml (5/31/88)
73   QUADY Port California 1985 $9.50 (8/31/89)
72   AUSTIN Sauvignon Blanc Late Harvest Santa Barbara County Botrytis Sierra Madre Vineyards 1985 $13/375ml (12/15/89)
68   ROBERT STEMMLER Sauvignon Blanc Late Harvest Sonoma County 1985 $10/375ml (9/30/88)
65   QUADY Port Amador County Frank's Vineyard 1985 $16 (8/31/89)

1984

94   HIDDEN CELLARS Riesling Late Harvest Mendocino Bailey Lovin Vineyard 1984 $10 (10/16/85)
92   DE LOACH Gewürztraminer Late Harvest Russian River Valley 1984 $10 (10/01/85) BB
88   QUADY Orange Muscat California Essensia 1984 $11 (7/01/85)
87   QUADY Black Muscat California Elysium 1984 $11 (8/01/85)

86　CHATEAU ST. JEAN Johannisberg Riesling Late Harvest Alexander Valley Robert Young Vineyard 1984 $15/375ml (3/16/86)
86　CHATEAU ST. JEAN Sémillon Late Harvest Sonoma Valley Sémillon D'Or St. Jean Vineyard Select 1984 $15 (11/30/86)
84　MAYACAMAS Zinfandel Late Harvest Napa Valley 1984 $18 (11/15/89)
82　QUADY Port Amador County 1984 $9 (10/01/85)
79　KENWOOD Johannisberg Riesling Late Harvest Sonoma Valley 1984 $8.50/375ml (9/16/85)
75　CHARLES LEFRANC Gewürztraminer Late Harvest San Benito County Selected 1984 $11 (3/16/86)

1983

92　CHATEAU ST. JEAN Gewürztraminer Late Harvest Alexander Valley Gewürztraminer Robert Young Vineyard 1983 $14/375ml (11/01/84)
92　CHATEAU ST. JEAN Johannisberg Riesling Late Harvest Alexander Valley Robert Young Vineyard 1983 $25/375ml (8/01/85) SS
88　FRANCISCAN Johannisberg Riesling Late Harvest Napa Valley Select 1983 $10/375ml (1/31/88)
87　JOSEPH PHELPS Scheurbe Late Harvest Napa Valley 1983 $15 (9/16/84)
85　STAG'S LEAP WINE CELLARS White Riesling Late Harvest Napa Valley Birkmyer Vineyards Selected Bunches 1983 $13.50/375ml (10/01/84)
79　MARK WEST Johannisberg Riesling Late Harvest Russian River Valley 1983 $10/375ml (3/16/86)
75　JOSEPH PHELPS Johannisberg Riesling Late Harvest Napa Valley Special Selection 1983 $25 (3/16/86)
66　RUTHERFORD HILL Port Napa Valley Vintage 1983 $18 (11/15/87)
61　JOSEPH PHELPS Sémillon Late Harvest Napa Valley Délice du Sémillon 1983 $15 (1/31/87)

1982

92　CHATEAU ST. JEAN Johannisberg Riesling Late Harvest Alexander Valley Robert Young Vineyard 1982 $22/375ml (9/01/84)
92　JOSEPH PHELPS Johannisberg Riesling Late Harvest Napa Valley Special Select 1982 $22.50/375ml (4/16/84)
91　CHATEAU ST. JEAN Gewürztraminer Late Harvest Alexander Valley Robert Young Vineyard 1982 $18/375ml (7/16/84)
90　JOSEPH PHELPS Scheurbe Late Harvest Napa Valley 1982 $15 (4/16/84) CS
88　JOSEPH PHELPS Scheurbe Late Harvest Napa Valley Special Select 1982 $25/375ml (5/16/85)
85　CHATEAU ST. JEAN Sauvignon Blanc Late Harvest Sonoma County Sauvignon d'Or Select 1982 $15 (7/01/84)

1981

91　WOODBURY Port Alexander Valley Old Vines 1981 $10 (1/01/86)

1980

84　FICKLIN Port California Special Bottling No. 5 1980 $19 (4/30/91)

1973

95　WENTE BROS. Riesling Late Harvest Arroyo Seco Auslese 1973 (NA) (2/28/87)
91　FREEMARK ABBEY Johannisberg Riesling Late Harvest Napa Valley Edelwein Gold 1973 (NA)/375ml (2/28/87)

NV

80　GEYSER PEAK Dessert California Opulence NV $7.50 (1/31/87)
78　FICKLIN Tinta Port California NV $10 (4/30/91)

GAMAY

1989

75　WEINSTOCK Gamay Sonoma County 1989 $8 (3/31/91)

1988

85　PRESTON Gamay Beaujolais Dry Creek Valley 1988 $7 (2/15/89)
84　BUENA VISTA Gamay Beaujolais Carneros 1988 $7.50 (7/15/89)
78　CHARLES SHAW Gamay Beaujolais Napa Valley 1988 $6.50 (7/15/89)
76　DUXOUP Napa Gamay Dry Creek Valley 1988 $7.50 (2/28/90)
74　FETZER Gamay Beaujolais Mendocino County 1988 $5 (7/15/89)
73　BEAULIEU Gamay Beaujolais Napa Valley 1988 $6.50 (8/31/89)

1987

86　DUXOUP Napa Gamay Dry Creek Valley 1987 $7 (2/28/89) BB
83　FETZER Gamay Beaujolais Mendocino 1987 $6 (7/15/88)
82　BUENA VISTA Gamay Beaujolais Sonoma Valley Carneros 1987 $7.25 (2/29/88)
78　J. LOHR Gamay Monterey County Monterey Gamay 1987 $5.50 (7/15/88)
78　PRESTON Gamay Beaujolais Dry Creek Valley 1987 $6.25 (1/31/88)
77　J. PEDRONCELLI Gamay Beaujolais Sonoma County 1987 $4.50 (1/31/88)
76　BEAULIEU Gamay Beaujolais Napa Valley 1987 $6.50 (9/30/88)

1986

88　PRESTON Gamay Beaujolais Dry Creek Valley 1986 $11 (2/15/87)
83　BUENA VISTA Gamay Beaujolais Sonoma Valley Carneros 1986 $7.25 (5/31/87)
80　FETZER Gamay Beaujolais Mendocino County 1986 $4.50 (1/31/88)
77　CHARLES SHAW Gamay Napa Valley 1986 $6 (5/31/87)

1985

88　PRESTON Gamay Beaujolais Dry Creek Valley 1985 $5.50 (2/01/86)

1984

87　J. PEDRONCELLI Gamay Beaujolais Sonoma County 1984 $4.50 (8/31/87) BB

1983

62　CHARLES KRUG Gamay Beaujolais Napa Valley 1983 $4.50 (5/31/87)

GEWÜRZTRAMINER

1990

83　THOMAS FOGARTY Gewürztraminer Monterey Ventana Vineyards 1990 $9 (6/15/91)
81　DE LOACH Gewürztraminer Russian River Valley Early Harvest 1990 $8 (4/30/91)
78　QUAFF Gewürztraminer Sonoma County 1990 $6.25 (4/30/91)
75　FETZER Gewürztraminer California 1990 $6.75 (4/30/91)

1989

89　NAVARRO Gewürztraminer Anderson Valley 1989 $8.50 (4/30/91) BB
84　BOUCHAINE Gewürztraminer Carneros 1989 $8.50 (6/15/91)
83　DE LOACH Gewürztraminer Russian River Valley Early Harvest 1989 $7.50 (6/30/90)
81　HUSCH Gewürztraminer Anderson Valley 1989 $8 (6/30/90)
79　FETZER Gewürztraminer California 1989 $6 (6/30/90)
79　ROUND HILL Gewürztraminer Napa Valley 1989 $6 (2/15/91)
76　CLOS DU BOIS Gewürztraminer Alexander Valley Early Harvest 1989 $8 (2/15/91)

1988

89　HANDLEY Gewürztraminer Anderson Valley 1988 $7 (1/31/90) BB
88　FETZER Gewürztraminer California 1988 $6.50 (2/28/89) BB
84　ROUND HILL Gewürztraminer Napa Valley 1988 $6.25 (1/31/90) BB
81　JOSEPH PHELPS Gewürztraminer Napa Valley 1988 $8.50 (6/30/90)
80　ST. FRANCIS Gewürztraminer Sonoma Valley 1988 $7.50 (1/31/90)
79　NAVARRO Gewürztraminer Anderson Valley 1988 $8.50 (1/31/90)
78　CHARLES KRUG Gewürztraminer Napa Valley 1988 $7.25 (1/31/90)
77　CLOS DU BOIS Gewürztraminer Alexander Valley Early Harvest 1988 $8 (11/15/89)
72　CHATEAU ST. JEAN Gewürztraminer Sonoma County 1988 $8 (1/31/90)
72　HOP KILN Gewürztraminer Russian River Valley 1988 $7.50 (1/31/90)
69　ALEXANDER VALLEY Gewürztraminer Alexander Valley 1988 $6.50 (6/30/90)

1987

90　HUSCH Gewürztraminer Anderson Valley 1987 $7 (9/15/88)
89　NAVARRO Gewürztraminer Anderson Valley 1987 $7.50 (2/28/89)
87　DAVIS BYNUM Gewürztraminer Russian River Valley McIlroy Vineyard Reserve 1987 $7 (6/15/88)
86　HANDLEY Gewürztraminer Anderson Valley 1987 $7 (2/28/89)
86　Z MOORE Gewürztraminer Russian River Valley 1987 $8.50 (2/28/89)
85　CLOS DU BOIS Gewürztraminer Alexander Valley Early Harvest 1987 $8 (5/31/88)
84　FETZER Gewürztraminer California 1987 $6 (7/15/88) BB
83　DE LOACH Gewürztraminer Russian River Valley Early Harvest 1987 $7 (9/30/88)
83　HIDDEN CELLARS Gewürztraminer Mendocino County 1987 $7 (2/28/89)
79　ST. FRANCIS Gewürztraminer Sonoma Valley 1987 $7.50 (10/31/88)
78　QUAFF Gewürztraminer Sonoma County 1987 $6.50 (2/28/89)
76　GRAND CRU Gewürztraminer Alexander Valley 1987 $8.50 (10/31/88)
75　HACIENDA Gewürztraminer Sonoma County 1987 $7 (10/31/88)
75　ROUND HILL Gewürztraminer Napa Valley 1987 $6.25 (7/15/88)
75　RODNEY STRONG Gewürztraminer Sonoma County 1987 $5.50 (2/28/89)
73　BABCOCK Gewürztraminer Santa Ynez Valley 1987 $6.50 (2/28/89)
71　LOUIS M. MARTINI Gewürztraminer Russian River Valley Los Vinedos del Rio 1987 $7 (1/31/90)
71　J. PEDRONCELLI Gewürztraminer Sonoma County 1987 $5.50 (2/28/89)
69　FIELD STONE Gewürztraminer Alexander Valley 1987 $7 (2/28/89)
64　WENTE BROS. Gewürztraminer Arroyo Seco Vintner Grown Arroyo Seco Vineyards 1987 $9 (12/15/89)

1986

87　NAVARRO Gewürztraminer Anderson Valley 1986 $7.50 (5/31/88)
87　ST. FRANCIS Gewürztraminer Sonoma Valley 1986 $7 (1/31/88)
85　ROUND HILL Gewürztraminer Napa Valley 1986 $4.75 (7/31/87) BB
82　BABCOCK Gewürztraminer Santa Ynez Valley 1986 $6.50 (12/31/87)
82　FETZER Gewürztraminer California 1986 $4.50 (2/15/88) BB
80　RUTHERFORD HILL Gewürztraminer Napa Valley 1986 $6.25 (12/31/87)
78　MARK WEST Gewürztraminer Russian River Valley 1986 $7.50 (7/15/88)
78　PAT PAULSEN Gewürztraminer Alexander Valley 1986 $7 (12/31/87)
77　CLOS DU BOIS Gewürztraminer Alexander Valley Early Harvest 1986 $7.50 (8/31/87)
77　HOP KILN Gewürztraminer Russian River Valley 1986 $7.50 (9/15/88)
76　MONTICELLO Gewürztraminer Napa Valley 1986 $7.50 (2/28/89)
73　CLAIBORNE & CHURCHILL Gewürztraminer Edna Valley Dry Alsatian Style 1986 $8 (7/15/88)
72　BUENA VISTA Gewürztraminer Sonoma Valley Carneros 1986 $7.25 (5/31/88)
69　ALEXANDER VALLEY Gewürztraminer Alexander Valley 1986 $6.50 (5/31/88)
68　WENTE BROS. Gewürztraminer Arroyo Seco Vintner Grown 1986 $7.50 (9/15/87)
67　J. PEDRONCELLI Gewürztraminer Sonoma County 1986 $5.50 (9/15/88)
62　GEYSER PEAK Gewürztraminer Sonoma County 1986 $5.50 (12/31/87)
61　CHATEAU ST. JEAN Gewürztraminer Russian River Valley Frank Johnson Vineyards 1986 $8 (9/15/87)

1985

91　CLOS DU BOIS Gewürztraminer Alexander Valley Early Harvest 1985 $7.50 (4/16/86)
91　HUSCH Gewürztraminer Anderson Valley 1985 $6.25 (4/01/86)
85　BELVEDERE Gewürztraminer Los Carneros Winery Lake 1985 $7 (6/15/87)
84　FETZER Gewürztraminer California 1985 $6 (5/16/86)
83　CHATEAU ST. JEAN Gewürztraminer Alexander Valley 1985 $8 (6/16/86)
83　NAVARRO Gewürztraminer Anderson Valley 1985 $7.50 (8/31/87)
81　MONTICELLO Gewürztraminer Napa Valley 1985 $7.50 (8/31/87)
79　GRAND CRU Gewürztraminer Alexander Valley 1985 $8.50 (12/31/87)
77　MARK WEST Gewürztraminer Russian River Valley 1985 $7.50 (3/15/87)
76　RODNEY STRONG Gewürztraminer Sonoma County 1985 $7.50 (1/31/87)
75　ROUND HILL Gewürztraminer Napa Valley 1985 $5.50 (6/16/86)
74　DE LOACH Gewürztraminer Russian River Valley Early Harvest 1985 $7 (3/15/87)
74　INGLENOOK Gewürztraminer Napa Valley 1985 $6.50 (5/31/88)
59　GUNDLACH BUNDSCHU Gewürztraminer Sonoma Valley Rhinefarm Vineyards 1985 $12 (6/16/86)
59　HACIENDA Gewürztraminer Sonoma County 1985 $7 (6/15/87)
55　ALEXANDER VALLEY Gewürztraminer Alexander Valley 1985 $6.50 (6/16/86)
51　CALLAWAY Gewürztraminer California 1985 $5.50 (9/15/86)

1984

90　HOP KILN Gewürztraminer Russian River Valley 1984 $7.50 (12/01/85)
87　CLOS DU BOIS Gewürztraminer Alexander Valley Early Harvest 1984 $7.50 (11/01/85)
86　DE LOACH Gewürztraminer Russian River Valley Early Harvest 1984 $7 (11/01/85)
83　WENTE BROS. Gewürztraminer Arroyo Seco Vintner Grown 1984 $7.50 (3/01/86)
82　CHATEAU ST. JEAN Gewürztraminer Alexander Valley 1984 $8 (5/16/85)
81　ST. FRANCIS Gewürztraminer Sonoma Valley 1984 $7 (5/16/85)
79　ROUND HILL Gewürztraminer Napa Valley 1984 $5 (10/16/85)
76　RUTHERFORD HILL Gewürztraminer Napa Valley 1984 $6.25 (5/16/86)
75　JOSEPH PHELPS Gewürztraminer Napa Valley 1984 $8 (11/01/85)

UNITED STATES
CALIFORNIA/*GEWÜRZTRAMINER*

74 BELVEDERE Gewürztraminer Los Carneros Winery Lake 1984 $7 (11/01/85)
70 HACIENDA Gewürztraminer Sonoma County 1984 $7 (3/01/86)
70 MONTICELLO Gewürztraminer Napa Valley 1984 $7.50 (3/01/86)
68 FIRESTONE Gewürztraminer Santa Ynez Valley 1984 $6.50 (8/31/86)
67 E.&J. GALLO Gewürztraminer California Limited Release Reserve 1984 $3.50 (9/30/86)
63 BUENA VISTA Gewürztraminer Sonoma Valley Carneros 1984 $7 (5/16/86)
55 KENWOOD Gewürztraminer Sonoma Valley 1984 $7.50 (9/15/86)

1983

77 ALEXANDER VALLEY Gewürztraminer Alexander Valley 1983 $6.50 (11/01/84)

MERLOT

1990

90+ CLOS DU VAL Merlot Stags Leap District 1990 (NR) (5/15/91) (BT)
90+ CHATEAU SOUVERAIN Merlot Alexander Valley 1990 (NR) (5/15/91) (BT)
90+ CAIN Merlot Napa Valley 1990 (NR) (5/15/91) (BT)
85+ STELTZNER Merlot Stags Leap District 1990 (NR) (5/15/91) (BT)
85+ ALEXANDER VALLEY Merlot Alexander Valley 1990 (NR) (5/15/91) (BT)
85+ DUCKHORN Merlot Napa Valley 1990 (NR) (5/15/91) (BT)
85+ FLORA SPRINGS Merlot Napa Valley 1990 (NR) (5/15/91) (BT)
85+ MARKHAM Merlot Napa Valley 1990 (NR) (5/15/91) (BT)
85+ PINE RIDGE Merlot Napa Valley Selected Cuvée 1990 (NR) (5/15/91) (BT)
85+ SHAFER Merlot Napa Valley 1990 (NR) (5/15/91) (BT)
85+ STERLING Merlot Napa Valley 1990 (NR) (5/15/91) (BT)
85+ STONEGATE Merlot Napa Valley Pershing Vineyard 1990 (NR) (5/15/91) (BT)

1989

90+ BERINGER Merlot Howell Mountain Bancroft Ranch 1989 (NR) (5/15/91) (BT)
85+ CLOS DU VAL Merlot Stags Leap District 1989 (NR) (5/15/91) (BT)
85+ ALEXANDER VALLEY Merlot Alexander Valley 1989 (NR) (5/15/91) (BT)
85+ COSENTINO Merlot Napa Valley 1989 (NR) (5/15/91) (BT)
84 RAVENSWOOD Merlot Sonoma County Vintners Blend 1989 $9 (3/31/91) BB
83 RICHARDSON Merlot Carneros Sonoma Valley Gregory 1989 $14 (3/31/91)
72 MOUNTAIN VIEW Merlot Napa County 1989 $6 (5/31/91)
70 NAPA CELLARS Merlot California 1989 $7 (5/31/91)

1988

90 MARKHAM Merlot Napa Valley 1988 $13.50 (4/15/91)
90+ SANTA CRUZ MOUNTAIN Merlot Central Coast 1988 (NR) (4/30/90) (BT)
90+ CONN CREEK Merlot Napa Valley 1988 (NR) (4/30/90) (BT)
89 CLOS DU VAL Merlot Stags Leap District 1988 $20 (3/31/91)
86 SILVERADO Merlot Stags Leap District 1988 $15.50 (5/31/91)
86 CUVAISON Merlot Napa Valley 1988 $24 (4/15/91)
86 DUCKHORN Merlot Napa Valley 1988 $19 (12/31/90)
85 MARILYN MERLOT Merlot Napa Valley 1988 $12.50 (5/31/91)
85+ BUENA VISTA Merlot Carneros Private Reserve 1988 (NR) (4/30/90) (BT)
85+ FLORA SPRINGS Merlot Napa Valley 1988 (NR) (4/30/90) (BT)
85+ GUNDLACH BUNDSCHU Merlot Sonoma Valley Rhinefarm Vineyards 1988 $16 (4/30/90) (BT)
85+ MARKHAM Merlot Napa Valley 1988 $13.50 (4/30/90) (BT)
85+ LOUIS M. MARTINI Merlot Russian River Valley Los Viendos del Rio 1988 (NR) (4/30/90) (BT)
85+ NEWTON Merlot Napa Valley 1988 $11 (4/30/90) (BT)
85+ PINE RIDGE Merlot Napa Valley Selected Cuvée 1988 (NR) (4/30/90) (BT)
85+ SHAFER Merlot Napa Valley 1988 $16.50 (4/30/90) (BT)
85+ STERLING Merlot Napa Valley 1988 $15 (4/30/90) (BT)
85+ VICHON Merlot Napa Valley 1988 $16 (4/30/90) (BT)
84 BEAUCANON Merlot Napa Valley 1988 $13 (3/31/91)
83 DRY CREEK Merlot Dry Creek Valley 1988 $15 (3/31/91)
83 KONOCTI Merlot Lake County 1988 $9.50 (3/31/91) BB
83 SHAFER Merlot Napa Valley 1988 $16.50 (12/31/90)
83 STERLING Merlot Napa Valley 1988 $15 (4/15/91)
82 COSENTINO Merlot Napa County 1988 $18 (4/15/91)
82 GAINEY Merlot Santa Barbara County 1988 $13 (4/15/91)
82 FIRESTONE Merlot Santa Ynez Valley 1988 $11 (3/31/91)
82 FOLIE A DEUX Merlot Napa Valley 1988 $18 (3/31/91)
82 HAVENS Merlot Napa Valley 1988 $14 (3/31/91)
82 STRAUS Merlot Napa Valley 1988 $14 (12/31/90)
82 WHITEHALL LANE Merlot Knights Valley Summers Ranch 1988 $18 (3/31/91)
81 CLOS DU BOIS Merlot Sonoma County 1988 $15 (5/31/91)
81 GUNDLACH BUNDSCHU Merlot Sonoma Valley Rhinefarm Vineyards 1988 $16 (5/31/91)
81 VICHON Merlot Napa Valley 1988 $16 (12/31/90)
80+ FRANCISCAN Merlot Napa Valley Oakville Estate 1988 (NR) (4/30/90) (BT)
78 BOEGER Merlot El Dorado 1988 $12.50 (3/31/91)
78 PARDUCCI Merlot North Coast 1988 $9.50 (4/30/91)
76 MONTEREY VINEYARD Merlot Monterey County Classic 1988 $6 (12/31/90)
76 SMITH & HOOK Merlot Monterey Santa Lucia Highlands 1988 $15 (3/31/91)
75 NAPA CREEK Merlot Napa Valley 1988 $13 (3/31/91)
74 CONGRESS SPRINGS Merlot Santa Clara County 1988 $14 (3/31/91)
74 TERRA Merlot Napa Valley 1988 $12 (5/31/91)

1987

93 GUNDLACH BUNDSCHU Merlot Sonoma Valley Rhinefarm Vineyards 1987 $13 (10/31/89) SS

92 MATANZAS CREEK Merlot Sonoma County 1987 Rel: $25 Cur: $32 (6/15/90) SS
92 DUCKHORN Merlot Napa Valley Three Palms Vineyard 1987 Rel: $25 Cur: $50 (7/31/90)
92 SHAFER Merlot Napa Valley 1987 $15 (10/15/89)
92 SILVERADO Merlot Napa Valley 1987 $14 (4/15/90)
91 BERINGER Merlot Howell Mountain Bancroft Ranch 1987 $29 (12/31/90)
91 DUCKHORN Merlot Napa Valley 1987 Rel: $18 Cur: $26 (12/31/89)
91 MARKHAM Merlot Napa Valley 1987 $13.50 (10/15/89)
91 VICHON Merlot Napa Valley 1987 $16 (2/15/90)
90 STRAUS Merlot Napa Valley 1987 $12 (2/15/90)
90 STERLING Merlot Carneros Winery Lake 1987 $25 (12/31/90)
90+ BERINGER Merlot Howell Mountain Bancroft Ranch 1988 (NR) (4/30/90) (BT)
90+ BERINGER Merlot Howell Mountain Bancroft Ranch 1987 $29 (4/15/89) (BT)
90+ COSENTINO Merlot Napa County 1987 (NR) (4/15/89) (BT)
90+ DUCKHORN Merlot Napa Valley Three Palms Vineyard 1987 Rel: $25 Cur: $50 (4/15/89) (BT)
90+ KEENAN Merlot Napa Valley 1987 Rel: $18 Cur: $20 (4/15/89) (BT)
90+ PINE RIDGE Merlot Napa Valley Selected Cuvée 1987 $15 (4/15/89) (BT)
90+ RAVENSWOOD Merlot Sonoma County 1987 $18 (4/15/89) (BT)
89 CHAPPELLET Merlot Napa Valley 1987 $15 (12/31/90)
89 CLOS DU BOIS Merlot Sonoma County 1987 $12 (4/15/90)
89 GEORIS Merlot Carmel Valley 1987 $27 (3/31/91)
89 HAVENS Merlot Napa Valley 1987 $14 (7/15/90)
88 FRANCISCAN Merlot Napa Valley Oakville Estate 1987 $12.50 (6/15/90)
88 KEENAN Merlot Napa Valley 1987 Rel: $18 Cur: $20 (3/31/90)
88 PINE RIDGE Merlot Napa Valley Selected Cuvée 1987 $15 (4/15/90)
88 ROBERT SINSKEY Merlot Napa Valley 1987 $18 (3/31/91)
87 CONN CREEK Merlot Napa Valley Collins Vineyard Barrel Select Limited Bottling 1987 $22 (12/31/90)
87 DUCKHORN Merlot Napa Valley Vine Hill Ranch 1987 $18 (7/31/90)
87 FLORA SPRINGS Merlot Napa Valley 1987 $16.50 (7/31/90)
87 KENDALL-JACKSON Merlot Sonoma County The Proprietor's 1987 $20 (12/31/90)
87 RAVENSWOOD Merlot Sonoma County 1987 $18 (1/31/90)
87 ROMBAUER Merlot Napa Valley 1987 $14 (2/15/90)
86 BENZIGER Merlot Sonoma Valley 1987 $12 (3/31/91)
86 BUENA VISTA Merlot Sonoma County 1987 $11 (7/31/90)
86 CAFARO Merlot Napa Valley 1987 $18 (12/31/90)
86 QUAIL RIDGE Merlot Napa Valley 1987 $15 (6/15/90)
86 STONEGATE Merlot Napa Valley Spaulding Vineyard 1987 $16.50 (3/31/91)
85 CLOS DU VAL Merlot Stags Leap District 1987 $17 (3/31/90)
85 LAKESPRING Merlot Napa Valley 1987 $14 (6/15/90)
85 ST. CLEMENT Merlot Napa Valley 1987 $16 (12/31/90)
85+ CUVAISON Merlot Napa Valley 1987 $20 (4/15/89) (BT)
85+ DUCKHORN Merlot Napa Valley 1987 Rel: $18 Cur: $26 (4/15/89) (BT)
85+ FRANCISCAN Merlot Napa Valley Oakville Estate 1987 $12.50 (4/15/89) (BT)
85+ GUNDLACH BUNDSCHU Merlot Sonoma Valley Rhinefarm Vineyards 1987 $13 (4/15/89) (BT)
85+ MATANZAS CREEK Merlot Sonoma County 1987 Rel: $25 Cur: $32 (4/15/89) (BT)
85+ NEWTON Merlot Napa Valley 1987 $17 (4/15/89) (BT)
85+ NEWTON Merlot Napa Valley Reserve 1987 (NR) (4/15/89) (BT)
85+ SHAFER Merlot Napa Valley 1987 $15 (4/15/89) (BT)
85+ SILVERADO Merlot Napa Valley 1987 $14 (4/15/89) (BT)
85+ WHITEHALL LANE Merlot Knights Valley 1987 $16 (4/15/89) (BT)
84 BRAREN PAULI Merlot Alexander Valley Mauritson Vineyard 1987 $11 (3/31/91)
84 BUENA VISTA Merlot Carneros Private Reserve 1987 $18 (3/31/91)
84 FERRARI-CARANO Merlot Alexander Valley 1987 $16.50 (7/31/90)
83 FIRESTONE Merlot Santa Ynez Valley 1987 $9 (12/15/89)
83 MASSON Merlot Monterey County Vintage Selection 1987 $8.50 (7/15/90)
83 SMITH & HOOK Merlot Napa County 1987 $15 (12/31/90)
83 STRATFORD Merlot California 1987 $13 (10/31/89)
83 NAPA CREEK Merlot Napa Valley 1987 $13.50 (6/15/90)
83 STERLING Merlot Napa Valley 1987 $13 (6/15/90)
83 STONEGATE Merlot Napa Valley Pershing Vineyard 1987 $16.50 (3/31/91)
82 GEYSER PEAK Merlot Alexander Valley 1987 $8 (7/15/90)
81 BOEGER Merlot El Dorado 1987 $12.50 (7/15/90)
81 NEWTON Merlot Napa Valley 1987 $17 (7/31/90)
80 COSENTINO Merlot Napa County Reserve 1987 $18 (7/31/90)
80 JOSEPH PHELPS Merlot Napa Valley 1987 $18 (7/31/90)
80 ST. FRANCIS Merlot Sonoma Valley 1987 $14 (6/15/90)
80+ BUENA VISTA Merlot Carneros 1987 (NR) (4/15/89) (BT)
80+ CHAPPELLET Merlot Napa Valley 1987 $15 (4/15/89) (BT)
80+ CONN CREEK Merlot Napa Valley 1987 (NR) (4/15/89) (BT)
80+ INGLENOOK Merlot Napa Valley 1987 (NR) (4/15/89) (BT)
80+ LAKESPRING Merlot Napa Valley 1987 $14 (4/15/89) (BT)
80+ LOUIS M. MARTINI Merlot Russian River Valley Los Viendos del Rio 1987 (NR) (4/15/89) (BT)
80+ RIDGE Merlot Sonoma County Bradford Mountain 1987 $17 (4/15/89) (BT)
80+ SANTA CRUZ MOUNTAIN Merlot Central Coast 1987 (NR) (4/15/89) (BT)
80+ STERLING Merlot Napa Valley 1987 $13 (4/15/89) (BT)
80+ VICHON Merlot Napa Valley 1987 $16 (4/15/89) (BT)
77 M.G. VALLEJO Merlot California 1987 $7 (6/15/90)
77 WHITEHALL LANE Merlot Knights Valley 1987 $16 (7/15/90)
75 SMITH & HOOK Merlot Napa County 1987 $15 (7/15/90)
75 RIDGE Merlot Sonoma County Bradford Mountain 1987 $17 (7/15/90)
75+ FLORA SPRINGS Merlot Napa Valley 1987 $16.50 (4/15/89) (BT)
74 RUTHERFORD HILL Merlot Napa Valley 1987 $14 (3/31/91)
73 KONOCTI Merlot Lake County 1987 $9.50 (12/31/90)
73 M.G. VALLEJO Merlot California 1987 $7 (10/31/89)

1986

94 ST. FRANCIS Merlot Sonoma Valley Reserve 1986 $20 (1/31/90)
93 KENDALL-JACKSON Merlot Alexander Valley 1986 $16 (12/31/88)
93 STRAUS Merlot Napa Valley 1986 $11 (2/28/89)
92 MATANZAS CREEK Merlot Sonoma County 1986 Rel: $20 Cur: $20 (6/30/89)
91 GUNDLACH BUNDSCHU Merlot Sonoma Valley Rhinefarm Vineyards 1986 $12 (12/31/88)
91 SHAFER Merlot Napa Valley 1986 $13 (12/31/88)
91 SILVERADO Merlot Napa Valley 1986 $12 (8/31/89)
90 KEENAN Merlot Napa Valley 1986 Rel: $18 Cur: $20 (6/30/89)
90 MURPHY-GOODE Merlot Alexander Valley Premier Vineyard 1986 $14 (1/31/89)
90+ DUCKHORN Merlot Napa Valley 1986 Rel: $17 Cur: $30 (4/15/88) (BT)

90+ DUCKHORN Merlot Napa Valley Three Palms Vineyard 1986 Rel: $20 Cur: $59 (4/15/88) (BT)
90+ KEENAN Merlot Napa Valley 1986 Rel: $18 Cur: $20 (4/15/88) (BT)
90+ MATANZAS CREEK Merlot Sonoma County 1986 Rel: $20 Cur: $20 (4/15/88) (BT)
90+ RAVENSWOOD Merlot Sonoma County 1986 $18 (4/15/88) (BT)
90+ WHITEHALL LANE Merlot Knights Valley 1986 (NR) (4/15/88) (BT)
90+ VICHON Merlot Napa Valley 1986 (NR) (4/15/88) (BT)
90+ ST. FRANCIS Merlot Sonoma Valley 1986 $14 (4/15/88) (BT)
88 R.W. DOLAN Merlot California 1986 $8 (1/31/89)
88 DUCKHORN Merlot Napa Valley Three Palms Vineyard 1986 Rel: $20 Cur: $59 (7/31/89)
87 BELVEDERE Merlot Alexander Valley Robert Young Vineyards 1986 $13 (6/30/89)
87 FERRARI-CARANO Merlot Alexander Valley 1986 $15 (6/30/89)
87 RUTHERFORD RANCH Merlot Napa Valley 1986 $11.75 (12/31/88)
86 BUENA VISTA Merlot Carneros Private Reserve 1986 $16.50 (10/31/89)
86 CLOS DU BOIS Merlot Sonoma County 1986 $10.75 (10/15/88)
86 CLOS DU VAL Merlot Napa Valley 1986 $16 (8/31/89)
86 DUCKHORN Merlot Napa Valley 1986 Rel: $17 Cur: $30 (1/31/89)
86 SMITH & HOOK Merlot Napa County 1986 $20 (8/31/89)
86 VICHON Merlot Napa Valley 1986 $16 (8/31/89)
85 COSENTINO Merlot Napa County 1986 $14 (9/30/88)
85 MARILYN MERLOT Merlot Napa Valley 1986 $13 (12/31/88)
85 ST. FRANCIS Merlot Sonoma Valley 1986 $14 (6/30/89)
85 STERLING Merlot Napa Valley 1986 $14 (3/31/89)
85+ BELVEDERE Merlot Alexander Valley Robert Young Vineyards 1986 $13 (4/15/88) (BT)
85+ BUENA VISTA Merlot Carneros Private Reserve 1986 $16.50 (4/15/88) (BT)
85+ CLOS DU BOIS Merlot Sonoma County 1986 $10.75 (4/15/88) (BT)
85+ DEHLINGER Merlot Sonoma County 1986 $13 (4/15/88) (BT)
85+ DRY CREEK Merlot Dry Creek Valley 1986 $15 (4/15/88) (BT)
85+ FLORA SPRINGS Merlot Napa Valley 1986 $16 (4/15/88) (BT)
85+ FRANCISCAN Merlot Napa Valley Oakville Estate 1986 (NR) (4/15/88) (BT)
85+ LOUIS M. MARTINI Merlot Russian River Valley Los Viendos del Rio 1986 $20 (4/15/88) (BT)
85+ NEWTON Merlot Napa Valley 1986 $15 (4/15/88) (BT)
85+ PINE RIDGE Merlot Napa Valley Selected Cuvée 1986 $15 (4/15/88) (BT)
84 BENZIGER Merlot Sonoma Valley 1986 $16 (7/31/89)
84 CAFARO Merlot Napa Valley 1986 $18 (12/31/89)
84 CLOS PEGASE Merlot Napa Valley 1986 $15.50 (7/15/90)
84 FITCH MOUNTAIN Merlot Napa Valley 1986 $9 (9/30/88)
84 GLEN ELLEN Merlot California Proprietor's Reserve 1986 $6 (1/31/89) BB
84 MONTEREY PENINSULA Merlot Monterey Doctors' Reserve 1986 $16 (3/31/91)
84 JOSEPH PHELPS Merlot Napa Valley 1986 $15 (6/30/88)
84 STAGS' LEAP WINERY Merlot Napa Valley 1986 $17 (12/31/90)
84 STONEGATE Merlot Napa Valley 1986 $15 (4/15/90)
83 CAIN Merlot Napa Valley 1986 $14 (2/28/89)
83 DEHLINGER Merlot Sonoma County 1986 $13 (7/31/89)
83 FENESTRA Merlot Sonoma County 1986 $11 (10/15/89)
83 FIRESTONE Merlot Santa Ynez Valley 1986 $9 (9/30/88)
83 JAEGER Merlot Napa Valley Inglewood Vineyard 1986 $19 (3/31/91)
83 NEWTON Merlot Napa Valley 1986 $15 (12/31/88)
83 ROBERT SINSKEY Merlot Napa Valley 1986 $17 (10/15/89)
82 J. CAREY Merlot Santa Ynez Valley La Cuesta Vineyard 1986 $12 (12/15/89)
82 ROUND HILL Merlot Napa Valley Reserve 1986 $12 (12/31/88)
81 INGLENOOK Merlot Napa Valley Reserve 1986 $12 (10/31/89)
80 CHAPPELLET Merlot Napa Valley 1986 $15 (1/31/90)
80 CHATEAU CHEVRE Merlot Napa Valley Reserve 1986 $25 (7/31/89)
80 DUCKHORN Merlot Napa Valley Vine Hill Ranch 1986 $18 (7/31/89)
80 FRANCISCAN Merlot Napa Valley Oakville Estate 1986 $12 (7/31/89)
80 GUENOC Merlot Lake-Napa Counties 1986 $12 (6/15/90)
80 PINE RIDGE Merlot Napa Valley Selected Cuvée 1986 $15 (6/30/89)
80 RAVENSWOOD Merlot Sonoma County 1986 $18 (12/31/88)
80 YORK MOUNTAIN Merlot San Luis Obispo County 1986 $10 (12/31/89)
80+ HAVENS Merlot Napa Valley Reserve 1986 (NR) (4/15/88) (BT)
80+ STERLING Merlot Napa Valley 1986 $14 (4/15/88) (BT)
79 LAKESPRING Merlot Napa Valley 1986 $14 (3/31/89)
79 LOUIS M. MARTINI Merlot North Coast 1986 $12 (10/31/89)
79 LOUIS M. MARTINI Merlot Russian River Valley Los Vinedos del Rio 1986 $20 (3/31/90)
78 DRY CREEK Merlot Sonoma County 1986 $15 (3/31/89)
78 CHATEAU NAPA-BEAUCANON Merlot Napa Valley 1986 $13 (12/31/88)
78 ROMBAUER Merlot Napa Valley 1986 $14 (7/31/89)
78 STRATFORD Merlot California 1986 $10 (1/31/89)
77 GEORIS Merlot Carmel 1986 $25 (12/31/90)
77 RANCHO SISQUOC Merlot Santa Maria Valley 1986 $9 (12/15/89)
77 WILD HORSE Merlot Central Coast 1986 $11 (7/31/89)
75+ HAVENS Merlot Napa Valley 1986 $13.50 (4/15/88) (BT)
75+ CHARLES KRUG Merlot Carneros Napa Valley 1986 (NR) (4/15/88) (BT)
74 ST. CLEMENT Merlot Napa Valley 1986 $15 (10/31/89)
74 CHATEAU SOUVERAIN Merlot Sonoma County 1986 $10 (3/31/89)
73 BOEGER Merlot El Dorado 1986 $12.50 (1/31/89)
73 VICHON Merlot Napa Valley 1986 $16 (6/30/89)
72 HAVENS Merlot Napa Valley 1986 $13.50 (3/31/90)
72 WHITEHALL LANE Merlot Knights Valley Reserve 1986 $15 (7/31/89)
69 BELLEROSE Merlot Sonoma County 1986 $16 (4/15/90)
68 RUTHERFORD HILL Merlot Napa Valley 1986 $13 (6/15/90)
64 RIDGE Merlot Sonoma County Bradford Mountain 1986 $16 (7/31/89)
60 CHATEAU JULIEN Merlot Monterey County 1986 $10 (4/15/89)

1985

93 DUCKHORN Merlot Napa Valley 1985 Rel: $16 Cur: $38 (12/31/87) CS
93 NEWTON Merlot Napa Valley 1985 $14 (3/31/88)
92 CLOS DU BOIS Merlot Sonoma County 1985 $10 (10/31/87) SS
92 GUNDLACH BUNDSCHU Merlot Sonoma Valley Rhinefarm Vineyards 1985 $12 (2/29/88) SS
92 RUTHERFORD HILL Merlot Napa Valley 1985 $12 (1/31/89)
92 RUTHERFORD RANCH Merlot Napa Valley 1985 $10.50 (4/30/88)
91 DUCKHORN Merlot Napa Valley Three Palms Vineyard 1985 Rel: $20 Cur: $63 (6/30/88)
91 DUCKHORN Merlot Napa Valley Vine Hill Ranch 1985 $18 (6/30/88)
91 INGLENOOK Merlot Napa Valley Reserve 1985 $10.50 (10/15/88) SS
91 LAKESPRING Merlot Napa Valley 1985 $12 (3/31/88) SS
91 PINE RIDGE Merlot Napa Valley Selected Cuvée 1985 $13 (2/15/88) SS
91 ST. CLEMENT Merlot Napa Valley 1985 $15 (3/31/89)

90 FREEMARK ABBEY Merlot Napa Valley 1985 $10 (12/31/88)
90 QUAIL RIDGE Merlot Napa Valley 1985 $13.50 (3/31/89)
90 SHAFER Merlot Napa Valley 1985 $12.50 (12/15/87)
90 VINA VISTA Merlot Alexander Valley 1985 $8 (10/31/87)
89 CUVAISON Merlot Napa Valley 1985 $19 (6/30/88)
89 DEHLINGER Merlot Sonoma County 1985 $10.50 (4/30/88)
89 FITCH MOUNTAIN Merlot Napa Valley 1985 $9 (12/15/87)
89 FRANCISCAN Merlot Napa Valley Oakville Estate 1985 $9.25 (5/31/88)
89 JAEGER Merlot Napa Valley Inglewood Vineyard 1985 $16 (2/15/90)
88 ALEXANDER VALLEY Merlot Alexander Valley 1985 $11 (10/31/87)
88 LEEWARD Merlot Napa Valley 1985 $10 (5/15/87)
88 MARKHAM Merlot Napa Valley 1985 $11 (4/30/88)
88 MATANZAS CREEK Merlot Sonoma Valley 1985 Rel: $18 Cur: $40 (5/31/88)
88 VICHON Merlot Napa Valley 1985 $14 (12/15/87)
87 CHATEAU CHEVRE Merlot Napa Valley 1985 $16 (8/31/88)
87 CLOS DU VAL Merlot Napa Valley 1985 $15.50 (4/30/88)
87 STERLING Merlot Napa Valley 1985 $14 (3/31/88)
86 STAG'S LEAP WINE CELLARS Merlot Napa Valley 1985 $16 (5/31/88)
85 GUENOC Merlot Guenoc Valley 1985 $15 (3/31/89)
85 SEBASTIANI Merlot Sonoma County Family Selection 1985 $7 (9/30/88)
84 CARNEROS CREEK Merlot Napa Valley 1985 $12.50 (2/15/88)
84 CHESTNUT HILL Merlot North Coast 1985 $8.50 (12/15/87)
84 CONN CREEK Merlot Napa Valley Collins Vineyard 1985 $14 (3/31/88)
84 HAVENS Merlot Napa Valley 1985 $12.50 (5/31/88)
84 HUNTER ASHBY Merlot Napa Valley 1985 $9.75 (7/31/89)
84 ROUND HILL Merlot Napa Valley Reserve 1985 $10 (5/31/88)
83 GEORIS Merlot Carmel Valley 1985 $20 (4/15/89)
83 KEENAN Merlot Napa Valley 1985 Rel: $18 Cur: $20 (5/31/88)
83 KONOCTI Merlot Lake County 1985 $8 (12/31/88)
83 MONTEREY PENINSULA Merlot Monterey Doctors' Reserve 1985 $14 (1/31/89)
83 TAFT STREET Merlot Sonoma County 1985 $10 (5/31/88)
82 BOEGER Merlot El Dorado 1985 $12.50 (2/15/88)
82 FLORA SPRINGS Merlot Napa Valley 1985 $15 (6/30/88)
81 ST. FRANCIS Merlot Sonoma Valley Reserve 1985 $14.50 (12/31/88)
81 STRAUS Merlot Napa Valley 1985 $10 (2/15/88)
80 BUENA VISTA Merlot Carneros 1985 $11 (6/30/88)
80 CHRISTIAN BROTHERS Merlot Napa Valley 1985 $8 (8/31/88)
80 DRY CREEK Merlot Dry Creek Valley 1985 $7.50 (2/15/88)
80+ MATANZAS CREEK Merlot Sonoma Valley 1985 Rel: $18 Cur: $40 (6/15/87) (BT)
79 RODNEY STRONG Merlot Russian River Valley River West Vineyard 1985 $12 (2/28/90)
78 CHAPPELLET Merlot Napa Valley 1985 $12 (12/31/88)
78 FIRESTONE Merlot Santa Ynez Valley 1985 $9 (4/30/88)
77 GEYSER PEAK Merlot Alexander Valley 1985 $7.75 (10/15/88)
73 BELLEROSE Merlot Sonoma County 1985 $16 (2/28/89)
69 LAMBERT BRIDGE Merlot Sonoma County 1985 $10 (12/15/87)
66 ST. FRANCIS Merlot Sonoma Valley 1985 $12 (10/15/88)

1984

94 DEHLINGER Merlot Sonoma County 1984 $12 (6/15/87) SS
94 DUCKHORN Merlot Napa Valley 1984 Rel: $15 Cur: $40 (12/31/86) SS
94 KEENAN Merlot Napa Valley 1984 Rel: $16.50 Cur: $20 (7/31/87) CS
93 STERLING Merlot Napa Valley 1984 $11.50 (4/30/87)
91 CHATEAU CHEVRE Merlot Napa Valley 1984 $12.50 (10/31/87)
91 MATANZAS CREEK Merlot Sonoma Valley 1984 Rel: $14.50 Cur: $25 (6/30/87)
90 BELVEDERE Merlot Alexander Valley Robert Young Vineyards 1984 $13 (8/31/88)
90 CUVAISON Merlot Napa Valley Anniversary Release 1984 $13.50 (8/31/87)
90 FRANCISCAN Merlot Napa Valley Oakville Estate 1984 $8.50 (6/30/87) SS
89 CAIN Merlot Napa Valley 1984 $12 (9/30/88)
89 DUCKHORN Merlot Napa Valley Three Palms Vineyard 1984 Rel: $18 Cur: $70 (7/31/87)
88 CLOS DU VAL Merlot Napa Valley 1984 $15 (7/31/87)
88 GUNDLACH BUNDSCHU Merlot Sonoma Valley Rhinefarm Vineyards 1984 $12 (2/28/87)
88 LAKESPRING Merlot Napa Valley 1984 $12 (5/15/87)
88 ST. FRANCIS Merlot Sonoma Valley 1984 $12 (10/31/87)
87 BUENA VISTA Merlot Carneros Private Reserve 1984 $14.50 (2/15/88)
87 CARNEROS CREEK Merlot Napa Valley 1984 $10.50 (8/31/87)
87 CLOS DU BOIS Merlot Sonoma County 1984 $9 (5/16/86)
87 ROUND HILL Merlot Napa Valley 1984 $9 (5/15/87)
87 SHAFER Merlot Napa Valley 1984 $12.50 (2/28/87)
87 WHITEHALL LANE Merlot Knights Valley 1984 $14 (12/31/87)
86 CHATEAU SOUVERAIN Merlot Sonoma County 1984 $8.50 (7/31/87)
85 RAVENSWOOD Merlot Sonoma County 1984 $11 (2/28/87)
85 STONEGATE Merlot Napa Valley Spaulding Vineyard Proprietor's Reserve 1984 $15 (12/31/88)
84 RUTHERFORD HILL Merlot Napa Valley 1984 $11 (4/30/88)
83 ACACIA Merlot Napa Valley 1984 $15 (2/28/87)
83 RUTHERFORD RANCH Merlot Napa Valley 1984 $9.75 (10/15/87)
82 LOUIS M. MARTINI Merlot Russian River Valley Los Vinedos del Rio 1984 $12 (2/15/88)
80 PINE RIDGE Merlot Napa Valley Selected Cuvée 1984 $13 (5/15/87)
79 LOUIS M. MARTINI Merlot North Coast 1984 $6.75 (2/15/88)
78 CHATEAU CHEVRE Merlot Napa Valley Reserve 1984 $15 (12/15/87)
78 SILVERADO Merlot Napa Valley 1984 $12.50 (12/15/87)
78 STAG'S LEAP WINE CELLARS Merlot Napa Valley 1984 $15 (5/15/87)
77 BELLEROSE Merlot Sonoma County 1984 $12 (12/31/87)
76 CHATEAU JULIEN Merlot Santa Barbara County Bien Nacido Vineyard 1984 $12 (2/29/88)
74 MONTEREY PENINSULA Merlot Monterey Doctors' Reserve 1984 $12 (12/15/87)
74 ST. FRANCIS Merlot Sonoma Valley Reserve 1984 $16 (2/15/88)
72 ESTATE WILLIAM BACCALA Merlot Alexander Valley 1984 $10 (2/28/87)
70 PAGOR Merlot Santa Maria Valley 1984 $10.25 (4/30/88)
70 CHARLES LEFRANC Merlot Monterey County San Lucas Ranch 1984 $8.50 (12/15/87)
69 GEYSER PEAK Merlot Alexander Valley 1984 $7 (2/29/88)
68 MILL CREEK Merlot Dry Creek Valley 1984 $8.50 (2/15/88)
66 SANFORD Merlot Santa Barbara County 1984 $18 (12/31/87)

1983

94 DUCKHORN Merlot Napa Valley 1983 Rel: $15 Cur: $45 (11/01/85) CS
93 SHAFER Merlot Napa Valley 1983 $10 (2/16/86)
92 CLOS DU VAL Merlot Napa Valley 1983 $14 (6/16/86)
92 GUNDLACH BUNDSCHU Merlot Sonoma Valley Rhinefarm Vineyards 1983 $12 (5/01/86)
92 ROUND HILL Merlot Napa Valley 1983 $7.50 (1/31/87) SS
91 STERLING Merlot Napa Valley 1983 $11 (6/01/86)

UNITED STATES
CALIFORNIA/*MERLOT*

90   NEWTON Merlot Napa Valley 1983 $11.50 (2/28/87)
88   FRANCISCAN Merlot Napa Valley Oakville Estate 1983 $8.50 (2/28/87)
87   JAEGER Merlot Napa Valley Inglewood Vineyard 1983 $14 (2/29/88)
87   LAKESPRING Merlot Napa Valley 1983 $11 (5/16/86)
87   RUTHERFORD HILL Merlot Napa Valley 1983 $10 (8/31/87)
86   CLOS DU BOIS Merlot Sonoma County 1983 $9 (10/01/85)
85   CHATEAU CHEVRE Merlot Napa Valley 1983 $12.50 (10/15/87)
85   INGLENOOK Merlot Napa Valley Reserve 1983 $9.50 (10/15/87)
85   WHITEHALL LANE Merlot Knights Valley 1983 $12 (10/01/85)
84   CARNEROS CREEK Merlot Napa Valley Truchard Vineyard 1983 $10 (10/01/85)
83   PINE RIDGE Merlot Napa Valley Selected Cuvée 1983 $13 (12/16/85)
82   SANTA CRUZ MOUNTAIN Merlot California 1983 $10 (10/01/85)
81   ST. CLEMENT Merlot Napa Valley 1983 $14.50 (5/31/88)
80   GEYSER PEAK Merlot Alexander Valley 1983 $7 (12/31/86)
80   MILL CREEK Merlot Dry Creek Valley 1983 $9 (10/01/85)
80   ST. FRANCIS Merlot Sonoma Valley 1983 $11 (7/31/87)
79   STRATFORD Merlot California 1983 $8.50 (9/30/86)
75   PARDUCCI Merlot Mendocino County 1983 $8 (12/15/87)
70   BELVEDERE Merlot Alexander Valley Robert Young Vineyards 1983 $12 (12/31/87)
61   RAVENSWOOD Merlot Sonoma County 1983 $11 (5/16/86)

1982
94   BELVEDERE Merlot Alexander Valley Robert Young Vineyards 1982 $12 (3/16/86)
92   DUCKHORN Merlot Napa Valley 1982 Rel: $13 Cur: $52 (12/16/84) SS
92   WHITEHALL LANE Merlot Knights Valley 1982 $10 (6/01/85) CS
90   PINE RIDGE Merlot Napa Valley Selected Cuvée 1982 $13 (10/01/85)
88   GUNDLACH BUNDSCHU Merlot Sonoma Valley Rhinefarm Vineyards 1982 $9.25 (10/01/85)
88   MATANZAS CREEK Merlot Sonoma Valley 1982 Rel: $13.50 Cur: $24 (10/01/85)
85   MILL CREEK Merlot Dry Creek Valley 1982 $8.50 (4/01/85)
84   STEPHEN ZELLERBACH Merlot Alexander Valley 1982 $8.50 (10/01/85)
84   CHATEAU CHEVRE Merlot Napa Valley 1982 $12 (10/01/85)
84   STONEGATE Merlot Napa Valley Spaulding Vineyard 1982 $14 (2/28/87)
83   NEWTON Merlot Napa Valley 1982 $12.50 (2/16/86)
83   NEWTON Merlot Napa Valley 1982 $12.50 (10/01/85)
83   STERLING Merlot Napa Valley 1982 $12 (10/01/85)
81   DUCKHORN Merlot Napa Valley 1982 Rel: $13 Cur: $52 (10/01/85)
80   DEVLIN Merlot Central Coast 1982 $8 (7/16/85)
80   CARNEROS CREEK Merlot Napa Valley 1982 $9.50 (2/16/86)
80   CLOS DU VAL Merlot Napa Valley 1982 $12.50 (10/01/85)
79   LAMBERT BRIDGE Merlot Sonoma County 1982 $11.50 (12/16/84)
79   RUTHERFORD HILL Merlot Napa Valley 1982 $10.50 (5/16/86)
78   CAIN Merlot Napa Valley 1982 $11 (2/01/85)
78   LAKESPRING Merlot Napa Valley 1982 $10 (10/01/85)
78   ST. FRANCIS Merlot Sonoma Valley 1982 $10.75 (10/01/85)
78   STAG'S LEAP WINE CELLARS Merlot Napa Valley 1982 $13.50 (10/01/85)
74   BOEGER Merlot El Dorado 1982 $10 (10/01/84)
71   LOUIS M. MARTINI Merlot North Coast 1982 $5.85 (2/16/86)
67   INGLENOOK Merlot Napa Valley Limited Bottling 1982 $8.50 (5/16/86)
65   HUNTER ASHBY Merlot Napa Valley 1982 $6.50 (12/15/87)
65   ROUND HILL Merlot Napa Valley 1982 $7.50 (2/16/86)
60   WOLTNER Merlot Alexander Valley Cask 465 1982 $4.75 (4/16/85)

1981
91   FRANCISCAN Merlot Napa Valley 1981 $8.50 (10/01/85)
91   NEWTON Merlot Napa Valley 1981 $12.50 (12/16/84)
89   CHATEAU SOUVERAIN Merlot North Coast 1981 $6.75 (10/01/85)
88   CAPARONE Merlot Santa Maria Valley Tepusquet Vineyard 1981 $10 (3/16/84)
88   CLOS DU VAL Merlot Napa Valley 1981 $13.50 (2/15/84)
86   MARKHAM Merlot Napa Valley 1981 $8.75 (8/01/84)
83   STAGS' LEAP WINERY Merlot Napa Valley 1981 $12 (2/16/85)
83   STERLING Merlot Napa Valley 1981 $11 (3/01/84)
82   PINE RIDGE Merlot Napa Valley Selected Cuvée 1981 $12.50 (3/16/84)
82   STAG'S LEAP WINE CELLARS Merlot Napa Valley 1981 $13.50 (4/16/84)
81   LOUIS M. MARTINI Merlot Russian River Valley Los Vinedos del Rio 1981 $10 (10/01/85)
80   INGLENOOK Merlot Napa Valley Limited Cask Reserve Selection 1981 $12 (2/16/85)
80   MATANZAS CREEK Merlot Sonoma Valley 1981 Rel: $12.50 Cur: $30 (4/16/84)
79   DIABLO VISTA Merlot Dry Creek Valley 1981 $7.50 (5/01/84)
78   RUTHERFORD HILL Merlot Napa Valley 1981 $10 (10/01/85)
77   INGLENOOK Merlot Napa Valley 1981 $12 (10/01/85)
50   FIRESTONE Merlot Santa Ynez Valley 1981 $6.50 (5/16/86)

1980
78   FARVIEW FARM Merlot California Templeton 1980 $6.50 (3/16/84)
68   STEPHEN ZELLERBACH Merlot Alexander Valley 1980 $8.50 (5/01/84)
68   STONEGATE Merlot Napa Valley Spaulding Vineyard 1980 $12 (10/01/85)

MUSCAT

1989
86   ROBERT PECOTA Muscato di Andrea Napa Valley 1989 $9.25 (7/15/90)
79   MARKHAM Muscat Blanc Napa Valley 1989 $9 (7/15/90)
75   ALDERBROOK Muscat Canelli Sonoma County 1989 $7.50 (7/15/90)

1988
84   MARKHAM Muscat Blanc Napa Valley Markham Vineyard 1988 $9 (4/30/89)
83   FOLIE A DEUX Muscat Canelli Napa Valley Muscat à Deux 1988 $7.50 (8/31/89)
78   ROBERT MONDAVI Moscato d'Oro Napa Valley 1988 $10 (4/30/90)
76   EBERLE Muscat Canelli Paso Robles 1988 $7.50 (12/15/89)
72   AUSTIN Muscat Canelli Santa Barbara County 1988 $8.50 (12/15/89)
68   MISSION VIEW Muscat Canelli Paso Robles 1988 $7 (12/15/89)
67   ARCIERO Muscat Canelli Paso Robles 1988 $6 (12/15/89)

1987
93   MARKHAM Muscat de Frontignan Napa Valley Markham Vineyard 1987 $9 (5/15/88)
85   ROBERT PECOTA Muscato di Andrea California 1987 $9.50 (7/15/88)
80   BENZIGER Muscat Canelli Sonoma County 1987 $10 (8/31/89)
79   ROBERT MONDAVI Moscato d'Oro Napa Valley 1987 $11 (11/15/89)
78   CLAIBORNE & CHURCHILL Muscat Canelli California Dry Alsatian Style 1987 $8 (12/15/89)
78   PRESTON Muscat Canelli Dry Creek Valley 1987 $7 (8/31/89)

1986
89   ROBERT PECOTA Muscato di Andrea California 1986 $8.50 (8/31/87)

1985
91   ROBERT PECOTA Muscato di Andrea California 1985 $8.50 (5/16/85)
83   KENDALL-JACKSON Muscat Canelli Lake County 1985 $7.50 (6/16/86)
76   FETZER Muscat Canelli Lake County 1985 $6 (10/31/86)

1984
83   ROBERT MONDAVI Moscato d'Oro Napa Valley 1984 $8.75 (12/31/86)

PETITE SIRAH

1988
86   FOPPIANO Petite Sirah Russian River Valley 1988 $8.25 (8/31/90)
85   FIELD STONE Petite Sirah Alexander Valley 1988 $15 (12/31/90)
81   KARLY Petite Sirah Amador County Not So Petite Sirah 1988 $14 (12/31/90)
70   BOGLE Petite Sirah Clarksburg 1988 $7 (10/31/89)

1987
87   STAG'S LEAP WINE CELLARS Petite Sirah Napa Valley 1987 $12 (8/31/90)
84   FIELD STONE Petite Sirah Alexander Valley 1987 $15 (12/31/90)
82   HOP KILN Petite Sirah Russian River Valley M. Griffin Vineyards 1987 $11 (2/28/90)
79   FOPPIANO Petite Sirah Russian River Valley Reserve Le Grande Petite 1987 $20 (8/31/90)

1986
83   FOPPIANO Petite Sirah Russian River Valley 1986 $8 (6/15/89)
81   LOUIS M. MARTINI Petite Sirah Napa Valley Reserve 1986 $12 (10/31/90)
79   FIELD STONE Petite Sirah Alexander Valley 1986 $15 (9/30/89)
74   FETZER Petite Sirah California Petite Syrah Reserve 1986 $14 (8/31/90)

1985
87   FRICK Petite Sirah Monterey County 1985 $8 (2/15/89)
87   RIDGE Petite Sirah Napa County York Creek 1985 $9 (10/31/89)
85   LOUIS M. MARTINI Petite Sirah Napa Valley 1985 $7 (10/31/89) BB
85   STAG'S LEAP WINE CELLARS Petite Sirah Napa Valley 1985 $9 (10/15/88)
83   FIELD STONE Petite Sirah Alexander Valley 1985 $11 (2/15/89)
83   GUENOC Petite Sirah Guenoc Valley 1985 $15 (2/15/89)
81   BLACK MOUNTAIN Petite Sirah Alexander Valley Bosun Crest 1985 $9 (2/15/89)
77   HOP KILN Petite Sirah Russian River Valley M. Griffin Vineyards 1985 $10.75 (3/31/88)

1984
90   HOP KILN Petite Sirah Russian River Valley M. Griffin Vineyards 1984 $10 (2/15/87)
88   FIELD STONE Petite Sirah Alexander Valley 1984 $11 (10/15/88)
84   FOPPIANO Petite Sirah Russian River Valley 1984 $7.50 (5/31/88)
84   ROUDON-SMITH Petite Sirah San Luis Obispo County 1984 $8 (9/30/88)
77   GUENOC Petite Sirah Guenoc Valley 1984 $7 (11/15/87)
73   R.&J. COOK Petite Sirah Clarksburg 1984 $6 (12/31/87)
70   RIDGE Petite Sirah Napa County York Creek 1984 $10 (1/31/88)

1983
86   RIDGE Petite Sirah Napa County York Creek 1983 $9 (3/15/87)
76   LOUIS M. MARTINI Petite Sirah Napa Valley 1983 $6 (12/31/87)

1982
87   INGLENOOK Petite Sirah Napa Valley 1982 $5.50 (12/31/86) BB
80   LOUIS M. MARTINI Petite Sirah Napa Valley 1982 $5.25 (9/15/86) BB
78   FETZER Petite Sirah Mendocino Petite Syrah 1982 $5.50 (4/16/85)
73   STAG'S LEAP WINE CELLARS Petite Sirah Napa Valley 1982 $7 (12/01/85)
69   FIELD STONE Petite Sirah Alexander Valley 1982 $8.50 (7/01/86)

1981
90   RIDGE Petite Sirah Napa County York Creek 1981 $8.50 (10/01/84)
86   R.&J. COOK Petite Sirah Clarksburg 1981 $5.50 (12/16/84)
86   INGLENOOK Petite Sirah Napa Valley 1981 $6 (2/01/85) BB
61   WENTE BROS. Petite Sirah Livermore Valley 1981 $5 (12/01/85)

1980
84   STAGS' LEAP WINERY Petite Sirah Napa Valley Petite Syrah 1980 $10 (3/01/85)
78   FREEMARK ABBEY Petite Sirah Napa Valley 1980 (NA) (2/01/88)

1979
87   FREEMARK ABBEY Petite Sirah Napa Valley 1979 (NA) (2/01/88)

1978
80   FREEMARK ABBEY Petite Sirah Napa Valley 1978 (NA) (2/01/88)

1977
82   FREEMARK ABBEY Petite Sirah Napa Valley 1977 (NA) (2/01/88)

1976
77   FREEMARK ABBEY Petite Sirah Napa Valley 1976 (NA) (2/01/88)

1975

73   FREEMARK ABBEY Petite Sirah Napa Valley 1975 (NA) (2/01/88)

1974

80   FREEMARK ABBEY Petite Sirah Napa Valley 1974 (NA) (2/01/88)

1973

86   FREEMARK ABBEY Petite Sirah Napa Valley 1973 (NA) (2/01/88)

1972

76   FREEMARK ABBEY Petite Sirah Napa Valley 1972 (NA) (2/01/88)

1971

90   FREEMARK ABBEY Petite Sirah Napa Valley 1971 (NA) (2/01/88)

1969

81   FREEMARK ABBEY Petite Sirah Napa Valley 1969 (NA) (2/01/88)

PINOT BLANC

1990

83   AU BON CLIMAT Pinot Blanc Santa Barbara County 1990 $12.50 (7/15/91)

1989

88   CHALONE Pinot Blanc Chalone 1989 $17 (11/30/90)
86   MIRASSOU Pinot Blanc Monterey County Limited Bottling Fifth Generation Harvest Reserve 1989 $12.50 (5/31/91)
78   CONGRESS SPRINGS Pinot Blanc Santa Clara County 1989 $9 (4/30/91)

1988

89   CHATEAU ST. JEAN Pinot Blanc Alexander Valley Robert Young Vineyards 1988 $9 (5/31/91) BB
88   CHALONE Pinot Blanc Chalone 1988 $17 (2/15/90)
87   MONTEREY PENINSULA Pinot Blanc Monterey Doctor's Reserve 1988 $12 (4/30/91)
84   BUEHLER Pinot Blanc Napa Valley Buehler Vineyards 1988 $9 (2/15/90)
84   CONGRESS SPRINGS Pinot Blanc Santa Clara County San Ysidro Vineyard 1988 $9.50 (8/31/89)

1987

88   CHATEAU ST. JEAN Pinot Blanc Alexander Valley Robert Young Vineyards 1987 $9 (5/31/90)
87   BUEHLER Pinot Blanc Napa Valley 1987 $9 (3/31/89)
87   CHALONE Pinot Blanc Chalone 1987 $17 (12/15/88)
87   CONGRESS SPRINGS Pinot Blanc Santa Clara County San Ysidro Vineyard 1987 $9 (12/15/88)
82   ELLISTON Pinot Blanc Central Coast Sunol Valley Vineyard 1987 $10 (5/31/91)
82   MERLION Pinot Blanc Napa Valley Coeur de Melon 1987 $9 (11/30/90)

1986

86   MONTEREY PENINSULA Pinot Blanc Arroyo Seco Cobblestone Vineyards 1986 $9 (1/31/88)
84   BUEHLER Pinot Blanc Napa Valley 1986 $9 (7/15/88)
83   MERLION Pinot Blanc Napa Valley Coeur de Melon 1986 $9.50 (1/31/88)

1985

85   CHATEAU ST. JEAN Pinot Blanc Alexander Valley Robert Young Vineyards 1985 $9 (12/15/89)
83   JEKEL Pinot Blanc Arroyo Seco Arroyo Blanc 1985 $6 (6/15/89) BB
79   BUEHLER Pinot Blanc Napa Valley 1985 $8 (2/15/87)
70   MIRASSOU Pinot Blanc Monterey County White Burgundy 1985 $5.50 (6/30/87)

1984

91   CHATEAU ST. JEAN Pinot Blanc Alexander Valley Robert Young Vineyards 1984 $9 (8/31/87)
85   BUEHLER Pinot Blanc Napa Valley 1984 $8 (2/01/86)
82   JEKEL Pinot Blanc Arroyo Seco Arroyo Blanc 1984 $6 (2/01/86)
81   JEKEL Pinot Blanc Arroyo Seco Home Vineyard 1984 $8 (3/31/89)

1983

88   CONGRESS SPRINGS Pinot Blanc Santa Cruz Mountains 1983 $9 (8/01/84)
81   CHATEAU ST. JEAN Pinot Blanc Alexander Valley Robert Young Vineyards 1983 $9 (2/01/86)

1982

84   CHATEAU ST. JEAN Pinot Blanc Sonoma County St. Jean Vineyards 1982 $10 (11/01/84)
76   CHATEAU ST. JEAN Pinot Blanc Alexander Valley Robert Young Vineyards 1982 $11 (10/01/84)

1981

75   BUEHLER Pinot Blanc Napa Valley 1981 $8 (10/01/84)

PINOT NOIR

1989

88   GARY FARRELL Pinot Noir Russian River Valley 1989 $16 (7/31/91)
88   SAINTSBURY Pinot Noir Carneros Garnet 1989 $9 (12/15/90)
87   GREENWOOD RIDGE Pinot Noir Anderson Valley 1989 $13.50 (6/30/91)
86   ROBERT MONDAVI Pinot Noir Napa Valley 1989 $15 (4/30/91)
86   RICHARDSON Pinot Noir Sonoma Valley Los Carneros Sangiacomo 1989 $14 (4/30/91)
85   BEAULIEU Pinot Noir Carneros Napa Valley Reserve 1989 $13 (4/30/91)
84   CONGRESS SPRINGS Pinot Noir Santa Clara County 1989 $10 (4/30/91)
84   INNISFREE Pinot Noir California 1989 $11 (4/30/91)
84   SANTA BARBARA Pinot Noir Santa Barbara County 1989 $11 (7/31/91)
82   CARNEROS CREEK Pinot Noir Carneros Fleur de Carneros 1989 $9 (4/30/91)
82   COSENTINO Pinot Noir Sonoma County 1989 $13 (6/30/91)
82   MOUNTAIN VIEW Pinot Noir Monterey-Napa Counties 1989 $6 (2/28/91) BB
82   NAPA RIDGE Pinot Noir North Coast Coastal 1989 $7.50 (7/31/91) BB
81   BUENA VISTA Pinot Noir Los Carneros 1989 $11 (7/31/91)
81   ROCHE Pinot Noir Carneros 1989 $15 (4/30/91)
78   ROCHE Pinot Noir Carneros Unfiltered 1989 $19 (4/30/91)
77   DOMAINE DE CLARCK Pinot Noir Monterey Première 1989 $15 (4/30/91)
75   WESTWOOD Pinot Noir California 1989 $9.75 (4/30/91)
74   MANISCHEWITZ Pinot Noir Russian River Valley 1989 $9 (3/31/91)
70   ARIES Pinot Noir Los Carneros Cuvée Vivace 1989 $8 (4/30/91)

1988

92   WILLIAMS SELYEM Pinot Noir Russian River Valley Rochioli Vineyard 1988 $40 (2/28/91)
92   WILLIAMS SELYEM Pinot Noir Sonoma Coast 1988 $40 (5/31/90)
91   ACACIA Pinot Noir Carneros Napa Valley St. Clair Vineyard 1988 $20 (2/28/91)
91   SAINTSBURY Pinot Noir Carneros 1988 $15 (12/15/90) SS
89   ACACIA Pinot Noir Carneros Napa Valley 1988 $14 (2/28/91)
89   CARNEROS CREEK Pinot Noir Carneros Signature Reserve 1988 $28 (10/31/90)
89   ROBERT MONDAVI Pinot Noir Napa Valley 1988 $13 (2/15/90)
89   ROCHE Pinot Noir Carneros 1988 $14 (12/31/89)
88   CAMBRIA Pinot Noir Santa Maria Valley Julia's Vineyard 1988 $16 (12/15/90)
88   GARY FARRELL Pinot Noir Russian River Valley 1988 $16 (10/31/90)
88   GUNDLACH BUNDSCHU Pinot Noir Sonoma Valley Rhinefarm Vineyards 1988 $12 (2/28/91)
88   WILLIAMS SELYEM Pinot Noir Russian River Valley Allen Vineyard 1988 $40 (5/31/90)
88   WILLIAMS SELYEM Pinot Noir Sonoma Coast Summa Vineyard 1988 $40 (5/31/90)
87   BEAULIEU Pinot Noir Napa Valley Carneros Reserve 1988 $9.50 (4/15/90)
87   CONGRESS SPRINGS Pinot Noir Santa Clara County San Ysidro Vineyard 1988 $9 (3/31/90)
87   GARY FARRELL Pinot Noir Russian River Valley Allen Vineyard 1988 $25 (10/31/90)
87   STERLING Pinot Noir Carneros Napa Valley Winery Lake 1988 $14 (4/30/91)
86   DAVIS BYNUM Pinot Noir Russian River Valley Limited Release 1988 $16 (4/30/91)
86   ETUDE Pinot Noir Napa Valley 1988 $20 (12/15/90)
86   THOMAS FOGARTY Pinot Noir Napa Valley 1988 $15 (2/28/91)
86   MERIDIAN Pinot Noir Santa Barbara County Riverbench Vineyard 1988 $14 (2/28/91)
86   ZACA MESA Pinot Noir Santa Barbara County Reserve 1988 $15.50 (10/31/90)
85   CARNEROS CREEK Pinot Noir Carneros Fleur de Carneros 1988 $10 (2/15/90)
85   LOUIS M. MARTINI Pinot Noir Los Carneros 1988 $8 (7/15/91) BB
85   OLIVET LANE Pinot Noir Russian River Valley 1988 $9 (6/30/91) BB
85   PARDUCCI Pinot Noir Mendocino County 1988 $7.50 (4/15/90) BB
85   ROCHIOLI Pinot Noir Russian River Valley 1988 $15 (10/31/90)
85   SIGNORELLO Pinot Noir Napa Valley 1988 $25 (2/28/91)
84   HUSCH Pinot Noir Anderson Valley 1988 $13 (12/15/90)
84   J. PEDRONCELLI Pinot Noir Dry Creek Valley 1988 $8 (2/28/91) BB
84   KENT RASMUSSEN Pinot Noir Carneros 1988 $22 (10/31/90)
84   SAINTSBURY Pinot Noir Carneros Garnet 1988 $9 (3/31/90)
83   AU BON CLIMAT Pinot Noir Santa Ynez Valley Rancho Vinedo Vineyard 1988 $12.50 (12/15/89)
83   BYINGTON Pinot Noir California 1988 $15 (4/30/91)
83   CARNEROS CREEK Pinot Noir Carneros 1988 $15.50 (10/31/90)
83   THOMAS FOGARTY Pinot Noir Santa Cruz Mountains Estate 1988 $15 (2/28/91)
82   BUENA VISTA Pinot Noir Carneros 1988 $11 (12/15/90)
82   ROBERT MONDAVI Pinot Noir Napa Valley Reserve 1988 Rel: $23 Cur: $26 (10/31/90)
82   VILLA MT. EDEN Pinot Noir Napa Valley 1988 $12 (2/28/91)
82   WHITEHALL LANE Pinot Noir Alexander Valley 1988 $13.50 (10/31/90)
82   ZD Pinot Noir Carneros Napa Valley 1988 $17 (6/30/91)
81   MIRASSOU Pinot Noir Monterey County Fifth Generation Family Selection 1988 $7.50 (4/30/91) BB
81   MONT ST. JOHN Pinot Noir Carneros Napa Valley 1988 $14 (4/30/91)
81   ROBERT SINSKEY Pinot Noir Carneros 1988 $18 (2/28/91)
80   AU BON CLIMAT Pinot Noir Santa Barbara County 1988 $16 (4/30/91)
80   CLOS DU BOIS Pinot Noir Sonoma County 1988 $12 (4/30/91)
80   DURNEY Pinot Noir Carmel Valley 1988 $16 (4/30/91)
80   MONTEREY VINEYARD Pinot Noir Monterey County Limited Release 1988 $9 (2/28/91)
79   JOSEPH SWAN Pinot Noir Sonoma Coast Russian River Valley 1988 $20 (6/30/91)
79   WILD HORSE Pinot Noir Santa Barbara County 1988 $14 (4/30/91)
78   BOUCHAINE Pinot Noir Carneros Napa Valley 1988 $15 (7/31/91)
78   SANFORD Pinot Noir Santa Barbara County 1988 $14.50 (6/30/91)
78   SOLIS Pinot Noir Santa Clara County 1988 $9 (4/30/91)
75   AUSTIN Pinot Noir Santa Barbara County Artist Series 1988 $10 (12/15/89)
75   MORGAN Pinot Noir California 1988 $14 (4/30/91)
74   CRESTON MANOR Pinot Noir San Luis Obispo County Petit d'Noir Maceration Carbonique 1988 $8 (12/15/89)
74   WEIBEL Pinot Noir Mendocino County 1988 $6 (2/28/91)
72   MOUNTAIN VIEW Pinot Noir Monterey-Napa Counties 1988 $6.50 (3/31/90)

1987

93   CALERA Pinot Noir San Benito County Jensen 1987 $30 (4/30/91)
92   CARNEROS CREEK Pinot Noir Carneros Fleur de Carneros 1987 $9 (2/28/89) SS
92   WILLIAMS SELYEM Pinot Noir Russian River Valley Allen Vineyard 1987 $20 (5/31/89)
91   DEHLINGER Pinot Noir Russian River Valley 1987 $14 (2/15/90)
91   SAINTSBURY Pinot Noir Carneros Garnet 1987 $9 (12/31/88)
90   BEAULIEU Pinot Noir Carneros Napa Valley Reserve 1987 $9.50 (12/31/88)
90   WILD HORSE Pinot Noir Paso Robles 1987 $14 (10/15/89)
89   ACACIA Pinot Noir Carneros Napa Valley St. Clair Vineyard 1987 Rel: $18 Cur: $21 (2/15/90)
89   ROCHIOLI Pinot Noir Russian River Valley 1987 $15 (5/31/90)
89   SANTA BARBARA Pinot Noir Santa Ynez Valley Reserve 1987 $20 (12/15/89)
88   AU BON CLIMAT Pinot Noir Santa Ynez Valley Benedict Vineyard 1987 $30 (12/15/89)
88   ROBERT MONDAVI Pinot Noir Napa Valley 1987 $12 (7/31/89)
88   RICHARDSON Pinot Noir Sonoma Valley Carneros Sangiacomo 1987 $12 (10/15/89)
88   WHITEHALL LANE Pinot Noir Napa Valley 1987 $12 (10/15/89)
88   WILLIAMS SELYEM Pinot Noir Sonoma County 1987 $16 (5/31/89)
87   ACACIA Pinot Noir Carneros Napa Valley 1987 Rel: $13 Cur: $15 (2/15/90)
87   CARNEROS CREEK Pinot Noir Carneros Signature Reserve First Release 1987 $28 (10/31/90)
87   CHARLES KRUG Pinot Noir Carneros 1987 $8.50 (2/28/91) BB
87   STAR HILL Pinot Noir Napa Valley Doc's Reserve 1987 $19 (5/31/90)
86   CAYMUS Pinot Noir Napa Valley Special Selection 1987 $14 (12/15/90)
86   MONTEREY PENINSULA Pinot Noir Monterey Sleepy Hollow 1987 $18 (2/28/91)
86   SAINTSBURY Pinot Noir Carneros 1987 $15 (7/31/89)
86   ROBERT SINSKEY Pinot Noir Carneros Napa Valley 1987 $14 (3/31/90)
86   STERLING Pinot Noir Carneros Napa Valley Winery Lake 1987 $18 (12/31/89)
85   BOUCHAINE Pinot Noir Carneros Reserve 1987 $20 (10/31/90)
85   BYRON Pinot Noir Santa Barbara County Reserve 1987 $16 (12/15/89)
85   CARNEROS CREEK Pinot Noir Napa Valley Los Carneros 1987 $15 (2/15/90)
85   KISTLER Pinot Noir Russian River Valley Dutton Ranch 1987 $15 (3/31/90)
85   MONTICELLO Pinot Noir Napa Valley 1987 $14.50 (10/15/89)
85   NAVARRO Pinot Noir Anderson Valley Méthode à l'Ancienne 1987 $14 (4/30/91)
85   PAGOR Pinot Noir Santa Barbara County 1987 $10.50 (12/15/89)
84   AU BON CLIMAT Pinot Noir Santa Barbara County 1987 $16 (12/15/89)
84   CLOS DU VAL Pinot Noir Napa Valley 1987 $13.50 (4/30/91)

UNITED STATES
CALIFORNIA/*PINOT NOIR*

84 GARY FARRELL Pinot Noir Sonoma County Howard Allen Vineyard 1987 $20 (2/15/90)
84 MONTEREY VINEYARD Pinot Noir Monterey County 1987 $8.50 (3/31/90)
84 PARDUCCI Pinot Noir Mendocino County Cellarmaster Selection 1987 $15 (4/30/91)
84 ROUDON-SMITH Pinot Noir Santa Cruz Mountains Cox Vineyard 1987 $15 (2/28/91)
84 SEGHESIO Pinot Noir Russian River Valley 1987 $8 (4/15/90)
83 SEGHESIO Pinot Noir Russian River Valley Reserve 1987 $13 (4/15/90)
82 BOUCHAINE Pinot Noir Carneros 1987 $13 (10/31/90)
82 CALERA Pinot Noir Central Coast 1987 $14 (2/15/90)
82 CASTORO Pinot Noir Central Coast 1987 $4.50 (12/15/89) BB
82 DE LOACH Pinot Noir Russian River Valley OFS 1987 $25 (10/31/90)
82 LOUIS M. MARTINI Pinot Noir Carneros 1987 $7 (2/28/91) BB
82 ROBERT STEMMLER Pinot Noir Sonoma County 1987 $19 (10/31/90)
82 WILD HORSE Pinot Noir Santa Barbara County 1987 $13.50 (3/31/90)
82 ZACA MESA Pinot Noir Santa Barbara County Reserve 1987 $15 (12/15/89)
81 LAWRENCE J. BARGETTO Pinot Noir Santa Maria Valley 1987 $16 (2/28/91)
81 MORGAN Pinot Noir California 1987 $15 (7/31/89)
81 NAVARRO Pinot Noir Anderson Valley Whole Berry Fermentation 1987 $9.75 (2/28/89)
81 NEWLAN Pinot Noir Napa Valley 1987 $16 (3/31/90)
81 SCHUG Pinot Noir Carneros Beckstoffer Vineyard 1987 $13 (2/28/91)
80 BUENA VISTA Pinot Noir Carneros Private Reserve 1987 $14 (6/30/91)
80 CALERA Pinot Noir San Benito County Reed 1987 $35 (4/30/91)
80 CRESTON MANOR Pinot Noir San Luis Obispo County Petit d'Noir 1987 $8 (8/31/88)
80 HUSCH Pinot Noir Anderson Valley 1987 $13 (2/15/90)
80 MAYACAMAS Pinot Noir Napa Valley 1987 $14 (4/30/91)
79 MOUNT EDEN Pinot Noir Santa Cruz Mountains 1987 Rel: $20 Cur: $30 (4/15/90)
78 FOXEN Pinot Noir Santa Maria Valley 1987 $16 (12/15/89)
78 HACIENDA Pinot Noir Sonoma Valley Estate Reserve 1987 $15 (10/31/90)
77 AUSTIN Pinot Noir Santa Barbara County 1987 $15 (12/15/89)
76 MONT ST. JOHN Pinot Noir Carneros Napa Valley 1987 $15 (3/31/90)
76 SANFORD Pinot Noir Santa Barbara County 1987 $14 (2/28/91)
74 ALEXANDER VALLEY Pinot Noir Alexander Valley 1987 $9 (5/31/90)
74 BYINGTON Pinot Noir Napa Valley 1987 $15 (4/30/91)
73 CLOS DU BOIS Pinot Noir Sonoma County 1987 $12 (5/31/90)
72 IRON HORSE Pinot Noir Sonoma County Green Valley 1987 $19 (10/31/90)
62 SANTA YNEZ VALLEY Pinot Noir Santa Maria Valley 1987 $13 (3/31/90)
61 BYINGTON Pinot Noir Napa Valley 1987 $15 (2/28/91)

1986

92 CARNEROS CREEK Pinot Noir Los Carneros 1986 $14.50 (12/31/88)
92 SAINTSBURY Pinot Noir Carneros 1986 $14 (6/15/88)
91 ACACIA Pinot Noir Carneros Napa Valley St. Clair Vineyard 1986 Rel: $18 Cur: $30 (6/15/88)
91 ROBERT MONDAVI Pinot Noir Napa Valley Reserve 1986 Rel: $22 Cur: $23 (10/15/89)
91 WILLIAMS SELYEM Pinot Noir Sonoma County 1986 $16 (6/15/88)
91 ZACA MESA Pinot Noir Santa Barbara County Reserve 1986 $15 (6/15/88)
90 DOMAINE LAURIER Pinot Noir Sonoma County Green Valley 1986 $10 (6/15/88)
90 GARY FARRELL Pinot Noir Russian River Valley 1986 $15 (6/15/88)
89 CHALONE Pinot Noir Chalone 1986 $25 (12/15/90)
89 GUNDLACH BUNDSCHU Pinot Noir Sonoma Valley Rhinefarm Vineyards 1986 $12 (6/15/88)
89 KISTLER Pinot Noir Russian River Valley Dutton Ranch 1986 $13.50 (6/15/88)
89 LA CREMA Pinot Noir California 1986 $11.75 (12/31/88)
89 MONTICELLO Pinot Noir Napa Valley 1986 $12 (6/15/88)
89 STERLING Pinot Noir Carneros Napa Valley Winery Lake 1986 $18 (2/28/89)
88 ACACIA Pinot Noir Carneros Napa Valley 1986 Rel: $15 Cur: $15 (6/15/88)
88 ACACIA Pinot Noir Carneros Napa Valley Madonna Vineyard 1986 Rel: $18 Cur: $18 (6/15/88)
88 BEAULIEU Pinot Noir Napa Valley Los Carneros Reserve 1986 $9.50 (9/15/88)
88 BYRON Pinot Noir Santa Barbara County 1986 $12 (6/15/88)
88 CALERA Pinot Noir San Benito County Jensen 1986 $25 (5/31/89)
88 DEHLINGER Pinot Noir Russian River Valley 1986 $13 (5/31/89)
88 GAINEY Pinot Noir Santa Barbara County 1986 $15 (12/15/89)
87 CLOS DU BOIS Pinot Noir Sonoma County 1986 $11 (10/15/89)
87 DE LOACH Pinot Noir Russian River Valley 1986 $12 (5/31/90)
87 FETZER Pinot Noir Mendocino County Reserve 1986 $17.50 (10/31/90)
87 FETZER Pinot Noir Mendocino County Reserve 1986 $17.50 (2/15/90)
87 NAVARRO Pinot Noir Anderson Valley Méthode à l'Ancienne 1986 $14 (3/31/90)
87 RICHARDSON Pinot Noir Sonoma Valley Carneros Sangiacomo 1986 $12 (6/15/88)
87 ROCHIOLI Pinot Noir Russian River Valley 1986 $14.25 (10/15/89)
87 SAINTSBURY Pinot Noir Carneros Garnet 1986 $8 (12/15/87)
87 SCHUG Pinot Noir Carneros Beckstoffer Vineyard 1986 $13 (10/31/90)
86 BOUCHAINE Pinot Noir Carneros Napa Valley 1986 $12 (5/31/89)
85 BUENA VISTA Pinot Noir Carneros Private Reserve 1986 $14 (3/31/90)
85 CALERA Pinot Noir San Benito County Selleck 1986 $30 (3/31/90)
85 LA CREMA Pinot Noir California Reserve 1986 $22 (5/31/89)
85 LOUIS M. MARTINI Pinot Noir Napa Valley 1986 $8 (12/31/89) BB
85 WILD HORSE Pinot Noir Santa Barbara County 1986 $13.50 (6/15/88)
84 BYRON Pinot Noir Santa Barbara County Reserve 1986 $12 (6/15/88)
84 HANZELL Pinot Noir Sonoma Valley 1986 Rel: $19 Cur: $19 (10/31/90)
84 MORGAN Pinot Noir California 1986 $14 (6/15/88)
84 ROBERT STEMMLER Pinot Noir Sonoma County 1986 $18 (6/15/88)
83 DAVIS BYNUM Pinot Noir Russian River Valley Limited Release 1986 $14 (3/31/90)
83 CORBETT CANYON Pinot Noir Central Coast Reserve 1986 $8 (12/15/89)
83 MONTEREY VINEYARD Pinot Noir Monterey County 1986 $7 (6/15/88)
82 DAVIS BYNUM Pinot Noir Sonoma County Reserve Bottling 1986 $9 (9/15/88)

Key to Symbols

The scores reported here are the results of blind tastings conducted by our panel of senior editors. Wines that carry the initials below are results of individual tastings.

THE WINE SPECTATOR 100-POINT SCALE *95-100*—Classic, a great wine; *90-94*—Outstanding, superior character and style; *80-89*—Good to very good, a wine with special qualities; *70-79*—Average, drinkable wine that may have minor flaws; *60-69*—Below average, drinkable but not recommended; *50-59*—Poor, undrinkable, not recommended. "+"—With a score indicates a range; used primarily with barrel tastings to indicate a preliminary score.

SPECIAL DESIGNATIONS SS—Spectator Selection, CS—Cellar Selection, BB—Best Buy.

TASTER'S INITIALS (JG)—Jim Gordon, (HS)—Harvey Steiman, (JL)—James Laube, (JS)—James Suckling, (TM)—Thomas Matthews, (TR)—Terry Robards, (BT)—Barrel Tasting (these wines were tasted blind from barrel samples), (CA-date)—*California's Great Cabernets* by James Laube, (CH-date)—*California's Great Chardonnays* by James Laube, (VP-date)—*Vintage Port* by James Suckling.

DATE TASTED Dates in parentheses represent the issue in which the rating was published.

82 CAYMUS Pinot Noir Napa Valley Special Selection 1986 $15 (12/31/89)
81 CARNEROS QUALITY ALLIANCE Pinot Noir Carneros 1986 $23 (7/31/89)
81 HUSCH Pinot Noir Anderson Valley 1986 $13 (10/15/89)
81 MARK WEST Pinot Noir Russian River Valley Ellis Vineyard 1986 $14 (3/31/90)
81 YORK MOUNTAIN Pinot Noir Central Coast 1986 $6 (6/15/88)
80 CLOS DU VAL Pinot Noir Napa Valley 1986 $16 (2/15/90)
80 HACIENDA Pinot Noir Sonoma Valley Estate Reserve 1986 $15 (6/15/88)
80 KALIN Pinot Noir Sonoma County Cuvée DD 1986 $20 (4/30/91)
80 MARK WEST Pinot Noir Sonoma County 1986 $8 (2/28/89)
80 MOUNTAIN VIEW Pinot Noir Carneros 1986 $6 (2/28/89) BB
80 SANTA BARBARA Pinot Noir Santa Barbara County 1986 $11 (6/15/88)
79 ROBERT SINSKEY Pinot Noir Carneros Napa Valley 1986 $12 (6/15/88)
78 MIRASSOU Pinot Noir Monterey Harvest Reserve 1986 $12 (4/30/91)
78 SANFORD Pinot Noir Santa Barbara County Barrel Select 1986 $20 (12/15/89)
77 CLOS DU BOIS Pinot Noir Sonoma County 1986 $11 (6/15/88)
77 FIRESTONE Pinot Noir Santa Ynez Valley 1986 $10 (12/15/89)
77 WATSON Pinot Noir Santa Maria Valley Bien Nacido Vineyard 1986 $9 (12/15/89)
76 BARROW GREEN Pinot Noir California 1986 $16 (10/15/89)
76 EDNA VALLEY Pinot Noir Edna Valley 1986 $15 (12/15/89)
76 JORY Pinot Noir Santa Clara County 1986 $19 (6/15/88)
76 NEWLAN Pinot Noir Napa Valley Vieilles Vignes 1986 $19 (3/31/90)
75 SANFORD Pinot Noir Santa Barbara County 1986 $14 (12/15/89)
74 BEAULIEU Pinot Noir Napa Valley Beaumont 1986 $7 (6/15/88)
74 CRYSTAL VALLEY Pinot Noir North Coast Reserve Edition 1986 $10.50 (6/15/88)
74 ST. FRANCIS Pinot Noir Sonoma Valley 1986 $14 (6/15/88)
70 PARDUCCI Pinot Noir Mendocino County 1986 $7 (6/15/88)
70 J. PEDRONCELLI Pinot Noir Dry Creek Valley 1986 $7 (5/31/90)
68 TREFETHEN Pinot Noir Napa Valley 1986 $13 (7/31/89)
67 MAYACAMAS Pinot Noir Napa Valley 1986 $14 (3/31/90)
66 MERLION Pinot Noir Los Carneros Hyde Vineyards 1986 $13.50 (2/28/89)
60 SUNRISE Pinot Noir Sonoma County Green Valley Dutton Ranch Vineyard 1986 $10 (6/15/88)
59 DAVID BRUCE Pinot Noir Santa Cruz Mountains 1986 $18 (3/31/90)

1985

92 ROBERT MONDAVI Pinot Noir Napa Valley Reserve 1985 Rel: $19 Cur: $22 (4/15/89) SS
92 ROCHIOLI Pinot Noir Russian River Valley 1985 $12.50 (6/15/88)
92 SAINTSBURY Pinot Noir Carneros 1985 $13 (11/30/87) (JL)
91 ACACIA Pinot Noir Carneros Napa Valley St. Clair Vineyard 1985 Rel: $16 Cur: $16 (12/15/87)
90 CARNEROS QUALITY ALLIANCE Pinot Noir Carneros 1985 $25 (12/31/87)
90 CAYMUS Pinot Noir Napa Valley Special Selection 1985 $15 (12/31/88)
90 LA CREMA Pinot Noir California 1985 $11 (9/30/87)
90 MOUNT EDEN Pinot Noir Santa Cruz Mountains 1985 Rel: $25 Cur: $25 (6/15/88)
89 MONTICELLO Pinot Noir Napa Valley 1985 $12 (12/15/87)
89 JOSEPH SWAN Pinot Noir Sonoma Coast 1985 $18 (6/15/88)
88 ACACIA Pinot Noir Carneros Napa Valley Madonna Vineyard 1985 Rel: $16 Cur: $16 (12/15/87)
88 CALERA Pinot Noir San Benito County Jensen 1985 $25 (6/15/88)
88 CARNEROS CREEK Pinot Noir Los Carneros 1985 $13 (4/15/88)
88 NEWLAN Pinot Noir Napa Valley 1985 $12 (6/15/88)
87 PAGE MILL Pinot Noir Santa Barbara County Bien Nacido Vineyard 1985 $12.50 (6/15/88)
86 HACIENDA Pinot Noir Sonoma Valley Estate Reserve 1985 $15 (6/15/88)
86 ROUDON-SMITH Pinot Noir Santa Cruz Mountains 1985 $15 (6/15/88)
86 SAINTSBURY Pinot Noir Carneros Garnet 1985 $9 (3/15/87)
86 WILD HORSE Pinot Noir Santa Barbara County 1985 $12.50 (6/15/88)
85 CHALONE Pinot Noir Chalone 1985 Rel: $17.50 Cur: $107 (2/15/90)
85 DEHLINGER Pinot Noir Russian River Valley 1985 $12 (2/15/88)
85 NAVARRO Pinot Noir Anderson Valley Méthode à l'Ancienne 1985 $14 (2/28/89)
84 ACACIA Pinot Noir Carneros Napa Valley 1985 Rel: $12 Cur: $14 (12/15/87)
84 HUSCH Pinot Noir Anderson Valley 1985 $10 (6/15/88)
83 LAWRENCE J. BARGETTO Pinot Noir Carneros Madonna Vineyard 1985 $12.50 (9/15/88)
83 ETUDE Pinot Noir Napa Valley 1985 $16 (6/15/88)
83 RODNEY STRONG Pinot Noir Russian River Valley River East Vineyard 1985 $10 (2/28/91)
83 TULOCAY Pinot Noir Napa Valley Haynes Vineyard 1985 $18 (2/28/91)
83 WINDSOR Pinot Noir Russian River Valley Winemaster's Private Reserve 1985 $8 (6/15/88)
82 BOUCHAINE Pinot Noir Carneros Napa Valley 1985 $11.50 (12/31/88)
82 DAVIS BYNUM Pinot Noir Russian River Valley Artist Series 1985 $15 (6/15/88)
82 CALERA Pinot Noir Santa Barbara County Bien Nacido Vineyard 1985 $12.50 (6/15/88)
82 GEYSER PEAK Pinot Noir Sonoma County Carneros 1985 $6 (6/15/88)
82 HANZELL Pinot Noir Sonoma Valley 1985 Rel: $19 Cur: $19 (3/31/90)
82 INGLENOOK Pinot Noir Napa Valley 1985 $9.50 (6/15/88)
82 LA CREMA Pinot Noir California Reserve 1985 $17.50 (12/31/87)
82 MONT ST. JOHN Pinot Noir Carneros Napa Valley 1985 $15 (10/15/89)
82 TULOCAY Pinot Noir Napa Valley Haynes Vineyard 1985 $18 (6/15/88)
82 WHITEHALL LANE Pinot Noir Napa Valley 1985 $7.50 (6/15/88)
81 ALEXANDER VALLEY Pinot Noir Alexander Valley 1985 $8 (4/15/88)
81 BYRON Pinot Noir Santa Barbara County 1985 $12 (6/15/88)
81 CORBETT CANYON Pinot Noir Santa Maria Valley Sierra Madre Vineyard Reserve 1985 $12 (2/15/88)
81 GUNDLACH BUNDSCHU Pinot Noir Sonoma Valley Rhinefarm Vineyards 1985 $12 (2/29/88)
81 CHARLES KRUG Pinot Noir Carneros Napa Valley 1985 $8.50 (2/15/90)
80 CLOS DU VAL Pinot Noir Napa Valley 1985 $12.50 (6/15/88)
80 NEWLAN Pinot Noir Napa Valley Vieilles Vignes 1985 $16 (6/15/88)
80 YORK MOUNTAIN Pinot Noir San Luis Obispo County 1985 $9 (6/15/88)
79 ROBERT MONDAVI Pinot Noir Napa Valley 1985 $10.50 (6/15/88)
79 ROBERT STEMMLER Pinot Noir Sonoma County 1985 $18 (9/30/87)
79 ZD Pinot Noir Carneros Napa Valley 1985 $14 (7/31/89)
78 BEAULIEU Pinot Noir Napa Valley Beaumont 1985 $6.25 (6/15/88)
78 EDNA VALLEY Pinot Noir Edna Valley 1985 $15 (6/15/88)
78 FETZER Pinot Noir Mendocino County Special Reserve 1985 $13 (6/15/88)
78 MONT ST. JOHN Pinot Noir Carneros Napa Valley Madonna Vineyard 1985 $11 (6/15/88)
77 BAY CELLARS Pinot Noir Los Carneros 1985 $15 (6/15/88)
77 CHATEAU DE LEU Pinot Noir Solano County Green Valley 1985 $7 (2/28/89)
77 ROLLING HILLS Pinot Noir Santa Maria Valley 1985 $6 (6/15/88)
76 BOUCHAINE Pinot Noir Los Carneros 1985 $7.50 (6/30/87)
76 PARDUCCI Pinot Noir Mendocino County 1985 $5.50 (11/15/87)
76 J. PEDRONCELLI Pinot Noir Dry Creek Valley 1985 $7.50 (6/15/88)
75 CHARLES KRUG Pinot Noir Carneros Napa Valley 1985 $8.50 (6/15/88)
75 MCHENRY Pinot Noir Santa Cruz Mountains 1985 $13 (6/15/88)

75 SANFORD Pinot Noir Santa Barbara County Barrel Select 1985 $20 (6/15/88)
74 BEAULIEU Pinot Noir Napa Valley Los Carneros Reserve 1985 $9.50 (1/31/88)
74 SANFORD Pinot Noir Santa Barbara County 1985 $14 (6/15/88)
74 TREFETHEN Pinot Noir Napa Valley 1985 $12 (6/15/88)
73 AU BON CLIMAT Pinot Noir Santa Barbara County 1985 $12 (6/15/88)
73 BELVEDERE Pinot Noir Sonoma County Bacigalupi 1985 $12 (6/15/88)
72 DE LOACH Pinot Noir Russian River Valley 1985 $12 (6/15/88)
72 MAYACAMAS Pinot Noir Napa Valley 1985 $12 (6/15/88)
71 SUNRISE Pinot Noir Santa Clara County San Ysidro Vineyard 1985 $12 (6/15/88)
70 CLOS DU BOIS Pinot Noir Sonoma County 1985 $10.50 (6/15/88)
67 DAVIS BYNUM Pinot Noir Sonoma County Reserve Bottling 1985 $7 (1/31/88)
62 GARY FARRELL Pinot Noir Russian River Valley 1985 $13.50 (6/15/88)

1984

95 ACACIA Pinot Noir Carneros Napa Valley 1984 Rel: $11 Cur: $11 (12/15/86) SS
93 ACACIA Pinot Noir Carneros Napa Valley St. Clair Vineyard 1984 Rel: $16 Cur: $30 (11/30/86)
93 SAINTSBURY Pinot Noir Carneros 1984 $12 (12/15/86)
93 ZACA MESA Pinot Noir Santa Barbara County American Reserve 1984 $12.75 (2/15/87)
92 CARNEROS CREEK Pinot Noir Los Carneros 1984 $15 (3/15/87)
91 NAVARRO Pinot Noir Anderson Valley 1984 $12 (1/31/88)
90 ROBERT STEMMLER Pinot Noir Sonoma County 1984 $16 (8/31/86)
89 DAVIS BYNUM Pinot Noir Russian River Valley Limited Release 1984 $14 (5/31/88)
89 DEHLINGER Pinot Noir Russian River Valley 1984 $11 (6/30/87)
89 LA CREMA Pinot Noir California 1984 $11 (3/15/87)
88 ACACIA Pinot Noir Carneros Napa Valley Madonna Vineyard 1984 Rel: $16 Cur: $16 (3/15/87)
88 CHALONE Pinot Noir Chalone 1984 Rel: $18.50 Cur: $24 (12/15/87)
87 ALEXANDER VALLEY Pinot Noir Alexander Valley 1984 $7 (2/15/88)
86 CLOS DU BOIS Pinot Noir Sonoma County 1984 $8 (8/31/86)
86 MOUNT EDEN Pinot Noir Santa Cruz Mountains 1984 Rel: $20 Cur: $21 (4/15/88)
86 WHITEHALL LANE Pinot Noir Napa Valley 1984 $7.50 (3/01/86)
85 BYRON Pinot Noir Santa Barbara County Sierra Madre Vineyards 1984 $12.50 (8/31/86)
85 EDNA VALLEY Pinot Noir Edna Valley 1984 $10 (12/15/87)
85 SANFORD Pinot Noir Central Coast 1984 $12 (5/15/87)
84 MARK WEST Pinot Noir Russian River Valley Ellis Vineyard 1984 $10 (3/15/87)
84 ROCHIOLI Pinot Noir Russian River Valley 1984 $12 (11/15/87)
84 SEGHESIO Pinot Noir Sonoma-Mendocino Counties 1984 $6.75 (5/31/88)
81 ACACIA Pinot Noir Carneros Napa Valley Iund Vineyard 1984 Rel: $15 Cur: $15 (3/15/87)
81 DAVID BRUCE Pinot Noir Santa Cruz Mountains 1984 $15 (6/30/87)
81 BUENA VISTA Pinot Noir Carneros Private Reserve 1984 $14.50 (2/15/88)
80 TREFETHEN Pinot Noir Napa Valley 1984 $9.25 (5/31/88)
79 CAYMUS Pinot Noir Napa Valley Special Selection 1984 $12.50 (2/15/88)
79 GARY FARRELL Pinot Noir Russian River Valley 1984 $12 (4/15/87)
78 CLOS DU VAL Pinot Noir Napa Valley 1984 $11.50 (9/30/87)
78 HANZELL Pinot Noir Sonoma Valley 1984 Rel: $17 Cur: $45 (5/31/89)
78 RODNEY STRONG Pinot Noir Russian River Valley River East Vineyard 1984 $8 (11/15/87)
77 FELTON EMPIRE Pinot Noir California Tonneaux Français 1984 $12 (5/15/87)
77 KENWOOD Pinot Noir Sonoma Valley Jack London Vineyard 1984 $15 (5/31/89)
76 SAINTSBURY Pinot Noir Carneros Garnet 1984 $8 (8/31/86)
75 FRICK Pinot Noir Santa Maria Valley 1984 $12 (2/28/89)
75 ROBERT MONDAVI Pinot Noir Napa Valley 1984 $8.25 (11/15/87)
71 MAYACAMAS Pinot Noir Napa Valley 1984 $12 (12/31/88)
65 SMITH-MADRONE Pinot Noir Napa Valley 1984 $10 (12/15/87)
53 GUNDLACH BUNDSCHU Pinot Noir Sonoma Valley Rhinefarm Vineyards 1984 $12 (6/30/87)

1983

95 ACACIA Pinot Noir Carneros Napa Valley St. Clair Vineyard 1983 Rel: $15 Cur: $30 (10/01/85) CS
93 ACACIA Pinot Noir Carneros Napa Valley Madonna Vineyard 1983 Rel: $15.50 Cur: $16 (8/31/86)
93 SAINTSBURY Pinot Noir Carneros 1983 $12 (12/01/85)
93 ROBERT STEMMLER Pinot Noir Sonoma County 1983 $15 (3/16/85) SS
92 CARNEROS CREEK Pinot Noir Carneros 1983 $12.50 (8/31/86)
89 ACACIA Pinot Noir Carneros Napa Valley Lee Vineyard 1983 Rel: $15.50 Cur: $20 (8/31/86)
89 CHALONE Pinot Noir Chalone 1983 Rel: $18.50 Cur: $32 (8/31/86)
89 DEHLINGER Pinot Noir Russian River Valley 1983 $10 (8/31/86)
88 GARY FARRELL Pinot Noir Russian River Valley 1983 $12 (8/31/86)
80 CALERA Pinot Noir San Benito County Jensen 1983 $22 (8/31/86)
80 ROBERT MONDAVI Pinot Noir Napa Valley Reserve 1983 Rel: $16 Cur: $22 (11/15/87)
78 ACACIA Pinot Noir Carneros Napa Valley Winery Lake Vineyard 1983 $15 (11/16/85)
78 AUSTIN Pinot Noir Santa Barbara County 1983 $25 (12/15/89)
78 DAVID BRUCE Pinot Noir Santa Cruz Mountains 1983 $15 (8/31/86)
77 ACACIA Pinot Noir Carneros Napa Valley Iund Vineyard 1983 Rel: $15.50 Cur: $16 (8/31/86)
77 MOUNT EDEN Pinot Noir Santa Cruz Mountains 1983 Rel: $18 Cur: $19 (8/31/86)
76 TAFT STREET Pinot Noir Santa Maria Valley 1983 $9 (4/15/87)
75 BUENA VISTA Pinot Noir Sonoma Valley Carneros 1983 $14 (8/31/86)
75 CHATEAU ST. JEAN Pinot Noir Sonoma Valley McCrea Vineyards 1983 $12 (9/30/87)
75 DE LOACH Pinot Noir Russian River Valley 1983 $10 (3/01/86)
74 HUSCH Pinot Noir Anderson Valley 1983 $9 (5/31/88)
73 BELVEDERE Pinot Noir Los Carneros Winery Lake 1983 $12 (12/15/87)
73 SAINTSBURY Pinot Noir Carneros Garnet 1983 (NA) (11/30/87) (JL)
72 SEGHESIO Pinot Noir Northern Sonoma 1983 $5 (4/15/87)
71 DAVIS BYNUM Pinot Noir Russian River Valley Westside Road 1983 $10 (7/16/86)
71 CHALONE Pinot Noir Chalone Red Table Wine 1983 $9 (8/31/86)
71 FIRESTONE Pinot Noir Santa Ynez Valley 1983 $9 (11/15/87)
70 CLOS DU BOIS Pinot Noir Sonoma County 1983 $8 (8/31/86)
70 HANZELL Pinot Noir Sonoma Valley 1983 Rel: $17 Cur: $38 (4/15/88)
67 MARK WEST Pinot Noir Russian River Valley 1983 $10 (5/16/86)
67 J. PEDRONCELLI Pinot Noir Sonoma County 1983 $6 (4/15/88)
66 CLOS DU VAL Pinot Noir Napa Valley 1983 $11.50 (8/31/86)
65 PARDUCCI Pinot Noir Mendocino County 1983 $6 (8/31/86)
60 ZACA MESA Pinot Noir Santa Barbara County American Reserve 1983 $13 (8/31/86)
57 EDNA VALLEY Pinot Noir Edna Valley 1983 $10 (4/15/87)

1982

91 ACACIA Pinot Noir Carneros Napa Valley Iund Vineyard 1982 Rel: $15 Cur: $29 (7/16/84) CS
91 BOUCHAINE Pinot Noir Napa Valley Los Carneros Winery Lake Vineyard 1982 $15 (3/01/86) CS
90 ACACIA Pinot Noir Carneros Napa Valley Lee Vineyard 1982 Rel: $15 Cur: $15 (7/16/84)
90 ACACIA Pinot Noir Carneros Napa Valley Winery Lake Vineyard 1982 $15 (7/16/84)
89 ACACIA Pinot Noir Carneros Napa Valley St. Clair Vineyard 1982 Rel: $15 Cur: $25 (7/16/84)
89 EDMEADES Pinot Noir Anderson Valley 1982 $10 (2/16/85)
89 ROCHIOLI Pinot Noir Russian River Valley 1982 $12.50 (8/31/86)
88 AUSTIN Pinot Noir Santa Barbara County Bien Nacido Vineyard 1982 $10 (3/16/85)
88 CALERA Pinot Noir California Jensen 1982 $23 (1/01/85)
88 HUSCH Pinot Noir Anderson Valley 1982 $9 (8/31/86)
87 AUSTIN Pinot Noir Santa Barbara County Sierra Madre Vineyards 1982 $12 (5/01/84)
87 BOUCHAINE Pinot Noir Napa Valley Los Carneros 1982 $12.50 (7/16/85)
86 BOUCHAINE Pinot Noir Napa Valley Los Carneros Winery Lake Vineyard 1982 $15 (8/31/86)
86 DEHLINGER Pinot Noir Russian River Valley 1982 $10 (10/01/85)
86 SAINTSBURY Pinot Noir Carneros 1982 $8 (11/30/87) (JL)
85 CAYMUS Pinot Noir Napa Valley Special Selection 1982 $12.50 (8/31/86)
85 HACIENDA Pinot Noir Sonoma Valley 1982 $12 (12/16/84)
85 LOUIS M. MARTINI Pinot Noir Carneros Napa Valley Las Amigas 1982 $12 (3/31/90)
82 NAVARRO Pinot Noir Anderson Valley 1982 $9.75 (4/15/87)
82 JOSEPH SWAN Pinot Noir 1982 $17 (8/31/86)
81 BOUCHAINE Pinot Noir Napa Valley 1982 $20 (6/30/87)
80 EDNA VALLEY Pinot Noir Edna Valley 1982 $11.50 (8/31/86)
80 SOLETERRA Pinot Noir Napa Valley Three Palms Vineyard 1982 $12 (10/16/84)
79 ROBERT MONDAVI Pinot Noir Napa Valley 1982 $9.50 (8/31/86)
78 ROBERT MONDAVI Pinot Noir Napa Valley Reserve 1982 Rel: $15 Cur: $23 (8/31/86)
76 DE LOACH Pinot Noir Russian River Valley 1982 $10 (8/31/86)
76 IRON HORSE Pinot Noir Sonoma County Green Valley 1982 $10 (10/01/85)
76 TAFT STREET Pinot Noir Monterey County 1982 $7.50 (5/01/84)
75 ALEXANDER VALLEY Pinot Noir Alexander Valley 1982 $6.50 (11/01/84)
75 CALERA Pinot Noir San Benito County Reed 1982 $23 (8/31/86)
75 CLOS DU VAL Pinot Noir Napa Valley 1982 $10.75 (9/01/84)
75 GUNDLACH BUNDSCHU Pinot Noir Sonoma Valley Rhinefarm Vineyards 1982 $9.25 (5/01/84)
75 ZD Pinot Noir Napa Valley 1982 $12.50 (8/31/86)
72 SEA RIDGE Pinot Noir Sonoma County 1982 $10.50 (8/31/86)
71 MILL CREEK Pinot Noir Dry Creek Valley 1982 $6 (8/31/86)
69 ALMADEN Pinot Noir San Benito County 1982 $5 (6/30/87)
68 J. PEDRONCELLI Pinot Noir Sonoma County 1982 $5.50 (6/30/87)
66 CHALONE Pinot Noir Chalone 1982 Rel: $20 Cur: $35 (8/31/86)
65 BELVEDERE Pinot Noir Sonoma County Bacigalupi 1982 $12 (11/16/85)
64 INGLENOOK Pinot Noir Napa Valley 1982 $7.50 (12/31/86)
63 DOMAINE LAURIER Pinot Noir Sonoma County Green Valley 1982 $10 (11/15/87)
63 SANFORD Pinot Noir Santa Maria Valley 1982 $11 (12/01/84)
62 CALERA Pinot Noir Santa Barbara County Los Alamos Vineyard 1982 $10 (11/16/85)
60 CLOS DU BOIS Pinot Noir Sonoma County 1982 $8 (7/16/85)
58 BELVEDERE Pinot Noir Los Carneros Winery Lake 1982 $12 (8/31/86)
57 JEKEL Pinot Noir Arroyo Seco Home Vineyard 1982 $9 (6/30/87)

1981

93 HANZELL Pinot Noir Sonoma Valley 1981 Rel: $17 Cur: $21 (8/31/86)
92 CHALONE Pinot Noir Chalone Reserve 1981 $28 (8/31/86)
89 FRICK Pinot Noir California 1981 $12 (8/31/86)
89 SANTA CRUZ MOUNTAIN Pinot Noir Santa Cruz Mountains Jarvis Vineyard 1981 $15 (8/31/86)
88 BUENA VISTA Pinot Noir Sonoma Valley Carneros Private Reserve 1981 $14 (8/31/86)
86 ROBERT MONDAVI Pinot Noir Napa Valley Reserve 1981 Rel: $14 Cur: $17 (8/31/86)
86 VILLA MT. EDEN Pinot Noir Napa Valley Tres Ninos Vineyard 1981 $5 (4/16/85) BB
85 CAYMUS Pinot Noir Napa Valley 1981 $7.50 (5/01/84) BB
83 CHALONE Pinot Noir Chalone 1981 Rel: $18.50 Cur: $35 (12/16/84)
82 GEYSER PEAK Pinot Noir Sonoma County Carneros 1981 $5.75 (8/31/86)
80 FETZER Pinot Noir Mendocino 1981 $5.50 (4/01/84)
80 ROBERT MONDAVI Pinot Noir Napa Valley 1981 $7.50 (11/01/84)
80 SAINTSBURY Pinot Noir Carneros Rancho 1981 (NA) (11/30/87) (JL)
79 DONNA MARIA Pinot Noir Chalk Hill 1981 $6 (9/16/84)
78 DOMAINE LAURIER Pinot Noir Sonoma County Green Valley 1981 $10 (2/16/85)
74 MAYACAMAS Pinot Noir California 1981 $12 (8/31/86)
73 FIRESTONE Pinot Noir Santa Ynez Valley 1981 $8.25 (5/16/86)
73 MONT ST. JOHN Pinot Noir Carneros Napa Valley 1981 $9.75 (5/16/84)
65 BONNY DOON Pinot Noir Sonoma County 1981 $9 (3/01/84)
64 SIMI Pinot Noir North Coast 1981 $7 (9/16/85)
63 RODNEY STRONG Pinot Noir Russian River Valley River East Vineyard 1981 $8.50 (8/31/86)
62 INGLENOOK Pinot Noir Napa Valley 1981 $7.50 (2/01/85)
59 ZACA MESA Pinot Noir Santa Ynez Valley 1981 $12 (4/01/84)

1980

88 BEAULIEU Pinot Noir Napa Valley Los Carneros 1980 $10 (8/31/86)
86 CLOS DU BOIS Pinot Noir Dry Creek Valley Proprietor's Reserve 1980 $10.75 (7/16/84)
82 MATANZAS CREEK Pinot Noir Sonoma County Quail Hill Ranch 1980 $9.50 (7/01/84)
81 CAYMUS Pinot Noir Napa Valley 1980 $6.50 (3/16/84)
81 ROBERT MONDAVI Pinot Noir Napa Valley Reserve 1980 Rel: $13.25 Cur: $14 (8/01/84)
78 RODNEY STRONG Pinot Noir Russian River Valley River East Vineyard 1980 $10 (7/01/84)
71 BUENA VISTA Pinot Noir Sonoma Valley Carneros 1980 $7 (4/16/84)
71 INGLENOOK Pinot Noir Napa Valley 1980 $6 (3/01/84)
68 LOUIS M. MARTINI Pinot Noir Napa Valley Las Amigas Vineyard Selection 1980 $10 (3/15/87)
65 FETZER Pinot Noir California Special Reserve 1980 $13 (8/31/86)
56 PARDUCCI Pinot Noir Mendocino County 1980 $5.65 (8/01/84)
55 HULTGREN & SAMPERTON Pinot Noir Sonoma County 1980 $5.75 (9/01/84)

1979

72 HMR Pinot Noir Paso Robles 1979 $6.50 (2/01/85)

RHONE-TYPE RED

1990

87 BONNY DOON Grenache California Clos de Gilroy 1990 $8 (2/15/91) BB

UNITED STATES
CALIFORNIA/RHONE-TYPE RED

1989

88   BONNY DOON Grenache California Clos de Gilroy Cuvée Tremblement de Terre 1989 $7.50 (2/15/90) BB
88   CLINE Oakley Cuvée Contra Costa County 1989 $12 (5/31/91)
85   JOSEPH PHELPS Vin du Mistral Rouge California 1989 $14 (7/15/91)
82   BONNY DOON Grahm Crew Vin Rouge California 1989 $7.50 (10/31/90) BB
80   CLINE Côtes d'Oakley Contra Costa County 1989 $7.50 (5/31/91)
79   EDMUNDS ST. JOHN Les Côtes Sauvages California 1989 $19 (7/15/91)
74   SHENANDOAH Serene Varietal Adventure Series Amador County 1989 $8 (3/31/91)

1988

91   CLINE Mourvèdre Contra Costa County 1988 $18 (4/30/90)
91   MERIDIAN Syrah Paso Robles 1988 $14 (3/31/91)
90   CLINE Oakley Cuvée Contra Costa County 1988 $12 (2/28/90)
90   QUPE Syrah Central Coast 1988 $10.25 (12/15/89)
89   SEAN H. THACKREY Syrah Napa Valley Orion 1988 $30 (9/30/90)
88   BONNY DOON Syrah Santa Cruz Mountains 1988 $25 (2/15/91)
86   BONNY DOON Le Cigare Volant California 1988 $19 (12/31/90)
86   CHATEAU LA GRANDE ROCHE Napa Valley 1988 $13 (10/15/90)
86   SEAN H. THACKREY Mourvèdre California Taurus 1988 $24 (9/30/90)
85   BONNY DOON Grenache California Clos de Gilroy 1988 $6.75 (2/15/89) BB
85   BONNY DOON Mourvèdre California Old Telegram 1988 $20 (12/31/90)
83   BONNY DOON Grahm Crew Vin Rouge California 1988 $7.50 (2/15/90)
83   CLINE Côtes d'Oakley Contra Costa County 1988 $9 (4/30/90)
83   WILLIAM WHEELER RS Reserve California 1988 $10 (8/31/90)
80   MCDOWELL Grenache McDowell Valley Rosé Les Vieux Cepages 1988 $6.50 (11/15/89) BB
80   SARAH'S Grenache California Cadenza 1988 (NA) (4/15/89)
74   R.H. PHILLIPS Mourvèdre California EXP 1988 $13/375ml (4/30/91)

1987

92   SEAN H. THACKREY Syrah Napa Valley Orion 1987 $30 (9/30/89)
90   KENDALL-JACKSON Syrah Sonoma Valley Durell Vineyard 1987 $17 (12/15/89)
88   QUPE Syrah Central Coast 1987 $9 (4/15/89)
87   BONNY DOON Grenache California Clos de Gilroy 1987 $6.50 (2/29/88) BB
87   DUXOUP Syrah Dry Creek Valley 1987 $12 (4/15/89)
85   BONNY DOON Le Cigare Volant California 1987 Rel: $15 Cur: $16 (12/15/89)
82   CLINE Mourvèdre Contra Costa County 1987 $18 (4/15/89)
82   MCDOWELL Les Vieux Cépages Les Trésor McDowell Valley 1987 $14 (8/31/90)
81   DAVID BRUCE Cote de Shandon Vin Rouge San Luis Obispo County 1987 $7.50 (12/31/88)
81   EDMUNDS ST. JOHN Syrah California 1987 $18 (12/15/89)
81   QUPE Syrah Santa Barbara County Bien Nacido Vineyard 1987 $20 (2/28/90)
80   R.H. PHILLIPS Syrah California Reserve 1987 $13 (12/31/90)
74   MCDOWELL Syrah McDowell Valley Les Vieux Cépages 1987 $16 (3/31/91)

1986

92   BONNY DOON Le Cigare Volant California 1986 Rel: $13.50 Cur: $25 (11/15/88)
92   KENDALL-JACKSON Syrah Sonoma Valley Durell Vineyard 1986 $14 (11/30/88)
91   EDMUNDS ST. JOHN Syrah Sonoma County 1986 $12 (4/15/89)
90   BONNY DOON Mourvèdre California Old Telegram 1986 Rel: $13.50 Cur: $40 (11/15/88)
90   PRESTON Syrah-Sirah Dry Creek Valley 1986 $11 (2/15/89)
89   DOMAINE DE LA TERRE ROUGE Sierra Foothills 1986 $12 (4/15/89)
88   EDMUNDS ST. JOHN Les Côtes Sauvages California 1986 $13.50 (4/15/89)
88   JOSEPH PHELPS Syrah Napa Valley Vin du Mistral 1986 $14 (10/31/90)
87   EDMUNDS ST. JOHN Mourvèdre Napa Valley 1986 $15 (4/15/89)
86   MCDOWELL Les Vieux Cépages Les Trésor McDowell Valley 1986 $13 (9/30/89)
85   DUXOUP Syrah Dry Creek Valley 1986 $9 (4/15/89)
85   SOTOYOME Syrah Russian River Valley 1986 $7 (4/15/89)
84   BONNY DOON Grenache California Clos de Gilroy 1986 $6.50 (4/30/87)
83   SEAN H. THACKREY Syrah Napa Valley Orion 1986 $26 (4/15/89)
82   ESTRELLA RIVER Syrah Paso Robles 1986 $8 (9/30/89)
82   FREY Syrah Mendocino Bulow Vineyard 1986 $10 (4/15/89)
80   MCDOWELL Syrah McDowell Valley Les Vieux Cépages 1986 $14 (8/31/90)
79   QUPE Syrah Central Coast 1986 $9.50 (4/15/89)
77   OJAI Syrah California 1986 $7.50 (4/15/89)
74   OJAI Cabernet Sauvignon Syrah Red California 1986 $7.50 (4/15/89)

1985

91   PRESTON Sirah-Syrah Dry Creek Valley 1985 $9.50 (1/31/88)
90   BONNY DOON Le Cigare Volant California 1985 Rel: $12.50 Cur: $25 (1/31/88)
90   MCDOWELL Syrah McDowell Valley 1985 $12 (9/30/89)
86   FRICK Grenache Napa County 1985 $7.50 (4/15/89)
85   MCDOWELL Syrah McDowell Valley 1985 $12 (4/15/89)
82   SIERRA VISTA Syrah El Dorado Sierra Syrah 1985 $9.75 (4/15/89)
80   BONNY DOON Grahm Crew Vin Rouge California 1985 $6.25 (9/30/87) BB
79   ESTRELLA RIVER Syrah Paso Robles 1985 $6.50 (3/31/88)
77   SOTOYOME Syrah Russian River Valley 1985 $7 (4/15/89)

1984

89   JOSEPH PHELPS Syrah Napa Valley 1984 $8.50 (11/15/88)
87   BONNY DOON Le Cigare Volant California 1984 Rel: $10.50 Cur: $30 (8/31/86)
86   MCDOWELL Syrah McDowell Valley 1984 $9.50 (2/15/89)

1983

89   SIERRA VISTA Syrah El Dorado Sierra Syrah 1983 $9 (4/15/89)

Key to Symbols

The scores reported here are the results of blind tastings conducted by our panel of senior editors. Wines that carry the initials below are results of individual tastings.

THE WINE SPECTATOR 100-POINT SCALE *95-100*—Classic, a great wine; *90-94*—Outstanding, superior character and style; *80-89*—Good to very good, a wine with special qualities; *70-79*—Average, drinkable wine that may have minor flaws; *60-69*—Below average, drinkable but not recommended; *50-59*—Poor, undrinkable, not recommended. "*+*"—With a score indicates a range; used primarily with barrel tastings to indicate a preliminary score.

SPECIAL DESIGNATIONS SS—Spectator Selection, CS—Cellar Selection, BB—Best Buy.

TASTER'S INITIALS (JG)—Jim Gordon, (HS)—Harvey Steiman, (JL)—James Laube, (JS)—James Suckling, (TM)—Thomas Matthews, (TR)—Terry Robards, (BT)—Barrel Tasting (these wines were tasted blind from barrel samples), (CA-date)—*California's Great Cabernets* by James Laube, (CH-date)—*California's Great Chardonnays* by James Laube, (VP-date)—*Vintage Port* by James Suckling.

DATE TASTED Dates in parentheses represent the issue in which the rating was published.

---

80   ESTRELLA RIVER Syrah Paso Robles 1983 $6.50 (1/31/88) BB
71   JOSEPH PHELPS Syrah Napa Valley 1983 $8.50 (11/15/87)
69   MCDOWELL Syrah McDowell Valley 1983 $10 (5/31/88)

1982

78   DUXOUP Syrah Sonoma County 1982 $9 (3/16/84)
75   MCDOWELL Syrah McDowell Valley 1982 $10 (1/31/87)

1981

90   MCDOWELL Syrah McDowell Valley 1981 $10 (12/16/84)

1979

78   JOSEPH PHELPS Syrah Napa Valley 1979 $7.50 (9/16/84)

NV

79   TRUMPETVINE Syrah California Berkeley Red NV $5 (4/15/89)
78   CLINE Oakley Cuvée Contra Costa County NV $12 (4/15/89)

RHONE-TYPE WHITE

1990

89   JOSEPH PHELPS Viognier Napa Valley Vin du Mistral 1990 $20 (6/15/91)

1989

90   BONNY DOON Le Sophiste Santa Cruz Mountains 1989 $25 (1/31/91)
88   LA JOTA Viognier Howell Mountain 1989 $25 (1/31/91)

1988

87   QUPE Marsanne Santa Barbara County 1988 $12.50 (12/15/89)

1987

89   RITCHIE CREEK Viognier Napa Valley 1987 $13 (4/15/89)
87   BONNY DOON Le Sophiste Santa Cruz Mountains 1987 (NA) (4/15/89)
86   CALERA Viognier San Benito County 1987 (NA) (4/15/89)
84   LA JOTA Viognier Howell Mountain 1987 $18 (4/15/89)

RIESLING

1990

85   FETZER Johannisberg Riesling California 1990 $6.75 (5/15/91) BB
85   FREEMARK ABBEY Johannisberg Riesling Napa Valley 1990 $8 (4/30/91) BB
85   HIDDEN CELLARS Johannisberg Riesling Potter Valley 1990 $7.50 (6/30/91) BB
84   FIRESTONE Johannisberg Riesling Santa Ynez Valley 1990 $7.50 (7/15/91)
82   CALLAWAY White Riesling Temecula 1990 $6.75 (5/15/91)
82   FIRESTONE Johannisberg Riesling Santa Barbara County Dry 1990 $9 (7/15/91)
82   GAINEY Johannisberg Riesling Santa Ynez Valley 1990 $8 (6/15/91)

1989

84   FIRESTONE Johannisberg Riesling Santa Ynez Valley 1989 $7.50 (12/31/90)
84   HAGAFEN Johannisberg Riesling Napa Valley 1989 $8.75 (7/31/90)
83   HIDDEN CELLARS Johannisberg Riesling Potter Valley 1989 $8 (9/15/90)
83   NAVARRO White Riesling Anderson Valley 1989 $8.50 (4/30/91)
83   RENAISSANCE Riesling North Yuba Dry 1989 $8 (5/15/91)
82   J. LOHR Johannisberg Riesling Monterey County Greenfield Vineyards 1989 $6.50 (12/31/90)
81   HAGAFEN Johannisberg Riesling Napa Valley 1989 $8.75 (3/31/91)
81   J. PEDRONCELLI White Riesling Dry Creek Valley 1989 $5.50 (9/30/90) BB
80   KENDALL-JACKSON Johannisberg Riesling Clear Lake Vintner's Reserve 1989 $9 (12/31/90)
76   GAINEY Johannisberg Riesling Santa Barbara County 1989 $7.75 (9/15/90)
75   BERINGER Johannisberg Riesling North Coast 1989 $8 (12/31/90)
73   CALLAWAY White Riesling Temecula 1989 $6.75 (5/31/90)
71   GEYSER PEAK Johannisberg Riesling California Soft 1989 $6 (7/31/90)
69   ROBERT MONDAVI Johannisberg Riesling Napa Valley 1989 $8.25 (5/15/91)

1988

90   FREEMARK ABBEY Johannisberg Riesling Napa Valley 1988 $8 (8/31/89)
87   J. PEDRONCELLI White Riesling Dry Creek Valley 1988 $5.50 (8/31/89) BB
87   TREFETHEN White Riesling Napa Valley 1988 $8.25 (7/31/89)
86   DRY CREEK Johannisberg Riesling Sonoma County 1988 $7 (7/31/89)
84   CALLAWAY White Riesling Temecula 1988 $6.25 (7/31/89)
84   GAINEY Johannisberg Riesling Santa Barbara County 1988 $7.50 (12/15/89)
82   FIRESTONE Johannisberg Riesling Santa Ynez Valley 1988 $7 (12/15/89)
81   FETZER Johannisberg Riesling California 1988 $6 (7/31/89) BB
81   RANCHO SISQUOC Franken Riesling Santa Maria Valley Sylvaner 1988 $7 (12/15/89)
80   ST. FRANCIS Johannisberg Riesling Sonoma Valley 1988 $7.50 (7/31/90)
79   MIRASSOU Monterey Riesling Monterey County 1988 $6.75 (7/31/89)
78   RANCHO SISQUOC Johannisberg Riesling Santa Maria Valley 1988 $6.50 (12/15/89)
77   FORTINO Johannisberg Riesling Santa Clara County 1988 $5.50 (7/31/89)
76   SANTA BARBARA Johannisberg Riesling Santa Ynez Valley 1988 $7.50 (12/15/89)
76   SMITH-MADRONE Riesling Napa Valley 1988 $8.50 (9/15/90)
75   BALLARD CANYON Johannisberg Riesling Santa Ynez Valley Reserve 1988 $9 (12/15/89)
74   BALLARD CANYON Johannisberg Riesling Santa Ynez Valley 1988 $7 (12/15/89)
74   HAGAFEN Johannisberg Riesling Napa Valley 1988 $8.75 (7/31/89)
71   ESTRELLA RIVER Johannisberg Riesling Paso Robles 1988 $6 (12/15/89)
55   ROBERT MONDAVI Johannisberg Riesling Napa Valley 1988 $8 (9/15/90)

1987

90   GRGICH HILLS Johannisberg Riesling Napa Valley 1987 $7.75 (8/31/89)
90   JEKEL White Riesling Arroyo Seco Gravelstone Vineyard Sweet Styled 1987 $11.50 (2/28/89)
89   KENWOOD Johannisberg Riesling Sonoma Valley 1987 $7.50 (9/30/88)
87   CLOS DU BOIS Johannisberg Riesling Alexander Valley Early Harvest 1987 $8 (5/31/88)
87   FREEMARK ABBEY Johannisberg Riesling Napa Valley 1987 $7.75 (5/31/88)
86   JOSEPH PHELPS Johannisberg Riesling Napa Valley 1987 $8.50 (2/28/89)
85   JEKEL White Riesling Arroyo Seco Gravelstone Vineyard Dry Styled 1987 $11.50 (2/28/89)
85   JOSEPH PHELPS Johannisberg Riesling Napa Valley Early Harvest 1987 $8 (8/31/89)
85   ZACA MESA Johannisberg Riesling Santa Barbara County 1987 $6 (12/15/89) BB
84   GEYSER PEAK Johannisberg Riesling Sonoma Valley Soft 1987 $5.50 (7/15/88)
84   SANTA BARBARA Johannisberg Riesling Santa Ynez Valley 1987 $7 (12/15/89)
83   AUSTIN White Riesling Santa Barbara County Los Alamos Vineyards 1987 $6.50 (12/15/89)
81   CONGRESS SPRINGS Johannisberg Riesling Santa Clara County San Ysidro Vineyard 1987 $7.50 (5/31/88)

80 CALLAWAY White Riesling California 1987 $5.50 (11/15/88)
80 HAYWOOD White Riesling Sonoma Valley 1987 $7.50 (9/30/88)
80 TREFETHEN White Riesling Napa Valley 1987 $7.75 (7/15/88)
79 MADRONA Johannisberg Riesling El Dorado 1987 $6 (7/31/89)
78 BUENA VISTA Johannisberg Riesling Carneros 1987 $7 (7/31/89)
78 ST. FRANCIS Johannisberg Riesling Sonoma Valley 1987 $7.50 (10/15/88)
77 BOEGER Johannisberg Riesling El Dorado 1987 $7 (5/31/88)
77 GREENWOOD RIDGE White Riesling Mendocino 1987 $8 (7/31/89)
77 HIDDEN CELLARS Johannisberg Riesling Potter Valley 1987 $7.50 (7/15/88)
76 CLAIBORNE & CHURCHILL Riesling Edna Valley Dry Alsatian Style 1987 $8 (12/15/89)
75 FETZER Johannisberg Riesling California 1987 $6 (7/15/88)
75 JEKEL White Riesling Arroyo Seco 1987 $6.75 (2/28/89)
74 FIRESTONE Johannisberg Riesling Santa Ynez Valley 1987 $6.50 (2/28/89)
74 MARION Johannisberg Riesling California 1987 $4.50 (2/28/89)

1986

92 JEKEL White Riesling Arroyo Seco Sweet Styled 1986 $10 (10/31/87)
90 NAVARRO White Riesling Anderson Valley 1986 $7.50 (4/30/88)
88 BABCOCK Johannisberg Riesling Santa Ynez Valley 1986 $6 (12/15/89)
88 FIRESTONE Johannisberg Riesling Santa Ynez Valley 1986 $6.50 (12/15/87) BB
87 ST. FRANCIS Johannisberg Riesling Sonoma Valley 1986 $6.50 (9/15/87)
85 JEKEL White Riesling Arroyo Seco 1986 $6.75 (9/15/87)
84 CLAIBORNE & CHURCHILL Riesling Edna Valley Dry Alsatian Style 1986 $8 (7/15/88)
82 CLOS DU BOIS Johannisberg Riesling Alexander Valley Early Harvest 1986 $7.50 (6/30/87)
82 TREFETHEN White Riesling Napa Valley 1986 $7 (4/30/88)
81 ALEXANDER VALLEY Johannisberg Riesling Alexander Valley 1986 $6 (4/30/88)
81 JOSEPH PHELPS Johannisberg Riesling Napa Valley 1986 $8.50 (12/15/87)
80 HAYWOOD White Riesling Sonoma Valley 1986 $7.50 (6/30/87)
79 BUENA VISTA Johannisberg Riesling Carneros 1986 $7.25 (4/30/88)
79 CALLAWAY White Riesling Temecula 1986 $5.50 (1/31/88)
78 ESTRELLA RIVER Johannisberg Riesling Paso Robles 1986 $5.50 (12/15/87)
78 STAG'S LEAP WINE CELLARS White Riesling Napa Valley 1986 $7.50 (9/15/87)
76 MARK WEST Johannisberg Riesling Russian River Valley 1986 $7 (9/15/87)
74 CHARLES KRUG Johannisberg Riesling Napa Valley 1986 $7 (10/31/87)
72 ZACA MESA Johannisberg Riesling Santa Barbara County 1986 $5.50 (11/15/88)
70 GEYSER PEAK Johannisberg Riesling Sonoma Valley Carneros Soft 1986 $5.50 (10/31/87)
68 FREEMARK ABBEY Johannisberg Riesling Napa Valley 1986 $7.75 (6/30/87)

1985

91 HIDDEN CELLARS Johannisberg Riesling Potter Valley 1985 $7 (3/31/87)
90 FETZER Johannisberg Riesling California 1985 $6 (7/01/86)
85 JEKEL Johannisberg Riesling Arroyo Seco 1985 $6.75 (11/15/86)
85 KENDALL-JACKSON Johannisberg Riesling Monterey County 1985 $7.50 (9/15/86)
85 ST. FRANCIS Johannisberg Riesling Sonoma Valley 1985 $6 (8/31/86) BB
84 INGLENOOK Johannisberg Riesling Napa Valley 1985 $6.50 (4/30/88) BB
83 FIRESTONE Johannisberg Riesling Santa Ynez Valley 1985 $6.50 (11/15/86)
82 CHATEAU ST. JEAN Johannisberg Riesling Sonoma County 1985 $8.50 (8/31/86)
82 FREEMARK ABBEY Johannisberg Riesling Napa Valley 1985 $7.25 (8/31/86)
82 SMITH-MADRONE Johannisberg Riesling Napa Valley 1985 $7.25 (6/15/87)
80 FRANCISCAN Johannisberg Riesling Napa Valley Oakville Estate 1985 $6.50 (5/31/88)
79 KENDALL-JACKSON Johannisberg Riesling Lake County 1985 $7.50 (8/31/86)
75 RAYMOND Riesling Monterey 1985 $6 (1/31/87)
75 SMITH-MADRONE Riesling Napa Valley 1985 $7.25 (11/15/86)
74 J. LOHR Johannisberg Riesling Monterey County Greenfield Vineyards 1985 $6 (9/15/86)
69 ROBERT MONDAVI Johannisberg Riesling Napa Valley Special Selection 1985 $8 (10/31/87)
69 JOSEPH PHELPS Johannisberg Riesling Napa Valley 1985 $8.50 (9/30/86)
68 MARK WEST Johannisberg Riesling Russian River Valley 1985 $7 (11/30/86)
63 MIRASSOU Johannisberg Riesling Monterey County Fifth Generation Family Selection 1985 $6.50 (6/30/87)
58 GRGICH HILLS Johannisberg Riesling Napa Valley 1985 $7.75 (8/31/86)

1984

89 BUENA VISTA Johannisberg Riesling Sonoma Valley Carneros 1984 $7.75 (3/16/86)
89 JOSEPH PHELPS Johannisberg Riesling Napa Valley 1984 $8 (11/16/85)
88 FIRESTONE Johannisberg Riesling Santa Ynez Valley 1984 $6.50 (10/16/85)
85 JEKEL Johannisberg Riesling Monterey 1984 $6.75 (1/01/86)
83 CLOS DU BOIS Johannisberg Riesling Alexander Valley Early Harvest 1984 $6.50 (10/16/85)
81 FRANCISCAN Johannisberg Riesling Napa Valley Oakville Estate 1984 $6.50 (5/15/87)
81 FREEMARK ABBEY Johannisberg Riesling Napa Valley 1984 $7 (9/01/85)
79 RAYMOND Johannisberg Riesling Napa Valley 1984 $6 (11/16/85)
72 E.&J. GALLO Johannisberg Riesling California Limited Release Reserve 1984 $3.50 (9/15/86) BB
70 STAG'S LEAP WINE CELLARS White Riesling Napa Valley Birkmyer Vineyards 1984 $7.50 (3/16/86)
60 SMITH-MADRONE Riesling Napa Valley 1984 $7.25 (8/31/86)

1983

88 RODNEY STRONG Johannisberg Riesling Russian River Valley Le Baron Vineyard 1983 $7.25 (7/16/84)
80 SMITH-MADRONE Riesling Napa Valley 1983 $7 (11/01/84)
73 HAYWOOD White Riesling Sonoma Valley Dry 1983 $7 (11/01/84)

SAUVIGNON BLANC

1990

87 FERRARI-CARANO Fumé Blanc Sonoma County 1990 $10 (7/15/91)
87 MURPHY-GOODE Fumé Blanc Alexander Valley Estate Vineyard 1990 $9 (7/15/91)
87 PRESTON Sauvignon Blanc Dry Creek Valley Cuvée de Fumé 1990 $9.50 (7/15/91)
80 GLEN ELLEN Sauvignon Blanc California Proprietor's Reserve 1990 $6 (7/31/91) BB

1989

90 HIDDEN CELLARS Sauvignon Blanc Mendocino County White Table Wine Alchemy 1989 $18 (7/31/91)
90 KENDALL-JACKSON Sauvignon Blanc Lake County Vintner's Reserve 1989 $9 (10/31/90)
88 CAYMUS Sauvignon Blanc Napa Valley 1989 $9 (10/31/90)
88 FLORA SPRINGS Sauvignon Blanc Napa Valley Soliloquy Special Select 1989 $20 (3/15/91)
88 ROBERT PEPI Sauvignon Blanc Napa Valley Two-Heart Canopy 1989 $9.50 (3/31/91)
87 DRY CREEK Sauvignon Blanc Sonoma County 1989 $9 (12/31/90)
87 DUCKHORN Sauvignon Blanc Napa Valley 1989 $10 (12/31/90)
87 FROG'S LEAP Sauvignon Blanc Napa Valley 1989 $9.50 (10/31/90)
87 HANNA Sauvignon Blanc Sonoma County 1989 $8.50 (7/15/91)
87 MARKHAM Sauvignon Blanc Napa Valley 1989 $7 (10/31/90) BB
86 PRESTON Sauvignon Blanc Dry Creek Valley Cuvée de Fumé 1989 $8 (5/15/90)
85 BERINGER Sauvignon Blanc Knights Valley 1989 $8.50 (7/31/91)
85 BUENA VISTA Sauvignon Blanc Lake County 1989 $7.50 (8/31/90)
85 CHALK HILL Sauvignon Blanc Chalk Hill 1989 $8 (7/31/91)
85 CHATEAU ST. JEAN Fumé Blanc Sonoma County 1989 $8 (4/30/91)
85 GRGICH HILLS Fumé Blanc Napa Valley 1989 $11 (3/15/91)
85 MATANZAS CREEK Sauvignon Blanc Sonoma County 1989 $12 (7/15/91)
84 BYRON Sauvignon Blanc Santa Barbara County 1989 $9 (4/30/91)
84 CHATEAU ST. JEAN Fumé Blanc Sonoma County La Petite Etoile 1989 $10.50 (4/30/91)
84 DE LOACH Sauvignon Blanc Russian River Valley 1989 $9 (5/15/90)
84 J. PEDRONCELLI Fumé Blanc Dry Creek Valley 1989 $7 (4/30/91) BB
84 SIMI Sauvignon Blanc Sonoma County 1989 $9.50 (4/30/91)
83 BARON HERZOG Sauvignon Blanc California 1989 $8 (3/31/91)
83 CAIN Sauvignon Blanc Napa Valley Musqué 1989 $12 (3/15/91)
83 ROBERT MONDAVI Fumé Blanc Napa Valley To-Kalon Vineyard Reserve 1989 $15 (7/15/91)
83 QUIVIRA Sauvignon Blanc Dry Creek Valley 1989 $9.25 (10/31/90)
83 ROUND HILL Fumé Blanc Napa Valley House 1989 $5.75 (11/30/90) BB
83 SILVERADO Sauvignon Blanc Napa Valley 1989 $9 (10/31/90)
82 E.&J. GALLO Sauvignon Blanc California Reserve 1989 $4 (7/31/91) BB
82 INNISFREE Sauvignon Blanc Napa Valley 1989 $7.50 (4/30/91)
82 PRESTON Sauvignon Blanc Dry Creek Valley Estate Reserve 1989 $12 (12/31/90)
82 ST. SUPERY Sauvignon Blanc Napa Valley Dollarhide Ranch 1989 $8 (3/15/91)
82 PHILIP TOGNI Sauvignon Blanc Napa Valley 1989 $12.50 (7/15/91)
82 STEPHEN ZELLERBACH Sauvignon Blanc Sonoma County 1989 $5.50 (12/31/90) BB
81 BEAULIEU Sauvignon Blanc Napa Valley Dry 1989 $8.50 (4/30/91)
81 CHIMNEY ROCK Fumé Blanc Stags Leap District 1989 $11 (7/31/91)
81 GROTH Sauvignon Blanc Napa Valley 1989 $8.50 (10/31/90)
81 ST. CLEMENT Sauvignon Blanc Napa Valley 1989 $9.50 (8/31/90)
81 SPOTTSWOODE Sauvignon Blanc Napa Valley 1989 $11 (8/31/90)
80 ADLER FELS Fumé Blanc Sonoma County 1989 $10 (4/30/91)
80 FERRARI-CARANO Fumé Blanc Sonoma County 1989 $10 (10/15/90)
80 HAWK CREST Sauvignon Blanc California 1989 $6 (8/31/90) BB
80 LOUIS M. MARTINI Sauvignon Blanc Napa Valley 1989 $8 (4/30/91)
80 MERRYVALE Sauvignon Blanc Napa Valley Meritage 1989 $12 (4/30/91)
80 ROBERT MONDAVI Sauvignon Blanc California Woodbridge 1989 $5 (4/30/91) BB
80 QUAIL RIDGE Sauvignon Blanc Napa Valley 1989 $8 (12/31/90)
80 RAYMOND Sauvignon Blanc Napa Valley 1989 $10 (4/30/91)
79 BRANDER Sauvignon Blanc Santa Ynez Valley Tête de Cuvée 1989 $9.50 (4/30/91)
79 CALLAWAY Sauvignon Blanc Temecula 1989 $8 (10/31/90)
79 ESTANCIA Sauvignon Blanc Alexander Valley 1989 $7 (3/15/91)
79 MONTEREY VINEYARD Sauvignon Blanc Monterey County Classic 1989 $5.50 (3/31/91)
79 STERLING Sauvignon Blanc Napa Valley 1989 $9 (3/15/91)
79 SUNNY ST. HELENA Sauvignon Blanc Napa Valley 1989 $9 (4/30/91)
79 SUTTER HOME Sauvignon Blanc California 1989 $4.50 (4/30/91)
78 LONG Sauvignon Blanc Napa Valley 1989 $12 (7/15/91)
78 ROBERT PECOTA Sauvignon Blanc Napa Valley 1989 $9.25 (8/31/90)
77 GLEN ELLEN Sauvignon Blanc California Proprietor's Reserve 1989 $5 (8/31/90)
77 GUENOC Sauvignon Blanc Guenoc Valley 1989 $10 (4/30/91)
77 IRON HORSE Fumé Blanc Alexander Valley Barrel Fermented 1989 $11 (8/31/90)
76 CLOS DU BOIS Sauvignon Blanc Alexander Valley 1989 $8 (8/31/90)
76 FETZER Fumé Blanc California Valley Oaks Fumé 1989 $6.50 (12/31/90)
65 SANFORD Sauvignon Blanc Santa Barbara County 1989 $9 (7/31/91)

1988

90 GRGICH HILLS Fumé Blanc Napa Valley 1988 $10 (3/31/90)
90 SILVERADO Sauvignon Blanc Napa Valley 1988 $8.50 (2/15/90) SS
90 SIMI Sauvignon Blanc Sonoma County 1988 $8 (10/31/90)
89 CHATEAU ST. JEAN Fumé Blanc Russian River Valley La Petite Etoile 1988 $10.50 (11/30/89)
89 KENDALL-JACKSON Sauvignon Blanc Lake County Vintner's Reserve 1988 $9 (3/31/90)
89 MURPHY-GOODE Fumé Blanc Alexander Valley Estate Vineyard 1988 $8 (11/30/89)
88 BUENA VISTA Sauvignon Blanc Lake County 1988 $7.50 (9/15/89)
88 FERRARI-CARANO Fumé Blanc Sonoma County 1988 $9 (9/15/89)
88 HAYWOOD Fumé Blanc Sonoma Valley 1988 $9.50 (11/30/89)
88 QUIVIRA Sauvignon Blanc Dry Creek Valley 1988 $9.50 (11/30/89)
88 RAYMOND Sauvignon Blanc Napa Valley 1988 $8.50 (11/30/89)
87 J. CAREY Sauvignon Blanc Santa Ynez Valley 1988 $8 (12/15/89)
87 ROBERT PEPI Sauvignon Blanc Napa Valley Two-Heart Canopy 1988 $9.50 (2/15/90)
87 PRESTON Sauvignon Blanc Dry Creek Valley Estate Reserve 1988 $10 (11/30/89)
87 ST. SUPERY Sauvignon Blanc Napa Valley Dollarhide Ranch 1988 $7.50 (10/31/89)
87 STONEGATE Sauvignon Blanc Napa Valley 1988 $8.50 (6/30/90)
86 DE LOACH Fumé Blanc Russian River Valley 1988 $9 (7/31/89)
86 DUCKHORN Sauvignon Blanc Napa Valley 1988 $10 (2/15/90)
86 MATANZAS CREEK Sauvignon Blanc Sonoma County 1988 $12 (2/15/90)
86 PRESTON Sauvignon Blanc Dry Creek Valley Cuvée de Fumé 1988 $8 (9/15/89)
85 ALDERBROOK Sauvignon Blanc Dry Creek Valley 1988 $9 (3/31/90)
85 BERINGER Sauvignon Blanc Knights Valley 1988 $8.50 (6/30/90)
85 BYRON Sauvignon Blanc Santa Barbara County 1988 $8.50 (12/15/89)
85 GROTH Sauvignon Blanc Napa Valley 1988 $8 (2/15/90)
85 KENWOOD Sauvignon Blanc Sonoma County 1988 $9 (11/30/89)
85 QUAIL RIDGE Sauvignon Blanc Napa Valley 1988 $8 (11/30/89)
84 BENZIGER Fumé Blanc Sonoma County 1988 $8.50 (10/31/89)
84 HANDLEY Sauvignon Blanc Dry Creek Valley 1988 $8 (8/31/90)
84 IRON HORSE Fumé Blanc Alexander Valley Barrel Fermented 1988 $11 (11/30/89)
84 ROBERT MONDAVI Fumé Blanc Napa Valley To-Kalon Vineyard Reserve 1988 $15 (8/31/90)
84 STERLING Sauvignon Blanc Napa Valley 1988 $9 (11/30/89)
83 BEAULIEU Sauvignon Blanc Napa Valley Dry 1988 $8.50 (9/15/89)
83 CAYMUS Sauvignon Blanc Napa Valley 1988 $9 (9/15/89)
83 MORGAN Sauvignon Blanc Alexander Valley 1988 $8.50 (11/30/89)
83 J. PEDRONCELLI Fumé Blanc Dry Creek Valley 1988 $6 (9/15/89) BB
83 STRATFORD Sauvignon Blanc California 1988 $8 (5/15/90)
82 CALLAWAY Sauvignon Blanc Temecula 1988 $8 (10/31/89)
82 ESTANCIA Sauvignon Blanc Alexander Valley 1988 $6 (5/15/90) BB
82 MARKHAM Sauvignon Blanc Napa Valley 1988 $7 (9/15/89)
82 PARDUCCI Fumé Blanc Mendocino County Cellarmaster Selection 1988 $12 (4/30/91)
81 DE LOACH Sauvignon Blanc Russian River Valley 1988 $9 (7/31/89)
81 M.G. VALLEJO Fumé Blanc California 1988 $5 (5/15/90) BB

UNITED STATES
CALIFORNIA/SAUVIGNON BLANC

81 VENTANA Sauvignon Blanc Monterey 1988 $8 (3/31/90)
79 FETZER Fumé Blanc California Valley Oaks Fumé 1988 $6.50 (7/31/89)
79 MCDOWELL Fumé Blanc Mendocino 1988 $7.50 (3/31/90)
78 CASTORO Fumé Blanc San Luis Obispo County 1988 $5.25 (12/15/89)
78 CLOS DU BOIS Sauvignon Blanc Alexander Valley 1988 $11 (7/31/89)
78 CORBETT CANYON Sauvignon Blanc Central Coast Coastal Classic 1988 $5.50/1.5L (12/15/89)
78 LOUIS HONIG Sauvignon Blanc Napa Valley 1988 $8.75 (5/15/90)
78 ROBERT MONDAVI Sauvignon Blanc California Woodbridge 1988 $5 (10/31/89)
78 PARDUCCI Sauvignon Blanc Mendocino County 1988 $7.50 (5/15/90)
78 ST. CLEMENT Sauvignon Blanc Napa Valley 1988 $9.50 (3/31/90)
78 M.G. VALLEJO Fumé Blanc California 1988 $5 (10/31/89)
77 CORBETT CANYON Sauvignon Blanc Central Coast Reserve 1988 $6 (12/15/89)
76 FROG'S LEAP Sauvignon Blanc Napa Valley 1988 $9.50 (11/30/89)
76 HAWK CREST Sauvignon Blanc California 1988 $6 (5/15/90)
76 LAKESPRING Sauvignon Blanc Napa Valley 1988 $8.50 (11/30/89)
76 STAG'S LEAP WINE CELLARS Sauvignon Blanc Napa Valley Rancho Chimiles 1988 $9 (11/30/89)
75 CANTERBURY Sauvignon Blanc California 1988 $5 (10/31/89)
74 BERINGER Fumé Blanc Napa Valley 1988 $7.50 (8/31/90)
74 ROBERT MONDAVI Fumé Blanc Napa Valley 1988 $9.50 (5/15/90)
73 BOGLE Fumé Blanc California 1988 $6/1.5L (7/31/89)
73 CHATEAU ST. JEAN Fumé Blanc Sonoma County 1988 $8 (5/15/90)
73 VIANSA Sauvignon Blanc Napa-Sonoma Counties 1988 $10 (10/31/90)
72 GAN EDEN Sauvignon Blanc Sonoma County 1988 $9 (3/31/91)
71 HANNA Sauvignon Blanc Sonoma County 1988 $8.75 (8/31/90)
71 ZACA MESA Sauvignon Blanc Santa Barbara County 1988 $8 (12/15/89)
68 CALLAWAY Fumé Blanc Temecula 1988 $8 (7/31/91)
67 BARON HERZOG Sauvignon Blanc Sonoma County Special Reserve 1988 $10 (3/31/91)
67 FLORA SPRINGS Sauvignon Blanc Napa Valley 1988 $8.50 (3/31/90)
66 MAYACAMAS Sauvignon Blanc Napa Valley 1988 $11 (8/31/90)
65 CHIMNEY ROCK Fumé Blanc Stags Leap District 1988 $15 (5/15/90)
55 JOSEPH PHELPS Sauvignon Blanc Napa Valley 1988 $9.50 (6/30/90)

1987

90 BUENA VISTA Sauvignon Blanc Lake County 1987 $7.50 (6/15/88)
89 FERRARI-CARANO Fumé Blanc Sonoma County 1987 $9 (3/15/89)
89 GRGICH HILLS Fumé Blanc Napa Valley 1987 $10 (7/31/89)
89 QUAIL RIDGE Sauvignon Blanc Napa Valley 1987 $7.50 (3/15/89)
89 QUIVIRA Sauvignon Blanc Dry Creek Valley 1987 $8.50 (10/15/88)
88 CLOS DU BOIS Sauvignon Blanc Alexander Valley 1987 $8 (6/15/88)
88 PHILIP TOGNI Sauvignon Blanc Napa Valley 1987 $10 (11/15/88)
87 DRY CREEK Fumé Blanc Sonoma County 1987 $8.75 (11/15/88)
87 FROG'S LEAP Sauvignon Blanc Napa Valley 1987 $9 (10/15/88)
87 LONG Sauvignon Blanc Sonoma County 1987 $11 (1/31/89)
87 MAYACAMAS Sauvignon Blanc Napa Valley 1987 $11 (9/15/89)
87 ROBERT MONDAVI Fumé Blanc Napa Valley 1987 $9.50 (7/31/89)
86 ALDERBROOK Sauvignon Blanc Dry Creek Valley 1987 $7.50 (4/15/89)
86 BUENA VISTA Fumé Blanc Alexander Valley 1987 $8.50 (3/15/89)
86 DE LOACH Fumé Blanc California 1987 $9 (12/31/88)
86 DUCKHORN Sauvignon Blanc Napa Valley 1987 $9.50 (12/31/88)
86 HUSCH Sauvignon Blanc Mendocino La Ribera Vineyards 1987 $7.50 (10/15/88)
86 IRON HORSE Fumé Blanc Alexander Valley 1987 $10 (7/31/88)
86 MARKHAM Sauvignon Blanc Napa Valley 1987 $7 (4/15/89)
86 PRESTON Sauvignon Blanc Dry Creek Valley Cuvée de Fumé 1987 $7.25 (8/31/88)
85 BRANDER Sauvignon Blanc Santa Ynez Valley 1987 $8 (3/15/89)
85 MATANZAS CREEK Sauvignon Blanc Sonoma County 1987 $12 (3/15/89)
85 RAYMOND Sauvignon Blanc Napa Valley 1987 $8 (1/31/89)
85 SANFORD Sauvignon Blanc Santa Barbara County 1987 $8.50 (12/15/89)
85 VENTANA Sauvignon Blanc Monterey 1987 $8 (10/31/89)
84 BENZIGER Fumé Blanc Sonoma County 1987 $8.50 (8/31/88)
84 CAYMUS Sauvignon Blanc Napa Valley 1987 $8 (7/15/88)
84 CLOS PEGASE Sauvignon Blanc Lake County 1987 $9.50 (5/15/90)
84 LOUIS HONIG Sauvignon Blanc Napa Valley 1987 $8.75 (7/31/89)
83 CONN CREEK Sauvignon Blanc Napa Valley Barrel Select 1987 $10 (4/30/89)
83 HAWK CREST Sauvignon Blanc California 1987 $6 (10/31/89) BB
83 KENDALL-JACKSON Sauvignon Blanc Lake County Jackson Vineyard 1987 $12 (12/31/88)
83 MORGAN Sauvignon Blanc Alexander Valley 1987 $8.50 (8/31/88)
82 BEAULIEU Sauvignon Blanc Napa Valley Dry 1987 $8.50 (12/31/88)
82 BRANDER Sauvignon Blanc Santa Ynez Valley Reserve 1987 $11 (12/15/89)
82 CHALK HILL Sauvignon Blanc Sonoma County 1987 $7 (10/31/89)
82 CHRISTOPHE Sauvignon Blanc California 1987 $7 (4/30/89) BB
82 GAINEY Sauvignon Blanc Santa Barbara County 1987 $8.50 (12/15/89)
82 KENWOOD Sauvignon Blanc Sonoma County 1987 $9 (11/15/88)
81 BELVEDERE Sauvignon Blanc Sonoma County Discovery Series 1987 $3.25 (8/31/88) BB
81 ESTRELLA RIVER Sauvignon Blanc Paso Robles 1987 $6 (12/15/89)
81 ROBERT MONDAVI Sauvignon Blanc California White 1987 $5 (3/15/89) BB
81 PRESTON Sauvignon Blanc Dry Creek Valley Private Reserve 1987 $9.50 (12/31/88)
81 VIANSA Sauvignon Blanc Sonoma-Napa Counties 1987 $9.50 (4/30/89)
80 HAYWOOD Fumé Blanc Sonoma Valley 1987 $9.50 (5/31/88)
80 ROBERT MONDAVI Fumé Blanc Napa Valley To-Kalon Vineyard Reserve 1987 $15 (3/31/90)
80 STAG'S LEAP WINE CELLARS Sauvignon Blanc Napa Valley Rancho Chimiles 1987 $9 (1/31/89)
79 J. PEDRONCELLI Fumé Blanc Dry Creek Valley 1987 $6 (4/30/89)
78 CALLAWAY Fumé Blanc Temecula 1987 $8.25 (6/30/90)
78 SIGNORELLO Sauvignon Blanc Napa Valley 1987 $8.25 (4/30/89)
77 BERINGER Sauvignon Blanc Knights Valley 1987 $8.50 (3/15/89)
77 CHIMNEY ROCK Fumé Blanc Stags Leap District 1987 $10 (1/31/89)
77 FIRESTONE Sauvignon Blanc Santa Ynez Valley 1987 $7.50 (12/15/89)
76 MURPHY-GOODE Fumé Blanc Alexander Valley 1987 $7.50 (3/15/89)
76 ROBERT PEPI Sauvignon Blanc Napa Valley 1987 $8.50 (11/30/89)
75 RUTHERFORD HILL Sauvignon Blanc Napa Valley 1987 $8 (7/31/89)
74 GROTH Sauvignon Blanc Napa Valley 1987 $7.50 (12/31/88)
73 CONCANNON Fumé Blanc California Selected Vineyards 1987 $9.50 (4/30/91)
73 HANNA Sauvignon Blanc Sonoma County 1987 $8.75 (10/15/88)
73 JOSEPH PHELPS Sauvignon Blanc Napa Valley 1987 $9 (12/31/88)
73 STERLING Sauvignon Blanc Napa Valley 1987 $10 (11/15/88)
72 CRESTON MANOR Sauvignon Blanc San Luis Obispo County 1987 $8.25 (12/15/89)
72 LIBERTY SCHOOL Sauvignon Blanc California Lot 6 1987 $5 (8/31/88)
72 SANTA BARBARA Sauvignon Blanc Santa Ynez Valley Valley View Vineyards 1987 $8.50 (12/15/89)
72 SIMI Sauvignon Blanc Sonoma County 1987 $9.50 (7/31/89)
71 CALLAWAY Sauvignon Blanc Temecula 1987 $8.25 (3/15/89)
70 CAKEBREAD Sauvignon Blanc Napa Valley 1987 $11 (12/31/88)
69 GLEN ELLEN Sauvignon Blanc California Proprietor's Reserve 1987 $4.50 (8/31/88)
68 ST. CLEMENT Sauvignon Blanc Napa Valley 1987 $9.50 (7/31/89)
68 SANTA BARBARA Sauvignon Blanc Santa Ynez Valley Reserve 1987 $11 (12/15/89)
67 R.H. PHILLIPS Sauvignon Blanc Yolo County Dunnigan Hills Night Harvest 1987 $4 (3/15/89)
66 JEPSON Sauvignon Blanc Mendocino 1987 $7 (7/31/89)
65 BABCOCK Sauvignon Blanc Santa Ynez Valley 1987 $8 (12/15/89)
56 BELLEROSE Sauvignon Blanc Sonoma County Barrel Fermented 1987 $10.50 (5/15/90)

1986

91 BUENA VISTA Sauvignon Blanc Lake County 1986 $7.25 (7/15/87) SS
91 CLOS DU BOIS Sauvignon Blanc Alexander Valley 1986 $7.50 (9/15/87)
89 GRGICH HILLS Fumé Blanc Napa Valley 1986 $10 (5/15/88)
89 PRESTON Sauvignon Blanc Dry Creek Valley Reserve 1986 $11 (10/15/87)
88 BEAULIEU Sauvignon Blanc Napa Valley Dry 1986 $8.50 (5/31/88)
88 KENWOOD Sauvignon Blanc Sonoma County 1986 $8.75 (8/31/87)
88 PRESTON Sauvignon Blanc Dry Creek Valley Cuvée de Fumé 1986 $11 (8/31/87)
87 CONCANNON Sauvignon Blanc Livermore Valley Reserve 1986 $9.50 (12/31/88)
87 VENTANA Sauvignon Blanc Monterey Ventana Vineyards 1986 $7.50 (11/15/87)
86 CHRISTOPHE Sauvignon Blanc California 1986 $5 (10/31/87) BB
86 CLOS PEGASE Fumé Blanc Napa Valley 1986 $9.50 (7/15/88)
86 FREMONT CREEK Sauvignon Blanc Mendocino-Napa Counties 1986 $9 (5/31/88)
86 IRON HORSE Fumé Blanc Alexander Valley Barrel Fermented 1986 $9.25 (8/31/87)
85 ADLER FELS Fumé Blanc Sonoma County 1986 $8.75 (10/31/87)
85 FLORA SPRINGS Sauvignon Blanc Napa Valley 1986 $8.50 (8/31/88)
85 LOUIS HONIG Sauvignon Blanc Napa Valley 1986 $8.25 (5/15/88)
85 CHARLES KRUG Sauvignon Blanc Napa Valley 1986 $7 (10/31/87)
84 CHATEAU ST. JEAN Fumé Blanc Sonoma County 1986 $8 (8/31/87)
84 HANNA Sauvignon Blanc Sonoma County 1986 $8.75 (11/15/87)
83 CAYMUS Sauvignon Blanc Napa Valley 1986 $7.50 (5/15/87)
83 GROTH Sauvignon Blanc Napa Valley 1986 $7 (3/15/88)
83 HIDDEN CELLARS Sauvignon Blanc Mendocino County Bock Vineyard 1986 $8 (8/31/88)
83 HUSCH Sauvignon Blanc Mendocino La Ribera Vineyards 1986 $7 (12/31/87)
83 STRATFORD Sauvignon Blanc California 1986 $6.75 (11/15/87)
82 FERRARI-CARANO Fumé Blanc Alexander Valley 1986 $9 (11/15/87)
82 GLEN ELLEN Fumé Blanc Sonoma County Benziger Family Selection 1986 $7 (11/15/87)
82 JEPSON Sauvignon Blanc Mendocino 1986 $7.50 (3/15/88)
82 MATANZAS CREEK Sauvignon Blanc Sonoma County 1986 $11 (5/15/88)
82 MURPHY-GOODE Fumé Blanc Alexander Valley 1986 $7 (10/15/87)
82 PARDUCCI Sauvignon Blanc Mendocino County 1986 $6.50 (10/15/87)
82 ROBERT PECOTA Sauvignon Blanc Napa Valley Barrel Fermented 1986 $9.25 (10/31/87)
82 ST. CLEMENT Sauvignon Blanc Napa Valley 1986 $9.50 (5/31/88)
82 M.G. VALLEJO Fumé Blanc California 1986 $4.50 (7/15/87) BB
82 VIANSA Sauvignon Blanc Napa-Sonoma Counties 1986 $8.75 (5/31/88)
81 BERINGER Sauvignon Blanc Knights Valley 1986 $8 (5/31/88)
81 BUENA VISTA Fumé Blanc Alexander Valley Wasson Vineyard 1986 $8.50 (3/15/88)
81 CLOS PEGASE Sauvignon Blanc Napa Valley 1986 $9.50 (11/30/87)
81 CONN CREEK Sauvignon Blanc Napa Valley Barrel Select 1986 $9.75 (3/15/88)
81 DUCKHORN Sauvignon Blanc Napa Valley 1986 $9.50 (12/31/87)
81 LIBERTY SCHOOL Sauvignon Blanc Napa Valley Lot 4 1986 $5 (11/15/87) BB
81 ROUND HILL Fumé Blanc Napa Valley House 1986 $5 (1/31/88) BB
80 CANTERBURY Sauvignon Blanc California 1986 $4.75 (5/15/87) BB
80 CHIMNEY ROCK Fumé Blanc Stags Leap District 1986 $9 (10/15/88)
80 KARLY Sauvignon Blanc Amador County 1986 $8 (3/15/88)
80 SHENANDOAH Sauvignon Blanc Amador County 1986 $7 (8/31/87)
80 SIGNORELLO Sauvignon Blanc Napa Valley 1986 $7.25 (3/15/88)
79 GLEN ELLEN Sauvignon Blanc California Proprietor's Reserve 1986 $4.50 (10/31/87)
79 RAYMOND Sauvignon Blanc Napa Valley 1986 $7.50 (12/31/87)
79 STERLING Sauvignon Blanc Napa Valley 1986 $9 (1/31/88)
78 AUDUBON Sauvignon Blanc Pope Valley 1986 $7 (5/31/88)
78 LAKESPRING Sauvignon Blanc California 1986 $7.50 (5/15/88)
78 QUIVIRA Sauvignon Blanc Dry Creek Valley 1986 $8 (11/30/87)
78 J. WILE & SONS Sauvignon Blanc Napa Valley 1986 $6 (10/31/87)
77 CLOS DU BOIS Sauvignon Blanc Dry Creek Valley Proprietor's Reserve 1986 $10.50 (8/31/87)
77 GUENOC Sauvignon Blanc Lake-Napa Counties 1986 $6.75 (3/15/88)
77 ROBERT MONDAVI Fumé Blanc Napa Valley To-Kalon Vineyard Reserve 1986 $15 (7/31/89)
77 TAFT STREET Sauvignon Blanc Napa Valley 1986 $5.50 (12/31/87)
76 MONTICELLO Sauvignon Blanc Napa Valley 1986 $7.50 (7/15/88)
76 ROBERT PEPI Sauvignon Blanc Napa Valley 1986 $8.50 (5/15/88)
76 RUTHERFORD HILL Sauvignon Blanc Napa Valley 1986 $7 (5/31/88)
75 DRY CREEK Fumé Blanc Sonoma County 1986 $8.75 (8/31/87)
75 ROBERT MONDAVI Sauvignon Blanc California 1986 $4 (10/15/87) BB
75 J. PEDRONCELLI Fumé Blanc Dry Creek Valley 1986 $6 (11/30/87)
75 ROCHIOLI Sauvignon Blanc Russian River Valley 1986 $8.50 (11/30/87)
75 WILLIAM WHEELER Sauvignon Blanc Sonoma County 1986 $8 (3/15/88)
74 DORE Fumé Blanc California 1986 $5 (3/15/88)
74 INGLENOOK Sauvignon Blanc Napa Valley 1986 $7.50 (5/31/88)
73 CLOS DU VAL Sauvignon Blanc Napa Valley 1986 $8 (5/31/88)

Key to Symbols

The scores reported here are the results of blind tastings conducted by our panel of senior editors. Wines that carry the initials below are results of individual tastings.

THE WINE SPECTATOR 100-POINT SCALE *95-100*—Classic, a great wine; *90-94*—Outstanding, superior character and style; *80-89*—Good to very good, a wine with special qualities; *70-79*—Average, drinkable wine that may have minor flaws; *60-69*—Below average, drinkable but not recommended; *50-59*—Poor, undrinkable, not recommended. "+"—With a score indicates a range; used primarily with barrel tastings to indicate a preliminary score.

SPECIAL DESIGNATIONS SS—Spectator Selection, CS—Cellar Selection, BB—Best Buy.

TASTER'S INITIALS (JG)—Jim Gordon, (HS)—Harvey Steiman, (JL)—James Laube, (JS)—James Suckling, (TM)—Thomas Matthews, (TR)—Terry Robards, (BT)—Barrel Tasting (these wines were tasted blind from barrel samples), (CA-date)—*California's Great Cabernets* by James Laube, (CH-date)—*California's Great Chardonnays* by James Laube, (VP-date)—*Vintage Port* by James Suckling.

DATE TASTED Dates in parentheses represent the issue in which the rating was published.

73 CYPRESS LANE Sauvignon Blanc California 1986 $4.50 (3/15/88)
73 SIMI Sauvignon Blanc Sonoma County 1986 $9 (10/15/88)
72 FETZER Sauvignon Blanc California Valley Oaks Fumé 1986 $6.50 (10/15/87)
72 GEYSER PEAK Fumé Blanc Alexander Valley 1986 $6 (3/31/88)
72 MERIDIAN Sauvignon Blanc Napa Valley 1986 $8 (5/31/88)
71 ROBERT MONDAVI Fumé Blanc Napa Valley 1986 $9.50 (7/15/88)
70 RUTHERFORD RANCH Sauvignon Blanc Napa Valley 1986 $6.75 (3/15/88)
69 CHATEAU SOUVERAIN Sauvignon Blanc Sonoma County 1986 $5 (3/15/88)
67 CAKEBREAD Sauvignon Blanc Napa Valley 1986 $26 (10/15/87)
64 SEBASTIANI Sauvignon Blanc Sonoma County Reserve 1986 $9 (12/31/87)
62 SUNNY ST. HELENA Sauvignon Blanc Napa Valley 1986 $6 (11/15/87)
59 JOSEPH PHELPS Sauvignon Blanc Napa Valley 1986 $9 (12/31/87)
58 AMIZETTA Sauvignon Blanc Napa Valley 1986 $8 (5/31/88)

1985

94 ROBERT PECOTA Sauvignon Blanc Napa Valley 1985 $9.25 (10/15/86) SS
90 PRESTON Sauvignon Blanc Dry Creek Valley 1985 $6.75 (9/15/86)
90 STRATFORD Sauvignon Blanc California 1985 $6.75 (11/15/86)
90 WILLIAM WHEELER Sauvignon Blanc Sonoma County 1985 $8 (2/28/87)
89 BERINGER Sauvignon Blanc Knights Valley 1985 $7.50 (4/15/87)
88 CHRISTOPHE Sauvignon Blanc California 1985 $6 (1/31/87) BB
88 HANNA Sauvignon Blanc Sonoma County 1985 $8.75 (10/31/86)
88 MURPHY-GOODE Fumé Blanc Alexander Valley Estate Vineyard 1985 $8 (7/01/86)
87 BERINGER Fumé Blanc Napa Valley 1985 $7.50 (4/15/87)
87 CLOS DU VAL Sauvignon Blanc California 1985 $7.50 (2/28/87)
87 PRESTON Sauvignon Blanc Dry Creek Valley Reserve 1985 $9 (5/15/87)
87 RAYMOND Sauvignon Blanc Napa Valley 1985 $7.50 (5/15/87)
86 CHATEAU ST. JEAN Fumé Blanc Sonoma County 1985 $8 (1/31/87)
86 MAYACAMAS Sauvignon Blanc Napa Valley 1985 $10 (8/31/87)
86 SILVERADO Sauvignon Blanc Napa Valley 1985 $8 (2/28/87)
85 BEAULIEU Sauvignon Blanc Napa Valley Dry 1985 $7 (5/15/87)
85 BUENA VISTA Sauvignon Blanc Lake County 1985 $7.50 (9/30/86)
85 SPOTTSWOODE Sauvignon Blanc Napa Valley 1985 $9 (1/31/87)
84 CAYMUS Sauvignon Blanc Napa Valley 1985 $7.50 (1/31/87)
84 IRON HORSE Fumé Blanc Alexander Valley Barrel Fermented 1985 $8.75 (11/30/86)
84 QUIVIRA Sauvignon Blanc Dry Creek Valley 1985 $8 (1/31/87)
84 SHENANDOAH Sauvignon Blanc Amador County 1985 $7 (10/31/86)
83 CHATEAU ST. JEAN Fumé Blanc Alexander Valley Robert Young Vineyards 1985 $9.50 (5/31/88)
83 CHATEAU ST. JEAN Fumé Blanc Russian River Valley La Petite Etoile 1985 $10.50 (1/31/87)
83 INGLENOOK Sauvignon Blanc Napa Valley Reserve 1985 $9.50 (3/15/88)
82 KENDALL-JACKSON Sauvignon Blanc Clear Lake 1985 $7.50 (2/15/87)
82 NAPA RIDGE Sauvignon Blanc California 1985 $4.75 (3/31/87) BB
82 ST. CLEMENT Sauvignon Blanc Napa Valley 1985 $9.50 (8/31/86)
79 BRANDER Sauvignon Blanc Santa Ynez Valley 1985 $8.50 (3/15/88)
79 CONCANNON Sauvignon Blanc Livermore Valley 1985 $9 (8/31/87)
79 DRY CREEK Fumé Blanc Sonoma County 1985 $8.50 (10/15/86)
79 J FRITZ Fumé Blanc Dry Creek Valley 1985 $7 (11/15/87)
78 KENWOOD Sauvignon Blanc Sonoma County 1985 $6 (1/31/87)
78 SIMI Sauvignon Blanc Sonoma County 1985 $10 (8/31/87)
77 BELLEROSE Sauvignon Blanc Sonoma County 1985 $8.50 (2/15/87)
77 GUENOC Sauvignon Blanc Lake-Napa Counties 1985 $15 (11/15/87)
76 CALLAWAY Fumé Blanc Temecula 1985 $7.50 (11/15/87)
76 CHATEAU DE LEU Sauvignon Blanc Solano County Green Valley 1985 $6 (11/15/87)
76 KONOCTI Fumé Blanc Lake County 1985 $6 (8/31/87)
76 SAM J. SEBASTIANI Sauvignon Blanc Sonoma-Napa Counties 1985 $10 (10/31/86)
75 CAIN Sauvignon Blanc Napa-Sonoma Counties 1985 $8 (10/15/87)
75 DE LOACH Sauvignon Blanc Russian River Valley 1985 $8.50 (8/31/87)
75 MONTICELLO Sauvignon Blanc Napa Valley 1985 $7.50 (10/15/87)
75 STERLING Sauvignon Blanc Napa Valley 1985 $10 (11/30/86)
73 CLOS DU BOIS Sauvignon Blanc Dry Creek Valley Proprietor's Reserve 1985 $12 (9/30/86)
73 FLORA SPRINGS Sauvignon Blanc Napa Valley 1985 $8 (2/28/87)
73 GLEN ELLEN Fumé Blanc Sonoma County Benziger Family Selection 1985 $7 (8/31/86)
72 EHLERS LANE Sauvignon Blanc Napa Valley 1985 $7.50 (3/15/88)
72 HIDDEN CELLARS Sauvignon Blanc Sonoma County 1985 $8 (3/31/88)
72 ROBERT MONDAVI Fumé Blanc Napa Valley 1985 $7.25 (2/28/87)
72 ROBERT PEPI Sauvignon Blanc Napa Valley 1985 $8.50 (12/31/87)
71 CLOS DU BOIS Sauvignon Blanc Alexander Valley Barrel Fermented 1985 $7.50 (6/01/87)
71 ST. VRAIN Sauvignon Blanc Alexander Valley 1985 $8 (5/15/87)
70 CLOS PEGASE Fumé Blanc Napa Valley 1985 $9 (8/31/87)
70 CORBETT CANYON Sauvignon Blanc Central Coast Select 1985 $6 (10/31/87)
70 MATANZAS CREEK Sauvignon Blanc Sonoma County 1985 $10.50 (5/15/87)
69 LAKESPRING Sauvignon Blanc California 1985 $7.50 (6/30/87)
68 DUCKHORN Sauvignon Blanc Napa Valley 1985 $9 (1/31/87)
67 FETZER Fumé Blanc California Valley Oaks Fume 1985 $6.50 (9/30/86)
63 GARY FARRELL Sauvignon Blanc Russian River Valley 1985 $8.50 (8/31/87)
61 RUTHERFORD HILL Sauvignon Blanc Napa Valley 1985 $7 (10/15/87)
60 GRGICH HILLS Sauvignon Blanc Napa Valley 1985 $9 (5/15/87)
60 NEWTON Sauvignon Blanc Napa Valley 1985 $9.50 (9/30/87)

1984

94 JOSEPH PHELPS Sauvignon Blanc Napa Valley 1984 $9 (2/01/86)
92 PRESTON Sauvignon Blanc Dry Creek Valley Reserve 1984 $9 (11/01/85)
91 QUIVIRA Sauvignon Blanc Dry Creek Valley 1984 $8 (10/01/85)
90 CONCANNON Sauvignon Blanc Livermore Valley 1984 $9 (4/30/87)
89 ESTATE WILLIAM BACCALA Sauvignon Blanc Mendocino 1984 $8.50 (11/30/86)
87 DUCKHORN Sauvignon Blanc Napa Valley 1984 $9 (12/01/85)
87 GRGICH HILLS Fumé Blanc Napa Valley 1984 $9 (2/16/86)
86 CHATEAU ST. JEAN Fumé Blanc Alexander Valley Robert Young Vineyards 1984 $9.75 (4/16/86)
86 MATANZAS CREEK Sauvignon Blanc Sonoma County 1984 $10.50 (7/01/86)
85 ADLER FELS Fumé Blanc Sonoma County 1984 $8.50 (10/16/85)
85 ROBERT PEPI Sauvignon Blanc Napa Valley 1984 $8 (1/31/87)
84 BOUCHAINE Sauvignon Blanc Napa Valley 1984 $8.50 (2/16/86)
84 CORBETT CANYON Sauvignon Blanc San Luis Obispo County 1984 $6 (4/01/86) BB
83 LOUIS HONIG Sauvignon Blanc Napa Valley 1984 $8.25 (12/01/85)
83 ST. CLEMENT Sauvignon Blanc Napa Valley 1984 $9.50 (10/16/85)
82 STRATFORD Sauvignon Blanc California 1984 $6.50 (12/01/85)
79 LAKESPRING Sauvignon Blanc California 1984 $7.50 (12/01/85)
78 INGLENOOK Sauvignon Blanc Napa Valley Reserve 1984 $9.50 (2/28/87)

77 DRY CREEK Fumé Blanc Sonoma County 1984 $8.50 (4/16/86)
77 E.&J. GALLO Sauvignon Blanc California Limited Release Reserve 1984 $3.50 (11/15/86) BB
77 ROBERT MONDAVI Fumé Blanc Napa Valley 1984 $10 (6/01/86)
77 ROBERT PECOTA Sauvignon Blanc Napa Valley 1984 $8.50 (11/16/85)
76 SIMI Sauvignon Blanc Sonoma County 1984 $10.50 (10/15/86)
76 DAVID S. STARE Fumé Blanc Dry Creek Valley Reserve 1984 $11 (1/31/87)
73 CHATEAU ST. JEAN Fumé Blanc Sonoma County 1984 $8.75 (10/16/85)
73 CHATEAU ST. JEAN Fumé Blanc Sonoma County La Petite Etoile 1984 $10.50 (11/16/85)
73 STERLING Sauvignon Blanc Napa Valley 1984 $9 (4/16/86)
72 ESTANCIA Sauvignon Blanc Alexander Valley 1984 $6 (7/01/86)
72 STAG'S LEAP WINE CELLARS Sauvignon Blanc Napa Valley 1984 $8.50 (6/01/86)
72 ZACA MESA Sauvignon Blanc Central Coast 1984 $7.50 (2/15/87)
70 CALLAWAY Fumé Blanc Temecula 1984 $7.50 (4/16/86)
70 CHATEAU SOUVERAIN Sauvignon Blanc Alexander Valley Wasson Vineyard 1984 $8 (1/31/87)
70 LIBERTY SCHOOL Sauvignon Blanc Napa Valley Lot 2 1984 $5.50 (12/01/85)
70 PARDUCCI Sauvignon Blanc Mendocino County 1984 $6 (11/01/85)
68 FLORA SPRINGS Sauvignon Blanc Napa Valley 1984 $8.50 (9/30/86)
68 HACIENDA Sauvignon Blanc Sonoma County 1984 $8 (10/16/85)
68 NEWTON Sauvignon Blanc Napa Valley 1984 $8 (5/15/87)
68 WHITEHALL LANE Sauvignon Blanc Napa Valley 1984 $8 (10/15/86)
67 RUTHERFORD HILL Sauvignon Blanc Napa Valley 1984 $7.50 (12/31/86)
66 SUTTER HOME Sauvignon Blanc North Coast 1984 $4.50 (2/16/86)
65 EHLERS LANE Sauvignon Blanc Napa Valley 1984 $9 (6/01/86)
65 MONTEREY VINEYARD Fumé Blanc Monterey County 1984 $6 (2/28/87)
64 GIRARD Sauvignon Blanc North Coast 1984 $8 (10/31/86)
61 CHALK HILL Sauvignon Blanc Sonoma County 1984 $7 (4/16/86)
61 PAT PAULSEN Sauvignon Blanc Sonoma County 1984 $8.50 (12/01/85)
51 DE LOACH Fumé Blanc Russian River Valley 1984 $8.50 (4/16/86)

1983

90 CHATEAU ST. JEAN Fumé Blanc Sonoma County 1983 $9.75 (4/16/84) SS
89 CONCANNON Sauvignon Blanc California 1983 $7 (3/01/85)
88 KENWOOD Sauvignon Blanc Sonoma County 1983 $8.50 (10/16/84)
86 MONTICELLO Sauvignon Blanc Napa Valley 1983 $7.50 (6/01/86)
81 ROBERT PEPI Sauvignon Blanc Napa Valley 1983 $8 (2/16/86)
79 WENTE BROS. Sauvignon Blanc Livermore Valley 1983 $6.50 (2/16/86)
65 SIMI Sauvignon Blanc Sonoma County 1983 $9.50 (11/16/85)
63 FOPPIANO Sauvignon Blanc Russian River Valley 1983 $8 (11/16/85)
58 NEWTON Sauvignon Blanc Napa Valley 1983 $9.50 (4/16/86)
56 BERINGER Sauvignon Blanc Sonoma County 1983 $8 (10/16/85)

1982

87 SIMI Sauvignon Blanc Sonoma County 1982 $9 (4/01/84)
77 ROBERT MONDAVI Fumé Blanc Napa Valley Reserve 1982 $12.50 (4/16/86)

SAUVIGNON BLENDS

1989

89 CAYMUS Conundrum California 1989 $18 (4/30/91)
81 VICHON Chevrignon Napa Valley 1989 $9.75 (5/31/91)

1988

89 BENZIGER A Tribute Sonoma Mountain 1988 $11.50 (12/31/90)
89 KONOCTI Meritage Clear Lake 1988 $14 (4/30/91)
89 LYETH White Alexander Valley 1988 $12 (10/31/90)
88 GUSTAVE NIEBAUM Chevrier Herrick Vineyard Napa Valley 1988 $11.50 (12/15/89)
86 VICHON Chevrignon Napa Valley 1988 $9.75 (1/31/91)
84 CARMENET Reserve Edna Valley 1988 $12 (1/31/91)
83 DE LORIMIER Spectrum Alexander Valley 1988 $8.50 (9/30/90)

1987

89 INGLENOOK Gravion Napa Valley 1987 $9.50 (2/28/89)
81 DE LORIMIER Spectrum Alexander Valley 1987 $8.50 (3/31/89)
77 CARMENET Sonoma County 1987 $9.50 (3/31/90)
70 MERLION Chevrier Hyde Vineyards Los Carneros 1987 $10 (8/31/90)

1986

91 INGLENOOK Gravion Napa Valley 1986 $9.50 (4/30/88) SS
88 MERLION Sauvrier Napa Valley 1986 $9 (9/15/88)
86 DE LORIMIER Spectrum Alexander Valley 1986 $8.50 (2/29/88)
85 CARMENET Sonoma County 1986 $9.50 (1/31/89)
78 LYETH White Alexander Valley 1986 $12 (9/15/89)
75 CARMENET Edna Valley 1986 $9 (12/15/88)
74 VICHON Chevrignon Napa Valley 1986 $9.75 (1/31/89)

1985

85 CARMENET Edna Valley 1985 $8.75 (4/15/88)
85 MERLION Sauvrier Napa Valley 1985 $9.50 (1/31/88)
81 KENDALL-JACKSON Chevriot Lake County 1985 $9 (9/30/87)
80 CARMENET Sonoma County 1985 $8.75 (12/31/87)
76 LYETH White Alexander Valley 1985 $10 (12/31/87)
70 VICHON Chevrignon Napa Valley 1985 $9.50 (8/31/87)

1984

63 VICHON Chevrignon Napa Valley 1984 $7.50 (9/15/86)

1983

91 VICHON Chevrignon Napa Valley 1983 $9.60 (1/01/85) SS
84 CARMENET Edna Valley 1983 $9 (3/16/85)
76 LYETH White Alexander Valley 1983 $10 (5/01/86)

SÉMILLON

1988

83 ALDERBROOK Sémillon Dry Creek Valley 1988 $9 (2/15/90)

1987

87 ALDERBROOK Sémillon Dry Creek Valley Rued Vineyard 1987 $7.50 (5/15/89) BB
82 CLOS DU VAL Sémillon California 1987 $10 (7/15/91)

UNITED STATES
CALIFORNIA/SÉMILLON

77   J. CAREY Sémillon Santa Ynez Valley Buttonwood Farm 1987 $8 (12/15/89)

1986

88   MERLION Sémillon Los Carneros Hyde Vineyards Chevrier 1986 $10 (9/15/88)
77   MONTICELLO Sémillon Napa Valley Chevrier Blanc 1986 $7.50 (1/31/89)
73   CLOS DU VAL Sémillon California 1986 $9 (10/31/88)

1985

76   CLOS DU VAL Sémillon California 1985 $8.50 (8/31/87)
75   ALDERBROOK Sémillon Dry Creek Valley 1985 $6.50 (4/30/88)

1984

87   MONTICELLO Sémillon Napa Valley Chevrier Blanc 1984 $7.50 (1/01/86)
86   CLOS DU VAL Sémillon California 1984 $8.50 (3/01/86)
71   R.H. PHILLIPS Sémillon Yolo County Dunnigan Hills 1984 $6.50 (3/01/86)

1983

90   CLOS DU VAL Sémillon California 1983 $7.50 (3/01/85) SS
76   WENTE BROS. Sémillon Livermore Valley 1983 $5 (3/01/86)

SPARKLING/BLANC DE BLANCS

1987

81   CHATEAU ST. JEAN Brut Blanc de Blancs Sonoma County 1987 $12 (12/31/89)

1986

91   SCHARFFENBERGER Blanc de Blancs Mendocino County 1986 $20 (3/15/91)
89   SCHRAMSBERG Blanc de Blancs Napa Valley 1986 $20 (12/31/90)
87   IRON HORSE Blanc de Blancs Sonoma County Green Valley 1986 $22 (12/31/90)
86   JEPSON Blanc de Blancs Mendocino 1986 $16 (4/30/91)
81   SCHARFFENBERGER Blanc de Blancs Mendocino County 1986 $18 (12/31/89)

1985

87   SCHRAMSBERG Blanc de Blancs Napa Valley Late Disgorged 1985 $27 (6/15/91)
85   IRON HORSE Blanc de Blancs Sonoma County Green Valley 1985 $21 (12/31/89)
85   IRON HORSE Blanc de Blancs Sonoma County Green Valley 1985 $20 (5/31/89)
85   SCHARFFENBERGER Blanc de Blancs Mendocino County 1985 $18 (12/31/88)
84   SCHRAMSBERG Blanc de Blancs Napa Valley 1985 $20 (5/31/89)
80   TIJSSELING Blanc de Blancs Mendocino Cuvée de Chardonnay 1985 $13 (12/31/89)

1984

89   FALCONER Brut Blanc de Blancs Russian River Valley 1984 $15 (3/15/91)
88   CHATEAU ST. JEAN Brut Blanc de Blancs Sonoma County 1984 $11 (5/31/89)
88   CHATEAU ST. JEAN Brut Blanc de Blancs Sonoma County 1984 $11 (8/31/88)
79   IRON HORSE Blanc de Blancs Sonoma County Green Valley 1984 $19 (12/31/88)
78   SCHARFFENBERGER Blanc de Blancs Mendocino County 1984 $17.50 (12/31/87)
77   SHADOW CREEK Blanc de Blancs California 1984 $14.50 (1/31/88)

1983

88   SHADOW CREEK Blanc de Blancs Sonoma County 1983 $15 (5/16/86)
82   SCHRAMSBERG Blanc de Blancs Napa Valley 1983 $17.50 (5/16/86)
81   ESTRELLA RIVER Blanc de Blancs Paso Robles Star Cuvée 1983 $13 (2/29/88)
76   CHATEAU ST. JEAN Brut Blanc de Blancs Sonoma County 1983 $11 (7/31/87)

1982

89   SHADOW CREEK Blanc de Blancs Sonoma County 1982 $15 (10/16/85)
85   IRON HORSE Blanc de Blancs Sonoma County Green Valley Late Disgorged 1982 $24 (12/31/87)
79   CHATEAU ST. JEAN Brut Blanc de Blancs Sonoma County 1982 $13 (5/16/86)
78   IRON HORSE Blanc de Blancs Sonoma County Green Valley 1982 $16.50 (5/16/86)
77   HANNS KORNELL Blanc de Blancs California 1982 $14.75 (11/30/86)

1981

86   IRON HORSE Blanc de Blancs Sonoma County Green Valley 1981 $18 (11/01/84)
82   CHATEAU ST. JEAN Brut Blanc de Blancs Sonoma County 1981 $14 (11/01/84)
69   KORBEL Blanc de Blancs California Private Reserve 1981 $34/1.5L (2/29/88)

NV

86   CHATEAU ST. JEAN Brut Blanc de Blancs Sonoma County NV $12 (5/15/91)
79   KORBEL Blanc de Blancs California NV $13 (6/15/91)
73   KORBEL Blanc de Blancs California NV $14.50 (8/31/89)
73   KORBEL Blanc de Blancs California NV $14.50 (5/16/86)
64   KORBEL Blanc de Blancs California NV $14.50 (3/15/88)

BLANC DE NOIRS

1987

87   HANNS KORNELL Blanc de Noirs California 1987 $15 (6/15/91)
86   S. ANDERSON Blanc de Noirs Napa Valley 1987 $19 (6/15/91)
83   PIPER SONOMA Blanc de Noirs Sonoma County 1987 $16 (6/15/91)

1986

90   IRON HORSE Blanc de Noirs Sonoma County Green Valley Wedding Cuvée 1986 $19 (5/31/89)
87   PIPER SONOMA Blanc de Noirs Sonoma County 1986 $15 (5/31/89)

83   S. ANDERSON Blanc de Noirs Napa Valley 1986 $20 (12/31/90)
71   CHATEAU DIANA Blanc de Noirs Monterey Special Reserve 1986 $7 (6/15/91)
69   HANNS KORNELL Blanc de Noirs California 1986 $15 (5/31/89)

1985

87   S. ANDERSON Blanc de Noirs Napa Valley 1985 $16 (5/31/89)
86   IRON HORSE Blanc de Noirs Sonoma County Green Valley Wedding Cuvée 1985 $17 (12/31/88)
79   FIRESTONE Blanc de Noirs Santa Ynez Valley 1985 $15 (12/31/88)

1984

86   SHADOW CREEK Blanc de Noirs California 1984 $12.50 (5/31/87)
85   IRON HORSE Blanc de Noirs Sonoma County Green Valley Wedding Cuvée 1984 $16.50 (12/31/87)
84   ROBERT HUNTER Blanc de Noirs Sonoma Valley Brut de Noirs 1984 $15 (10/15/88)
83   PAUL MASSON Blanc de Noirs Monterey Centennial Cuvée 1984 $9 (12/31/87)
82   SCHRAMSBERG Blanc de Noirs Napa Valley 1984 $22 (12/31/90)
79   S. ANDERSON Blanc de Noirs Napa Valley 1984 $16 (10/15/88)
71   MARK WEST Blanc de Noirs Russian River Valley 1984 $16.50 (12/31/88)

1983

90   SCHRAMSBERG Blanc de Noirs Napa Valley 1983 $21 (5/31/89)
88   S. ANDERSON Blanc de Noirs Napa Valley 1983 $28 (5/31/87)
88   PIPER SONOMA Blanc de Noirs Sonoma County 1983 $15 (12/31/86)
87   SCHRAMSBERG Blanc de Noirs Napa Valley Late Disgorged 12/90 1983 $28 (6/15/91)
85   S. ANDERSON Blanc de Noirs Napa Valley 1983 $28 (5/31/89)
84   ROBERT HUNTER Blanc de Noirs Sonoma Valley Brut de Noirs 1983 $15 (1/31/88)
82   IRON HORSE Blanc de Noirs Sonoma County Green Valley Wedding Cuvée 1983 $16.50 (12/31/86)
78   WENTE BROS. Blanc de Noirs Arroyo Seco 1983 $15 (3/31/89)
69   MIRASSOU Blanc de Noirs Monterey 1983 $11 (12/31/88)
68   CULBERTSON Blanc de Noirs California 1983 $14 (5/16/86)

1982

90   ROBERT HUNTER Blanc de Noirs Sonoma Valley Brut de Noirs 1982 $14 (12/31/86)
86   PIPER SONOMA Blanc de Noirs Sonoma County 1982 $15 (4/01/86)
79   SHADOW CREEK Blanc de Noirs Sonoma County 1982 $13 (5/16/86)
66   MIRASSOU Blanc de Noirs Monterey 1982 $10 (8/31/87)

1981

91   SCHRAMSBERG Blanc de Noirs Napa Valley 1981 $20 (5/16/86)
87   ROBERT HUNTER Blanc de Noirs Sonoma Valley Brut de Noirs 1981 $14 (12/16/84)
69   ROBERT HUNTER Blanc de Noirs Sonoma Valley Brut de Noirs Late Disgorged 1981 $14 (2/01/86)

NV

84   CHANDON Blanc de Noirs Napa Valley NV $14 (5/31/89)
83   DOMAINE MUMM Blanc de Noirs Napa Valley Cuvée Napa NV $15 (11/15/90)
83   SHADOW CREEK Blanc de Noirs California NV $13 (5/31/89)
80   CHANDON Blanc de Noirs Napa Valley NV $27/1.5L (5/16/86)
80   CHANDON Blanc de Noirs Napa-Sonoma Counties NV $15 (12/31/89)
80   SHADOW CREEK Blanc de Noirs California NV $11 (6/15/91)
77   CULBERTSON Blanc de Noirs California NV $14 (12/31/90)
77   SEBASTIANI Blanc de Noirs Sonoma County Five Star NV $11 (4/30/90)
77   SHADOW CREEK Blanc de Noirs California NV $13 (5/31/89)
76   CHANDON Blanc de Noirs Napa Valley NV $14 (5/16/86)
71   KORBEL Blanc de Noirs California NV $14 (12/31/89)

BRUT

1989

81   FOLIE A DEUX Brut Napa Valley Fantasie 1989 $18 (6/15/91)

1988

84   CHATEAU DE BAUN Brut Sonoma County Symphony Romance 1988 $11 (7/15/91)

1987

91   DOMAINE MUMM Brut Carneros Winery Lake Cuvée Napa 1987 $22 (11/15/90)
89   IRON HORSE Brut Sonoma County Green Valley 1987 $21 (11/15/90)
87   DOMAINE MUMM Brut Napa Valley Reserve Cuvée Napa 1987 $22 (12/31/90)
87   PIPER SONOMA Brut Sonoma County 1987 $16 (6/15/91)
82   CHATEAU ST. JEAN Brut Sonoma County 1987 $12 (4/30/90)

1986

89   TIJSSELING Brut Mendocino 1986 $11.50 (12/31/89)
87   CHATEAU ST. JEAN Brut Sonoma County 1986 $12 (12/31/89)
87   DOMAINE MUMM Brut Carneros Winery Lake Cuvée Napa 1986 $23 (5/31/89)
84   GLORIA FERRER Brut Sonoma County Royal Cuvée 1986 $16 (4/30/91)
82   IRON HORSE Brut Sonoma County Green Valley 1986 $20 (12/31/89)
82   PIPER SONOMA Brut Sonoma County 1986 $14 (5/31/89)
77   CONGRESS SPRINGS Brut Santa Clara County Brut de Pinot 1986 $8 (3/31/88)
77   MAISON DEUTZ Brut San Luis Obispo County Reserve 1986 $22 (4/30/91)
74   CHATEAU DE BAUN Brut Sonoma County Symphony Romance 1986 $12 (7/31/88)

1985

91   MICHEL TRIBAUT Brut Monterey County 1985 $13 (5/31/89)
89   DOMAINE MUMM Brut Napa Valley Reserve Cuvée Napa 1985 $21 (12/31/88)
87   S. ANDERSON Brut Napa Valley 1985 $18 (6/15/91)
87   GLORIA FERRER Brut Sonoma County Royal Cuvée 1985 $15 (5/31/89)
86   CHATEAU ST. JEAN Brut Sonoma County 1985 $11 (12/31/88)
86   DOMAINE MUMM Brut Napa Valley Reserve Cuvée Napa 1985 $21 (5/31/89)
83   CULBERTSON Brut California 1985 $14 (5/31/89)
83   GLORIA FERRER Brut Sonoma County Royal Cuvée 1985 $16 (3/15/91)
83   IRON HORSE Brut Sonoma County Green Valley 1985 $17.50 (12/31/88)
82   JEPSON Brut Mendocino 1985 $16 (12/31/88)
81   GLORIA FERRER Brut Carneros Carneros Cuvée 1985 $20 (4/30/90)
79   MONTREAUX Brut Napa Valley 1985 $32 (12/31/90)
79   PIPER SONOMA Brut Sonoma County 1985 $14 (7/15/88)
77   MONTREAUX Brut Napa Valley 1985 $32 (12/31/88)

1984

89 GLORIA FERRER Brut Sonoma County Royal Cuvée 1984 $15 (4/15/88)
86 VAN DER KAMP Brut Sonoma Valley 1984 $15 (5/31/89)
85 MICHEL TRIBAUT Brut Monterey County 1984 $14 (12/31/87)
84 CHATEAU ST. JEAN Brut Sonoma County 1984 $11 (7/15/88)
84 MIRASSOU Brut Monterey Cuvée 1984 $12 (6/15/91)
82 S. ANDERSON Brut Napa Valley 1984 $18 (10/15/88)
82 ST. FRANCIS Brut Sonoma Valley 1984 $9.50 (12/16/85)
81 HANDLEY Brut Anderson Valley 1984 $15 (10/15/88)
80 IRON HORSE Brut Sonoma County Green Valley Late Disgorged 1984 $23 (12/31/89)
79 IRON HORSE Brut Sonoma County Green Valley 1984 $16.50 (12/31/87)

1983

87 IRON HORSE Brut Sonoma County Green Valley 1983 $16.50 (12/31/86)
87 SHADOW CREEK Brut California Reserve Cuvée 1983 $20 (5/31/89)
86 VAN DER KAMP Brut Sonoma Valley 1983 $17.50 (12/31/87)
84 SCHARFFENBERGER Brut Mendocino County 1983 $13 (9/30/87)
82 SCHRAMSBERG Brut Napa Valley Reserve 1983 $29 (12/31/90)
81 MICHEL TRIBAUT Brut Monterey County 1983 $14 (2/15/87)
79 PIPER SONOMA Brut Sonoma County 1983 $13 (12/31/86)
79 WENTE BROS. Brut Arroyo Seco 1983 $10 (8/31/88)
76 MIRASSOU Brut Monterey Reserve 1983 $15 (12/31/89)
74 PIPER SONOMA Brut Sonoma County 1983 $22/1.5L (1/31/88)
72 S. ANDERSON Brut Napa Valley 1983 $16 (5/31/87)
67 CHATEAU ST. JEAN Brut Sonoma County 1983 $11 (5/31/87)
66 CULBERTSON Brut California 1983 $14 (5/16/86)
66 MIRASSOU Brut Monterey 1983 $10 (7/31/88)

1982

93 PIPER SONOMA Brut Sonoma County Reserve 1982 $20 (12/31/89)
88 PIPER SONOMA Brut Sonoma County Reserve 1982 $20 (5/31/89)
87 BEAULIEU Brut Napa Valley Champagne de Chardonnay 1982 $16 (5/31/89)
85 SCHARFFENBERGER Brut Mendocino County 1982 $12.50 (2/01/86)
85 SCHRAMSBERG Brut Napa Valley Reserve 1982 $28 (5/31/89)
84 WENTE BROS. Brut Arroyo Seco 1982 $8 (12/31/86)
81 BEAULIEU Brut Napa Valley 1982 $12 (5/31/89)
80 CHATEAU ST. JEAN Brut Sonoma County Grande Cuvée 1982 $19 (6/15/91)
80 IRON HORSE Brut Sonoma County Green Valley 1982 $16.50 (5/16/86)
78 MIRASSOU Brut Monterey 1982 $12 (9/16/85)
77 WEIBEL Brut Mendocino County 1982 $13 (9/15/86)
67 CHATEAU ST. JEAN Brut Sonoma County 1982 $13 (5/16/86)
62 PIPER SONOMA Brut Sonoma County 1982 $13 (5/01/86)

1981

88 PIPER SONOMA Brut Sonoma County Tête de Cuvée 1981 $29 (5/31/89)
81 CHATEAU ST. JEAN Brut Sonoma County 1981 $14 (11/01/84)
81 PIPER SONOMA Brut Sonoma County Tête de Cuvée 1981 $29 (5/16/86)
78 SCHRAMSBERG Brut Napa Valley Reserve 1981 $27 (7/31/87)
78 WENTE BROS. Brut Arroyo Seco 1981 $8 (4/01/86)

1980

61 SCHRAMSBERG Brut Napa Valley Reserve 1980 $30 (5/16/86)

NV

89 CHANDON Brut Napa Valley Reserve NV $38/1.5L (5/31/89)
89 DOMAINE MUMM Brut Napa Valley Cuvée Napa NV $14 (12/31/87)
89 DOMAINE MUMM Brut Napa Valley Cuvée Napa NV $14 (7/01/86)
89 GLORIA FERRER Brut Sonoma County NV $14 (5/31/89)
89 MAISON DEUTZ Brut Santa Barbara County Cuvée NV $15 (10/31/86)
89 MAISON DEUTZ Brut Santa Barbara County Cuvée 3 NV $17 (5/31/89)
89 ROEDERER ESTATE Brut Anderson Valley NV $16 (12/31/88)
88 DOMAINE CARNEROS Brut Carneros NV $14 (11/15/90)
88 DOMAINE MUMM Brut Napa Valley Prestige Cuvée Napa NV $14 (12/31/88)
88 GLORIA FERRER Brut Sonoma County NV $14 (1/31/88)
88 ROEDERER ESTATE Brut Anderson Valley NV $16 (5/31/89)
87 CHANDON Brut Napa Valley Reserve NV $19 (4/15/88)
87 DOMAINE MUMM Brut Napa Valley Prestige Cuvée Napa NV $15 (5/31/89)
86 CHATEAU ST. JEAN Brut Sonoma County NV $12 (5/15/91)
86 GLORIA FERRER Brut Sonoma County NV $14 (12/31/90)
85 CHANDON Brut Napa Valley NV $28/1.5L (5/31/89)
85 CHANDON Brut Napa Valley NV $14 (5/16/86)
85 SCHARFFENBERGER Brut Mendocino County NV $18 (6/15/91)
85 SHADOW CREEK Brut California NV $13 (5/31/89)
83 KORBEL Brut California NV $10 (6/15/91)
82 DOMAINE MUMM Brut Napa Valley Prestige Cuvée Napa NV $15 (12/31/90)
81 CHANDON Brut Napa Valley Reserve NV $19 (12/31/89)
80 CHANDON Brut Napa Valley Reserve NV $38/1.5L (5/16/86)
80 CHANDON Brut Napa-Sonoma Counties NV $15 (12/31/89)
80 TOTT'S Brut California Reserve Cuvée NV $8 (5/31/89)
79 HANNS KORNELL Brut California NV $11.50 (6/15/91)
79 PARSONS CREEK Brut Mendocino County Reserve NV $15 (5/31/89)
78 KORBEL Brut California NV $11.50 (8/31/89)
78 SHADOW CREEK Brut California NV $13 (12/31/89)
77 CHANDON Brut Napa Valley Club Cuvée NV $17 (6/15/91)
77 SCHARFFENBERGER Brut Mendocino County NV $14 (10/15/88)
76 SHADOW CREEK Brut California NV $11 (6/15/91)
76 STANFORD Brut California Governor's Cuvée NV $5 (12/31/90)
75 KORBEL Brut California NV $11.50 (5/16/86)
74 SCHARFFENBERGER Brut Mendocino County NV $14 (5/16/86)
72 CHASE-LIMOGERE Brut California NV $7 (5/31/89)
72 SEBASTIANI Brut Sonoma County Five Star NV $11 (4/30/90)
70 HANNS KORNELL Brut California NV $11.25 (10/15/88)
68 HANNS KORNELL Brut California NV $11.25 (5/31/89)
67 LE DOMAINE Brut California NV $5 (2/28/89)
58 TOTT'S Brut California Reserve Cuvée NV $8 (12/31/88)

Rosé

1988

83 CHATEAU DE BAUN Brut Rosé Sonoma County Symphony Rhapsody 1988 $11 (7/15/91)

1987

84 IRON HORSE Brut Rosé Sonoma County Green Valley 1987 $28 (12/31/90)
81 SCHRAMSBERG Brut Rosé Napa Valley Cuvée de Pinot 1987 $20 (12/31/90)
81 VAN DER KAMP Brut Rosé Sonoma Valley Midnight Cuvée 1987 $15 (11/15/90)

1986

88 CHATEAU DE BAUN Rosé Sonoma County Symphony Rhapsody Sec 1986 $12 (9/15/88)
84 J. PEDRONCELLI Brut Rosé Sonoma County 1986 $10 (7/31/89)
83 VAN DER KAMP Brut Rosé Sonoma Valley Midnight Cuvée 1986 $15 (5/31/89)
80 CULBERTSON Brut Rosé California 1986 $17.50 (5/31/89)
80 IRON HORSE Brut Rosé Sonoma County Green Valley 1986 $23 (12/31/89)
76 SCHRAMSBERG Brut Rosé Napa Valley Cuvée de Pinot 1986 $19 (5/31/89)

1985

88 IRON HORSE Brut Rosé Sonoma County Green Valley 1985 $20 (12/31/88)
84 VAN DER KAMP Brut Rosé Sonoma Valley Midnight Cuvée 1985 $17.50 (12/31/87)
80 SCHRAMSBERG Brut Rosé Napa Valley Cuvée de Pinot 1985 $17 (4/30/88)

1984

83 SCHRAMSBERG Brut Rosé Napa Valley Cuvée de Pinot 1984 $17 (5/31/87)
80 MICHEL TRIBAUT Rosé Monterey County 1984 $14 (12/31/87)
75 HANDLEY Rosé Anderson Valley 1984 $16.75 (12/31/88)

NV

84 SCHARFFENBERGER Brut Rosé Mendocino County NV $18 (3/15/91)
82 KORBEL Brut Rosé California NV $10.50 (8/31/89)
78 KORBEL Brut Rosé California NV $10 (6/15/91)
76 SCHARFFENBERGER Brut Rosé Mendocino County NV $16 (12/31/88)
68 CHASE-LIMOGERE Brut Rosé California NV $7 (12/31/89)

Other Sparkling

1987

88 JORDAN Sparkling Sonoma County J 1987 $22 (5/15/91)

1986

77 SCHRAMSBERG Demi-Sec Crémant Napa Valley 1986 $20 (12/31/90)
74 CULBERTSON Natural California 1986 $18.50 (12/31/90)

1985

85 SCHRAMSBERG Demi-Sec Crémant Napa Valley 1985 $19 (5/31/89)
81 CULBERTSON Natural California 1985 $17.50 (5/31/89)
74 ADLER FELS Sparkling Sonoma County Melange à Deux 1985 $15 (10/15/87)

1984

83 MIRASSOU Natural Monterey Cuvée Au Naturel 1984 $15 (6/15/91)
74 HANNS KORNELL Sparkling California Sehr Trocken 1984 $14.50 (6/15/91)

1983

72 CULBERTSON Natural California 1983 $16.50 (5/16/86)

NV

89 GLORIA FERRER Natural Sonoma County Cuvée Emerald NV $11 (5/16/86)
87 BALLATORE Sparkling California NV $4 (5/01/86) BB
81 KORBEL Natural California NV $13 (6/15/91)
81 SCHARFFENBERGER Demi-Sec Crémant Mendocino County NV $16.50 (12/31/88)
80 CULBERTSON Sparkling California Cuvée Rouge NV $12 (3/31/89)
80 KORBEL Natural California NV $13 (6/15/91)
79 CULBERTSON Sparkling California Cuvée Rouge NV $14 (12/31/90)
78 KORBEL Natural California NV $13 (8/31/89)
77 KORBEL Extra Dry California NV $10 (8/31/89)
77 KORBEL Natural California NV $12.50 (2/15/88)
68 KORBEL Natural California NV $12.50 (5/16/86)
75 KORBEL Extra Dry California NV $10 (6/15/91)
75 TOTT'S Extra Dry California Reserve Cuvée NV $8 (2/28/89)
74 CULBERTSON Demi-Sec California Cuvée de Frontignan NV $18.50 (12/31/90)
73 S. ANDERSON Brut Napa Valley Tivoli Brut Noir NV $12 (6/15/91)
73 KORBEL Sec California NV $10 (8/31/89)
73 HANNS KORNELL Extra Dry California NV $11 (5/31/89)
73 STANFORD Extra Dry California Governor's Cuvée NV $5 (12/31/90)

Zinfandel

1989

88 FRANCISCAN Zinfandel Napa Valley Oakville Estate 1989 $10 (7/31/91)
87 GUNDLACH BUNDSCHU Zinfandel Sonoma Valley Rhinefarm Vineyards 1989 $12 (7/31/91)
86 CLINE Zinfandel Contra Costa County 1989 $9 (5/15/91)
86 HALLCREST Zinfandel California Doe Mill Cuvée 1989 $7 (4/30/91)
85 NALLE Zinfandel Dry Creek Valley 1989 $13.50 (7/31/91)
85 SUTTER HOME Zinfandel California 1989 $5 (5/15/91) BB
84 GUNDLACH BUNDSCHU Zinfandel Sonoma Valley 1989 $7.50 (7/31/91)
84 QUIVIRA Zinfandel Dry Creek Valley 1989 $13 (7/31/91)
83 CHARLES KRUG Zinfandel Napa Valley 1989 $6 (12/15/90) BB
83 RAVENSWOOD Zinfandel North Coast Vintners Blend 1989 $7.50 (7/31/91) BB
82 SHENANDOAH Zinfandel Amador County Classico Varietal Adventure Series 1989 $6 (4/30/91) BB
77 DOMAINE ST. GEORGE Zinfandel California 1989 $5 (2/15/91)
76 FETZER Zinfandel California 1989 $6.50 (11/30/90)

1988

90 LYTTON SPRINGS Zinfandel Sonoma County 1988 $12 (7/31/90)
90 A. RAFANELLI Zinfandel Dry Creek Valley 1988 $9.75 (9/15/90)
90 RIDGE Zinfandel Sonoma County Geyserville 1988 $14 (11/30/90) SS
89 HAYWOOD Zinfandel Sonoma Valley Los Chamizal Vineyards 1988 $12.50 (11/30/90)
89 HOP KILN Zinfandel Sonoma County Primitivo 1988 $14 (12/31/90)
89 LAMBORN FAMILY Zinfandel Howell Mountain 1988 $11 (2/15/91)
89 MAZZOCCO Zinfandel Sonoma County Traditional Style 1988 $13 (10/15/90)
89 NALLE Zinfandel Dry Creek Valley 1988 Rel: $12.50 Cur: $16 (7/31/90)
89 ROUND HILL Zinfandel Napa Valley 1988 $6.50 (2/15/91) BB
88 ADELAIDA Zinfandel Paso Robles 1988 $12 (4/30/91)

UNITED STATES
CALIFORNIA/*ZINFANDEL*

88 FROG'S LEAP Zinfandel Napa Valley 1988 $11.50 (12/15/90)
88 GUNDLACH BUNDSCHU Zinfandel Sonoma Valley 1988 $7 (5/31/90) BB
88 GUNDLACH BUNDSCHU Zinfandel Sonoma Valley Rhinefarm Vineyards 1988 $10 (12/15/90)
88 HOP KILN Zinfandel Russian River Valley 1988 $12 (12/15/90)
88 QUIVIRA Zinfandel Dry Creek Valley 1988 $12 (5/31/90)
88 RIDGE Zinfandel Sonoma County 1988 $8.50 (2/15/91) BB
88 SAUSAL Zinfandel Alexander Valley Private Reserve 1988 $14 (4/30/91)
88 SOBON ESTATE Zinfandel Shenandoah Valley 1988 $10 (11/30/90)
87 FRANCISCAN Zinfandel Napa Valley Oakville Estate 1988 $9 (5/31/90)
87 RAVENSWOOD Zinfandel Sonoma County Old Vine 1988 $11 (11/30/90)
87 ROUDON-SMITH Zinfandel Sonoma County 1988 $12 (2/15/91)
86 DRY CREEK Zinfandel Dry Creek Valley Old Vines 1988 $11 (2/15/91)
86 GREENWOOD RIDGE Zinfandel Sonoma County 1988 $11 (5/15/91)
86 PRESTON Zinfandel Dry Creek Valley 1988 $10 (10/15/90)
86 RABBIT RIDGE Zinfandel Russian River Valley Rabbit Ridge Ranch 1988 $8 (4/30/91)
85 BOEGER Zinfandel El Dorado Walker Vineyard 1988 $8.50 (2/15/91)
85 HIDDEN CELLARS Zinfandel Mendocino County Pacini Vineyard 1988 $10 (12/31/90)
85 MARTINELLI Zinfandel Russian River Valley 1988 $11 (4/30/91)
85 MILANO Zinfandel Mendocino County Sanel Valley Vineyard 1988 $8 (4/30/91)
84 J. PEDRONCELLI Zinfandel Dry Creek Valley 1988 $7 (11/30/90) BB
84 ROSENBLUM Zinfandel Napa Valley Hendry Vineyard Reserve 1988 $14 (4/30/91)
83 KARLY Zinfandel Amador County 1988 $9.50 (12/31/90)
82 BALDINELLI Zinfandel Shenandoah Valley 1988 $7.75 (12/31/90)
82 DOMAINE BRETON Zinfandel Lake County 1988 $8 (2/15/91)
82 KENWOOD Zinfandel Sonoma Valley 1988 $11 (12/31/90)
82 RIDGE Zinfandel Howell Mountain 1988 $12 (7/31/91)
82 RIDGE Zinfandel Sonoma County Lytton Springs 1988 $12 (11/30/90)
82 SAUSAL Zinfandel Alexander Valley 1988 $8.50 (4/30/91)
81 RAVENSWOOD Zinfandel North Coast Vintners Blend 1988 $7.25 (10/15/90) BB
81 SARAFORNIA Zinfandel Napa Valley 1988 $8 (2/15/91)
80 BURGESS Zinfandel Napa Valley 1988 $12 (7/31/91)
80 CAYMUS Zinfandel Napa Valley 1988 $9 (10/15/90)
80 MCDOWELL Zinfandel McDowell Valley 1988 $9.50 (12/31/90)
80 SANTA BARBARA Zinfandel Santa Ynez Valley Beaujour 1988 $7 (12/15/89)
79 J FRITZ Zinfandel Dry Creek Valley 80-Year-Old Vines 1988 $10 (7/31/91)
78 DE LOACH Zinfandel Russian River Valley 1988 $11 (9/15/90)
76 GUENOC Zinfandel California 1988 $7.50 (9/15/90)
75 STORYBOOK MOUNTAIN Zinfandel Napa Valley 1988 $12.50 (12/31/90)
72 DE MOOR Zinfandel Napa Valley 1988 $10 (4/30/91)
72 SUTTER HOME Zinfandel California 1988 $5 (3/31/91)

1987

92 NALLE Zinfandel Dry Creek Valley 1987 Rel: $10 Cur: $10 (5/31/89) SS
91 RIDGE Zinfandel Sonoma County Lytton Springs 1987 Rel: $11 Cur: $11 (10/31/89)
90 CASTORO Zinfandel Paso Robles 1987 $7.50 (12/15/89)
90 DE LOACH Zinfandel Russian River Valley 1987 $10 (9/15/89)
90 KENDALL-JACKSON Zinfandel Anderson Valley DuPratt Vineyard 1987 $20 (7/31/91)
90 KENWOOD Zinfandel Sonoma Valley 1987 $11 (10/31/89)
90 RIDGE Zinfandel Sonoma County Geyserville 1987 Rel: $14 Cur: $14 (10/31/89)
90 SKY Zinfandel Napa Valley 1987 Rel: $12 Cur: $17 (10/15/90)
89 BUEHLER Zinfandel Napa Valley 1987 $9.50 (5/15/90)
89 CLINE Zinfandel Contra Costa County 1987 $9 (5/15/90)
89 STORYBOOK MOUNTAIN Zinfandel Napa Valley Reserve 1987 $17.50 (12/31/90)
89 TERRACES Zinfandel Napa Valley 1987 $12.50 (2/15/91)
88 KENDALL-JACKSON Zinfandel Mendocino 1987 $9 (3/15/90)
88 KENWOOD Zinfandel Sonoma Valley Jack London Vineyard 1987 $12 (12/15/89)
88 LYTTON SPRINGS Zinfandel Sonoma County 1987 $12 (5/31/89)
88 QUIVIRA Zinfandel Dry Creek Valley 1987 $11 (7/31/89)
88 RAVENSWOOD Zinfandel Sonoma County 1987 $11 (3/15/90)
88 RAVENSWOOD Zinfandel Sonoma County Vintners Blend 1987 $6 (6/15/89) BB
88 STORYBOOK MOUNTAIN Zinfandel Napa Valley 1987 $11.50 (12/15/89)
87 CLINE Zinfandel Contra Costa County Reserve 1987 $12 (5/15/90)
87 GUNDLACH BUNDSCHU Zinfandel Sonoma Valley 1987 $7.75 (3/31/89)
87 MCDOWELL Zinfandel McDowell Valley 1987 $8 (12/15/89) BB
87 RAVENSWOOD Zinfandel Sonoma Valley Old Hill Vineyard 1987 $15 (3/15/90)
87 SUMMIT LAKE Zinfandel Howell Mountain 1987 $11 (2/15/91)
86 BERINGER Zinfandel North Coast 1987 $8 (9/15/90)
86 BOEGER Zinfandel El Dorado Walker Vineyard 1987 $8.50 (3/31/90)
86 FOPPIANO Zinfandel Dry Creek Valley Proprietor's Reserve 1987 $12 (12/31/90)
86 FROG'S LEAP Zinfandel Napa Valley 1987 $10.50 (3/15/90)
86 RAVENSWOOD Zinfandel Napa Valley Dickerson 1987 $13 (3/15/90)
86 JOSEPH SWAN Zinfandel Sonoma Coast Ziegler Vineyard 1987 $12.50 (9/15/90)
86 JOSEPH SWAN Zinfandel Sonoma County 1987 $12.50 (7/31/90)
86 JOSEPH SWAN Zinfandel Sonoma Valley Stellwagen Vineyard 1987 $12.50 (9/15/90)
85 BALDINELLI Zinfandel Shenandoah Valley 1987 $8 (5/15/90)
85 CAYMUS Zinfandel Napa Valley 1987 $9.75 (10/31/89)
85 CHATEAU SOUVERAIN Zinfandel Dry Creek Valley Bradford Mountain Vineyard 1987 $15 (5/15/90)
85 MEEKER Zinfandel Dry Creek Valley 1987 $10 (3/31/90)
85 RIDGE Zinfandel Paso Robles 1987 $10 (3/15/90)
85 SEGHESIO Zinfandel Northern Sonoma 1987 $6.50 (7/31/90) BB
84 GRGICH HILLS Zinfandel Sonoma County 1987 Rel: $12 Cur: $15 (10/15/90)
84 GUENOC Zinfandel Guenoc Valley 1987 $8 (5/15/90)
84 LAMBORN FAMILY Zinfandel Howell Mountain 1987 $10 (3/15/90)
84 A. RAFANELLI Zinfandel Dry Creek Valley 1987 $9 (12/15/89)
84 RAVENSWOOD Zinfandel Sonoma Valley Cooke 1987 $13 (3/15/90)
84 ROUND HILL Zinfandel Napa Valley Select 1987 $6 (3/31/90) BB
84 SANTA YNEZ VALLEY Zinfandel Paso Robles 1987 $8 (3/31/90)
84 STORY Zinfandel Amador County 1987 $8.50 (4/30/91)
83 CLOS DU VAL Zinfandel Stags Leap District 1987 $12.50 (5/31/90)
83 CONGRESS SPRINGS Zinfandel Santa Cruz Mountains 1987 $12 (3/15/90)
83 KARLY Zinfandel Amador County 1987 $9.50 (3/31/90)
83 LA JOTA Zinfandel Howell Mountain 1987 $12 (10/31/89)
83 MONTEREY PENINSULA Zinfandel Amador County Ferrero Ranch Doctors' Reserve 1987 $15 (5/15/91)
83 PRESTON Zinfandel Dry Creek Valley 1987 $10 (3/15/90)
83 RIDGE Zinfandel Howell Mountain 1987 $10 (5/31/90)
83 SAUSAL Zinfandel Alexander Valley 1987 $7.75 (9/15/89)
82 ALEXANDER VALLEY Zinfandel Alexander Valley 1987 $9 (3/31/90)
82 BURGESS Zinfandel Napa Valley 1987 $10 (5/31/90)
82 CHATEAU SOUVERAIN Zinfandel Dry Creek Valley 1987 $9.50 (5/15/90)
82 SANTA BARBARA Zinfandel Santa Ynez Valley 1987 $8.50 (12/15/89)
81 SHENANDOAH Zinfandel Amador County Special Reserve 1987 $8.50 (7/31/89)
79 MARIETTA Zinfandel Sonoma County 1987 $8 (11/30/90)
79 SUTTER HOME Zinfandel Amador County Reserve 1987 $9.50 (5/15/91)
78 SARAFORNIA Zinfandel Napa Valley 1987 $7 (3/15/90)
78 SUTTER HOME Zinfandel California 1987 $5.50 (7/31/89)
78 VENDANGE Zinfandel California 1987 $5.50 (9/15/90)
77 GREEN & RED Zinfandel Napa Valley 1987 $9.50 (2/15/91)
77 ROSENBLUM Zinfandel Napa Valley 1987 $9 (10/31/89)
75 MONTEVINA Zinfandel Amador County 1987 $7.50 (3/31/90)
72 ESTRELLA RIVER Zinfandel Paso Robles 1987 $8 (12/15/89)
71 GUNDLACH BUNDSCHU Zinfandel Sonoma Valley Rhinefarm Vineyards 1987 $8.50 (9/15/89)
69 CHATEAU MONTELENA Zinfandel Napa Valley 1987 Rel: $10 Cur: $10 (7/31/90)
65 J. PEDRONCELLI Zinfandel Dry Creek Valley 1987 $7 (7/31/90)

1986

92 RAVENSWOOD Zinfandel Sonoma Valley Old Hill Vineyard 1986 $13 (12/15/88)
91 A. RAFANELLI Zinfandel Dry Creek Valley 1986 $7 (9/15/88)
90 GUNDLACH BUNDSCHU Zinfandel Sonoma Valley Rhinefarm Vineyards 1986 $12 (9/15/88)
90 MAZZOCCO Zinfandel Sonoma County Traditional Style 1986 $10 (12/15/88)
90 NALLE Zinfandel Dry Creek Valley 1986 Rel: $9 Cur: $9 (6/30/88)
90 RAVENSWOOD Zinfandel Sonoma County 1986 $9 (12/15/88)
90 SAUSAL Zinfandel Alexander Valley 1986 $6.75 (3/31/89) SS
90 VILLA MT. EDEN Zinfandel Napa Valley 1986 $8.50 (12/15/88)
89 CAYMUS Zinfandel Napa Valley 1986 $9 (12/15/88)
89 HAYWOOD Zinfandel Sonoma Valley 1986 $11 (9/15/88)
89 LA JOTA Zinfandel Howell Mountain 1986 $10 (10/31/88)
89 QUIVIRA Zinfandel Dry Creek Valley 1986 $9.75 (12/31/87)
89 JOSEPH SWAN Zinfandel Sonoma Coast 1986 Rel: $12.50 Cur: $17 (3/15/90)
88 DE LOACH Zinfandel Russian River Valley 1986 $9 (10/15/88)
88 FETZER Zinfandel Mendocino County Reserve 1986 $14 (12/15/89)
88 QUIVIRA Zinfandel Dry Creek Valley 1986 $9.75 (12/15/88)
88 RAVENSWOOD Zinfandel Napa Valley Dickerson 1986 $12 (12/15/88)
88 RIDGE Zinfandel Sonoma County Lytton Springs 1986 Rel: $10 Cur: $14 (10/15/88)
88 STORYBOOK MOUNTAIN Zinfandel Napa Valley 1986 $10.50 (12/15/88)
87 CLOS DU VAL Zinfandel Napa Valley 1986 $12 (5/31/89)
87 LYTTON SPRINGS Zinfandel Sonoma County 1986 $10 (10/15/88)
87 SAUCELITO CANYON Zinfandel San Luis Obispo County 1986 $9.50 (12/15/89)
87 STORYBOOK MOUNTAIN Zinfandel Sonoma County 1986 $8.50 (10/15/88)
86 CONN CREEK Zinfandel Napa Valley Barrel Select 1986 $9 (10/15/90)
86 J FRITZ Zinfandel Dry Creek Valley 1986 $9 (3/15/89)
86 HIDDEN CELLARS Zinfandel Mendocino Pacini Vineyard 1986 $7.50 (10/31/88)
86 KENDALL-JACKSON Zinfandel Mendocino 1986 $9 (9/15/88)
86 J. PEDRONCELLI Zinfandel Dry Creek Valley 1986 $6 (3/31/89) BB
86 SHENANDOAH Zinfandel Amador County Special Reserve 1986 $7.50 (7/15/88)
85 CUVAISON Zinfandel Napa Valley 1986 $10 (3/15/89)
85 DRY CREEK Zinfandel Dry Creek Valley 1986 $9 (4/15/89)
85 FROG'S LEAP Zinfandel Napa Valley 1986 $10 (12/15/88)
85 GRGICH HILLS Zinfandel Alexander Valley 1986 Rel: $12 Cur: $15 (5/15/90)
85 HOP KILN Zinfandel Russian River Valley 1986 $10 (6/15/89)
85 KENDALL-JACKSON Zinfandel Anderson Valley DePatie-DuPratt Vineyard 1986 $16 (12/15/89)
85 RAVENSWOOD Zinfandel Sonoma-Napa Counties Vintners Blend 1986 $5.75 (6/30/88) BB
85 YORK MOUNTAIN Zinfandel San Luis Obispo County 1986 $8 (12/15/89)
84 DALLA VALLE Zinfandel Napa Valley 1986 $25 (2/15/91)
84 PRESTON Zinfandel Dry Creek Valley 1986 $11 (12/15/88)
84 SIERRA VISTA Zinfandel El Dorado Herbert Vineyards 1986 $8 (3/31/89)
84 STEVENOT Zinfandel Calaveras County 1986 $7.50 (7/31/89) BB
84 SUMMIT LAKE Zinfandel Howell Mountain 1986 $11 (3/15/90)
83 BALDINELLI Zinfandel Shenandoah Valley Reserve 1986 $6.75 (12/15/88) BB
83 BUEHLER Zinfandel Napa Valley 1986 $8.50 (12/15/88)
83 FETZER Zinfandel Lake County 1986 $6 (2/15/88) BB
83 FETZER Zinfandel Mendocino County Reserve 1986 $14 (7/31/90)
83 MARK WEST Zinfandel Sonoma County Robert Rue Vineyard 1986 $14 (3/15/90)
83 MEEKER Zinfandel Dry Creek Valley 1986 $9 (3/15/89)
82 AMADOR FOOTHILL Zinfandel Fiddletown Eschen Vineyard 1986 $9 (6/15/89)
82 BLACK MOUNTAIN Zinfandel Alexander Valley Cramer Ridge 1986 $9 (3/31/90)
82 BURGESS Zinfandel Napa Valley 1986 $9.50 (7/31/89)
82 STORYBOOK MOUNTAIN Zinfandel Napa Valley Reserve 1986 Rel: $17.50 Cur: $21 (5/15/90)
81 CHATEAU SOUVERAIN Zinfandel Dry Creek Valley 1986 $5 (3/31/89) BB
81 RAVENSWOOD Zinfandel Napa Valley Canard 1986 $11 (3/15/90)
81 RIDGE Zinfandel Paso Robles 1986 $7.25 (10/31/88)
80 BLACK MOUNTAIN Zinfandel Alexander Valley Cramer Ridge 1986 $9 (3/31/89)
80 CHATEAU MONTELENA Zinfandel Napa Valley 1986 Rel: $10 Cur: $12 (9/15/89)
80 PARDUCCI Zinfandel Mendocino County 1986 $5.75 (7/15/88)
80 SEGHESIO Zinfandel Alexander Valley Reserve 1986 $9 (10/31/89)
80 SEGHESIO Zinfandel Northern Sonoma 1986 $6.50 (5/15/90) BB
79 CHRISTIAN BROTHERS Zinfandel Napa Valley 1986 $5.50 (6/30/88)
79 KARLY Zinfandel Amador County 1986 $9 (3/31/89)
79 LOUIS M. MARTINI Zinfandel Sonoma County 1986 $7 (10/31/89)

Key to Symbols

The scores reported here are the results of blind tastings conducted by our panel of senior editors. Wines that carry the initials below are results of individual tastings.

THE WINE SPECTATOR 100-POINT SCALE ***95-100***—Classic, a great wine; ***90-94***—Outstanding, superior character and style; ***80-89***—Good to very good, a wine with special qualities; ***70-79***—Average, drinkable wine that may have minor flaws; ***60-69***—Below average, drinkable but not recommended; ***50-59***—Poor, undrinkable, not recommended. "+"—With a score indicates a range; used primarily with barrel tastings to indicate a preliminary score.

SPECIAL DESIGNATIONS SS—Spectator Selection, CS—Cellar Selection, BB—Best Buy.

TASTER'S INITIALS (JG)—Jim Gordon, (HS)—Harvey Steiman, (JL)—James Laube, (JS)—James Suckling, (TM)—Thomas Matthews, (TR)—Terry Robards, (BT)—Barrel Tasting (these wines were tasted blind from barrel samples), (CA-date)—*California's Great Cabernets* by James Laube, (CH-date)—*California's Great Chardonnays* by James Laube, (VP-date)—*Vintage Port* by James Suckling.

DATE TASTED Dates in parentheses represent the issue in which the rating was published.

79 RIDGE Zinfandel Sonoma County Geyserville 1986 Rel: $12 Cur: $18 (10/31/88)
79 RODNEY STRONG Zinfandel Sonoma County 1986 $5.50 (3/31/89)
78 FETZER Zinfandel California 1986 $6 (9/15/88)
78 MARTIN Zinfandel Paso Robles 1986 $8 (12/15/89)
76 GREEN & RED Zinfandel Napa Valley 1986 $9 (3/15/90)
76 SUTTER HOME Zinfandel California 1986 $7 (10/15/88)
74 FETZER Zinfandel Mendocino Ricetti Vineyard Reserve 1986 $14 (7/31/90)
73 BOEGER Zinfandel El Dorado Walker Vineyard 1986 $7 (7/31/88)
73 INGLENOOK Zinfandel Napa Valley 1986 $8 (4/30/91)
62 RUTHERFORD RANCH Zinfandel Napa Valley 1986 $7.75 (10/31/88)

1985

91 GARY FARRELL Zinfandel Sonoma County 1985 $10 (4/30/88)
91 NALLE Zinfandel Dry Creek Valley 1985 Rel: $8 Cur: $8 (9/15/87)
91 PRESTON Zinfandel Dry Creek Valley 1985 $8.50 (11/15/87)
90 CHATEAU MONTELENA Zinfandel Napa Valley 1985 Rel: $10 Cur: $10 (4/30/88)
90 CLOS DU VAL Zinfandel Napa Valley 1985 $12 (4/30/88)
90 HOP KILN Zinfandel Russian River Valley Primitivo Reserve 1985 $12 (6/15/89)
90 LYTTON SPRINGS Zinfandel Sonoma County 1985 $8 (8/31/87)
90 MEEKER Zinfandel Dry Creek Valley 1985 $8 (5/15/88)
90 STORYBOOK MOUNTAIN Zinfandel Napa Valley 1985 $10 (12/31/87)
89 BUEHLER Zinfandel Napa Valley 1985 $8 (12/31/87)
89 KENWOOD Zinfandel Sonoma Valley 1985 $9.50 (5/15/88)
89 RUTHERFORD RANCH Zinfandel Napa Valley 1985 $7.75 (3/15/88)
88 MARIETTA Zinfandel Sonoma County Reserve 1985 $10 (12/31/87)
88 SEBASTIANI Zinfandel Sonoma County Family Selection 1985 $5 (9/15/88) BB
88 SKY Zinfandel Napa Valley 1985 Rel: $9 Cur: $9 (10/31/88)
88 STORYBOOK MOUNTAIN Zinfandel Napa Valley Reserve 1985 Rel: $16.50 Cur: $22 (5/31/89)
88 SUMMIT LAKE Zinfandel Howell Mountain 1985 $9.50 (12/15/88)
87 BERINGER Zinfandel North Coast 1985 $6 (4/30/88) BB
87 BURGESS Zinfandel Napa Valley 1985 $9 (6/30/88)
87 MARIETTA Zinfandel Sonoma County 1985 $7.50 (12/31/87)
87 RAVENSWOOD Zinfandel Sonoma Valley Old Hill Vineyard 1985 $12 (12/31/87)
87 TERRACES Zinfandel Napa Valley Hogue Vineyard 1985 $12.50 (10/31/88)
85 CAYMUS Zinfandel Napa Valley 1985 $8 (12/31/87)
85 HAYWOOD Zinfandel Sonoma Valley 1985 $9.50 (11/15/87)
85 LA JOTA Zinfandel Howell Mountain 1985 $10 (4/30/88)
85 MARK WEST Zinfandel Sonoma County Robert Rue Vineyard 1985 $14 (7/31/88)
85 RAVENSWOOD Zinfandel Napa Valley Canard 1985 $10 (3/15/89)
85 SHENANDOAH Zinfandel Amador County Special Reserve 1985 $7.50 (2/15/88)
84 GRGICH HILLS Zinfandel Alexander Valley 1985 Rel: $12 Cur: $16 (7/31/89)
84 GUNDLACH BUNDSCHU Zinfandel Sonoma Valley Rhinefarm Vineyards 1985 $12 (2/29/88)
83 MARTIN Zinfandel Paso Robles 1985 $6.50 (2/15/88)
83 RIDGE Zinfandel Sonoma County Geyserville 1985 Rel: $10.50 Cur: $15 (9/15/87)
82 JOSEPH PHELPS Zinfandel Napa Valley 1985 $6 (12/31/86)
82 RIDGE Zinfandel Napa County York Creek 1985 $10.50 (12/31/87)
82 ROUND HILL Zinfandel Napa Valley 1985 $5.50 (5/15/88) BB
82 JOSEPH SWAN Zinfandel Sonoma Coast 1985 Rel: $12 Cur: $17 (3/15/89)
81 FETZER Zinfandel Mendocino Special Reserve 1985 $14 (12/15/88)
81 RIDGE Zinfandel Sonoma County Lytton Springs 1985 Rel: $9 Cur: $9 (9/15/87)
81 SUTTER HOME Zinfandel Amador County Reserve 1985 $8.75 (11/30/90)
80 HOP KILN Zinfandel Russian River Valley Primitivo 1985 $12 (3/15/88)
80 LOUIS M. MARTINI Zinfandel North Coast 1985 $6.25 (3/31/89)
80 RAVENSWOOD Zinfandel Napa Valley Dickerson 1985 $10.50 (12/31/87)
80 RAVENSWOOD Zinfandel Napa Valley Vintners Blend 1985 $6.25 (5/31/87)
80 RAVENSWOOD Zinfandel Sonoma County 1985 $8.25 (12/31/87)
80 ROUDON-SMITH Zinfandel Sonoma Valley Chauvet Vineyard 1985 $8.50 (3/31/89)
80 SEGHESIO Zinfandel Northern Sonoma 1985 $5.50 (3/15/89) BB
79 FETZER Zinfandel Mendocino Ricetti Vineyard 1985 $14 (10/15/88)
79 FROG'S LEAP Zinfandel Napa Valley 1985 $9 (11/15/87)
79 GUENOC Zinfandel Lake County 1985 $15 (3/31/89)
79 MENDOCINO ESTATE Zinfandel Mendocino 1985 $4.75 (2/15/88)
79 WILLIAMS SELYEM Zinfandel Russian River Valley Leno Martinelli Vineyard 1985 $10 (7/31/88)
78 ARCIERO Zinfandel Paso Robles 1985 $7.50 (12/15/89)
77 A. RAFANELLI Zinfandel Dry Creek Valley 1985 $6.25 (12/31/87)
77 WENTE BROS. Zinfandel Livermore Valley Special Selection Raboli Vineyards 1985 $10 (12/15/89)
75 MONTEVINA Zinfandel Shenandoah Valley Montino 1985 $5.50 (10/15/88)
74 JOSEPH PHELPS Zinfandel Alexander Valley 1985 $10 (7/31/87)
73 GREEN & RED Zinfandel Napa Valley 1985 $8.50 (6/15/89)
73 RIDGE Zinfandel Howell Mountain 1985 $9 (5/15/88)
73 SIERRA VISTA Zinfandel El Dorado Reeves Vineyard Special Reserve 1985 $12 (4/30/88)
72 KARLY Zinfandel Amador County 1985 $8.50 (12/31/87)
72 SAUSAL Zinfandel Alexander Valley 1985 $6.25 (10/15/88)
72 STEVENOT Zinfandel Amador County Grand Reserve 1985 $7.50 (12/31/87)

1984

92 HAYWOOD Zinfandel Sonoma Valley 1984 $9 (5/31/87)
92 STORYBOOK MOUNTAIN Zinfandel Napa Valley Reserve 1984 Rel: $14.50 Cur: $24 (4/30/88)
91 CHATEAU MONTELENA Zinfandel Napa Valley John Rolleri Vineyard 1984 Rel: $10 Cur: $15 (5/15/87)
91 NALLE Zinfandel Dry Creek Valley 1984 Rel: $7.50 Cur: $8 (10/15/86)
90 CAYMUS Zinfandel Napa Valley 1984 $8 (5/15/87)
90 GRGICH HILLS Zinfandel Alexander Valley 1984 Rel: $10 Cur: $16 (3/15/87)
90 KENWOOD Zinfandel Sonoma Valley 1984 $8.50 (9/15/87)
90 MARIETTA Zinfandel Sonoma County 1984 $7.50 (1/31/87)
90 SUMMIT LAKE Zinfandel Howell Mountain 1984 $8.50 (4/30/88)
89 BURGESS Zinfandel Napa Valley 1984 $8 (11/15/87)
88 HIDDEN CELLARS Zinfandel Mendocino County Pacini Vineyard 1984 $7.50 (4/15/87)
88 LA JOTA Zinfandel Howell Mountain 1984 $10 (11/15/87)
88 J. PEDRONCELLI Zinfandel Dry Creek Valley 1984 $5.50 (7/15/88) BB
88 QUIVIRA Zinfandel Dry Creek Valley 1984 $7 (4/15/87)
87 CORBETT CANYON Zinfandel San Luis Obispo County Select 1984 $7.50 (5/15/88)
87 GUNDLACH BUNDSCHU Zinfandel Sonoma Valley Rhinefarm Vineyards 1984 $12 (4/30/87) BB
86 AMADOR FOOTHILL Zinfandel Fiddletown Eschen Vineyard 1984 $9 (10/15/88)
86 GRGICH HILLS Zinfandel Sonoma County 1984 $11 (10/31/88)
86 KENDALL-JACKSON Zinfandel Mendocino Ciapusci Vineyard 1984 $16 (12/15/89)
86 RIDGE Zinfandel Napa County York Creek 1984 $10.50 (3/15/87)
86 SAUSAL Zinfandel Alexander Valley Private Reserve 1984 $10 (2/15/88)
84 DE LOACH Zinfandel Russian River Valley 1984 $8.50 (7/31/87)
84 J FRITZ Zinfandel Dry Creek Valley 1984 $7 (2/15/88)
84 LOUIS M. MARTINI Zinfandel North Coast 1984 $6 (2/15/88) BB
82 GREEN & RED Zinfandel Napa Valley 1984 $7.75 (11/15/87)
82 SUTTER HOME Zinfandel Amador County Reserve 1984 $9.50 (7/31/89)
81 CLOS DU VAL Zinfandel Napa Valley 1984 $12 (5/31/87)
81 FETZER Zinfandel Lake County 1984 $5 (4/15/87)
81 RIDGE Zinfandel Howell Mountain 1984 $9 (6/30/87)
80 PRESTON Zinfandel Dry Creek Valley 1984 $8 (12/31/86)
80 STORYBOOK MOUNTAIN Zinfandel Napa Valley 1984 $9.50 (3/15/87)
79 GEYSER PEAK Zinfandel Alexander Valley 1984 $7.75 (7/31/88)
79 PESENTI Zinfandel San Luis Obispo County Family Reserve 1984 $6 (12/15/89)
79 RIDGE Zinfandel Sonoma County Geyserville 1984 Rel: $10.50 Cur: $11 (12/31/86)
79 RIDGE Zinfandel Sonoma County Lytton Springs 1984 Rel: $9 Cur: $17 (11/15/86)
79 STORY Zinfandel Amador County Shenandoah Valley Private Reserve 1984 $14 (4/30/91)
79 SUTTER HOME Zinfandel Amador County Reserve 1984 $9.50 (7/31/88)
78 SAUSAL Zinfandel Alexander Valley 1984 $6.75 (5/31/88)
77 BUENA VISTA Zinfandel North Coast 1984 $7.25 (4/30/88)
77 SUTTER HOME Zinfandel California 1984 $6 (12/31/86)
76 SEGHESIO Zinfandel Northern Sonoma 1984 $5.50 (6/30/88)
76 VALLEY OF THE MOON Zinfandel Sonoma Valley 1984 $9 (3/15/90)
75 MONTEVINA Zinfandel Shenandoah Valley Winemaker's Choice 1984 $9 (8/31/87)
73 MASTANTUONO Zinfandel San Luis Obispo County Dante Dusi Vineyards Unfined & Unfiltered 1984 $18 (7/31/91)
73 STEVENOT Zinfandel Calaveras County 1984 $6 (6/30/87)
70 LYTTON SPRINGS Zinfandel Sonoma County 1984 $8 (10/31/86)
70 SANDERLING Zinfandel Amador County 1984 $6 (5/01/86)
68 MENDOCINO ESTATE Zinfandel Mendocino 1984 $4.25 (5/31/87)
67 GUENOC Zinfandel Guenoc Valley 1984 $5.50 (9/15/87)
67 SANTINO Zinfandel Amador County Aged Release 1984 $7 (3/31/89)

1983

91 A. RAFANELLI Zinfandel Dry Creek Valley 1983 $6.50 (3/01/86) BB
90 STORYBOOK MOUNTAIN Zinfandel Napa Valley 1983 $8.75 (4/16/86)
89 RIDGE Zinfandel Howell Mountain 1983 $9 (5/01/86)
88 KENWOOD Zinfandel Sonoma Valley 1983 $7.50 (11/15/86)
87 LOUIS M. MARTINI Zinfandel North Coast 1983 $7.75 (10/15/86)
85 GRGICH HILLS Zinfandel Alexander Valley 1983 Rel: $10 Cur: $15 (5/01/86)
85 HAYWOOD Zinfandel Sonoma Valley 1983 $8 (1/01/86)
84 AUDUBON Zinfandel San Luis Obispo County 1983 $7 (7/15/88)
84 CHATEAU MONTELENA Zinfandel Napa Valley 1983 Rel: $10 Cur: $11 (5/01/86)
84 CONN CREEK Zinfandel Napa Valley Collins Vineyard 1983 $10 (12/15/88)
84 SANTINO Zinfandel Fiddletown Eschen Vineyards 1983 $7.50 (4/15/87)
83 FETZER Zinfandel Lake County 1983 $4.50 (7/16/86) BB
82 FETZER Zinfandel Mendocino Ricetti Vineyard 1983 $8.50 (2/16/86)
82 SAUSAL Zinfandel Alexander Valley 1983 $5.75 (9/15/87) BB
81 BURGESS Zinfandel Napa Valley 1983 $7.50 (10/31/86)
81 INGLENOOK Zinfandel Napa Valley 1983 $7.50 (3/15/88)
81 STORYBOOK MOUNTAIN Zinfandel Napa Valley Reserve 1983 Rel: $12.50 Cur: $22 (7/31/87)
80 KENDALL-JACKSON Zinfandel Clear Lake Vina Las Lomas Vineyard 1983 $7 (6/01/85)
79 CAYMUS Zinfandel Napa Valley 1983 $7.50 (12/31/86)
77 J. PEDRONCELLI Zinfandel Sonoma County 1983 $4.50 (9/15/87)
76 KENDALL-JACKSON Zinfandel Anderson Valley DuPratt-DePatie Vineyard 1983 $10 (11/01/85)
75 CUVAISON Zinfandel Napa Valley 1983 $8.50 (9/15/87)
75 QUIVIRA Zinfandel Dry Creek Valley 1983 $7 (1/01/86)
74 SHENANDOAH Zinfandel Fiddletown Special Reserve 1983 $7 (10/15/86)
73 DEHLINGER Zinfandel Sonoma County 1983 $8 (7/31/87)
73 SHAFER Zinfandel Napa Valley Last Chance 1983 $7 (2/16/86)
71 BUEHLER Zinfandel Napa Valley 1983 $6.50 (3/15/87)
69 DE LOACH Zinfandel Russian River Valley 1983 $8 (10/15/86)
64 GREEN & RED Zinfandel Napa Valley 1983 $7.25 (7/31/87)
63 FETZER Zinfandel Mendocino Special Reserve 1983 $8.50 (5/01/86)
57 RAVENSWOOD Zinfandel Sonoma County 1983 $8 (5/01/86)

1982

92 CAYMUS Zinfandel Napa Valley 1982 $7.50 (5/16/86)
91 BUEHLER Zinfandel Napa Valley 1982 $6 (3/01/85)
91 CHATEAU MONTELENA Zinfandel Napa Valley 1982 Rel: $10 Cur: $18 (5/01/84)
91 GRGICH HILLS Zinfandel Alexander Valley 1982 Rel: $10 Cur: $17 (5/16/85) SS
91 RIDGE Zinfandel Napa County York Creek 1982 $10.50 (7/16/85) SS
90 KENWOOD Zinfandel Sonoma Valley 1982 $7.50 (7/16/86)
90 RIDGE Zinfandel Paso Robles 1982 $8.50 (1/01/85)
89 RIDGE Zinfandel Sonoma County Geyserville 1982 Rel: $9.50 Cur: $10 (9/16/84)
89 HAYWOOD Zinfandel Sonoma Valley 1982 $8 (11/01/84)
87 GUNDLACH BUNDSCHU Zinfandel Sonoma Valley Rhinefarm Vineyards 1982 $9.25 (2/16/86)
87 SYCAMORE CREEK Zinfandel California 1982 $9 (6/16/84)
86 MOUNT VEEDER Zinfandel Napa County 1982 $8.50 (3/16/85)
86 STORYBOOK MOUNTAIN Zinfandel Napa Valley 1982 $8.50 (12/01/84)
85 BURGESS Zinfandel Napa Valley 1982 $6.50 (7/16/85)
85 FETZER Zinfandel Mendocino Scharffenberger Vineyard 1982 $8 (10/16/84)
85 HOP KILN Zinfandel Russian River Valley 1982 $8.50 (11/01/85)
85 RIDGE Zinfandel Howell Mountain 1982 $9 (6/01/85)
83 MONTEREY PENINSULA Zinfandel Amador County Ferrero Ranch Doctors' Reserve 1982 $10 (2/29/88)
82 GREEN & RED Zinfandel Napa Valley 1982 $7.50 (12/16/85)
81 FETZER Zinfandel Mendocino 1982 $5.50 (4/01/85)
81 IRON HORSE Zinfandel Alexander Valley 1982 $7 (10/16/84)
81 STORYBOOK MOUNTAIN Zinfandel Sonoma County 1982 $7.50 (9/16/85)
80 BUENA VISTA Zinfandel Sonoma County 1982 $6 (4/01/85)
80 RUTHERFORD RANCH Zinfandel Napa Valley 1982 $6 (9/16/85)
79 FETZER Zinfandel Mendocino Lolonis Vineyards 1982 $8 (11/01/84)
79 FETZER Zinfandel Mendocino Ricetti Vineyard 1982 $8 (10/16/84)
79 J. PEDRONCELLI Zinfandel Sonoma County 1982 $4.50 (10/31/86) BB
77 DE LOACH Zinfandel Russian River Valley 1982 $8 (11/01/85)

UNITED STATES
CALIFORNIA/ZINFANDEL

77   FETZER Zinfandel Mendocino Home Vineyard 1982 $8 (11/01/84)
74   AMADOR FOOTHILL Zinfandel Fiddletown Eschen Vineyard Special Selection 1982 $9 (4/15/87)
73   MARIETTA Zinfandel Sonoma County 1982 $6.50 (6/16/84)
70   RODNEY STRONG Zinfandel Sonoma County 1982 $5.50 (12/31/87)
60   SIMI Zinfandel Sonoma County 1982 $6.25 (5/01/86)

1981
90   CLOS DU VAL Zinfandel Napa Valley 1981 Rel: $9 Cur: $18 (5/16/84) CS
89   DE LOACH Zinfandel Russian River Valley 1981 $7.50 (6/01/85)
89   RIDGE Zinfandel Napa County York Creek 1981 $9.50 (1/01/84)
87   EDMEADES Zinfandel Mendocino Ciapusci Vineyard 1981 $9 (3/01/85)
86   STORYBOOK MOUNTAIN Zinfandel Napa Valley Reserve 1981 Rel: $9.50 Cur: $10 (4/16/84)
85   LYTTON SPRINGS Zinfandel Sonoma County Valley Vista Vineyard Private Reserve 1981 $12 (1/01/85)
85   SHOWN AND SONS Zinfandel Napa Valley 1981 $7.50 (4/16/84)
84   CAYMUS Zinfandel Napa Valley 1981 $6.50 (12/01/84)
84   ROUND HILL Zinfandel Napa Valley 1981 $5 (4/16/84)
82   CALERA Zinfandel Cienega Valley Reserve 1981 $8.50 (1/01/85)
82   J. PEDRONCELLI Zinfandel Sonoma County Reserve 1981 $8 (11/15/87)
81   BURGESS Zinfandel Napa Valley 1981 $6 (4/16/84)
81   CALERA Zinfandel Cienega Valley 1981 $7 (4/16/84)
81   RAVENSWOOD Zinfandel Sonoma County Dry Creek Benchland 1981 $6.50 (4/01/84)
80   BUEHLER Zinfandel Napa Valley 1981 $8 (9/16/84)
80   CHATEAU MONTELENA Zinfandel Napa Valley 1981 Rel: $8 Cur: $20 (4/16/84)
80   GRGICH HILLS Zinfandel Sonoma County 1981 $10 (4/01/84)
80   MILANO Zinfandel Mendocino County 1981 $6 (10/01/84)
80   JOSEPH PHELPS Zinfandel Alexander Valley 1981 $6.75 (4/16/85)
80   SUTTER HOME Zinfandel Amador County 1981 $6.25 (5/16/84)
79   INGLENOOK Zinfandel Napa Valley 1981 $7 (2/01/85)
78   GUENOC Zinfandel Lake County 1981 $5 (5/16/84)
78   J. PEDRONCELLI Zinfandel Sonoma County 1981 $4.50 (1/01/85)
76   BOEGER Zinfandel El Dorado Walker Vineyard 1981 $6 (7/16/85)
68   RAVENSWOOD Zinfandel Sonoma County Vogensen Vineyard 1981 $8 (4/16/84)

1980
85   JOSEPH PHELPS Zinfandel Alexander Valley 1980 $6.75 (7/16/84)
78   AHERN Zinfandel Amador County 1980 $6.50 (2/15/84)
78   FETZER Zinfandel Mendocino 1980 $5.50 (4/01/84)
78   MONTEVINA Zinfandel Shenandoah Valley Winemaker's Choice 1980 $9 (4/16/84)
77   ESTRELLA RIVER Zinfandel San Luis Obispo County 1980 $6 (12/01/84)
76   SEBASTIANI Zinfandel Sonoma Valley Proprietor's Reserve Black Beauty 1980 $9 (12/16/85)
75   STONY RIDGE Zinfandel Livermore Valley 1980 $7 (6/16/84)
73   STORY Zinfandel Amador County 1980 $6 (4/01/84)
68   RODNEY STRONG Zinfandel Russian River Valley Old Vines River West Vineyard 1980 $12 (11/15/87)
62   FARVIEW FARM Zinfandel San Luis Obispo Reserve 1980 $7 (3/16/84)
60   JOSEPH PHELPS Zinfandel Napa Valley 1980 $6.75 (1/01/86)
55   FRANCISCAN Zinfandel Napa Valley 1980 $6.50 (3/16/85)

1979
71   RODNEY STRONG Zinfandel Russian River Valley Old Vines River West Vineyard 1979 $10 (3/15/87)
60   CONN CREEK Zinfandel Napa Valley 1979 $7.50 (3/16/84)
60   JOSEPH PHELPS Zinfandel Napa Valley 1979 $6.75 (4/16/84)

1976
79   CAYMUS Zinfandel California 1976 (NA) (6/16/85)
78   CHATEAU MONTELENA Zinfandel North Coast 1976 Cur: $25 (6/16/85)

1975
77   CAYMUS Zinfandel California Lot 31-J 1975 (NA) (6/16/85)
67   RIDGE Zinfandel Sonoma County Geyserville 1975 Cur: $33 (6/16/85)

1974
92   CHATEAU MONTELENA Zinfandel Napa-Alexander Valleys 1974 Cur: $40 (6/16/85)
83   CAYMUS Zinfandel California 1974 (NA) (6/16/85)
79   RIDGE Zinfandel Sonoma County Geyserville 1974 Cur: $45 (6/16/85)
78   LOUIS M. MARTINI Zinfandel California 1974 Cur: $22 (6/16/85)
77   CLOS DU VAL Zinfandel Napa Valley 1974 Cur: $45 (6/16/85)

1973
90   CHATEAU MONTELENA Zinfandel Napa Valley 1973 Cur: $50 (6/16/85)
87   LOUIS M. MARTINI Zinfandel California 1973 Cur: $25 (6/16/85)
86   CLOS DU VAL Zinfandel Napa Valley 1973 Cur: $50 (6/16/85)
86   SUTTER HOME Zinfandel Amador County 1973 Cur: $30 (6/16/85)
84   JOSEPH SWAN Zinfandel California 1973 Cur: $55 (6/16/85)
80   RIDGE Zinfandel Sonoma County Geyserville 1973 Cur: $55 (6/16/85)

1972
90   CLOS DU VAL Zinfandel Napa Valley 1972 (NA) (6/16/85)
85   SUTTER HOME Zinfandel Amador County 1972 Cur: $25 (6/16/85)

1970
80   SUTTER HOME Zinfandel Amador County 1970 Cur: $25 (6/16/85)

1969
83   JOSEPH SWAN Zinfandel California 1969 Cur: $80 (6/16/85)

NV
81   MIRASSOU Zinfandel California Lot No. 4 NV $5.50 (7/31/91) BB
76   RICHARDSON Zinfandel Sonoma Valley NV $9 (7/31/89)
73   MIRASSOU Zinfandel California Dry Red Lot No. 3 NV $5 (7/31/91)
71   CALERA Zinfandel California NV $5 (7/31/88)

OTHER CALIFORNIA RED

1989
77   PRESTON Estate Red Dry Creek Valley 1989 $5.50 (6/30/90)

1988
87   GLEN ELLEN Petite Verdot Alexander Valley Imagery Series 1988 $14.50 (7/15/91)
85   HOP KILN Marty Griffin's Big Red Russian River Valley 1988 $7.50 (11/30/90) BB
82   PRESTON Estate Red Dry Creek Valley 1988 $5 (8/31/89) BB
79   DICKERSON Ruby Cabernet Napa Valley 1988 $9 (2/28/91)
79   MASTANTUONO Carminello California 1988 $7 (7/15/91)
78   BOEGER Hangtown Red California 1988 $5.25 (8/31/90)
77   KENWOOD Vintage Red California 1988 $5 (12/31/90)

1987
89   HOP KILN Marty Griffin's Big Red Russian River Valley 1987 $7.50 (12/15/89) BB
89   MONTEVINA Barbera Amador County Reserve Selection 1987 $14 (5/31/91)
88   DUXOUP Charbono Napa Valley 1987 $9.50 (6/15/89)
87   CLOS DU BOIS Malbec Alexander Valley L'Etranger Winemaker's Reserve 1987 $20 (1/31/91)
86   SEBASTIANI Barbera Sonoma Valley 1987 $11 (4/30/91)
85   MARTIN Nebbiolo Paso Robles 1987 $12 (12/15/89)
83   LOUIS M. MARTINI Barbera California 1987 $6 (12/31/90) BB
82   BOEGER Hangtown Red California 1987 $5.25 (2/28/90) BB
80   BEAULIEU Burgundy Napa Valley 1987 $5 (1/31/91) BB
79   CHRISTOPHE Joliesse California 1987 $5 (2/28/90)
77   GEYSER PEAK Trione Vineyards California 1987 $3.25 (2/28/90)
75   MARTIN Nebbiolo California 1987 $12 (12/15/89)
70   J.W. MORRIS Private Reserve California 1987 $3.50 (6/30/90)

1986
85   HOP KILN Marty Griffin's Big Red Russian River Valley 1986 $6.50 (6/15/89) BB
83   HIDDEN CELLARS Pinot Noir Petite Syrah California Côte du Nord 1986 $7.50 (11/15/88)
78   J.W. MORRIS Private Reserve California 1986 $3.50 (12/31/88)
75   MARTIN Nebbiolo California 1986 $12 (12/15/89)
74   KENWOOD Vintage Red California 1986 $5 (11/30/88)

1985
85   PRESTON Barbera Dry Creek Valley 1985 $8 (1/31/88)
78   FETZER Premium Red California 1985 $4.25 (3/15/88)
73   BOEGER Hangtown Red California 1985 $5 (12/31/88)
68   DEHLINGER Young Vines Russian River Valley 1985 $9 (4/15/89)

1984
82   INGLENOOK Charbono Napa Valley 1984 $8 (4/15/88)
80   LOUIS M. MARTINI Barbera California 1984 $7 (11/15/89)
80   PAT PAULSEN American Gothic California 1984 $8.50 (12/31/86) BB
79   J.W. MORRIS Private Reserve California 1984 $3 (11/15/87) BB
78   BEAULIEU Burgundy Napa Valley 1984 $5 (8/31/89)
78   MONTEVINA Barbera Shenandoah Valley 1984 $6 (10/15/88)
77   BOEGER Hangtown Red California 1984 $4.75 (1/31/88)
75   ROBERT MONDAVI Red California 1984 $5 (1/31/87)
75   RAYMOND Vintage Select Red California 1984 $4.25 (2/15/88)
74   MONTEREY VINEYARD Classic Red Monterey 1984 $4.25 (11/15/87)
68   HOP KILN Marty Griffin's Big Red Russian River Valley 1984 $5.75 (12/31/87)

1983
78   BELVEDERE Discovery Series Red Table Wine Sonoma County 1983 $3 (7/31/88)
77   KENWOOD Vintage Red Sonoma County 1983 $4 (5/31/88)
71   BOEGER Hangtown Red California 1983 $4.50 (6/30/87)
71   STAGS' LEAP WINERY Burgundy Napa Valley 1983 $5 (9/15/87)
69   RAYMOND Vintage Select Red California 1983 $4.25 (8/31/87)

1982
82   RAYMOND Vintage Select Red North Coast 1982 $4.25 (4/01/86) BB
79   ALMADEN Premium California 1982 $7 (12/31/86)
79   BEAULIEU Burgundy Napa Valley 1982 $5 (10/15/88)
78   MARTIN Nebbiolo California 1982 $7 (4/01/84)
74   MONTEREY VINEYARD Classic Red California 1982 $4.25 (6/16/86)

1981
80   LOUIS M. MARTINI Barbera Napa Valley 1981 $6 (12/31/87) BB

1980
84   VERITE Bourguignon Noir Cuvée Ancienne Alexander Valley 1980 $6 (1/01/85)
79   INGLENOOK Charbono Napa Valley 1980 $8.50 (3/01/85)

NV
86   R.H. PHILLIPS Night Harvest Cuvée California NV $5 (5/15/89) BB
86   TREFETHEN Eshcol Red Blend 184 Napa Valley NV $4.25 (2/01/86) BB
85   CLOS DU VAL Le Clos Napa Valley NV $5.50 (8/31/90) BB
85   MARIETTA Old Vine Red Lot III Sonoma County NV $4.50 (4/16/86) BB
84   R.H. PHILLIPS Cuvée Rouge Night Harvest California NV $6 (5/31/91) BB
84   M.G. VALLEJO Red M.G.V. California NV $3 (3/31/88) BB
83   TREFETHEN Eshcol Red Napa Valley NV $5.25 (2/29/88) BB
82   HEITZ Ryan's Red Napa Valley NV $6 (6/16/86) BB
82   MARIETTA Old Vine Red Lot 7 Sonoma County NV $6 (11/15/89) BB
82   MONTEREY PENINSULA California NV $6.50 (7/15/91) BB
81   MARIETTA Old Vine Red Lot Number Eight Sonoma County NV $5.50 (5/31/90) BB
80   CALERA Rouge de Rouge California NV $4 (1/31/87) BB

80   E.&J. GALLO Hearty Burgundy Limited Release California NV $2.75 (3/15/88) BB
80   TREFETHEN #3 Eshcol Red Napa Valley NV $6.25 (11/15/89) BB
79   AUDUBON Audubon Rouge California NV $4.50 (10/15/88)
79   TREFETHEN Eschol Red Napa Valley NV $6 (2/15/91)
78   ROUDON-SMITH Claret Cuvée Five California NV $4.50 (3/31/89)
78   SEGHESIO Sonoma Red Lot 3 Sonoma County NV $4 (5/31/88)
77   GUNDLACH BUNDSCHU #2 Sonoma Red Sonoma Valley NV $5 (11/15/89)
77   MARIETTA Old Vine Red Lot Number Five Sonoma County NV $5 (12/31/87)
76   DUNNEWOOD Reserve Red California NV $3.75 (2/28/89)
75   R. & J. COOK Delta Red Table Wine Clarksburg NV $3.50 (11/15/87)
75   SEGHESIO Sonoma Red Lot 4 Sonoma County NV $5 (6/30/90)
74   HAYWOOD Spaghetti Red California NV $6 (2/15/90)
74   HAYWOOD Spaghetti Red Sonoma County NV $4.50 (4/30/87)
74   HEITZ Ryan's Red Napa Valley NV $6 (2/28/89)
74   M.G. VALLEJO M.G.V. Red California NV $3 (5/31/90)

OTHER CALIFORNIA WHITE

1990

84   BONNY DOON Malvasia Bianca Ca' del Solo Monterey 1990 $8 (6/15/91) BB
83   BUENA VISTA Bistro Style Napa Valley 1990 $11 (7/15/91)

1989

87   GEYSER PEAK Semchard California 1989 $8 (2/15/91) BB
83   LIBERTY SCHOOL Three Valley Select Series One California 1989 $4.50 (6/15/91) BB
82   CHATEAU DE BAUN Château Blanc Reserve Sonoma County 1989 $5 (6/15/91) BB
82   RABBIT RIDGE Mystique Sonoma County 1989 $7 (6/30/91) BB
80   CHATEAU ST. JEAN Vin Blanc Sonoma County 1989 $5 (2/15/91) BB

1988

83   LA CREMA Crème de Tête Select White California 1988 $5.50 (12/15/89) BB
83   PRESTON Estate White Dry Creek Valley 1988 $5 (9/15/89) BB
79   SEBASTIANI La Sorella California 1988 $4 (3/31/90)
73   CLOS DU VAL Le Clos Napa Valley 1988 $5.50 (12/31/90)
72   BEAULIEU Chablis Napa Valley 1988 $5 (12/31/90)

1987

82   GUNDLACH BUNDSCHU Sonoma White Wine (Chardonnay) Sonoma Valley 1987 $5 (10/31/88) BB
81   CHATEAU ST. JEAN Vin Blanc Sonoma County 1987 $4 (6/15/88) BB
80   CHATEAU DE BAUN Symphony Sonoma Valley Prelude Off-Dry 1987 $8.50 (3/31/90)
80   CHATEAU DE BAUN Symphony Sonoma Romance Brut 1987 $12 (4/30/90)
80   KENWOOD Vintage White California 1987 $5 (6/15/88)
79   PAT PAULSEN Refrigerator White Sonoma County 1987 $6 (10/31/88)
78   CHATEAU DE BAUN Symphony Sonoma County Rhapsody Sec Rosé 1987 $12 (5/31/90)
76   RAYMOND Vintage Select White California 1987 $4.25 (2/28/89)
75   CHATEAU DE BAUN Symphony Sonoma County Dry Overture 1987 $8.50 (4/30/90)
74   BELVEDERE Discovery Series White Table Wine Sonoma County 1987 $3 (7/31/88)
71   GLEN ELLEN Proprietor's Reserve White California 1987 $3.50 (7/31/88)

1986

88   CHATEAU DE BAUN Symphony Sonoma County Theme Semi Sweet 1986 $10.50 (9/15/87)
86   PAT PAULSEN Refrigerator White Sonoma County 1986 $6 (4/30/87) BB
83   CHATEAU ST. JEAN Vin Blanc Sonoma County 1986 $4 (7/15/87) BB
78   M.G. VALLEJO M.G.V. White California 1986 $3 (4/15/88) BB
77   CHATEAU DE BAUN Symphony Sonoma County Overture Dry 1986 $8.50 (9/15/87)
77   CHRISTOPHE Joliesse California 1986 $4.75 (12/31/87)
77   RAYMOND Vintage Select White California 1986 $4.25 (6/30/87)
76   BEAULIEU Chablis Napa Valley 1986 $5 (10/31/88)
76   CALLAWAZY Spring Wine Vin Blanc California 1986 $4.75 (6/15/87)
75   CHATEAU DE BAUN Symphony Sonoma County Prelude Off-Dry 1986 $8.50 (9/15/87)
75   FETZER Premium White California 1986 $4.25 (3/15/88)
75   GUENOC Lillie's White Wine North Coast 1986 $5.50 (3/15/88)
74   HUSCH La Ribera Blanc Mendocino 1986 $5 (1/31/88)
73   CARMENET Columbard Cyril Saviez Vineyard Old Vines BF Napa Valley 1986 $5 (1/31/88)
71   WENTE BROS. Le Blanc de Blanc California 1986 $5 (11/15/87)
70   CHATEAU DE BAUN Symphony Sonoma County Classical Jazz 1986 $6.50 (9/15/87)
70   SAUSAL Blanc Alexander Valley 1986 $4.75 (3/15/88)
64   J.W. MORRIS Private Reserve California 1986 $3 (1/31/88)

1985

88   HAYWOOD White Wine Sonoma Valley 1985 $5 (4/15/87) BB
82   BUENA VISTA Chaarblanc Carneros 1985 $6 (5/31/88)
82   PAT PAULSEN Refrigerator White Sonoma County 1985 $6 (5/16/86) BB
81   BUENA VISTA Spiceling Carneros 1985 $5 (5/31/88) BB

1984

79   BUENA VISTA Spiceling Sonoma County 1984 $5.50 (4/16/86)
74   INGLENOOK Napa Valley 1984 $5 (7/01/86)
72   WENTE BROS. Chablis California 1984 $3.25 (6/01/86) BB
54   HOP KILN A Thousand Flowers Sonoma County 1984 $5 (12/01/85)

NV

84   TREFETHEN Eshcol White Napa Valley NV $6.25 (2/29/88) BB
84   TREFETHEN Eshcol White Napa Valley NV $6.25 (6/01/86) BB
83   HEITZ Joe's White Napa Valley NV $5 (4/30/89) BB
81   TREFETHEN Eschol White Napa Valley NV $6.50 (1/31/91) BB
80   HAYWOOD Linguini White Sonoma County NV $4.50 (9/30/87) BB
78   CHRISTOPHE Joliesse California NV $4 (6/15/89)
78   TREFETHEN Eschol White Napa Valley NV $6.25 (9/15/89)
78   TREFETHEN Eschol White Napa Valley NV $6.25 (7/31/88)
69   PESENTI Grey Riesling San Luis Obispo County French Camp Vineyards NV $6 (12/15/89)

NEW YORK/BLUSH

1987

83   HAMPTON Sunset Blush North Fork of Long Island 1987 $6 (12/15/88) (JL)

NV

75   PALMER Pinot Noir Blanc North Fork of Long Island NV $6 (12/15/88) (JL)

CABERNET FRANC

1988

81   HARGRAVE Cabernet Franc North Fork of Long Island 1988 $14 (6/30/91) (TM)

CABERNET SAUVIGNON

1988

90   GRISTINA Cabernet Sauvignon North Fork of Long Island 1988 $14 (6/30/91) (TM)
86   BEDELL Cabernet Sauvignon North Fork of Long Island 1988 $15 (6/30/91) (TM)
85   PINDAR Cabernet Sauvignon North Fork of Long Island Reserve 1988 $14 (6/30/91) (TM)
84   BRIDGEHAMPTON Cabernet Sauvignon Long Island 1988 $14 (6/30/91) (TM)
83   PALMER Cabernet Sauvignon North Fork of Long Island 1988 $13.50 (6/30/91) (TM)
82   BIDWELL Cabernet Sauvignon North Fork of Long Island 1988 $12 (6/30/91) (TM)
81   PECONIC BAY Cabernet Sauvignon North Fork of Long Island 1988 $13 (6/30/91) (TM)

1987

87   BRIDGEHAMPTON Cabernet Sauvignon Long Island 1987 $14 (6/30/91) (TM)
82   MATTITUCK HILLS Cabernet Sauvignon North Fork of Long Island 1987 $9 (6/30/91) (TM)
81   BIDWELL Cabernet Sauvignon North Fork of Long Island 1987 $12 (6/30/91) (TM)
78   JAMESPORT Cabernet Sauvignon North Fork of Long Island North House 1987 $10 (6/30/91) (TM)
78   PECONIC BAY Cabernet Sauvignon North Fork of Long Island 1987 $13 (6/30/91) (TM)
76   BIDWELL Cabernet Sauvignon North Fork of Long Island 1987 $12 (6/15/90)

1986

87   HARGRAVE Cabernet Sauvignon North Fork of Long Island 1986 $22 (12/15/88) (JL)
86   PINDAR Cabernet Sauvignon North Fork of Long Island 1986 $13 (12/15/88) (JL)
84   PECONIC BAY Cabernet Sauvignon North Fork of Long Island 1986 $11 (12/15/88) (JL)
82   PALMER Cabernet Sauvignon North Fork of Long Island 1986 $10 (12/15/88) (JL)
79   BRIDGEHAMPTON Cabernet Sauvignon Long Island 1986 $12 (12/15/88) (JL)
78   LA REVE Cabernet Sauvignon North Fork of Long Island American Series 1986 $12 (12/15/88) (JL)

1985

82   HARGRAVE Cabernet Sauvignon North Fork of Long Island 1985 $22 (12/15/88) (JL)
78   PECONIC BAY Cabernet Sauvignon North Fork of Long Island 1985 $11 (12/15/88) (JL)

1984

71   PINDAR Cabernet Sauvignon North Fork of Long Island 1984 $9 (3/16/86)
51   FOUR CHIMNEYS Cabernet Sauvignon New York 1984 $17 (3/16/86)

1983

86   HARGRAVE Cabernet Sauvignon North Fork of Long Island 1983 $22 (12/15/88) (JL)

1982

70   HARGRAVE Cabernet Sauvignon North Fork of Long Island Reserve 1982 $22 (12/15/88) (JL)
52   KNAPP Cabernet Sauvignon New York 1982 $16 (3/16/86)

1981

78   HARGRAVE Cabernet Sauvignon North Fork of Long Island Vintner's Signature 1981 $29 (12/15/88) (JL)

1980

79   HARGRAVE Cabernet Sauvignon North Fork of Long Island Vintner's Signature 1980 (NA) (12/15/88) (JL)

NV

79   PETITE CHATEAU Cabernet Sauvignon North Fork of Long Island NV $10 (6/30/91) (TM)

CABERNET BLENDS

1988

83   PINDAR Mythology North Fork of Long Island 1988 $20 (6/30/91) (TM)

1987

86   PINDAR Mythology North Fork of Long Island 1987 $20 (3/31/90)
81   PINDAR Mythology North Fork of Long Island 1987 $20 (6/30/91) (TM)
80   BRIDGEHAMPTON Reserve Red Grand Vineyard North Fork of Long Island 1987 $17 (6/30/91) (TM)

CHARDONNAY

1989

90   GRISTINA Chardonnay North Fork of Long Island 1989 $13 (6/30/91) (TM)
86   RIVENDELL Chardonnay New York Reserve 1989 $17 (6/30/91)
85   RIVENDELL Chardonnay New York Barrel Selection 1989 $14 (6/30/91) (TM)
84   LENZ Chardonnay North Fork of Long Island Barrel Fermented 1989 $15 (6/30/91) (TM)
84   PALMER Chardonnay North Fork of Long Island 1989 $11.50 (6/30/91) (TM)
83   BEDELL Chardonnay North Fork of Long Island 1989 $12 (6/30/91) (TM)
82   PALMER Chardonnay North Fork of Long Island Barrel Fermented 1989 $15 (6/30/91) (TM)
81   BRIDGEHAMPTON Chardonnay Long Island Grand Vineyard Selection 1989 $17 (6/30/91) (TM)
81   LENZ Chardonnay North Fork of Long Island 1989 $10 (6/30/91) (TM)
80   PAUMANOK Chardonnay North Fork of Long Island 1989 $10 (6/30/91) (TM)
80   PECONIC BAY Chardonnay North Fork of Long Island 1989 $11 (6/30/91) (TM)
80   RIVENDELL Chardonnay New York 1989 $12 (6/30/91)
79   PECONIC BAY Chardonnay North Fork of Long Island Reserve 1989 $15 (6/30/91) (TM)
78   BRIDGEHAMPTON Chardonnay Long Island The Hamptons Estate Reserve 1989 $14.50 (6/30/91) (TM)

1988

91   BRIDGEHAMPTON Chardonnay Long Island Grand Vineyard Selection 1988 $18 (3/31/90)
87   PINDAR Chardonnay North Fork of Long Island 1988 $9 (12/15/90)
87   RIVENDELL Chardonnay North Fork of Long Island Cuvée 1988 $12 (6/30/91) (TM)
86   PINDAR Chardonnay North Fork of Long Island 1988 $9 (6/30/91) (TM)
82   HARGRAVE Chardonnay North Fork of Long Island 1988 $15 (6/30/91) (TM)
82   PINDAR Chardonnay North Fork of Long Island Reserve 1988 $12 (6/30/91) (TM)
81   BEDELL Chardonnay North Fork of Long Island Reserve 1988 $14 (12/15/90)
81   BIDWELL Chardonnay North Fork of Long Island 1988 $9 (6/30/91) (TM)

UNITED STATES
NEW YORK/CHARDONNAY

78   PUGLIESE Chardonnay North Fork of Long Island 1988 $10 (6/30/91) (TM)
77   MATTITUCK HILLS Chardonnay North Fork of Long Island 1988 $11 (6/30/91) (TM)
70   BANFI Chardonnay Nassau County Old Brookville 1988 $11 (6/30/91) (TM)

1987
90   BRIDGEHAMPTON Chardonnay Long Island Grand Vineyard Selection 1987 $15 (12/15/88) (JL)
88   BEDELL Chardonnay North Fork of Long Island 1987 $11 (12/15/88) (JL)
86   LENZ Chardonnay North Fork of Long Island Gold Label 1987 $13 (12/15/88) (JL)
85   BANFI Chardonnay Nassau County Old Brookville 1987 $11.50 (12/15/90)
85   PECONIC BAY Chardonnay North Fork of Long Island 1987 $11 (12/15/88) (JL)
84   BRIDGEHAMPTON Chardonnay Long Island 1987 $10 (12/15/88) (JL)
80   LENZ Chardonnay North Fork of Long Island White Label 1987 $10 (12/15/88) (JL)

1986
89   BEDELL Chardonnay North Fork of Long Island Reserve 1986 $13 (12/15/88) (JL)
89   LA REVE Chardonnay North Fork of Long Island 1986 $11 (12/15/88) (JL)
89   LA REVE Chardonnay North Fork of Long Island American Series 1986 $12 (12/15/88) (JL)
88   PINDAR Chardonnay North Fork of Long Island 1986 $8 (12/15/88) (JL)
87   BIDWELL Chardonnay North Fork of Long Island 1986 $9 (3/31/90)
87   HARGRAVE Chardonnay North Fork of Long Island 1986 $11 (12/15/88) (JL)
86   BEDELL Chardonnay North Fork of Long Island 1986 $9 (12/15/88) (JL)
86   BEDELL Chardonnay North Fork of Long Island 1986 $9 (12/15/88) (JL)
84   PALMER Chardonnay North Fork of Long Island Barrel Fermented 1986 $11 (12/15/88) (JL)
84   PINDAR Chardonnay North Fork of Long Island Poetry Barrel Fermented 1986 $11 (12/15/88) (JL)
80   BRIDGEHAMPTON Chardonnay Long Island Reserve 1986 $11 (12/15/88) (JL)
80   PALMER Chardonnay North Fork of Long Island 1986 $11 (12/15/88) (JL)

1985
87   BRIDGEHAMPTON Chardonnay Long Island 1985 $15 (12/15/88) (JL)
87   HARGRAVE Chardonnay North Fork of Long Island Collector's Series 1985 $15 (12/15/88) (JL)
83   BRIDGEHAMPTON Chardonnay Long Island Reserve 1985 $15 (12/15/88) (JL)

1984
86   HERMANN J. WIEMER Chardonnay Finger Lakes 1984 $10 (3/16/86)
83   GLENORA Chardonnay Finger Lakes 1984 $9 (3/16/86)
79   WAGNER Chardonnay Finger Lakes 1984 $11 (3/16/86)
76   FINGER LAKES Chardonnay Finger Lakes 1984 $9 (3/16/86)
72   HERON HILL Chardonnay Finger Lakes 1984 $8 (3/16/86)
69   BRIDGEHAMPTON Chardonnay Long Island 1984 $9 (3/16/86)
66   PLANE'S CAYUGA Chardonnay Finger Lakes 1984 $10 (3/16/86)
61   POPLAR RIDGE Chardonnay Finger Lakes 1984 $9.50 (3/16/86)
61   WICKHAM Chardonnay Finger Lakes 1984 $7 (3/16/86)
59   FOUR CHIMNEYS Chardonnay Finger Lakes 1984 $15 (3/16/86)
54   PINDAR Chardonnay North Fork of Long Island First Release Poetry Edition 1984 $11 (3/16/86)
48   MCGREGOR Chardonnay Finger Lakes 1984 $8 (3/16/86)

1983
63   KNAPP Chardonnay Finger Lakes 1983 $8 (3/16/86)

1981
92   HARGRAVE Chardonnay North Fork of Long Island 1981 $22 (12/15/88) (JL)
80   HARGRAVE Chardonnay North Fork of Long Island Collector's Series 1981 $22 (12/15/88) (JL)

1980
73   DR. KONSTANTIN FRANK Chardonnay Finger Lakes 1980 $8 (3/16/86)

DESSERT
1984
82   HERMANN J. WIEMER Finger Lakes 1984 $9 (3/16/86)

1983
64   HERON HILL Ingles Vineyard Finger Lakes 1983 $6 (3/16/86)

GEWÜZTRAMINER
1987
79   PALMER Gewürztraminer North Fork of Long Island 1987 $8 (12/15/88) (JL)
78   LENZ Gewürztraminer North Fork of Long Island 1987 $7 (12/15/88) (JL)

1986
82   BEDELL Gewürztraminer North Fork of Long Island 1986 $6.50 (12/15/88) (JL)
80   PINDAR Gewürztraminer North Fork of Long Island 1986 $7 (12/15/88) (JL)

LATE HARVEST
1984
57   BALDWIN Late Harvest New York Vignoles Select 1984 $6/375ml (3/16/86)
68   GREAT WESTERN Late Harvest Finger Lakes Vidal Blanc Laursen Farm Vineyard Special Select 1984 $5 (3/16/86)

63   WICKHAM Late Harvest Finger Lakes Ravat Vignoles Select 1984 $6.50/375ml (3/16/86)
62   GLENORA Late Harvest Finger Lakes Ravat Blanc Select 1984 $7/375ml (3/16/86)
61   FINGER LAKES Late Harvest Finger Lakes Ravat 1984 $8/375ml (3/16/86)

1987
85   BEDELL Late Harvest North Fork of Long Island 1987 $15/375ml (12/15/88) (JL)

1986
90   PINDAR Late Harvest Gewürztraminer North Fork of Long Island 1986 $20 (12/15/88) (JL)

MERLOT
1989
78   PECONIC BAY Merlot North Fork of Long Island 1989 $13 (6/30/91) (TM)

1988
90   BEDELL Merlot North Fork of Long Island Reserve 1988 $14 (6/30/91) (TM)
89   BRIDGEHAMPTON Merlot Long Island 1988 $16 (6/30/91) (TM)
86   PALMER Merlot North Fork of Long Island 1988 $13 (6/30/91) (TM)
85   BIDWELL Merlot North Fork of Long Island 1988 $11 (6/30/91) (TM)
83   PINDAR Merlot North Fork of Long Island Reserve 1988 $14 (6/30/91) (TM)
81   GRISTINA Merlot North Fork of Long Island 1988 $13 (6/30/91) (TM)
81   HARGRAVE Merlot North Fork of Long Island 1988 $17.50 (6/30/91) (TM)

1987
90   BEDELL Merlot North Fork of Long Island 1987 $18 (3/31/90)
83   BIDWELL Merlot North Fork of Long Island Reserve 1987 $16 (3/31/90)
80   LENZ Merlot North Fork of Long Island 1987 $12 (6/30/91) (TM)
80   PINDAR Merlot North Fork of Long Island 1987 $13 (12/15/90)

1986
88   BEDELL Merlot North Fork of Long Island 1986 $11 (12/15/88) (JL)
86   LA REVE Merlot North Fork of Long Island American 1986 $13 (12/15/88) (JL)
84   PINDAR Merlot North Fork of Long Island 1986 $13 (12/15/88) (JL)
83   LENZ Merlot North Fork of Long Island 1986 $12 (12/15/88) (JL)
80   PALMER Merlot North Fork of Long Island 1986 $10 (12/15/88) (JL)
78   BRIDGEHAMPTON Merlot Long Island 1986 $11 (12/15/88) (JL)
72   JAMESPORT Merlot North Fork of Long Island 1986 $9 (6/30/91) (TM)

1985
85   HARGRAVE Merlot North Fork of Long Island 1985 $19 (12/15/88) (JL)
84   LENZ Merlot North Fork of Long Island 1985 $11 (12/15/88) (JL)
79   BRIDGEHAMPTON Merlot Long Island 1985 $11 (12/15/88) (JL)

1984
74   LENZ Merlot North Fork of Long Island 1984 $12 (12/15/88) (JL)

1980
78   HARGRAVE Merlot North Fork of Long Island 1980 (NA) (12/15/88) (JL)

PINOT NOIR
1986
70   MCGREGOR Pinot Noir Finger Lakes 1986 $13 (6/15/88)

1985
75   DR. KONSTANTIN FRANK Pinot Noir Finger Lakes 1985 $15 (6/15/88)
56   PINDAR Pinot Noir North Fork of Long Island 1985 $15 (6/15/88)

1984
75   BRIDGEHAMPTON Pinot Noir Long Island 1984 $8 (3/16/86)

1983
67   MCGREGOR Pinot Noir Finger Lakes Reserve 1983 $14 (3/16/86)

RIESLING
1987
84   LA REVE White Riesling North Fork of Long Island 1987 $8 (12/15/88) (JL)
81   PECONIC BAY Riesling North Fork of Long Island White 1987 $8 (12/15/88) (JL)
80   BEDELL Riesling North Fork of Long Island 1987 $7.50 (12/15/88) (JL)
78   BRIDGEHAMPTON Riesling Long Island 1987 $8 (12/15/88) (JL)
76   PALMER Riesling North Fork of Long Island 1987 $7 (12/15/88) (JL)

1985
76   WIDMER Johannisberg Riesling Finger Lakes Private Reserve 1985 $7 (3/16/86)
59   BARON HERZOG Johannisberg Riesling New York Selection 1985 $7 (3/16/86)

1984
91   HAZLITT 1852 Johannisberg Riesling Finger Lakes 1984 $6 (3/16/86)
91   HERMANN J. WIEMER Johannisberg Riesling Finger Lakes 1984 $7.50 (3/16/86)
88   FINGER LAKES Johannisberg Riesling Finger Lakes 1984 $7 (3/16/86)
85   PINDAR Riesling North Fork of Long Island Select Berry Late Harvest 1984 $30/375ml (3/16/86)
84   WOODBURY Johannisberg Riesling New York 1984 $8 (3/16/86)
74   WICKHAM Johannisberg Riesling Finger Lakes 1984 $6 (3/16/86)
73   MCGREGOR Riesling Finger Lakes 1984 $7.50 (3/16/86)
69   BRIDGEHAMPTON Riesling Long Island 1984 $7.50 (3/16/86)
69   PLANE'S CAYUGA Johannisberg Riesling Finger Lakes 1984 $7 (3/16/86)
68   KNAPP Johannisberg Riesling Finger Lakes 1984 $7 (3/16/86)
68   WAGNER Johannisberg Riesling Finger Lakes 1984 $6.75 (3/16/86)
65   BALDWIN Riesling New York Reserve 1984 $7 (3/16/86)
63   GLENORA Johannisberg Riesling Finger Lakes 1984 $6 (3/16/86)
55   GREAT WESTERN Johannisberg Riesling Finger Lakes Special Selection 1984 $6 (3/16/86)

1982
56   DR. KONSTANTIN FRANK Johannisberg Riesling Finger Lakes 1982 $6 (3/16/86)

NV
57   CASCADE MOUNTAIN Riesling New York NV $7 (3/16/86)

Key to Symbols
The scores reported here are the results of blind tastings conducted by our panel of senior editors. Wines that carry the initials below are results of individual tastings.

THE WINE SPECTATOR 100-POINT SCALE **95-100**—Classic, a great wine; **90-94**—Outstanding, superior character and style; **80-89**—Good to very good, a wine with special qualities; **70-79**—Average, drinkable wine that may have minor flaws; **60-69**—Below average, drinkable but not recommended; **50-59**—Poor, undrinkable, not recommended. "**+**"—With a score indicates a range; used primarily with barrel tastings to indicate a preliminary score.

SPECIAL DESIGNATIONS SS—Spectator Selection, CS—Cellar Selection, BB—Best Buy.

TASTER'S INITIALS (JG)—Jim Gordon, (HS)—Harvey Steiman, (JL)—James Laube, (JS)—James Suckling, (TM)—Thomas Matthews, (TR)—Terry Robards, (BT)—Barrel Tasting (these wines were tasted blind from barrel samples), (CA-date)—*California's Great Cabernets* by James Laube, (CH-date)—*California's Great Chardonnays* by James Laube, (VP-date)—*Vintage Port* by James Suckling.

DATE TASTED Dates in parentheses represent the issue in which the rating was published.

SAUVIGNON BLANC

1987

77   HARGRAVE Sauvignon Blanc North Fork of Long Island 1987 $9 (12/15/88) (JL)

1986

87   LA REVE Sauvignon Blanc North Fork of Long Island American Series 1986 $10 (12/15/88) (JL)

77   BRIDGEHAMPTON Sauvignon Blanc Long Island 1986 $10 (12/15/88) (JL)

1981

83   HARGRAVE Sauvignon Blanc North Fork of Long Island 1981 $19 (12/15/88) (JL)

SEYVAL BLANC

1985

80   HERON HILL Seyval Blanc Finger Lakes Ingle Vineyard 1985 $5 (3/16/86)
72   WIDMER Seyval Blanc Finger Lakes Private Reserve 1985 $6.25 (3/16/86)

1984

89   GLENORA Seyval Blanc Finger Lakes 1984 $5 (3/16/86)
87   WOODBURY Seyval Blanc New York Proprietor's 1984 $5 (3/16/86)
77   WALKER VALLEY Seyval Blanc Hudson River Region 1984 $5 (3/16/86)
70   WAGNER Seyval Blanc Finger Lakes Barrel Fermented 1984 $5 (3/16/86)
58   FINGER LAKES Seyval Blanc Finger Lakes 1984 $5 (3/16/86)
54   BENMARL Seyval Blanc Hudson River Region Estate Reserve 1984 $8 (3/16/86)
51   FOUR CHIMNEYS Seyval Blanc Finger Lakes 1984 $6 (3/16/86)

1983

55   KEDEM Seyval Blanc New York Estate Brand 1983 $5 (3/16/86)
51   CLINTON Seyval Blanc Hudson River Region 1983 $8.50 (3/16/86)
47   BALDWIN Seyval Blanc New York Proprietor's Reserve 1983 $6 (3/16/86)

SPARKLING

1988

74   BULLY HILL Brut Seyval Blanc Finger Lakes 1988 $15 (12/31/90)

1987

85   GLENORA Blanc de Blancs Finger Lakes 1987 $12 (12/31/90)
82   WOODBURY Brut Blanc de Blancs New York 1987 $12 (12/31/90)
81   GLENORA Brut New York 1987 $12 (12/31/90)
70   WOODBURY Blanc de Noirs New York 1987 $12 (12/31/90)

1986

80   PINDAR Brut North Fork Premier Cuvée North Fork of Long Island 1986 $13 (12/31/90)
68   LENZ North Fork North Fork of Long Island 1986 $17.50 (12/31/90)

1985

80   CHATEAU FRANK Brut Finger Lakes 1985 $18 (12/31/90)
64   MCGREGOR Blanc de Blancs Finger Lakes 1985 $15 (12/31/90)

NV

86   PINDAR Champagne North Fork of Long Island NV $13 (12/15/88) (JL)
78   CASA LARGA Blanc de Blancs Finger Lakes NV $13 (12/31/90)
77   CASA LARGA Brut Blanc de Blancs Finger Lakes NV $11 (12/31/90)
76   GREAT WESTERN Blanc de Blancs New York NV $14 (6/30/90)
74   GREAT WESTERN Natural New York NV $14 (6/30/90)
72   KEDEM Charmat Kosher New York NV $6 (12/31/90)
71   GREAT WESTERN Rosé New York NV $9.75 (12/31/90)
69   GOLD SEAL Brut Bottle Fermented New York NV $7 (12/31/90)
69   GREAT WESTERN Brut Very Dry New York NV $9.75 (12/31/90)
68   GREAT WESTERN Extra Dry New York NV $9.75 (12/31/90)
61   TAYLOR Brut Bottle Fermented New York NV $6.50 (12/31/90)

OTHER NEW YORK RED

1983

76   PLANE'S CAYUGA Chancellor Finger Lakes 1983 $5 (3/16/86)

1982

95   BALDWIN Landot Noir New York 1982 $6 (3/16/86)
68   BENMARL Marlboro Village Red Reserve New York 1982 $10 (3/16/86)

1981

54   POPLAR RIDGE Foch New York 1981 $7.50 (3/16/86)

OTHER NEW YORK WHITE

1989

84   RIVENDELL Sarabande Sur Lie New York 1989 $7.50 (6/30/91)
83   HARGRAVE Pinot En Blanc North Fork of Long Island 1989 $10 (6/30/91) (TM)

1987

85   PECONIC BAY Vin di L'Ile North Fork of Long Island 1987 $8 (12/15/88) (JL)
83   HAMPTON Blanc de Mers North Fork of Long Island 1987 $5 (12/15/88) (JL)
80   PINDAR Pinot Meunier New York 1987 $25 (12/31/90)

NV

83   BEDELL Cygnet North Fork of Long Island NV $6 (12/15/88) (JL)

OREGON/CHARDONNAY

1989

84   BRIDGEVIEW Chardonnay Oregon Barrel Select 1989 $12 (3/31/91)

1988

91   TUALATIN Chardonnay Willamette Valley Barrel Fermented Private Reserve 1988 $20 (3/31/91)
90   ARTERBERRY Chardonnay Willamette Valley 1988 $10 (1/31/91)
87   SOKOL BLOSSER Chardonnay Yamhill County Redland 1988 $12 (3/31/91)

86   TUALATIN Chardonnay Willamette Valley Barrel Fermented 1988 $14 (3/31/91)
84   YAMHILL VALLEY Chardonnay Willamette Valley 1988 $12 (3/31/91)
83   OAK KNOLL Chardonnay Willamette Valley 1988 $11 (3/31/91)
83   VERITAS Chardonnay Willamette Valley 1988 $12 (3/31/91)
83   YAMHILL VALLEY Chardonnay Willamette Valley 1988 $12 (12/15/90)
81   BRIDGEVIEW Chardonnay Oregon Barrel Select 1988 $12 (3/31/91)
81   VALLEY VIEW Chardonnay Oregon Barrel Select 1988 $12 (3/31/91)
77   MONTINORE Chardonnay Washington County 1988 $11 (3/31/91)
75   ELK COVE Chardonnay Willamette Valley 1988 $12 (3/31/91)

1987

93   ARGYLE Chardonnay Oregon Barrel Fermented 1987 $18.50 (12/15/90)

1986

86   GIRARDET Chardonnay Oregon 1986 (NA) (9/30/87)
70   ELK COVE Chardonnay Willamette Valley 1986 $12 (5/31/88)
64   VALLEY VIEW Chardonnay Oregon 1986 $6 (5/31/88)

1985

92   TUALATIN Chardonnay Willamette Valley Private Reserve 1985 (NA) (9/30/87)
91   VERITAS Chardonnay Oregon 1985 (NA) (9/30/87)
90   EYRIE Chardonnay Willamette Valley Yamhill County 1985 $12.50 (7/31/87)
89   ADAMS Chardonnay Willamette Valley Reserve 1985 (NA) (9/30/87)
87   ARTERBERRY Chardonnay Willamette Valley Red Hills Vineyard 1985 (NA) (9/30/87)
85   PONZI Chardonnay Willamette Valley 1985 $10.50 (7/31/87)
84   HENRY Chardonnay Umpqua Valley 1985 (NA) (9/30/87)
84   VALLEY VIEW Chardonnay Oregon 1985 $15 (2/15/87)
79   YAMHILL VALLEY Chardonnay Oregon 1985 $12.50 (7/31/87)
78   ELK COVE Chardonnay Willamette Valley 1985 $9.75 (7/31/87)
76   ADELSHEIM Chardonnay Oregon 1985 $12 (7/31/87)
71   CAMERON Chardonnay Willamette Valley Reserve 1985 $16.50 (7/31/87)
71   SOKOL BLOSSER Chardonnay Yamhill County Reserve 1985 $15 (7/31/87)
69   BETHEL HEIGHTS Chardonnay Willamette Valley 1985 $12 (7/31/87)
69   OAK KNOLL Chardonnay Oregon 1985 $12 (7/31/87)
69   REX HILL Chardonnay Willamette Valley 1985 $15 (5/31/88)

PINOT NOIR

1988

90   MCKINLAY Pinot Noir Willamette Valley 1988 $13 (4/15/91)
89   ADELSHEIM Pinot Noir Willamette Valley 1988 $13 (4/15/91)
89   DOMAINE DROUHIN Pinot Noir Oregon 1988 $32 (5/31/91)
88   BRIDGEVIEW Pinot Noir Oregon Estate Bottled 1988 $8 (2/15/90)
88   MONTINORE Pinot Noir Washington County 1988 $13.50 (4/15/91)
88   REX HILL Pinot Noir Willamette Valley 1988 $18 (4/15/91)
87   BETHEL HEIGHTS Pinot Noir Willamette Valley Estate Grown 1988 $15 (4/15/91)
87   VERITAS Pinot Noir Willamette Valley 1988 $15 (5/31/91)
86   BETHEL HEIGHTS Pinot Noir Willamette Valley Estate Grown Reserve 1988 $18 (4/15/91)
86   PONZI Pinot Noir Willamette Valley Reserve 1988 $25 (4/15/91)
84   AMITY Pinot Noir Oregon Gamay Noir 1988 $9 (2/15/90)
83   COOPER MOUNTAIN Pinot Noir Willamette Valley 1988 $13 (4/15/91) (JL)
83   COOPER MOUNTAIN Pinot Noir Willamette Valley Reserve 1988 $20 (4/15/91)
82   AMITY Pinot Noir Oregon 1988 $10 (5/31/91)
82   KNUDSEN ERATH Pinot Noir Willamette Valley 1988 $11 (5/31/91)
82   SOKOL BLOSSER Pinot Noir Yamhill County Redland 1988 $13 (4/15/91)
81   OAK KNOLL Pinot Noir Willamette Valley 1988 $11 (4/15/91)
81   OAK KNOLL Pinot Noir Willamette Valley Vintage Select 1988 $18 (5/31/91)
80   AUTUMN WIND Pinot Noir Willamette Valley 1988 $12 (4/15/91)
80   ELK COVE Pinot Noir Willamette Valley Wind Hills Vineyard 1988 $18 (1/31/91)
79   ARTERBERRY Pinot Noir Willamette Valley Winemaker's Reserve 1988 $14 (1/31/91)
78   ELK COVE Pinot Noir Willamette Valley 1988 $15 (1/31/91)
76   PONZI Pinot Noir Willamette Valley 1988 $16 (5/31/91)
76   YAMHILL VALLEY Pinot Noir Willamette Valley 1988 $12 (1/31/91)
75   PANTHER CREEK Pinot Noir Willamette Valley 1988 $15 (4/15/91)

1987

91   PONZI Pinot Noir Willamette Valley Reserve 1987 $20 (2/15/90)
90   ARTERBERRY Pinot Noir Yamhill County Weber Vineyards Winemaker's Reserve 1987 $14 (2/15/90)
89   BRIDGEVIEW Pinot Noir Oregon Winemaker's Reserve 1987 $15 (2/15/90)
89   KNUDSEN ERATH Pinot Noir Willamette Valley Leland Vineyards Reserve 1987 $24 (2/15/90)
88   BROADLEY Pinot Noir Oregon Reserve 1987 $12 (2/15/90)
88   CALLAHAN RIDGE Pinot Noir Oregon Elkton Vineyards 1987 $8 (2/15/90)
88   PONZI Pinot Noir Willamette Valley 1987 $15 (2/15/90)
87   COOPER MOUNTAIN Pinot Noir Willamette Valley 1987 $13 (2/15/90)
86   BETHEL HEIGHTS Pinot Noir Willamette Valley 1987 $12 (2/15/90)
86   CAMERON Pinot Noir Willamette Valley Vintage Reserve 1987 $18 (2/15/90)
86   EYRIE Pinot Noir Willamette Valley Reserve 1987 $25 (2/15/90)
85   ELK COVE Pinot Noir Willamette Valley Reserve 1987 $15 (12/15/90)
84   STATON HILLS Pinot Noir Oregon 1987 $13 (4/15/91)
83   AMITY Pinot Noir Willamette Valley Winemaker's Reserve 1987 $30 (2/15/90)
83   AUTUMN WIND Pinot Noir Willamette Valley 1987 $15 (2/15/90)
81   AMITY Pinot Noir Willamette Valley 1987 $15 (2/15/90)
81   CAMERON Pinot Noir Willamette Valley 1987 $14 (2/15/90)
81   ELK COVE Pinot Noir Willamette Valley Dundee Hills Vineyard 1987 $15 (2/15/90)
81   MONTINORE Pinot Noir Washington County 1987 $12.50 (2/15/90)
80   BRIDGEVIEW Pinot Noir Oregon Special Reserve 1987 $12 (2/15/90)
80   EYRIE Pinot Noir Willamette Valley 1987 $20 (2/15/90)
80   SISKIYOU Pinot Noir Oregon Estate 1987 $13 (2/15/90)
79   AMITY Pinot Noir Willamette Valley Estate 1987 $25 (2/15/90)
79   TUALATIN Pinot Noir Willamette Valley Estate Bottled 1987 $14 (2/15/90)
78   ELK COVE Pinot Noir Willamette Valley Estate Bottled 1987 $15 (2/15/90)
77   OAK KNOLL Pinot Noir Willamette Valley Vintage Select 1987 $17.50 (2/15/90)
77   VERITAS Pinot Noir Willamette Valley 1987 $15 (2/15/90)
76   BROADLEY Pinot Noir Oregon 1987 $8 (2/15/90)
76   EOLA HILLS Pinot Noir Oregon 1987 $12 (2/15/90)
76   FORGERON Pinot Noir Oregon Vinters Reserve 1987 $12 (2/15/90)
76   ST. JOSEF'S WEINKELLER Pinot Noir Oregon 1987 $8 (4/15/91)
75   AIRLIE Pinot Noir Willamette Valley 1987 $9 (2/15/90)

UNITED STATES
OREGON/*PINOT NOIR*

75	ELK COVE Pinot Noir Willamette Valley Wind Hills Vineyard 1987 $15 (2/15/90)
75	GIRARDET Pinot Noir Umpqua Valley 1987 $12 (2/15/90)
75	SILVER FALLS Pinot Noir Willamette Valley 1987 $10 (2/15/90)
75	STATON HILLS Pinot Noir Oregon 1987 $13 (2/15/90)
74	PANTHER CREEK Pinot Noir Willamette Valley 1987 $17 (4/15/90)
73	ADELSHEIM Pinot Noir Yamhill County Elizabeth's Reserve 1987 $19 (2/15/90)
72	ADELSHEIM Pinot Noir Oregon 1987 $13 (2/15/90)
70	ADELSHEIM Pinot Noir Polk County The Eola Hills 1987 $16 (2/15/90)
70	SCHWARZENBERG Pinot Noir Oregon 1987 $13.50 (2/15/90)
67	GIRARD Pinot Noir Oregon 1987 $12 (2/15/90)
66	SOKOL BLOSSER Pinot Noir Yamhill County Redland 1987 $13 (2/15/90)
65	KNUDSEN ERATH Pinot Noir Willamette Valley 1987 $11 (2/15/90)
58	PANTHER CREEK Pinot Noir Willamette Valley Oak Knoll and Freedom Hill Vyds 1987 $17 (2/15/90)

1986

87	ADELSHEIM Pinot Noir Polk County 1986 $15 (6/15/88)
87	BRIDGEVIEW Pinot Noir Oregon Estate Bottled 1986 $8 (6/15/88)
87	ELK COVE Pinot Noir Willamette Valley Estate Bottled 1986 $15 (6/15/88)
87	KNUDSEN ERATH Pinot Noir Willamette Valley Vintage Select 1986 $15 (6/15/88)
86	BETHEL HEIGHTS Pinot Noir Willamette Valley 1986 $15 (6/15/88)
86	CAMERON Pinot Noir Willamette Valley 1986 $15 (6/15/88)
86	HONEYWOOD Pinot Noir Willamette Valley 1986 $9 (6/15/88)
85	ELK COVE Pinot Noir Willamette Valley Wind Hills Vineyard 1986 $15 (6/15/88)
85	TUALATIN Pinot Noir Willamette Valley Estate Bottled 1986 $13.50 (6/15/88)
84	EVESHAM WOOD Pinot Noir Willamette Valley 1986 $12 (6/15/88)
83	EYRIE Pinot Noir Willamette Valley 1986 $19.50 (6/15/88)
81	EOLA HILLS Pinot Noir Oregon 1986 $15 (6/15/88)
81	HENRY Pinot Noir Umpqua Valley 1986 $10 (4/15/91)
81	PONZI Pinot Noir Willamette Valley Reserve 1986 $15 (6/15/88)
80	CAMERON Pinot Noir Willamette Valley Reserve 1986 $18 (2/15/90)
79	BRIDGEVIEW Pinot Noir Oregon 1986 $8 (2/15/90)
79	SOKOL BLOSSER Pinot Noir Yamhill County Hyland Vineyards 1986 $15 (6/15/88)
78	ELK COVE Pinot Noir Willamette Valley Dundee Hills Vineyard 1986 $15 (6/15/88)
77	EOLA HILLS Pinot Noir Oregon 1986 $15 (2/15/90)
77	SOKOL BLOSSER Pinot Noir Yamhill County Red Hills 1986 $15 (6/15/88)
74	AMITY Pinot Noir Willamette Valley 1986 $12.50 (2/15/90)
73	BROADLEY Pinot Noir Oregon Reserve 1986 $11.50 (6/15/88)
71	ELLENDALE Pinot Noir Willamette Valley Estate Bottled 1986 $12 (6/15/88)
71	KNUDSEN ERATH Pinot Noir Willamette Valley 1986 $10 (6/15/88)
70	ARTERBERRY Pinot Noir Yamhill County Red Hills Vineyard Winemaker's Reserve 1986 $14.75 (6/15/88)
69	PANTHER CREEK Pinot Noir Willamette Valley Oak Grove Vineyard Abbey Ridge Vineyard 1986 $15 (6/15/88)
68	ANKENY Pinot Noir Willamette Valley Estate Bottled 1986 $9 (6/15/88)
68	EVESHAM WOOD Pinot Noir Willamette Valley 1986 $12 (2/15/90)
65	ELK COVE Pinot Noir Willamette Valley Estate Bottled 1986 $15 (2/15/90)
64	KNUDSEN ERATH Pinot Noir Willamette Valley 1986 $10 (2/15/90)
64	STATON HILLS Pinot Noir Oregon 1986 $13 (2/15/90)
59	SOKOL BLOSSER Pinot Noir Yamhill County 1986 $10 (6/15/88)
55	CHATEAU BENOIT Pinot Noir Oregon 1986 $15 (6/15/88)

1985

95	ARTERBERRY Pinot Noir Yamhill County Red Hills Vineyard Winemaker's Reserve 1985 $16 (6/15/87)
93	KNUDSEN ERATH Pinot Noir Yamhill County Vintage Select 1985 $20 (6/15/87)
93	WASSON BROS Pinot Noir Oregon 1985 (NA) (9/30/87)
92	SOKOL BLOSSER Pinot Noir Willamette Valley Red Hills Vineyard 1985 (NA) (9/30/87)
91	CAMERON Pinot Noir Willamette Valley 1985 $14 (6/15/87)
91	ELK COVE Pinot Noir Willamette Valley Wind Hills Vineyard 1985 $15 (6/15/87)
91	EYRIE Pinot Noir Willamette Valley 1985 $25 (2/15/90)
90	BONNY DOON Pinot Noir Oregon Bethel Heights Vineyard 1985 $18 (6/15/88)
90	KNUDSEN ERATH Pinot Noir Willamette Valley Vintage Select 1985 (NA) (9/30/87)
90	PONZI Pinot Noir Willamette Valley 1985 $20 (6/15/87)
89	ADAMS Pinot Noir Yamhill County 1985 $25 (2/15/90)
89	ADAMS Pinot Noir Yamhill County 1985 $25 (6/15/87)
89	FORGERON Pinot Noir Oregon 1985 $19 (2/15/90)
89	ST. JOSEF'S WEINKELLER Pinot Noir Oregon 1985 $16 (2/15/90)
89	TUALATIN Pinot Noir Willamette Valley Private Reserve 1985 $14 (6/15/87)
88	ADELSHEIM Pinot Noir Yamhill County 1985 $16 (6/15/87)
88	BONNY DOON Pinot Noir Oregon Temperance Hill Vineyard 1985 $18 (6/15/88)
88	VERITAS Pinot Noir Oregon 1985 $15 (6/15/87)
87	AMITY Pinot Noir Willamette Valley 1985 $25 (6/15/88)
87	EYRIE Pinot Noir Willamette Valley 1985 $25 (6/15/88)
86	BETHEL HEIGHTS Pinot Noir Willamette Valley Unfiltered 1985 $12 (2/15/90)
86	SOKOL BLOSSER Pinot Noir Yamhill County Hyland Vineyards 1985 $15 (6/15/87)
86	SOKOL BLOSSER Pinot Noir Yamhill County Hyland Vineyards Reserve 1985 $18 (6/15/88)
86	YAMHILL VALLEY Pinot Noir Oregon 1985 $16 (6/15/87)
85	AMITY Pinot Noir Willamette Valley 1985 $25 (2/15/90)
85	BAY CELLARS Pinot Noir Willamette Valley 1985 $18 (6/15/88)
85	ELK COVE Pinot Noir Willamette Valley Dundee Hills Vineyard 1985 $15 (6/15/87)
85	HENRY Pinot Noir Umpqua Valley 1985 $15 (2/15/90)
84	PONZI Pinot Noir Willamette Valley 1985 $20 (2/15/90)
84	REX HILL Pinot Noir Oregon Archibald Vineyards 1985 $30 (2/15/90)

84	TUALATIN Pinot Noir Willamette Valley Private Reserve 1985 $14 (2/15/90)
82	CAMERON Pinot Noir Willamette Valley 1985 $14 (2/15/90)
82	SOKOL BLOSSER Pinot Noir Yamhill County Red Hills Reserve 1985 $30 (6/15/88)
81	REX HILL Pinot Noir Oregon 1985 $15 (2/15/90)
80	ALPINE Pinot Noir Willamette Valley Vintage Select 1985 $17 (6/15/87)
80	AMITY Pinot Noir Oregon Winemaker's Reserve 1985 (NA) (2/15/90)
80	HENRY Pinot Noir Umpqua Valley 1985 $15 (6/15/88)
80	SOKOL BLOSSER Pinot Noir Yamhill County Red Hills 1985 $15 (6/15/87)
79	AMITY Pinot Noir Willamette Valley Estate 1985 $25 (2/15/90)
79	BETHEL HEIGHTS Pinot Noir Willamette Valley 1985 $15 (2/15/90)
79	ELK COVE Pinot Noir Willamette Valley Reserve 1985 $15 (2/15/90)
79	REX HILL Pinot Noir Oregon Maresh Vineyards 1985 $40 (6/15/88)
79	REX HILL Pinot Noir Oregon Wirtz Vineyards 1985 $18 (6/15/88)
79	REX HILL Pinot Noir Willamette Valley 1985 $15 (6/15/88)
79	ST. JOSEF'S WEINKELLER Pinot Noir Oregon 1985 $16 (6/15/88)
78	BETHEL HEIGHTS Pinot Noir Willamette Valley 1985 $15 (6/15/87)
78	ELLENDALE Pinot Noir Willamette Valley Estate Bottled 1985 $15 (6/15/88)
78	HIDDEN SPRINGS Pinot Noir Oregon 1985 $12 (6/15/88)
78	REX HILL Pinot Noir Oregon Archibald Vineyards 1985 $30 (6/15/88)
77	REX HILL Pinot Noir Oregon 1985 $15 (6/15/88)
77	REX HILL Pinot Noir Oregon Medici Vineyard 1985 $28 (2/15/90)
76	REX HILL Pinot Noir Oregon Medici Vineyard 1985 $28 (6/15/88)
75	ADELSHEIM Pinot Noir Oregon 1985 $25 (2/15/90)
75	KNUDSEN ERATH Pinot Noir Yamhill County Vintage Select 1985 $20 (2/15/90)
74	REX HILL Pinot Noir Oregon Dundee Hills Vineyards 1985 $25 (2/15/90)
74	SOKOL BLOSSER Pinot Noir Yamhill County Red Hills Reserve 1985 $30 (2/15/90)
73	PELLIER Pinot Noir Willamette Valley 1985 $8 (6/15/88)
72	REX HILL Pinot Noir Oregon Dundee Hills Vineyards 1985 $25 (6/15/88)
70	OAK KNOLL Pinot Noir Willamette Valley Vintage Select 1985 $17.50 (6/15/87)
66	REX HILL Pinot Noir Oregon Maresh Vineyards 1985 $40 (2/15/90)
65	OAK KNOLL Pinot Noir Willamette Valley 1985 $10 (6/15/87)
63	CAMERON Pinot Noir Willamette Valley Reserve 1985 $25 (2/15/90)
59	OAK KNOLL Pinot Noir Willamette Valley Vintage Select 1985 $17.50 (2/15/90)
55	CHATEAU BENOIT Pinot Noir Oregon 1985 $14 (6/15/88)

1984

84	EYRIE Pinot Noir Willamette Valley 1984 $15 (8/31/86)

1983

94	EYRIE Pinot Noir Willamette Valley 1983 $20 (8/31/86)
94	KNUDSEN ERATH Pinot Noir Yamhill County Vintage Select 1983 $35 (8/31/86)
94	KNUDSEN ERATH Pinot Noir Yamhill County Vintage Select 1983 $35 (7/01/86) SS
92	YAMHILL VALLEY Pinot Noir Oregon 1983 $17 (8/31/86)
91	PETER F. ADAMS Pinot Noir Oregon 1983 (NA) (2/15/90)
87	EYRIE Pinot Noir Willamette Valley 1983 $30 (2/15/90)
87	YAMHILL VALLEY Pinot Noir Willamette Valley 1983 $35 (2/15/90)
86	ARTERBERRY Pinot Noir Yamhill County Red Hills Vineyard Winemaker's Reserve 1983 $16 (2/15/90)
86	REX HILL Pinot Noir Oregon Dundee Hills Vineyards 1983 $35 (8/31/86)
85	AMITY Pinot Noir Oregon 1983 $30 (8/31/86)
82	SOKOL BLOSSER Pinot Noir Yamhill County Hyland Vineyards 1983 $14 (8/31/86)
81	ELK COVE Pinot Noir Willamette Valley Reserve 1983 $20 (8/31/86)
81	KNUDSEN ERATH Pinot Noir Yamhill County Vintage Select 1983 $35 (2/15/90)
79	ELK COVE Pinot Noir Willamette Valley Reserve 1983 $20 (2/15/90)
78	OAK KNOLL Pinot Noir Oregon Vintage Select 1983 $20 (2/15/90)
77	REX HILL Pinot Noir Oregon Dundee Hills Vineyards 1983 $35 (2/15/90)
76	AMITY Pinot Noir Willamette Valley Estate Bottled 1983 $30 (2/15/90)
75	AMITY Pinot Noir Oregon Winemaker's Reserve 1983 $30 (2/15/90)
73	AMITY Pinot Noir Oregon 1983 $30 (2/15/90)
70	ADELSHEIM Pinot Noir Yamhill County 1983 $40 (2/15/90)
67	SOKOL BLOSSER Pinot Noir Yamhill County Hyland Vineyards Reserve 1983 $30 (2/15/90)
64	REX HILL Pinot Noir Oregon Maresh Vineyards 1983 $40 (2/15/90)
64	TUALATIN Pinot Noir Willamette Valley 1983 $10 (8/31/86)

1982

77	AMITY Pinot Noir Willamette Valley 1982 $9.50 (3/01/86)
77	OAK KNOLL Pinot Noir Oregon Vintage Select 1982 $25 (2/15/90)
73	VALLEY VIEW Pinot Noir Oregon 1982 $8.50 (3/01/86)
63	SOKOL BLOSSER Pinot Noir Yamhill County 1982 $8.95 (2/16/85)

1980

76	VALLEY VIEW Pinot Noir Oregon 1980 $7.50 (9/16/84)

NV

81	KNUDSEN ERATH Pinot Noir Willamette Valley NV $6 (6/16/86) BB

OTHER OREGON

1990

85	YAMHILL VALLEY Pinot Gris Willamette Valley 1990 $10 (6/30/91)

1989

84	MONTINORE White Riesling Late Harvest Yamhill County 1989 $7 (3/31/91)
81	KNUDSEN ERATH Gewürztraminer Willamette Valley Dry 1989 $7 (6/30/91)
80	TUALATIN White Riesling Willamette Valley 1989 $6.50 (6/30/91)

1988

89	TUALATIN White Riesling Willamette Valley 1988 $6 (7/31/89) BB

1987

83	MONTINORE White Riesling Late Harvest Oregon Ultra Late Harvest 1987 $22/375ml (3/31/91)
82	ARGYLE Sparkling Brut Oregon Cuvée Limited 1987 $18.50 (12/31/90)
80	ELK COVE Cabernet Sauvignon Willamette Valley Dundee Hills Vineyard Commander's Cabernet 1987 $15 (3/31/91)
69	FORGERON Chenin Blanc Oregon 1987 $7.50 (7/31/89)

1986

60	ELK COVE Gewürztraminer Willamette Valley 1986 $6.75 (7/15/88)

1985

87 ST. JOSEF'S WEINKELLER Cabernet Sauvignon Oregon 1985 $15 (3/31/91)

1983

78 VALLEY VIEW Merlot Oregon 1983 $10 (5/31/88)

NV

74 VALLEY VIEW Rogue Red Oregon NV $3.75 (2/15/88)

WASHINGTON/CABERNET SAUVIGNON & BLENDS

1989

85 PRESTON WINE CELLARS Cabernet Sauvignon Washington Oak Aged 1989 $10 (5/15/91)
80 PAUL THOMAS Cabernet Sauvignon Washington 1989 $11 (12/31/90)

1988

86 COLUMBIA Cabernet Sauvignon Columbia Valley 1988 $10 (3/31/91)

1987

95 WOODWARD CANYON Cabernet Sauvignon Columbia Valley 1987 $18.50 (12/31/90)
91 LEONETTI Cabernet Sauvignon Washington 1987 $22 (6/15/90)
90 SNOQUALMIE Cabernet Sauvignon Columbia Valley 1987 $10 (9/30/90)
89 WOODWARD CANYON Charbonneau Walla Walla County 1987 $20 (12/31/90)
88 HOGUE Cabernet Sauvignon Washington Reserve 1987 $19 (3/31/91)
87 COLUMBIA Cabernet Sauvignon Columbia Valley 1987 $9.50 (6/15/90)
86 STATON HILLS Cabernet Sauvignon Washington 1987 $13 (3/31/91)
85 CHATEAU STE. MICHELLE Cabernet Sauvignon Columbia Valley Twentieth Vintage 1987 $12 (9/30/90)
83 LATAH CREEK Cabernet Sauvignon Washington Limited Bottling 1987 $13 (10/15/89)
83 LATAH CREEK Cabernet Sauvignon Washington Limited Bottling 1987 $13 (7/31/89)
62 PRESTON WINE CELLARS Cabernet Sauvignon Washington Preston Vineyard Selected Reserve 1987 $13.50 (10/15/89)

1986

93 WOODWARD CANYON Cabernet Sauvignon Columbia Valley 1986 $18.50 (10/15/89)
89 KIONA Cabernet Sauvignon Yakima Valley Estate Bottled 1986 $14 (10/15/89)
88 CHATEAU STE. MICHELLE Cabernet Sauvignon Columbia Valley 1986 $12 (9/30/90)
88 COLUMBIA CREST Cabernet Sauvignon Columbia Valley 1986 $8 (1/31/91) BB
88 COLUMBIA CREST Cabernet Sauvignon Columbia Valley 1986 $8 (12/15/90)
85 COLUMBIA Cabernet Sauvignon Columbia Valley 1986 $10 (10/15/89)
85 COLUMBIA Cabernet Sauvignon Columbia Valley David Lake Sagemoor Vineyards 1986 $16 (5/15/91)
84 PAUL THOMAS Cabernet Sauvignon Washington 1986 $14 (9/30/90)
83 STATON HILLS Cabernet Sauvignon Washington Estate Bottled 1986 $20 (3/31/91)
81 LEONETTI Cabernet Sauvignon Columbia Valley 1986 $20 (10/15/89)
80 COVEY RUN Cabernet Sauvignon Yakima Valley 1986 $10 (10/15/89)
80 LATAH CREEK Cabernet Sauvignon Washington 1986 $13 (10/15/88)
80 STATON HILLS Cabernet Sauvignon Washington 1986 $12 (10/15/89)
78 QUARRY LAKE Cabernet Sauvignon Washington 1986 $10 (10/15/89)

1985

91 COLUMBIA Cabernet Sauvignon Yakima Valley Otis Vineyard 1985 $15 (10/15/89)
90 CHATEAU STE. MICHELLE Cabernet Sauvignon Washington River Ridge Vineyard Limited Bottling 1985 $17 (11/30/90)
88 CHATEAU STE. MICHELLE Cabernet Sauvignon Washington River Ridge Vineyard Limited Bottling 1985 $16 (10/15/89)
88 PAUL THOMAS Cabernet Sauvignon Washington 1985 $20 (10/15/89)
88 PAUL THOMAS Cabernet Sauvignon Washington 1985 $20 (7/31/89)
85 CHATEAU STE. MICHELLE Cabernet Sauvignon Washington 1985 $11.50 (10/15/89)
85 COLUMBIA Cabernet Sauvignon Columbia Valley Sagemoor Vineyards 1985 $15 (10/15/89)
85 LEONETTI Cabernet Sauvignon Walla Walla Valley Seven Hills Vineyard 1985 $22 (10/15/89)
84 LEONETTI Cabernet Sauvignon Washington Reserve 1985 $40 (6/15/91)
83 CHATEAU STE. MICHELLE Cabernet Sauvignon Washington Cold Creek Vineyard Limited Bottling 1985 $19 (12/15/90)
82 CHATEAU STE. MICHELLE Cabernet Sauvignon Washington Cold Creek Vineyard Limited Bottling 1985 $16 (10/15/89)
82 COLUMBIA Cabernet Sauvignon Yakima Valley Red Willow Vineyard 1985 $15 (10/15/89)
82 FRENCH CREEK Cabernet Sauvignon Washington 1985 $8 (10/15/88)
81 COLUMBIA CREST Cabernet Sauvignon Columbia Valley 1985 $8 (10/15/89)
81 HOGUE Cabernet Sauvignon Washington Reserve 1985 $18 (10/15/89)
81 MERCER RANCH Cabernet Sauvignon Columbia Valley Mercer Ranch Vineyard Block 1 1985 $13 (10/15/89)
80 ARBOR CREST Cabernet Sauvignon Columbia Valley Bacchus Vineyard 1985 $11 (10/15/89)
79 COLUMBIA Cabernet Sauvignon Columbia Valley 1985 $9.50 (7/15/88)
78 COLUMBIA CREST Cabernet Sauvignon Columbia Valley 1985 $8 (7/31/89)
74 QUILCEDA CREEK Cabernet Sauvignon Washington 1985 $16.50 (10/15/89)

1984

89 CHATEAU STE. MICHELLE Cabernet Sauvignon Washington 1984 $11 (12/31/88)
79 COLUMBIA CREST Cabernet Sauvignon Columbia Valley 1984 $7.50 (7/15/88)

1983

81 CHATEAU STE. MICHELLE Cabernet Sauvignon Washington 1983 $10 (11/15/87)
77 ARBOR CREST Cabernet Sauvignon Columbia Valley Bacchus Vineyard 1983 $12.50 (12/15/87)
77 STE. CHAPELLE Cabernet Sauvignon Washington 1983 $9 (4/30/88)

1982

84 PRESTON WINE CELLARS Cabernet Sauvignon Washington 1982 $8 (5/31/88)

1981

86 COLUMBIA Cabernet Sauvignon Washington Bacchus Vineyard 1981 $12 (8/01/84)
84 COLUMBIA Cabernet Sauvignon Yakima Valley Red Willow Vineyard 1981 $35 (10/15/89)
83 COLUMBIA Cabernet Sauvignon Yakima Valley Otis Vineyard 1981 $13 (8/01/84)
81 STE. CHAPELLE Cabernet Sauvignon Washington Collectors' Series 1981 $18 (10/15/89)
80 STE. CHAPELLE Cabernet Sauvignon Washington 1981 $9 (5/15/87)
76 COLUMBIA Cabernet Sauvignon Yakima Valley 1981 $8 (8/01/84)

1980

85 CHATEAU STE. MICHELLE Cabernet Sauvignon Benton County Cold Creek Vineyards Château Reserve 1980 $21 (10/15/89)
75 CHATEAU STE. MICHELLE Cabernet Sauvignon Benton County Cold Creek Vineyards Château Reserve 1980 $20 (12/15/86)
65 CHATEAU STE. MICHELLE Cabernet Sauvignon Washington 1980 $9 (3/01/85)

CHARDONNAY

1989

91 PRESTON WINE CELLARS Chardonnay Washington Barrel Fermented 1989 $12 (5/31/91)
89 COLUMBIA Chardonnay Columbia Valley Sagemoor Vineyards Barrel Fermented The Woodburne Collection 1989 $10 (3/31/91)
89 COVEY RUN Chardonnay Yakima Valley Reserve 1989 $15 (7/15/91)
88 SILVER LAKE Chardonnay Columbia Valley Reserve 1989 $16 (5/31/91)
86 COLUMBIA CREST Chardonnay Columbia Valley 1989 $7 (9/30/90) BB
86 COLUMBIA CREST Chardonnay Columbia Valley Barrel Select 1989 $15 (5/31/91)
86 COVEY RUN Chardonnay Yakima Valley 1989 $10 (3/31/91)
86 HOGUE Chardonnay Washington Reserve 1989 $13 (5/31/91)
82 STATON HILLS Chardonnay Washington 1989 $10 (7/15/91)
78 COLUMBIA Chardonnay Columbia Valley 1989 $7 (5/31/91)

1988

89 PAUL THOMAS Chardonnay Washington 1988 $11 (10/15/89)
85 ARBOR CREST Chardonnay Columbia Valley 1988 $9.50 (3/31/90)
85 STEWART Chardonnay Columbia Valley 1988 $10 (3/31/91)
84 CHATEAU STE. MICHELLE Chardonnay Columbia Valley 1988 $10 (9/30/90)
80 HOGUE Chardonnay Washington 1988 $8 (6/15/90)
80 LATAH CREEK Chardonnay Washington Feather 1988 $6 (10/15/89)
79 COLUMBIA Chardonnay Columbia Valley 1988 $8.50 (9/30/90)
79 STATON HILLS Chardonnay Washington 1988 $10 (5/31/91)
78 STEWART Chardonnay Columbia Valley Reserve 1988 $17 (5/31/91)

1987

91 KIONA Chardonnay Yakima Valley Barrel Fermented 1987 $10 (10/15/89)
90 STEWART Chardonnay Columbia Valley Reserve 1987 $15 (3/31/90)
88 HOGUE Chardonnay Yakima Valley Reserve 1987 $10 (10/15/89)
87 CHATEAU STE. MICHELLE Chardonnay Washington Cold Creek Vineyard Limited Bottling 1987 $13 (10/15/89)
85 CHATEAU STE. MICHELLE Chardonnay Washington River Ridge Vineyard Limited Bottling 1987 $13 (10/15/89)
85 SNOQUALMIE Chardonnay Columbia Valley Reserve 1987 $13 (10/15/89)
85 PAUL THOMAS Chardonnay Washington Private Reserve 1987 $18 (10/15/89)
84 ARBOR CREST Chardonnay Columbia Valley 1987 $9.25 (10/15/89)
83 HOGUE Chardonnay Washington 1987 $8 (10/15/89)
83 SNOQUALMIE Chardonnay Columbia Valley 1987 $8 (10/15/89)
82 CHINOOK Chardonnay Washington 1987 $11 (10/15/89)
82 COVEY RUN Chardonnay Yakima Valley 1987 $9 (10/15/89)
82 LATAH CREEK Chardonnay Washington 1987 $9 (10/15/89)
82 PRESTON WINE CELLARS Chardonnay Washington Preston Vineyard Hand Harvested 1987 $10 (10/15/89)
81 CHATEAU STE. MICHELLE Chardonnay Washington 1987 $10 (10/15/89)
81 STATON HILLS Chardonnay Washington 1987 $10 (10/15/89)
81 PAUL THOMAS Chardonnay Washington 1987 $10 (10/15/89)
81 WOODWARD CANYON Chardonnay Columbia Valley 1987 $18 (10/15/89)
80 COLUMBIA Chardonnay Yakima Valley Brookside Vineyards 1987 $15 (10/15/89)
80 COLUMBIA CREST Chardonnay Columbia Valley 1987 $7 (12/31/88)
77 COLUMBIA CREST Chardonnay Columbia Valley Vintage Select 1987 $7 (10/15/89)
74 QUARRY LAKE Chardonnay Washington 1987 $10 (10/15/89)

1986

85 WOODWARD CANYON Chardonnay Washington 1986 $16 (4/30/88)
82 CHATEAU STE. MICHELLE Chardonnay Washington Cold Creek Vineyard Limited Bottling 1986 $13 (12/31/88)
81 HOGUE Chardonnay Washington 1986 $8 (12/31/87)
79 COLUMBIA CREST Chardonnay Columbia Valley 1986 $8 (12/31/87)
70 LATAH CREEK Chardonnay Washington 1986 $8.50 (12/31/87)

1985

79 COLUMBIA Chardonnay Washington 1985 $8 (7/31/87)

1984

81 WOODWARD CANYON Chardonnay Washington 1984 $21 (5/15/87)
78 ARBOR CREST Chardonnay Columbia Valley 1984 $9.25 (7/31/87)
70 SNOQUALMIE Chardonnay Yakima Valley Early Release 1984 $7 (4/16/86)
67 CHATEAU STE. MICHELLE Chardonnay Washington 1984 $10 (7/31/87)
53 SNOQUALMIE Chardonnay Yakima Valley 1984 $9 (4/16/86)

1983

81 CHATEAU STE. MICHELLE Chardonnay Washington River Ridge Vineyard Château Reserve 1983 $18 (7/31/87)
69 ARBOR CREST Chardonnay Washington Sagemoore Vineyards 1983 $10 (11/01/85)
46 COLUMBIA Chardonnay Yakima Valley Wyckoff Vineyard 1983 $8.50 (4/16/86)

1982

85 ARBOR CREST Chardonnay Washington Sagemoore Vineyards 1982 $14 (1/01/85)
80 COLUMBIA Chardonnay Washington Jolona Vineyard 1982 $12 (9/01/84)
73 CHATEAU STE. MICHELLE Chardonnay Washington 1982 $9 (4/16/86)

CHENIN BLANC

1988

88 CHATEAU STE. MICHELLE Chenin Blanc Columbia Valley 1988 $6 (7/31/89)
84 PAUL THOMAS Chenin Blanc Washington 1988 $7 (10/15/89)
81 WORDEN Chenin Blanc Washington 1988 $6 (10/15/89)
80 SNOQUALMIE Chenin Blanc Columbia Valley 1988 $6.50 (10/15/89)
78 BOOKWALTER Chenin Blanc Washington Joseph Roberts Vineyards 1988 $6 (10/15/89)
76 KIONA Chenin Blanc Yakima Valley Estate Bottled 1988 $5.75 (10/15/89)
76 SADDLE MOUNTAIN Chenin Blanc Columbia Valley 1988 $5 (10/15/89)
74 HOGUE Chenin Blanc Washington 1988 $6 (10/15/89)

UNITED STATES
WASHINGTON/CHENIN BLANC

71 SALISHAN Chenin Blanc Washington Dry 1988 $6.25 (10/15/89)
68 SNOQUALMIE Chenin Blanc Columbia Valley 1988 $6.50 (7/31/89)

1987

83 QUARRY LAKE Chenin Blanc Washington 1987 $5.50 (10/15/89)
80 CHATEAU STE. MICHELLE Chenin Blanc Washington 1987 $6 (10/15/89)
75 CASCADE MOUNTAIN Chenin Blanc Washington Vouvray 1987 $5.25 (10/15/89)

1986

84 CHATEAU STE. MICHELLE Chenin Blanc Washington 1986 $4 (7/31/89)
77 COLUMBIA CREST Chenin Blanc Columbia Valley 1986 $5.25 (10/15/89)

1985

82 CHATEAU STE. MICHELLE Chenin Blanc Washington 1985 $5 (1/31/87)

NV

68 LAKESIDE Chenin Blanc Washington NV $6 (7/31/89)

DESSERT

1989

85 SILVER LAKE Ice Wine Columbia Valley 1989 $25/375ml (6/15/91)
75 KIONA Ice Wine Yakima Valley 1989 $15/375ml (6/15/91)

1988

85 COLUMBIA Johannisberg Riesling Late Harvest Columbia Valley Cellarmaster's Reserve 1988 $7 (10/15/89) BB
84 SNOQUALMIE White Riesling Late Harvest Columbia Valley 1988 $7 (10/15/89)

1987

87 COVEY RUN White Riesling Late Harvest Yakima Valley Ice Wine 1987 $24/375ml (10/15/89)
87 HYATT Riesling Late Harvest Yakima Valley 1987 $8 (10/15/89)
85 THURSTON WOLFE Dessert Washington Black Muscat 1987 $9 (10/15/89)
83 STEWART White Riesling Late Harvest Columbia Valley 1987 $8/375ml (7/31/89)
83 THURSTON WOLFE Sauvignon Blanc Late Harvest Washington Sweet Rebecca 1987 $9 (10/15/89)
79 HOGUE White Riesling Late Harvest Yakima Valley Markin Vineyard 1987 $7.50 (10/15/89)
78 BOOKWALTER White Riesling Late Harvest Washington 1987 $5.50/375ml (10/15/89)
71 BAINBRIDGE ISLAND Dessert Washington Siegerrebe Botrytis Affected 1987 $15/375ml (10/15/89)

1986

83 COVEY RUN White Riesling Late Harvest Yakima Valley Mahre Vineyards Botrytis 1986 $7 (10/15/89)
80 PRESTON WINE CELLARS White Riesling Late Harvest Washington Ice Wine 1986 $38 (10/15/89)
80 STEWART White Riesling Late Harvest Columbia Valley Select 1986 $6.50/375ml (10/15/89)

1985

91 CHATEAU STE. MICHELLE White Riesling Late Harvest Yakima Valley Château Reserve Hand-Selected Cluster 1985 $22 (7/31/89)
82 HINZERLING Gewürztraminer Late Harvest Yakima Valley Selected Cluster Die Sonne 1985 $12/375ml (10/15/89)

1982

58 ARBOR CREST Dessert Washington Dionysius Vineyard 1982 $6/375ml (4/16/84)

GEWÜRZTRAMINER

1989

76 COVEY RUN Gewürztraminer Yakima Valley 1989 $7 (6/15/91)

1988

85 HOODSPORT Gewürztraminer Washington 1988 $6 (10/15/89) BB
79 CHATEAU STE. MICHELLE Gewürztraminer Columbia Valley 1988 $6.50 (10/15/89)
79 SNOQUALMIE Gewürztraminer Columbia Valley 1988 $6 (10/15/89)
77 COVEY RUN Gewürztraminer Yakima Valley 1988 $5.50 (10/15/89)
69 STEWART Gewürztraminer Yakima Valley 1988 $5.50 (10/15/89)

1987

81 COLUMBIA CREST Gewürztraminer Columbia Valley 1987 $6 (10/15/89)

1986

80 COLUMBIA CREST Gewürztraminer Columbia Valley 1986 $6 (12/15/87)

1985

74 COLUMBIA Gewürztraminer Washington 1985 $6 (5/15/87)

MERLOT

1989

93 LEONETTI Merlot Washington 1989 $18 (5/31/91)
86 STONE CREEK Merlot Columbia Valley 1989 $7 (5/31/91) BB

1988

90 LEONETTI Merlot Washington 1988 $17 (4/15/90)
87 COVEY RUN Merlot Yakima Valley 1988 $10 (3/31/91)
84 KIONA Merlot Columbia Valley 1988 $12 (5/31/91)
82 COLUMBIA Merlot Yakima Valley Red Willow Vineyard Milestone David Lake 1988 $16 (3/31/91)
81 COLUMBIA Merlot Columbia Valley 1988 $10 (3/31/91)
78 STONE CREEK Merlot Columbia Valley 1988 $6 (9/30/90)

1987

91 SNOQUALMIE Merlot Columbia Valley Reserve 1987 $12 (9/30/90)
90 LATAH CREEK Merlot Washington Limited Bottling 1987 $10 (10/15/89)
89 HOGUE Merlot Washington Reserve 1987 $19 (3/31/91)
89 PAUL THOMAS Merlot Washington 1987 $16 (9/30/90)
88 LEONETTI Merlot Columbia Valley 1987 $16 (10/15/89)
86 COLUMBIA CREST Merlot Columbia Valley 1987 $8 (9/30/90) BB
85 ARBOR CREST Merlot Columbia Valley Cameo Reserve 1987 $11 (6/15/90)
84 CHATEAU STE. MICHELLE Merlot Columbia Valley 1987 $12 (9/30/90)
84 COLUMBIA CREST Merlot Columbia Valley Barrel Select 1987 $15 (5/31/91)
83 ARBOR CREST Merlot Columbia Valley 1987 $8 (10/15/89)
80 COLUMBIA Merlot Yakima Valley Red Willow Vineyard Milestone 1987 $15 (10/15/89)
76 STATON HILLS Merlot Washington 1987 $12 (10/15/89)
73 STE. CHAPELLE Merlot Washington 1987 $10 (9/30/90)

1986

89 LATAH CREEK Merlot Washington 1986 $10 (5/31/88)
85 HOGUE Merlot Washington 1986 $12 (4/15/89)
84 CHATEAU STE. MICHELLE Merlot Columbia Valley 1986 $12 (9/30/90)
84 COLUMBIA Merlot Columbia Valley 1986 $10 (10/15/89)
83 CHINOOK Merlot Washington 1986 $12.50 (10/15/89)
82 COVEY RUN Merlot Yakima Valley 1986 $9 (10/15/89)
82 HOGUE Merlot Washington 1986 $12 (10/15/89)
81 QUARRY LAKE Merlot Washington 1986 $10 (10/15/89)
81 STE. CHAPELLE Merlot Washington Dionysus Vineyard 1986 $12 (5/31/88)

1985

89 CHATEAU STE. MICHELLE Merlot Columbia Valley River Ridge Vineyard 1985 $17.50 (9/30/90)
87 CHATEAU STE. MICHELLE Merlot Washington River Ridge Vineyard 1985 $14 (10/15/89)
86 COLUMBIA Merlot Columbia Valley 1985 $9.50 (5/31/88)
85 COLUMBIA CREST Merlot Columbia Valley 1985 $8 (10/15/89)
85 COVEY RUN Merlot Yakima Valley 1985 $9 (4/15/89)
83 ARBOR CREST Merlot Columbia Valley Bacchus Vineyard Cameo Reserve 1985 $10 (12/15/87)
83 FRENCH CREEK Merlot Washington 1985 $11.50 (12/31/88)
80 COLUMBIA CREST Merlot Columbia Valley 1985 $8 (7/31/89)
80 HOGUE Merlot Washington 1985 $12 (11/15/87)
75 ARBOR CREST Merlot Columbia Valley Bacchus Vineyard 1985 $8 (7/31/87)

1984

82 COVEY RUN Merlot Yakima Valley 1984 $8.50 (11/15/87)
78 COLUMBIA CREST Merlot Columbia Valley 1984 $7.50 (5/31/88)
75 COLUMBIA Merlot Washington 1984 $9 (5/15/87)

1983

87 CHATEAU STE. MICHELLE Merlot Washington River Ridge Vineyard Château Reserve 1983 $15 (12/31/88)
80 CHATEAU STE. MICHELLE Merlot Washington 1983 $10 (12/31/88)

1982

82 ARBOR CREST Merlot Washington Bacchus Vineyard 1982 $8.25 (11/01/84)
76 HAVILAND Merlot Washington 1982 $8 (10/01/84)

1981

87 COLUMBIA Merlot Washington 1981 $25 (10/15/89)
78 COLUMBIA Merlot Washington 1981 $25 (8/01/84)

RIESLING

1990

85 CHATEAU STE. MICHELLE Riesling Columbia Valley Dry River Ridge Vineyard 1990 $7 (6/15/91) BB

1989

88 COVEY RUN Johannisberg Riesling Yakima Valley 1989 $7 (8/31/90) BB
87 SILVER LAKE Riesling Columbia Valley Dry 1989 $6 (6/15/91) BB
80 HOGUE Riesling Washington Dry Schwartzman Vineyard Reserve 1989 $8.50 (6/15/91)

1988

90 HOGUE Johannisberg Riesling Yakima Valley 1988 $6 (10/15/89) BB
87 HOODSPORT Johannisberg Riesling Washington 1988 $6 (10/15/89) BB
85 CHATEAU STE. MICHELLE Johannisberg Riesling Columbia Valley 1988 $6.50 (10/15/89)
85 PAUL THOMAS Johannisberg Riesling Washington 1988 $7 (10/15/89)
85 PAUL THOMAS Riesling Washington Dry 1988 $7 (10/15/89)
85 WORDEN Johannisberg Riesling Washington Charbonneau Vineyards 1988 $6 (10/15/89)
85 WORDEN Johannisberg Riesling Washington Charbonneau Vineyards 1988 $6 (7/31/89)
84 HOGUE Johannisberg Riesling Yakima Valley Dry Schwartzman Vineyard 1988 $6.50 (10/15/89)
81 SNOQUALMIE Johannisberg Riesling Columbia Valley RS 1.9% 1988 $6 (10/15/89)
80 HOGUE Johannisberg Riesling Yakima Valley Dry Schwartzman Vineyard 1988 $6.50 (10/15/89)
80 HOGUE Johannisberg Riesling Yakima Valley Dry Schwartzman Vineyard 1988 $6.50 (7/31/89)
80 SNOQUALMIE Johannisberg Riesling Columbia Valley 1988 $6 (10/15/89)
79 COVEY RUN Johannisberg Riesling Washington 1988 $5.50 (10/15/89)
79 SALISHAN White Riesling Washington Dry 1988 $5 (10/15/89)
78 CHATEAU STE. MICHELLE White Riesling Columbia Valley Sweet Select 1988 $7 (10/15/89)
78 FACELLI Johannisberg Riesling Washington Dry 1988 $7.50 (10/15/89)
74 KIONA White Riesling Columbia Valley 1988 $6 (10/15/89)
72 STEWART Johannisberg Riesling Columbia Valley 1988 $6.50 (10/15/89)

68   STEWART White Riesling Columbia Valley 1988 $15/375ml (10/15/89)

1987

88   BARNARD GRIFFIN Johannisberg Riesling Columbia Valley 1987 $6.50 (10/15/89) BB
83   HOGUE Johannisberg Riesling Yakima Valley Classic 1987 $5.50 (7/15/88)
82   CHATEAU STE. MICHELLE Johannisberg Riesling Washington 1987 $6 (4/15/89)
82   LATAH CREEK Johannisberg Riesling Washington 1987 $5.50 (4/15/89) BB
80   STEWART Johannisberg Riesling Columbia Valley 1987 $6 (4/15/89)
77   PAUL THOMAS Riesling Washington Dry 1987 $7 (7/31/89)
75   CASCADE CREST Johannisberg Riesling Yakima Valley 1987 $6 (10/15/89)
74   BONAIR Johannisberg Riesling Yakima Valley 1987 $5.50 (10/15/89)
73   COLUMBIA Johannisberg Riesling Columbia Valley Cellarmaster's Reserve 1987 $7 (5/31/88)
71   PRESTON WINE CELLARS Johannisberg Riesling Washington Preston Vineyard Hand Harvested 1987 $5.75 (10/15/89)
68   WHITE HERON Johannisberg Riesling Washington 1987 $5 (7/31/89)
66   BLACKWOOD CANYON White Riesling Columbia Valley Claar Vineyard Dry 1987 $9 (10/15/89)
65   NEUHARTH Johannisberg Riesling Washington 1987 $8.75 (10/15/89)

1986

87   COLUMBIA Johannisberg Riesling Washington 1986 $6 (5/15/87)
84   COVEY RUN Johannisberg Riesling Yakima Valley 1986 $6 (11/15/87)
83   HOGUE Johannisberg Riesling Washington 1986 $6 (11/15/87)
83   LATAH CREEK Johannisberg Riesling Washington 1986 $5.50 (11/15/87)
81   F.W. LANGGUTH Johannisberg Riesling Columbia Valley 1986 $6 (7/15/88)
80   COLUMBIA CREST Johannisberg Riesling Columbia Valley 1986 $6 (11/15/87)
75   CHATEAU STE. MICHELLE Johannisberg Riesling Washington 1986 $5.50 (11/15/87)
75   SNOQUALMIE Johannisberg Riesling Washington 1986 $6 (7/15/88)
70   COLUMBIA CREST Johannisberg Riesling Columbia Valley 1986 $6 (10/15/89)

1985

60   HOGUE Johannisberg Riesling Yakima Valley 1985 $6 (5/15/87)

1984

88   ARBOR CREST Johannisberg Riesling Washington 1984 $6.50 (9/01/85)
79   HOGUE Riesling Yakima Valley Markin Vineyard 1984 $7 (1/01/86)
74   CHATEAU STE. MICHELLE Riesling Washington Reserve Hahn Hill Vineyards Hand-Selected 1984 $14 (12/15/87)

1983

88   F.W. LANGGUTH Johannisberg Riesling Washington Anders Gyving Vineyard 1983 $7 (10/16/84)
87   F.W. LANGGUTH Johannisberg Riesling Columbia Valley Select Harvest 1983 $8 (10/01/84)
76   HAVILAND Riesling Washington 1983 $6 (10/01/84)

1982

80   ARBOR CREST Johannisberg Riesling Washington Stewart's Sunnyside Vineyard Select Late H 1982 $7.15 (3/16/84)

SAUVIGNON BLANC

1989

78   PRESTON Fumé Blanc Washington Oak Aged 1989 $7 (7/15/91)

1988

88   HOGUE Fumé Blanc Washington 1988 $8 (10/15/89)
86   SADDLE MOUNTAIN Fumé Blanc Columbia Valley 1988 $5 (10/15/89) BB
80   COVEY RUN Fumé Blanc Washington 1988 $8 (10/15/89)
78   CHATEAU STE. MICHELLE Sauvignon Blanc Columbia Valley 1988 $7 (12/31/90)
78   STEWART Sauvignon Blanc Yakima Valley 1988 $8 (10/15/89)
76   TAGARIS Fumé Blanc Washington 1988 $8 (10/15/89)

1987

89   CHINOOK Sauvignon Blanc Washington 1987 $8.25 (10/15/89)
88   SNOQUALMIE Fumé Blanc Columbia Valley 1987 $7 (10/15/89) BB
85   ARBOR CREST Sauvignon Blanc Columbia Valley Wahluke Slope 1987 $7.50 (10/15/89)
85   PAUL THOMAS Sauvignon Blanc Washington 1987 $9 (10/15/89)
85   WATERBROOK Sauvignon Blanc Washington 1987 $9 (10/15/89)
75   BARNARD GRIFFIN Fumé Blanc Washington Barrel Fermented 1987 $9 (10/15/89)
73   WORDEN Fumé Blanc Washington 1987 $7 (10/15/89)
71   STATON HILLS Sauvignon Blanc Washington 1987 $8 (10/15/89)
68   QUARRY LAKE Sauvignon Blanc Washington 1987 $7.50 (10/15/89)

1986

82   COLUMBIA CREST Sauvignon Blanc Columbia Valley 1986 $7 (10/15/89)
78   ARBOR CREST Sauvignon Blanc Columbia Valley 1986 $7.50 (11/15/87)

1985

87   ARBOR CREST Fumé Blanc Columbia Valley 1985 $7.50 (8/31/86)

1984

95   ARBOR CREST Sauvignon Blanc Washington 1984 $7.50 (11/16/85)

SÉMILLON

1988

84   COLUMBIA Sémillon Columbia Valley 1988 $6 (10/15/89) BB
82   FACELLI Sémillon Washington 1988 $8 (10/15/89)
74   SNOQUALMIE Sémillon Columbia Valley 1988 $6 (10/15/89)

1987

87   CASCADE CREST Sémillon Yakima Valley Blanc 1987 $5.50 (10/15/89) BB
83   BLACKWOOD CANYON Sémillon Yakima Valley Barrel Fermented 1987 $9 (10/15/89)
67   PORTTEUS Sémillon Yakima Valley 1987 $7 (10/15/89)

1986

79   LATAH CREEK Sémillon Washington 1986 $6 (10/15/89)
78   COLUMBIA CREST Sémillon Columbia Valley 1986 $5.75 (10/15/89)
72   HOGUE Sémillon Washington Reserve 1986 $8 (10/15/89)

SPARKLING

1986

85   DOMAINE STE. MICHELLE Sparkling Columbia Valley Blanc de Blanc 1986 $15 (12/31/90)

1985

86   DOMAINE STE. MICHELLE Sparkling Columbia Valley Blanc de Noir 1985 $20 (12/31/90)

NV

82   HOGUE Sparkling Yakima Valley Brut NV $12 (10/15/89)
80   STE. CHAPELLE Sparkling Washington Brut Chardonnay Champagne NV $9 (3/15/88)
78   DOMAINE STE. MICHELLE Sparkling Columbia Valley Brut NV $13 (12/31/90)
78   DOMAINE STE. MICHELLE Sparkling Columbia Valley Brut NV $13 (10/15/89)
77   STATON HILLS Sparkling Washington Blanc de Noir NV $16 (10/15/89)
76   STE. CHAPELLE Sparkling Washington Sec Johannisberg Riesling Champagne NV $7 (3/15/88)

OTHER WASHINGTON RED

1988

90   COLUMBIA Syrah Yakima Valley Red Willow Vineyard 1988 $25 (5/15/91)
83   CAVATAPPI Nebbiolo Maddalena Red Willow Vineyards Washington 1988 $19 (6/15/91)

1987

88   COLUMBIA Pinot Noir Washington The Woodburne Collection 1987 $10 (3/31/91)
83   COLUMBIA Pinot Noir Washington Barrel Fermented The Woodburne Collection 1987 $10 (3/31/91)

1981

71   COLUMBIA Pinot Noir Washington Yakima County 1981 $7 (9/01/84)

OTHER WASHINGTON WHITE

1989

73   COLUMBIA CREST Sémillon-Chardonnay Columbia Valley 1989 $7 (7/15/91)

1988

82   HOGUE Washington 1988 $6 (10/15/89)
80   PONTIN DEL ROZA Roza Sunset Yakima Valley 1988 $6 (10/15/89)
75   CHATEAU STE. MICHELLE Blush Riesling Columbia Valley 1988 $5 (10/15/89)
63   MOUNT BAKER Müller-Thurgau Washington 1988 $6 (10/15/89)
59   SADDLE MOUNTAIN Blush White Riesling Columbia Valley 1988 $5 (10/15/89)

1987

84   BAINBRIDGE ISLAND Müller-Thurgau Washington 1987 $6 (10/15/89)
81   LATAH CREEK Muscat Washington 1987 $6 (10/15/89)
77   BAINBRIDGE ISLAND Müller-Thurgau Washington Dry 1987 $6 (10/15/89)

1986

64   COLUMBIA CREST Vineyard Reserve Columbia Valley 1986 $5 (10/15/89)

OTHER UNITED STATES/AMERICAN

NV

83   PRINCE MICHEL Red Le Ducq Lot 87 NV $50 (6/30/90)
82   BEL ARBORS Cabernet Sauvignon American Founder's Selection NV $5 (10/15/89) BB
82   GRAYSON White Zinfandel American NV $4 (6/15/89)
81   BEL ARBORS Chardonnay American Founder's Selection NV $5 (10/31/89) BB
81   BEL ARBORS Sauvignon Blanc American Founder's Selection NV $5 (10/15/89) BB
77   GOLD SEAL Blanc de Blanc American Charles Fournier Special Selection NV $10 (6/30/90)
75   COOK'S Brut American Imperial Grand Reserve Extremely Dry NV $6 (12/31/87)
72   BEL ARBORS Merlot American Founder's Selection American Grown NV $5 (6/15/90)
72   COOK'S Sparkling Rosé Blush NV $4 (10/15/88)
70   GREAT WESTERN Blanc de Noirs American NV $14 (3/31/90)

IDAHO

1989

81   STE. CHAPELLE Johannisberg Riesling Idaho 1989 $6 (12/15/90) BB

1988

88   STE. CHAPELLE Johannisberg Riesling Idaho 1988 $6 (7/31/89) BB
83   STE. CHAPELLE Chardonnay Idaho 1988 $10 (12/15/90)
83   STE. CHAPELLE Chardonnay Idaho Reserve 1988 $15 (3/31/91)

1987

79   STE. CHAPELLE Johannisberg Riesling Idaho 1987 $6 10/15/88)

1986

81   STE. CHAPELLE Riesling Idaho Special Harvest Winery Block 1986 $10 (7/31/87)
79   STE. CHAPELLE Johannisberg Riesling Late Harvest Idaho Botrytis 1986 $15 (2/15/88)
74   STE. CHAPELLE Chardonnay Idaho 1986 $10 (4/30/88)

1985

62   STE. CHAPELLE Chardonnay Idaho Canyon 1985 $7 (4/30/88)

1983

74   STE. CHAPELLE Chardonnay Idaho Symms Family Vineyard 1983 $10 (10/01/85)

1982

87   STE. CHAPELLE Chardonnay Idaho Symms Family Vineyard 1982 $10 (1/01/85)
83   STE. CHAPELLE Chardonnay Idaho Symms Family Vineyard 1982 $10 (4/16/86)

NEW ENGLAND

77   CROSSWOODS Chardonnay Southeastern New England 1986 $15 (10/31/89)

NEW MEXICO

1987

79   ANDERSON VALLEY Chardonnay New Mexico Barrel Fermented 1987 $8.50 (4/15/89)

UNITED STATES
OTHER UNITED STATES/NEW MEXICO

79   ANDERSON VALLEY Sauvignon Blanc New Mexico 1987 $7 (4/15/89)

1986

80   ANDERSON VALLEY Cabernet Sauvignon New Mexico 1986 $11 (7/31/89)
70   ANDERSON VALLEY Chardonnay New Mexico Barrel Fermented 1986 $7 (3/15/88)

NV

80   DOMAINE CHEURLIN Extra Dry New Mexico NV $12 (9/15/87)
80   GRUET Brut Blanc de Noirs New Mexico NV $13 (3/31/90)
79   GRUET Brut New Mexico NV $13 (3/31/90)
77   DOMAINE CHEURLIN Brut New Mexico NV $12 (9/15/87)

TEXAS

1989

83   FALL CREEK Sauvignon Blanc Texas 1989 $8.50 (7/15/91)

1988

86   MESSINA HOF Chenin Blanc Brazos Valley 1988 $7 (7/31/89)
82   LLANO ESTACADO Chenin Blanc Texas 1988 $6.50 (7/31/89)
78   FALL CREEK Cabernet Sauvignon Texas 1988 $13 (7/15/91)
73   FALL CREEK Carnelian Llano County 1988 $13 (7/15/91)

NV

79   MOYER Brut Natural Texas NV $11 (7/31/89)

VIRGINIA

1988

87   PRINCE MICHEL Chardonnay Virginia Barrel Select 1988 $15 (6/30/90)

NV

83   PRINCE MICHEL Virginia Le Ducq Lot 87 NV $50 (6/30/90)

NOTES

NOTES

NOTES

NOTES

NOTES

NOTES